THE MERCERS' SERIES

Oil Paintings in Public Ownership in
Glasgow Museums

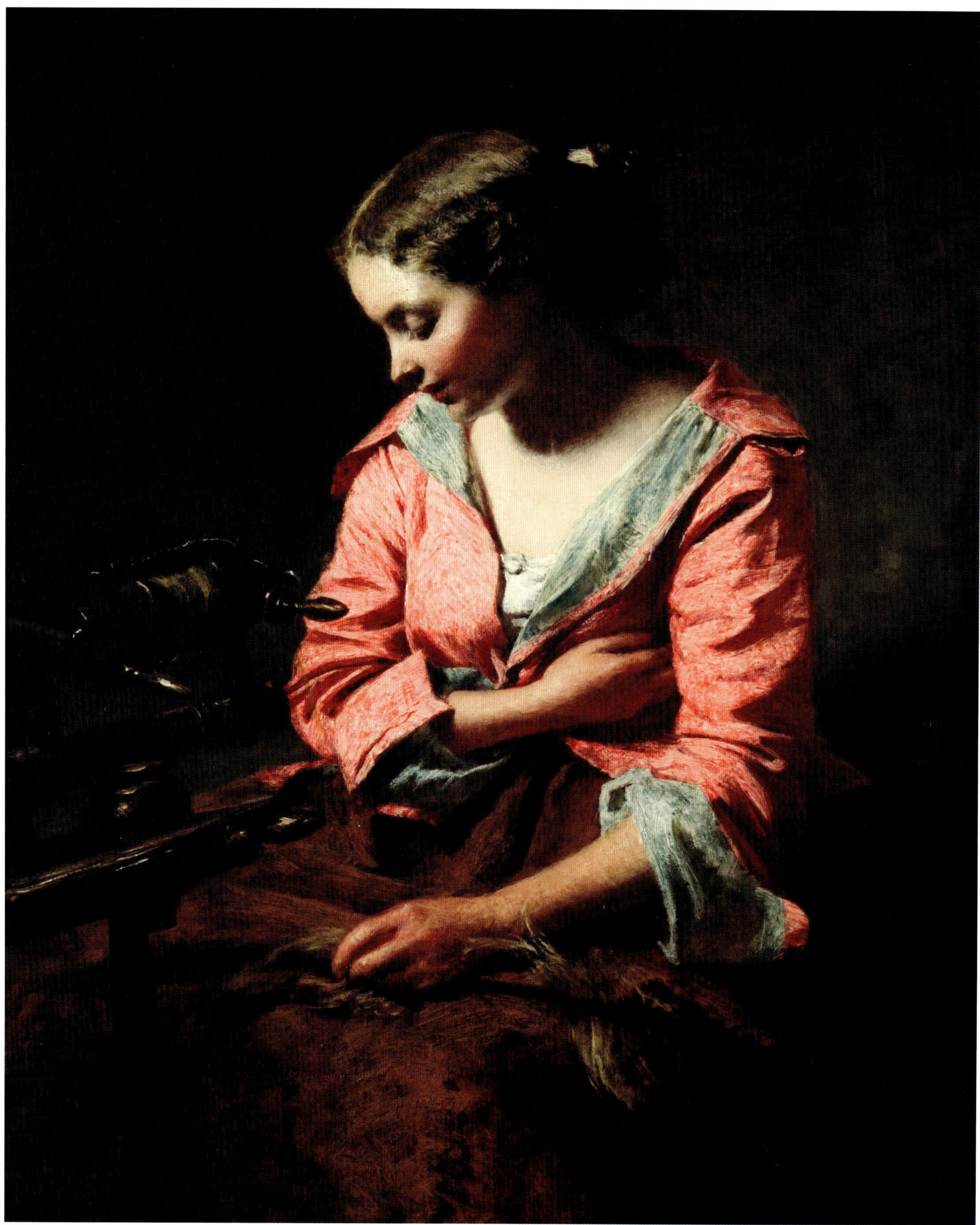

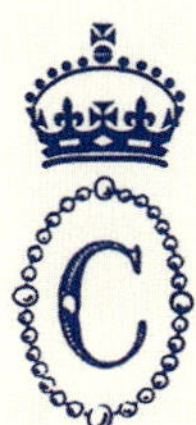

The *Oil Paintings in Public Ownership* series of catalogues is an extraordinary work in progress. Published by The Public Catalogue Foundation, it is the result of the determined efforts of a small team of administrative staff, researchers and photographers spread across the United Kingdom.

Our national collection of oil paintings in public ownership is probably one of the finest anywhere in the world. It is held not just by our museums and galleries but is also to be found in hospitals, universities and other civic buildings throughout the United Kingdom. A large proportion of these paintings are not on display and many have never before been reproduced.

This series of books for the first time allows the public to see an entire photographic record of these works – a collection likely to number some 200,000 in total. In doing so, these volumes provide a unique insight into our nation's artistic and cultural history.

As Patron of The Public Catalogue Foundation, my visits to collections across the country have highlighted to me not only the desire of curators to publicise their paintings, but also the limited resources at their disposal. The Foundation's work goes a long way towards helping to create access to these collections, while at the same time giving the British public the opportunity to see and enjoy *all* the paintings that they own.

I wish The Public Catalogue Foundation every success in its continuing endeavours.

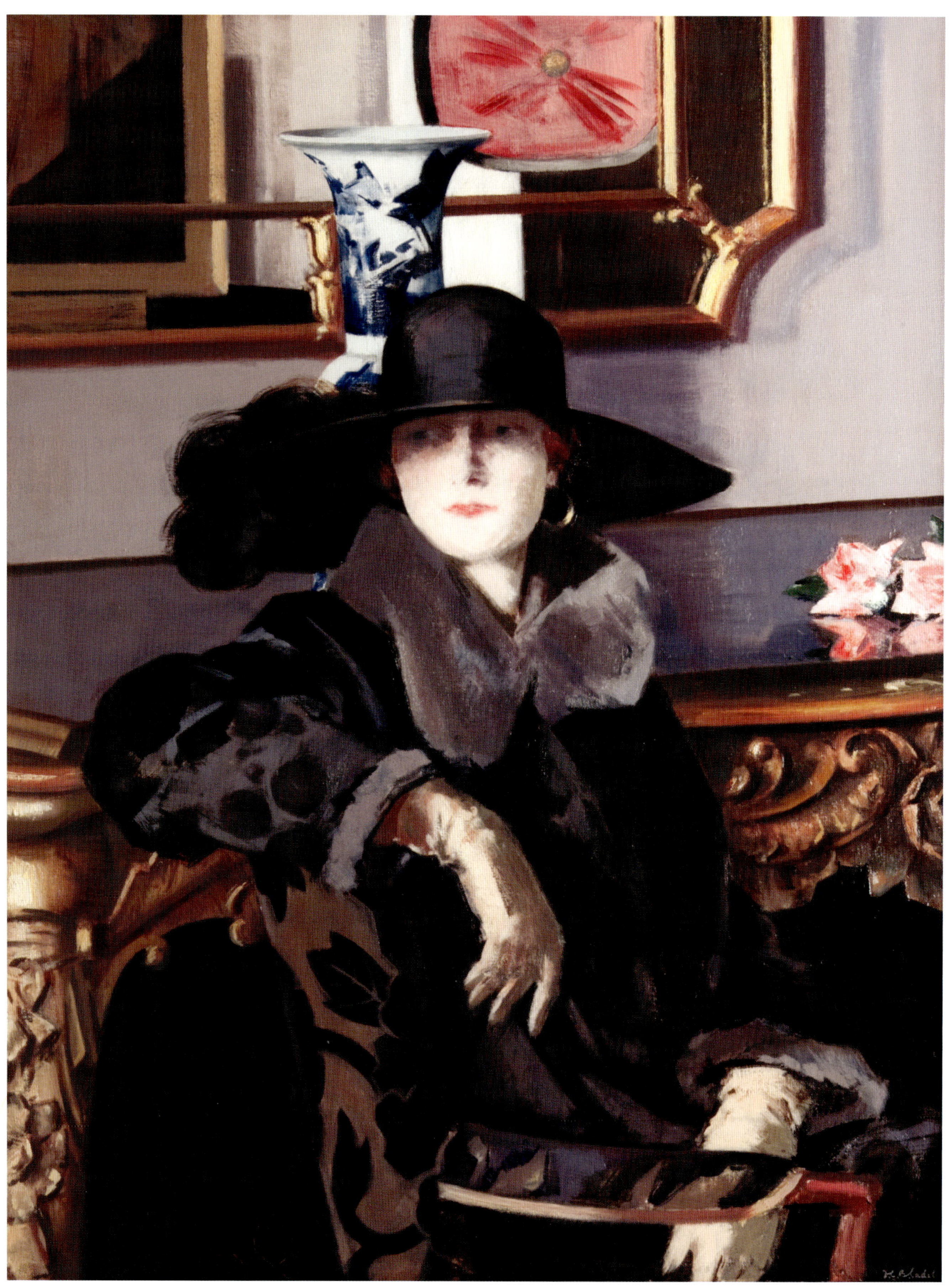

Oil Paintings in Public Ownership

in

Glasgow Museums

Master Patron (Scotland)
Magnus Linklater

Honorary Patrons
Bridget McConnell
Mark O'Neill

Funding Patron
The Mercers' Company

Coordinators: Dr Sam Maddra, Dr Joanna Meacock & Lisa Pearson
Photographer: Iona Shepherd

The Public Catalogue Foundation
Patron
HRH The Duchess of Cornwall

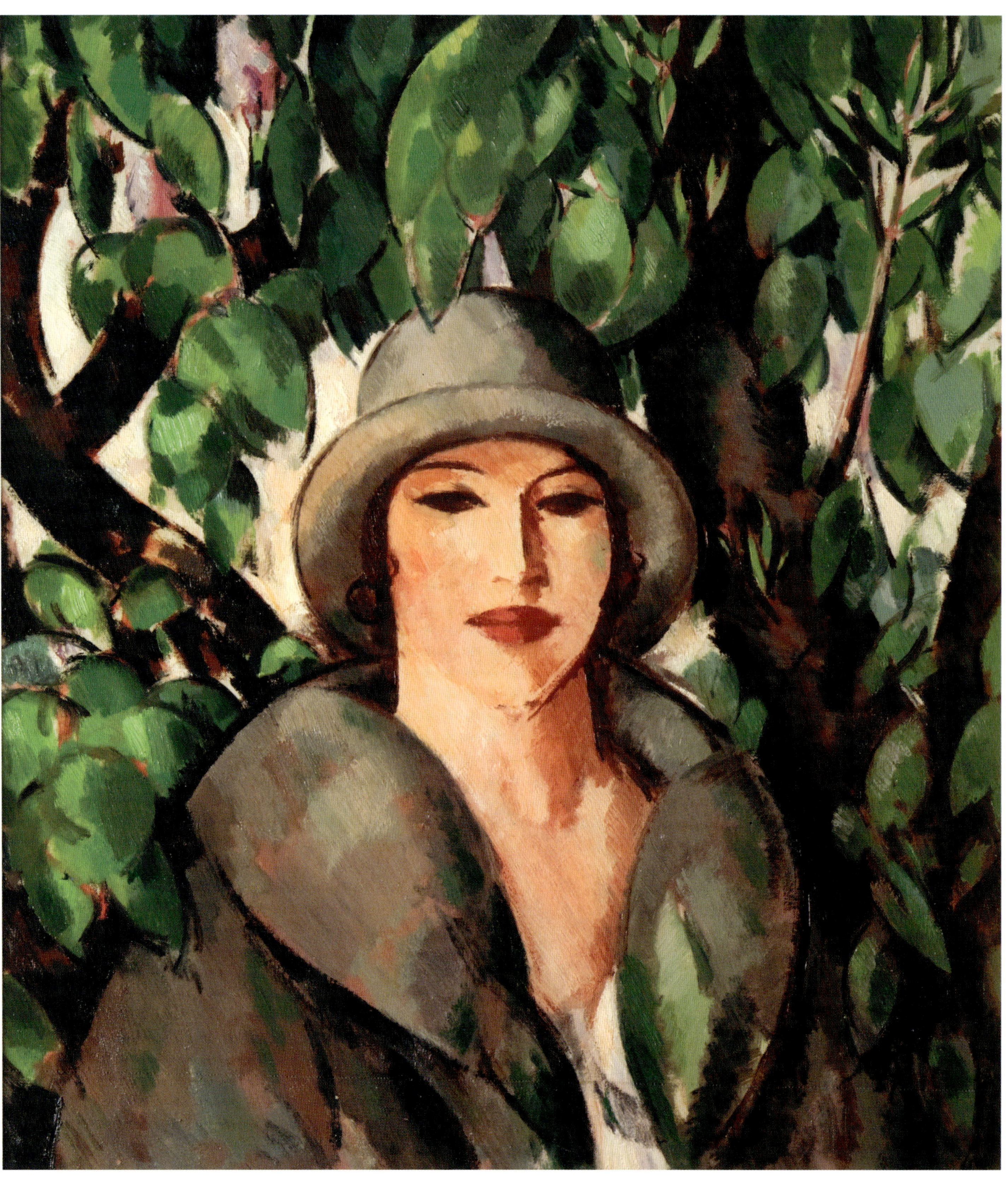

Contents

THE PAINTINGS

Facing page: Fergusson, John Duncan, 1874–1961, *In the Boltons: The Artist's Wife*, c.1927–1928, (p. 135)

Image opposite HRH The Duchess of Cornwall's statement: Phillip, John, 1817–1867, *The Spinning Wheel*, 1859, (p. 350)
Image opposite title page: Cadell, Francis Campbell Boileau, 1883–1937, *A Lady in Black*, c.1926, (p. 70)

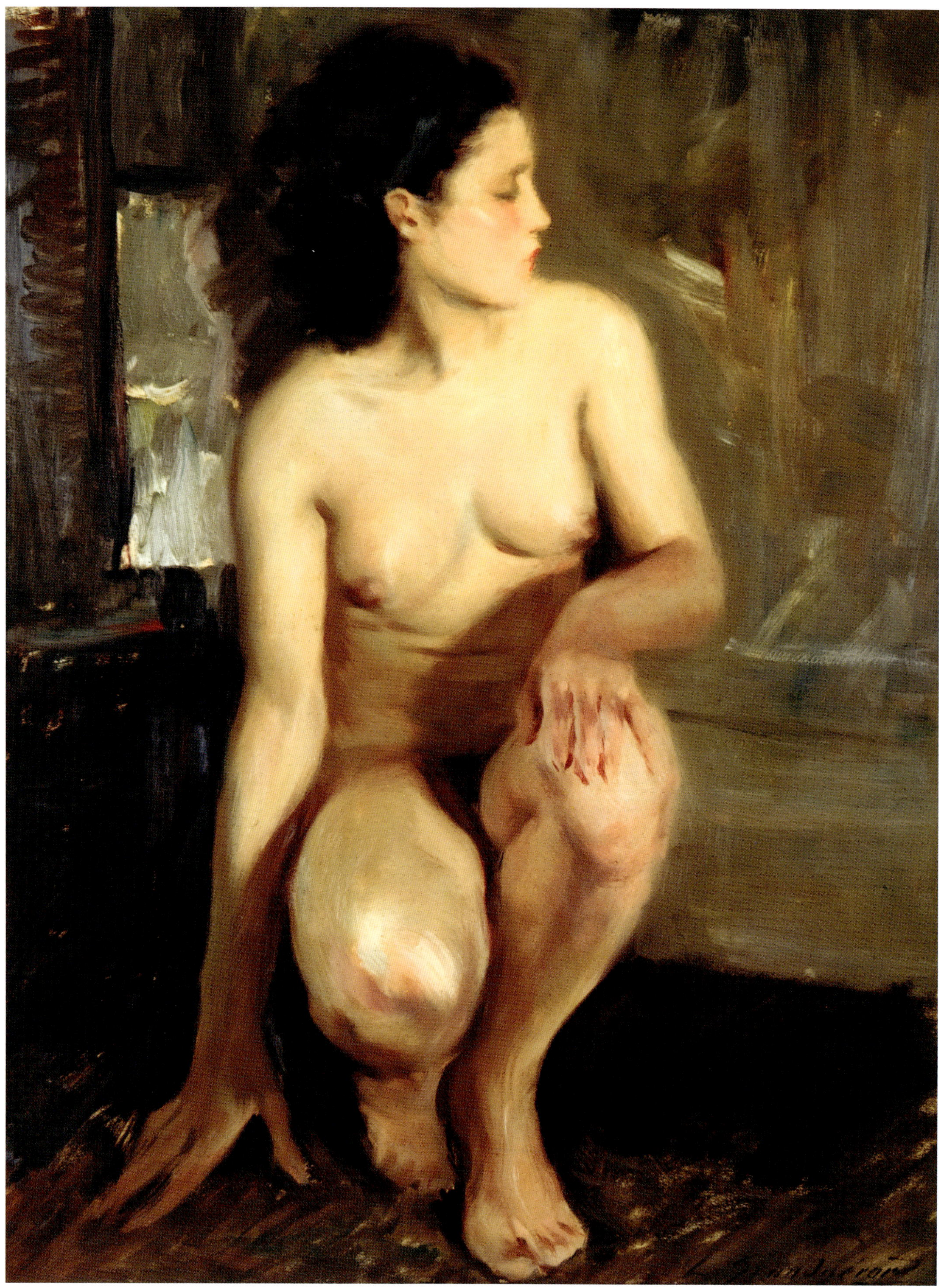

Foreword

Glasgow owes a very great deal to Bridget McConnell, the Chief Executive of Glasgow Lifeand I owe a great deal both to her and to Mark O'Neill, her Director of Policy and Research. That the inhabitants of the Isle of Raasay have yet to owe anything tangible to either of them is not their fault, nor Mark's, nor Bridget's. The blame is part mine but it can more palpably be left at the feet of those authorities in their region who failed to see the benefit for the Island of the Boswell Project. Recognising the need for swift action, Bridget McConnell lent instant support to the Boswell Project which aimed to reverse the decline of the fast-fading economy of Raasay through the creation of a new National Gallery for the Highlands in a disused early nineteenth-century steading on the island. Glasgow Life would provide the paintings and the technical support. This gallery would be the only substantial public gallery in the Western Highland region and would offer locals and visitors alike an entirely new cultural experience. Its economic impact would be wide and in particular it would offer a unique educational provision in the visual arts for children in schools throughout the region. Bridget's dedicated agent in this venture was Mark O'Neill. A phoenix gallery may still rise from these ashes. It needs to.

Bridget's instant and vital support for this project at first hearing was not just characteristic of the person who has done more than anyone to transform the cultural environment of Glasgow. It demonstrated an understanding of the historic link between Glasgow and Raasay and a key commitment to helping the less privileged around her. Equally extraordinary was the dedication and commitment to the project demonstrated by Mark. The energy and the generosity of spirit that drove them both was humbling to witness and it is to applaud and thank both of them that I have chosen, uniquely, to dedicate this Glasgow volume to them. Thank you.

All the volumes in our Scottish series should record my gratitude to Magnus Linklater, our Scottish Patron. Alert from the outset to the value of the project to Scotland as a whole, Magnus' hospitality, constant support, and guidance have greatly eased the tasks of all of us who have worked to bring this series to life. The Foundation is truly grateful to him.

Financial support for the Scottish project has come from many individuals, trusts and corporations and the generosity of their support for the public good is recorded in the front of this volume. The printing of this and other Scottish titles has however been made possible to a significant extent by the Mercer's Company in London, whose multi-faceted support and financial generosity I salute.

Fred Hohler, Founder

Facing page: Grandgérard, Lucien Henri, 1880–1970, *Adolescence*, 1935 (p. 172)

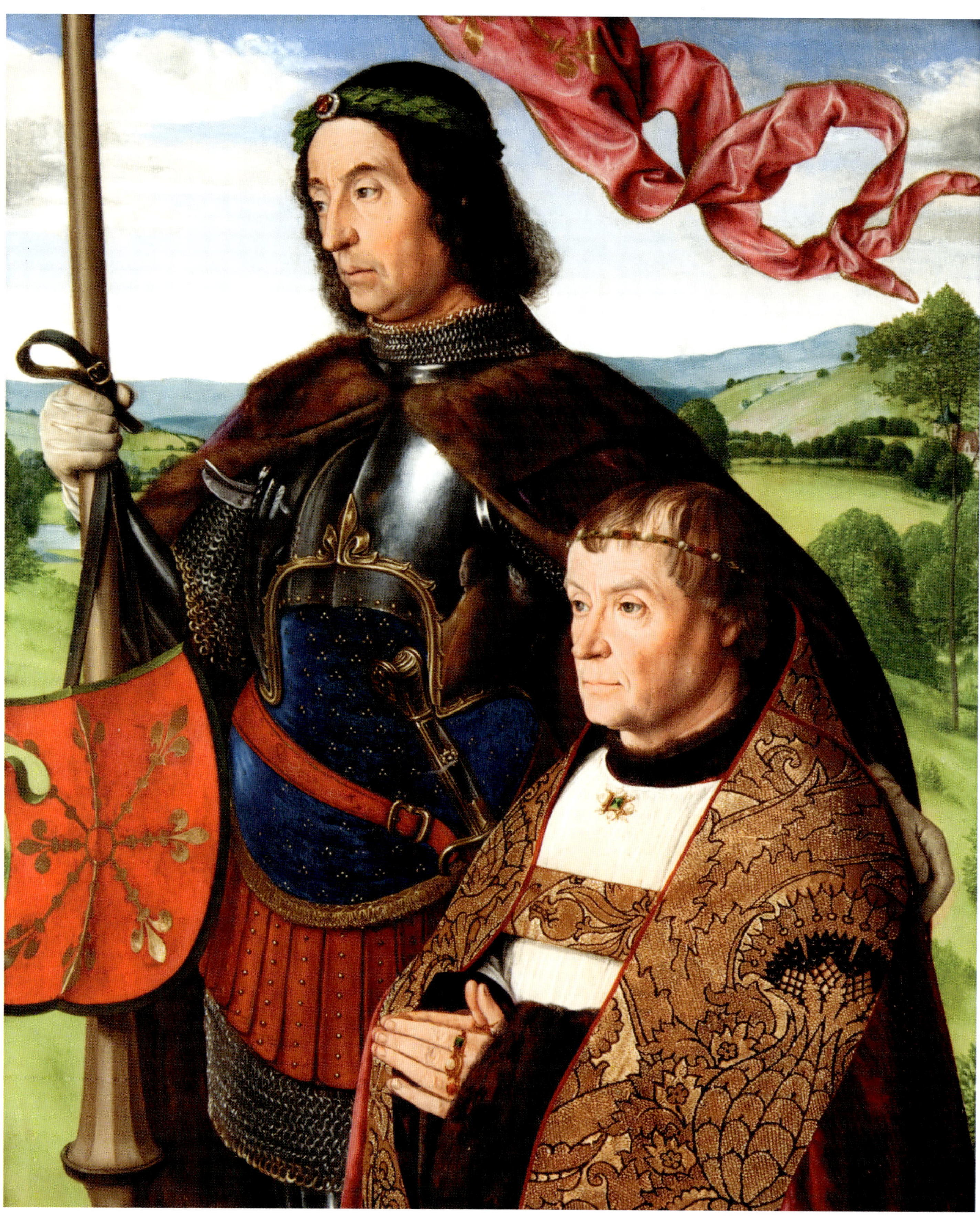

Preface

The City of Glasgow is extremely proud of its art collection and of its museums in general. From 1857 onwards, despite the inevitable fluctuations in civic finances, Glasgow citizens have funded the preservation, display and acquisition of works of art and have come to see them frequently and in large numbers. The result is that Glasgow's is the largest civic museum service in the UK, in terms of the number of venues, the scale of the collection and perhaps above all, in terms of visitor numbers. Together, the City's museums receive well over three million visits a year. More than a million of these are made by Glaswegians; from a population of 600,000, this is the highest level of museum visitation of any city in Britain. The service flagship, Kelvingrove Art Gallery and Museum, is the most visited museum in Britain outside London, while the Burrell Collection is world famous both for the range and quality of exquisite objects gathered by one man, and for the generosity of his gift to his native city. Though Sir William Burrell's gift was exceptional in its scale and quality, it was not so in spirit, as the spirit of generosity was shared by the thousands of donors who contributed to the creation of the collection. The numbers of gifts and visits are not separate; they both reflect the City's strong sense of identity and are mutually reinforcing. It would be no exaggeration to describe the collection and the museums in which it is housed as the collective creation of the citizens of Glasgow. The great variety of paintings donated, bequeathed and purchased reflect the City's high cultural ambitions and intense local, Scottish and international interests over a period of over 150 years. Just as we are delighted to welcome tourists (2.4 million in the past year) to see our treasures, we are very grateful to The Public Catalogue Foundation for enabling the world, for the first time, to see all of Glasgow's paintings in one publication.

Bailie Liz Cameron, Chair, Culture and Sport Glasgow

Facing page: Master of Moulins, active c.1475–c.1505, *Saint Maurice (or Saint Victor) with a Donor,* c.1500–1505 (p. 283)

The Public Catalogue Foundation: People Involved

Trustees & Advisors

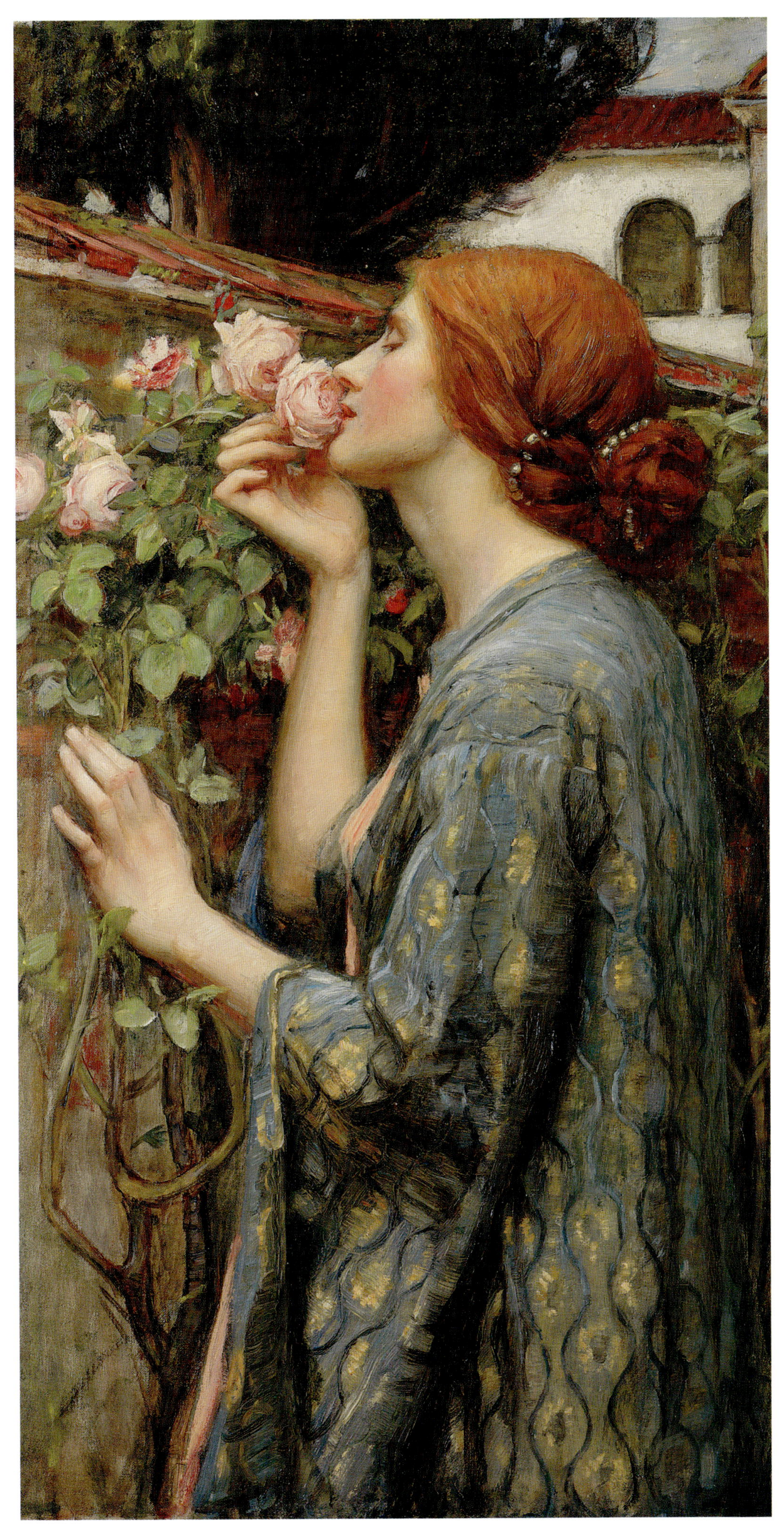

Christie's is proud to be the sponsor of The Public Catalogue Foundation in its pursuit to improve public access to paintings held in public collections in the UK.

Christie's is a name and place that speaks of extraordinary art. Founded in 1766 by James Christie, the company is now the world's leading art business. Many of the finest works of art in UK public collections have safely passed through Christie's, as the company has had the privilege of handling the safe cultural passage of some of the greatest paintings and objects ever created. Christie's today remains a popular showcase for the unique and the beautiful.
In addition to acquisition through auction sales, Christie's regularly negotiates private sales to the nation, often in lieu of tax, and remains committed to leading the auction world in the area of Heritage sales.

CHRISTIE'S

Financial Supporters for Scotland

The Public Catalogue Foundation would like to express its profound appreciation to the following organisations and individuals, who alongside the Mercers' Company, have supported the Scottish series.

Creative Scotland
Museums Galleries
   Scotland
NADFAS Scotland &
   Northern Ireland
   Area
Scottish Government

Binks Trust
Dunard Fund
The Hope Scott Trust
ICAP plc
The MacRobert Trust
Marc Fitch Fund
Nancie Massey
   Charitable Trust
P .F. Charitable Trust
Swire Charitable Trust

Marion Blythman
Janey Buchan
Rhona Callander
Lord William Douglas,
   Cullen of Whitekirk
James Ferguson
Mrs Patricia Grayburn
   MBE DL
Edward and Anna
   Hocknell
Allan and Carol
   Murray
Alexander Stewart

Catalogue Scope and Organisation

Medium and Support

The principal focus of this series is oil paintings. However, tempera and acrylic are also included as well as mixed media, where oil is the predominant constituent. Paintings on all forms of support (e.g. canvas, panel, etc.) are included as long as the support is portable. The principal exclusions are miniatures, hatchments or other purely heraldic paintings and wall paintings *in situ*.

Public Ownership

Public ownership has been taken to mean any paintings that are directly owned by the public purse, made accessible to the public by means of public subsidy or generally perceived to be in public ownership. The term 'public' refers to both central government and local government. Paintings held by national museums, local authority museums, English Heritage and independent museums, where there is at least some form of public subsidy, are included. Paintings held in civic buildings such as local government offices, town halls, guildhalls, public libraries, universities, hospitals, crematoria, fire stations and police stations are also included.

Geographical Boundaries of Catalogues

The geographical boundary of each county is the 'ceremonial county' boundary. This county definition includes all unitary authorities. Counties that have a particularly large number of paintings are divided between two or more catalogues on a geographical basis.

Criteria for Inclusion

As long as paintings meet the requirements above, all paintings are included irrespective of their condition and perceived quality. However, painting reproductions can only be included with the agreement of the participating collections and, where appropriate, the relevant copyright owner. It is rare that a collection forbids the inclusion of its paintings. Where this is the case and it is possible to obtain a list of paintings, this list is given in the Paintings Without Reproductions section. Where copyright consent is refused, the paintings are also listed in the Paintings Without Reproductions section. All paintings in collections' stacks and stores are included, as well as those on display. Paintings which have been lent to other institutions, whether for short-term exhibition or long-term loan, are listed under the owner collection. In addition, paintings on long-term loan are also included under the borrowing institution when they are likely to remain there for at least another five years from the date of publication of this catalogue. Information relating to owners and borrowers is listed in the Further Information section.

Layout

Collections are grouped together under their home town. These locations are listed in alphabetical order. In some cases collections that are spread over a number of locations are included under a single owner collection. A number of collections, principally the larger ones, are preceded by curatorial forewords. Within each collection paintings are listed in order of artist surname. Where there is more than one painting by the same artist, the paintings are listed chronologically, according to their execution date.

The few paintings that are not accompanied by photographs are listed in the Paintings Without Reproductions section.

There is additional reference material in the Further Information section at the back of the catalogue. This gives the full names of artists, titles and media if it has not been possible to include these in full in the main section. It also provides acquisition credit lines and information about loans in and out, as well as copyright and photographic credits for each painting. Finally, there is an index of artists' surnames.

Key to Painting Information

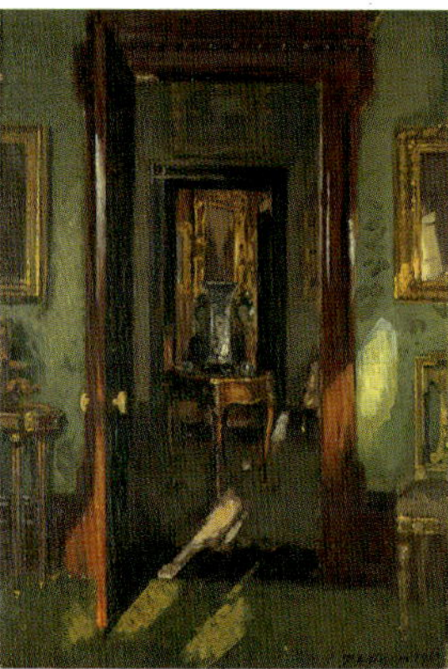

Adam, **Patrick William** 1854–1929
Interior, Rutland Lodge: Vista through Open Doors 1920
oil on canvas 67.3 × 45.7
LEEAG.PA.1925.0671.LACF

Almost all paintings are reproduced in the catalogue. Where this is not the case they are listed in the Paintings Without Reproductions section. Where paintings are missing or have been stolen, the best possible photograph on record has been reproduced. In some cases this may be black and white. Paintings that have been stolen are highlighted with a red border. Some paintings are shown with conservation tissue attached to parts of the painting surface.

Artist name This is shown with the surname first. Where the artist is listed on the Getty Union List of Artist Names (ULAN), ULAN's preferred presentation of the name is given. In a number of cases the name may not be a firm attribution and this is made clear. Where the artist name is not known, a school may be given instead. Where the school is not known, the painter name is listed as *unknown artist*. If the artist name is too long for the space, as much of the name is given as possible followed by (…). This indicates the full name is given at the rear of the catalogue in the Further Information section.

Painting title A painting title followed by *(?)* indicates that the title is in doubt. Where the alternative title to the painting is considered to be better known than the original, the alternative title is given in parentheses. Where the collection has not given a painting a title, the publisher does so instead and marks this with an asterisk. If the title is too long for the space, as much of the title is given as possible followed by *(…)* and the full title is given in the Further Information section.

Execution date In some cases the precise year of execution may not be known for certain. Instead an approximate date will be given or no date at all.

Artist dates Where known, the years of birth and death of the artist are given. In some cases one or both dates may not be known with certainty, and this is marked. No date indicates that even an approximate date is not known. Where only the period in which the artist was active is known, these dates are given and preceded with the word *active*.

Medium and support Where the precise material used in the support is known, this is given.

Dimensions All measurements refer to the unframed painting and are given in cm with up to one decimal point. In all cases the height is shown before the width. An (E) indicates where a painting has not been measured and its size has been calculated by sight only. If the painting is circular, the single dimension is the diameter. If the painting is oval, the dimensions are height and width.

Collection inventory number In the case of paintings owned by museums, this number will always be the accession number. In all other cases it will be a unique inventory number of the owner institution. (P) indicates that a painting is a private loan. Details can be found in the Further Information section. Accession numbers preceded by 'PCF' indicate that the collection did not have an accession number at the time of catalogue production and therefore the number given has been temporarily allocated by The Public Catalogue Foundation. The symbol indicates that the reproduction is based on a Bridgeman Art Library transparency (go to www.bridgemanart.com) or that Bridgeman administers the copyright for that artist.

Facing page: French (Amiens) School, *Angel of the Annunciation*, (p. 144)

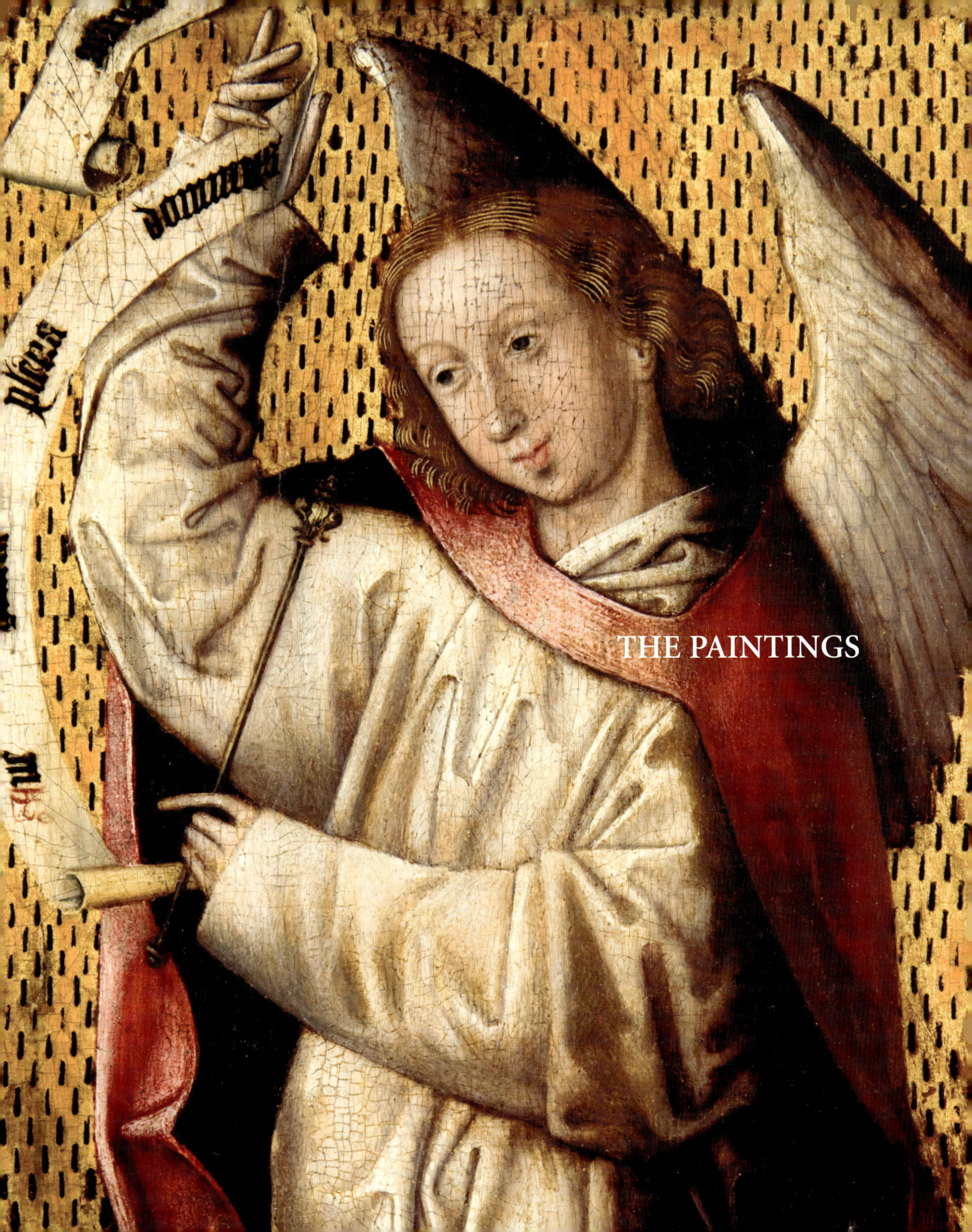
THE PAINTINGS

Glasgow Museums

The City of Glasgow owns one of the finest museum collections in Europe, consisting of approximately one million objects cared for by Culture and Sport Glasgow. These encompass a broad spectrum of art and design, human history, natural history, and transport and technology. The art collection is recognised as one of the best in the UK, and covers a wide range of media including paintings, drawings, prints, sculpture, metalwork, ceramics, glass, jewellery, furniture and textiles. It provides a comprehensive overview of the history of European art and design, with masterpieces by major artists such as Rembrandt, Van Gogh, Whistler and Dalí. Works from non-European cultures include an internationally renowned collection of Chinese art.

The development of the art collection began with the 1854 bequest of 510 paintings by Glasgow coachbuilder Archibald McLellan (1795–1854). He was a prolific collector of Italian, Dutch and Flemish art, and his gift included gems such as *The Annunciation* by Botticelli and studio, and Titian's *Christ and the Adulteress*. Unfortunately, McLellan was insolvent at the time of his death, and there were numerous claims on his property by his creditors. Before the City could acquire the collection, it had to pay off his debts and it was only after more than a year of debate and a narrow vote in Council that the collection was acquired. One of those who argued strongly for the acquisition was the philanthropist and collector William Euing (1788–1874), who donated 30 paintings from his own collection shortly after McLellan's collection was purchased. He later bequeathed the remainder of his collection of some 200 works to the City. Among the paintings he bequeathed is Saenredam's *Interior of St Bavo's, Haarlem, with a Catholic Baptism*.

Another major acquisition came in 1877, when Jane Graham-Gilbert, widow of the portrait painter John Graham-Gilbert (1794–1866), died and bequeathed her husband's collection and all his unfinished works. Among the 70 works are copies of Italian paintings made during his training, as well as Italian and Dutch Old Masters such as Rembrandt's *A Man in Armour*, one of the greatest works in the Collection.

While the Collection itself was growing and improving, the gallery in which it was displayed was becoming something of an embarrassment to the city. Archibald McLellan's partially-completed gallery was acquired along with his collection and was used as the Corporation's art gallery. In order to recoup the cost it was hired out for balls and soirées, and the physical damage incurred during these gatherings was compounded by poor ventilation, dirty gas lighting and a lack of maintenance. By the late nineteenth century, Glasgow had become one of the principal manufacturing and commercial centres in the country and was styling itself as the Second City of the Empire. In order to reflect this status, the City decided to create a new combined museum and art gallery, which, in the words of the Convener of the Museums and Galleries Committee, would be 'adequate for the necessities and dignity of the great commercial and industrial city of Glasgow'. In 1888, the city's first International Exhibition was held expressly to raise funds for the new museum. This was followed in 1901 with a second International Exhibition, to celebrate the newly constructed Kelvingrove Art Gallery and Museum and to raise funds for future acquisitions.

Glasgow's massive expansion in the late nineteenth century saw the rise of an industrial elite who developed a taste for collecting art. Many were extremely discerning and knowledgeable, and their gifts now form the backbone of the collection. Their motivations for giving were a mixture of civic pride, philanthropy and status aggrandizement, but most adhered to McLellan's belief that 'the study of what are called the "fine arts" is eminently conducive to the elevation and refinement of all classes, as well as intimately connected with the manufacturing and mercantile prosperity of this community.' Among the industrialist collectors who donated paintings were the shipbuilder Isabella Elder, the chemical manufacturer William J. Chrystal and the engineer Sir John Richmond.

Dr T. J. Honeyman, Director of the Museums Service from 1939 to 1954, was highly influential in encouraging industrialist collectors to donate to the City. He courted William McInnes, a shipping company owner with a particular fondness for French art, for many years. McInnes bequeathed over 70 paintings in 1944 including Monet's *Vétheuil*, Van Gogh's *The Blute-Fin Windmill, Montmartre* and Picasso's *The Flower Seller*.

However, the greatest gift came from shipping magnate Sir William Burrell and his wife. Their collection of nearly 9,000 objects included a vast array of works from every period from all over the world, including important medieval tapestries, stained glass, English oak furniture, European paintings and sculpture, and important collections of Chinese and Islamic art. Significant paintings in his collection include Rembrandt's *Self Portrait*, Degas' *The Rehearsal*, and Cézanne's *The Château of Médan*. One of the remarkable strengths of the Burrells' collection is that Sir William deliberately purchased groups of works by specific artists including Géricault, Millet, Daumier, Courbet, Manet and Degas. However, some of the most important works by Millet, Manet and Degas are pastels and they are out of the remit of this catalogue.

As well as receiving gifts from private collectors, the Museums Service has been very active in purchasing art. The most high-profile acquisition was undoubtedly Dalí's *Christ of St John of the Cross*. This was an inspired purchase by Dr Honeyman, a friend of Dalí's, who managed to secure the work despite major opposition in the Council and from students of the Glasgow School of Art. However, it received major public acclaim and has remained one of the most iconic and loved paintings in Glasgow's Collection. The painting was purchased from the remainder of the 1901 Exhibition purchase fund, but other major acquisitions have been made possible using funds from the Hamilton Bequest, which derives from the combined estates of the storekeeper John Hamilton and his two sisters, Elizabeth and Christina. They gave a sum of money in 1927 solely for the purchase of oil paintings for Kelvingrove. The fund is still administered by the Hamilton Trustees, and has presented some 80 paintings including Rossetti's *Regina cordium*, Gauguin's *Østre Anlæg Park, Copenhagen* and Monet's *View of Ventimiglia*.

Thus, with a combination of generous gifts and judicious purchasing, Glasgow Museums has established an internationally significant art collection with major strengths in European and Scottish art.

The collection of Italian paintings is among the finest, both intellectually and aesthetically, held by any municipal museum service in the UK. It includes works ranging from the fourteenth to the late ninteenth century, originating from the main artistic centres of Italy such as Venice, Bologna,

Rome, Florence and Naples. A number of important fifteenth- and sixteenth-century Venetian School works by major artists such as Giovanni Bellini, Titian and Paris Bordon form the backbone of the collection. It also includes paintings closely associated with the workshops of Botticelli and Pesellino, and boasts seventeenth- and eighteenth-century works of particularly high quality and importance by Carlo Dolci, Domenichino, Francesco Guardi and Salvator Rosa.

The Spanish collection is the second largest in the UK. The majority of the paintings date from the late sixteenth and seventeenth centuries, and include works by El Greco, Cano, Murillo, Velázquez (school of), and Ribera (studio of). Later works include paintings by Goya, Juan Gris and Dalí. The collection of Spanish paintings is of particular historical interest, having been formed largely by the pioneering local collector William Stirling-Maxwell (1818–1878). The substantial group of Habsburg portraits, which reflects Stirling-Maxwell's preoccupation with the history of Spain, is the finest outside Madrid and Vienna.

The Dutch and Flemish collection is of unusual depth and breadth, and is among the largest in the world outside the great national or princely collections. It includes paintings, watercolours and gouaches made between c.1450 and c.1960. Dutch art forms the largest part of this collection. Old Masters include Rembrandt, Lairesse and works attributed to, or after, Rubens. Later works include a significant collection of nineteenth-century Dutch School paintings. The majority of the works from the southern Netherlands date from the seventeenth century, as well as the fine sixteenth-century work *Virgin and Child by a Fountain* by Bernaert van Orley and studio.

The collection of French nineteenth-century oils is one of the largest, finest and most important in the UK. It covers some of the key artistic movements of this time, with stunning individual masterpieces and works by many of the most important French artists working in the period from 1800 to 1950. The collection ranges from early nineteenth-century works by Théodore Géricault to paintings by Braque and Matisse from the early twentieth century. It covers a wide range of styles, including the Barbizon School, Impressionism, Post-Impressionism and Fauvism.

The British collection is more patchy, but includes some outstanding individual masterpieces by key artists. Most of the works are of high artistic quality, and the collection as a whole provides a substantial contribution towards an overview of British art. Among the more significant works are Turner's *Modern Italy: The Pifferari* and Whistler's internationally important *Arrangement in Grey and Black, No.2: Portrait of Thomas Carlyle*, the first painting by the artist to enter a public collection.

The Scottish collection, in contrast, is one of the most comprehensive in the country, being especially rich in nineteenth- and twentieth-century painting. It includes works by many of the key figures in Scottish art, including Henry Raeburn, Horatio McCulloch, William McTaggart and Joan Eardley. It includes eighteenth- and nineteenth-century portraits, eighteenth- and nineteenth-century landscapes, and Scottish Victorian narrative and history paintings.

The collection of works by the Glasgow Boys is of great significance, and the overall aesthetic quality of the works is extremely high. The most significant areas of the collection include an excellent group of 'rustic realist' pictures painted in the early 1880s by James Guthrie, James Paterson and William Kennedy, including Guthrie's *Old Willie: The Village Worthy* and *A Funeral Service in the Highlands*. The group of 'symbolist' pictures from the 1890s includes *The Druids: Bringing in the Mistletoe*, a joint collaboration by Henry and Hornel. The breadth of the collection is such that many lesser known Glasgow Boy artists are also represented by significant works in their careers.

The collection of Scottish Colourists also has excellent breadth and depth, and includes a fine group of early landscapes painted in Scotland and France by Fergusson and Peploe, a series of mature landscapes mainly of Scottish views by Peploe, Cadell and Hunter, a group of Cadell 'ladies in interiors', an excellent group of Peploe still lifes, and some strong figurative compositions painted in Paris by Fergusson.

More recent Scottish artists such as John Bellany and John Byrne are also well represented in the collection. Their work paved the way for a renewed interest in figurative and narrative painting exemplified by the New Glasgow Boys – Peter Howson, Ken Currie, Adrian Wiszniewski and Steven Campbell. The collection contains some rare and unique examples of their work, including Currie's monumental and eerie *The Bathers* and Howson's popular *The Glorious Game*. Glasgow has established its reputation as an international centre for contemporary visual arts, and the collection contains a number of important works by Glasgow-based artists who have become internationally significant, including a number of Turner Prize winners, although few of these contemporary artists are currently working in oil.

As with most municipal collections, some works are important for their high artistic merit, while others are important because their subject matter provides an important historical record of local people and places.

The principal museums in which the collection is displayed are Kelvingrove Art Gallery and Museum, which has comprehensive displays of the major Scottish and European paintings, the Burrell Collection, where Sir William Burrell's collection can be seen, and the Gallery of Modern Art, which displays elements of the permanent collection alongside temporary exhibitions. Paintings of a local character can be seen at the People's Palace and Winter Gardens, which has an important early commission from Ken Currie. Glasgow's Spanish paintings can still be seen in Pollok House, the former home of William Stirling-Maxwell, now run on the City's behalf by the National Trust for Scotland. Paintings not on display can be accessed at Glasgow Museums Resource Centre, which now includes one of the largest painting stores in Europe.

This is the first time that the whole collection of Glasgow Museums' oil paintings has been brought together and we are very grateful to The Public Catalogue Foundation for the chance to do so.

Martin Bellamy, Major Projects and Research Manager

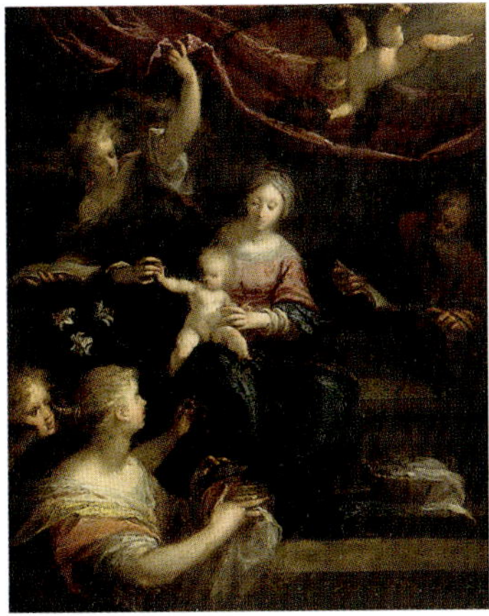

Aachen, Hans von 1552–1615
The Holy Family with Angels c.1572
oil on copper 26.7 x 21.6
129

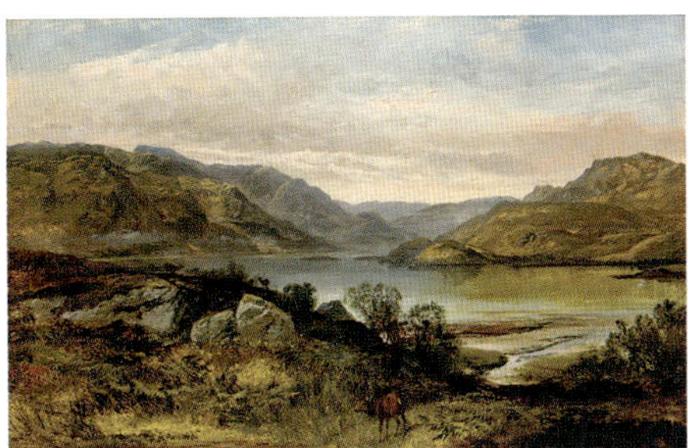

Adam, Joseph 1819–1886
Overlooking Glendaruel, Kyles of Bute
oil on canvas 33 x 50.8
880

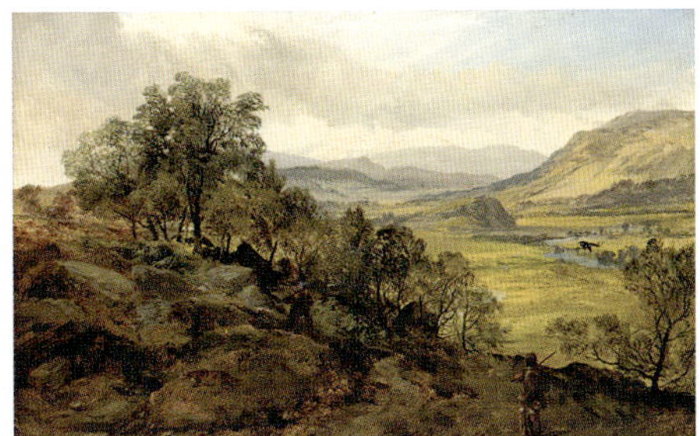

Adam, Joseph 1819–1886 & **Roe, Robert Henry** 1822–1905
Strathblane
oil on canvas 33 x 50.8
878

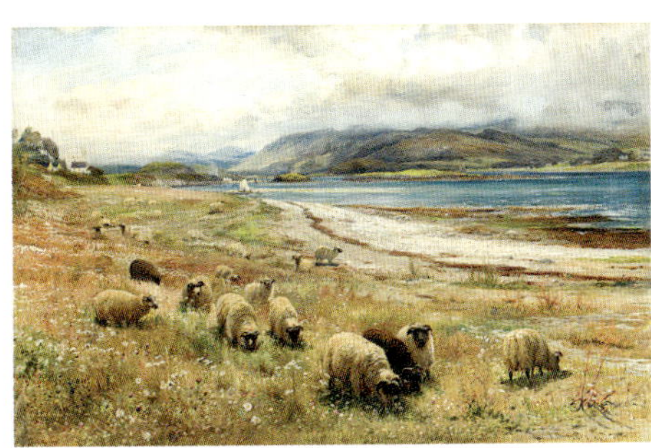

Adam, Joseph Denovan 1841–1896
In Clover 1885
oil on canvas 90.2 x 137.2
768

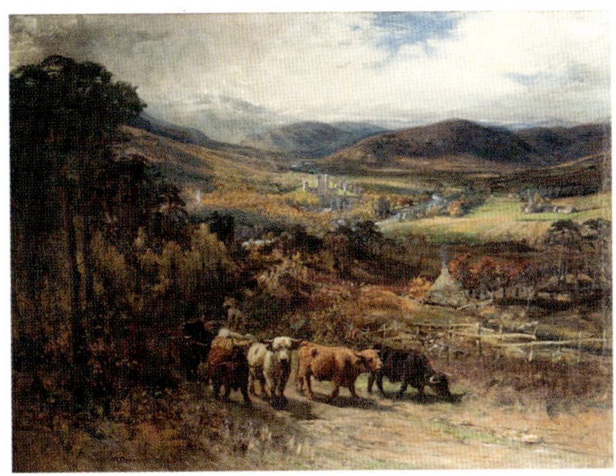

Adam, Joseph Denovan 1841–1896
Balmoral, Autumn
oil on canvas 172.7 x 228.6
748

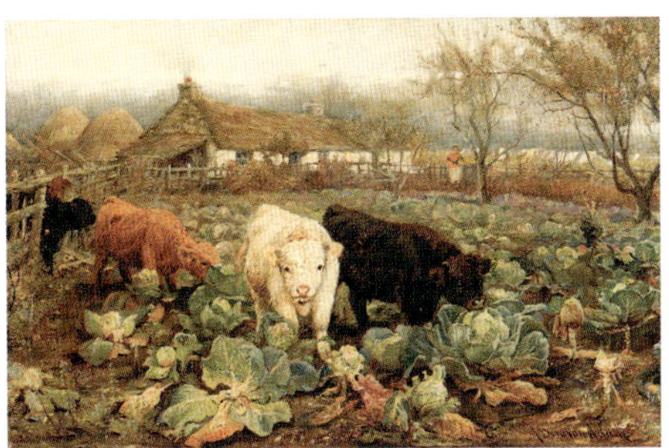

Adam, Joseph Denovan 1841–1896
Calves in the Cabbage Patch
oil on canvas 91.4 x 141
3442

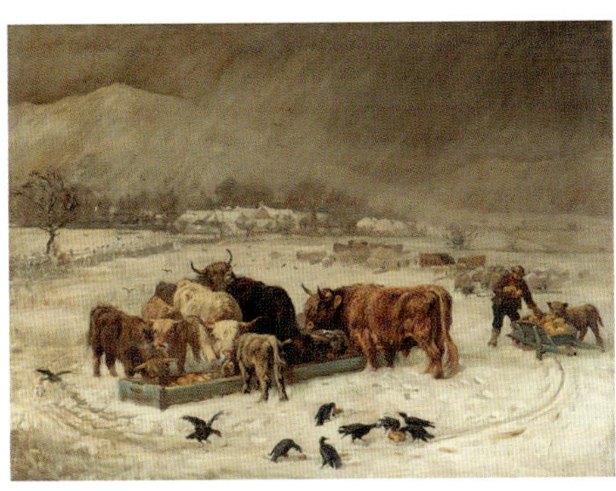

Adam, Joseph Denovan 1841–1896
December, near Callander
oil on canvas 116.8 x 152.4
2311

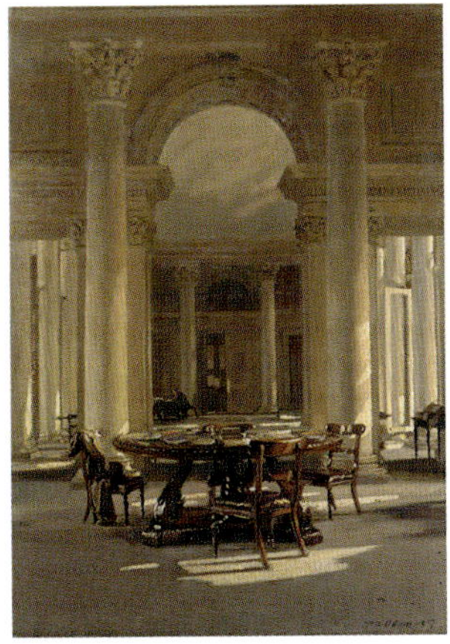

Adam, Patrick William 1854–1929
Interior: The Signet Library, Edinburgh 1917
oil on canvas 114.3 x 77.5
1459

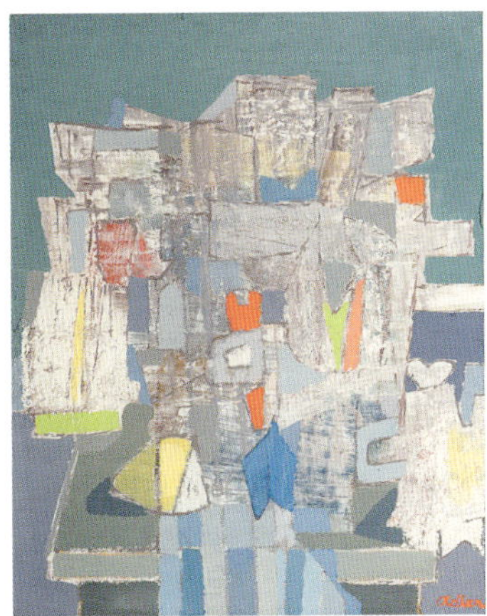

Adler, Jankel 1895–1949
Composition
oil on board 63.5 x 50.8
2981

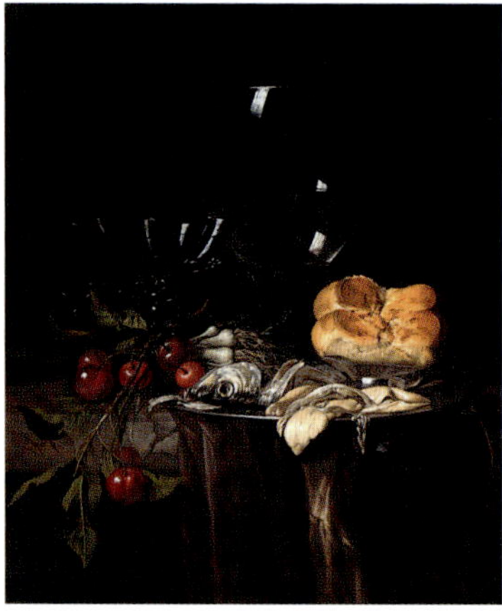

Aelst, Willem van 1627–after 1687
*Still Life: Herring, Cherries and
Glassware* 1680
oil on canvas 50.2 x 42.5
307

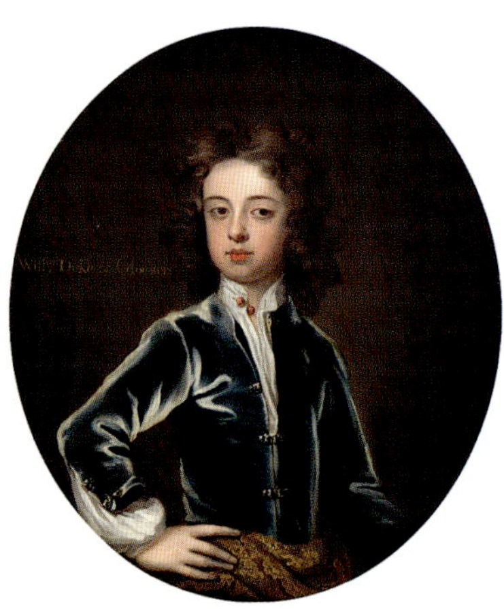

Agar, Charles d' (attributed to) 1669–1723
Portrait of a Boy
oil on canvas 76.8 x 66.1
35.295

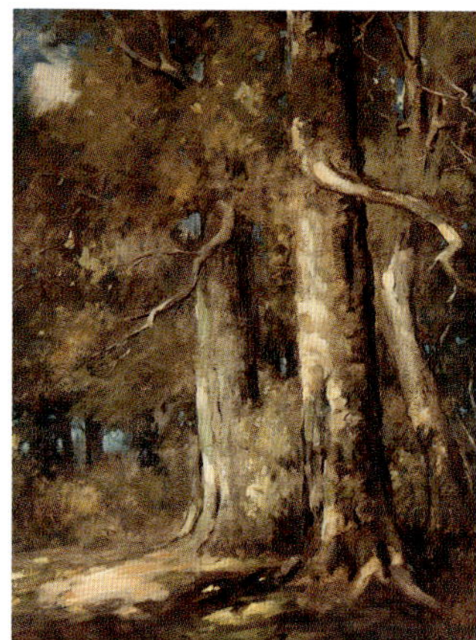

Ahrens, Carl 1864–1938
The Glade
oil on canvas 61 x 35.5
3427

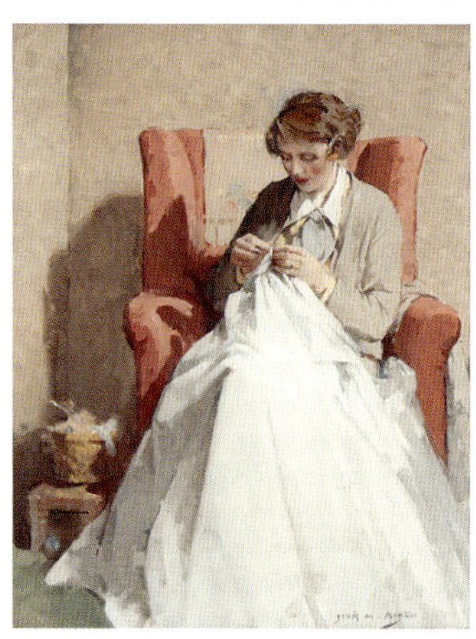

Aiken, John MacDonald 1880–1961
The Seamstress c.1939
oil on canvas 91.4 x 71.1
2158

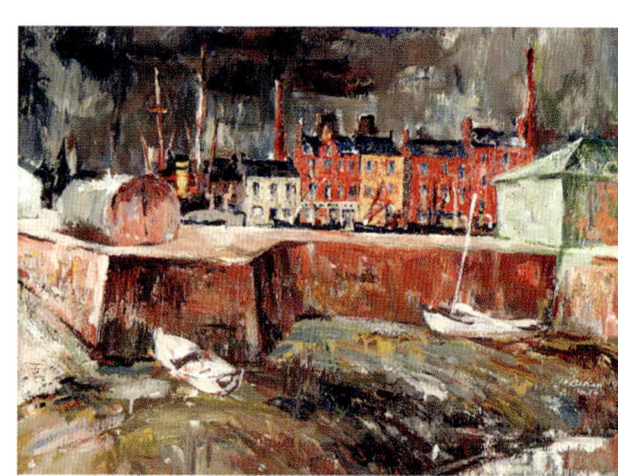

Aiken, John P. 1919–1966
Low Tide, Arbroath 1954
oil on panel 50.8 x 70.5
3021

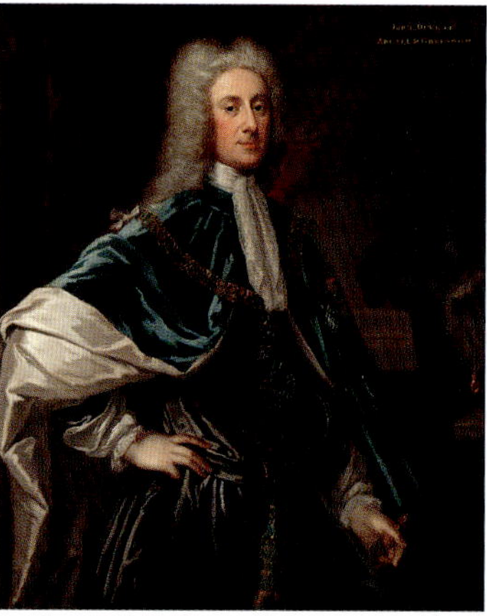

Aikman, William 1682–1731
*John Dalrymple (1673–1747), 2nd Earl of Stair
or John Campbell (1680–1743), Duke of Argyll
and Greenwich*
oil on canvas 128.2 x 99.7
3139

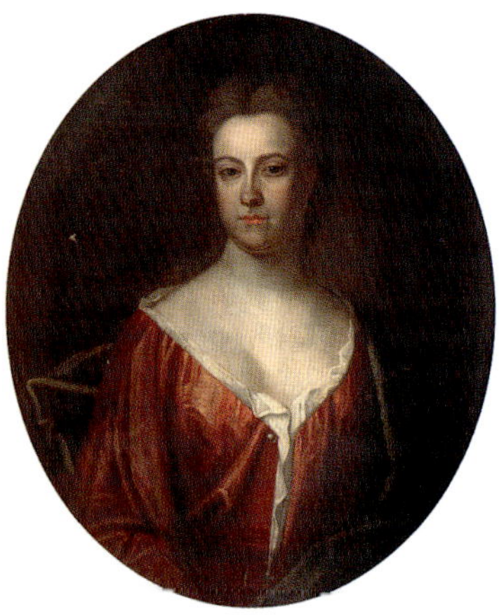

Aikman, William (attributed to) 1682–1731
Lady Anne Maxwell (d.1720)
oil on canvas 76 x 63.3
PL.171 (P)

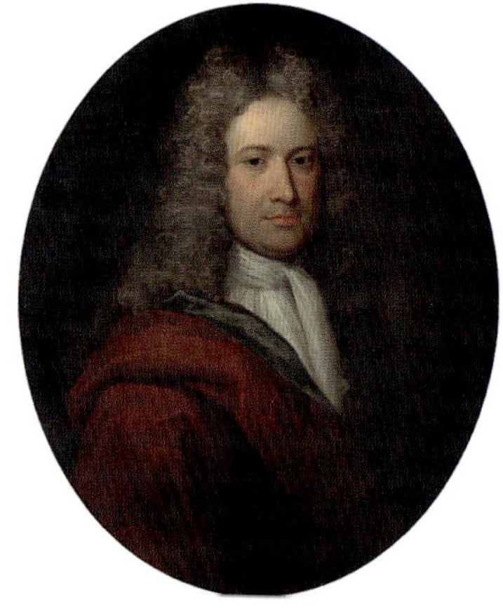

Aikman, William (attributed to) 1682–1731
Sir John Maxwell (1686–1752), 2nd Bt
oil on canvas 74.4 x 62.5
PL.170 (P)

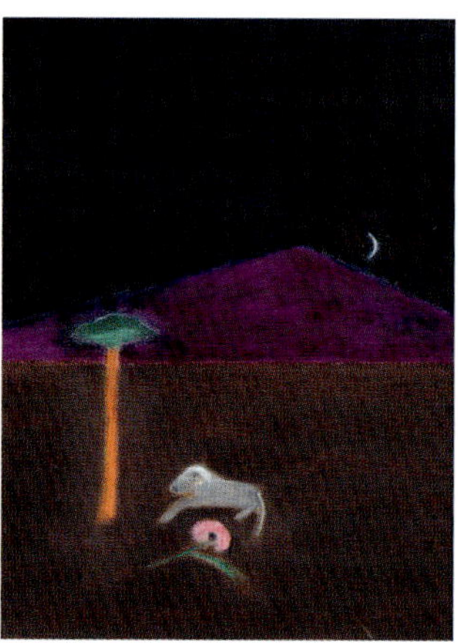

Aitchison, Craigie Ronald John 1926–2009
Wayney Dead 2 1986
oil on board 34.9 x 27.3
3417

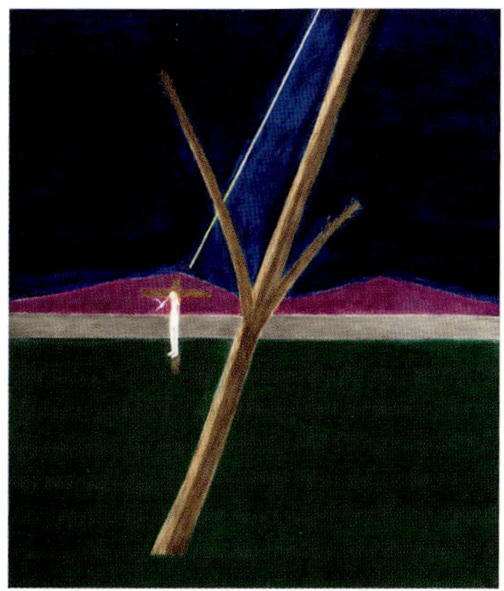

Aitchison, Craigie Ronald John 1926–2009
Crucifixion VII 1988–1989
oil on canvas 213 x 177.8
3467

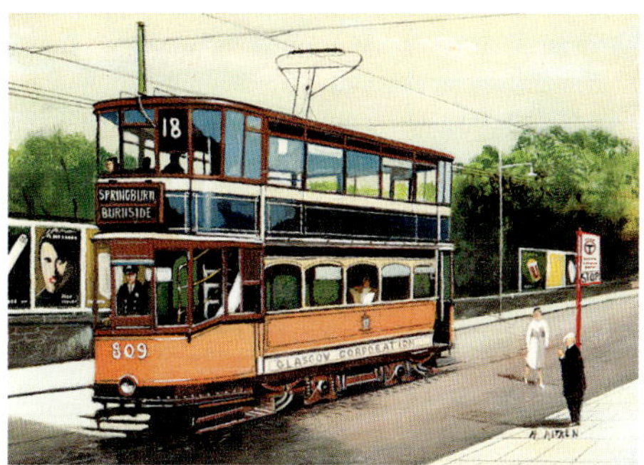

Aitken, Henry
Springburn Tram
oil on canvas 29.5 x 39.5
TEMP.15448

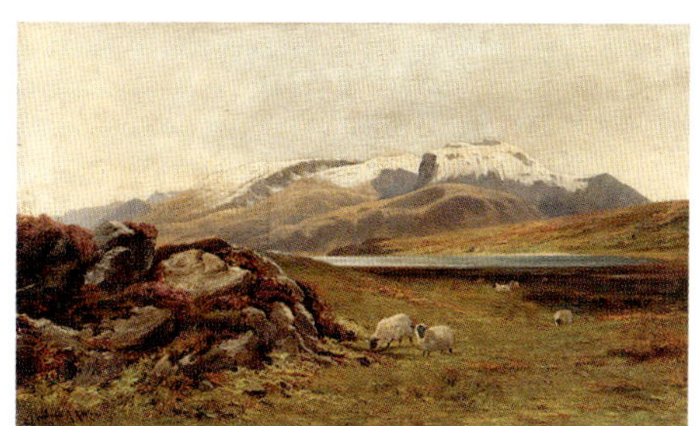

Aitken, James Alfred 1846–1897
Ben Nevis: The First Snow
oil on canvas 76.2 x 127
3448

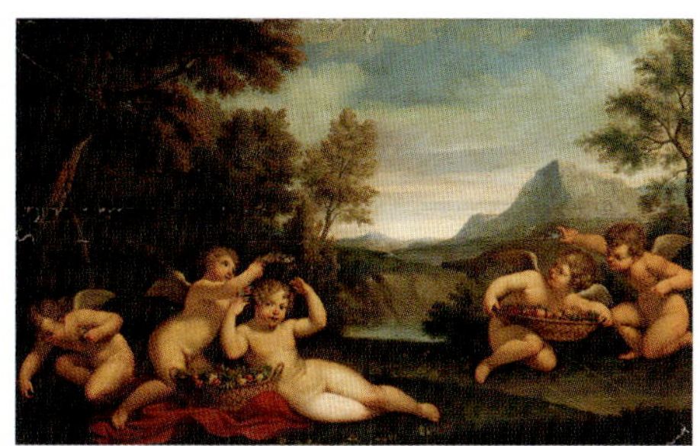

Albani, Francesco (after) 1578–1660
Cupids at Play 18th C (?)
oil on copper 61.2 x 103.5
136

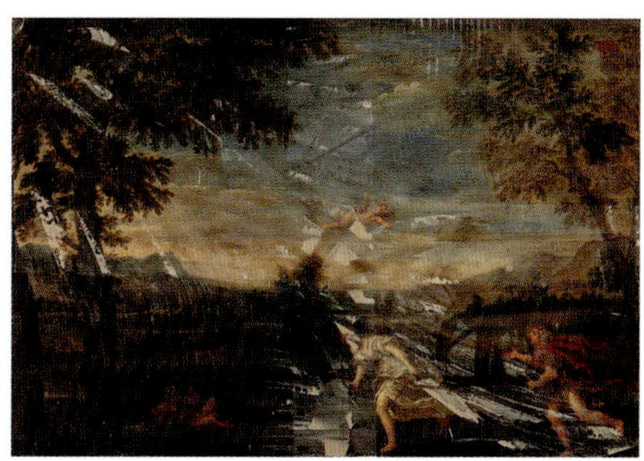

Albani, Francesco (studio of) 1578–1660
Apollo and Daphne c.1640–1650
oil on copper 31.8 x 42.7
133

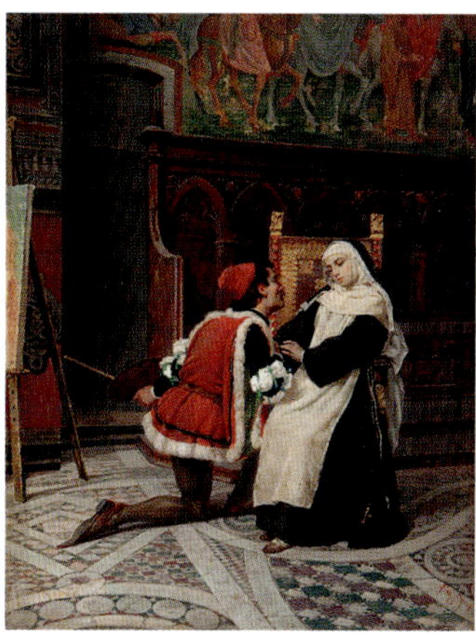

Aldi, Pietro 1852–1888
A Painter and His Model 1879
oil on panel 27.1 x 20.2
2146

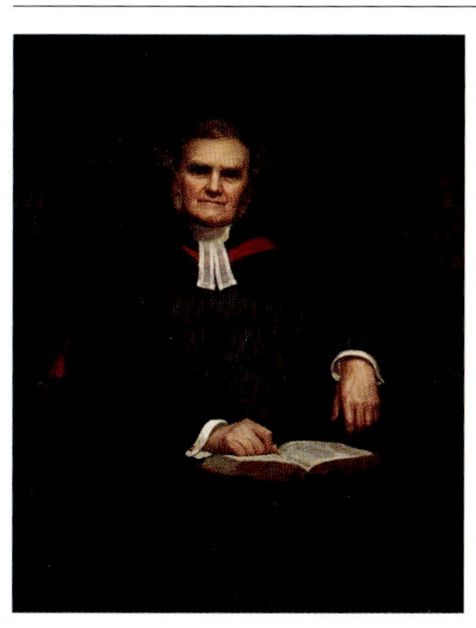

Alexander, Ella Hean 1862–1951
Reverend Dr George Reith (b.1842) 1909
oil on canvas 127 x 101.6
3295

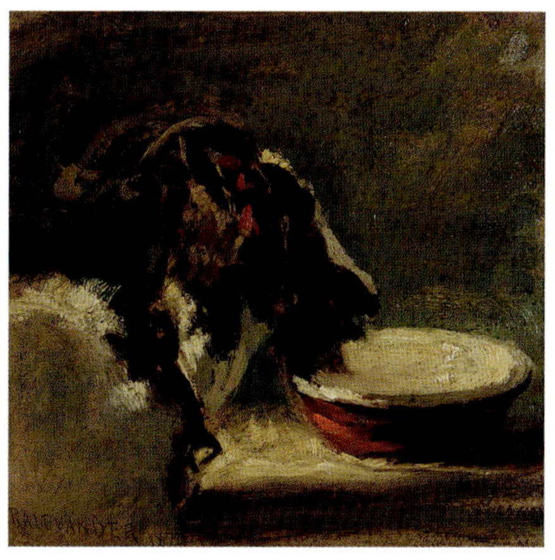

Alexander, Robert L. 1840–1923
Head of a Goat 1874
oil on millboard 17.8 x 17.8
1579

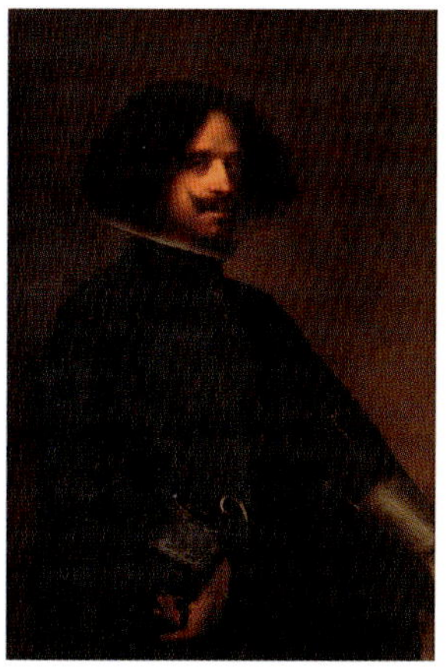

Alfaro y Gámez, Juan de 1643–1688
Diego Velázquez (1599–1660)
oil on canvas 101 x 66
PC.106

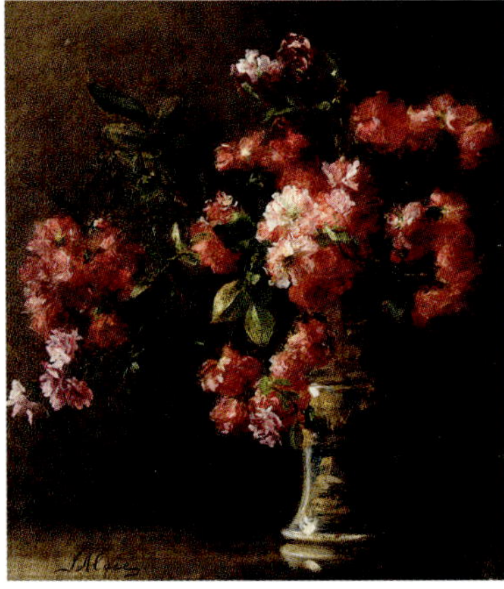

Algie, Jessie 1859–1927
Rambler Roses
oil on canvas 45.7 x 40.6
2871

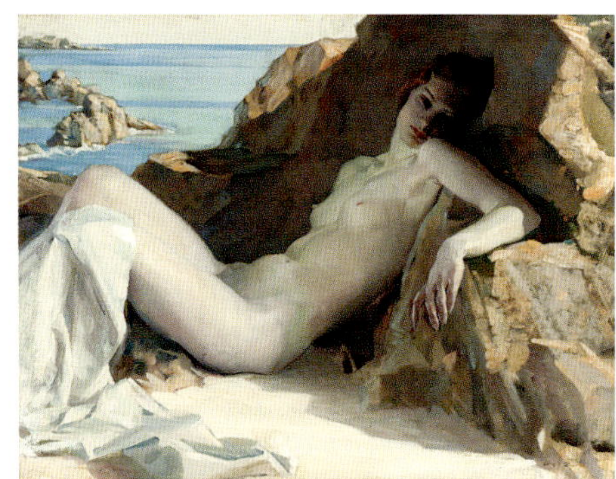

Alison, Henry Young 1889–1972
Youth c.1936
oil on canvas 86.4 x 112.4
2065

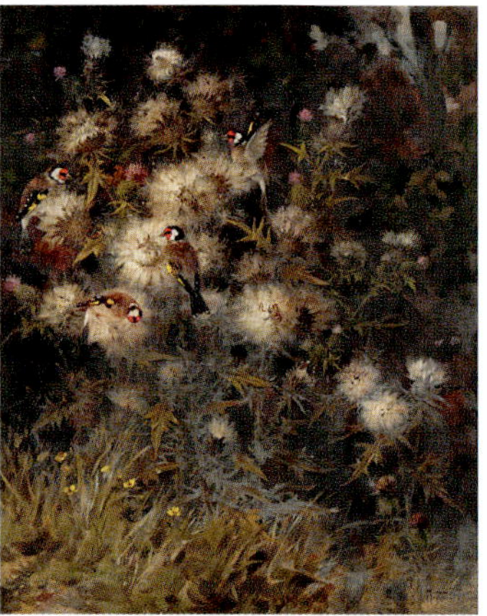

Allan, Andrew 1863–1942
Thistledown
oil on canvas 76.2 x 60.9
2318

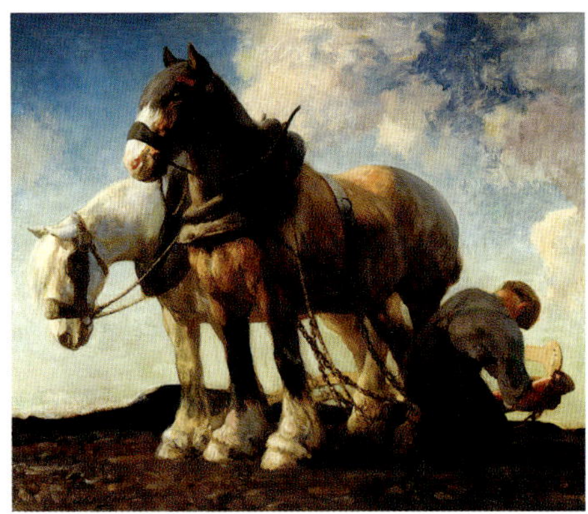

Allan, Archibald Russell Watson 1878–1959
The Top of the Hill c.1924
oil on canvas 130.8 x 154.9
1600

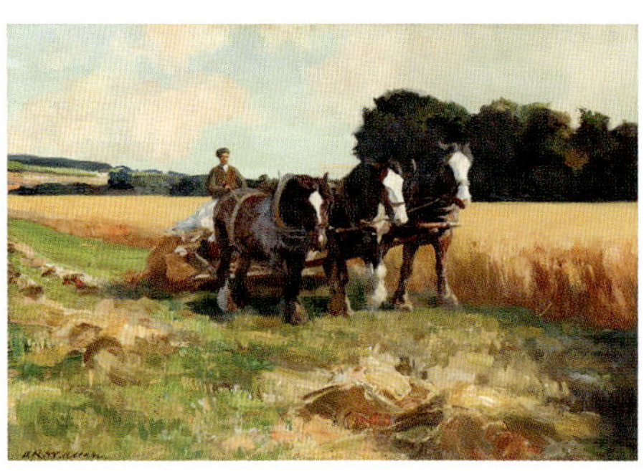

Allan, Archibald Russell Watson 1878–1959
Harvest Time
oil on canvas 60.9 x 91.4
2643

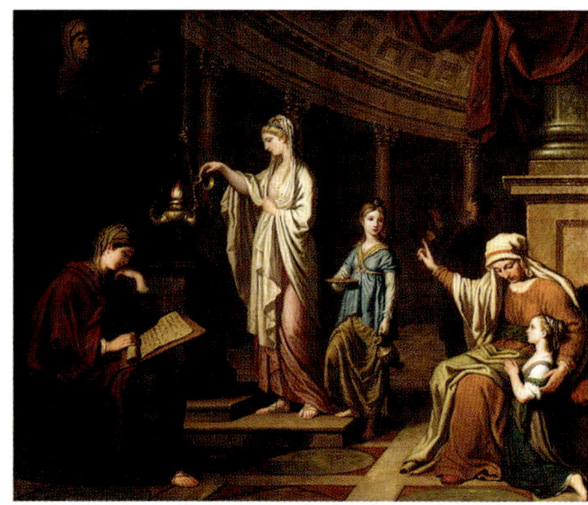

Allan, David 1744–1796
The Vestals Attending the Sacred Fire 1772
oil on canvas 148.6 x 174
3402

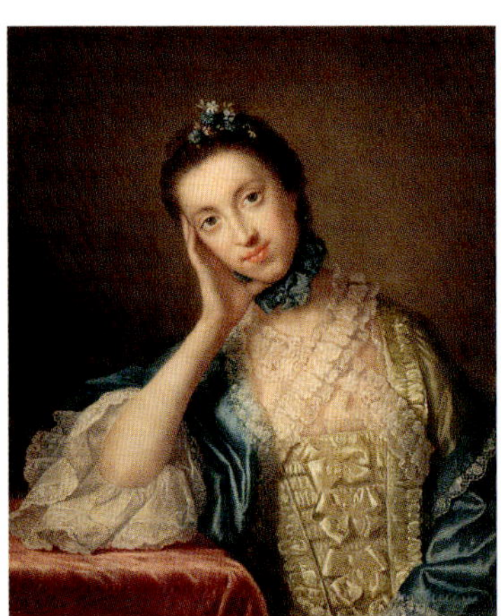

Allan, David 1744–1796
Jean Duff (1746–1805), Lady Grant c.1780
oil on canvas 73.7 x 60.9
2204

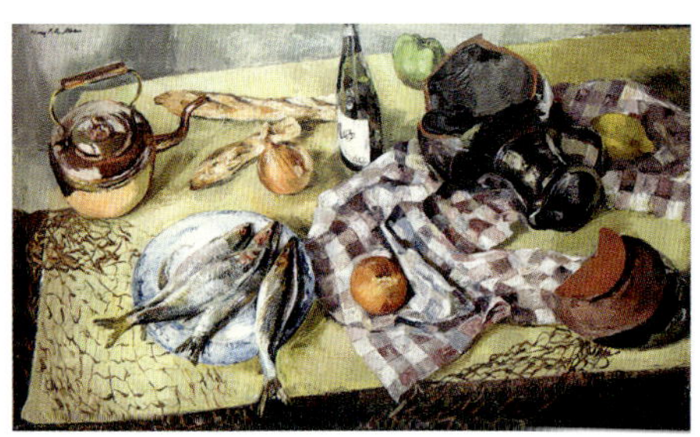

Allan, Mary Parsons Reid 1917–2002
Still Life with Fish c.1953
oil on canvas 55.9 x 91.4
3033

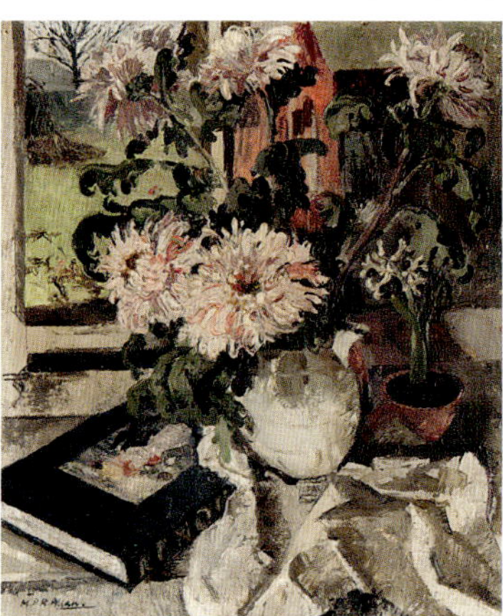

Allan, Mary Parsons Reid 1917–2002
Still Life with Flowers and 'Renoir' Book
oil on canvas 52 x 43
ME.2007.1.155

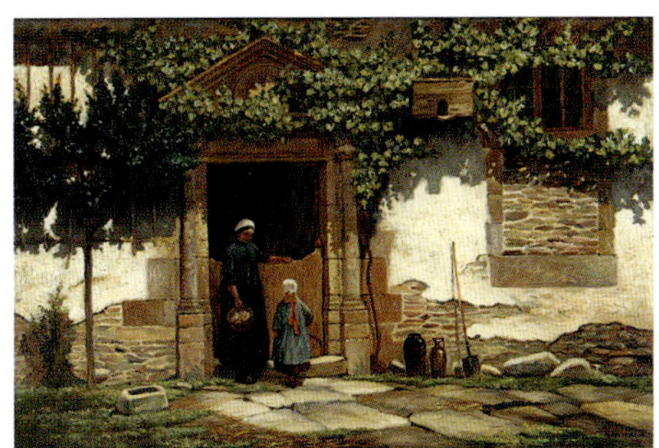

Allan, Robert Weir 1852–1942
Doorway and Figures 1875
oil on canvas 39.4 x 59.7
873

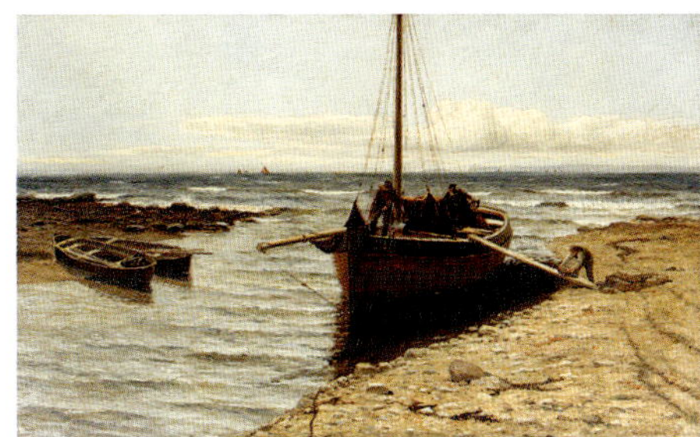

Allan, Robert Weir 1852–1942
Home from the Herring Fishing 1876
oil on canvas 85.1 x 137.2
793

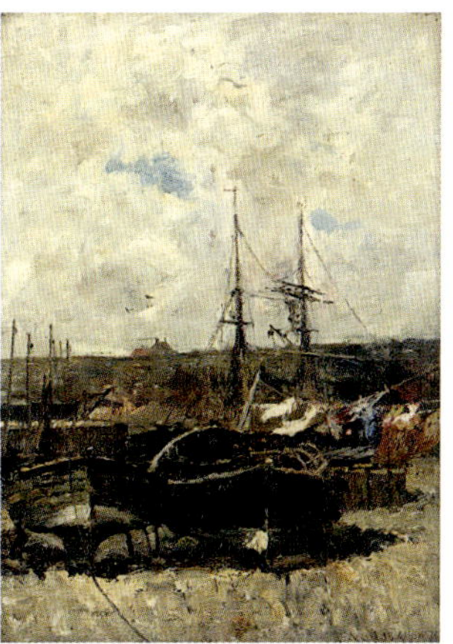

Allan, Robert Weir 1852–1942
Crail Harbour 1879
oil on canvas 52.1 x 36.8
1250

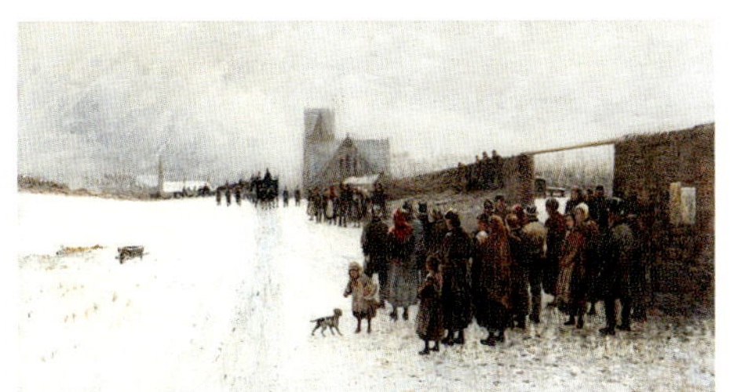

Allan, Robert Weir 1852–1942
The Funeral of Thomas Carlyle 1881
oil on canvas 66 x 124.5
1286

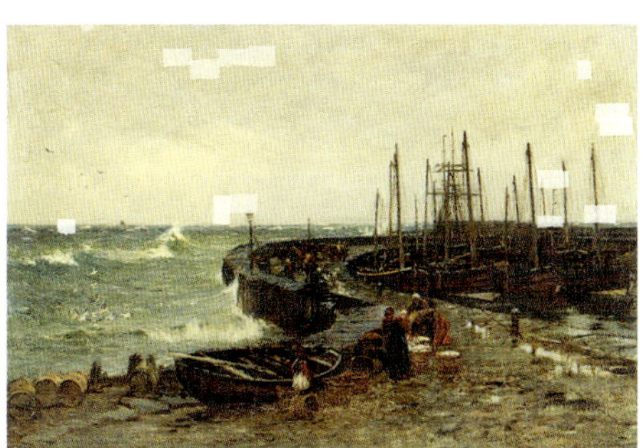

Allan, Robert Weir 1852–1942
Sheltered from the Stormy Sea 1904
oil on canvas 123.2 x 184.2
1078

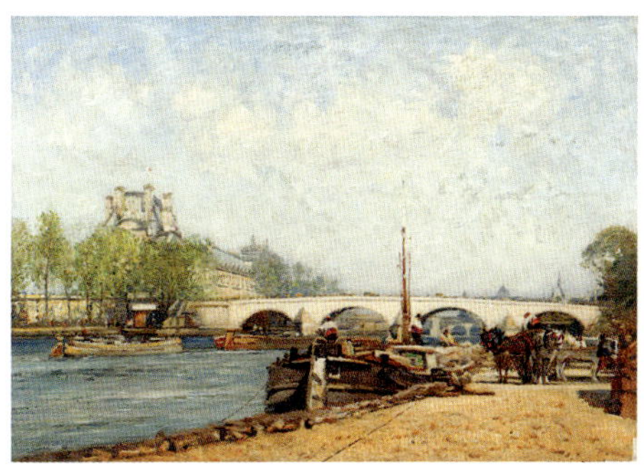

Allan, Robert Weir 1852–1942
Paris, River Scene 1925
oil on canvas 96.5 x 121.9
NR.54

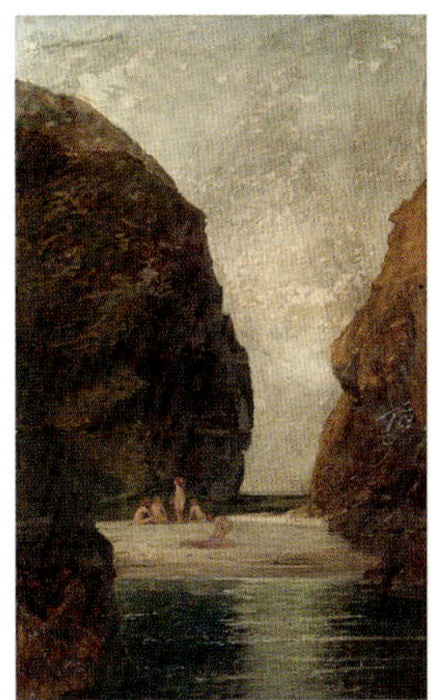

Allan, Robert Weir 1852–1942
Bathing Scene
oil on canvas 152.4 x 91.4
NR.116

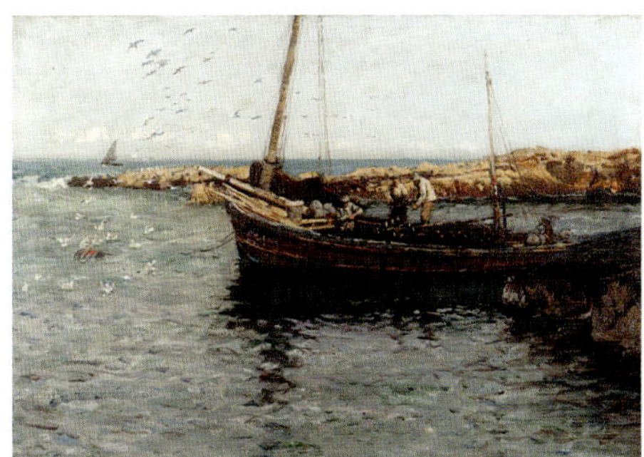

Allan, Robert Weir 1852–1942
Home with a Good Fishing
oil on canvas 86.4 x 109.2
NR.55

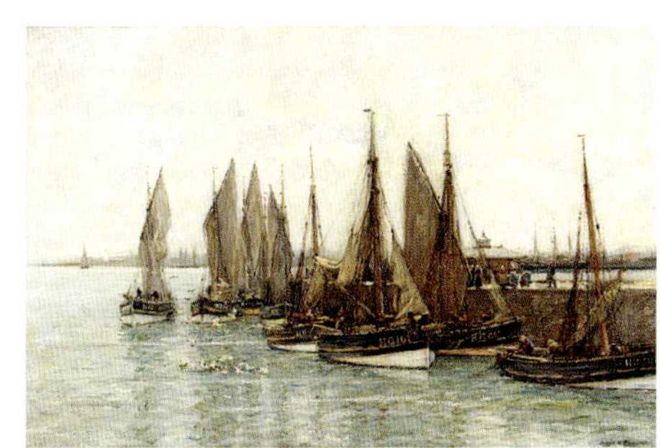

Allan, Robert Weir 1852–1942
In from the Sea
oil on canvas 121.9 x 182.9
2299

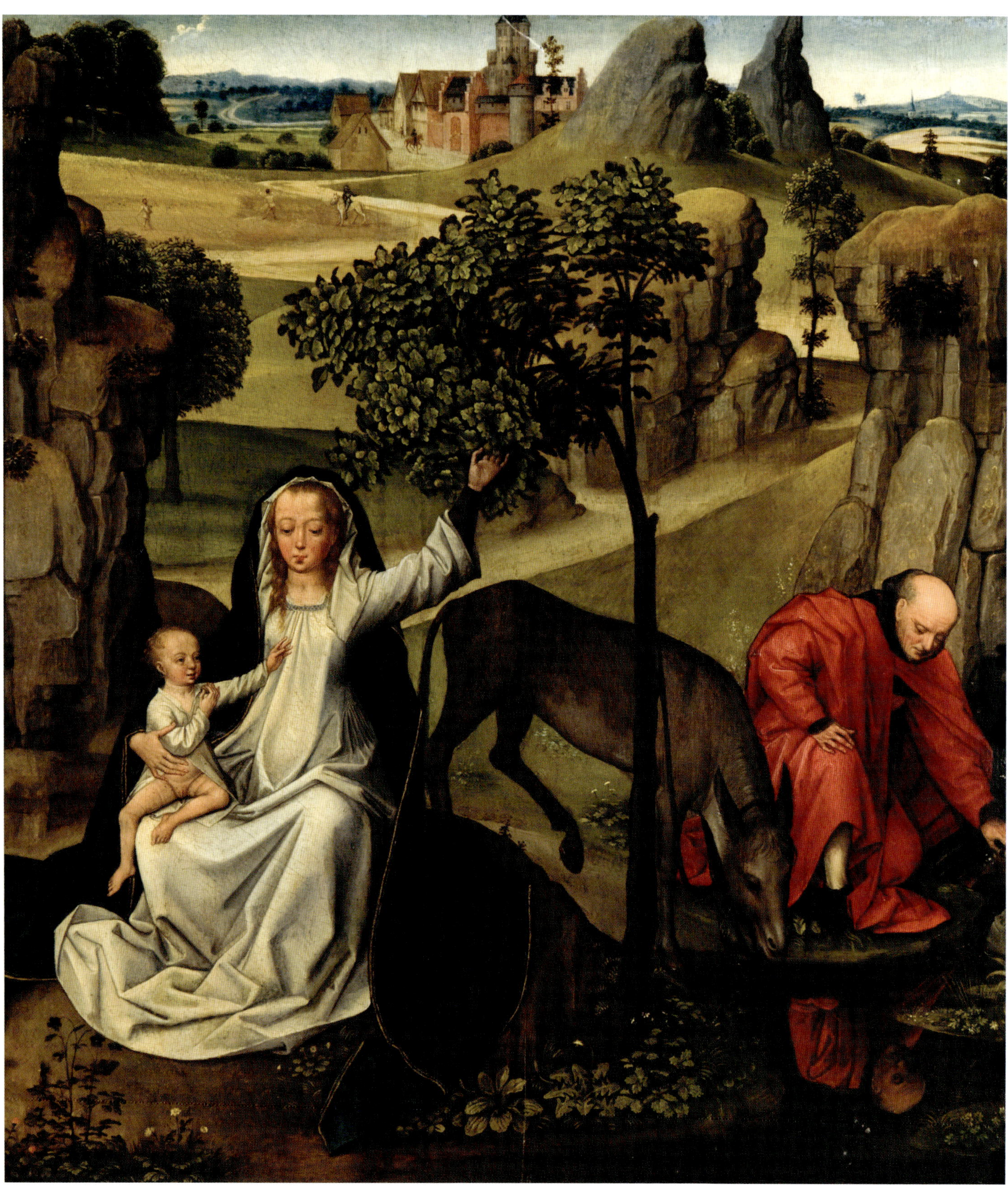

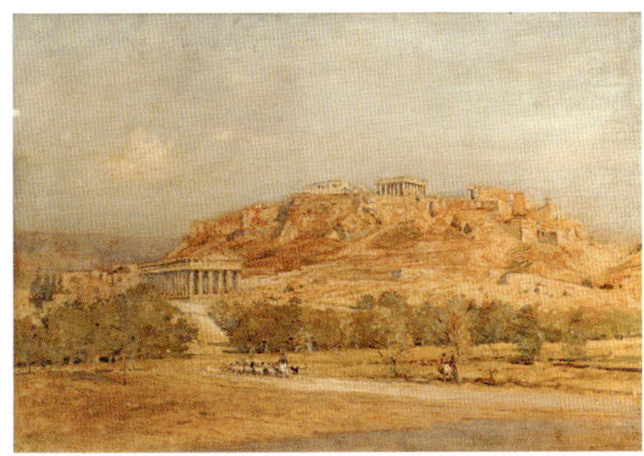

Allan, Robert Weir 1852–1942
Near Athens
oil on canvas 86.4 x 121.9
L.1.1944.1 (P)

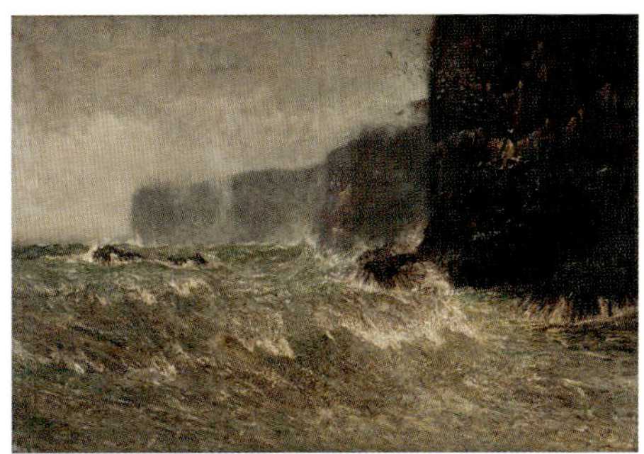

Allan, Robert Weir 1852–1942
North-Easter Gale
oil on canvas 132.8 x 208.2
2300

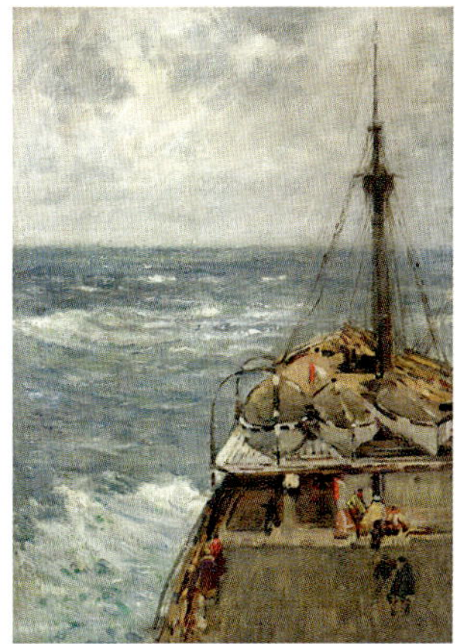

Allan, Robert Weir 1852–1942
Sea Piece
oil on canvas 76.2 x 53.3
2301

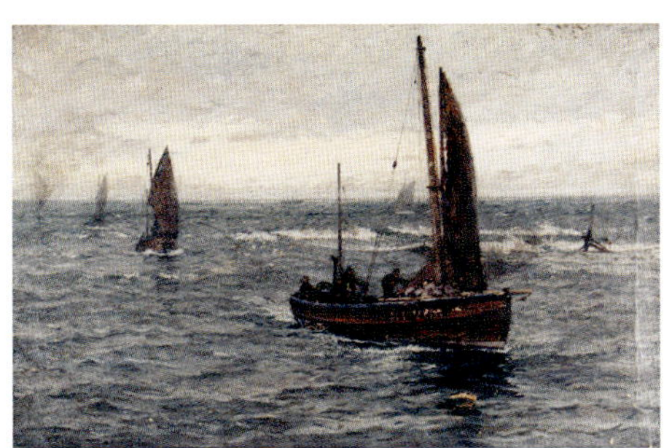

Allan, Robert Weir 1852–1942
Seascape, Fishing Boats Returning
oil on canvas 91.4 x 137.2
NR.115

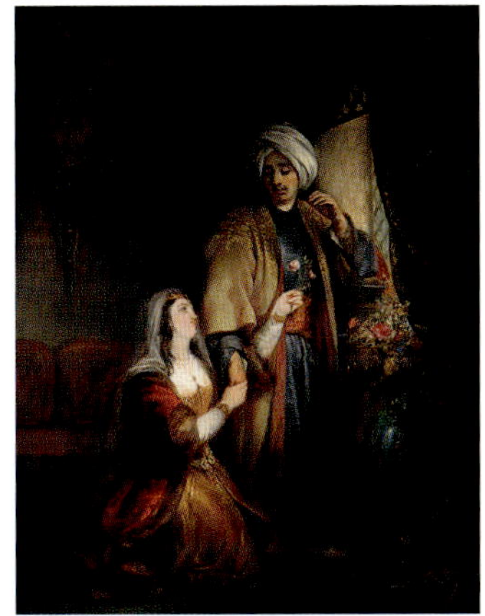

Allan, William 1782–1850
The Bride of Abydos (from the poem by
Byron) 1836
oil on canvas 60.9 x 47
254

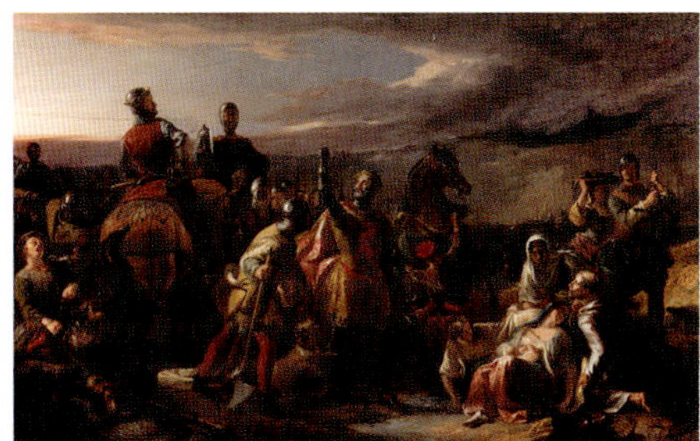

Allan, William 1782–1850
Heroism and Humanity c.1840
oil on canvas 127 x 196.9
1233

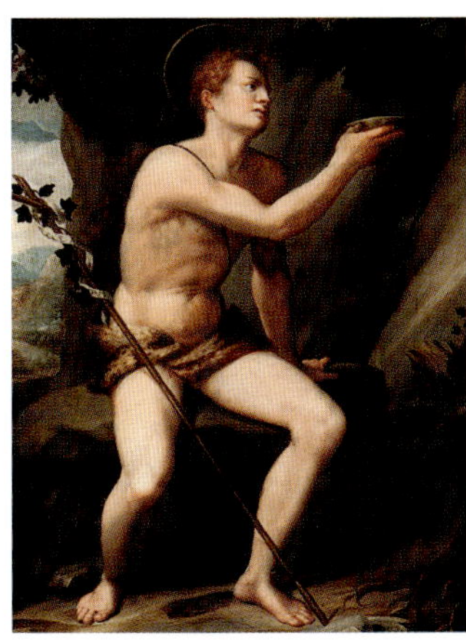

Allori, Alessandro (attributed to)
1535–1607
St John the Baptist late 16th C
oil on panel 53.3 x 40.6
1588

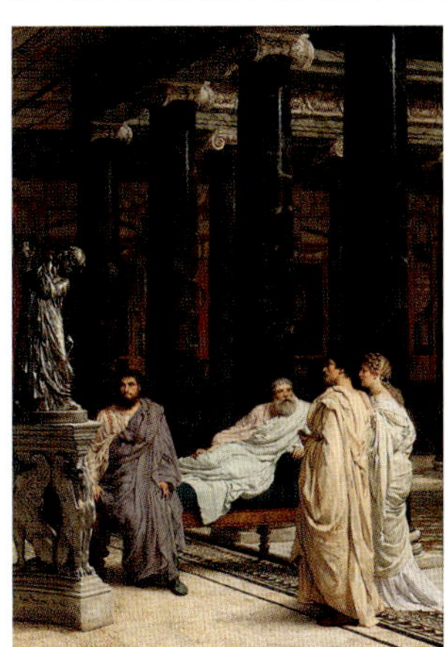

Alma-Tadema, Lawrence 1836–1912
A Lover of Art 1868
oil on canvas 78.7 x 55.9
736

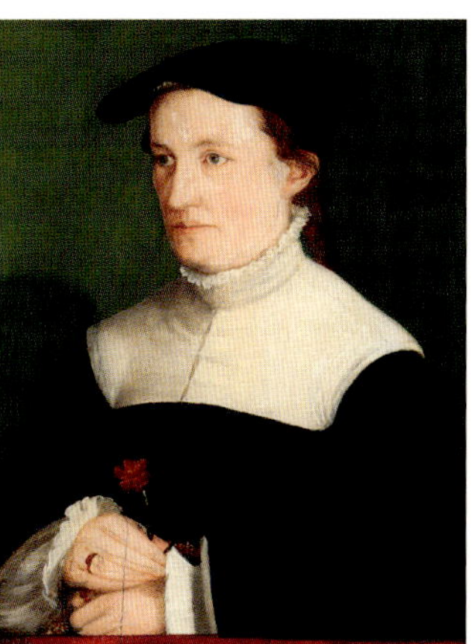

Amberger, Christoph c.1505–1561/1562
Portrait of a Lady c.1530–1550
oil on panel 53.6 x 41.9
200

Facing page: Master of the Prado Adoration of the Magi, active c.1450–1475,
The Flight into Egypt, c.1465–1470 (p. 260)

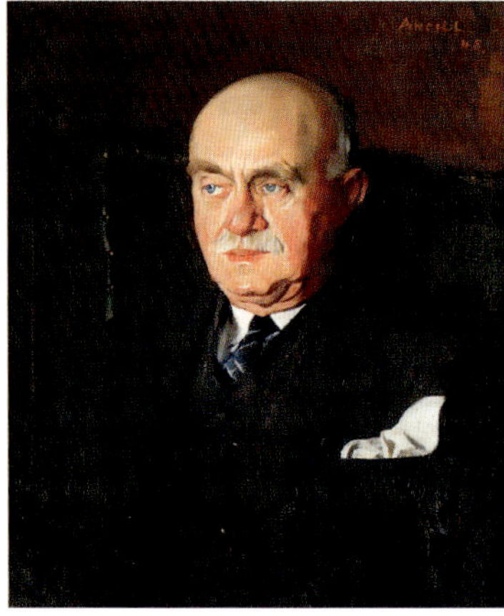

Ancill, Joseph 1896–c.1976
*James Welsh, Lord Provost of Glasgow
(1943–1945)* 1945
oil on canvas 69.2 x 57.1
2597

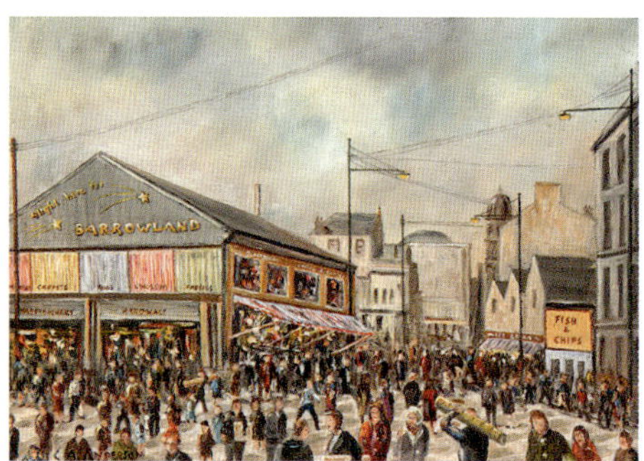

Anderson, Charles
The Barras, Glasgow
oil on canvas 30.7 x 41.4
PP.1986.2

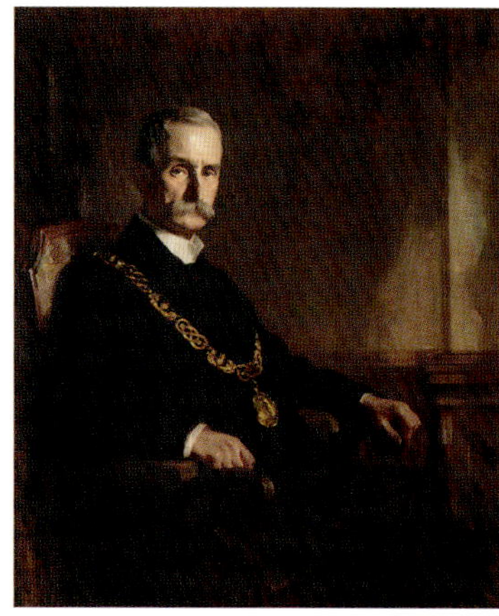

Anderson, James Bell 1886–1938
*Sir Daniel Macaulay Stevenson (1851–1944),
Lord Provost of Glasgow (1911–1914)* 1914
oil on canvas 125.7 x 100.3
1357

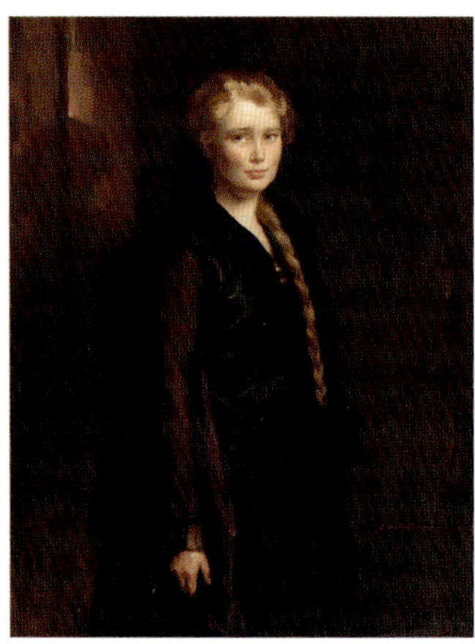

Anderson, James Bell 1886–1938
Miss Muriel Sterling 1917
oil on canvas 133 x 102
ME.2007.1.15

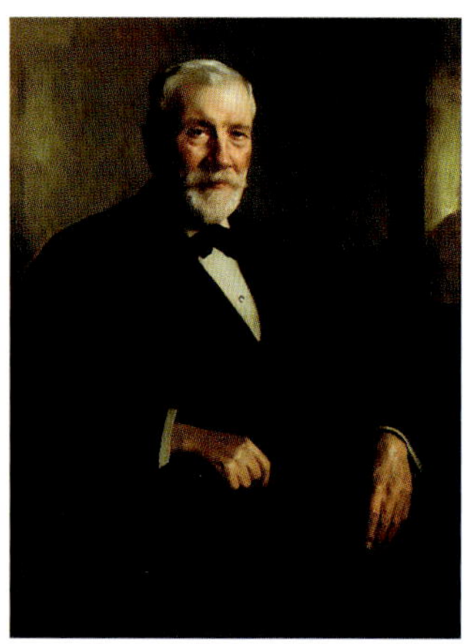

Anderson, James Bell 1886–1938
Former Bailie James Steele 1928
oil on canvas 101.6 x 76.2
1750

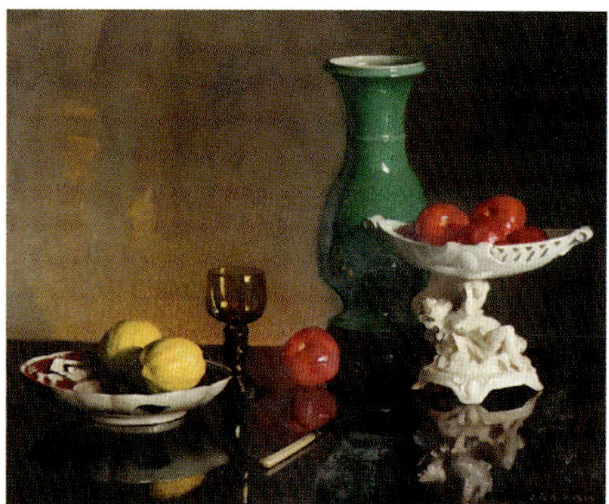

Anderson, James Bell 1886–1938
Still Life c.1932–1933
oil on canvas 50.8 x 60.9
1861

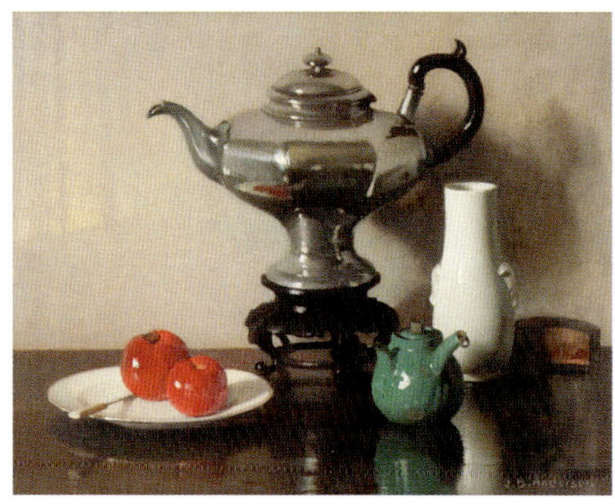

Anderson, James Bell 1886–1938
Still Life
oil on canvas 40.6 x 50.8
2647

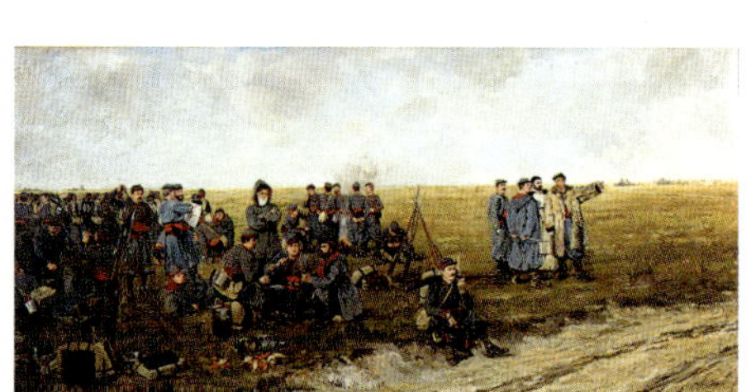

André, Edmond 1837–1877
Awaiting Orders
oil on canvas 48.2 x 98.2
811

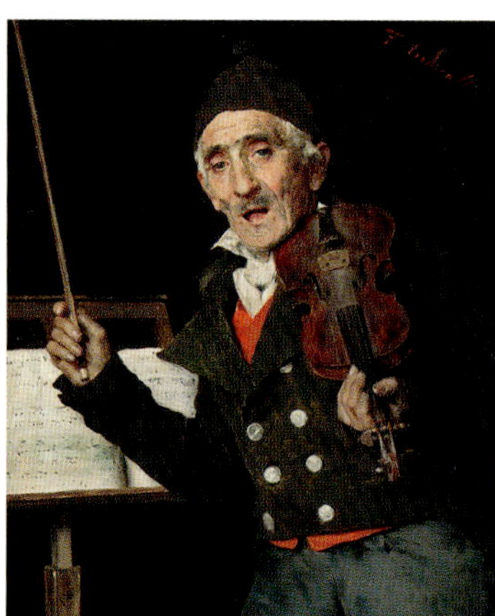

Andreotti, Federico 1847–1930
The Violin Teacher c.1875–1890
oil on canvas 31.4 x 25.7
2598

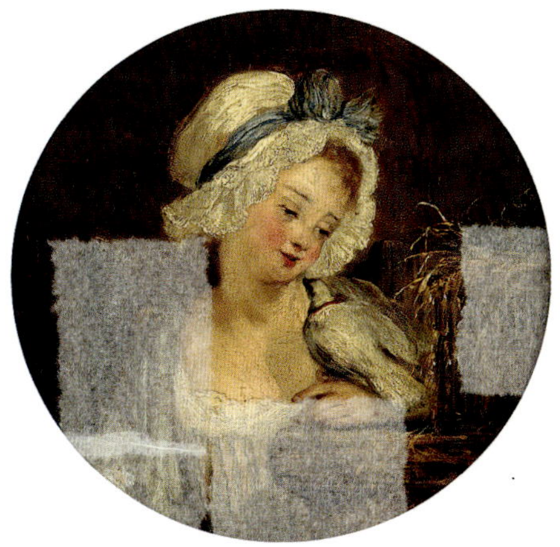

Andrews, Henry 1794–1868
The Pet Dove
oil on canvas 27.9
414

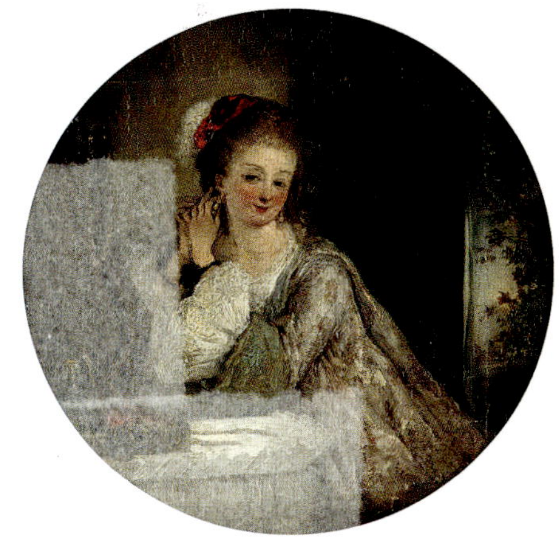

Andrews, Henry 1794–1868
The Toilet
oil on canvas 27.9
416

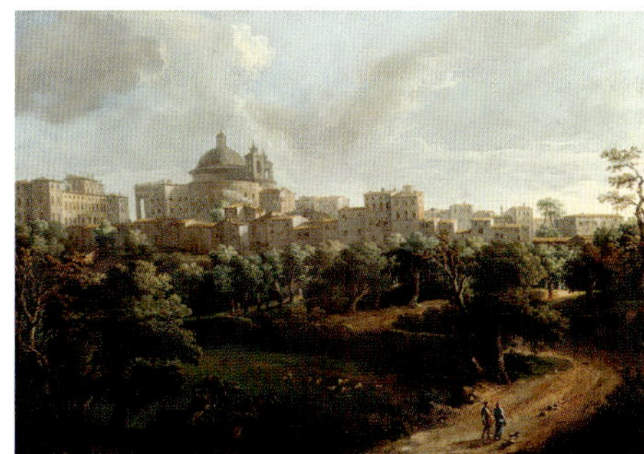

Anesi, Paolo 1697–1773
View of Ariccia c.1760–1765
oil on canvas 59 x 85.1
213

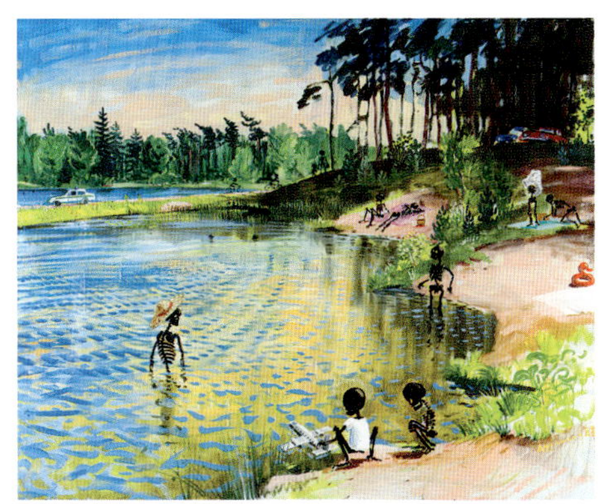

Angermann, Peter b.1945
Baggersee 1988
oil on canvas 170.2 x 220.6
3562

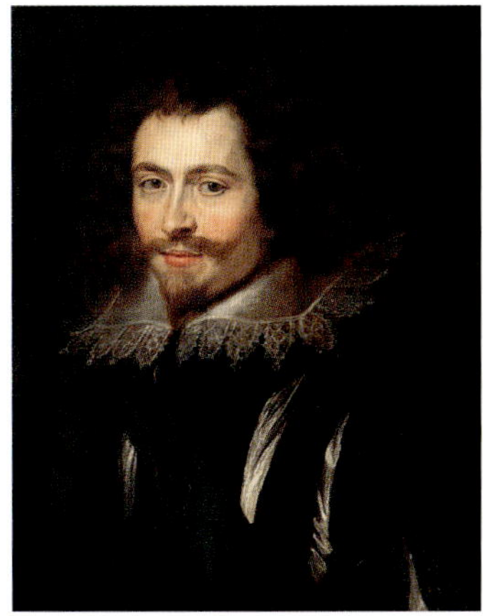

Anglo/Flemish School 17th C
*George Villiers (1592–1628), 1st Duke of
Buckingham* (after Peter Paul Rubens)
oil on panel 60.9 x 47.3
PC.49

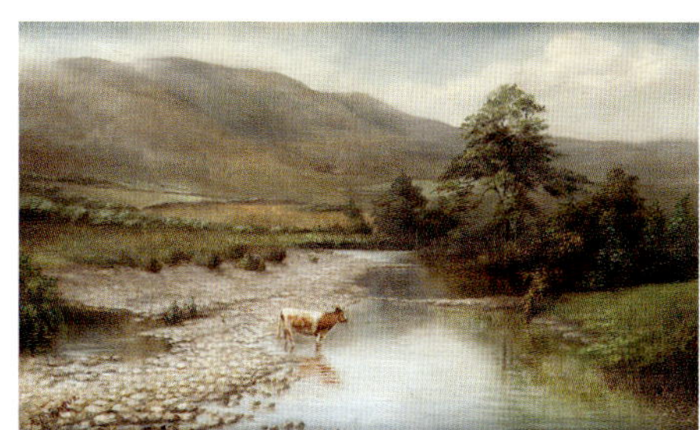

Angus, A. M. active 19th C
Landscape and Cattle
oil on canvas 48.5 x 76
NR.34

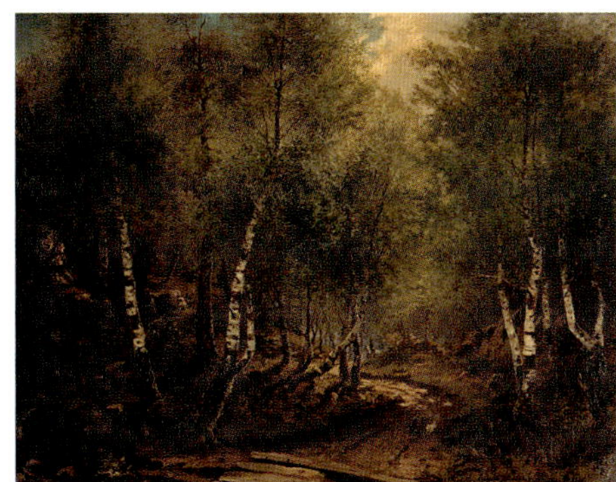

Ankarcrona, Alexis 1825–1901
Woody Landscape
oil on canvas 91.4 x 116.8
2474

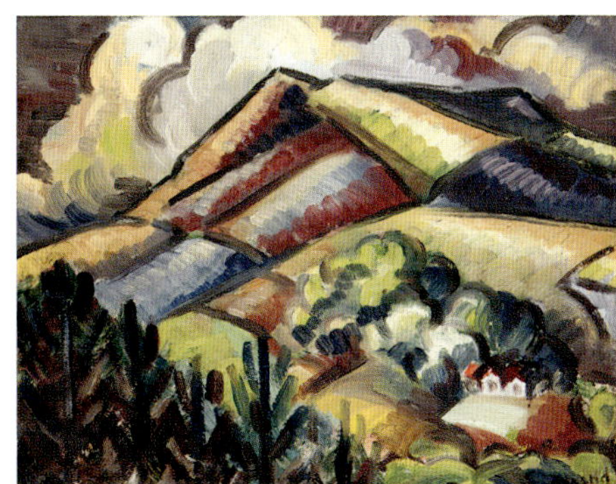

Annand, Louise Gibson b.1915
Border Landscape c.1943
oil on board 38.1 x 45.7
2331

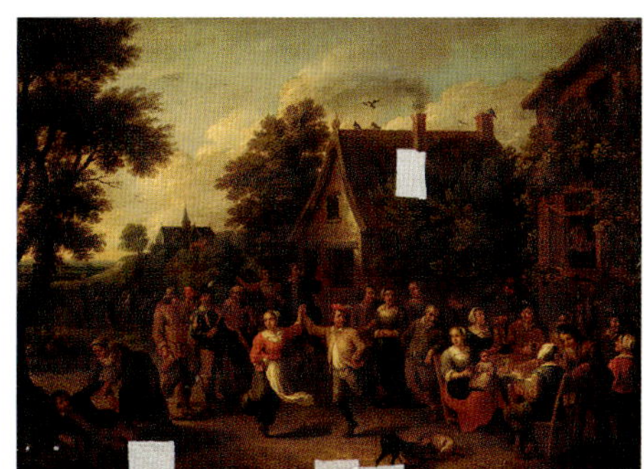

Apshoven, Thomas van (attributed to)
1622–1664
A Village Festival c.1650–1664
oil on canvas 66.7 x 91.4
24

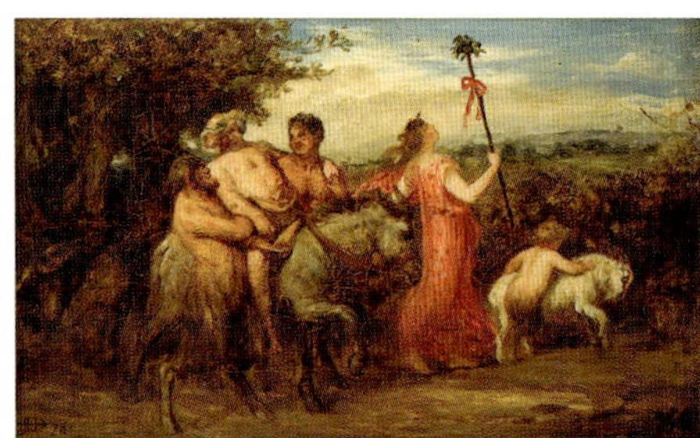

Archer, James 1822–1904
Classical Subject 1878
oil on canvas 35.6 x 45.7
789

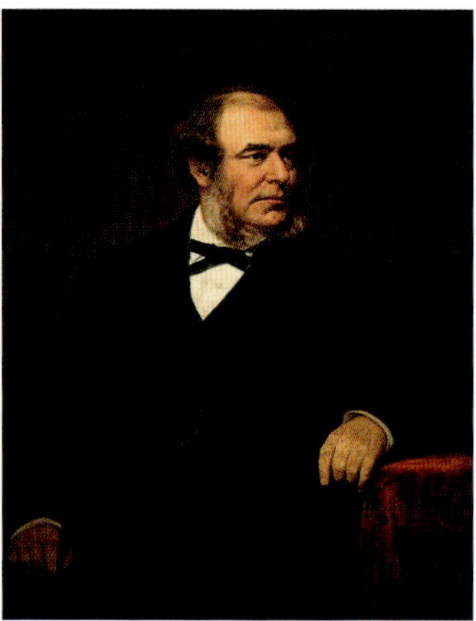

Archer, James 1822–1904
John Francis Ure (1820–1883) 1884
oil on canvas 111.8 x 86.4
1171

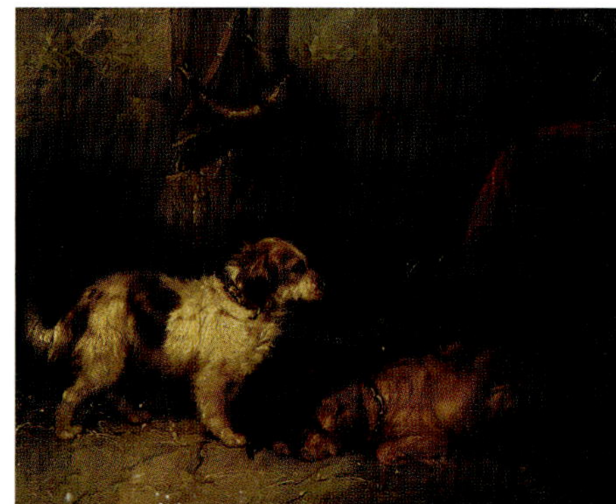

Armfield, George 1810–1893
Dogs
oil on canvas 25.4 x 30.5
444

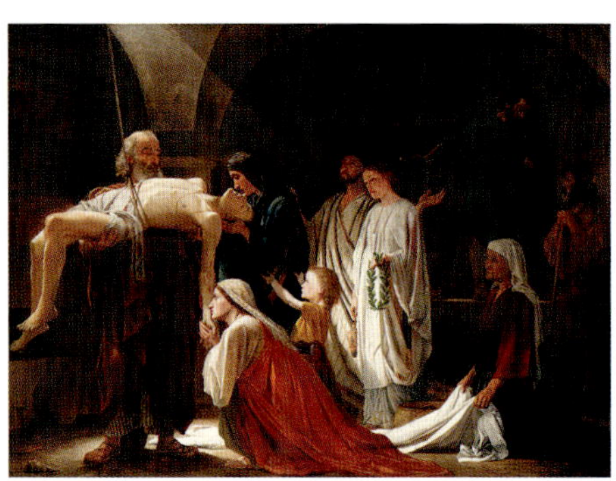

Armitage, Edward 1817–1896
The Christian Martyr 1863
oil on canvas 114.3 x 152.4
850

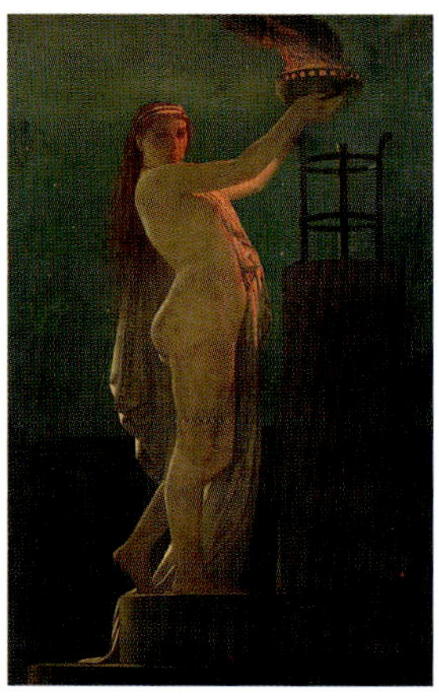

Armitage, Edward 1817–1896
Hero 1869
oil on canvas 243.8 x 152.4
1154

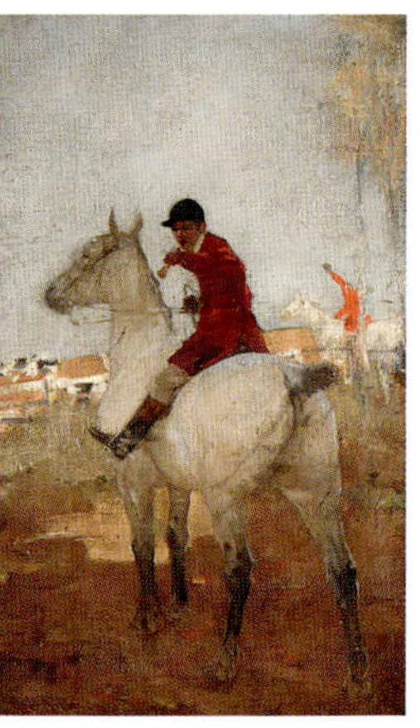

Armour, George Denholm 1864–1949
Two Huntsmen on Horseback, One Blowing a Horn
oil on canvas 48.3 x 28.9
3215

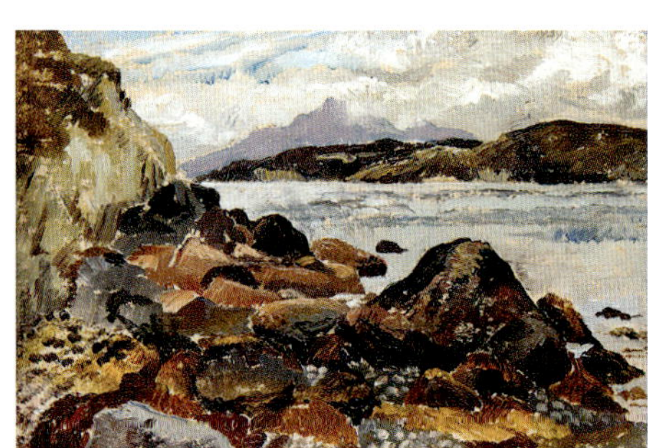

Armour, Mary 1902–2000
Rhum from Skye 1939
oil on laminated paper board 27.6 x 40.3
3242

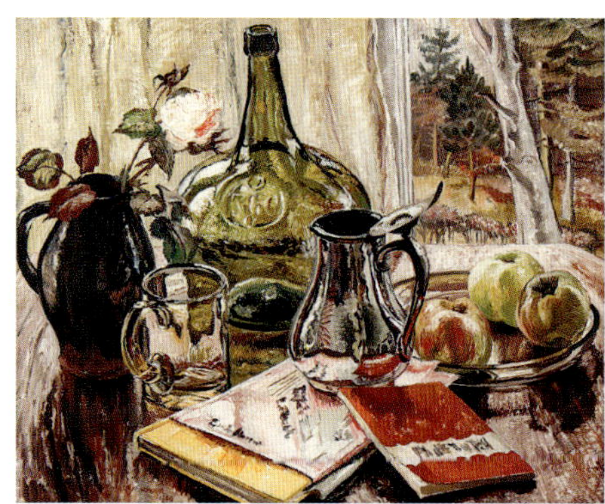

Armour, Mary 1902–2000
Still Life (Lustre Jug) 1940
oil on canvas 55.9 x 68.6
2282

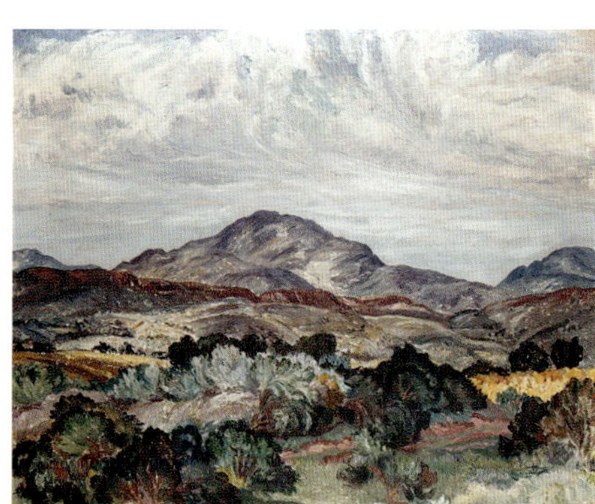

Armour, Mary 1902–2000
Ben Ledi 1948
oil on canvas 63.5 x 76.2
2696

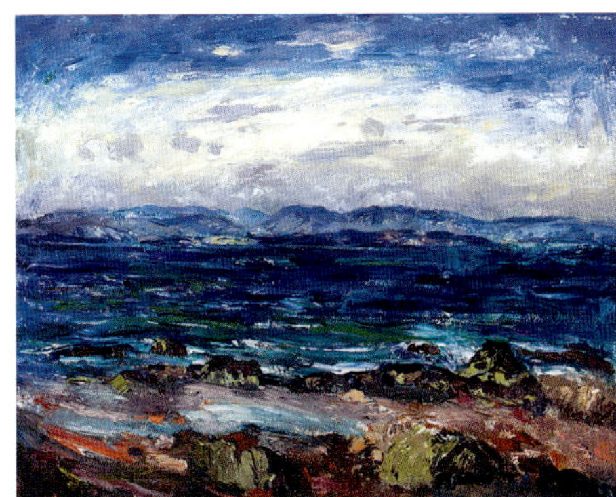

Armour, Mary 1902–2000
The Clyde from Corrie, Arran 1964
oil on canvas 65.4 x 80.9
3218

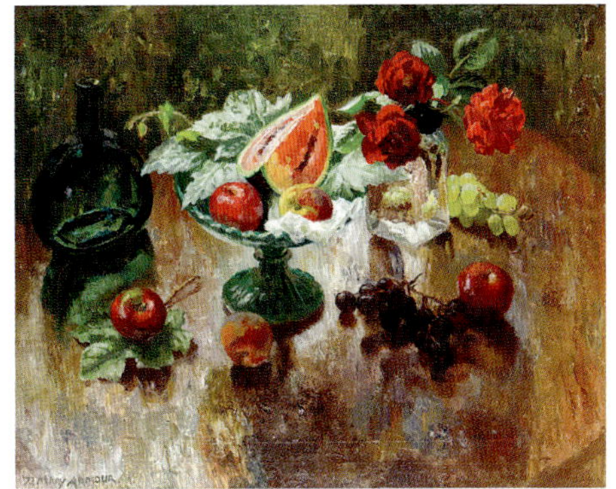

Armour, Mary 1902–2000
Green Dish with Melon 1972
oil on canvas 63.4 x 76
3299

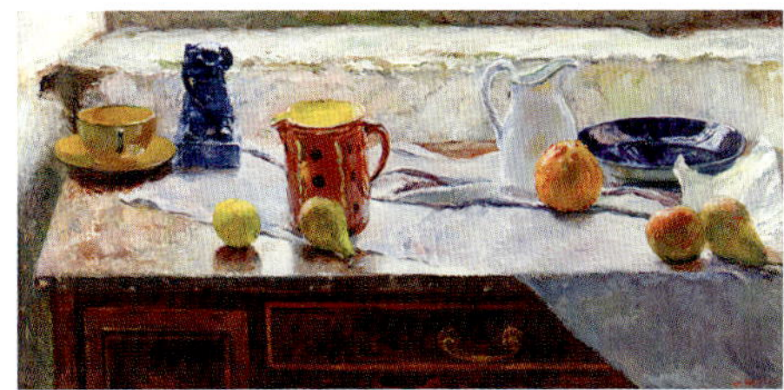

Armour, William 1903–1979
Still Life with Gourd 1954
oil on hardboard 50.7 x 104.1
3092

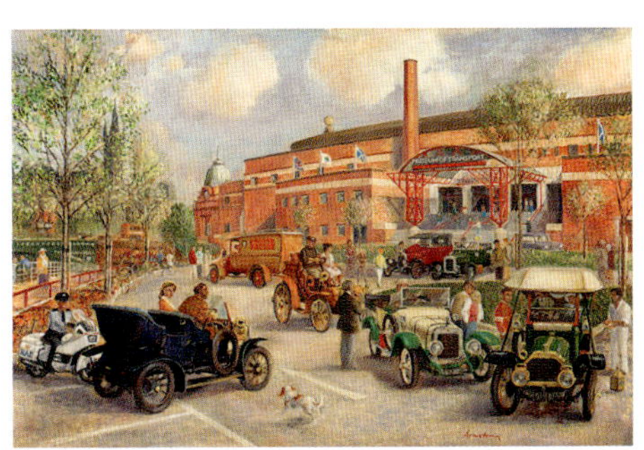

Armstrong, Anthony b.1935
Preparing for the Rally
oil on canvas (?) 124.5 x 175
T.1990.9

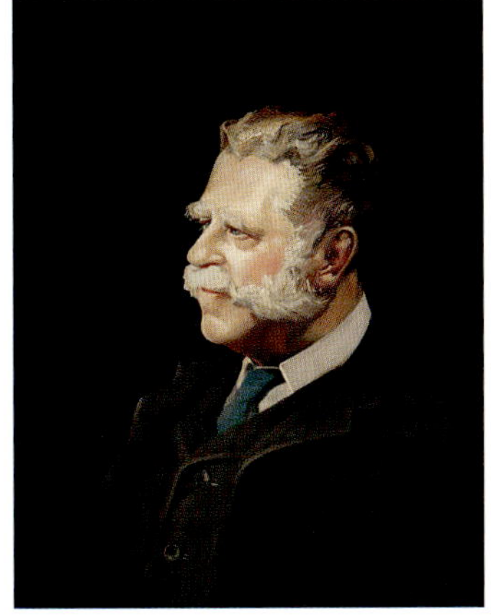

Armstrong, James active 1932–1933
Portrait of a Man 1933
oil on canvas 76.5 x 58.5
TEMP.2779

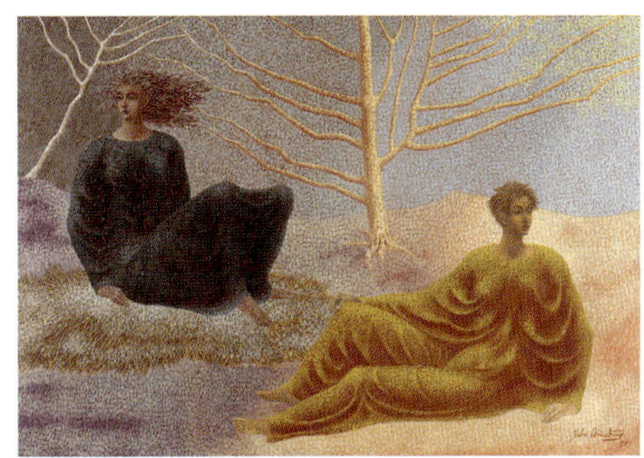

Armstrong, John 1893–1973
Spring and Winter 1955
oil on canvas 96 x 136.5
3059

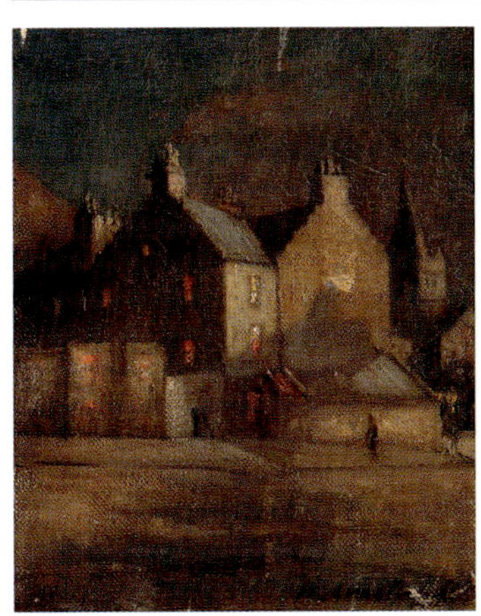

Armstrong, William active 1887–1896
Provand's Lordship
oil on canvas 27 x 20.9
PL.1945.255

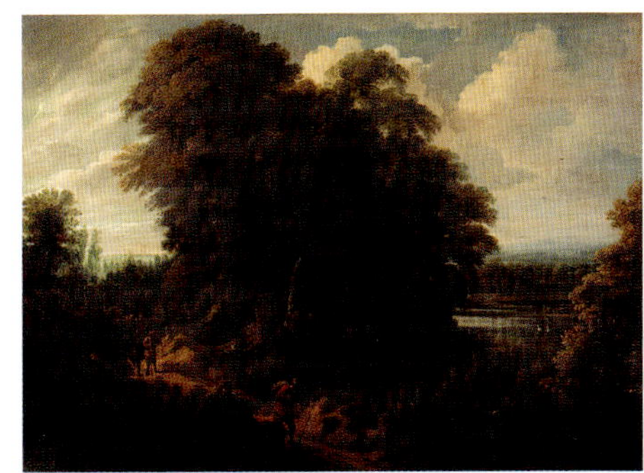

Arthois, Jacques d' 1613–1686
A Wooded Landscape
oil on canvas 120.6 x 170.2
1170

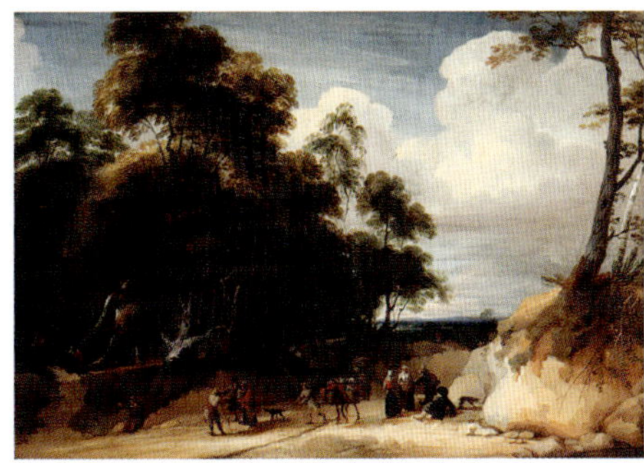

Arthois, Jacques d' 1613–1686
Peasants at the Edge of a Forest
oil on canvas 54.9 x 79
54

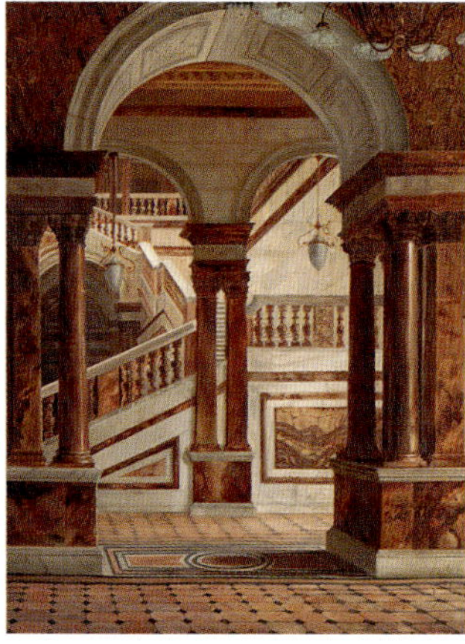

Arthur, G. G.
City Chambers Staircase c.1907–1908
oil on canvas 76.8 x 56.5
OG.1954.35

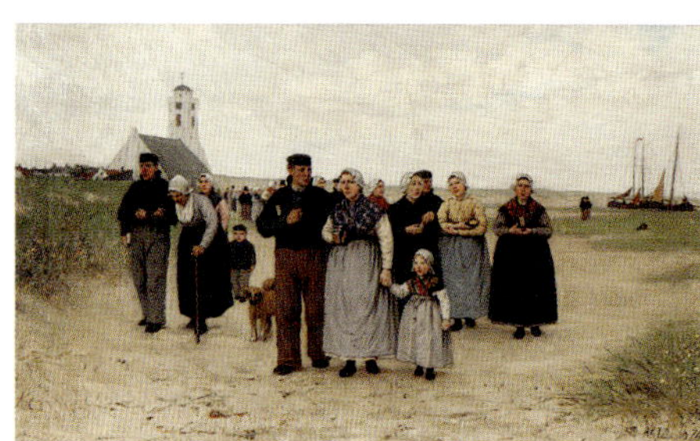

Artz, David Adolph Constant 1837–1890
Coming from Church 1874
oil on canvas 47.5 x 75
1255

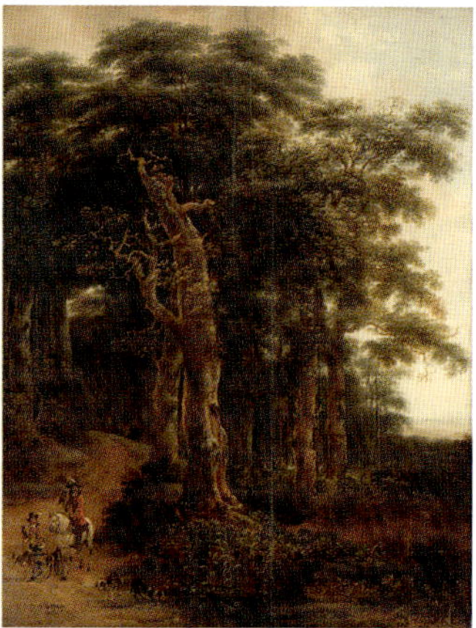

Asch, Pieter Jansz. van 1603–1678
A Hawking Party at the Edge of a Forest
oil on panel 54.6 x 42.5
91

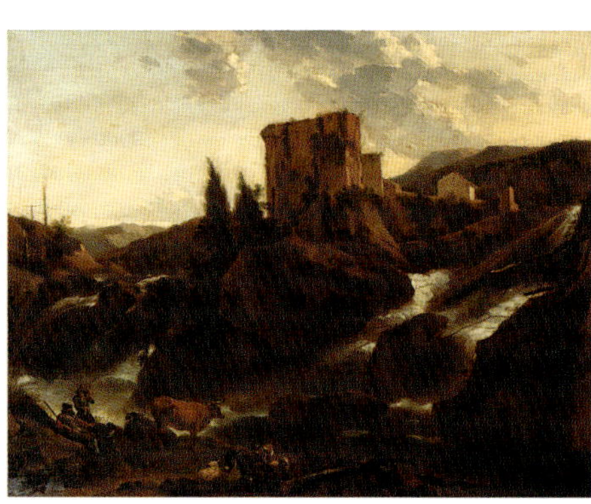

Asselyn, Jan (attributed to) after 1610–1652
Mountain Landscape with a Castle
c.1640–1652
oil on canvas 88.2 x 110.8
93

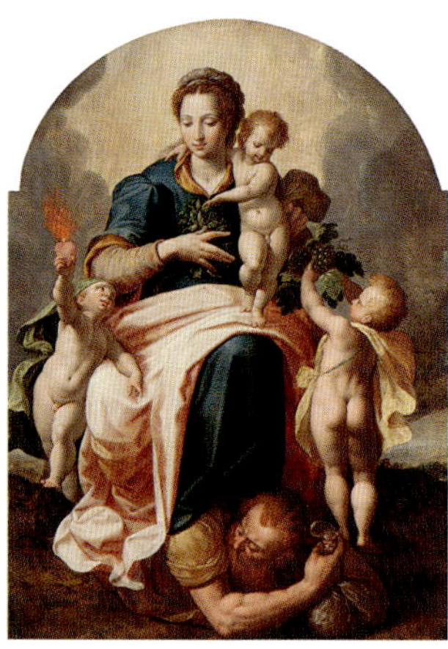

Backer, Jacques de 1540/1545–before 1600
Charity c.1580–1590
oil on panel 84.2 x 61.8
142

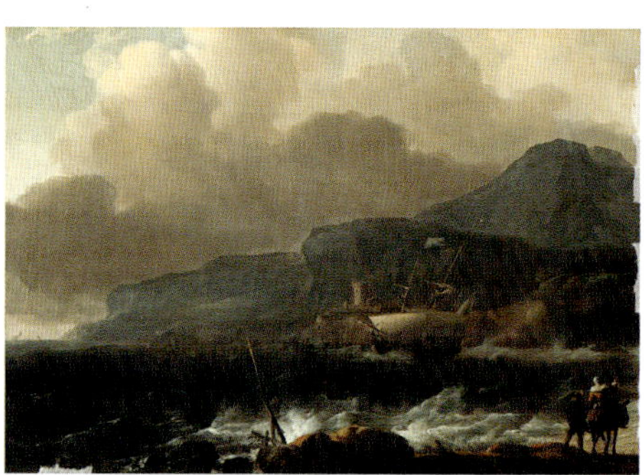

Backhuysen, Ludolf I (attributed to)
1630–1708
A Dutch Ship Clawing off a High Coast in a Gale
oil on canvas 47.9 x 67.6
115

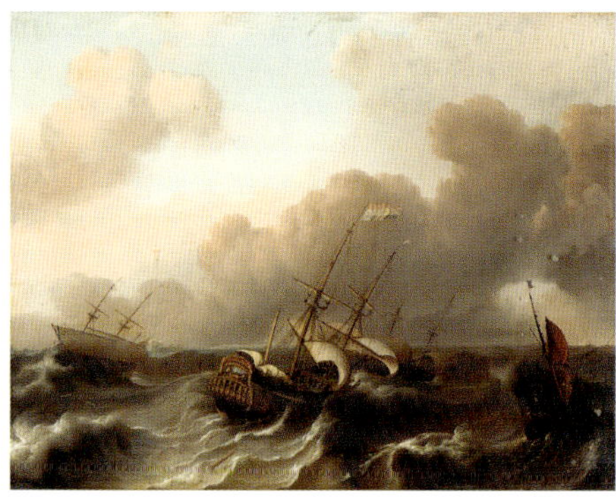

Backhuysen, Ludolf I (imitator of)
1630–1708
A Dutch Flagship and Other Vessels Running before a Gale
oil on canvas 67.9 x 88.2
105

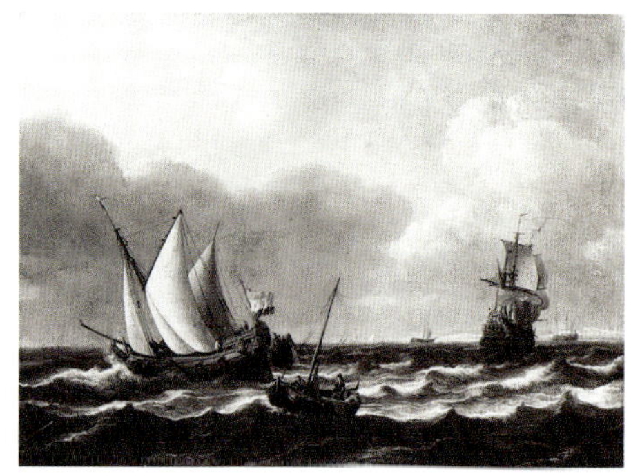

Backhuysen, Ludolf I (imitator of)
1630–1708
A Dutch States Yacht Beating to Windward off the Coast, and Other Vessels
oil on canvas 54.3 x 73
19

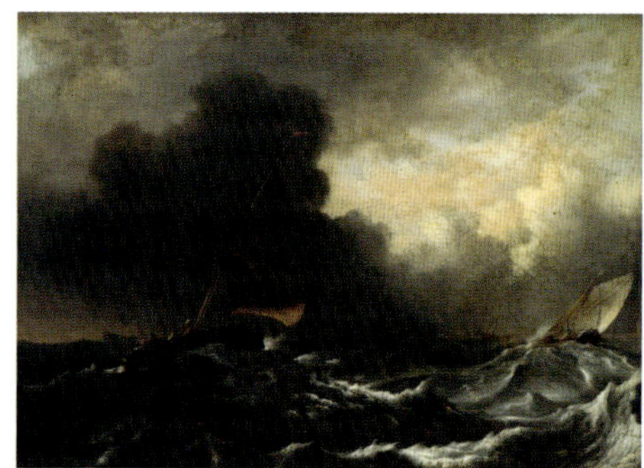

Backhuysen, Ludolf I (style of)
1630–1708
Fishing Boats off the Coast in a Gale
oil on canvas 34.3 x 47.6
565

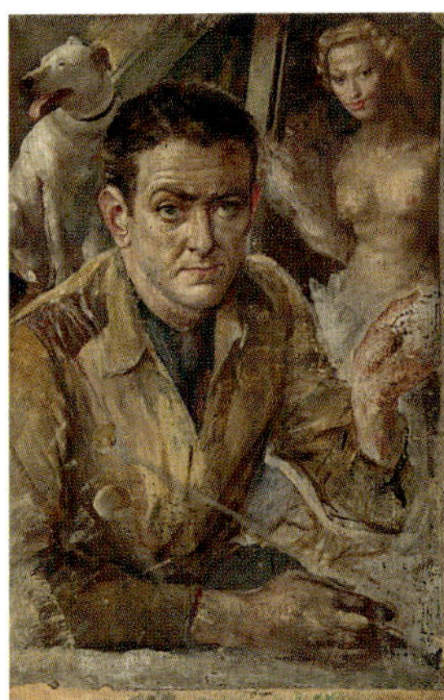

Baillie, Charles Cameron 1901–1960
Self Portrait
oil on canvas 68.7 x 44.5
PP.1981.39

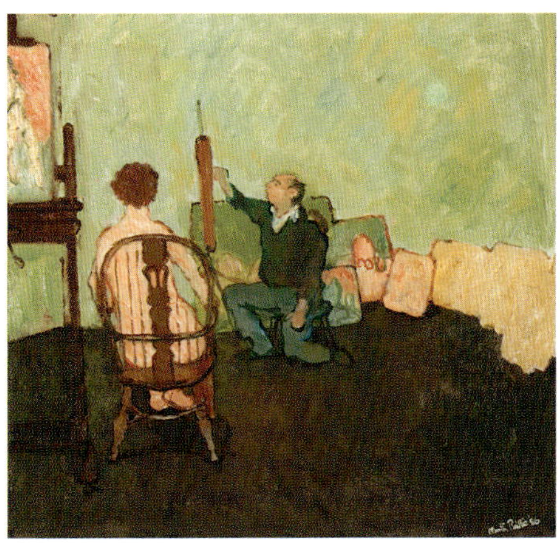

Baillie, Martin b.1920
Painter Drawing from the Model 1986
oil on canvas 73.5 x 73.3
3682

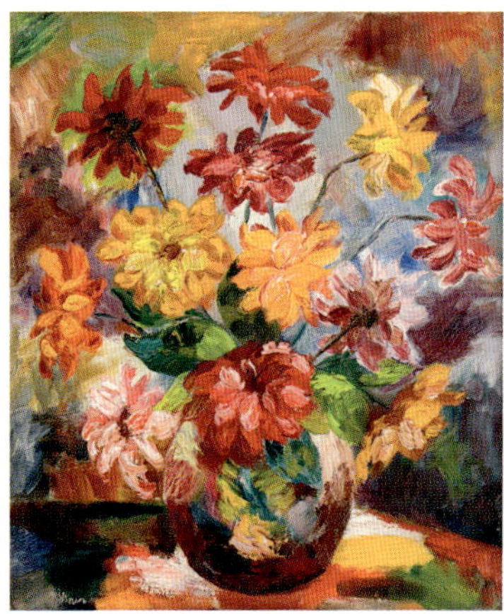

Bain, Donald 1904–1979
Flower Piece 1943
oil on canvas 60.6 x 50.8
2456

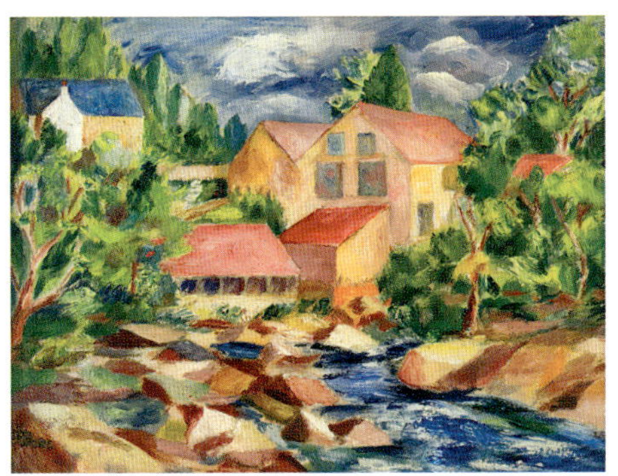

Bain, Donald 1904–1979
Old Tweed Mill 1944
oil on canvas 60.5 x 91.4
2832

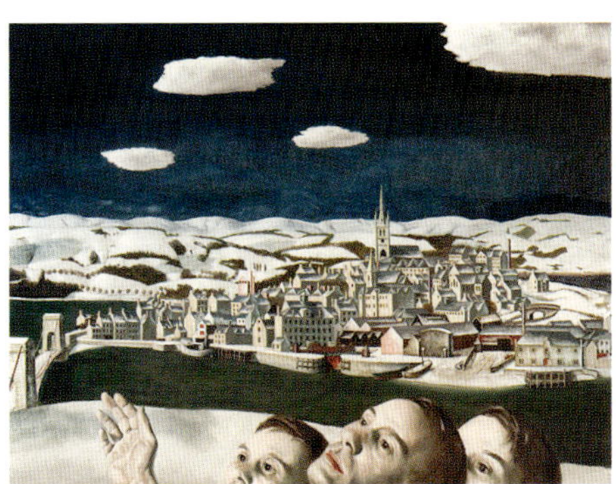

Baird, Edward 1904–1949
Unidentified Aircraft (over Montrose) 1942
oil on canvas 71.1 x 91.4
2315

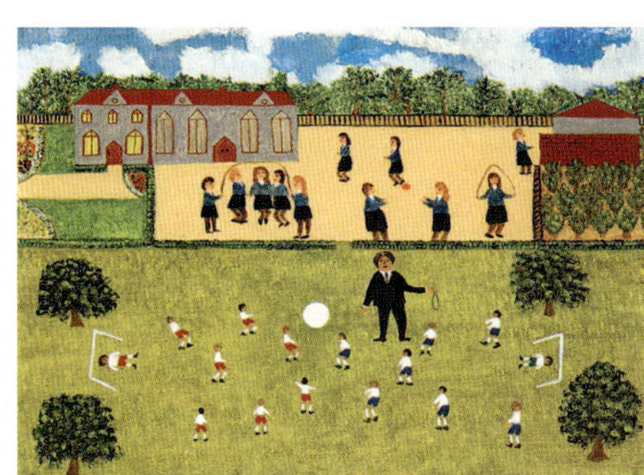

Baird, Margaret 1891–1979
School Days 1967
oil on hardboard 31.7 x 44.2
3573

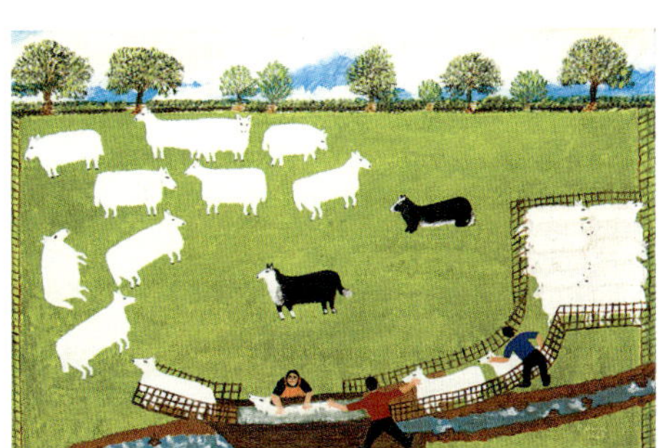

Baird, Margaret 1891–1979
Sheep Dipping 1967
oil on hardboard 38.1 x 55.6
3575

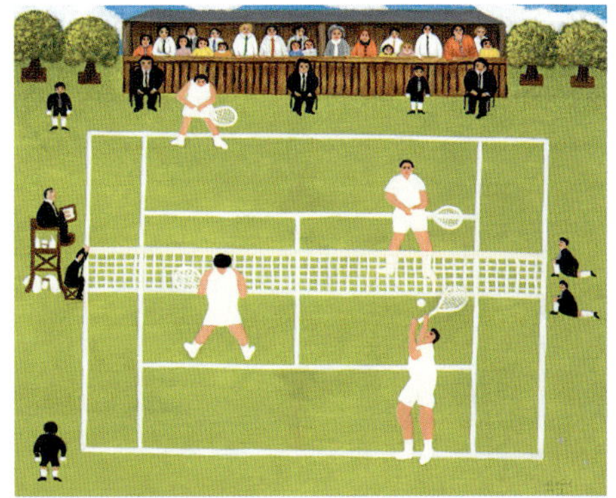

Baird, Margaret 1891–1979
Doubles 1971
oil on hardboard 37.4 x 44.4
3574

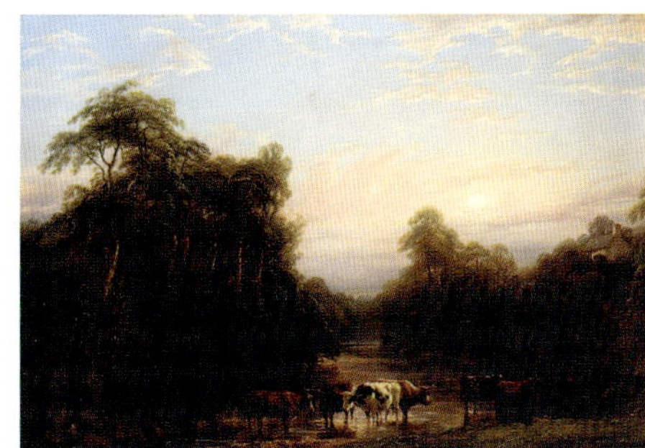

Baker, Thomas 1809–1869
Landscape and Cattle 1831
oil on canvas 38.1 x 54.6
107

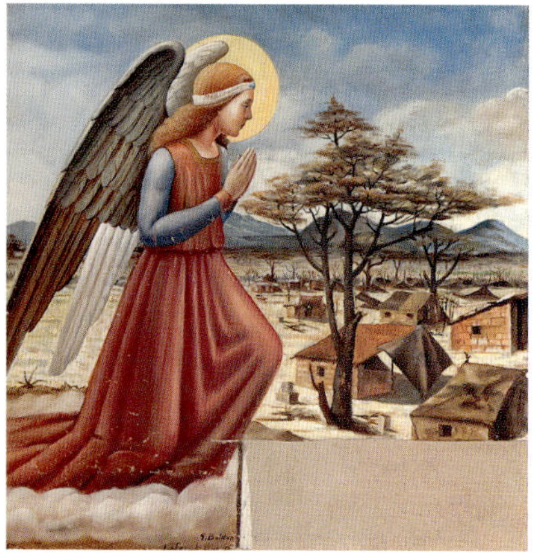

Baldan, Giuseppe active 20th C
La Faruk Madonna (triptych, left wing)
oil on flour bag 113.9 x 107
PP.1995.16.a

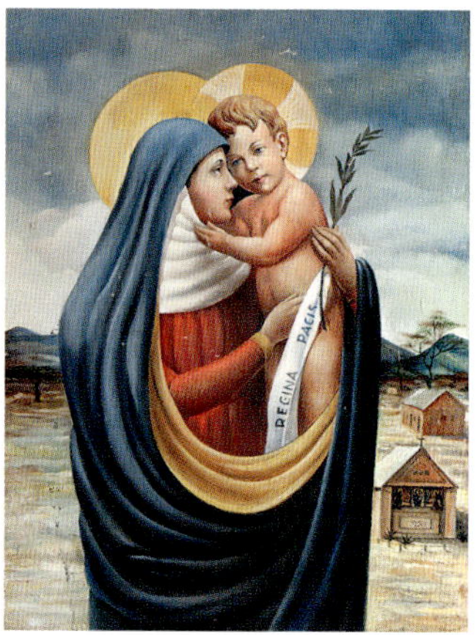

Baldan, Giuseppe active 20th C
La Faruk Madonna (triptych, centre panel)
oil on flour bag 94.3 x 73.2
PP.1995.16.b

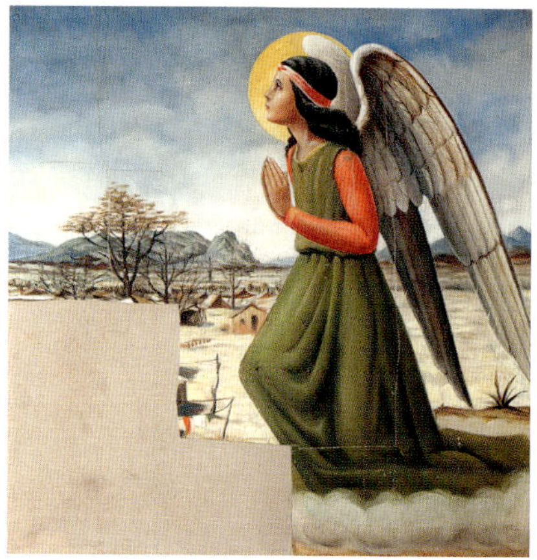

Baldan, Giuseppe active 20th C
La Faruk Madonna (triptych, right wing)
oil on flour bag 113.8 x 107.2
PP.1995.16.c

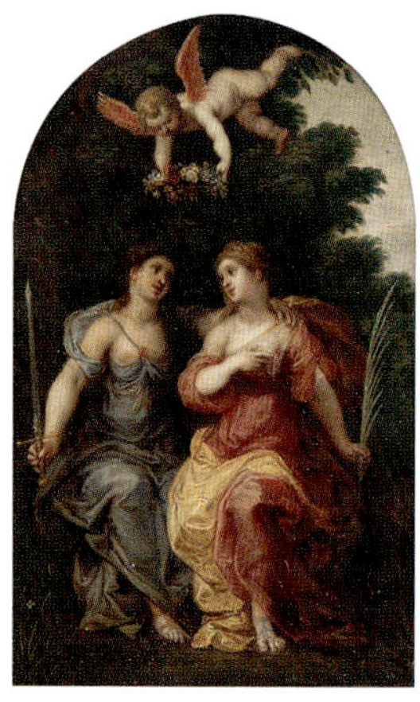

Balen, Hendrik van I 1575–1632
Justice and Peace c.1600–1609
oil on copper 27.6 x 17.8
119

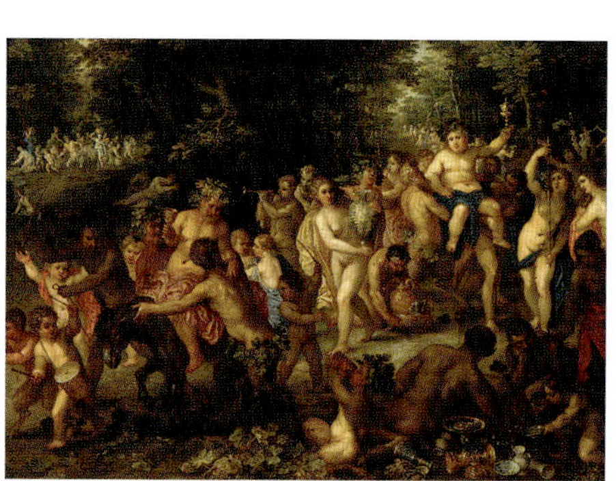

Balen, Hendrik van I 1575–1632
A Bacchic Procession c.1605–1608
oil on copper 28.7 x 39.5
57

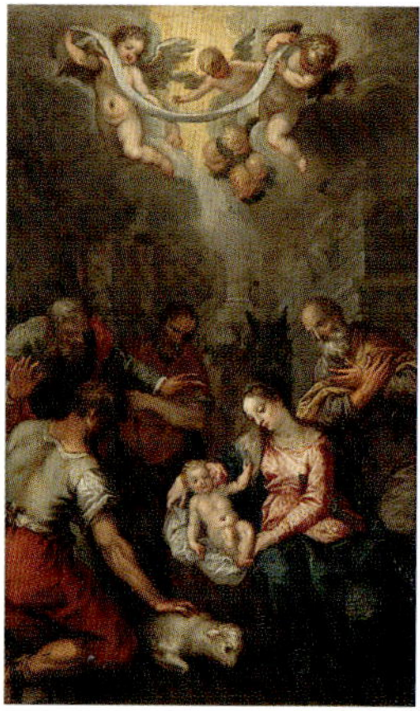

Balen, Hendrik van I 1575–1632
The Adoration of the Shepherds
oil on copper 33.3 x 21.3
198

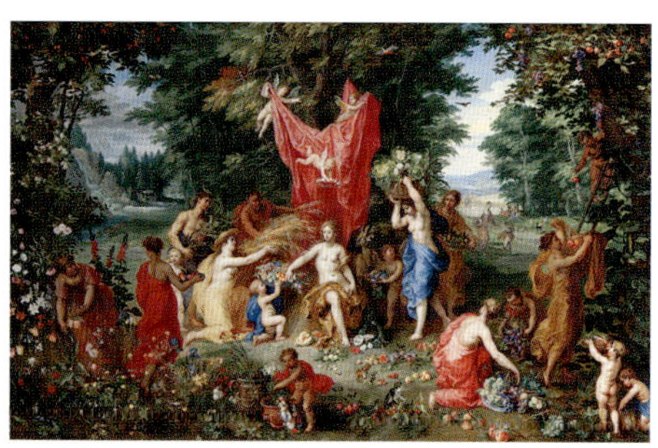

Balen, Hendrick van I 1575–1632 &
Brueghel, Jan the younger 1601–1678
An Allegory of Abundance c.1631/1632
oil on panel 73.6 x 114.6
43

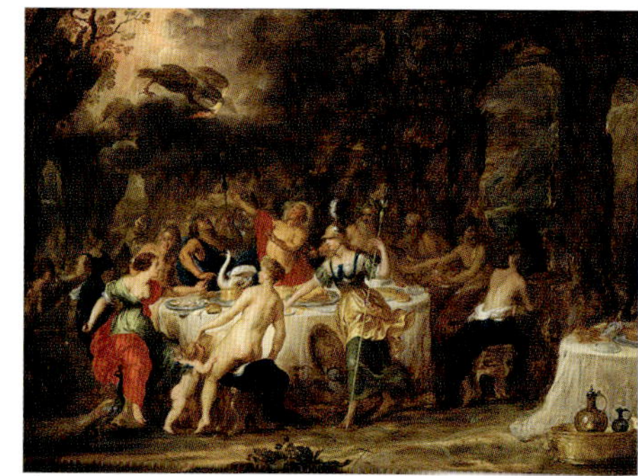

Balen, Jan van (attributed to) c.1611–1654
The Marriage Feast of Peleus and Thetis c.1630
oil on panel 53.3 x 72.7
75

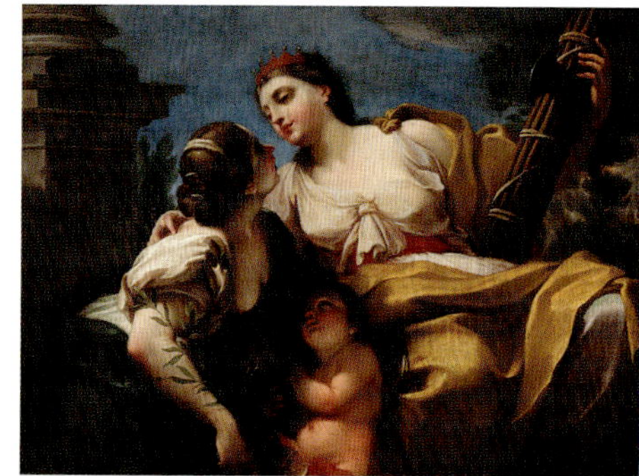

Balestra, Antonio 1666–1740
Justice and Peace Embracing c.1700
oil on canvas 105.4 x 138.7
266

Facing page: Cesari, Giuseppe, 1568–1640, *The Archangel Michael and the Rebel Angels*, c.1592–1593 (p. 260)

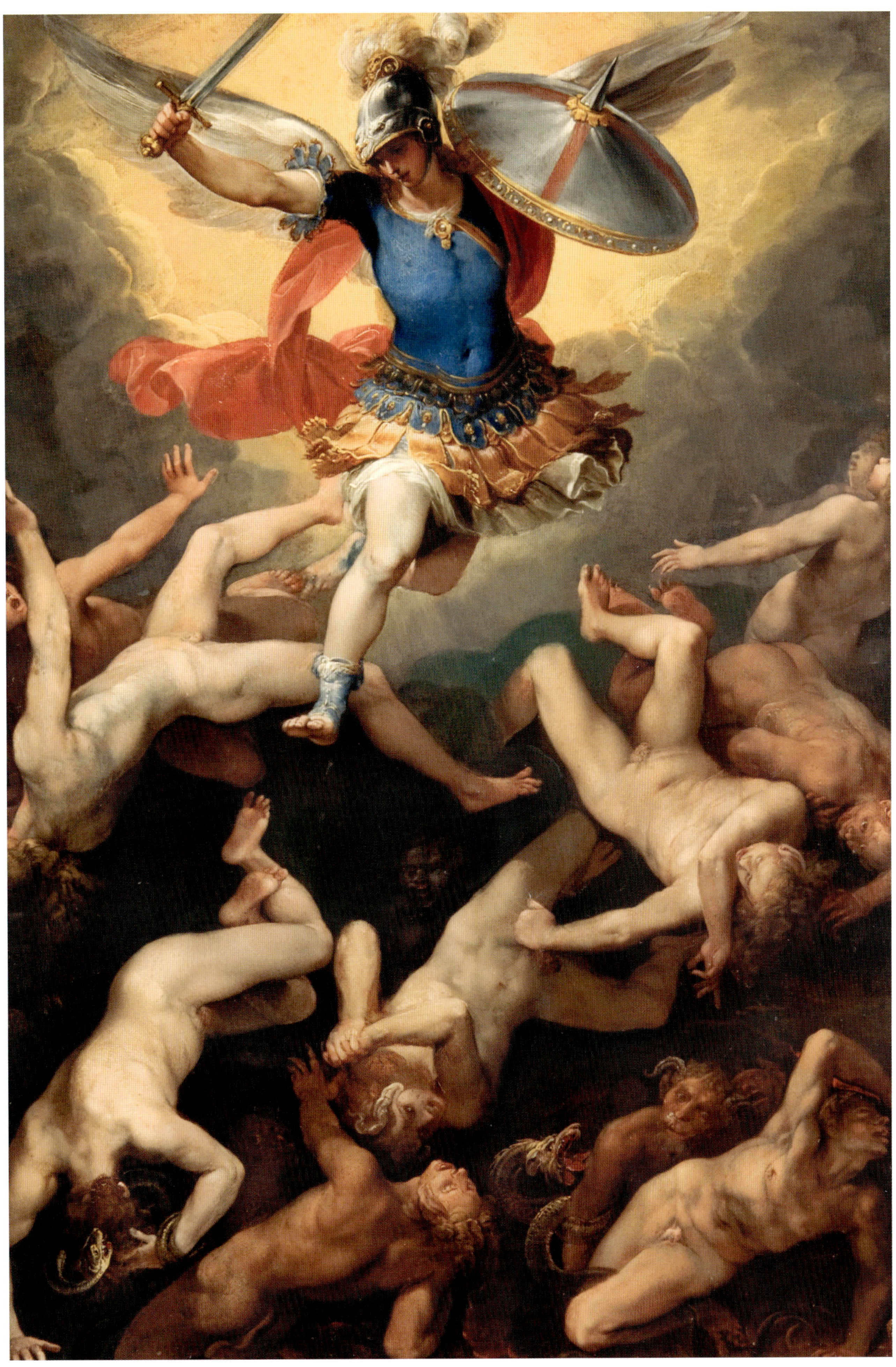

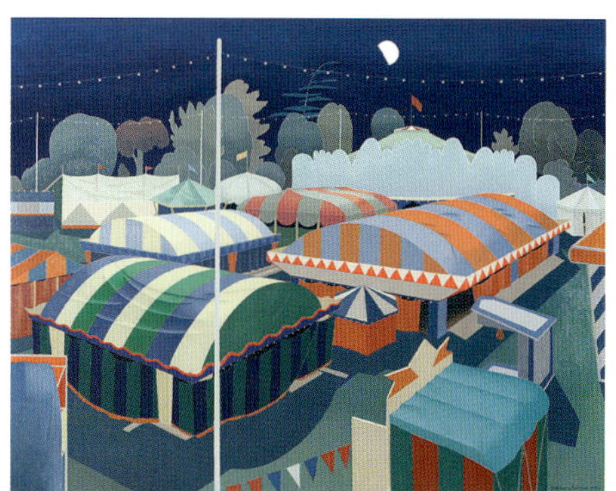

Balmer, Barbara b.1929
Sleeping Fairground 1979
oil on canvas 122 x 153
3377

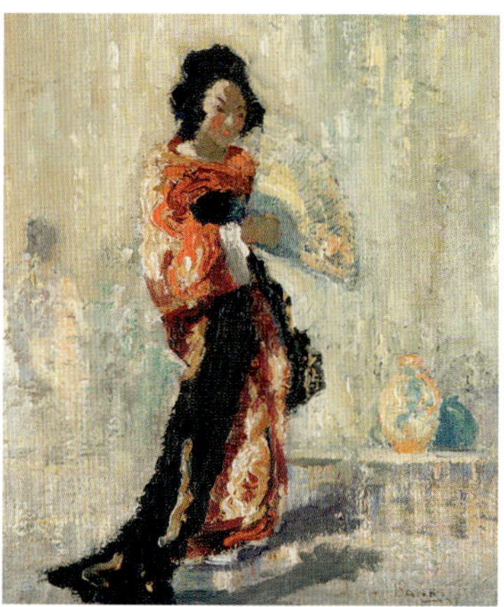

Banks, John 1883–1945
Fuji San
oil on millboard 33 x 27.9
2119

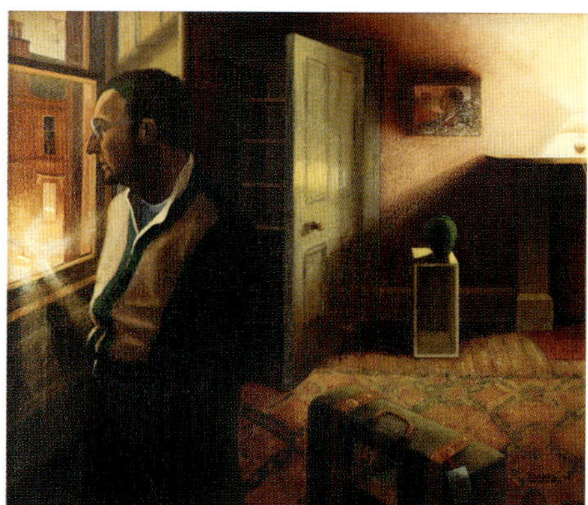

Banks, Lesley b.1962
Leaving 1990
oil on canvas 58.7 x 64.6
3688

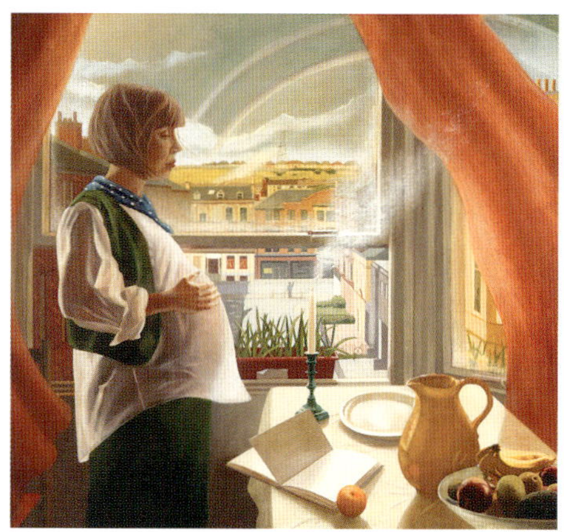

Banks, Lesley b.1962
The 39th Week – Counting 1993
oil on canvas 76.2 x 81.3
3556

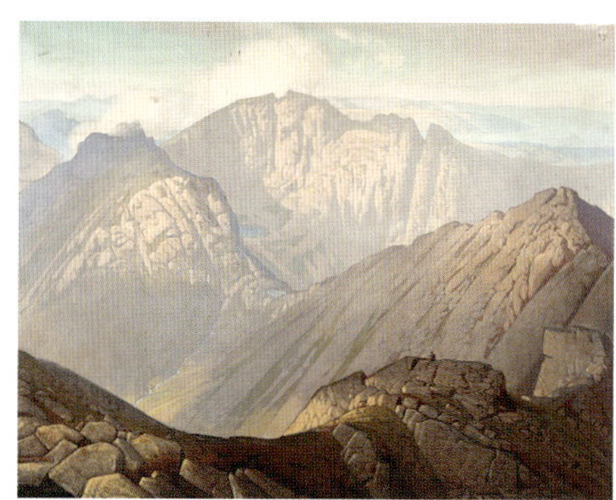

Banner, Delmar Harmond 1896–1983
On Top of Goatfell, Arran 1948
oil on canvas 101.6 x 127
2687

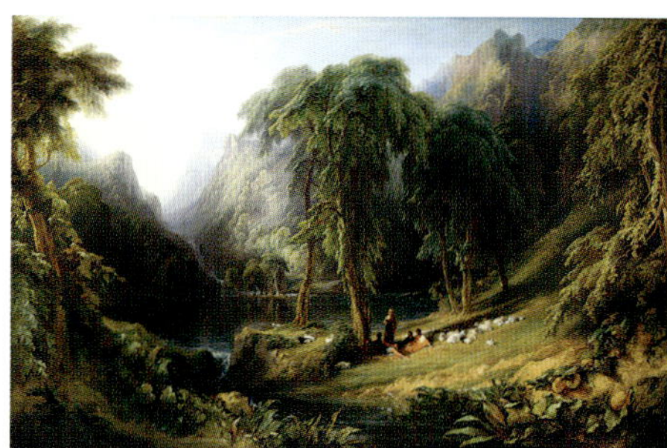

Barber, Joseph Vincent 1788–1838
Landscape: The Golden Age c.1828
oil on canvas 99 x 147.3
261

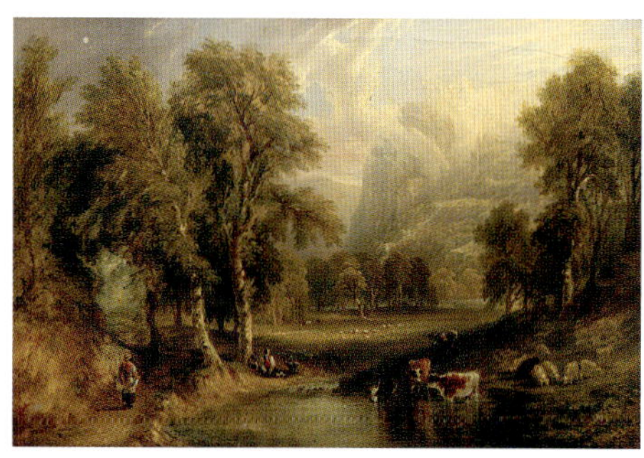

Barber, Joseph Vincent 1788–1838
Landscape with Cattle
oil on canvas 33 x 48.2
240

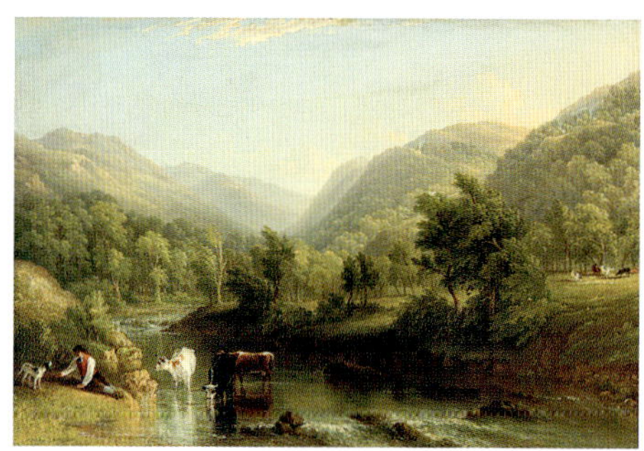

Barber, Joseph Vincent 1788–1838
Landscape with Cattle
oil on canvas 33 x 48.2
255

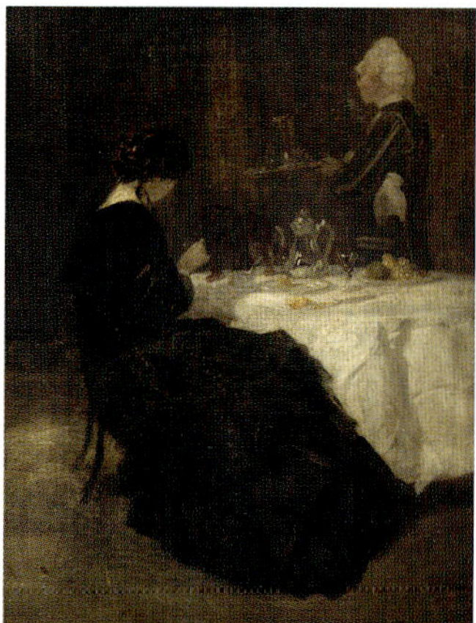

Bargue, Charles 1826–1883
Lady at a Table
oil on canvas 40.6 x 32.4
35.2

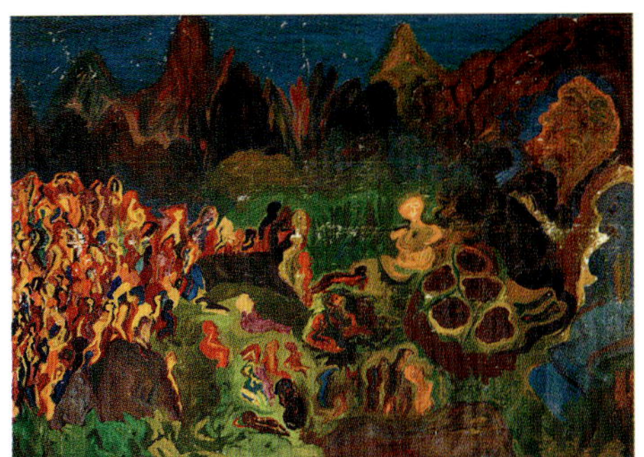

Barnes, Mary 1923–2001
Feeding the Five Thousand 1966
oil on canvas 147 x 209
3616

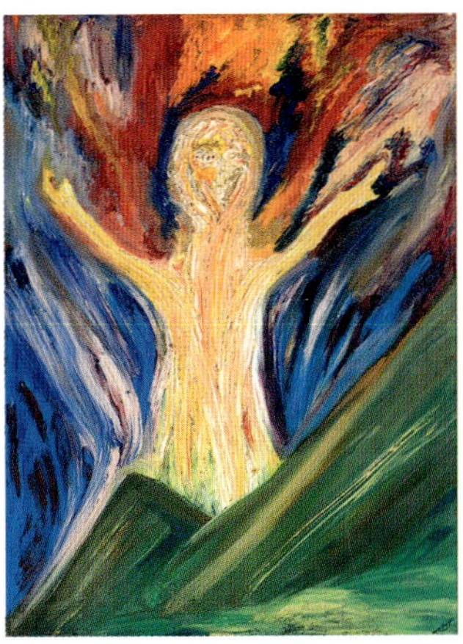

Barnes, Mary 1923–2001
The Transfiguration 1969
oil on canvas 127 x 91.3
3617

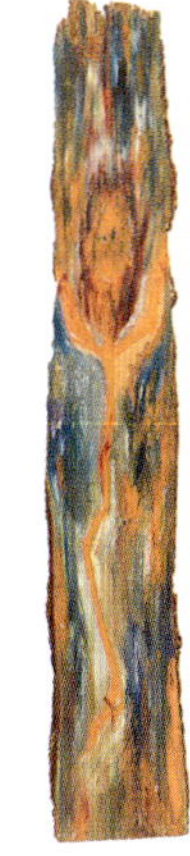

Barnes, Mary 1923–2001
Crucifixion 1977
oil on bark 141.3 x 23
3618

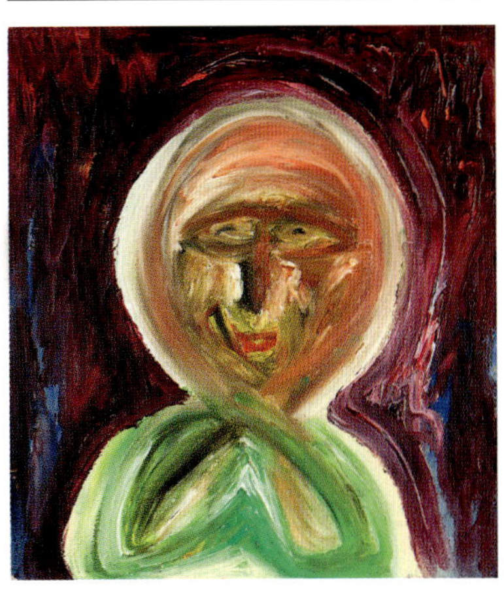

Barnes, Mary 1923–2001
Our Lady 1980
oil on canvas on board 36.7 x 31.7
3619

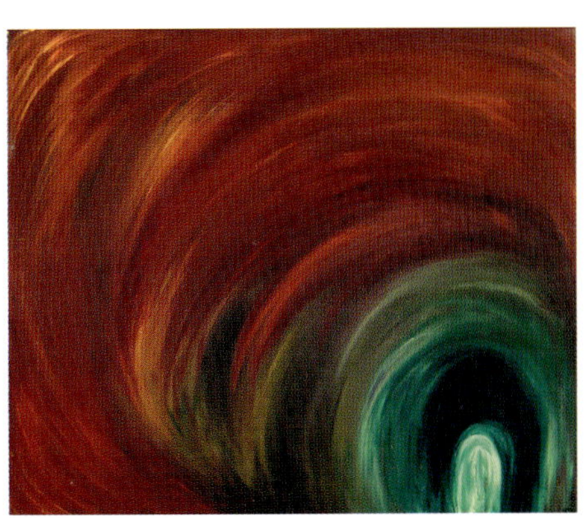

Barnes, Mary 1923–2001
Tunnel 1988
oil on board 53 x 61
3620

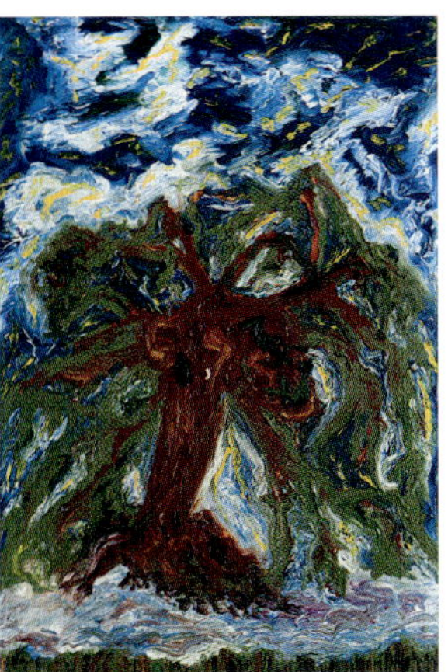

Barnes, Mary 1923–2001
Willow 1988
oil on board 58.1 x 38.5
3621

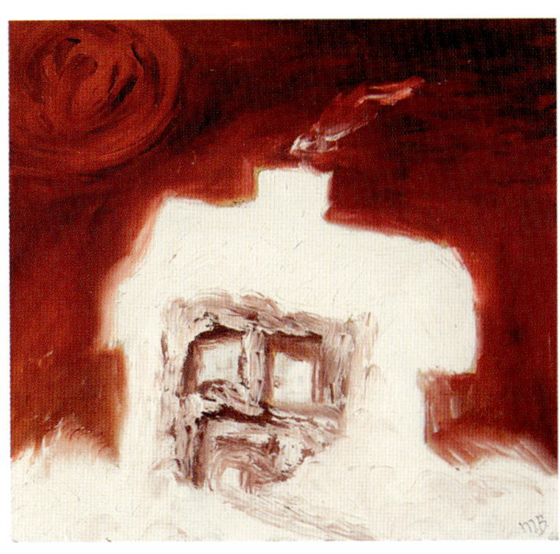

Barnes, Mary 1923–2001
Heavy Snowfall 1996
oil on board 20.6 x 21
3622

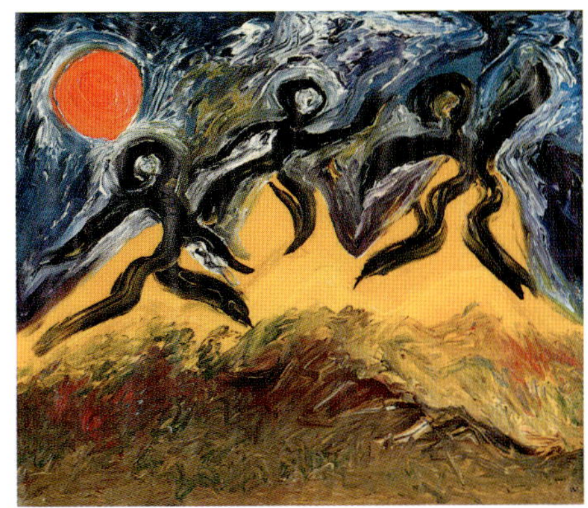

Barnes, Mary 1923–2001
Dancers of the Dunes 1997
oil on canvas 29 x 46.2
TEMP.15774

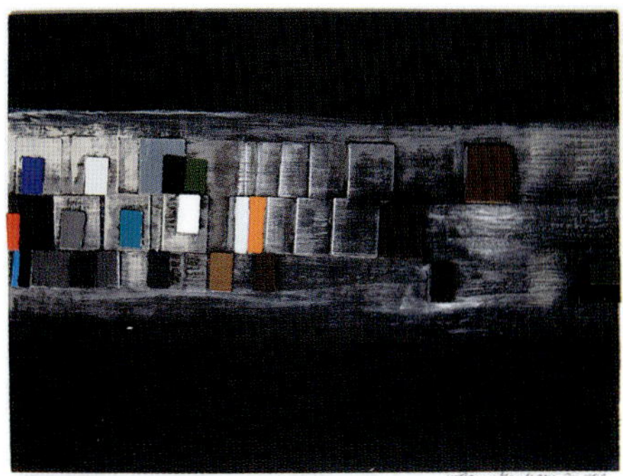

Barns-Graham, Wilhelmina 1912–2004
November (Collage 179) 1983
acrylic on board 19.5 x 25.9
3458

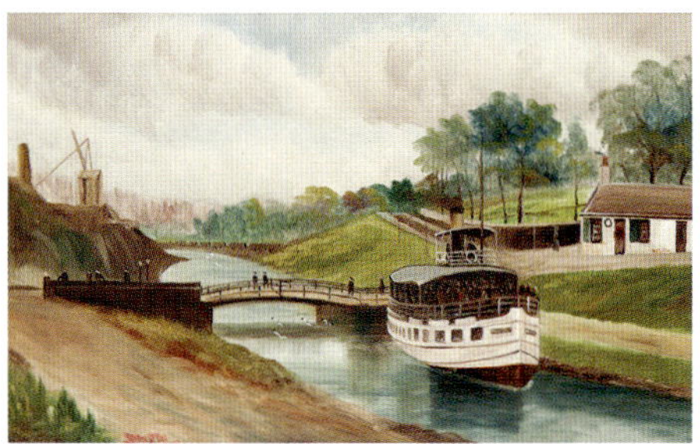

Barnston, J.
Old Lambhill Bridge, Glasgow 1913
oil on canvas 28.5 x 44
TEMP.1663

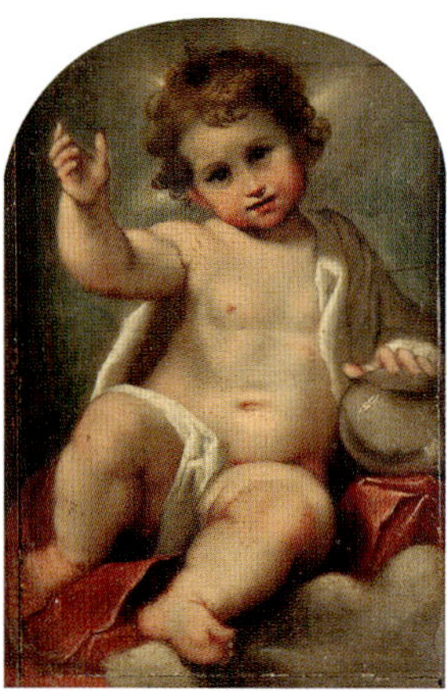

Barocci, Federico (after) 1535–1612
The Infant Saviour after c.1596
oil on panel 18.4 x 12.6
162

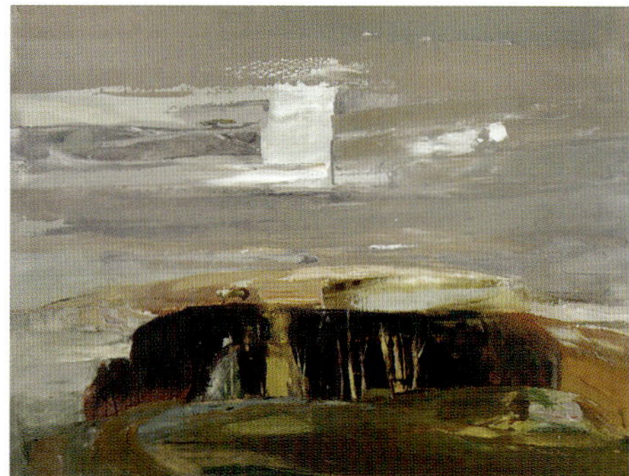

Barrie, Mardi 1931–2004
Across a Dark Wood 1963
oil on canvas 76.5 x 101.9
3196

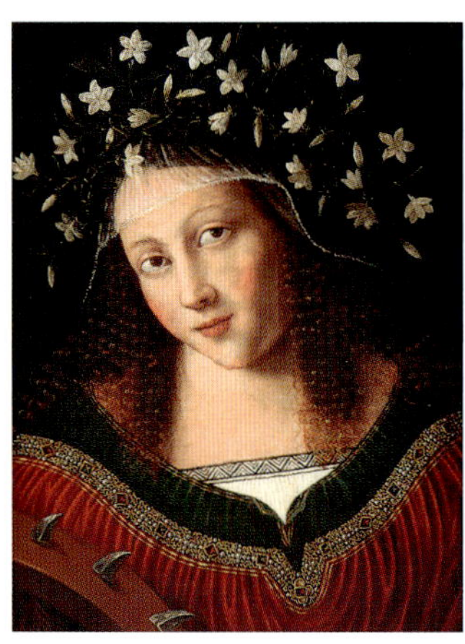

Bartolomeo Veneto c.1480–1531
Saint Catherine c.1520
oil on panel 35.2 x 27.9
210

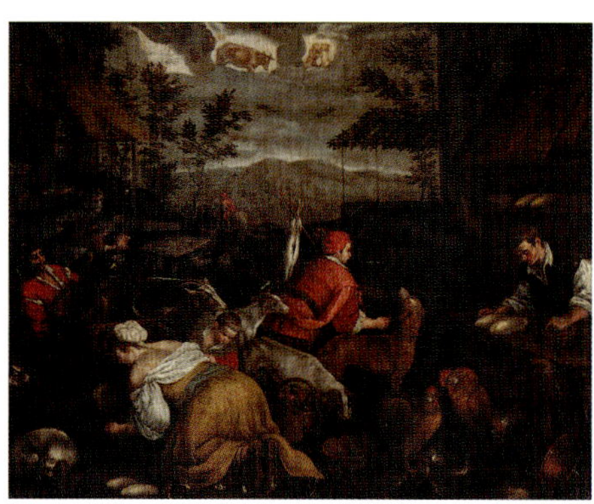

Bassano, Francesco II (after) 1549–1592
Spring c.1630 or later
oil on canvas 115.7 x 140.2
179

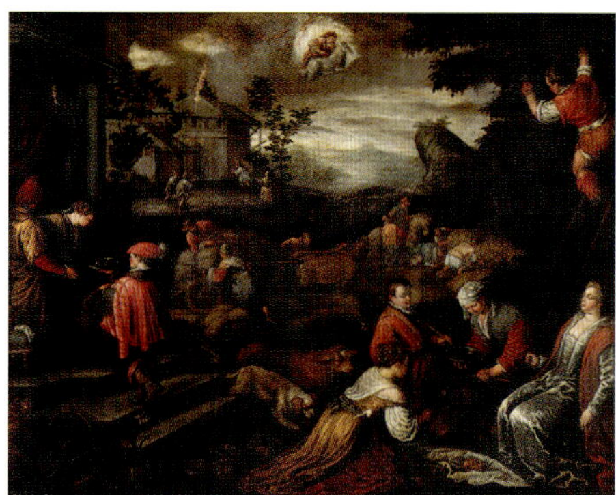

Bassano, Francesco II (after) 1549–1592
Summer c.1630 or later
oil on canvas 114 x 141.5
177

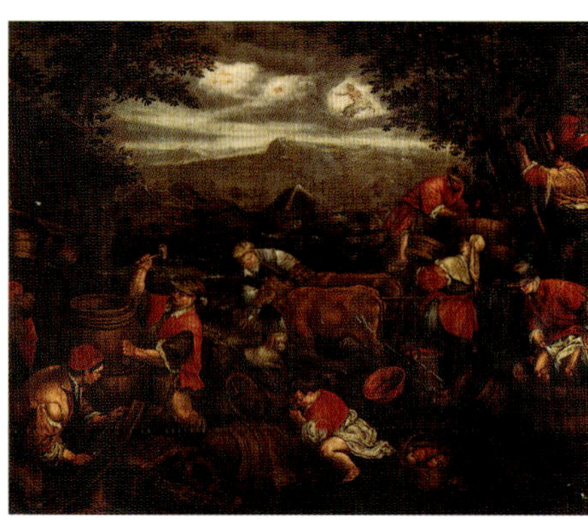

Bassano, Francesco II (after) 1549–1592
Autumn c.1630 or later
oil on canvas 116.1 x 140.9
180

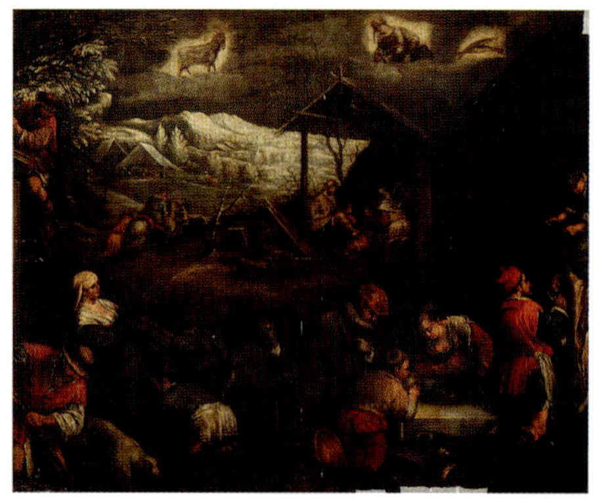

Bassano, Francesco II (after) 1549–1592
Winter c.1630 or later
oil on canvas 116.2 x 142.4
178

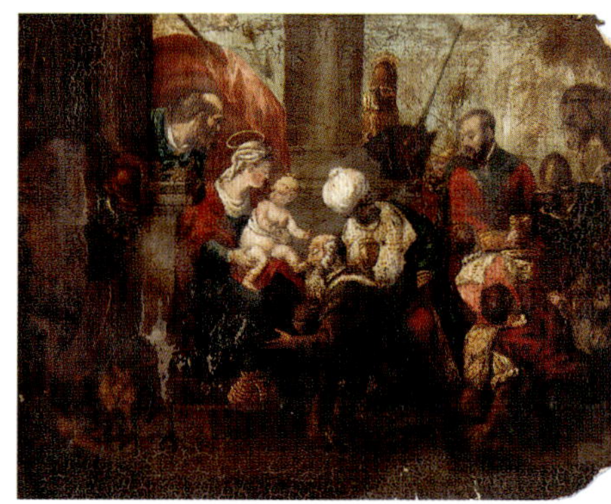

Bassano, Jacopo the elder (after)
c.1510–1592
The Adoration of the Magi 19th C
oil on paper 27.8 x 33.9
TEMP.20410

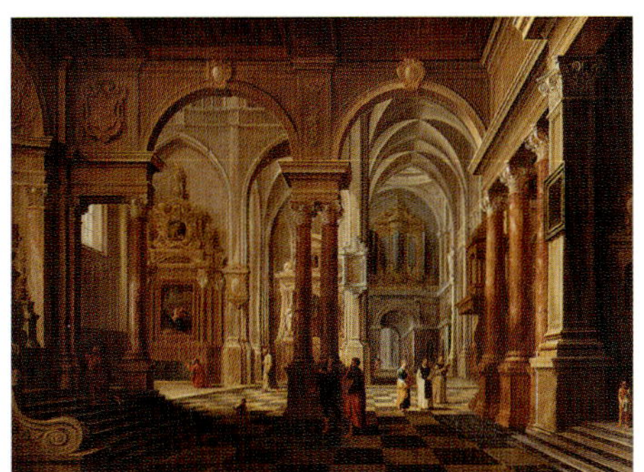

Bassen, Bartholomeus van c.1590–1652
An Imaginary Church Interior 1645
oil on canvas 100.3 x 135.8
2

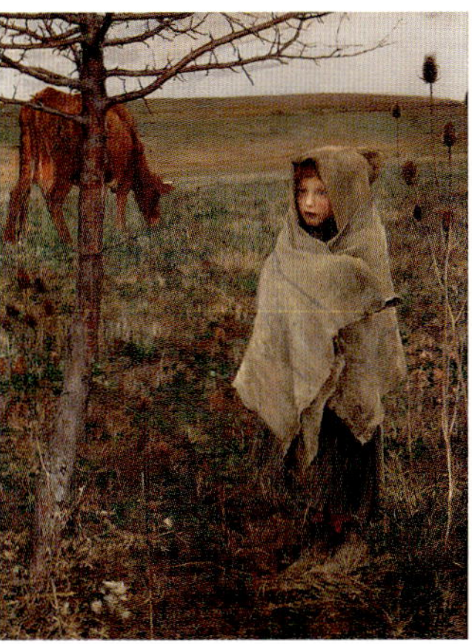

Bastien-Lepage, Jules 1848–1884
Poor Fauvette 1881
oil on canvas 162.5 x 125.7
1323

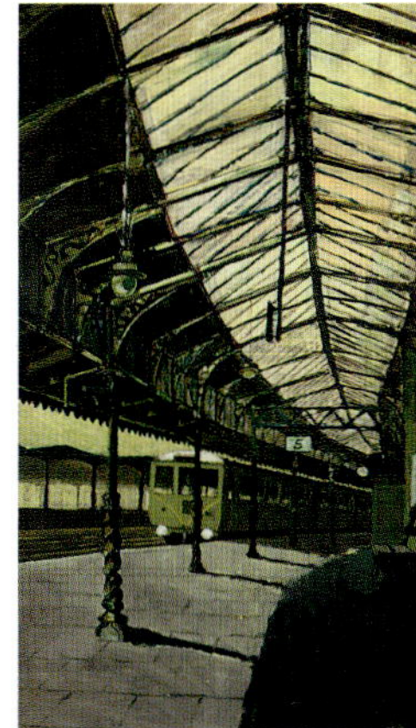

Bateman, Anthony Robert b.1942
Gloucester Central 1961
oil on hardboard 117.8 x 65.4
3179

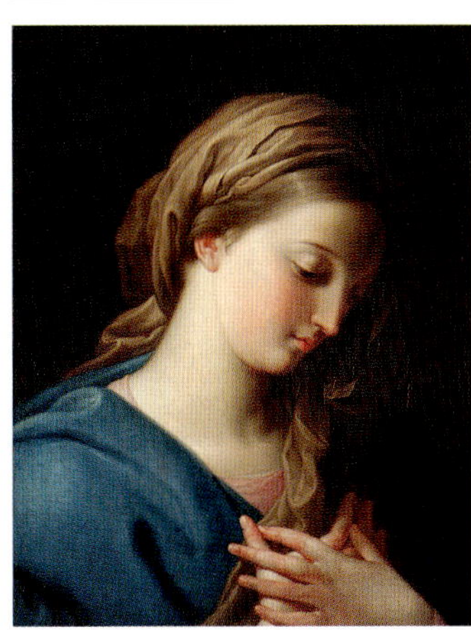

Batoni, Pompeo (studio of) 1708–1787
Virgin Annunciate
oil on canvas 49.5 x 38.4
916

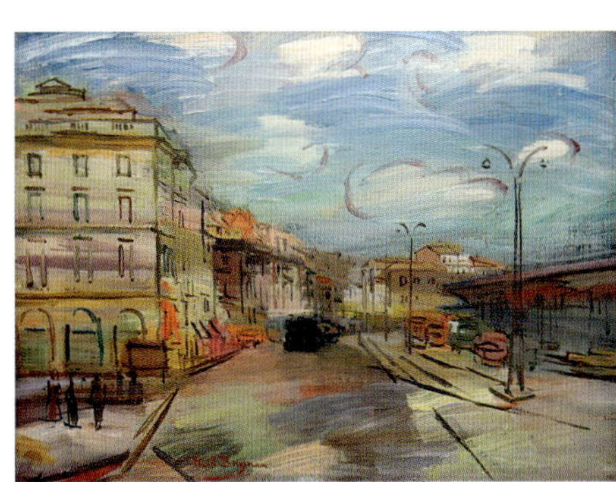

Baynes, Keith 1887–1977
Quai des Chartrons, Bordeaux c.1949
oil on canvas 35.6 x 45.7
2892

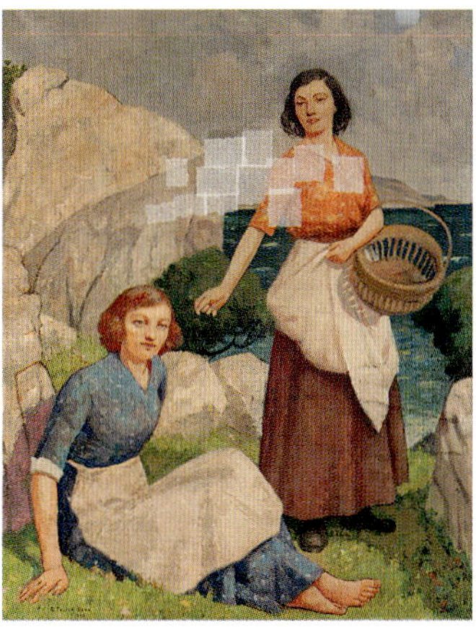

Bear, George Telfer 1876–1973
Figures in a Landscape 1940
oil on canvas 122 x 91.4
3443

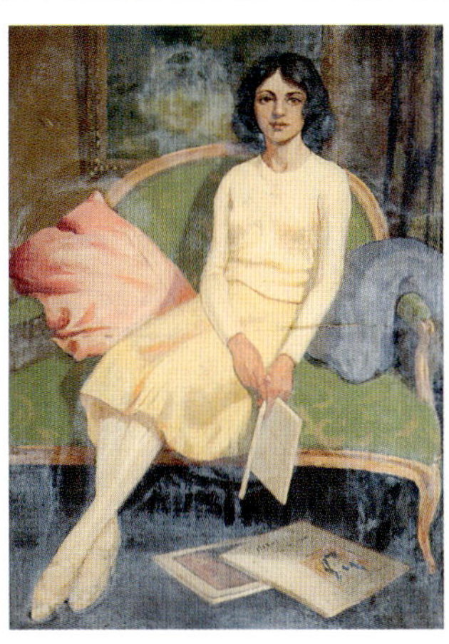

Bear, George Telfer 1876–1973
La jeunesse c.1940
oil on canvas 101.6 x 76.2
2152

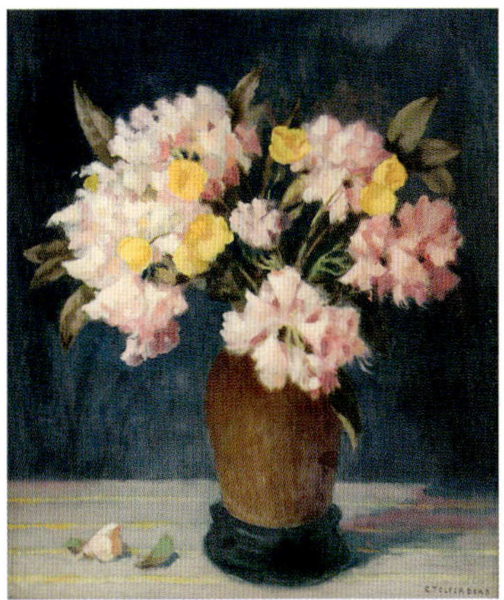

Bear, George Telfer 1876–1973
Rhododendron and Icelandic Poppies
oil on board 66 x 55.9
2594

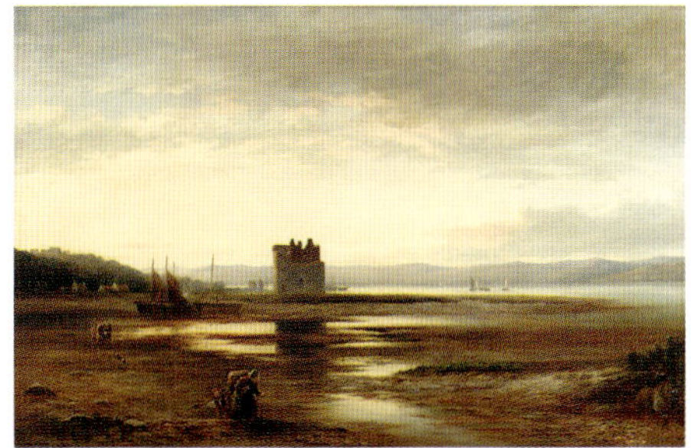

Beattie-Brown, William 1831–1909
Lochranza Castle c.1871
oil on canvas 85.1 x 135.9
1714

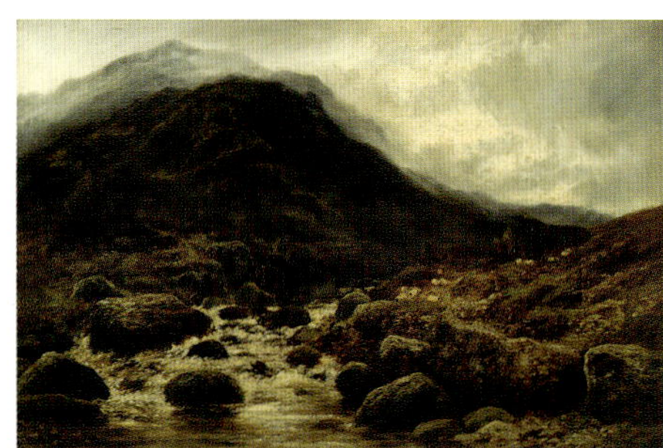

Beattie-Brown, William 1831–1909
*A Mountain Burn, Glen Shieldaig,
Ross-shire* c.1871–1884
oil on canvas 50.8 x 76.2
1852

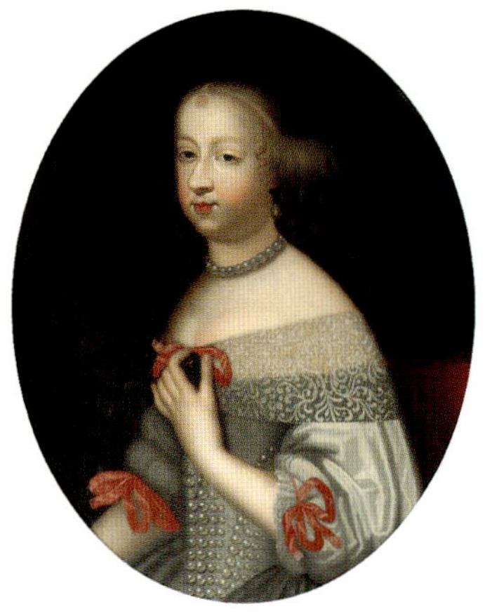

Beaubrun, Charles 1604–1692
Maria Theresa of Spain (1638–1683) 1659
oil on canvas 73 x 58.7
PC.109

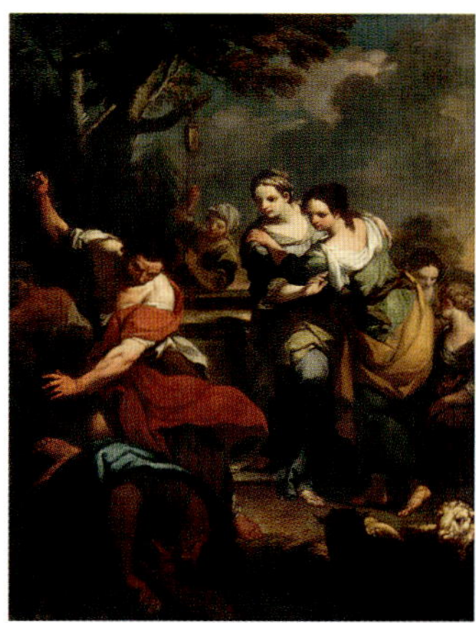

**Beaumont, Claudio Francesco
(attributed to)** 1694–1766
Moses and the Daughters of Jethro
c.1730–1740
oil on canvas 111.5 x 84.8
151

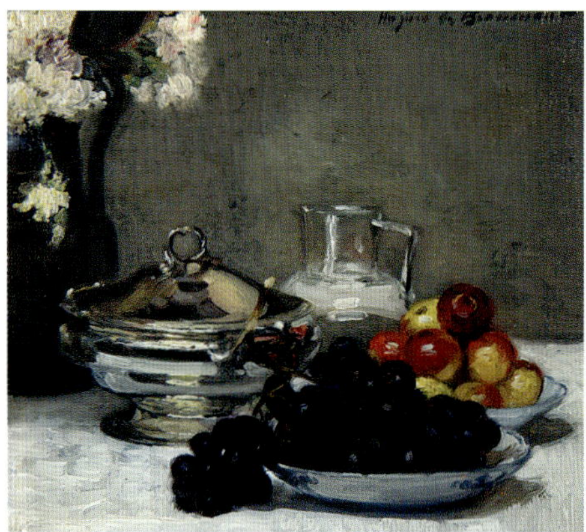

Beaumont, Hugues de 1874–1947
Still Life
oil on panel 17.5 x 19.8
2375

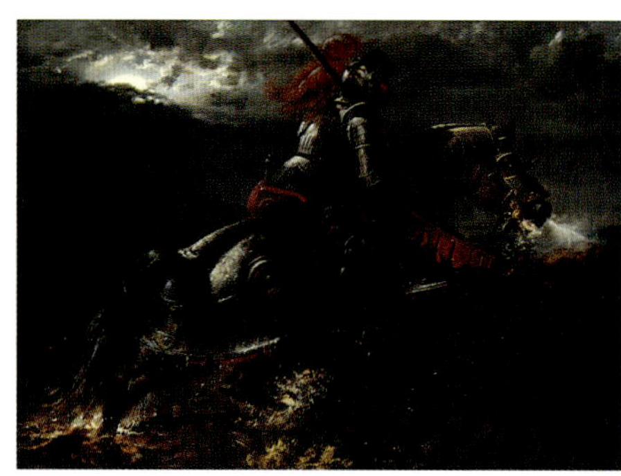

Beavis, Richard 1824–1896
The Midnight Ride of Deloraine 1869
oil on canvas 49.5 x 67.3
868

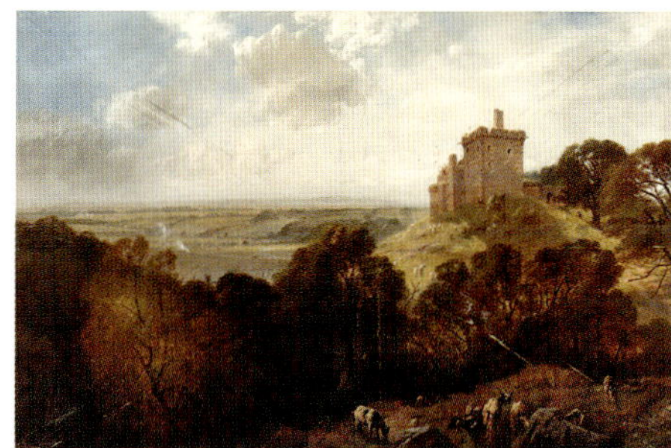

Beavis, Richard 1824–1896
Castle Campbell, near Dollar
oil on canvas 101.6 x 154.9
2239

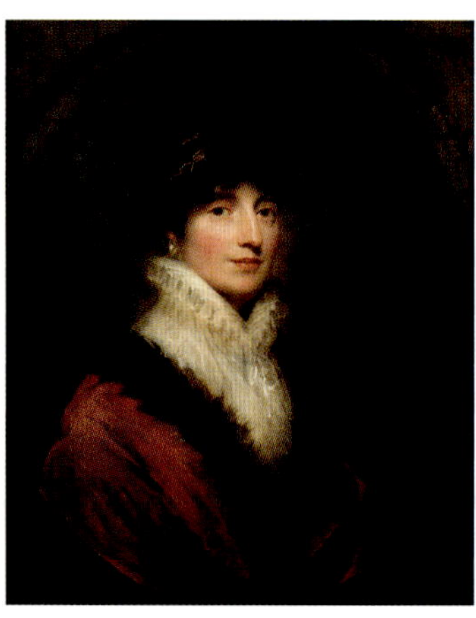

Beechey, William 1753–1839
Margaret Stirling of Ardoch (c.1754–c.1825)
oil on canvas 76.2 x 63.5
L.4.1971 (P)

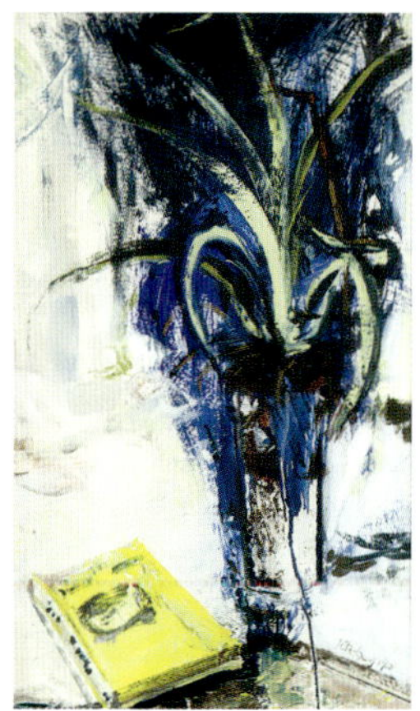

Begg, Nita b.1920
Exotic Plant 1968
oil on cardboard 76.6 x 45.1
3260

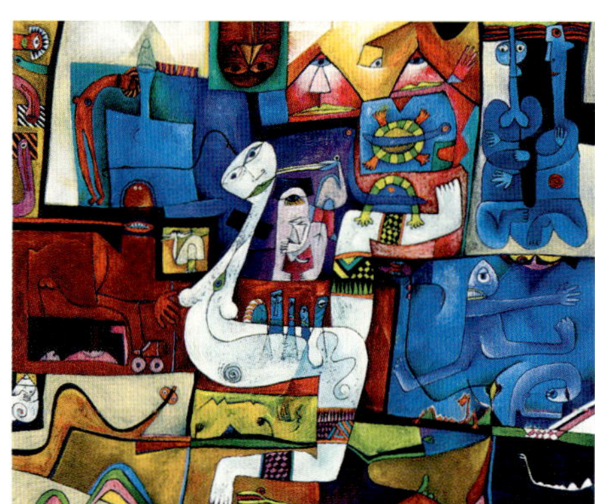

Beier, Georgina b.1938
Untitled 1988
oil on hardboard 60.9 x 69.4
3563

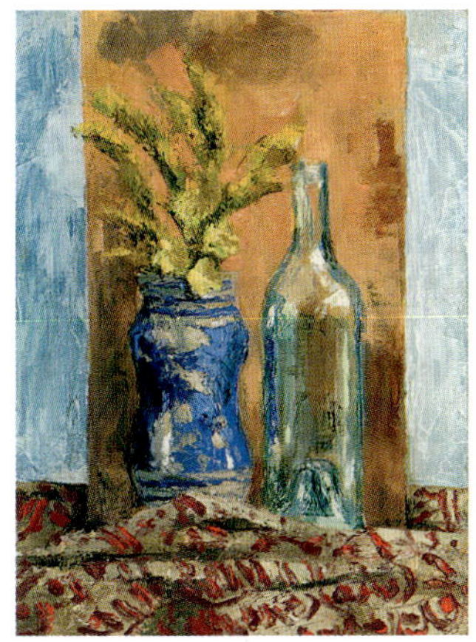

Bell, Quentin 1910–1996
Still Life
oil on canvas 50.8 x 36.8
3199

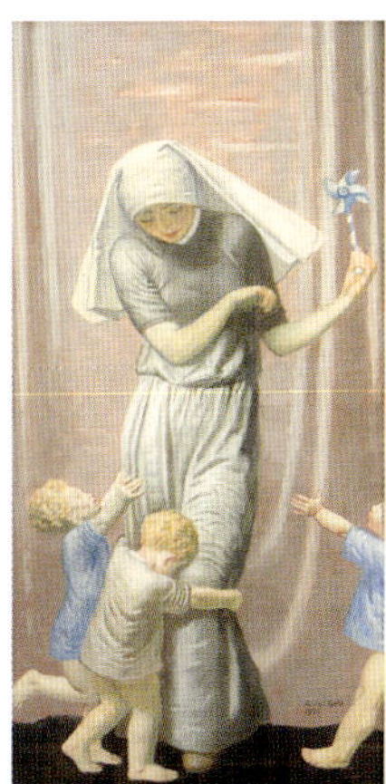

Bell, Robert Anning 1863–1933
The Toy Windmill 1931
oil on panel 72.4 x 36.8
1842

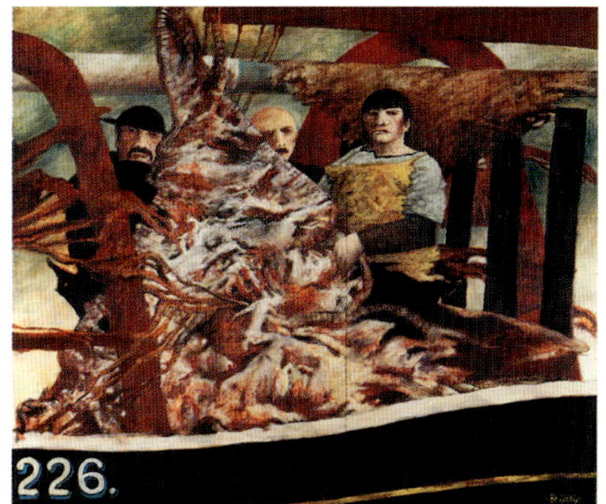

Bellany, John b.1942
The Fishers 1966
oil on hardboard 183.2 x 213.4
3466 ✴

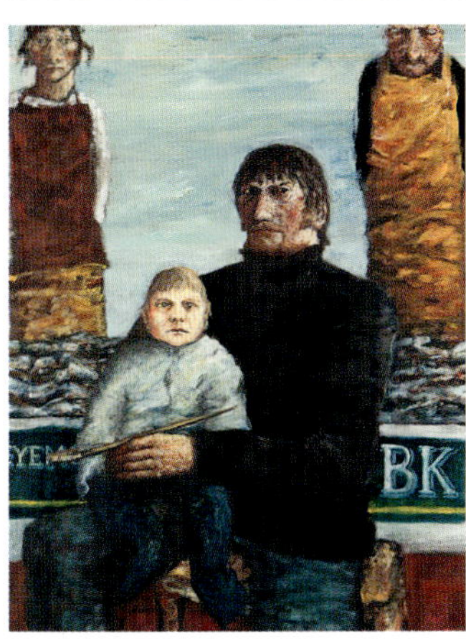

Bellany, John b.1942
Self Portrait with Jonathan 1967
oil on hardboard 122 x 91.3
3411 ✴

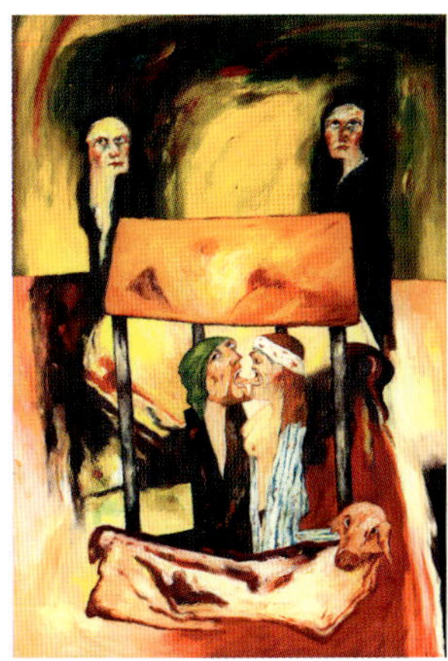

Bellany, John b.1942
Journey to the End of the Night (triptych, left wing) 1972
oil on hardboard 209.5 x 138.4
3481.1 (left) ✴

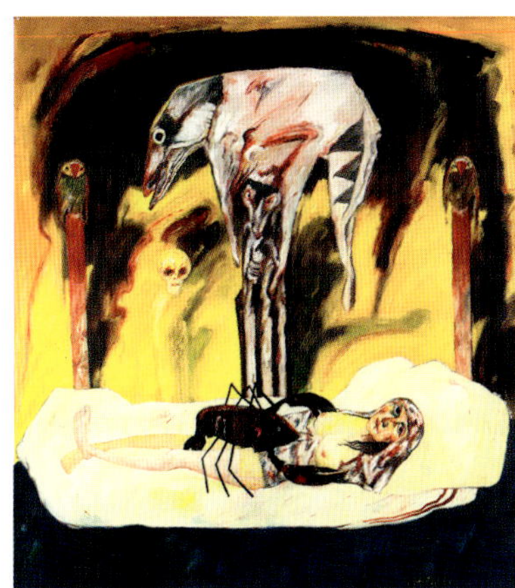

Bellany, John b.1942
Journey to the End of the Night (triptych, centre panel) 1972
oil on hardboard 209.5 x 184.1
3481.2 (centre) ✴

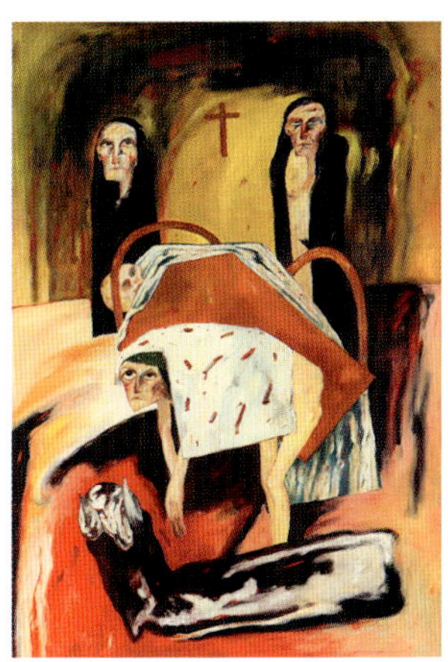

Bellany, John b.1942
Journey to the End of the Night (triptych, right wing) 1972
oil on hardboard 209.5 x 138.4
3481.3 (right) ✴

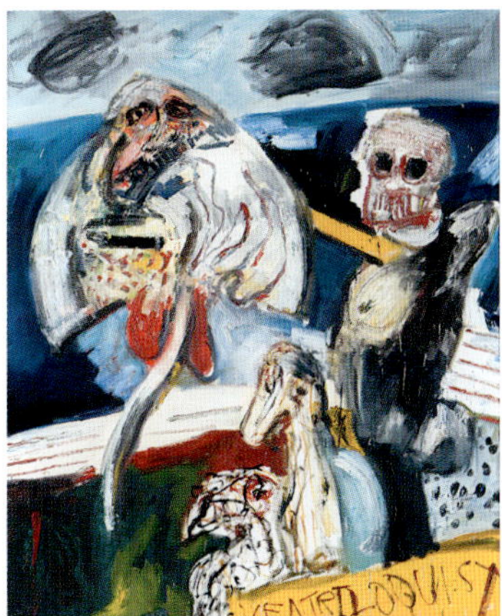

Bellany, John b.1942
The Ventriloquist 1983
oil on canvas 181.1 x 151.5
3488 ✴

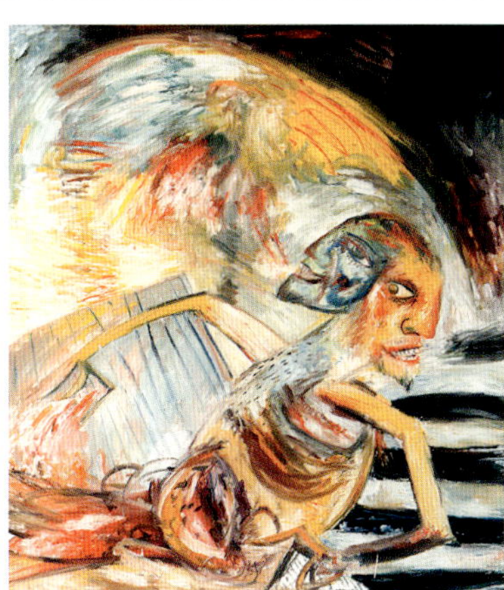

Bellany, John b.1942
Prometheus II 1988
oil on canvas 172.8 x 152.4
3462 ✴

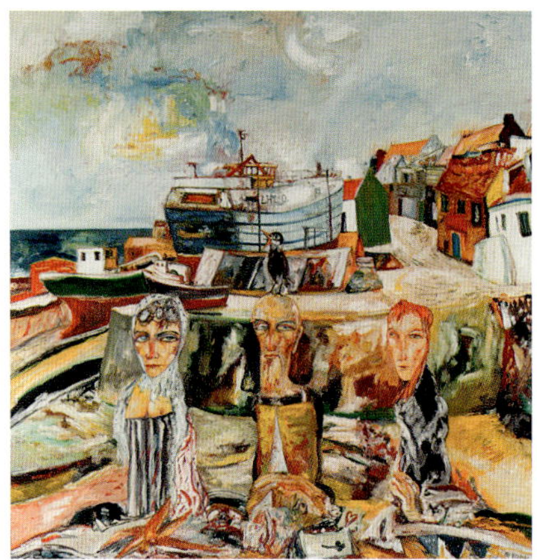

Bellany, John b.1942
Scottish Gothic 1990
oil on canvas 203.2 x 214
3465

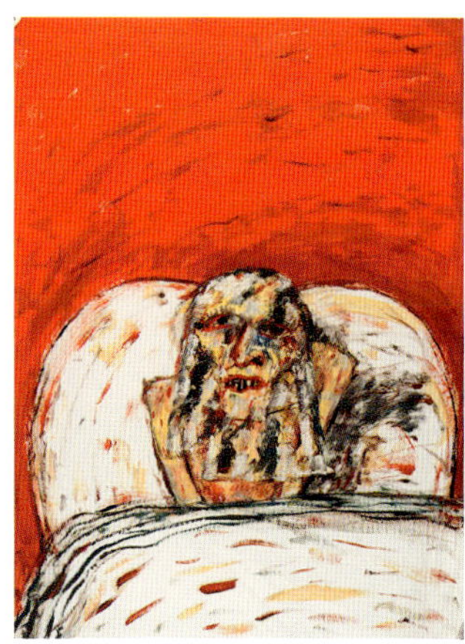

Bellany, John b.1942
Old Woman 1991
oil on paper 76.2 x 55.9
3489

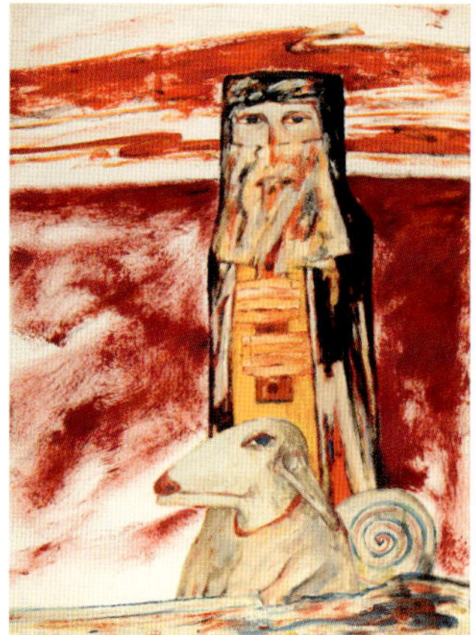

Bellany, John b.1942
Top Hat Masquerade 1991
oil on paper 79.4 x 57
3490

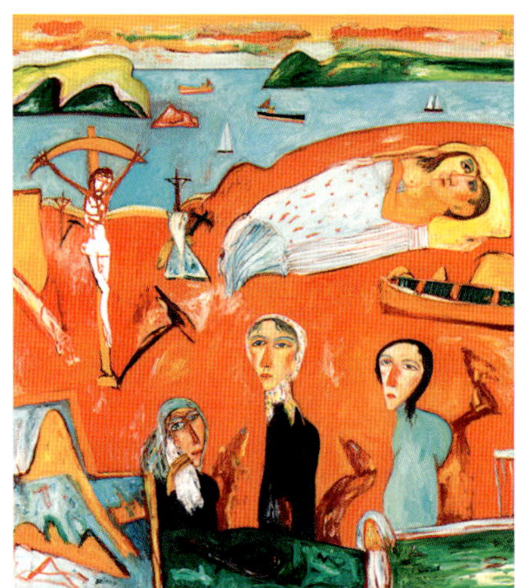

Bellany, John b.1942
Untitled 1999
oil on canvas 201.3 x 176.2
3631

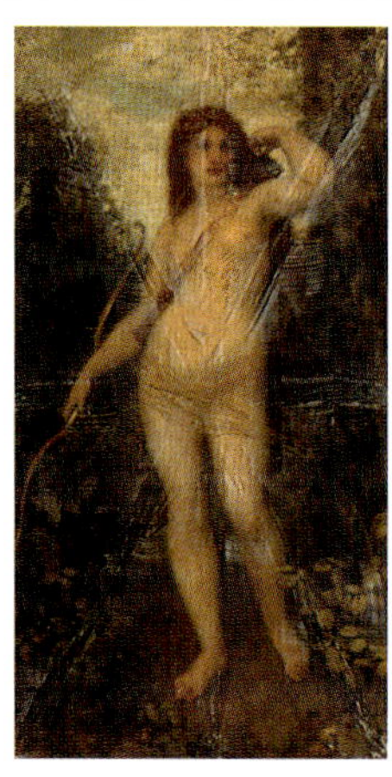

Bellenger, Georges 1847–1915 & **Maris, Matthijs** 1839–1917
Diana c.1878–1883
oil on canvas 199.4 x 103.8
1727

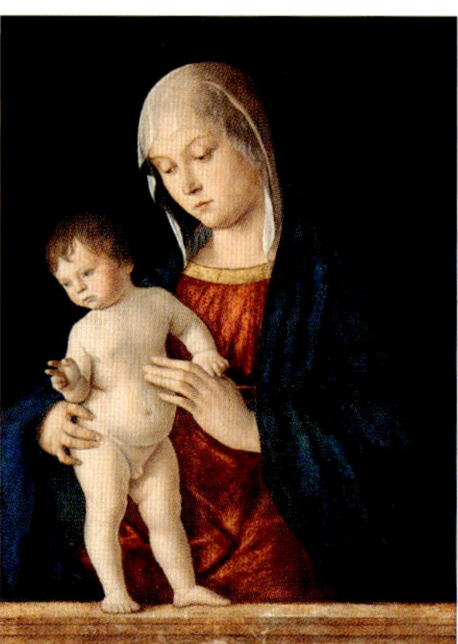

Bellini, Giovanni c.1438 (?)–1516
Virgin and Child c.1480–1485
oil on panel 62.2 x 46.4
575

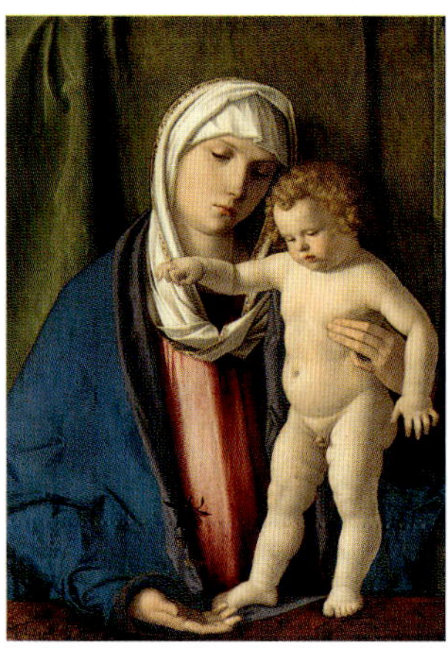

Bellini, Giovanni c.1438 (?)–1516
Virgin and Child c.1485–1488
oil on panel 62.3 x 47.7
35.4

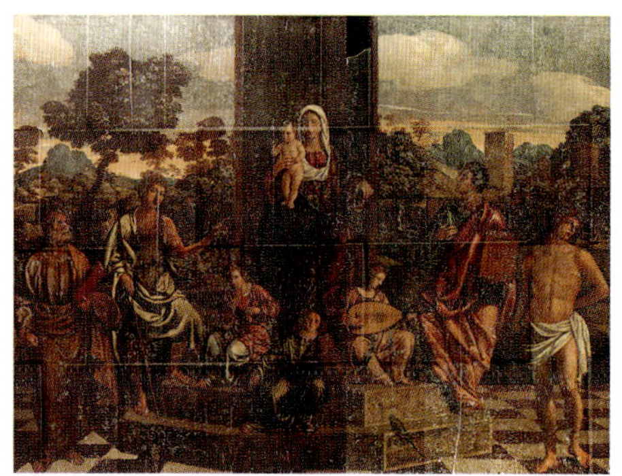

Bellini, Giovanni (follower of)
c.1438 (?)–1516
Virgin and Child Enthroned with Saints Peter, John the Baptist, John the (...) c.1520–1530
oil on panel 304 x 391
188

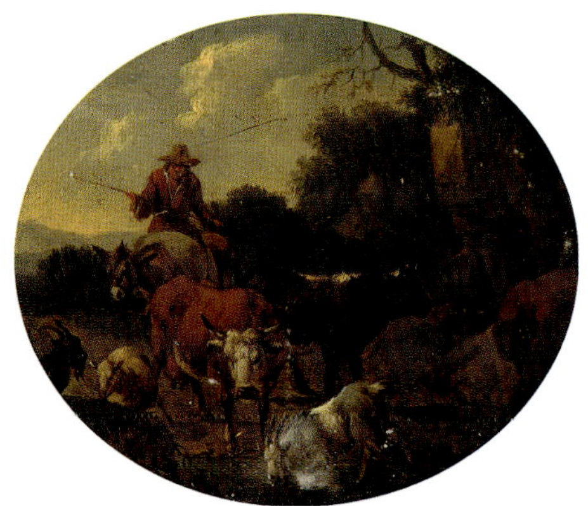

Berchem, Nicolaes 1620–1683
Landscape with Cattle 1650
oil on copper 8.9 x 10.8
PL.107 (P)

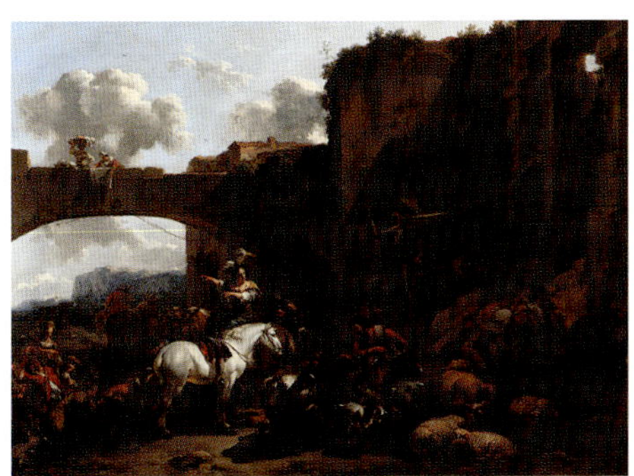

Berchem, Nicolaes 1620–1683
A Country Gathering by a Bridge c.1660–1665
oil on canvas 73.3 x 98.7
566

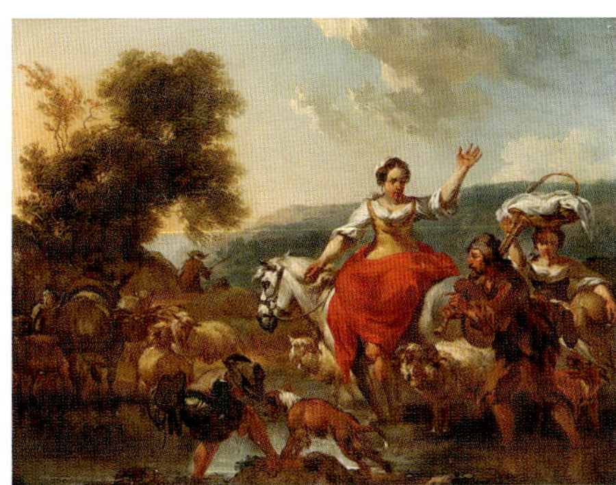

Berchem, Nicolaes 1620–1683
Peasants and Animals Crossing a Ford
oil on panel 26.6 x 31.8
53

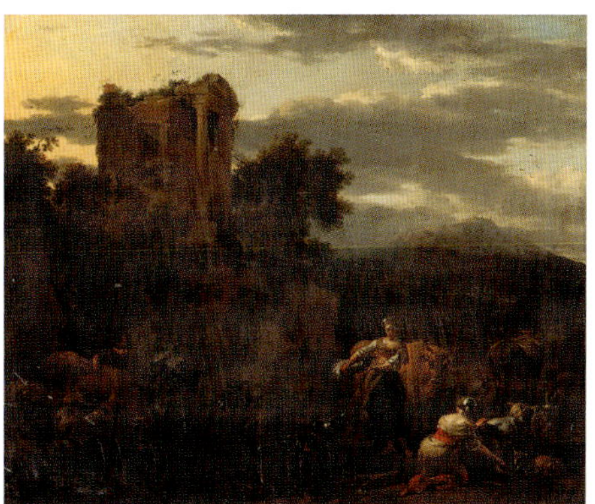

Berchem, Nicolaes (after) 1620–1683
*Landscape with a Ruined Temple, Peasants
and Cattle* 17th C–18th C
oil on canvas 55.2 x 64.1
569

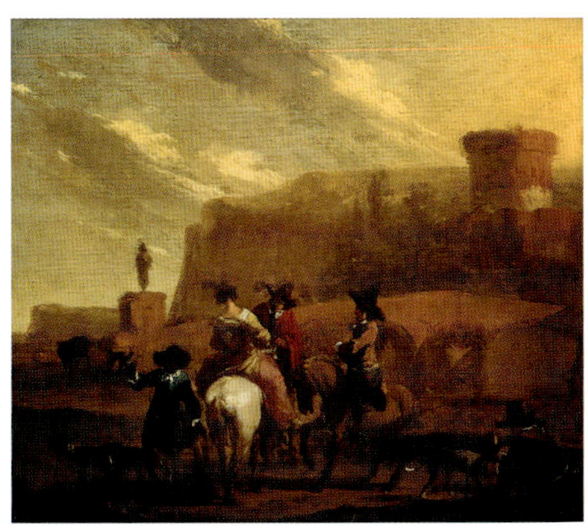

Berchem, Nicolaes (after) 1620–1683
Landscape with a Hawking Party late 18th C
oil on panel 22.2 x 26.7
1

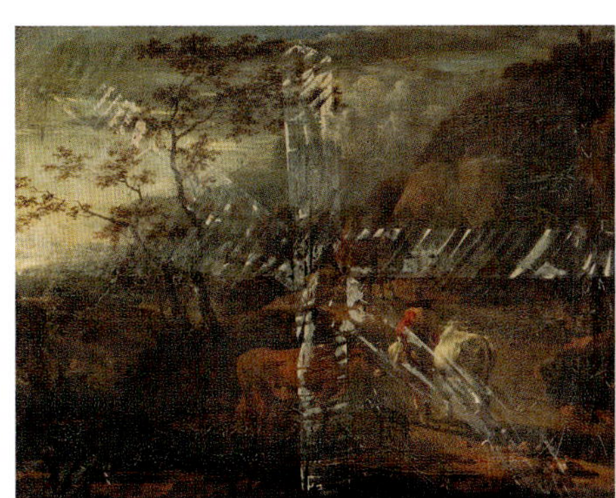

Berchem, Nicolaes (after) 1620–1683
*Landscape with Cattle and Figures on a
Mountain Path*
oil on canvas 51.1 x 65.7
41

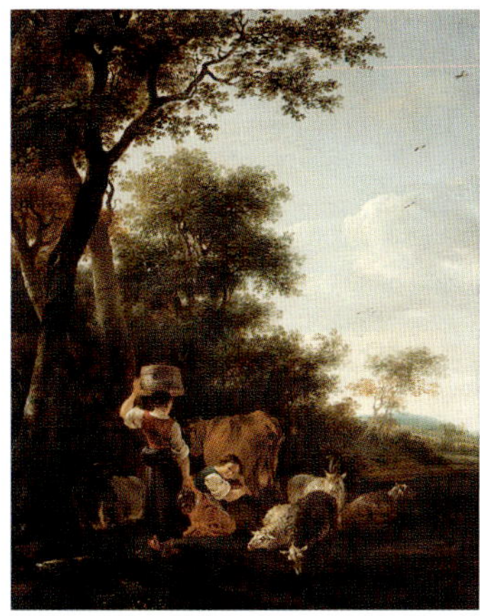

Berchem, Nicolaes (attributed to)
1620–1683
Milkmaids and Cattle by a Spinney c.1645
oil on panel 55.2 x 43.3
568

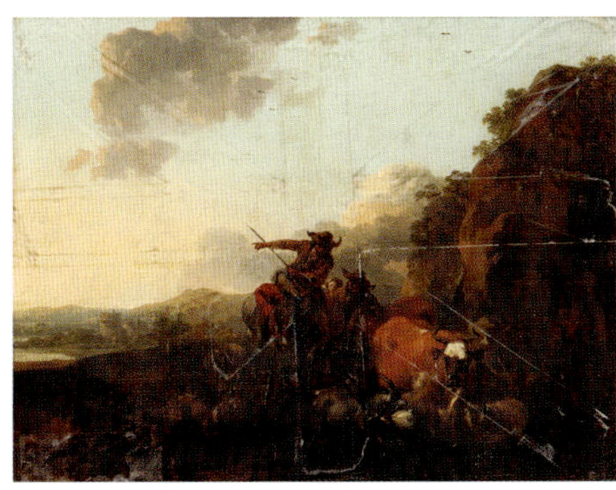

Berchem, Nicolaes (attributed to)
1620–1683
*Landscape with Peasants Driving
Cattle* c.1647–1683
oil on canvas 37.5 x 47
567

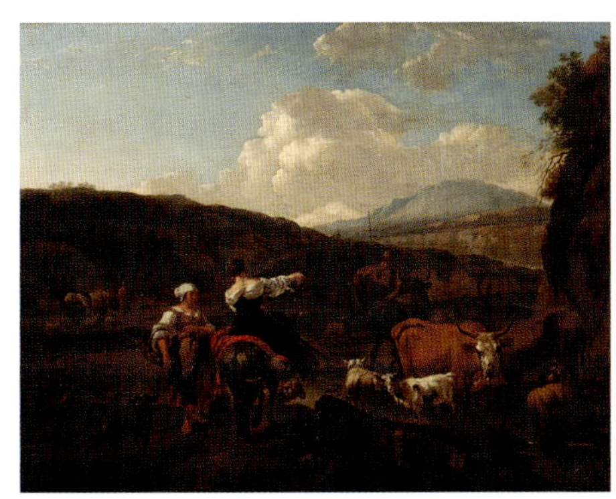

Berchem, Nicolaes (imitator of) 1620–1683
*Landscape with Cattle and Figures at a
Ford* 17th C–18th C
oil on canvas 57.4 x 71.7
117

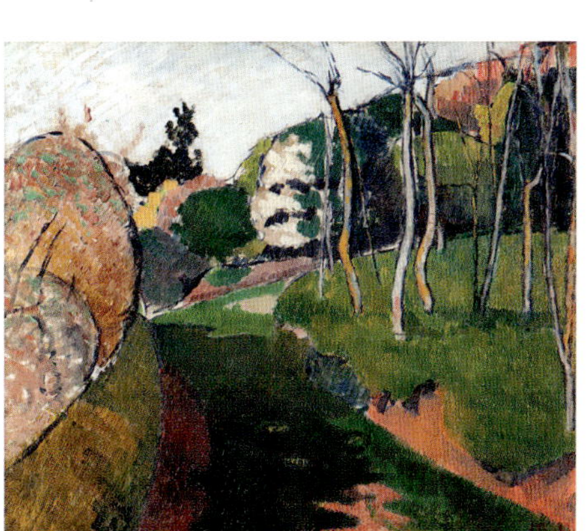

Bernard, Émile 1868–1941
Landscape, Saint-Briac c.1887–1889
oil on canvas 54 x 65
3401

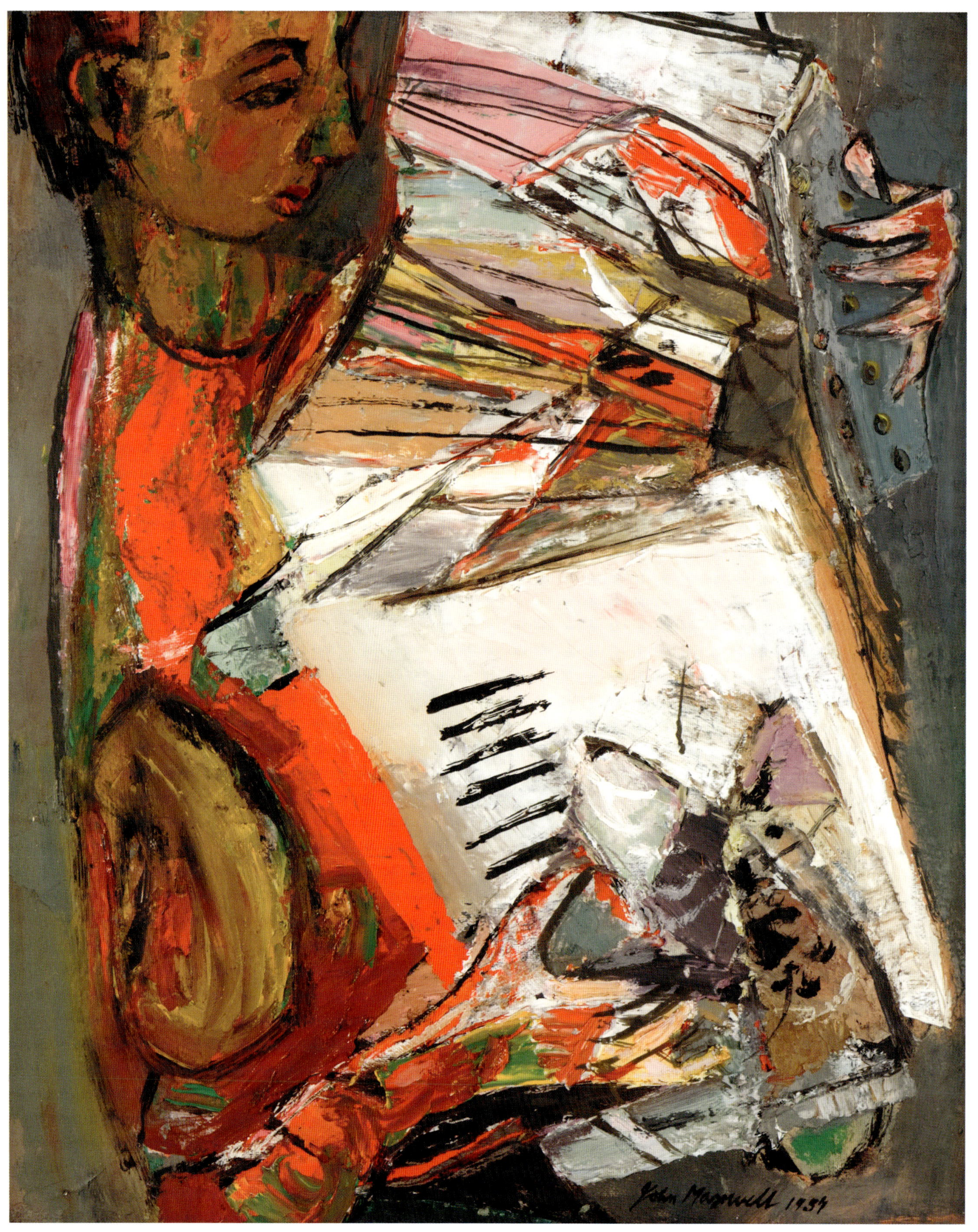

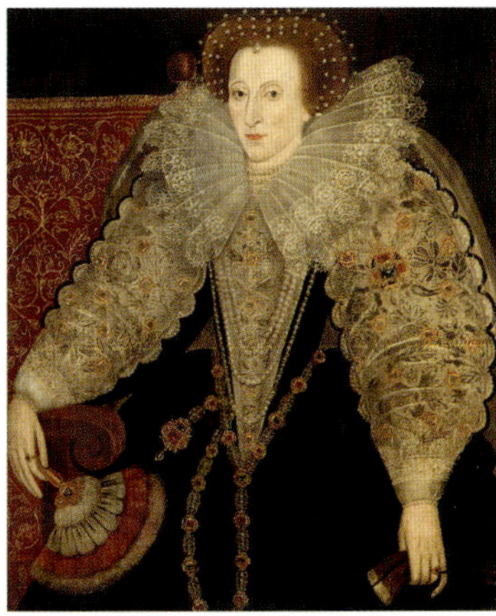

Bettes, John the younger d.1615
Queen Elizabeth (1533–1603) c.1590
oil on canvas on panel 89.2 x 72.4
PL.4 (P)

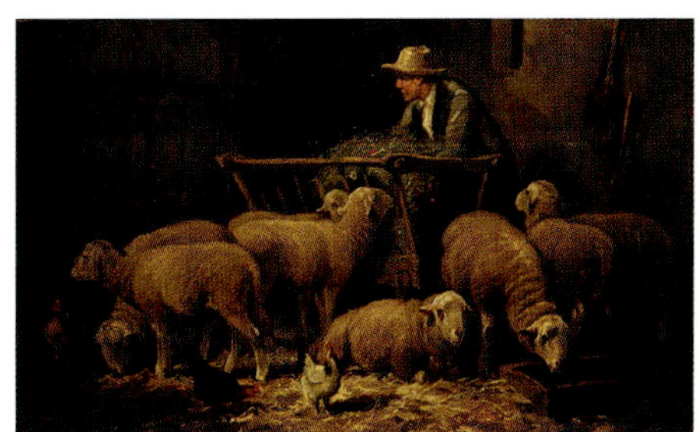

Beul, Franz de 1849–1919
Feeding Sheep
oil on panel 24 x 34
822

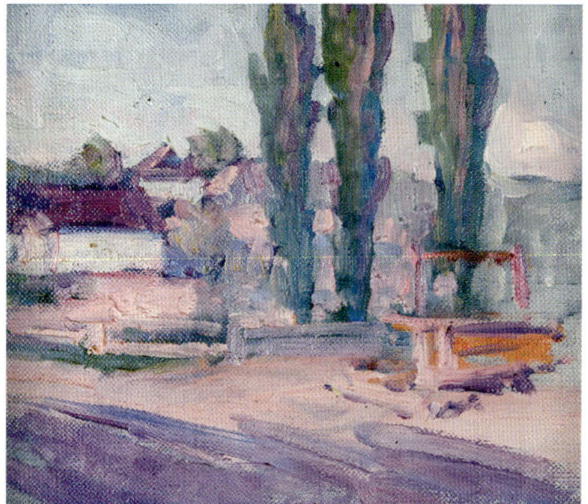

Bevan, Robert Polhill 1865–1925
Three Poplars and a Well c.1908
oil on canvas on hardboard 26.7 x 32.4
3255

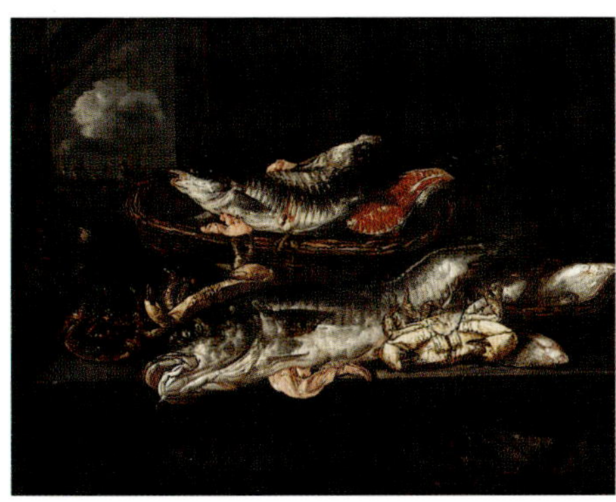

Beyeren, Abraham van 1620/1621–1690
*Still Life: Haddock, Plaice, Crabs and
Lobster* c.1650–1670
oil on canvas 99.4 x 125
935

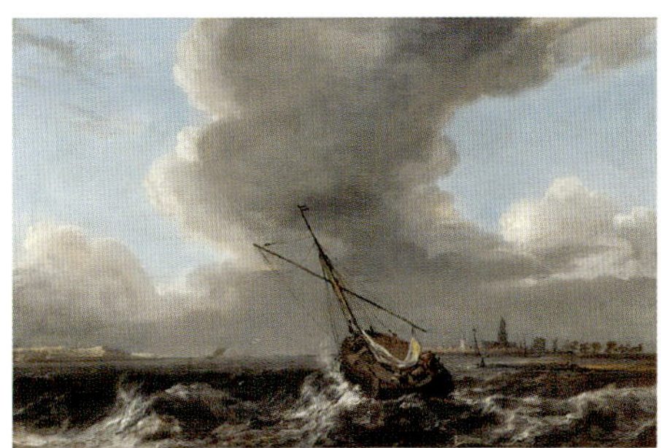

Beyeren, Abraham van (attributed to)
1620/1621–1690
*A Small Dutch Vessel at Anchor off the Coast
in a Rough Sea*
oil on canvas 46.3 x 67.9
613

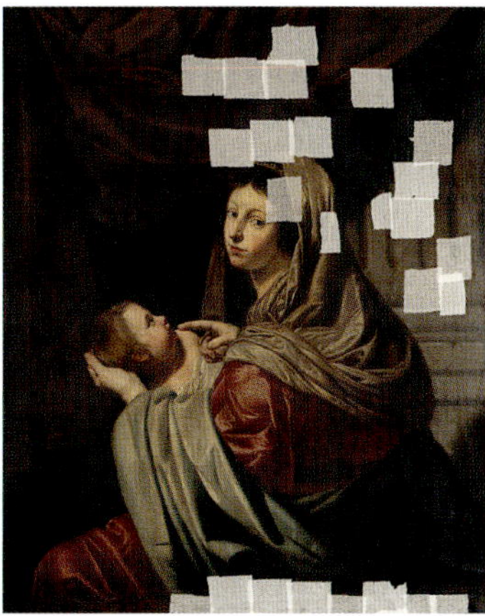

Bijlert, Jan van (after) 1597–1671
Virgin and Child 17th C
oil on canvas 117.7 x 94
273

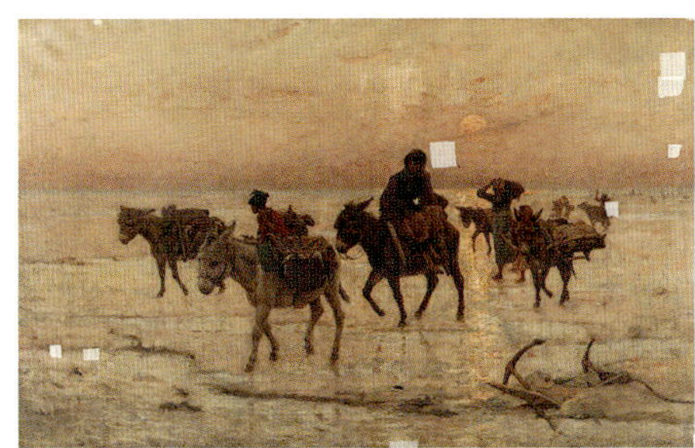

Billet, Pierre 1837–1922
Bringing in the Catch 1885
oil on canvas 117 x 182.9
2632

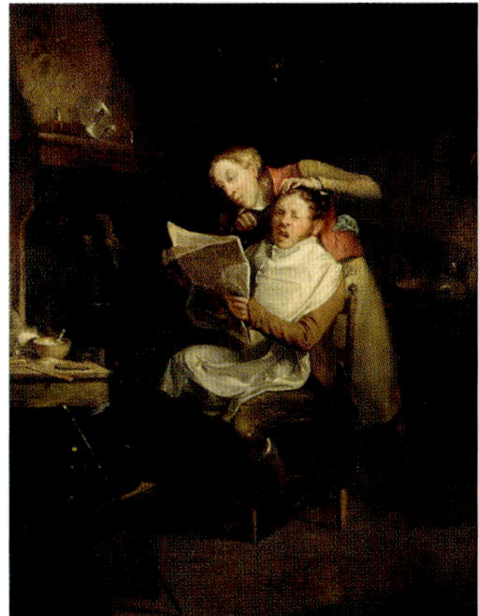

Bird, Edward 1772–1819
A Man at a Barber's Shop, Reading a Paper
oil on canvas 61 x 45.5
NR.23

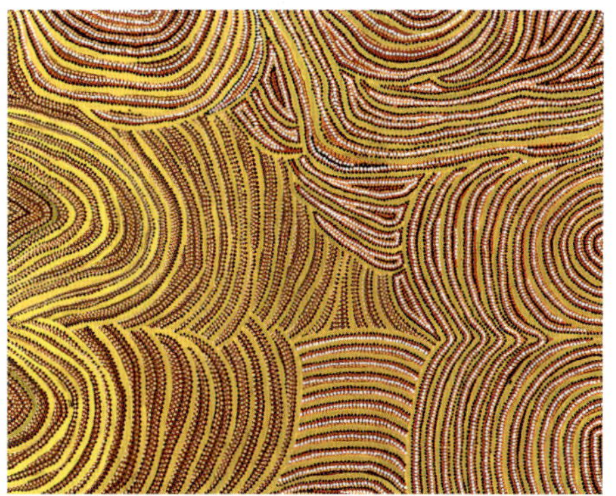

Bird Petyarre, June b.c.1960
Arnkerrthe, Sacred Lands 1992
acrylic on canvas 120.7 x 149.2
3514

Facing page: Maxwell, John, 1905–1962, *Boy with an Accordion*, 1957, (p. 260)

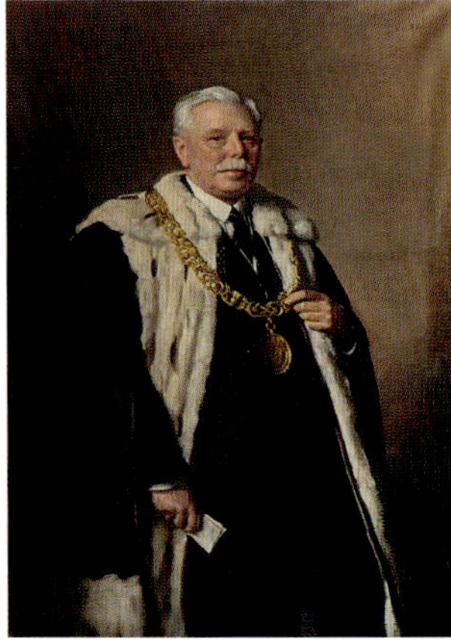

Birley, Oswald Hornby Joseph 1880–1952
*Sir Thomas Kelly, Lord Provost of Glasgow
(1929–1932)* 1932
oil on canvas 152.3 x 101.6
1841

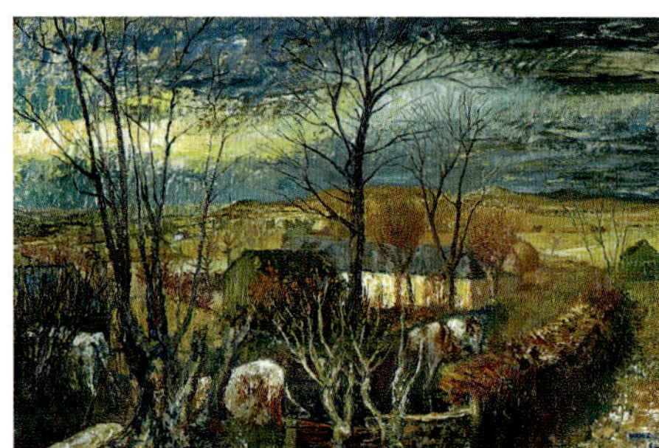

Birnie, William 1929–2006
The Rinnans Road, Balfron 1956
oil on hardboard 60.9 x 92.1
3058

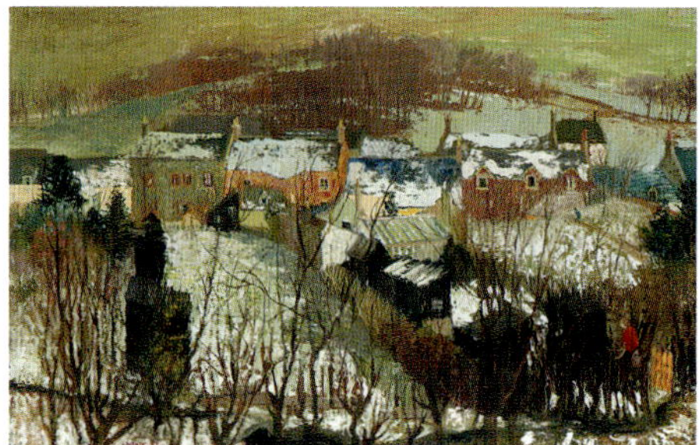

Birnie, William 1929–2006
Melting Snow, Kilbarchan 1957
oil on hardboard 60.9 x 91.4
3081

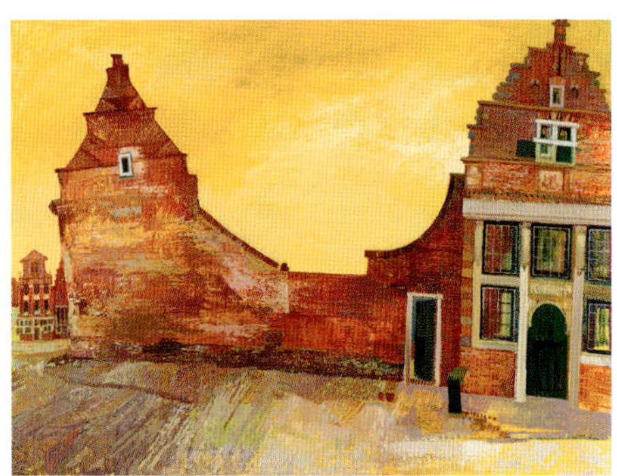

Birnie, William 1929–2006
Brick Galleons 1973
oil on hardboard 97.8 x 128.3
NR.90

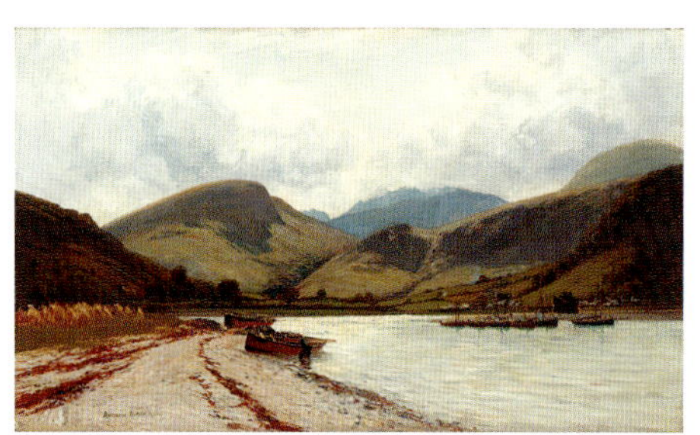

Black, Andrew 1850–1916
Lochranza
oil on canvas 76.2 x 127
1758

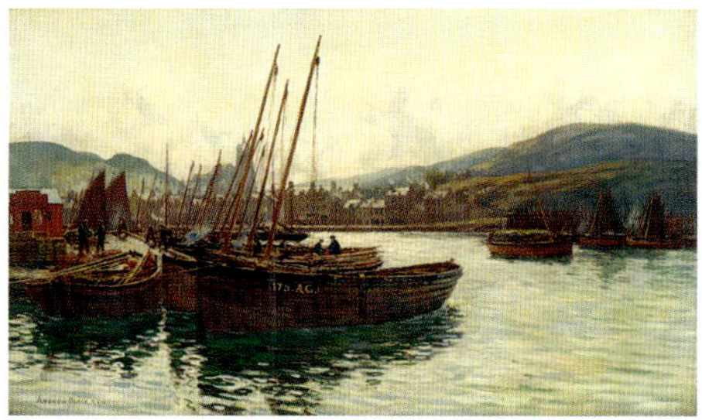

Black, Andrew 1850–1916
Tarbert, Loch Fyne
oil on canvas 76.2 x 127
1412

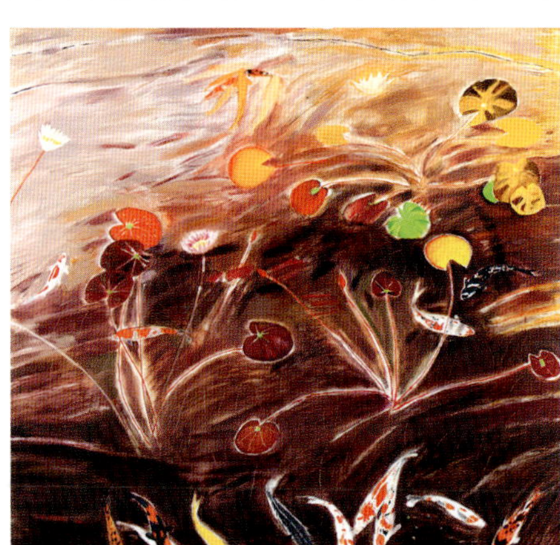

Blackadder, Elizabeth V. b.1931
Water Lilies and Koi Carp 1993
oil on canvas 172.2 x 182.7
3548

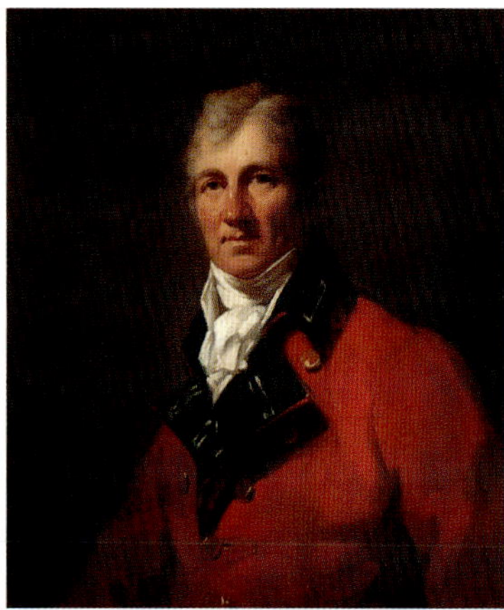

Blackburn, Samuel active 1838–1857
*Sir Michael Shaw-Stewart (1766–1825), 5th Bt
of Ardgowan (after Henry Raeburn)* 1839
oil on canvas 76 x 63.3
PL.174 (P)

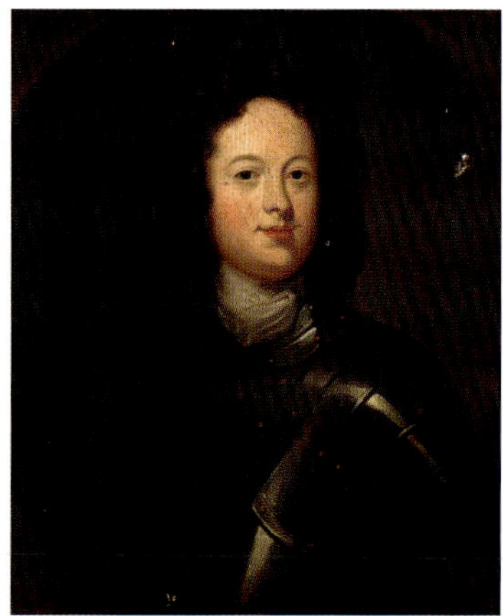

Blackburn, Samuel (attributed to) active
1838–1857
Sir John Maxwell (1648–1732), 1st Bt 1838
oil on canvas 78.1 x 65.4
PL.161 (P)

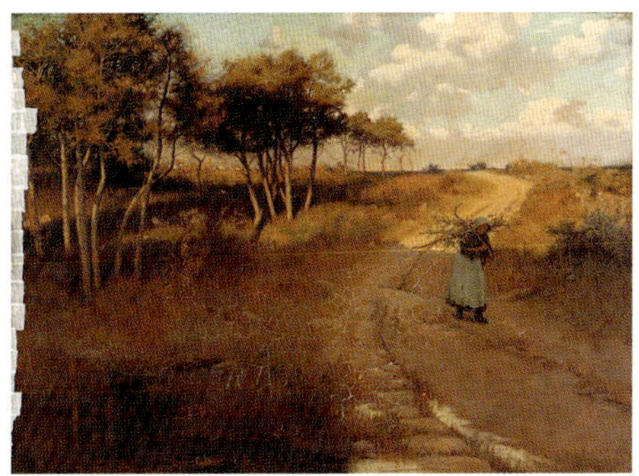

Blackburne, Ernest Robert Ireland 1864–1947
Lengthening Shadows 1894
oil on canvas 114.3 x 152.4
2129

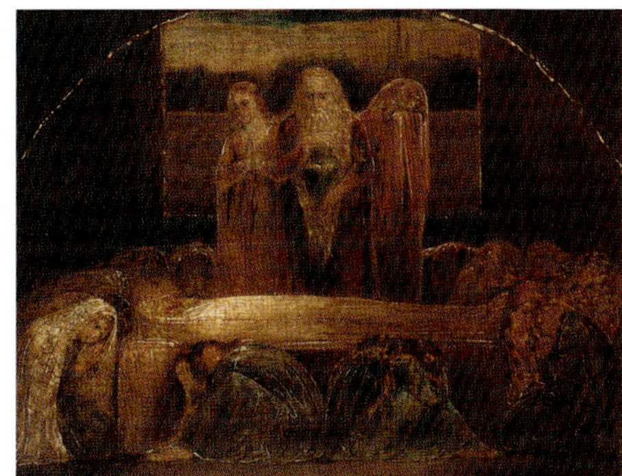

Blake, William 1757–1827
The Entombment 1799–1800
tempera on canvas 26 x 36.2
PC.91

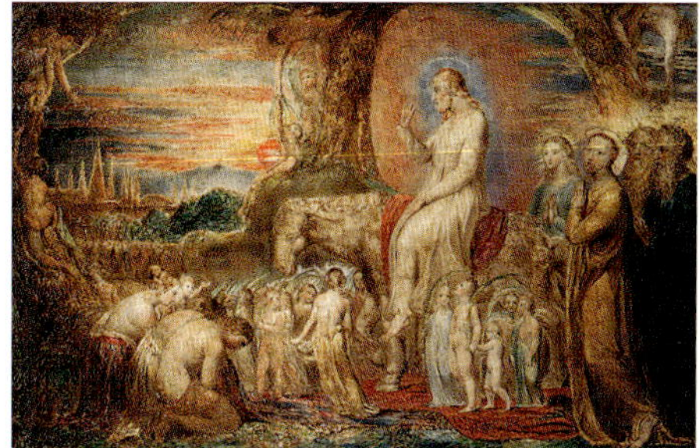

Blake, William 1757–1827
Christ's Entry into Jerusalem 1800
oil on copper 31.1 x 47.9
PC.86

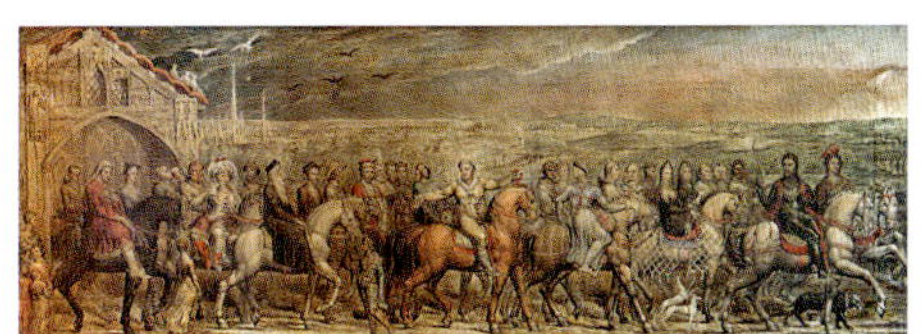

Blake, William 1757–1827
The Canterbury Pilgrims 1808
tempera on canvas 46.8 x 137
PC.89

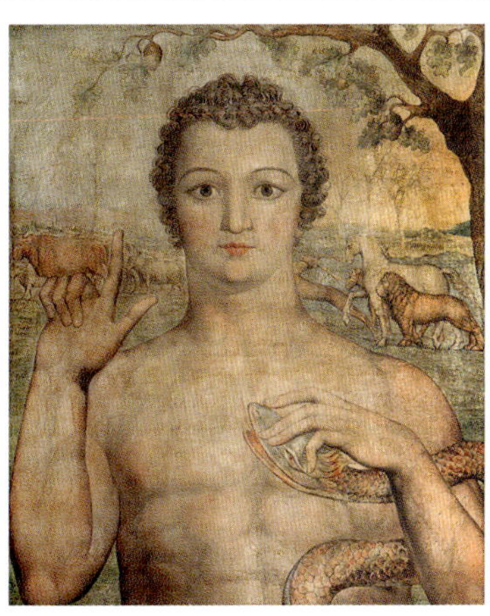

Blake, William 1757–1827
Adam Naming the Beasts 1810
tempera on canvas 74.9 x 61.6
PC.95

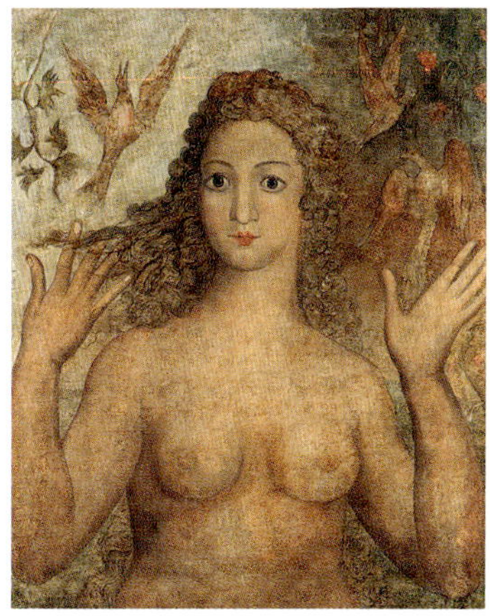

Blake, William 1757–1827
Eve Naming the Birds c.1810
tempera on canvas 74.3 x 61.6
PC.94

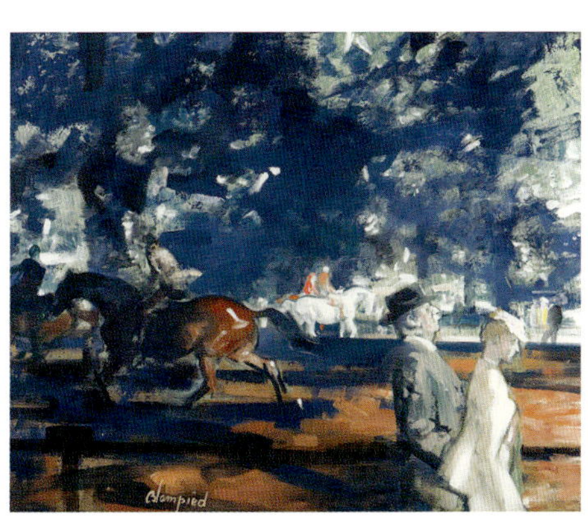

Blampied, Edmund 1886–1966
The Row c.1939
oil on canvas 63.5 x 76.2
2157

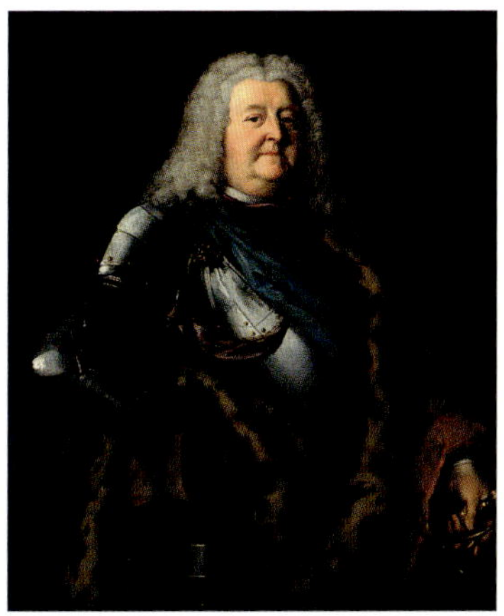

Blanchet, Louis Gabriel (attributed to)
1705–1777
Archibald Stuart of Torrance (d.1767)
c.1739–1740
oil on canvas 135.7 x 99.9
3150

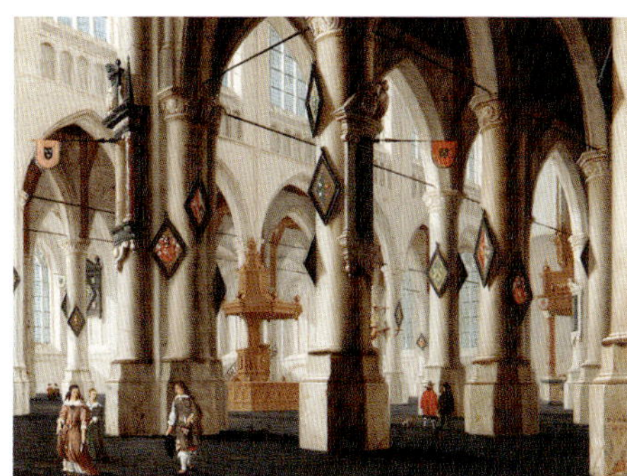

Blieck, Daniel de active c.1630–1673
Interior of an Imaginary Gothic Church 1656
oil on panel 23.8 x 31.7
5

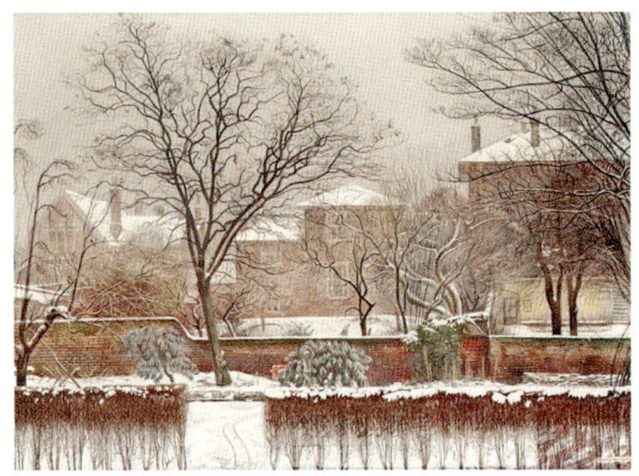

Bliss, Douglas Percy 1900–1984
Urban Garden under Snow c.1946
oil on canvas 76.2 x 101.6
2593

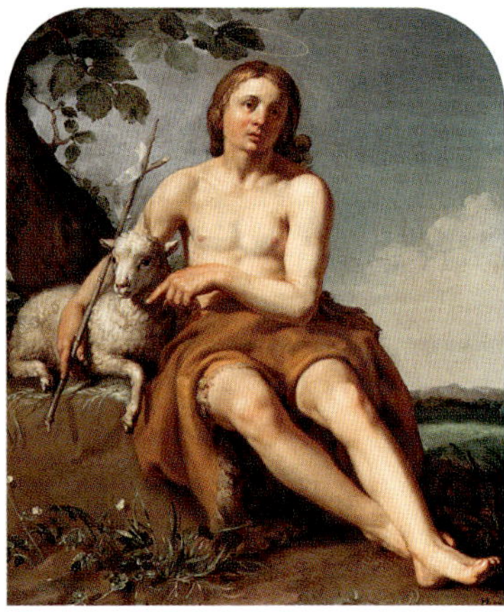

Bloemaert, Hendrick c.1601–1672
Saint John the Baptist 1624
oil on canvas 81.2 x 66.3
32

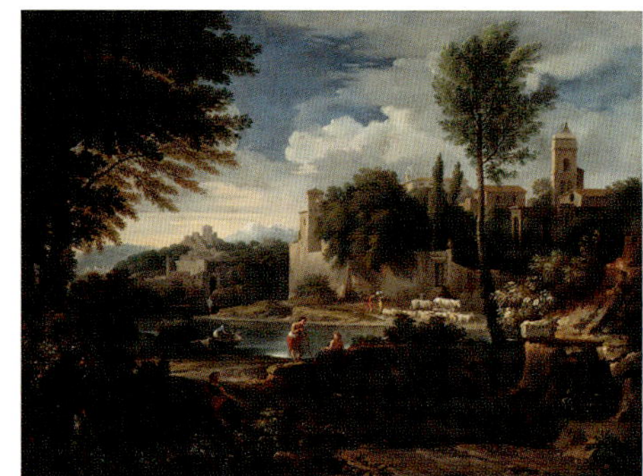

Bloemen, Jan Frans van 1662–1749
*Landscape with a River and a Walled
Town* c.1688–1700
oil on canvas 73.6 x 97.8
159

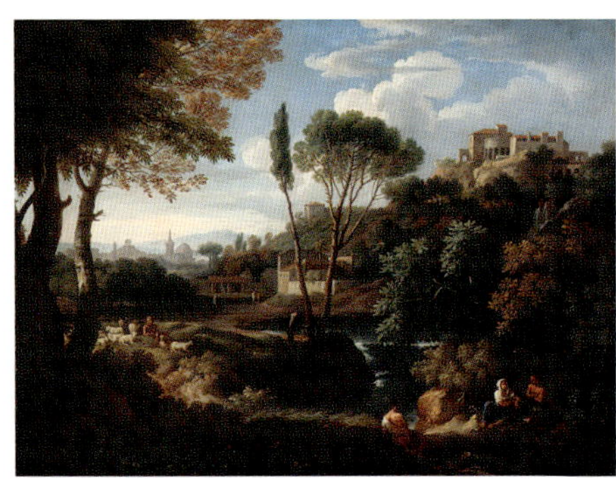

Bloemen, Jan Frans van 1662–1749
Landscape with a Waterfall and Buildings
c.1688–1700
oil on canvas 73 x 97.8
168

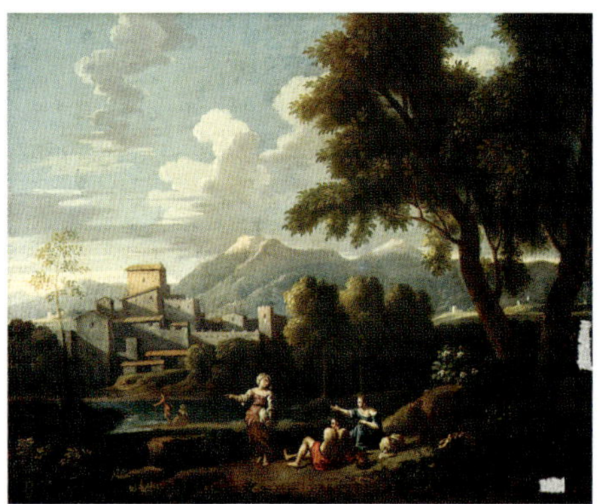

Bloemen, Jan Frans van 1662–1749
*Landscape with a Building and Distant
Mountains*
oil on canvas 61.6 x 74.3
917

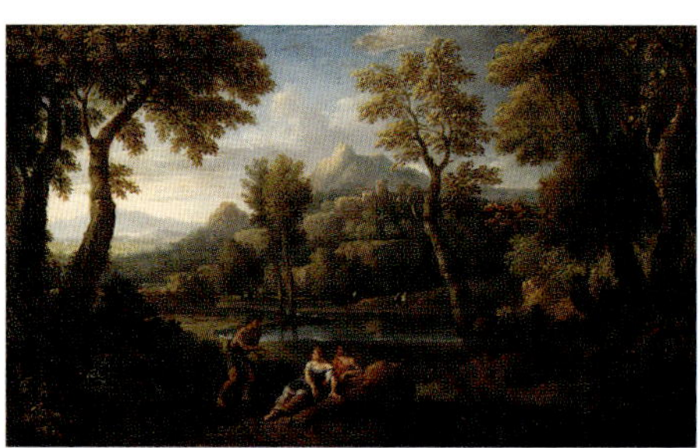

Bloemen, Jan Frans van (attributed to)
1662–1749
Landscape with a River
oil on canvas 47.3 x 74.2
175

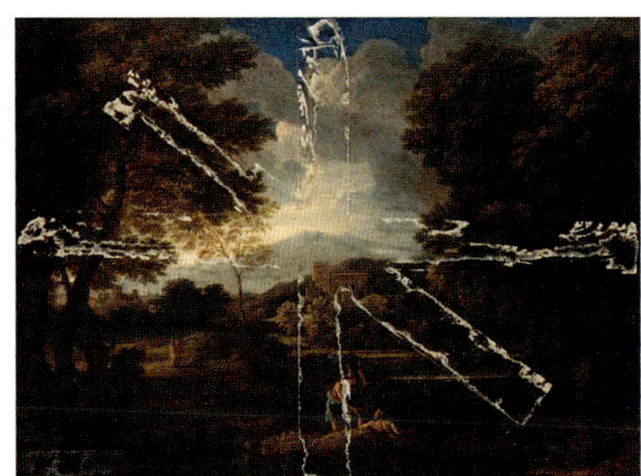

Bloemen, Jan Frans van (circle of)
1662–1749
An Italian Landscape
oil on canvas 47.9 x 62.5
150

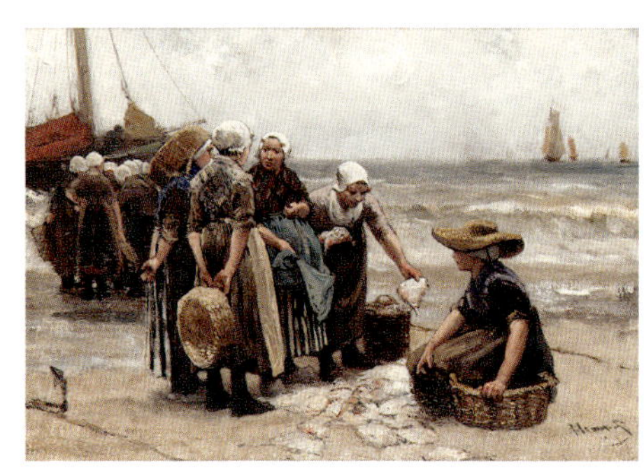

Blommers, Bernardus Johannes 1845–1914
Fishwives by the Sea c.1875–1888
oil on panel 27.6 x 37.8
1239

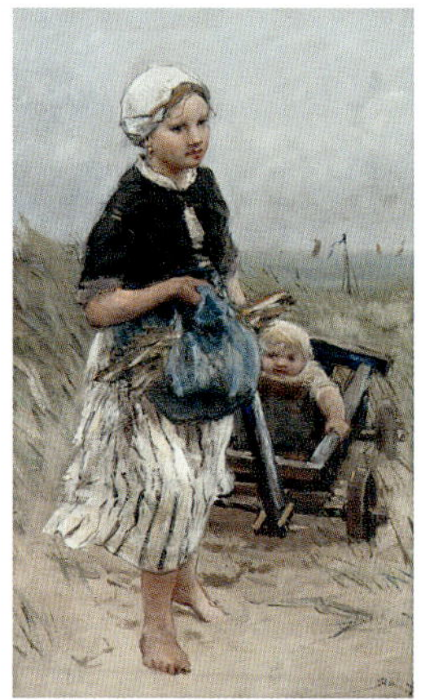

Blommers, Bernardus Johannes 1845–1914
On the Dunes c.1875–1901
oil on panel 30.8 x 19.7
958

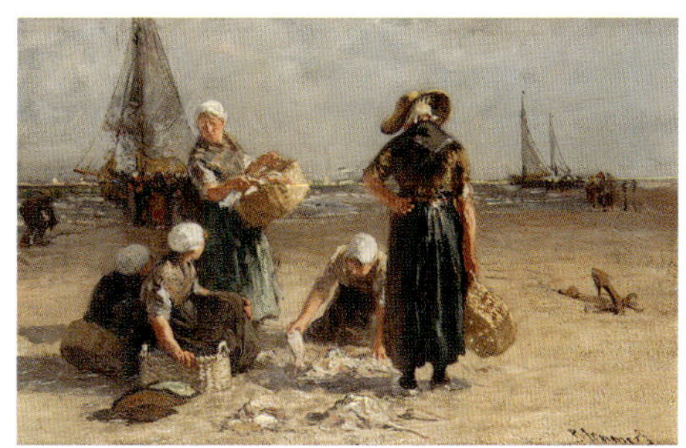

Blommers, Bernardus Johannes 1845–1914
Fishwives on the Beach
oil on canvas 28.2 x 40
825

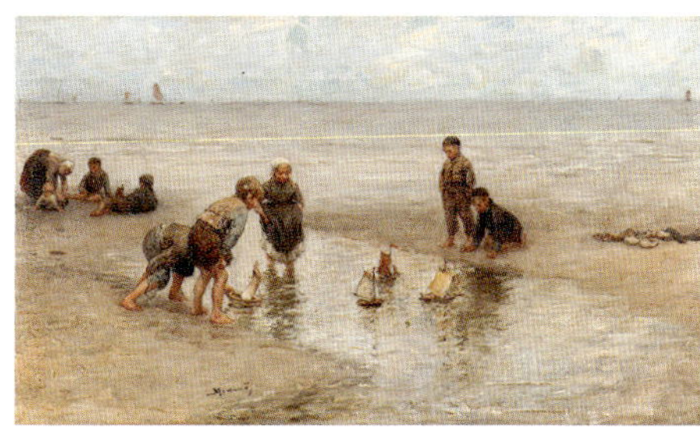

Blommers, Bernardus Johannes 1845–1914
The Regatta
oil on canvas 74.6 x 124.4
2450

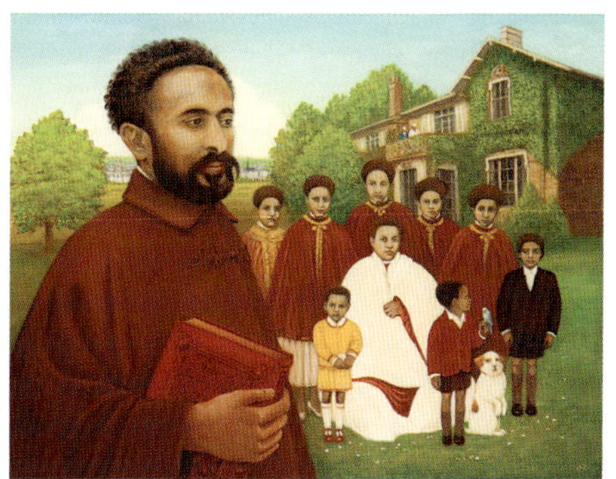

Bloomfield, Francis
Haile Selassie (1892–1975), and His Family
1936–1940
oil on canvas 20 x 25.5
A.1993.9

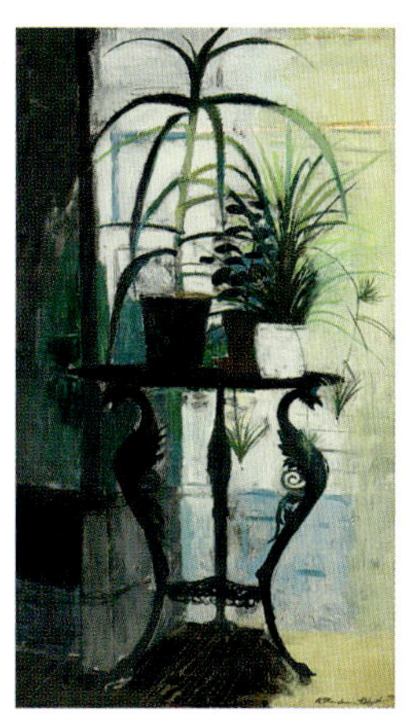

Blyth, Robert Henderson 1919–1970
Victorian Cast Iron 1959
oil on canvas 90.8 x 49.8
3114

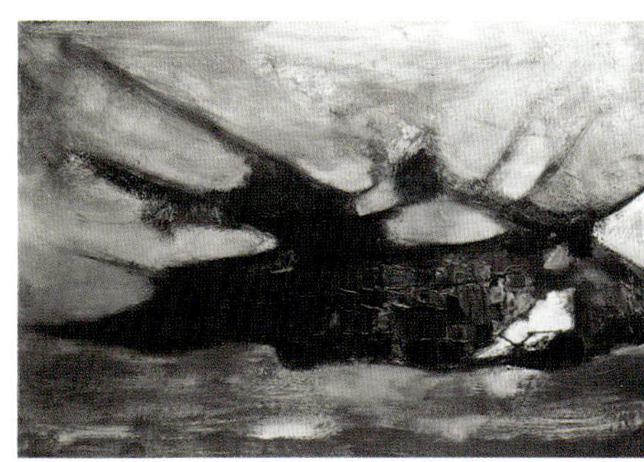

Blyth, Robert Henderson 1919–1970
Aberdeenshire Hillside c.1961
oil on hardboard 76.1 x 106.7
3154

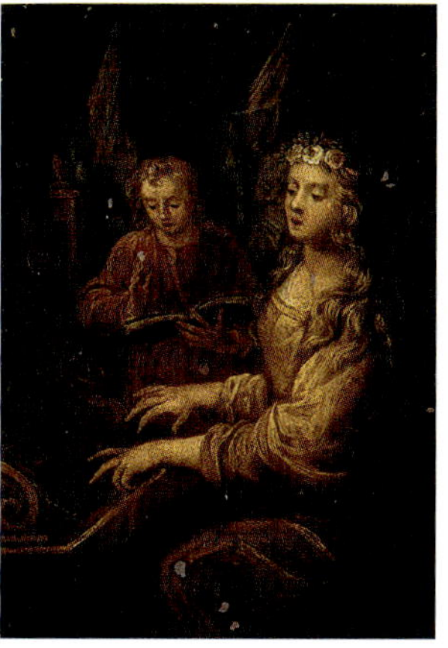

Bocanegra, Pedro Atanasio c.1638–1689
Saint Cecilia with an Angel
oil on copper 20.9 x 15.2
PL.118 (P)

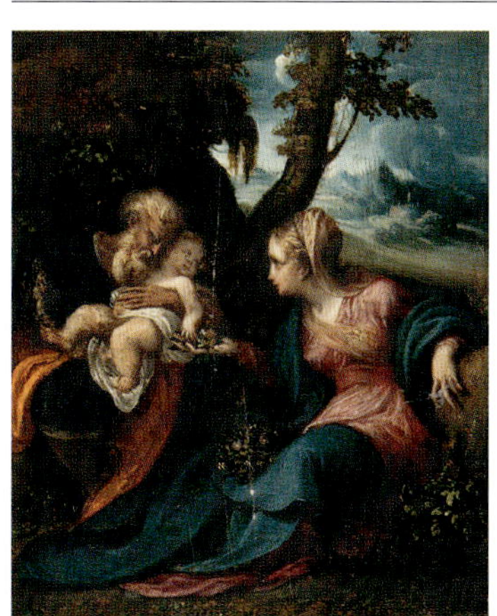

Boccaccino, Camillo 1504/1505–1546
Holy Family in a Landscape c.1535–1540
oil on panel 28.9 x 23.3
125

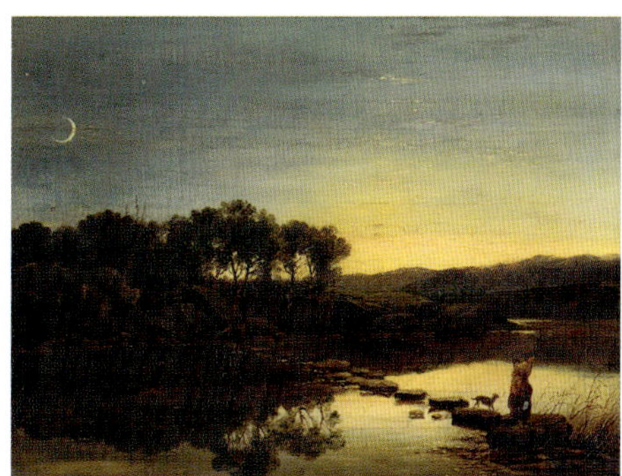

Boddington, Edwin Henry 1836–1905
Landscape, Sunset
oil on canvas 29.2 x 39.8
369

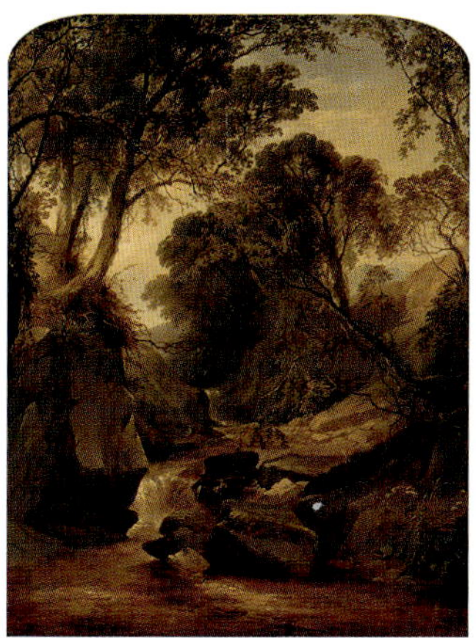

Boddington, Henry John 1811–1865
A Rocky Landscape, View in Wales 1847
oil on canvas 106.7 x 82.6
357

Boddington, Henry John 1811–1865
Loch Ericht 1857
oil on canvas 76.2 x 127
2111

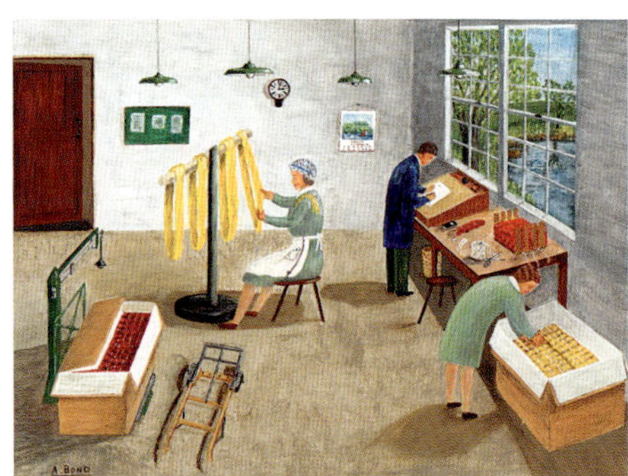

Bond, Albert b.1905
Examining and Packing Silk Yarns 1972
oil on hardboard 30.2 x 40.6
3594

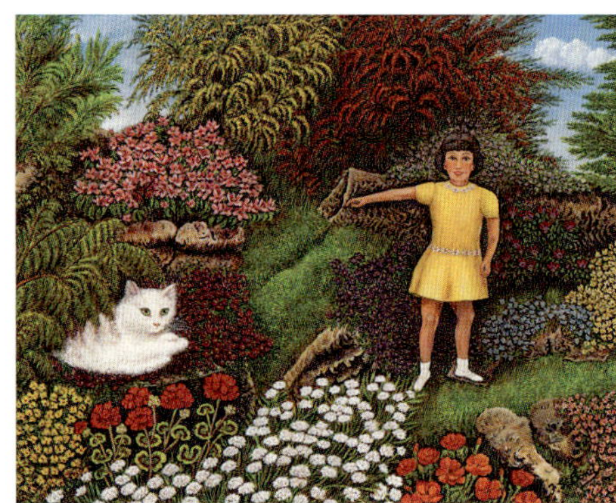

Bond, Frances 1905–1978
Discovered 1969
acrylic on board 37.5 x 45.5
3593

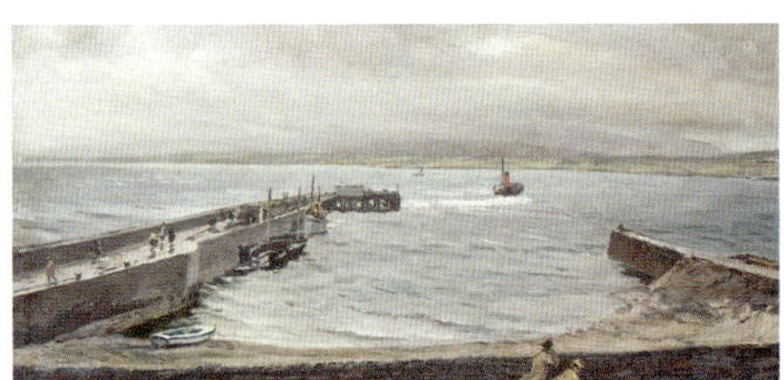

Bone, Muirhead 1876–1953
Broadford Pier, Skye c.1929
oil on canvas 31.1 x 60.9
1775

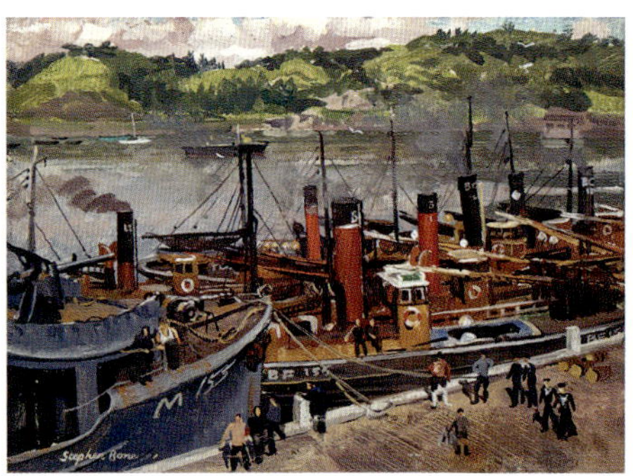

Bone, Stephen 1904–1958
Admiralty Trawlers and Drifters c.1940–1945
oil on board 30.5 x 40.6
2720

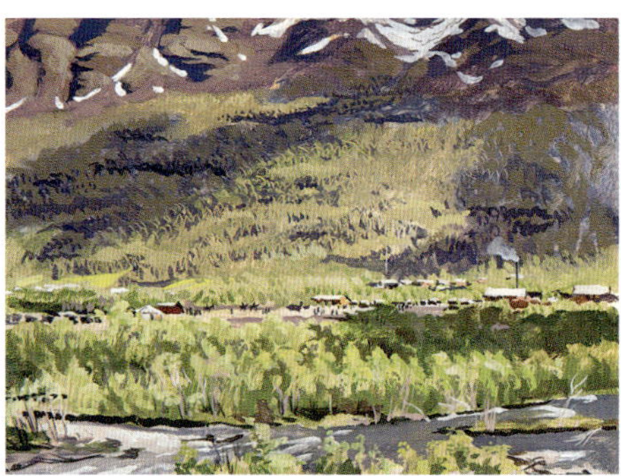

Bone, Stephen 1904–1958
German Camp at Kvesmenes in the Birch Forest c.1940–1945
oil on paper 25.4 x 35.6
2727

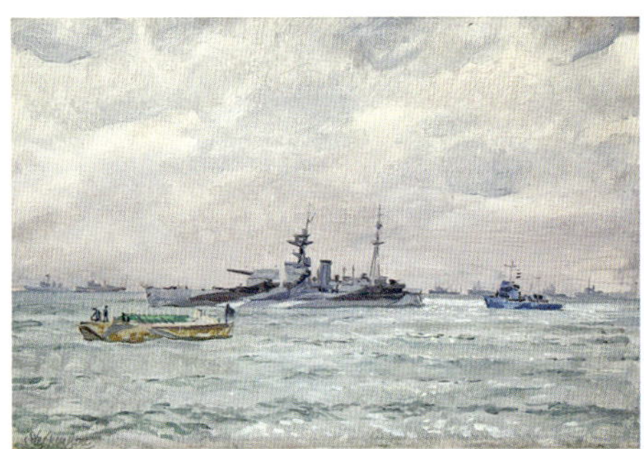

Bone, Stephen 1904–1958
HMS 'Roberts' c.1940–1945
oil on board 25.4 x 35.6
2726

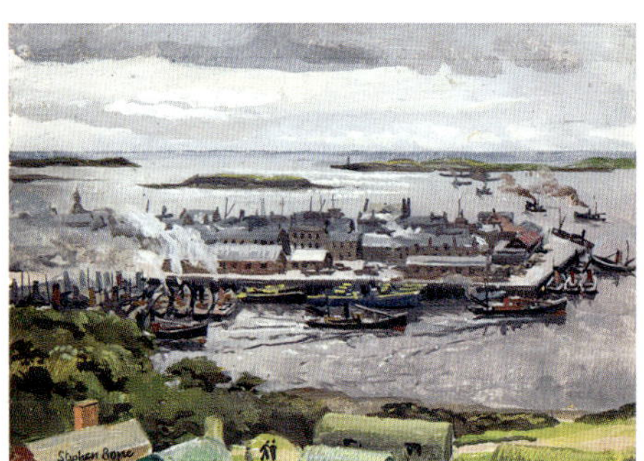

Bone, Stephen 1904–1958
Stornoway, 6pm, Drifters Setting Out for the Fishing Grounds c.1940–1945
oil on paper 25.4 x 35.6
2722

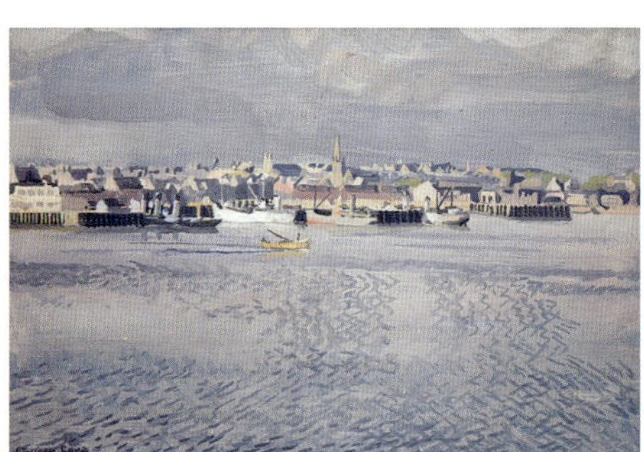

Bone, Stephen 1904–1958
Stornoway Harbour, Evening, Minesweepers and Coasting Vessels c.1940–1945
oil on board 25.4 x 35.6
2723

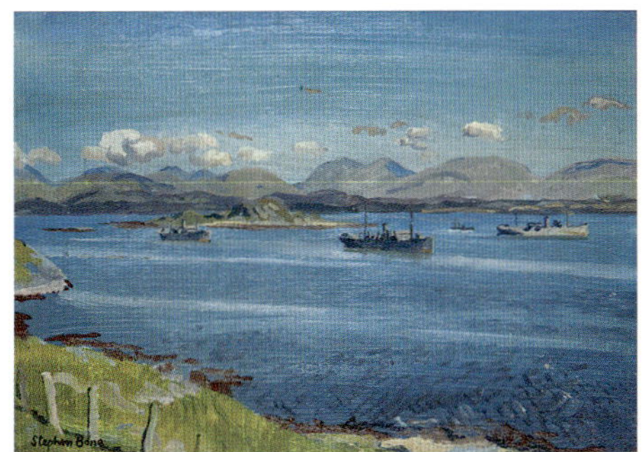

Bone, Stephen 1904–1958
The Convoy Anchorage from Lismore
c.1940–1945
oil on paper 30.5 x 40.6
2721

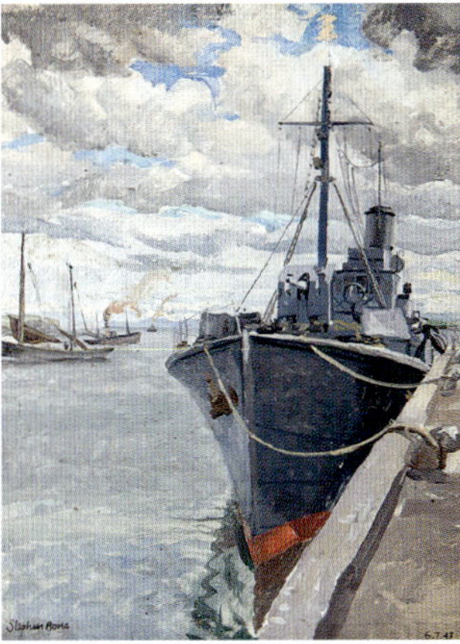

Bone, Stephen 1904–1958
HMS Trawler 'Stella Pegasi' 1943
oil on paper 35.6 x 25.4
2724

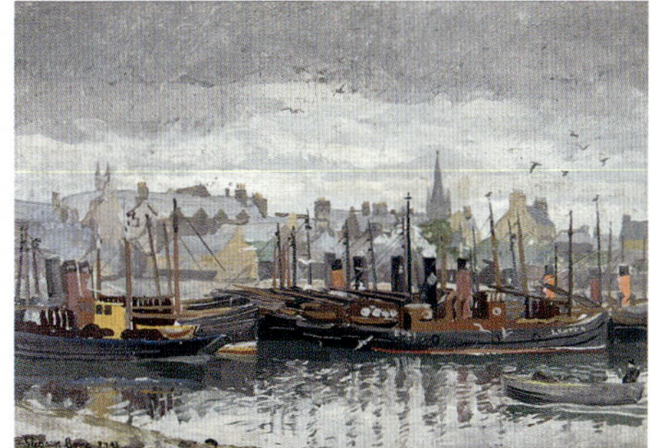

Bone, Stephen 1904–1958
Stornoway, Drifters in Harbour, Saturday Afternoon 1943
oil on board 25.4 x 35.6
2719

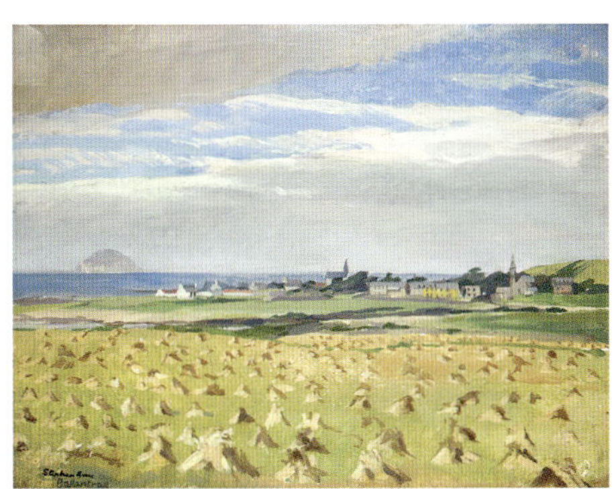

Bone, Stephen 1904–1958
Ballantrae
oil on panel 33 x 41.3
2480

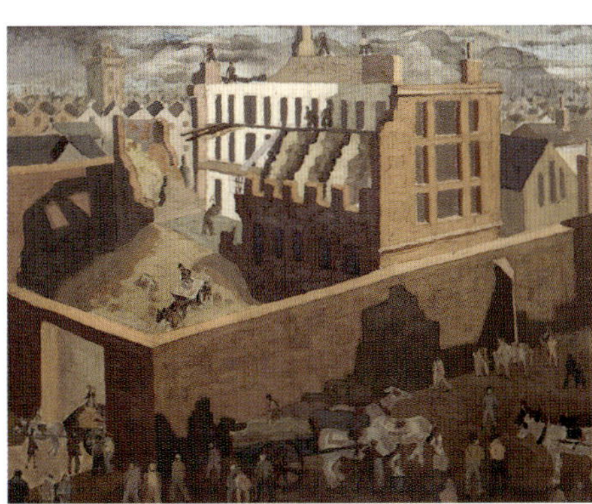

Bone, William Drummond 1907–1979
The Demolition of Ayr Jail
oil on canvas 63.5 x 76.2
3416

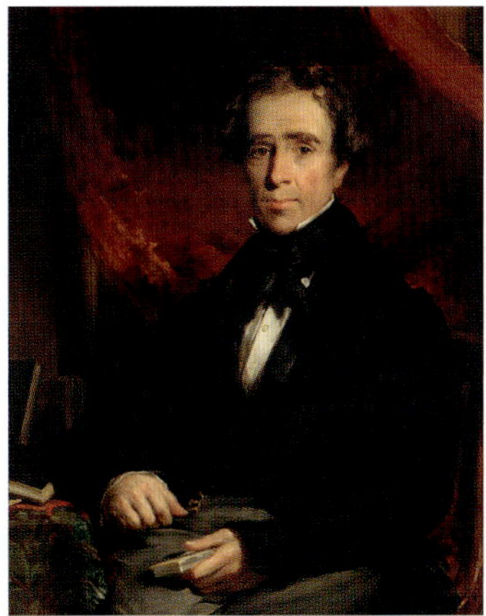

Bonnar, Wiliam 1800–1855
John Blackie, Senior, Glasgow Publisher
c.1846
oil on canvas 93.9 x 77.5
1848

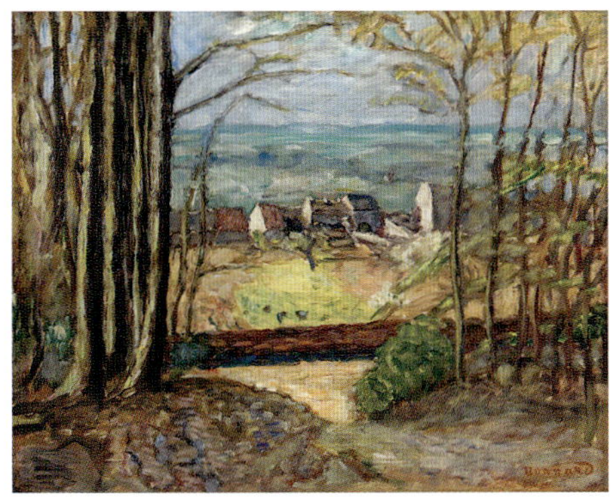

Bonnard, Pierre 1867–1947
The Edge of the Forest c.1918
oil on panel 37.3 x 45.9
2376

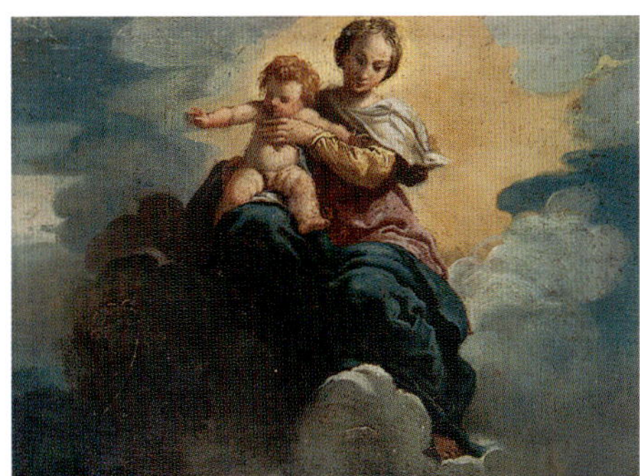

Bononi, Carlo 1569–1632
Virgin and Child in Glory c.1615–1632
oil on copper 15.7 x 21.3
131

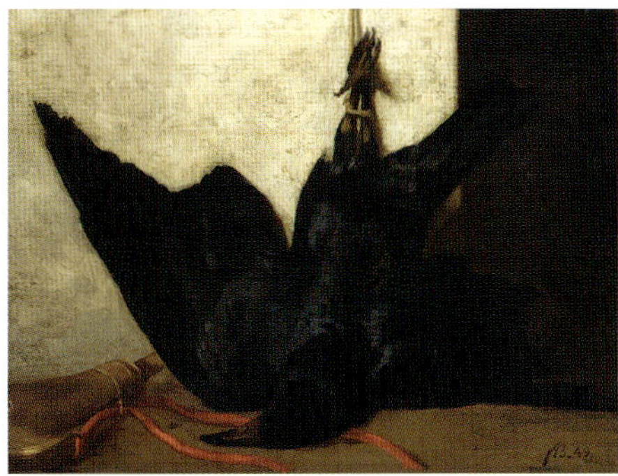

Bonvin, François 1817–1887
The Crow 1849
oil on panel 41.9 x 49.5
35.8

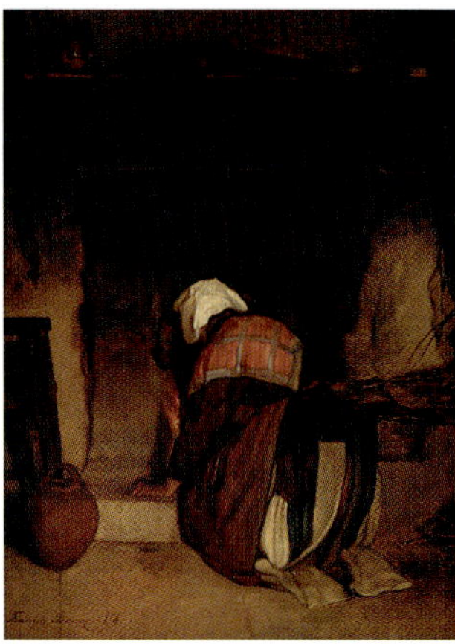

Bonvin, François 1817–1887
Interior with an Old Woman Kneeling 1854
oil on panel 37.4 x 28.6
2853

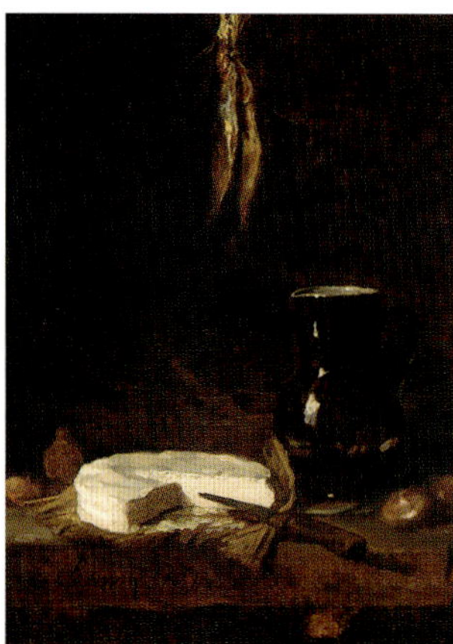

Bonvin, François 1817–1887
Still Life with a Jug, Cheese, Onions, Fish and a Knife 1854
oil on canvas 34.9 x 28.3
35.16

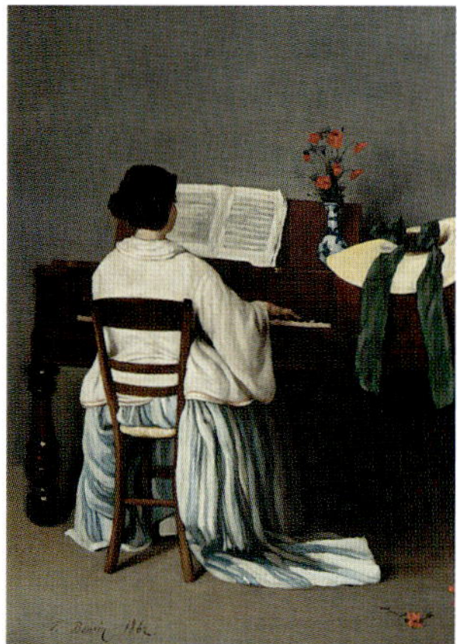

Bonvin, François 1817–1887
Woman at a Spinet 1862
oil on canvas 43.8 x 33.6
35.1

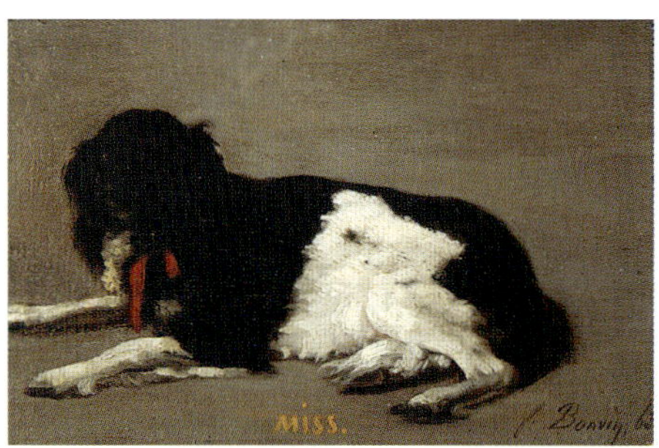

Bonvin, François 1817–1887
'Miss' 1863
oil on panel 11.4 x 16.5
35.9

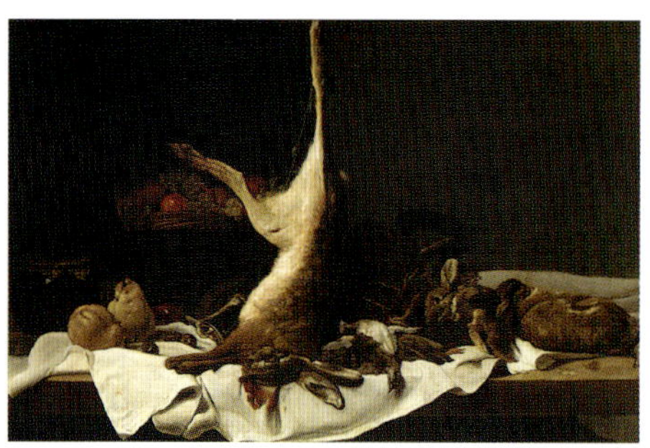

Bonvin, François 1817–1887
Still Life with Game 1874
oil on canvas 88.9 x 132
35.11

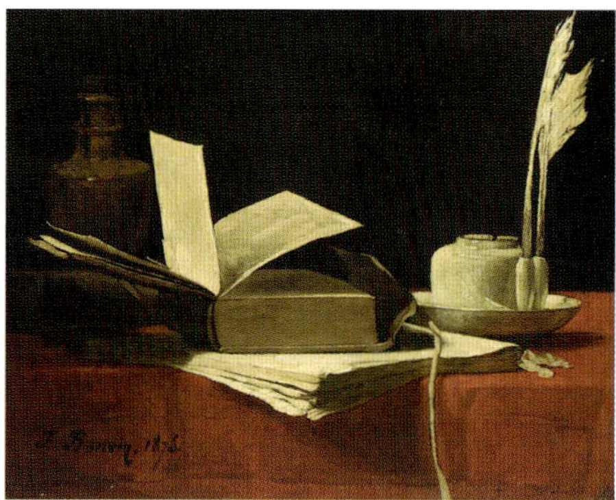

Bonvin, François 1817–1887
Still Life with a Book and an Ink Well 1875
oil on millboard 34.9 x 41.9
35.15

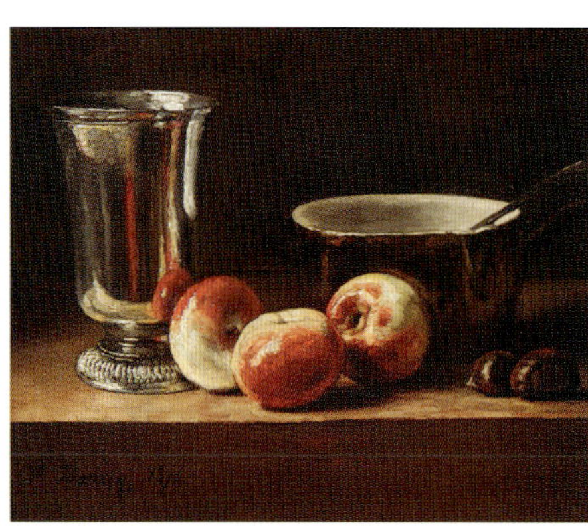

Bonvin, François 1817–1887
Still Life with Apples and a Silver Goblet 1876
oil on canvas 32.1 x 40.3
2377

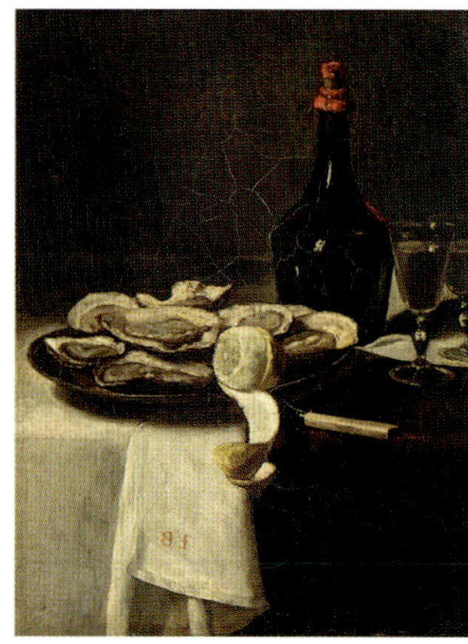

Bonvin, François 1817–1887
Still Life with Oysters, a Wine Bottle and a Glass of Wine 1876
oil on canvas 63.5 x 48.2
35.17

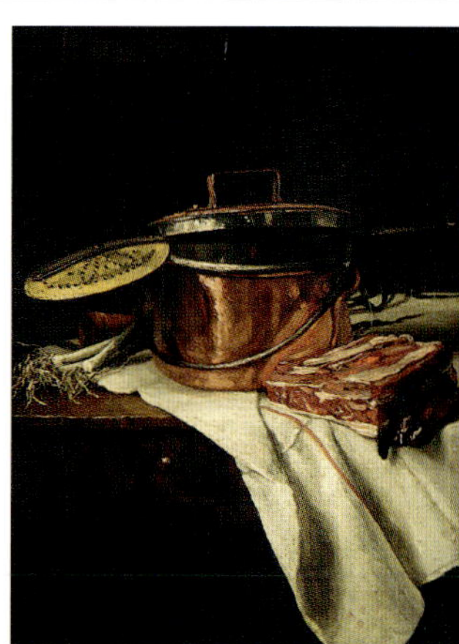

Bonvin, François 1817–1887
Still Life with a Copper Pot 1879
oil on panel 26.7 x 19
35.14

Facing page: Shee, Martin Archer, 1769–1850, *Ariadne Deserted by Theseus*, 1834, (p. 260)

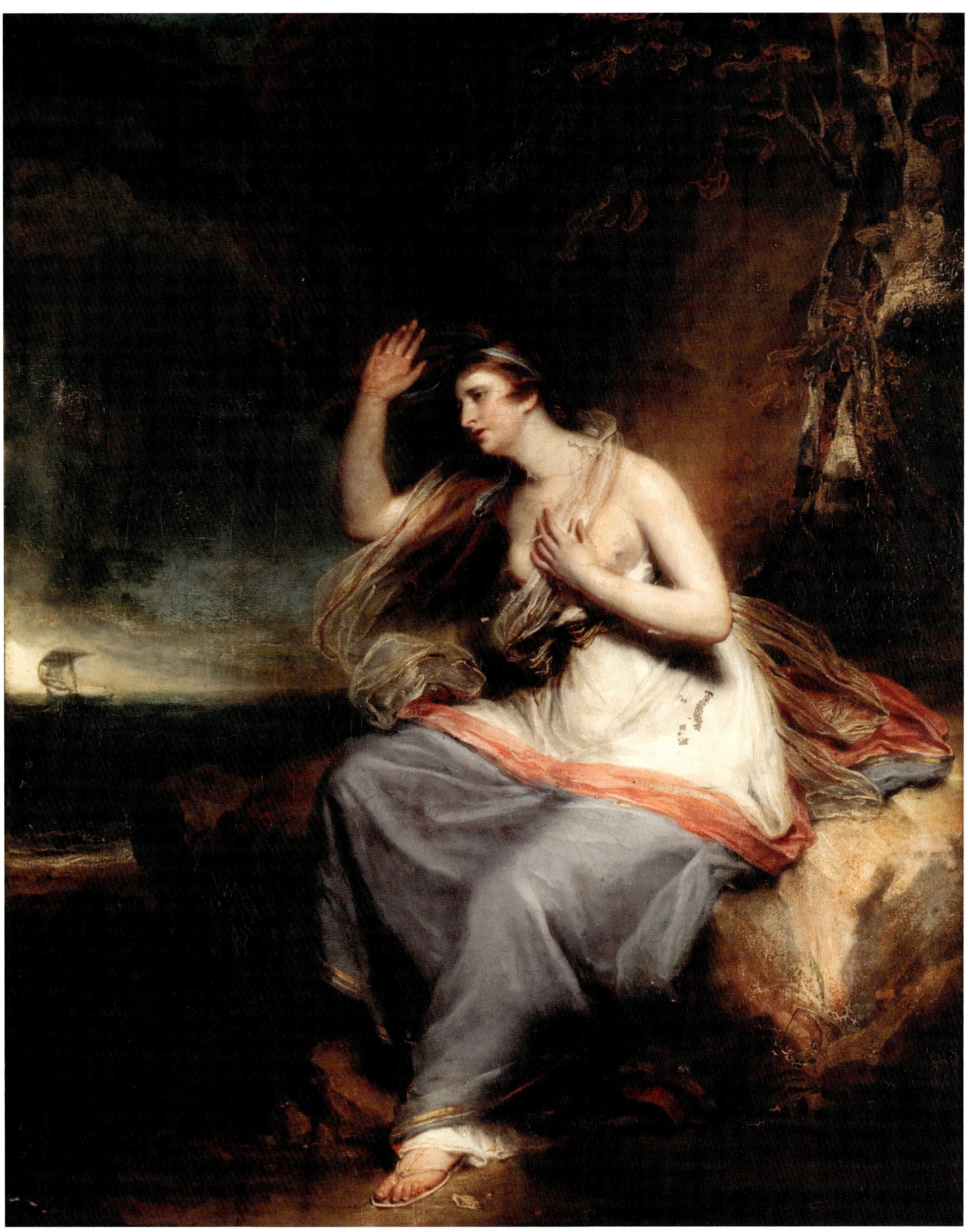

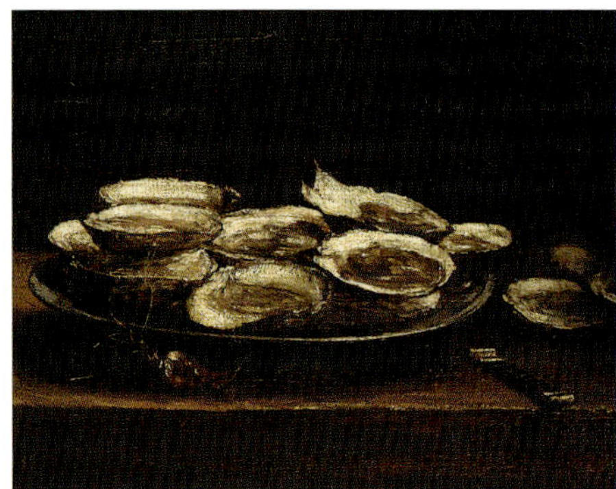

Bonvin, François 1817–1887
Oysters 1883
oil on canvas 31.1 x 40.6
35.12

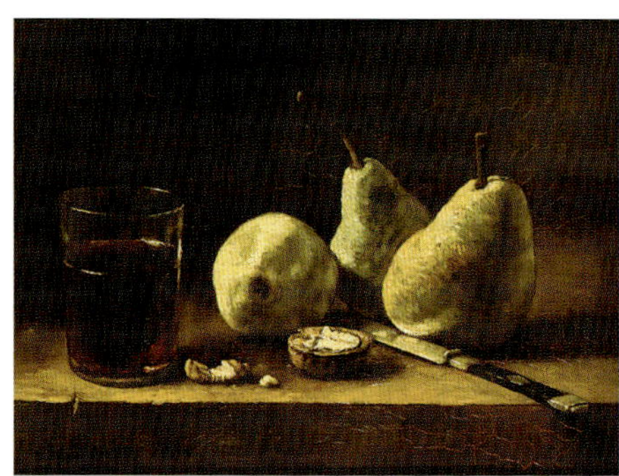

Bonvin, François 1817–1887
Still Life with a Glass, Pears and a Knife 1884
oil on canvas 32.4 x 42.5
35.13

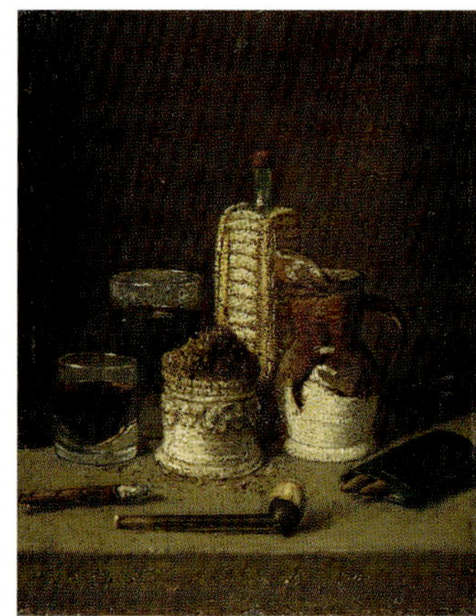

Bonvin, François 1817–1887
Still Life with a Tobacco Pot and a Pipe
oil on panel 21.6 x 17.8
35.18

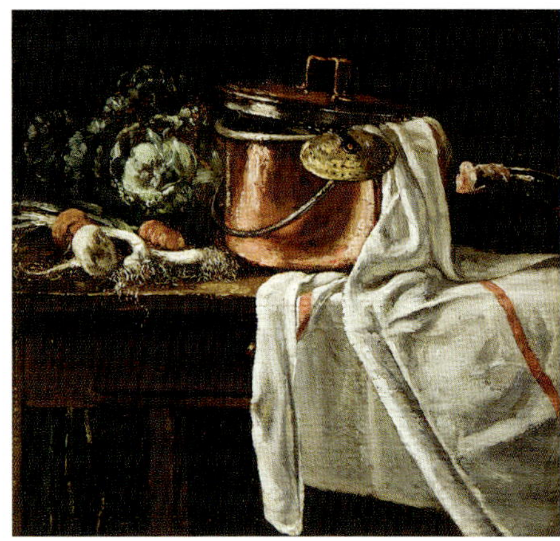

Bonvin, François 1817–1887
Still Life with Vegetables and Cooking Utensils
oil on canvas 20.3 x 22.8
35.19

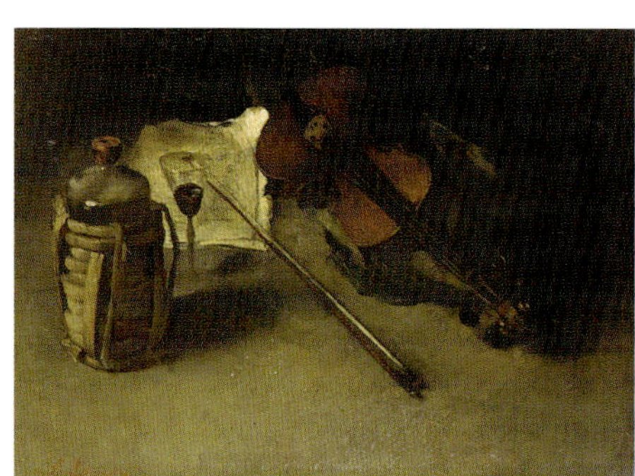

Bonvin, François 1817–1887
The Violin
oil on panel 28.5 x 37.8
35.2

Boonen, Arnold (attributed to) 1669–1729
A Woman in Bed Extinguishing a Candle
oil on canvas 38.7 x 33
110

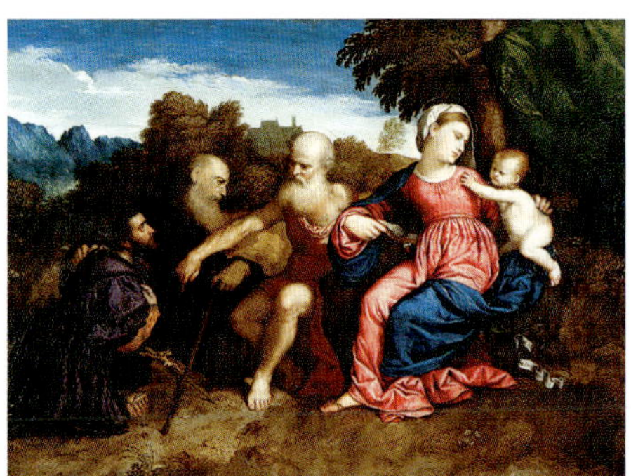

Bordon, Paris 1500–1571
Virgin Mary and Child with Saints Jerome and Anthony Abbot and a Donor c.1522
oil on panel 61 x 82.9
570

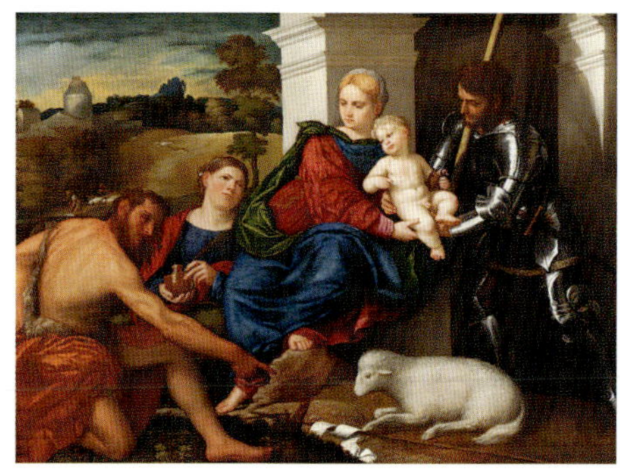

Bordon, Paris 1500–1571
Virgin and Child with Saints John the Baptist, Mary Magdalene and George (?) c.1524
oil on panel 85.4 x 117.5
191

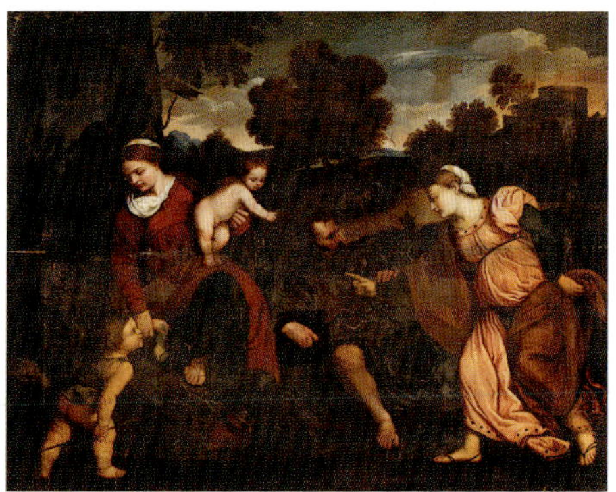

Bordon, Paris (after) 1500–1571
The Mystic Marriage of Saint Catherine
c.1675–1700
oil on canvas 190.5 x 236.2
3432

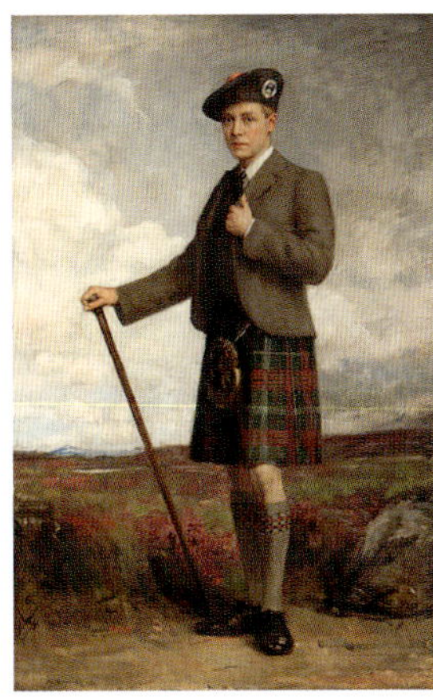

Borthwick, Alfred Edward 1871–1955
Edward, Prince of Wales (1894–1972), in Highland Costume 1923
oil on canvas 203 x 127
3064

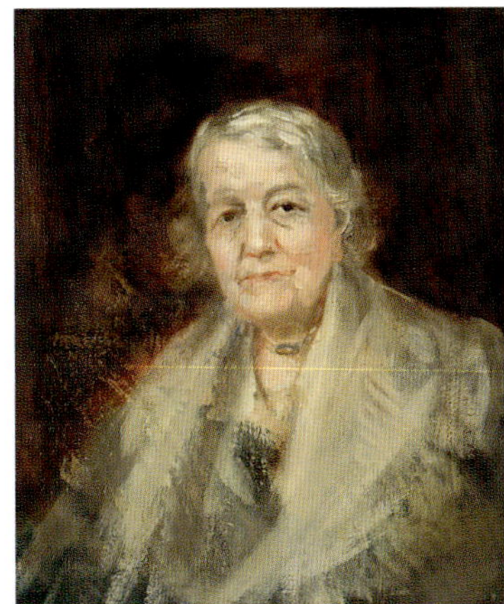

Borthwick, Alfred Edward 1871–1955
Lady Fairfax-Lucy (1866–1943) c.1942
oil on canvas 61.5 x 51.5
3066

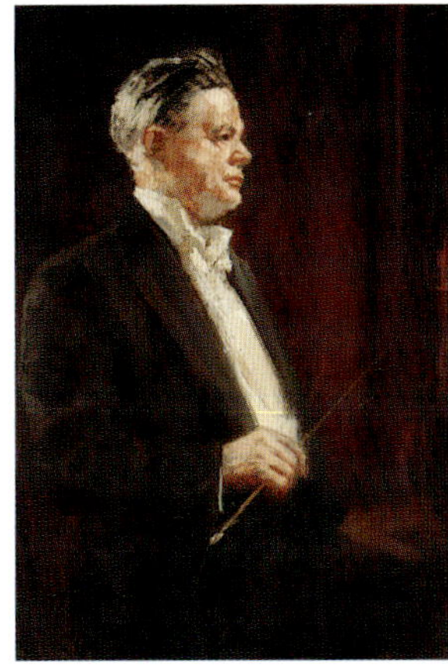

Borthwick, Alfred Edward 1871–1955
Sir Ernest C. MacMillan (1893–1973) 1949
oil on canvas on board 105.3 x 71.1
3065

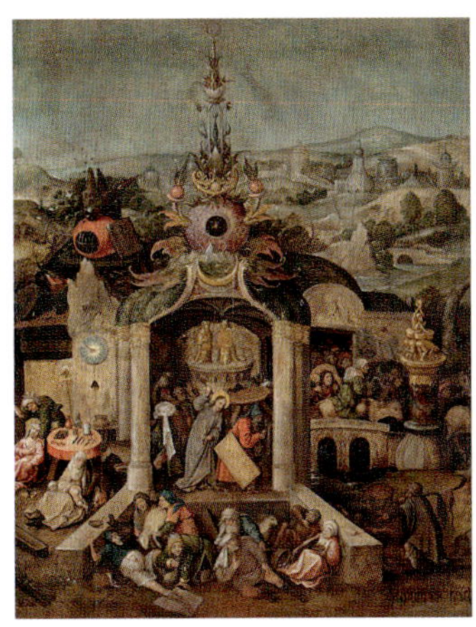

Bosch, Hieronymus (imitator of)
c.1450–1516
Christ Driving the Money-Lenders from the Temple late 16th C
oil on panel 77.7 x 60
1586

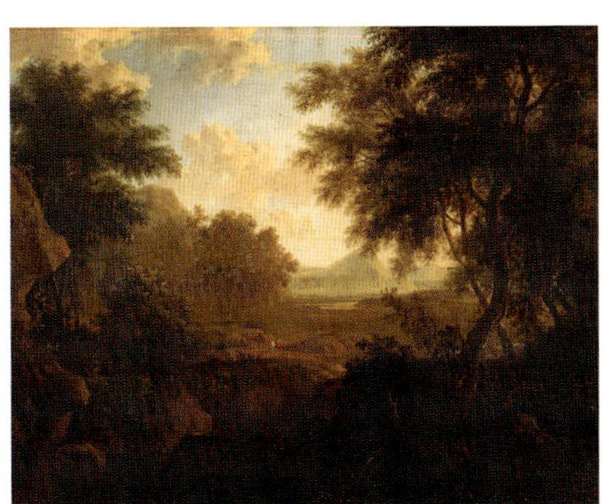

Both, Jan (school of) c.1618–1652
A Mountain Landscape with a River Valley
c.1637–1652
oil on canvas 111.1 x 134.6
1184

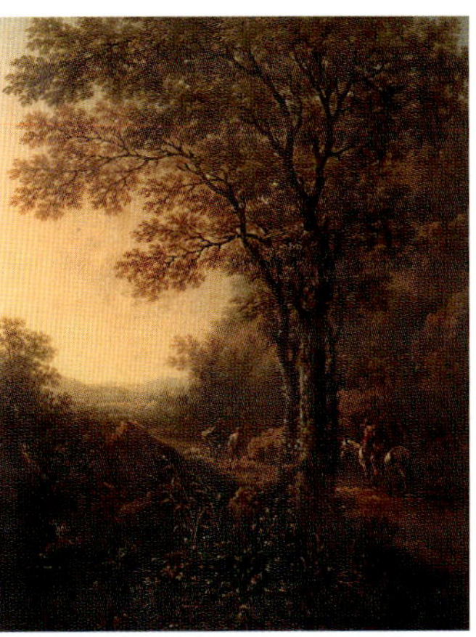

Both, Jan (style of) c.1618–1652
Evening Landscape
oil on canvas 39.7 x 29.8
PL.36 (P)

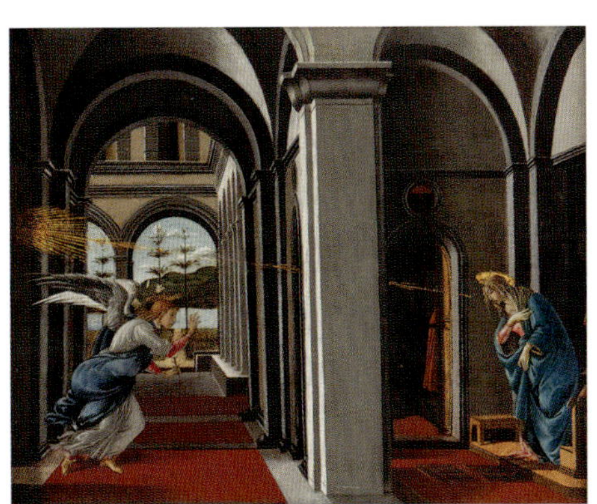

Botticelli, Sandro (and studio)
1444/1445–1510
The Annunciation c.1490–1495
tempera on panel 49.5 x 61.9
174

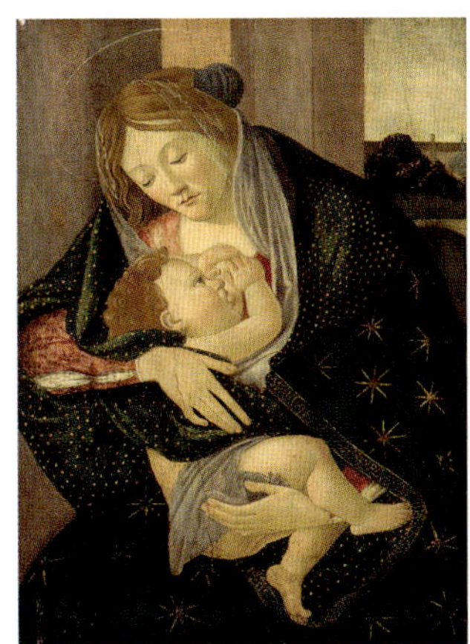

Botticelli, Sandro (school of)
1444/1445–1510
Virgin and Child c.1490–1510
tempera with oil glazes (?) on panel 61 x 43.2
35.39

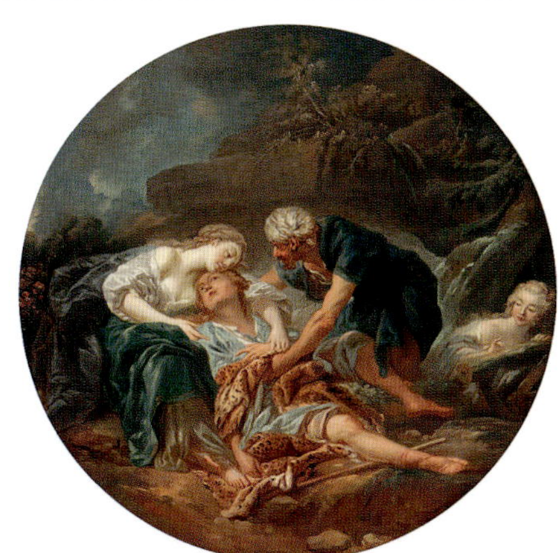

Boucher, François (after) 1703–1770
Amintas Revived by Sylvia 18th C
oil on canvas 134
2959

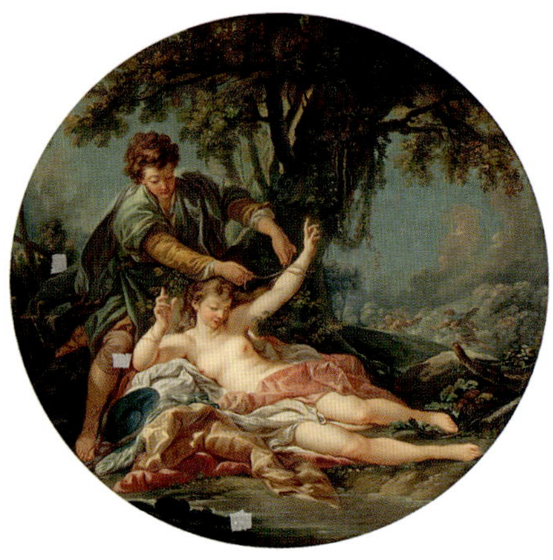

Boucher, François (after) 1703–1770
Sylvia Saved by Amintas 18th C
oil on canvas 134
2958

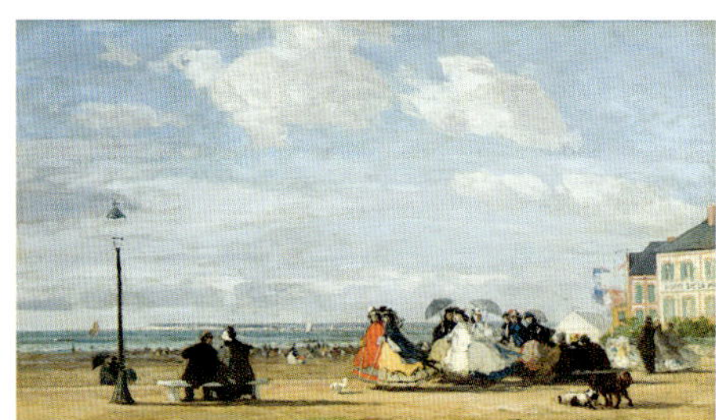

Boudin, Eugène Louis 1824–1898
The Beach at Trouville, the Empress Eugénie
1863
oil on panel 34.3 x 57.8
35.45

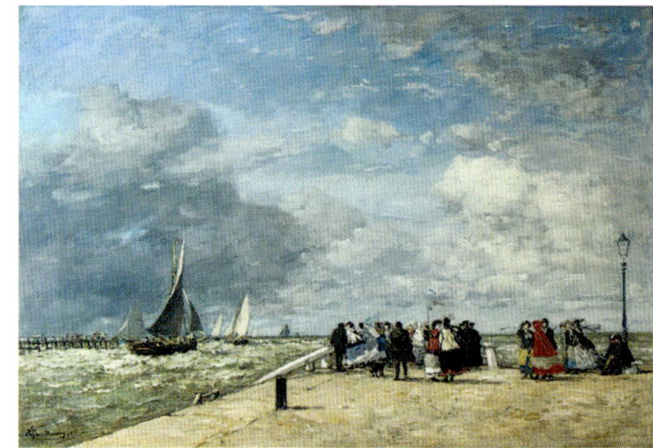

Boudin, Eugène Louis 1824–1898
The Jetty at Trouville 1869
oil on canvas 64.8 x 92.8
35.43

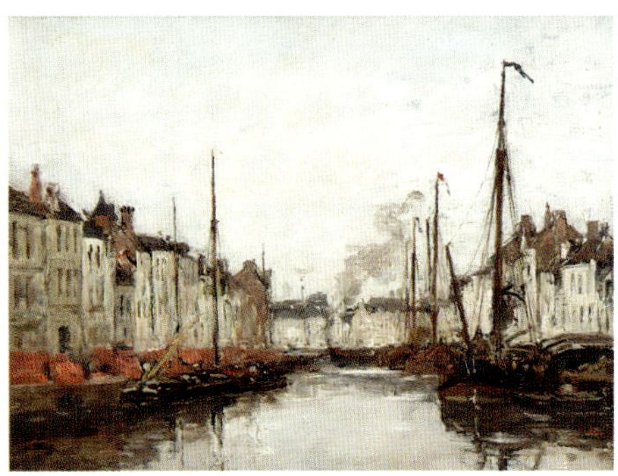

Boudin, Eugène Louis 1824–1898
A Dutch Canal 1871
oil on panel 26 x 34.3
35.4

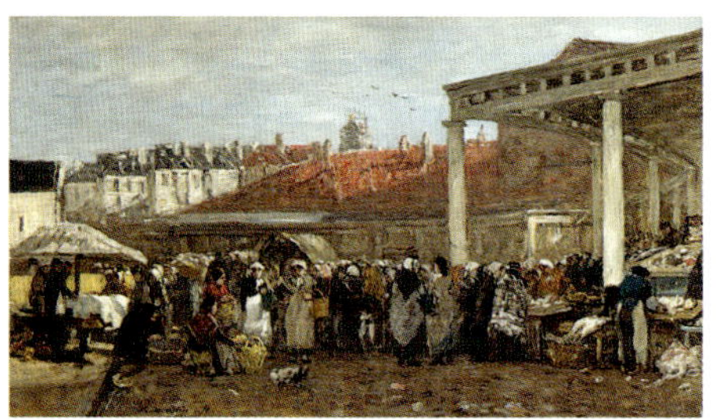

Boudin, Eugène Louis 1824–1898
The Old Fish Market, Brussels 1871
oil on panel 25.7 x 46.3
35.44

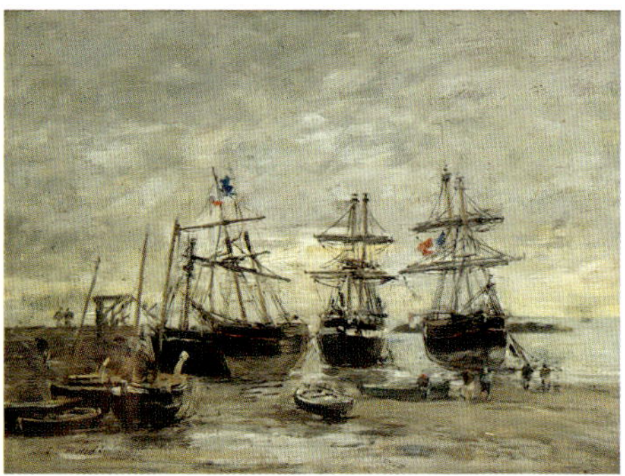

Boudin, Eugène Louis 1824–1898
The Port of Portrieux at Low Tide
c.1871–1873
oil on panel 24.1 x 32.3
35.49

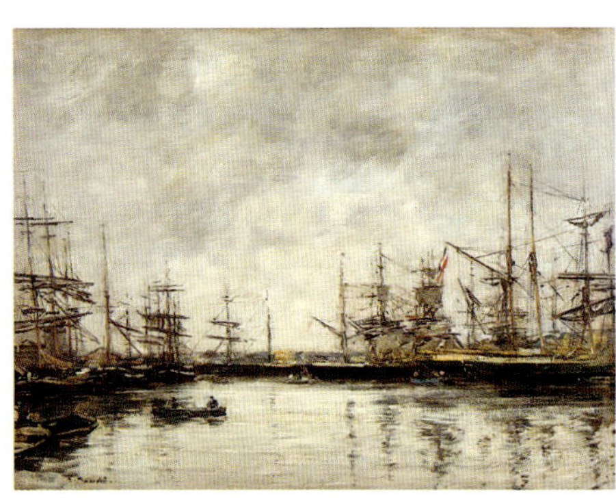

Boudin, Eugène Louis 1824–1898
The Port of Deauville c.1880–1884
oil on canvas 41 x 55.3
2379

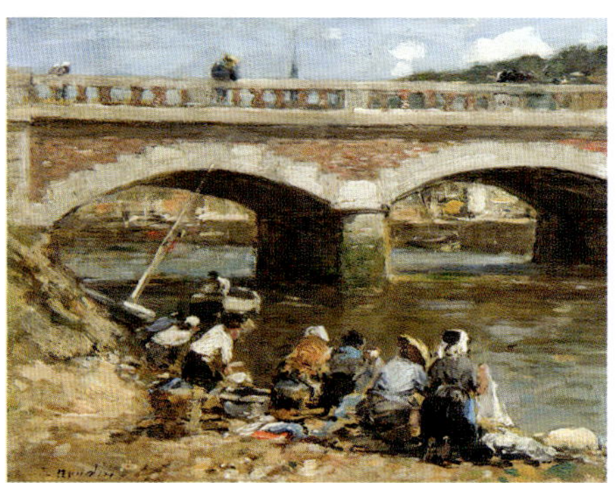

Boudin, Eugène Louis 1824–1898
*Washerwomen on the Banks of the River
Touques* c.1883–1887
oil on panel 16.5 x 21.6
35.46

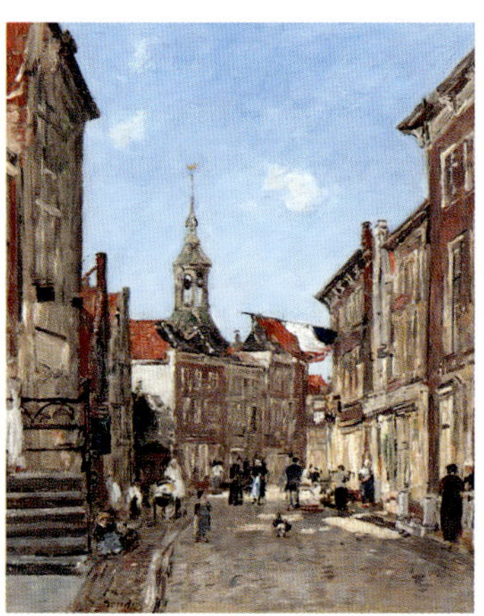

Boudin, Eugène Louis 1824–1898
A Street in Dordrecht 1884
oil on panel 41 x 32.7
2378

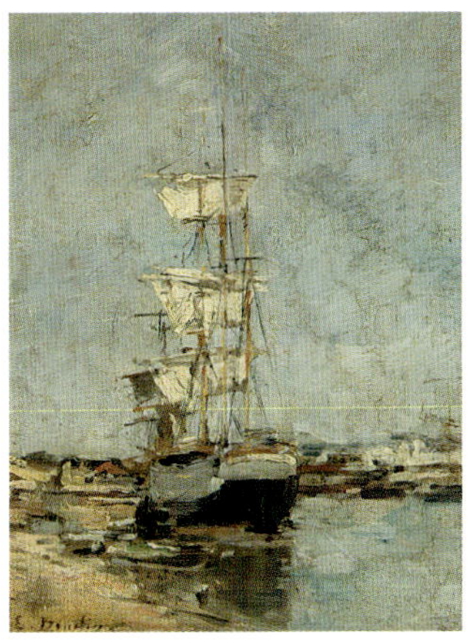

Boudin, Eugène Louis 1824–1898
Large Sailing Ship in Port, Deauville
c.1885–1888
oil on panel 25.4 x 20.3
35.42

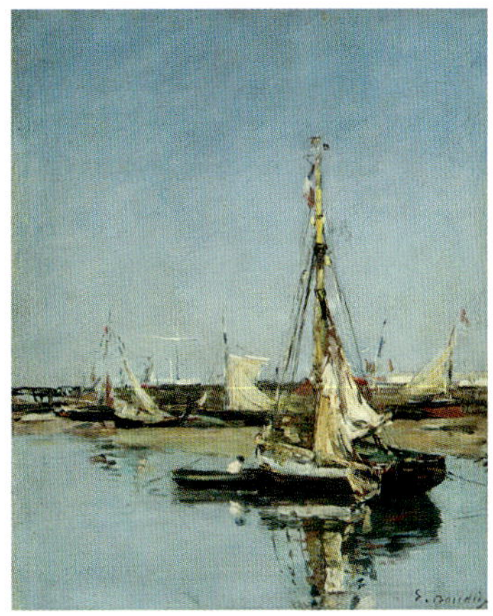

Boudin, Eugène Louis 1824–1898
Trouville, the Jetties at Low Tide c.1885–1890
oil on panel 26.3 x 21.3
35.41

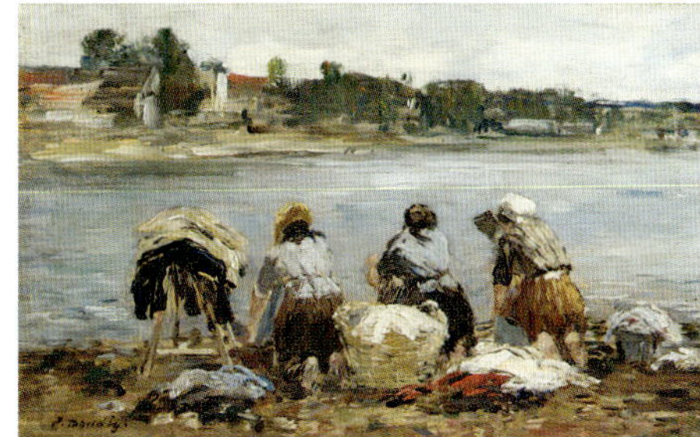

Boudin, Eugène Louis 1824–1898
Washerwomen on the Banks of the River Touques c.1888–1895
oil on panel 20.6 x 33
35.5

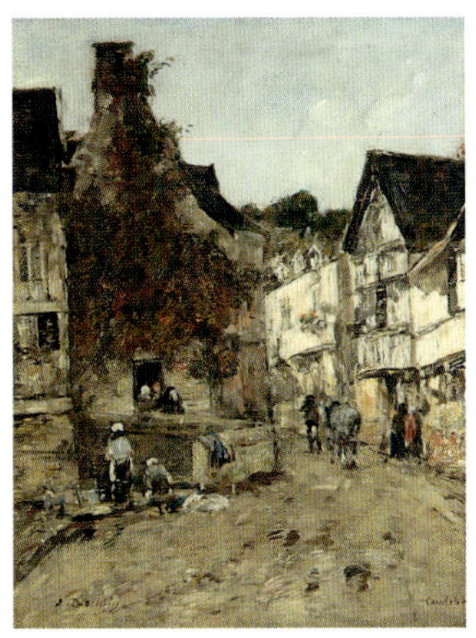

Boudin, Eugène Louis 1824–1898
A Street in Caudebec-en-Caux c.1889–1892
oil on panel 36.8 x 27.9
35.47

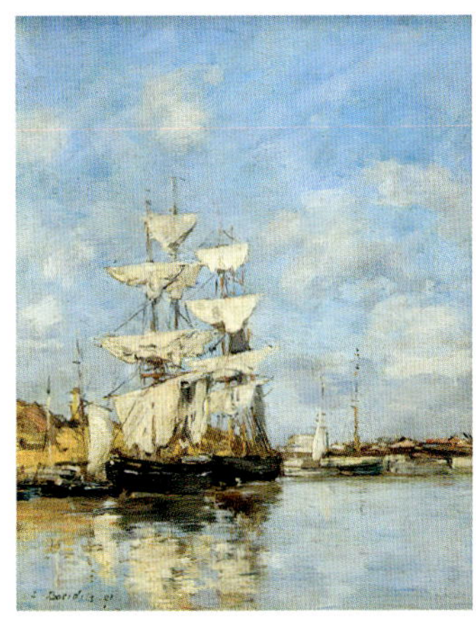

Boudin, Eugène Louis 1824–1898
Deauville, the Dock 1891
oil on panel 27.9 x 21.9
35.48

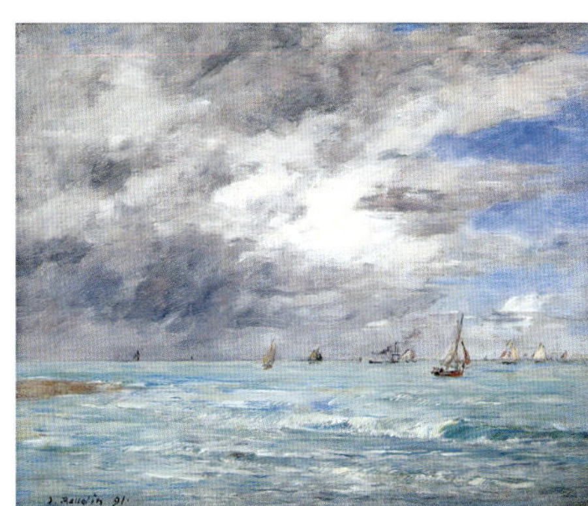

Boudin, Eugène Louis 1824–1898
The Shore at Deauville 1891
oil on panel 37.4 x 46.3
2916

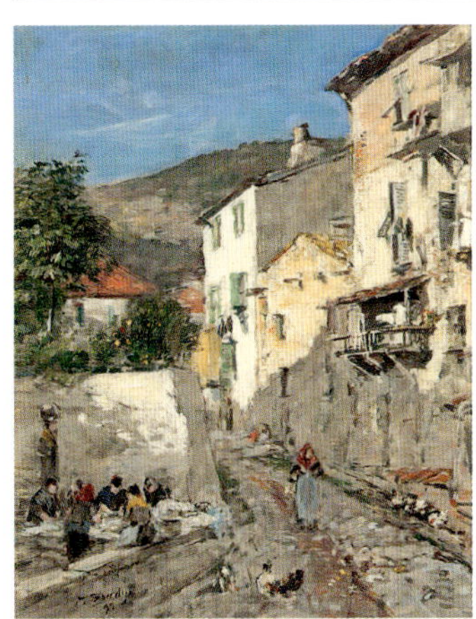

Boudin, Eugène Louis 1824–1898
Villefranche 1892
oil on board 39.1 x 32.8
3660

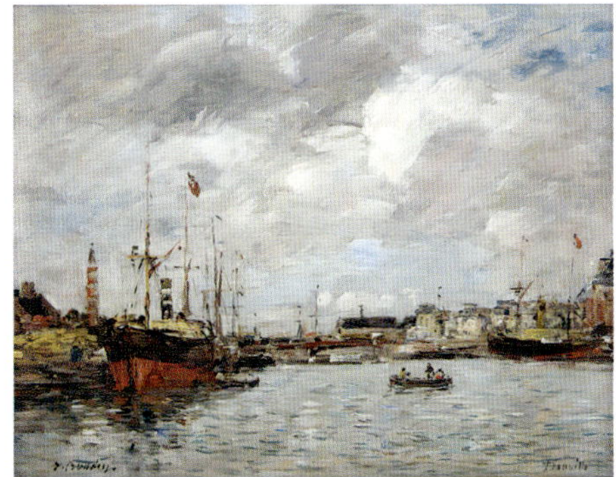

Boudin, Eugène Louis 1824–1898
The Port of Trouville c.1894–1897
oil on panel 32.5 x 41
3642

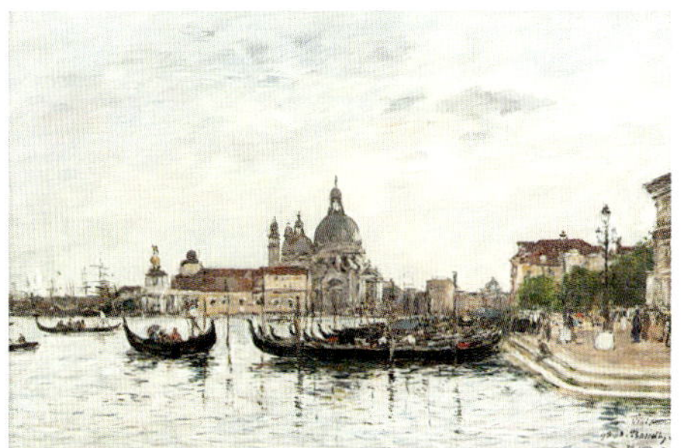

Boudin, Eugène Louis 1824–1898
Venice: Santa Maria della Salute and the Dogana Seen from across the Grand Canal 1895
oil on canvas 36 x 55
3605

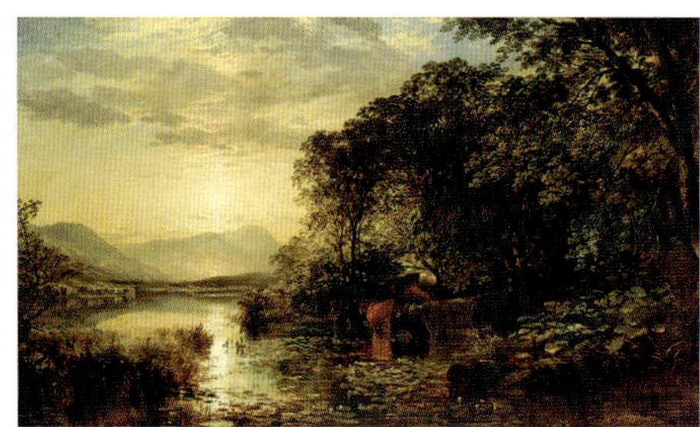

Bough, Samuel 1822–1878
By the Lake, Cumberland 1855
oil on canvas 54.6 x 90.2
758

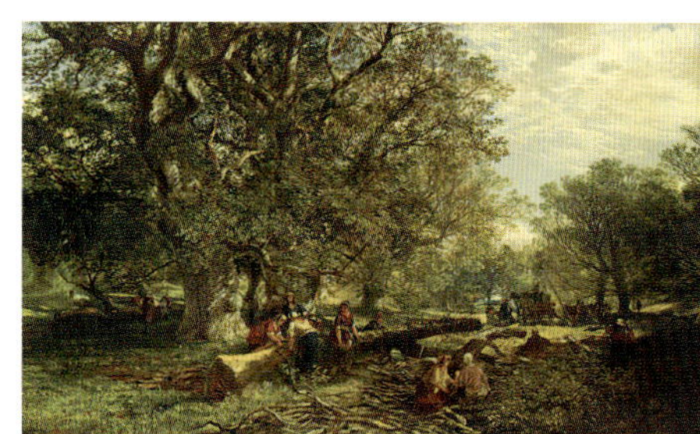

Bough, Samuel 1822–1878
Cadzow Forest 1855
oil on canvas 54.6 x 90.2
755

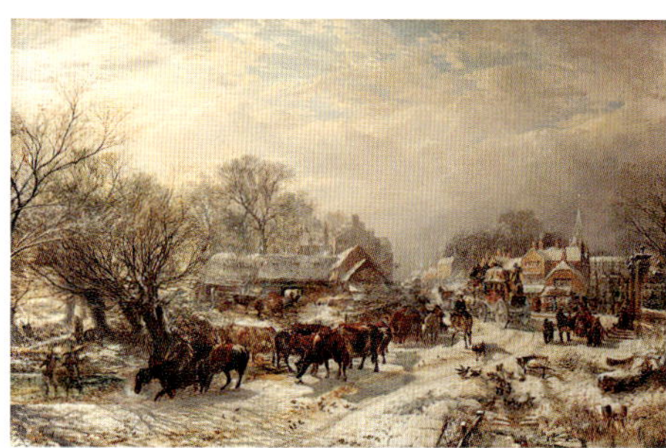

Bough, Samuel 1822–1878
The Mail Coach 1855
oil on canvas 101.6 x 152.4
1719

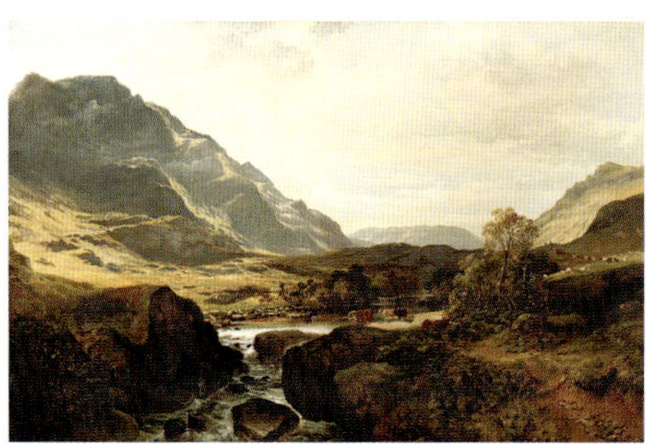

Bough, Samuel 1822–1878
In Glen Massan 1856
oil on canvas 59.7 x 90.2
756

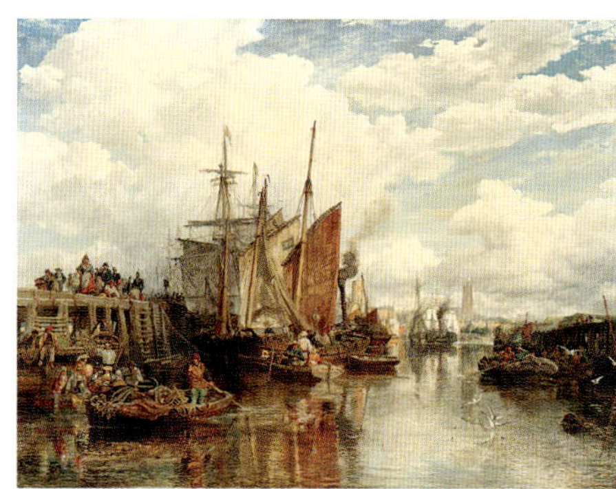

Bough, Samuel 1822–1878
Dunkirk Harbour 1863
oil on canvas 102.9 x 124.6
938

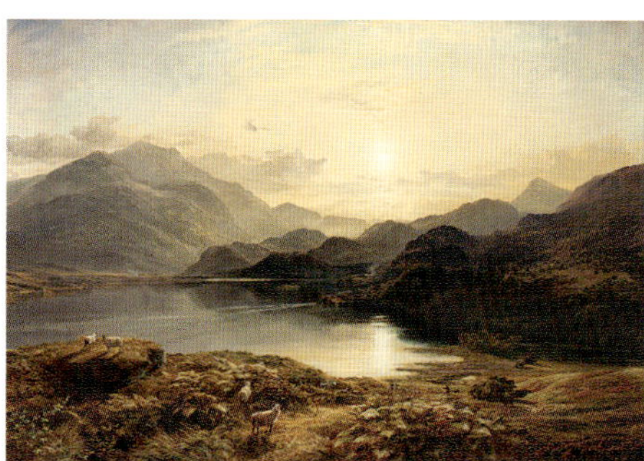

Bough, Samuel 1822–1878
Loch Achray 1869
oil on canvas 95.6 x 137.2
1166

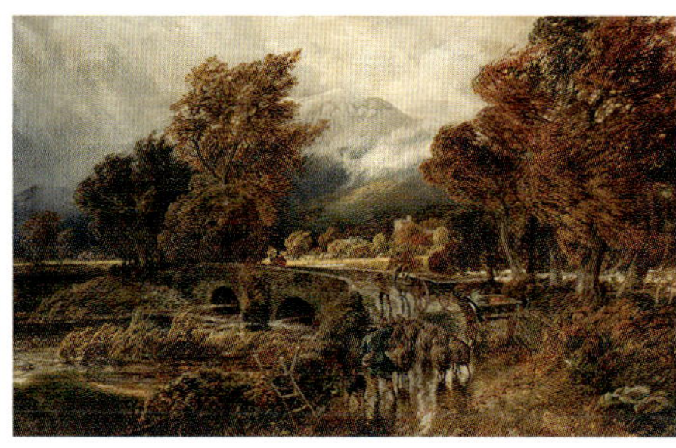

Bough, Samuel 1822–1878
Crossthwaite Bridge, near Keswick 1874
oil on canvas 94 x 154.9
1504

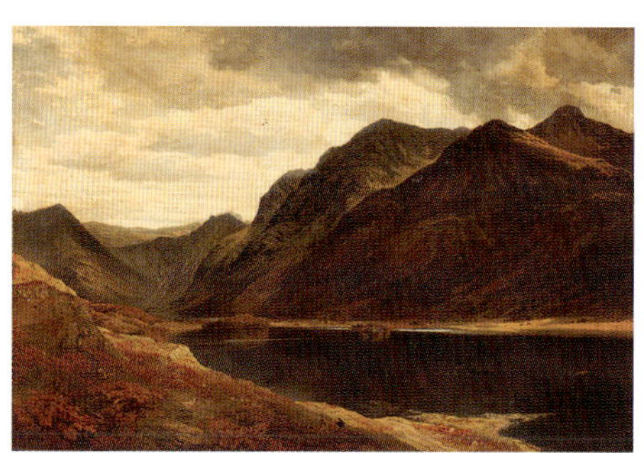

Bough, Samuel 1822–1878
Crummock Water, Cumberland 1875
oil on canvas 101.6 x 139.6
3447

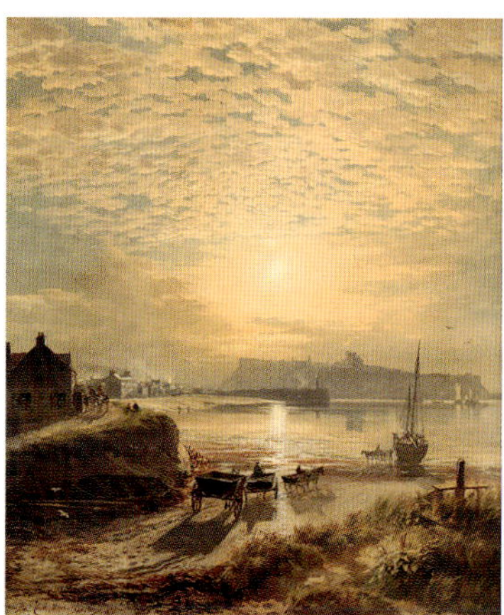

Bough, Samuel 1822–1878
Peel Castle, Mona 1875
oil on canvas 88.9 x 74.9
772

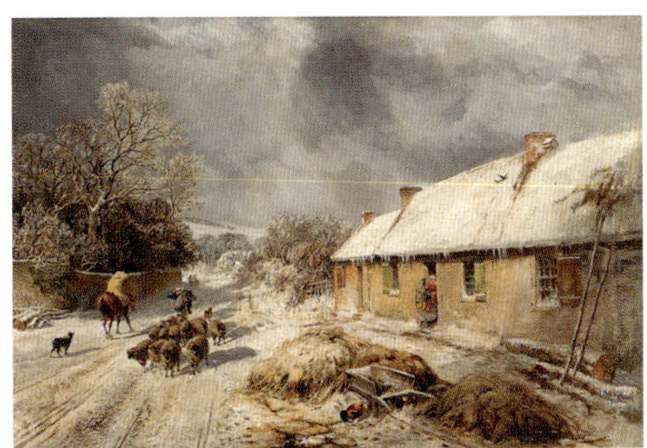

Bough, Samuel 1822–1878
Burns's Cottage, Alloway 1876
oil on canvas 101.8 x 145.7
2048

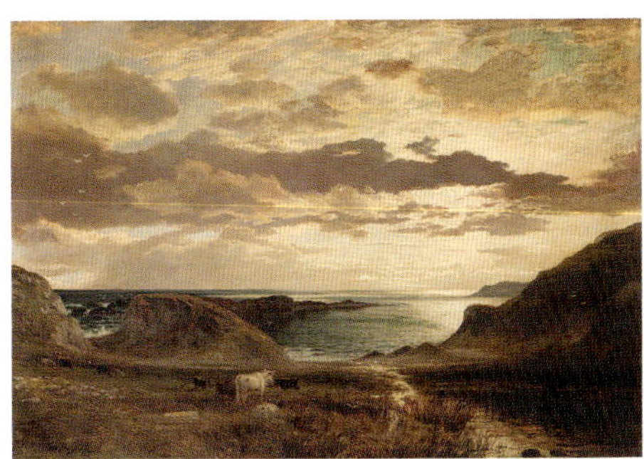

Bough, Samuel 1822–1878
Scottish Landscape 1878
oil on canvas 96.5 x 137.2
2360

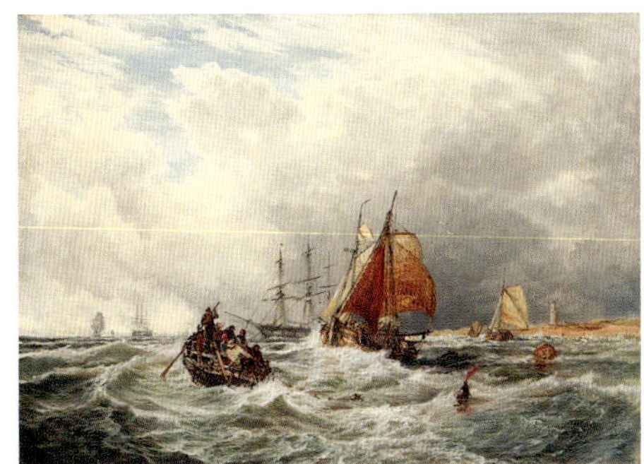

Bough, Samuel 1822–1878
Dutch Lugger Entering the Thames
oil on canvas 72.4 x 99.1
757

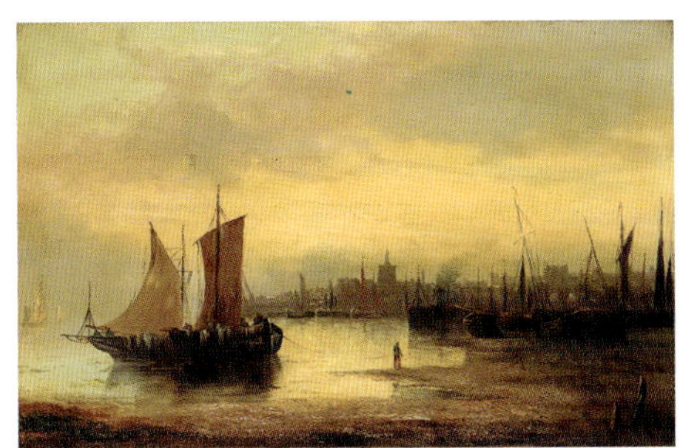

Bough, Samuel 1822–1878
Sea Piece
oil on canvas 40.6 x 60.3
1511

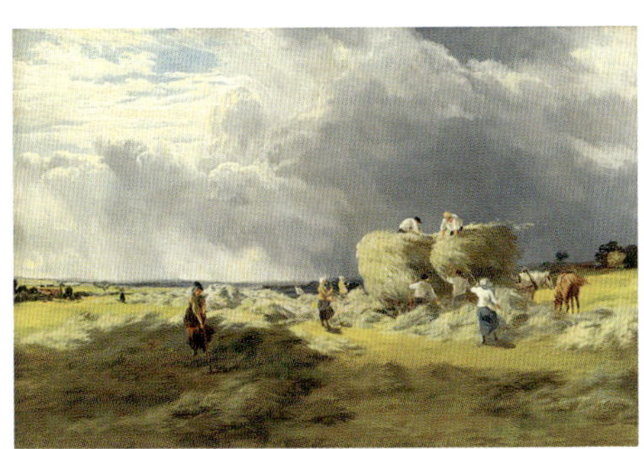

Bough, Samuel 1822–1878
The Hayfield, Coming Storm
oil on canvas 59.7 x 90.2
977

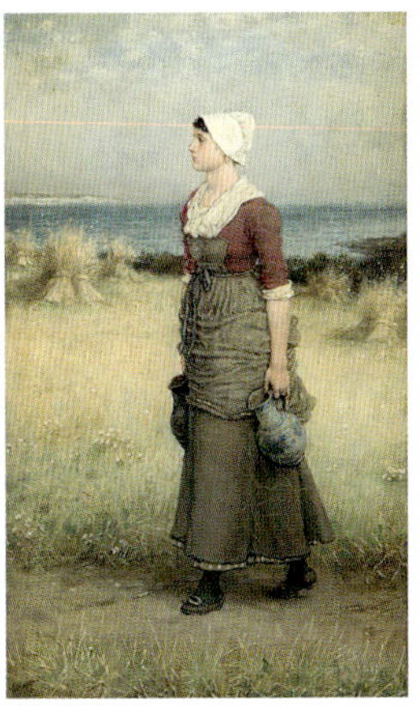

Boughton, George Henry 1833–1905
Girl with Pitchers, Summer Scene
c.1883–1887
oil on panel 53.3 x 35.6
2631

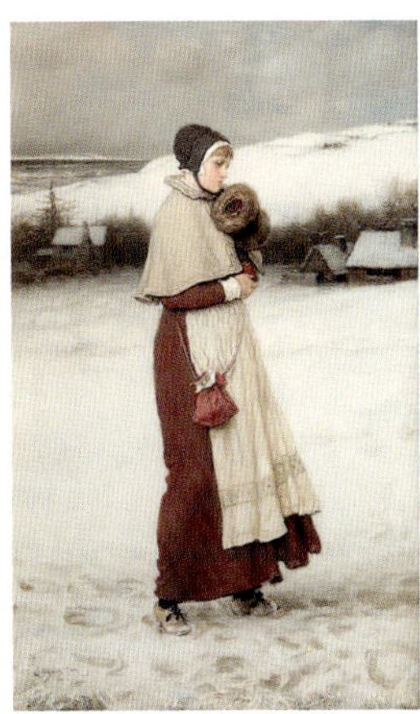

Boughton, George Henry 1833–1905
Girl with a Muff, Winter Scene
oil on panel 53.3 x 35.6
2630

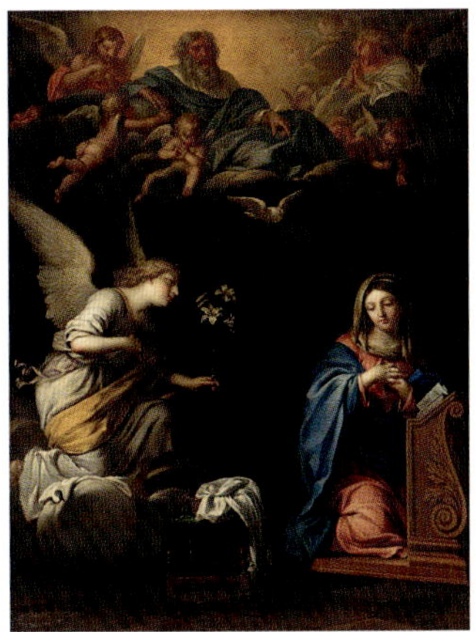

Boullogne, Bon (after) 1649–1717
The Annunciation
oil on canvas 100 x 72.3
217

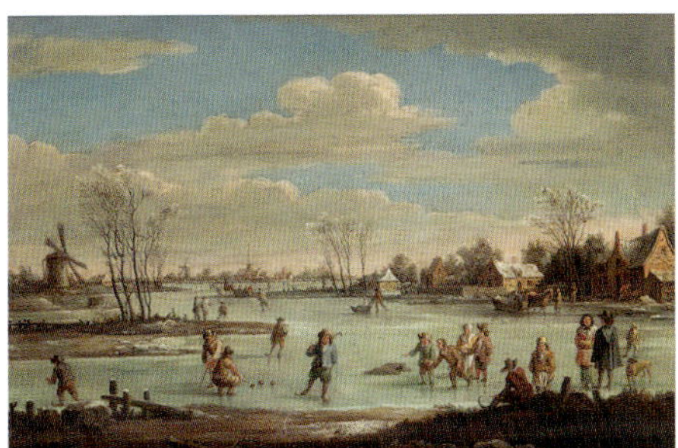

Bout, Peeter (after) 1658–1719
Skaters on a Frozen River 17th C–18th C
oil on copper 27.3 x 39
1464

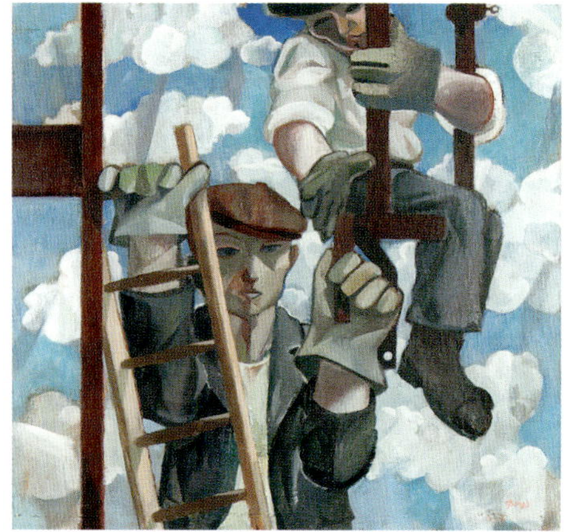

Boyd, John
The Scaffolders 1979
oil on board 49.6 x 49.7
PP.1980.124.dup1

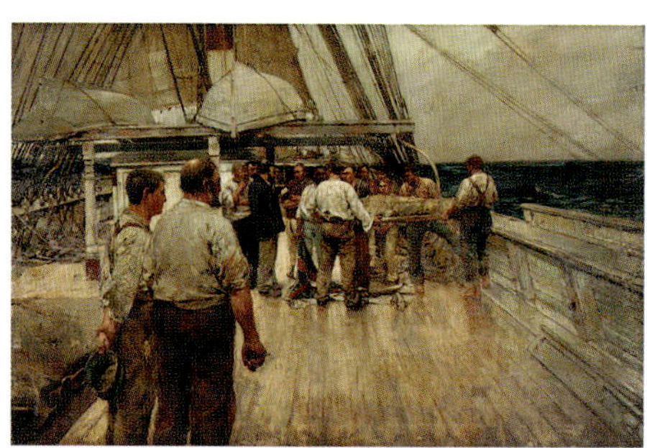

Brangwyn, Frank 1867–1956
The Burial at Sea 1890
oil on canvas 154.9 x 233.7
1077

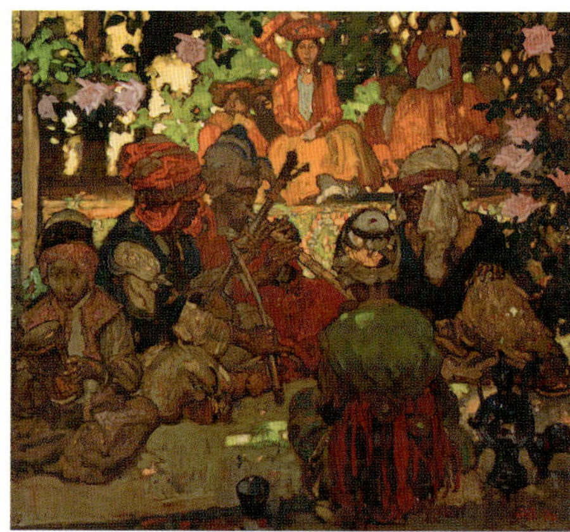

Brangwyn, Frank 1867–1956
Arab Musicians 1896
oil on canvas 144.8 x 157.5
1747

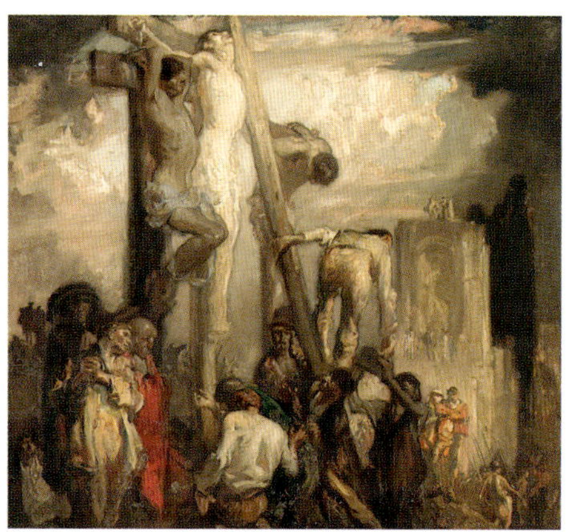

Brangwyn, Frank 1867–1956
The Crucifixion 1911
oil on canvas 147.3 x 160
1814

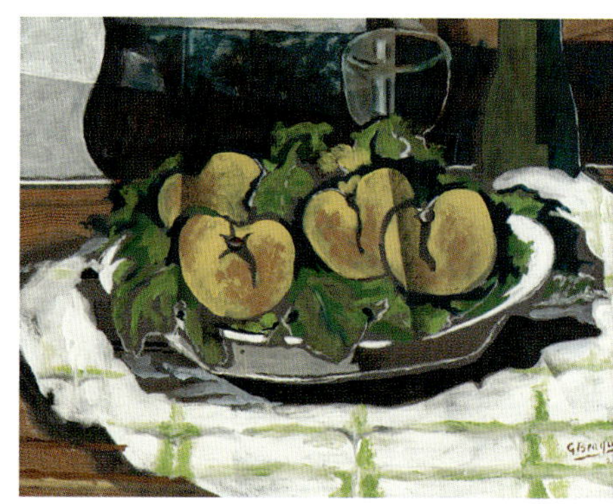

Braque, Georges 1882–1963
A Dish of Fruit, a Glass and a Bottle 1926
oil on plywood 44 x 54.6
2380

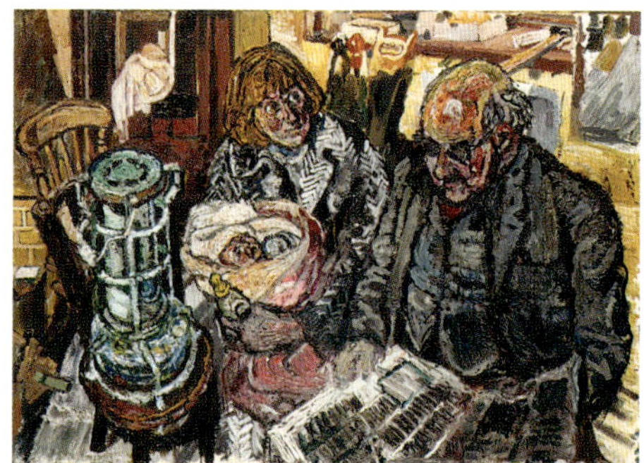

Bratby, John Randall 1928–1992
A Carlisle City Councillor with Jean and David Bratby 1955
oil on board 89.9 x 120.6
3116

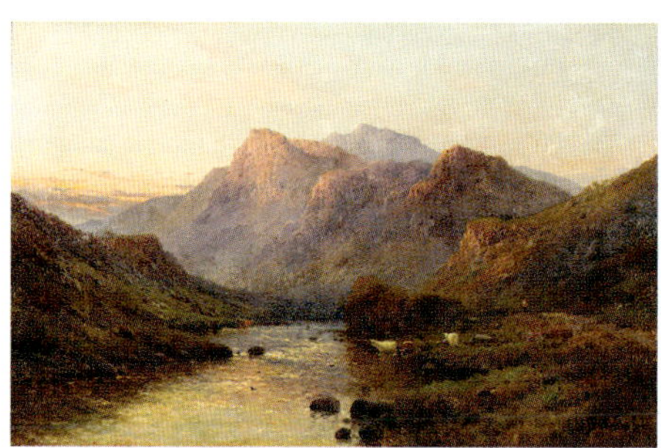

Breanski, Alfred de 1852–1928
Evening on a Perthshire River
oil on canvas 40.6 x 61
NR.130

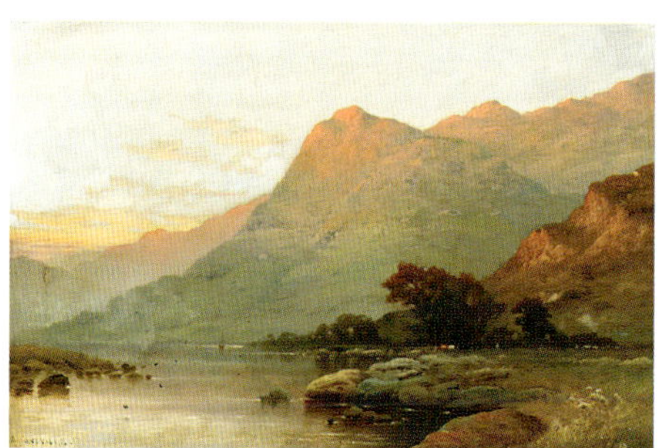

Breanski, Alfred de 1852–1928
Highland Loch
oil on canvas 52.1 x 78.7
NR.35

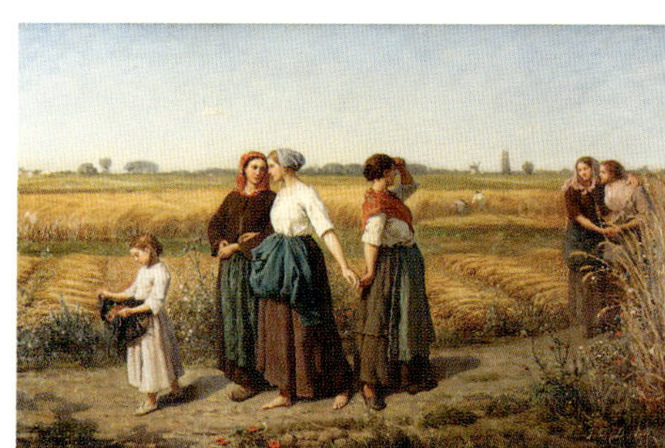

Breton, Jules Adolphe Aimé Louis 1827–1906
The Reapers 1860
oil on canvas 74.9 x 111.7
3396

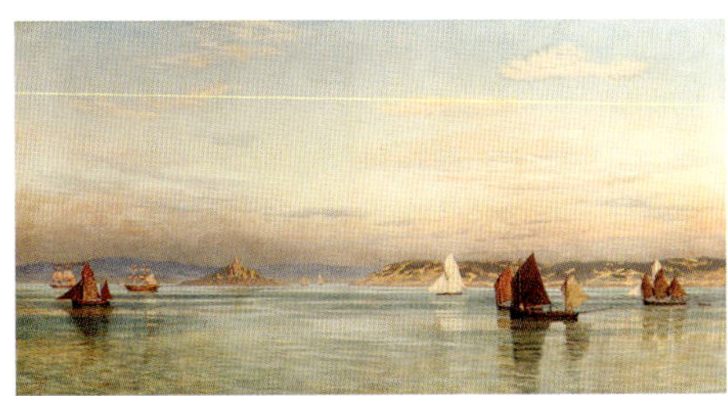

Brett, John 1830–1902
St Ives Bay 1878
oil on canvas 70.5 x 134.6
1733

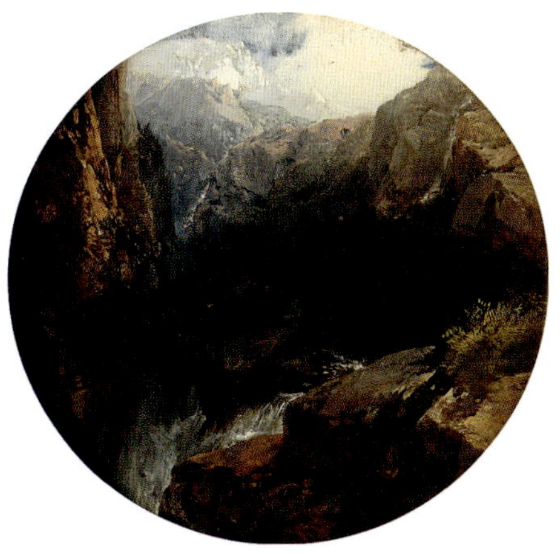

Bright, Henry 1810–1873
Rocky Landscape, Val d'Aosta 1849
oil on panel 27.9
427

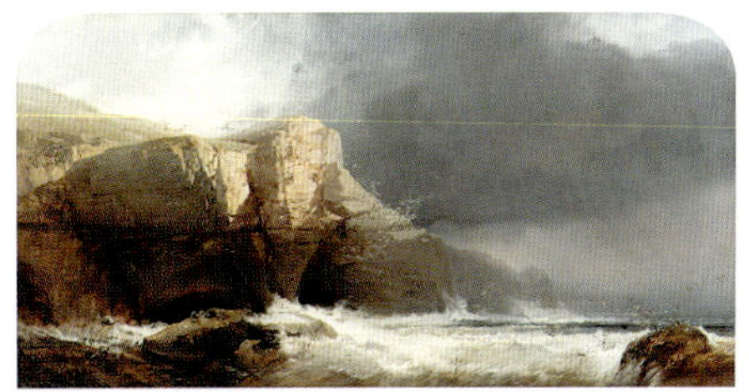

Bright, Henry 1810–1873
A Rock-Bound Coast
oil on canvas 39.4 x 77.5
353

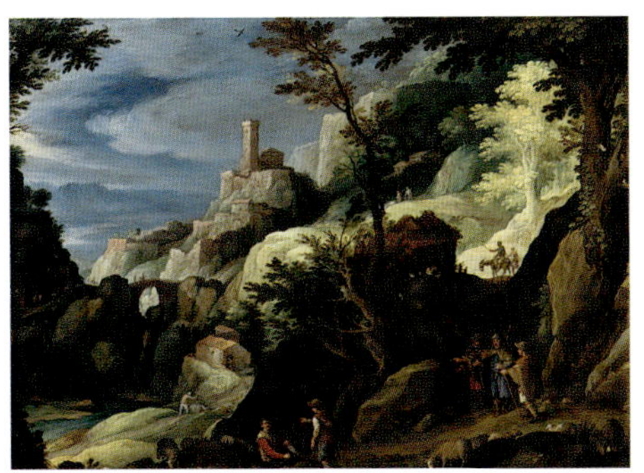

Bril, Paul 1554–1626
A Mountain Landscape with the Journey to Emmaus 1602
oil on copper 28.6 x 39.5
10

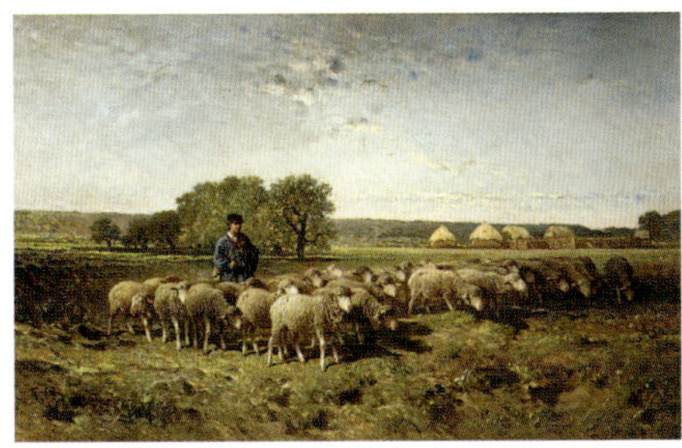

Brissot, Frank active 1879–1881
Landscape with a Shepherd and Sheep
oil on panel 54.6 x 85.1
765

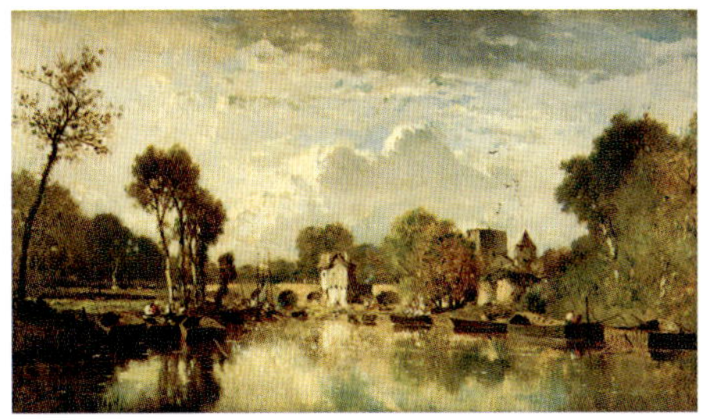

Brissot, Frank active 1879–1881
River Scene
oil on panel 19.1 x 33
2233

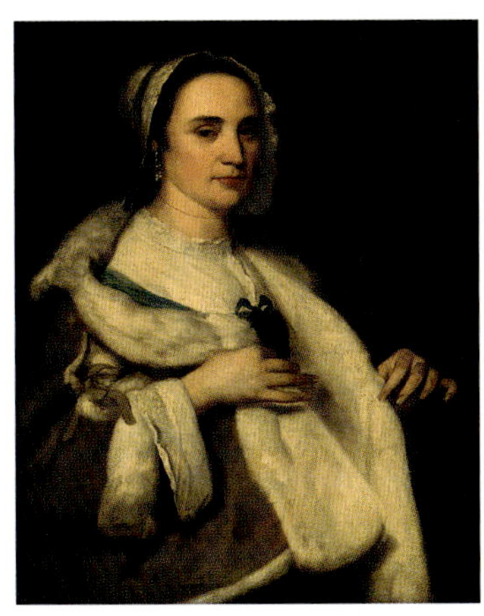

British (English) School (attributed to)
Portrait of a Lady 1720s
oil on canvas 82.5 x 64.8
35.292

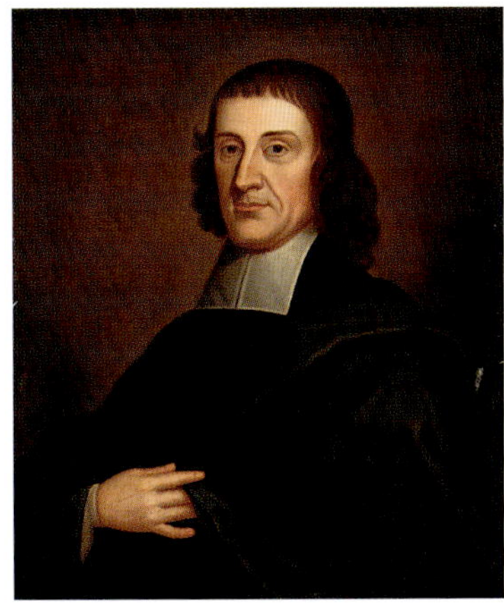

British (Scottish) School
John Anderson of Dowhill (1611–1689), Provost 1650s
oil on canvas 74 x 62.4
TEMP.9384

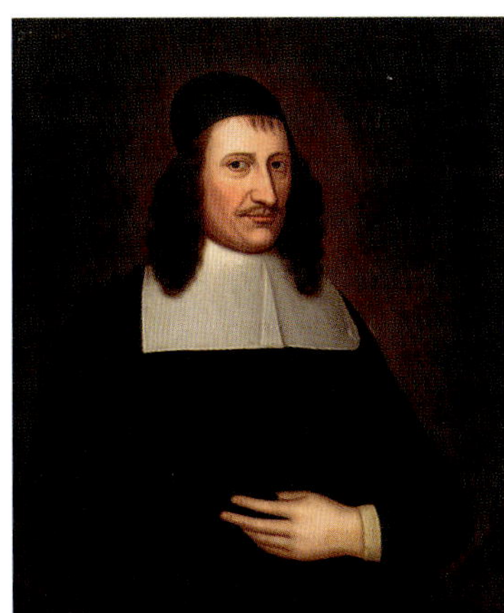

British (Scottish) School
John Luke of Claythorn (1627–1686) 1650s–1660s
oil on canvas 74.5 x 62
TEMP.9382

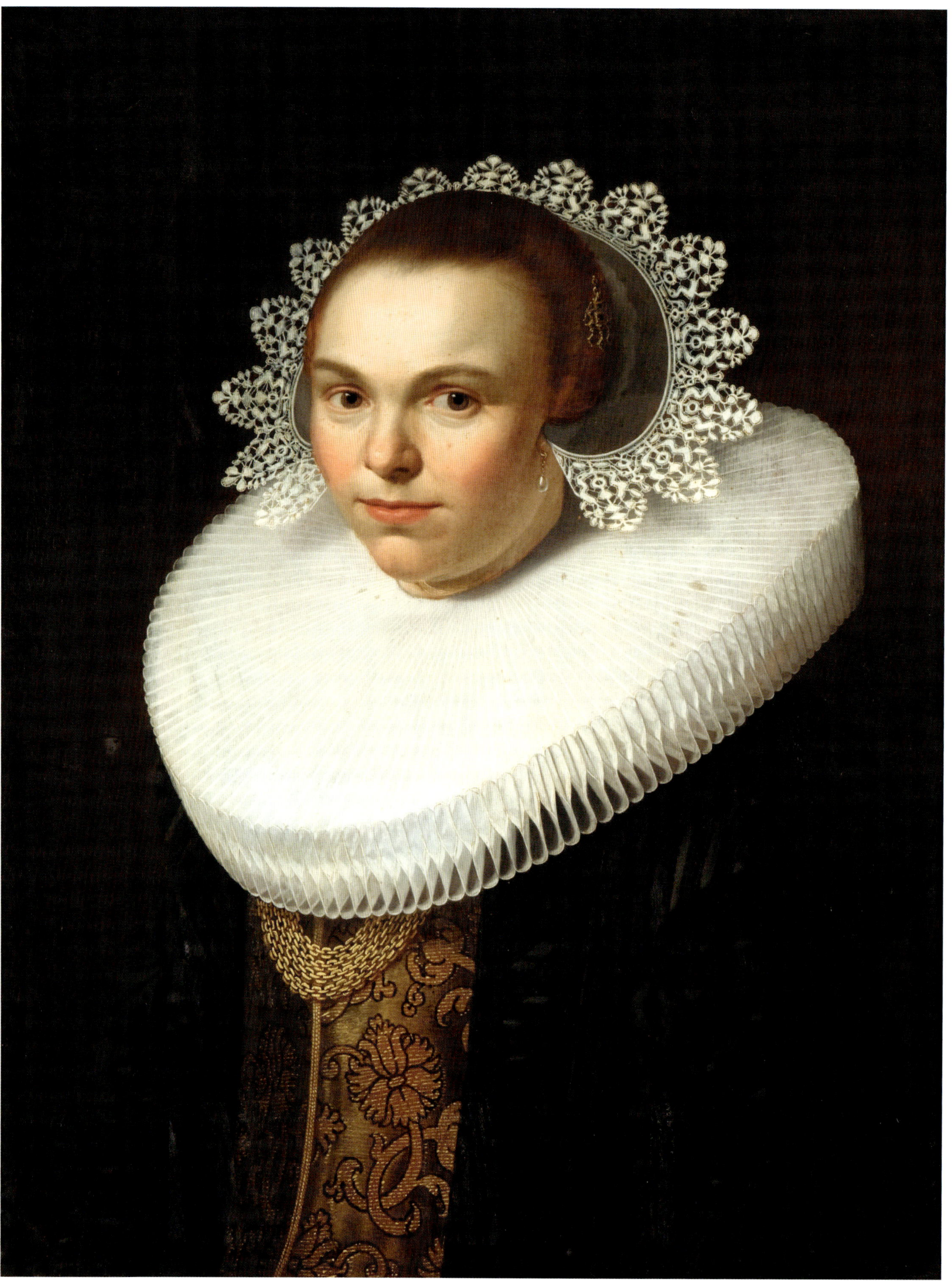

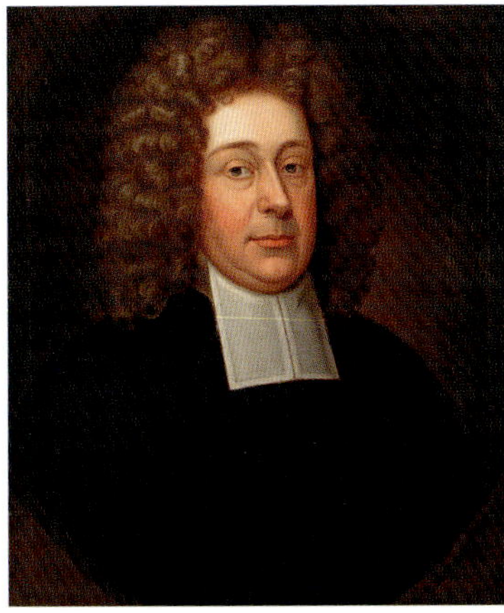

British (Scottish) School
Robert Cross (or Corse) *(1639–1705)*
c.1660–1680s
oil on canvas 76.5 x 64
TEMP.9383

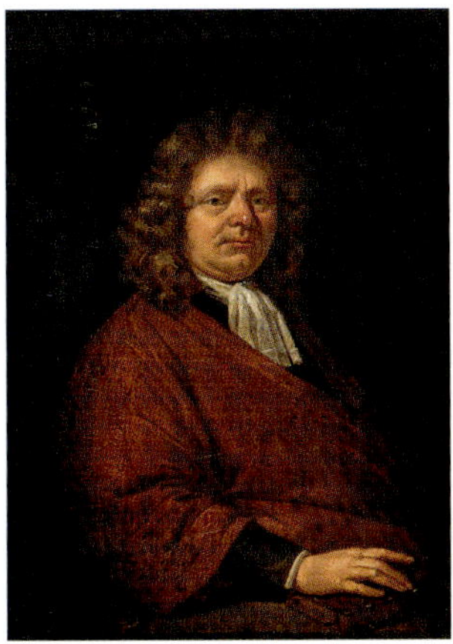

British (Scottish) School
William Carstares (1649–1715) c.1710–1715
oil on canvas 35.5 x 26
OG.1961.10.u

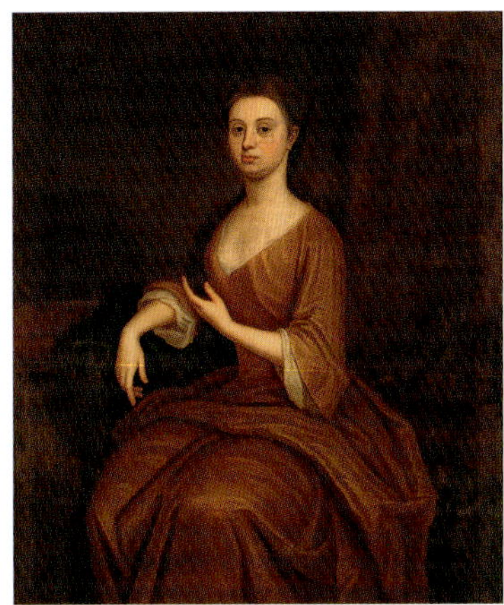

British (Scottish) School
Helen Smith Orr of Barrowfield 1710s
oil on canvas 106.7 x 101.6
NR.45

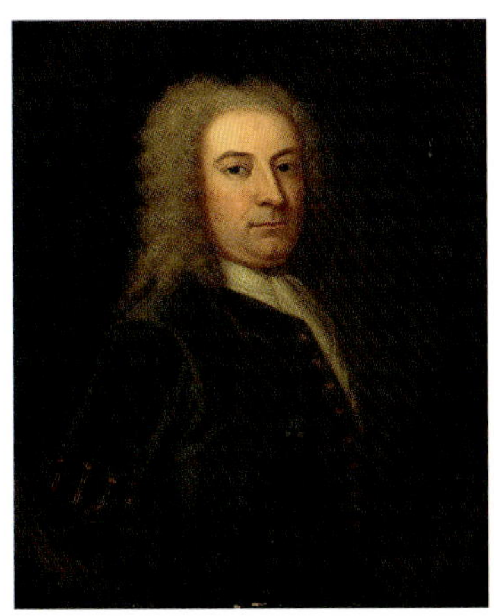

British (Scottish) School
George Bogle of Daldowie c.1730–1740
oil on canvas 76.2 x 63.5
2516

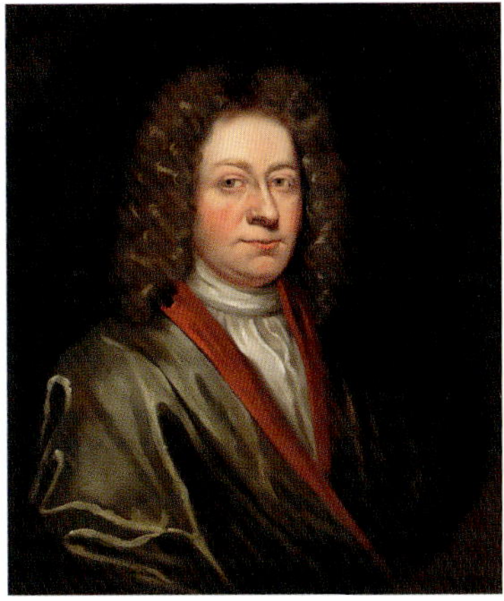

British (Scottish) School
Alexander Dunlop (1682–1747) 1740s
oil on canvas 74.9 x 61
OG.1961.10.r

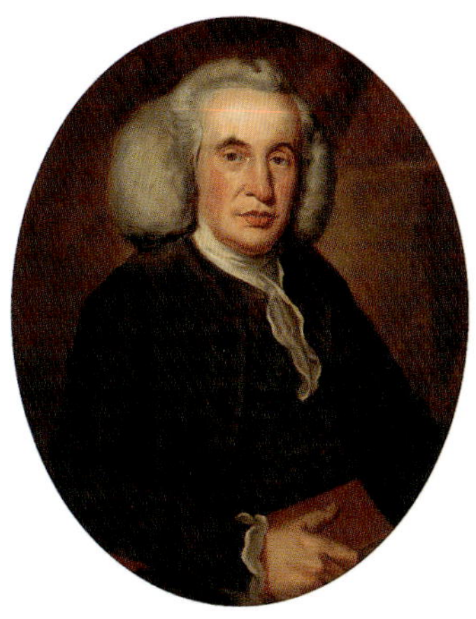

British (Scottish) School
Professor William Cullen (1710–1790) c.1765
oil on canvas 56 x 43.2
OG.1962.31.a

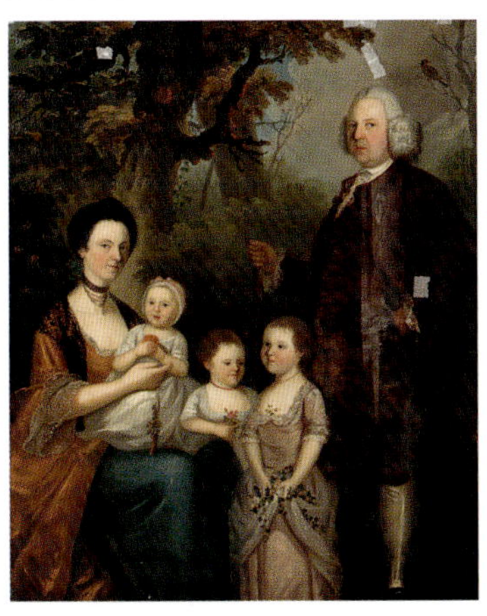

British (Scottish) School
*John McCall of Belvidere and Family (The
Dennistoun)* c.1765–1769
oil on canvas 181.7 x 145.5
OG.1965.1

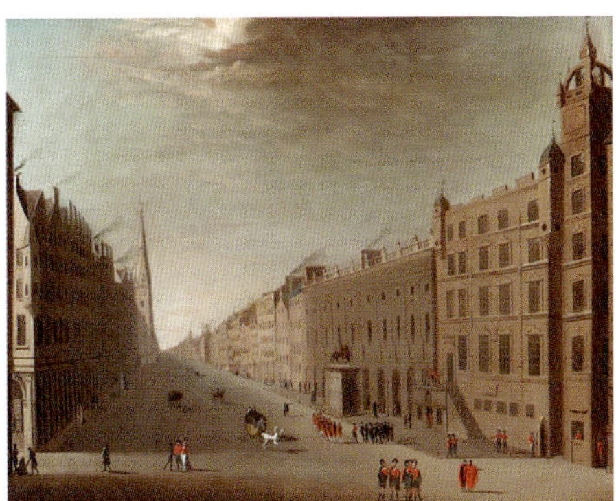

British (Scottish) School
*Trongate, Glasgow, Looking West from
Glasgow Cross (after the Foulis Academy)*
c.1770–1780
oil on canvas 43.2 x 55.9
OG.1959.54

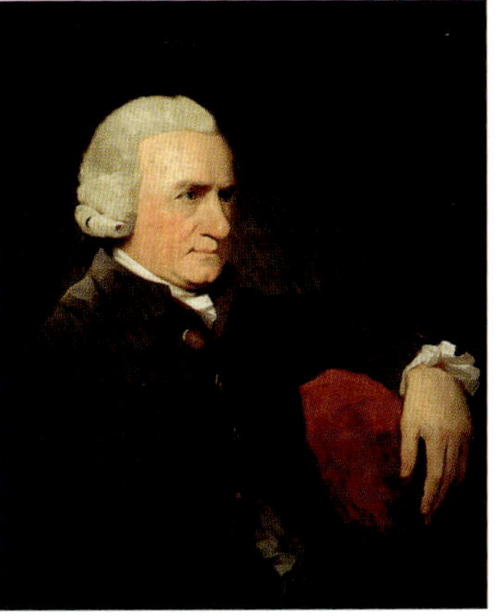

British (Scottish) School
Mungo Campbell of Hundleshope (1731–1793)
c.1785–1793
oil on canvas 76.2 x 63.5
1415

Facing page: Pickenoy, Nicolaes Eliasz., c.1588–c.1655, *Portrait of a Young Woman*, c.1625–1635, (p. 260)

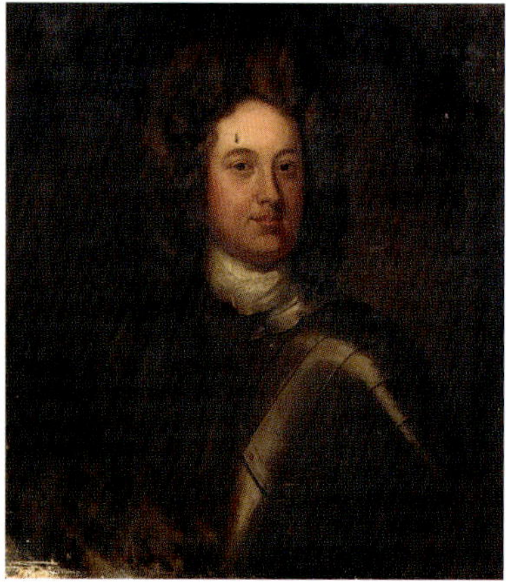

British (Scottish) School 18th C
Sir John Maxwell (1648–1732), 1st Bt
oil on canvas 78 x 65.4
PL.155 (P)

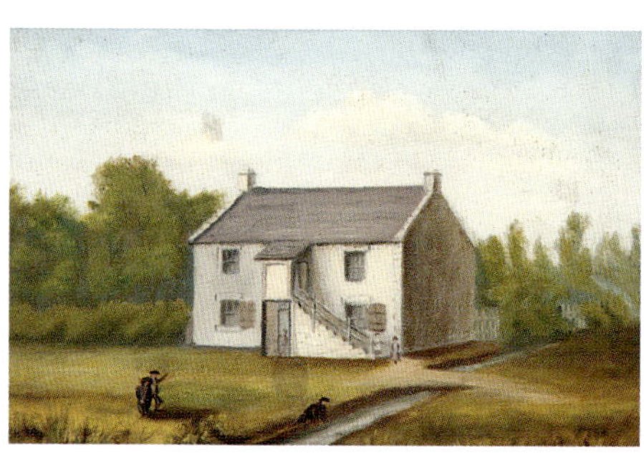

British (Scottish) School
Penny a Week School, Goat Burn c.1800
oil on canvas 17 x 24.6
PP.1978.101.8

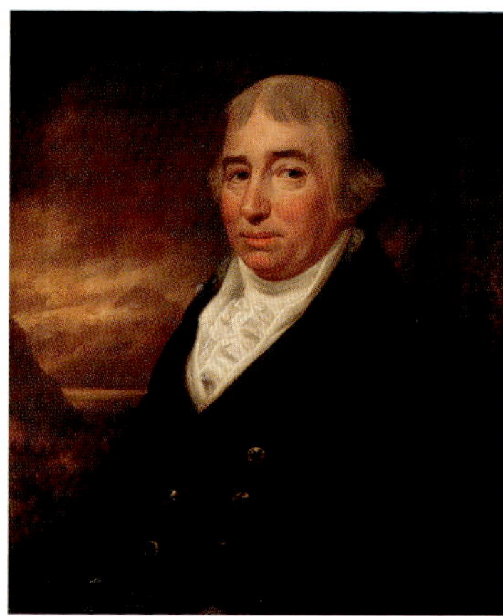

British (Scottish) School
George MacIntosh (1739–1807) c.1800–1807
oil on canvas 76.2 x 63.5
1903

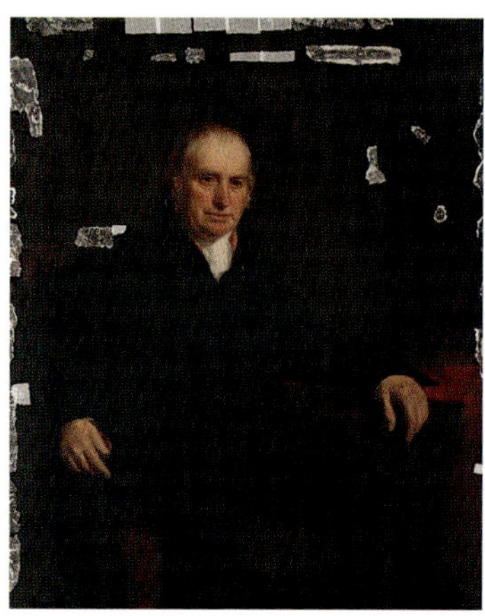

British (Scottish) School
John Bartholomew c.1810–1830
oil on canvas 125.1 x 100.3
NR.97

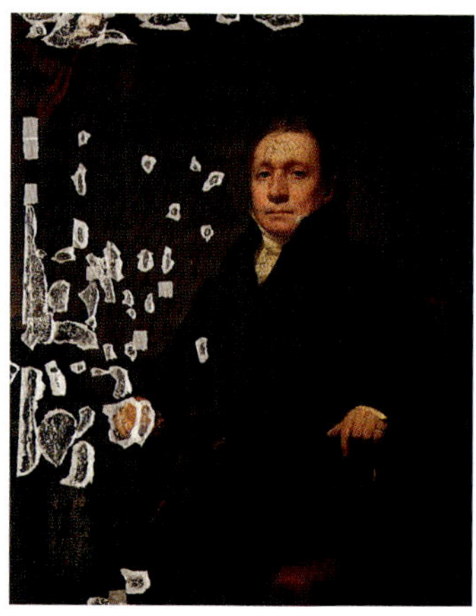

British (Scottish) School
*Alex Campbell of Haylodge, Peeblesshire
(1780–1849)* c.1818
oil on canvas 127 x 101.6
1423

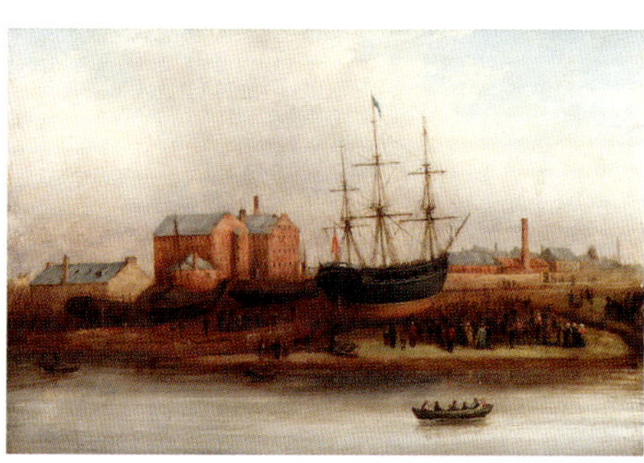

British (Scottish) School
Barclay Curle's Shipyard at Stobcross c.1830
oil on paper 43.3 x 61.7
PP.1977.126.2

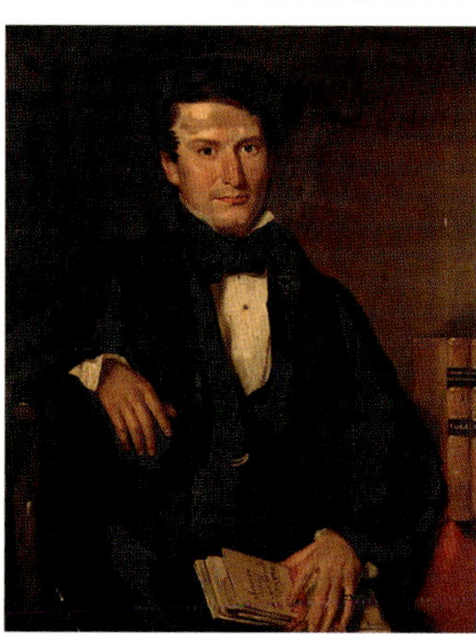

British (Scottish) School
Andrew Gemmill c.1836
oil on canvas 91.4 x 71.1
NR.65

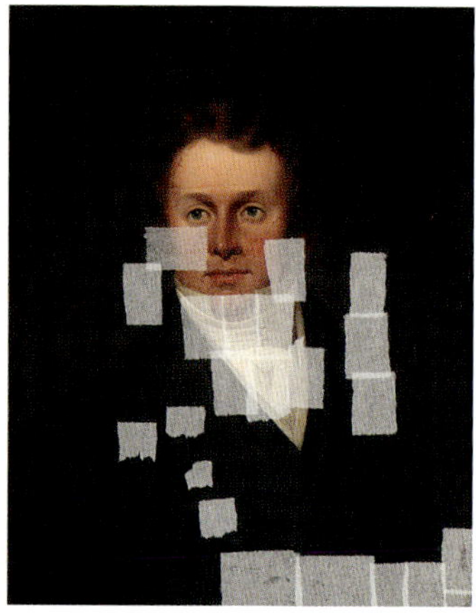

British (Scottish) School
*Joseph Reid, Town Clerk Depute of Glasgow
(1820–1832)* 1850s
oil on canvas 76.2 x 63.5
NR.73

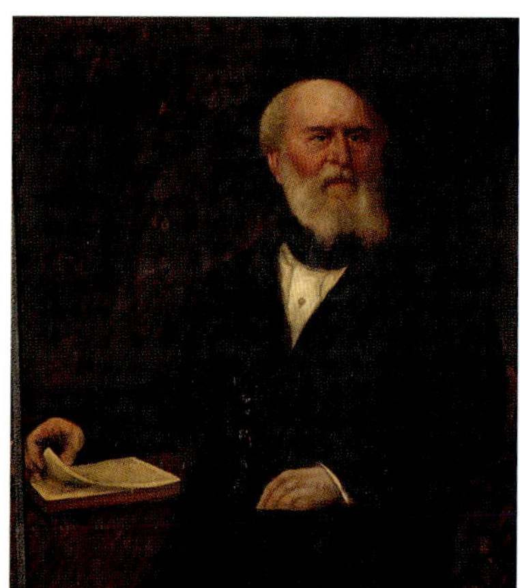

British (Scottish) School
John Dunlop (1789–1865) c.1855–1865
oil on canvas 107.5 x 91.5
TEMP.2738

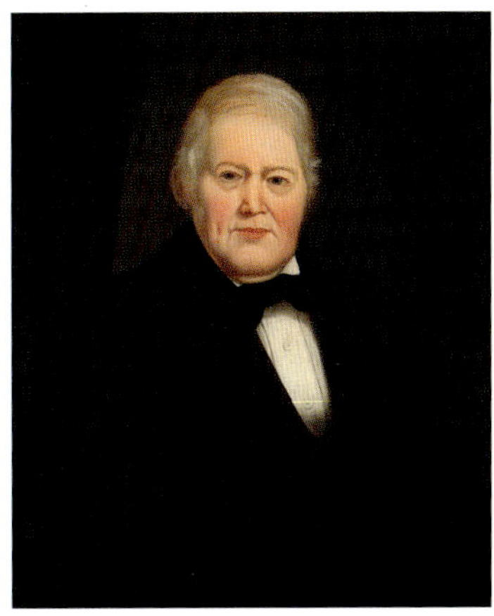

British (Scottish) School
John Robertson (1782–1863) c.1866
oil on canvas 124 x 93.5
1894.137

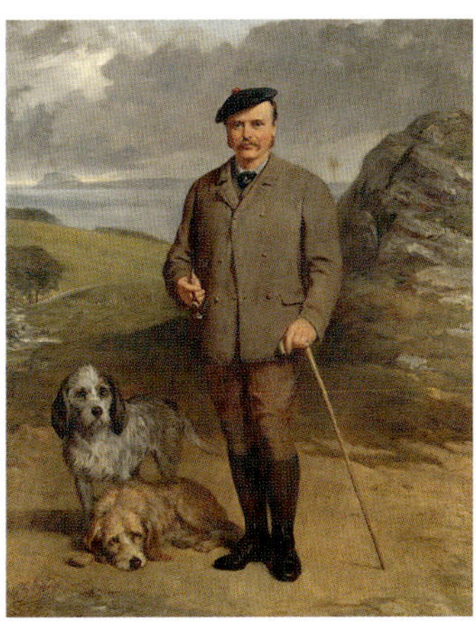

British (Scottish) School
Portrait of a Man 1880
oil on canvas 113 x 87.6
NR.87

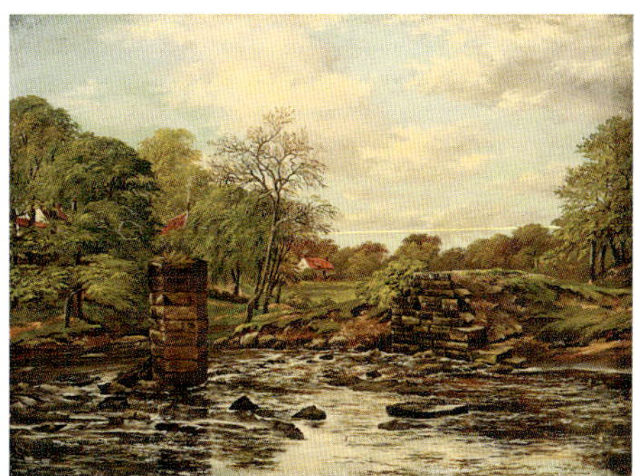

British (Scottish) School
The River Kelvin at, or below, the Pear Tree Well c.1880
oil on canvas 30.5 x 40.9
TEMP.8394

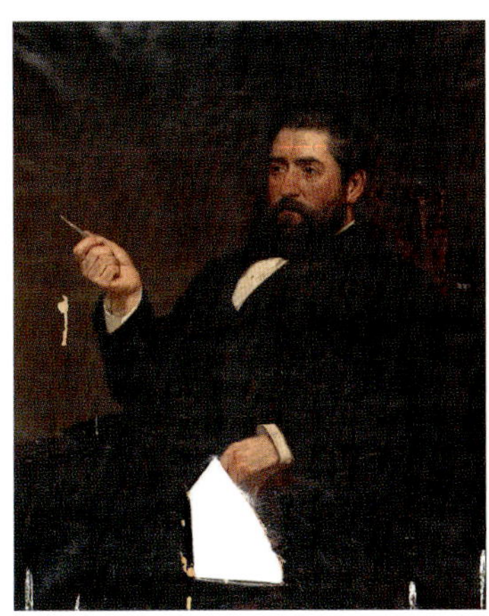

British (Scottish) School
John Turnbull, Junior 1882
oil on canvas 112 x 86
TEMP.20120

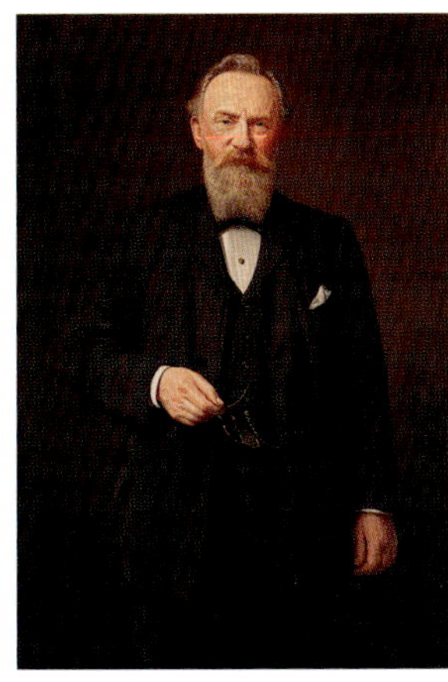

British (Scottish) School
Portrait of a Man 1890s
oil on canvas 132.1 x 83.8
NR.164

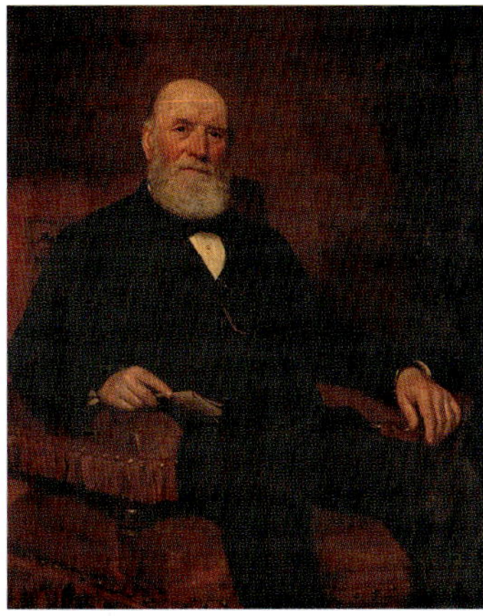

British (Scottish) School
John White, Provost of Partick c.1891
oil on canvas 162 x 138
NR.172

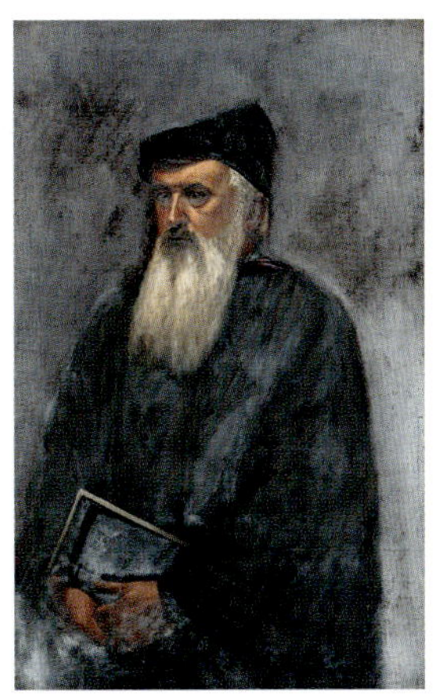

British (Scottish) School
Principal Robert Herbert Story c.1898–1907
oil on canvas 61 x 40.5
NR.21

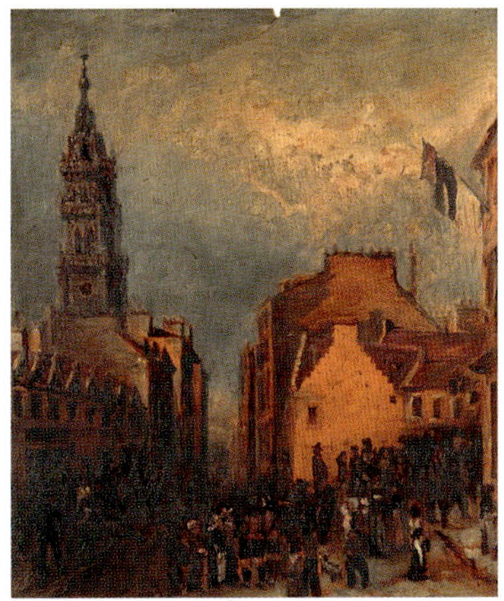

British (Scottish) School 19th C
Bridge Gate
oil on canvas 30.5 x 25.5
TEMP.1664

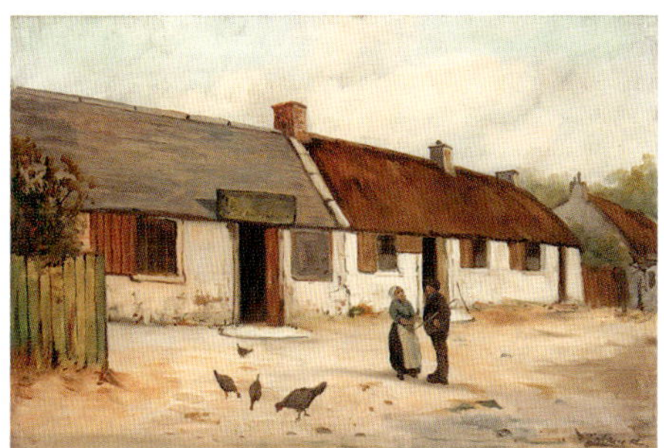

British (Scottish) School 19th C
Cottage Scene
oil on canvas 40.5 x 61.2
TEMP.1732

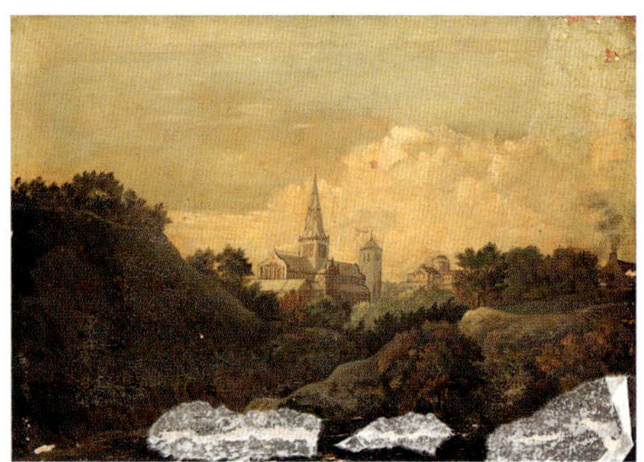

British (Scottish) School 19th C
Glasgow Cathedral
oil on canvas 35.8 x 49.8
TEMP.19236

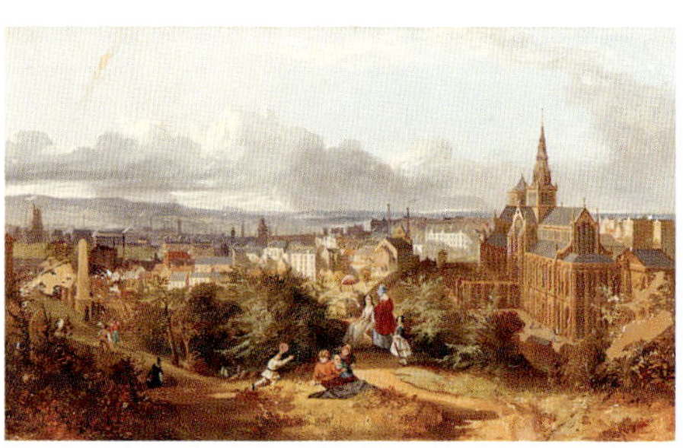

British (Scottish) School 19th C
Glasgow Cathedral from the Necropolis (after
J. A. Houston)
oil on canvas 38.1 x 61
TEMP.14928

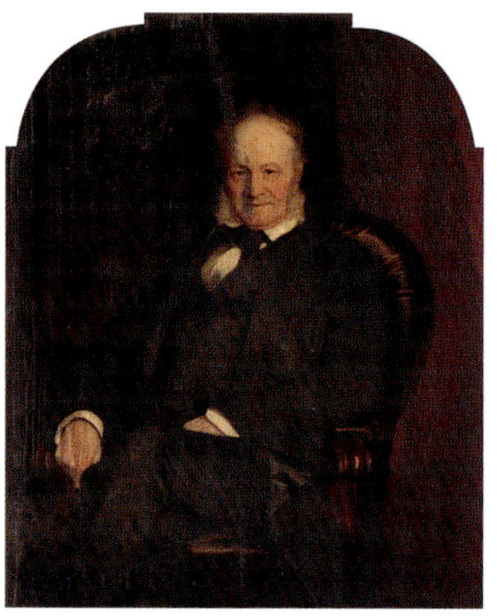

British (Scottish) School 19th C
Mr Campbell
oil on canvas 127 x 101.6
L.1.1949 (P)

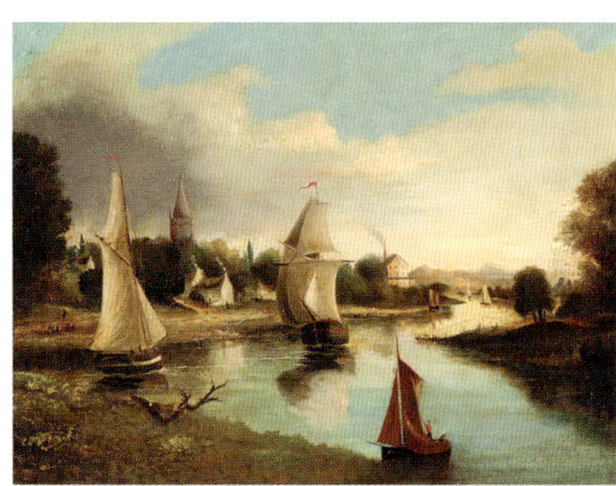

British (Scottish) School 19th C
Salmon Fishing at Govan
oil on canvas 92 x 117.7
TEMP.5899

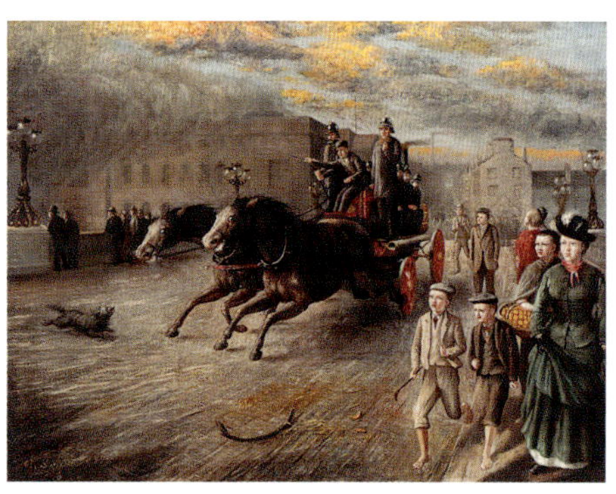

British (Scottish) School 19th C–20th C
*Glasgow Fire Brigade Crossing the Albert
Bridge*
oil on canvas 89 x 110
OG.1961.33

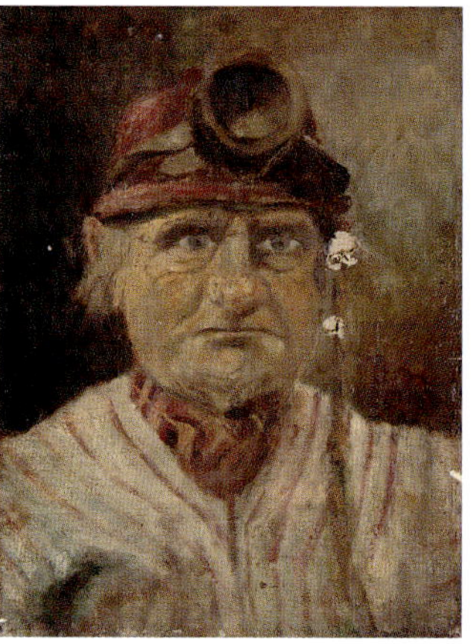

British (Scottish) School 19th C–20th C
Old Malabar
oil on canvas 35.8 x 25.2
OG.1955.154

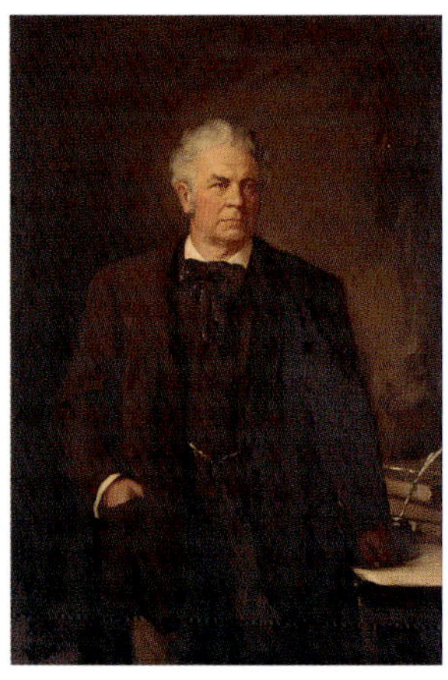

British (Scottish) School
Sir Renny Watson of Braco 1900
oil on canvas 149.9 x 104.1
NR.68

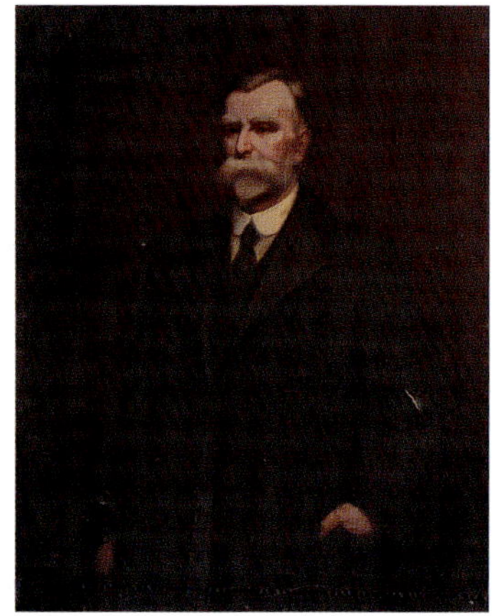

British (Scottish) School
James Dalrymple 1919
oil on canvas 128.3 x 101
NR.168

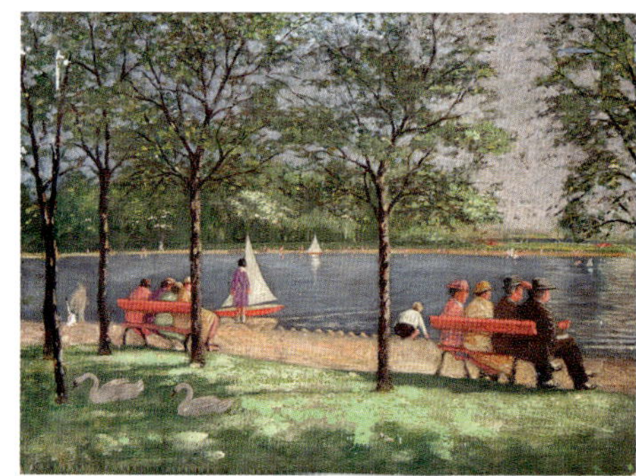

British (Scottish) School
Boating Scene in Queen's Park c.1925–1930
oil on canvas 51 x 66.5
PP.1977.22.1

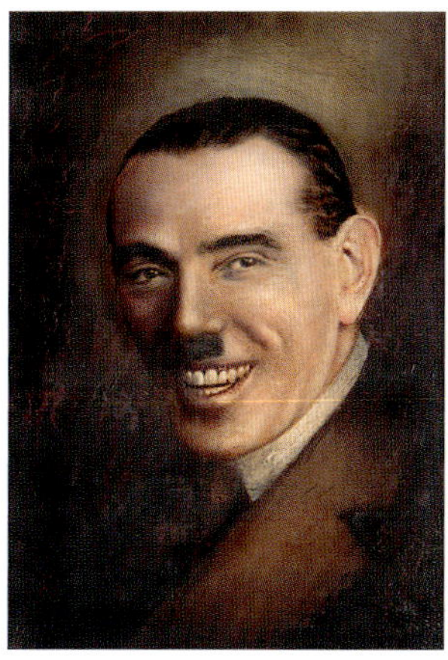

British (Scottish) School
Dave Willis (1895–1973) 1930s
oil on canvas 34.4 x 23.9
PP.1978.3.1

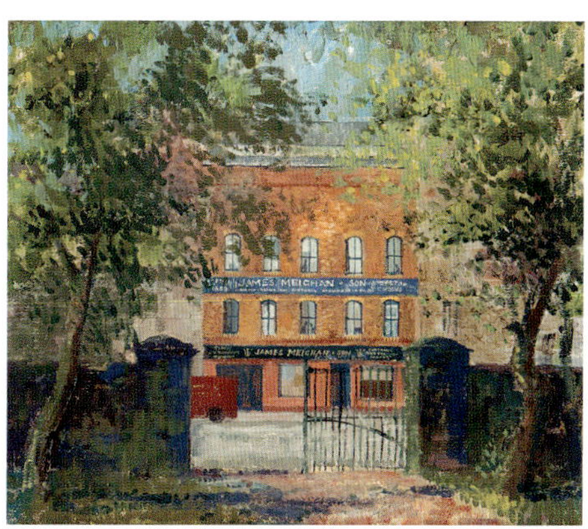

British (Scottish) School
Meighan's Premises c.1930–1940
oil on board 36.4 x 40.3
PP.1977.43

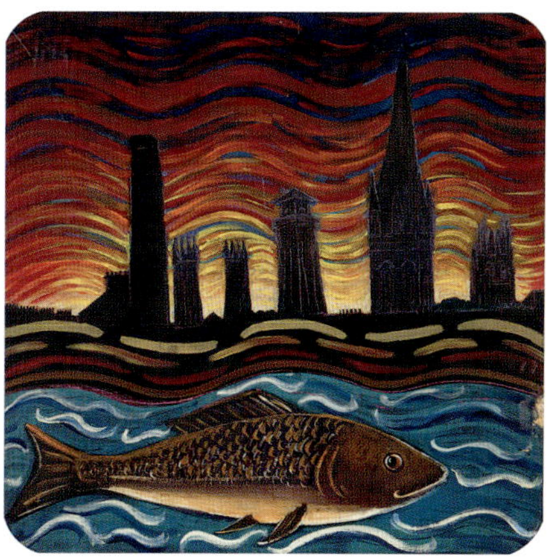

British (Scottish) School
Fish and Towers 1990
acrylic on panel 60 x 60
TEMP.15537

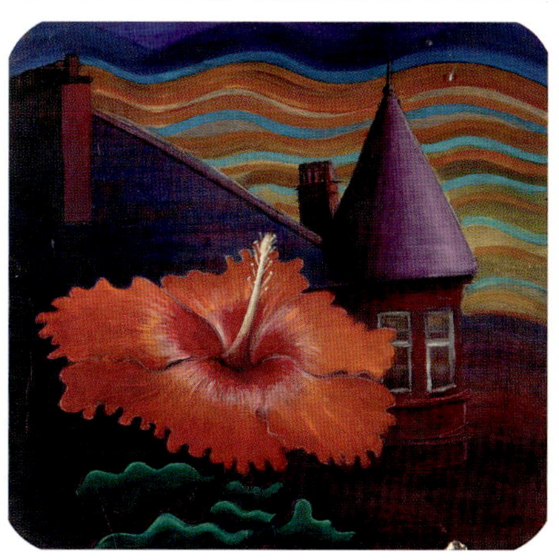

British (Scottish) School
Turret Tower 1990
acrylic on panel 61 x 62
TEMP.15521

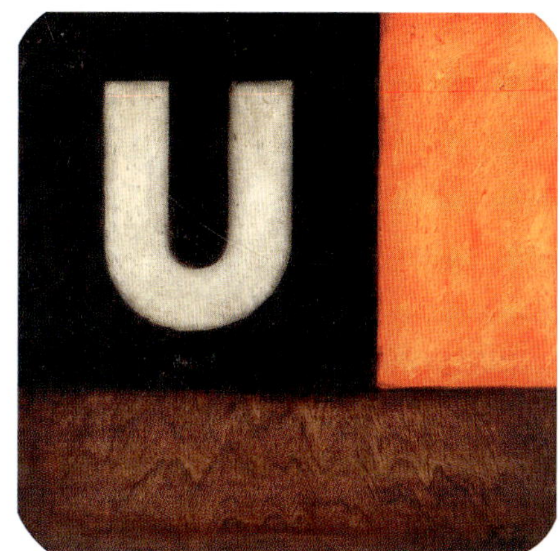

British (Scottish) School
U 1990
acrylic on panel 60 x 60
TEMP.15531

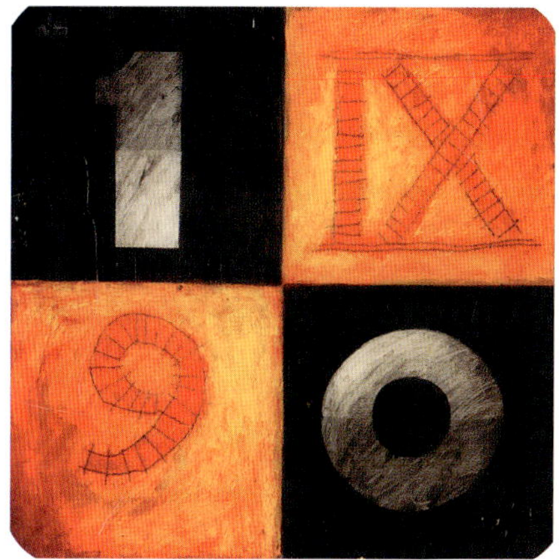

British (Scottish) School
1 IX 9 0 c.1990
acrylic on panel 60 x 60
TEMP.15541

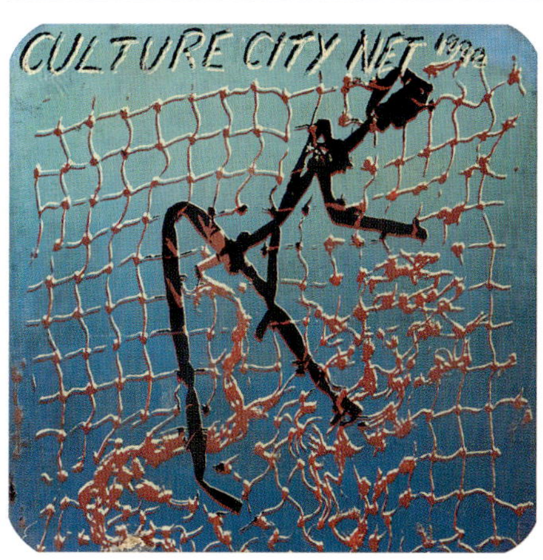

British (Scottish) School
Culture City Net 1990 c.1990
acrylic on panel 60 x 60
TEMP.15526

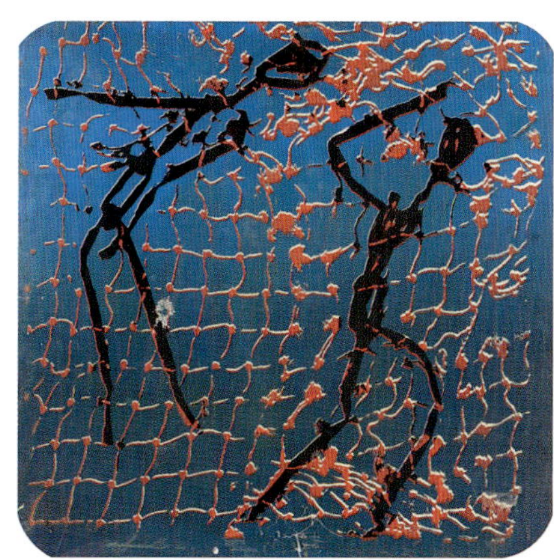

British (Scottish) School
Culture City Net 1990 c.1990
acrylic on panel 60 x 60
TEMP.15530

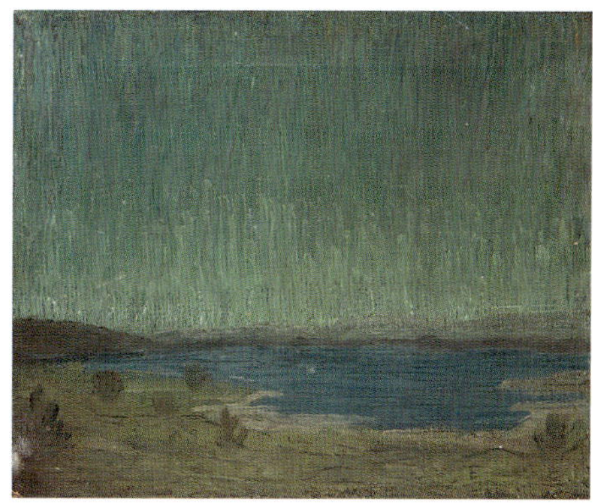

British (Scottish) School 20th C
Loch Landscape
oil on canvas 25.8 x 30.7
TEMP.1774

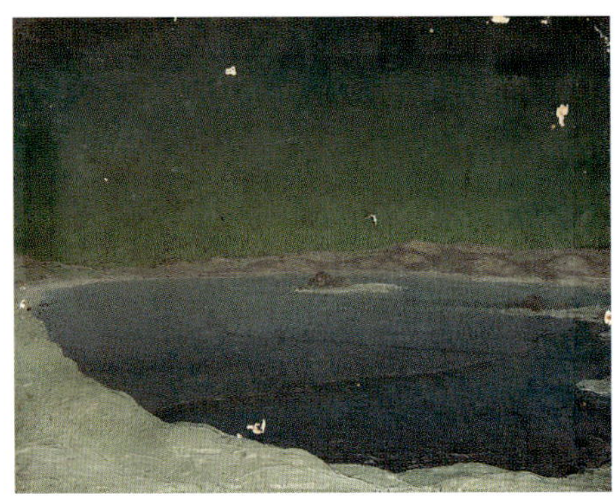

British (Scottish) School 20th C
Loch Scene Landscape
oil on canvas 43 x 53.1
TEMP.1731

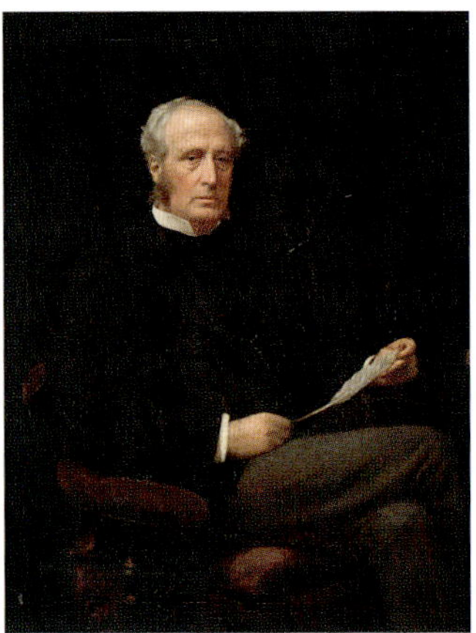

British (Scottish) School 20th C
Sir George MacLeod
oil on canvas 91 x 71
NR.86

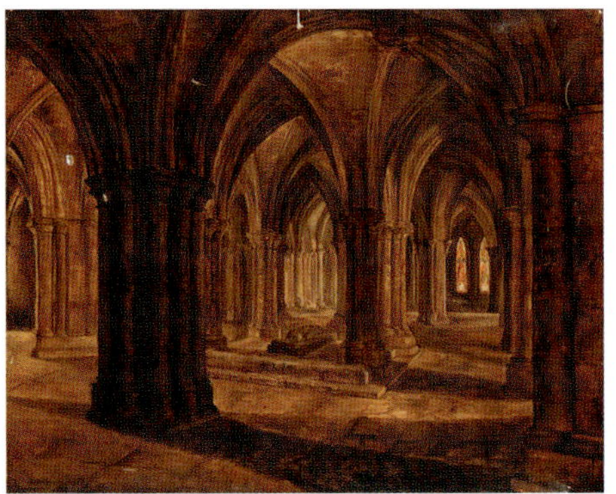

British (Scottish) School 20th C
The Lower Church of Glasgow Cathedral
oil on canvas 51 x 61.3
TEMP.1727

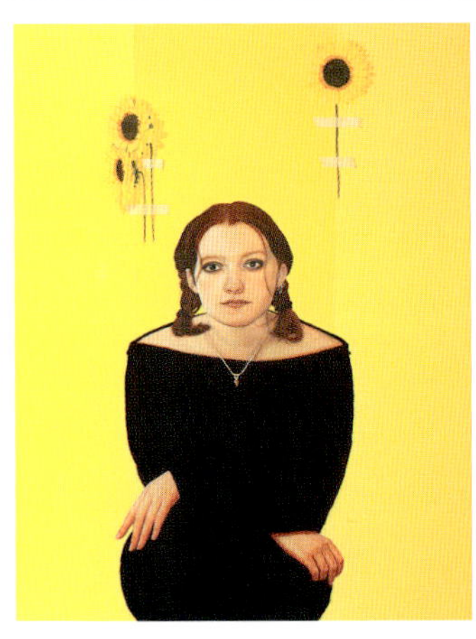

British (Scottish) School
Girl with Sunflowers c.2009
acrylic on canvas 121.8 x 91.6
SP.2010.2

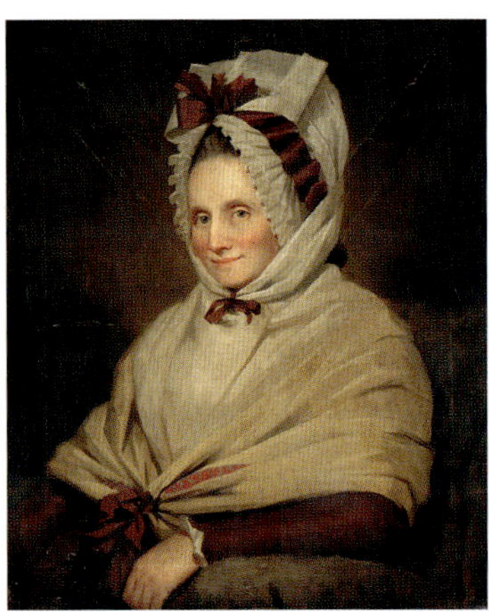

British (Scottish) School
Mrs Elizabeth Campbell
oil on canvas 76.2 x 63.5
1416

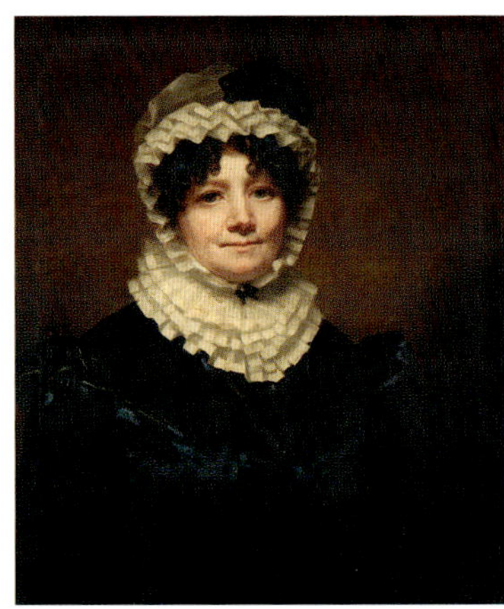

British (Scottish) School
Mrs General Campbell
oil on canvas 76.2 x 63.5
1425

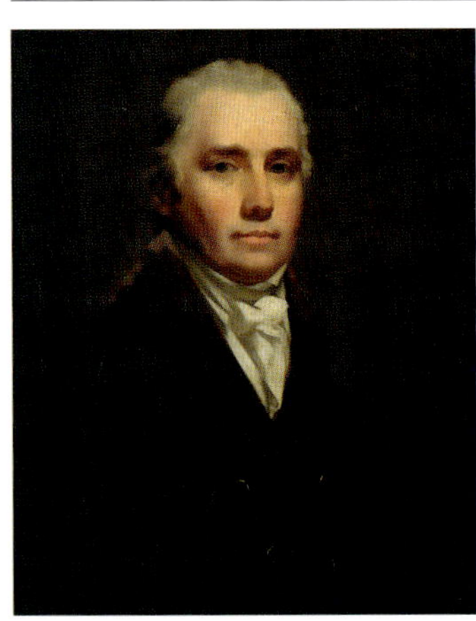

British (Scottish) School
Portrait of a Gentleman
oil on canvas 61 x 48.3
436

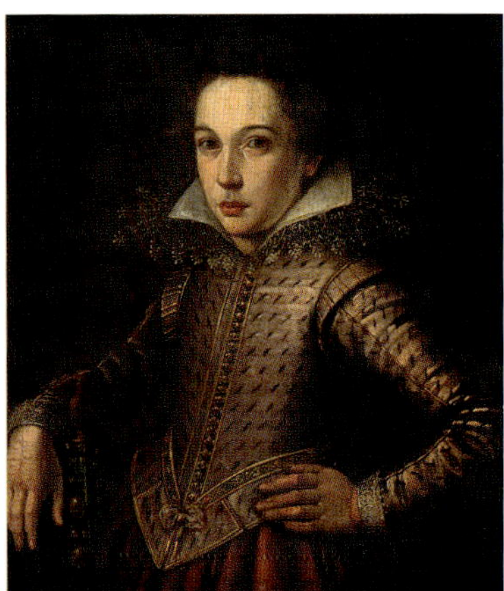

British School
Portrait of a Man (said to be Henry Frederick
Stuart, 1594–1612, Prince of Wales)
c.1608–1612
oil on canvas 64.5 x 52.5
PC.52

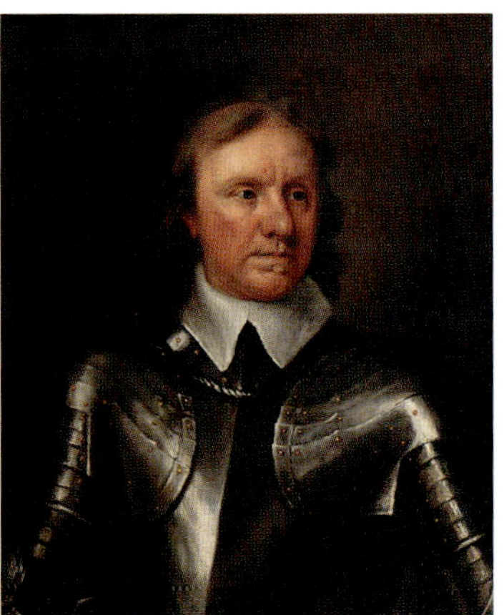

British School 17th C
Oliver Cromwell (1599–1658) (after Peter
Lely)
oil on canvas 74.3 x 61
PC.60

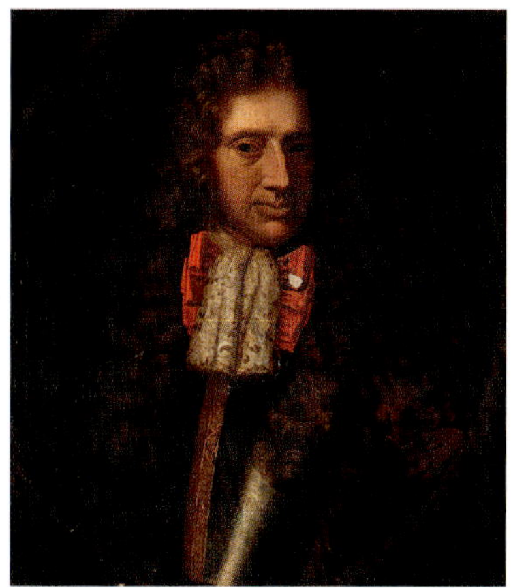

British School 17th C
Portrait of a Man
oil on canvas 71.1 x 63.5
L.4.1944.2 (P)

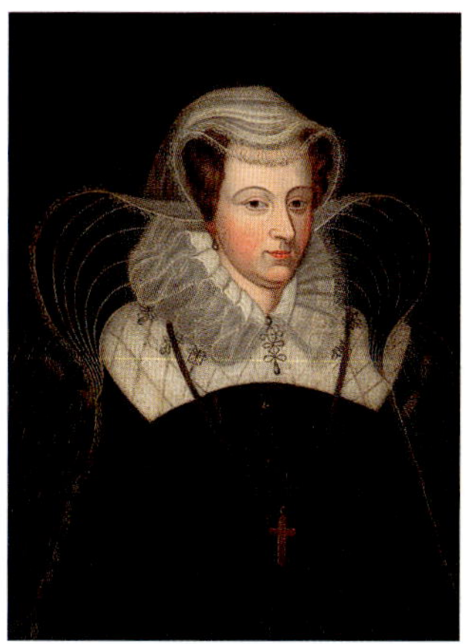

British School 17th C
Mary Queen of Scots (1542–1587)
oil on canvas 75.9 x 55.2
1086

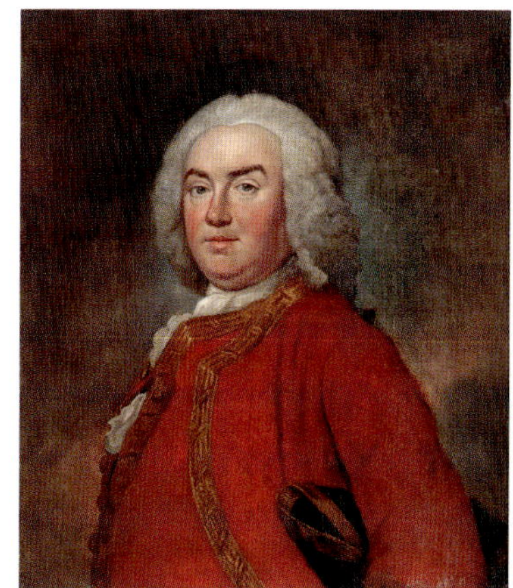

British School
Colonel Archer c.1755–1780
oil on canvas 76.2 x 62.9
NR.108

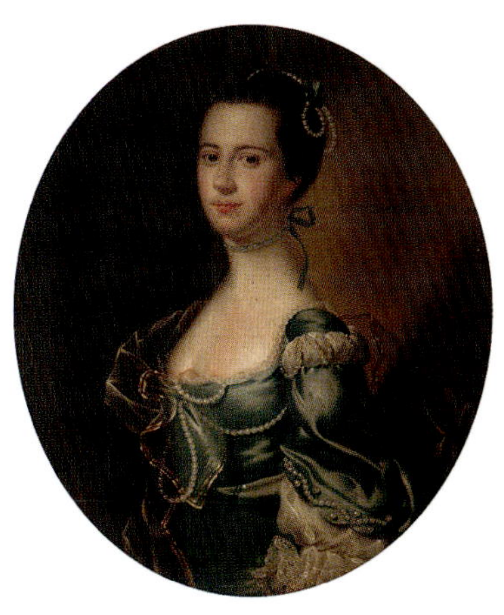

British School
Portrait of a Lady c.1760
oil on canvas 71.7 x 61.6
PL.167 (P)

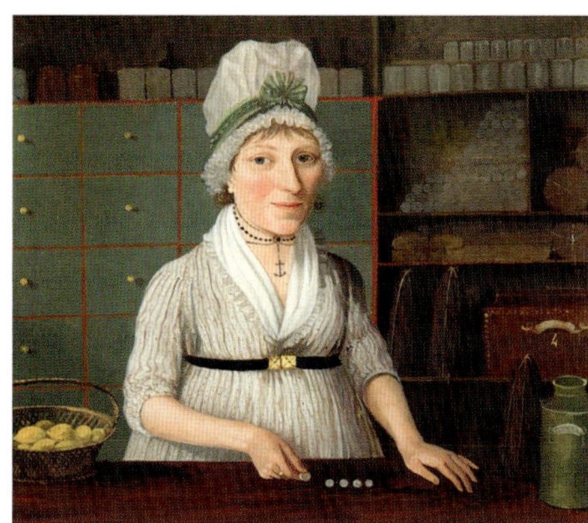

British School
The Woman Shopkeeper c.1790–1800
oil on board 26.5 x 32.7
TEMP.7685

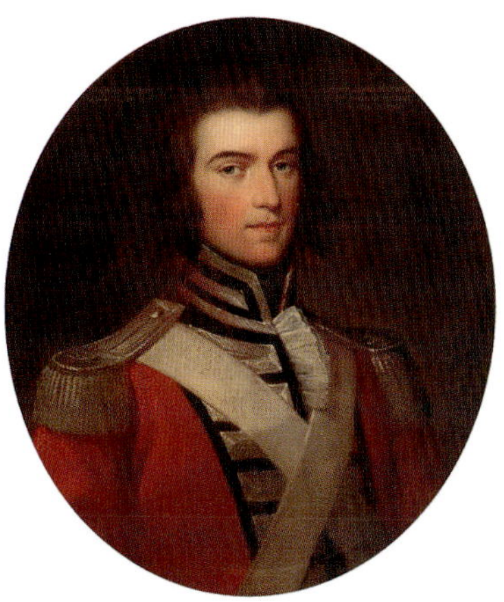

British School 18th C
Captain Robert Maxwell (1770–1796)
oil on canvas 75.8 x 63.3
PL.175 (P)

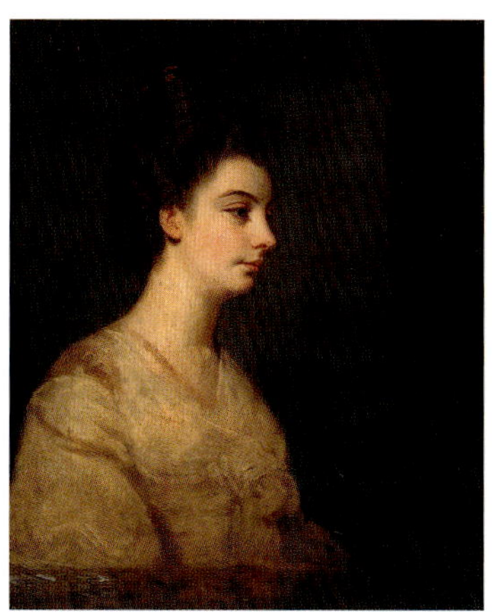

British School 18th C
Elizabeth A. Linley
oil on panel 74.9 x 62.2
253

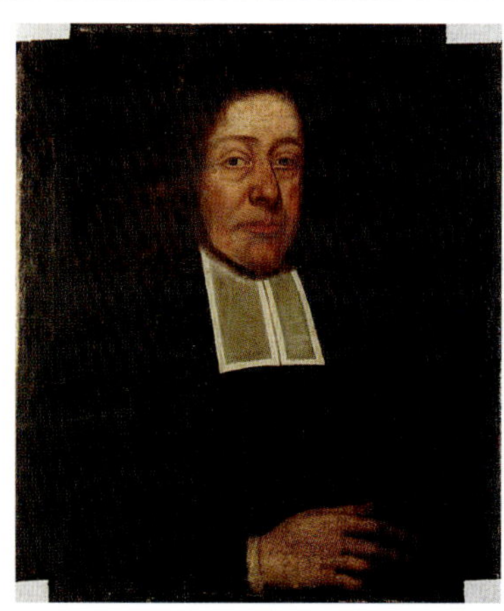

British School 18th C
Portrait of a Clergyman, Half-Length
oil on canvas 73.7 x 61
NR.60

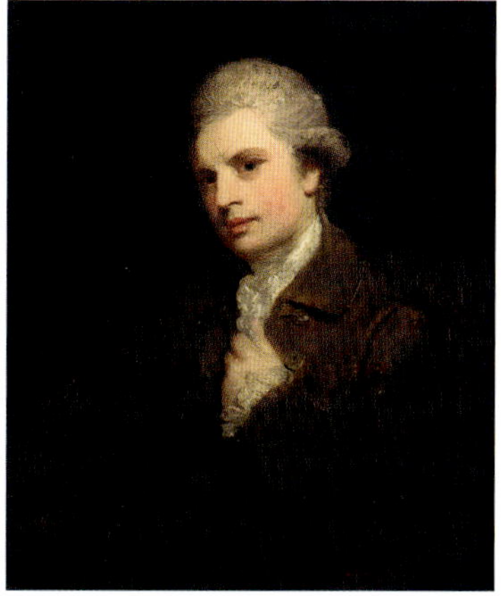

British School 18th C
Portrait of a Gentleman
oil on canvas 73.7 x 61
604

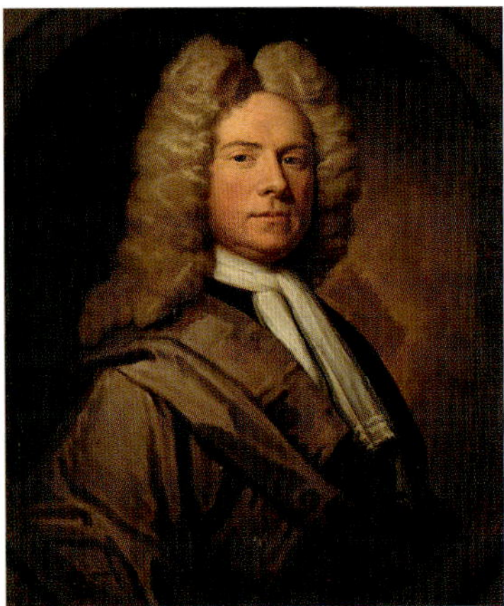

British School 18th C
Portrait of a Man
oil on canvas 76.2 x 63.5
L.4.1944.1 (P)

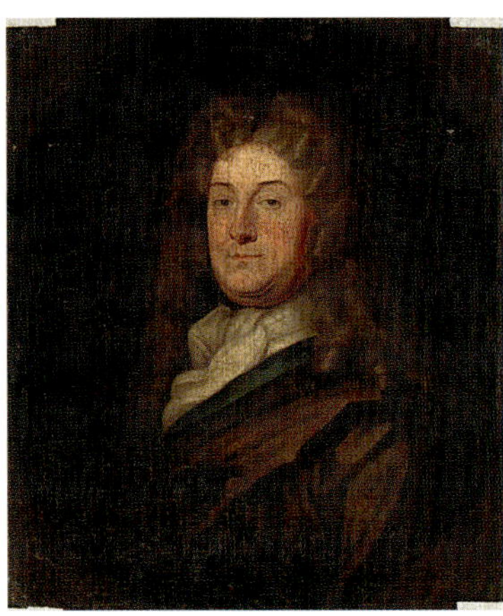

British School 18th C
Portrait of a Man
oil on canvas 73.7 x 61
NR.59

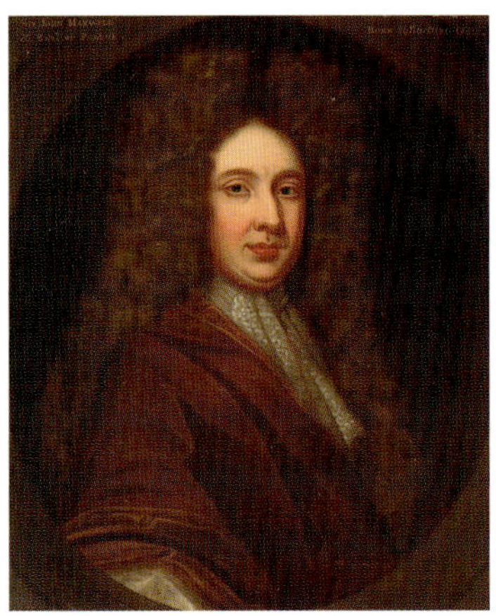

British School 18th C
Sir John Maxwell (1686–1752), 2nd Bt
oil on canvas 76.5 x 61.8
PL.180 (P)

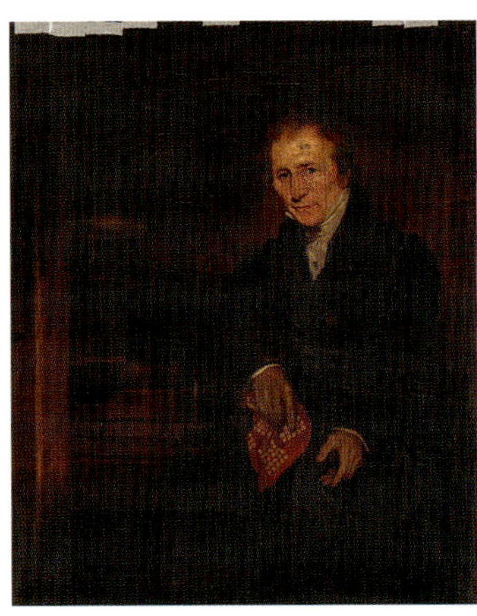

British School
Portrait of a Man c.1810–1830
oil on canvas 124.5 x 99.1
NR.70

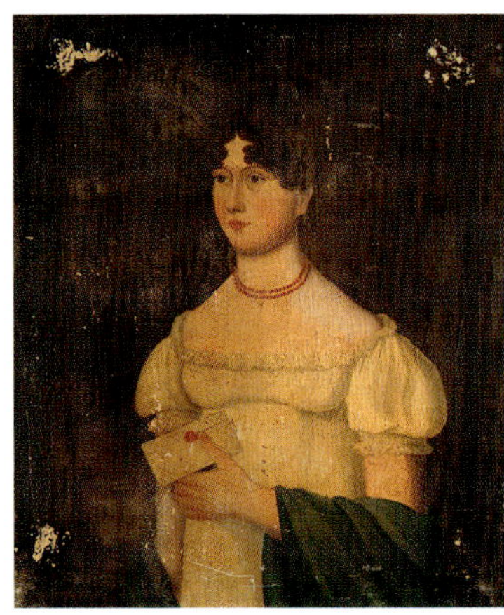

British School
Portrait of a Woman in a White Dress
c.1815–1820
oil on canvas 64.6 x 53.2
TEMP.19216

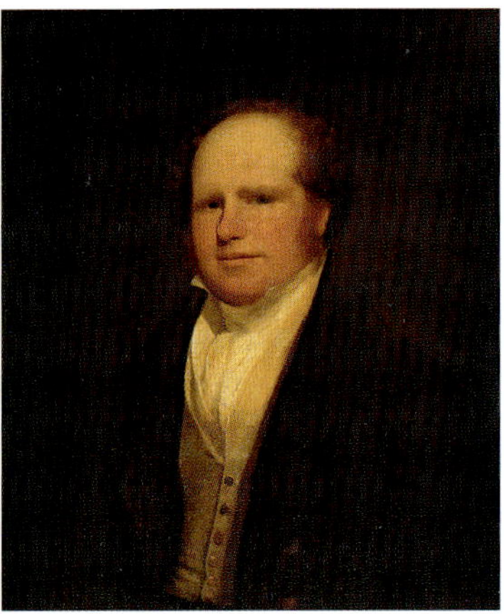

British School
Mr W. S. Dixon c.1820–1840
oil on canvas 75 x 61.5
NR.2

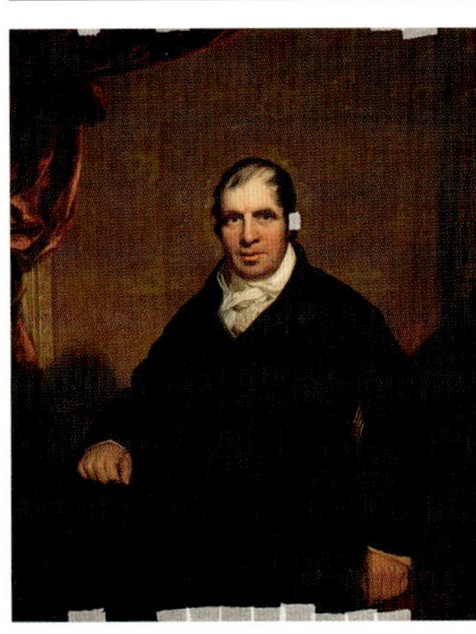

British School
Portrait of a Man c.1820–1840
oil on canvas 127 x 101.6
NR.80

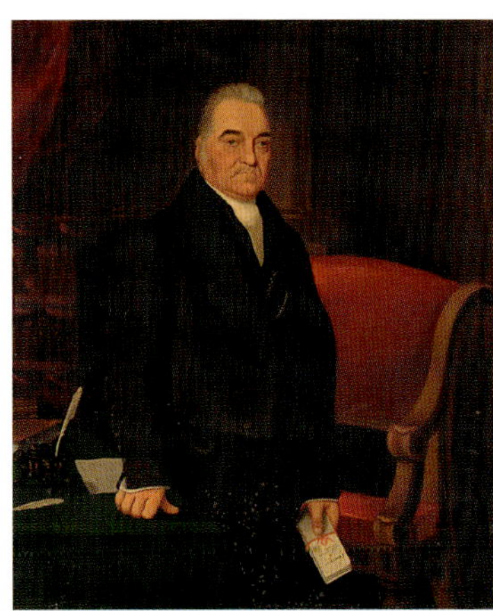

British School
Portrait of a Man 1825
oil on canvas 127 x 104.1
NR.125

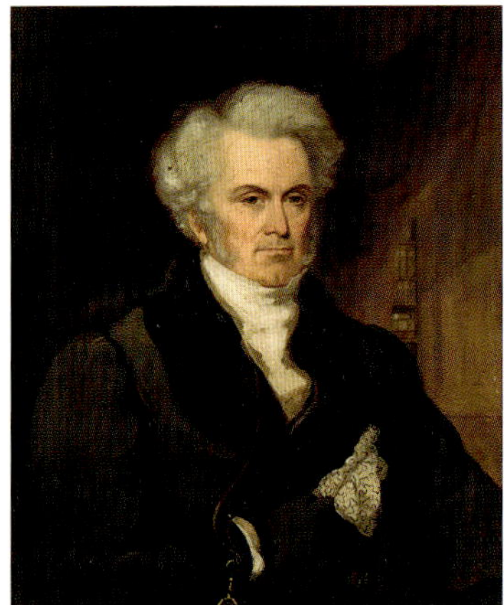

British School
Portrait of a Man c.1830–1850
oil on canvas 42 x 35
NR.16

Facing page: Reesbroeck, Jacob van, 1620–1704, *Portrait of a Man with a Lute*, c.1655–1660, (p. 260)

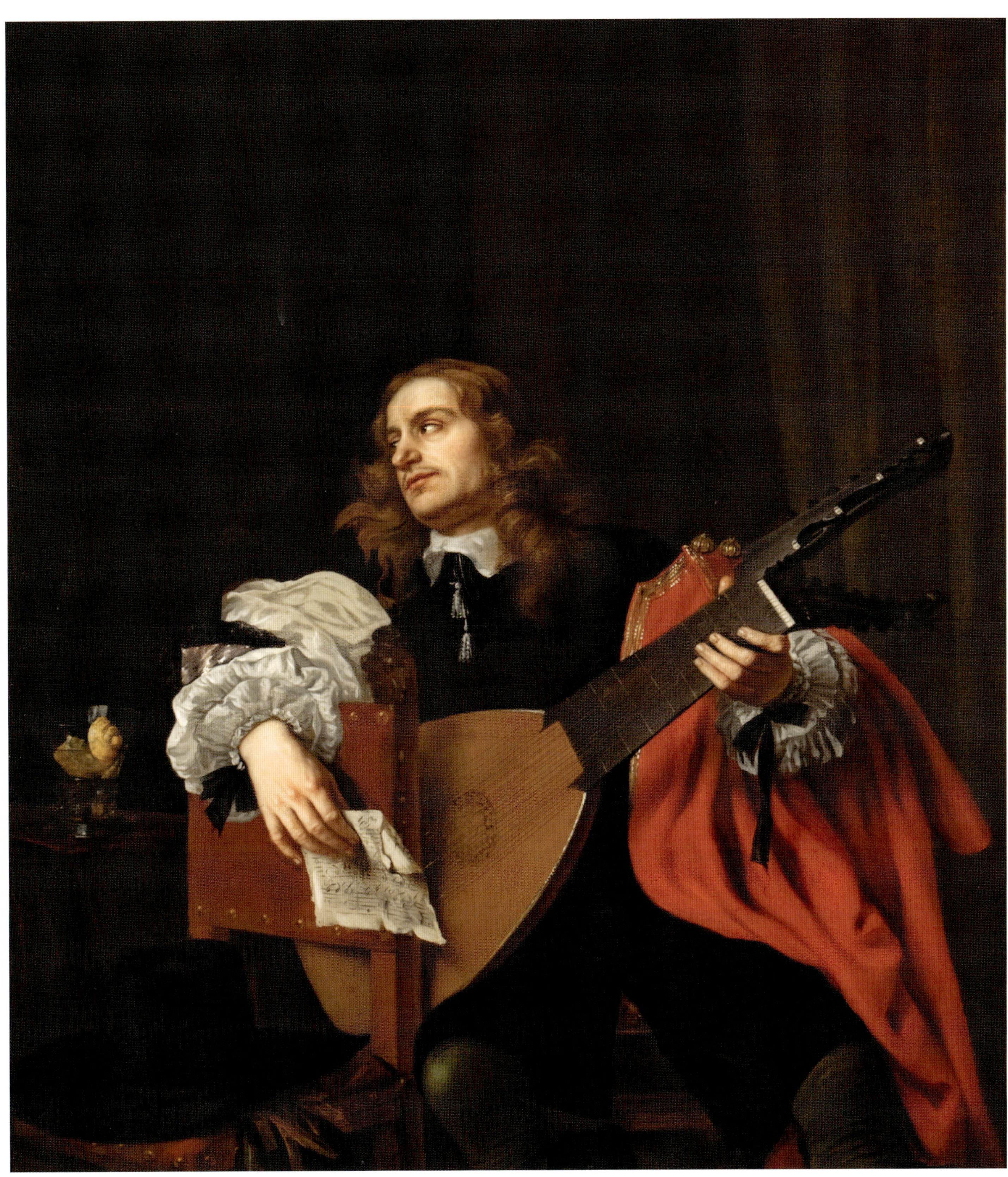

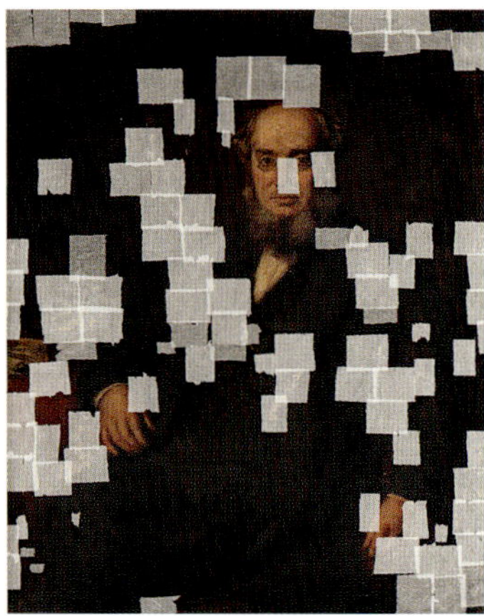

British School
Portrait of a Gentleman c.1860–1880
oil on canvas 127 x 101.6
NR.157

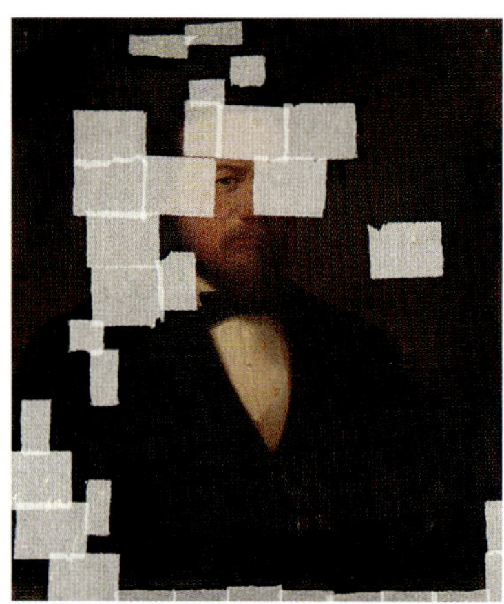

British School
Portrait of a Man c.1870–1890
oil on canvas 76.2 x 63.5
NR.66

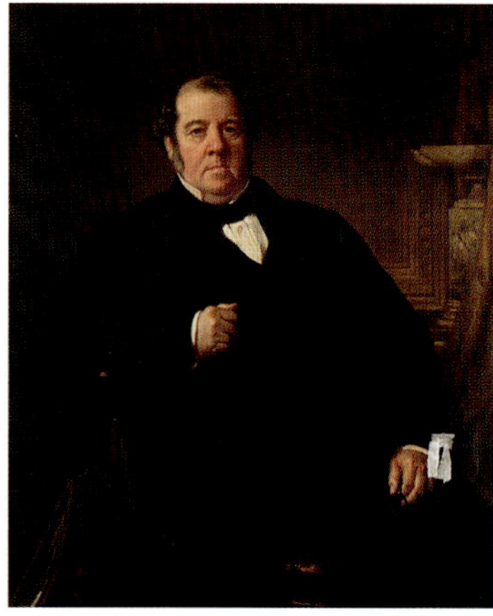

British School
Portrait of a Man c.1870–1890
oil on canvas 127 x 101.6
NR.83

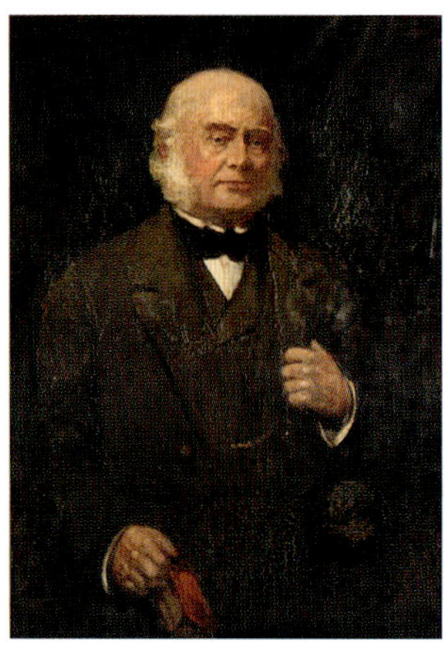

British School
Portrait of a Man c.1880–1900
oil on canvas 106.7 x 86.4
NR.72

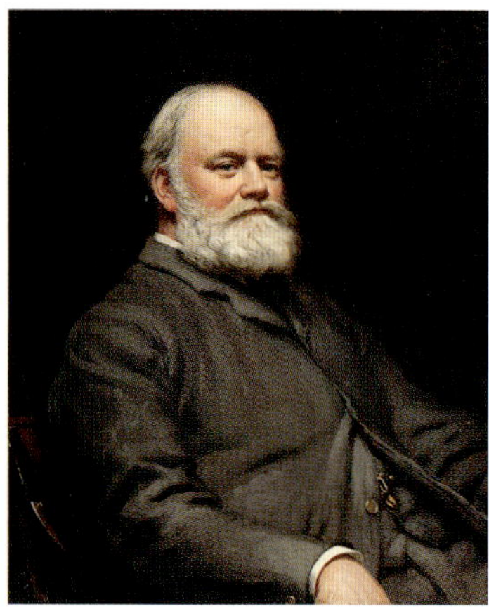

British School
Portrait of a Man c.1890–1910
oil on canvas 74 x 59
NR.1

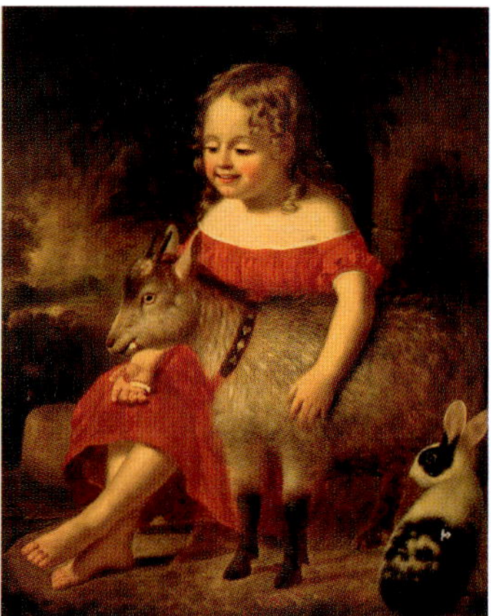

British School 19th C
Child with Animals
oil on canvas 91.4 x 71.1
NR.51

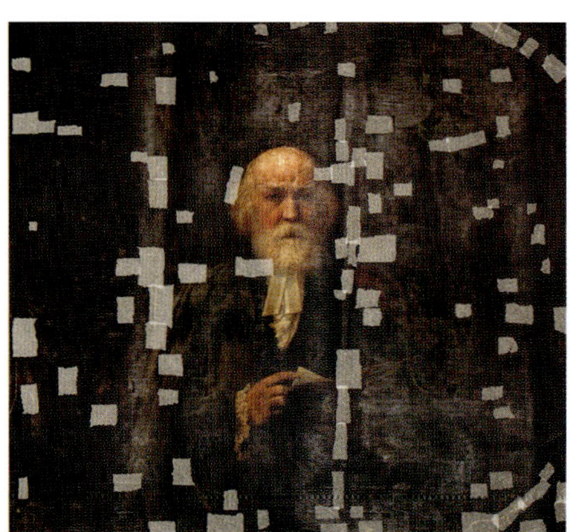

British School 19th C
Doctor of Divinity
oil on canvas 128.3 x 145
PP.1978.121.7

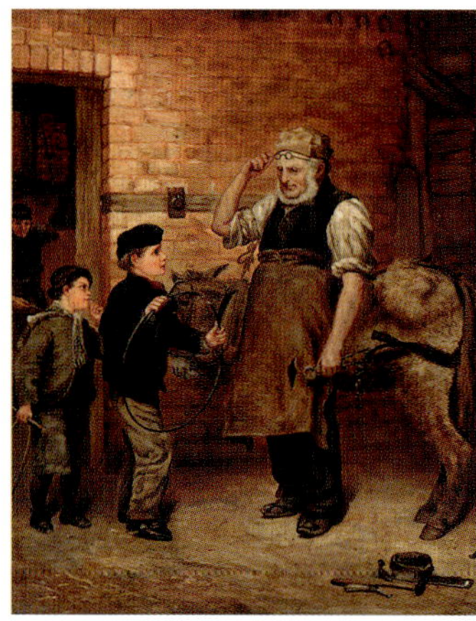

British School 19th C
Genre Scene with a Blacksmith
oil on plywood 61 x 48
NR.28

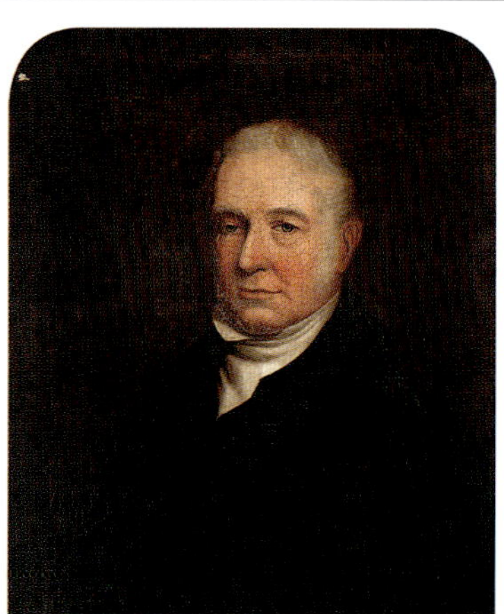

British School 19th C
George Stephenson (1781–1848)
oil on canvas 76.2 x 63.5
NR.119

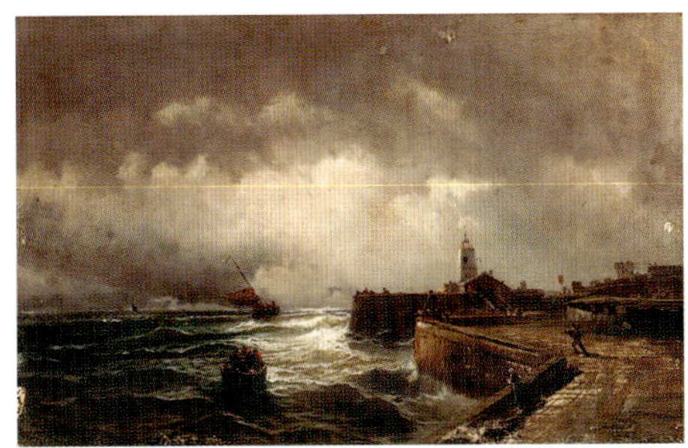

British School 19th C
Harbour Scene
oil on canvas 61 x 91
NR.136

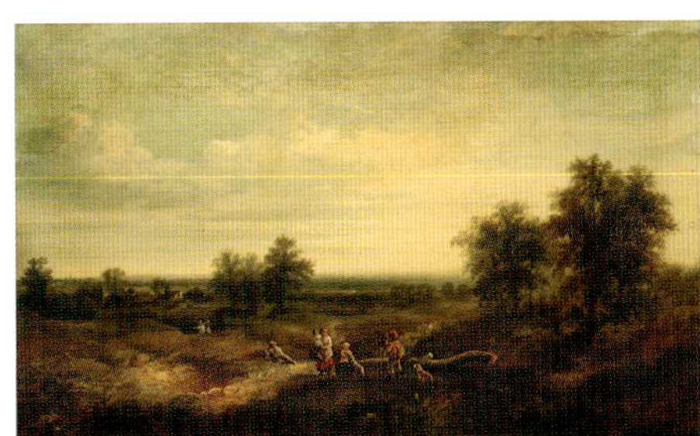

British School 19th C
Landscape
oil on canvas 64.7 x 104.9
TEMP.2973

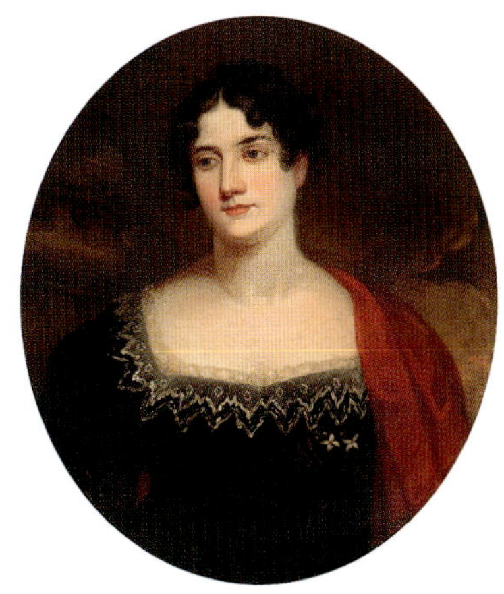

British School 19th C
Mrs Stirling of Keir (1793–1822)
oil on canvas 75 x 63
PL.178 (P)

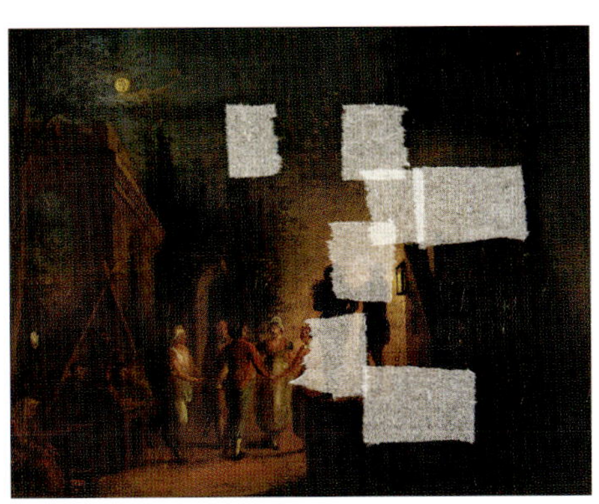

British School 19th C
Night Scene: Dancing near Classical Ruins
oil on canvas 32.5 x 41
NR.4

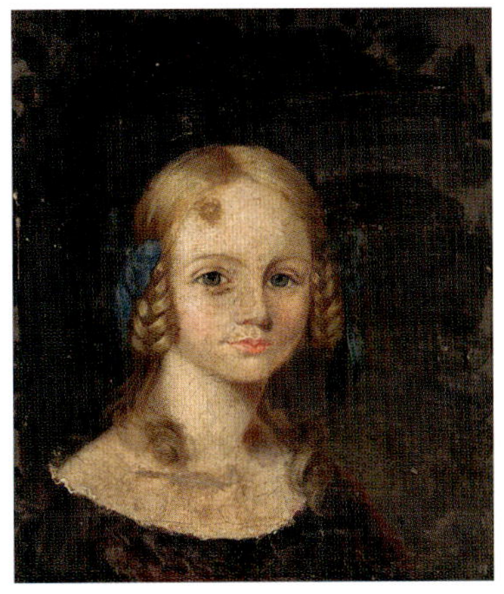

British School 19th C
Portrait of a Blonde Girl
oil on canvas 35.7 x 31
TEMP.2483

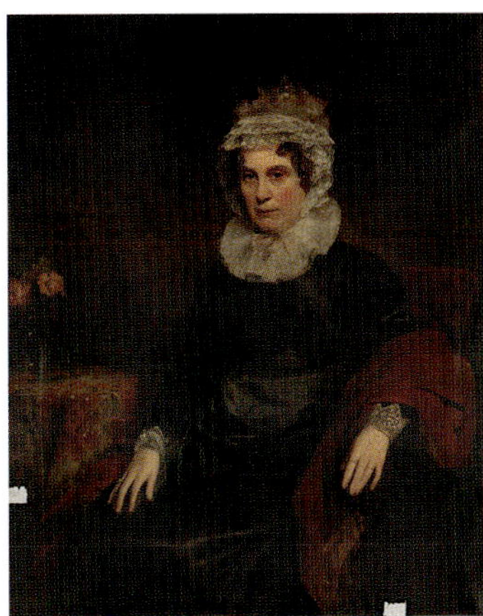

British School 19th C
Portrait of a Lady
oil on canvas 127 x 101.6
NR.69

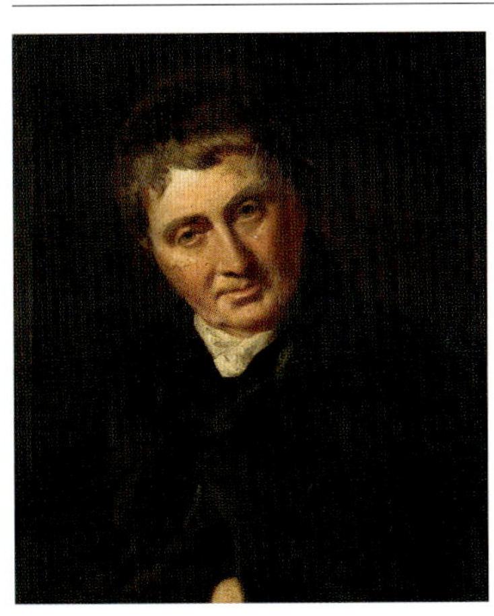

British School 19th C
Portrait of a Man
oil on canvas 57 x 48
NR.27

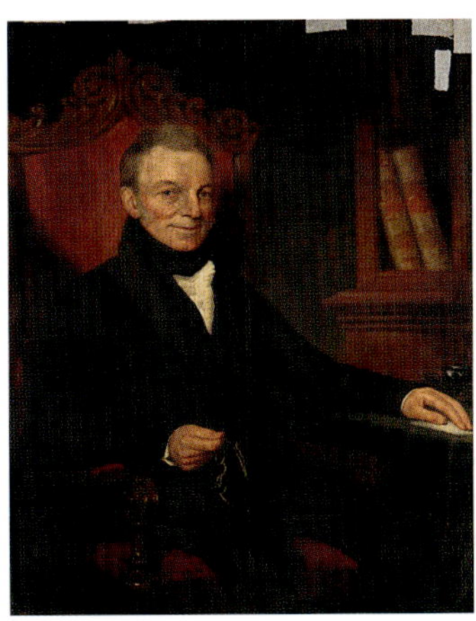

British School 19th C
Portrait of a Man
oil on canvas 111.8 x 87.6
NR.44

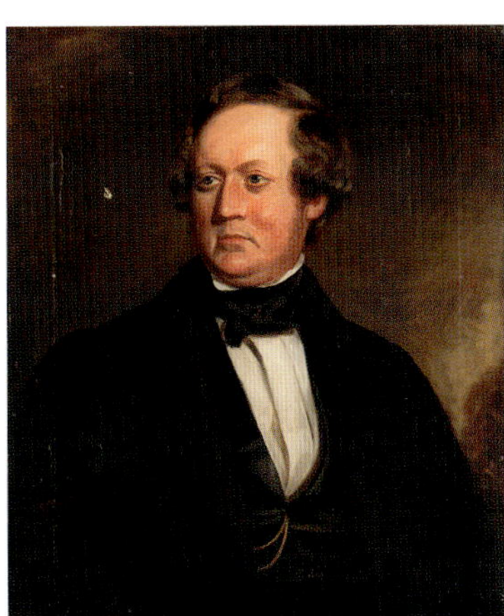

British School 19th C
Portrait of a Man
oil on canvas 75.6 x 64.7
NR.75

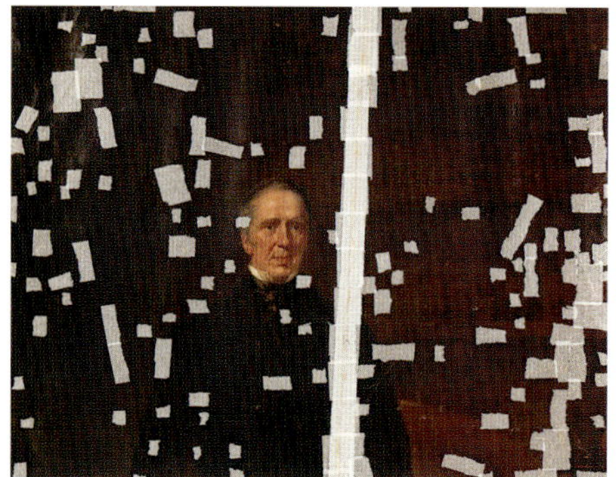

British School 19th C
Portrait of a Man
oil on canvas 116 x 147.8
PP.1978.121.6

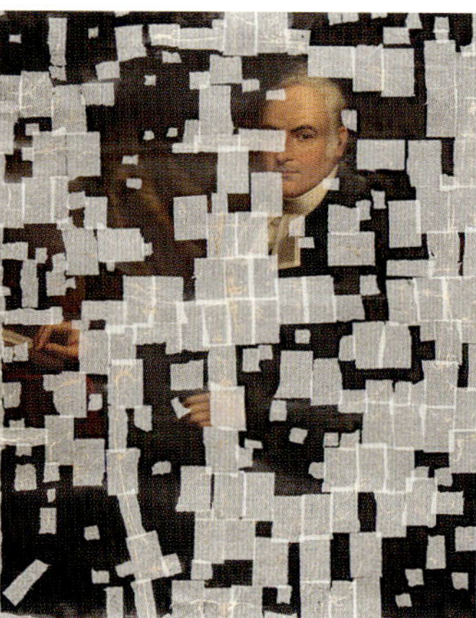

British School 19th C
Portrait of a Man
oil on canvas 128 x 102
TEMP.1386

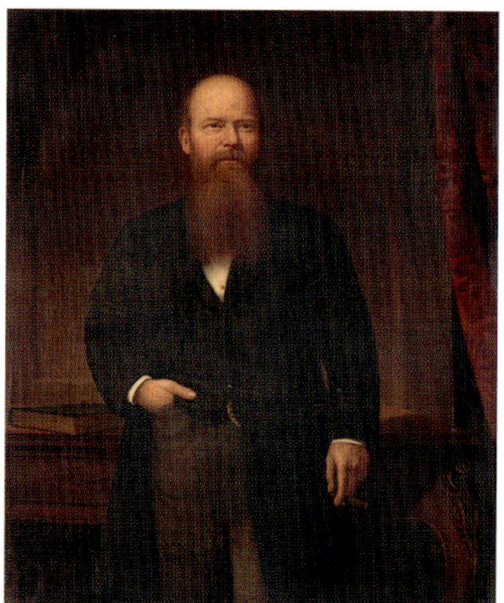

British School 19th C
Portrait of a Man
oil on canvas 127 x 101.6
TEMP.14953

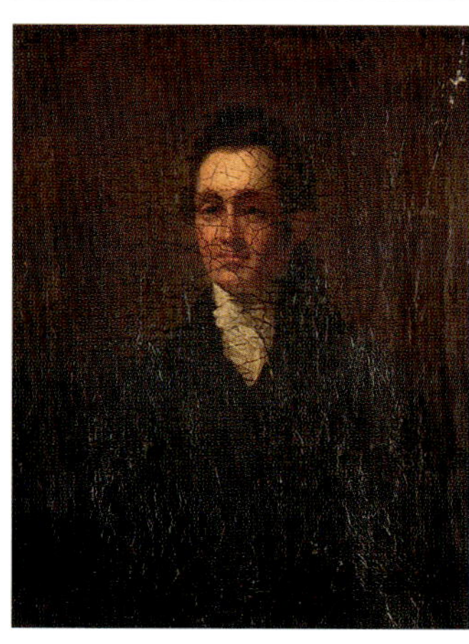

British School 19th C
Portrait of a Man with a White Stock
oil on canvas 25 x 19
NR.10

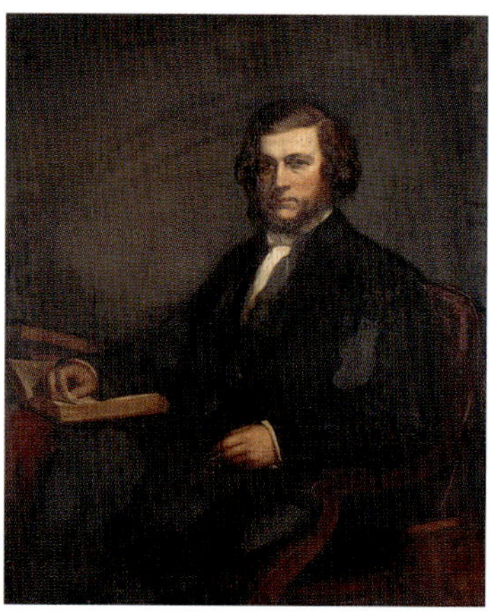

British School 19th C
Portrait of a Young Minister
oil on canvas 127 x 101
TEMP.7432

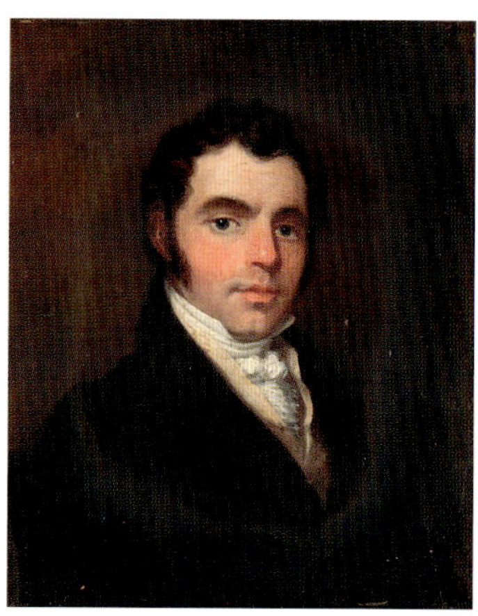

British School 19th C
Portrait of an Unknown Man
oil on canvas 31 x 23.5
TEMP.1474

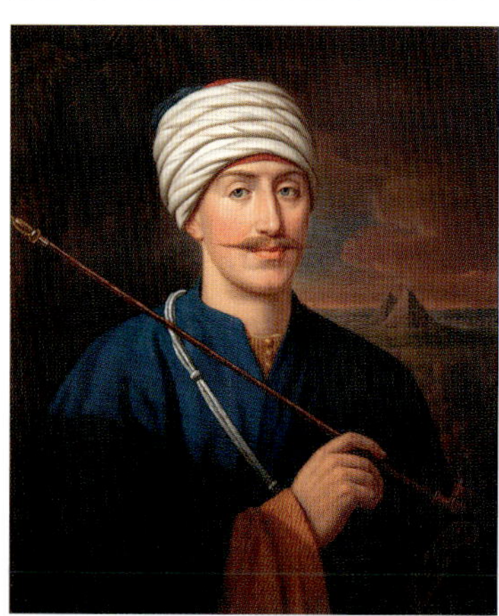

British School 19th C
Sir John Maxwell (1791–1865), 8th Bt
oil on canvas 74.3 x 62.2
PL.160 (P)

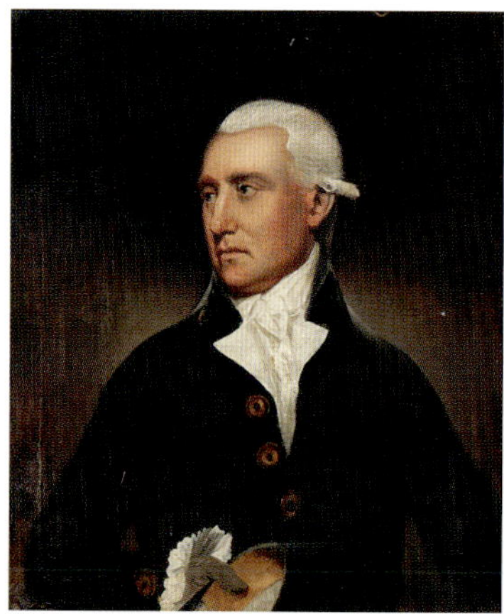

British School 19th C
Thomas Campbell
oil on canvas 76.2 x 63.5
1420

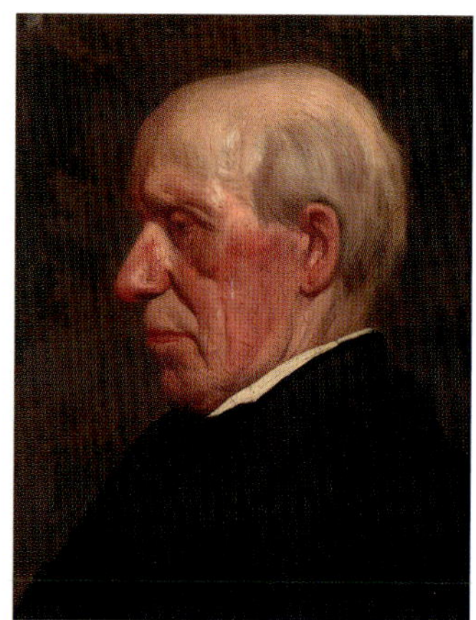

British School 19th C–20th C
J. M. Gass
oil on canvas 46 x 35.8
TEMP.8361

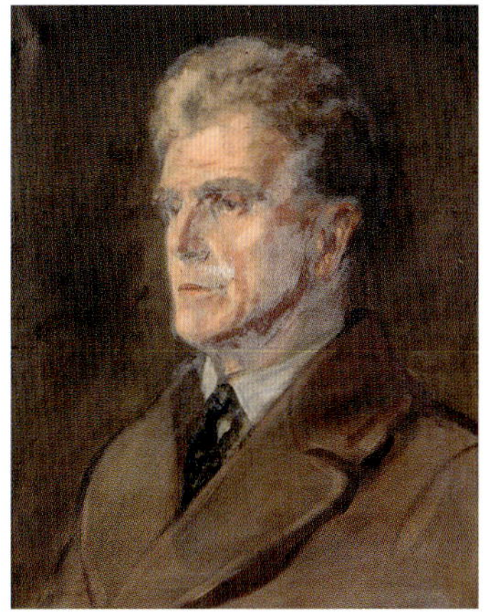

British School 20th C
Portrait of a Man
oil on canvas 52 x 40
NR.18

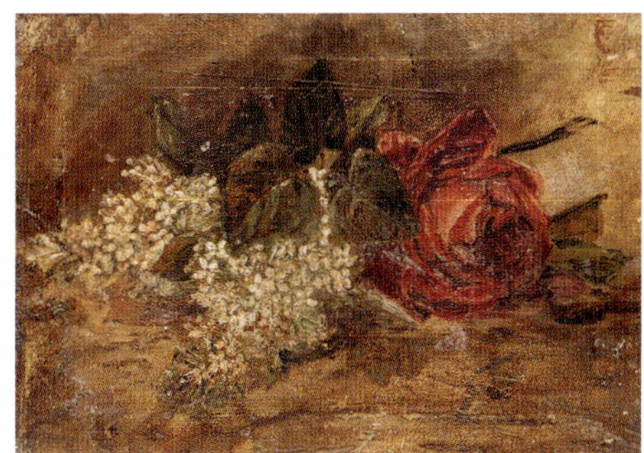

British School 20th C
Still Life with a Rose and Lilacs
oil on canvas 25.4 x 36.2
NR.160

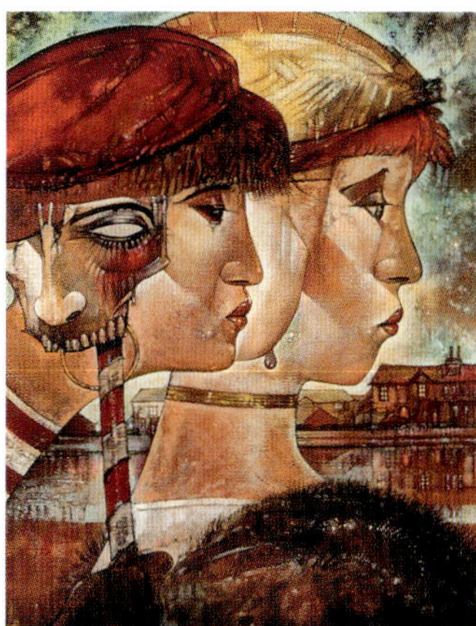

British School 20th C
Two Profiles of Girls and a Mask
oil on board 67 x 55
3694

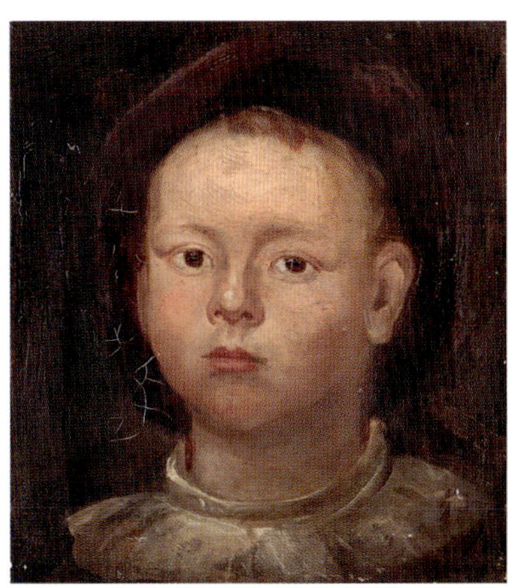

British School 20th C (?)
Portrait of a Child
oil on canvas 35.7 x 30.5
TEMP.1775

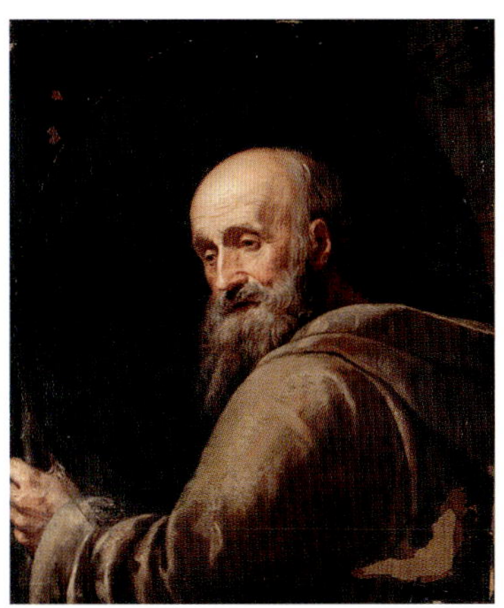

British School
An Old Pilgrim
oil on canvas 72.4 x 59.7
439

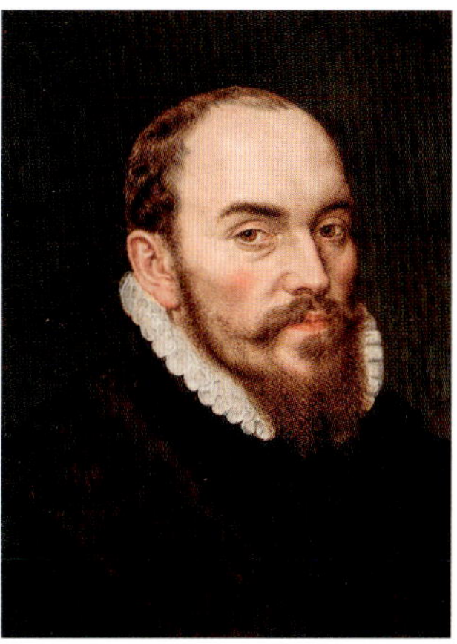

British School
Henry Rich (1590–1649), 1st Earl of Holland
oil on panel 44.4 x 33
PC.53

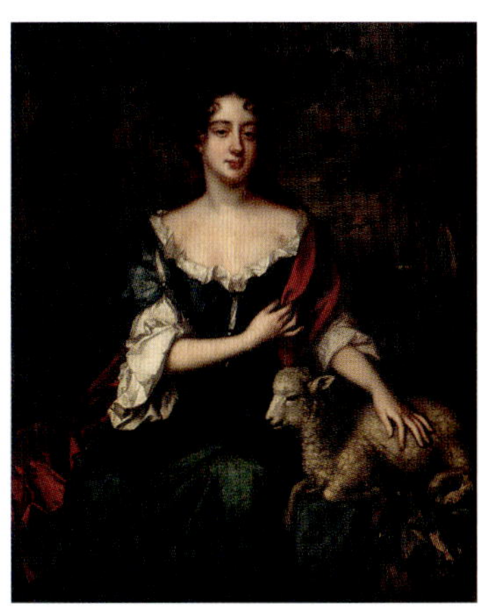

British School
Nell Gwynn (1650–1687) (?)
oil on canvas 127.6 x 101.6
1158

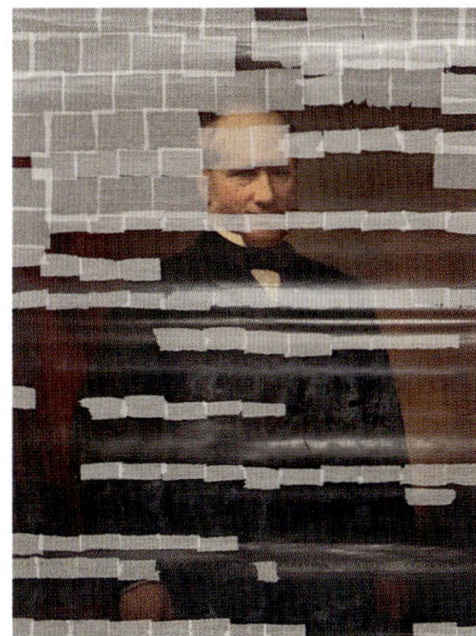

British School
Portrait of a Man
oil on canvas 109.2 x 80.6
NR.117

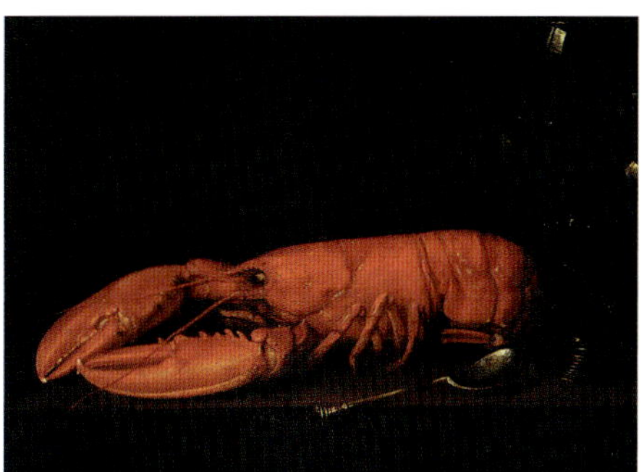

British School (attributed to) 18th C (?)
Lobster, Wine Glass and Spoon
oil on canvas 42.5 x 55.9
35.5

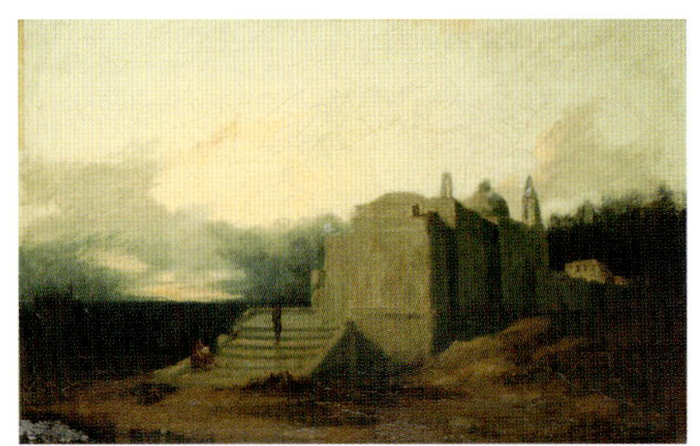

British School (attributed to) 19th C
The Convent (Church of San Vitale, Posillipo, near Naples)
oil on canvas 61 x 94
252

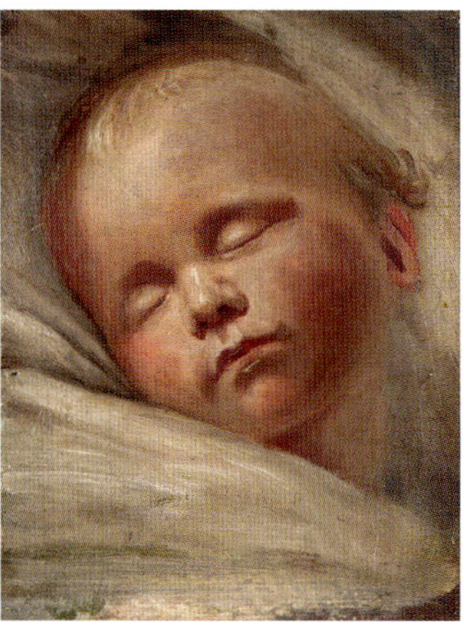

British School (attributed to) 19th C (?)
Portrait of a Sleeping Baby
oil on canvas 33.5 x 24.4
TEMP.1776

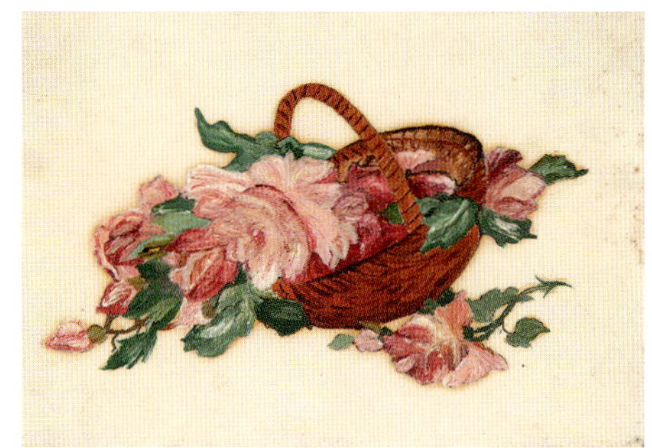

British School (attributed to) 20th C
Pink Flowers
oil on board 17.8 x 25.5
TEMP.19198

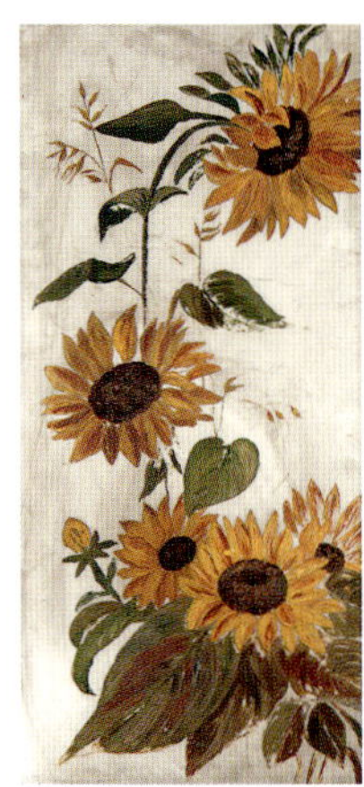

British School (attributed to) 20th C
Sunflowers and Foliage
oil on bakelite 57.3 x 27.1
TEMP.19219

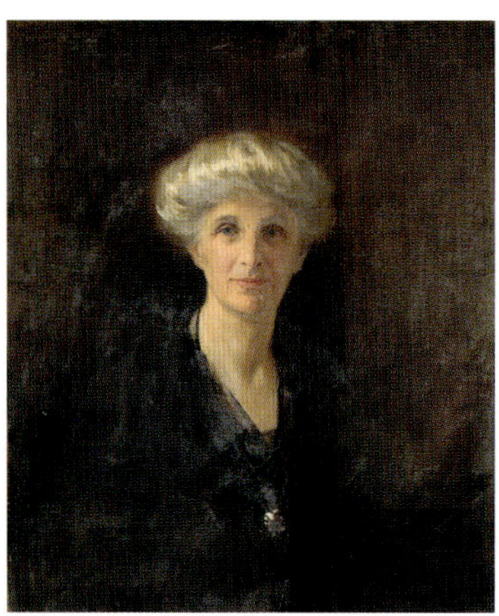

Brock, Edmond b.1882
Marion L. Chrystal (b.1855)
oil on canvas 76.2 x 63.5
2224

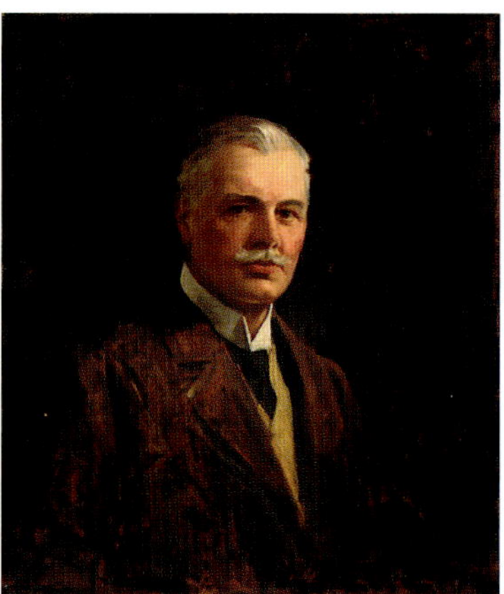

Brock, Edmond b.1882
William J. Chrystal (1854–1921)
oil on canvas 76.2 x 63.5
2223

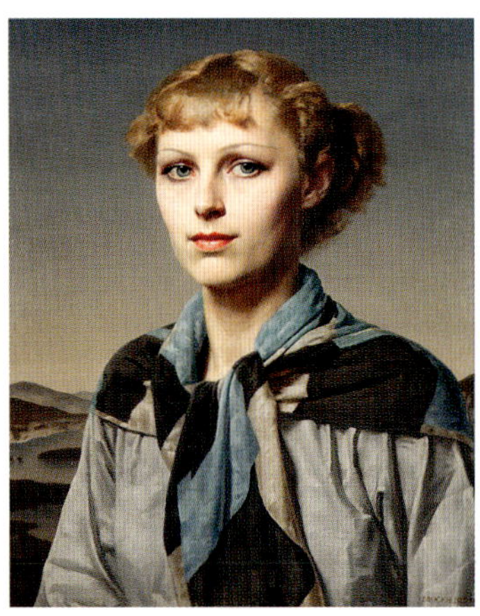

Brockhurst, Gerald Leslie 1890–1978
Gillian 1934
oil on canvas 60.9 x 55.9
1923

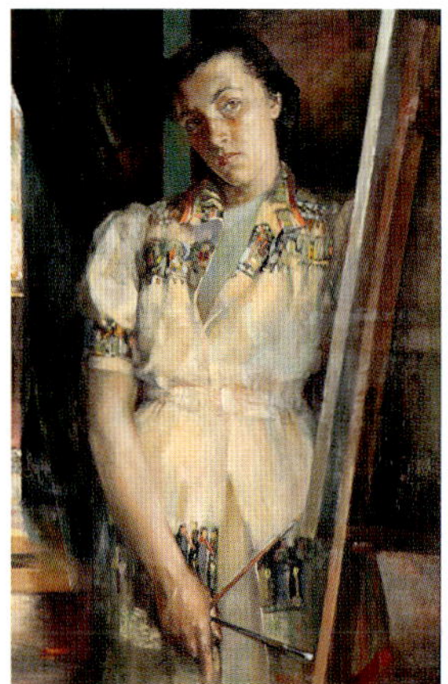

Brodie, Isabel Babianska 1920–2006
Reflection (Self Portrait) 1939
oil on canvas 91.4 x 60.9
2156

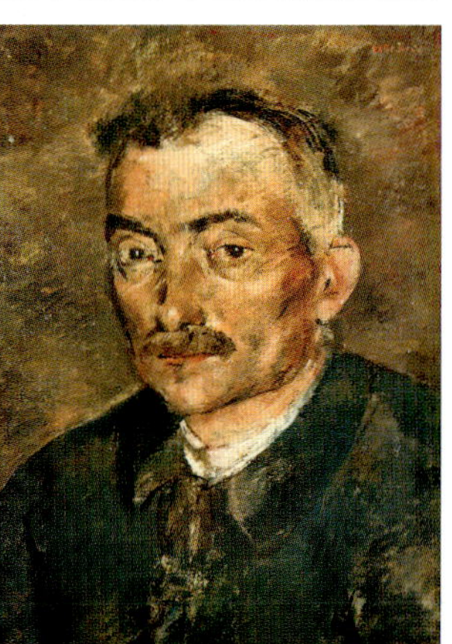

Brooker, Peter Alfred 1900–1965
Emile Plantin
oil on canvas 40.6 x 30.5
2100

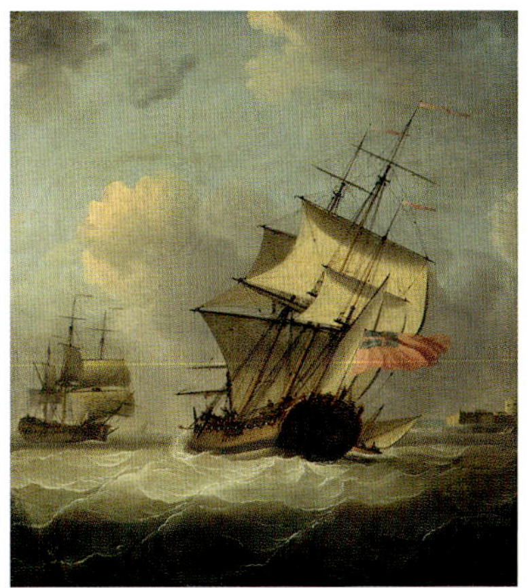

Brooking, Charles 1723–1759
Sea Piece
oil on canvas 50.8 x 45.7
461

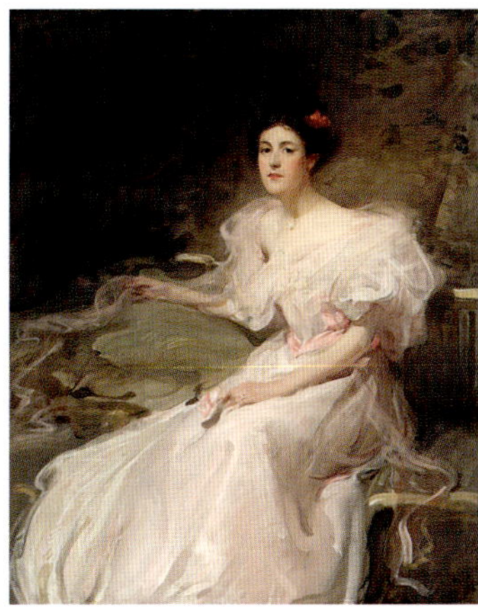

Brough, Robert 1872–1905
Miss Maud Lawrence 1898
oil on canvas 142.2 x 111.8
3444

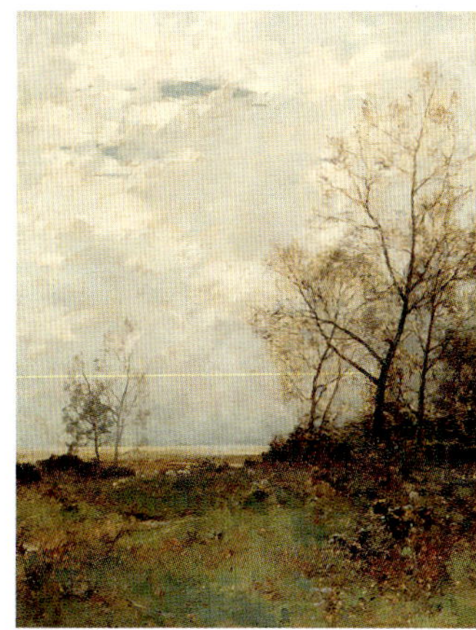

Brown, Alexander Kellock 1849–1922
Springtime c.1898
oil on canvas 110.4 x 85.1
762

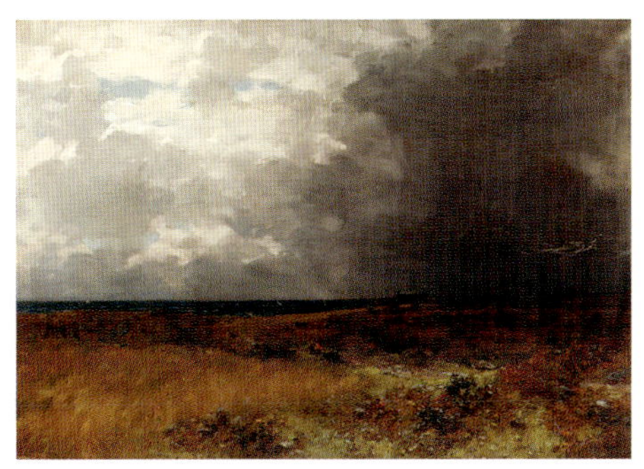

Brown, Alexander Kellock 1849–1922
A Dagger Day c.1907
oil on canvas 73.7 x 99.1
1530

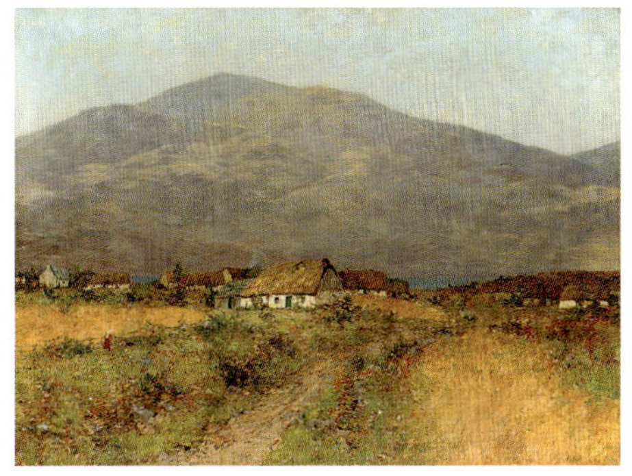

Brown, Alexander Kellock 1849–1922
Ben Lawers
oil on canvas 86.4 x 111.8
1667

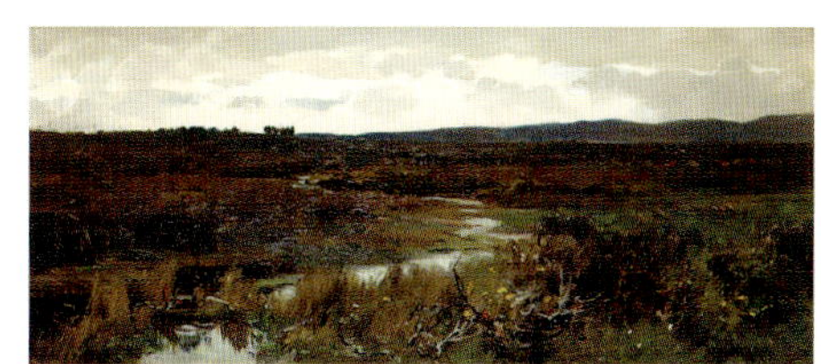

Brown, Alexander Kellock 1849–1922
Landscape
oil on canvas 29.7 x 68.6
860

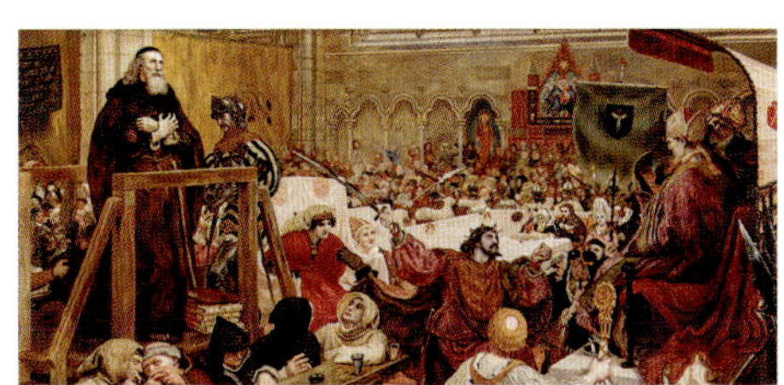

Brown, Ford Madox 1821–1893
Wycliffe on Trial 1885
oil on canvas 55.9 x 114.3
1776

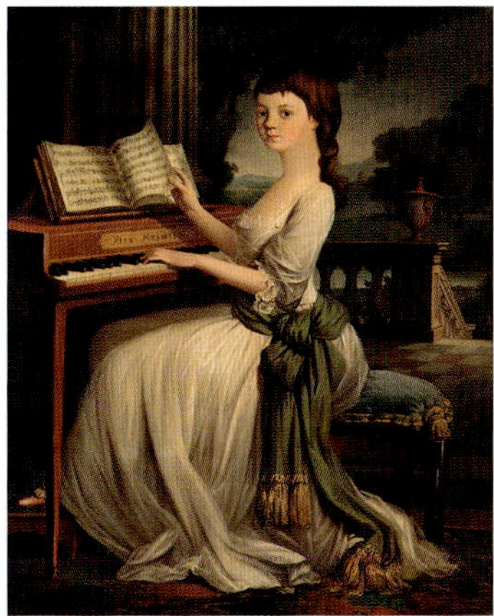

Brown, Mather (attributed to) 1761–1831
A Girl at a Harpsichord c.1782
oil on canvas 127 x 101.6
2970

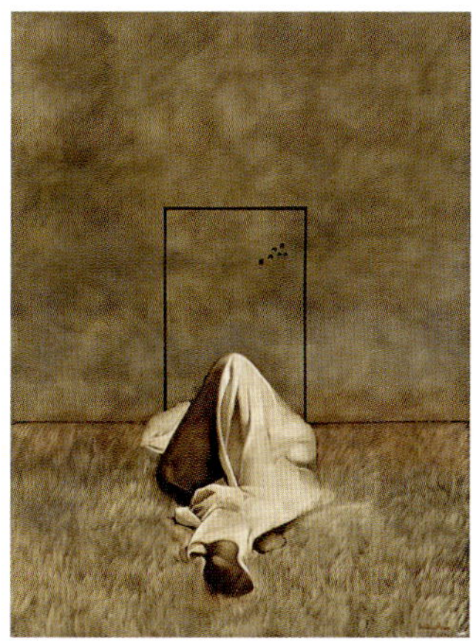

Brown, Neil Dallas 1938–2003
Shroud 1975
oil on hardboard 213.6 x 160
3657

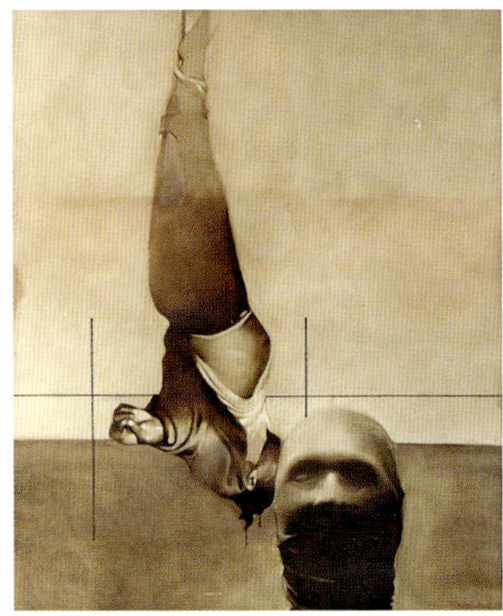

Brown, Neil Dallas 1938–2003
The Indictment 1976–1977
oil on hardboard 198 x 161.5
3654

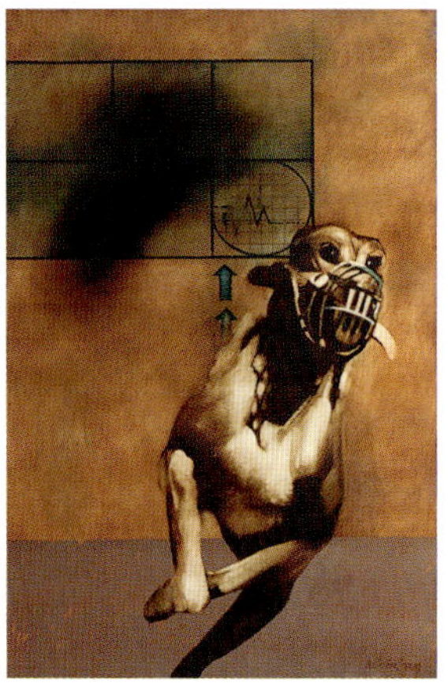

Brown, Neil Dallas 1938–2003
Alarm (Danger Zone) 1982
oil & pencil on panel 144.5 x 92.5
3655

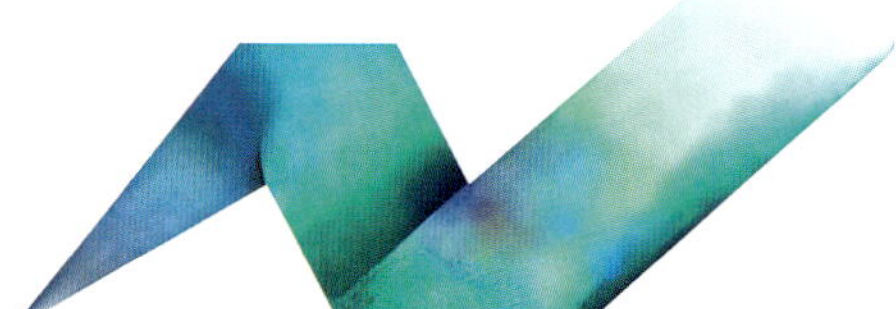

Brown, Neil Dallas 1938–2003
Fast Glide (Impact) 2002
oil, alkyd & sand on canvas 97 x 269.8
3656

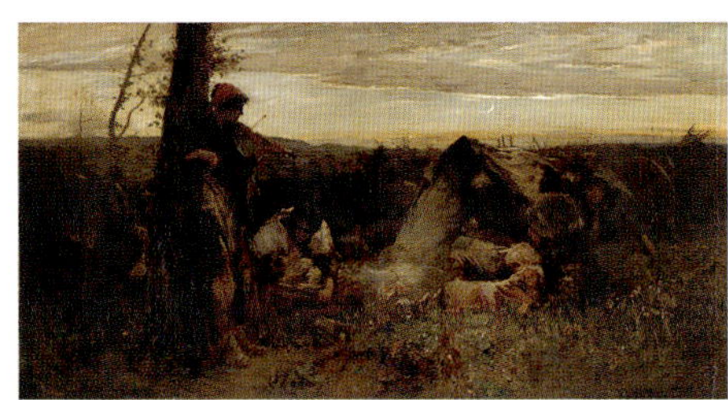

Brown, Thomas Austen 1859–1924
A Gypsy Encampment 1887
oil on canvas 118.1 x 224.8
1094

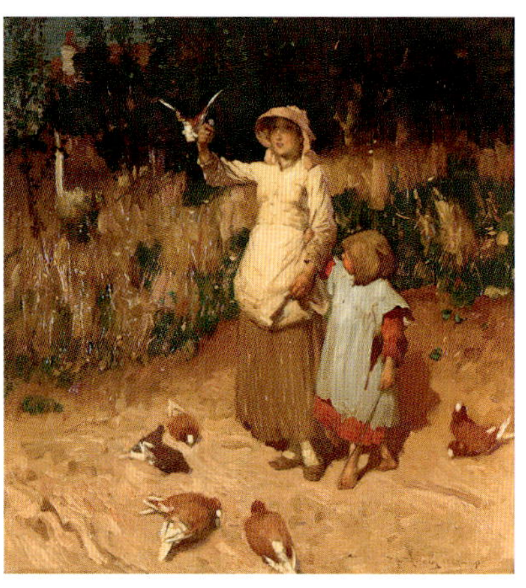

Brown, Thomas Austen 1859–1924
Feeding the Pigeons 1887
oil on canvas 71.1 x 64.8
1447

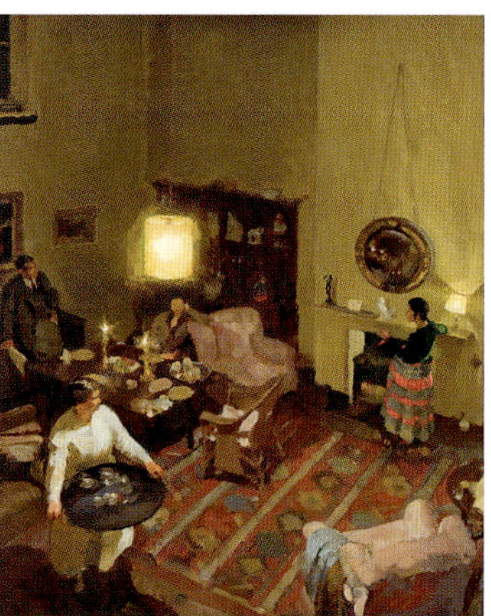

Browning, Amy Katherine 1881–1978
Interior: Studio Supper 1930
oil on canvas 76.2 x 63.5
2109

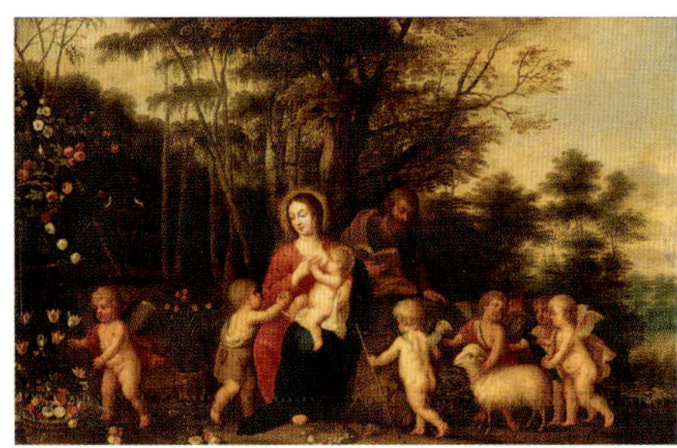

Brueghel, Jan the elder (attributed to)
1568–1625 & **Avont, Peeter van** 1600–1652
*The Holy Family in a Wooded
Landscape* c.1622–1632
oil on panel 68.6 x 99.7
35

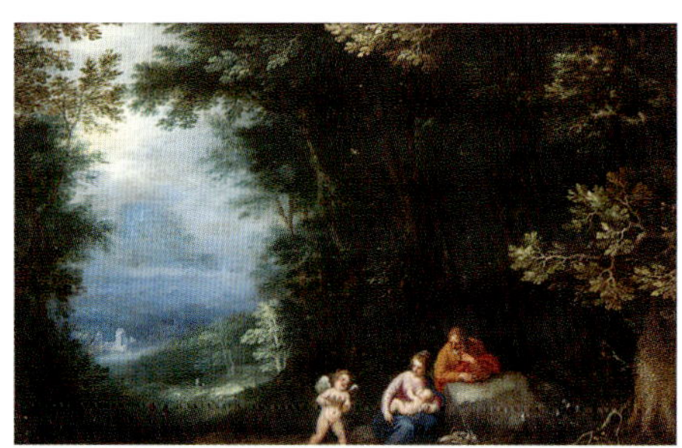

Brueghel, Jan the elder (attributed to)
1568–1625 & **Rottenhammer, Hans I
(attributed to)** 1564–1625
A Wooded Landscape with (...) c.1594–1625
oil on copper 20.3 x 31.7
25

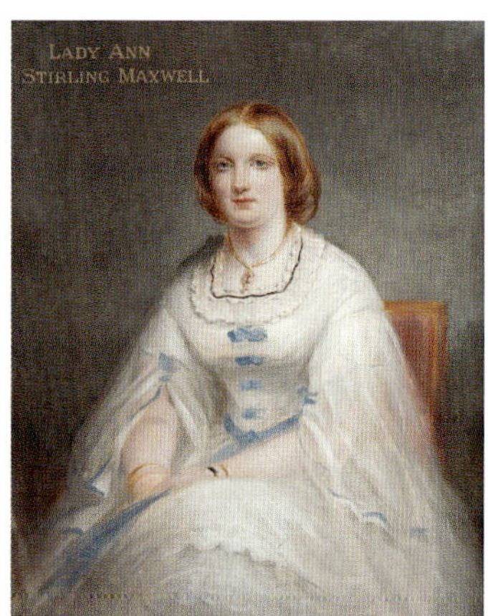

Brydall, Robert 1839–1907
Lady Anna Stirling Maxwell (d.1874)
oil on canvas 26 x 20
PL.123 (P)

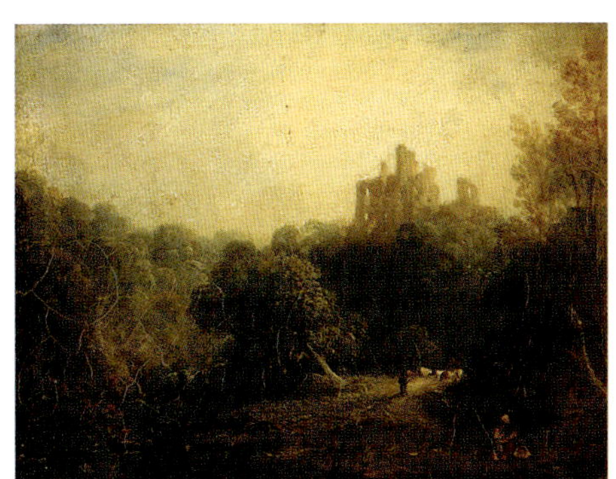

Buchanan, George F. 1800–1864
Greenan Castle
oil on panel 18.7 x 24.1
1089

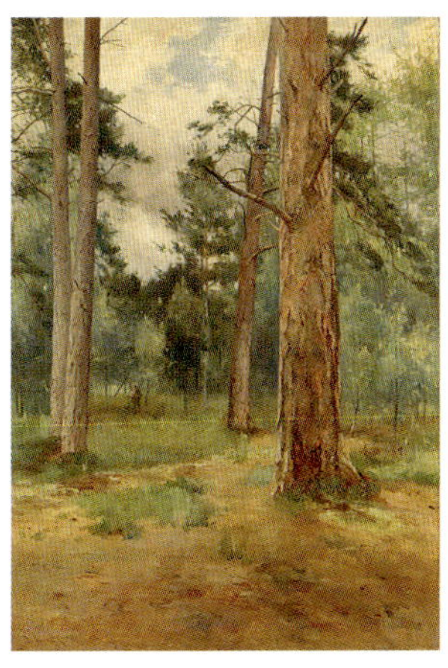

Bunting, Thomas 1851–1928
Landscape, Woodland Scene
oil on canvas 91.5 x 60.8
NR.33

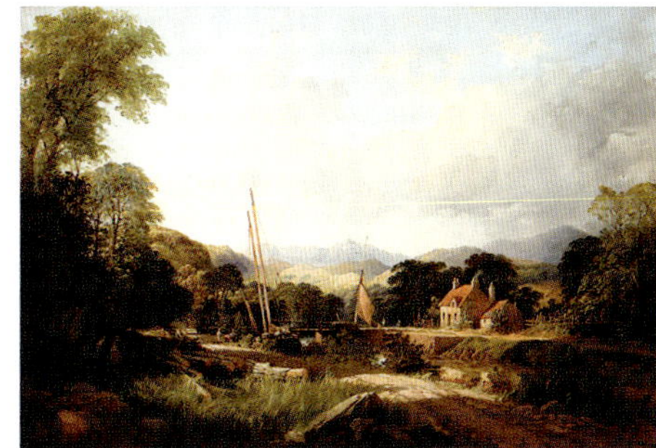

Burbidge, John active c.1855–1894
Crinan Canal
oil on canvas 57.2 x 82.6
405

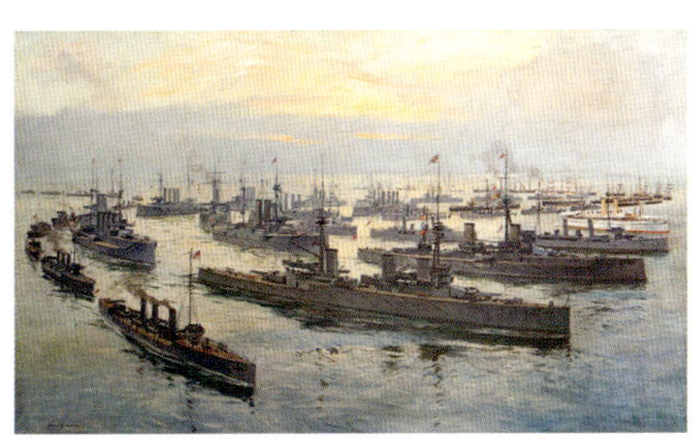

Burgess, Arthur James Wetherall
1879–1957
The Fairfield Fleet 1907
oil on canvas 102 x 162.5
T.1977.33

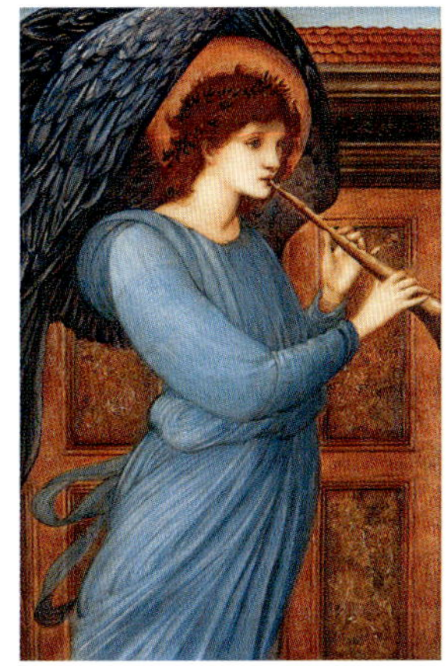

Burne-Jones, Edward 1833–1898
The Angel 1881
oil on panel 26.7 x 19.1
1742

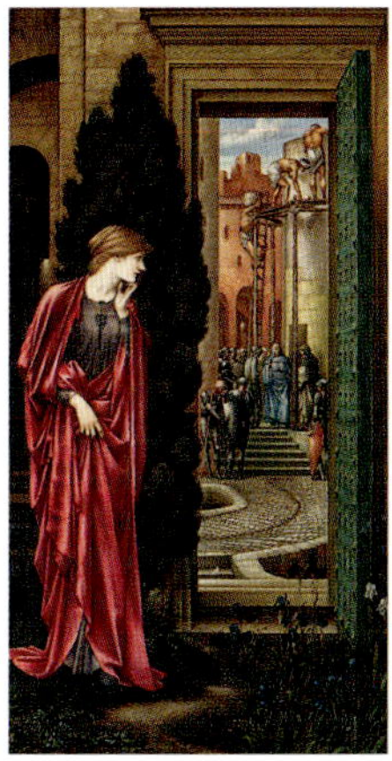

Burne-Jones, Edward 1833–1898
Danaë (The Tower of Brass) 1887–1888
oil on panel 231.1 x 113
936

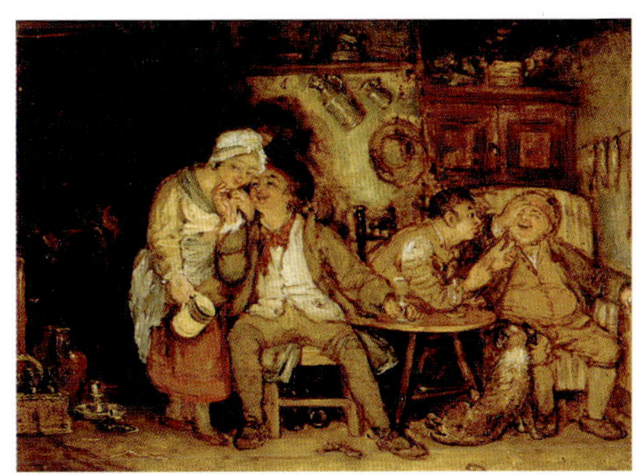

Burnet, John 1784–1868
Tam o' Shanter
oil on canvas 21.6 x 29.2
403

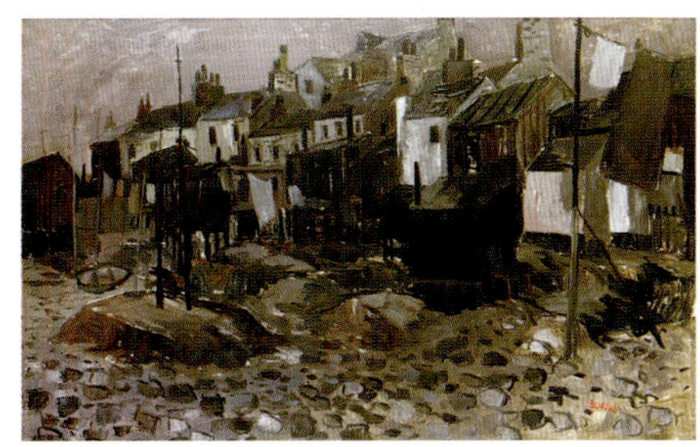

Burns, William 1921–1972
Ferryden c.1952
oil on canvas 66 x 101.6
2973

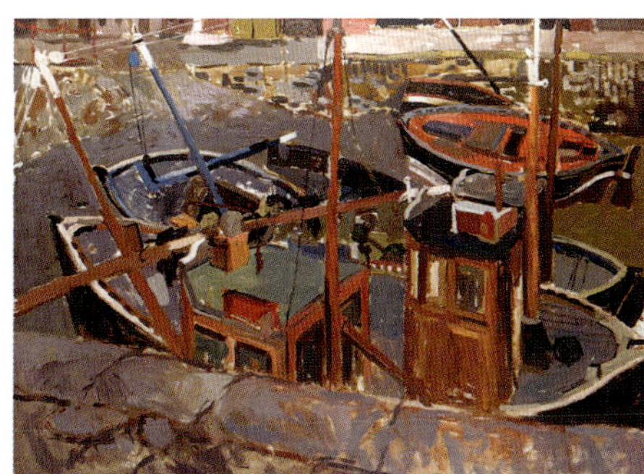

Burns, William 1921–1972
Boats, Gourdon c.1954
oil on canvas 76.2 x 101.6
3022

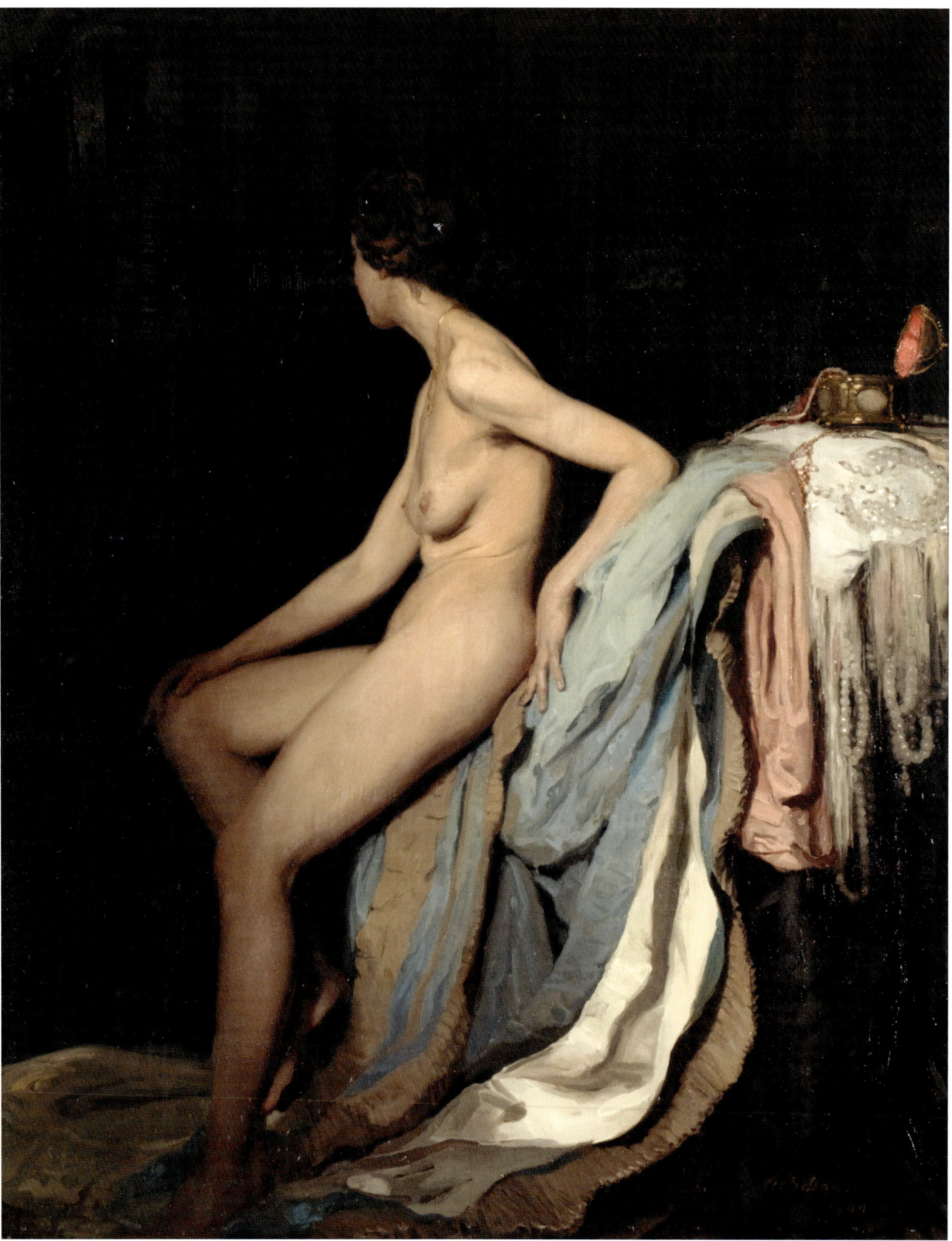

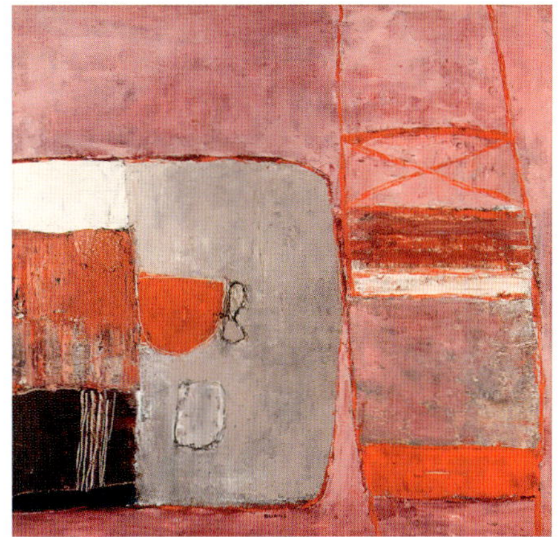

Burns, William 1921–1972
Sea-Crane c.1968
oil on board 60.8 x 60.8
3392

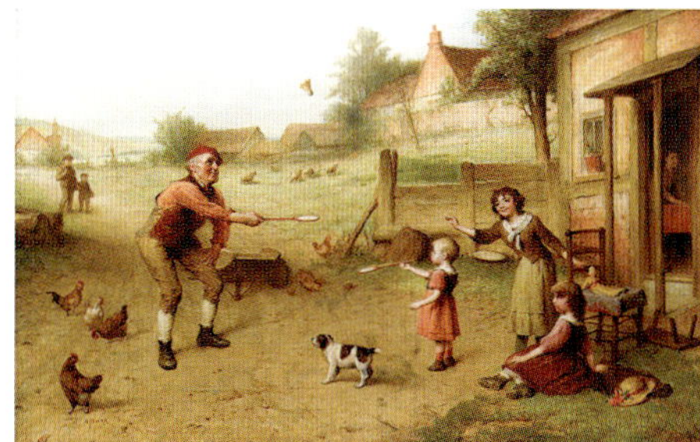

Burr, Alexander Hohenlohe 1835–1898
Shuttlecock
oil on canvas 49.5 x 73.7
784

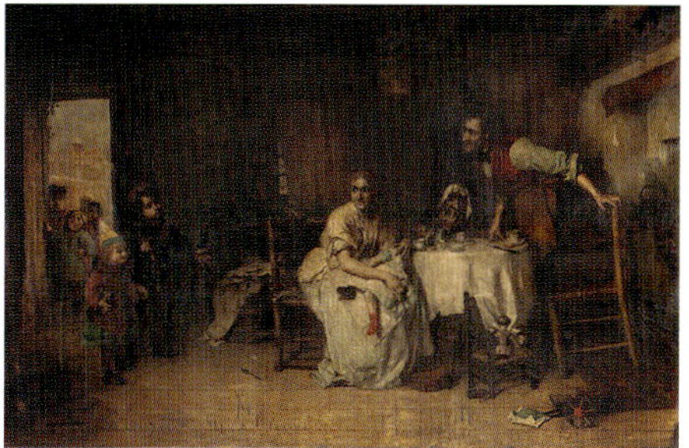

Burr, John P. 1831–1893
The Fifth of November 1871
oil on canvas 121.9 x 182.9
1024

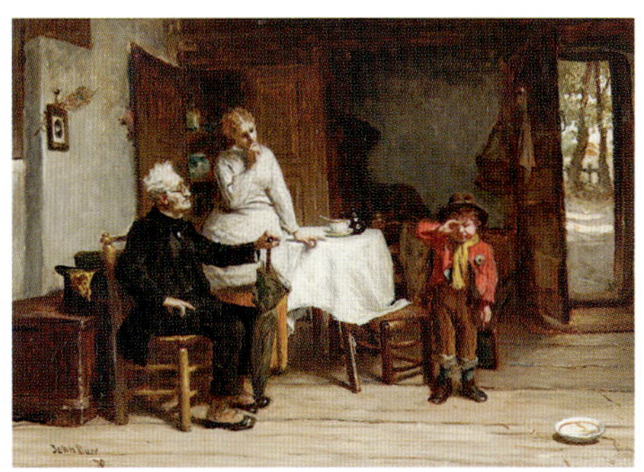

Burr, John P. 1831–1893
The Dominie's Visit 1879
oil on canvas 23.5 x 33.7
979

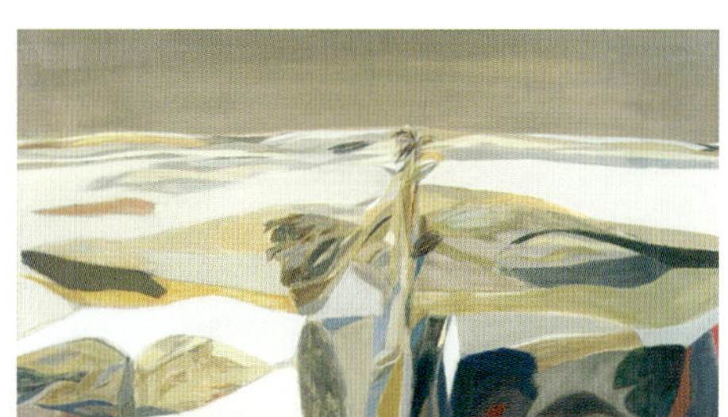

Busby, John Philip b.1928
Landscape Silence 1964
oil on plywood 70.8 x 126
3212

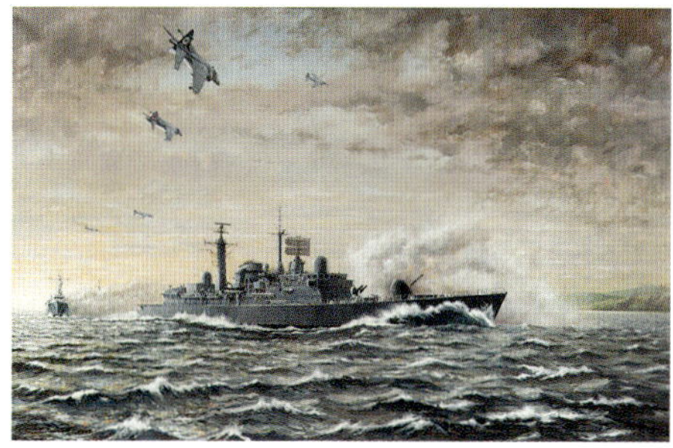

Butts, Malcolm 1943–2009
Sheffield Class Destroyer on South Atlantic Patrol
oil on canvas 58.5 x 89.5
TEMP.17864

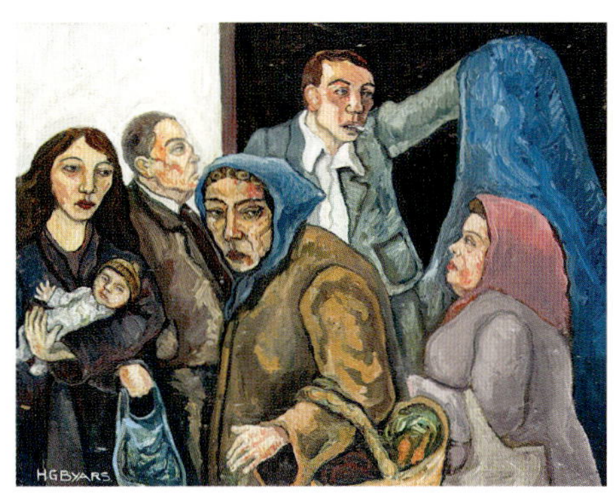

Byars, Hugh Gerard b.1957
Market Scene c.1970–1990
oil on canvas 61.5 x 76.2
TEMP.2981

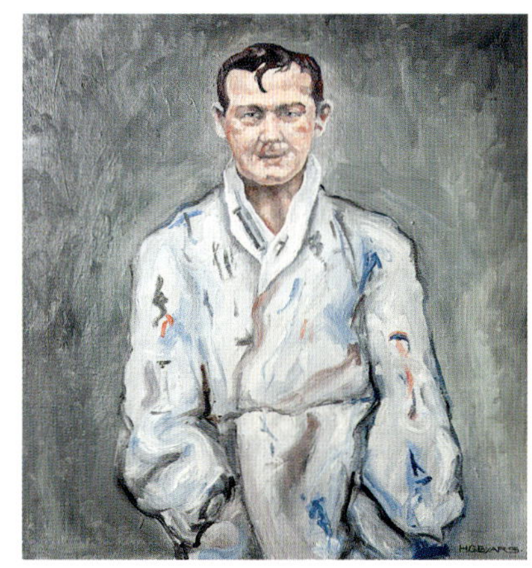

Byars, Hugh Gerard b.1957
Benny Lynch (1913–1946)
oil on canvas 81.3 x 74.9
PP.1983.118.dup1

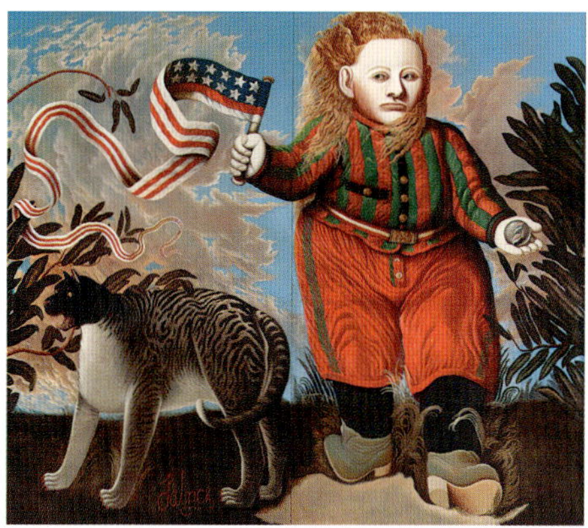

Byrne, John b.1940
The American Boy 1971
oil on board 213.3 x 243.9
3495

Facing page: Nicholson, William, 1872–1949, *Carlina*, 1909, (p. 260)

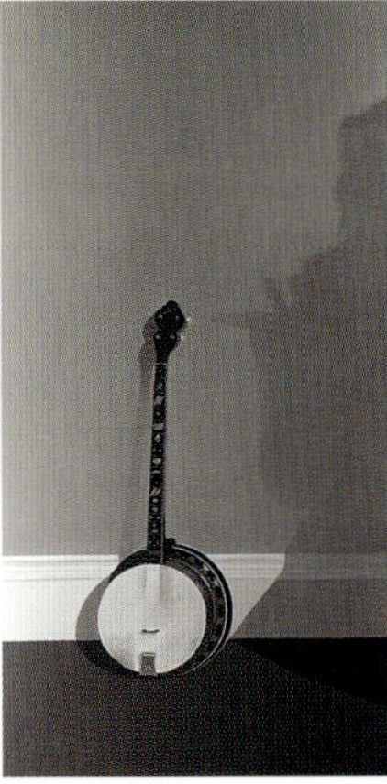

Byrne, John b.1940
Billy Connolly's Banjo (b.1942) (diptych, left
panel) c.1974
oil on panel 243.4 x 120.2 (E)
PP.1977.26.2

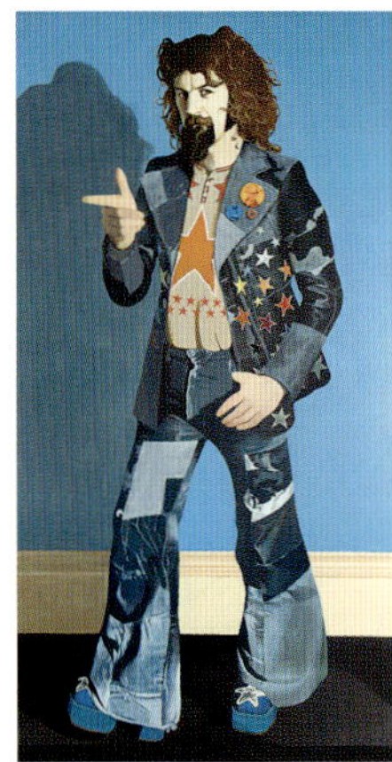

Byrne, John b.1940
Billy Connolly (b.1942) (diptych, right
panel) c.1974
oil on panel 243.4 x 120.2
PP.1977.26

Byrne, John b.1940
Self Portrait with Red Palette (diptych, left
panel) c.1974–1975
oil & acrylic on plywood 244.4 x 122.2
3623.1 (left)

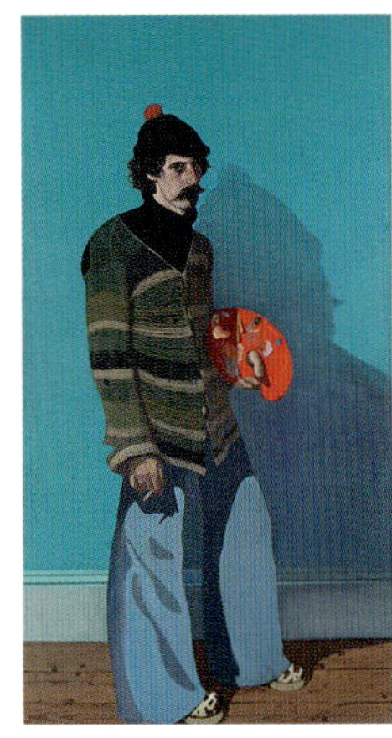

Byrne, John b.1940
Self Portrait with Red Palette (diptych, right
panel) c.1974–1975
oil & acrylic on plywood 244.4 x 122.2
3623.2 (right)

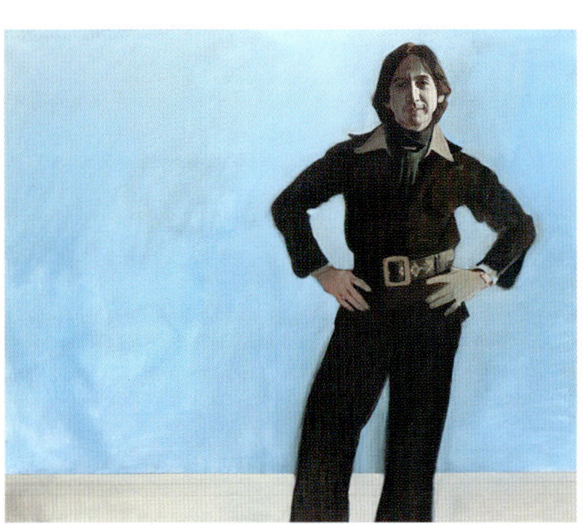

Byrne, John b.1940
Stuart Hopps (b.1942) 1975
oil on paper 62.6 x 73
3333

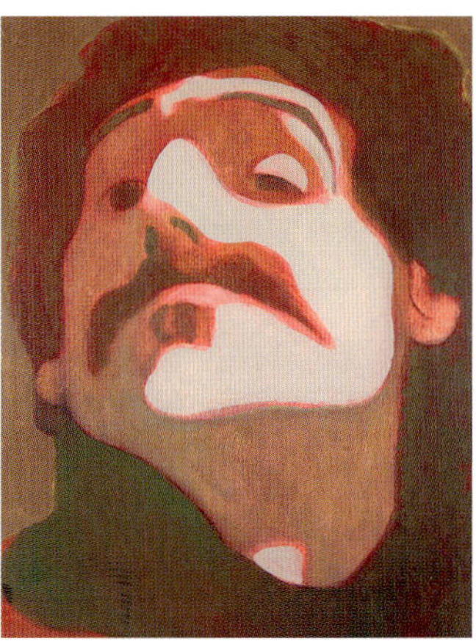

Byrne, John b.1940
To Be Continued (polyptych, panel 1 of 9)
1975
acrylic on panel 30.4 x 24
3334.a

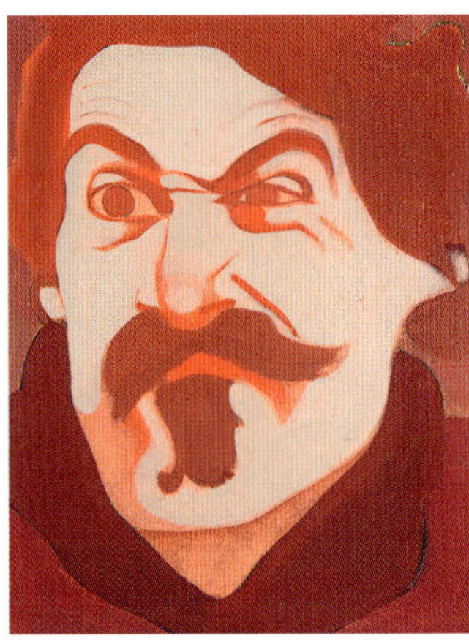

Byrne, John b.1940
To Be Continued (polyptych, panel 2 of 9)
1975
acrylic on panel 30.4 x 24
3334.b

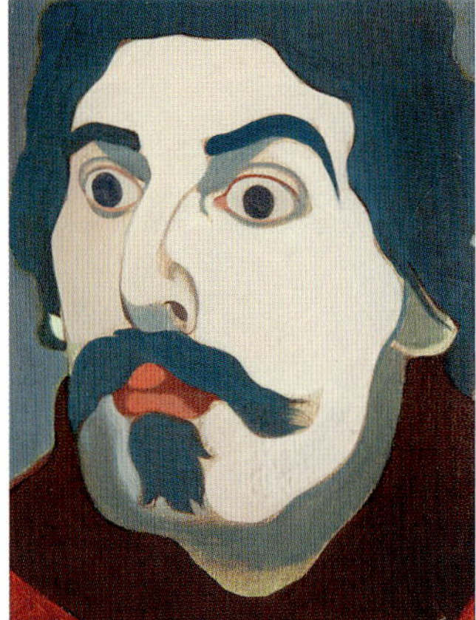

Byrne, John b.1940
To Be Continued (polyptych, panel 3 of 9)
1975
acrylic on panel 30.4 x 24
3334.c

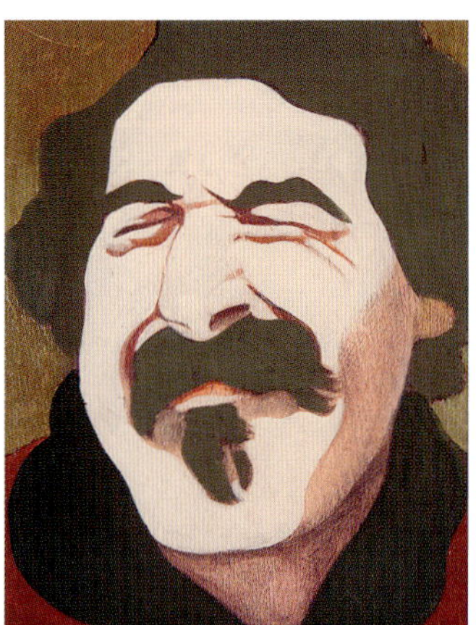

Byrne, John b.1940
To Be Continued (polyptych, panel 4 of 9)
1975
acrylic on panel 30.4 x 24
3334.d

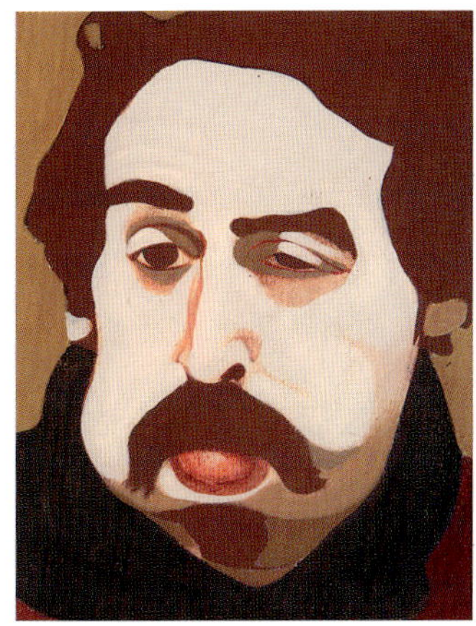

Byrne, John b.1940
To Be Continued (polyptych, panel 5 of 9)
1975
acrylic on panel 30.4 x 24
3334.e

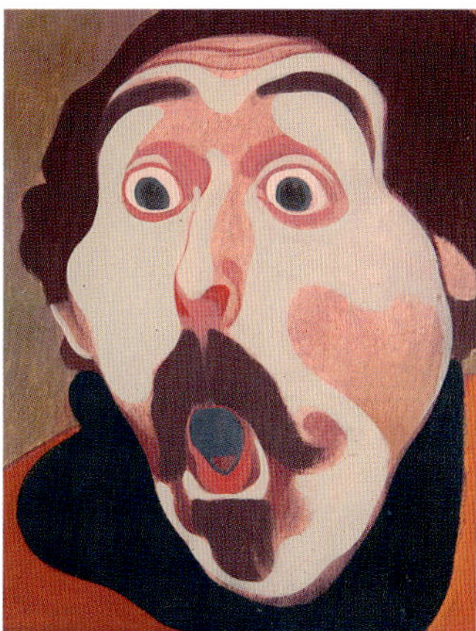

Byrne, John b.1940
To Be Continued (polyptych, panel 6 of 9)
1975
acrylic on panel 30.4 x 24
3334.f

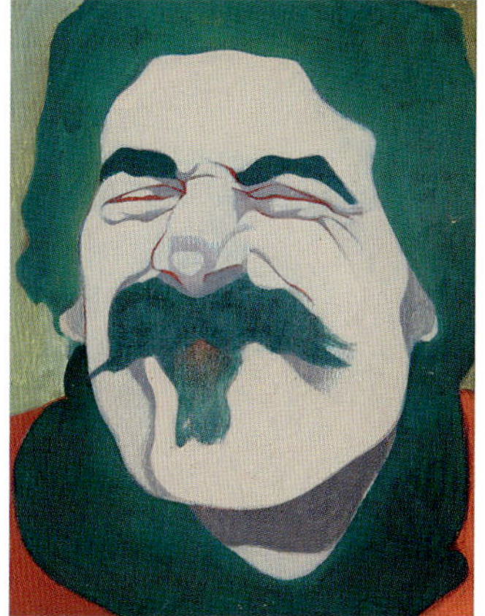

Byrne, John b.1940
To Be Continued (polyptych, panel 7 of 9)
1975
acrylic on panel 30.4 x 24
3334.g

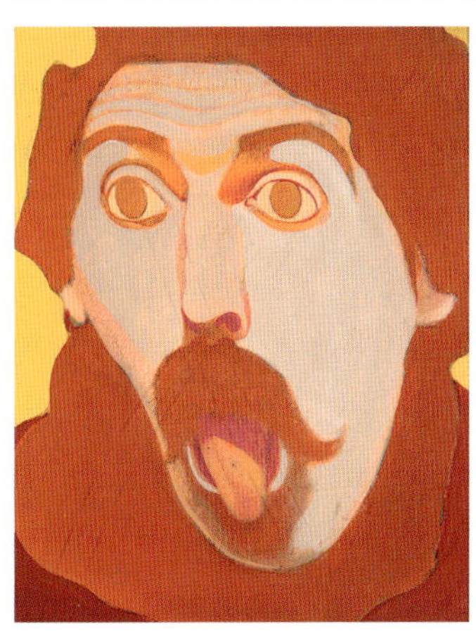

Byrne, John b.1940
To Be Continued (polyptych, panel 8 of 9)
1975
acrylic on panel 30.4 x 24
3334.h

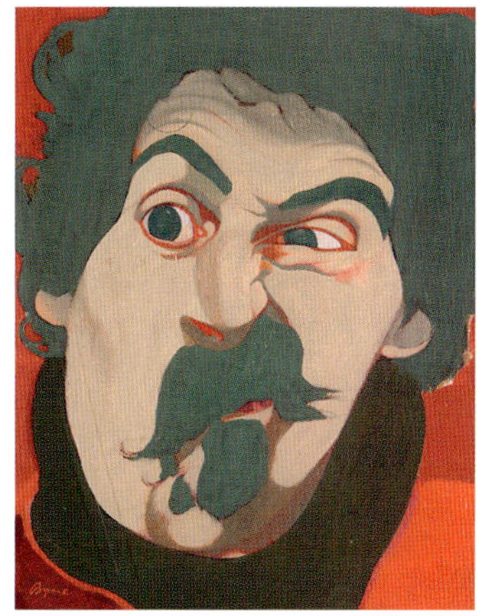

Byrne, John b.1940
To Be Continued (polyptych, panel 9 of 9)
1975
acrylic on panel 30.4 x 24
3334.i

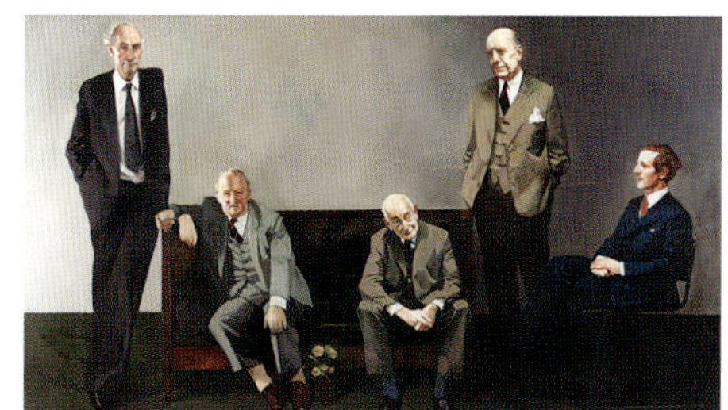

Byrne, John b.1940
The Trustees of the Hamilton Bequest 1977
oil on panel 122.2 x 213.8
3335

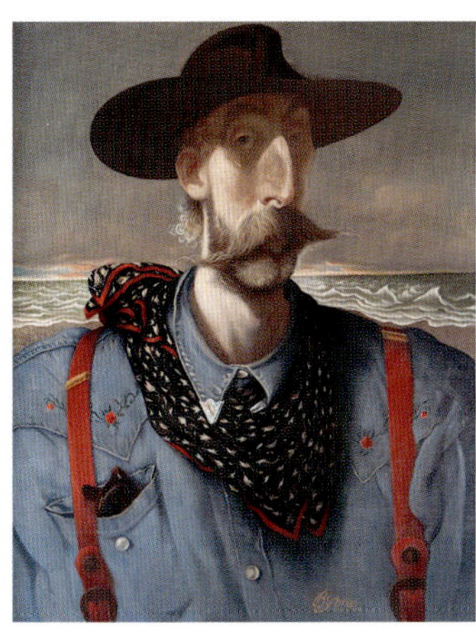

Byrne, John b.1940
Self Portrait in Stetson 1989
oil on canvas 90.2 x 70.5
3469

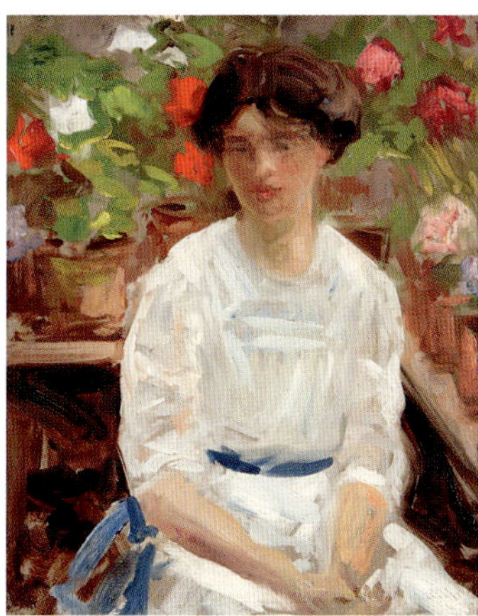

Cadell, Francis Campbell Boileau
1883–1937
Lady in White c.1910
oil on panel 43.2 x 35.6
2381

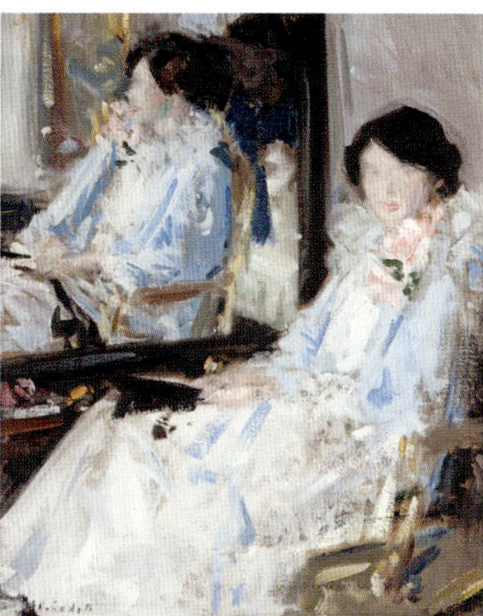

Cadell, Francis Campbell Boileau
1883–1937
Girl in Blue (Reflections) c.1912
oil on canvas 61 x 50.8
2798

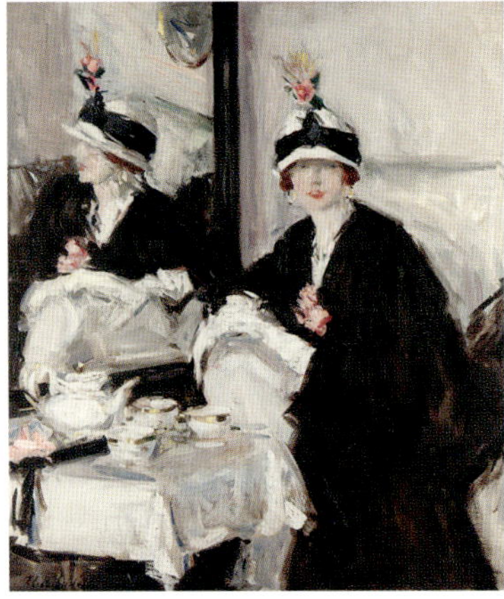

Cadell, Francis Campbell Boileau
1883–1937
Reflections c.1915
oil on canvas 116.8 x 101.6
2194

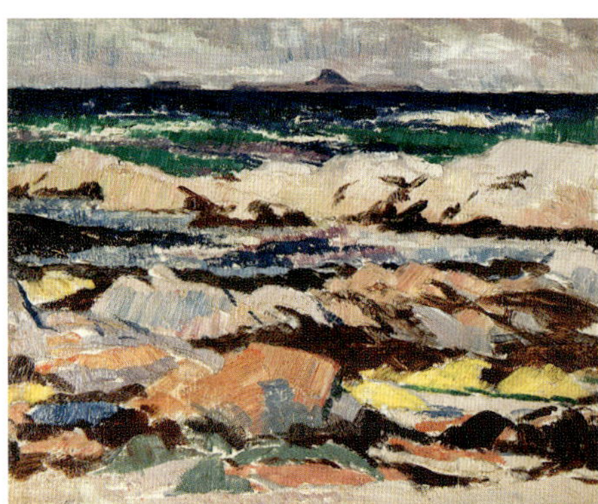

Cadell, Francis Campbell Boileau
1883–1937
The Dutchman's Cap from Iona c.1919
oil on panel 37.1 x 44.7
3413

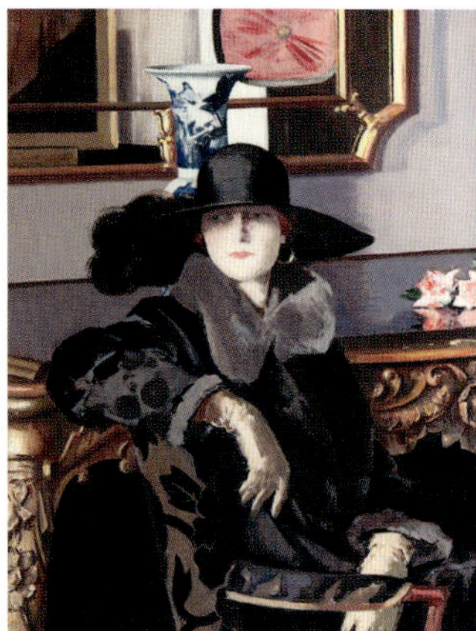

Cadell, Francis Campbell Boileau
1883–1937
A Lady in Black c.1926
oil on canvas 101.6 x 76.2
1680

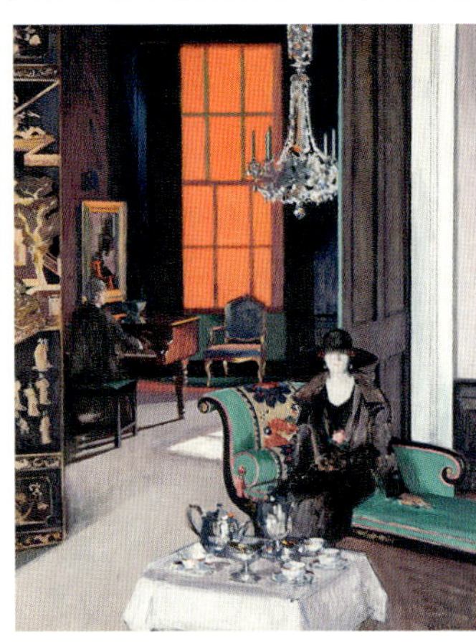

Cadell, Francis Campbell Boileau
1883–1937
Interior: The Orange Blind c.1927
oil on canvas 111.8 x 86.4
1763

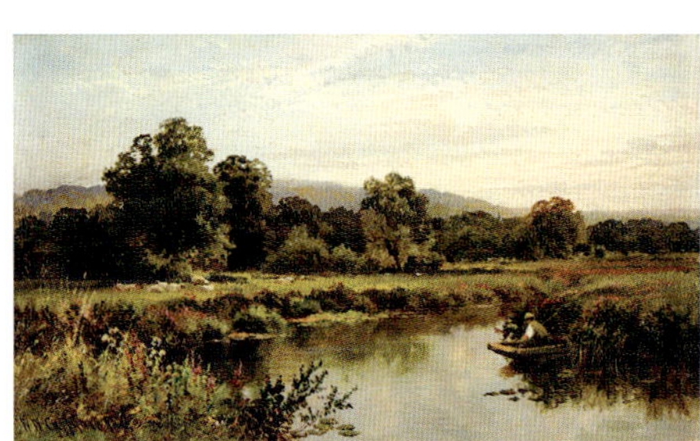

Caffyn, Walter Wallor 1850–1897
On the Rother, Fittleworth, Sussex 1894
oil on canvas 33 x 53.3
1514

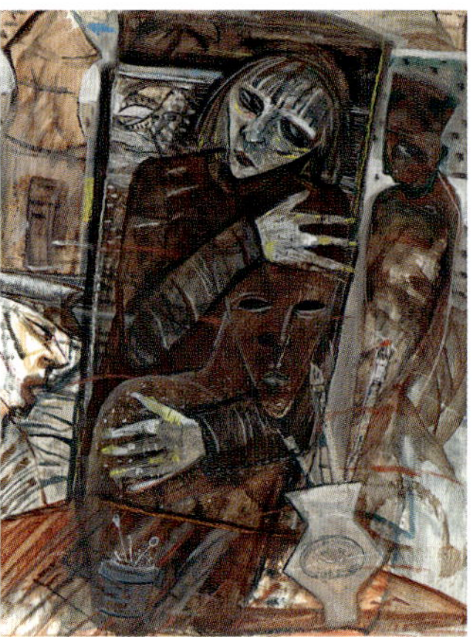

Cairns, Joyce W. b.1947
The Wounded Heart 1988
oil & oil pastel on paper 135.9 x 100
3485

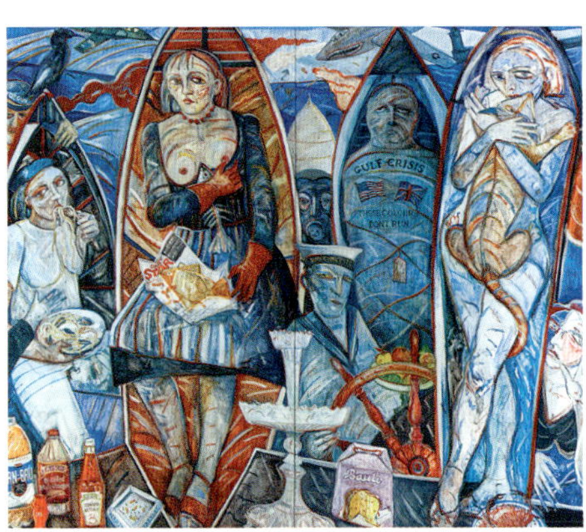

Cairns, Joyce W. b.1947
TV Dinners 1991
oil on board 213.5 x 244.6
3484

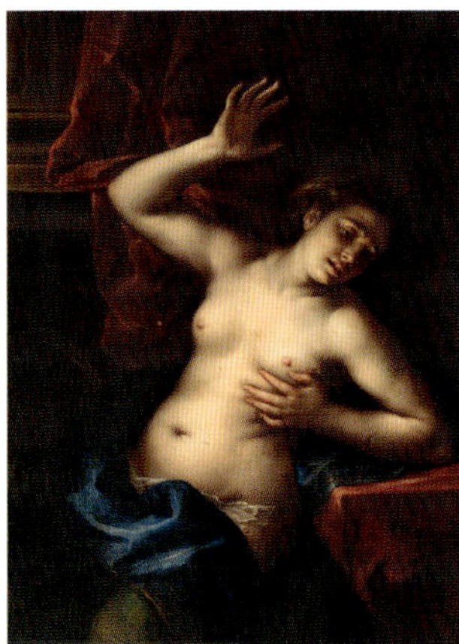

Cairo, Francesco del 1607–1665
The Death of Cleopatra c.1645–1650
oil on canvas 129.5 x 97.7
134

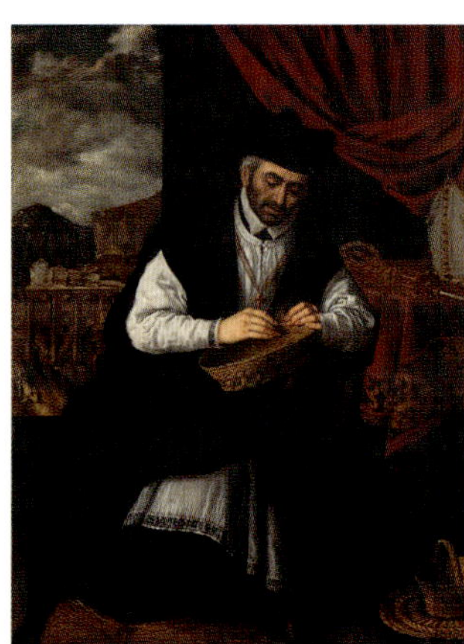

Cajés, Eugenio 1575–1634
San Julián, Bishop of Cuenca c.1604
oil on canvas 189.8 x 143.5
PC.98

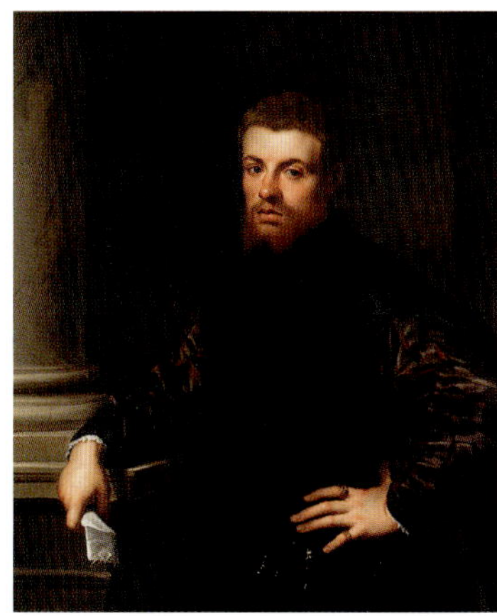

Calcar, Jan Stephan van (after)
c.1499–c.1546
Portrait of a Young Man (possibly Melchior von Brauweiler, 1515–1569)
oil on canvas 95.3 x 77.5
621

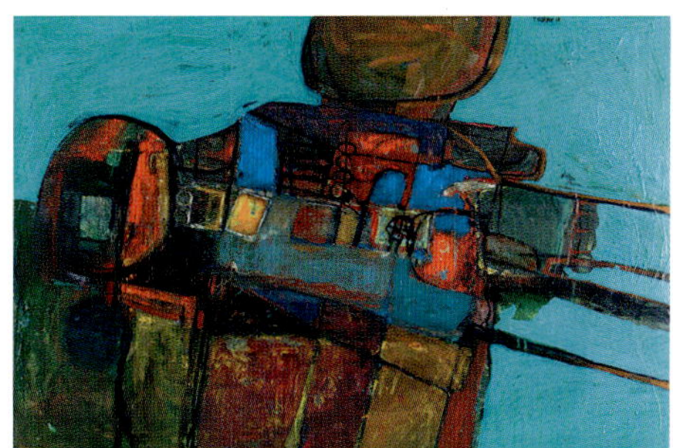

Calder, Thomas 1927–1984
Street Busker 1968
oil on board 122 x 183
3305

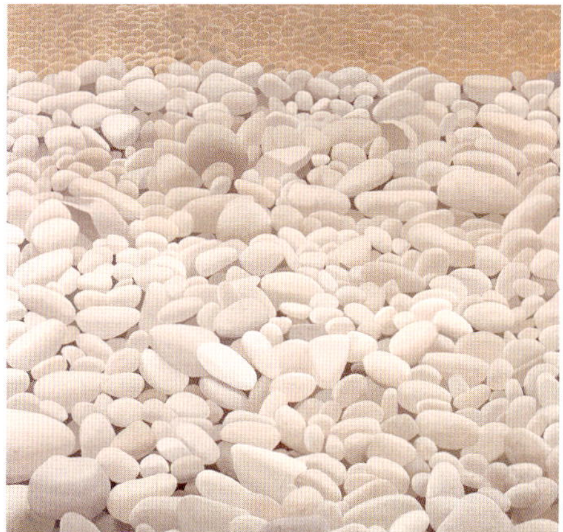

Callender, Robert b.1932
Tidebank 1980
oil on canvas 164 x 164
3364

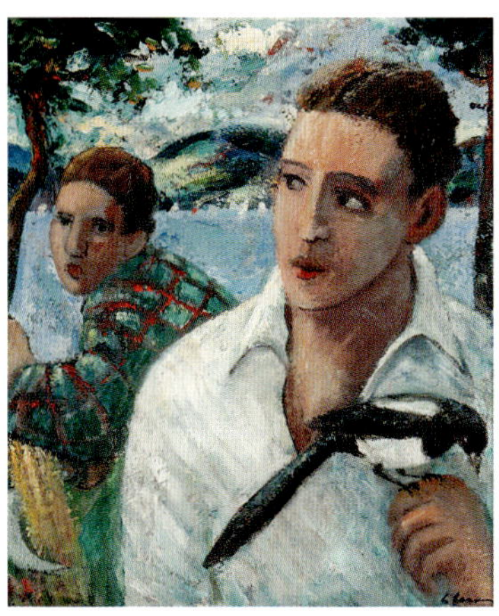

Cameron, Christie
One and Two
oil on canvas 73.8 x 61.9
PR.2007.2.14

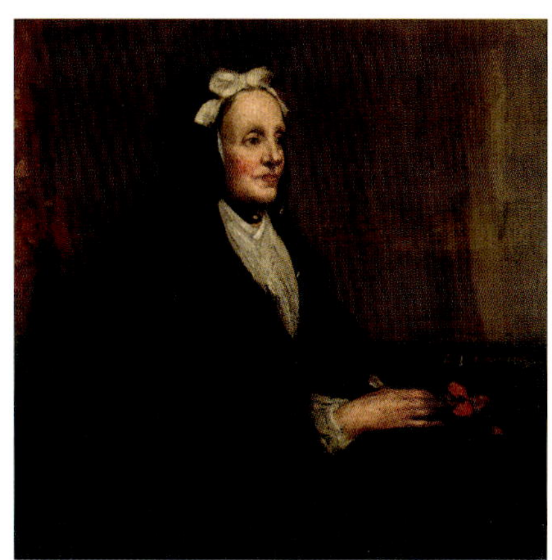

Cameron, David Young 1865–1945
Mrs Thomas Annan 1894
oil on canvas 86.4 x 86.4
3353

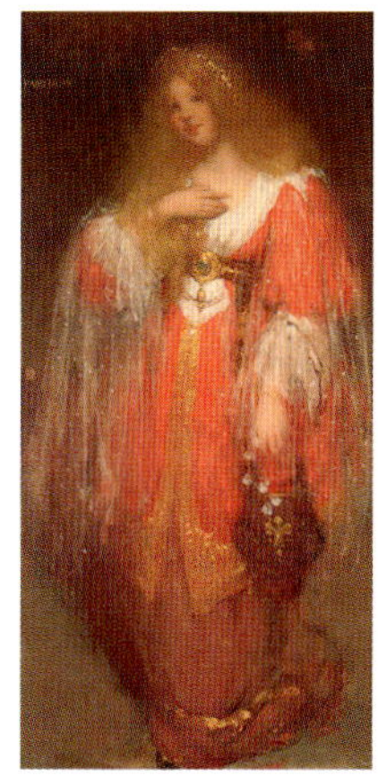

Cameron, David Young 1865–1945
Fairy Lilian 1894–1895
oil on canvas 87.6 x 60
1238

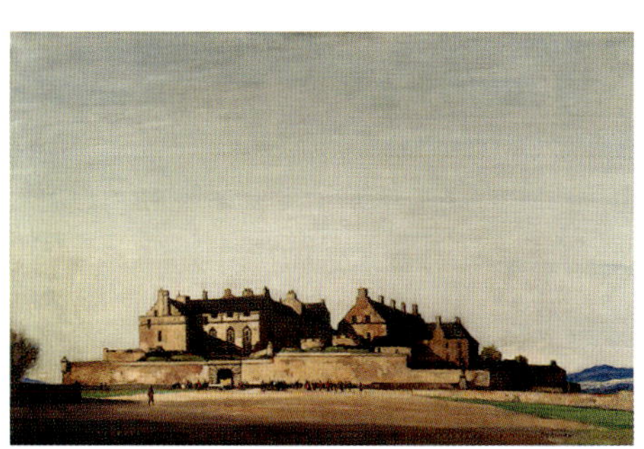

Cameron, David Young 1865–1945
Stirling Castle 1905
oil on canvas 81.3 x 121.9
1880

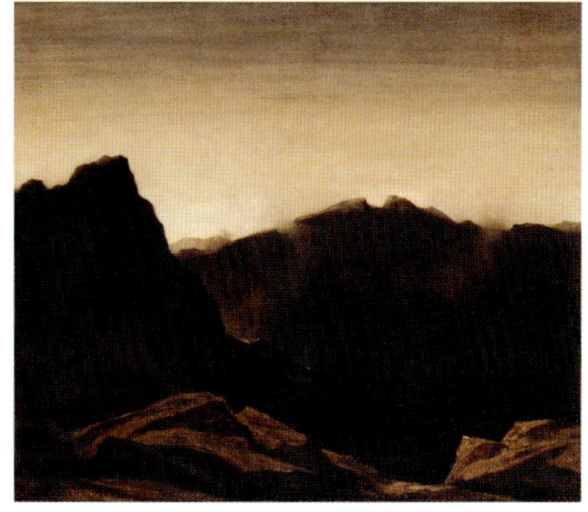

Cameron, David Young 1865–1945
Cir Mhòr (The Large Comb) 1912
oil on canvas 114.9 x 130.2
1301

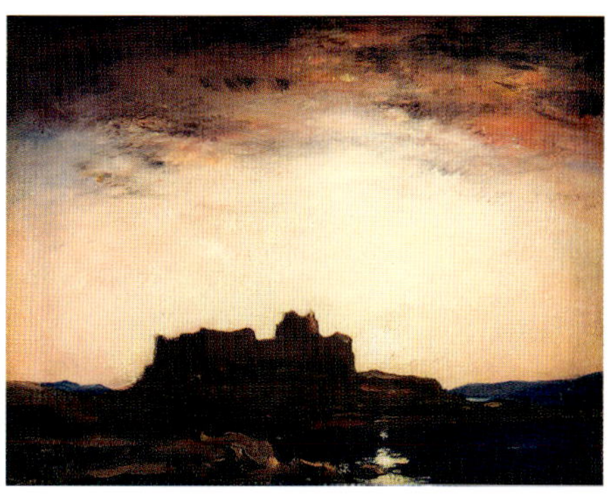

Cameron, David Young 1865–1945
A Castle in Morven
oil on canvas 24.1 x 30.5
2923

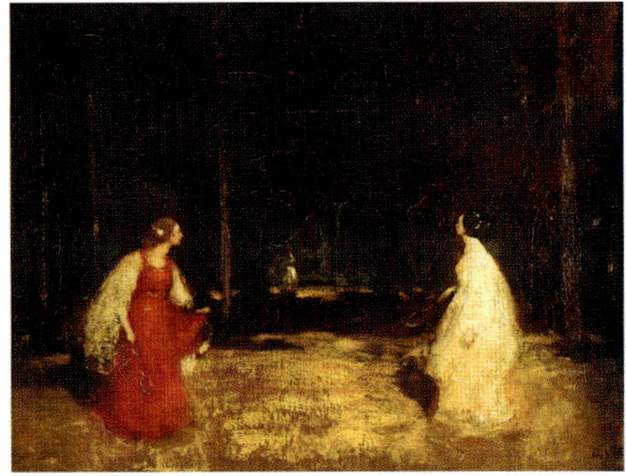

Cameron, David Young 1865–1945
Battledore and Shuttlecock
oil on canvas 34.3 x 42.5
2852

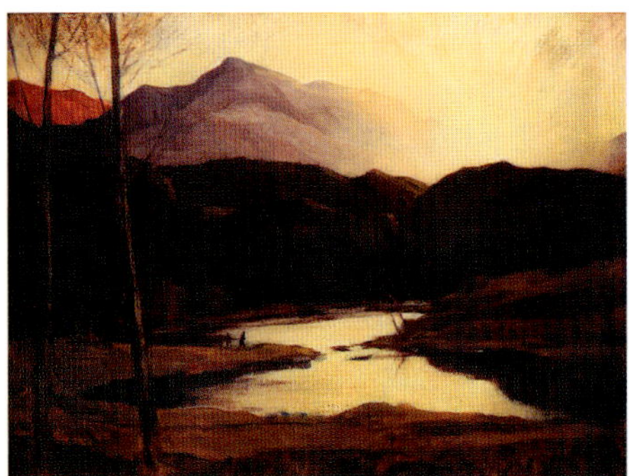

Cameron, David Young 1865–1945
Dawn on Rannoch
oil on canvas 35.6 x 48.3
2925

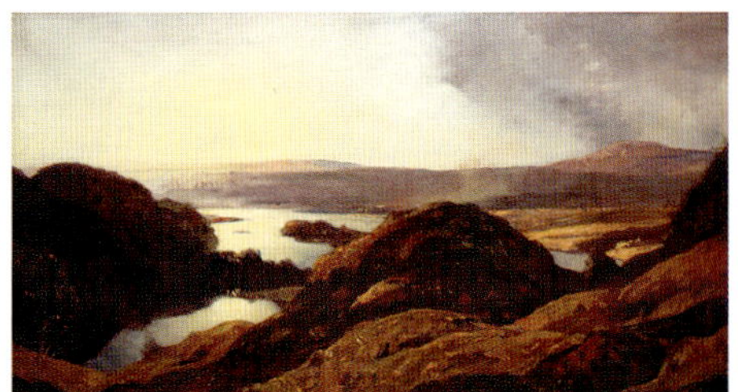

Cameron, David Young 1865–1945
Loch Trool
oil on canvas 61 x 106.7
2924

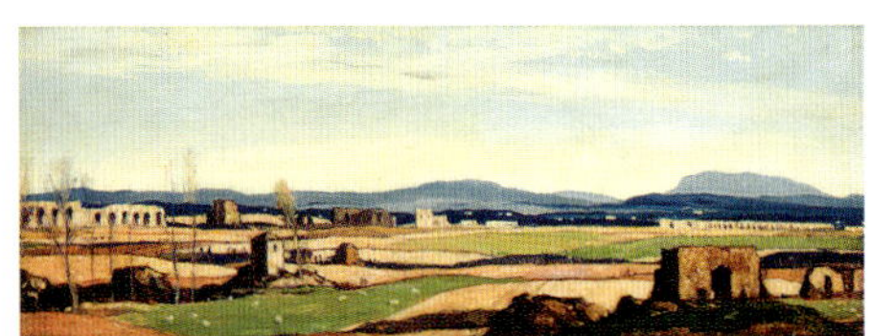

Cameron, David Young 1865–1945
Roman Campagna, Italy
oil on canvas 22.9 x 61.6
2918

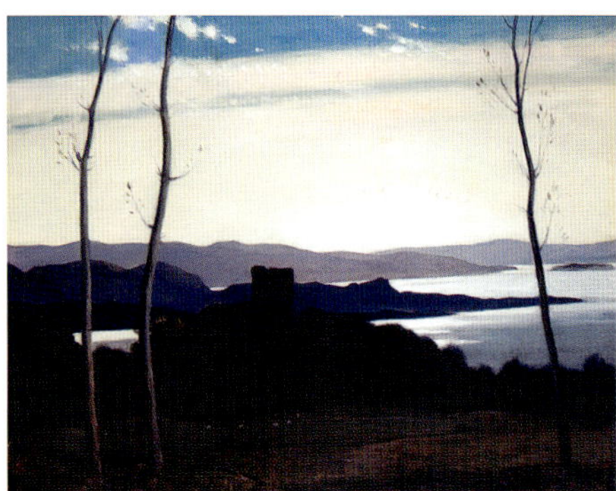

Cameron, David Young 1865–1945
Sundown in Lorne
oil on canvas 55.9 x 68.6
1606

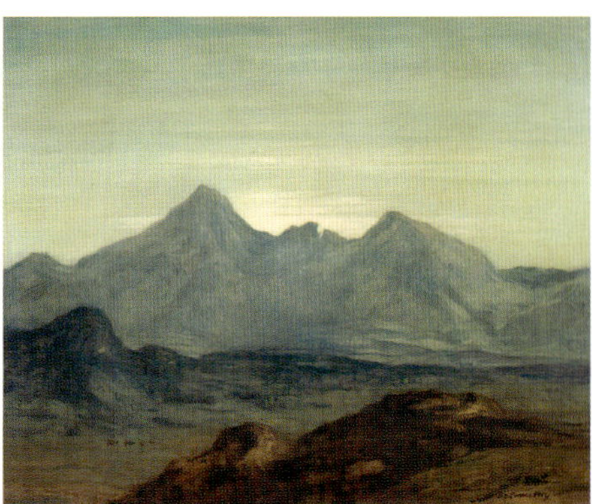

Cameron, David Young 1865–1945
The Hills of Skye
oil on canvas 106.7 x 127
1759

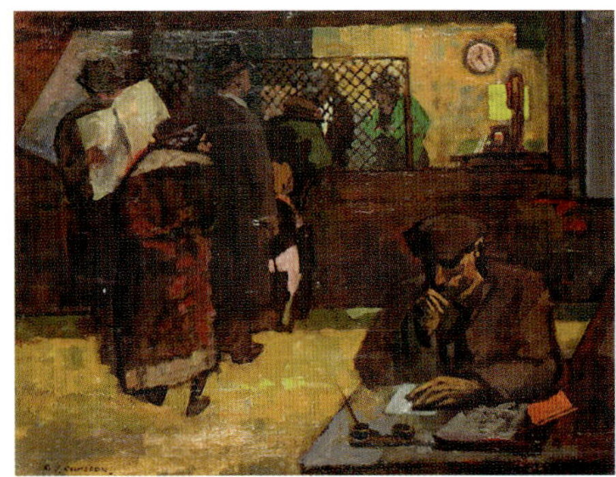

Cameron, Gordon Stewart 1916–1994
The Post Office 1960
oil on canvas 75.9 x 86.2
3274

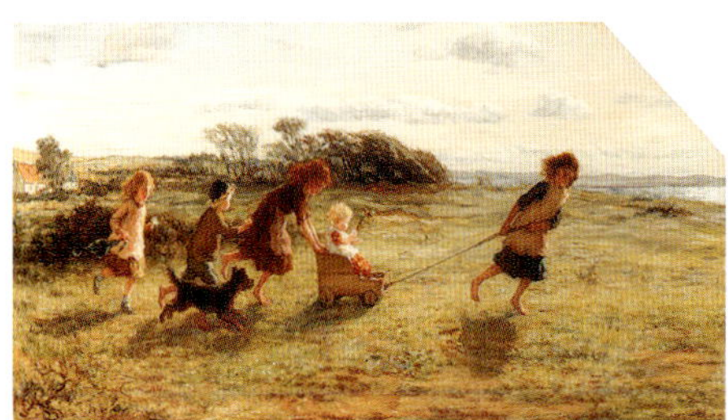

Cameron, Hugh 1835–1918
The Go-Cart 1885
oil on canvas 39.4 x 87.6
1728

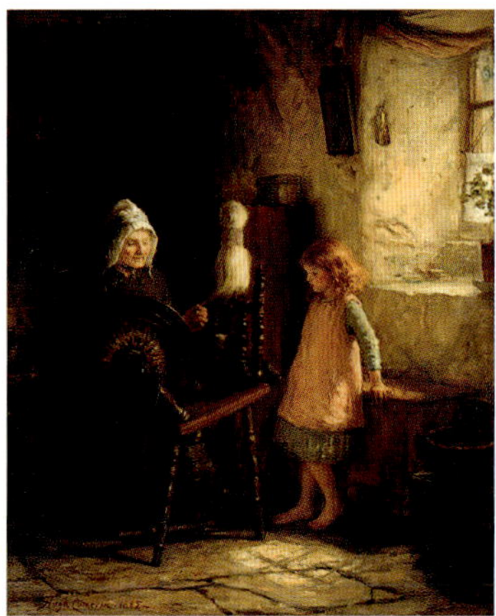

Cameron, Hugh 1835–1918
The Spinning Lesson 1885
oil on canvas 63.5 x 50.8
795

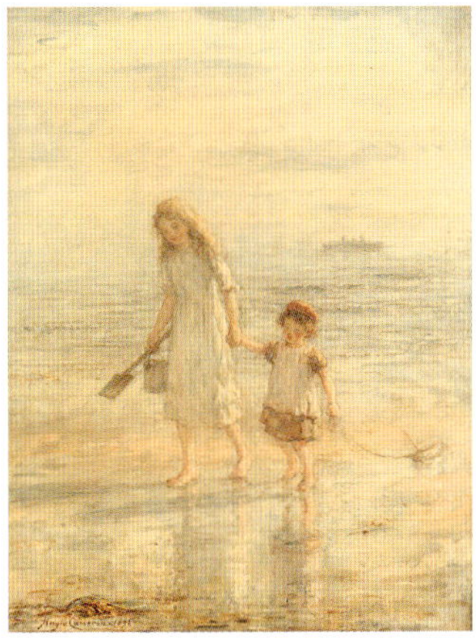

Cameron, Hugh 1835–1918
The Careful Sister 1892
oil on canvas 50.8 x 38.1
1449

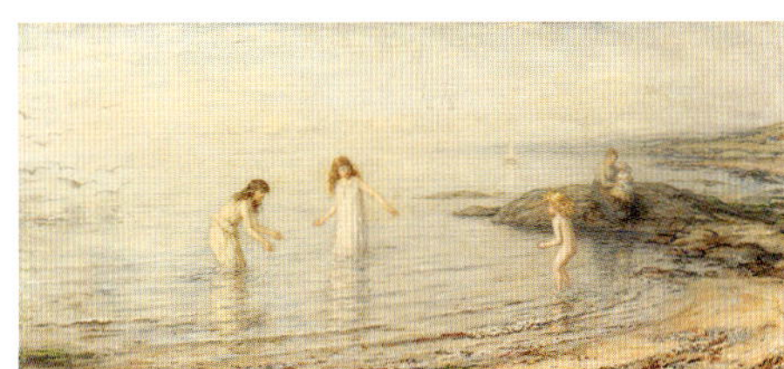

Cameron, Hugh 1835–1918
The Timid Bather 1898–1900
oil on canvas 61 x 127
1194

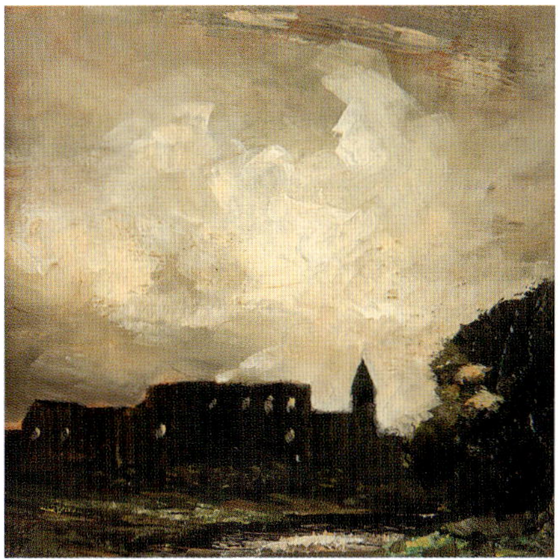

Cameron, J. Bone active 1902–1939
Castle by a River, Evening
oil on card 13.9 x 13.2
NR.147

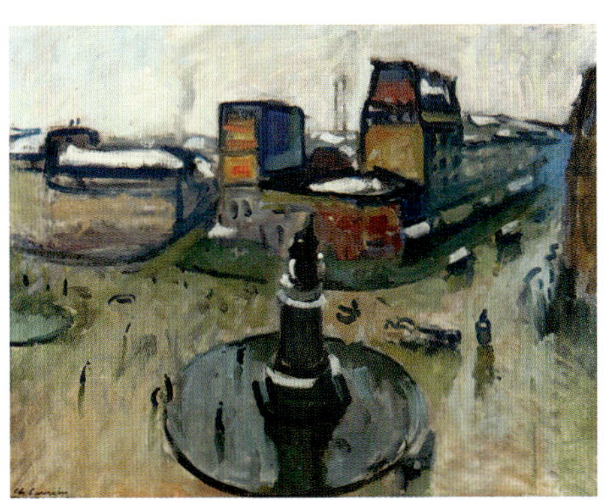

Camoin, Charles 1879–1965
Place de Clichy, Paris 1910
oil on canvas 65.1 x 81.3
3063

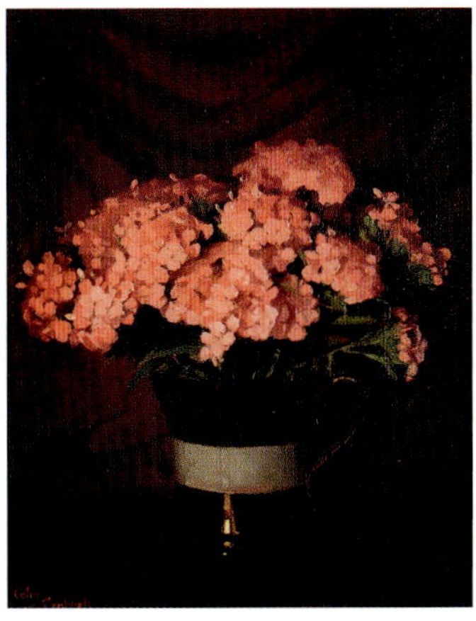

Campbell, Colin Cairns Clinton 1894–1970
Sweet William in a Lustre Jug
oil on canvas 45.7 x 35.6
2869

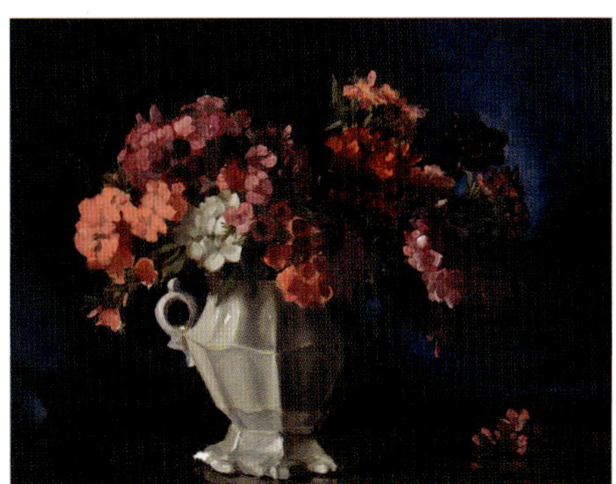

Campbell, Colin Cairns Clinton 1894–1970
Sweet William in a White Vase
oil on canvas 36.2 x 46.3
2868

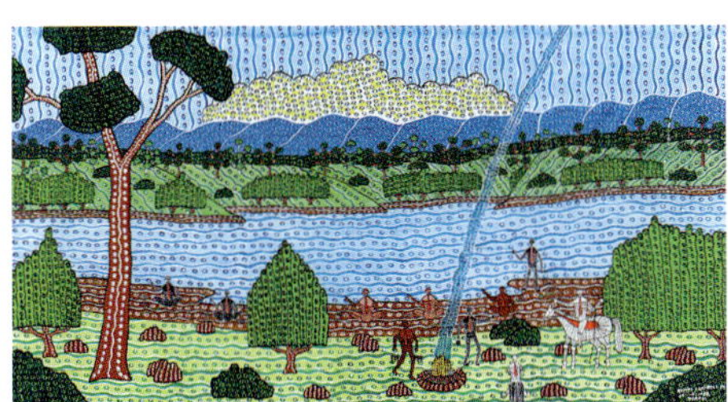

Campbell, Robert junior 1944–1994
Who Said You Could Fish Here? 1988
acrylic on canvas 121 x 225
3560

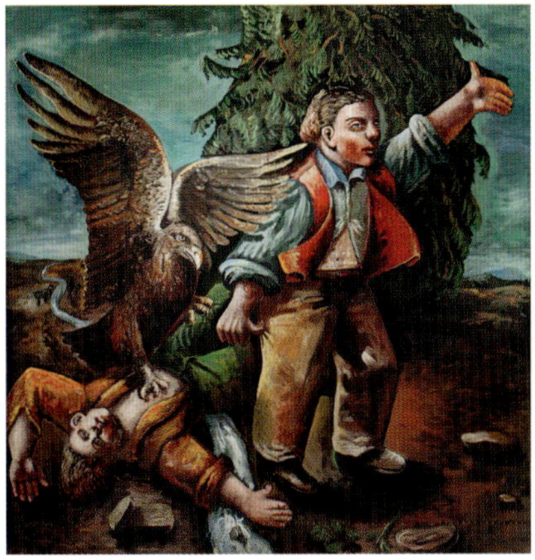

Campbell, Steven 1953–2007
Young Man Surrendering to the Landscape
1983
oil on canvas 254 x 243
3455

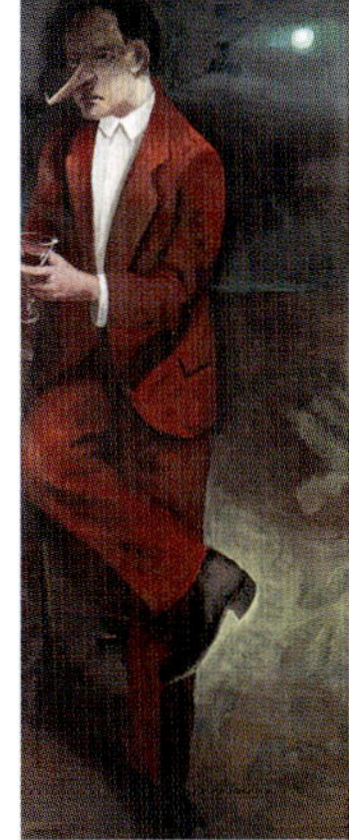

Campbell, Steven 1953–2007
Pinocchio in Exile, Alone 1992
acrylic on paper 162.5 x 66.3
3524

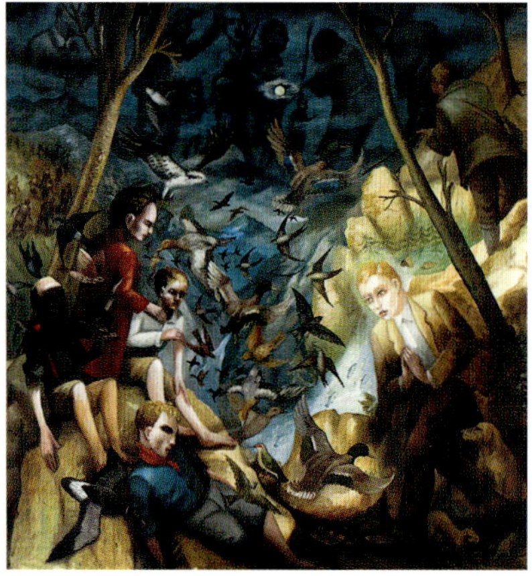

Campbell, Steven 1953–2007
Painting in Defence of Migrants 1993
oil on canvas 271.5 x 256
3523

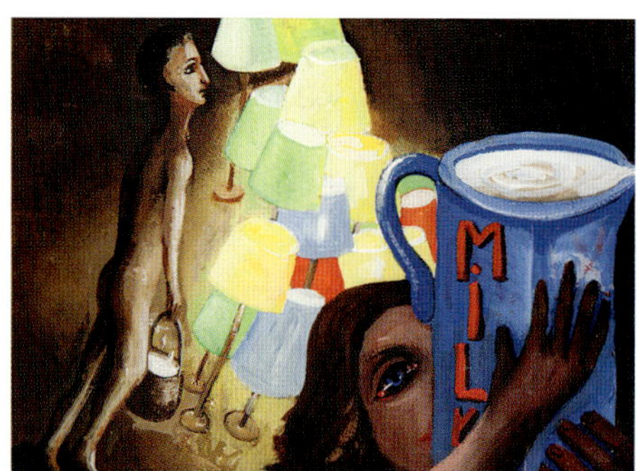

Campbell, Steven 1953–2007
Milkman 1994
acrylic on paper 22.5 x 30
PR.1994.24

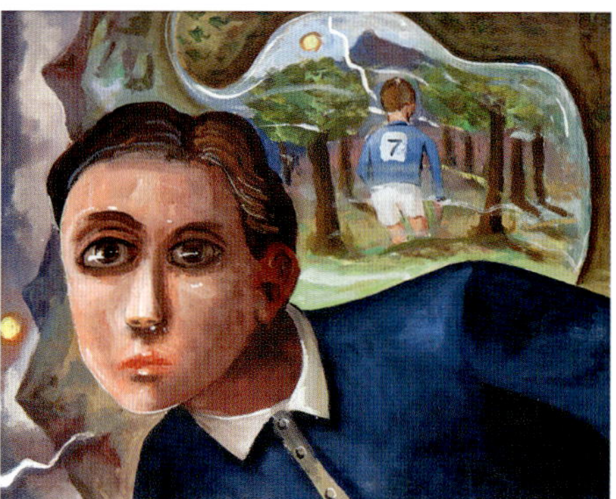

Campbell, Steven 1953–2007
Rising at 7.01 1994
acrylic on paper 37.8 x 45.2
PR.1994.23

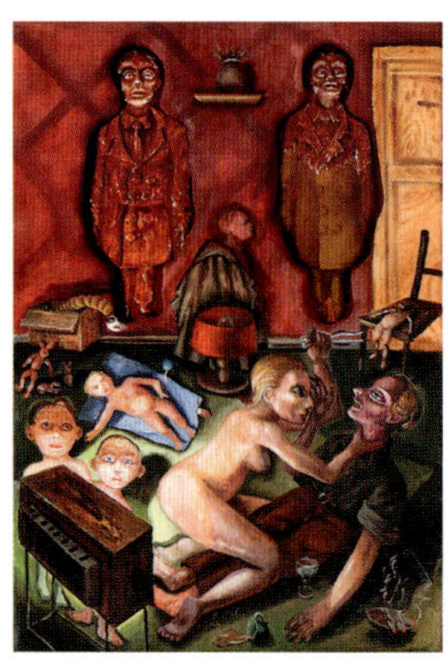

Campbell, Steven 1953–2007
The Emotional Detectives 1996
acrylic, oil & ceramic on canvas 183 x 122
3611

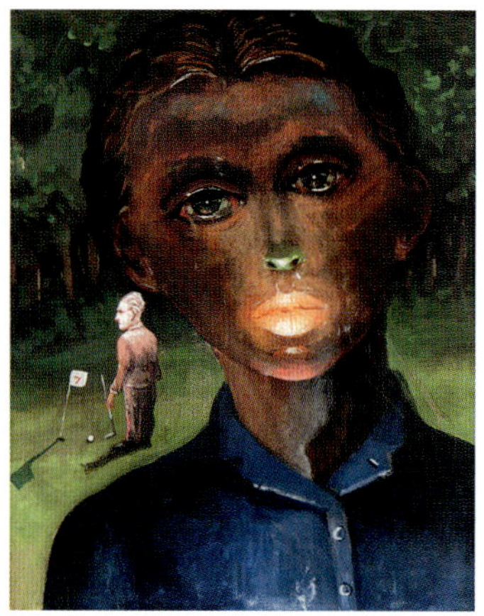

Campbell, Steven 1953–2007
The Light from the Grounds
acrylic on paper 50.7 x 40.5
PR.1994.22

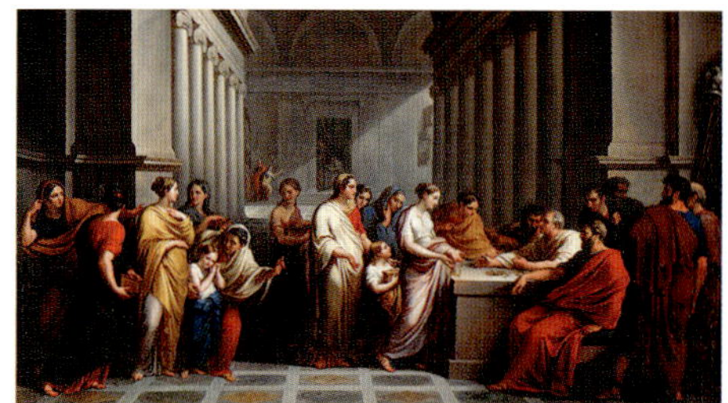

Camuccini, Vincenzo 1771–1844
Roman Women Offering Their Jewellery in Defence of the State c.1825–1829
oil on canvas 72.4 x 128.9
319

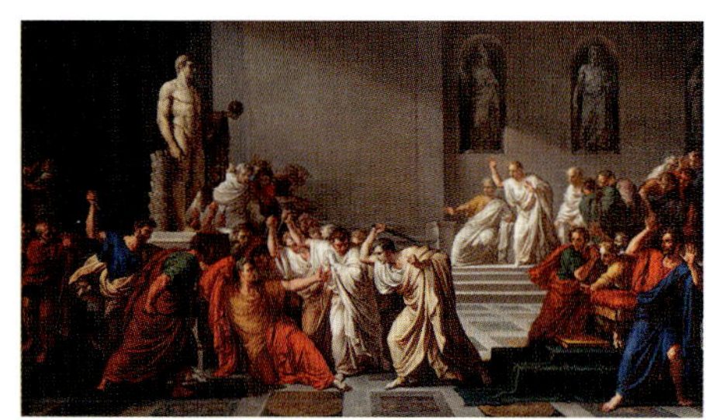

Camuccini, Vincenzo 1771–1844
The Death of Julius Caesar c.1825–1829
oil on canvas 72.7 x 129.1
318

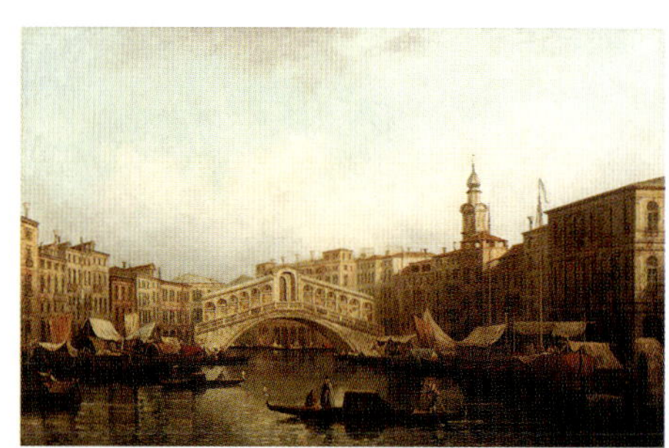

Canaletto (imitator of) 1697–1768
Venice: The Grand Canal, with the Rialto Bridge from the South late 18th C
oil on canvas 66 x 102.6
PC.90

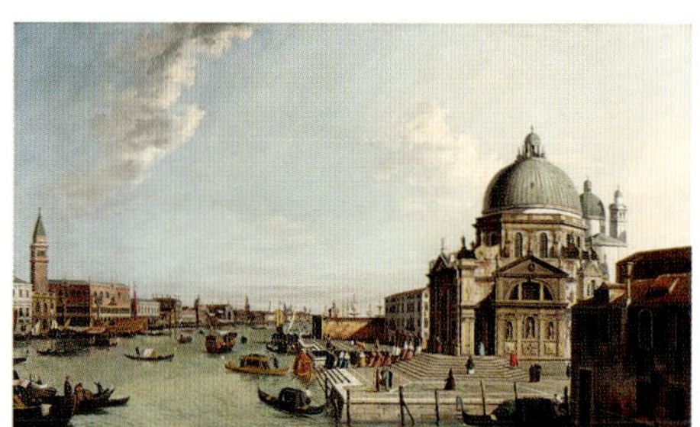

Canaletto (imitator of) 1697–1768
Venice: The Grand Canal Looking East, with the Church of Santa Maria della Salute
early 19th C
oil on canvas 74.9 x 126.6
1156

Facing page: Russell, Walter Westley, 1867–1949, *The Flower Girl*, c.1938 (p. 383)

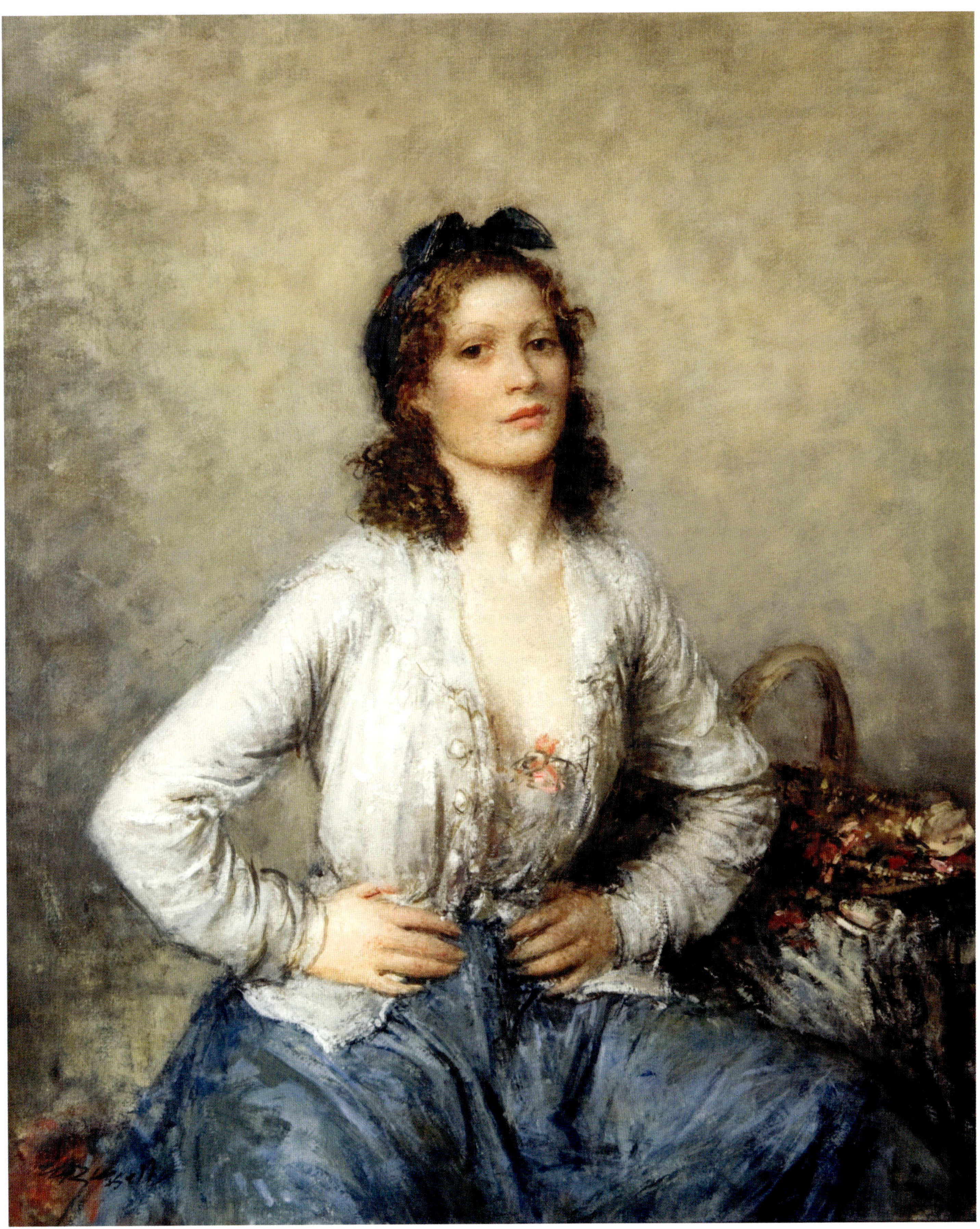

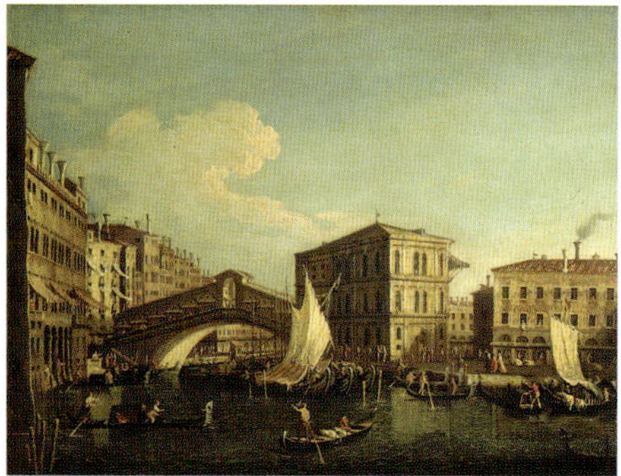

Canaletto (studio of) 1697–1768
Venice: The Rialto Bridge from the North
c.1730–1735
oil on canvas 54 x 72.4
35.52

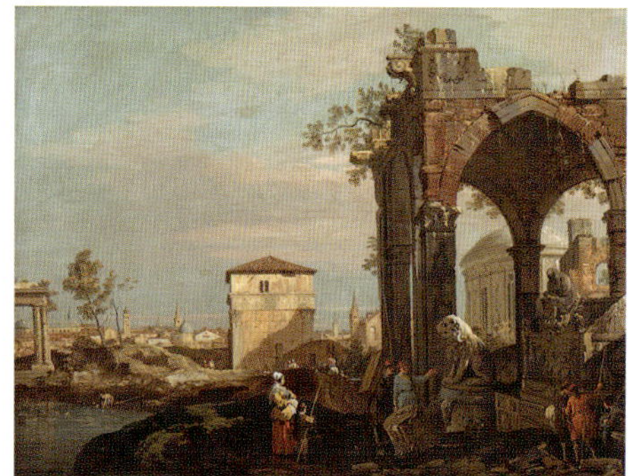

Canaletto (studio of) 1697–1768
Capriccio Landscape of Ruins c.1740–1750
oil on canvas 54.9 x 72.4
182

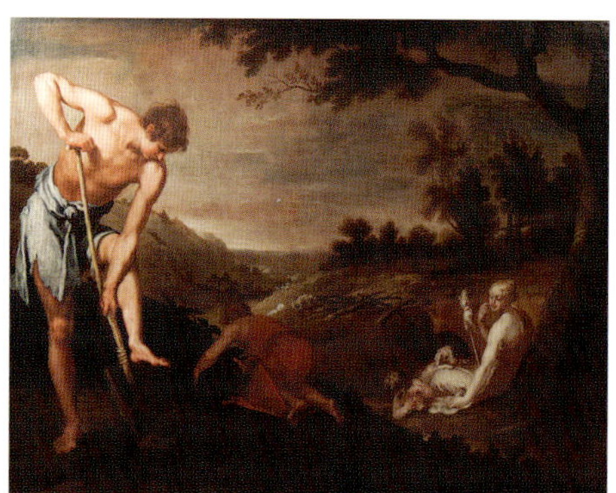

Cano, Alonso 1601–1667
The First Labours of Adam and Eve
c.1650/1652
oil on canvas 164.5 x 203.8
PC.43

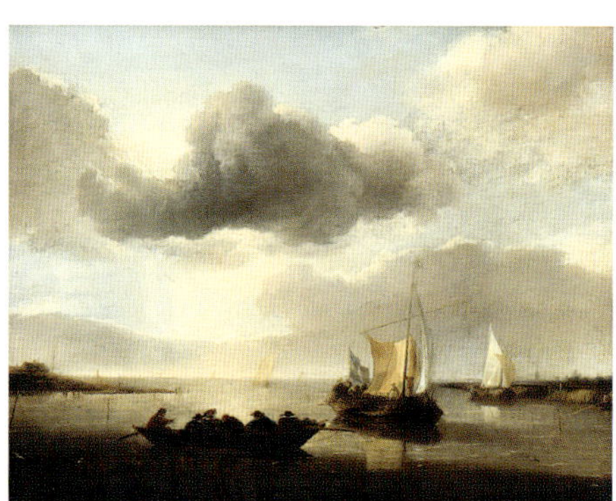

Cappelle, Jan van de (attributed to)
1624/1626–1679
Vessels in the Mouth of a River
oil on panel 35.5 x 45.1
38

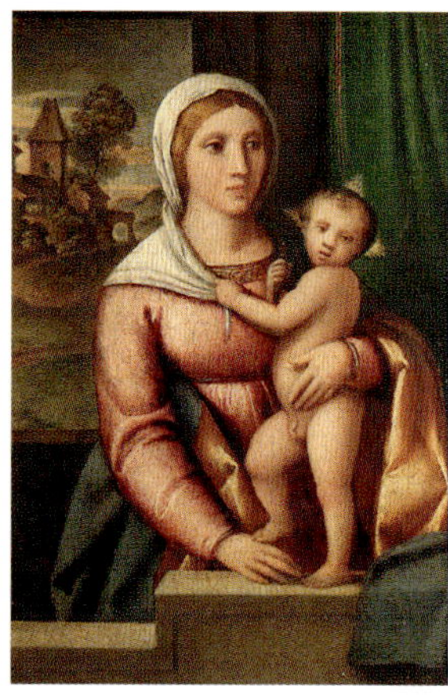

Capriolo, Domenico c.1494–1528
Virgin and Child c.1515
oil on canvas 33 x 22.9
3182

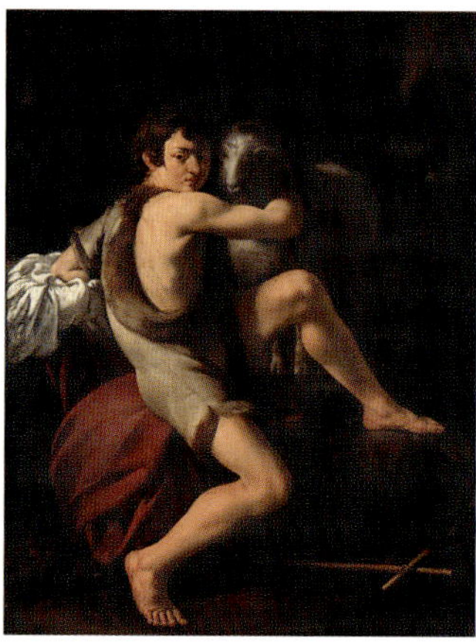

Caravaggio, Michelangelo Merisi da (after)
1571–1610
Saint John the Baptist c.1615–1630
oil on canvas 115.4 x 85.9
140

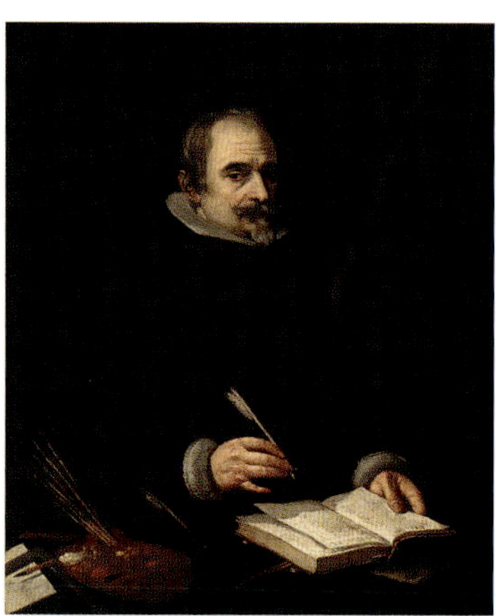

Carducho, Vicente 1576–1638
Self Portrait c.1633/1638
oil on canvas 91.9 x 85
PC.116

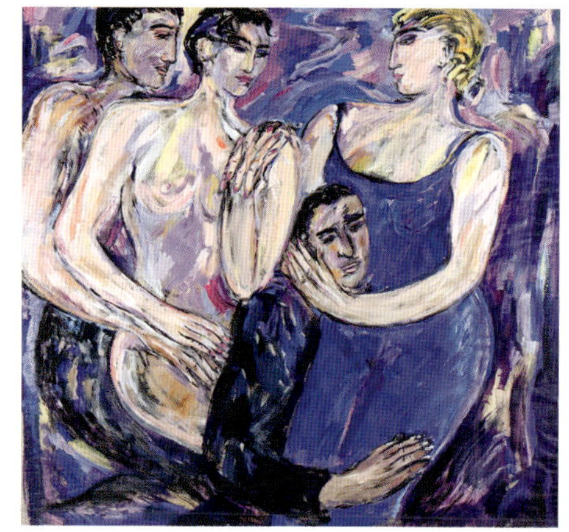

Carlisle, Fionna b.1954
Anterastes III
acrylic on paper 199.3 x 202
PR.1991.17

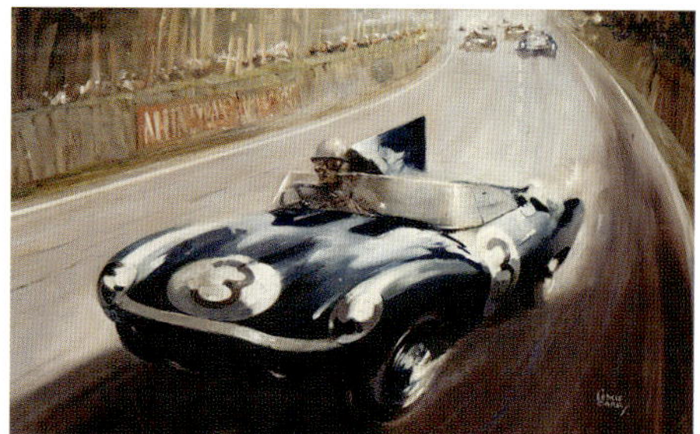

Carr, Leslie 1891– 1961
D-Type Jaguar at Le Mans 1957 1957
oil on hardboard 41.8 x 60.3
T.1957.30

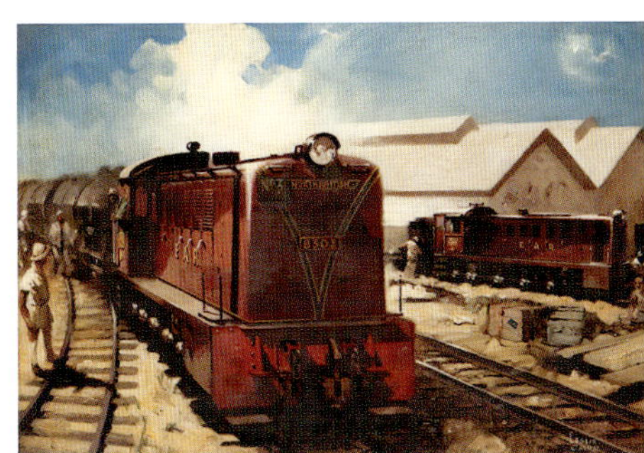 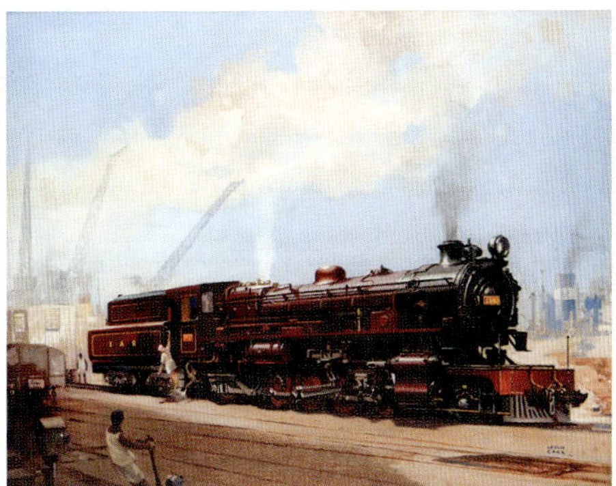 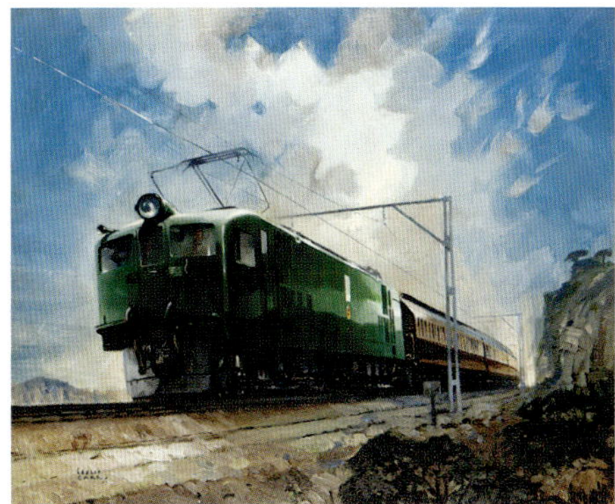

Carr, Leslie 1891– 1961
East African Railway Northern British Diesel Locomotive No.8303
oil on board 36.8 x 49.8
T.1965.6.4

Carr, Leslie 1891– 1961
East African Railway Tribal Class Locomotive No.2903
oil on board 49.8 x 59.7
T.1965.6.3

Carr, Leslie 1891– 1961
Electric Train
oil on board 55 x 66
T.1965.6.2

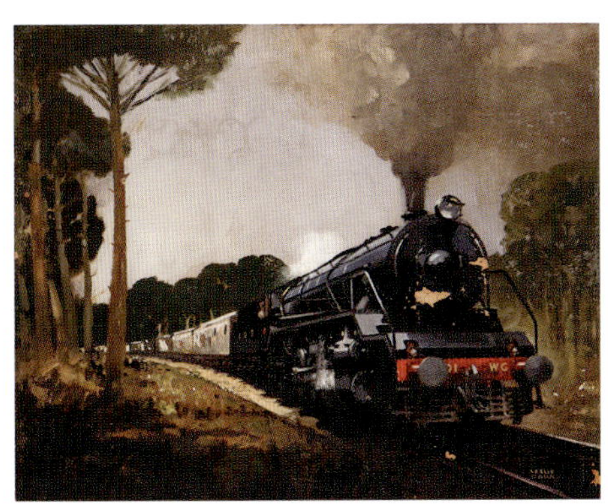 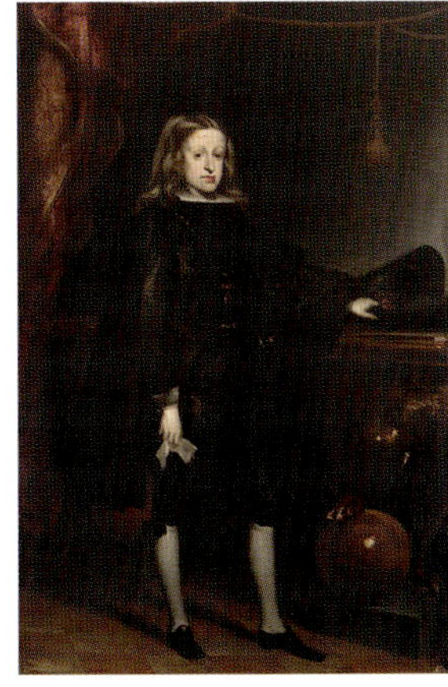 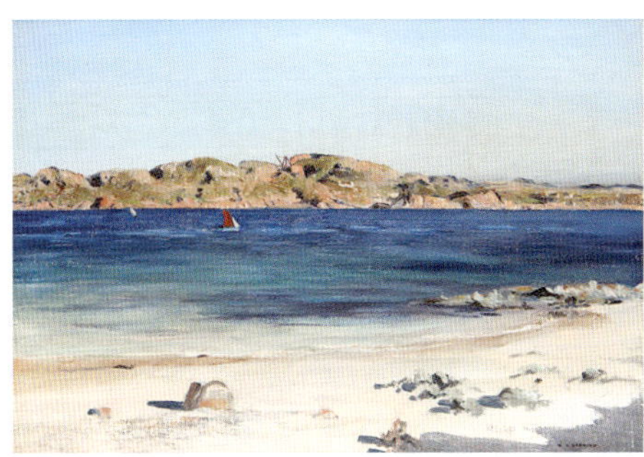

Carr, Leslie 1891– 1961
IGR Steam Locomotive
oil on board 50.4 x 60.8
T.1965.6.1

Carreño de Miranda, Juan 1614–1685
Charles II (1661–1700), King of Spain c.1673
oil on canvas 175.3 x 110.5
PC.2

Carrick, William Arthur Laurie 1879–1964
Iona
oil on canvas 36.2 x 48.3
2886

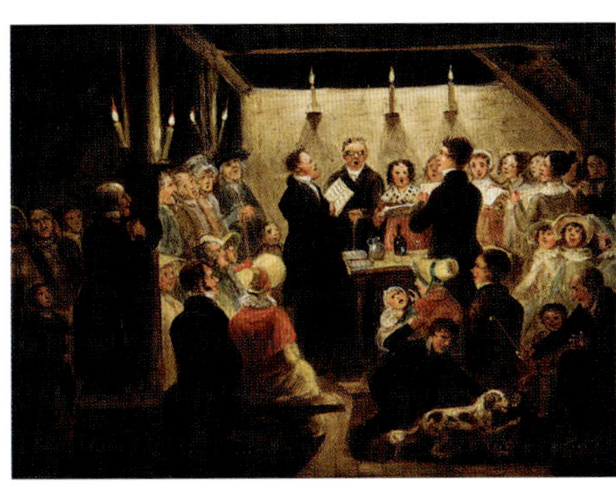 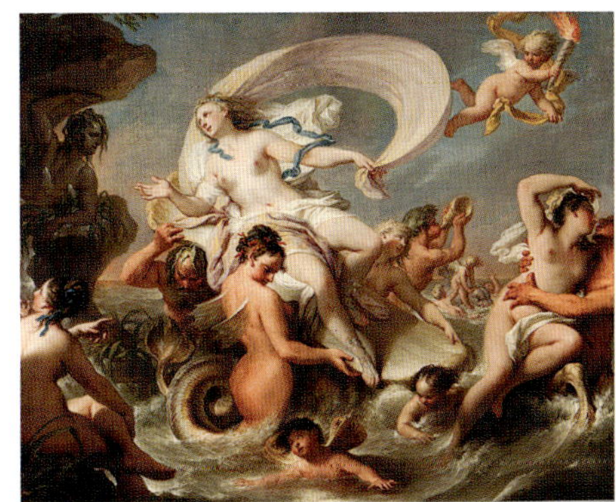 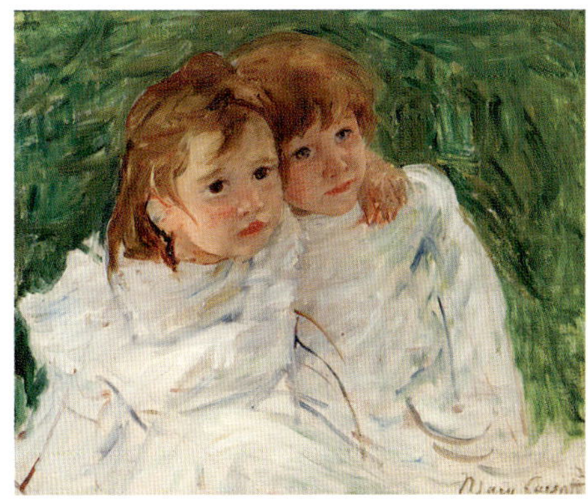

Carse, Alexander (attributed to) 1770–1843
A Village Concert
oil on panel 17.8 x 22.9
3262

Casali, Andrea 1705–1784
The Triumph of Galatea c.1730–1760
oil on canvas 72.4 x 87
195

Cassatt, Mary 1844–1926
The Young Girls c.1885
oil on canvas 46.3 x 55.5
2980

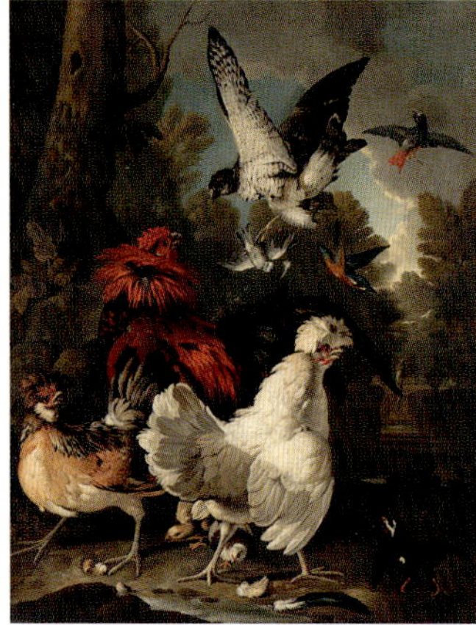

Casteels, Pieter 1684–1749
A Falcon Attacking Poultry c.1719
oil on canvas 137.1 x 101.6
393

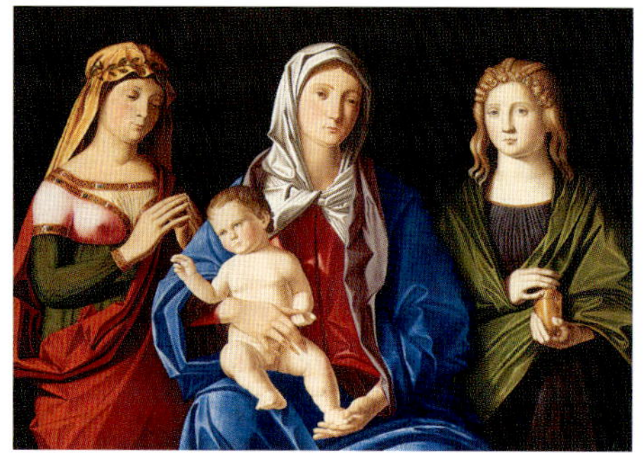

Catena, Vincenzo 1470–1531
*Virgin and Child with Saint Mary Magdalene
and Another Female Saint* c.1500–1505
oil on panel 61.6 x 83.5
199

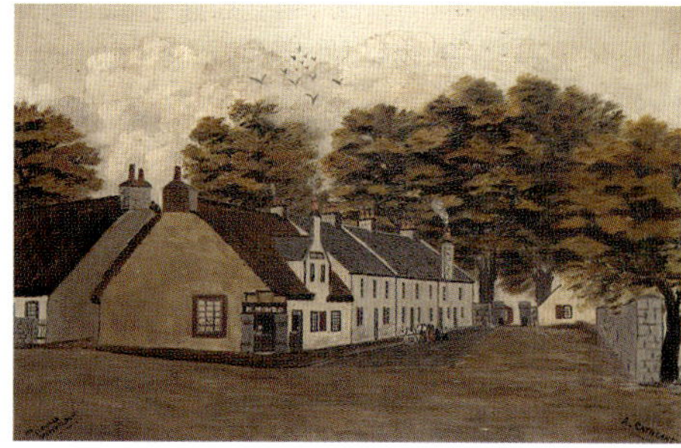

Cathcart, A. active 19th C
Old Clachan, Crossmyloof
oil on canvas 35.8 x 53.8
TEMP.1662

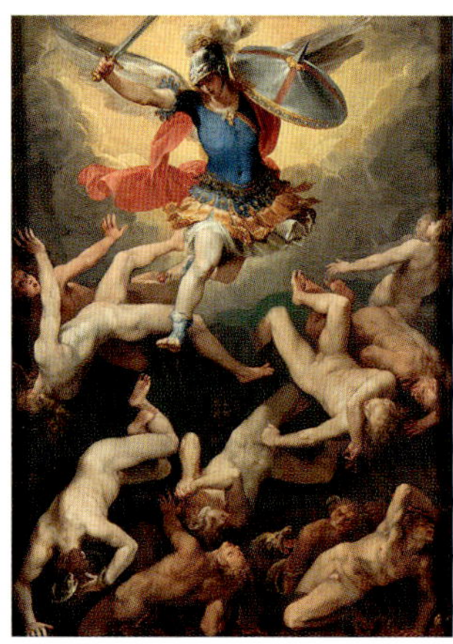

Cesari, Giuseppe 1568–1640
*The Archangel Michael and the Rebel
Angels* c.1592–1593
oil on copper 47.8 x 41.8
153

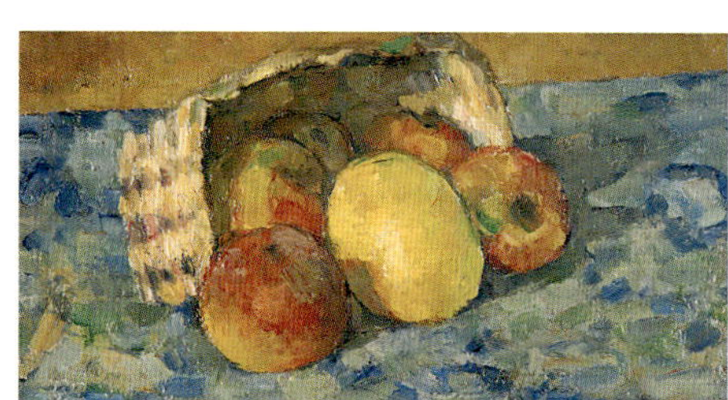

Cézanne, Paul 1839–1906
Overturned Basket of Fruit c.1877
oil on canvas 16 x 32.3
2382

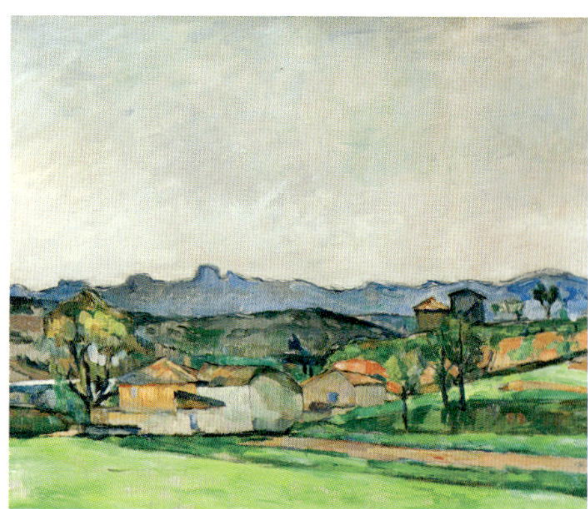

Cézanne, Paul 1839–1906
The Star Ridge with the King's Peak
c.1878–1879
oil on canvas 49.2 x 59
2932

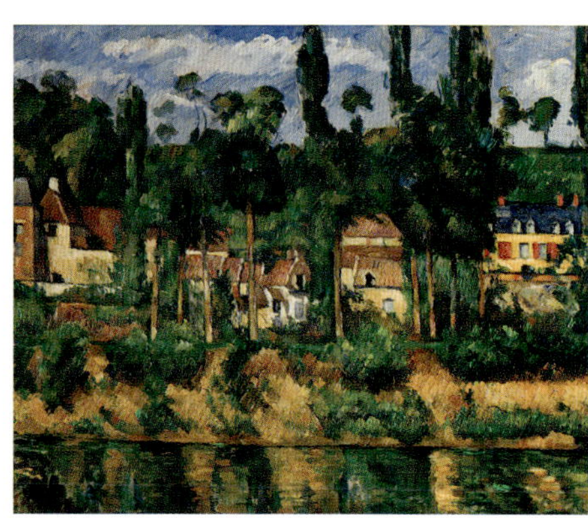

Cézanne, Paul 1839–1906
The Château of Médan c.1879–1880
oil on canvas 59.1 x 72.4
35.53

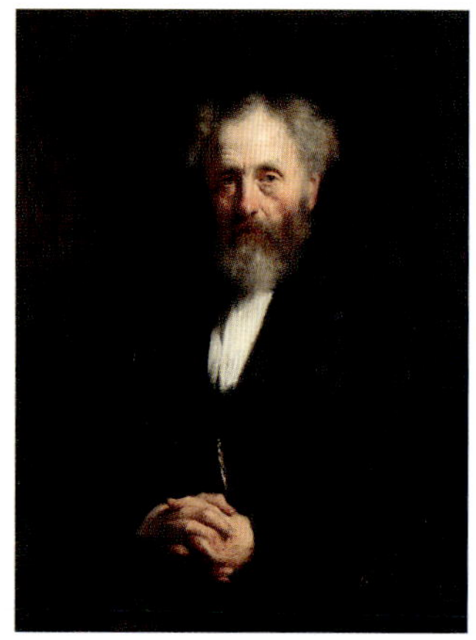

Chalmers, George Paul 1833–1878
John McGavin 1875
oil on canvas 106.7 x 81.3
709

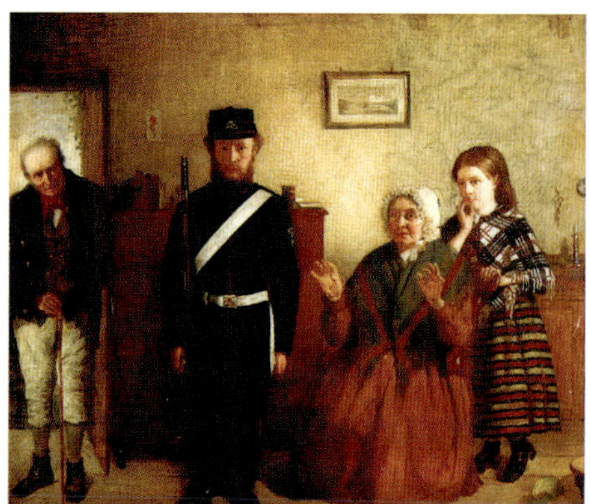

Chalmers, George Paul 1833–1878
A Volunteer Reviewed
oil on canvas 30.5 x 35.5
3327

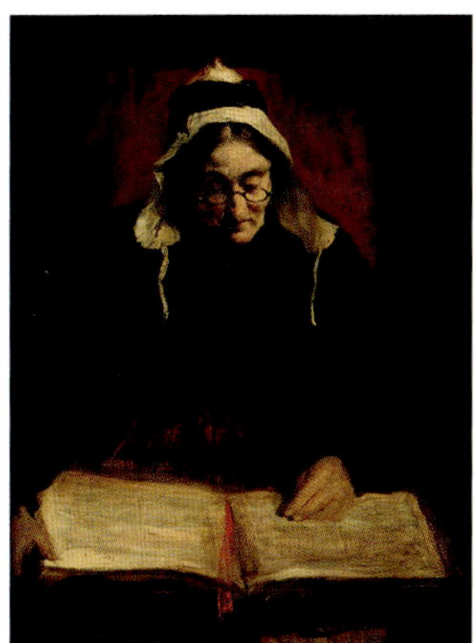

Chalmers, George Paul 1833–1878
Old Woman Reading
oil on wood 56.5 x 41.3
3004

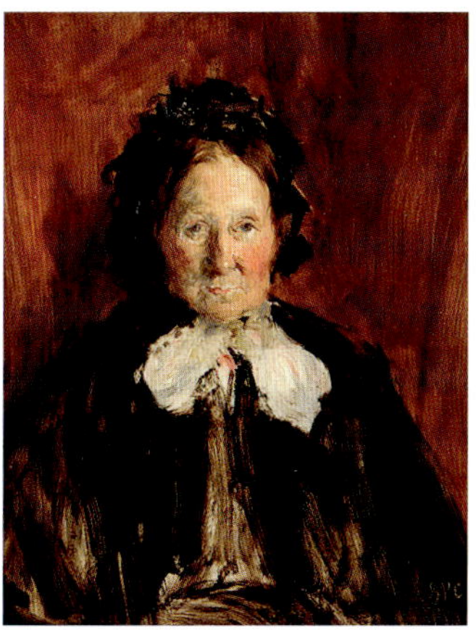

Chalmers, George Paul 1833–1878
The Artist's Mother
oil on canvas 30.5 x 23.5
3175

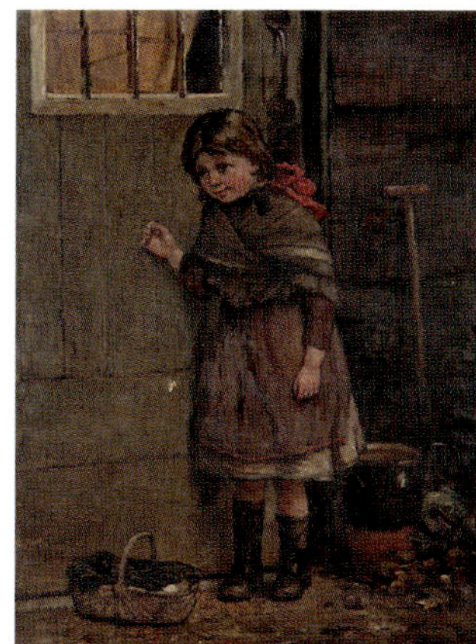

Chalmers, Hector 1849–1943
Genre Scene with a Little Girl 1880/1889
oil on canvas 41.9 x 30.5
NR.161

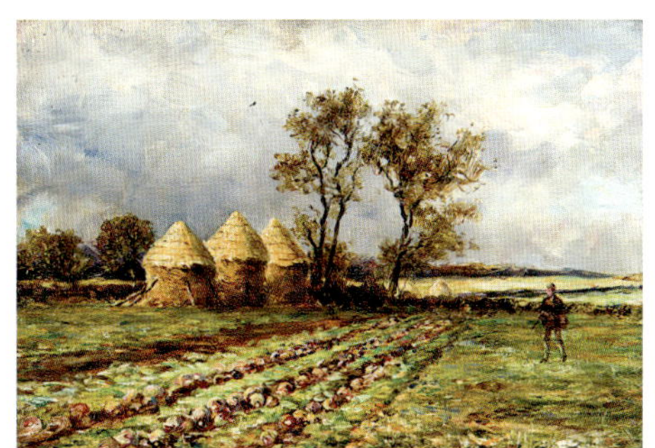

Chalmers, Hector 1849–1943
A Turnip Field
oil on canvas 25.4 x 34.3
848

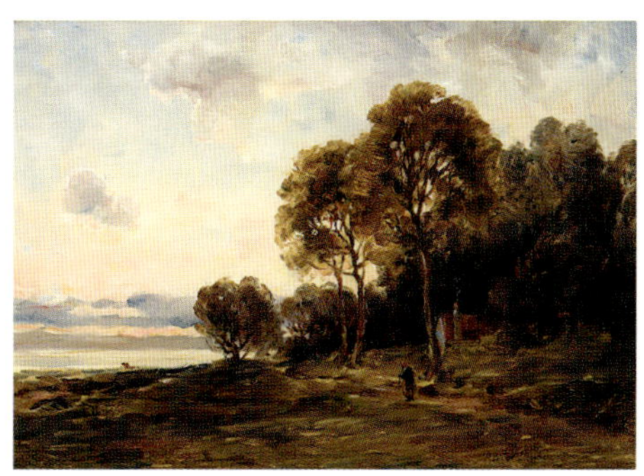

Chalmers, Hector 1849–1943
Landscape
oil on canvas 24.1 x 34.3
876

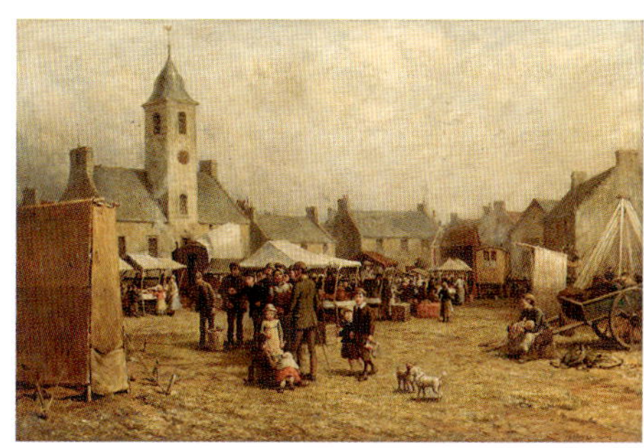

Chalmers, Hector 1849–1943
The Fair
oil on canvas 94 x 139.7
854

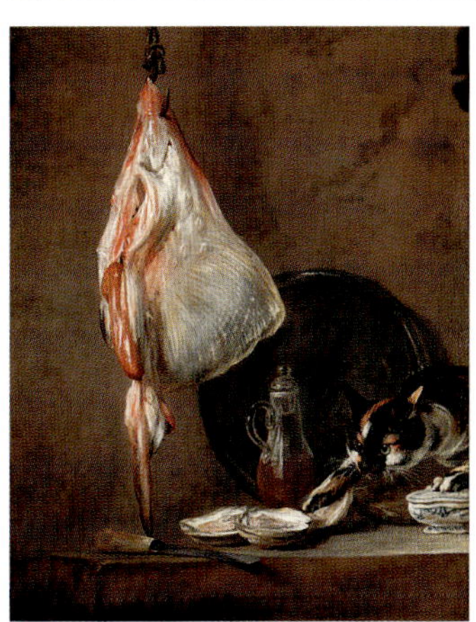

Chardin, Jean-Baptiste Siméon 1699–1779
The Ray c.1728
oil on canvas 81.2 x 64.1
35.57

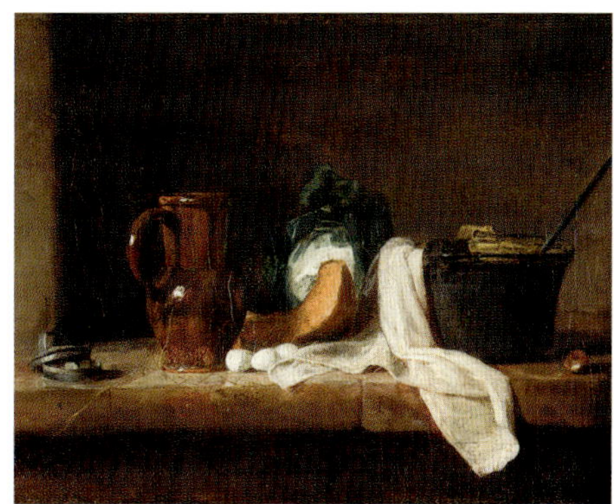

Chardin, Jean-Baptiste Siméon 1699–1779
Still Life c.1728–1730
oil on canvas 27.9 x 36.8
35.54

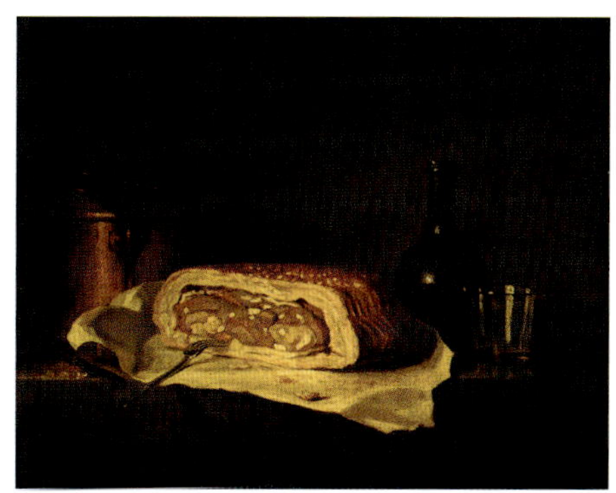

Chardin, Jean-Baptiste Siméon (style of)
1699–1779
Still Life late 18th C/9th C
oil on canvas 71.1 x 90.2
35.55

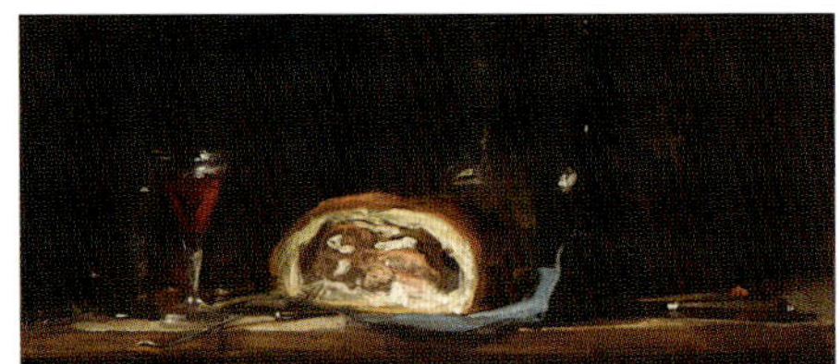

Chardin, Jean-Baptiste Siméon (style of)
1699–1779
Still Life late 18th C/19th C
oil on canvas 33 x 71.2
35.58

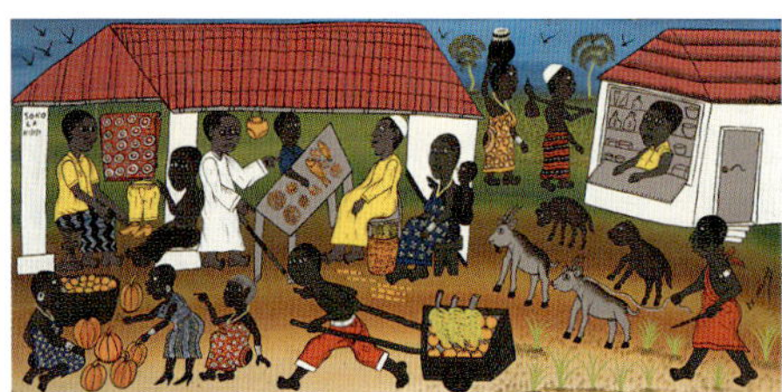

Charinda, Mohamed Wasia b.1947
Street Scene
enamel paint on hardboard 61 x 123.2
A.1989.23.f

Christie, James Elder 1847–1914
Mr Glover 1883
oil on canvas 76.5 x 51.3
TEMP.19292

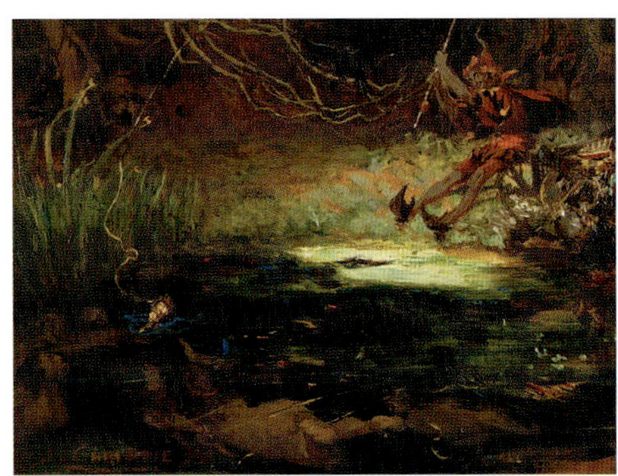

Christie, James Elder 1847–1914
The Red Fisherman 1893
oil on canvas 29.2 x 39.4
1283

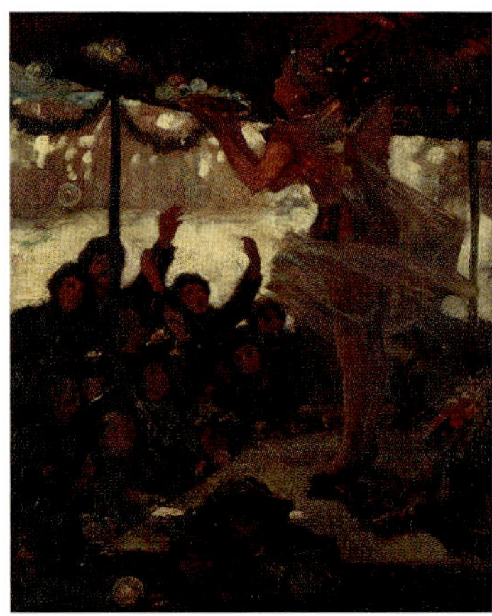

Christie, James Elder 1847–1914
Vanity Fair (study of children's heads)
c.1895
oil on canvas 61 x 50.8
3360

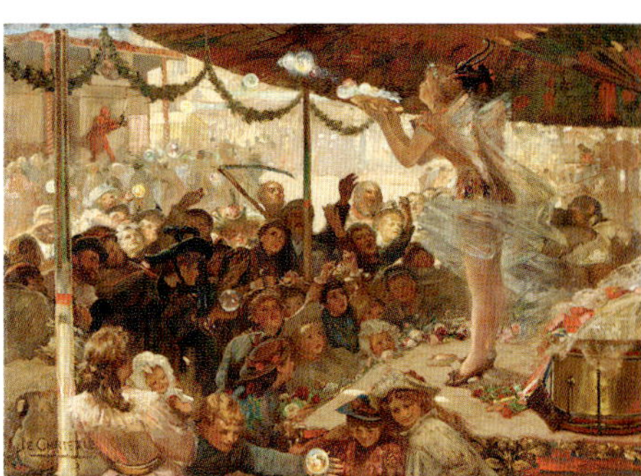

Christie, James Elder 1847–1914
Vanity Fair c.1895
oil on canvas 147.3 x 198.1
723

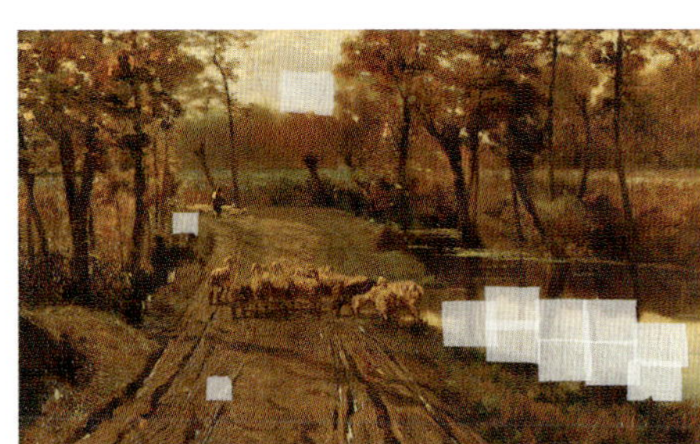

Ciardi, Guglielmo 1842–1917
October in the Venetian Countryside c.1900
oil on canvas 68.3 x 114
1080

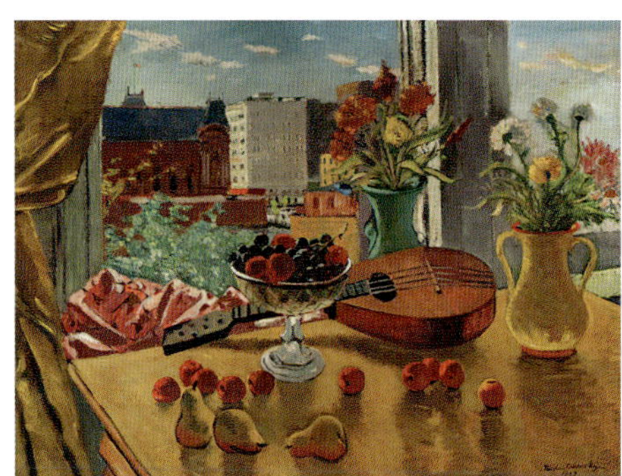

Cikovsky, Nicolai 1894–1987
Mandolin and the Old Corcoran Gallery 1939
oil on canvas 76.2 x 101.6
2482

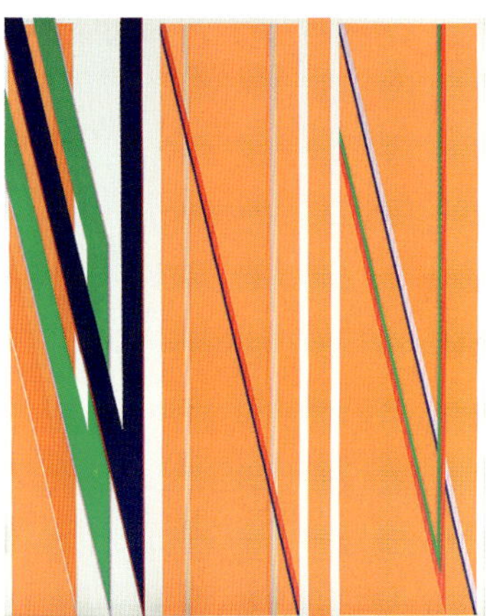

Cina, Colin b.1943
MH9 1970
acrylic on canvas 274.3 x 213.4
3394

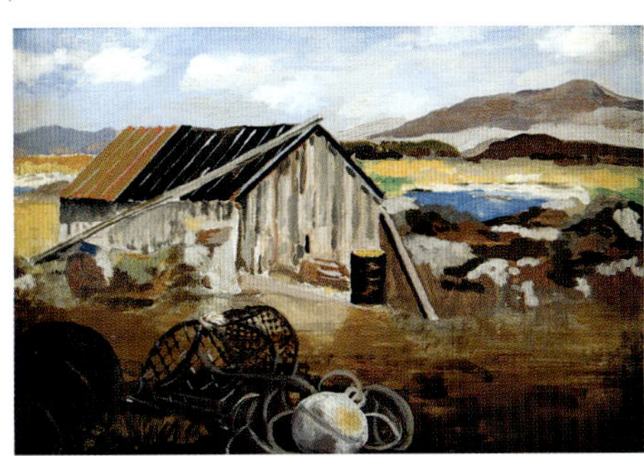

Clark, Georges 1896–1990
Back of Keppoch 1956
oil on hardboard 40.4 x 58.2
3072

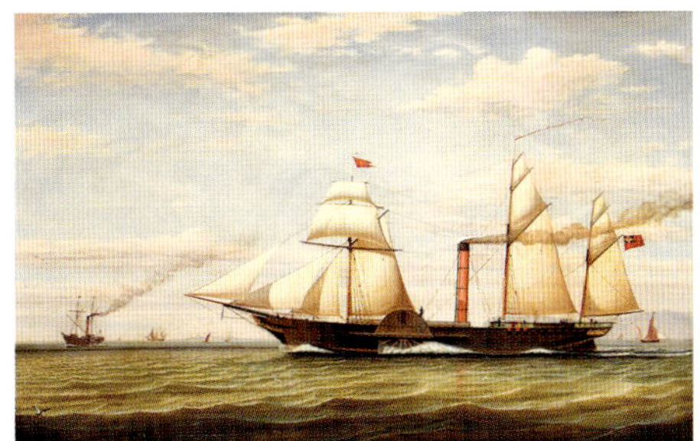

Clark, William 1803–1883
Paddle Steamer 1834
oil on canvas 76.2 x 116.8
TEMP.14937

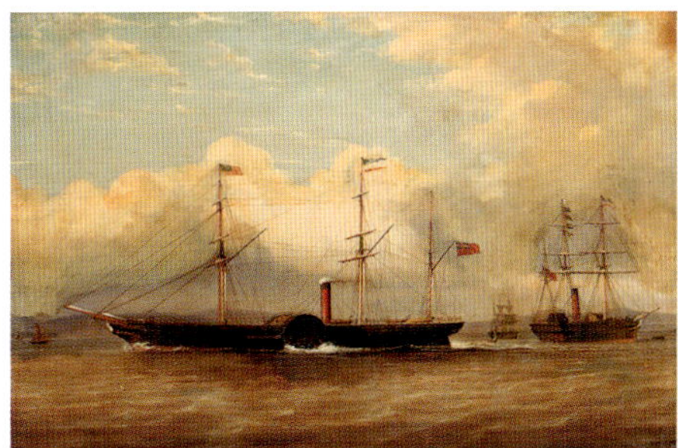

Clark, William 1803–1883
*The British and North American Royal Mail
Steam Ships 'Europa' and 'Niagara' off the
Tail of the Bank* 1848
oil on canvas 92 x 128.5
1877.137.b

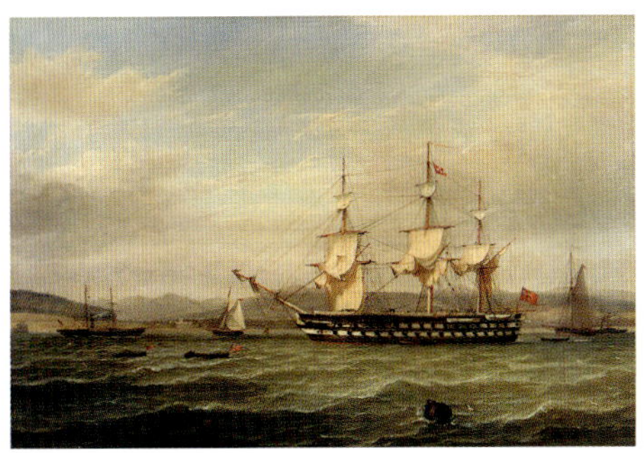

Clark, William 1803–1883
HMS 'Hogue' 1862
oil on canvas 49 x 74.5
T.1960.5

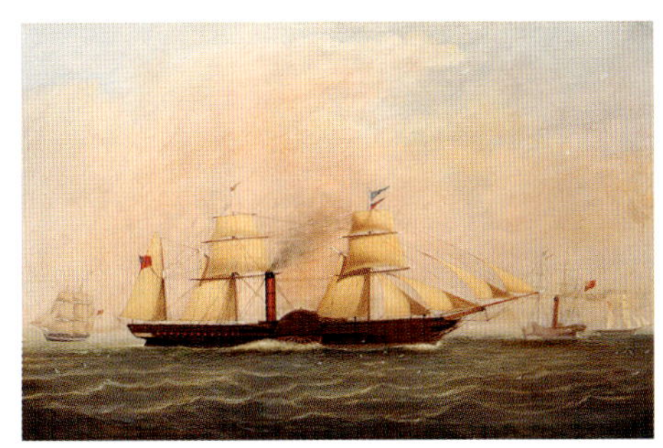

Clark, William (after) 1803–1883
'Britannia': First of the Cunard Line c.1882
oil on board 31.1 x 46.7
1882.39

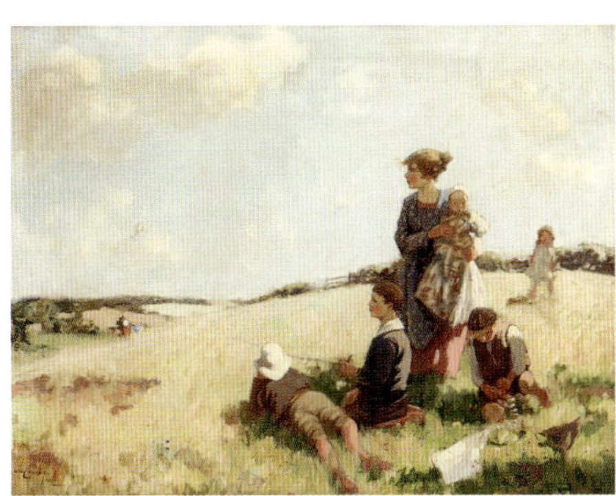

Clarke, William Hanna 1882–1924
Flying the Kite 1918
oil on canvas 76.2 x 101.6
2558

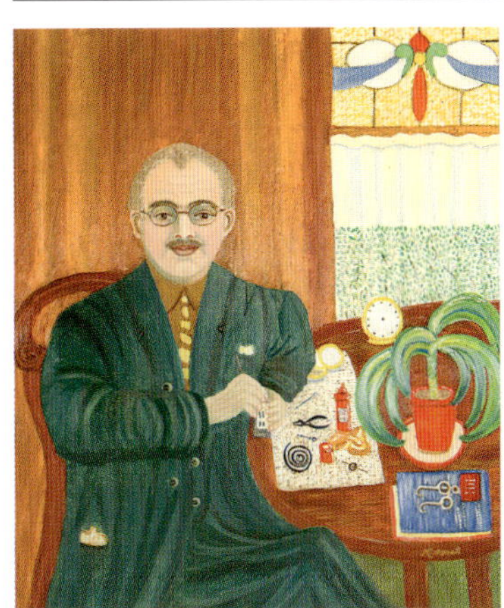

Clarkson, Marjorie b.1898
The Broken Spring 1971
oil on hardboard 60 x 50.2
3582

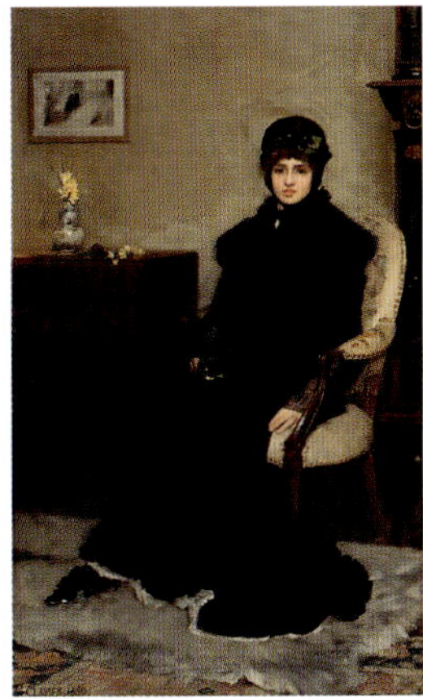

Clausen, George 1852–1944
La pensée 1880
oil on canvas 124.5 x 73.7
728

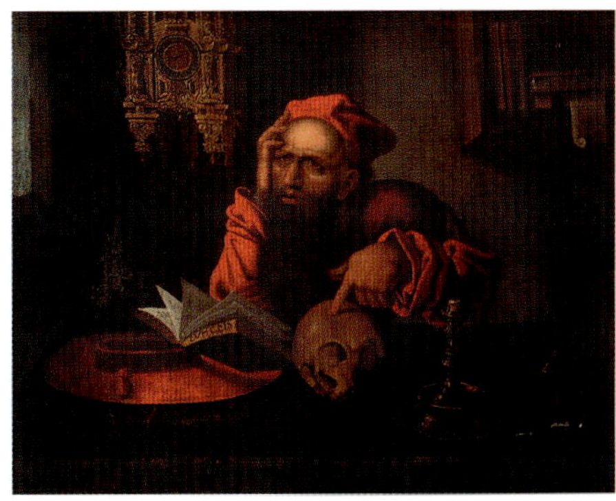

Cleve, Joos van (school of) 1464–1540
Saint Jerome in His Study c.1530–1540
oil on canvas 55.2 x 69.5
PC.31

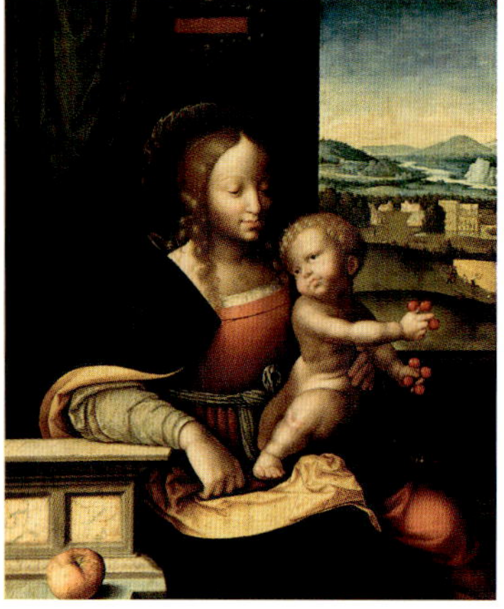

Cleve, Joos van (studio of) 1464–1540
Virgin and Child 1529
oil on panel 71.1 x 55.9
35.303

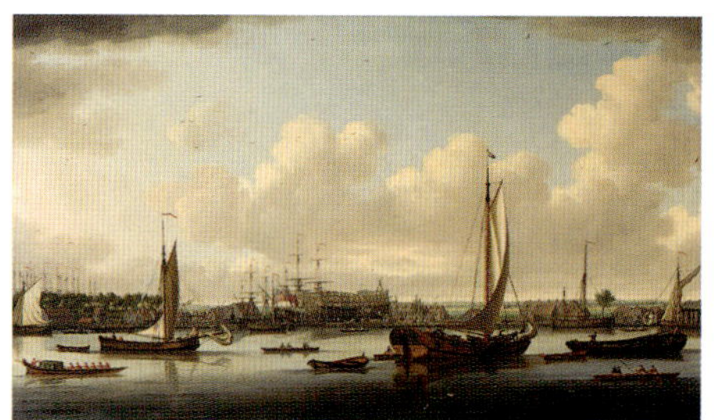

Cleveley, John 1712–1777
A Shipyard on the Thames 1762
oil on canvas 55.6 x 95.3
3282

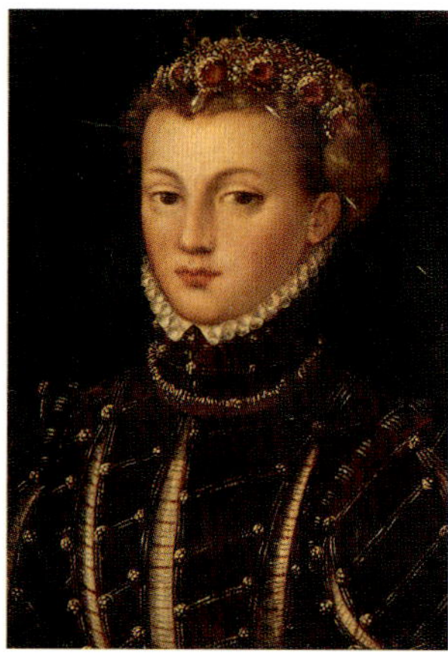

Clouet, François (style of) 1515–1572
Portrait of a Lady c.1560–1575
oil on panel 26.7 x 19.7
152

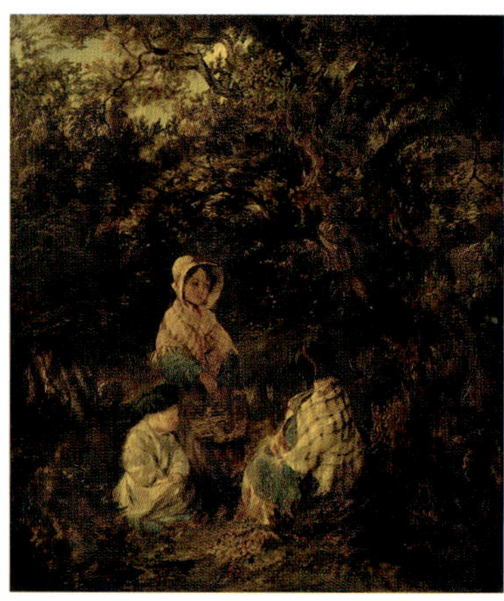

Cobbett, Edward John 1815–1899
Forest Scene
oil on canvas 43.2 x 38.1
423

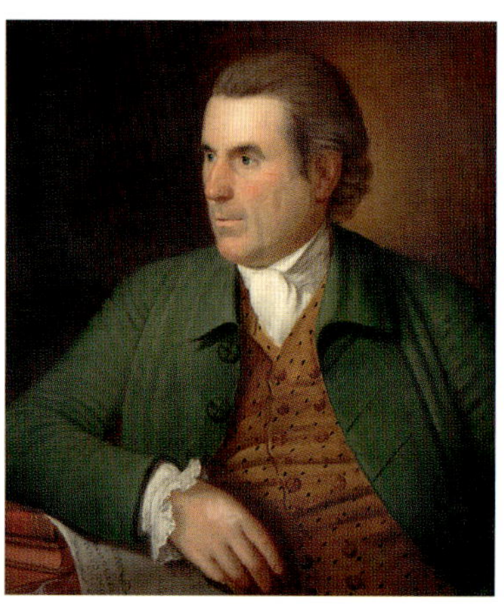

Cochran, William 1738–1785
Portrait of a Man (formerly said to be James Watt) c.1780
oil on canvas 72.4 x 63.5
2295

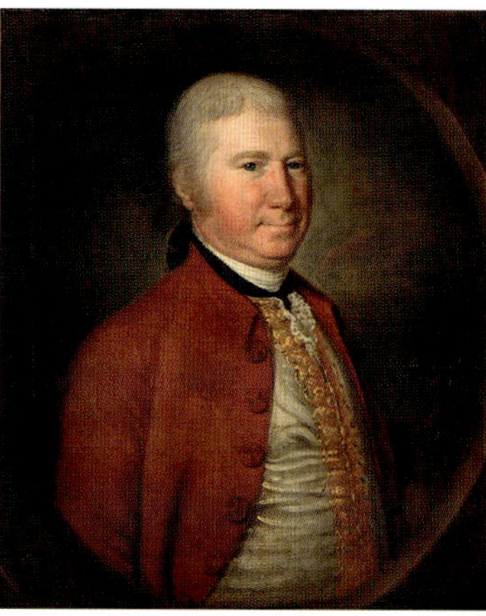

Cochran, William 1738–1785
Sir James Dunbar of Mochrum (d.1782)
oil on canvas 76.2 x 63.5
3001

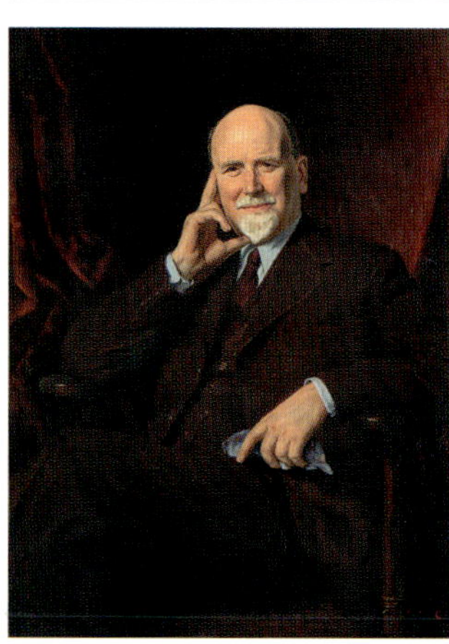

Codner, Maurice Frederick 1888–1958
Sir Hugh Roberton (1874–1952) 1938
oil on canvas 101.6 x 76.2
2573

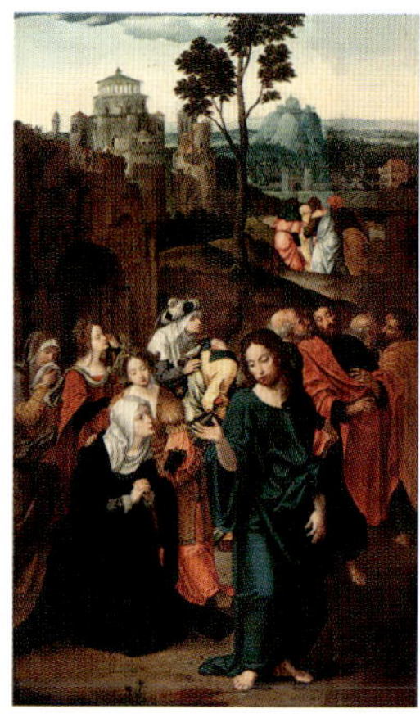

Coecke van Aelst, Pieter the elder (attributed to) 1502–1550
Christ Taking Leave of His Mother c.1530–1535
oil on panel 84.8 x 49.5
207

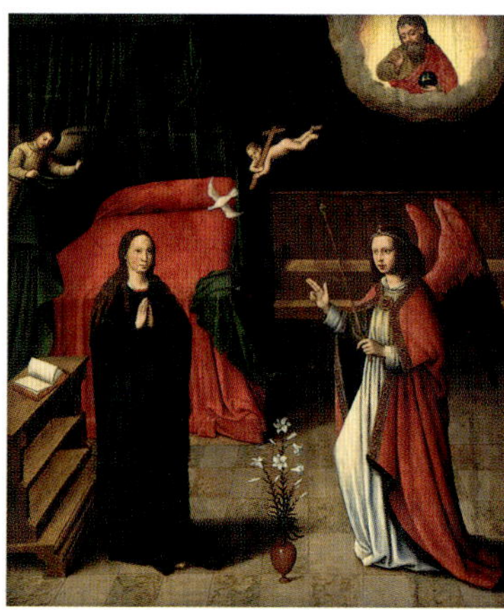

Coffermans, Marcellus 1520/1530–c.1578
The Annunciation c.1549–1578
oil on panel 69.9 x 57.8
35.296

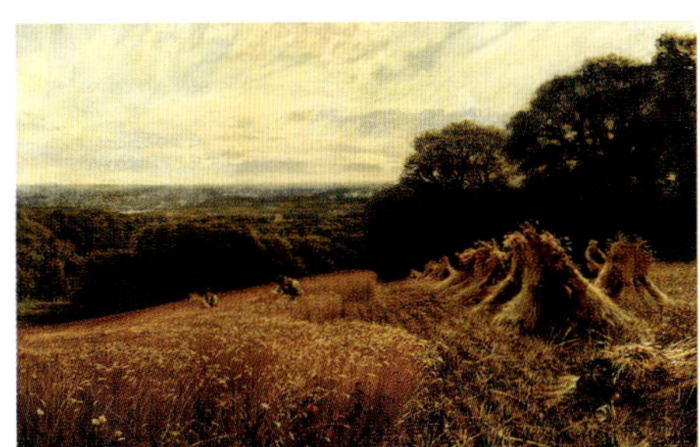

Cole, George Vicat 1833–1893
A Harvest Field 1890
oil on canvas 66 x 101.6
1875

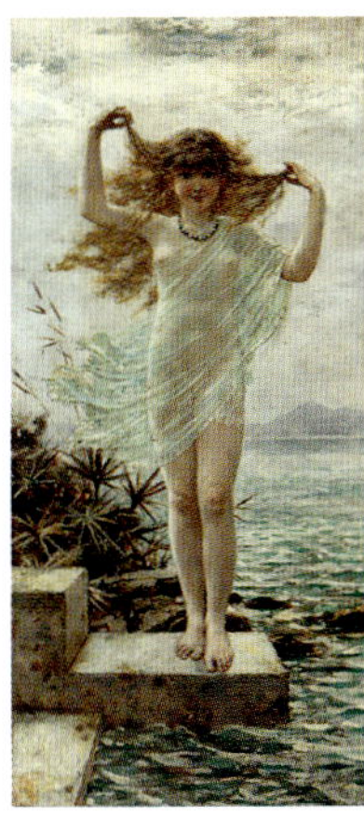

Coleman, William Stephen 1829–1904
A Naiad
oil on canvas 72 x 33
844

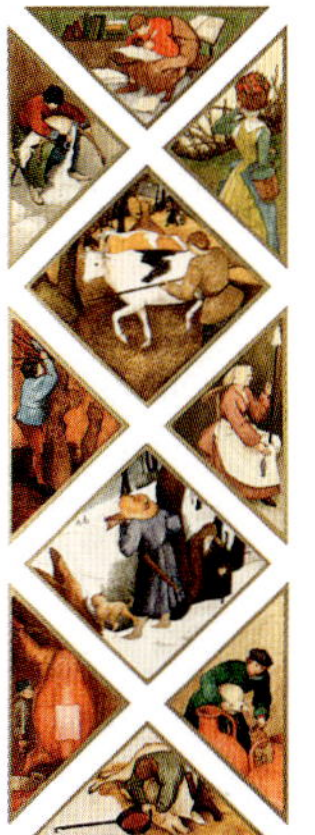

Colley, Virginia
Peasants at Work 1980s
acrylic on panel 182 x 61.9
TEMP.15786

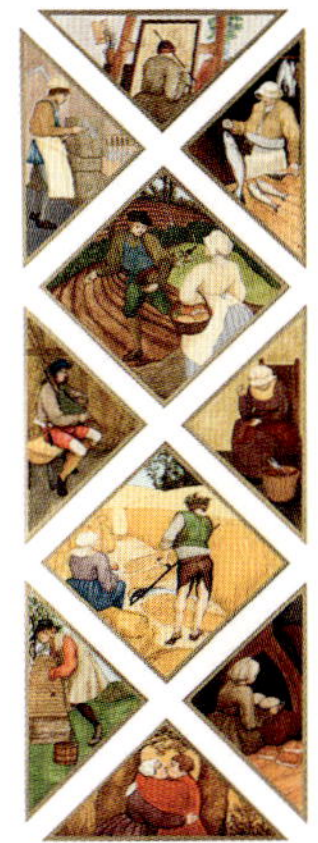

Colley, Virginia
Peasants at Work 1980s
acrylic on panel 182 x 61.9
TEMP.15787

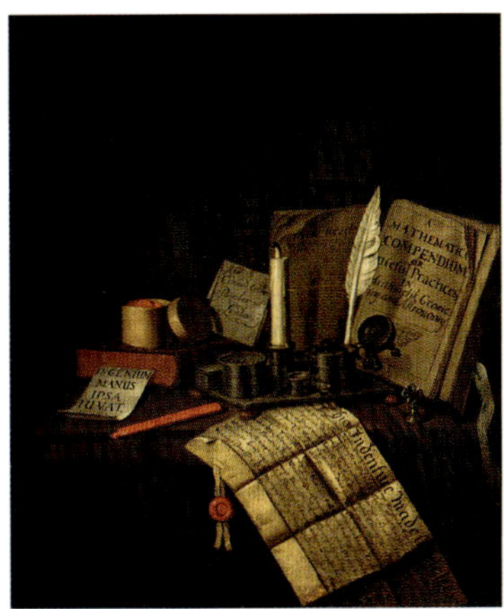

Collier, Edwaert c.1640–c.1707
Still Life c.1693–1700
oil on canvas 76.2 x 63.5
35.59

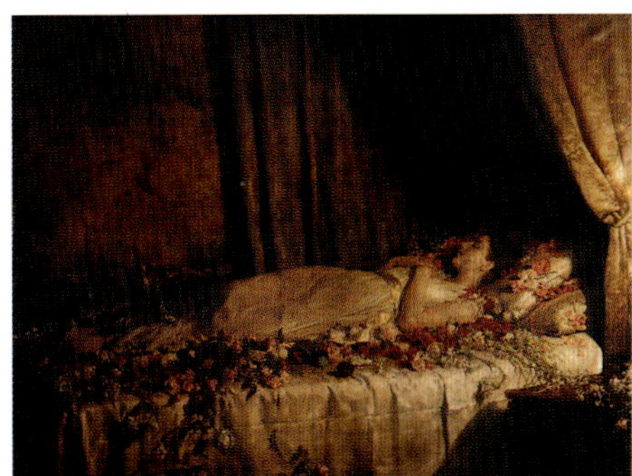

Collier, John 1850–1934
The Death of Albine 1898
oil on canvas 137.2 x 182.9
1501

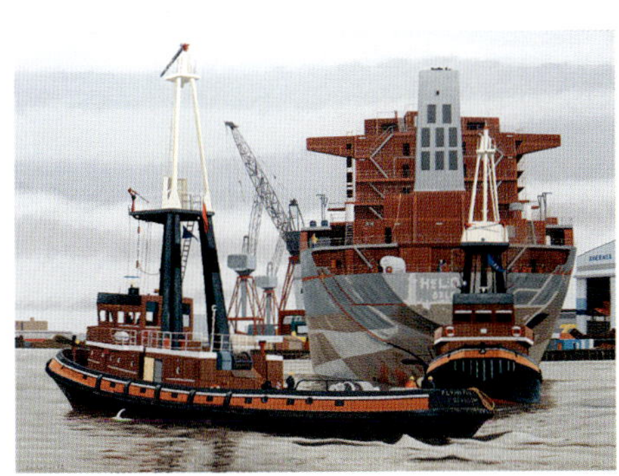

Collins, Jim b.1947
Guardians of Helios
oil on canvas 75.4 x 100.7
SP.2010.1

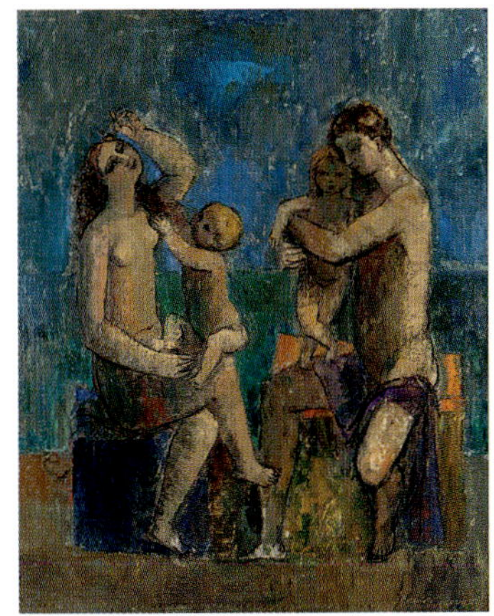

Collins, Peter b.1935
Family Group 1963
oil on canvas 91.4 x 71.1
3198

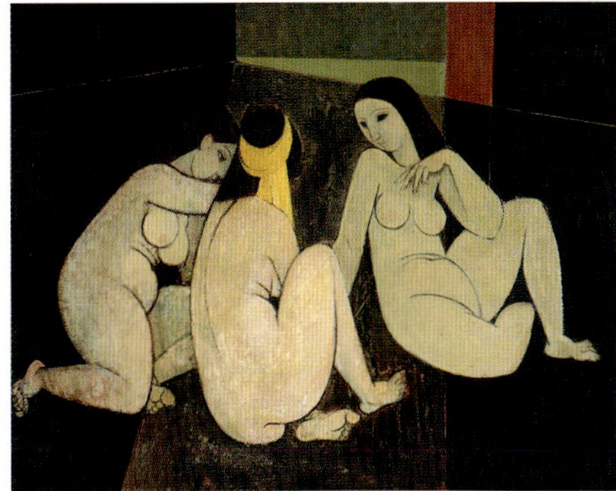

Collins, Peter b.1935
The Yellow Bandana 1964
oil on canvas 101.3 x 126.7
3211

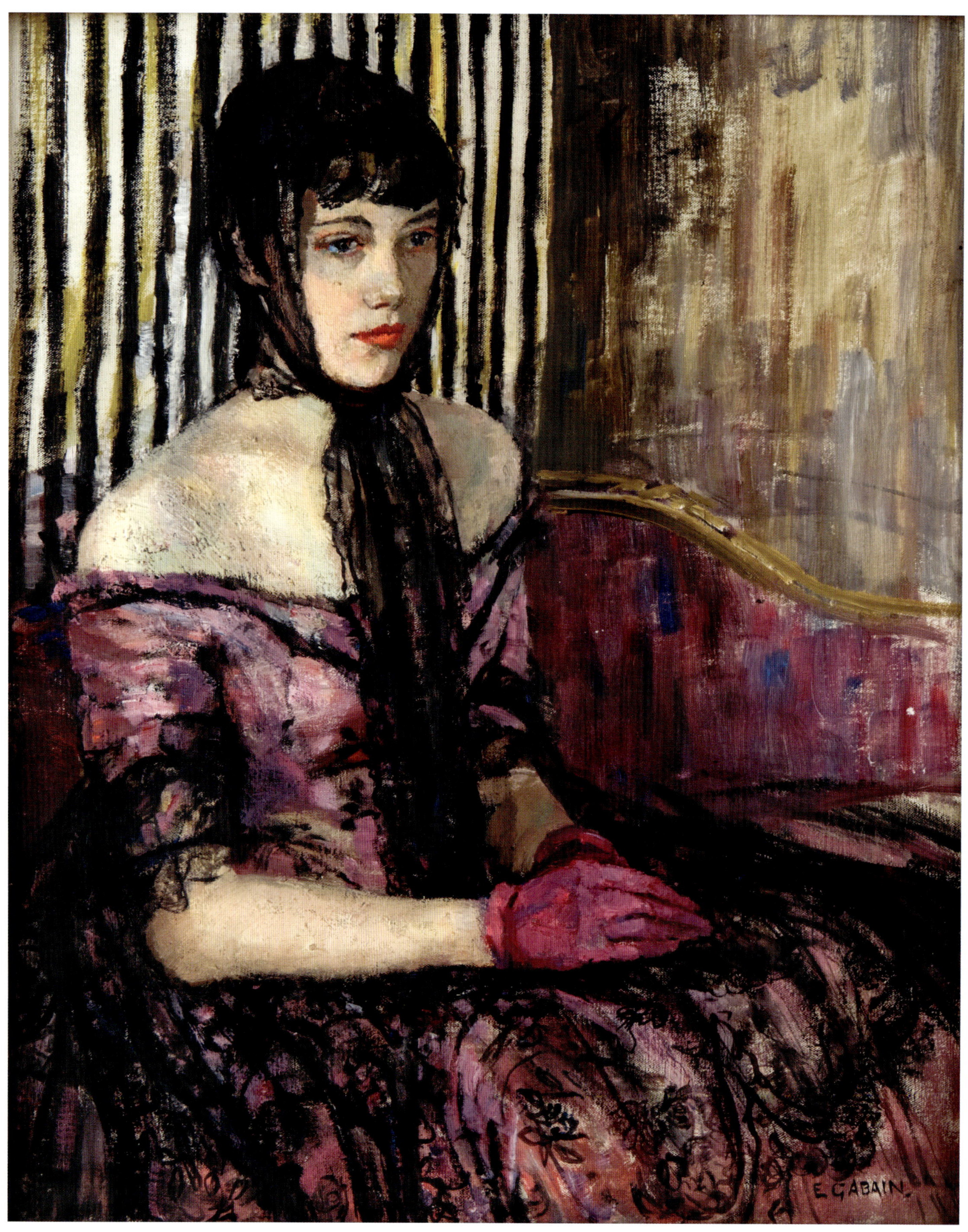
E GABAIN.

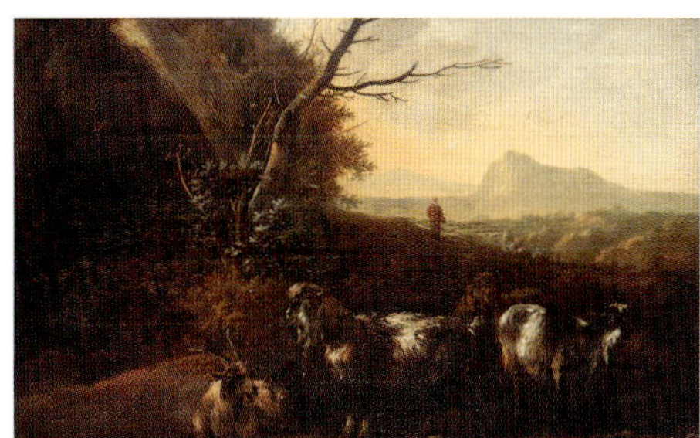

Colonia, Adam (attributed to) 1634–1685
A Landscape with Goats c.1660–1670
oil on panel 31.7 x 48.7
346

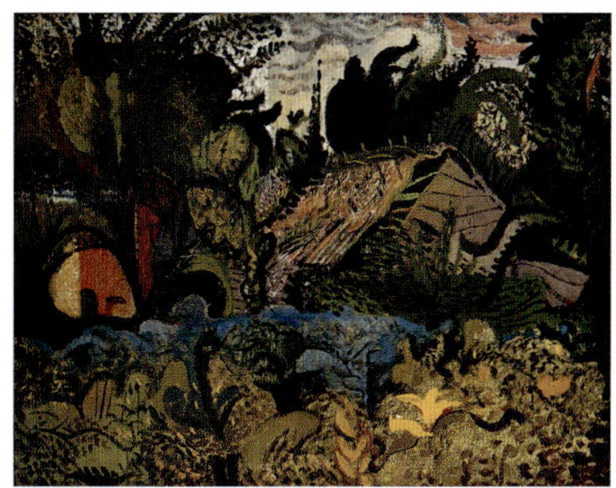

Colquhoun, Robert 1914–1962
Marrowfield, Worcestershire 1941
oil on canvas 35.6 x 45.7
2461

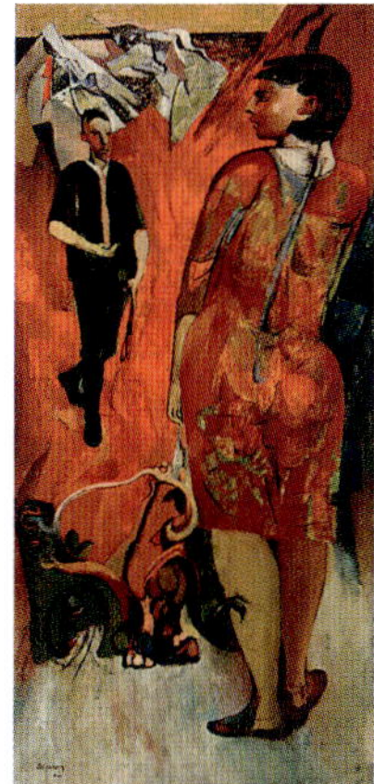

Colquhoun, Robert 1914–1962
Encounter 1942
oil on canvas 97.5 x 47
3339

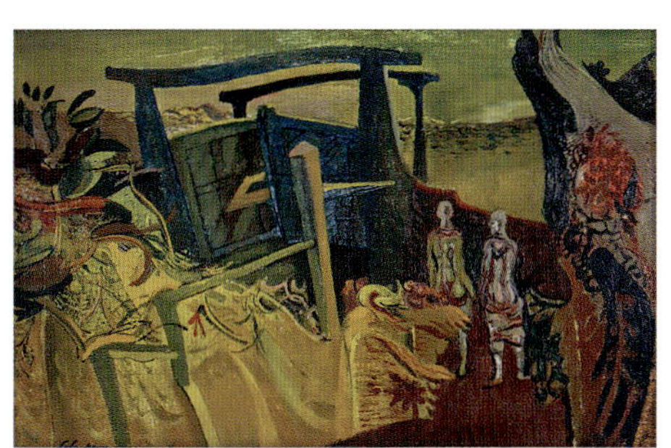

Colquhoun, Robert 1914–1962
The Lock Gate 1942
oil on canvas 39 x 58.4
2936

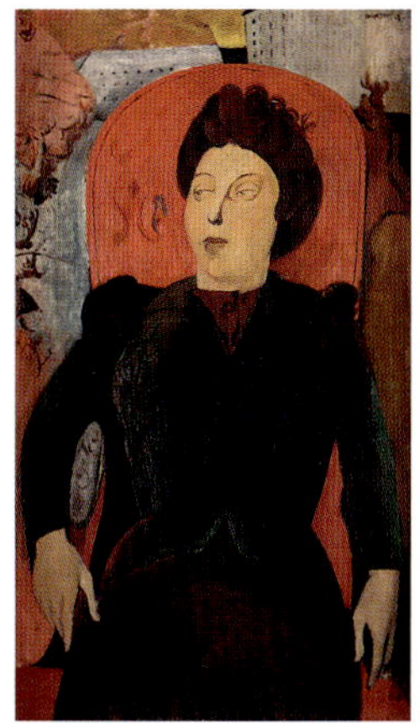

Colquhoun, Robert 1914–1962
Thea Neu 1943
oil on canvas 91.3 x 50.8
3089

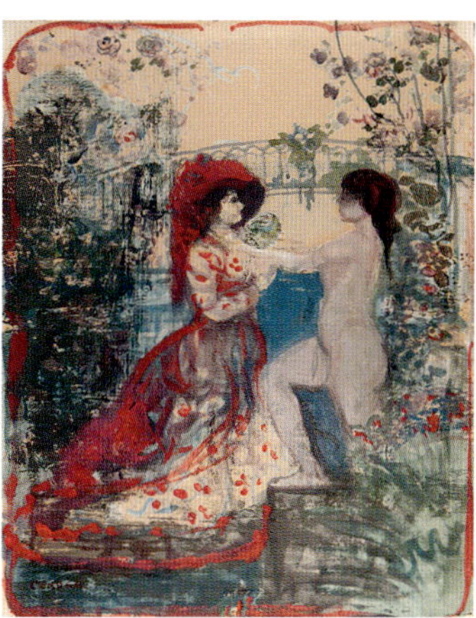

Conder, Charles 1868–1909
The Bridge
oil on board 55.9 x 44.1
2990

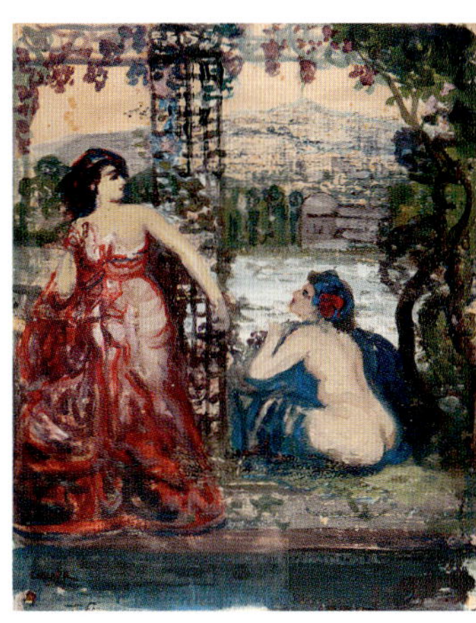

Conder, Charles 1868–1909
The Trellis
oil on board 55.9 x 44.1
2989

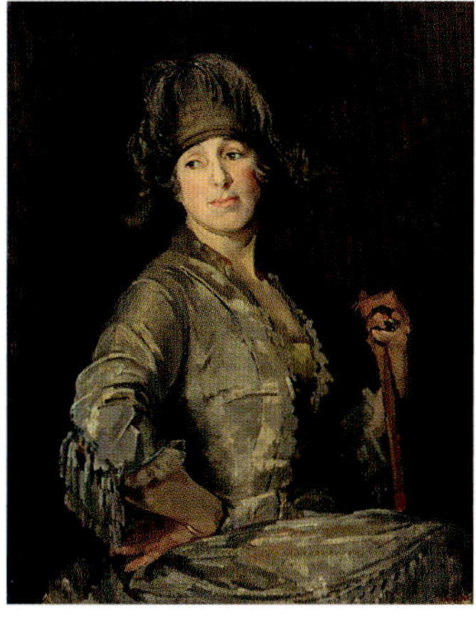

Connard, Philip 1875–1958
Portrait of a Lady in Grey (Mrs Benge)
oil on canvas 91.4 x 71.1
2286

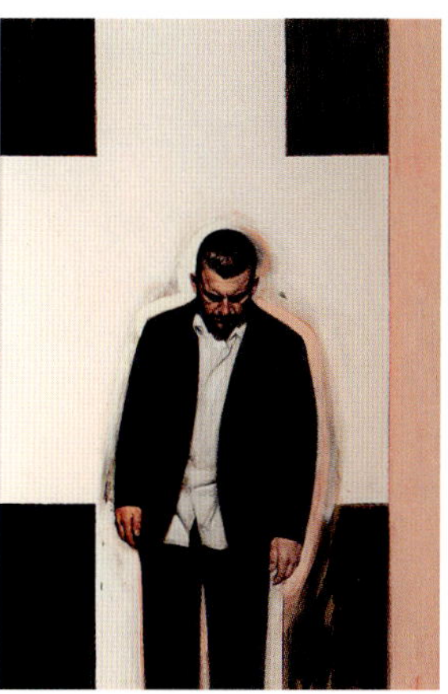

Conroy, Stephen b.1964
Self Portrait 1 2005
oil on canvas 183 x 122
3652

Facing page: Gabain, Ethel Leontine, 1883–1950, *Stripes and Lace*, (p. 146)

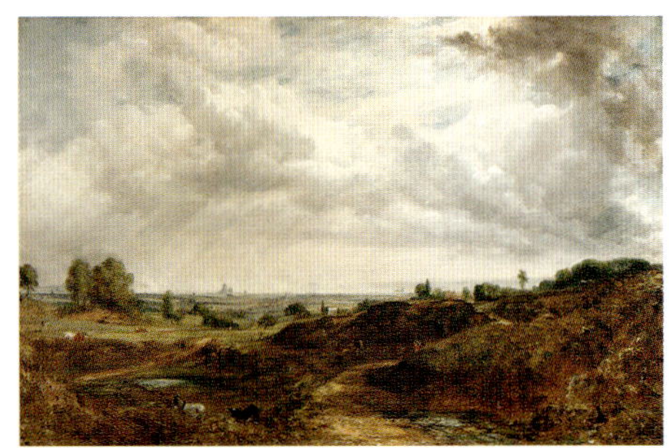

Constable, John 1776–1837
Hampstead Heath c.1830
oil on canvas 63.5 x 96.5
734

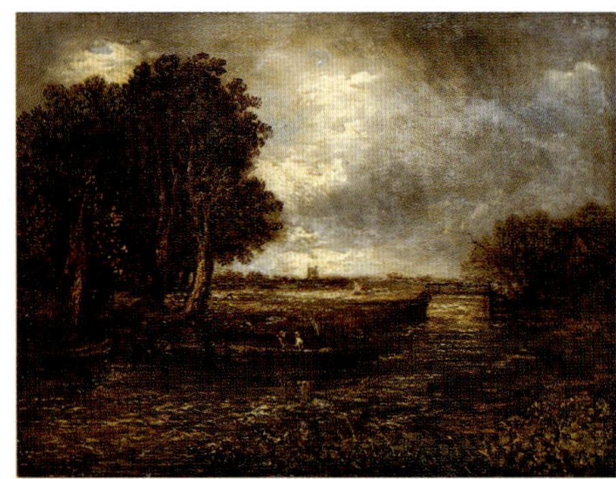

Constable, John (imitator of) 1776–1837
Landscape with Barges on a River
oil on canvas 71.1 x 91.4
NR.91

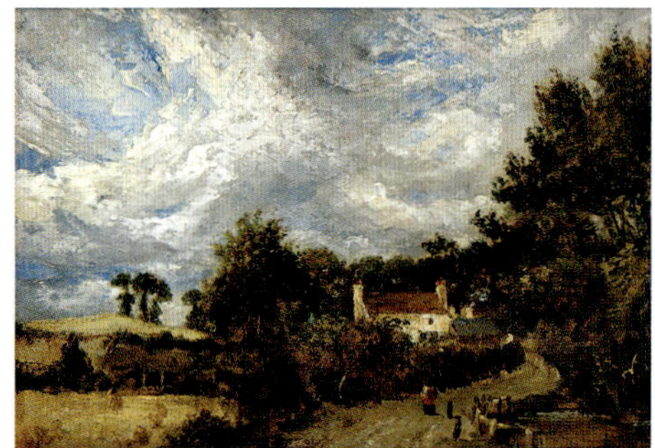

Constable, John (style of) 1776–1837
House by the Road
oil on panel 22.9 x 34.3
1142

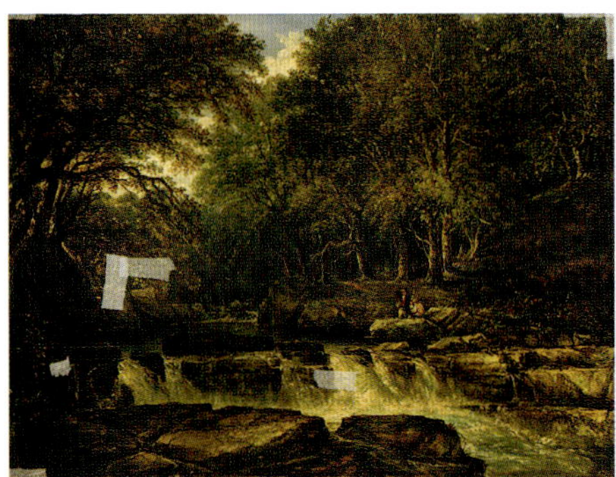

Constable, John (style of) 1776–1837
On the Wye, Herefordshire
oil on canvas 71.1 x 91.4
2626

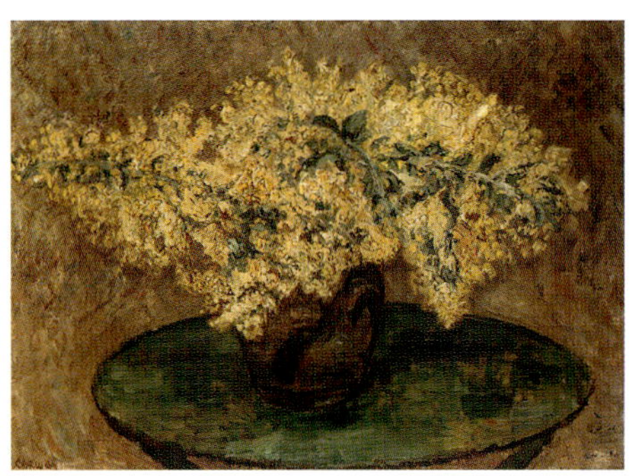

Conway, F. J. active 20th C
Mimosa
oil on canvas 46.4 x 61
2863

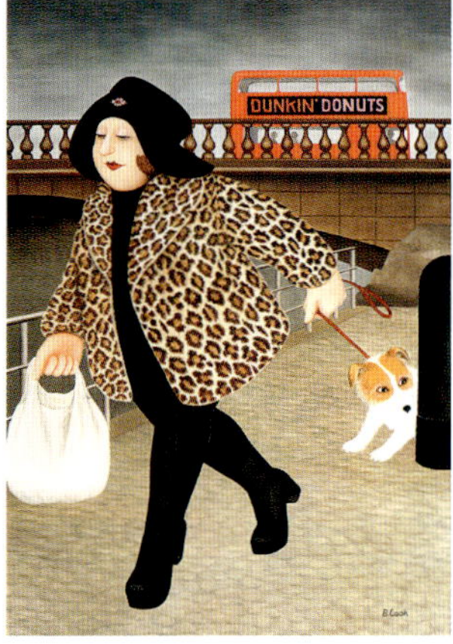

Cook, Beryl 1926–2008
By the Clyde 1992
oil on board 87.9 x 59.6
3512

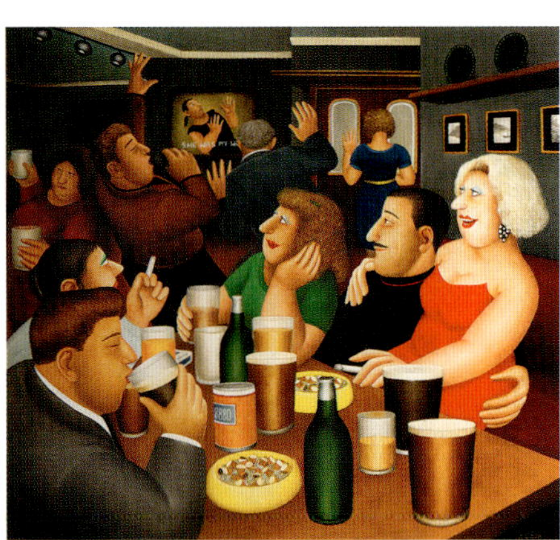

Cook, Beryl 1926–2008
Karaoke 1992
oil on board 81.5 x 88.9
3511

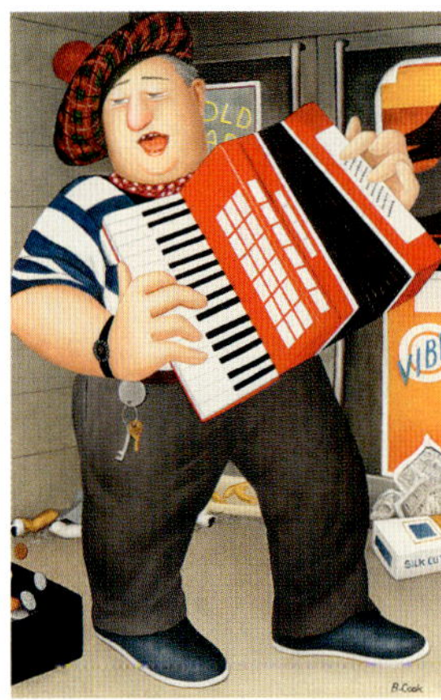

Cook, Beryl 1926–2008
The Accordion Player 1992
oil on board 55 x 36.2
3513

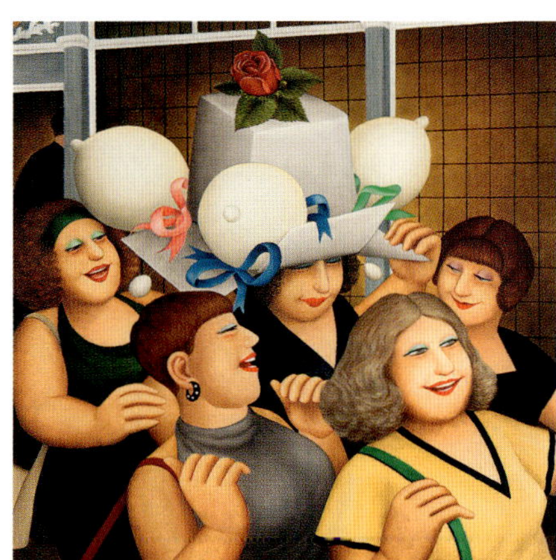

Cook, Beryl 1926–2008
Hen Party II 1995
oil on board 62.2 x 62.2
3598

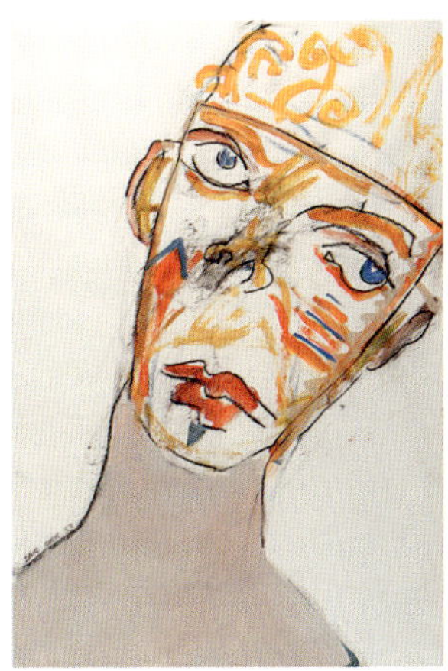

Cook, David b.1957
Mask 1983
acrylic & chalk on paper 76 x 50.8
PR.1994.20

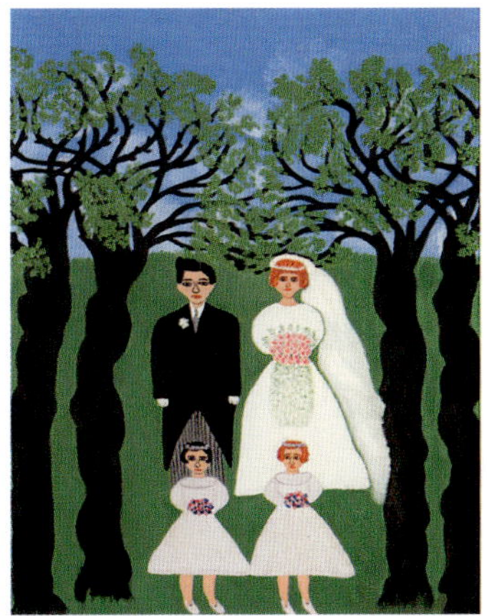

Cooper, Gladys 1899–1975
The Bridal Group 1959
oil on hardboard 76.2 x 61
3577

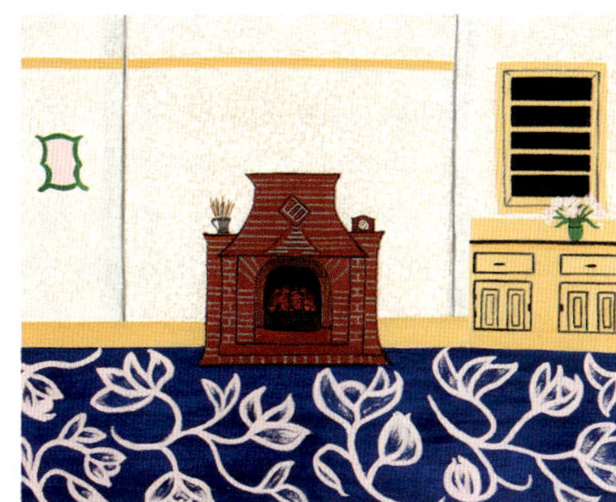

Cooper, Gladys 1899–1975
The New Carpet 1961
oil on hardboard 60.3 x 75.7
3578

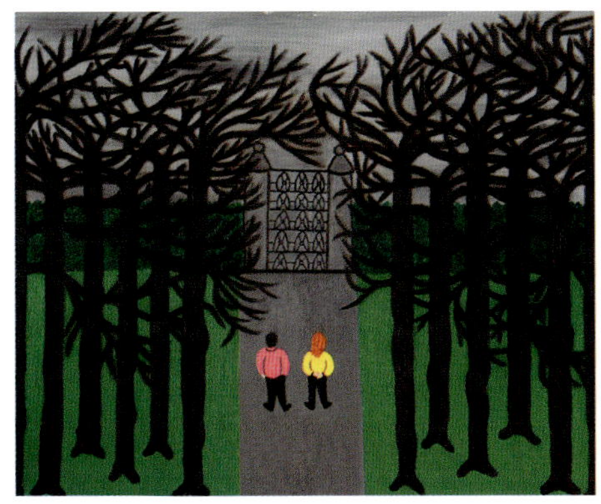

Cooper, Gladys 1899–1975
The Gate 1964
oil on hardboard 61 x 76.2
3576

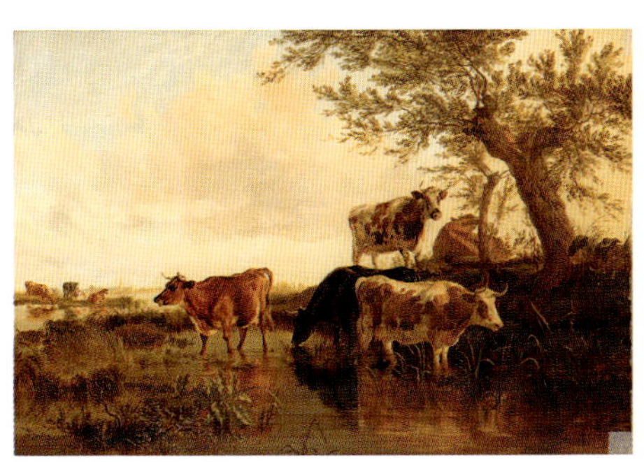

Cooper, Thomas Sidney 1803–1902
Landscape with Cattle 1852
oil on canvas 76.2 x 106.7
1167

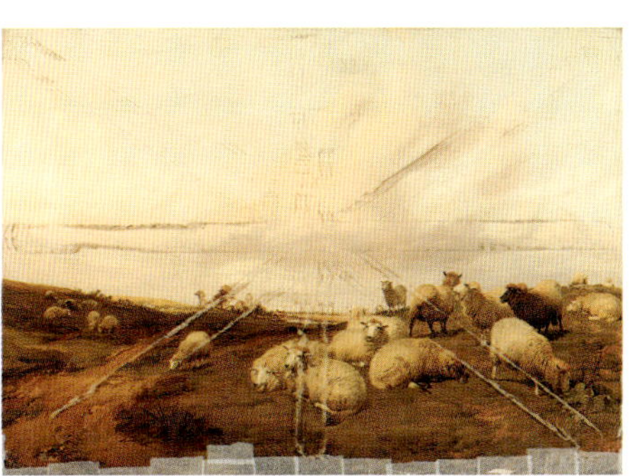

Cooper, Thomas Sidney 1803–1902
Landscape with Sheep 1864
oil on canvas 76.2 x 106.7
1168

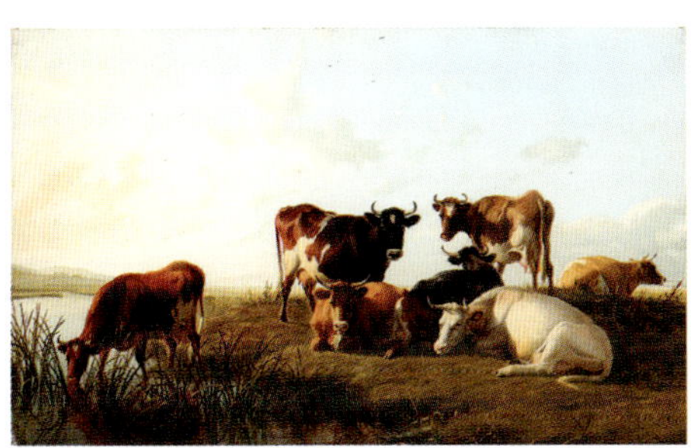

Cooper, Thomas Sidney 1803–1902
Canterbury Meadows 1879
oil on wood 32.4 x 53.3
985

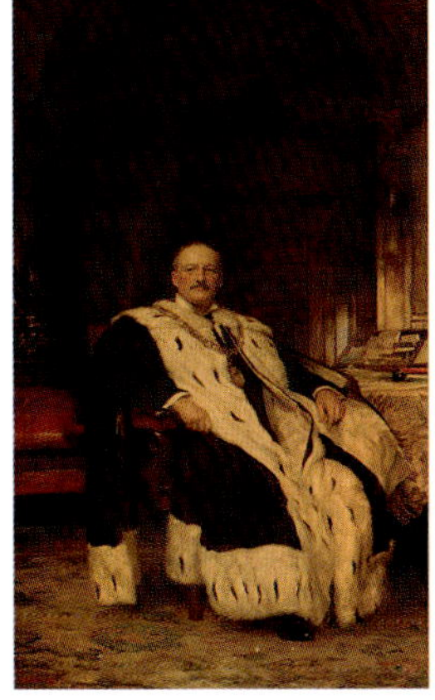

Cope, Arthur Stockdale 1857–1940
Sir John Ure Primrose (1847–1924), Lord Provost of Glasgow (1902–1905) 1906
oil on canvas 243.8 x 127
1185

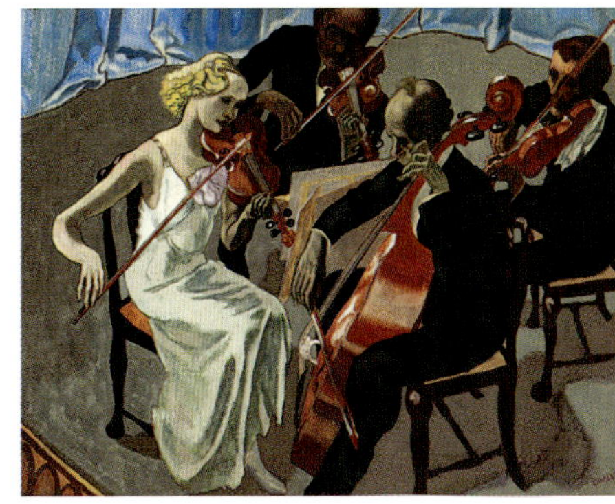

Copley, John 1875–1950
String Quartet c.1943
oil on canvas 96.5 x 121.9
2355

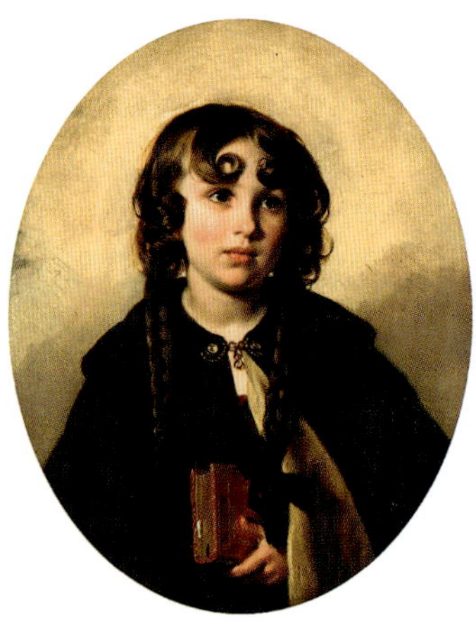

Corbet, Philip 1801–1877
Going to Chapel: Edith Corbet (1833–1904)
1847
oil on panel 43.2 x 34.9
440

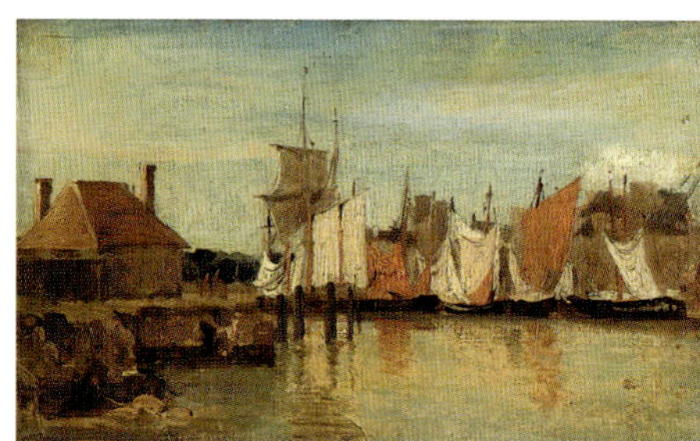

Corot, Jean-Baptiste-Camille 1796–1875
Shipping c.1830–1840
oil on canvas 17.1 x 27.3
35.63

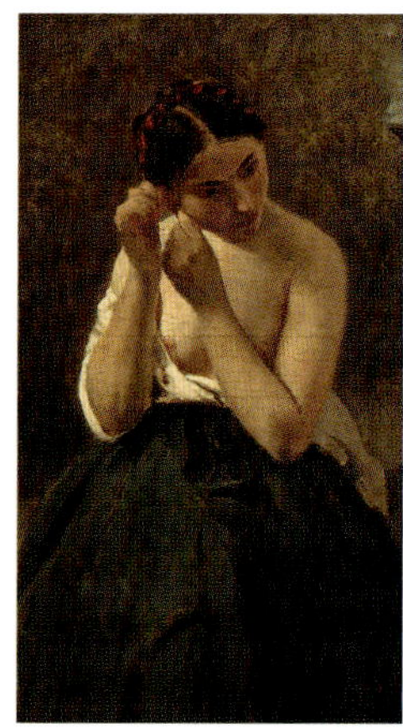

Corot, Jean-Baptiste-Camille 1796–1875
Portrait of a Woman c.1850–1855
oil on canvas 44.5 x 26
35.62

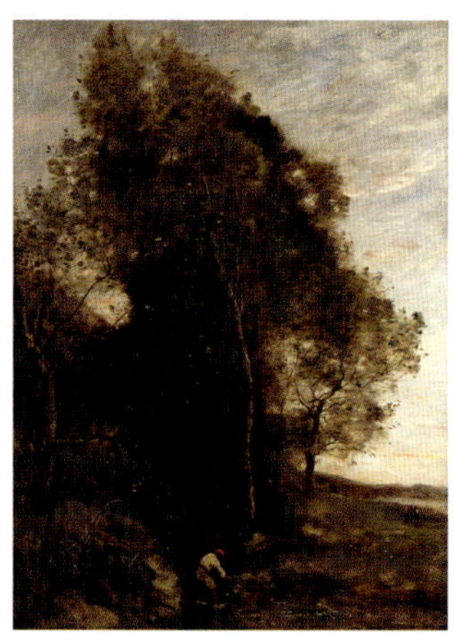

Corot, Jean-Baptiste-Camille 1796–1875
The Crayfisher c.1865–1870
oil on canvas 103.5 x 76.5
1120

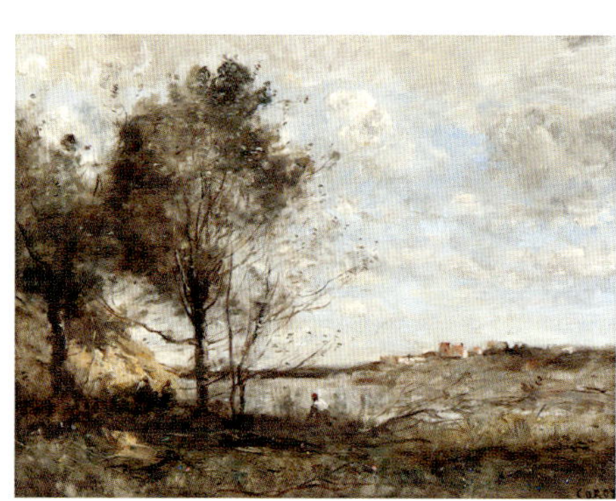

Corot, Jean-Baptiste-Camille 1796–1875
The Woodcutter c.1865–1870
oil on canvas 49.8 x 64.8
1115

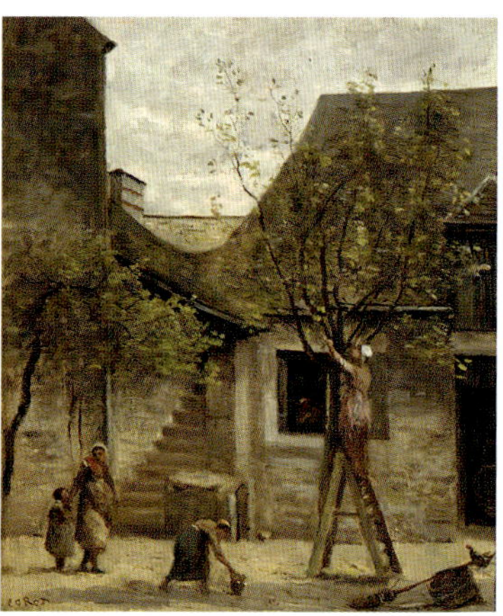

Corot, Jean-Baptiste-Camille 1796–1875
Peasants' Houses, Fontainebleau c.1865–1872
oil on canvas 55.9 x 46.3
35.61

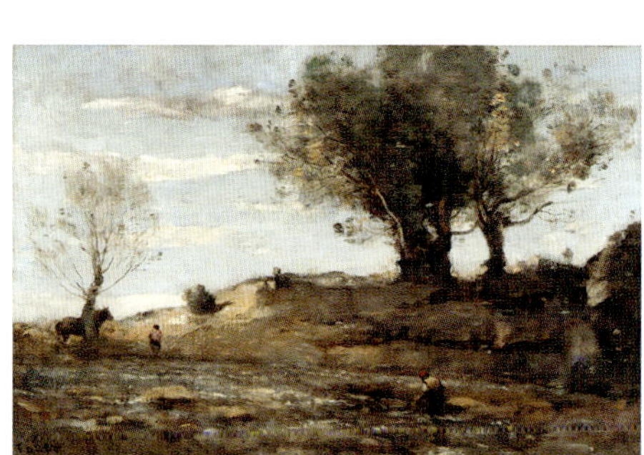

Corot, Jean-Baptiste-Camille 1796–1875
The Riverbank c.1870
oil on canvas 40 x 60.1
2383

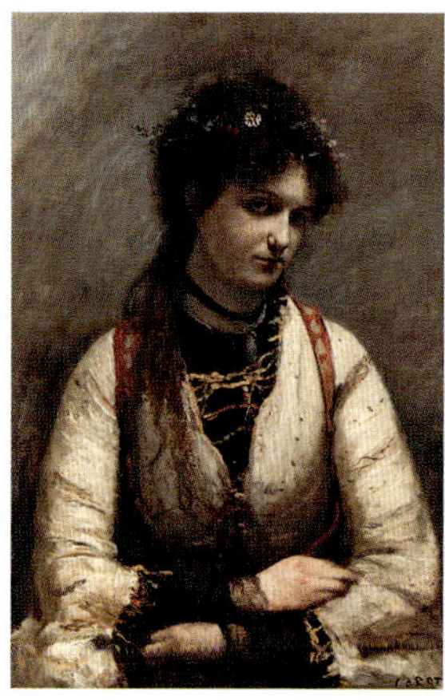

Corot, Jean-Baptiste-Camille 1796–1875
Mademoiselle de Foudras 1872
oil on canvas 89 x 59.7
2858

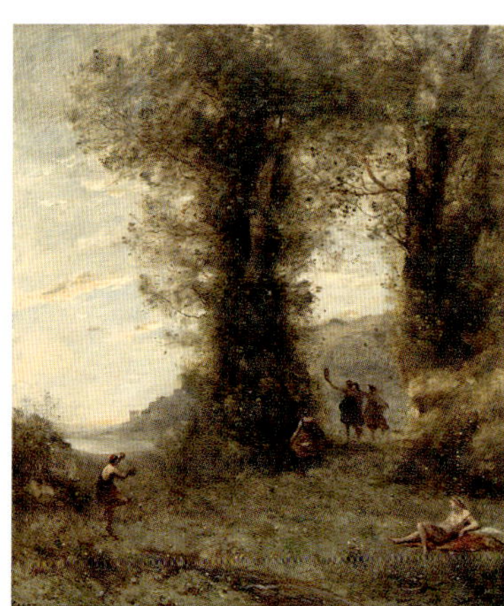

Corot, Jean-Baptiste-Camille 1796–1875
Pastorale 1873
oil on canvas 172.7 x 144.4
732

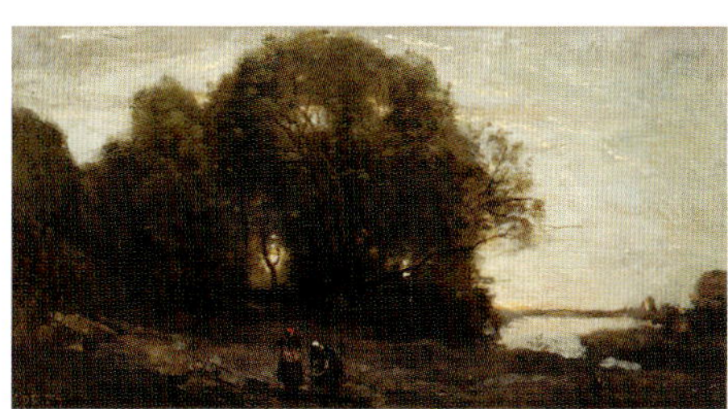

Corot, Jean-Baptiste-Camille (attributed to)
1796–1875
Evening
oil on canvas 33 x 57.7
1112

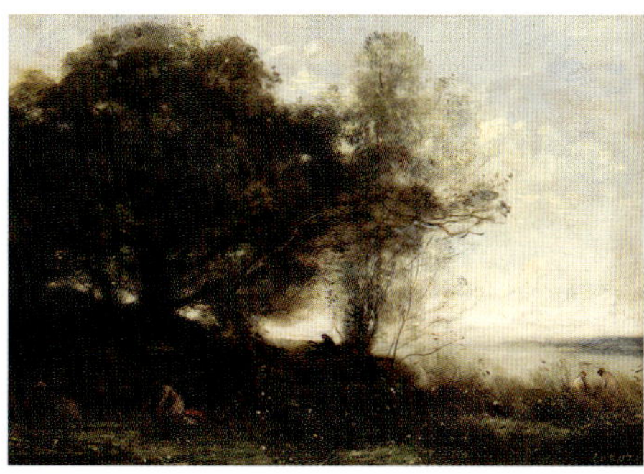

Corot, Jean-Baptiste-Camille (attributed to)
1796–1875
The Bathers
oil on canvas 32.5 x 46.1
2135

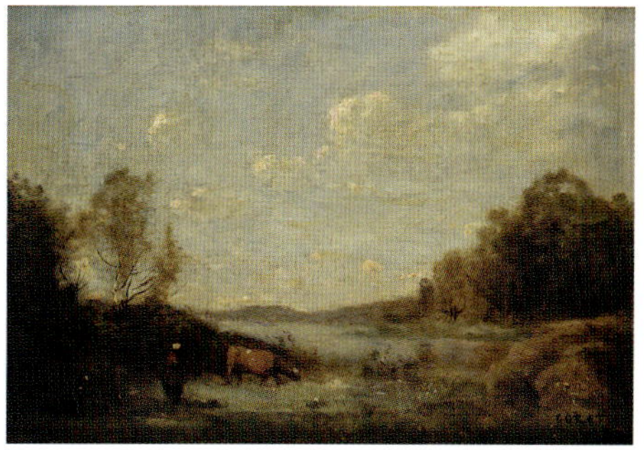

Corot, Jean-Baptiste-Camille (attributed to)
1796–1875
The Lake
oil on canvas 24.5 x 35.5
1148

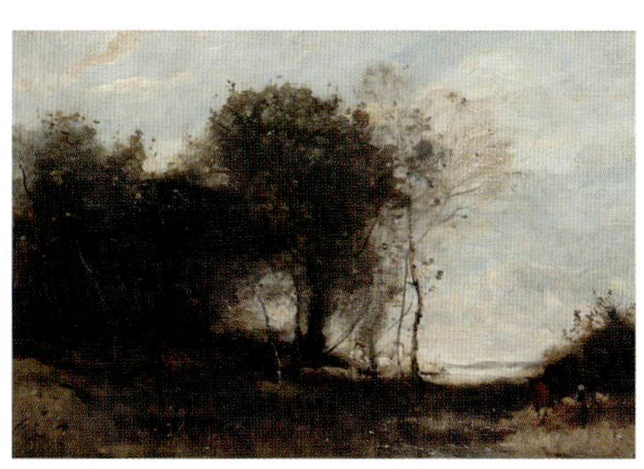

Corot, Jean-Baptiste-Camille (attributed to)
1796–1875
Wooded Landscape with Figures
oil on canvas 32 x 45.3
1160

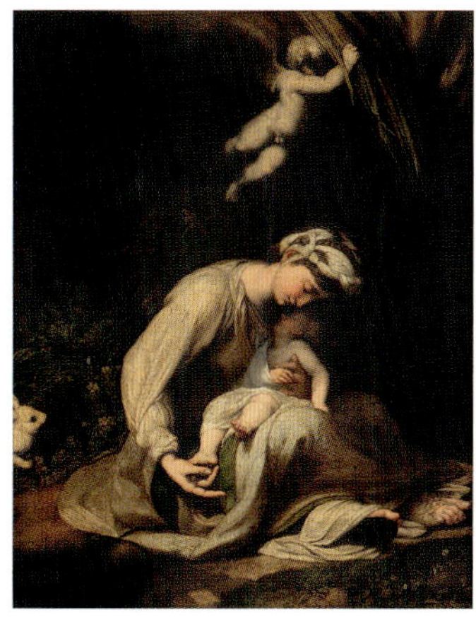

Correggio (after) c.1489–1534
Madonna and Child with a Rabbit
mid-16th C
oil on canvas 50.4 x 40.2
126

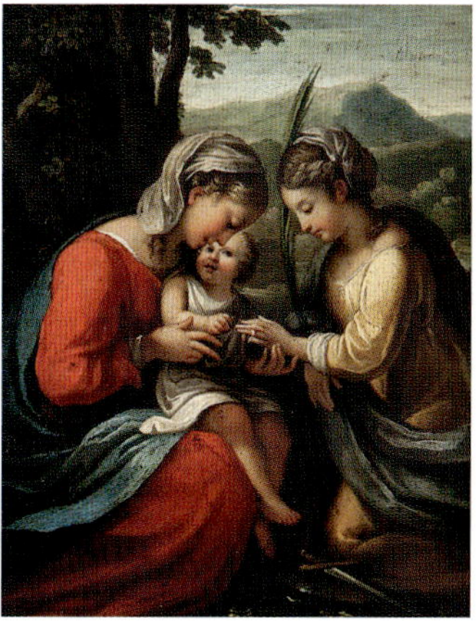

Correggio (after) c.1489–1534
The Mystic Marriage of Saint Catherine
mid-16th C (?)
oil on panel 30.9 x 24.4
127

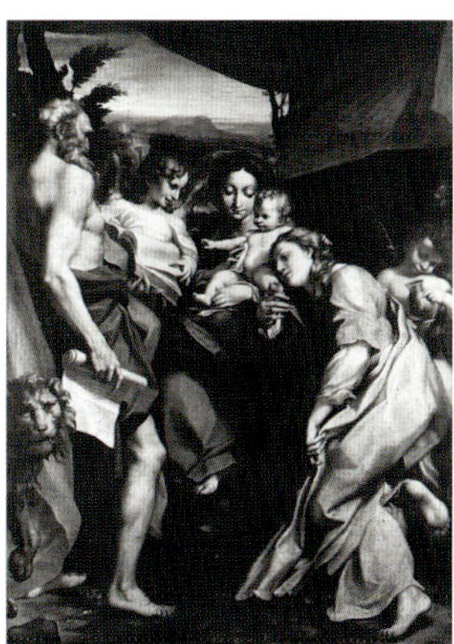

Correggio (after) c.1489–1534
Madonna of Saint Jerome 17th C (?)
oil on panel 180.2 x 128.2
128

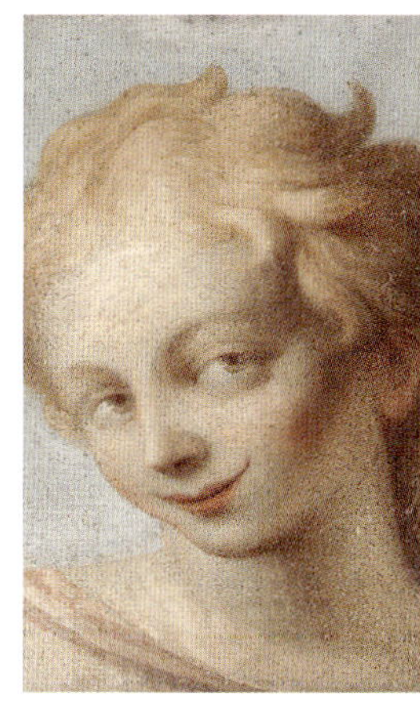

Correggio (imitator of) c.1489–1534
Head of an Angel 18th C (?)
fresco fragment 61.6 x 37.1
124

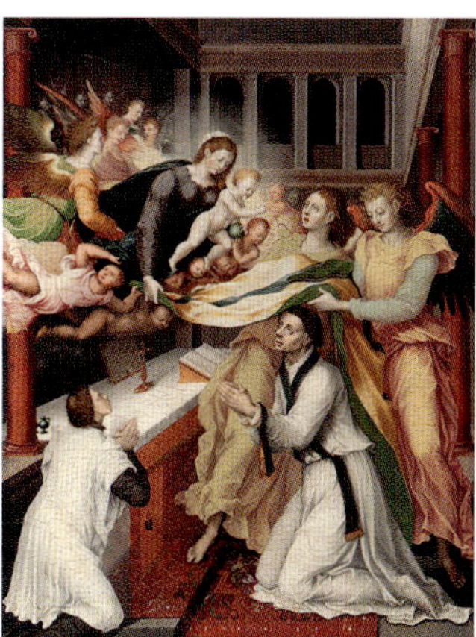

Cosida, Jerónimo c.1516–1592
San Ildefonso Receiving the Chasuble c.1550–1590
oil on canvas 75.2 x 56.4
PC.68

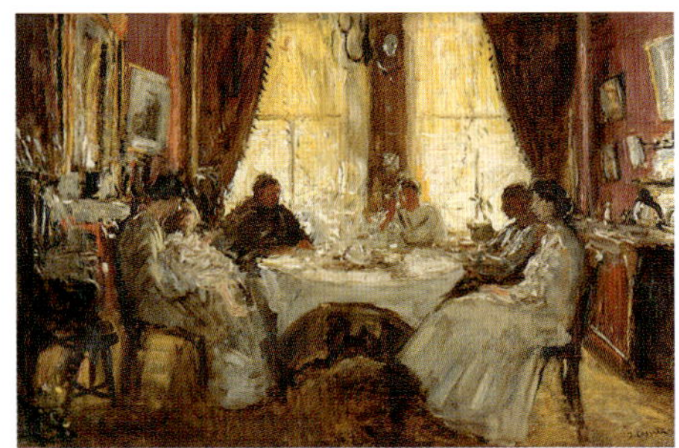

Cossaar, Jacobus Cornelis Wyand
1874–1966
Interior with Figures c.1890–1910
oil on canvas 50.5 x 76.5
2800

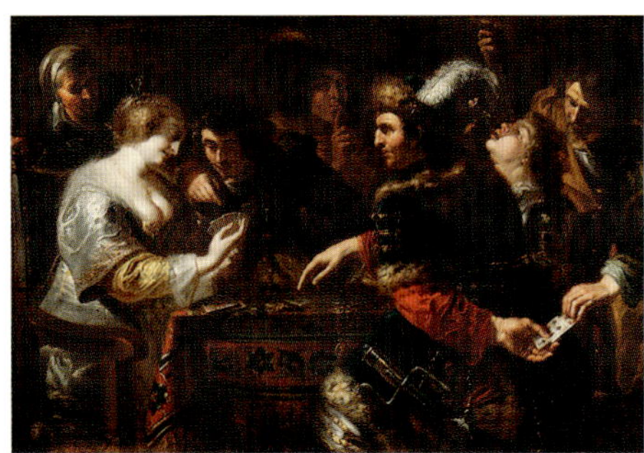

Cossiers, Jan (style of) 1600–1671
A Gambling Party
oil on canvas 118.7 x 168
121

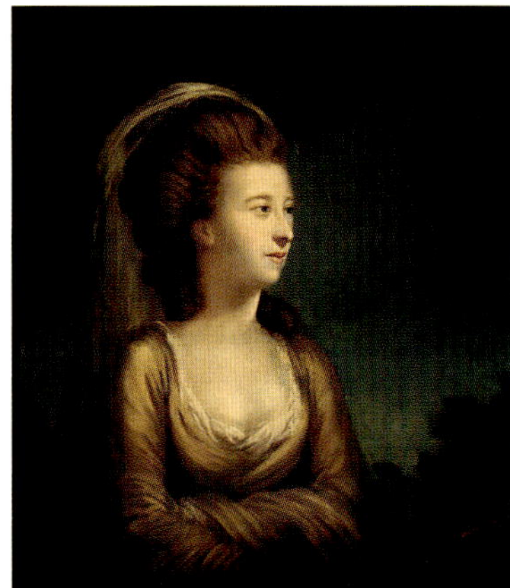

Cotes, Francis (circle of) 1726–1770
Henrietta Archer (1754–1794)
oil on canvas 74.9 x 62.2
L.3.1973 (P)

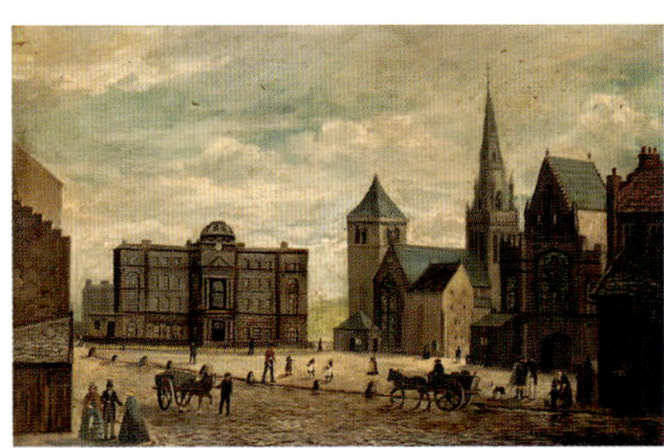

Cottrel, A.
Glasgow Cathedral and Infirmary 1821
oil on canvas 61 x 91.4
NR.64

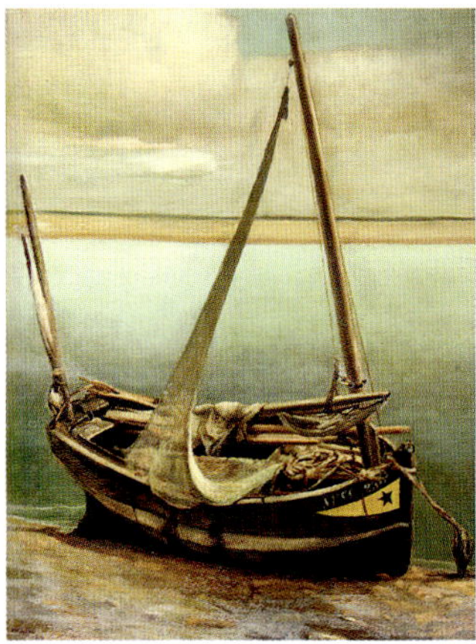

Couling, Arthur Vivian 1890–1962
Le bateau à la moustache jaune 1925
oil on canvas 51.3 x 40.9
1779

Courbet, Gustave 1819–1877
Baskets of Flowers 1863
oil on canvas 75.9 x 100.8
2859

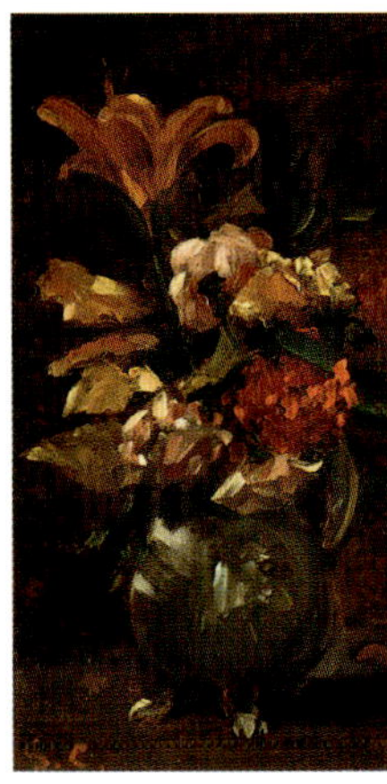

Courbet, Gustave 1819–1877
Lily and Gillyflower c.1863
oil on canvas 40.6 x 21.6
35.68

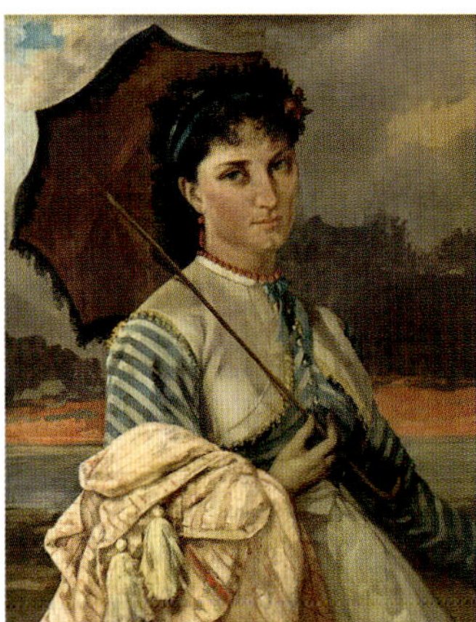

Courbet, Gustave 1819–1877
Woman with a Parasol, Mademoiselle Aubé de la Holde 1865
oil on canvas 92.1 x 73.7
35.65

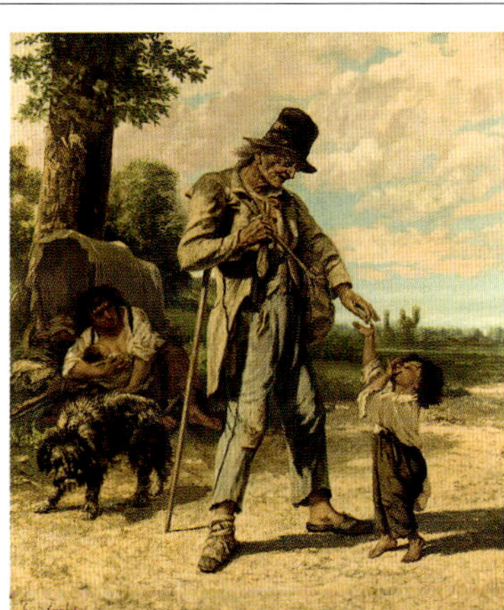

Courbet, Gustave 1819–1877
The Charity of a Beggar at Ornans 1868
oil on canvas 210.9 x 175.3
35.64

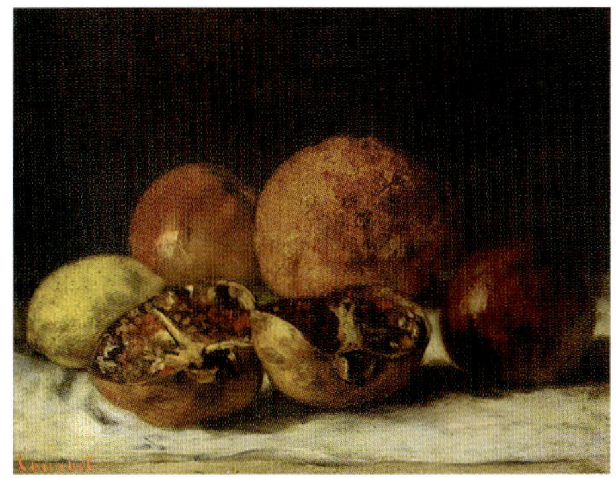

Courbet, Gustave 1819–1877
Pomegranates 1871
oil on panel 26.7 x 34.9
35.67

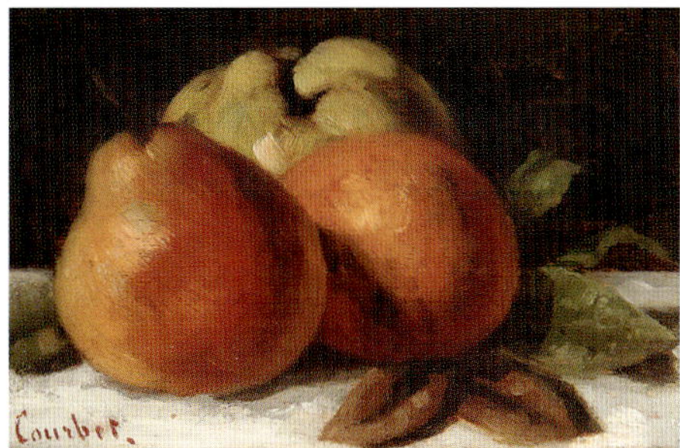

Courbet, Gustave 1819–1877
Apple, Pear and Orange c.1871–1872
oil on panel 13 x 20.7
2384

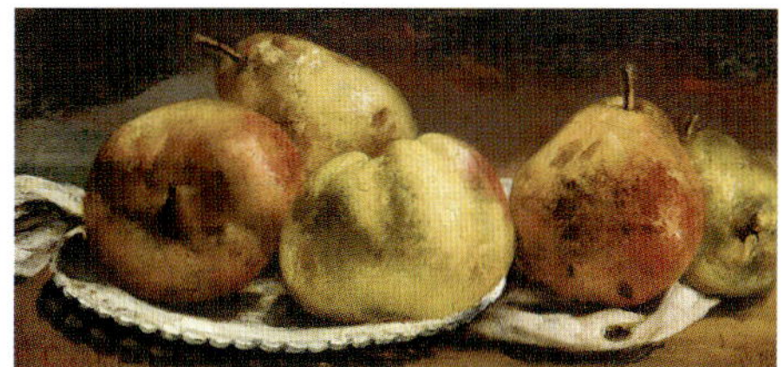

Courbet, Gustave 1819–1877
Fruit c.1871–1872
oil on panel 17.8 x 36.8
35.66

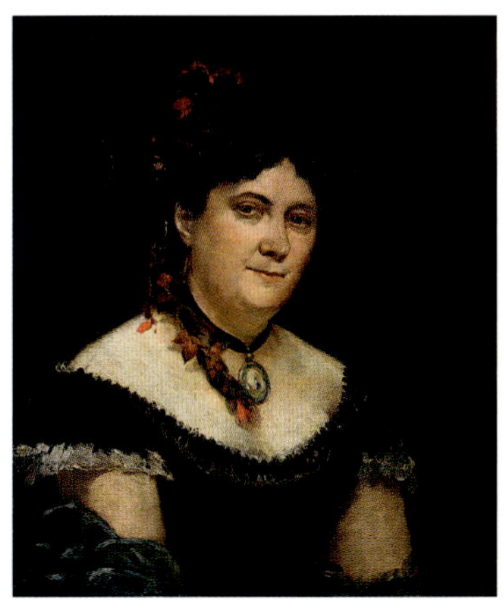

Courbet, Gustave (attributed to) 1819–1877
Portrait of a Woman
oil on canvas 61 x 49.8
2775

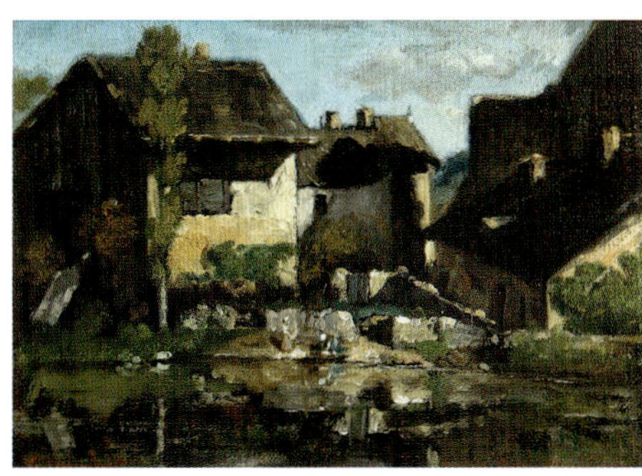

Courbet, Gustave (attributed to) 1819–1877
The Washerwomen
oil on canvas 20.3 x 27.9
35.69

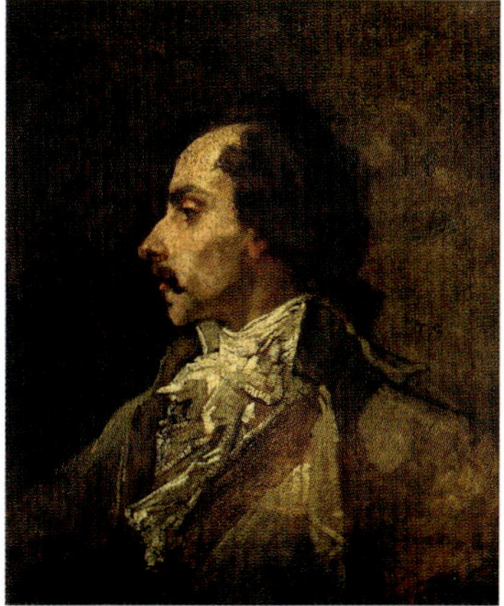

Couture, Thomas 1815–1879
A Volunteer c.1848
oil on canvas 66.7 x 56.5
35.7

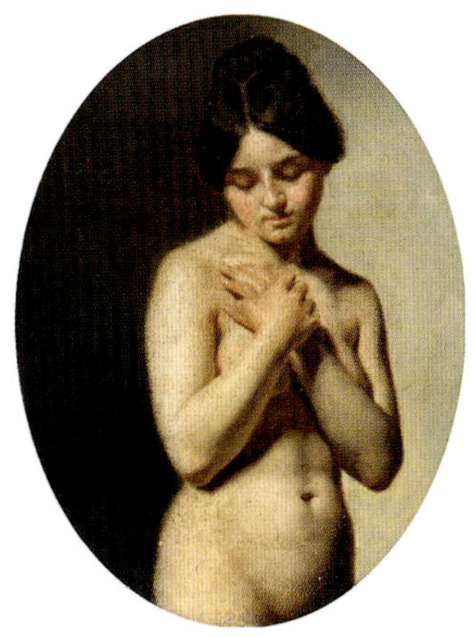

Couture, Thomas (attributed to) 1815–1879
Girl
oil on canvas 31.7 x 24.1
35.71

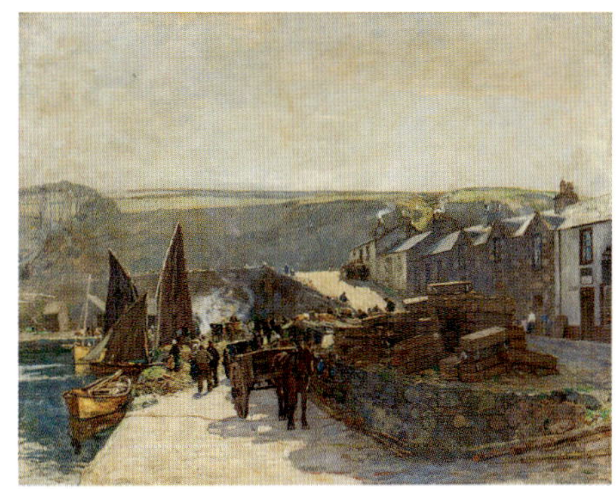

Coventry, Robert McGown 1855–1914
The Haven c.1908
oil on canvas 101.6 x 125.7
1220

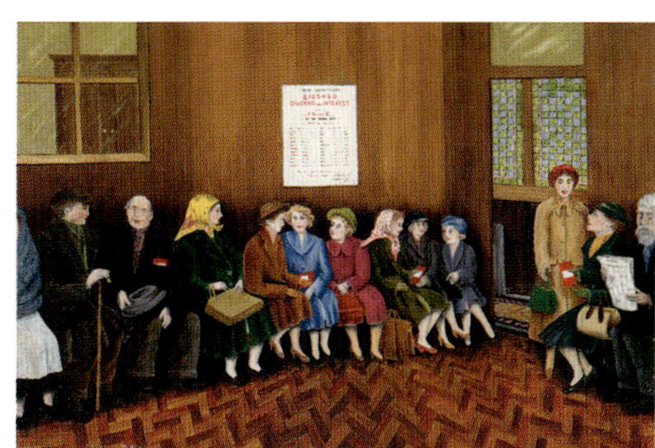

Cowell, Margaret 1899–1970
Collecting the Divi 1961
oil on board 35.9 x 50.8
3595

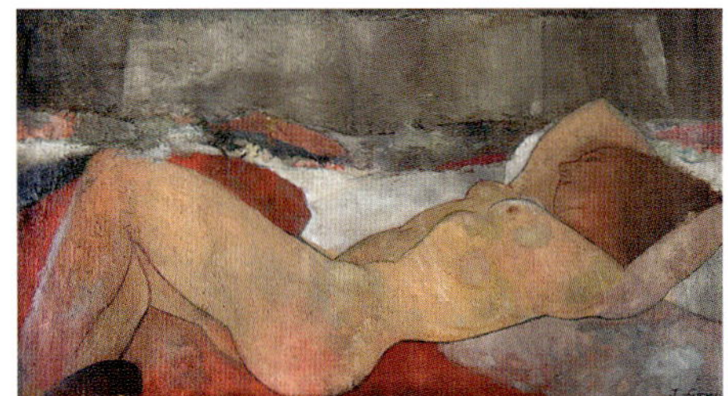

Cowie, James 1886–1956
Nude 1933
oil on canvas 29.8 x 52.7
2684

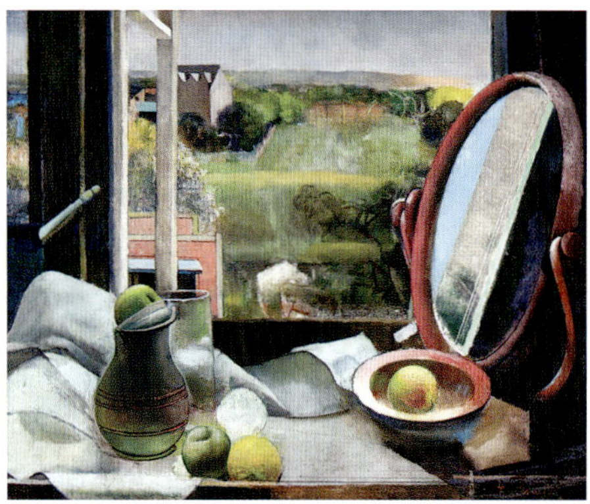

Cowie, James 1886–1956
The Looking-Glass c.1940–1950
oil on canvas 50.8 x 60.7
3056

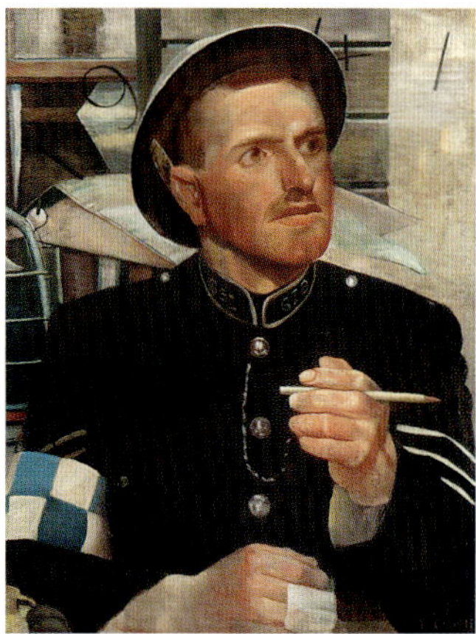

Cowie, James 1886–1956
Scottish Policeman 1941–1942
oil on canvas 66 x 49.5
2728

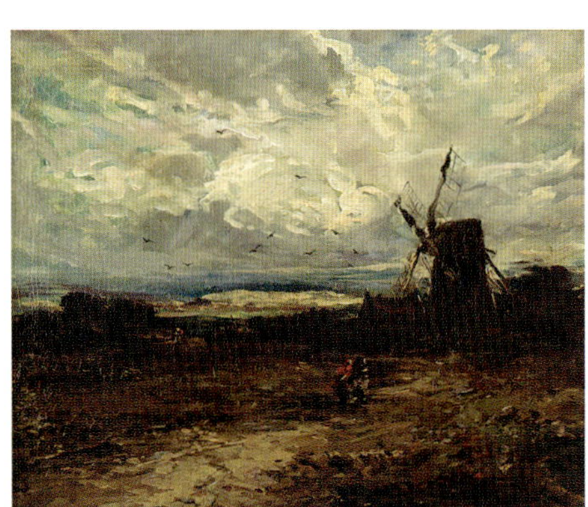

Cox, David the elder 1783–1859
Landscape with a Windmill 1852
oil on canvas 31.8 x 38.1
3036

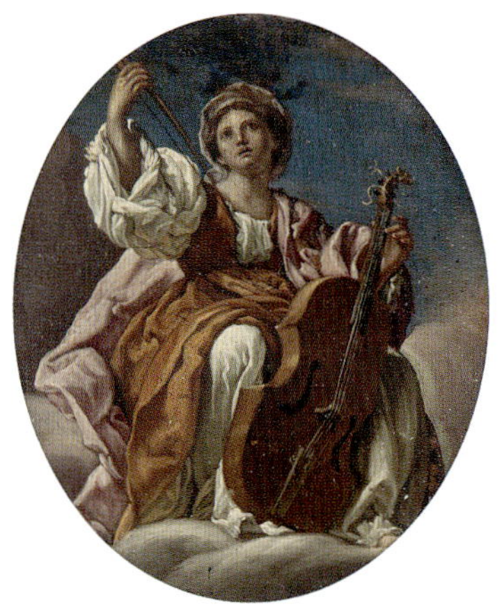

Cozza, Francesco 1605–1682
Music c.1660–1670
oil on copper 16.2 x 14.3
144

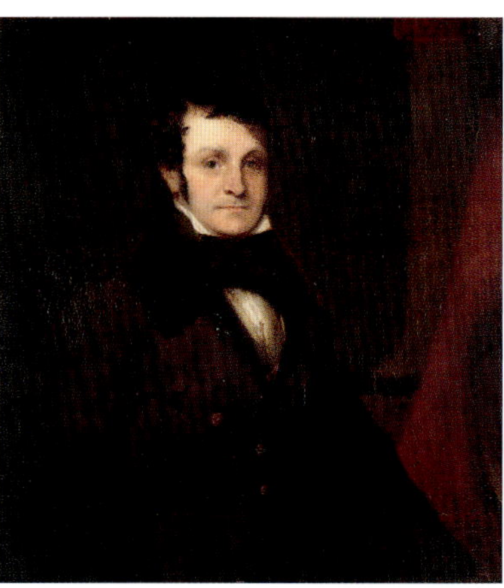

Craig, Alexander d.1878
Thomas Campbell (1777–1844), Poet c.1837
oil on canvas 91.4 x 81.2
497

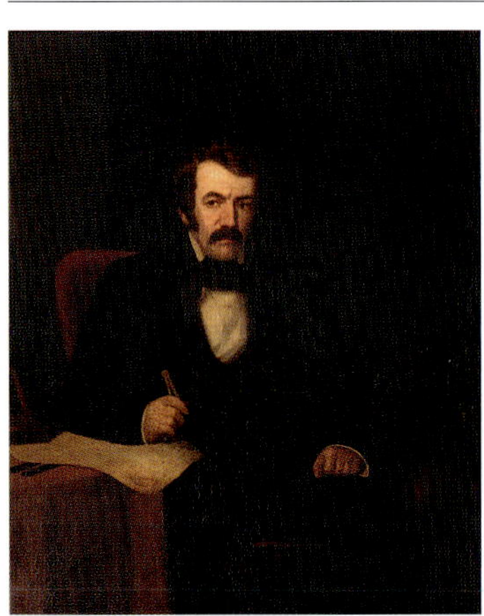

Craig, Alexander d.1878
Dr Livingstone (1813–1873)
oil on canvas 127 x 101.6
L.2.1944 (P)

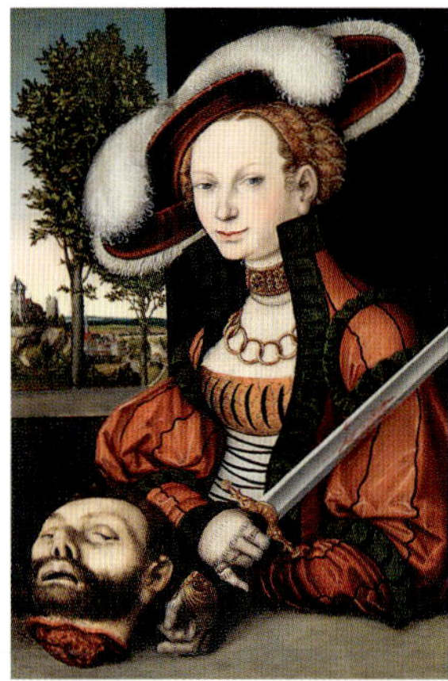

Cranach, Lucas the elder 1472–1553
Judith with the Head of Holofernes 1530
oil on panel 76.7 x 55.8
35.671

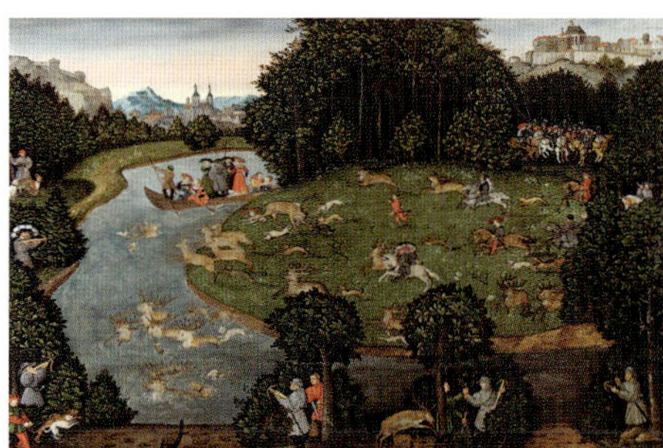

Cranach, Lucas the elder (studio of)
1472–1553
The Stag Hunt 1529
oil on panel 83.2 x 119.5
35.73

Facing page: Sutherland, Graham Vivian, 1903–1980, *Landscape with Rocks*, (p. 410)

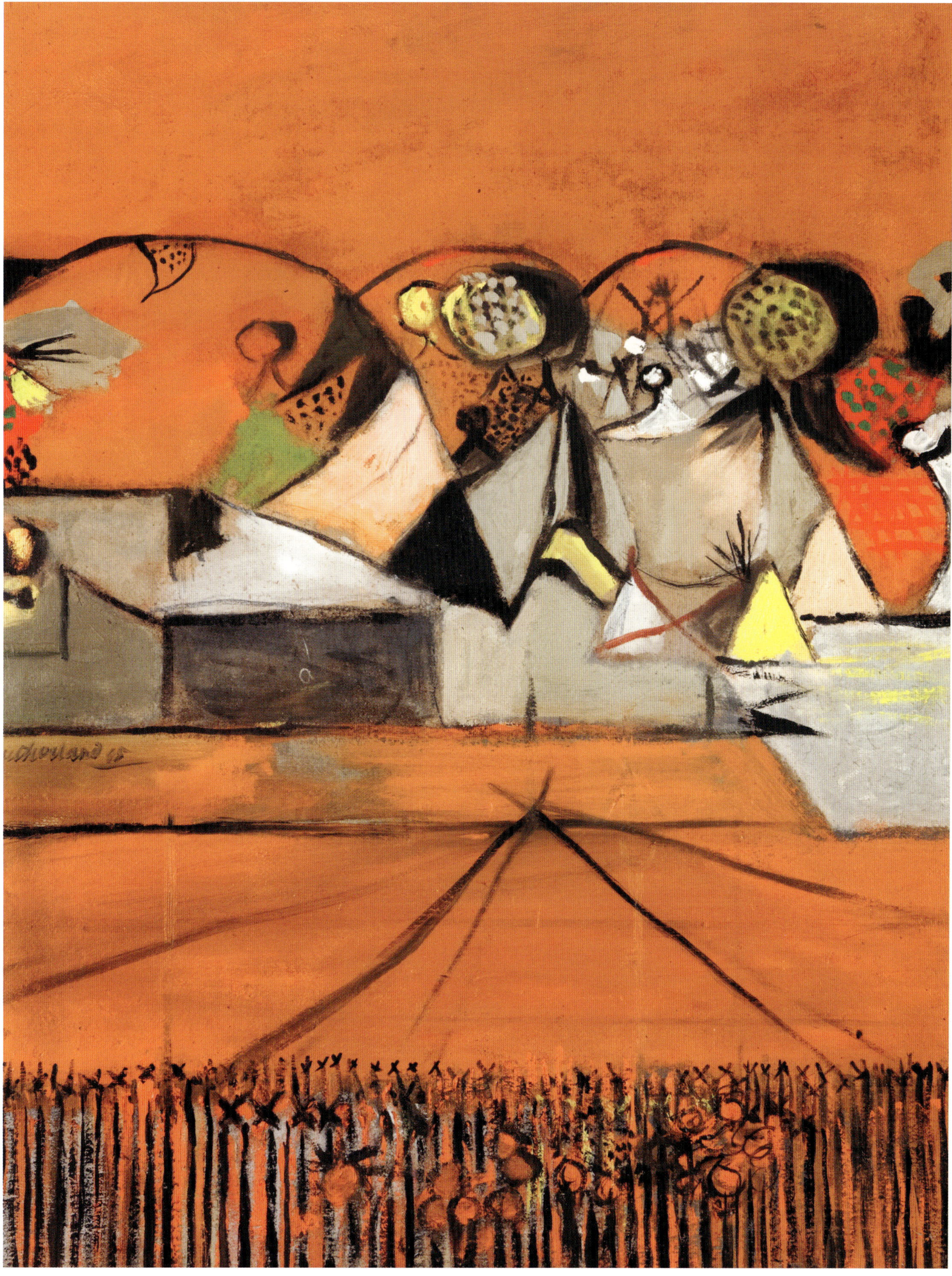

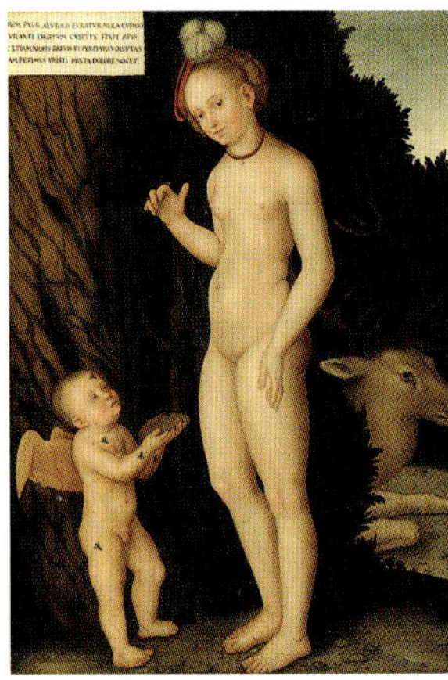

Cranach, Lucas the elder (studio of)
1472–1553
Venus and Cupid, the Honey Thief 1545
oil on panel 51.5 x 36.2
35.74

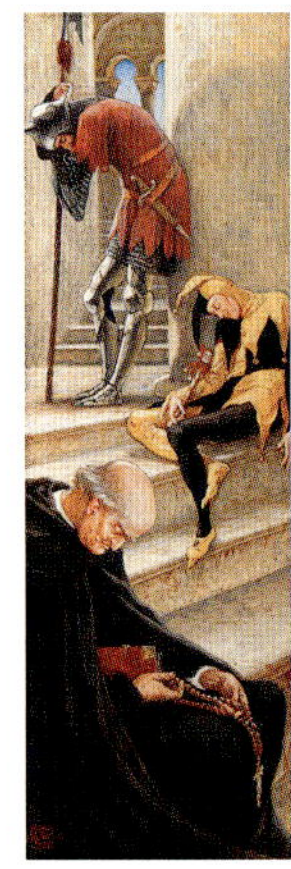

Crane, Walter 1845–1915
The Briar Rose (triptych, left wing) 1905
tempera on panel 59.1 x 21
1520 (left)

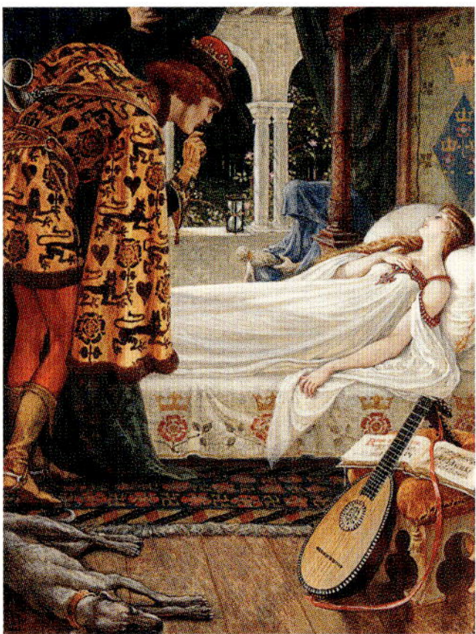

Crane, Walter 1845–1915
The Briar Rose (triptych, centre panel) 1905
tempera on panel 59.1 x 43.2
1520 (centre)

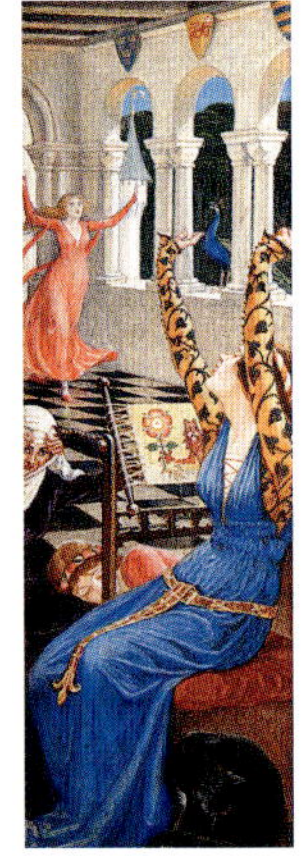

Crane, Walter 1845–1915
The Briar Rose (triptych, right wing) 1905
tempera on panel 59.1 x 21
1520 (right)

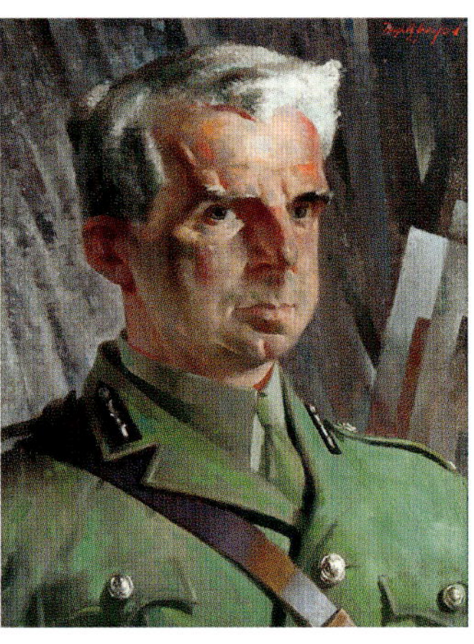

Crawford, Hugh Adam 1898–1982
*Sir Patrick Dollan (1885–1963), Lord Provost
of Glasgow (1938–1941)* 1941
oil on canvas 92.1 x 71.1
2729

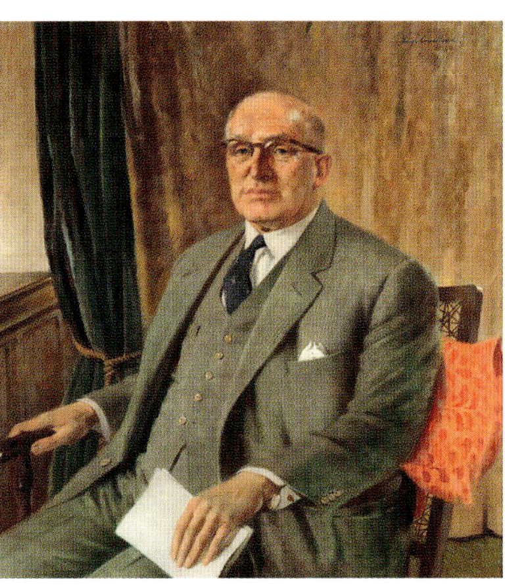

Crawford, Hugh Adam 1898–1982
Sir Alexander King (1888–1973)
oil on canvas 114.5 x 109.2
LT.1988.8.4 (P)

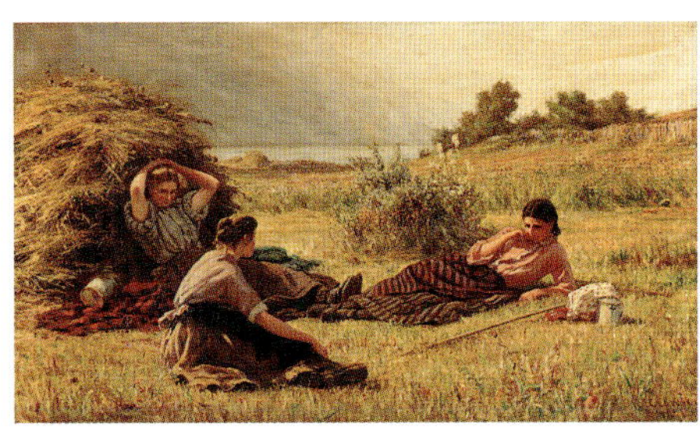

Crawford, Robert Cree 1842–1924
Midday Rest 1878
oil on canvas 81.3 x 142.2
2343

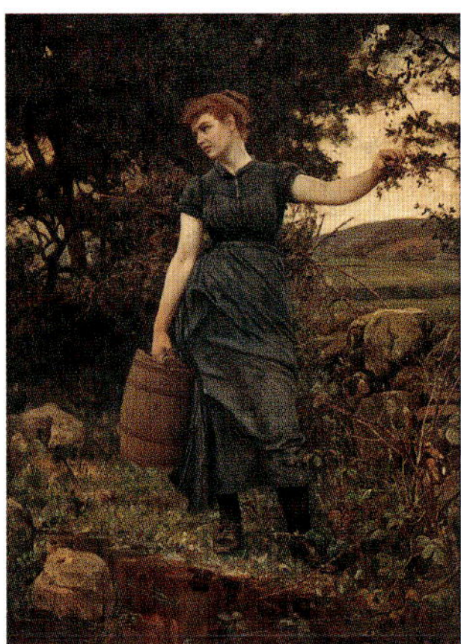

Crawford, Robert Cree 1842–1924
The Water Stoup 1892
oil on canvas 152.4 x 111.8
1211

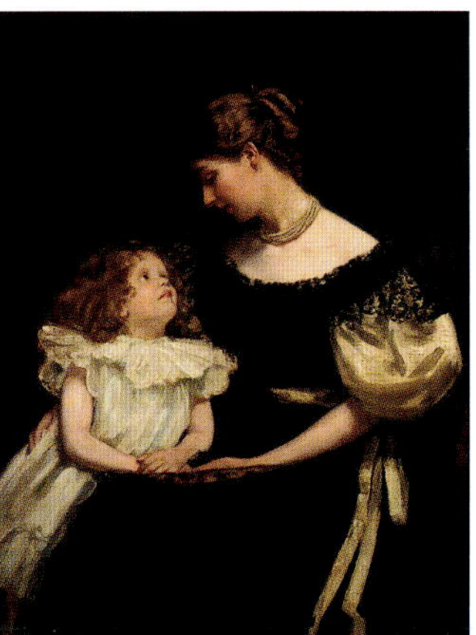

Crawford, Robert Cree 1842–1924
Woman and Child c.1895–1897
oil on canvas 123.2 x 92.7
2557

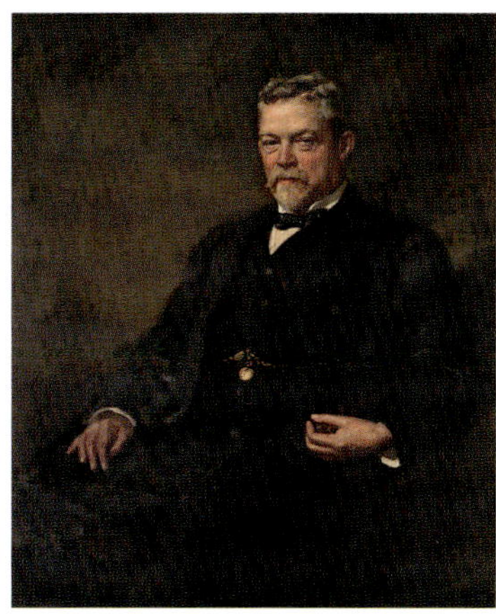

Crawford, Robert Cree 1842–1924
Sir James Thompson, Chairman of the
Caledonian Railway (1901–1906) 1901–1906
oil on canvas 132.1 x 104.1
T.1972.3

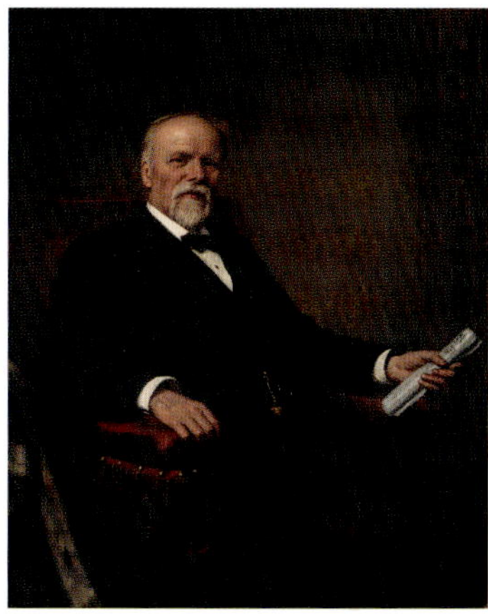

Crawford, Robert Cree 1842–1924
Former Bailie Walter Paton (1838–1906) 1905
oil on canvas 139.7 x 111.8
1104

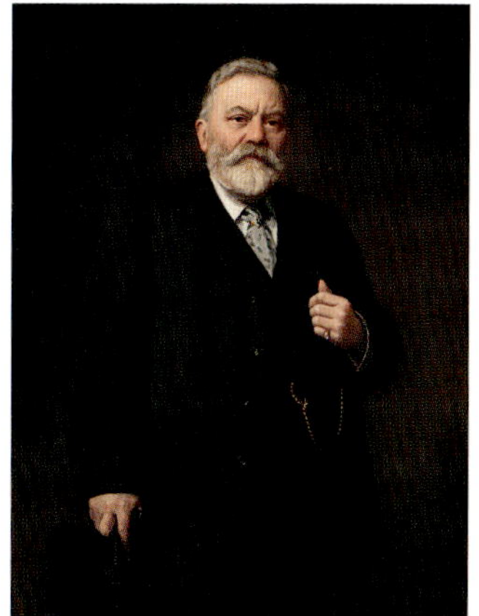

Crawford, Robert Cree 1842–1924
Portrait of a Man 1905
oil on canvas 142.2 x 111.8
NR.174

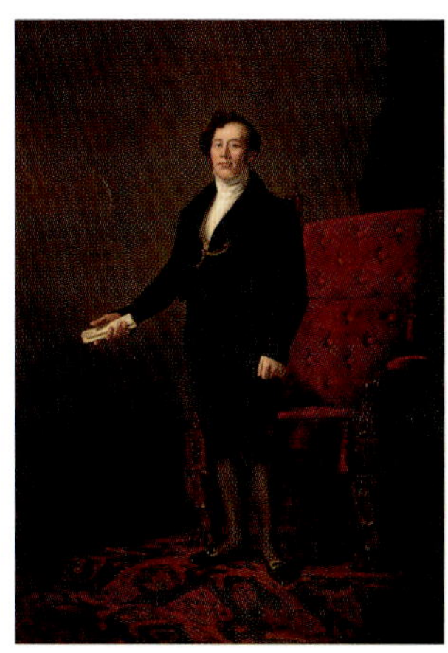

Crawford, Robert Cree 1842–1924
Archibald McLellan (1795–1854) (after John
Graham-Gilbert) 1906
oil on canvas 247.6 x 165.1
1191

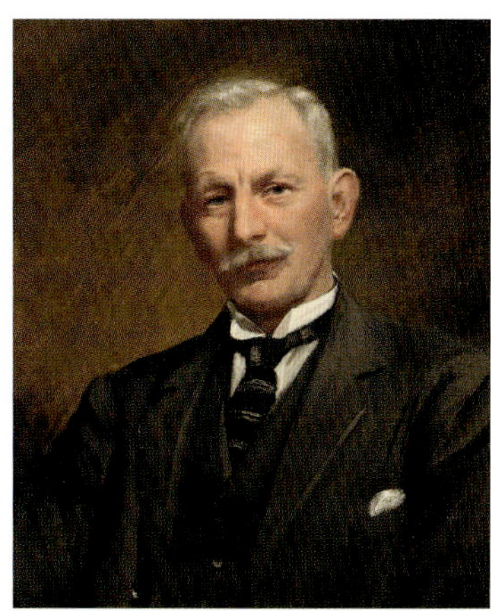

Crawford, Robert Cree 1842–1924
Portrait of a Man 1923
oil on canvas 66 x 54
NR.162

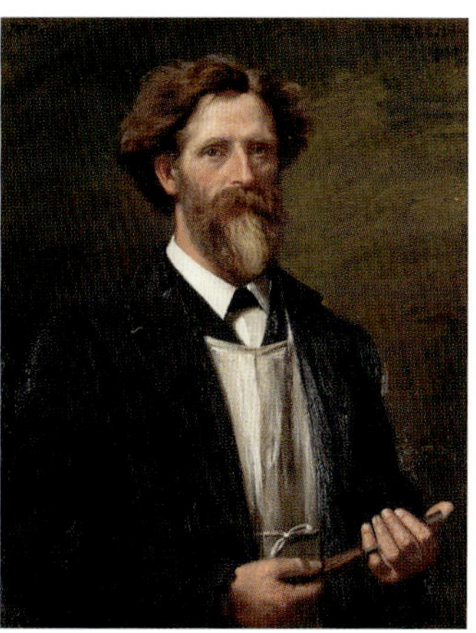

Crawford, Robert Cree 1842–1924
James W. Briggs, Violin Maker in Glasgow
oil on canvas 91.4 x 71.1
2150

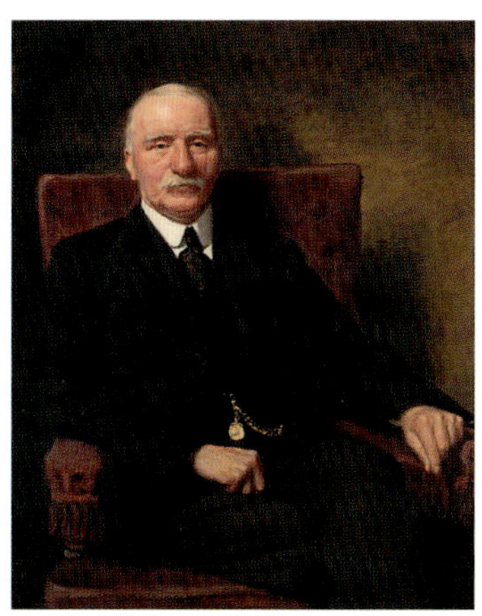

Crawford, Robert Cree 1842–1924
John Arnott (1814–1898)
oil on canvas 116.8 x 91.4
2321

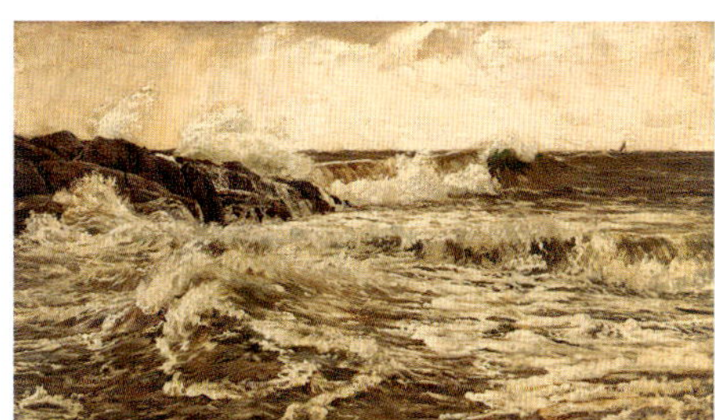

Crawford, Robert Cree 1842–1924
Storm at Portincross
oil on canvas 132.1 x 223.5
1210

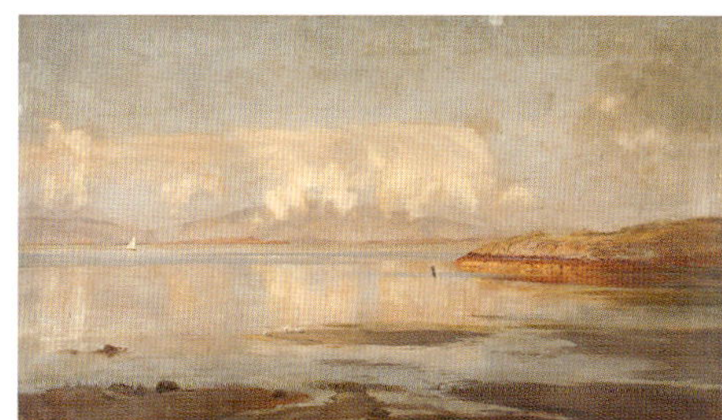

Crawford, Robert Cree 1842–1924
The Gates of the North
oil on canvas 73.7 x 142.2
1688

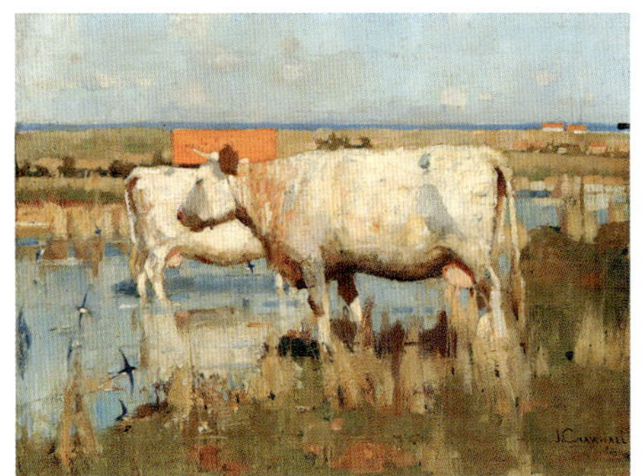

Crawhall, Joseph E. 1861–1913
Landscape with Cattle c.1883–1885
oil on canvas 43.2 x 57.8
3042

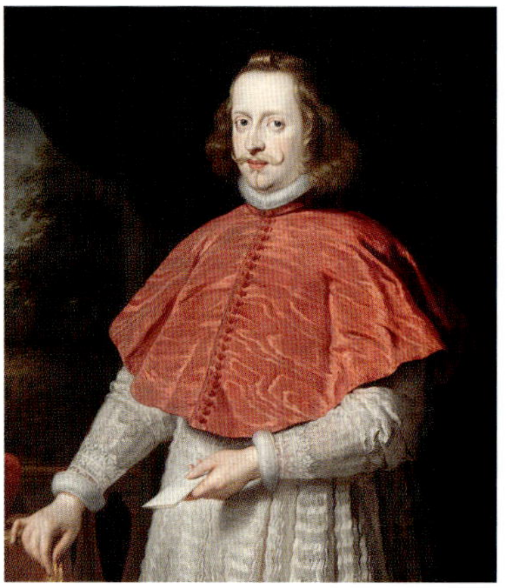

Crayer, Gaspar de (and studio) 1584–1669
*Cardinal Infante Fernando of Austria
(1609–1641)* c.1639–1641
oil on canvas 91.4 x 81.9
PC.124

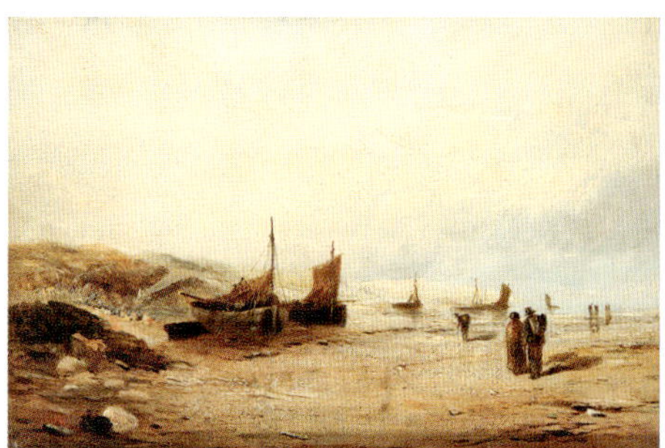

Creswick, Thomas 1811–1869
Coast Scene
oil on canvas 24.1 x 34.3
994

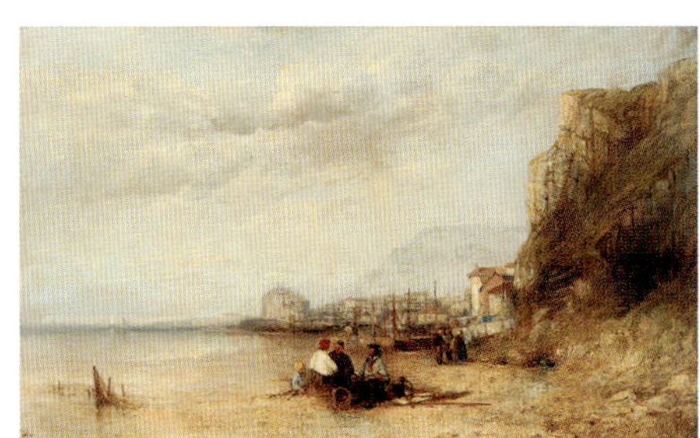

Creswick, Thomas 1811–1869
Sea Beach Scene
oil on canvas 45.7 x 74.9
356

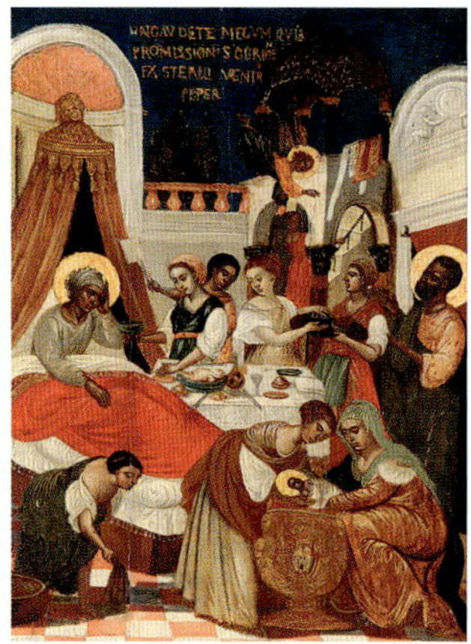

Cretan School early 17th C
The Birth of the Virgin
oil on panel 40.7 x 31.1
156

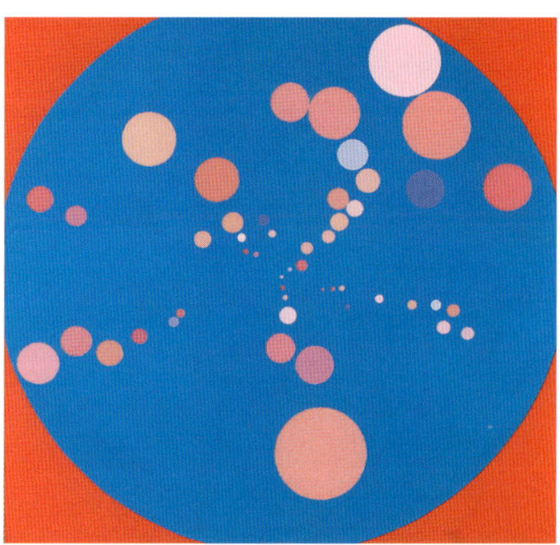

Croft-Smith, David A. b.1934
Polarization 1972
PVA on canvas 142 x 142
3290

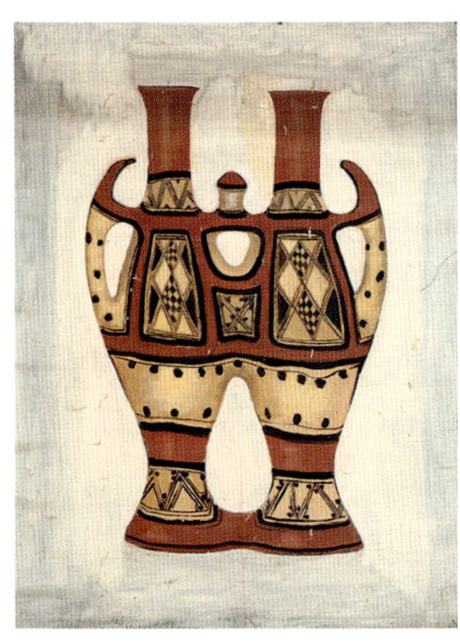

Crosbie, William 1915–1999
A Kabyle Pot 1943
oil on canvas 129.5 x 96.5
ETHNN.1275

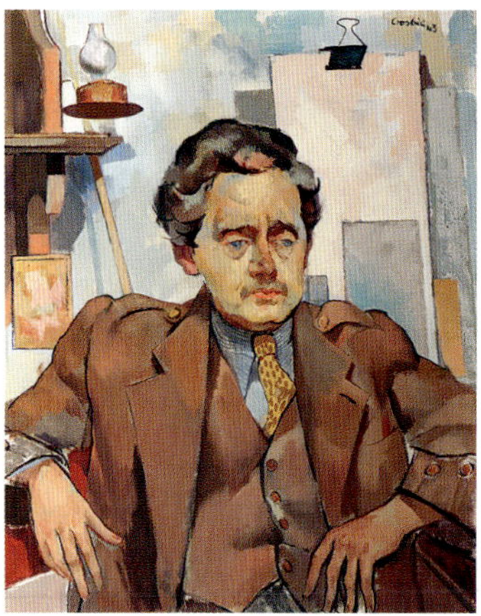

Crosbie, William 1915–1999
Hugh MacDiarmid (1892–1978) 1943
oil on canvas 91.4 x 71.1
2471

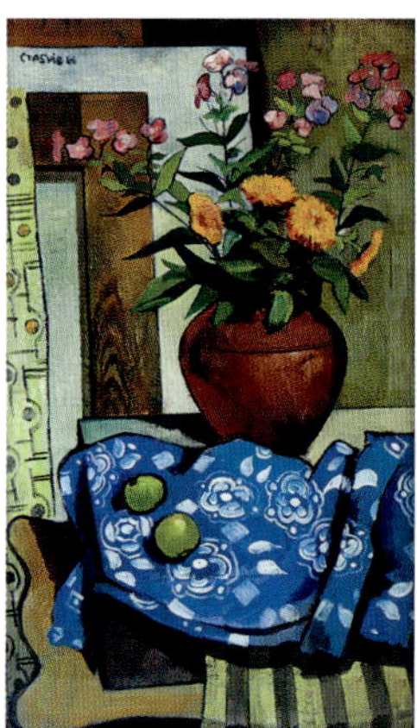

Crosbie, William 1915–1999
Composition, Flowers 1944
oil on canvas 105.5 x 59.8
3143

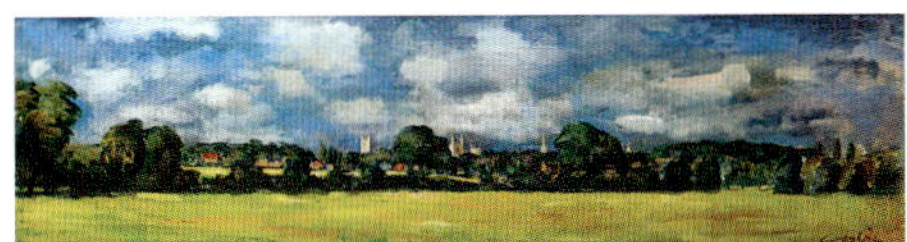

Crosbie, William 1915–1999
Cambridge from Grantchester c.1952
oil on board 26.4 x 92.4
2974

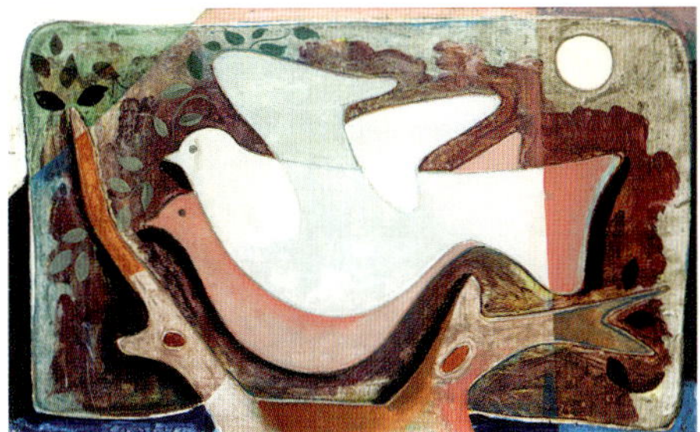

Crosbie, William 1915–1999
Birds and Tree 1969–1970
oil on board 38 x 59.1
3272

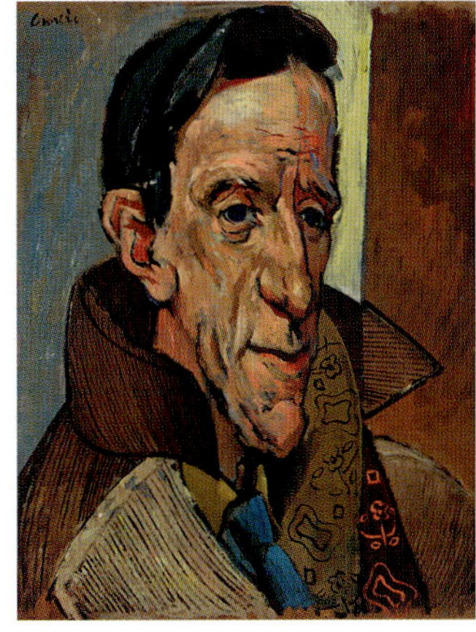

Crosbie, William 1915–1999
Halbert Tatlock (d.1963)
oil on hardboard 59 x 45.6
3087

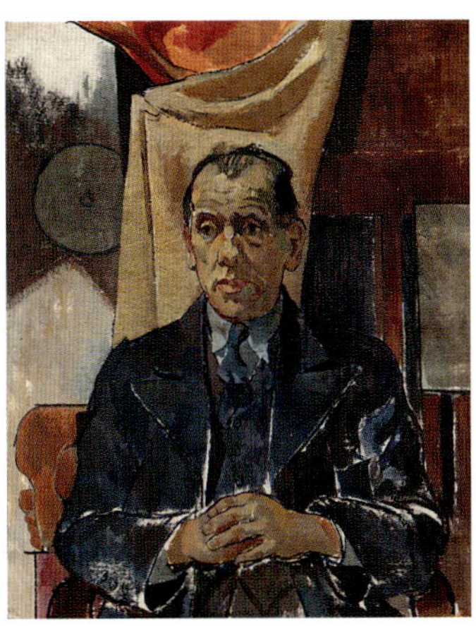

Crosbie, William 1915–1999
John Morton, Radio Personality
oil on canvas 92 x 69.6
TEMP.2977

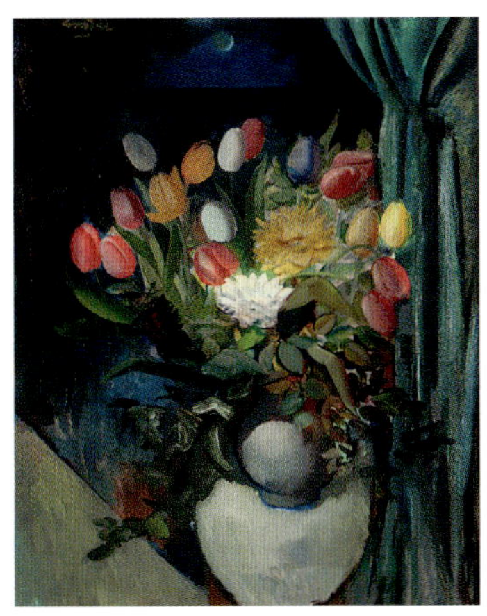

Crosbie, William 1915–1999
Moonlight and Flowers
oil on hardboard 90.8 x 70.5
3253

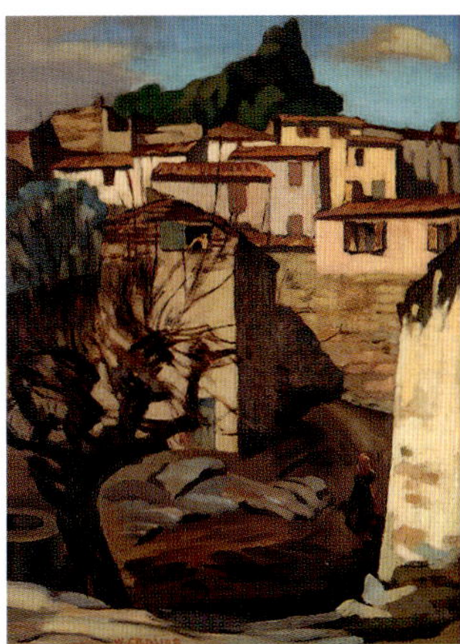

Crozier, William 1893–1930
The Well c.1929
oil on plywood 61 x 45.7
1780

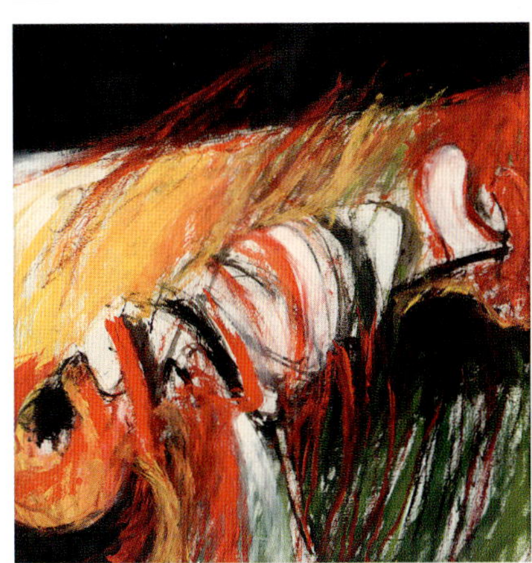

Crozier, William b.1930
Fallen Man II 1961
oil on canvas 91.4 x 90.8
3224

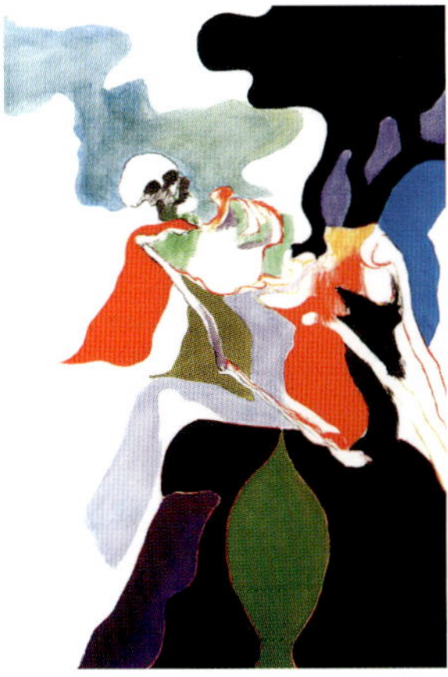

Crozier, William b.1930
Aviator 1967
oil on canvas 182.9 x 122.2
3250

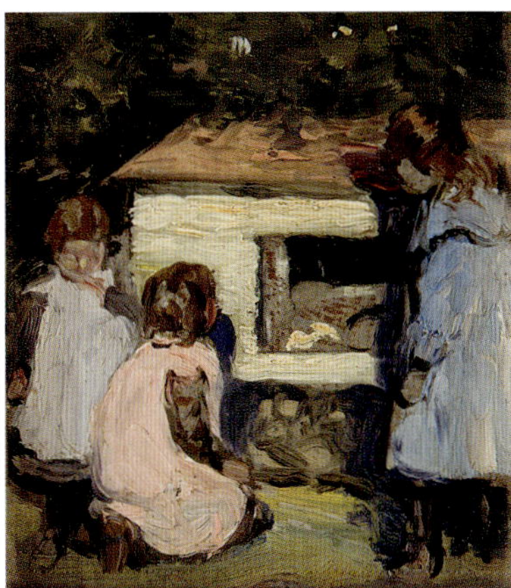

Cruickshank, George active 1895–1909
Girls at a Rabbit Hutch at Ravelston
oil on cardboard 14.3 x 12.7
3161

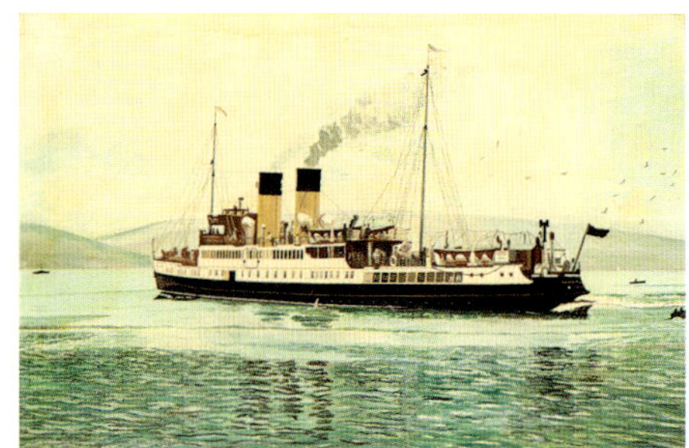

Cruickshank, R. S.
'Duchess of Montrose'
oil on board 56.2 x 81.7
T.1992.13

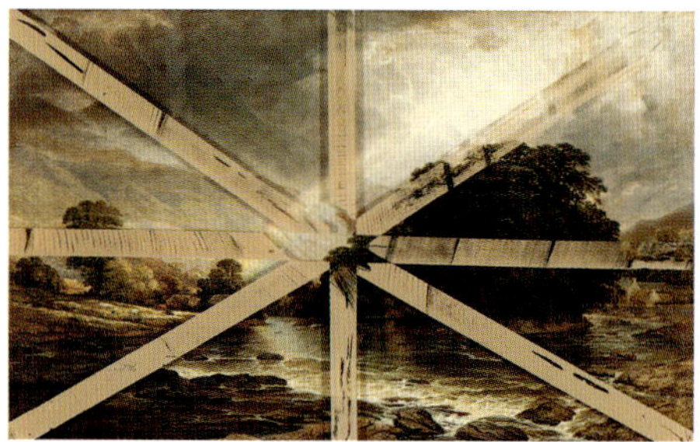

Cubley, William Harold 1816–1896
Killin, Perthshire
oil on canvas 81.3 x 127
1673

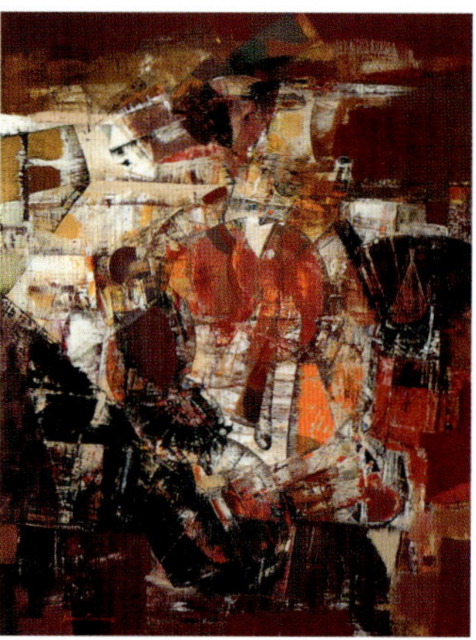

Cumming, James 1922–1991
The Hill Farmer 1962–1963
oil on canvas 101.2 x 76.2
3181

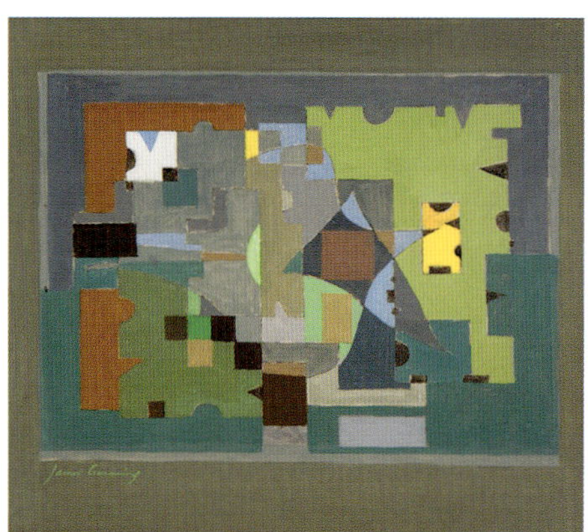

Cumming, James 1922–1991
Points of Contact
oil on panel 19 x 21.6
3453

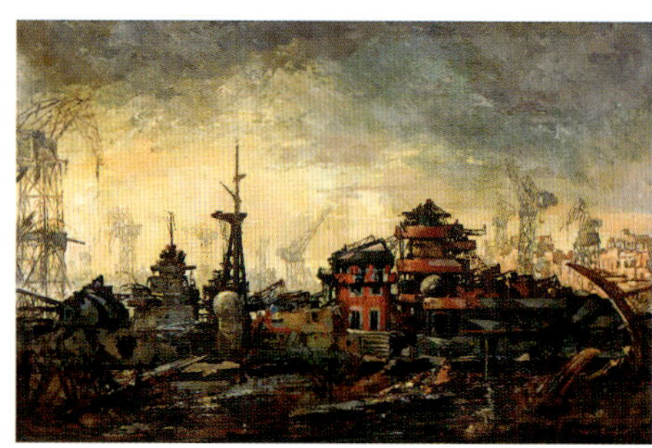

Cundall, Charles Ernest 1890–1971
The Hipper at Kiel 1945
oil on canvas 81.3 x 121.9
2730

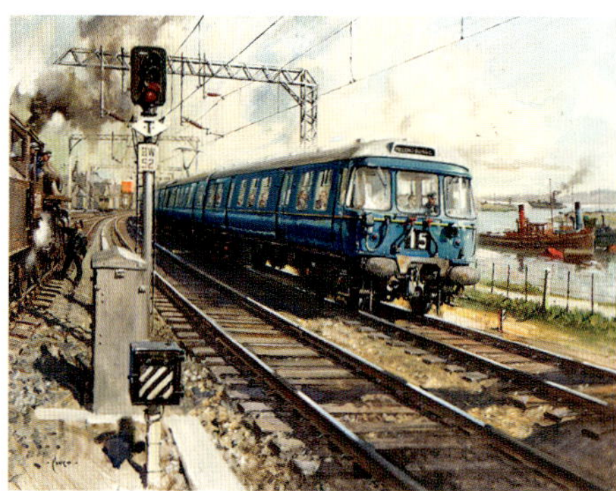

Cuneo, Terence Tenison 1907–1996
Blue Train at Bowling Harbour 1965
oil on canvas 94 x 119.5
T.2009.3

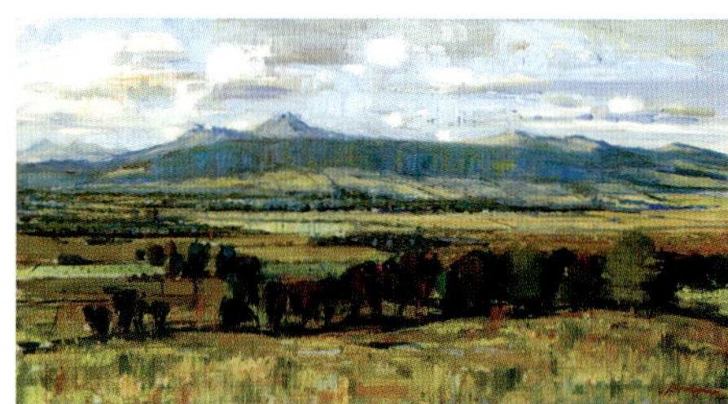

Cunningham, John 1926–1998
Flanders Moss 1961
oil on canvas 63.3 x 114.5
3153

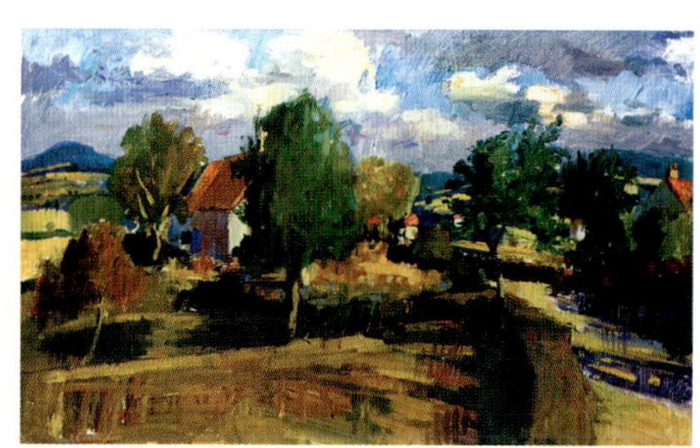

Cunningham, John 1926–1998
Farm near Charolles c.1964
oil on canvas 63.3 x 101.3
3220

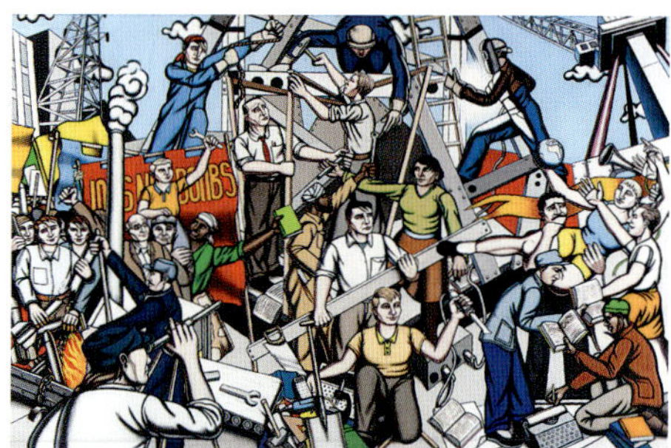

Currie, Ken b.1960
Peace 1983
acrylic on canvas 213.4 x 320
PP.1984.53.2

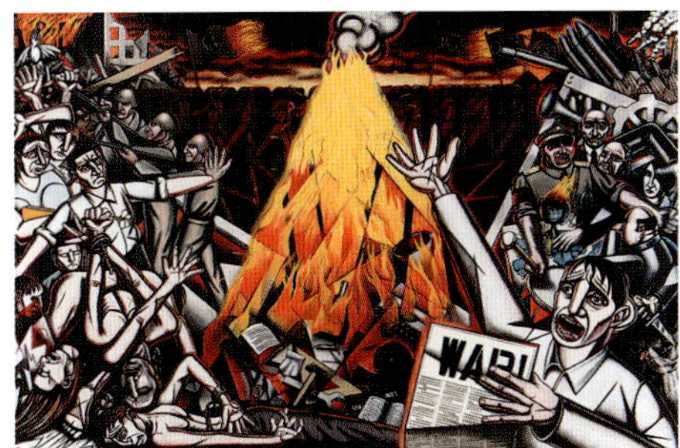

Currie, Ken b.1960
War 1983
acrylic on canvas 213.4 x 320
PP.1984.53.1

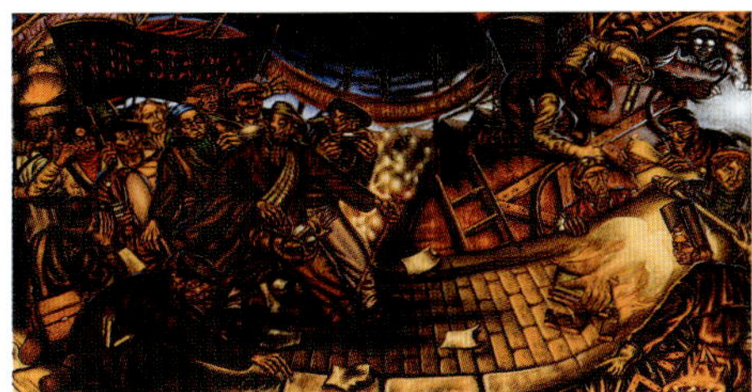

Currie, Ken b.1960
*Weavers' Struggles ... The Calton Weavers'
Massacre* 1986–1987
oil on canvas 218 x 251
PP.1987.203.1

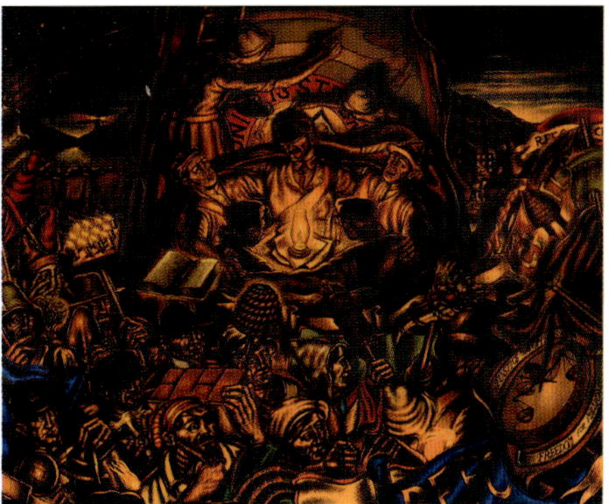

Currie, Ken b.1960
*Radical Wars ... Let Truth and Justice Be
Woven Together, Liberty Is Our Fabric*
1986–1987
oil on canvas 218 x 381
PP.1987.203.2

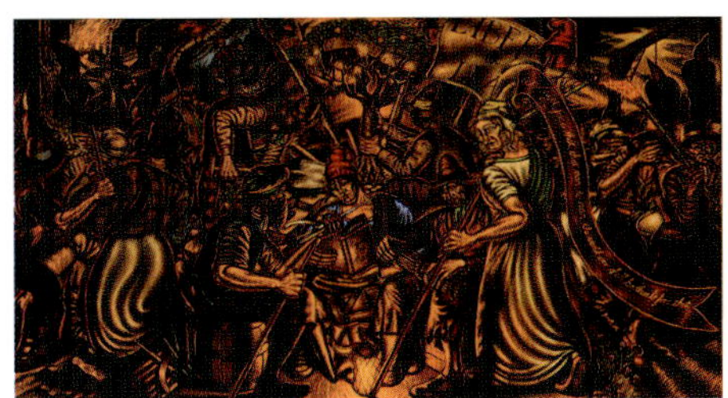

Currie, Ken b.1960
Great Reform Agitation ... Union Is Strength
1986–1987
oil on canvas 218 x 251
PP.1987.203.3

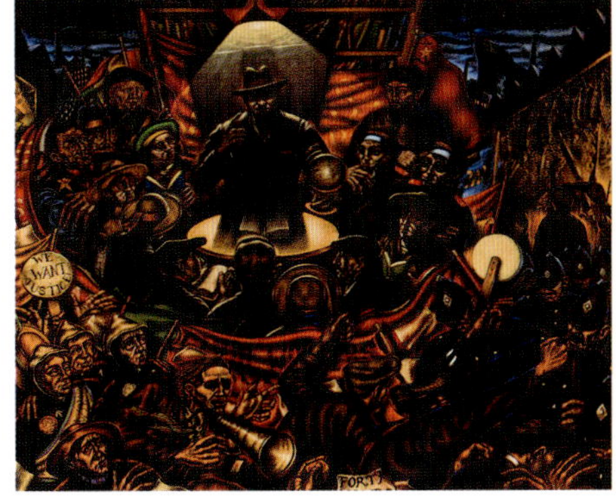

Currie, Ken b.1960
The Socialist Vision ... Workers of the World
1986–1987
oil on canvas 218 x 381
PP.1987.203.4

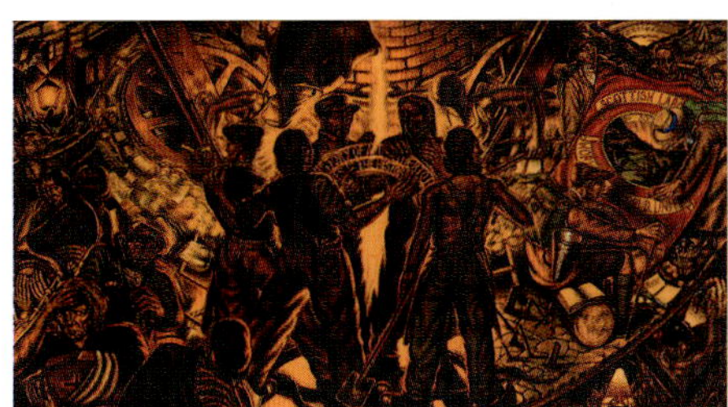

Currie, Ken b.1960
*Red Clyde ... 'We Can Make Glasgow a
Petrograd, a Revolutionary Storm Centre
Second to None'* 1986–1987
oil on canvas 218 x 251
PP.1987.203.5

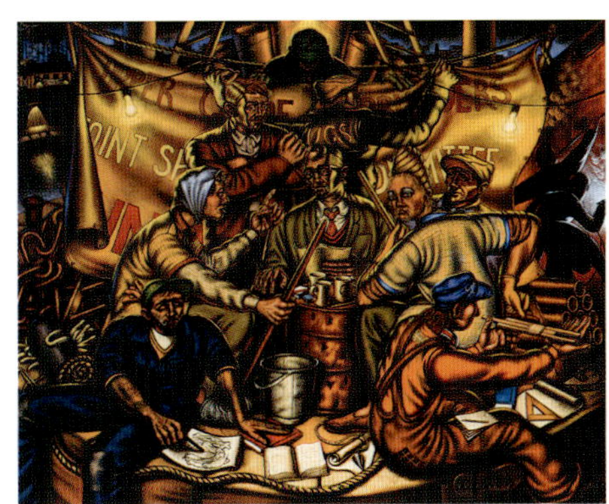

Currie, Ken b.1960
*Fight or Starve ... Wandering through the
Thirties* 1986–1987
oil on canvas 218 x 381
PP.1987.203.6

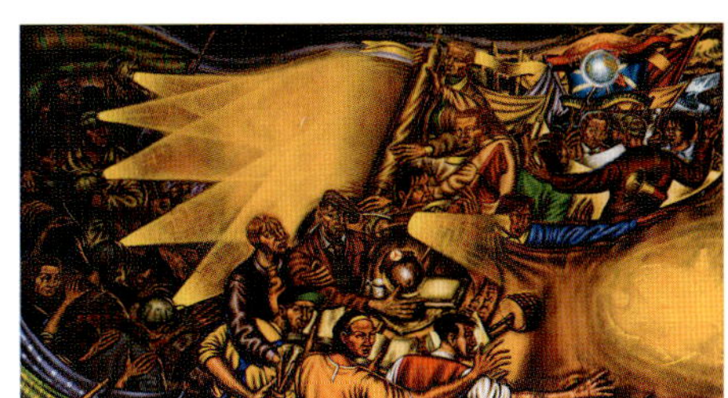

Currie, Ken b.1960
The UCS 1986–1987
oil on canvas 218 x 251
PP.1987.203.7

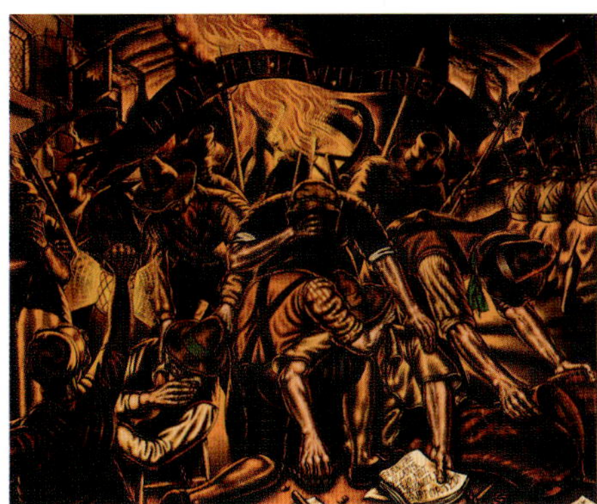

Currie, Ken b.1960
Unfurling Our History ... Our Future! 1986–
1987
oil on canvas 218 x 381
PP.1987.203.8

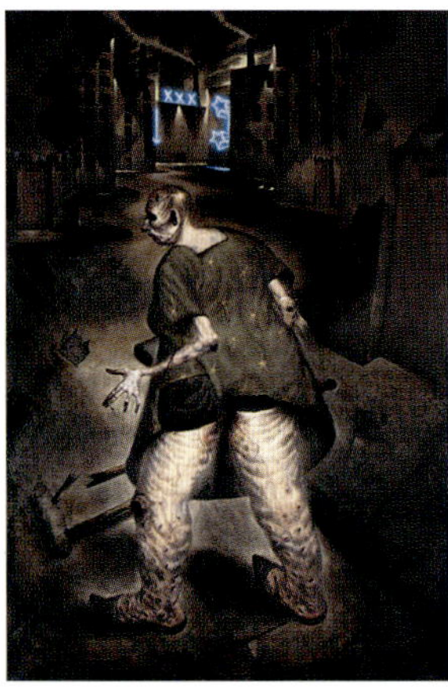

Currie, Ken b.1960
Scottish Stoics: A Prostitute (triptych, left wing) 1989
oil on canvas 274.3 x 182.2
3464.1

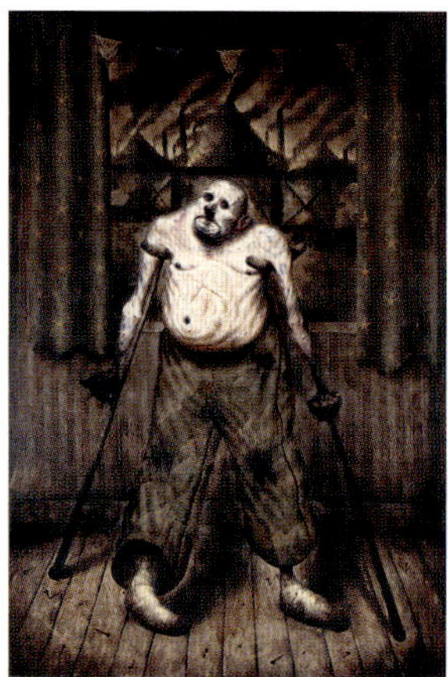

Currie, Ken b.1960
Scottish Stoics: A Cripple (triptych, centre panel) 1989
oil on canvas 274.3 x 182.2
3464.2

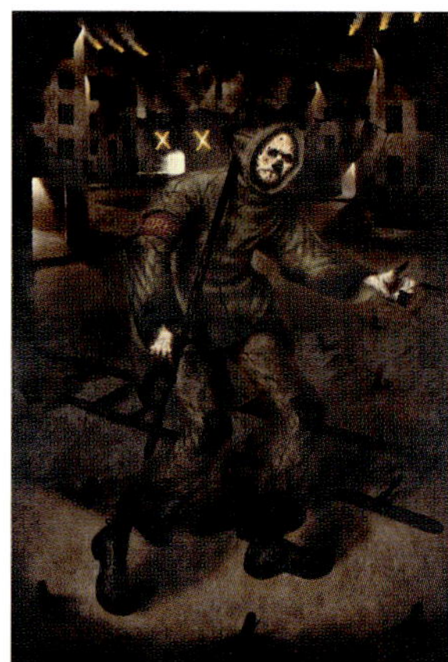

Currie, Ken b.1960
Scottish Stoics: A Worker (triptych, right wing) 1989
oil on canvas 274.3 x 182.2
3464.3

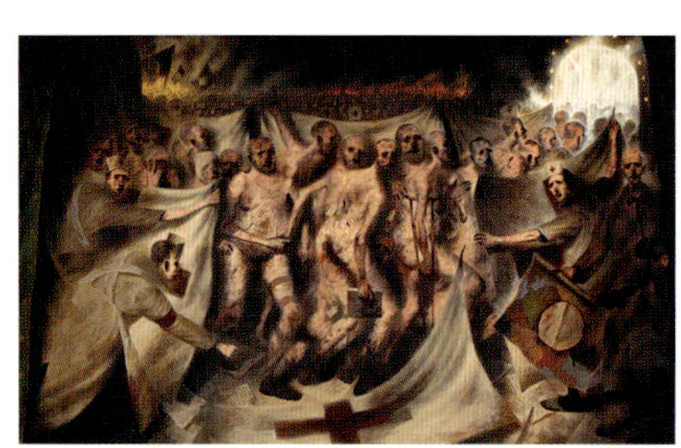

Currie, Ken b.1960
The Bathers 1992–1993
oil on linen 259 x 420.4
3525

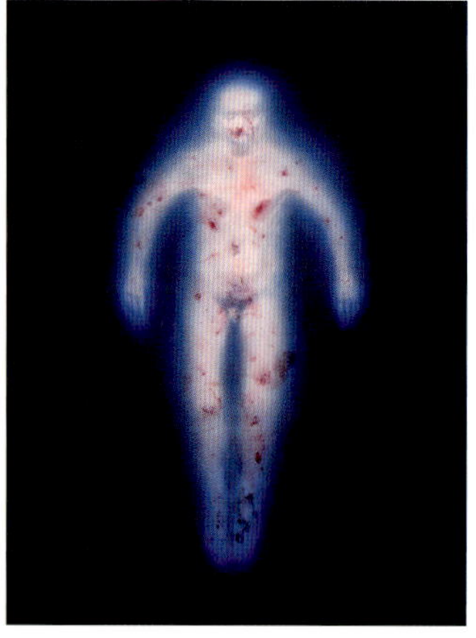

Currie, Ken b.1960
Untitled 2000
oil on paper 78.3 x 60.3
3632

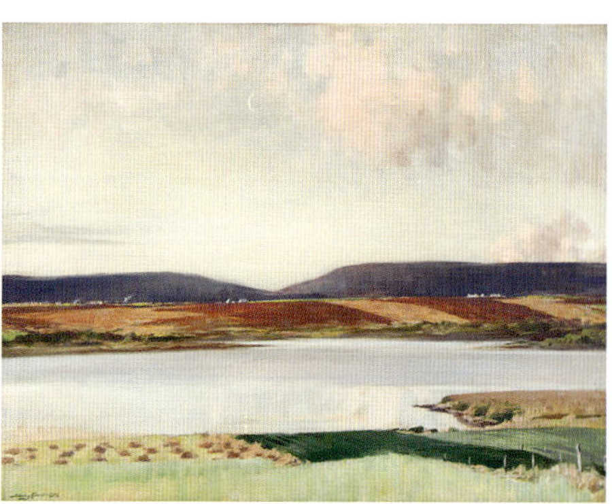

Cursiter, Stanley 1887–1976
Evening on the Loch 1949
oil on canvas 71.1 x 91.4
2842

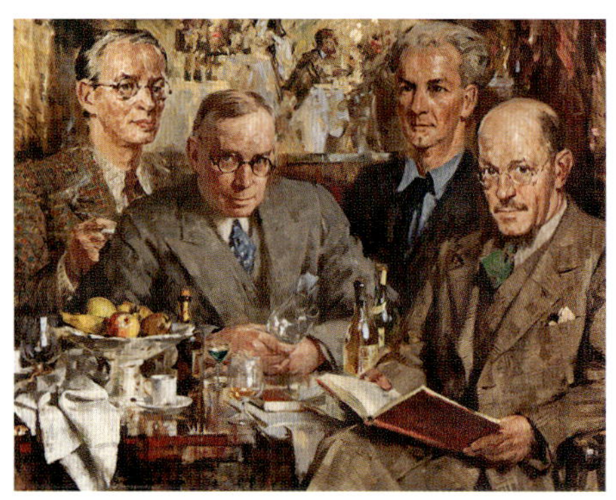

Cursiter, Stanley 1887–1976
Authors in Session 1950
oil on canvas 96.5 x 120.7
2935

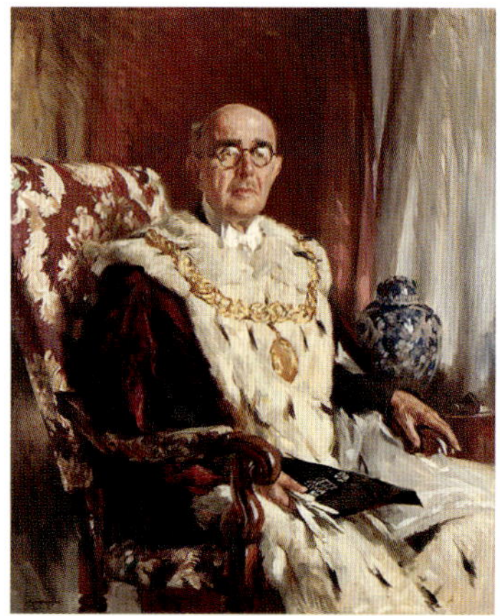

Cursiter, Stanley 1887–1976
Andrew Hood, Lord Provost of Glasgow (1955–1958) 1958
oil on canvas 126.8 x 101.5
3095

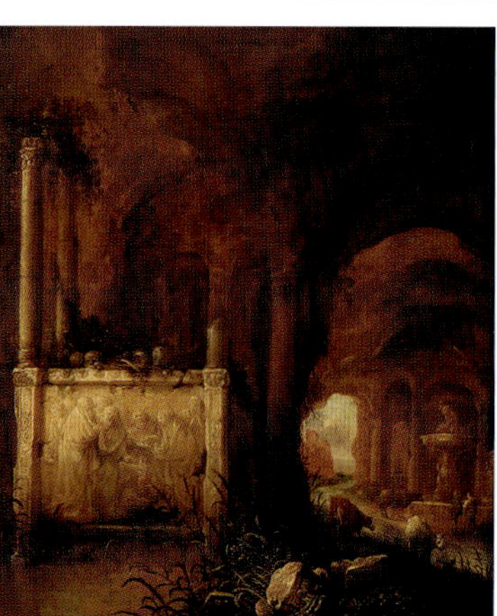

Cuylenborch, Abraham van c.1610–1658
A Tomb in a Grotto 1641
oil on panel 41 x 33.6
437

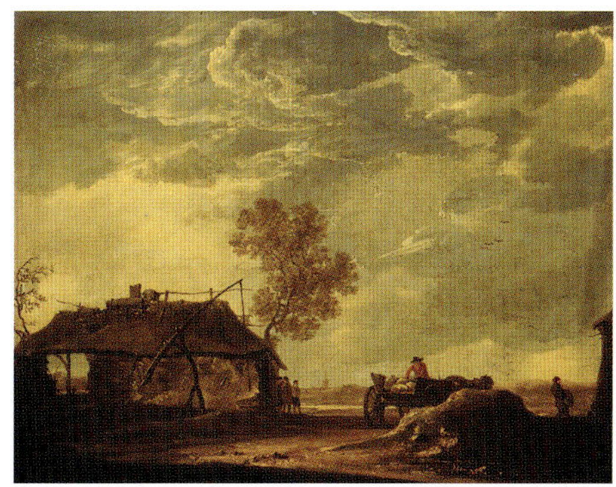

Cuyp, Aelbert (imitator of) 1620–1691
Farm Buildings and Figures
oil on panel 33.3 x 42.5
1147

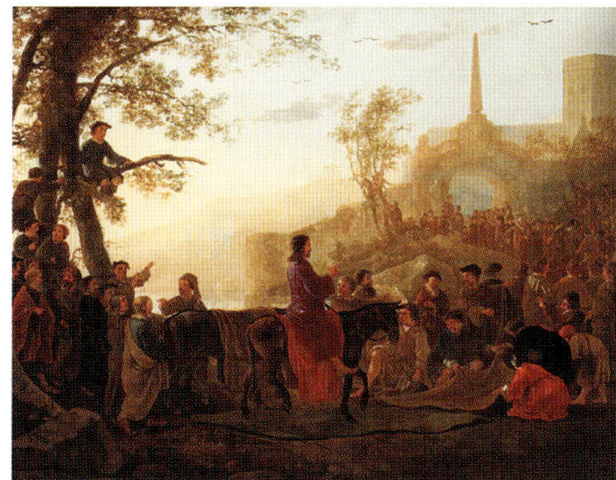

Cuyp, Aelbert (school of) 1620–1691
Christ Riding into Jerusalem c.1640–1700
oil on panel 70.8 x 90.8
31

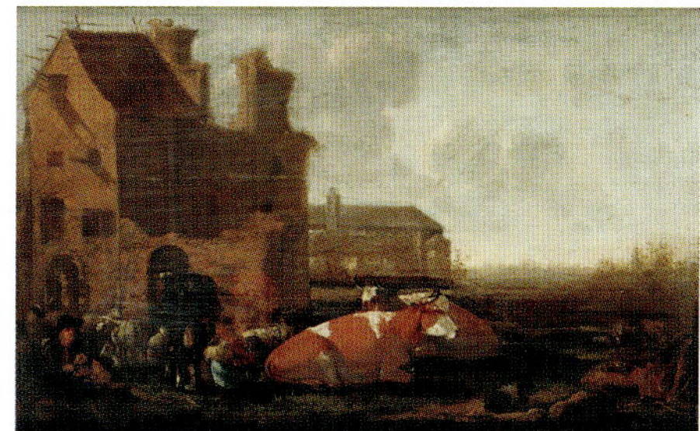

Cuyp, Aelbert (style of) 1620–1691
Landscape with Cattle and Figures late 17th C
oil on panel 33.6 x 52.7
573

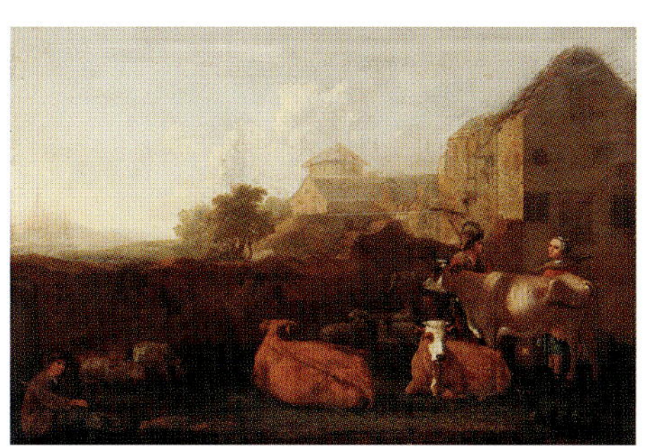

Cuyp, Aelbert (style of) 1620–1691
Landscape with Cattle and Figures late 17th C
oil on panel 35.5 x 52.7
574

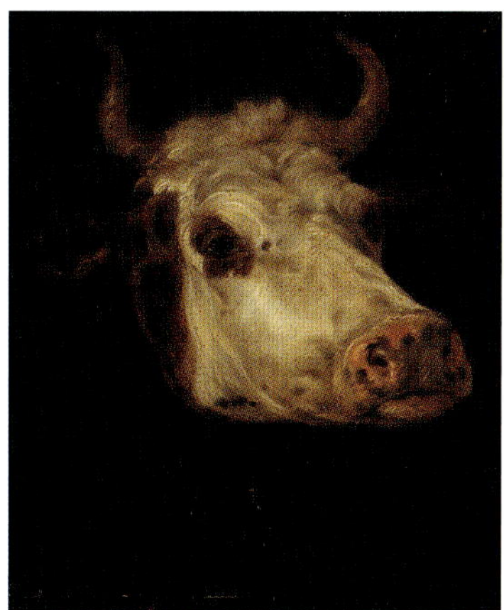

Cuyp, Aelbert (style of) 1620–1691
The Head of a Cow 18th C
oil on canvas 19.4 x 16.2
402

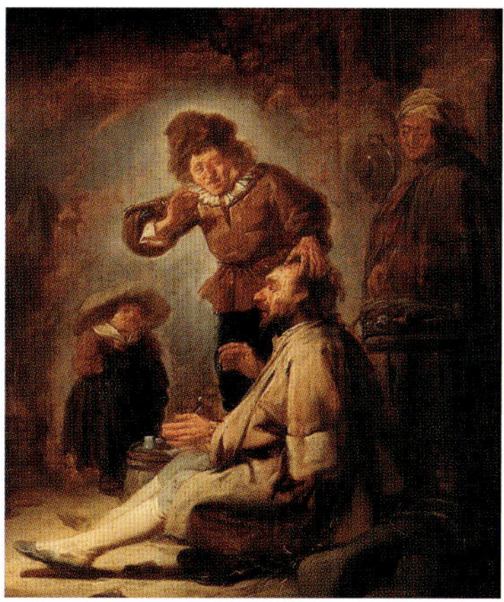

Cuyp, Benjamin Gerritsz. 1612–1652
The Quack Doctor 1645
oil on panel 45.7 x 38.1
407

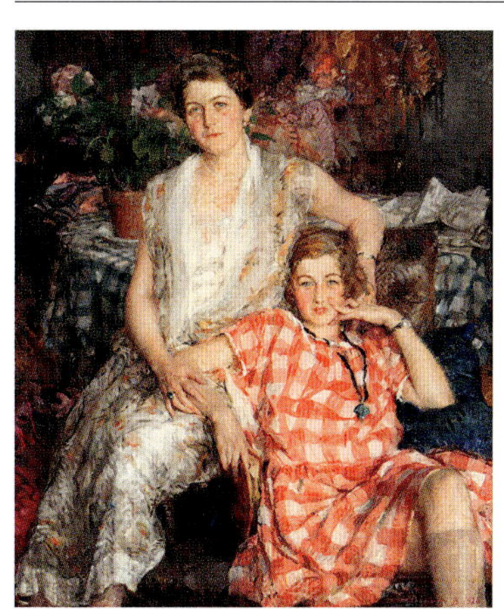

Czedekowski, Bloleslaw Jan 1885–1969
The Artist's Family 1926
oil on canvas 132.1 x 110.5
1762

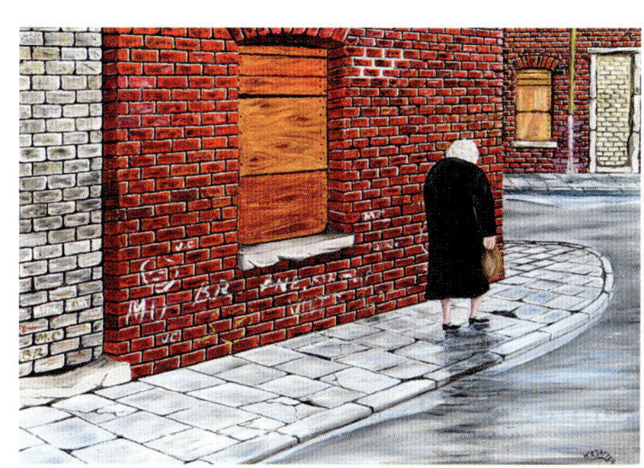

Dafter, William R. b.1901
Nearing the End 1982
oil on board 33.9 x 48
3579

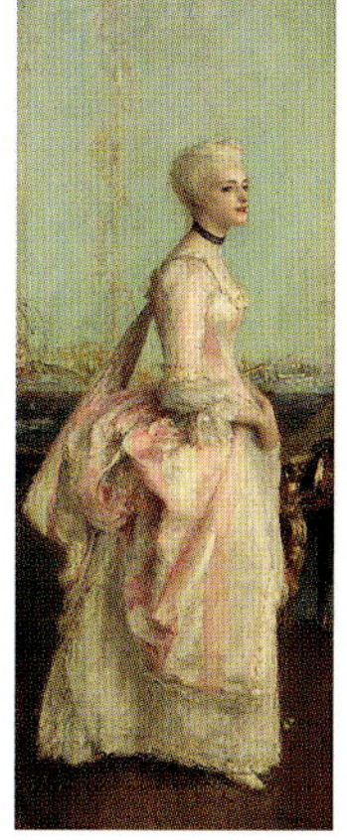

Dagnan-Bouveret, Pascal Adolphe Jean
1852–1929
Portrait of a Lady c.1878–1885
oil on canvas 51 x 19.6
3126

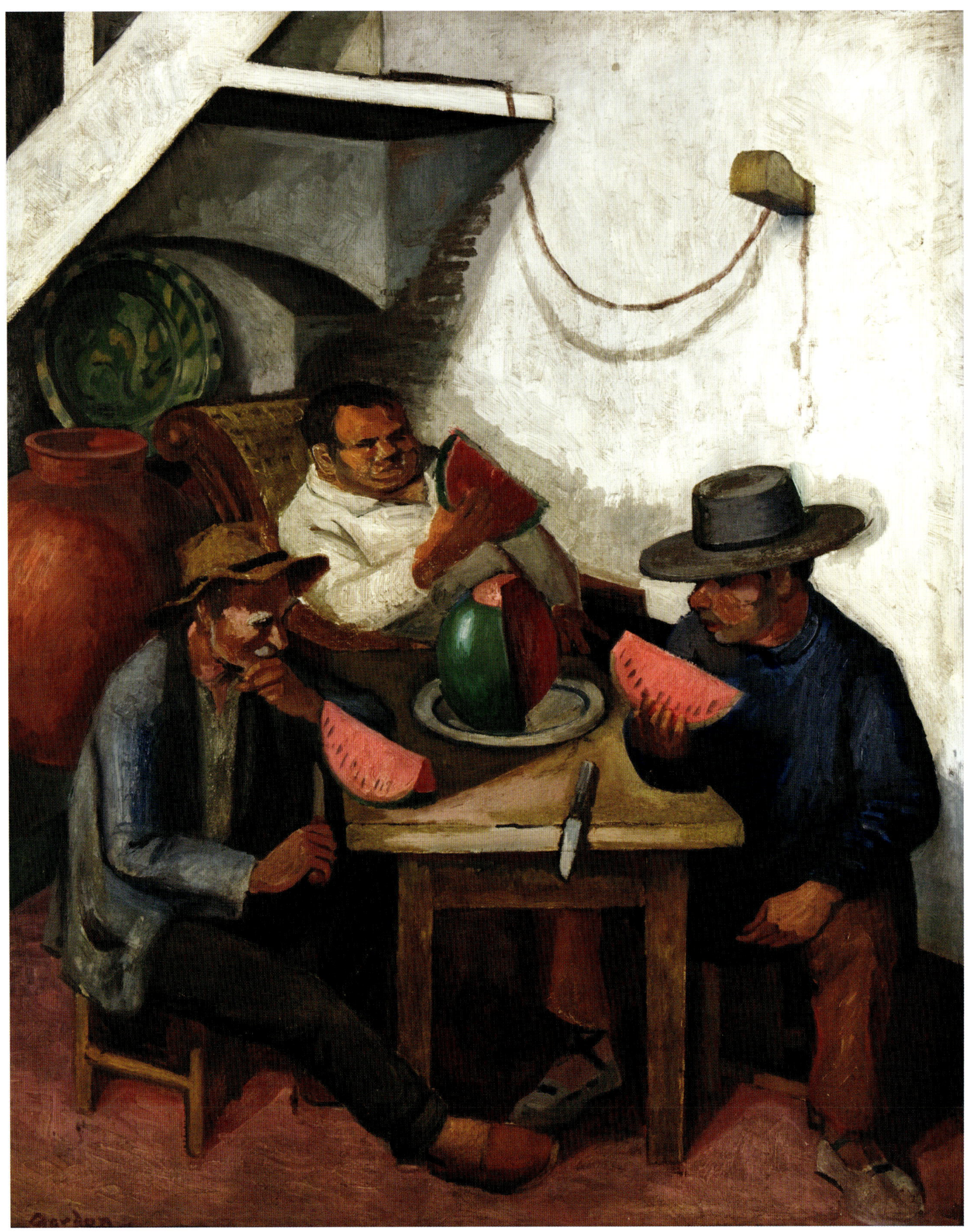

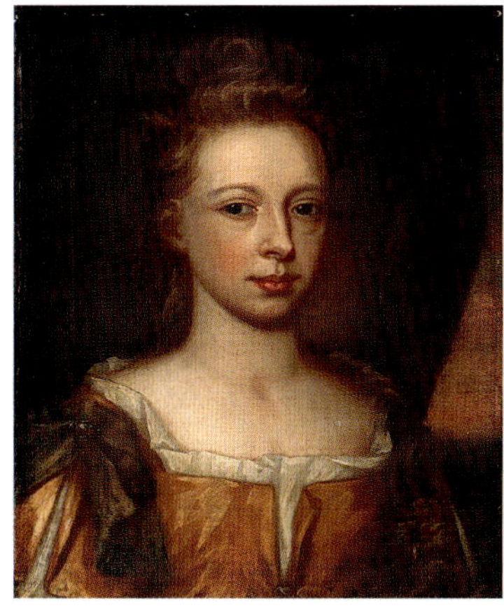

Dahl, Michael I 1656/1659–1743
Mrs Salisbury
oil on canvas 44.1 x 41.6
PC.48

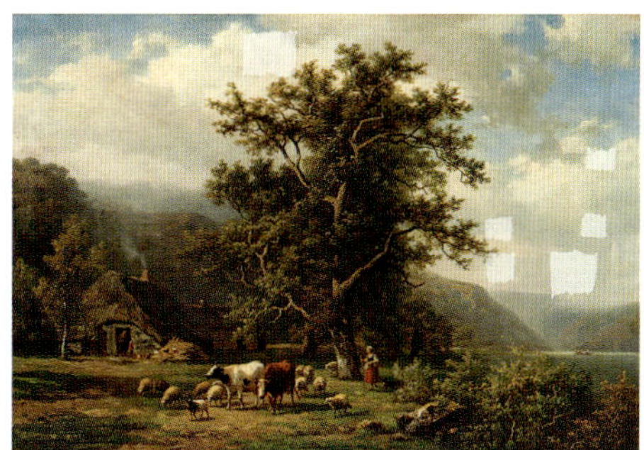

Daiwaille, Alexander Joseph 1818–1888 &
Verboeckhoven, Eugène Joseph 1799–1881
Landscape with Cattle 1877
oil on canvas 57.8 x 80
1507

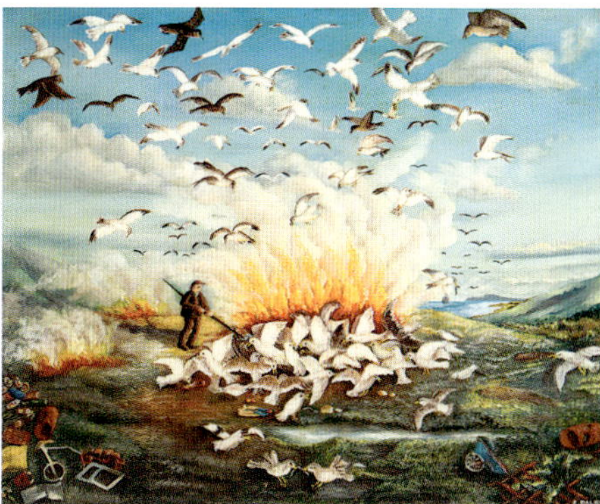

Dalby, Eva b.1915
Operation Salvage 1968
oil on canvas 46.3 x 55.9
3584

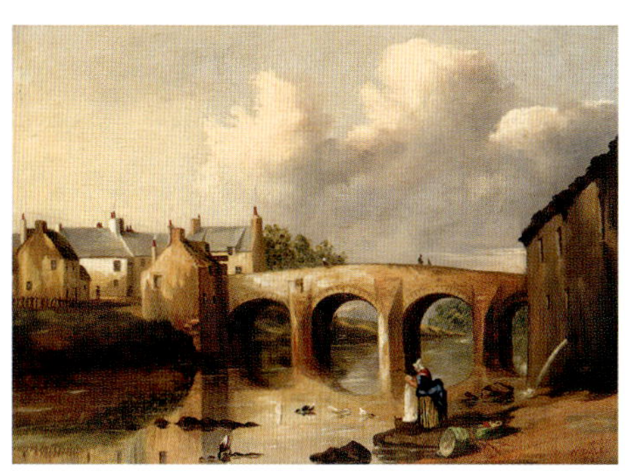

Dale, William
Old Partick Bridge 1863
oil on canvas 36.8 x 49.5
OG.1948.131

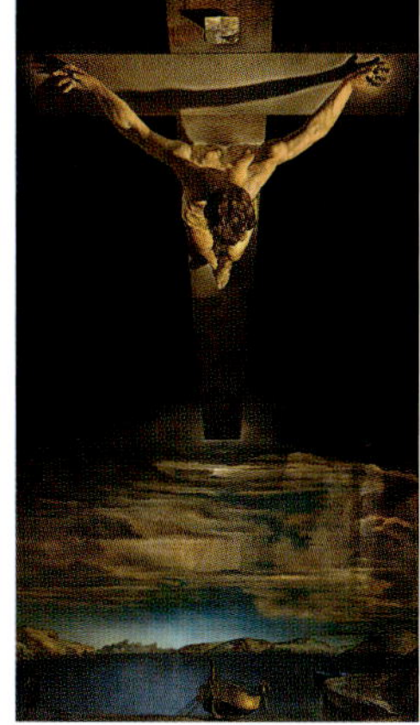

Dalí, Salvador 1904–1989
Christ of St John of the Cross 1951
oil on canvas 238.5 x 148.8
2964

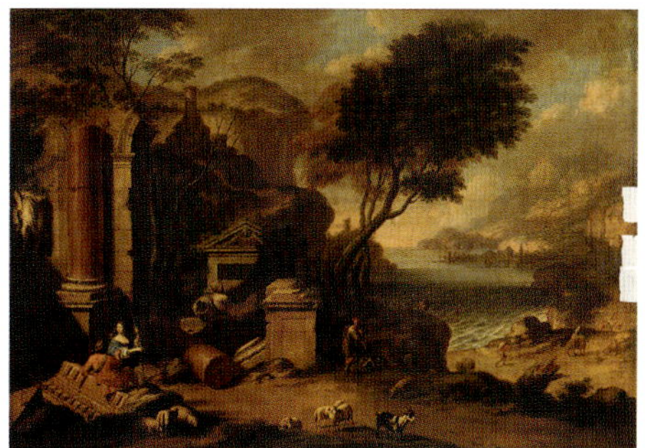

Daret, Jean 1613/1615–1668
*A Mountainous Coastal Landscape with
Classical Ruins and Shepherds* 1661
oil on canvas 99.7 x 138.7
212

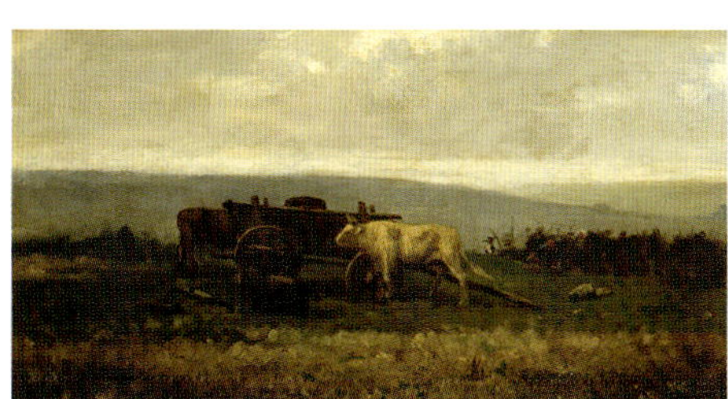

Daubigny, Charles-François 1817–1878
Landscape with Cattle c.1863–1866
oil on panel 24.8 x 44.5
35.207

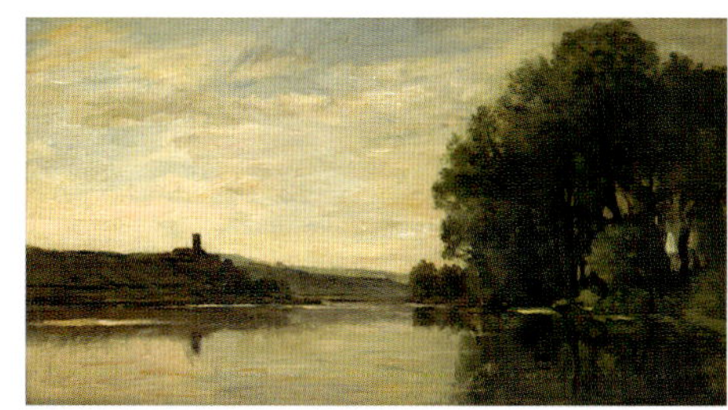

Daubigny, Charles-François 1817–1878
*Château Gaillard, the Seine at Roche
Guyon* c.1870–1874
oil on panel 38.1 x 68.6
35.206

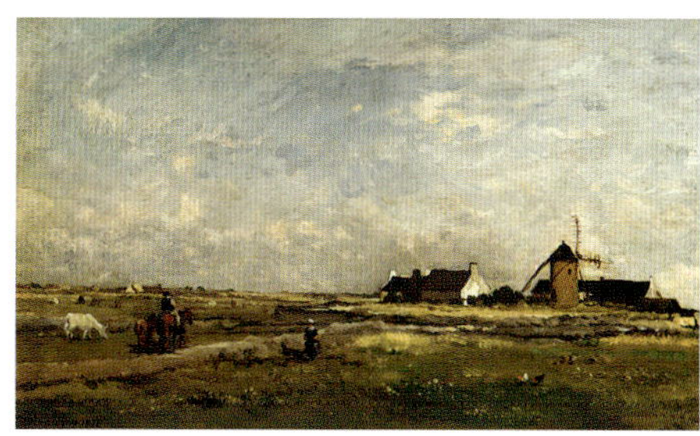

Daubigny, Charles-François 1817–1878
Landscape with a Mill 1872
oil on panel 30.4 x 51.8
35.209

Facing page: Gordon, Jan (Godfrey Jervis), 1882–1944, *The Melon Guzzlers*, (p. 159)

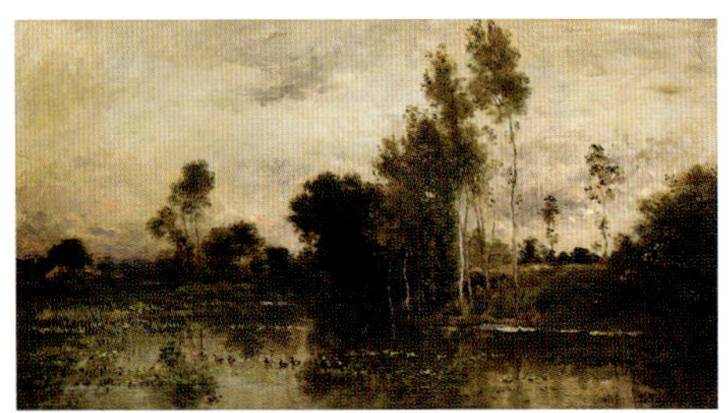

Daubigny, Charles-François 1817–1878
Lake with Ducks 1873
oil on panel 37.9 x 67.3
1141

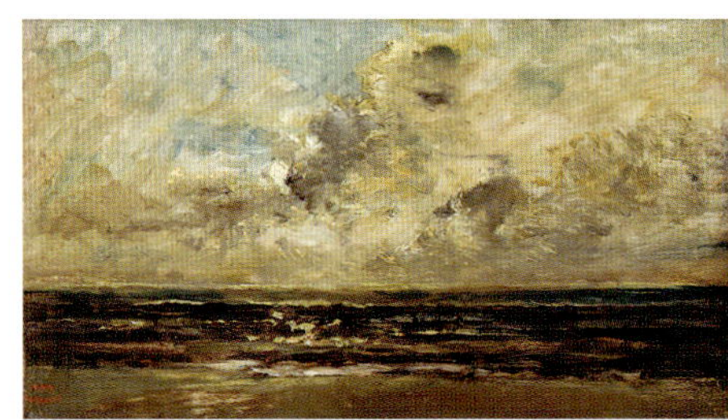

Daubigny, Charles-François 1817–1878
Seascape at Villerville 1876
oil on panel 33 x 56.7
2136

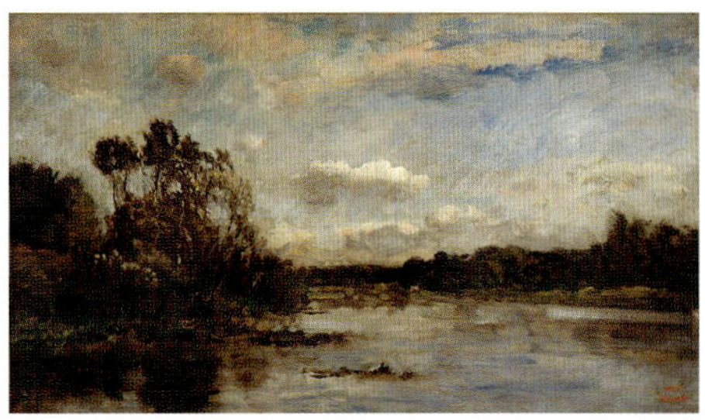

Daubigny, Charles-François 1817–1878
River Scene with Wooded Banks
oil on panel 39 x 67
2137

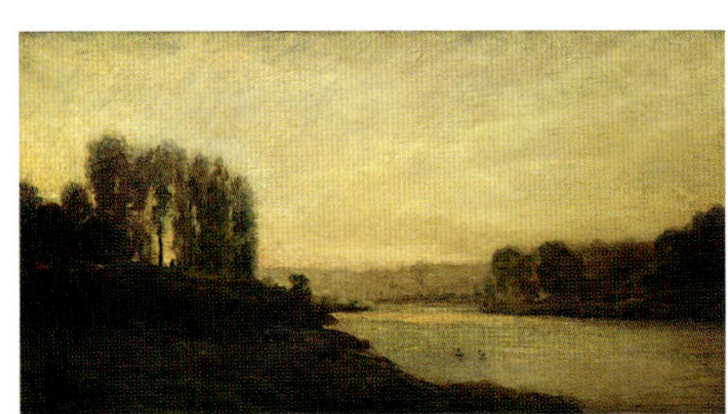

Daubigny, Charles-François (attributed to)
1817–1878
River Scene, Sunset
oil on panel 25.7 x 47.6
2230

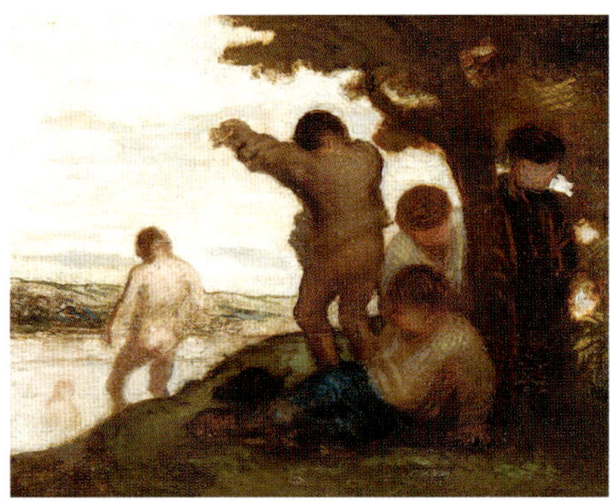

Daumier, Honoré 1808–1879
The Bathers c.1846–1848
oil on panel 25.4 x 32.1
35.212

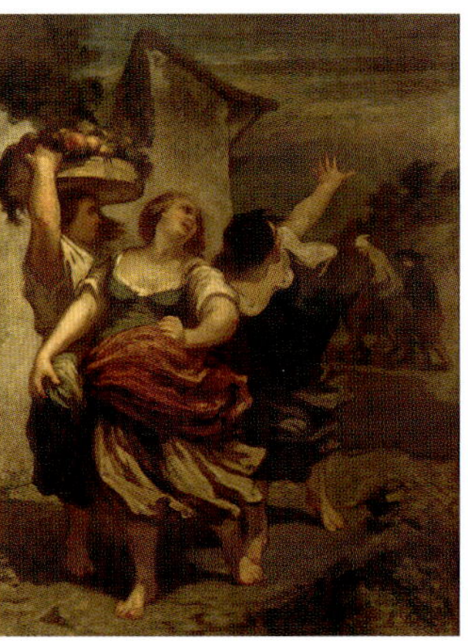

Daumier, Honoré 1808–1879
The Miller, His Son and the Ass 1849
oil on canvas 132.2 x 97.9
35.222

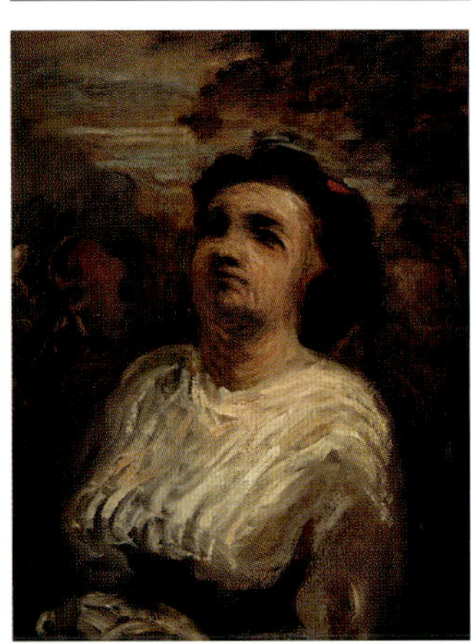

Daumier, Honoré 1808–1879
The Gossip c.1850–1855
oil on canvas 40 x 32
2385

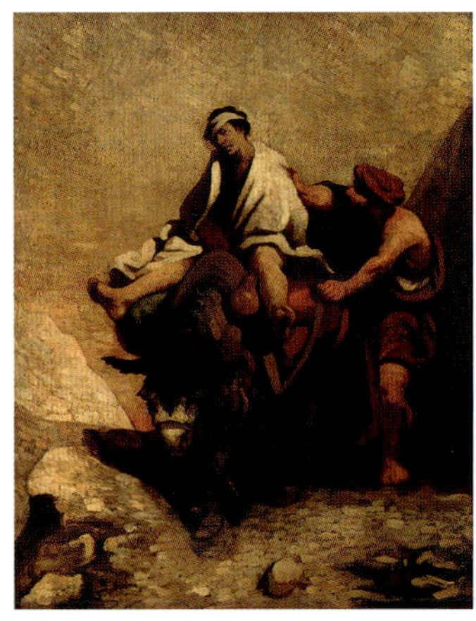

Daumier, Honoré 1808–1879
The Good Samaritan c.1850–1860
oil on canvas 166.2 x 114.3
35.215

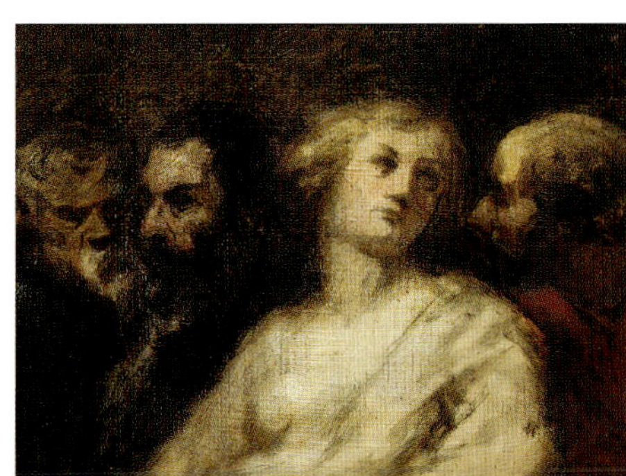

Daumier, Honoré 1808–1879
Susannah and the Elders 1853
oil on panel 19.1 x 25.4
35.227

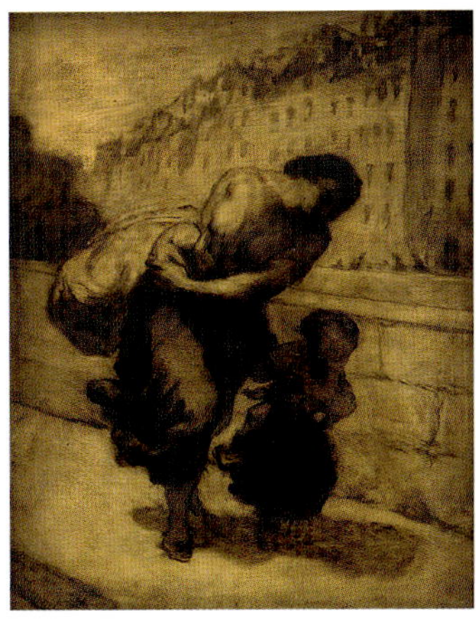

Daumier, Honoré 1808–1879
The Burden c.1855–1856
oil on panel 39.3 x 31.3
35.213

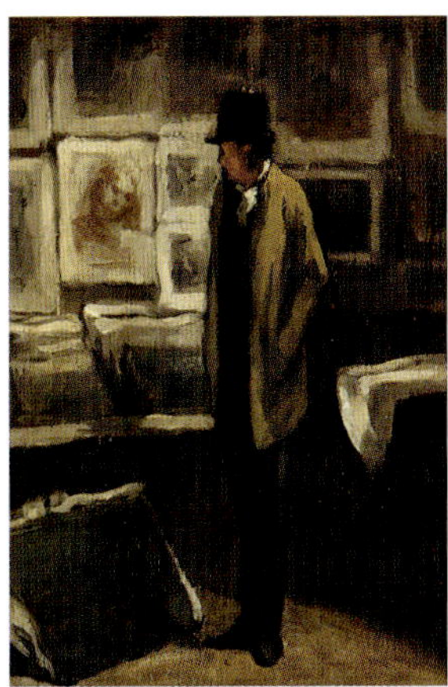

Daumier, Honoré 1808–1879
The Print Collector c.1860–1863
oil on canvas 35.5 x 25.4
35.21

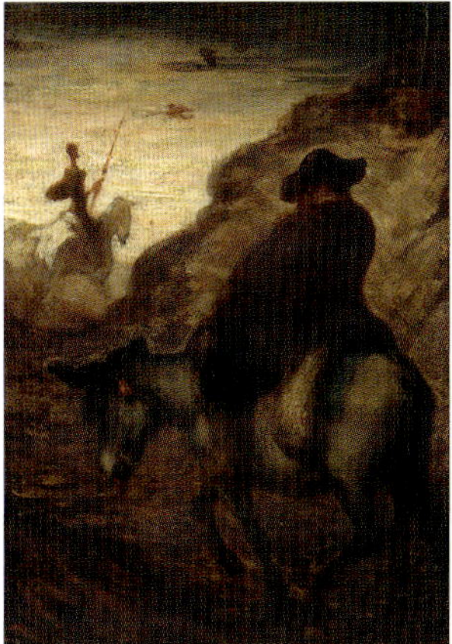

Daumier, Honoré 1808–1879
Don Quixote and Sancho Panza (from the
novel by Cervantes) c.1864–1865
oil on panel 32.4 x 24.1
35.217

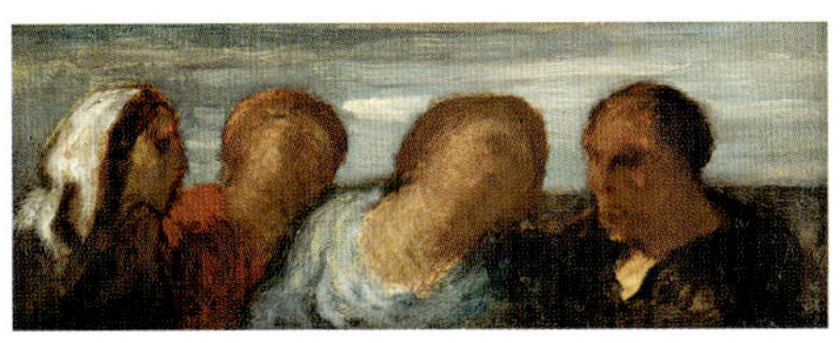

Daumier, Honoré (attributed to)
1808–1879
Four Heads c.1857
oil on panel 10.8 x 25.4
35.226

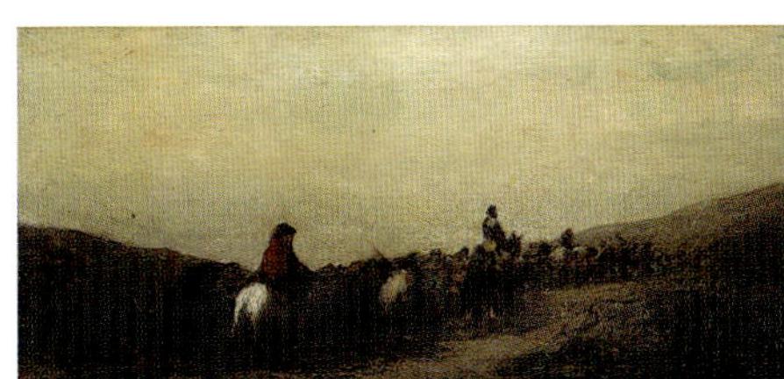

Daumier, Honoré (attributed to)
1808–1879
The Fugitives
oil on panel 15.5 x 31.1
35.218

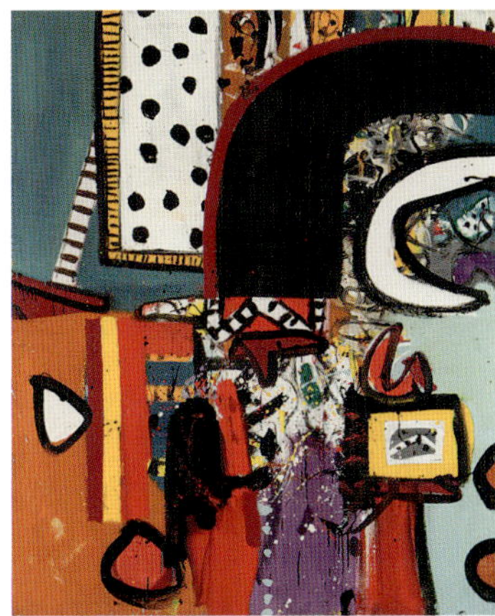

Davie, Alan b.1920
Cornucopia 1960
oil on canvas 213.3 x 172.7
3503

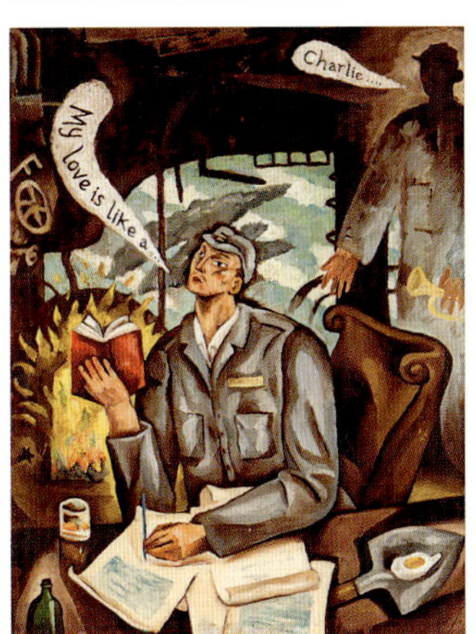

Davie, Joseph b.1965
The Poetic Stoker 1988
oil on paper 132 x 98
PR.2007.2.25

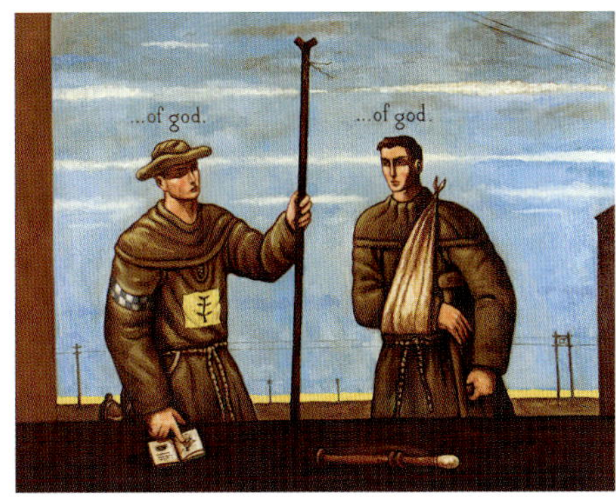

Davie, Joseph b.1965
Apostleship 1991
oil on canvas 182.9 x 228.6
3480

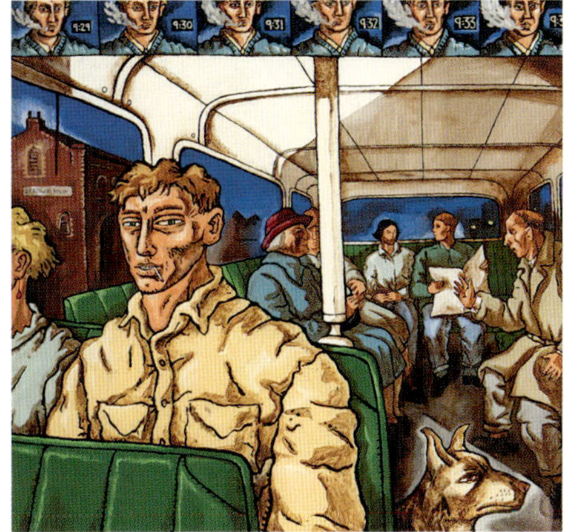

Davie, Joseph b.1965
The 37 Bus
enamel on canvas 59.5 x 59.6
1990.68.3

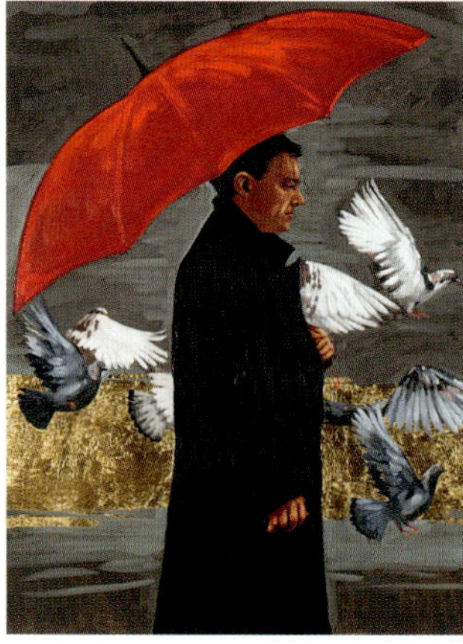

Davis, Jason Pyper b.1973
Flutter c.2003
oil on canvas 121.5 x 90.2
3649

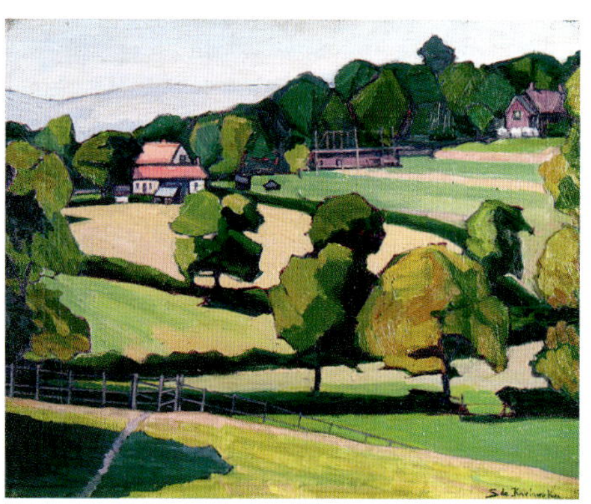

De Karlowska, Stanislawa 1876–1952
Cottages at Cuckfield, Sussex c.1914
oil on canvas 50.5 x 61
3254

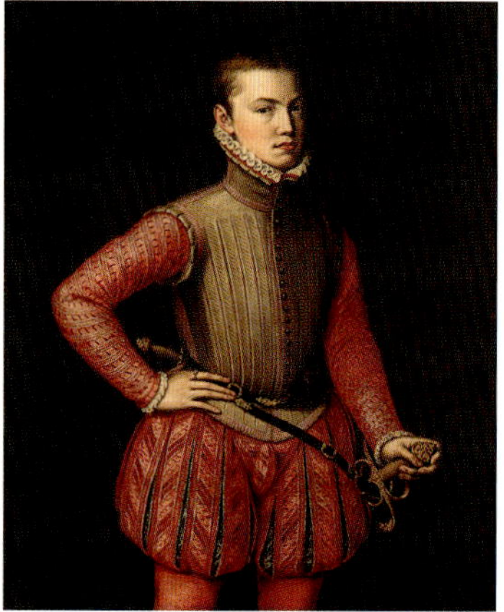

de la Rua, Jorge active 1552–1578
Don John of Austria (1547–1578)
oil on canvas 97.5 x 76.5
PC.6

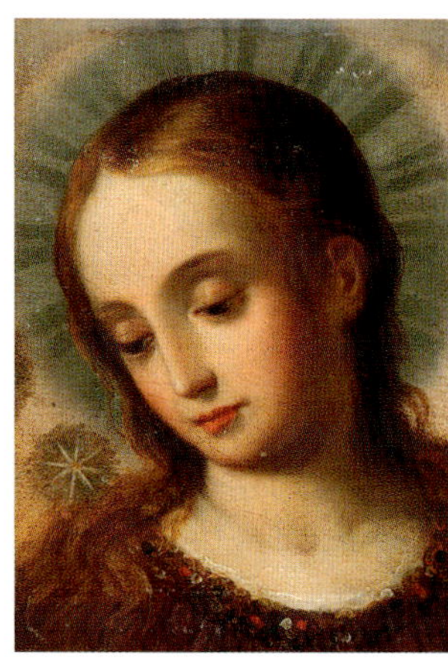

de Roelas, Juan (style of) c.1558–1625
Head of a Female Saint c.1600–1620
oil on canvas laid on board 27 x 18
NR.7

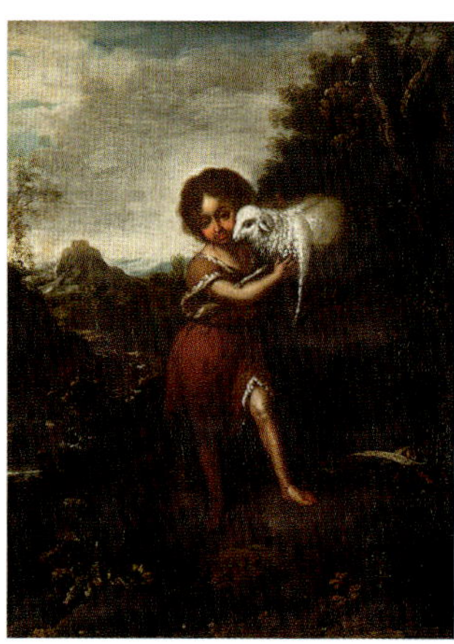

de Tobar, Alonso Miguel 1678–1758
The Infant Saint John with the Lamb (after
Bartolomé Esteban Murillo)
oil on canvas 80.6 x 60.3
PC.9

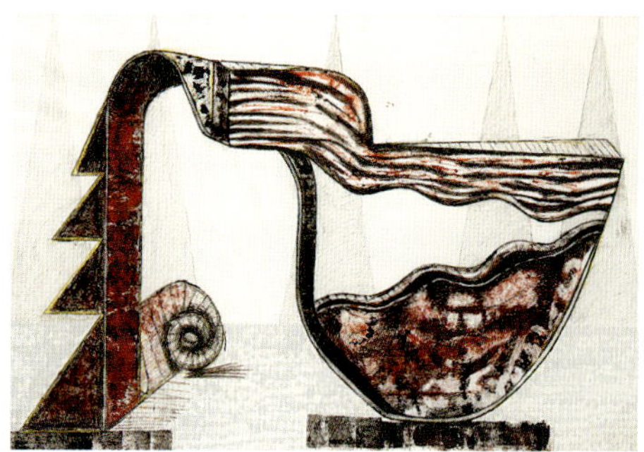

Dean, Fiona b.1962
Water Dipper
oil, conté, ink, gouache & pastel on paper
59 x 83
PR.2007.2.30

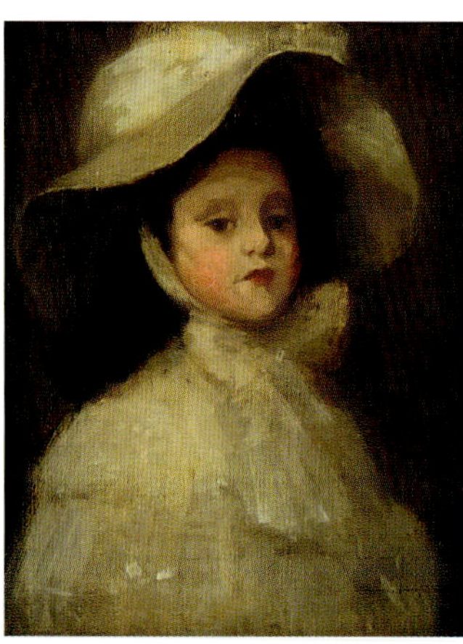

Dean, Stansmore Richmond Leslie
1866–1944
Jean Macaulay Stevenson
oil on canvas 53.3 x 43.2
3390

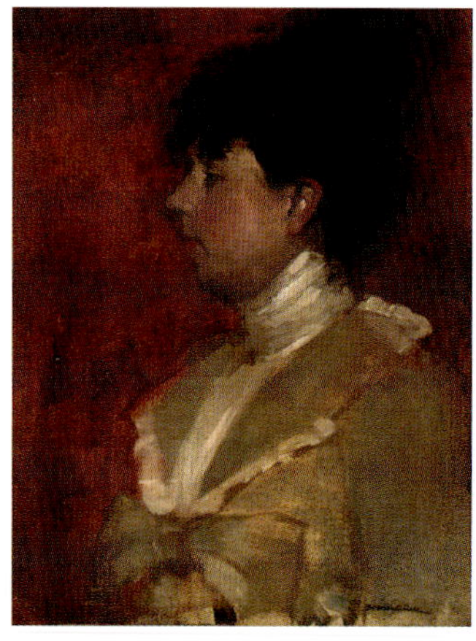

Dean, Stansmore Richmond Leslie
1866–1944
Portrait of a Lady
oil on canvas 60.8 x 46.3
3391

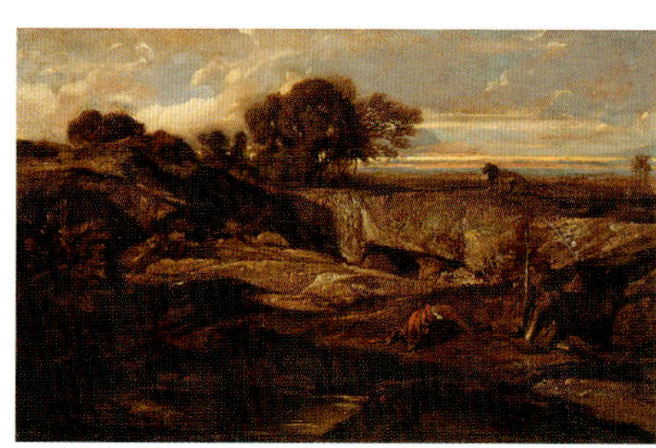

Decamps, Alexandre-Gabriel 1803–1860
Saint Jerome in the Wilderness 1842
oil on paper on canvas 45.7 x 69.2
1129

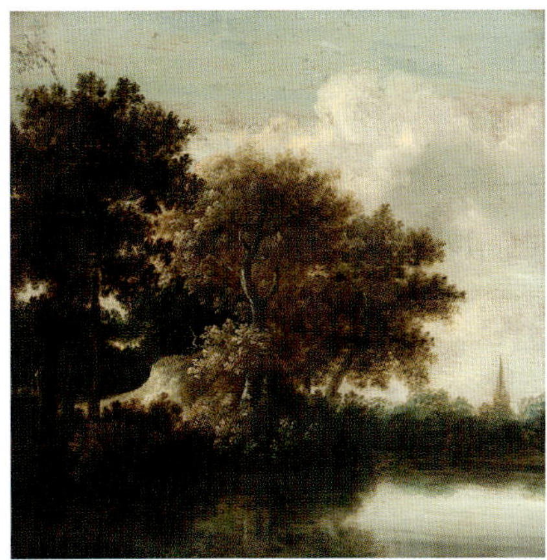

Decker, Cornelis Gerritsz. (style of)
before 1625–1678
A Landscape 17th C
oil on panel 30.1 x 29.8
615

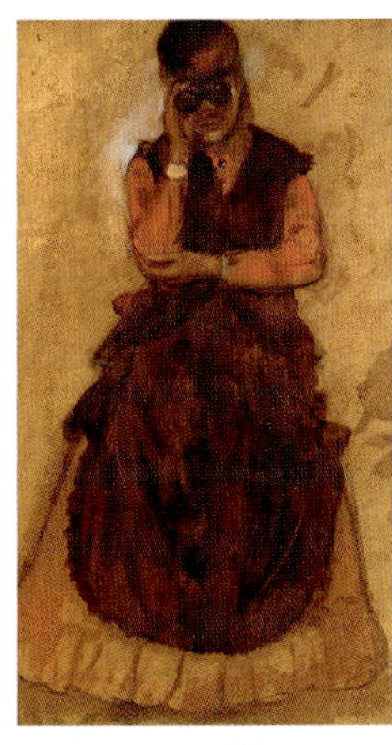

Degas, Edgar 1834–1917
Girl Looking through Field Glasses
c.1865–1872
oil & pencil on paper on canvas 32 x 18.5
35.239

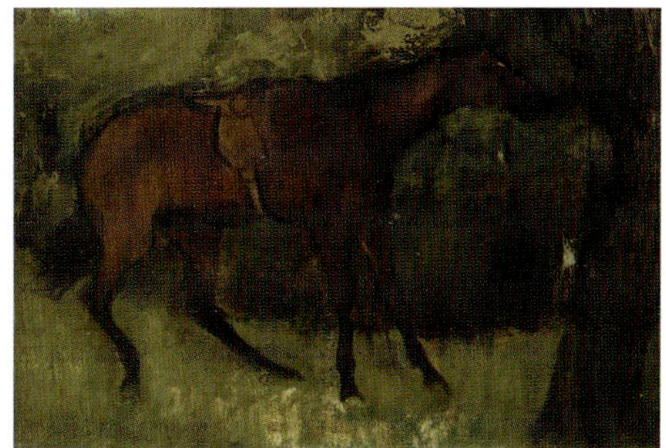

Degas, Edgar 1834–1917
Horse Tied to a Tree c.1873–1880
oil on linen 22.2 x 31.7
35.24

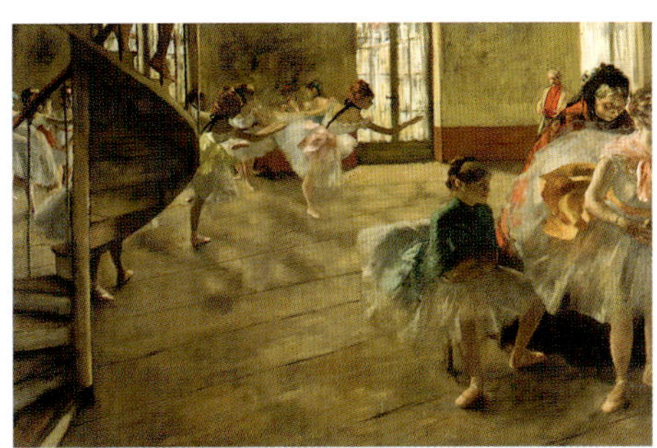

Degas, Edgar 1834–1917
The Rehearsal c.1874
oil on canvas 58.4 x 83.8
35.246

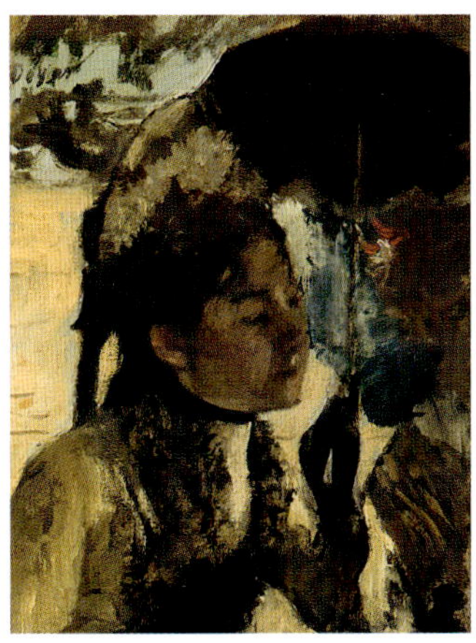

Degas, Edgar 1834–1917
In the Tuileries, Woman with a Parasol c.1880
oil on canvas 27.3 x 20.3
35.234

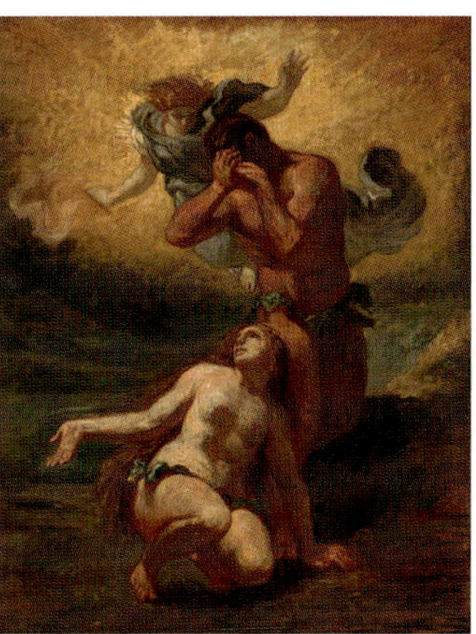

Delacroix, Eugène (studio of) 1798–1863
The Expulsion of Adam and Eve from Paradise
oil on canvas 136.5 x 104.5
1873

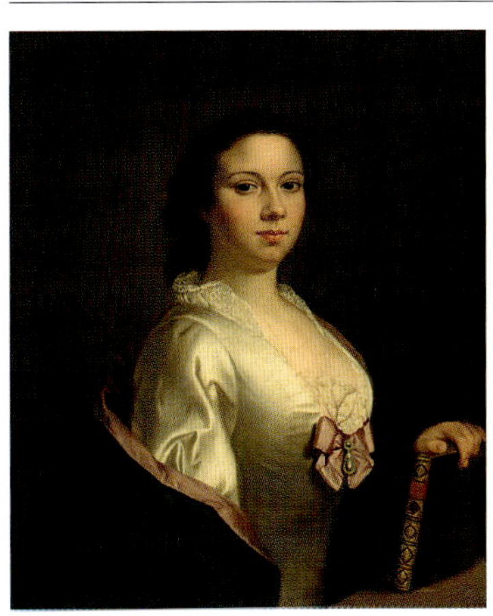

Denune, William c.1712–1750
Portrait of a Lady in White c.1733–1750
oil on canvas 76.2 x 63.5
35.597

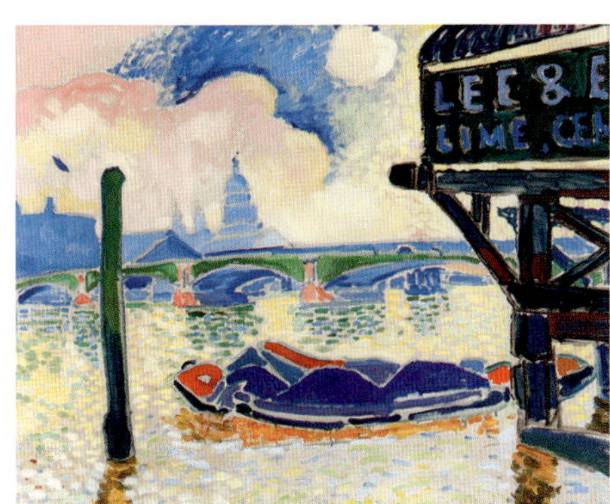

Derain, André 1880–1954
Blackfriars Bridge, London 1906
oil on canvas 80.7 x 99.5
2283

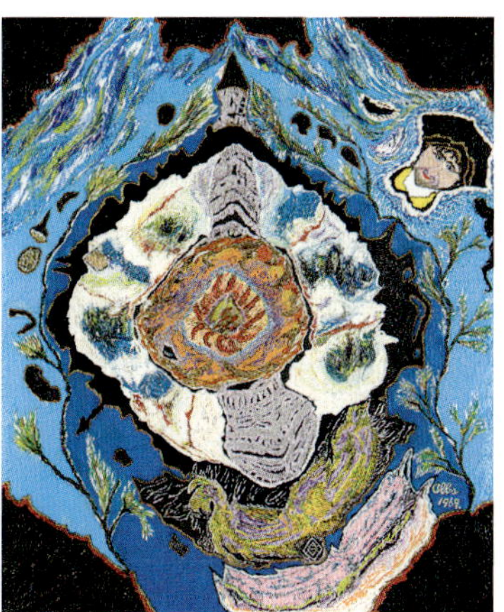

Derbyshire, Florence Abba 1922–1975
Black Jack 1969
oil on hardboard 57.1 x 47.6
3588

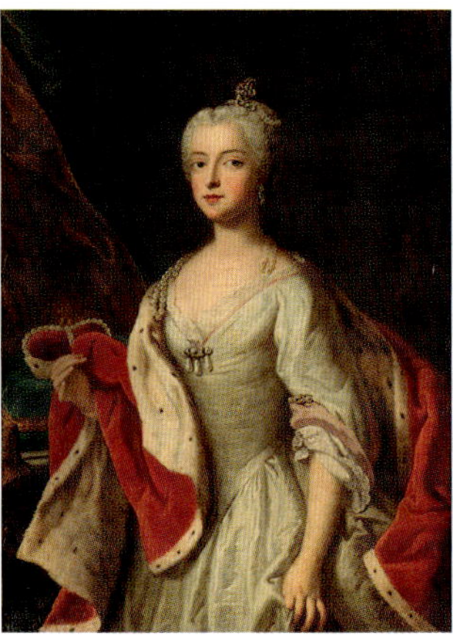

Desmarées, George (studio of) 1697–1776
*Princess Theresia Benedikta Maria of Bavaria
(1725–1743)*
oil on canvas 109.5 x 79
2452

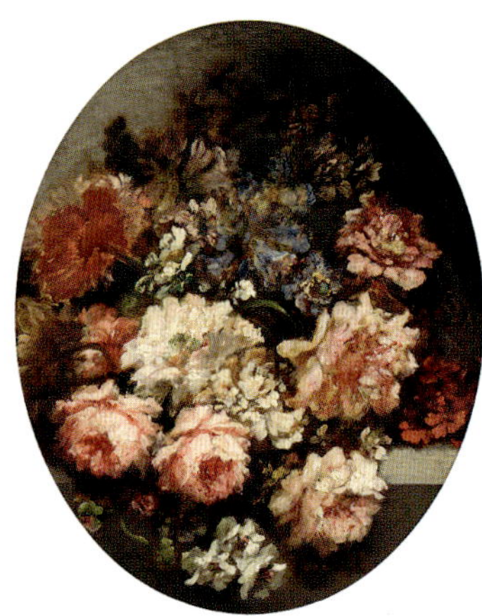

Diaz de la Peña, Narcisse Virgile 1808–1876
Roses and Other Flowers c.1845–1850
oil on canvas 61.8 x 49.5
1159

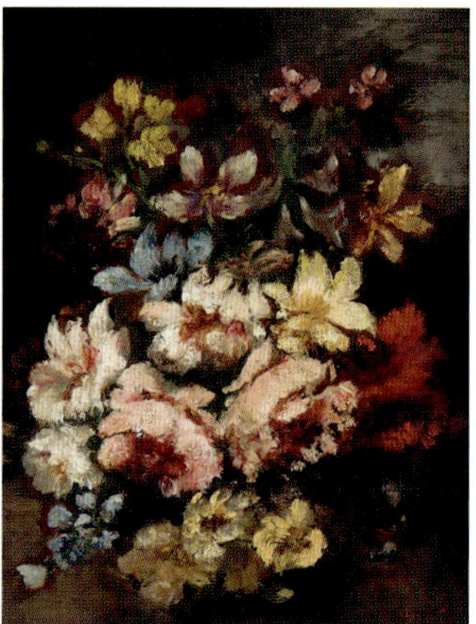

Diaz de la Peña, Narcisse Virgile 1808–1876
Flower Piece
oil on panel 35.6 x 27.2
1114

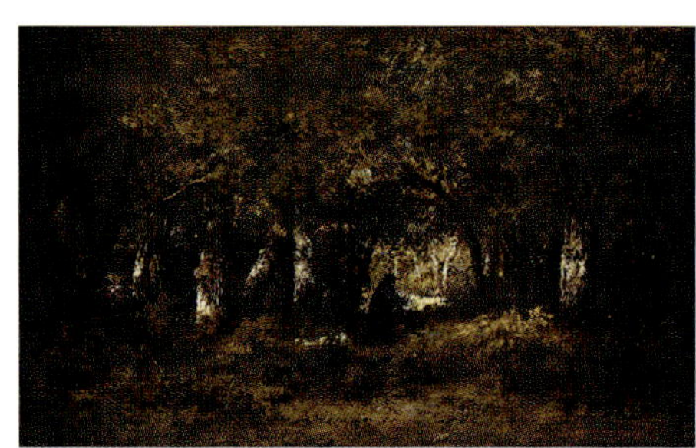

Diaz de la Peña, Narcisse Virgile 1808–1876
In the Forest
oil on millboard 22.8 x 36.5
1117

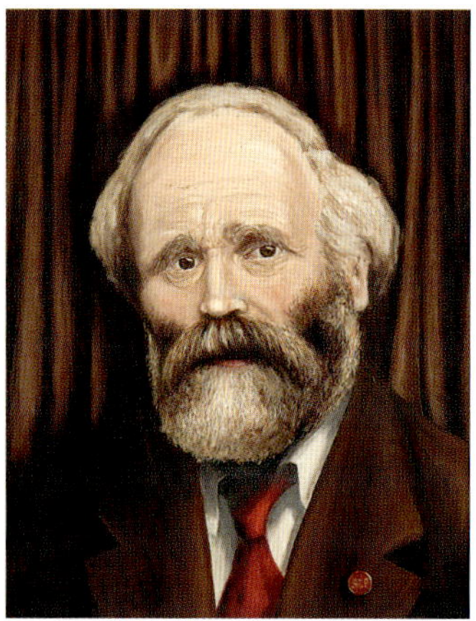

Dick, Bill
James Keir Hardie (1856–1915) 1984
oil on board 44 x 34.2
PP.1984.159

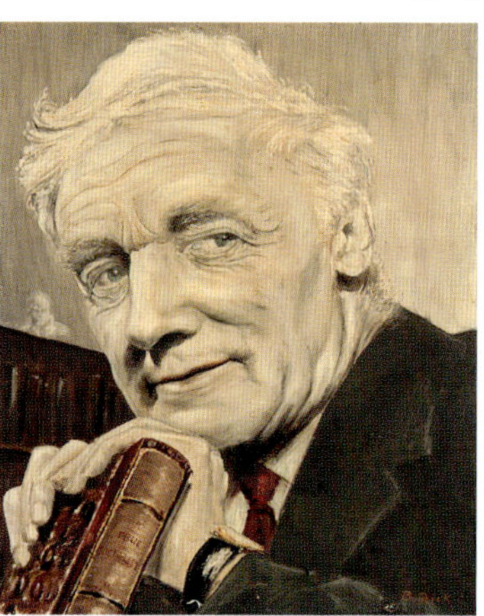

Dick, Bill
Emrys Hughes (1894–1969)
oil on canvas 50.5 x 40.5
PP.1977.3

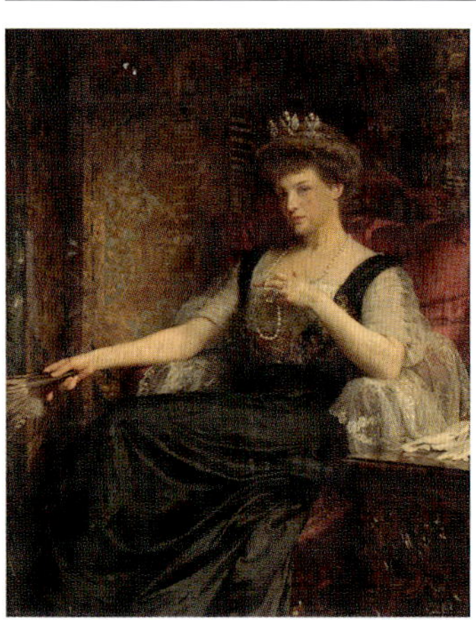

Dicksee, Frank 1853–1928
*Charlotte Mary Emily Nugent-Dunbar
(d.1951), Wife of 3rd Baron Inverclyde* 1910
oil on canvas 137.8 x 109.2
3082

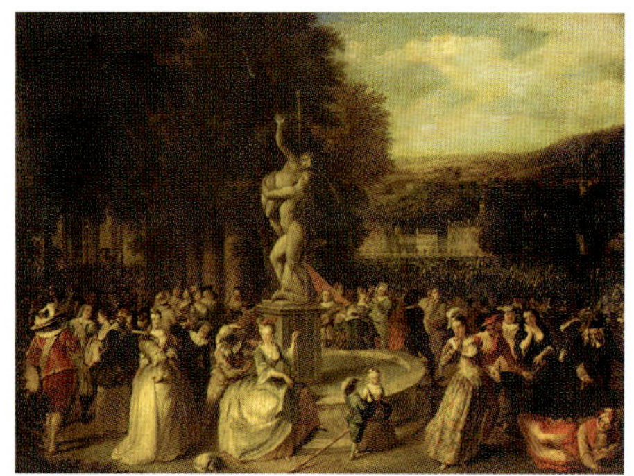

**Dietrich, Christian Wilhelm Ernst
(attributed to)** 1712–1774
A Festive Gathering in a Park
oil on copper 47 x 62.2
215

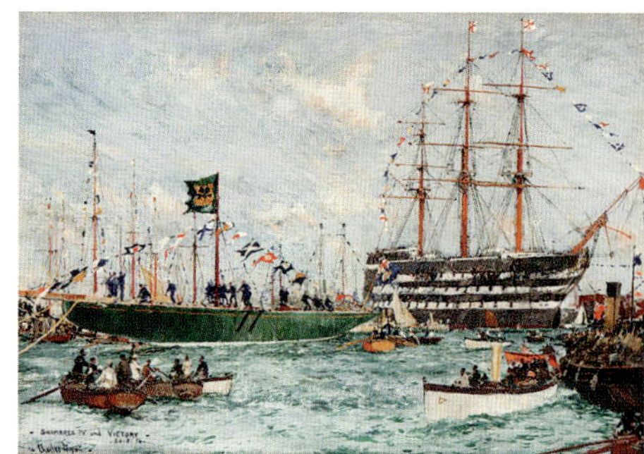

Dixon, Charles 1872–1934
*'Shamrock IV' and 'Victory', 26 May
1914* 1914
oil on canvas 39.8 x 50.4
1932.29.gt

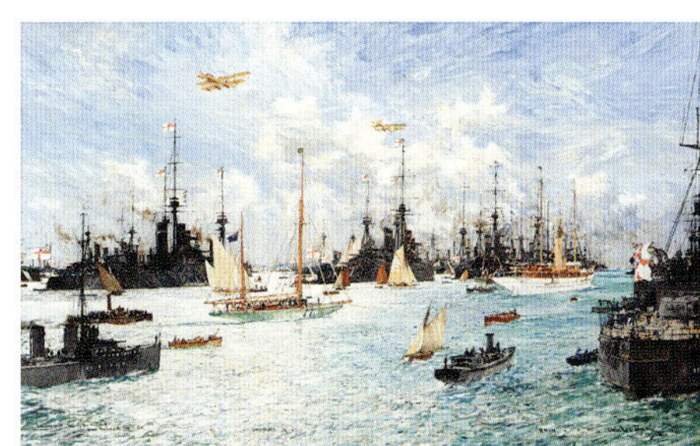

Dixon, Charles 1872–1934
'Shamrock IV' Leaving for New York from Portsmouth, 18 July 1914 1914
oil on canvas 45.5 x 71.5
1932.29.gu

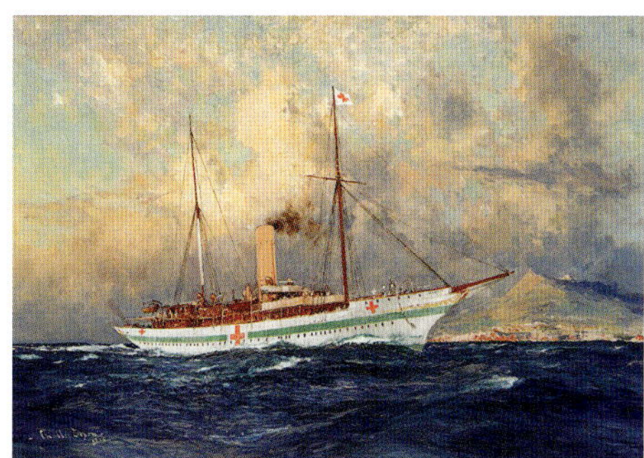

Dixon, Charles 1872–1934
SY 'Erin' as a Hospital Ship 1916
oil on board 27.1 x 37.3
1932.29.gv

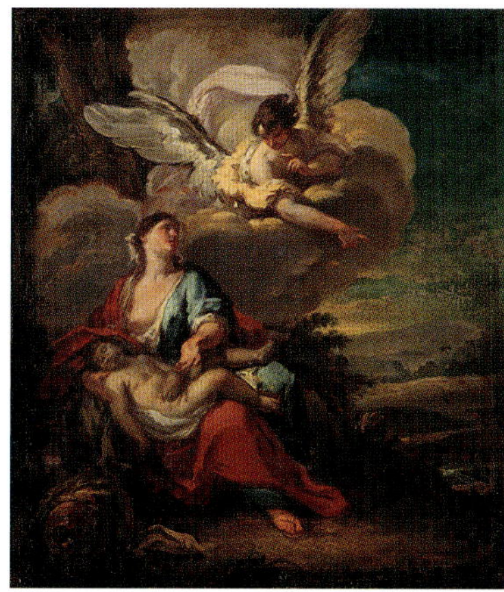

Diziani, Gaspare (attributed to) 1689–1767
Hagar and the Angel
oil on canvas 38.1 x 31.8
194

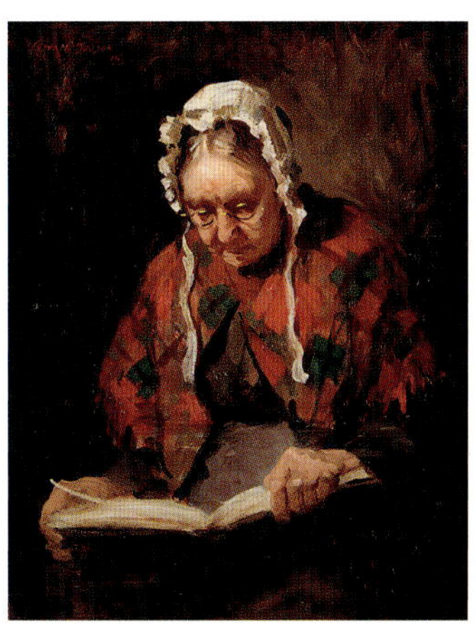

Dobson, Cowan 1894–1980
Old Lady Reading 1915
oil on canvas 40.9 x 30.5
2874

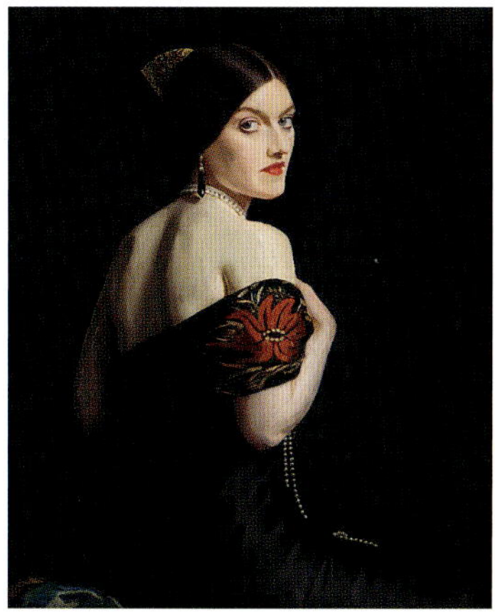

Dobson, Cowan 1894–1980
Mrs Cowan Dobson 1931
oil on canvas 85.1 x 67.3
1845

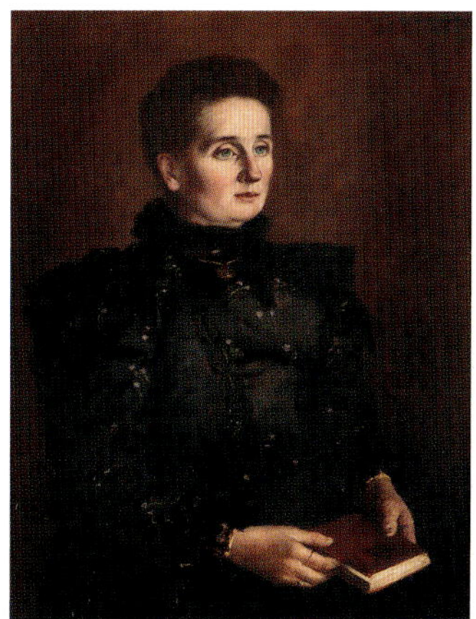

Dobson, Henry John 1858–1928
Mrs Hamilton 1899
oil on canvas 124 x 104
OG.1958.10.2

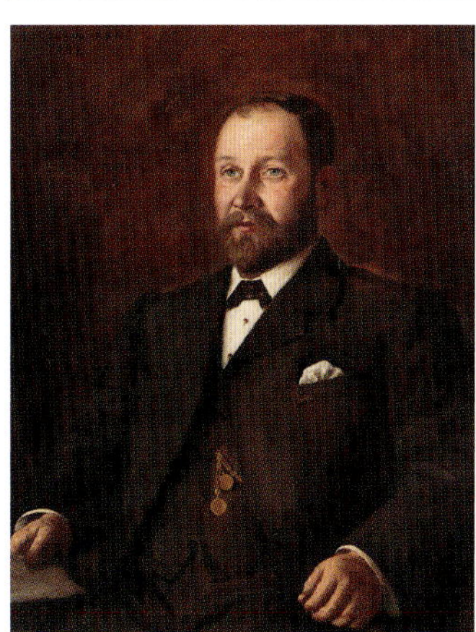

Dobson, Henry John 1858–1928
George Hamilton (1855–1935) 1899
oil on canvas 122.5 x 102
OG.1958.10.1

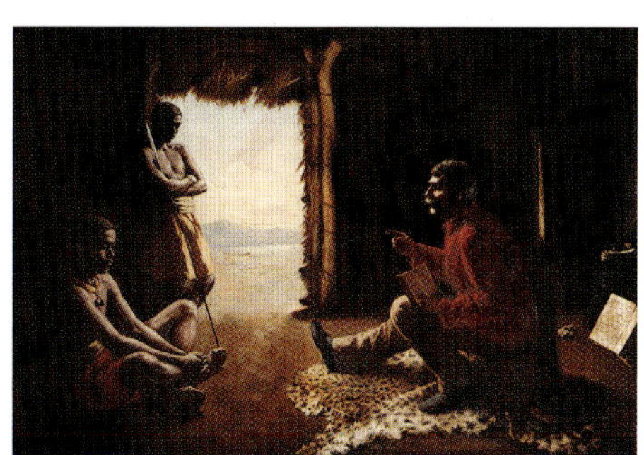

Dobson, Henry John 1858–1928
Dr Livingstone Teaching the Natives
oil on canvas 104.2 x 157.1
3440

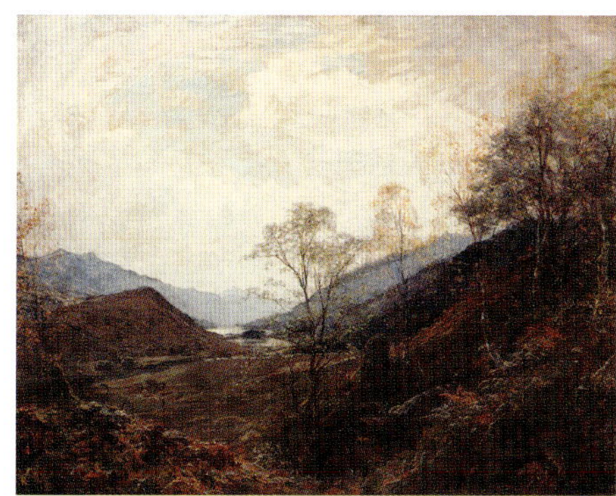

Docharty, Alexander Brownlie 1862–1940
September, Glen Falloch c.1907
oil on canvas 99.1 x 125.7
1205

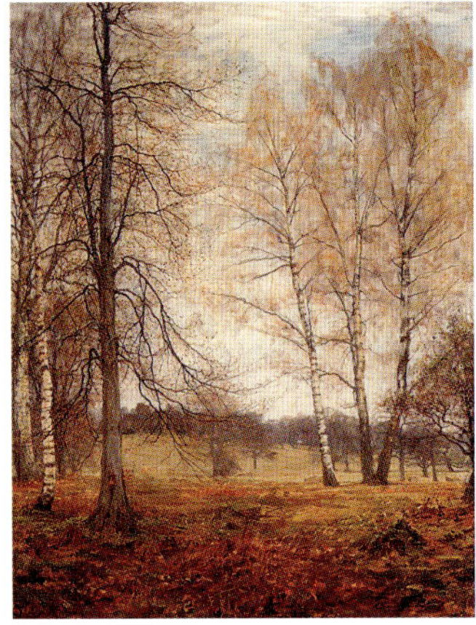

Docharty, Alexander Brownlie 1862–1940
In the Woods, Early Spring c.1914
oil on canvas 121.9 x 91.4
1436

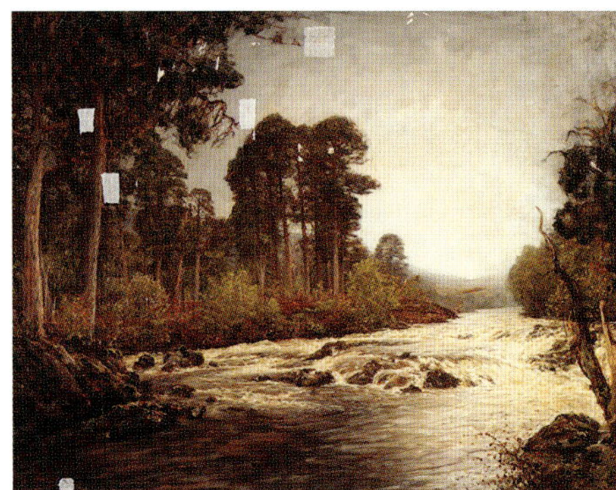

Docharty, Alexander Brownlie 1862–1940
Lochiel's Country c.1914
oil on canvas 100.3 x 125.7
1354

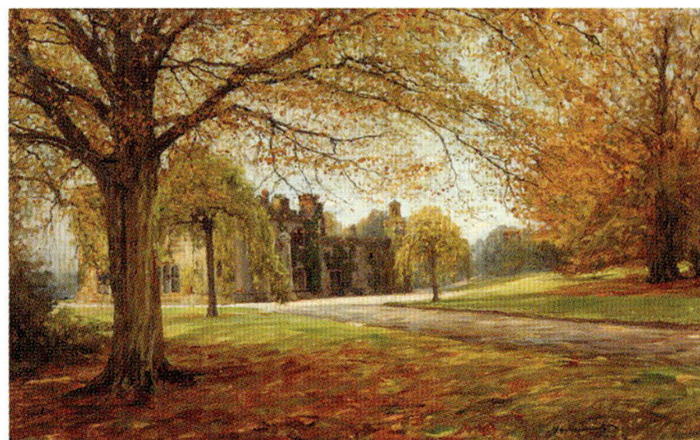

Docharty, Alexander Brownlie 1862–1940
An Autumn Day c.1917
oil on canvas 71.1 x 111.8
1437

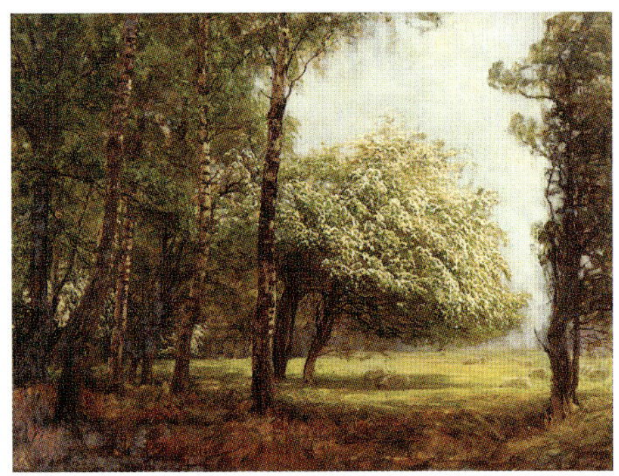

Docharty, Alexander Brownlie 1862–1940
Springtime, Hawthorn Blossom c.1917
oil on canvas 50.8 x 66
1440

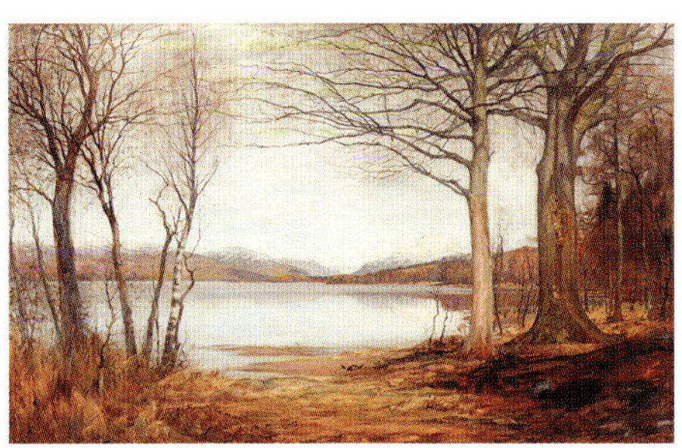

Docharty, Alexander Brownlie 1862–1940
Winter Sunshine c.1917
oil on canvas 77.5 x 125.7
1438

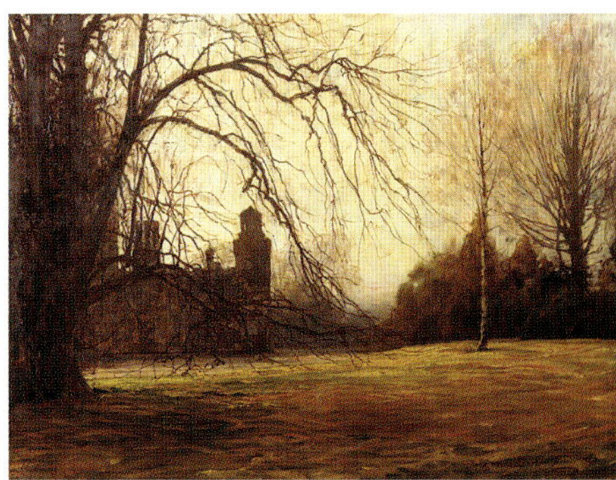

Docharty, Alexander Brownlie 1862–1940
The Old Clock Tower
oil on canvas 50.8 x 66
1439

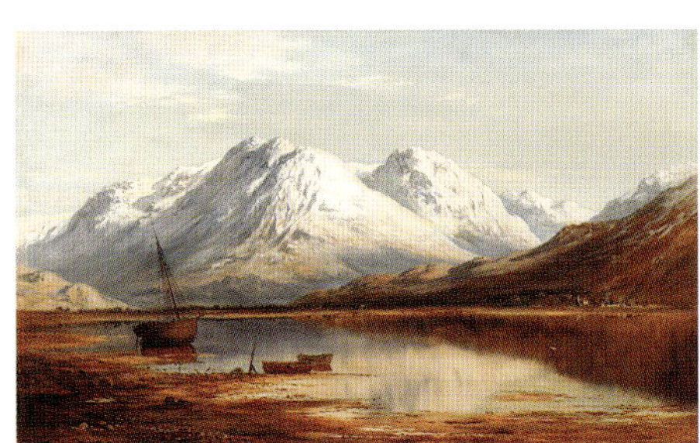

Docharty, James 1829–1878
Head of the Holy Loch 1868
oil on canvas 44.5 x 77.5
834

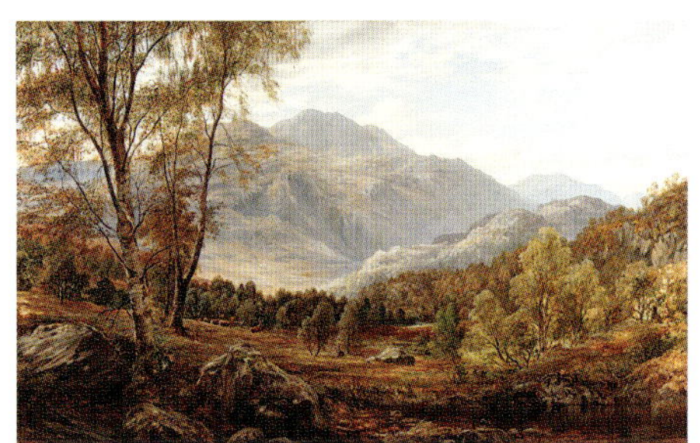

Docharty, James 1829–1878
The Heart of the Trossachs 1868
oil on canvas 91.4 x 142.2
777

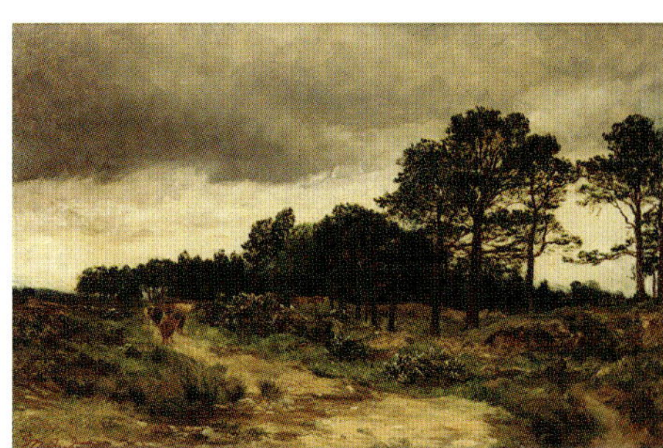

Docharty, James 1829–1878
Moorland Road with Cattle 1870
oil on canvas 38.7 x 59.7
981

Facing page: Weight, Carel Victor Morlais, 1908–1997, *Palazzo Vecchio, Florence, August 1945*, (p. 451)

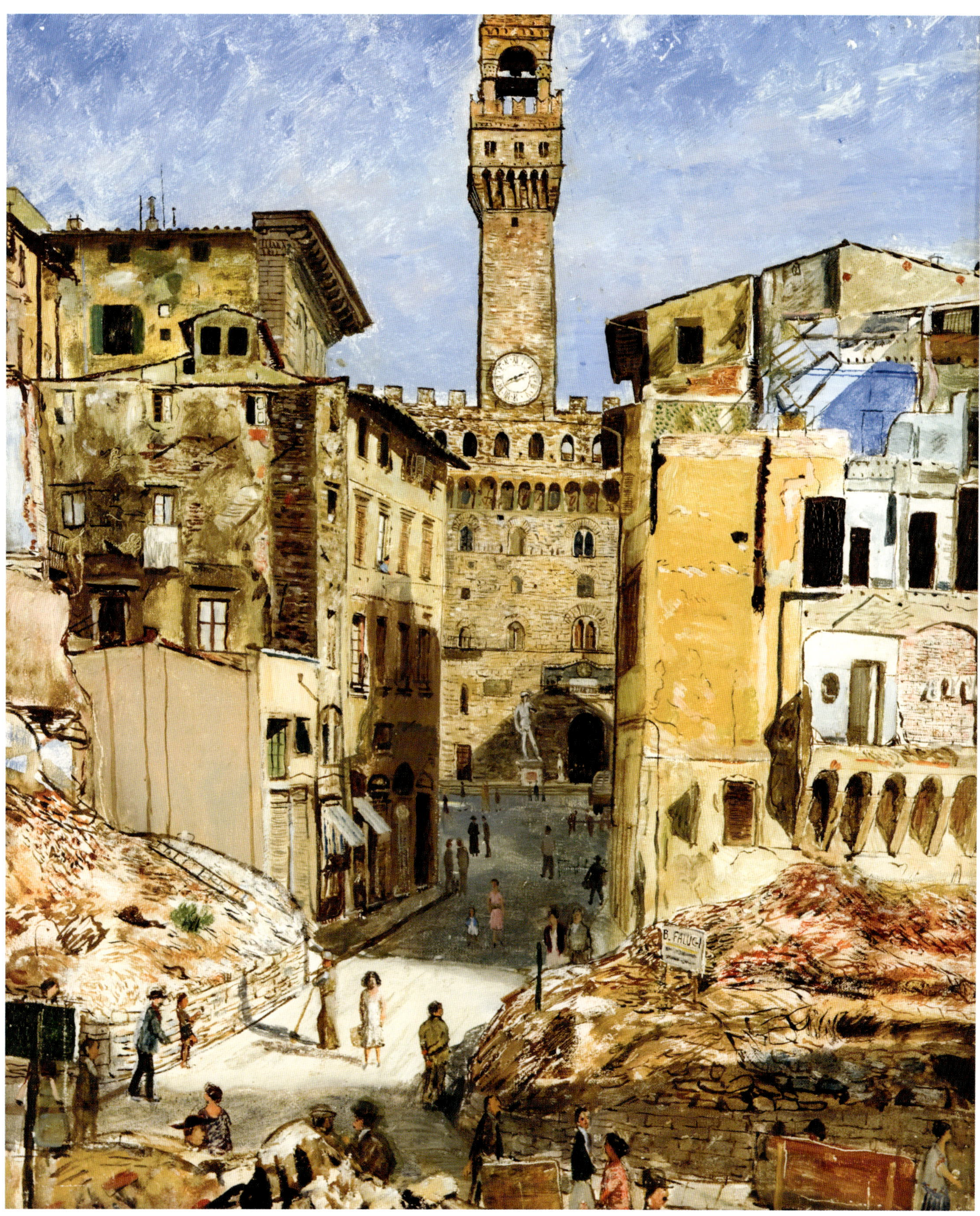
B. FALUGI

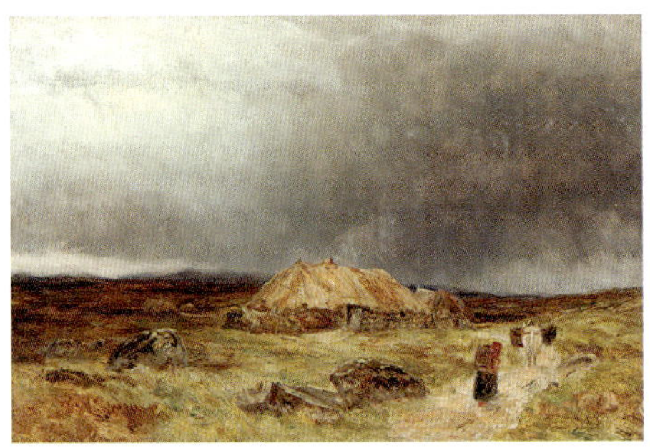

Docharty, James 1829–1878
The Lone Shieling on the Misty Island 1870
oil on canvas 28.6 x 45.1
980

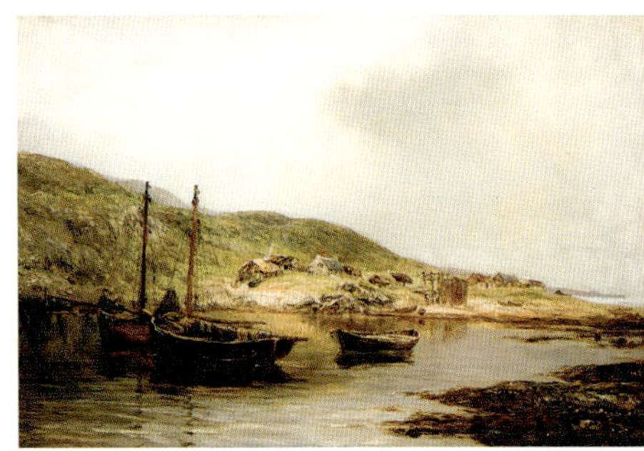

Docharty, James 1829–1878
A Fishing Village, Skye 1873
oil on canvas 45.7 x 66
1070

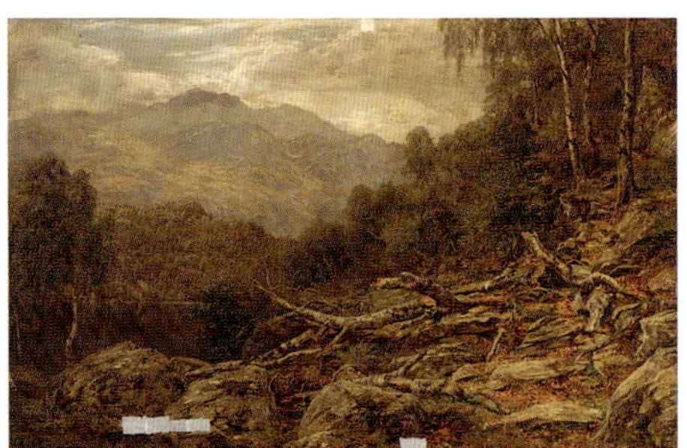

Docharty, James 1829–1878
In the Trossachs 1876
oil on canvas 131.4 x 200
1466

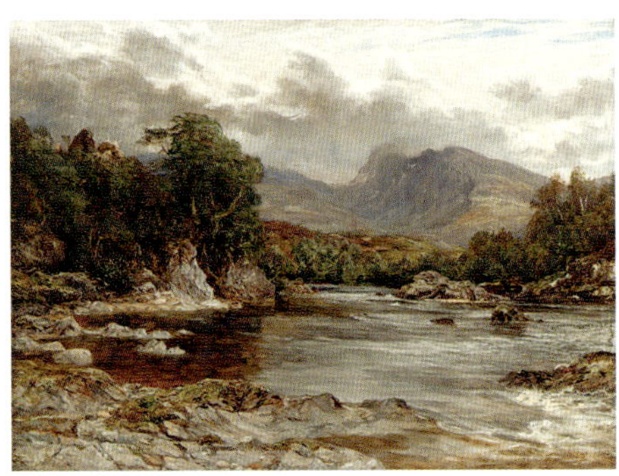

Docharty, James 1829–1878
A Salmon Stream 1878
oil on canvas 88.9 x 119.4
1069

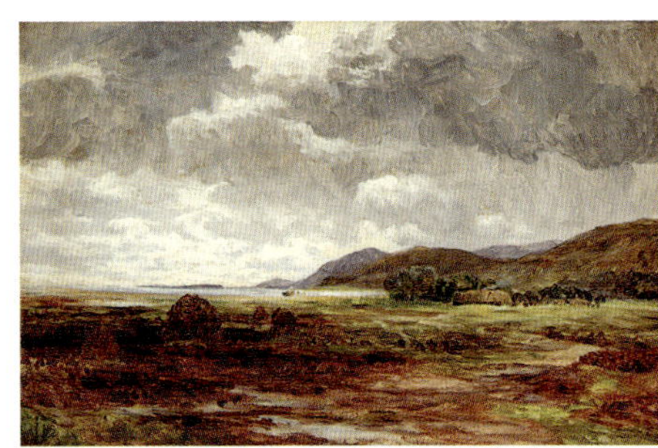

Docharty, James 1829–1878
Head of Loch Eil
oil on canvas 40.6 x 61
3128

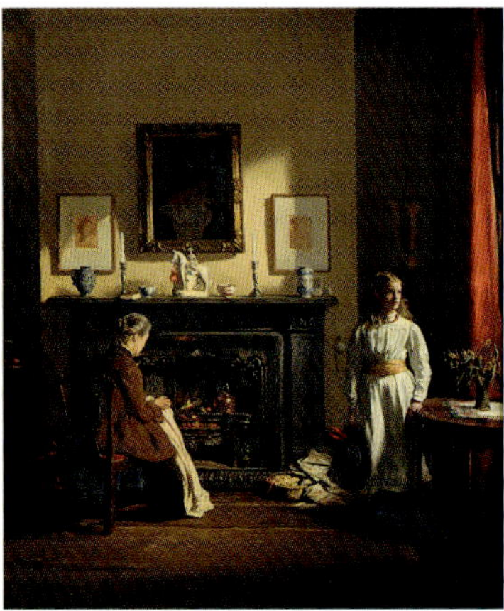

Dodd, Francis 1874–1949
Afternoon in the Parlour 1903
oil on canvas 76.2 x 63.5
2821

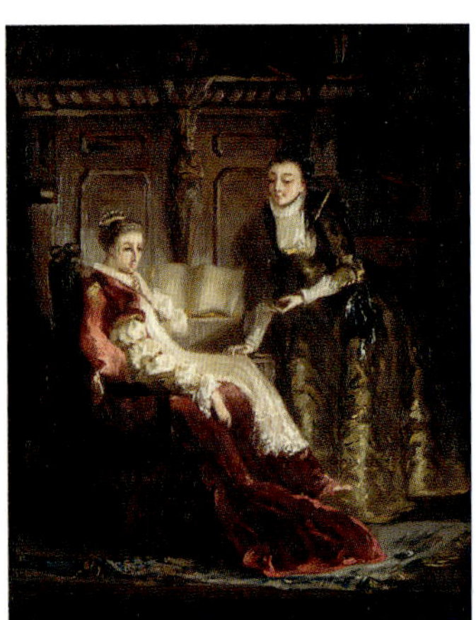

Dodson, Sarah Paxton Ball 1847–1906
The Duenna 1880s
oil on canvas 26.7 x 20.3
1483

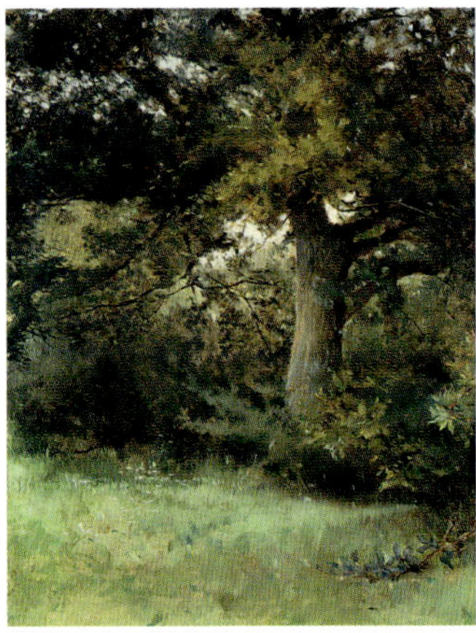

Dodson, Sarah Paxton Ball 1847–1906
An Oak Tree, Green Hedges, East Grinstead, Sussex 1896
oil on canvas 61 x 45.7
1482

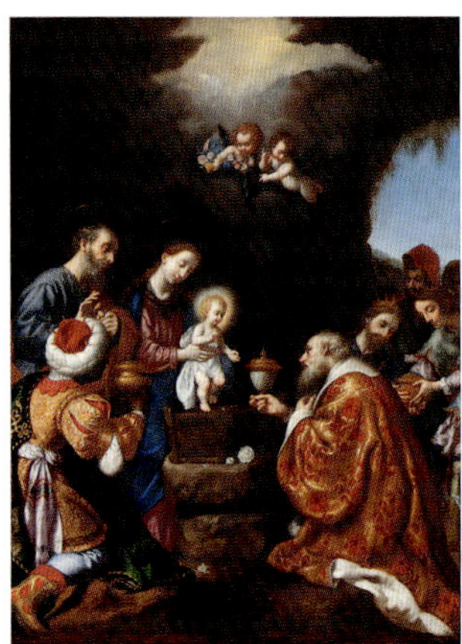

Dolci, Carlo 1616–1686
The Adoration of the Magi c.1633–1634
oil on canvas 128.9 x 100.3
154

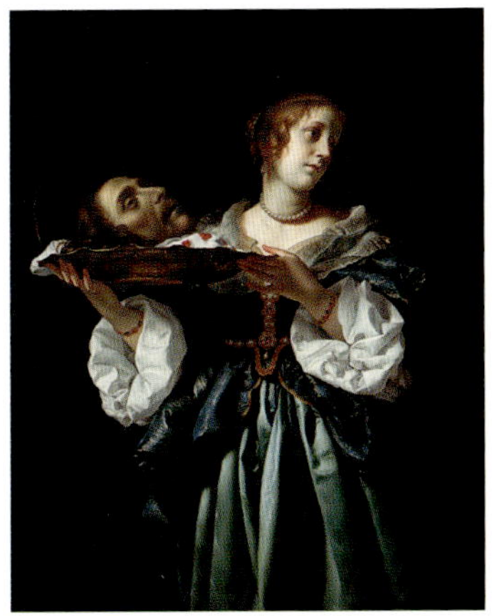

Dolci, Carlo 1616–1686
Salome c.1681–1685
oil on canvas 123.1 x 95.2
656

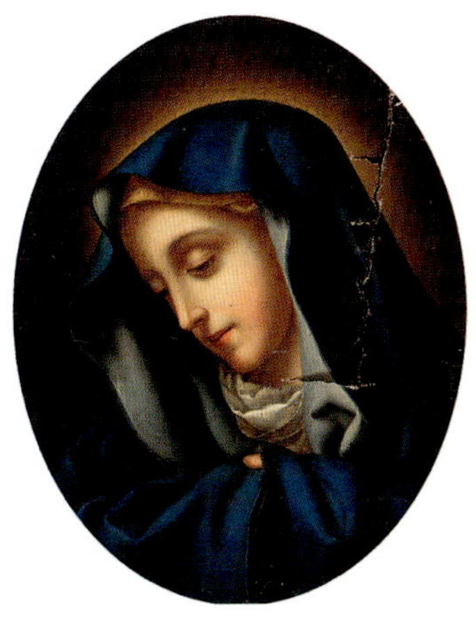

Dolci, Carlo (after) 1616–1686
Head of the Virgin 1823
oil on canvas 27.9 x 20.3
315

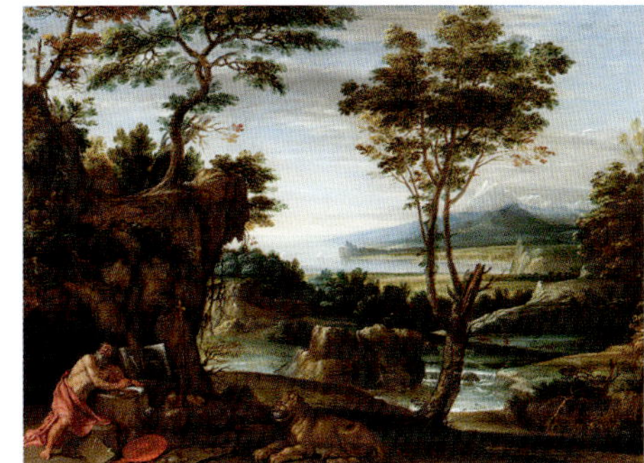

Domenichino 1581–1641
Landscape with Saint Jerome c.1610
oil on panel 44 x 59.8
139

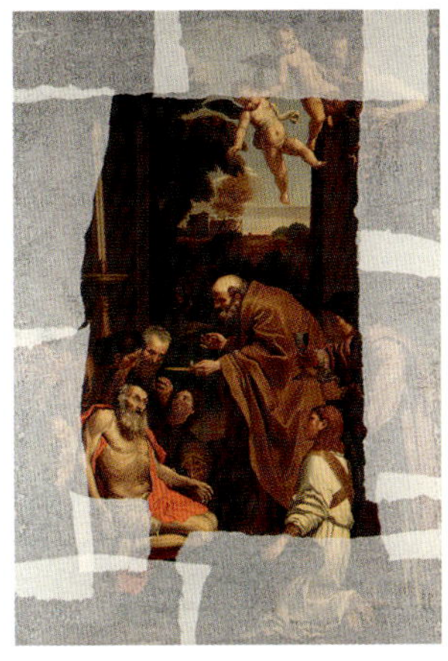

Domenichino (after) 1581–1641
The Last Communion of Saint Jerome c.1823
oil on canvas 170.2 x 114.3
310

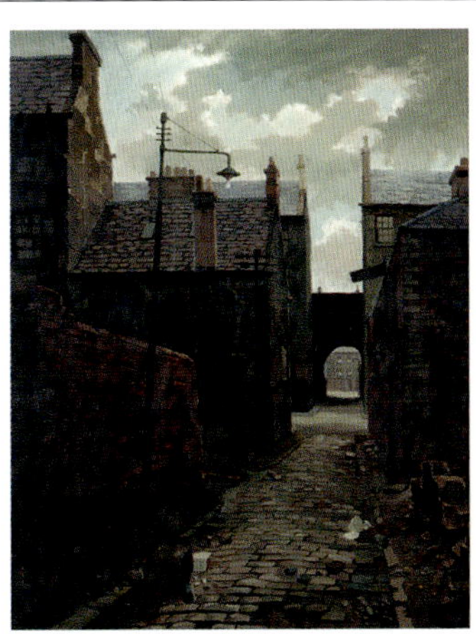

Donald, Anne b.1941
Abbotsford Lane, Gorbals 1964
oil on canvas 91.2 x 70.8
3207

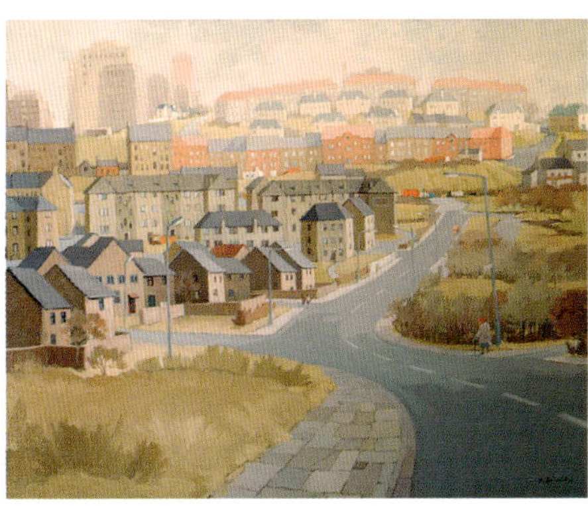

Donald, Anne b.1941
Maryhill, Old and New, January 1994
oil on canvas 101.6 x 121.9
PP.2001.11

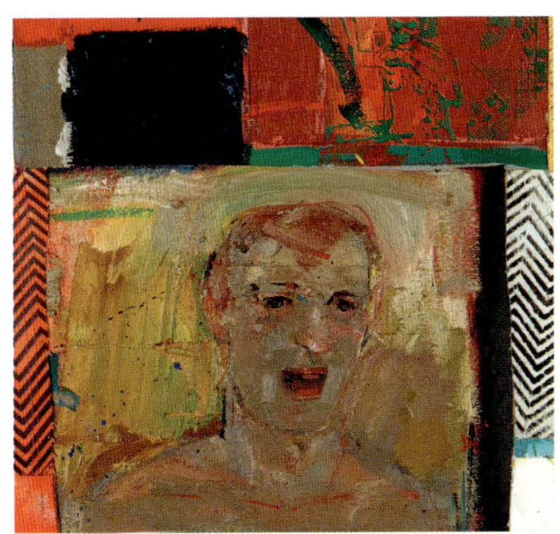

Donald, George Malcolm b.1943
Singer 1987
oil on canvas 32.3 x 32.5
3668

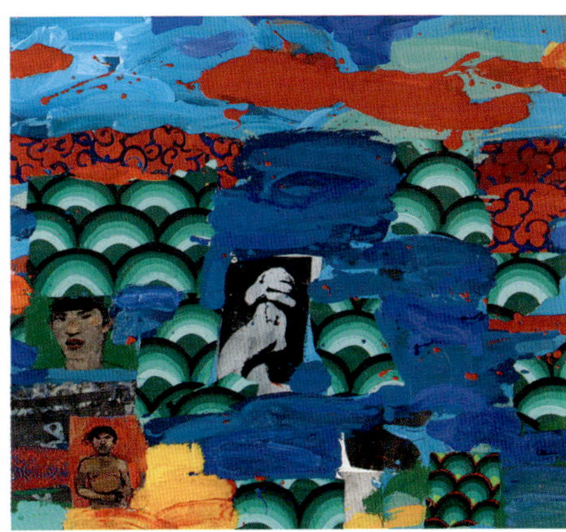

Donald, George Malcolm b.1943
Red Dragon over West Lake
acrylic & mixed media on board 90.2 x 97.7
3693

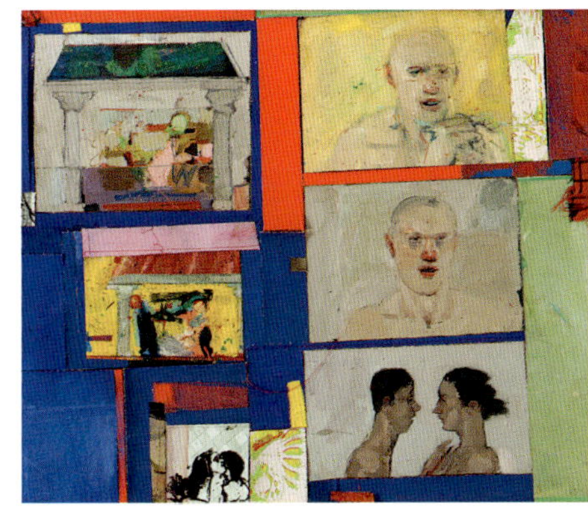

Donald, George Malcolm b.1943
Temples
oil on board 75 x 87.5
3667

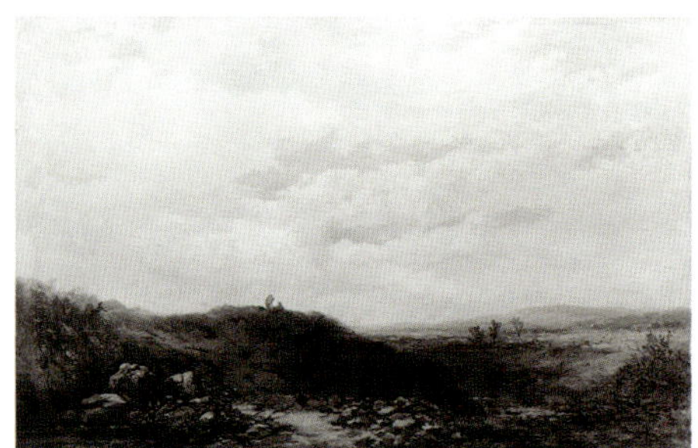

Donald, John Milne 1819–1866
Moorland Landscape 1855
oil on canvas 39.4 x 59.7
973

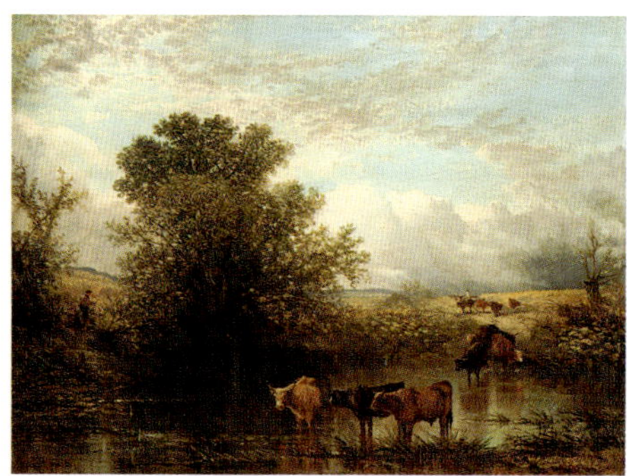

Donald, John Milne 1819–1866
Cattle in a Pool 1858
oil on canvas 45.7 x 61
2629

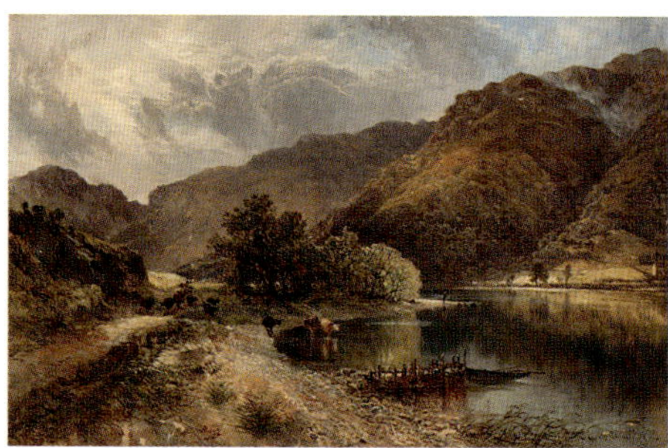

Donald, John Milne 1819–1866
Loch Eck 1863
oil on canvas 39.4 x 59.7
886

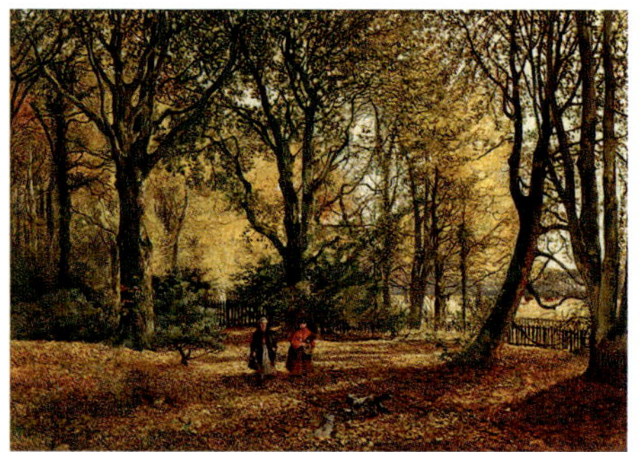

Donald, John Milne 1819–1866
Autumn Leaves 1864
oil on canvas 63.5 x 91.4
887

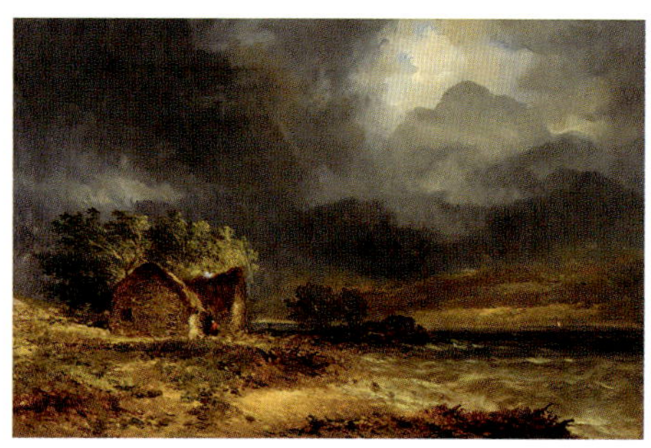

Donald, John Milne 1819–1866
A Brooding Storm
oil on canvas 30.5 x 45.7
769

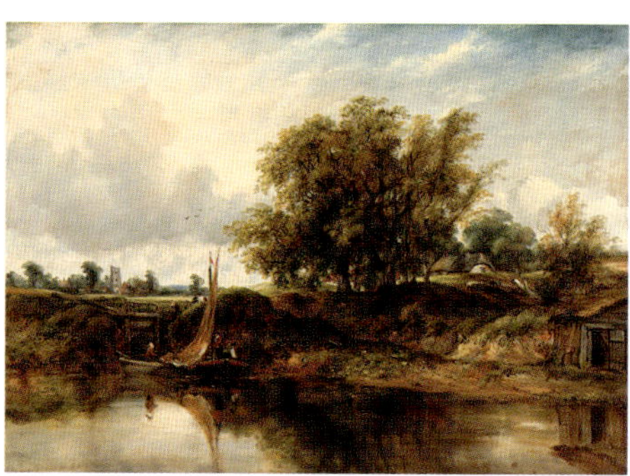

Donald, John Milne 1819–1866
Canal Scene, Boats and Figures
oil on canvas 49.5 x 67.3
803

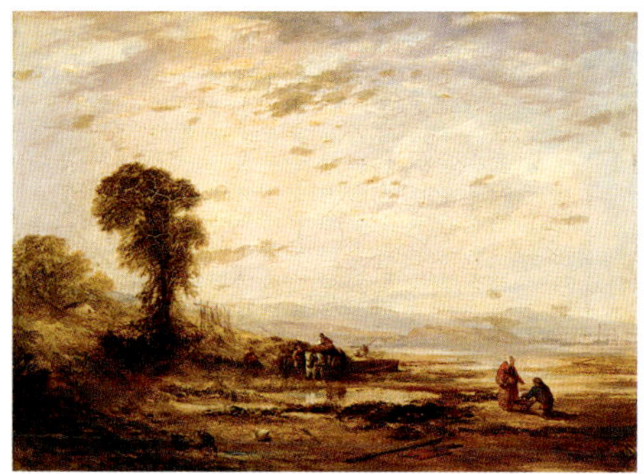

Donald, John Milne 1819–1866
Highland Loch Scene
oil on canvas 34.3 x 47
800

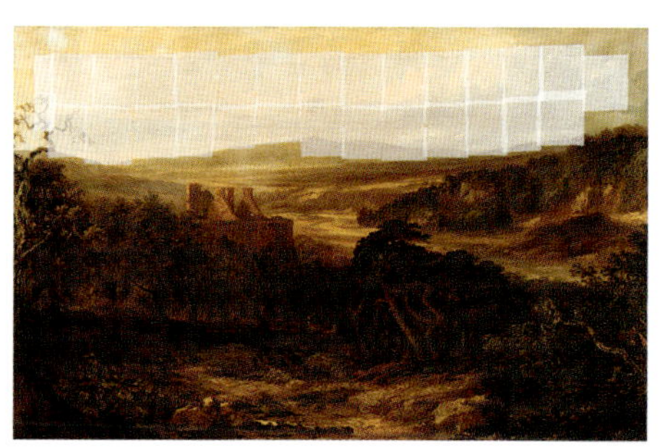

Donald, John Milne 1819–1866
Landscape with a Ruined Castle
oil on canvas 80.6 x 123.2
1055

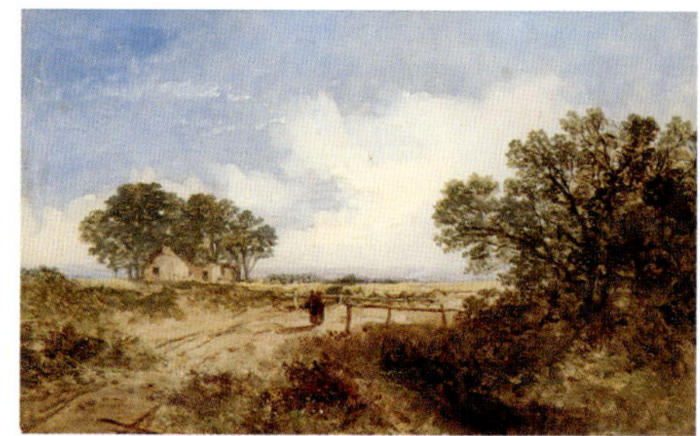

Donald, John Milne 1819–1866
Landscape with Figures
oil on canvas 29.2 x 44.5
986

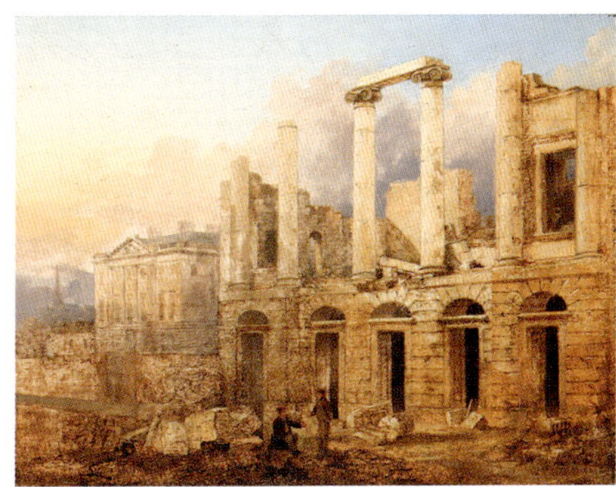

Donaldson, Andrew 1790–1846
*Old Theatre Royal, Queen Street, after the Fire
in January 1829* 1829
oil on canvas 45.7 x 61
275

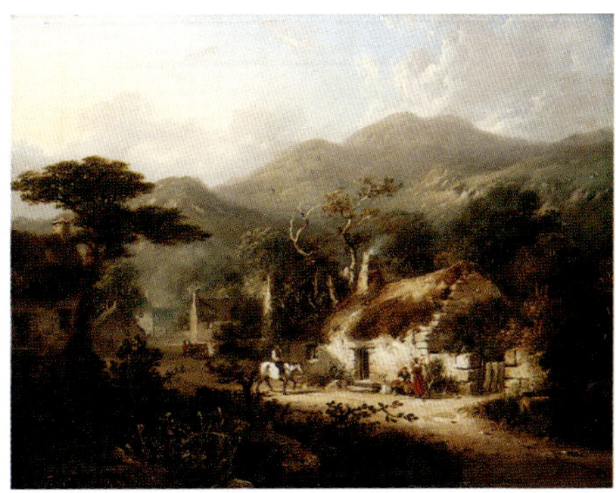

Donaldson, Andrew 1790–1846
A Scotch Highland Village
oil on canvas 48.3 x 61
243

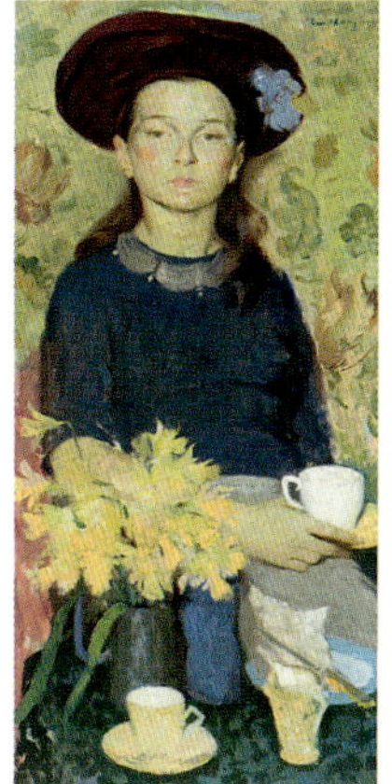

Donaldson, David Abercrombie 1916–1996
Maria 1948
oil on canvas 127 x 59.7
2841

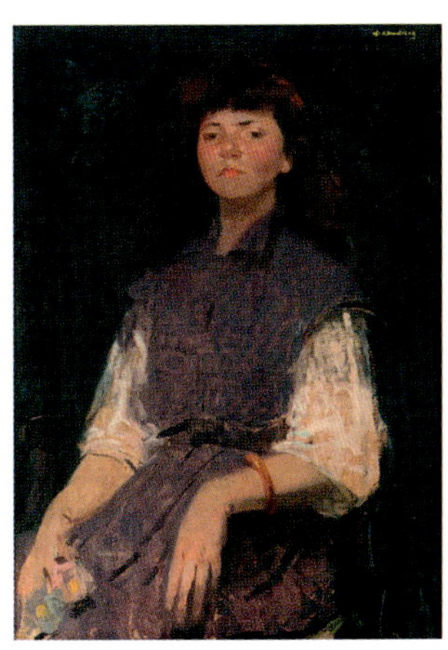

Donaldson, David Abercrombie 1916–1996
Miss Barrie 1953
oil on canvas 101.1 x 70.9
3055

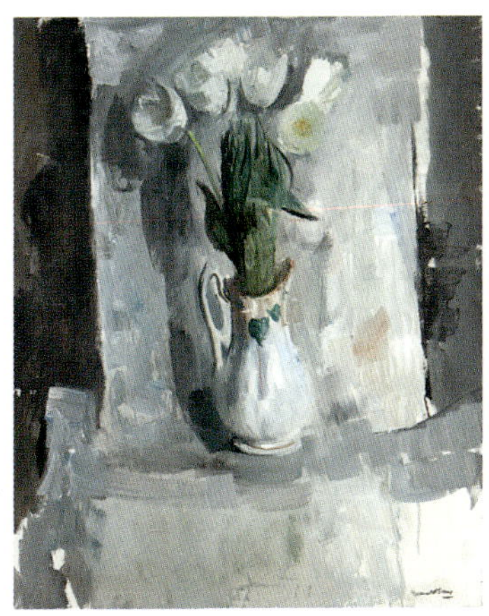

Donaldson, David Abercrombie 1916–1996
White Tulips 1964
oil on canvas 91.4 x 71.1
3639

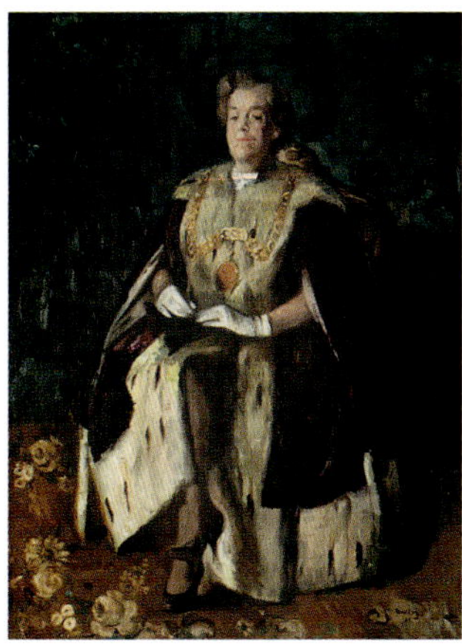

Donaldson, David Abercrombie 1916–1996
*Dame Jean Roberts (1895–1988), Lord Provost
of Glasgow (1960–1963)* 1965
oil on canvas 167.6 x 121.9
3232

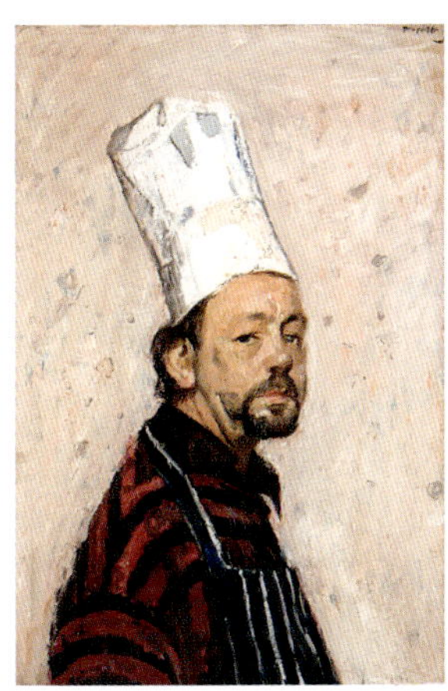

Donaldson, David Abercrombie 1916–1996
Self Portrait 1967
oil on canvas 75.6 x 50.5
3252

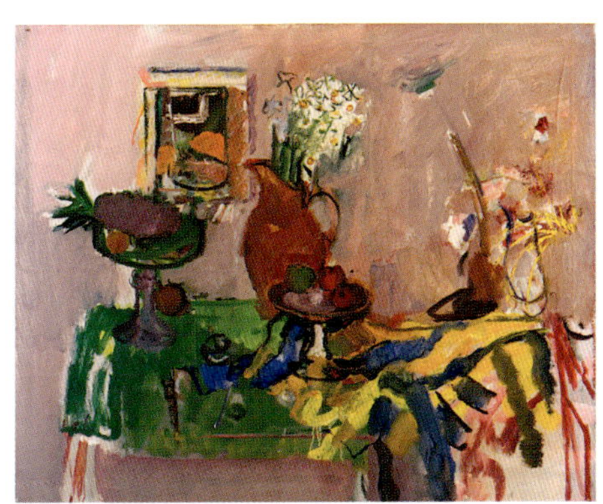

Donaldson, David Abercrombie 1916–1996
Narcissi c.1973
oil on canvas 91.3 x 106.5
3298

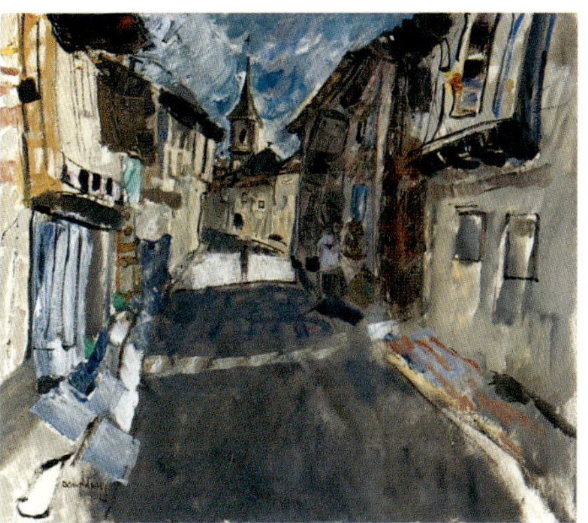

Donaldson, David Abercrombie 1916–1996
Montjoi c.1982
oil on canvas 76.2 x 86.3
3381

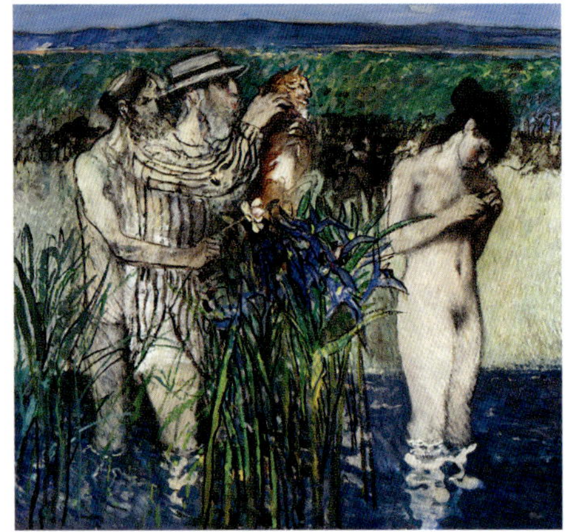

Donaldson, David Abercrombie 1916–1996
Susannah and the Elders c.1982
oil on canvas 153 x 153
3380

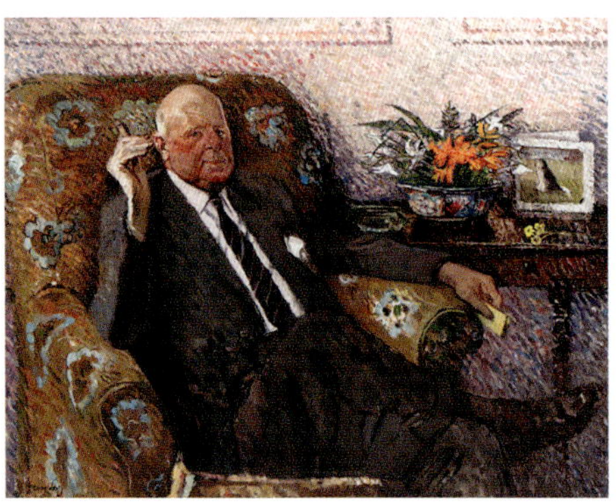

Donaldson, David Abercrombie 1916–1996
Ronald J. P. Cowan (d.1922), Chairman of the Trustees of the Hamilton Bequest 1984
oil on canvas 101.6 x 127
3399

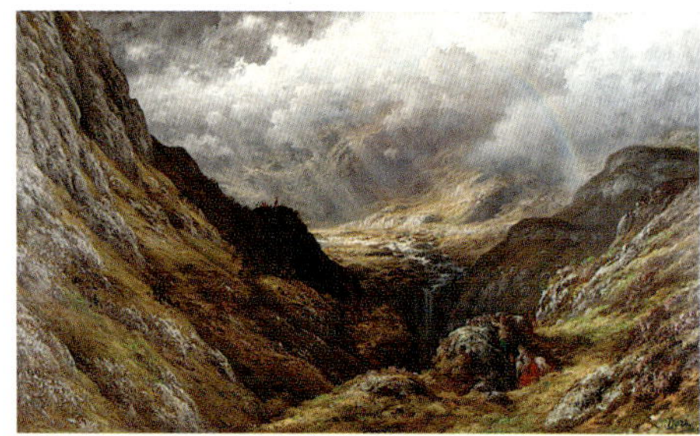

Doré, Gustave 1832–1883
Glen Massan
oil on canvas 112.7 x 184.8
3352

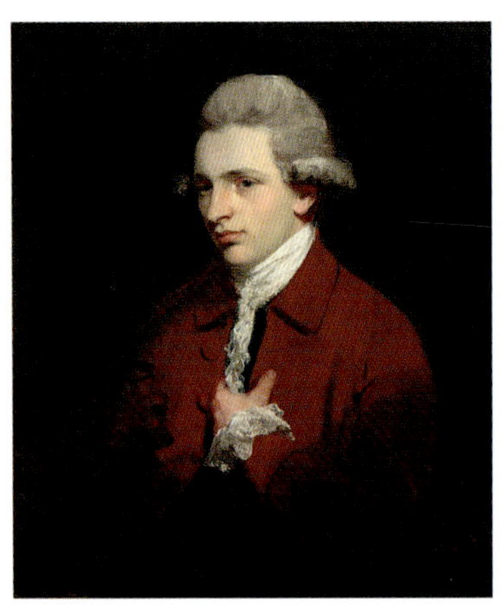

Doughty, William (attributed to) 1757–1782
Mr Palmer c.1778
oil on canvas 101 x 88.9
35.603

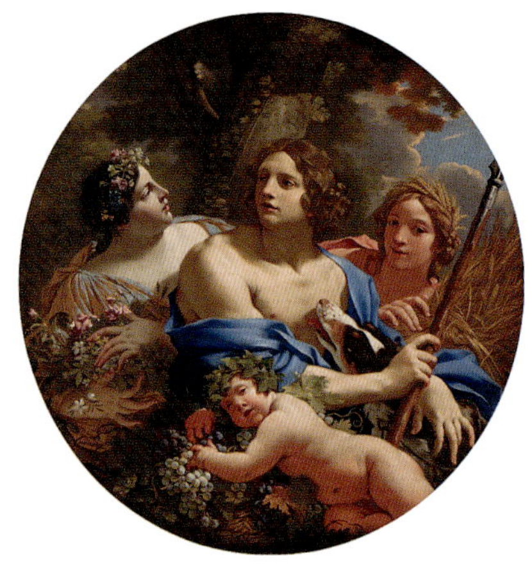

Dorigny, Michel (attributed to) 1617–1665
The Four Seasons
oil on canvas 140.3 x 129.5
218

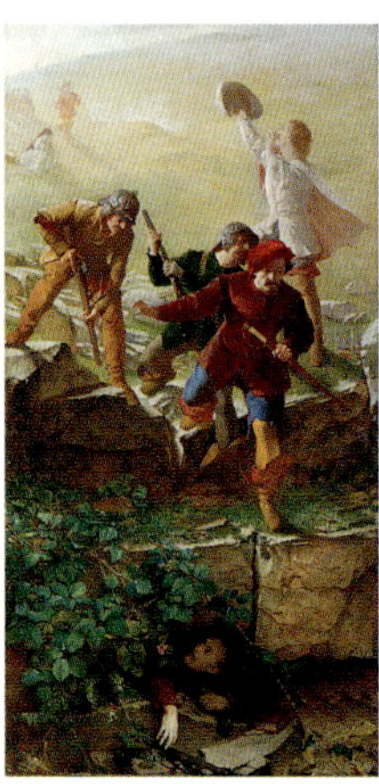

Douglas, William Fettes 1822–1891
The Recusant's Concealment Discovered 1859
oil on canvas 101.2 x 50.5
3208

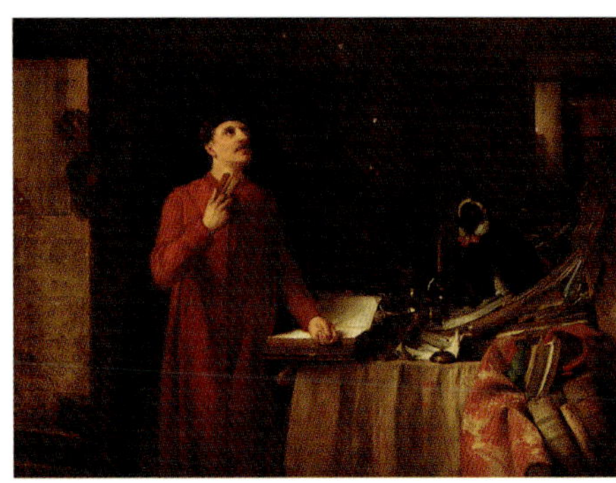

Douglas, William Fettes 1822–1891
The Rosicrucian c.1872
oil on canvas 45.7 x 61
3188

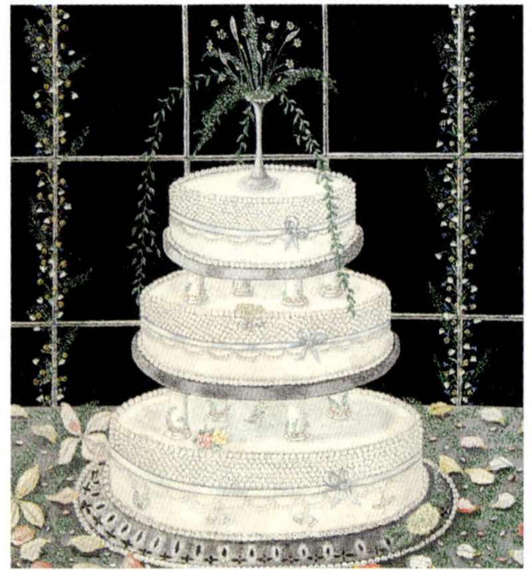

Douglass, Lilian 1903–1982
Orchids for the Bride 1965
oil on hardboard 52 x 49.3
3586

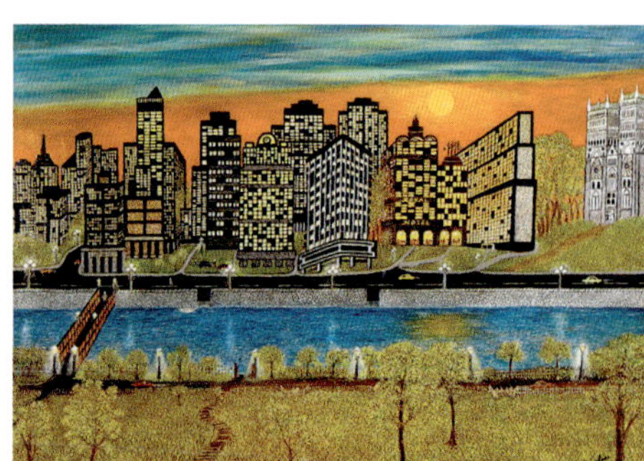

Douglass, Lilian 1903–1982
Sundown 1973
oil on panel 46.2 x 64.4
3585

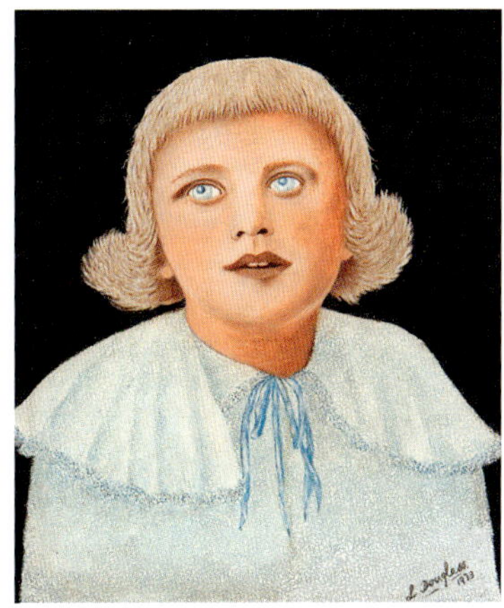

Douglass, Lilian 1903–1982
Who Art in Heaven 1973
oil on panel 38.4 x 33.4
3587

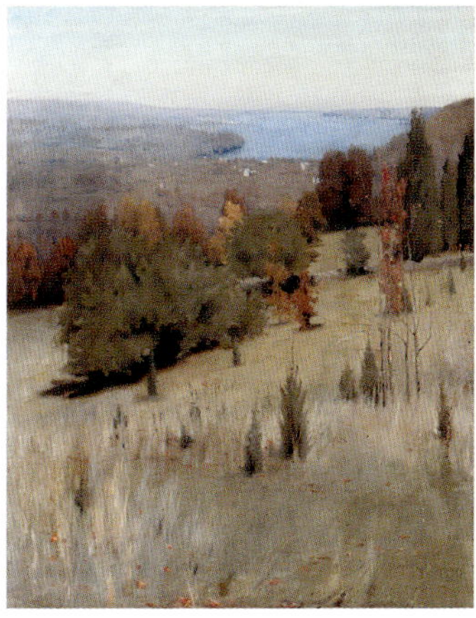

Dow, Thomas Millie 1848–1919
The Hudson River 1884
oil on canvas 123.2 x 97.8
1739

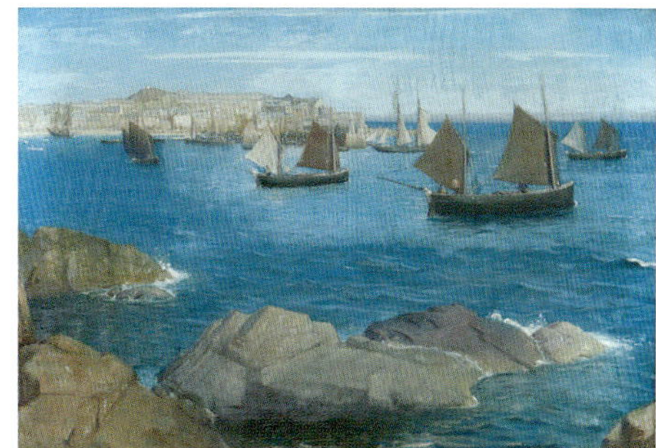

Dow, Thomas Millie 1848–1919
St Ives, Cornwall
oil on canvas 91.4 x 127
1738

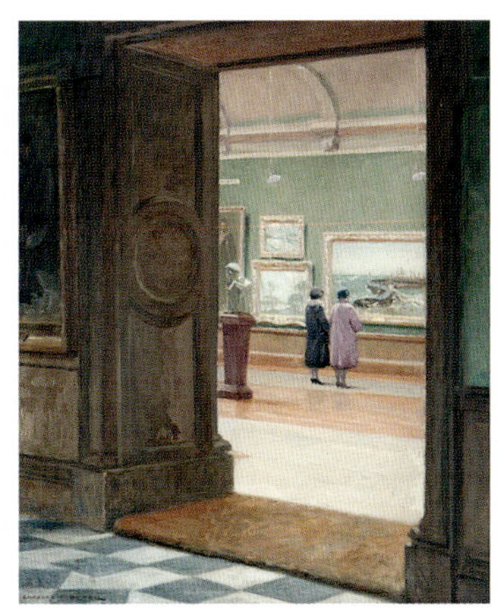

Dowell, Charles R. c.1876–1935
*Interior of Glasgow Corporation Art
Galleries* c.1926
oil on canvas 74.9 x 62.2
1671

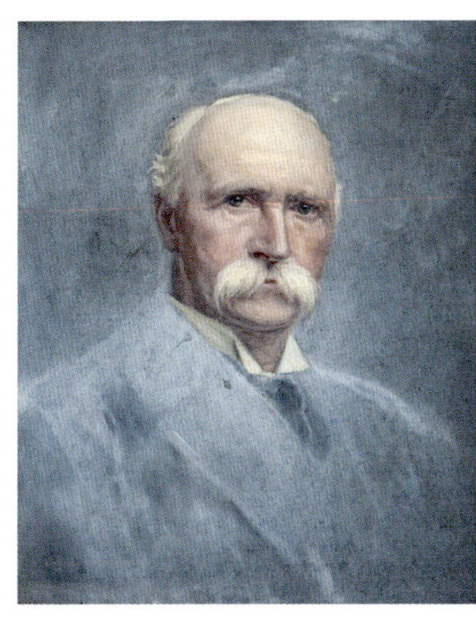

Dowell, Charles R. c.1876–1935
Sir William MacEwan (1848–1924)
oil on canvas 50.8 x 41.7
1760

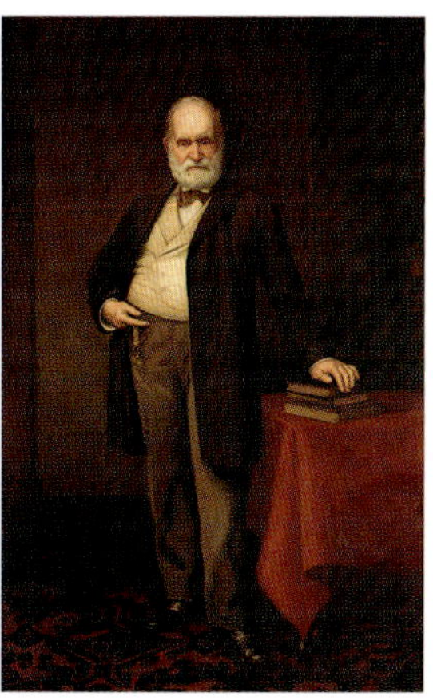

Downie, John Patrick 1871–1945
John Burns (b.1815), MD 1898
oil on canvas 236.2 x 144.8
891

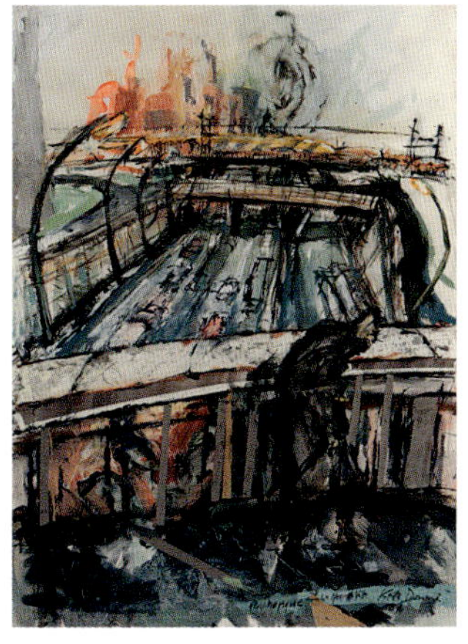

Downie, Kate b.1958
Périphérique, la nouvelle ville 1989
acrylic on canvas 107.5 x 75
PR.1992.10

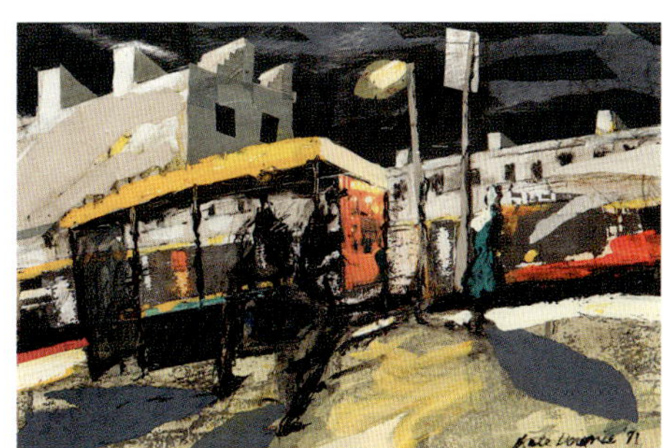

Downie, Kate b.1958
Blue Night, Yellow Roof 1991
acrylic & collage on paper 45.5 x 68.5
PR.1992.10.a

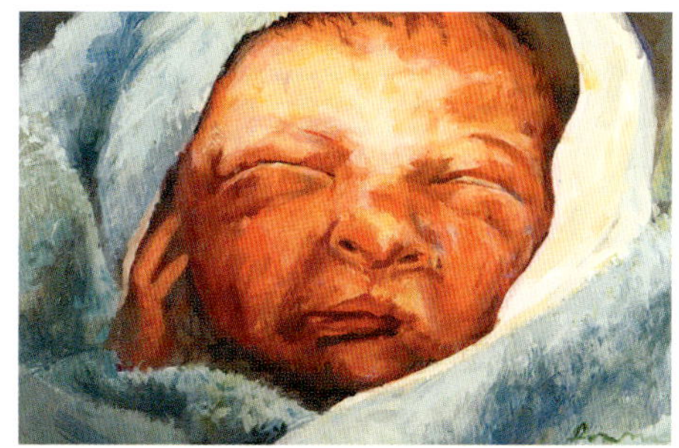

Downie, Kate b.1958
12 Minute Baby 1993
oil on canvas 76.2 x 115.6
TEMP.14954

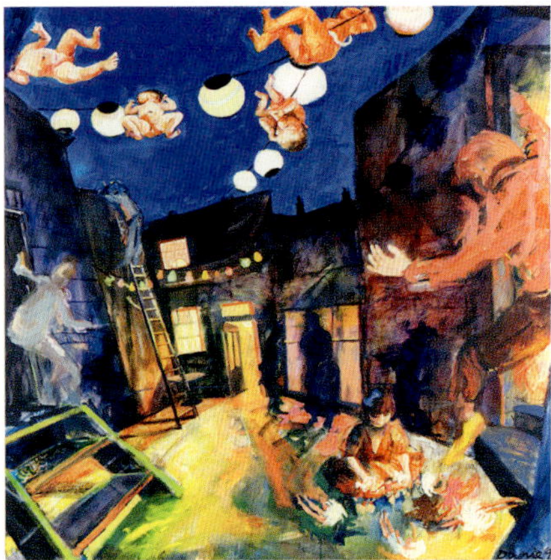

Downie, Kate b.1958
The Mother Pool 1993
acrylic on canvas 177.5 x 169.8
3530

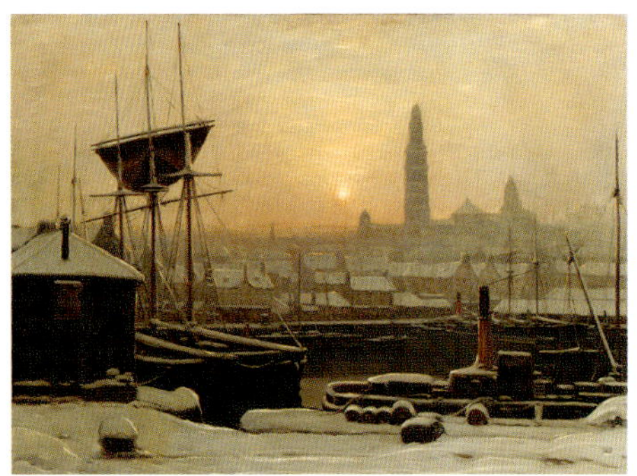

Downie, Patrick 1854–1945
The Day of Rest, Winter 1904
oil on canvas 135.9 x 181.6
1180

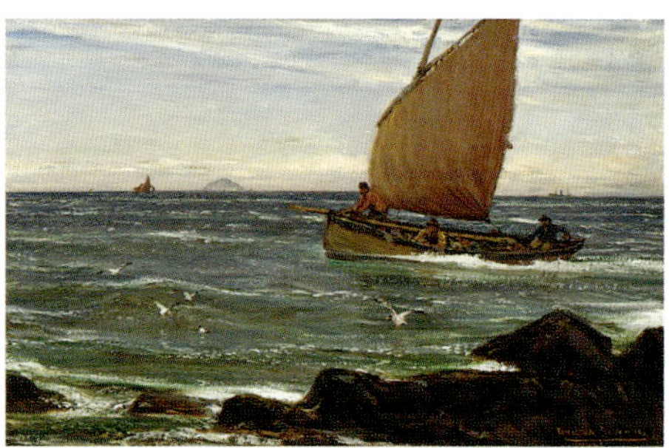

Downie, Patrick 1854–1945
Haddock Fishers, Ballantrae
oil on canvas 50.5 x 76.3
3131

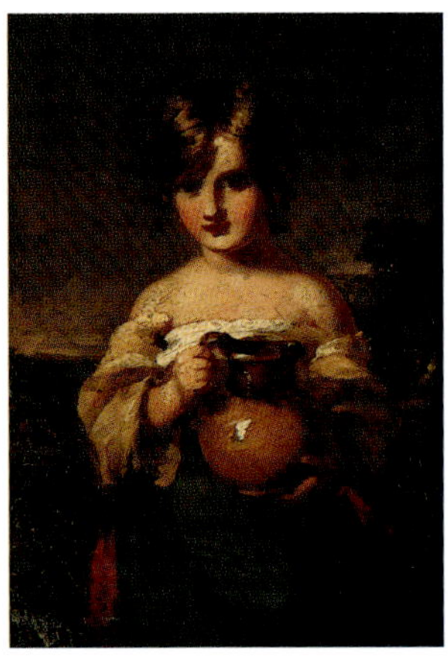

Drew, J. P. active 1835–1861
Study of a Girl 1850
oil on canvas 23.5 x 16.5
450

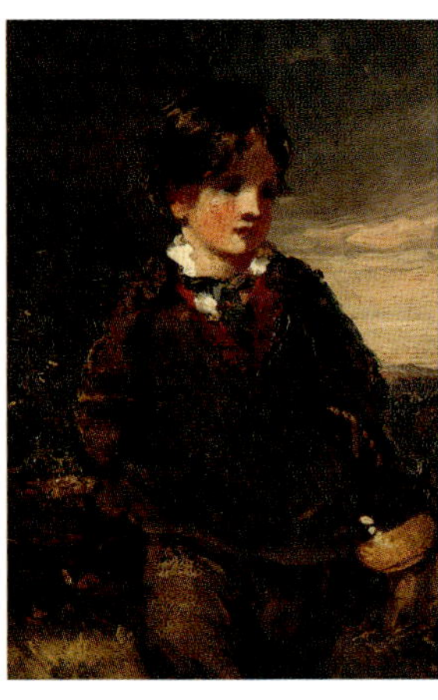

Drew, J. P. active 1835–1861
Study of a Boy
oil on canvas 23.5 x 16.5
449

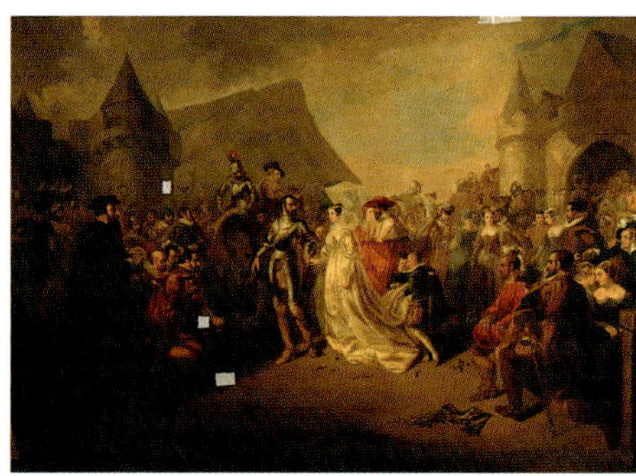

Drummond, James 1816–1877
*The Marriage of Mary, Queen of Scots, and the
Earl of Bothwell*
oil on panel 139.7 x 190.5
2079

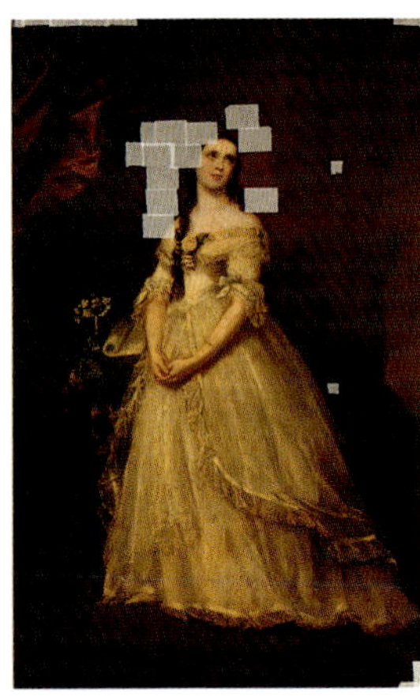

Drummond, Rose Myra active 1833–1849
*Helena Saville Faucit (1817–1898), Lady
Martin*
oil on canvas 238.8 x 146.1
1260

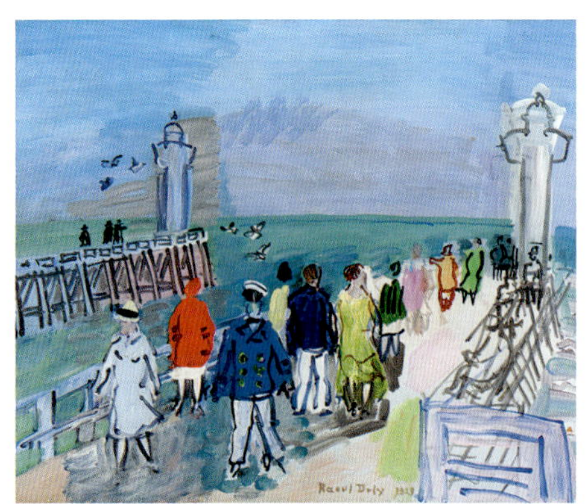

Dufy, Raoul 1877–1953
The Jetties of Trouville-Deauville 1929
oil on canvas 46.2 x 54.8
3120

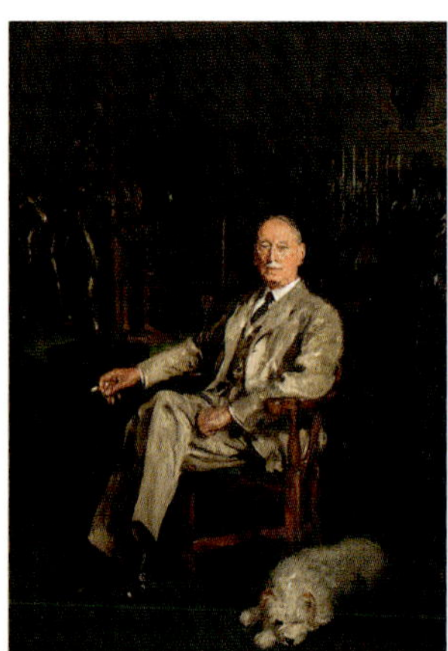

Dugdale, Thomas Cantrell 1880–1952
Robert L. Scott (1871–1939) 1936–1937
oil on canvas 218.4 x 152.4
2277

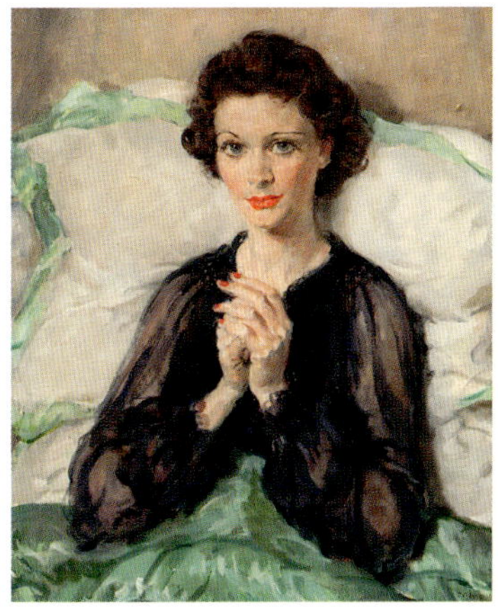

Dugdale, Thomas Cantrell 1880–1952
Vivien Leigh (1913–1967) c.1936
oil on canvas 76.1 x 64
2066

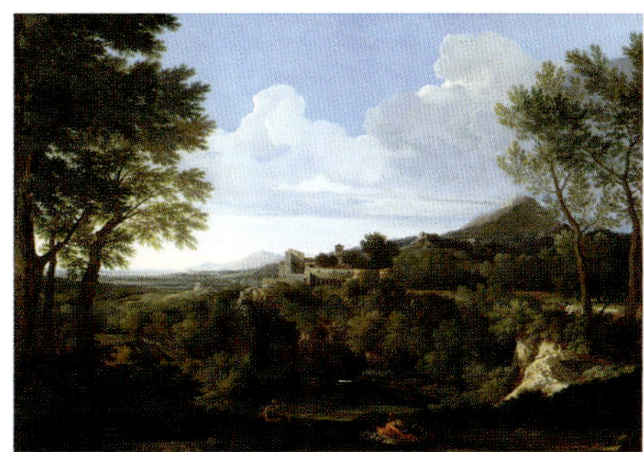

Dughet, Gaspard 1615–1675
Ideal Landscape c.1658–1660
oil on canvas 95.5 x 135.2
596

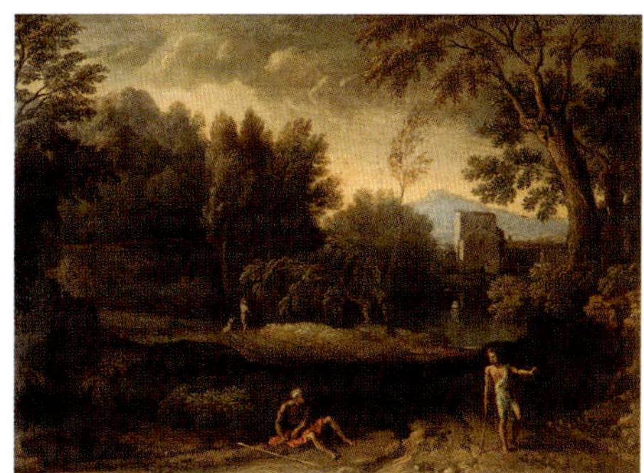

Dughet, Gaspard 1615–1675
Landscape with Figures
oil on canvas 40.3 x 51.4
PC.85

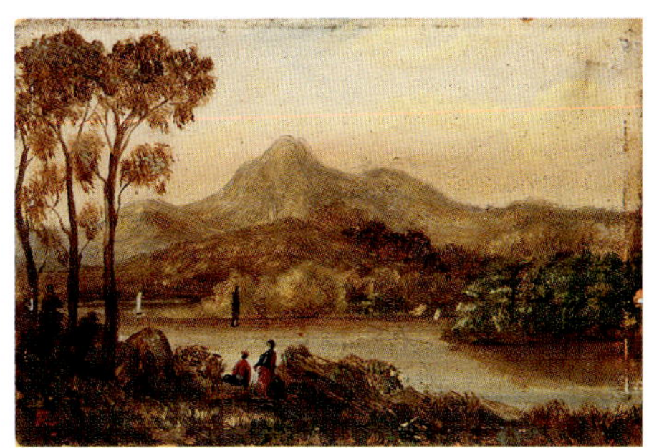

Duguid, David 1832–1907
Landscape
oil on millboard 15.7 x 23
OG.1963.19.1

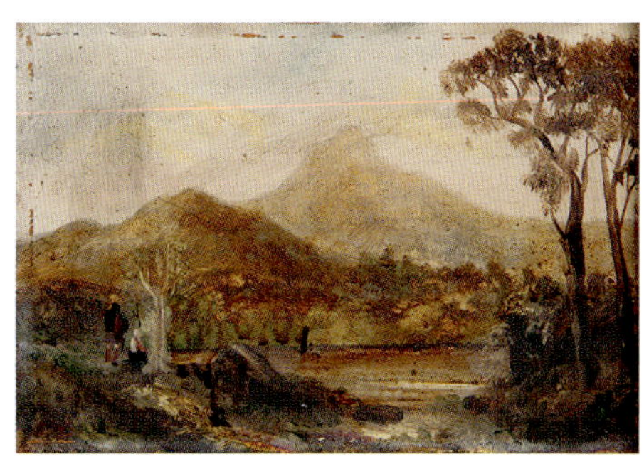

Duguid, David 1832–1907
Landscape
oil on millboard 15.9 x 23
OG.1963.19.2

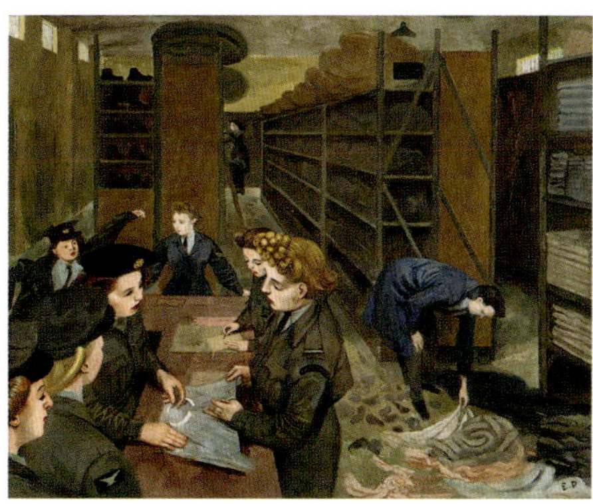

Dunbar, Evelyn Mary 1906–1960
Women's Auxiliary Air Force Store
c.1940–1945
oil on canvas 40.6 x 50.8
2733

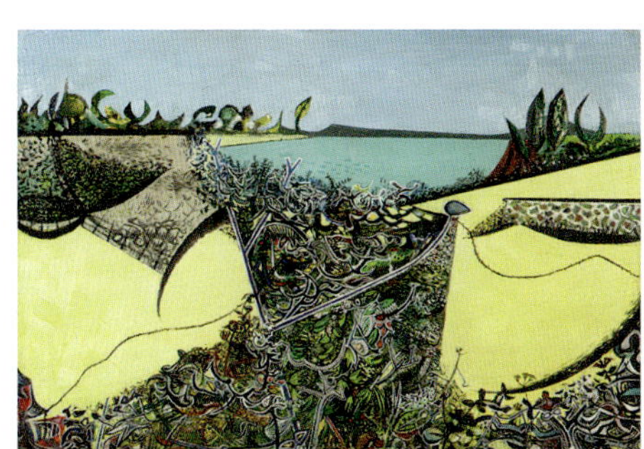

Dunbar, Peter 1929–1983
Seashore 1951
oil on canvas 50.4 x 76.2
3045

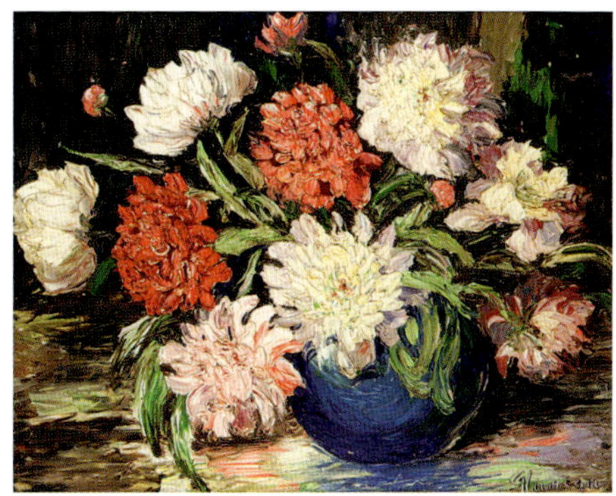

Duncan, E. active 20th C
Peonies
oil on canvas 58.4 x 69.8
1908

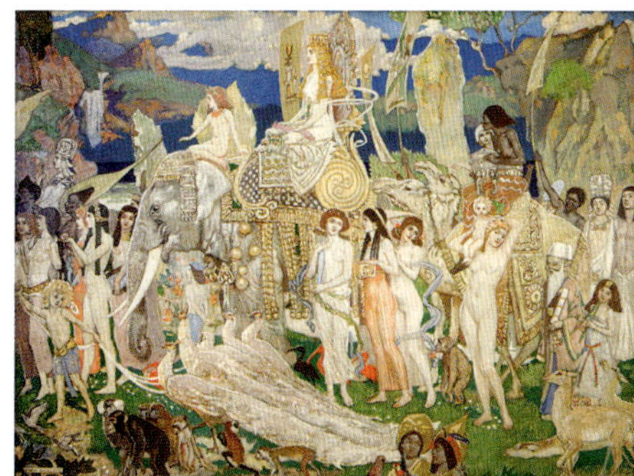

Duncan, John 1866–1945
Ivory, Apes and Peacocks (The Queen of Sheba) 1909–1920
tempera on canvas 44.9 x 61.2
3410

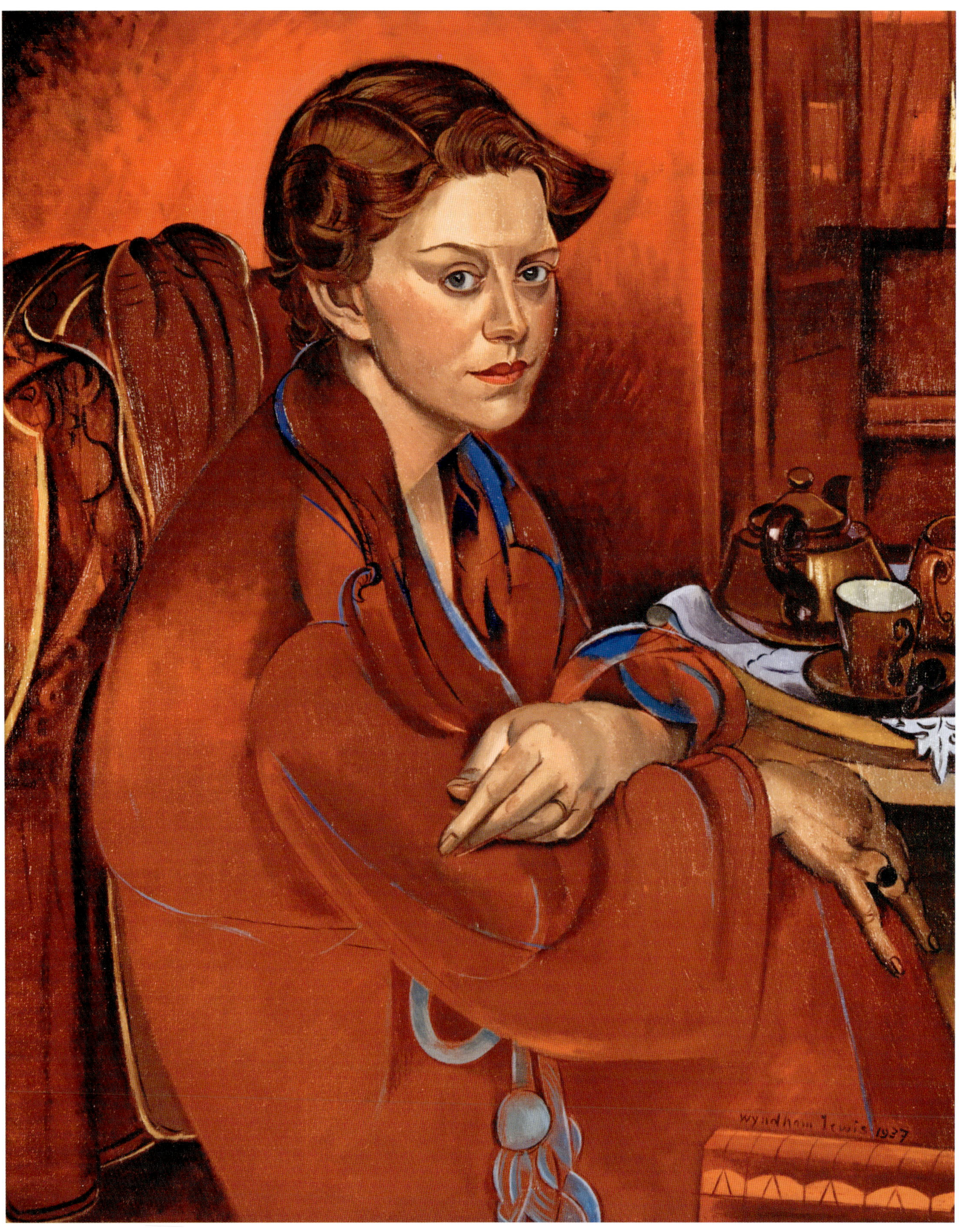

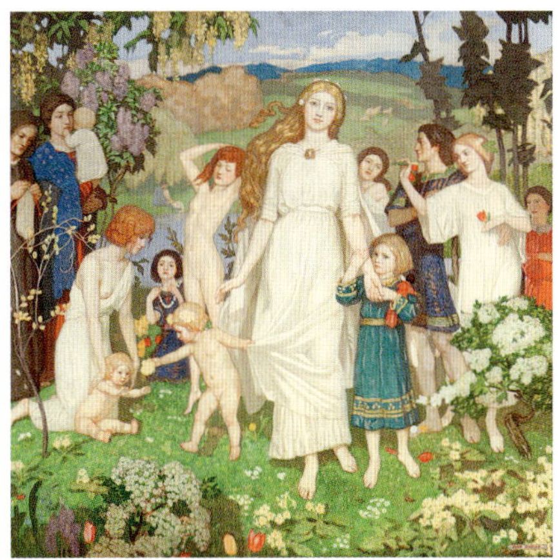

Duncan, John 1866–1945
The Coming of Bride 1917
tempera on canvas 151.1 x 151.1
1457

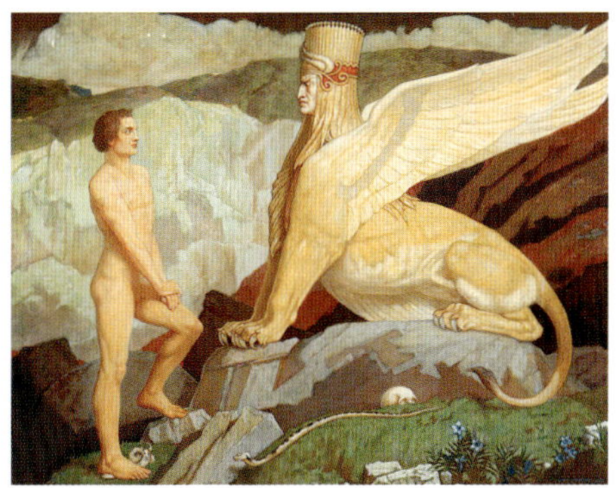

Duncan, John 1866–1945
Force and Reason 1939
oil on canvas on board 121.6 x 152.4
2545

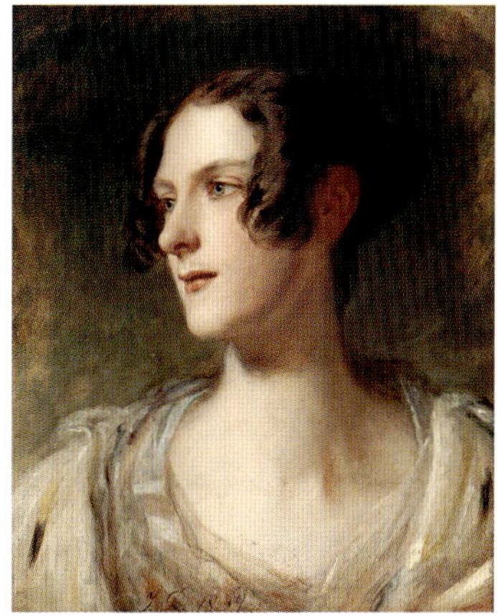

Duncan, Thomas 1807–1845
*Christina Mitchell McNeil, the Mother of Ina,
Dowager Duchess of Argyll* 1839
oil on canvas 49.5 x 39.4
1664

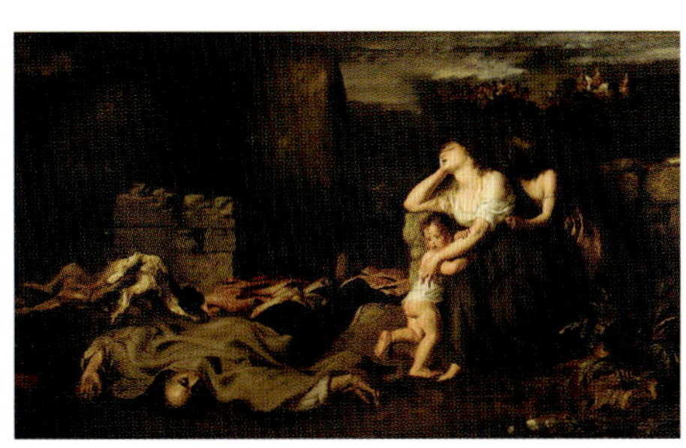

Duncan, Thomas 1807–1845
*The Martyrdom of John Brown of Priesthill,
1685* 1844
oil on canvas 132.1 x 208.3
302

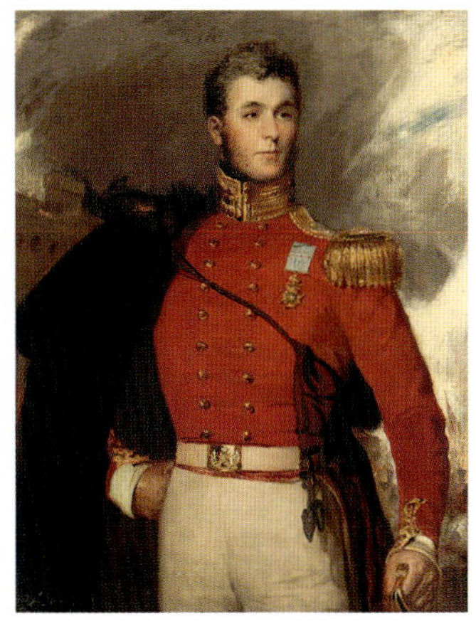

Duncan, Thomas 1807–1845
*Lieutenant Colonel A. Hope Pattison (1785–
1824)*
oil on canvas 120.7 x 91.4
2532

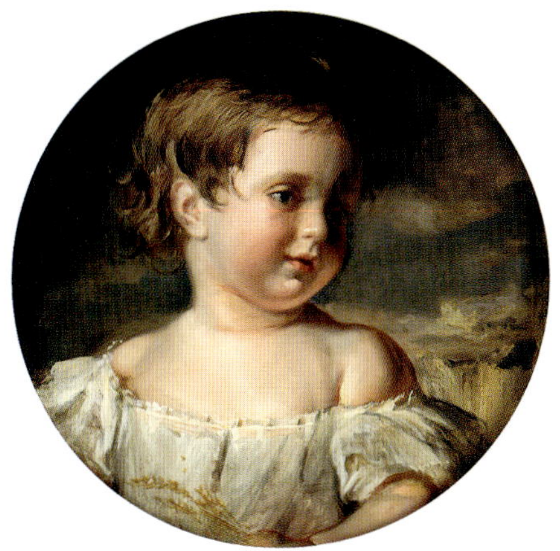

Duncan, Thomas 1807–1845
*The Brother of Ina, Dowager Duchess of Argyll,
as a Boy*
oil on panel 40.6
1665

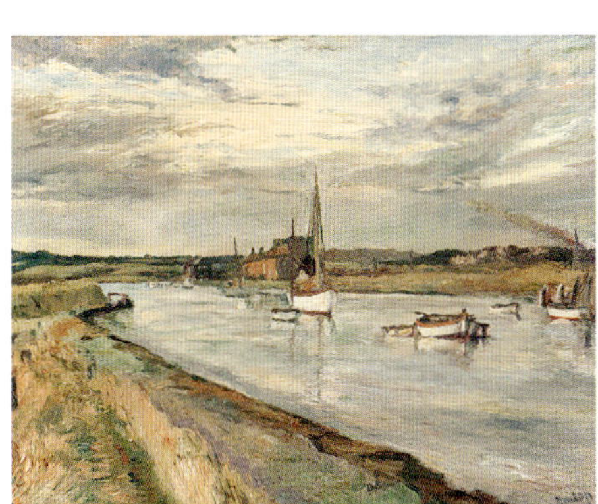

Dunlop, Ronald Ossory 1894–1973
Walberswick c.1937
oil on canvas 101.6 x 127
2078

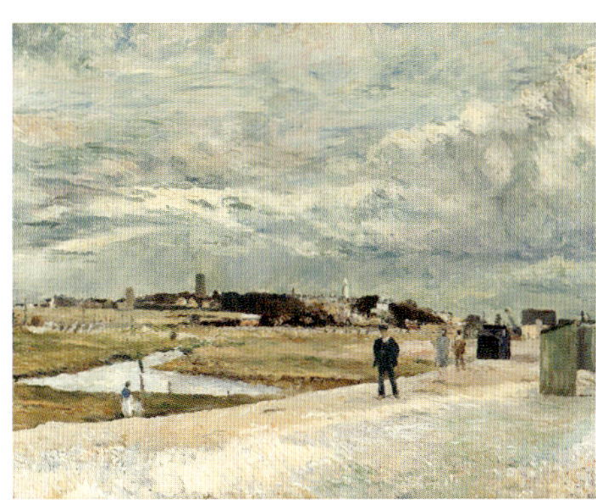

Dunlop, Ronald Ossory 1894–1973
Southwold from Walberswick Beach c.1938
oil on canvas 101.6 x 127
2107

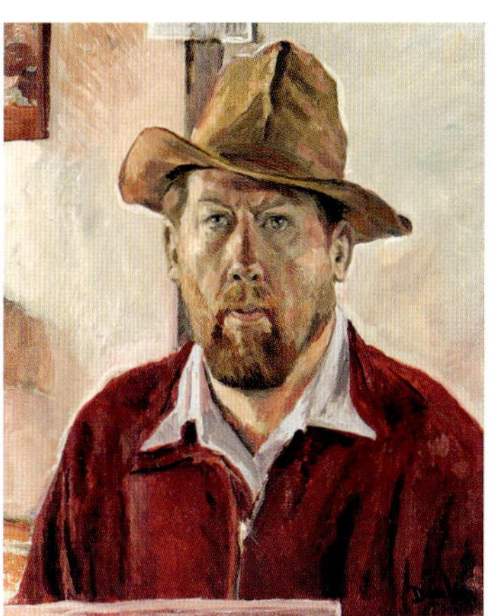

Dunlop, Ronald Ossory 1894–1973
Myself in a French Hat 1951
oil on canvas 61 x 50.8
2975

Facing page: Lewis, Wyndham, 1882–1957, *Froanna, the Artist's Wife,* (p. 260)

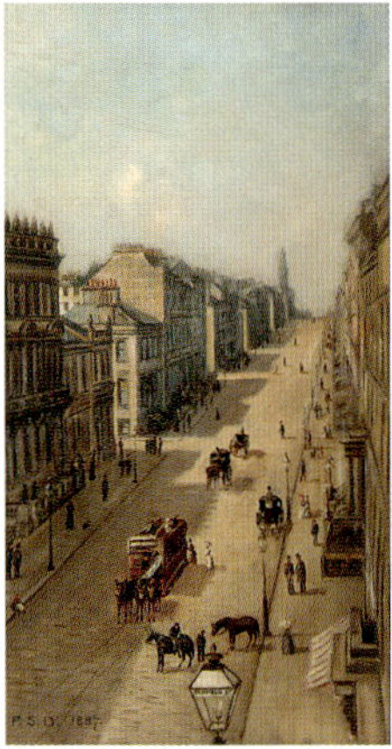

Dunn, Patrick S. active 1880–1918
Renfield Street 1887
oil on canvas 37.4 x 19.7
TEMP.1666

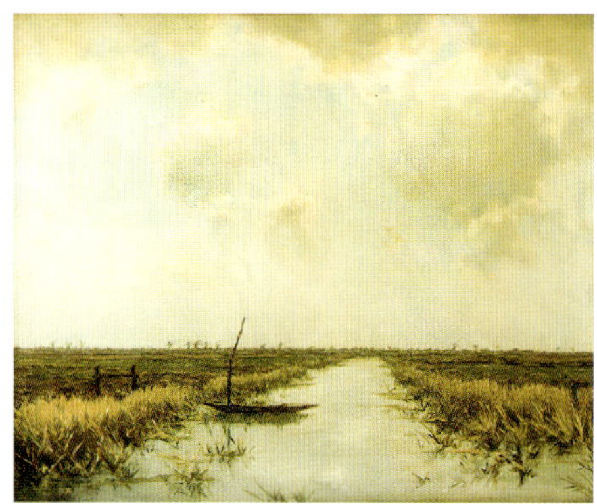

Dunn, William 1862–c.1932
A Spring Morning in Marshland
oil on canvas 41.9 x 50.8
1602

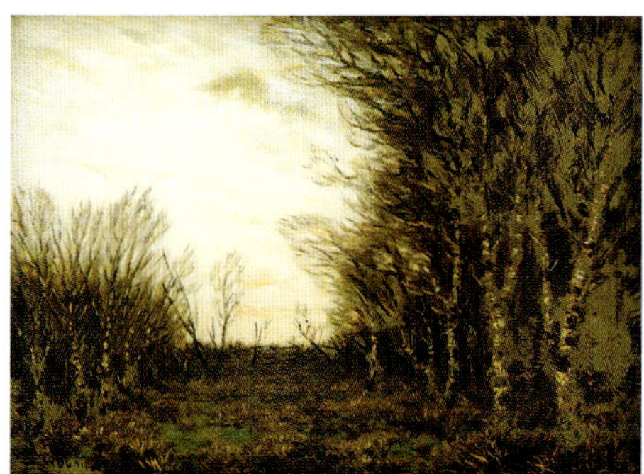

Dunn, William 1862–c.1932
Marshy Land, Kent
oil on canvas 30.5 x 40.6
2577

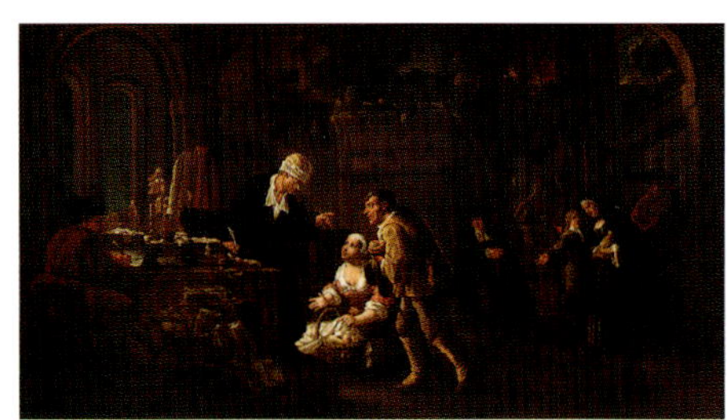

Duplessis, Jacques Vigoroux 1680–1732
In a Notary Public's Office 1719
oil on canvas 111.6 x 194.3
2077

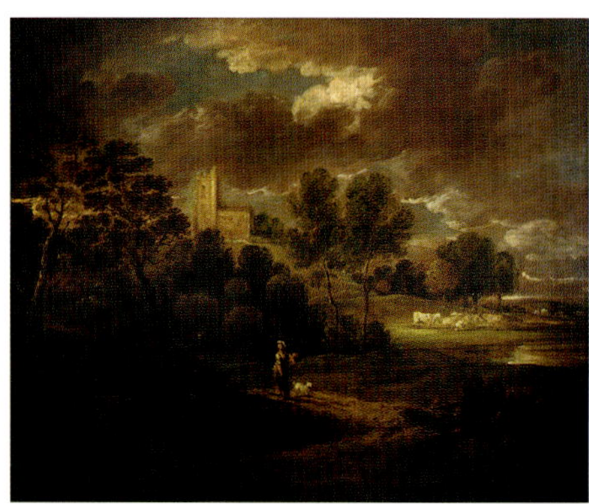

Dupont, Gainsborough 1754–1797
Woody Landscape near Bath 1790s
oil on canvas 63.5 x 76.2
2591

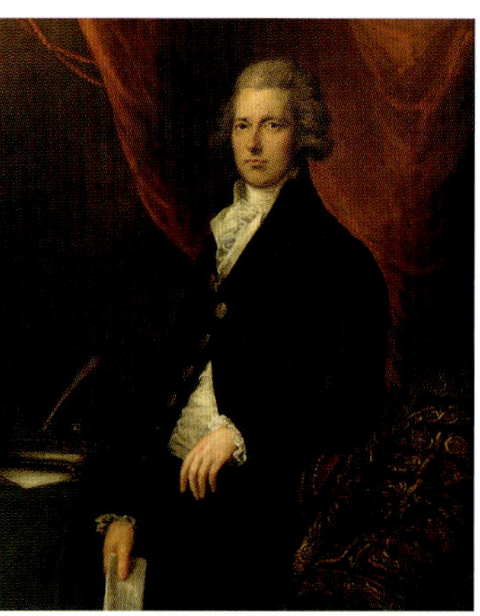

Dupont, Gainsborough (and studio) 1754–1797
William Pitt the Younger (1759–1806) c.1787
oil on canvas 127 x 101.6
35.263

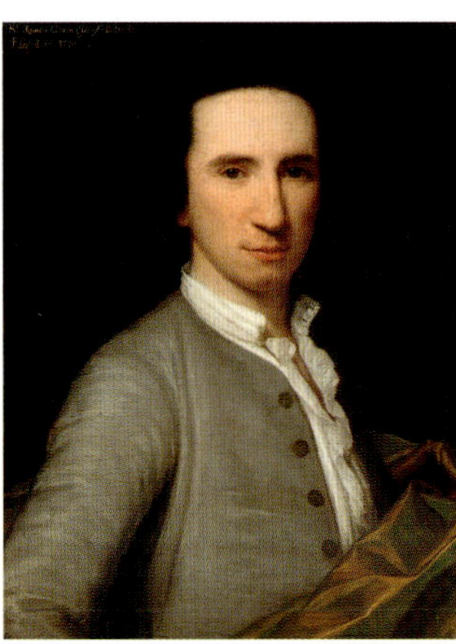

Duprà, Domenico 1689–1770
James Carnegie of Boysack (c.1714–1770) 1739
oil on canvas 62.2 x 48.3
3020

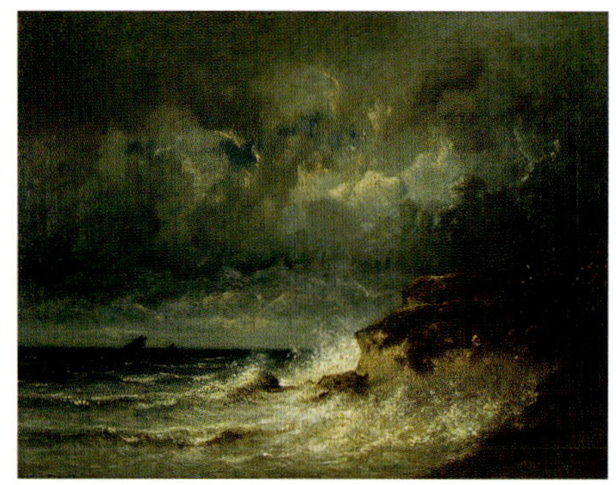

Dupré, Jules 1811–1889
The Headland
oil on canvas 72.4 x 91.4
1130

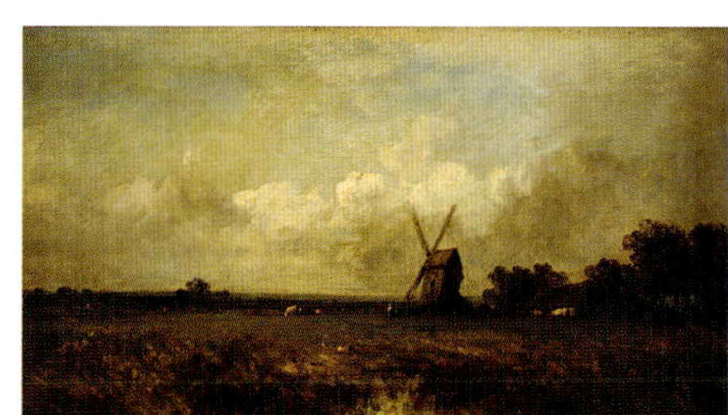

Dupré, Léon Victor 1816–1879
Landscape c.1870–1872
oil on panel 25.5 x 45.7
1529

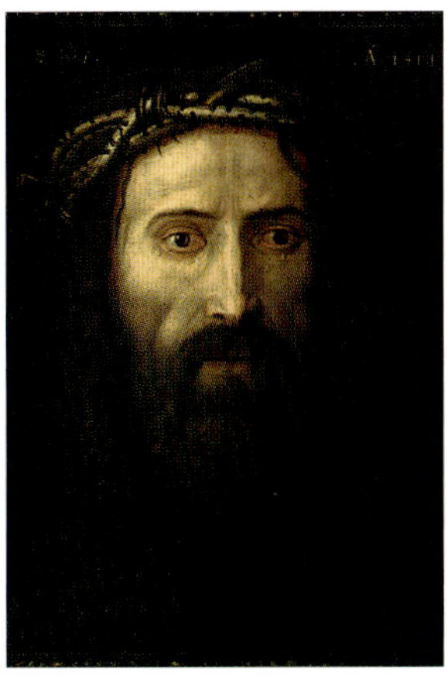

Dürer, Albrecht (imitator of) 1471–1528
*The Head of Christ Crowned with
Thorns* c.1584–1591
oil on panel 45.4 x 35.9
209

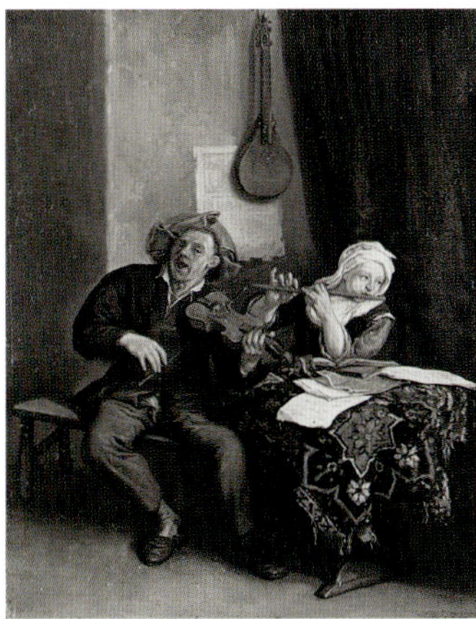

Dusart, Cornelis (imitator of) 1660–1704
A Man and a Woman Making Music
late 18th C
oil on copper 20.8 x 16
406

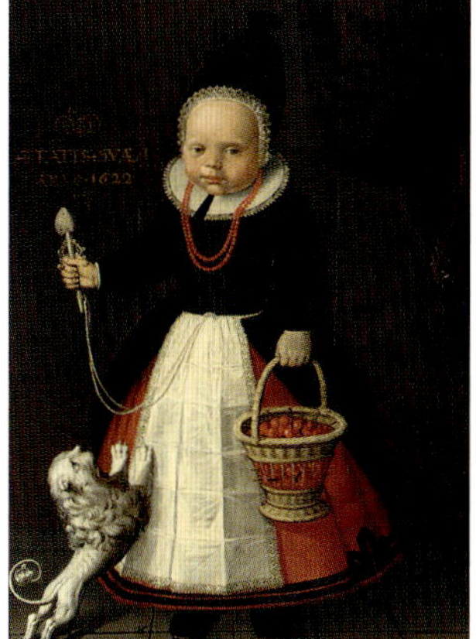

Dutch (Friesland) School
*Portrait of a Girl, Aged One, with a Basket of
Strawberries* 1622
oil on panel 125.8 x 67.3
35.252

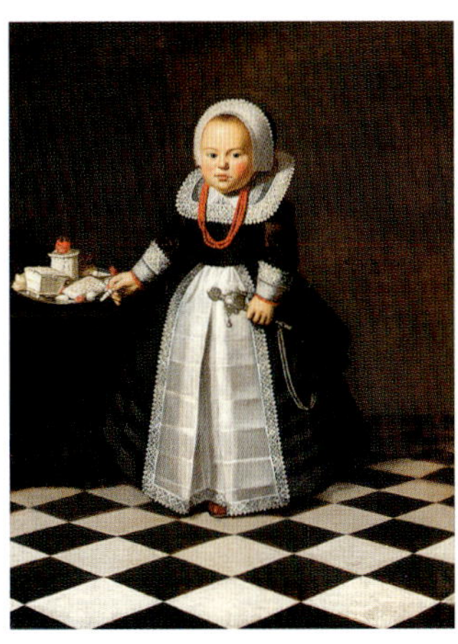

Dutch (Friesland) School
Portrait of a Girl, Aged One, with a Rattle
1635
oil on panel 106.7 x 83.8
35.253

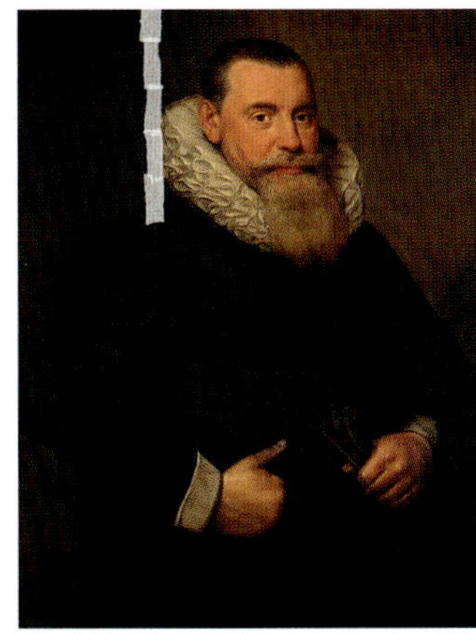

Dutch School
Portrait of a Bearded Man, Aged 54
c.1625–1639
oil on panel 94 x 68.9
1327

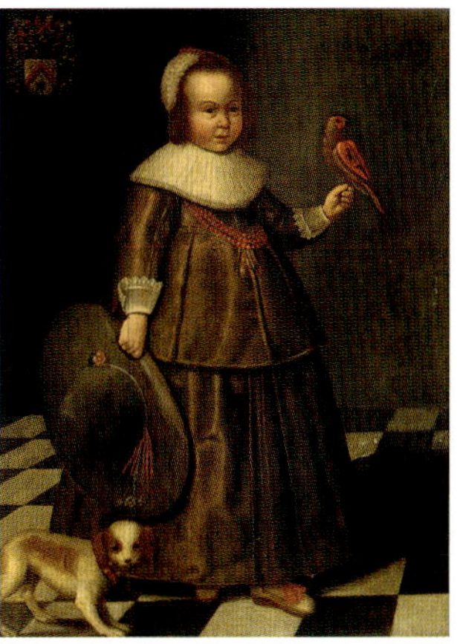

Dutch School
*Portrait of a Boy, Aged Three, with a Large Hat
and a Parrot* 1644
oil on panel 110.5 x 84.5
35.254

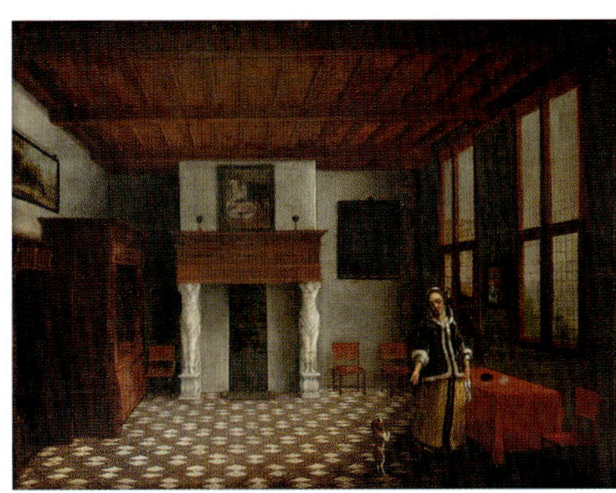

Dutch School 17th C
Interior of a Living Room
oil on panel 38.1 x 50.5
377

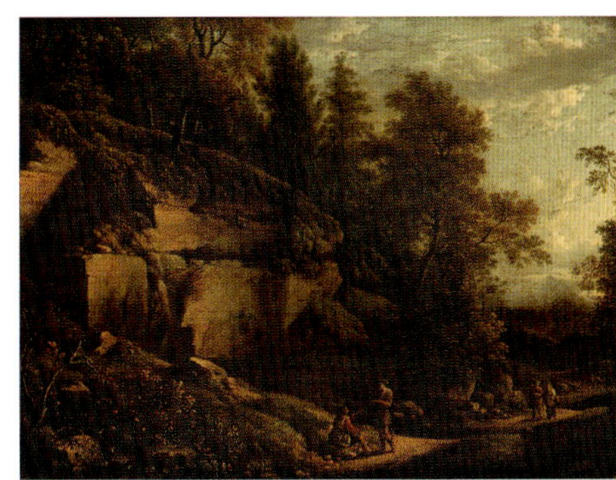

Dutch School late 17th C
A Disused Quarry in a Wood, with Figures
oil on canvas 32.7 x 41
67

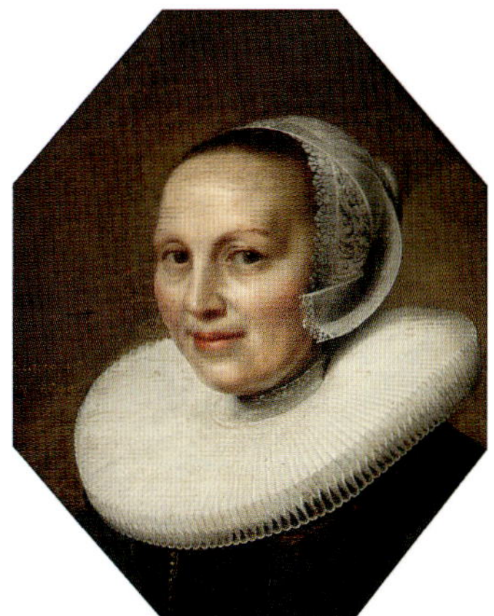

Dutch School (attributed to)
Portrait of a Woman, Aged 46 1640
oil on panel 32.4 x 27
103

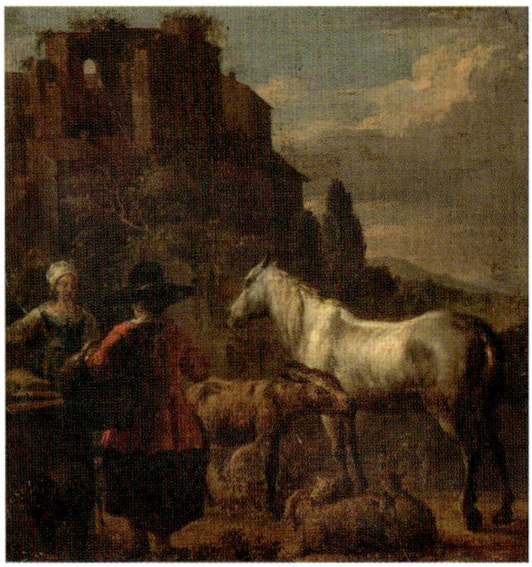

Dutch School (attributed to) 17th C
Landscape with Ruins, Figures and Animals
oil on canvas 45.8 x 42
3429

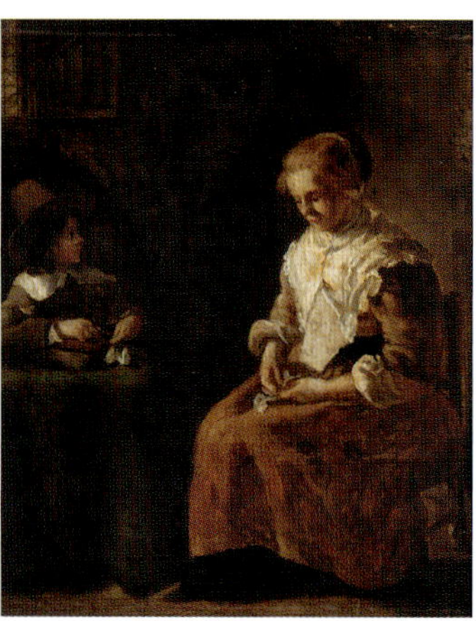

Dutch School (attributed to) 18th C–19th C
Interior with a Young Woman and a Boy
oil on panel 29.2 x 23.2
211

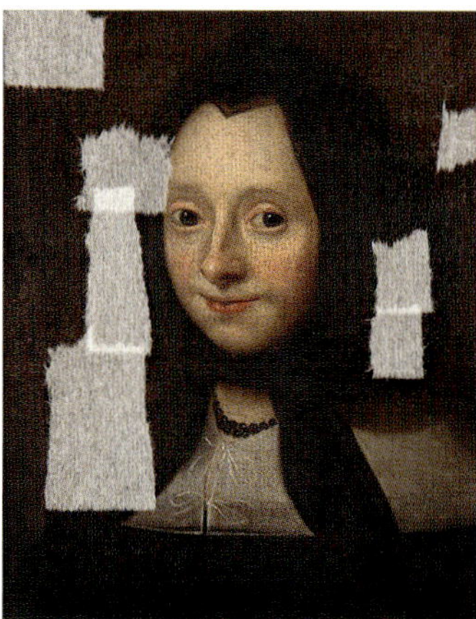

Dutch School (attributed to) 18th C–19th C
The Head of a Young Woman
oil on canvas 27.6 x 21
2187

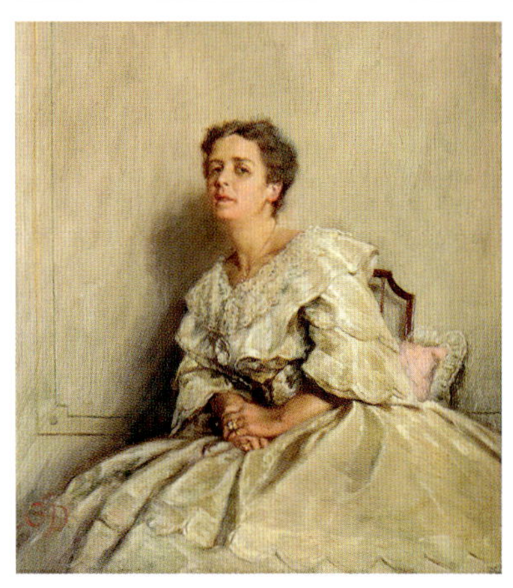

Duthie, Alexander Spottiswoode active
1885–1930
Mrs Ruby McLennan
oil on panel 23.5 x 21
2566

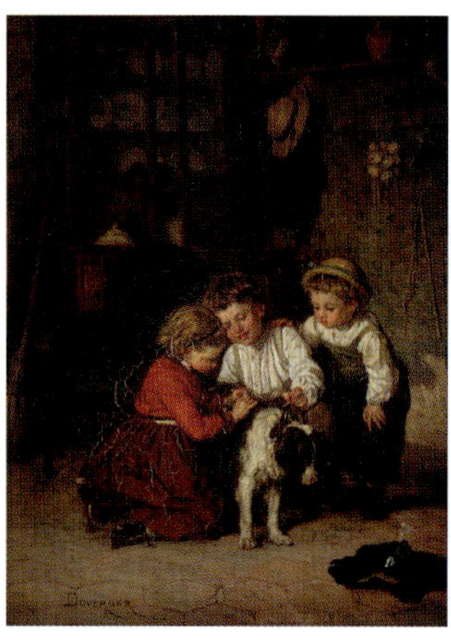

Duverger, Théophile Emmanuel 1821–1901
Playmates
oil on panel 32.4 x 24.1
1164

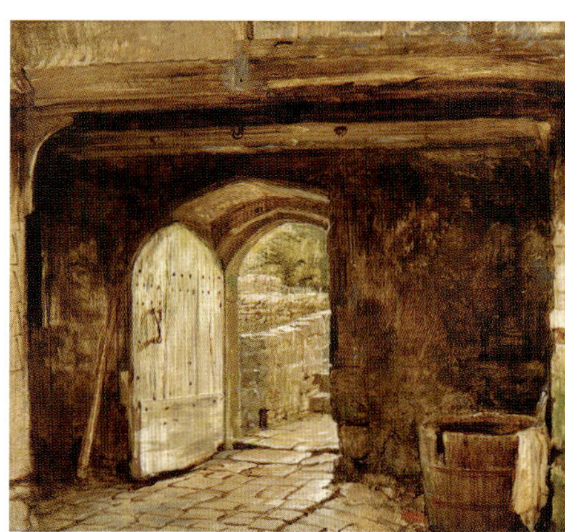

Dyce, William 1806–1864
*Sketch of a Doorway with a Water
Barrel* c.1830–1840
oil on board 25.4 x 27.9
3210

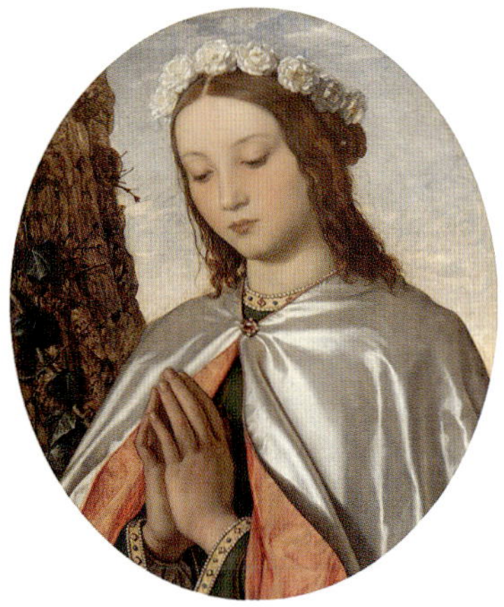

Dyce, William 1806–1864
Christabel c.1855
oil on panel 54 x 44.8
3221

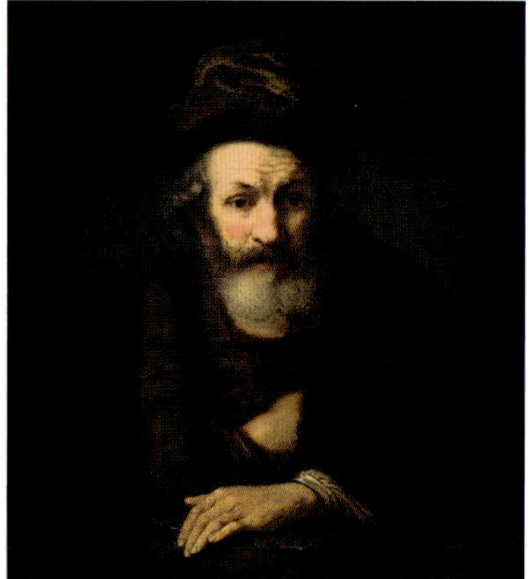

Dyck, Abraham van (attributed to)
c.1635–1672
*A Bearded Man in a Fur Hat with a
Book* c.1651–1672
oil on canvas 73.7 x 63.5
35.256

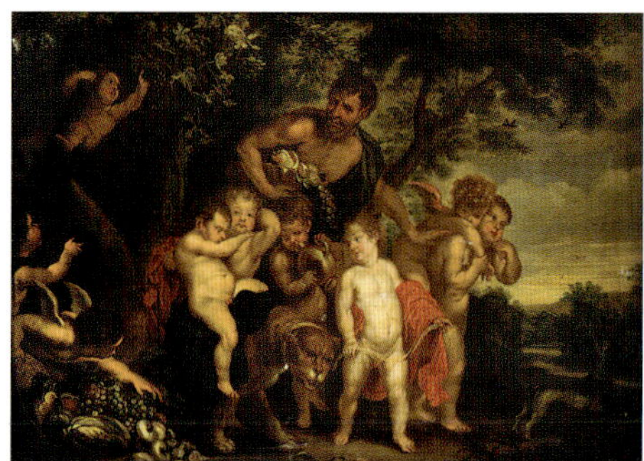

Dyck, Anthony van (after) 1599–1641
A Bacchic Procession 17th C
oil on copper 35.5 x 49.8
390

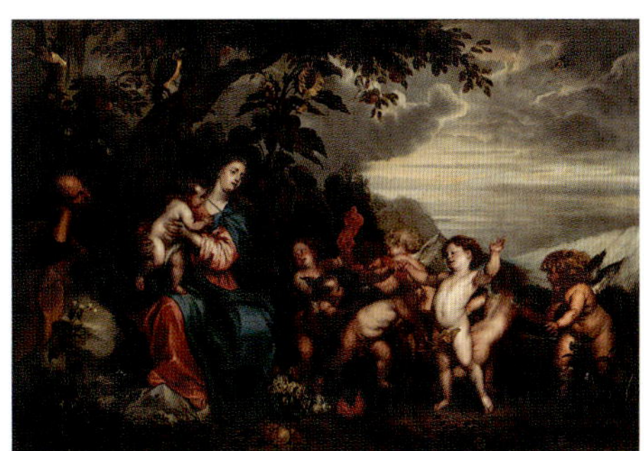

Dyck, Anthony van (after) 1599–1641
The Rest on the Flight into Egypt 18th C (?)
oil on canvas 175.3 x 250.8
298

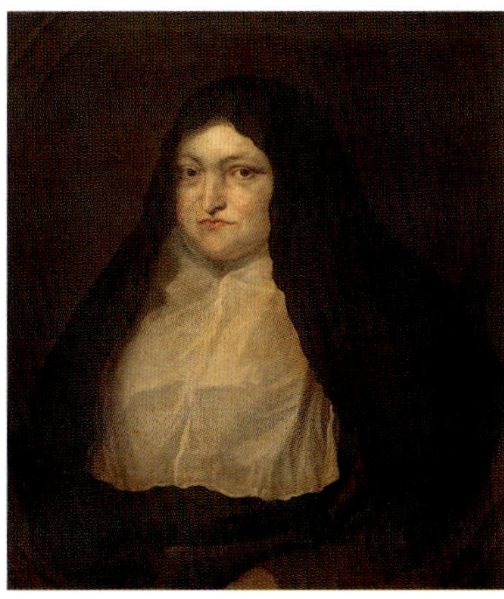

Dyck, Anthony van (after) 1599–1641
Infanta Isabella Clara Eugenia (1566–1633)
oil on canvas 67.6 x 56.5
PC.1

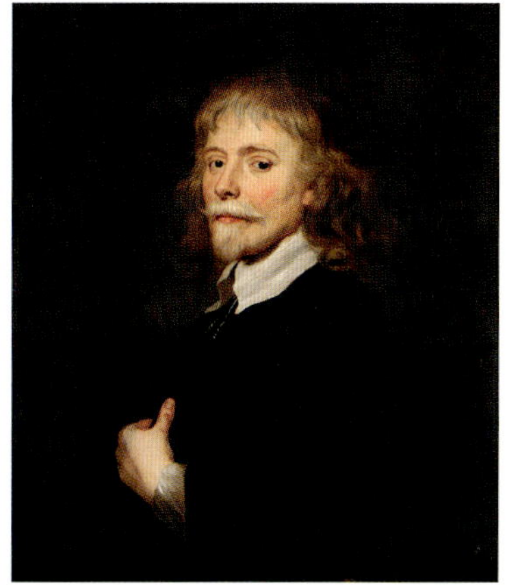

Dyck, Anthony van (follower of) 1599–1641
Portrait of a Young Bearded Man c.1640–1660
oil on canvas 76.2 x 63.5
50

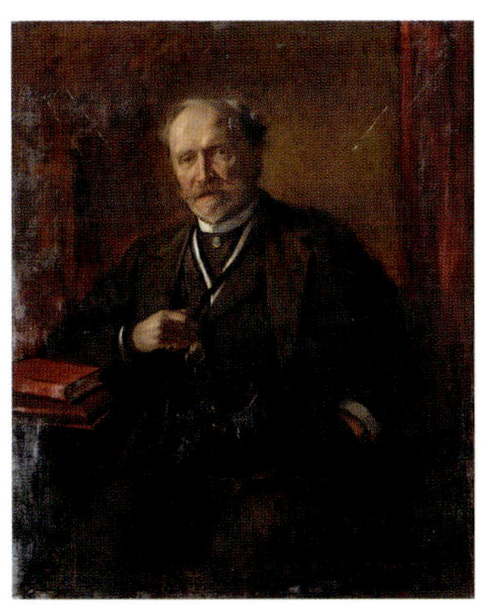

Eadie, Robert 1877–1954
J. Shaw Maxwell (1855–1928), JP 1917
oil on canvas 110.5 x 87.6
1697

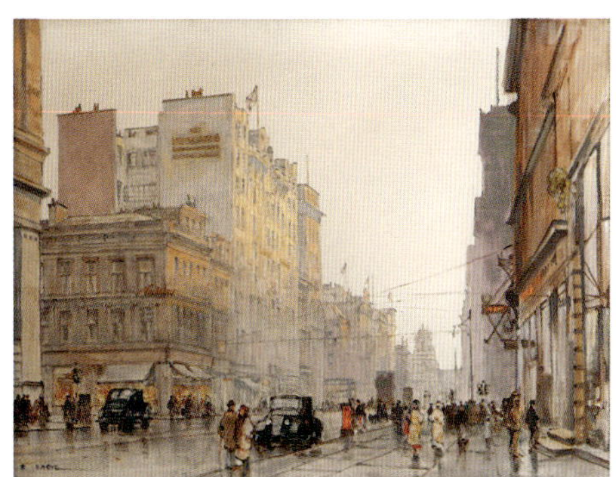

Eadie, Robert 1877–1954
St Vincent Street c.1941
oil on canvas 71.1 x 91.4
2258

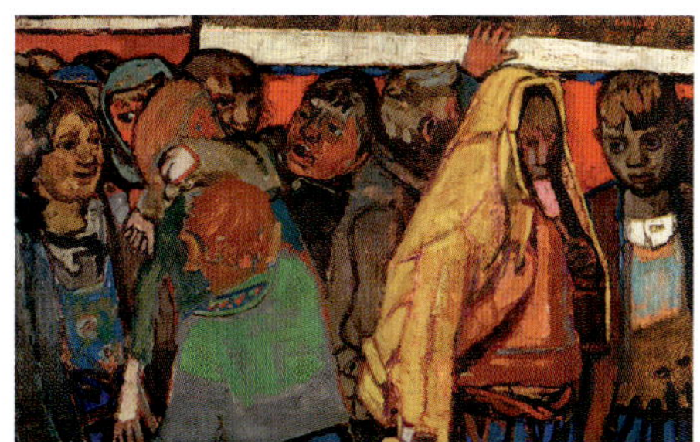

Eardley, Joan Kathleen Harding 1921–1963
Glasgow Kids, a Saturday Matinée Picture Queue c.1949
oil on canvas 70.8 x 114.5
3240

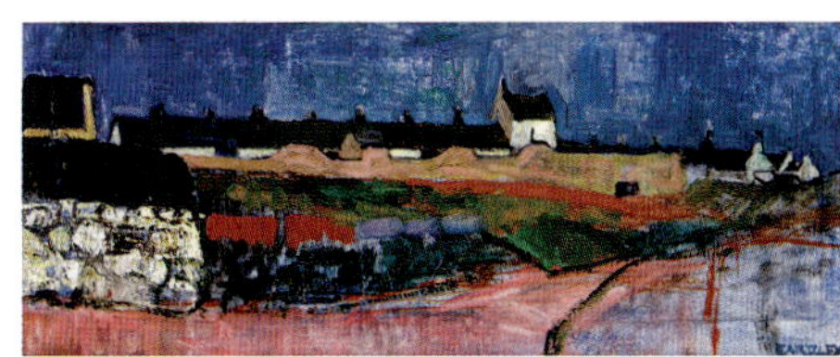

Eardley, Joan Kathleen Harding 1921–1963
Catterline Coastguard Cottages c.1952
oil on canvas 35.6 x 83.8
2963

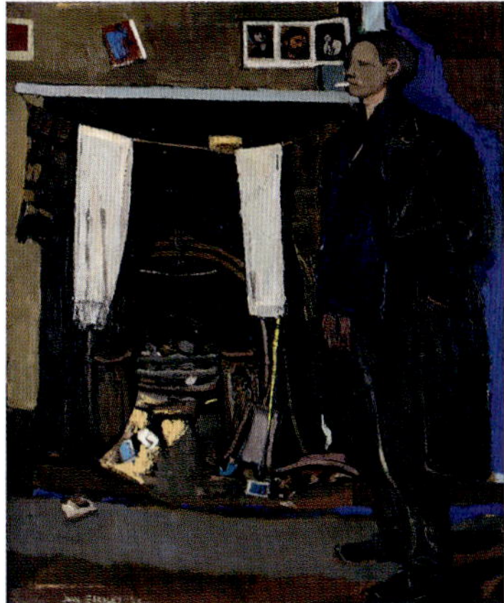

Eardley, Joan Kathleen Harding 1921–1963
A Glasgow Lodging 1953
oil on canvas 112.9 x 92.8
3320

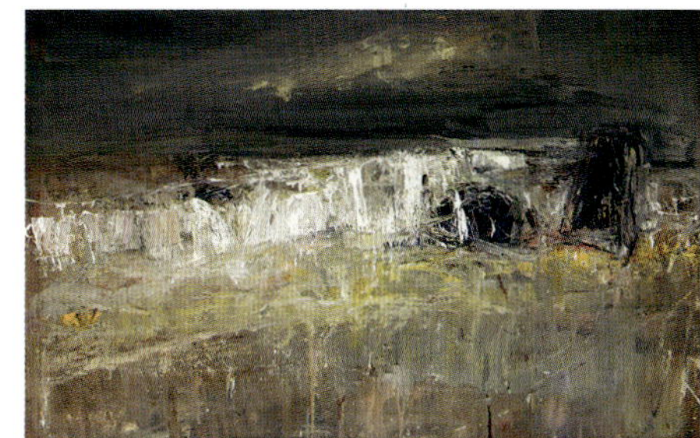

Eardley, Joan Kathleen Harding 1921–1963
A Stormy Sea No.1 1960
oil on hardboard 96.5 x 145.5
3146

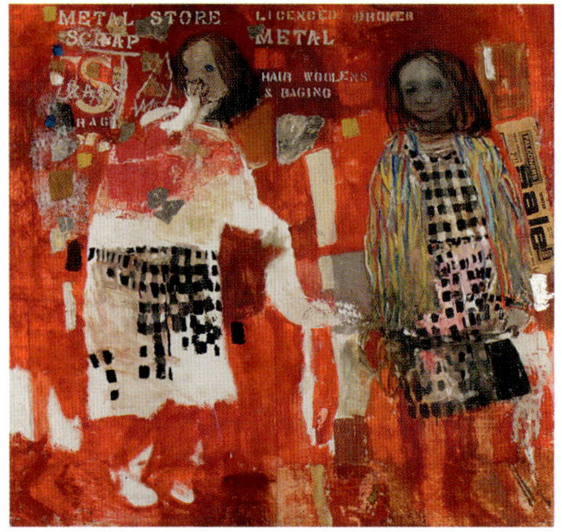

Eardley, Joan Kathleen Harding 1921–1963
Two Children 1963
oil & collage on canvas 134.7 x 134.7
3532

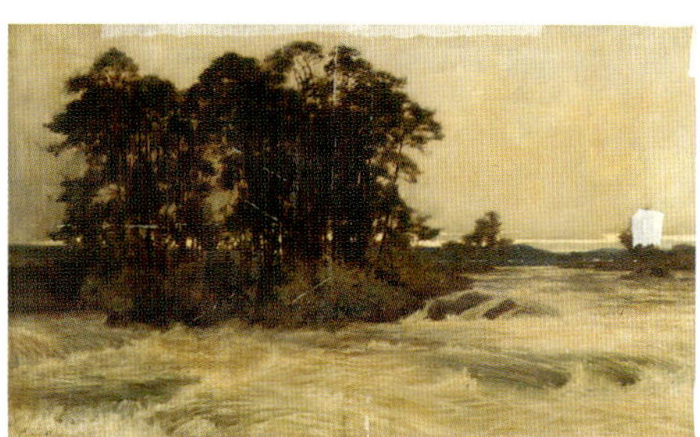

East, Alfred 1844–1913
Falls of Dochart, Killin 1884
oil on canvas 55.9 x 91.4
1454

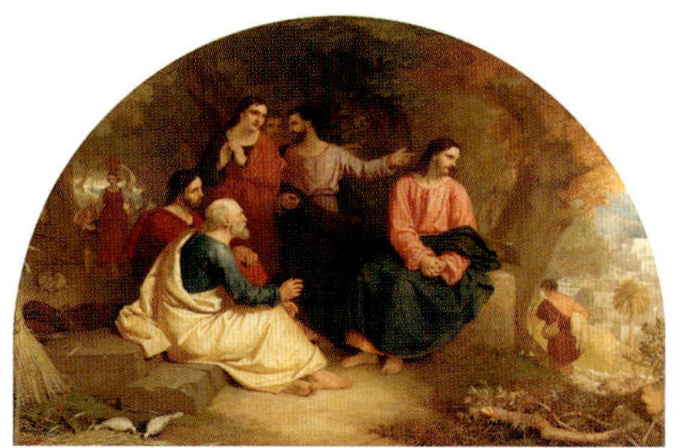

Eastlake, Charles Lock 1793–1865
Christ Lamenting over Jerusalem 1855
oil on canvas 49.9 x 99.1
1731

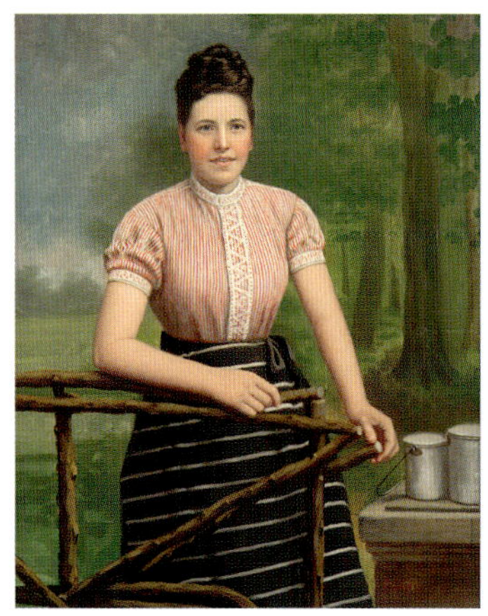

Edwards
Mary Millar, Dairy Girl 1887
oil on canvas 44 x 36.5
PP.1977.45.2

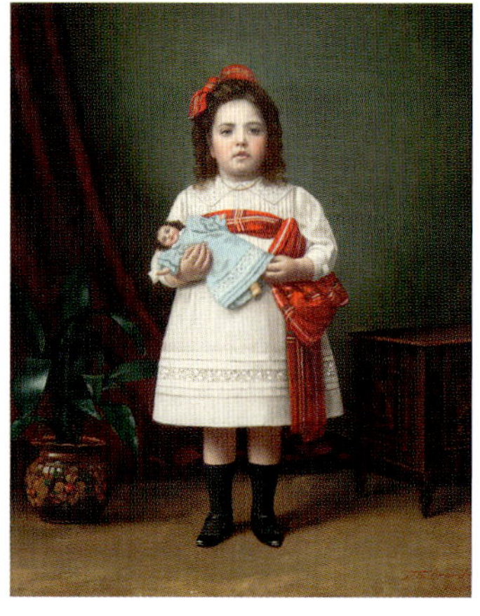

Edwards, J.
Portrait of a Girl with a Doll 1914
oil on canvas 49.1 x 39.1
TEMP.2929

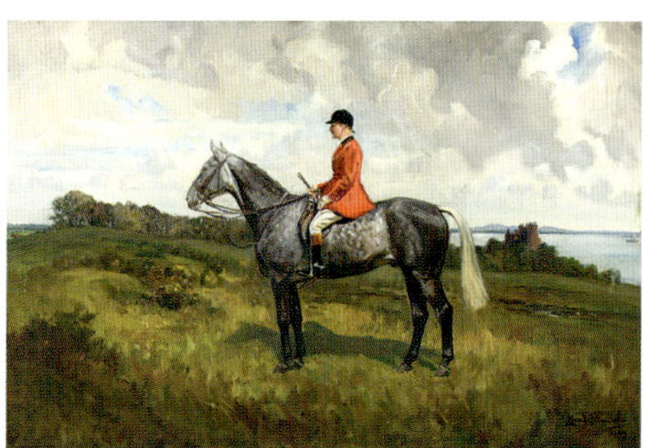

Edwards, Lionel D. R. 1878–1966
*John Alan Burns (1897–1957), 4th Lord
Inverclyde* 1949
oil on canvas 61 x 91.4
3083

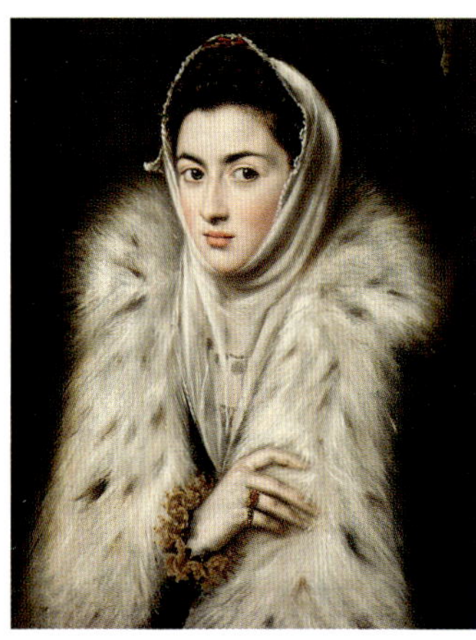

El Greco 1541–1614
Lady in a Fur Wrap c.1577–1579
oil on canvas 79.8 x 65.7
PC.18

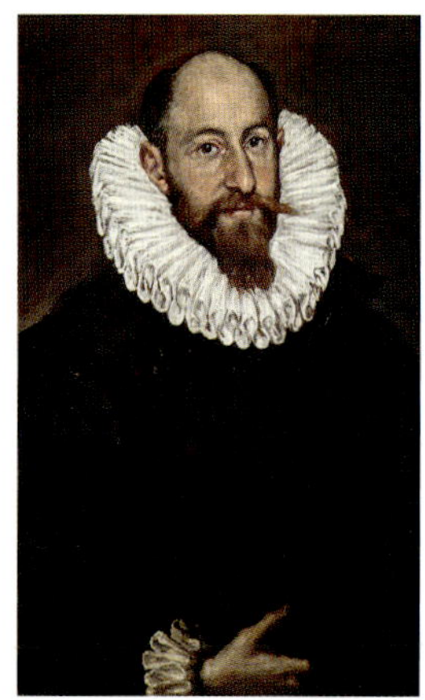

El Greco 1541–1614
Portrait of a Man c.1590
oil on canvas 73.3 x 46.5
PC.17

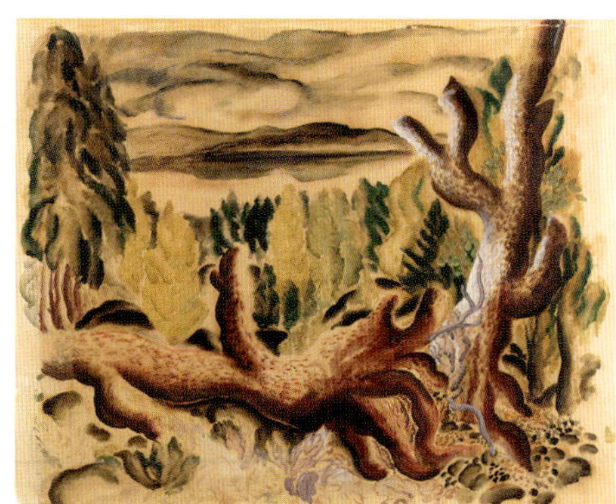

Elder, Andrew Taylor 1908–1966
Scottish Loch
oil on paper 56.2 x 71
2195

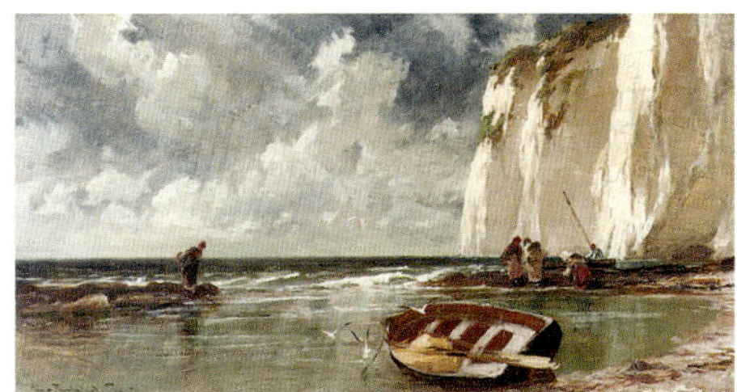

Ellis, Edwin 1841–1895
On the South Coast of England
oil on canvas 44.5 x 82.6
820

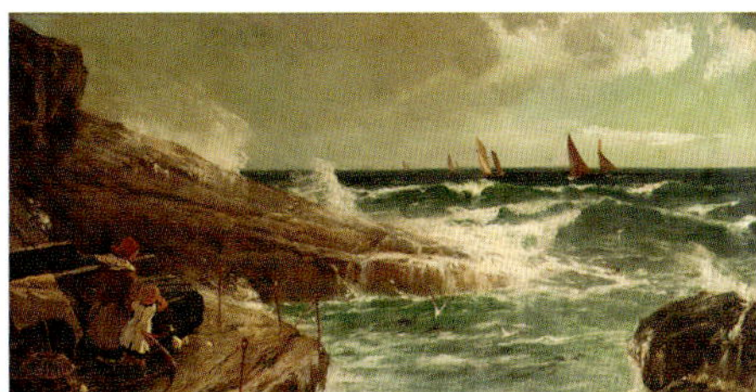

Ellis, Edwin 1841–1895
Seascape
oil on canvas 66 x 129.5
1791

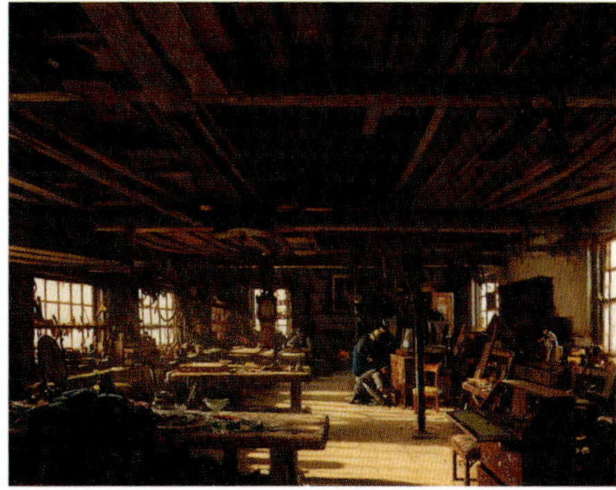

Elwell, Frederick William 1870–1958
Widdall's 1928
oil on canvas 101.6 x 127
1810

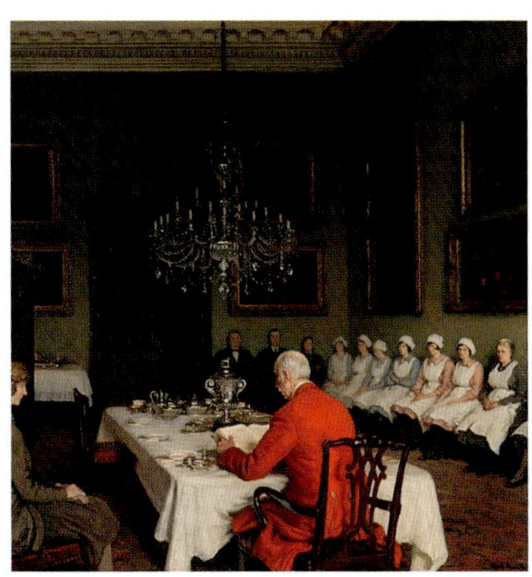

Elwell, Frederick William 1870–1958
The Squire 1931
oil on canvas 114.3 x 109.2
2644

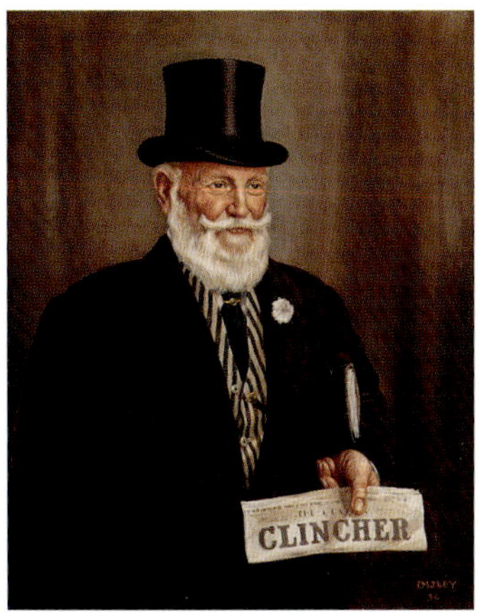

Emsley, Walter 1860–1938
The Clincher 1936
oil on canvas 90.6 x 69.6
TEMP.4051

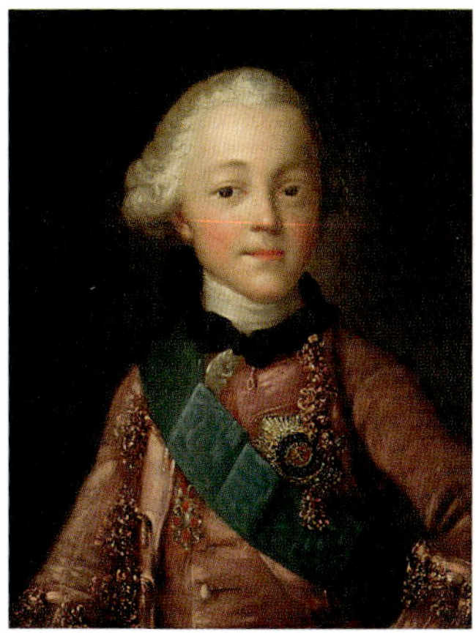

Erichsen, Vigilius (after) 1722–1783
Prince Paul of Russia (1754–1801)
oil on canvas 59.7 x 46.8
425

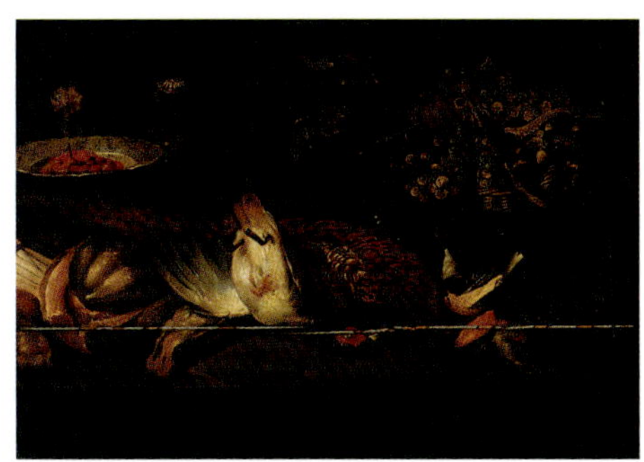

Es, Jacob Foppens van c.1596–1666
Still Life with Game and Fruit
oil on panel 75.9 x 106.7
391

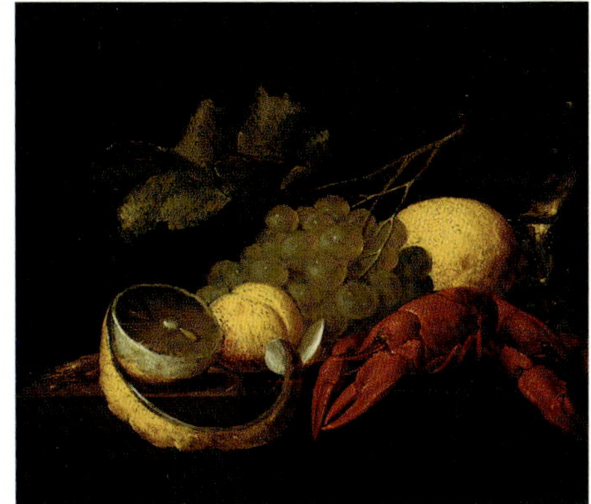

Es, Jacob Foppens van (attributed to)
c.1596–1666
Still Life with Fruit and Crayfish
oil on copper 24.4 x 29.2
81

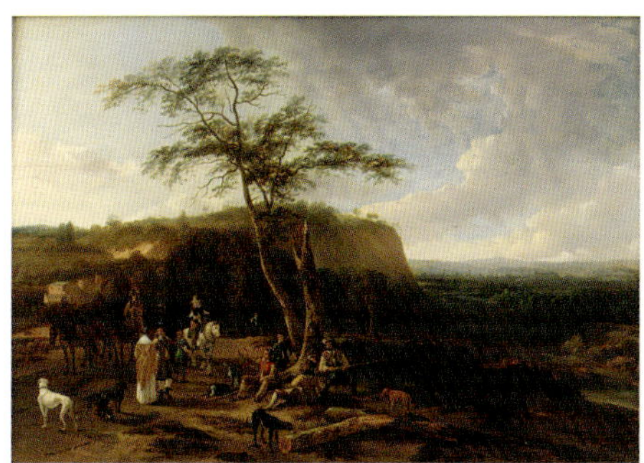

Esselens, Jacob 1626–1687
Landscape with a Fowling Party c.1650–1670
oil on panel 59.7 x 83.2
114

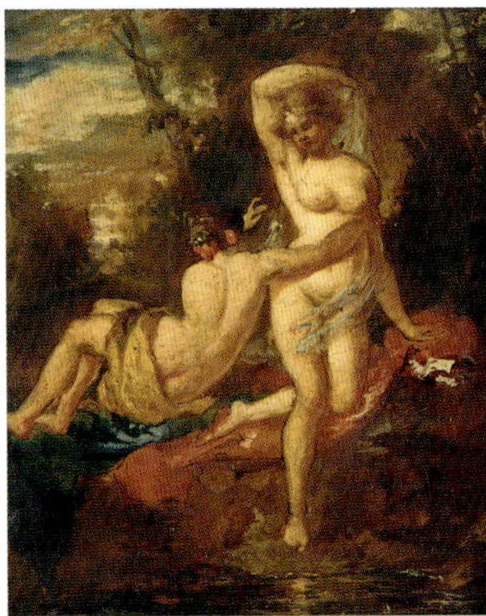

Etty, William 1787–1849
The Bathers
oil on paper on canvas 15.9 x 13.3
454

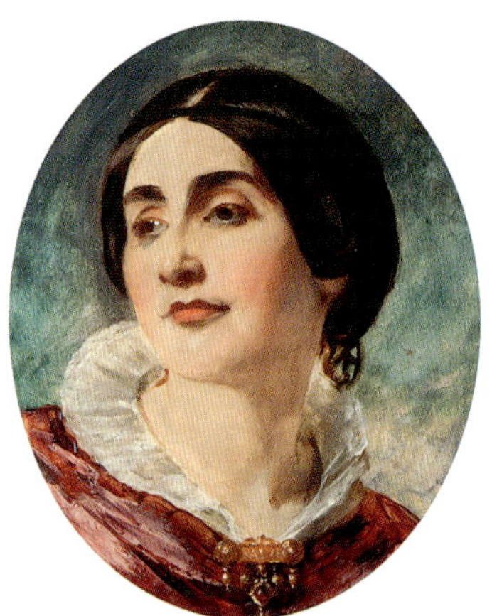

Etty, William 1787–1849
*The Honourable Mrs Caroline Norton
(d.1877), Lady Stirling Maxwell*
oil on copper 44.5 x 33.6
PL.16 (P)

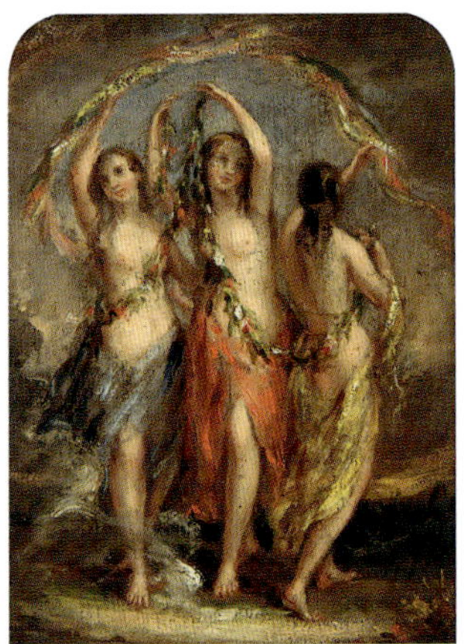

Etty, William 1787–1849
The Three Graces
oil on panel 17.7 x 12.7
453

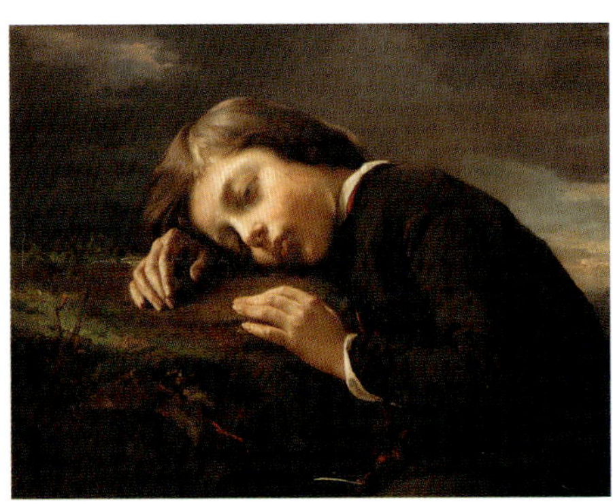

Eudes de Guimard, Louisa 1827–1904
Boy Asleep
oil on canvas 50 x 60.7
435

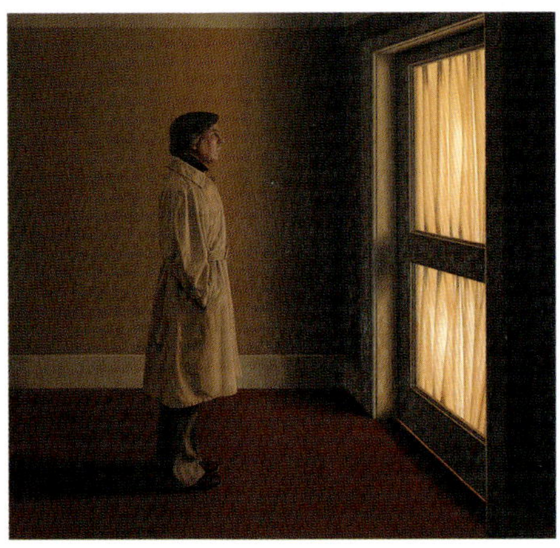

Evans, David Pugh b.1942
North Corridor 1979
oil on canvas 153 x 156.2
3379

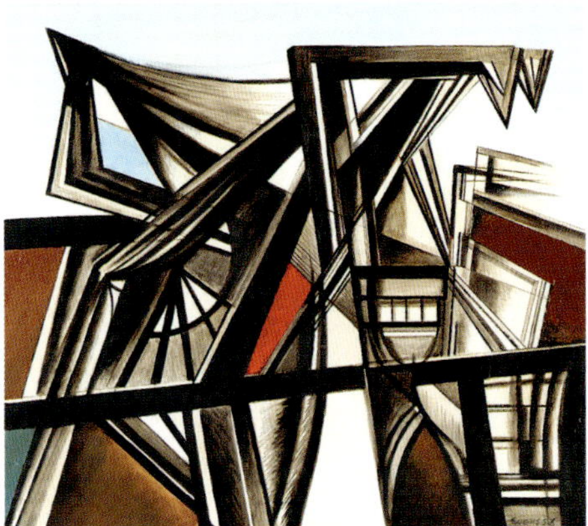

Evans, Merlyn Oliver 1910–1973
Wharfside Construction, Morning 1953
oil on canvas on hardboard 83.5 x 91
3113

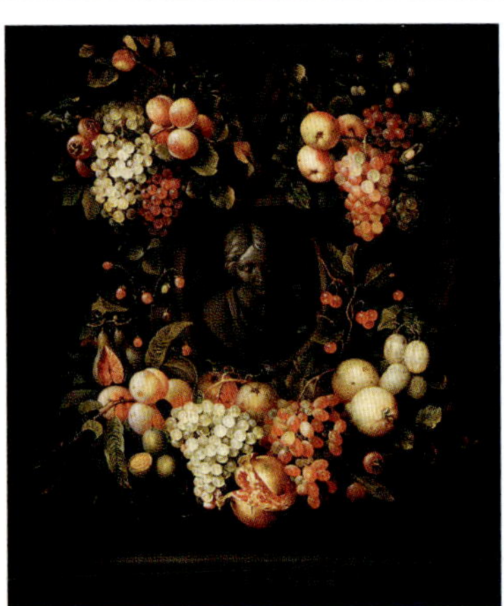

Everbroeck, Frans van (attributed to) active
1654–1672
*A Garland of Fruit around the Sculpted Bust of
a Girl* c.1654–1672
oil on canvas 105 x 89.5
51

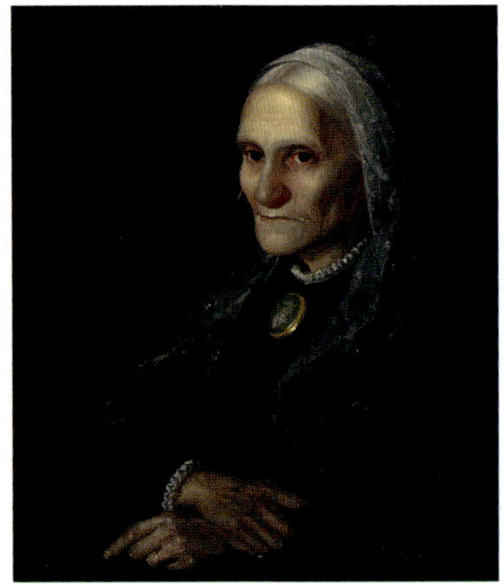

Ewart, David Shanks 1901–1965
A Scots Lady 1929
oil on canvas 61 x 50.8
1792

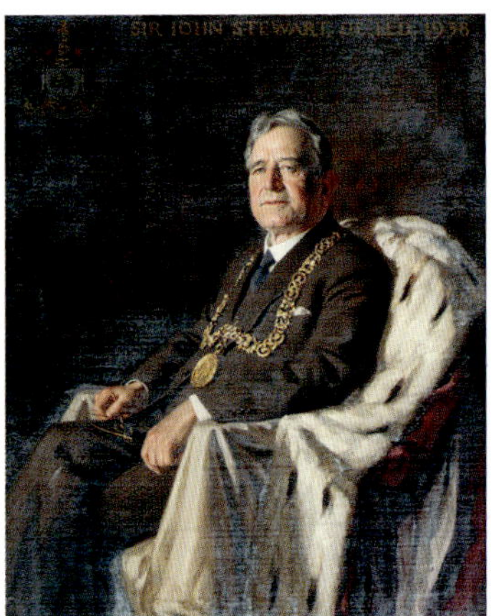

Ewart, David Shanks 1901–1965
*Sir John Stewart, Lord Provost of Glasgow
(1935–1938)* 1938
oil on canvas 127 x 101.6
2118

Facing page: Matisse, Henri, 1869–1954, *Woman in Oriental Dress*, 1919 (p. 284)

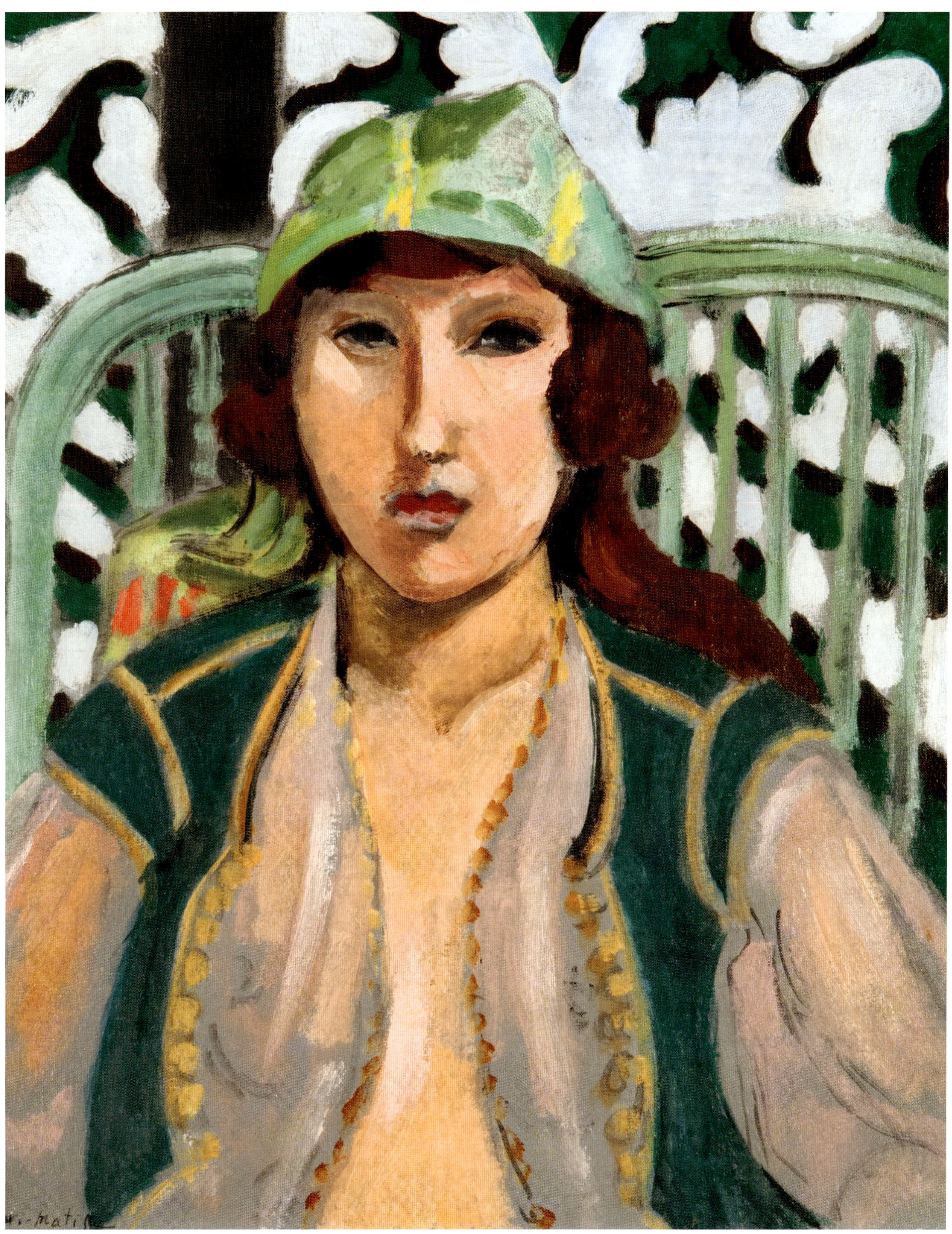

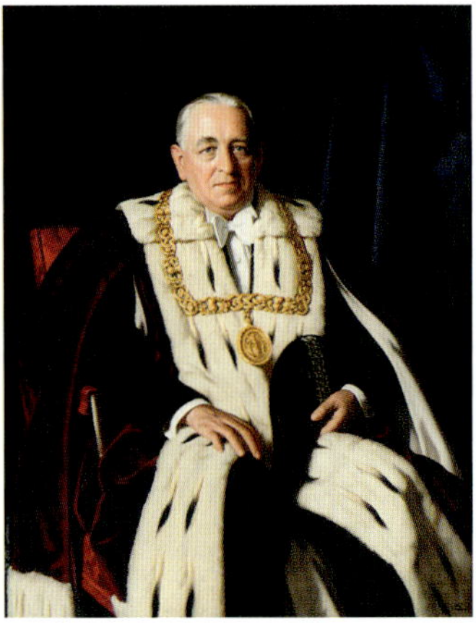

Ewart, David Shanks 1901–1965
Sir Hector McNeil, Lord Provost of Glasgow (1945–1949) c.1949–1950
oil on canvas 127 x 101.6
2860

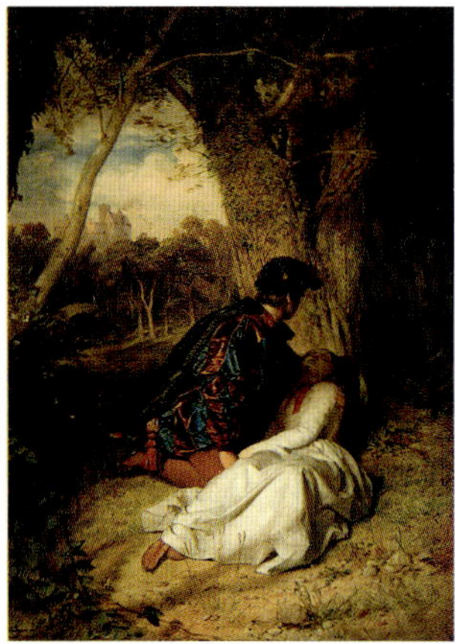

Faed, John 1819–1902
The Death of Burd Ellen c.1860
oil on canvas 29.2 x 21.6
987

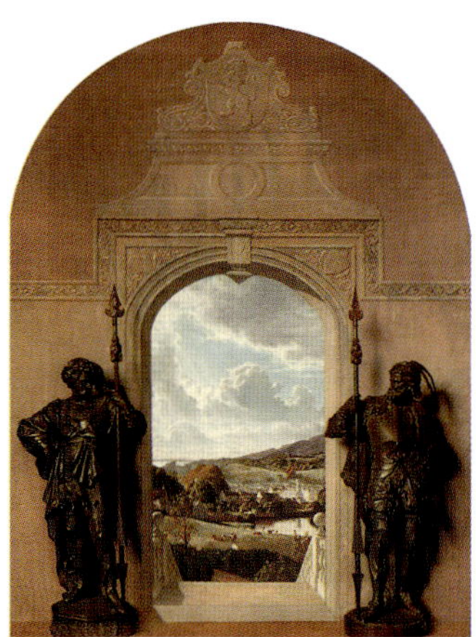

Faed, John 1819–1902
View of Gatehouse of Fleet 1885
oil on canvas 104.5 x 76.8
3343

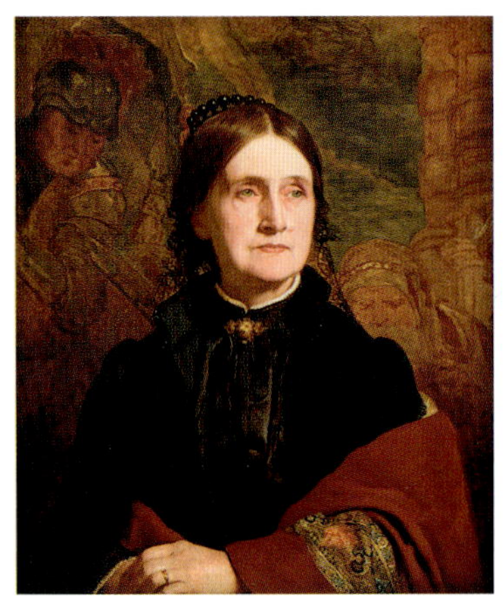

Faed, John 1819–1902
The Artist's Wife, Jane Macdonald (1820–1897) 1890
oil on canvas 76.2 x 63.5
2986

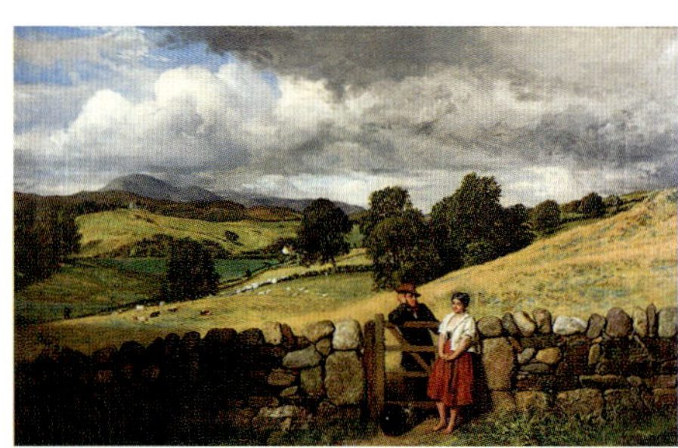

Faed, John 1819–1902
Trysting Place, Landscape with Cattle and Sheep
oil on canvas 38.1 x 61
794

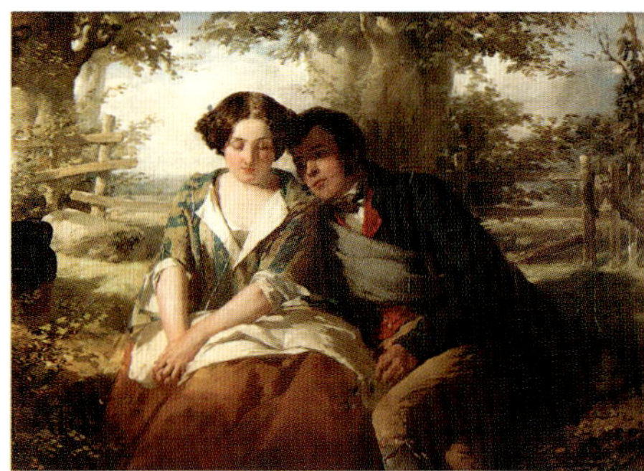

Faed, Thomas 1826–1900
Burns and Highland Mary c.1850
oil on panel 47.3 x 66
1748

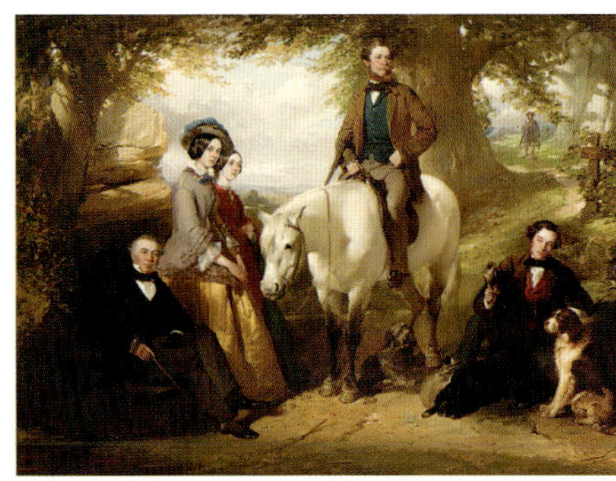

Faed, Thomas 1826–1900
Alexander Dennistoun of Golfhill (1790–1874), and Family 1851
oil on canvas 101.6 x 133.3
3439

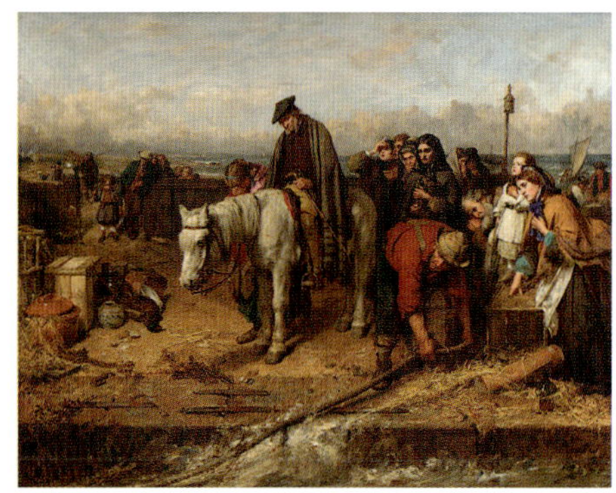

Faed, Thomas 1826–1900
The Last of the Clan 1865
oil on canvas 144.8 x 182.9
3366

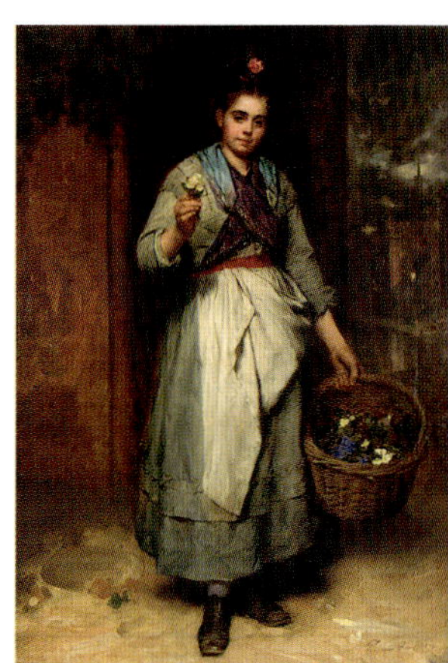

Faed, Thomas 1826–1900
Violets and Primroses 1874
oil on canvas 78.7 x 54.6
783

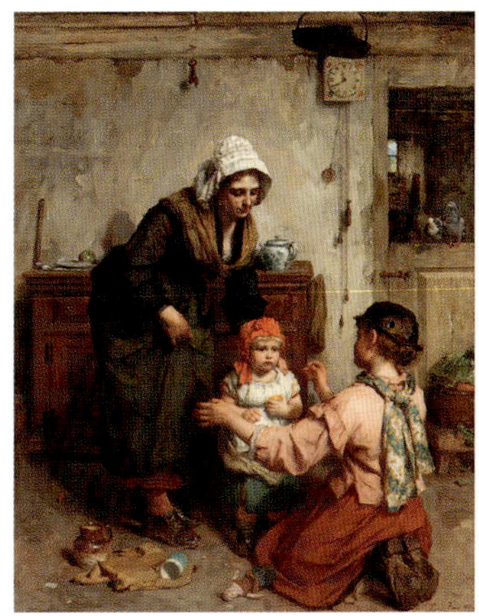

Faed, Thomas 1826–1900
Where's My Good Little Girl? 1882
oil on canvas 104.1 x 81.3
2110

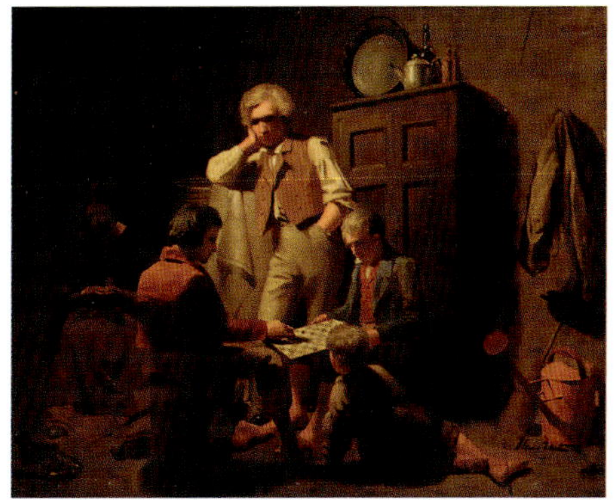

Faed, Thomas 1826–1900
Interior with Figures
oil on canvas 40 x 48.9
2985

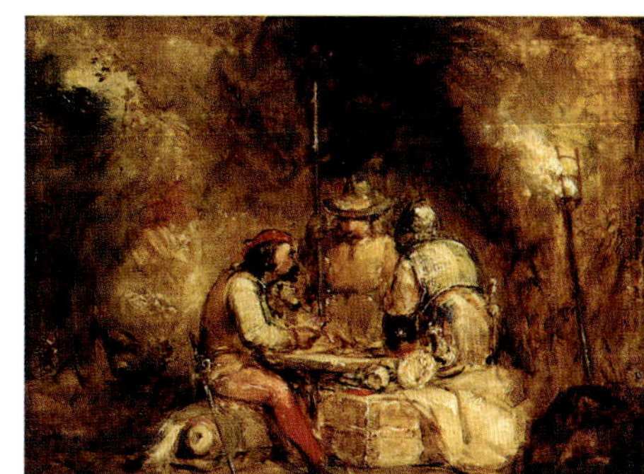

Faed, Thomas 1826–1900
Spanish Bandits in a Cave
oil on canvas 22.9 x 30.5
856

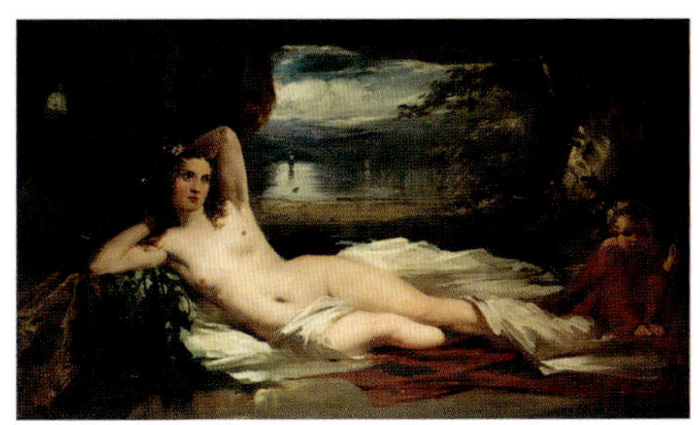

Faed, Thomas 1826–1900
Venus and Cupid
oil on canvas 44.5 x 64.8
813

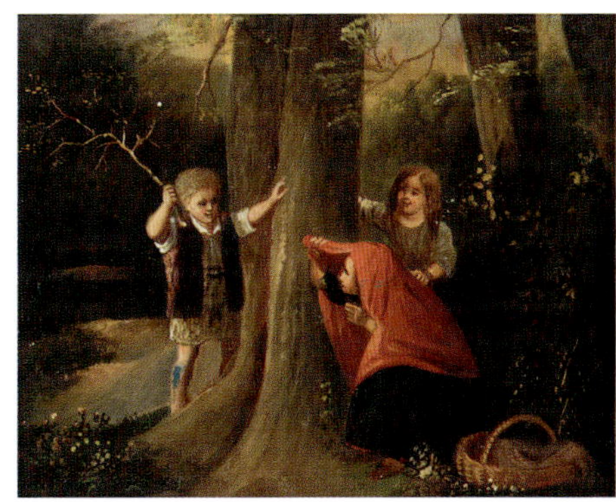

Faed, Thomas (after) 1826–1900
Three Children Playing in a Wood 1851
oil on metal 16.5 x 21.6
3012

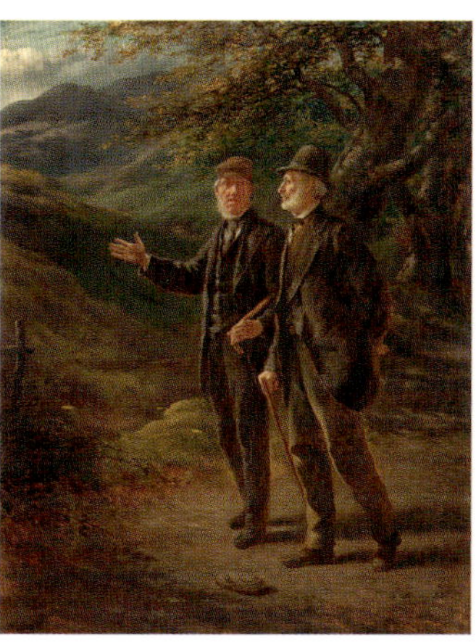

Fairbairn, Thomas 1820–1885
'We twa hae paddled i' the burn'
oil on canvas 91.7 x 71.4
1730

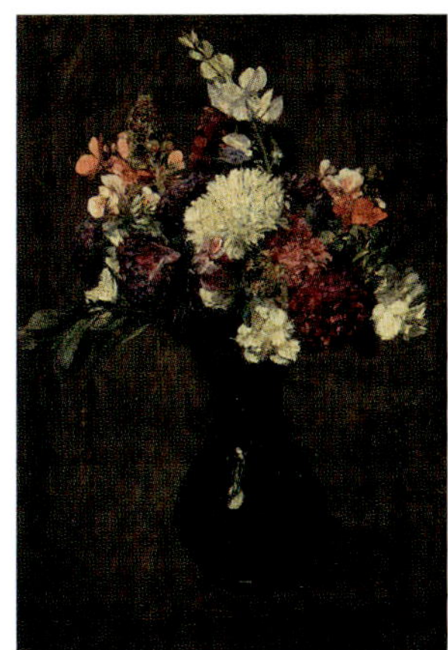

Fantin-Latour, Henri 1836–1904
A Mixed Bunch 1872
oil on canvas 39.1 x 27.5
2917

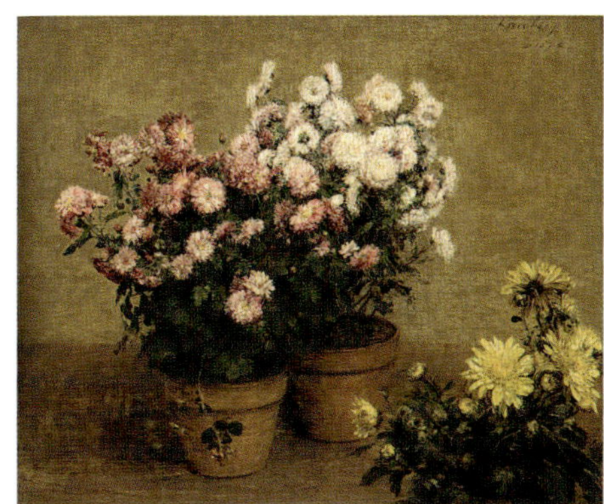

Fantin-Latour, Henri 1836–1904
Chrysanthemums 1874
oil on canvas 55.2 x 64.8
35.26

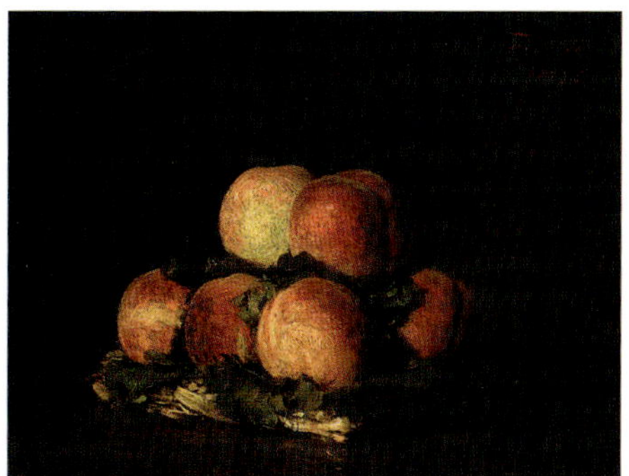

Fantin-Latour, Henri 1836–1904
Basket of Peaches 1875
oil on canvas 26 x 33
35.259

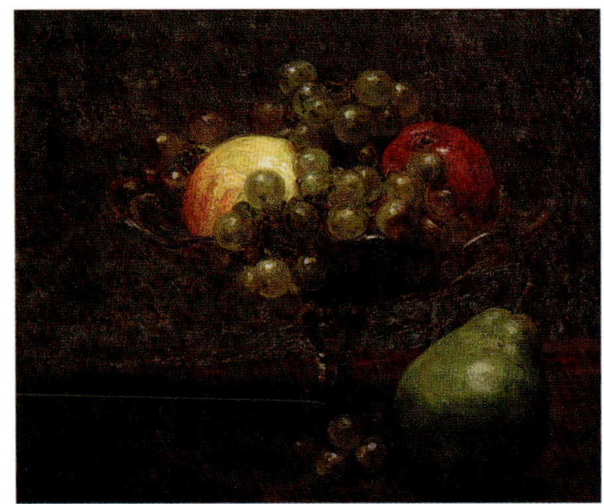

Fantin-Latour, Henri 1836–1904
Still Life 1877
oil on canvas 25.8 x 30.7
2387

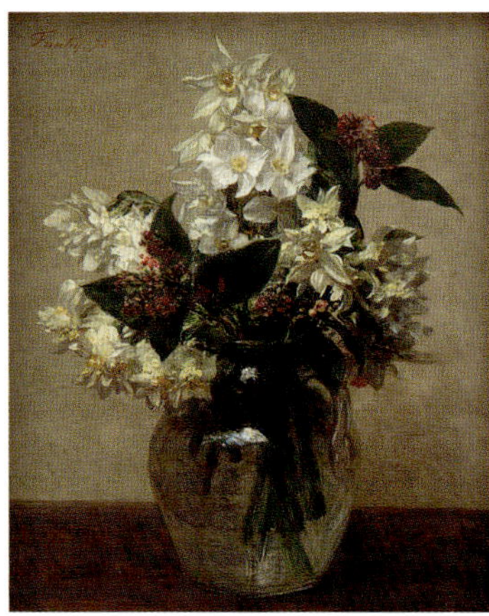

Fantin-Latour, Henri 1836–1904
Spring Flowers 1878
oil on canvas 29.2 x 24.1
35.261

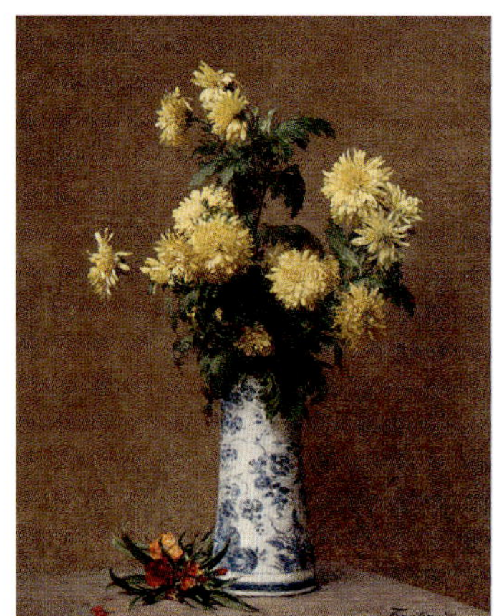

Fantin-Latour, Henri 1836–1904
Yellow Chrysanthemums 1879
oil on canvas 61 x 48.4
1795

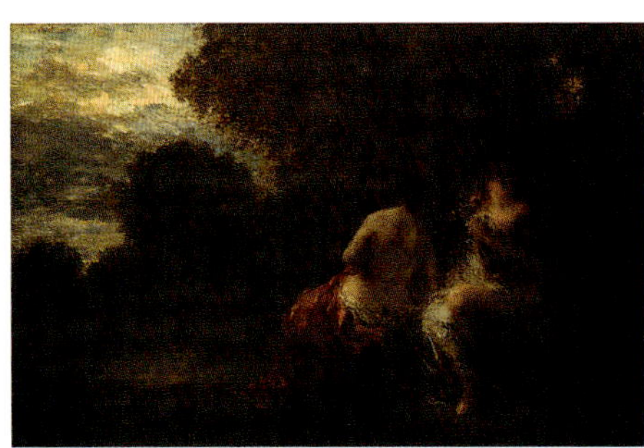

Fantin-Latour, Henri 1836–1904
The Bathers 1883
oil on canvas 27.3 x 41
2933

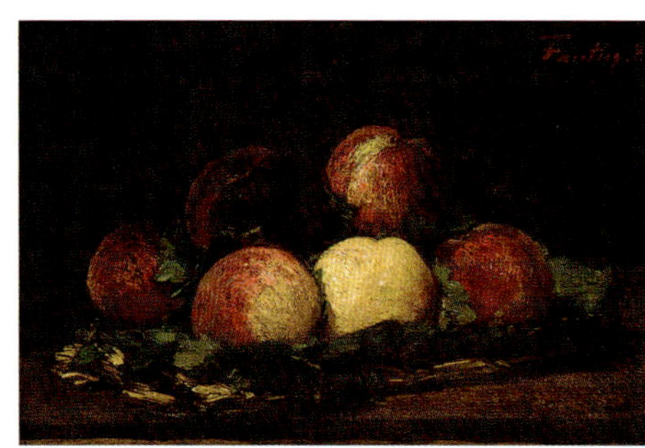

Fantin-Latour, Henri 1836–1904
Basket of Peaches 1884
oil on canvas 22.2 x 33
35.258

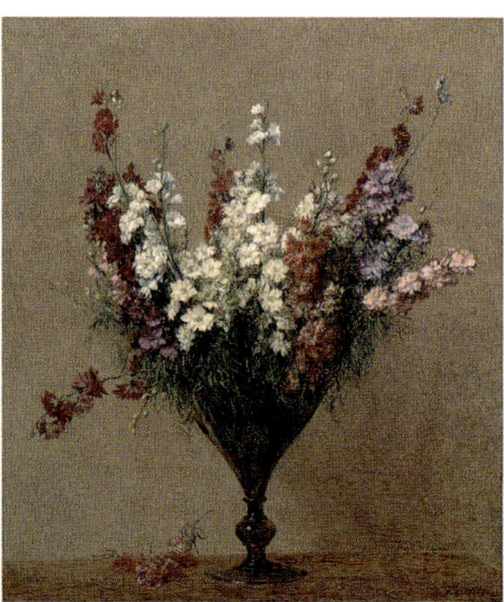

Fantin-Latour, Henri 1836–1904
Larkspur 1892
oil on canvas 68.6 x 57.9
2139

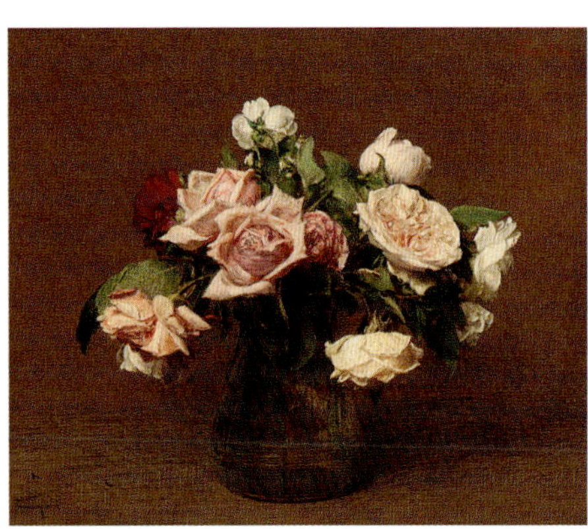

Fantin-Latour, Henri 1836–1904
Roses 'La France' 1895
oil on canvas 40.2 x 46
2138

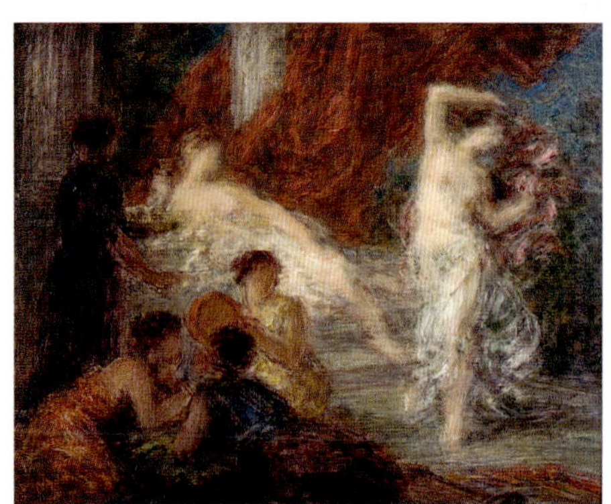

Fantin-Latour, Henri 1836–1904
The Dance 1898
oil on canvas 60.4 x 73.1
2386

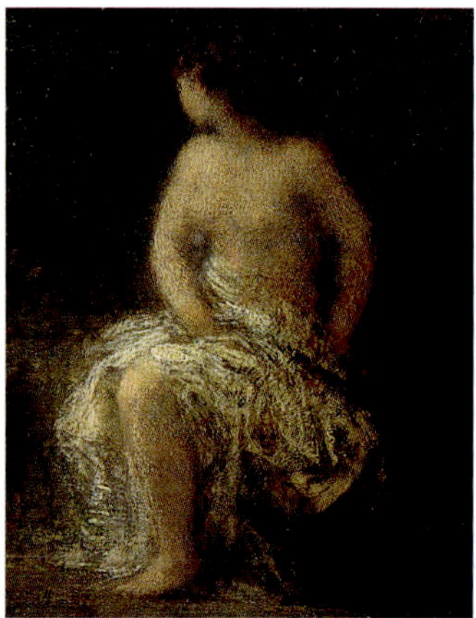

Fantin-Latour, Henri 1836–1904
The Bather
oil on canvas 19 x 14.6
35.257

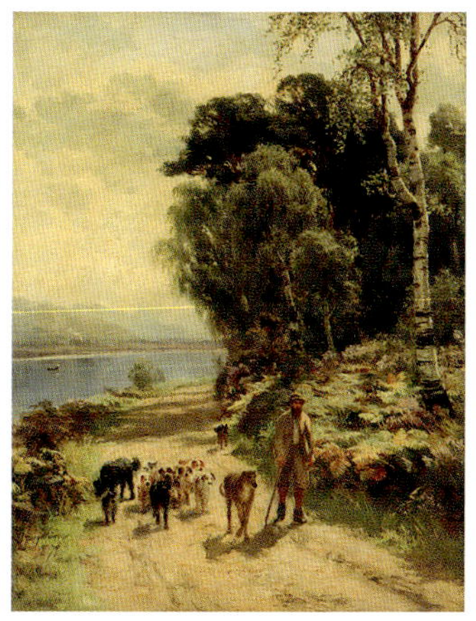

Farquharson, David 1839–1907
The Wayside, Loch Maree 1879
oil on canvas 45.7 x 35.6
1448

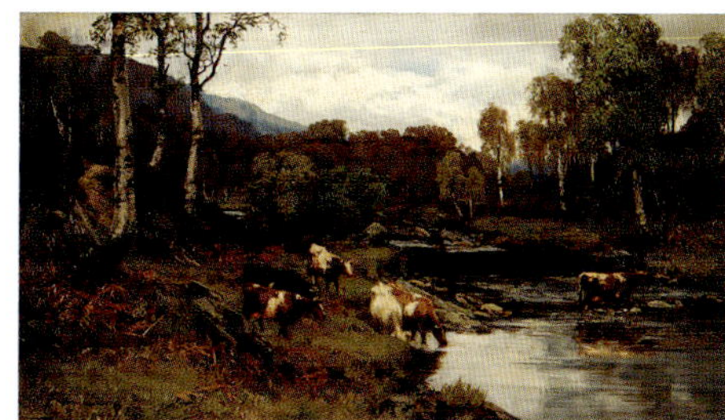

Farquharson, David 1839–1907
On the Achray 1884
oil on canvas 29.2 x 49.5
989

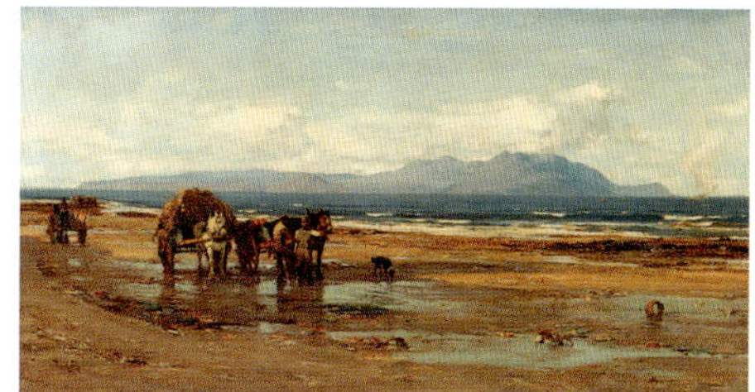

Farquharson, David 1839–1907
Arran from the Ayrshire Coast
oil on canvas 81.3 x 152.4
857

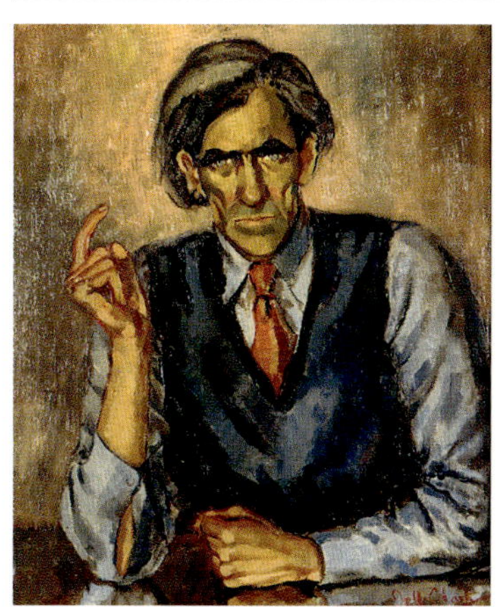

Fell-Clark, Patricia 1914–2001
James Maxton (1885–1946), MP 1940s
oil on canvas 96 x 83.5
OG.1955.117

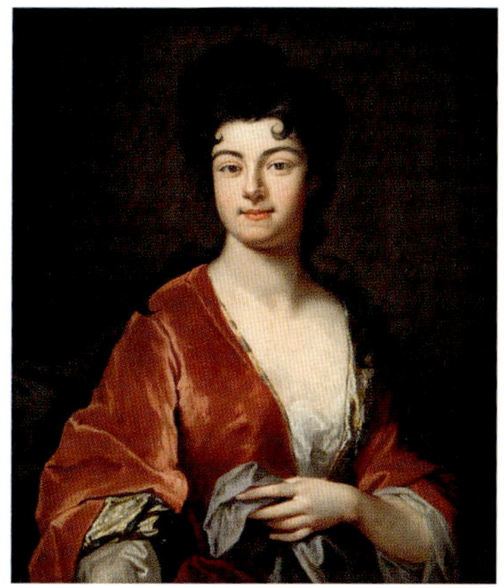

Fellowes, James (attributed to)
c.1690–c.1760
Lady Villiers
oil on canvas 73.7 x 61
35.286

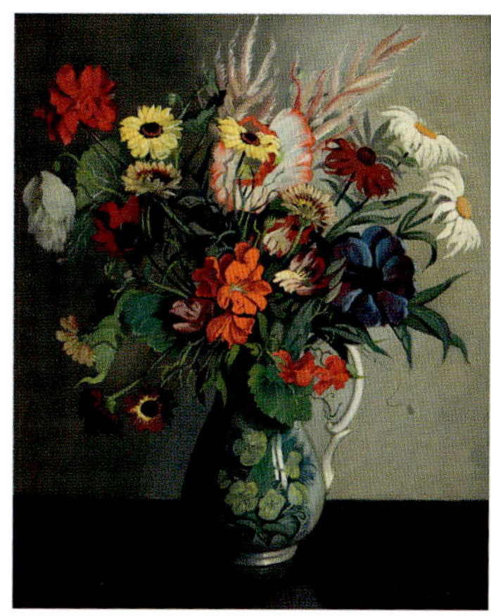

Ferguson, Dan 1910–1992
Flowers in a Jug c.1951
oil on canvas 55.2 x 44.5
2942

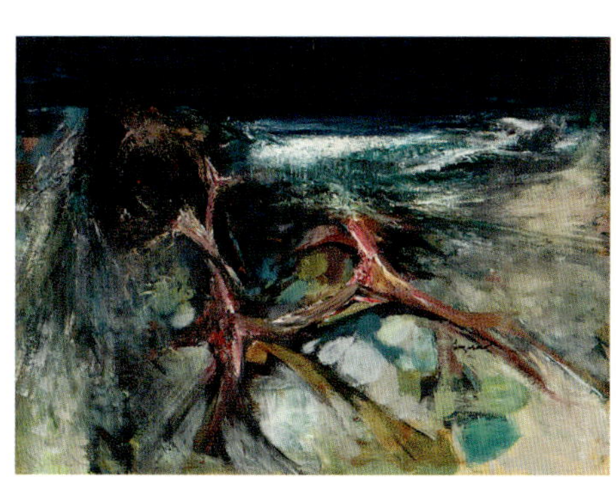

Ferguson, Dan 1910–1992
Breaking Wave c.1965
oil on hardboard 91.4 x 121.9
3238

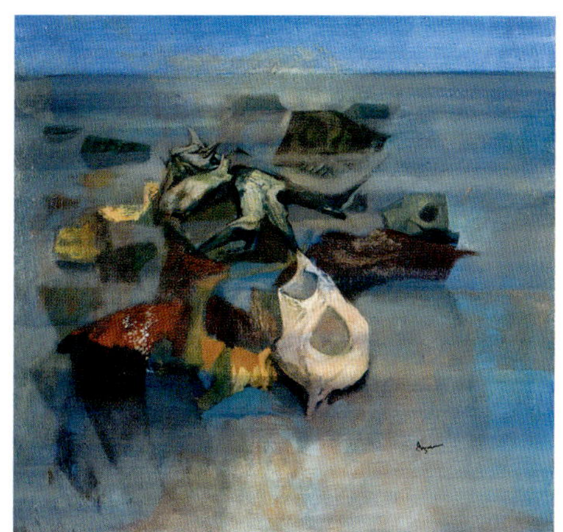

Ferguson, Dan 1910–1992
Sea Edge c.1971
oil on canvas 90.9 x 90.7
3285

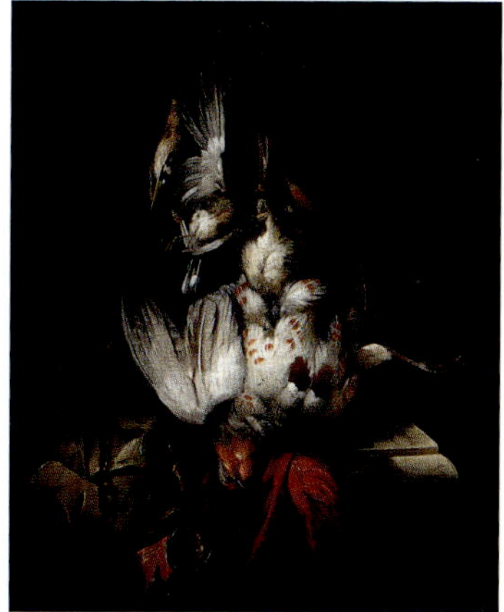

Ferguson, William Gowe
c.1632/1633–c.1695
Still Life
oil on canvas 59.1 x 48.3
912

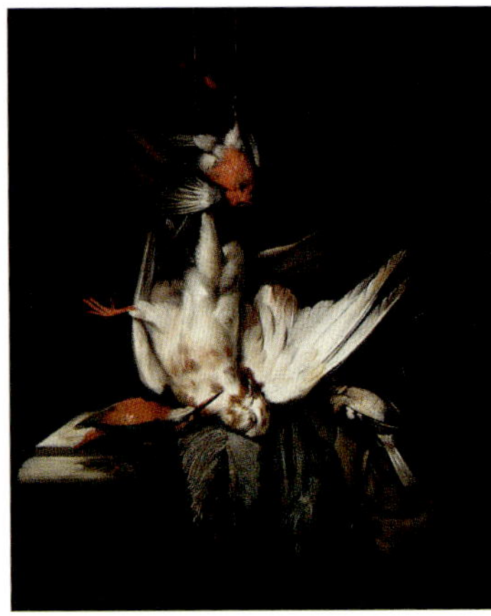

Ferguson, William Gowe
c.1632/1633–c.1695
Still Life
oil on canvas 59.1 x 48.3
913

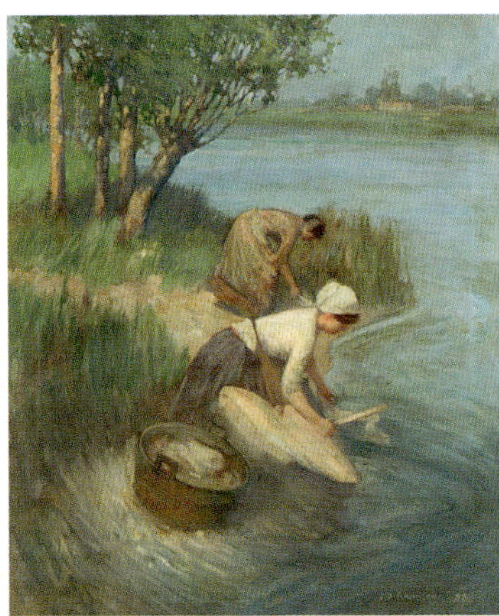

Fergusson, John Duncan 1874–1961
On the Loing 1898
oil on canvas 76.2 x 63.4
3331

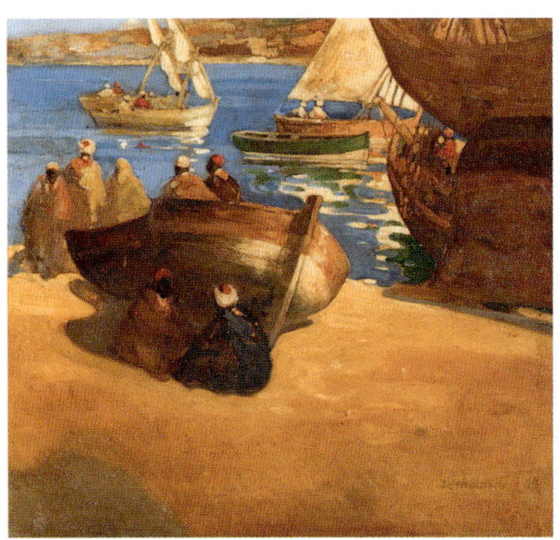

Fergusson, John Duncan 1874–1961
On the Beach at Tangier 1899
oil on canvas 75.9 x 75.9
3163

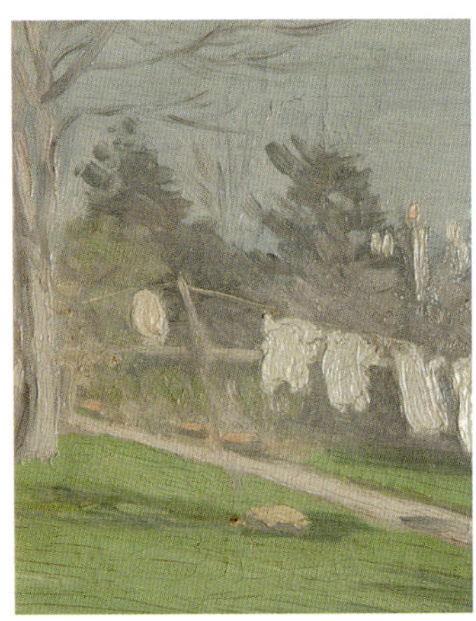

Fergusson, John Duncan 1874–1961
Garden Scene with Clothes Drying on a Line
c.1900
oil on canvas 25.7 x 20.6
3160

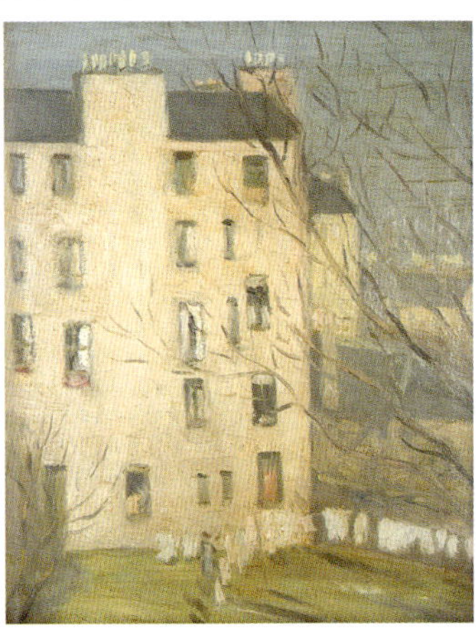

Fergusson, John Duncan 1874–1961
Tenements, Edinburgh c.1900
oil on canvas 50.8 x 40.6
3159

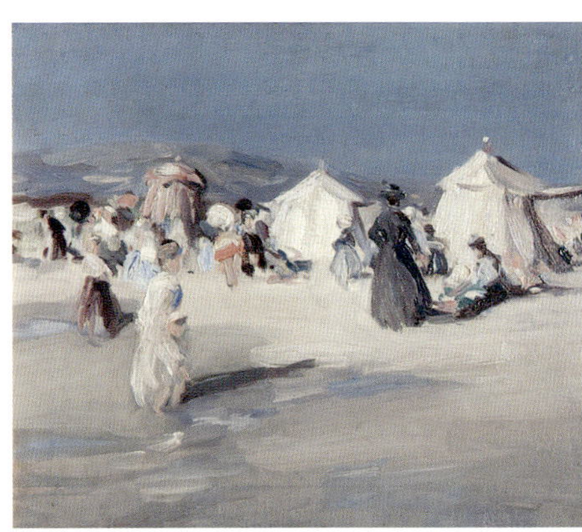

Fergusson, John Duncan 1874–1961
Grey Day, Paris Plage c.1906
oil on canvas 35.6 x 45.7
3370

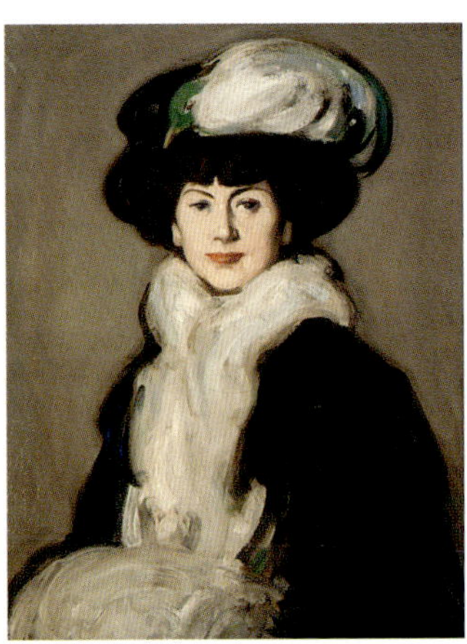

Fergusson, John Duncan 1874–1961
Hat with Bird: Anne Estelle Rice 1907
oil on canvas 86.4 x 66
3173

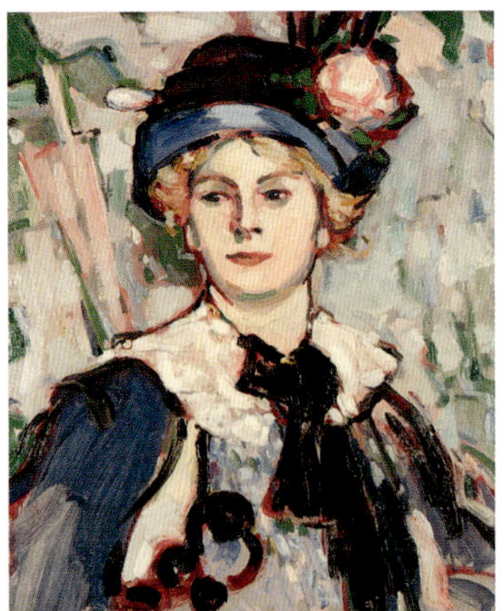

Fergusson, John Duncan 1874–1961
The Pink Parasol: Bertha Case 1908
oil on millboard 75.2 x 63.5
3090

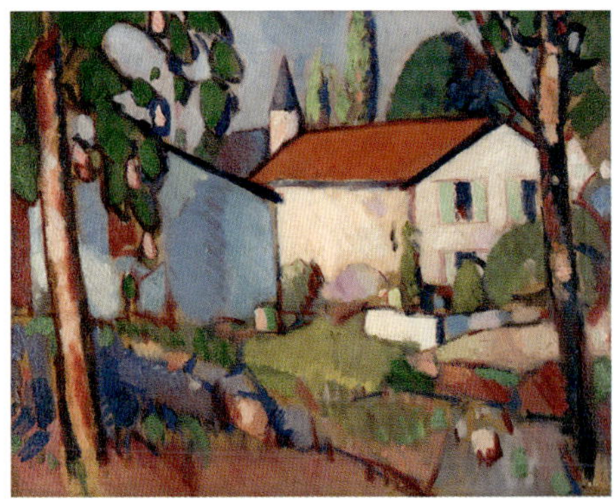

Fergusson, John Duncan 1874–1961
Montgeron 1909
oil on canvas 66 x 81.3
3172

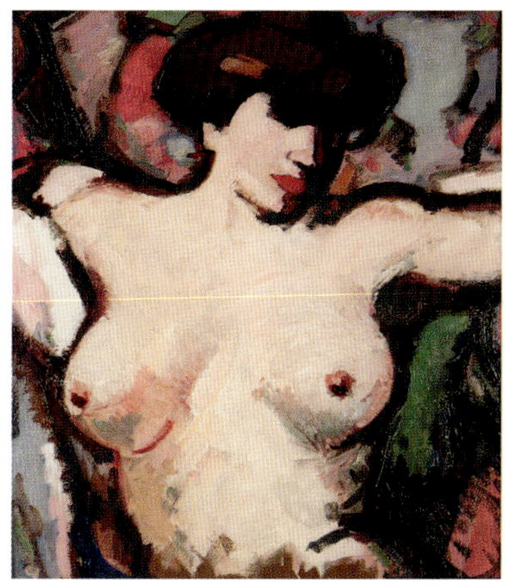

Fergusson, John Duncan 1874–1961
Torse de femme c.1911
oil on board 66 x 55.9
3171

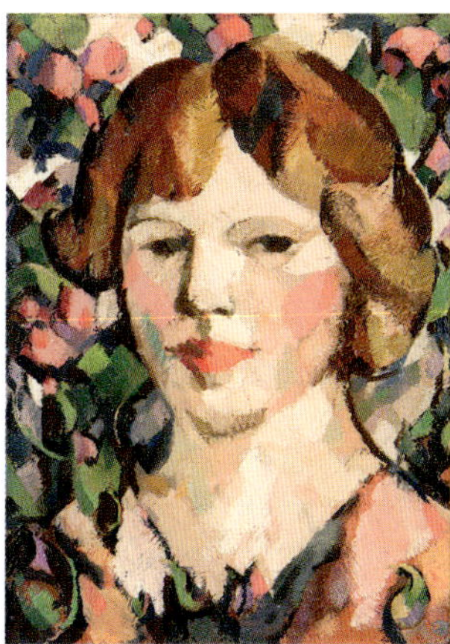

Fergusson, John Duncan 1874–1961
Head of a Girl 1917
oil on panel 34.6 x 24.8
1571

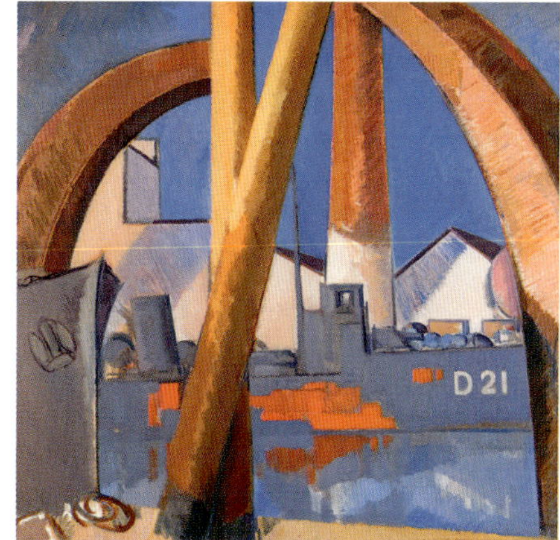

Fergusson, John Duncan 1874–1961
Damaged Destroyer 1918
oil on canvas 73.6 x 76.2
3330

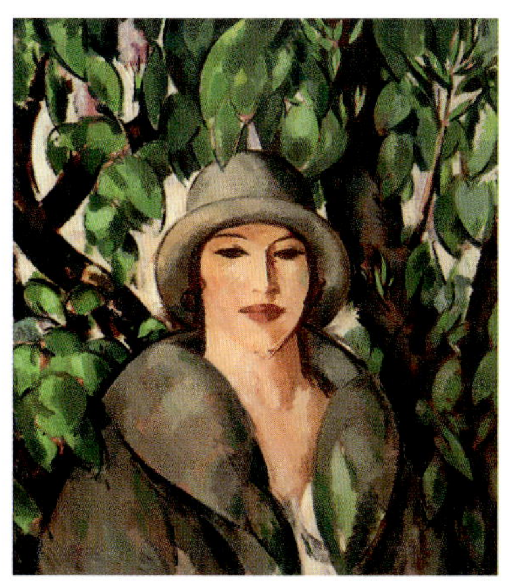

Fergusson, John Duncan 1874–1961
In the Boltons: The Artist's Wife c.1927–1928
oil on canvas 71.1 x 60.6
1751

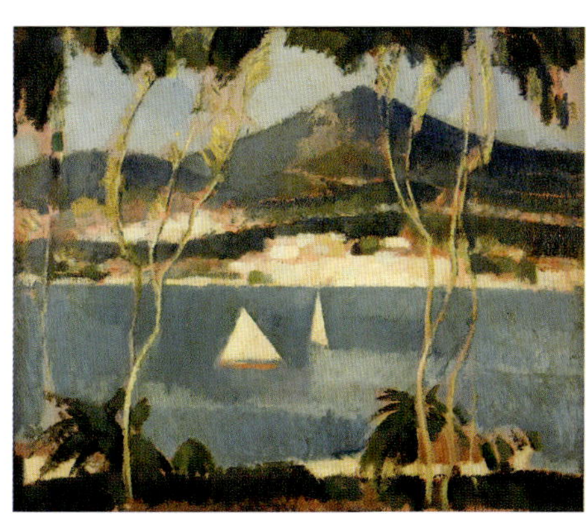

Fergusson, John Duncan 1874–1961
Golfe-Juan 1937
oil on canvas 54.6 x 65.4
2792

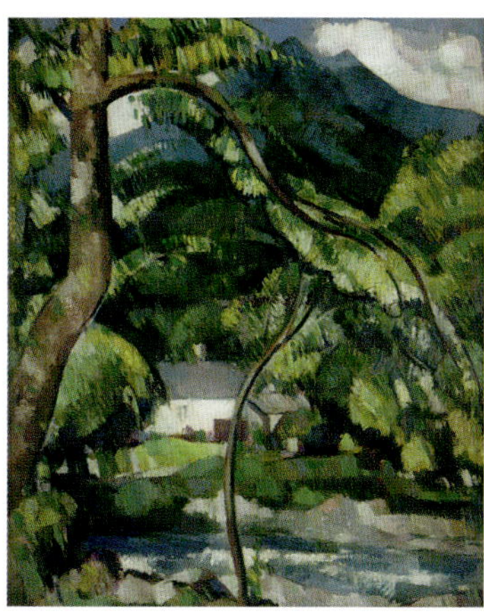

Fergusson, John Duncan 1874–1961
The Roadman's House, St Fillans 1944
oil on canvas 64.8 x 53.3
2793

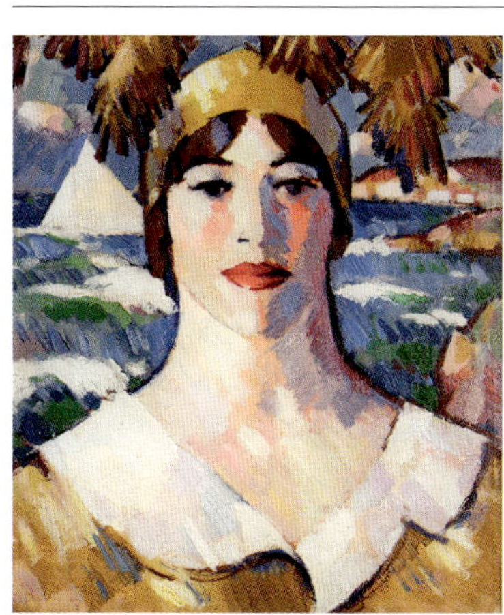

Fergusson, John Duncan 1874–1961
Sun, Wind and Sea, and the Smell of the Pines
oil on canvas 50.2 x 43
3200

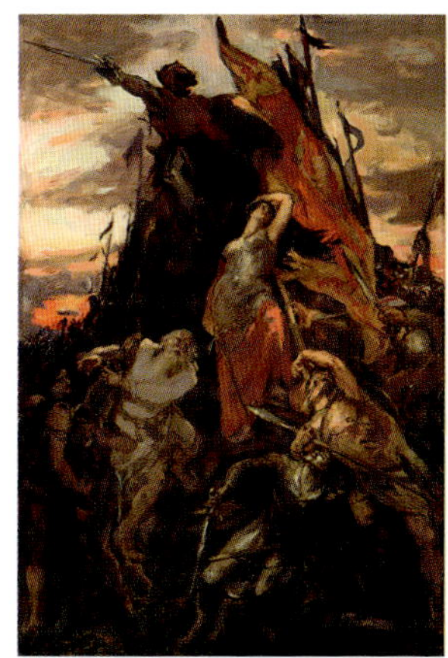

Findlay, William 1875–1960
The Liberation of Scotland (The Battle of Bannockburn) 1914
oil on canvas 91.4 x 61
1353

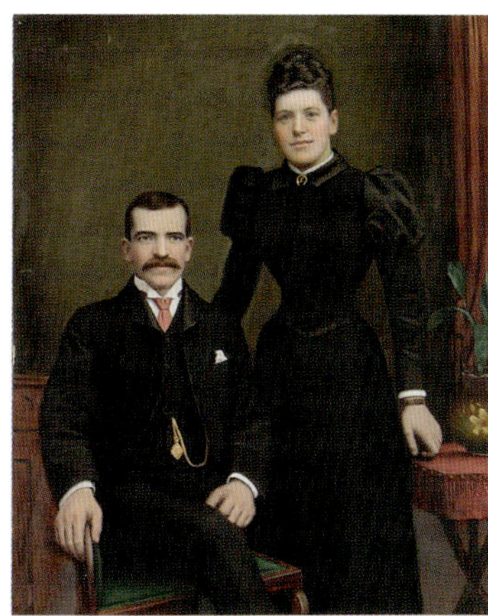

Finlayson
John and Mary Carmichael 1888
oil on board 45.7 x 35.6
PP.1977.45.1

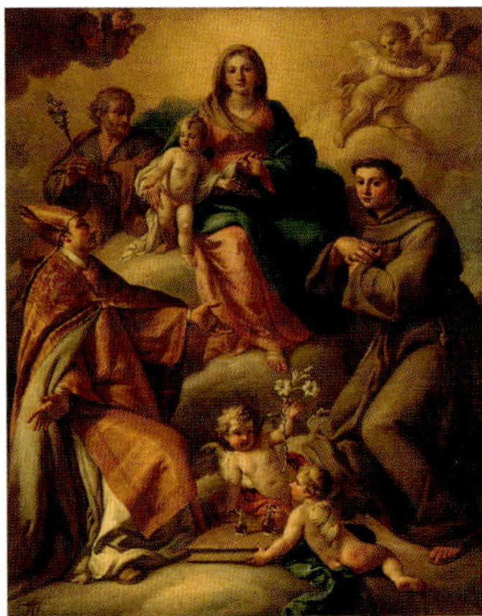

Fischetti, Fedele 1734–1789
The Holy Family with Saints Januarius and Anthony of Padua c.1773–1775
oil on canvas 128.6 x 102
170

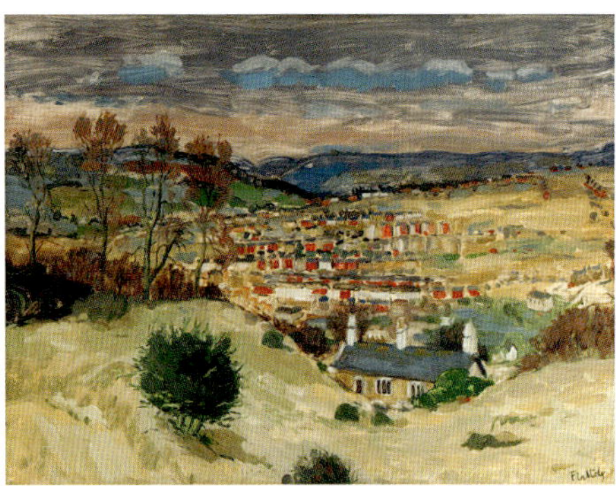

Flattely, Alastair Frederick 1922–2009
View of Stroud, from Rodborough Common
1961
oil on hardboard 91.2 x 121.9
3165

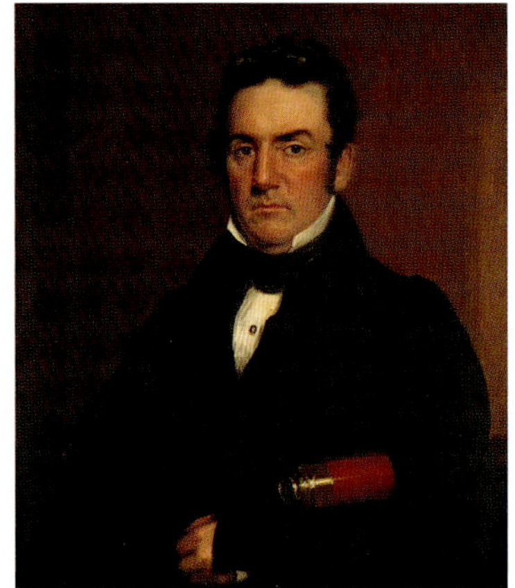

Fleming
Captain John Orkney 1833
oil on canvas 92.8 x 80.1
PP.2000.13.2

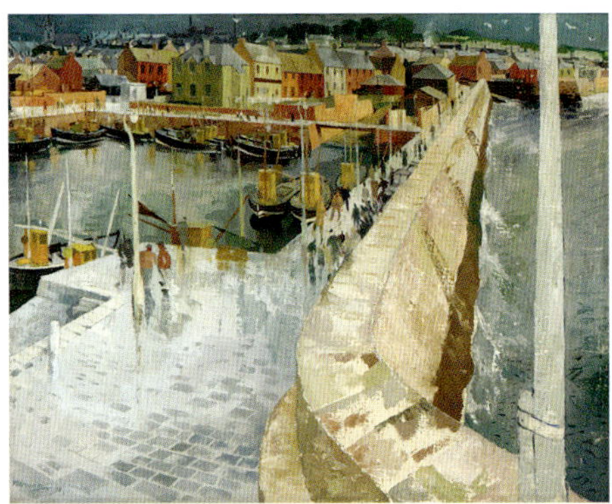

Fleming, Ian 1906–1994
Arbroath Harbour 1951
oil on canvas 71.1 x 91.4
2943

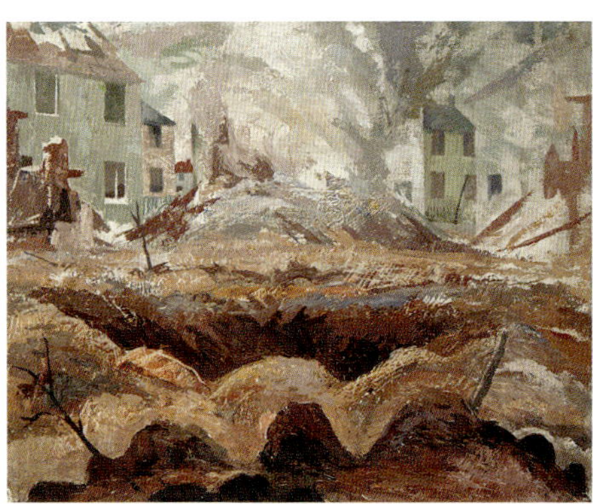

Fleming, Ian 1906–1994
Bomb Crater, Knightswood
oil on board 50.5 x 60
PP.1986.311

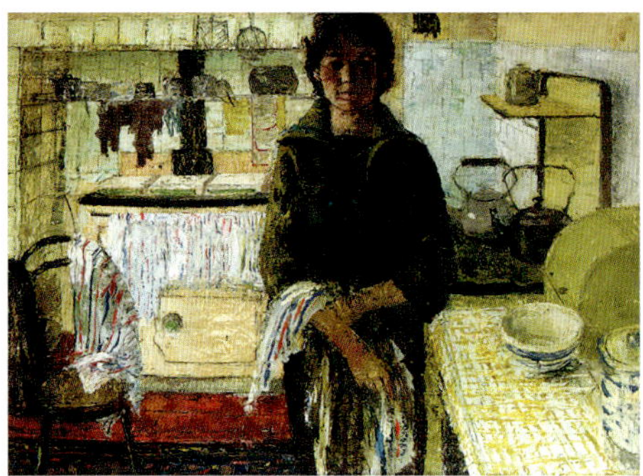

Fleming, Jean 1937–1988
Self Portrait 1958
oil on board 75.9 x 101
3094

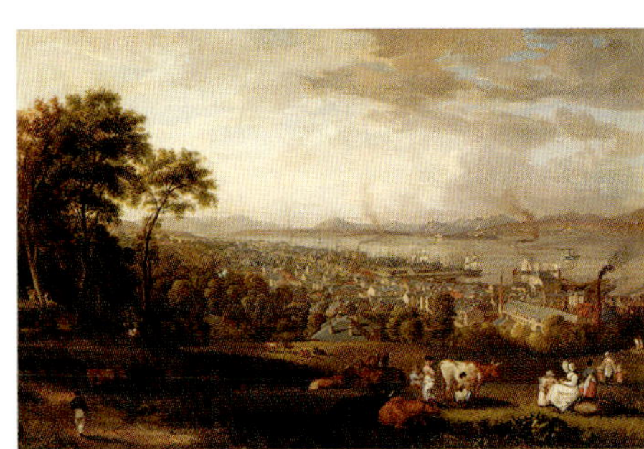

Fleming, John B. 1792–1845
View of Greenock 1827
oil on canvas 86.4 x 127
432

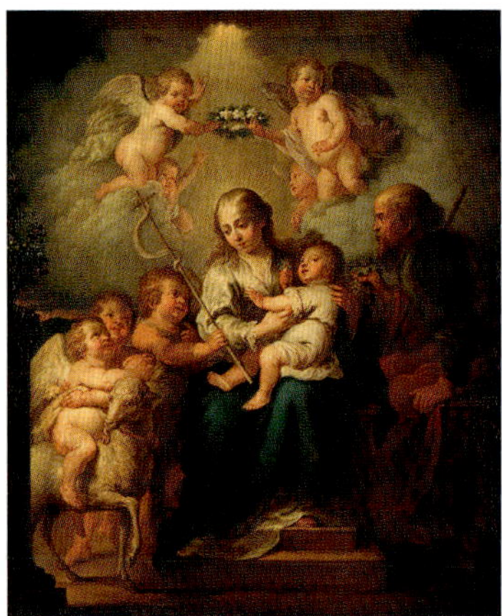

Flemish School early 17th C
The Holy Family, Saint John and Angels
oil on canvas 120 x 96.8
284

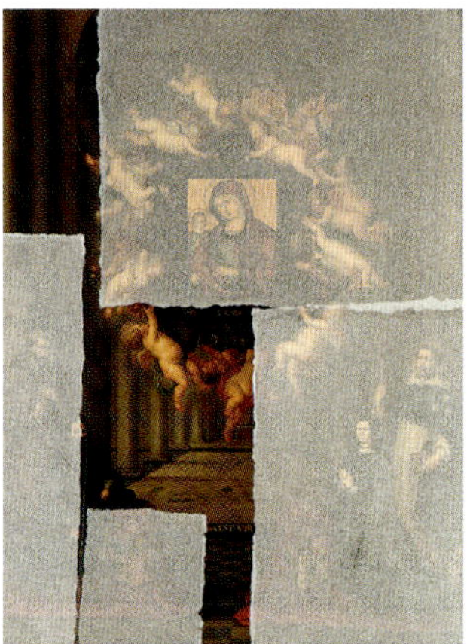

Flemish School 17th C
*A Portrait of the Madonna, Supported by
Cherubs, with Donors and Saints*
oil on panel 102.2 x 75.6
401

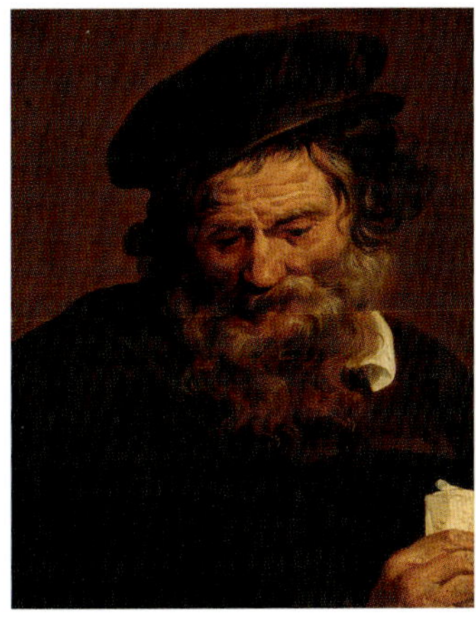

Flemish School 17th C
Bust of a Bearded Man Wearing a Cap
oil on panel 64.2 x 49.3
606

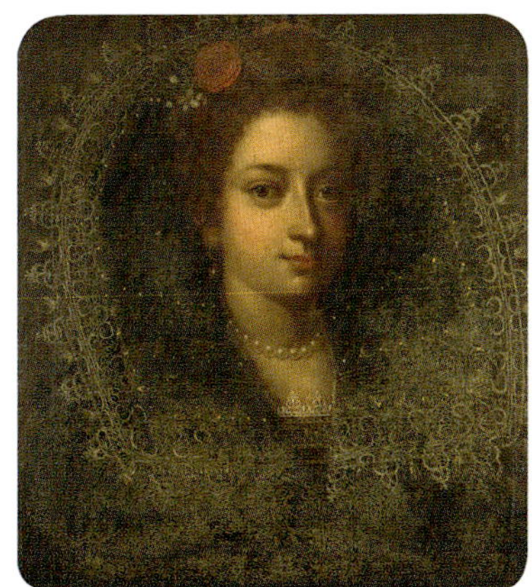

Flemish School 17th C
Portrait of a Lady with a Ruff
oil on canvas 50.8 x 46
PC.61

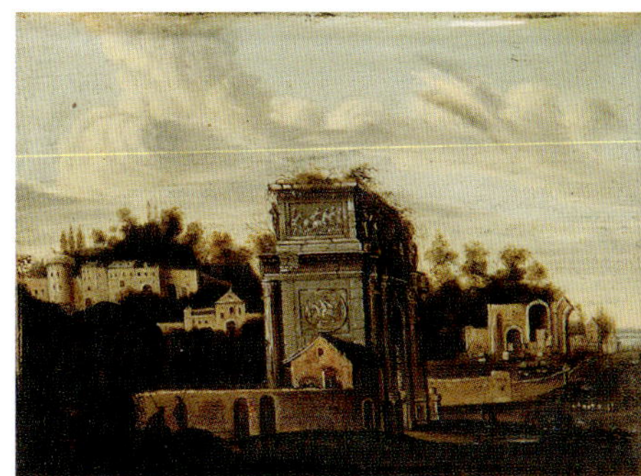

Flemish School 17th C
The Arch of Constantine, Rome
oil on panel 10.8 x 14.6
976

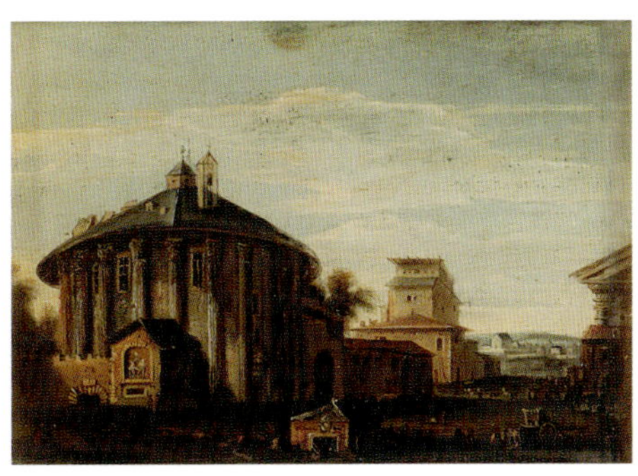

Flemish School 17th C
The Temple in the Piazza della Bocca della Verità, Rome
oil on panel 10.8 x 14.6
975

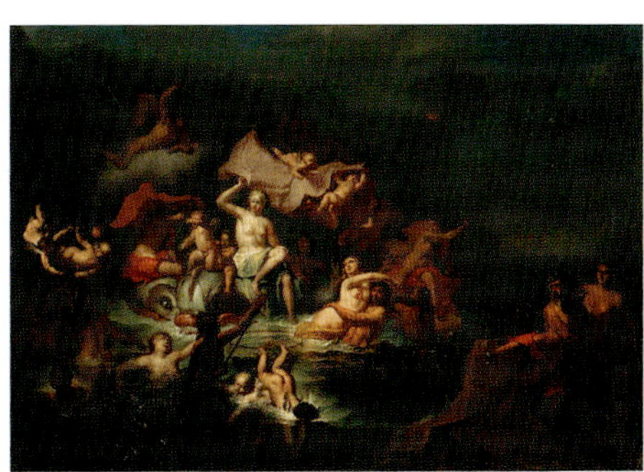

Flemish School
The Triumph of Amphitrite
oil on panel 55 x 74.9
274

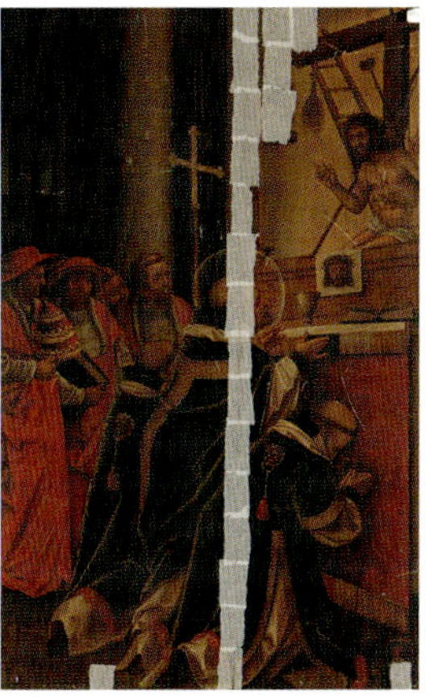

Flemish School (attributed to) 16th C
The Mass of Saint Gregory
oil on panel 96.5 x 61
3423

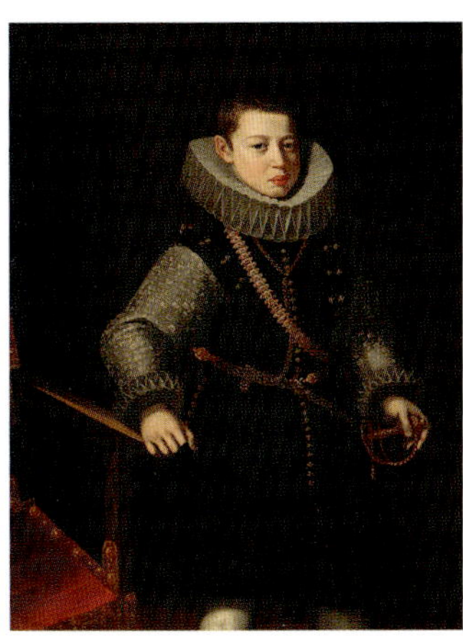

Flemish School (attributed to)
Portrait of a Boy c.1600
oil on canvas 105.4 x 78.1
PC.134

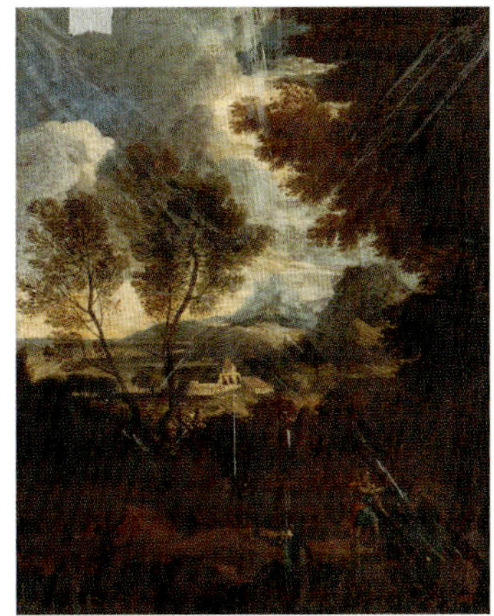

Flemish School (attributed to) 17th C
Italian Landscape with Figures
oil on canvas 57.1 x 44.4
169

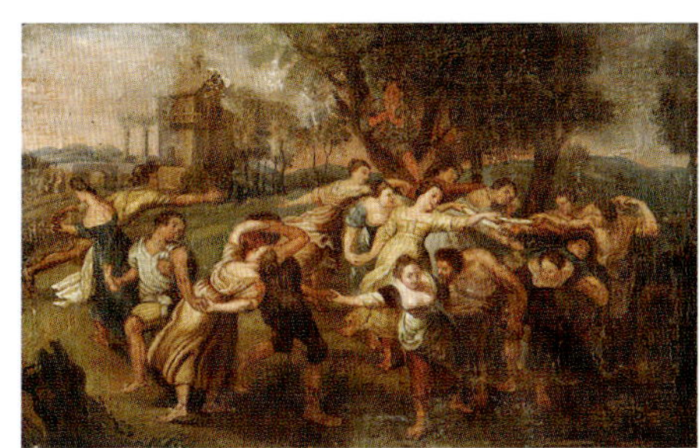

Flemish School (attributed to) 17th C
Kermesse
oil on canvas 25.4 x 41
NR.149

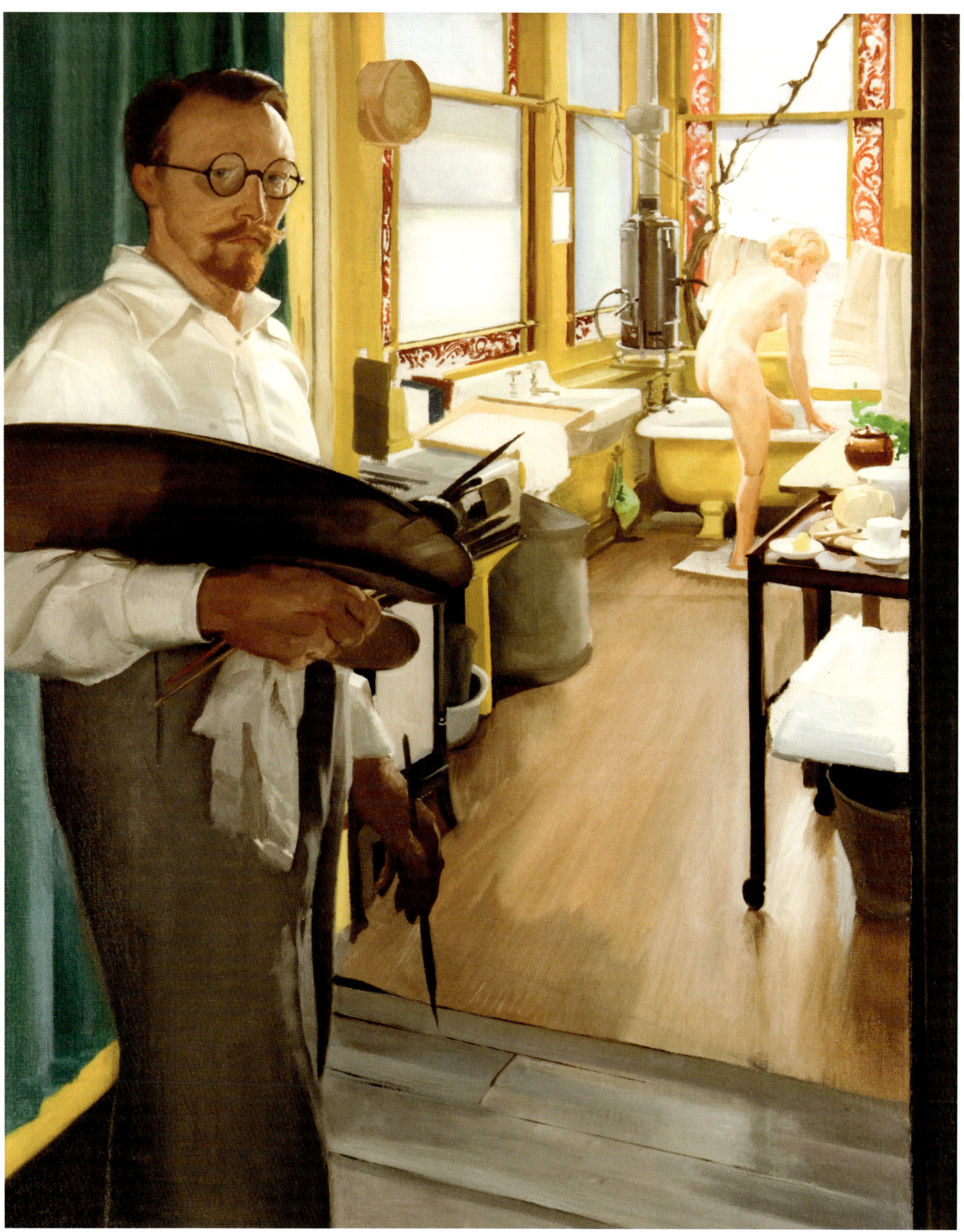

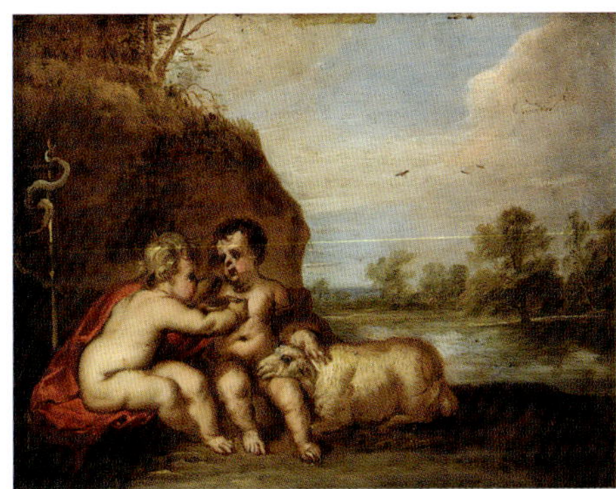

Flemish School (attributed to) 17th C
*The Infant Christ and Saint John in a
Landscape*
oil on copper 16.5 x 21.2
618

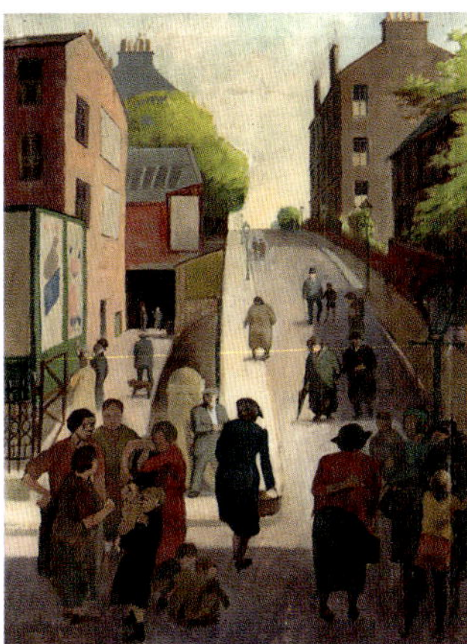

Fletcher, Alan 1936–1958
Hill Street from George's Road, Glasgow
(recto) 1956
oil on canvas 86.4 x 64
PP.1989.57

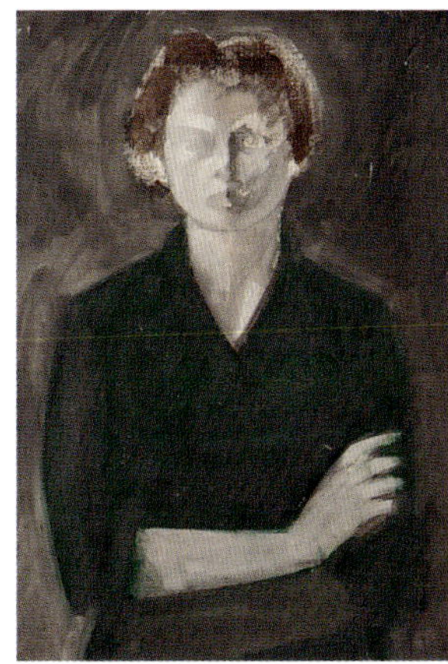

Fletcher, Alan 1936–1958
Study of an Art School Model (verso) 1956
oil on canvas 86.4 x 64
PP.1989.57 (verso)

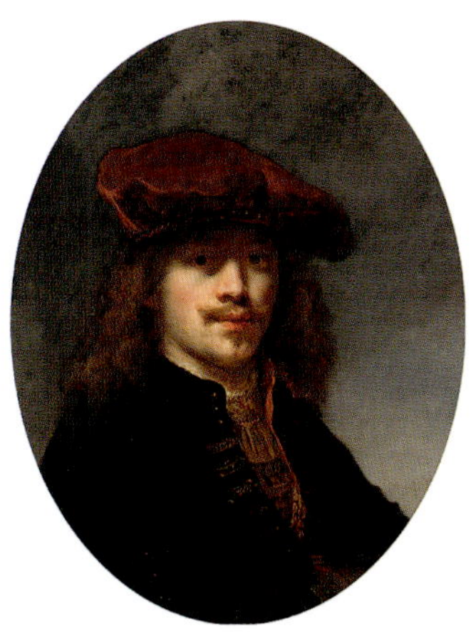

Flinck, Govaert 1615–1660
Self Portrait with Beret c.1638–1643
oil on panel 66 x 51.4
44

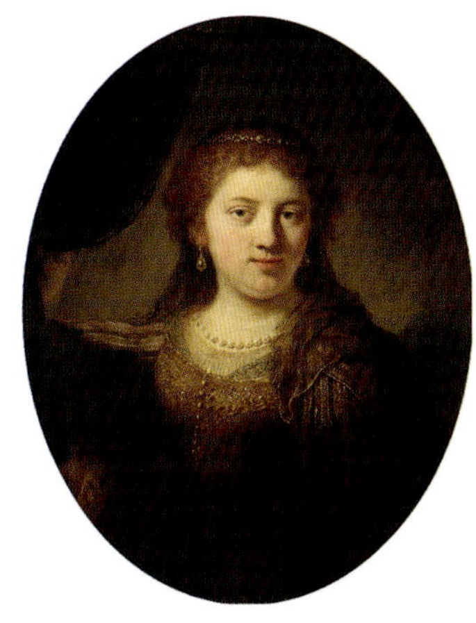

Flinck, Govaert (attributed to) 1615–1660
Portrait of a Woman (possibly Saskia
Uylenburgh, 1612–1642) 1634 (?)
oil on panel 67.3 x 51.5
35.599

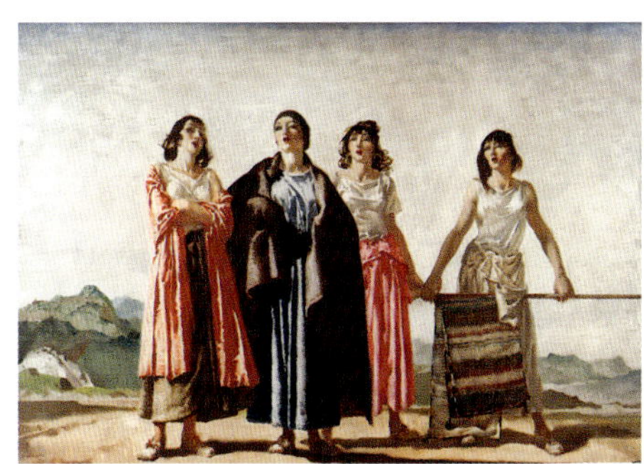

Flint, William Russell 1880–1969
The Four Singers of Vera 1931
oil on canvas 88.9 x 127
2053

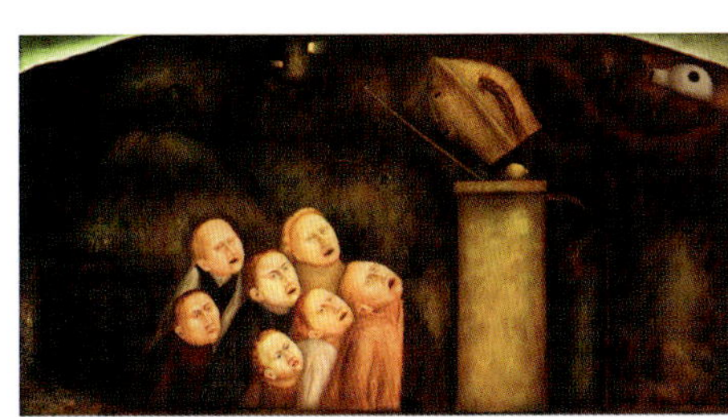

Flockhart, Helen b.1963
Dwelling Place c.1998
oil on canvas 96.5 x 178.2
3629

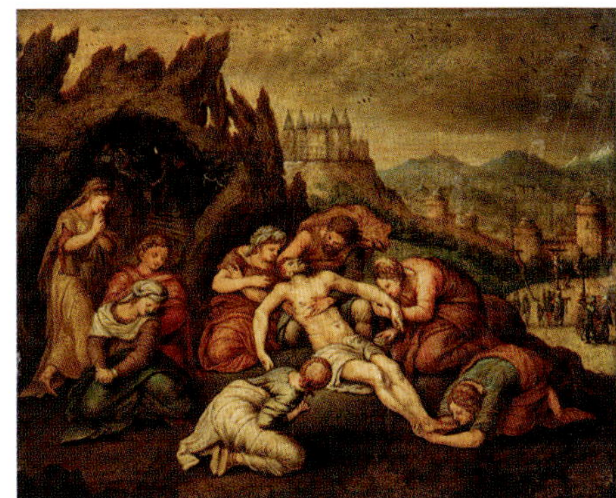

Floris, Frans the elder (follower of)
c.1517–1570
*A Pietà, with the Crucifixion and the
Entombment*
oil on panel 22.8 x 28.5
221

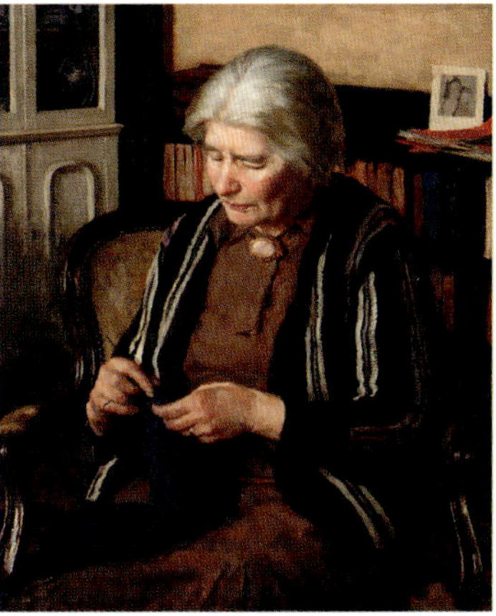

Foggie, David Simpson 1878–1948
Grandmother Knits 1943
oil on canvas 88.9 x 63.5
2358

Facing page: Hutchison, William Oliphant, 1889–1970, *The Kitchen Bathroom*,
1932 (p. 217)

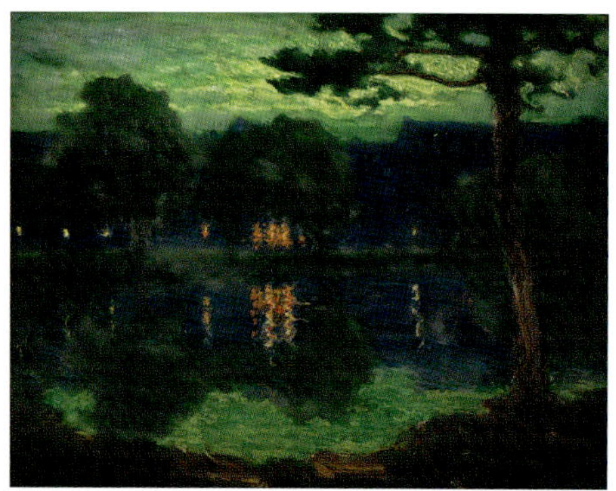

Foottet, Frederick Francis 1850–1935
Barnes, Surrey by Twilight
oil on canvas 50.8 x 68.6
1930

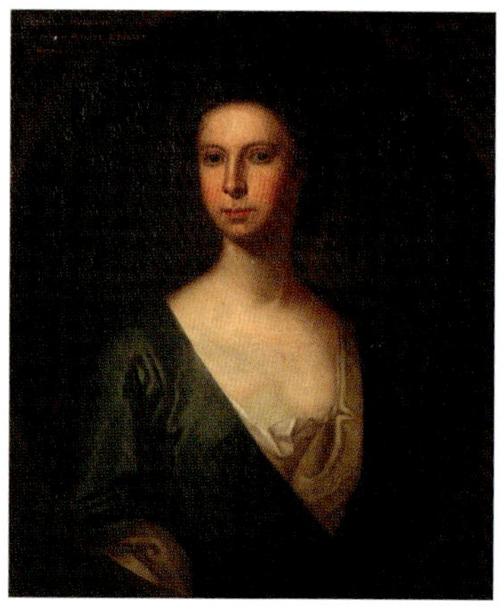

Ford, John A. active 1880–1923
Lady Barbara Steuart Maxwell (d.1737)
oil on canvas 78 x 65.4
PL.162 (P)

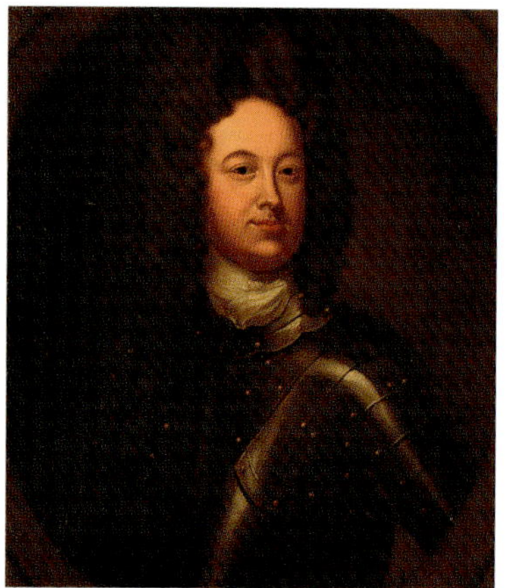

Ford, John A. active 1880–1924
Sir John Maxwell (1648–1732), 1st Bt
oil on canvas 78 x 65.4
PL.152 (P)

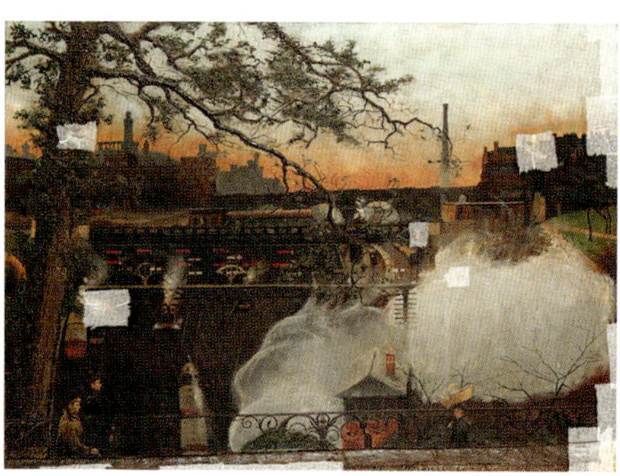

Forrester, W.
Waverley Station, Edinburgh c.1890
oil & plaster on canvas 54.8 x 73.3
T.1967.33.aj

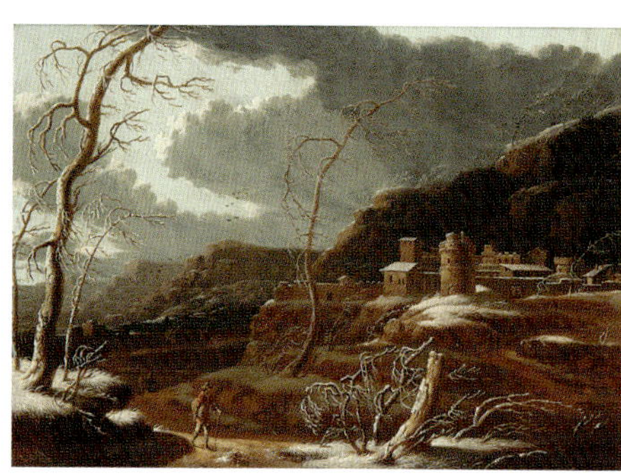

Foschi, Francesco 1710–1780
*A Winter Landscape with Fortified
Buildings* c.1770–1780
oil on panel 40.6 x 54.6
378

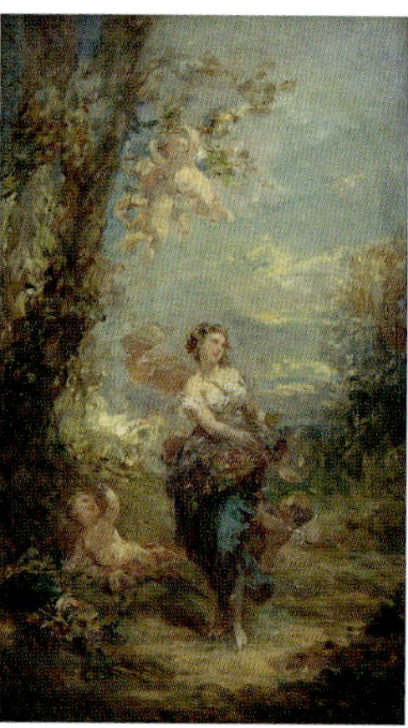

Fragonard, Jean-Honoré (follower of)
1732–1806
Spring c.1790–1810
oil on panel 31 x 18.5
2692

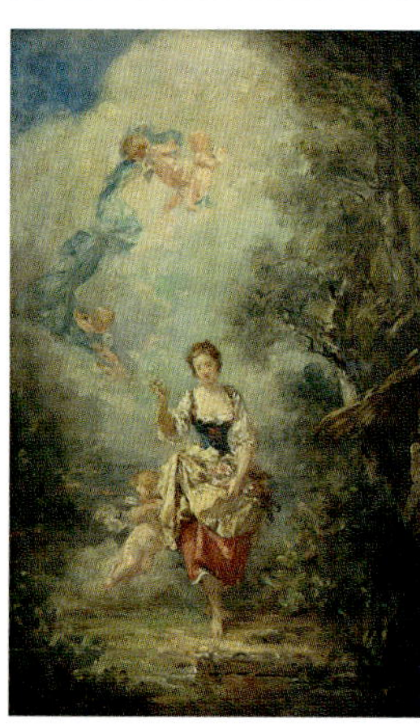

Fragonard, Jean-Honoré (follower of)
1732–1806
Summer c.1790–1810
oil on panel 31 x 20
2693

Fragonard, Jean-Honoré (follower of)
1732–1806
Autumn c.1790–1810
oil on panel 31 x 18.5
2694

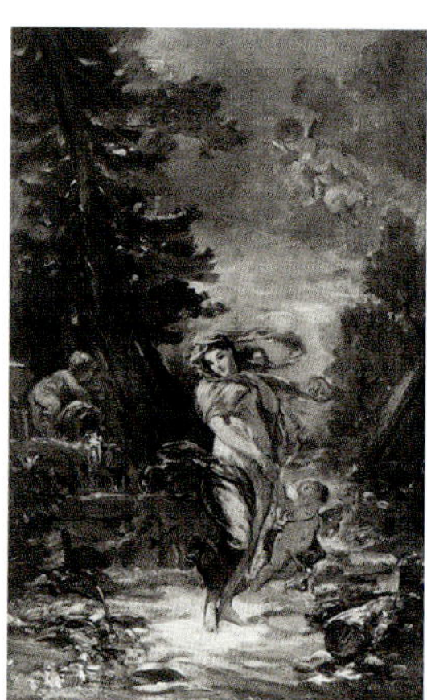

Fragonard, Jean-Honoré (follower of)
1732–1806
Winter c.1790–1810
oil on panel 31.1 x 18.4
2695

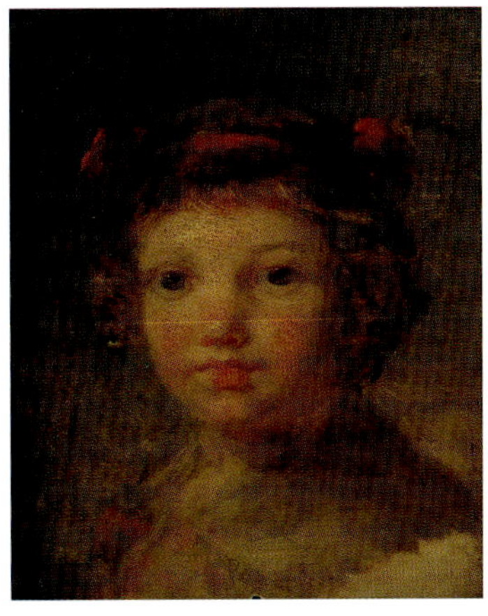

Fragonard, Jean-Honoré (school of)
1732–1806
A Child's Head
oil on panel 18.4 x 15.6
225

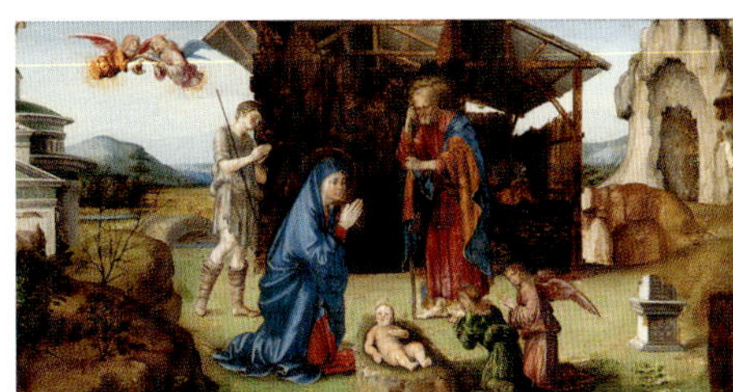

Francia, Francesco c.1450–1517
The Nativity of Christ c.1490
oil on panel 28.9 x 54.9
146

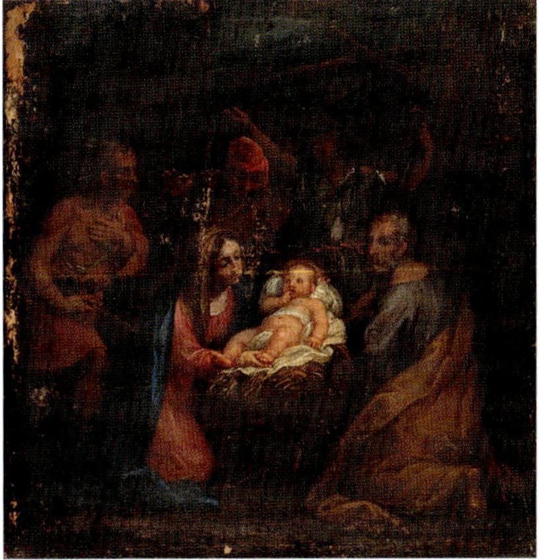

Francken, Frans I (circle of) 1542–1616
The Adoration of the Shepherds
oil on canvas 37.5 x 35.6
56

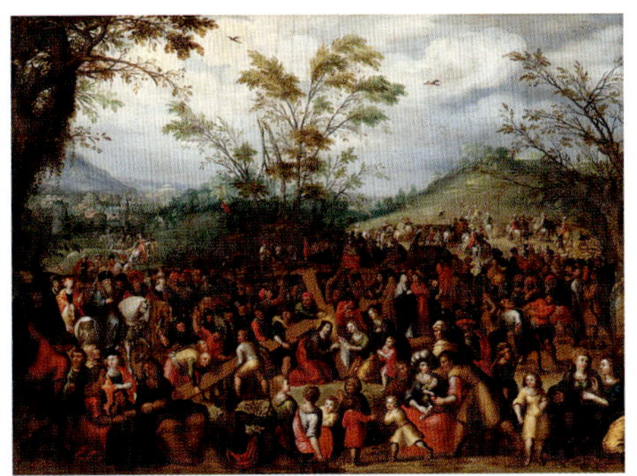

Francken, Frans II 1581–1642
The Procession to Calvary 1642
oil on panel 72.7 x 102.8
15

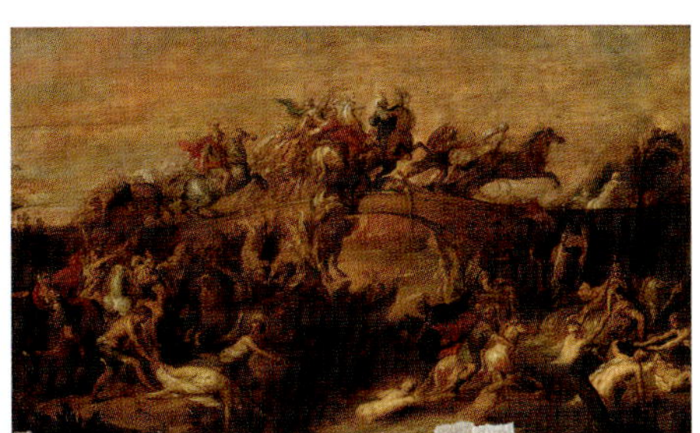

Francken, Frans III (attributed to)
1607–1667
The Battle of the Amazons (after Peter Paul
Rubens)
oil on panel 63.5 x 105.1
88

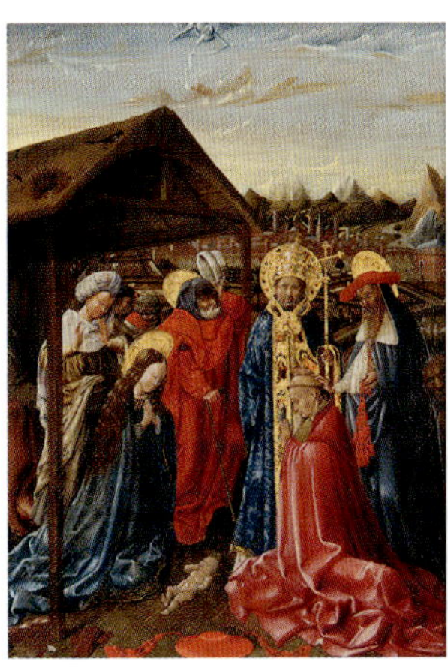

Franco-Italian (Savoy) School
*The Nativity with Saint Sixtus (?), Saint
Jerome and a Cardinal* c.1440–1450
oil on panel 52.2 x 41.8
158

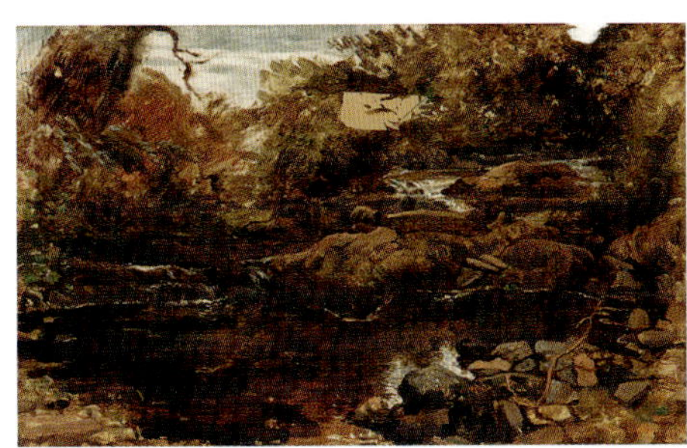

Fraser, Alexander 1827–1899
A Highland Burn (A Brooklet Stream)
oil on canvas 22.9 x 35.6
879

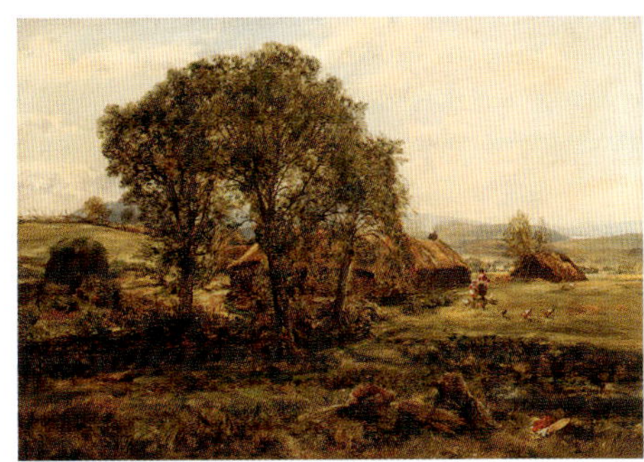

Fraser, Alexander 1827–1899
A Highland Croft
oil on canvas 76.2 x 106.7
2552

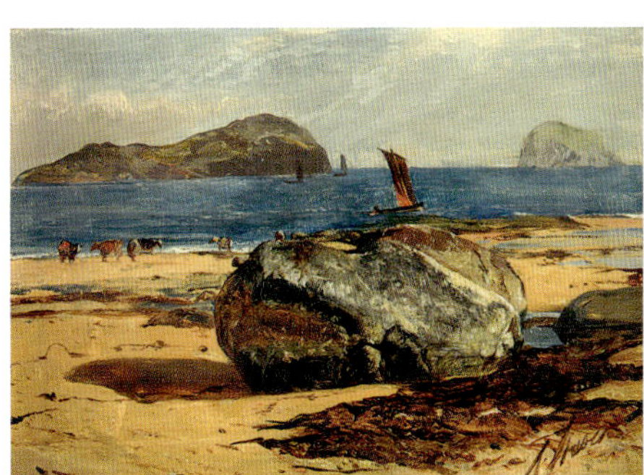

Fraser, Alexander 1827–1899
At North Berwick, Sunshine
oil on canvas 24.1 x 34.3
855

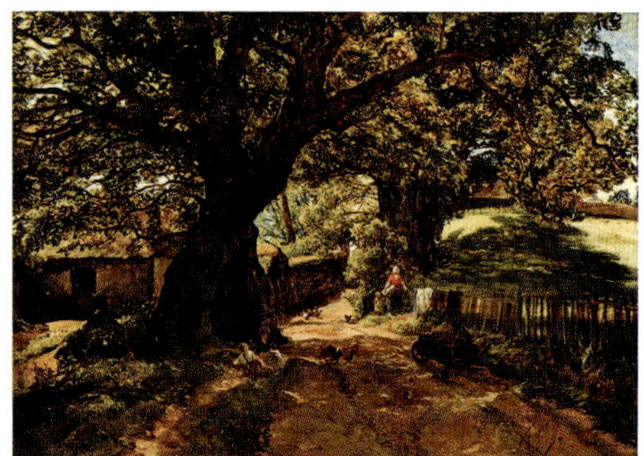

Fraser, Alexander 1827–1899
Barncluith
oil on canvas 40.3 x 54
1237

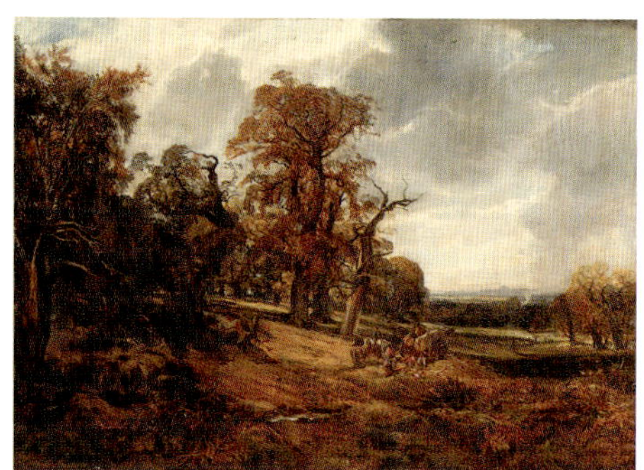

Fraser, Alexander 1827–1899
Cadzow Forest, Autumn
oil on canvas 95.3 x 125.7
881

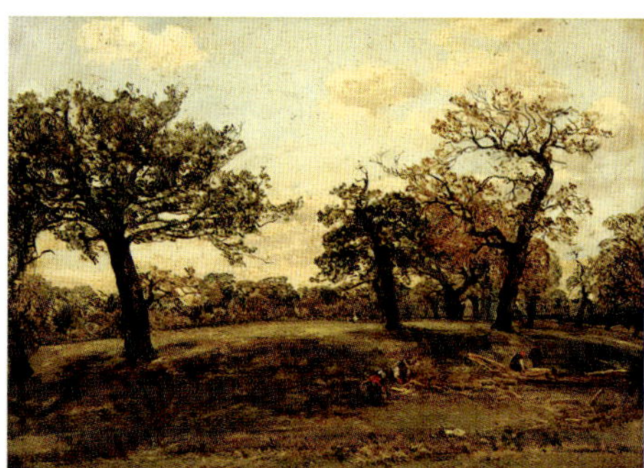

Fraser, Alexander 1827–1899
Cadzow Forest in Springtime
oil on panel 26.7 x 34.3
806

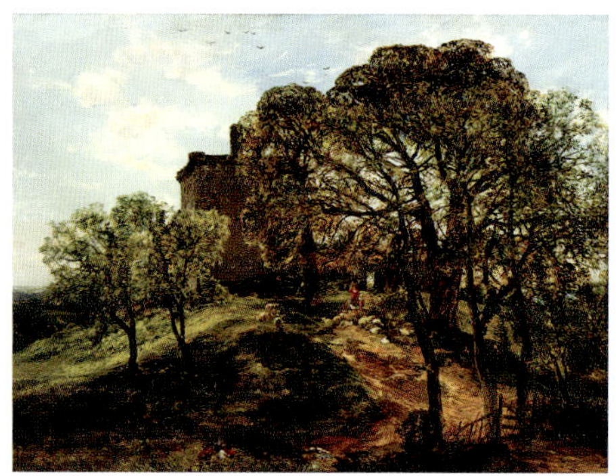

Fraser, Alexander 1827–1899
Castle Campbell, Springtime
oil on canvas 44.5 x 59.7
782

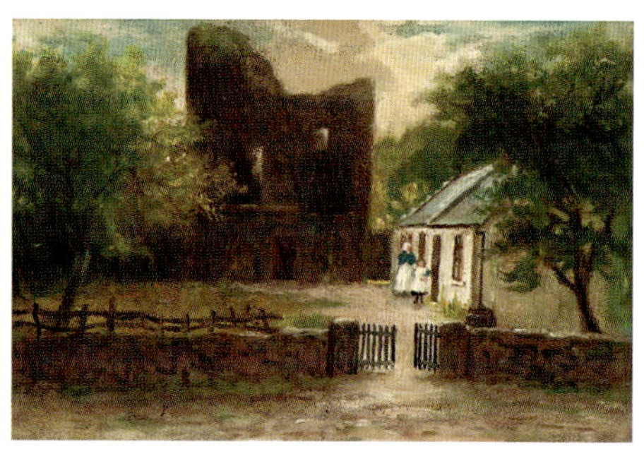

Fraser, Alexander 1827–1899
Cathcart Castle
oil on canvas 25.7 x 35.6
OG.1967.16.2.1

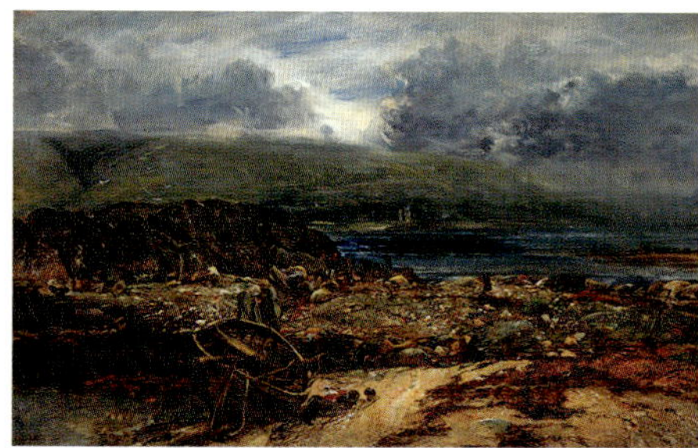

Fraser, Alexander 1827–1899
Dundarave Castle, Loch Fyne
oil on canvas 41.9 x 64.8
866

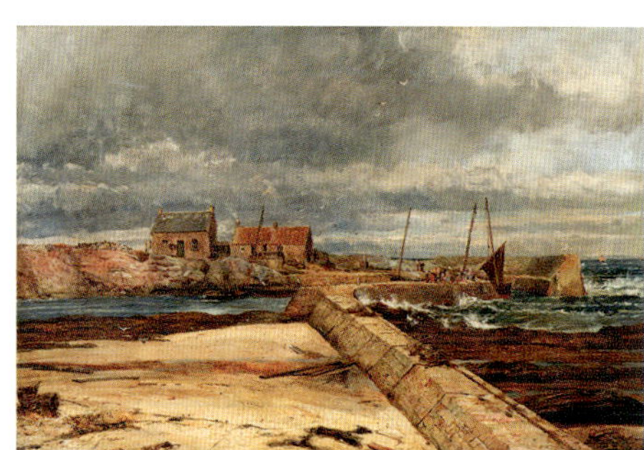

Fraser, Alexander 1827–1899
East Coast Harbour Scene
oil on canvas 74.9 x 110.5
835

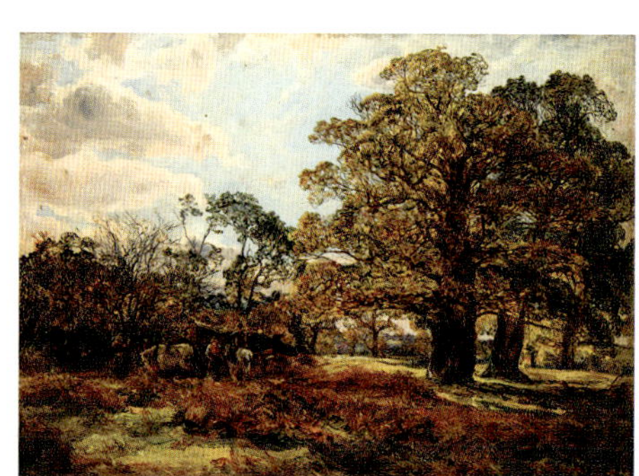

Fraser, Alexander 1827–1899
Gathering Logs in Cadzow Forest
oil on canvas 24.1 x 34.3
842

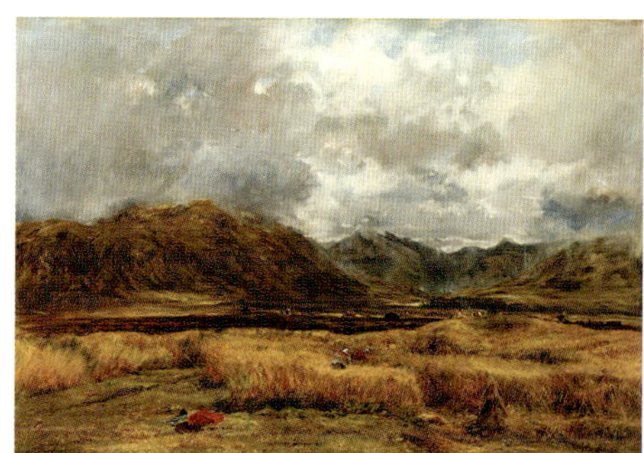

Fraser, Alexander 1827–1899
Harvest in the Highlands
oil on canvas 74.9 x 105.4
1299

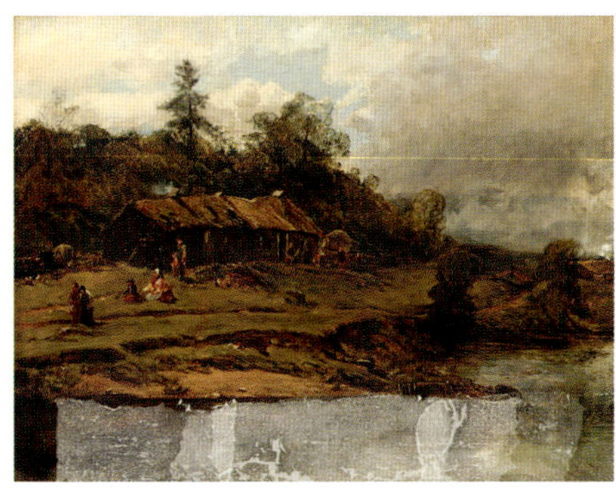

Fraser, Alexander 1827–1899
Highland Flitting
oil on canvas 83.8 x 108
988

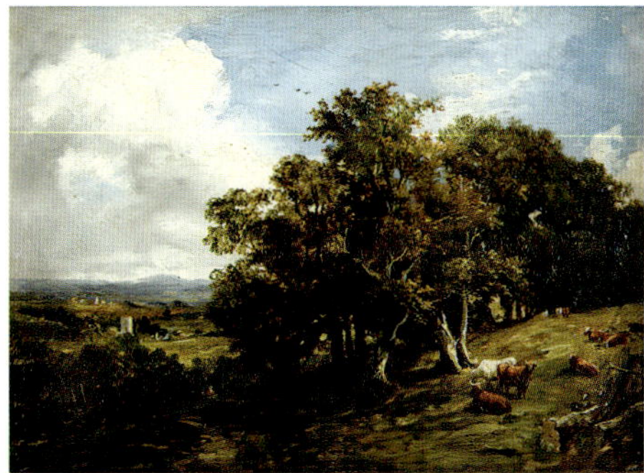

Fraser, Alexander 1827–1899
Landscape and Cattle
oil on millboard 20.3 x 26.7
847

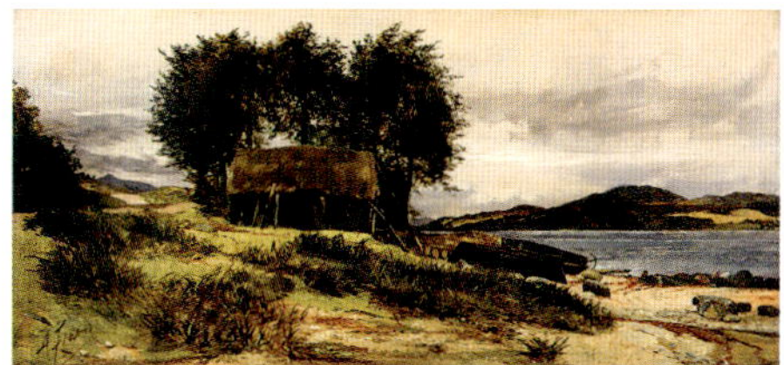

Fraser, Alexander 1827–1899
On Loch Fyne
oil on panel 26.7 x 57.2
831

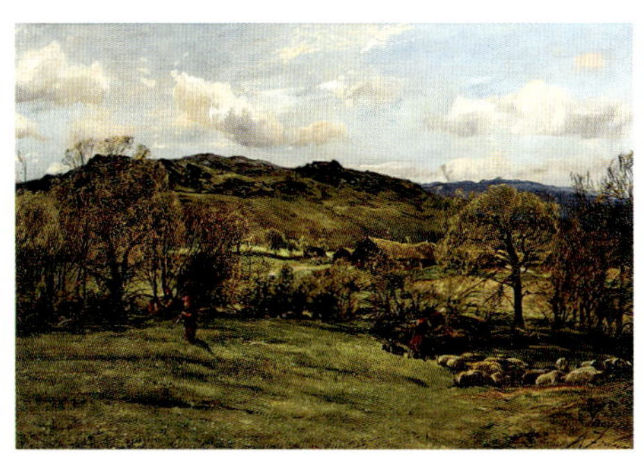

Fraser, Alexander 1827–1899
Springtime, Dundarroch, Brig o' Turk
oil on canvas 44.5 x 64.8
814

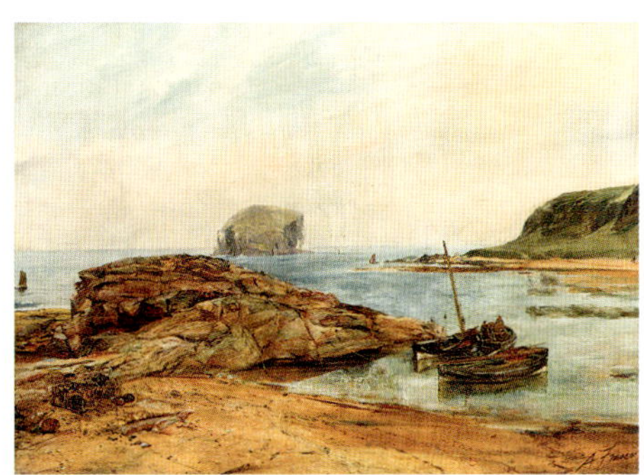

Fraser, Alexander 1827–1899
The Bass Rock from Canty Bay
oil on canvas 64.8 x 91.4
864

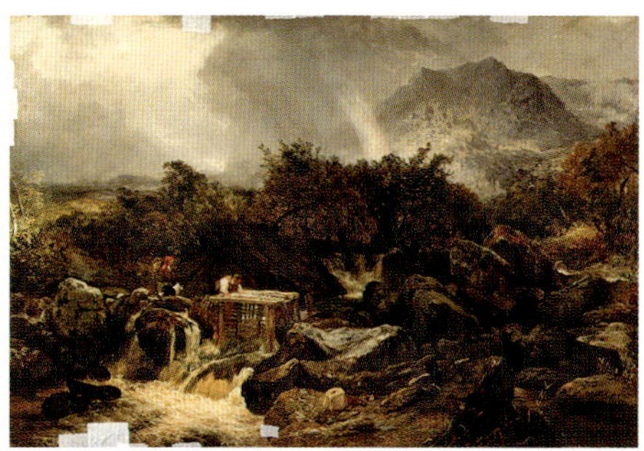

Fraser, Alexander 1827–1899
The Salmon Trap
oil on canvas 104.1 x 152.4
1789

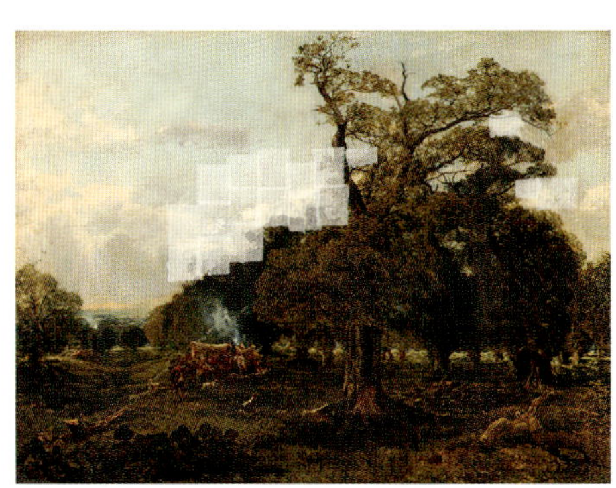

Fraser, Alexander 1827–1899
View in Cadzow Forest
oil on canvas 94 x 127
858

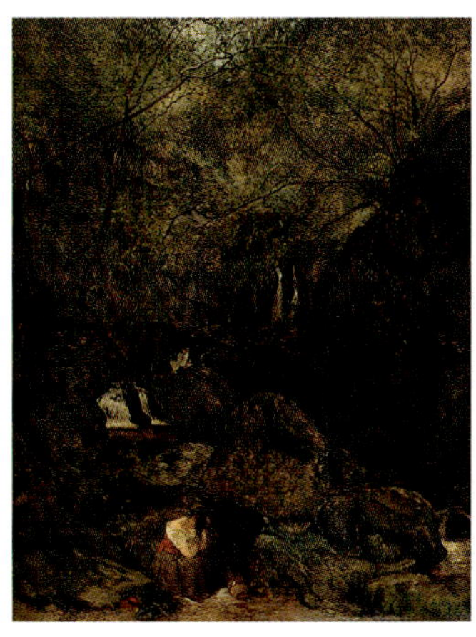

Fraser, Alexander 1827–1899
Waterfall
oil on canvas 91.4 x 69.8
859

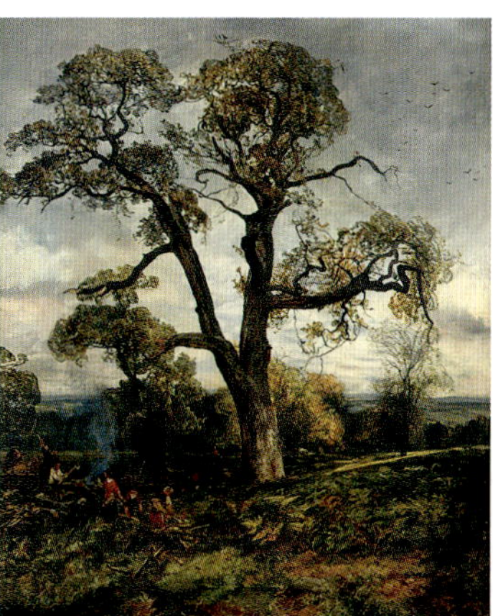

Fraser, Alexander 1827–1899
Woodcutters in Cadzow Forest
oil on canvas 67.3 x 54.6
805

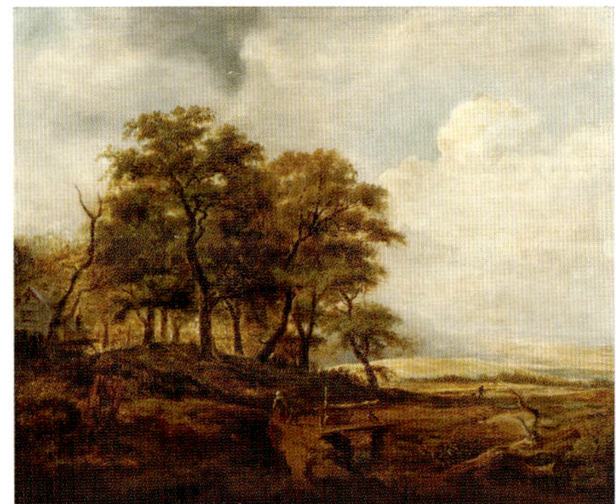

Fraser, Alexander (attributed to) 1827–1899
Landscape with a Rustic Bridge
oil on panel 39 x 46
NR.3

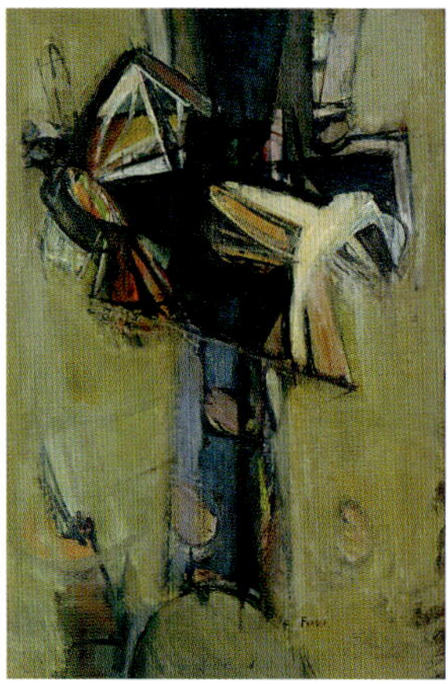

Fraser, Alexander b.1940
Celtic Cross and Birds 1962
oil on hardboard 77.7 x 52.7
3170

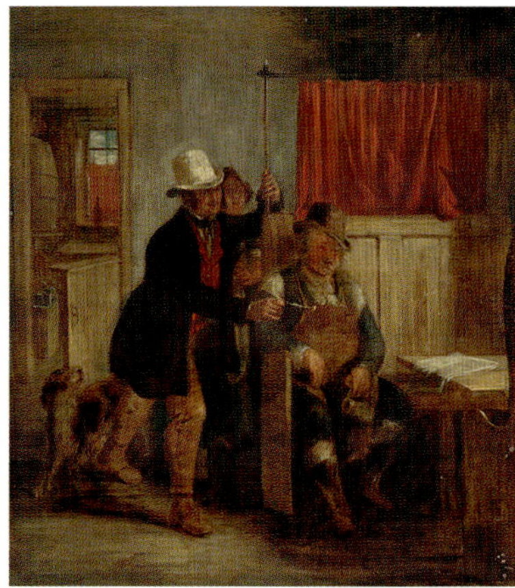

Fraser, Alexander George 1786–1865
Smoking the Cobbler
oil on panel 39.7 x 34
PC.145

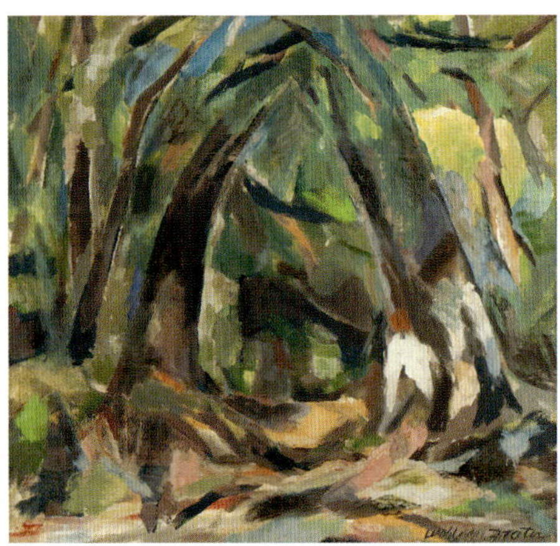

Frater, William 1890–1974
Bush Landscape, Wandong, Victoria 1966
oil on hardboard 88.3 x 90.5
3259

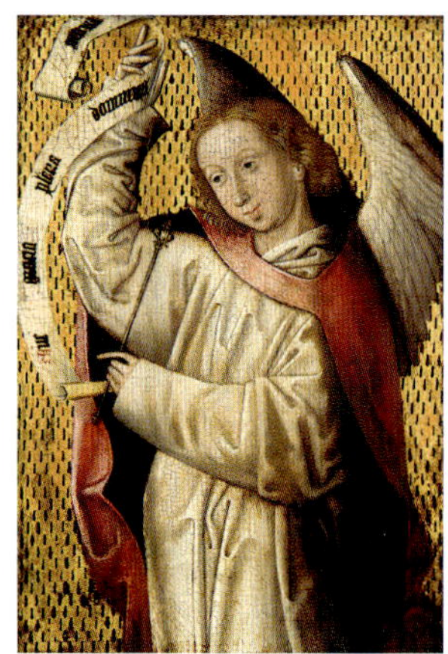

French (Amiens) School late 15th C
Angel of the Annunciation
oil on panel 22.8 x 15.2
35.1

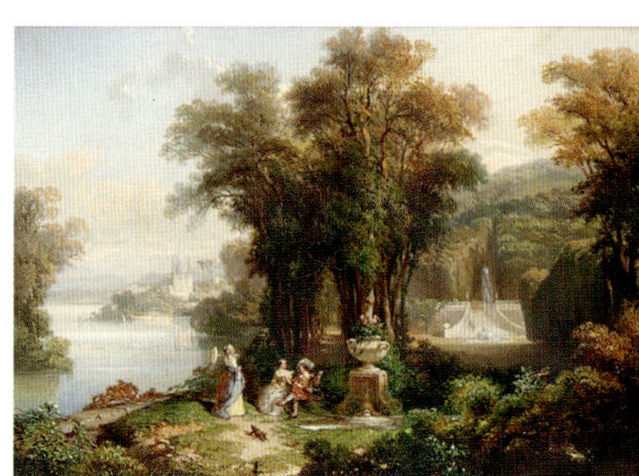

French School
Figures in a Park c.1815–1830
oil on canvas 27.3 x 35.6
246

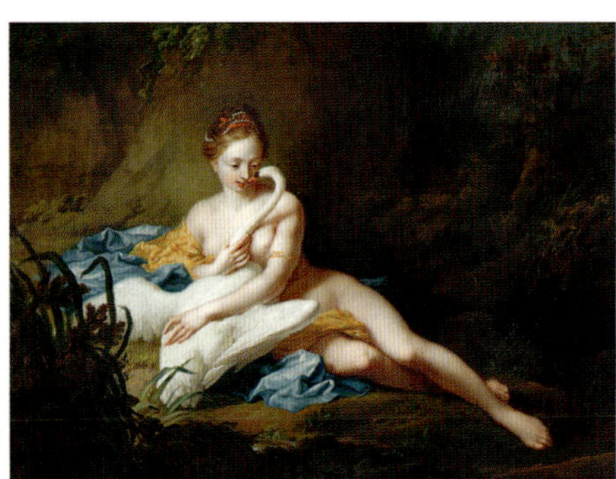

French School (attributed to)
Leda and the Swan c.1760–1780
oil on canvas 71.8 x 97.9
220

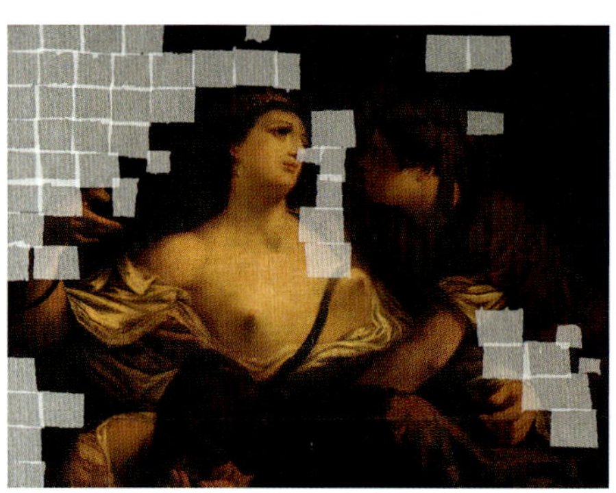

French School (attributed to) 18th C
The Death of Cleopatra
oil on canvas 87.6 x 115.5
237

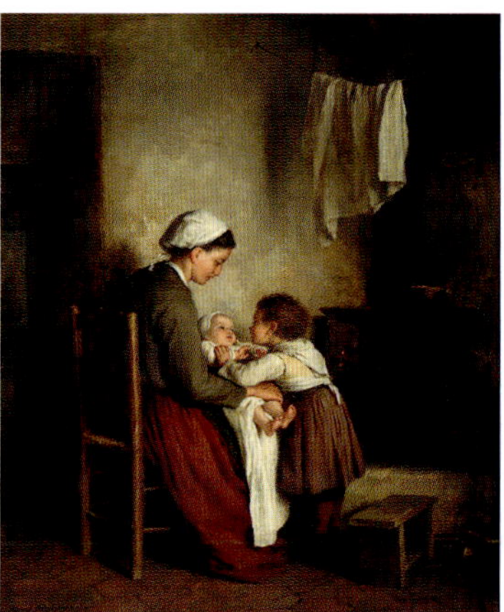

Frère, Pierre Edouard 1819–1886
Mother and Children 1877
oil on panel 45.8 x 37.5
1134

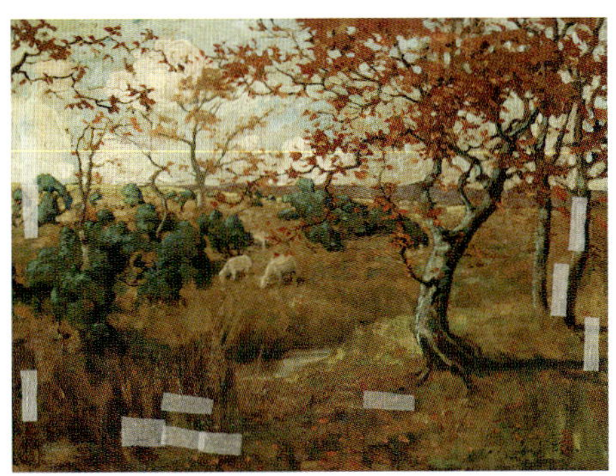

Frew, Alexander d.1908
Landscape 1893
oil on canvas 72.6 x 101.6
2913

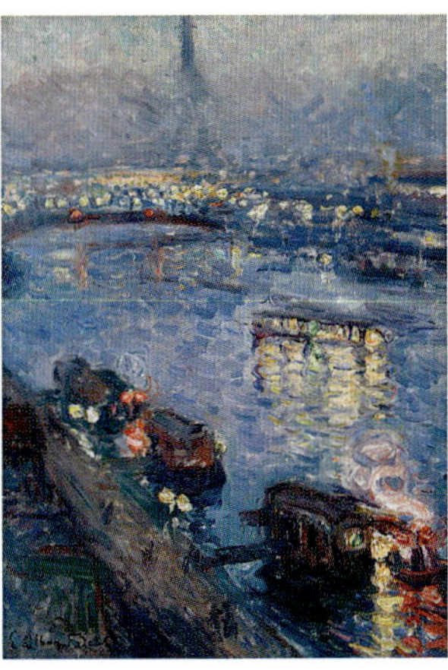

Friesz, Othon 1879–1949
The Seine at Paris, Pont de Grenelle 1901
oil on canvas 46.2 x 33.1
3110

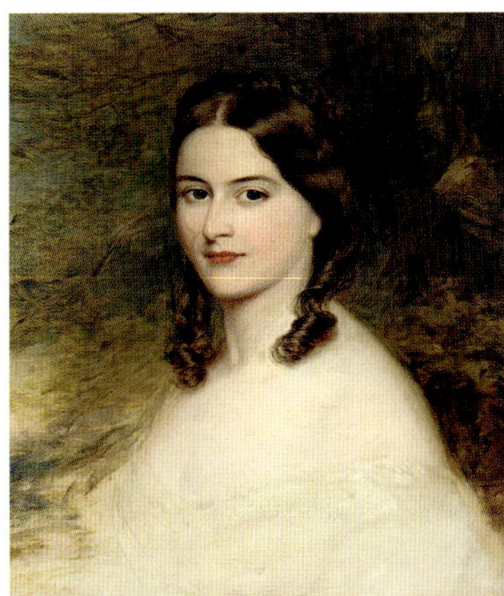

Frith, William Powell 1819–1909
A Royal Princess
oil on canvas 66 x 55.9
2329

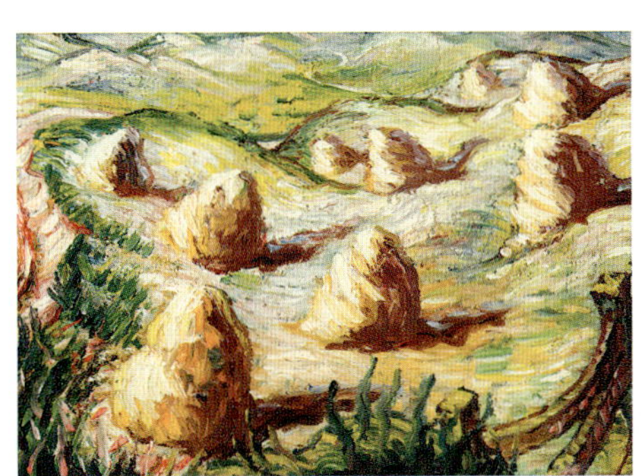

Frood, Millie 1900–1988
Hayricks
oil on panel 40 x 55.9
2298

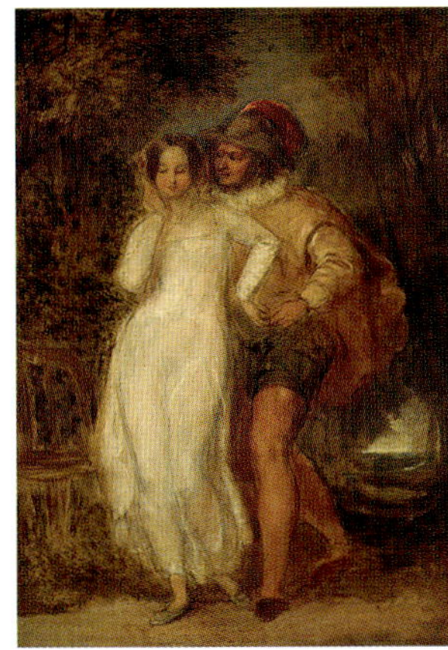

Frost, George 1754–1821
Courtship
oil on panel 24.1 x 18.4
431

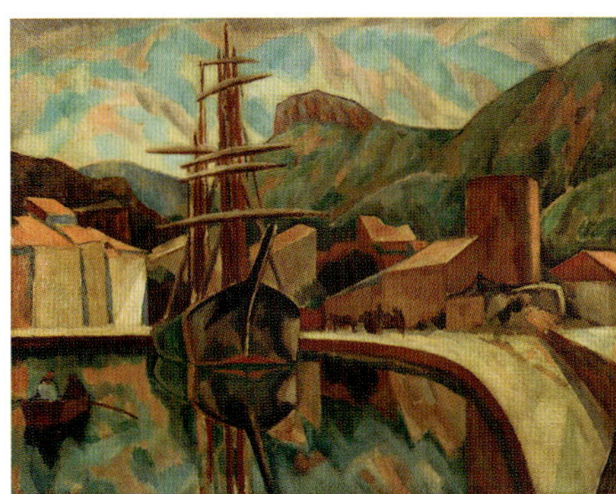

Fry, Roger Eliot 1866–1934
A Provençal Harbour 1915
oil on canvas 70.5 x 90.6
3103

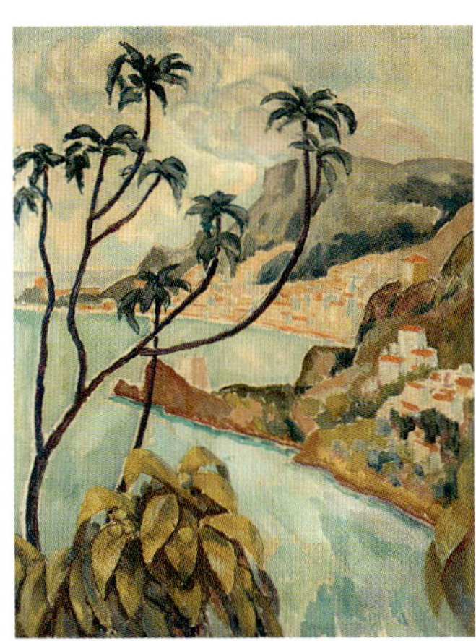

Fry, Roger Eliot 1866–1934
Roquebrune and Monte Carlo from Palm Beach c.1915
oil on canvas 91.4 x 70.8
3263

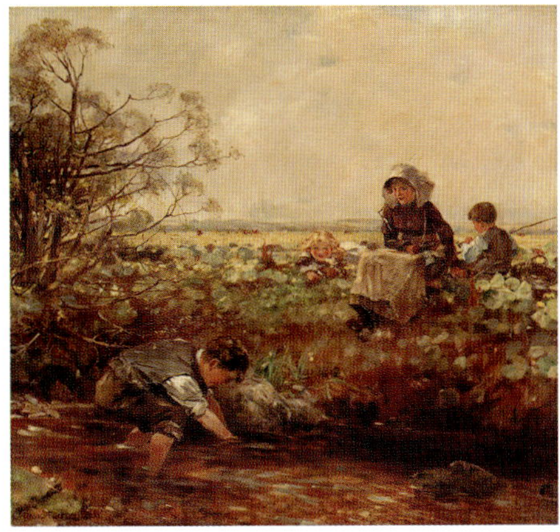

Fulton, David 1848–1930
By the Burnside c.1912
oil on canvas 113 x 120.7
1294

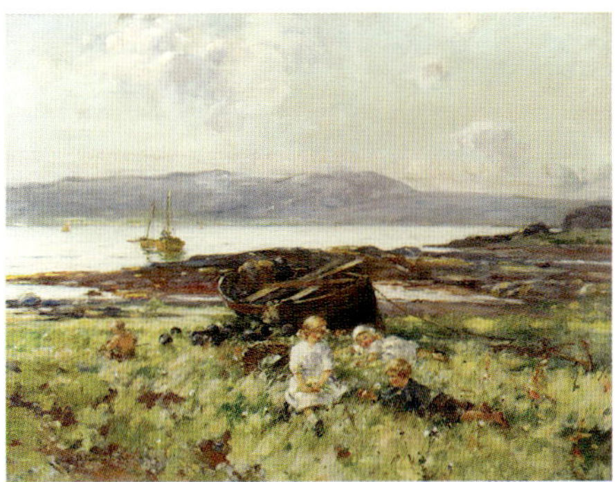

Fulton, David 1848–1930
Morning Time, Grogport, Kintyre c.1928
oil on canvas 71.1 x 91.4
2060

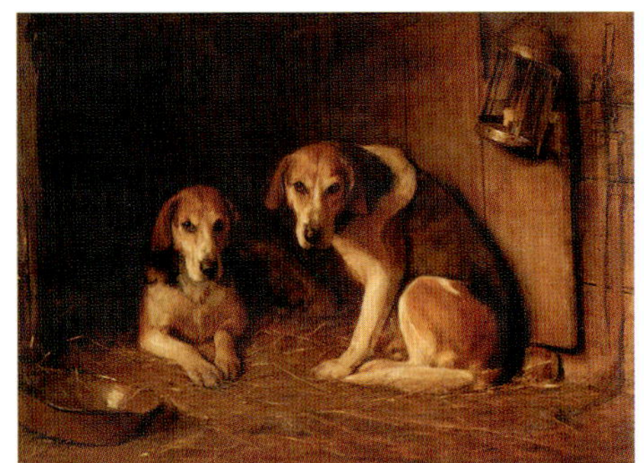

Fulton, Samuel 1855–1941
Foxhounds c.1910
oil on canvas 76.2 x 105.4
1265

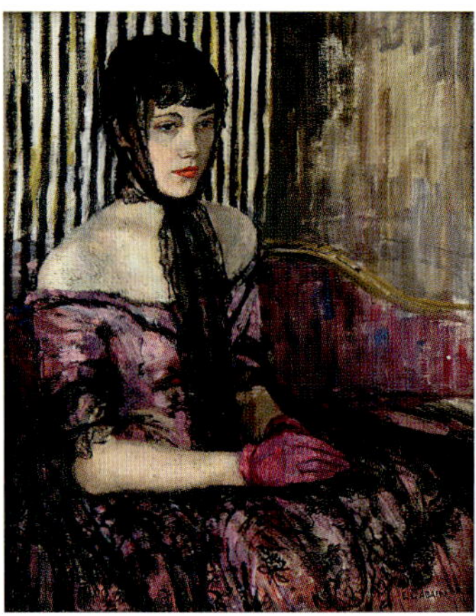

Gabain, Ethel Leontine 1883–1950
Stripes and Lace
oil on canvas 50.2 x 40.6
2851

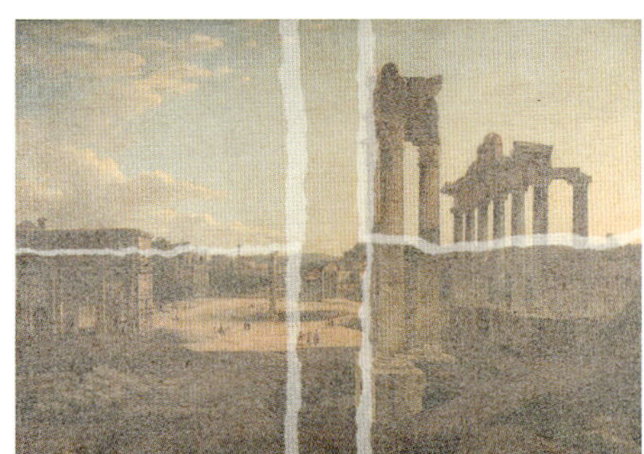

Gabrielli, Gaspare 1770–1828
View of the Roman Forum 1824
oil on canvas 67.3 x 97.8
317

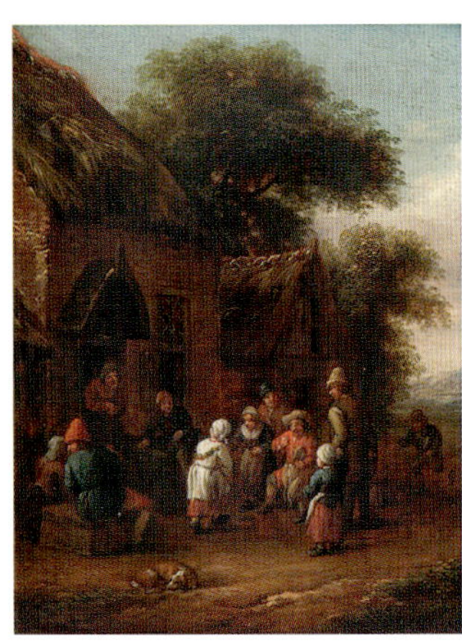

Gael, Barend c.1635–1698
Peasants before a Cottage
oil on panel 23.5 x 18.1
94

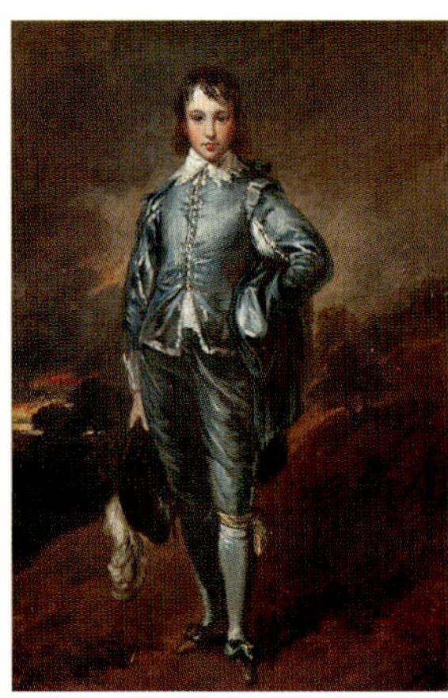

Gainsborough, Thomas (after) 1727–1788
The Blue Boy 18th C (?)
oil on millboard 33.3 x 22.8
PC.117

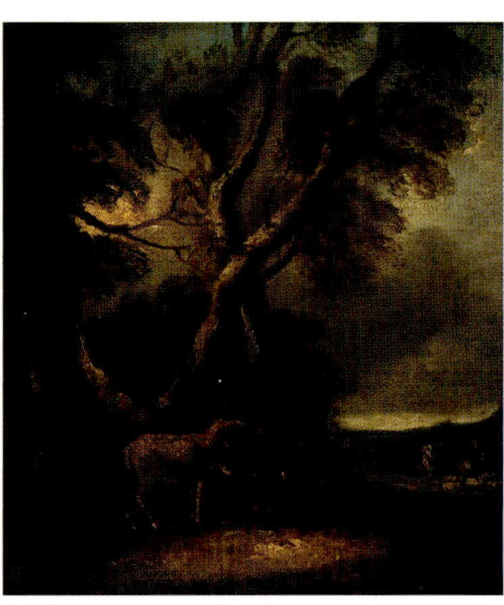

Gainsborough, Thomas (attributed to)
1727–1788
Donkeys in a Storm
oil on canvas 38.1 x 33.7
230

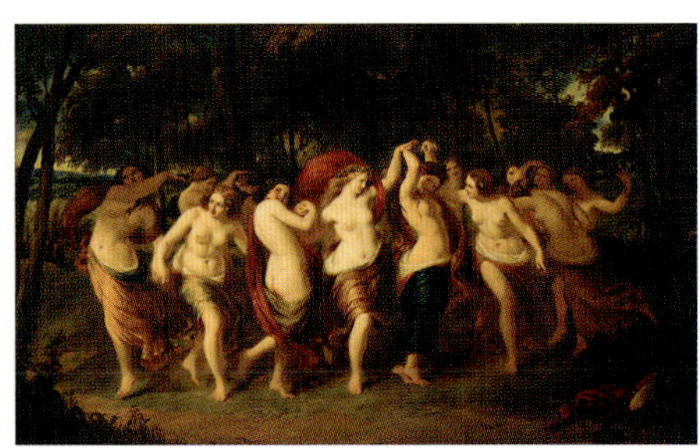

Gale, William 1823–1909
The Dance of Nymphs 1855
oil on canvas 53.3 x 91.4
1045

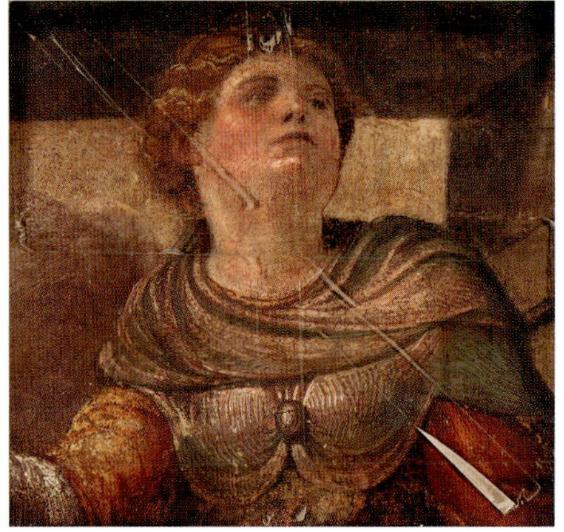

Gambara, Lattanzio c.1530–1574
Agrippine Sibyl c.1555–1560
fresco transferred to canvas 64.7 x 65
483

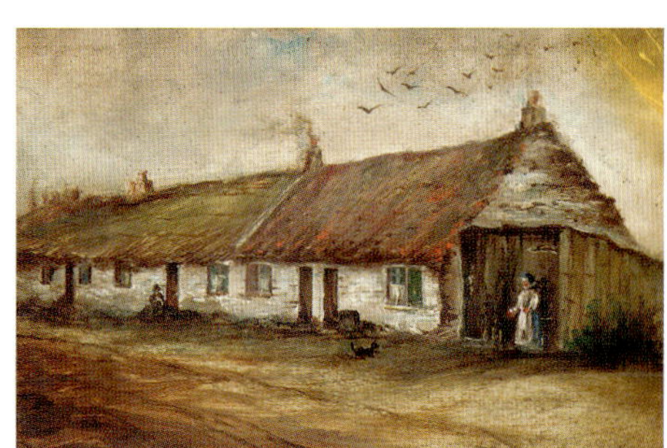

Gardner, A. active 19th C
Auld Shettleston Road, Glasgow
oil on canvas 18.7 x 26.7
TEMP.1668

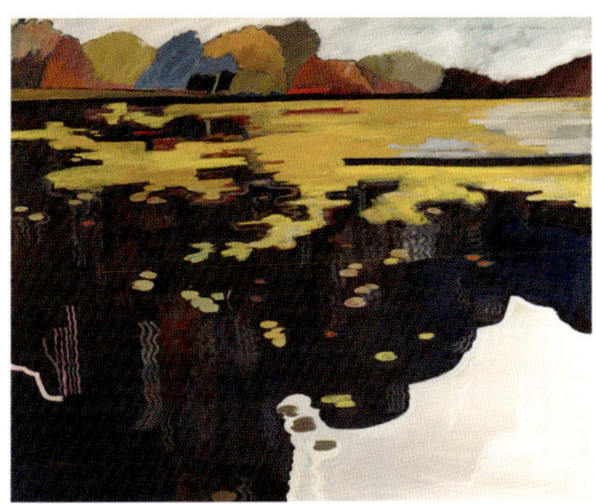

Gardner, Alexandra b.1945
Yellow Pond 1973–1975
oil on canvas 152.1 x 182.7
3323

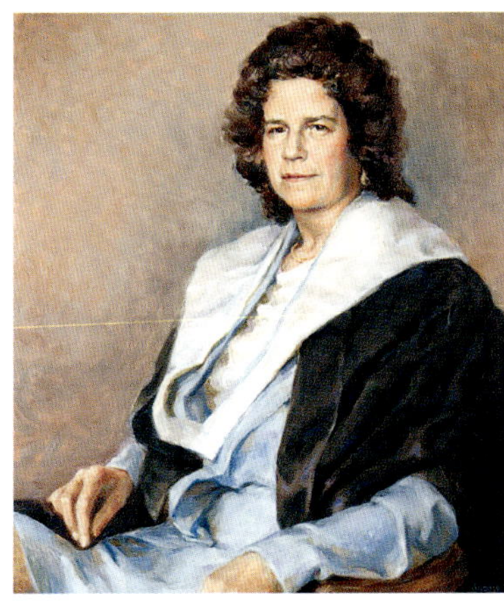

Gardner, Audrey R.
Mrs Gray, Headmistress of Park School (1995)
oil on canvas 78 x 66
ME.2007.1.9

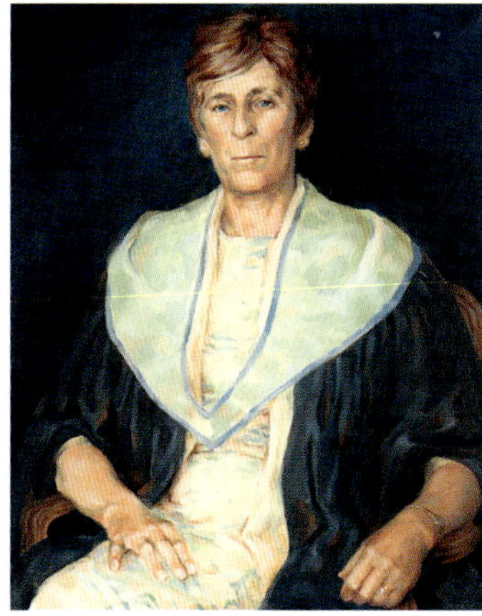

Gardner, Audrey R.
*Mrs Myatt, Headmistress of Park School
(1986–1995)*
oil on canvas 81 x 64
ME.2007.1.8

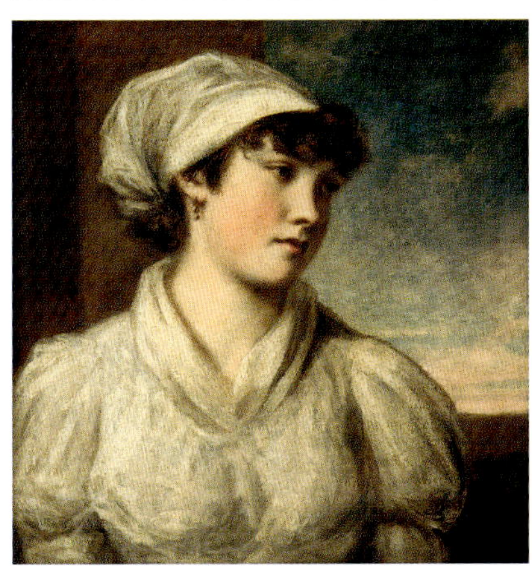

Gardner, Daniel 1750–1805
Agnes Pennington
oil on canvas 52.1 x 50.8
1820

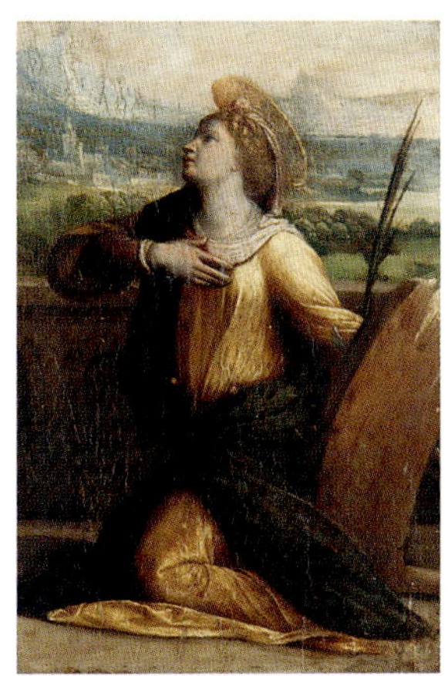

Garofalo c.1481–1559
Saint Catherine of Alexandria c.1530–1535
oil on panel 27.6 x 18.9
171

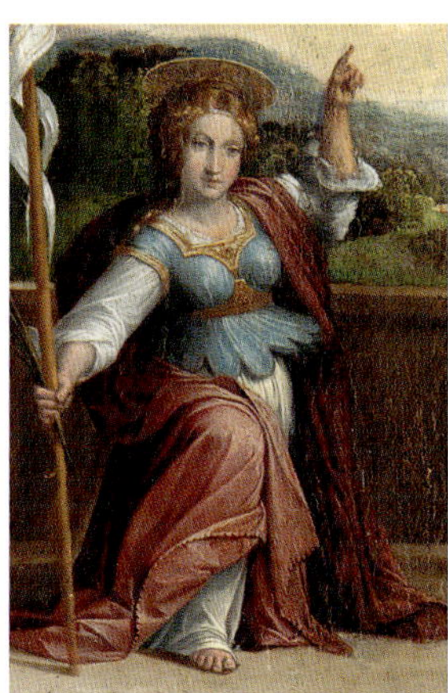

Garofalo c.1481–1559
Saint Ursula c.1530–1535
oil on panel 27.6 x 19.1
167

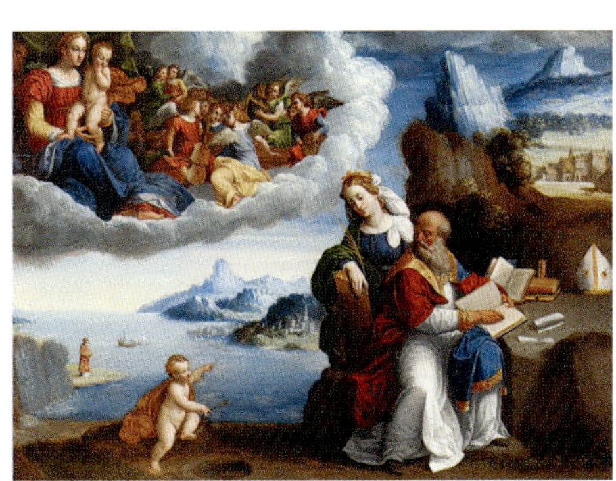

Garofalo (after) c.1481–1559
The Vision of Saint Augustine
oil on panel 61.6 x 82.6
155

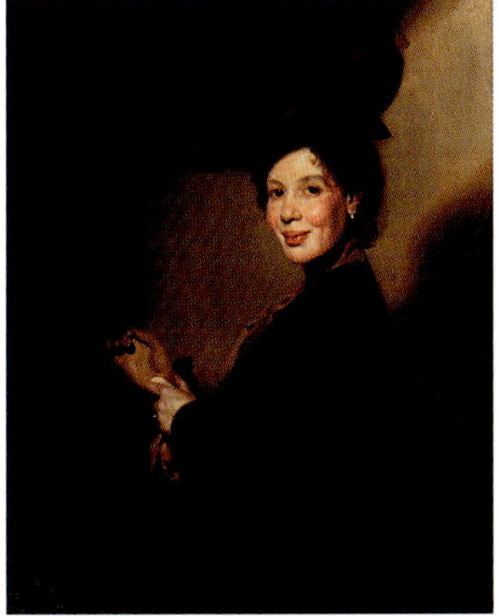

Garrido, Leandro Ramón 1868–1909
The Lady with the Gloves 1901
oil on canvas 95.3 x 75.6
1085

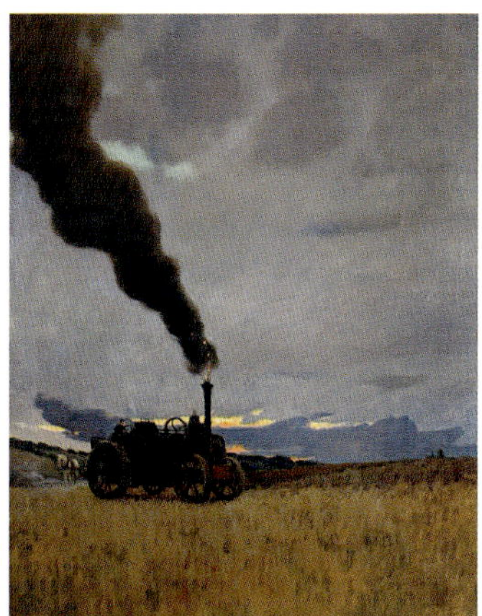

Garstin, Norman 1847–1926
The Last Furrow 1915
oil on canvas 127 x 101.6
1709

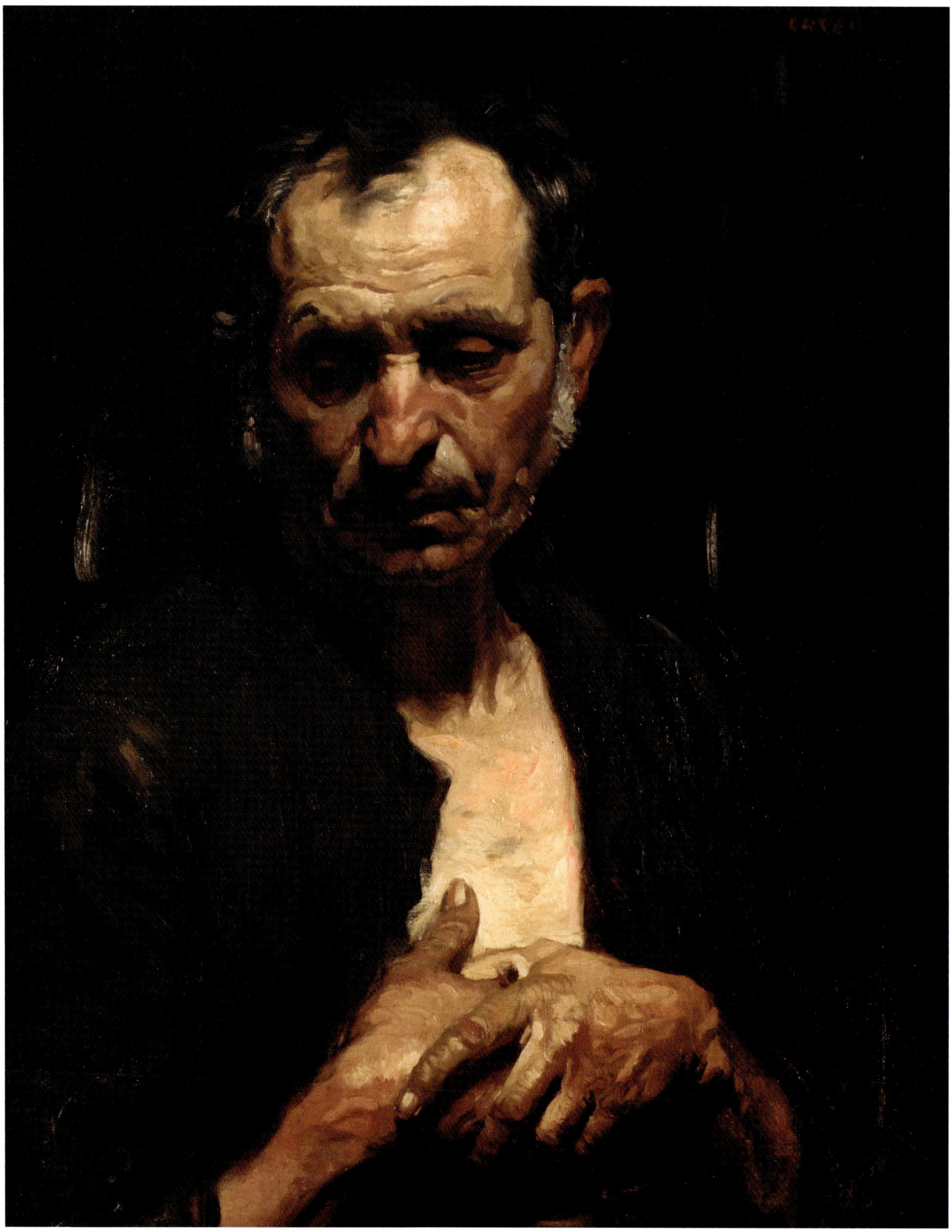

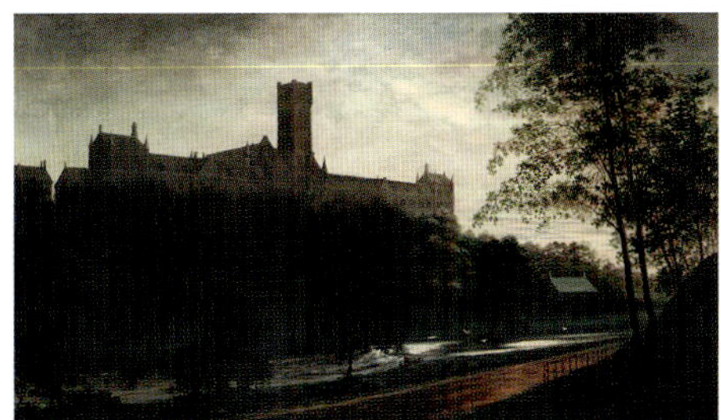

Gartside, Fred
Glasgow University, Sunrise 1887
oil on canvas 76.2 x 127
1872

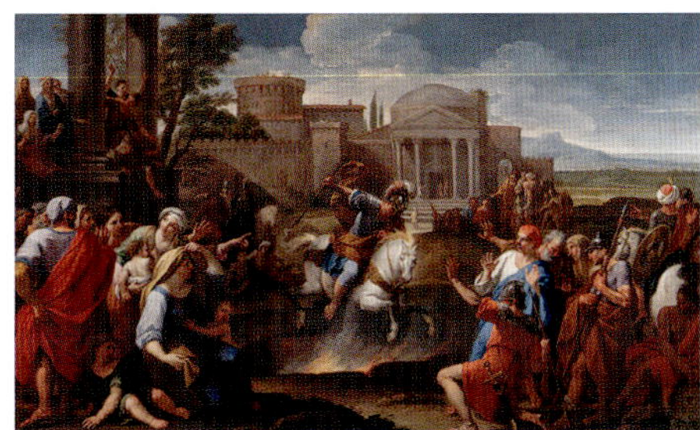

Garzi, Luigi 1638–1721
The Sacrifice of Marcus Curtius c.1715–1720
oil on canvas 105.8 x 172.3
900

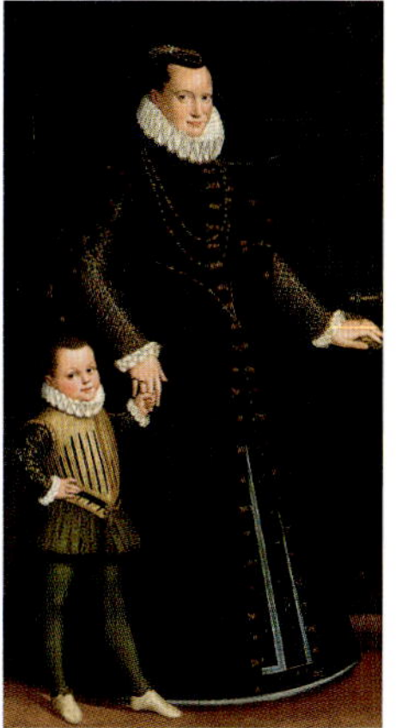

Gatti, Gervasio (attributed to) 1549–1631
Mother and Child c.1575
oil on canvas 190.5 x 104.1
35.56

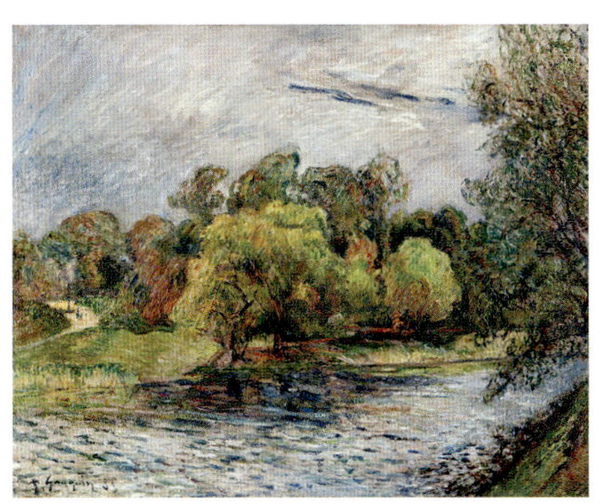

Gauguin, Paul 1848–1903
Østre Anlæg Park, Copenhagen 1885
oil on canvas 59.1 x 72.8
2465

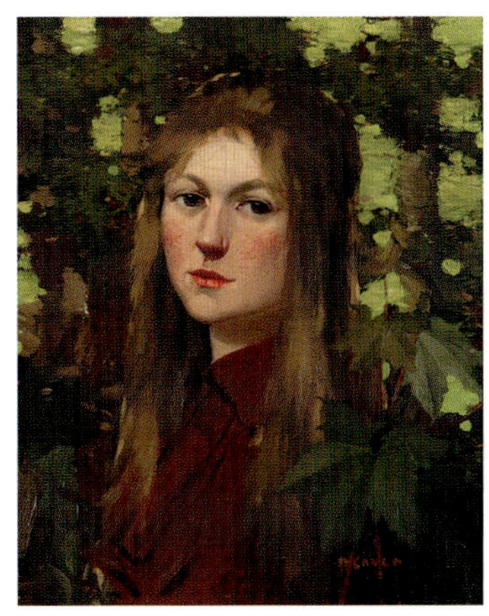

Gauld, David 1865–1936
Portrait Head c.1893–1894
oil on canvas 50.8 x 40.6
2802

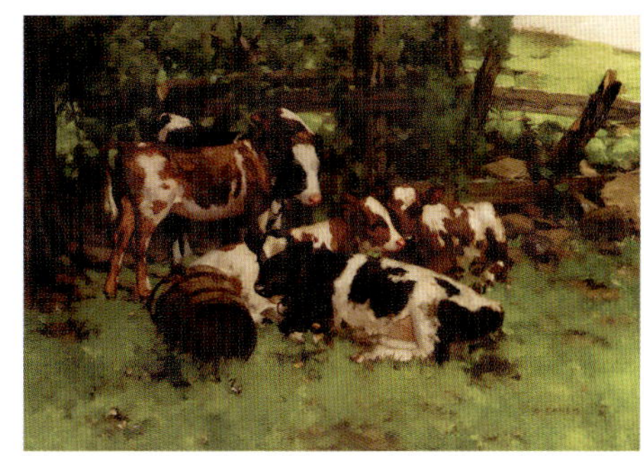

Gauld, David 1865–1936
Contentment c.1903
oil on canvas 106.7 x 152.4
1061

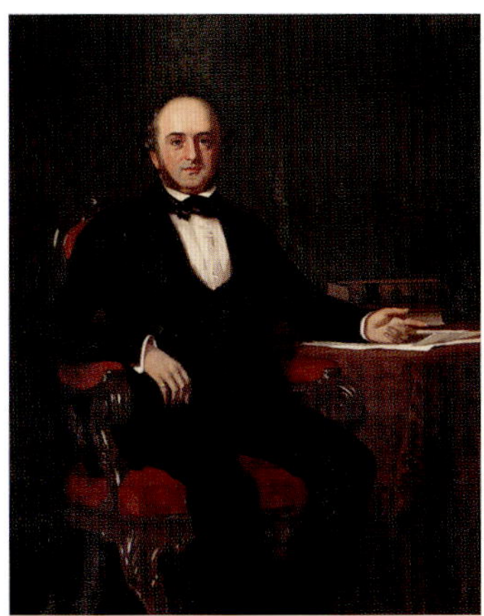

Gauld, David 1865–1936
*Robert Stewart, Lord Provost of Glasgow
(1851–1854) (after Daniel Macnee)* c.1909
oil on canvas 149.9 x 114.3
1256

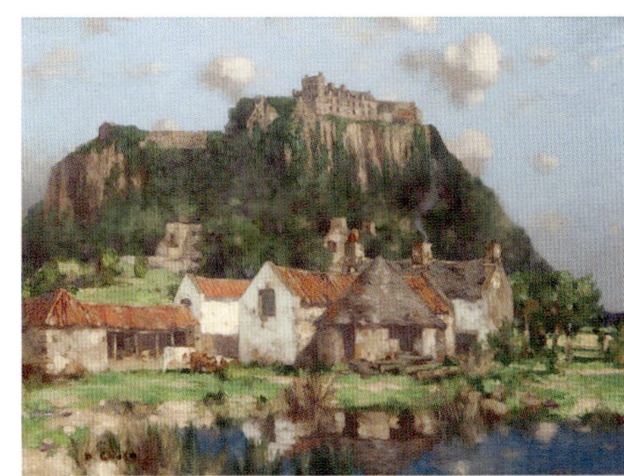

Gauld, David 1865–1936
Raploch, Stirling c.1931
oil on canvas 76.2 x 101.6
1825

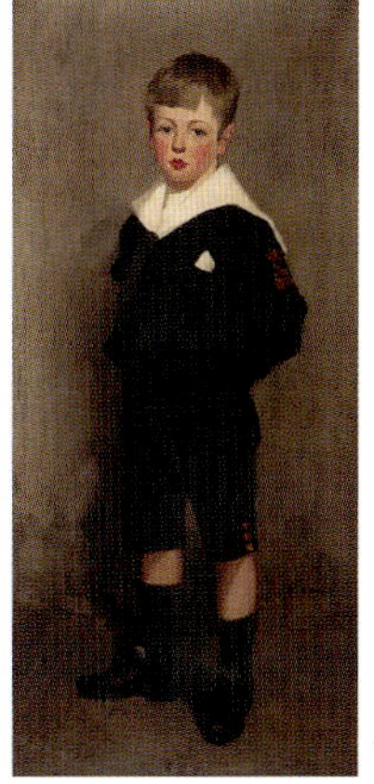

Gauld, David 1865–1936
A Boy
oil on canvas 142.2 x 66
2304

Facing page: Orpen, William, 1878–1931, *A Saint of the Poor*, c.1905 (p. 333)

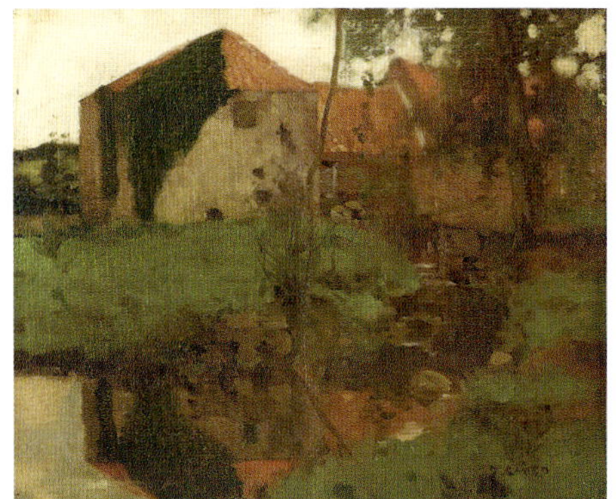

Gauld, David 1865–1936
East Linton Mill
oil on canvas 50.8 x 61
2801

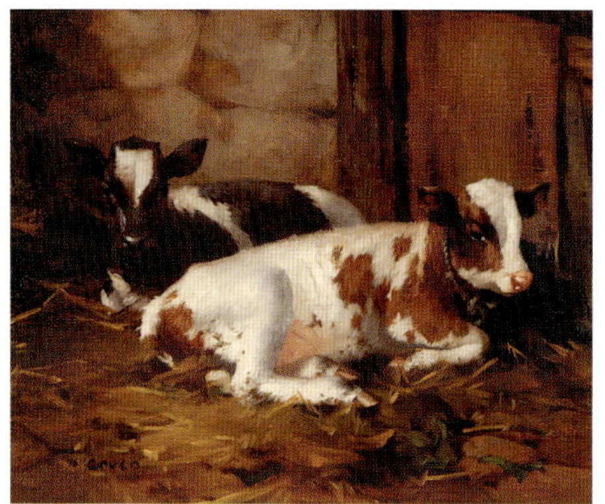

Gauld, David 1865–1936
Two Calves
oil on canvas 50.8 x 61
2803

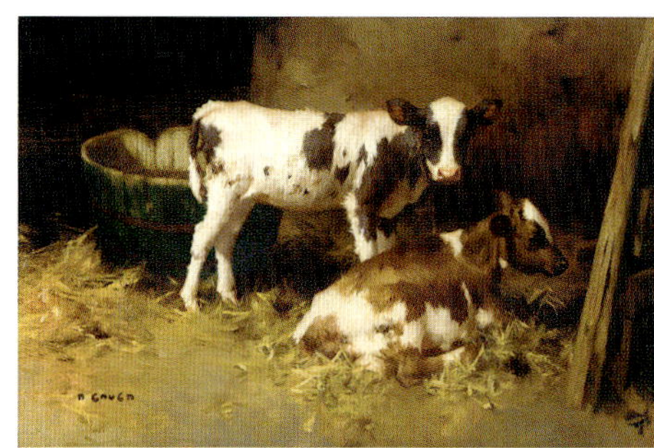

Gauld, David 1865–1936
Two Calves
oil on canvas 61 x 91.4
3093

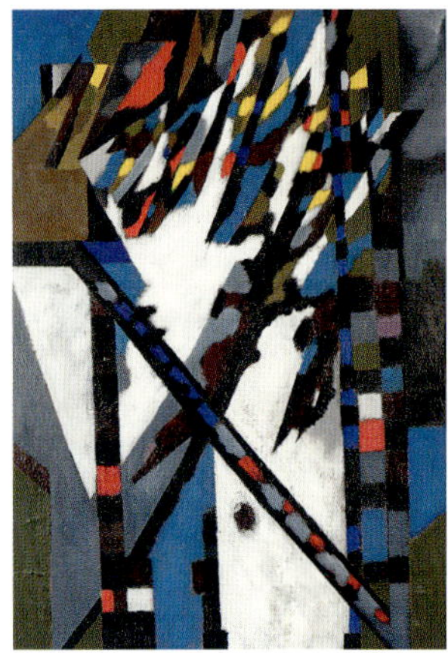

Gear, William 1915–1997
Summer Garden 1951
oil on canvas 122 x 81.2
3378

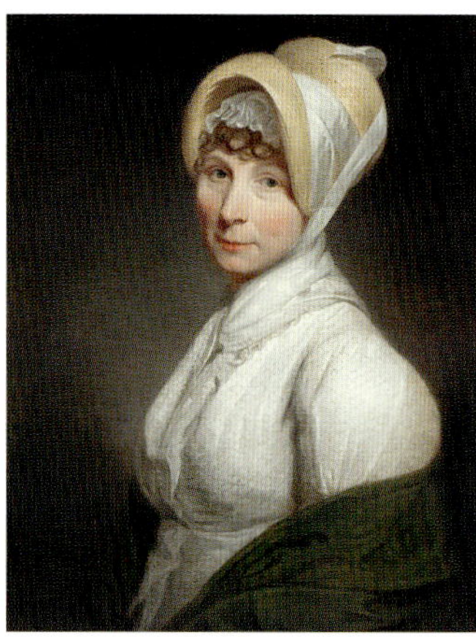

Geddes, Andrew 1783–1844
Portrait of a Lady c.1803–1810
oil on canvas 63.5 x 50.8
1797

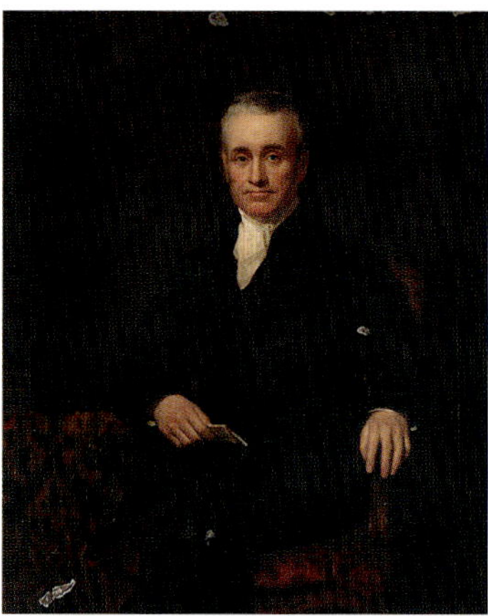

Geddes, Andrew 1783–1844
Charles Tennant (1768–1838) c.1820–1830
oil on canvas 127.6 x 101.6
1491

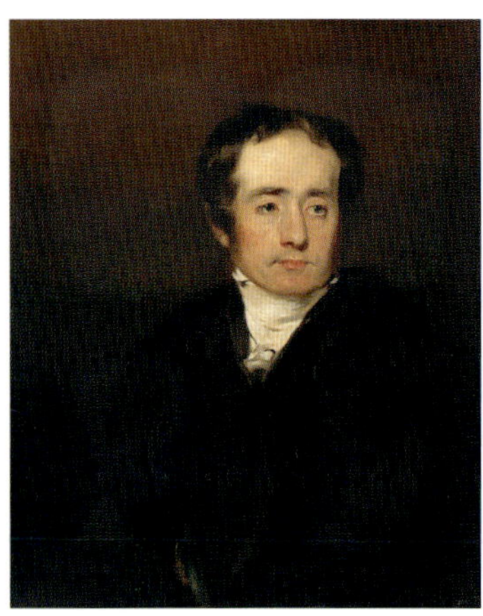

Geddes, Andrew 1783–1844
Alexander Oswald of Changue (1777–1821)
oil on canvas 76.2 x 63.5
2849

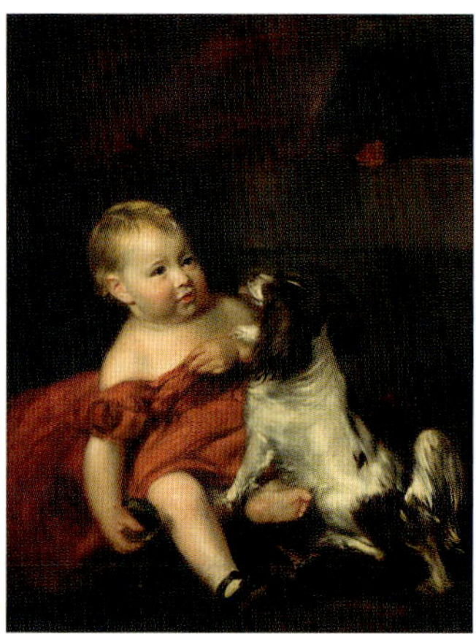

Geddes, Andrew 1783–1844
Child with a Spaniel
oil on canvas 91.2 x 70.6
3052

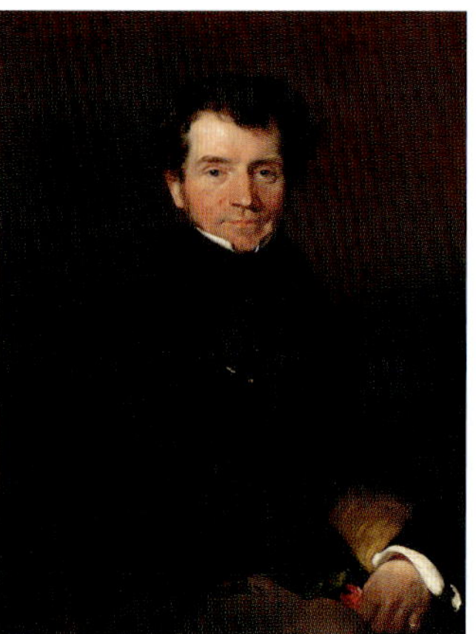

Geddes, Andrew 1783–1844
Jeremiah Greatorex (1768–1877)
oil on canvas 90.2 x 70.5
2850

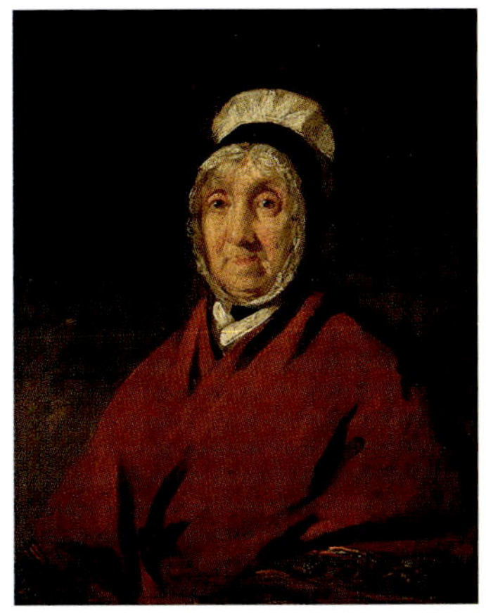

Geddes, Andrew 1783–1844
Portrait of an Old Scottish Lady
oil on canvas 31.8 x 26.7
1403

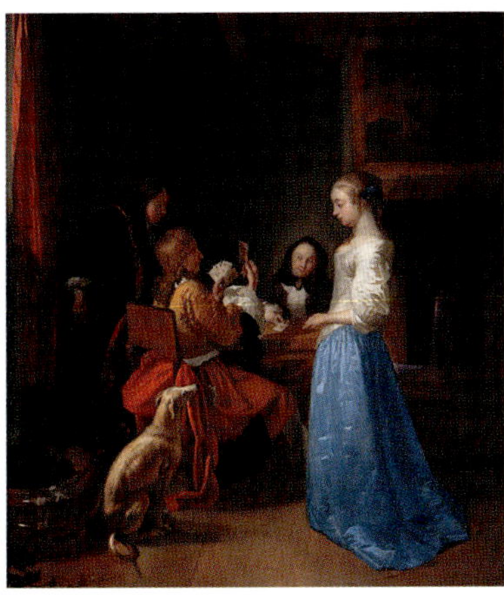

Geel, Joost van 1631–1698
The Queen of Hearts c.1660–1680
oil on canvas 44.4 x 39
1365

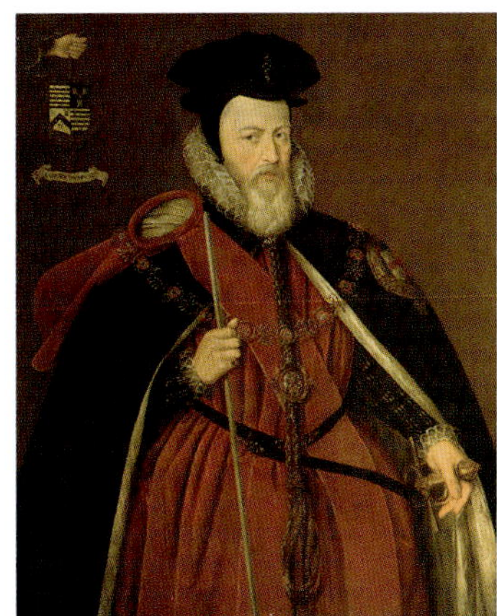

Geeraerts, Marcus the younger (school of)
1561–1635
William Cecil (1520–1598), Lord Burghley
c.1585
oil on panel 111.8 x 86.4
35.274

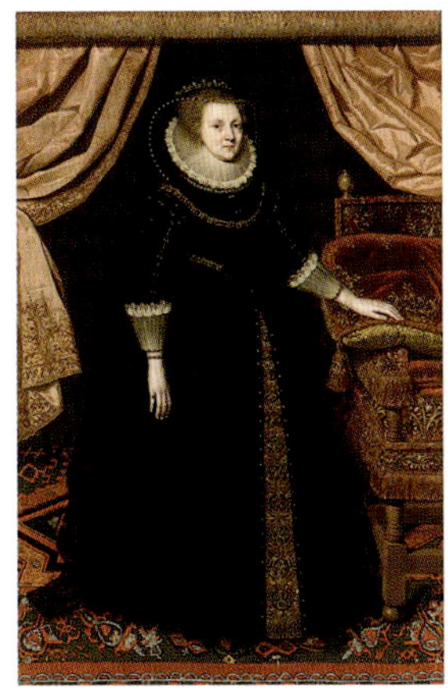

Geeraerts, Marcus the younger (school of)
1561–1635
*Elizabeth Vernon (1572–1655), Countess of
Southampton* 1622
oil on canvas 200 x 129
35.672

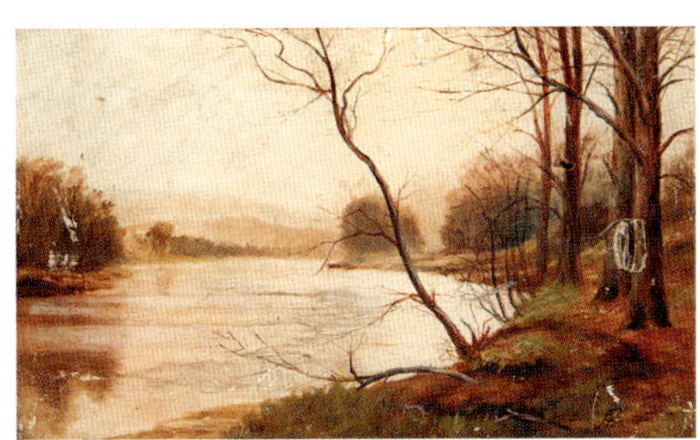

Gemmell, A. active 19th C
The Clyde at Carmyle, Glasgow
oil on canvas 22.7 x 37.3
TEMP.1472

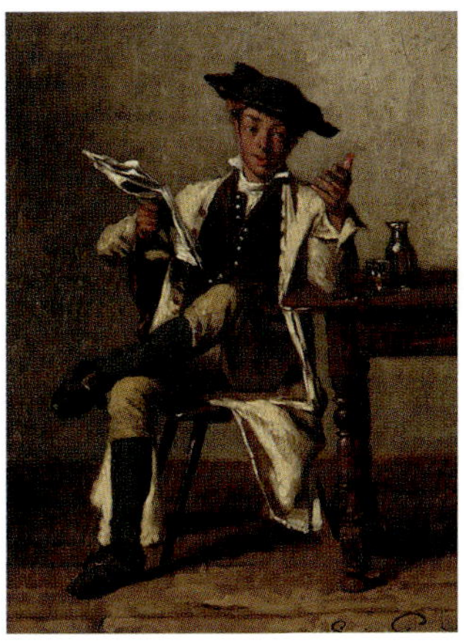

Gérard, Lucien 1852–1935
Young Man Reading
oil on panel 22.2 x 17.1
2600

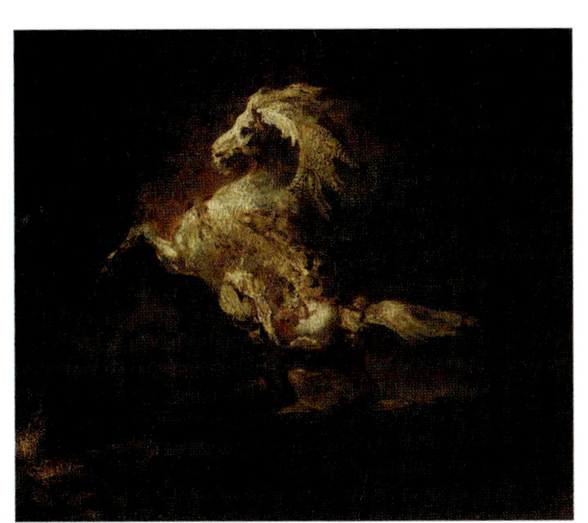

Géricault, Théodore 1791–1824
A Prancing Grey Horse 1812
oil on canvas 45.1 x 54.6
35.271

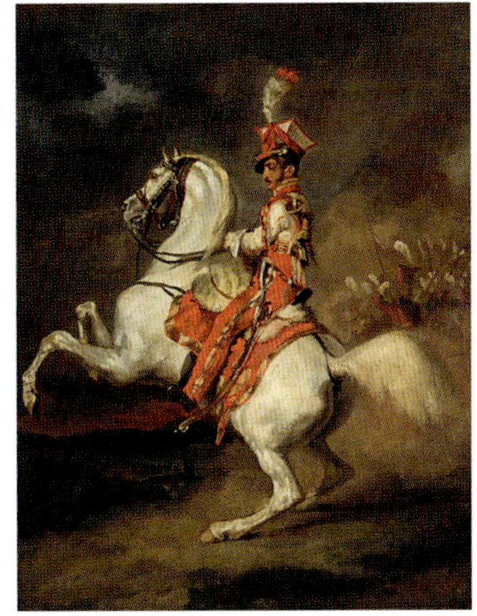

Géricault, Théodore 1791–1824
The Trumpeter of the Lancers of the Guard
c.1812–1815
oil on canvas 40.6 x 32.6
35.27

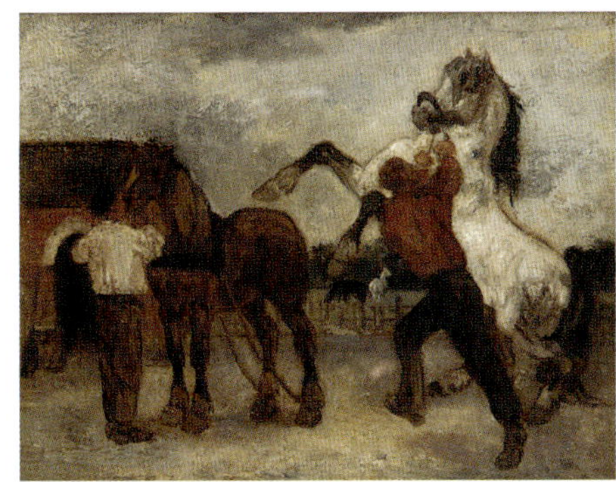

Géricault, Théodore (after) 1791–1824
The Stud Farm
oil on canvas 19 x 24.5
35.268

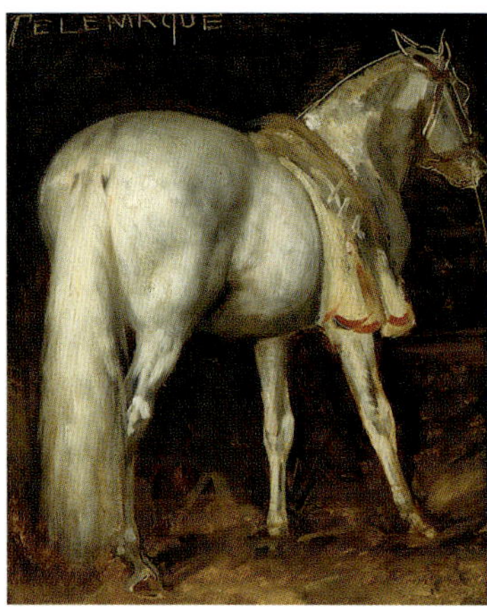

Géricault, Théodore (attributed to)
1791–1824
The Grey Horse 'Telemachus'
oil on paper on panel 31.5 x 24.5
35.273

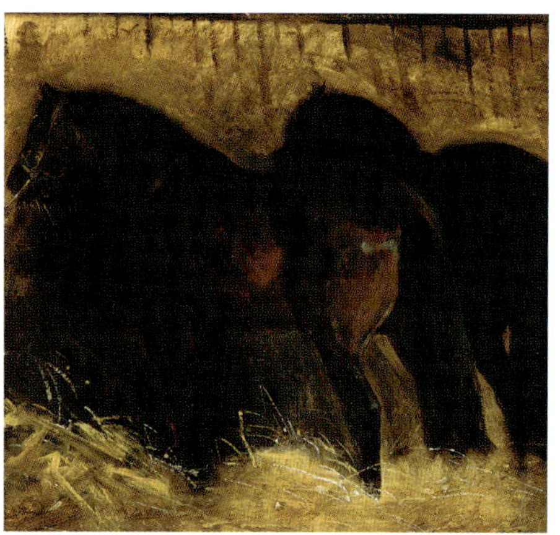

Géricault, Théodore (attributed to)
1791–1824
Two Brown Horses in a Stall
oil on panel 31.5 x 32.3
35.265

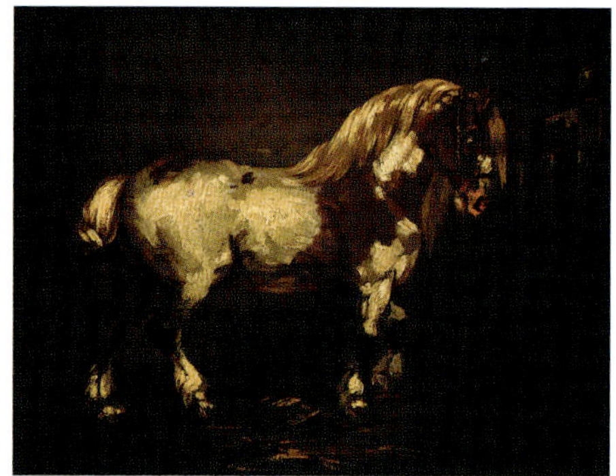

Géricault, Théodore (style of) 1791–1824
A Piebald Stallion
oil on canvas 31.7 x 40
35.269

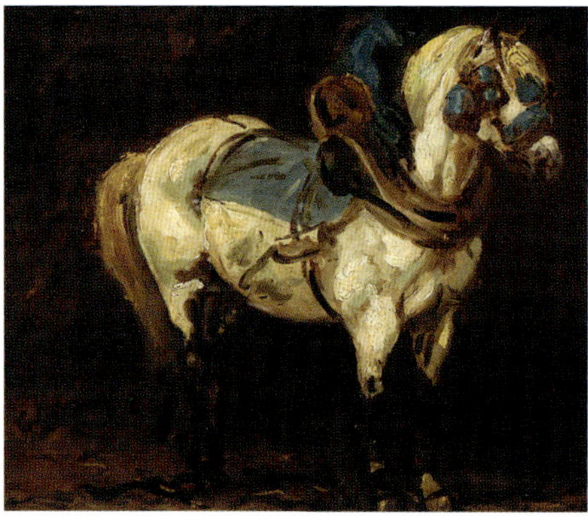

Géricault, Théodore (style of) 1791–1824
Grey Charger Harnessed with Blue Trappings
oil on paper mounted on canvas 31 x 35.5
35.267

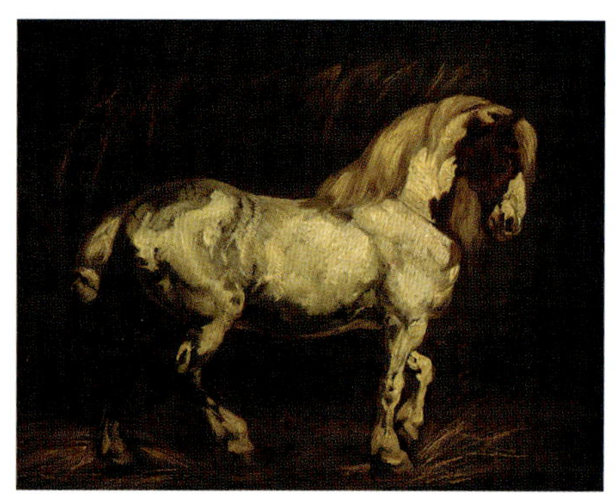

Géricault, Théodore (style of) 1791–1824
The Stallion
oil on canvas 30 x 40.6
35.272

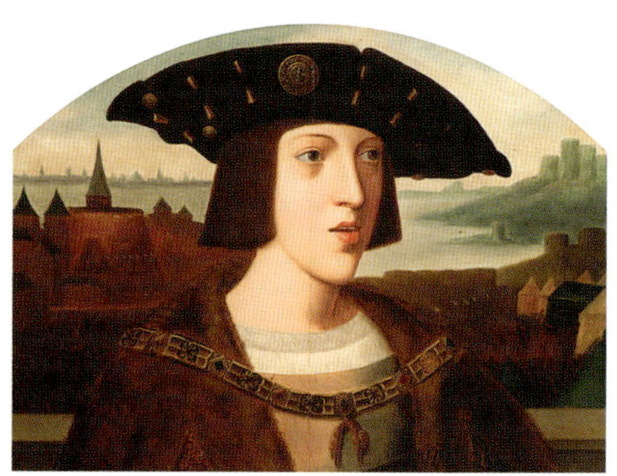

German School
The Emperor Ferdinand I (1503–1564)
1527–1576
oil on panel 35.5 x 46.9
PC.69

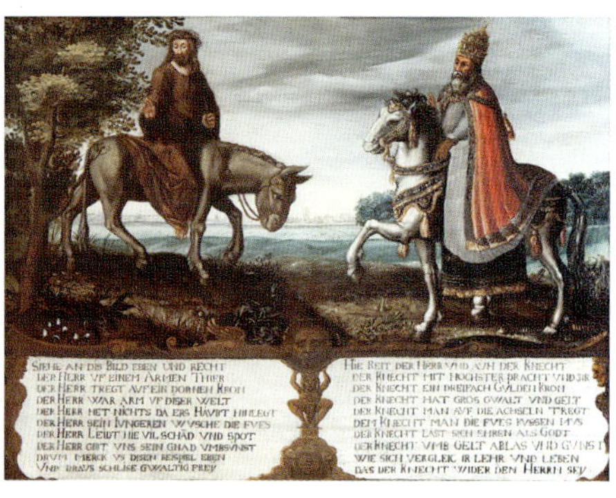

German School
Christ and the Pope 1550–1600
oil on panel 56.8 x 77.8
PC.157

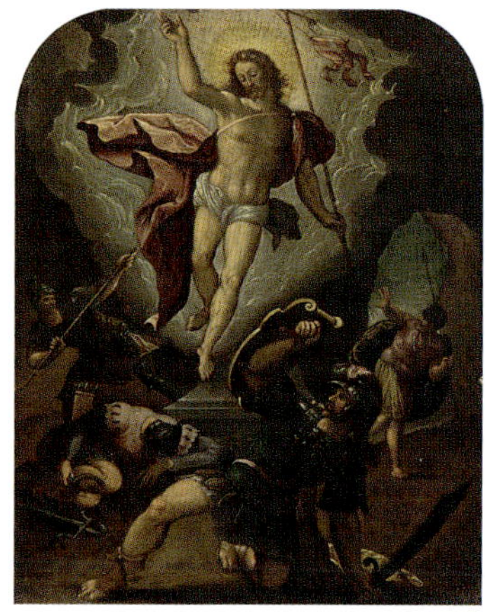

German School
The Resurrection c.1570–1600
oil on copper 25.1 x 20
202

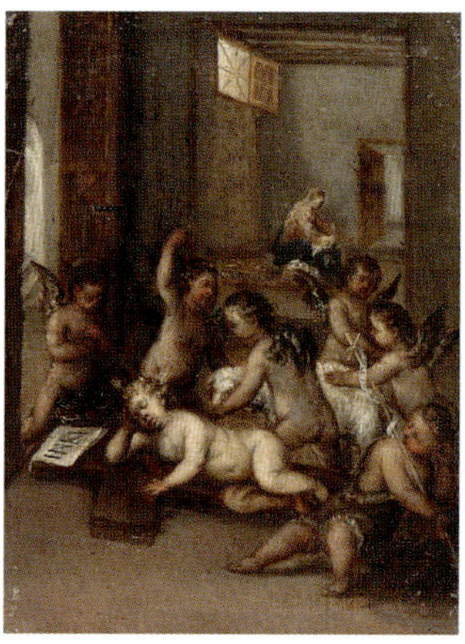

German School 17th C (?)
The Christ Child Sleeping on the Cross, with Saint John
oil on canvas 34.3 x 24.8
208

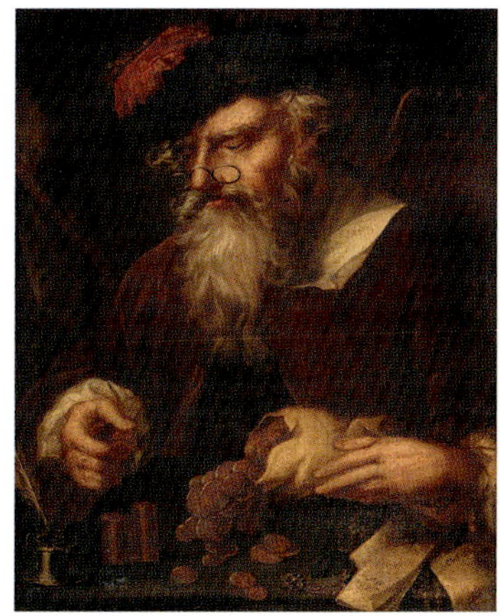

German School (attributed to) 18th C
A Miser
oil on canvas 78.1 x 71.5
2367

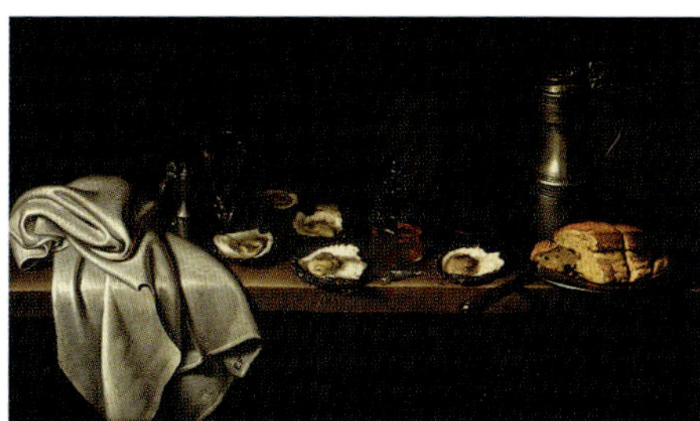

German School (attributed to) 18th C
Still Life: Oysters, a Glass and a Decanter
oil on canvas 58.4 x 97.9
35.255

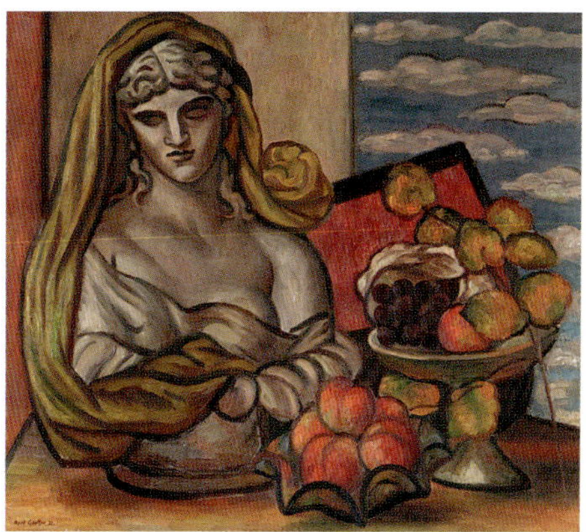

Gertler, Mark 1891–1939
Clytie and Autumn Leaves 1932
oil on canvas 78.7 x 86.4
2929

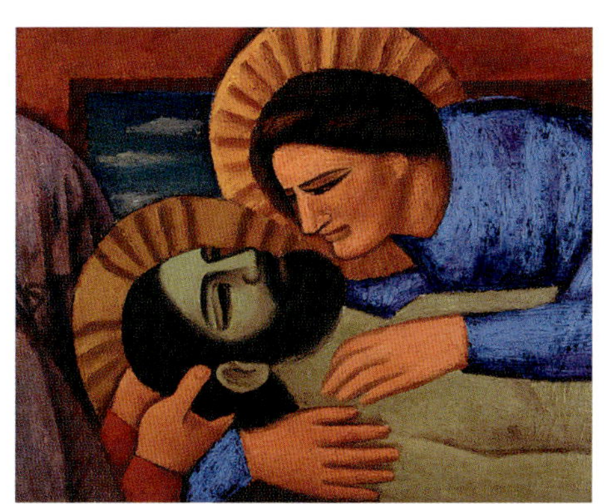

Gertler, Mark 1891–1939
After Giotto
oil on canvas 67.3 x 79.4
2928

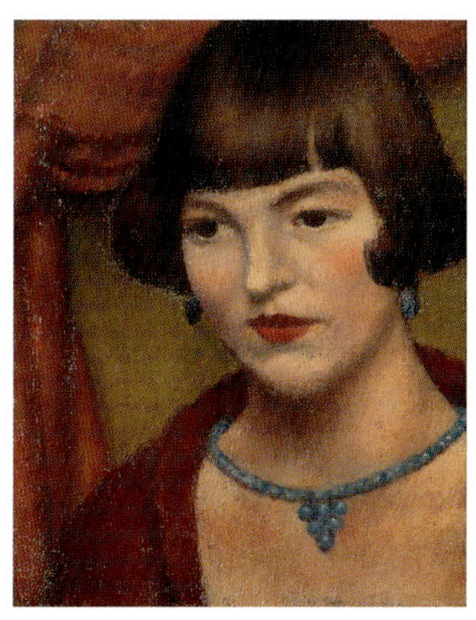

Gertler, Mark 1891–1939
Head of a Girl
oil on canvas 43.2 x 35.6
1929

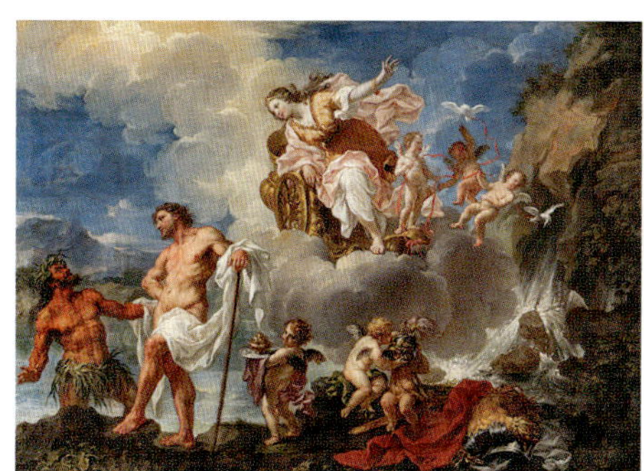

Ghezzi, Pier Leone 1674–1755
The Purification of Aeneas in the River Numicius c.1725
oil on canvas 96.5 x 135.5
3233

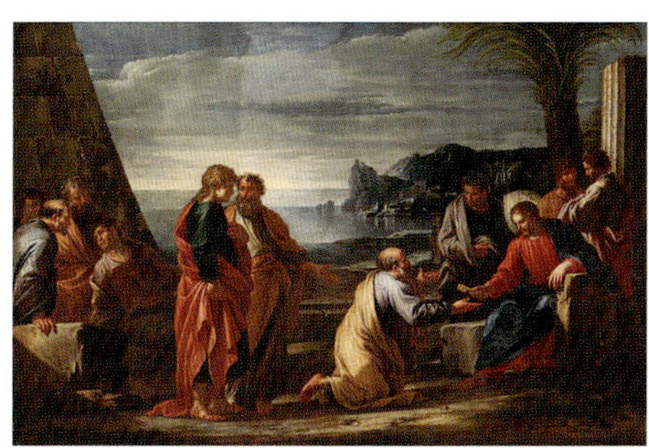

Ghisolfi, Giovanni (attributed to)
c.1623–1683
Christ Giving the Keys to Saint Peter
c.1655–1680
oil on canvas 78.1 x 115.8
222

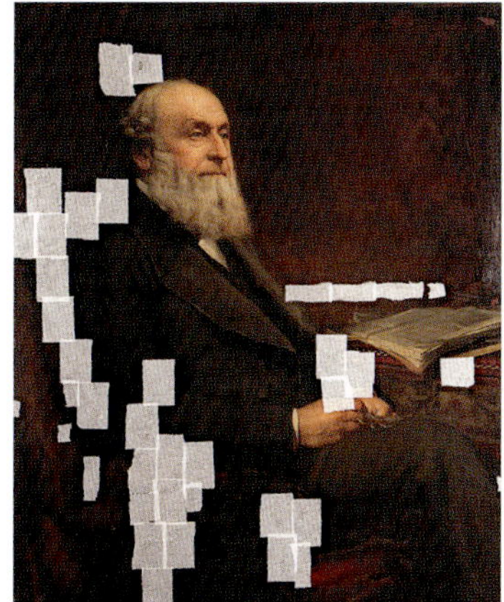

Gibb, Robert II 1845–1932
Portrait of a Seated Man 1883
oil on canvas 127.3 x 101.5
PP.1978.121.8

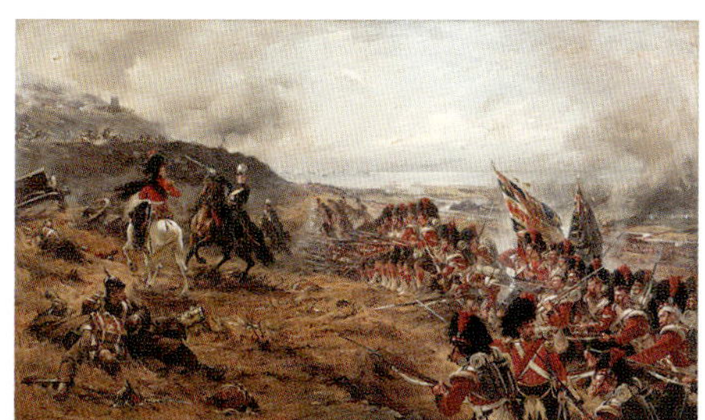

Gibb, Robert II 1845–1932
Alma: Forward the 42nd 1888
oil on canvas 127 x 218.4
1570

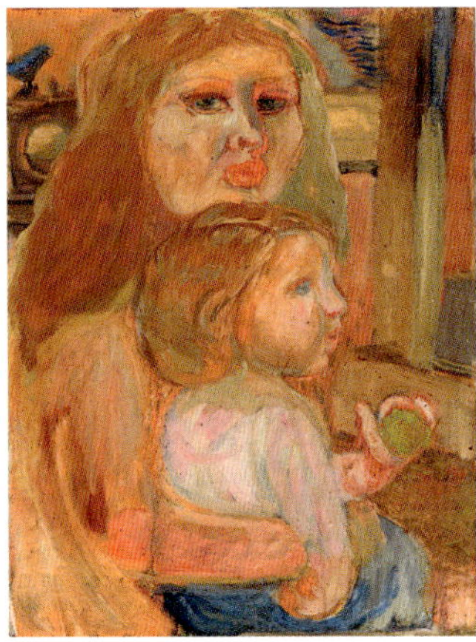

Gibbons, Carole b.1935
Self Portrait with Henry c.1973–1974
oil on canvas 62.3 x 47.6
3493

Gibson, John 1768–1852
Reverend William Kidston, DD
oil on canvas 127.8 x 102.2
PP.1978.121.5

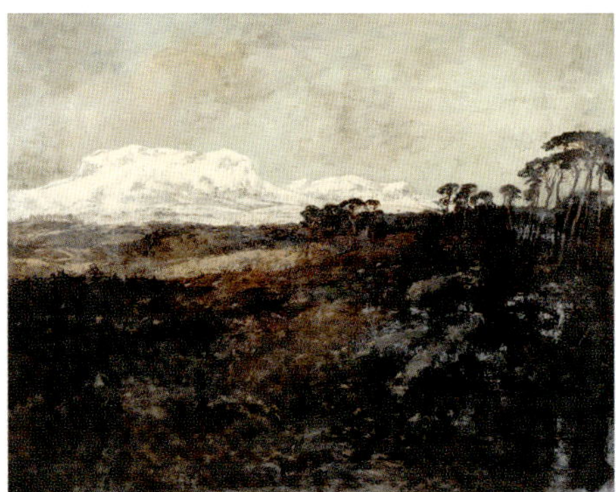

Gibson, William Alfred 1866–1931
The Passing of Autumn c.1913
oil on canvas 120.7 x 151.3
1330

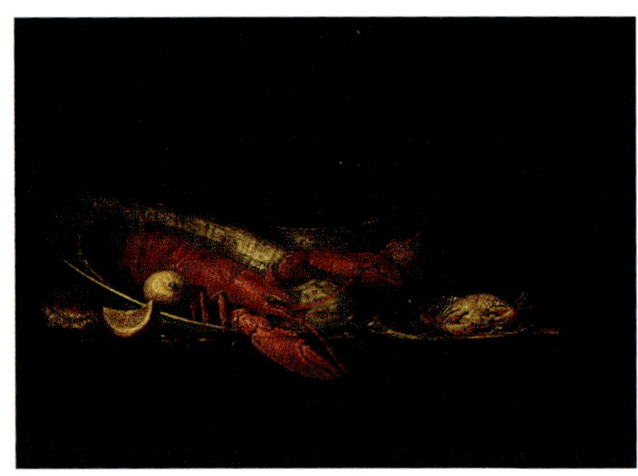

Gijsels, Philips (attributed to)
active 1642–1663
Still Life: Lobster, Fruit and Glasses 1642
oil on panel 57.8 x 78.7
35.277

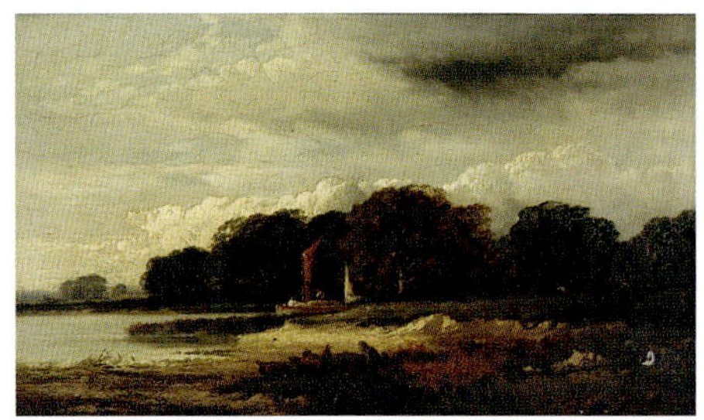

Gilbert, Arthur 1819–1895
Landscape 1850
oil on canvas 22.9 x 38.1
349

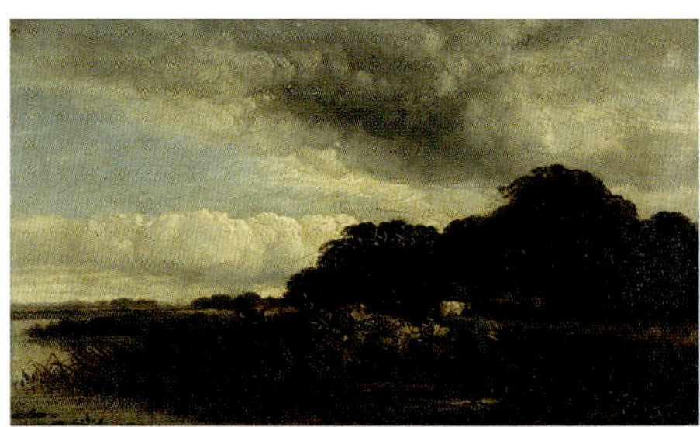

Gilbert, Arthur 1819–1895
Landscape 1850
oil on canvas 22.9 x 38.1
352

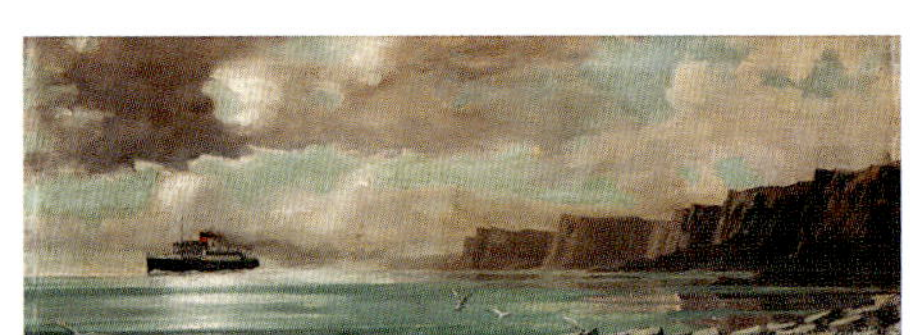

Gilfillan, James active 20th C
Ferry off the Antrim Coast
oil on canvas 30.5 x 78.7
TEMP.15495

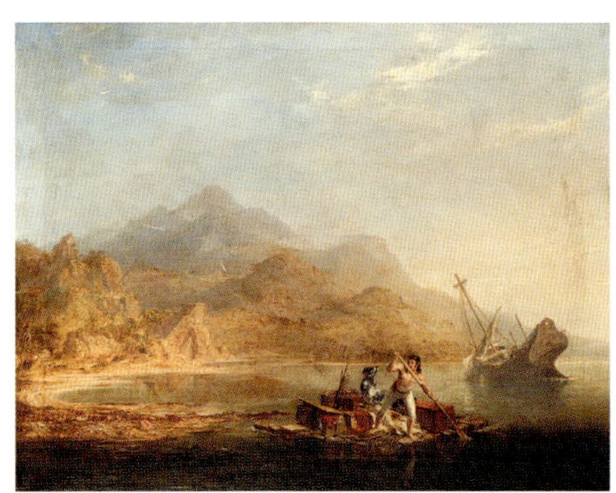

Gilfillan, John Alexander 1793–1864
Robinson Crusoe Landing Stores from the Wreck
oil on canvas 99.1 x 124.5
438

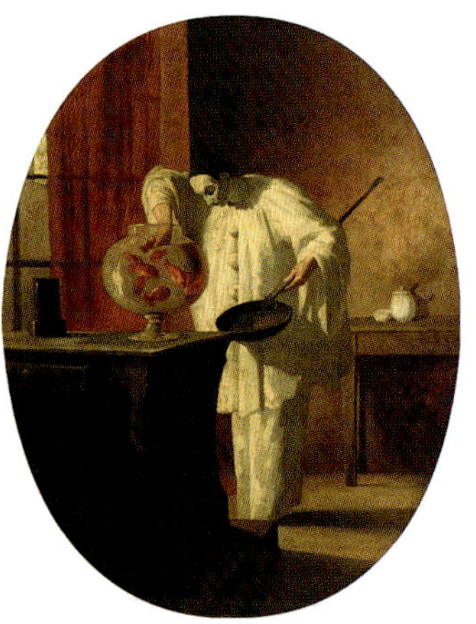

Gill, André (attributed to) 1840–1885
Pierrot voleur
oil on canvas 121.9 x 86.4
35.56

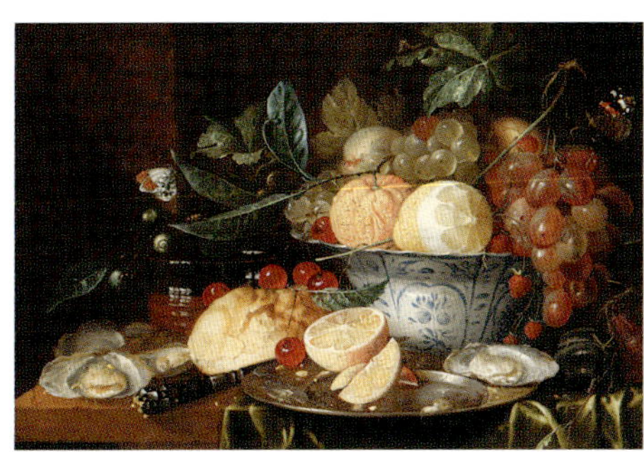

Gillemans, Jan Pauwel I (attributed to)
1618–1675
Still Life with Fruit and Oysters
oil on canvas 36.5 x 52.7
11

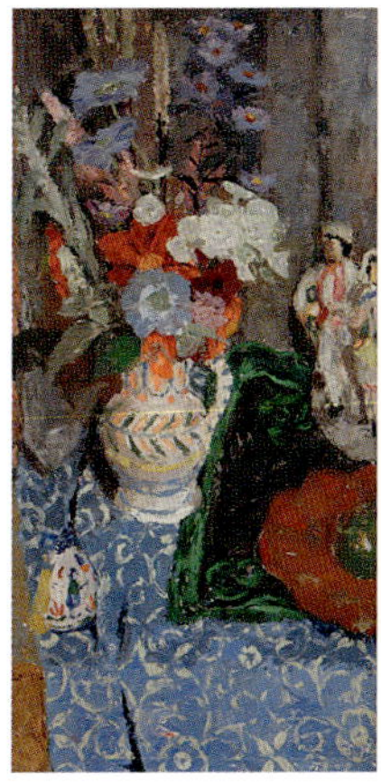

Gillies, William George 1898–1973
Still Life, Flowers and Figures c.1943
oil on canvas 96.5 x 45.7
2308

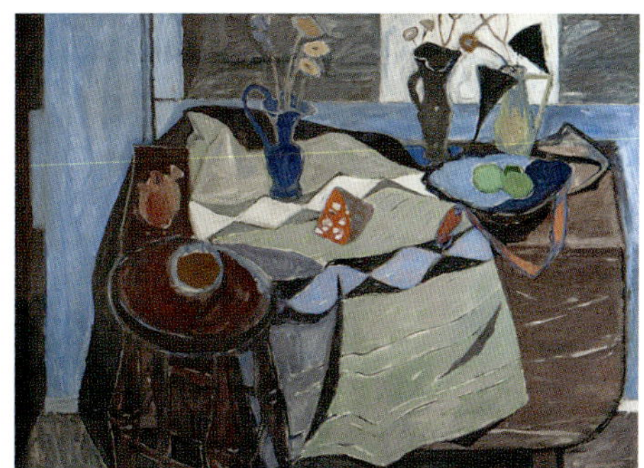

Gillies, William George 1898–1973
Still Life, Blue and Brown 1952
oil on canvas 99.1 x 137.2
2994

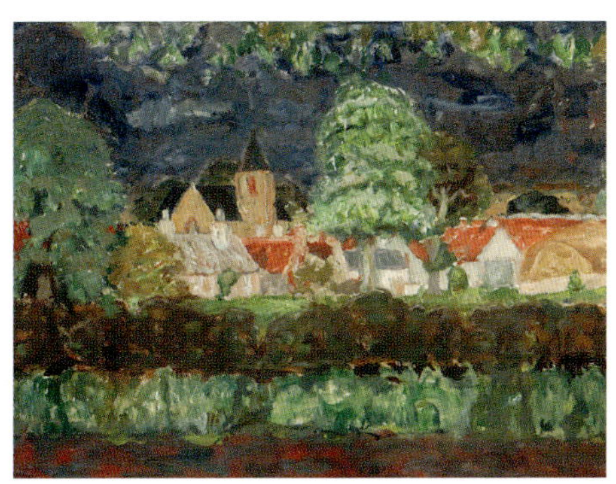

Gillies, William George 1898–1973
Carrington 1953
oil on canvas 52.2 x 66.8
3386

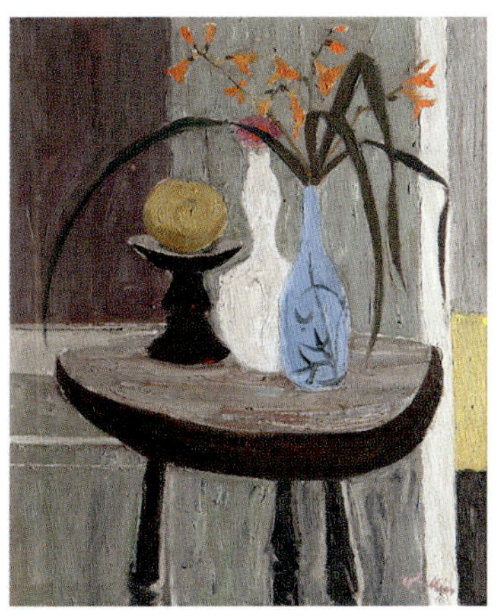

Gillies, William George 1898–1973
Interior c.1959
oil on canvas 47 x 38.1
3222

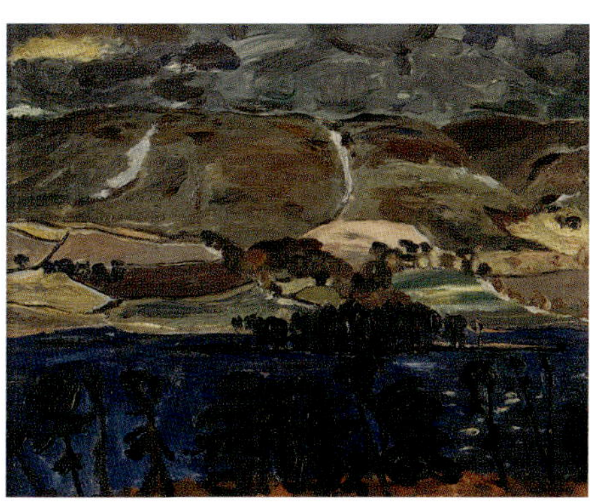

Gillies, William George 1898–1973
Storm over Gladhouse
oil on canvas 46.1 x 57.5
3452

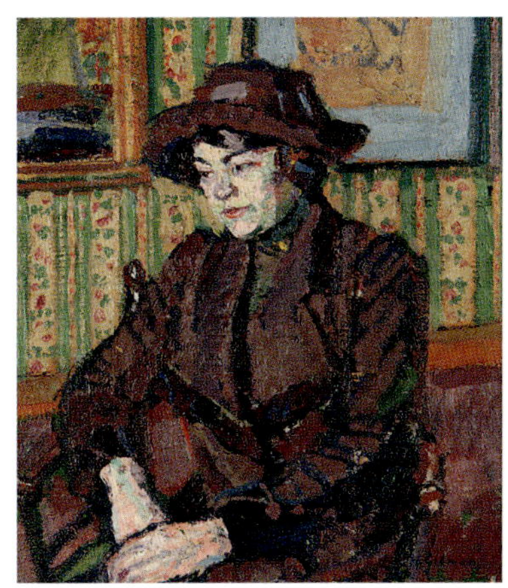

Gilman, Harold 1876–1919
Contemplation c.1915
oil on canvas 35.5 x 30.4
3309

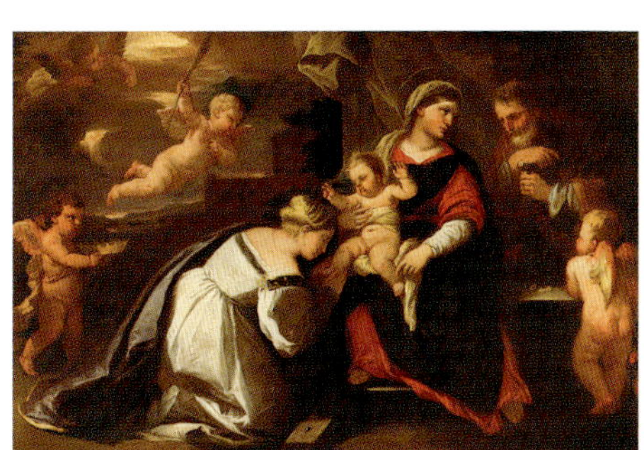

Giordano, Luca 1634–1705
*The Holy Family with Saint Catherine of
Alexandria* c.1675
oil on canvas 159.6 x 232.1
1056

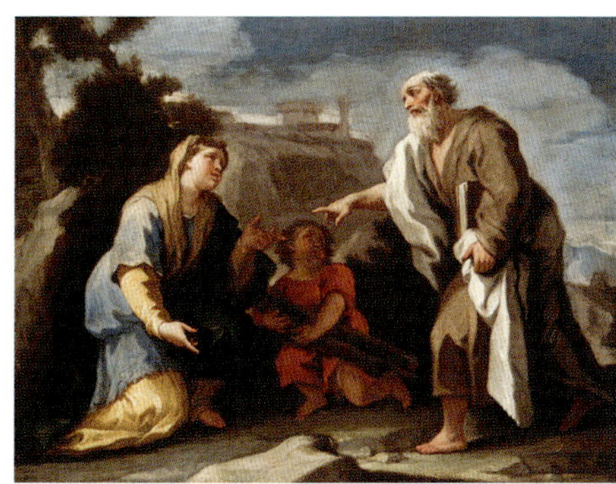

Giordano, Luca (follower of) 1634–1705
Elijah and the Widow of Zarephath
early 18th C
oil on canvas 37.8 x 49.5
193

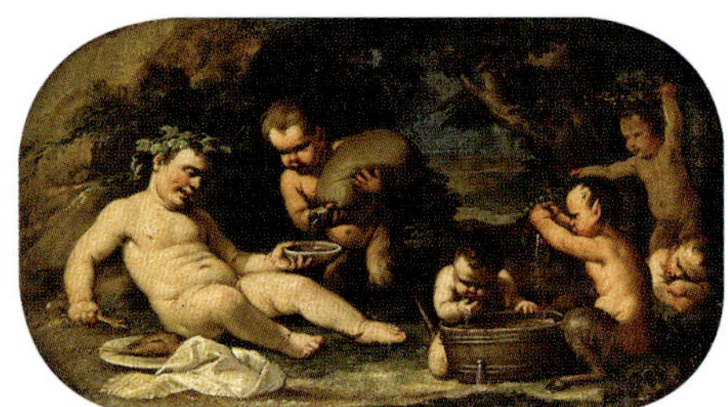

Giordano, Luca (follower of) 1634–1705
Bacchus and Infant Fauns 18th C
oil on canvas 15.2 x 26.7
186

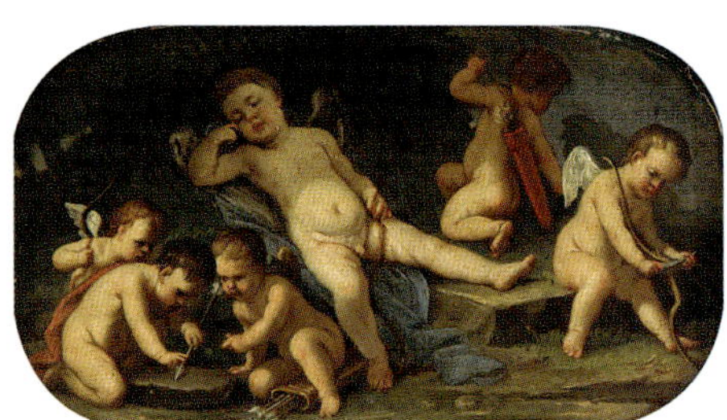

Giordano, Luca (follower of) 1634–1705
Cupids at Play 18th C
oil on canvas 15.2 x 26.7
185

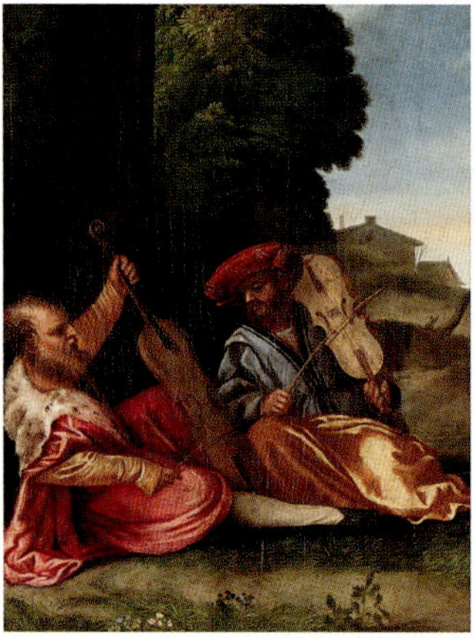

Giovanni da Asola (attributed to) d.1531
Musicians in a Landscape c.1516
oil on panel 56 x 43.2
579

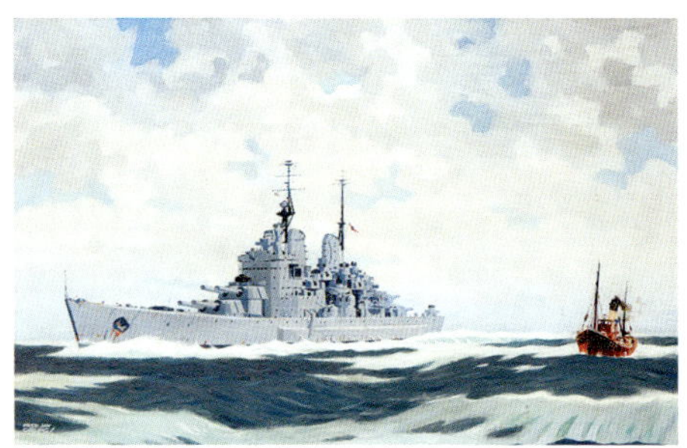

Girling, Fred Jay 1900–1982
HMS 'Vanguard' after 1943
oil on canvas 55.2 x 86.3
T.1973.10.ai

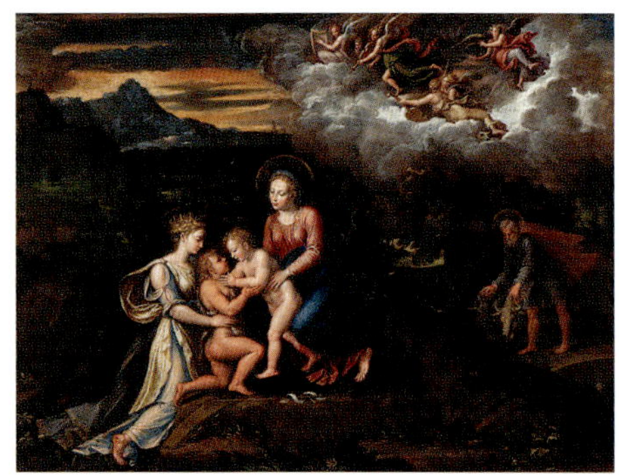

Girolamo da Carpi c.1501–1556
*Virgin and Child in a Landscape with the
Child Baptist and Saint Catherine of
Alexandria* c.1545
oil on panel 61.5 x 82
1587

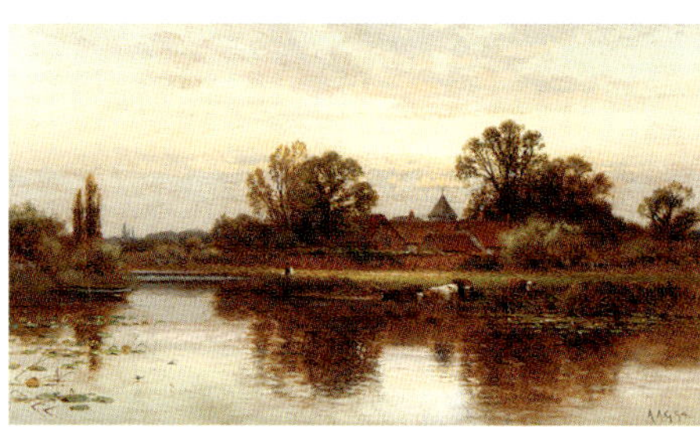

Glendening, Alfred Augustus 1840–1921
Lady Place, Hurley-on-Thames 1894
oil on canvas 33 x 53.3
1513

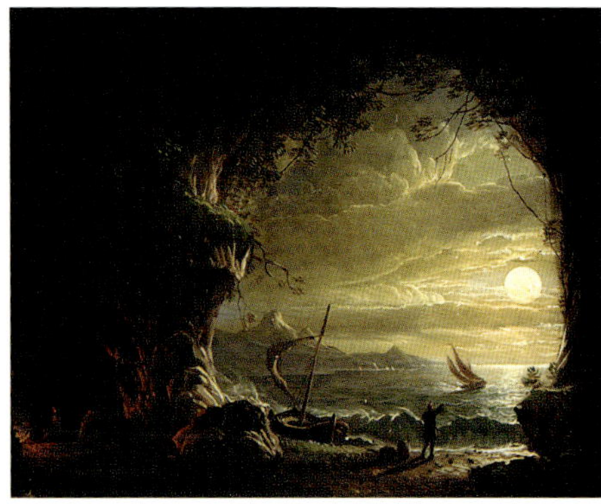

Glover, Edmund 1816–1860
Landscape, Moonlight
oil on panel 17.8 x 20.3
1088

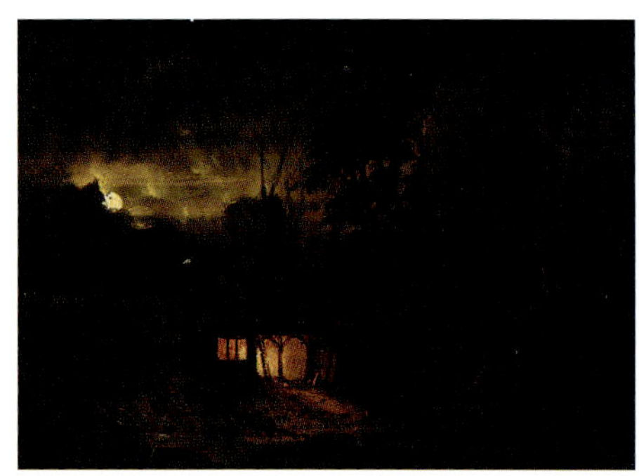

Glover, Edmund 1816–1860
Rothesay Castle, Moonlight
oil on canvas 25.4 x 35.6
426

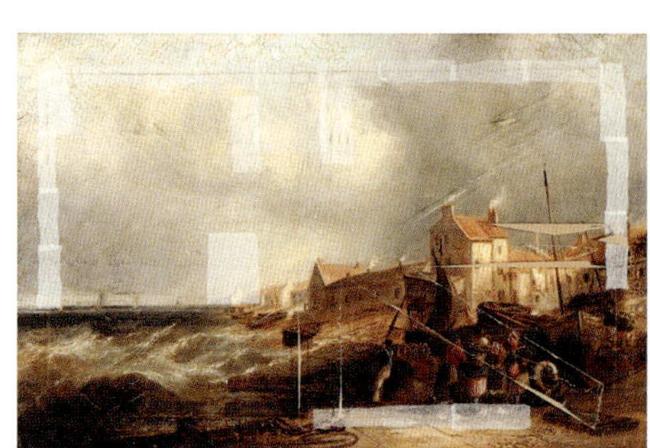

Glover, Edmund 1816–1860
Village of Newhaven, near Edinburgh
oil on canvas 49.5 x 74.9
375

Facing page: Hutchison, Robert Gemmell, 1855–1936, *When the Day Is Done*, (p. 216)

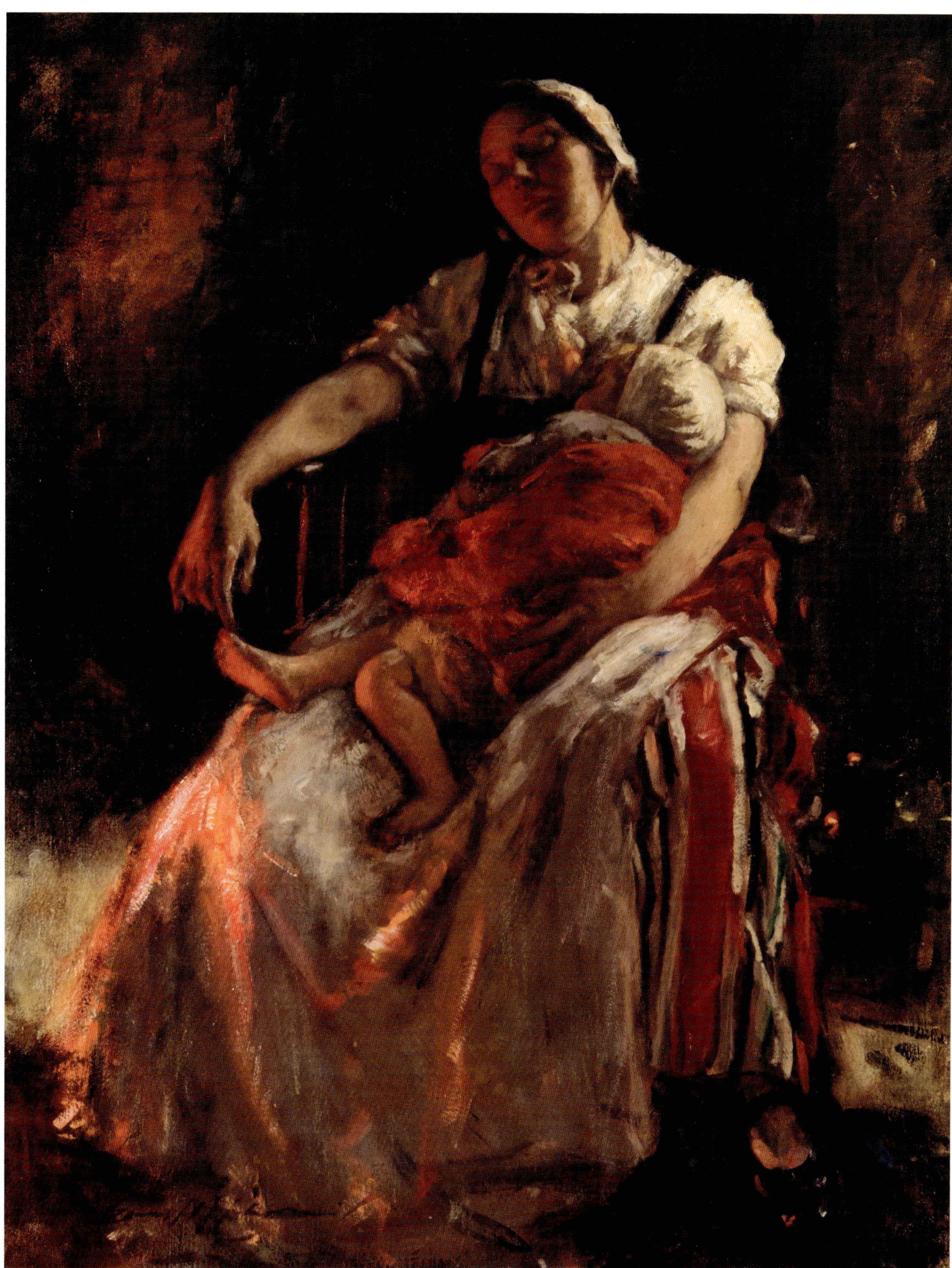

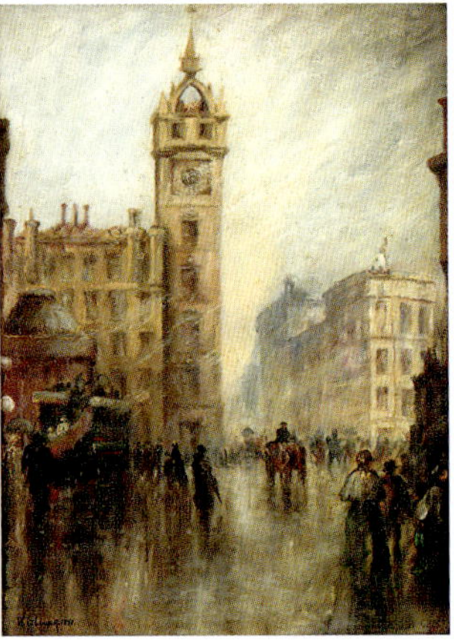

Glover, William 1836–1916
Glasgow Cross from the Saltmarket 1871
oil on canvas 74.9 x 59.1
OG.1960.14

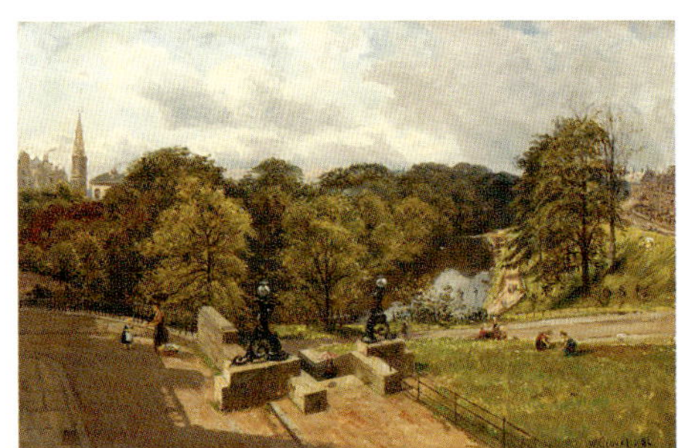

Glover, William 1836–1916
The River Kelvin from the North at the Botanic Gardens 1884
oil on canvas 55.9 x 83.8
1871

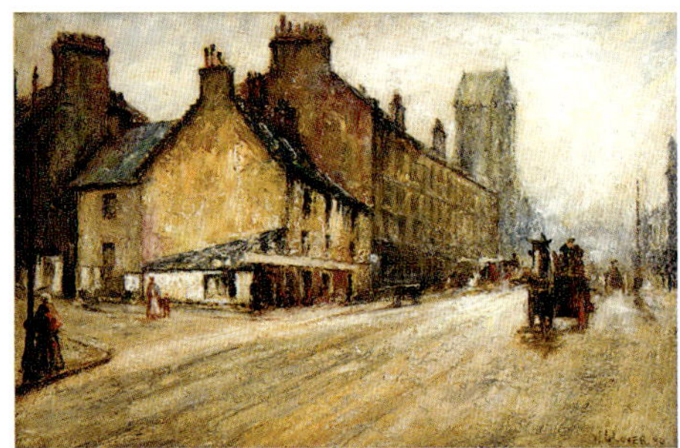

Glover, William 1836–1916
Castle Street, Glasgow 1890
oil on canvas 56.7 x 74.5
OG.1960.13

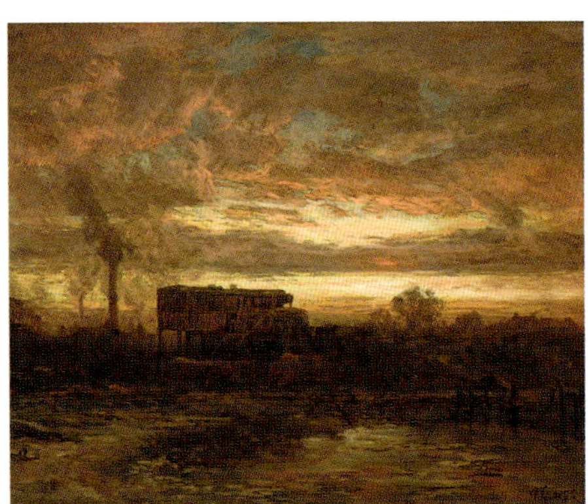

Glover, William 1836–1916
Glenboig Clay Mill
oil on millboard 45.7 x 53.3
2166

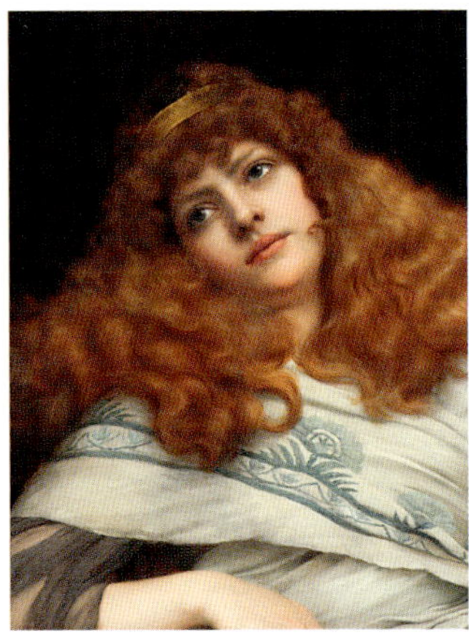

Godward, John William 1861–1922
A Lady 1895
oil on canvas 55.9 x 43.2
1496

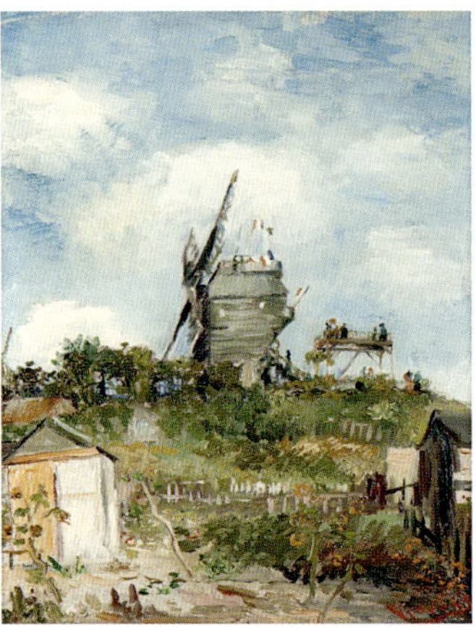

Gogh, Vincent van 1853–1890
The Blute-Fin Windmill, Montmartre 1886
oil on canvas 45.4 x 37.5
2425

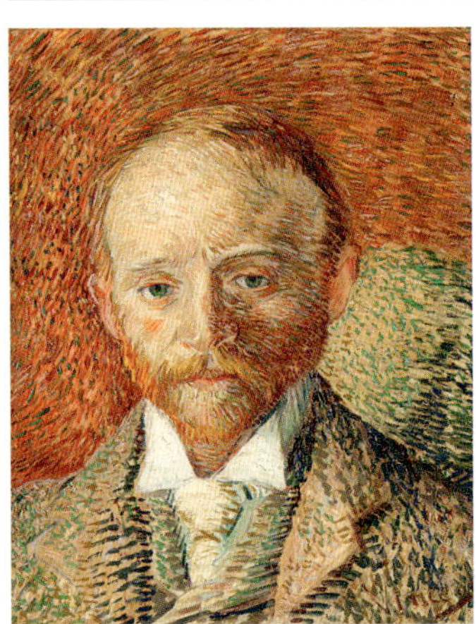

Gogh, Vincent van 1853–1890
Alexander Reid (1854–1928) 1887
oil on board 42 x 33
3315

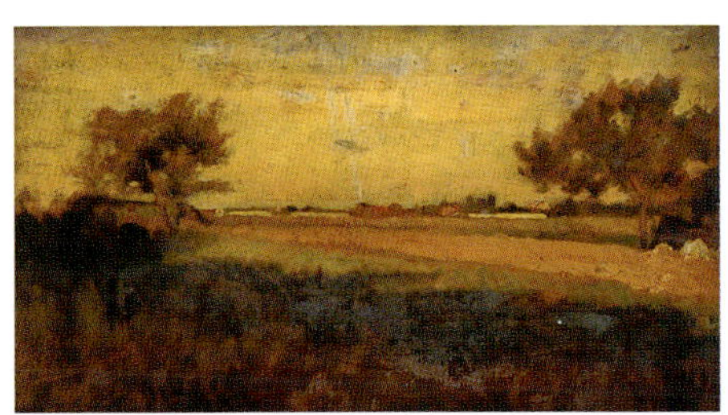

Gogin, Charles 1844–1931
A Road in France
oil on panel 25.4 x 39.4
2372

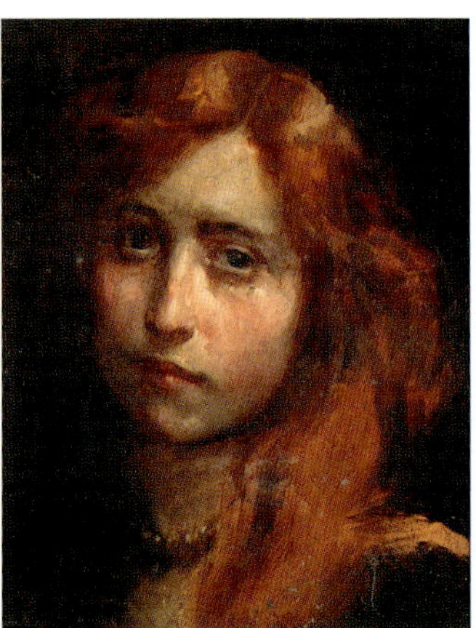

Gogin, Charles 1844–1931
Thelma
oil on canvas 38.7 x 30.5
2371

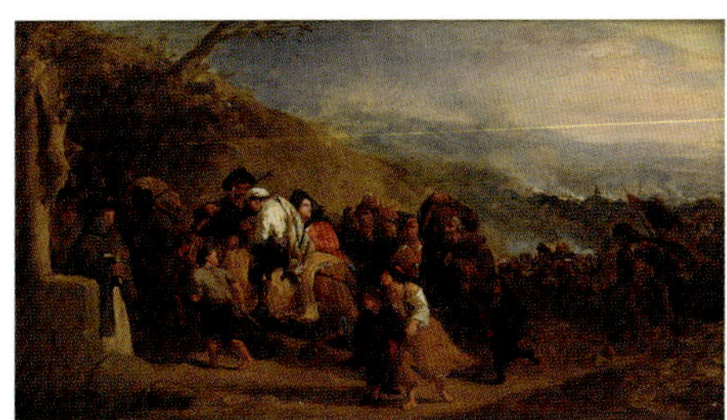

Goodall, Frederick 1822–1904
*Spanish Peasants Retreating from the French
Army* 1846
oil on canvas 15.2 x 27.9
1162

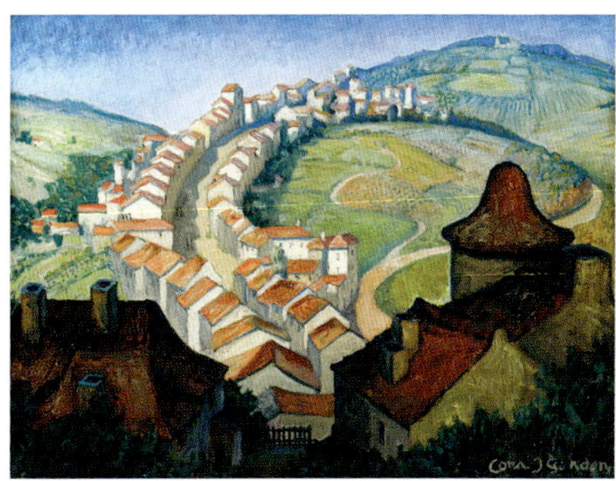

Gordon, Cora Josephine 1879–1950
France: The Village on the Hills
oil on canvas 71.1 x 91.4
2865

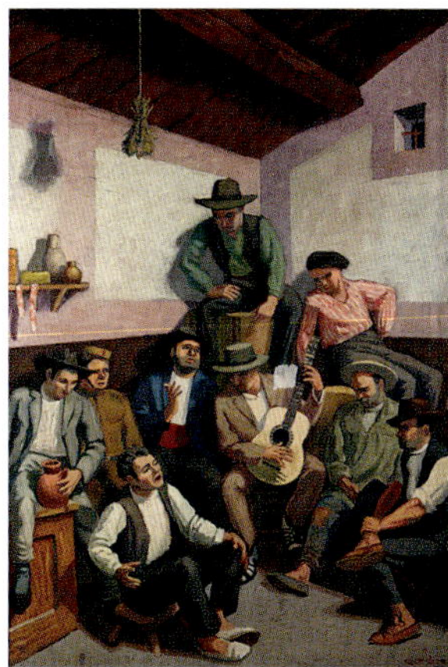

Gordon, Jan (Godfrey Jervis) 1882–1944
The Gipsy Singer
oil on canvas 130.8 x 88.9
2867

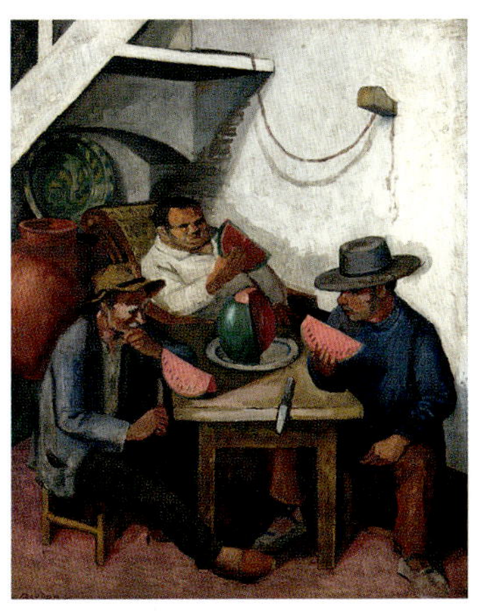

Gordon, Jan (Godfrey Jervis) 1882–1944
The Melon Guzzlers
oil on canvas 92.1 x 73
2866

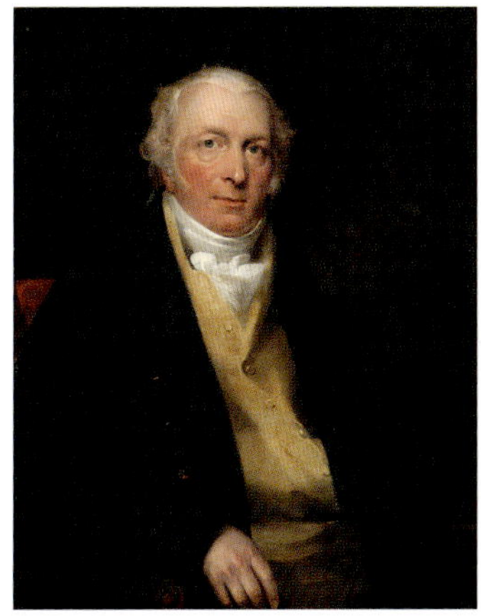

Gordon, John Watson 1788–1864
Alexander Dunlop of Keppoch (1766–1840)
c.1800–1825
oil on canvas 89.5 x 67.9
OG.1961.10.s

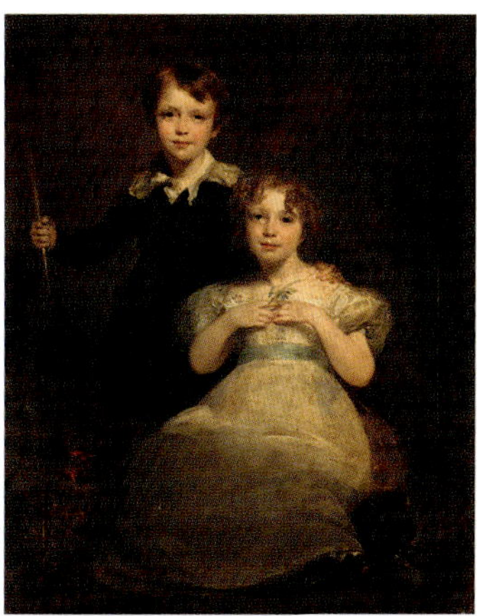

Gordon, John Watson 1788–1864
A Boy and a Girl 1820s
oil on canvas 127 x 101.6
1296

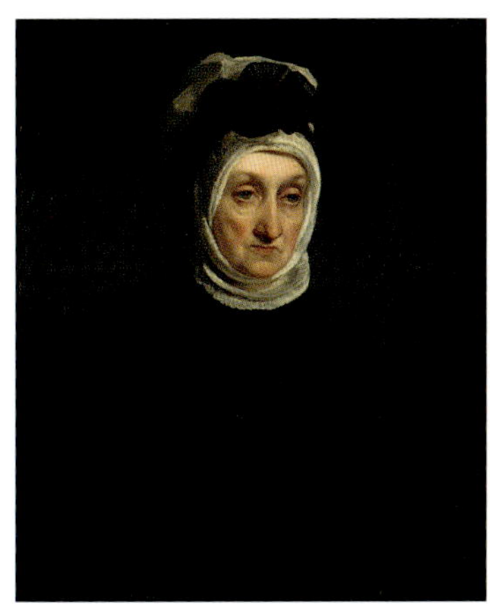

Gordon, John Watson 1788–1864
Elizabeth Galloway (or Grieve), *of Sandyhills*
(d.1826) 1820s
oil on canvas 76.2 x 63.5
1067

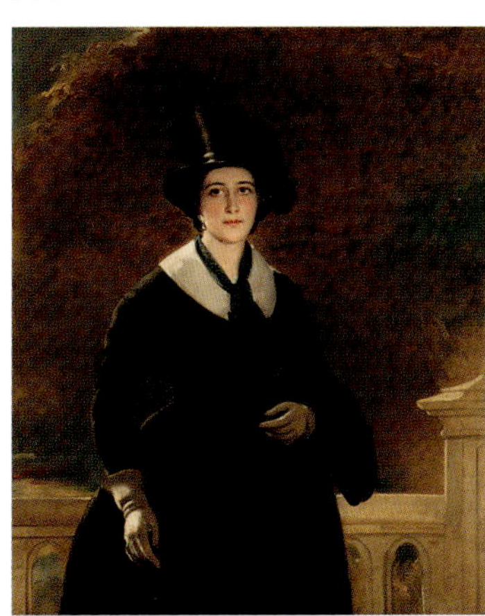

Gordon, John Watson 1788–1864
The Honourable Mrs Alexander Macalister
1843
oil on canvas 127 x 101.6
2823

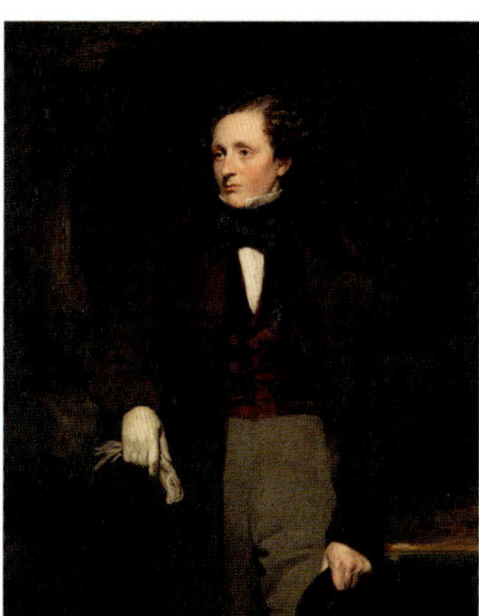

Gordon, John Watson 1788–1864
*Alexander Macalister of Loup, Torrisdale and
Strathaird (1802–1876)*
oil on canvas 127 x 101.6
2822

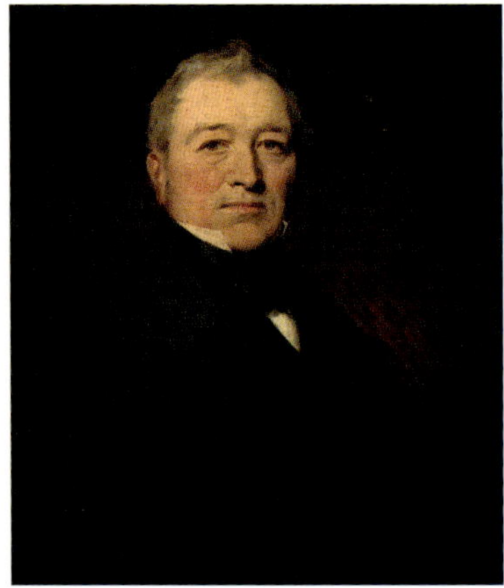

Gordon, John Watson 1788–1864
Andrew Vannan
oil on canvas 76.2 x 63.5
2554

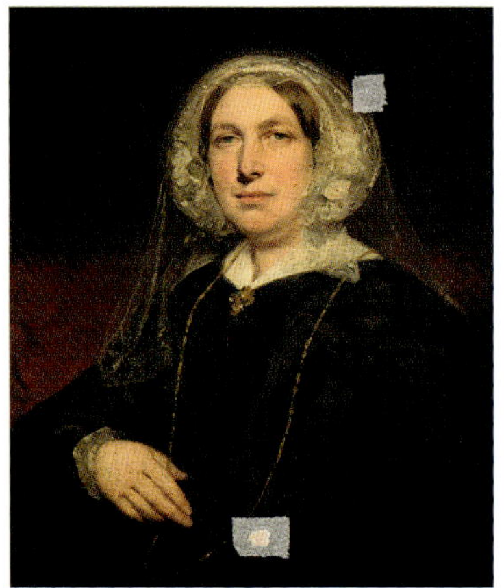

Gordon, John Watson 1788–1864
Mrs Janet D. Vannan
oil on canvas 76.2 x 63.5
2555

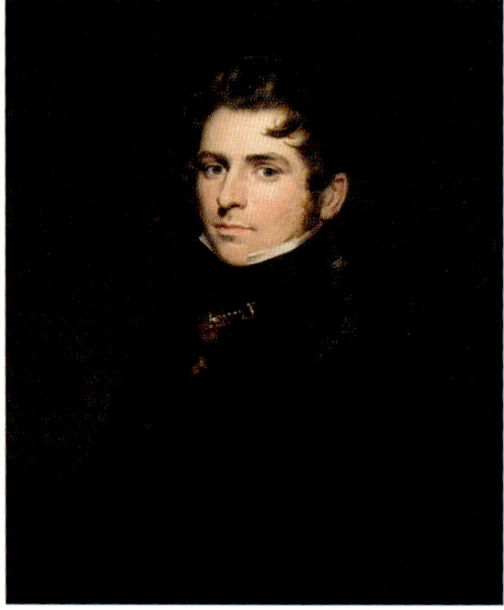

Gordon, John Watson 1788–1864
Charles Heath Wilson (1809–1882)
oil on canvas 73.7 x 61
1362

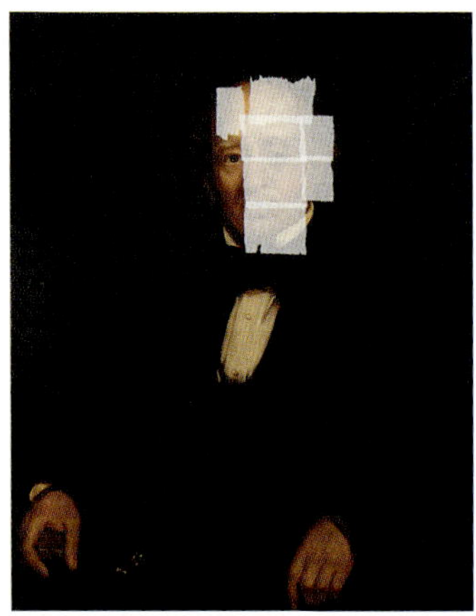

Gordon, John Watson 1788–1864
James Grant
oil on canvas 91.4 x 71.1
2595

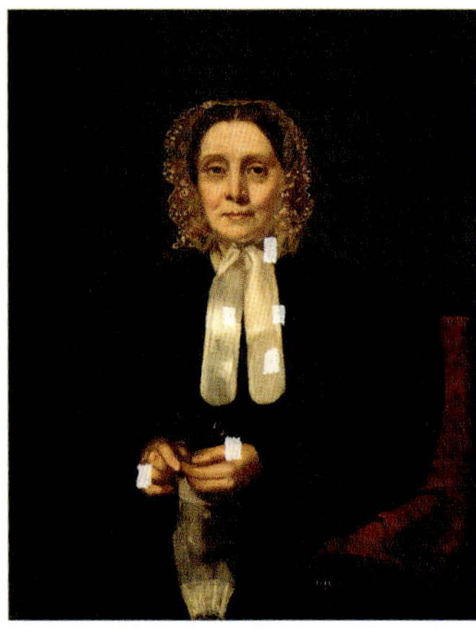

Gordon, John Watson 1788–1864
Mrs James Grant
oil on canvas 91.4 x 71.1
2596

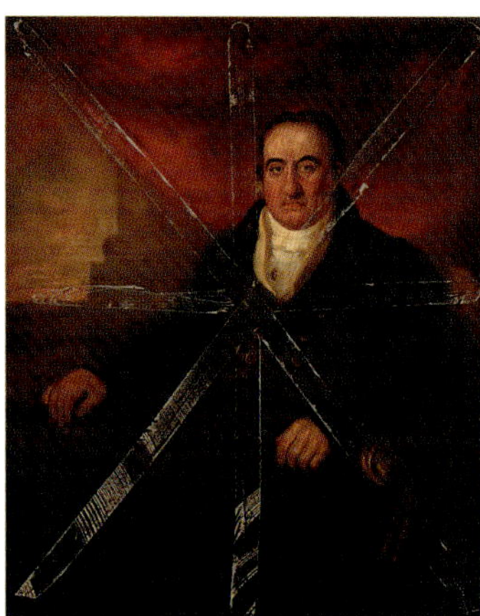

Gordon, John Watson 1788–1864
*John Geddes of Verreville Pottery and
Glassworks, Anderston*
oil on canvas 127 x 101.6
L.1.1947 (P)

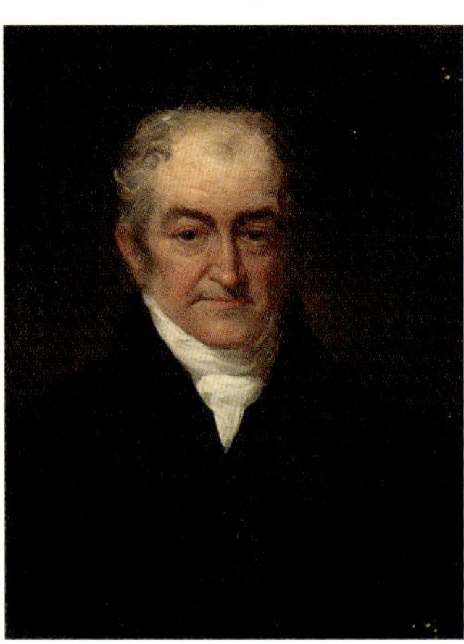

Gordon, John Watson 1788–1864
Portrait of a Gentleman
oil on canvas 61 x 45.7
2910

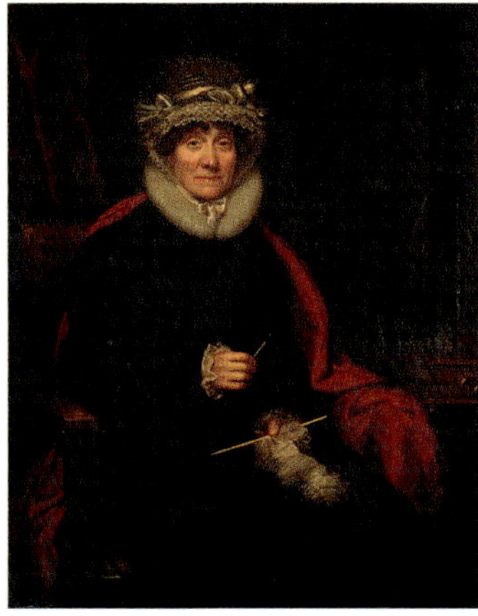

Gordon, John Watson 1788–1864
Portrait of a Lady
oil on canvas 125.7 x 99.7
1360

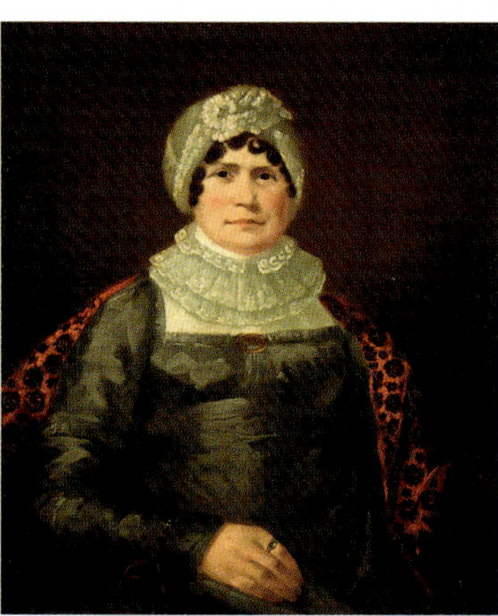

Gordon, John Watson 1788–1864
Mrs William Scott of Sandyfaulds
oil on canvas 76.2 x 63.5
2830

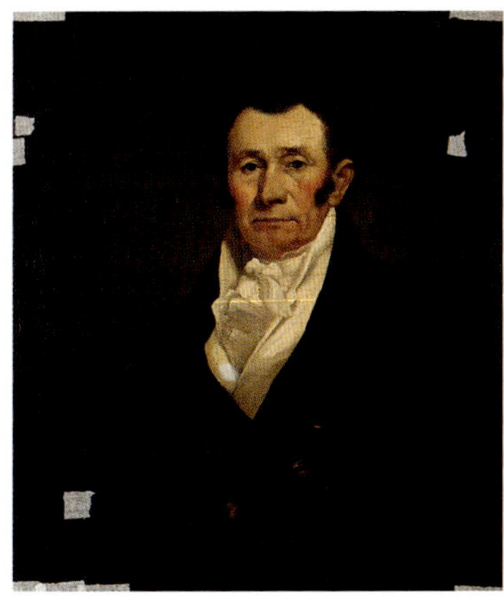

Gordon, John Watson 1788–1864
William Scott of Sandyfaulds
oil on canvas 76.2 x 63.5
2829

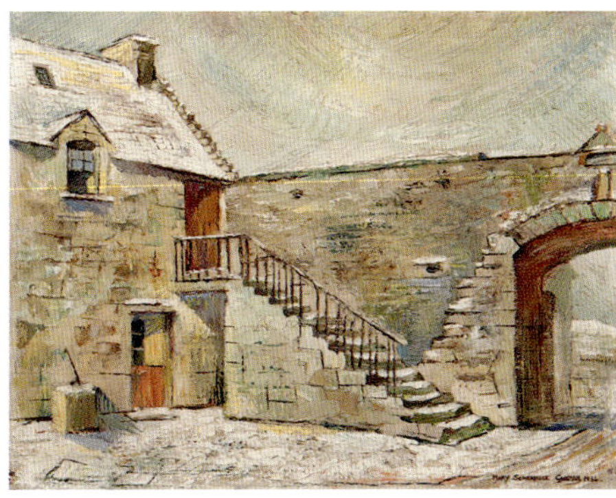

Gossman, Mary Hislop Somerville
Provan Hall, Glasgow 1934
oil on canvas 40.7 x 51
TEMP.8504

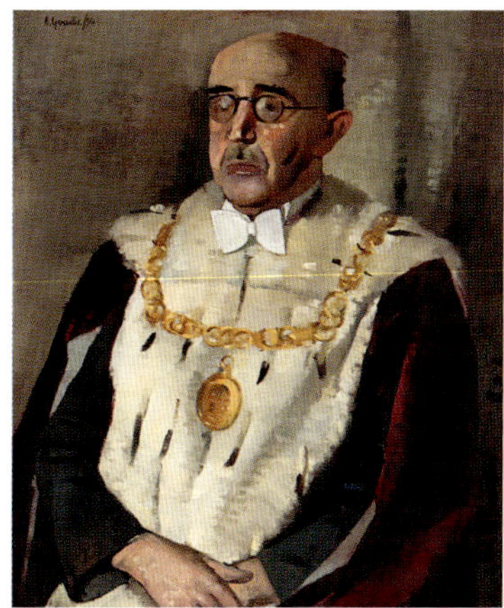

Goudie, Alexander 1933–2004
Andrew Hood (b.1887), LLD, Lord Provost of Glasgow (1955–1958) 1956
acrylic on canvas 76.2 x 63.5
OG.1962.42.a

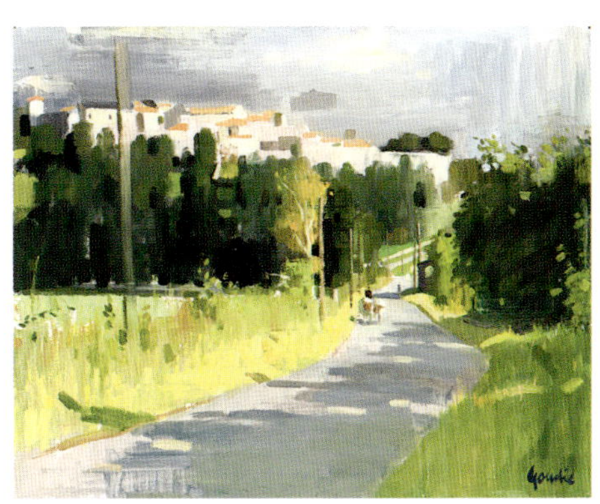

Goudie, Alexander 1933–2004
Evening Light, Saint-Lizier 1959
oil on canvas 50.8 x 60.8
3118

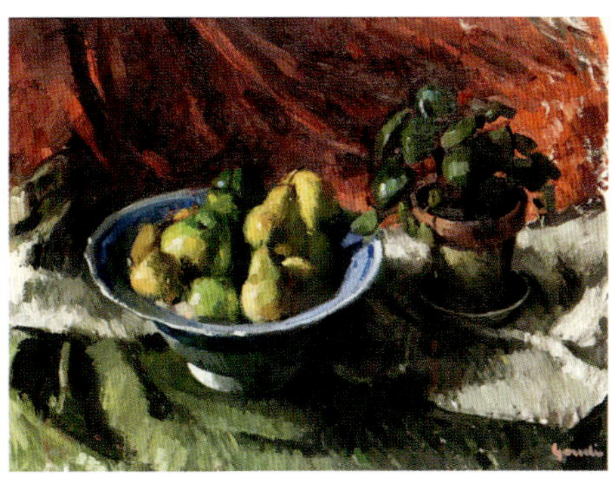

Goudie, Alexander 1933–2004
Still Life with a Bowl of Fruit c.1964
oil on canvas 71.1 x 91.1
3219

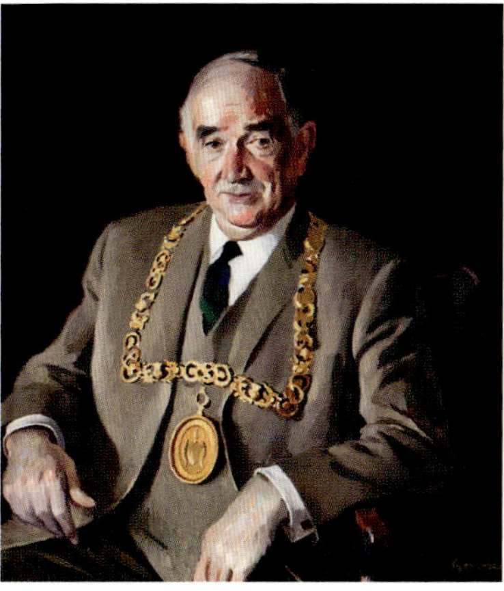

Goudie, Alexander 1933–2004
John Johnston, Lord Provost of Glasgow (1965–1969) 1970
oil on canvas 86.7 x 76.2
3271

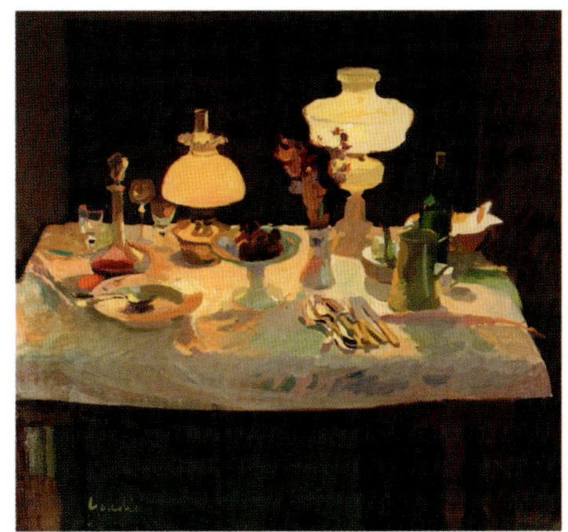

Goudie, Alexander 1933–2004
Après le repas du soir c.1972
oil on canvas 121.5 x 127
3289

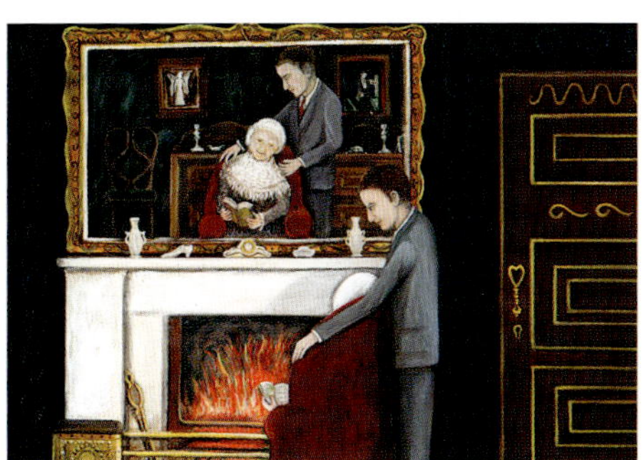

Goulding, Arthur b.1921
Reflections
oil on hardboard 37.7 x 53
3589

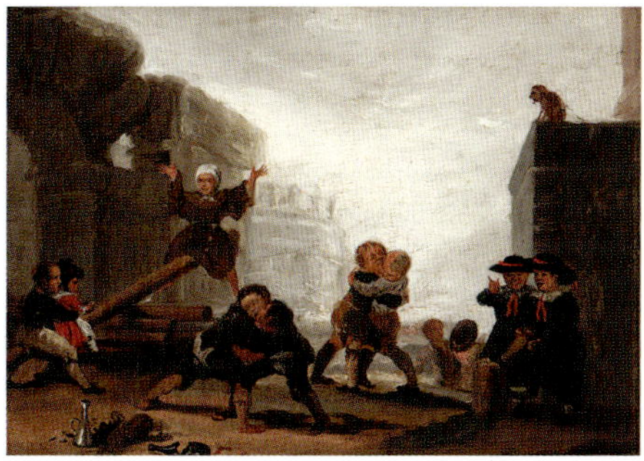

Goya, Francisco de 1746–1828
Boys Playing at See-Saw c.1775–1799
oil on canvas 29.8 x 41.9
PC.24

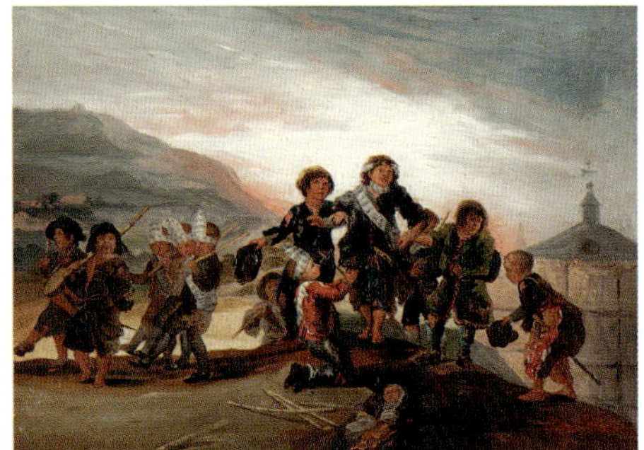

Goya, Francisco de 1746–1828
Boys Playing at Soldiers c.1775–1799
oil on canvas 29.2 x 41.9
PC.27

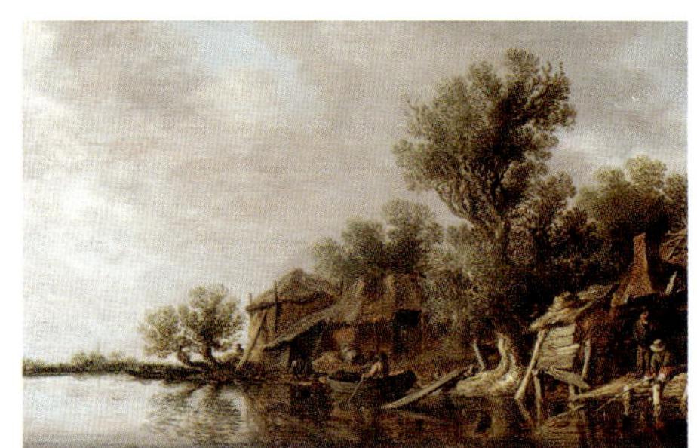

Goyen, Jan van 1596–1656
Cottages and Fishermen by a River 1631
oil on panel 29.2 x 45.7
4

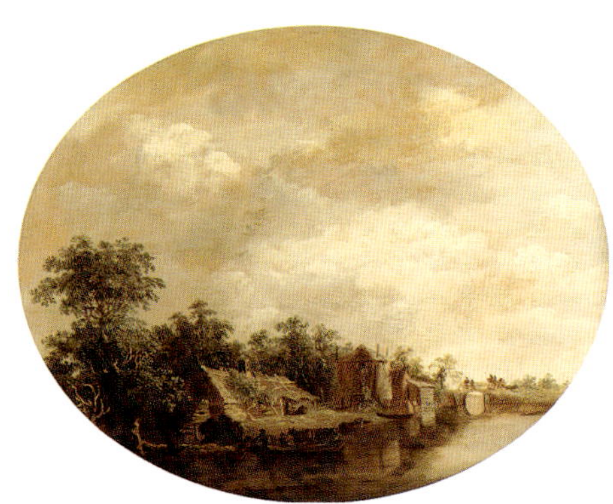

Goyen, Jan van (after) 1596–1656
Cottages by a Canal c.1752–1766
oil on panel 45.4 x 55.9
276

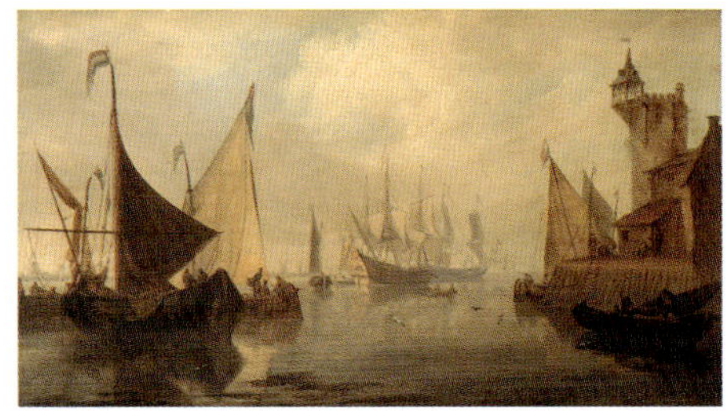

Goyen, Jan van (follower of) 1596–1656
Shipping Scene
oil on panel 15.6 x 31.8
PL.114 (P)

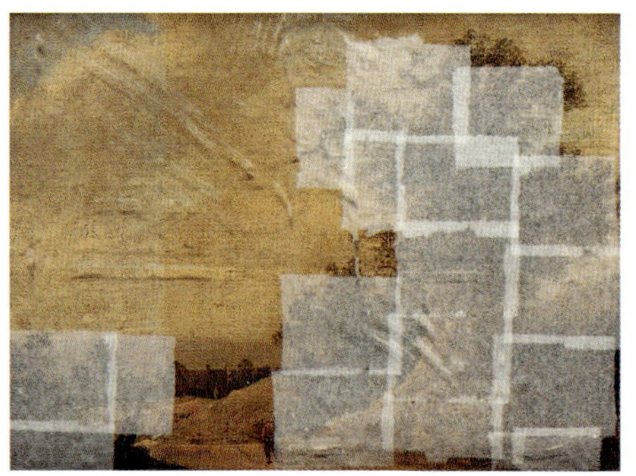

Goyen, Jan van (style of) 1596–1656
Landscape with an Old Oak Tree
17th C–18th C
oil on canvas 37.8 x 47.6
619

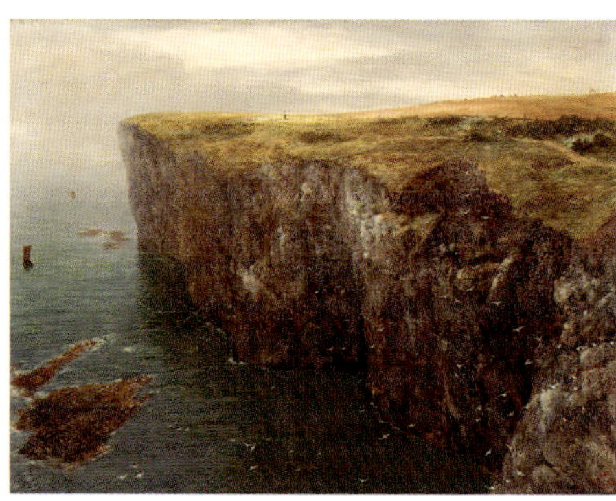

Graham, Peter 1836–1921
Along the Cliffs 1868
oil on canvas 88.9 x 106.7
1165

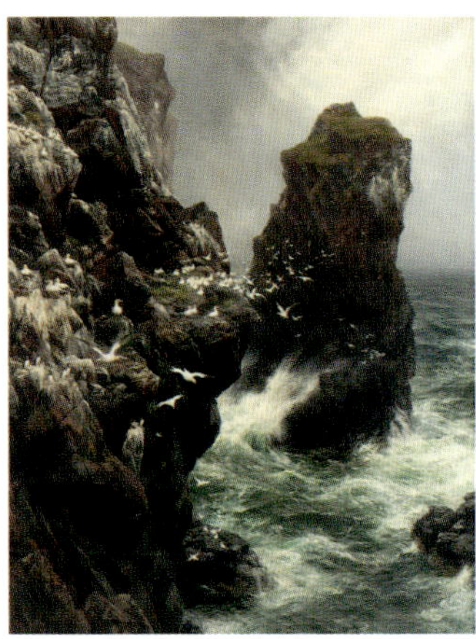

Graham, Peter 1836–1921
Where Gannets Build 1896
oil on canvas 172.7 x 129.5
1876

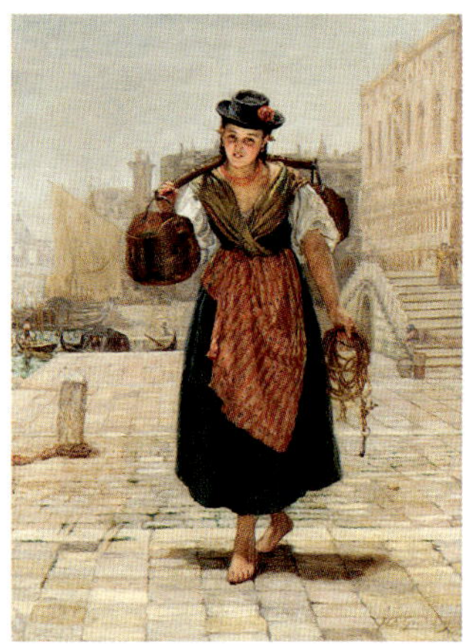

Graham, Thomas Alexander Ferguson
1840–1906
Venetian Water Girl
oil on canvas 77.5 x 57.2
927

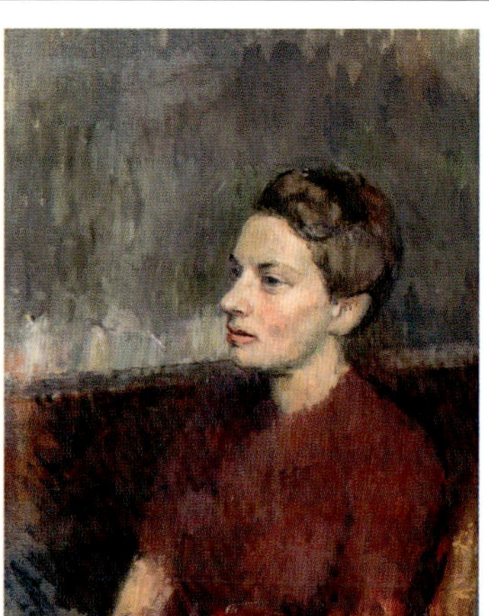

Graham Bell, Frank 1910–1943
Miss Pool
oil on canvas 61 x 50
2460

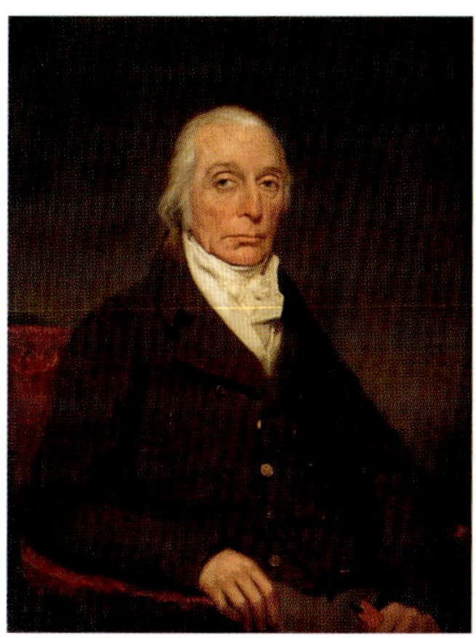

Graham-Gilbert, John 1794–1866
James Hopkirk of Dalbeth (1749–1836)
c.1814–1835
oil on canvas 91.4 x 69.9
894

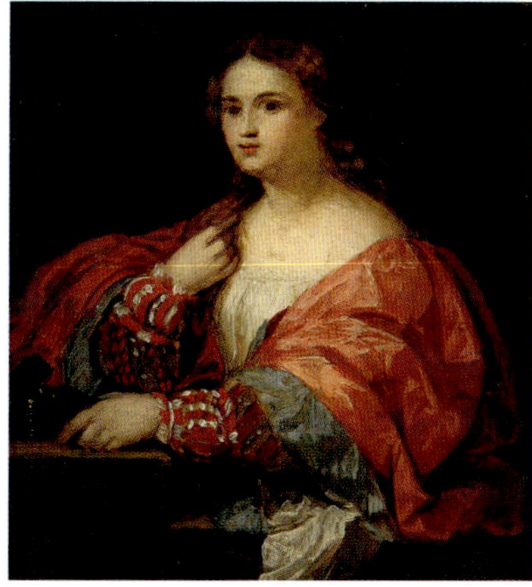

Graham-Gilbert, John 1794–1866
Figure of a Lady (after Jacopo Palma il
vecchio) c.1820–1825
oil on panel 22.2 x 17.8
547

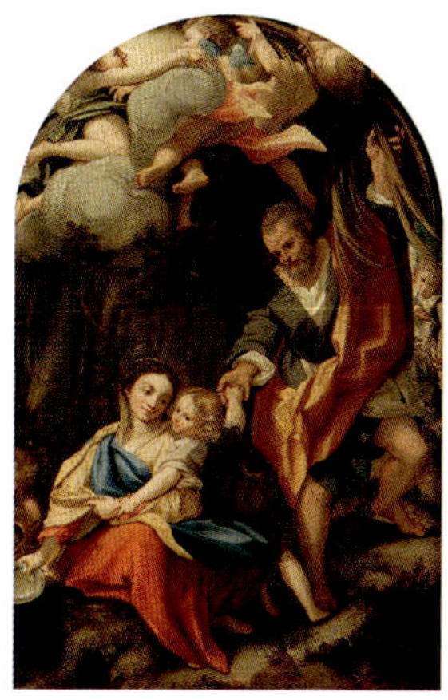

Graham-Gilbert, John 1794–1866
Madonna della scodella (after Correggio)
c.1820–1825
oil on paper on canvas 50.8 x 33
541

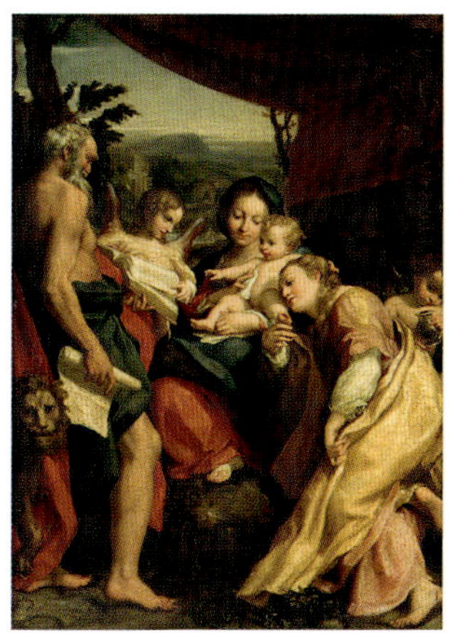

Graham-Gilbert, John 1794–1866
Madonna with Saint Jerome (after Correggio)
c.1820–1825
oil on paper on canvas 48.9 x 34.9
542

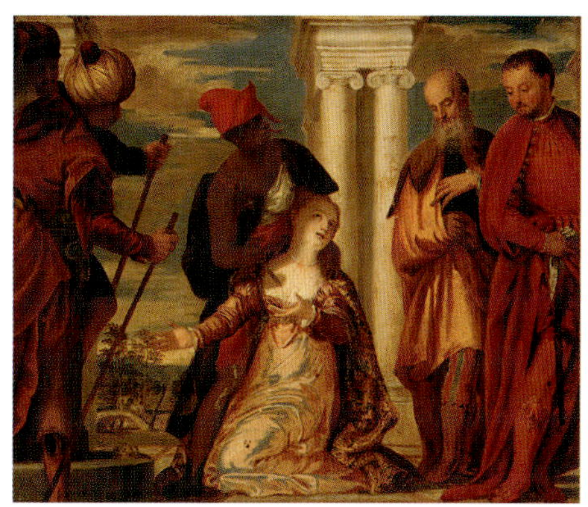

Graham-Gilbert, John 1794–1866
The Martyrdom of Saint Justina (after Paolo
Veronese) c.1820–1825
oil on canvas 45.7 x 51.1
564

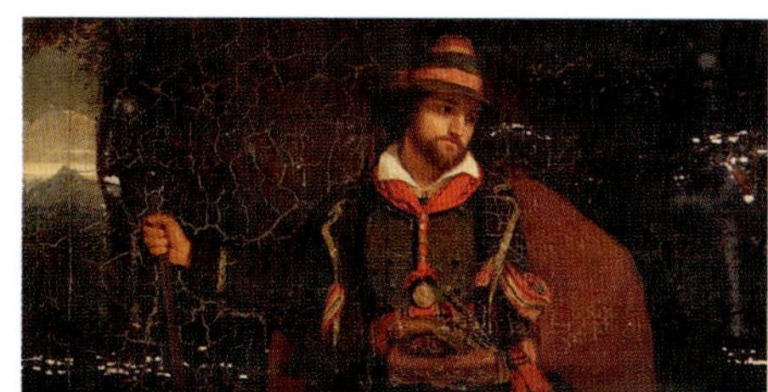

Graham-Gilbert, John 1794–1866
A Tyrolese Hunter 1826
oil on canvas 76.2 x 62.2
501

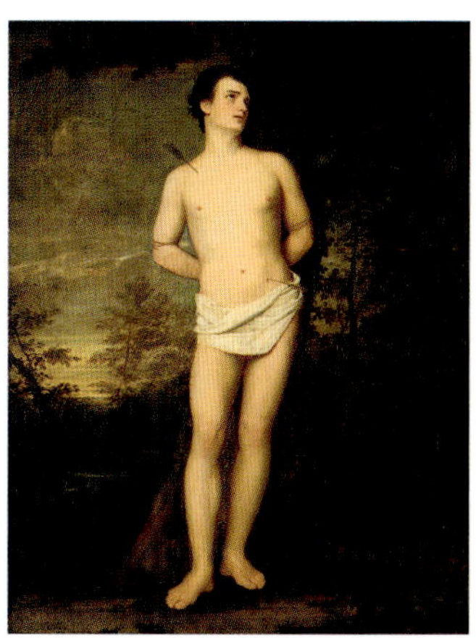

Graham-Gilbert, John 1794–1866
Saint Sebastian 1826
oil on canvas 96.5 x 72.4
525

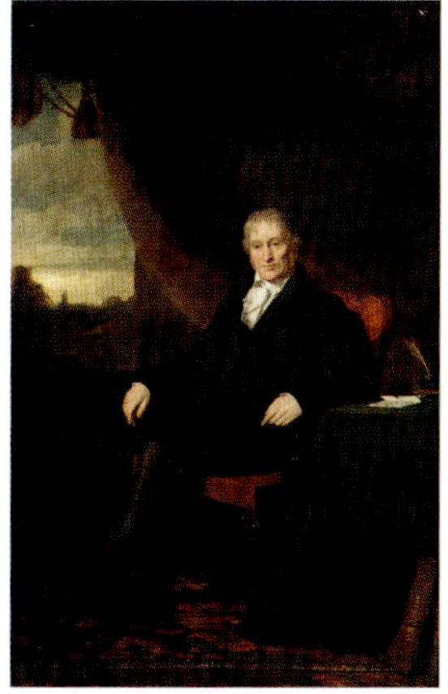

Graham-Gilbert, John 1794–1866
*James Dennistoun, Esq. of Golfhill
(1758–1835)* 1829
oil on canvas 238.7 x 147.3
NR.102

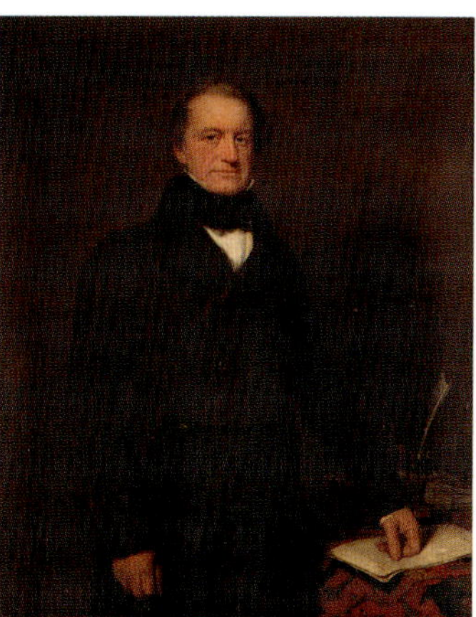

Graham-Gilbert, John 1794–1866
*John T. Alston (1780–1857), Provost of
Glasgow (1820–1821)* 1832
oil on canvas 127 x 101.6
1808

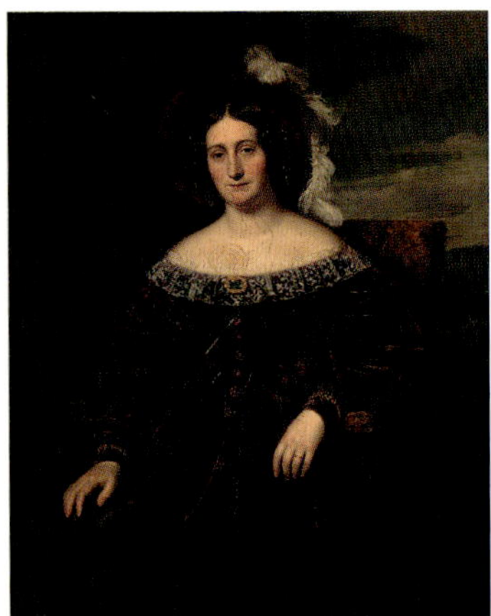

Graham-Gilbert, John 1794–1866
Mrs Hugh Robertson of Gartloch (1798–1846)
1841
oil on canvas 127 x 101.6
3048

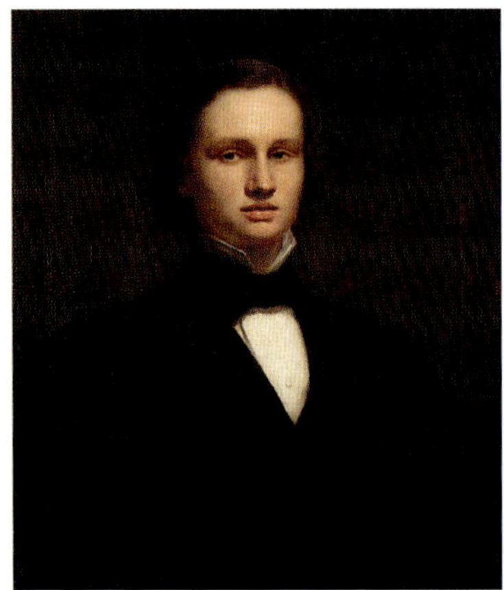

Graham-Gilbert, John 1794–1866
Lord Kelvin William Thomson (1824–1907), at the Age of 22 c.1846
oil on canvas 76.2 x 63.5
1484

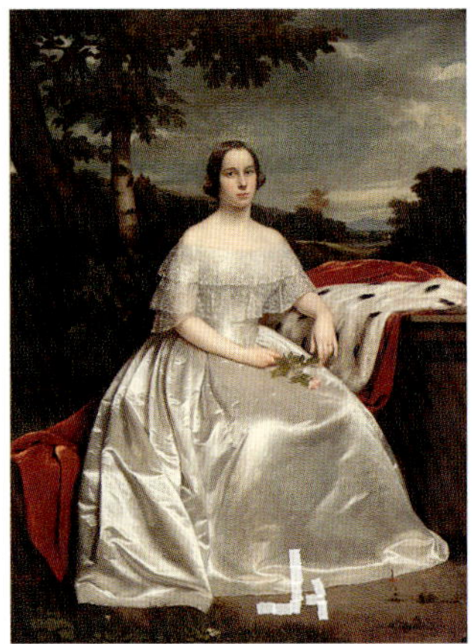

Graham-Gilbert, John 1794–1866
Mrs James Scott of Kelly 1850
oil on canvas 203.2 x 147.3
2590

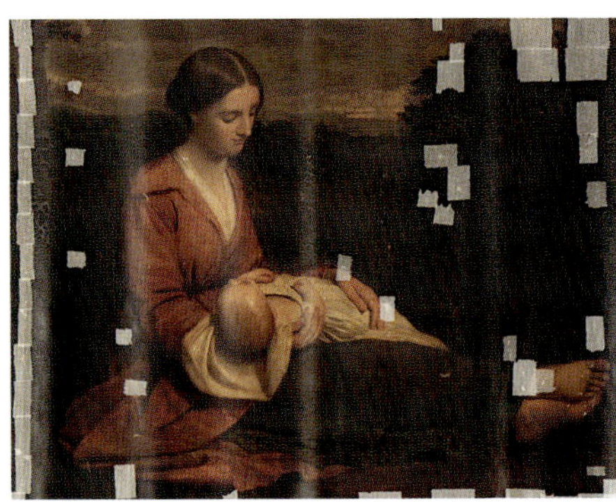

Graham-Gilbert, John 1794–1866
The First Born 1853
oil on canvas 110.5 x 148
534

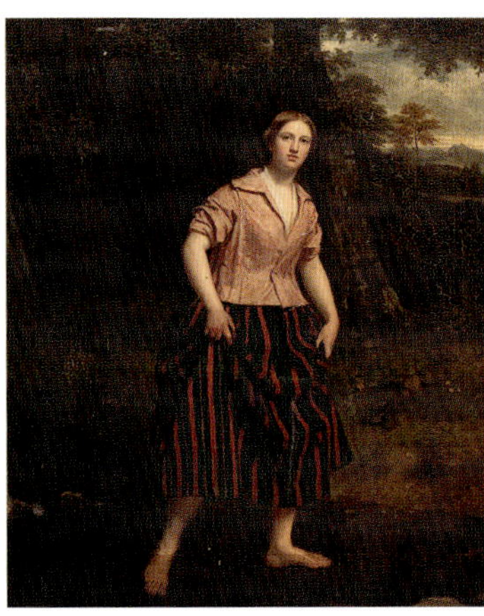

Graham-Gilbert, John 1794–1866
Crossing the Ford 1859
oil on canvas 127 x 91.4
505

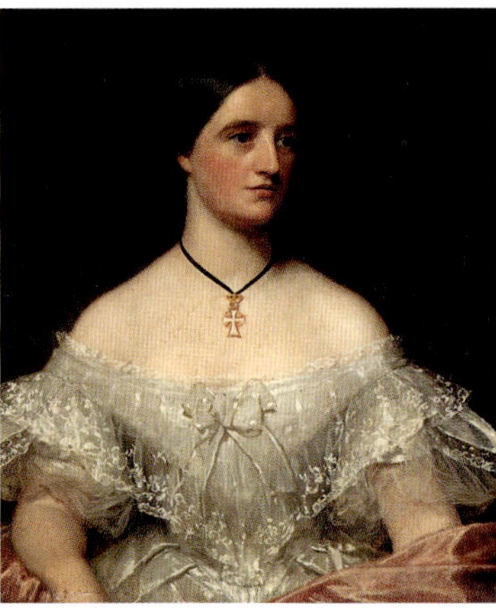

Graham-Gilbert, John 1794–1866
Mrs John Jarvie 1850s
oil on canvas 76.2 x 63.5
2862

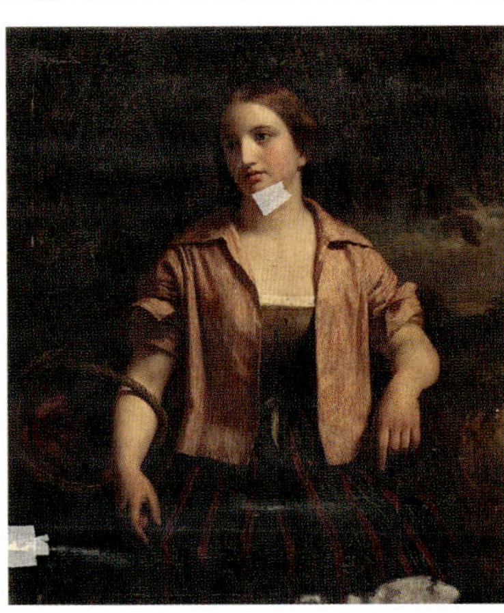

Graham-Gilbert, John 1794–1866
Going to Market 1860
oil on canvas 114.3 x 90.8
507

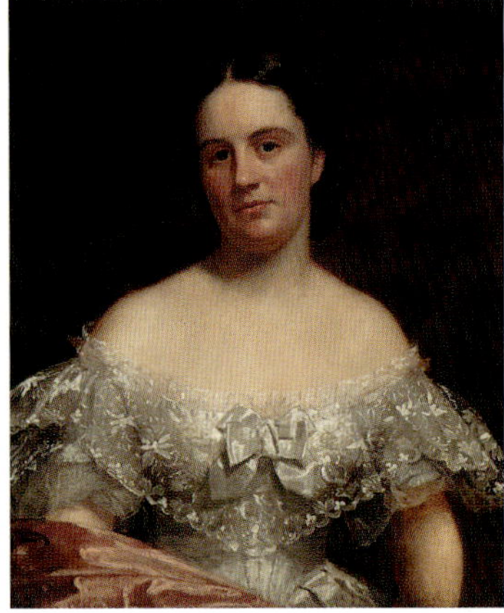

Graham-Gilbert, John 1794–1866
Mrs Agnes D'Arcy Jarvie c.1860–1866
oil on canvas 76.2 x 63.5
3166

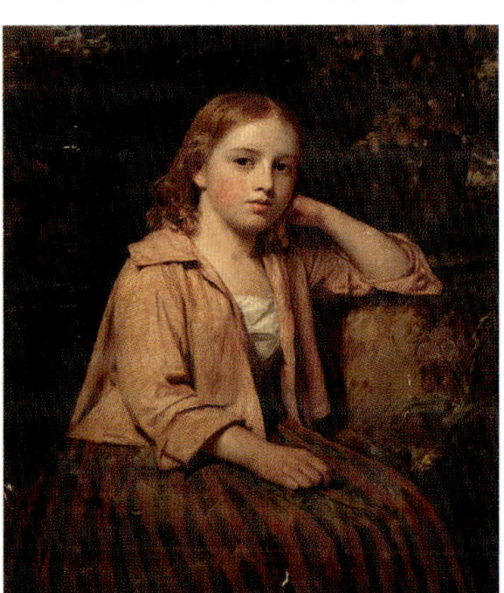

Graham-Gilbert, John 1794–1866
A Country Maid
oil on canvas 88.9 x 68.6
515

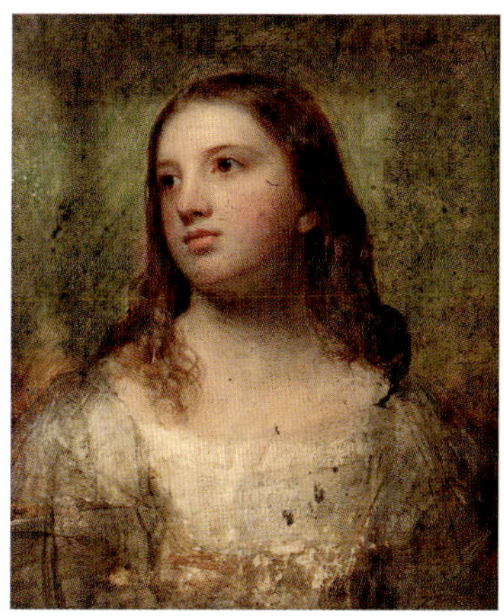

Graham-Gilbert, John 1794–1866
A Girl
oil on panel 45.7 x 38.1
532

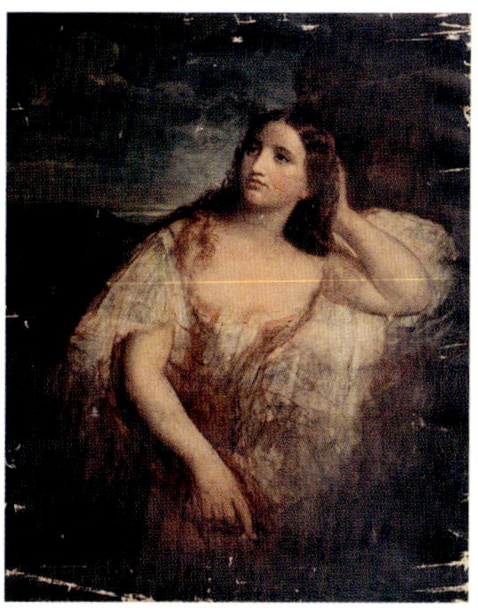

Graham-Gilbert, John 1794–1866
A Grecian Girl
oil on canvas 121.9 x 97.8
513

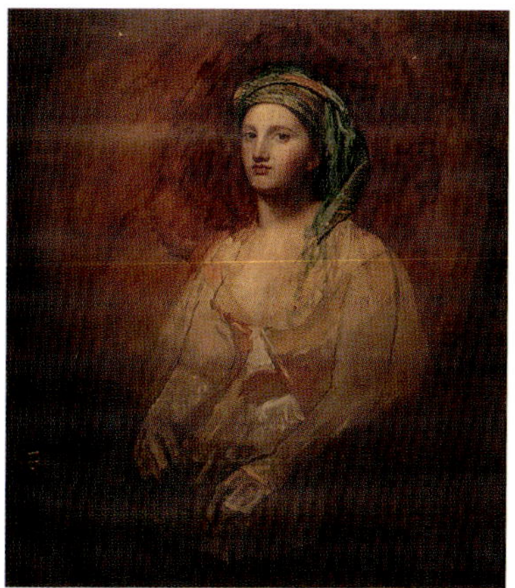

Graham-Gilbert, John 1794–1866
A Grecian Girl
oil on canvas 123.2 x 99.1
516

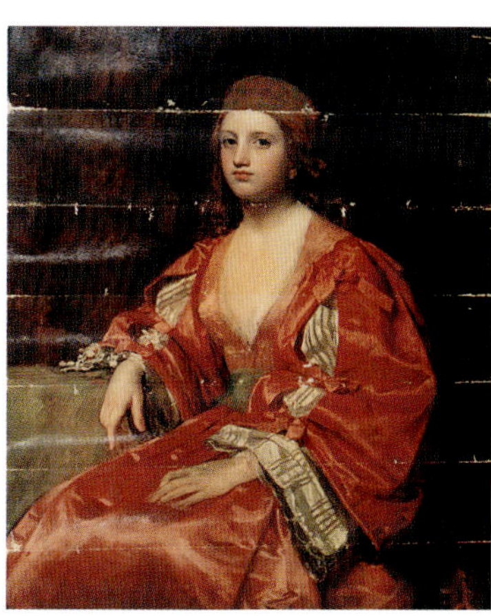

Graham-Gilbert, John 1794–1866
A Grecian Girl
oil on canvas 113 x 88.9
536

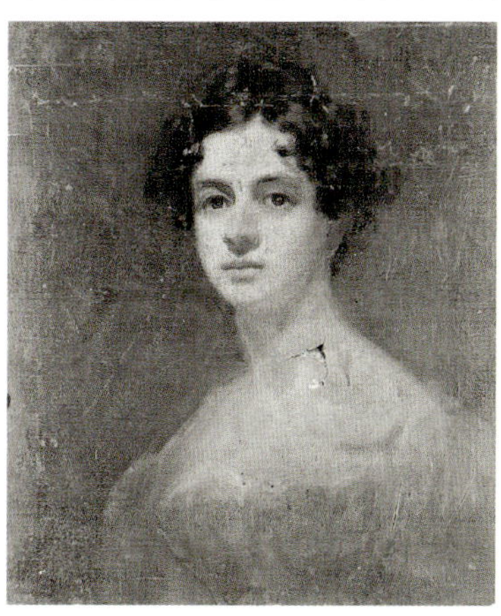

Graham-Gilbert, John 1794–1866
A Lady (after Henry Raeburn)
oil on canvas 45.7 x 38.1
548

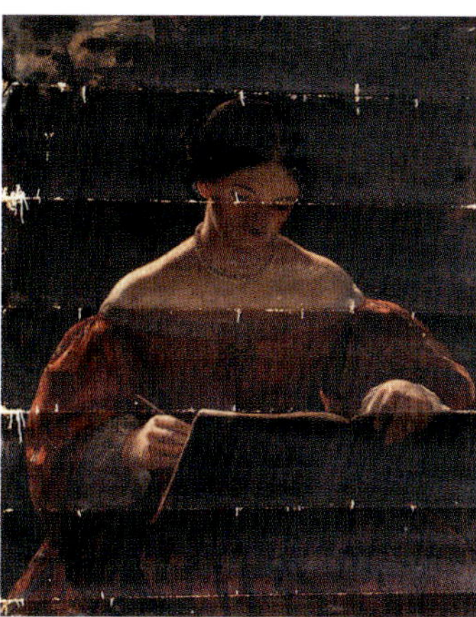

Graham-Gilbert, John 1794–1866
A Lady Sketching
oil on canvas 91.4 x 71.1
510

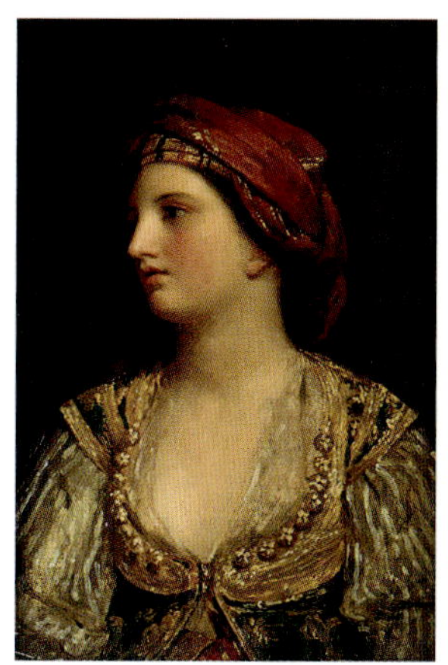

Graham-Gilbert, John 1794–1866
A Woman of Lonico
oil on panel 33.7 x 23.5
508

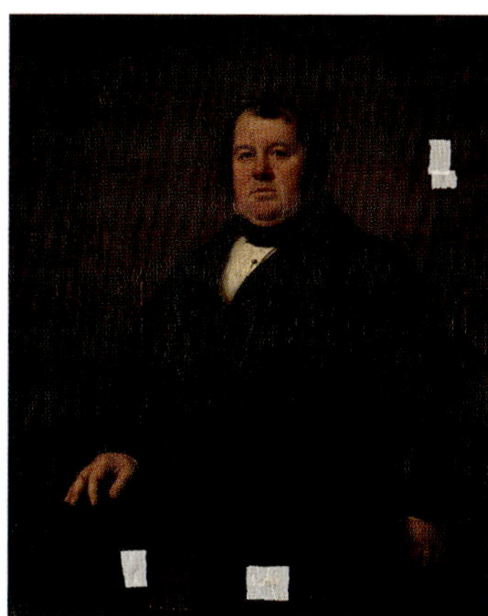

Graham-Gilbert, John 1794–1866
Andrew Stevenson Dalglish (1793–1858)
oil on canvas 127 x 101.6
NR.81

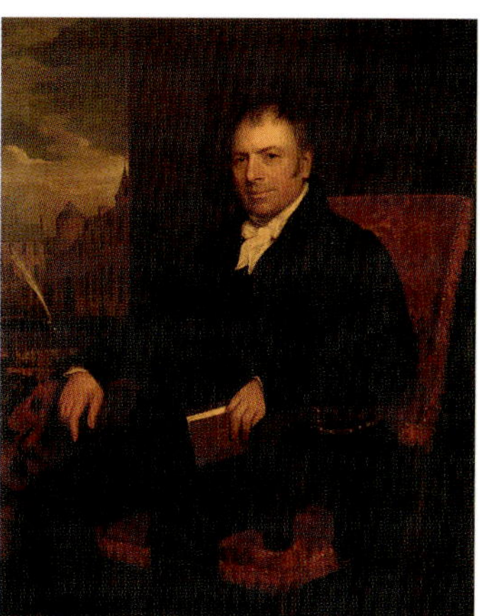

Graham-Gilbert, John 1794–1866
Bailie John Alston of Rosemount (1778–1846)
oil on canvas 127 x 101.6
2993

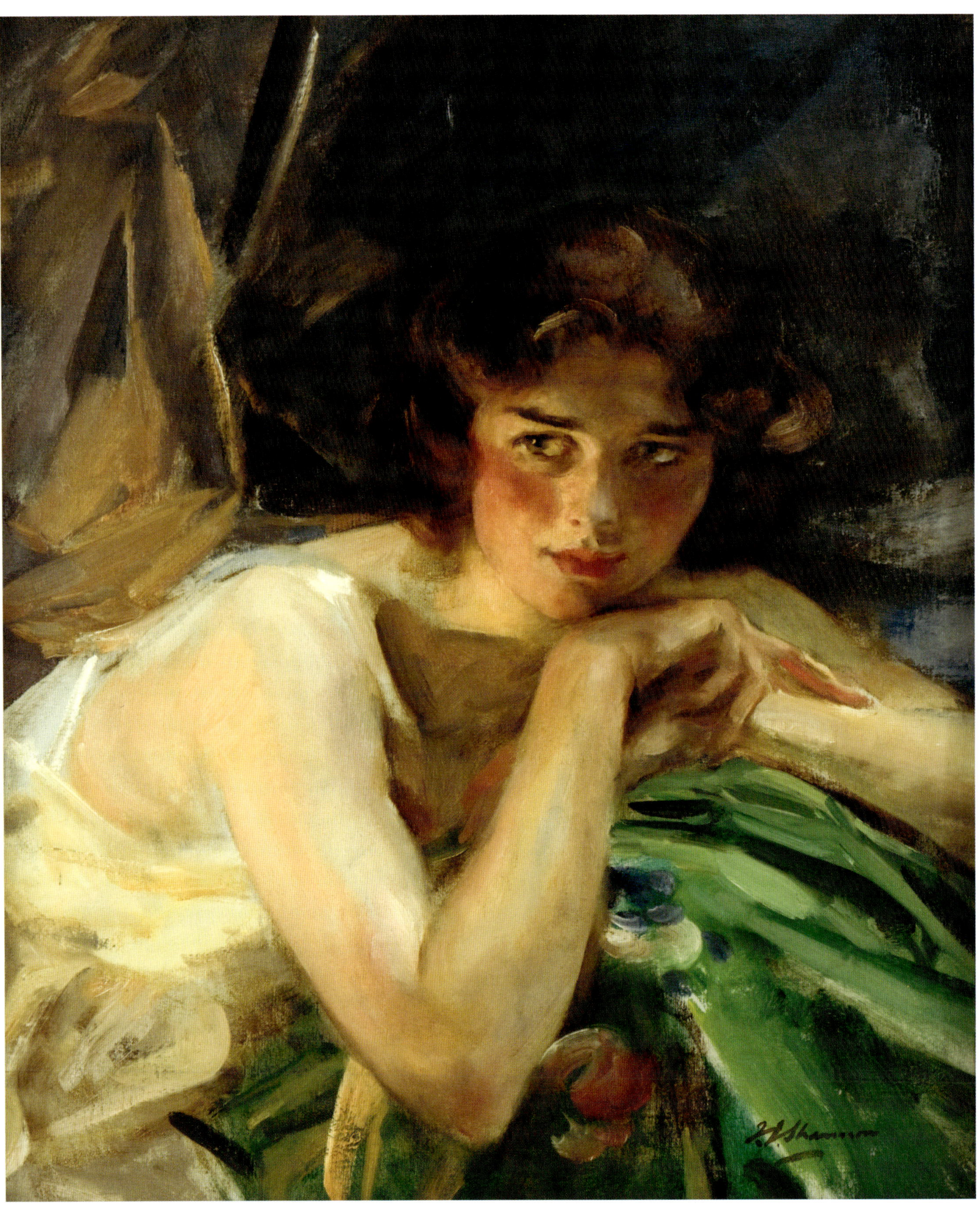

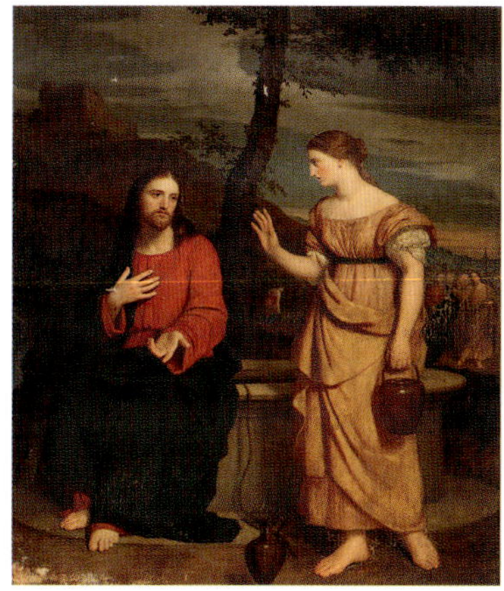

Graham-Gilbert, John 1794–1866
Christ and the Woman of Samaria
oil on canvas 125.7 x 99.1
523

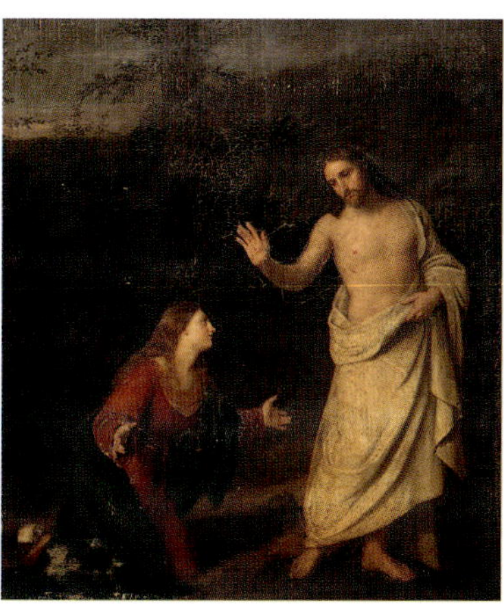

Graham-Gilbert, John 1794–1866
Christ Appearing to Mary Magdalene
oil on canvas 125.7 x 99.1
520

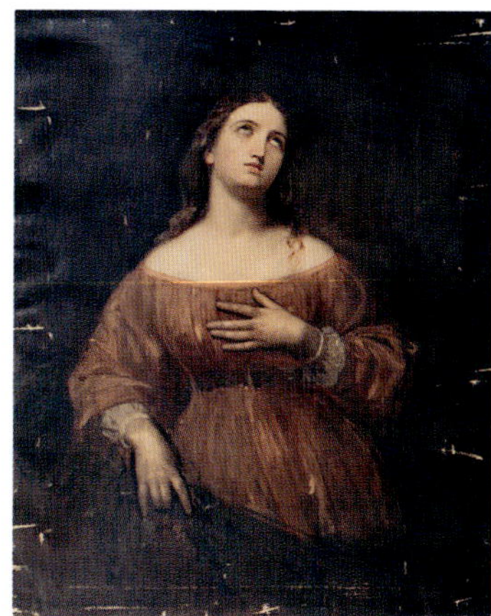

Graham-Gilbert, John 1794–1866
Contemplation
oil on canvas 115.5 x 88.9
511

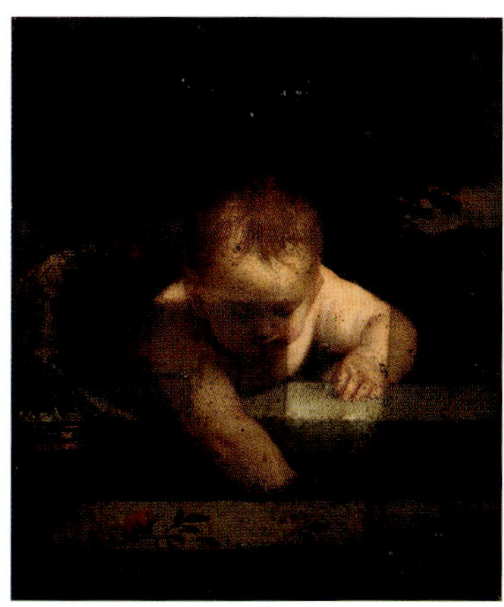

Graham-Gilbert, John 1794–1866
Cupid (after Titian)
oil on canvas 47 x 39.4
560

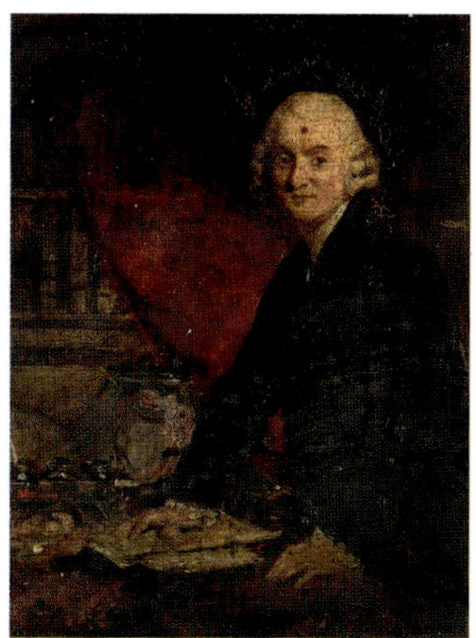

Graham-Gilbert, John 1794–1866
Dr William Hunter (1718–1783) (after Joshua
Reynolds)
oil on panel 21.6 x 17.1
553

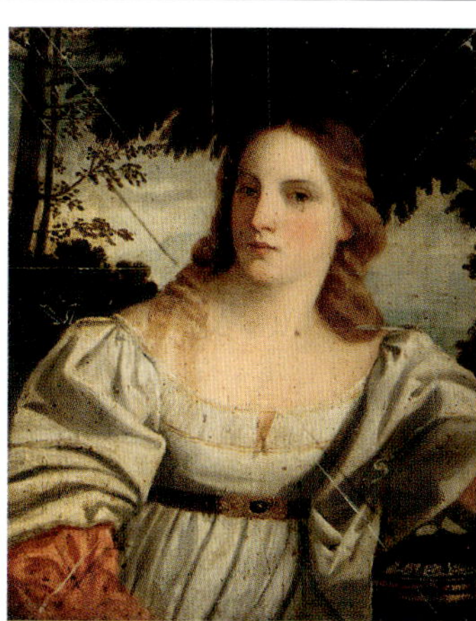

Graham-Gilbert, John 1794–1866
Female Figure (after Titian)
oil on canvas 53.3 x 43.2
559

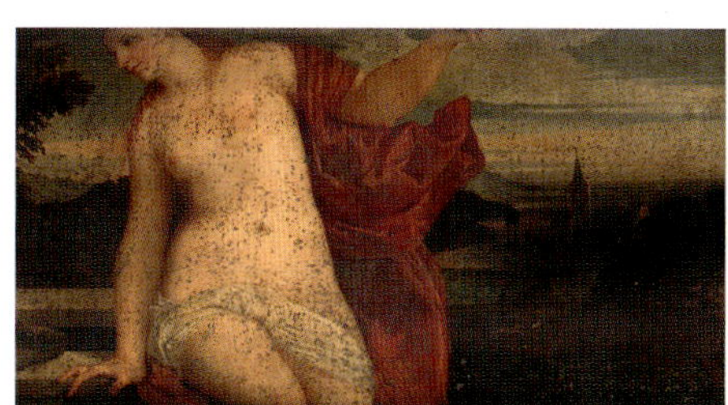

Graham-Gilbert, John 1794–1866
Female Figure (after Titian)
oil on canvas 104.8 x 164.5
561

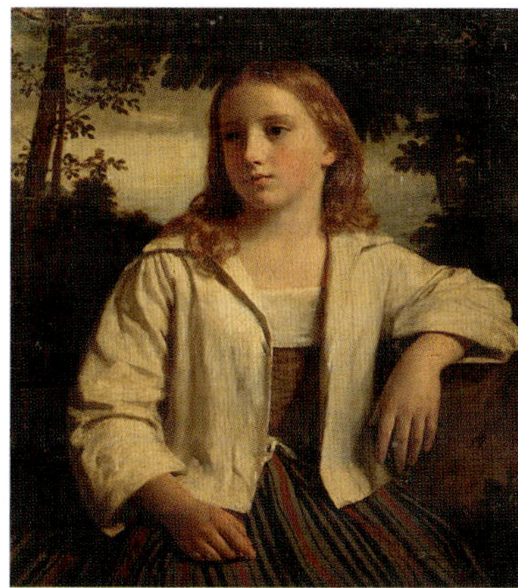

Graham-Gilbert, John 1794–1866
Female Portrait
oil on canvas
TEMP.14959

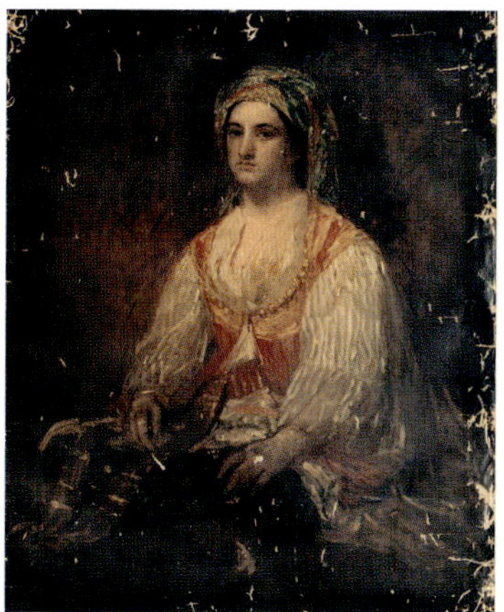

Graham-Gilbert, John 1794–1866
Figure Study
oil on canvas 173.9 x 88.9
517

Facing page: Shannon, James Jebusa, 1862–1923, *Flora*, c.1922 (p. 392)

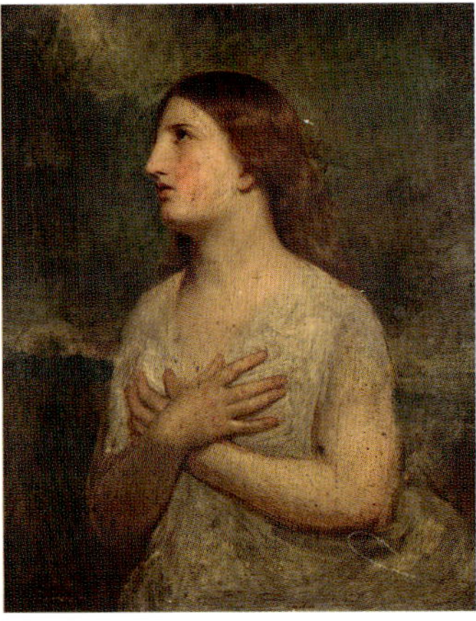

Graham-Gilbert, John 1794–1866
Figure Study
oil on panel 76.2 x 66
535

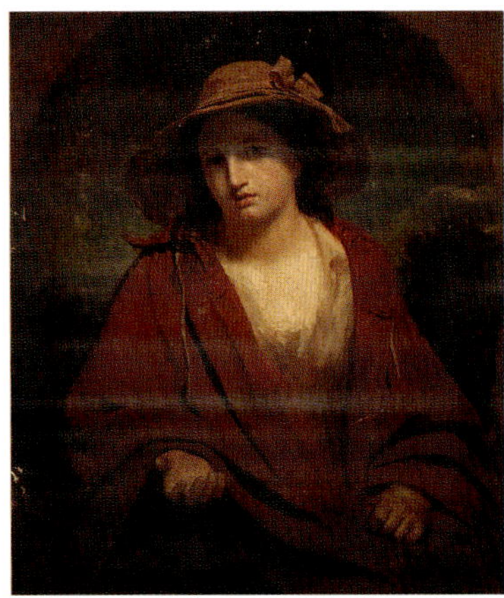

Graham-Gilbert, John 1794–1866
Gipsy Girl
oil on canvas 91.4 x 71.1
531

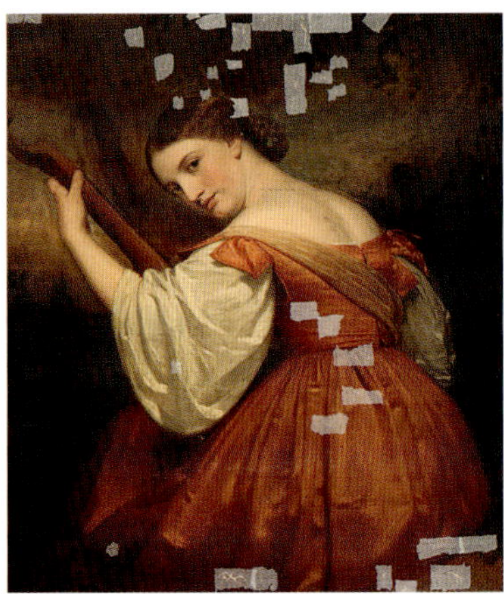

Graham-Gilbert, John 1794–1866
Girl Playing the Guitar
oil on canvas 114.3 x 91.4
527

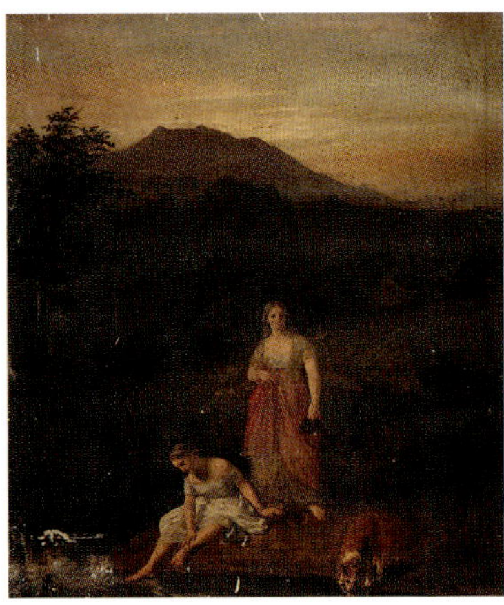

Graham-Gilbert, John 1794–1866
Girls at a Stream
oil on canvas 137.2 x 106.7
530

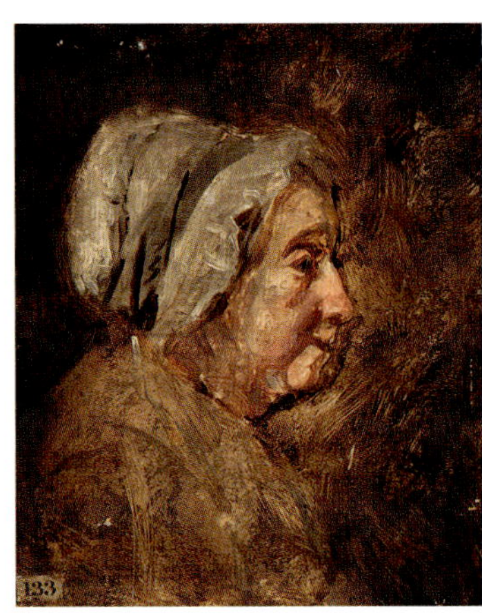

Graham-Gilbert, John 1794–1866
Head of an Old Woman with a Cap, in Profile to the Right
oil on panel 25.4 x 20.3
528

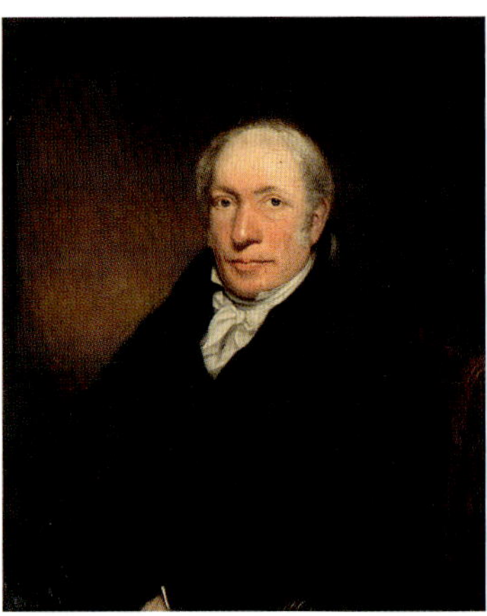

Graham-Gilbert, John 1794–1866
Humphrey E. Maclae of Cathkin (1773–1860)
oil on canvas 76.2 x 63.5
3017

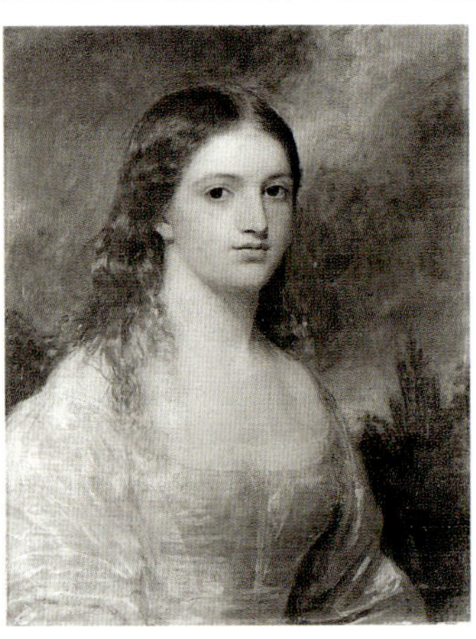

Graham-Gilbert, John 1794–1866
Ideal Portrait
oil on canvas 63.5 x 50.8
519

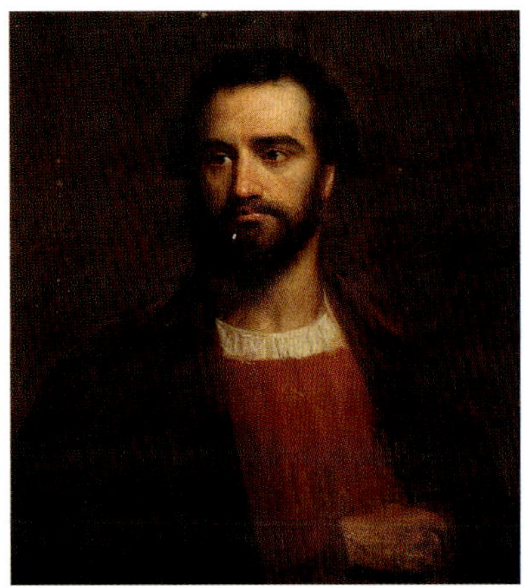

Graham-Gilbert, John 1794–1866
Italian Gentleman
oil on canvas 76.2 x 62.2
509

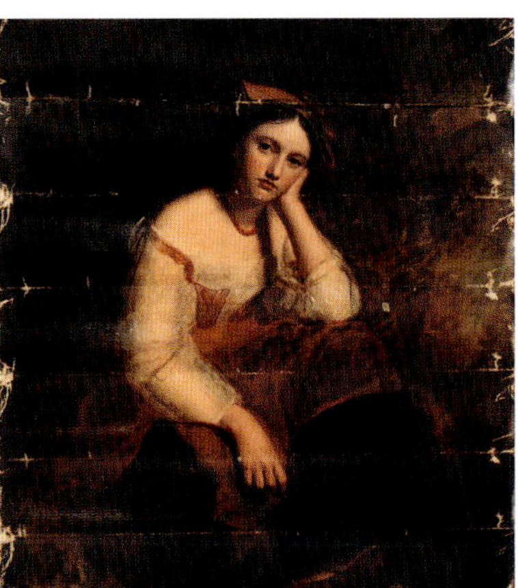

Graham-Gilbert, John 1794–1866
Italian Girl
oil on canvas 123.2 x 99.1
503

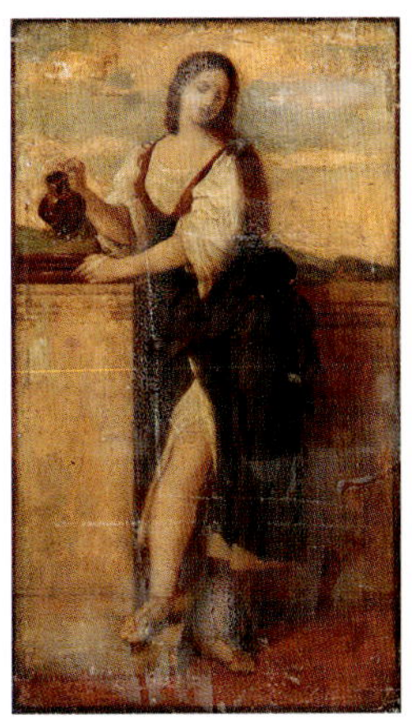

Graham-Gilbert, John 1794–1866
Italian Study
oil on panel 34.3 x 19
526

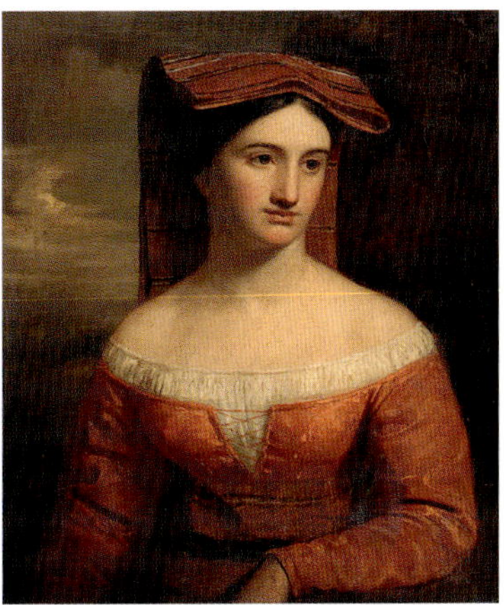

Graham-Gilbert, John 1794–1866
Italian Woman
oil on canvas 81.3 x 66
538

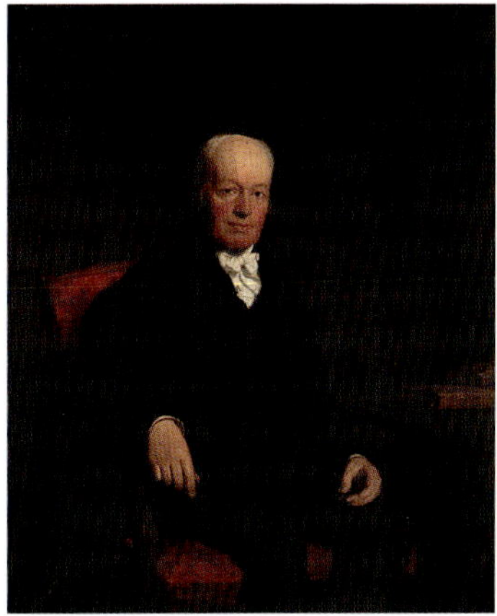

Graham-Gilbert, John 1794–1866
James Buchanan of Dowanhill (1756–1844)
oil on canvas 125.7 x 100.3
1385

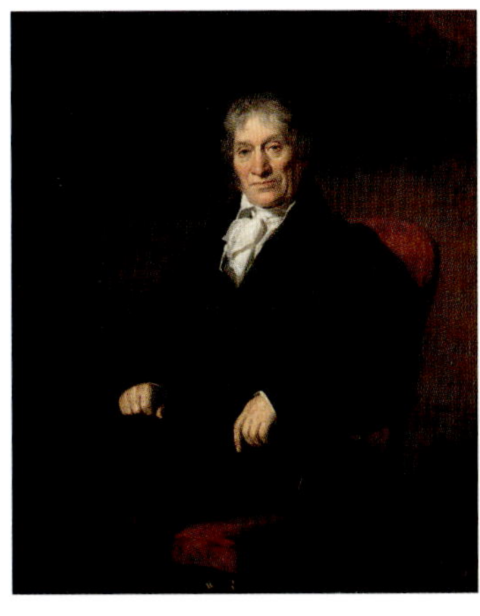

Graham-Gilbert, John 1794–1866
*James Dennistoun, Esq., of Golfhill
(1758–1835)*
oil on canvas 127 x 101.6
L.1.1912.1 (P)

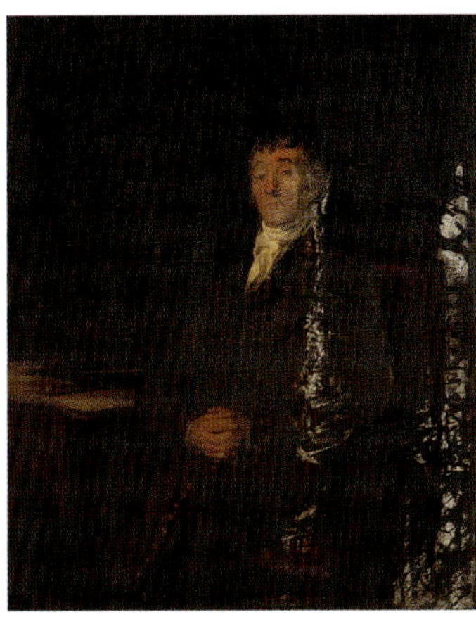

Graham-Gilbert, John 1794–1866
James Hamilton
oil on canvas 141 x 110.5
653

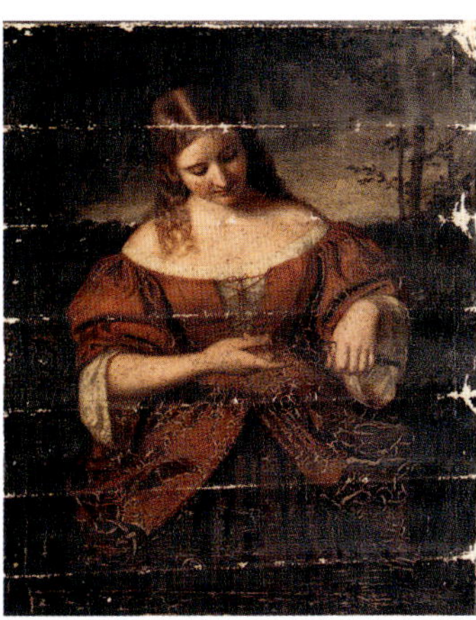

Graham-Gilbert, John 1794–1866
Lady with a Finch
oil on canvas 111.8 x 86.4
358

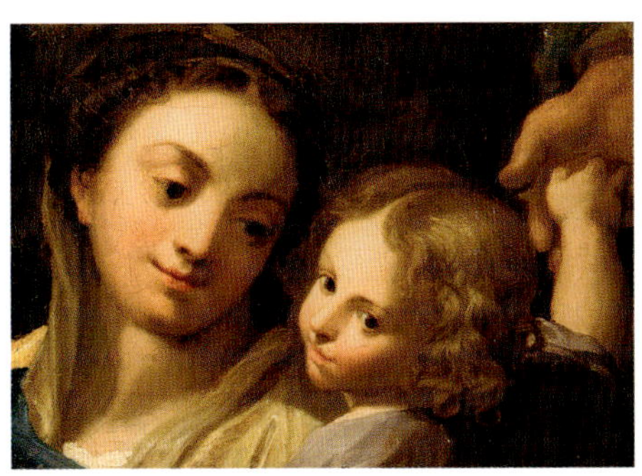

Graham-Gilbert, John 1794–1866
Madonna and Child (after Correggio)
oil on canvas 29.5 x 41.6
544

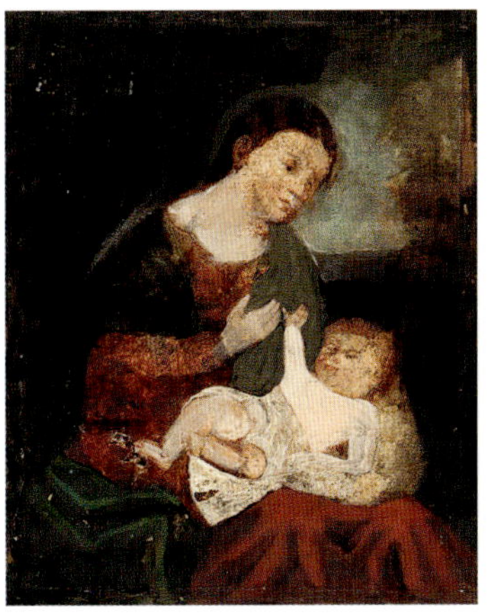

Graham-Gilbert, John 1794–1866
Madonna and Child (after Correggio)
oil on canvas 30.5 x 24.1
546

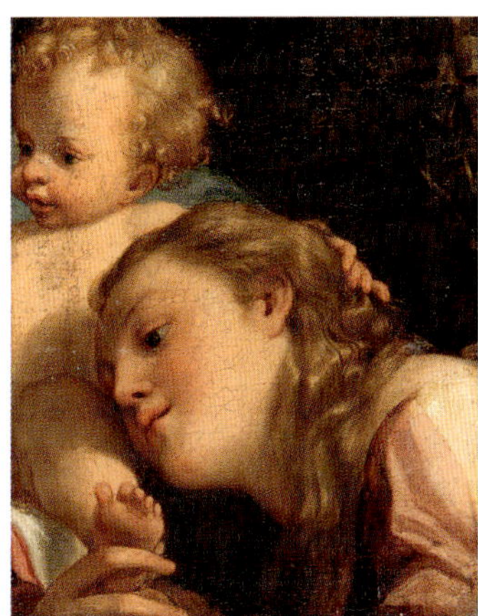

Graham-Gilbert, John 1794–1866
Magdalene and Child (after Correggio)
oil on canvas 38.1 x 30.2
543

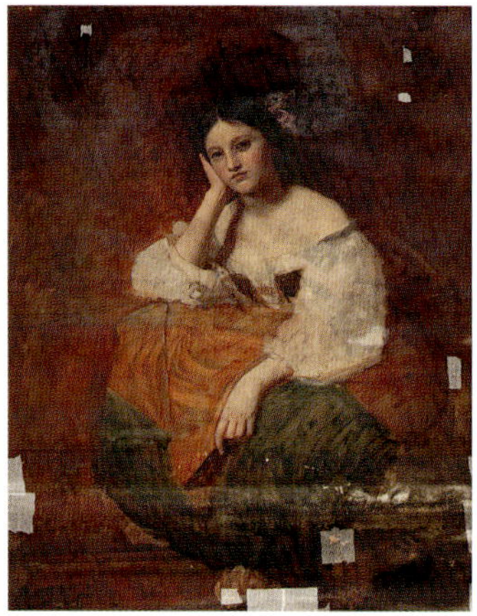

Graham-Gilbert, John 1794–1866
Meditation
oil on canvas 147.3 x 110.5
539

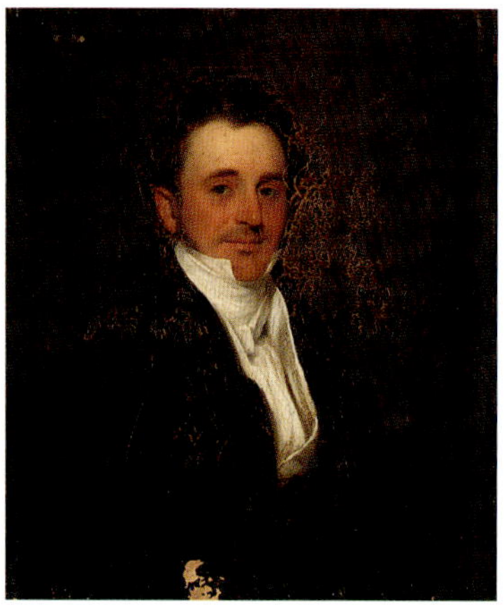

Graham-Gilbert, John 1794–1866
Mungo Campbell
oil on canvas 76.2 x 63.5
1427

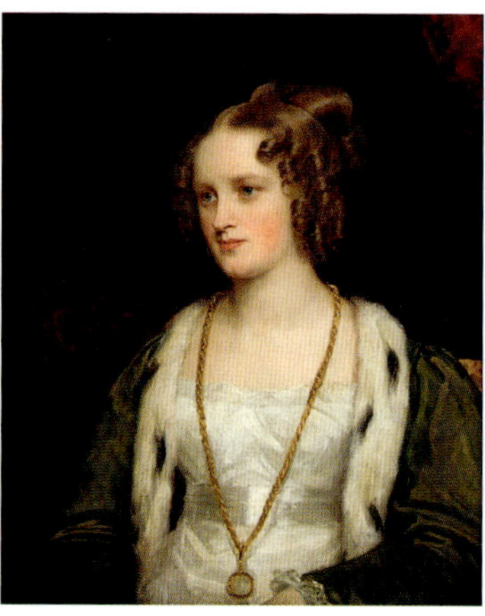

Graham-Gilbert, John 1794–1866
Mrs Isabella C. Campbell
oil on canvas 76.2 x 63.5
1428

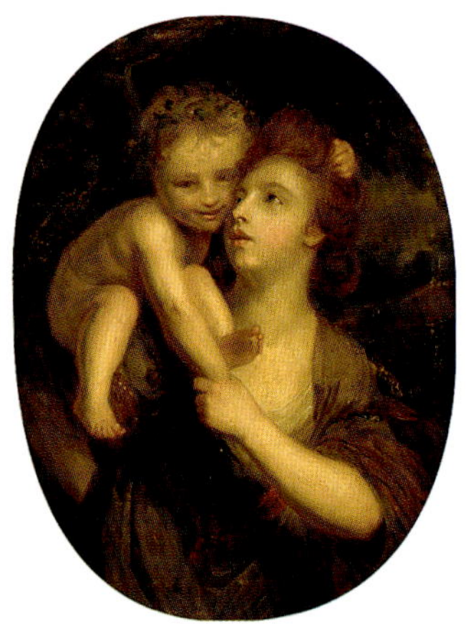

Graham-Gilbert, John 1794–1866
Nymph with Infant Bacchus (after Joshua
Reynolds)
oil on panel 43.2 x 34.3
552

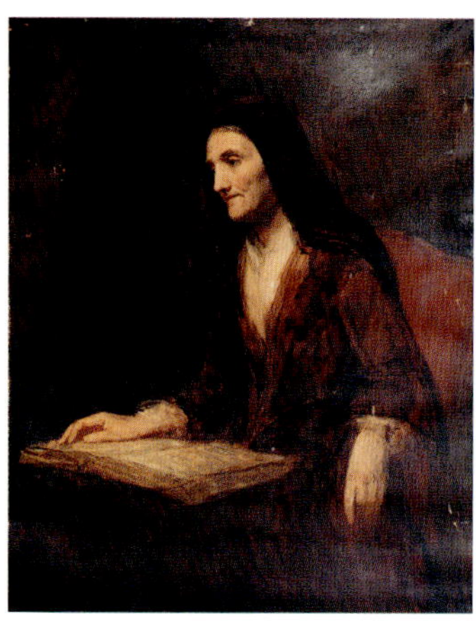

Graham-Gilbert, John 1794–1866
Old Lady Reading
oil on canvas 115.5 x 87.6
512

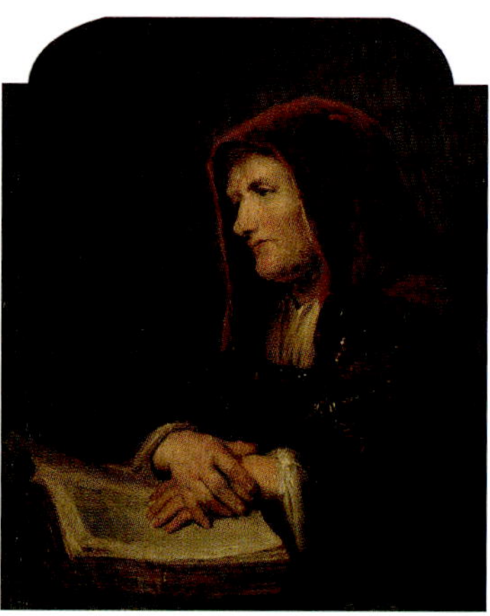

Graham-Gilbert, John 1794–1866
Old Woman Reading (after Rembrandt van
Rijn)
oil on panel 33 x 26
558

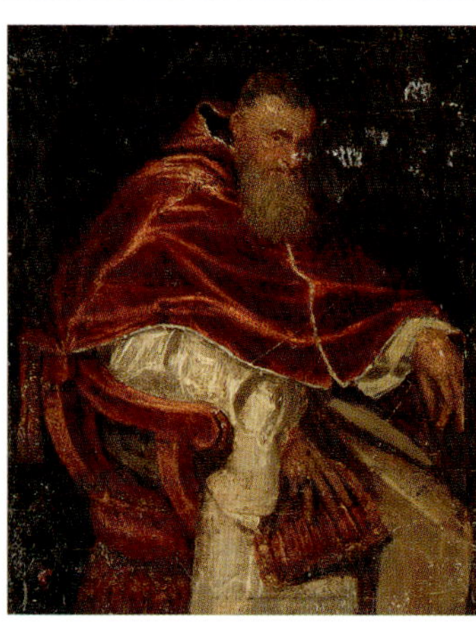

Graham-Gilbert, John 1794–1866
Pope Paul III (after Titian)
oil on panel 26.7 x 21
562

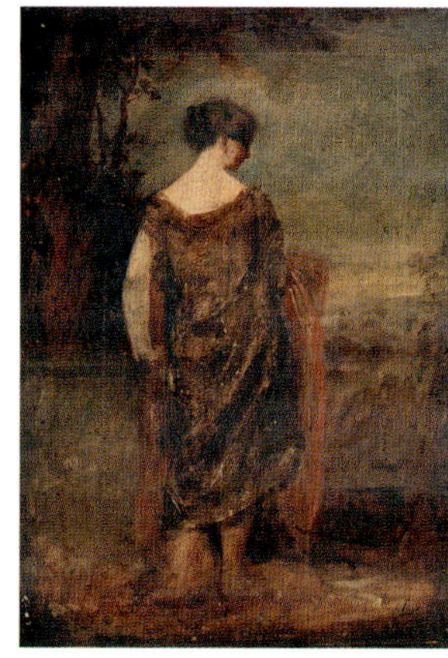

Graham-Gilbert, John 1794–1866
Study of a Female Figure
oil on canvas 63.5 x 43.2
514

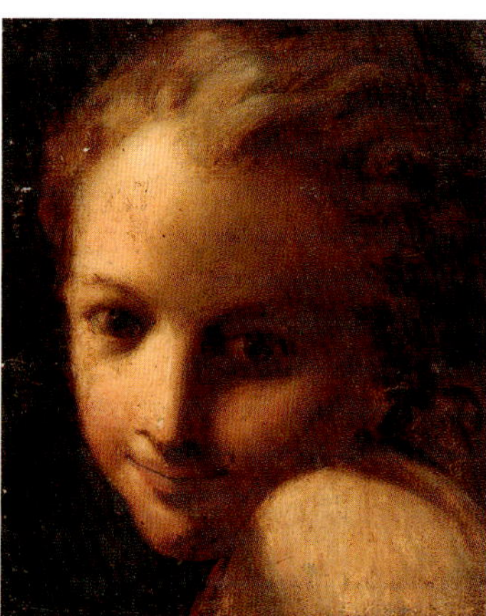

Graham-Gilbert, John 1794–1866
Study of a Head
oil on canvas 31.7 x 25.4
529

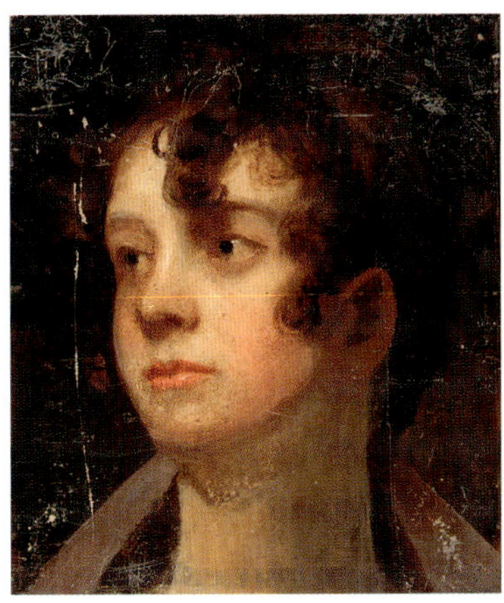

Graham-Gilbert, John 1794–1866
Study of a Head (after Henry Raeburn)
oil on panel 31.1 x 26
551

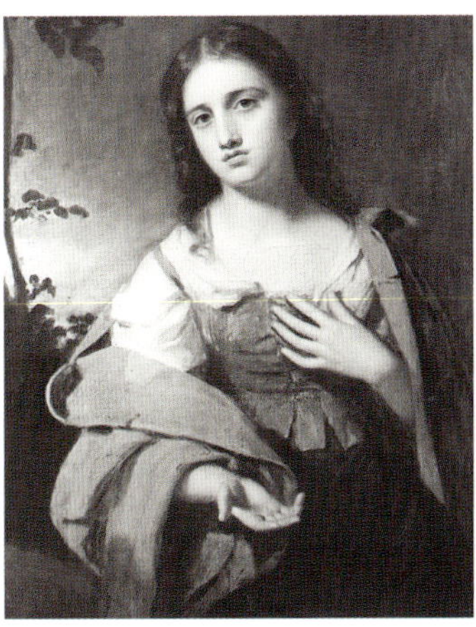

Graham-Gilbert, John 1794–1866
The Beggar Maid
oil on canvas 105.4 x 82.2
338

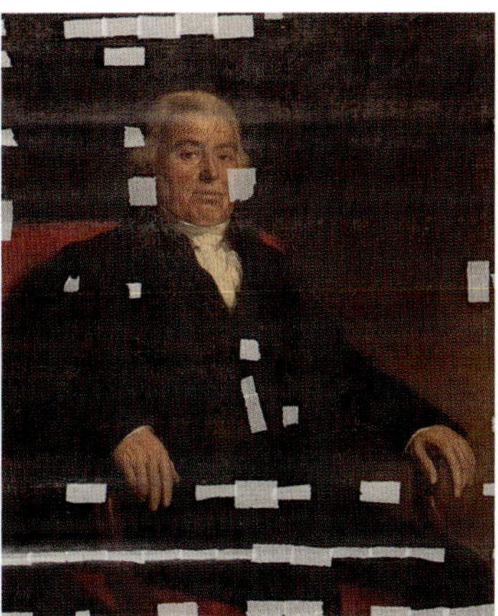

Graham-Gilbert, John 1794–1866
The Father of Archibald McLellan
oil on canvas 124.5 x 99.1
241

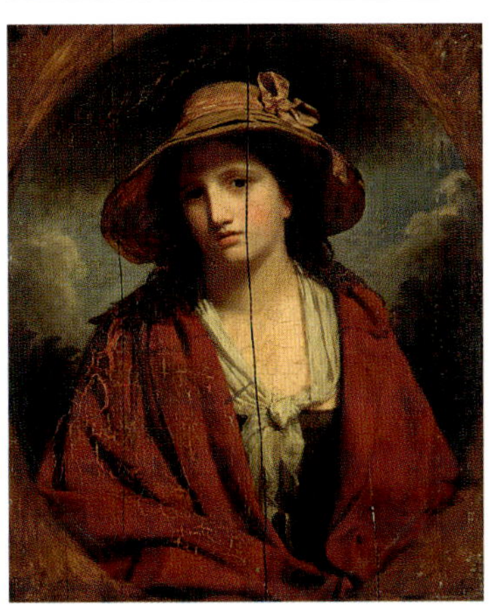

Graham-Gilbert, John 1794–1866
The Gipsy
oil on panel 77.8 x 64.8
521

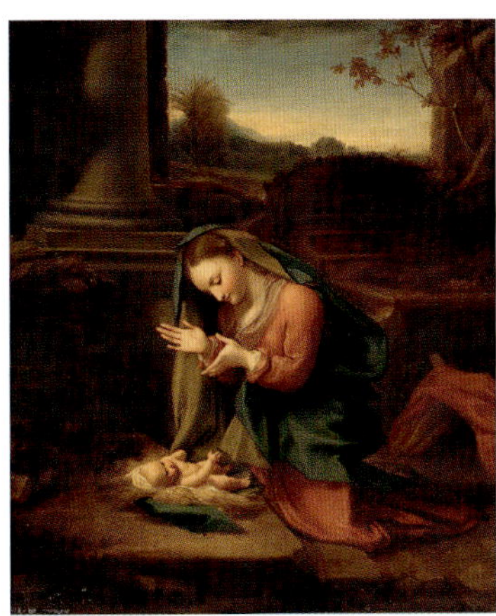

Graham-Gilbert, John 1794–1866
The Madonna Adoring the Infant Christ (after Correggio)
oil on canvas 80.9 x 67.3
545

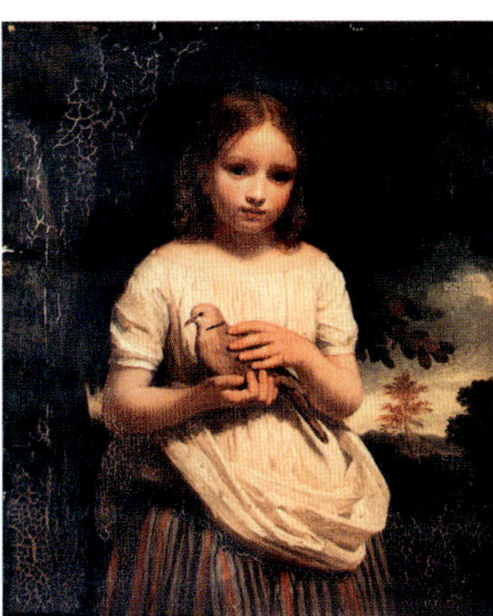

Graham-Gilbert, John 1794–1866
The Pet Dove
oil on canvas 73.7 x 61
504

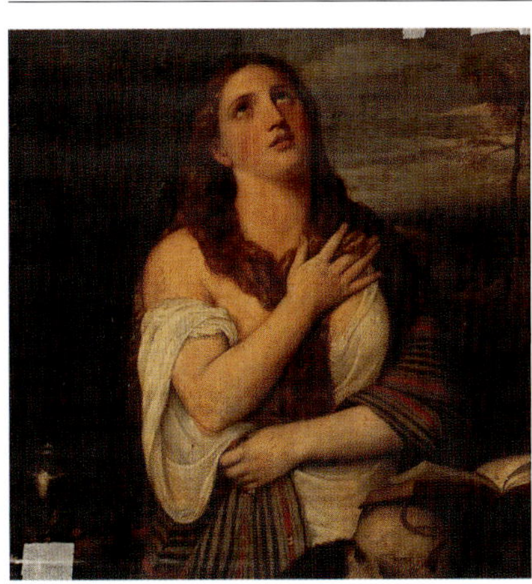

Graham-Gilbert, John 1794–1866
The Reading Magdalene (after Titian)
oil on canvas 106.7 x 91.4
540

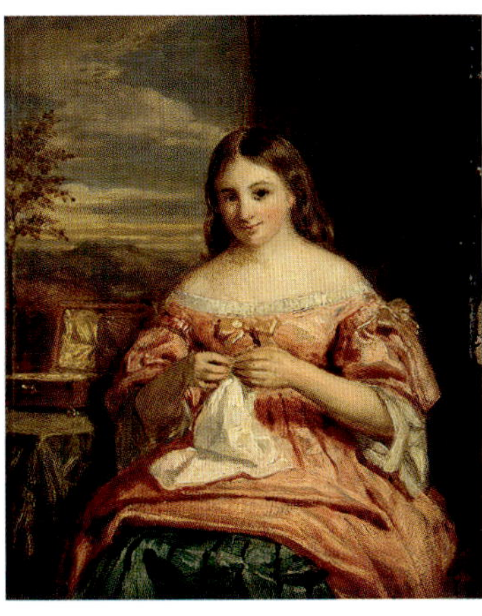

Graham-Gilbert, John 1794–1866
The Young Seamstress
oil on canvas 24.1 x 19.1
231

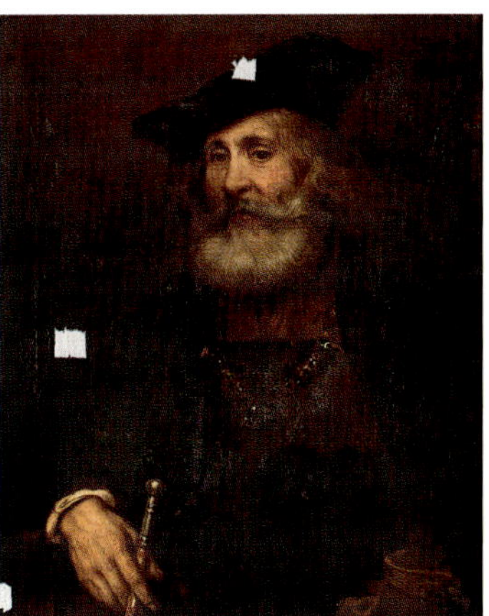

Graham-Gilbert, John (attributed to)
1794–1866
A Rabbi
oil on canvas 90.1 x 73
602

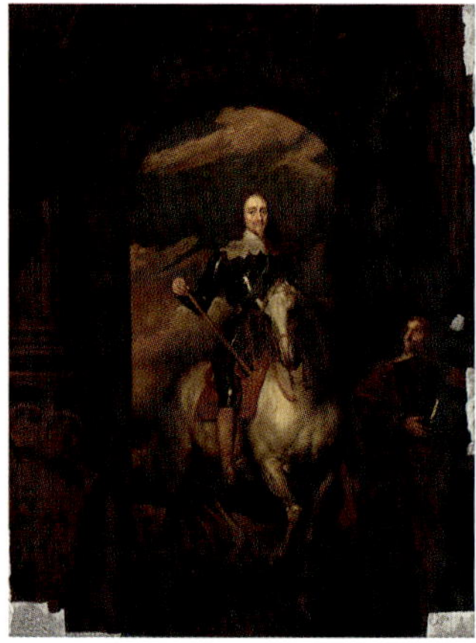

Graham-Gilbert, John (attributed to)
1794–1866
Charles I with M. de St Antoine (after
Anthony van Dyck)
oil on canvas 120.3 x 89.2
563

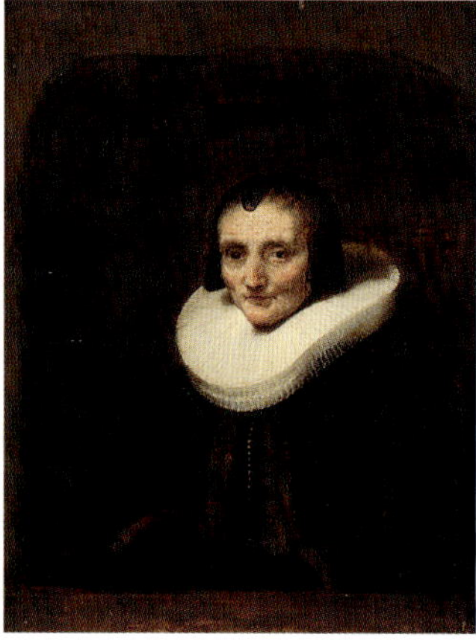

Graham-Gilbert, John (attributed to)
1794–1866
Margaretha de Geer, Wife of Jacob Trip (after
Rembrandt van Rijn)
oil on canvas 47 x 36.8
557

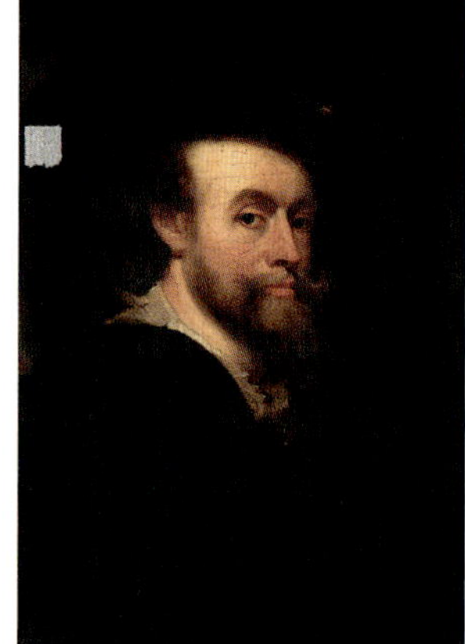

Graham-Gilbert, John (attributed to)
1794–1866
Self Portrait (after Peter Paul Rubens)
oil on canvas 87.6 x 63.5
608

Graham-Gilbert, John (attributed to)
1794–1866
Self Portrait (after Rembrandt van Rijn)
oil on canvas 68.6 x 62.2
598

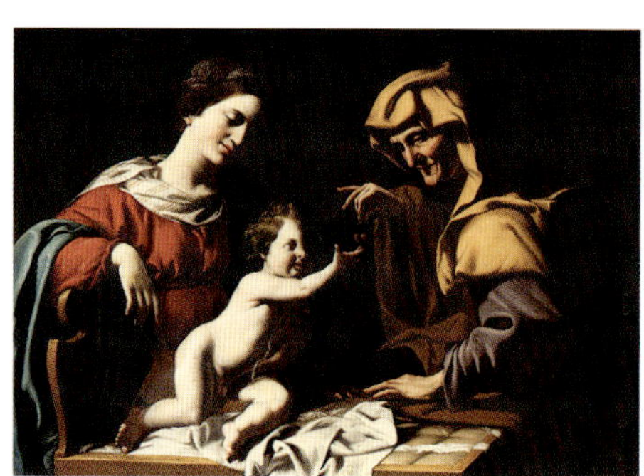

Grammatica, Antiveduto 1571–1626
Madonna and Child with Saint Anne
c.1614–1617
oil on canvas 95.4 x 133
141

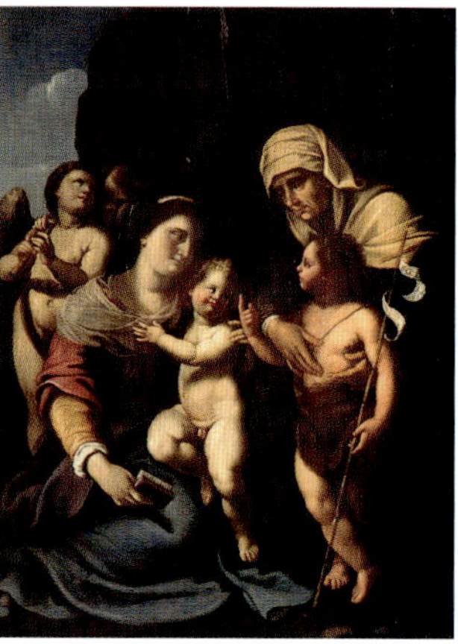

Grammatica, Antiveduto (circle of)
1571–1626
*Madonna and Child, with Saint Elizabeth and
Saint John* (after Andrea del Sarto) 17th C
oil on panel 49.8 x 36.2
PC.93

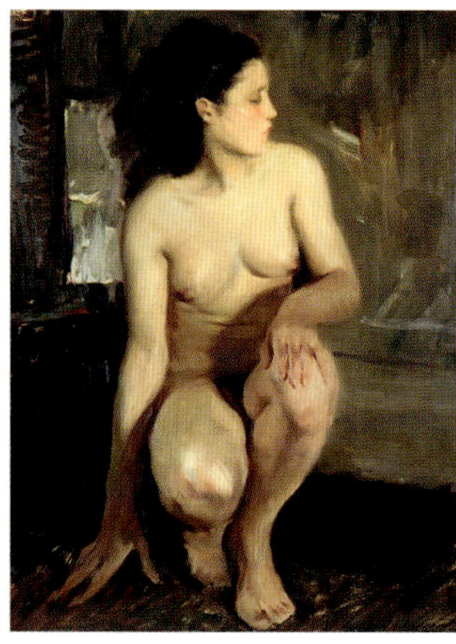

Grandgérard, Lucien Henri 1880–1970
Adolescence 1935
oil on panel 67 x 50
2116

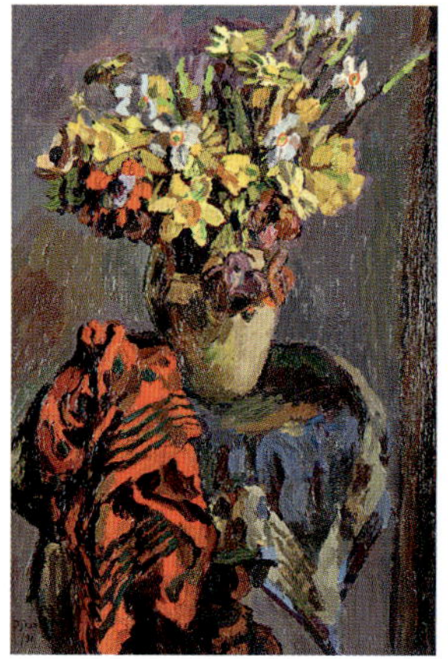

Grant, Duncan 1885–1978
Daffodils 1931
oil on canvas 76.2 x 50.8
1900

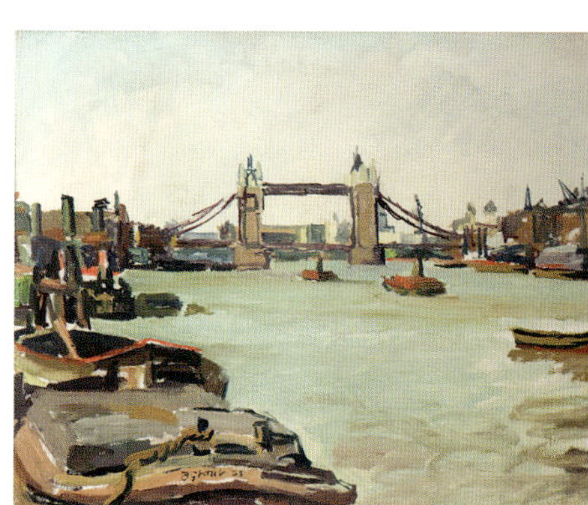

Grant, Duncan 1885–1978
Tower Bridge 1933
oil on canvas 50.8 x 61
3013

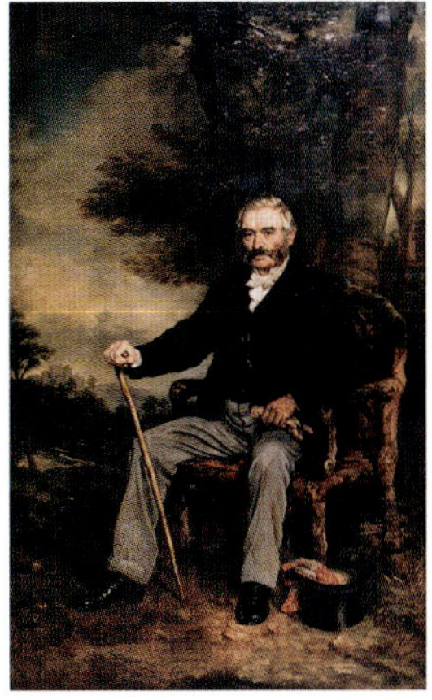

Grant, Francis 1803–1878
Sir Andrew Orr of Harvieston and Castle Campbell, Lord Provost of Glasgow (1854–1857) c.1857
oil on canvas 236.2 x 144.8
895

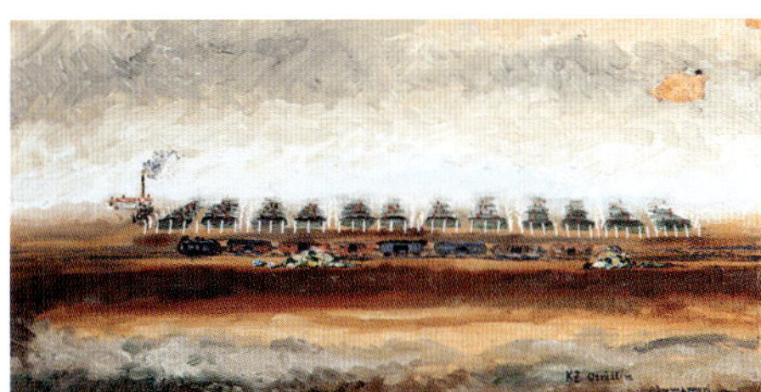

Grant, Marianne 1921–2007
KZ Osvěčěim 1952
oil on paper 26 x 50
PP.2005.38.26

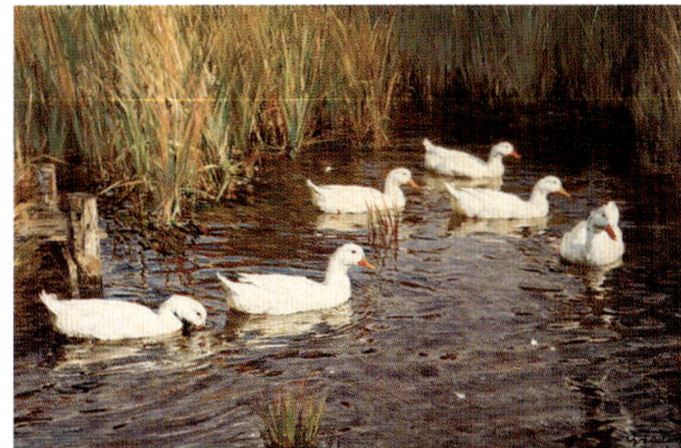

Grässel, Franz 1861–1948
Ducks 1903
oil on canvas 43 x 65
1079

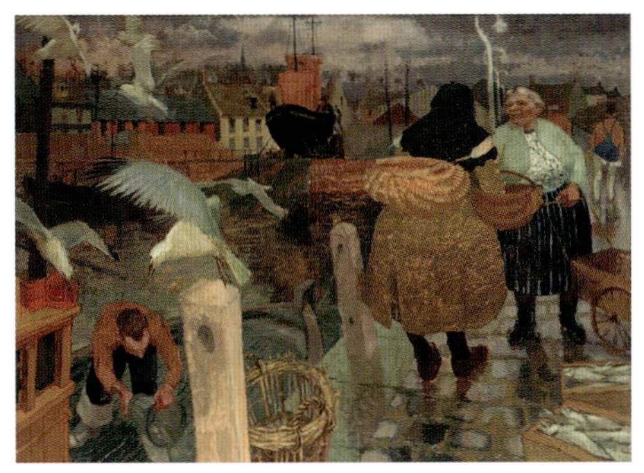

Grassie, Morris b.1931
Muckle Meg 1953–1954
oil on panel 76.2 x 101.6
3041

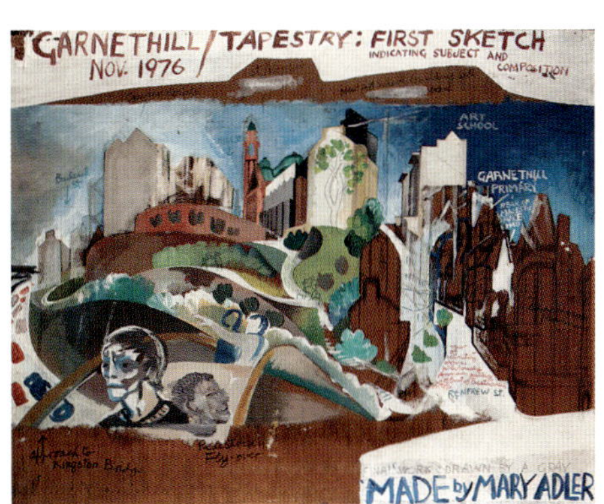

Gray, Alasdair b.1934
Garnethill Tapestry: First Sketch 1976
oil on board 74.1 x 90
TEMP.2739

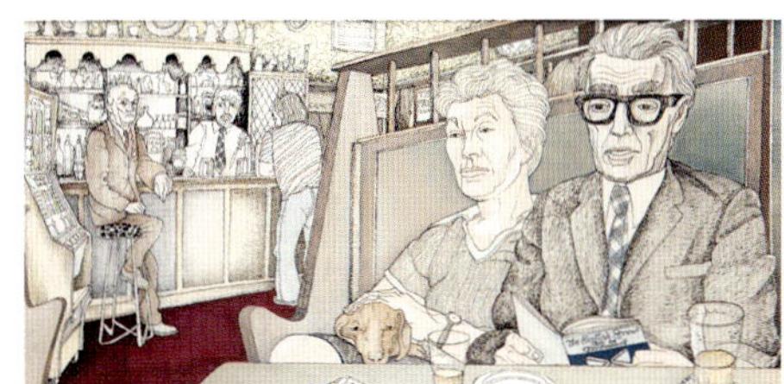

Gray, Alasdair b.1934
Alex Scott in the 'Pewter Pot' Pub 1977
acrylic & ink on paper 31 x 61
PP.1977.128.5

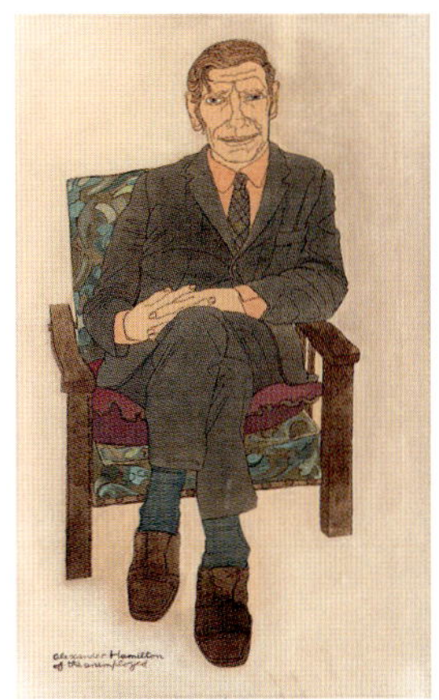

Gray, Alasdair b.1934
Alexander Hamilton of the Unemployed 1977
acrylic & pen on paper 76.8 x 48.3
PP.1977.128.12

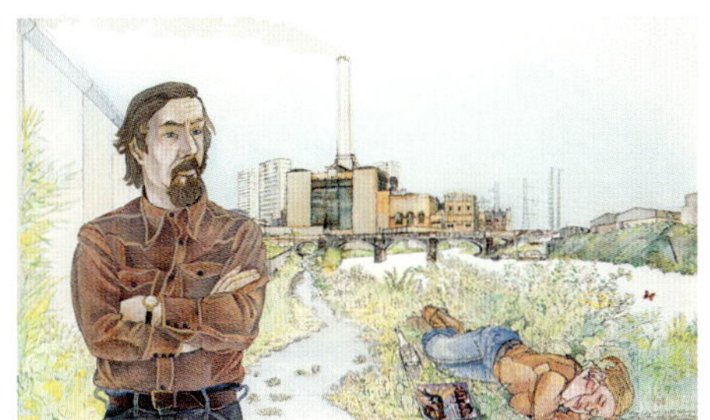

Gray, Alasdair b.1934
Archie Hind (1928–2008), and the Dalmarnock Power Station 1977
acrylic, pencil & ink on board 54.5 x 89
PP.1977.128.14

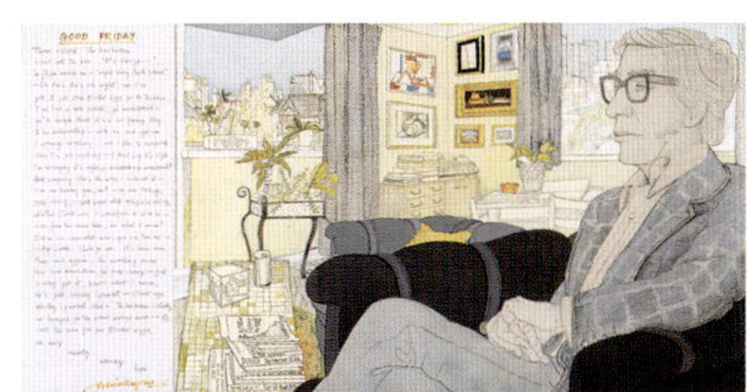

Gray, Alasdair b.1934
Edwin Morgan (1920–2010), Writer 1977
acrylic on paper 33 x 61.6
PP.1977.128.20

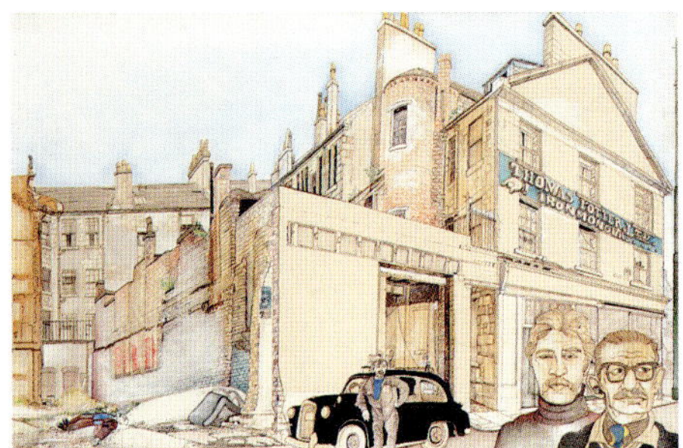

Gray, Alasdair b.1934
End of Arcadia Street (one) 1977
acrylic on paper 71.5 x 103.4
PP.1977.128.3

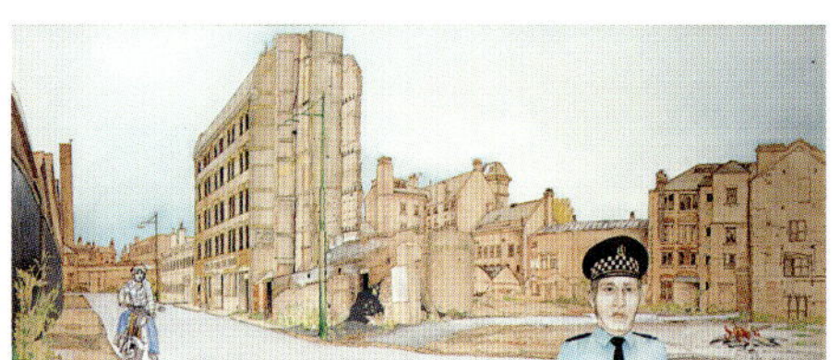

Gray, Alasdair b.1934
End of Arcadia Street (two) 1977
acrylic, pen & ink on paper 74.3 x 168.3
PP.1977.128.11

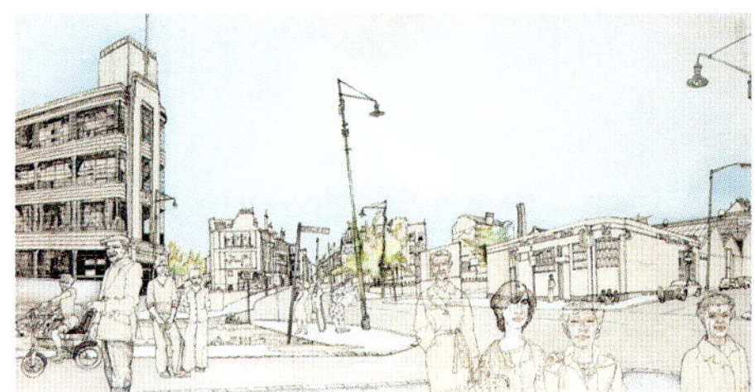

Gray, Alasdair b.1934
End of Arcadia Street (three) 1977
acrylic & ink on paper 70.7 x 132.7
PP.1977.128.26

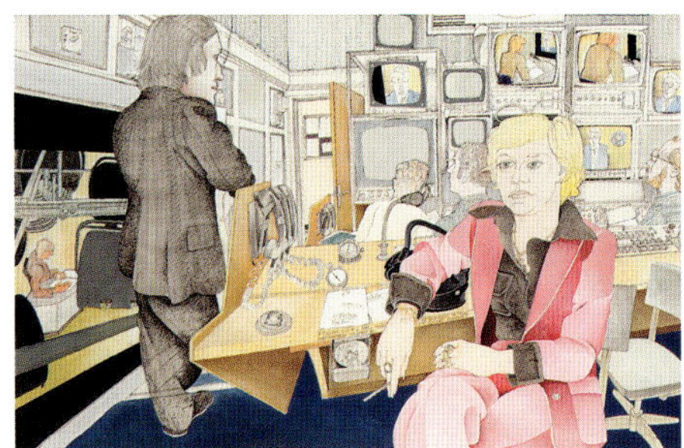

Gray, Alasdair b.1934
Fidelma Cook (b.1953), in the BBC News Gallery 1977
acrylic, pencil & ink on paper 52.5 x 77.4
PP.1977.128.15

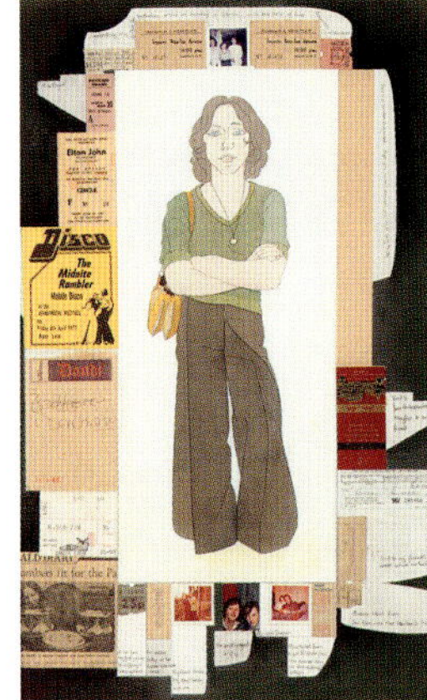

Gray, Alasdair b.1934
Frances Gordon, Glasgow Teenager 1977
acrylic on paper & collage on board 75.7 x 47.3
PP.1977.128.9

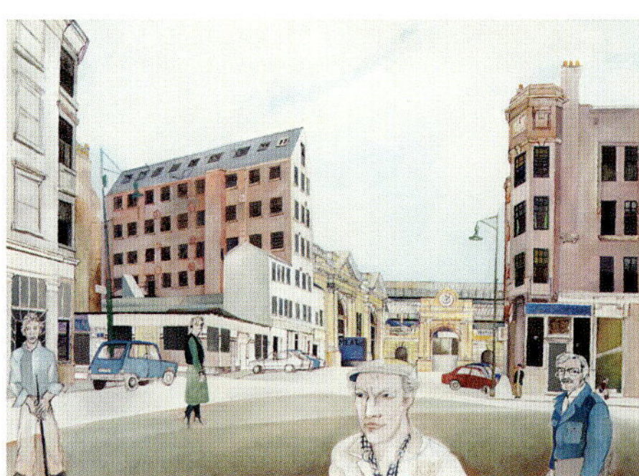

Gray, Alasdair b.1934
Graham Square Cotton Mill 1977
acrylic, pen & pencil on paper 66 x 88.4
PP.1977.128.16

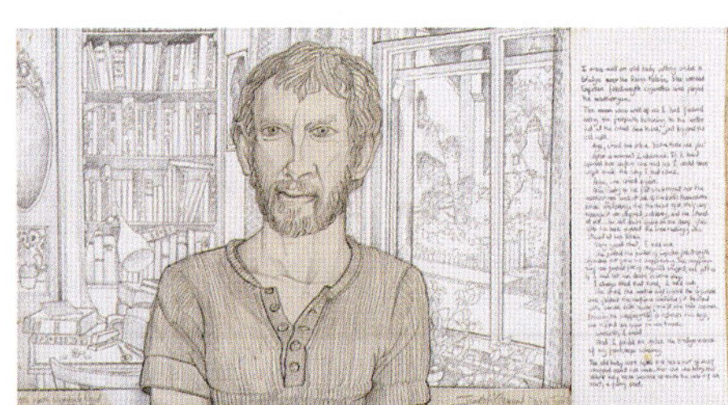

Gray, Alasdair b.1934
James Kelman (b.1946) 1977
acrylic & pencil on paper on board
30.5 x 55.9
PP.1977.128.7

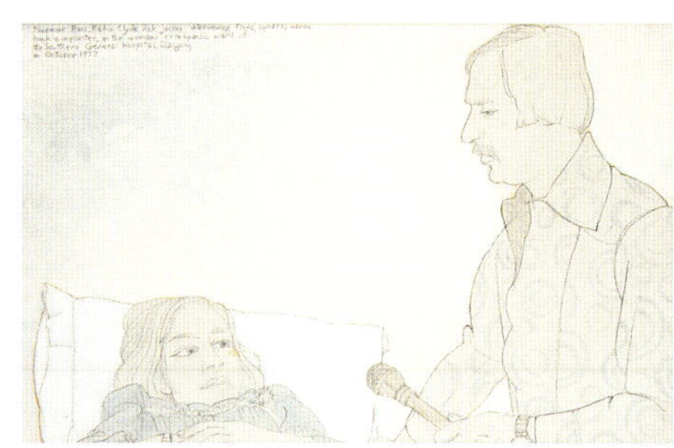

Gray, Alasdair b.1934
Norman Ross, Hospital Broadcaster 1977
acrylic, pen & pencil on paper 40 x 60.7
PP.1977.128.29

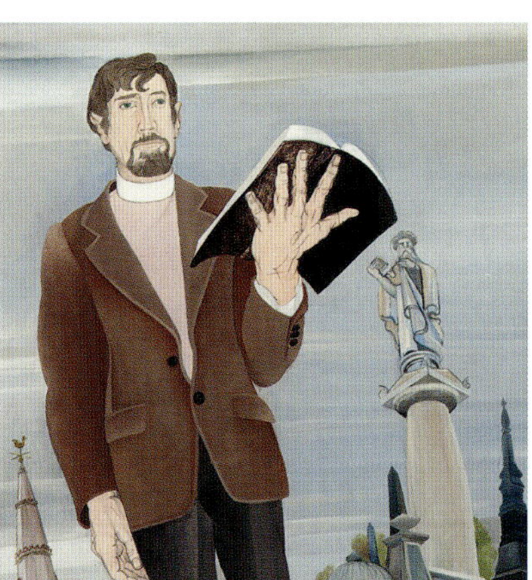

Gray, Alasdair b.1934
Pastor Jack Glass (1936–2004) 1977
acrylic, ink, graphite & paper collage on
plywood 53.3 x 50.8
PP.1977.128.10

Facing page: Raeburn, Henry, 1756–1823, *Mrs Anne Campbell*, (p. 361)

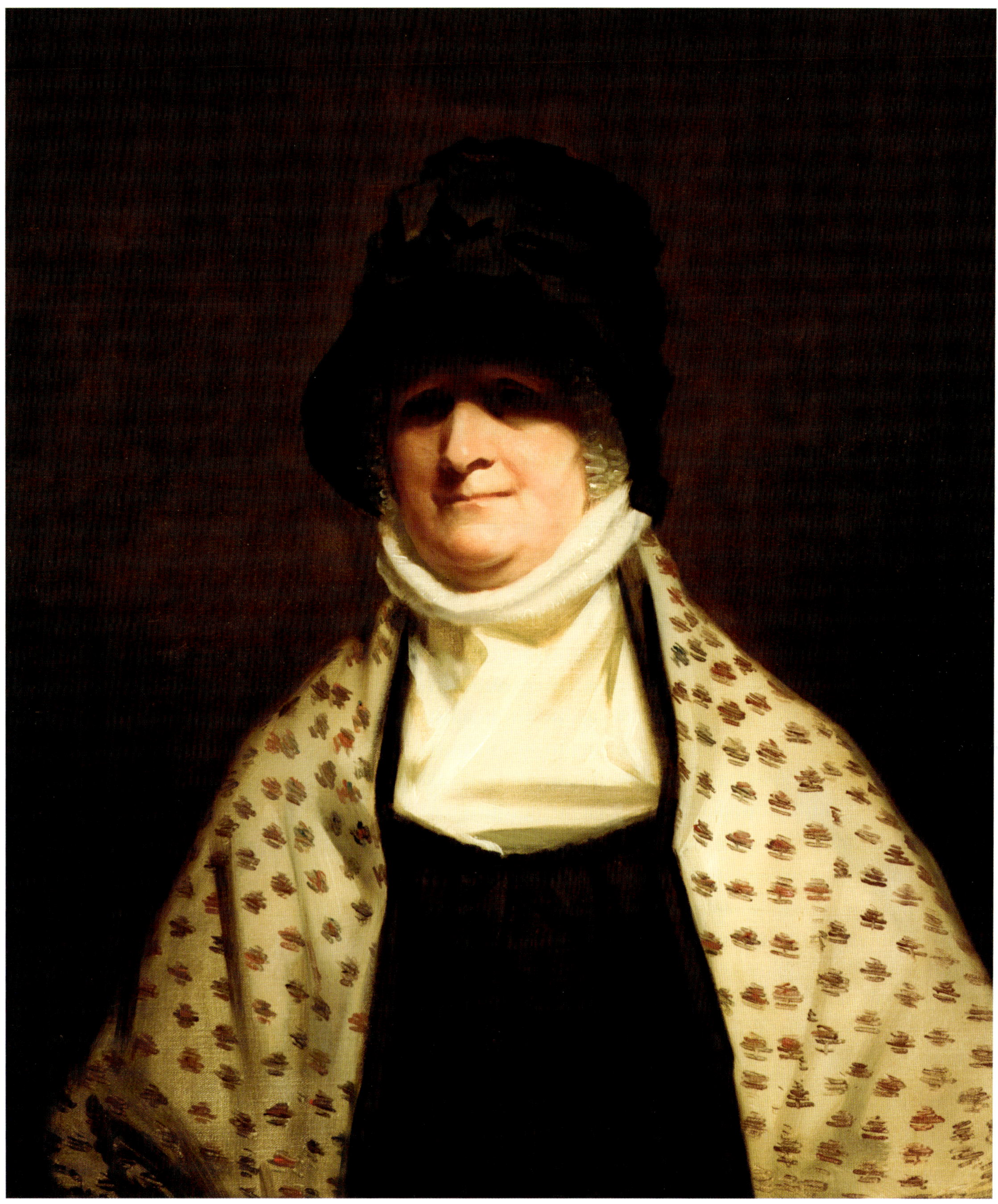

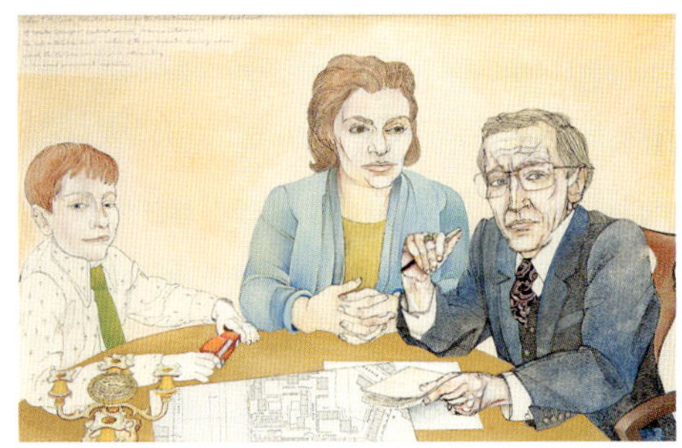

Gray, Alasdair b.1934
Provost McCann and Family 1977
acrylic, pen, pencil & collage on board
52.2 x 77
PP.1977.128.24

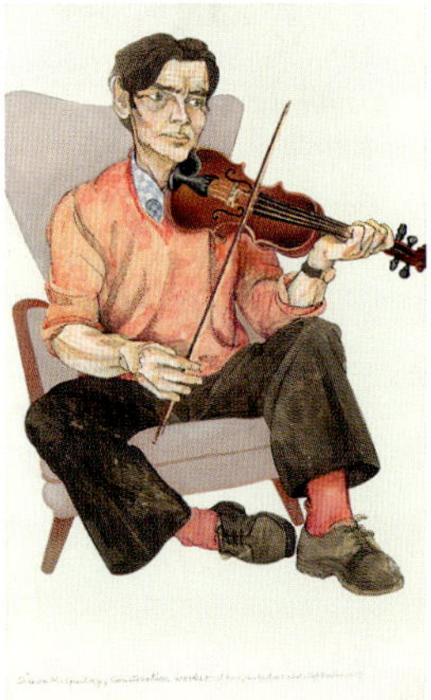

Gray, Alasdair b.1934
Simon McGinlay, Construction Worker 1977
acrylic & ink on paper 76.3 x 47.8
PP.1977.128.13

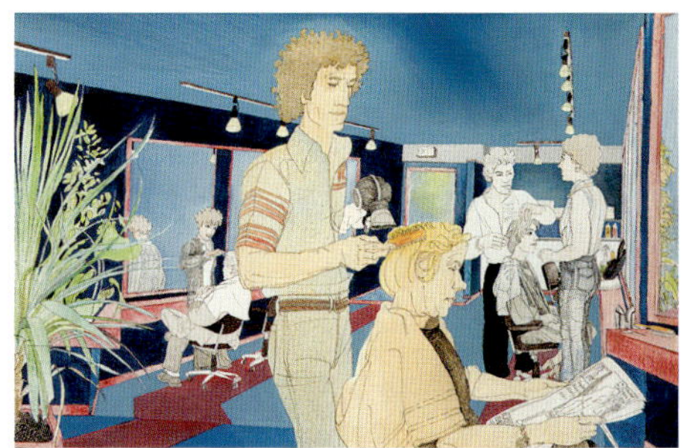

Gray, Alasdair b.1934
Sweeney Todd Hairdressing Salon 1977
acrylic on paper 52.3 x 76.5
PP.1977.128.21

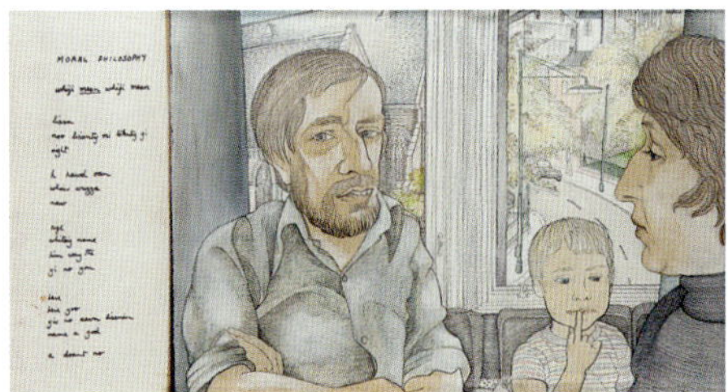

Gray, Alasdair b.1934
Tom Leonard (b.1944), Writer 1977
acrylic, pen & pencil on paper 30.5 x 43.1
PP.1977.128.8

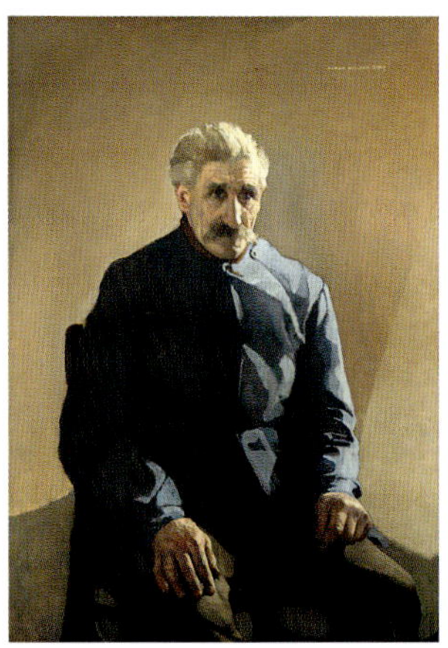

Gray, Norah Neilson 1882–1931
A Belgian Refugee c.1915–1921
oil on canvas 125.7 x 87
3348

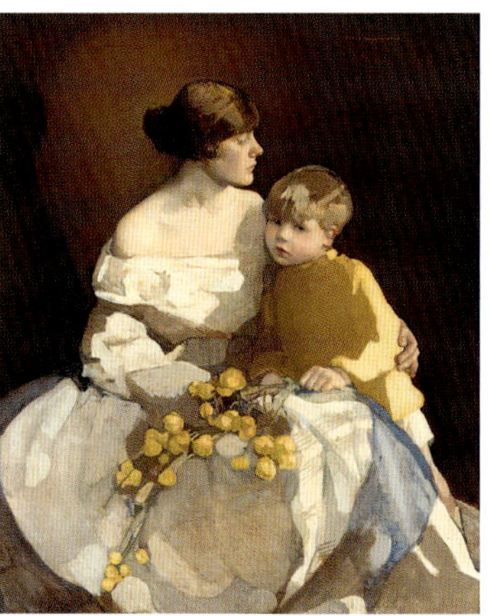

Gray, Norah Neilson 1882–1931
Little Brother 1920–1922
oil on canvas 127 x 101.6
1836

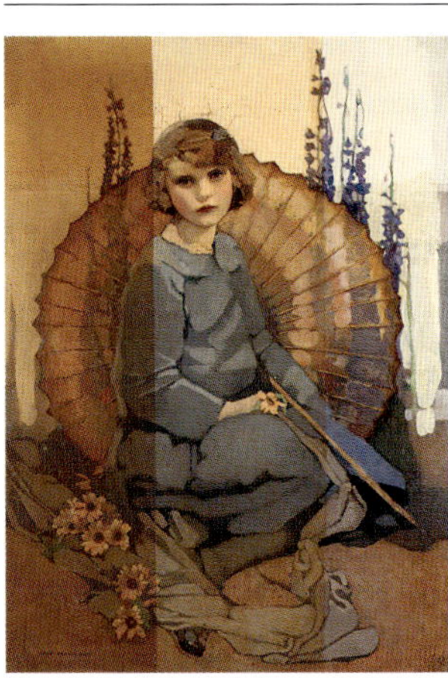

Gray, Norah Neilson 1882–1931
Portrait of a Girl in Blue c.1920–1925
oil on canvas 127 x 101.6
3476

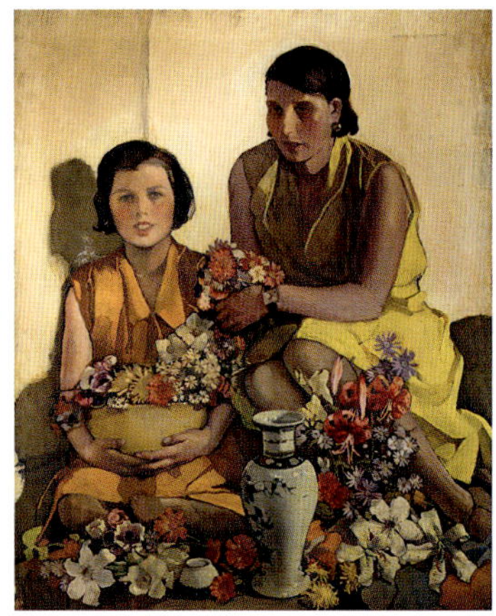

Gray, Norah Neilson 1882–1931
Salopian Cup and Chinese Vase c.1930
oil on canvas 127 x 101.6
3477

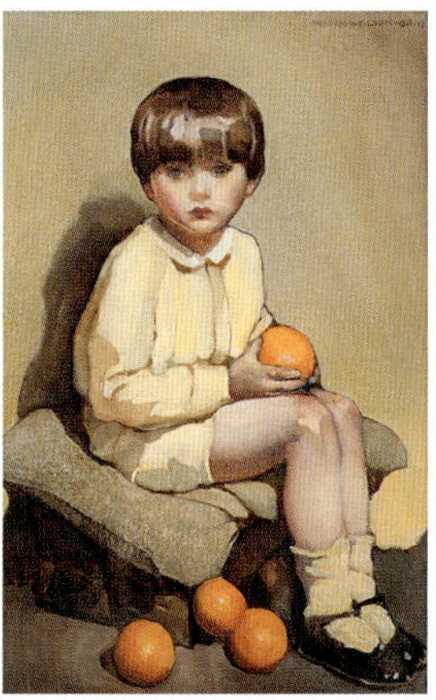

Gray, Norah Neilson 1882–1931
Little Boy with Oranges
oil on canvas 50.8 x 35.6
1837

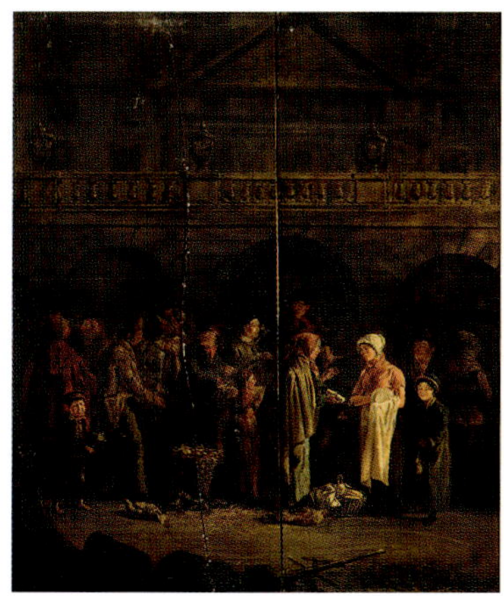

Green active 19th C
Royal Exchange and John's Coffee House, Edinburgh
oil on panel 73.7 x 62.2
397

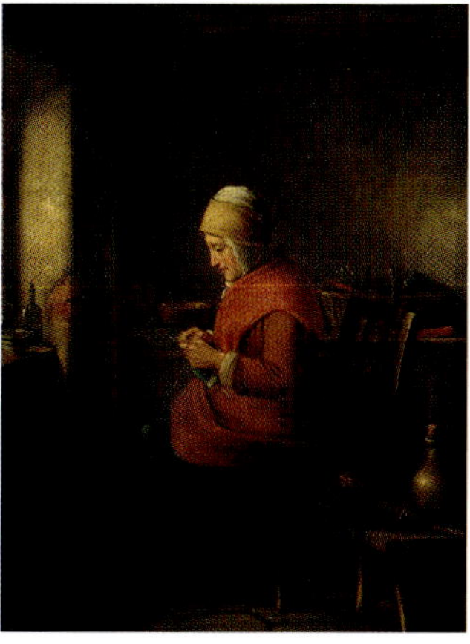

Green, A. P. active 19th C
Interior with an Old Woman Knitting
oil on panel 29.7 x 22.9
2948

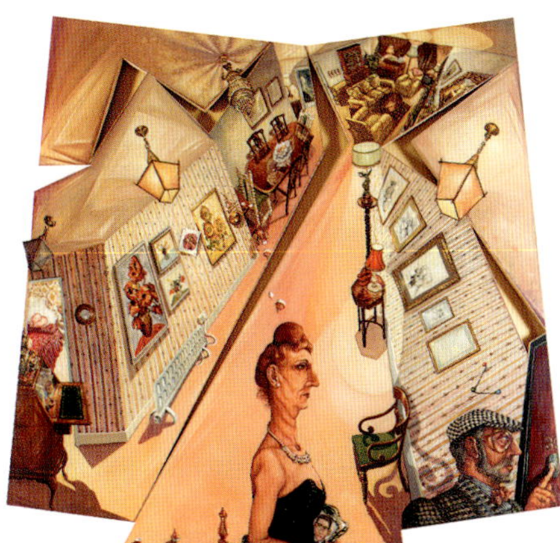

Green, Anthony b.1939
Embassy Lodge 1990
oil on board 232 x 253.3
3603

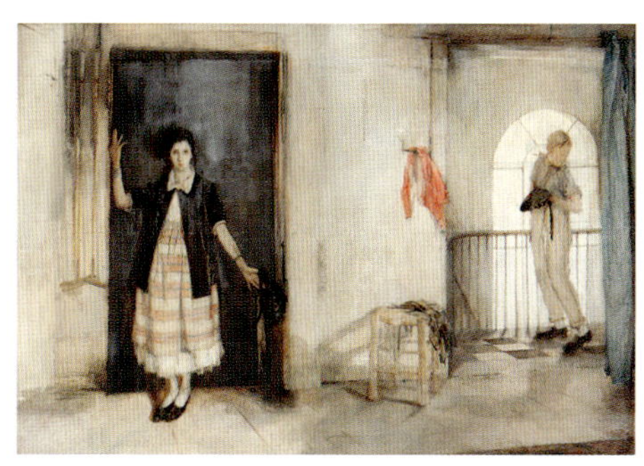

Green, Madeline 1884–1947
The Young Man
oil on canvas 61 x 91.4
2114

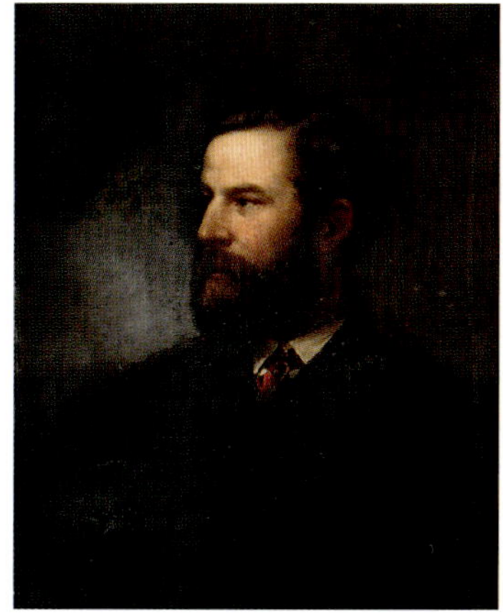

Greenlees, Georgina Mossmen 1849–1932
James Sellars (1843–1888), Architect 1880
oil on canvas 76.2 x 63.5
2915

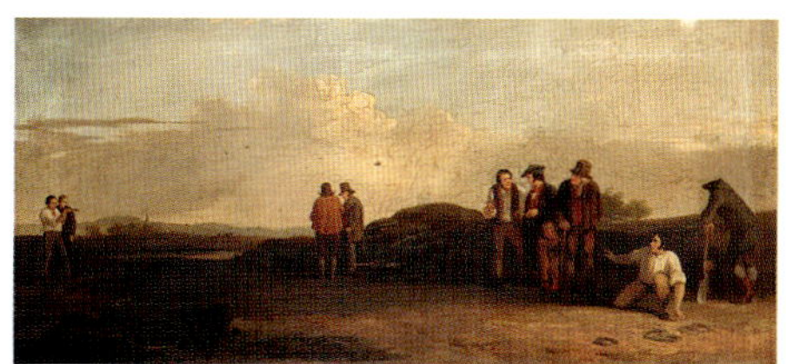

Greenlees, Robert M. 1820–1896
Playing Quoits 1845
oil on canvas 55.9 x 121.9
2366

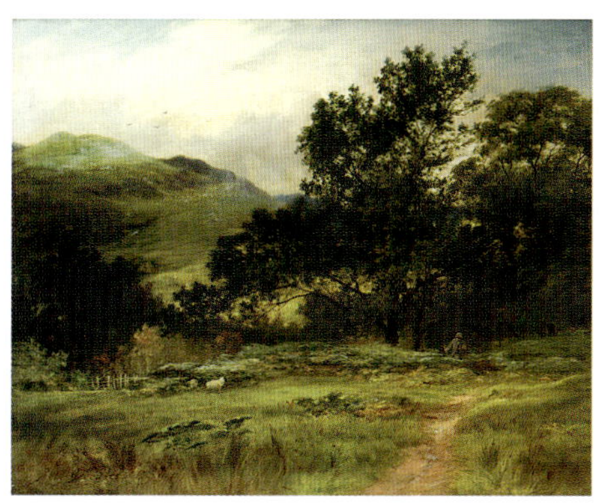

Greenlees, Robert M. 1820–1896
Hillside at Luss
oil on canvas 43 x 52
1103

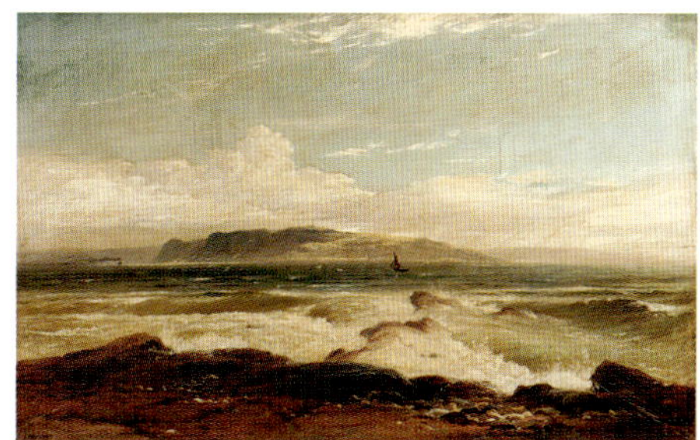

Greenlees, Robert M. 1820–1896
The Little Cumbrae from Corrie, Arran
oil on canvas 81.3 x 127
1840

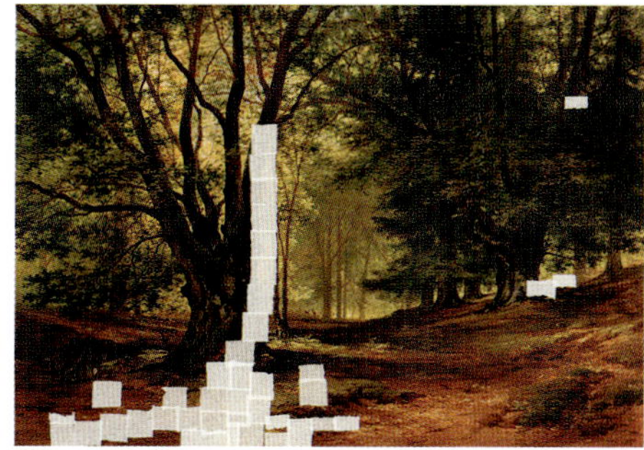

Greenlees, Robert M. 1820–1896
Woods at Inverary
oil on canvas 106.7 x 153.7
3438

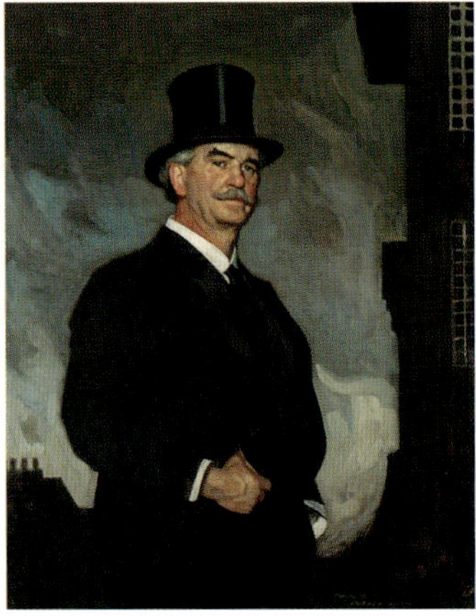

Greiffenhagen, Maurice 1862–1931
Fra Newbery (1855–1946) 1913
oil on canvas 132.1 x 102.2
2154

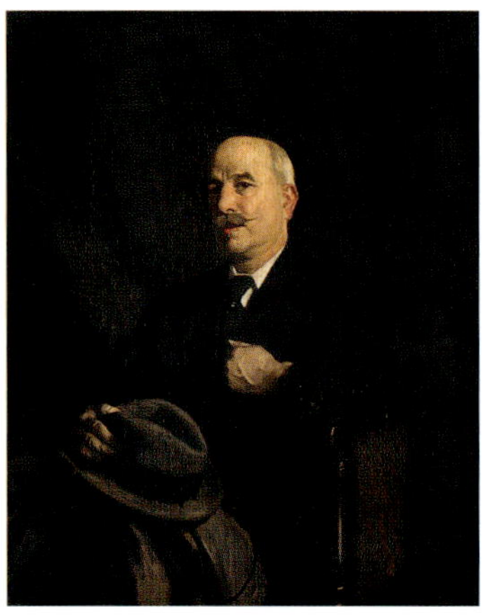

Greiffenhagen, Maurice 1862–1931
Adam C. Hay 1920
oil on canvas 119.4 x 94
2606

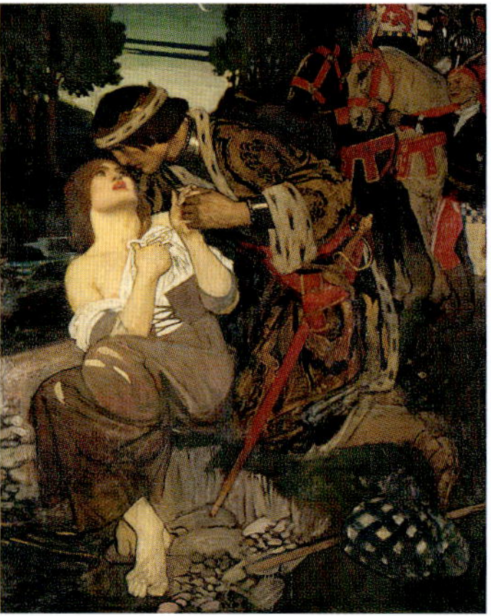

Greiffenhagen, Maurice 1862–1931
Cophetua c.1920–1925
oil on canvas 134 x 106
2076

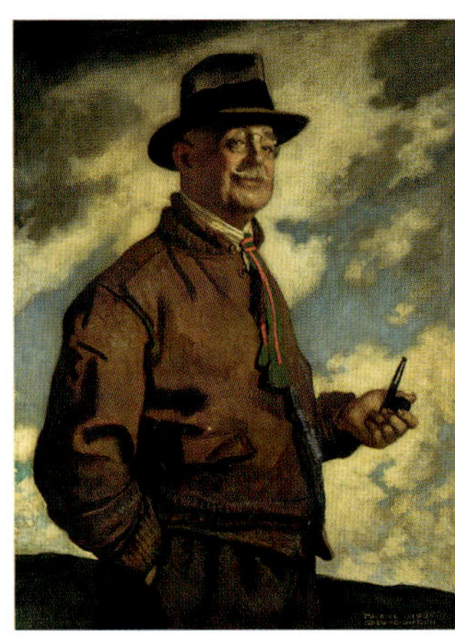

Greiffenhagen, Maurice 1862–1931
*Leonard Raven-Hill (1867–1942), of 'Punch'
Magazine* 1927
oil on canvas 111.8 x 86.4
2168

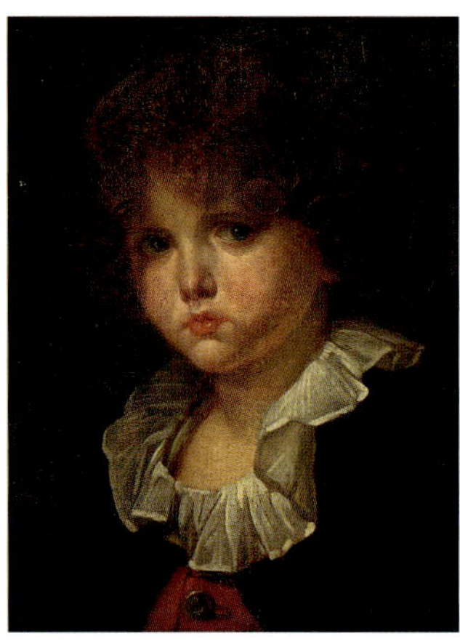

Greuze, Jean-Baptiste (after) 1725–1805
The Sulky Boy c.1780–1800
oil on canvas 38 x 27.9
433

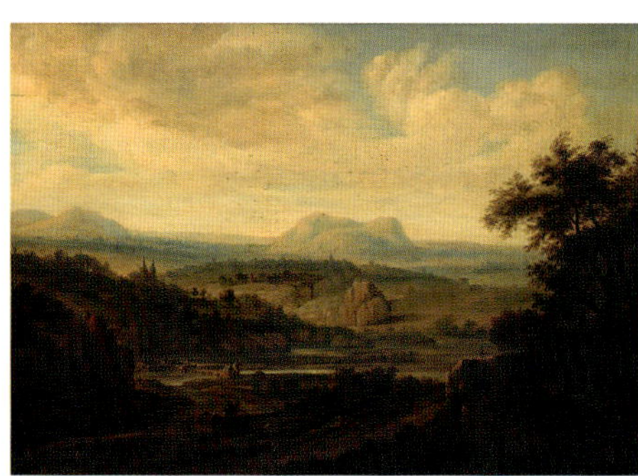

Griffier, Jan I (attributed to) c.1645–1718
A River Landscape
oil on panel 30.7 x 43.5
339

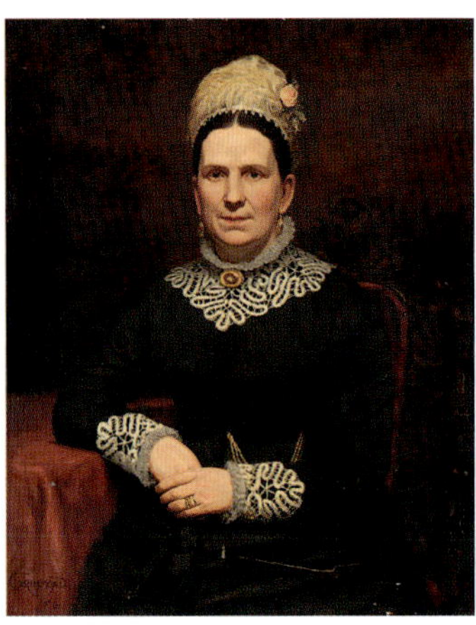

Grimmond
Portrait of a Woman, Half-Length 1880
oil on canvas 91.4 x 71.1
NR.61

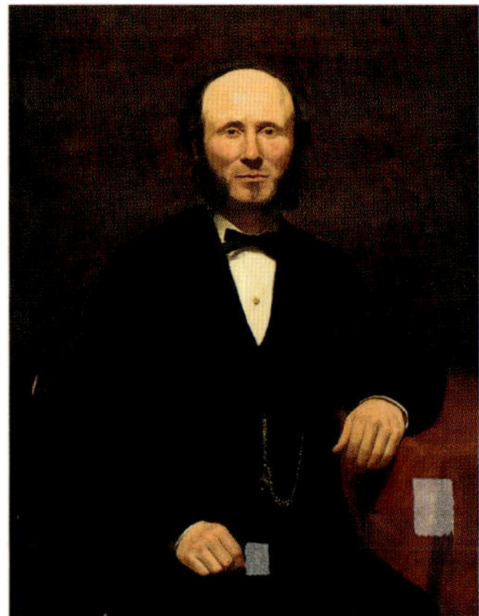

Grimmond
Portrait of a Man, Half-Length c.1880
oil on canvas 91.4 x 71.1
NR.62

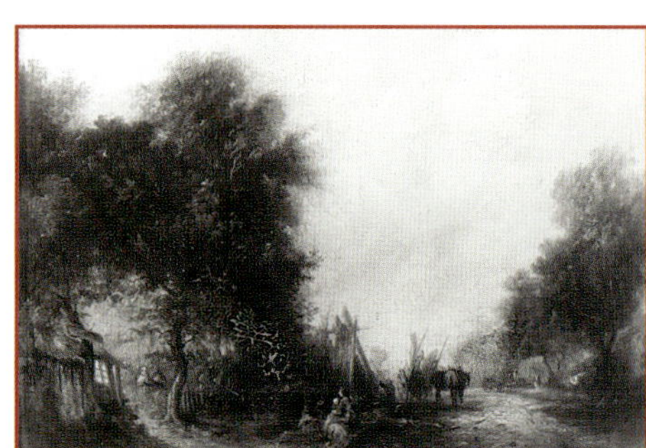

Grimson, A. active 19th C
Landscape
oil on canvas 20.3 x 28.6
239
STOLEN

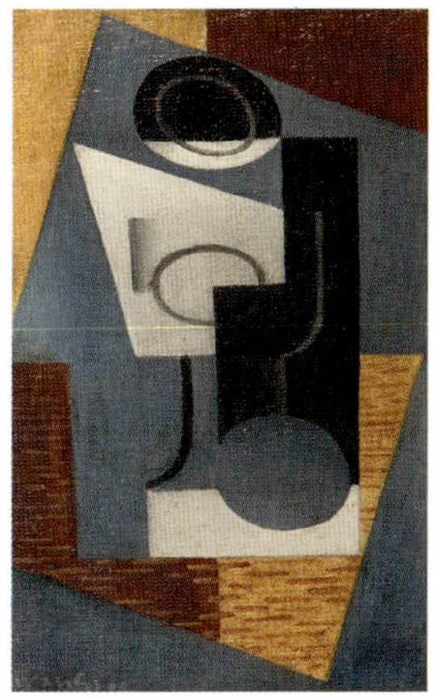

Gris, Juan 1887–1927
The Glass 1918
oil on canvas 26.6 x 15.8
3329

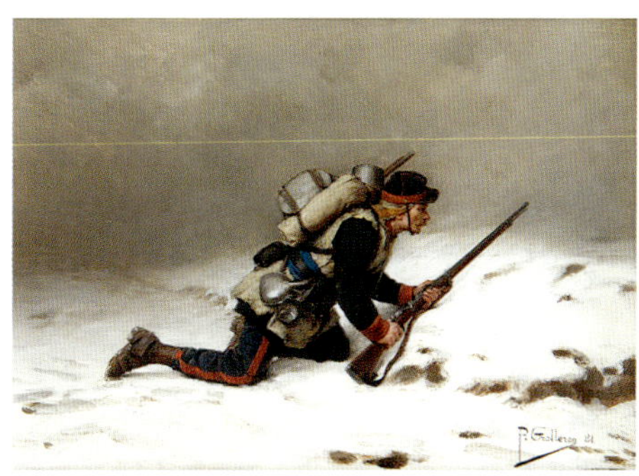

Grolleron, Paul Louis Narcisse 1848–1901
The Scout 1881
oil on panel 15.9 x 21.9
2601

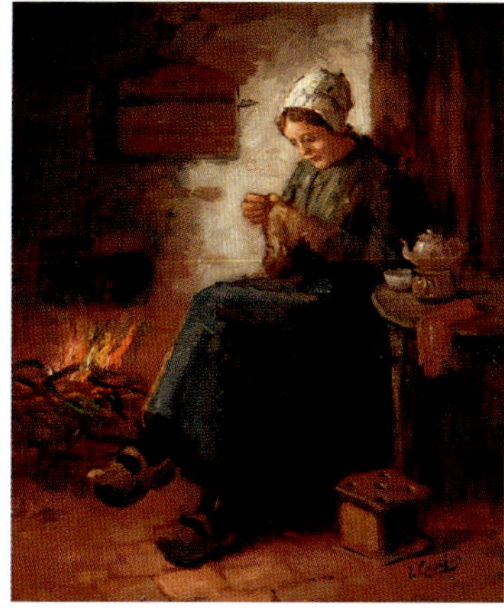

Grossen, L. active 19th C
Interior with a Woman Sewing
oil on canvas 60.3 x 50.8
NR.131

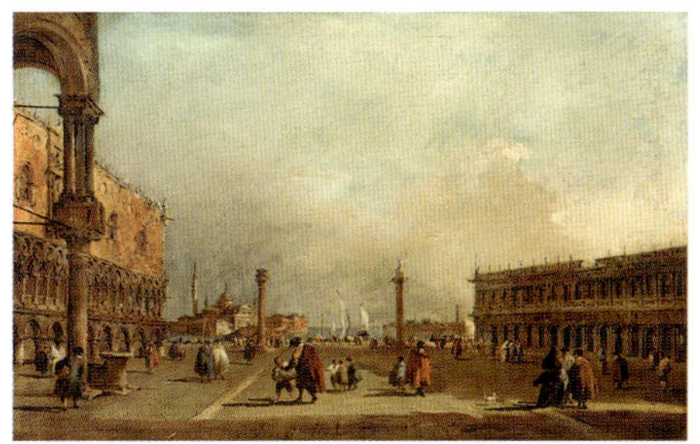

Guardi, Francesco 1712–1793
Venice: The Piazzetta di San Marco c.1760
oil on canvas 48.7 x 77.8
196

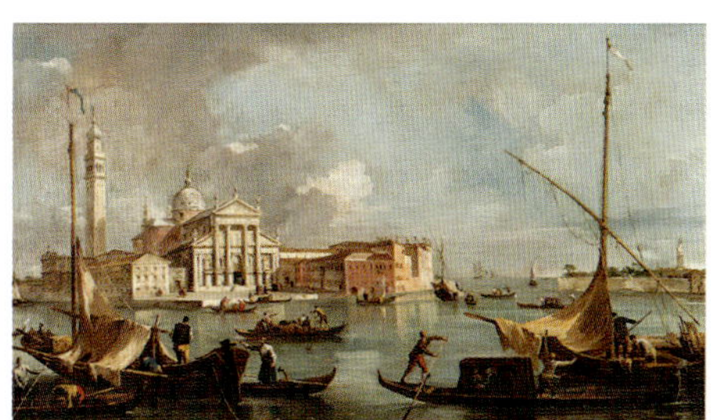

Guardi, Francesco (studio of) 1712–1793
View of San Giorgio Maggiore, Venice c.1760
oil on canvas 71.1 x 119.7
184

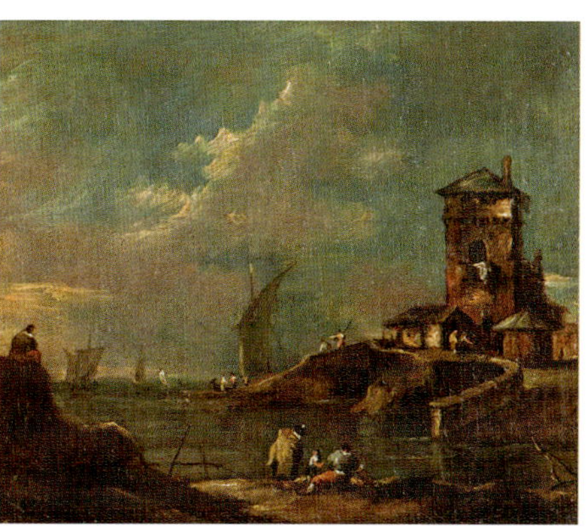

Guardi, Francesco (studio of) 1712–1793
*Capriccio with Rustic Tower, Houses and
Boats* c.1775–1780
oil on canvas 17.1 x 18.1
PL.87 (P)

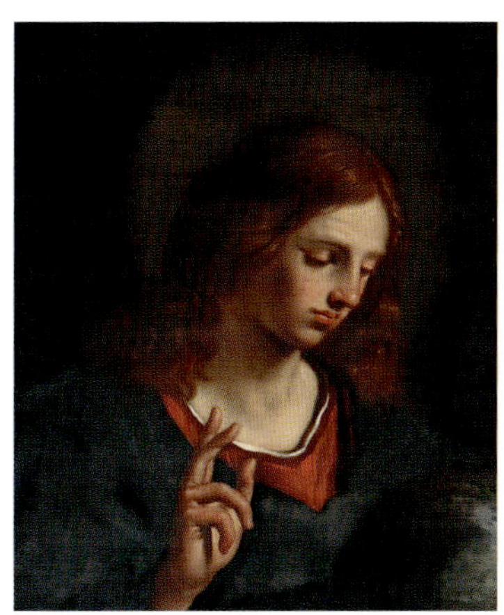

Guercino (follower of) 1591–1666
The Saviour of the World
oil on canvas 59.8 x 55
135

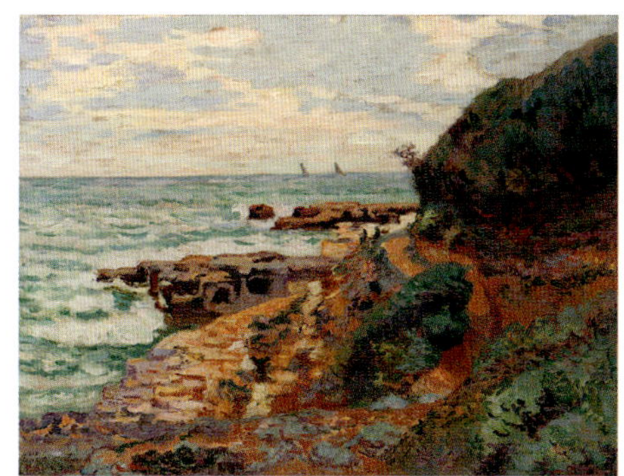

Guillaumin, Armand 1841–1927
The Coast at St Palais 1893
oil on canvas 65.1 x 89
2909

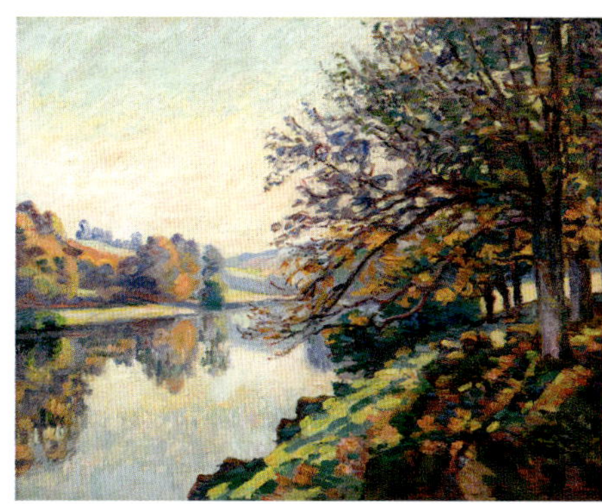

Guillaumin, Armand 1841–1927
Riverbank, Autumn c.1910
oil on canvas 64 x 80
2897

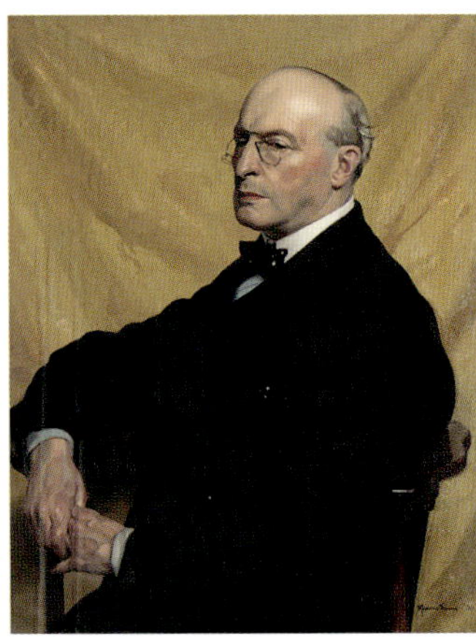

Gunn, Herbert James 1893–1964
Arthur Kay (c.1862–1939) 1930
oil on canvas 89.9 x 69.8
TEMP.3068

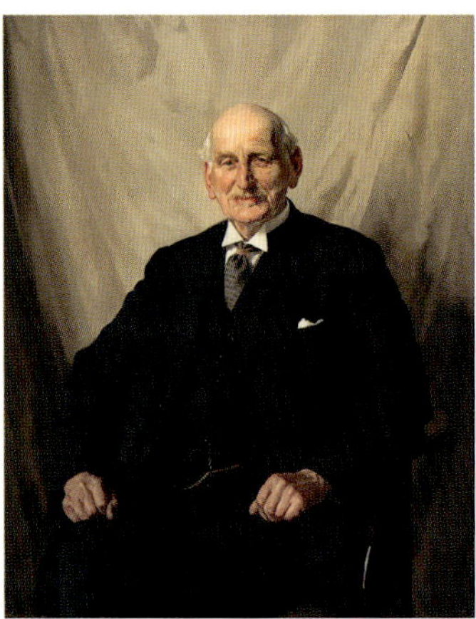

Gunn, Herbert James 1893–1964
William Primrose (1849–1935), JP, Chairman of the Trustees of the Hamilton Bequest 1935
oil on canvas 127 x 101.6
1911

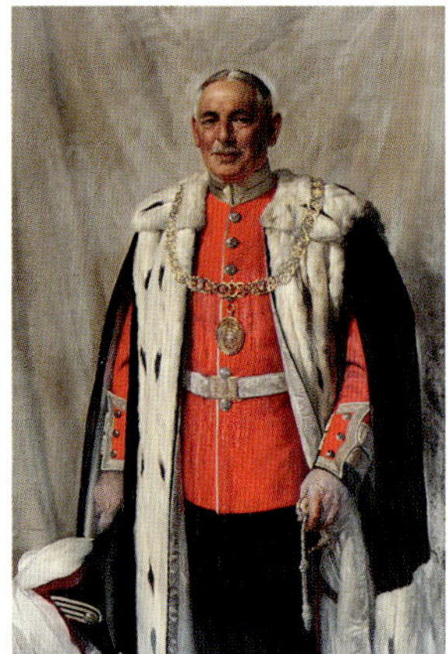

Gunn, Herbert James 1893–1964
Sir Alexander B. Swan, Lord Provost of Glasgow (1932–1935) c.1935
oil on canvas 152.4 x 101.6
1921

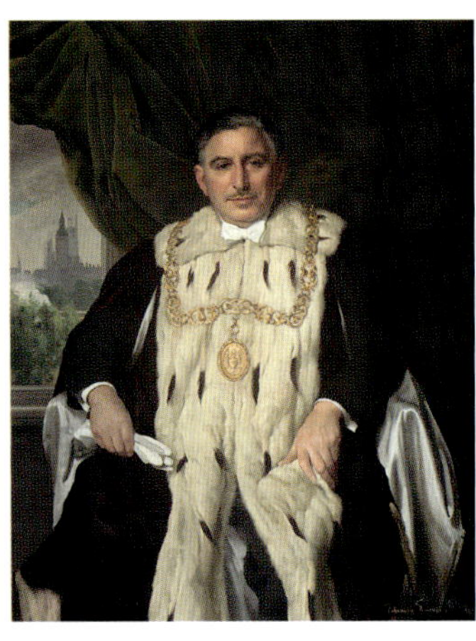

Gunn, Herbert James 1893–1964
Sir Myer Galpern (1903–1993), Lord Provost of Glasgow (1958–1960) 1961
oil on canvas 126.7 x 101.6
3183

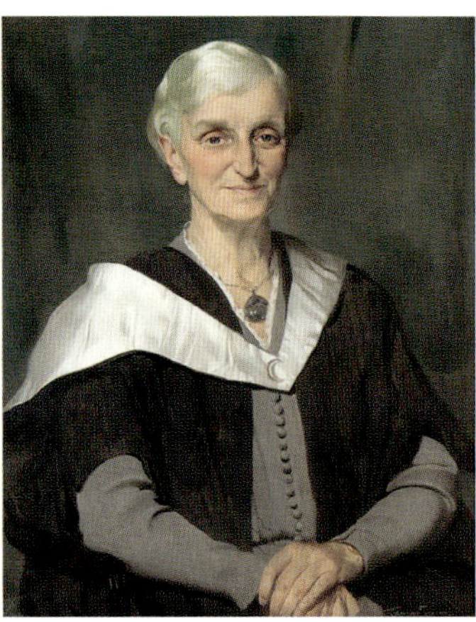

Gunn, Herbert James 1893–1964
Jane M. Robertson, Headmistress of Park School (1929–1944)
oil on canvas 94 x 79
ME.2007.1.4

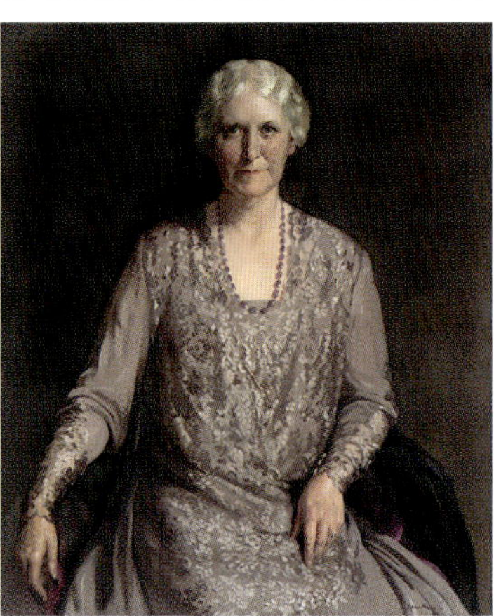

Gunn, Herbert James 1893–1964
Margaret P. Young, Headmistress of Park School (1900–1929)
oil on canvas 128 x 114
ME.2007.1.1

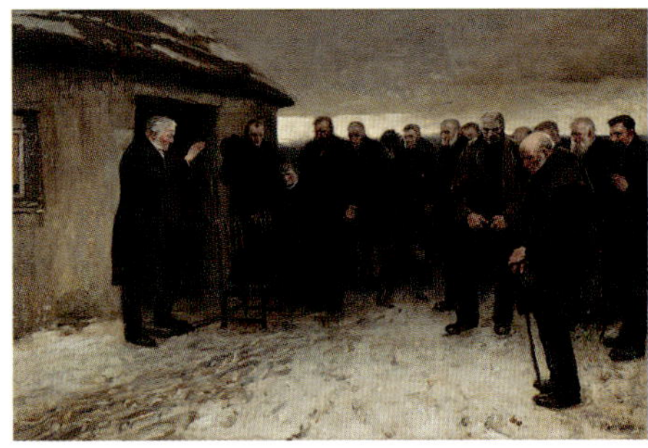

Guthrie, James 1859–1930
A Funeral Service in the Highlands 1882
oil on canvas 129.5 x 193
1060

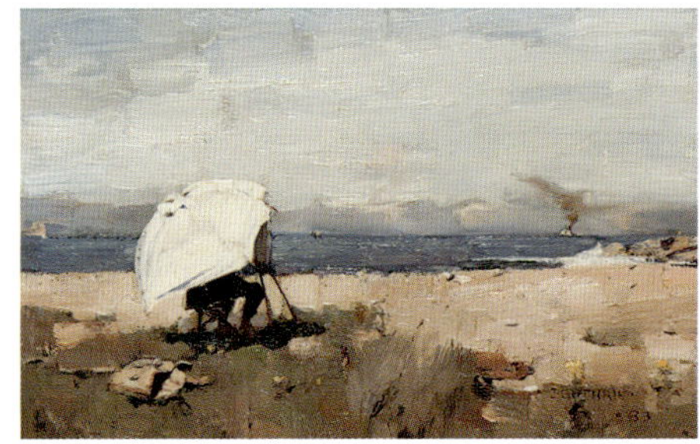

Guthrie, James 1859–1930
Hard at It 1883
oil on canvas 31 x 46
3248

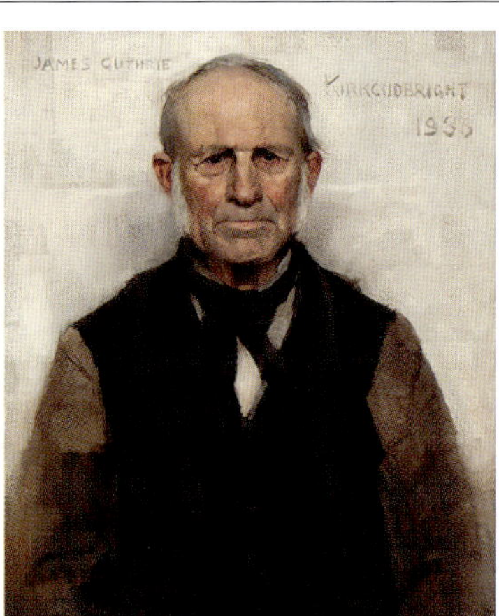

Guthrie, James 1859–1930
Old Willie: The Village Worthy 1886
oil on canvas 60.8 x 50.8
3314

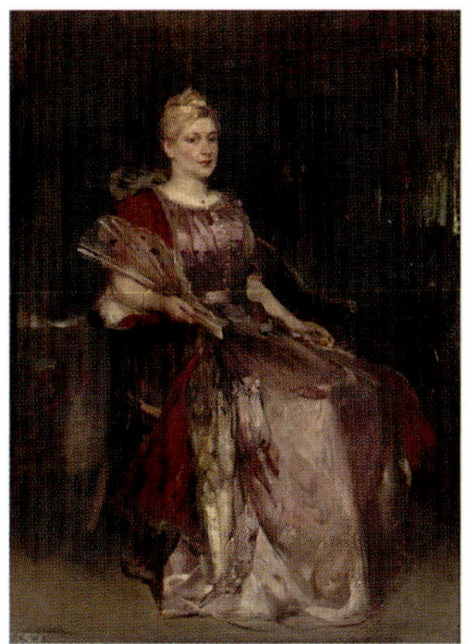

Guthrie, James 1859–1930
Mrs William Fergus 1889
oil on canvas 180.3 x 128.3
2938

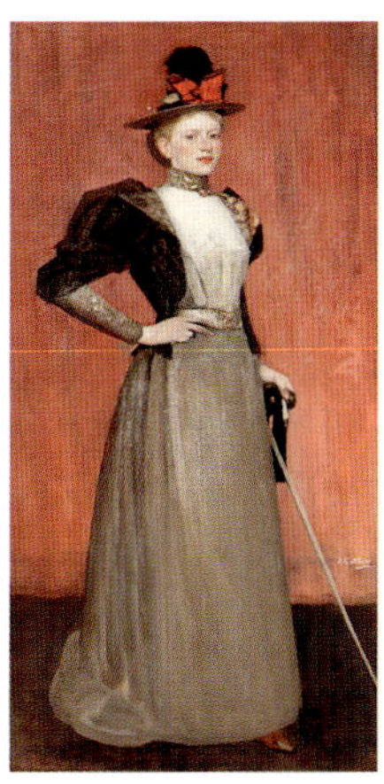

Guthrie, James 1859–1930
Maggie Hamilton (Mrs A. N. Paterson)
(1867–1952) 1892–1893
oil on canvas 195.6 x 87.6
2907

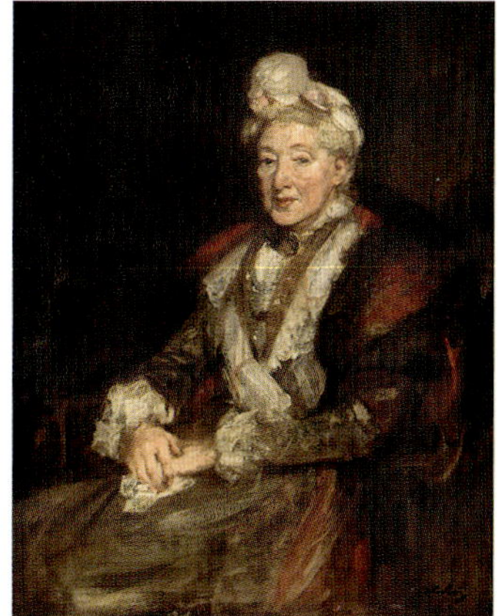

Guthrie, James 1859–1930
Mrs Marie A. Watson 1898
oil on canvas 105.4 x 83.8
2949

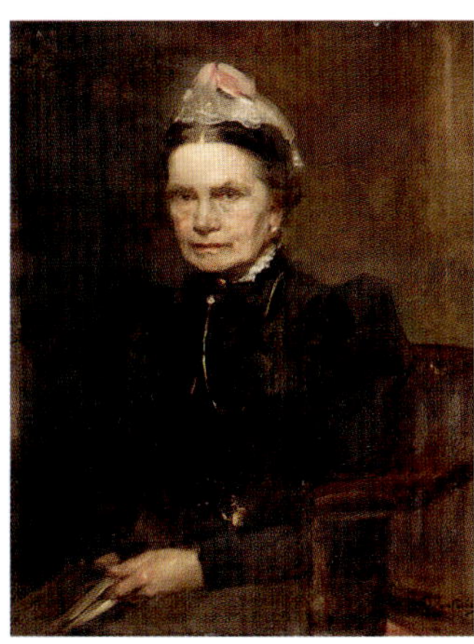

Guthrie, James 1859–1930
Miss Kinnear 1904
oil on canvas 106 x 87
ME.2007.1.2

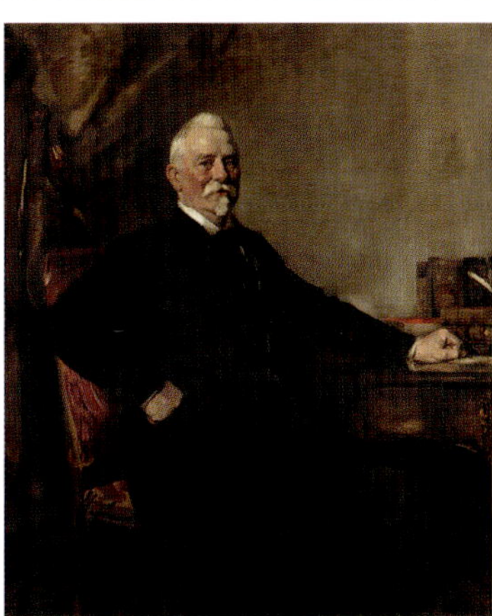

Guthrie, James 1859–1930
Sir John Shearer c.1905
oil on canvas 141 x 116.8
1150

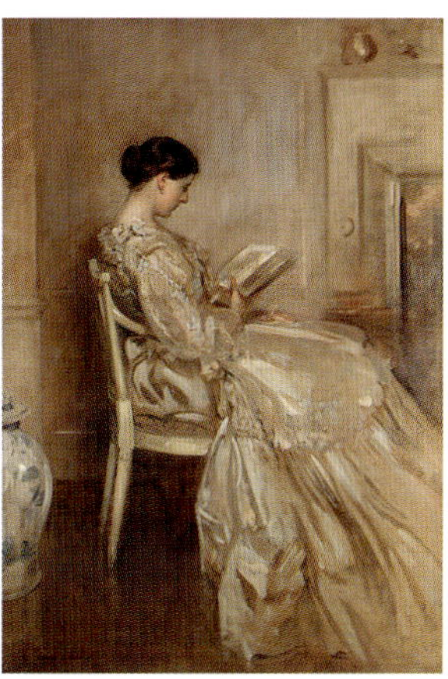

Guthrie, James 1859–1930
Lady Stirling Maxwell 1908
oil on canvas 185 x 125.3
PL.79 (P)

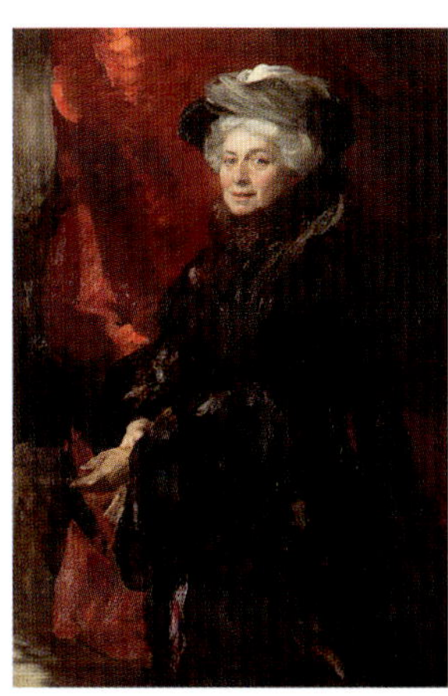

Guthrie, James 1859–1930
Lady E. M. Gardiner 1914
oil on canvas 134.6 x 90.2
2652

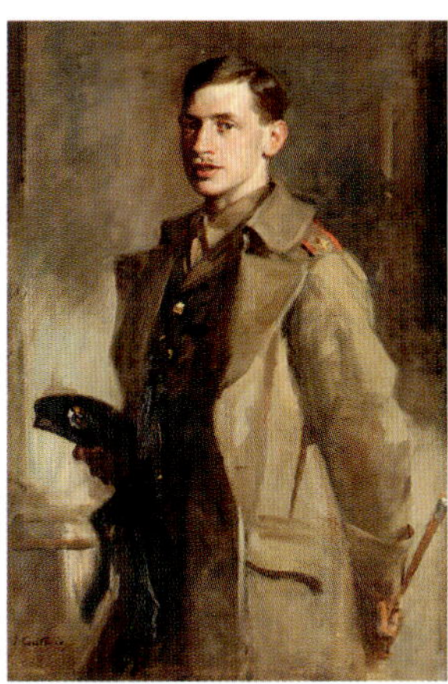

Guthrie, James 1859–1930
Lieutenant A. Leslie Hamilton (1893–1918)
1916
oil on canvas 116.8 x 80
3043

Guthrie, James 1859–1930
Sir Frederick C. Gardiner (1855–1937) 1920
oil on canvas 135.9 x 90.2
2651

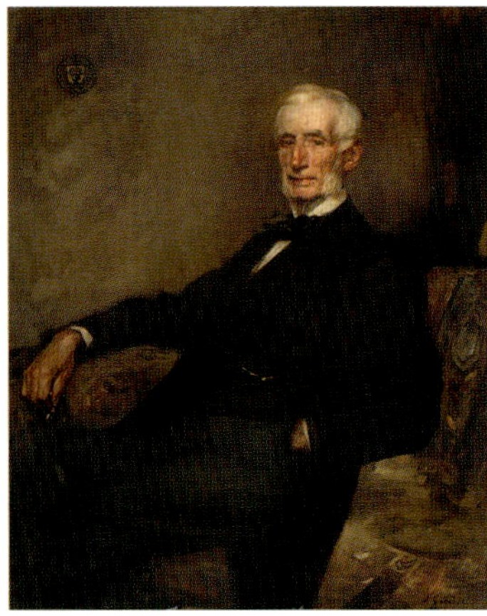

Guthrie, James 1859–1930
Former Bailie Alexander Osborne
oil on canvas 134.6 x 109.2
759

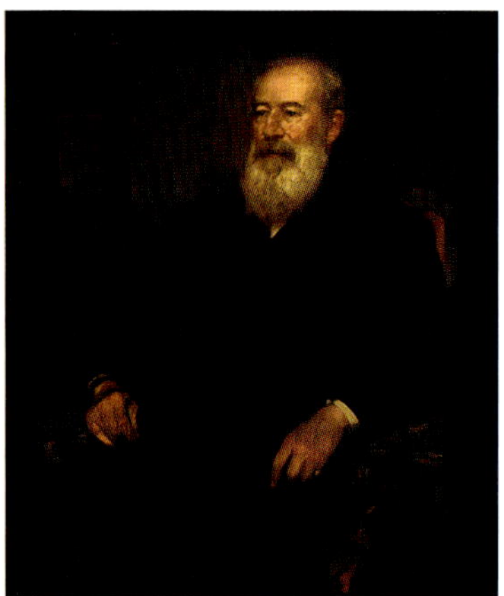

Guthrie, James 1859–1930
William Ritchie
oil on canvas 114.3 x 99.1
2704

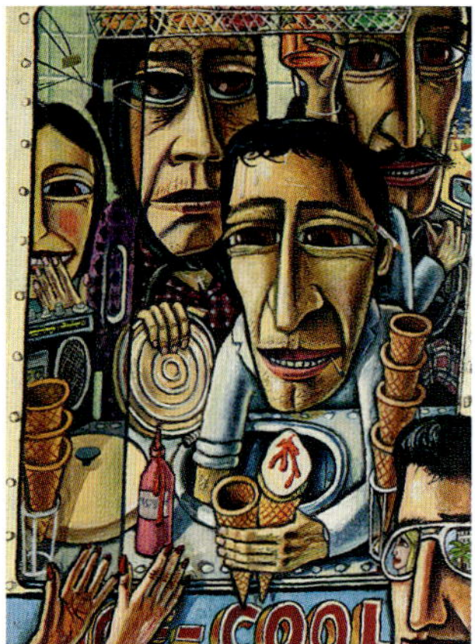

Guy, Alexander b.1962
The Ice-Cream Van 1984
oil on canvas 136.9 x 96.5
PP.1985.52

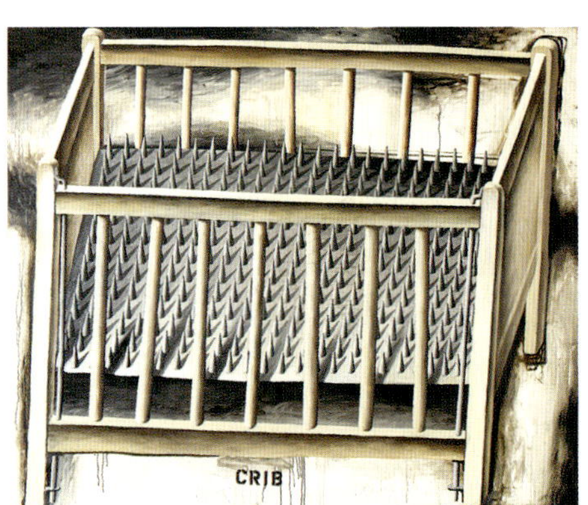

Guy, Alexander b.1962
Crib 1992
oil on canvas 172.8 x 203.1
3506

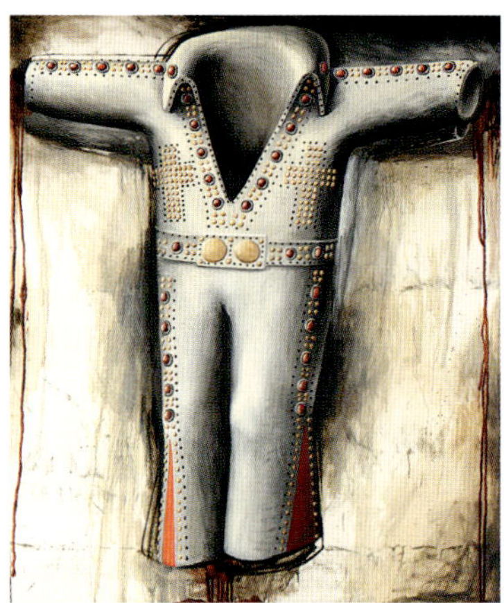

Guy, Alexander b.1962
Crucifixion 1992
oil on canvas 208.3 x 175.3
3507

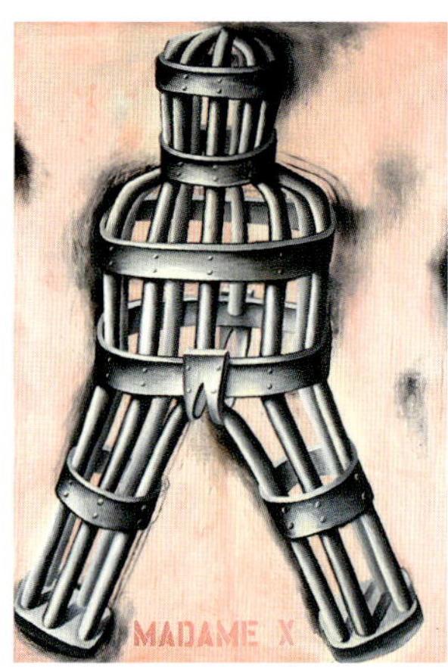

Guy, Alexander b.1962
Madame X II 1992
oil on canvas 264.1 x 172.7
3508

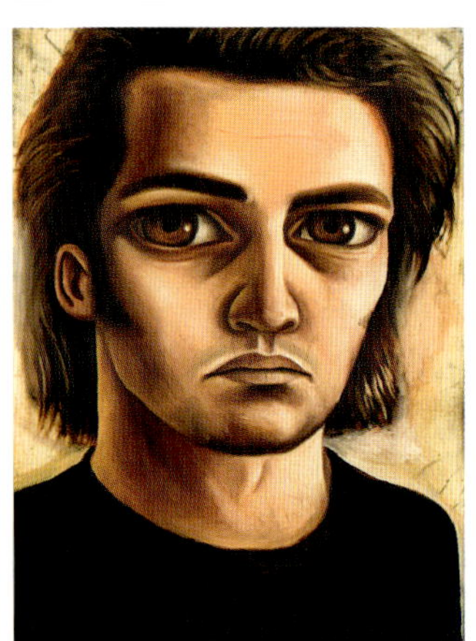

Guy, Alexander b.1962
Me 1992
oil on canvas 93 x 66
3510

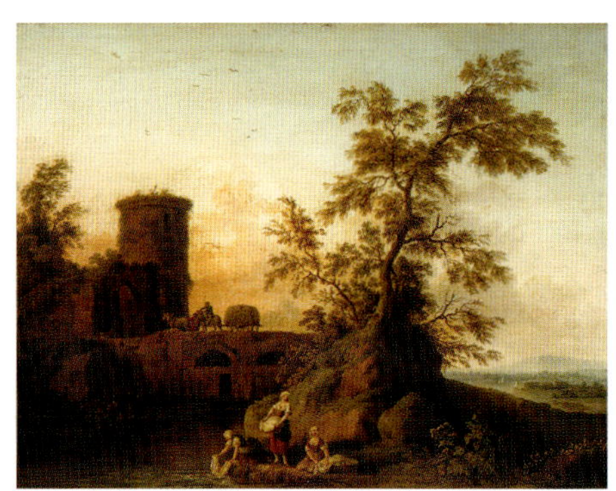

Hackert, Jacob Philipp 1737–1807
Landscape with Washerwomen 1768
oil on canvas 48.9 x 64.8
345

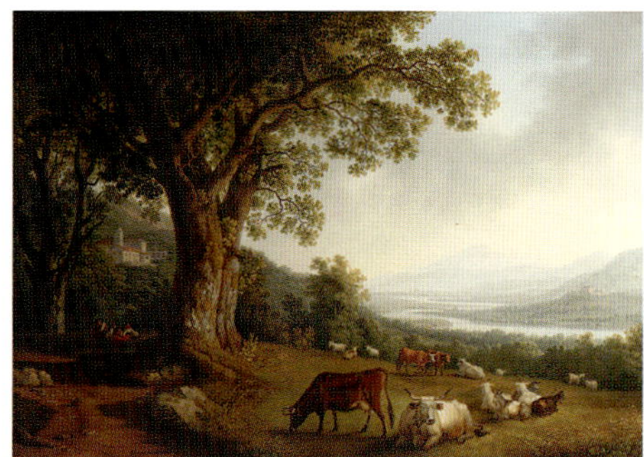

Hackert, Jacob Philipp 1737–1807
Landscape with Cattle and Goats 1799
oil on canvas 63.5 x 87.3
PC.44

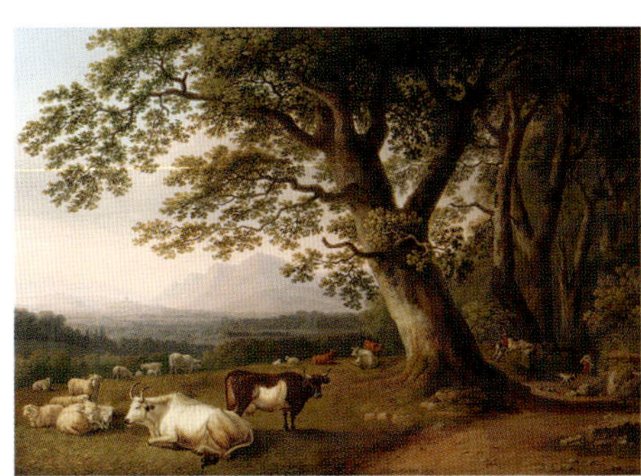 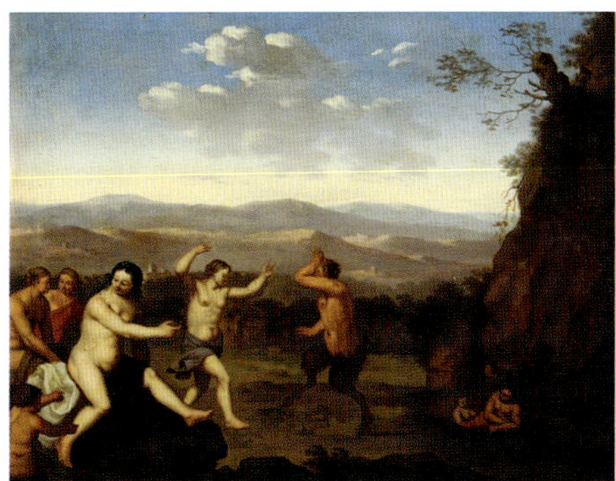 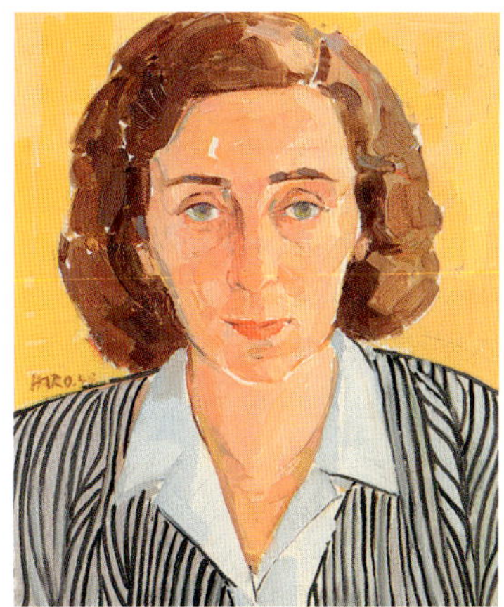

Hackert, Jacob Philipp 1737–1807
Landscape with Cattle and Sheep 1799
oil on canvas 63.8 x 86.9
PC.42

Haensbergen, Johan van (attributed to)
1642–1705
Landscape with Nymphs and Satyrs Dancing
c.1680–1705
oil on panel 26.7 x 34.3
116

Hako
Helen D. Leitch (1914–2000) 1948
oil on canvas 47 x 39
TEMP.19906

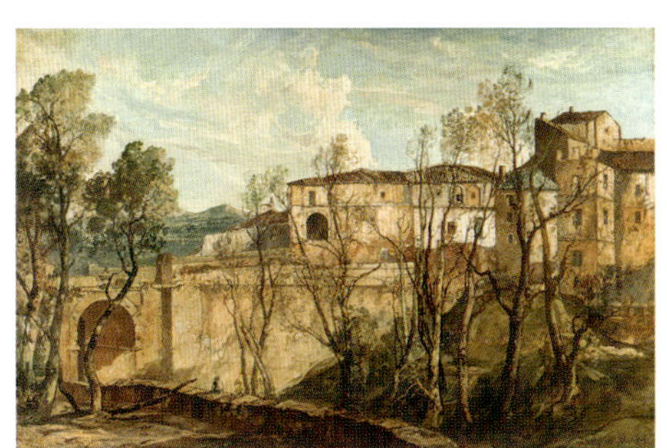 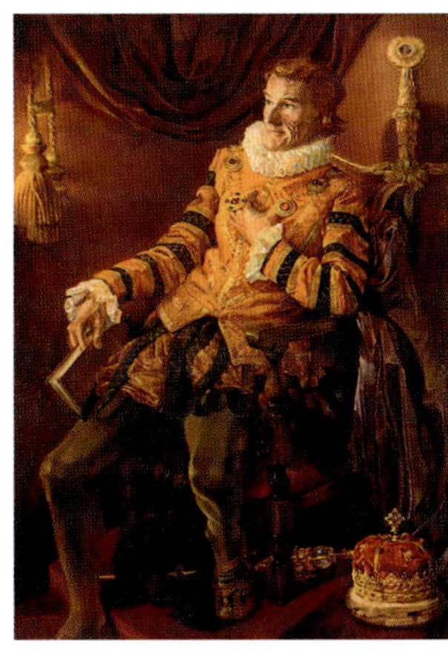 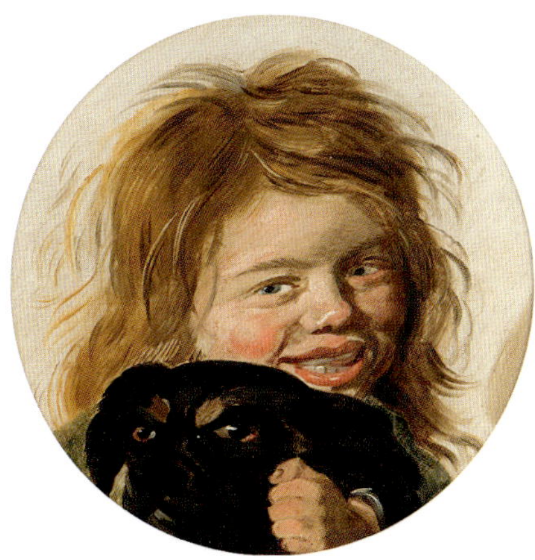

Hall, Oliver 1869–1957
Reminiscence of a Spanish Town
oil on canvas 101.6 x 152.4
1901

Halliday, Dorothy 1923–2001
Duncan Macrae (1905–1967), as Jamie the Saxt 1953
oil on canvas 151.2 x 97.5
LPP.1977.166.1

Hals, Frans (imitator of) c.1581–1666
Head of a Boy with a Dog 19th C
oil on panel 29.2
716

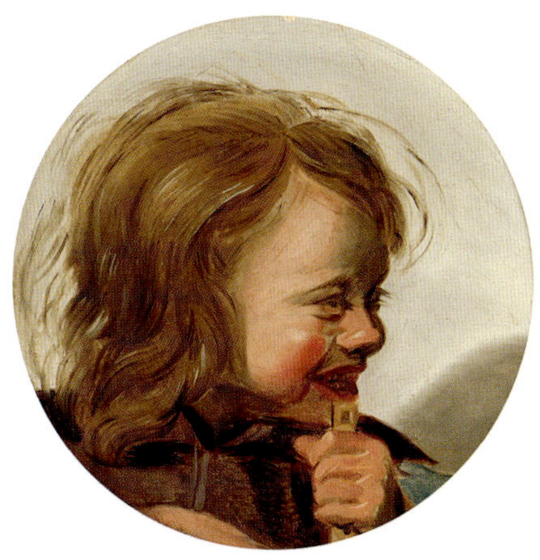 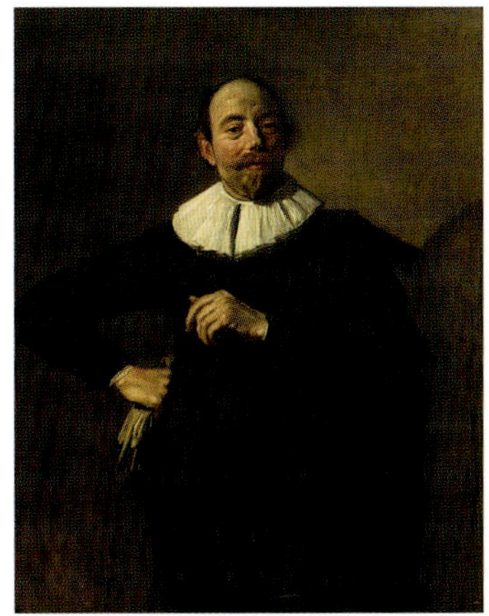 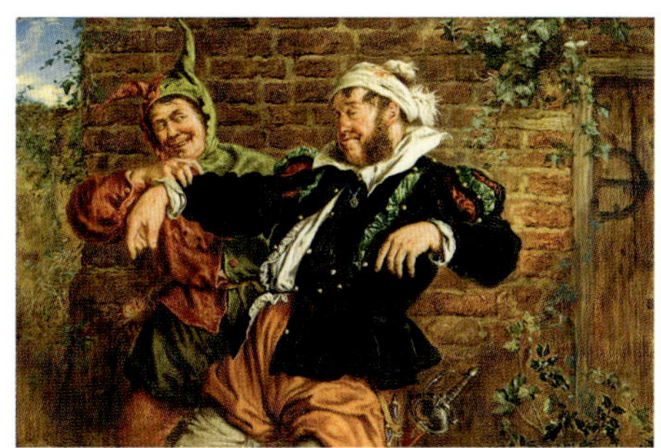

Hals, Frans (imitator of) c.1581–1666
Head of a Boy with a Whistle 19th C
oil on panel 29.2
717

Hals, Frans (studio of) c.1581–1666
Portrait of a Man 1630s
oil on canvas 117 x 91.5
35.276

Halswelle, Keeley 1832–1891
Sir Toby Belch and the Clown (from William Shakespeare's 'Twelfth Night') 1860
oil on canvas 35.6 x 55.9
1062

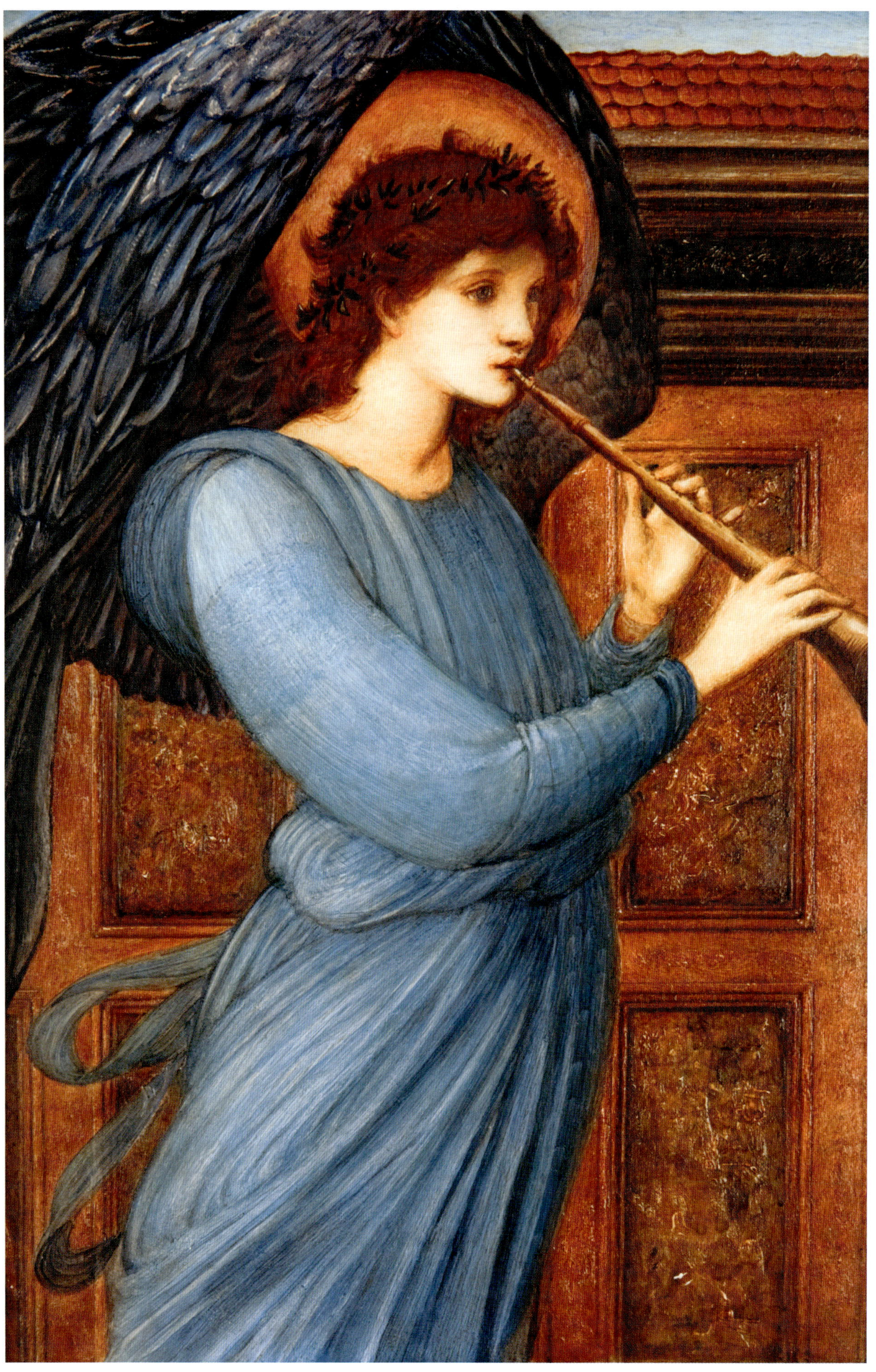

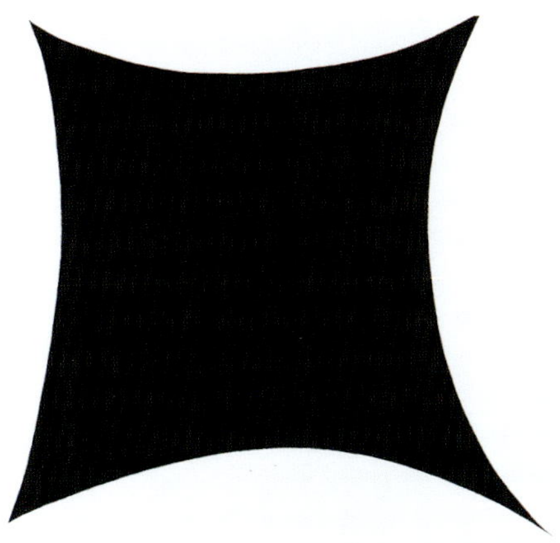

Hamersma, Cyril 1919–1994
Squircle No.1032 1993
acrylic on canvas 122 x 122
3628

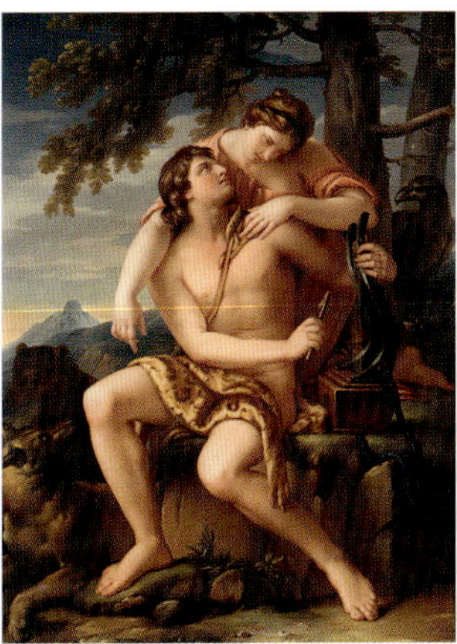

Hamilton, Gavin 1723–1798
Apollo and Artemis c.1770
oil on canvas 170.5 x 121
3297

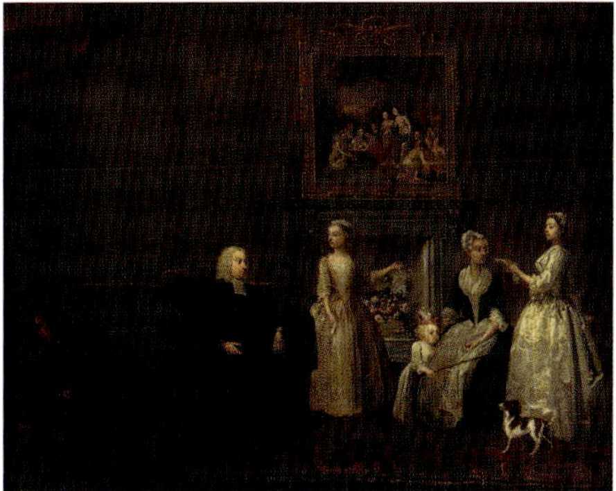

Hamilton, Gawen (attributed to)
1697–1737
*The Vicar of the Parish Visits the Infant
Squire* c.1730
oil on canvas 74.9 x 94.6
3029

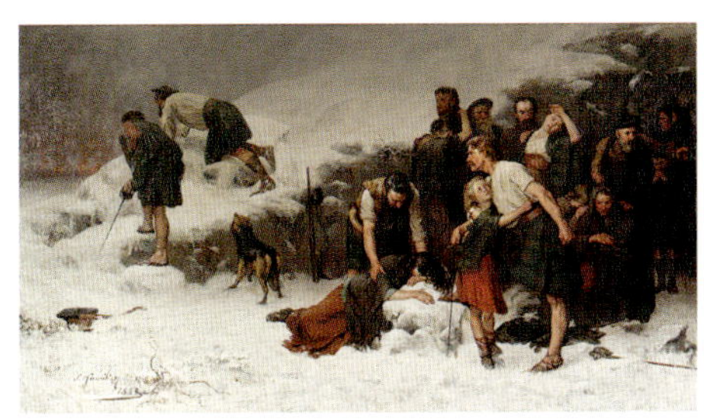

Hamilton, James 1853–1894
The Massacre of Glencoe 1883–1886
oil on canvas 106.7 x 182.9
1790

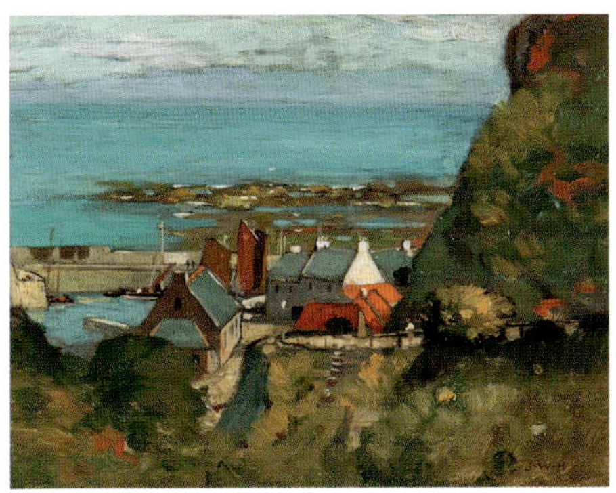

Hamilton, James Whitelaw 1860–1932
View of a Harbour c.1890
oil on panel 18.4 x 23.5
3368

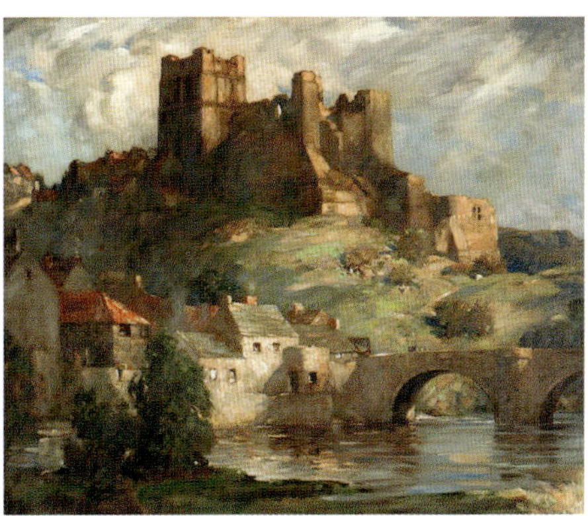

Hamilton, James Whitelaw 1860–1932
Richmond Castle c.1916
oil on canvas 105.4 x 125.1
1392

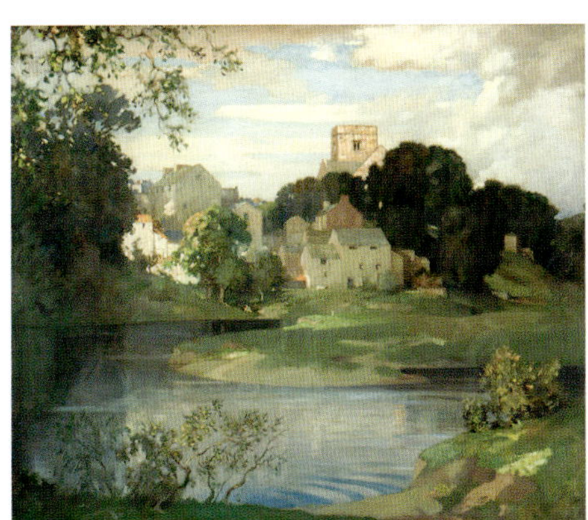

Hamilton, James Whitelaw 1860–1932
Kirkby Lonsdale, Westmorland
oil on canvas 106.7 x 122.1
3044

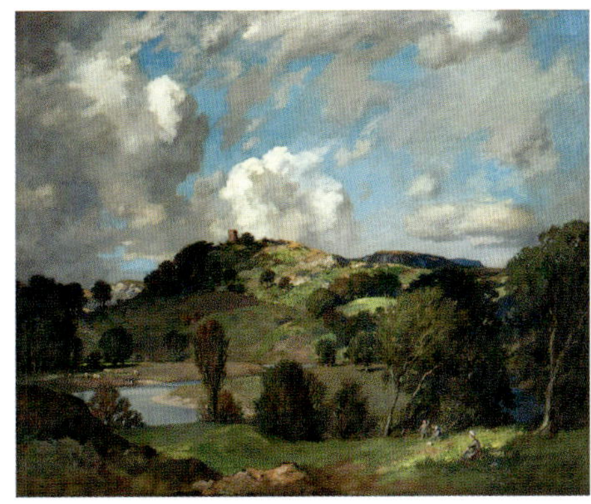

Hamilton, James Whitelaw 1860–1932
The Windings of the Lune
oil on canvas 106.7 x 127
1757

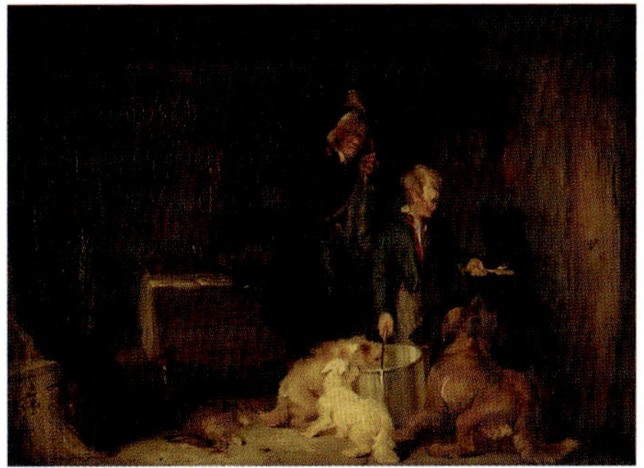

Hancock, Charles 1802–1877
The Gamekeeper's Home 1830
oil on canvas 22.9 x 30.5
457

Facing page: Burne-Jones, Edward, 1833–1898, *The Angel*, (p. 65)

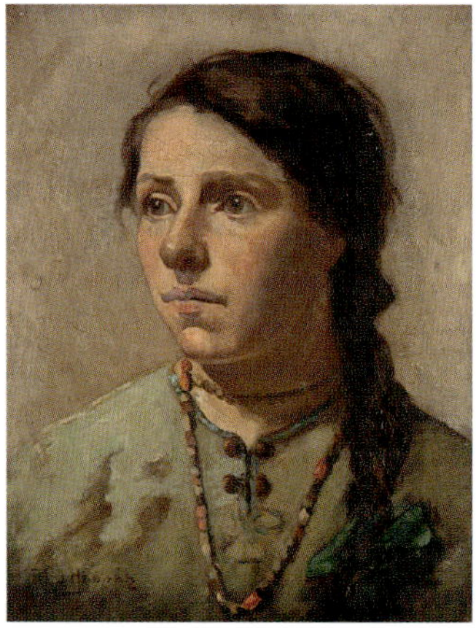

Hannah, Andrew G. 1872/1873–1955
Head of a Woman
oil on canvas 40.7 x 30.5
3431

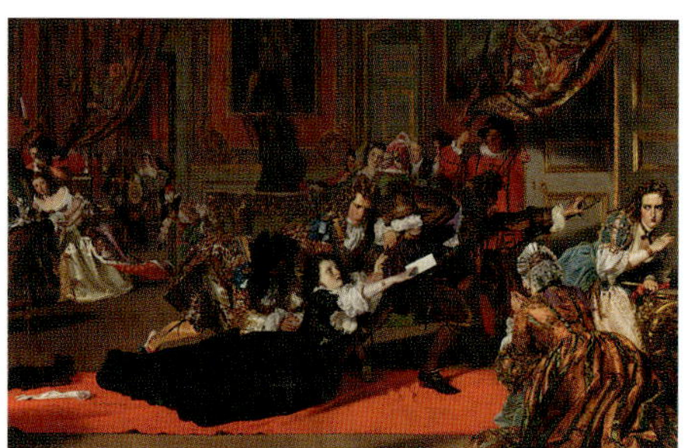

Hannah, Robert 1812–1909
The Countess of Nithsdale Petitioning George I on Behalf of Her Husband c.1854
oil on canvas 114.3 x 182.9
1177

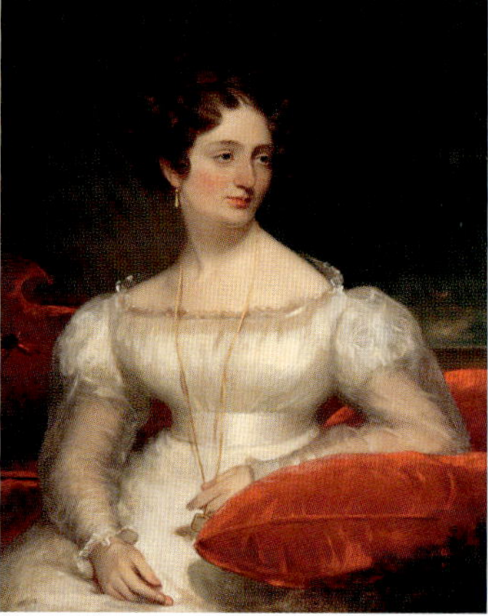

Harding, Chester 1792–1866
Hannah Finlay of Castle Toward (d.1834) 1825–1826
oil on canvas 91.4 x 71.1
3019

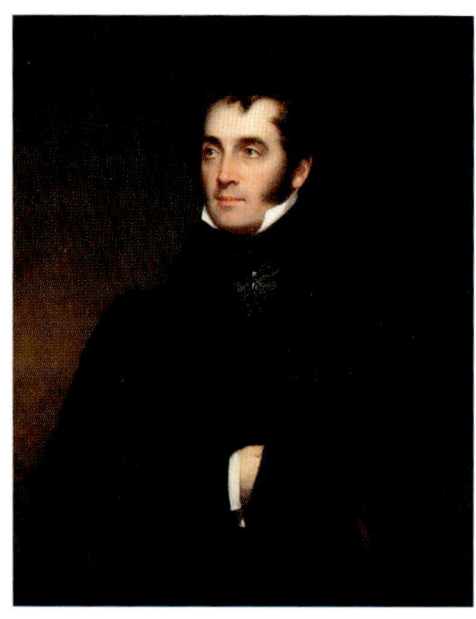

Harding, Chester 1792–1866
Thomas Grahame of Whitehill (1791–1870) c.1825
oil on canvas 91.4 x 71.1
3018

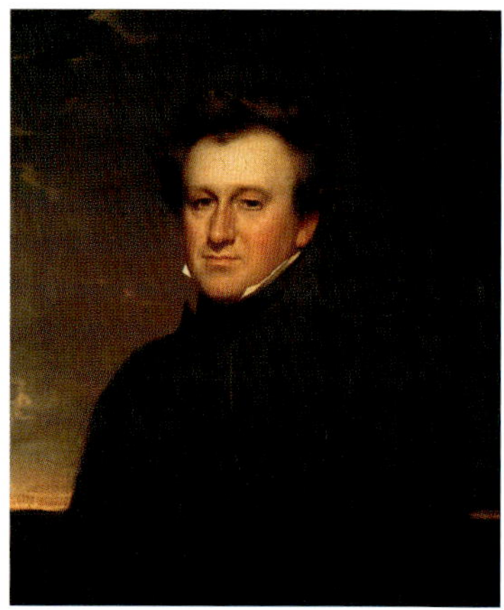

Harding, Chester 1792–1866
John Pattison (1783–1867)
oil on canvas 76.2 x 63.5
2535

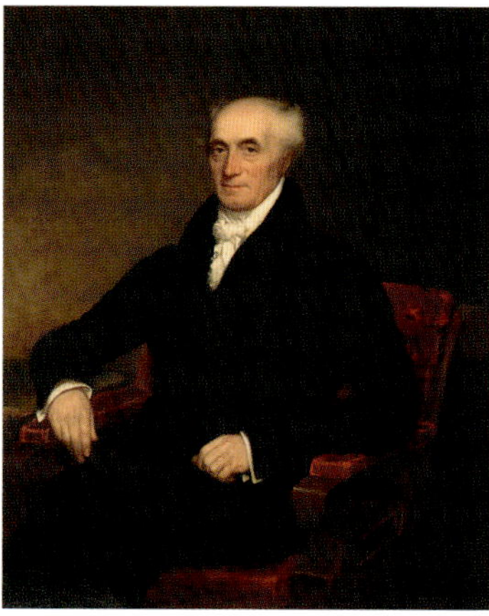

Harding, Chester 1792–1866
Robert Grahame (1759–1851), Lord Provost of Glasgow (1833–1834)
oil on canvas 127 x 101.6
2683

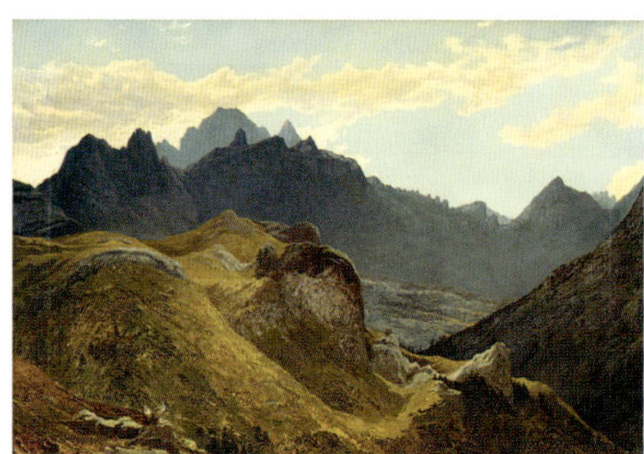

Hargitt, Edward 1835–1895
Mountain Landscape 1859
oil on canvas 54.5 x 80
3119

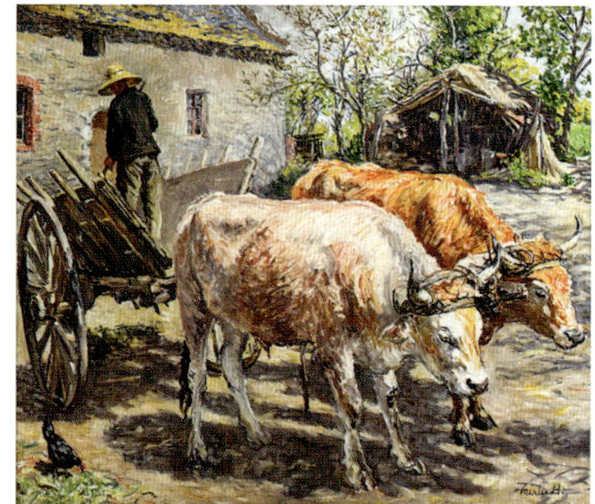

Harmar, Fairlie 1876–1945
Oxen in Brittany
oil on canvas 76.2 x 88.9
2106

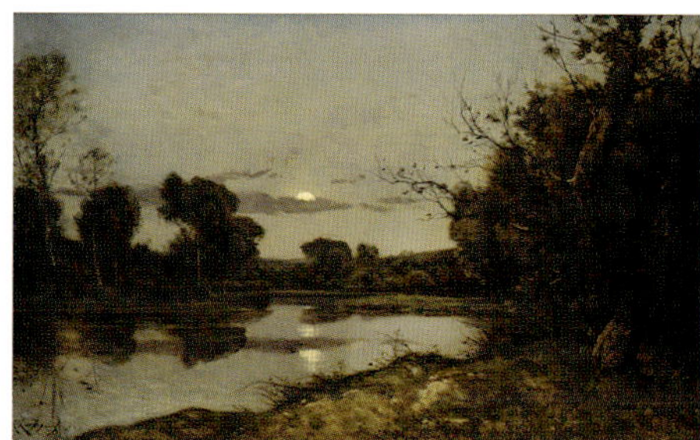

Harpignies, Henri-Joseph 1819–1916
Moonrise 1892
oil on canvas 52.5 x 84.2
1832

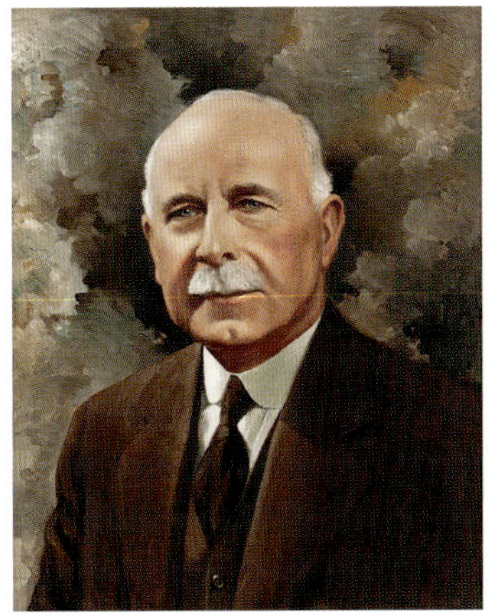

Harris, H. active 19th C
William C. Honeyman
oil on canvas 78 x 65.5
T.1996.19

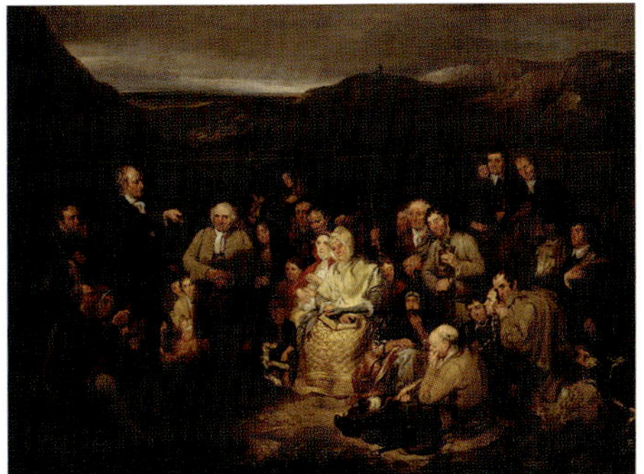

Harvey, George 1806–1876
The Covenanters' Preaching c.1830
oil on panel 82.6 x 106.7
485

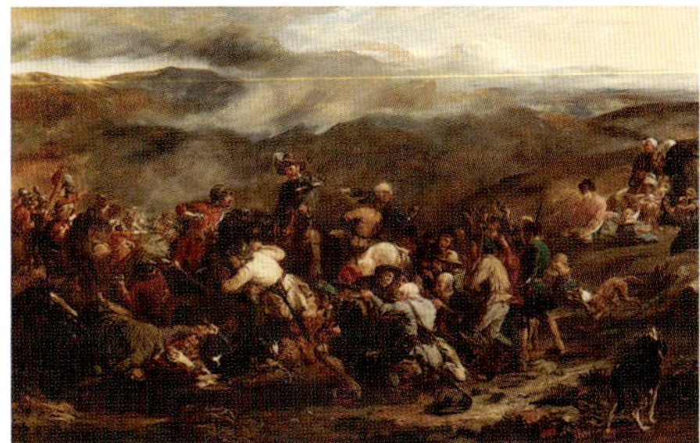

Harvey, George 1806–1876
Drumclog 1836
oil on panel 100.9 x 159.2
3099

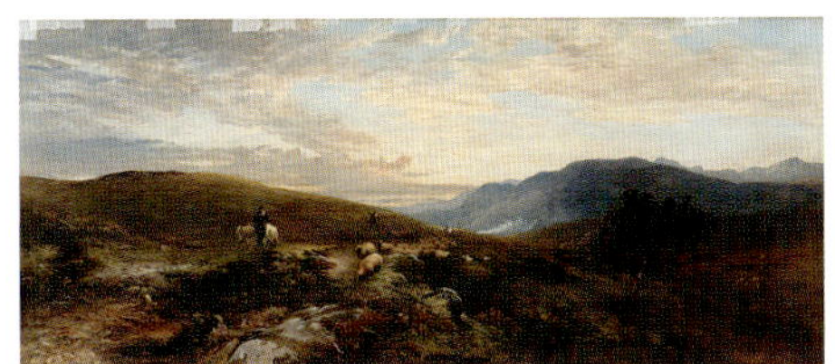

Harvey, George 1806–1876
The Drove Road 1865
oil on canvas 76.2 x 182.9
924

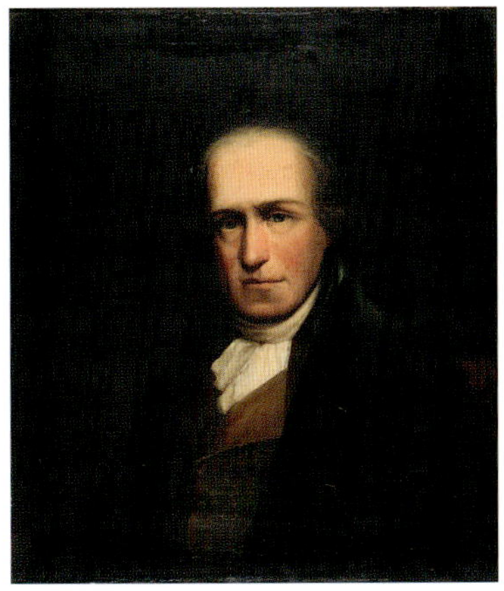

Harvey, R.
*James Watt (1736–1819), Engineer,
Greenock* 1854
oil on canvas 95 x 83
TEMP.21579

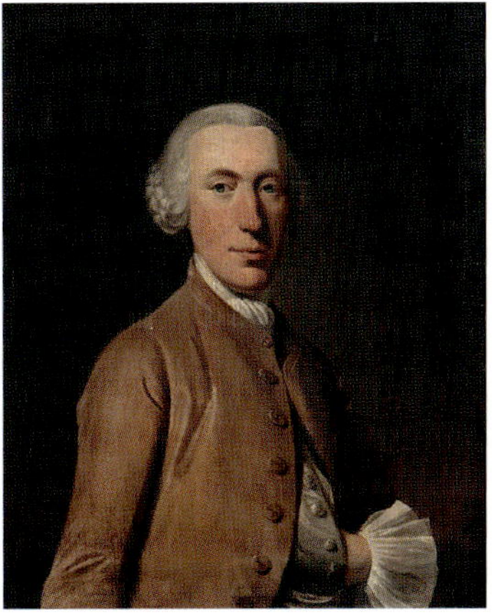

Harvie, Robert d.1781
*Arthur Connell (1717–1775), Provost of
Glasgow (1772–1773)* 1758
oil on canvas 79.5 x 64
2609

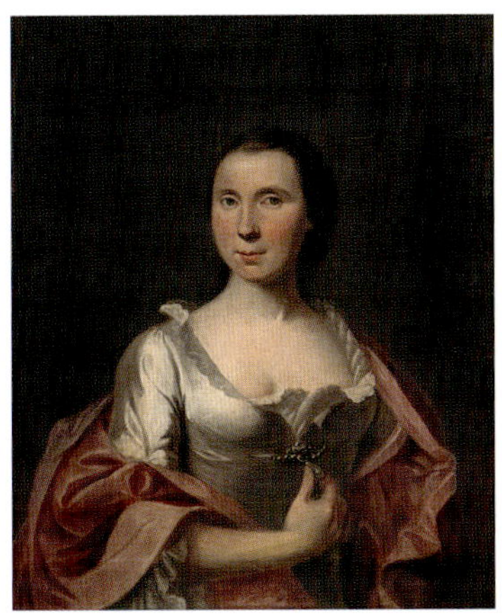

Harvie, Robert d.1781
Mrs Magdalene Connell (d.1803) 1758
oil on canvas 77.6 x 63.8
2610

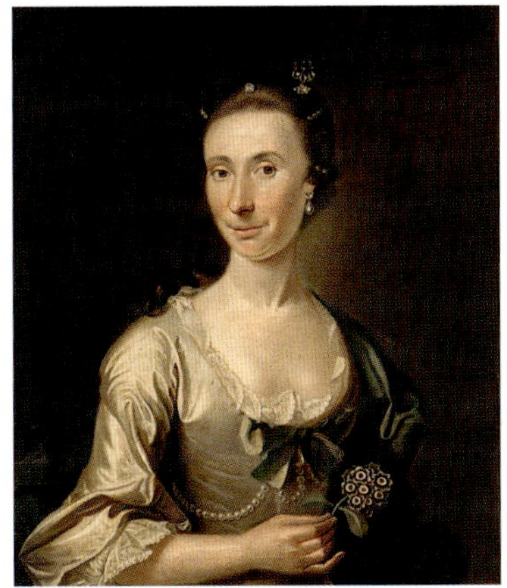

Harvie, Robert d.1781
Mrs George McCall
oil on canvas 76.2 x 63.5
2523

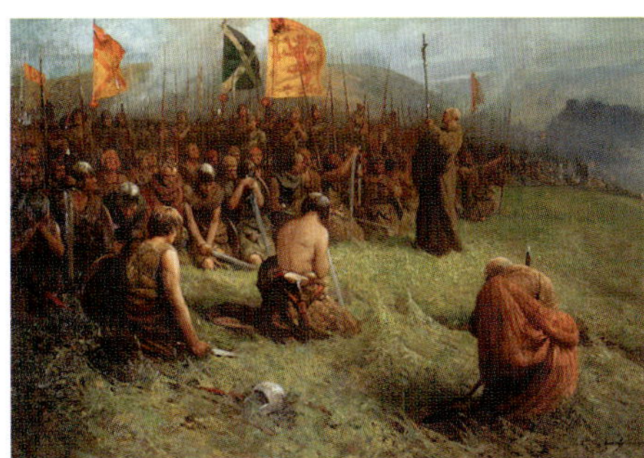

Hassall, John 1868–1948
Bannockburn 1914–1915
oil on canvas 125.7 x 180.3
1386

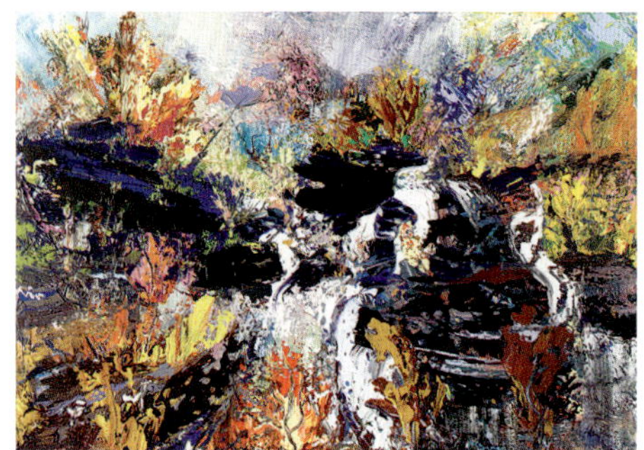

Hawkins, James b.1954
The Black Rock Falls 1992
acrylic on canvas 182.9 x 254
3502

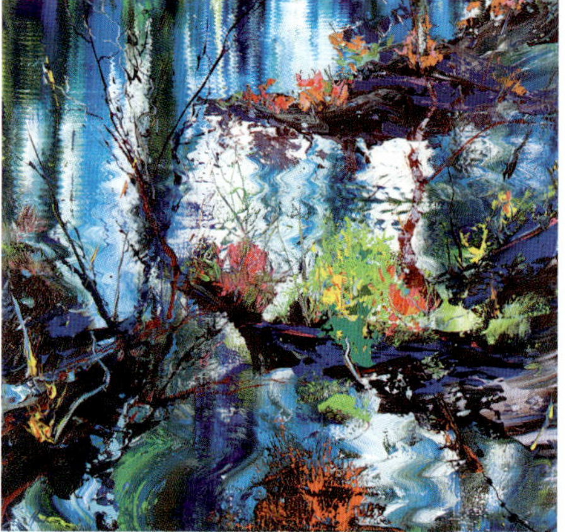

Hawkins, James b.1954
Galleon Rock 1996
acrylic on canvas 121.5 x 121.5
3601

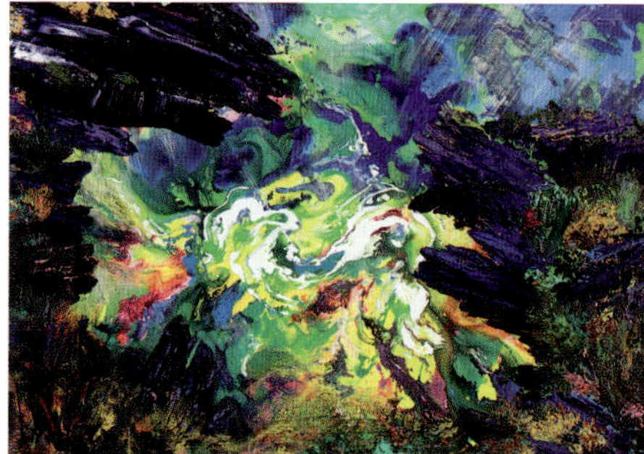

Hawkins, James b.1954
Vertigo 1996
acrylic on canvas 184.1 x 254.3
3606

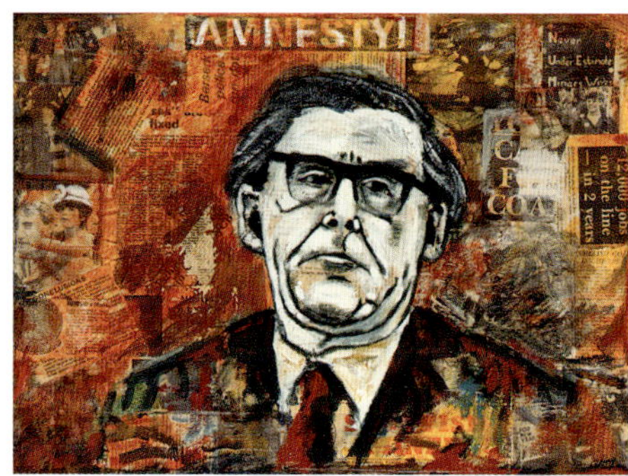

Hay, Andrew b.1944
Michael McGahey (1925–1999) 1984
cryla on paper 55.8 x 74.6
PP.1985.64.8

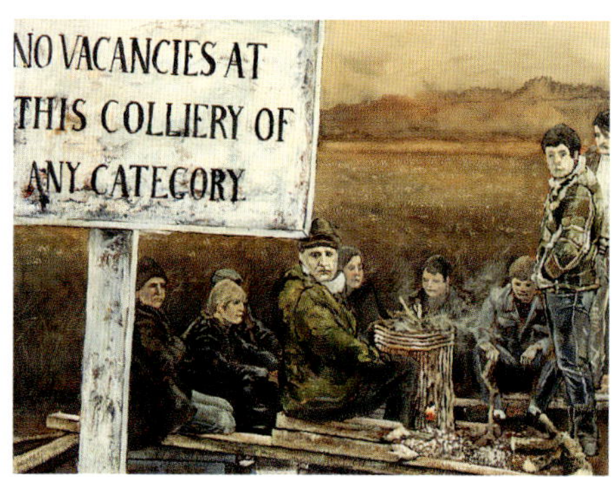

Hay, Andrew b.1944
No Vacancies at This Colliery of Any Category
1984
acrylic on paper 60.4 x 78.6
PP.1985.64.2

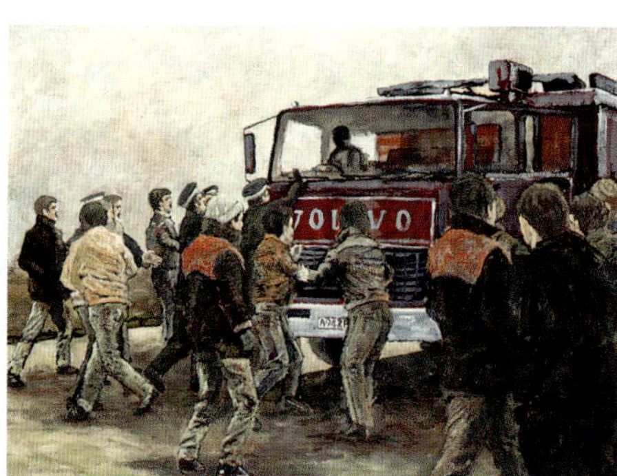

Hay, Andrew b.1944
Pickets and 'Yuill and Dodds' Lorry 1984
acrylic on paper 56.2 x 74.1
PP.1985.64.3

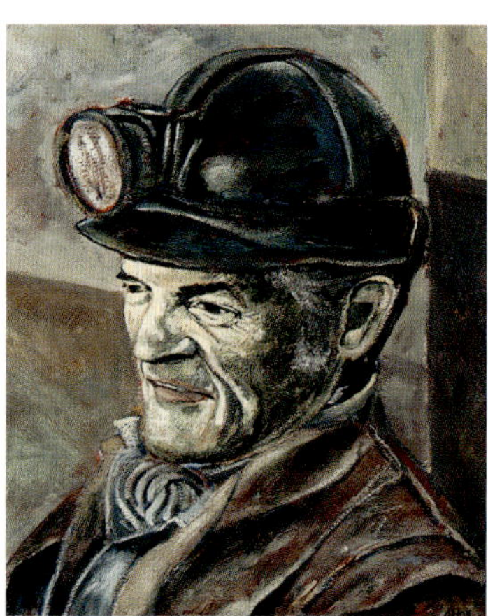

Hay, Andrew b.1944
Portrait of a Miner 1984
acrylic on paper 56.4 x 47.7
PP.1985.64.9

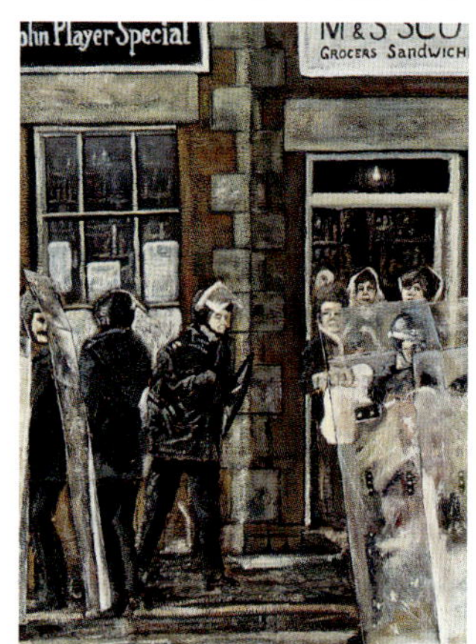

Hay, Andrew b.1944
Riot Police at the Newsagents 1984
cryla on paper 70.7 x 50.7
PP.1985.64.5

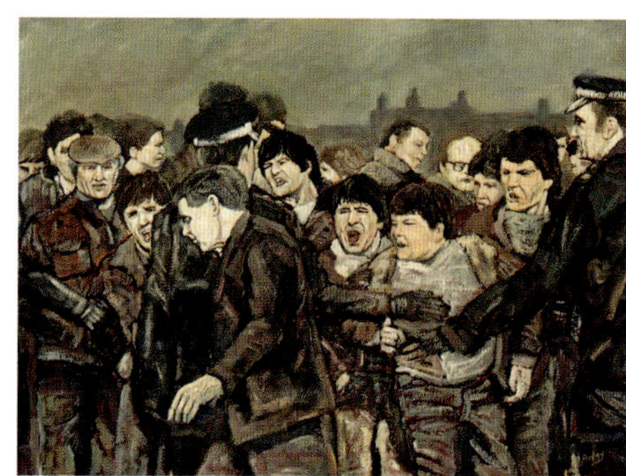

Hay, Andrew b.1944
The Police and the Picket Lines 1984
acrylic on paper 56 x 74.2
PP.1985.64.4

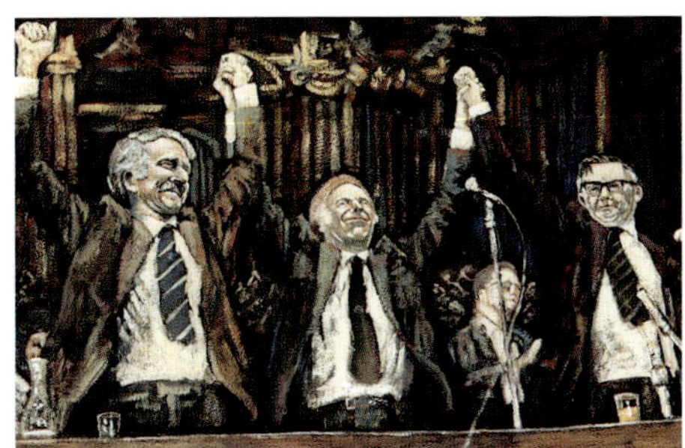

Hay, Andrew b.1944
The Strike Leaders 1984
cryla on paper 47 x 70.5
PP.1985.64.6

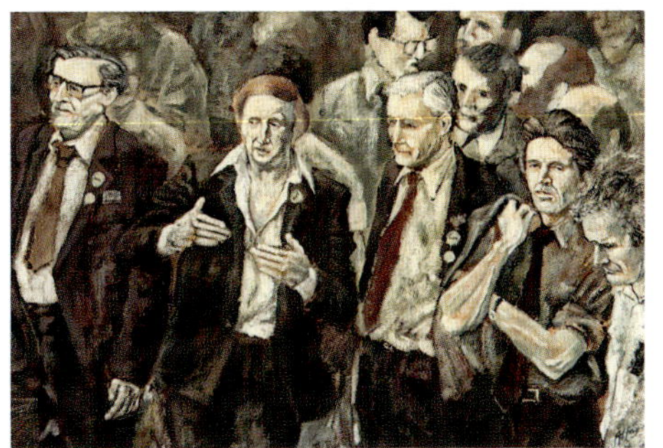

Hay, Andrew b.1944
The Strike Leaders and Supporters 1984
cryla on paper 52.7 x 74.4
PP.1985.64.7

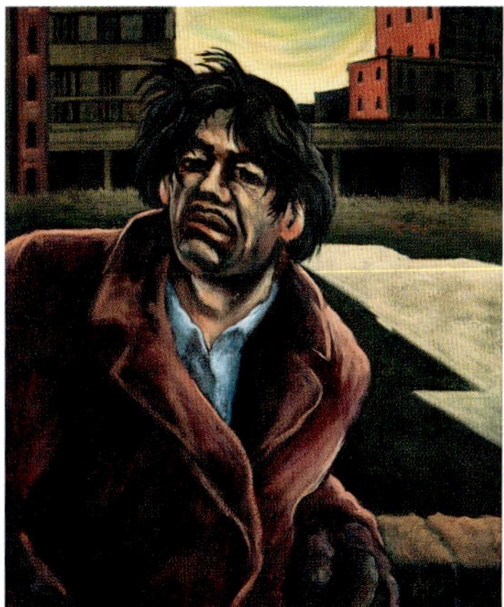

Hay, Andrew b.1944
Harry 1990
oil on canvas 61 x 50.8
3472

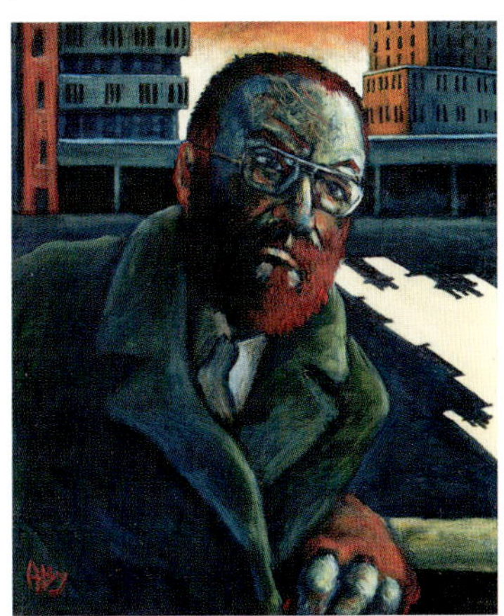

Hay, Andrew b.1944
Self Portrait c.1994
oil on canvas 89 x 73.5
3554

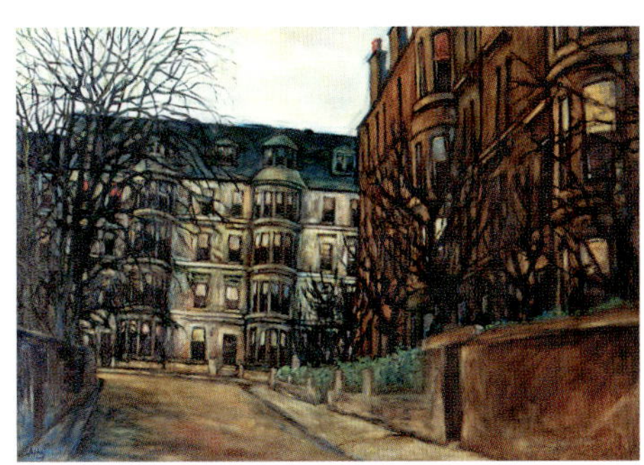

Hay, Andrew b.1944
Streets I Walked with My Father c.1994
oil on canvas 105.4 x 152.1
3553

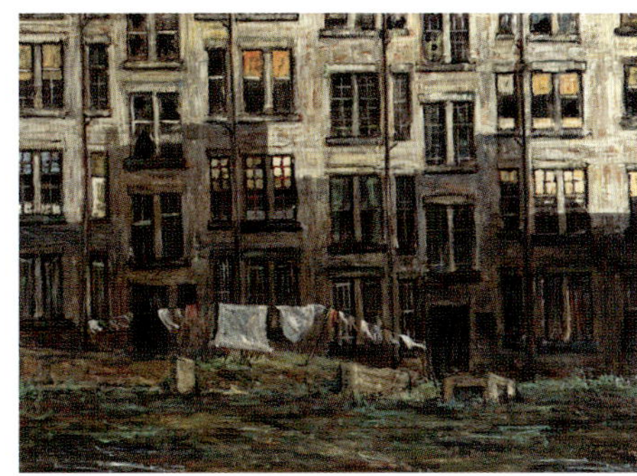

Hay, Andrew b.1944
A Mean Wind Wanders through the Backcourt Trash
acrylic on canvas 91.4 x 121.9
1997.68

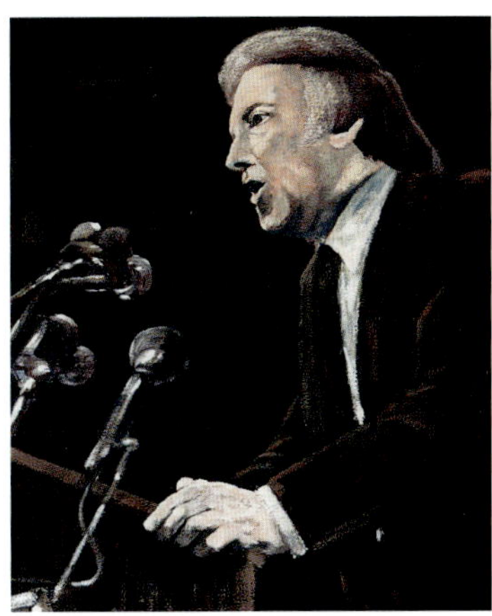

Hay, Andrew b.1944
Arthur Scargill (b.1938), Miners' Leader
acrylic on paper 61.3 x 48
PP.1985.64.10

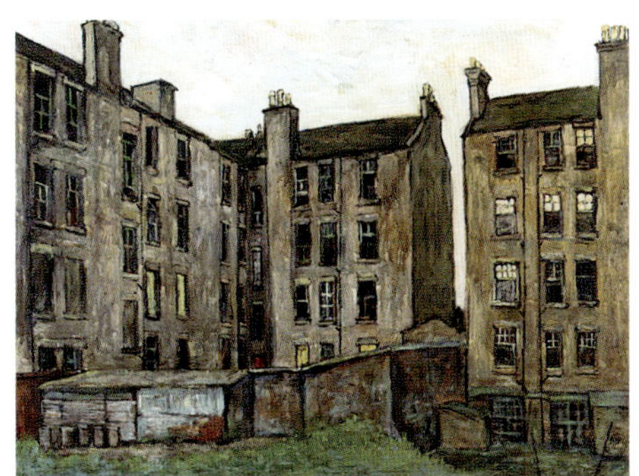

Hay, Andrew b.1944
Springburn Tenement
acrylic on canvas 91.4 x 121.9
1990.68.4

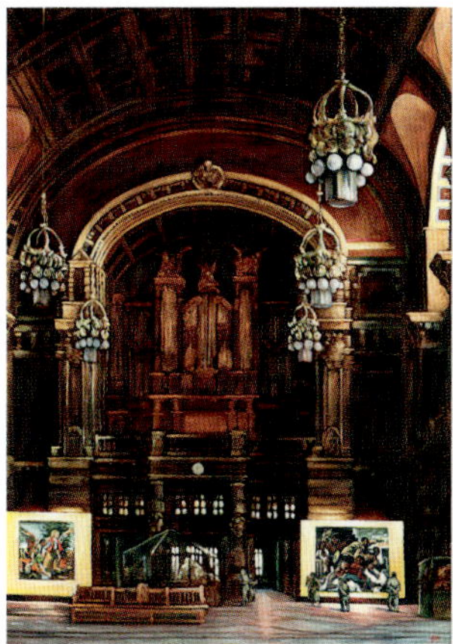

Hay, Andrew b.1944
The Hierarchy of Art
oil on canvas 148 x 103.2
3555

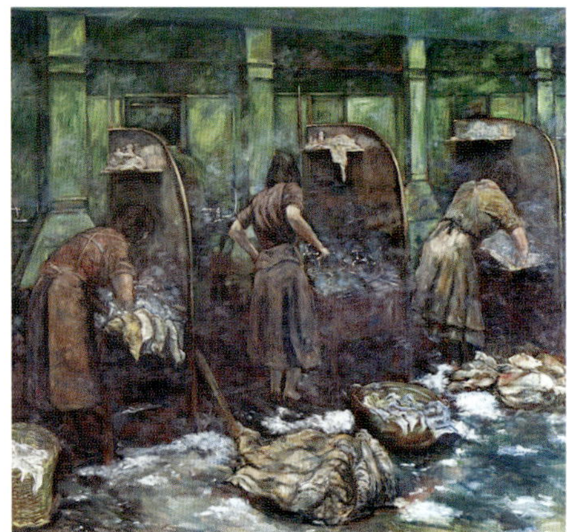

Hay, Andrew b.1944
The Steamie
oil on canvas 190.5 x 220.4
LPP.1997.2 (P)

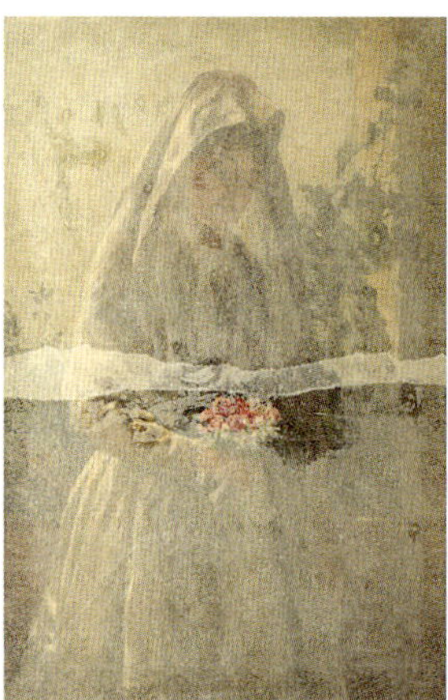

Haynes-Williams, John 1836–1908
The Spanish Bride 1877
oil on canvas 74.9 x 50.8
888

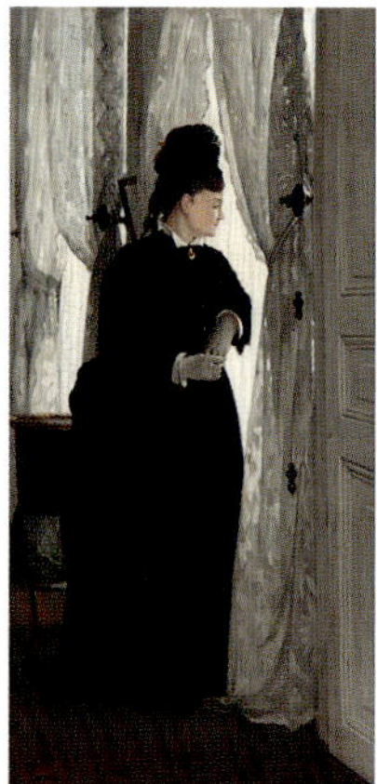

Hayon, Léon-Albert 1840–1895
Young Woman at Her Window 1874
oil on canvas 54.3 x 27
3534

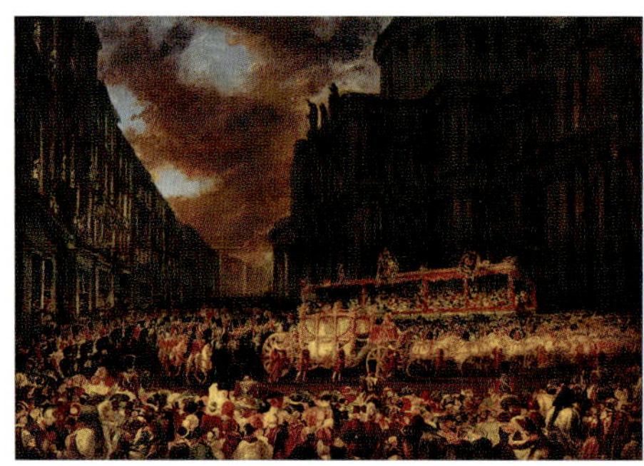

Hayter, George 1792–1871
First State Visit of Queen Victoria to the City of London, November 1837, Passing St Paul's 1837
oil on panel 43.2 x 59.7
1021

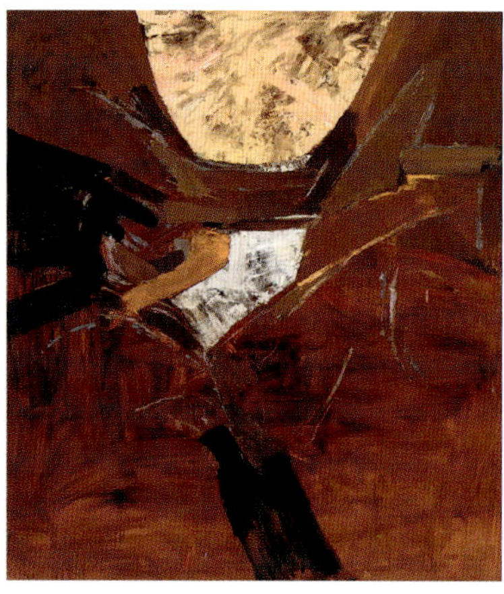

Heath, Adrian 1920–1992
Brown Painting 1960–1961
oil on canvas 188 x 162.6
3258

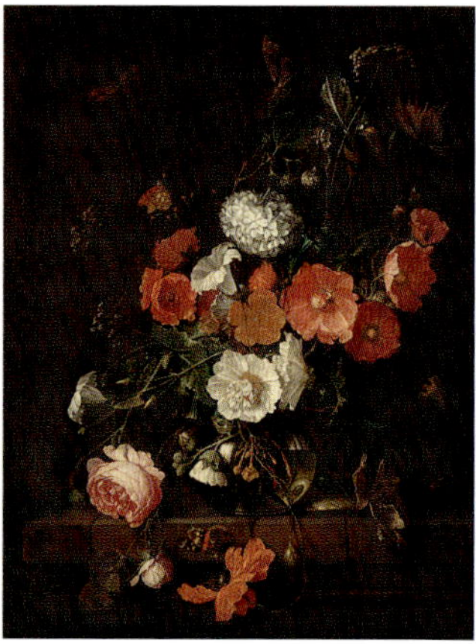

Heem, Cornelis de (attributed to) 1631–1695
Still Life: Flowers in a Glass Vase
oil on canvas 62.5 x 50.8
96

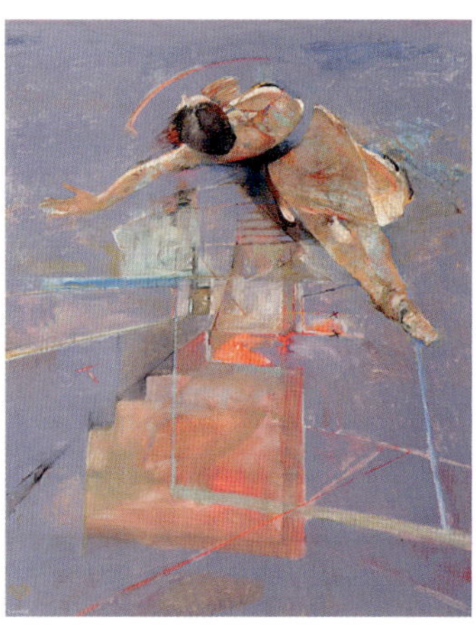

Heindel, Robert 1938–2005
The Last Obstacle 1990
acrylic & oil pastel on canvas 121.9 x 95.3
3646

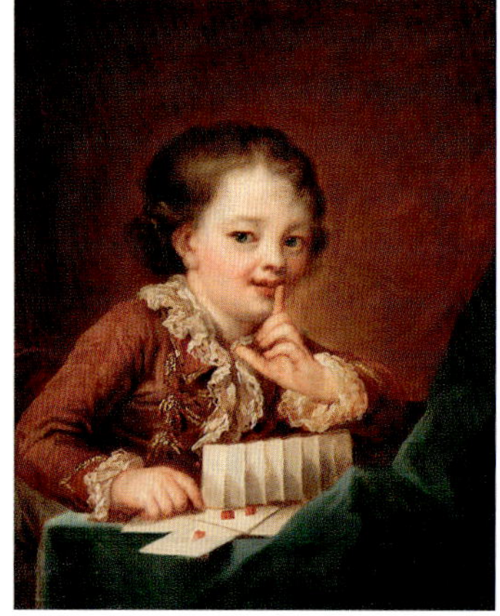

Heinsius, Johann Ernst (after) 1740–1812
A Small Boy with a House of Cards c.1781–1789
oil on canvas 64.5 x 53.3
224

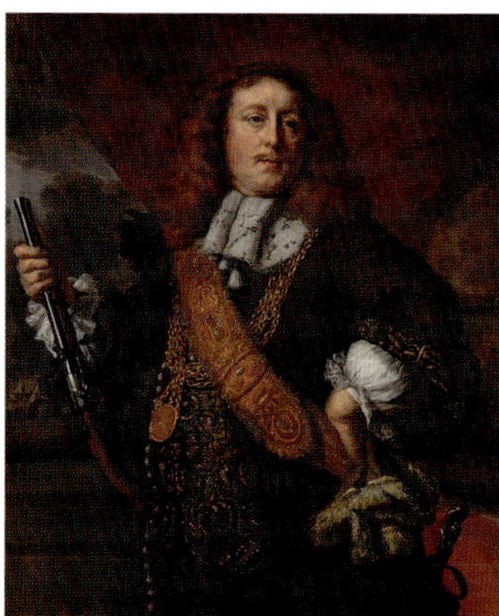

Helst, Bartholomeus van der 1613–1670
Captain Willem van der Zaan (1621–1669) 1662
oil on canvas 113 x 91.4
725

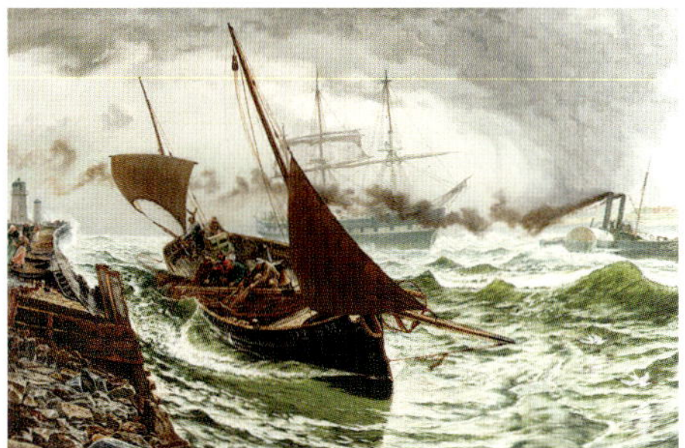

Hemy, Charles Napier 1841–1917
Saved 1880
oil on canvas 124.5 x 185.4
1722

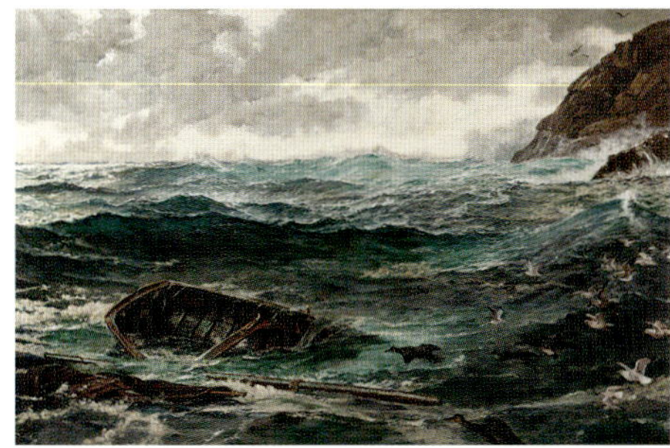

Hemy, Charles Napier 1841–1917
Lost 1897
oil on canvas 122 x 183.2
1721

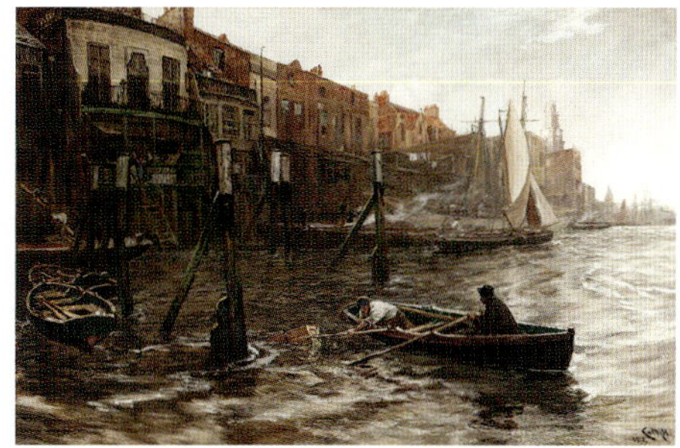

Hemy, Charles Napier 1841–1917
Limehouse Hole 1910
tempera on canvas 120.7 x 181.6
1278

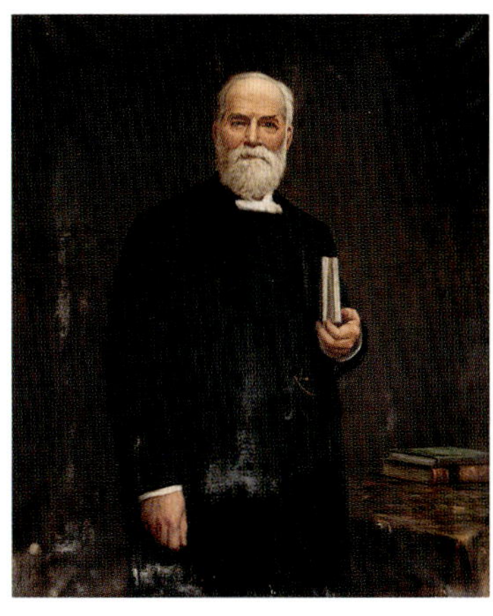

Henderson, J.
Male in Clerical Dress 1900
oil on canvas 128 x 102.6
TEMP.2737

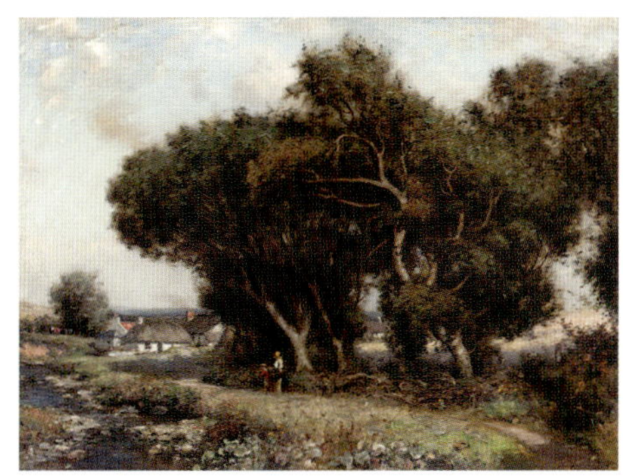

Henderson, John 1860–1924
The Path by the Stream c.1912
oil on canvas 127.7 x 151.1
1293

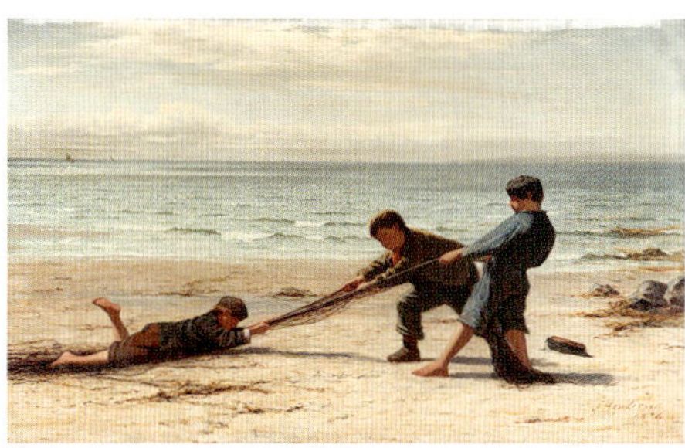

Henderson, Joseph 1832–1908
Haul on the Sands 1874
oil on canvas 105.4 x 172.7
1854

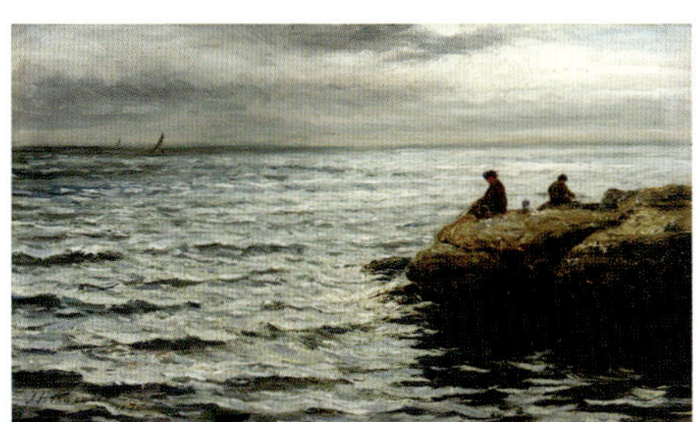

Henderson, Joseph 1832–1908
Sea Piece 1875
oil on canvas 29.2 x 49.5
877

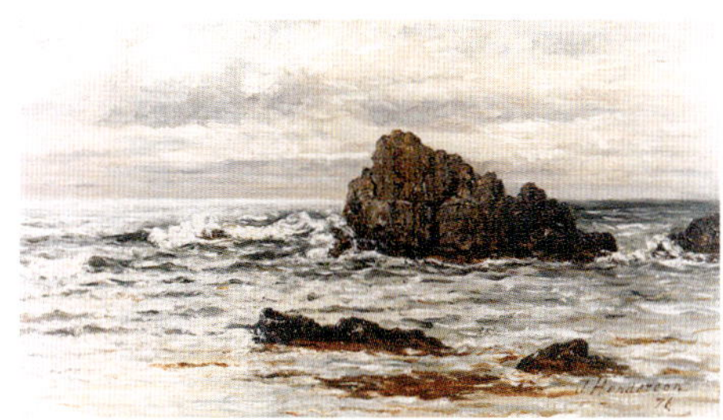

Henderson, Joseph 1832–1908
Sea Piece 1876
oil on canvas 34.3 x 59.7
874

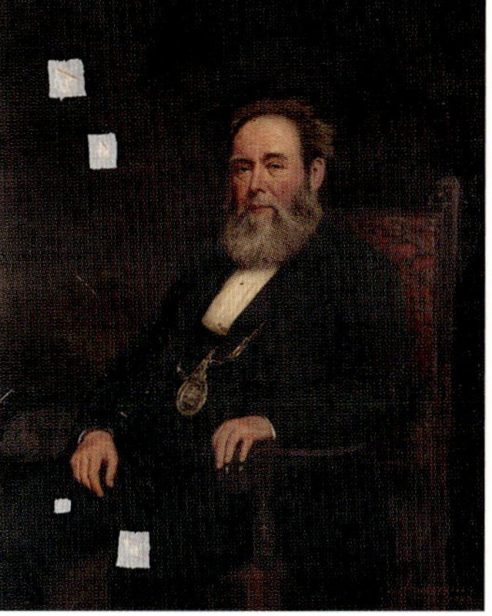

Henderson, Joseph 1832–1908
James Wilson 1882
oil on canvas 127 x 101.6
NR.166

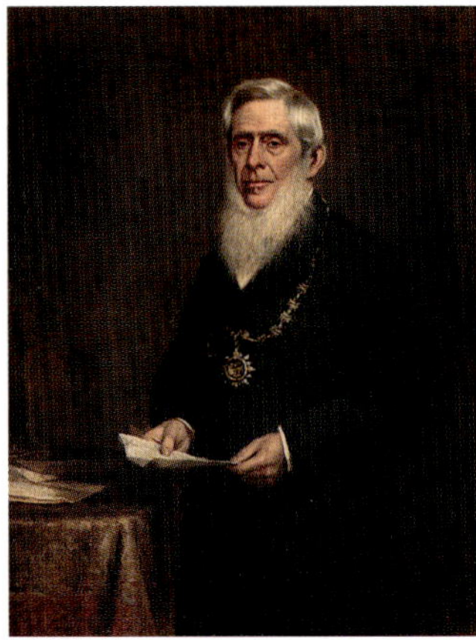

Henderson, Joseph 1832–1908
Councillor Alexander Waddell 1893
oil on canvas 119.4 x 88.9
731

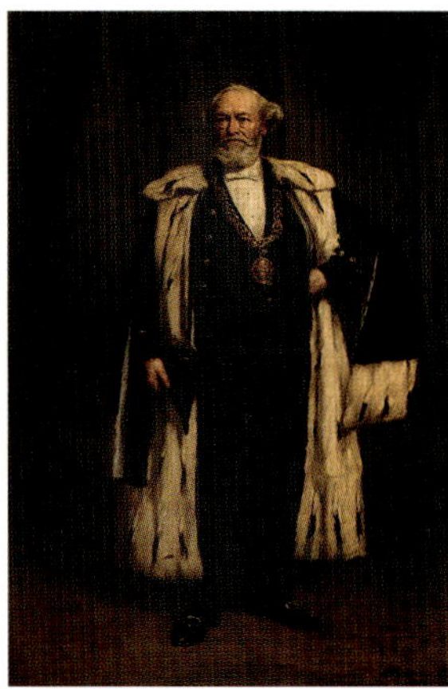

Henderson, Joseph 1832–1908
*Sir John Muir (1828–1903), Lord Provost of
Glasgow (1889–1892)* 1893
oil on canvas 223.5 x 134.6
713

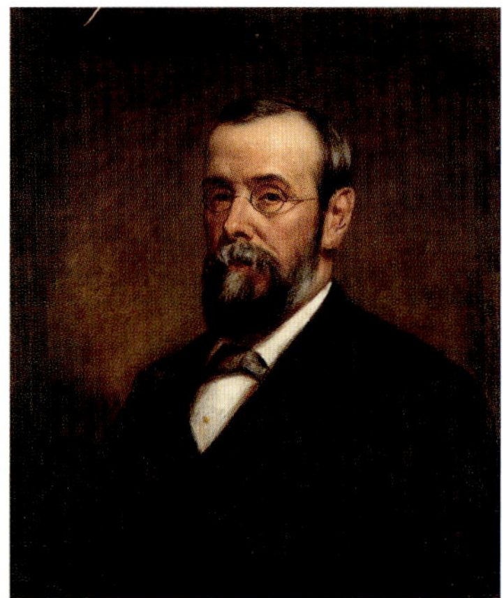

Henderson, Joseph 1832–1908
*James Paton (1843–1921), Superintendent of
Glasgow Art Gallery and Museum (1876–1914)*
1897
oil on canvas 68.6 x 57.2
1864

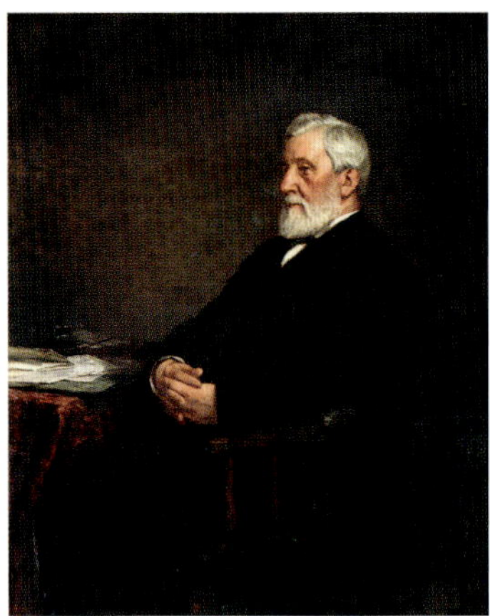

Henderson, Joseph 1832–1908
Portrait of a Man 1897
oil on canvas 127 x 101.6
NR.99

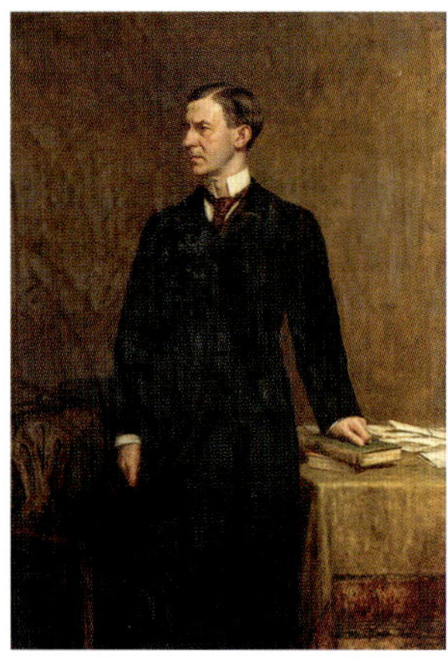

Henderson, Joseph 1832–1908
*The Right Honourable Lord Charles Scott
Dickson (1850–1922), Lord Justice Clerk
(1915–1922)* 1897
oil on canvas 166.4 x 111.8
1878

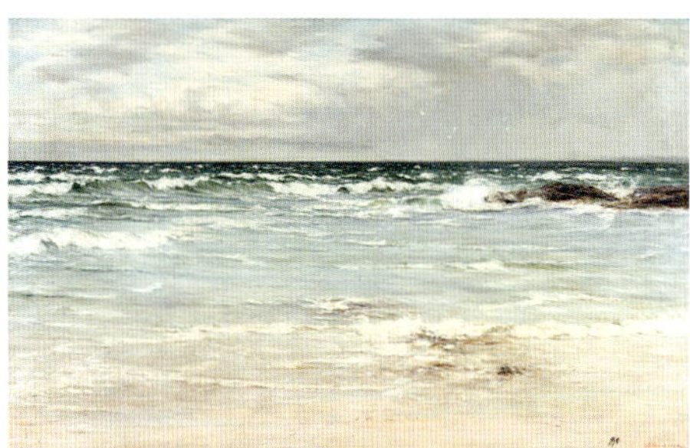

Henderson, Joseph 1832–1908
The Flowing Tide c.1897
oil on canvas 121.9 x 182.9
751

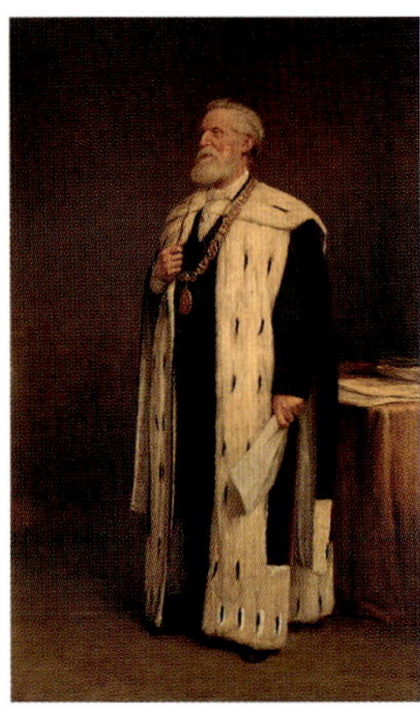

Henderson, Joseph 1832–1908
*Sir Samuel Chisholm (1836–1923), Lord
Provost of Glasgow (1899–1902)* 1902
oil on canvas 227.3 x 135.9
1026

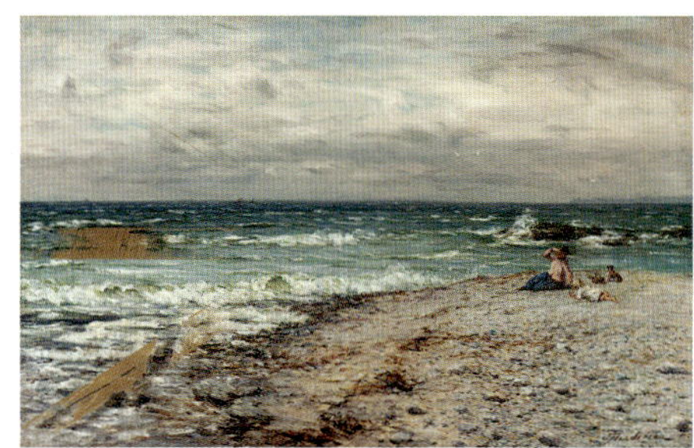

Henderson, Joseph 1832–1908
A Fresh Breeze
oil on canvas 71.1 x 111.8
2059

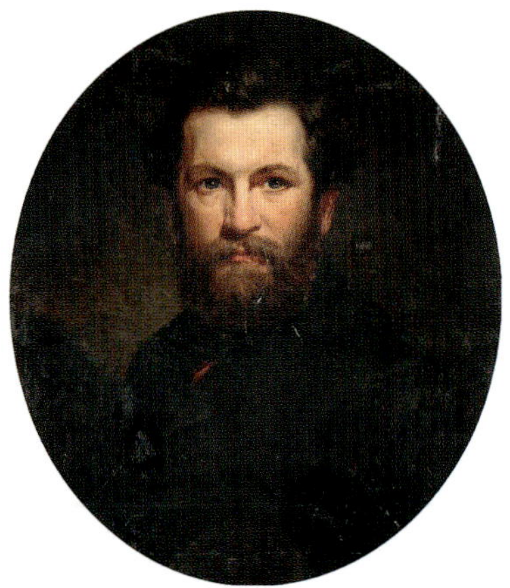

Henderson, Joseph 1832–1908
James Docharty (1829–1878)
oil on canvas 61 x 50.8
1699

Facing page: Mann, Cathleen, 1896–1959, *Ballerina*, (p. 275)

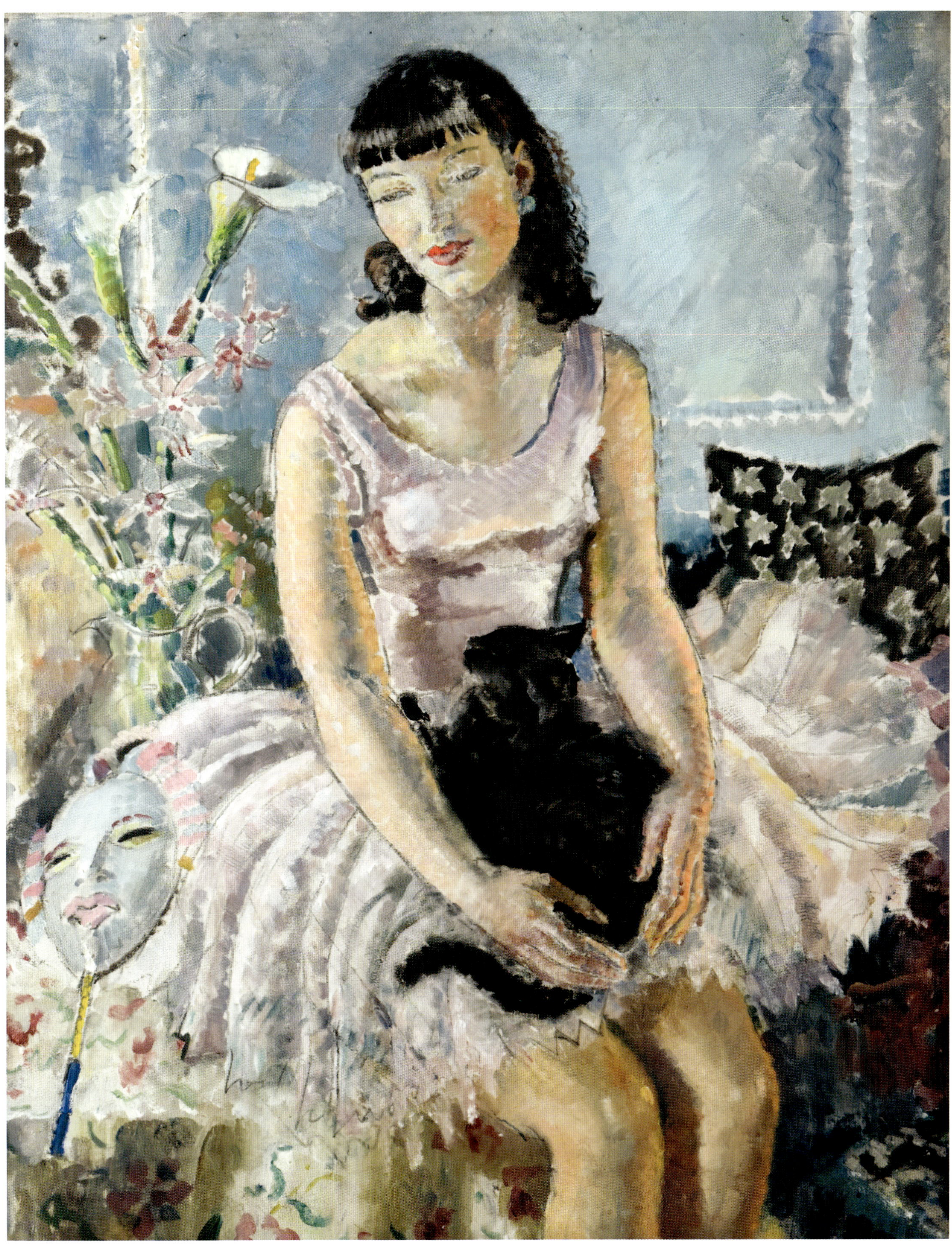

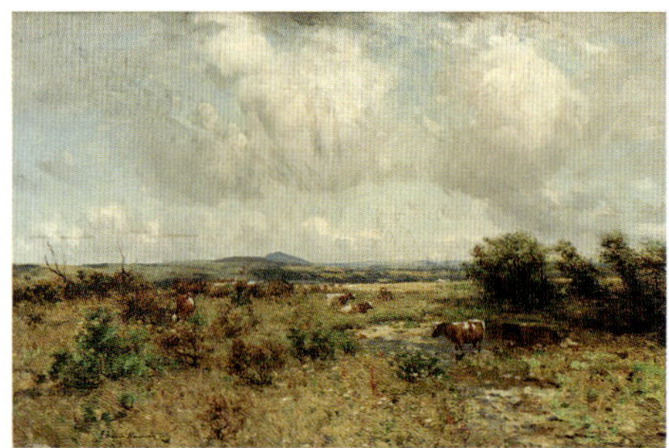

Henderson, Joseph Morris 1863–1936
In the Meadow c.1909
oil on canvas 80 x 119.4
1228

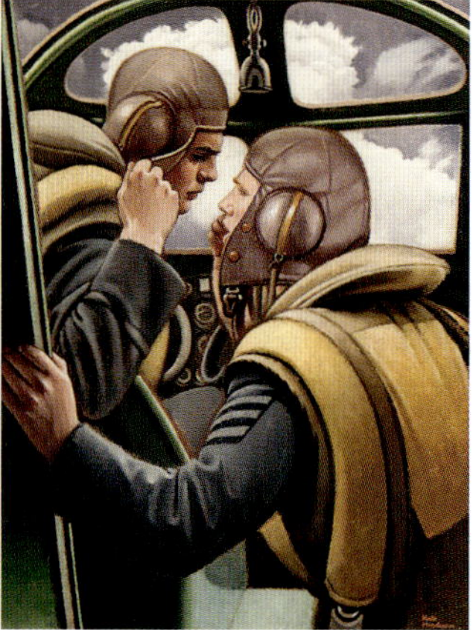

Henderson, Keith 1883–1982
Pilot and Navigator Confer c.1940–1945
oil on canvas 101.6 x 76.2
2742

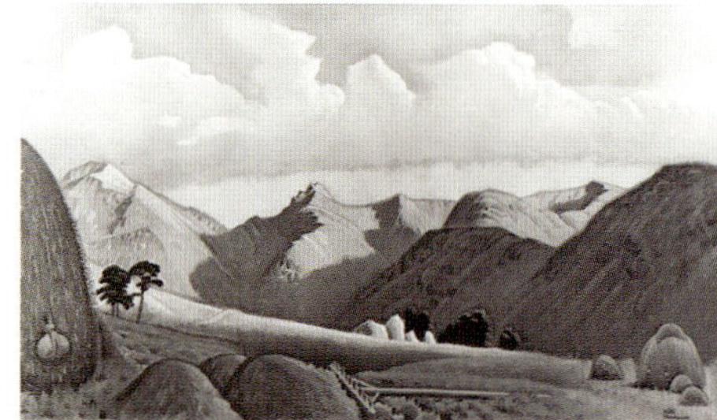

Henderson, Keith 1883–1982
Glen Nevis, Inverness-shire c.1944
oil on canvas 63.5 x 101.6
2470

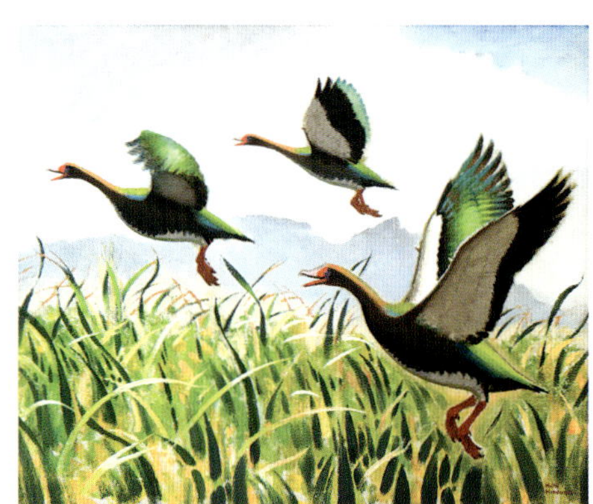

Henderson, Keith 1883–1982
Spur-Winged Geese
oil on canvas 78 x 90
NH.1972.42.a

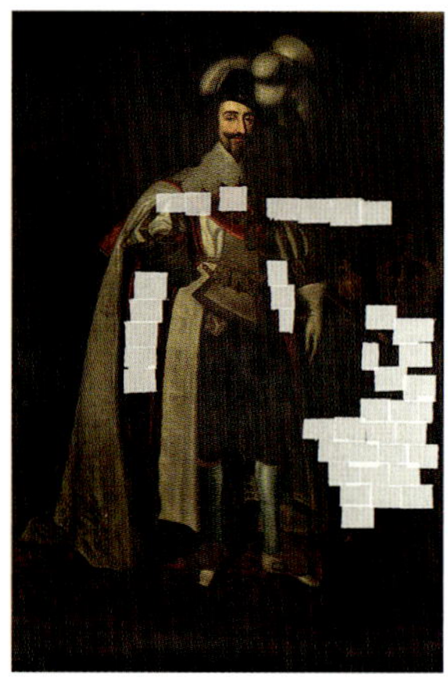

Hendrie, John active 1665–1677
Charles I (1600–1649) (after Daniel Mytens I)
1677
oil on canvas 238.8 x 156.2
473

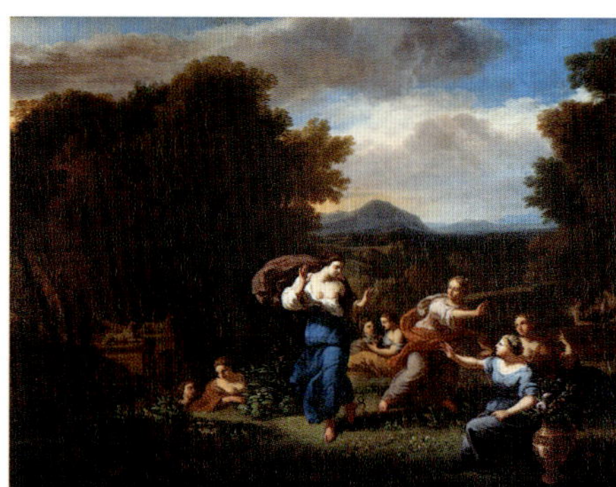

Hennin, Adriaen de active 1664–1710
Landscape with the Death of Eurydice
oil on canvas 42.2 x 55.2
580

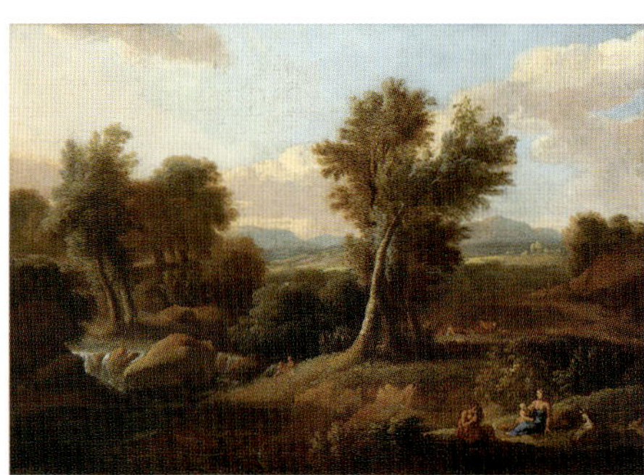

Hennin, Adriaen de (attributed to) active
1664–1710
Pastoral Landscape with Figures
oil on canvas 29 x 39
589

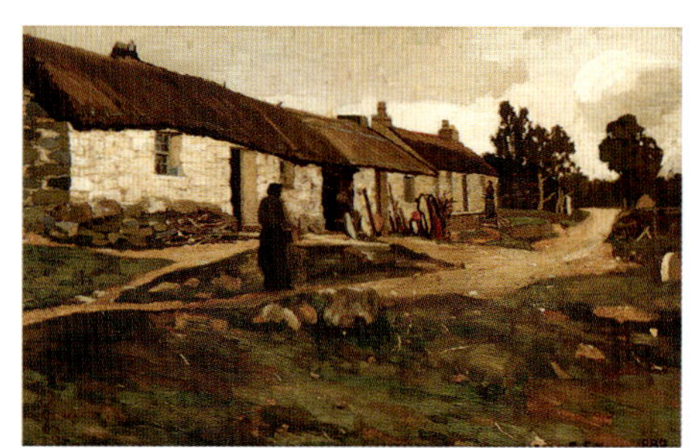

Henry, George 1858–1943
Brig o' Turk 1882
oil on canvas 30.4 x 47
3337

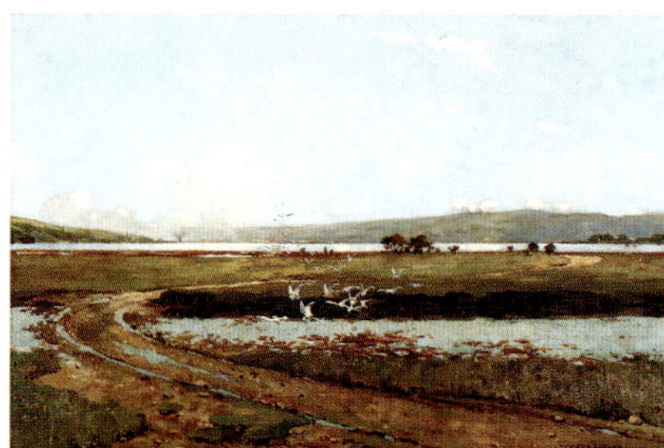

Henry, George 1858–1943
Head of the Holy Loch 1882
oil on canvas 59.1 x 89.5
1355

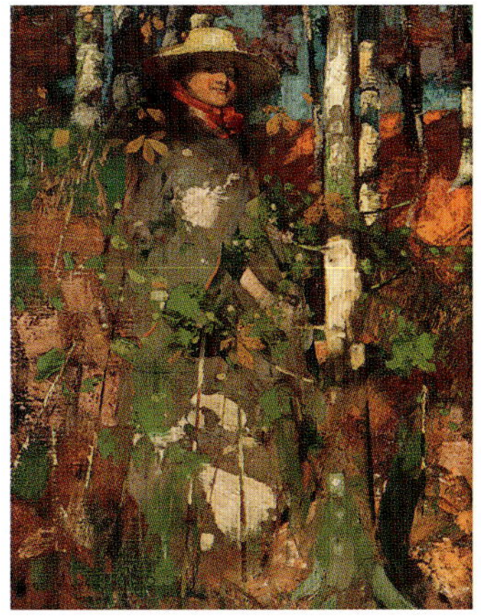

Henry, George 1858–1943
Autumn 1888
oil on canvas 45.7 x 38.1
2388

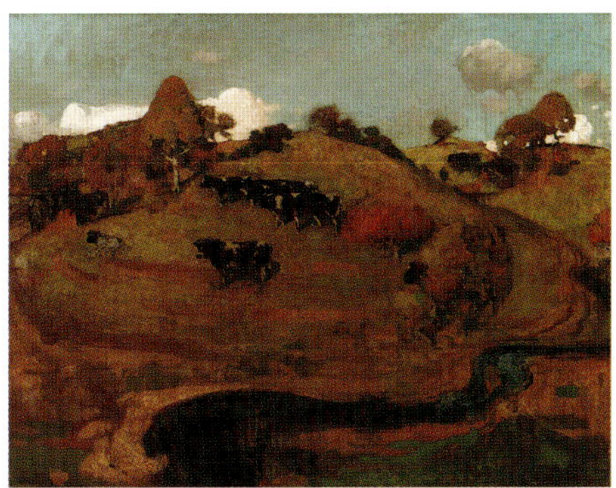

Henry, George 1858–1943
A Galloway Landscape 1889
oil on canvas 121.9 x 152.4
2208

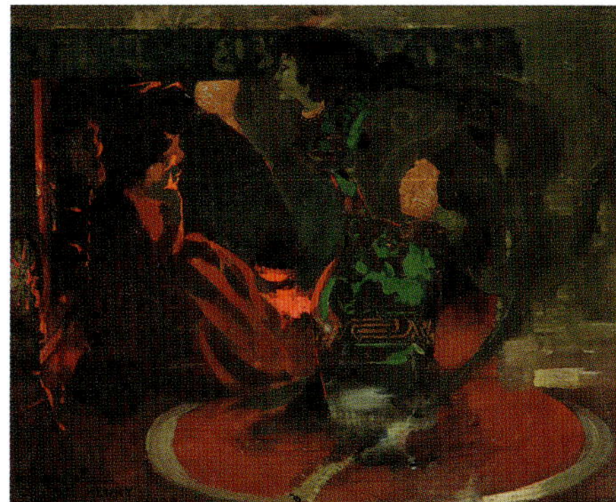

Henry, George 1858–1943
Gloamin' 1889
oil on panel 24.4 x 30.8
3361

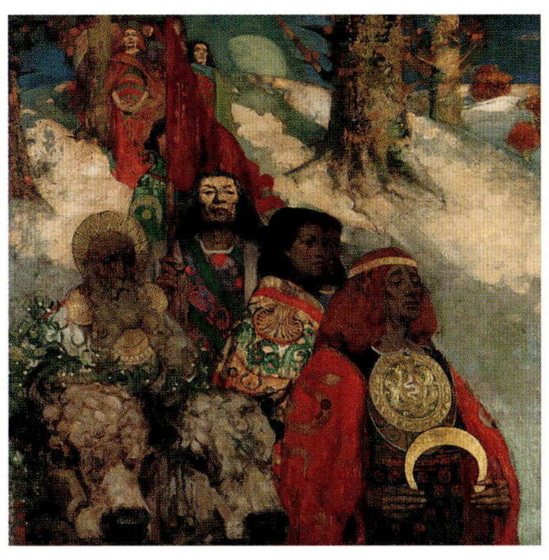

Henry, George 1858–1943 & **Hornel, Edward Atkinson** 1864–1933
The Druids: Bringing in the Mistletoe 1890
oil on canvas 152.4 x 152.4
1534

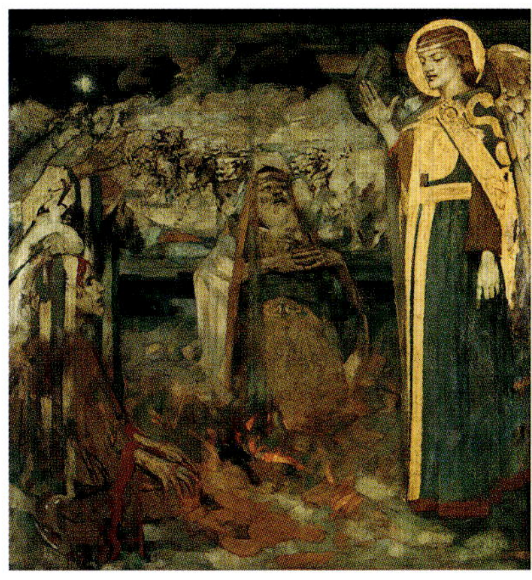

Henry, George 1858–1943 & **Hornel, Edward Atkinson** 1864–1933
The Star in the East 1891
oil on canvas 198.4 x 182.9
3137

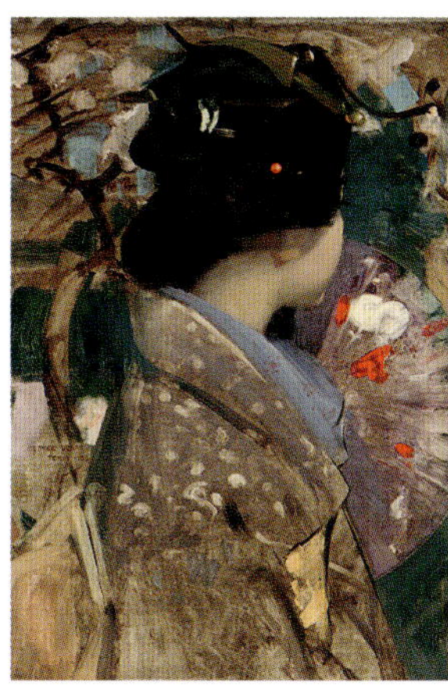

Henry, George 1858–1943
Japanese Lady with a Fan 1893–1894
oil on canvas 61 x 40.6
1704

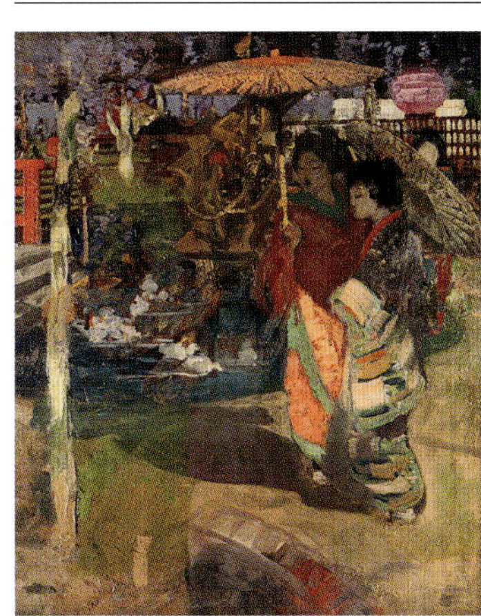

Henry, George 1858–1943
In a Japanese Garden c.1894
oil on canvas 76.2 x 63.5
2463

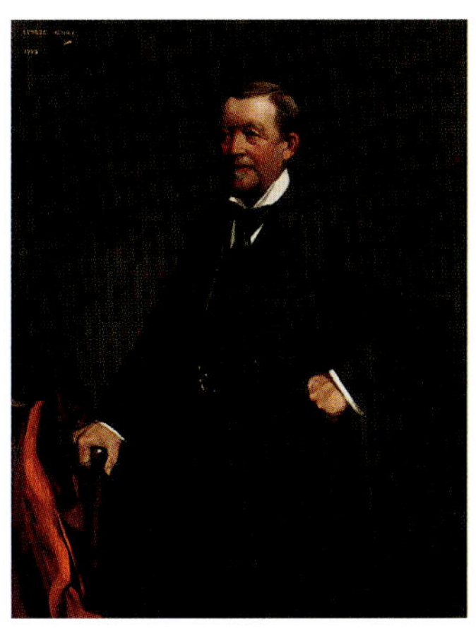

Henry, George 1858–1943
Councillor Robert Crawford (b.1845) 1903
oil on canvas 139.7 x 104.1
1073

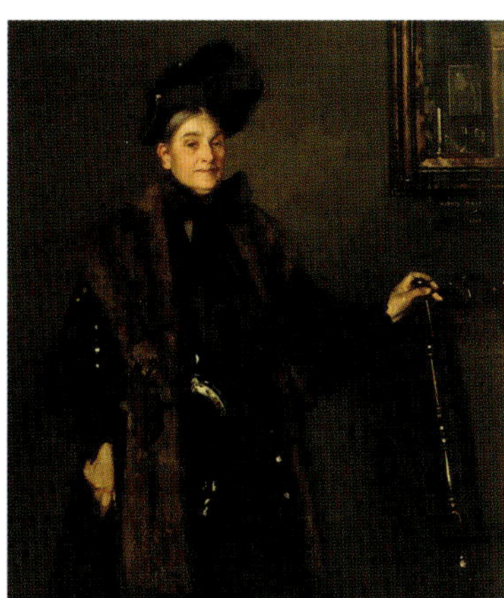

Henry, George 1858–1943
Mrs Burrell 1903
oil on canvas 150.6 x 125.1
35.278

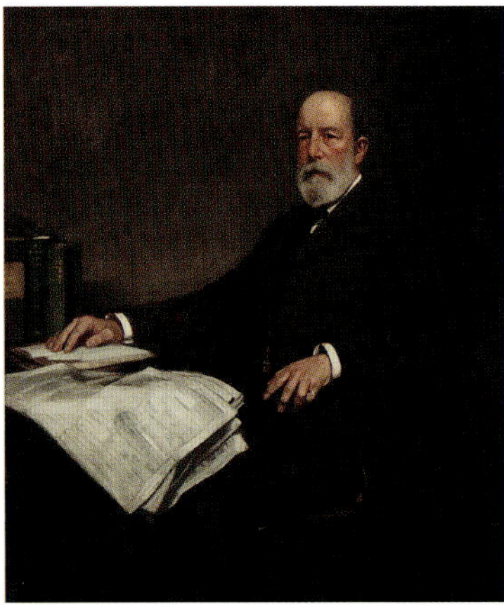

Henry, George 1858–1943
*Sir John Neilson Cuthbertson (1829–1905),
LLD, DL* c.1903
oil on canvas 141 x 121.9
1074

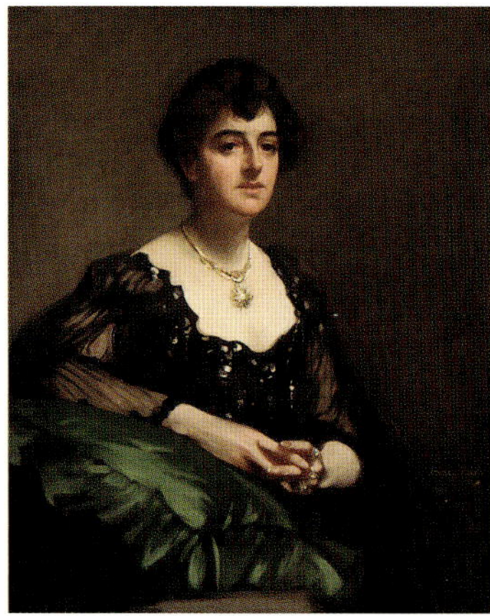

Henry, George 1858–1943
Mrs Isabella Sandilands (1865–1925) 1904
oil on canvas 91.8 x 76.4
3311

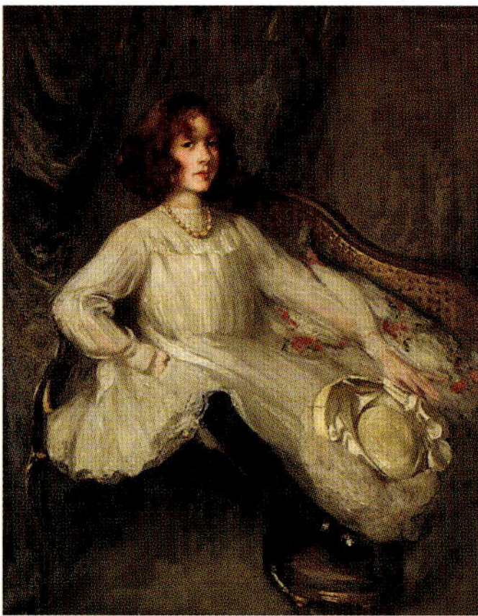

Henry, George 1858–1943
*Helen Stirling Stuart of Castlemilk (1896–
1985)* 1906
oil on canvas 127 x 101.6
3191

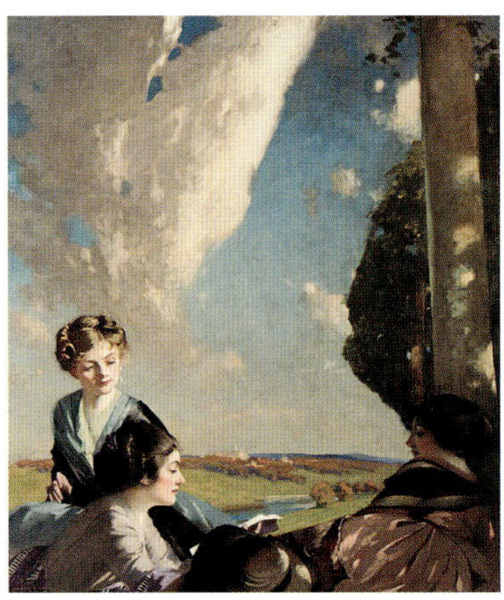

Henry, George 1858–1943
The Reading c.1913
oil on canvas 174 x 151.1
1329

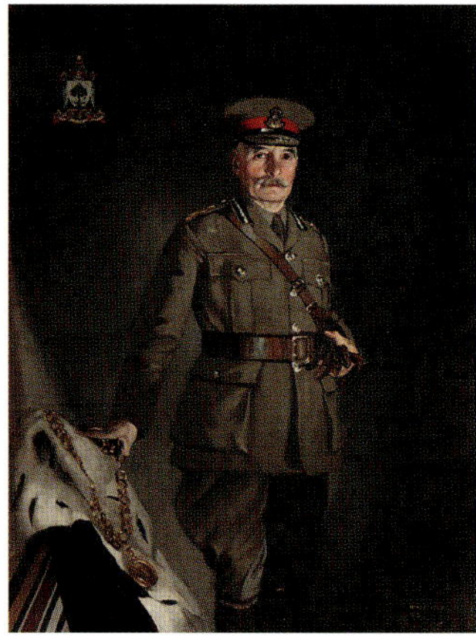

Henry, George 1858–1943
*Sir Thomas Dunlop (1855–1938), Lord Provost
of Glasgow (1914–1917)* 1917
oil on canvas 166.4 x 125.7
1441

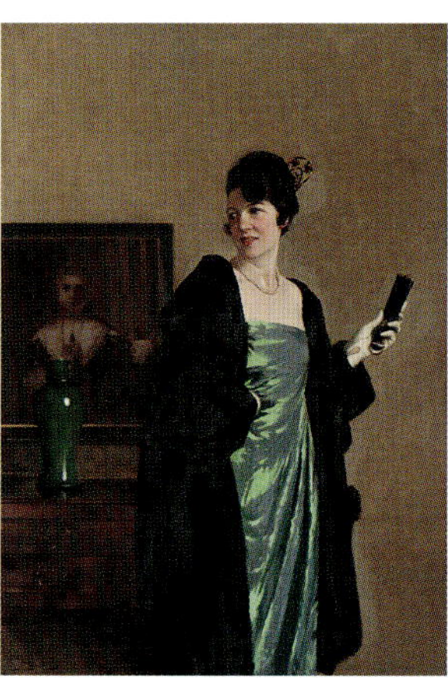

Henry, George 1858–1943
Lady in a Green Dress
oil on canvas 152.4 x 109.2
2188

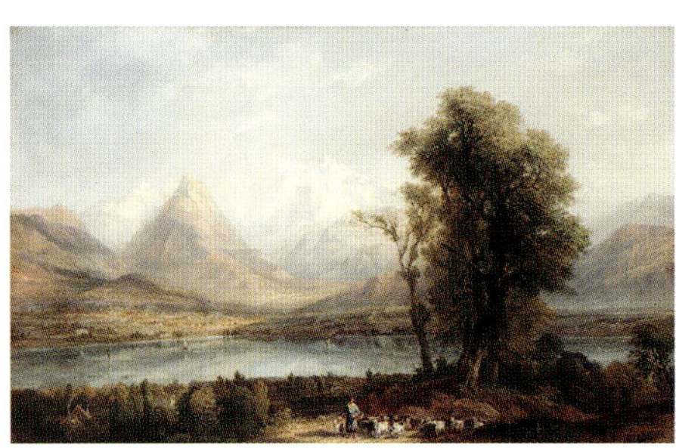

Henshaw, Frederick Henry 1807–1891
Swiss Landscape
oil on canvas 63.5 x 99.1
262

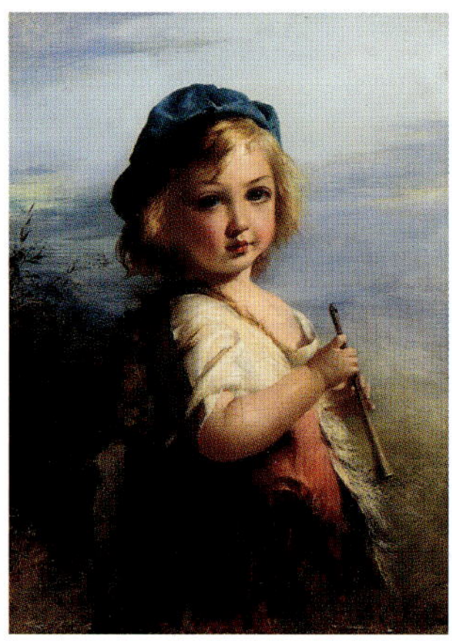

Herdman, Robert Inerarity 1829–1888
Morning 1861
oil on panel 30.5 x 22.9
1047

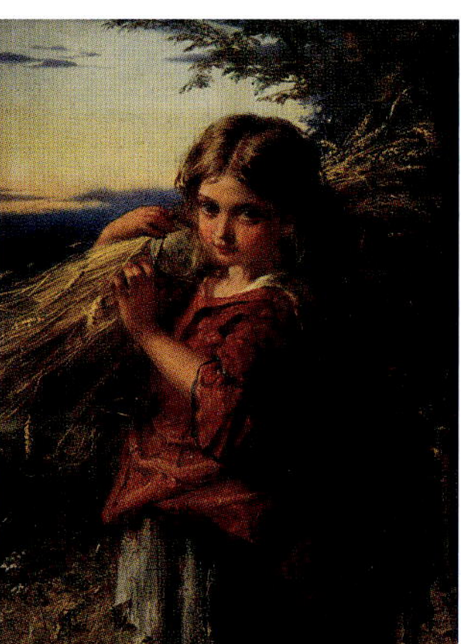

Herdman, Robert Inerarity 1829–1888
Evening 1862
oil on panel 30.5 x 22.9
1048

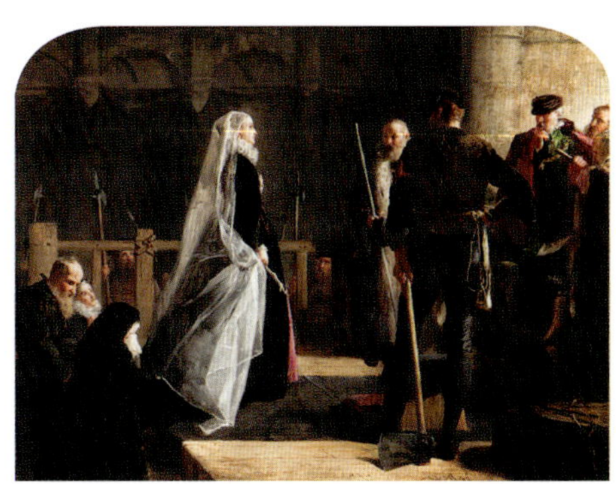

Herdman, Robert Inerarity 1829–1888
Execution of Mary, Queen of Scots 1867
oil on canvas 74.9 x 95.3
812

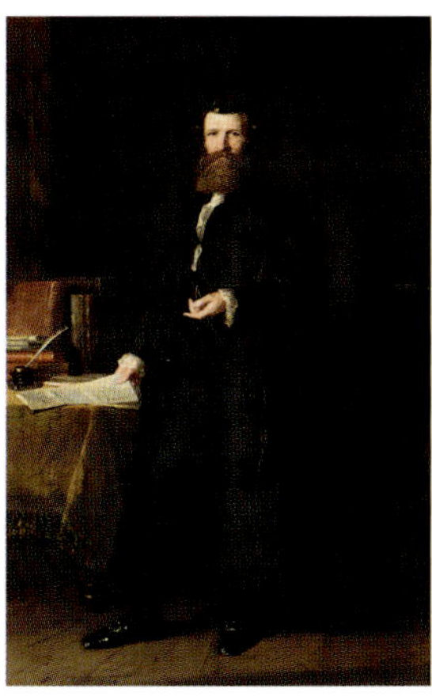

Herdman, Robert Inerarity 1829–1888
*Sir James David Marwick (1826–1908), Town
Clerk of Glasgow (1873–1903)* 1873
oil on canvas 241.1 x 143.5
1850

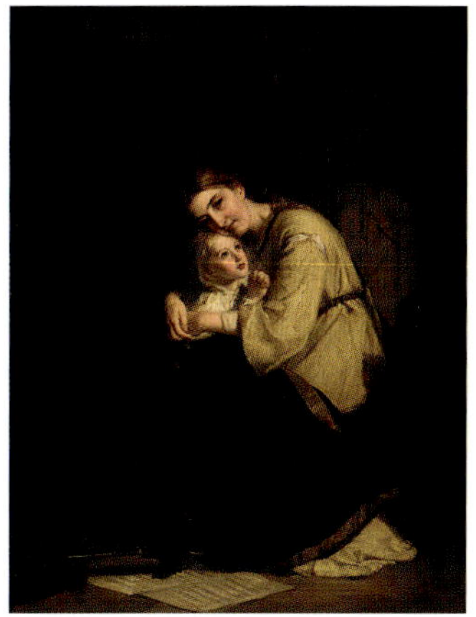

Herdman, Robert Inerarity 1829–1888
Pleasures of Hope 1877
oil on canvas 91.4 x 71.1
2344

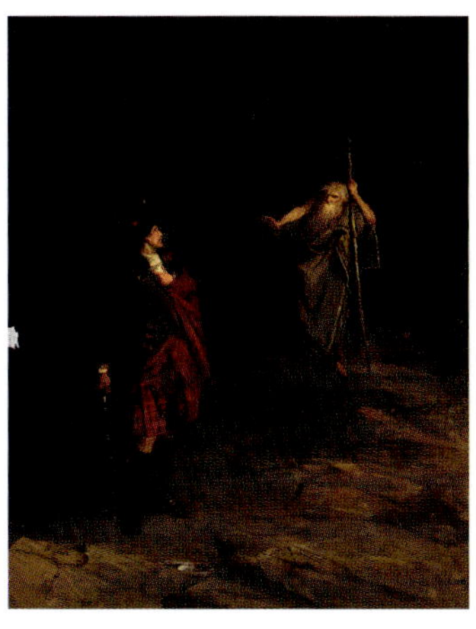

Herdman, Robert Inerarity 1829–1888
Lochiel's Warning 1878
oil on canvas 91.4 x 71.1
2345

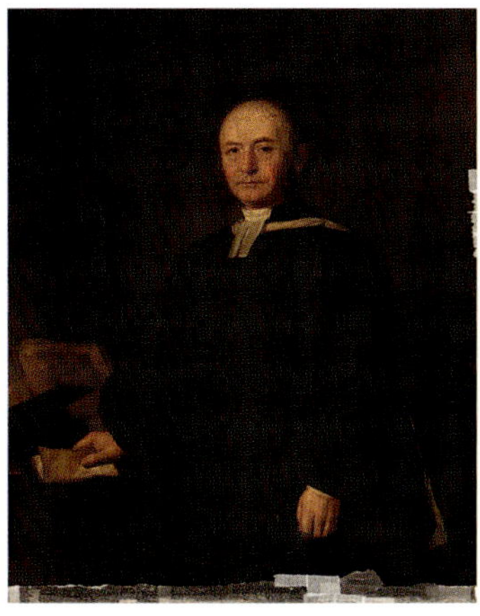

Herdman, Robert Inerarity 1829–1888
*Reverend George S. Burns, Minister of Glasgow
Cathedral* 1881
oil on canvas 137.2 x 106.7
650

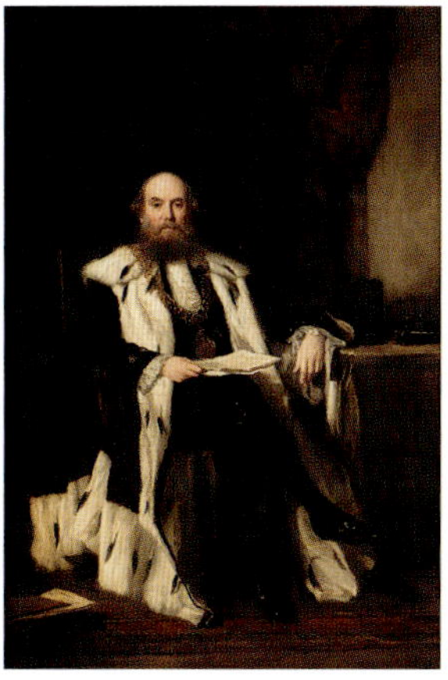

Herdman, Robert Inerarity 1829–1888
*Sir William Collins (1817–1895), Lord Provost
of Glasgow (1877–1880)* 1881
oil on canvas 228.6 x 152.4
646

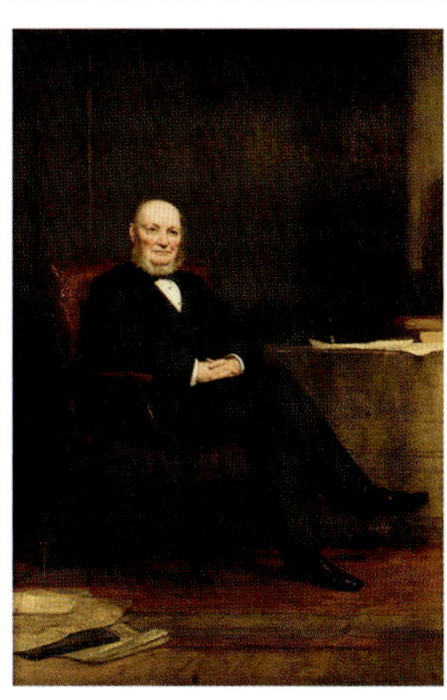

Herdman, Robert Inerarity 1829–1888
*Sir James Watson (1801–1889), Lord Provost of
Glasgow (1871–1874)* 1882
oil on canvas 236.2 x 147.3
651

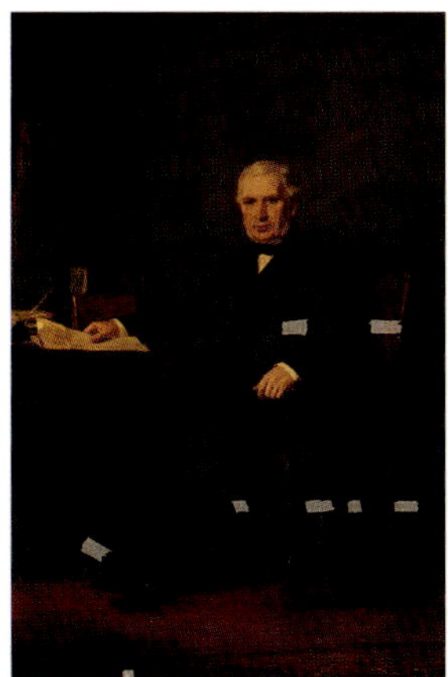

Herdman, Robert Inerarity 1829–1888
*Peter Clouston, Lord Provost of Glasgow
(1860–1863)* 1883
oil on canvas 218.4 x 139.7
654

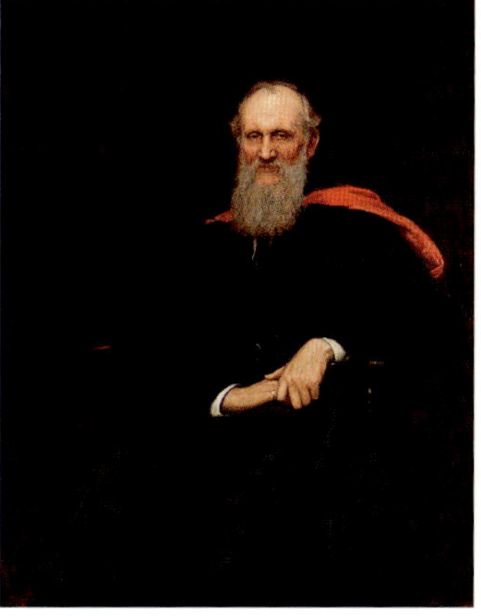

Herkomer, Hubert von 1849–1914
Lord Kelvin (1824–1907) 1896
oil on canvas 142.2 x 109.2
1675

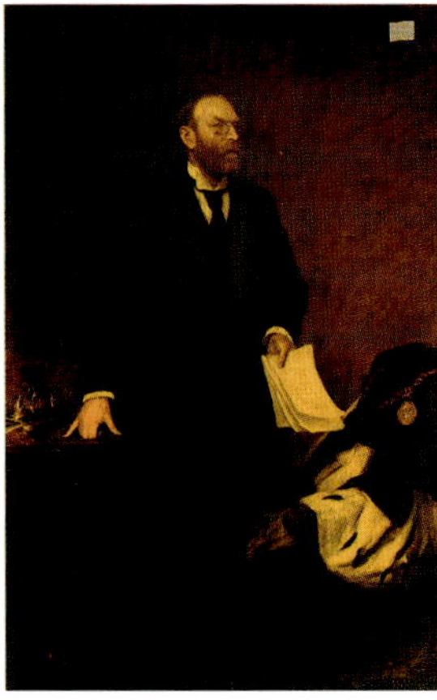

Herkomer, Hubert von 1849–1914
*Sir James Bell (b.1850), Lord Provost of
Glasgow (1892–1896)* 1896
oil on canvas 238.8 x 147.3
1076

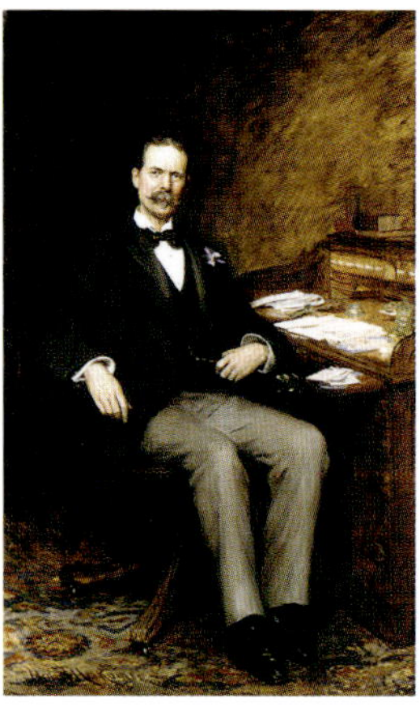

Herkomer, Hubert von 1849–1914
Sir Thomas J. Lipton (1850–1931) 1896
oil on canvas 228.6 x 138.4
1932.29

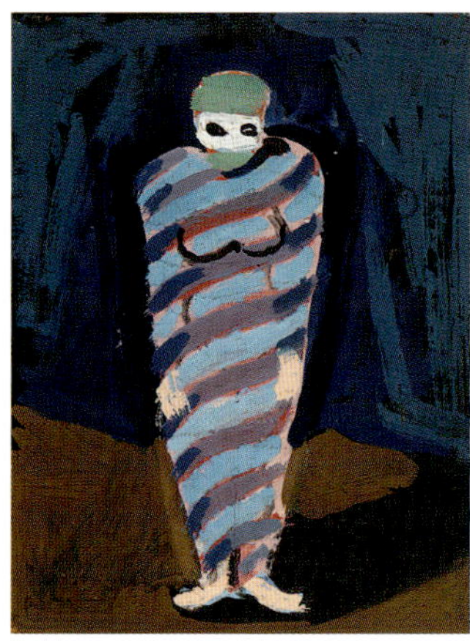

Herman, Josef 1911–2000
Blue-Costume for 'Ballet of the Palette' 1942
oil on paper 24.8 x 19
3356

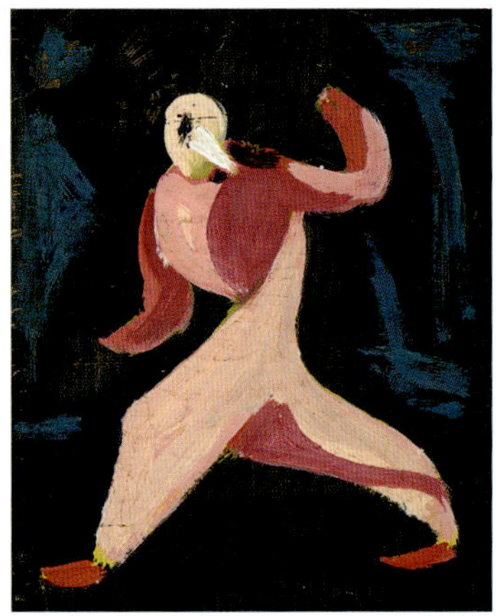

Herman, Josef 1911–2000
Pink-Costume for 'Ballet of the Palette' 1942
oil on paper 24.8 x 19
3355

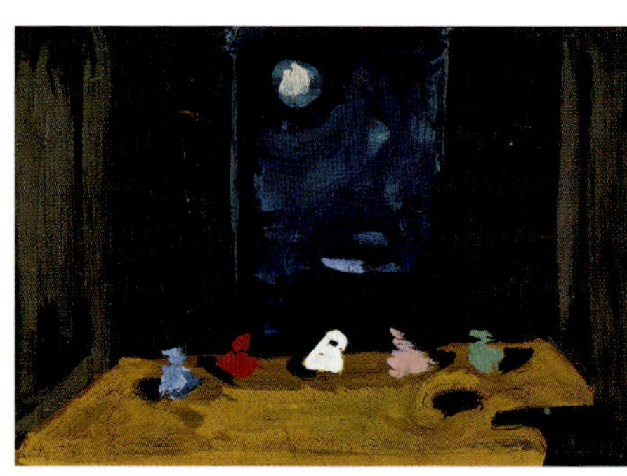

Herman, Josef 1911–2000
Set Design for 'Ballet of the Palette' 1942
oil on paper 19 x 24.1
3354

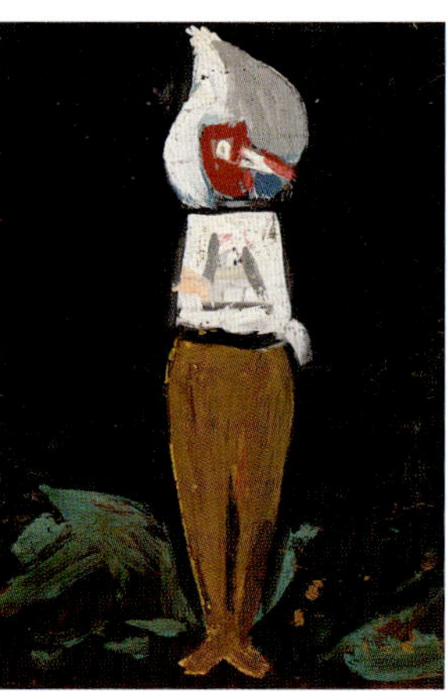

Herman, Josef 1911–2000
The Big Brush for 'Ballet of the Palette' 1942
oil on paper 30.5 x 19.7
3357

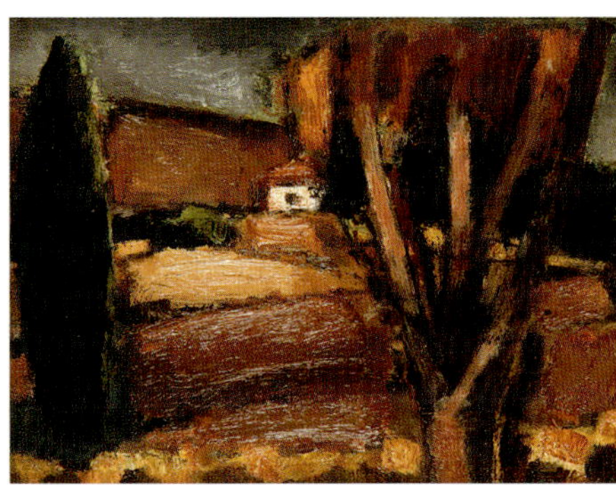

Herman, Josef 1911–2000
Southern Landscape c.1951–1952
oil on paper on hardboard 17.6 x 22.8
3100

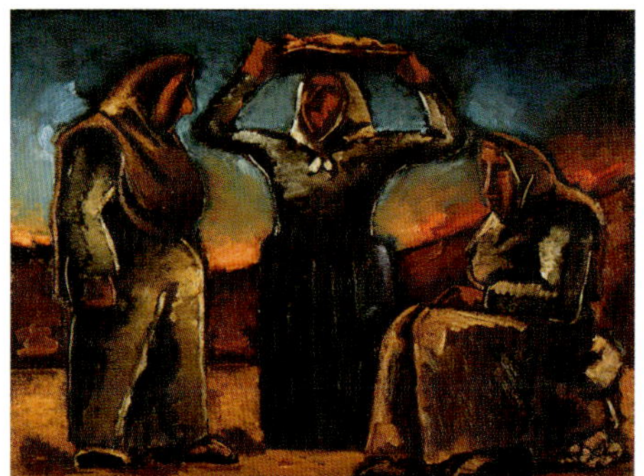

Herman, Josef 1911–2000
Three Mexican Women 1968
oil on canvas 88.8 x 121.8
3307

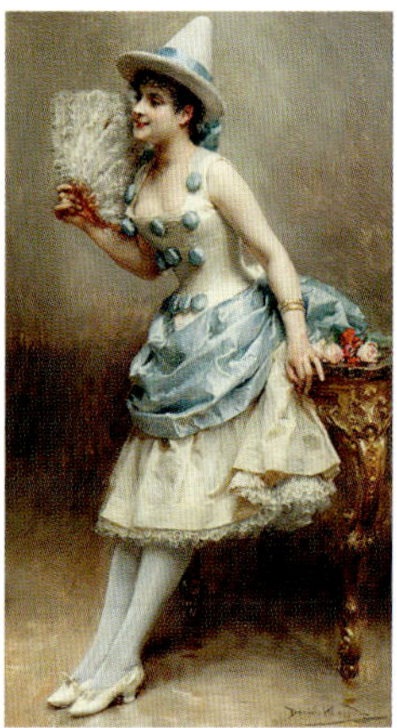

Hernández, Daniel 1856–1932
Pierrette
oil on panel 66 x 35.2
808

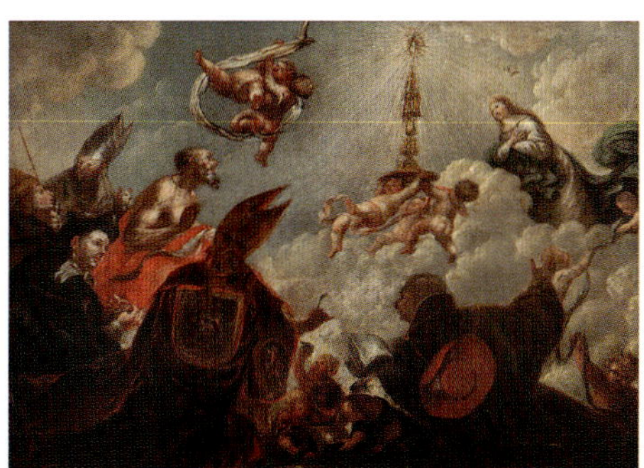

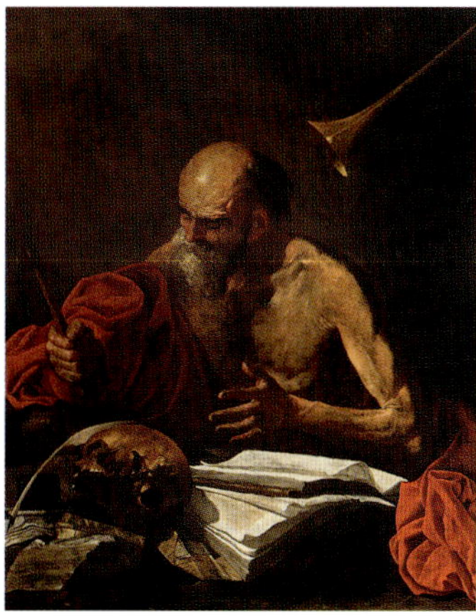

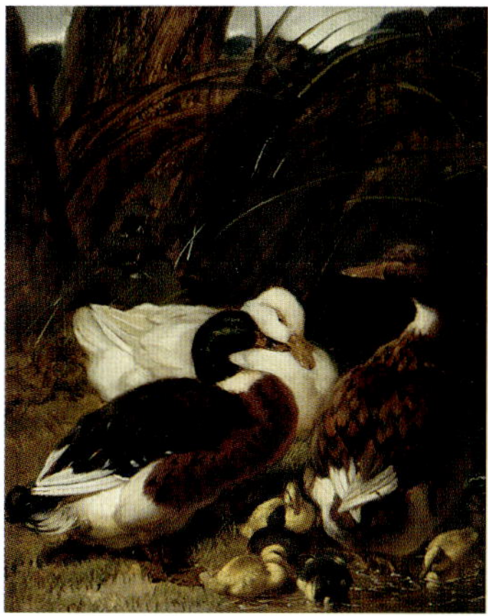

Herrera, Francisco de 1622–1685
The Adoration of the Blessed Sacrament
c.1655/1656
oil on canvas 40.5 x 56.8
PC.70

Herrera, Francisco de (attributed to)
1622–1685
Saint Jerome (after Jusepe de Ribera)
oil on canvas 120 x 93.9
PC.141

Herring, John Frederick I 1795–1865
A Group of Ducks 1852
oil on panel 29.2 x 23.5
367

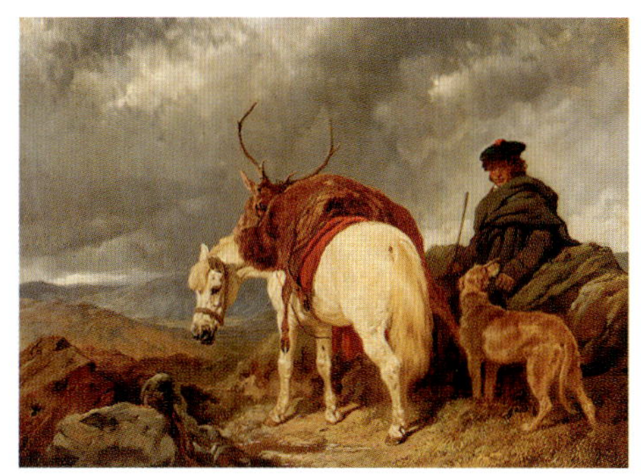

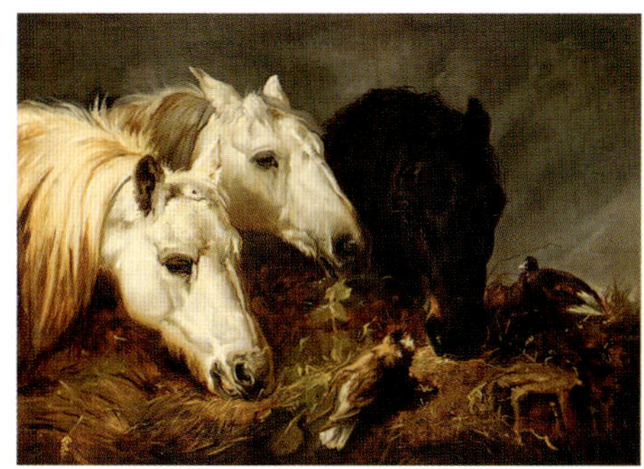

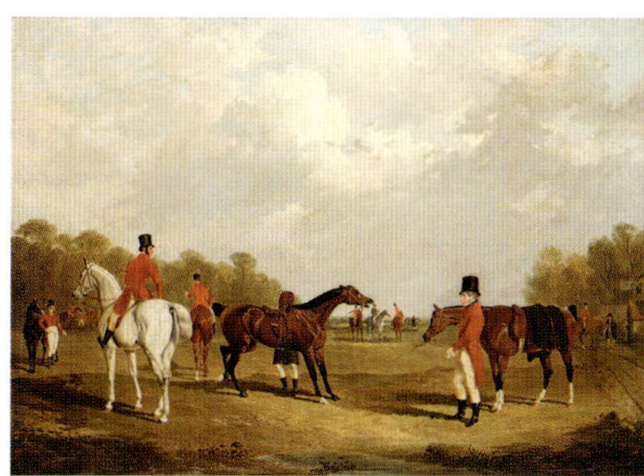

Herring, John Frederick I 1795–1865
The Deer-Stalker 1852
oil on canvas 44.5 x 59.7
363

Herring, John Frederick I 1795–1865
The Frugal Meal 1852
oil on canvas 55.9 x 81.3
1583

Herring, John Frederick I 1795–1865
The Meet
oil on canvas 88.9 x 124.5
1254

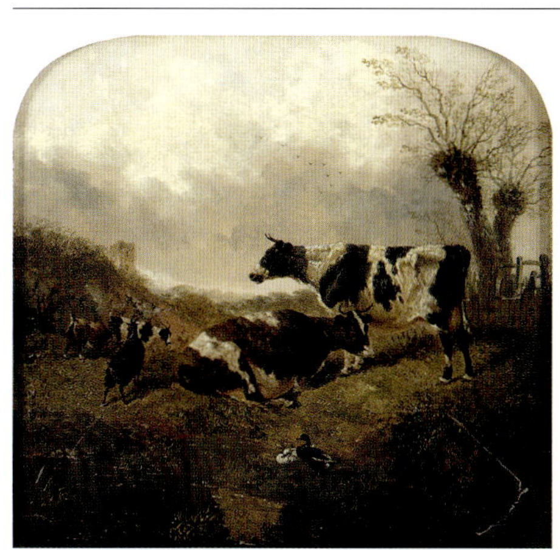

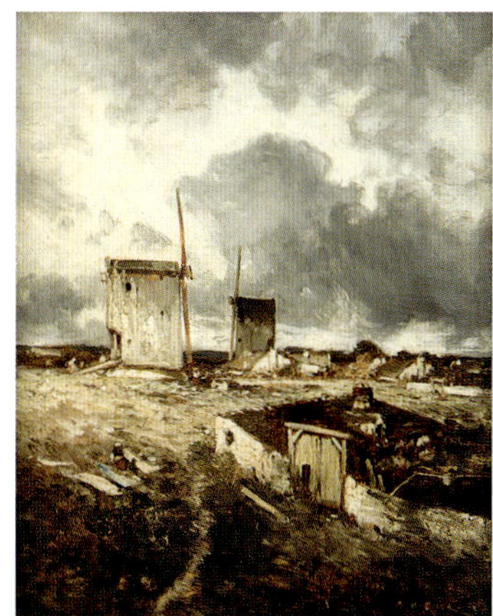

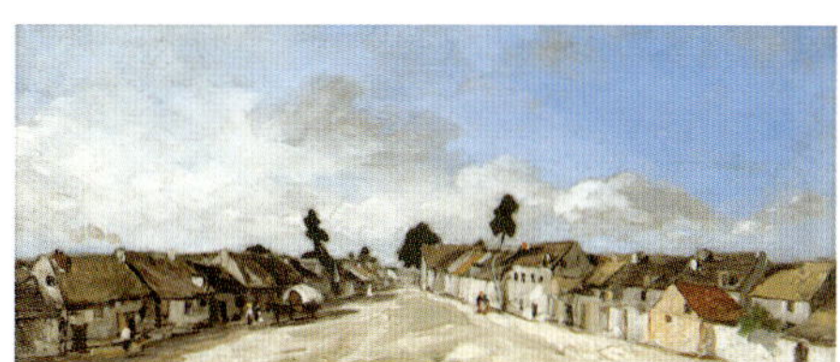

Herring, John Frederick I 1795–1865
*Two Cows with Goats and Ducks in a
Landscape*
oil on canvas 38.7 x 38.7
1366

Hervier, Louis Adolphe 1818–1879
Windmills 1850
oil on panel 34.9 x 26.9
35.281

Hervier, Louis Adolphe 1818–1879
Village Scene, Barbizon c.1850–1860
oil on panel 13 x 30.6
2389

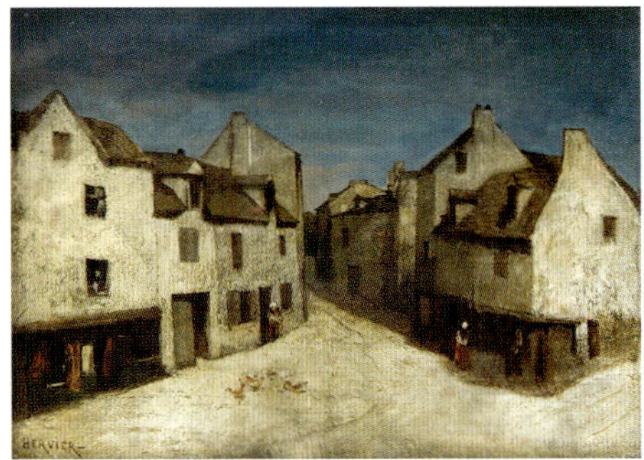

Hervier, Louis Adolphe 1818–1879
Village Street with Poultry
oil on panel 22.2 x 30.7
35.279

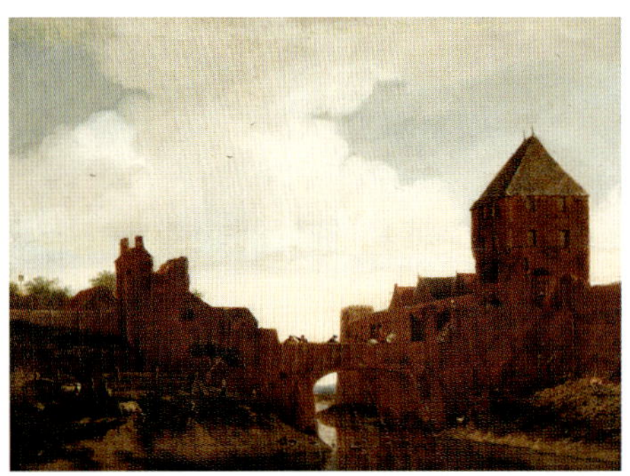

Heyden, Jan van der (imitator of)
1637–1712
A Bridge into a Fortified Town
oil on panel 40 x 54
52

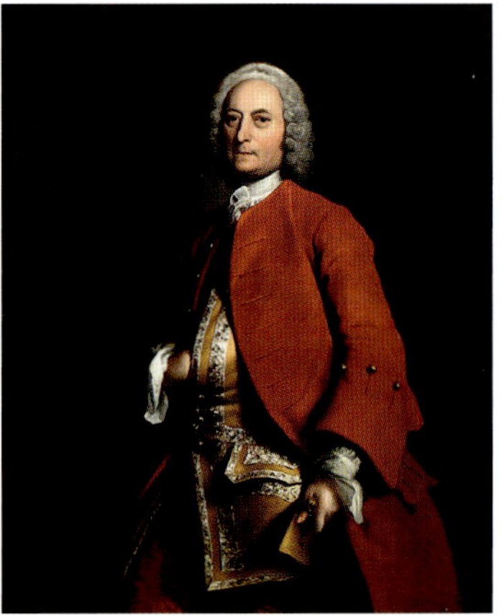

Highmore, Joseph 1692–1780
Portrait of a Man c.1730–1740
oil on canvas 126.8 x 101.7
3321

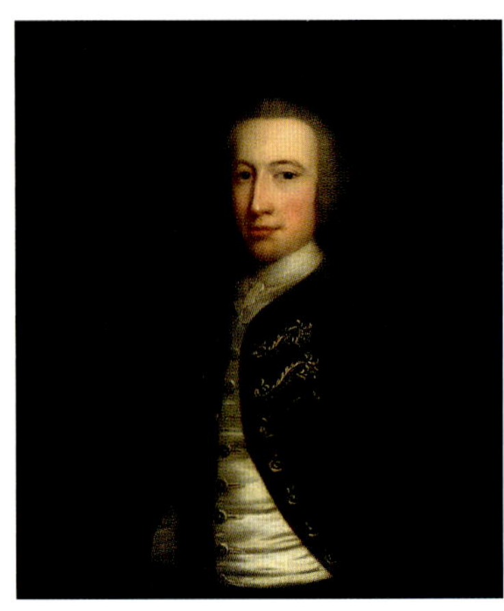

Highmore, Joseph (attributed to)
1692–1780
Portrait of a Man (said to be William Pitt,
1708–1778, 1st Earl of Chatham) c.1748
oil on canvas 75.5 x 62.5
3091

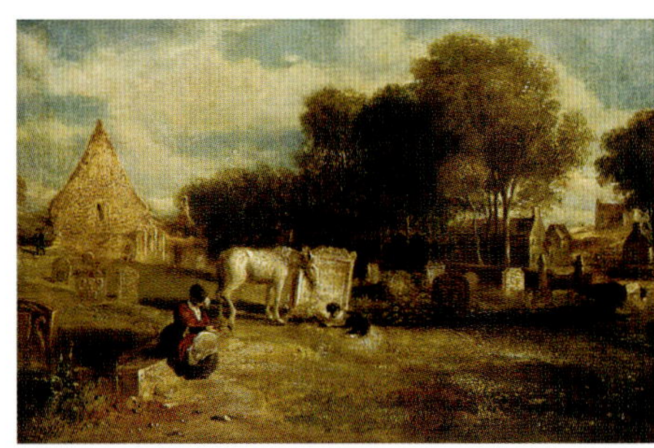

Hill, David Octavius 1802–1870
Kirkoswald, Tam o' Shanter's Grave c.1835
oil on paper on canvas 29.5 x 45.1
978

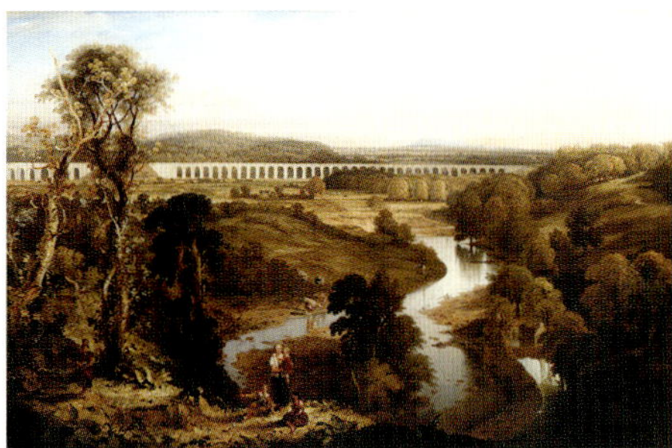

Hill, David Octavius 1802–1870
Viaduct over the River Almond, West Lothian
after 1841
oil on canvas 94 x 132
T.1967.33.al

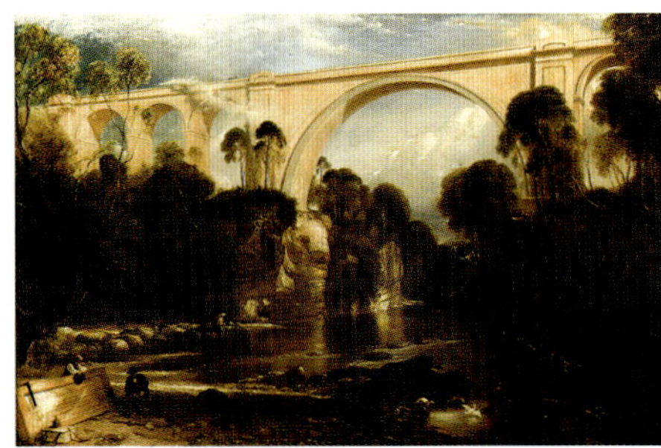

Hill, David Octavius 1802–1870
Ballochmyle Viaduct over the River Ayr 1851
oil on canvas 130.8 x 197.4
T.1967.28

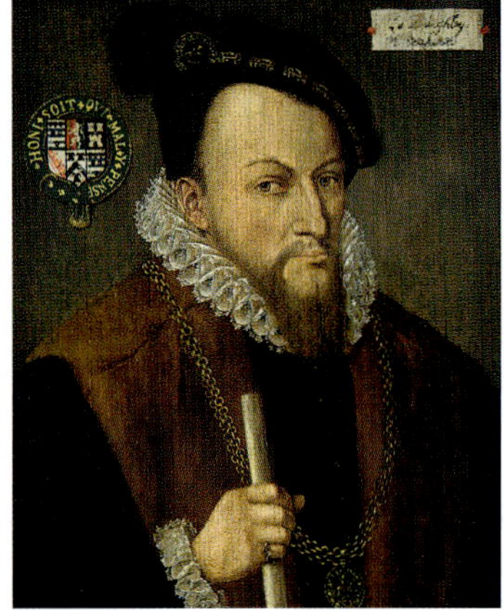

Hilliard, Nicholas (attributed to)
1537–1619
William Cecil (1520–1598), Lord Burghley
c.1560–1570
oil on panel 27.3 x 22.2
35.282

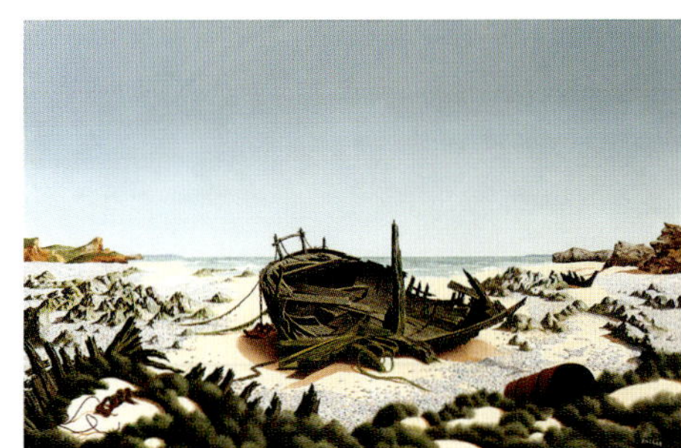

Hillier, Tristram Paul 1905–1983
Hulks 1957
oil on canvas 50.7 x 76
3108

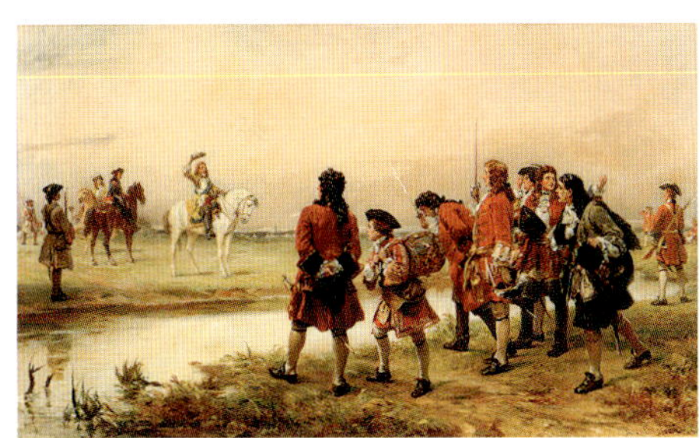

Hillingford, Robert Alexander 1825–1904
'Yet Still a King' c.1888
oil on canvas 78.7 x 129.5
708

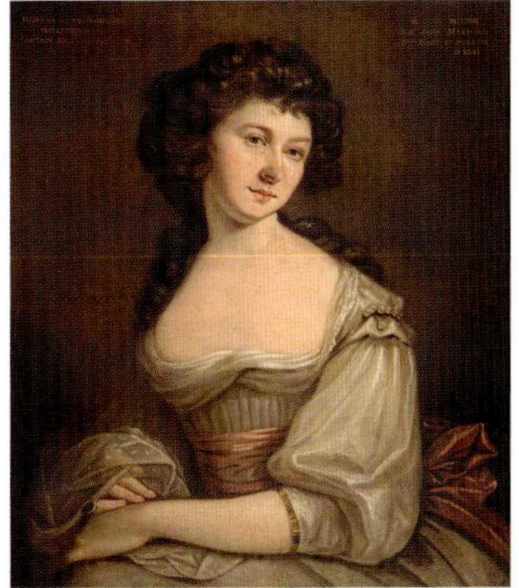

Hilton, William (attributed to) active
c.1780–1820
*Hannah Anne Gardiner (1764–1841), Lady
Maxwell* c.1800
oil on canvas 75.5 x 62.7
PL.176 (P)

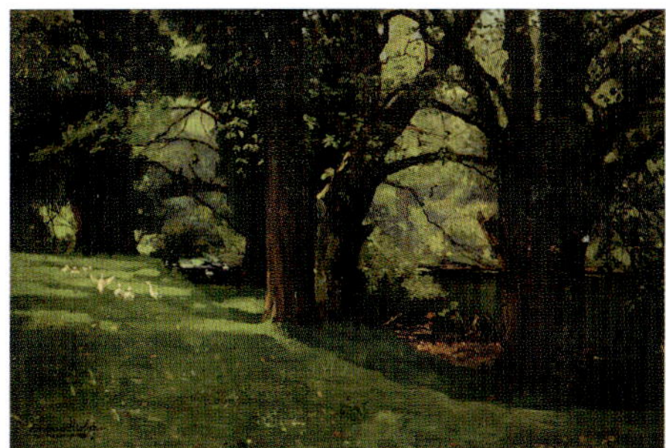

Hislop, Andrew active 1880–1903
The Cart at the Linn
oil on canvas 41.3 x 61
3303

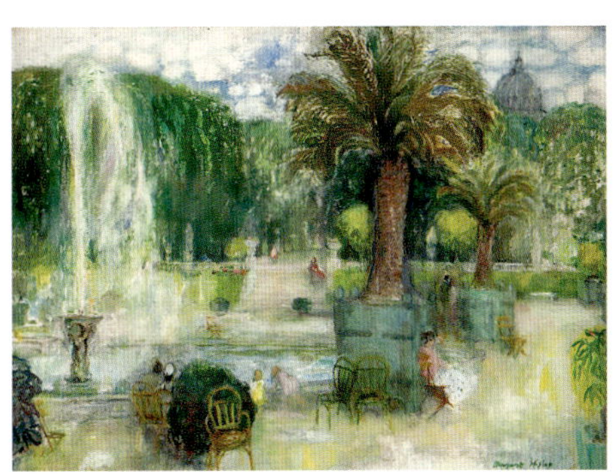

Hislop, Margaret 1894–1972
Jardin du Luxembourg c.1955
oil on panel 71.1 x 91.4
3034

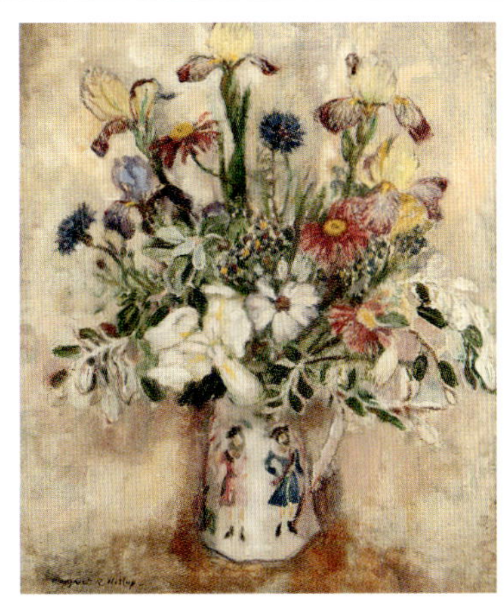

Hislop, Margaret 1894–1972
Flower Piece
oil on board 61 x 50.8
2779

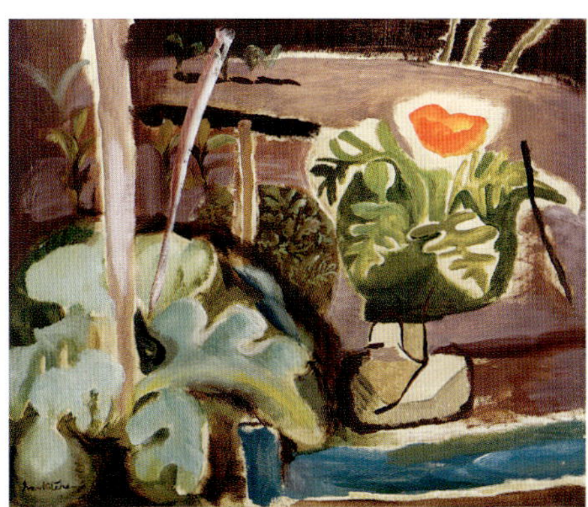

Hitchens, Ivon 1893–1979
Garden with a Poppy
oil on canvas 55.9 x 66
2572

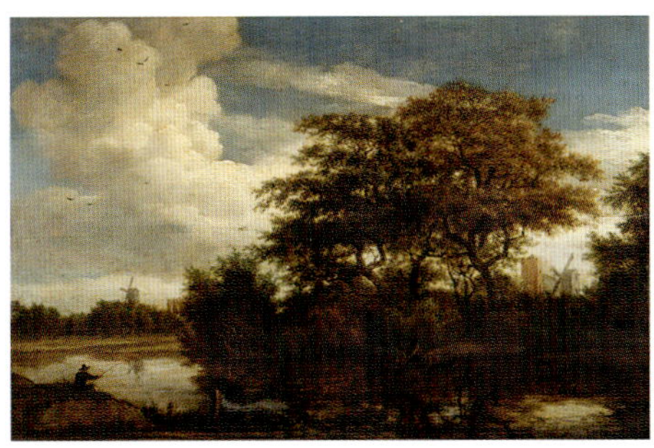

Hobbema, Meindert 1638–1709
River Landscape with Fishermen c.1659–1660
oil on panel 46.7 x 67.3
30

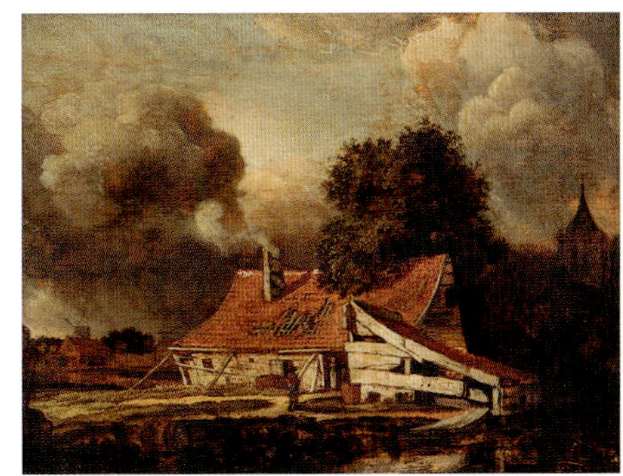

Hobbema, Meindert (imitator of)
1638–1709
A Ruined Cottage
oil on panel 27.6 x 36.2
7

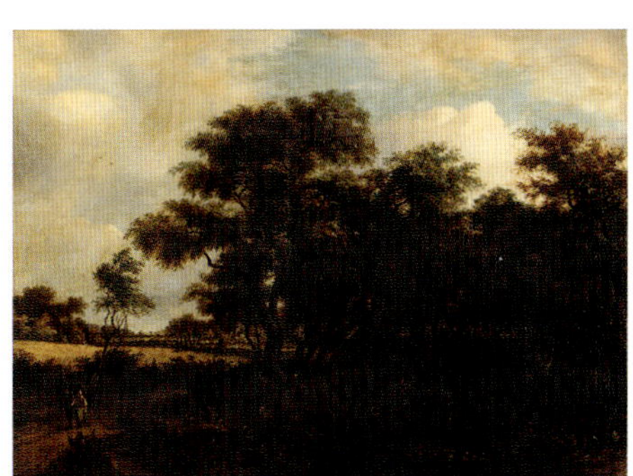

Hobbema, Meindert (imitator of)
1638–1709
A Wooded Landscape with a Pond
oil on panel 62.8 x 86.3
60

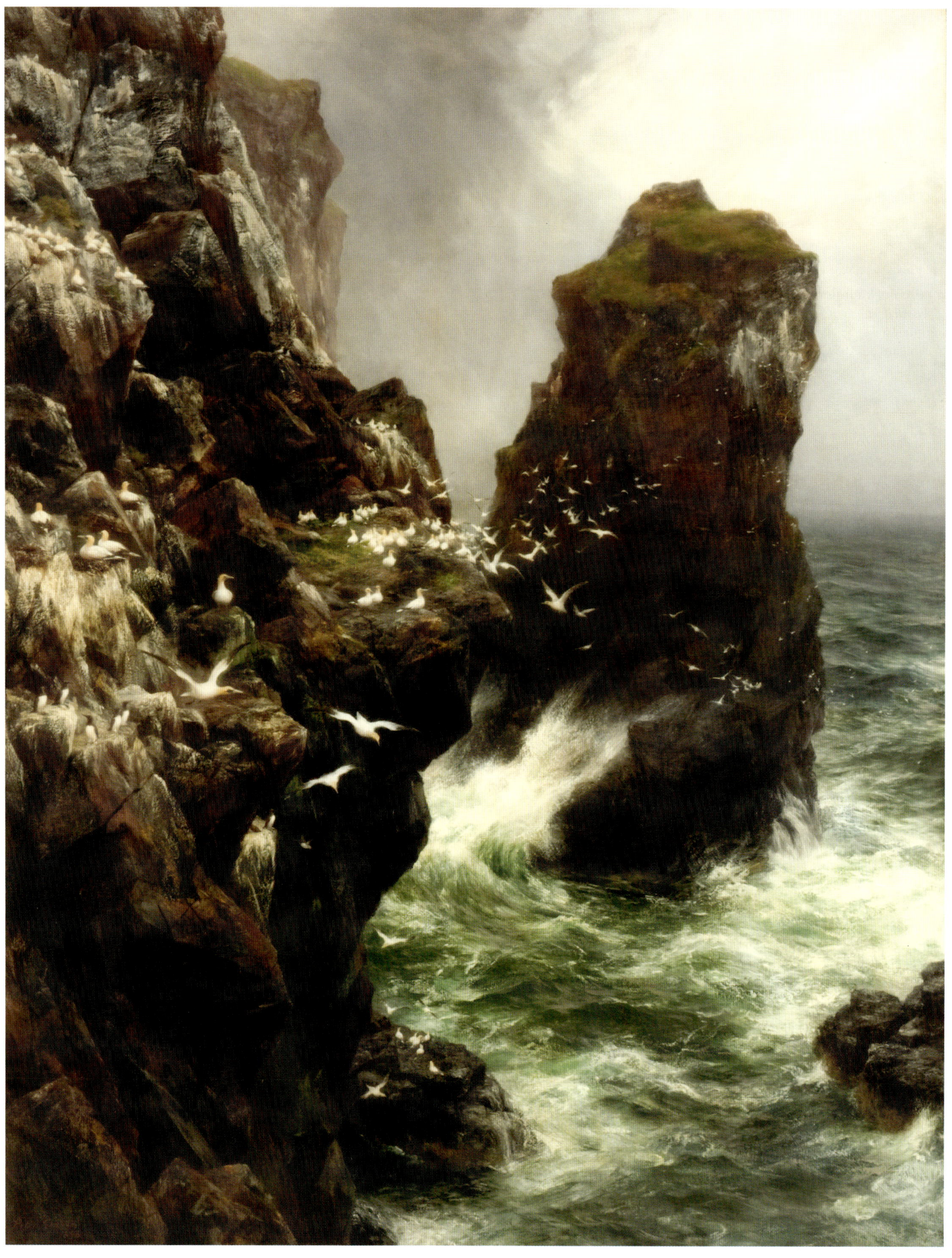

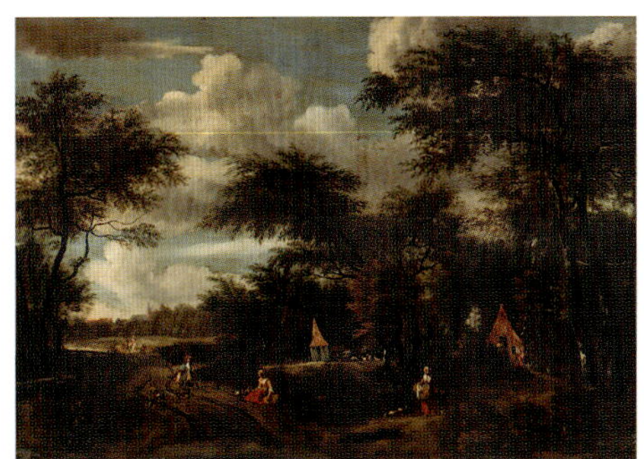

Hobbema, Meindert (school of) 1638–1709
A Wooded Landscape with Cottages
c.1650–1670
oil on canvas 109.2 x 150.5
18

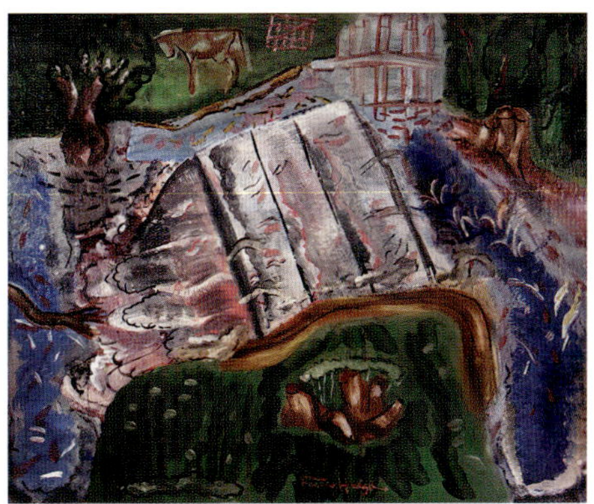

Hodgkins, Frances 1869–1947
The Weir
oil on canvas 64.1 x 76.2
2846

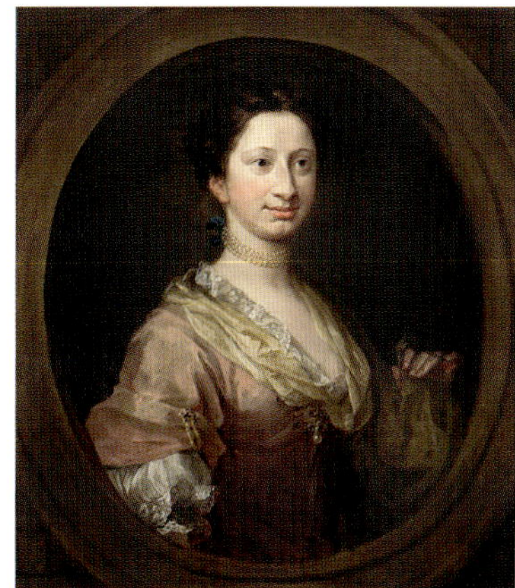

Hogarth, William 1697–1764
Mrs Ann Lloyd (1717–1757) c.1744
oil on canvas 76.2 x 63.5
35.283

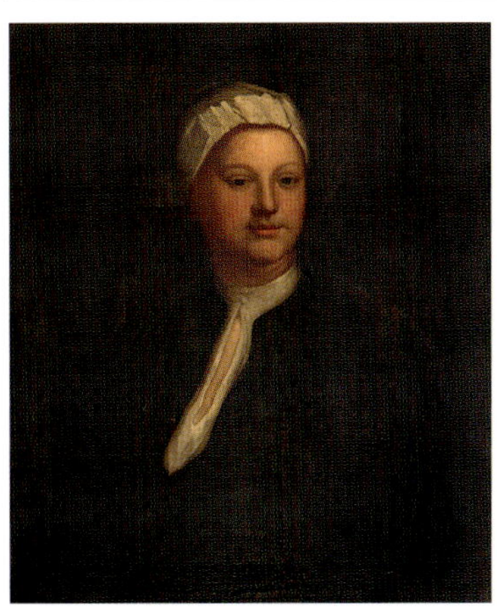

Hogarth, William (after) 1697–1764
James Thomson (1700–1748)
oil on canvas 73.6 x 61
PC.46

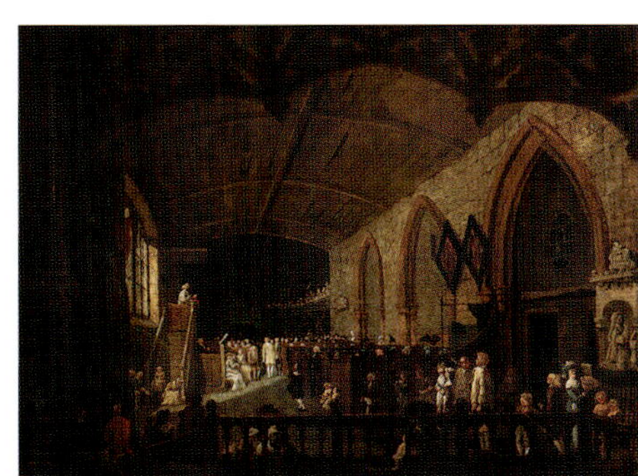

Hogarth, William (attributed to) 1697–1764
St Peter's Chapel in the Tower of London
oil on canvas 40.6 x 55.5
PC.58

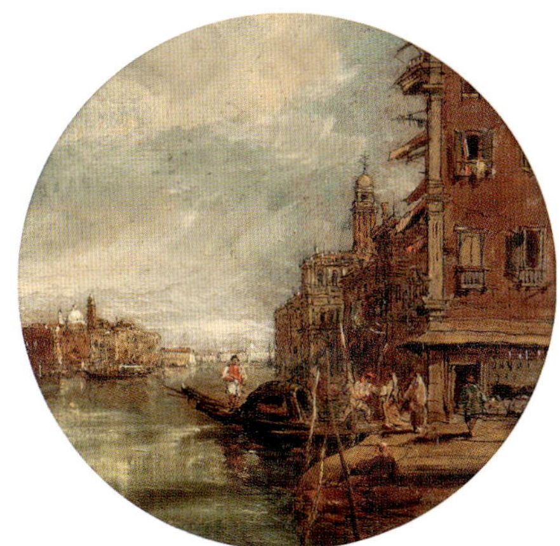

Holland, James 1800–1870
Grand Canal, Venice 1850
oil on cardboard 32.4
1137

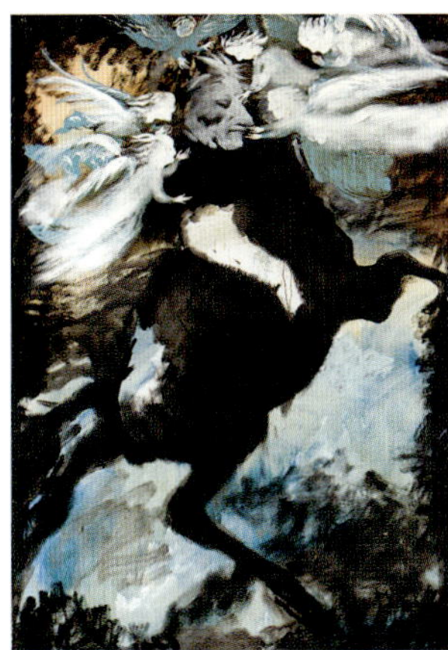

Holosiy, Oleg 1965–1993
Adagio 1990
oil on canvas 259.9 x 197.5
3558

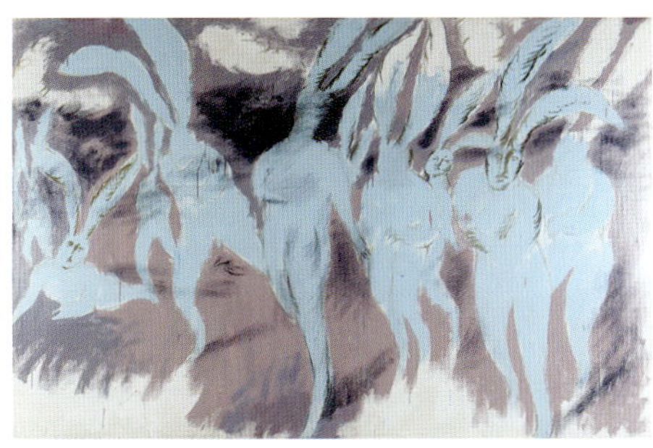

Holosiy, Oleg 1965–1993
Psychedelic Attack of the Blue Rabbits 1990
oil on canvas 200 x 300
3486

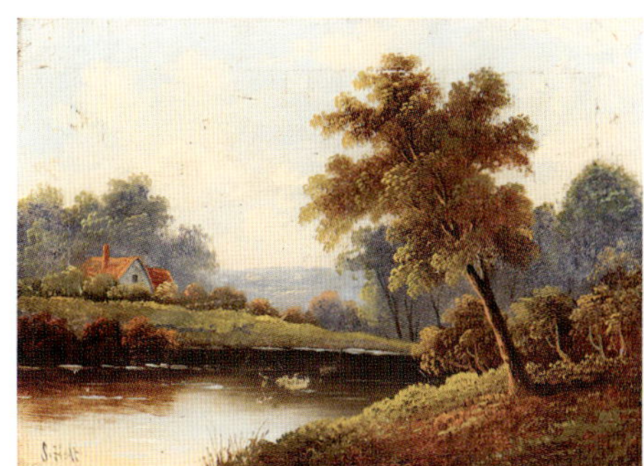

Holt, S.
Landscape with Trees, a Pond and a Cottage
c.1984
oil on canvas 25.4 x 35.6
NR.152

Facing page: Graham, Peter, 1836–1921, *Where Gannets Build*, 1896 (p. 162)

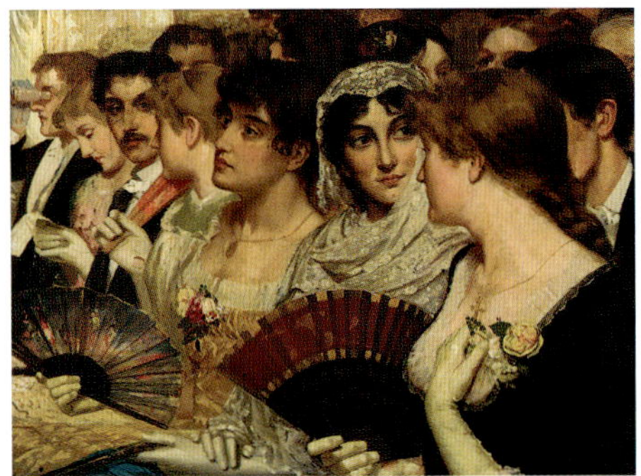

Holyoake, William 1834–1894
In the Front Row at the Opera c.1880
oil on canvas 62.2 x 81.3
764

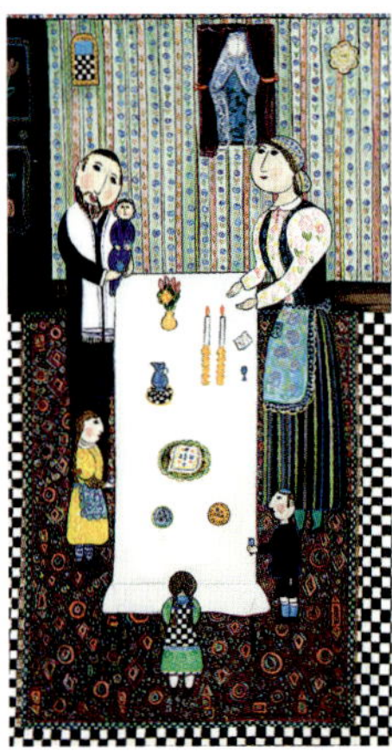

Holzhandler, Dora b.1928
The Sabbath Candles c.1992
oil on canvas 107.7 x 60
3505

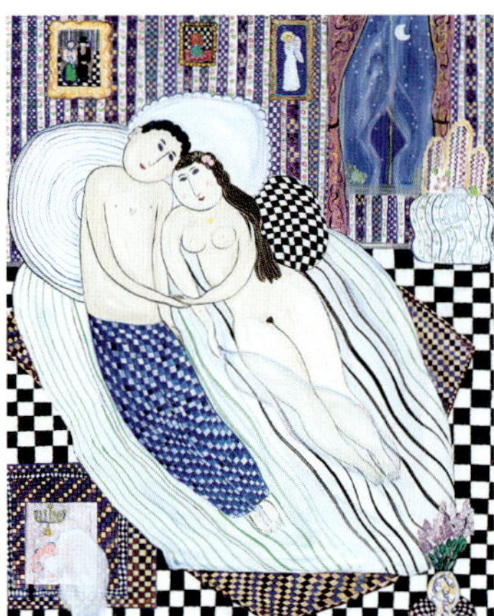

Holzhandler, Dora b.1928
Wedding Night c.1993
oil on canvas 129.3 x 102.6
3557

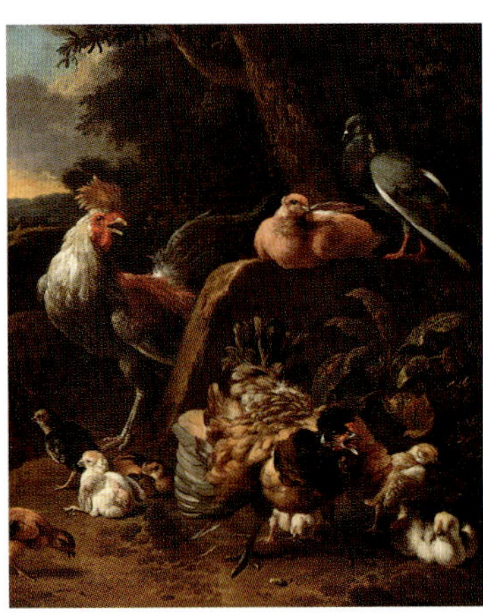

Hondecoeter, Melchior de 1636–1695
Poultry and Pigeons
oil on canvas 87.3 x 72.7
76

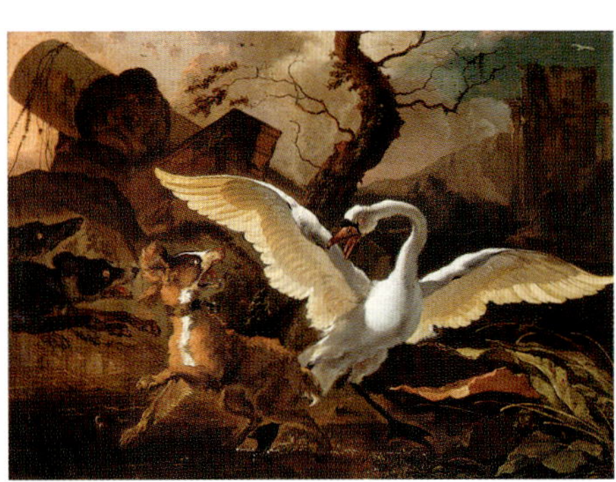

Hondius, Abraham c.1625–1691
A Swan Enraged by Dogs
oil on panel 25.4 x 34.9
22

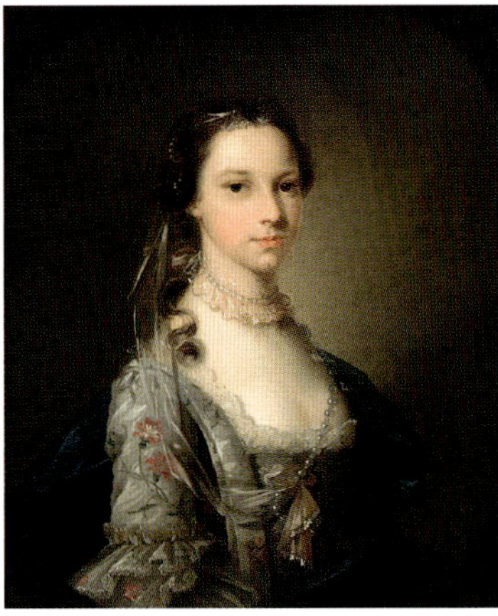

Hone, Nathaniel I 1718–1784
Antonina Willoughby c.1765
oil on canvas 66.1 x 52.7
35.284

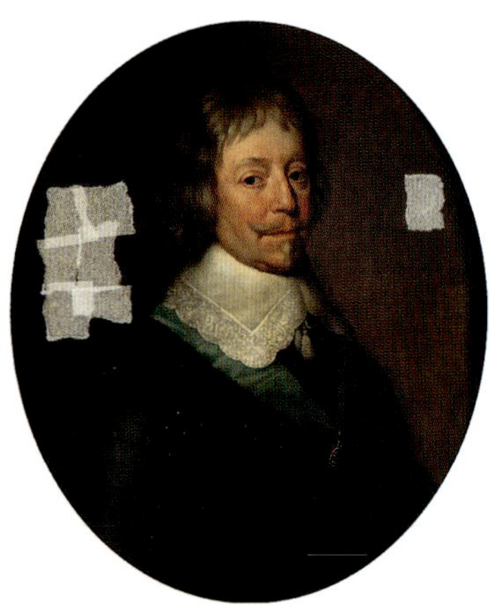

Honthorst, Gerrit van (after) 1590–1656
*Frederick Henry (1584–1647), Prince of
Orange* 17th C
oil on canvas 76.8 x 62.2
464

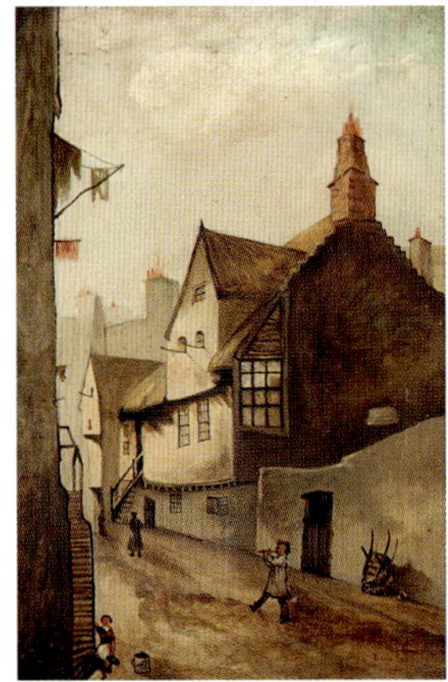

Hood, David
Fiddler's Close 1884
oil on canvas 46 x 30.5
PL.1979.256

Hood, Ernest 1932–1988
Self Portrait 1977
oil on canvas 29.5 x 24.5
PP.1988.45.2

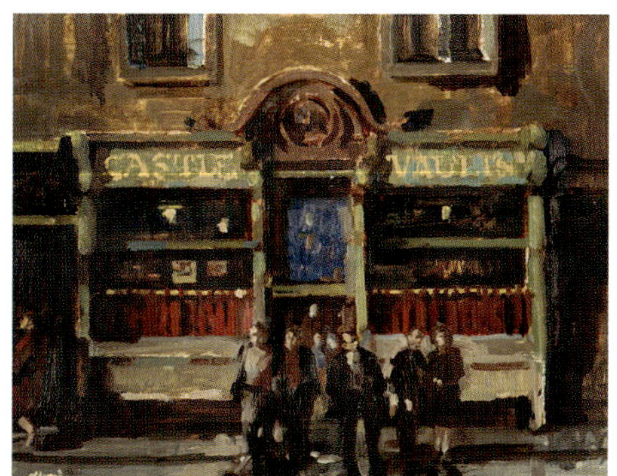

Hood, Ernest 1932–1988
'Castle Vaults' c.1978
oil on board 40.1 x 50.7
3345

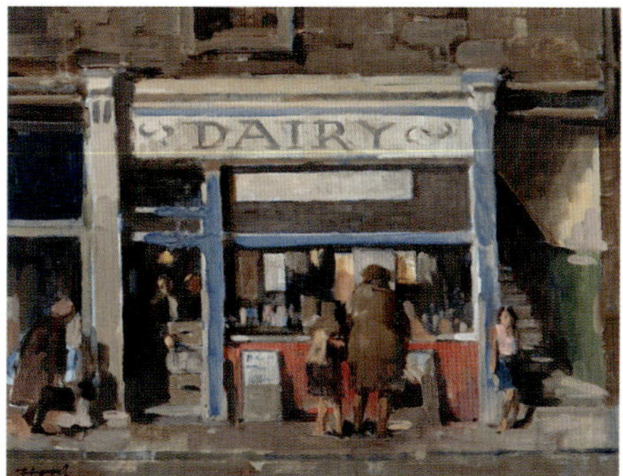

Hood, Ernest 1932–1988
The Dairy c.1978
oil on canvas board 40.1 x 50.7
3344

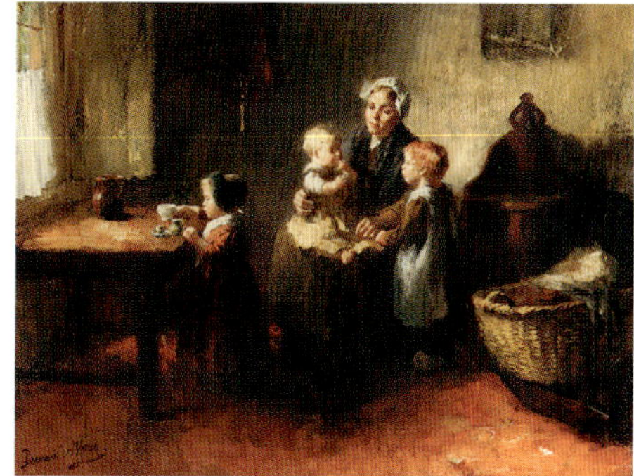

Hoog, Bernard de 1867–1943
Tea Time
oil on canvas 49.8 x 66
2637

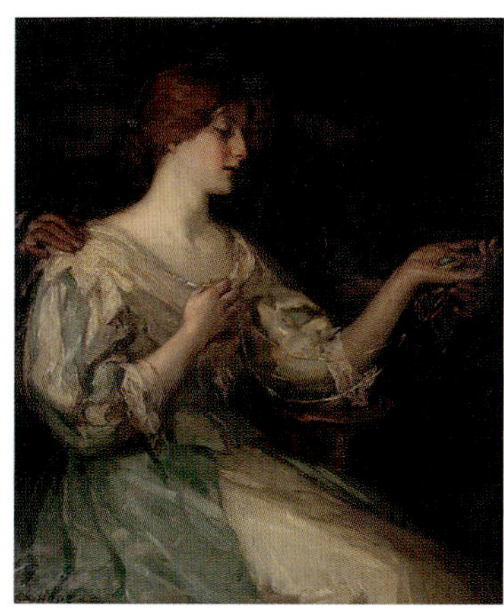

Hope, Robert 1869–1936
The Charm
oil on canvas 74.9 x 62.2
1462

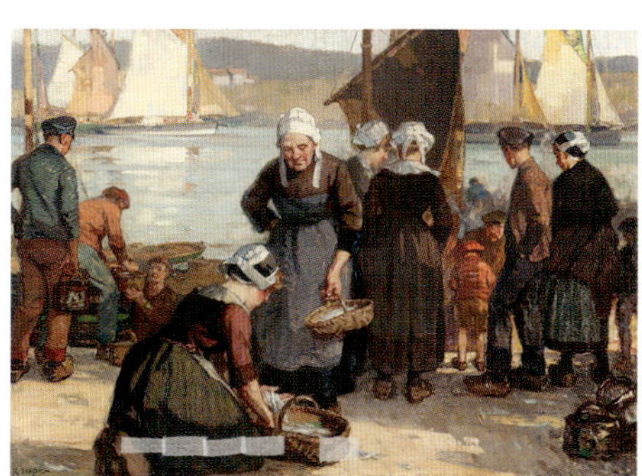

Hope, Robert 1869–1936
The Return of the Sardine Fishers, Concarneau
oil on canvas 91.4 x 127
2074

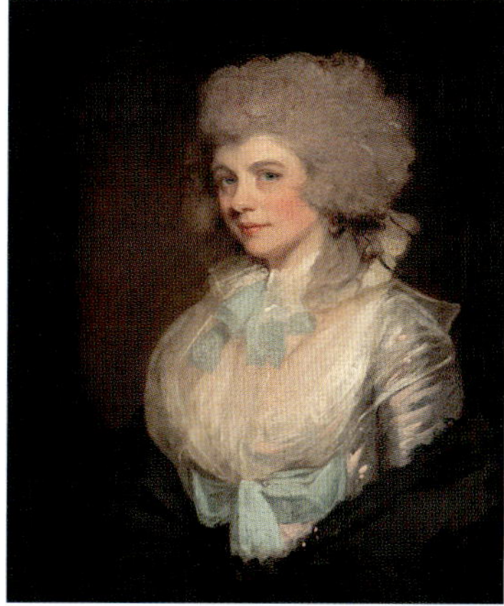

Hoppner, John 1758–1810
Mrs Errington c.1790–1810
oil on canvas 76.2 x 63.5
2071

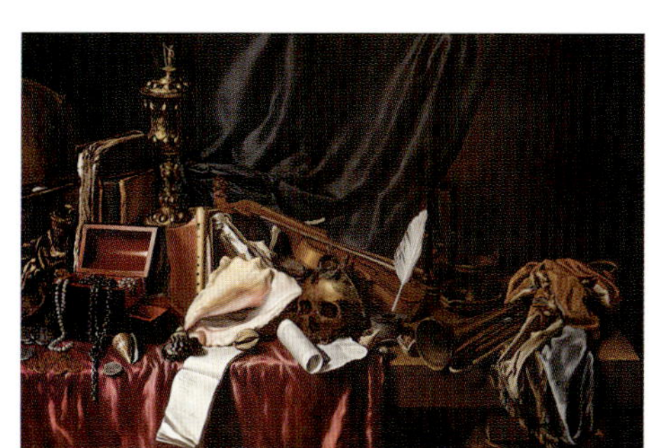

Horn, David active 19th C
Still Life
oil on canvas 99.1 x 143.5
2537

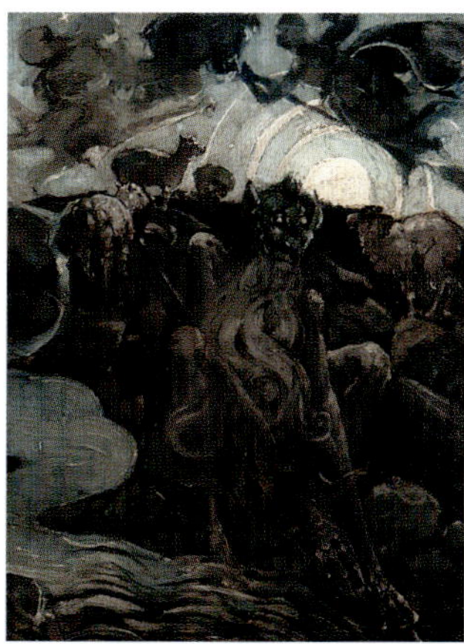

Hornel, Edward Atkinson 1864–1933
The Brownie of Blednoch 1889
oil on canvas 61 x 45.7
2479

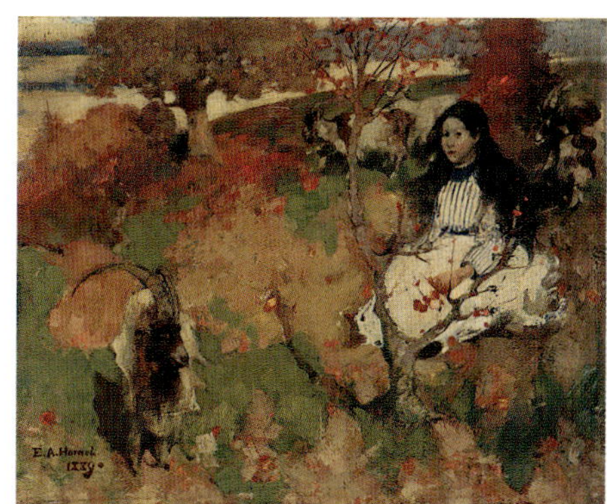

Hornel, Edward Atkinson 1864–1933
The Goatherd 1889
oil on canvas 52 x 60.4
LI.2008.016.1 (P)

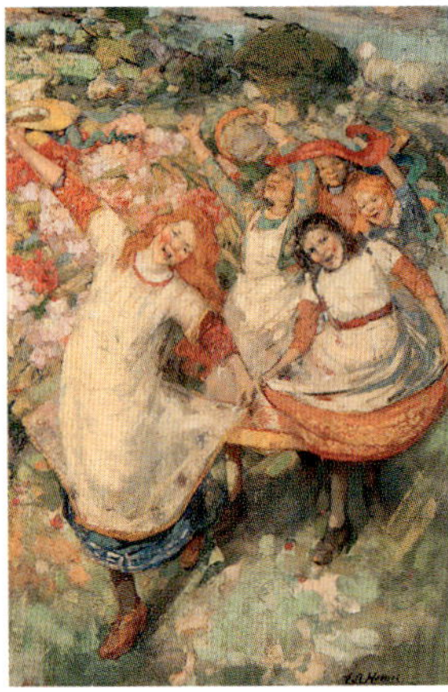

Hornel, Edward Atkinson 1864–1933
The Dance of Spring c.1891
oil on canvas 142.4 x 95.2
3138

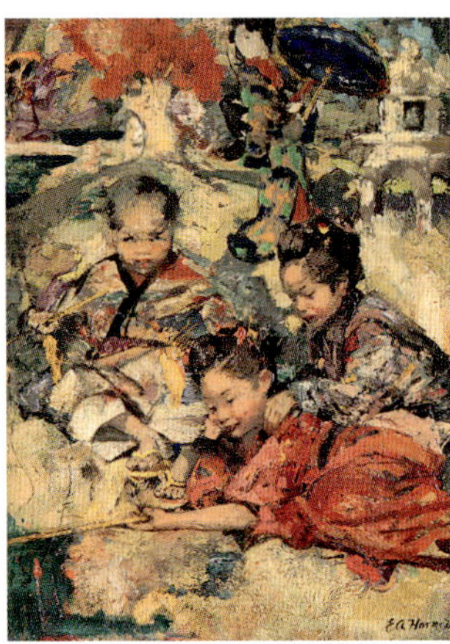

Hornel, Edward Atkinson 1864–1933
The Fish Pool 1894
oil on canvas 45.1 x 35.6
2906

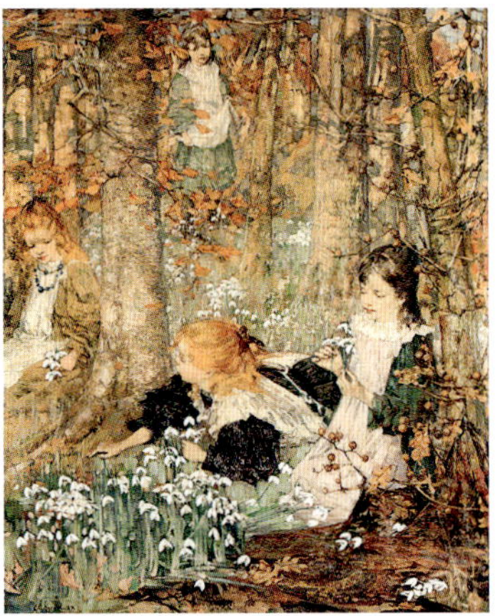

Hornel, Edward Atkinson 1864–1933
The Coming of Spring 1899
oil on canvas 152.4 x 121.9
909

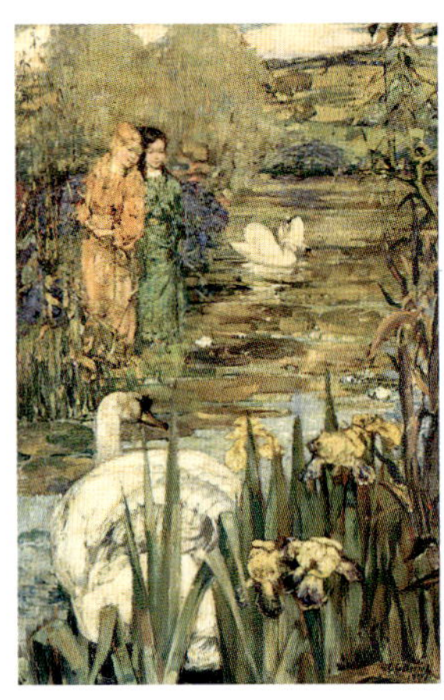

Hornel, Edward Atkinson 1864–1933
The Swans 1899
oil on canvas 111.8 x 72.4
2926

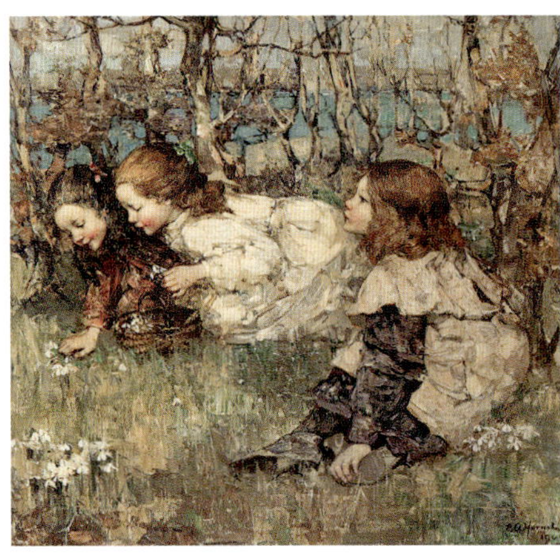

Hornel, Edward Atkinson 1864–1933
Gathering Snowdrops 1906
oil on canvas 61 x 61
2804

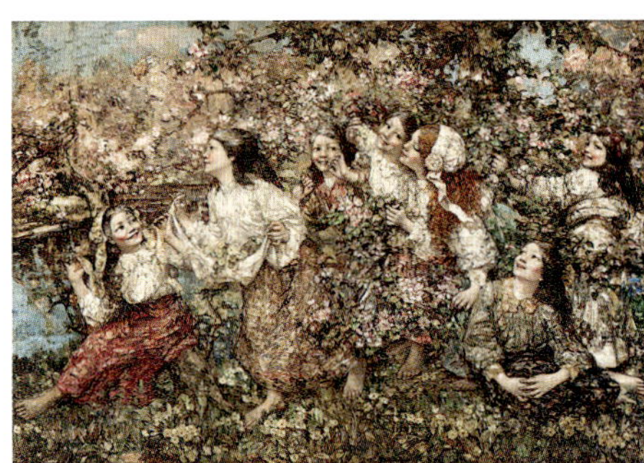

Hornel, Edward Atkinson 1864–1933
A Spring Roundelay 1910
oil on canvas 150.5 x 211.4
1349

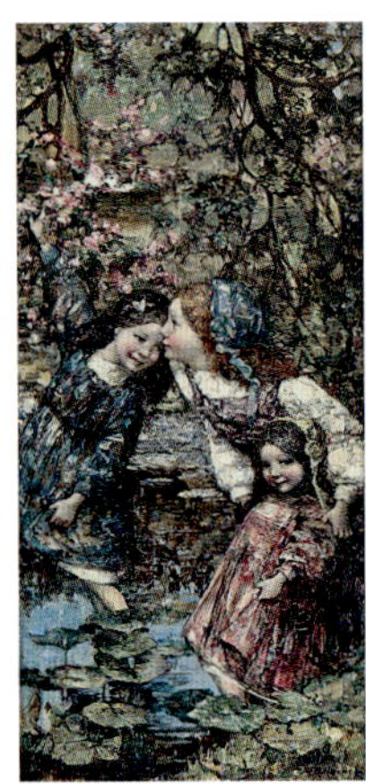

Hornel, Edward Atkinson 1864–1933
The Lily Pond 1912
oil on canvas 76.2 x 35.6
2920

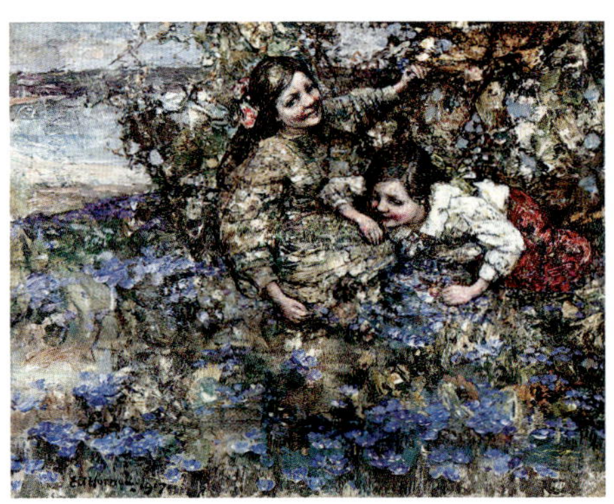

Hornel, Edward Atkinson 1864–1933
Blue Flax 1917
oil on canvas on board 40.6 x 50.8
3005

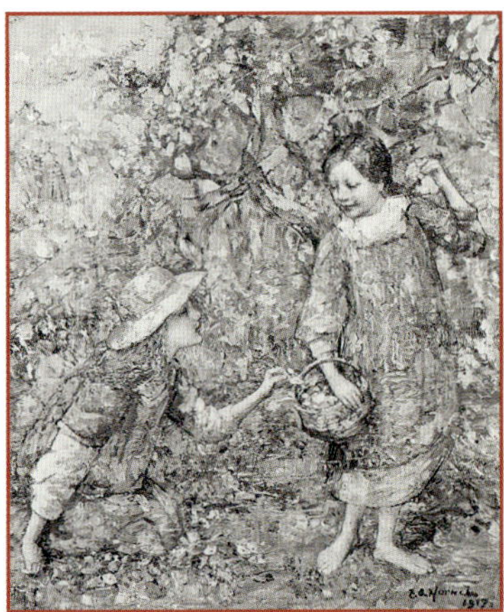

Hornel, Edward Atkinson 1864–1933
Gathering Primroses 1917
oil on canvas 50.7 x 40.6
3127
STOLEN

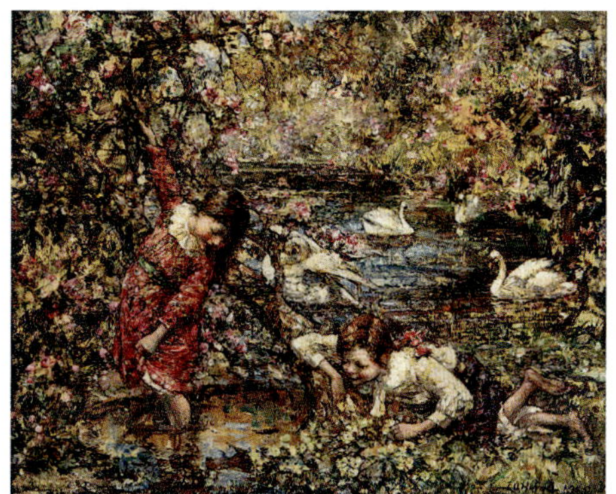

Hornel, Edward Atkinson 1864–1933
Two Girls and Swans at a Pool 1925
oil on canvas 63.5 x 76.2
2878

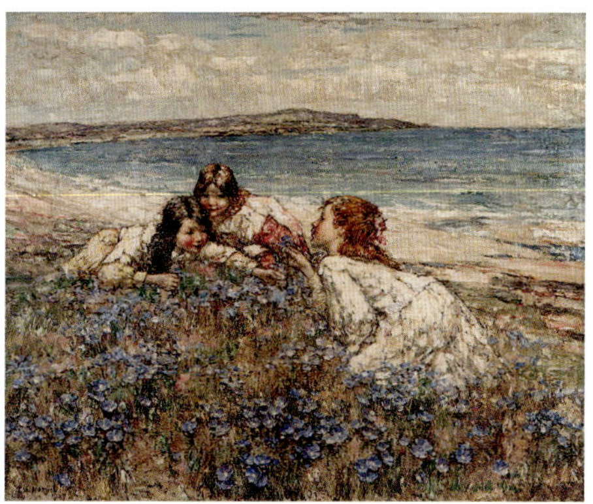

Hornel, Edward Atkinson 1864–1933
Blue Flax 1927
oil on canvas 76.2 x 91.4
2919

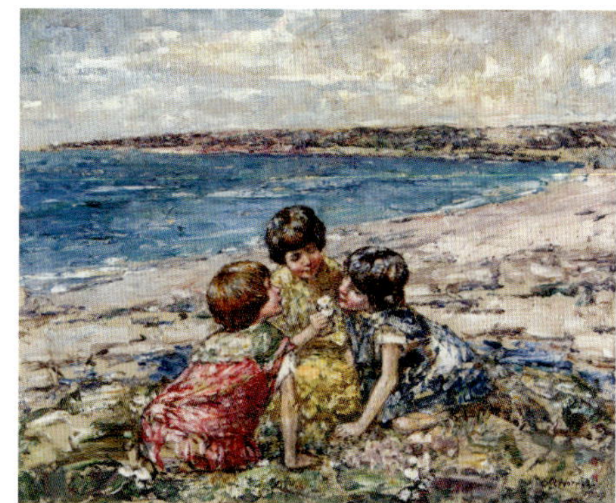

Hornel, Edward Atkinson 1864–1933
Children on the Sands 1927
oil on canvas 52.1 x 62.2
2877

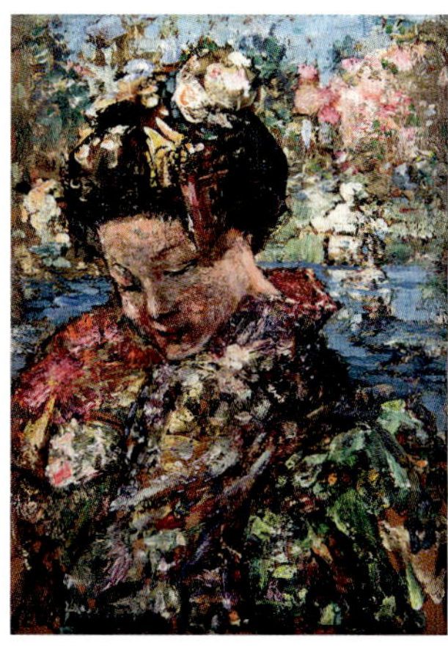

Hornel, Edward Atkinson (after) 1864–1933
In a Japanese Garden 1920
oil on canvas 32.4 x 22.2
2642

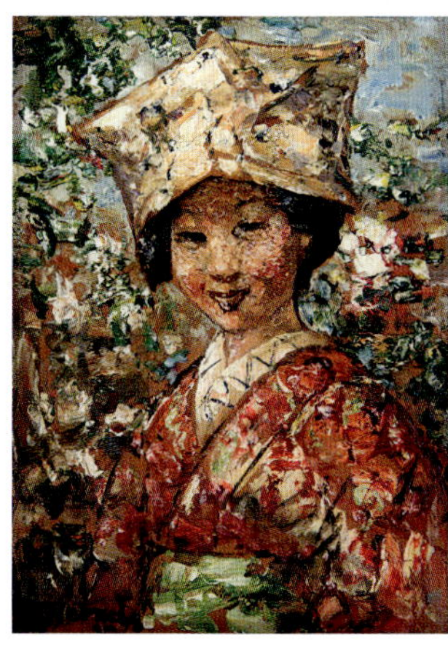

Hornel, Edward Atkinson (after) 1864–1933
The Paper Hat
oil on canvas 32.4 x 21.6
2641

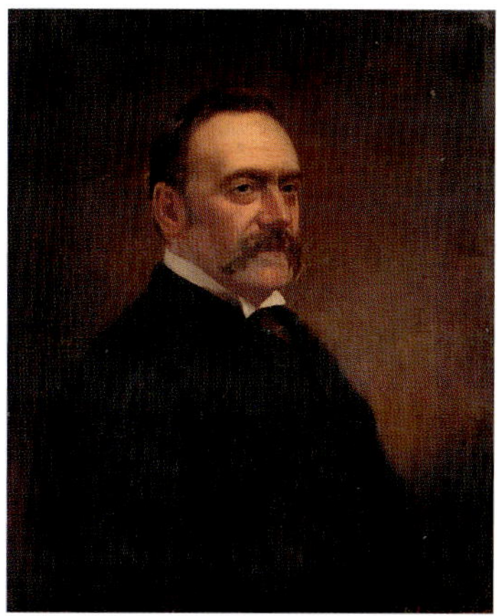

Horsburgh, Edward active 19th C
David Jones (1834–1906) 1887
oil on canvas 85 x 72
TEMP.15474

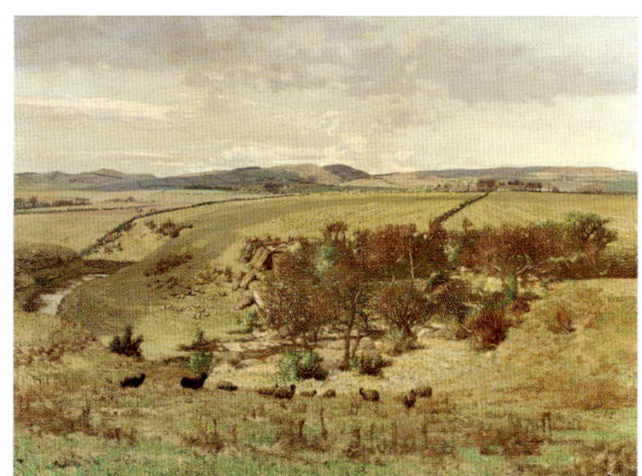

Houston, George 1869–1947
Ayrshire Landscape c.1904
oil on canvas 135.9 x 181.6
1082

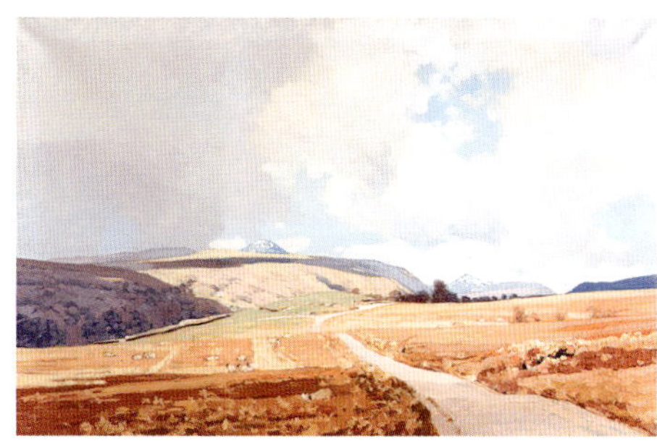

Houston, George 1869–1947
Heart of Argyll c.1936
oil on canvas 101.3 x 152.3
2067

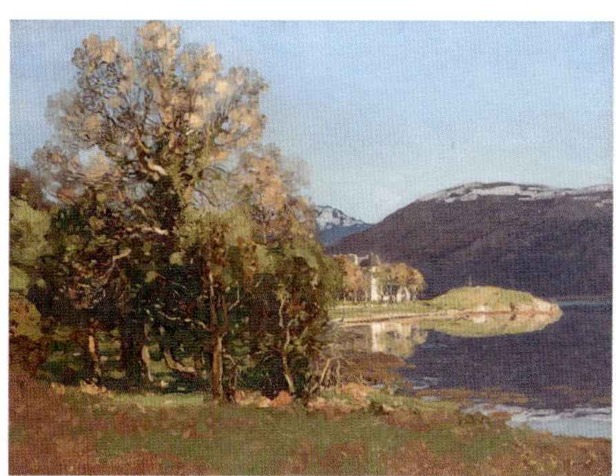

Houston, George 1869–1947
Dundarave Castle, Loch Fyne
oil on canvas 71 x 91
3133

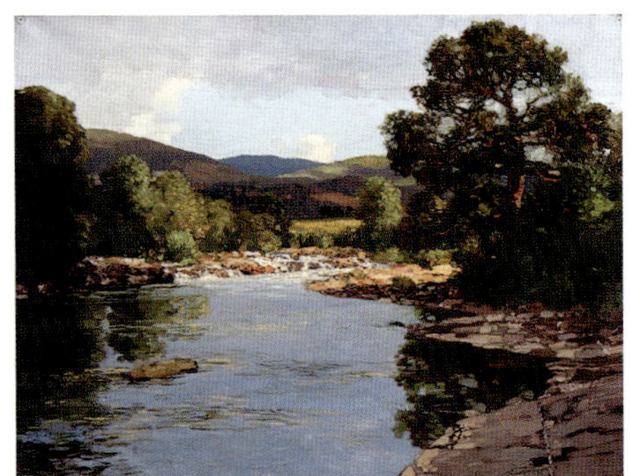

Houston, George 1869–1947
Glen Orchy
oil on canvas 70.8 x 90.8
3134

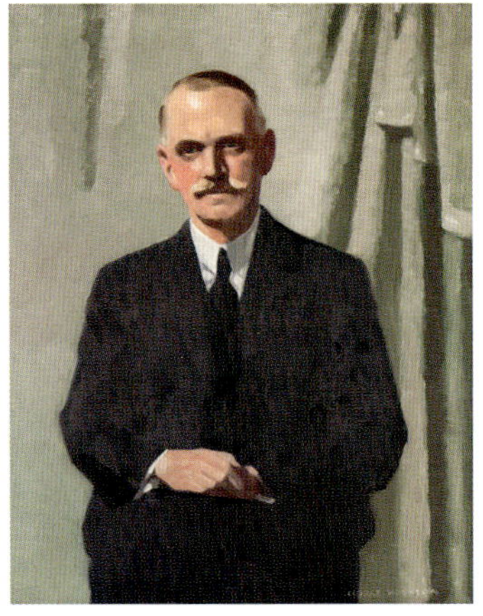

Houston, George 1869–1947
James D. Paterson (1879–1949)
oil on canvas 91.5 x 71
PP.1983.207.1

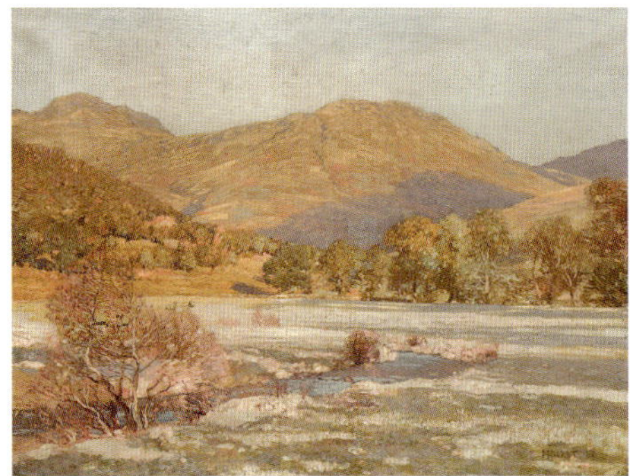

Houston, George 1869–1947
Landscape
oil on canvas 71.1 x 91.4
2163

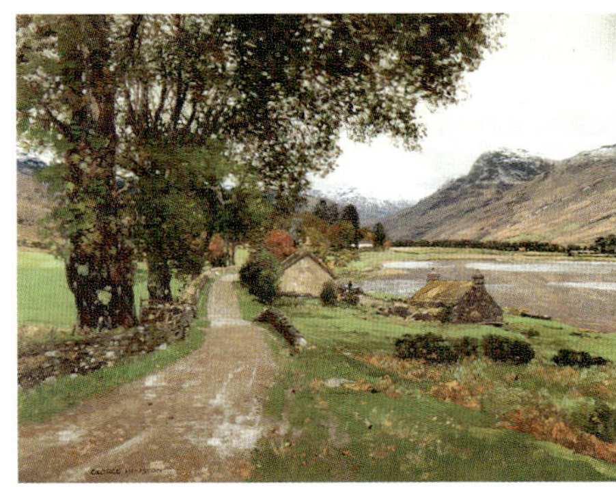

Houston, George 1869–1947
Loch Fyne Head
oil on canvas 70.8 x 91.1
3135

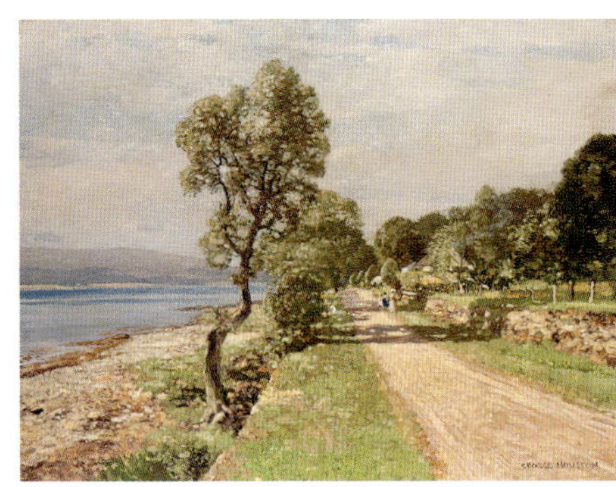

Houston, George 1869–1947
Summer Green, Loch Fyne Side
oil on canvas 70.8 x 91.1
3136

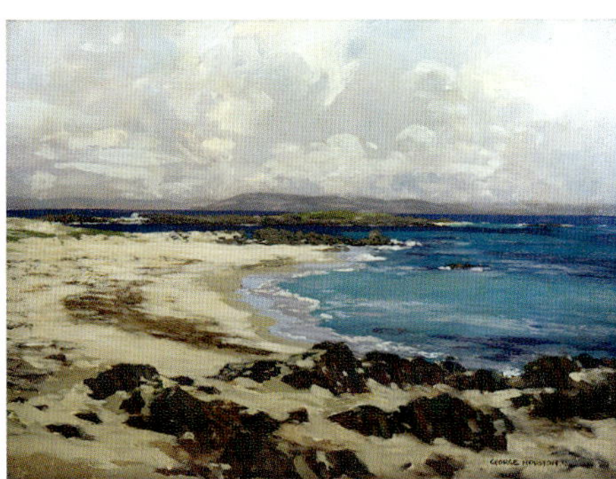

Houston, George 1869–1947
White Sands of Iona
oil on canvas 45.7 x 61.3
1708

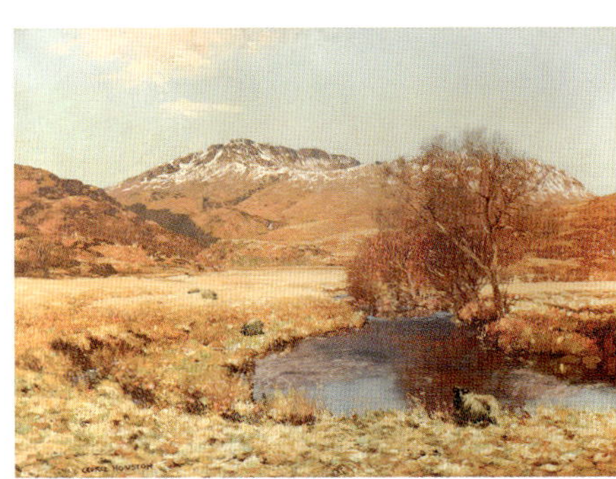

Houston, George 1869–1947
Winter Sunshine, Lochgoilhead
oil on canvas 71.1 x 91.4
1554

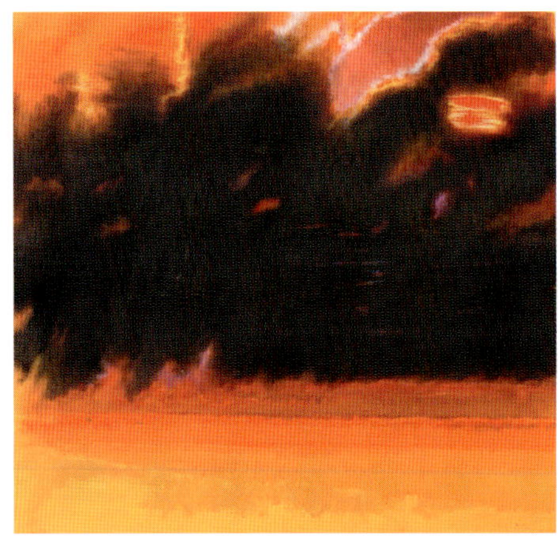

Houston, John 1930–2008
October Sunset 1972–1973
oil on canvas 152.4 x 152.4
3300

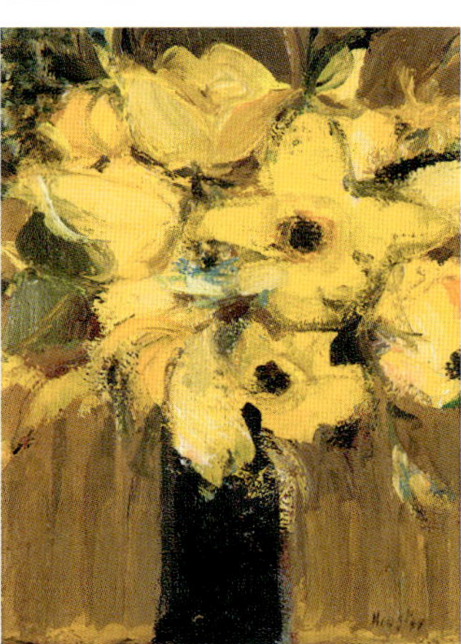

Houston, John 1930–2008
Yellow Flowers in a Black Jug
oil on board 22.3 x 16.5
3533

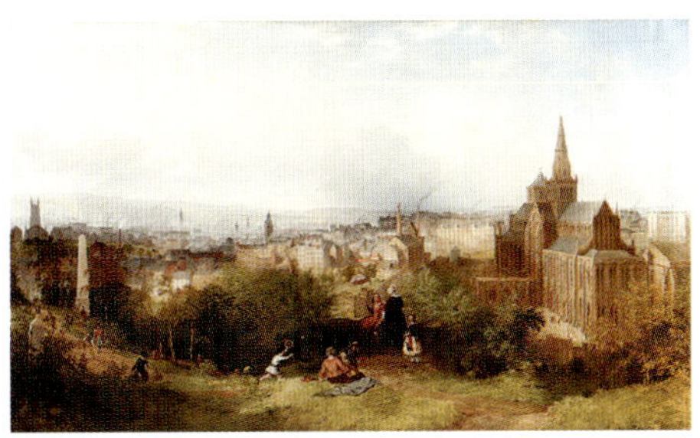

Houston, John Adam 1812–1884
View of Glasgow and the Cathedral c.1840
oil on canvas 111.8 x 182.9
484

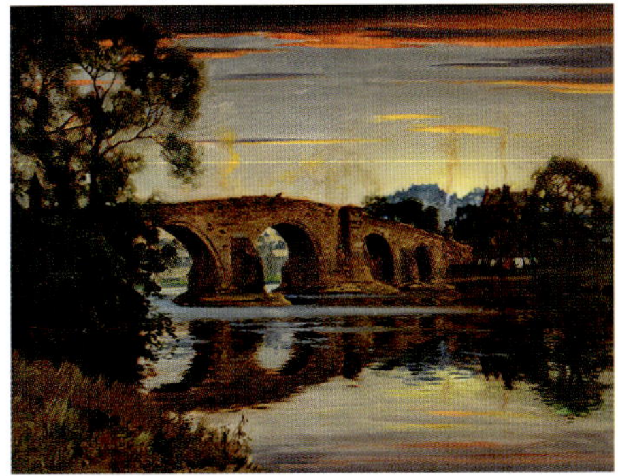

Houston, Robert 1891–1940
Stirling Brig
oil on canvas 86.6 x 106.7
TEMP.3067

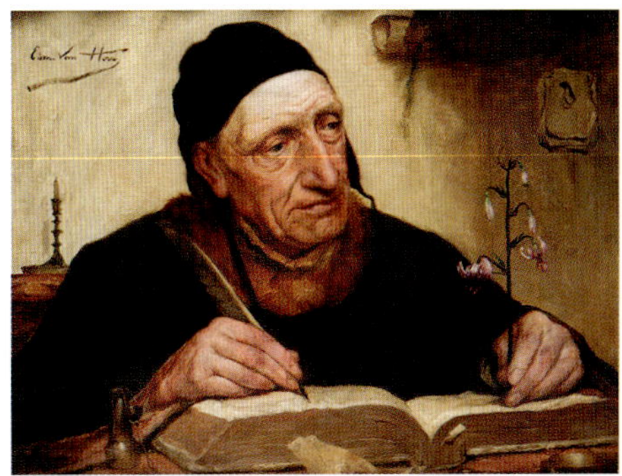

Hove, Edmond Theodor van 1853–1913
The Botanist
oil on panel 31.4 x 39.7
1203

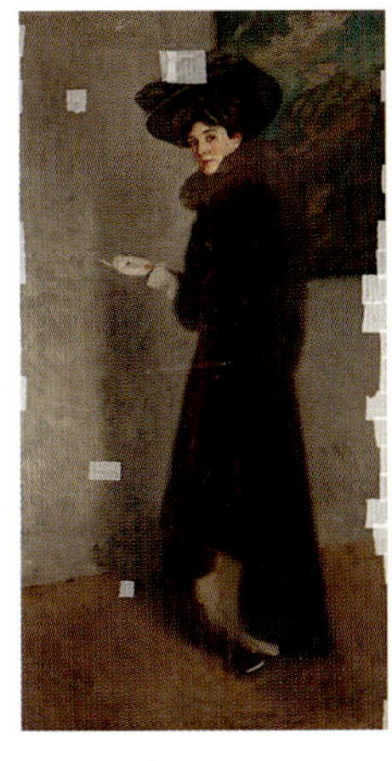

Howard, Francis 1874–1954
Mrs Francis Howard
oil on canvas 201.2 x 104.4
3105

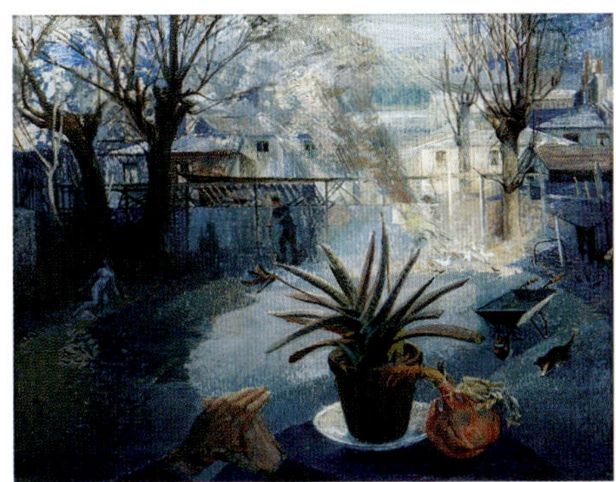

Howard-Jones, Ray 1903–1996
Homage to James Cowie 1945–1946
oil on hardboard 71.2 x 91.5
3291

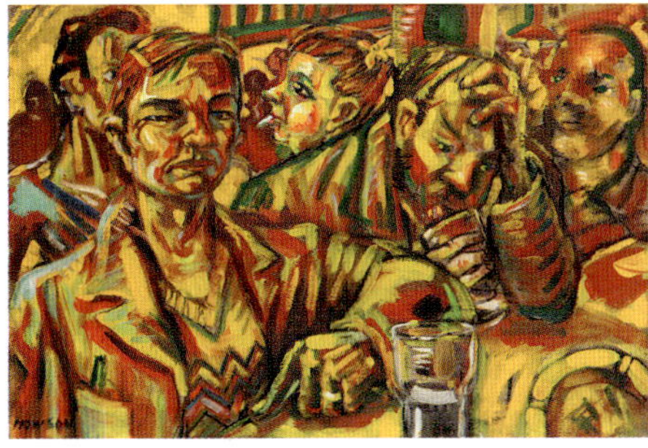

Howson, Peter b.1958
City Bar c.1984
oil on canvas 61.7 x 91.5
PP.1985.99

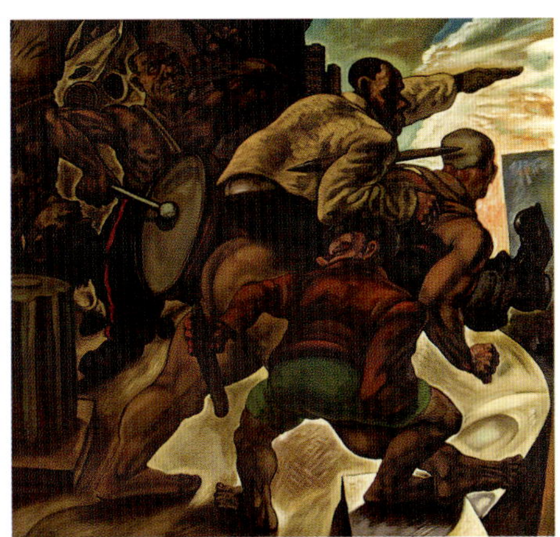

Howson, Peter b.1958
The Final Parade c.1987
oil on canvas 254 x 254
3415

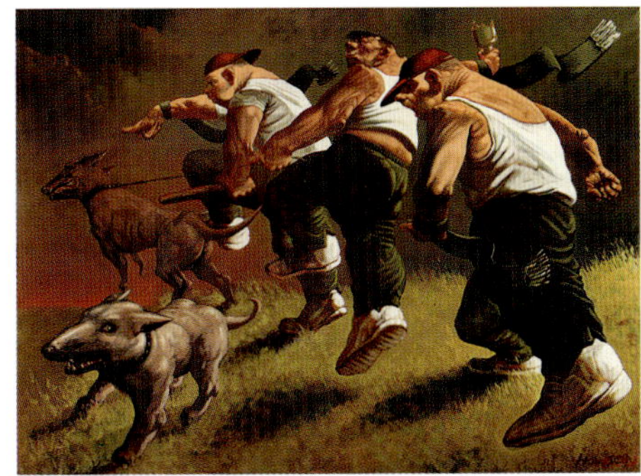

Howson, Peter b.1958
Patriots 1991
oil on canvas 206 x 274.5
3509

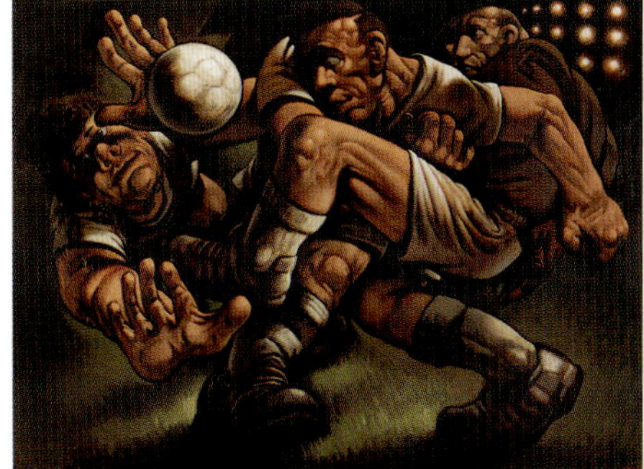

Howson, Peter b.1958
The Glorious Game 1997
oil on canvas 183 x 244
3612

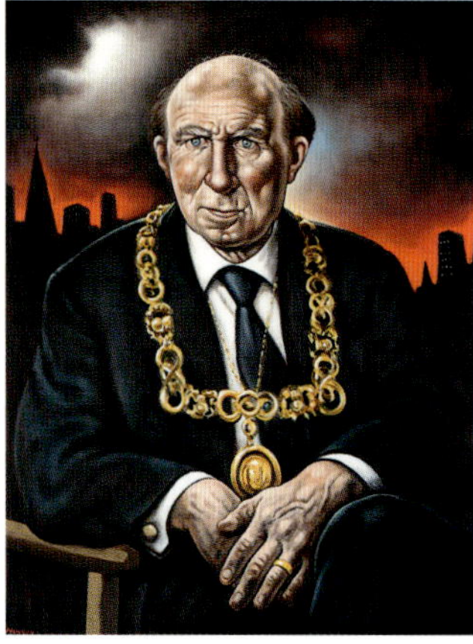

Howson, Peter b.1958
*Patrick Lally (b.1926), Lord Provost of the City
of Glasgow (1996–1999)* c.2000
oil on canvas 121.9 x 91.4
3634

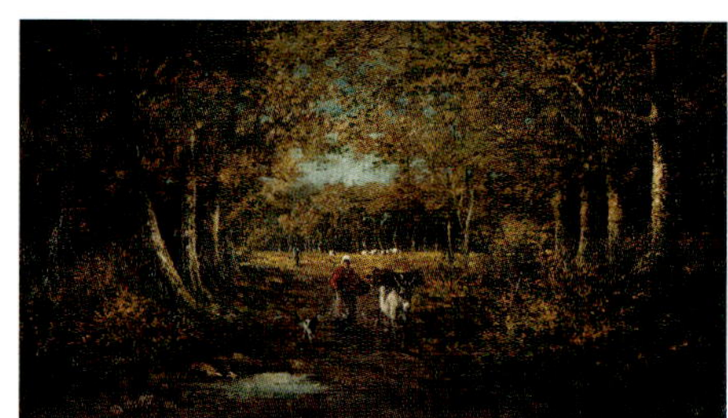

Hubert, F. active 19th C
A Forest Glade
oil on panel 42.8 x 73.6
780

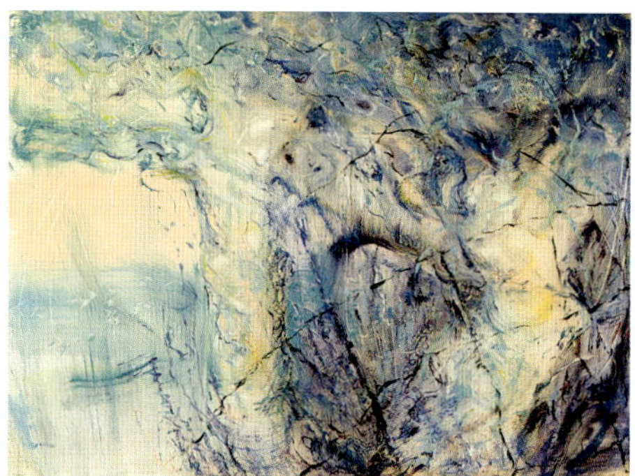

Hughes, Jean
Echoes
oil on canvas 99.5 x 129
3680

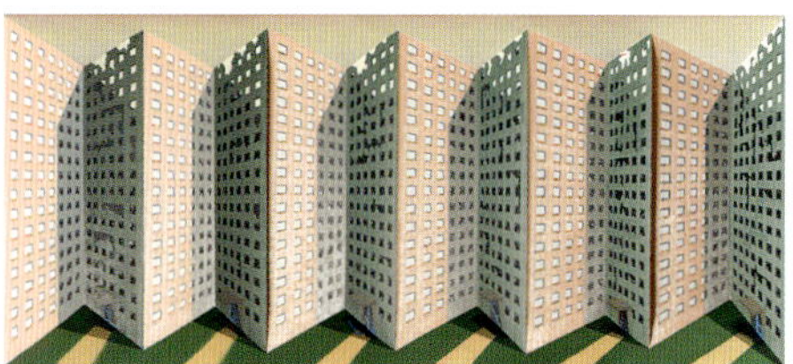

Hughes, Patrick b.1939
The Shadow of War 1993
oil on board 85.4 x 189 x 16.8
3531

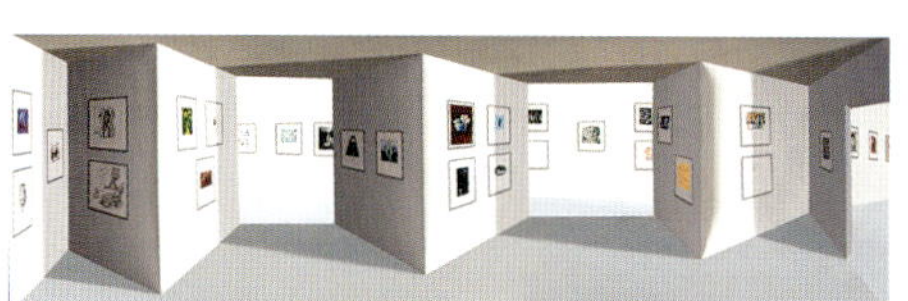

Hughes, Patrick b.1939
Jubilee 1995
oil on board 119 x 338 x 17.5
3597

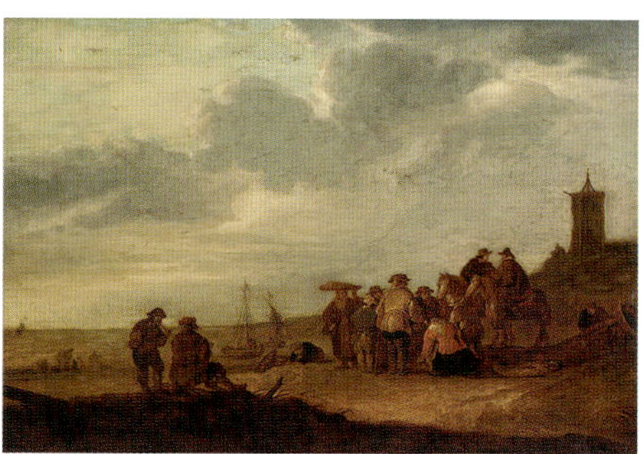

Hulst, Maerten Fransz. van der (after)
1605–1645
Fish Selling on the Dunes c.1630–1645
oil on panel 37.9 x 51.8
301

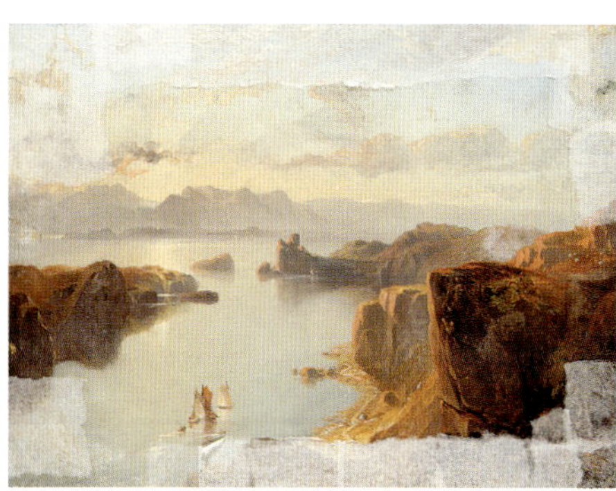

Hunt, Alfred William 1830–1896
The Sound of Kerrera 1852
oil on canvas 34.3 x 44.5
1049

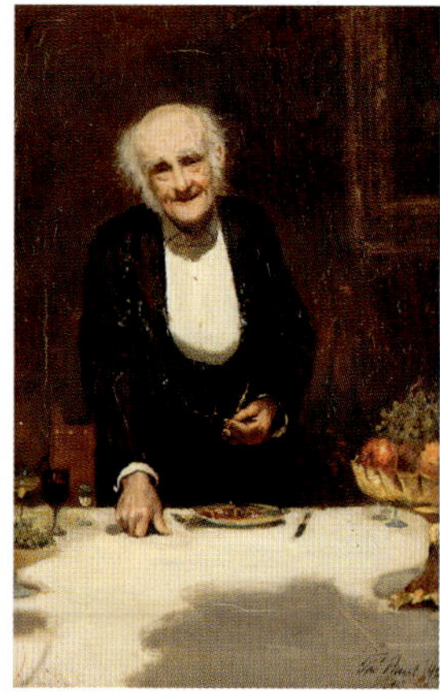

Hunt, Thomas 1854–1929
A Few Remarks 1914
oil on canvas 55.9 x 36.8
2124

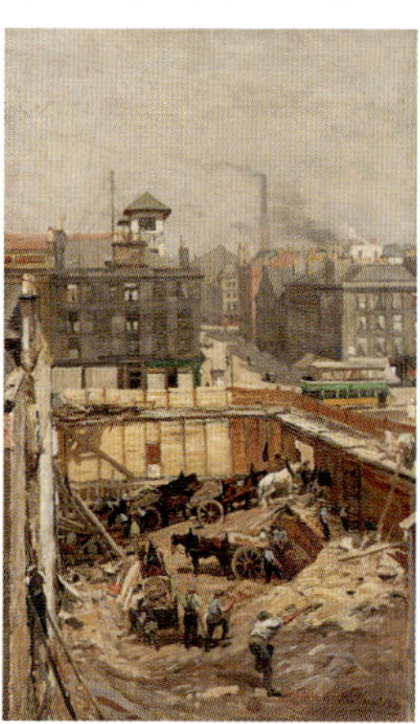

Hunt, Thomas 1854–1929
*Alterations, Corner of Hope Street and
Sauchiehall Street, Glasgow* 1914
oil on canvas 125.7 x 74.9
1444

Facing page: Kelly, Gerald Festus, 1879–1972, *The Blue Door (Consuelo VII)*, 1919 (p. 227)

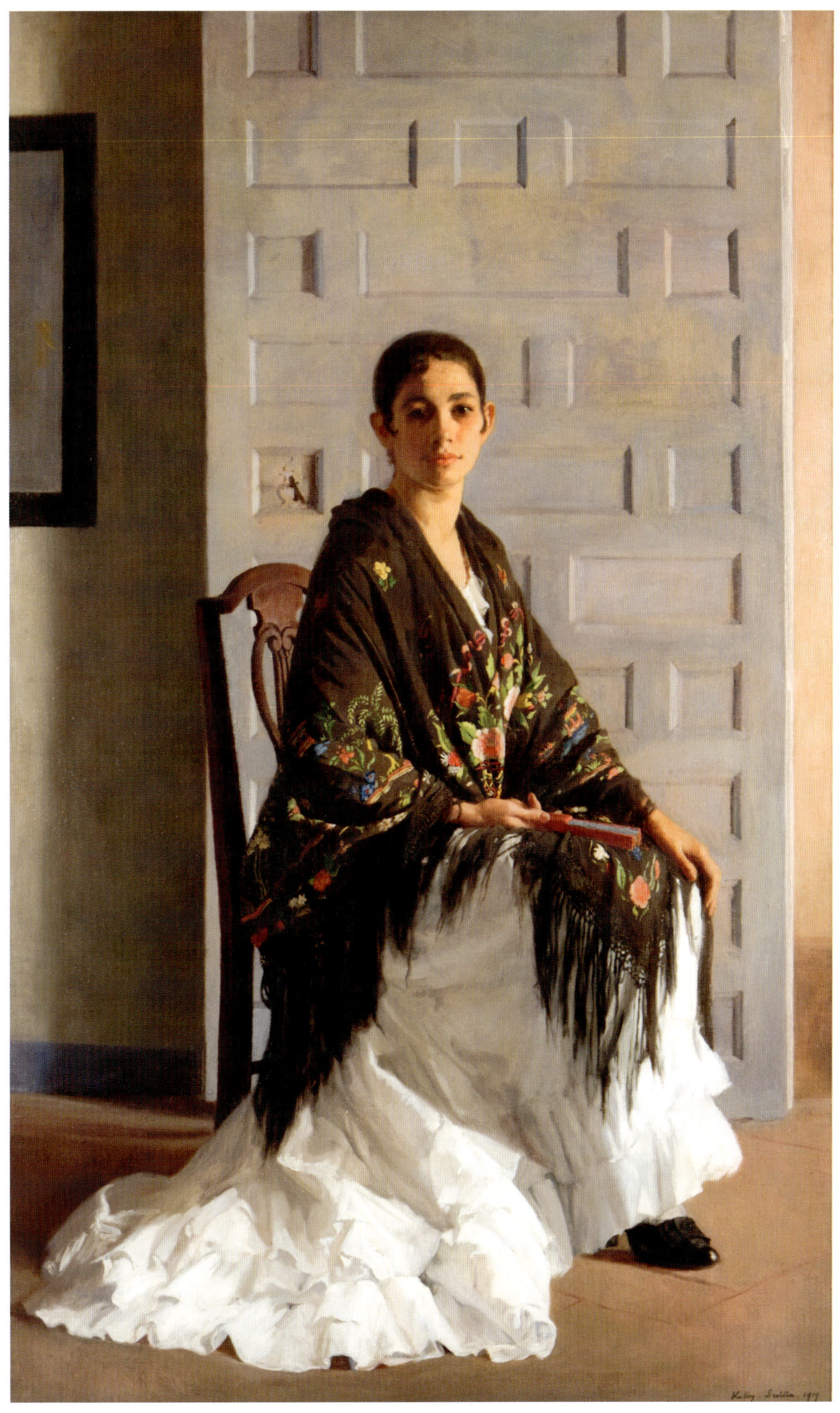

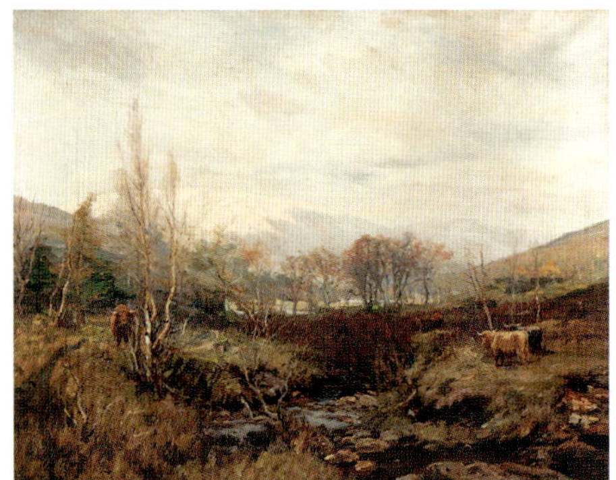

Hunt, Thomas 1854–1929
November, Braes of Balquhidder 1914
oil on canvas 101.6 x 126.4
1343

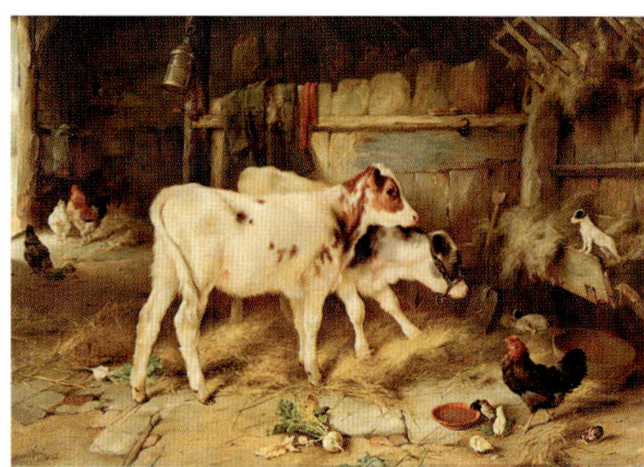

Hunt, Walter 1861–1941
Dog in the Manger 1885
oil on canvas 76.2 x 106.7
2112

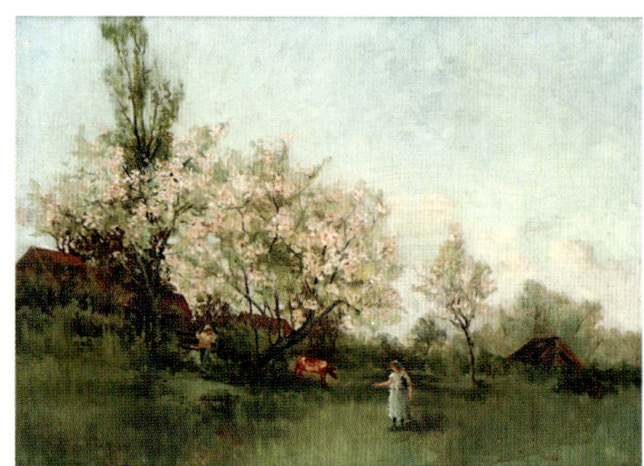

Hunt, William active 1888–1911
In Full Blossom 1889
oil on canvas 74.9 x 101.6
845

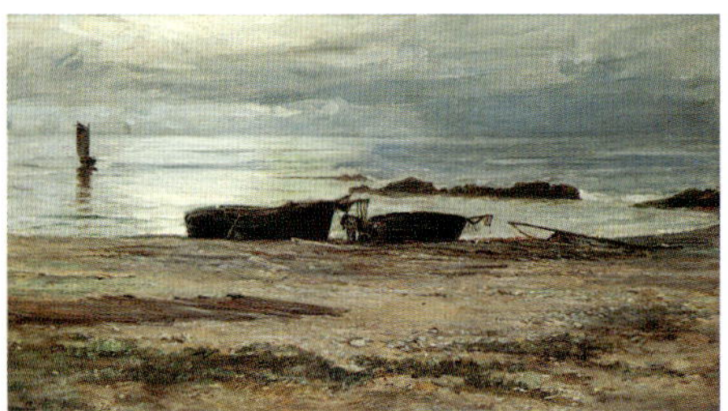

Hunter, Colin 1841–1904
Beach Scene 1874
oil on canvas 35.7 x 61.2
3054

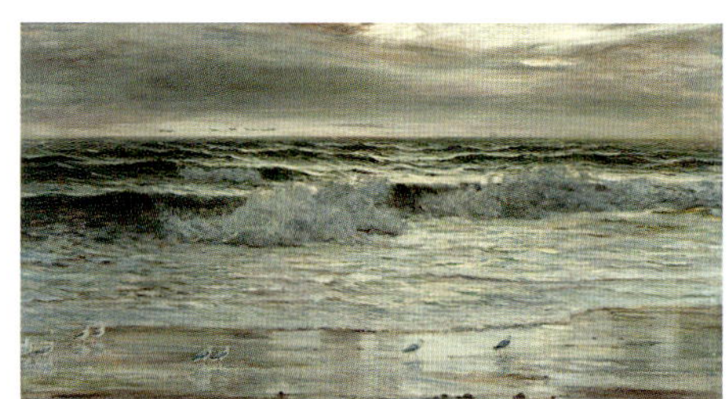

Hunter, Colin 1841–1904
Sea Piece, Dawn 1875
oil on canvas 64.8 x 120.7
797

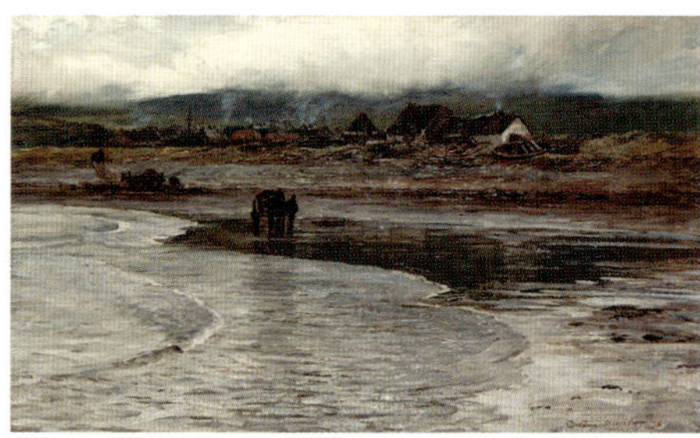

Hunter, Colin 1841–1904
Ebbing Tide 1878
oil on canvas 54.6 x 90.2
829

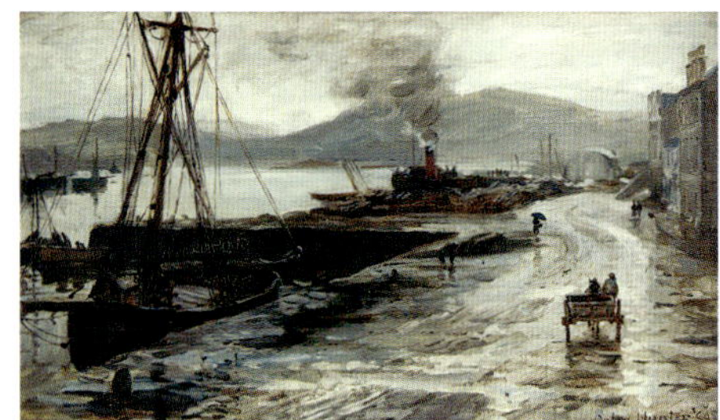

Hunter, Colin 1841–1904
Wet Day on the Clyde 1880
oil on canvas 30.8 x 50.8
3003

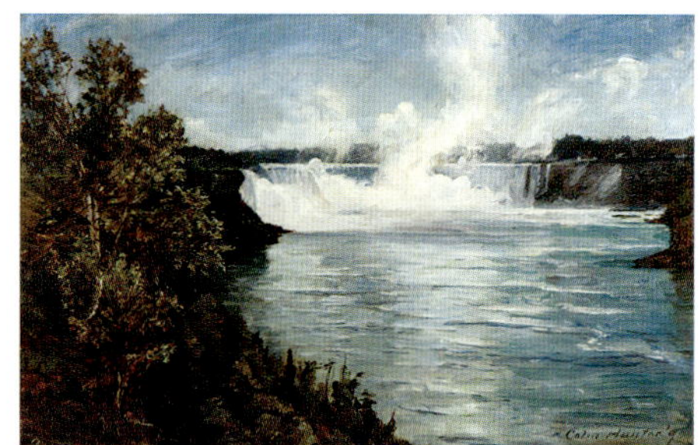

Hunter, Colin 1841–1904
Falls of Niagara 1890
oil on canvas 44.5 x 69.9
862

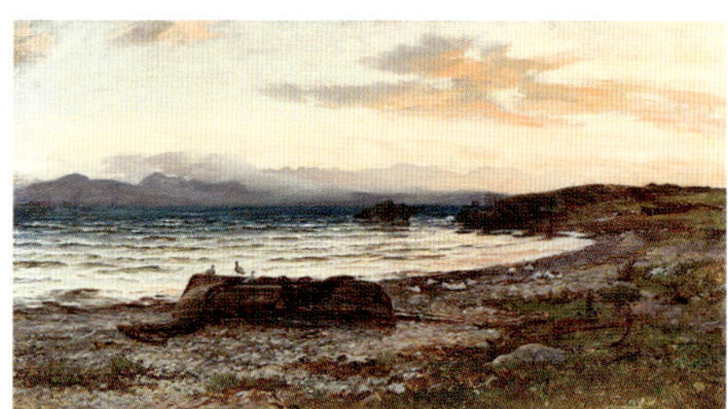

Hunter, Colin 1841–1904
Good-Night to Skye 1895
oil on canvas 99.1 x 180.3
727

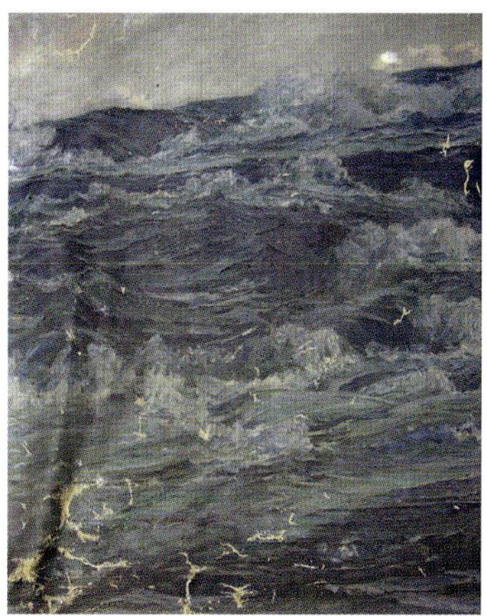

Hunter, Colin 1841–1904
Niagara Rapids (detail) 1901
oil on canvas 147.3 x 330.2
942

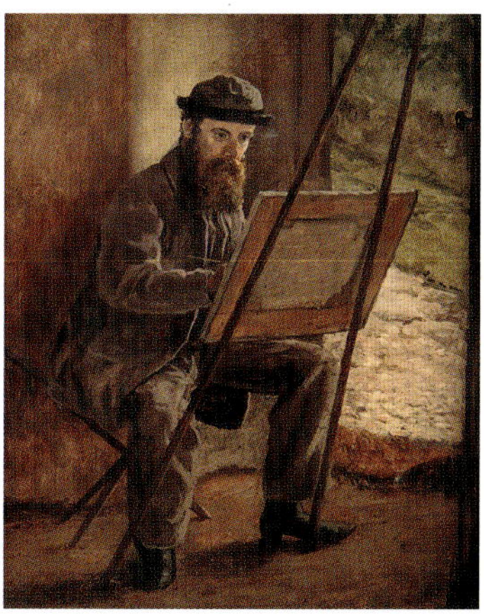

Hunter, Colin 1841–1904
J. Milne Donald (1819–1866), Sketching
oil on millboard 25.4 x 20.3
2167

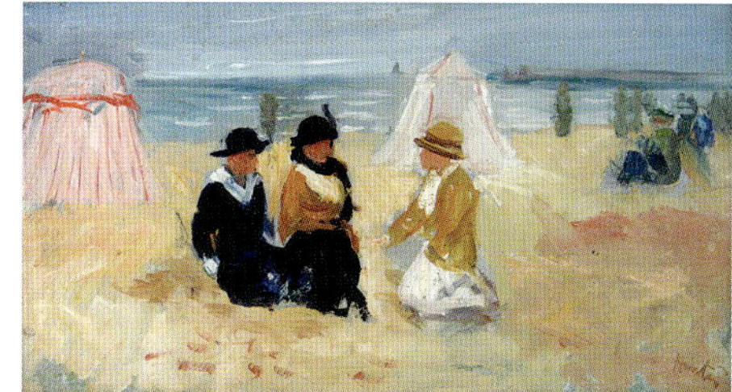

Hunter, George Leslie 1877–1931
On the Shore c.1910–1914
oil on millboard 24.1 x 43.2
2203

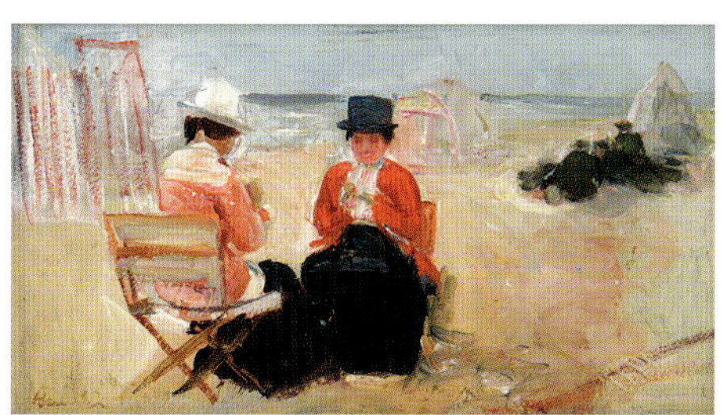

Hunter, George Leslie 1877–1931
The Red Jacket c.1910–1914
oil on millboard 24.1 x 43.2
2202

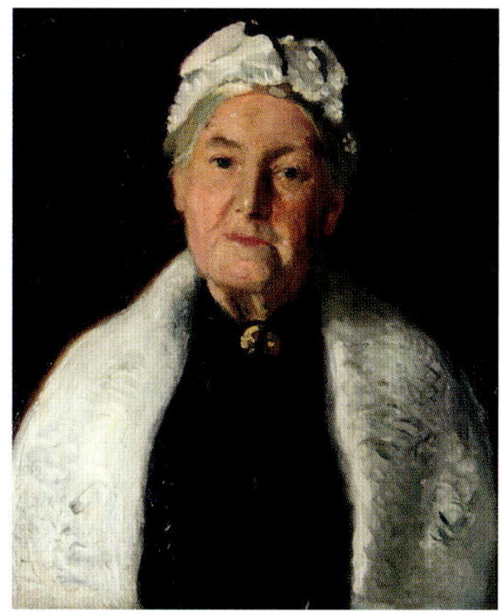

Hunter, George Leslie 1877–1931
Mrs Helen Meldrum (1829–1924) c.1917
oil on canvas 53.9 x 44
3288

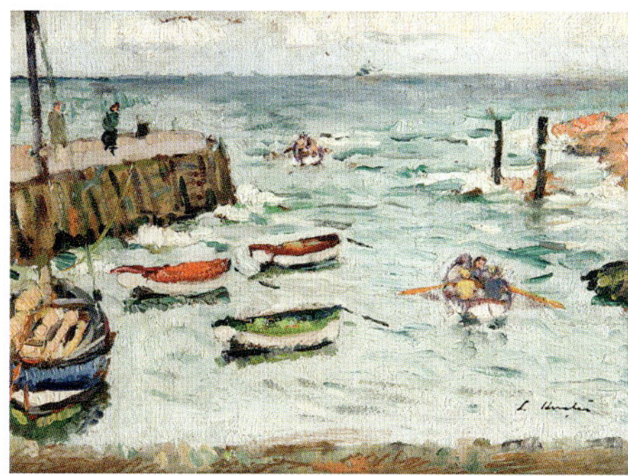

Hunter, George Leslie 1877–1931
A Summer Day, Largo c.1918–1926
oil on panel 22.9 x 30.5
2391

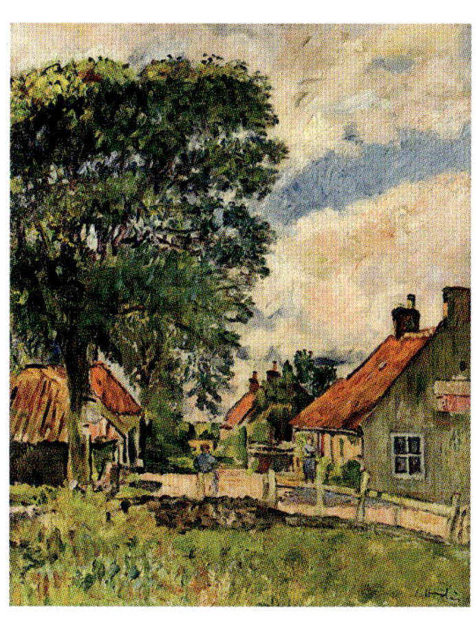

Hunter, George Leslie 1877–1931
A Village in Fife c.1918–1926
oil on canvas 101.6 x 81.3
3269

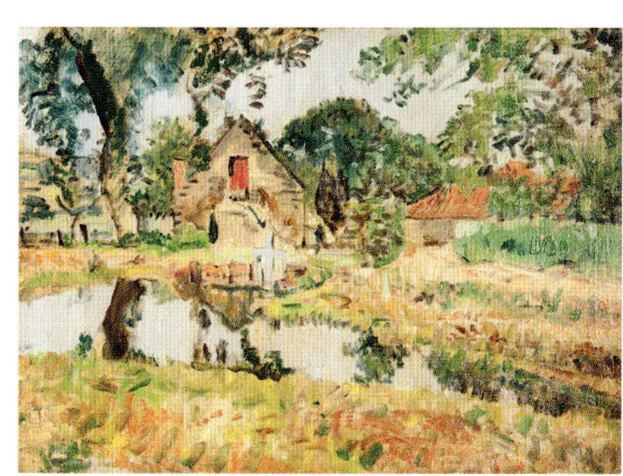

Hunter, George Leslie 1877–1931
Old Mill, Fifeshire c.1920
oil on canvas 50.8 x 68.6
1526

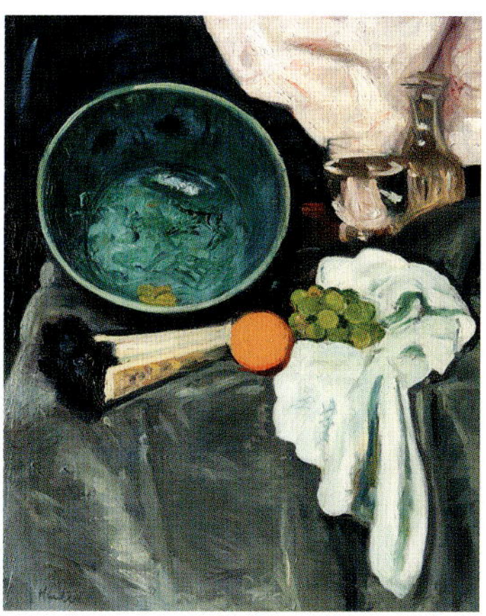

Hunter, George Leslie 1877–1931
The Green Bowl c.1920
oil on canvas 68.6 x 55.9
2242

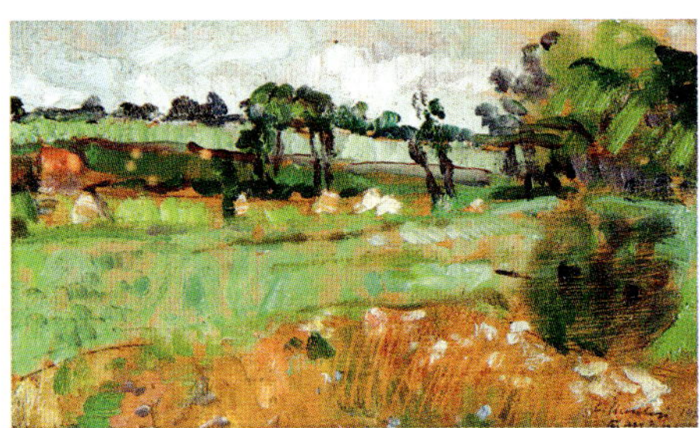

Hunter, George Leslie 1877–1931
Ceres, Fife 1921
oil on panel 12.7 x 20.3
2395

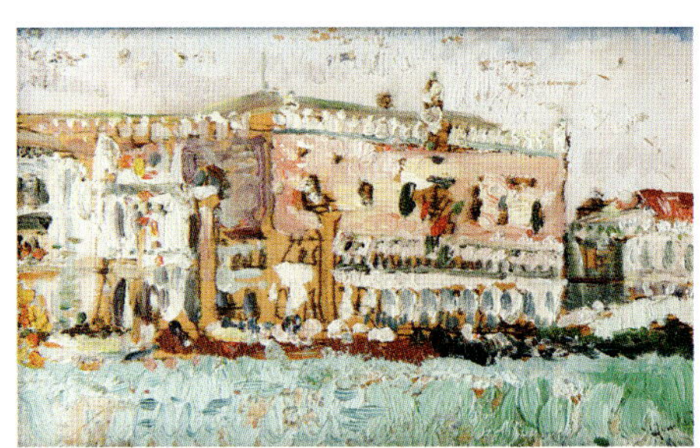

Hunter, George Leslie 1877–1931
Doge's Palace, Venice c.1922
oil on panel 12.7 x 20.3
2399

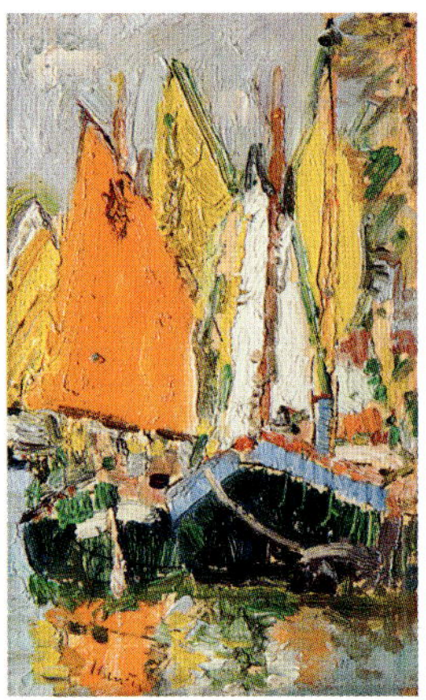

Hunter, George Leslie 1877–1931
Sails, Venice c.1922
oil on panel 21.6 x 12.7
2398

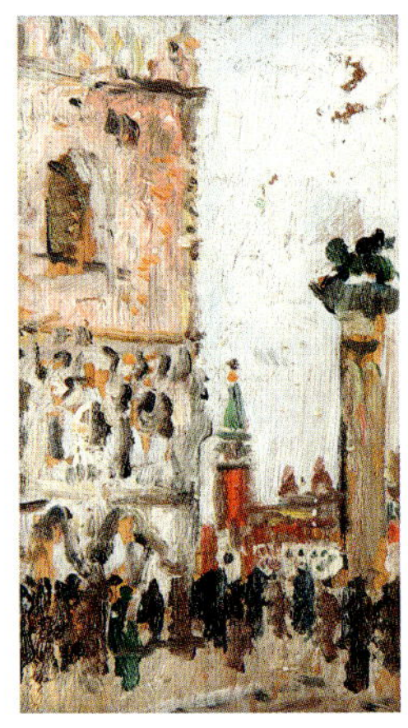

Hunter, George Leslie 1877–1931
Souvenir de Venise c.1922
oil on panel 21.6 x 12.7
2397

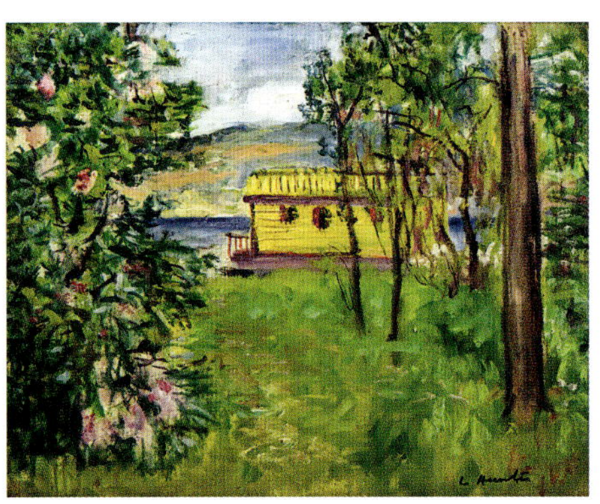

Hunter, George Leslie 1877–1931
Houseboat, Loch Lomond c.1924–1931
oil on canvas 43.2 x 53.3
2307

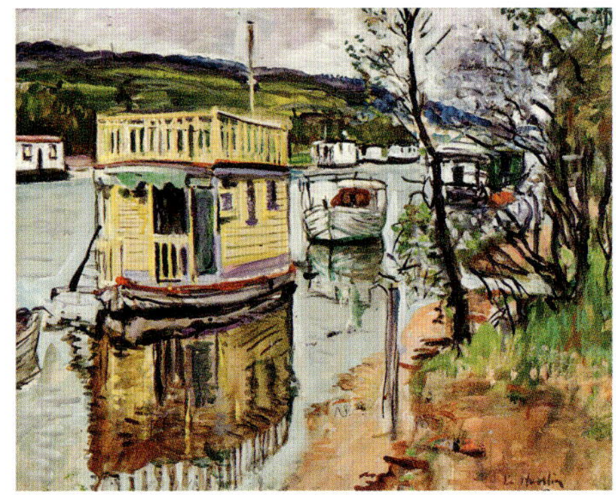

Hunter, George Leslie 1877–1931
Houseboats, Loch Lomond c.1924–1931
oil on canvas 45.7 x 55.9
2392

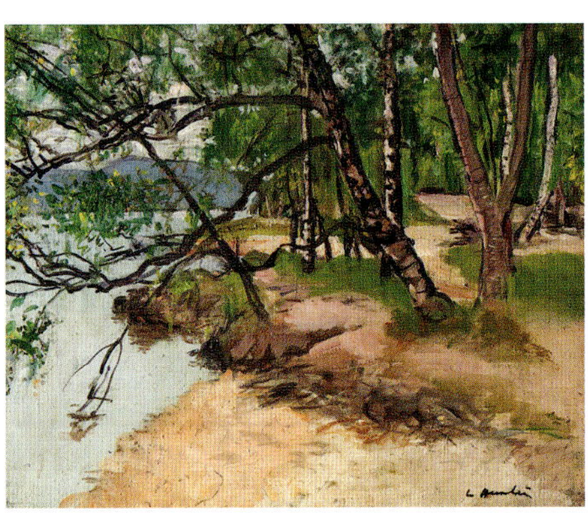

Hunter, George Leslie 1877–1931
Loch Lomond c.1924–1931
oil on canvas 50.8 x 62.2
2394

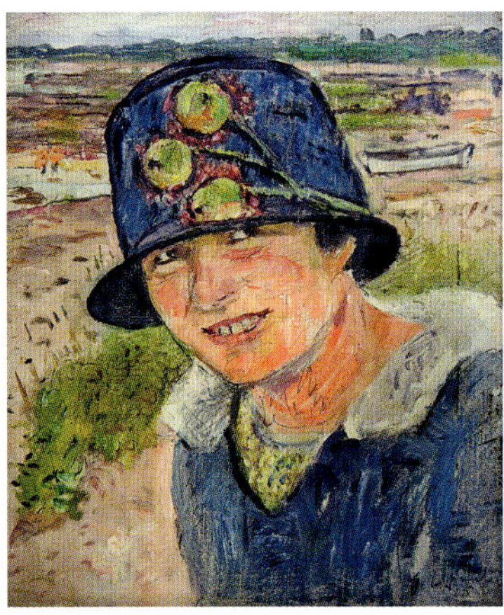

Hunter, George Leslie 1877–1931
The Blue Hat 1925
oil on canvas 35.6 x 30.5
2393

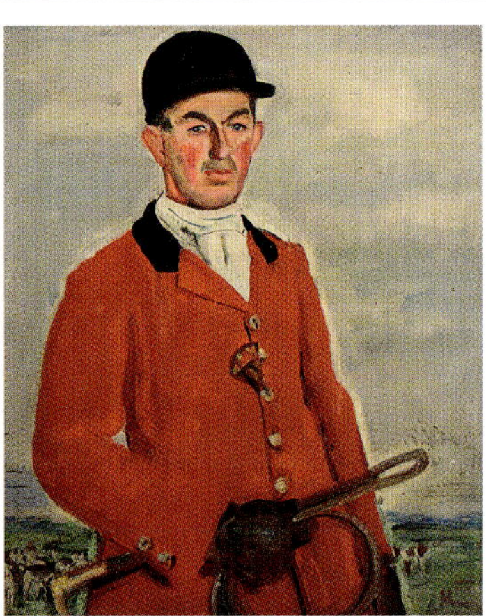

Hunter, George Leslie 1877–1931
The Huntsman c.1929–1931
oil on canvas 76.2 x 63.5
2891

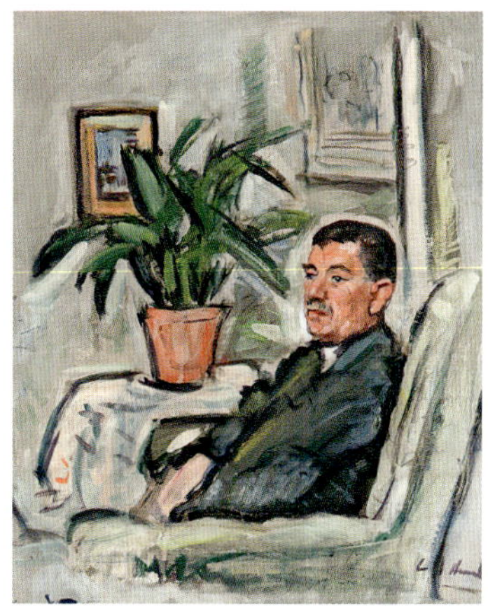

Hunter, George Leslie 1877–1931
William McInnes (1868–1944) c.1929–1931
oil on canvas 45.7 x 38.1
3404

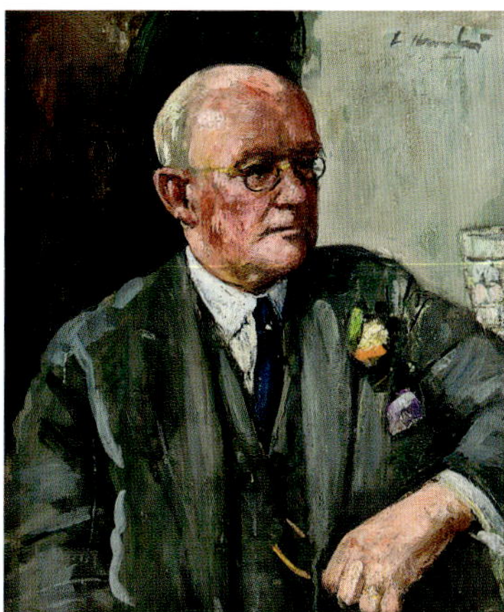

Hunter, George Leslie 1877–1931
William McNair c.1929–1931
oil on canvas 61 x 50.8
3157

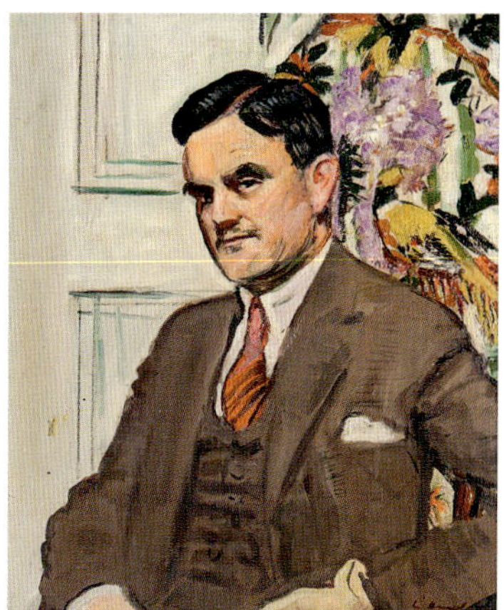

Hunter, George Leslie 1877–1931
*Dr Tom J. Honeyman (1891–1971), Director of
Glasgow Art Galleries (1939–1954)* c.1930
oil on canvas 61 x 50.8
3658

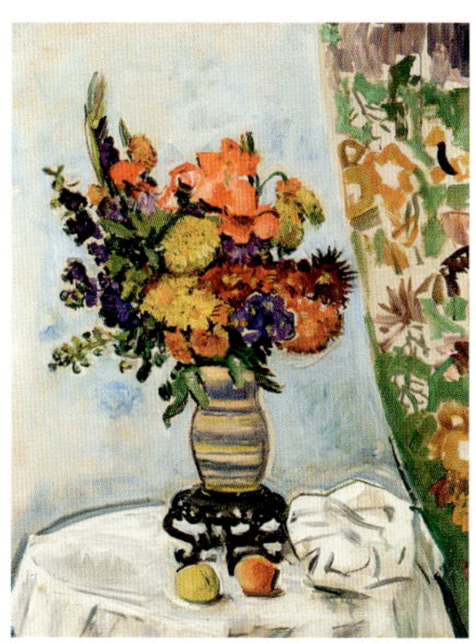

Hunter, George Leslie 1877–1931
Flowers in a Chinese Vase 1931
oil on canvas 101.6 x 76.5
3287

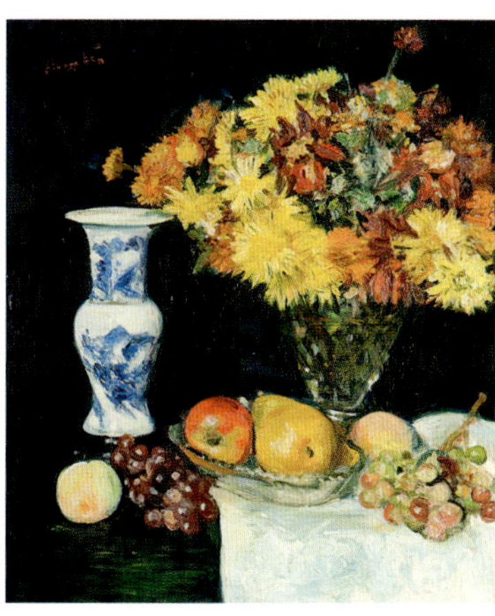

Hunter, George Leslie 1877–1931
Flowers in a Vase and Fruit
oil on canvas 61 x 50.8
2396

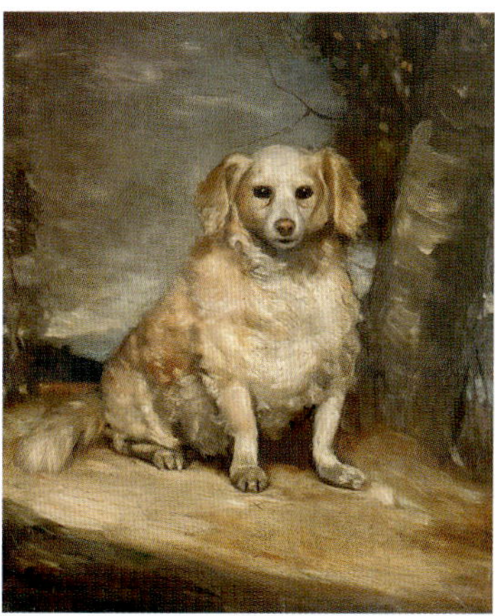

Hunter, George Leslie 1877–1931
Old Dog Seated by a Tree
oil on canvas 61 x 50.8
2571

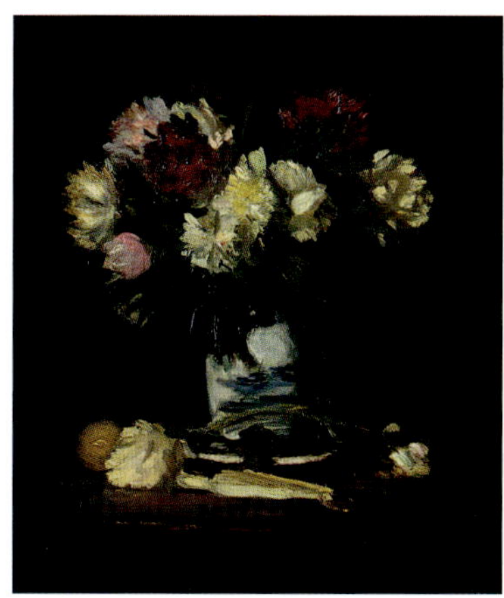

Hunter, George Leslie 1877–1931
Roses in a White and Blue Vase
oil on canvas 66 x 55.2
3209

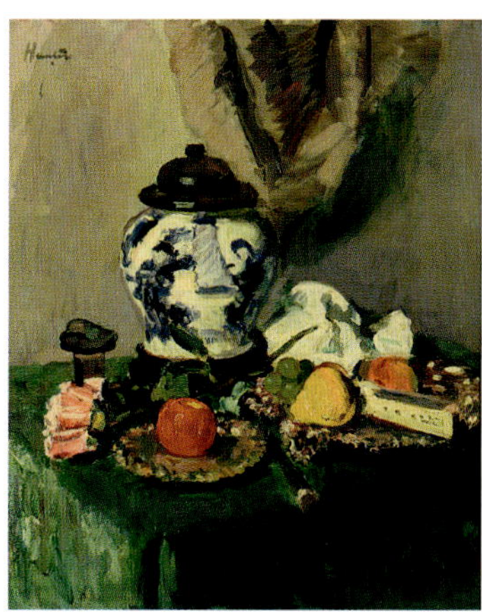

Hunter, George Leslie 1877–1931
Still Life
oil on canvas 68.6 x 55.8
1523

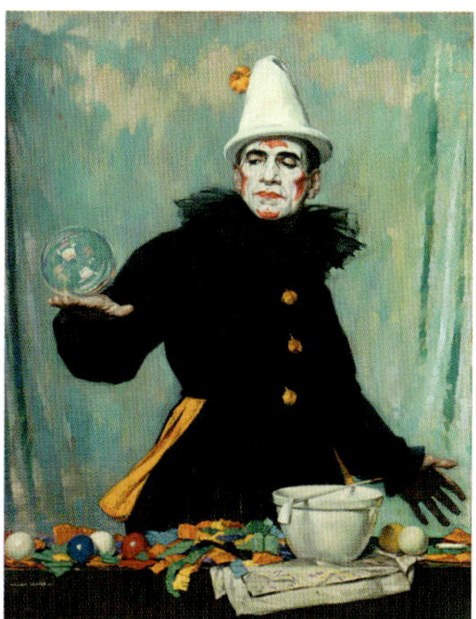

Hunter, William 1890–1967
The Bubble Reputation 1928
oil on canvas 127 x 101.6
2151

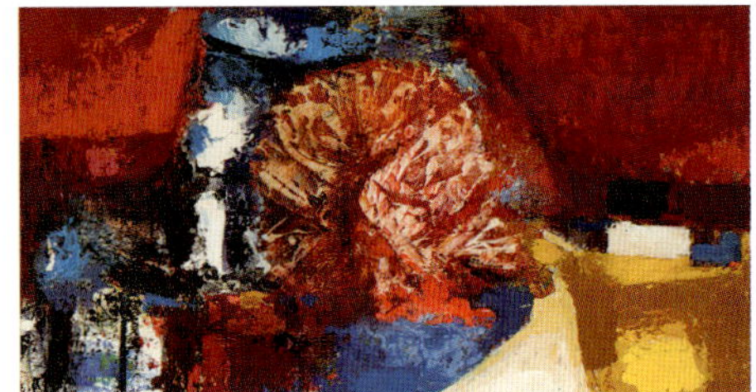

Hutcheson, Tom 1922–1999
Red Blaze Bing 1964
oil on hardboard 51.4 x 91.4
3217

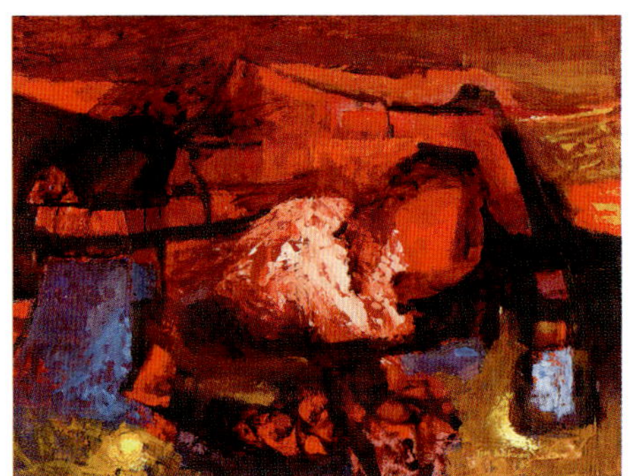

Hutcheson, Tom 1922–1999
Red Landscape, Lanarkshire 1965
oil on hardboard 74.9 x 96.2
3236

Hutcheson, Tom 1922–1999
Pier, West Coast 1969
oil on canvas 93.9 x 76.2
3268

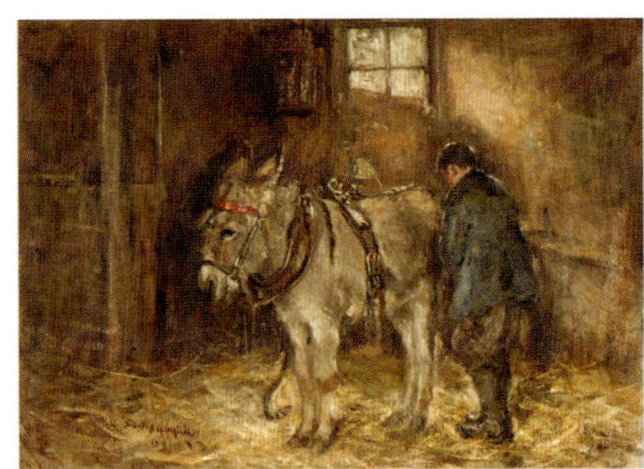

Hutchison, George Jackson 1896–1918
Getting Ready 1916
oil on canvas 76.2 x 101.6
1460

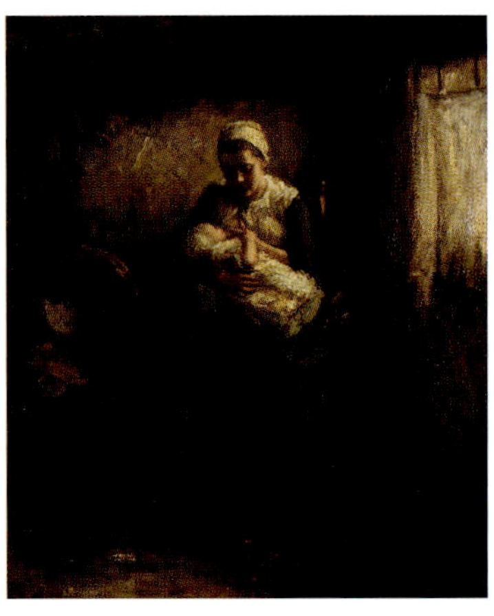

Hutchison, Robert Gemmell 1855–1936
A Dutch Mother c.1911
oil on canvas 59.7 x 49.5
1277

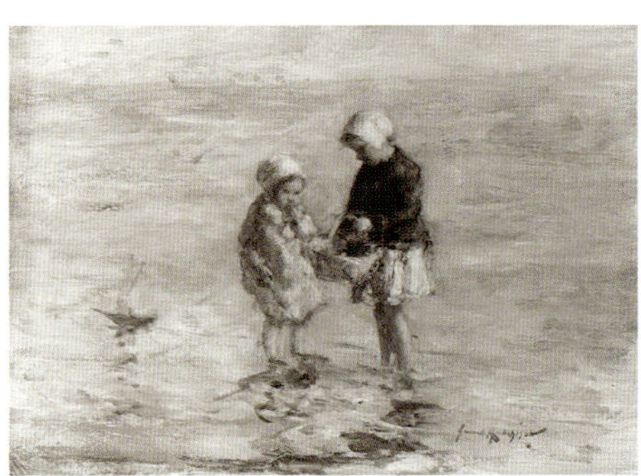

Hutchison, Robert Gemmell 1855–1936
Children Wading 1918
oil on cardboard 23.2 x 30.8
3129

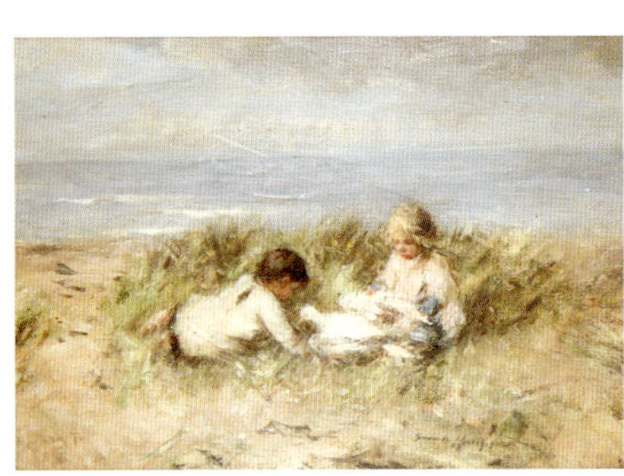

Hutchison, Robert Gemmell 1855–1936
The Dead Seagull
oil on cardboard 22.9 x 30.5
3130

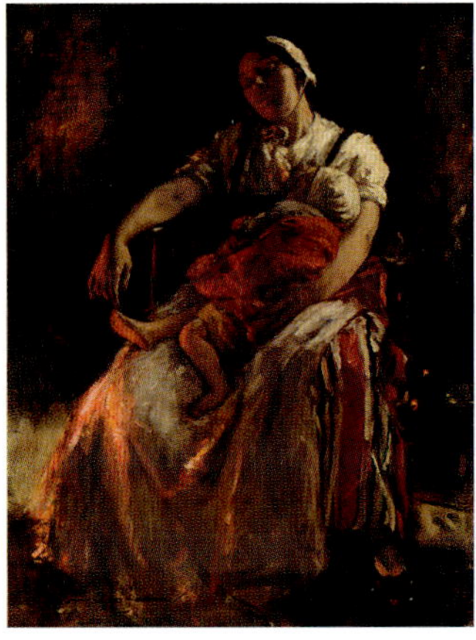

Hutchison, Robert Gemmell 1855–1936
When the Day Is Done
oil on canvas 101.6 x 76.2
1784

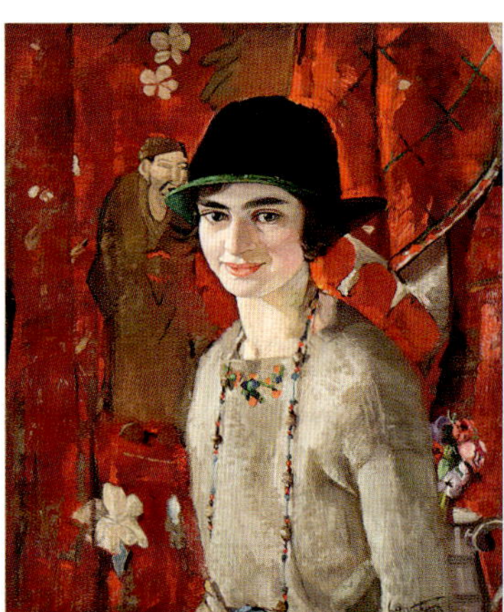

Hutchison, William Oliphant 1889–1970
Humoresque, 1919: The Artist's Wife 1919
oil on canvas 76.5 x 63.5
3276

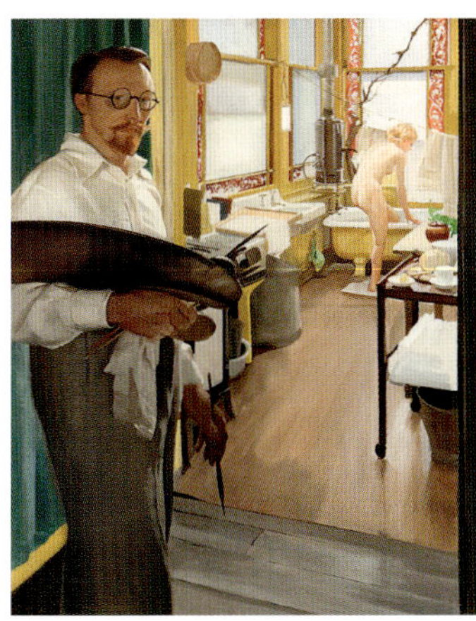

Hutchison, William Oliphant 1889–1970
The Kitchen Bathroom 1932
oil on canvas 91.4 x 71.1
2068

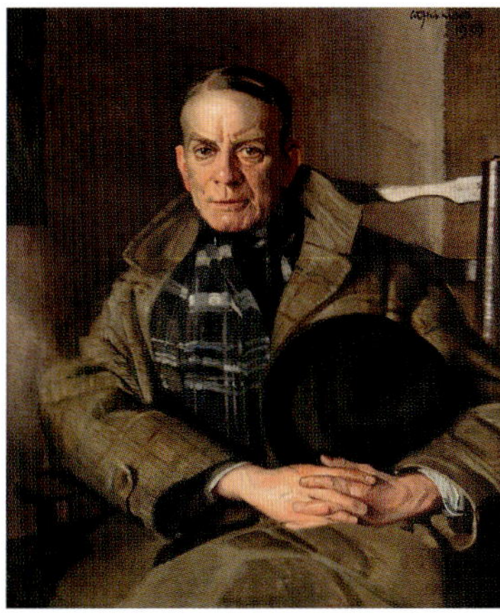

Hutchison, William Oliphant 1889–1970
Hugh Munro (1870–1916) 1939
oil on canvas 91.7 x 75.6
2183

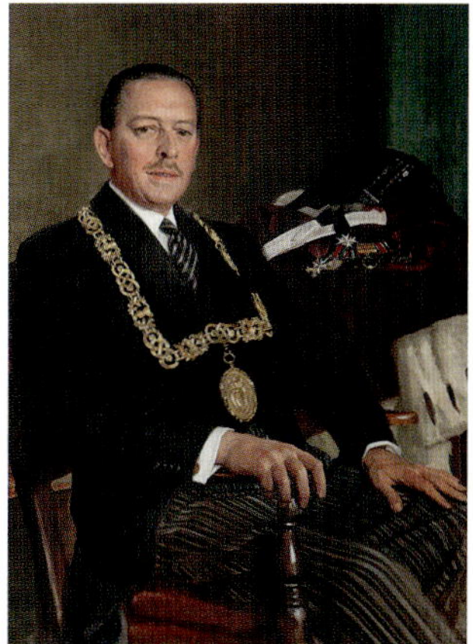

Hutchison, William Oliphant 1889–1970
*Sir Victor Warren (1903–1953), Lord Provost
of Glasgow (1949–1952)* 1952–1953
oil on canvas 113 x 82.6
3011

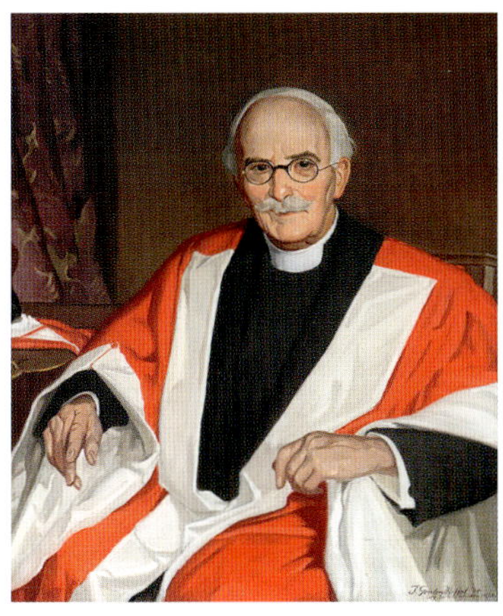

Hutchison, William Oliphant 1889–1970
J. Gordon Moffat 1954
oil on canvas 90.4 x 75.3
PP.1978.121.4

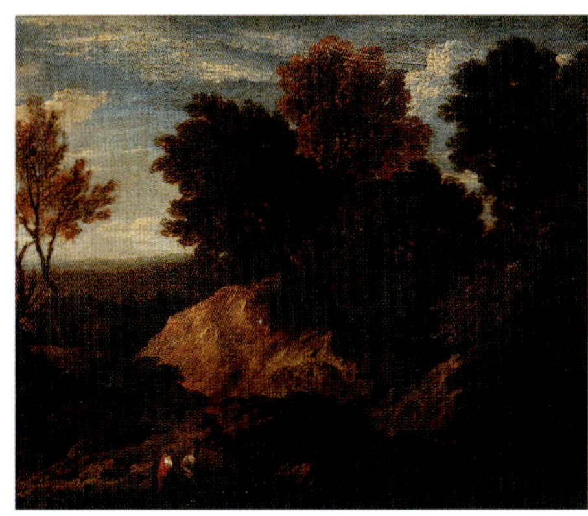

Huysmans, Cornelis 1648–1727
Wooded Landscape with Figures
oil on canvas 29.5 x 35.2
635

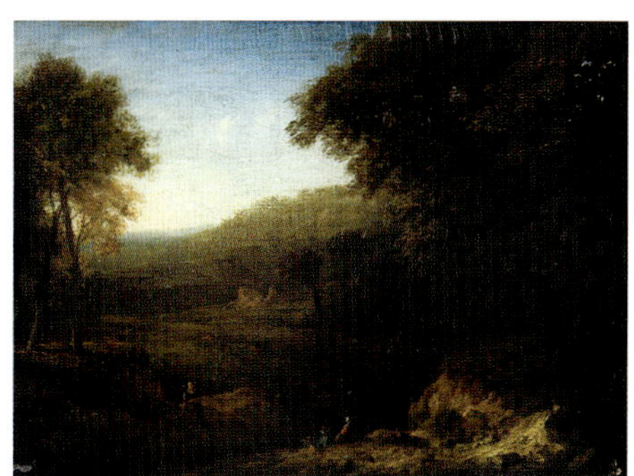

Huysmans, Cornelis 1648–1727
Wooded Landscape with Figures
oil on canvas 21.3 x 28.6
636

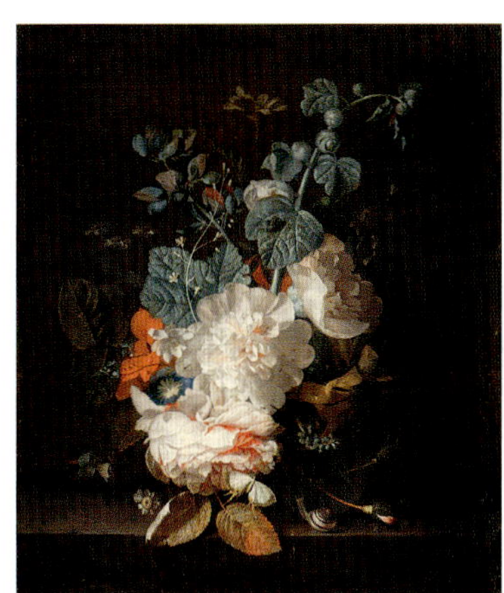

Huysum, Jan van 1682–1749
Still Life: Flowers in a Glass Vase c.1710–1716
oil on canvas 42.8 x 35.9
77

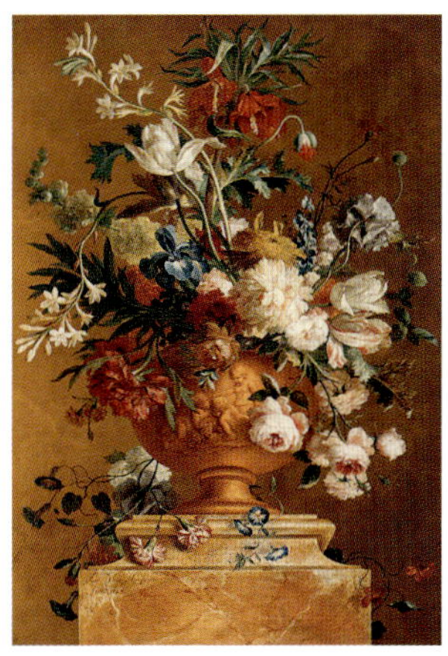

Huysum, Jan van 1682–1749
Still Life: Flowers in a Terracotta Urn 1727
oil on canvas 157.5 x 109.2
62

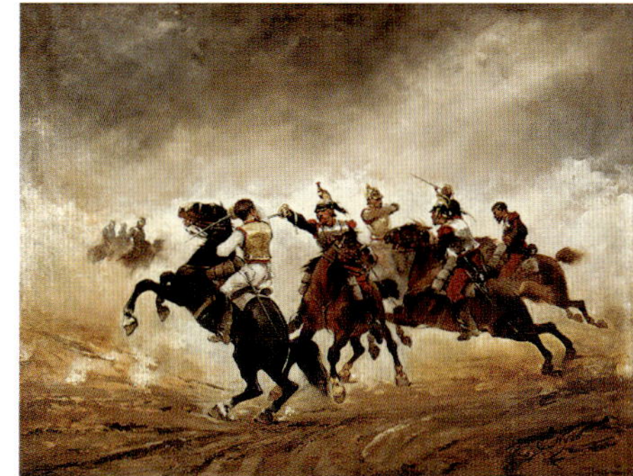

Hyon, Georges Louis 1840–1909
An Episode in the Franco-Prussian War
oil on canvas 92.3 x 119.5
1495

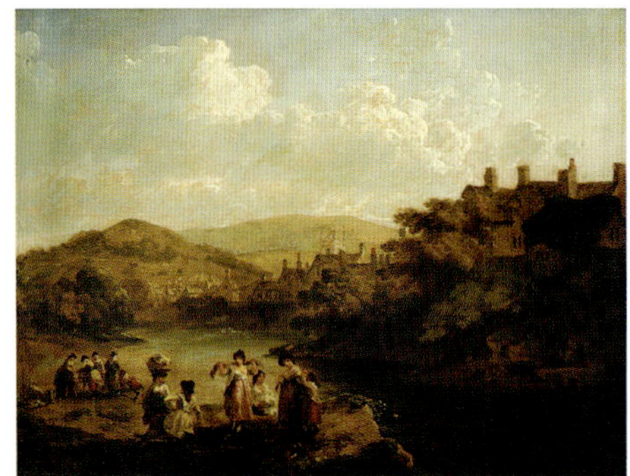

Ibbetson, Julius Caesar 1759–1817
Women Washing Clothes in a Welsh Stream 1790
oil on canvas 33 x 43.2
2689

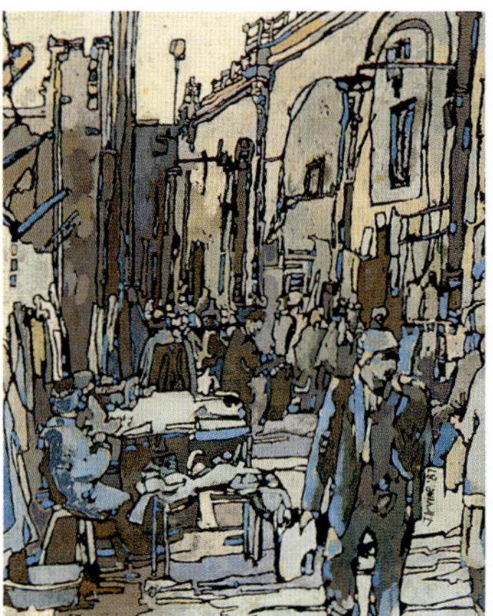

Irvine, Jennifer b.1956
Paddy's Market 1987
oil on board 27.6 x 21.8
PP.1988.59

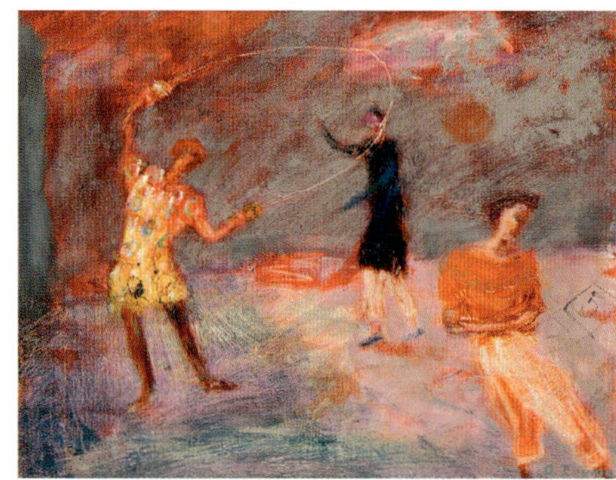

Irvine, Olivia b.1960
Catching the Sky 1988
oil on canvas 40.5 x 50
3670

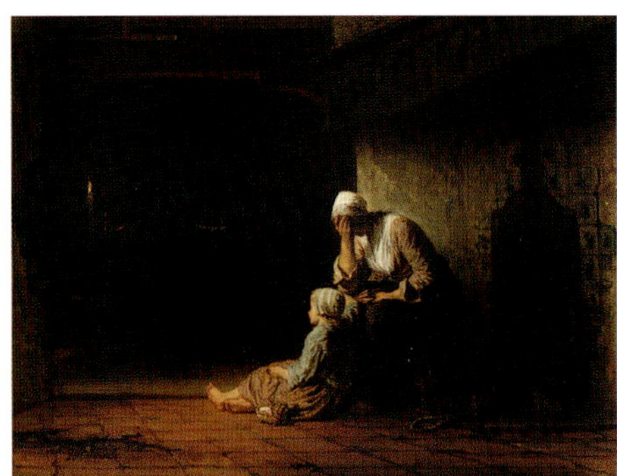

Israëls, Jozef 1824–1911
Grief c.1870–1875
oil on canvas 46 x 58
2912

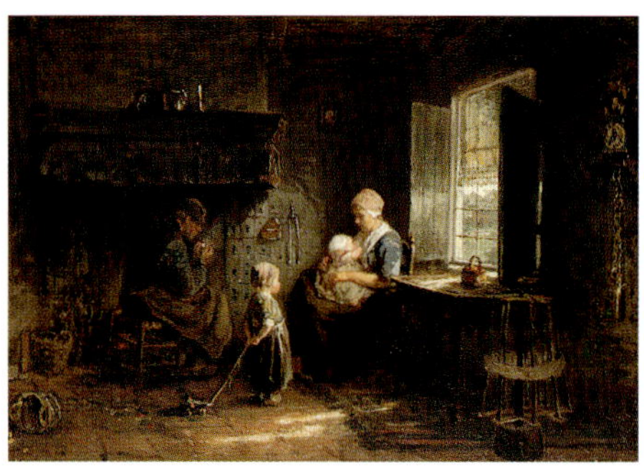

Israëls, Jozef 1824–1911
The Happy Family c.1870–1885
oil on canvas 41.6 x 57.8
1143

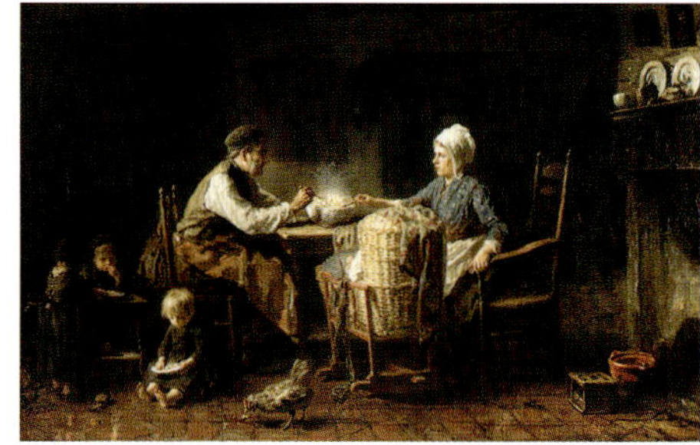

Israëls, Jozef 1824–1911
The Frugal Meal c.1876
oil on canvas 88.9 x 138.7
737

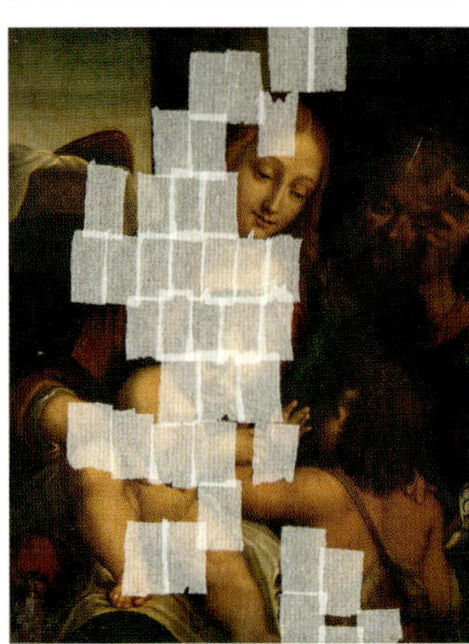

Italian (Lombard) School 16th C
The Holy Family with the Child Baptist
oil on panel 64.5 x 49.9
285

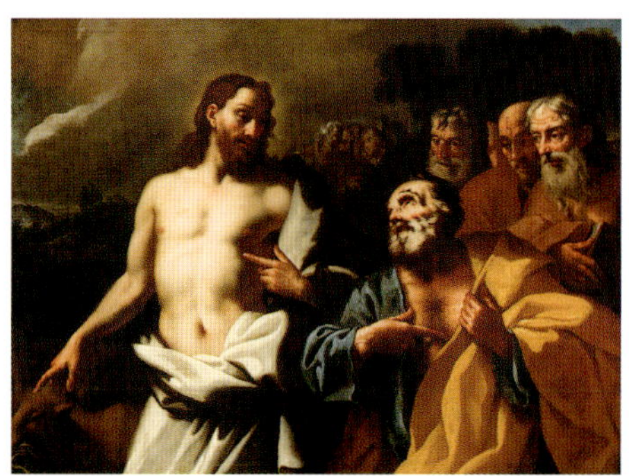

Italian (Neapolitan) School 17th C
Christ's Charge to Saint Peter
oil on canvas 152.6 x 205.7
226

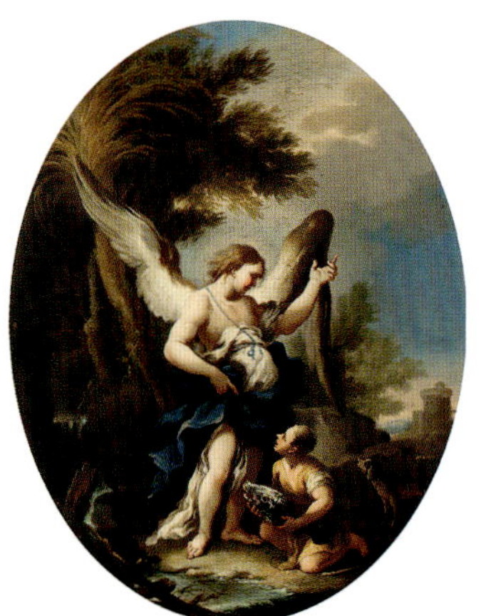

Italian (Neapolitan) School
Tobias and the Angel c.1738
oil on canvas 49 x 36.8
270

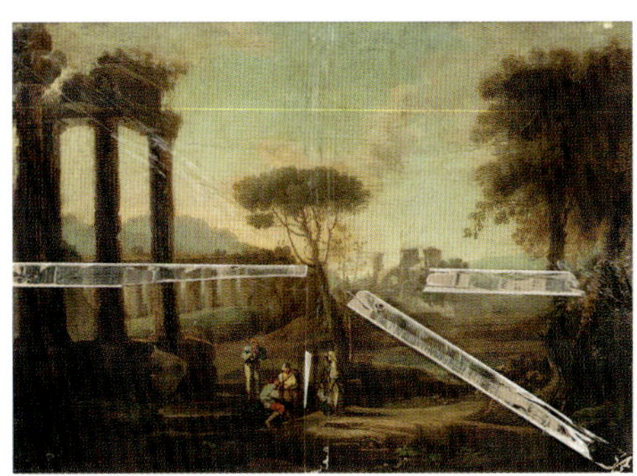

Italian (Neapolitan) School 18th C
Landscape with Figures beside a Ruined Colonnade
oil on canvas 97.5 x 134.6
920

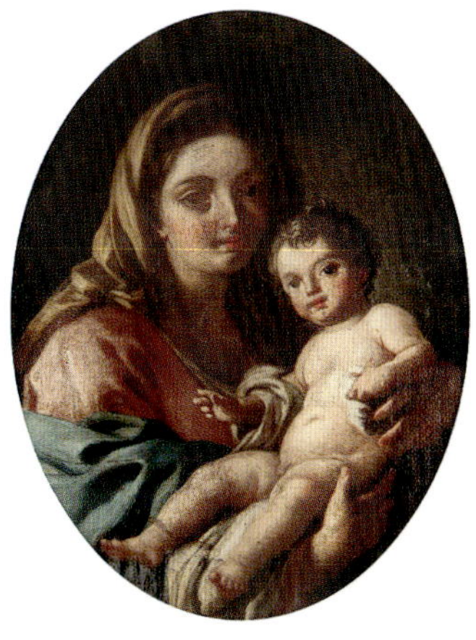

Italian (Neapolitan) School 18th C
Virgin and Child
oil on canvas 26.7 x 21
3430

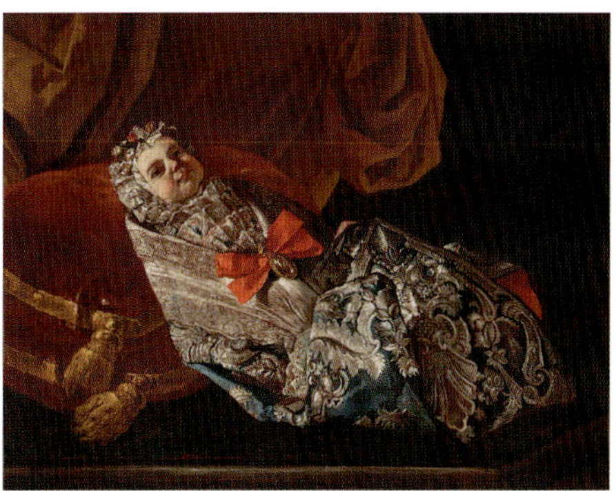

Italian (Neapolitan) School (attributed to)
18th C
Portrait of a Royal Infant
oil on canvas 74.3 x 101.6
PC.136

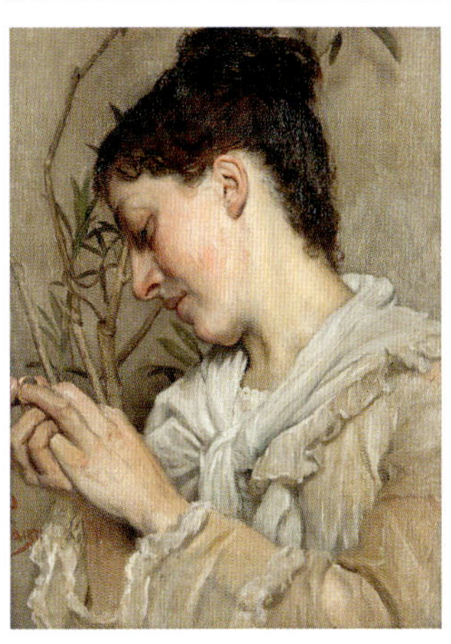

Italian (Roman) School
Engaged 1875
oil on canvas 27.7 x 21.8
846

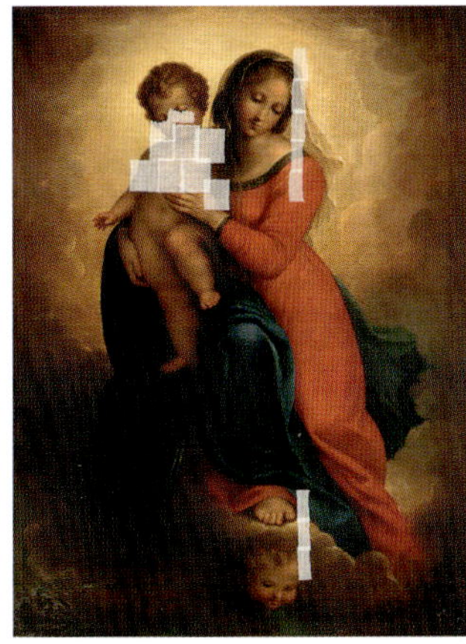

Italian (Roman) School 19th C
Madonna and Child in Glory
oil on canvas 149.5 x 106
163

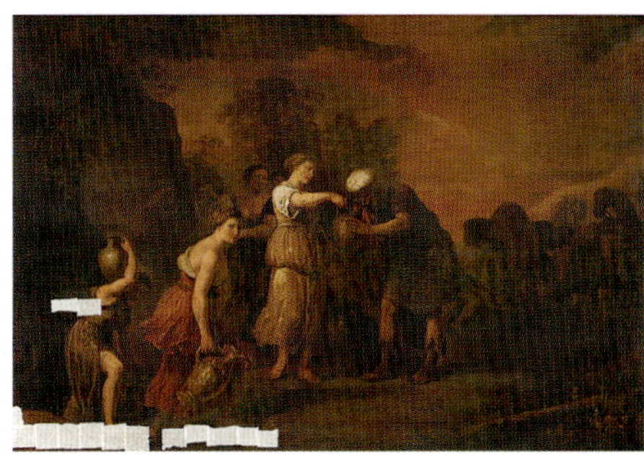

Italian (Roman) School (attributed to)
17th C
Rebekah at the Well
oil on canvas 114.3 x 163.8
1178

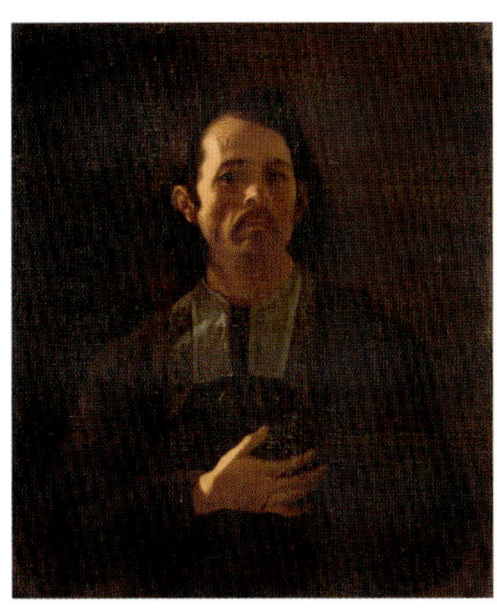

Italian School 17th C
Portrait of a Man (possibly a cleric)
oil on canvas 75.2 x 60.9
PC.76

Italian School early 18th C
Rocky Landscape with a River and a Bridge
oil on canvas 142.2 x 127
3435

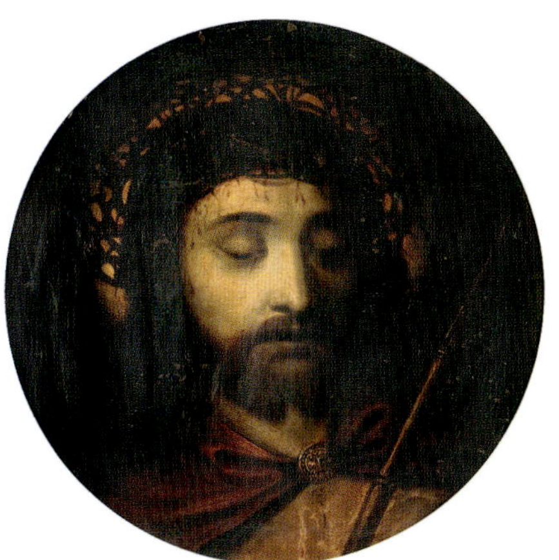

Italian School (attributed to) 16th C/17th C
Ecce Homo
oil on copper 33.5
572

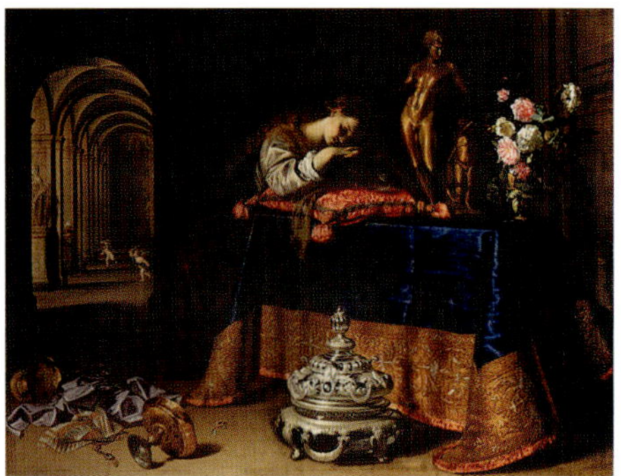

Italian School (attributed to) late 17th C
An Allegory of Repentance
oil on canvas 158.7 x 203.8
PC.26

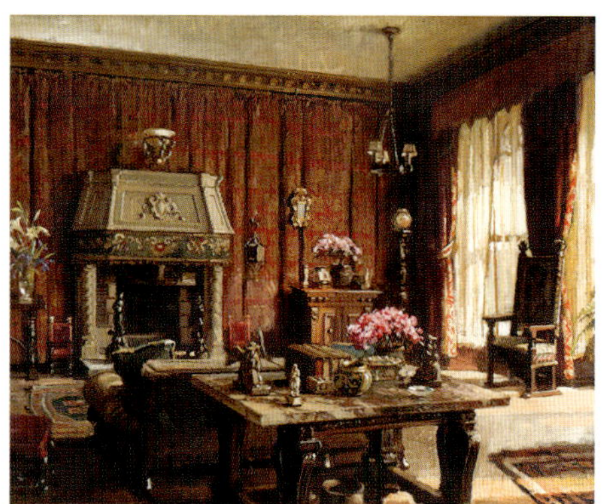

Jack, Richard 1866–1952
The Italian Room, 42 Hyde Park Gate, London
c.1930
oil on canvas 63.5 x 76.2
1811

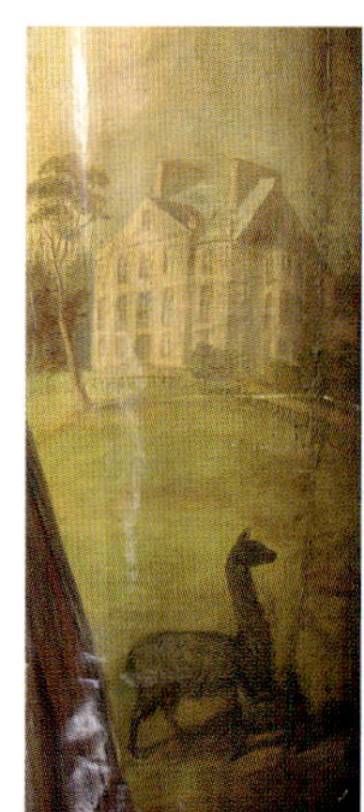

Jacob, Julius I 1811–1882
Alexander Gartshore Stirling of Craigbarnet Returning from Shooting (detail) c.1850
oil on canvas 243.8 x 304.8
NR.38

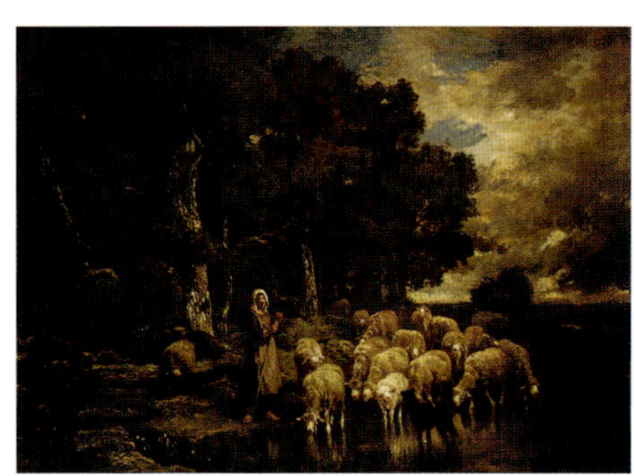

Jacque, Charles Émile 1813–1894
The Wane of Day 1881
oil on canvas 72 x 99.5
740

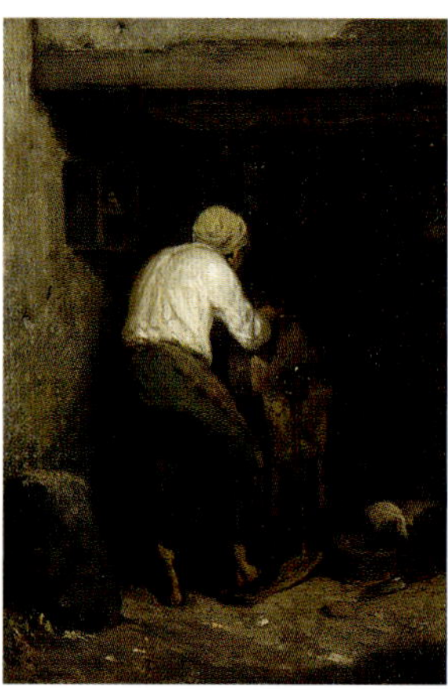

Jacque, Charles Émile 1813–1894
The Knife Grinder
oil on panel 21.6 x 16.5
35.291

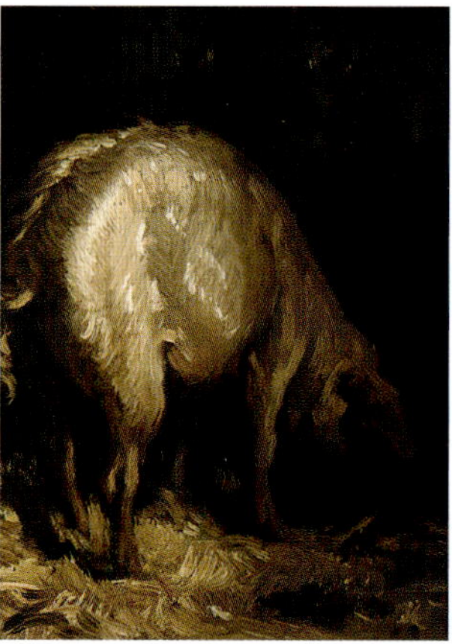

Jacque, Charles Émile 1813–1894
The Pig
oil on panel 21.6 x 16.5
35.288

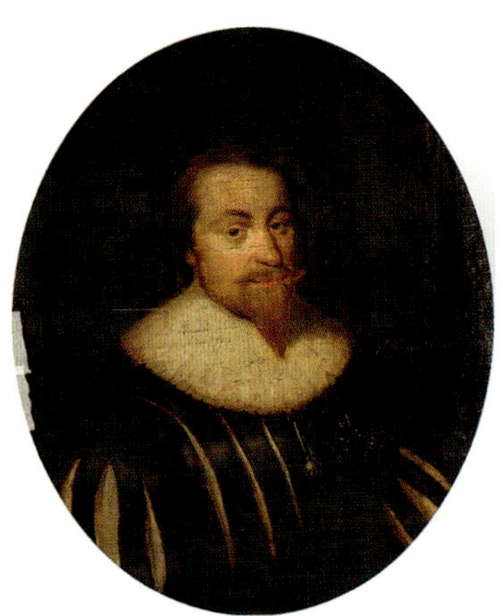

Jamesone, George c.1586–1644
Portrait of a Man c.1630–1640
oil on canvas 76.5 x 64.1
3038

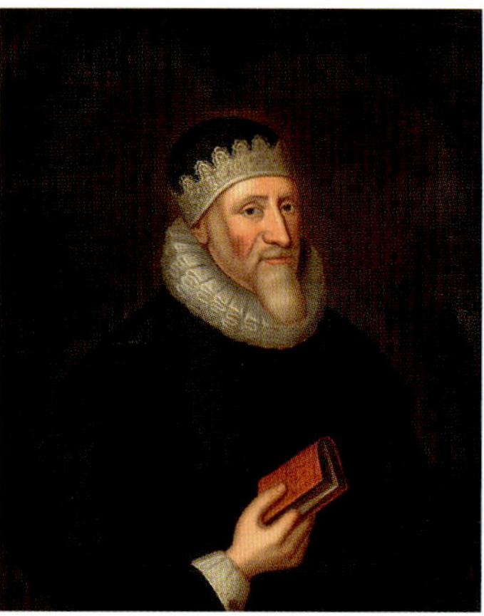

Jamesone, George (after) c.1586–1644
John Bell, Minister 1640
oil on canvas 76.2 x 63.5
2363

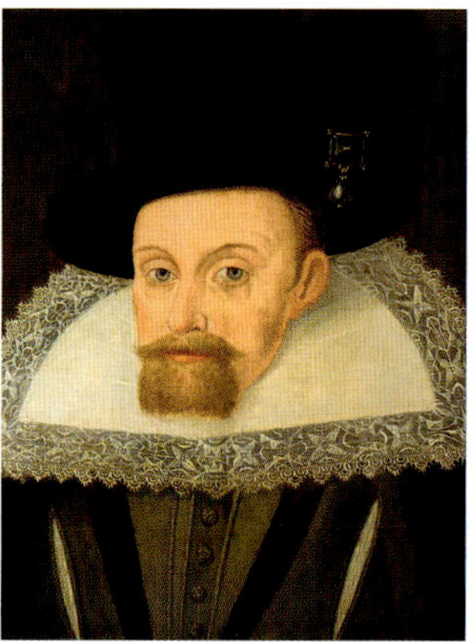

Jamesone, George (attributed to)
c.1586–1644
King James VI and I (1566–1625)
oil on panel 47 x 36.4
PL.1934.254

Facing page: Hornel, Edward Atkinson, 1864–1933, *The Coming of Spring*, 1899 (p. 206)

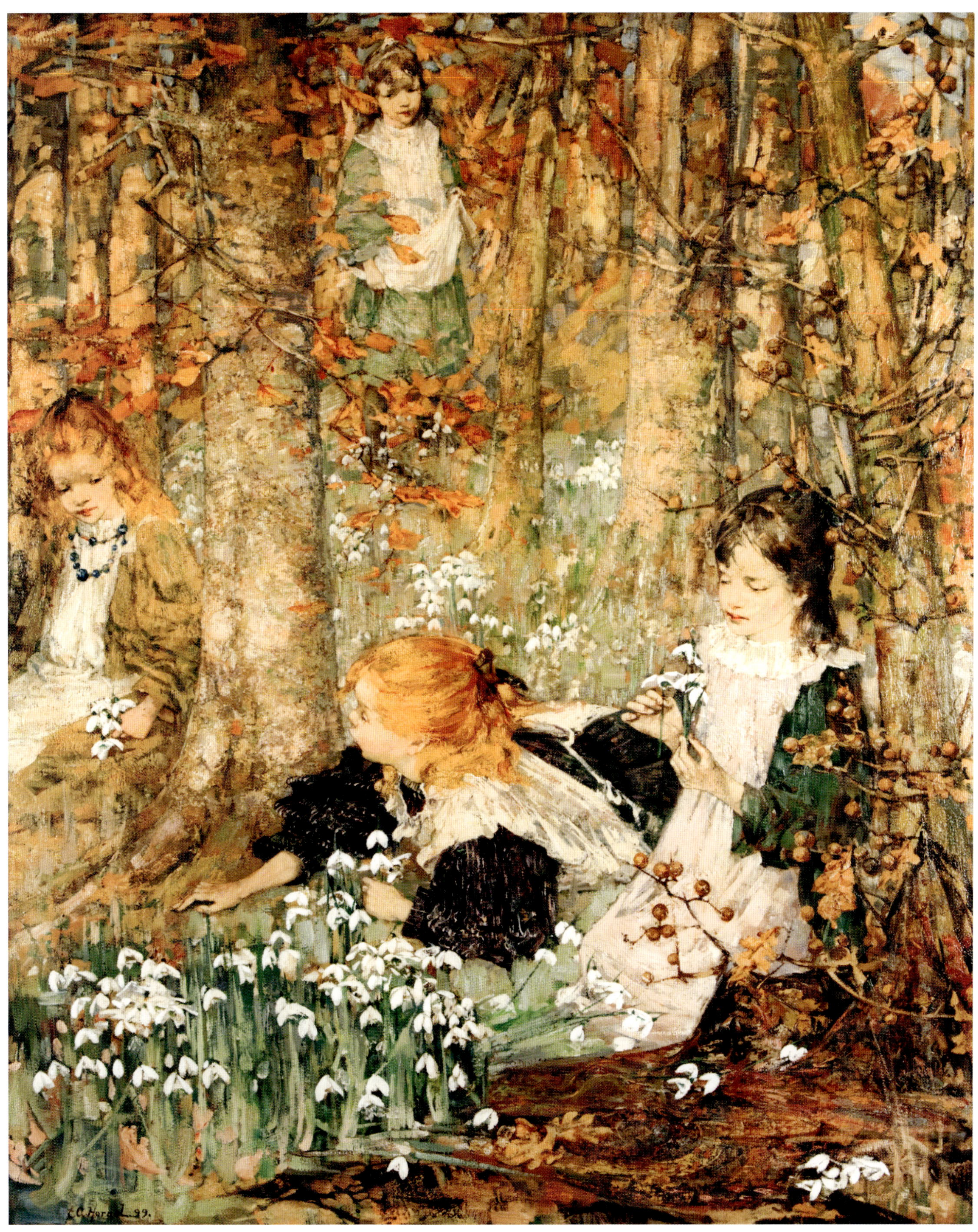

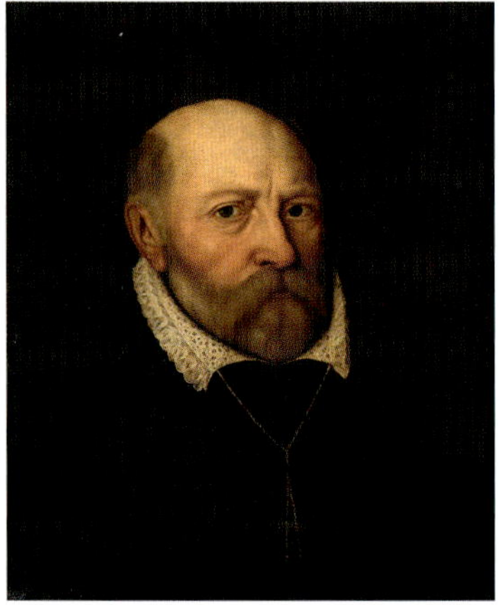

Jamesone, George (style of) c.1586–1644
Thomas Hutcheson 19th C
oil on canvas 47 x 39.4
1328

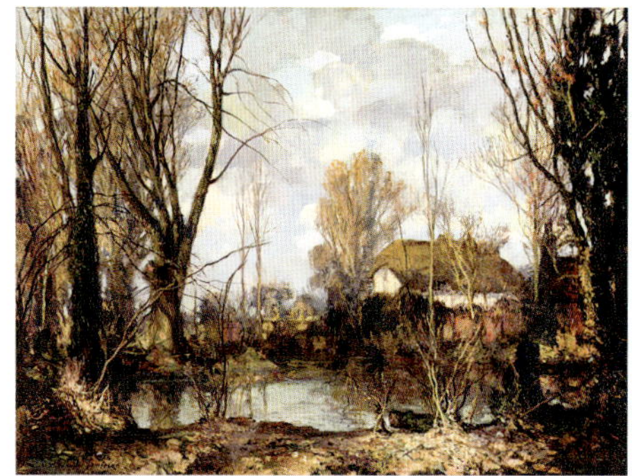

Jamieson, Alexander 1873–1937
Our Pond c.1937
oil on canvas 87 x 112.1
2081

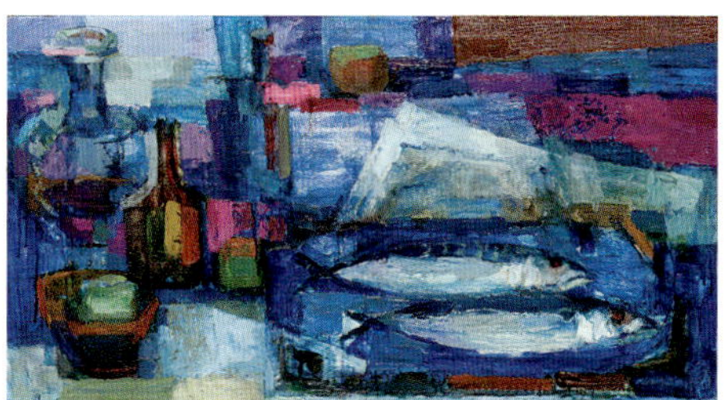

Jamieson, Florence b.1925
Mackerel Still Life 1960–1961
oil on hardboard 60.7 x 106.7
3151

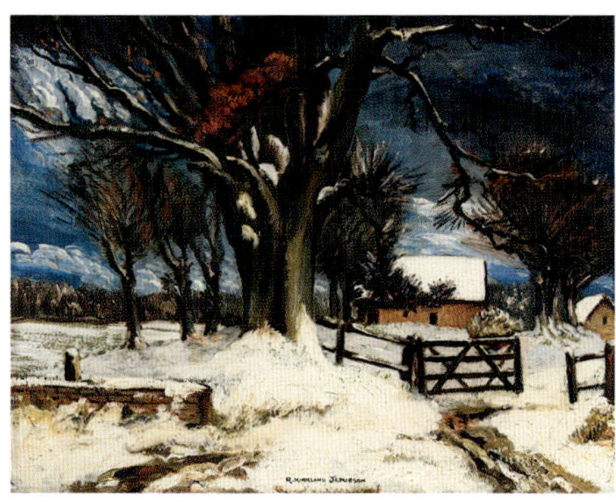

Jamieson, Robert Kirkland 1881–1950
Winter c.1942
oil on canvas 71.1 x 91.4
2256

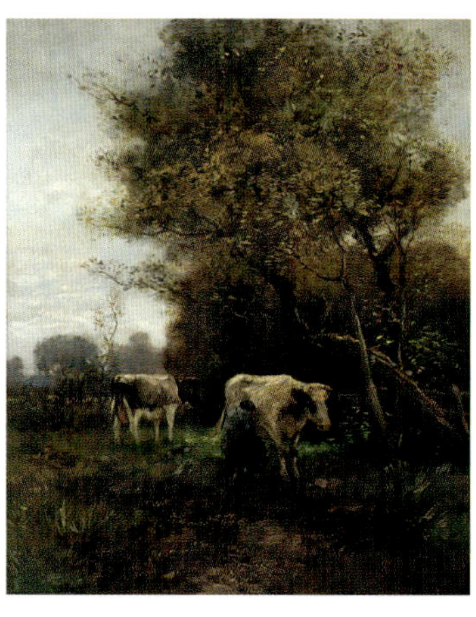

Jansen, Willem George Frederik 1871–1949
Milking Time
oil on canvas 73.2 x 59.2
2646

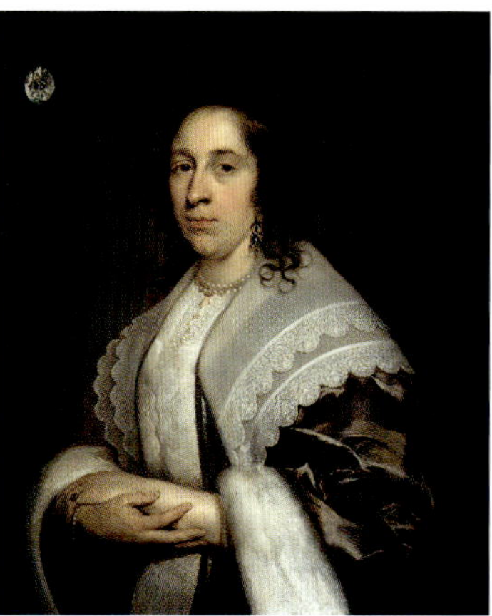

Janssens van Ceulen, Cornelis 1593–1661
Portrait of a Woman c.1644
oil on canvas 78.7 x 64.4
69

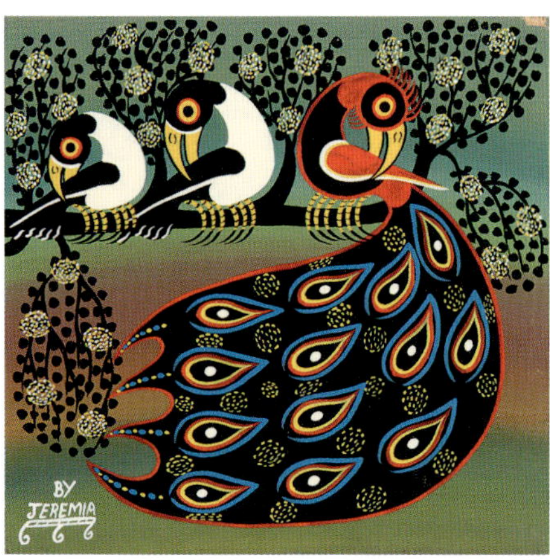

Jeremiah, Emanuel b.1975
Three Birds on a Tree Branch
enamel paint on hardboard 30 x 30
A.1989.23.c

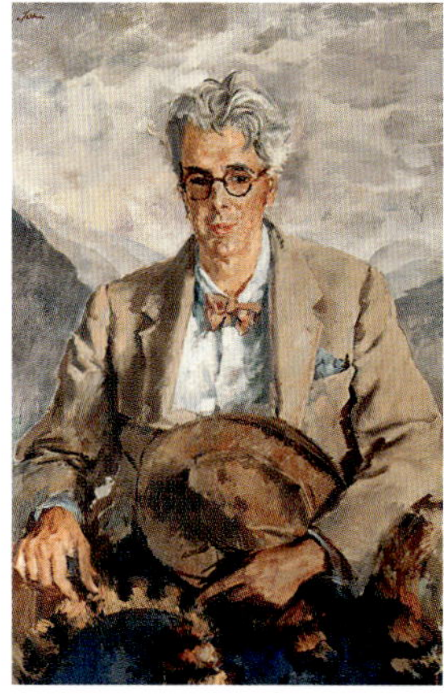

John, Augustus Edwin 1878–1961
*William Butler Yeats (1865–1939), Irish Poet
and Patriot* 1930
oil on canvas 121.9 x 76.2
1817

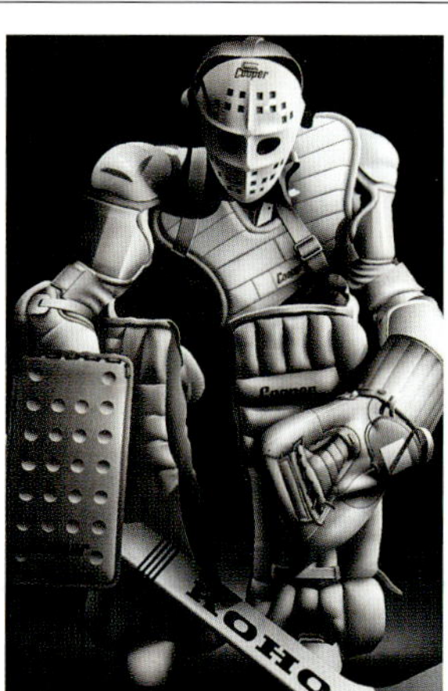

Johnson, Ben b.1946
The Keeper 1977
oil on canvas 205.1 x 134.4
3342

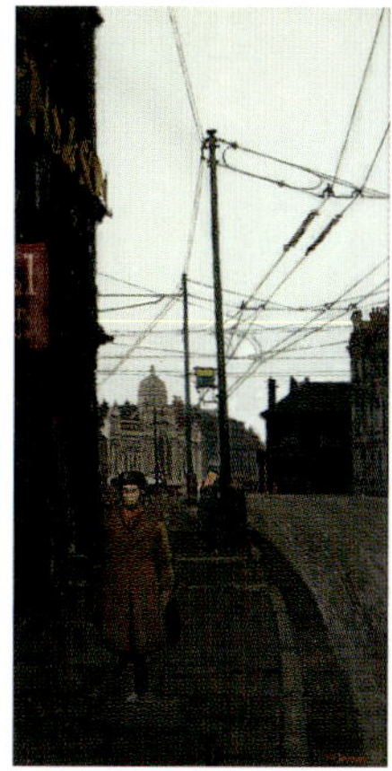

Johnson, Frank 1917–1998
Manor Row, Bradford c.1954
oil on board 101.6 x 50.8
3023

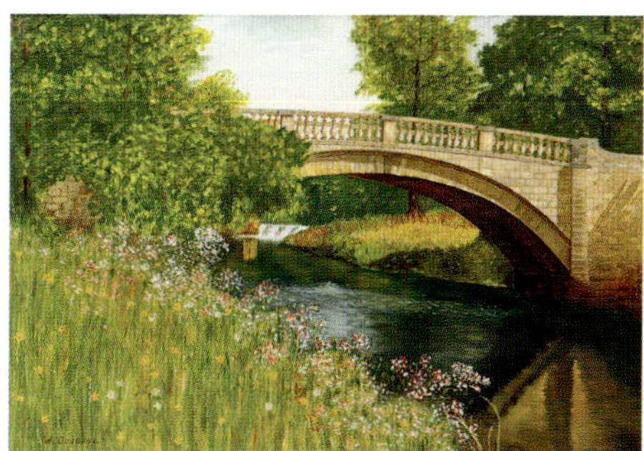

Johnson, W.
Bridge over the River Cart c.1997
oil on board 40 x 57
E.1997.19.2

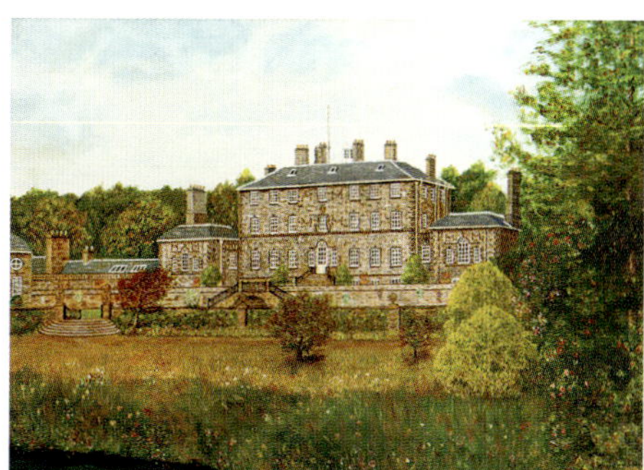

Johnson, W.
Pollok House c.1997
oil on board 44 x 60
E.1997.19.1

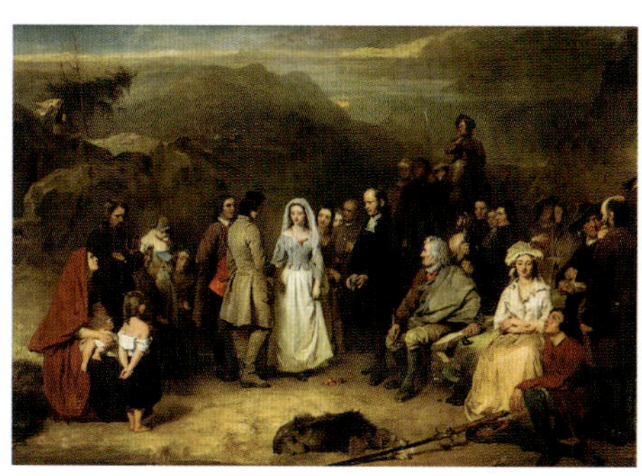

Johnston, Alexander 1815–1891
The Marriage of the Covenanter 1842
oil on canvas 110.8 x 157.1
3016

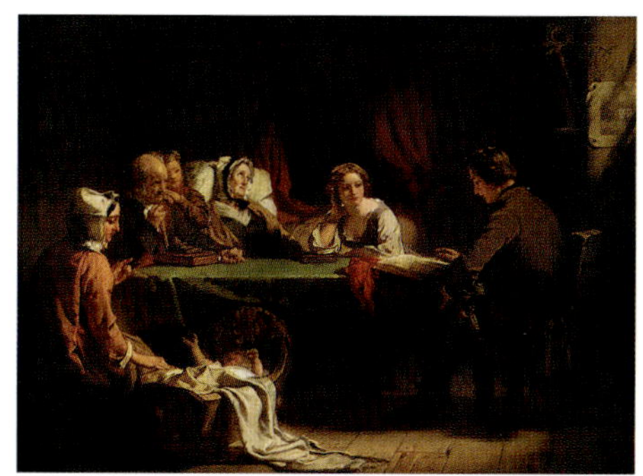

Johnston, Alexander 1815–1891
Family Devotions
oil on canvas 30.5 x 40.6
1553

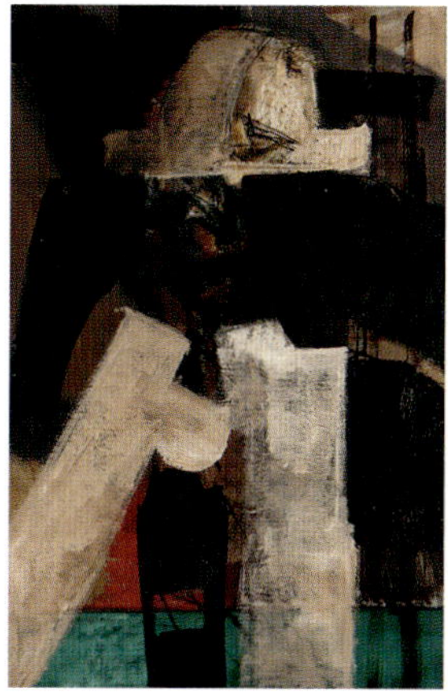

Johnstone, William 1897–1981
Border Farmer c.1927–1931
oil on canvas 75.9 x 50.5
3281

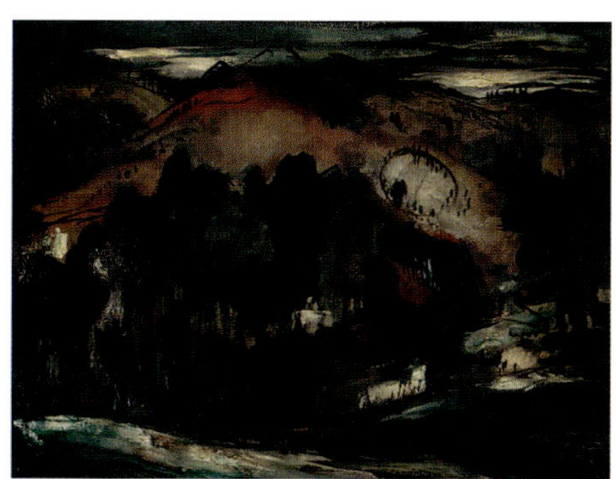

Johnstone, William 1897–1981
Border Landscape: The Eildon Hills c.1929
oil on canvas 71 x 91
3278

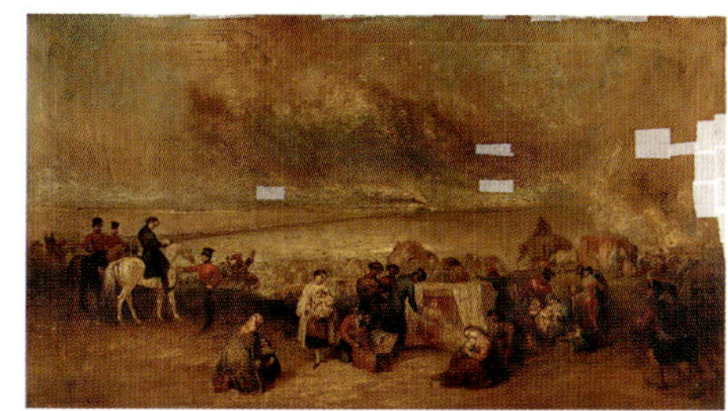

Jones, George 1786–1869
Cawnpore, Passage of the Ganges c.1865–1869
oil on canvas 101.6 x 177.8
643

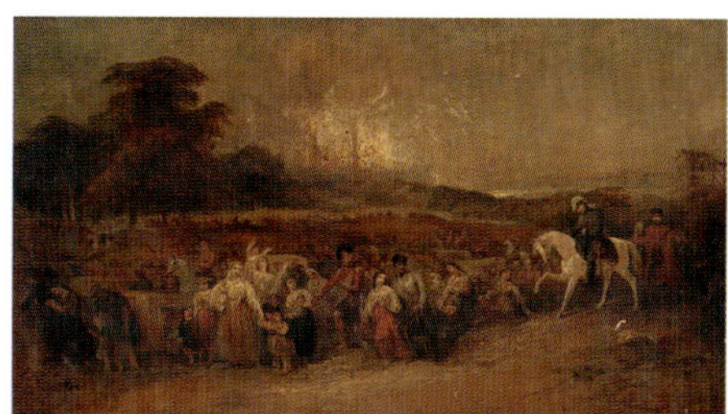

Jones, George 1786–1869
The Relief of Lucknow c.1869
oil on canvas 101.6 x 177.8
642

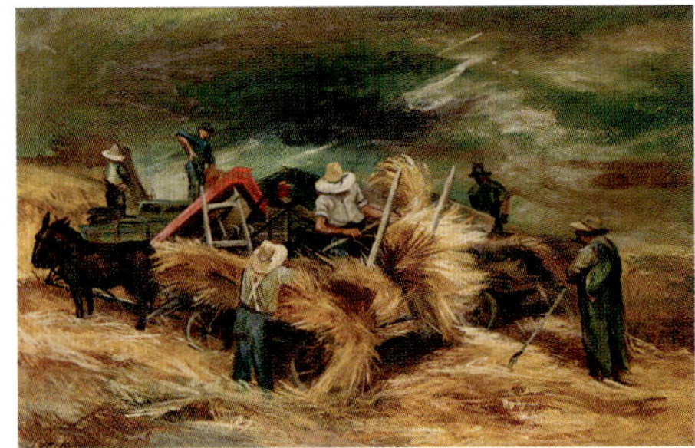

Jones, Joe active 20th C
The Wheat Farmer
oil on canvas 61 x 91.4
3007

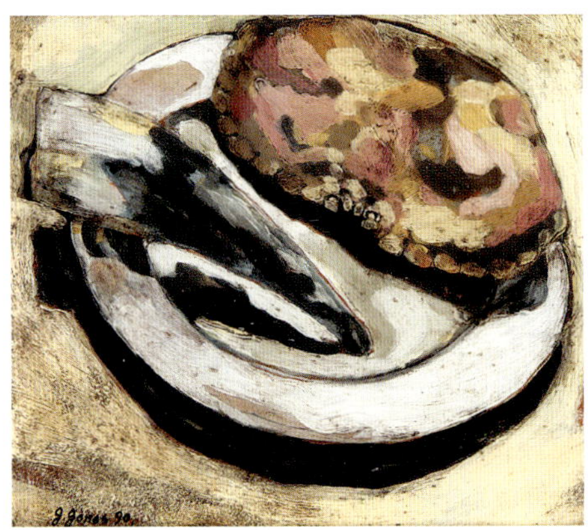

Joney, James W. G.
Bull's Horn with Crab Shell 1990
oil on board 30.5 x 32.5
3665

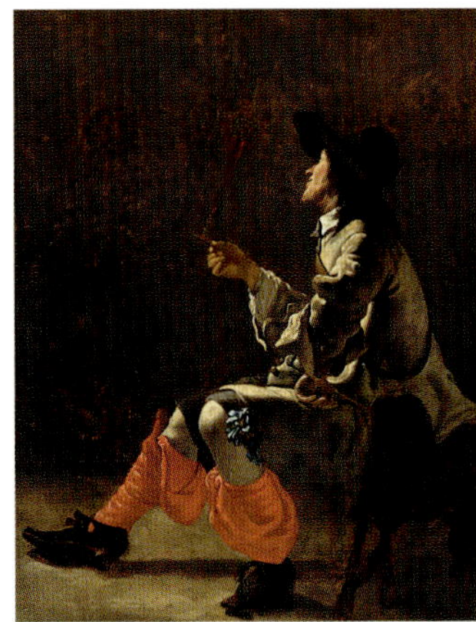

Jongh, Ludolf de (attributed to) 1616–1679
The Huntsman's Toast c.1650–1679
oil on panel 38.1 x 29.8
35.251

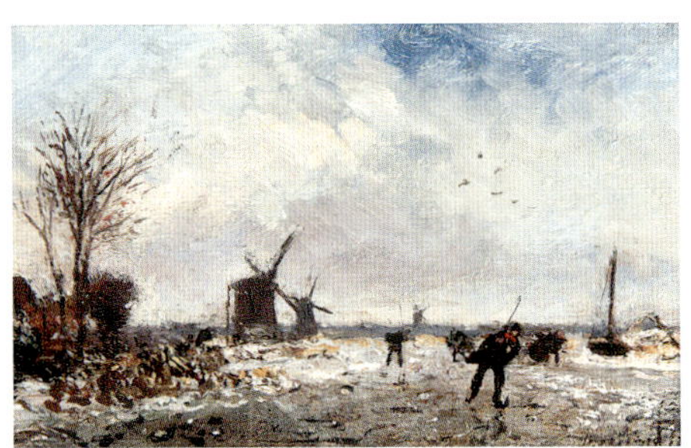

Jongkind, Johan Barthold 1819–1891
Winter Scene in Holland 1865
oil on panel 14.5 x 23.1
2400

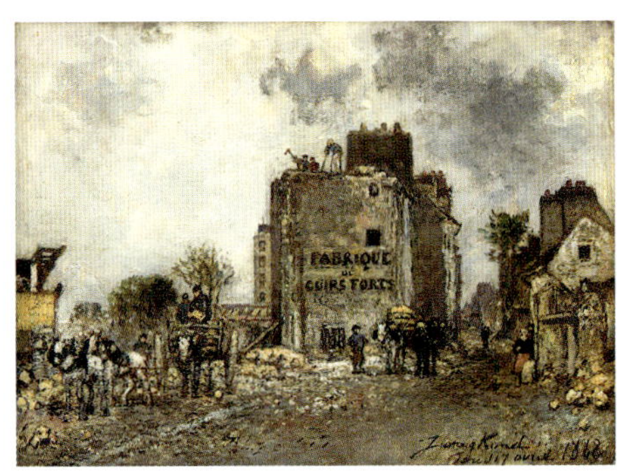

Jongkind, Johan Barthold 1819–1891
Paris, Demolition of the Rue des Francs-Bourgeois 1868
oil on canvas 34.3 x 42.5
35.293

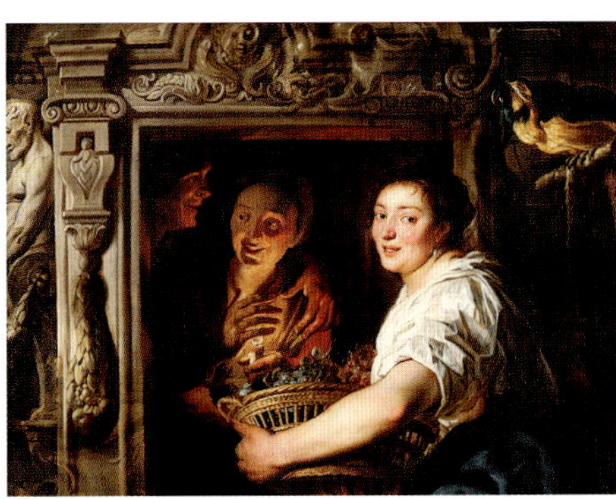

Jordaens, Jacob 1593–1678
A Maidservant with a Basket of Fruit and Two Lovers c.1630–1635
oil on canvas 119.7 x 156.5
84

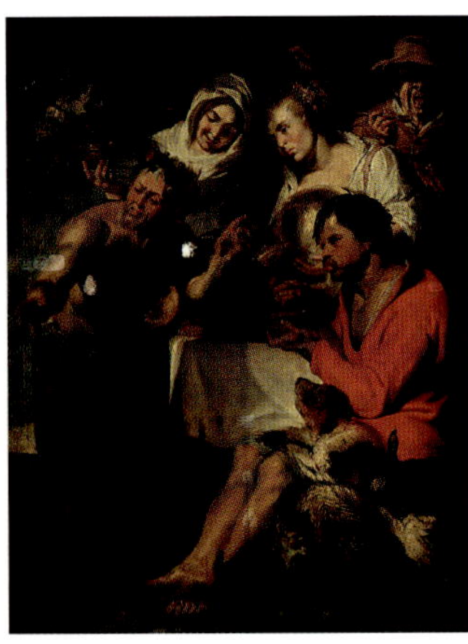

Jordaens, Jacob (attributed to) 1593–1678
The Satyr and the Peasant c.1615–1616
oil on canvas 67.3 x 51.1
PC.100

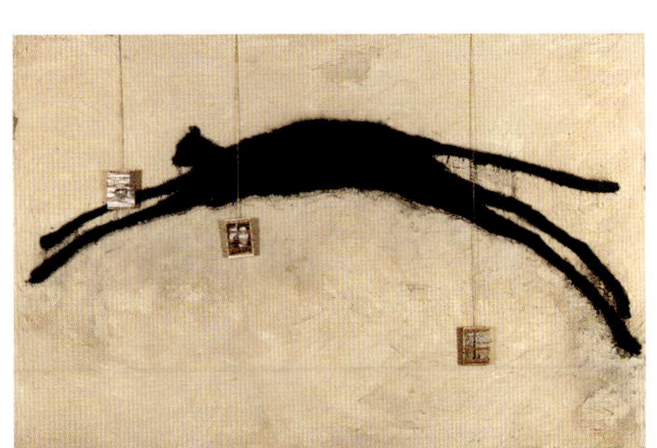

Joseph, Tam b.1947
Timespan 1987
acrylic, sand & pigment on canvas
166.4 x 250.8
3500

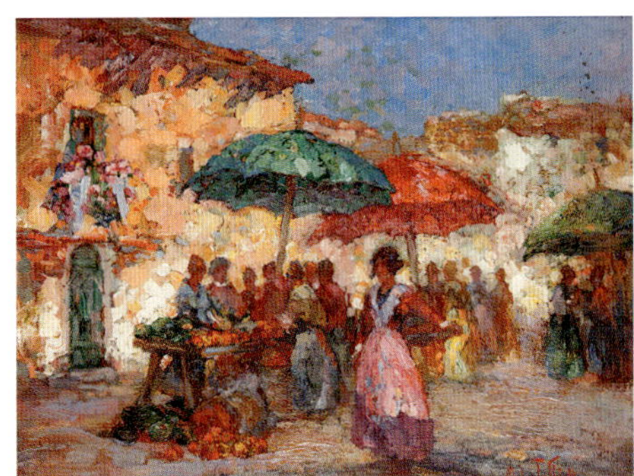

Julliotte, Madeleine Camille 1887–1948
Market in Spain 1928
oil on plywood 32.7 x 40.8
3132

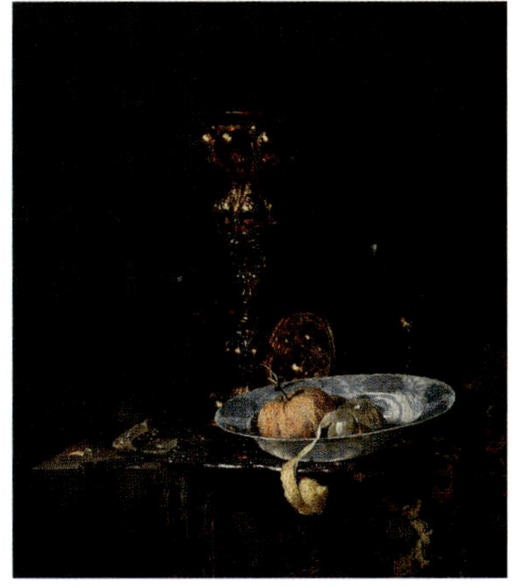

Kalf, Willem 1619–1693
Still Life: Silver-Gilt Goblet and Bowl of Fruit c.1656–1660
oil on canvas 83.8 x 69.8
1128

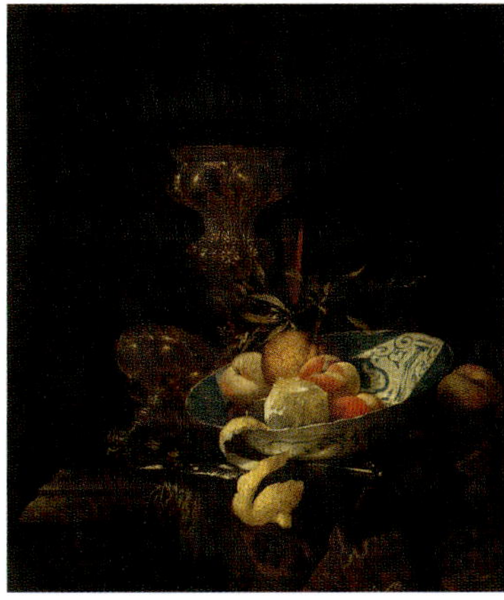

Kalf, Willem 1619–1693
Still Life: Silver-Gilt Goblet, Porcelain Bowl, Glassware and Peeled Orange c.1660–1665
oil on canvas 68.9 x 56.8
1127

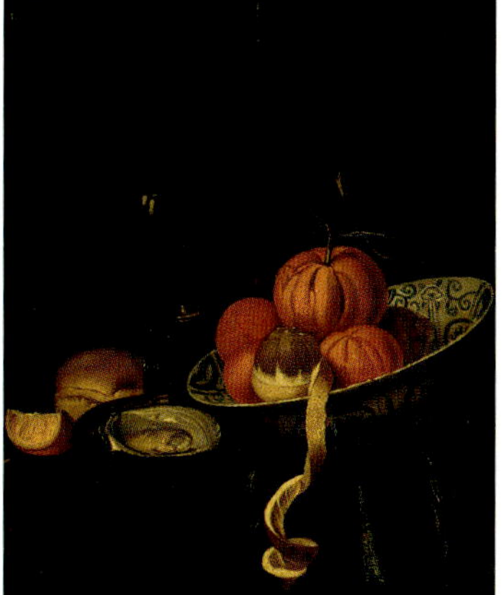

Kalf, Willem (after) 1619–1693
Still Life: Fruit, Oyster and Glasses
oil on canvas 53.3 x 41.9
35.294

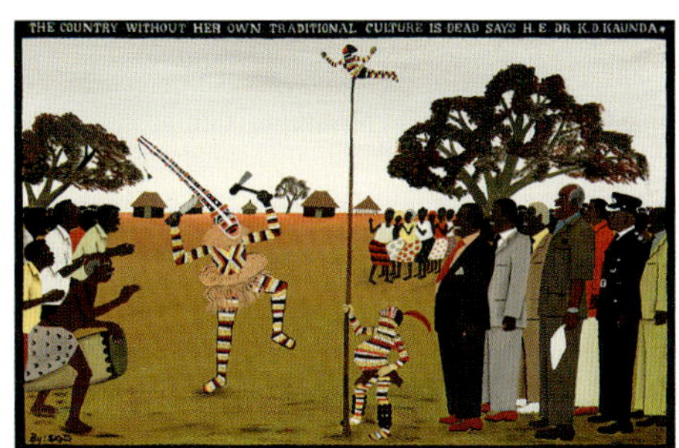

Kappata, Stephen b.1936
Likishi
oil on canvas 46 x 68.5
A.1990.41

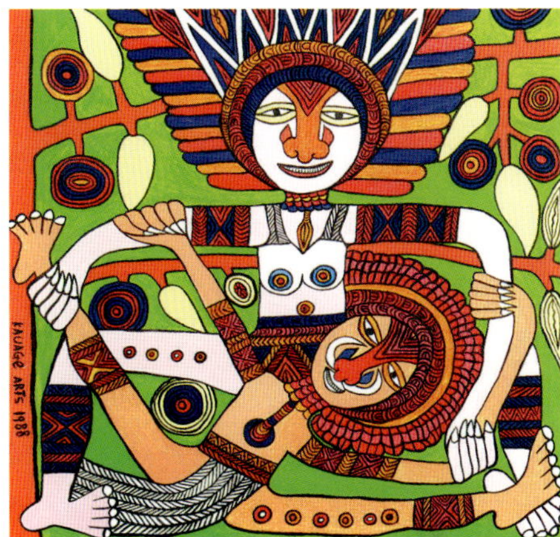

Kauage, Mathias 1944–2003
Carry Leg 1988
acrylic on canvas 98 x 93.2
3544

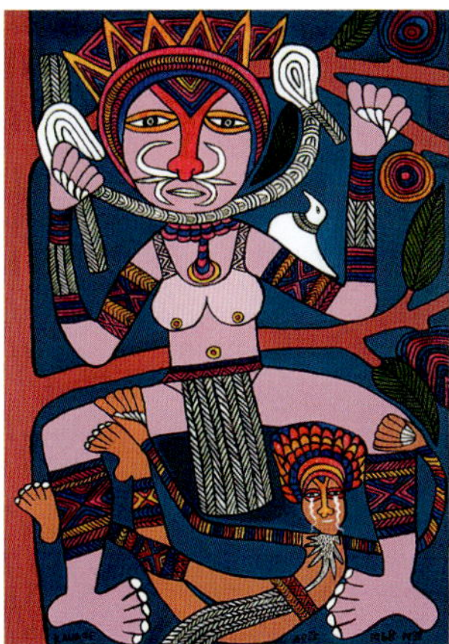

Kauage, Mathias 1944–2003
Suicide 1988
acrylic on canvas 96 x 67.3
3543

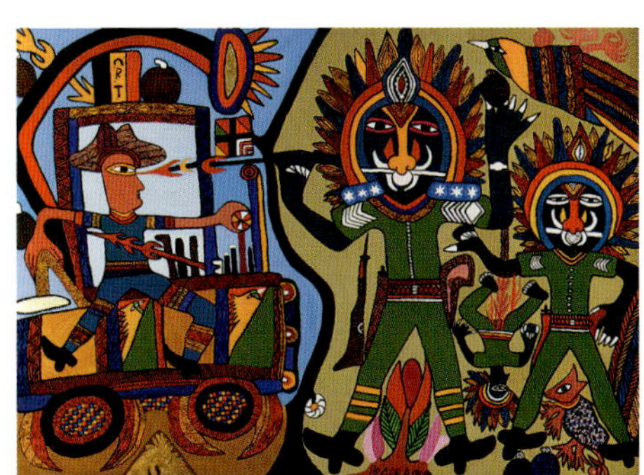

Kauage, Mathias 1944–2003
Buka War 1990
acrylic on canvas 125 x 175.5
3546

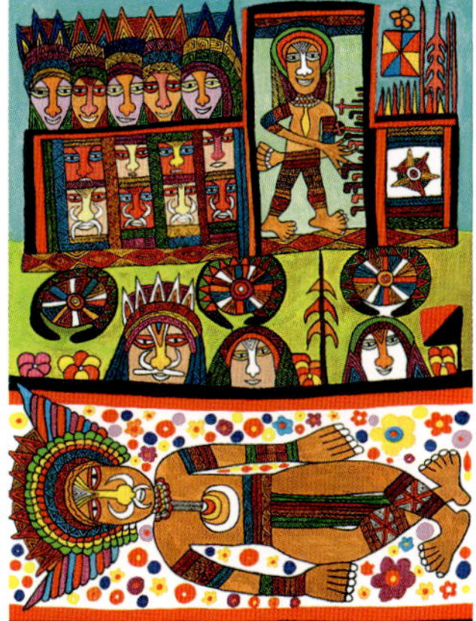

Kauage, Mathias 1944–2003
Burial 1990
acrylic on canvas 175.2 x 125.2
3545

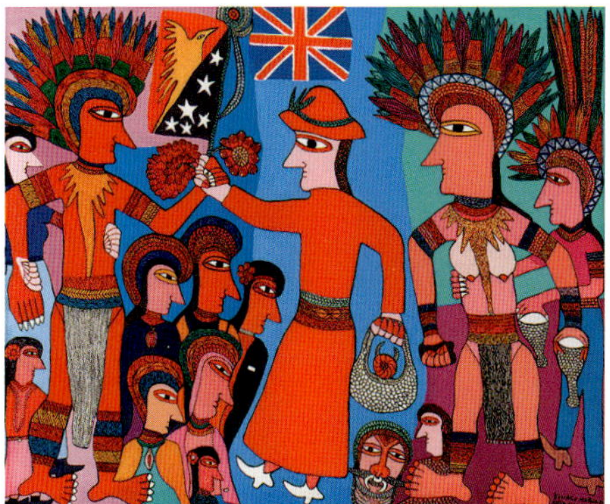

Kauage, Mathias 1944–2003
Misis Kwin 1996
acrylic on canvas 152.6 x 183.3
3607

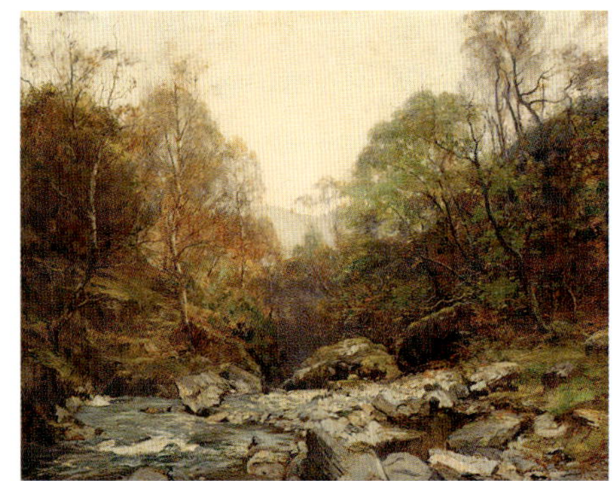

Kay, Archibald 1860–1935
The Rhymer's Glen c.1909
oil on canvas 100.3 x 125.7
1230

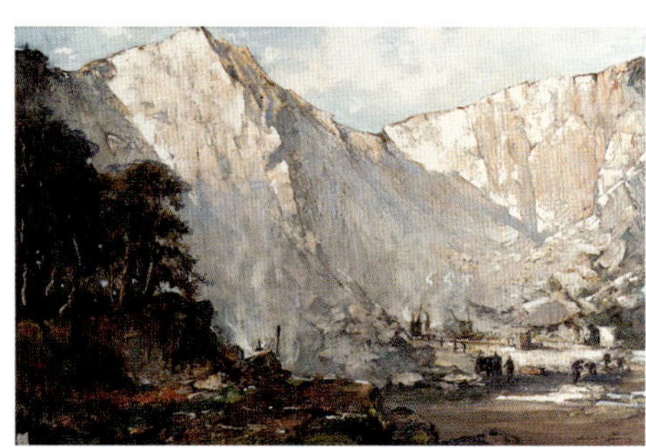

Kay, Archibald 1860–1935
Furnace Quarries, Streets of a Great City
c.1925–1930
oil on canvas 121.7 x 182.9
2057

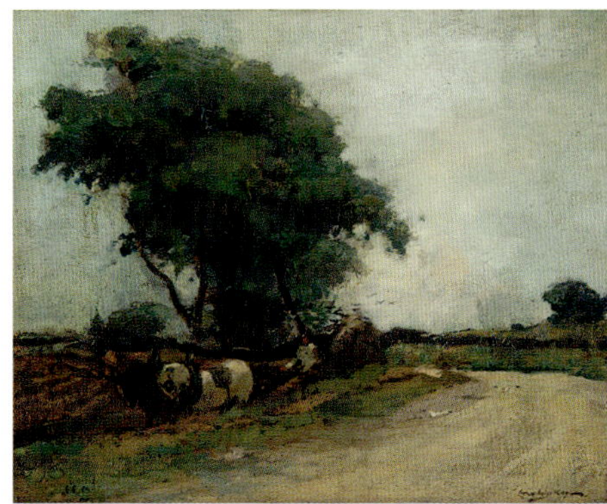

Kay, Archibald 1860–1935
Ploughing at Crail
oil on canvas 26.7 x 31.8
2578

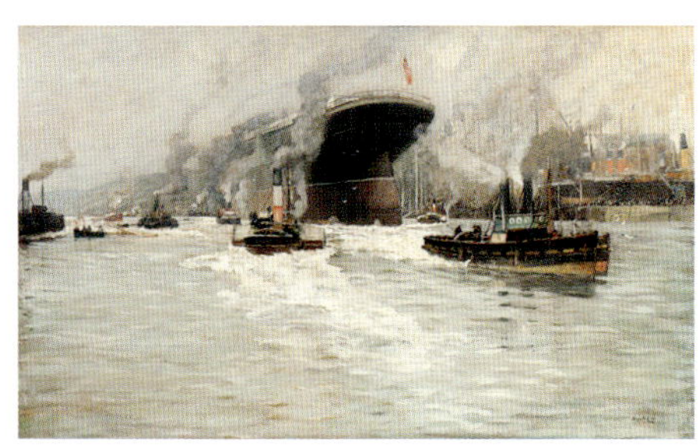

Kay, James 1858–1942
The Launch of the 'Lusitania' c.1907
oil on canvas 120.7 x 196.8
1200

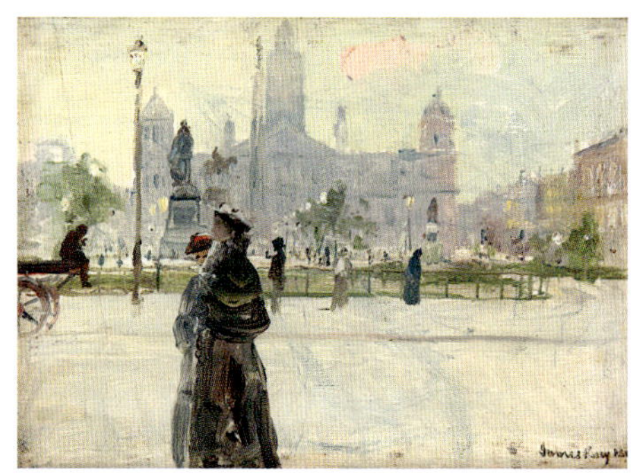

Kay, James 1858–1942
George Square, Glasgow
oil on board 15.2 x 20.3
NR.153

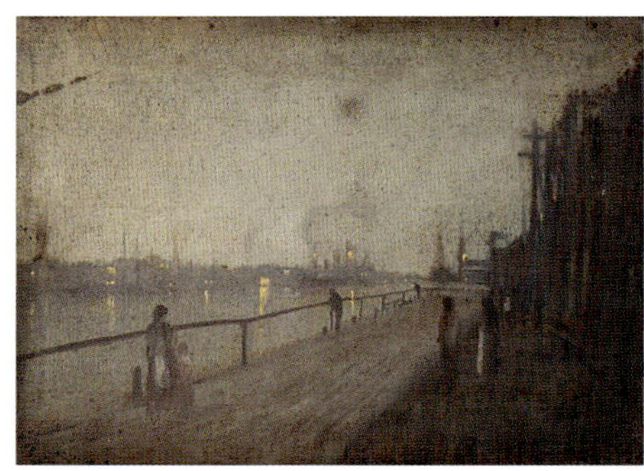

Kay, James 1858–1942
Harbour Scene
oil on canvas board 26.7 x 37
3608

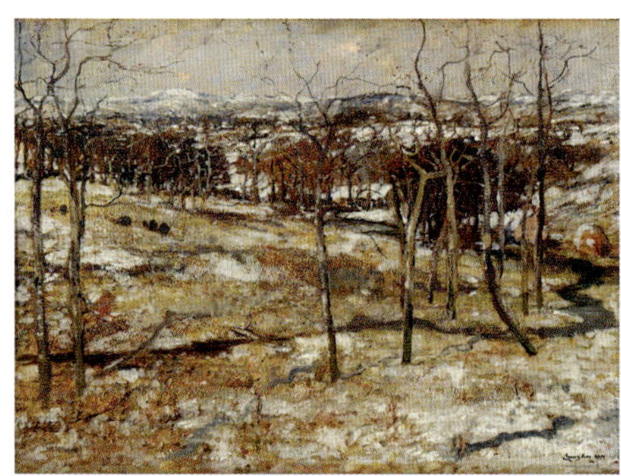

Kay, James 1858–1942
Thaw
oil on canvas 68.6 x 93.9
3264

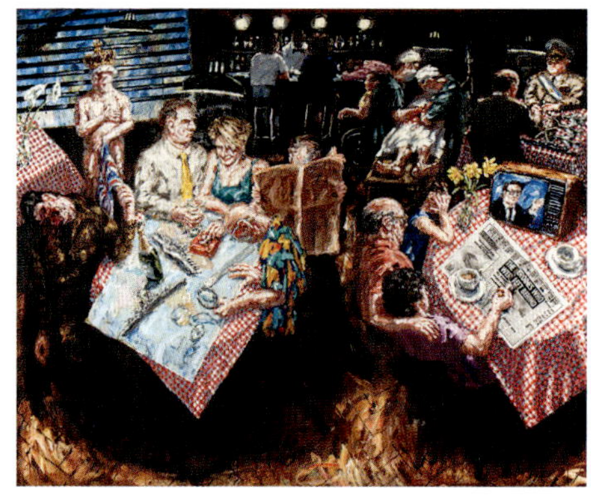

Keane, John b.1954
The Old Lie Café 1989
oil on canvas 248 x 300
3491

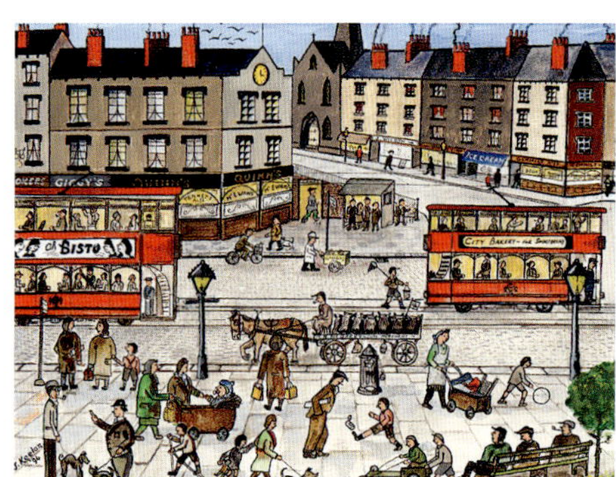

Keelan, J. active 1994
Memories of Springburn
oil & pencil on board 49 x 58.5
1994.84

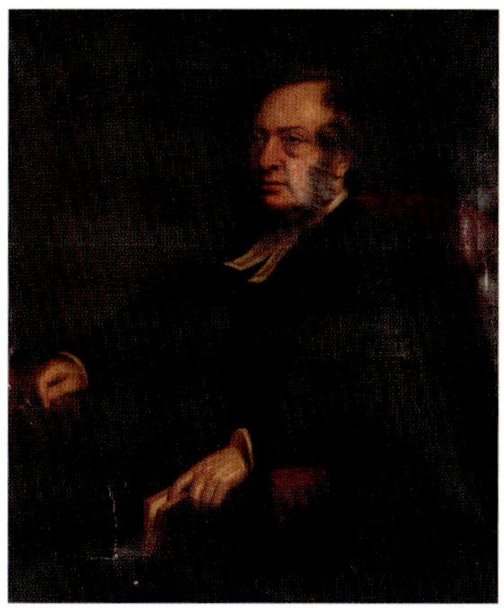

Keith, Alexander active 1808–1874
Reverend Dr Norman McLeod (1780–1866)
c.1863
oil on canvas 98 x 80
PP.1985.222.25

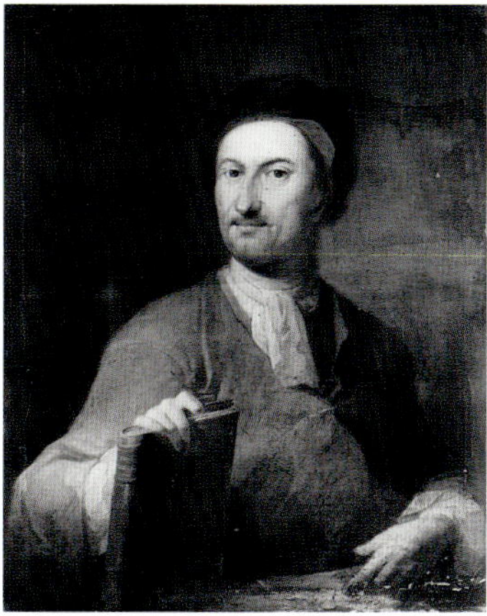

Keller, Johann Heinrich (attributed to)
1692–1765
Gottfried Wilhelm Leibniz (1646–1716)
c.1710–1730
oil on canvas 83.8 x 67.3
675

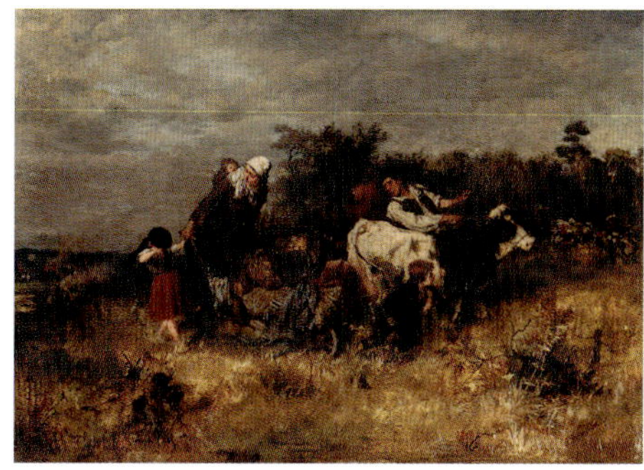

Kellner, Hermann II 1849–1926
The Ravages of War 1876–1898
oil on canvas 90.1 x 125.7
804

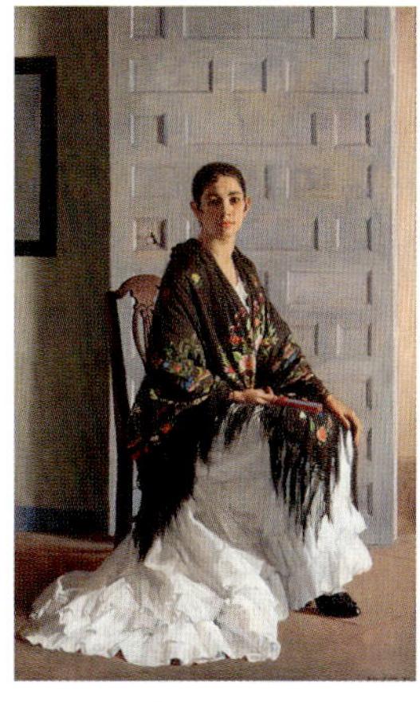

Kelly, Gerald Festus 1879–1972
The Blue Door (Consuelo VII) 1919
oil on canvas 127 x 76.2
1862

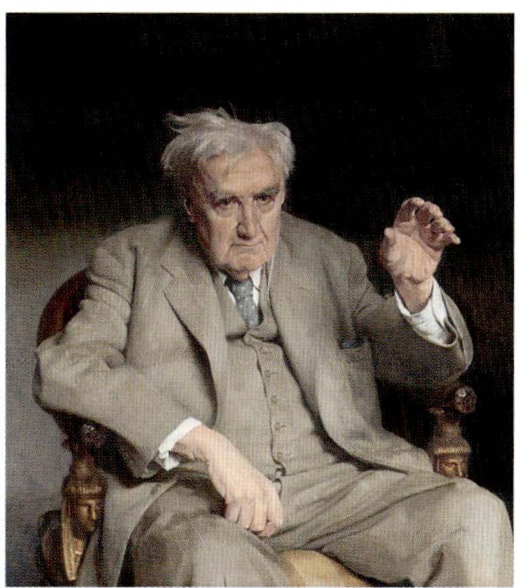

Kelly, Gerald Festus 1879–1972
Dr Ralph Vaughan Williams (1872–1958)
1959
oil on canvas 95.9 x 87.3
3115

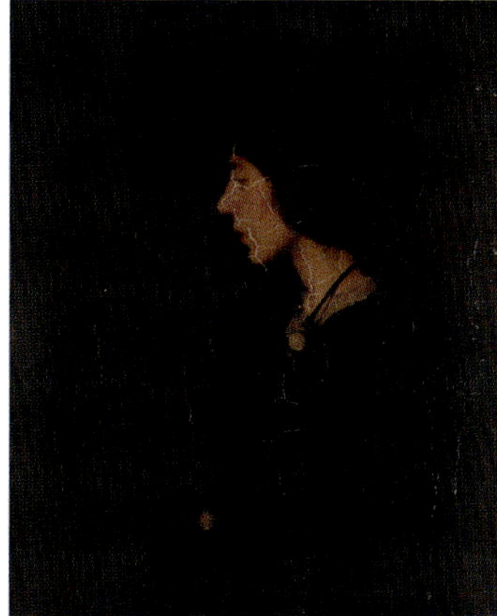

Kelly, Gerald Festus 1879–1972
Mademoiselle
oil on canvas 62.9 x 50.2
2492

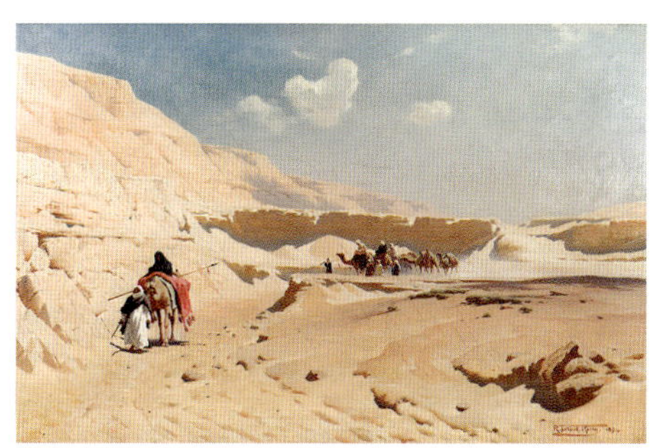

Kelly, Robert George Talbot 1861–1934
'In a dry and thirsty land, where no water is'
1894
oil on canvas 67 x 98
828

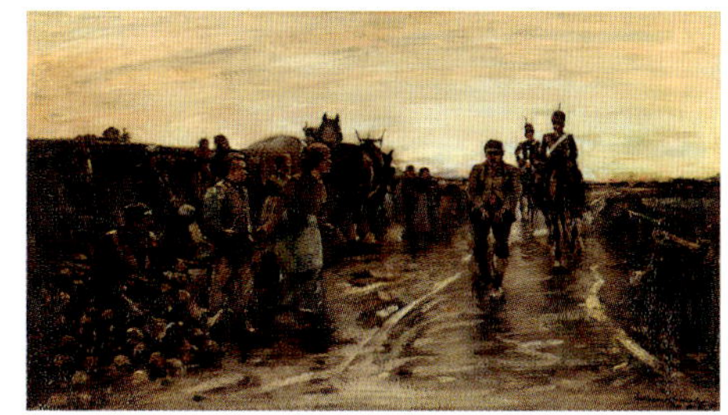

Kennedy, William 1859–1918
The Deserter 1886
oil on canvas 88.9 x 152.4
3374

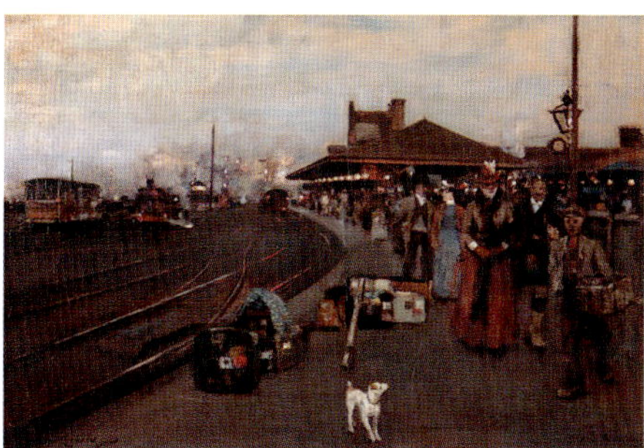

Kennedy, William 1859–1918
Stirling Station 1887–1888
oil on canvas 54 x 81.6
3664

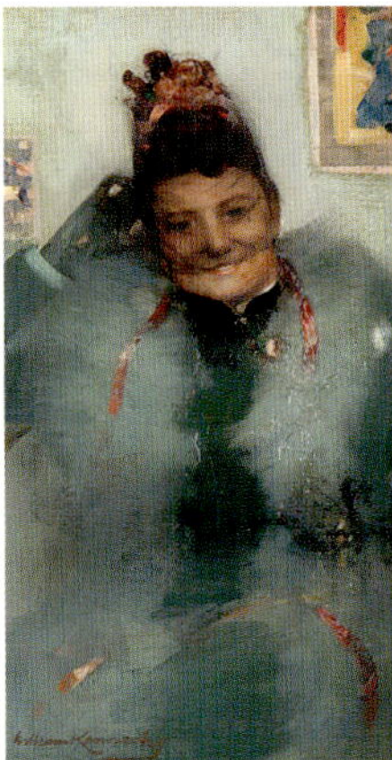

Kennedy, William 1859–1918
The Fur Boa c.1890–1893
oil on canvas 53.3 x 28.6
2446

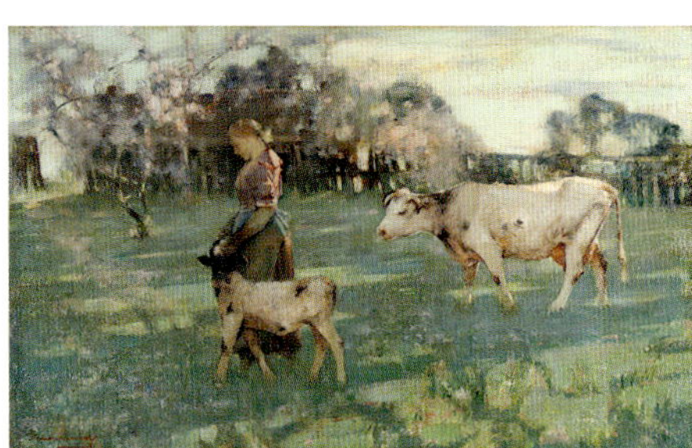

Kennedy, William 1859–1918
Homewards c.1891
oil on canvas 89.2 x 141.8
3124

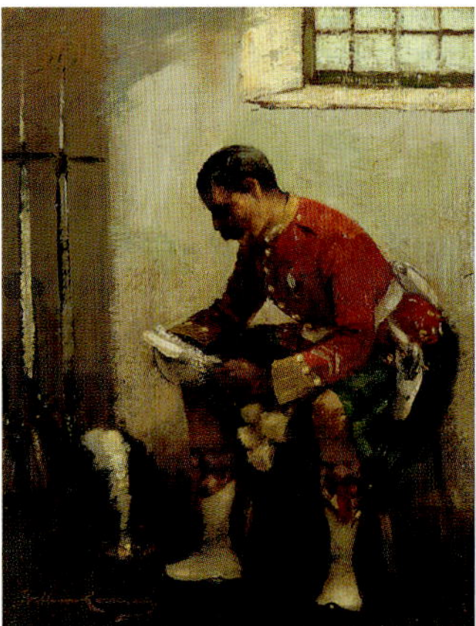

Kennedy, William 1859–1918
The Highlander c.1892
oil on panel 38.1 x 30.5
2243

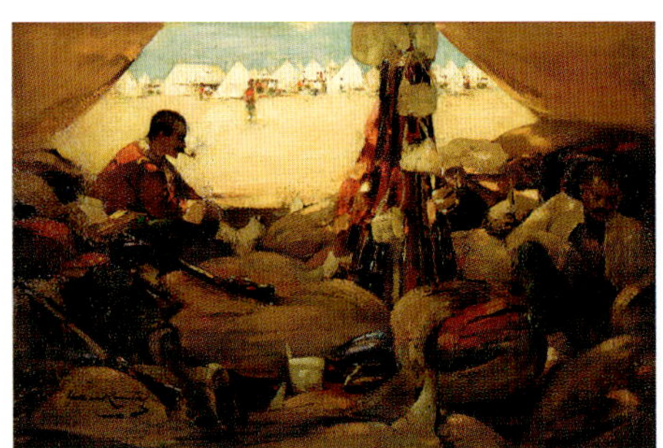

Kennedy, William 1859–1918
Midday Rest c.1892–1893
oil on canvas 61.3 x 91.7
3190

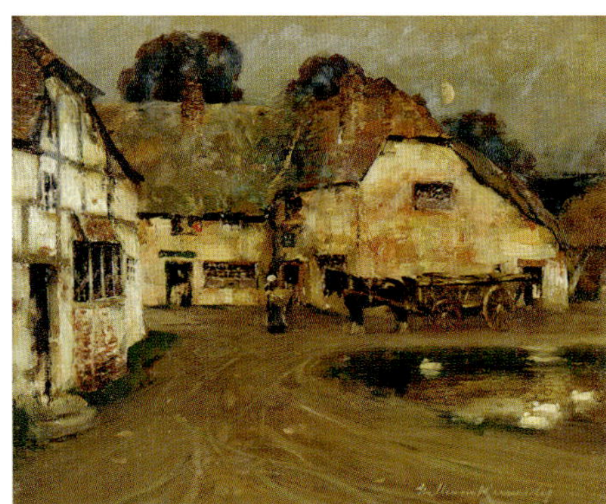

Kennedy, William 1859–1918
Evening in Berkshire c.1900–1910
oil on canvas 50.8 x 62.2
2806

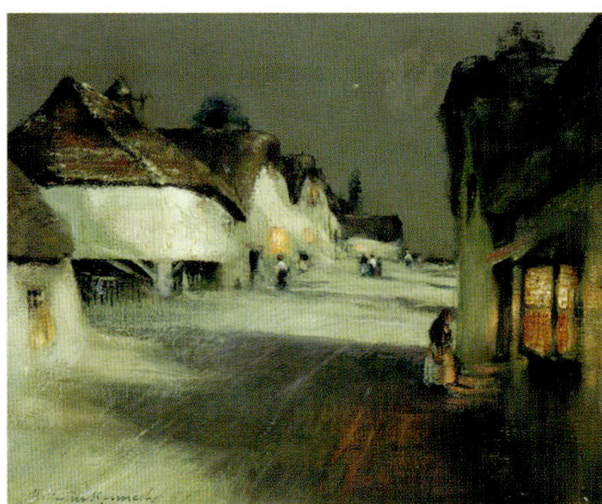

Kennedy, William 1859–1918
Moonlight c.1900–1910
oil on canvas 50.8 x 61
2127

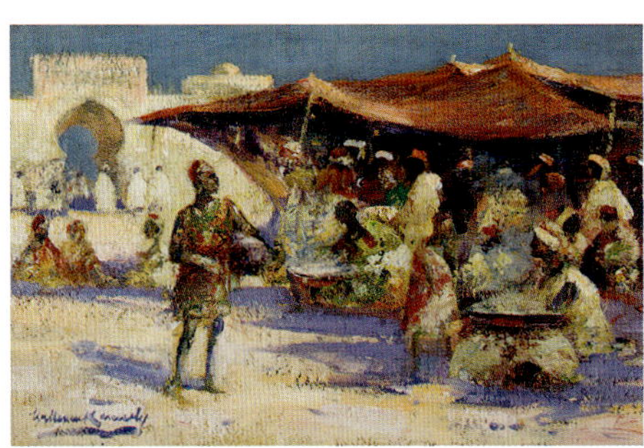

Kennedy, William 1859–1918
Restaurant in Tangier c.1912–1918
oil on canvas 40.6 x 62.2
1920

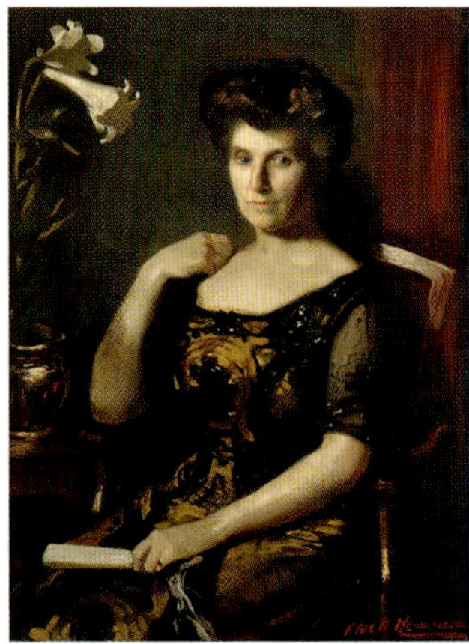

Kennington, Eric Henri 1888–1960
Mrs George Struthers (1856–1946) c.1910
oil on canvas 101 x 75.6
3213

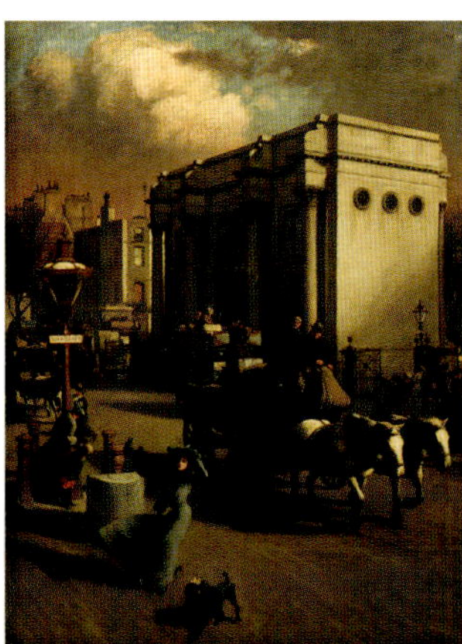

Kerr, Charles Henry Malcolm 1858–1907
March Winds, the Marble Arch c.1890–1900
oil on canvas 102.9 x 76.2
1815

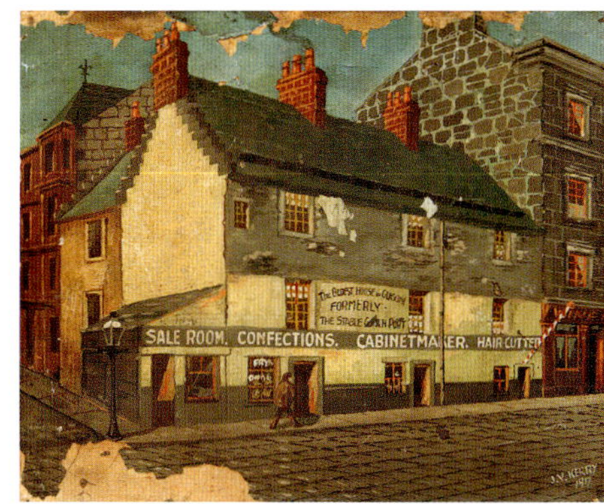

Kerry, J. Vincent active 1917–1935
Provand's Lordship from the East 1917
oil on canvas 30.4 x 35.5
TEMP.1957

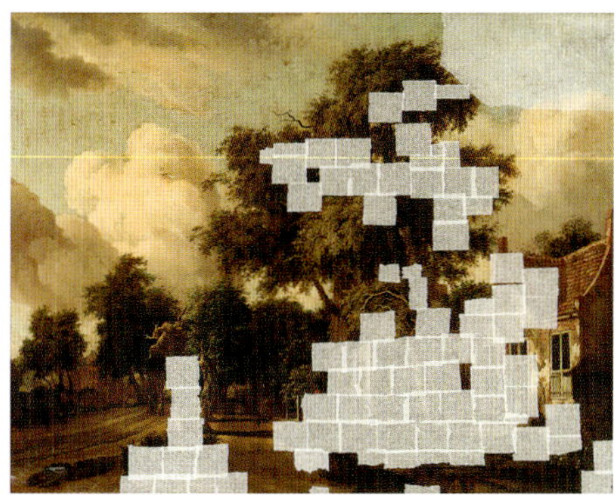

Kessel, Jan van II 1641–1680
Wooded Landscape with an Inn c.1664
oil on canvas 74.9 x 118.1
68

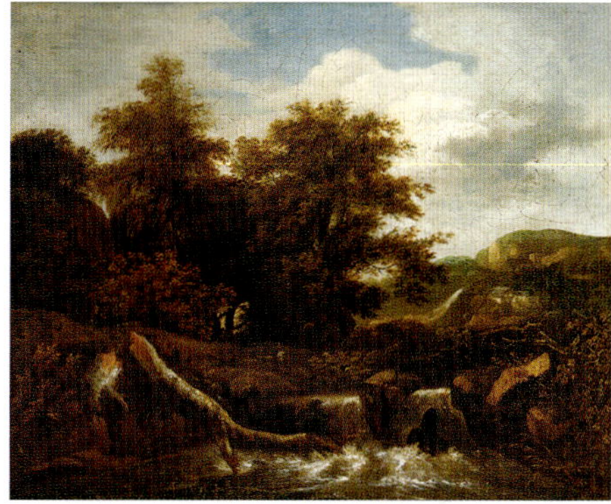

Kessel, Jan van II (attributed to) 1641–1680
Landscape with a Waterfall c.1664
oil on canvas 51 x 60.4
419

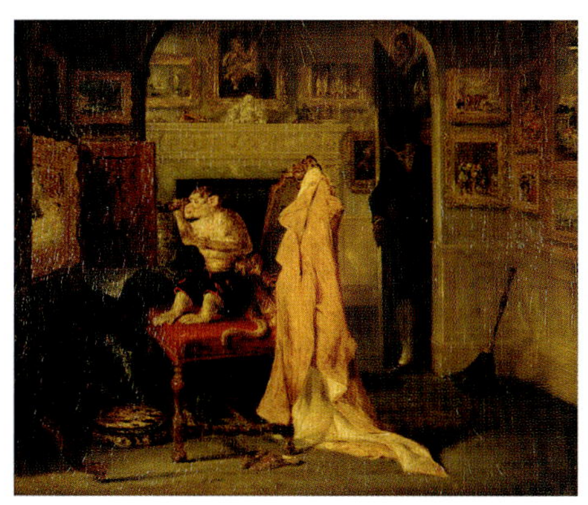

Kidd, William 1790–1863
An Art Connoisseur
oil on panel 29.2 x 34.3
934

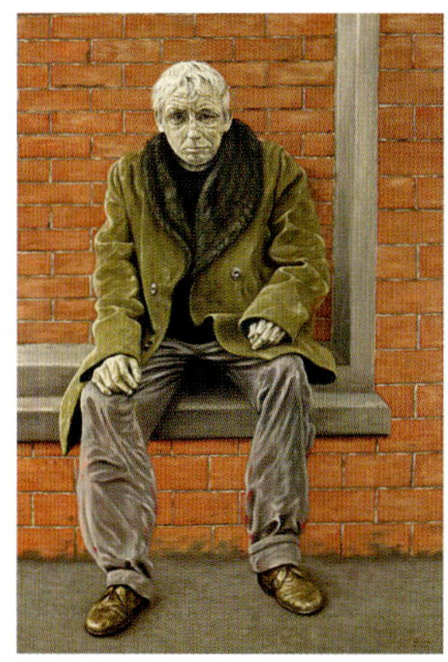

Kilmartin, John b.1964
Outside the Mission 1993
oil on canvas 148 x 102
PP.1994.31

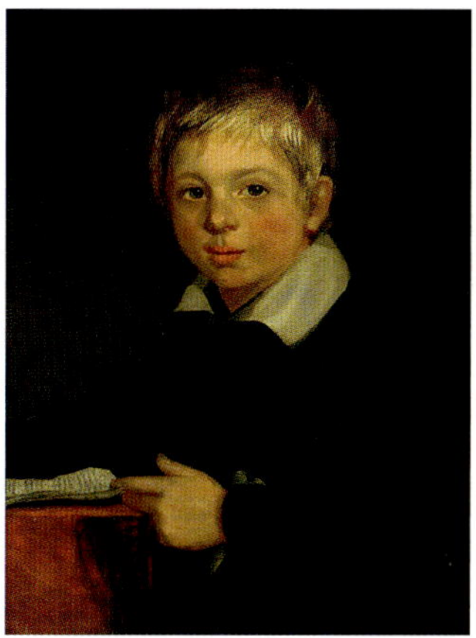

Kilpatrick
William Ross c.1846–1850
oil on canvas 50.2 x 40
2062

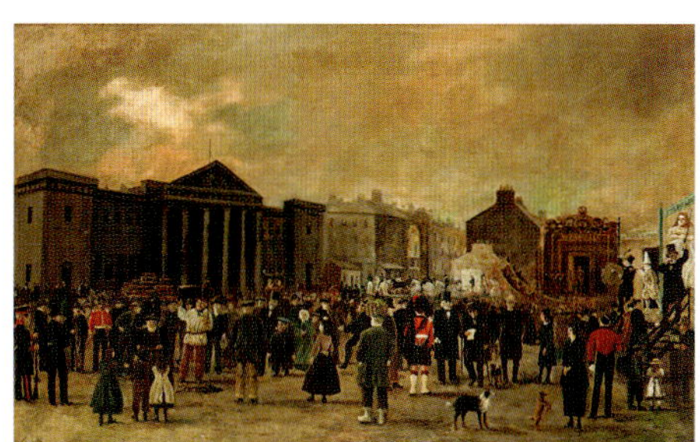

King, A.
Glasgow Fair in the Saltmarket 1849
oil on canvas 87.5 x 126
TEMP.14946

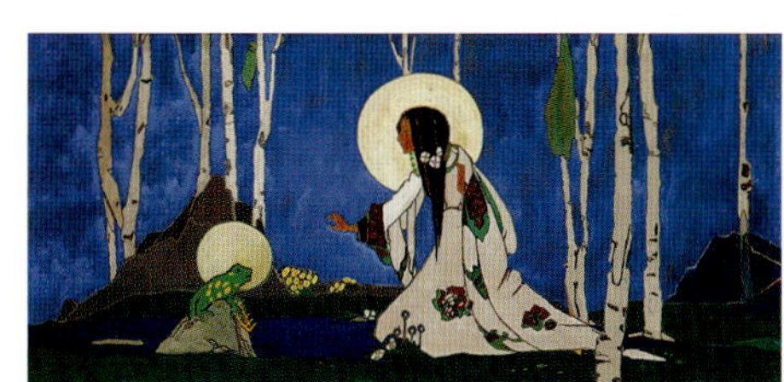

King, Jessie Marion 1875–1949
The Frog Prince 1913
oil on panel 35.5 x 67.7
E.2005.1.53

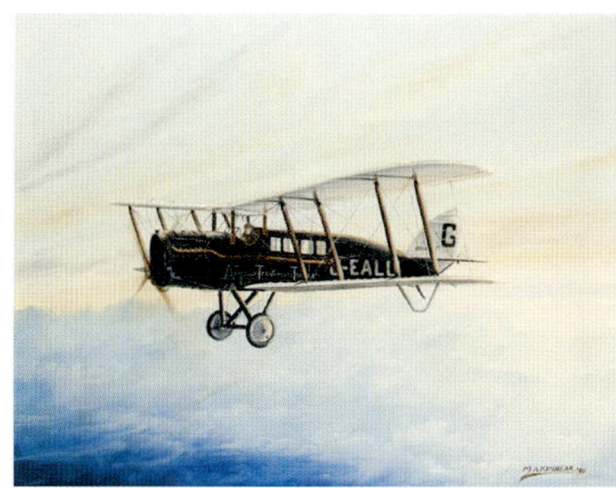

Kinnear, M. A.
Aircraft in Flight 1990
acrylic on canvas 45.5 x 55
T.1995.46.489

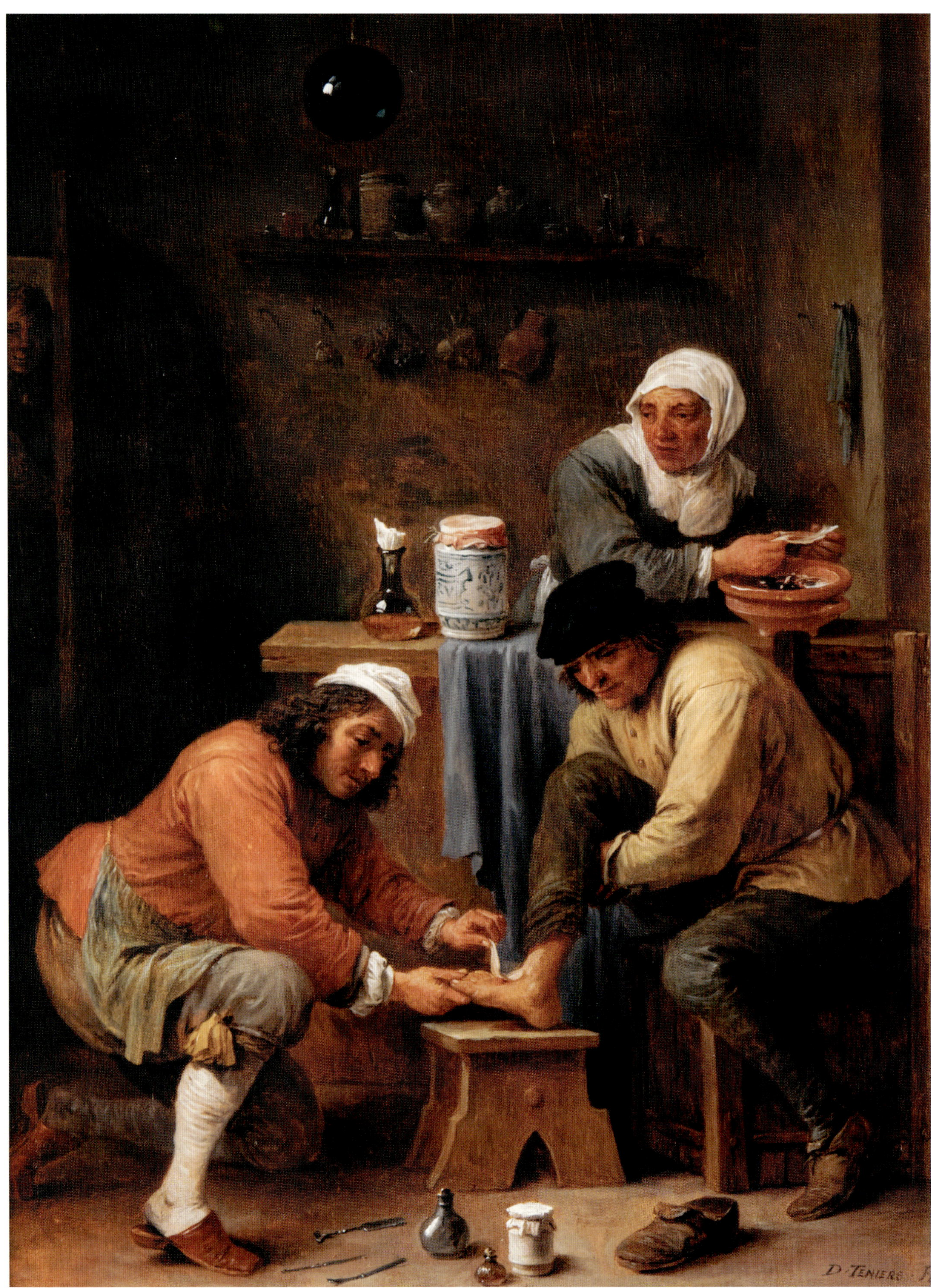

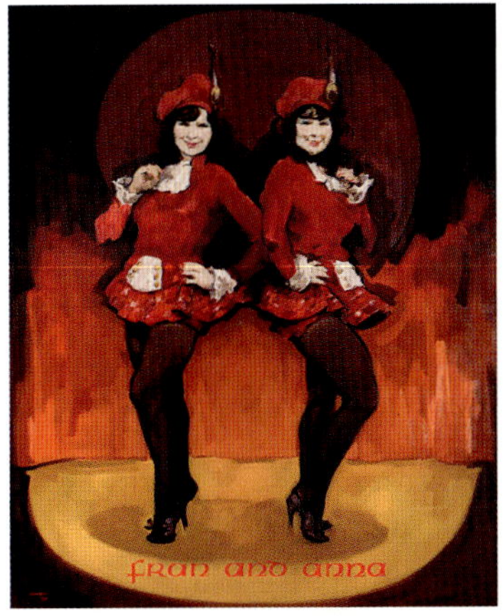

Kirkham, Norman b.1936
Fran and Anna 1980
oil on canvas 211 x 175.5
PP.1985.176

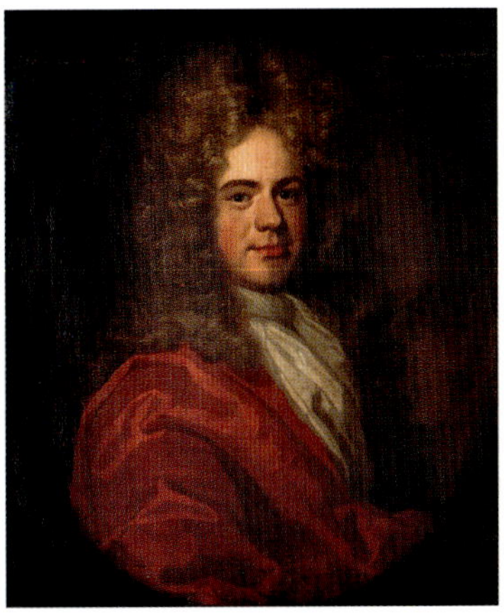

Kneller, Godfrey (attributed to) 1646–1723
Thomas Betterton (1635?–1710)
oil on canvas 73.6 x 60.6
PC.47

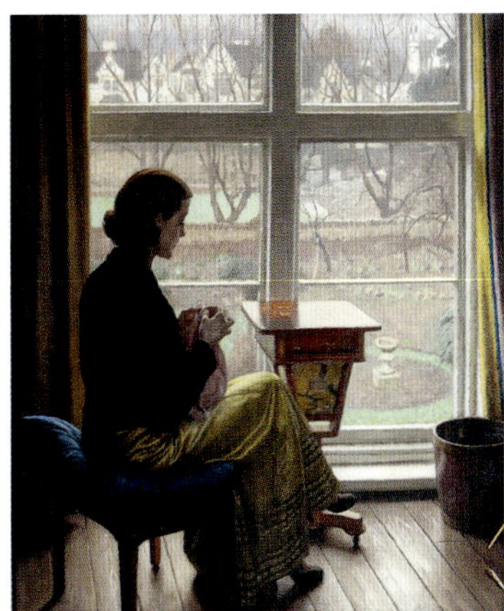

Knight, Harold 1874–1961
A Window in St John's Wood c.1932
oil on canvas 76.2 x 63.5
2105

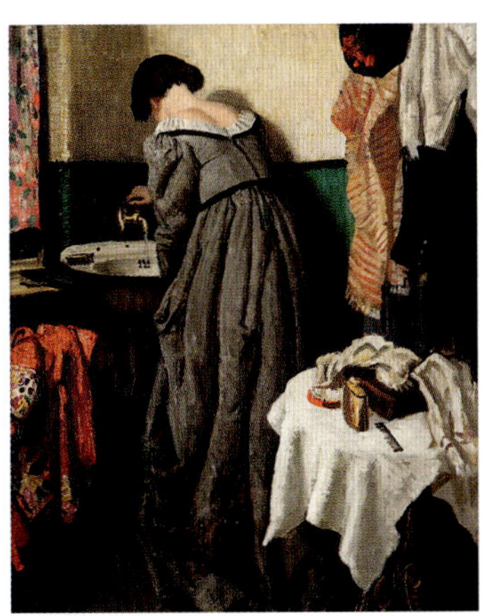

Knight, Laura 1877–1970
A Theatre Dressing Room c.1935
oil on canvas 74.3 x 62.9
1924

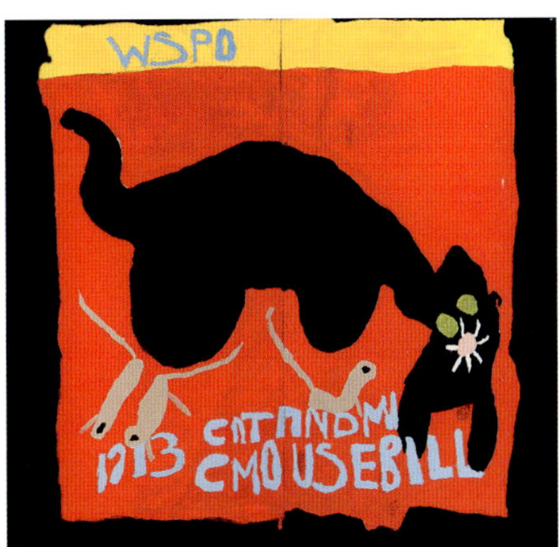

Knowles, John b.1966
*A Big Cat with a Bit of Writing
Underneath* c.1991
acrylic on board 178.4 x 178.7
3499

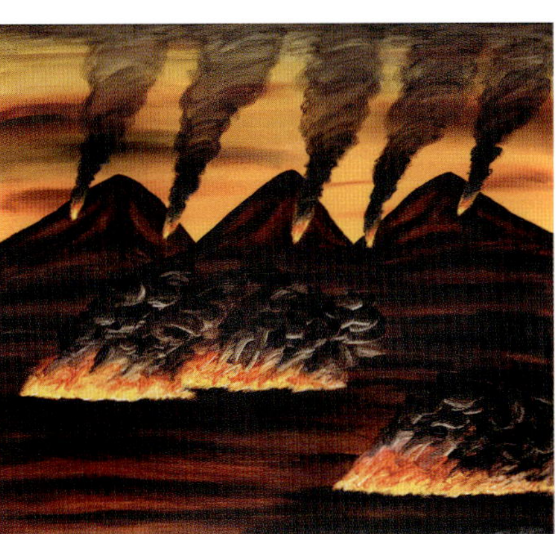

Knox, Jack b.1936
Burning the Heather c.1988
oil on canvas 112 x 122
3454

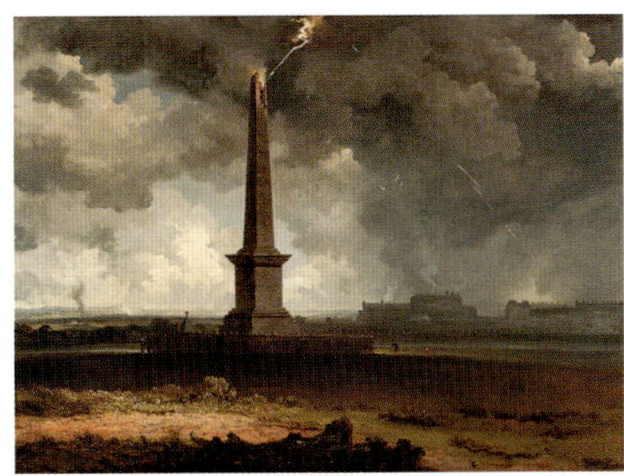

Knox, John 1778–1845
*The Nelson Monument on Glasgow Green
Struck by Lightning* c.1810
oil on canvas 67.6 x 90.5
3338

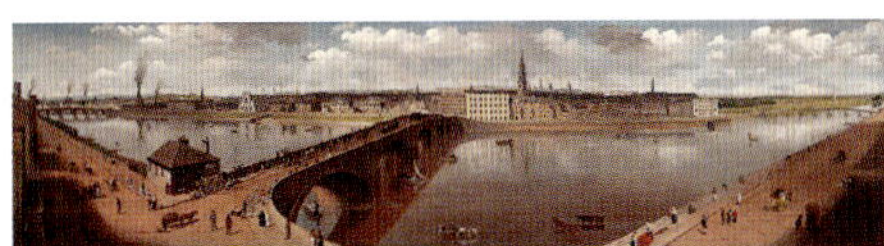

Knox, John 1778–1845
Old Glasgow Bridge c.1817
oil on canvas 30.5 x 119.4
OG.1955.119

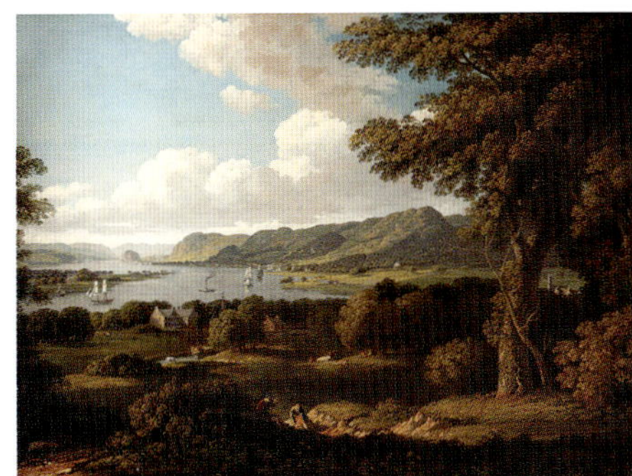

Knox, John 1778–1845
First Steamboat on the Clyde c.1820
oil on canvas 111.8 x 158.5
2342

Facing page: Teniers II, David, 1610–1690, *A Surgeon Treating a Peasant's Foot*, 1640s (p. 413)

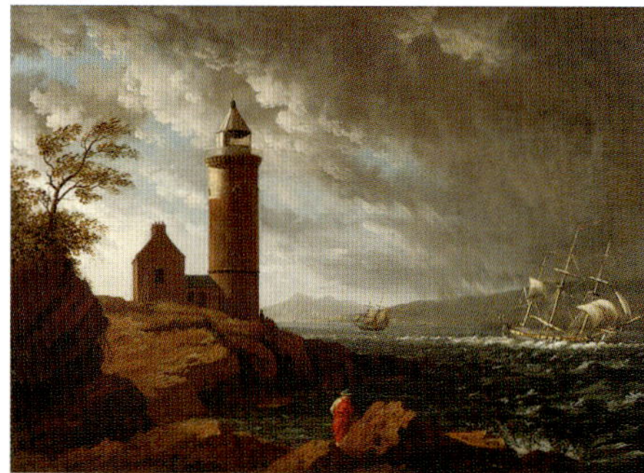

Knox, John 1778–1845
The Cloch Lighthouse c.1822
oil on canvas 53.3 x 73.7
1525

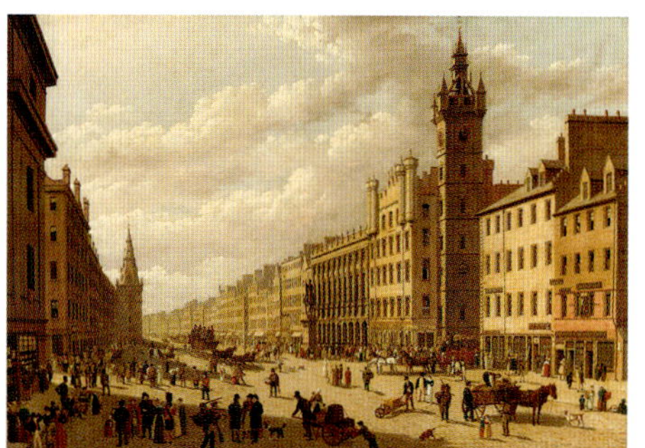

Knox, John 1778–1845
Old Glasgow Cross or the Trongate 1826
oil on canvas 90.2 x 125.1
1352

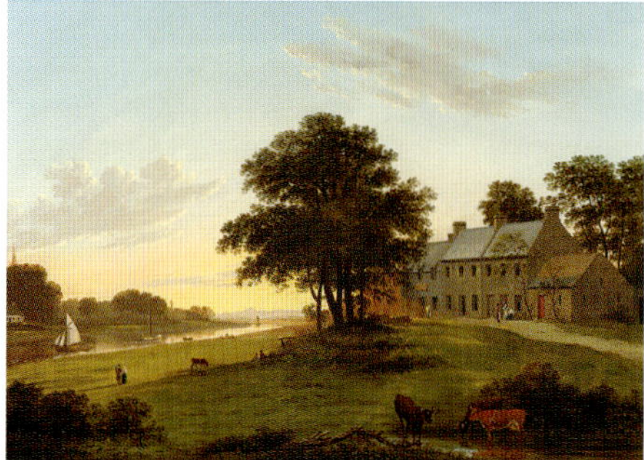

Knox, John 1778–1845
Govan Ferry c.1831
oil on canvas 54.2 x 76
3322

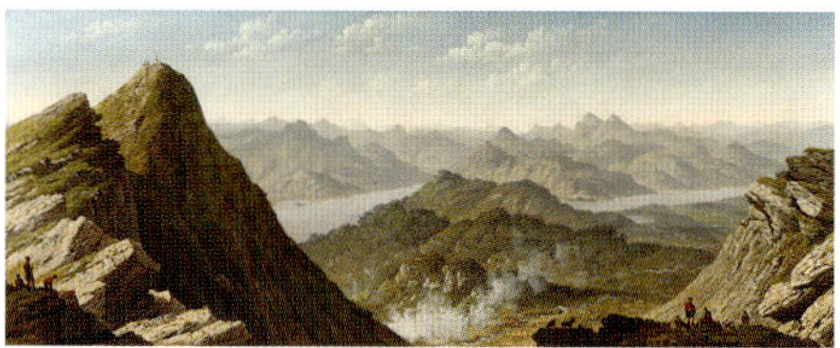

Knox, John 1778–1845
North Western View from Ben Lomond c.1834
oil on canvas 62.2 x 157.5
460

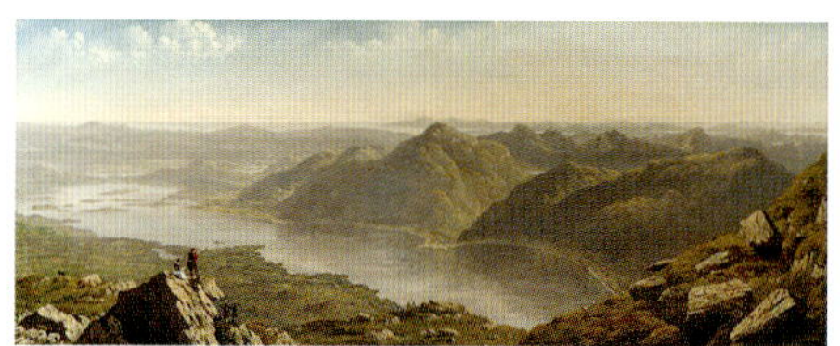

Knox, John 1778–1845
South Western View from Ben Lomond c.1834
oil on canvas 62.2 x 157.5
448

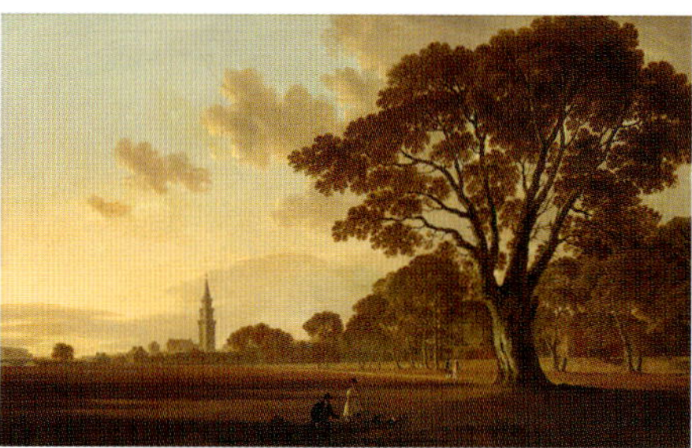

Knox, John 1778–1845
Glasgow Green
oil on canvas 74 x 105.5
OG.1950.117

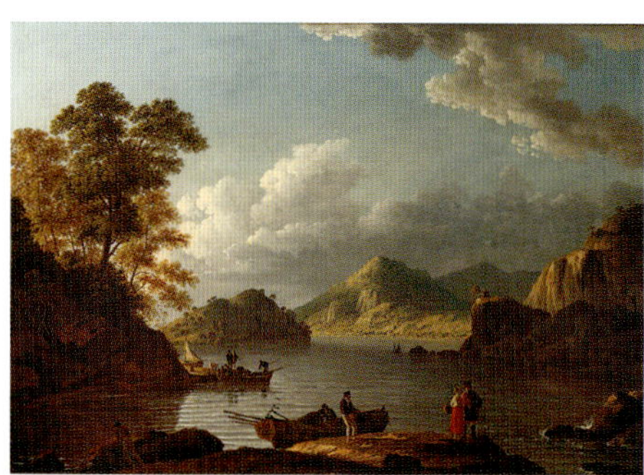

Knox, John 1778–1845
Highland Loch Scene
oil on canvas 62.2 x 87.6
PC.131

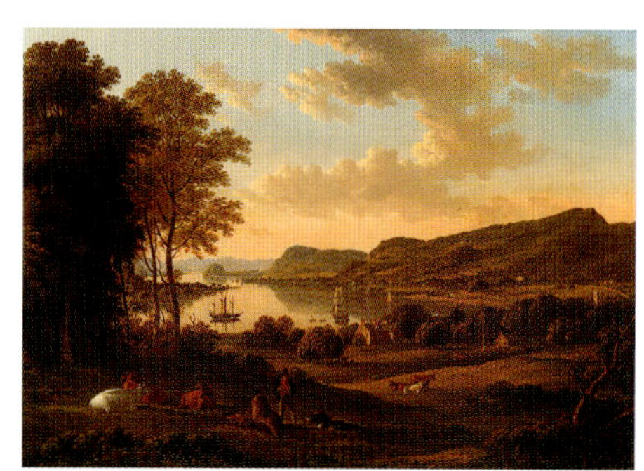

Knox, John 1778–1845
The Clyde from Dalnottar Hill
oil on canvas 63.5 x 88.9
1527

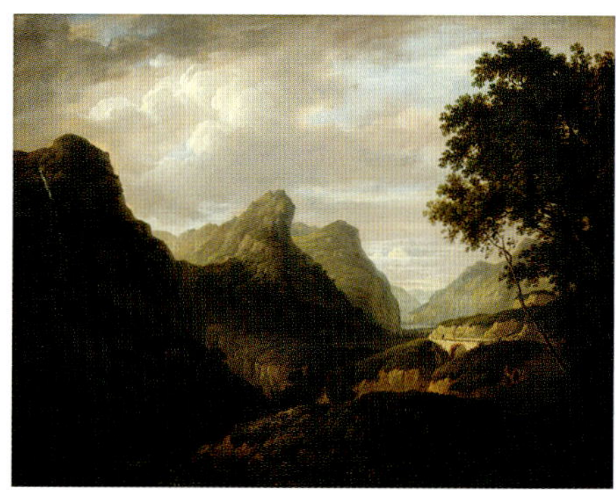

Knox, John 1778–1845
View of Glencoe
oil on canvas 67 x 88
3389

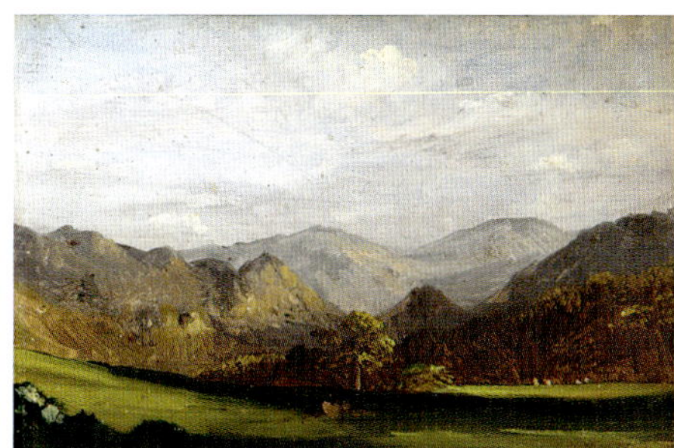

Knox, John
Hilly Landscape
oil on cardboard 15.2 x 23.5
1197

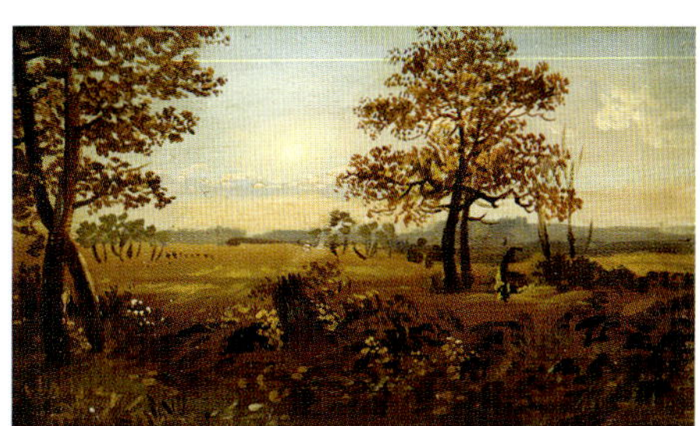

Knox, John
Landscape with Trees
oil on cardboard 11.4 x 19
1196

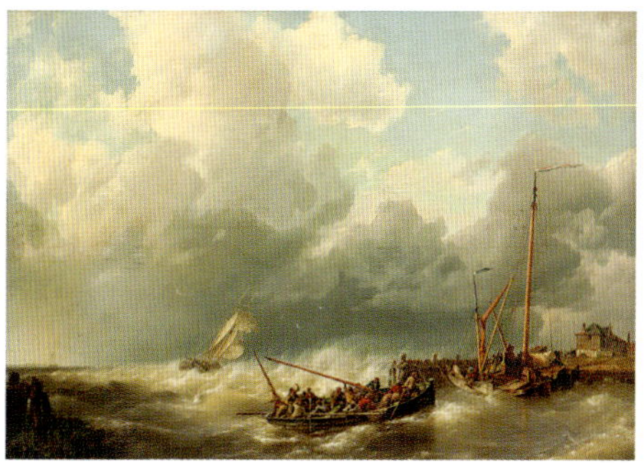

Koekkoek, Hermanus the elder 1815–1882
Boats Taking Haven from a Storm 1853
oil on canvas 64.4 x 87.5
421

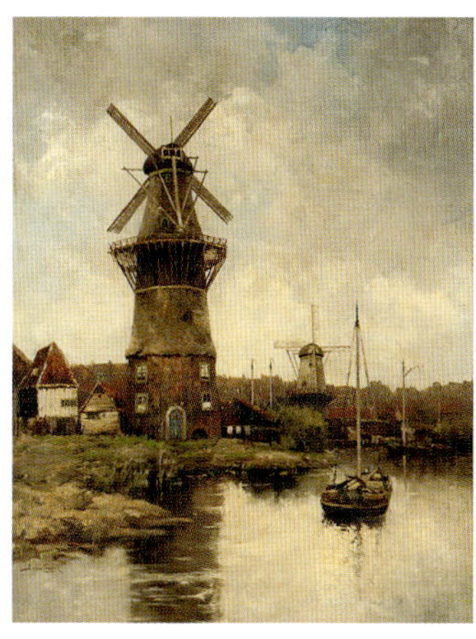

Koekkoek, Hermanus the younger 1836–1909
Windmills
oil on canvas 112 x 86.7
1573

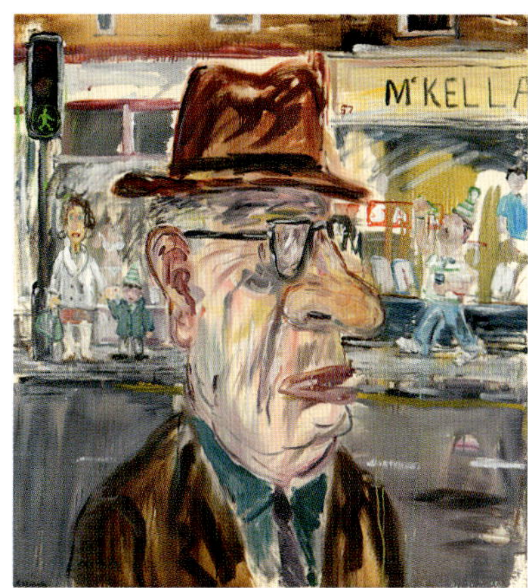

Kondracki, Henry b.1953
Old Man 1991
oil on canvas 137.5 x 122
3568

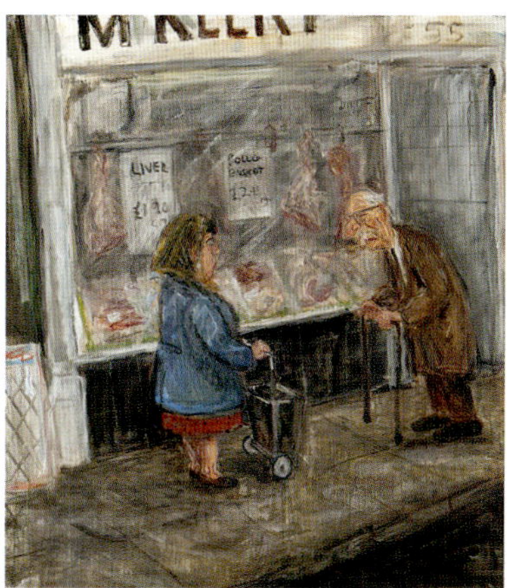

Kondracki, Henry b.1953
Passing the Butcher Shop 1994–1995
oil on canvas 122.2 x 107
3569

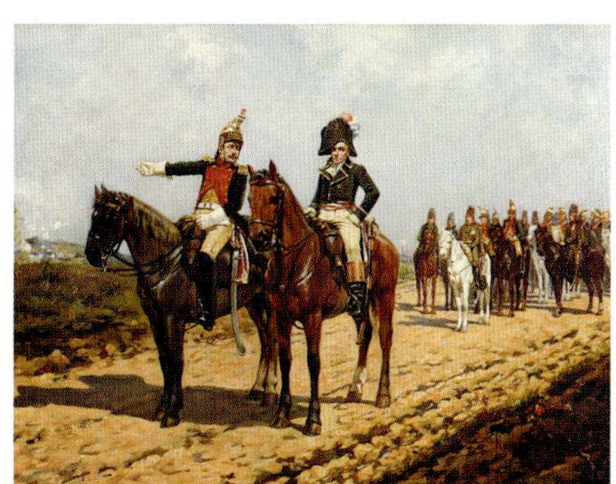

Kratké, Charles Louis 1848–1921
French Army on the March 1877
oil on canvas 53 x 70.5
2602

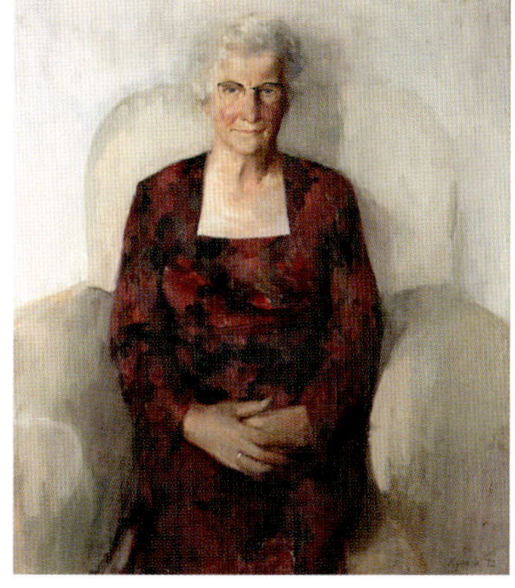

Kynoch, Kathryn b.1942
Lillian McDonald, Headmistress of Park School (1944–1962) c.1962
oil on canvas 100 x 90
ME.2007.1.5

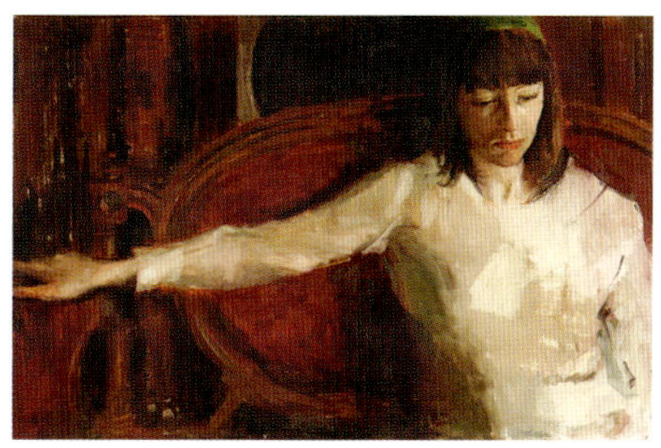

Kynoch, Kathryn b.1942
Girl in a White Blouse 1966
oil on canvas 60.6 x 91.1
3244

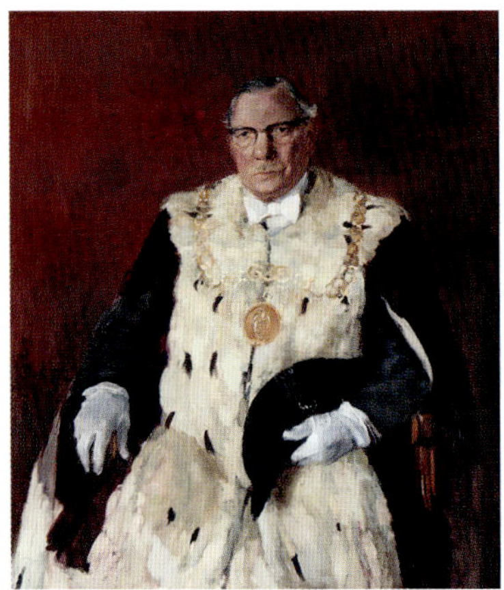

Kynoch, Kathryn b.1942
*Sir Donald Liddle, Lord Provost of Glasgow
(1969–1972)* 1974
oil on canvas 116.3 x 96.5
3312

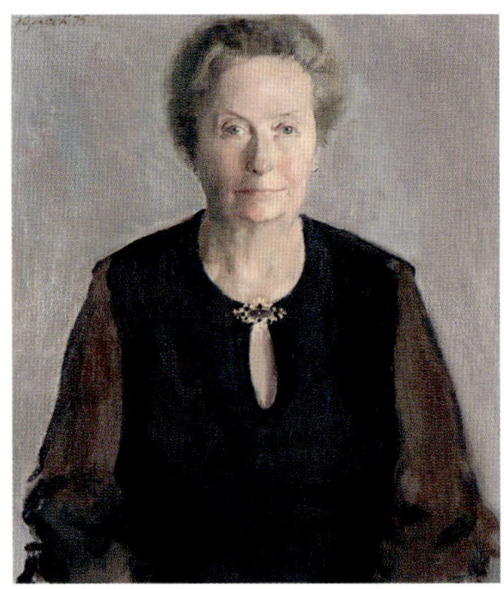

Kynoch, Kathryn b.1942
*Joan Lightwood, Headmistress of Park School
(1962–1974)* c.1974
oil on canvas 88 x 77
ME.2007.1.3

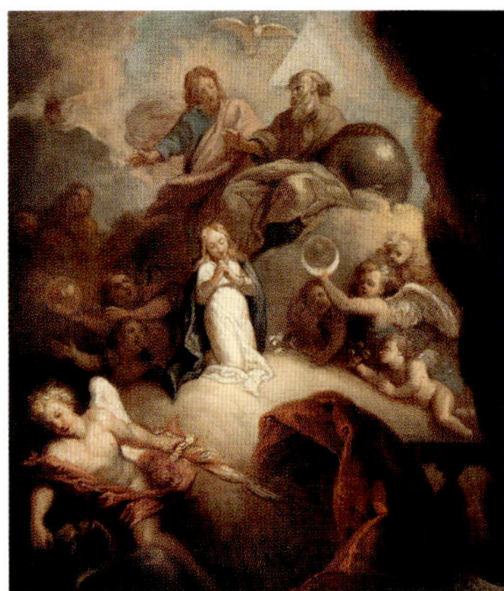

La Fosse, Charles de 1636–1716
The Assumption of the Virgin c.1700–1716
oil on canvas 43.8 x 35
268

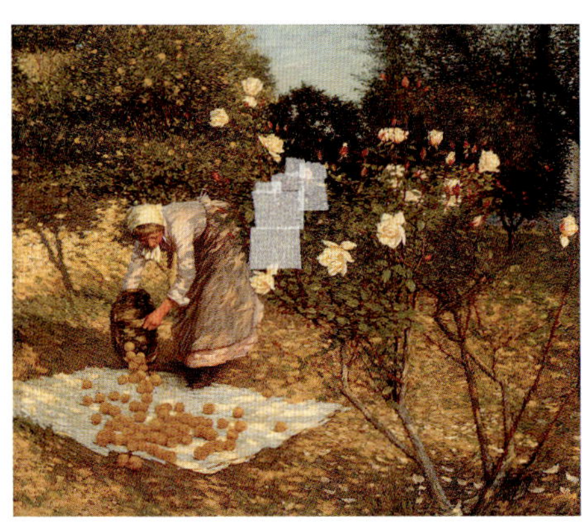

La Thangue, Henry Herbert 1859–1929
Provençal Winter c.1903
oil on canvas 78.7 x 94
1084

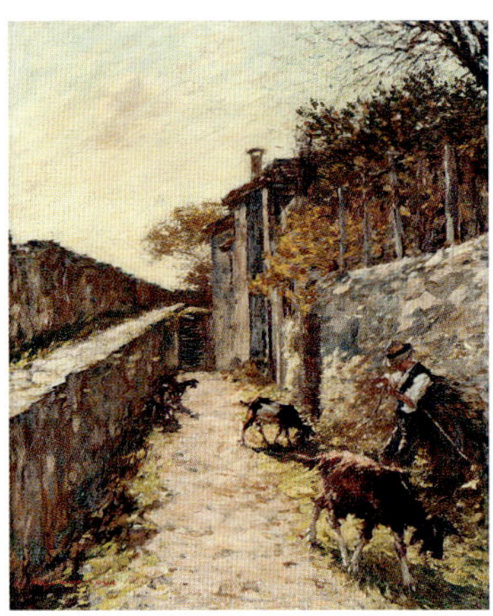

La Thangue, Henry Herbert 1859–1929
On the Ramparts
oil on canvas 63.5 x 50.8
2291

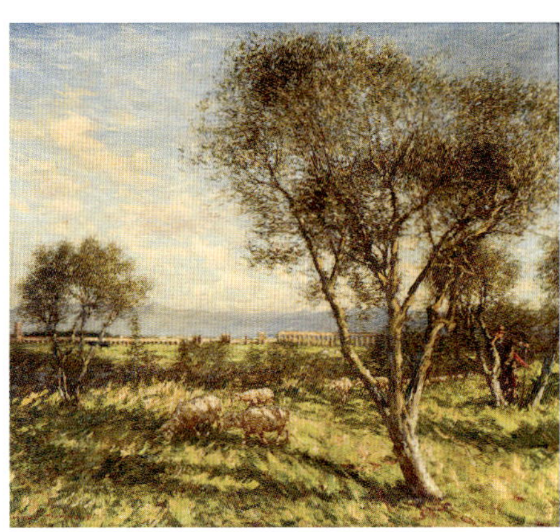

La Thangue, Henry Herbert 1859–1929
Roman Campagna
oil on canvas 73.7 x 82.6
2290

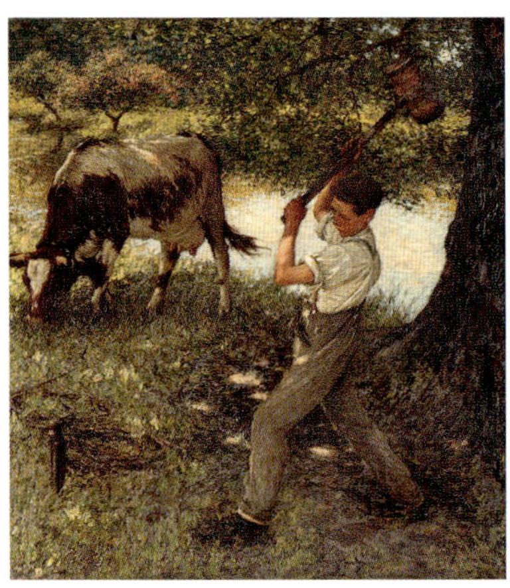

La Thangue, Henry Herbert 1859–1929
Stumping the Cow
oil on canvas 110.5 x 101.6
2292

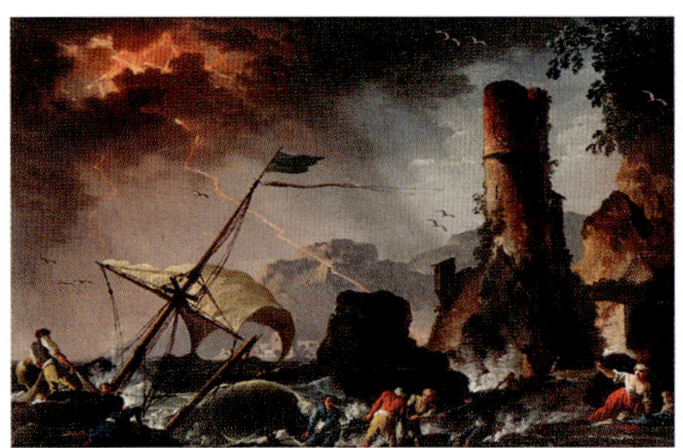

**Lacroix de Marseille, Charles FranÁois
(attributed to)** c.1700–1782
A Storm c.1755–1770
oil on canvas 25.4 x 36.8
1589

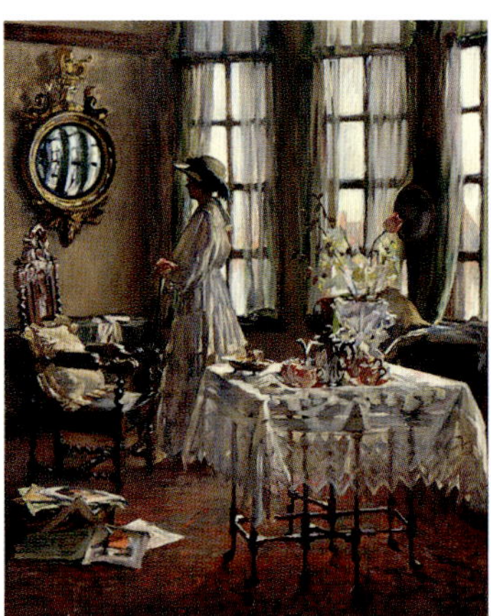

Laing, Annie Rose 1869–1946
The Mirror c.1919
oil on canvas 66 x 53.3
1474

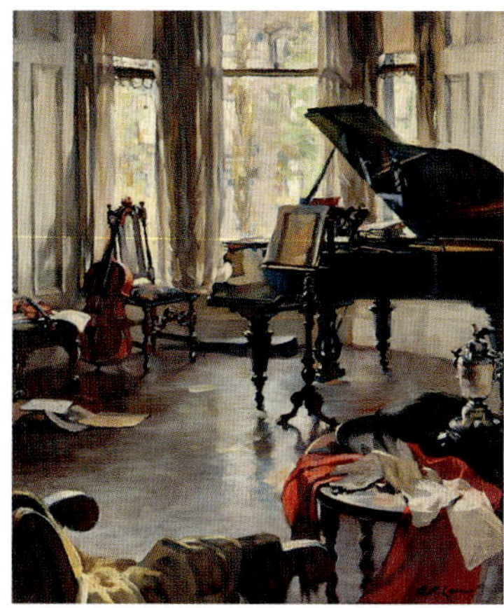

Laing, Annie Rose 1869–1946
After Rehearsal c.1922
oil on canvas 74 x 61.4
3098

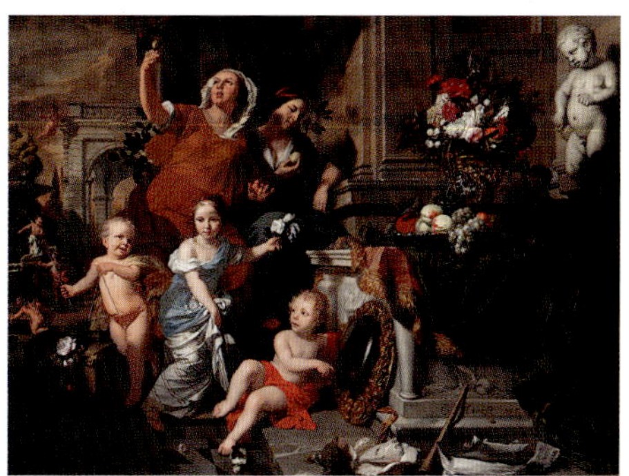

Lairesse, Gerard de 1640–1711
An Allegory of the Senses 1668
oil on canvas 137.2 x 182.9
3635

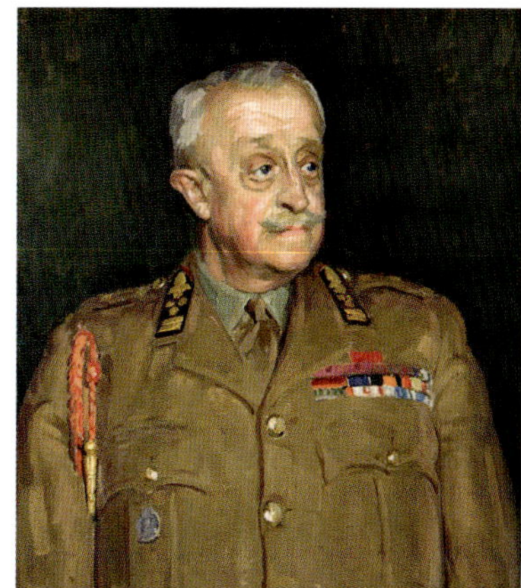

Lamb, Henry 1883–1960
Lieutenant General Le Chevalier Van Strydonck de Burkel (1879–1961)
c.1940–1945
oil on canvas 72.4 x 63.5
2751

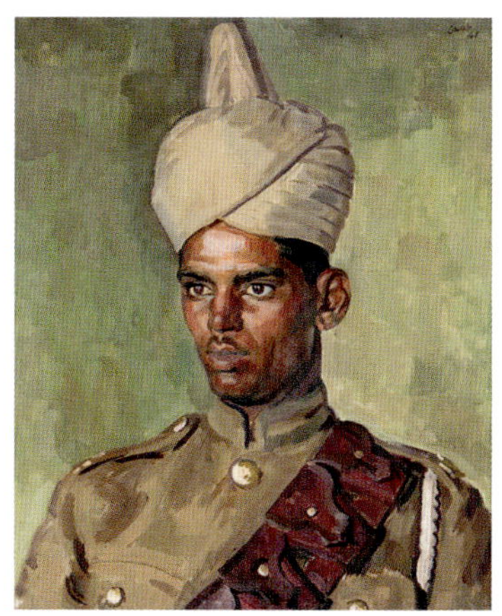

Lamb, Henry 1883–1960
Driver Abdul Ghani 1941
oil on canvas 61 x 50.8
2750

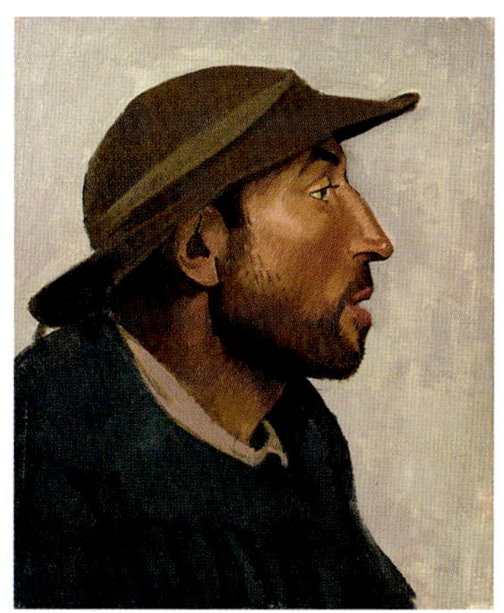

Lamb, Henry 1883–1960
Breton Peasant
oil on canvas 43.2 x 35.6
1753

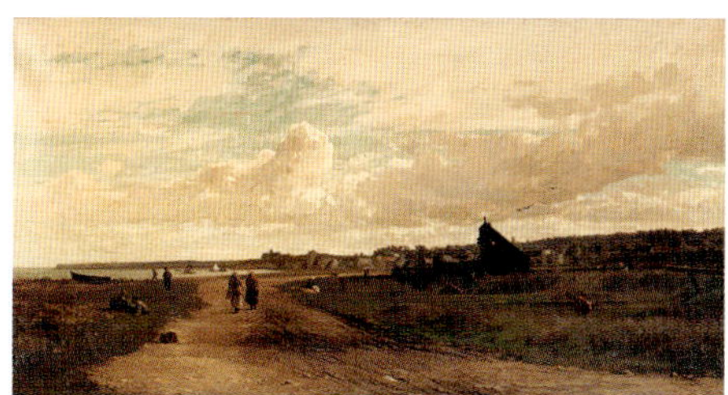

Lambinet, Emile Charles 1815–1877
Coast Scene 1867
oil on canvas 74.3 x 139.4
1157

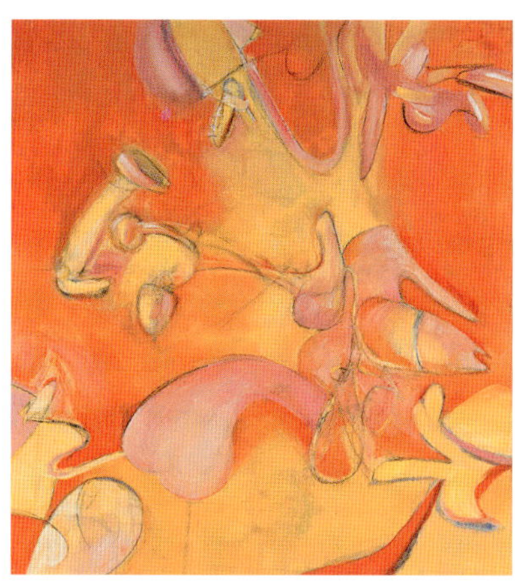

Lander, Heather Rose b.1976
Take a Seat 1999
acrylic on canvas 123 x 110.5
3676

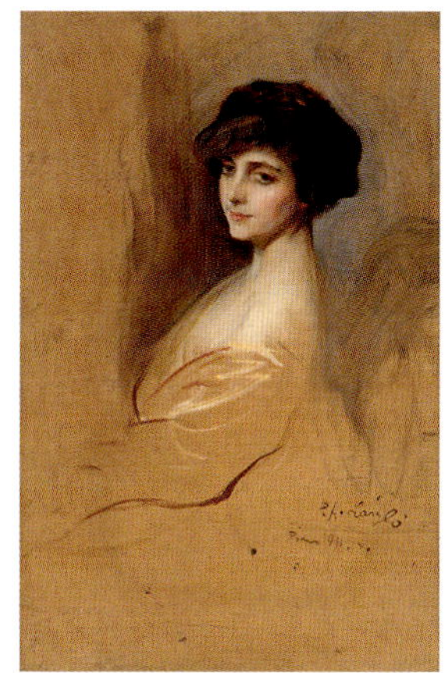

László, Philip Alexius de 1869–1937
Portrait Study: Madame Montague Yaunez
1911
oil on strawboard 97.8 x 63.5
1332

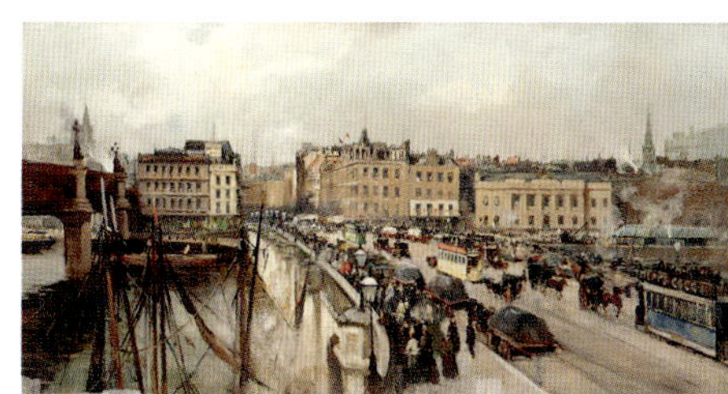

Lauder, Charles James 1841–1920
Glasgow Bridge c.1890
oil on canvas 61 x 109.2
OG.1963.44

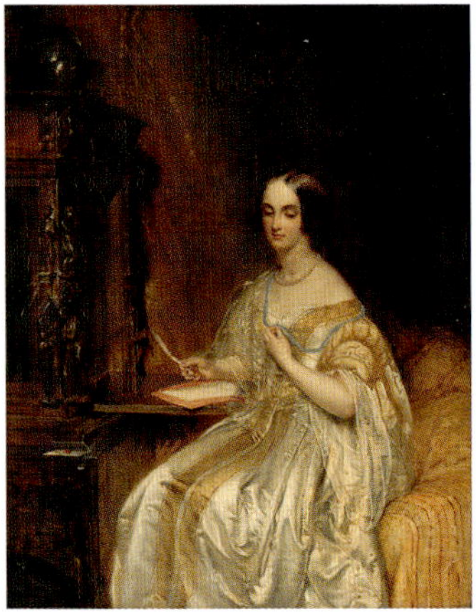

Lauder, Robert Scott 1803–1869
Portrait of a Lady
oil on canvas 63.5 x 49.5
350

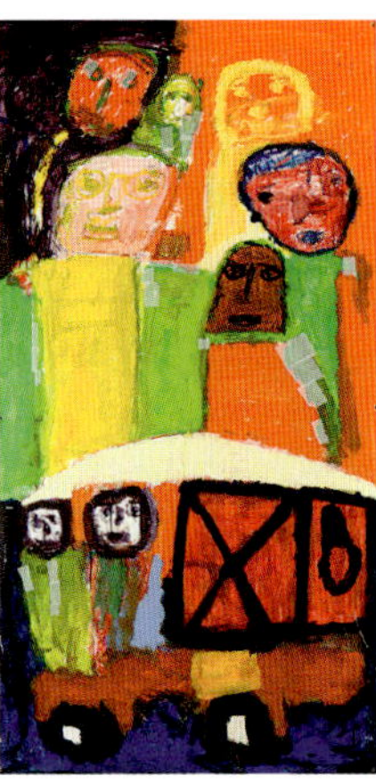

Laughlin, Alex b.1930
Untitled c.1992
acrylic on board 244 x 122.2
3497

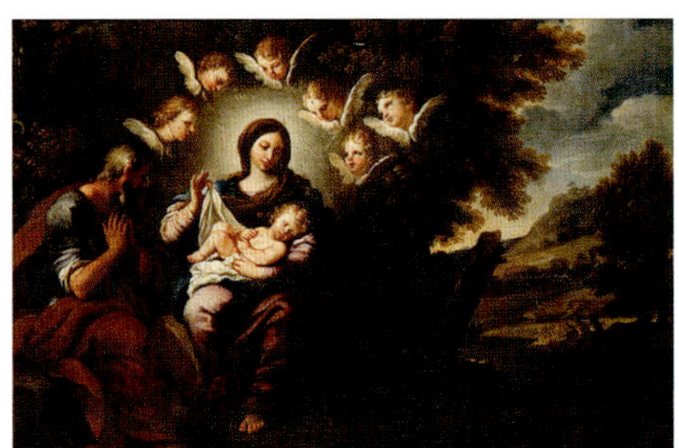

Lauri, Filippo 1623–1694
The Holy Family c.1670–1690
oil on canvas 24.4 x 34
161

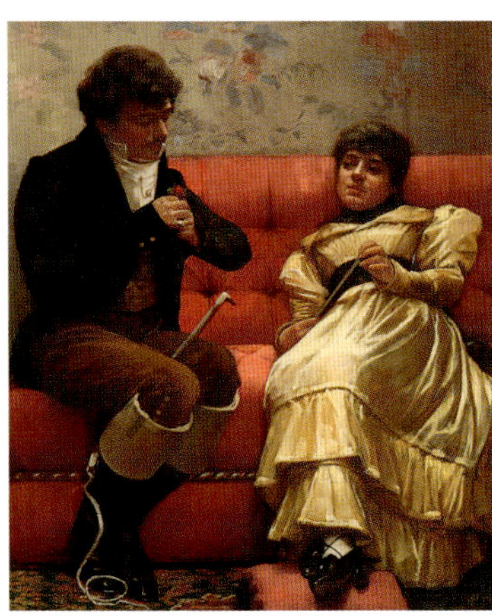

Lavery, John 1856–1941
A Conquest, a Heart for a Rose 1882
oil on canvas 61 x 50.8
2365

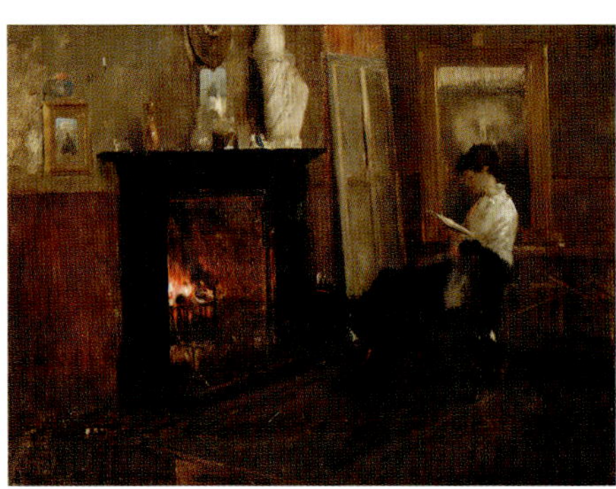

Lavery, John 1856–1941
A Quiet Day in the Studio 1885
oil on canvas 41.9 x 52.1
2364

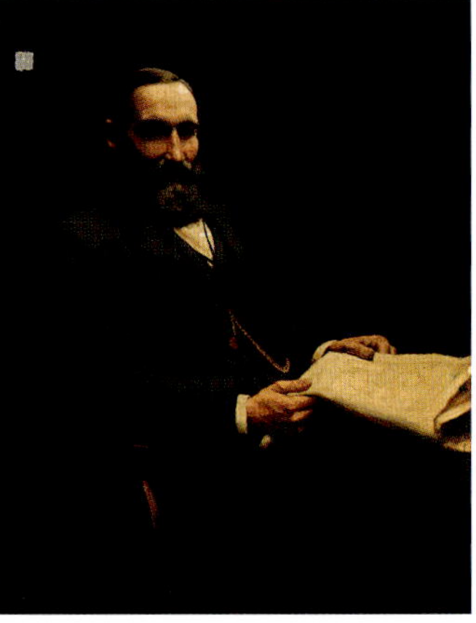

Lavery, John 1856–1941
George U. Baird 1885
oil on canvas 127 x 101.6
2361

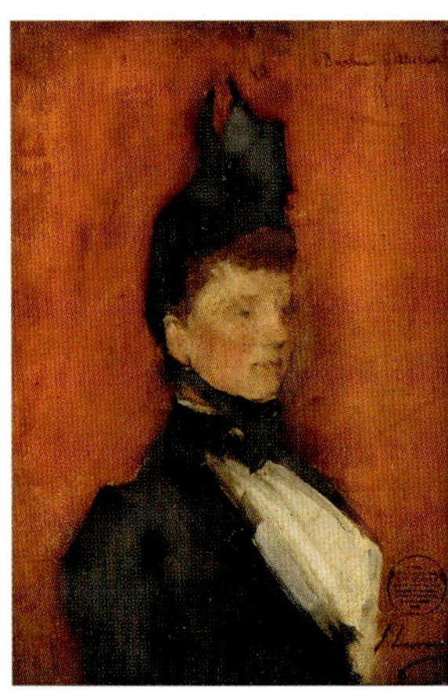

Lavery, John 1856–1941
Duchess of Abercorn (sketch) 1888
oil on panel 35.5 x 25.7
1933

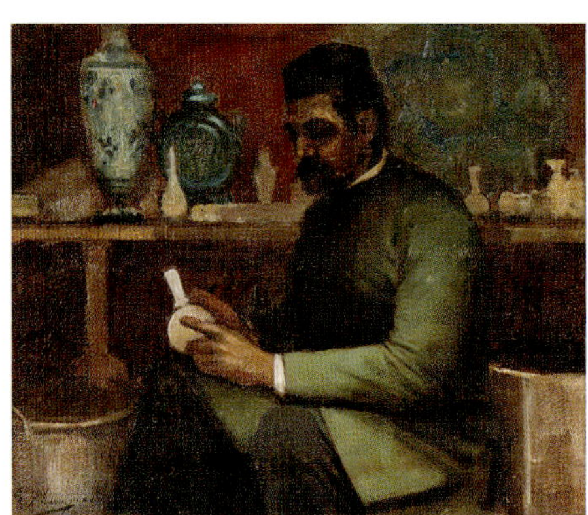

Lavery, John 1856–1941
Potter at Work 1888
oil on canvas 38.1 x 45.7
2835

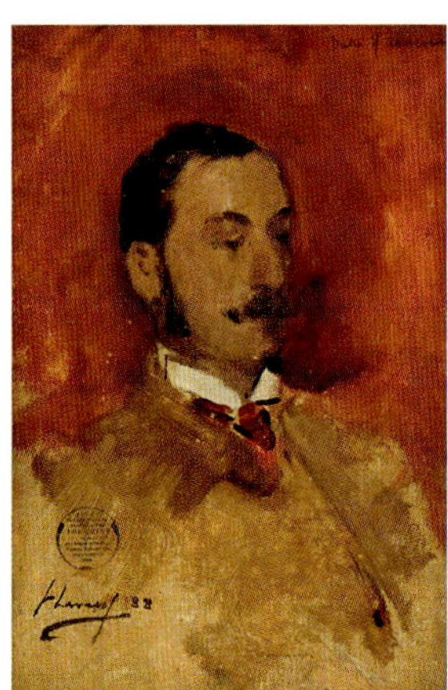

Lavery, John 1856–1941
The Duke of Abercorn, KP (sketch) 1888
oil on panel 35.6 x 25.4
1932

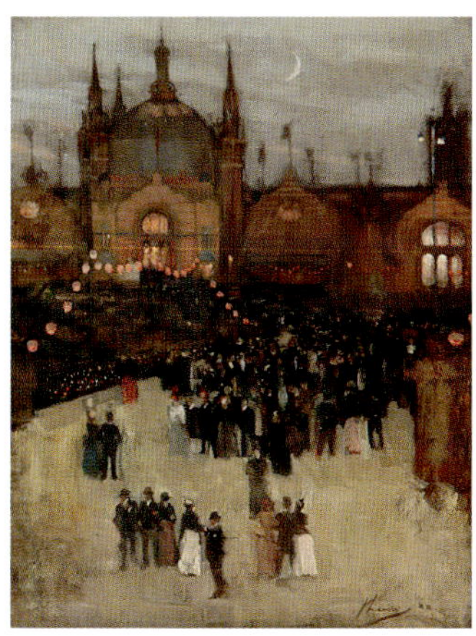

Lavery, John 1856–1941
The Glasgow International Exhibition 1888
oil on canvas 61 x 45.7
2504

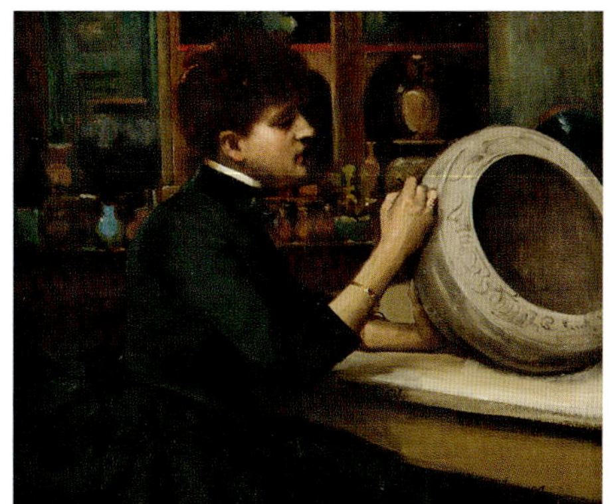

Lavery, John 1856–1941
Woman Painting a Pot 1888
oil on canvas 38.1 x 45.7
2834

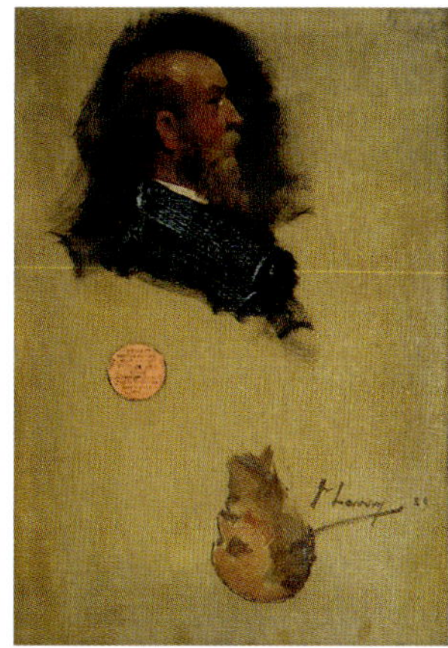

Lavery, John 1856–1941
Alexander Clapperton (sketch) 1889
oil on canvas 35.5 x 25.4
1954

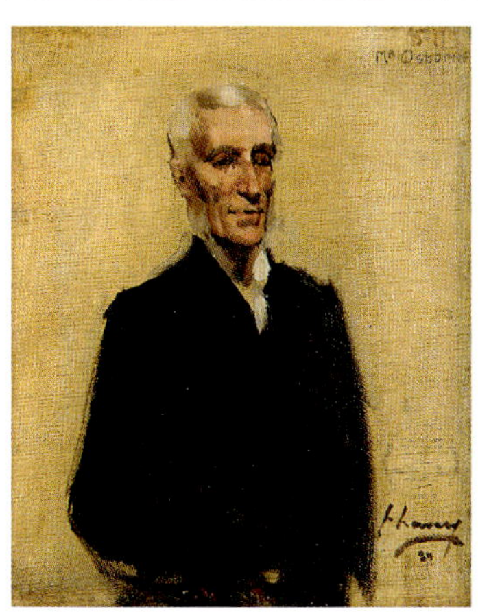

Lavery, John 1856–1941
Alexander Osborne (sketch) 1889
oil on canvas 25.4 x 20.3
2016

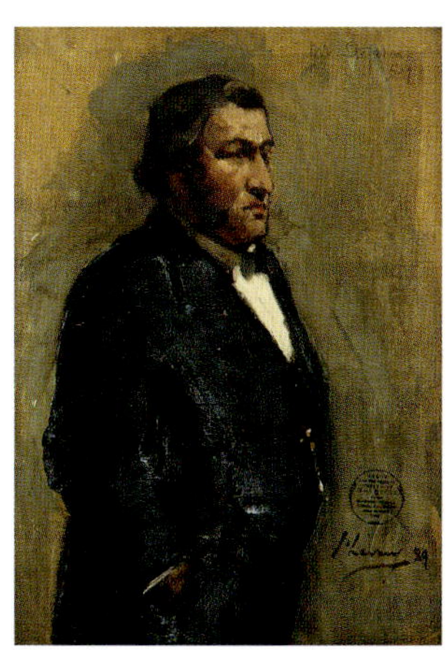

Lavery, John 1856–1941
Alexander Stephen (sketch) 1889
oil on canvas 35.5 x 25.4
2035

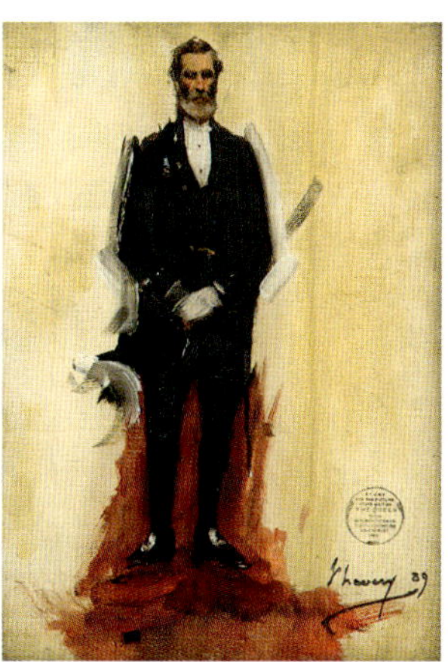

Lavery, John 1856–1941
*Bailie James Hunter Dickson (b.1824),
Vice-Chairman of Glasgow International
Exhibition (1888)* (sketch) 1889
oil on canvas 35.6 x 25.4
1967

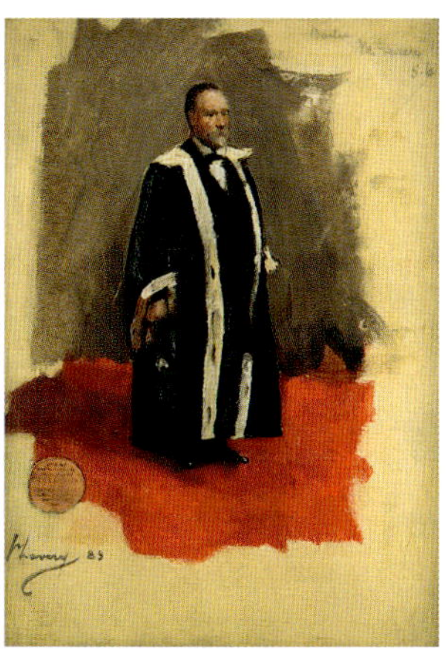

Lavery, John 1856–1941
Bailie MacLaren (sketch) 1889
oil on canvas 35.5 x 25.4
2007

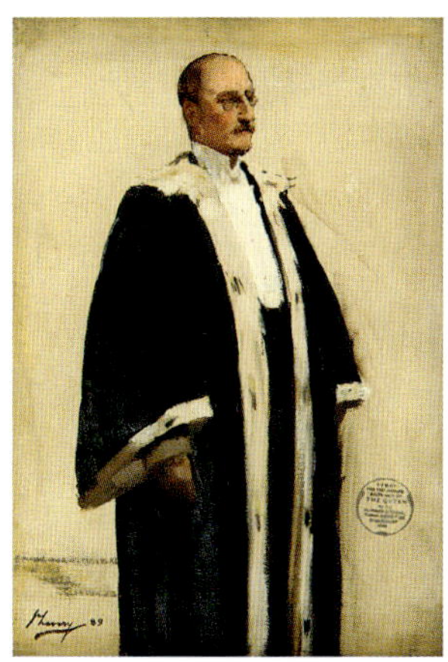

Lavery, John 1856–1941
Bailie Simons (sketch) 1889
oil on canvas 35.5 x 25.4
2033

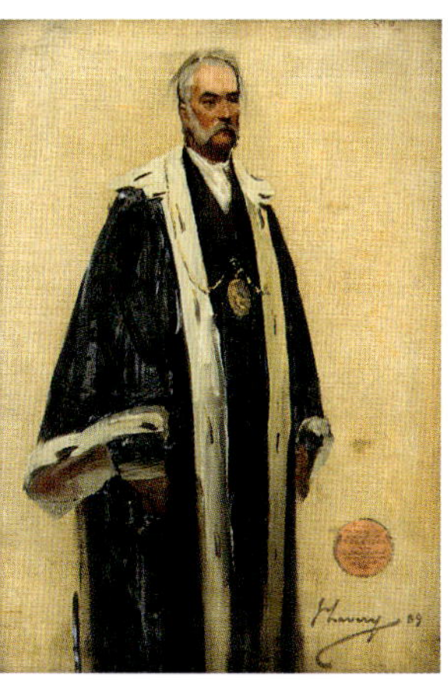

Lavery, John 1856–1941
Bailie Watson (sketch) 1889
oil on canvas 35.6 x 25.4
2041

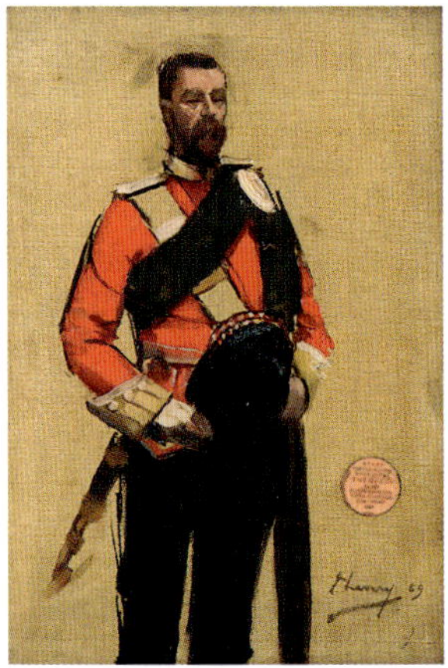

Lavery, John 1856–1941
Captain Shaw, Contractor (sketch) 1889
oil on canvas 35.5 x 25.4
2028

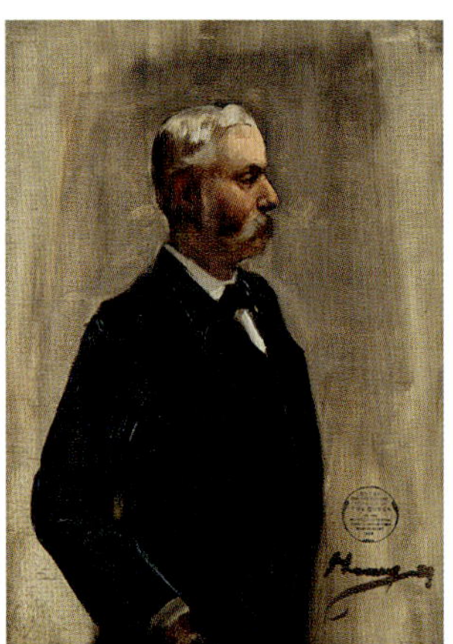

Lavery, John 1856–1941
Charles Howatson (sketch) 1889
oil on canvas 35.5 x 25.4
1986

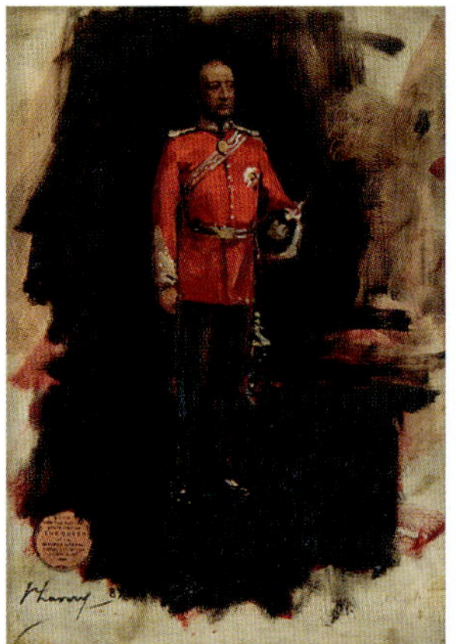

Lavery, John 1856–1941
*Colonel Sir D. Matheson, KCB, Grand
Marshal* (sketch) 1889
oil on canvas 35.5 x 25.4
1996

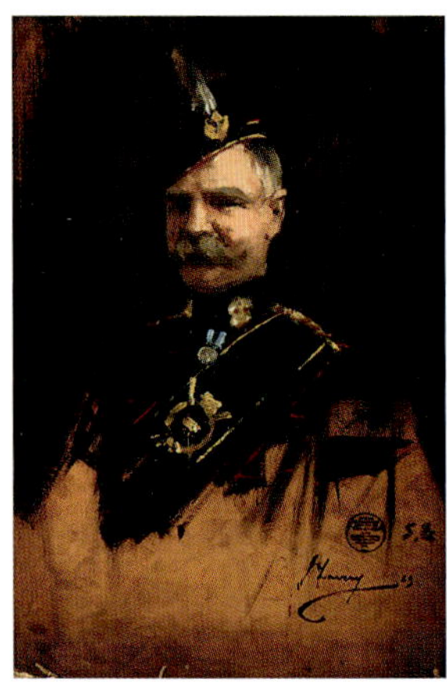

Lavery, John 1856–1941
Colonel Walker, ADC (sketch) 1889
oil on canvas 35.5 x 25.4
2039

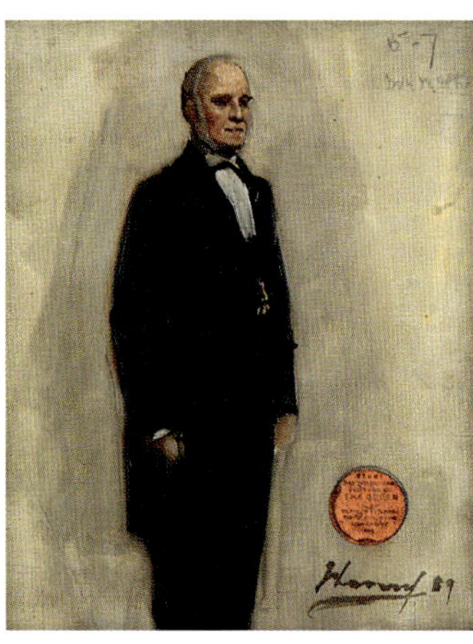

Lavery, John 1856–1941
Duncan McPherson (sketch) 1889
oil on panel 25.4 x 20.2
2013

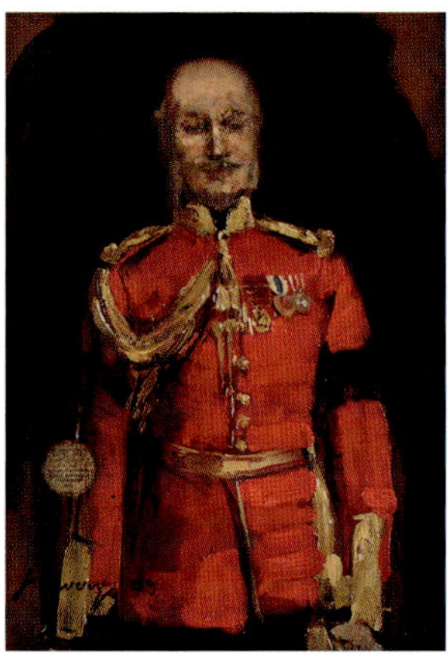

Lavery, John 1856–1941
General Gardiner (sketch) 1889
oil on canvas 35.5 x 25.4
1975

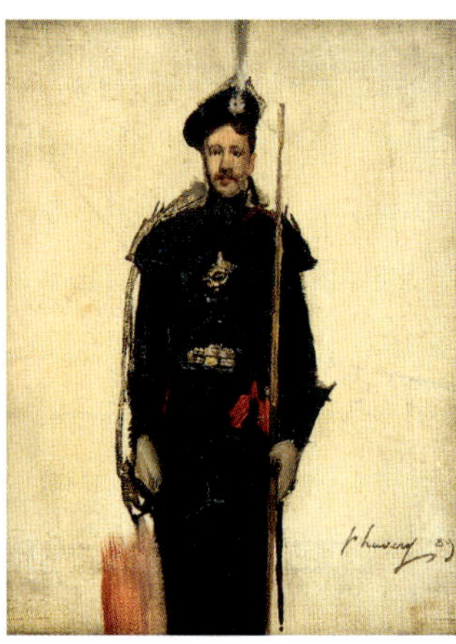

Lavery, John 1856–1941
Harry Younger (sketch) 1889
oil on canvas 25.5 x 20.3
2046

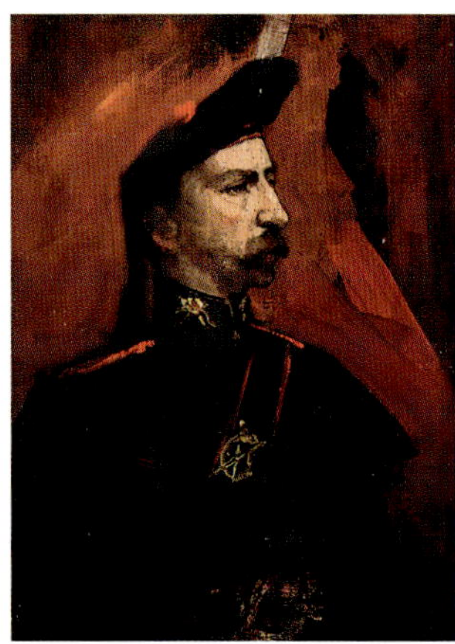

Lavery, John 1856–1941
Henry Cook (sketch) 1889
oil on canvas 35.5 x 25.4
1962

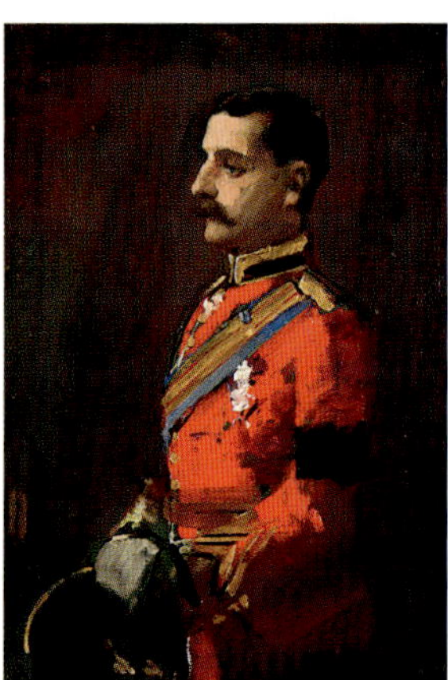

Lavery, John 1856–1941
*HRH Prince Henry of Battenberg (1858–1896),
KG* (sketch) 1889
oil on canvas 53.3 x 35.6
1940

Facing page: Bellini, Giovanni, 1431/1436–1516, *Virgin and Child*, c.1485–1488 (p. 28)

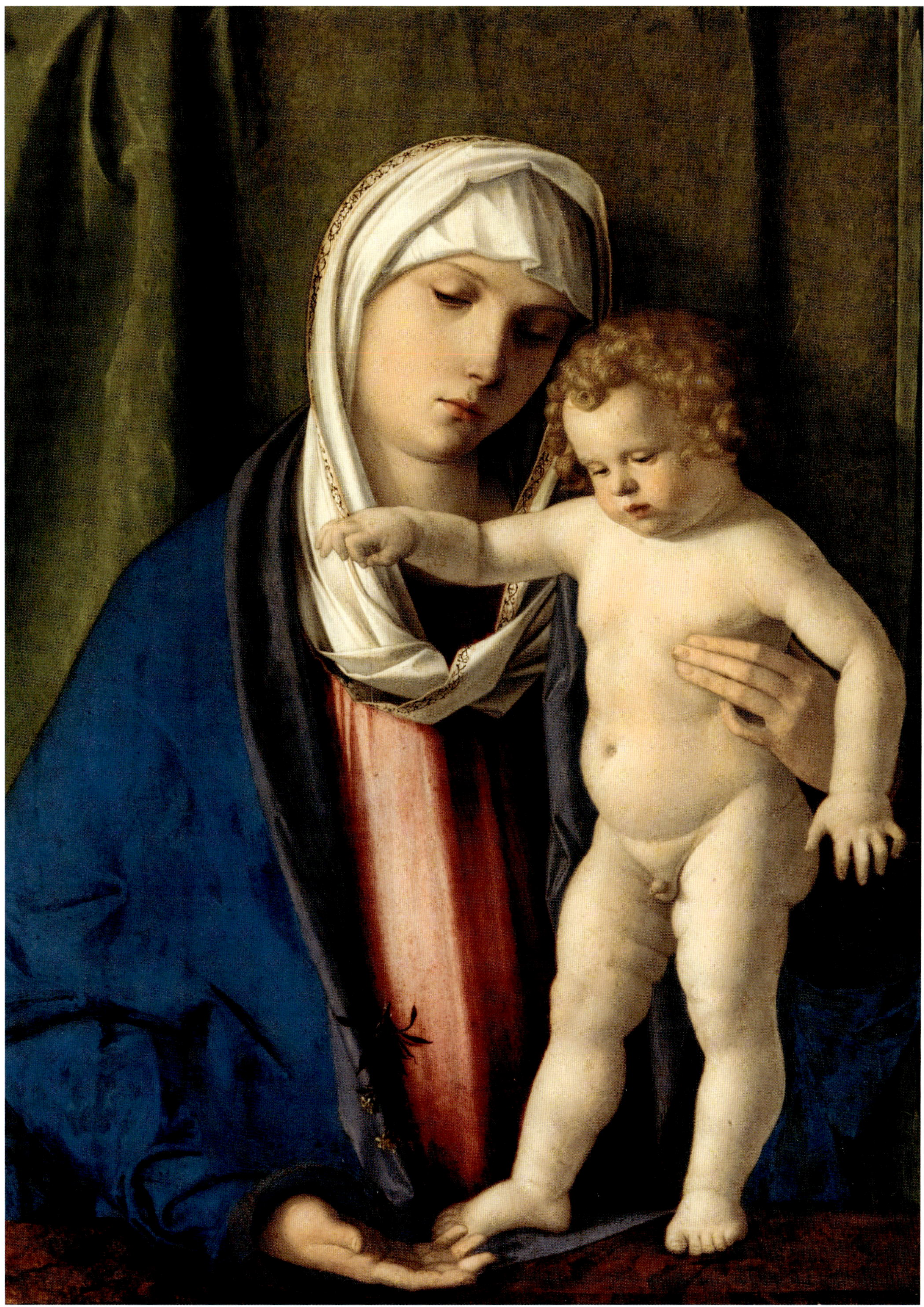

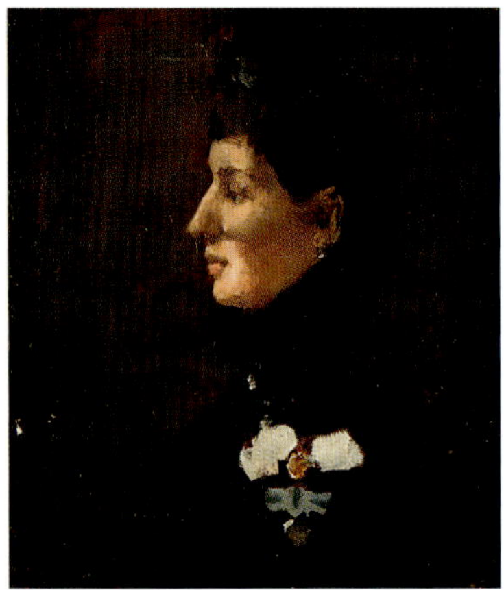

Lavery, John 1856–1941
HRH Princess Alix of Hesse (1872–1918)
(sketch) 1889
oil on canvas 35.8 x 30.7
1985

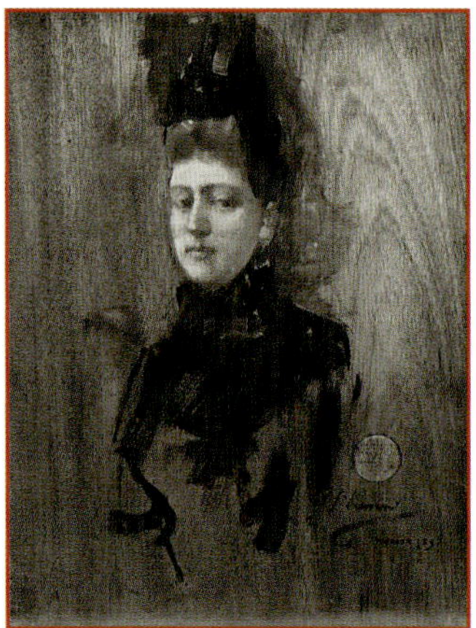

Lavery, John 1856–1941
HRH Princess Henry (Beatrice) of Battenberg
(1857–1944) (sketch) 1889
oil on panel 40.6 x 29.8
1941
STOLEN

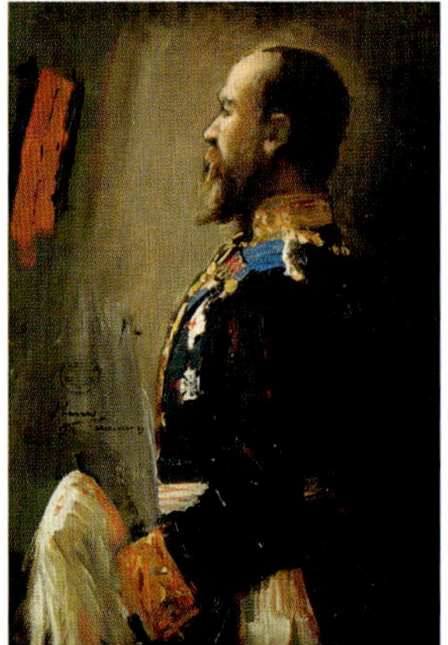

Lavery, John 1856–1941
HRH the Grand Duke of Hesse, KG
(sketch) 1889
oil on canvas 53.3 x 35.5
1983

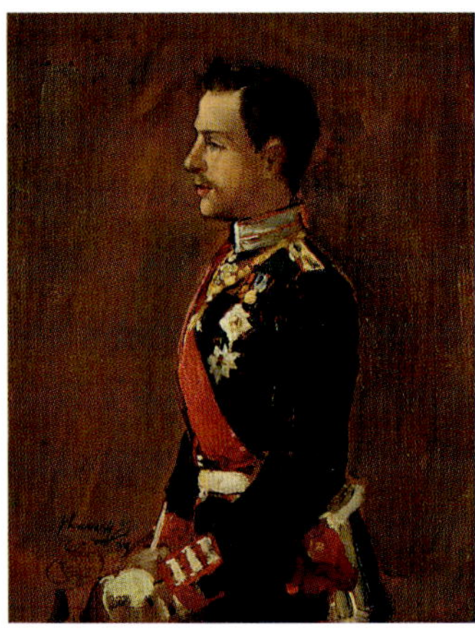

Lavery, John 1856–1941
HRH the Hereditary Grand Duke of Hesse
(sketch) 1889
oil on canvas 45.7 x 35.7
1984

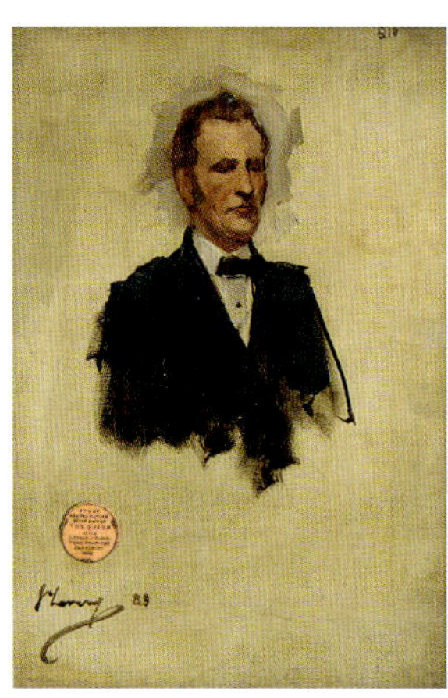

Lavery, John 1856–1941
Hugh Brechin (b.1846) (sketch) 1889
oil on canvas 35.5 x 25.4
1945

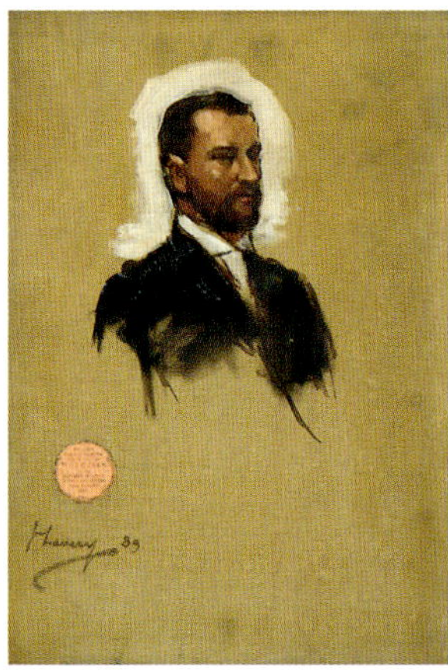

Lavery, John 1856–1941
J. F. X. King (1855–1933) (sketch) 1889
oil on canvas 35.5 x 25.4
1987

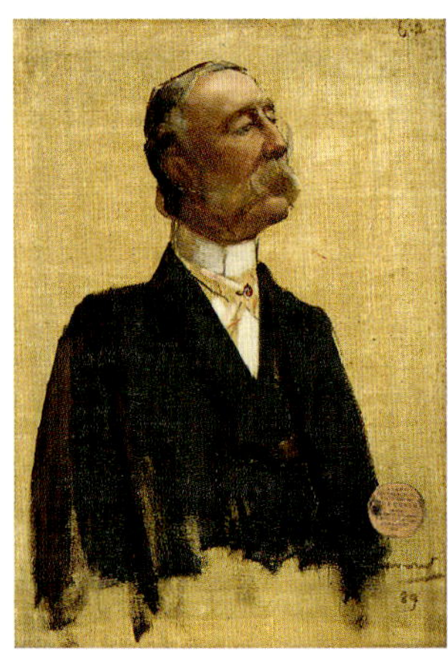

Lavery, John 1856–1941
J. L. Mitchell (sketch) 1889
oil on canvas 35.5 x 25.4
2001

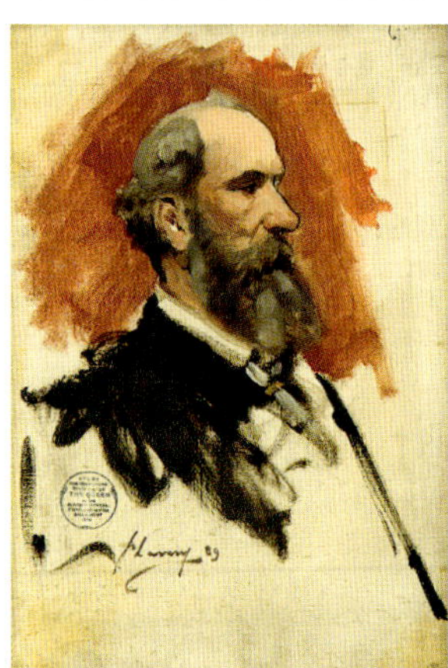

Lavery, John 1856–1941
J. Wyllie Guild (sketch) 1889
oil on canvas 35.5 x 25.4
1979

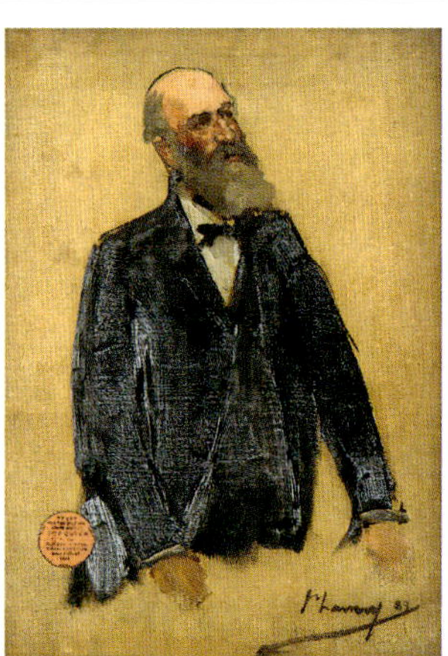

Lavery, John 1856–1941
James B. Russell (1837–1904) (sketch) 1889
oil on canvas 35.5 x 25.4
2026

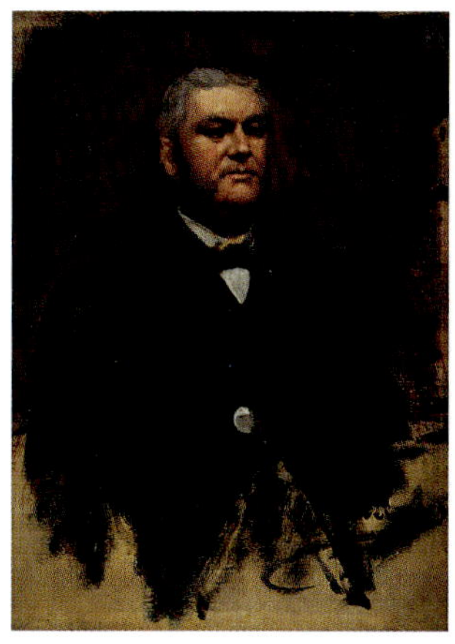

Lavery, John 1856–1941
James Barr, Architectural Engineer
(sketch) 1889
oil on canvas 35.5 x 25.4
1939

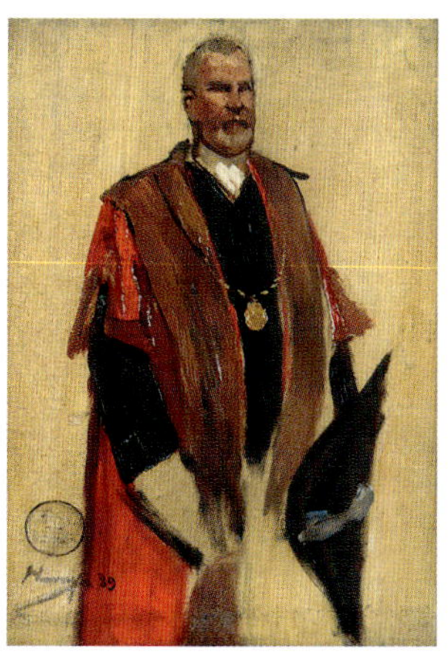

Lavery, John 1856–1941
James Black, Provost of Elgin (sketch) 1889
oil on canvas 35.5 x 25.4
1943

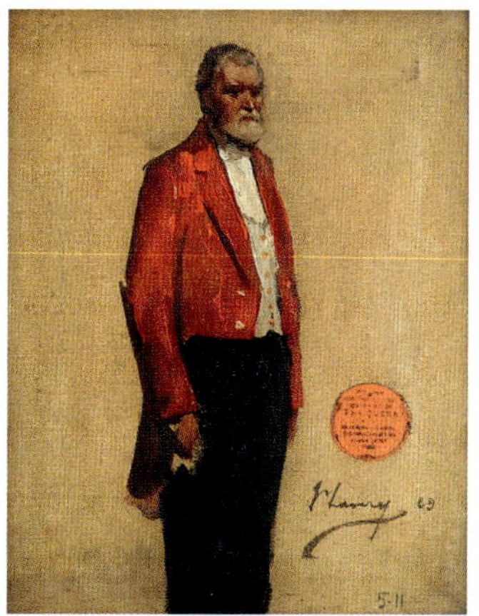

Lavery, John 1856–1941
James Brown, Council Officer (sketch) 1889
oil on canvas 25.4 x 20.3
1946

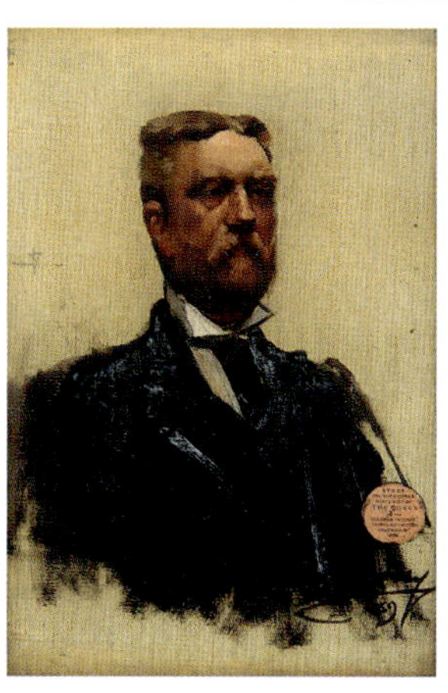

Lavery, John 1856–1941
James Muir (sketch) 1889
oil on canvas 33 x 22.8
2003

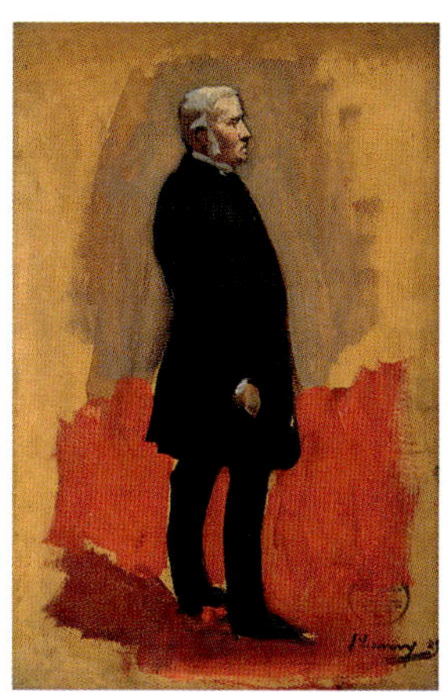

Lavery, John 1856–1941
James Murray (sketch) 1889
oil on canvas 35.7 x 22.8
2005

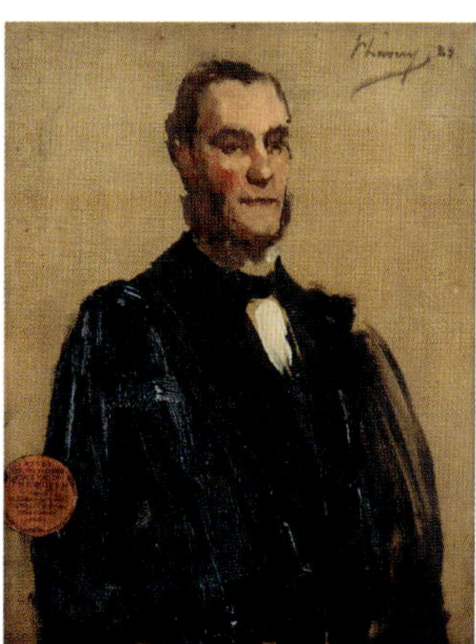

Lavery, John 1856–1941
James Nicol (1833–1911), City Chamberlain,
Glasgow (sketch) 1889
oil on canvas 25.4 x 20.3
2015

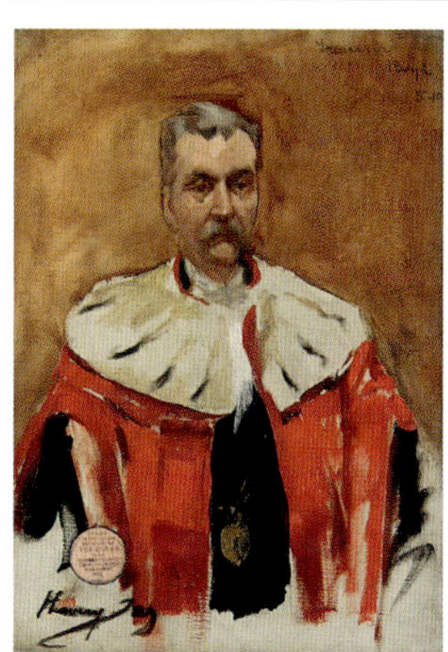

Lavery, John 1856–1941
John Boyd, City Treasurer, Edinburgh
(sketch) 1889
oil on canvas 35.5 x 25.4
1944

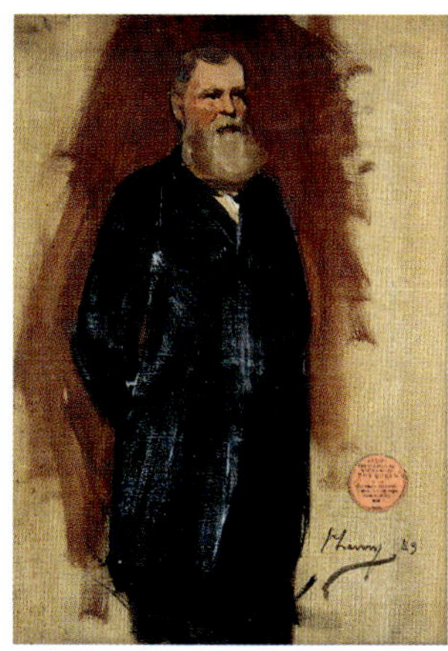

Lavery, John 1856–1941
John Filshill (sketch) 1889
oil on canvas 35.5 x 25.4
1973

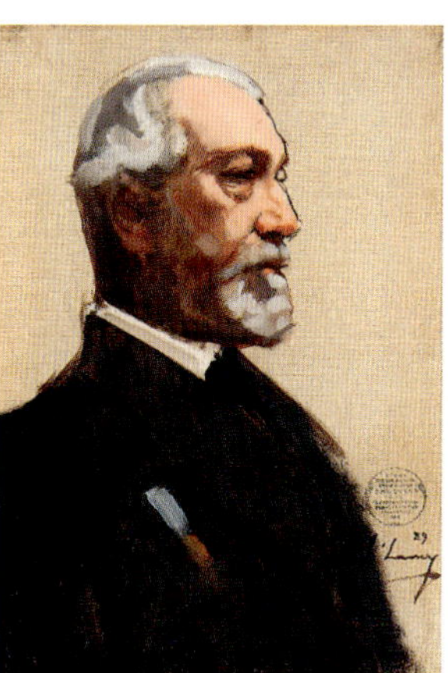

Lavery, John 1856–1941
John Muir of Deanston (1828–1903), 1st Bt,
Lord Provost of Glasgow (1889–1892)
(sketch) 1889
oil on canvas 35.5 x 25.4
2004

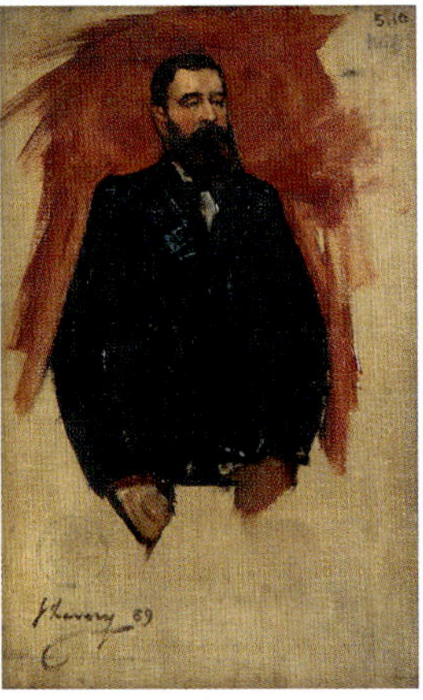

Lavery, John 1856–1941
John Neil (sketch) 1889
oil on canvas 30.4 x 20.3
2014

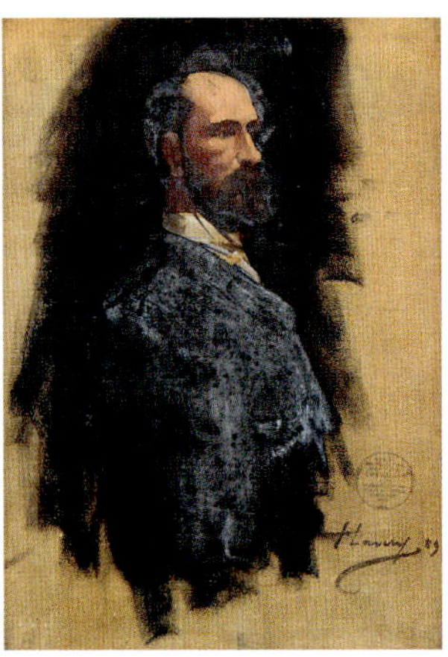

Lavery, John 1856–1941
John S. Templeton (sketch) 1889
oil on canvas 35.5 x 25.4
2036

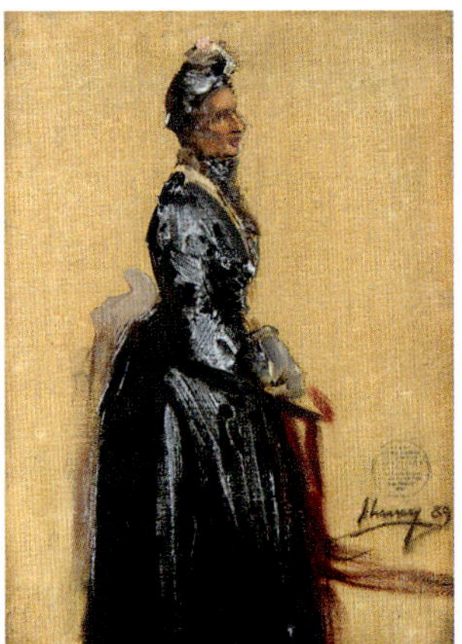

Lavery, John 1856–1941
Lady Octavia Shaw-Stewart (sketch) 1889
oil on canvas 35.5 x 25.4
2030

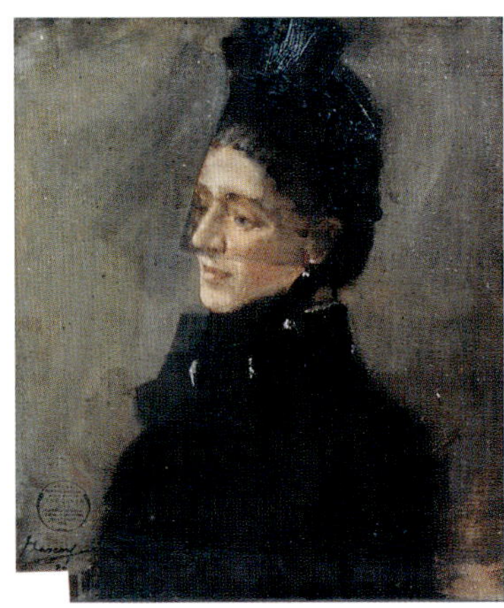

Lavery, John 1856–1941
Lady Southampton (sketch) 1889
oil on canvas 35.8 x 30.4
2034

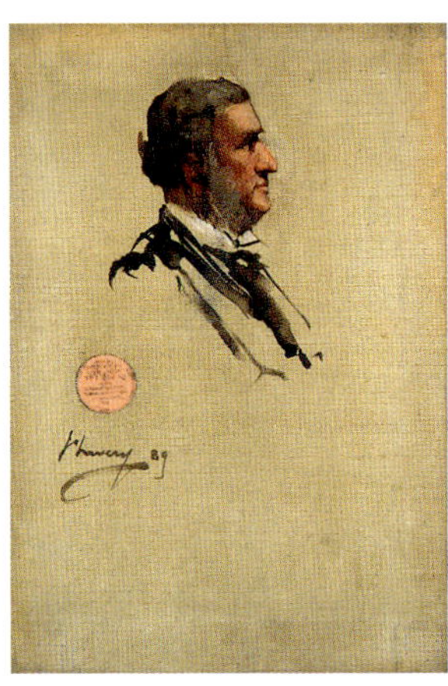

Lavery, John 1856–1941
Leonard Gow (1859–1936) (sketch) 1889
oil on canvas 35.5 x 25.4
1976

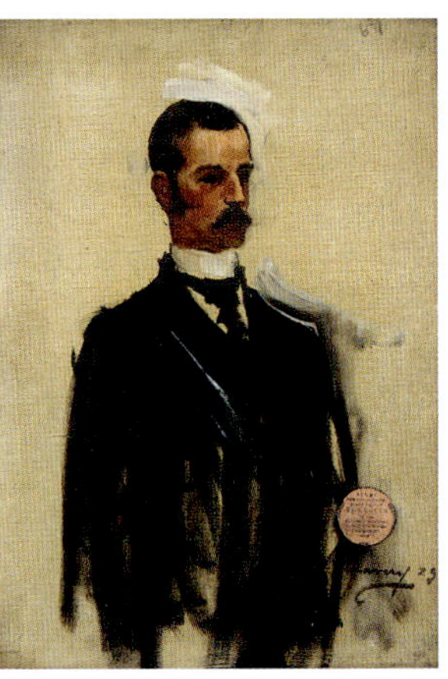

Lavery, John 1856–1941
*Lieutenant-General Douglas Mackinnon
Baillie Hamilton Cochrane (1852–1935), 12th
Earl of Dundonald, KGB, (…)* (sketch) 1889
oil on canvas 35.5 x 25.4
1968

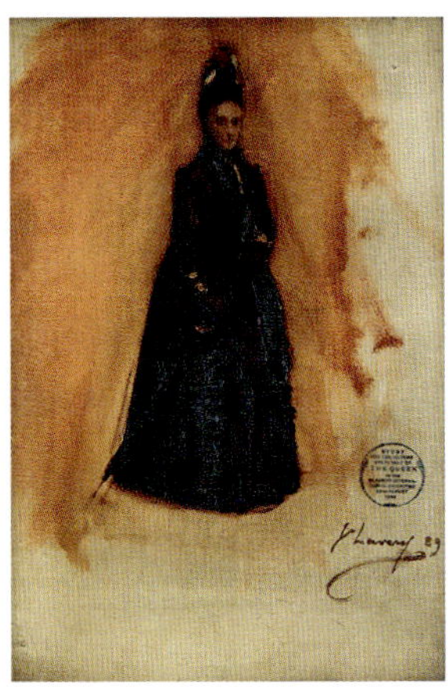

Lavery, John 1856–1941
Mrs Francis Powell (sketch) 1889
oil on canvas 33 x 23.2
2020

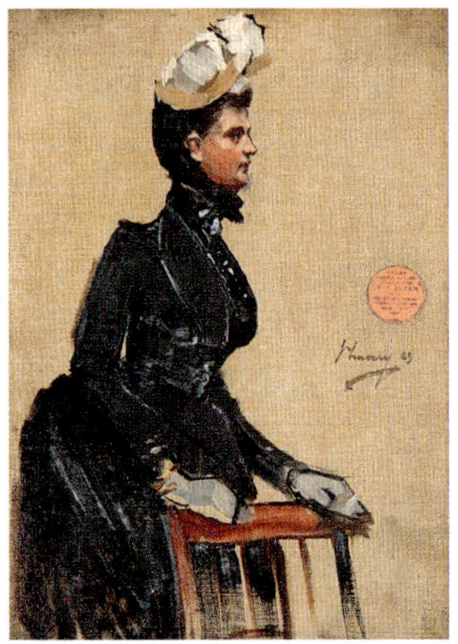

Lavery, John 1856–1941
Mrs John Shearer (sketch) 1889
oil on canvas 35.5 x 25.4
2032

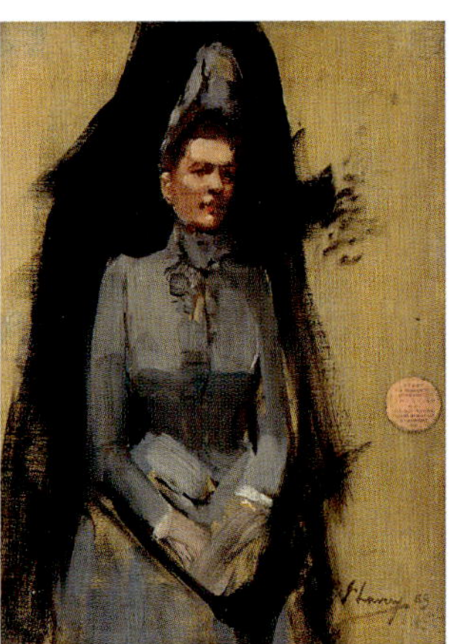

Lavery, John 1856–1941
Mrs Macleod (sketch) 1889
oil on canvas 35.5 x 25.4
2011

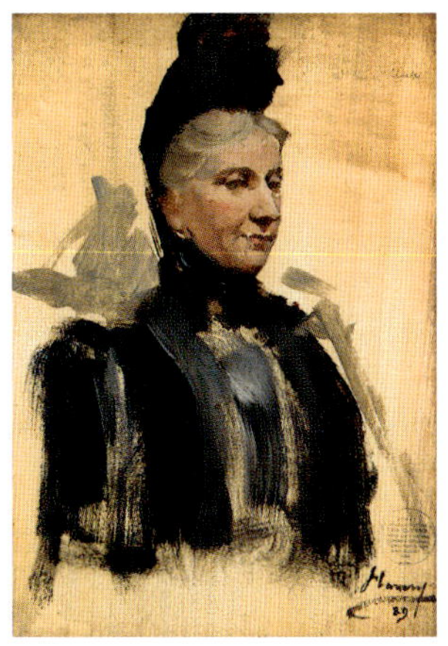

Lavery, John 1856–1941
Mrs Stewart Clark (sketch) 1889
oil on canvas 35.5 x 25.4
1958

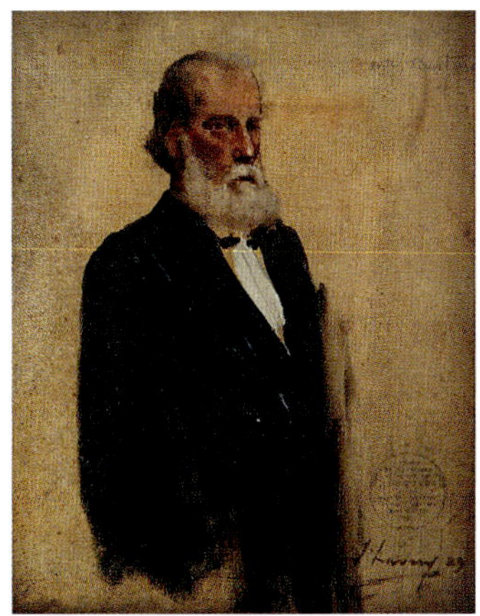

Lavery, John 1856–1941
Peter Bertram (sketch) 1889
oil on canvas 25.4 x 19.8
1942

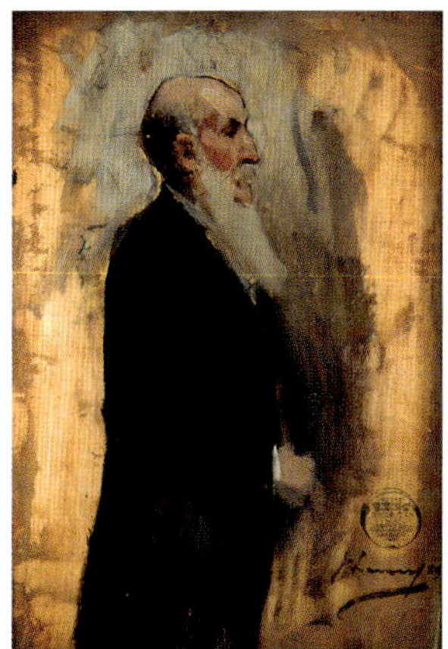

Lavery, John 1856–1941
Peter Denny (1821–1895) (sketch) 1889
oil on panel 35.5 x 24.6
1994

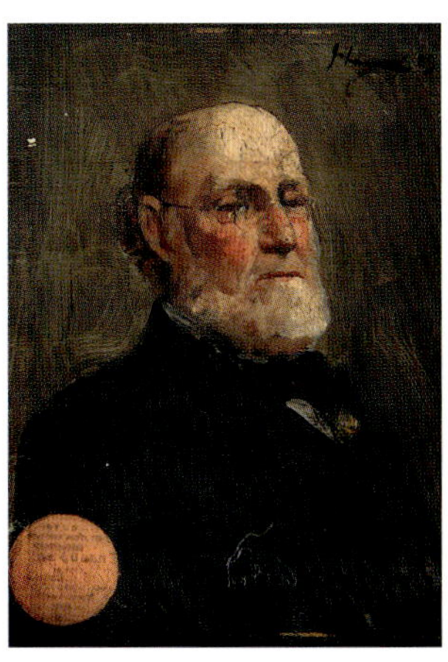

Lavery, John 1856–1941
Portrait of a Man (possibly John Martin)
(sketch) 1889
oil on panel 18.6 x 14.6
3539

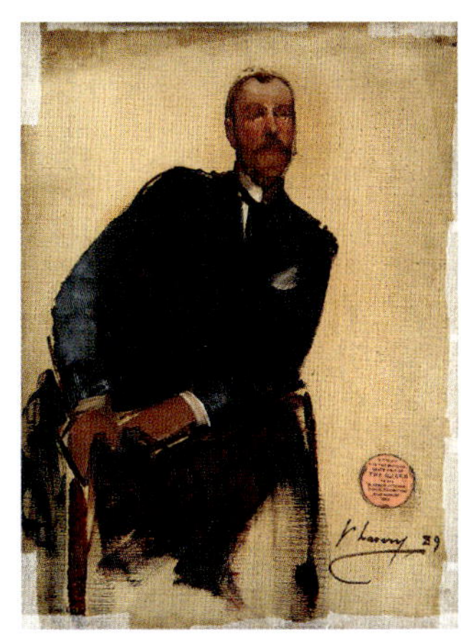

Lavery, John 1856–1941
Portrait of a Man (thought to be Archibald
Henderson) (sketch) 1889
oil on canvas 35.6 x 25.4
3537

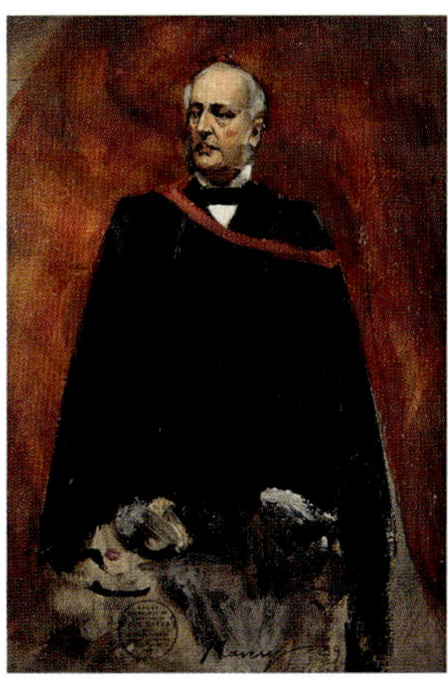

Lavery, John 1856–1941
*Professor Sir George H. B. Macleod (1828–
1892), MD, the Queen's Surgeon* (sketch)
1889
oil on canvas 35.5 x 25.4
2010

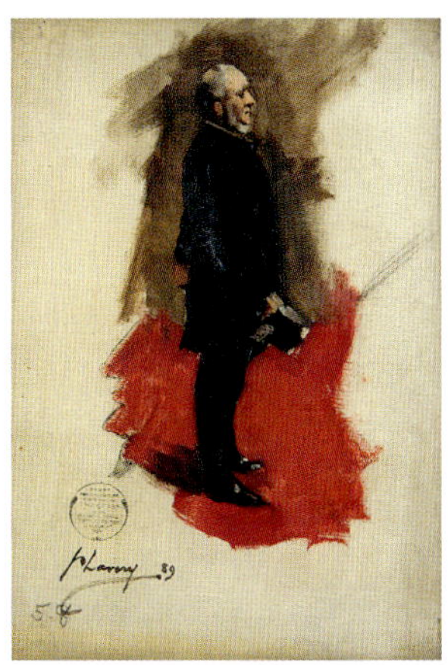

Lavery, John 1856–1941
*Reverend Donald Macleod, DD, the Queen's
Chaplin* (sketch) 1889
oil on canvas 35.5 x 25.4
2009

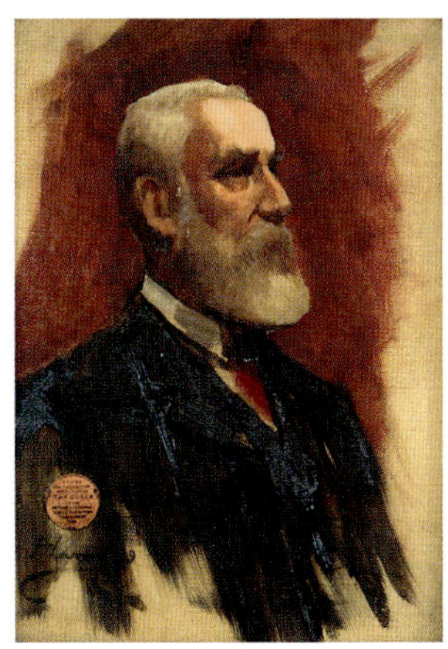

Lavery, John 1856–1941
Reverend F. L. Robertson, DD (sketch) 1889
oil on canvas 35.5 x 25.4
2023

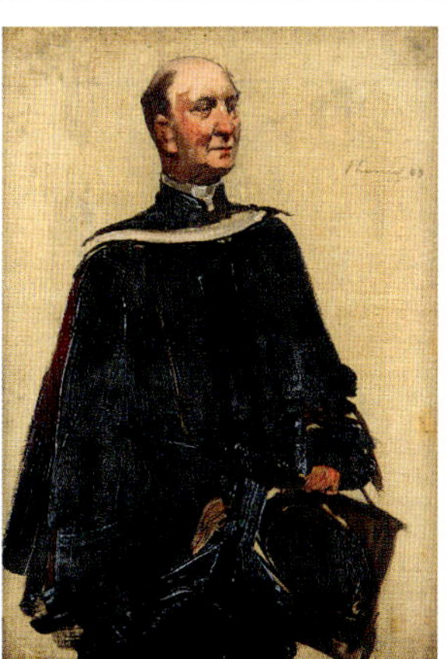

Lavery, John 1856–1941
Reverend George Stewart Burns, DD (sketch)
1889
oil on canvas 35.5 x 25.4
1949

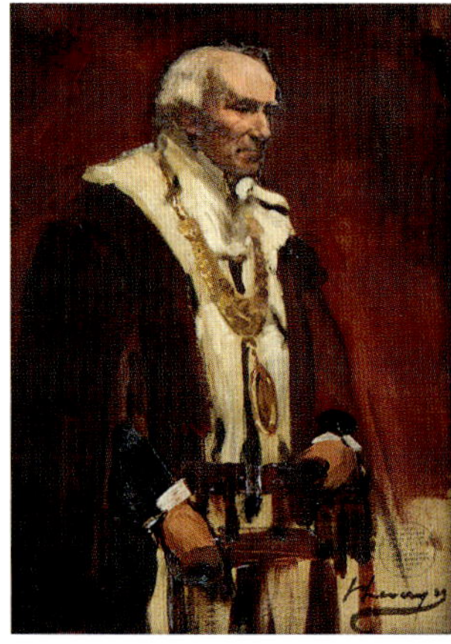

Lavery, John 1856–1941
Robert Cochrane, Provost of Paisley (sketch)
1889
oil on canvas 35.5 x 25.4
1959

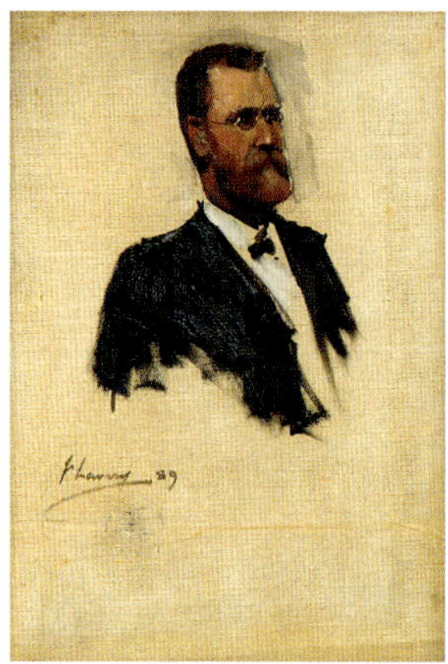

Lavery, John 1856–1941
Robert Graham (sketch) 1889
oil on canvas 35.5 x 25.4
1977

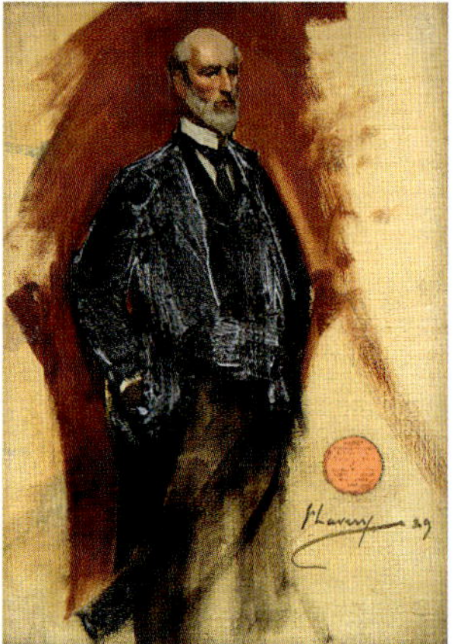

Lavery, John 1856–1941
Sir Charles Tennant (1823–1906), Bt (sketch)
1889
oil on canvas 35.5 x 25.4
2037

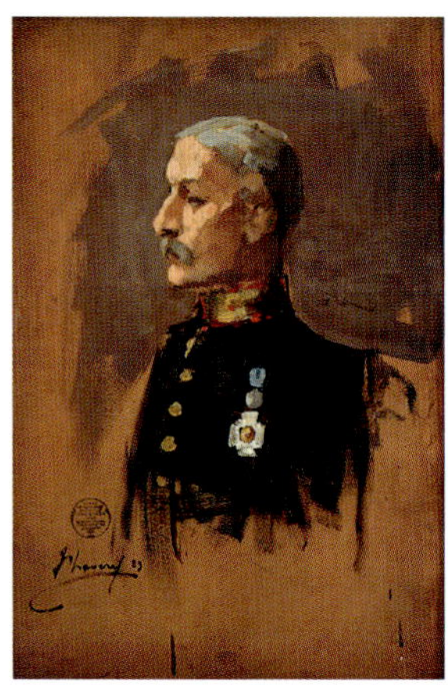

Lavery, John 1856–1941
Sir Fleetwood Edwards, KCB (sketch) 1889
oil on canvas 53.3 x 35.5
1971

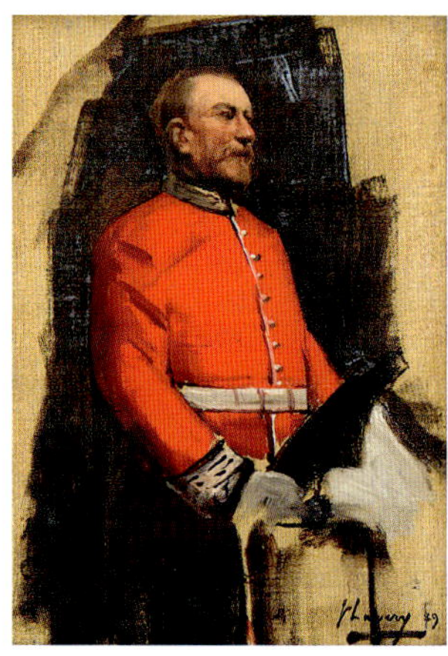

Lavery, John 1856–1941
Sir James Bain (sketch) 1889
oil on canvas 35.5 x 25.4
1936

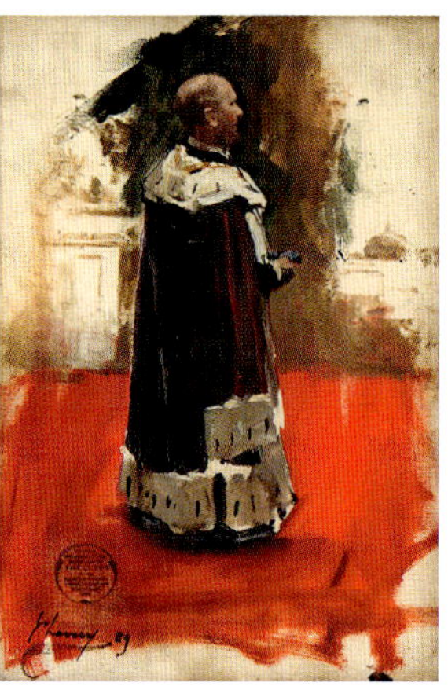

Lavery, John 1856–1941
*Sir James King (1830–1911), Lord Provost of
Glasgow (1886–1889)* (sketch) 1889
oil on canvas 35.6 x 25.4
3540

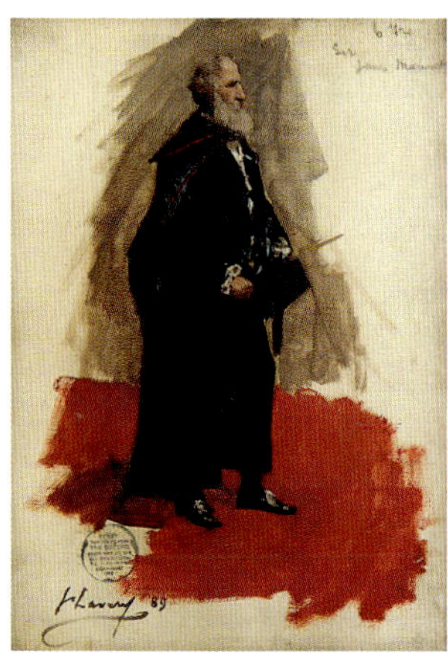

Lavery, John 1856–1941
*Sir James Marwick (1826–1908), Town Clerk
of Glasgow (1873–1903)* (sketch) 1889
oil on canvas 35.5 x 25.4
1995

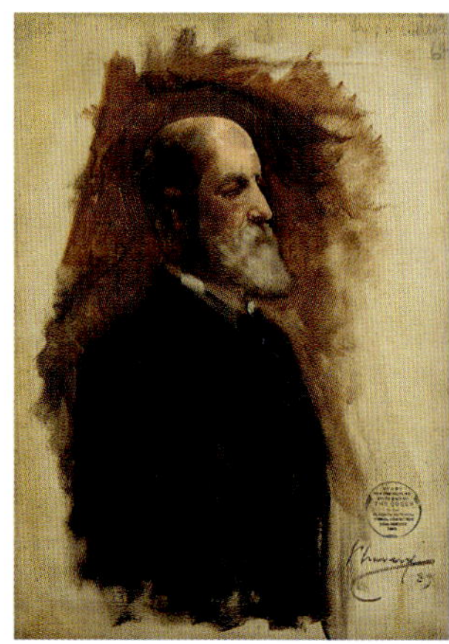

Lavery, John 1856–1941
*Sir John Neilson Cuthbertson (1829–1905),
LLD, DL* (sketch) 1889
oil on canvas 35.5 x 25.4
1966

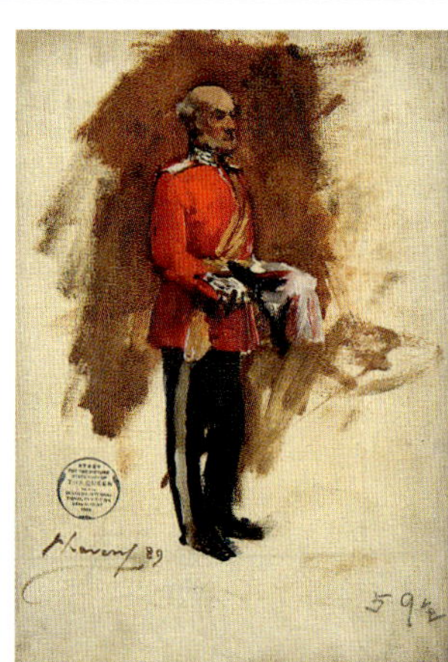

Lavery, John 1856–1941
*Sir Thomas Clark (1832–1900), Bt, Lord
Provost of Edinburgh* (sketch) 1889
oil on canvas 33 x 23
1956

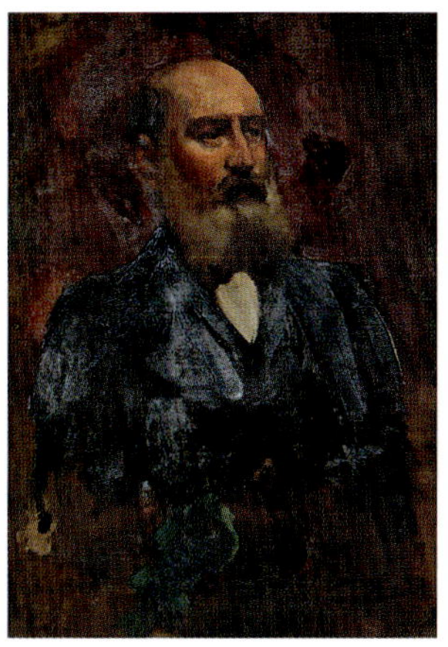

Lavery, John 1856–1941
Stewart Clarke (sketch) 1889
oil on canvas 35.5 x 25.4
1957

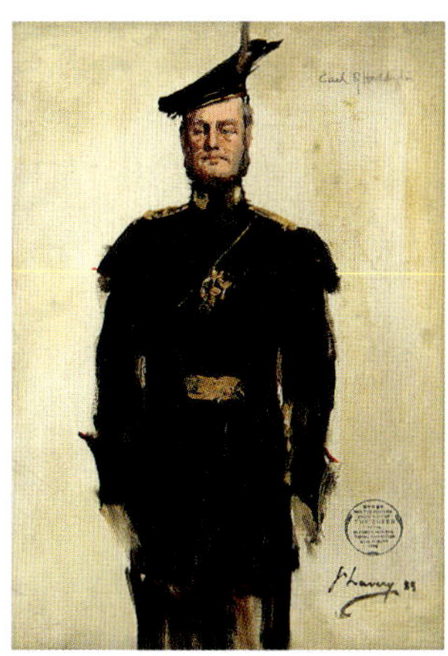

Lavery, John 1856–1941
The Earl of Haddington (sketch) 1889
oil on canvas 35.5 x 25.4
1980

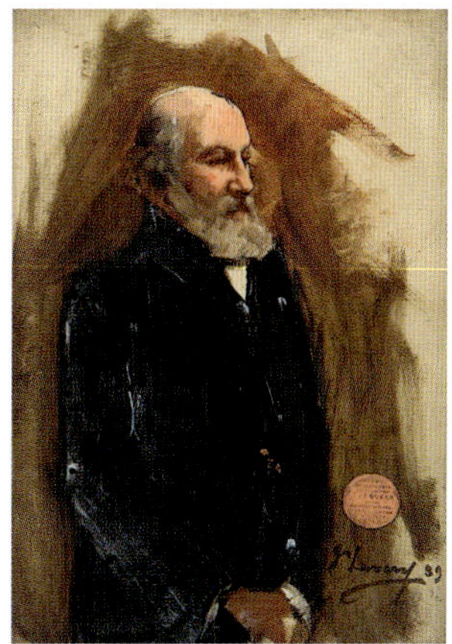

Lavery, John 1856–1941
The Earl of Lindsay (sketch) 1889
oil on canvas 35.5 x 25.4
1990

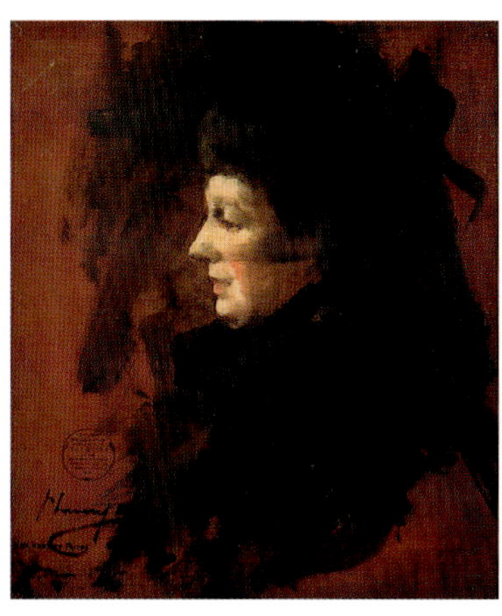

Lavery, John 1856–1941
*The Honourable Harriet Lepel Phipps
(1841–1922)* (sketch) 1889
oil on canvas 35.8 x 30.4
2019

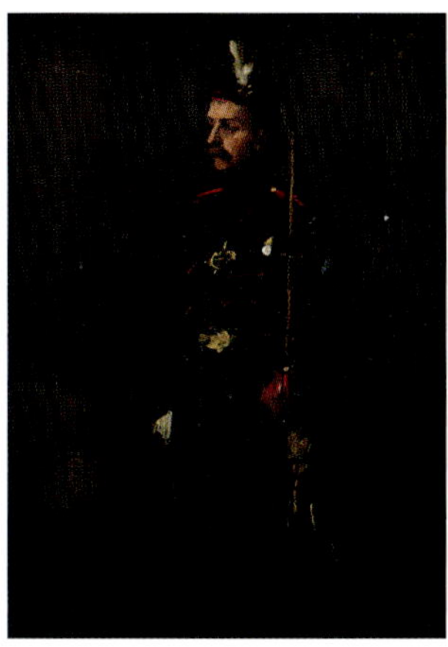

Lavery, John 1856–1941
The Honourable J. C. Maxwell-Scott (sketch)
1889
oil on canvas 35.5 x 25.4
1997

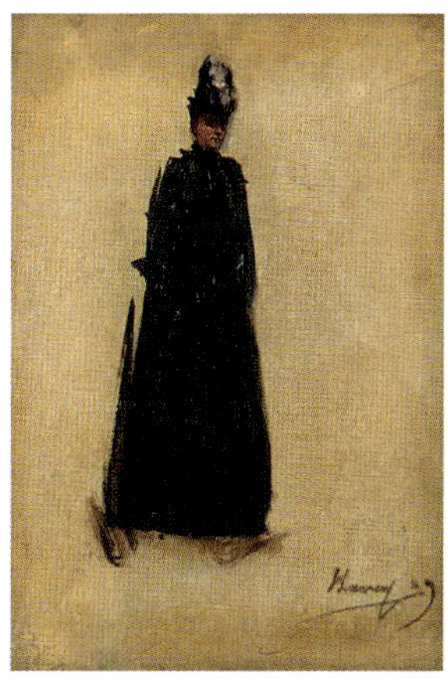

Lavery, John 1856–1941
The Honourable Mrs Maxwell-Scott (sketch)
1889
oil on canvas 35.6 x 26.7
1998

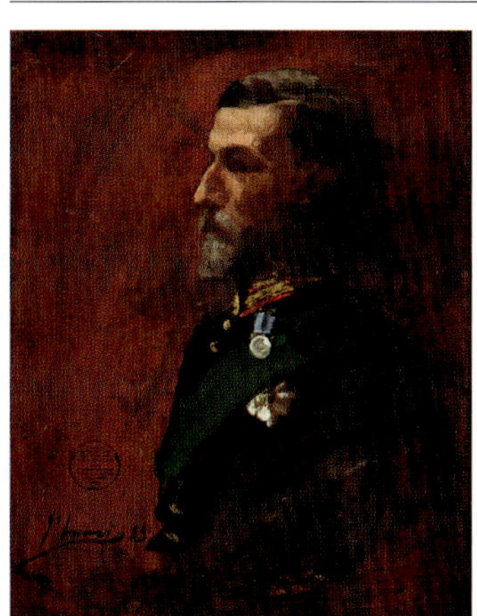

Lavery, John 1856–1941
The Marquis of Lothian, KT (sketch) 1889
oil on canvas 38.1 x 30.4
1992

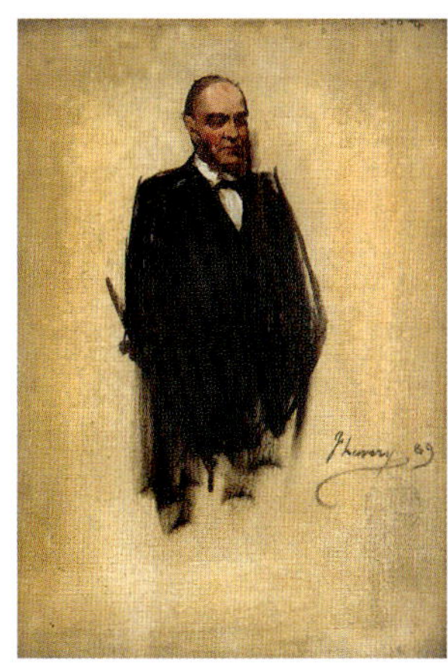

Lavery, John 1856–1941
William Ure (sketch) 1889
oil on canvas 35.6 x 25.4
2038

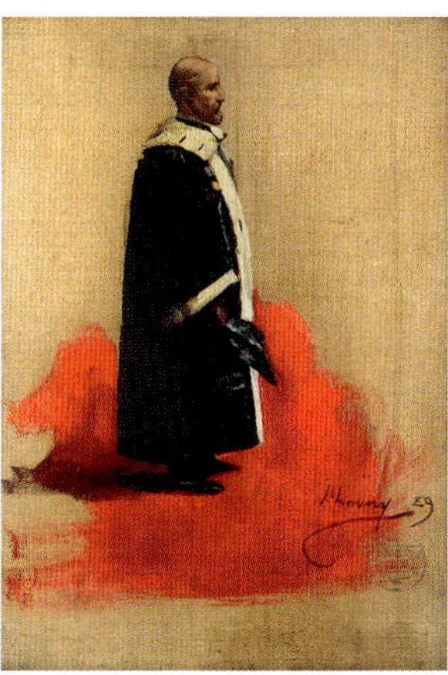

Lavery, John 1856–1941
William Walls (1819–1893) (sketch) 1889
oil on canvas 35.5 x 25.4
2040

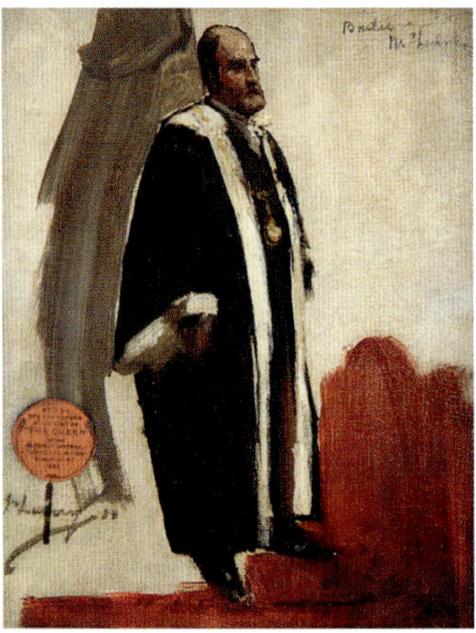

Lavery, John 1856–1941
Bailie McLennan (sketch) c.1889
oil on canvas 25.4 x 20.3
2008

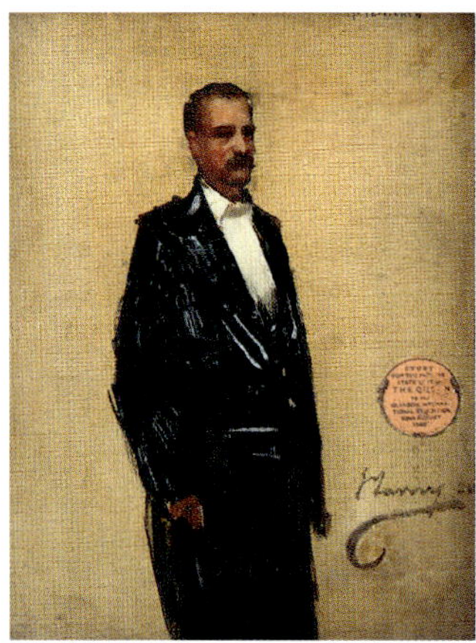

Lavery, John 1856–1941
William Pettigrew (sketch) c.1889
oil on canvas 25.4 x 20.3
2018

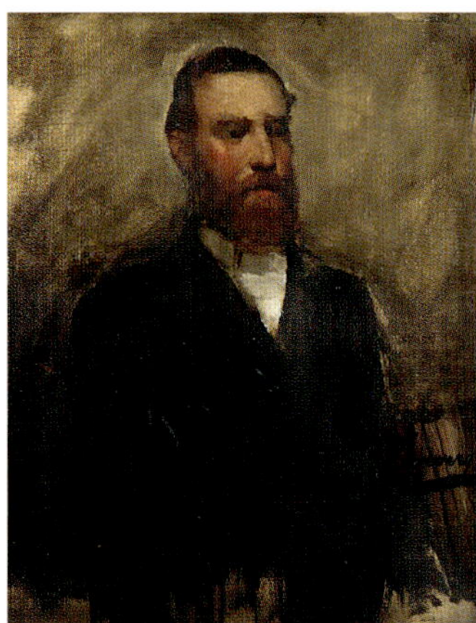

Lavery, John 1856–1941
Arthur Mechem (sketch) c.1889–1890
oil on canvas 25.4 x 20.3
1999

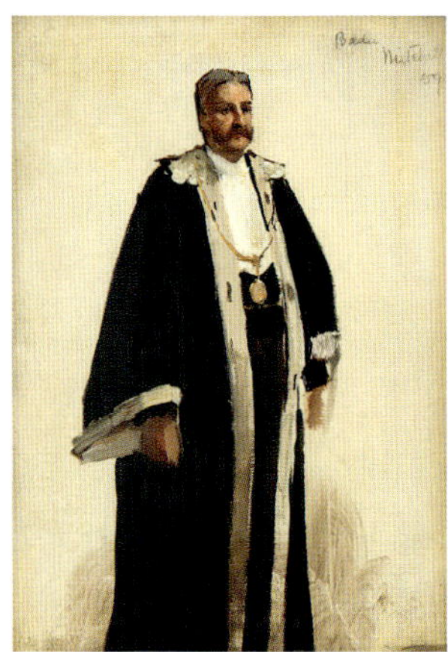

Lavery, John 1856–1941
Bailie Mitchell (sketch) c.1889–1890
oil on canvas 35.5 x 25.4
2000

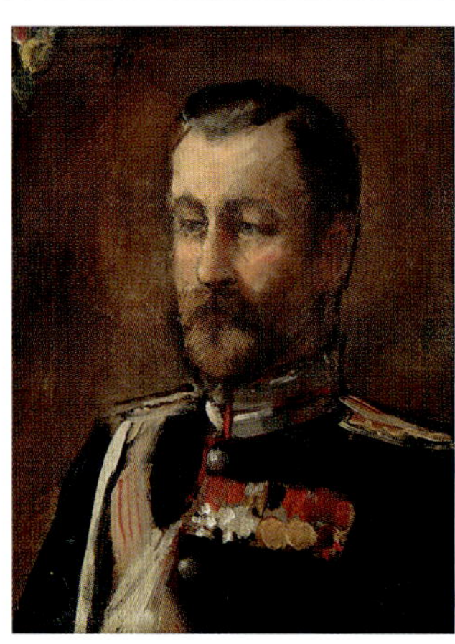

Lavery, John 1856–1941
Baron Grancy (sketch) c.1889–1890
oil on canvas 25.4 x 20.3
1978

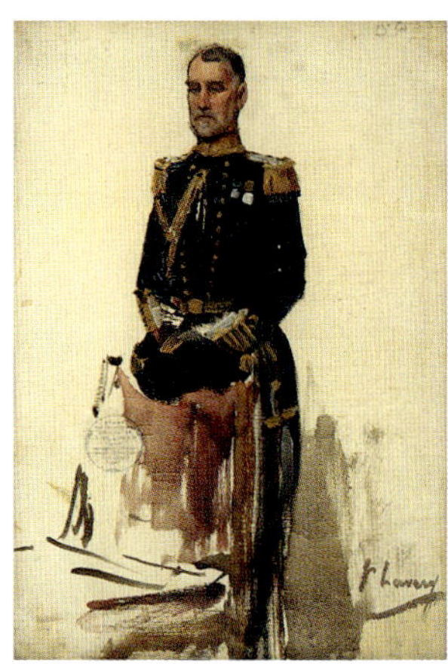

Lavery, John 1856–1941
Captain Fullerton, ADC (sketch)
c.1889–1890
oil on canvas 35.5 x 25.4
1974

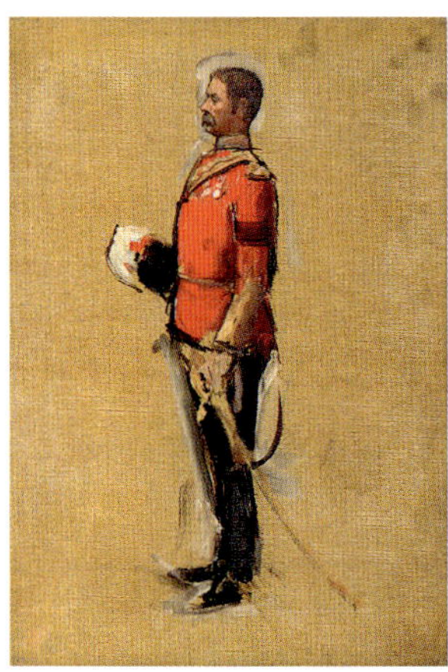

Lavery, John 1856–1941
Colonel Malcolm, CB (sketch) c.1889–1890
oil on canvas 35.5 x 25.4
1993

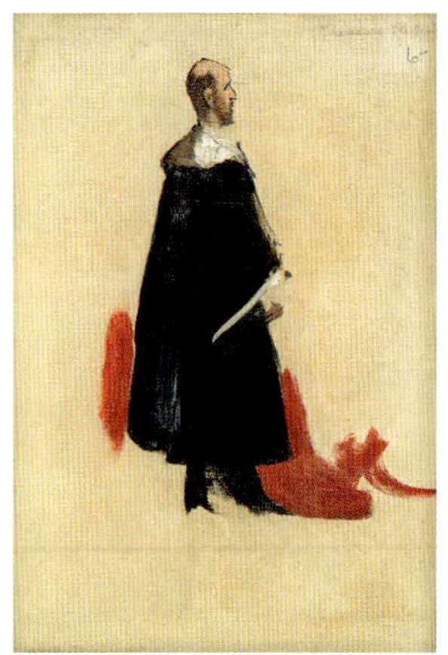

Lavery, John 1856–1941
*David Richmond (1843–1908), City Treasurer
of Glasgow (1887–1890)* (sketch) c.1889–1890
oil on canvas 35.6 x 25.4
2022

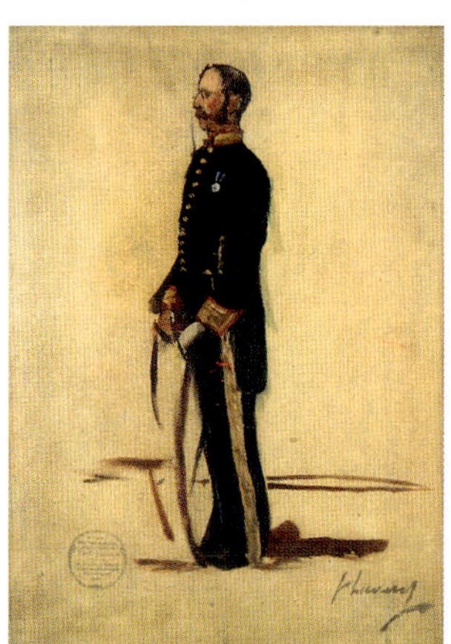

Lavery, John 1856–1941
Dr Reid (sketch) c.1889–1890
oil on canvas 35.5 x 25.4
2021

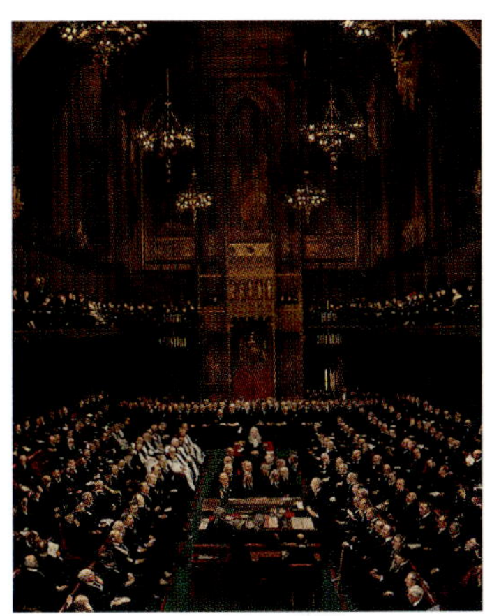

Lavery, John 1856–1941
Earl Morley Addressing the House of Lords
c.1889–1890
oil on canvas 127 x 101.6
1544

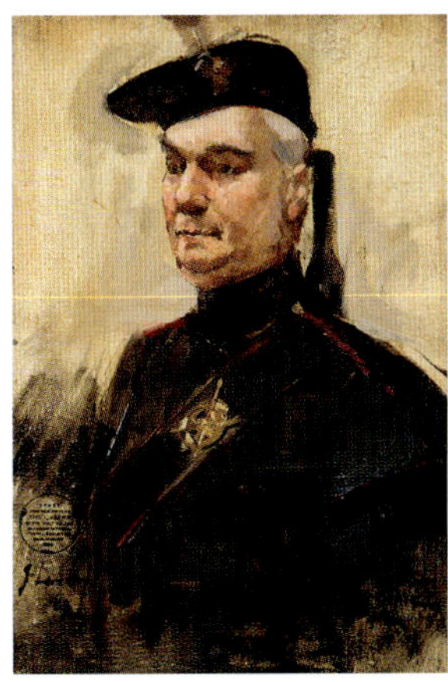

Lavery, John 1856–1941
G. Millar Cunningham, CE (sketch) c.1889–1890
oil on panel 35.5 x 24.4
1964

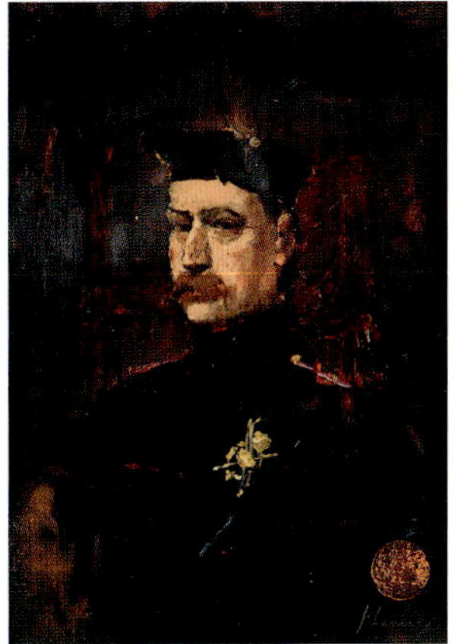

Lavery, John 1856–1941
Harry Cheyne (sketch) c.1889–1890
oil on panel 35.5 x 25.1
1953

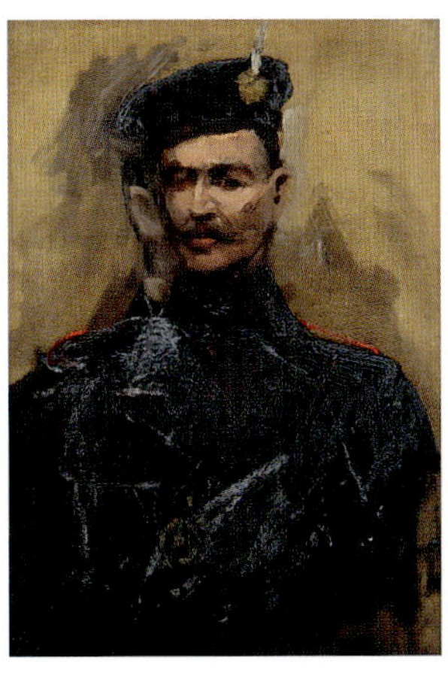

Lavery, John 1856–1941
James Clark (sketch) c.1889–1890
oil on canvas 35.5 x 25.4
1955

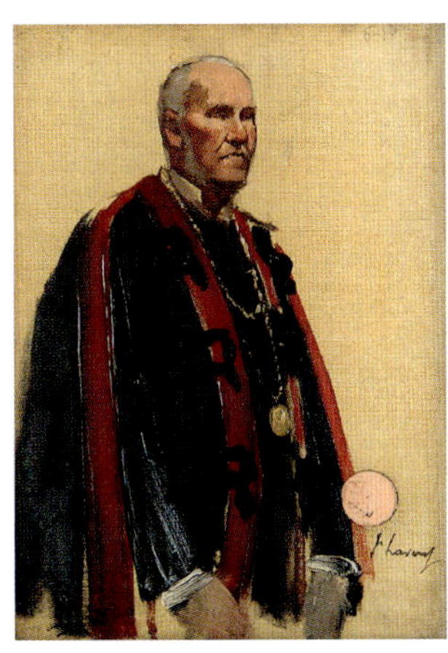

Lavery, John 1856–1941
James Watt, Provost of Haddington (sketch)
c.1889–1890
oil on canvas 35.5 x 25.4
2042

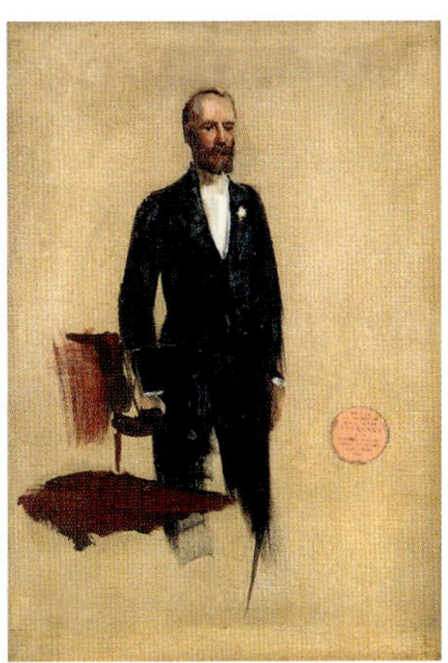

Lavery, John 1856–1941
John A. Campbell (sketch) c.1889–1890
oil on canvas 35.5 x 25.4
1950

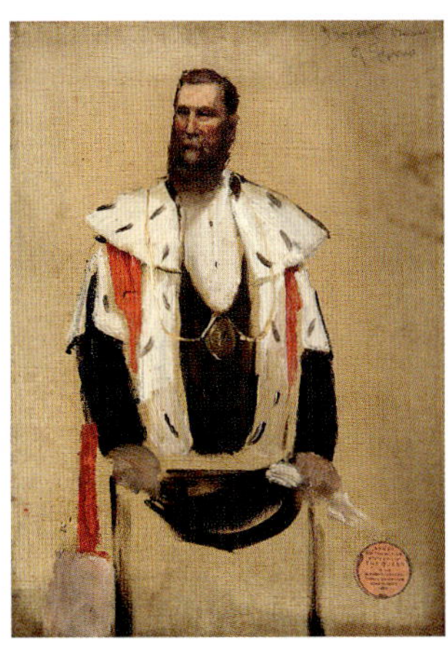

Lavery, John 1856–1941
John Burns, Provost of Forres (sketch)
c.1889–1890
oil on canvas 35.6 x 25.4
3538

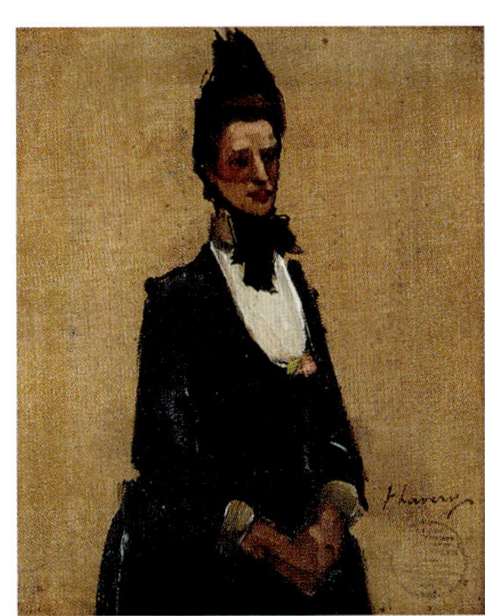

Lavery, John 1856–1941
Lady Balfour of Burleigh (sketch)
c.1889–1890
oil on canvas 25.4 x 20.3
1938

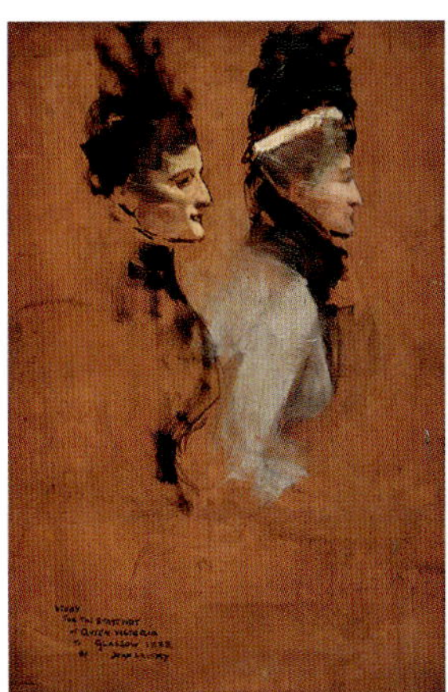

Lavery, John 1856–1941
Lady King (sketch) c.1889–1890
oil on canvas 53.3 x 35.5
1988

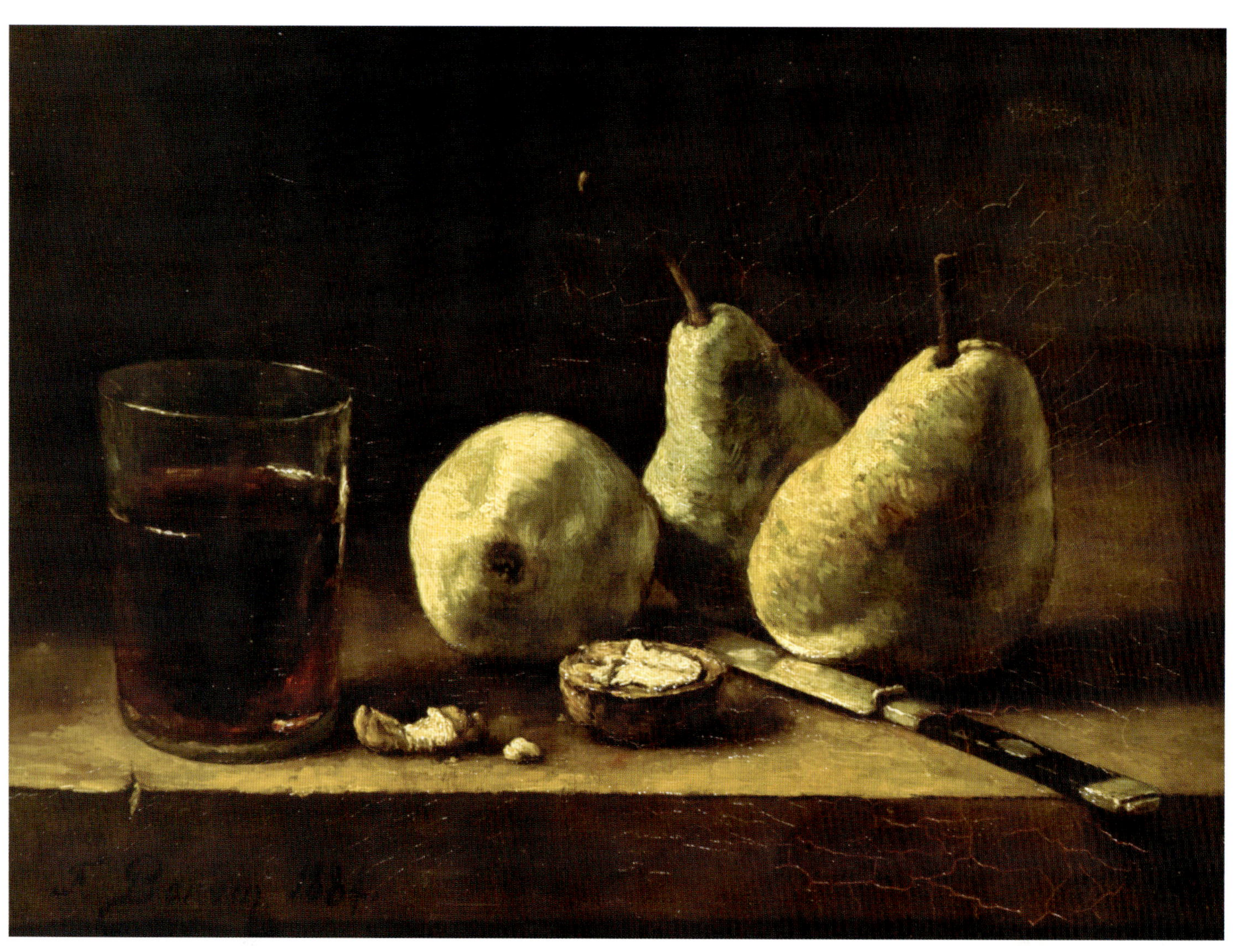

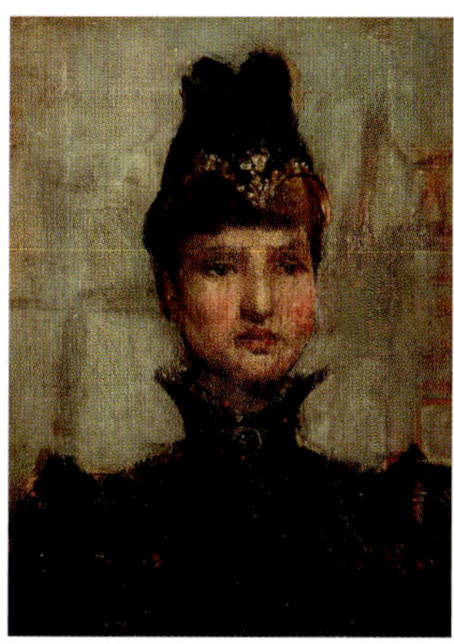

Lavery, John 1856–1941
Lady's Head c.1889–1890
oil on canvas 20.3 x 15.2
2451

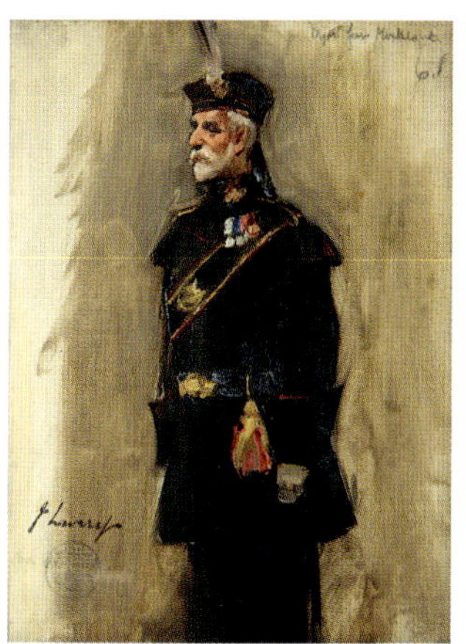

Lavery, John 1856–1941
Major General Kirkland (sketch)
c.1889–1890
oil on canvas 35.5 x 25.4
1989

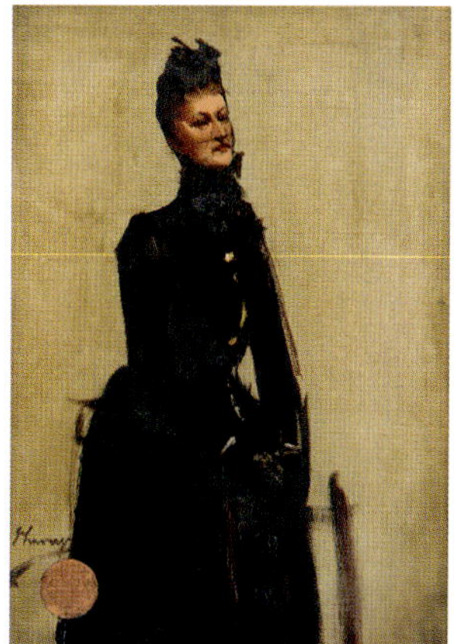

Lavery, John 1856–1941
Miss Bain (sketch) c.1889–1890
oil on canvas 35.5 x 25.4
1937

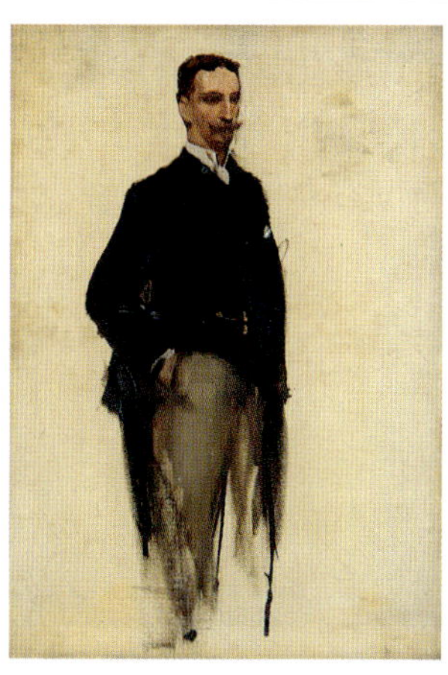

Lavery, John 1856–1941
Patrick S. Dunn (sketch) c.1889–1890
oil on canvas 35.5 x 25.4
1970

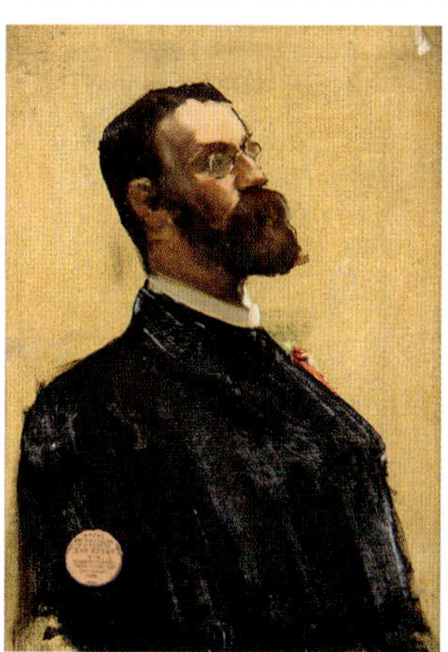

Lavery, John 1856–1941
Paul Rottenburg (sketch) c.1889–1890
oil on canvas 35.5 x 25.4
2025

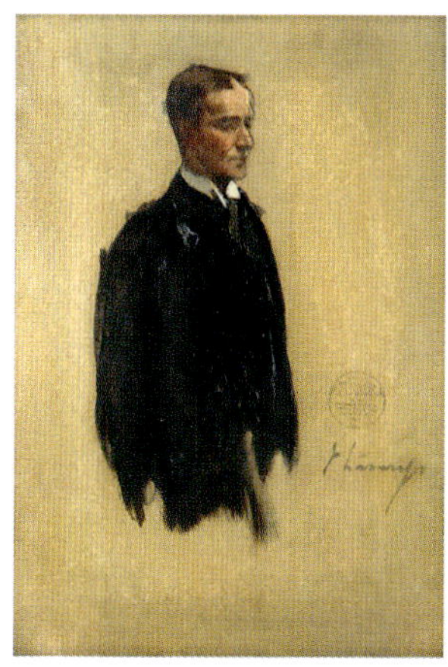

Lavery, John 1856–1941
*Right Honourable J. P. B. Robertson, Solicitor
General for Scotland* (sketch) c.1889–1890
oil on canvas 35.5 x 25.4
2024

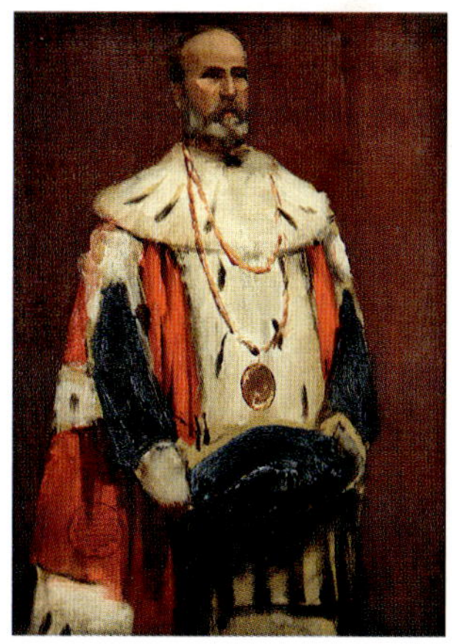

Lavery, John 1856–1941
Robert Yellowlees, Provost of Stirling (sketch)
c.1889–1890
oil on canvas 35.5 x 25.4
2045

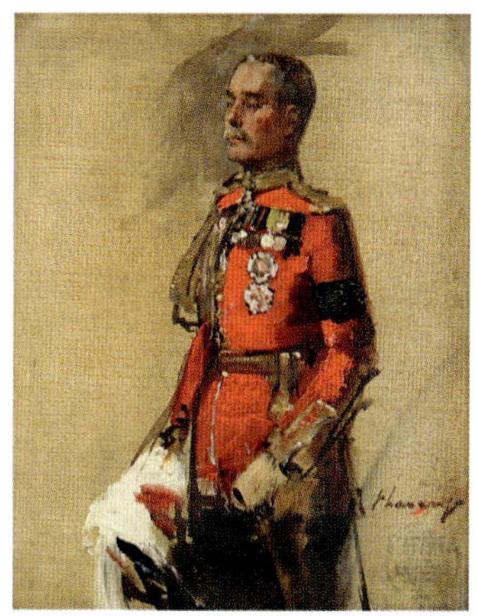

Lavery, John 1856–1941
Sir John MacNeil, KCB, VC (sketch)
c.1889–1890
oil on canvas 25.4 x 20.3
2012

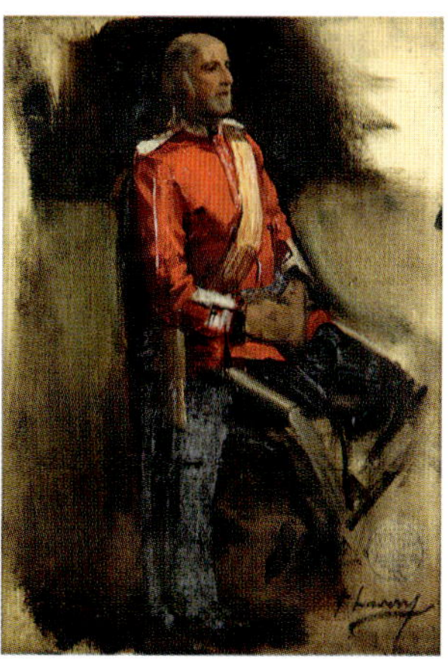

Lavery, John 1856–1941
*Sir Michael Robert Shaw-Stewart (1826–1903),
7th Bt* (sketch) c.1889–1890
oil on canvas 35.5 x 25.4
2029

Facing page: Bonvin, François, 1817–1887, *Still Life with a Glass, Pears and a Knife*, 1884 (p. 40)

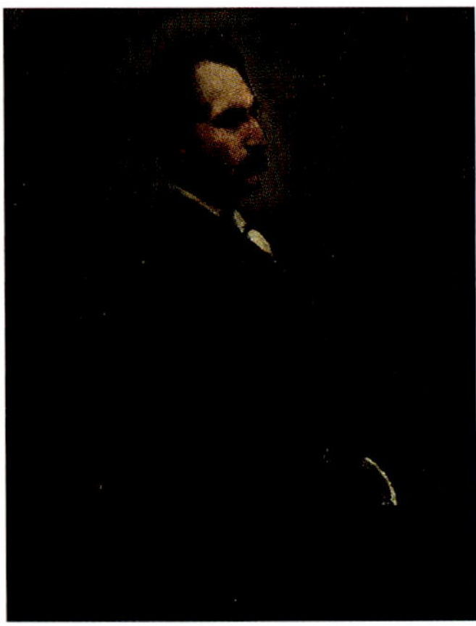

Lavery, John 1856–1941
Stephen Alley (sketch) c.1889–1890
oil on canvas 24.4 x 20.3
1934

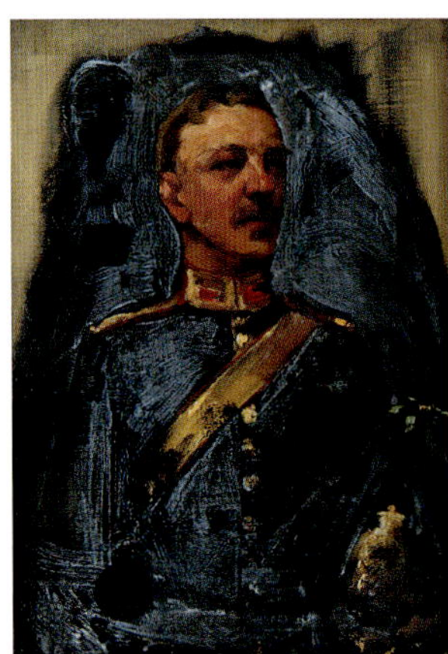

Lavery, John 1856–1941
T. G. Arthur (sketch) c.1889–1890
oil on canvas 35.6 x 25.4
1935

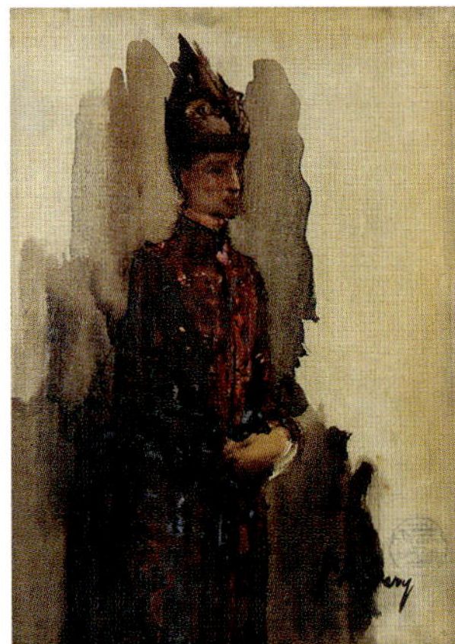

Lavery, John 1856–1941
The Countess of Dundonald (sketch)
c.1889–1890
oil on canvas 35.5 x 25.4
1969

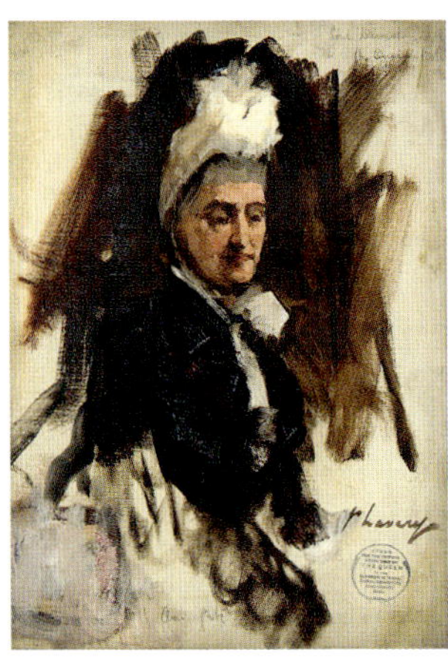

Lavery, John 1856–1941
The Countess of Lindsay (sketch) c.1889–
1890
oil on canvas 35.5 x 25.4
1991

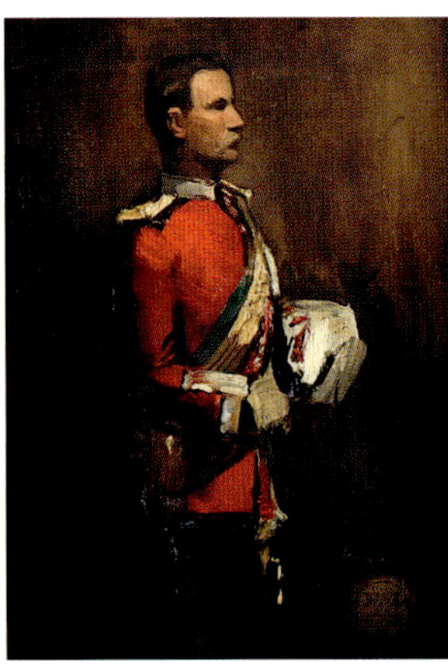

Lavery, John 1856–1941
The Duke of Montrose (sketch) c.1889–1890
oil on canvas 35.5 x 25.4
2002

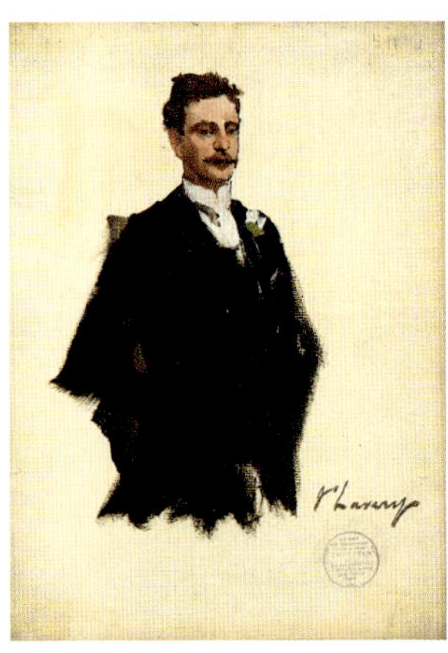

Lavery, John 1856–1941
*The Honourable Charles W. A. N. Cochrane-
Baillie, Lord Lamington* (sketch) c.1889–1890
oil on canvas 35.5 x 25.4
1960

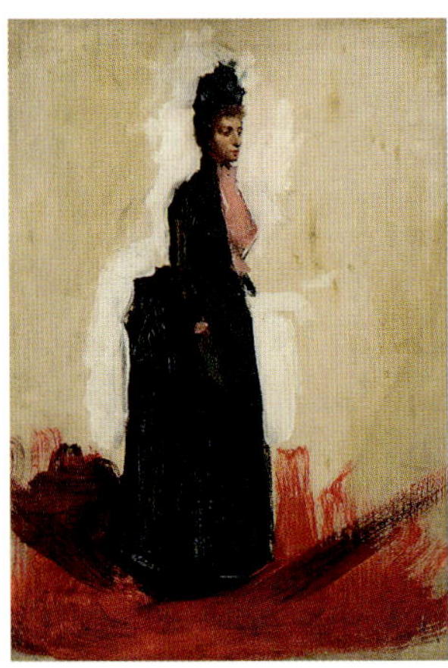

Lavery, John 1856–1941
The Honourable Mabel Hamilton of Dalzell
(sketch) c.1889–1890
oil on canvas 35.5 x 25.4
1981

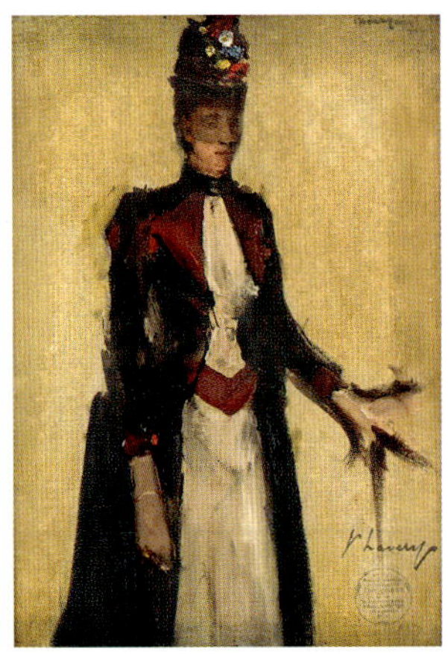

Lavery, John 1856–1941
The Honourable Miss Cochrane-Baillie
(sketch) c.1889–1890
oil on canvas 35.5 x 25.4
1961

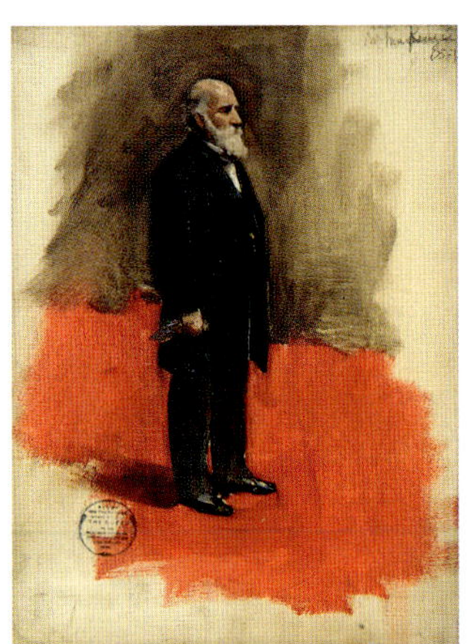

Lavery, John 1856–1941
Walter Mackenzie (sketch) c.1889–1890
oil on canvas 35.5 x 25.4
2006

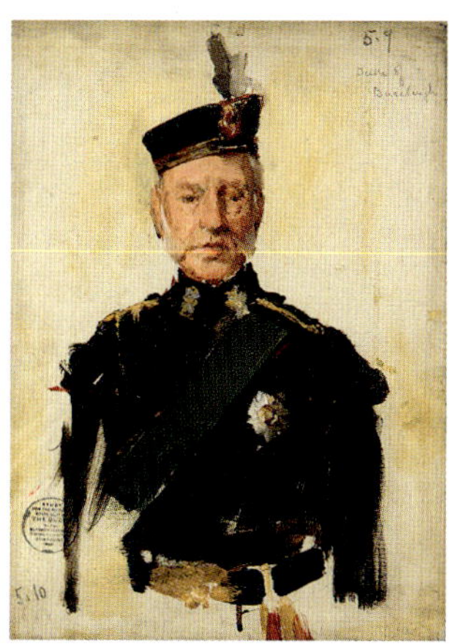

Lavery, John 1856–1941
*William Henry Walter Montagu Douglas Scott
(1831–1914), 6th Duke of Buccleuch and 8th
Duke of Queensberry, KG, KT, (...)* (sketch)
c.1889–1890
oil on canvas 35.5 x 25.4

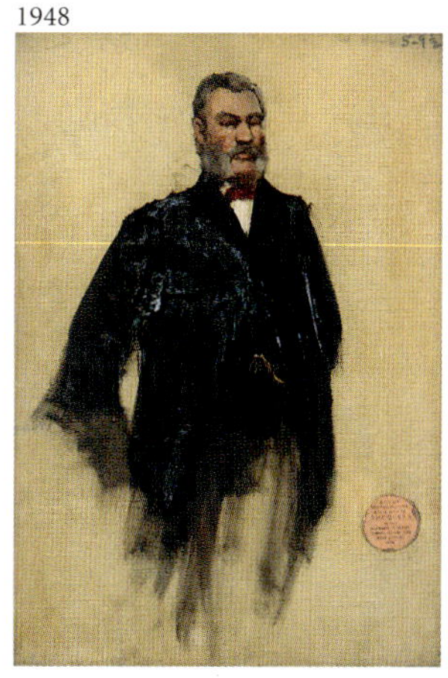

Lavery, John 1856–1941
William Wilson (sketch) c.1889–1890
oil on canvas 35.5 x 25.4
2044

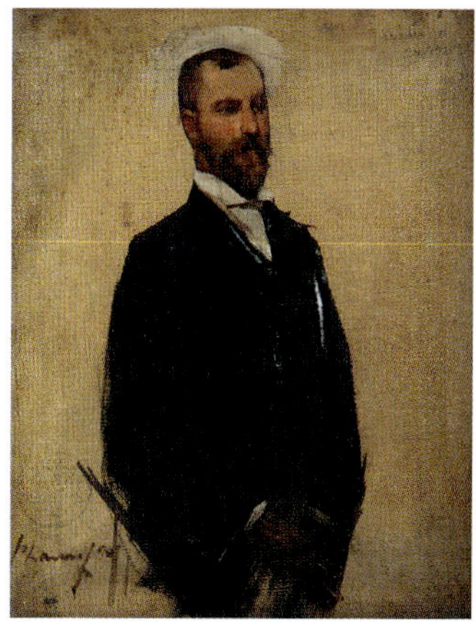

Lavery, John 1856–1941
Alexander Henderson (sketch) 1890
oil on canvas 25.4 x 20.3
1982

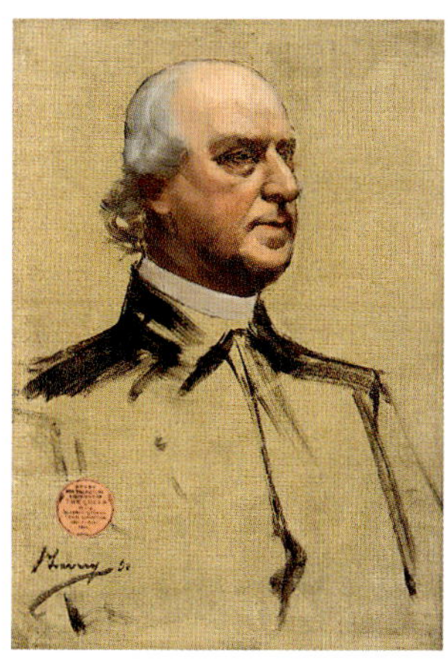

Lavery, John 1856–1941
Archbishop Eyre (1817–1902) (sketch) 1890
oil on canvas 35.5 x 25.4
1972

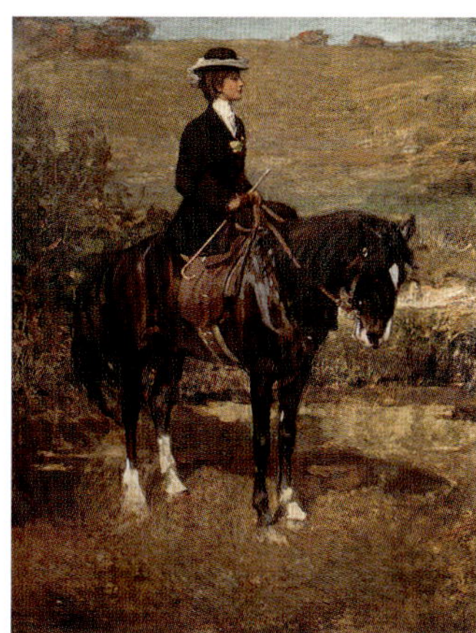

Lavery, John 1856–1941
Idonia in Morocco: The Equestrian Lady 1890
oil on canvas 243.8 x 182.9
2244

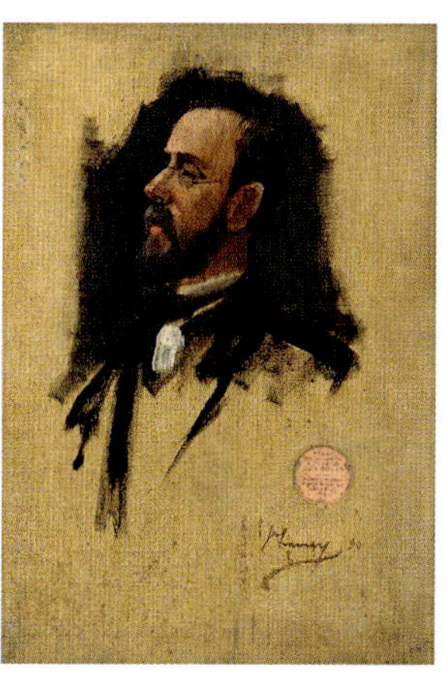

Lavery, John 1856–1941
James Paton (1843–1921) (sketch) 1890
oil on canvas 35.5 x 25.4
2017

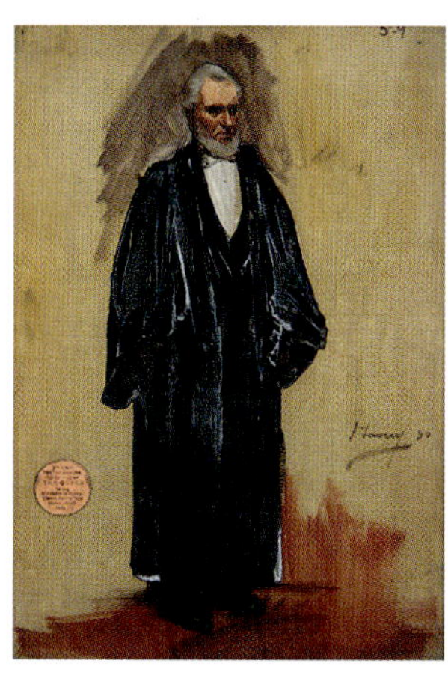

Lavery, John 1856–1941
John Carrick (1819–1890), City Architect
(sketch) 1890
oil on canvas 35.5 x 25.4
1952

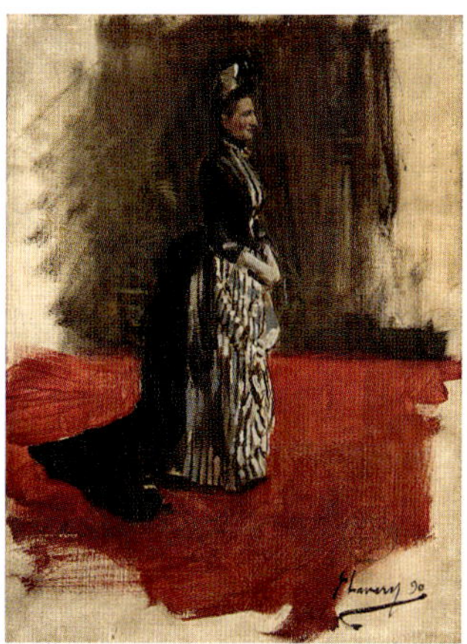

Lavery, John 1856–1941
Lady King (second sketch) 1890
oil on canvas 35.6 x 25.4
3541

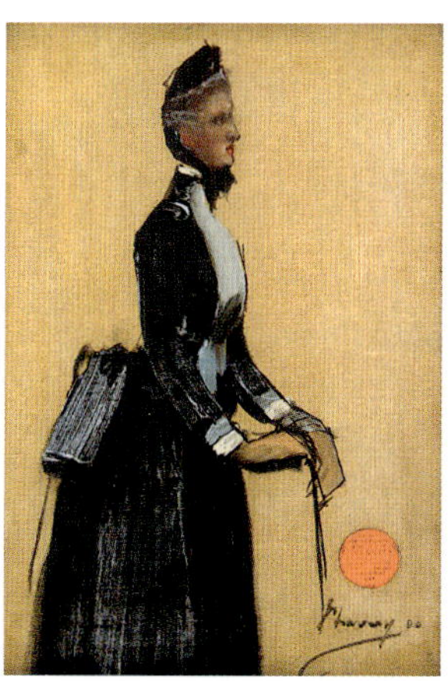

Lavery, John 1856–1941
Miss Shaw-Stewart (sketch) 1890
oil on canvas 35.5 x 25.4
2031

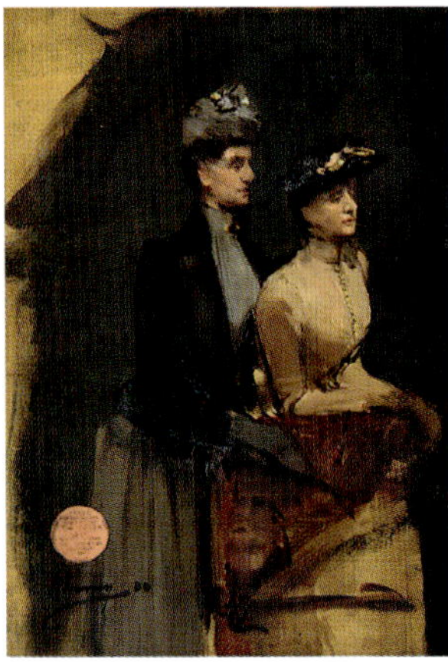

Lavery, John 1856–1941
Mrs Cunningham and Mrs Wedderspoon
(sketch) 1890
oil on canvas 35.5 x 25.4
1965

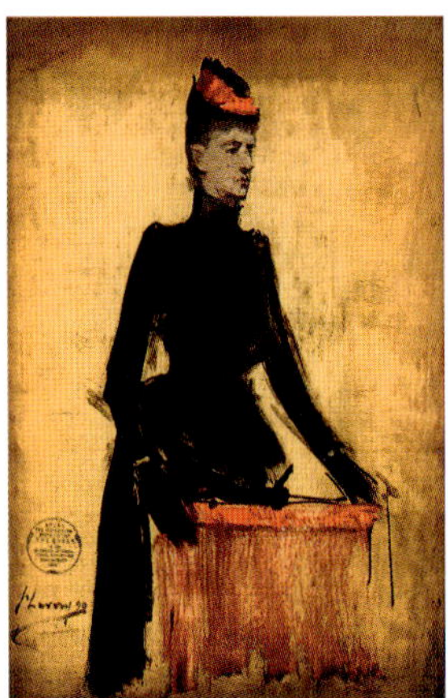

Lavery, John 1856–1941
Mrs Sargeant (sketch) 1890
oil on panel 38.2 x 25.2
2027

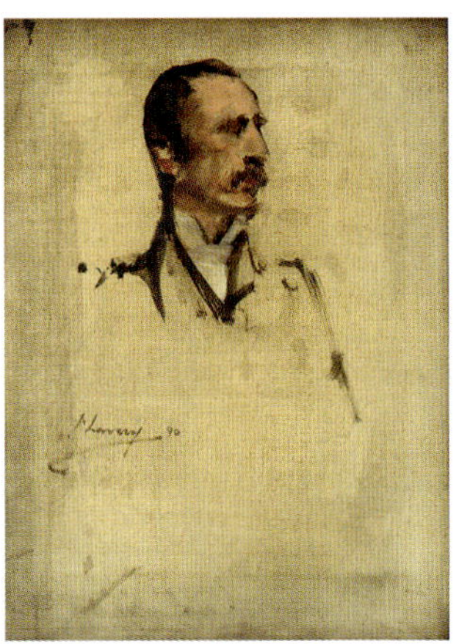

Lavery, John 1856–1941
*Sir Archibald Cameron Corbett (1856–1933),
1st Baron Rowallan, MP* (sketch) 1890
oil on canvas 38.1 x 28
1963

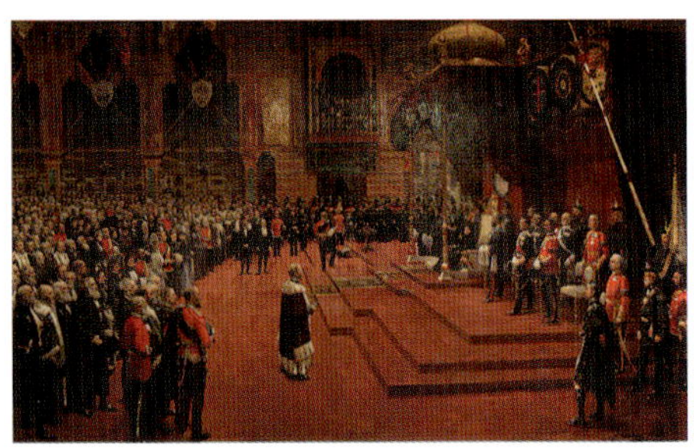

Lavery, John 1856–1941
*State Visit of Her Majesty, Queen Victoria to
the Glasgow International Exhibition, 1888*
1890
oil on canvas 256.5 x 406.4
710

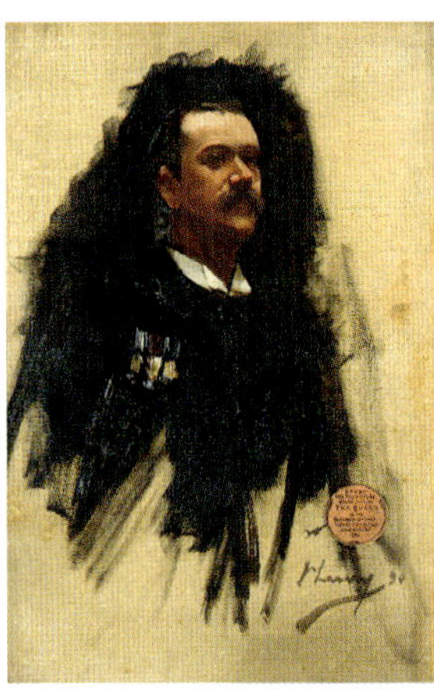

Lavery, John 1856–1941
W. A. Bryson, Engineer and Electrician
(sketch) 1890
oil on canvas 35.5 x 25.4
1947

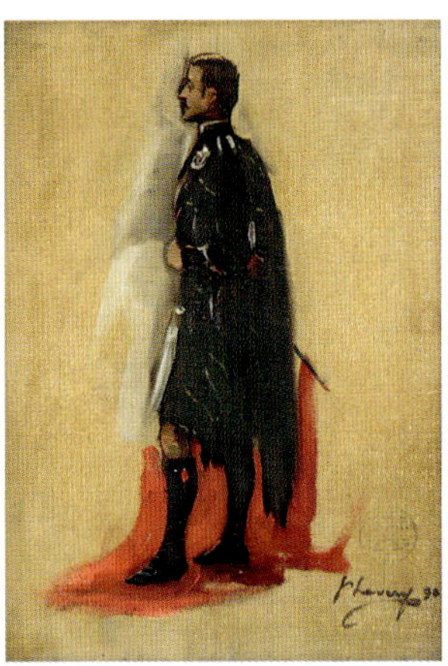

Lavery, John 1856–1941
Walter Douglas Campbell (sketch) 1890
oil on canvas 35.5 x 25.4
1951

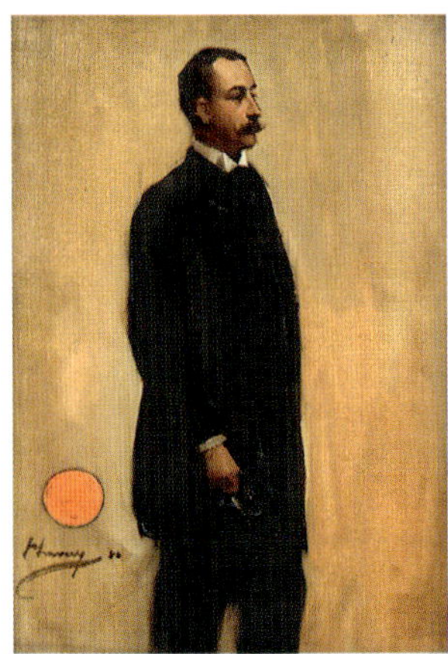

Lavery, John 1856–1941
Walter Wilson (sketch) 1890
oil on canvas 35.5 x 25
2043

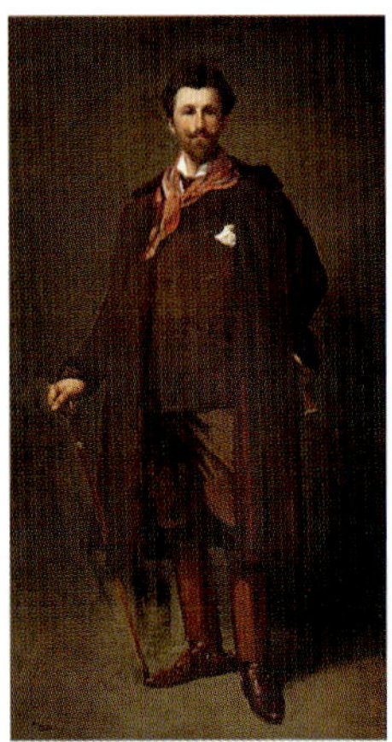

Lavery, John 1856–1941
*Robert Bontine Cunninghame Graham
(1852–1936)* 1893
oil on canvas 203.2 x 108.2
1181

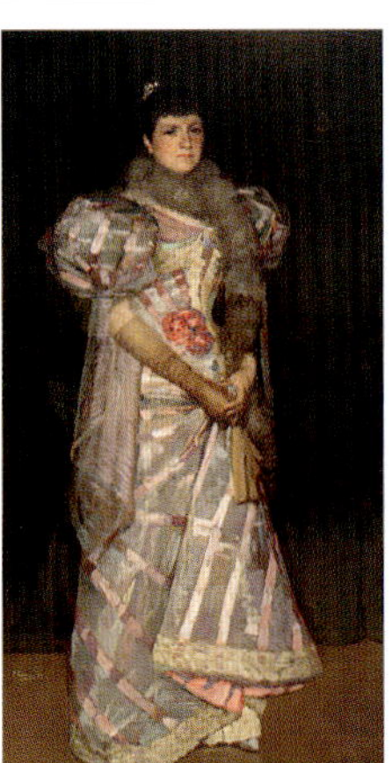

Lavery, John 1856–1941
Mrs Fitzroy Bell 1894
oil on canvas 182.9 x 91.4
1350

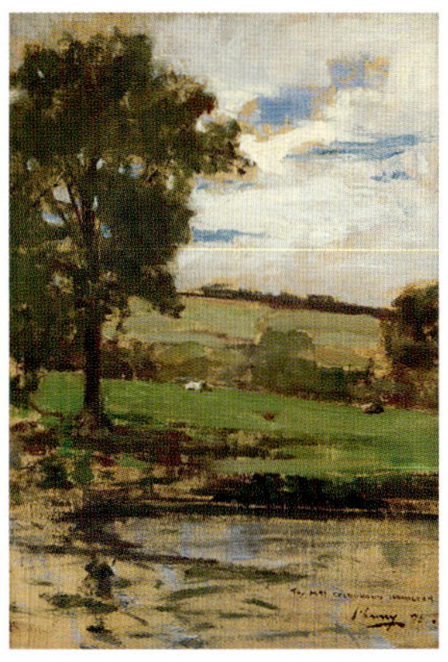

Lavery, John 1856–1941
Landscape 1895
oil on board 33 x 24.8
2838

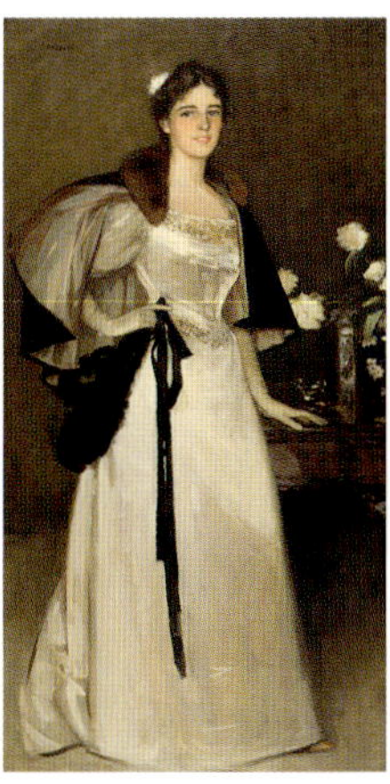

Lavery, John 1856–1941
Miss Mary Burrell 1895
oil on canvas 183 x 91.5
35.297

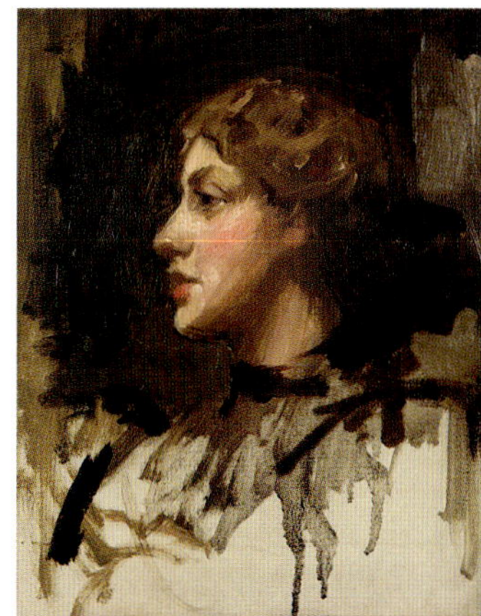

Lavery, John 1856–1941
Girl's Head (sketch) c.1895
oil on board 38.1 x 30.5
2347

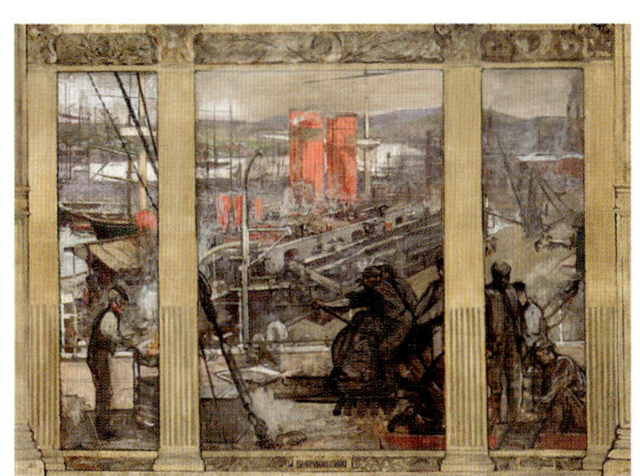

Lavery, John 1856–1941
Shipbuilding on the Clyde (sketch) 1900
oil on canvas 116.8 x 160
1458

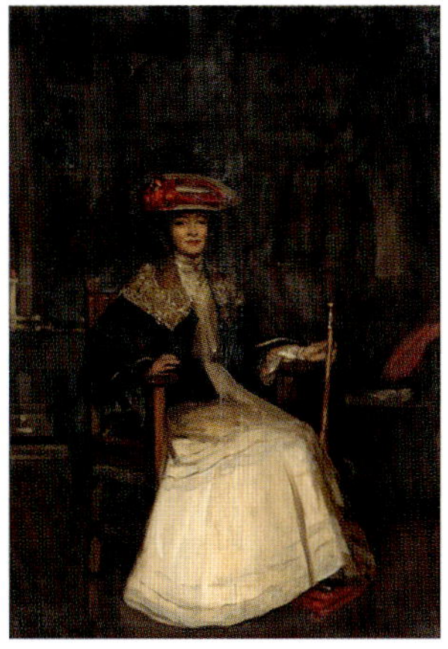

Lavery, John 1856–1941
*Mrs Robert Bontine Cunninghame Graham
(d.1906)* 1903
oil on canvas 137.2 x 95.3
1384

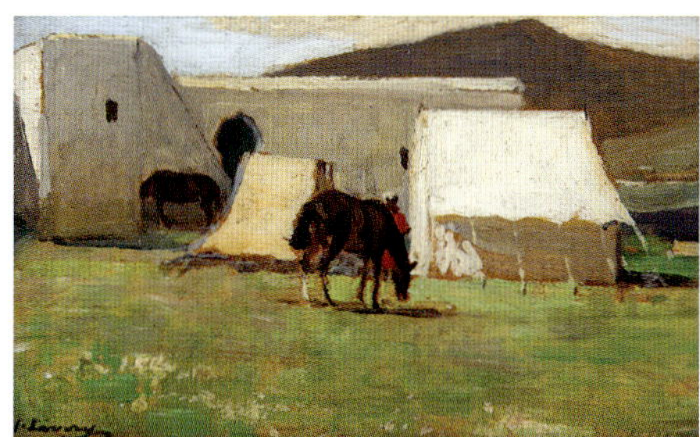

Lavery, John 1856–1941
Souvenir of Morocco 1904
oil on panel 13.7 x 21.9
2939

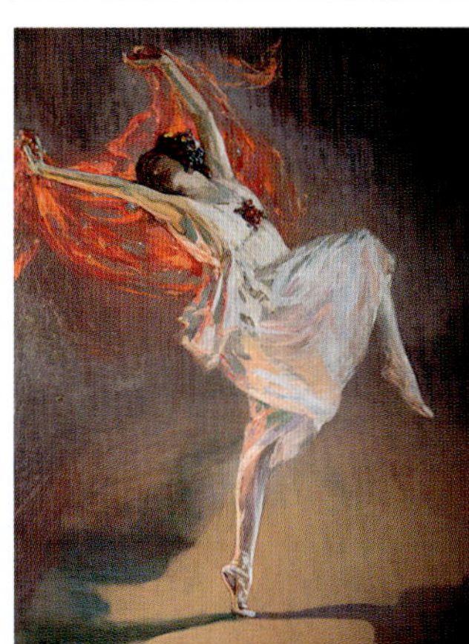

Lavery, John 1856–1941
Anna Pavlova (1881–1931) 1910–1923
oil on canvas 198.1 x 144.8
1581

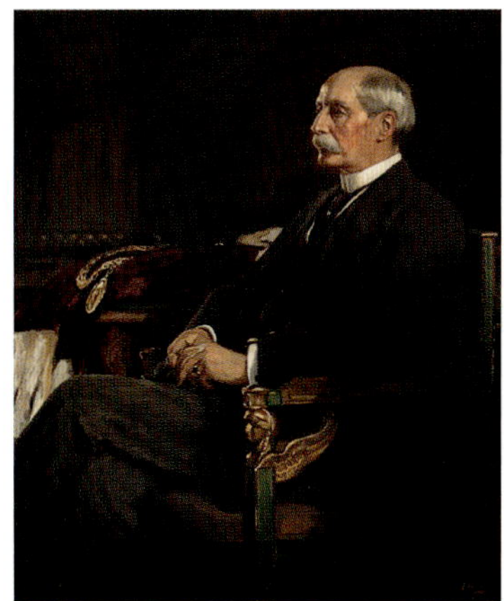

Lavery, John 1856–1941
*Sir James Watson Stewart, Lord Provost of
Glasgow (1917–1920)* 1921
oil on canvas 127 x 101.6
1518

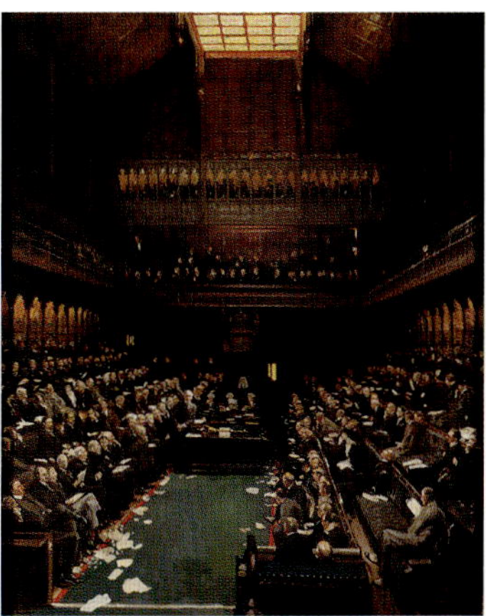

Lavery, John 1856–1941
*The Right Honourable J. Ramsay Macdonald
Addressing the House of Commons* 1923
oil on canvas 127 x 101.6
1809

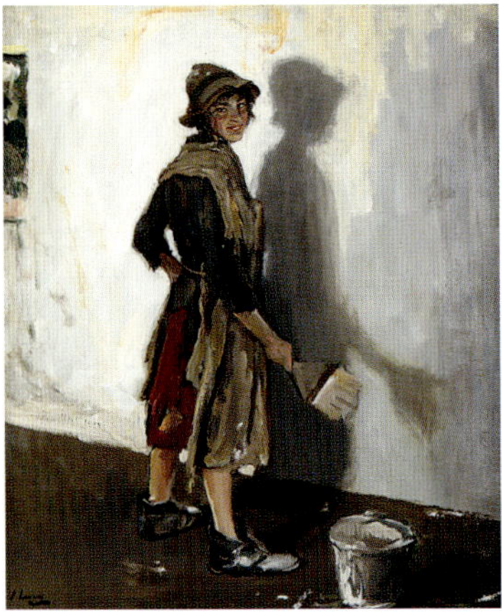

Lavery, John 1856–1941
Whitewashing c.1925
oil on canvas on board 61 x 50.8
2185

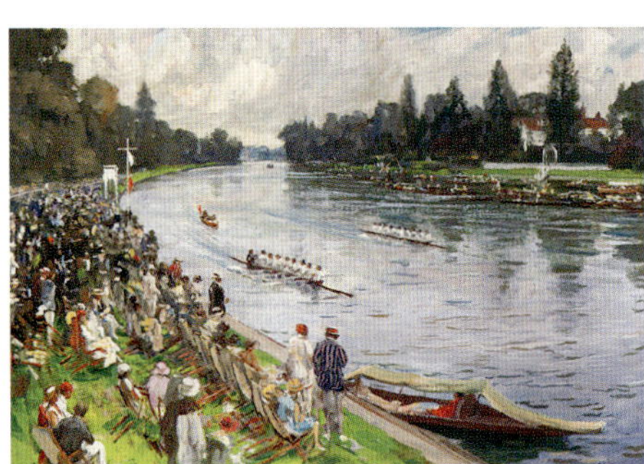

Lavery, John 1856–1941
Maidenhead Regatta 1932
oil on canvas 81.3 x 116.8
2070

Law, Andrew 1873–1967
The Tron Steeple, Glasgow 1927
oil on canvas 76.2 x 63.5
1725

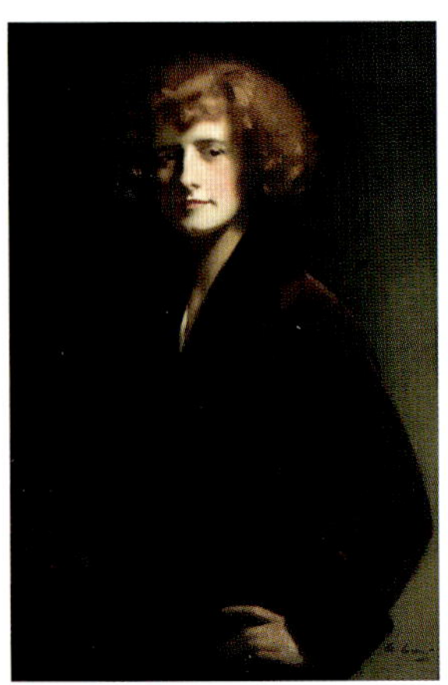

Law, Andrew 1873–1967
Stella Cameron c.1928
oil on canvas 91.5 x 61.2
3057

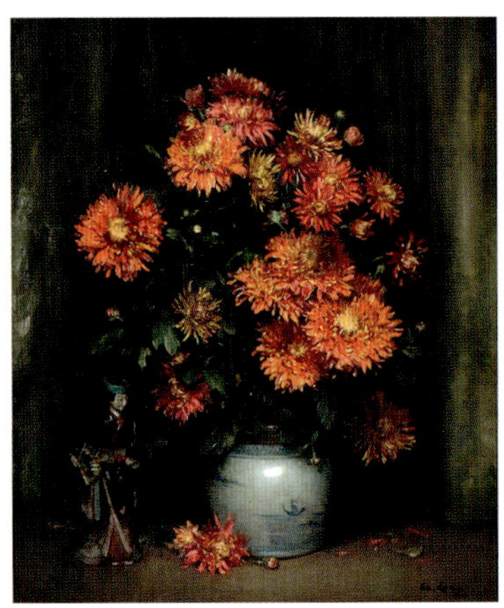

Law, Andrew 1873–1967
Chrysanthemums 1943
oil on canvas 76.2 x 63.5
2357

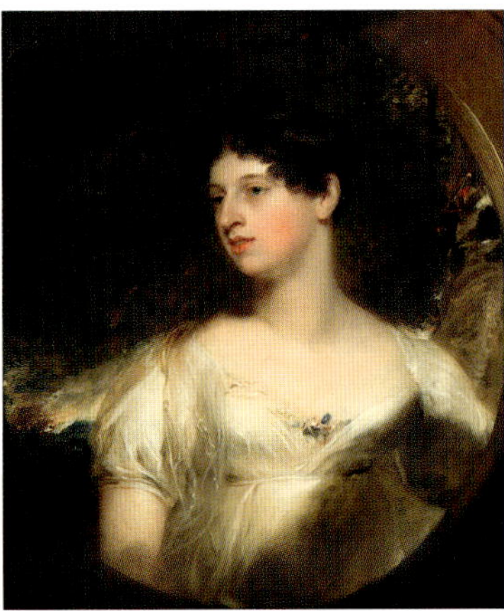

Lawrence, Thomas 1769–1830
Mrs John Trower (1782/1783–1809)
1803–1809
oil on canvas 75.2 x 62.5
3249

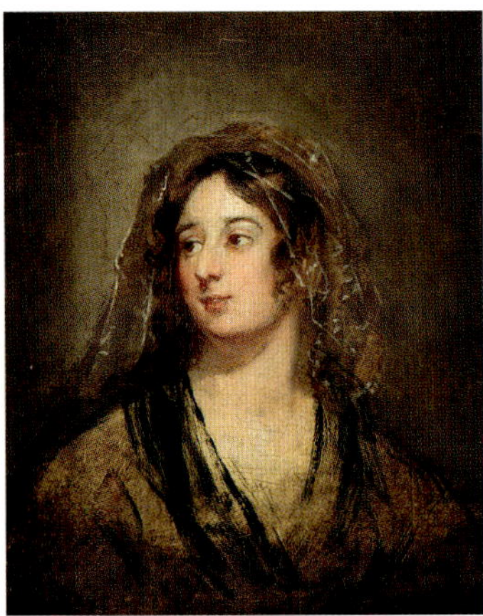

Lawrence, Thomas (attributed to)
1769–1830
Sketch of a Lady
oil on canvas 30.5 x 25.4
2054

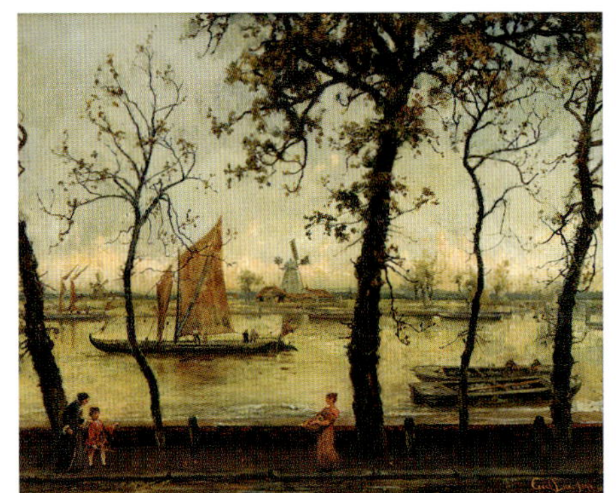

Lawson, Cecil Gordon 1851–1882
Don Saltero's Walk 1877
oil on canvas 50.8 x 61
35.298

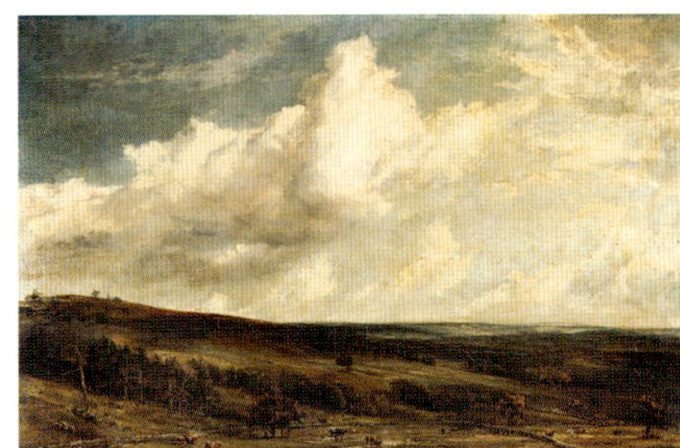

Lawson, Cecil Gordon 1851–1882
Barden Moor, Yorkshire 1881
oil on canvas 121.9 x 185.4
1572

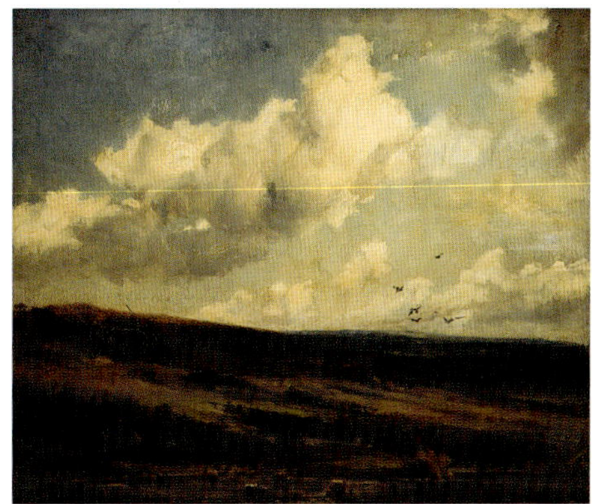

Lawson, Cecil Gordon 1851–1882
Landscape with Clouds 1881
oil on canvas 30.4 x 35.5
35.299

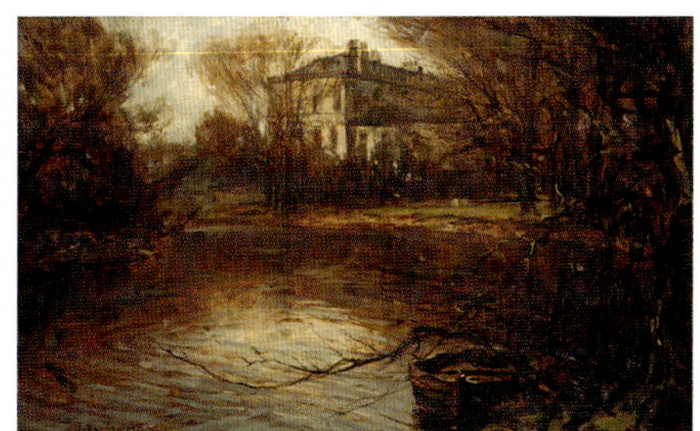

Lawson, John 1868–1909
Killermont House c.1889–1909
oil on canvas 30.8 x 45.8
OG.1951.417.v

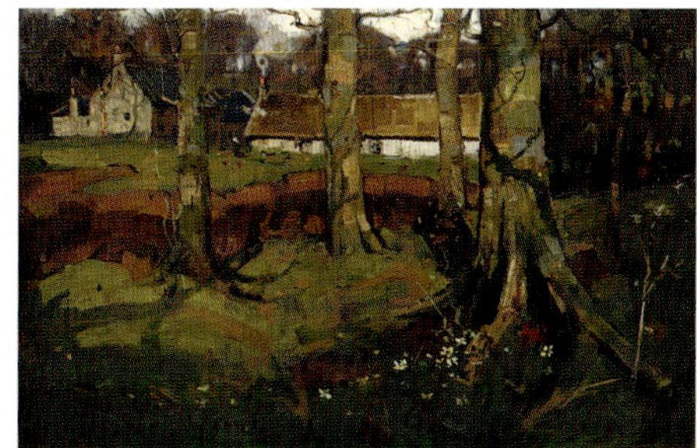

Lawson, John 1868–1909
Landscape, Dunlop c.1889–1909
oil on canvas 41.9 x 61
2807

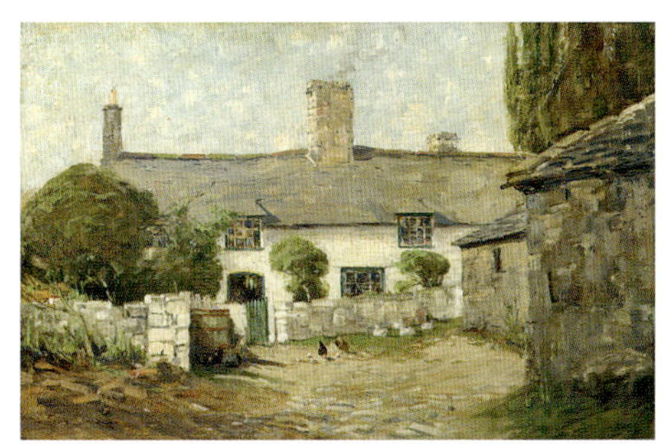

Lawson, John 1868–1909
Whitewashed Farmstead c.1889–1909
oil on canvas 40.6 x 61
2889

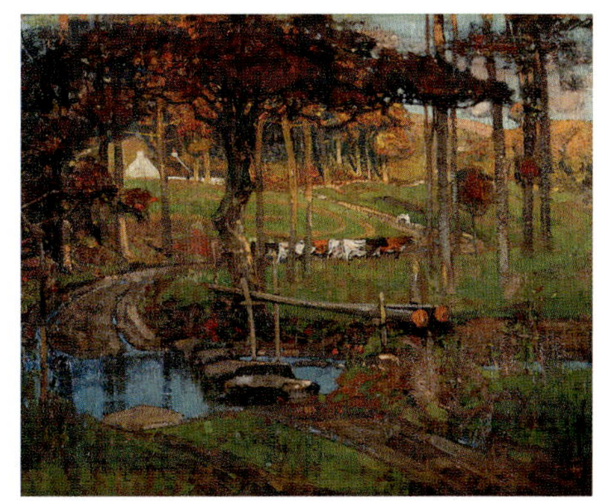

Lawson, John 1868–1909
An Ayrshire Stream c.1893
oil on canvas 83.8 x 101.6
2815

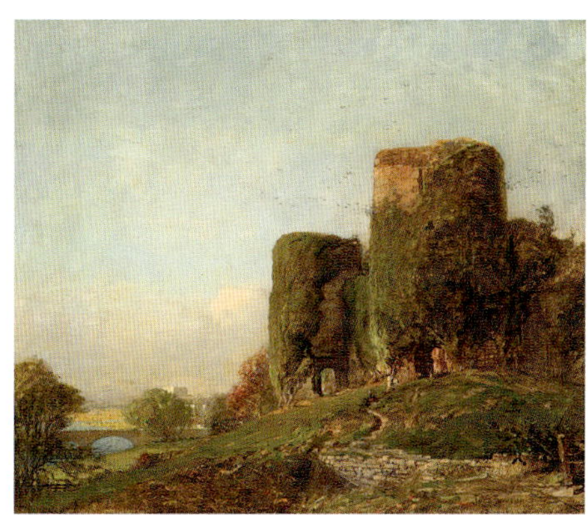

Lawson, John 1868–1909
Rhuddlan Castle, North Wales c.1909
oil on canvas 91.4 x 106.7
1262

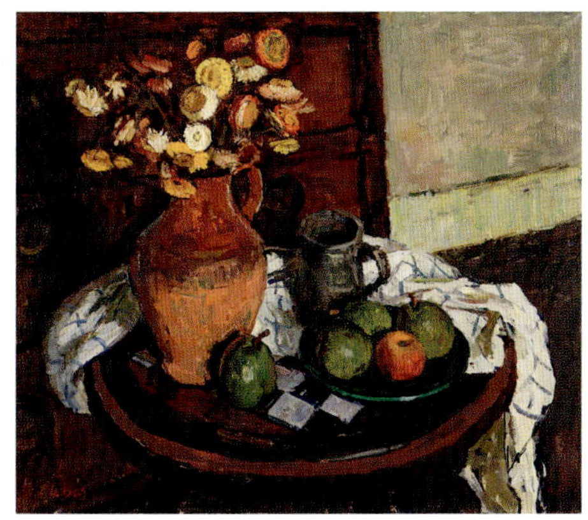

Le Bas, Edward 1904–1966
Still Life, No.4 c.1951
oil on canvas 66 x 76.2
2894

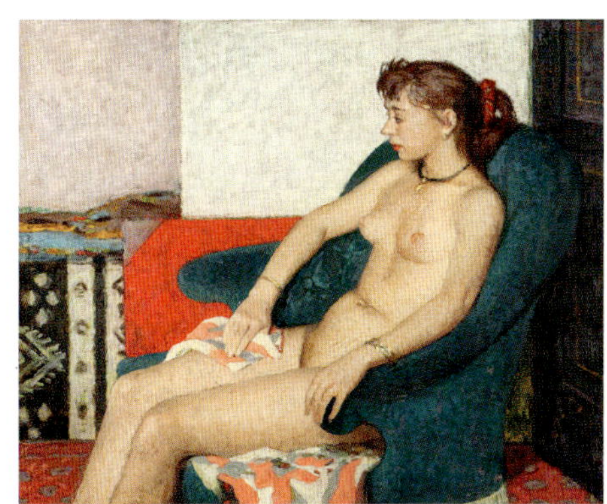

Le Bas, Edward 1904–1966
Model Resting c.1955
oil on board 91.4 x 109.2
3031

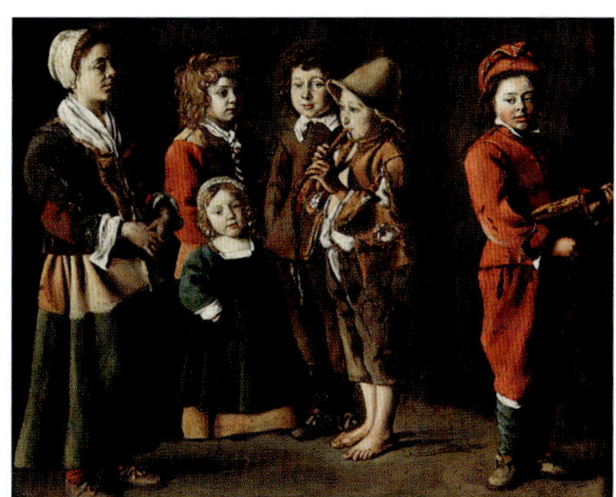

Le Nain, Antoine (attributed to)
c.1588–1648
Peasant Children c.1630–1640
oil on copper 21.6 x 27.9
35.578

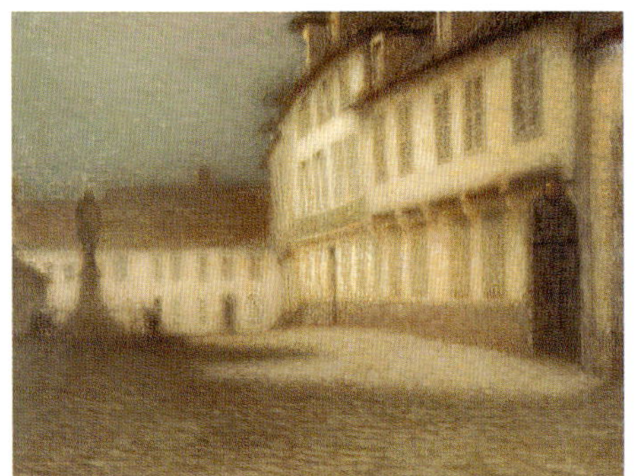

Le Sidaner, Henri Eugène 1862–1939
A Beauvais Square by Moonlight 1900
oil on canvas 70.2 x 92.4
2193

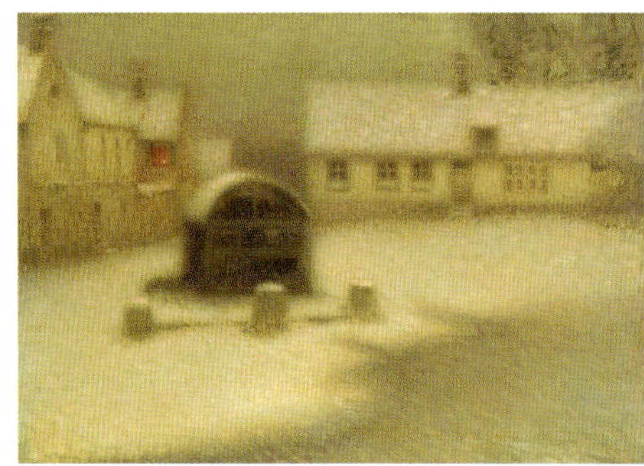

Le Sidaner, Henri Eugène 1862–1939
The Snow 1901
oil on canvas 55.9 x 74.9
35.621

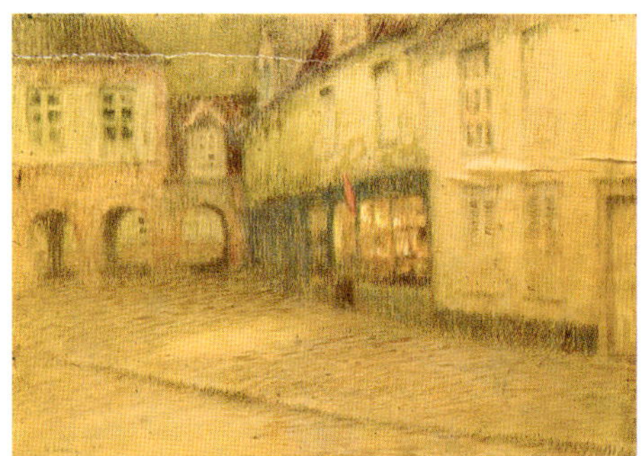

Le Sidaner, Henri Eugène 1862–1939
The Lighted Window c.1905–1906
oil & chalk on paper on mahogany panel
30.5 x 40.6
35.619

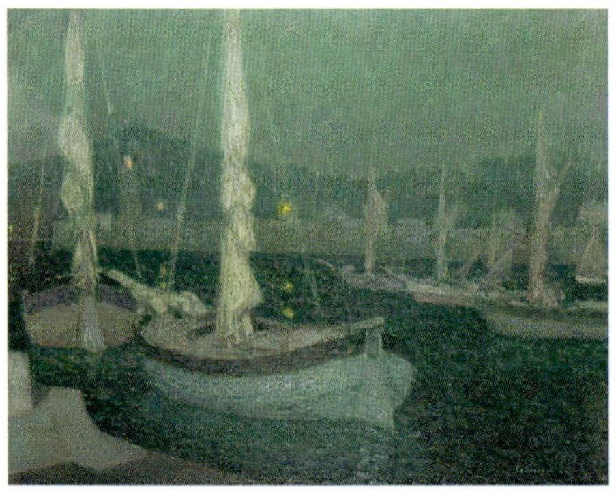

Le Sidaner, Henri Eugène 1862–1939
Rocky Inlets by Moonlight 1928
oil on canvas 64.5 x 81.3
35.618

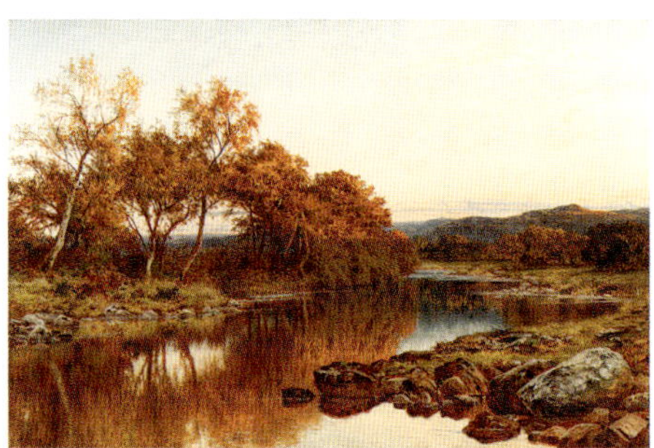

Leader, Benjamin Williams 1831–1923
A Golden Eve 1896
oil on canvas 121.9 x 182.8
2130

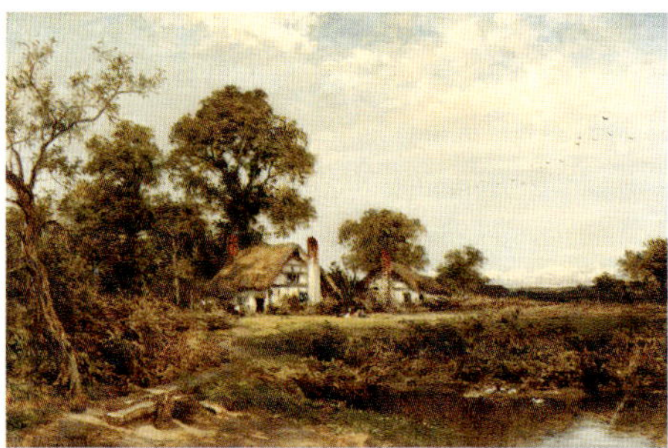

Leader, Benjamin Williams 1831–1923
Worcestershire Cottages 1901
oil on canvas 50.8 x 76.2
1508

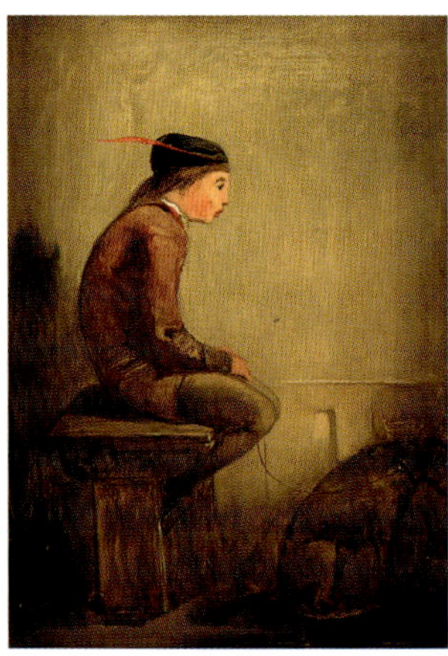

Lear, Edward 1812–1888
Launce and His Dog
oil on millboard 31.1 x 24.1
398

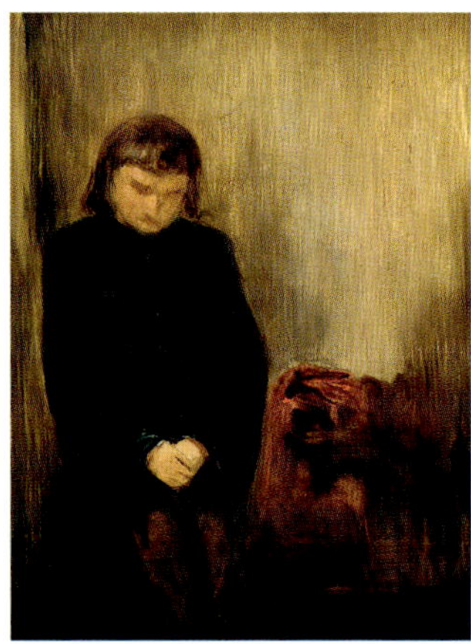

Lear, Edward 1812–1888
Valentine
oil on panel 29.8 x 21.6
400

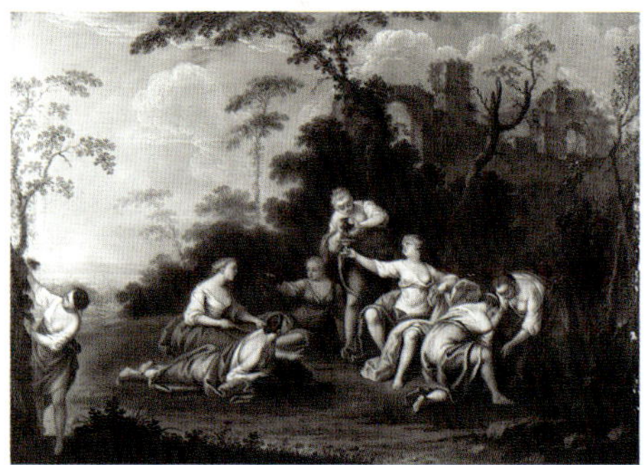

Leclerc, Jacques Sébastien (attributed to)
c.1734–1785
Autumn
oil on panel 27 x 35.6
411

Facing page: Dutch (Friesland) School, *Portrait of a Girl, Aged One, with a Rattle*, 1635 (p. 123)

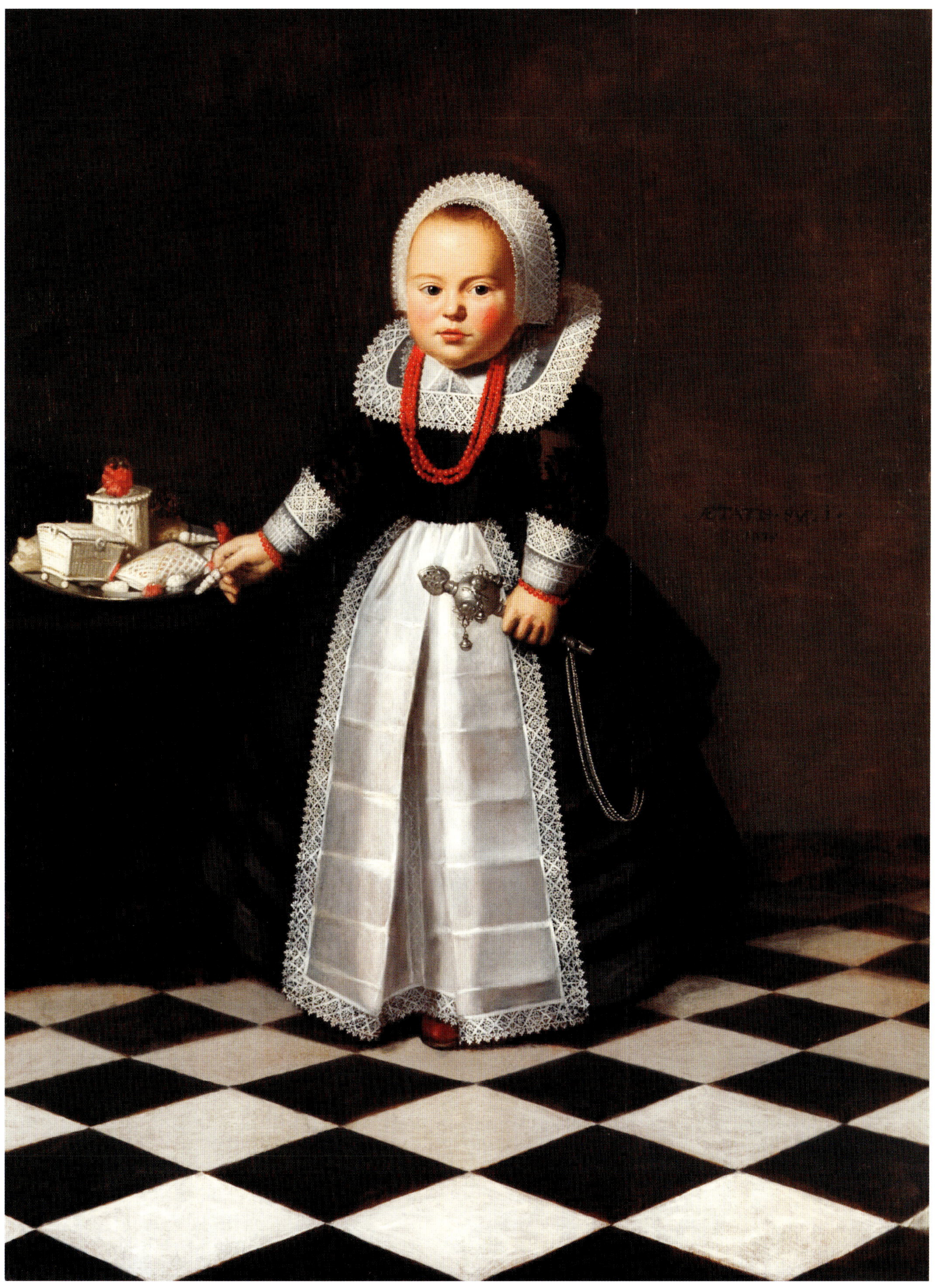

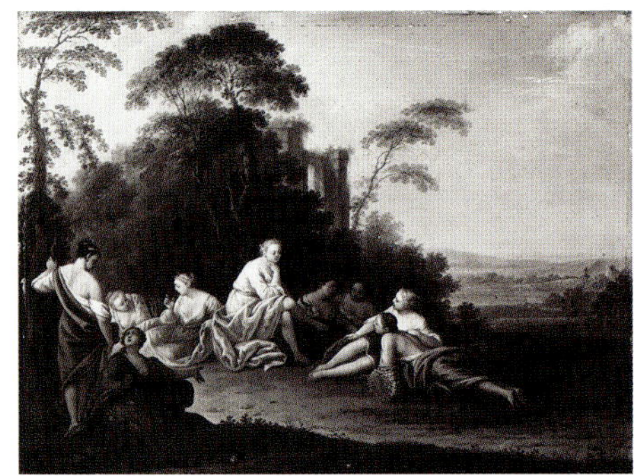

Leclerc, Jacques Sébastien (attributed to)
c.1734–1785
Summer
oil on panel 27 x 35.6
420

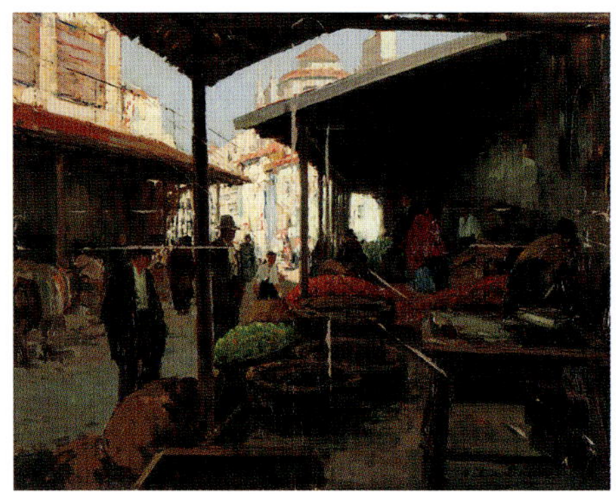

Lecomte, Paul Émile 1877–1950
The End of the Market, Granada, Spain
oil on canvas 65 x 80.8
2083

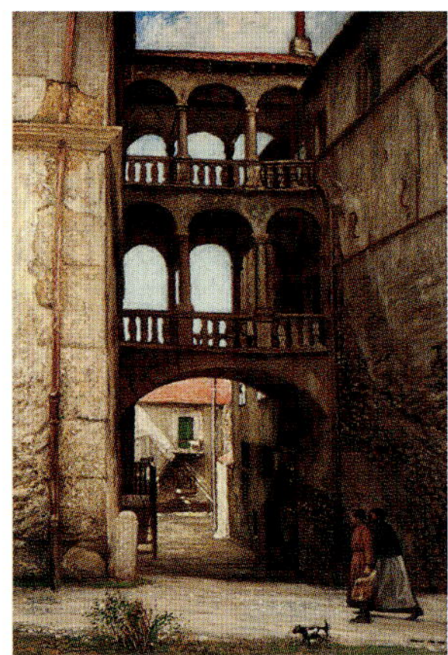

Lee, Sydney 1866–1949
The Gallery 1928
oil on canvas 132 x 88.9
1796

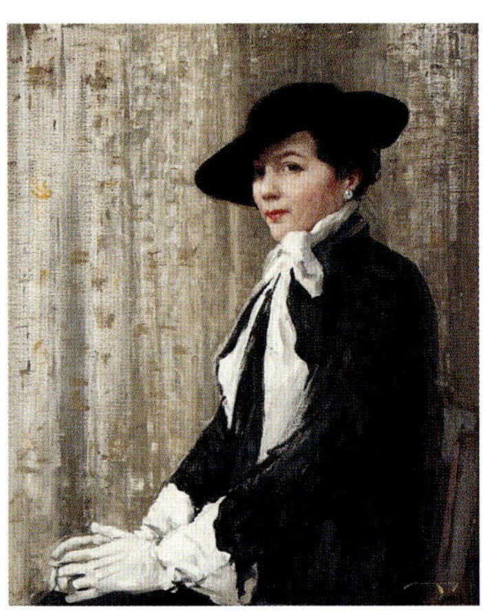

Lee-Hankey, William 1869–1952
Mrs John de la Valette c.1934
oil on canvas 76.2 x 63.5
1895

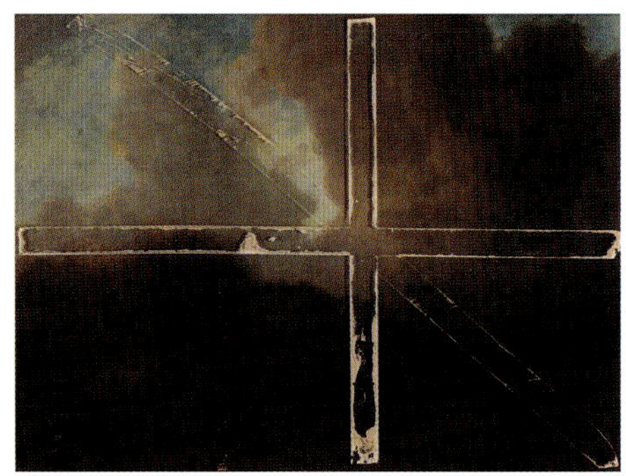

Legros, Alphonse 1837–1911
An Approaching Storm 1897
oil on canvas 85 x 112
1463

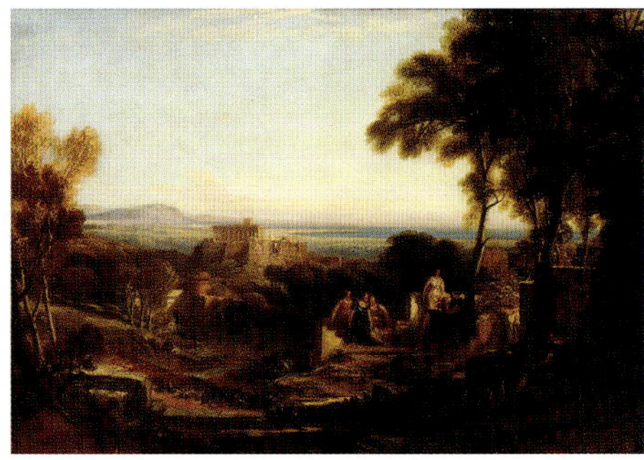

Leitch, William Leighton 1804–1883
Classical Composition
oil on canvas 30.5 x 43.2
1054

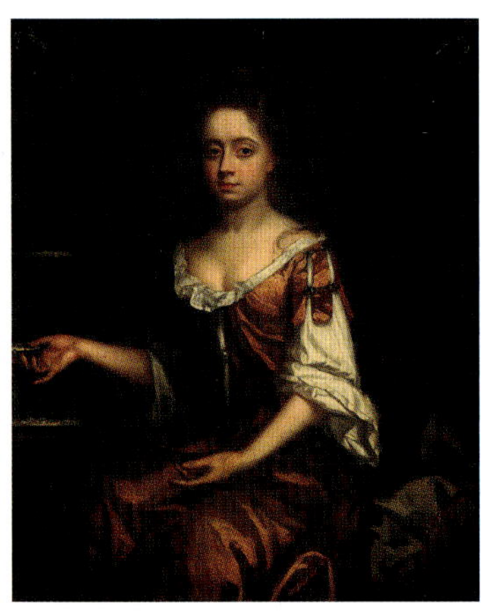

Lely, Peter (after) 1618–1680
The Duchess of Lauderdale c.1671–1680
oil on canvas 114.3 x 94
260

Lely, Peter (after) 1618–1680
Edward Hyde (1609–1674), Earl of Clarendon 17th C
oil on canvas 127 x 104.1
PC.135

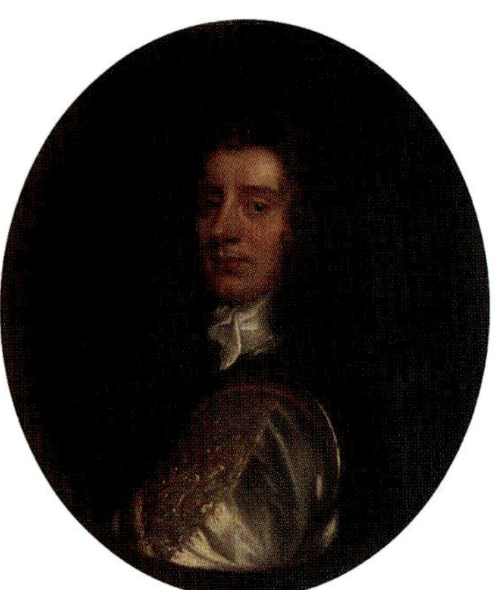

Lely, Peter (attributed to) 1618–1680
Portrait of a Man c.1675
oil on canvas 71.7 x 60.9
PL.166 (P)

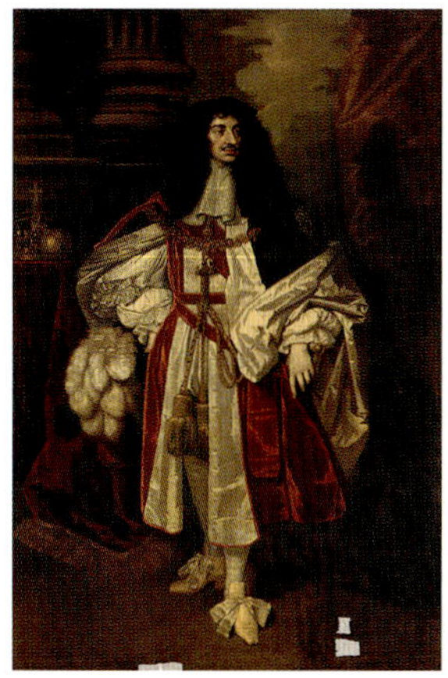

Lely, Peter (studio of) 1618–1680
Charles II (1630–1685) 1670
oil on canvas 238.8 x 157.5
474

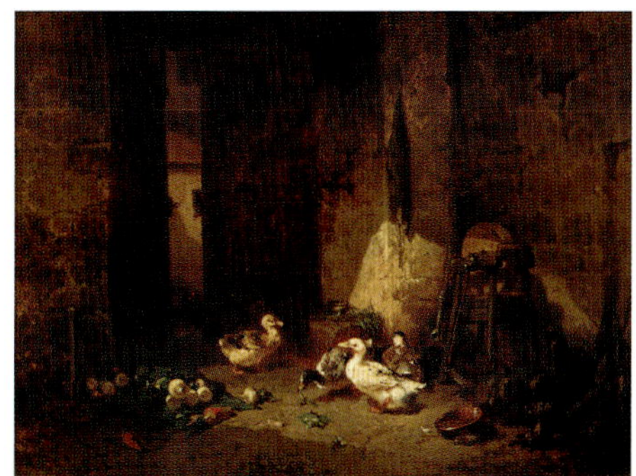

Lemmens, Theophile Victor Émile
1821–1867
Poultry 1857
oil on canvas 24.3 x 32.6
837

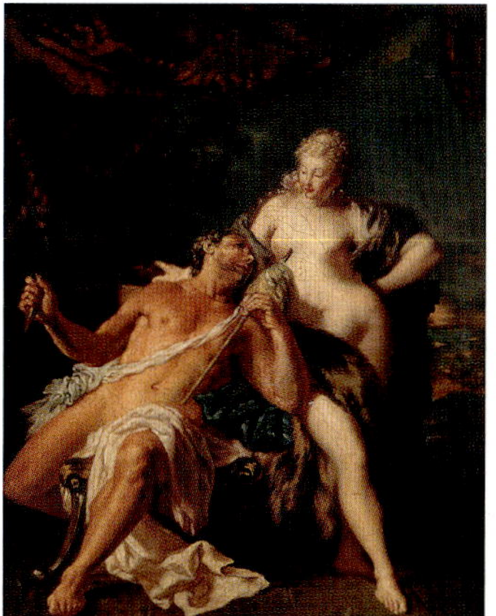

Lemoine, François (after) 1688–1737
Hercules and Omphale c.1734–1750
oil on canvas 68.6 x 54.6
2999

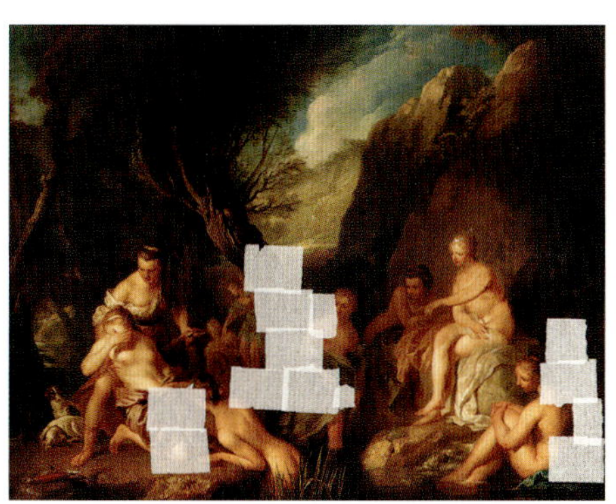

Lemoine, François (after) 1688–1737
The Guilt of Callisto 18th C
oil on canvas 74.8 x 92.5
48

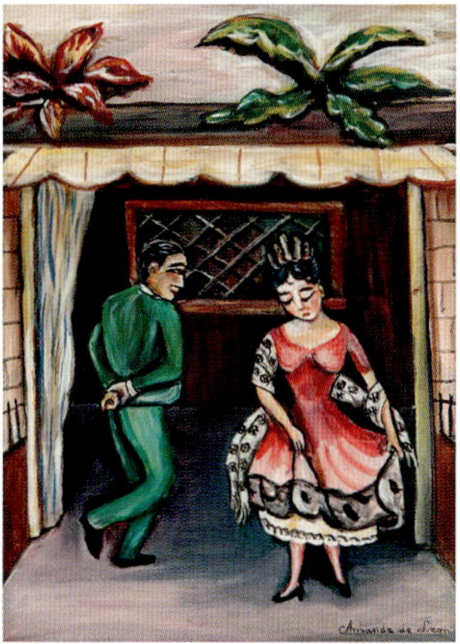

Leon, Amanda de b.1908
Spanish Dancers
oil on panel 40.6 x 30.5
3015

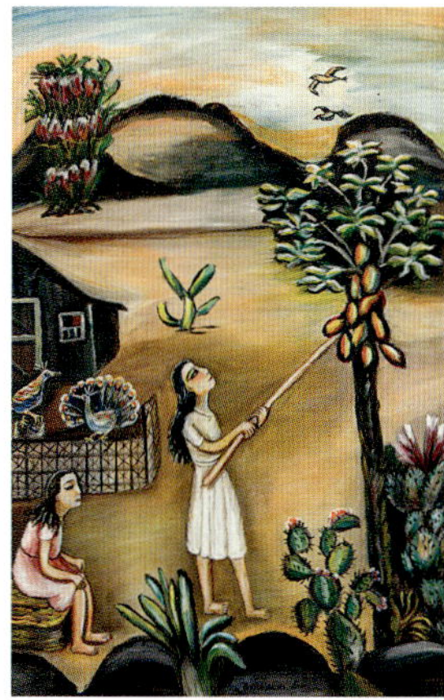

Leon, Amanda de b.1908
The Papaya Tree
oil on panel 76.8 x 50.8
3014

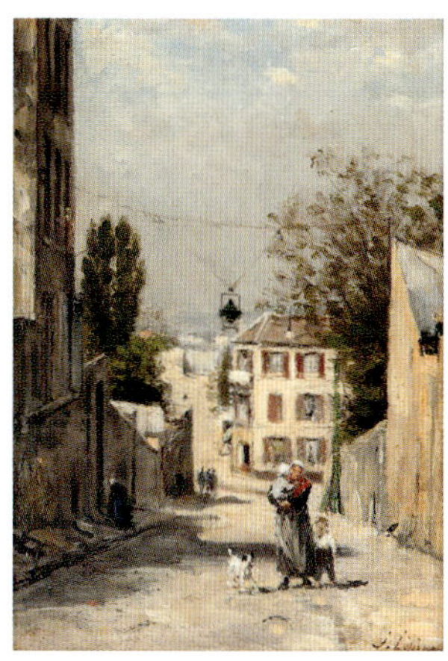

Lépine, Stanislas 1835–1892
The Rue de Norvins, Montmartre c.1876–1880
oil on canvas 32.1 x 23.7
2401

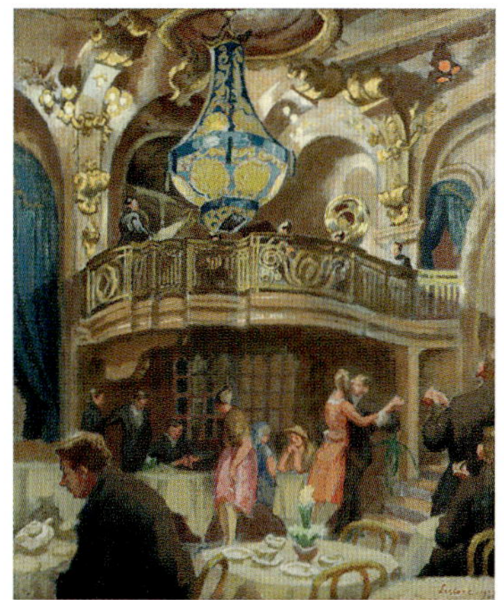

Lessore, Thérèse 1884–1945
Thé dansant 1932
oil on canvas 76.2 x 63.5
2611

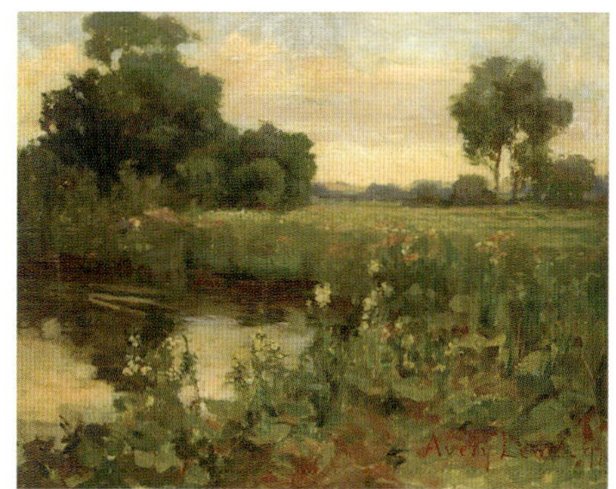

Lewis, Leonard Avery 1866–1906
Berkshire Landscape 1897
oil on canvas 40.6 x 55.9
2575

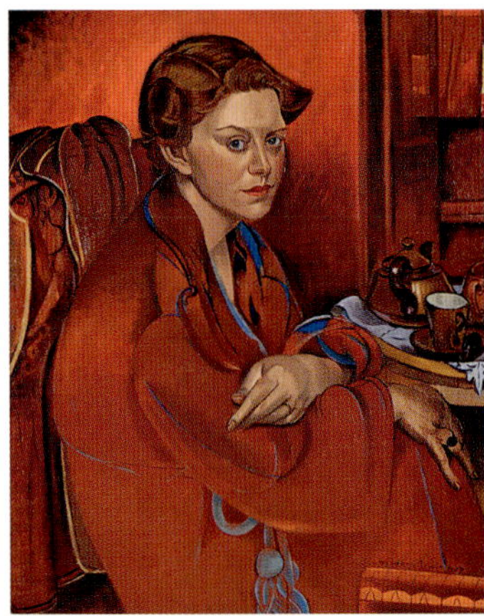

Lewis, Wyndham 1882–1957
Froanna, the Artist's Wife 1937
oil on canvas 76.2 x 63.5
2155

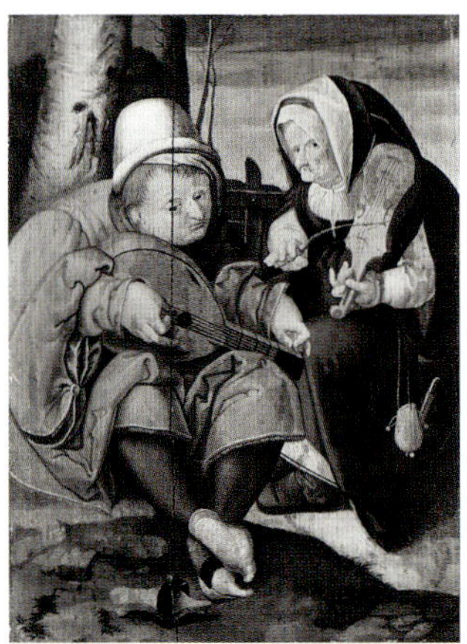

Leyden, Lucas van (after) c.1494–1533
Musicians: An Old Man and an Old Woman
18th C/early 19th C
oil on panel 47.9 x 34.9
587

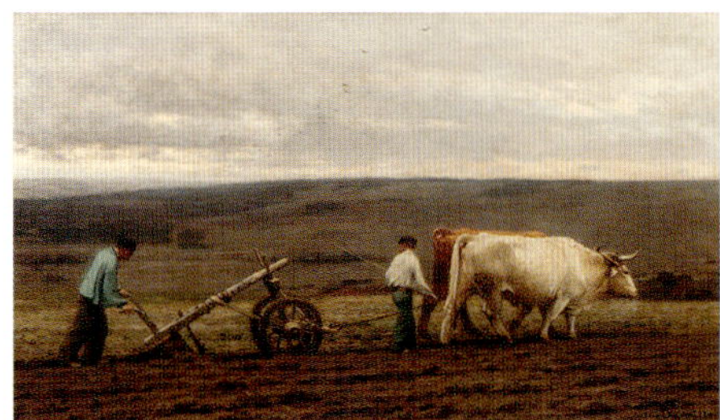

Lhermitte, Léon-Augustin 1844–1925
Ploughing with Oxen c.1871
oil on canvas 60 x 103
2229

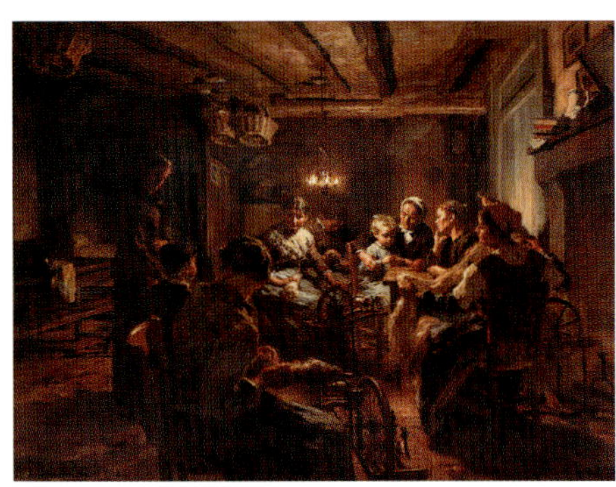

Lhermitte, Léon-Augustin 1844–1925
Evening Work 1888
oil on canvas 93.5 x 122
2140

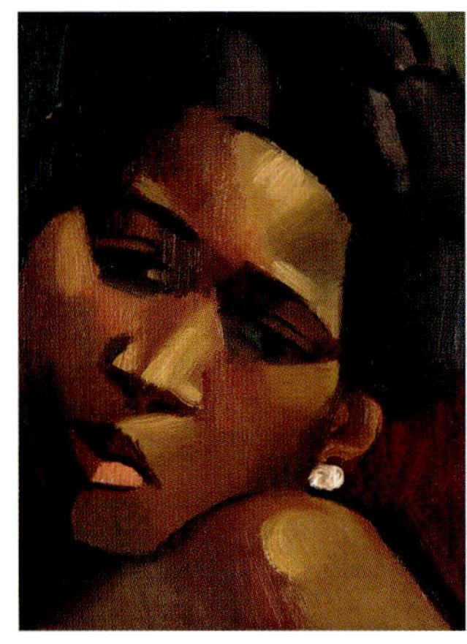

Lhote, André 1885–1962
Negress
oil on canvas 35.2 x 27
2930

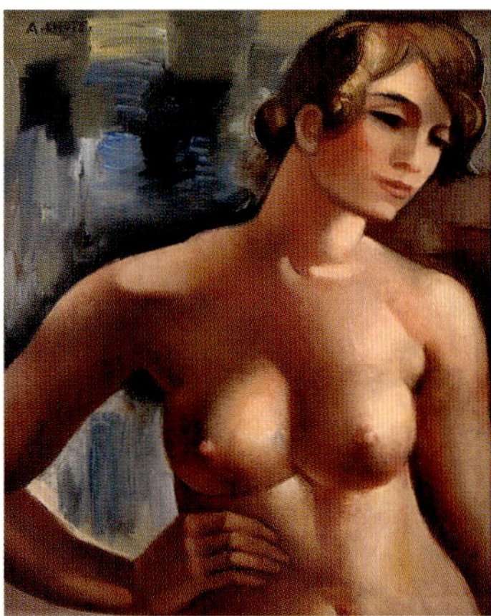

Lhote, André 1885–1962
Nude
oil on canvas 72.8 x 59
2931

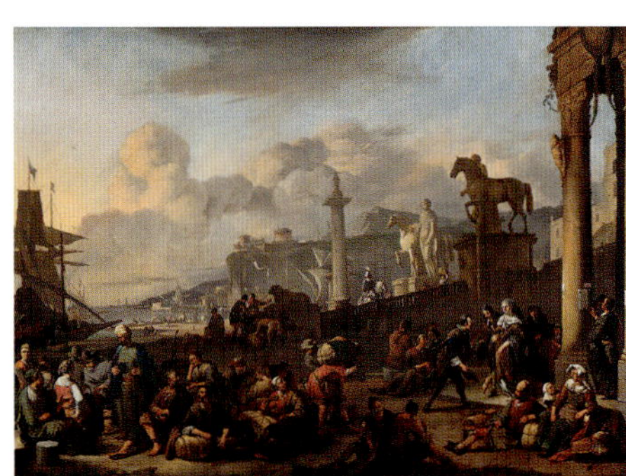

Lingelbach, Johannes 1622–1674
An Imaginary Mediterranean Seaport 1668
oil on canvas 76.2 x 104.4
588

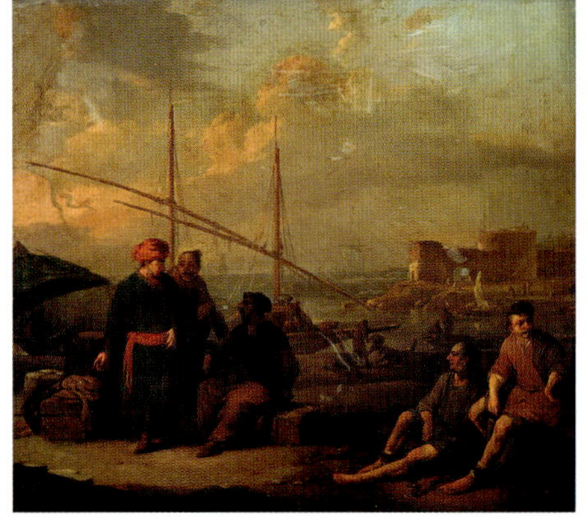

Lingelbach, Johannes 1622–1674
A Harbour, with Figures in Oriental Costume
oil on canvas 33.3 x 39
342

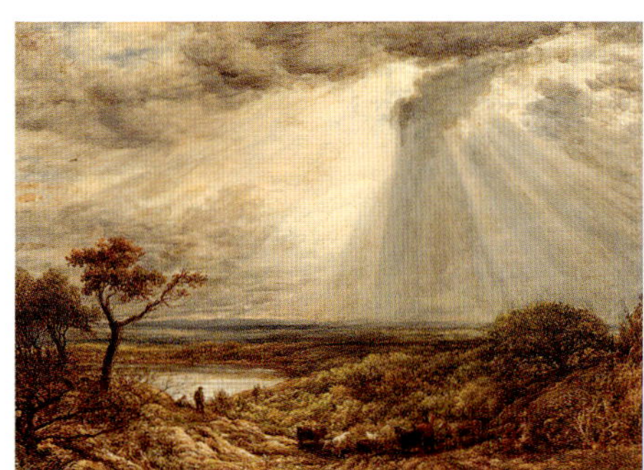

Linnell, John 1792–1882
Downward Rays 1872
oil on canvas 69.9 x 97.8
739

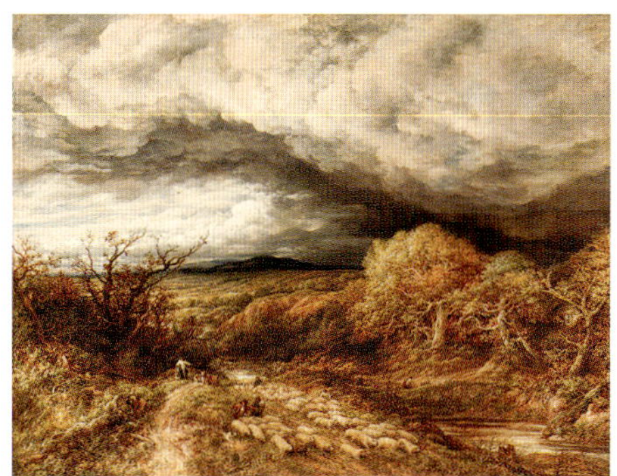

Linnell, John 1792–1882
A Coming Storm 1873
oil on canvas 127 x 167.7
648

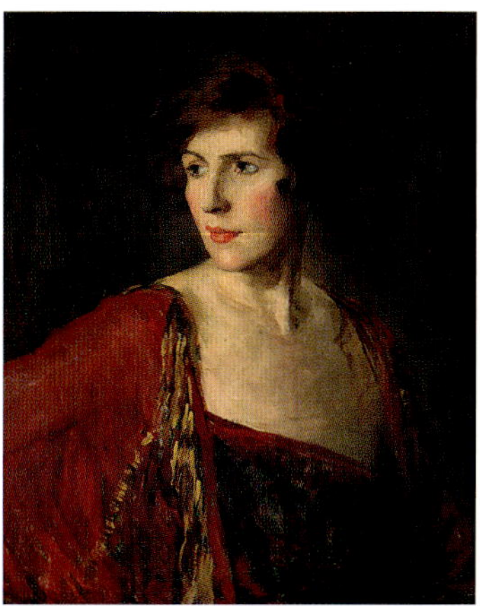

Lion, Flora 1878–1958
Mrs Ralph Peto 1921
oil on canvas 60.8 x 50.7
3142

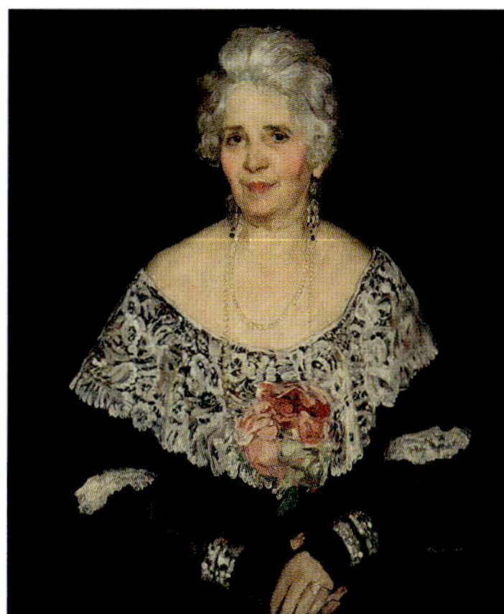

Lion, Flora 1878–1958
Mrs Hunter Crawford
oil on canvas 76.5 x 63.3
3141

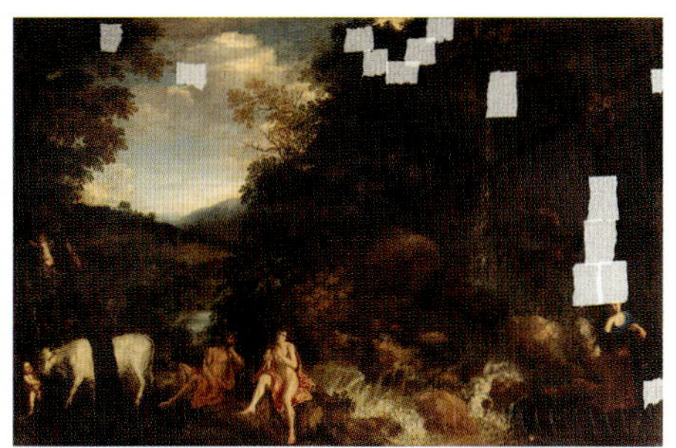

Lisse, Dirck van der 1586–1669
Landscape with Mercury, Argus and Io
oil on canvas 67.3 x 104.4
595

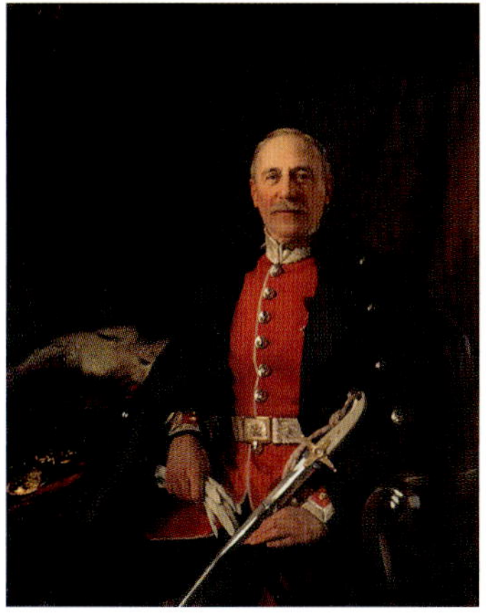

Llewellyn, William Samuel Henry
1858–1941
*Sir David Mason (1862–1940), Lord Provost of
Glasgow (1926–1929)* c.1930
oil on canvas 127 x 101.6
1807

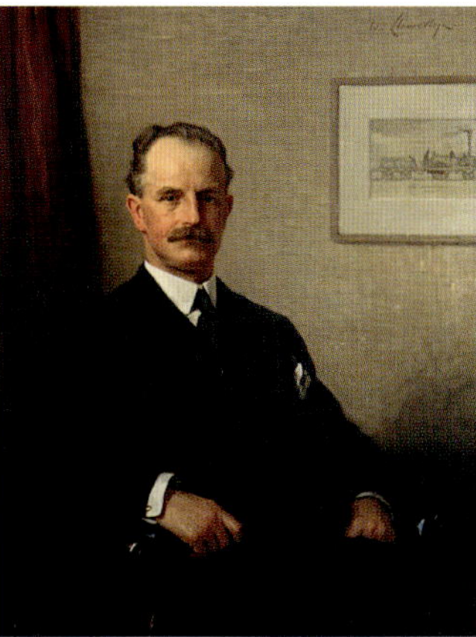

Llewellyn, William Samuel Henry
1858–1941
Sir Hugh Reid (1860–1935)
oil on canvas 109.9 x 85.1
OG.1962.23

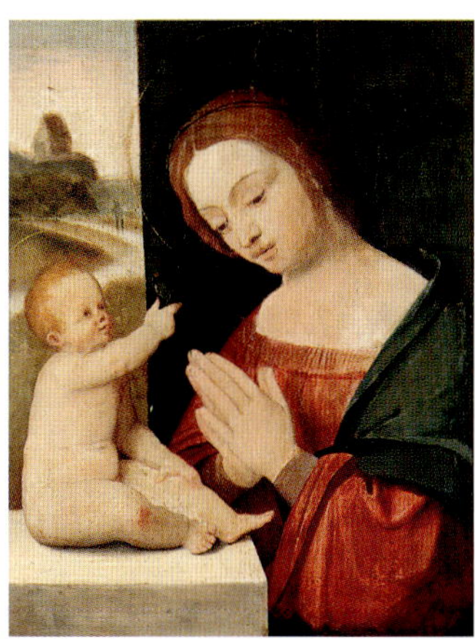

L'Ortolano 1485–c.1527
Madonna and Child c.1505
oil on panel 38.2 x 29.5
624

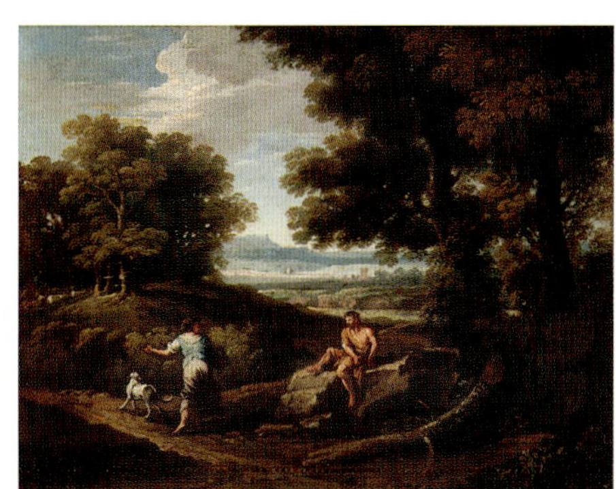

Locatelli, Andrea 1695–1741
Landscape and Figures c.1720–1725
oil on canvas 27.9 x 34.9
173

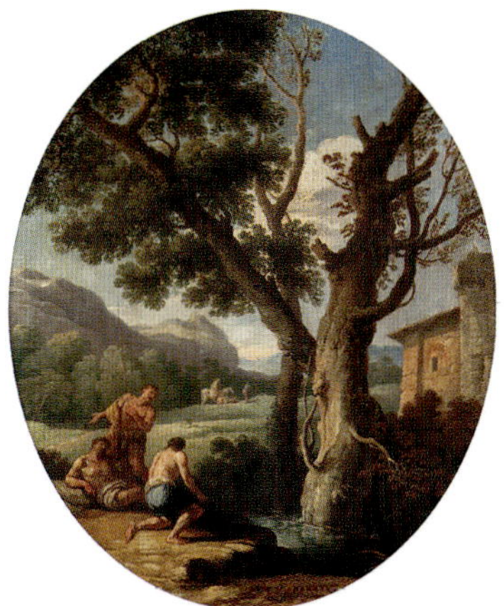

Locatelli, Andrea 1695–1741
Landscape with Three Fishermen by a Stream
c.1730
oil on canvas 46.3 x 37.8
160

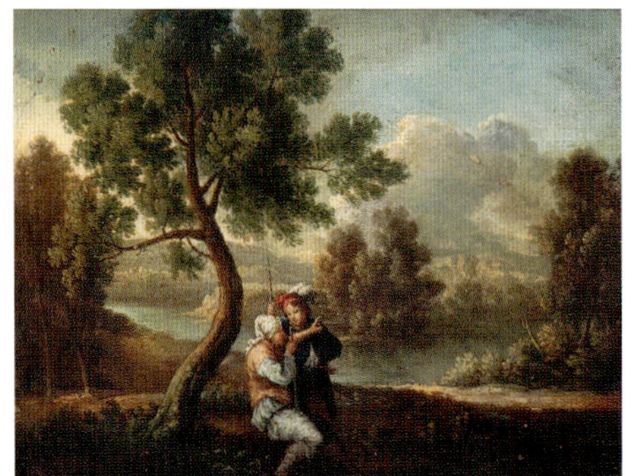

Locatelli, Andrea 1695–1741
Landscape with Figures
oil on canvas 27 x 34
NR.12

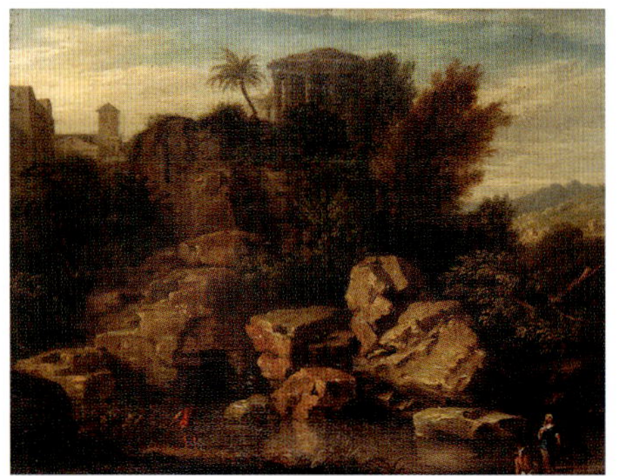

Locatelli, Andrea (style of) 1695–1741
Landscape with a Caprice View of the Temple of Vesta at Tivoli
oil on canvas 38.3 x 46.5
3060

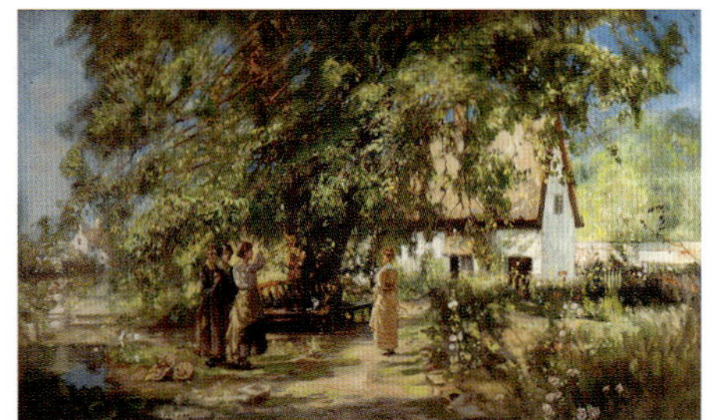

Lochhead, John 1866–1921
An Old World Garden c.1919
oil on canvas 76.2 x 127
1519

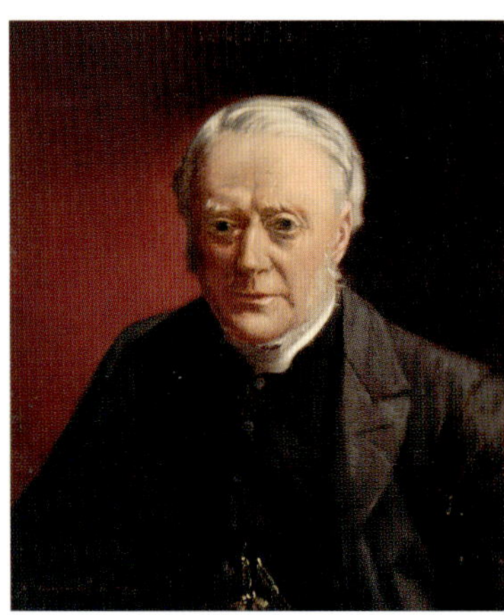

Lochhead, John 1866–1921
Reverend Monteith
oil on canvas 91 x 80.5
PP.1985.228

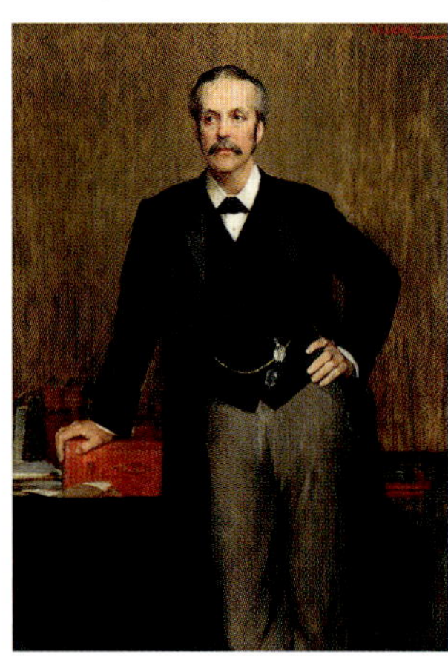

Lockhart, William Ewart 1846–1900
The Right Honourable Arthur J. Balfour (1848–1930), MP c.1898
oil on canvas 141 x 100.3
884

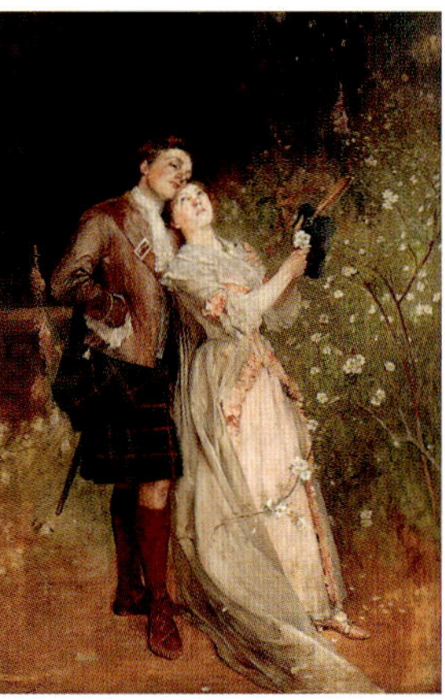

Lockhart, William Ewart 1846–1900
The White Cockade 1899
oil on canvas 182.9 x 121.9
1879

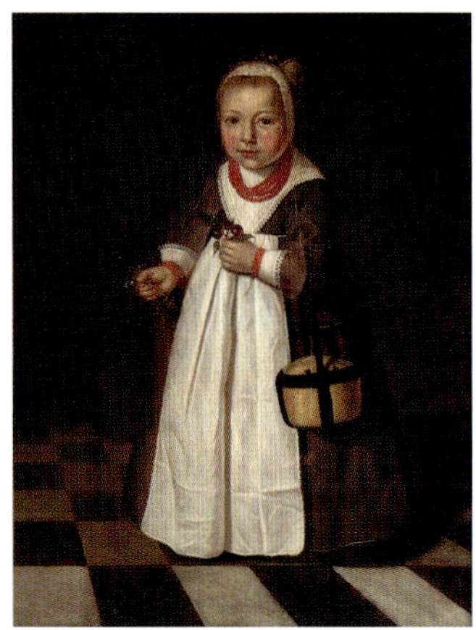

Loenen, Johan Cornelisz. van
c.1590–c.1643/1663
Portrait of a Little Girl 1630s
oil on panel 90.2 x 67.7
PL.75 (P)

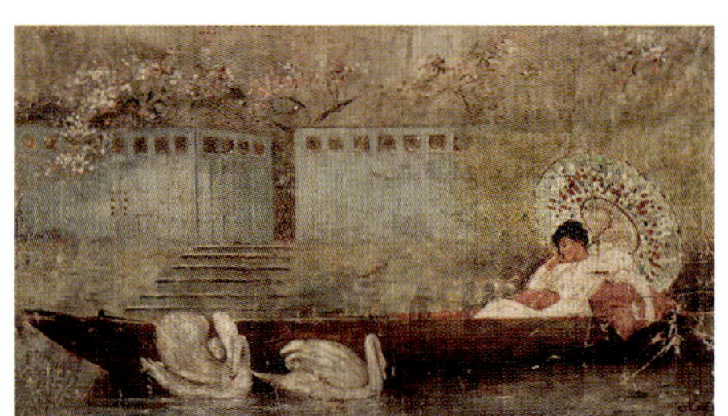

Logan, George 1866–1939
Lady Lying in a Punt with a Parasol
oil on canvas 55.2 x 90.5
E.1983.12.5

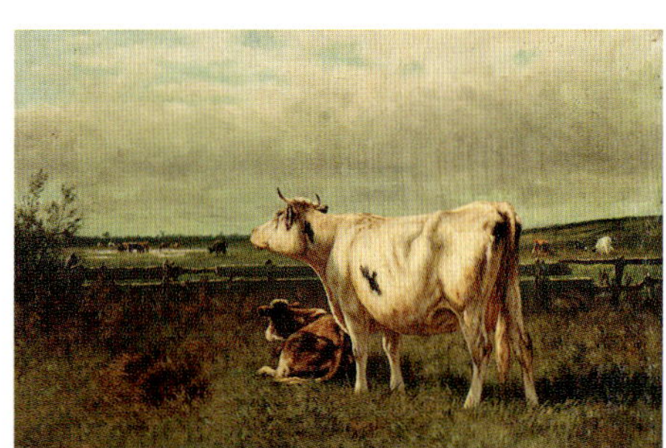

Lokhorst, Dirk Peter van (attributed to)
1848–1894
Landscape with Cattle
oil on canvas 61 x 91
785

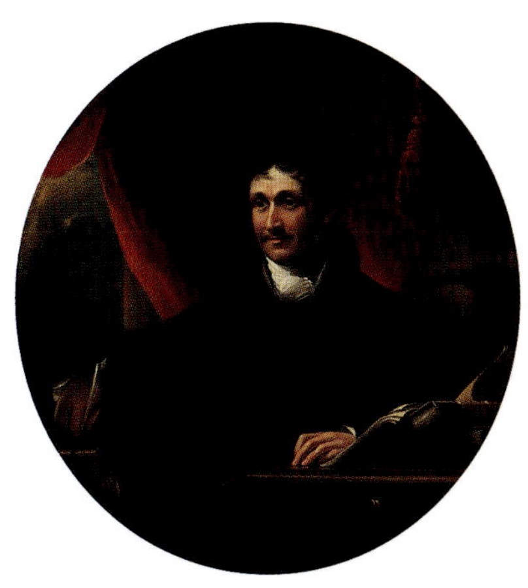

Lonsdale, James 1777–1839
Thomas Campbell (1777–1844), Poet c.1835
oil on canvas 109.2 x 99.1
1313

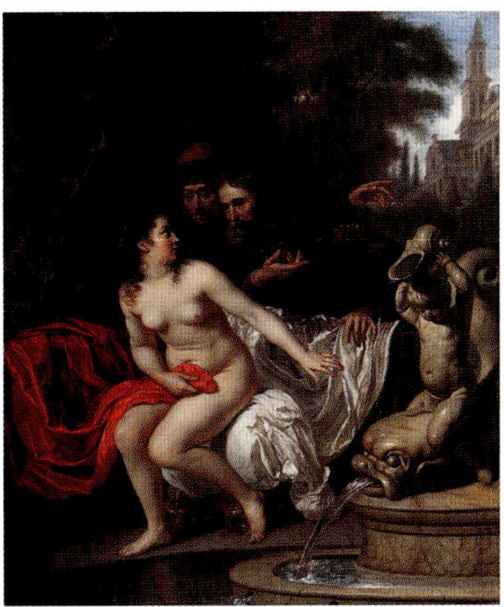

Loo, Jacob van c.1614–1670
Susannah and the Elders 1658
oil on canvas 77.5 x 65.1
623

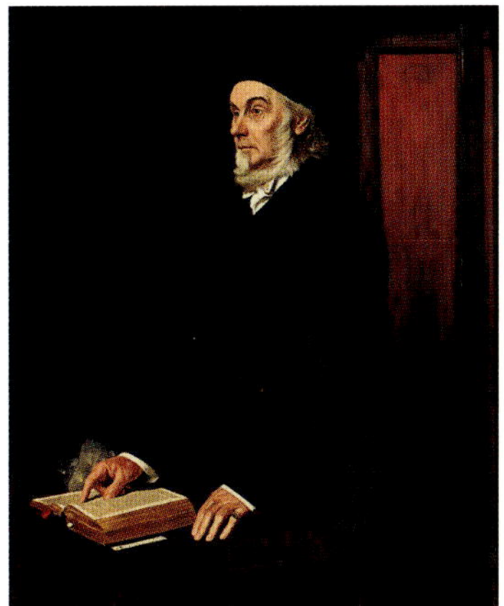

Lorimer, John Henry 1856–1936
Reverend Peter H. Waddell 1884–1893
oil on canvas 127 x 101.6
1063

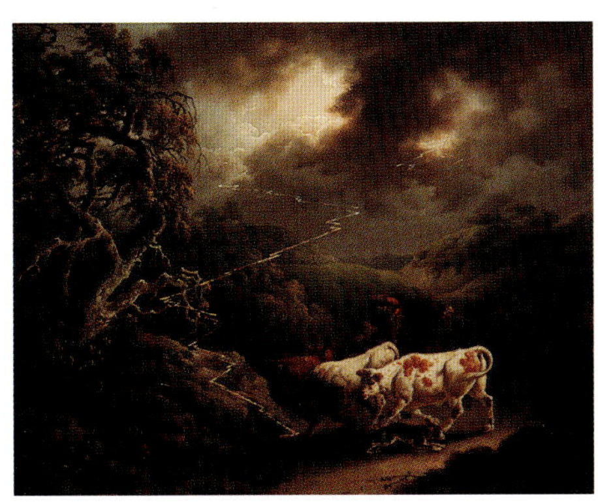

Loutherbourg, Philip James de 1740–1812
Horseman and Cattle in a Thunderstorm
c.1770–1780
oil on panel 27.3 x 33
371

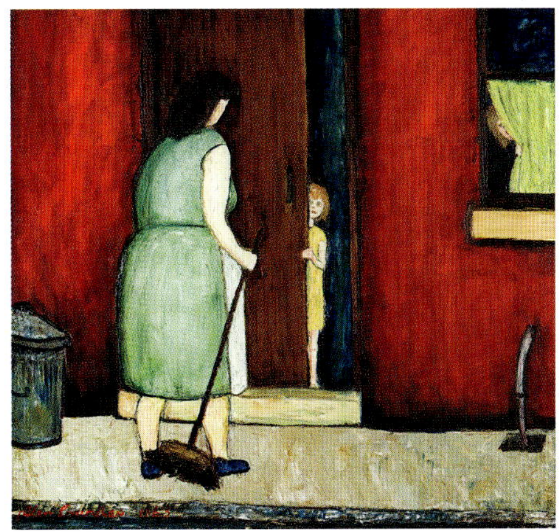

Lowndes, Alan 1921–1978
Mum Sweeping 1963
oil on canvas 89.5 x 89.5
3473

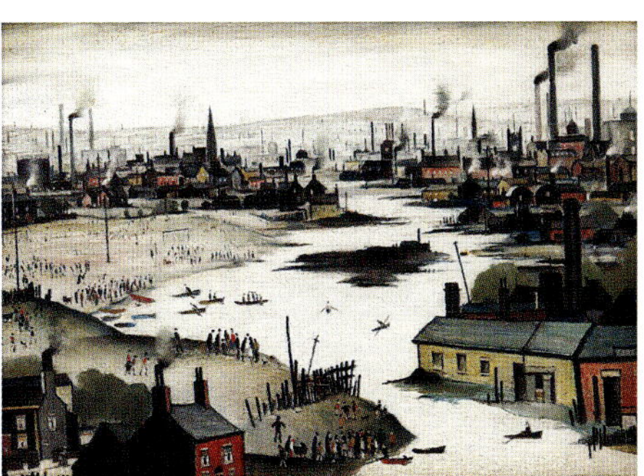

Lowry, Laurence Stephen 1887–1976
River Scene 1942
oil on plywood 45.7 x 63.5
2333

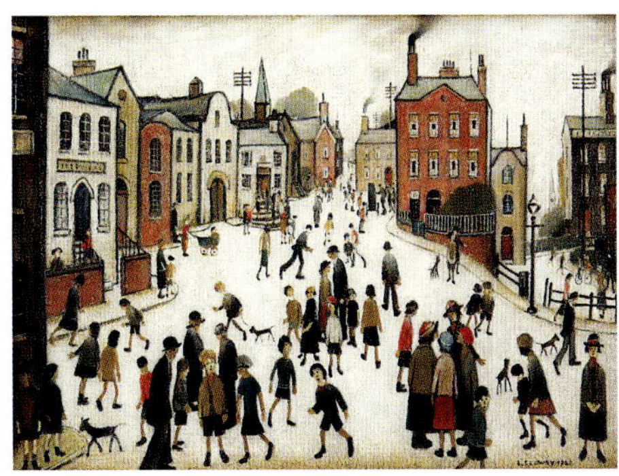

Lowry, Laurence Stephen 1887–1976
A Village Square 1943
oil on canvas 45.7 x 61
3235

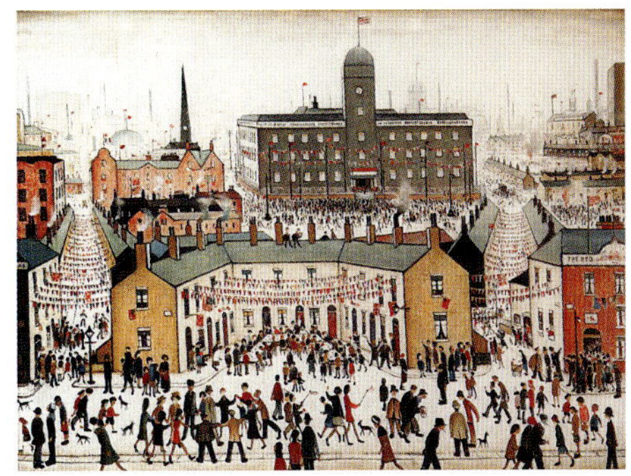

Lowry, Laurence Stephen 1887–1976
VE Day 1945
oil on canvas 78.7 x 101.6
2551

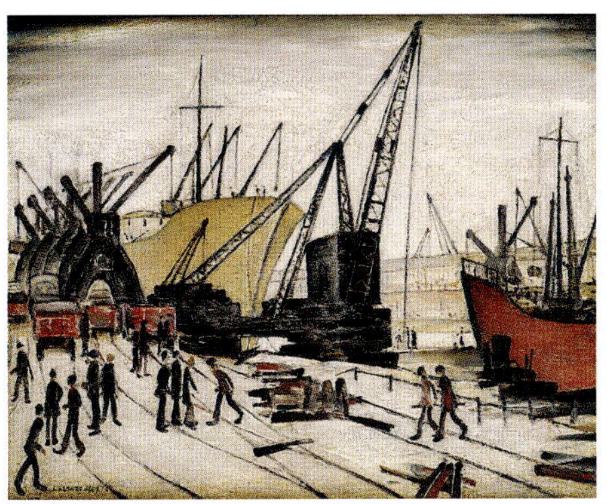

Lowry, Laurence Stephen 1887–1976
Cranes and Ships, Glasgow Docks 1947
oil on canvas 46.3 x 56.5
3651

Lowry, Laurence Stephen 1887–1976
Seascape 1950
oil on canvas 63.5 x 76.2
3487

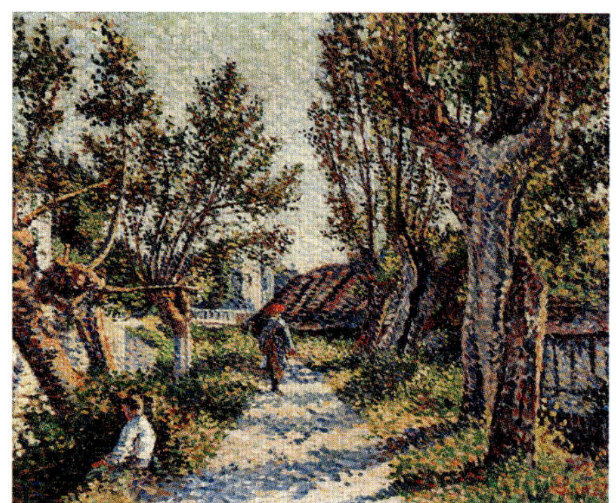

Luce, Maximilien 1858–1941
Landscape with Willow Trees 1887
oil on canvas 49.7 x 61.2
3318

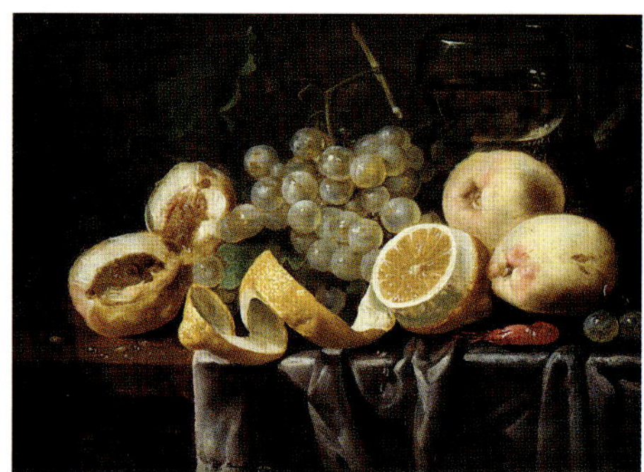

Luyckx, Carstian (after) 1623–c.1653
Still Life with Fruit
oil on panel 24.7 x 34.9
21

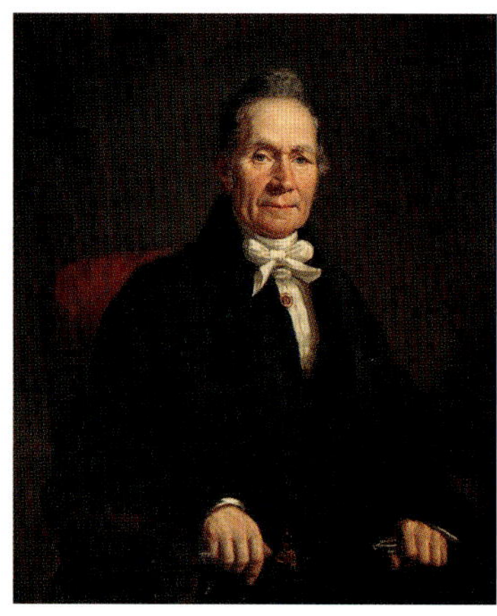

Macbeth, Norman 1821–1888
*James Turner of Thrushgrove (1768–1858), a
Former Magistrate of the City*
oil on canvas 91.4 x 76.2
1724

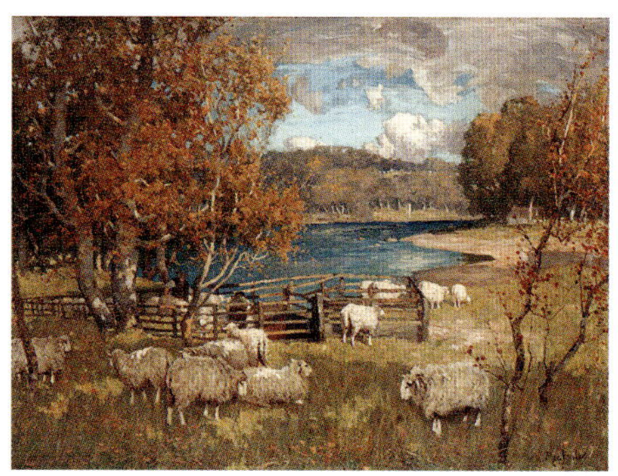

Macbride, William 1856–1913
Sheep Dipping, River Dee, Kirkcudbright
c.1907
oil on canvas 79.6 x 104.7
1204

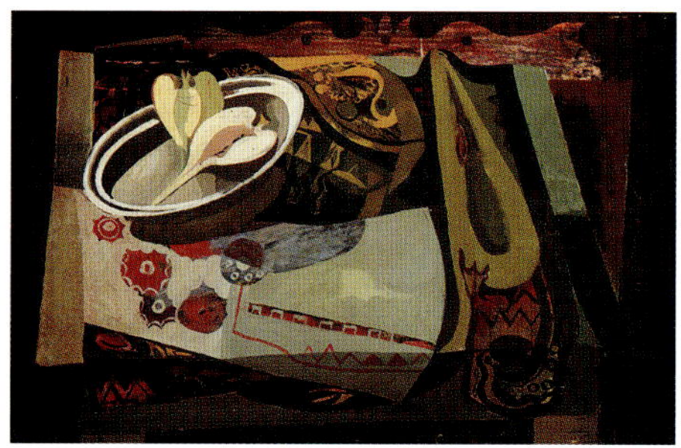

MacBryde, Robert 1913–1966
Still Life c.1942
oil on canvas 50.8 x 76.2
2937

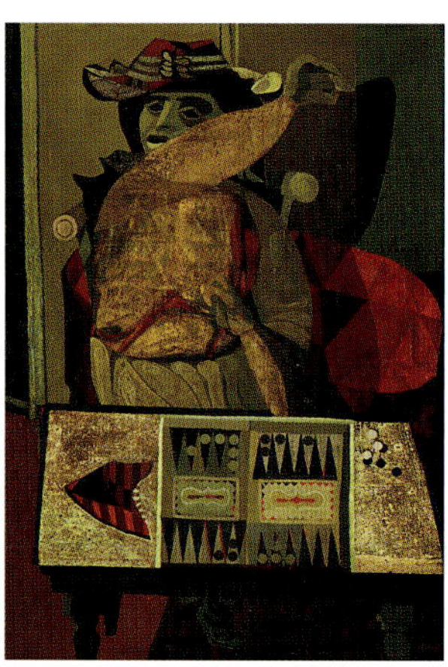

MacBryde, Robert 1913–1966
The Backgammon Player c.1947
oil on canvas 106.7 x 76.2
3376

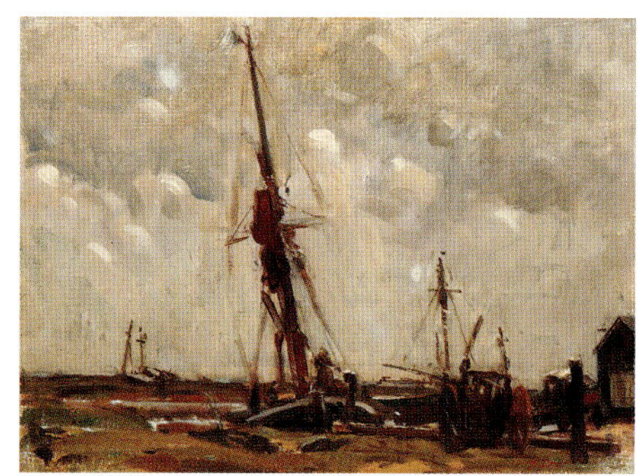

MacColl, Dugald Sutherland 1859–1948
Wardrope Hard, Tollesbury
oil on canvas 22.9 x 30.5
1777

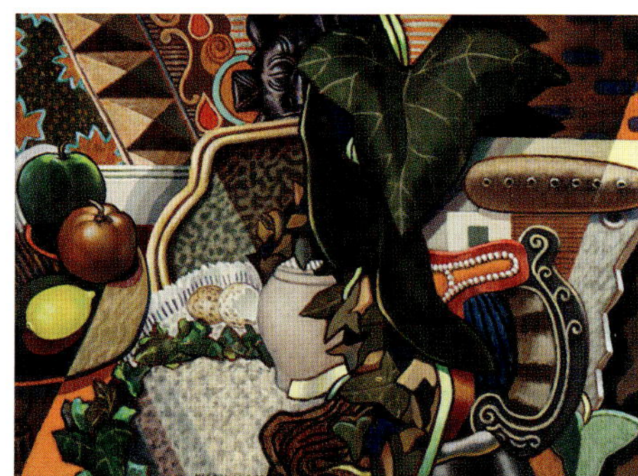

MacDonald, Tom 1914–1985
Still Life with a Plant 1979
oil on hardboard 76.2 x 101.6
3350

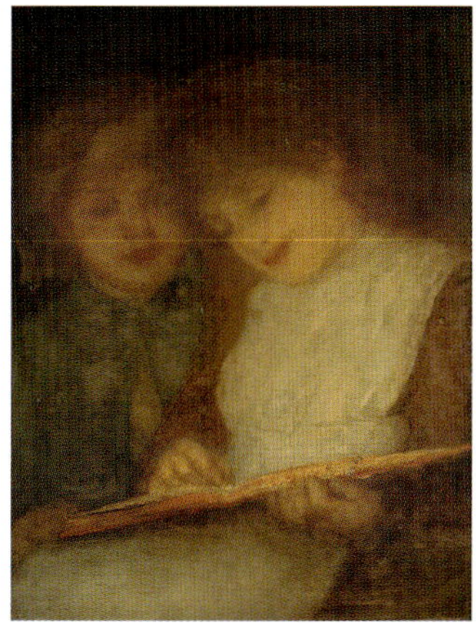

MacDougall, Norman McLeod 1849/1850–
1937 & **Maris Matthijs** 1839–1917
Girls Reading c.1885–1886
oil on canvas 52.1 x 40.6
35.344

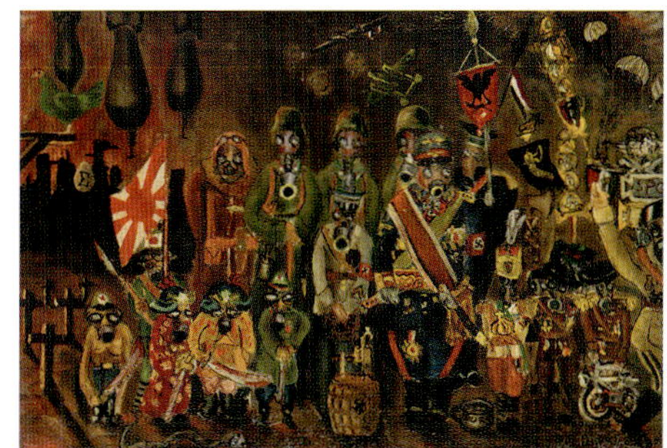

Macedo, Urbano de b.1912
Huns and Bersaglieri 1943
oil on canvas 38.7 x 54.9
2845

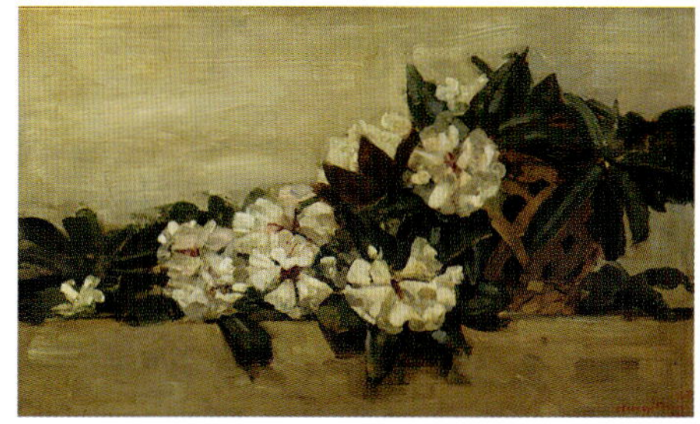

Macgillivray, James Pittendrigh 1856–1938
Rhododendrons 1887
oil on canvas 45.8 x 76.4
3347

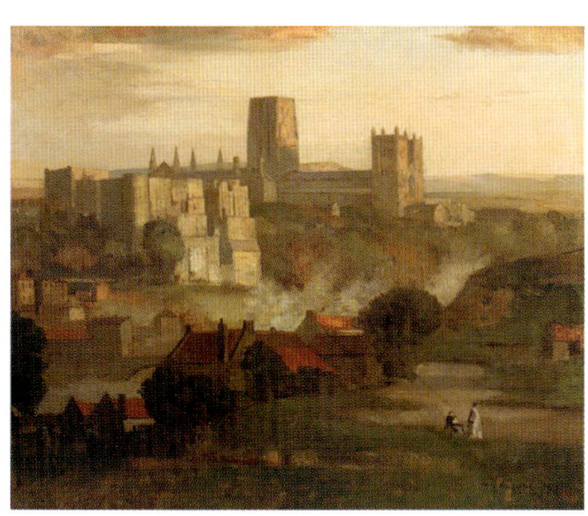

MacGregor, William York 1855–1923
Durham, Evening 1903
oil on canvas 116.8 x 142.2
1083

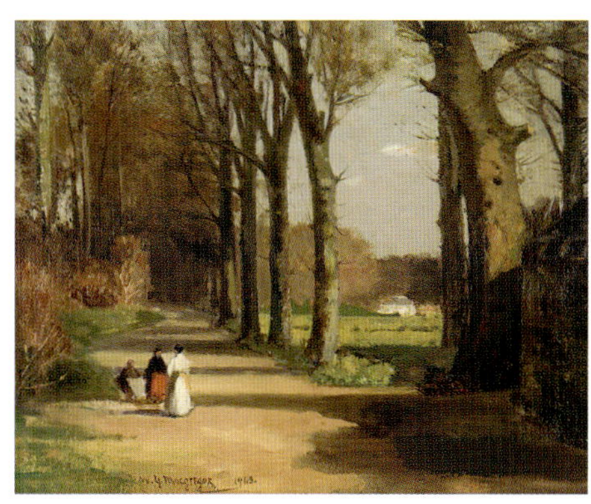

MacGregor, William York 1855–1923
Westerton, Bridge of Allan 1903
oil on canvas 57.2 x 69.2
3174

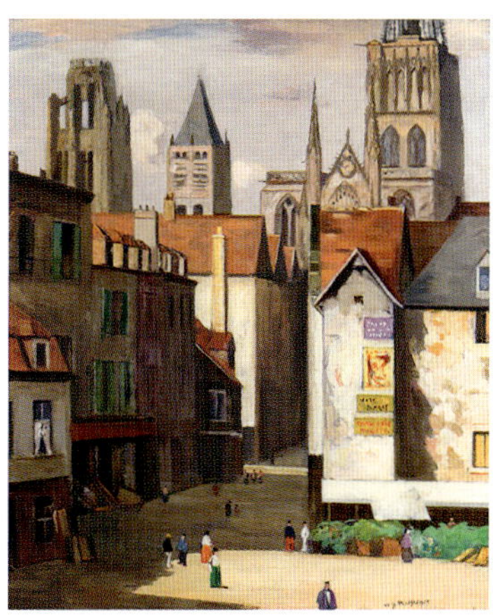

MacGregor, William York 1855–1923
A Street in Rouen
oil on canvas 71.1 x 58.4
3636

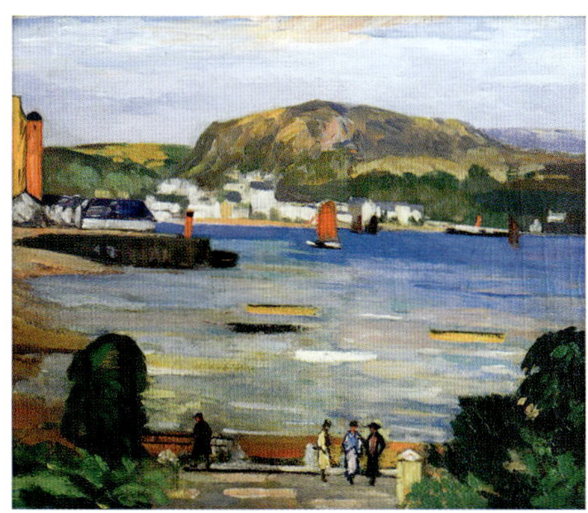

MacGregor, William York 1855–1923
Oban Bay
oil on canvas 64.8 x 77.5
2281

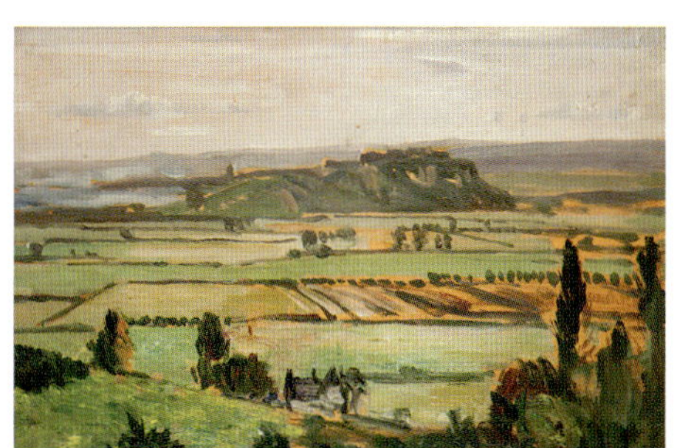

MacGregor, William York 1855–1923
Stirling Castle
oil on panel 25.4 x 35.6
2406

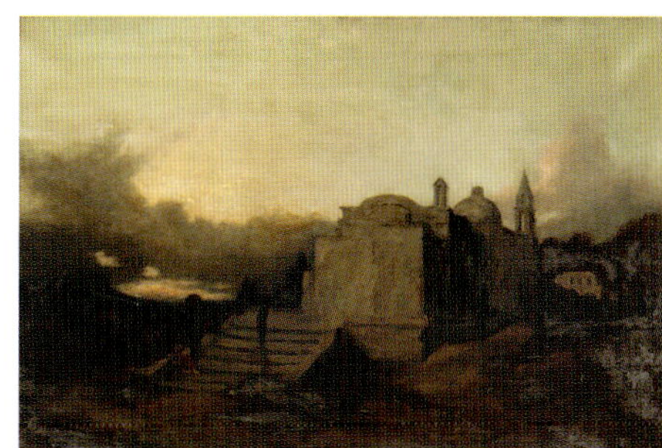

MacGregor, William York 1855–1923
The Convent, Twilight
oil on canvas 61 x 94
2267

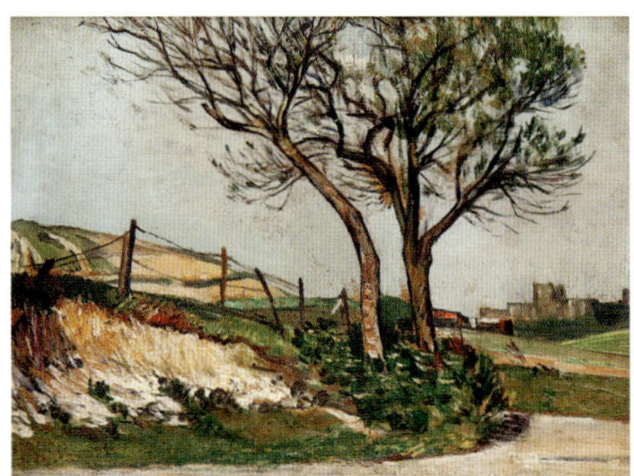

MacGregor, William York 1855–1923
Trees
oil on canvas 25.4 x 30.5
2272

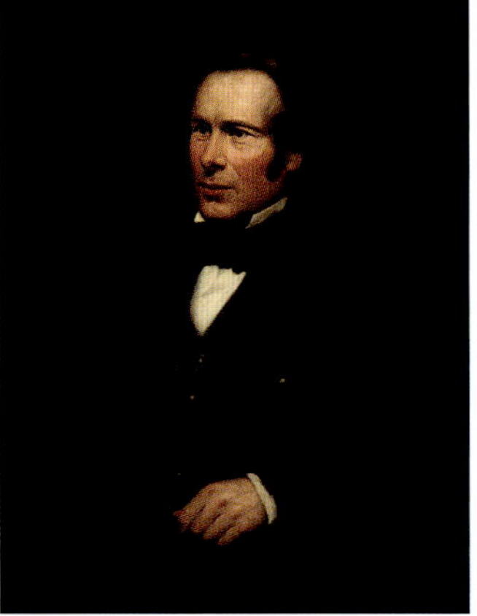

Mackay, Alexander S. 1832–1899
*Hugh Macdonald (1817–1860), the Glasgow
Rambler*
oil on canvas 91.4 x 71.4
1547

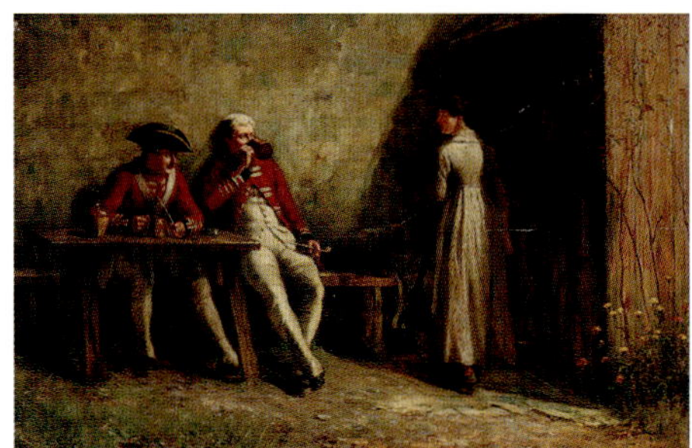

Mackellar, Duncan 1849–1908
*'The bee that sips the honey gets lost in the
sweets'* 1882
oil on canvas 66 x 101.6
2199

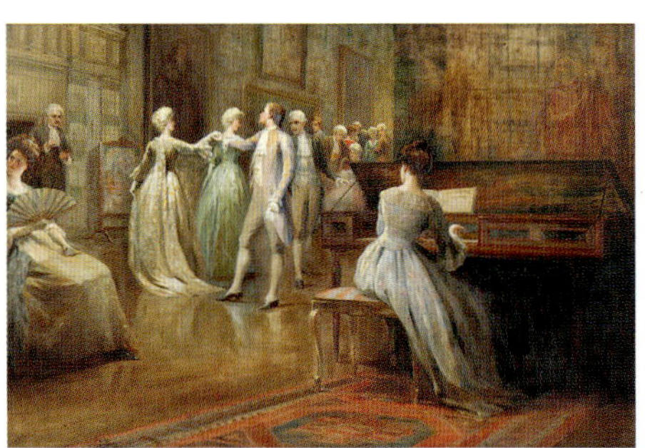

Mackellar, Duncan 1849–1908
The Minuet c.1908
oil on canvas 78.7 x 119.4
1221

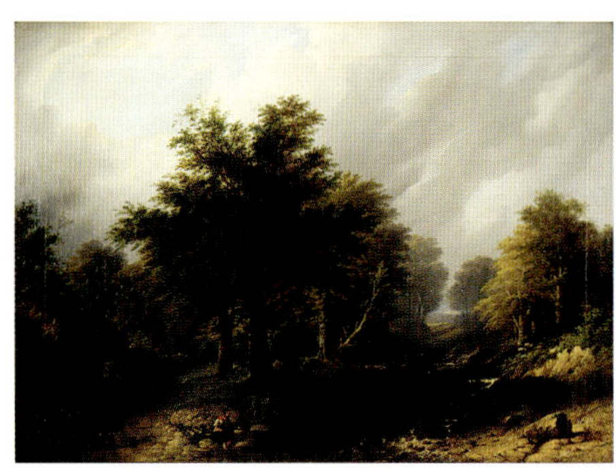

MacKenzie, David M. active 1832–1875
Braidburn, near Edinburgh 1845
oil on canvas 63.8 x 86.7
264

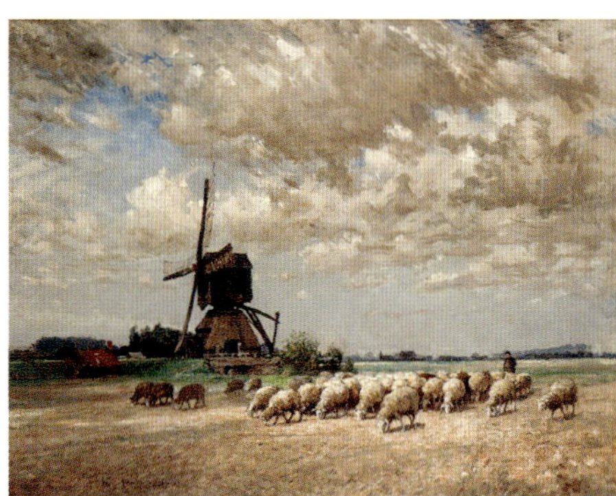

Mackenzie, James Hamilton 1875–1926
Fleeting Shadows c.1913
oil on canvas 99.1 x 125.7
1331

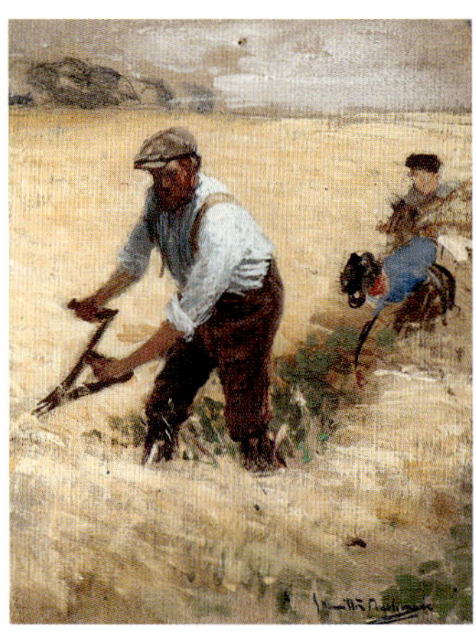

Mackenzie, James Hamilton 1875–1926
Reaper
oil on canvas 27.9 x 21.6
2411

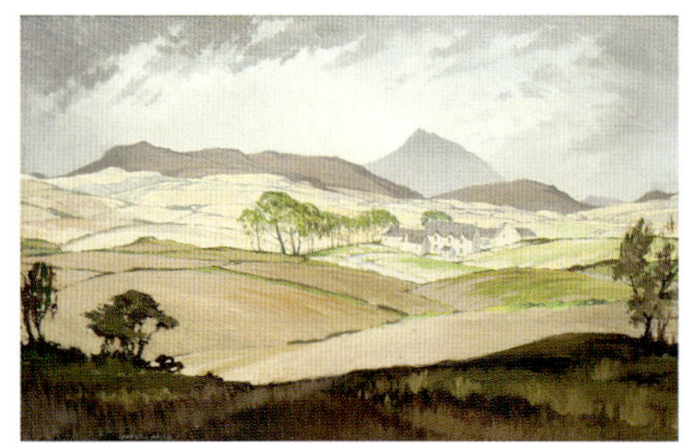

Mackie, Campbell 1886–1952
Ben Ledi
oil on canvas 61 x 91.4
2354

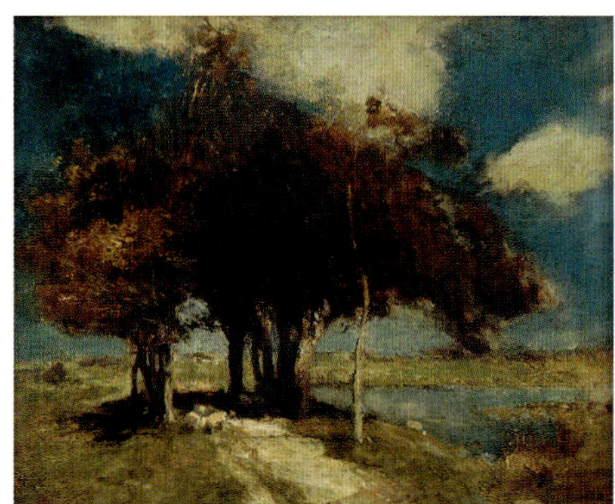

Mackie, Charles Hodge 1862–1920
Landscape with Sheep under Trees 1891
oil on canvas 32.9 x 40.6
3145

Facing page: Courbet, Gustave, 1819–1877, *The Charity of a Beggar at Ornans*, 1868 (p. 90)

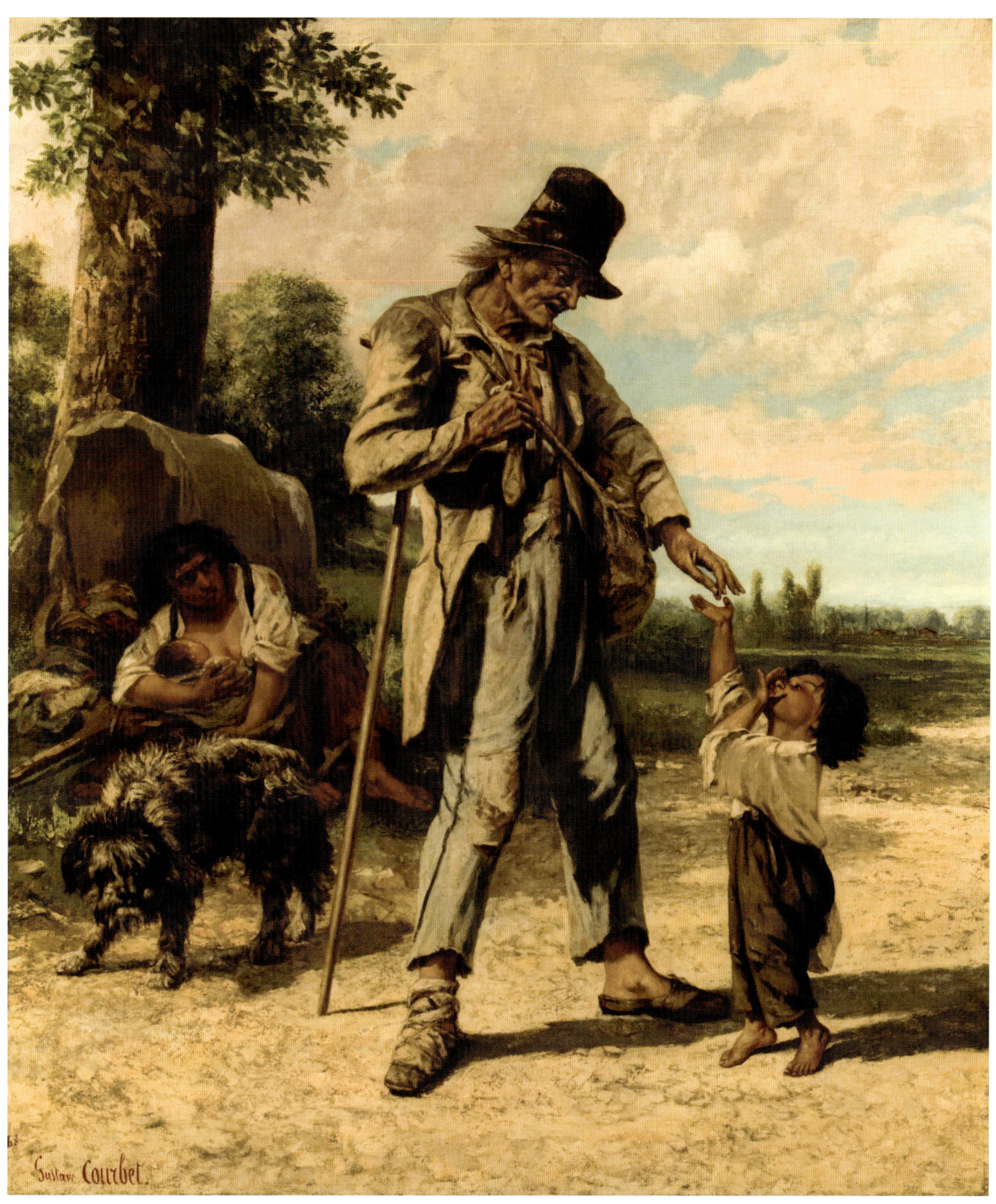

Gustave Courbet.

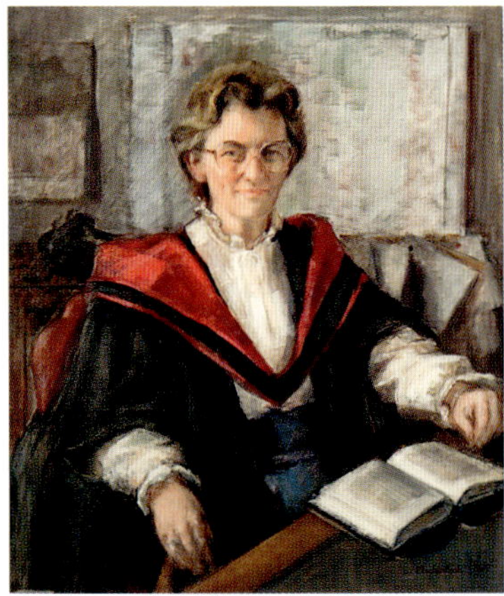

Mackintosh, Anne H. b.1944
Miss Jean Rutherford 1986
oil on canvas 105 x 99
ME.2007.1.6

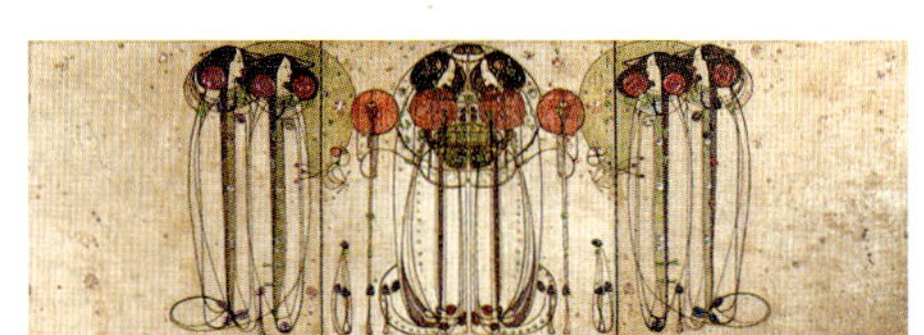

Mackintosh, Charles Rennie 1868–1928
The Wassail 1900
gesso, hessian, scrim, twine, glass beads,
thread, mother of pearl & tin leaf on
panel 158.2 x 462
E.1981.177.1-3

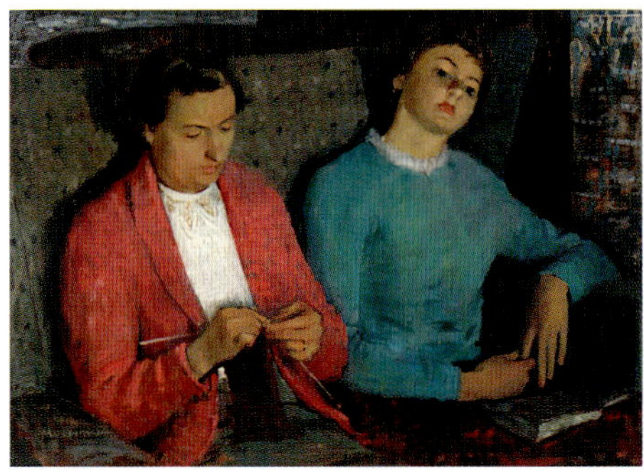

Mackintosh, John 1931–1966
Sunday Afternoon 1955
oil on canvas 66 x 91.4
3040

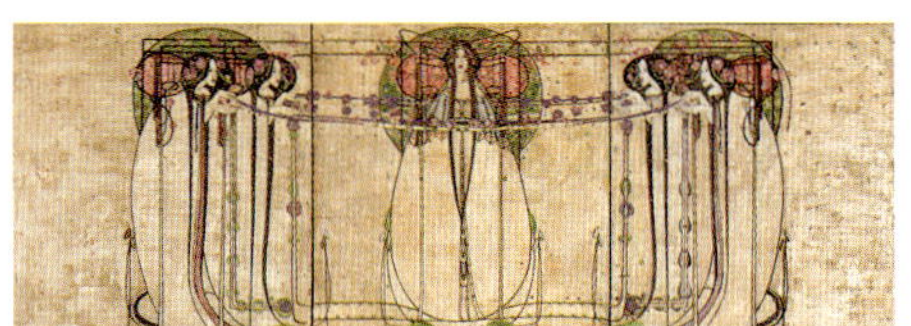

Mackintosh, Margaret Macdonald
1865–1933
The May Queen 1900
gesso, hessian, scrim, twine, glass beads,
thread, mother of pearl & (...)   158.8 x 457
E.1981.178.1-3

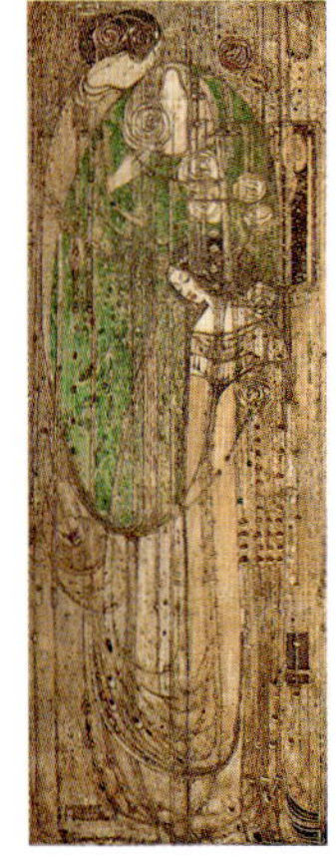

Mackintosh, Margaret Macdonald
1865–1933
'O ye, all ye that walk in Willowwood' 1903
oil painted gesso & pencil on board with glass
& enamelled glass 164.5 x 58.5
E.2001.6

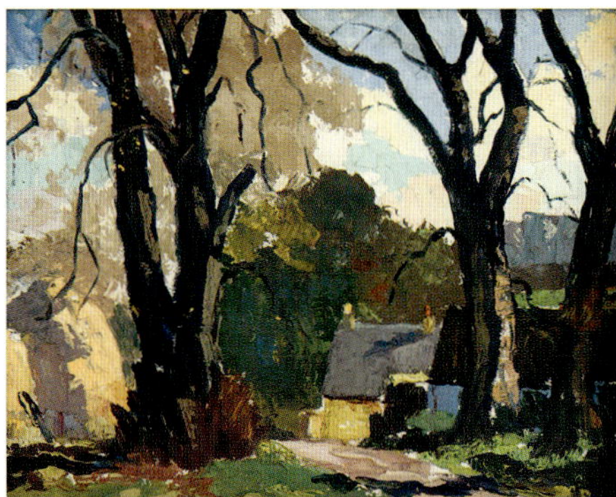

MacLellan, Malcolm b.1908
Lochermill, near Bridge of Weir 1957
oil on hardboard 33 x 40.9
3073

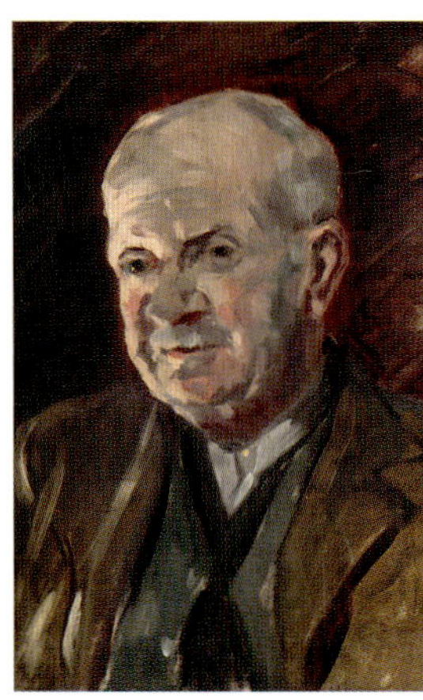

MacLellan, Malcolm b.1908
Oor Jamie
oil on canvas 46 x 30.9
TEMP.2041

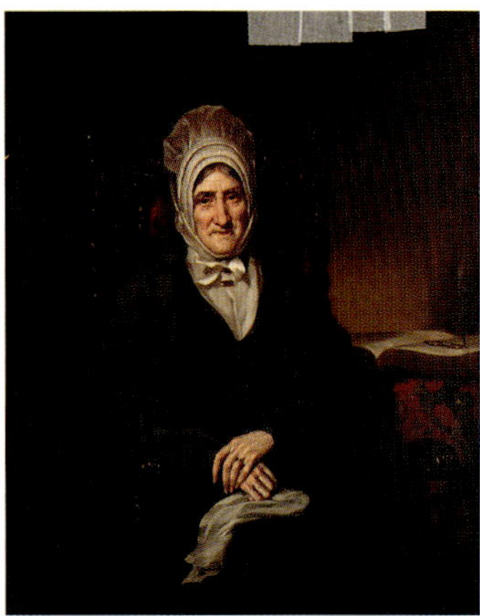

Macnee, Daniel 1806–1882
Mrs Agnes W. Whyte of Newbury c.1830–
1840
oil on canvas 127 x 101.6
1295

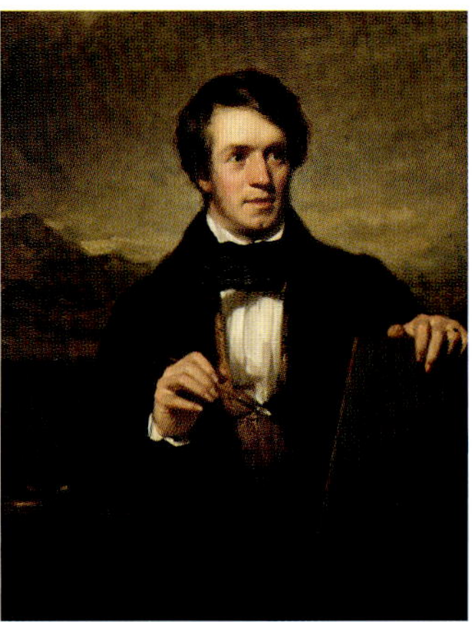

Macnee, Daniel 1806–1882
Horatio McCulloch (1805–1867), RSA 1842
oil on canvas 91.4 x 71.1
492

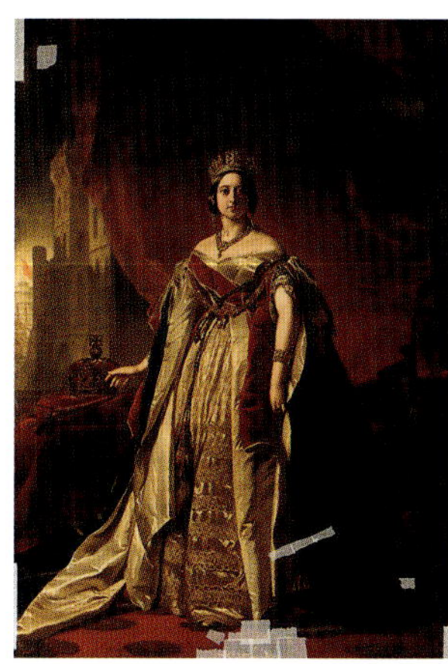

Macnee, Daniel 1806–1882
Queen Victoria (1819–1901) c.1845
oil on canvas 248.9 x 162.5
NR.92

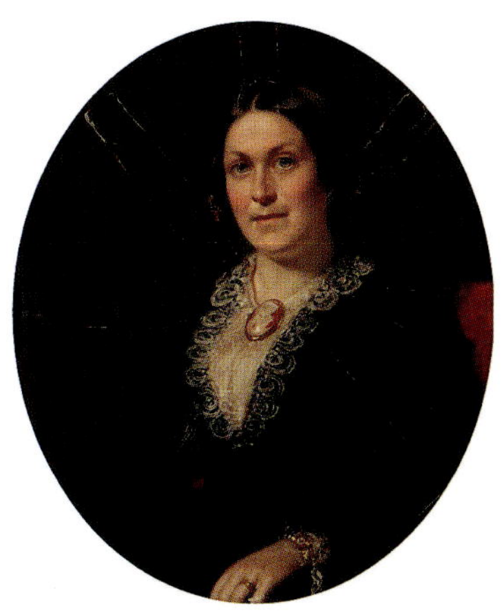

Macnee, Daniel 1806–1882
Mrs Thomas McGuffie (1842–1908) 1850s
oil on canvas 76.2 x 63.5
1771

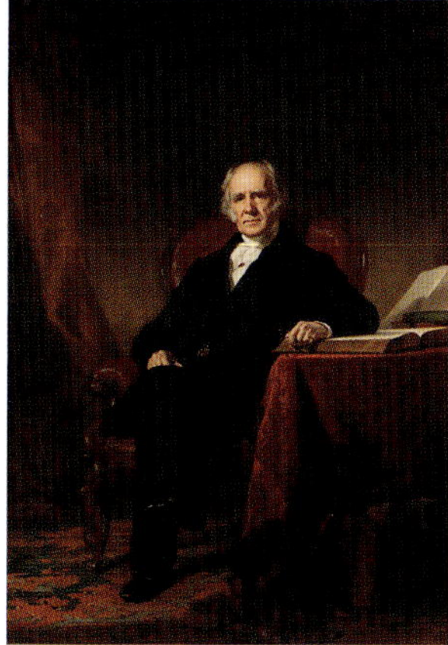

Macnee, Daniel 1806–1882
Reverend Dr Ralph Wardlaw (1779–1853)
1851
oil on canvas 213.4 x 147.3
1674

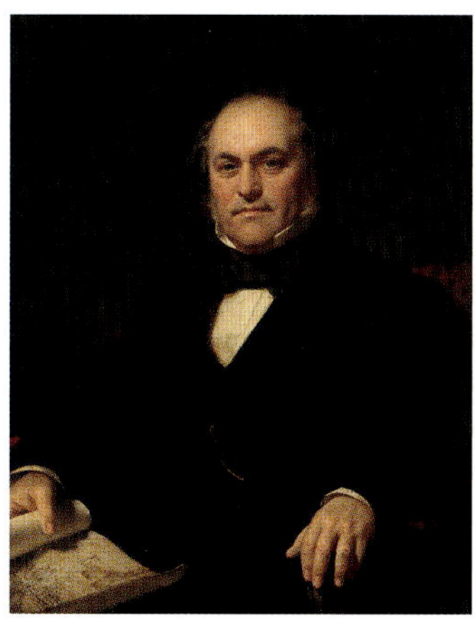

Macnee, Daniel 1806–1882
*John Erskine, Manager of William Dunn's
Machine Works, John Street, Glasgow* 1859
oil on canvas 91.4 x 71.1
2174

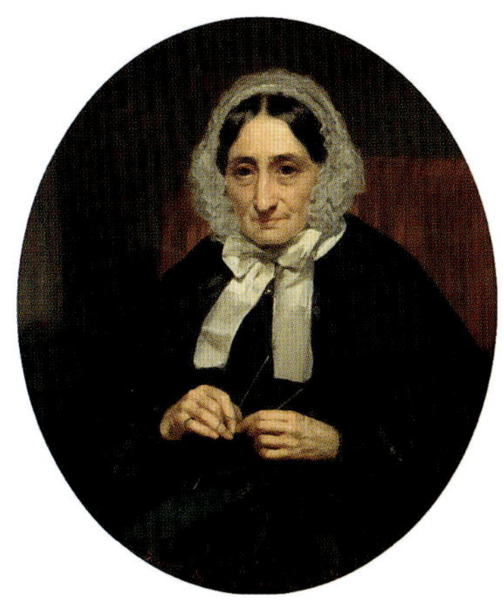

Macnee, Daniel 1806–1882
Portrait of an Old Lady 1864
oil on canvas 73.7 x 61
1102

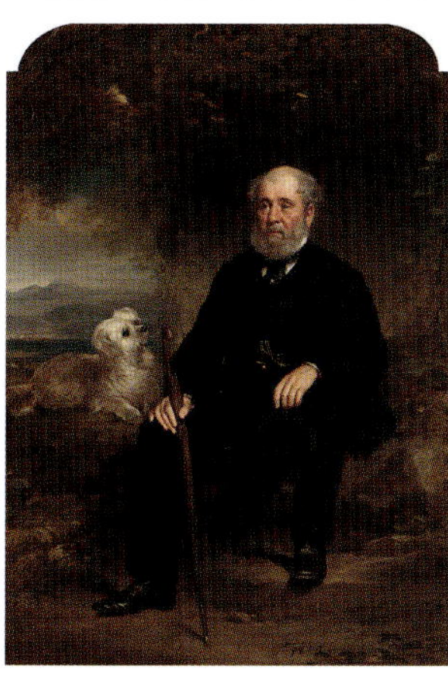

Macnee, Daniel 1806–1882
David Hutcheson (1799–1880) 1869
oil on canvas 190.5 x 134.6
657

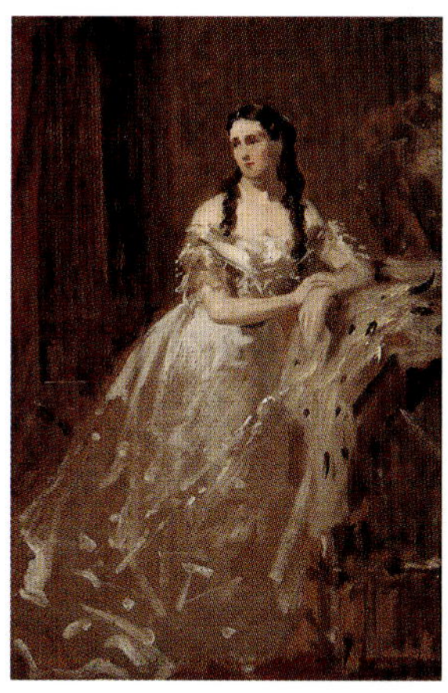

Macnee, Daniel 1806–1882
Lady Macnee c.1870
oil on board 40.6 x 26.4
NR.123

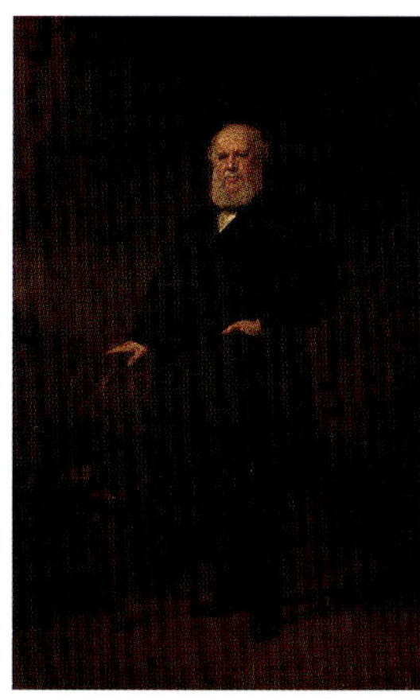

Macnee, Daniel 1806–1882
Robert Dalglish (1808–1880), MP 1874
oil on canvas 213.4 x 147.3
493

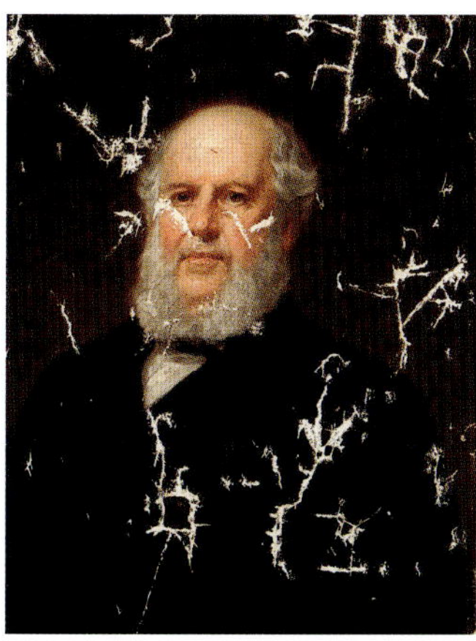

Macnee, Daniel 1806–1882
Robert Dalglish (1808–1880), MP 1874
oil on canvas 57.8 x 33.7
TEMP.14929

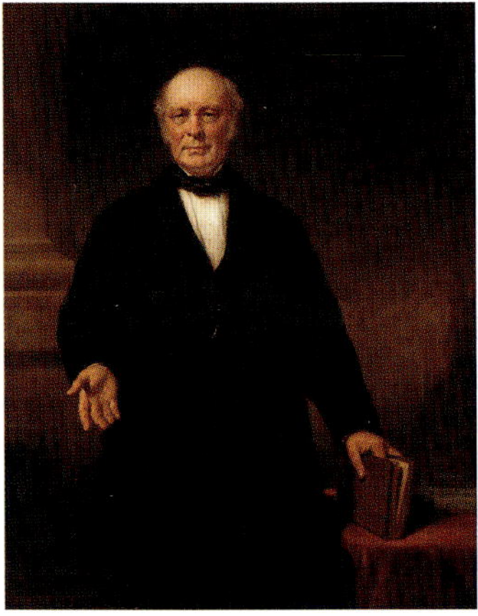

Macnee, Daniel 1806–1882
Bailie James Moir (1806–1880) 1877
oil on canvas 142.2 x 110.5
494

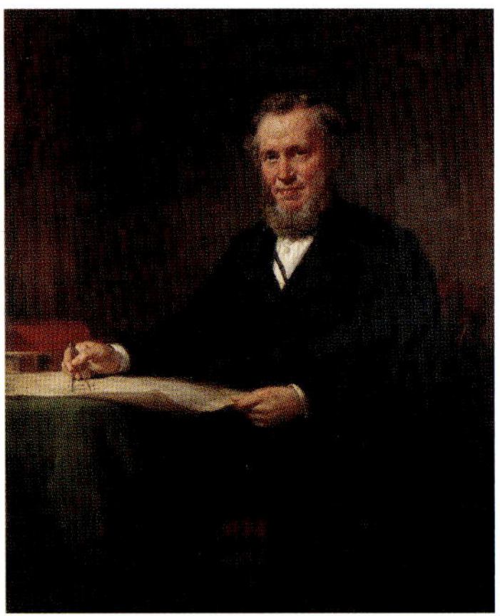

Macnee, Daniel 1806–1882
John Carrick (1819–1890), Glasgow City Architect 1877
oil on canvas 127 x 101.6
1488

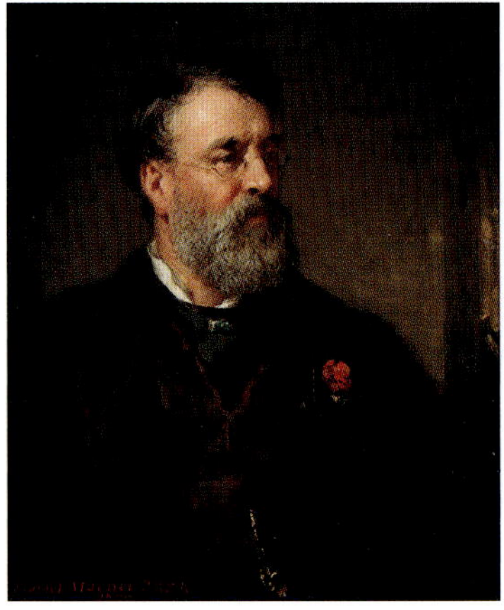

Macnee, Daniel 1806–1882
Sam Bough (1822–1878) 1878
oil on canvas 74.9 x 62.2
1022

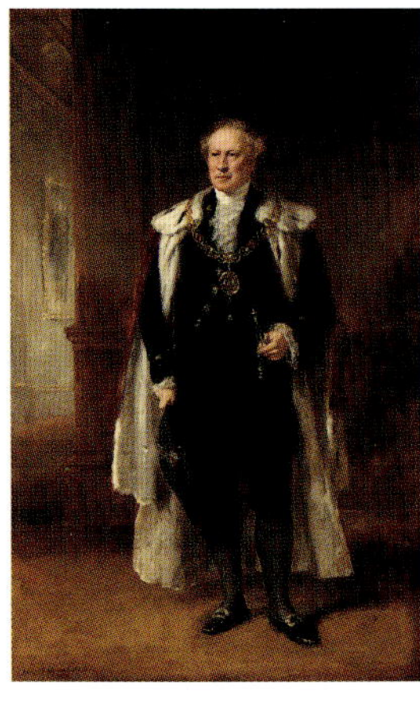

Macnee, Daniel 1806–1882
Sir James Bain (1818–1898), Lord Provost of Glasgow (1874–1877) 1878
oil on canvas 127 x 101.6
495

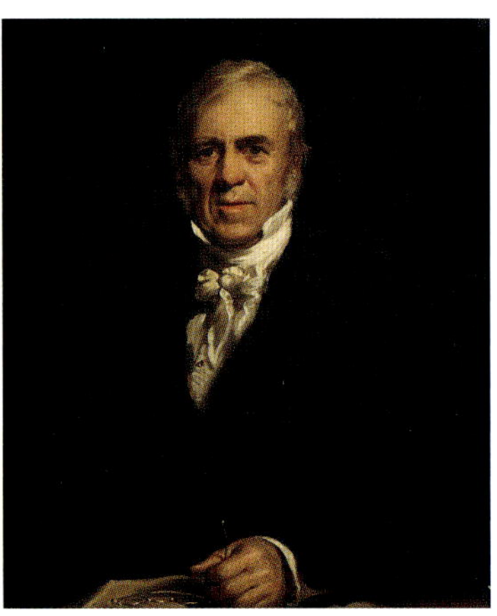

Macnee, Daniel 1806–1882
James Donaldson, Builder
oil on canvas 76.2 x 63.5
OG.1957.45

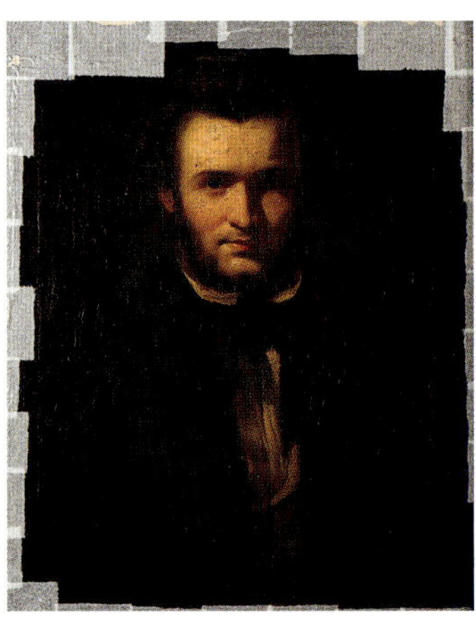

Macnee, Daniel 1806–1882
James Fillans (1808–1852), Sculptor
oil on canvas 71.1 x 55.9
487

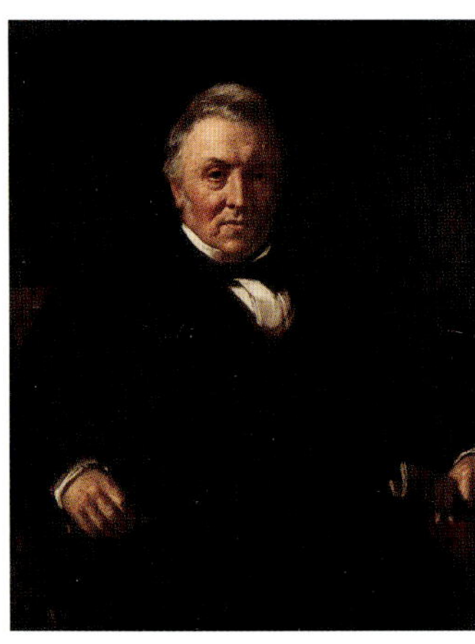

Macnee, Daniel 1806–1882
John Aitchison (1769–1859)
oil on canvas 88.9 x 68.5
661

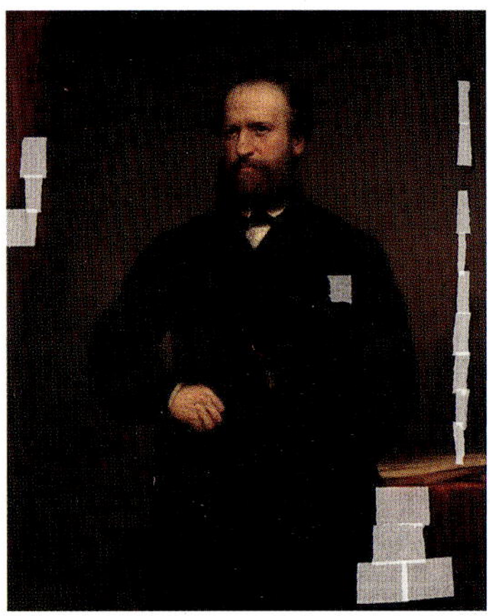

Macnee, Daniel 1806–1882
John Elder (1824–1869)
oil on canvas 127 x 101.6
1172

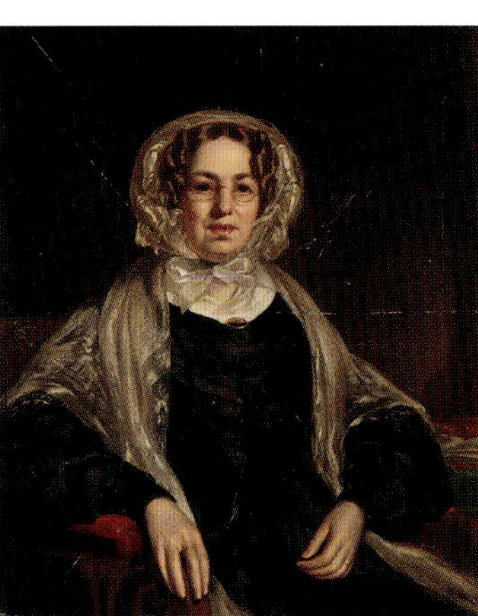

Macnee, Daniel 1806–1882
Mrs Catherine D. Blackie (1774–1847)
oil on canvas 92.7 x 72.4
1849

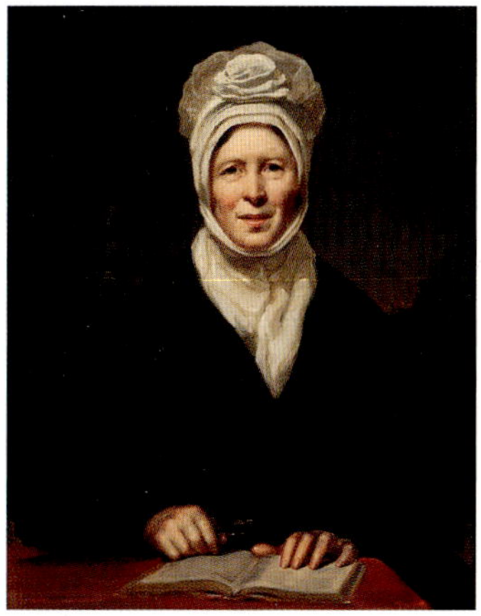

Macnee, Daniel 1806–1882
Mrs George Kerr
oil on canvas 91.4 x 71.1
1833

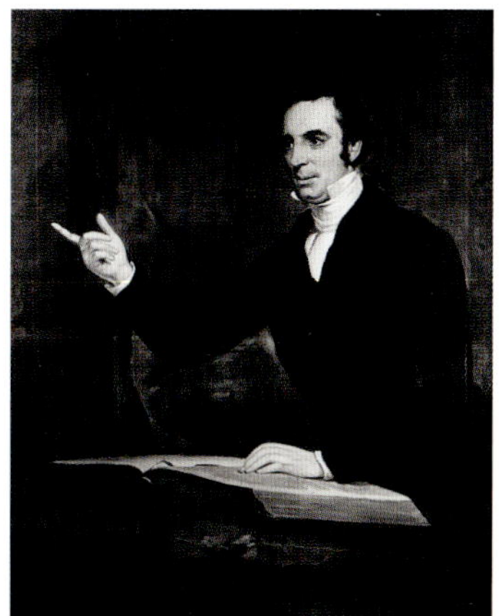

Macnee, Daniel 1806–1882
Reverend Dr William Anderson (1799–1873)
oil on canvas 127 x 101.6
1838

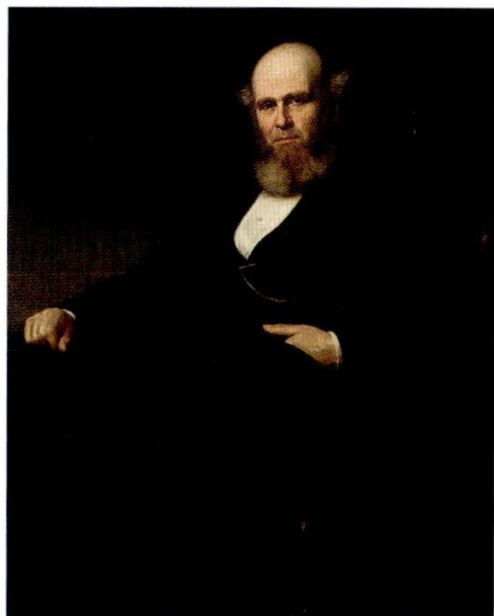

Macnee, Daniel 1806–1882
Sir John Whitehead
oil on canvas 127 x 101.6
NR.56

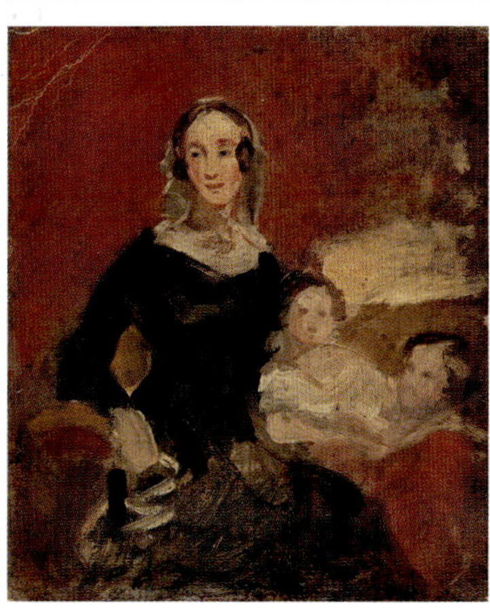

Macnee, Daniel 1806–1882
Sketch of a Lady with Two Children
oil on cardboard 28.6 x 23.5
NR.132

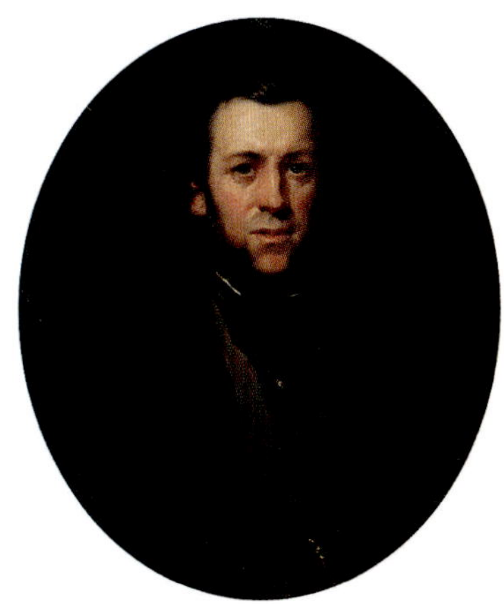

Macnee, Daniel 1806–1882
Thomas McGuffie (c.1831–1895)
oil on canvas 76.2 x 63.5
1770

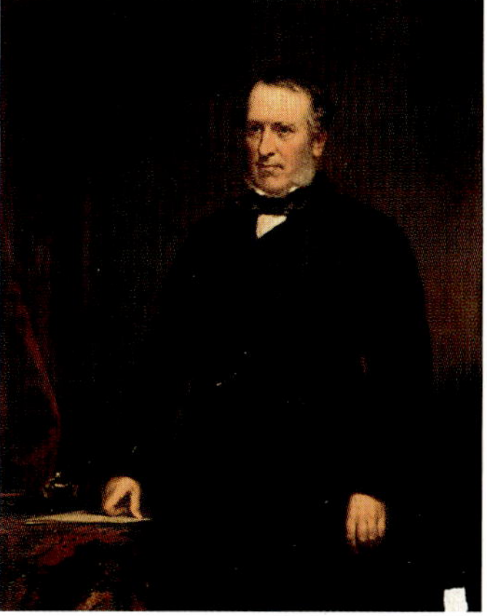

Macnee, Daniel 1806–1882
William Johnstone of Glenorchard (1806–1864)
oil on canvas 127 x 101.6
2506

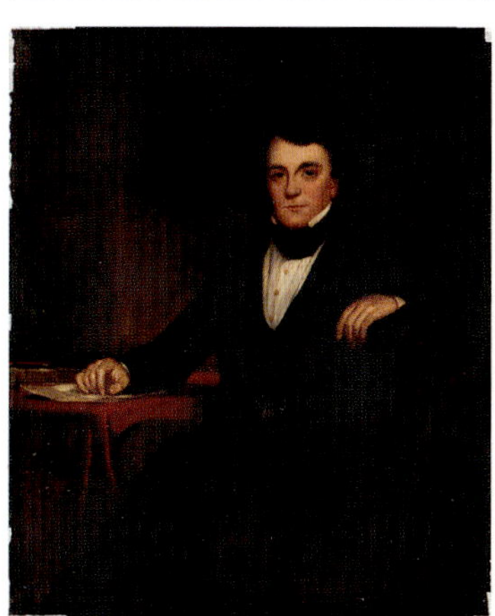

Macnee, Daniel 1806–1882
William Mathieson
oil on canvas 127 x 101.6
2828

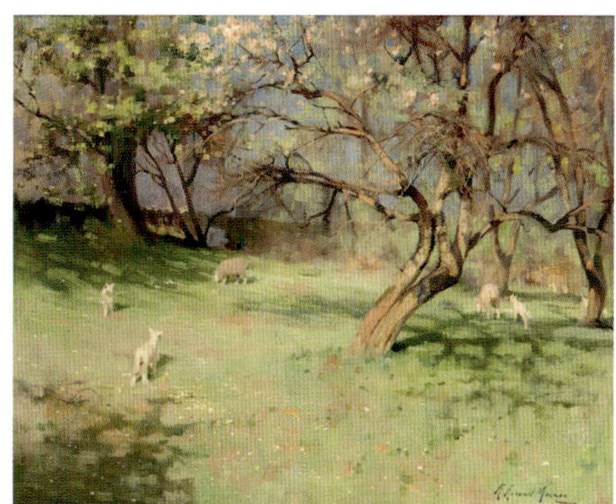

MacNee, Robert Russell c.1863–1952
Maytime
oil on canvas 63.5 x 76.2
2126

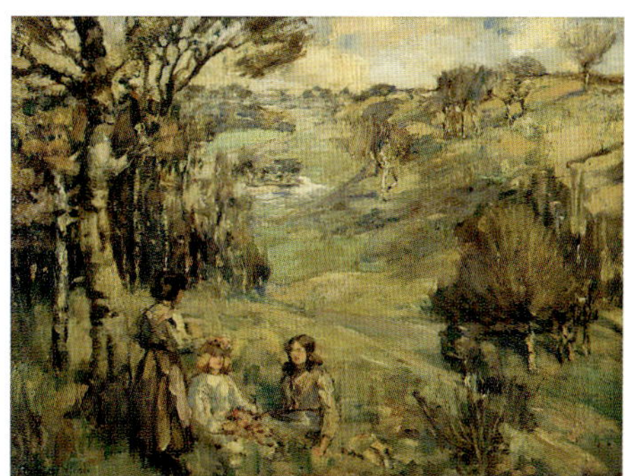

MacNicol, Bessie 1869–1904
A Galloway Landscape 1889
oil on canvas 50.8 x 68.6
2914

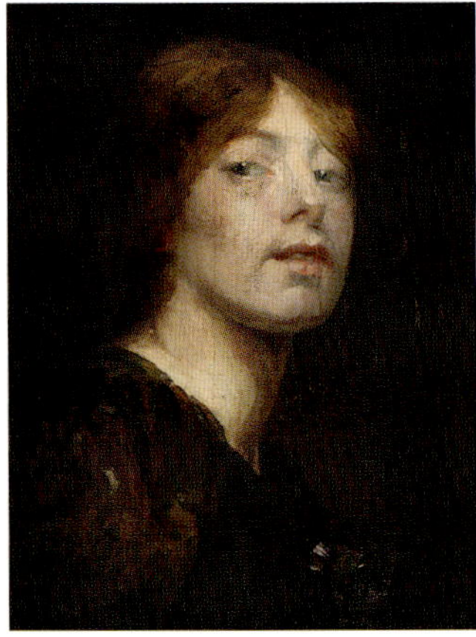

MacNicol, Bessie 1869–1904
Self Portrait c.1893
oil on canvas 40.7 x 30.5
2494

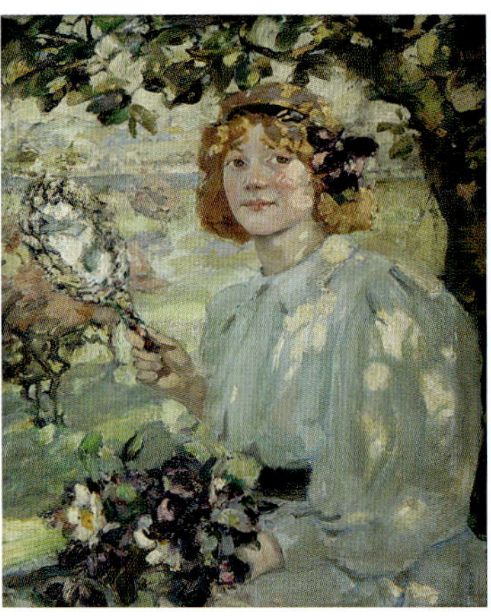

MacNicol, Bessie 1869–1904
Under the Apple Tree 1896–1898
oil on canvas 75.2 x 64.1
3184

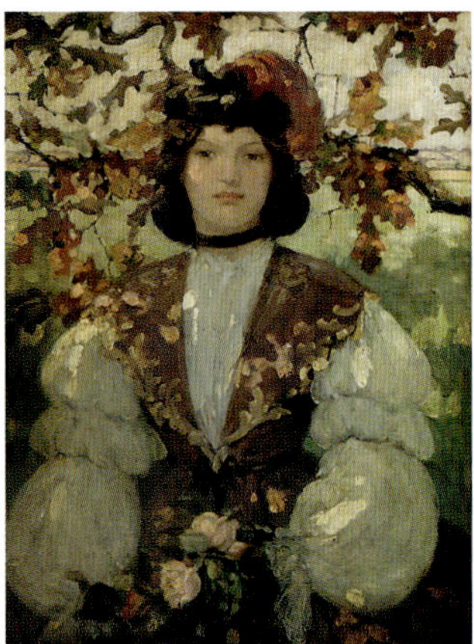

MacNicol, Bessie 1869–1904
A Girl of the Sixties c.1900
oil on canvas 81.3 x 61
2493

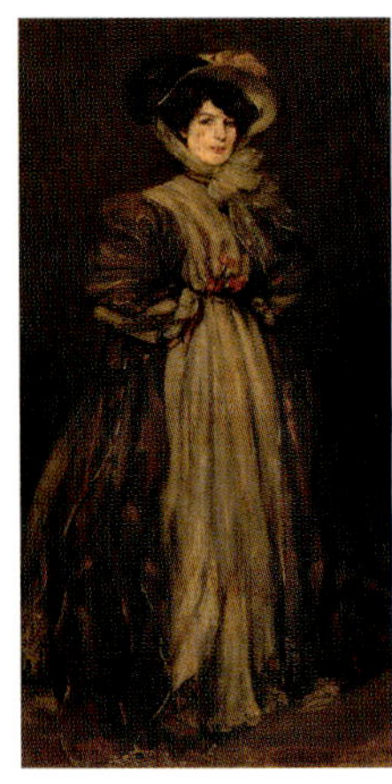

MacNicol, Bessie 1869–1904
Deborah 1904
oil on canvas 151.1 x 90.2
1223

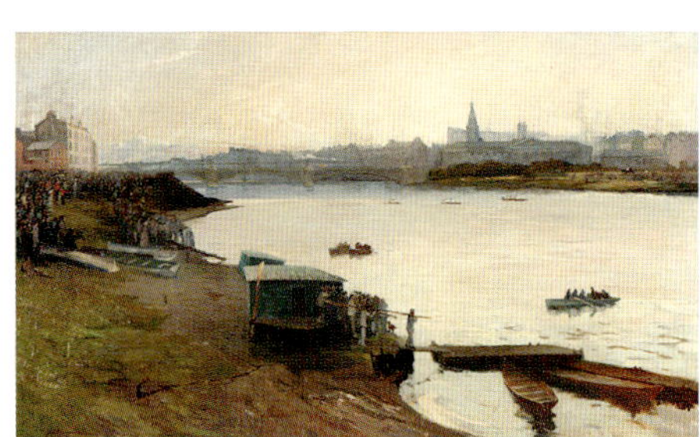

MacNiven, John 1819–1895
Glasgow Regatta, the Closing Stages 1880
oil on canvas 81.2 x 127
1576

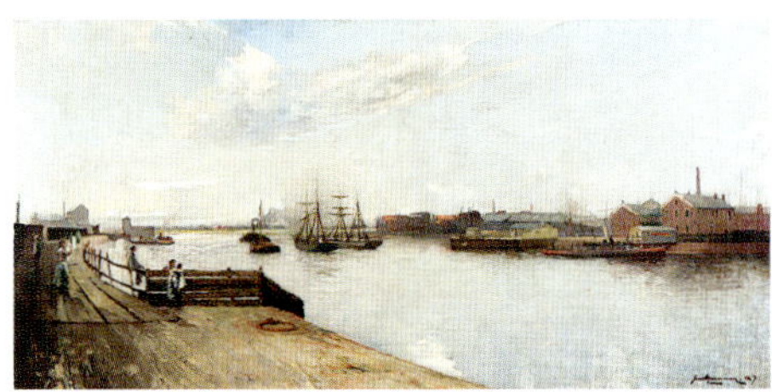

MacNiven, John 1819–1895
A Clutha Ferry at Pointhouse 1887
oil on canvas 44 x 89.5
TEMP.5874

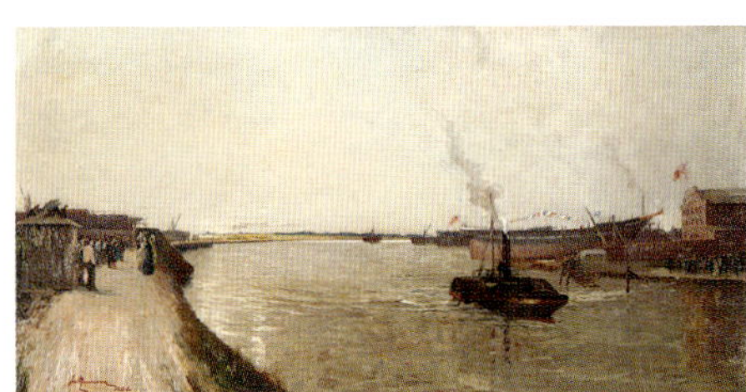

MacNiven, John 1819–1895
Launch of the 'County of Roxburgh'
oil on canvas 52 x 97
TEMP.5903

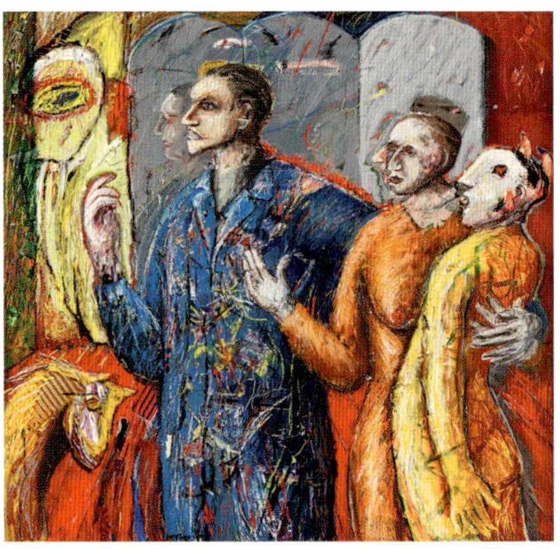

MacPherson, Neil b.1954
The Dance Master's Blue Coat c.1987
oil on canvas 122 x 122
3461

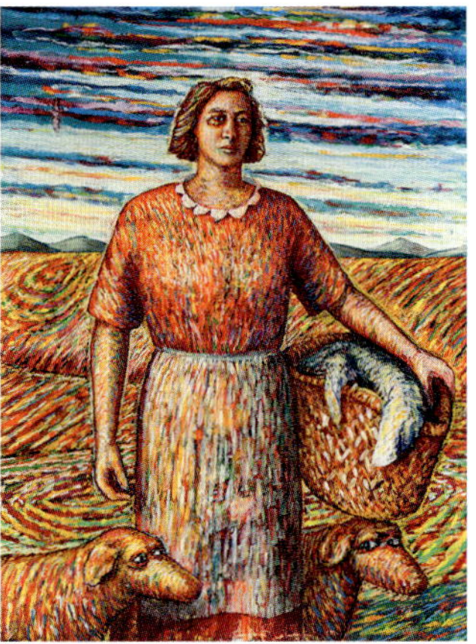

MacPherson, Neil b.1954
The Washer Woman 1988
acrylic & oil pastel on paper 113.5 x 84
PR.2007.2.59

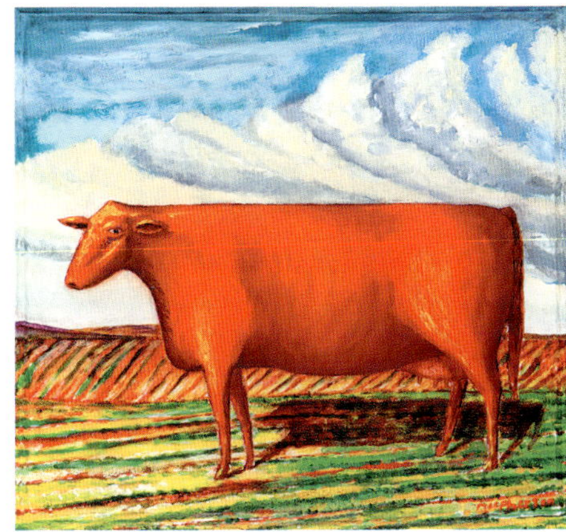

MacPherson, Neil b.1954
Painting of a Cow c.2008
acrylic on board 62.5 x 64
3684

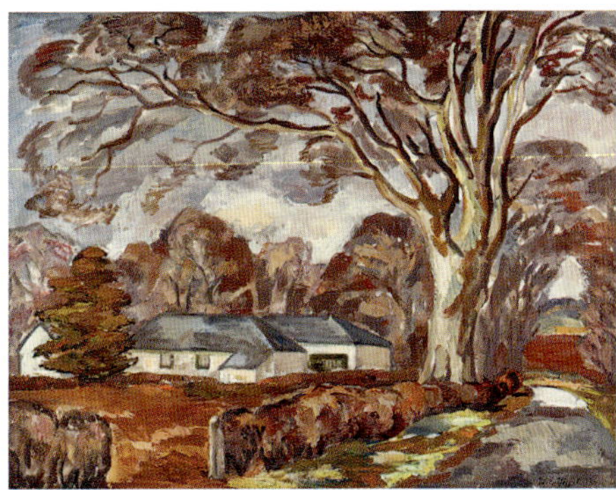

MacTaggart, William 1903–1981
Spring Landscape c.1941
oil on canvas 71.1 x 91.4
2262

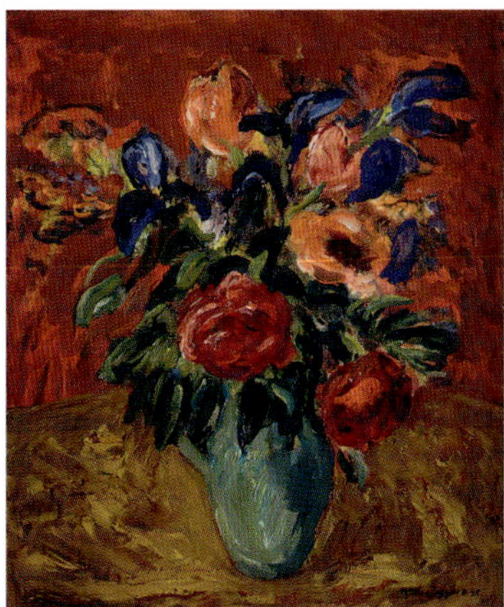

MacTaggart, William 1903–1981
The Gay Bouquet c.1950
oil on canvas 61 x 50.8
2895

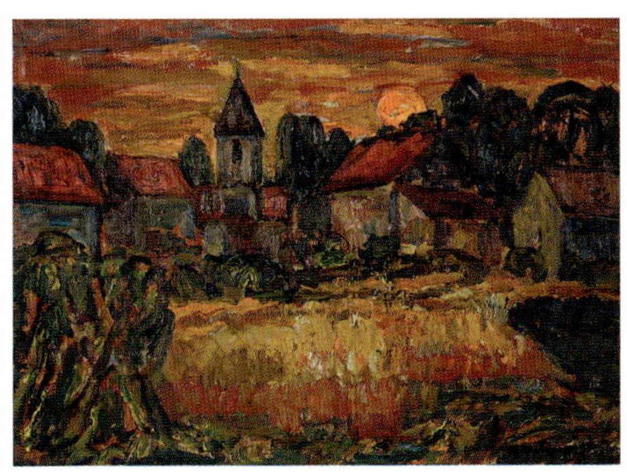

MacTaggart, William 1903–1981
Sunset, Pontarme 1953–1954
oil on canvas 71 x 91.4
3079

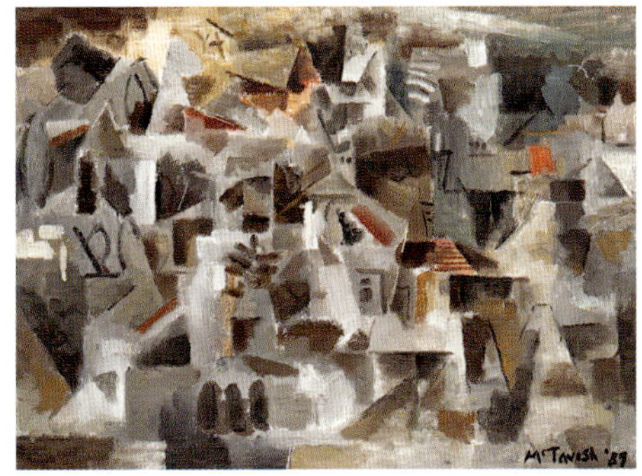

MacTavish, Grant
Towards Glasgow I 1989
oil on canvas 34.9 x 45
TEMP.14933

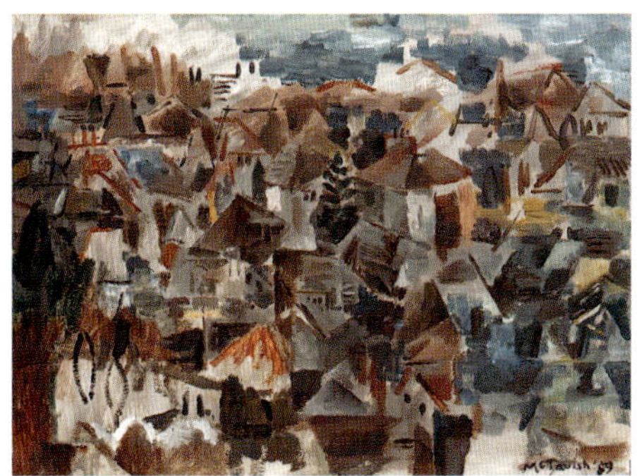

MacTavish, Grant
Towards Glasgow II 1989
oil on canvas 45.4 x 60.3
TEMP.14934

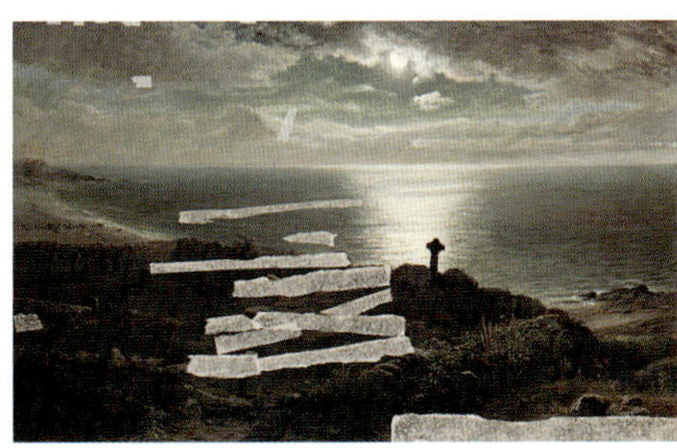

MacWhirter, John 1839–1911
Iona by Moonlight
oil on canvas 87 x 134.6
2466

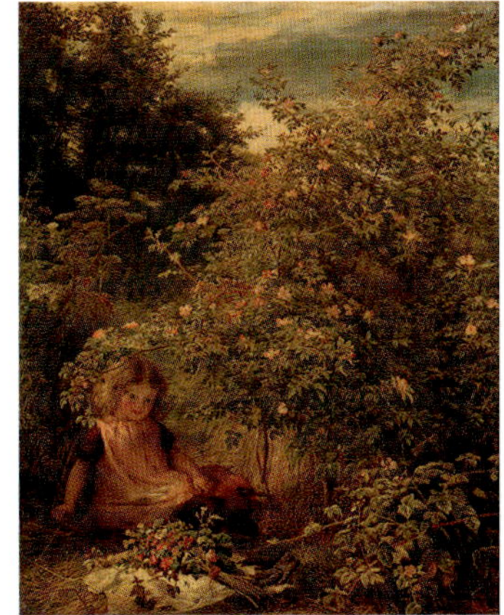

MacWhirter, John 1839–1911
Love among the Roses
oil on canvas 77.5 x 62
3425

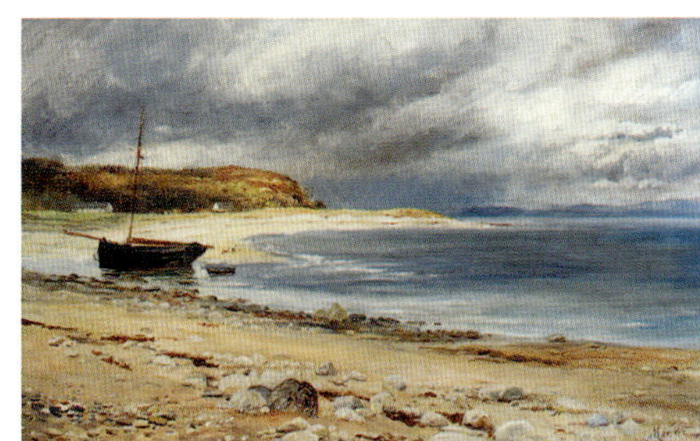

MacWhirter, John 1839–1911
Sannox Bay, Arran
oil on canvas 45.7 x 73.7
781

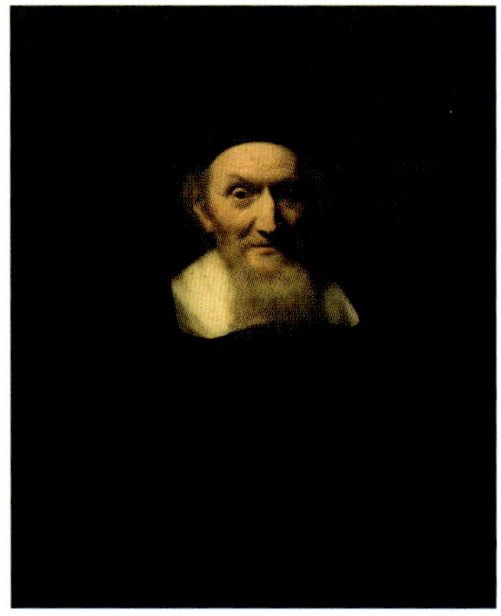

Maes, Nicolaes (attributed to) 1634–1693
Jacob Trip (1576–1661?) 1657
oil on canvas 74.3 x 59.1
35.304

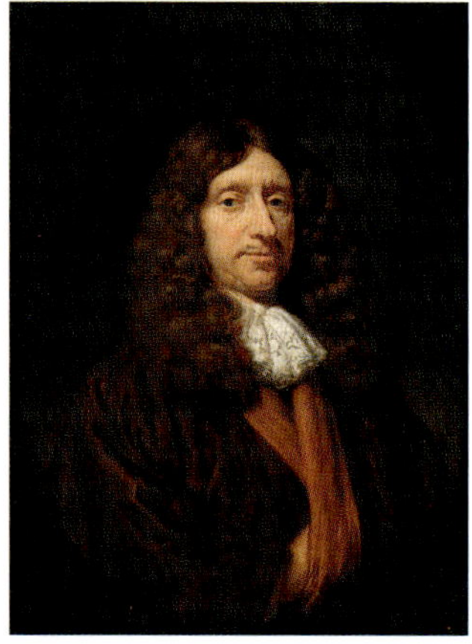

Maes, Nicolaes (attributed to) 1634–1693
Portrait of a Man c.1670–1680
oil on panel 41.9 x 30.5
591

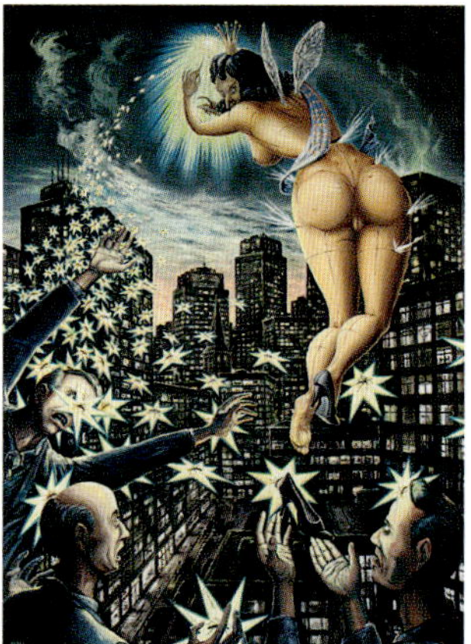

Maieu, Frank b.1952
Miss Liberty 1993
oil on canvas 296 x 203.5
3613

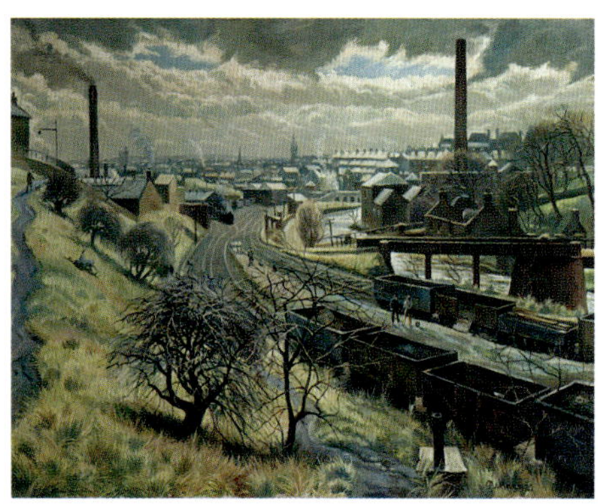

Makinson, Trevor b.1926
Maryhill Goods Yard
oil on canvas 61 x 73.7
OG.1962.00

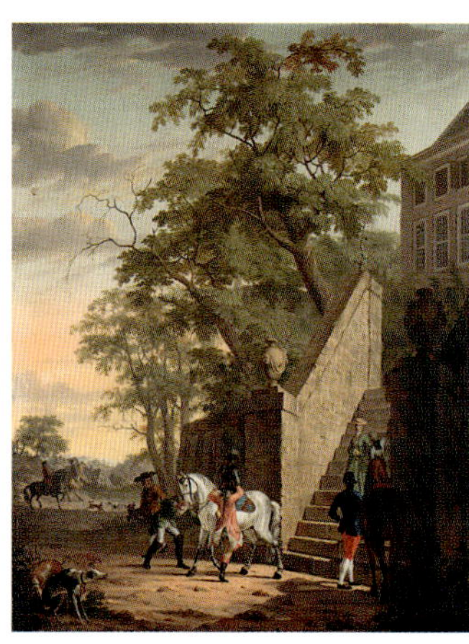

Malleyn, Gerrit 1753–1816
A Hawking Party Preparing to Depart 1779
oil on canvas 261 x 203 (E)
PC.158.2

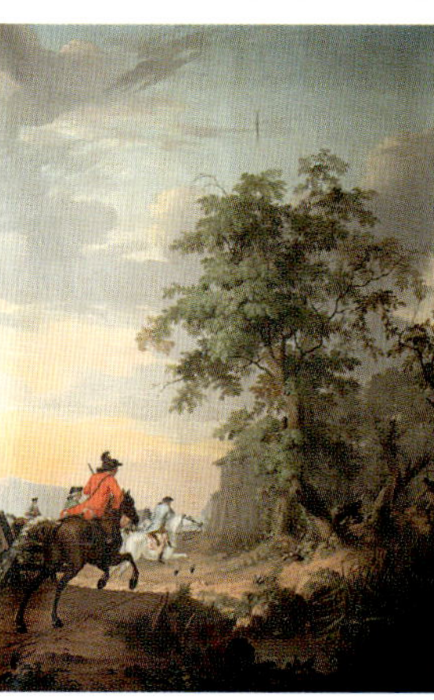

Malleyn, Gerrit 1753–1816
A Boar Hunt c.1779
oil on canvas 262 x 153 (E)
PC.158.1

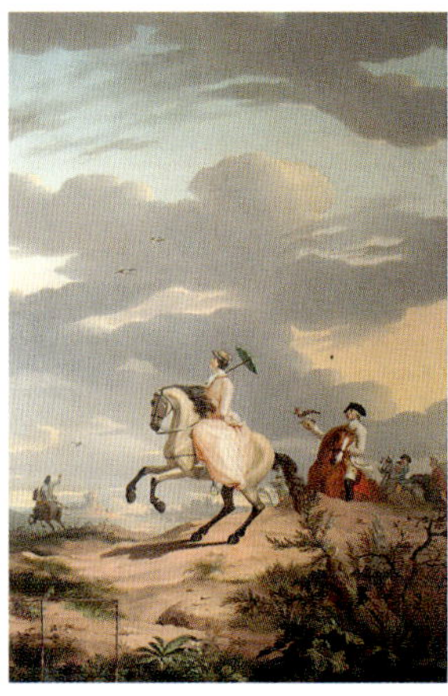

Malleyn, Gerrit 1753–1816
A Hawking Party c.1779
oil on canvas 261 x 153 (E)
PC.158.5

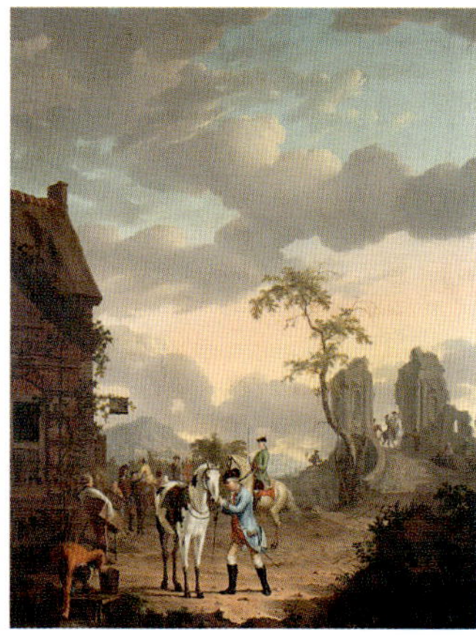

Malleyn, Gerrit 1753–1816
A Hunting Party at Rest by an Inn c.1779
oil on canvas 261 x 203 (E)
PC.158.4

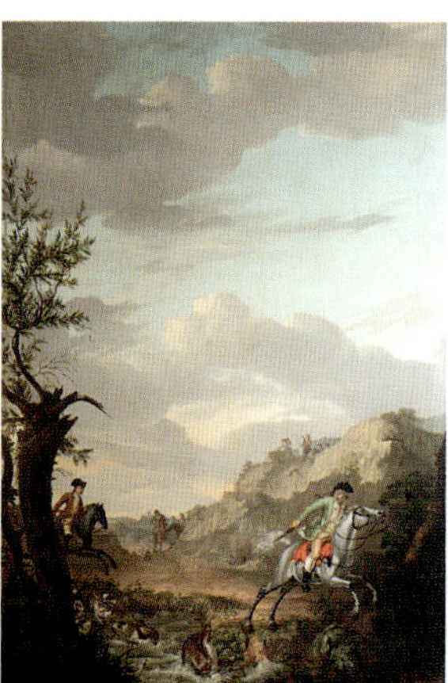

Malleyn, Gerrit 1753–1816
A Stag Hunt c.1779
oil on canvas 261 x 153 (E)
PC.158.3

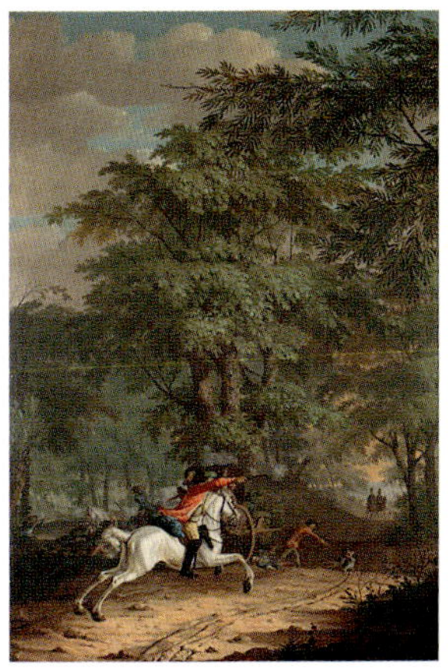

Malleyn, Gerrit 1753–1816
An Ambush in the Woods c.1779
oil on canvas 261 x 153 (E)
PC.158.6

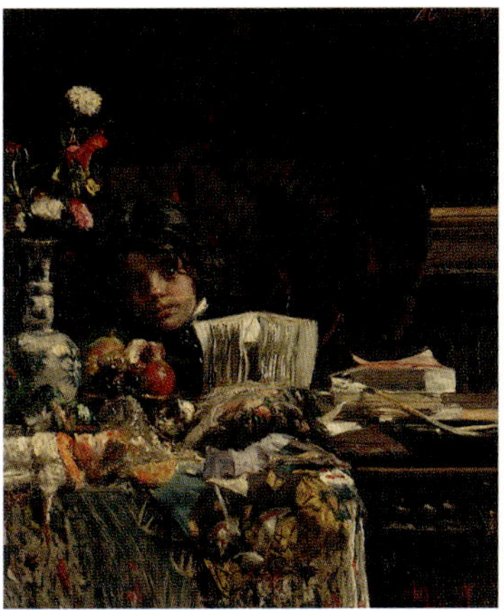

Mancini, Antonio 1852–1930
The Sulky Boy c.1875
oil on canvas 87.8 x 72
2191

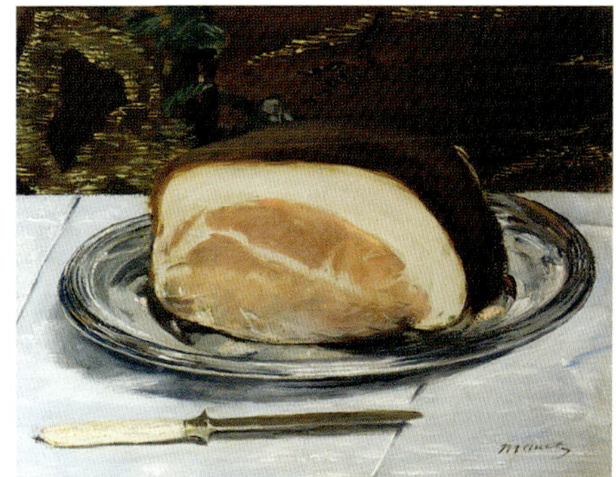

Manet, Édouard 1832–1883
The Ham c.1875–1878
oil on canvas 32.4 x 41.2
35.308

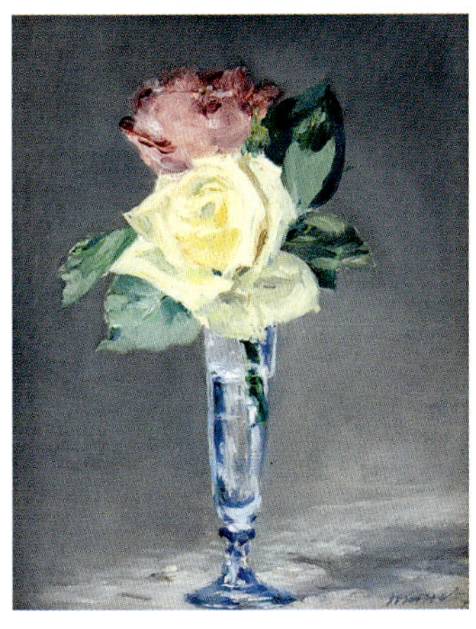

Manet, Édouard 1832–1883
Roses in a Champagne Glass 1882
oil on canvas 32.4 x 24.8
35.31

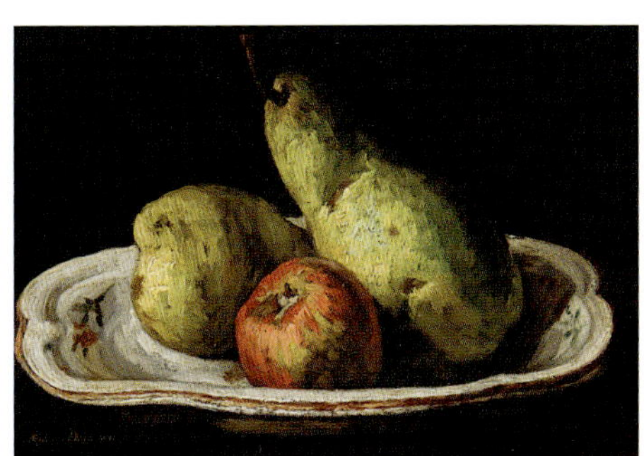

Manet, Édouard (attributed to) 1832–1883
Fruit
oil on canvas 21.6 x 29.5
35.307

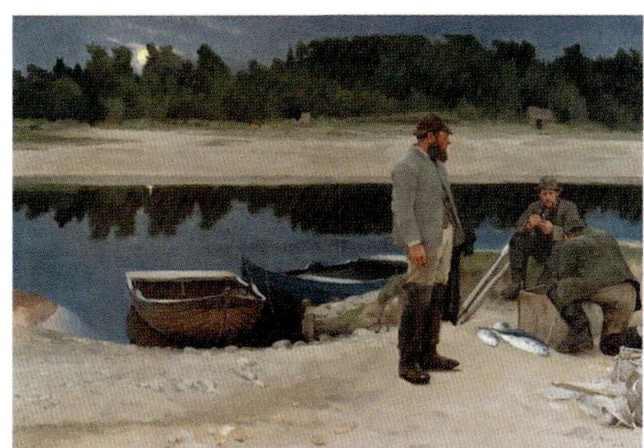

Mann, Alexander 1853–1908
By the Findhorn 1886
oil on canvas 89 x 129.7
3647

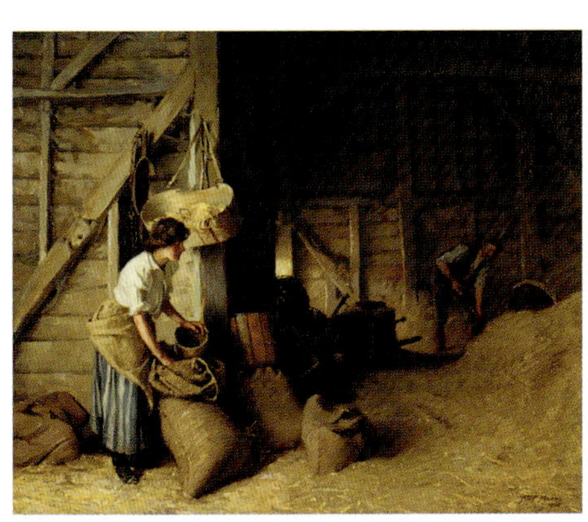

Mann, Alexander 1853–1908
Chaff 1905
oil on canvas 73.7 x 90.2
1219

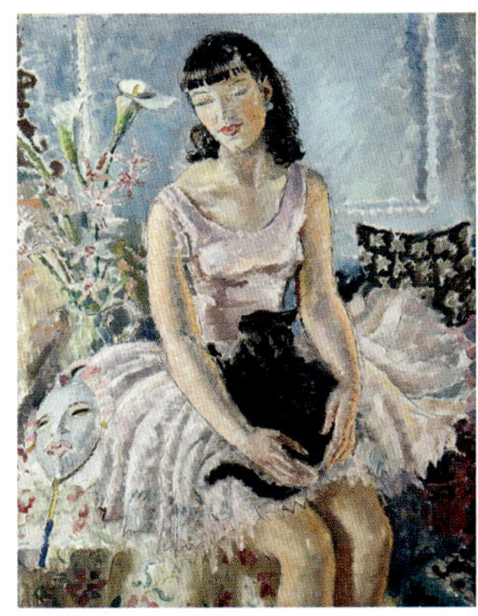

Mann, Cathleen 1896–1959
Ballerina c.1934
oil on canvas 91.4 x 71.1
1896

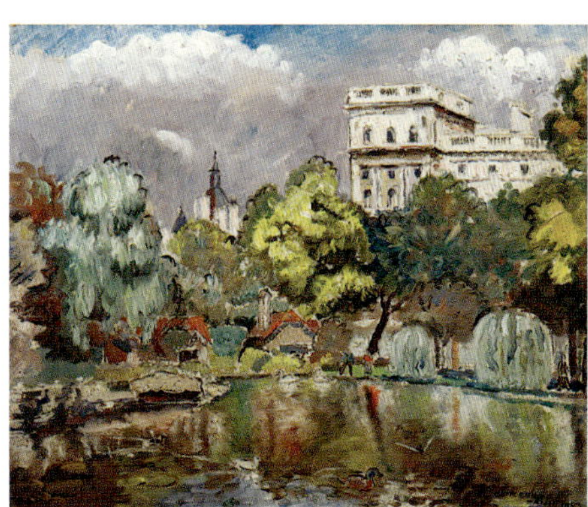

Mann, Cathleen 1896–1959
St James's Park 1943
oil on canvas 50.8 x 61
2362

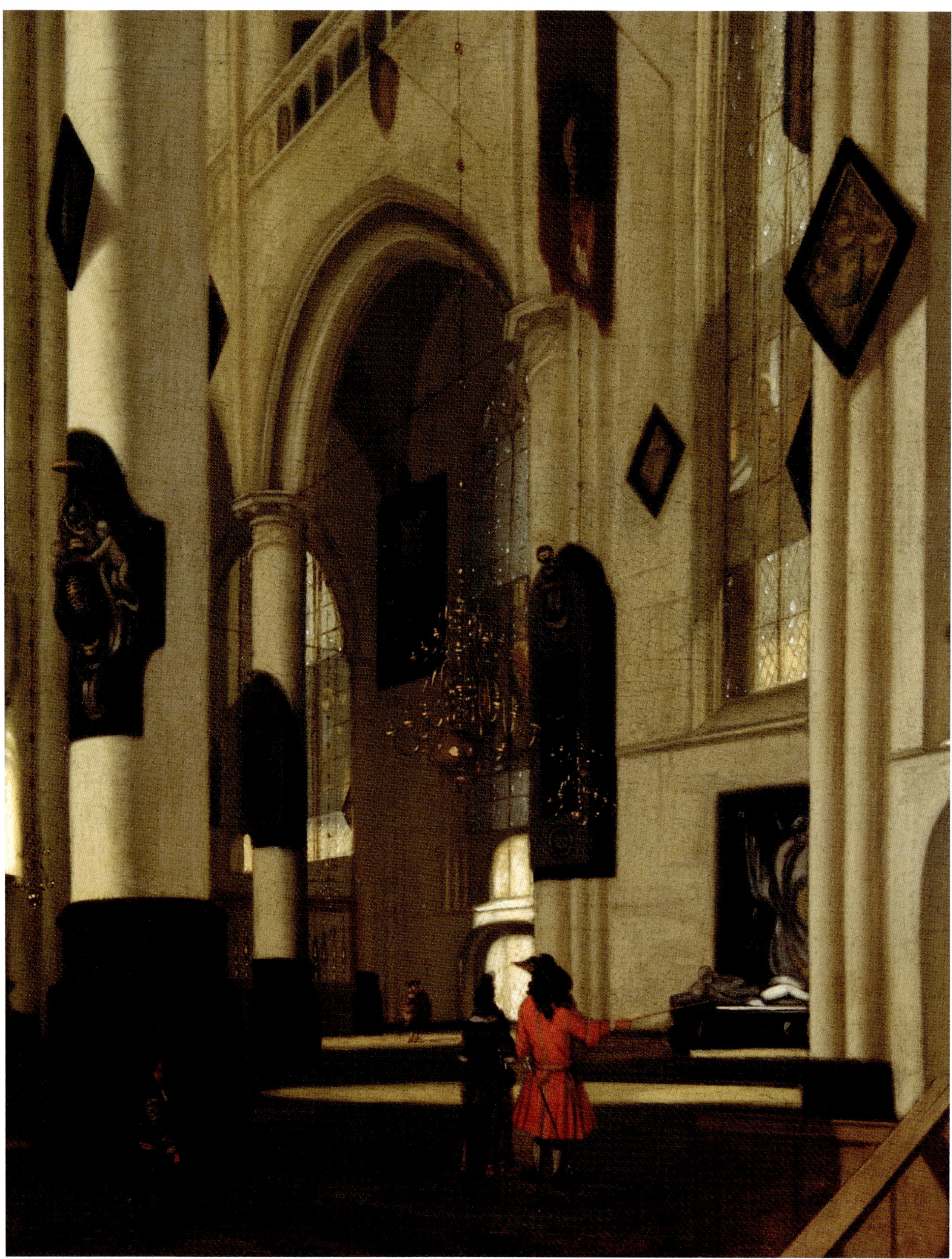

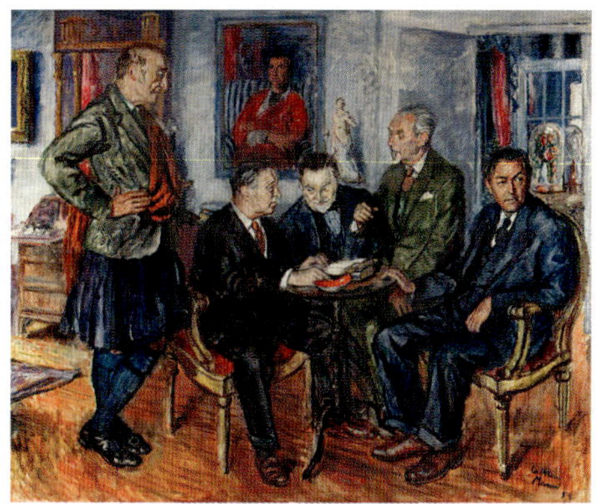

Mann, Cathleen 1896–1959
A Group of Writers (Shane Leslie, Compton Mackenzie, Henry Green, James Laver and Vyvyan Holland) 1958
oil on canvas 205.7 x 241.3
3104

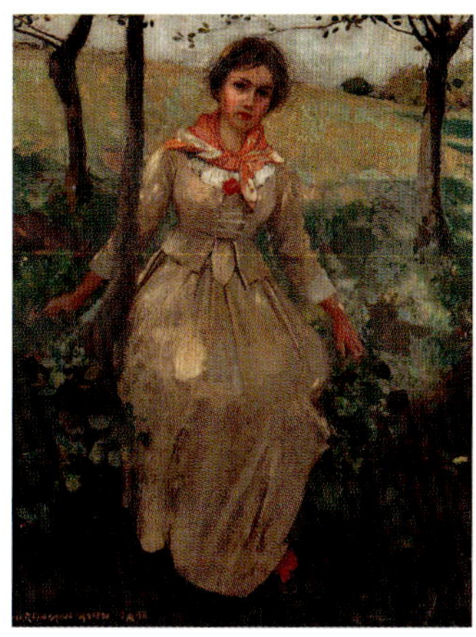

Mann, Harrington 1864–1936
A Young Woman 1891
oil on canvas 73.7 x 55.9
2476

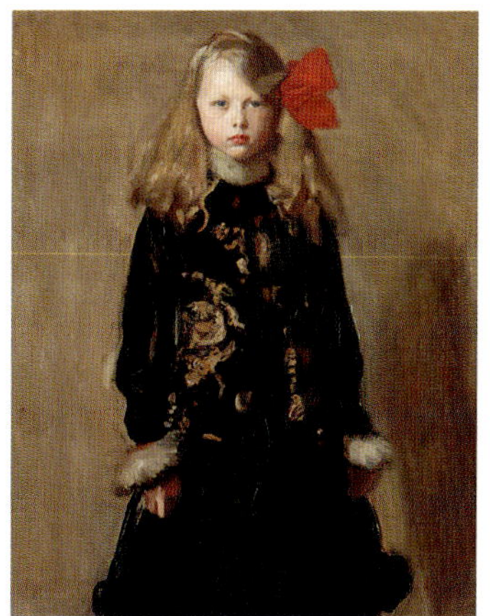

Mann, Harrington 1864–1936
Jinny Carpenter c.1911
oil on canvas 101.6 x 80.3
3125

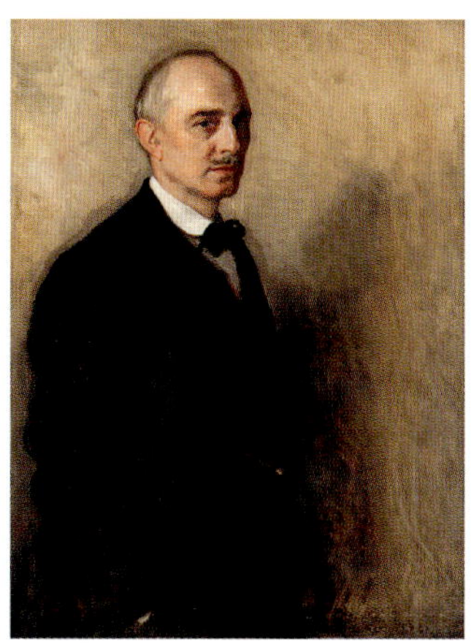

Mann, Harrington 1864–1936
Francis Howard 1924
oil on canvas 100.3 x 75.6
3106

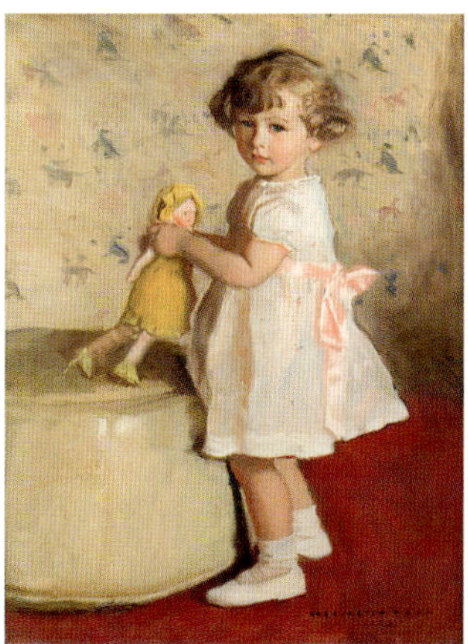

Mann, Harrington 1864–1936
Christine 1934
oil on canvas 99.1 x 73.7
1925

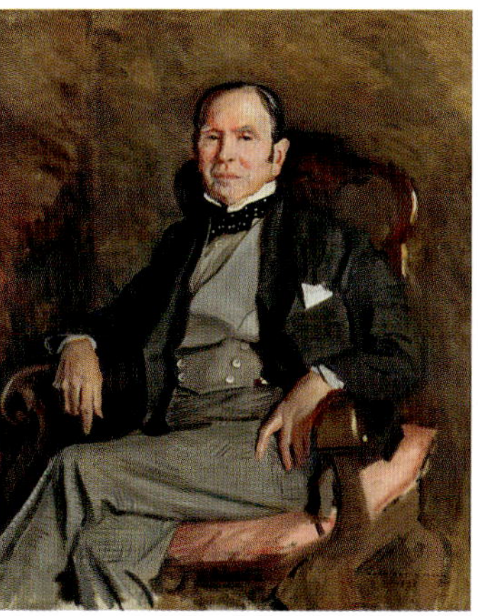

Mann, Harrington 1864–1936
Sir John Lavery (1856–1941), RA, RSA 1936
oil on canvas 101.6 x 81.3
2075

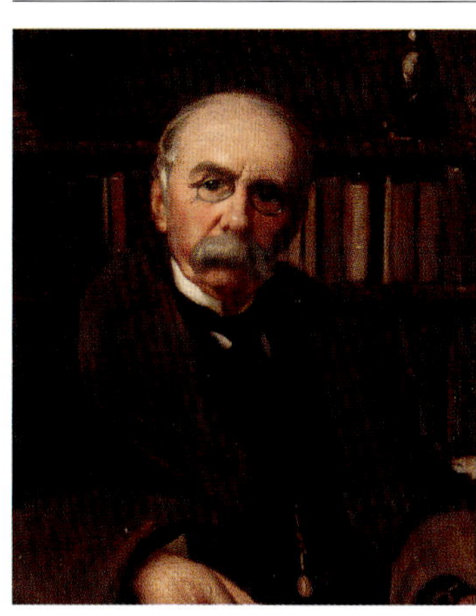

Mann, Harrington 1864–1936
Alexander Fergusson
oil on canvas 75 x 64.6
PP.1994.94.3

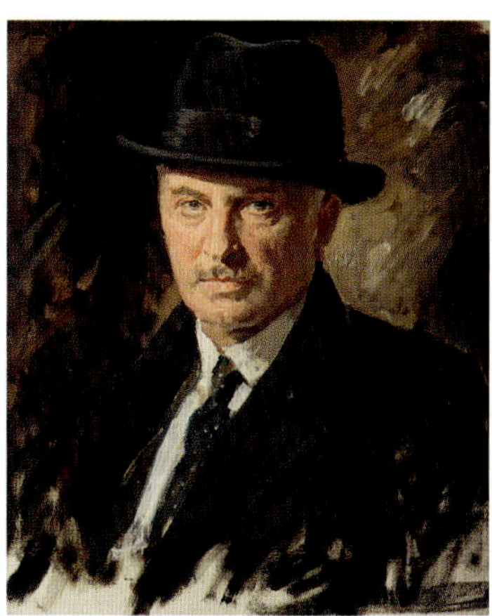

Mann, Harrington 1864–1936
Francis Howard
oil on canvas 60.7 x 50.3
3107

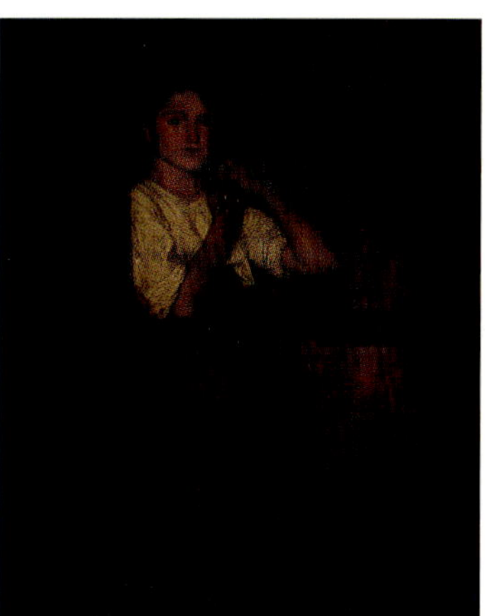

Mann, Harrington 1864–1936
Study of a Young Girl
oil on canvas 34.3 x 28
2475

Facing page: Vliet, Hendrick Cornelisz. van, c.1611–1675, *Interior of the Oude Kerk, Delft,* c.1660–1675 (p. 444)

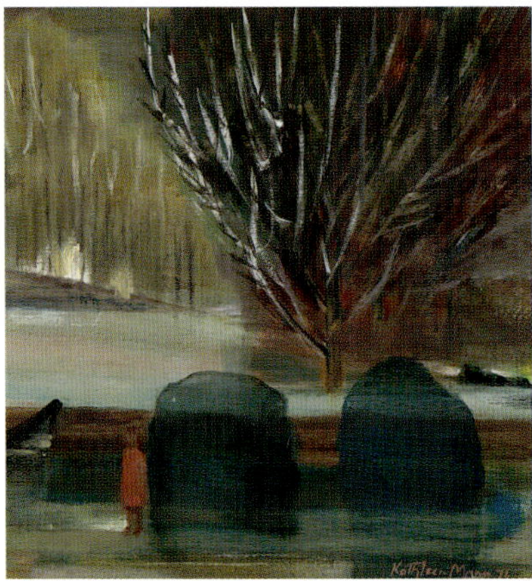

Mann, Kathleen b.1906
February 1971
oil on canvas 45.5 x 42.2
3292

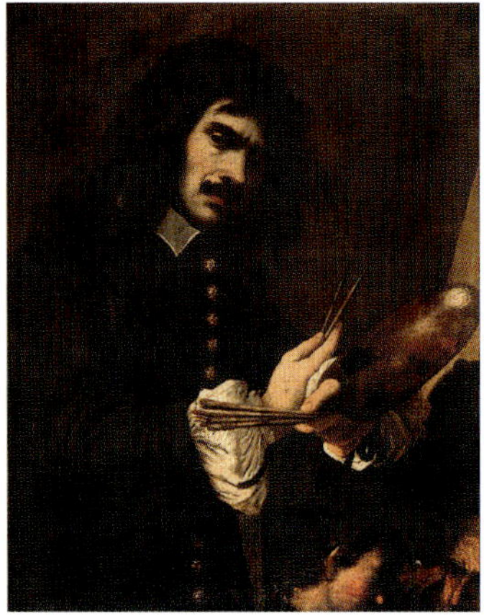

March, Esteban 1610–1660
Self Portrait
oil on canvas 88.9 x 69.2
PL.105 (P)

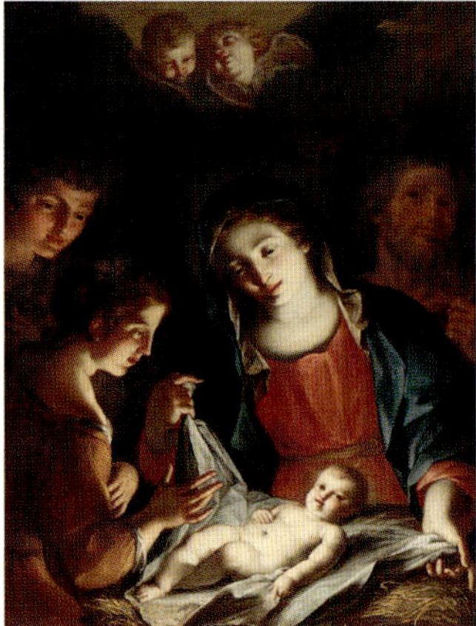

Marchesi, Giuseppe 1699–1771
Virgin Adoring the Infant Christ c.1730
oil on canvas 103.7 x 75.2
187

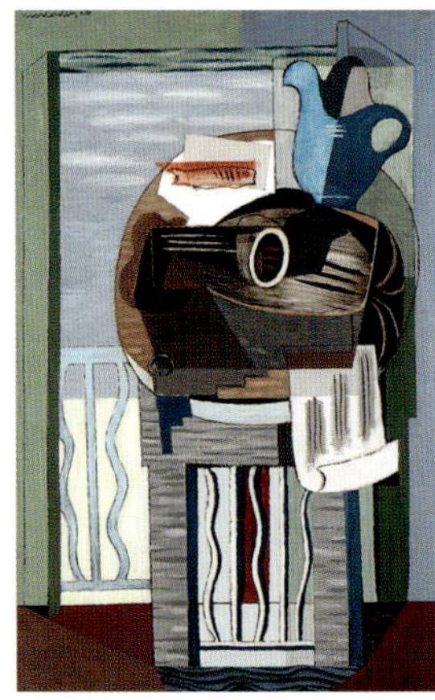

Marcoussis, Louis 1883–1941
Still Life in front of a Balcony 1928
oil on canvas 121.6 x 86.4
2902

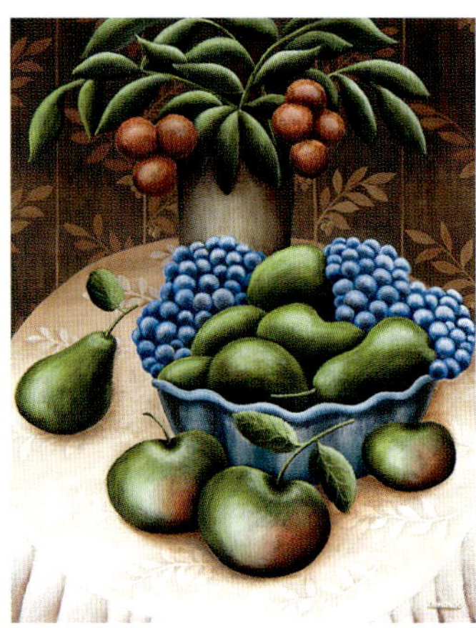

Marek, Jerzy b.1925
Still Life 1978
oil on hardboard 45.4 x 34.9
3592

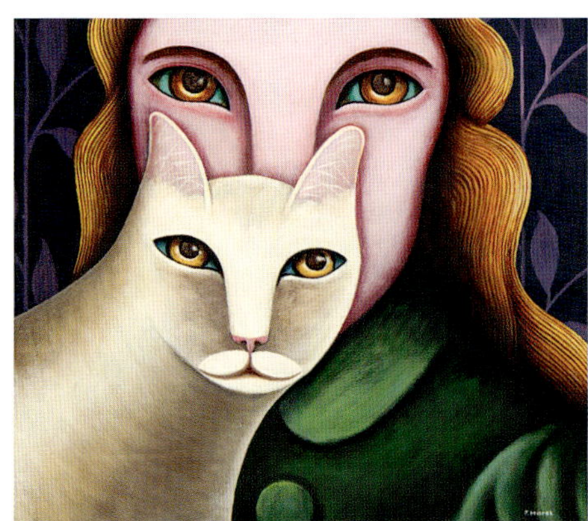

Marek, Jerzy b.1925
The Conspirators 1989–1991
oil on board 33.3 x 38.5
3591

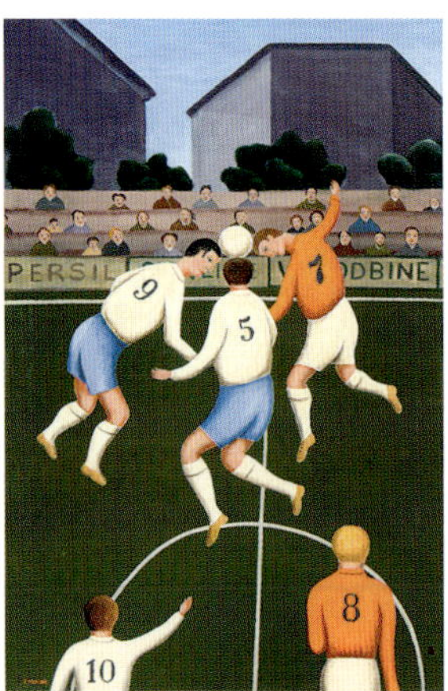

Marek, Jerzy b.1925
Football
oil on canvas 76.2 x 51.1
3590

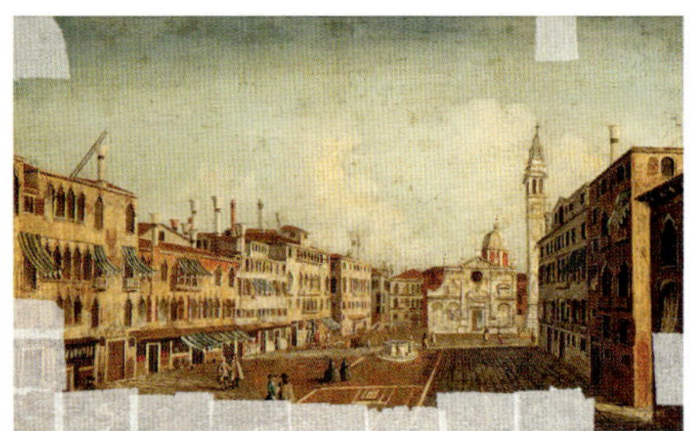

Marieschi, Michele Giovanni (after)
1710–1743
*Venice: View of the Campo Santa Maria
Formosa* 19th C
oil on canvas 47 x 71.8
921

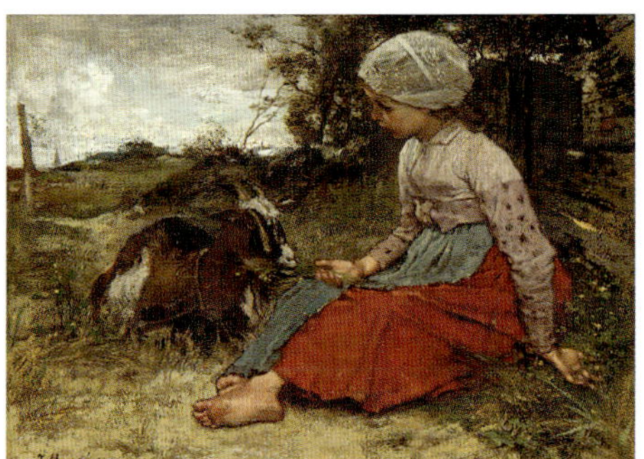

Maris, Jacob Henricus 1837–1899
The Pet Goat 1871
oil on canvas 22.8 x 29.8
35.322

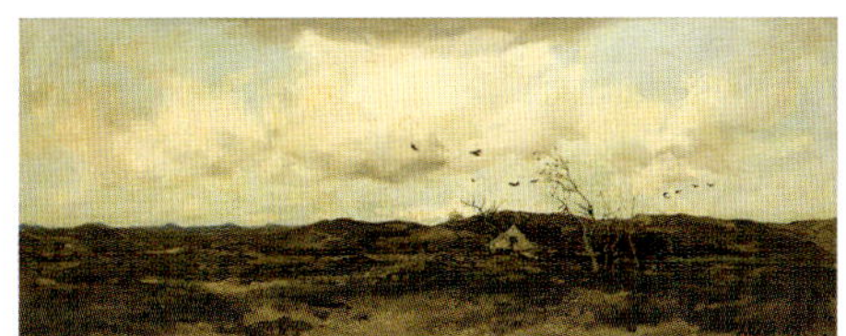

Maris, Jacob Henricus 1837–1899
Breezy Downs 1875
oil on canvas 45.7 x 111.8
35.316

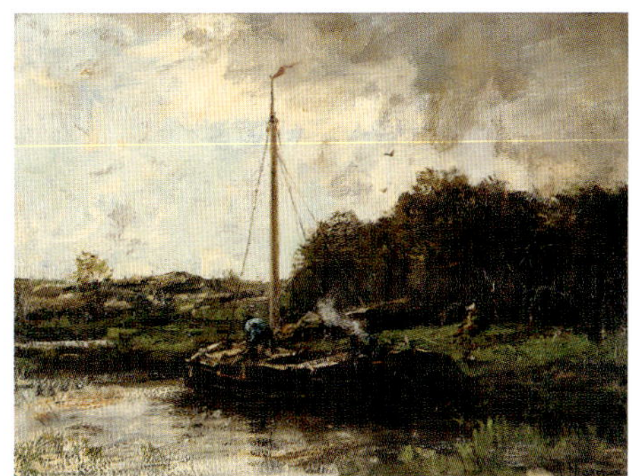

Maris, Jacob Henricus 1837–1899
A Quiet Berth, Morning Glow c.1875–1885
oil on canvas 55.3 x 71.1
1234

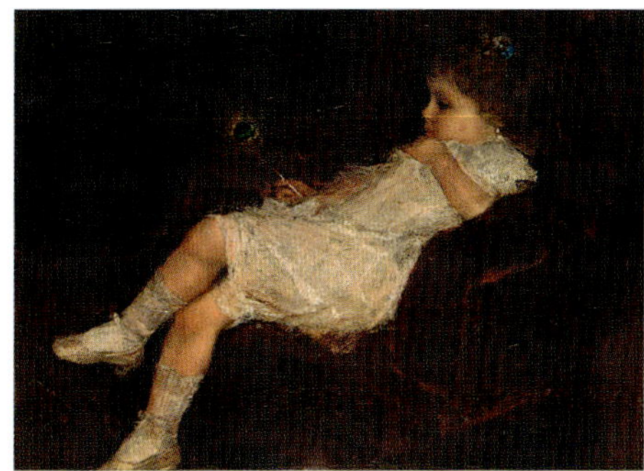

Maris, Jacob Henricus 1837–1899
Girl with a Peacock Feather c.1879
oil on canvas 22.8 x 31.7
35.321

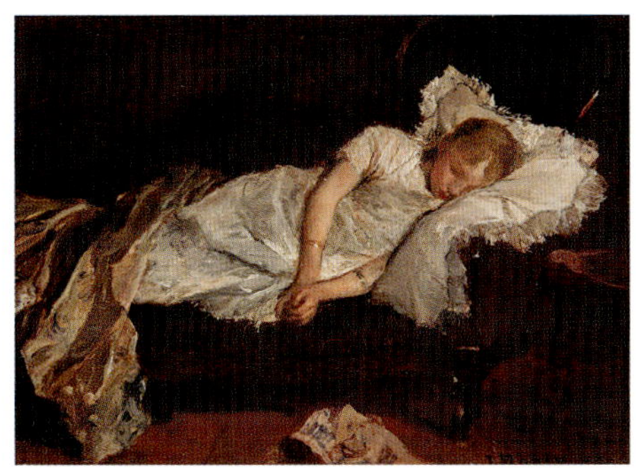

Maris, Jacob Henricus 1837–1899
A Girl Asleep on a Sofa 1880
oil on canvas 18.7 x 25.4
1113

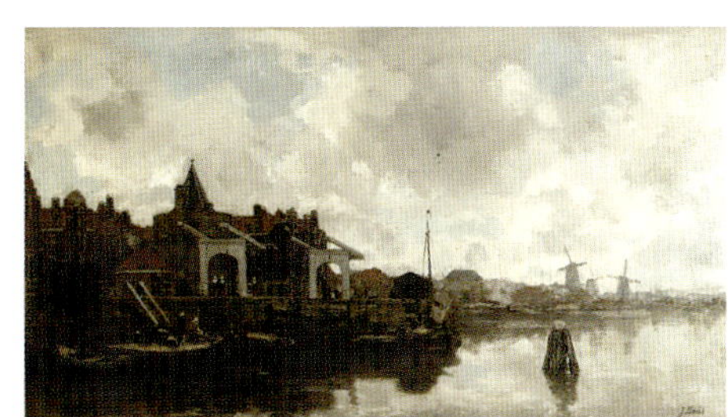

Maris, Jacob Henricus 1837–1899
Amsterdam c.1880–1885
oil on canvas 81.3 x 146.1
35.315

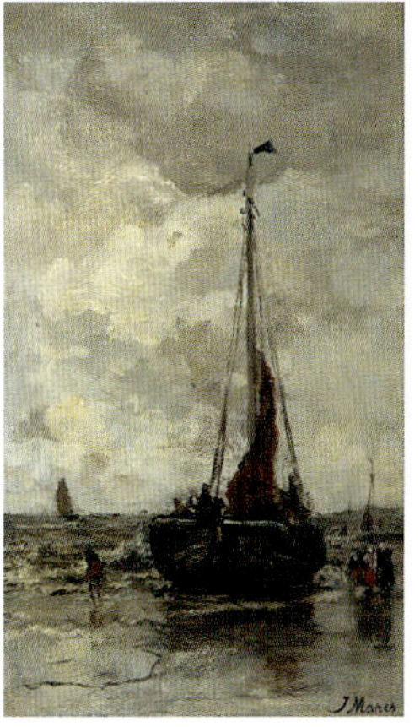

Maris, Jacob Henricus 1837–1899
Beach Scene with a Grounded Boat c.1880–
1885
oil on canvas 35.5 x 23
1136

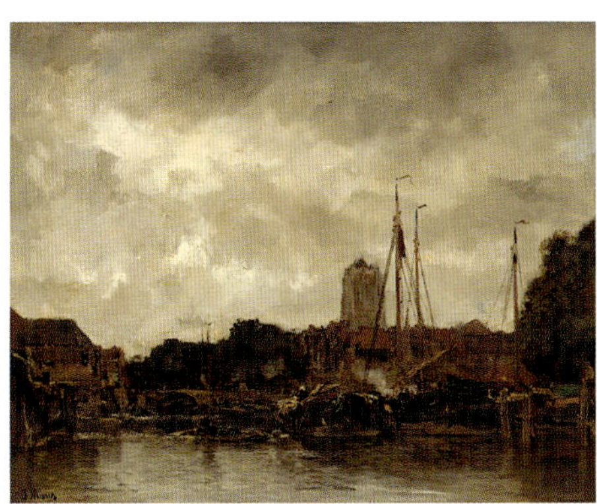

Maris, Jacob Henricus 1837–1899
Dordrecht c.1880–1885
oil on canvas 92.1 x 110.5
35.318

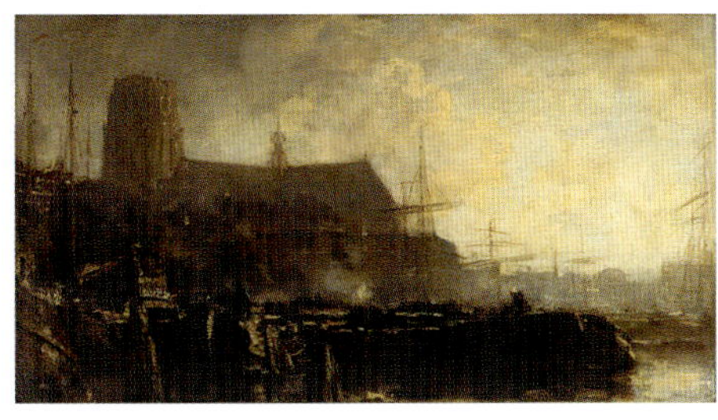

Maris, Jacob Henricus 1837–1899
A Souvenir of Dordrecht c.1884
oil on canvas 71.1 x 124.5
35.324

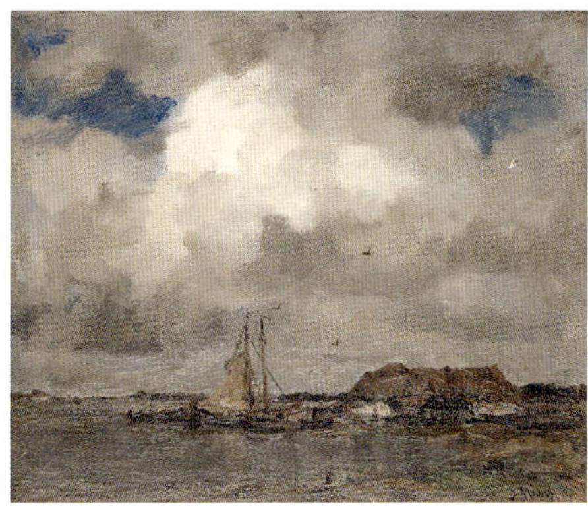

Maris, Jacob Henricus 1837–1899
River Scene with a Storm Cloud c.1885–1892
oil on canvas 40.6 x 48.6
1235

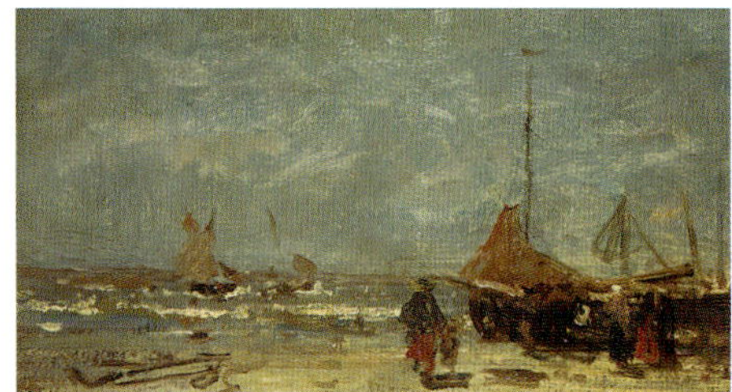

Maris, Jacob Henricus 1837–1899
The Stranded Boat c.1885–1895
oil on panel 19 x 33.6
35.325

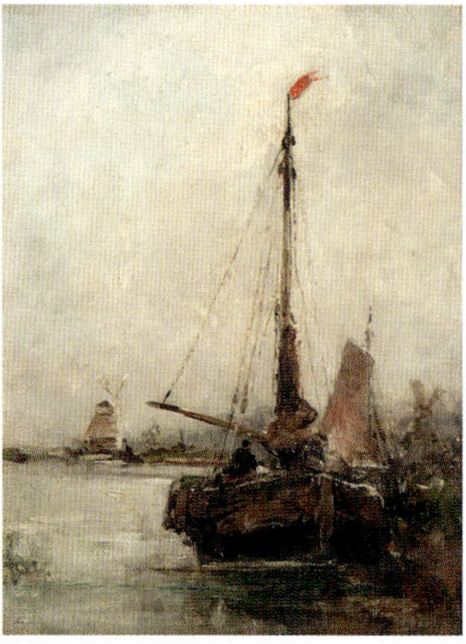

Maris, Jacob Henricus (style of) 1837–1899
A Dutch Lugger
oil on canvas 40.5 x 30.1
3270

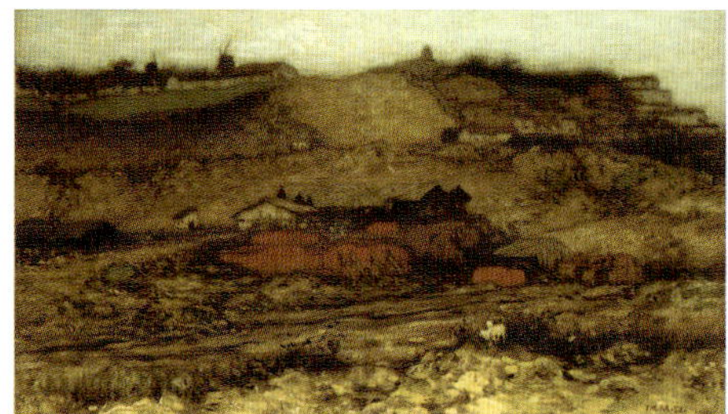

Maris, Matthijs 1839–1917
Montmartre 1872
oil on canvas 36.8 x 58.4
35.357

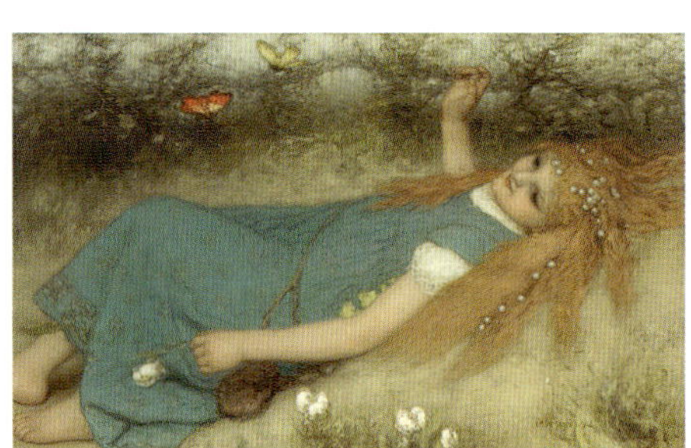

Maris, Matthijs 1839–1917
Butterflies 1874
oil on canvas 64.8 x 99.1
35.33

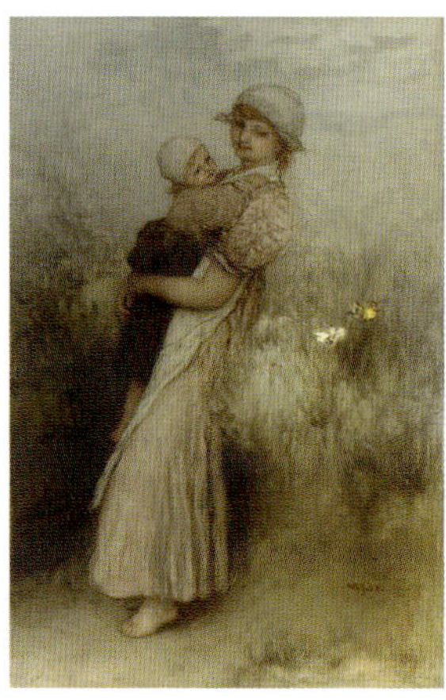

Maris, Matthijs 1839–1917
The Sisters 1875
oil on canvas 99.1 x 62.2
35.364

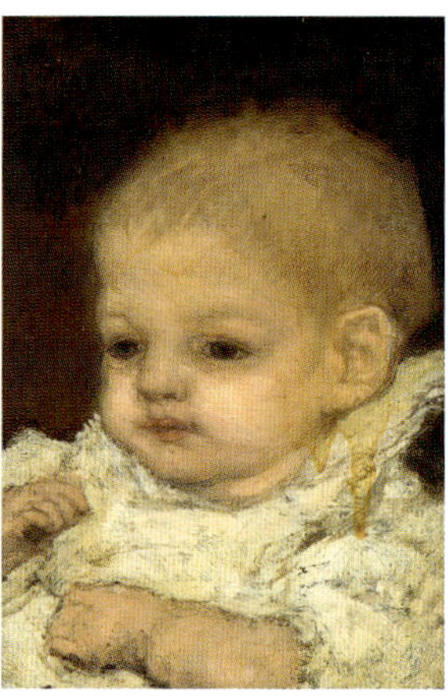

Maris, Matthijs 1839–1917
Lessore's Child 1879
oil on board 26 x 18.4
35.356

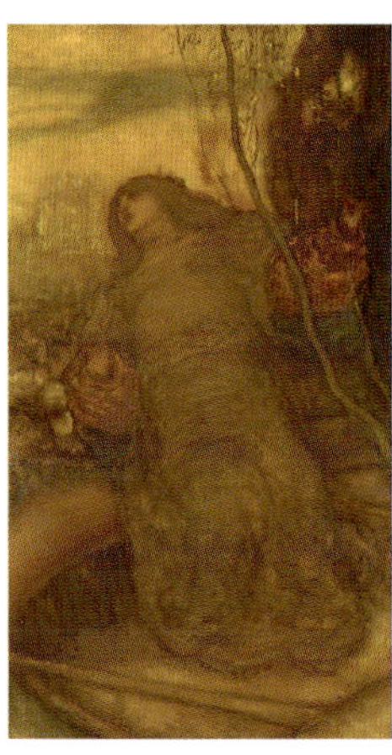

Maris, Matthijs 1839–1917
The Lady of Shalott c.1879–1882
oil on canvas 55.9 x 26.7
35.352

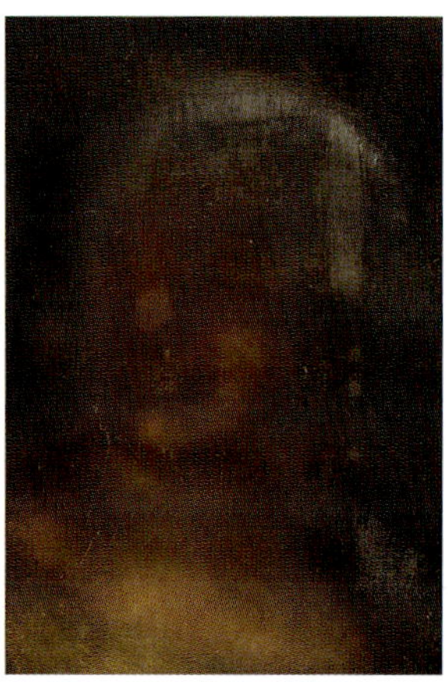

Maris, Matthijs 1839–1917
The Dark Beauty c.1880–1882
oil on canvas 38.1 x 27.3
35.335

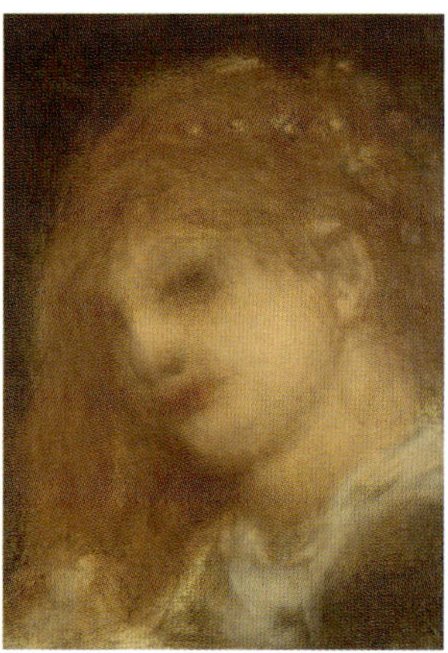

Maris, Matthijs 1839–1917
The Fair Beauty c.1880–1890
oil on canvas 38.1 x 27.9
35.341

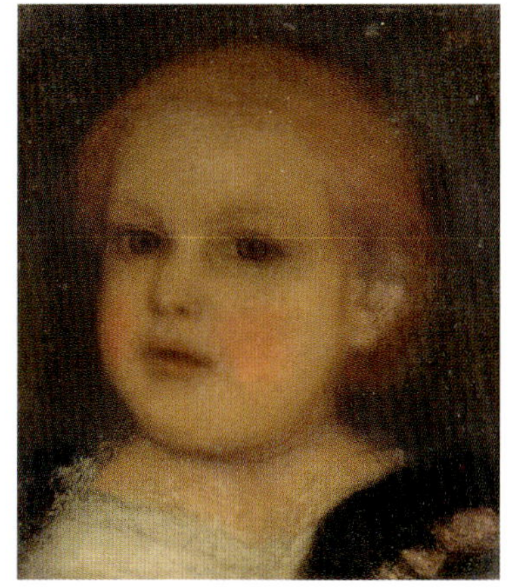

Maris, Matthijs 1839–1917
Girl with Auburn Hair c.1881
oil on canvas 26.7 x 22.8
35.345

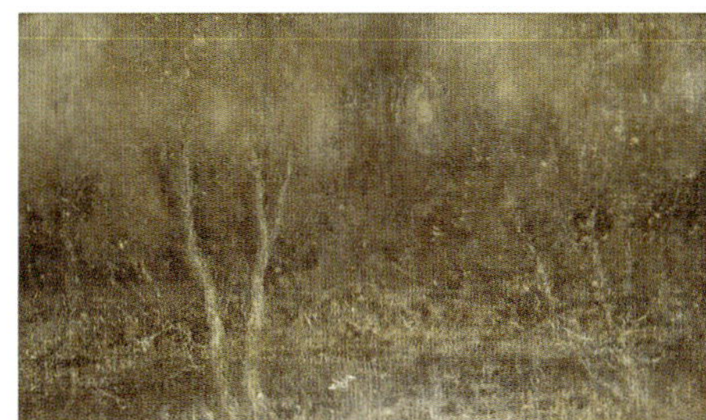

Maris, Matthijs 1839–1917
The Pond c.1885–1890
oil on canvas 30.4 x 45.7
35.359

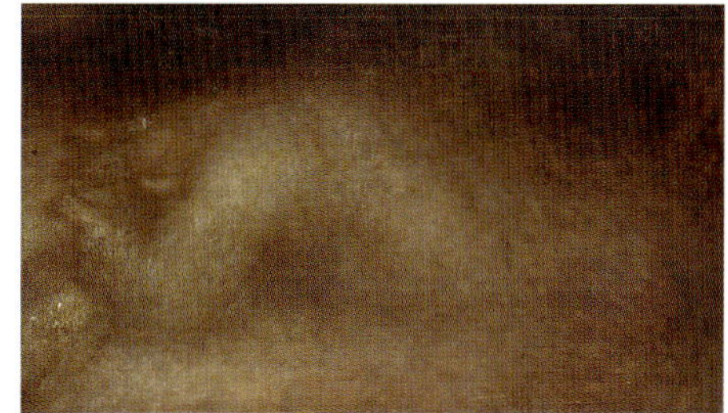

Maris, Matthijs 1839–1917
Grief c.1887
oil on canvas 34.3 x 58.8
35.346

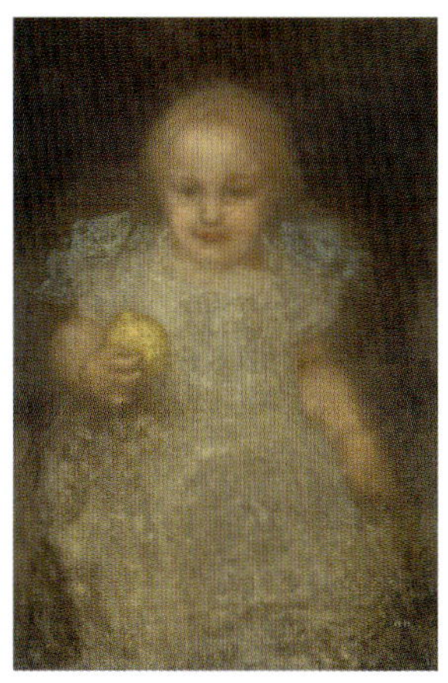

Maris, Matthijs 1839–1917
Child with a Lemon: Barye Swan c.1887–1890
oil on canvas 76.2 x 50.8
35.333

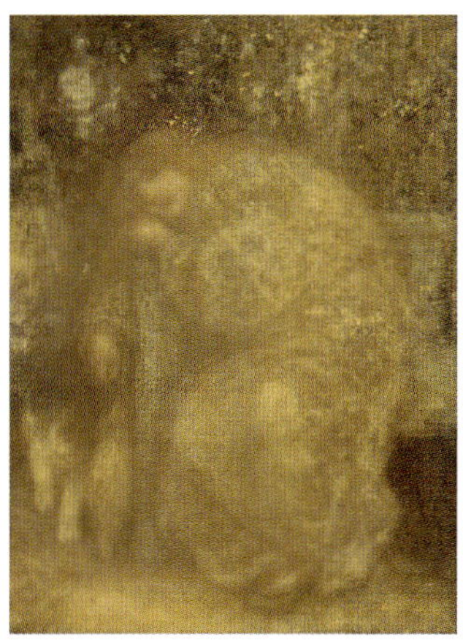

Maris, Matthijs 1839–1917
The Dreamer c.1887–1892
oil on canvas 54.6 x 39.4
35.337

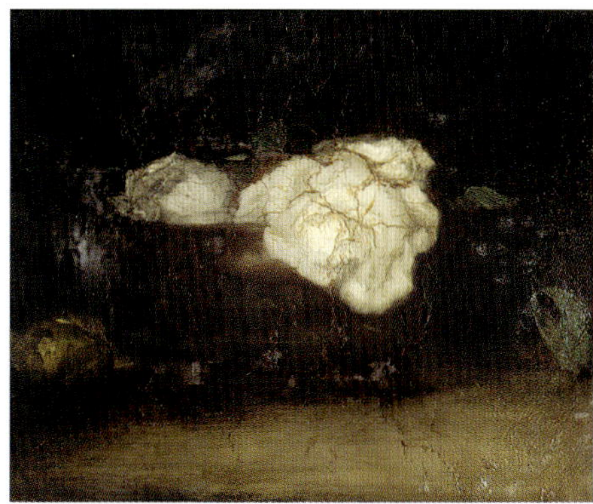

Maris, Matthijs 1839–1917
Roses 1890
oil on canvas 36.8 x 45.7
35.362

Maris, Matthijs 1839–1917
At the Altar c.1894–1895
oil on canvas 59.7 x 35.5
35.327

Maris, Matthijs 1839–1917
The Princess c.1895–1900
oil on canvas 61 x 45.7
35.36

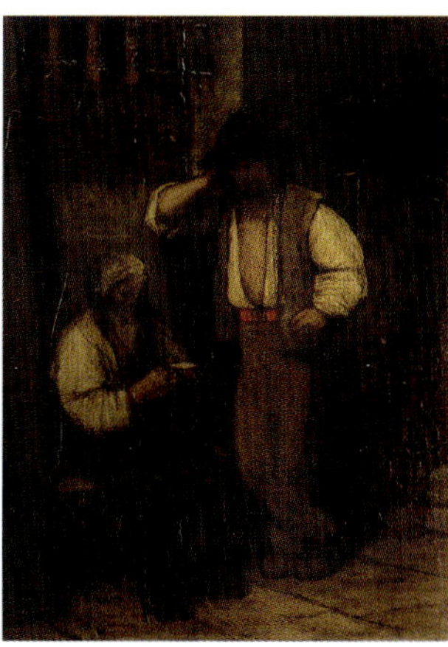

Maris, Matthijs 1839–1917
The Prisoners
oil on canvas 66.1 x 49.5
35.361

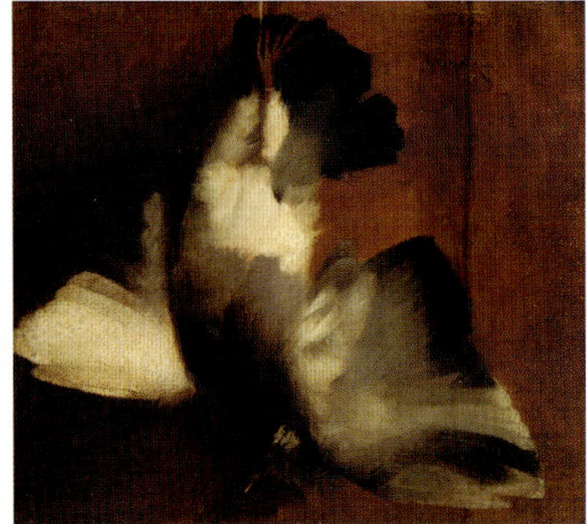

Maris, Willem 1844–1910
Dead Bird 1887
oil on canvas 20.3 x 22.8
35.371

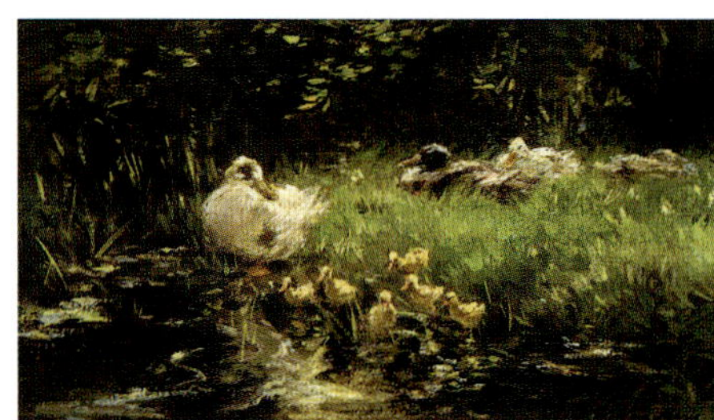

Maris, Willem 1844–1910
Ducks
oil on panel 16.5 x 26.7
35.372

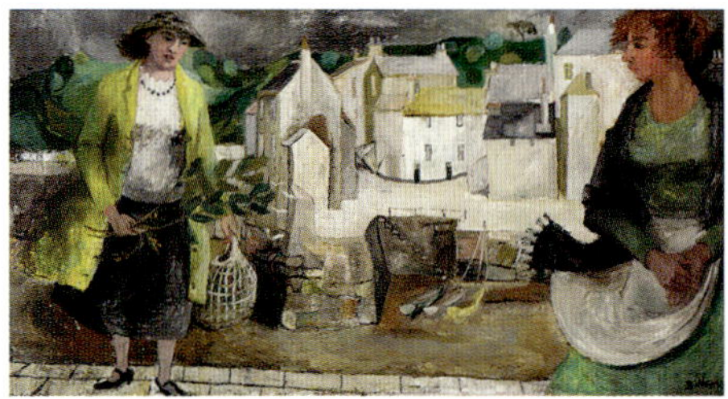

Mark, Brenda 1922–1960
Conversation at Polperro
oil on canvas 52.5 x 95.7
3624

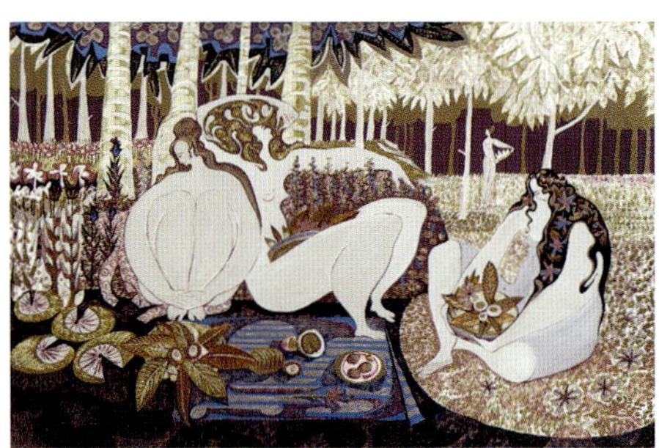

Marle, Edward b.1949
Lotus Eaters 1970
cryla on paper 61 x 91.1
3294

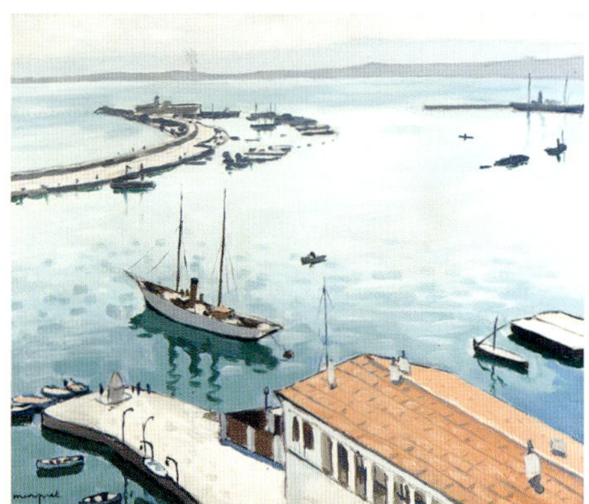

Marquet, Albert 1875–1947
The Port of Algiers c.1922
oil on canvas 54 x 65
3030

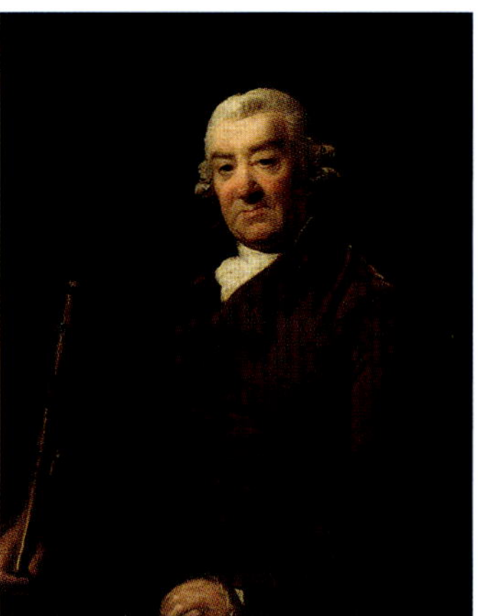

Martin, David 1736/1737–1798
*George Murdoch (1715–1795), Provost of
Glasgow (1754–1755 & 1766–1767)* 1793
oil on canvas 91.4 x 71.1
2352

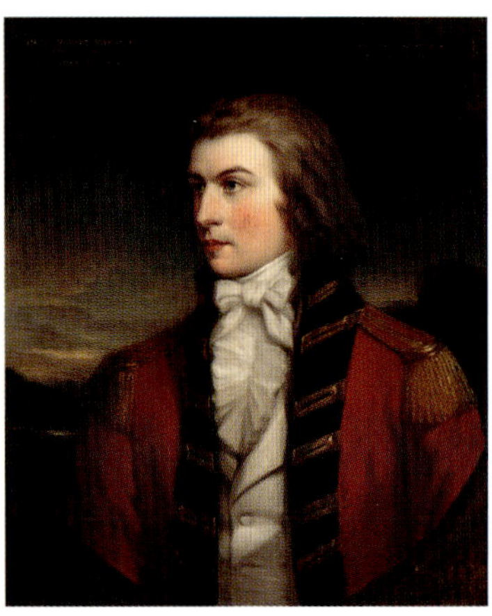

Martin, David 1736/1737–1798
Captain Robert Maxwell (1770–1796)
oil on canvas 75.5 x 62.5
PL.181 (P)

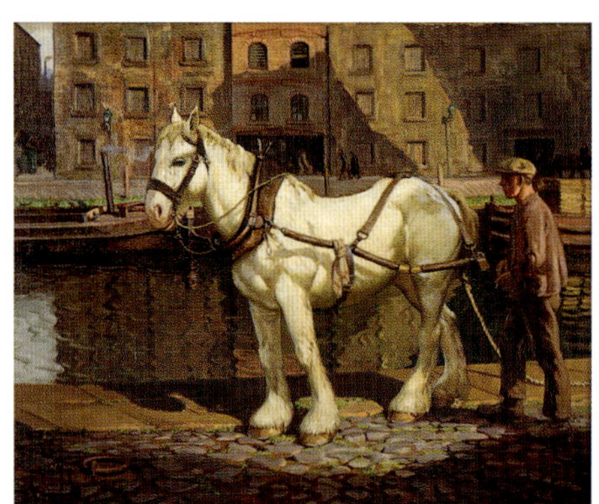

Martin, Francis Patrick 1883–1966
The Old Tow Horse 1937
oil on canvas 63.7 x 76.2
3088

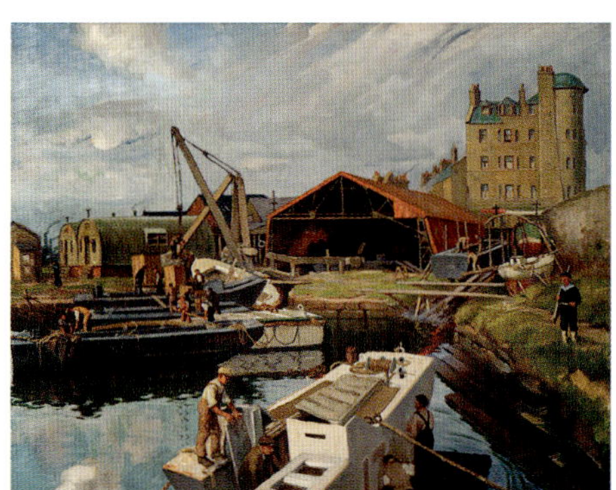

Martin, Francis Patrick 1883–1966
Maryhill Dock, Forth and Clyde Canal
c.1939–1945
oil on canvas 80.9 x 93.9
TEMP.2679

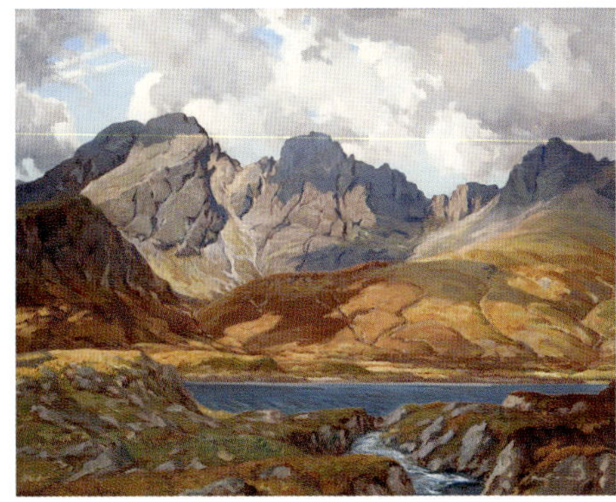

Martin, Francis Patrick 1883–1966
Spring Morning, Blaven c.1953
oil on canvas 63.5 x 76.2
3008

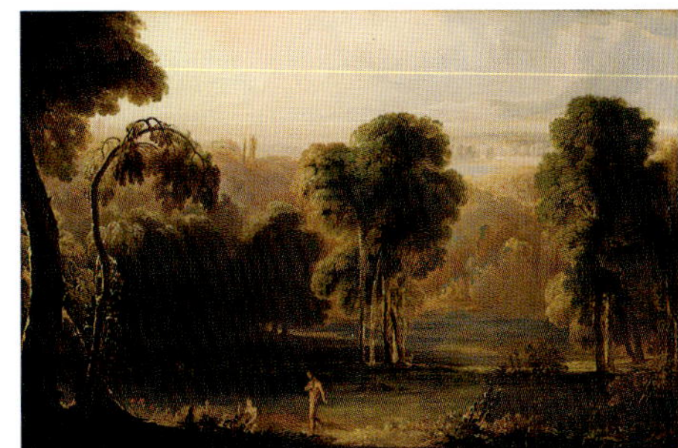

Martin, John 1789–1854
Adam's First Sight of Eve 1812
oil on canvas 70.2 x 105.7
2570

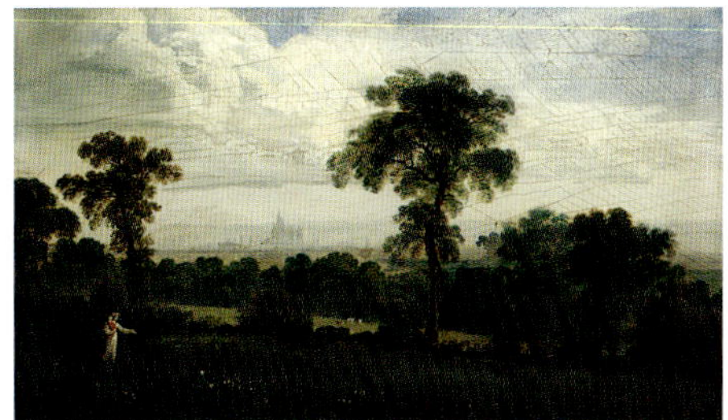

Martin, John 1789–1854
Distant View of London 1815
oil on panel 17.8 x 30.5
235

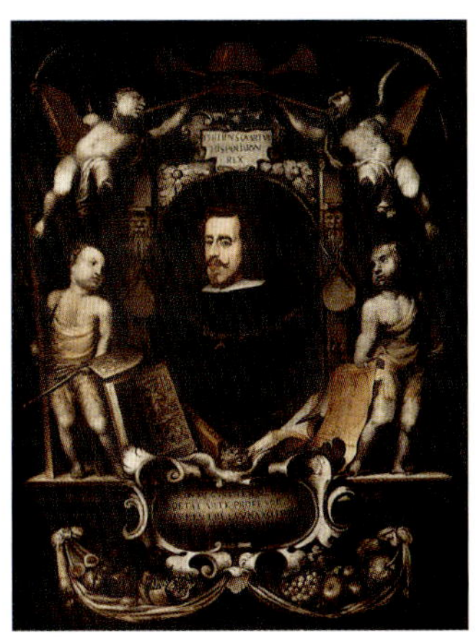

Martínez de Gradilla, Juan
active 1660–1682
Philip IV (1605–1665), King of Spain
1665–1666
oil on canvas 178.1 x 131.4
PC.144

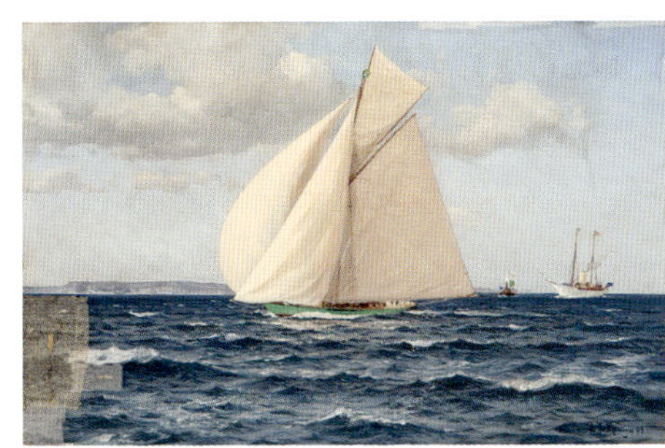

Martino, Edoardo de 1838–1912
Yacht 'Shamrock' 1899
oil on canvas 35.8 x 53.5
1932.29.gr

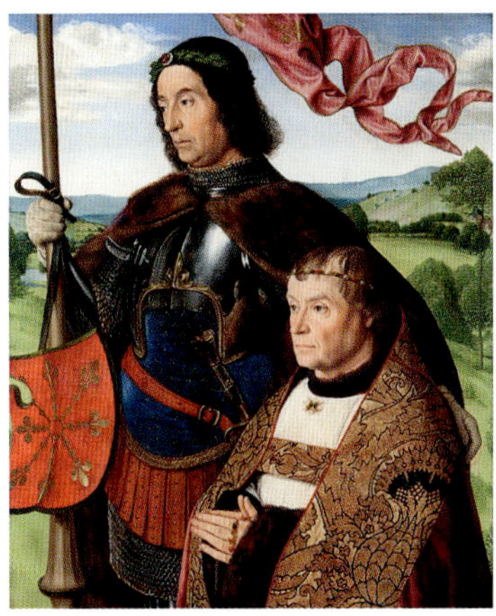

Master of Moulins active c.1475–c.1505
Saint Maurice (or Saint Victor) with a Donor
c.1500–1505
oil on panel 58.4 x 49.5
203

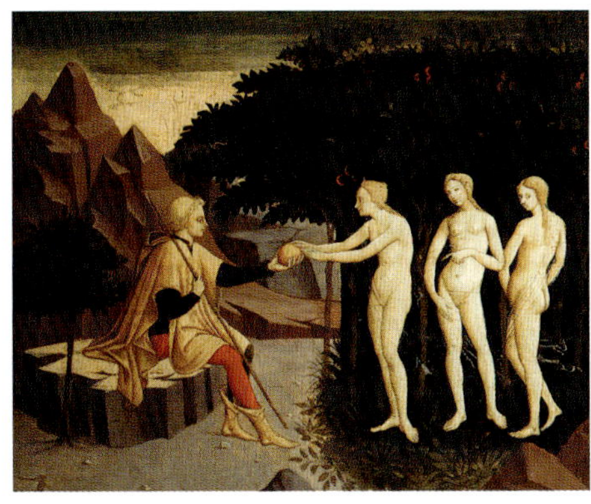

Master of Paris active c.1440–1460
The Judgement of Paris c.1450–1455
oil & tempera on panel 39.7 x 49.8
35.634

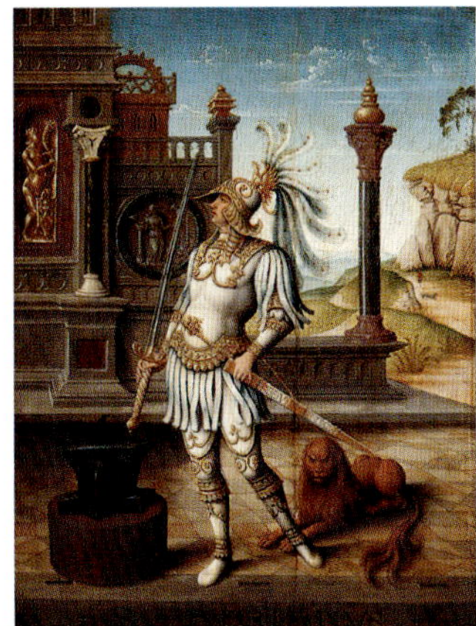

**Master of the Beyghem Altarpiece
(attributed to)** active 16th C
Saint Adrian c.1510–1530
oil on panel 31 x 23.2
206

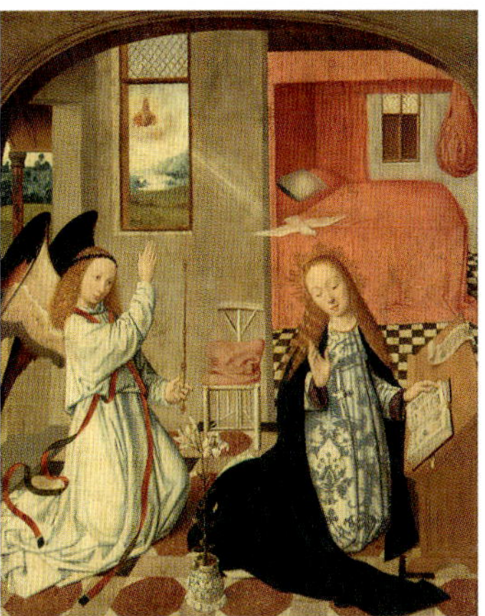

**Master of the Brunswick Diptych
(attributed to)** active c.1480–1510
The Annunciation c.1500
oil on panel 44.5 x 35.6
35.639

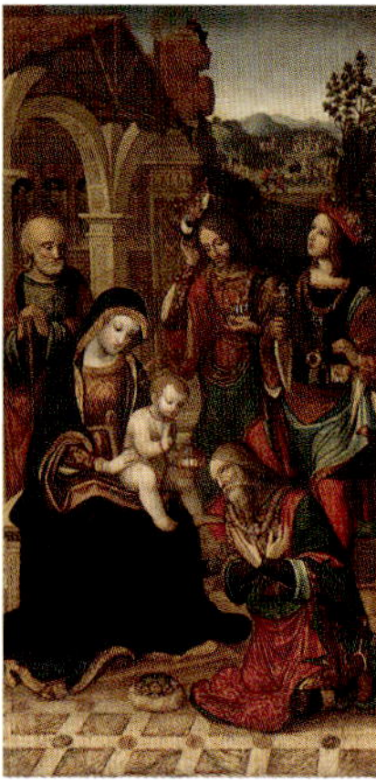

Master of the Glasgow Adoration
active c.1490–1520
The Adoration of the Magi c.1503–1510
oil on panel 174 x 69
586

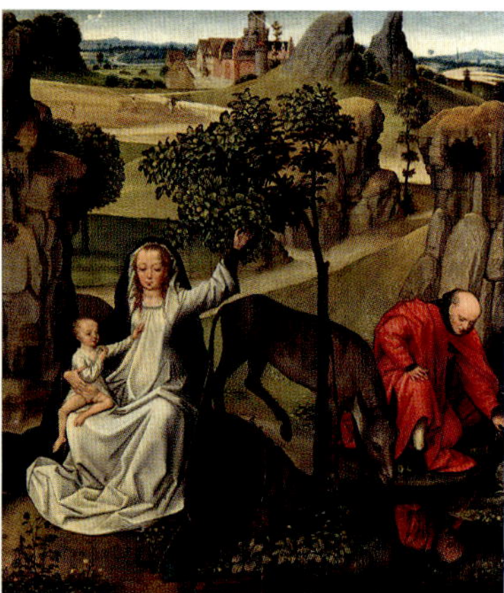

**Master of the Prado Adoration of the Magi
(attributed to)** active c.1450–1475
The Flight into Egypt c.1465–1470
oil on panel 58.4 x 50.8
35.532

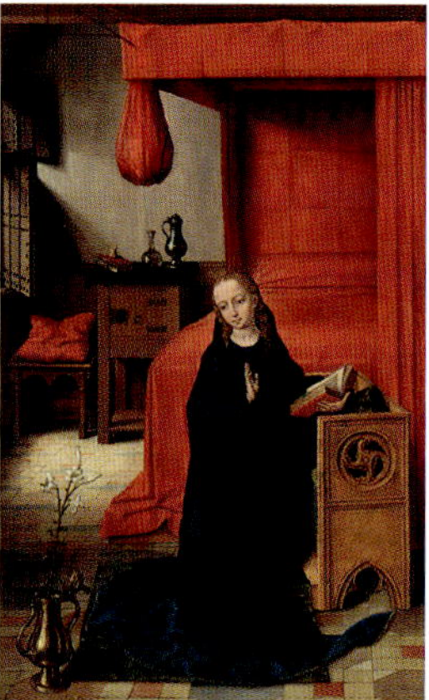

**Master of the Prado Adoration of the Magi
(attributed to)** active c.1450–1475
Virgin Annunciate c.1465–1470
oil on panel 58.4 x 35.6
35.533

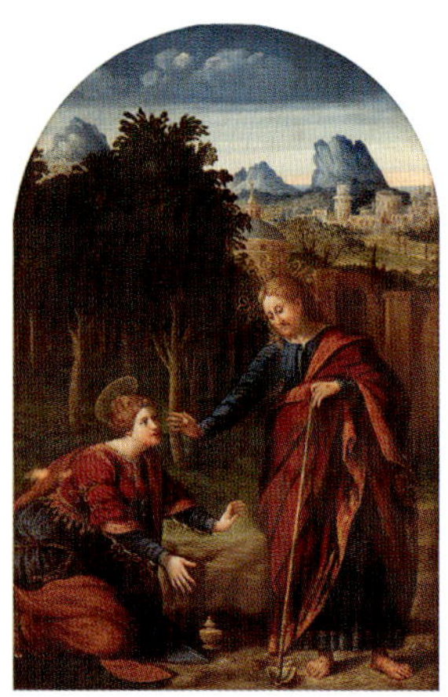

Master of the Twelve Apostles active
c.1527–1542
'Noli me tangere' c.1530–1540
oil on panel 45.7 x 30.8
172

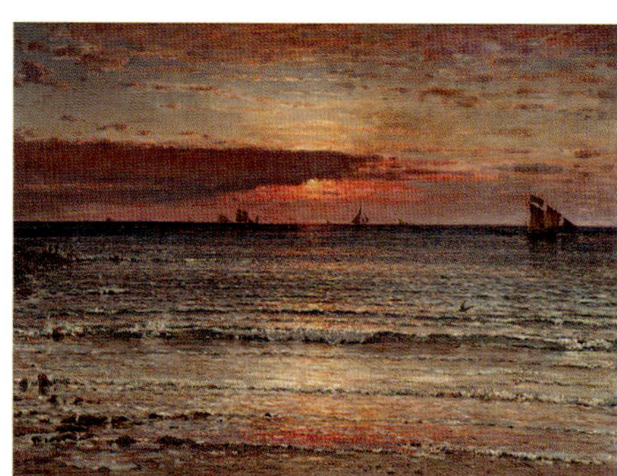

Masuré, Jules 1819–1910
Sunset c.1881
oil on canvas 88.1 x 117.9
2346

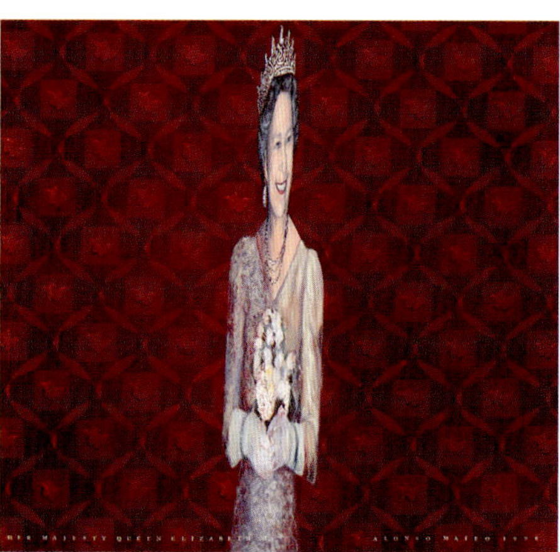

Mateo, José Luis Alonso b.1964
Reina Isabel 1996
acrylic on canvas 101.5 x 100.5
3614

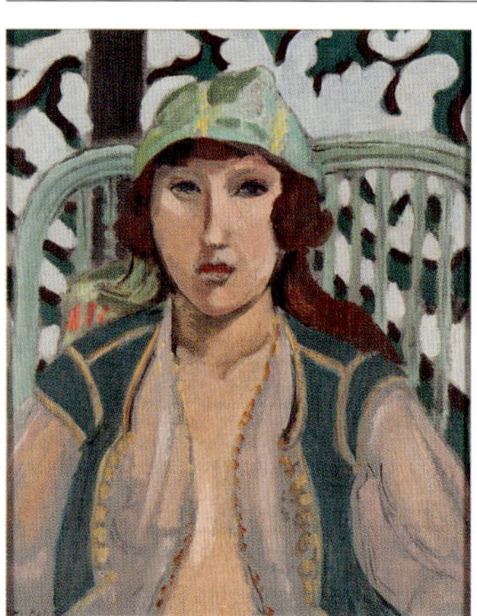

Matisse, Henri 1869–1954
Woman in Oriental Dress 1919
oil on canvas 40.8 x 32.7
2197

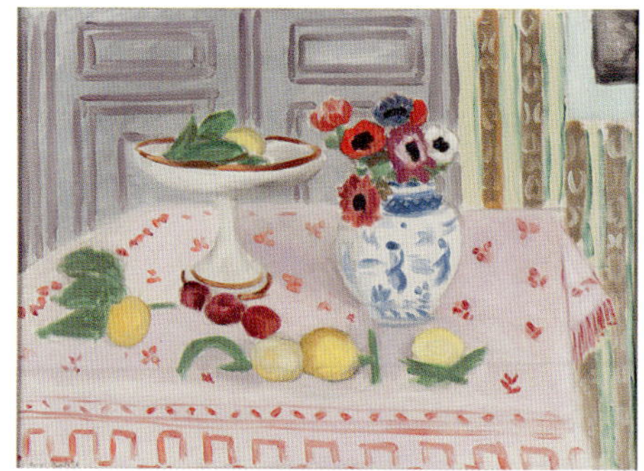

Matisse, Henri 1869–1954
The Pink Tablecloth c.1924–1925
oil on canvas 60.3 x 81
2402

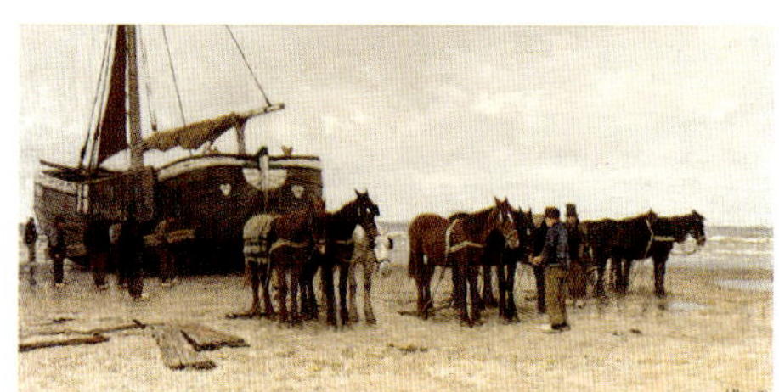

Mauve, Anton 1838–1888
Scheveningen 1874
oil on canvas 91.5 x 183
35.377

Facing page: Master of the Brunswick Diptych (attributed to), active c.1480–1510,
The Annunciation, Delft, c.1500 (p. 283)

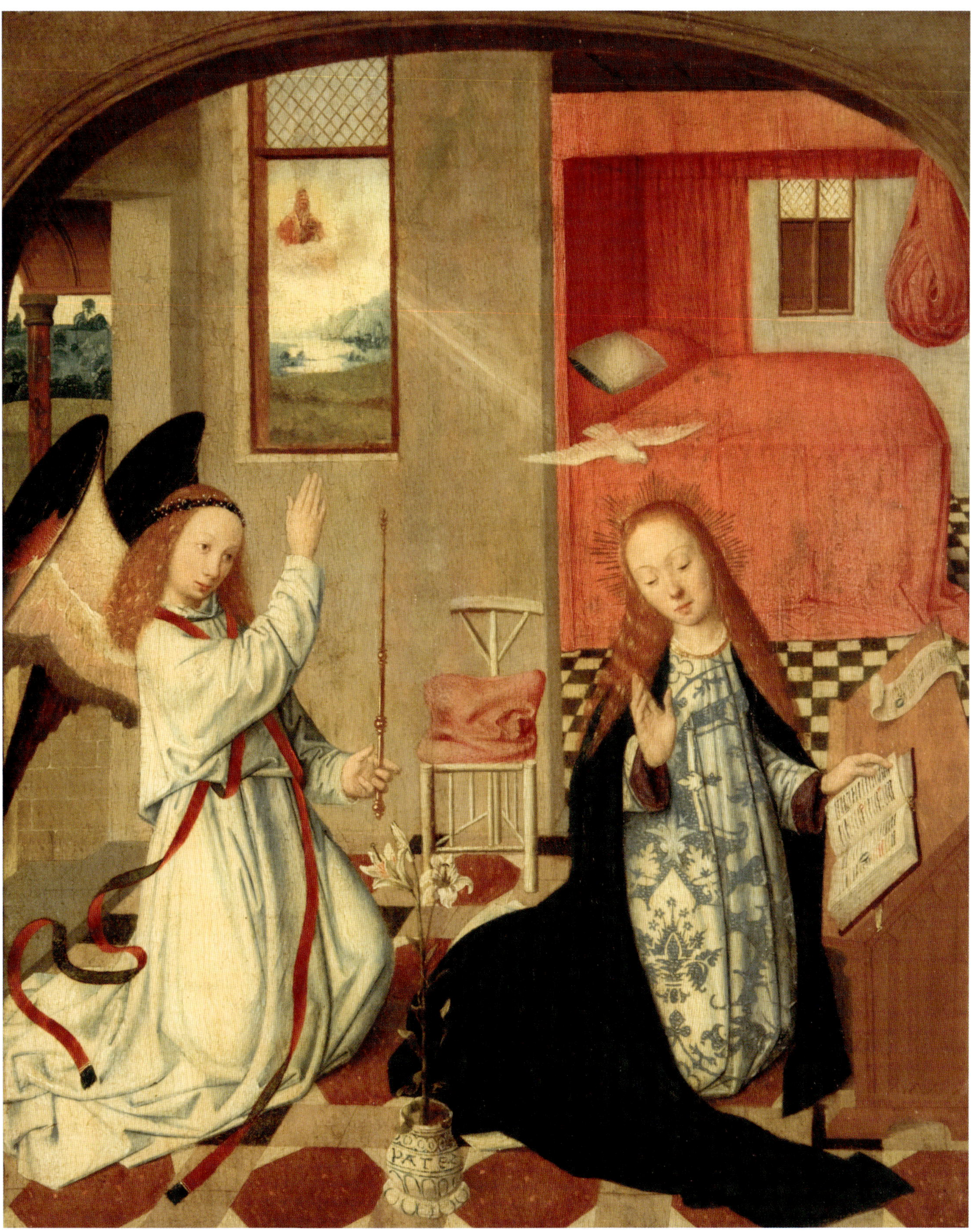

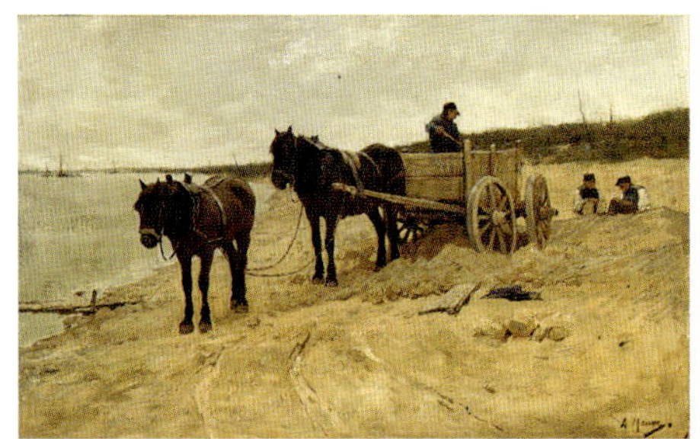

Mauve, Anton 1838–1888
Carting Sand c.1875–1880
oil on canvas 35.5 x 53.3
35.373

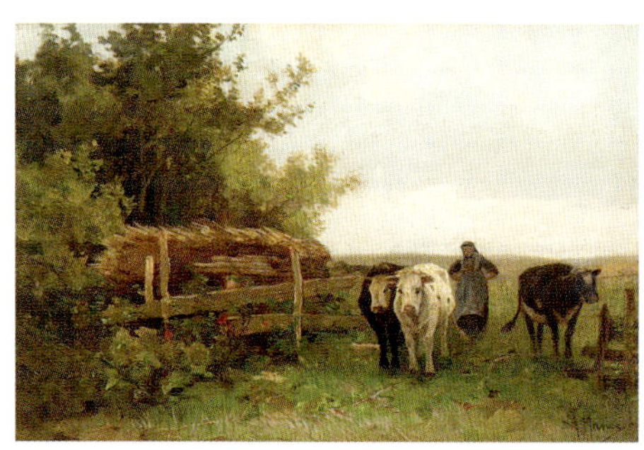

Mauve, Anton 1838–1888
A Woman Driving Cattle c.1878–1885
oil on panel 28.9 x 42.5
2691

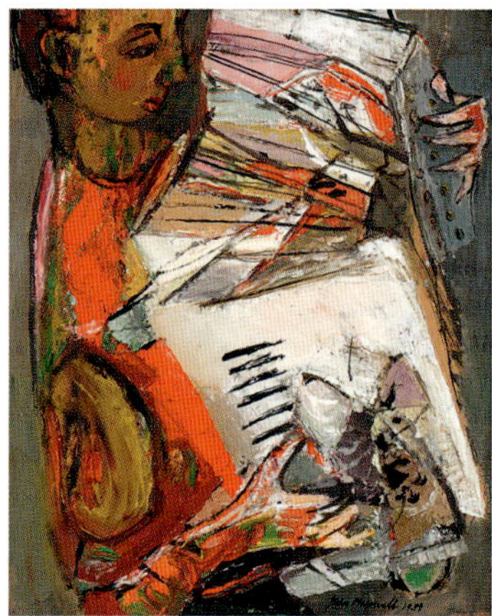

Maxwell, John 1905–1962
Boy with an Accordion 1957
oil on canvas 61 x 50.5
3075

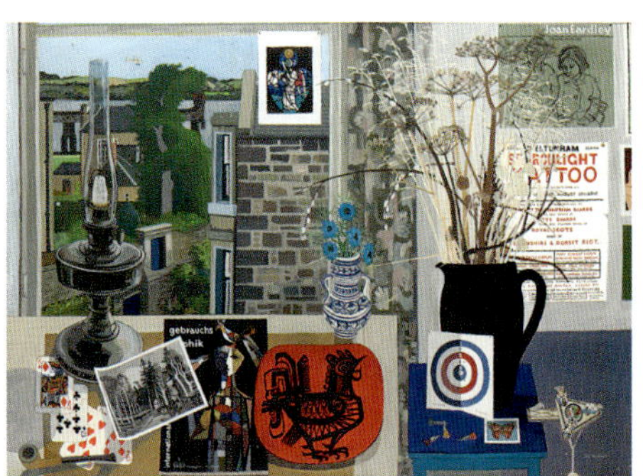

Maxwell, Joseph b.1925
'Extra Yankee' over the Tay Bridge 1965
oil on hardboard 76.2 x 101.6
3243

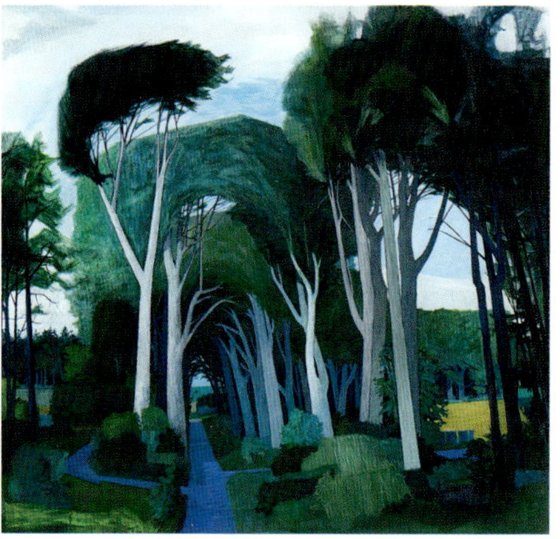

Maxwell, Joseph b.1925
Piper's Brae, Culzean 1969
oil & PVA on hardboard 121.9 x 121.9
3273

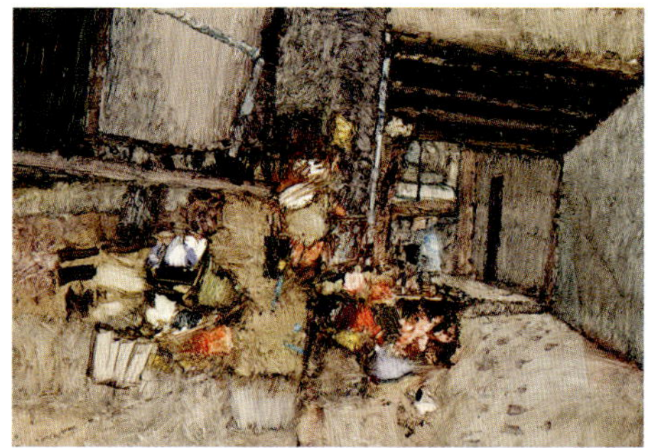

Mayo, Drummond b.1929
Vennel 1989
oil on card 47 x 67
3669

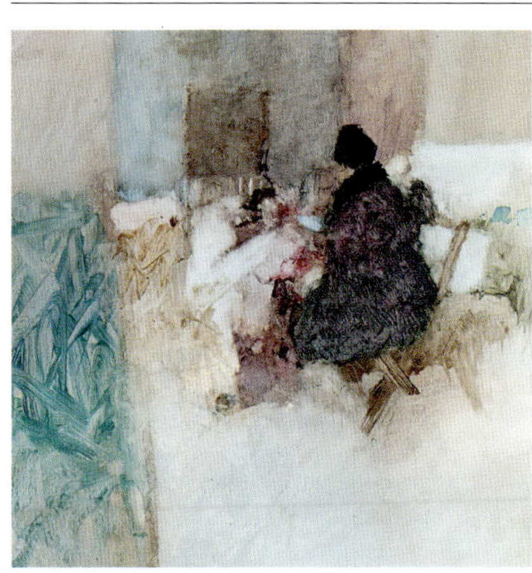

Mayo, Drummond b.1929
The Visitors
oil on board 38 x 37.5
PR.2007.2.64

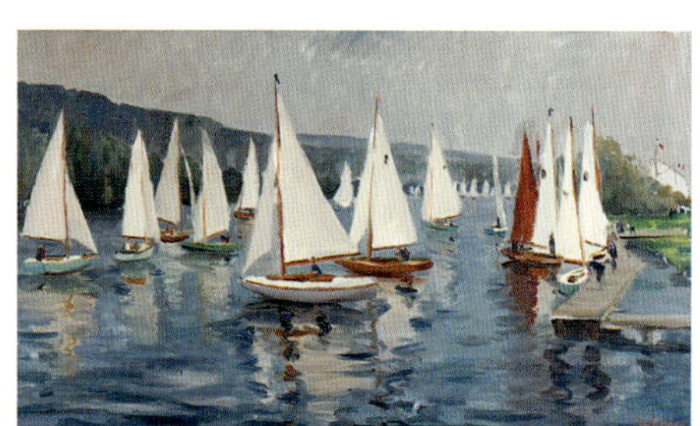

Maze, Paul Lucien 1887–1979
Regatta at Meulan
oil on canvas 43 x 72.7
2200

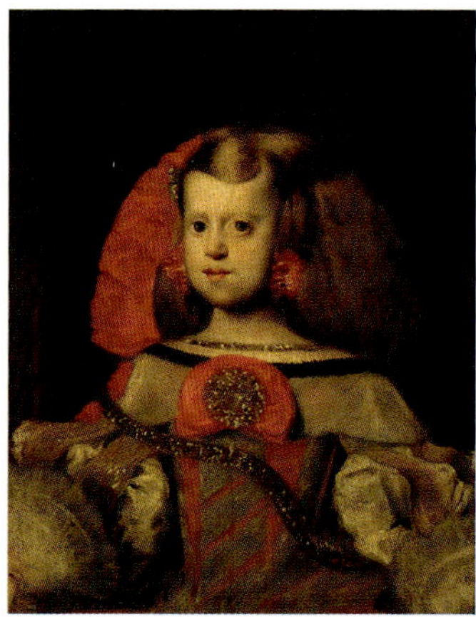

Mazo, Juan Bautista Martínez del (after)
1612–1667
The Infanta Margarita (1651–1673) c.1662
oil on canvas 68.6 x 57.2
35.633

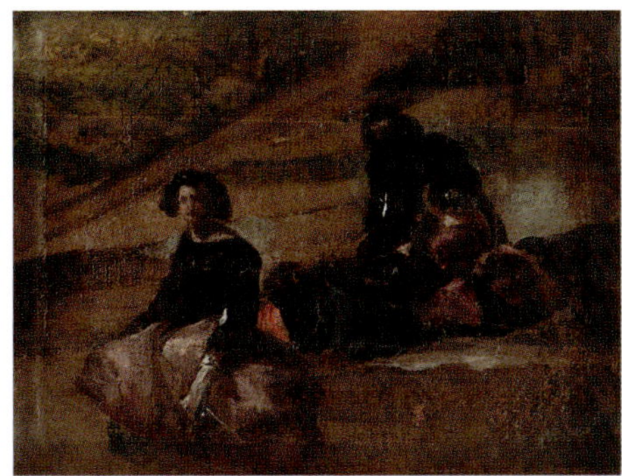

Mazo, Juan Bautista Martínez del (attributed to) 1612–1667
Landscape with Figures c.1657
oil on canvas 17.8 x 25.7
PC.92

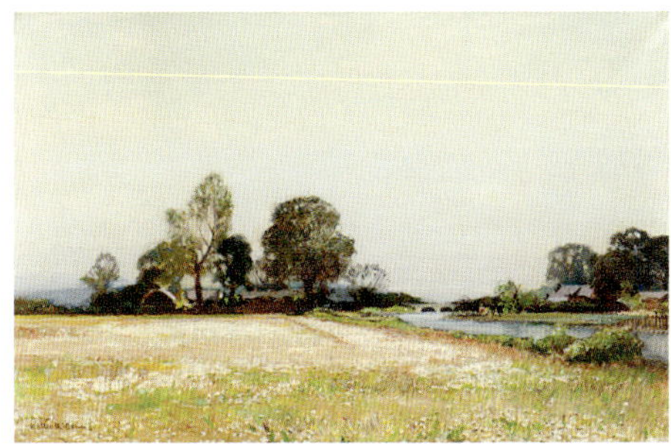

McAdam, Walter 1866–1935
Flowers in the Meadow c.1909
oil on canvas 59.7 x 90.2
1229

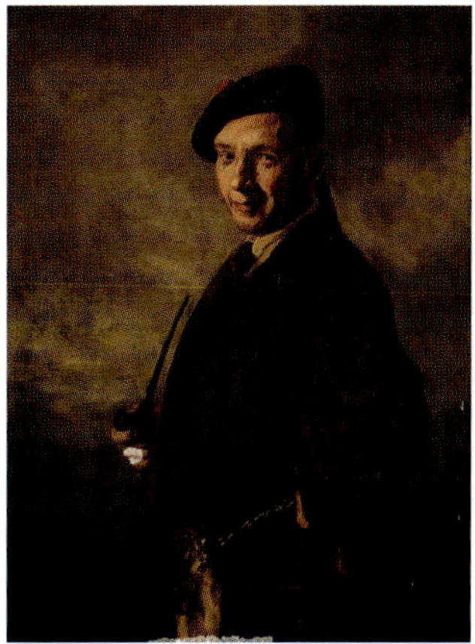

McBey, James 1883–1959
Sir Harry Lauder (1870–1950) 1921
oil on canvas 101.6 x 76.2
1806

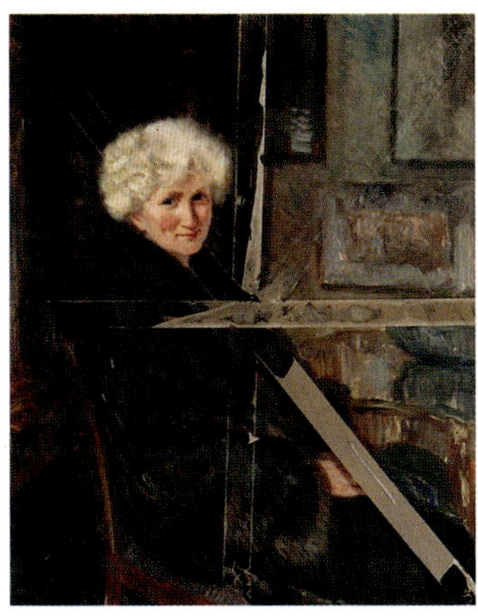

McBey, James 1883–1959
Mrs John Arnott 1927
oil on canvas 111.8 x 86.4
2322

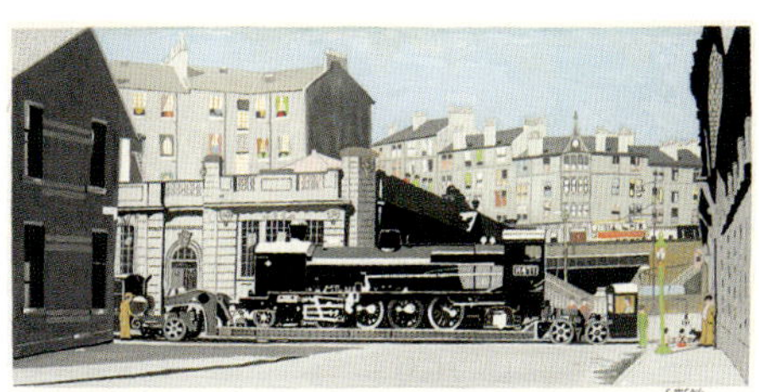

McCaig, Charles active 20th C
Train
acrylic on board 27.6 x 56.8
1997.47.4

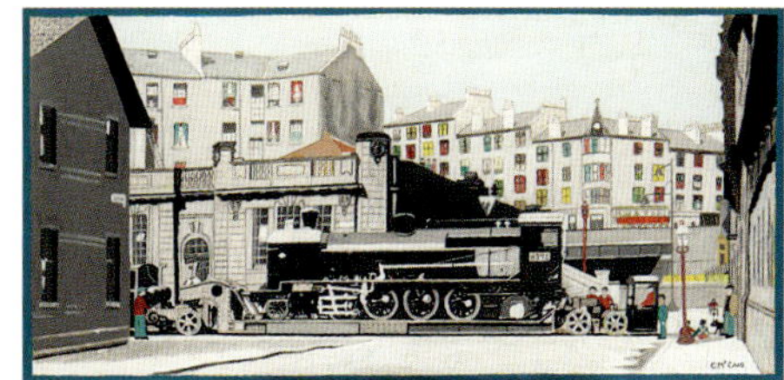

McCaig, Charles active 20th C
Train
oil on board 28.2 x 58.4
1997.47.5

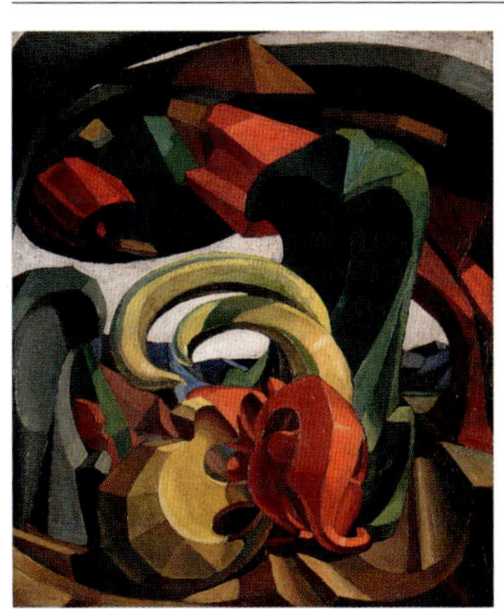

McCance, William 1894–1970
Conflict 1922
oil on canvas 76 x 63.5
3296

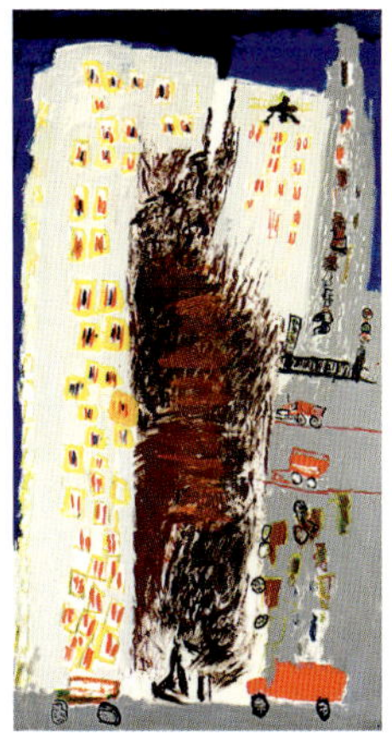

McCann, Frank b.1946
Untitled
acrylic on board 244 x 122.2
3498

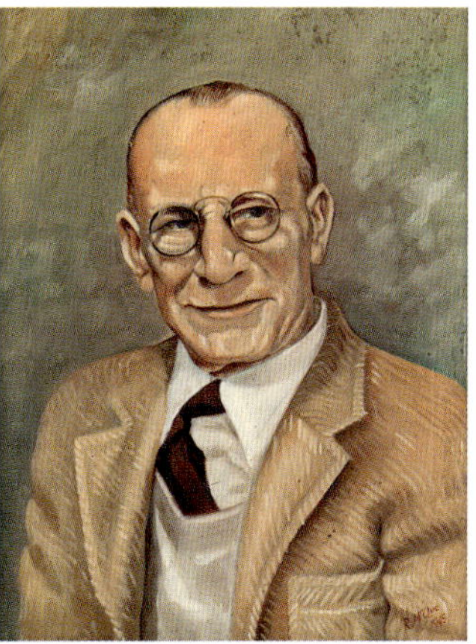

McClue, R.
Albert Ernest Pickard (1874–1964), of Albert Ernest Pickard Limited 1945
oil on canvas 60 x 44.5
TEMP.19232

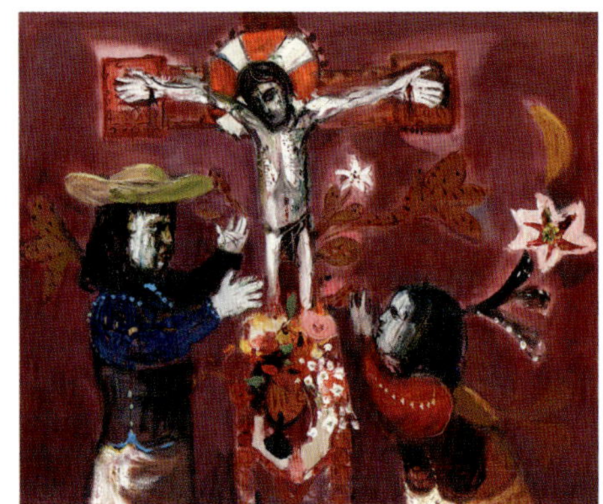

McClure, David 1926–1998
The Shrine 1963
oil on canvas 81.3 x 91.4
3197

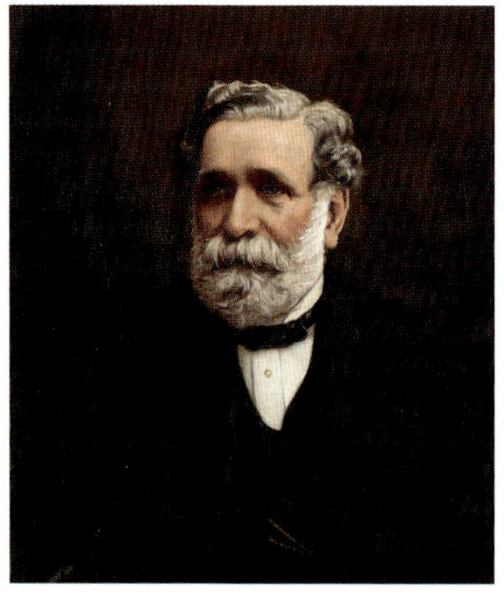

McClymant
William Strang (1859–1921) 1902
oil on canvas 73.5 x 61.6
PP.1975.283

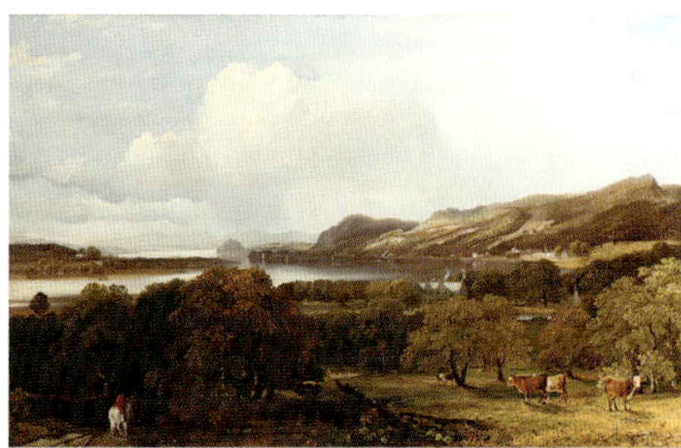

McCulloch, Horatio 1805–1867
Bowling c.1830–1835
oil on canvas 81.3 x 127
1834

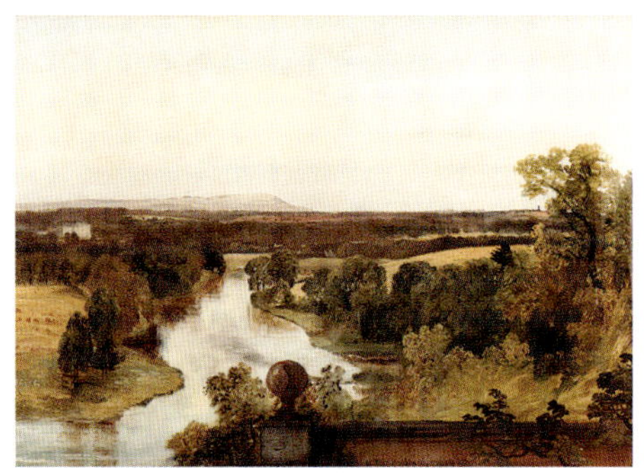

McCulloch, Horatio 1805–1867
View from the Roman Camp at Dalzell near Hamilton 1835
oil on canvas 56 x 76.2
3408

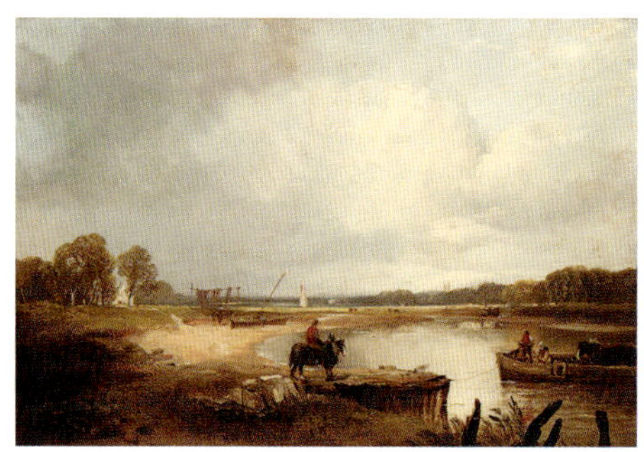

McCulloch, Horatio 1805–1867
The Clyde near Erskine Ferry c.1845
oil on panel 32.4 x 45.7
690

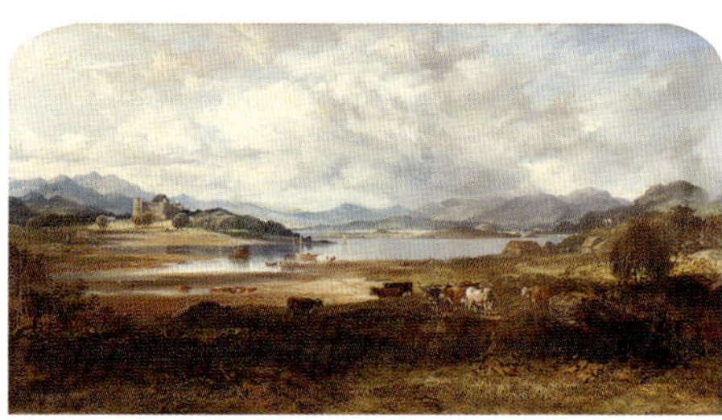

McCulloch, Horatio 1805–1867
Dunstaffnage Castle 1854
oil on canvas 64.8 x 120.7
997

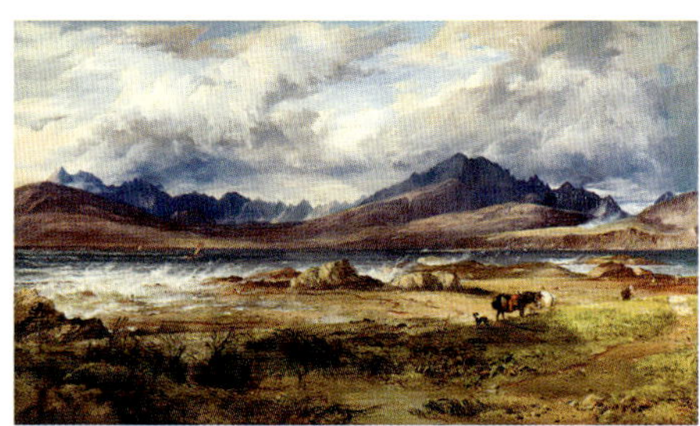

McCulloch, Horatio 1805–1867
The Cuillin from Ord, Skye c.1854
oil on canvas 71.1 x 121.9
1052

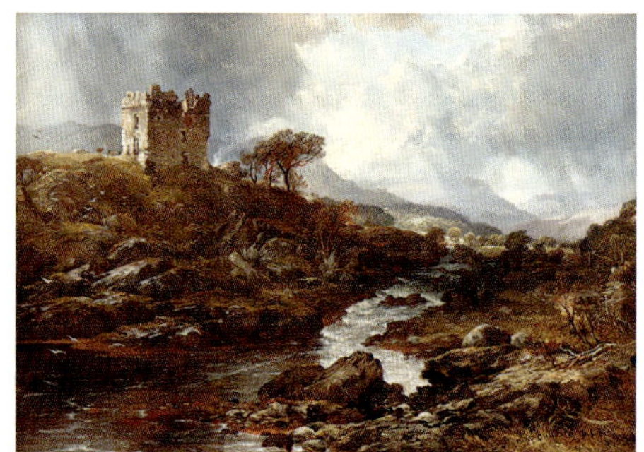

McCulloch, Horatio 1805–1867
Kinlochaline Castle, Morvern 1855
oil on canvas 53.6 x 76.5
3122

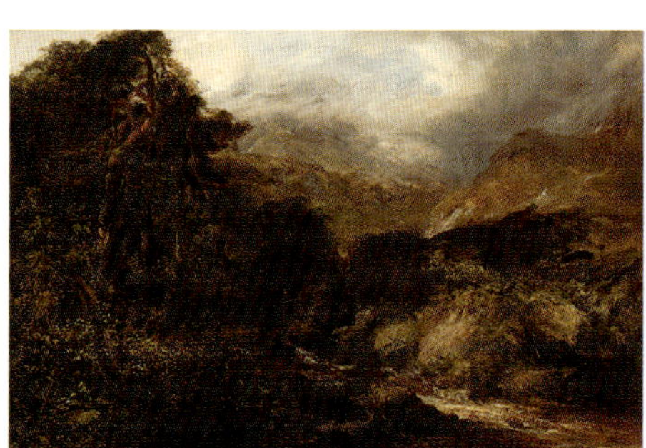

McCulloch, Horatio 1805–1867
Glen Affric 1857
oil on canvas 83.8 x 121.9
1713

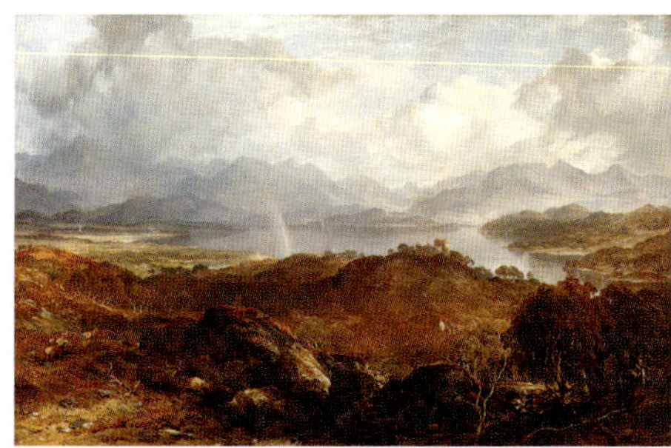

McCulloch, Horatio 1805–1867
'My heart's in the Highlands' 1860
oil on canvas 61 x 91.4
1001

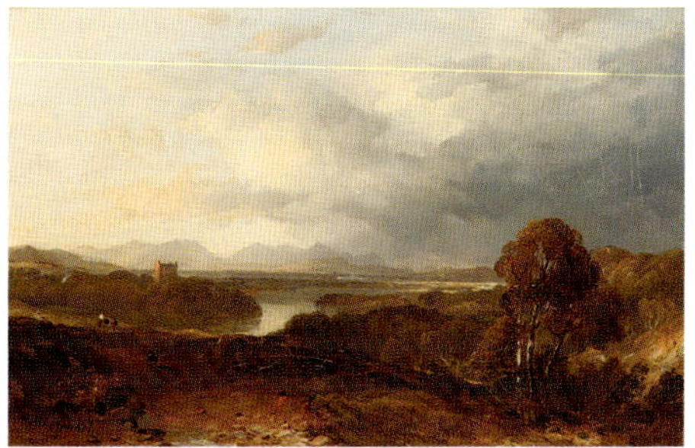

McCulloch, Horatio 1805–1867
Ross-shire Landscape c.1860
oil on canvas 28.6 x 44.5
974

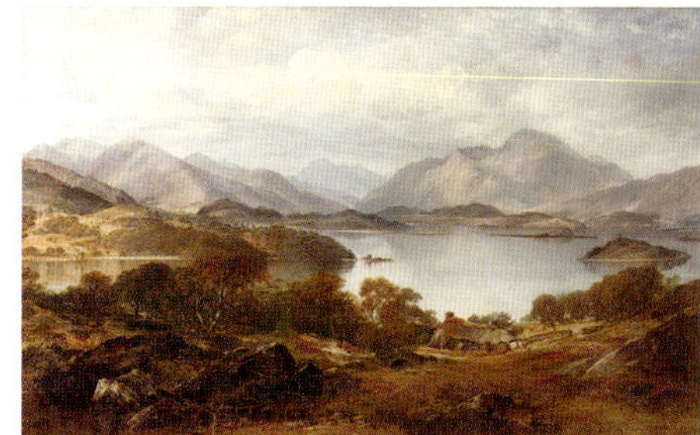

McCulloch, Horatio 1805–1867
Loch Lomond 1861
oil on canvas 84.5 x 135.9
1053

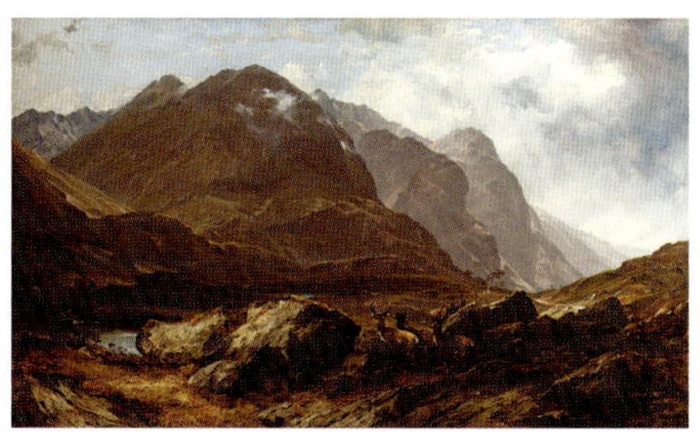

McCulloch, Horatio 1805–1867
Glencoe 1864
oil on canvas 110.5 x 182.9
1003

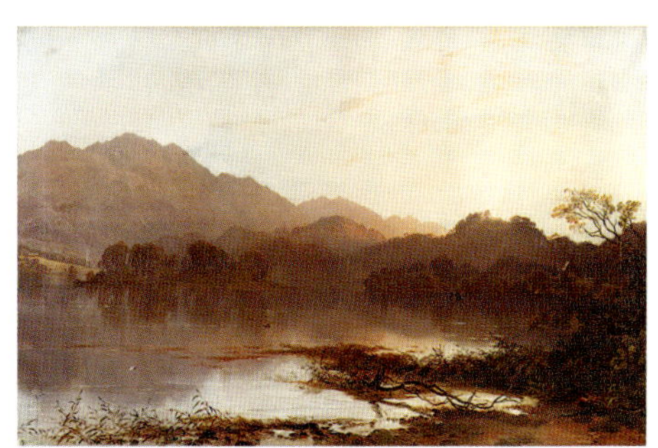

McCulloch, Horatio 1805–1867
Loch Achray, Evening 1864
oil on canvas 80 x 124.5
998

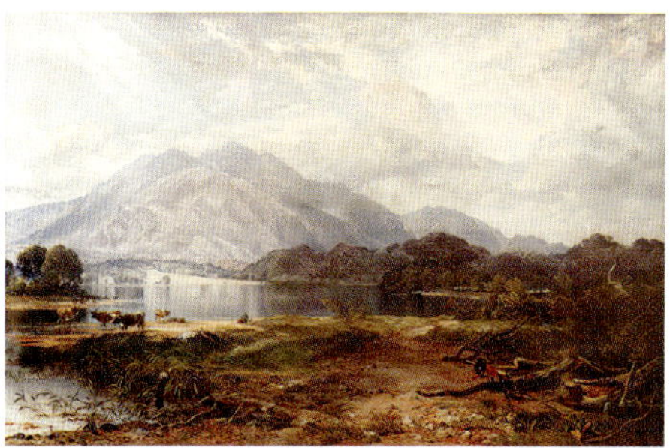

McCulloch, Horatio 1805–1867
Loch Achray, Morning 1865
oil on canvas 80 x 124.5
999

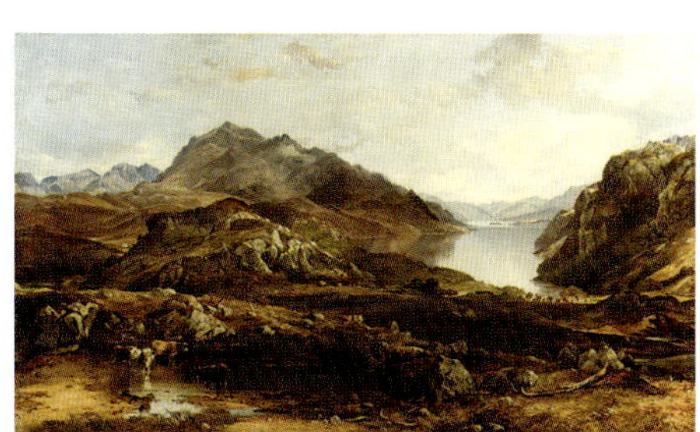

McCulloch, Horatio 1805–1867
Loch Maree 1866
oil on canvas 110.5 x 182.9
1002

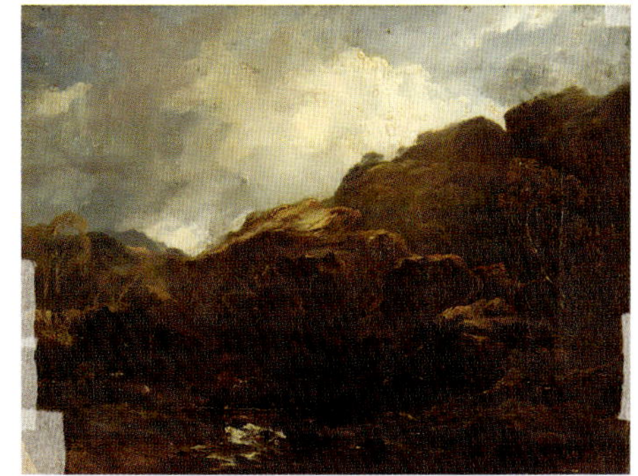

McCulloch, Horatio 1805–1867
Mountain Scenery
oil on canvas 35.5 x 45.8
NR.134

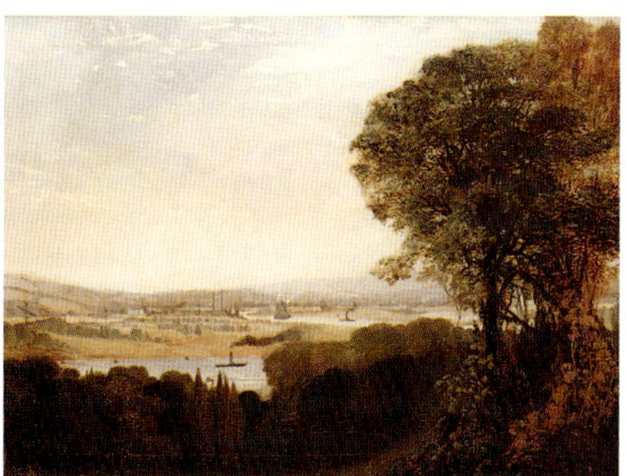

McCulloch, Horatio (after) 1805–1867
Bowling
oil on canvas 73.7 x 99.1
2289

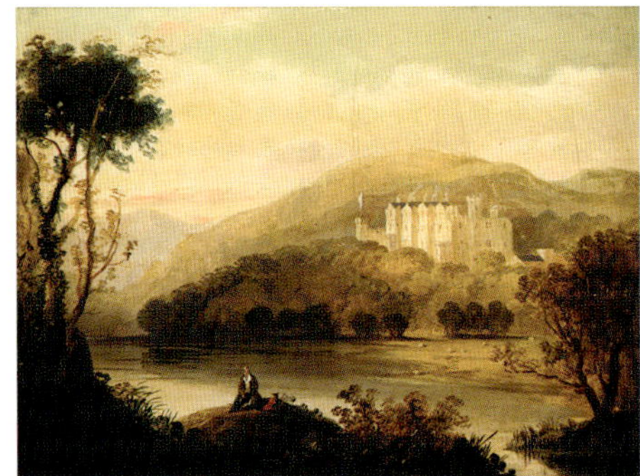

McCulloch, Horatio (attributed to)
1805–1867
Abbotsford from the Tweed
oil on board 22.7 x 30
3650

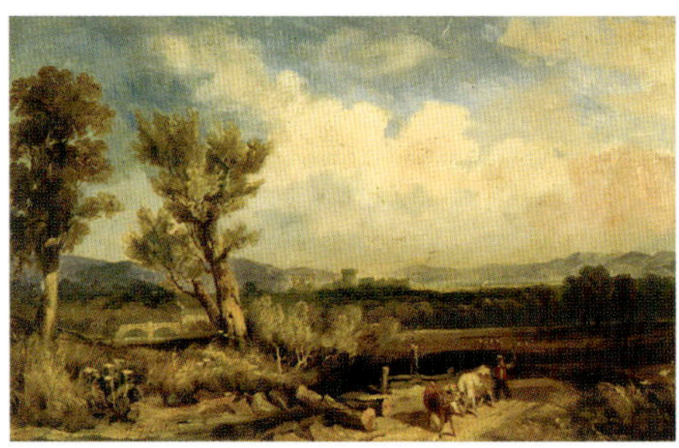

McCulloch, Horatio (attributed to)
1805–1867
Landscape
oil on board 30.5 x 48.3
2996

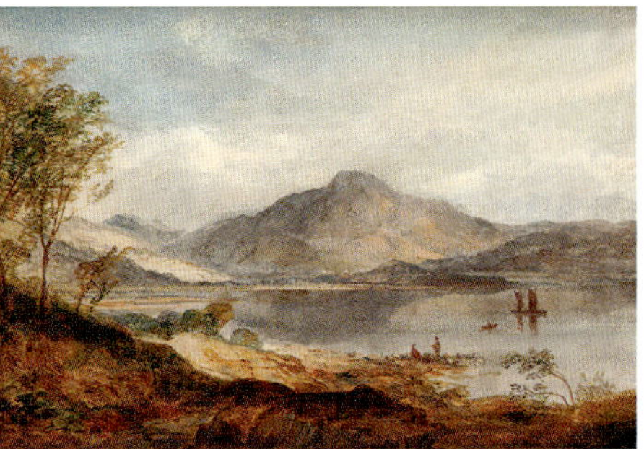

McCulloch, Horatio (attributed to)
1805–1867
Loch Lomond
oil on paper on canvas 25.4 x 35.6
3407

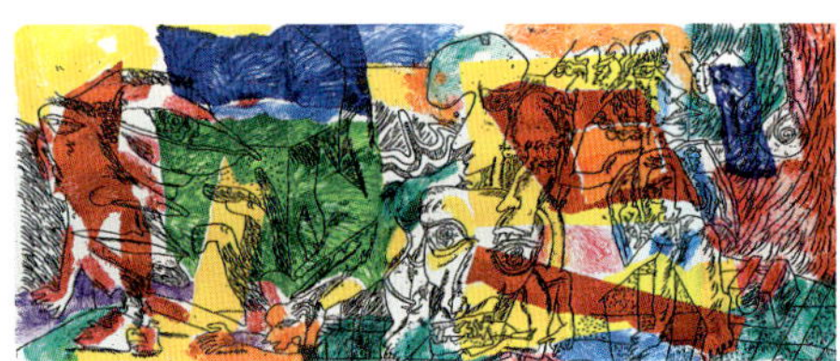

McCulloch, Ian b.1935
Strathclyde (diptych, left panel) 1990
acrylic on canvas 330.2 x 716.4
3696.g–3696.l

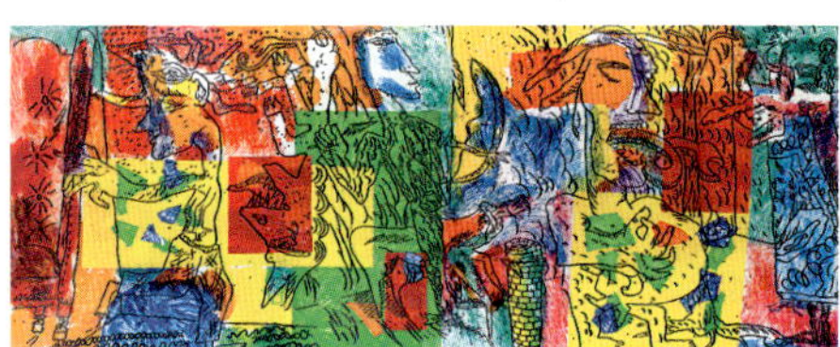

McCulloch, Ian b.1935
Strathclyde (diptych, right panel) 1990
acrylic on canvas 330.2 x 716.4
3696.a–3696.f

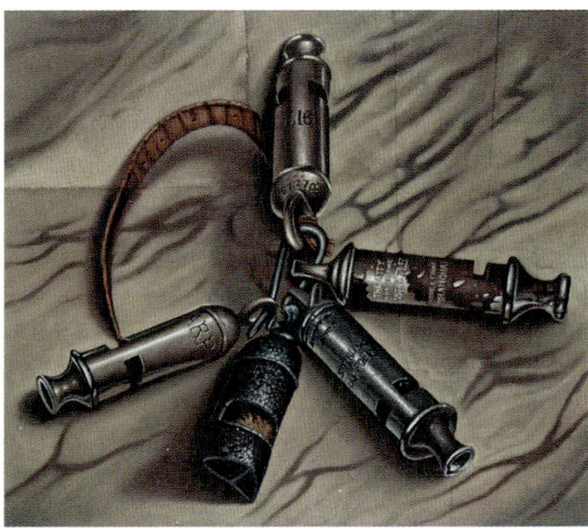

McDonald, James b.1956
Whistles 1989
oil & collage on paper 45 x 50
PR.2007.2.66

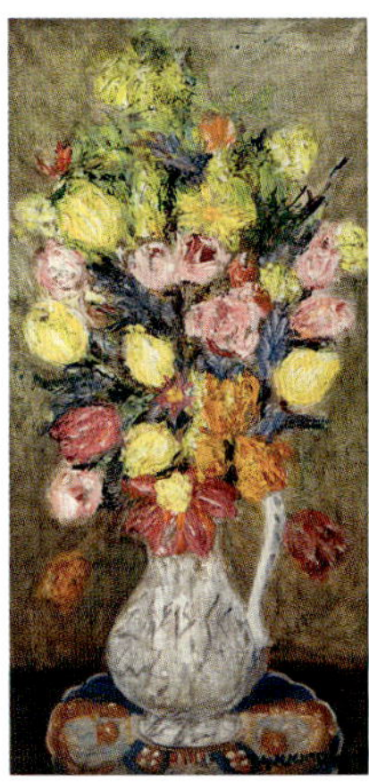

McDougall, Lily Martha Maud 1875–1958
The Marbled Jug
oil on canvas 91.4 x 45.7
3027

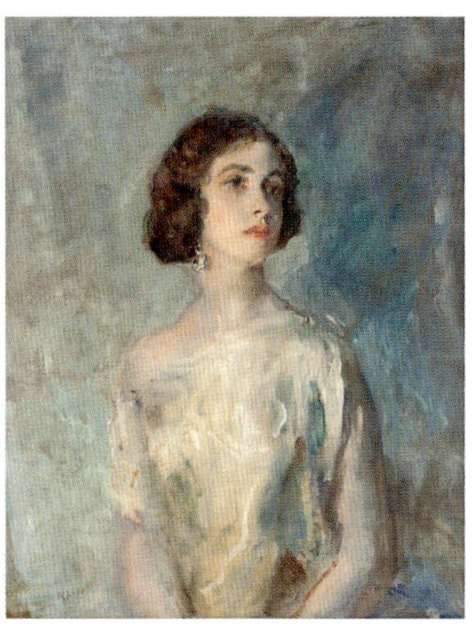

McEvoy, Ambrose 1878–1927
Elizabeth Johnson c.1920
oil on canvas 91.4 x 71.1
1863

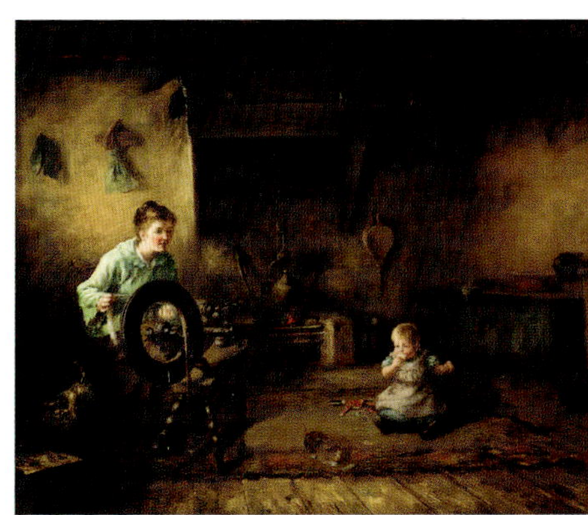

McEwan, Thomas 1846–1914
Interior: The Spinning Wheel 1896
oil on canvas 50.8 x 61
2268

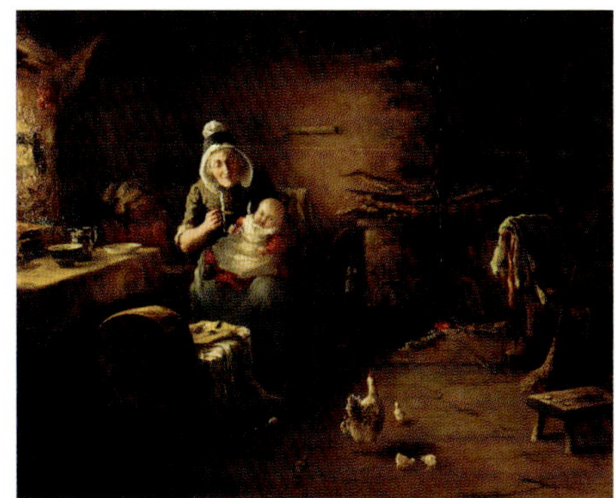

McEwan, Thomas 1846–1914
An Interior 1898
oil on canvas 61 x 74.9
763

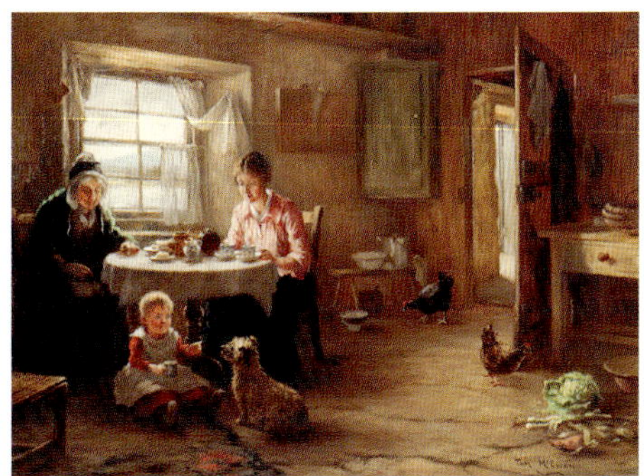

McEwan, Thomas 1846–1914
Tea Time
oil on canvas 45.7 x 61
2638

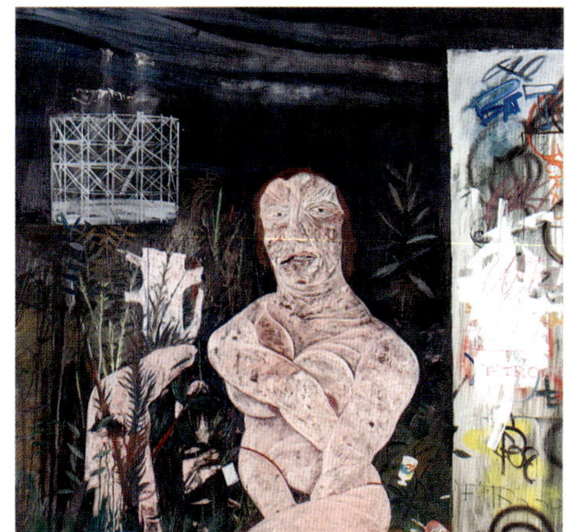

McFadyen, Jock b.1950
Depression 1990
oil on canvas 198.1 x 198.1
3470

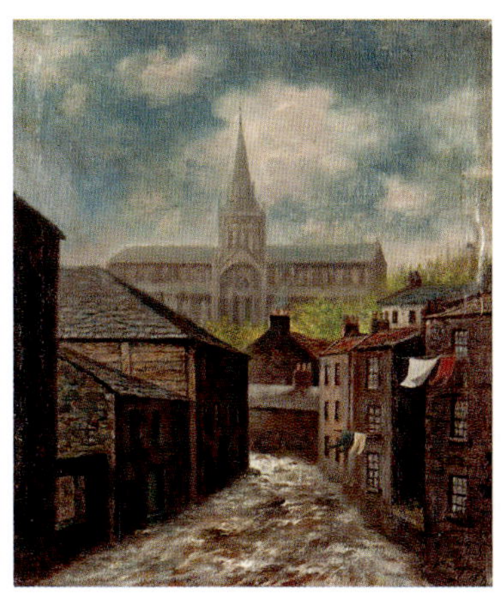

McFarlane, A.
Glasgow Cathedral and Molendinar Burn 1872
oil on canvas 46.7 x 38.2
TEMP.19217

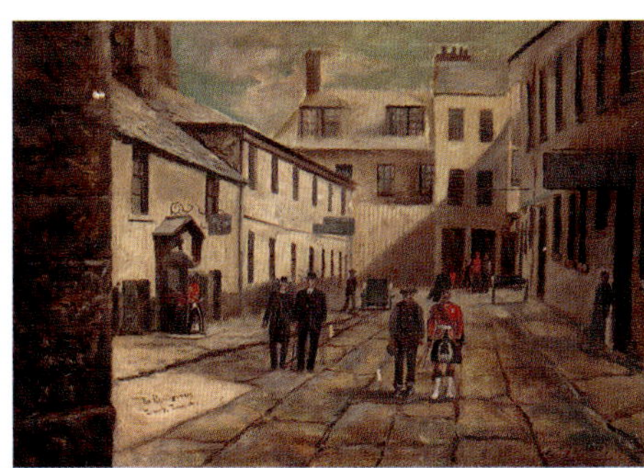

McFarlane, J.
Rendezvous Court 1869
oil on canvas 40 x 56
OG.1958.34.f

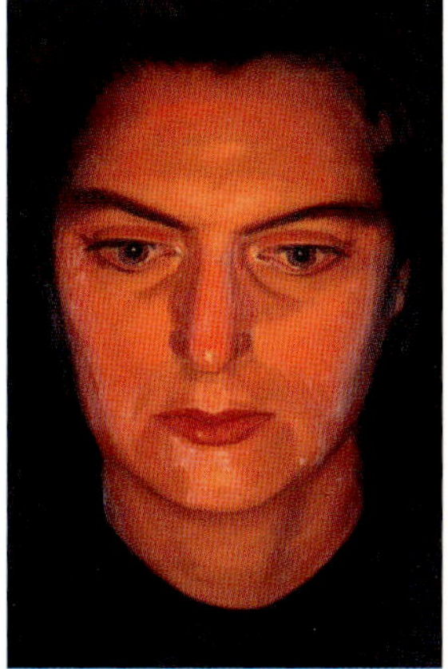

McGarvey, Don
Peripheral Reflection I c.2008
oil on canvas 62 x 42.5
3671

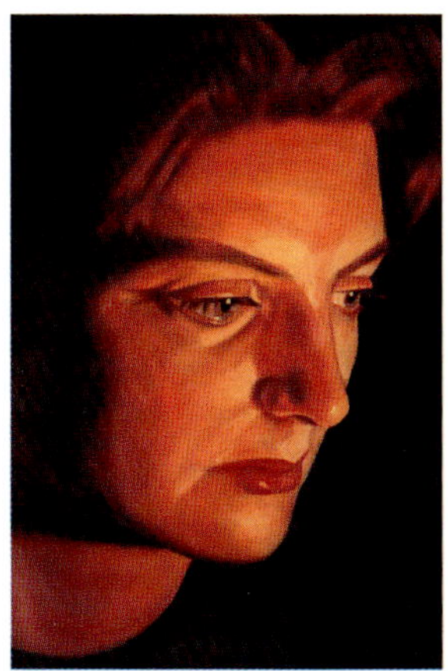

McGarvey, Don
Peripheral Reflection II c.2008
oil on canvas 62 x 42.5
3672

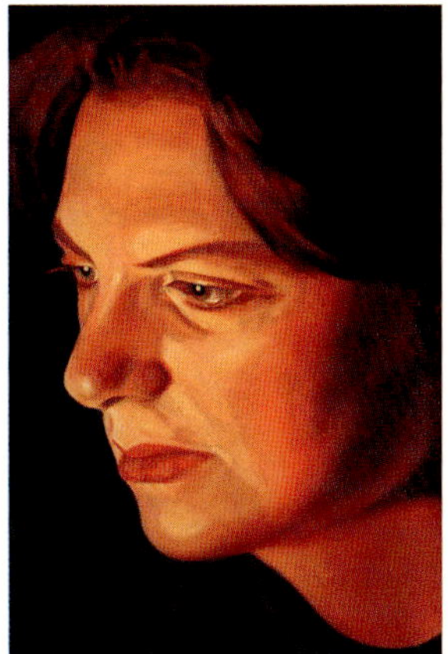

McGarvey, Don
Peripheral Reflection III c.2008
oil on canvas 62 x 42.5
3673

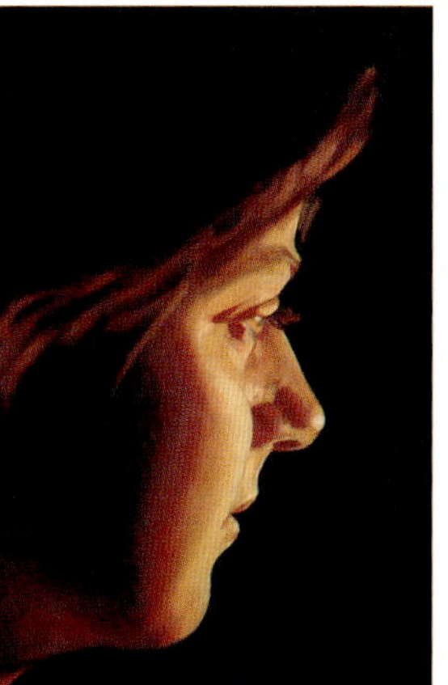

McGarvey, Don
Peripheral Reflection IV c.2008
oil on canvas 62 x 42.5
3674

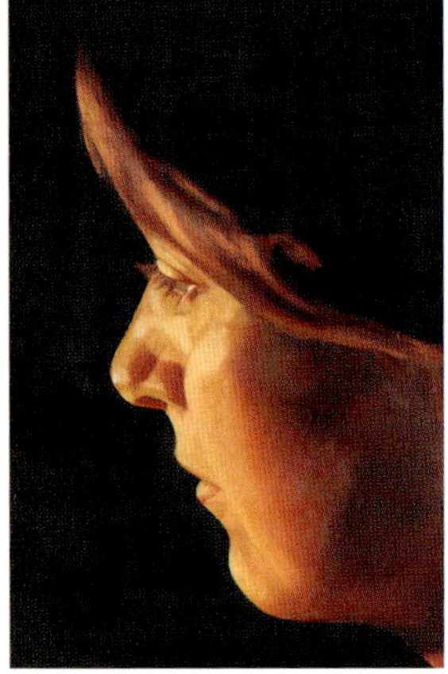

McGarvey, Don
Peripheral Reflection V c.2008
oil on canvas 62 x 42.5
3675

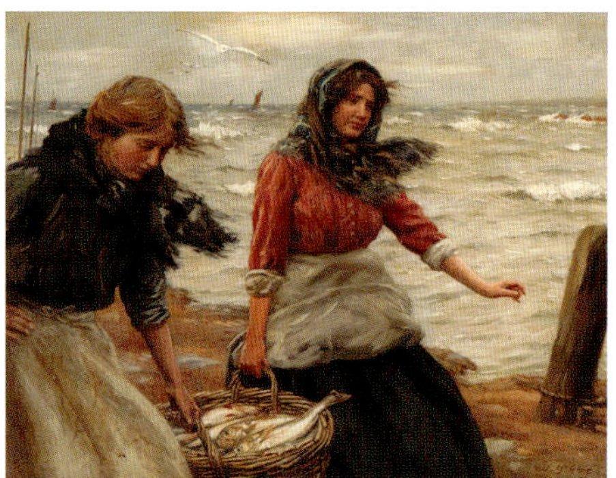

McGhie, John 1867–1952
Fresh from the Sea c.1911
oil on canvas 101.6 x 127
1275

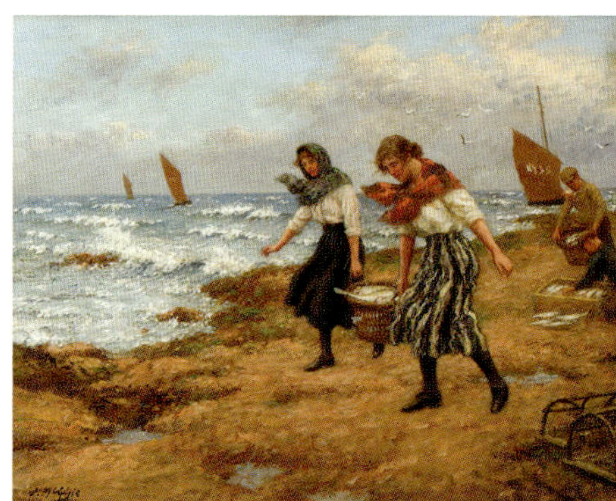

McGhie, John 1867–1952
Fisher Girls Landing the Catch
oil on canvas 40.6 x 50.8
2639

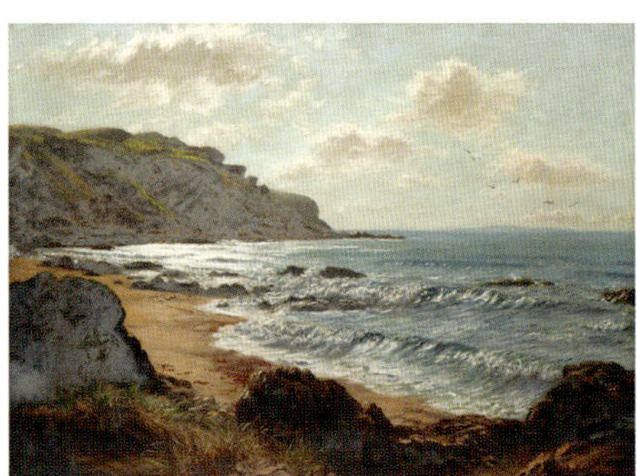

McGhie, John 1867–1952
Rocky Seascape
oil on canvas 71.1 x 91.4
2879

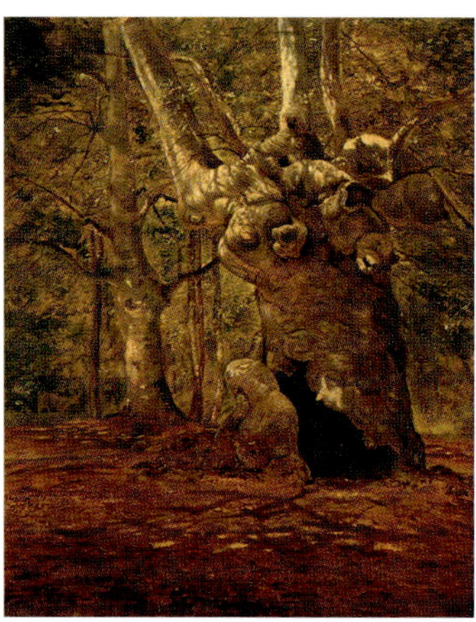

McGlashan, Alexander 1853–1880
Burnam Beeches 1874
oil on canvas 52.1 x 41.9
1786

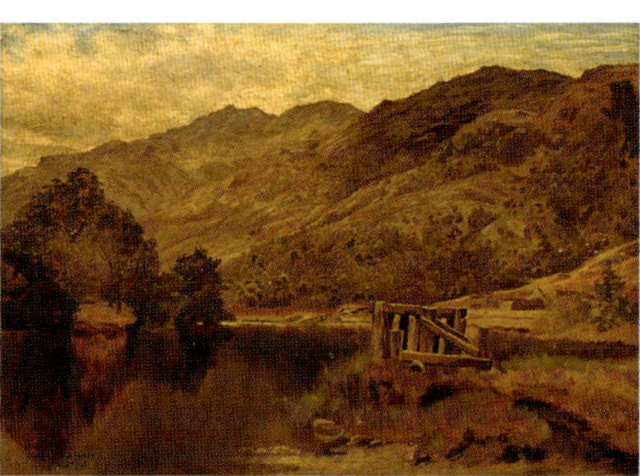

McGlashan, Alexander 1853–1880
Midday, Glen Falloch 1875
oil on canvas 40.6 x 55.9
1787

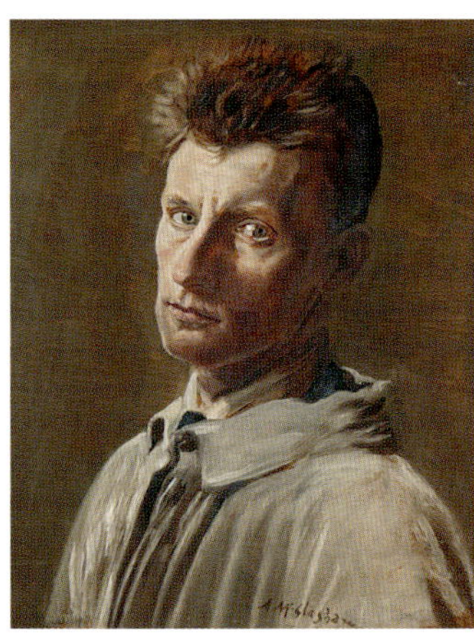

McGlashan, Archibald A. 1888–1980
Self Portrait as a Young Man c.1910–1920
oil on panel 47.5 x 38.6
3332

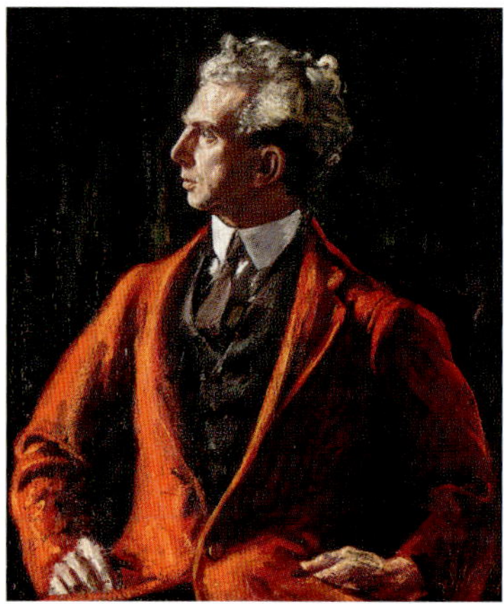

McGlashan, Archibald A. 1888–1980
*Sir Patrick Dollan (1885–1963), Wearing 'The
Red Jacket'* 1930
oil on canvas 76.6 x 66.1
3265

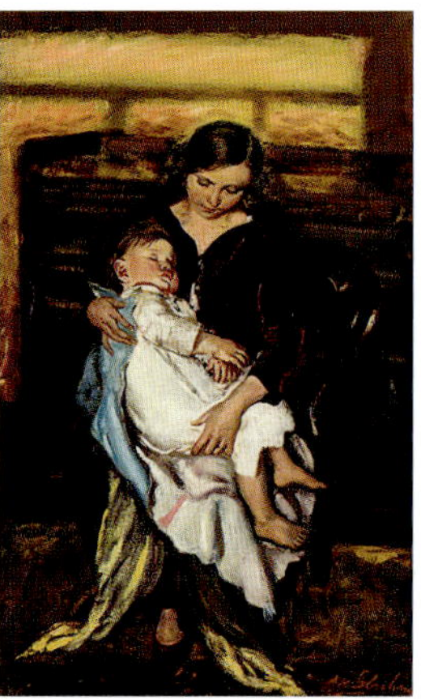

McGlashan, Archibald A. 1888–1980
Mother and Child c.1931
oil on canvas 149.9 x 91.4
1826

McGlashan, Archibald A. 1888–1980
Lachlan Mackinnon, JP c.1936
oil on canvas 106.7 x 97.8
NR.165

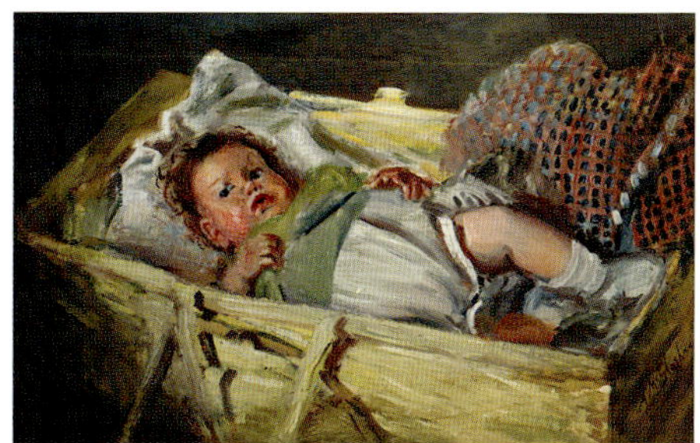

McGlashan, Archibald A. 1888–1980
Child in a Cot c.1955
oil on canvas 64.1 x 99.7
3032

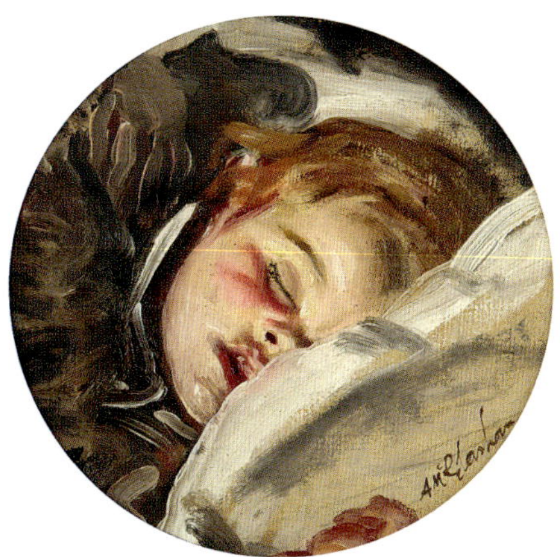

McGlashan, Archibald A. 1888–1980
Child's Head
oil on canvas 25.4
2808

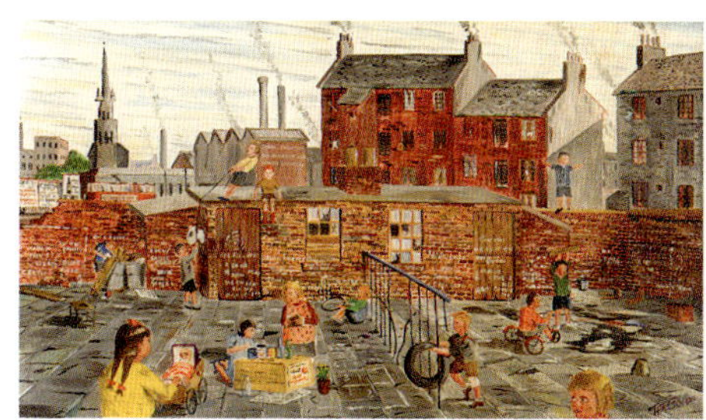

McGoran, Thomas b.1927
Back Court Games c.1956
acrylic on canvas 47 x 78
PP.1999.3.9

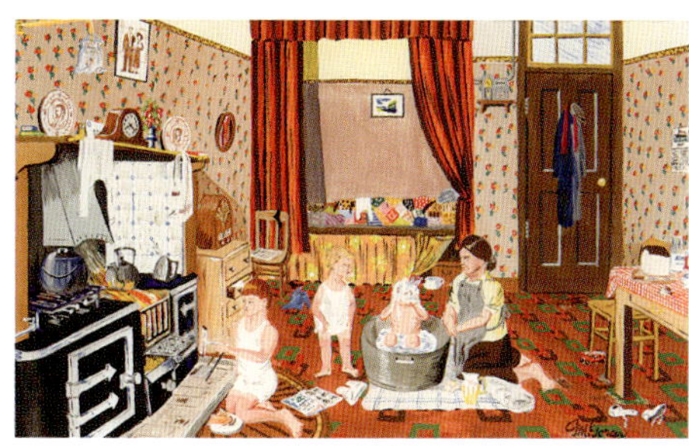

McGoran, Thomas b.1927
Bathtime c.1956
oil on board 32 x 51.7
PP.1996.68.4

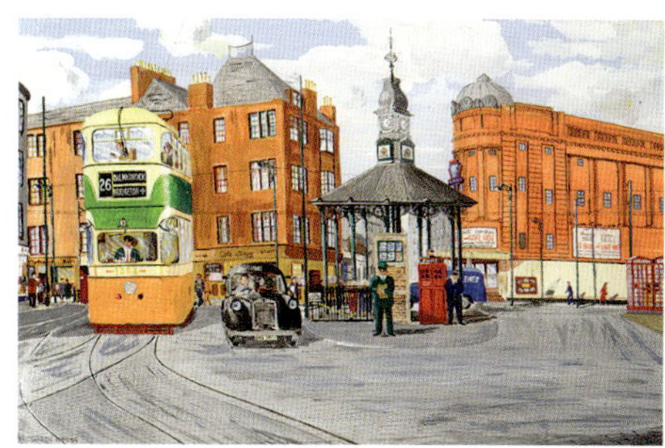

McGoran, Thomas b.1927
Bridgeton Cross c.1956
acrylic on canvas 56 x 75
PP.1999.3.1

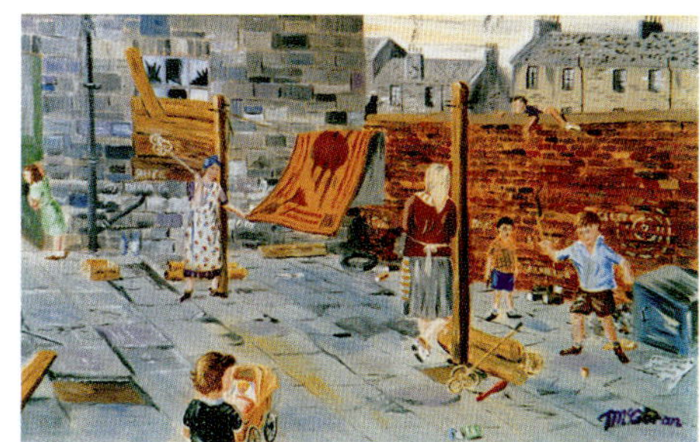

McGoran, Thomas b.1927
Carpet Beaters c.1956
acrylic on canvas 41 x 63
PP.1999.3.5

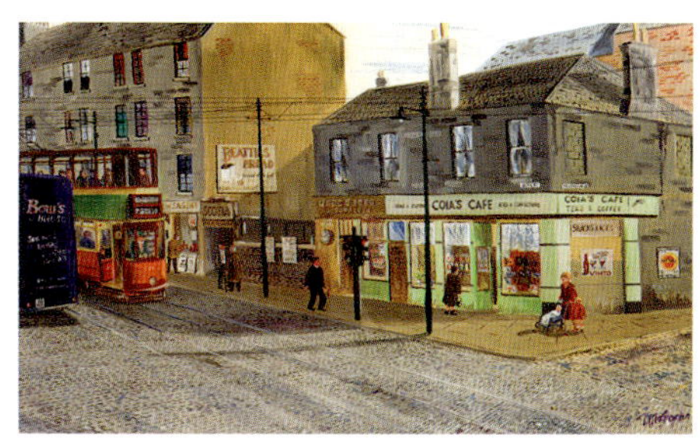

McGoran, Thomas b.1927
Coia's Corner c.1956
acrylic on canvas 47 x 75
PP.1999.3.2

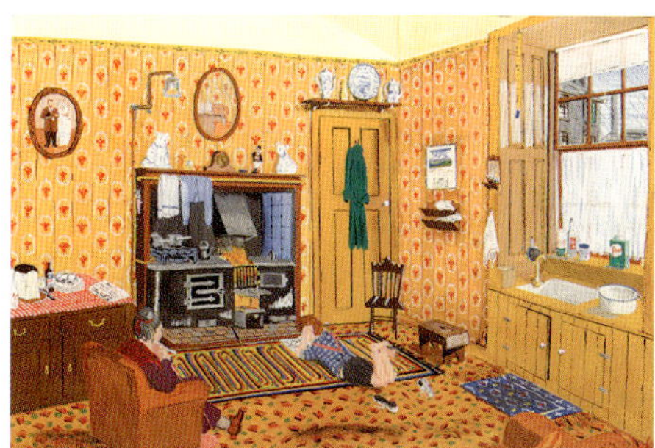

McGoran, Thomas b.1927
Half a Kitchen c.1956
oil on board 36.4 x 54.4
PP.1996.68.2

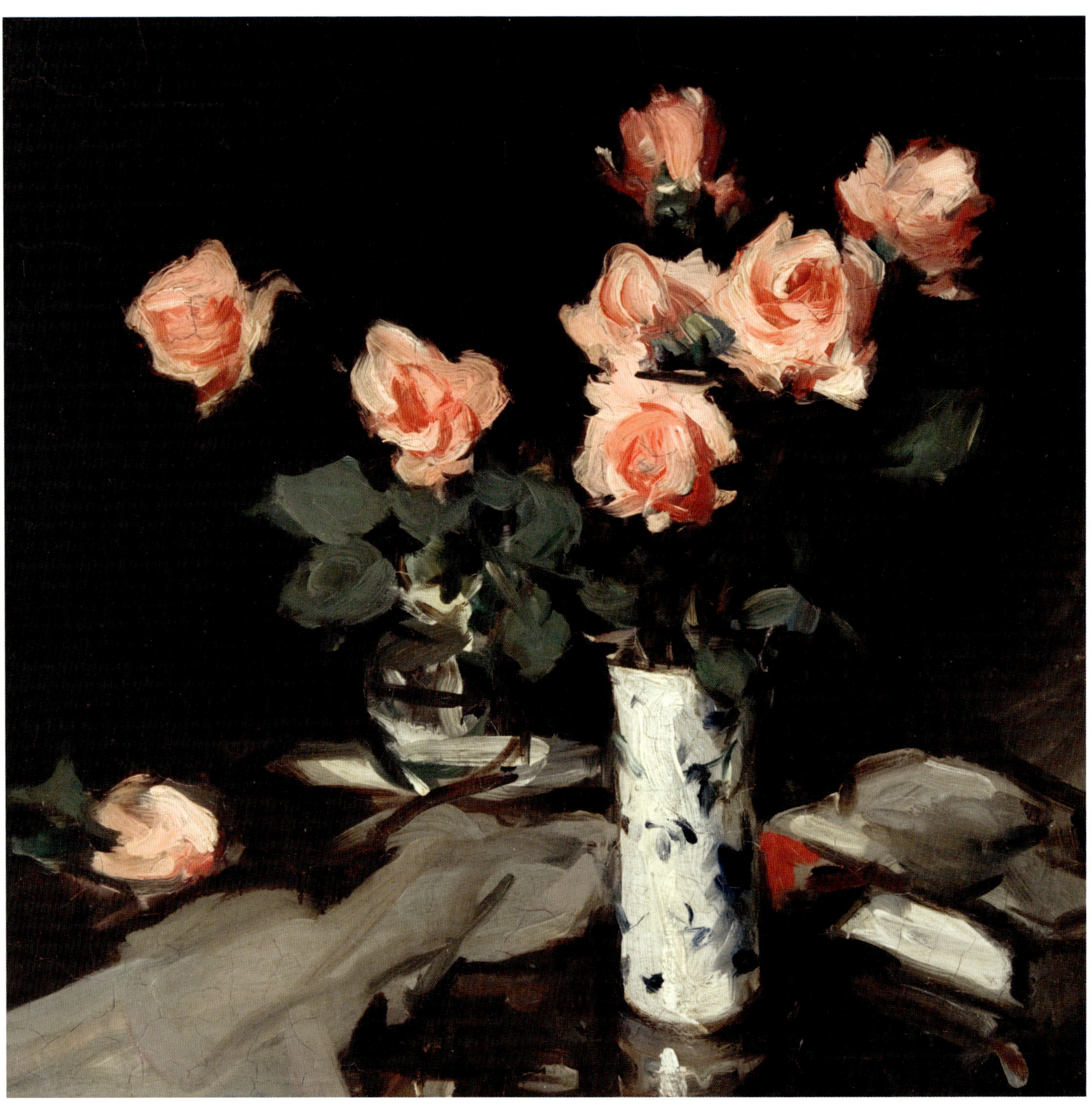

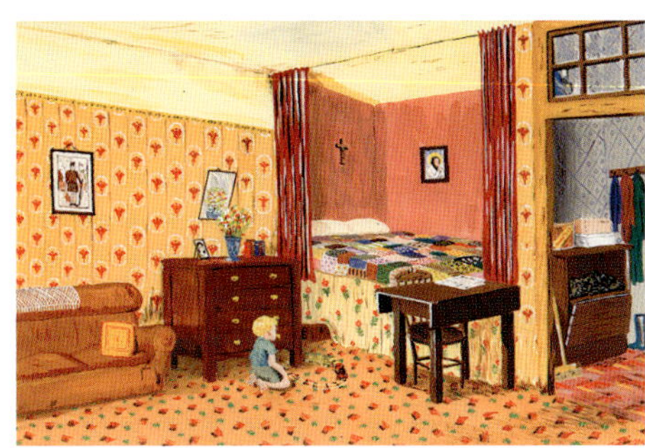

McGoran, Thomas b.1927
The Other Half c.1956
oil on board 35.2 x 52.4
PP.1996.68.1

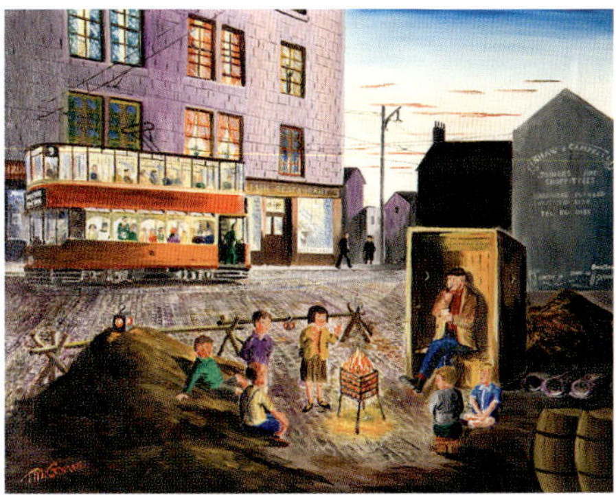

McGoran, Thomas b.1927
Night Watchman c.1956
acrylic on canvas 47 x 57
PP.1999.3.8

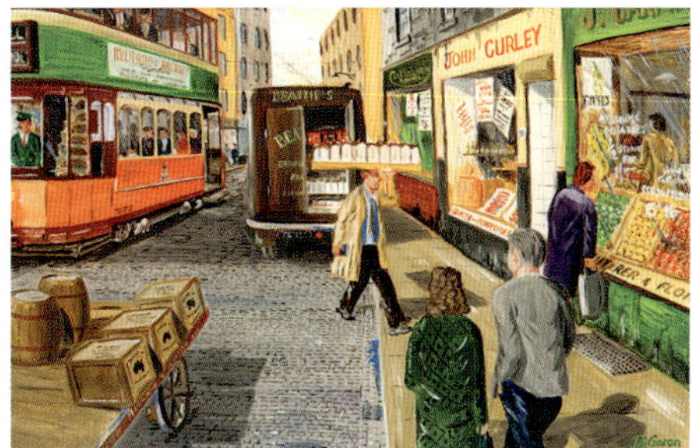

McGoran, Thomas b.1927
Our Daily Bread c.1956
oil on board 36.9 x 55
PP.1999.3.14

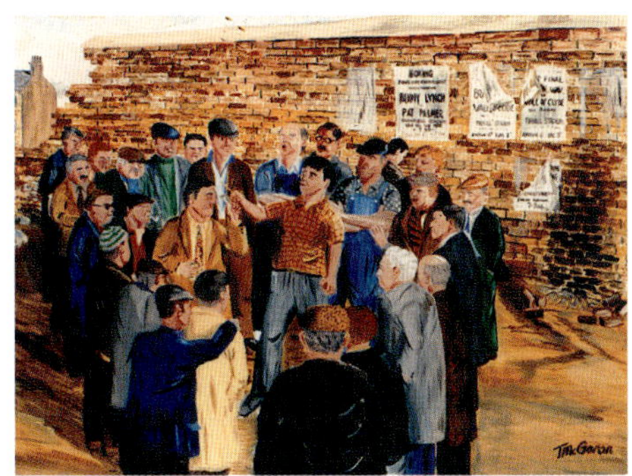

McGoran, Thomas b.1927
Pitch and Toss c.1956
acrylic on canvas 38 x 56
PP.1999.3.10

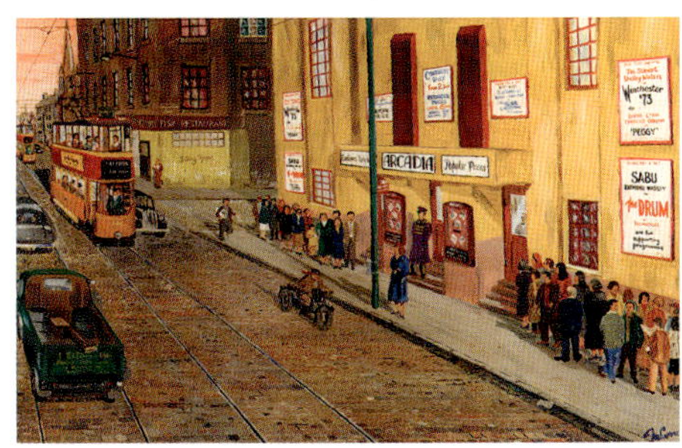

McGoran, Thomas b.1927
Saturday Night at the Movies c.1956
acrylic on canvas 47 x 72
PP.1999.3.4

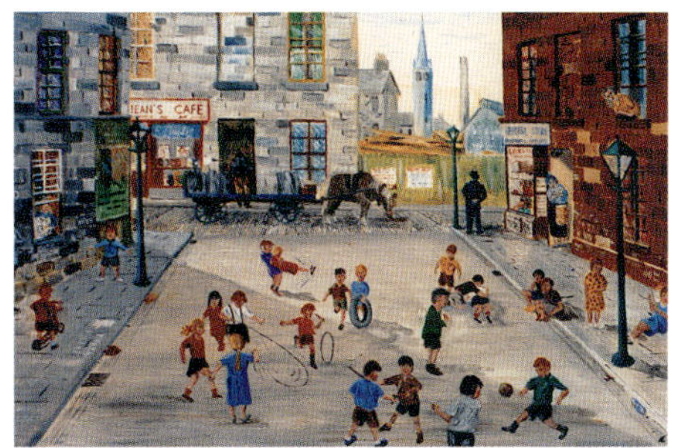

McGoran, Thomas b.1927
Street Games c.1956
acrylic on canvas 47 x 72
PP.1999.3.3

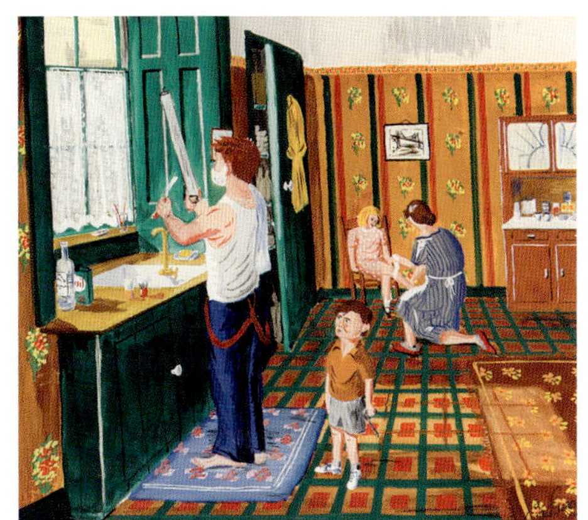

McGoran, Thomas b.1927
Sunday Morning c.1956
oil on board 34.4 x 37.2
PP.1996.68.3

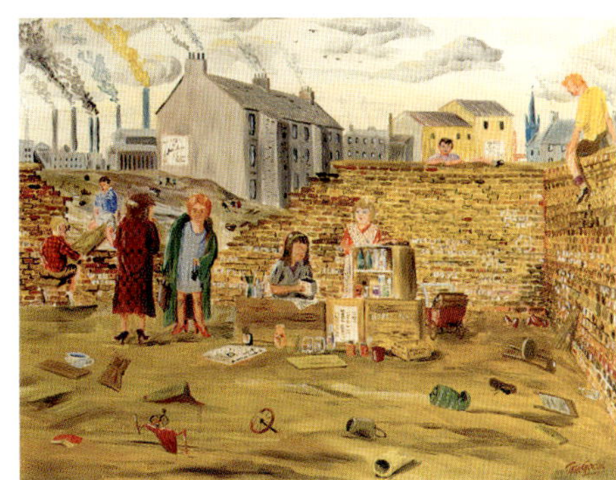

McGoran, Thomas b.1927
The Big Store c.1956
acrylic on canvas 46 x 59
PP.1999.3.6

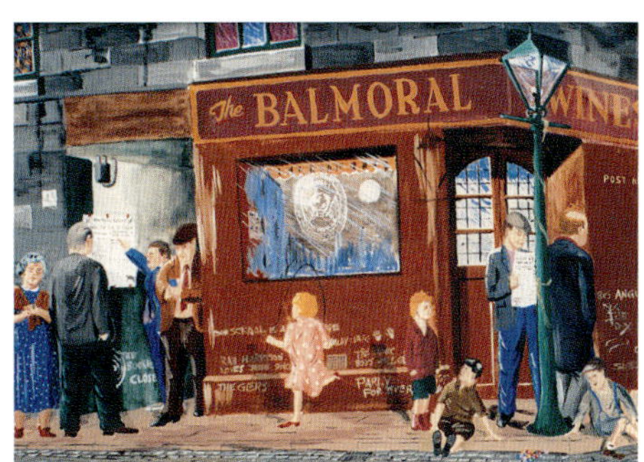

McGoran, Thomas b.1927
The Bookies' Close c.1956
acrylic on canvas 40 x 56
PP.1999.3.7

Facing page: Peploe, Samuel John, 1871–1935, *Roses,* (p. 345)

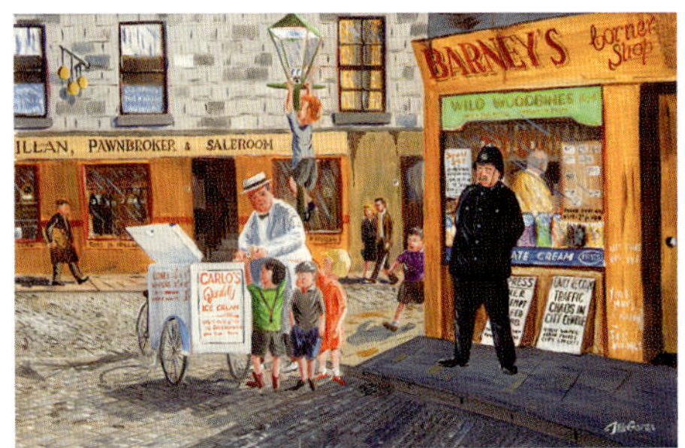

McGoran, Thomas b.1927
The Pokey Hat Man c.1956
acrylic on board 37.4 x 56
PP.1999.3.13

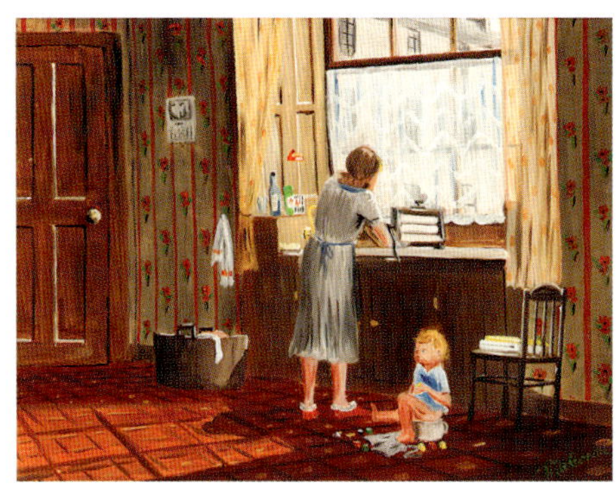

McGoran, Thomas b.1927
Wash Day c.1956
oil on board 38.3 x 48.5
PP.1999.3.12

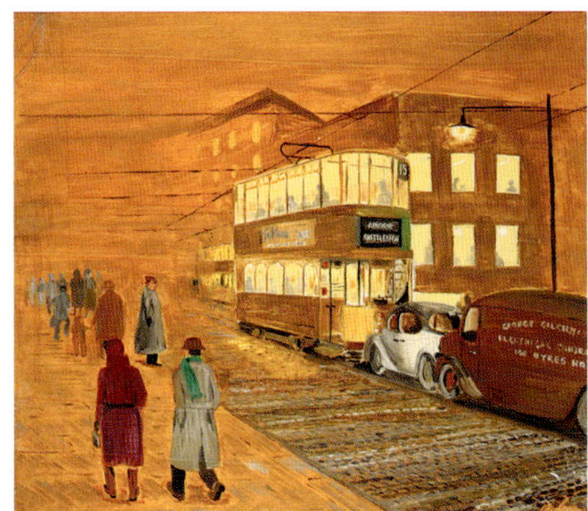

McGoran, Thomas b.1927
Foggy Day in Glasgow 1991
oil on paper 52.3 x 57.8
PP.1999.3.11

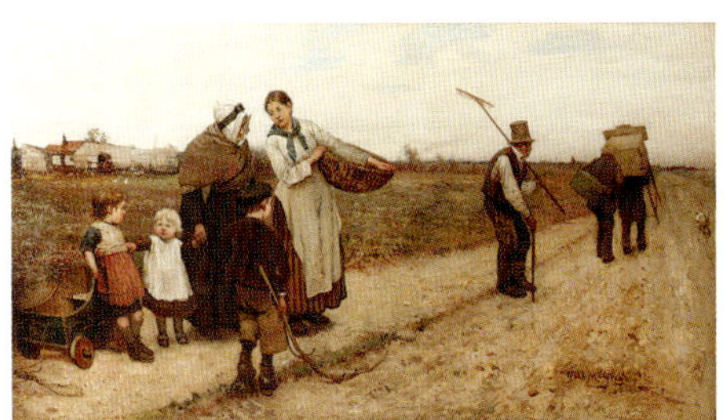

McGregor, Robert 1847–1922
Doing the Provinces c.1880
oil on canvas 73.7 x 137.2
809

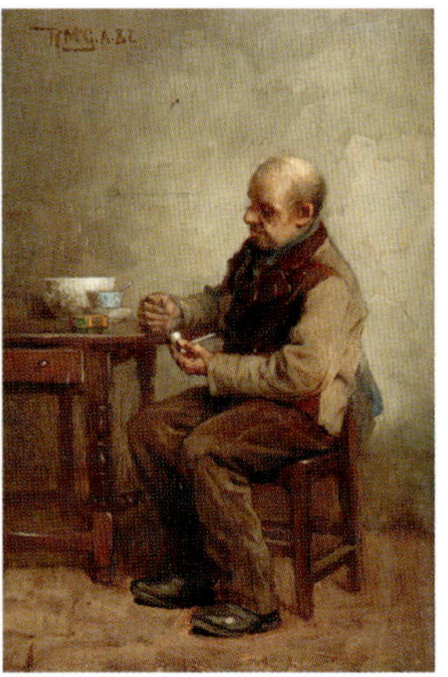

McGregor, Robert 1847–1922
A Smoker 1882
oil on canvas 19.1 x 14
826

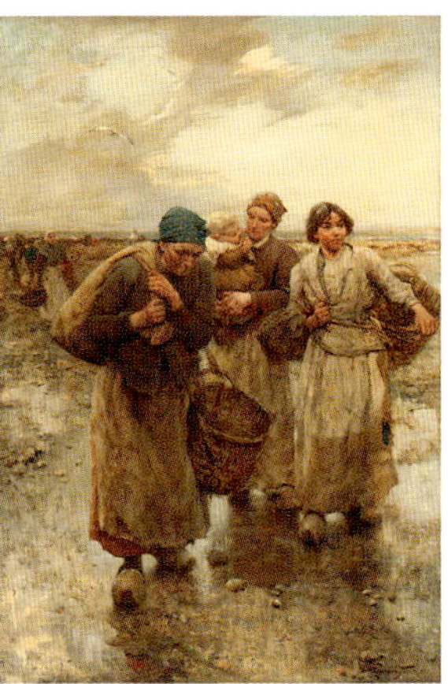

McGregor, Robert 1847–1922
Breadwinners c.1904
oil on canvas 142.2 x 97.8
1106

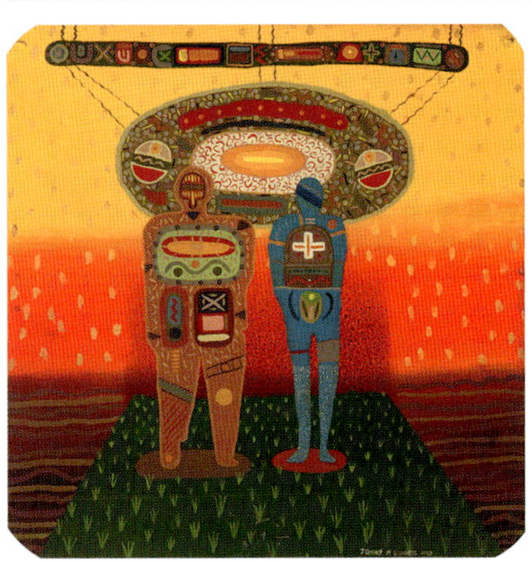

McGuinness, Johnny b.1955
The Field c.1990
oil on board 60 x 60
TEMP.15553

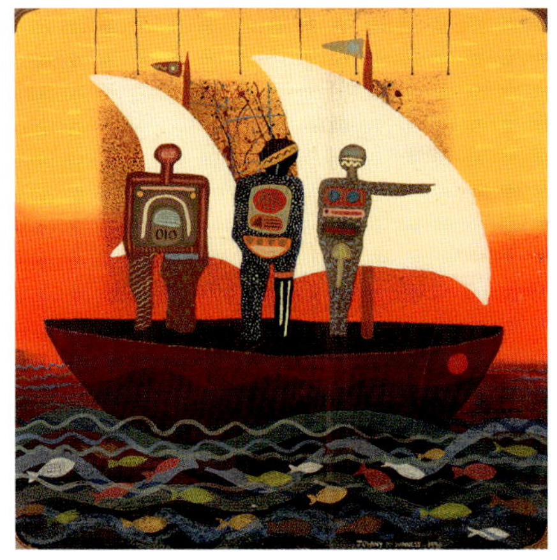

McGuinness, Johnny b.1955
White Sails c.1990
acrylic on panel 60 x 60
TEMP.15538

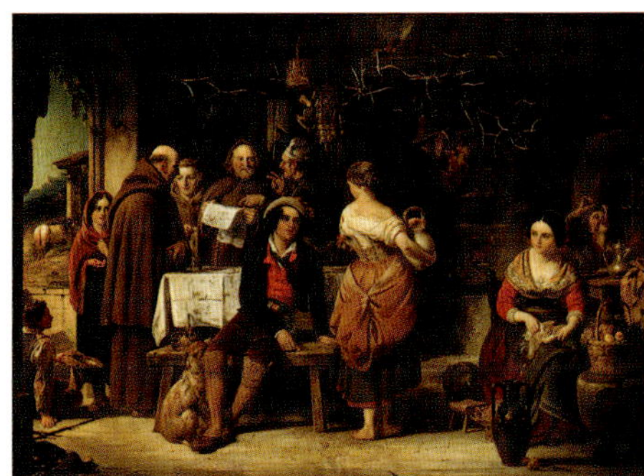

McInnes, Robert 1801–1886
An Italian Hostelry 1849
oil on canvas 91.4 x 127
370

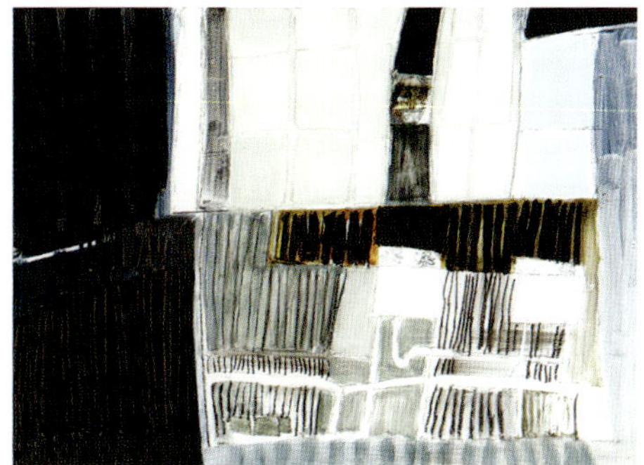

McIntosh, Archibald Dunbar b.1936
Windows and Sinks 1966
oil on hardboard 91.4 x 121.9
3245

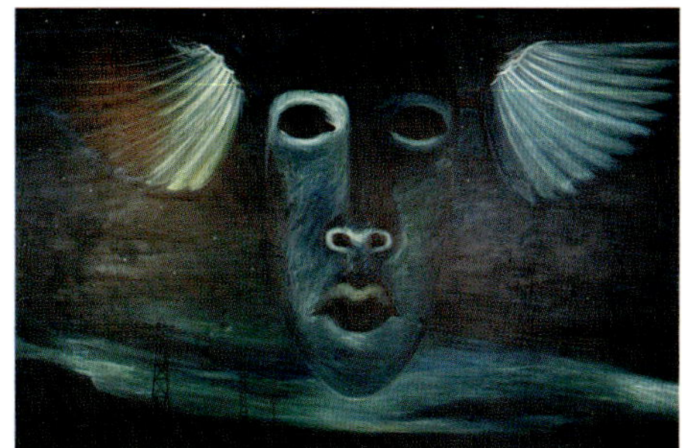

McIntyre, Keith b.1959
Psalms of the Shadows Opus II 1991
oil on canvas & metal construction
183.5 x 274
3492.1

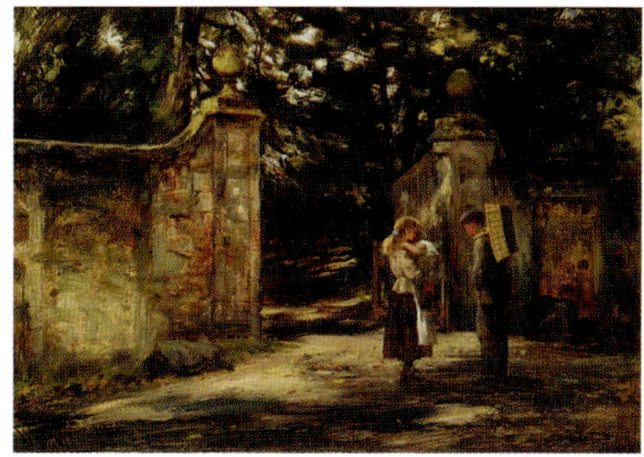

McKay, William Darling 1844–1924
The Old Gateway
oil on canvas 24.1 x 34.3
838

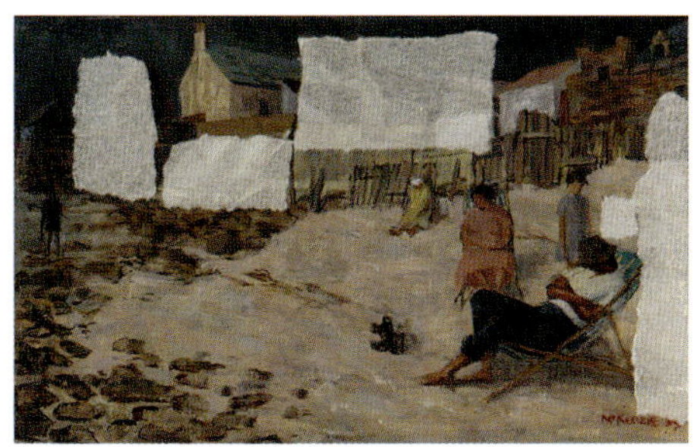

McKenzie, Elizabeth H. b.1931
Noon 1953
oil on canvas 45.7 x 71.1
3024

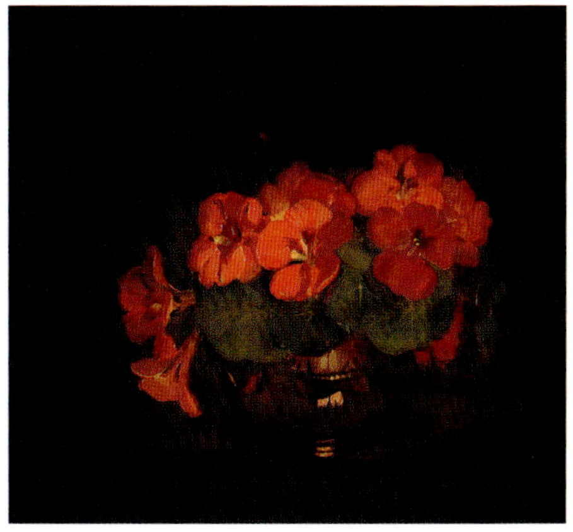

McKinna, Mary E. Tait active 1930–1952
Nasturtiums in a Lustre Jug
oil on canvas 30.5 x 35.6
2883

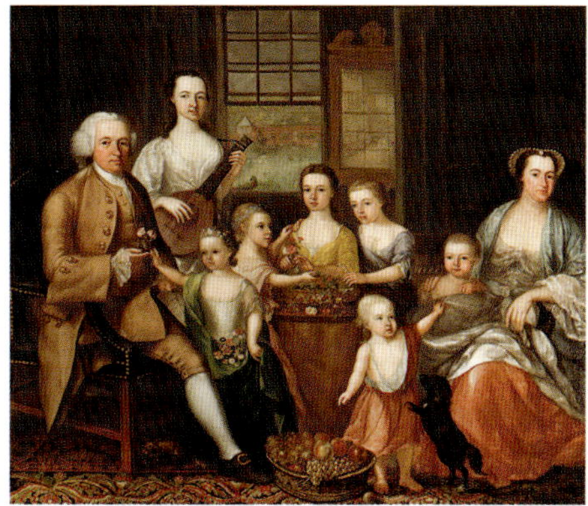

McLauchlan, Archibald active 1752–after
1770
John Glassford (1715–1783), and His Family
c.1767
oil on canvas 198.1 x 221
2887

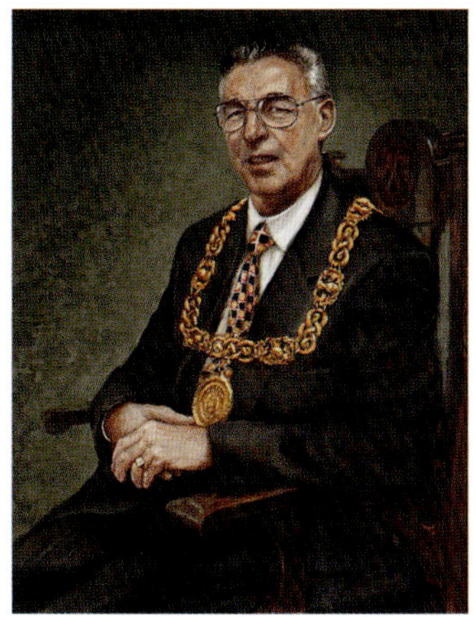

McLaughlin, Brian b.1966
*Thomas Dingwall, Lord Provost of the City of
Glasgow (1995–1996)* c.1997
oil on canvas 102 x 77.4
3633

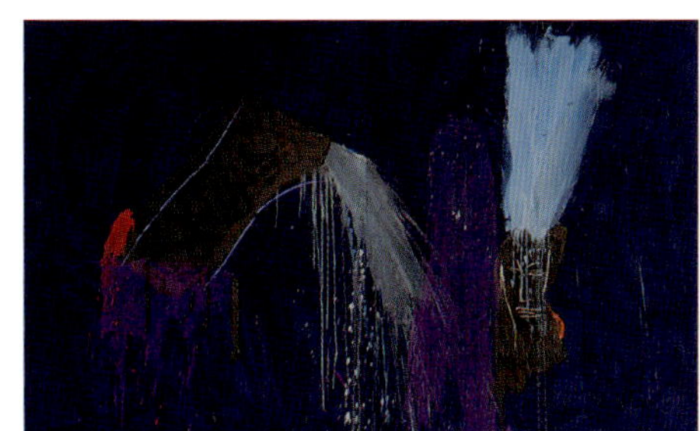

McLean, Bruce b.1944
Untitled 1984
acrylic on canvas 212.8 x 334
3403.a-b

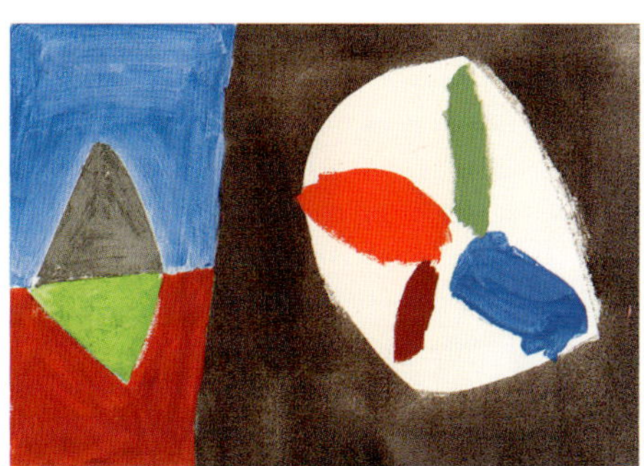

McLean, John b.1939
Gaillac 1993
acrylic on canvas 78 x 111.2
3528

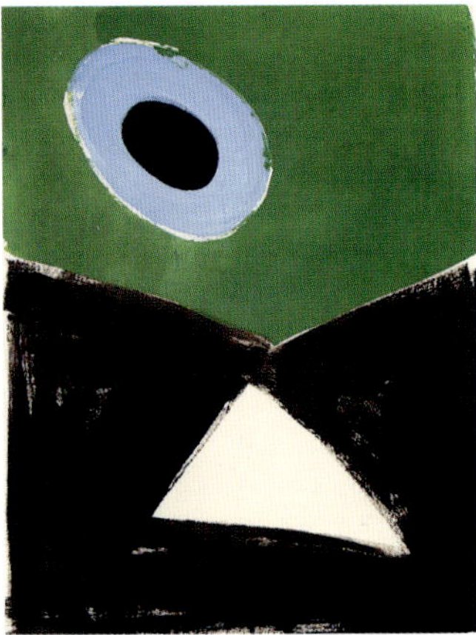

McLean, John b.1939
Hunter 1993
acrylic on canvas 114.9 x 86.1
3527

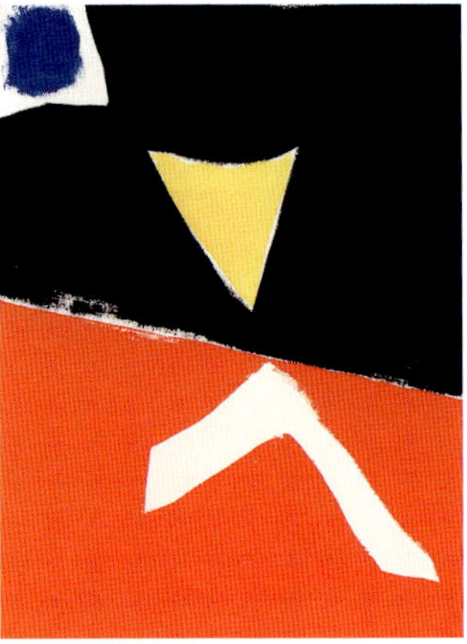

McLean, John b.1939
Inchcape 1993
acrylic on canvas 108 x 80
3526

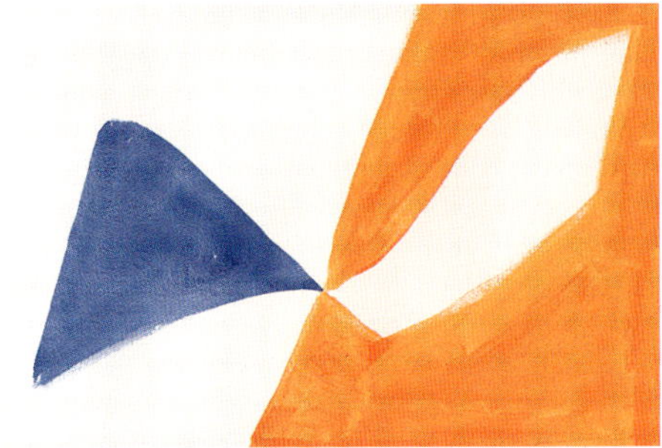

McLean, John b.1939
Peninsula 1993
acrylic on canvas 71.8 x 106.5
3529

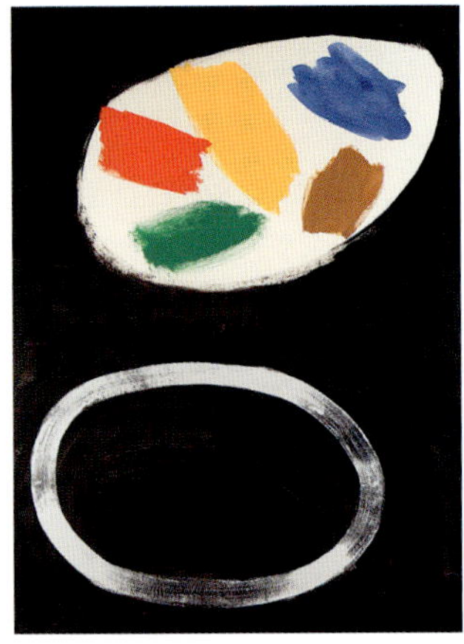

McLean, John b.1939
Strathspey 1994
acrylic on canvas 224.5 x 157.7
3547

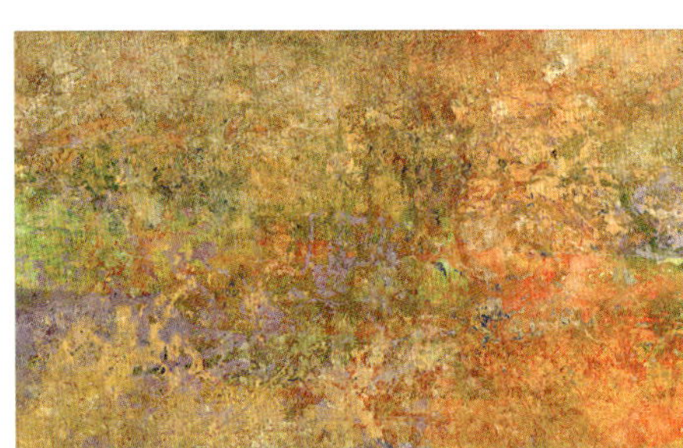

McLean, Talbert 1906–1992
Scree 1976
acrylic & paper collage on canvas
117.4 x 188.6
3384

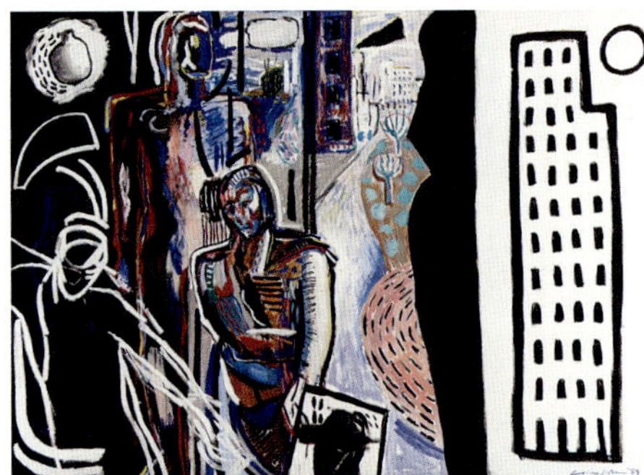

McNairn, Caroline 1955–2010
In a Foreign Country 1989
oil on canvas 172.8 x 231.1
3478

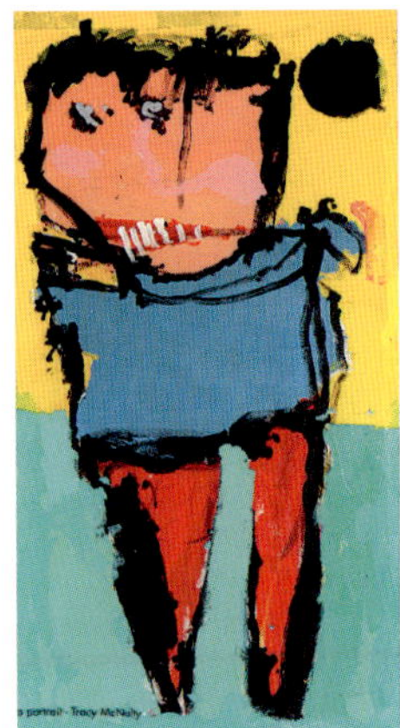

McNulty, Tracy b.1970
Portrait c.1992
acrylic on canvas 166.4 x 89.2
3496

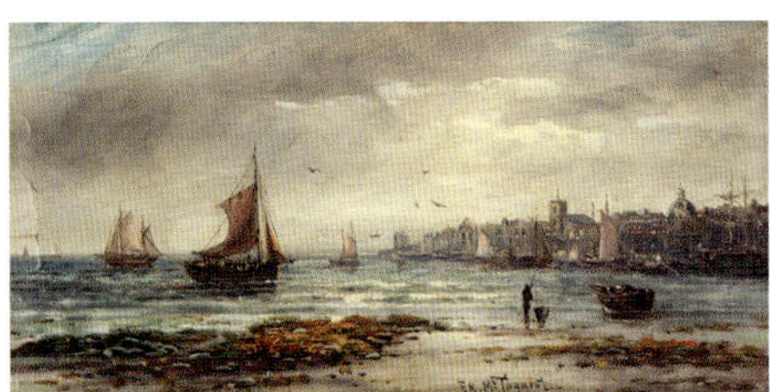

McTaggart, F. R. active 19th C
A Port by the Sea
oil on canvas 20.3 x 40.6
NR.110

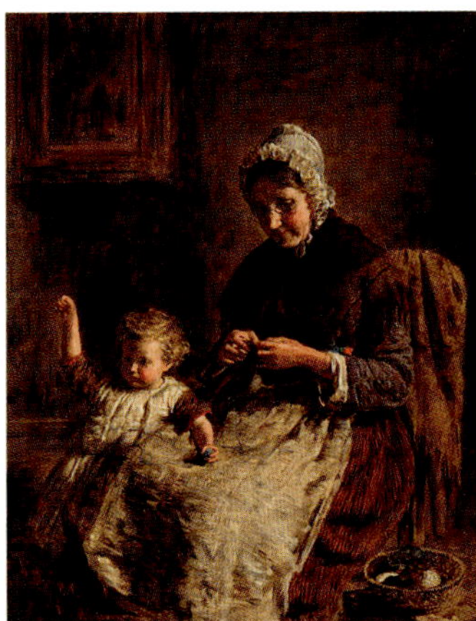

McTaggart, William 1835–1910
Grandmother's Pet 1864
oil on canvas 45.7 x 35.6
1552

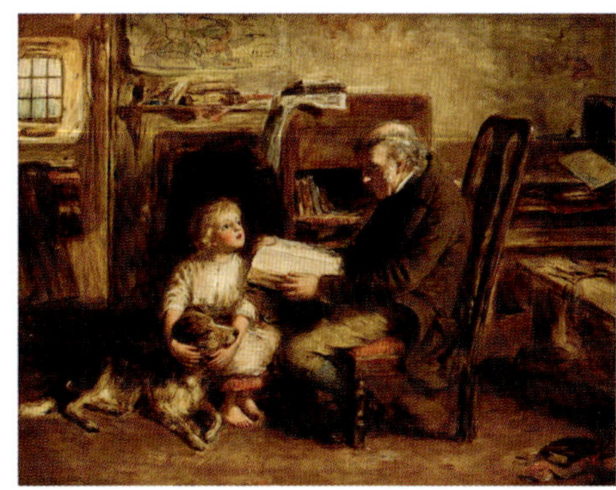

McTaggart, William 1835–1910
Do Doggies Gang tae Heaven? 1867
oil on canvas 33 x 40.6
2927

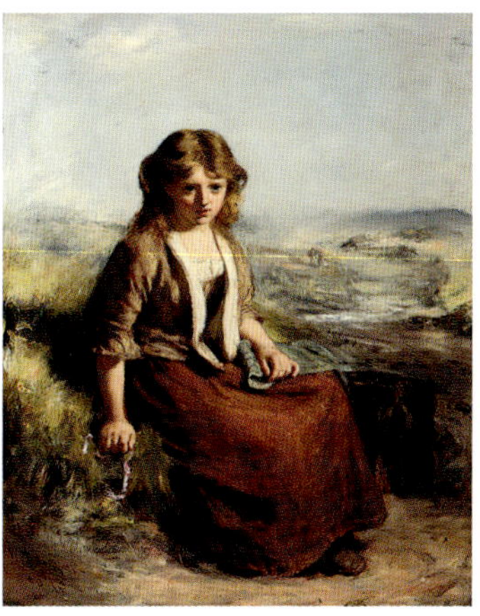

McTaggart, William 1835–1910
Lucy's Flitting 1873
oil on canvas 91.4 x 76.2
1788

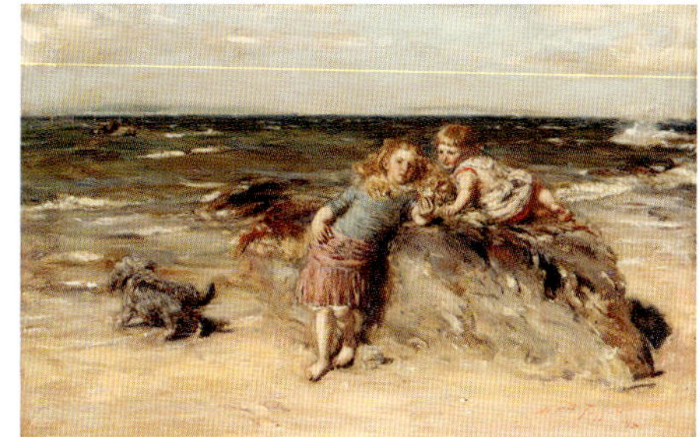

McTaggart, William 1835–1910
Summer Breezes 1881
oil on canvas 61 x 91.4
2368

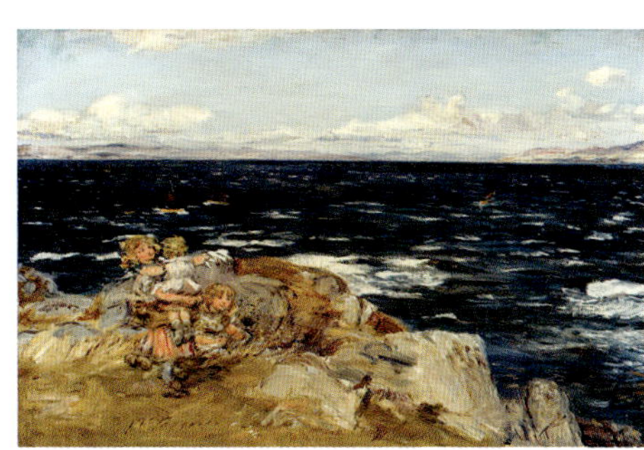

McTaggart, William 1835–1910
North Wind, Kilbrannan Sound 1883
oil on canvas 81.3 x 121.9
2407

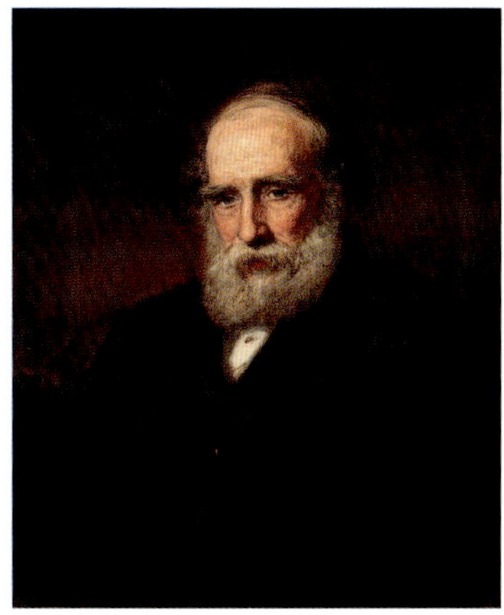

McTaggart, William 1835–1910
Robert Greenlees (1820–1894) 1883
oil on canvas 74.9 x 62.2
720

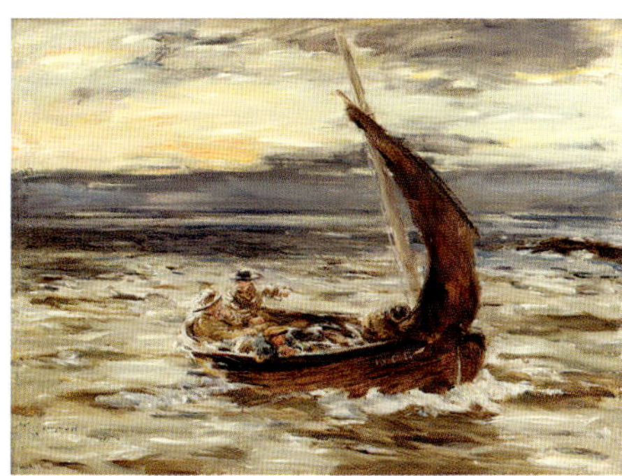

McTaggart, William 1835–1910
Dawn at Sea, Homewards 1891
oil on canvas 93.3 x 128.3
2049

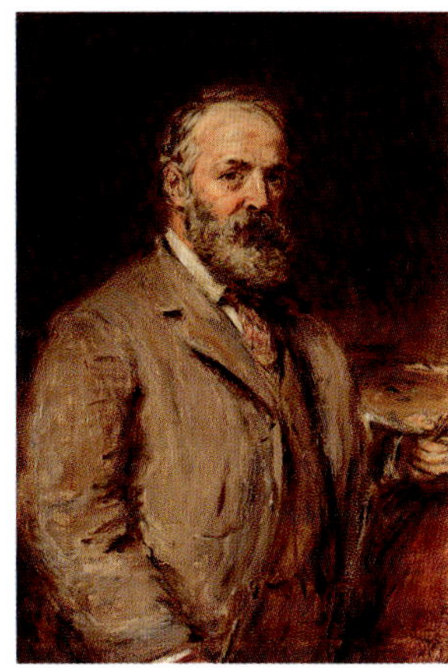

McTaggart, William 1835–1910
Joseph Henderson (1832–1908), RSW 1894
oil on canvas 105.4 x 69.9
1891

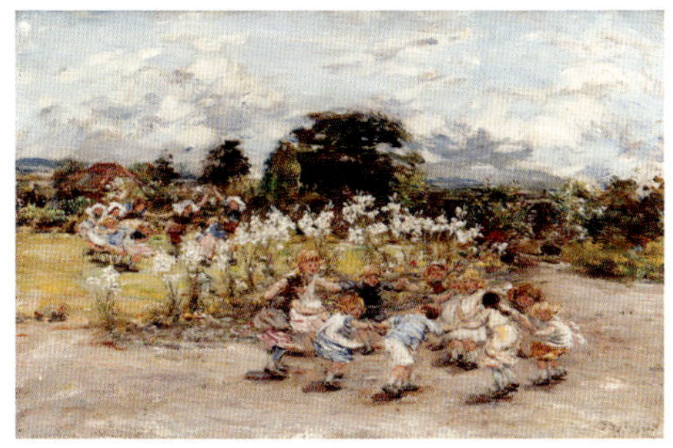

McTaggart, William 1835–1910
The Lilies 1896
oil on canvas 50.8 x 76.2
2408

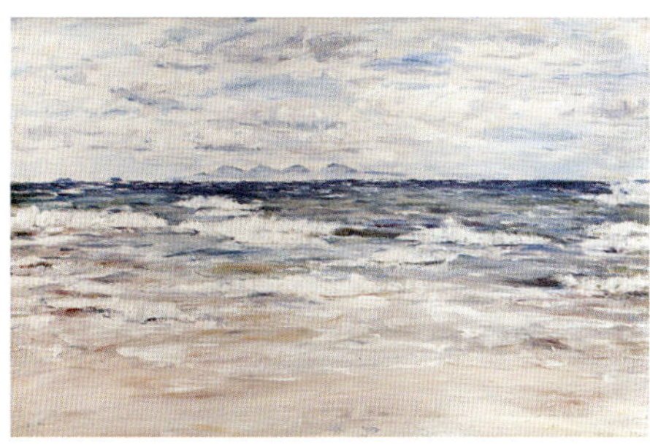

McTaggart, William 1835–1910
The Paps of Jura 1902
oil on canvas 137.5 x 208.3
1539

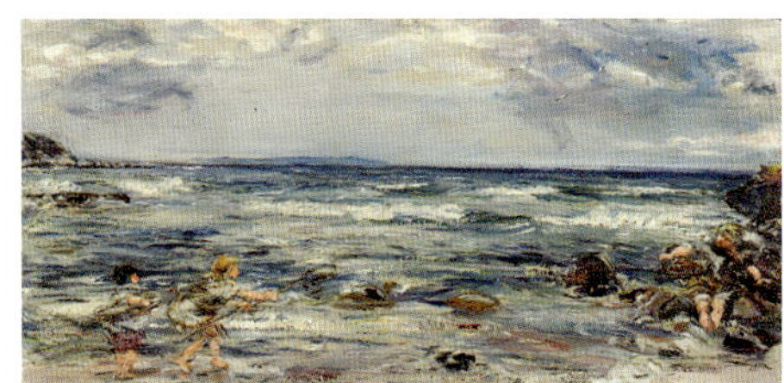

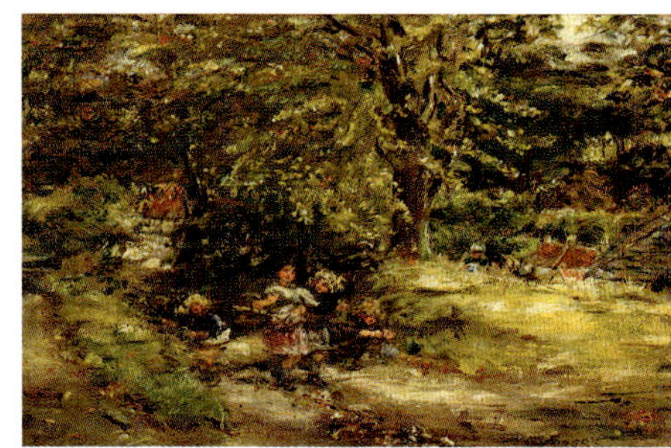

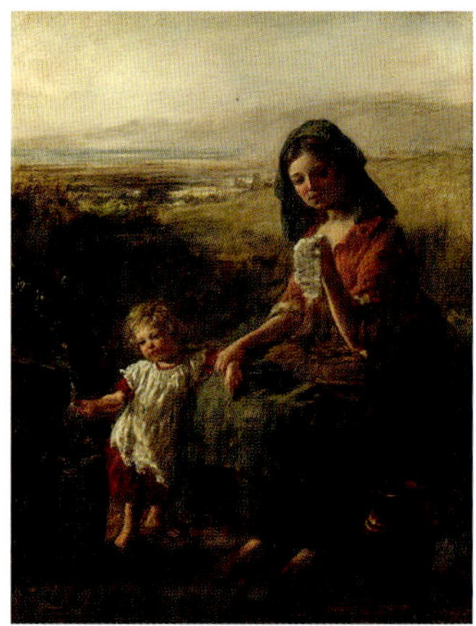

McTaggart, William 1835–1910
Along the Shore 1904
oil on canvas 43.2 x 85.1
2409

McTaggart, William 1835–1910
Gathering Brambles: Kevoch Mill
oil on canvas 51.5 x 76.9
3637

McTaggart, William 1835–1910
The Ballad
oil on canvas 31.1 x 24.8
3002

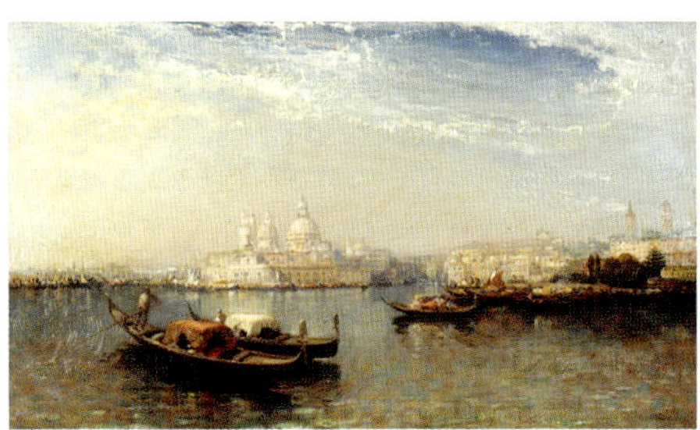

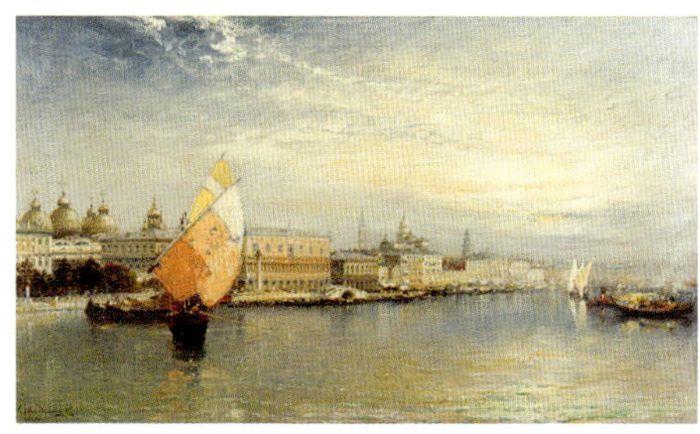

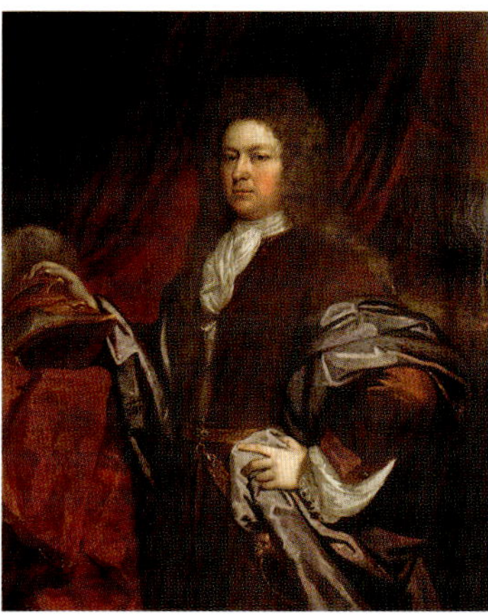

Meadows, Arthur Joseph 1843–1907
Venice, Morning 1899
oil on canvas 31.8 x 52.1
1510

Meadows, Arthur Joseph 1843–1907
Venice with the Doge's Palace 1899
oil on canvas 31.8 x 52.1
1509

Medina, John Baptist de 1659–1710
Sir John Maxwell (1648–1732), 1st Bt 1695
oil on canvas 124.5 x 99.1
PL.164 (P)

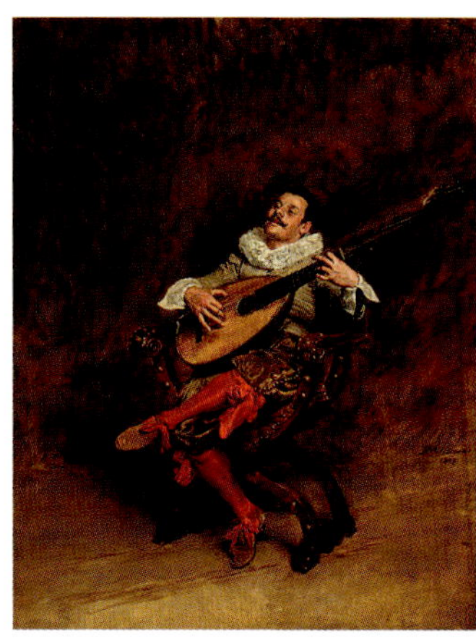

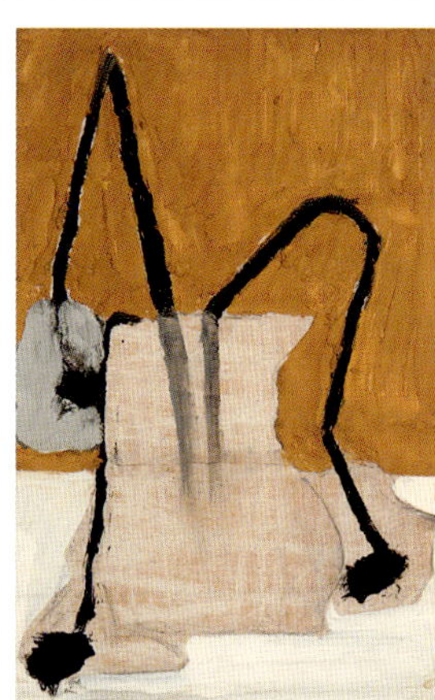

Medina, John Baptist de (after) 1659–1710
Self Portrait 17th C–18th C
oil on canvas 35.6 x 30.5
PC.59

Meissonier, Jean Louis Ernest 1815–1891
Pasquale 1888
oil on panel 46 x 35.5
2330

Mellis, Margaret 1914–2009
Three Faded Flowers 1957
oil on hardboard 33 x 21.5
3482

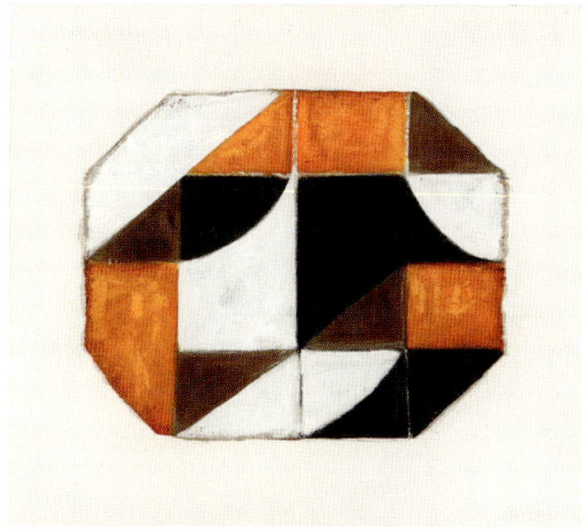

Mellis, Margaret 1914–2009
Burnt Out 1975–1976
oil on canvas 22.9 x 35
3483

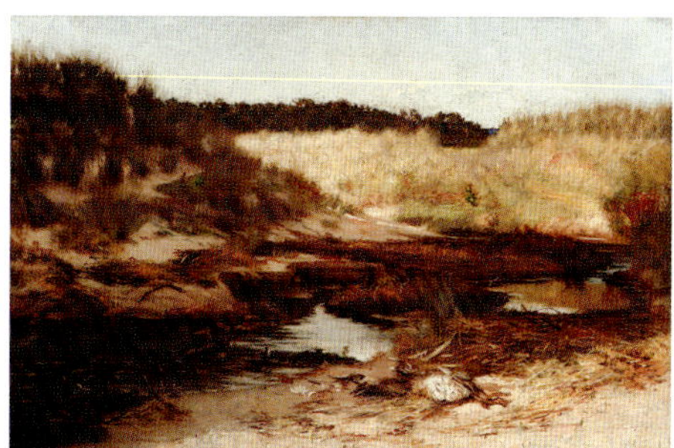

Melville, Arthur 1855–1904
The Tragedy of the Morn 1877
oil on canvas 61 x 91.4
2447

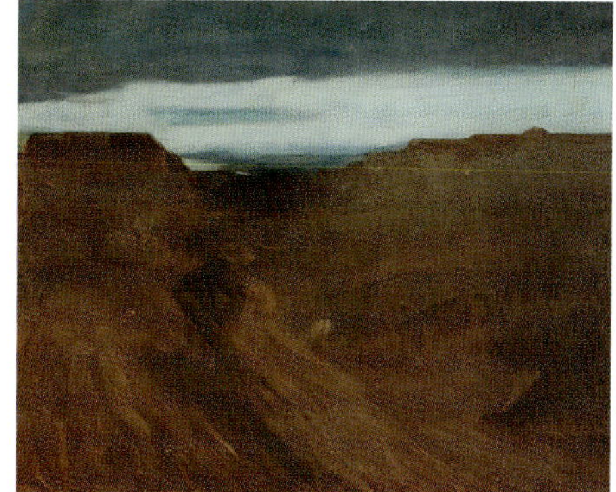

Melville, Arthur 1855–1904
Night, Spain c.1891
oil on canvas 81.2 x 96.8
3375

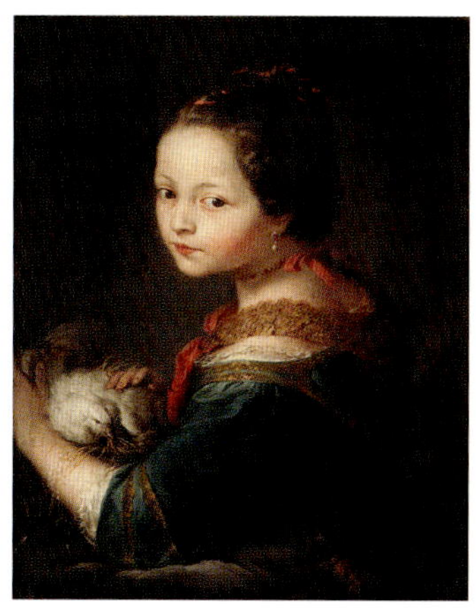

Mengs, Anton Raphael 1728–1779
Girl with a Dove
oil on canvas 60.5 x 50.5
PL.104 (P)

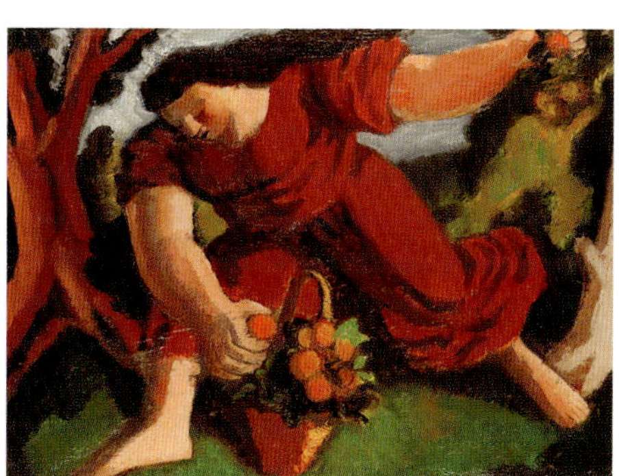

Meninsky, Bernard 1891–1950
Woman with a Basket of Fruit
oil on canvas 40.6 x 50.8
2861

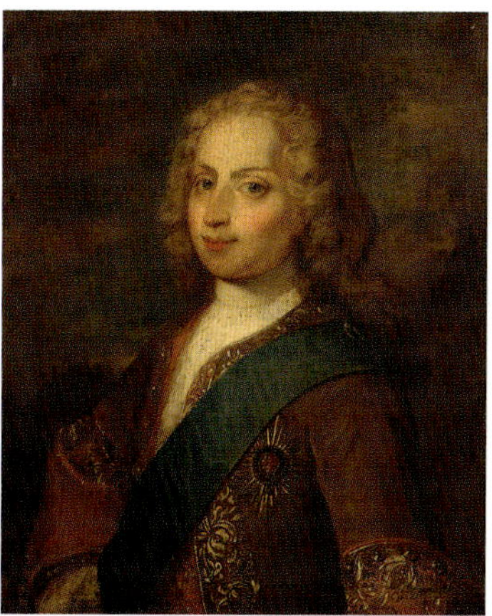

Mercier, Philippe (after) 1689–1760
Frederick, Prince of Wales (1707–1751)
oil on canvas 73.7 x 61
PC.55

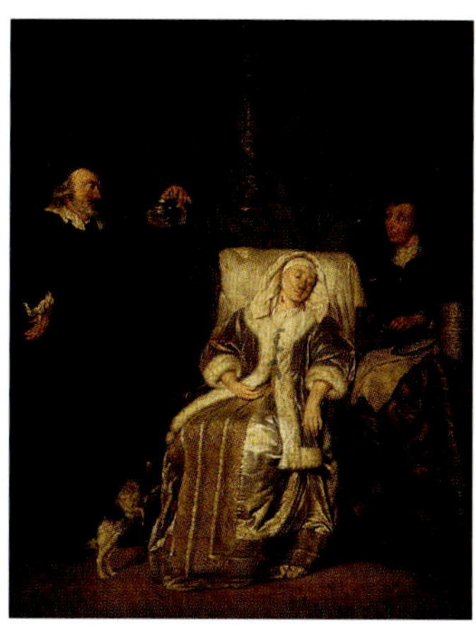

Metsu, Gabriel (after) 1629–1667
The Doctor's Visit 17th C–18th C
oil on canvas 33 x 26
92

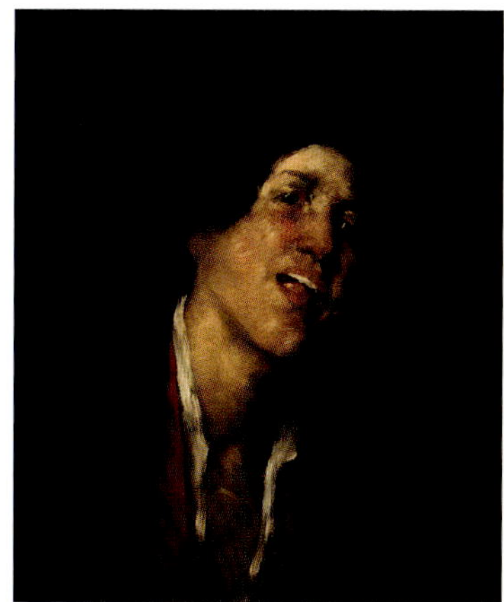

Mettling, Louis 1847–1904
Boy's Head c.1870–1880
oil on canvas 55.5 x 46.1
2189

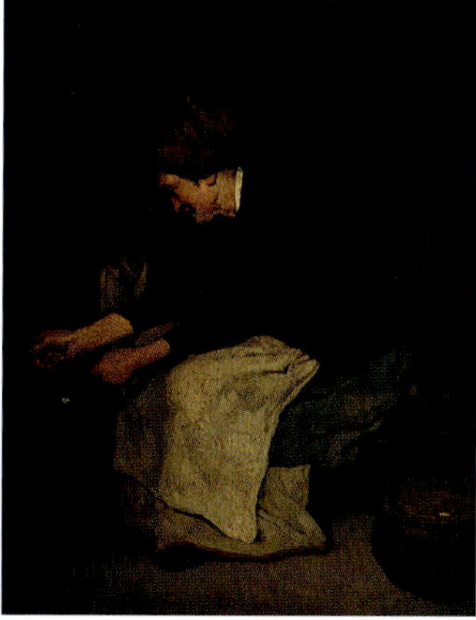

Mettling, Louis 1847–1904
Woman Cooking at a Stove
oil on canvas 45.6 x 38
1561

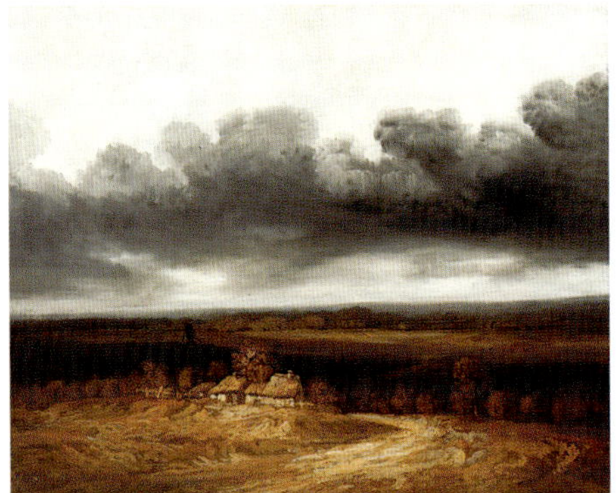

Michel, Georges 1763–1843
Landscape with Cottages after 1830
oil on canvas 78.5 x 99.2
3111

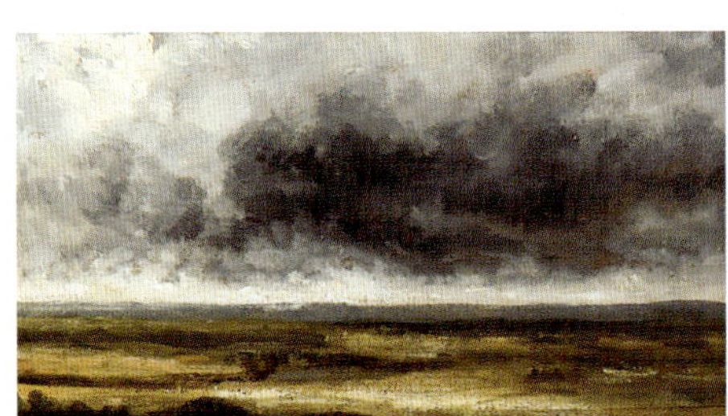

Michel, Georges 1763–1843
Moorland: The Storm Cloud
oil on canvas 17.8 x 31.1
35.534

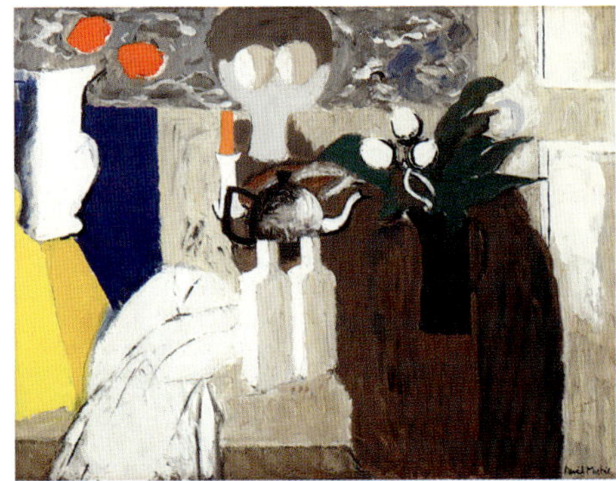

Michie, David Alan Redpath b.1928
E. P. N. S. Teapot 1958–1959
oil on hardboard 71.1 x 91.5
3102

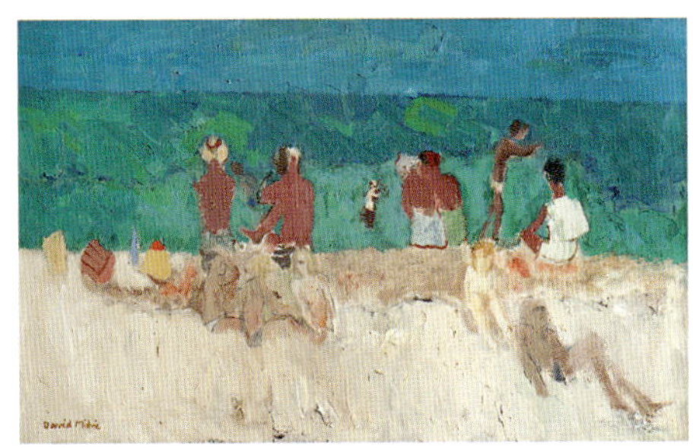

Michie, David Alan Redpath b.1928
Edge of the Sea 1964
oil on canvas 45.4 x 70.8
3223

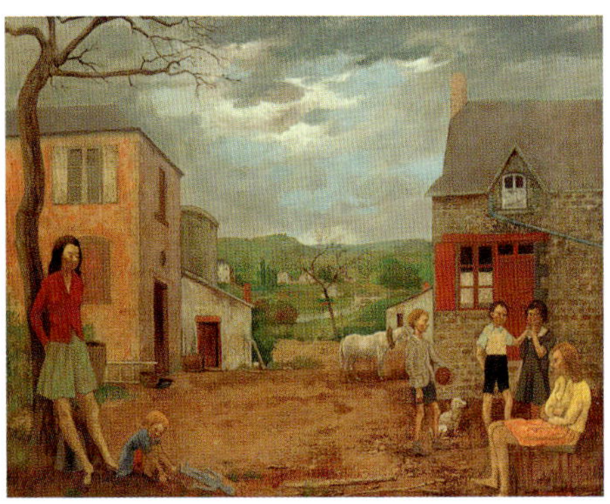

Michonze, Grégoire 1902–1982
Children at Play 1946–1947
oil on canvas 37.3 x 45.2
2825

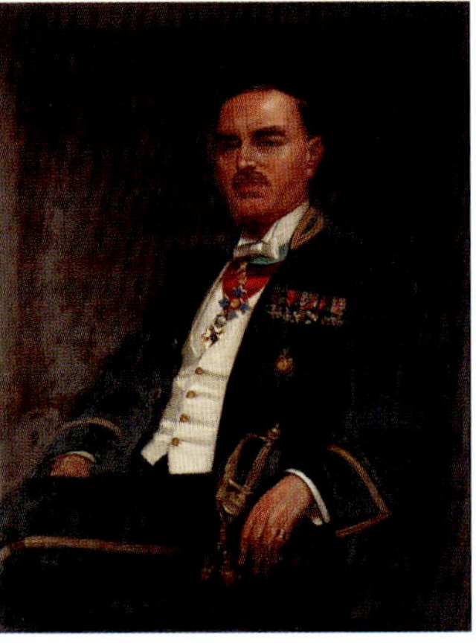

Middleton, James Raeburn 1855–1931
*Sir John S. Samuel, Secretary to the Lord
Provost of Glasgow* 1901
oil on canvas 111 x 84.9
OG.1963.42

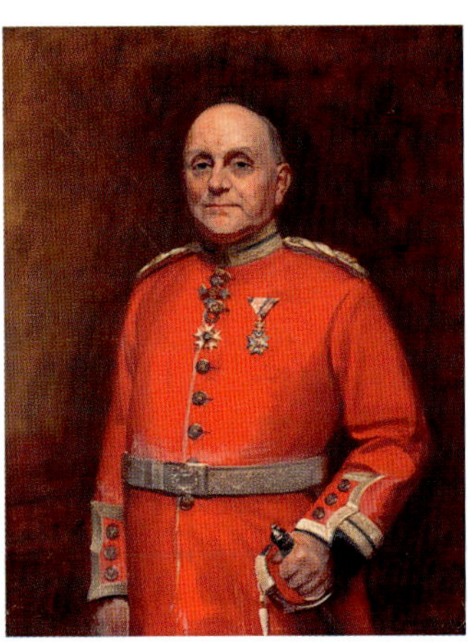

Middleton, James Raeburn 1855–1931
Alexander Walker
oil on canvas 111.8 x 81.3
2341

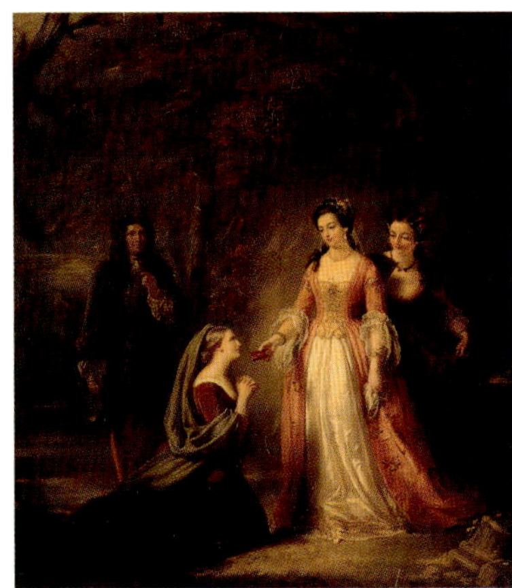

Middleton, James Raeburn 1855–1931
Jeanie Deans and the Queen
oil on canvas 121.9 x 106.7
2309

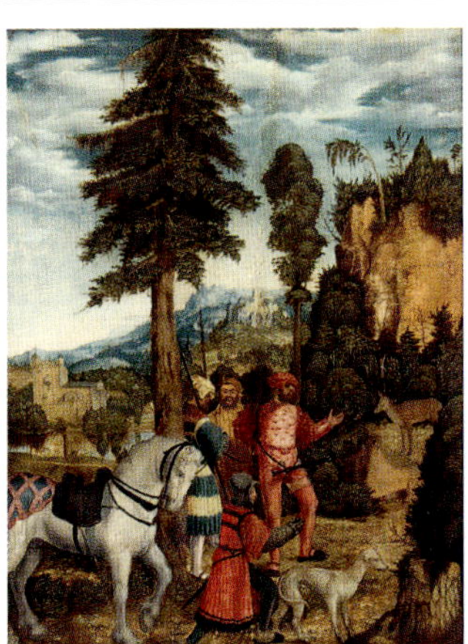

Mielich, Hans 1516–1573
The Conversion of Saint Eustace (or Saint
Hubert) c.1535–1540
oil on panel 55.9 x 41.3
205

Facing page: Cézanne, Paul, 1839–1906, *The Château of Médan*, c.1879–1880 (p. 78)

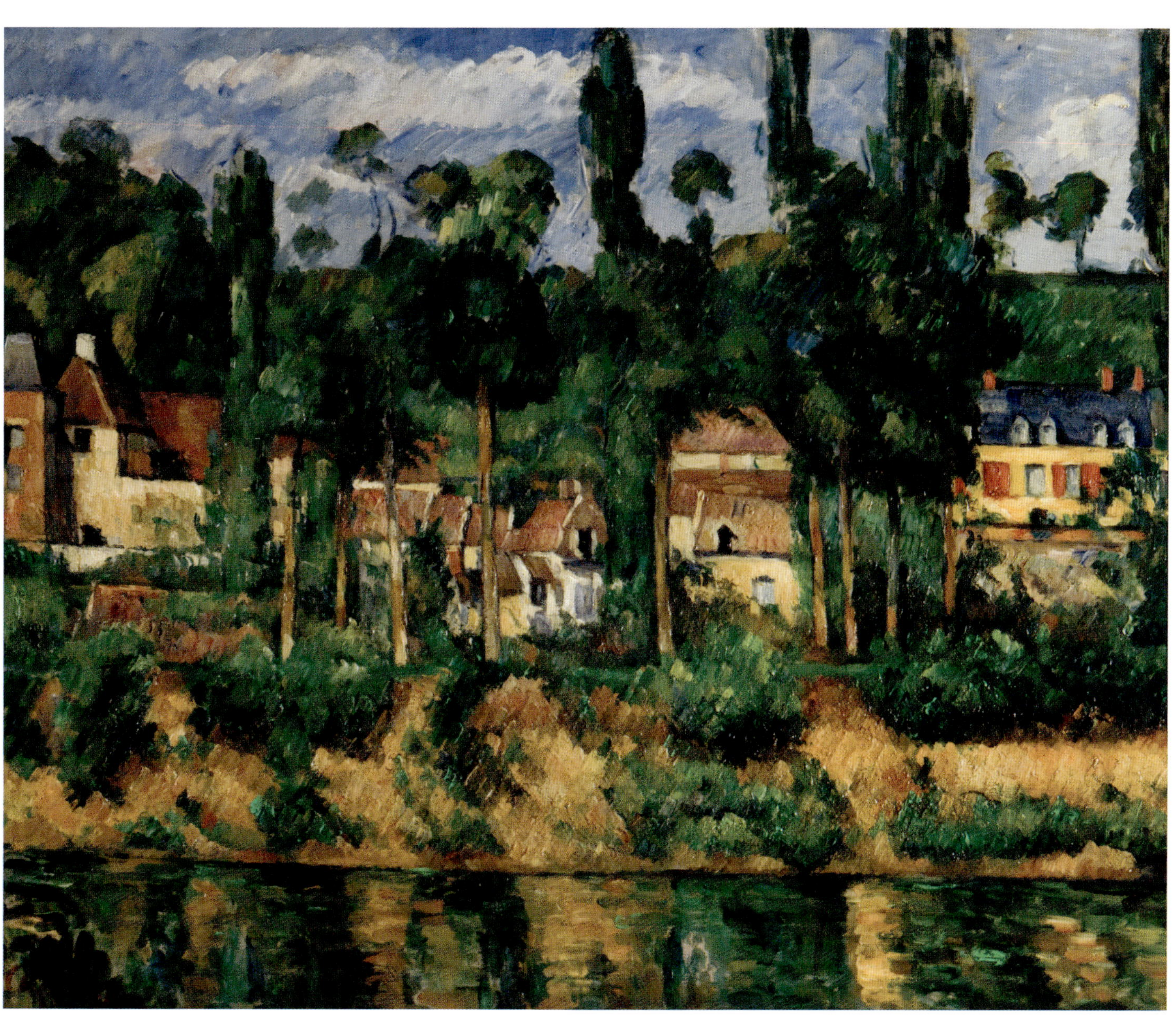

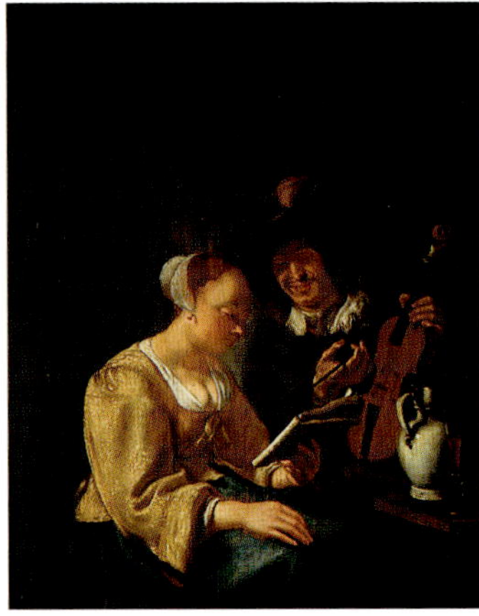

Mieris, Frans van the elder (after)
1635–1681
The Music Lesson 17th C–18th C
oil on panel 31.1 x 25.7
113

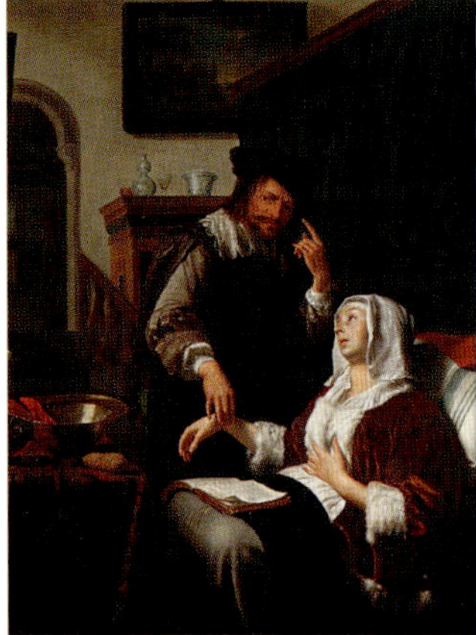

Mieris, Frans van the elder (studio of)
1635–1681
A Sick Woman and Her Doctor 1657
oil on copper 34.3 x 27.3
108

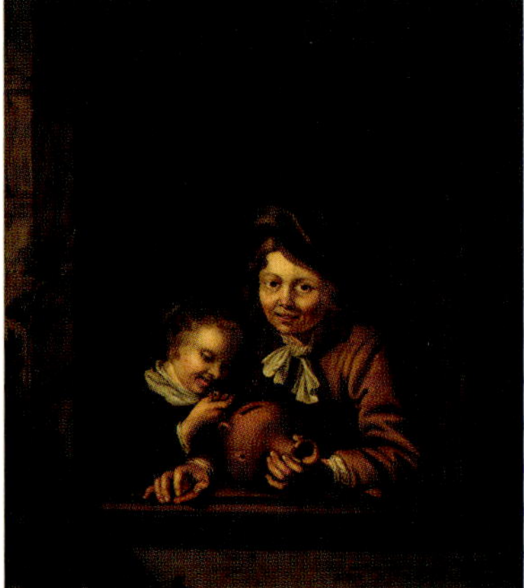

Mieris, Frans van the younger (after)
1689–1763
A Boy and a Girl at a Window
late 18th C–19th C
oil on panel 27.6 x 23.8
950

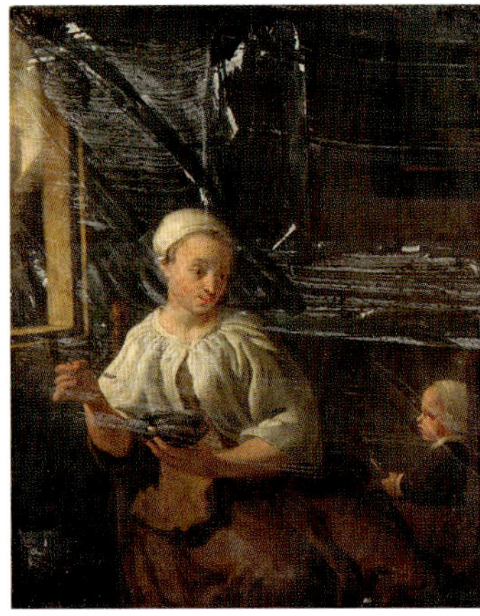

Mieris, Frans van the younger (style of)
1689–1763
A Woman and a Child by a Window
early 19th C
oil on panel 34 x 27.9
384

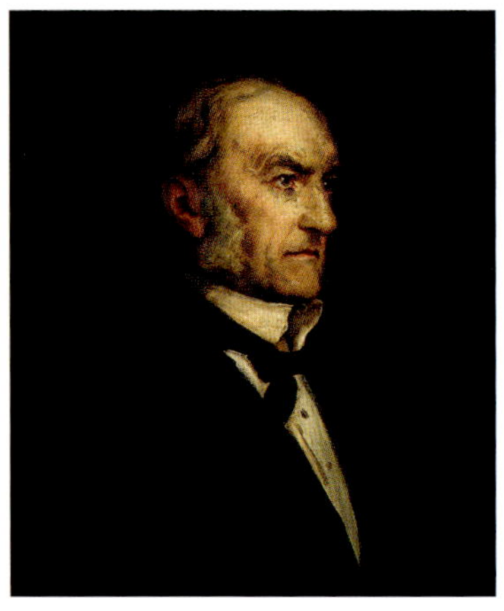

Millais, John Everett 1829–1896
William E. Gladstone (1809–1898) c.1879
oil on canvas 61 x 50.8
2848

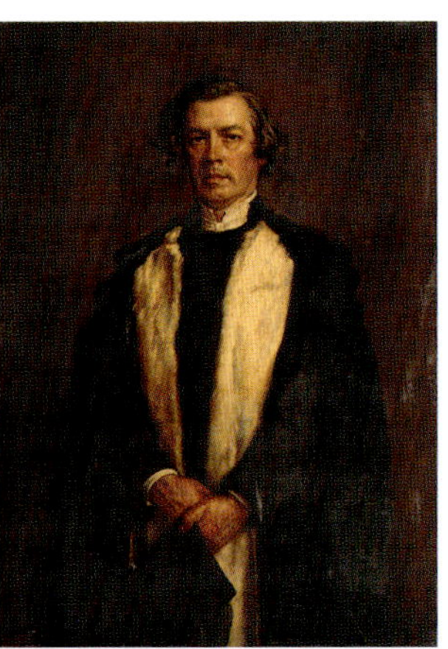

Millais, John Everett 1829–1896
Reverend John Caird (1820–1898), Principal of Glasgow University (1873–1898) c.1880
oil on canvas 127 x 91.4
1340

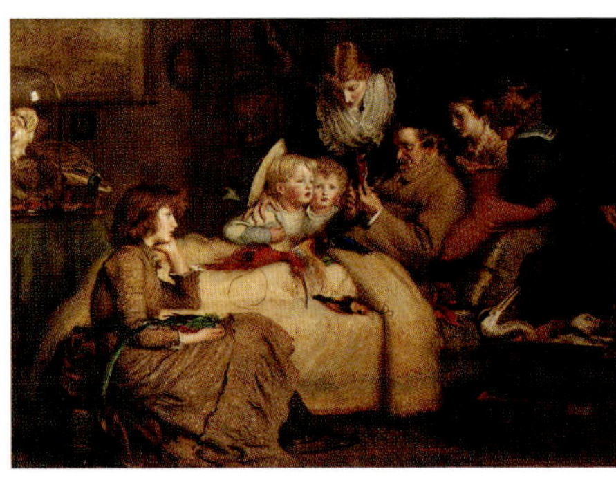

Millais, John Everett 1829–1896
The Ornithologist 1885
oil on canvas 160.7 x 215.9
1207

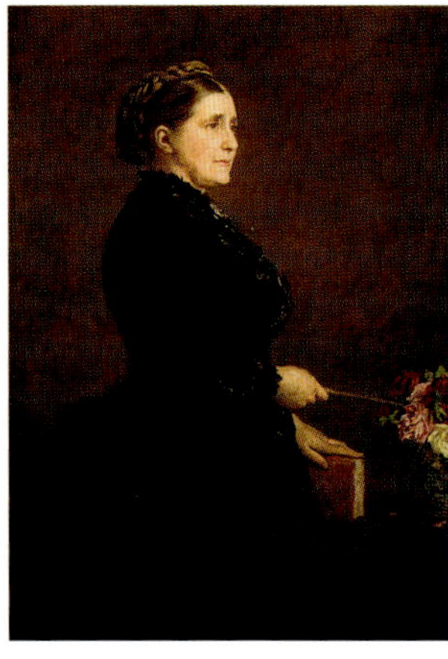

Millais, John Everett 1829–1896
Mrs Isabella Elder (1828–1905) 1886
oil on canvas 127.6 x 84.5
1414

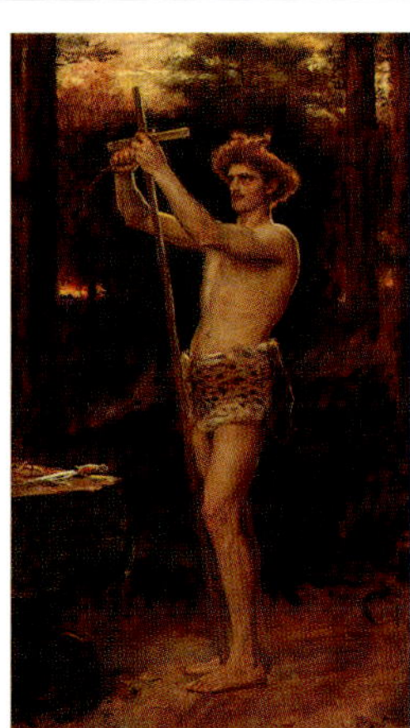

Millais, John Everett 1829–1896
The Forerunner 1896
oil on canvas 141.2 x 82.2
1032

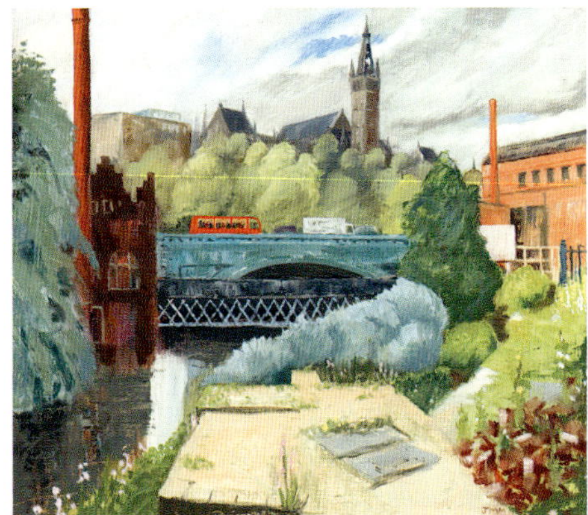

Millar, Jean M. 1932–2006
Glasgow University from Bunhouse Road 1984
oil on board 88.5 x 98.5
NH.1984.216

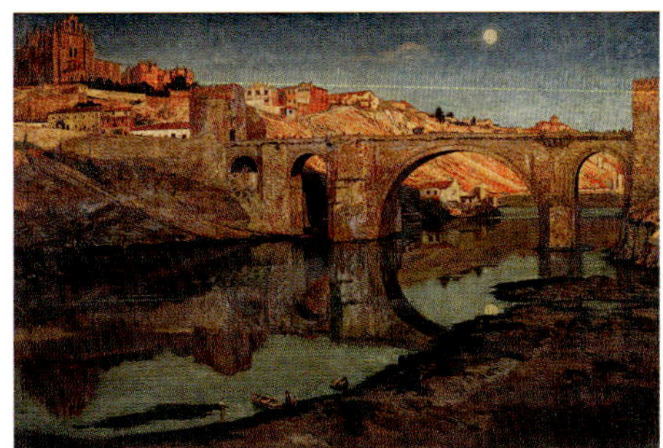

Miller, Archibald Elliot Haswell 1887–1979
The Bridge of St Martin, Toledo 1926
oil on canvas 114.3 x 167.6
1679

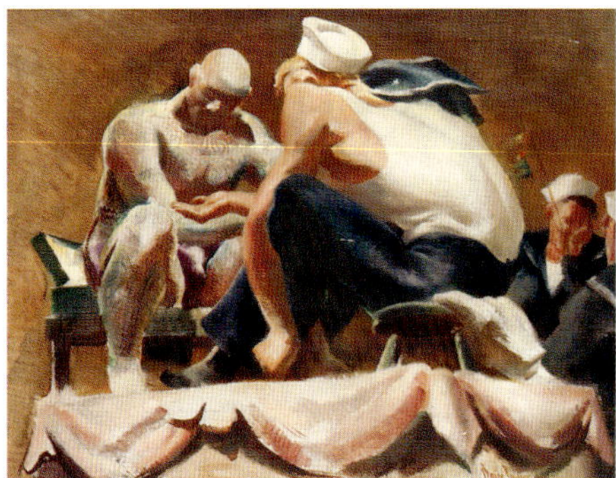

Miller, Barse 1904–1973
Tattoo Artist 1941
oil on canvas 48.9 x 61.6
2481

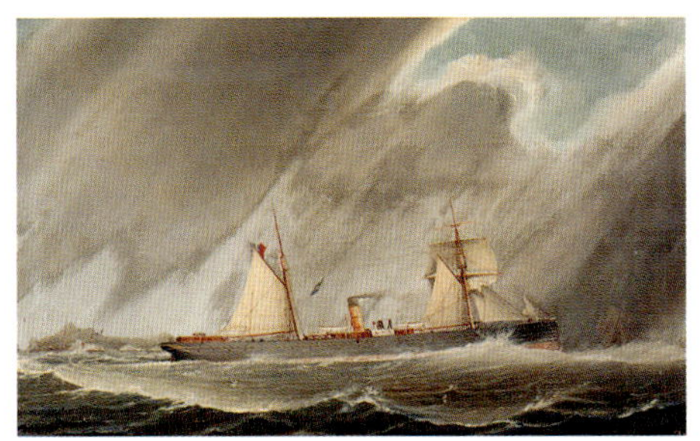

Miller, Charles Keith 1836–1907
In a Storm 1873
oil on canvas 72.5 x 111.5
T.1973.10.af

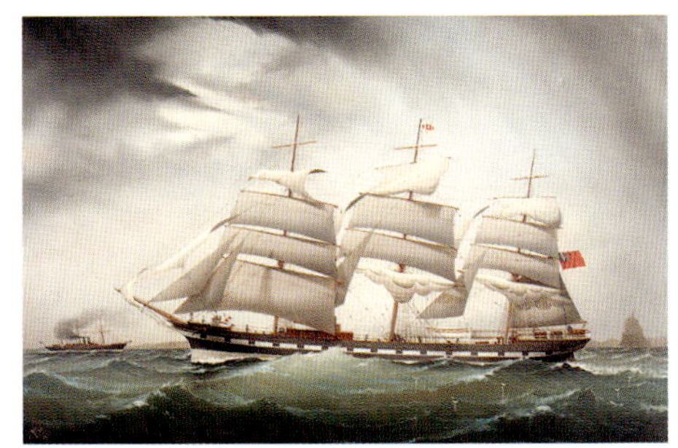

Miller, Charles Keith 1836–1907
'Marion Inglis' 1888
oil on canvas 64.8 x 97.8
T.1948.88

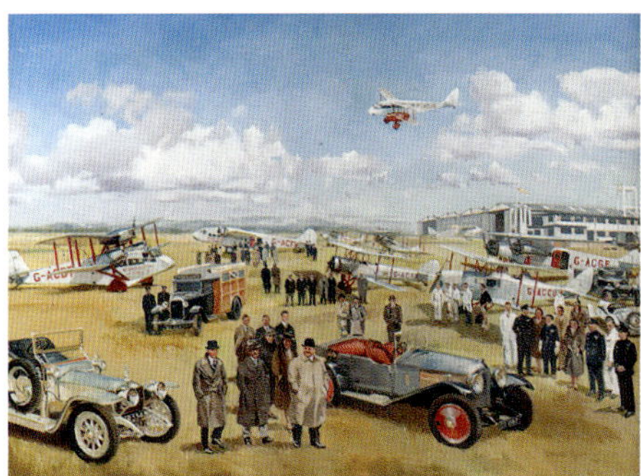

Miller, Edmund b.1929
Sword in the Sky
oil on hardboard 85 x 117.9
T.1990.13

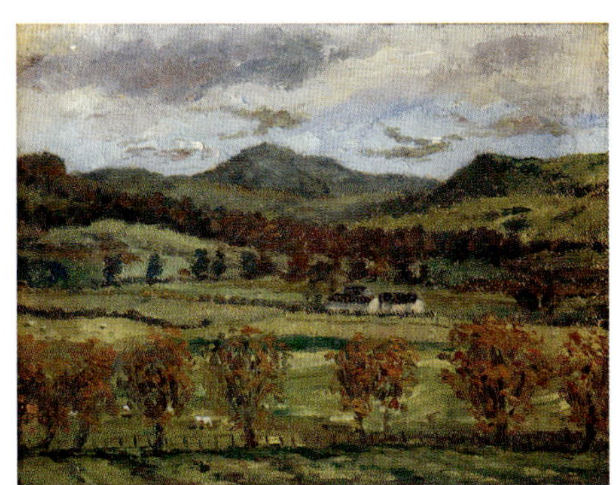

Miller, John 1911–1975
Landscape near Fintry c.1945
oil on canvas 44.5 x 55.9
2477

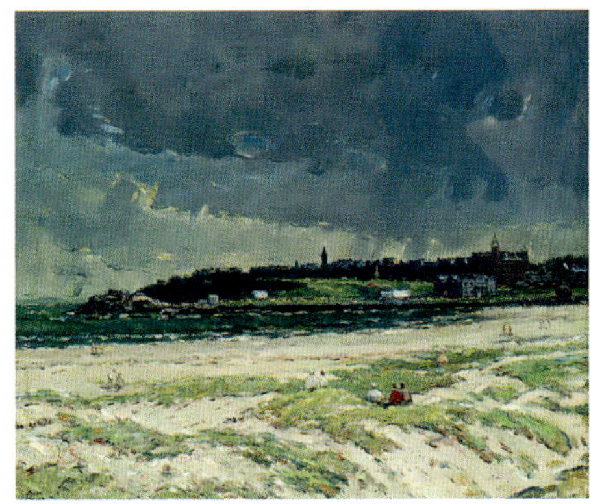

Miller, John 1911–1975
Showery Weather, St Andrews c.1969
oil on canvas board 50.8 x 60.3
3267

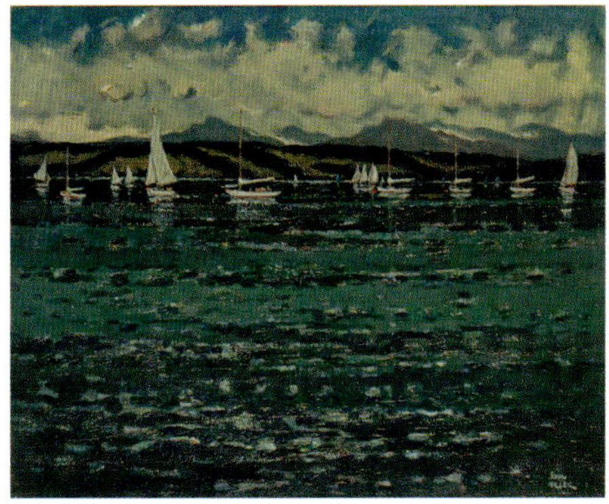

Miller, John 1911–1975
Spring on the Gareloch 1972
oil on canvas 63.5 x 81.3
3302

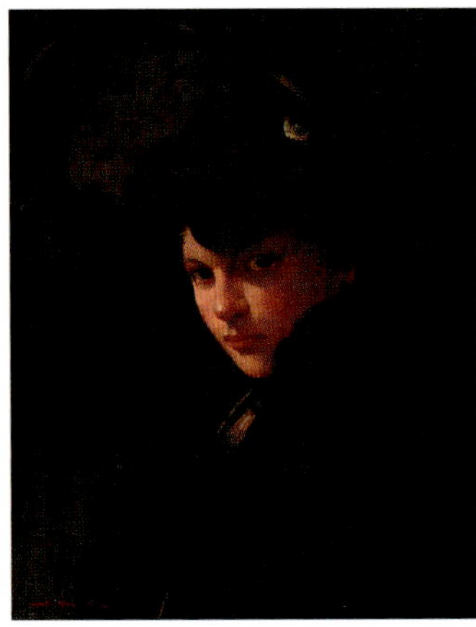

Miller, Walter active 1894–1949
Memory of the Past
oil on canvas 50.8 x 40.6
2236

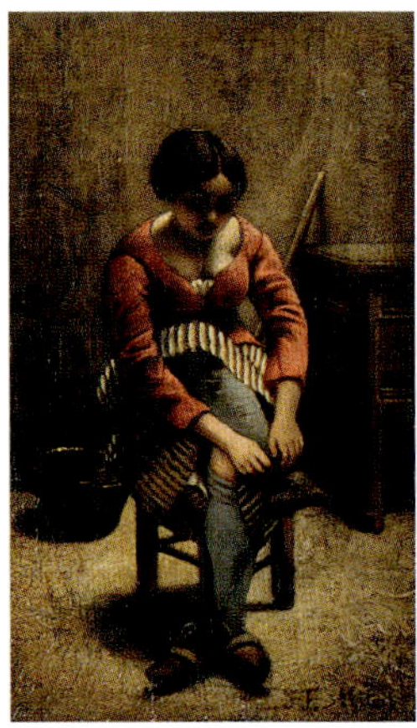

Millet, Jean-François 1814–1875
A Woman Adjusting Her Stocking c.1848
oil on panel 21.6 x 12.7
35.541

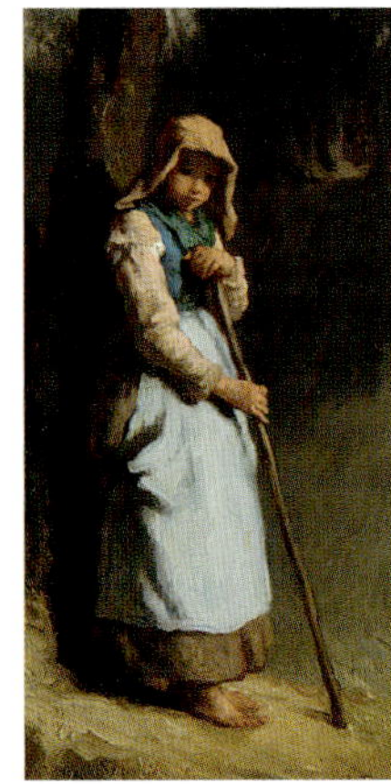

Millet, Jean-François 1814–1875
A Shepherdess 1849
oil on panel 29.8 x 16.5
35.544

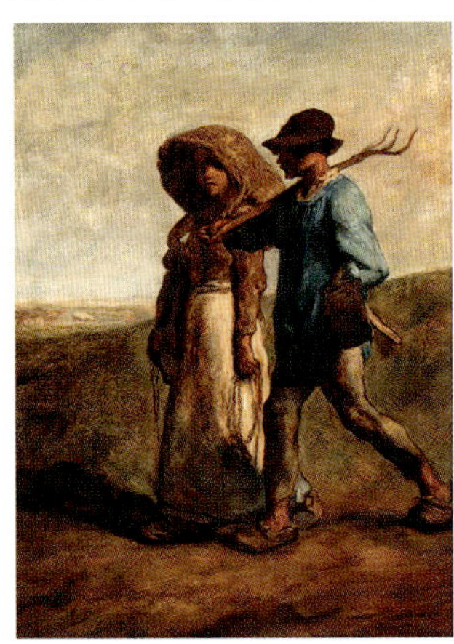

Millet, Jean-François 1814–1875
Going to Work c.1850–1851
oil on canvas 56 x 46
1111

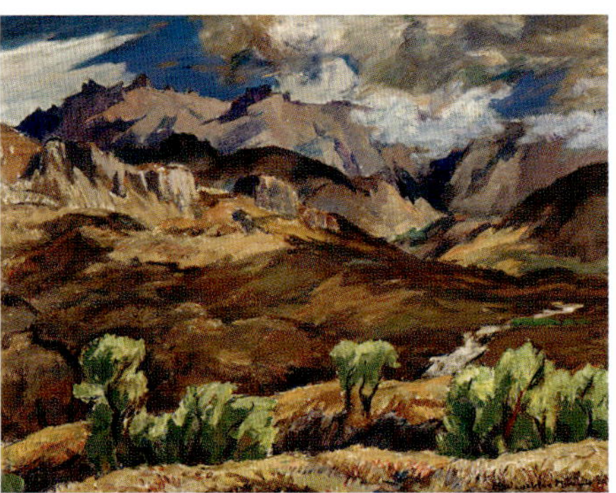

Milne, John Maclauchlan 1885–1957
North Glen Sannox c.1940
oil on canvas 71.1 x 91.4
2213

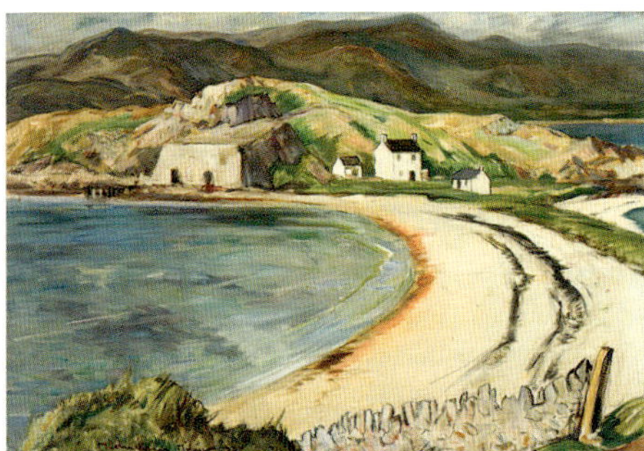

Milne, John Maclauchlan 1885–1957
Loch Eriboll
oil on canvas 66 x 91.4
1909

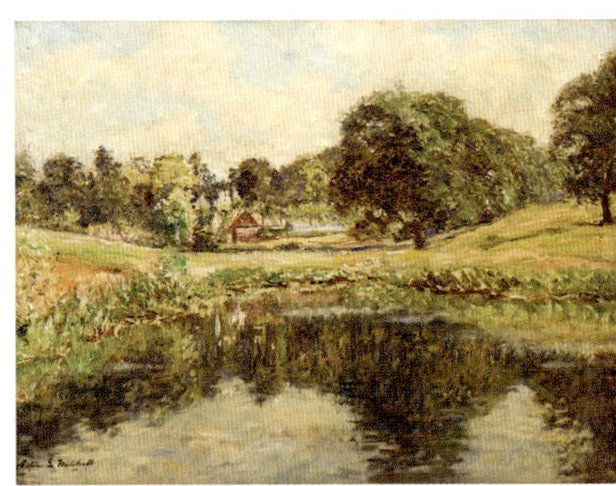

Mitchell, Colin Gillespie c.1870–c.1938
Reflections
oil on canvas 45.7 x 61
2182

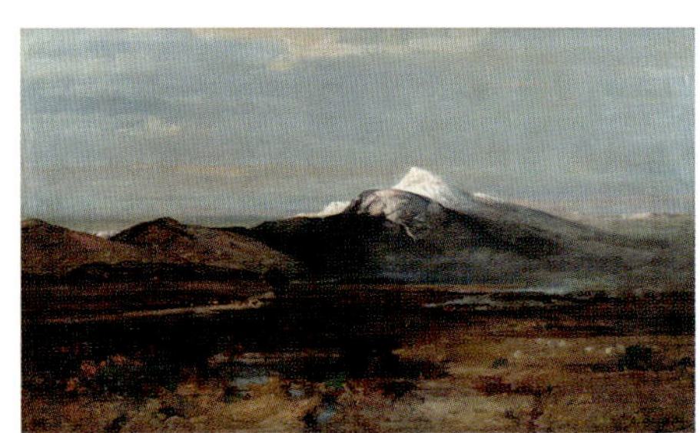

Mitchell, John Campbell 1865–1922
Cruachan
oil on canvas 76.2 x 152.4
2995

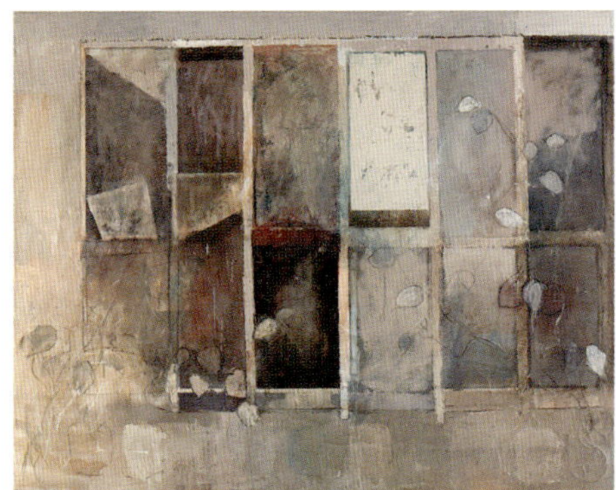

Mitchell, Meg
Finlay Stone Windows c.2008
oil on canvas 147.5 x 178
3678

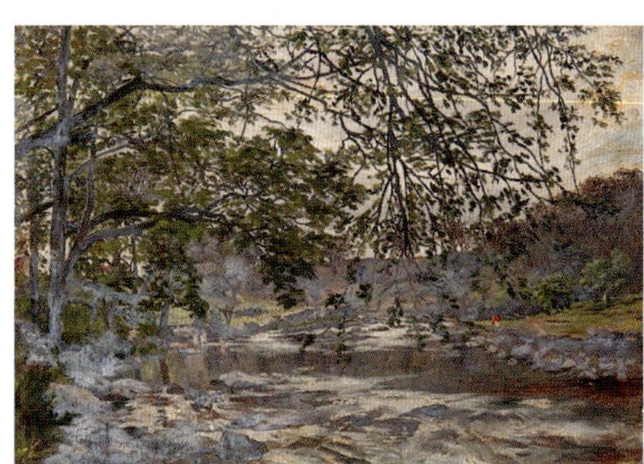

Mitchell, T.
The Kelvin at the Three Tree Well 1880
oil on paper 17.2 x 25
OG.1951.409.ob

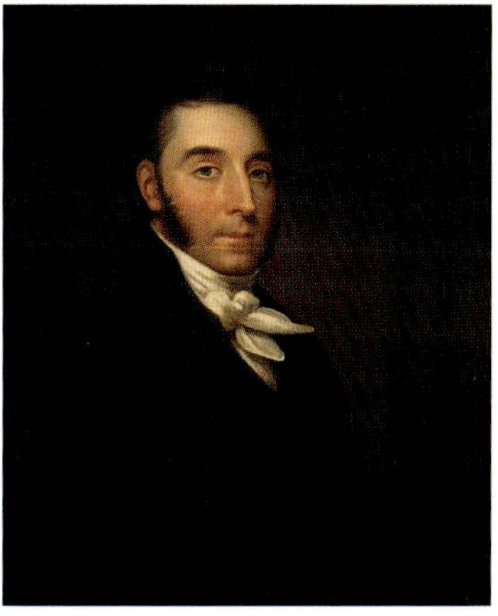

Moir, John 1776–1857
John M. Robertson 1815
oil on canvas 76.2 x 63.5
1431

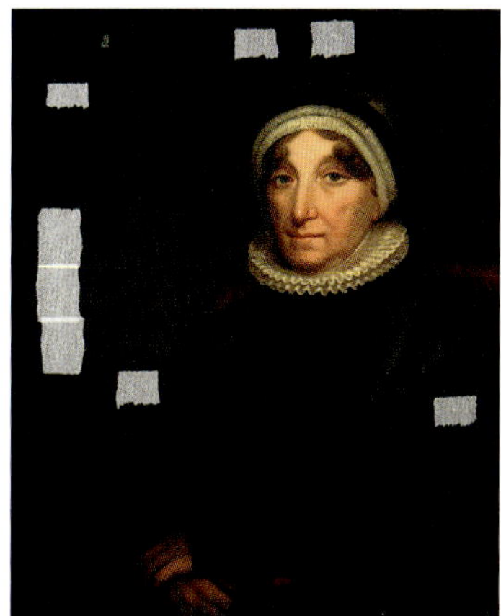

Moir, John 1776–1857
Mrs J. M. Robertson, Mother of John M. Robertson c.1815
oil on canvas 76.2 x 63.5
1430

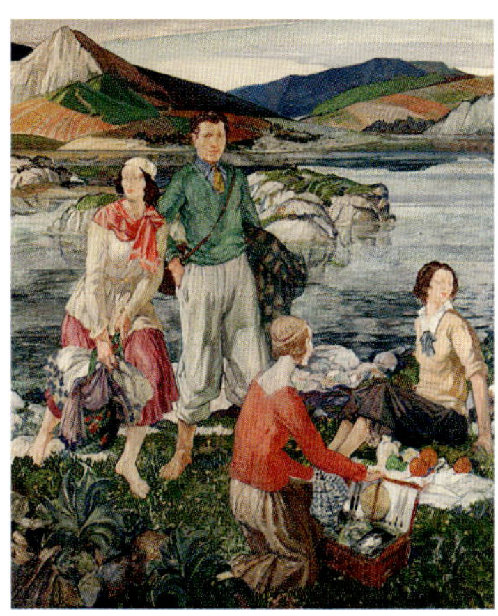

Moira, Gerald 1867–1959
Highland Landscape 1933
tempera on canvas on board 175.3 x 142.2
1860

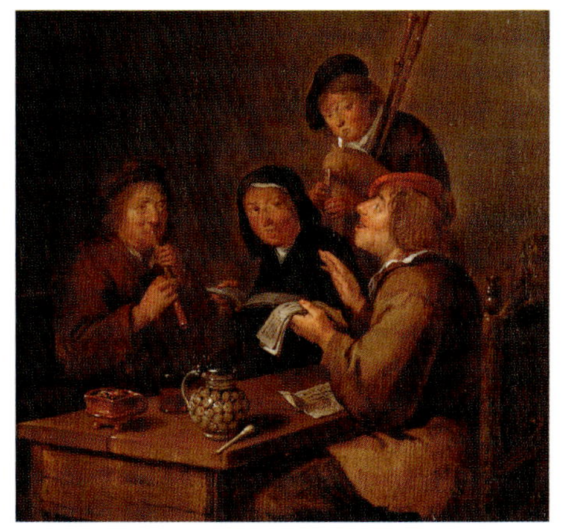

Molenaer, Klaes (attributed to) c.1630–1676
The Musicians
oil on panel 19.7 x 20.3
385

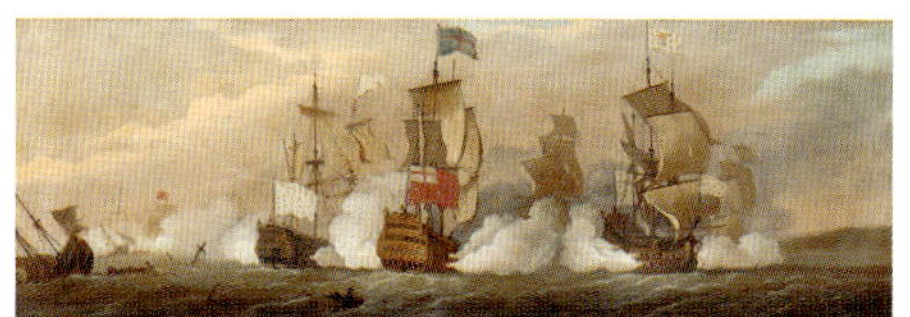

Monamy, Peter 1681–1749
The Battle of Barfleur, 19 May 1692
oil on canvas 35.6 x 101.3
101.a

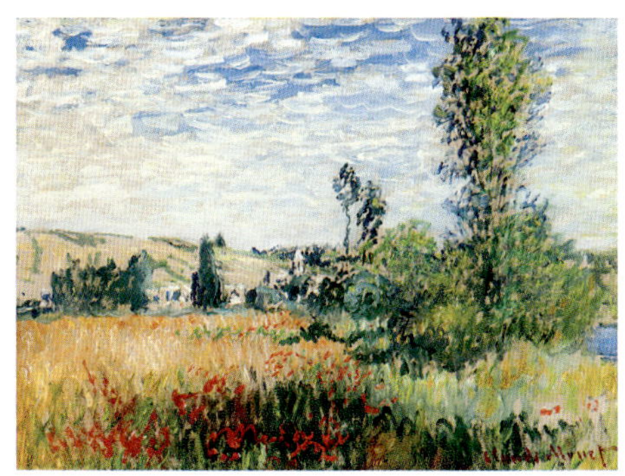

Monet, Claude 1840–1926
Vétheuil 1880
oil on canvas 59.7 x 80
2403

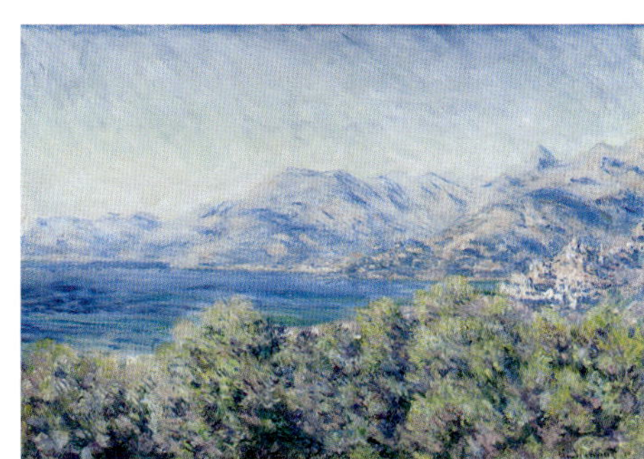

Monet, Claude 1840–1926
View of Ventimiglia 1884
oil on canvas 65.1 x 91.7
2336

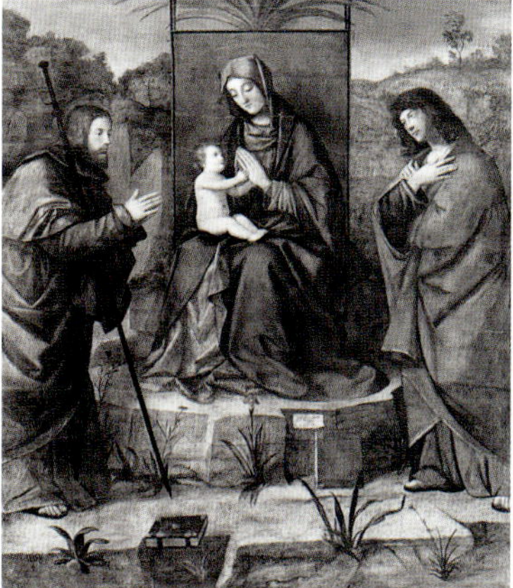

Montagna, Bartolomeo c.1450–1523
Virgin and Child Enthroned with Saint James Major and Saint John the Evangelist 1499
oil on panel 182.9 x 151.1
1193

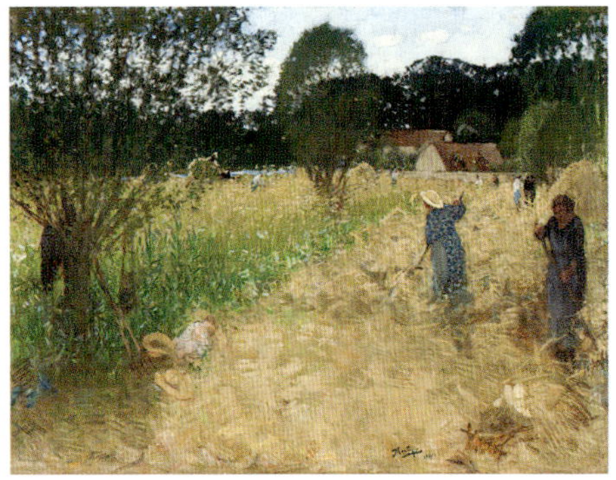

Montézin, Pierre Eugène 1874–1946
The Meadow in June 1937
oil on canvas 114.5 x 146.6
2084

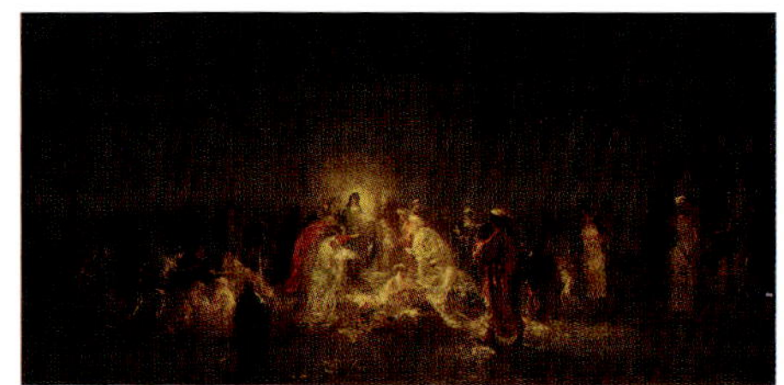

Monticelli, Adolphe Joseph Thomas
1824–1886
The Adoration of the Magi c.1860–1865
oil on canvas 50.2 x 99.7
1135

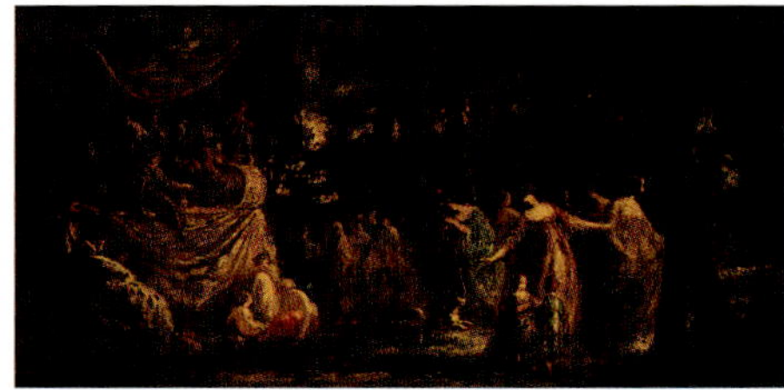

Monticelli, Adolphe Joseph Thomas
1824–1886
Strolling Players 1861
oil on canvas 52.1 x 101.6
35.55

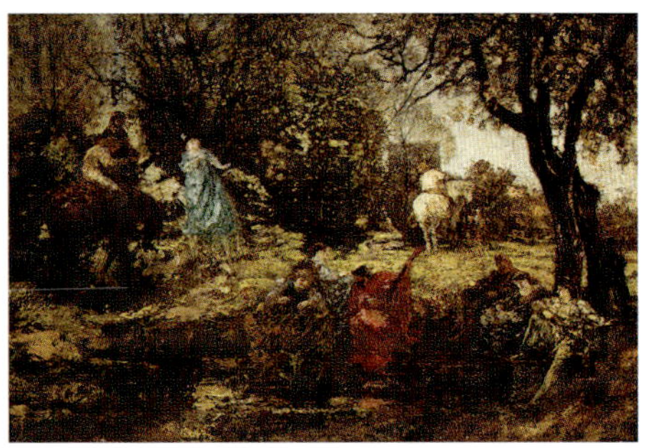

Monticelli, Adolphe Joseph Thomas
1824–1886
Garden Fête: The White Horse c.1863
oil on panel 39.8 x 59
1236

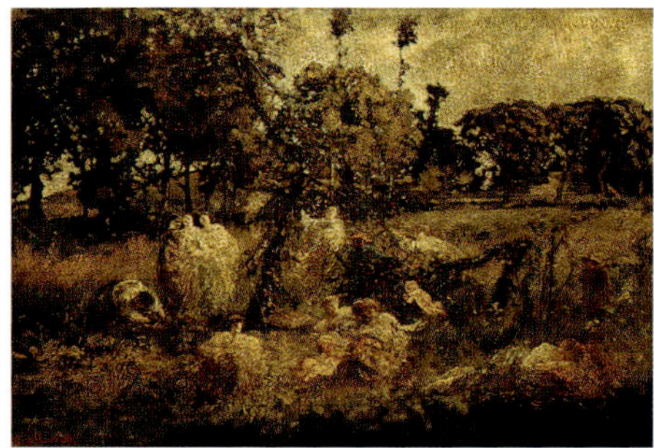

Monticelli, Adolphe Joseph Thomas
1824–1886
Autumn in the Field 1865
oil on panel 45.7 x 66
35.548

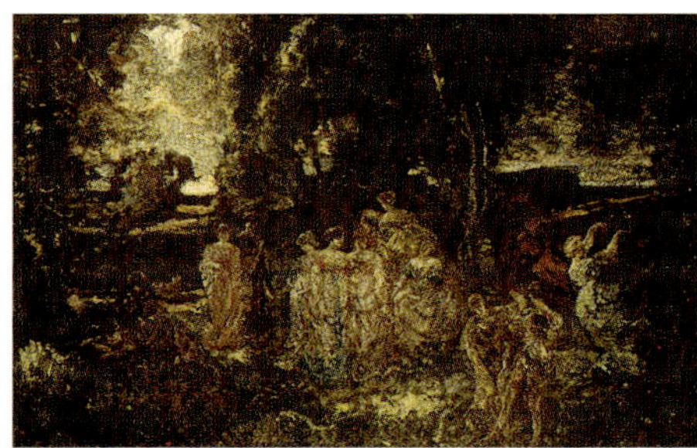

Monticelli, Adolphe Joseph Thomas
1824–1886
Scene from 'The Decameron' (by Giovanni
Boccaccio) c.1865
oil on panel 40.6 x 61.6
35.555

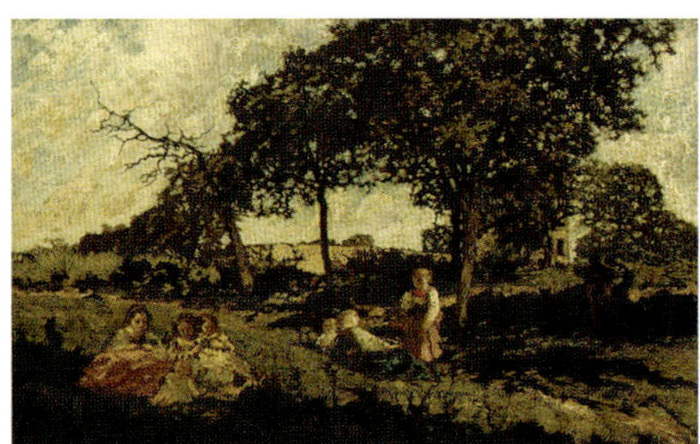

Monticelli, Adolphe Joseph Thomas
1824–1886
Children Playing in a Park c.1867
oil on panel 39.4 x 59.7
35.551

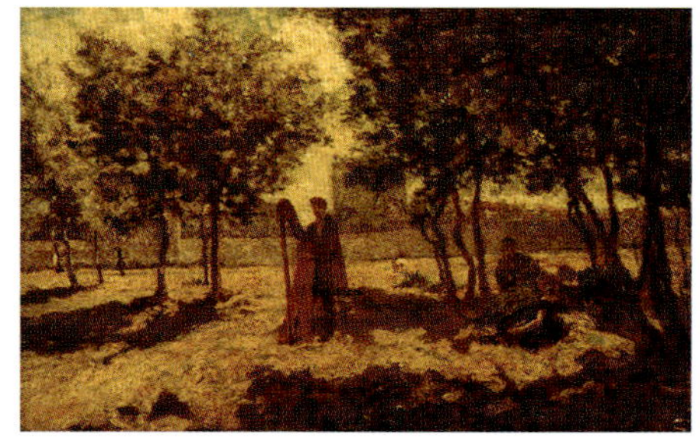

Monticelli, Adolphe Joseph Thomas
1824–1886
The Harpist c.1867
oil on panel 41.9 x 63.5
35.556

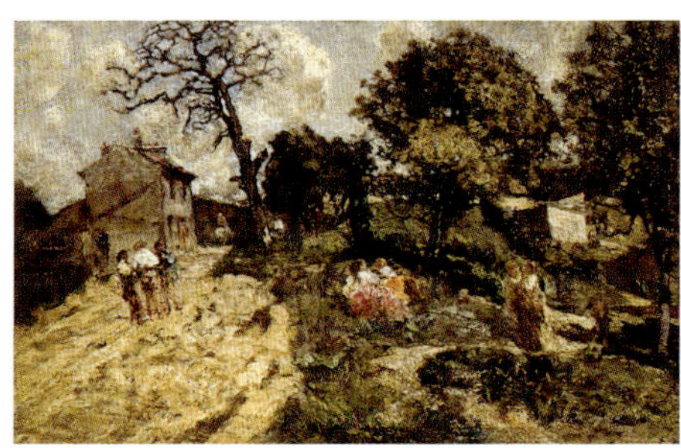

Monticelli, Adolphe Joseph Thomas
1824–1886
The New Vintage c.1868
oil on panel 40.6 x 59.7
35.558

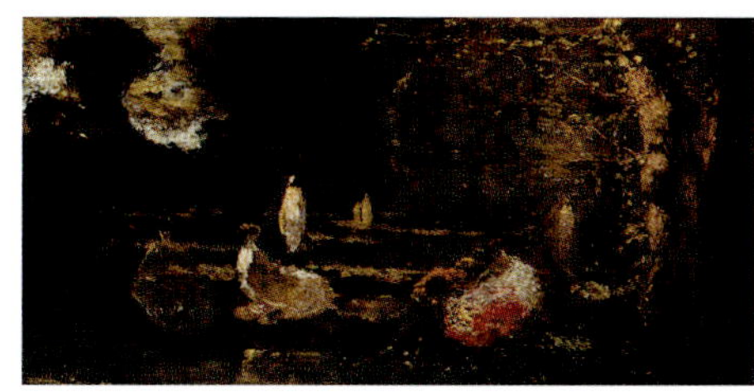

Monticelli, Adolphe Joseph Thomas
1824–1886
Ladies of Quality c.1870
oil on panel 14.3 x 27.9
2404

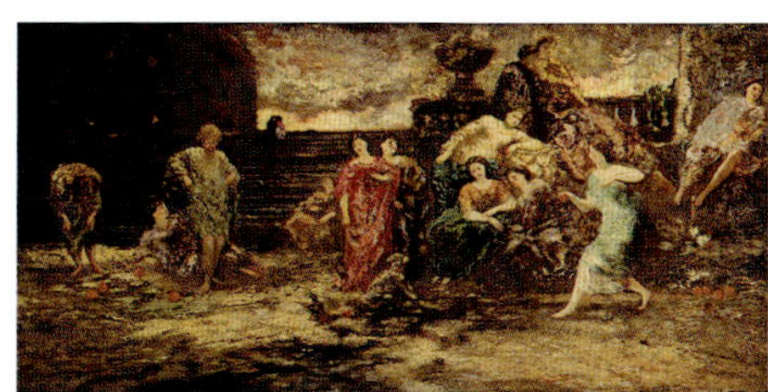

Monticelli, Adolphe Joseph Thomas
1824–1886
The Orange Game c.1885
oil on panel 25.5 x 52.4
2142

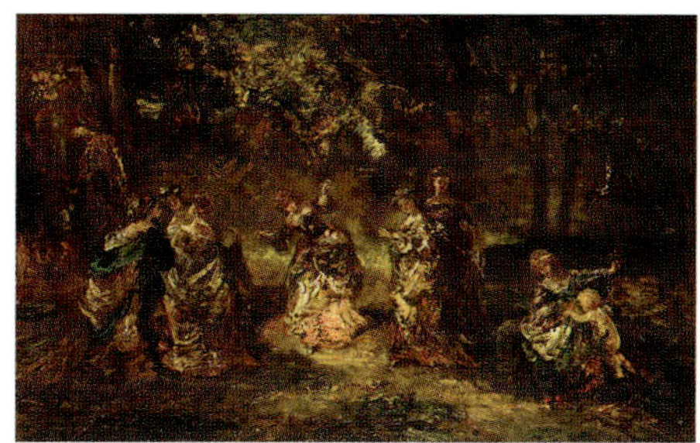

Monticelli, Adolphe Joseph Thomas
1824–1886
A Woodland Dance
oil on panel 39.4 x 60.3
35.647

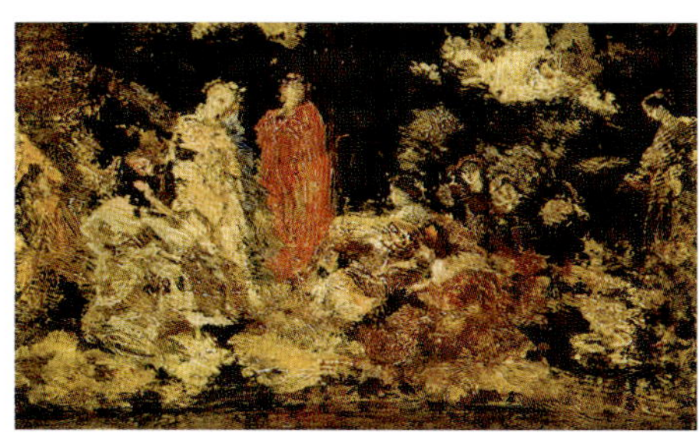

Monticelli, Adolphe Joseph Thomas
1824–1886
Alfresco
oil on panel 13.3 x 21
35.547

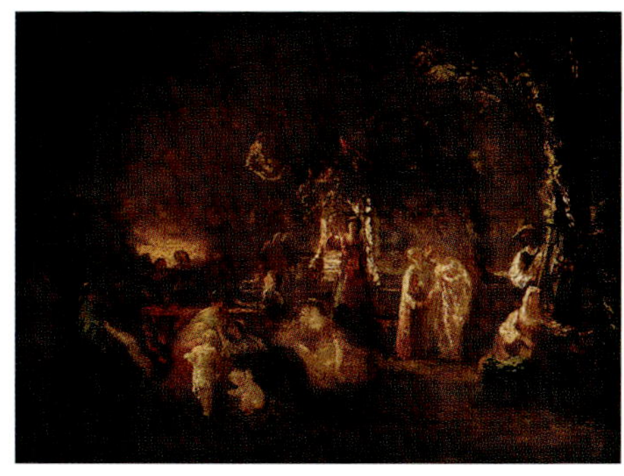

Monticelli, Adolphe Joseph Thomas
1824–1886
Fête champêtre
oil on canvas 48 x 66
2141

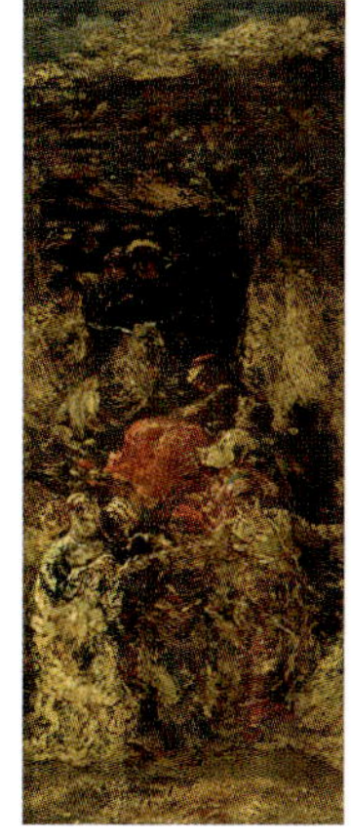

Monticelli, Adolphe Joseph Thomas
1824–1886
Forest Glade
oil on panel 35.6 x 14
35.552

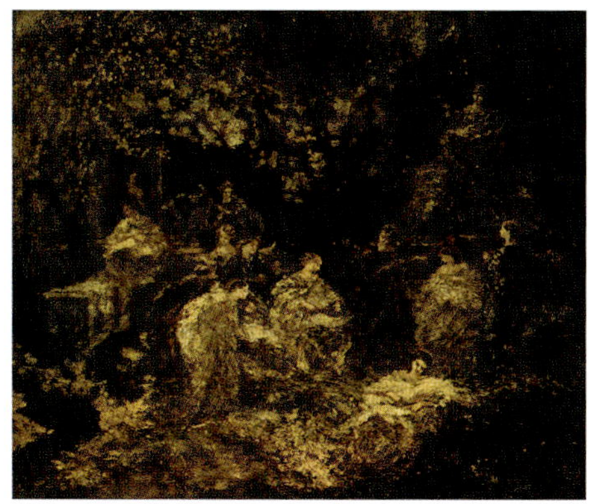

Monticelli, Adolphe Joseph Thomas
1824–1886
In the Forest
oil on panel 43.2 x 48.3
35.553

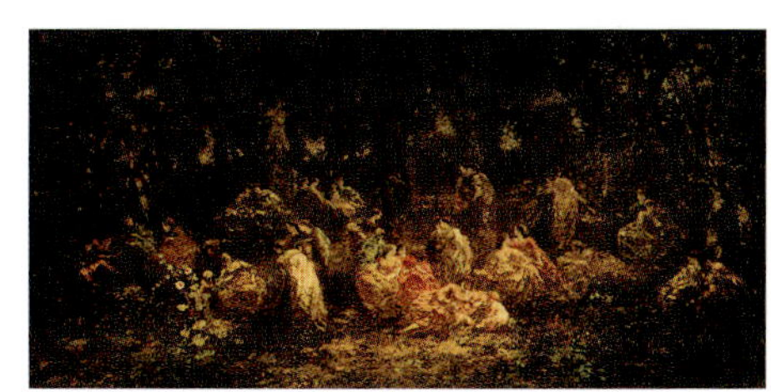

Monticelli, Adolphe Joseph Thomas
1824–1886
Ladies in a Glade near a Statue of Venus
oil on panel 50.8 x 99.1
35.557

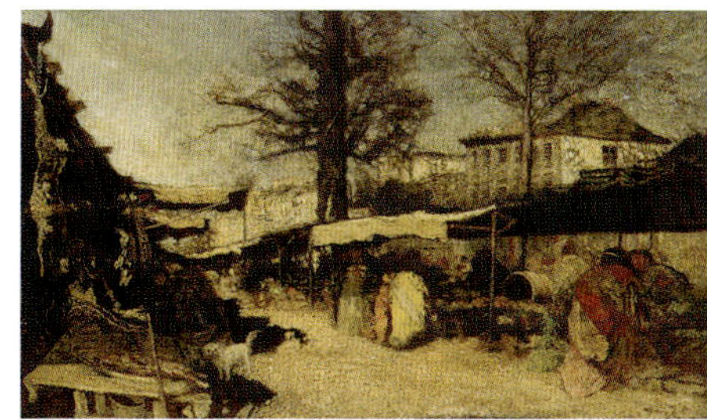

Monticelli, Adolphe Joseph Thomas
1824–1886
The Bazaar, Marseilles
oil on board 37.5 x 60.3
35.549

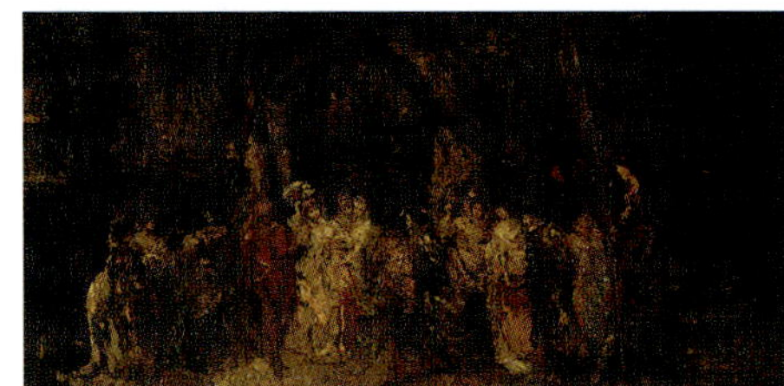

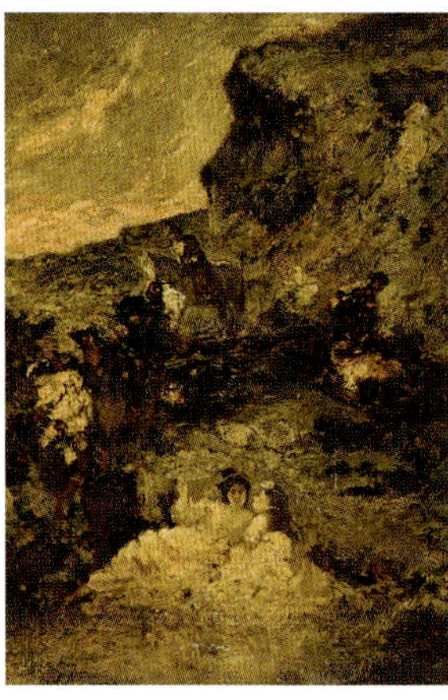

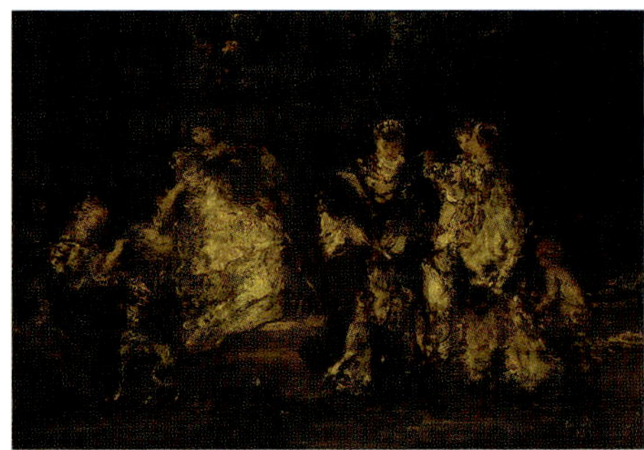

Monticelli, Adolphe Joseph Thomas
1824–1886
The Marriage Procession
oil on canvas 49.7 x 99.7
939

Monticelli, Adolphe Joseph Thomas
1824–1886
The Ravine
oil on panel 36.8 x 26.7
35.559

Monticelli, Adolphe Joseph Thomas
1824–1886 & **Maris, Matthijs** 1839–1917
In the Forest 1893
oil on panel 34.3 x 45.7
35.336

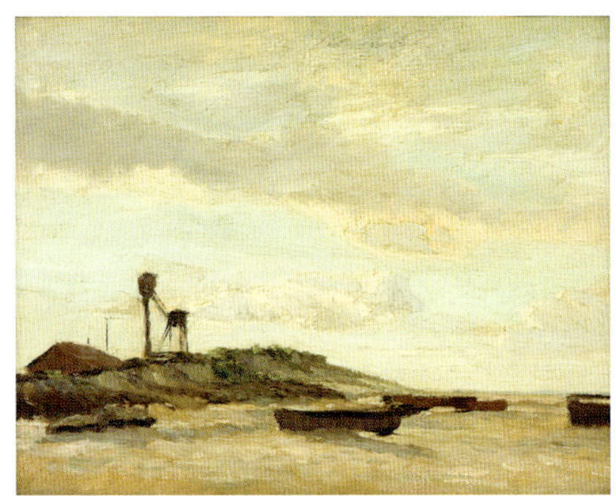

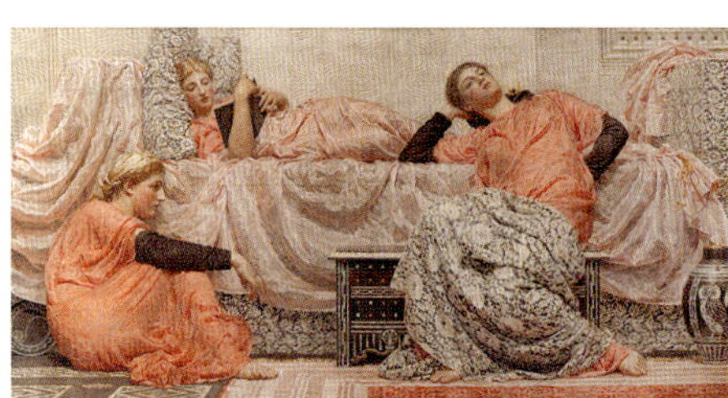

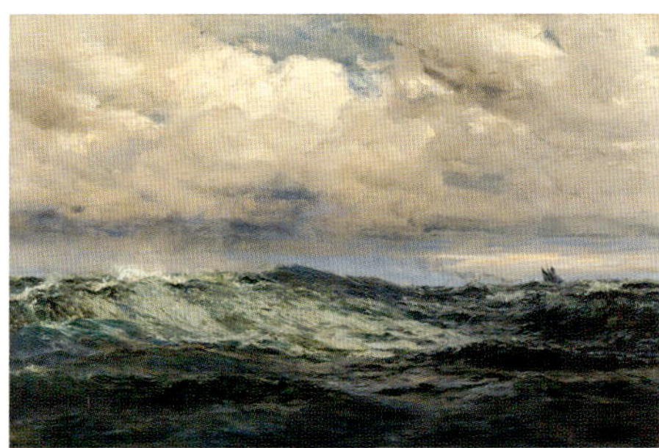

Moon, Henry George 1857–1905
The Outlook, Palling, Norfolk
oil on canvas 38.1 x 48.9
2334

Moore, Albert Joseph 1841–1893
Reading Aloud 1884
tempera/oil on canvas 107.3 x 205.7
1218

Moore, Henry 1831–1895
St Alban's Race
oil on canvas 123.8 x 184.1
1176

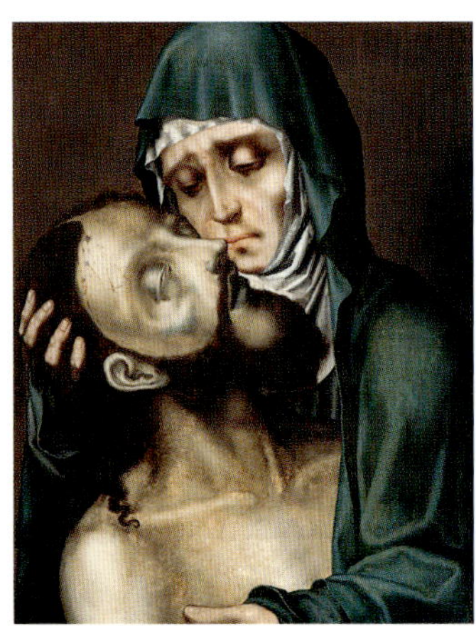

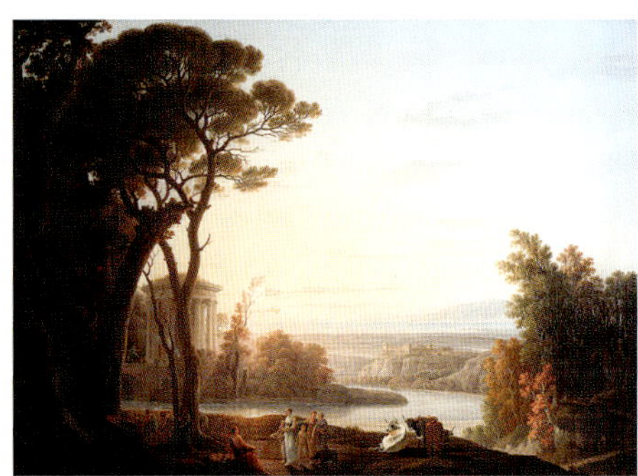

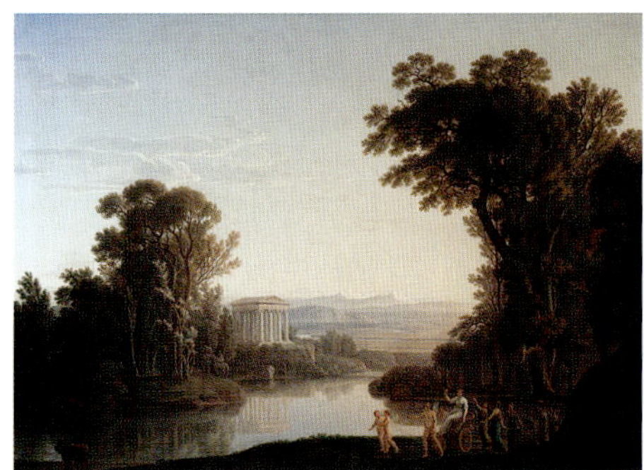

Morales, Luis de c.1509–c.1586
Pietà
oil on panel 53.3 x 40.6
PC.39

More, Jacob 1740–1793
Evening 1785
oil on canvas 152.2 x 203
3317

More, Jacob 1740–1793
Morning 1785
oil on canvas 155.2 x 202
3316

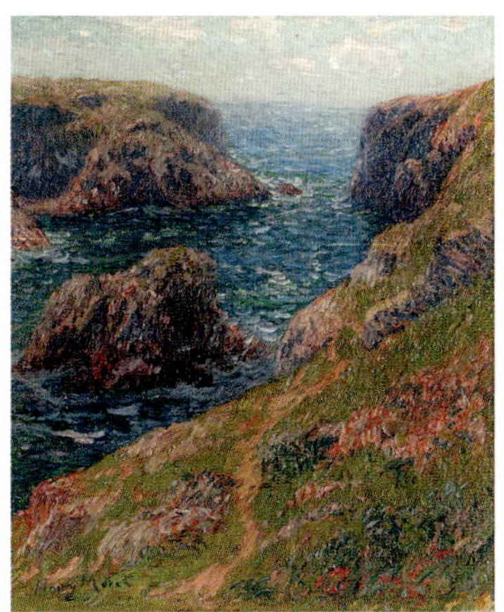

Moret, Henry 1856–1913
Cliffs at Port-Domois, Belle-Île c.1890
oil on canvas 72.7 x 59.7
3168

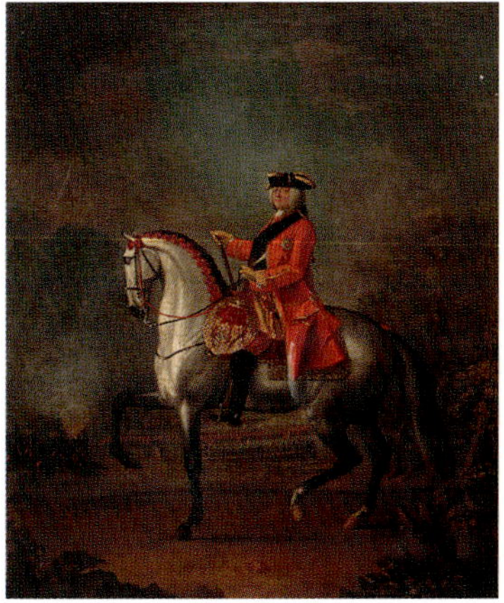

Morier, David 1705–1770
George II (1683–1760) c.1745–1770
oil on canvas 51.8 x 41.9
PC.128

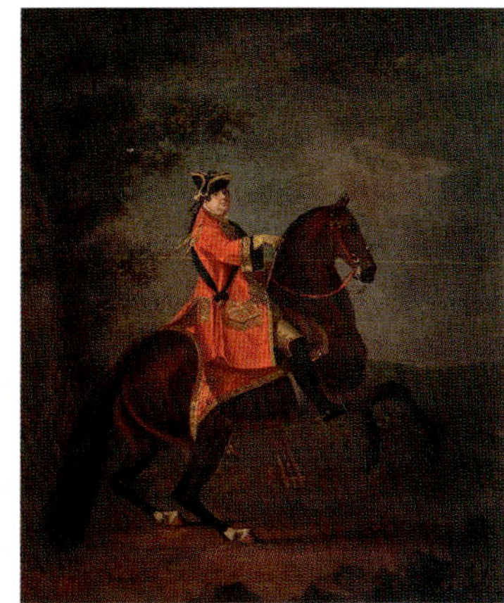

Morier, David 1705–1770
*HRH William Augustus (1721–1765), Duke of
Cumberland* c.1745–1770
oil on canvas 51.8 x 41.9
PC.126

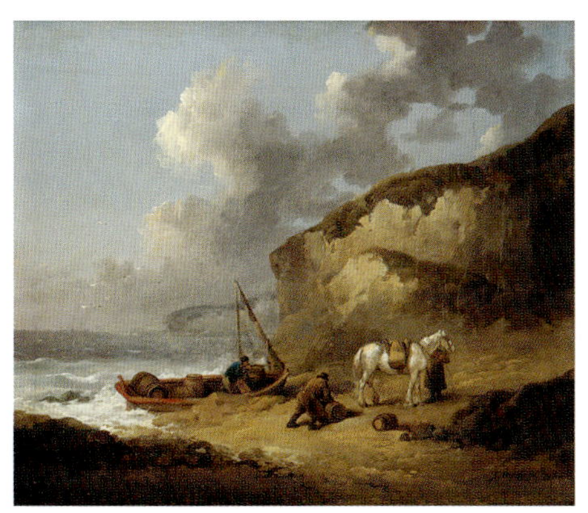

Morland, George 1763–1804
Sea-Coast Scene, Smugglers 1793
oil on canvas 31.8 x 38.1
248

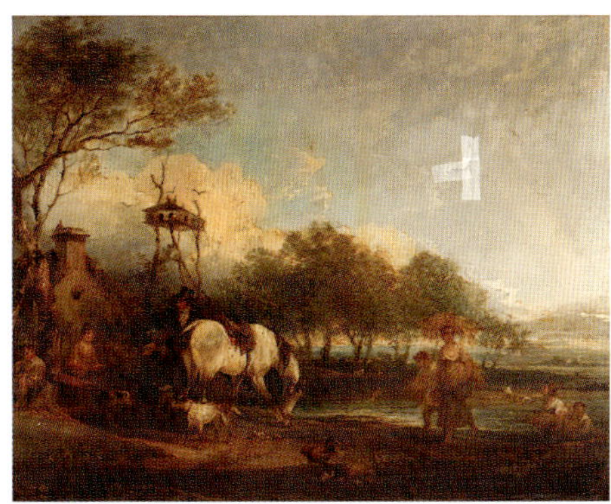

Morland, George (attributed to) 1763–1804
An English Homestead
oil on canvas 99.1 x 121.9
1064

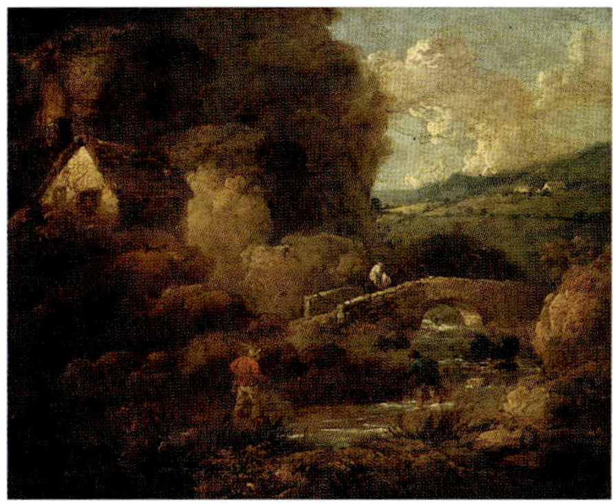

Morland, George (attributed to) 1763–1804
Landscape, an Inland Stream
oil on canvas 27.9 x 36.8
277

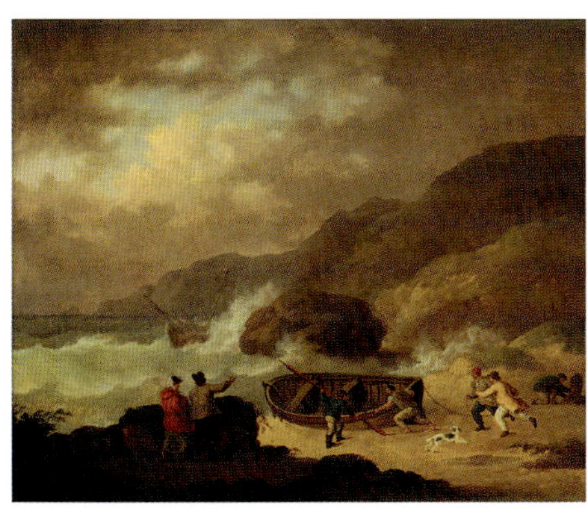

Morland, George (attributed to) 1763–1804
Storm and Wreck
oil on canvas 50.8 x 61
361

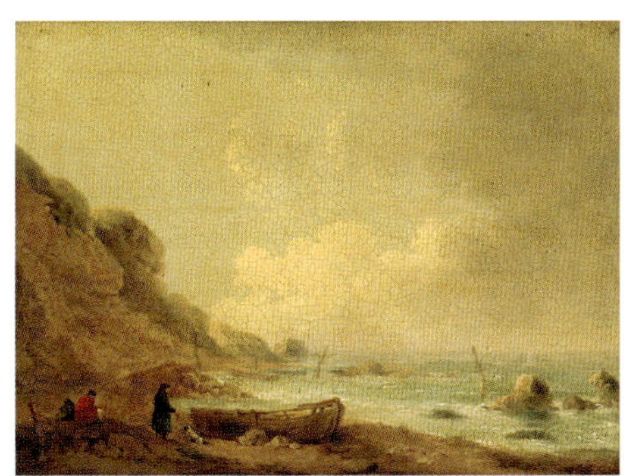

Morland, George (style of) 1763–1804
Sea Piece
oil on canvas 31.8 x 41.9
434

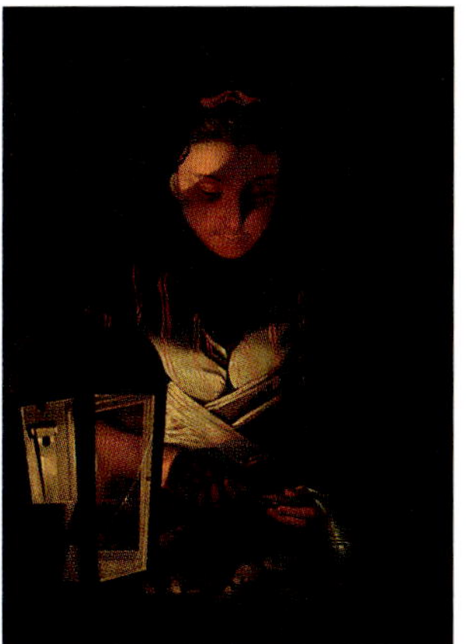

Morland, Henry Robert c.1716–1797
The Oyster Seller c.1769–1783
oil on metal 33.4 x 24.9
238

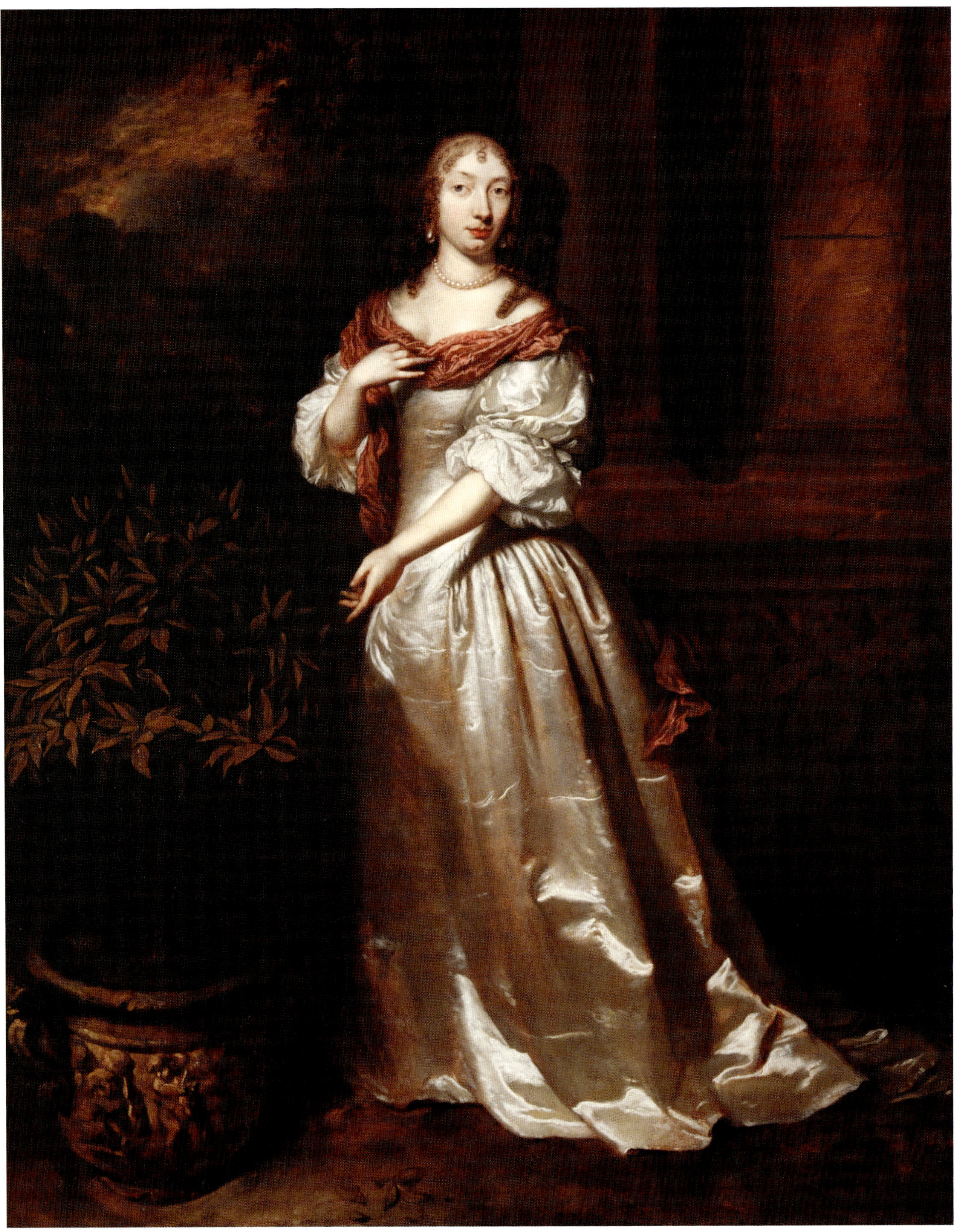

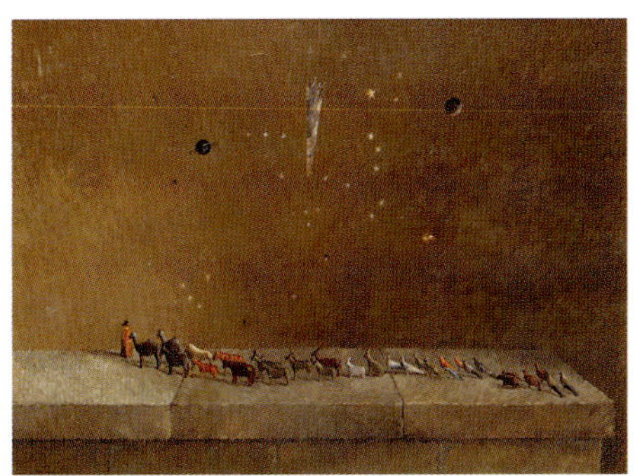

Morley, John b.1942
Noah and the Animals 1976
oil on canvas 45.7 x 59.7
3471

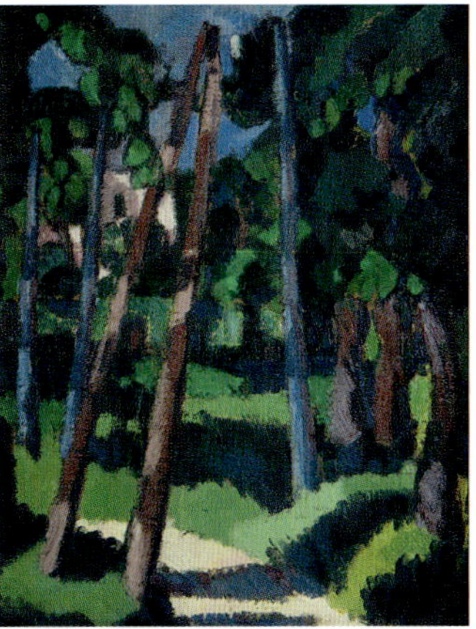

Morris, Margaret 1891–1980
Near Dieppe
oil on board 35.6 x 27.9
2332

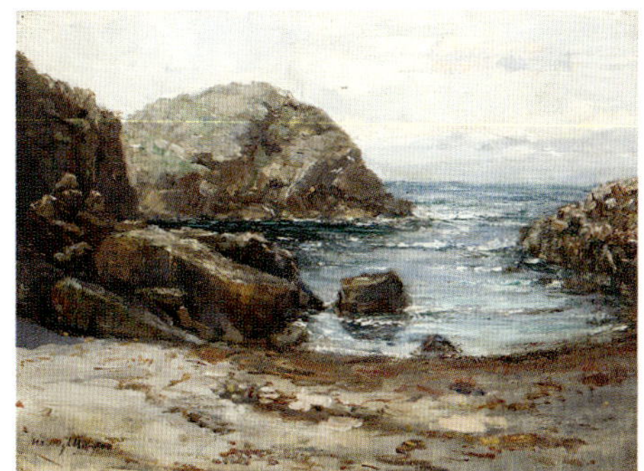

Morris, May active 1893–1950
Rocky Cove
oil on canvas 45.7 x 61
2875

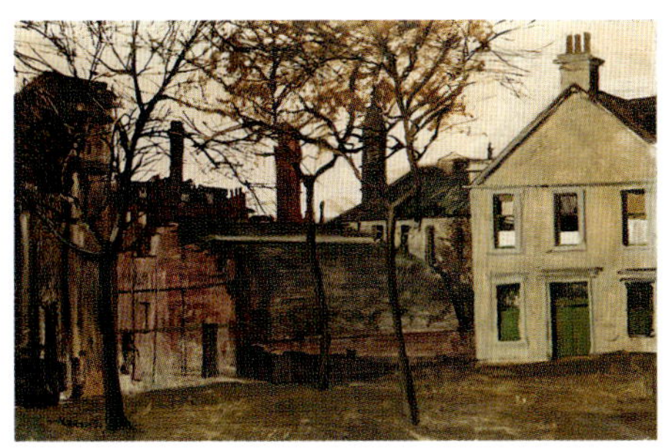

Morrison, James b.1932
Camp Coffee Works, Charlotte Street, Glasgow
1954
oil on canvas 60 x 90
PP.1983.207.2

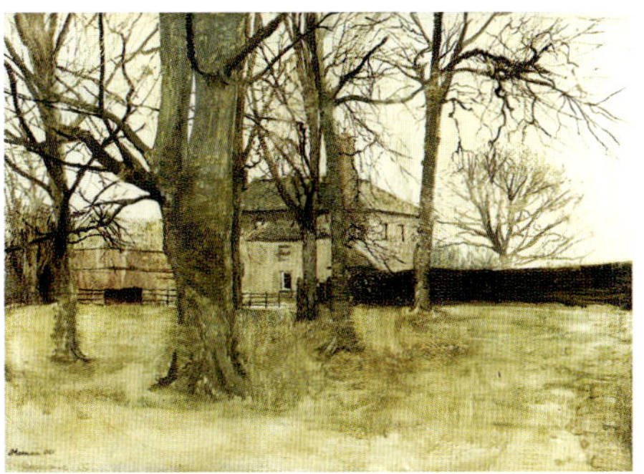

Morrison, James b.1932
Binney House c.1957
oil on canvas 91.6 x 127
3074

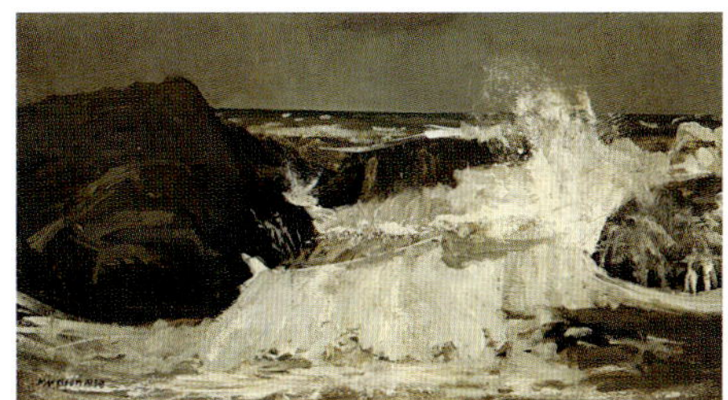

Morrison, James b.1932
Seascape I 1959
oil on board 47.6 x 86.8
3367

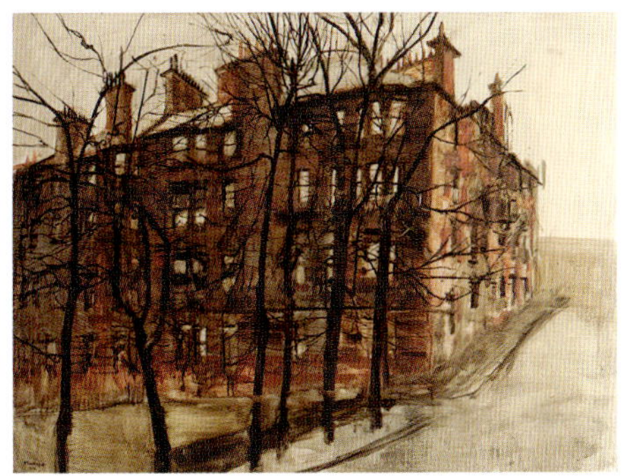

Morrison, James b.1932
Apsley Street, Glasgow 1960
oil on canvas 91.7 x 119.4
3152

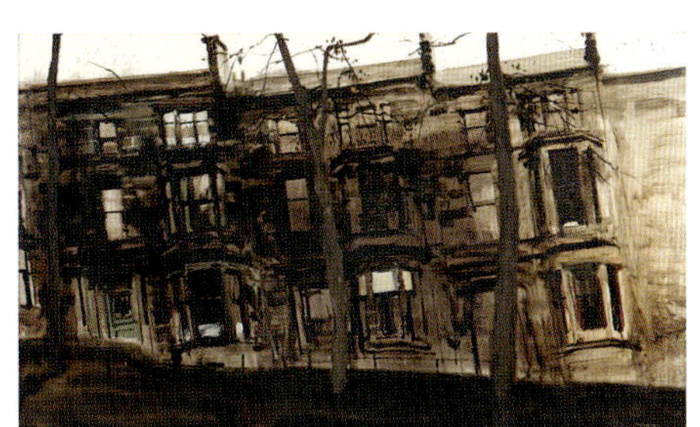

Morrison, James b.1932
Athole Gardens, Glasgow 1964
oil on canvas 91.4 x 151.8
3237

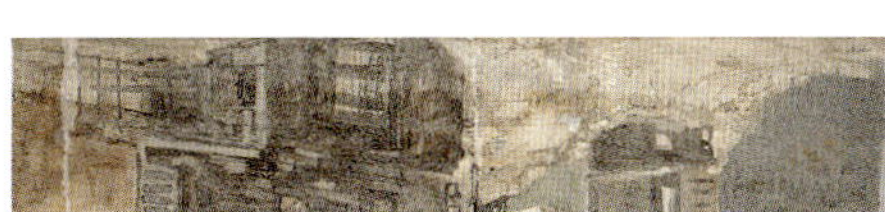

Morrison, James b.1932
Half-Demolished Tenements 1964
oil on canvas 31.7 x 153.6
NR.155

Facing page: Netscher, Caspar, 1639–1684, *Portrait of a Young Woman by an Orange Tree,* 1668 (p. 325)

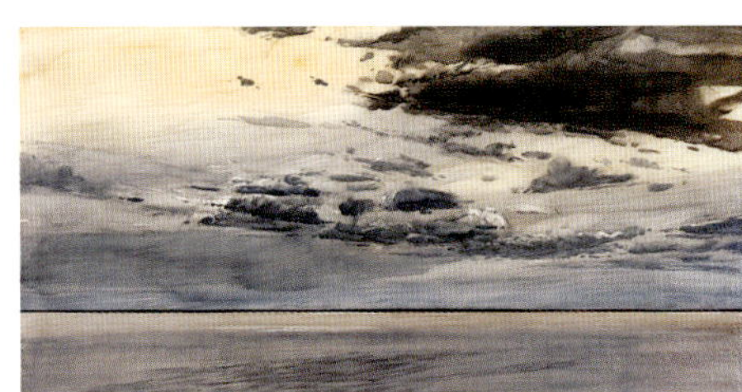

Morrison, James b.1932
Edge of the Storm, Turtle Lake 1987
oil on board 121 x 243
3456

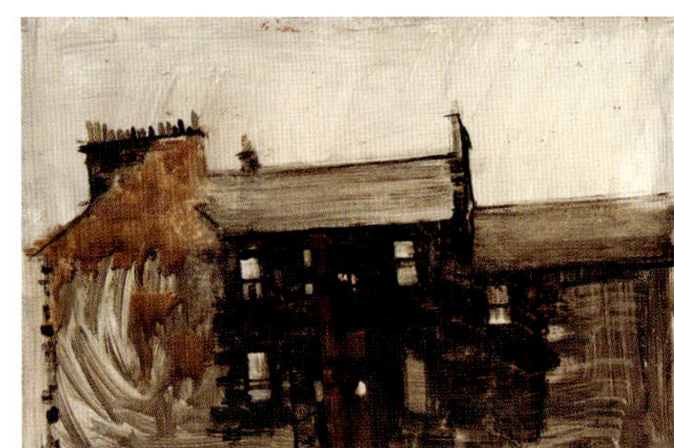

Morrison, James b.1932
Tenements
oil on hardboard 60.8 x 91.2
NR.154

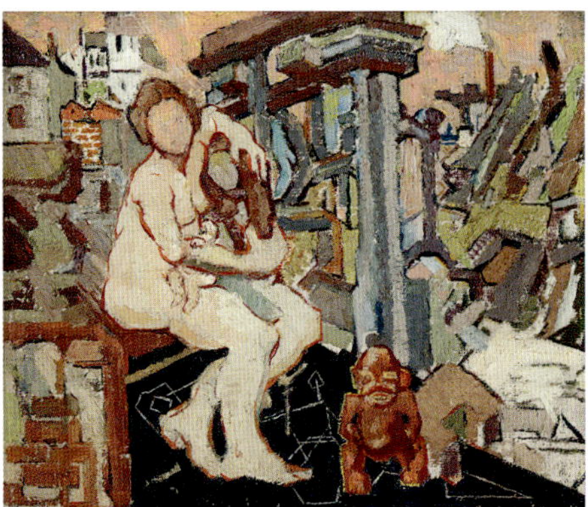

Morrison, John b.1904
Design c.1944
oil on canvas on board 45.7 x 53.3
2374

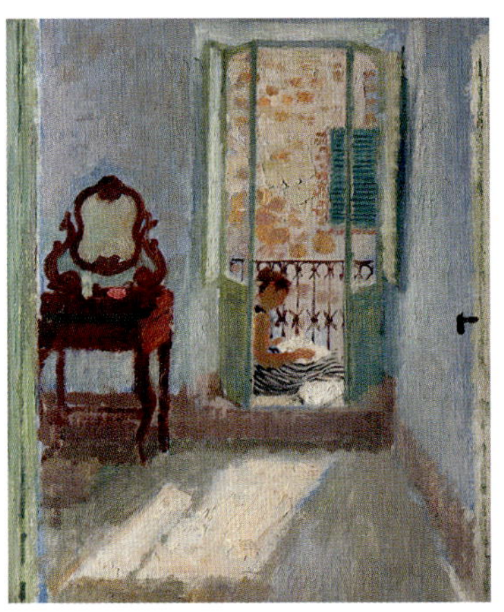

Morrocco, Alberto 1917–1998
The Blue Bedroom 1954
oil on plywood 56.1 x 46
3080

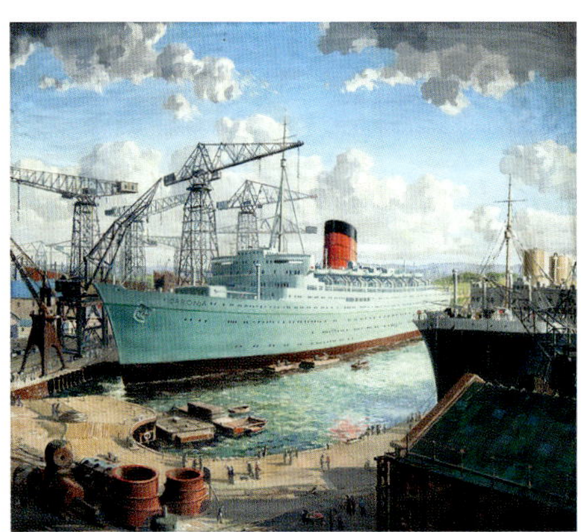

Morton, Cavendish b.1911
TSS 'Caronia' Fitting Out at Clydebank
c.1948
oil on canvas 53.8 x 57.8
T.1973.10.ac

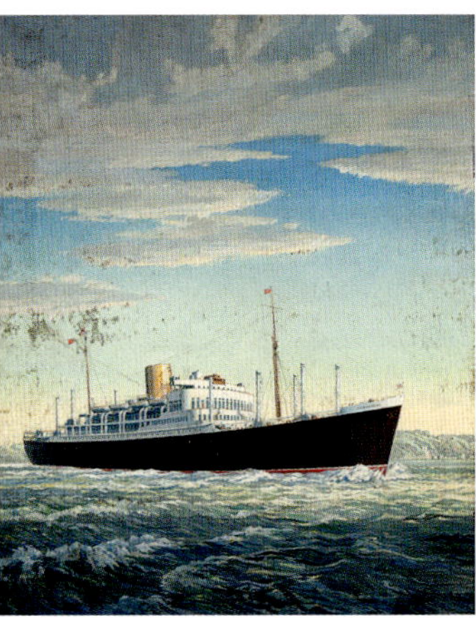

Morton, Cavendish b.1911
Passenger-Cargo Motor Vessel 'Rangitane'
after 1948
oil on canvas 76.3 x 61.1
T.1973.10.aa

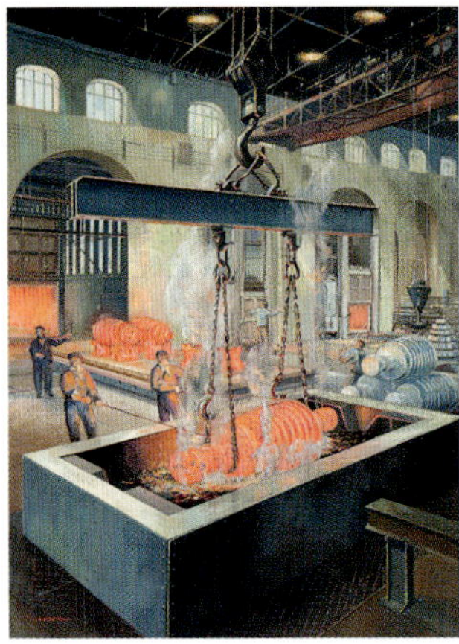

Morton, Cavendish b.1911
*Rotors Being Hardened, Beardmore Forge,
Glasgow* c.1950
oil on board 66.1 x 48.1
PP.1991.21.3

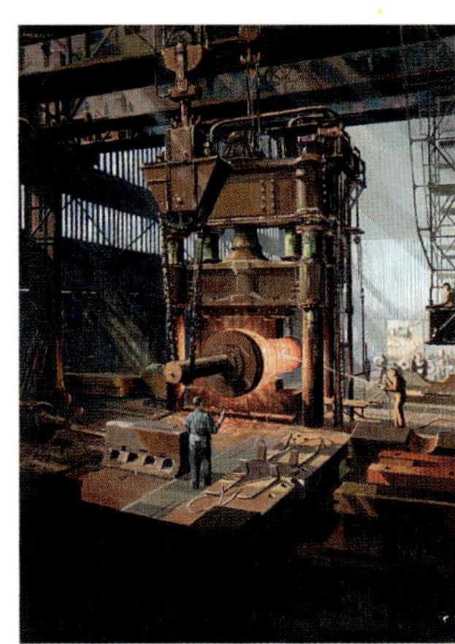

Morton, Cavendish b.1911
*Steam Hammer and Ingot, Beardmore Forge,
Glasgow* c.1950
oil on board 65.6 x 47
PP.1991.21.2

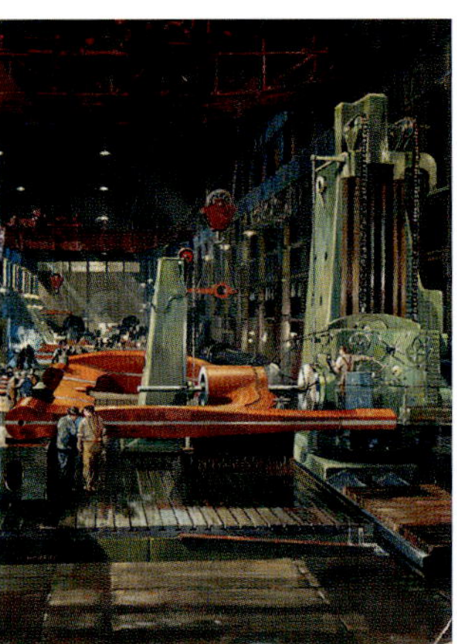

Morton, Cavendish b.1911
*Stern Iron Being Bored, Beardmore Forge,
Glasgow* c.1950
oil on board 63.5 x 45.7
PP.1991.21.1

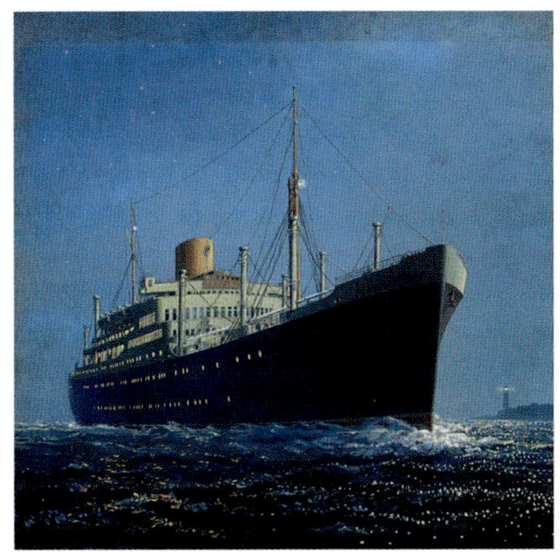

Morton, Cavendish b.1911
Passenger-Cargo Motor Vessel 'Ruahine'
after 1950
oil on panel 60.6 x 58.8
T.1973.10.ab

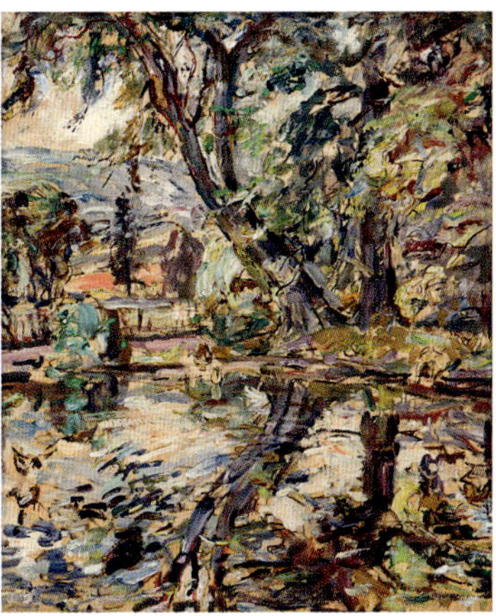

Morton, Robert Harold 1893–1965
St Thomas's Well c.1948
oil on panel 61 x 50.8
2778

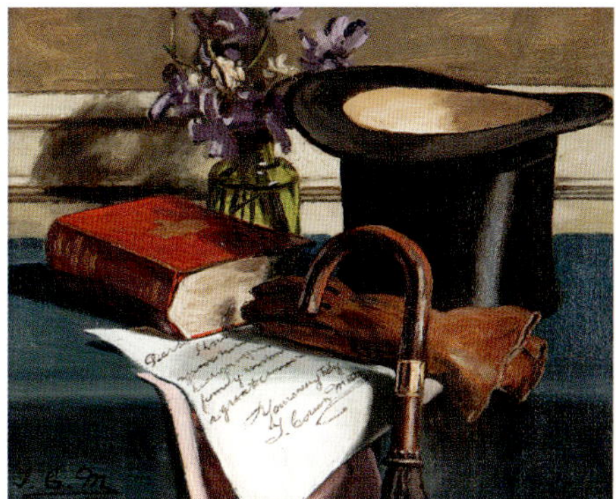

Morton, Thomas Corsan 1859–1928
Souvenir de Manet c.1900–1920
oil on canvas 40.6 x 50.8
1798

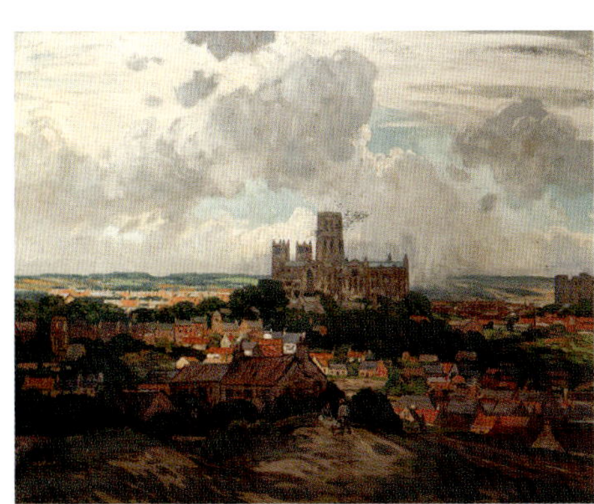

Morton, Thomas Corsan 1859–1928
A Cathedral City, Durham
oil on canvas 83.8 x 101.6
1774

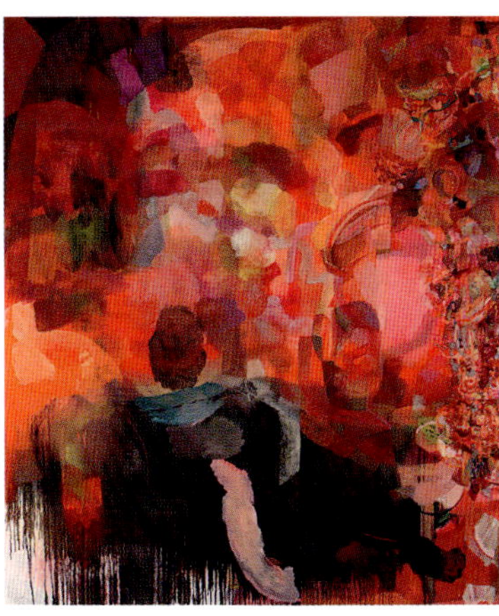

Morton, Victoria b.1971
Compartments for Isis (diptych, left
panel) 2007
oil on canvas & metal stands 180 x 125
3662.a

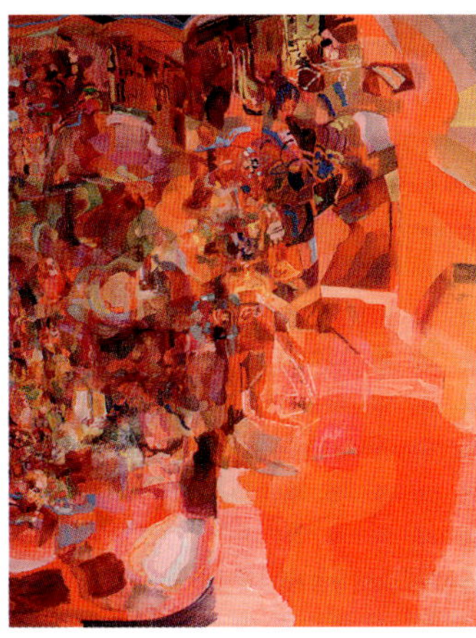

Morton, Victoria b.1971
Compartments for Isis (diptych, right
panel) 2007
oil on canvas & metal stands 180 x 125
3662.b

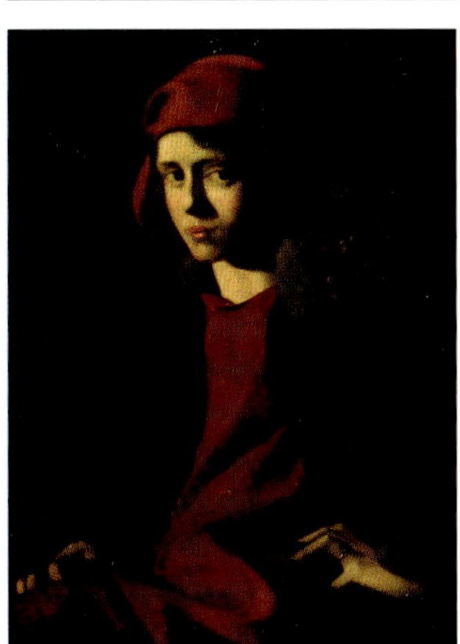

Moser, Oswald 1874–1953
Girl in Red 1930
oil on millboard 64.8 x 48.3
1812

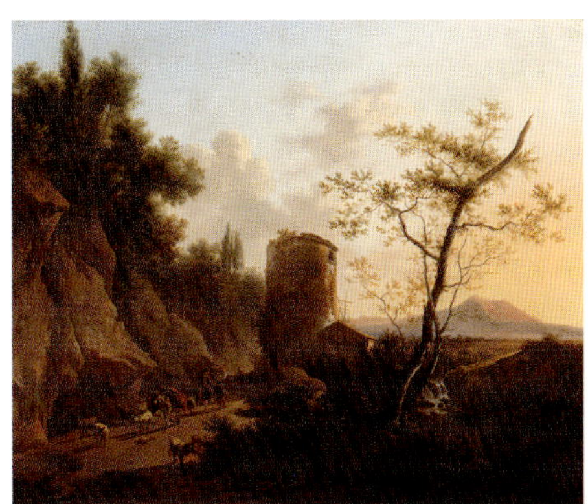

Moucheron, Frederick de 1633–1686
Landscape with a Ruined Tower and Figures
c.1660–1670
oil on panel 66 x 77.1
49

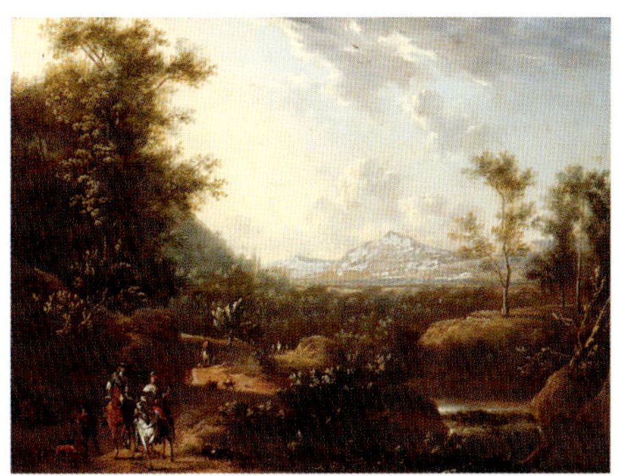

Moucheron, Frederick de (attributed to)
1633–1686
Landscape with a Hawking Party
c.1660–1686
oil on panel 30.5 x 59.3
23

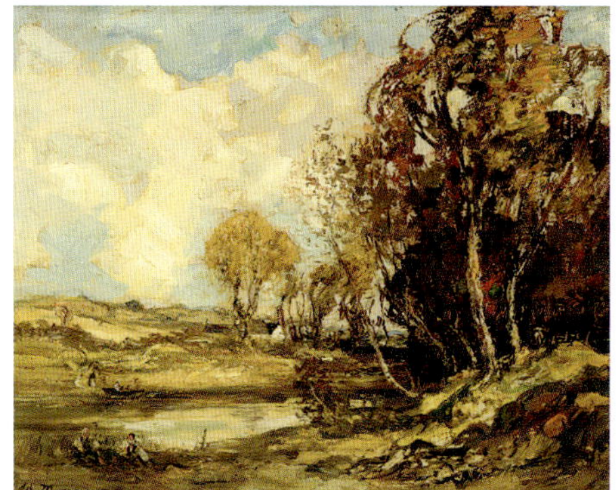

Mouncey, William 1852–1901
Autumn in Galloway
oil on canvas 50.2 x 61
3140

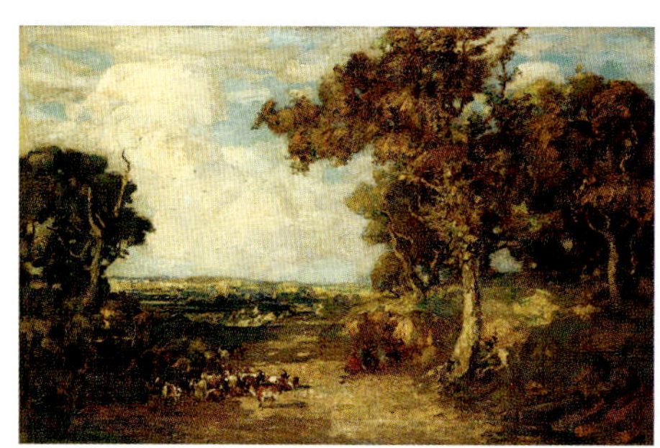

Mouncey, William 1852–1901
Kirkcudbrightshire Landscape
oil on canvas 100.3 x 148.6
2131

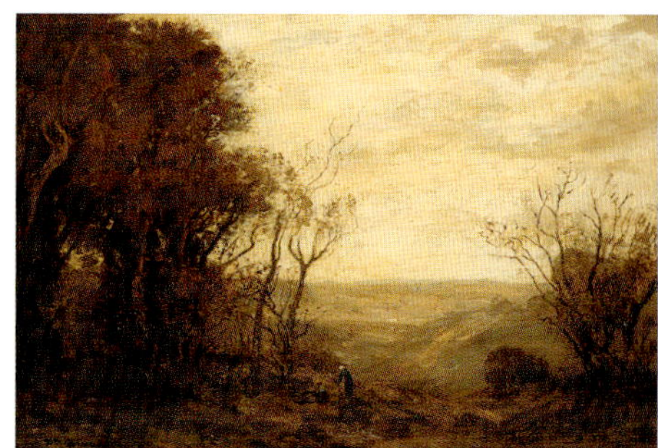

Mouncey, William 1852–1901
Landscape
oil on canvas 91.4 x 127
2279

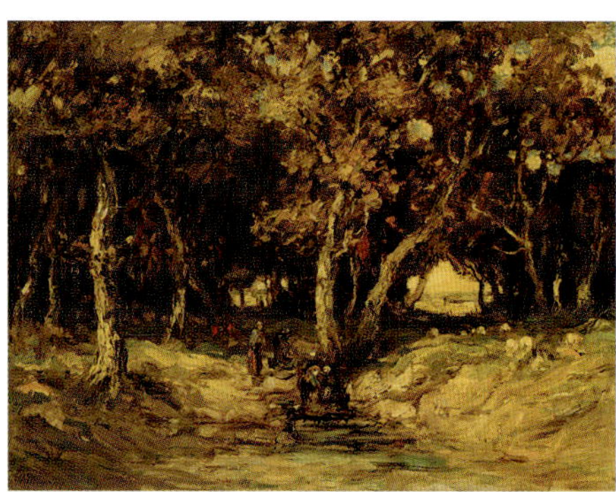

Mouncey, William 1852–1901
Wooded Landscape
oil on canvas 71.1 x 91.4
1894

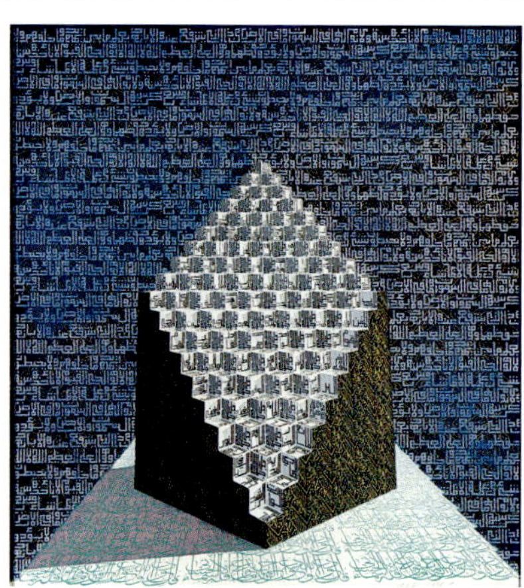

Moustafa, Ahmed b.1943
The Attributes of Divine Perception c.1994
oil & watercolour on paper 129 x 115
3535

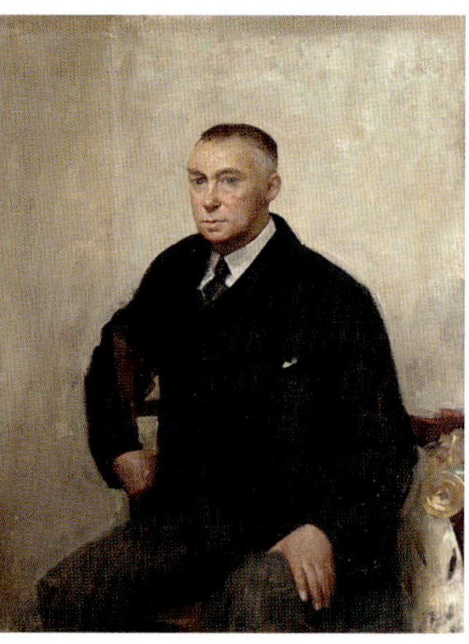

Moynihan, Rodrigo 1910–1990
Sir Garnet Wilson (1885–1975)
oil on canvas 121.9 x 91.4
2840

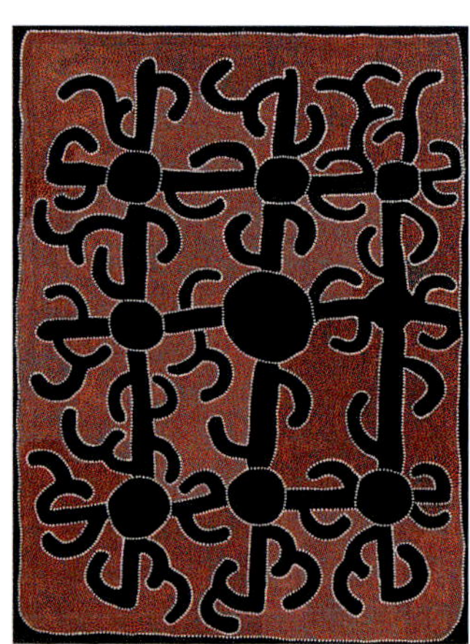

Mpetyane, Lindsay Bird b.1935
Anarkakula 1993
acrylic on canvas 132 x 91.4
3521

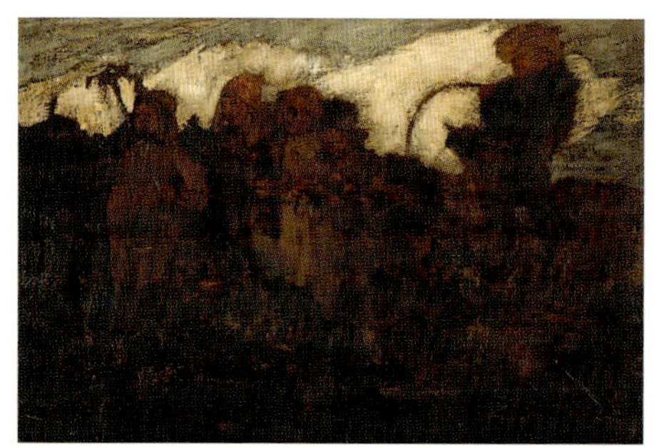

Muhrmann, Henry 1854–1916
Maying
oil on canvas 61 x 91.4
2495

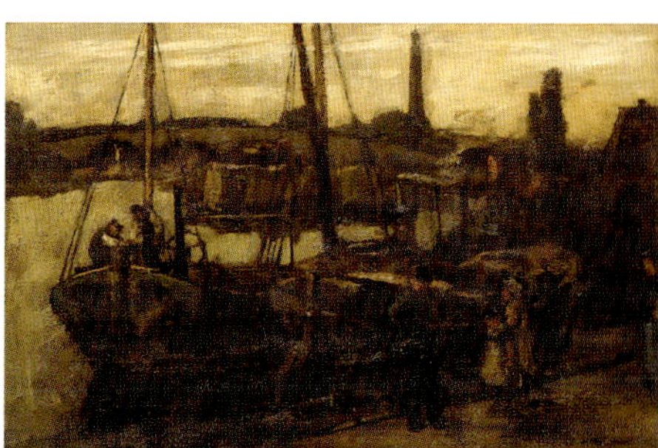

Muhrmann, Henry 1854–1916
The Thames
oil on canvas 61 x 92.7
35.576

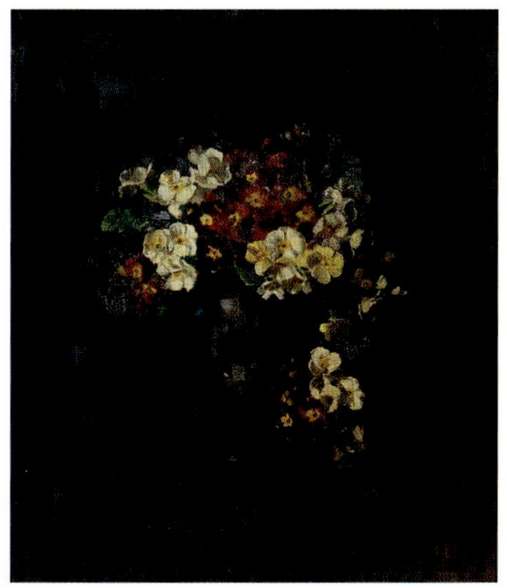

Muir, Anne Davidson 1875–1951
Primulas in a Blue and White Vase
oil on canvas 50.8 x 43.2
2872

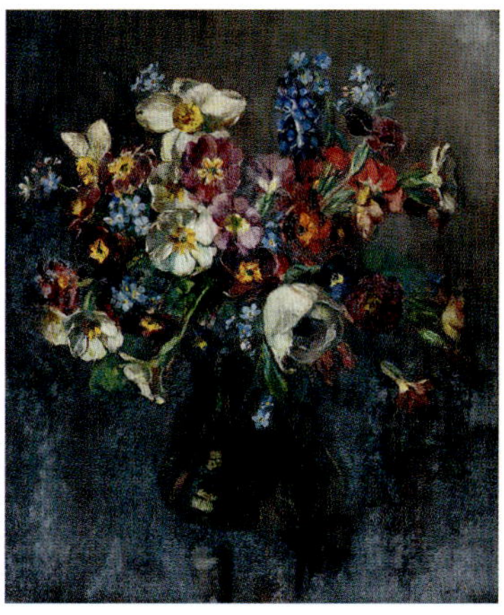

Muir, Anne Davidson 1875–1951
Spring Bouquet
oil on canvas 30.5 x 25.4
2873

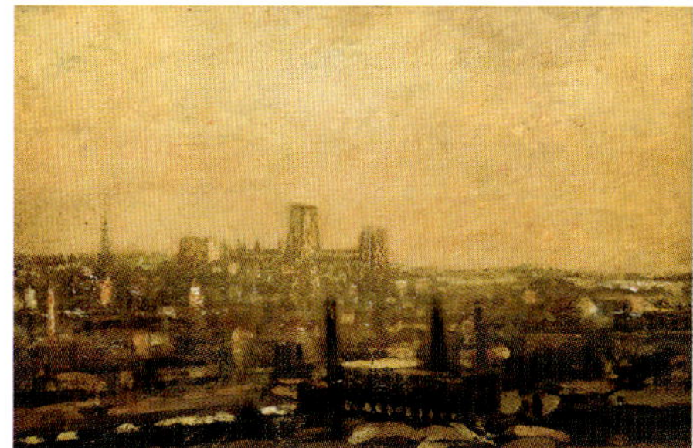

Muirhead, David 1867–1930
Durham Cathedral
oil on canvas 30.5 x 45.7
3067

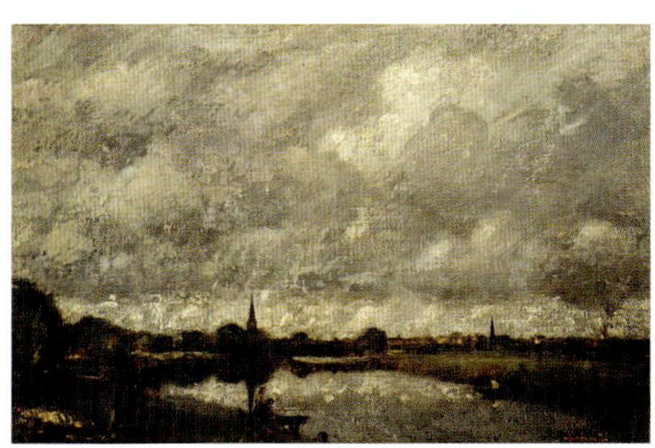

Muirhead, David 1867–1930
Landscape
oil on canvas 50.8 x 76.2
2288

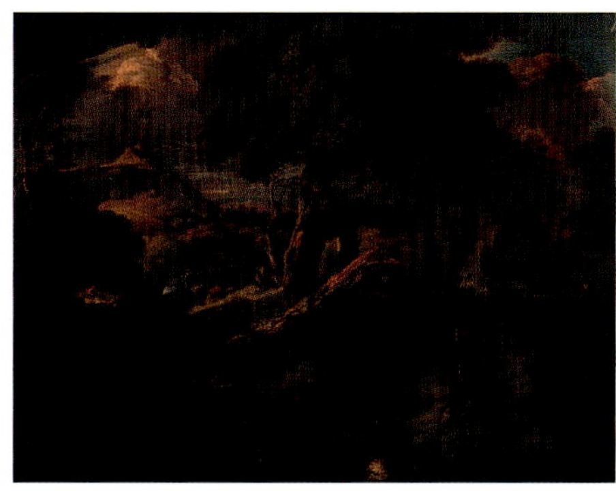

Mulier, Pieter the younger (attributed to)
c.1637–1701
Stormy Landscape with a Fallen Tree
oil on canvas 97.3 x 123.5
306

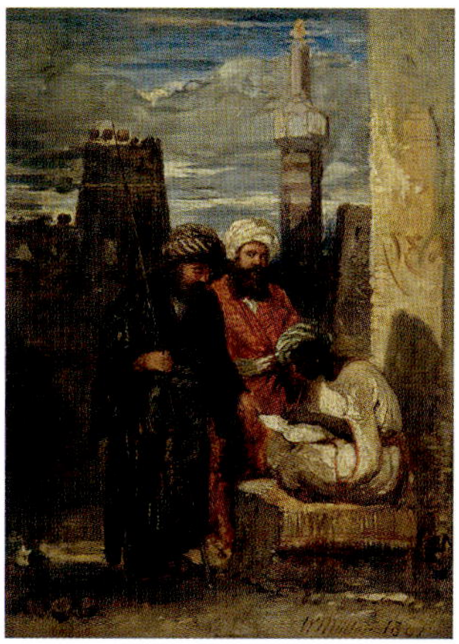

Muller, William James 1812–1845
Eastern Letter Writer 1841
oil on canvas 31.8 x 24.1
1139

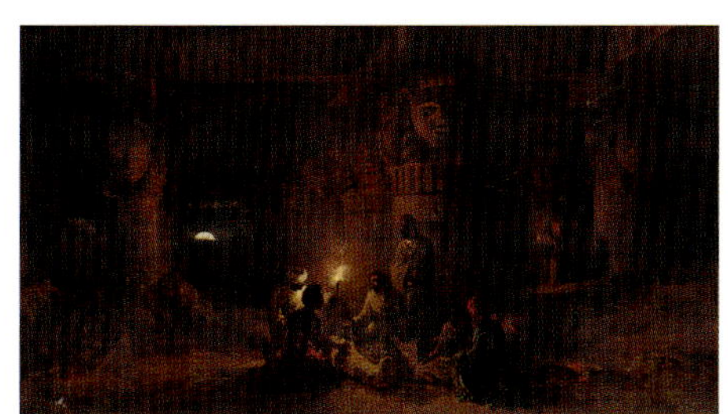

Muller, William James 1812–1845
The Treasure Finders 1843
oil on canvas 74.9 x 135.9
1212

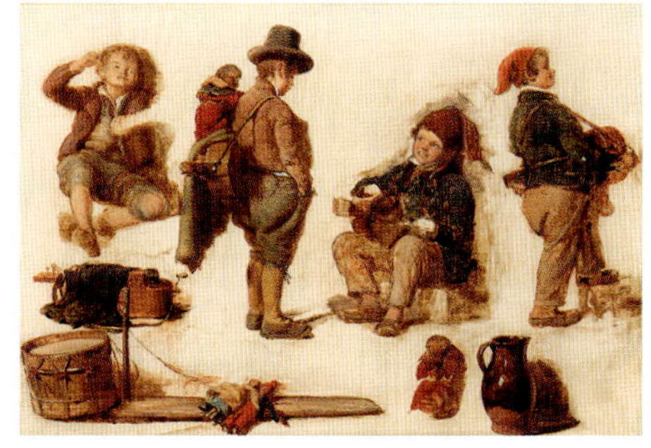

Mulready, William (attributed to)
1786–1863
*Studies of Italian Organ Boys and Their
Monkeys*
oil on canvas 46.3 x 64.7
3328

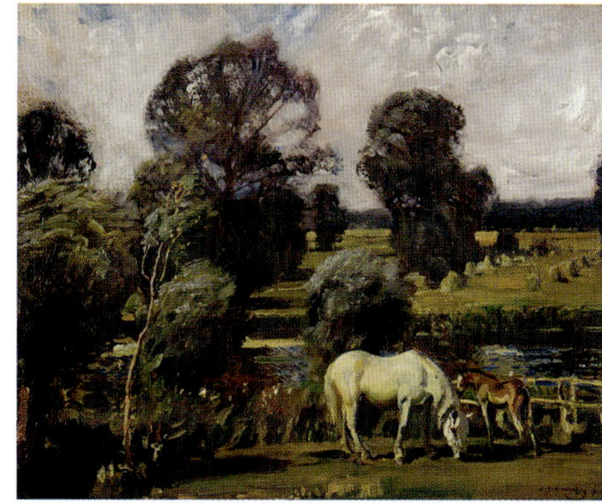

Munnings, Alfred James 1878–1959
By the River: A Mare and a Foal 1912
oil on canvas 51.1 x 61.4
3641

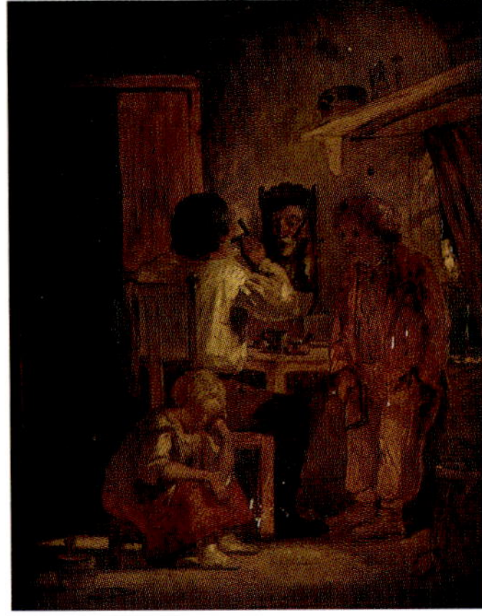

Munro, Daniel active 1846–1873
The Shaving Lesson
oil on panel 27.9 x 22.9
387

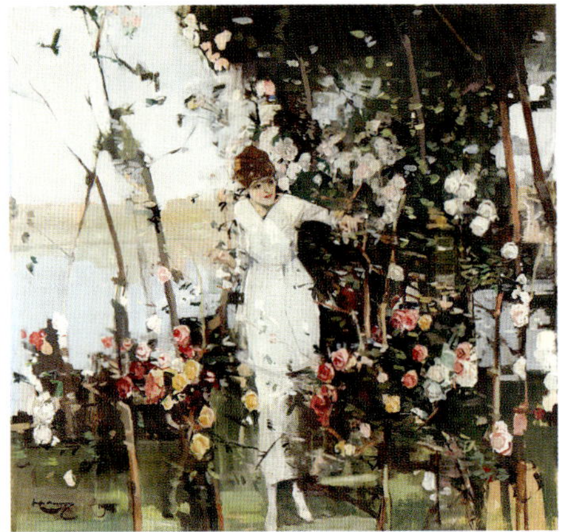

Munro, Hugh 1873–1939
Roses and My Morning Walk 1919
oil on canvas 86.4 x 86.4
1472

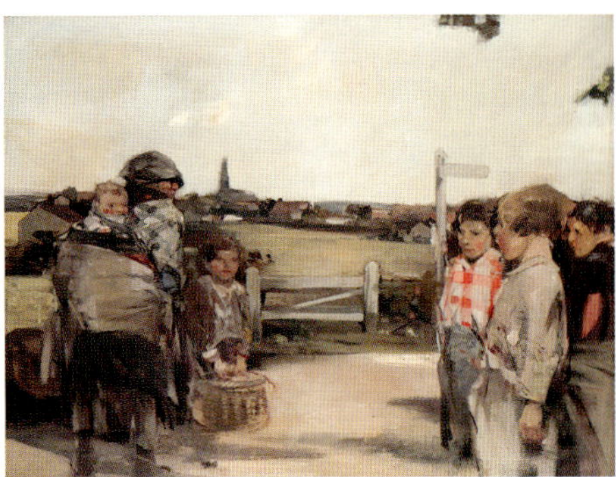

Munro, Hugh 1873–1939
The Stranger c.1931
oil on canvas 99.1 x 127
1827

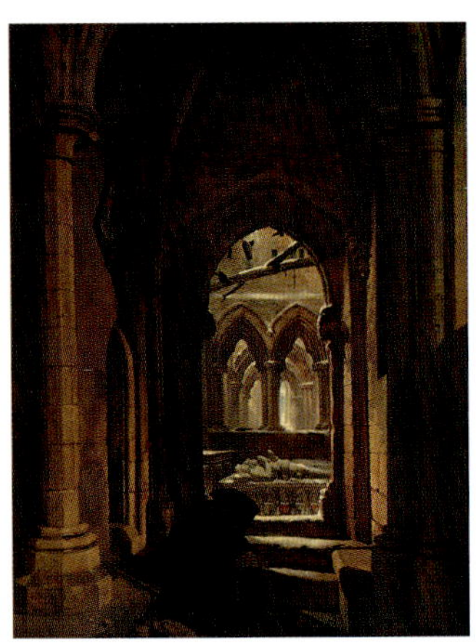

Murdoch, John S.
A Ruined Cloister 1853
oil on canvas 76.2 x 57.8
NR.137

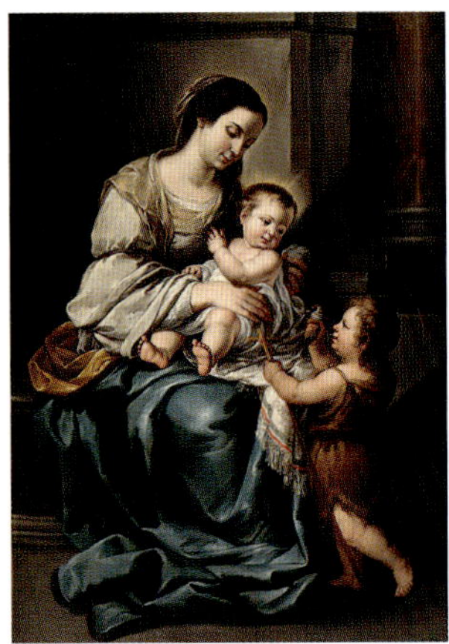

Murillo, Bartolomé Esteban 1618–1682
*Madonna and Child with Infant Saint John,
'La serrana'* 1645–1650
oil on canvas 160.7 x 109.2
PC.63

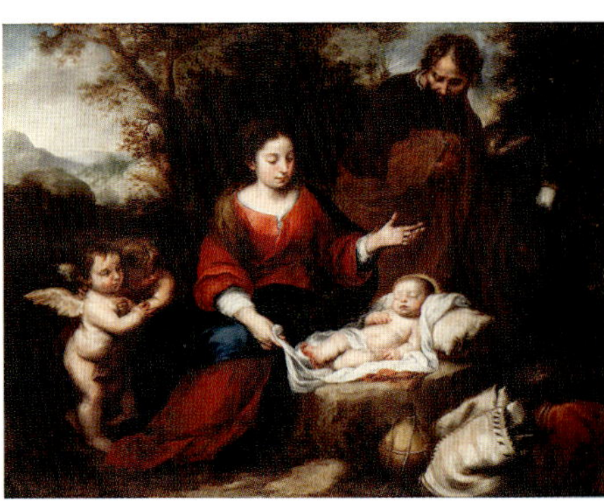

Murillo, Bartolomé Esteban (after)
1618–1682
The Rest on the Flight into Egypt c.1650–1680
oil on canvas 96.5 x 123.8
271

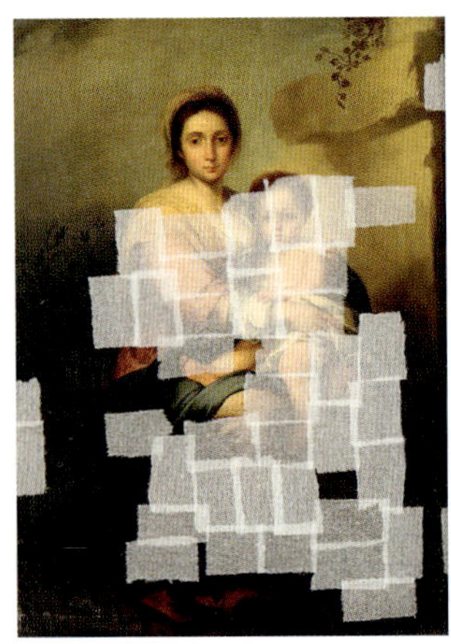

Murillo, Bartolomé Esteban (after)
1618–1682
Virgin and Child 18th C–19th C
oil on canvas 51.2 x 38.1
272

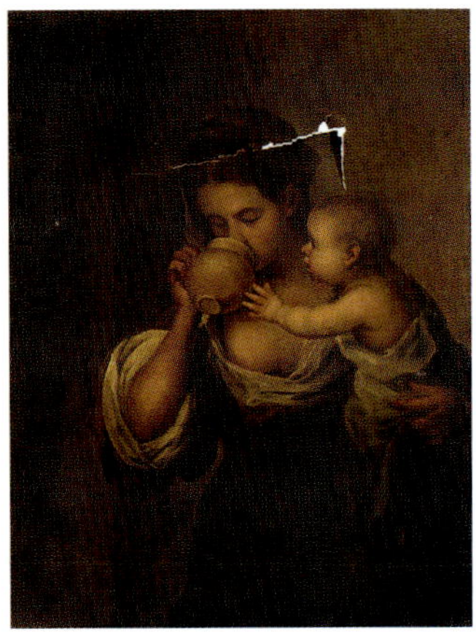

Murillo, Bartolomé Esteban (after)
1618–1682
Girl Drinking with a Child on Her Arm
oil on canvas 97.8 x 73.7
PC.140

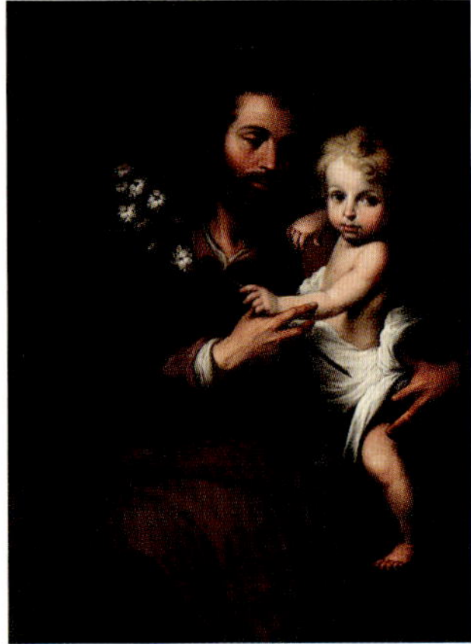

Murillo, Bartolomé Esteban (after)
1618–1682
Saint Joseph with the Infant Jesus
oil on canvas 123 x 92.7
269

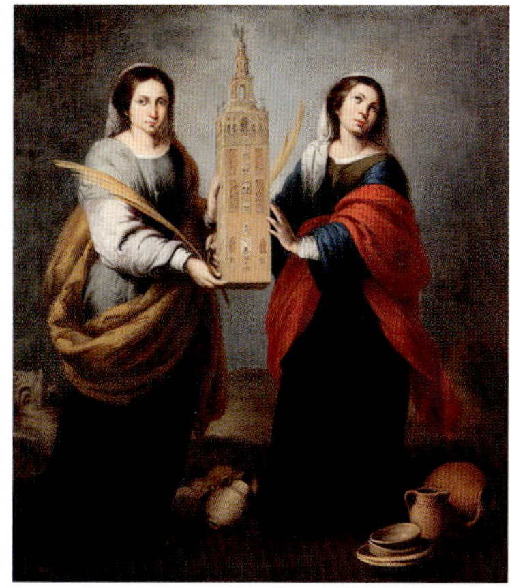

Murillo, Bartolomé Esteban (after)
1618–1682
Santa Justa and Santa Rufina
oil on canvas 65.7 x 57.2
PC.32

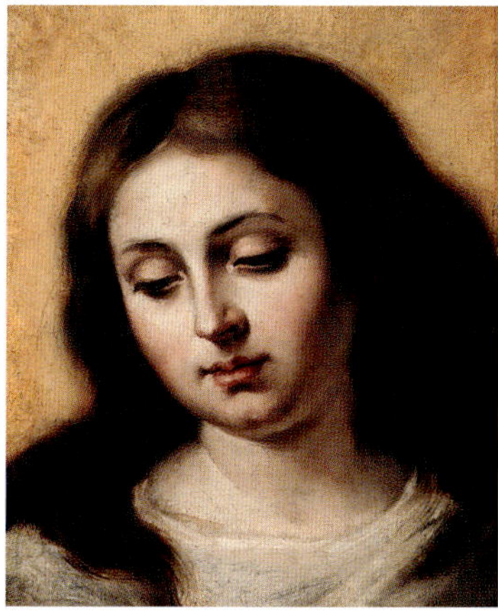

Murillo, Bartolomé Esteban (attributed to)
1618–1682
Head of the Madonna
oil on canvas 60.3 x 41.9
PC.23

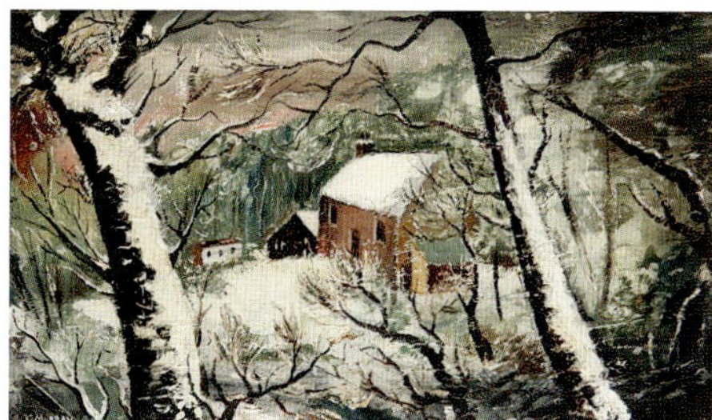

Murray, Charles 1894–1954
Winter 1949–1951
oil on board 33 x 50.8
2900

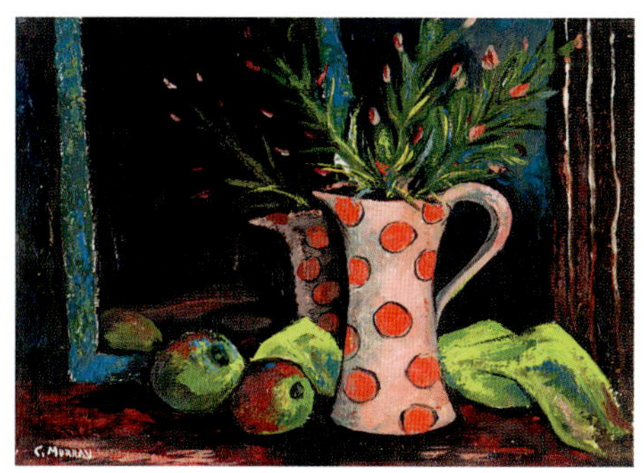

Murray, Charles 1894–1954
The Spotted Jug 1952
oil on laminated paper board 56.5 x 75.6
3203

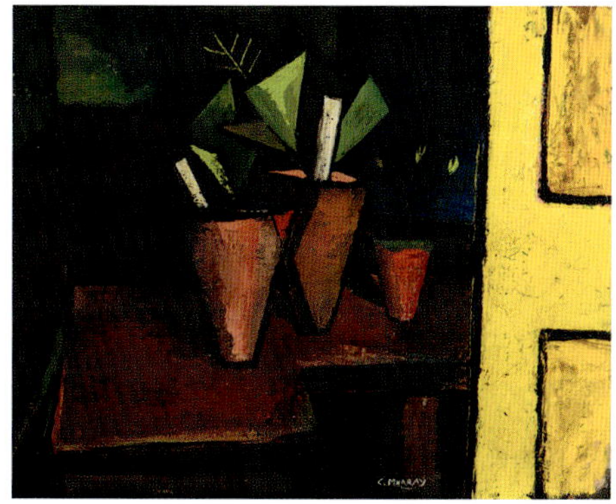

Murray, Charles 1894–1954
The Yellow Door 1952
oil on canvas 63.2 x 76
3202

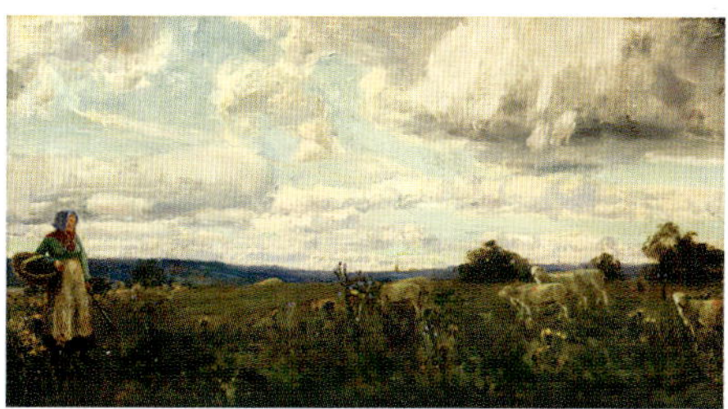

Murray, David 1849–1933
Landscape with a Figure and Sheep 1879
oil on canvas 24.1 x 44.5
816

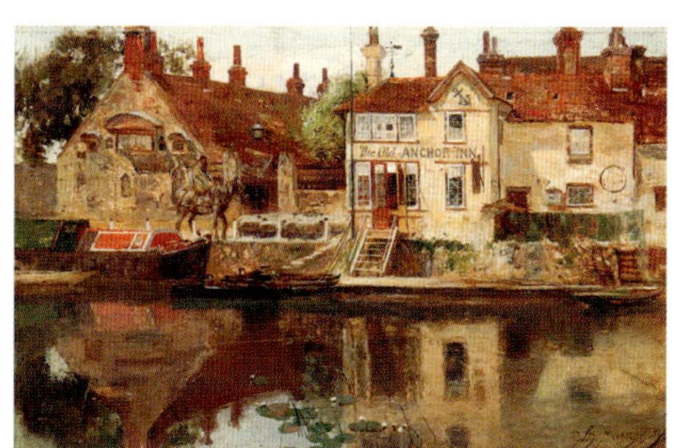

Murray, David 1849–1933
The 'Old Anchor' Inn 1881
oil on canvas 29.2 x 44.5
791

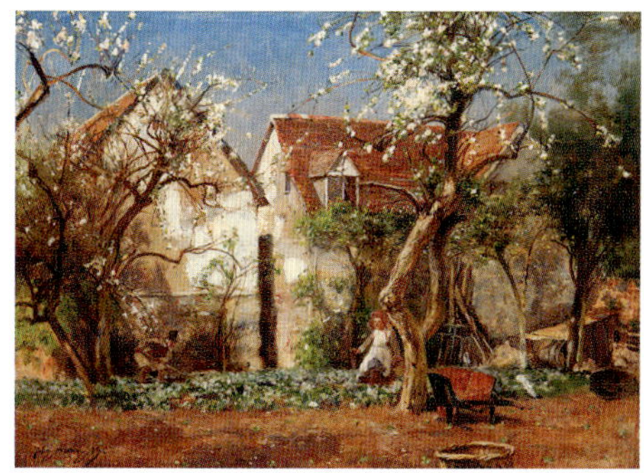

Murray, David 1849–1933
The Orchard 1883
oil on canvas 44.5 x 59.7
786

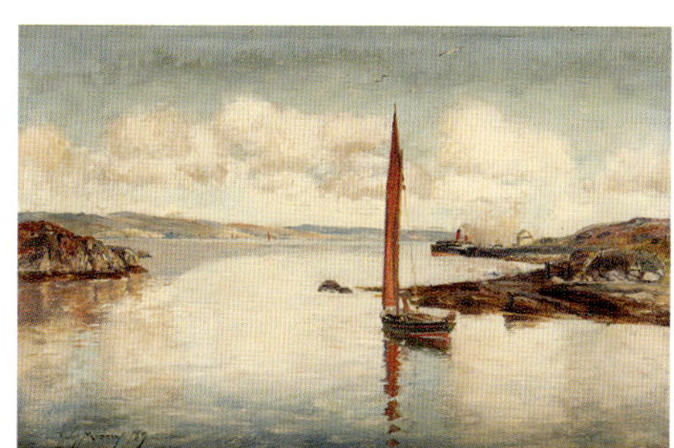

Murray, David 1849–1933
Tarbert, Loch Fyne 1887
oil on canvas 29.2 x 44.5
801

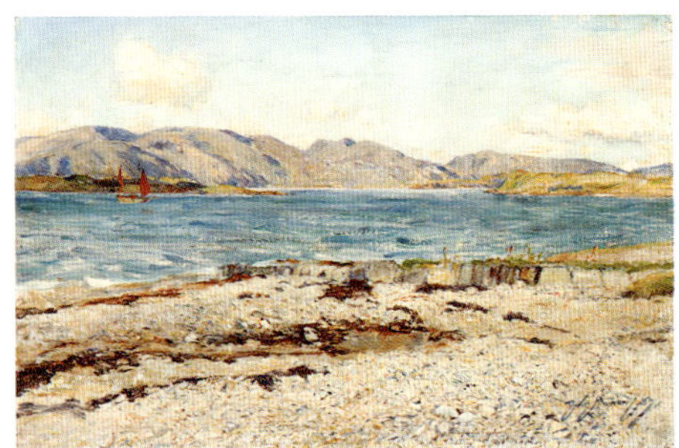

Murray, David 1849–1933
A Highland Loch 1889
oil on canvas 29.2 x 45.7
767

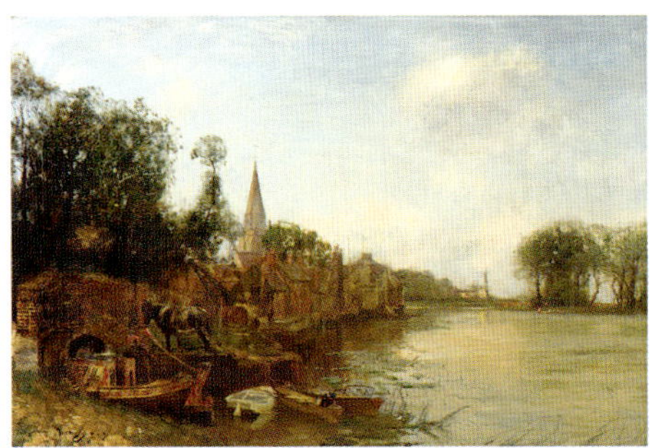

Murray, David 1849–1933
Abingdon-on-Thames 1889–1890
oil on canvas 59.7 x 90.2
869

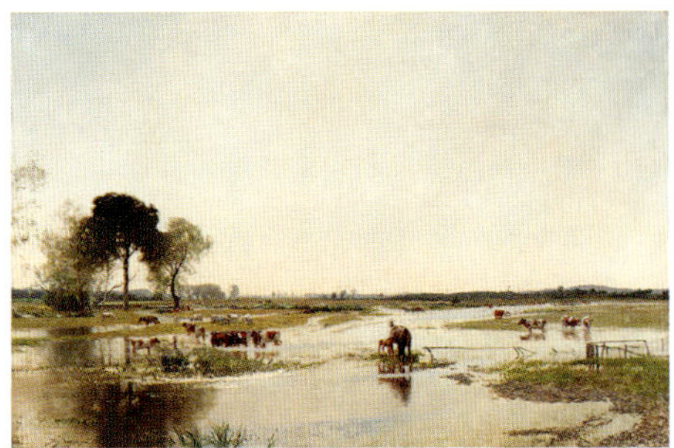

Murray, David 1849–1933
The White Heat 1892
oil on canvas 120.7 x 182.9
1324

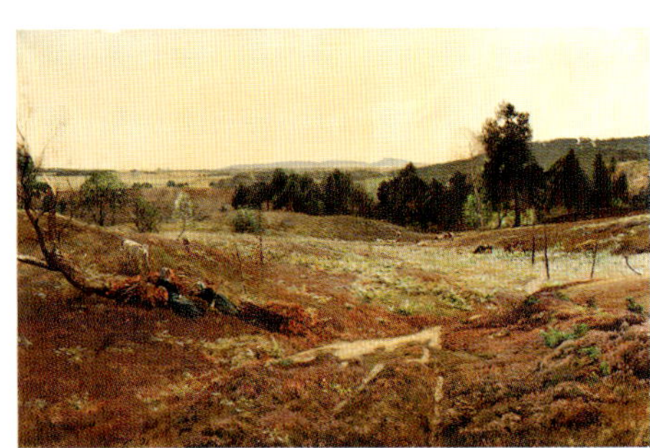

Murray, David 1849–1933
Fir Faggots: A Hampshire Landscape 1893
oil on canvas 119.4 x 181.6
714

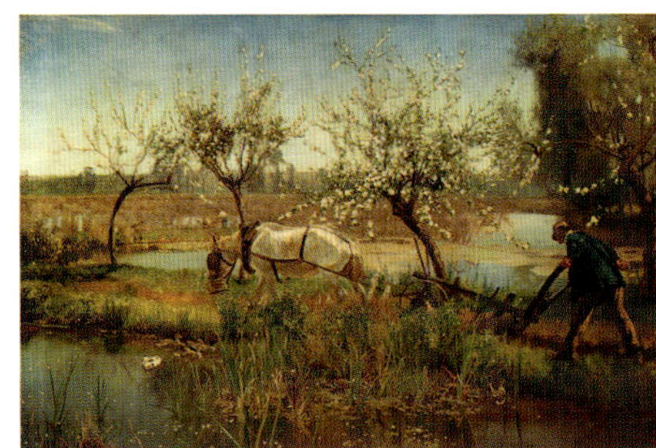

Murray, David 1849–1933
A Little Farm, Well Tilled
oil on canvas 102.9 x 153
2090

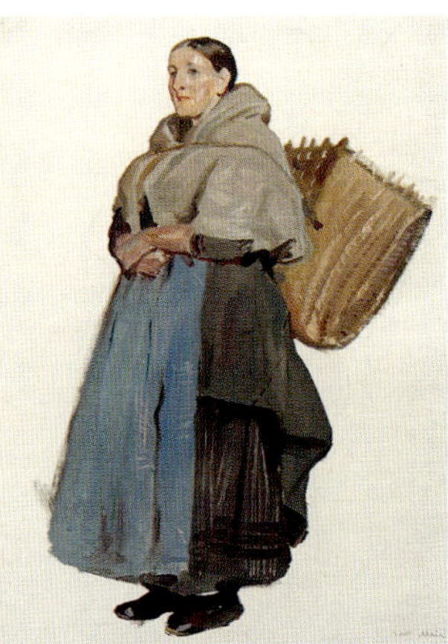

Murray, George 1875–1933
Fisherwoman, Portsoy
oil on canvas 35.6 x 26.7
1884

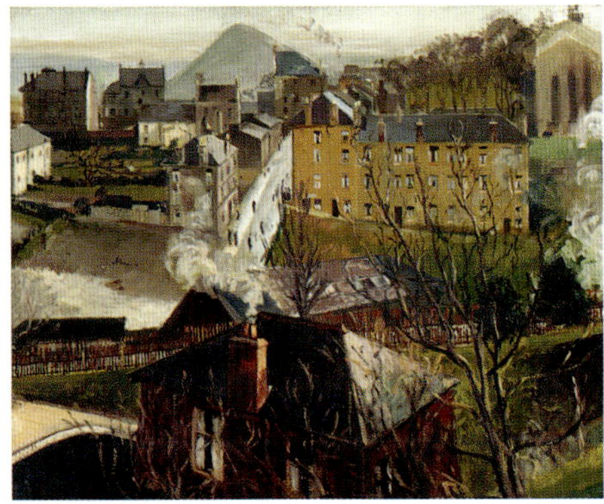

Murray, Graham 1907–1987
Kirkhill 1930
oil on canvas 61 x 76.2
3070

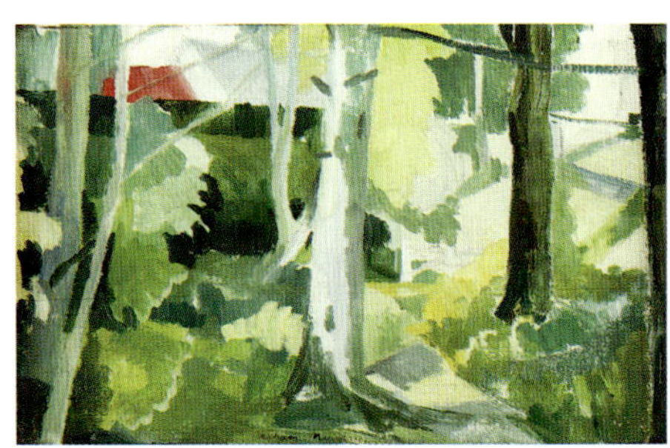

Murray, Graham 1907–1987
Liberty Wood 1932
oil on panel 26.7 x 41.9
2405

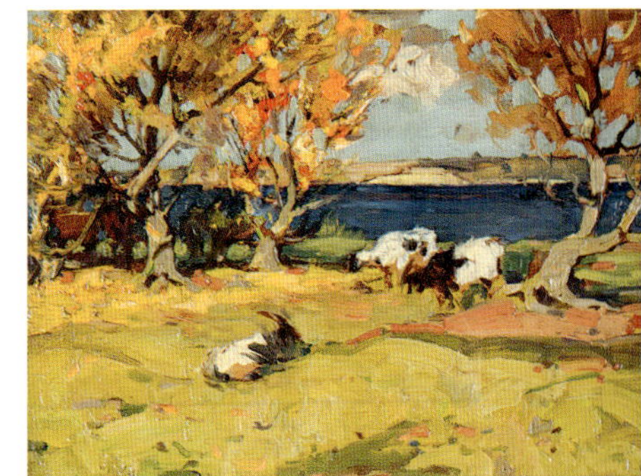

Murray, John Reid 1861–1906
Landscape with Goats c.1890–1900
oil on panel 26.7 x 34.9
3261

Facing page: Cranach the elder, Lucas, 1472–1553, *Judith with the Head of Holofernes*, 1530 (p. 92)

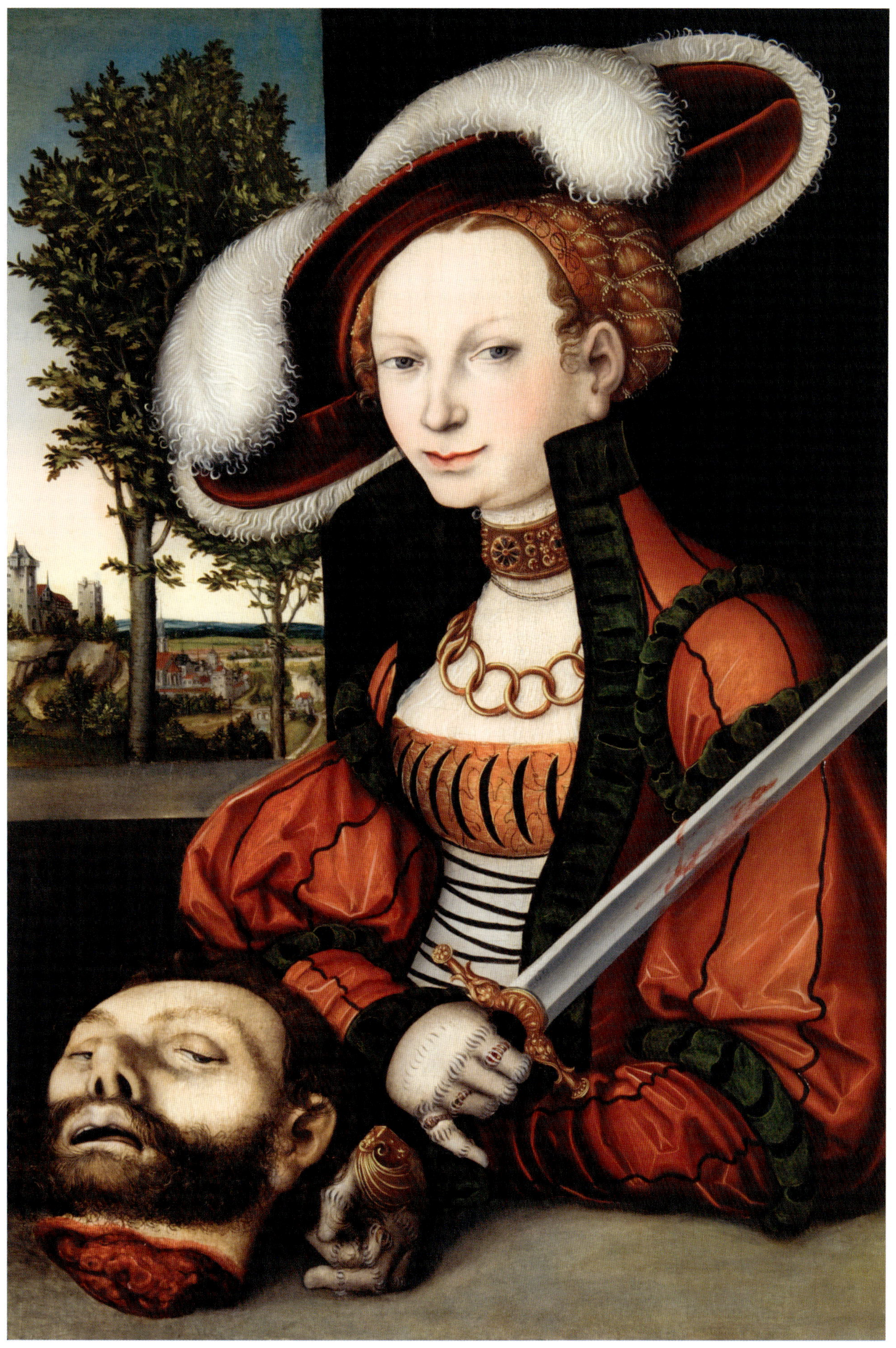

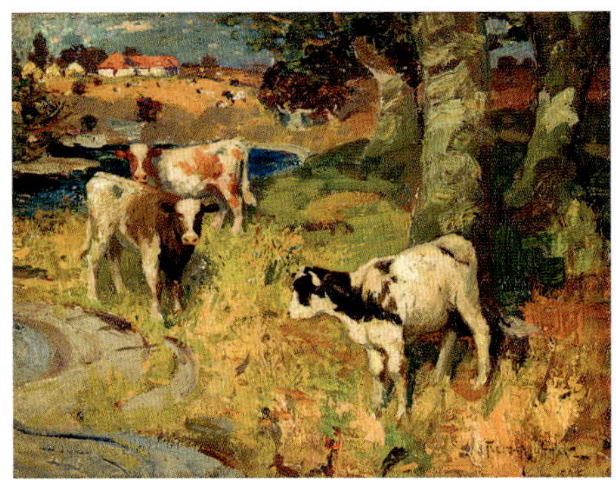

Murray, John Reid 1861–1906
Autumn 1895
oil on millboard on wood 30.8 x 40.6
3256

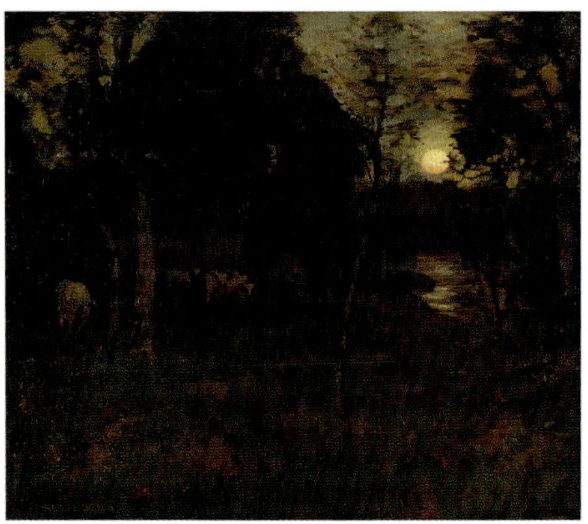

Murray, John Reid 1861–1906
Moonrise 1897
oil on canvas 88.9 x 105.4
1195

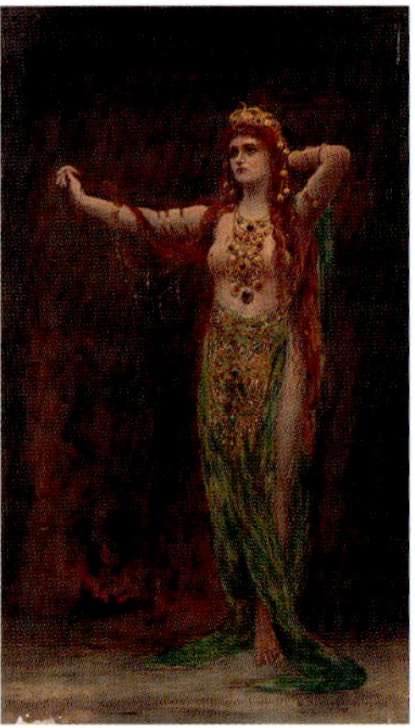

Murray-Cookesley, Margaret c.1850–1927
Circe resplendens 1913
oil on canvas 65.8 x 38.3
TEMP.19212

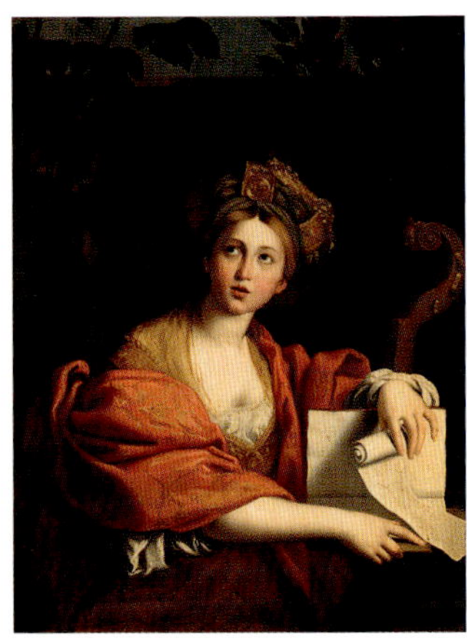

Muschi, Anna
Cumaean Sibyl (after Domenichino) 1823
oil on canvas 121 x 88.8
311

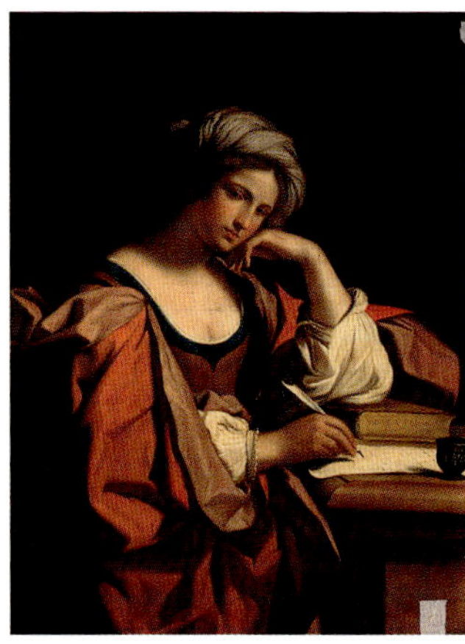

Muschi, Anna
The Persian Sibyl (after Guercino) 1823
oil on canvas 118.6 x 97.7
312

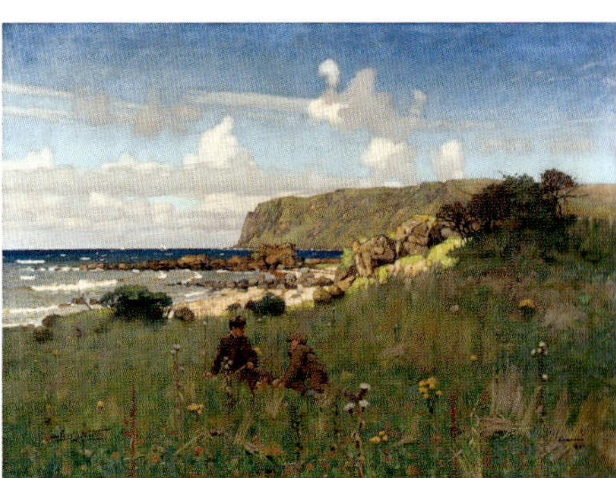

Nairn, James McLachlan 1859–1904
Kildonan 1886
oil on canvas 86.4 x 116.8
1199

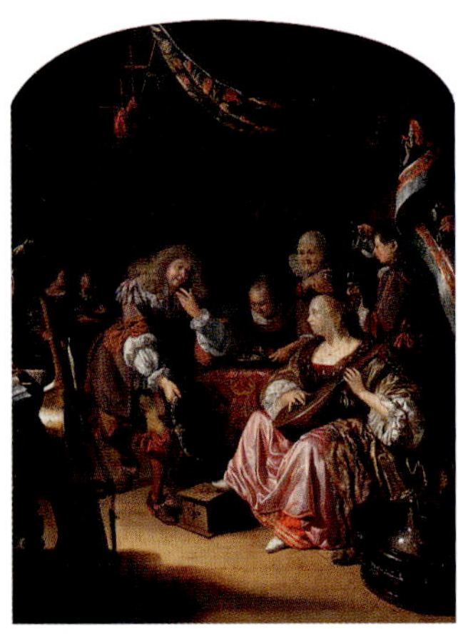

Naiveu, Matthys 1647–1726
A Brothel Scene 1672 (?)
oil on panel 51.7 x 40.3
300

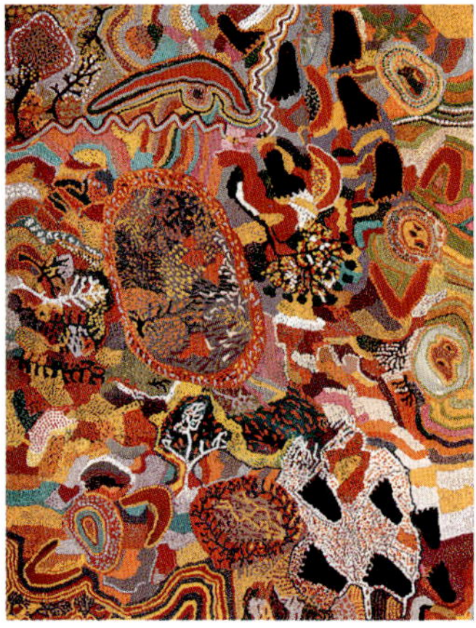

Napanangka, Marti c.1935–2003
Artist's Country 1989
acrylic on canvas 100 x 76
3522

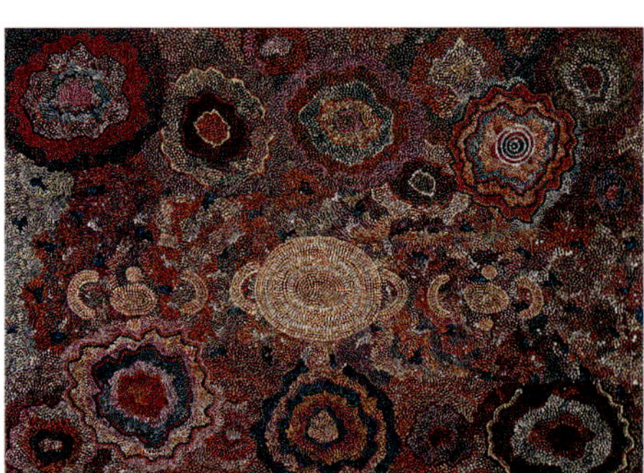

Napangati, Pansy b.c.1940
Hailstorm Dreaming 1992
acrylic on canvas 98.4 x 148.5
3536

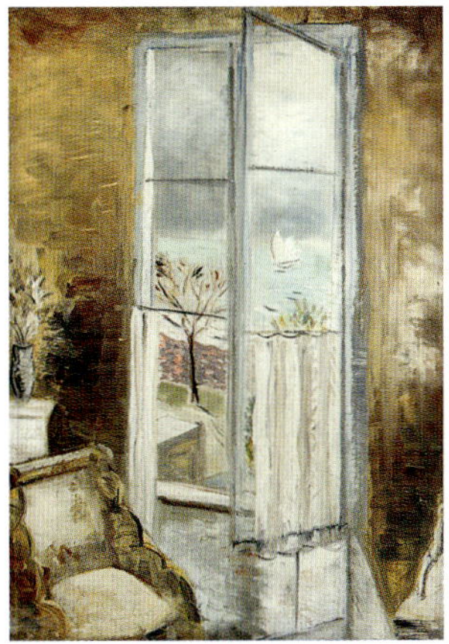

Nash, Paul 1889–1946
Through a Window, Riviera c.1927
oil on canvas 72.5 x 49.2
1821

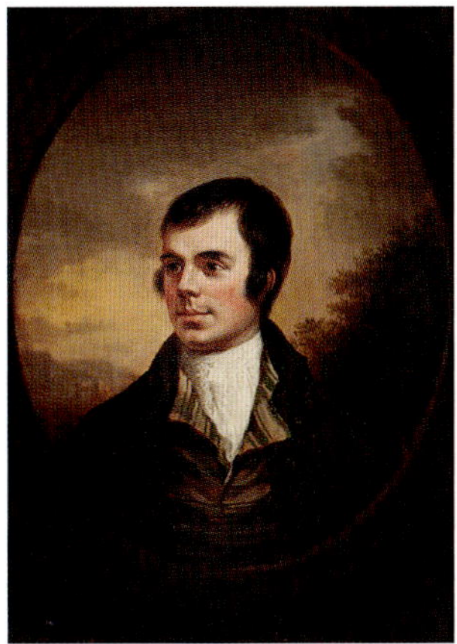

Nasmyth, Alexander 1758–1840
Robert Burns (1759–1796) c.1792–1824
oil on canvas 40.6 x 30.5
1783

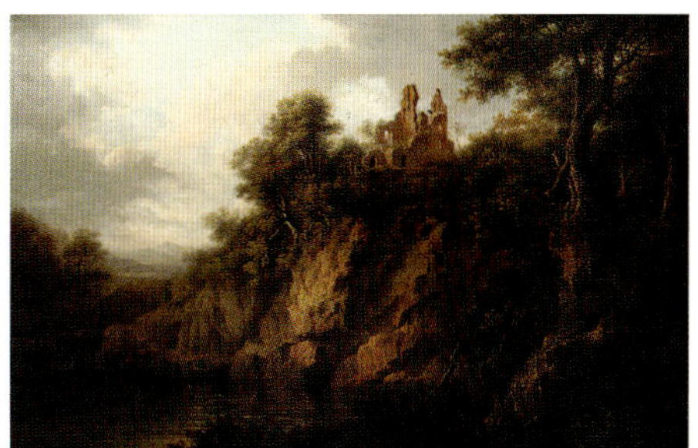

Nasmyth, Alexander 1758–1840
A Rocky Wooded Landscape with a Ruined Castle by a Loch 1817
oil on canvas 76.5 x 115.4
3121

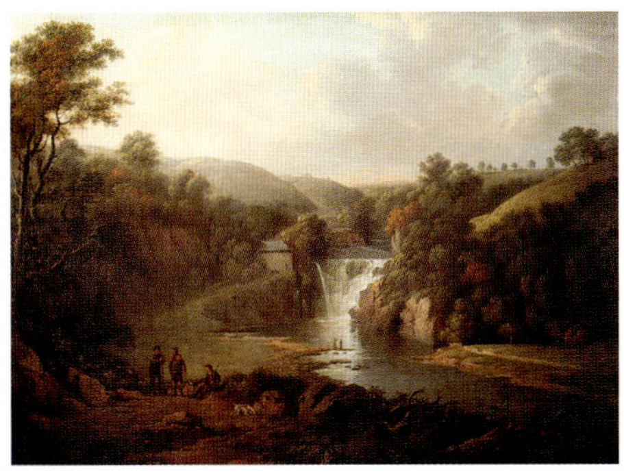

Nasmyth, Alexander 1758–1840
Falls of Clyde
oil on canvas 45 x 61
3051

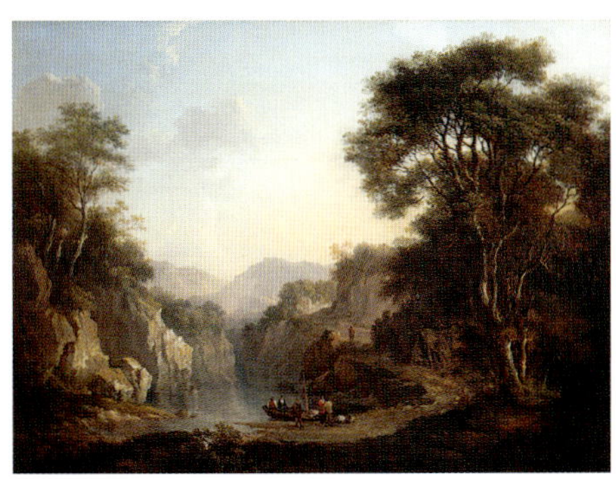

Nasmyth, Alexander 1758–1840
Highland Landscape
oil on canvas 43.2 x 58.4
PC.133

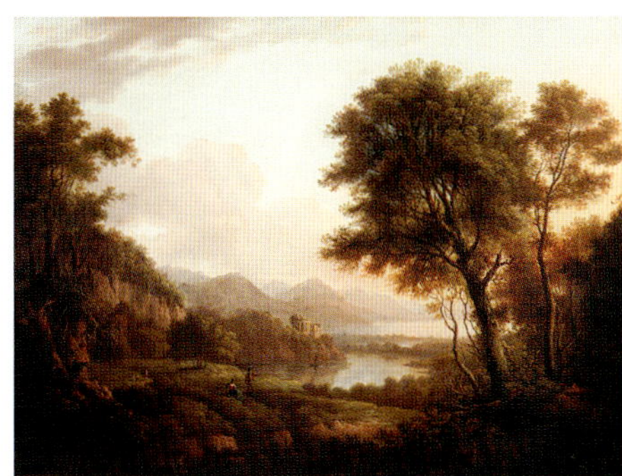

Nasmyth, Alexander 1758–1840
Landscape, Loch Katrine
oil on canvas 68.6 x 90.2
2561

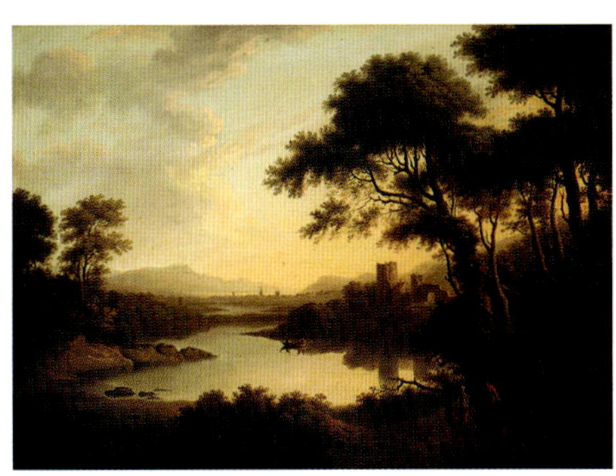

Nasmyth, Alexander (attributed to) 1758–1840
Wooded Landscape with a Castle
oil on canvas 67.3 x 87.6
265

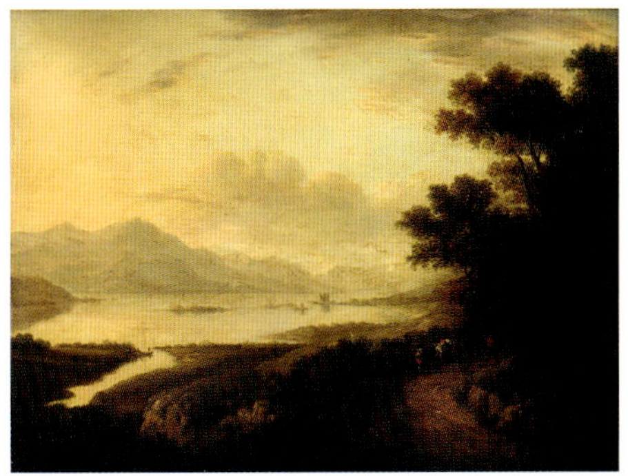

Nasmyth, Alexander (style of) 1758–1840
Landscape with a Distant Castle on a Loch
oil on canvas 50.8 x 63.4
3426

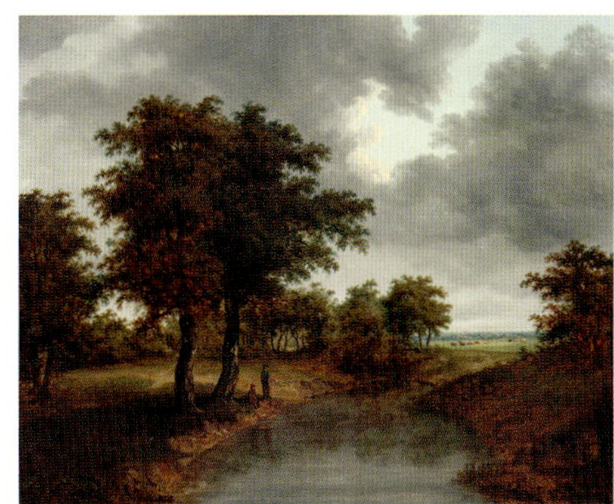

Nasmyth, Patrick 1787–1831
Landscape and River Scene 1827
oil on canvas 49.5 x 59.7
799

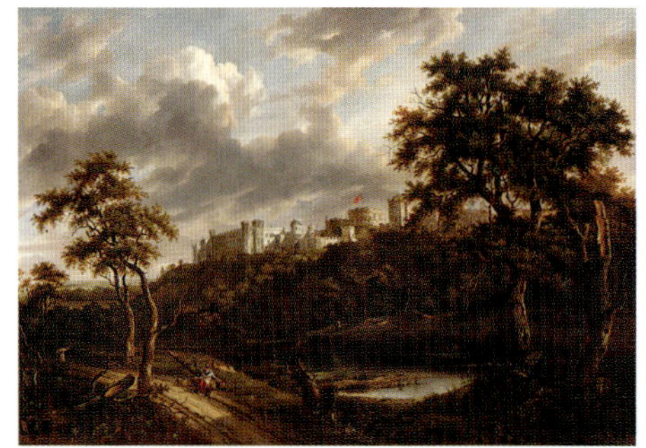

Nasmyth, Patrick 1787–1831
Windsor Castle 1830
oil on canvas 69.9 x 101.6
741

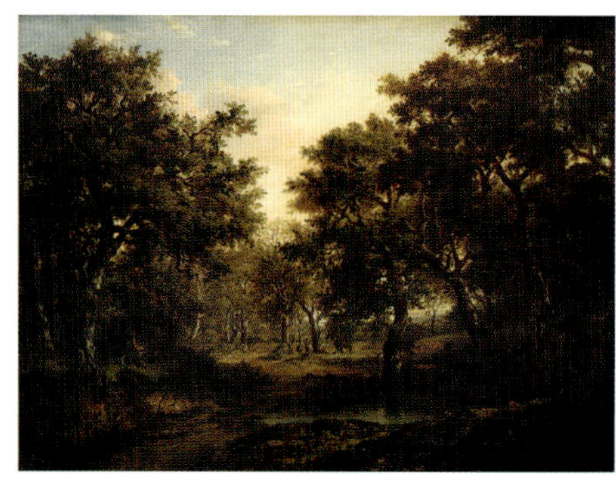

Nasmyth, Patrick 1787–1831
The Edge of the Wood
oil on canvas 45.7 x 60.3
2688

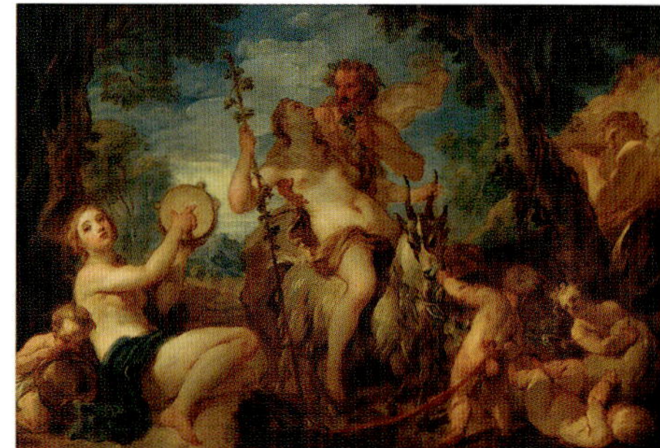

Natoire, Charles Joseph 1700–1777
Bacchantes and Satyrs c.1738–1750
oil on canvas 63.5 x 91.5
176

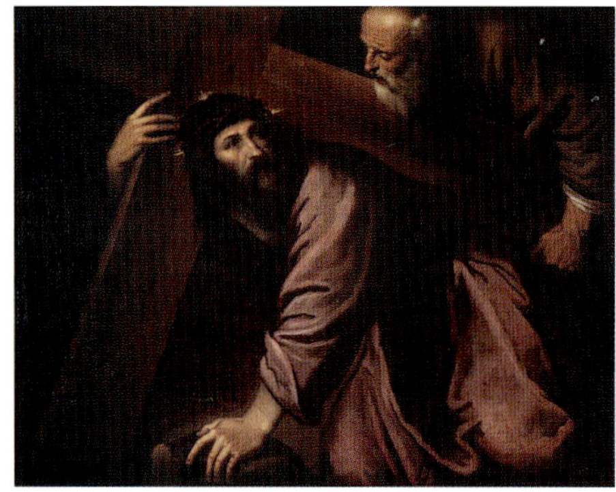

Navarrete, Juan Fernández de c.1526–1579
Christ Carrying the Cross (after Titian)
oil on canvas 95.9 x 119.1
PC.37

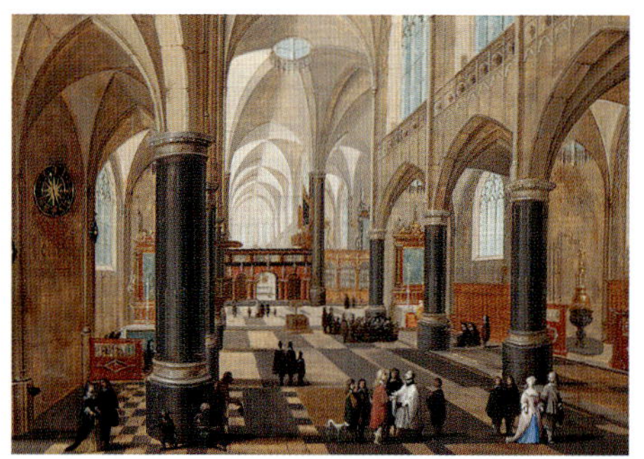

Neeffs, Peeter the younger (attributed to)
1620–1675
An Imaginary Cathedral Interior c.1650–1660
oil on panel 39 x 52
592

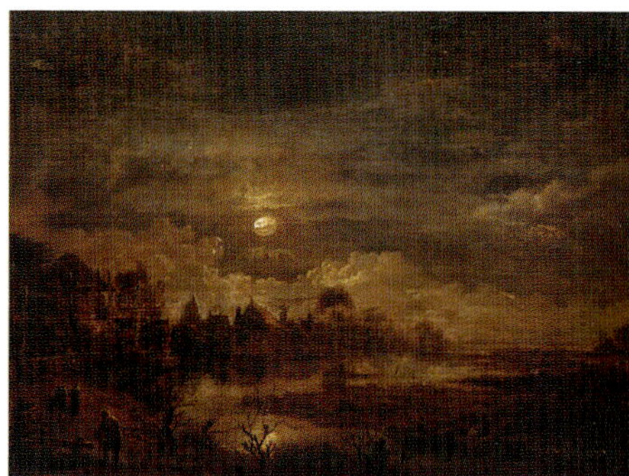

Neer, Aert van der 1603–1677
A Village and Marshland by Moonlight
oil on panel 31.1 x 40.5
299

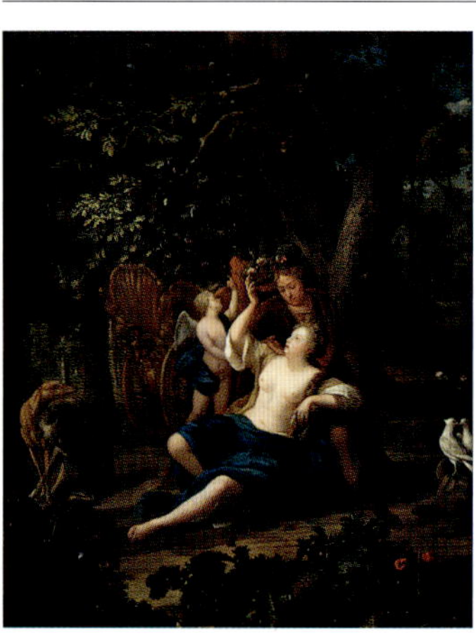

Neer, Eglon Hendrik van der 1634–1703
Venus and Adonis c.1685–1698
oil on canvas 63.5 x 53
59

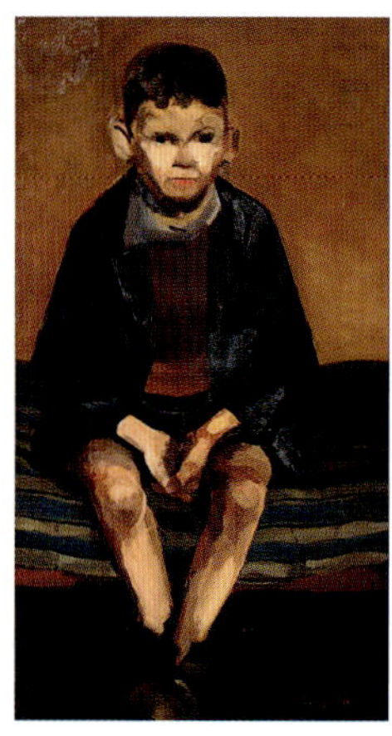

Neil, Angus 1924–1992
A Boy 1954
oil on board 85.1 x 49.5
3025

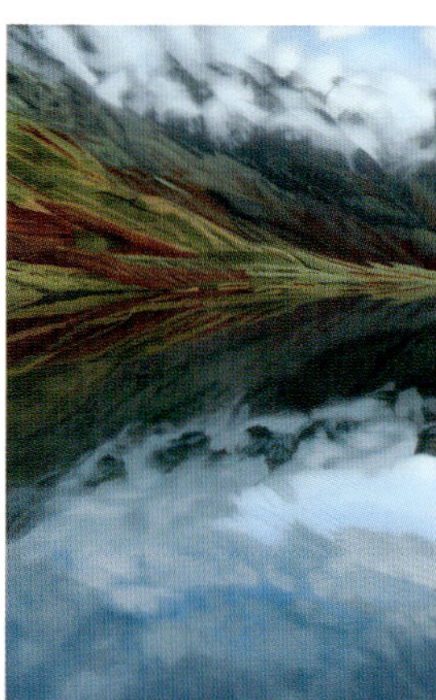

Neiland, Brendan b.1941
Glencoe
acrylic on canvas 99.5 x 63.5
T.2009.21.6

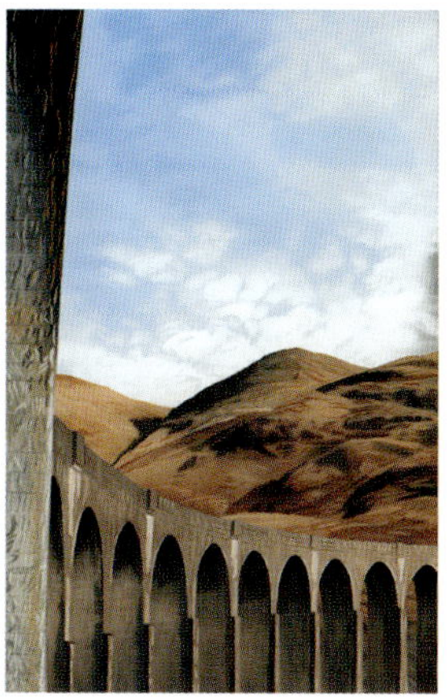

Neiland, Brendan b.1941
Glenfinnan
acrylic on canvas 99.5 x 63.5
T.2009.21.4

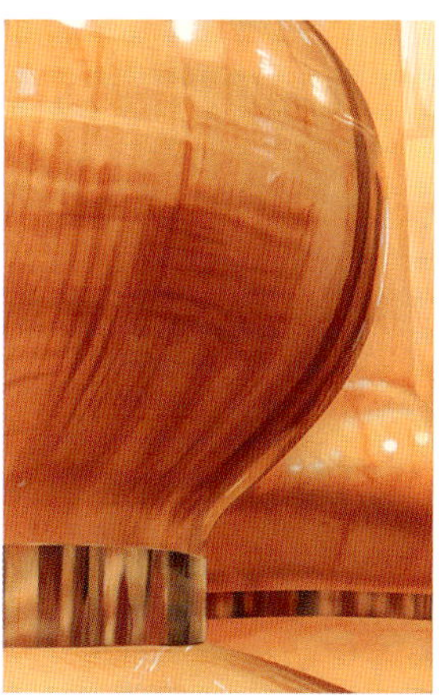

Neiland, Brendan b.1941
Glenmorangie
acrylic on canvas 99.5 x 63.5
T.2009.21.3

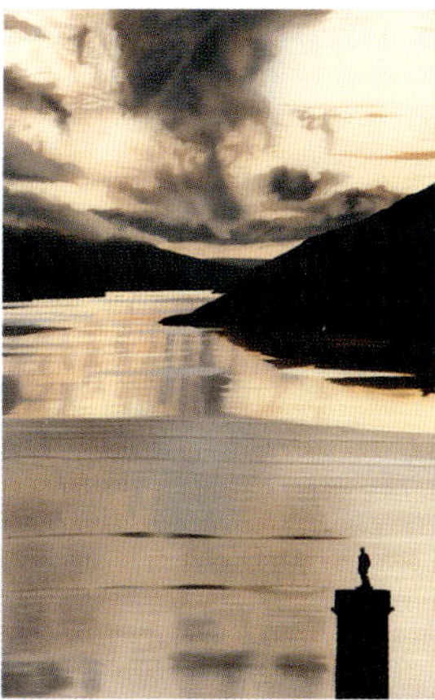

Neiland, Brendan b.1941
Loch Shiel
acrylic on canvas 99.5 x 63.5
T.2009.21.5

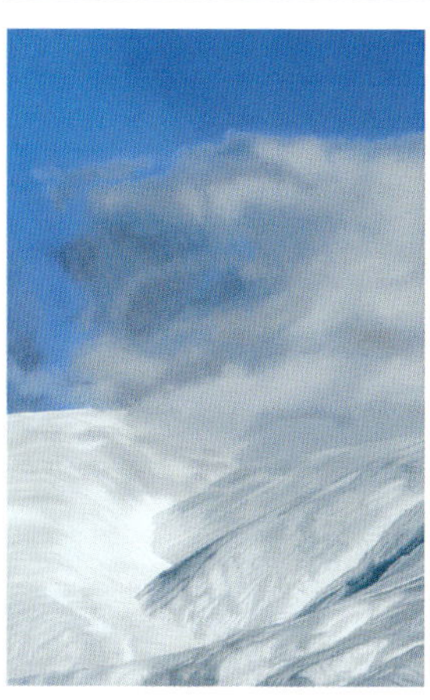

Neiland, Brendan b.1941
Nevis Range
acrylic on canvas 99.5 x 63.5
T.2009.21.2

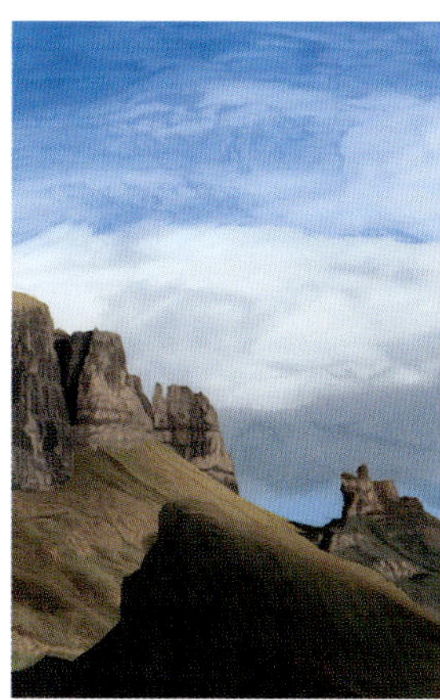

Neiland, Brendan b.1941
Quiraing
acrylic on canvas 99.5 x 63.5
T.2009.21.1

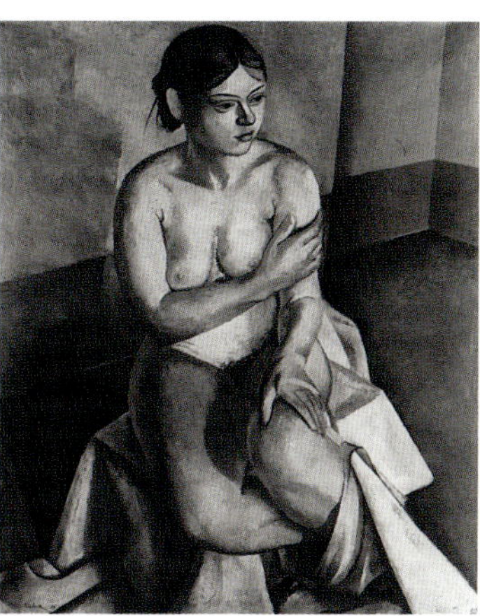

Nelson, H.
Nude 1925
oil on canvas 80.7 x 65
3201

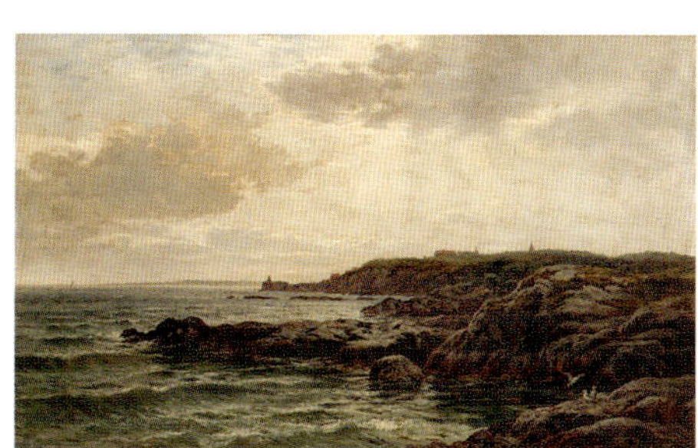

Nesbitt, John 1831–1904
Fife Coast near Anstruther 1874
oil on canvas 94 x 152.4
1502

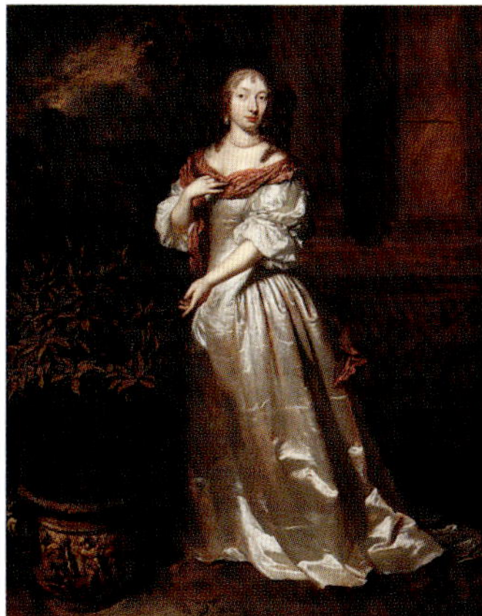

Netscher, Caspar 1639–1684
Portrait of a Young Woman by an Orange Tree 1668
oil on canvas 86.7 x 67.9
74

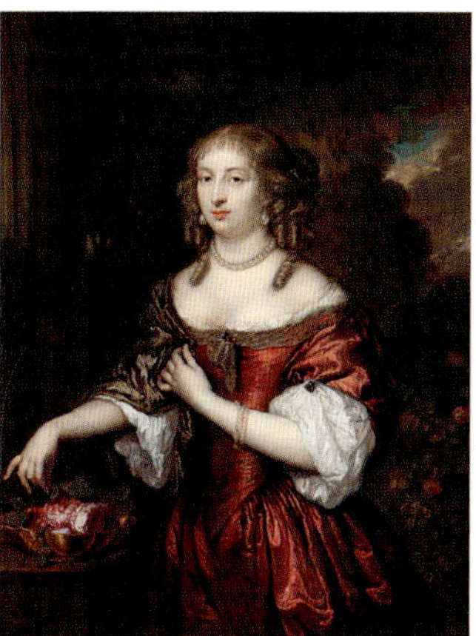

Netscher, Caspar 1639–1684
Portrait of a Woman 1671
oil on canvas 51.1 x 39.7
61

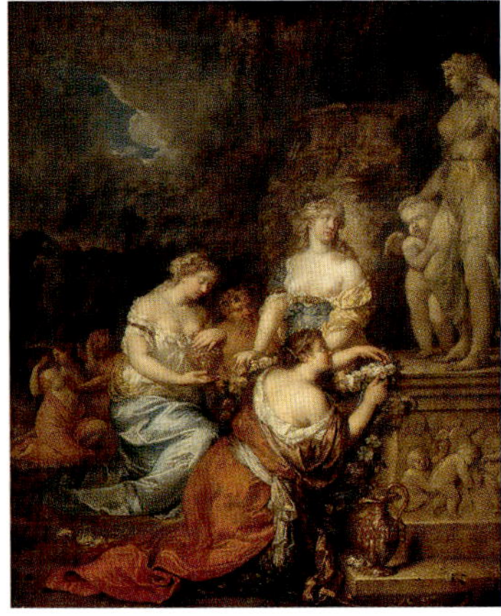

Netscher, Constantin (attributed to)
1668–1723
*Nymphs Laying Offerings before a Statue of
Venus and Cupid*
oil on canvas 52.7 x 44.1
80

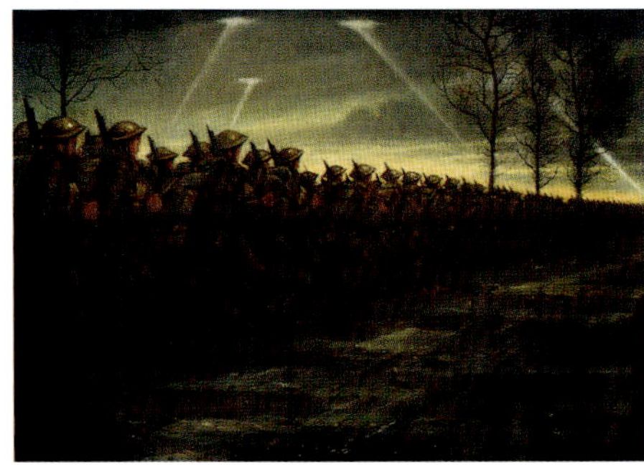

Nevinson, Christopher 1889–1946
March of Civilisation 1940
oil on canvas 71.1 x 101.6
2214

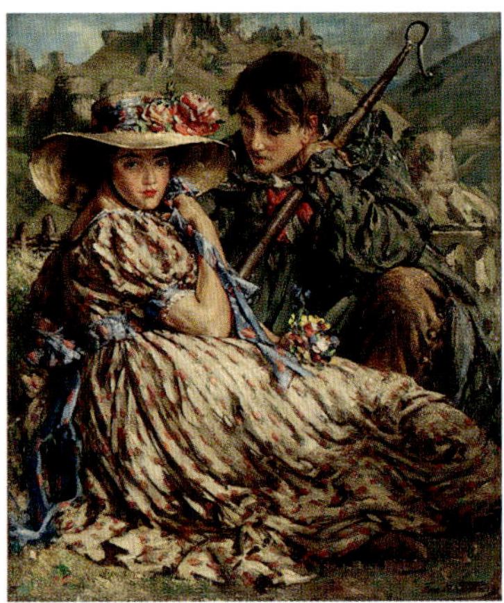

Newbery, Francis Henry 1855–1946
Castles in the Air c.1924
oil on canvas 134.6 x 116.8
1593

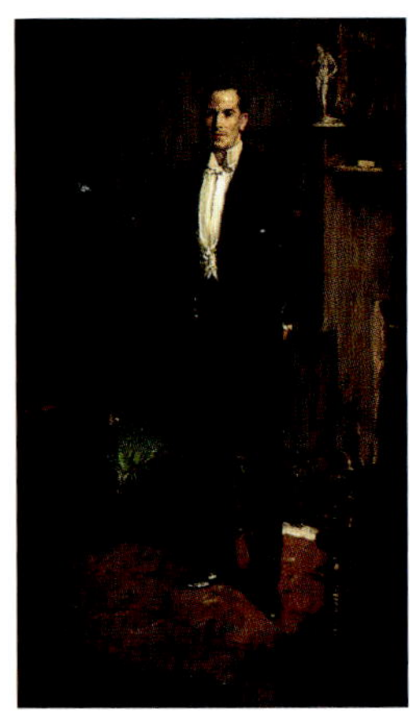

Newbery, Francis Henry (attributed to)
1855–1946
Graham Price
oil on canvas 103.5 x 59
TEMP.11806

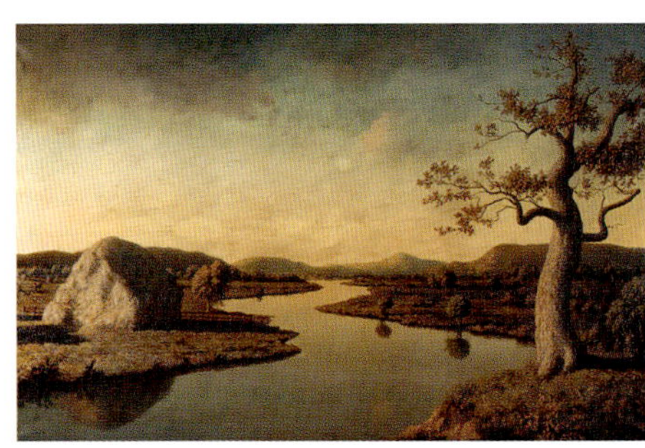

Newton, Algernon Cecil 1880–1968
River Scene
oil on canvas 182.9 x 274.3
2108

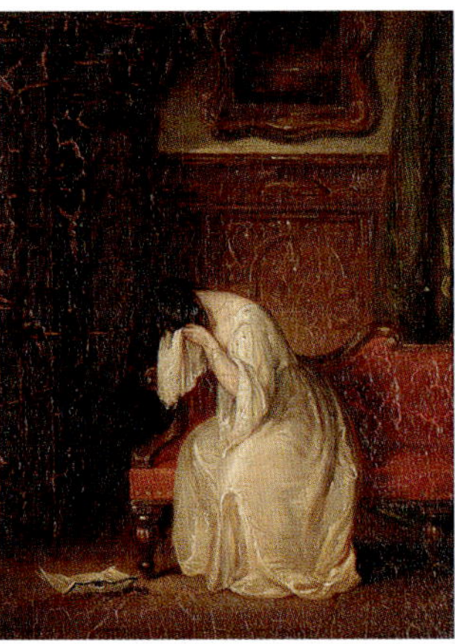

Newton, Gilbert Stuart 1794–1835
The Disconsolate
oil on panel 22.9 x 18.4
365

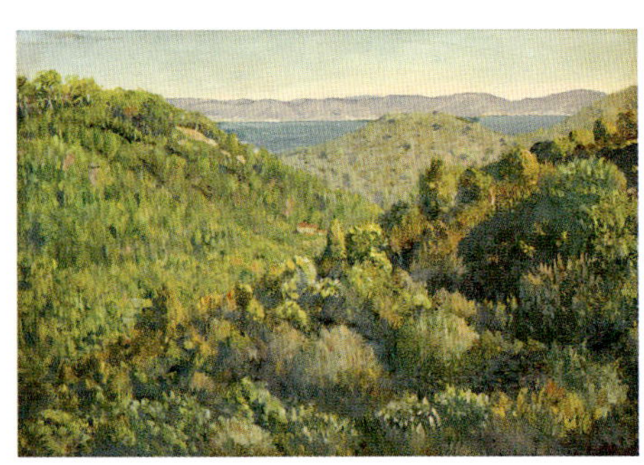

Newton, Herbert H. 1881–1959
Looking over Hills and Sea
oil on canvas 40.6 x 61
1755

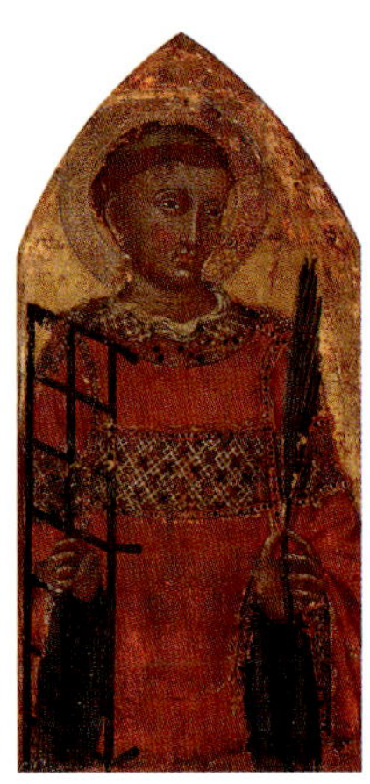

Niccolò di Buonaccorso c.1348–1388
Saint Lawrence c.1370–1375
tempera on panel 58.8 x 27.6
3359

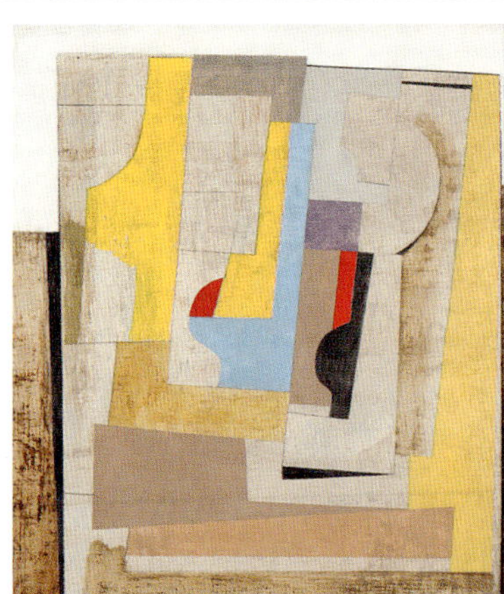

Nicholson, Ben 1894–1982
1946 - 50 (still life) 1946–1950
oil on canvas 61 x 50.8
2984

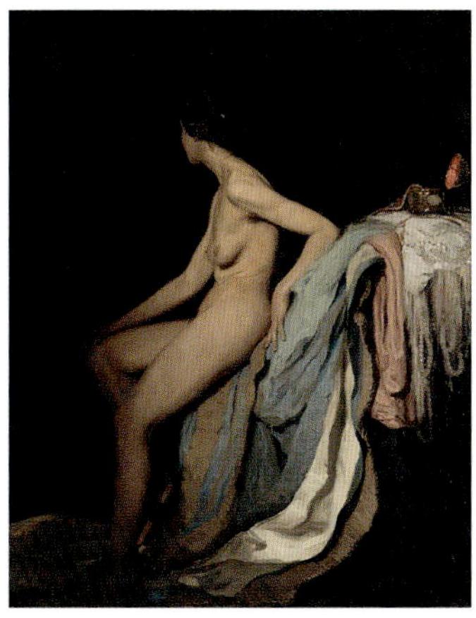

Nicholson, William 1872–1949
Carlina 1909
oil on canvas 157.5 x 121.9
1494

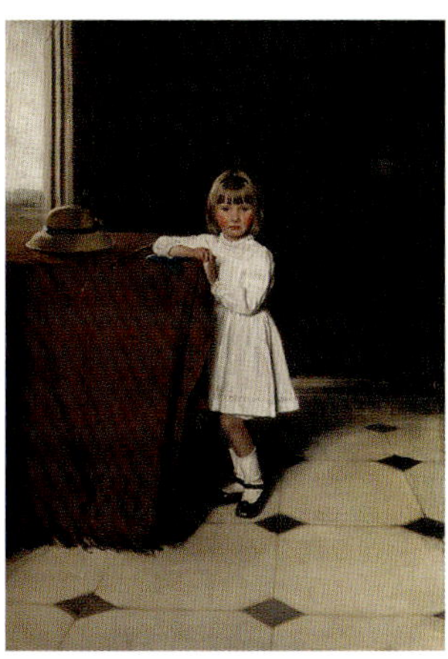

Nicholson, William 1872–1949
Anne Stirling Maxwell (b.1906) 1910–1911
oil on canvas 166.4 x 113
PL.19 (P)

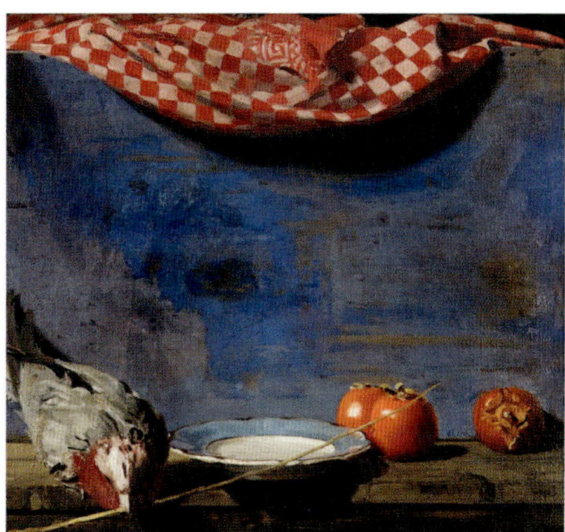

Nicholson, William 1872–1949
Parrot and Persimmons 1915
oil on canvas 53.3 x 59.1
35.581

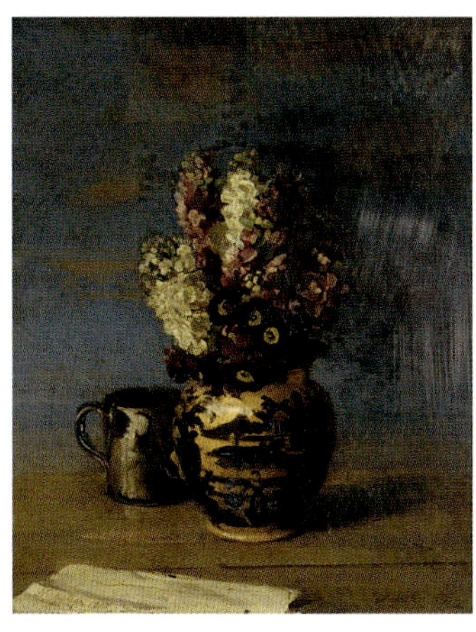

Nicholson, William 1872–1949
The Leeds Vase 1917
oil on canvas 55.9 x 45.7
35.58

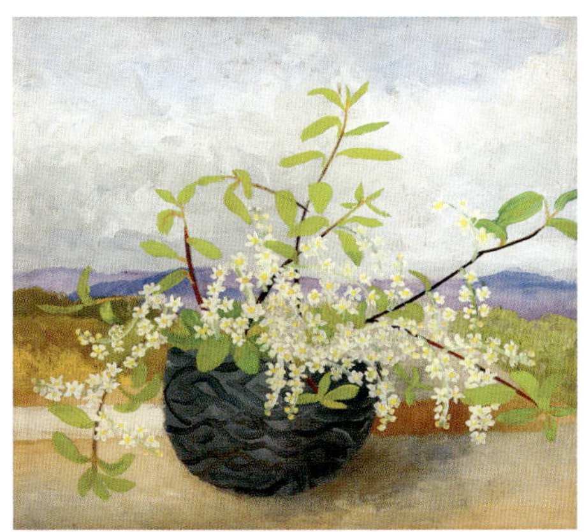

Nicholson, Winifred 1893–1981
Cumberland Landscape with Flowers 1946
oil on composite board 55.9 x 62.9
2608

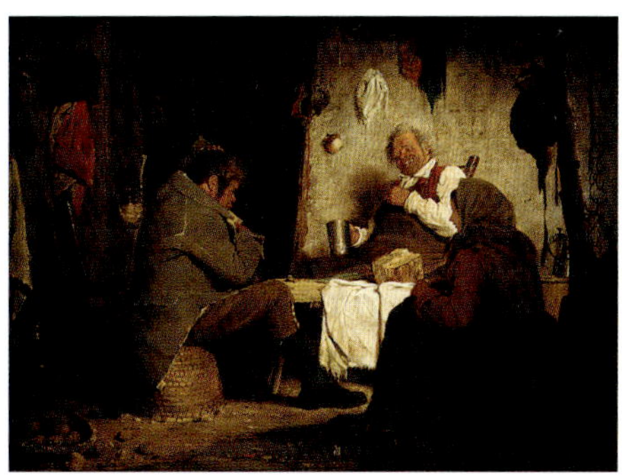

Nicol, Erskine 1825–1904
Beggar My Neighbour 1855
oil on canvas 31.8 x 43.2
770

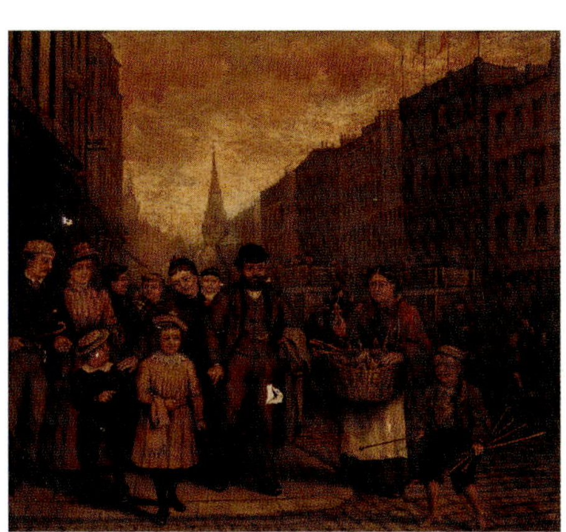

Nicol, J. active late 19th C
Trongate, Glasgow 1891
oil on canvas 56 x 61.2
OG.1960.30.1

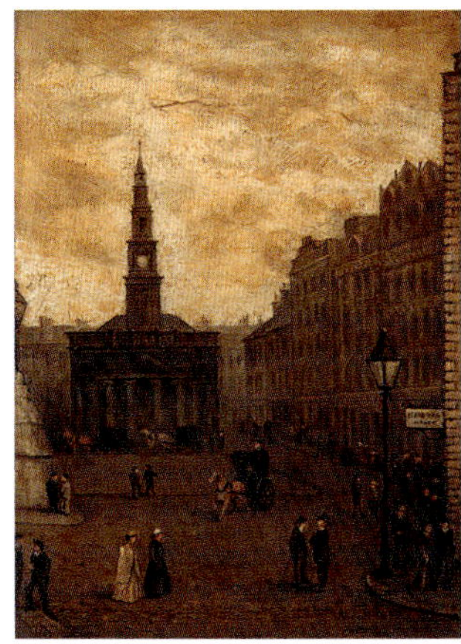

Nicol, J. active late 19th C
St Enoch Square 1892
oil on canvas 35.5 x 25.8
OG.1960.30.2

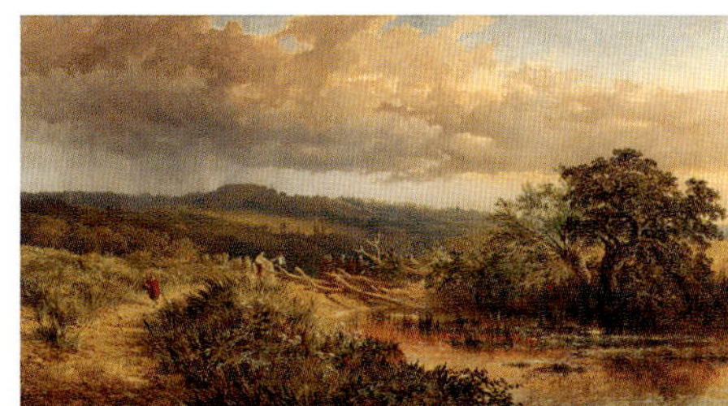

Niemann, Edmund John 1813–1876
Shooters' Hill, Kent 1866
oil on canvas 63.5 x 115.6
1505

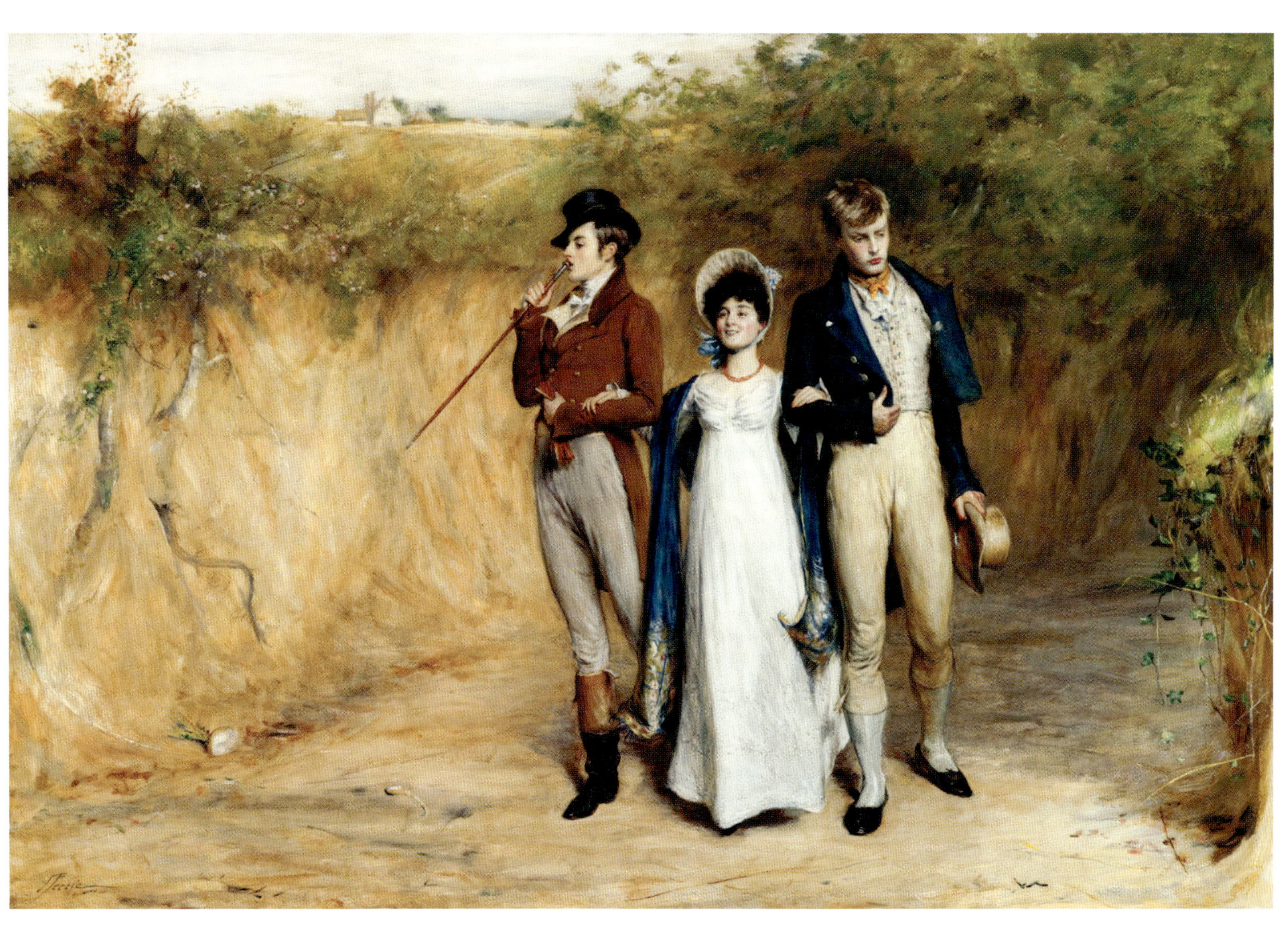

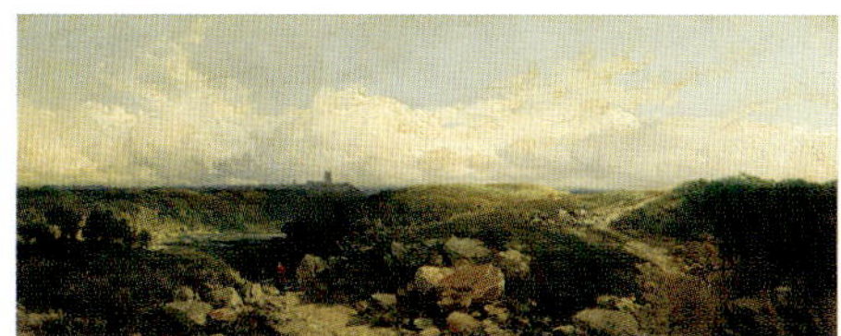

Niemann, Edmund John 1813–1876
Landscape, Richmond 1868
oil on canvas 19.7 x 47.6
944

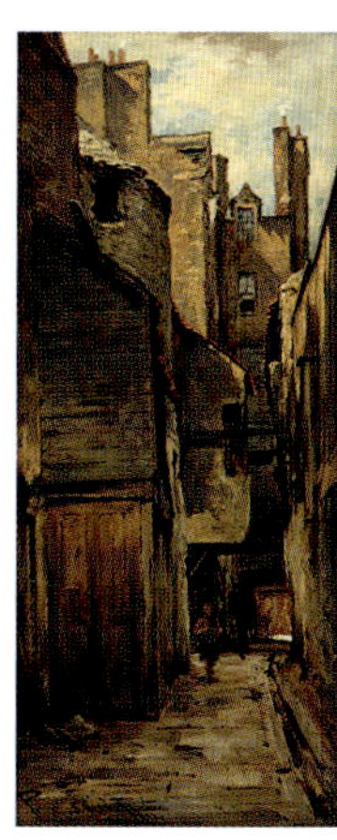

Nisbet, Pollok Sinclair 1848–1922
Plainstanes Close, Edinburgh 1881
oil on panel 45.5 x 19.1
817

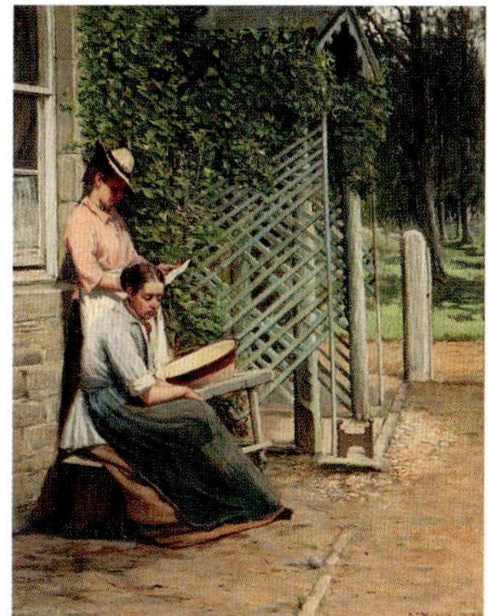

Noble, James Campbell 1846–1913
A Study 1877
oil on canvas 61 x 44.5
863

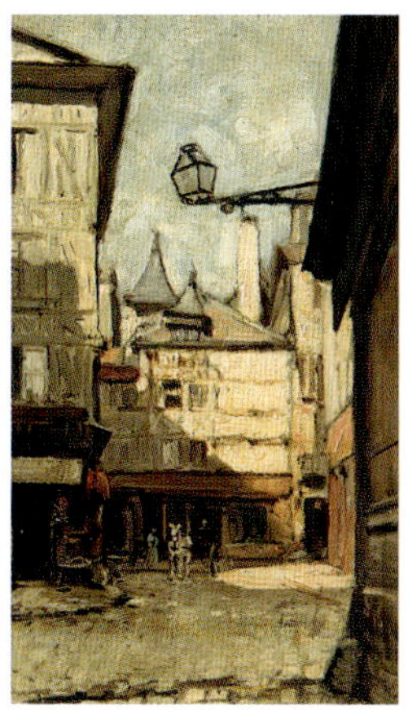

Noble, Robert 1857–1917
Rouen
oil on canvas 23.8 x 13
35.582

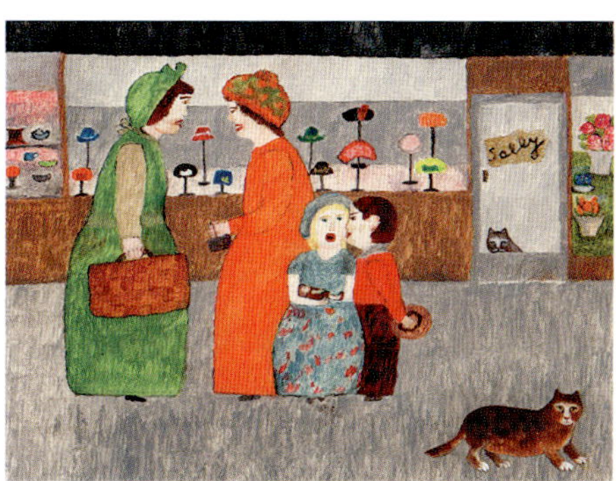

Nolan, Alice b.1910
The Gossip 1972
oil on hardboard 33 x 39
3583

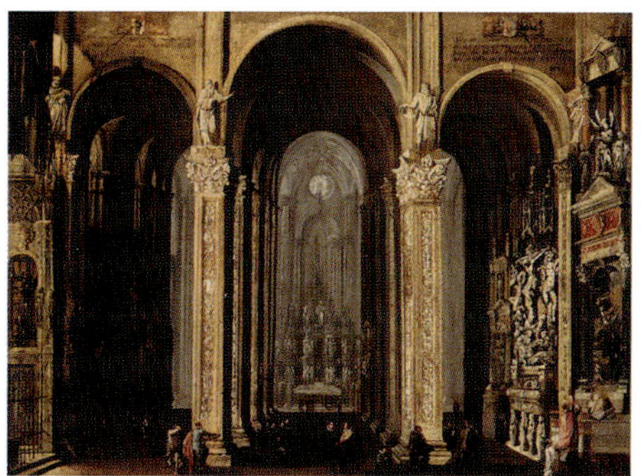

Nomé, François de c.1593–after 1644
Interior of a Cathedral
oil on canvas 74.9 x 100.6
PC.132

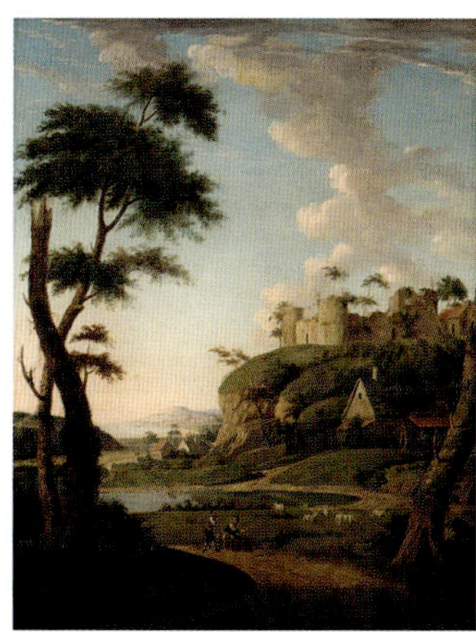

Norie, James 1684–1757
*Landscape with Rustics and Sheep near a
Castle* c.1730
oil on canvas 118 x 92
3400

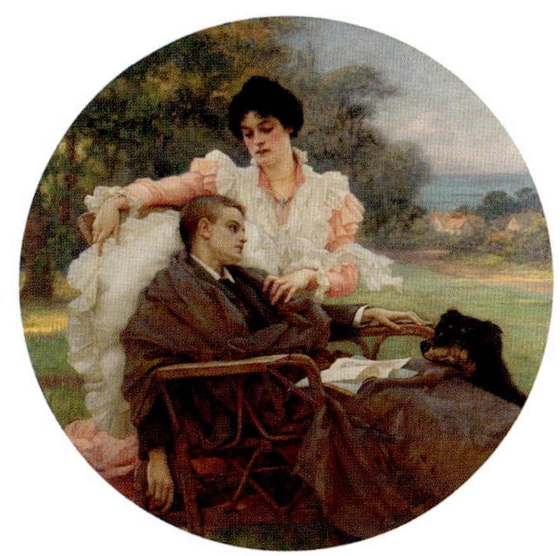

Normand, Ernest 1857–1923
On the Threshold 1903
oil on canvas 137.2
1803

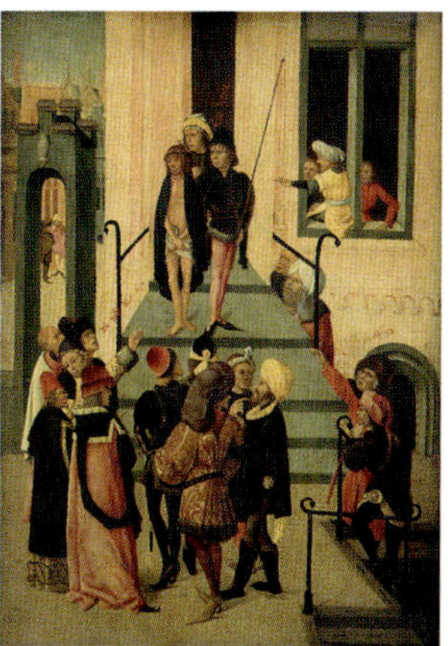

North Netherlandish School
Ecce Homo c.1470
oil on panel 54 x 39.3
35.3

Facing page: Pettie, John, 1839–1893, *Two Strings to Her Bow*, 1887 (p. 348)

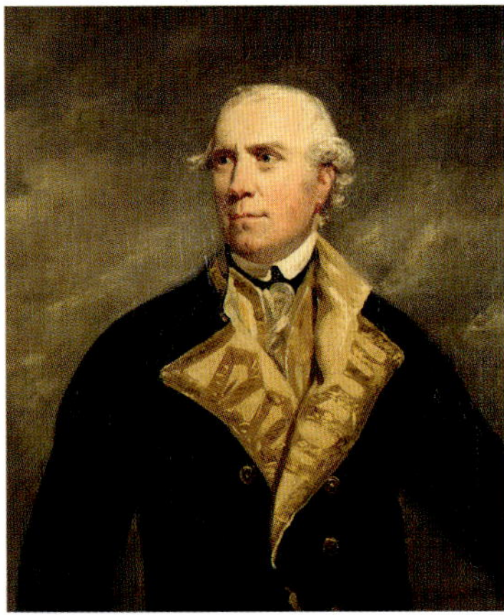

Northcote, James (attributed to) 1746–1831
Admiral Barrington (1729–1800) (after Joshua Reynolds)
oil on canvas 76.2 x 63.5
35.583

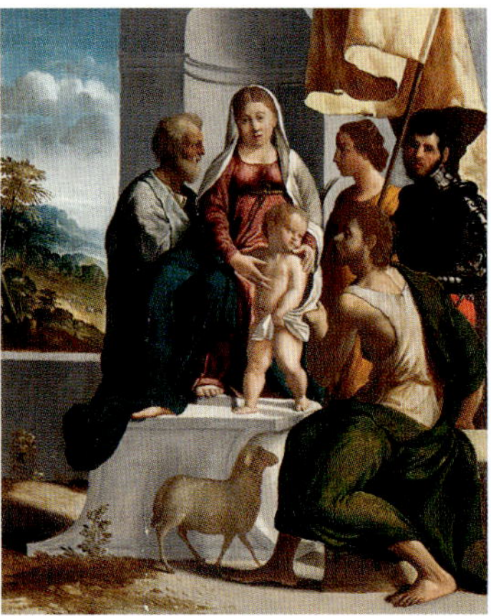

Northern Italian School
The Holy Family with a Virgin Martyr, Saint John the Baptist and Saint George (?)
c.1510–1520
oil on panel 43.5 x 35
197

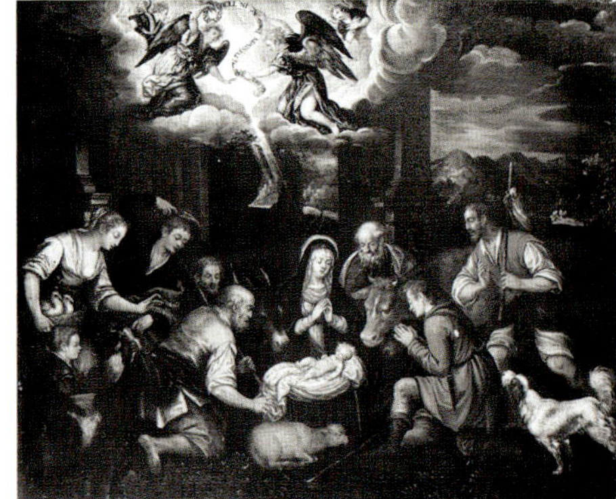

Northern Italian School 16th C
The Adoration of the Shepherds
oil on canvas 74.9 x 87
915

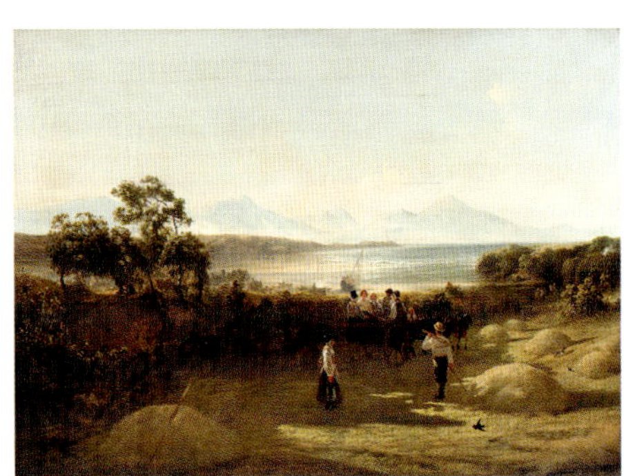

Oakes, John Wright 1820–1887
Barmouth 1870
oil on canvas 121.9 x 170.2
1732

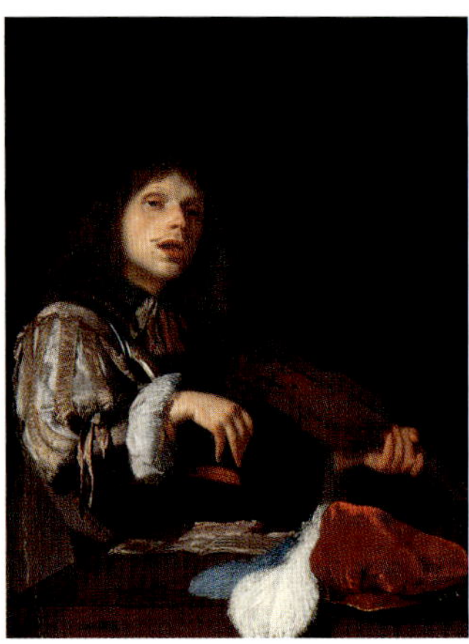

Ochtervelt, Jacob 1634–1682
A Young Man Singing to a Violin 1666
oil on panel 25.7 x 20.6
590

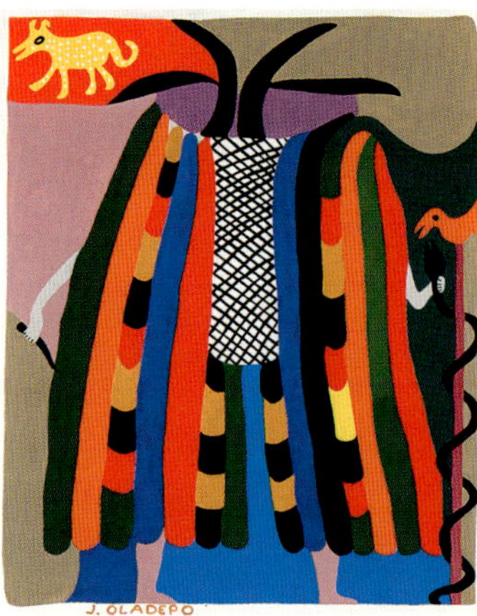

Oladepo, Jinadu b.1918
Untitled c.1995
oil on hardboard 76.2 x 59.7
3564

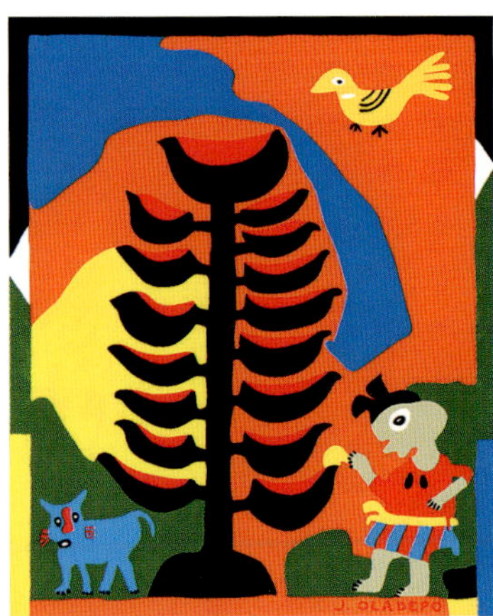

Oladepo, Jinadu b.1918
Untitled c.1995
oil on hardboard 76.2 x 61.2
3565

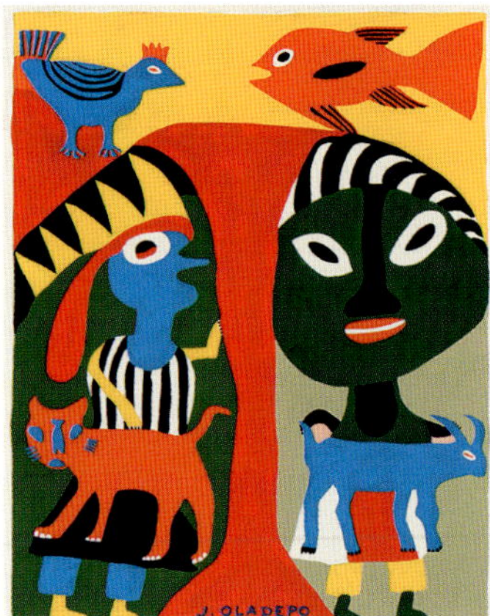

Oladepo, Jinadu b.1918
Untitled c.1995
oil on hardboard 75.9 x 60.1
3566

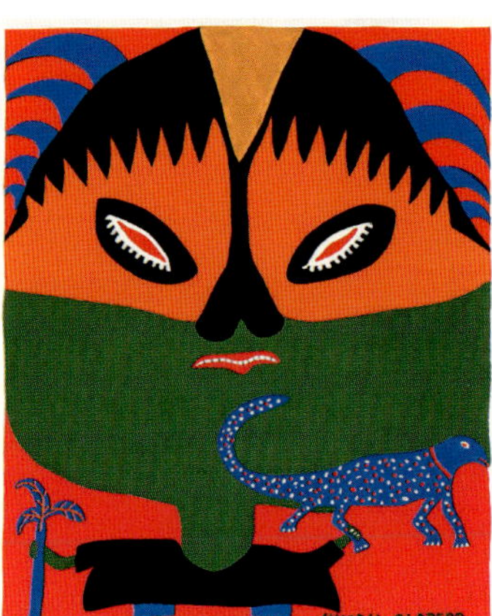

Oladepo, Jinadu b.1918
Untitled c.1995
oil on hardboard 76.2 x 60.9
3567

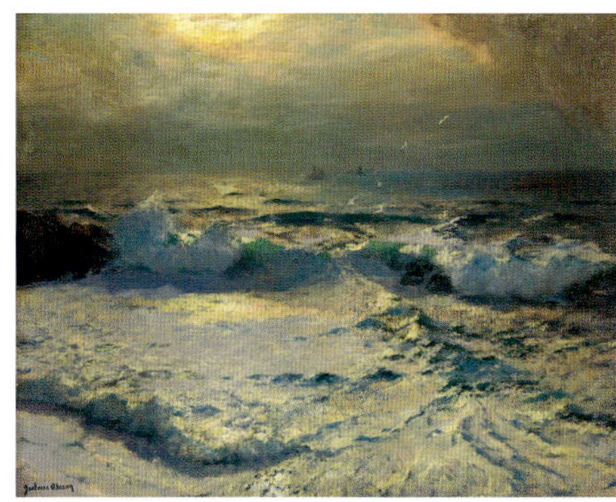

Olsson, Albert Julius 1864–1942
The Clouded Moon c.1910
oil on canvas 59.7 x 74.9
1263

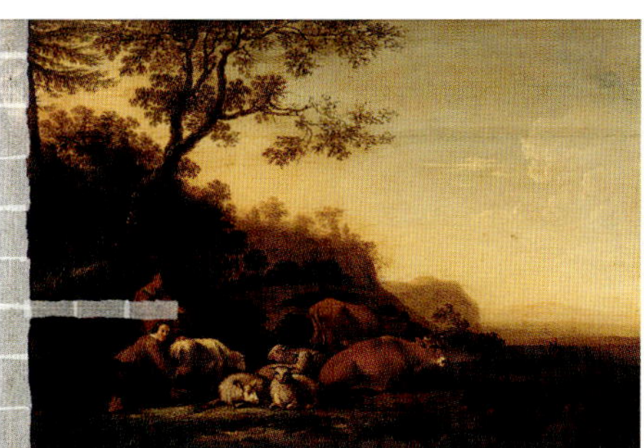

Ommeganck, Balthazar Paul (style of)
1755–1826
Landscape with Peasants and Cattle 19th C
oil on panel 59 x 86.3
278

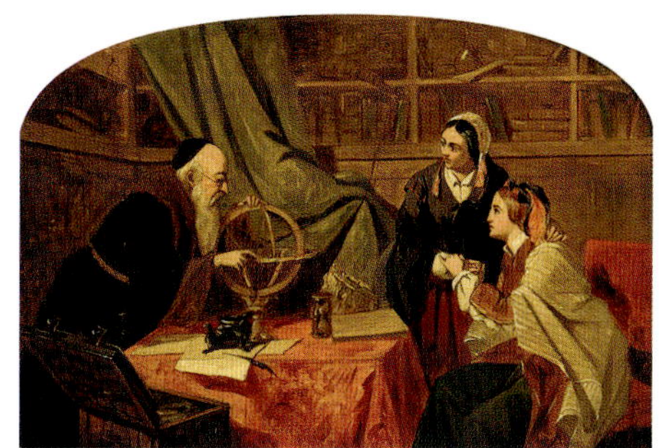

O'Neil, Henry Nelson 1817–1880
Consulting the Oracle
oil on canvas 20.3 x 30.5
415

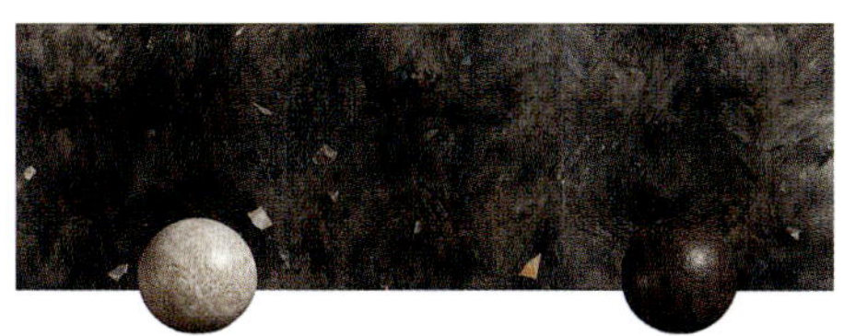

Onwin, Glen b.1947
Unthinkable (from the series 'Revenges of
Nature') 1985
oil, earth, metal, glass, stone (…) 244 x 732
3460.1

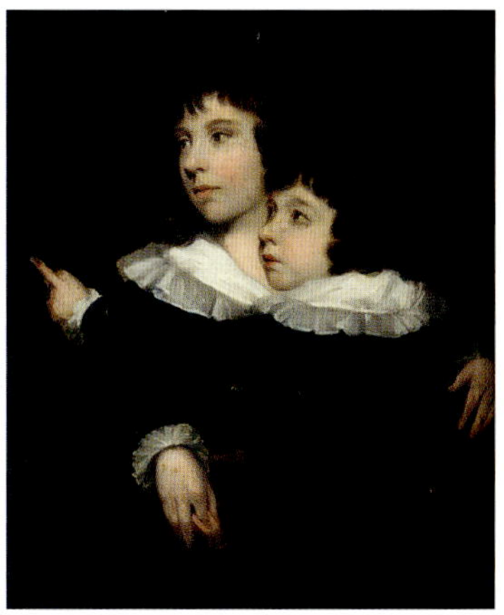

Opie, John 1761–1807
*Master Benjamin Smith (1783–1860), and His
Younger Brother* c.1796
oil on canvas 76.2 x 63.2
3205

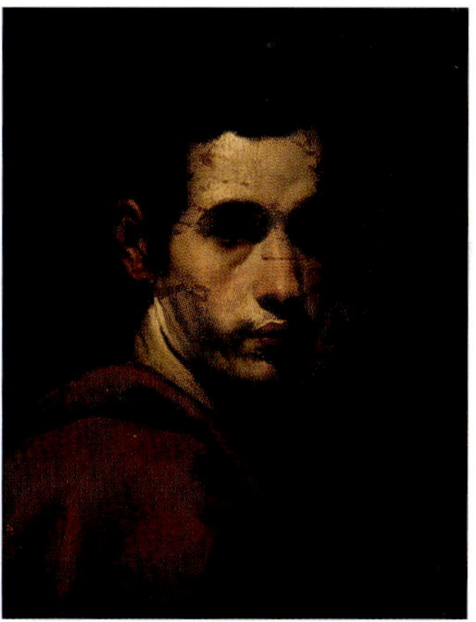

Opie, John (attributed to) 1761–1807
Portrait of a Man (said to be a self portrait)
oil on canvas 52.1 x 39.4
362

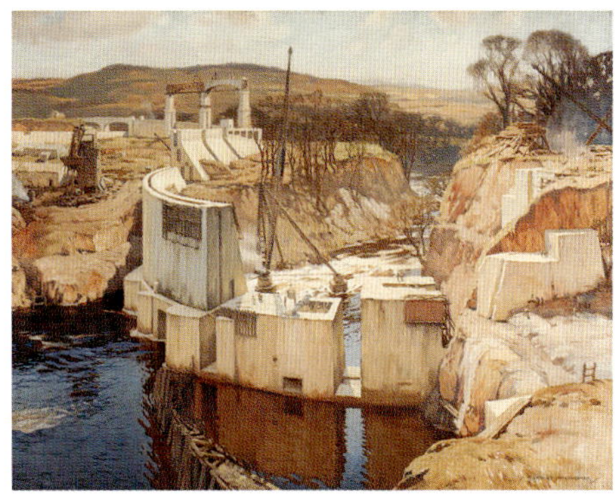

Oppenheimer, Charles 1875–1961
Harnessing the Dee, Galloway c.1934
oil on canvas 121.9 x 152.4
1897

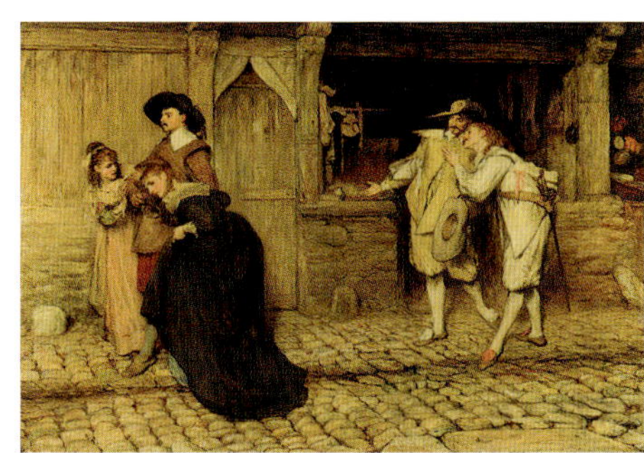

Orchardson, William Quiller 1832–1910
*'Casus belli': Scene from Walter Scott's 'Peveril
of the Peak'* c.1872
oil on canvas 76.2 x 111.8
1110

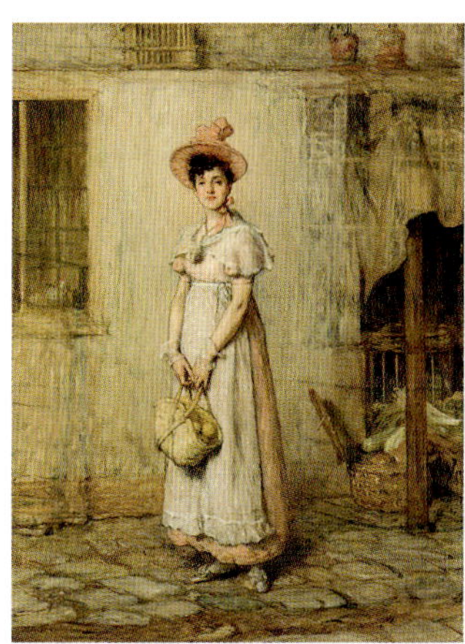

Orchardson, William Quiller 1832–1910
The Young Housewife 1878
oil on canvas 68.6 x 49.5
1121

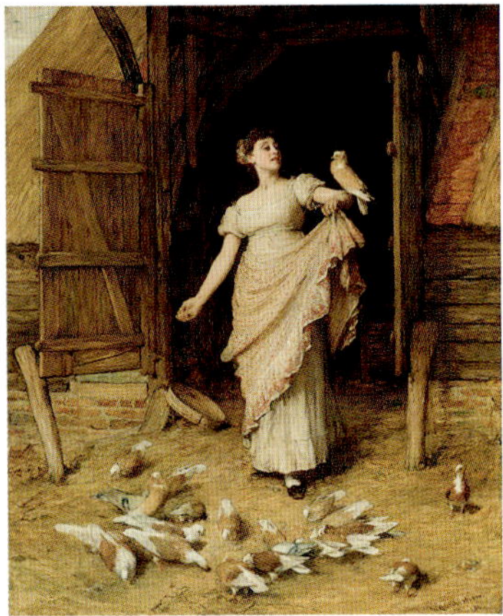

Orchardson, William Quiller 1832–1910
The Farmer's Daughter 1881
oil on canvas 104.1 x 83.8
738

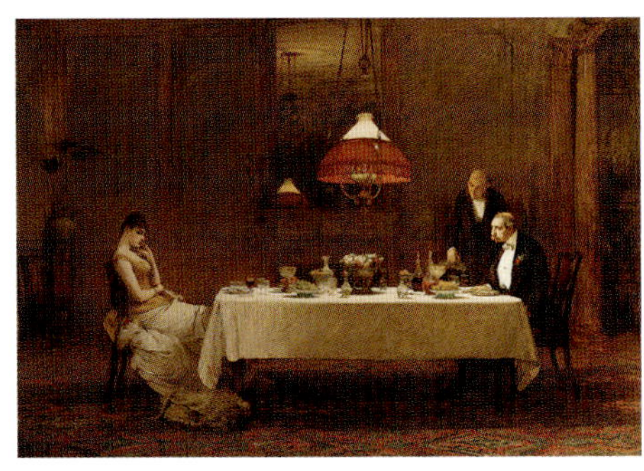

Orchardson, William Quiller 1832–1910
Le mariage de convenance 1883
oil on canvas 104.8 x 154.3
1666

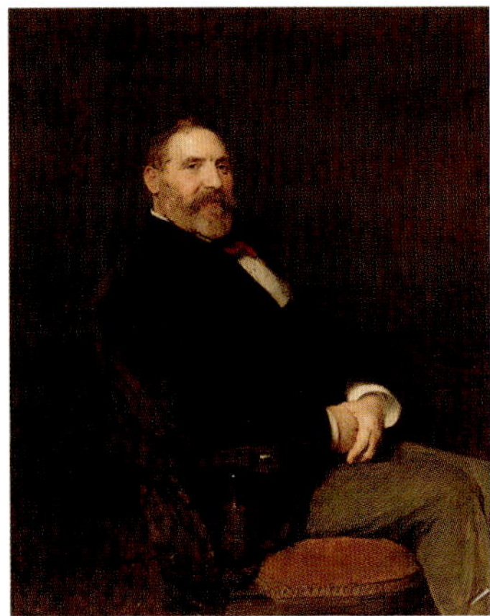

Orchardson, William Quiller 1832–1910
James T. Tullis (1842–1910) 1896
oil on canvas 127 x 101.6
1284

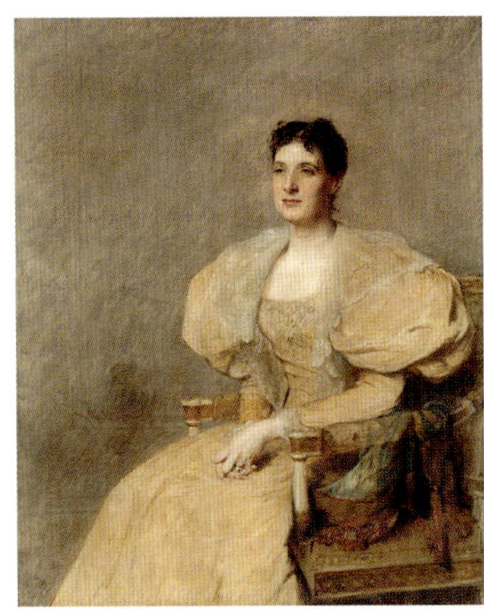

Orchardson, William Quiller 1832–1910
Mrs James T. Tullis 1896
oil on canvas 127 x 101.6
1285

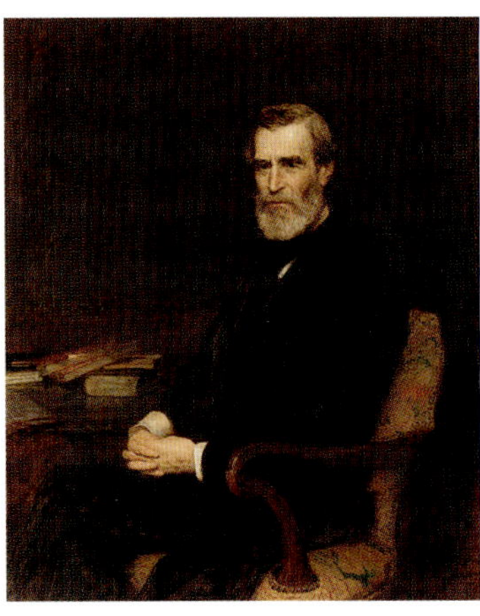

Orchardson, William Quiller 1832–1910
Former Bailie James H. Dickson (b.1824) 1897
oil on canvas 127 x 101.6
752

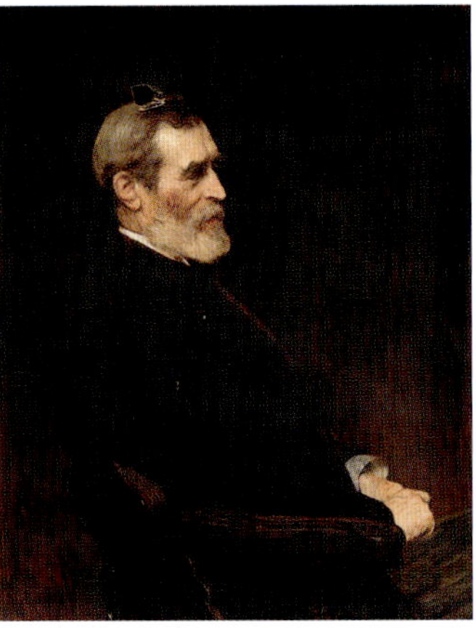

Orchardson, William Quiller 1832–1910
James Hunter Dixon (b.1824), DL 1897
oil on canvas 98.2 x 78.3
PP.1978.121.12

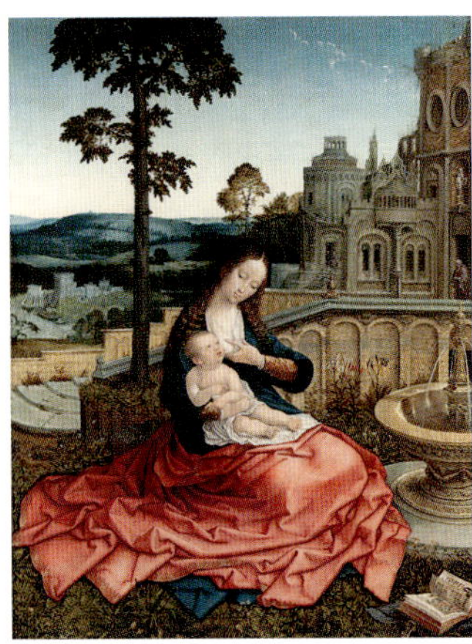

Orley, Bernaert van (and studio)
c.1492–1541
The Virgin and Child by a Fountain
c.1515–1540
oil on panel 105.4 x 82.2
201

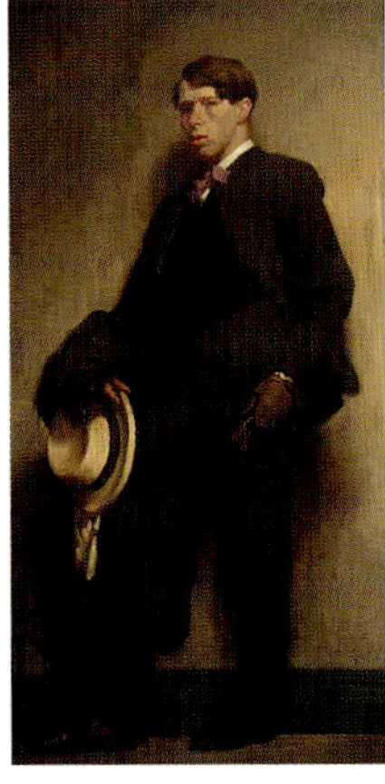

Orpen, William 1878–1931
The Artist as a Young Man c.1899–1900
oil on canvas 108 x 53.3
1843

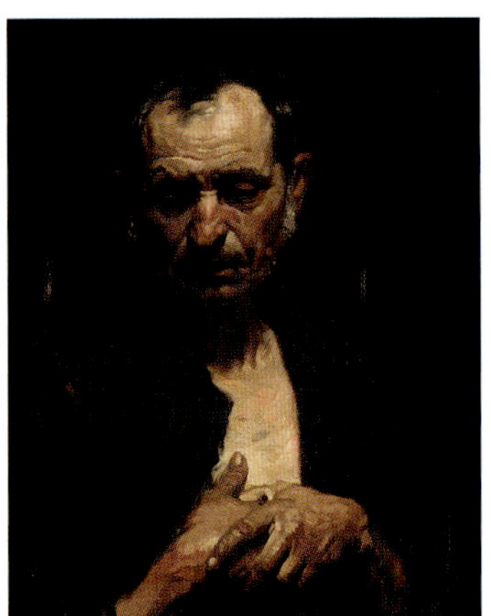

Orpen, William 1878–1931
A Saint of the Poor c.1905
oil on canvas 68.6 x 54.5
2096

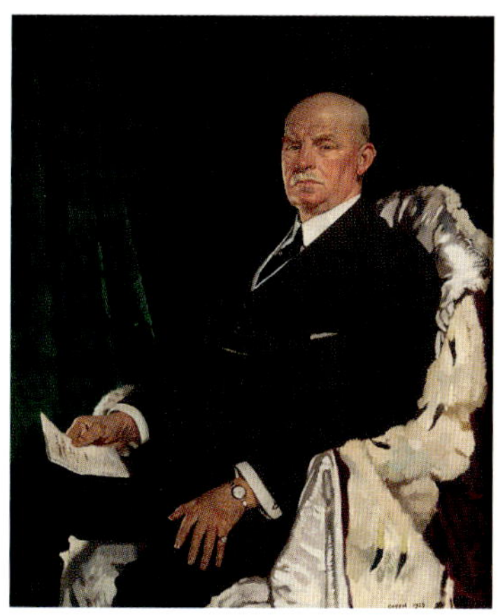

Orpen, William 1878–1931
*Sir Thomas Paxton (1860–1930), Lord Provost
of Glasgow (1920–1923)* 1923
oil on canvas 127 x 101.6
1851

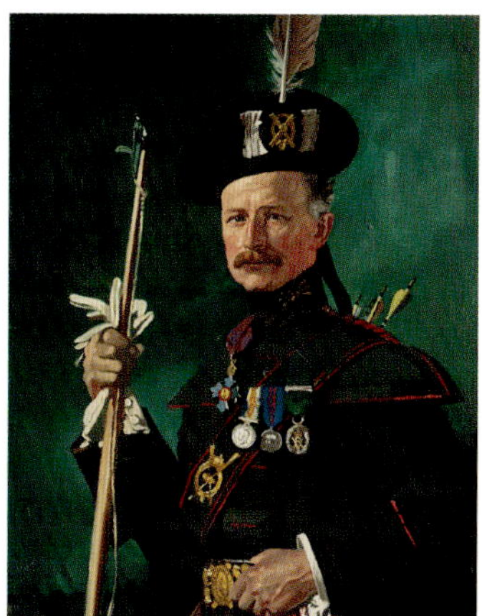

Orpen, William 1878–1931
*Sir Hugh Reid (1860–1935), in the Uniform of
the Scottish Archers* c.1929
oil on canvas 106.7 x 81.3
1922

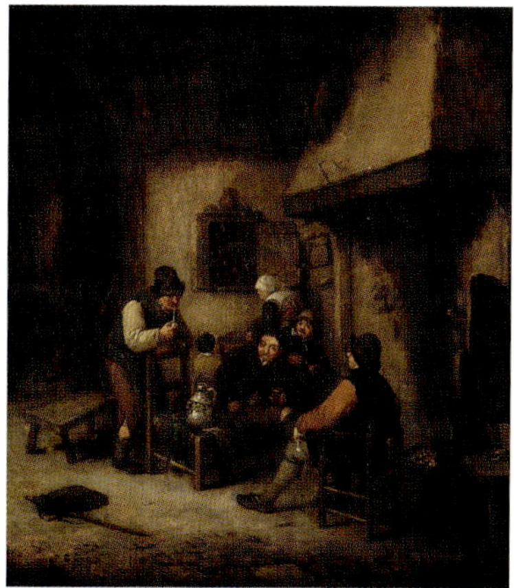

Ostade, Adriaen van (after) 1610–1685
Interior with Peasants by a Fire 17th C
oil on panel 36.2 x 32.7
78

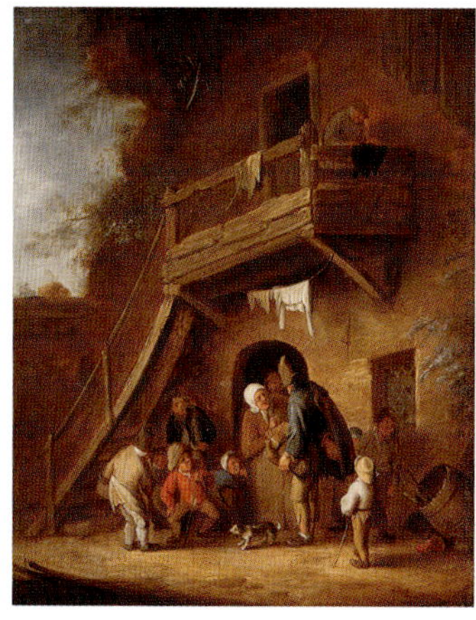

Ostade, Adriaen van (after) 1610–1685
*A Hurdy-Gurdy Player at a Cottage
Door* 17th C–18th C
oil on panel 32.1 x 25.7
120

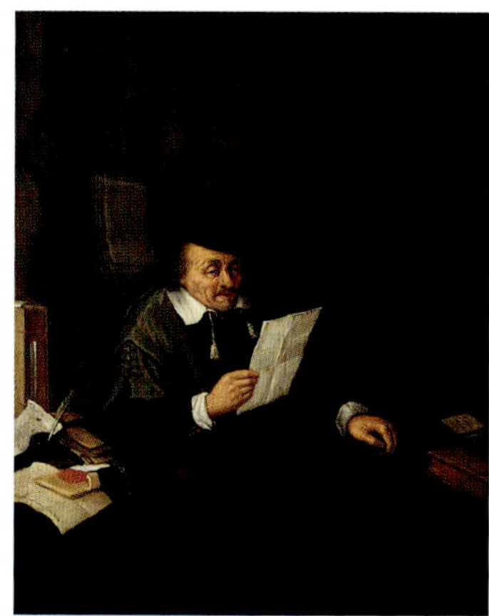

Ostade, Adriaen van (after) 1610–1685
A Lawyer in His Study 17th C–18th C
oil on panel 30.5 x 24.8
90

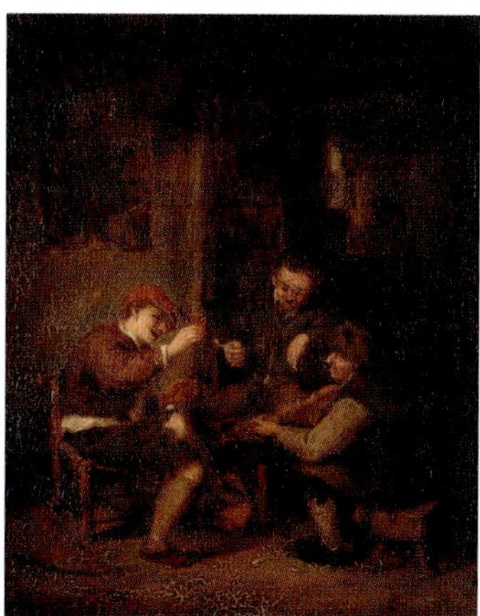

Ostade, Adriaen van (after) 1610–1685
Interior with Three Roistering Peasants
late 18th C/19th C
oil on panel 27.9 x 22.5
594

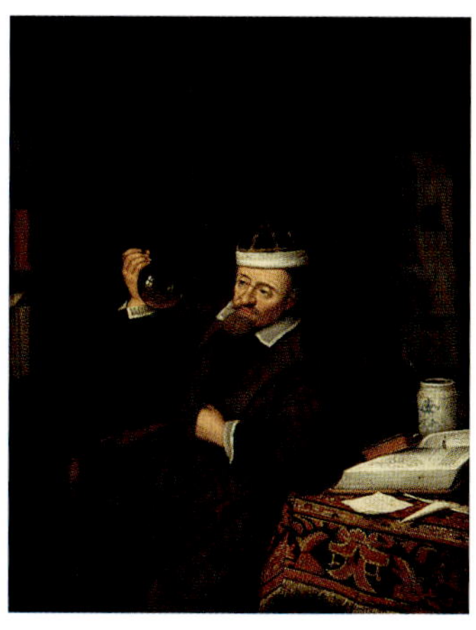

Ostade, Adriaen van (after) 1610–1685
A Doctor in His Cabinet
oil on canvas 29.2 x 24.1
112

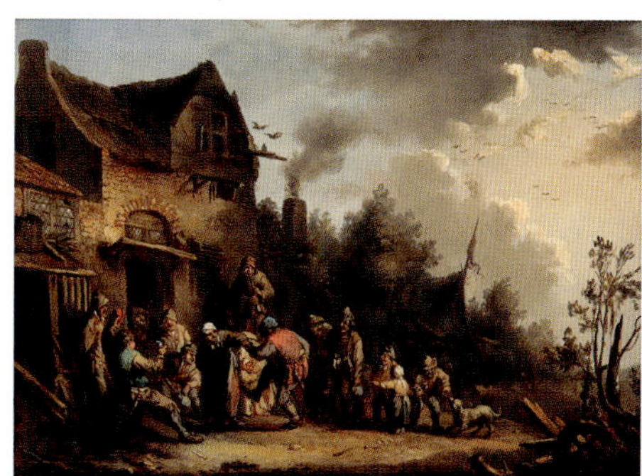

Ostade, Adriaen van (after) 1610–1685
A Village Festival
oil on panel 31.1 x 40
1367

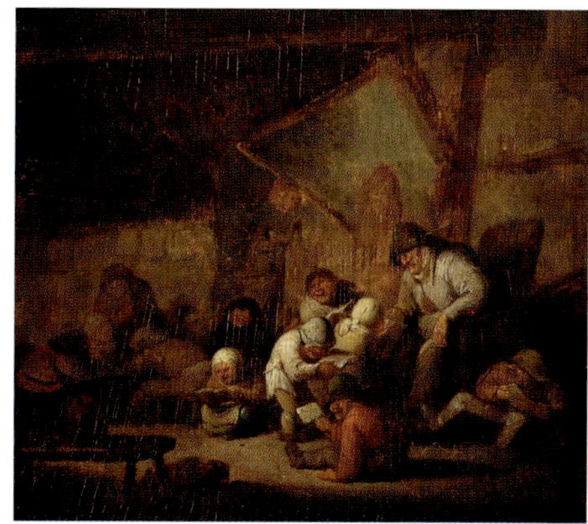

Ostade, Adriaen van (after) 1610–1685
A Village School Room
oil on panel 19.3 x 22.2
14

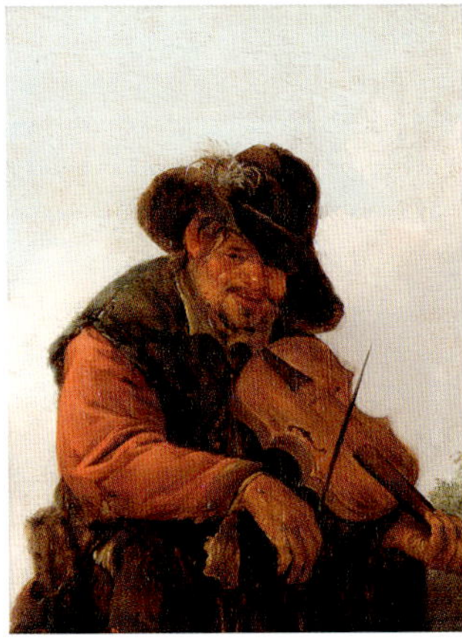

Ostade, Adriaen van (attributed to) 1610–1685
An Itinerant Musician c.1640–1660
oil on panel 27.3 x 21.9
593

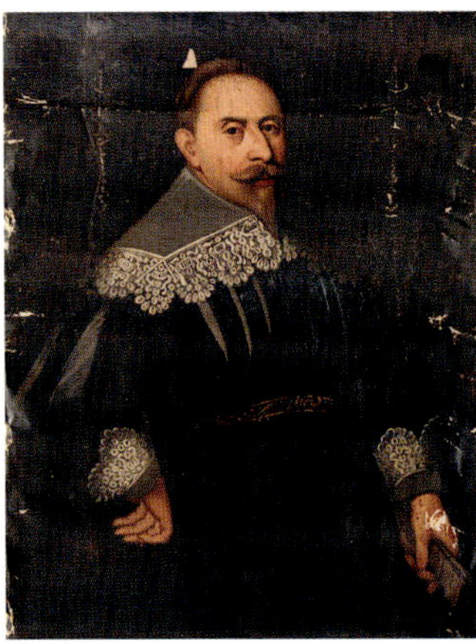

Österlund, John (after) 1875–1953
Gustavus Adolphus II (1594–1632), King of Sweden c.1900–1911
oil on canvas 102.9 x 78.1
1289

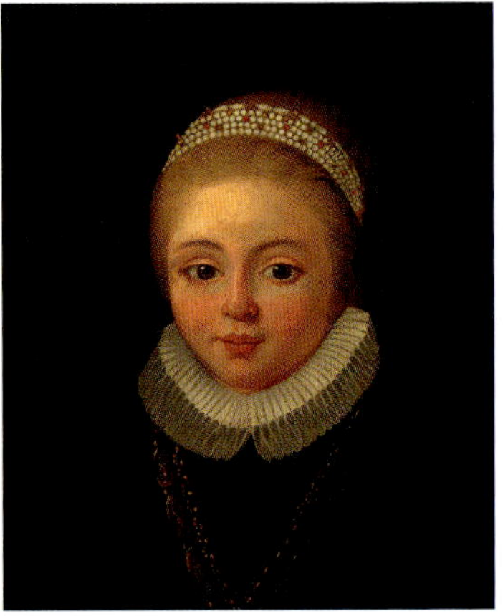

Österlund, John (after) 1875–1953
Mary Queen of Scots (1542–1587), as a Child c.1900–1911
oil on canvas 39.4 x 32.4
1288

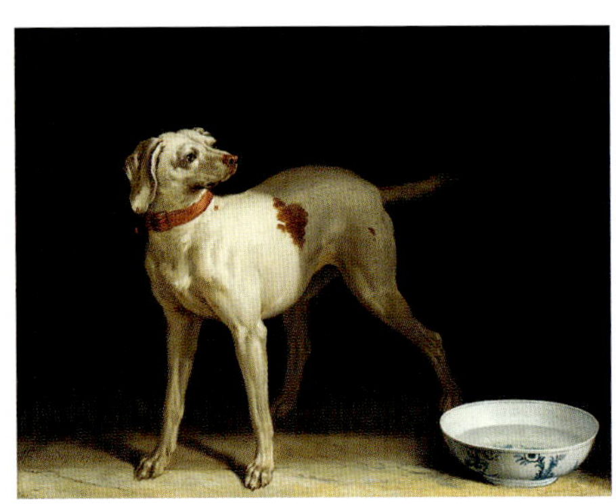

Oudry, Jean-Baptiste 1686–1755
The Dog 1751
oil on canvas 90.2 x 113
35.585

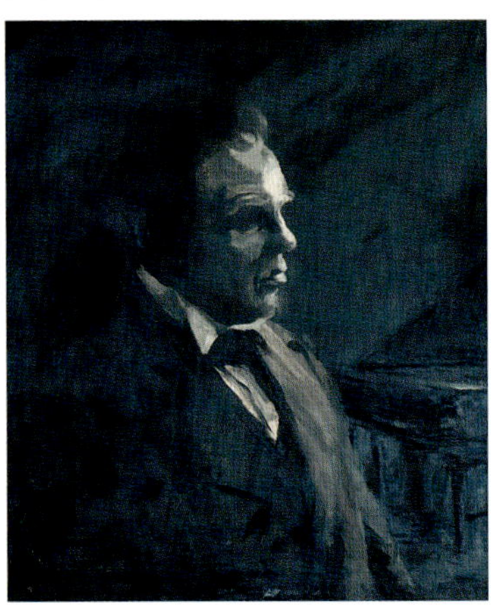

C. W. P.
Frederic Archibald Lamond (1868–1948)
oil on canvas 76.4 x 63.8
OG.1965.35

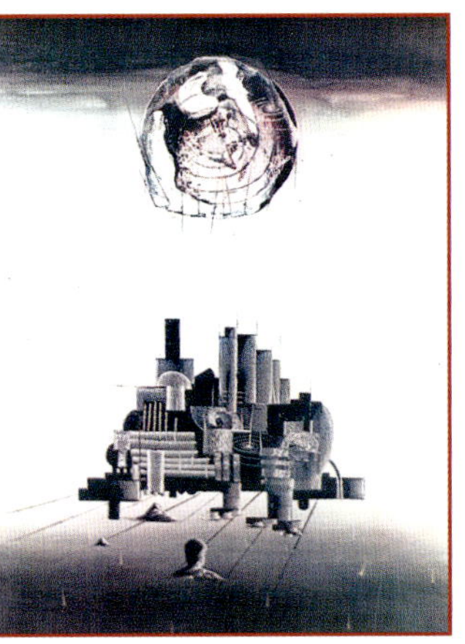

Pacheco, Pedro b.1943
From a Moment of Silence
oil on canvas 130 x 81
3310
STOLEN

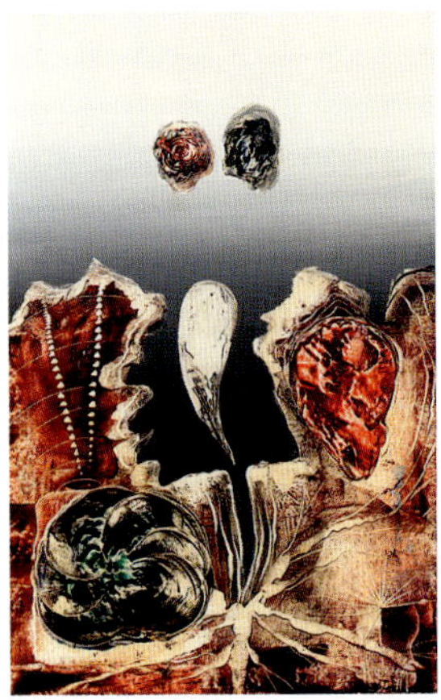

Pacheco, Pedro b.1943
Towards the Point of Convergence
oil on canvas 130 x 81
3286

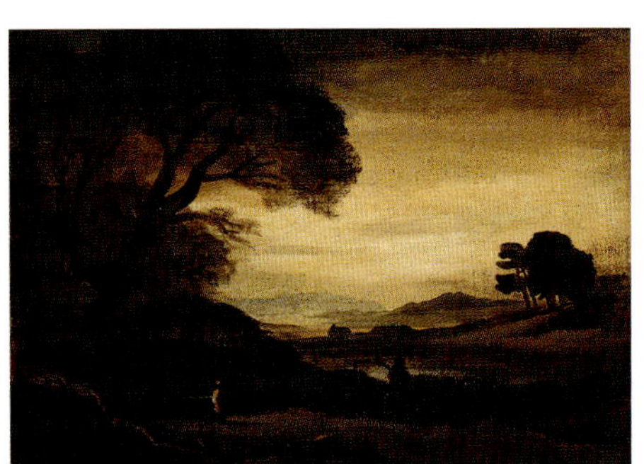

Padwick, Philip Hugh 1876–1958
Evening on the Lake
oil on canvas 45.7 x 61
2091

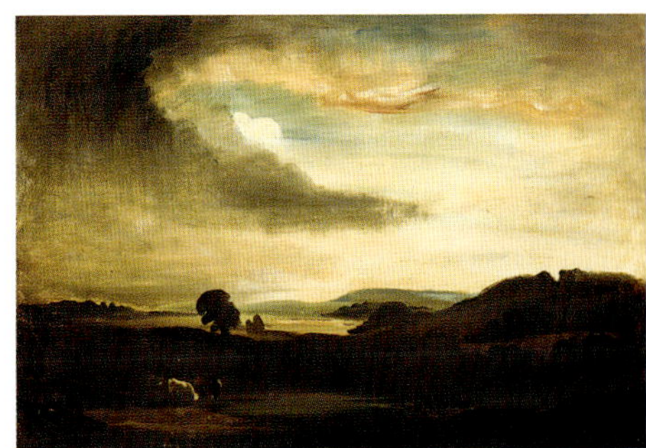

Padwick, Philip Hugh 1876–1958
The Heath, Petersfield
oil on canvas 50.8 x 63.5
2092

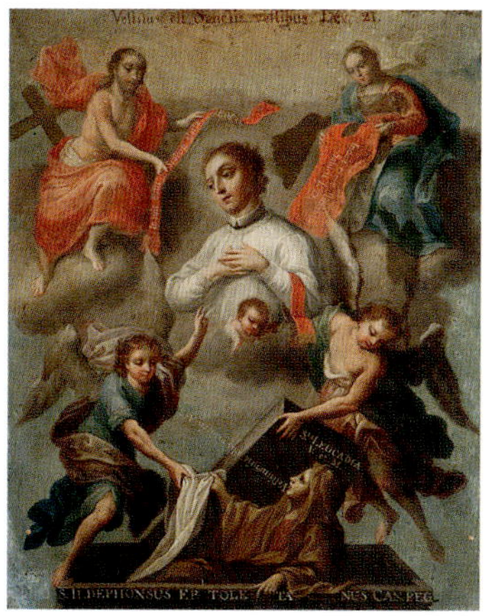

Paez, José de 1720–1790
San Ildefonso Receiving the Chasuble
oil on panel 26.4 x 20.9
PC.33

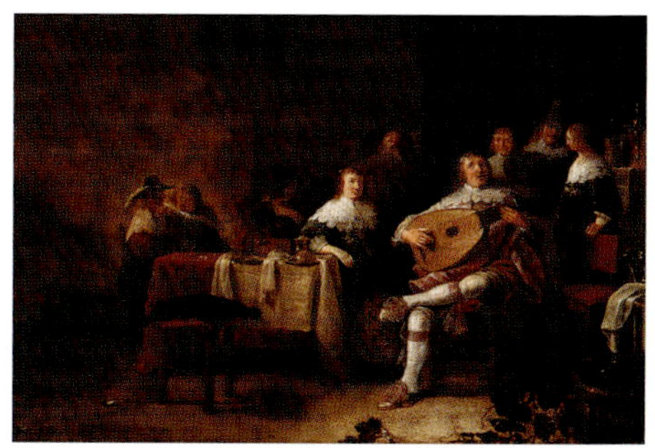

Palamedesz., Anthonie 1601–1673
A Musical Party c.1645–1650
oil on panel 37.1 x 55.2
344

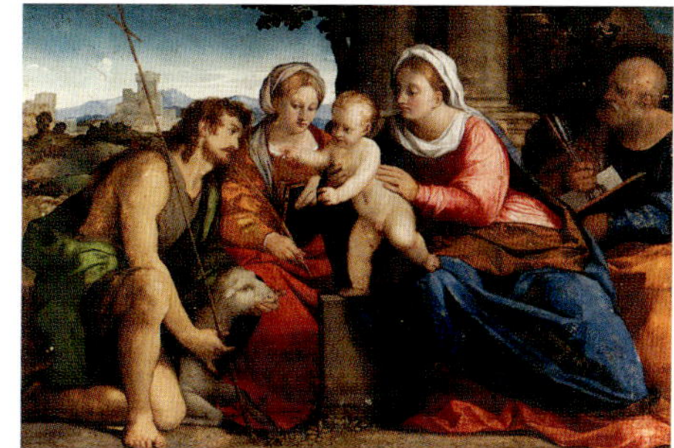

Palma, Jacopo il Vecchio c.1479–1528
*Virgin and Child with Saints John the Baptist,
Peter and a Female Saint* c.1523–1526
oil on panel 92.7 x 138.4
585

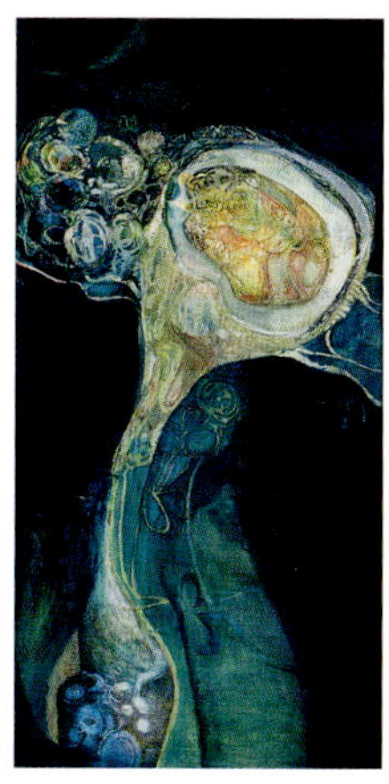

Palmer, Joan 1941–1984
Seed Head 1969
oil & PVA on hardboard 121.9 x 61
3266

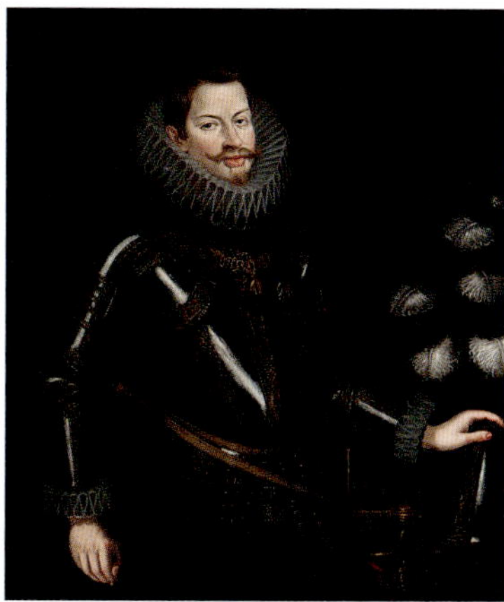

Pantoja de la Cruz, Juan 1553–1608
Philip III (1578–1621), King of Spain c.1605
oil on canvas 109.8 x 93
PC.139

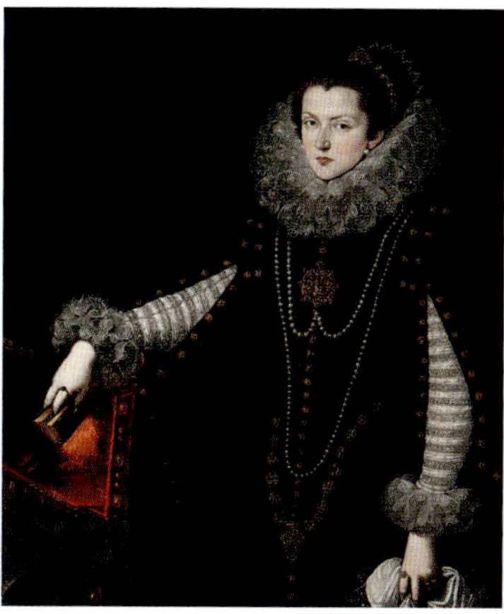

Pantoja de la Cruz, Juan (attributed to)
1553–1608
Portrait of a Lady
oil on canvas 109.2 x 92.4
PC.138

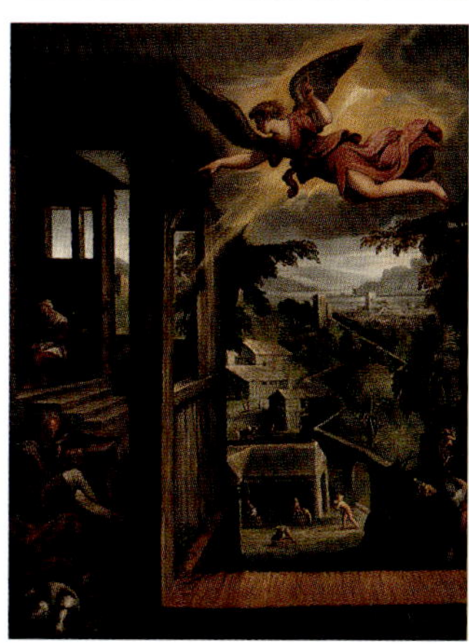

Paolo Fiammingo 1540–1596
The Dream of Joseph c.1587–1596
oil on canvas 160 x 116.8
1591

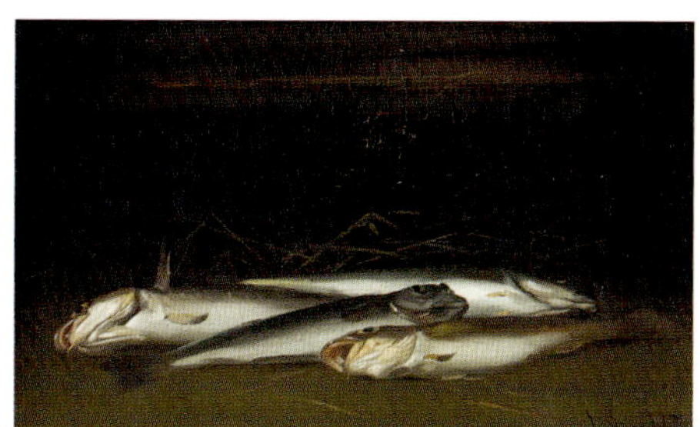

Park, Stuart 1862–1933
A Slippery Subject 1886
oil on canvas 25.7 x 40.6
3325

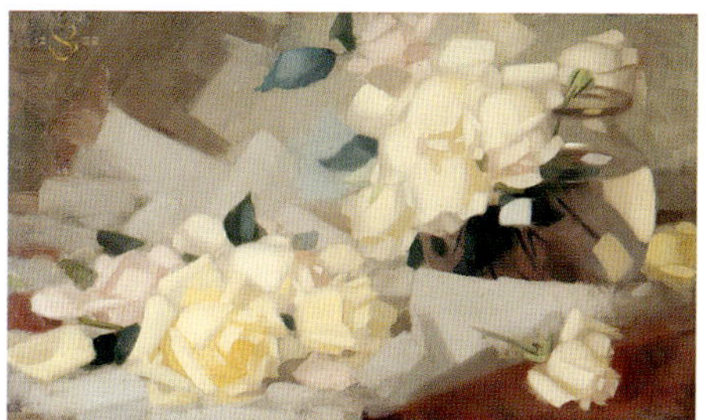

Park, Stuart 1862–1933
Roses 1889
oil on canvas 40.6 x 66
2503

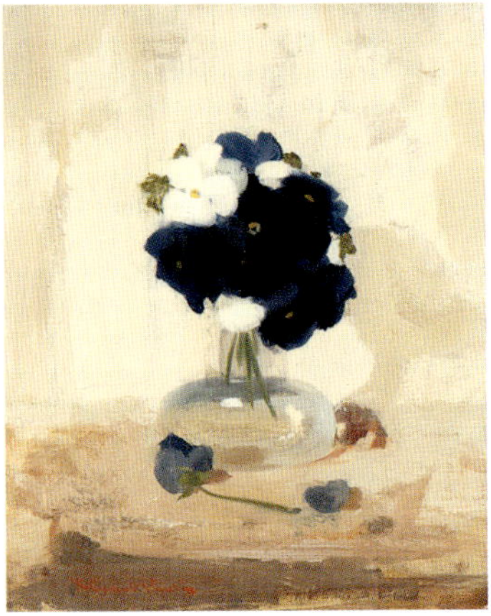

Park, Stuart 1862–1933
Violets c.1890–1900
oil on canvas 38.1 x 30.5
2809

Park, Stuart 1862–1933
Dr John Macintyre (1857?–1928) c.1904
oil on canvas 40.5 x 50.5
3096

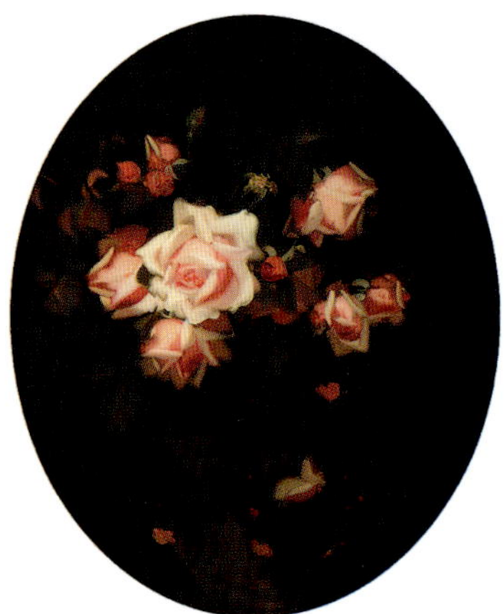

Park, Stuart 1862–1933
Roses 'La France' c.1907
oil on canvas 61 x 50.8
1201

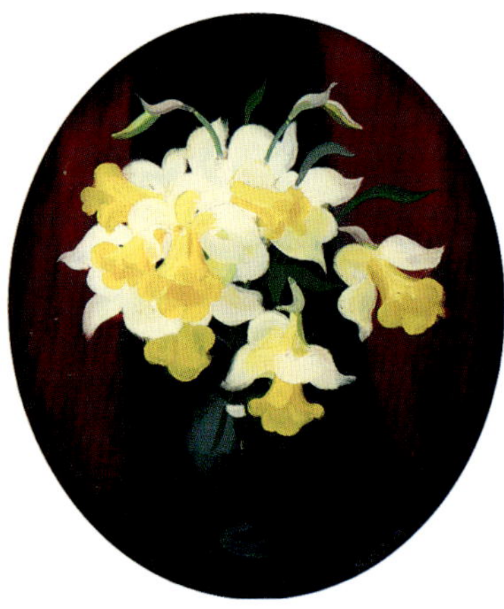

Park, Stuart 1862–1933
Daffodils
oil on canvas 50.8 x 43.2
2650

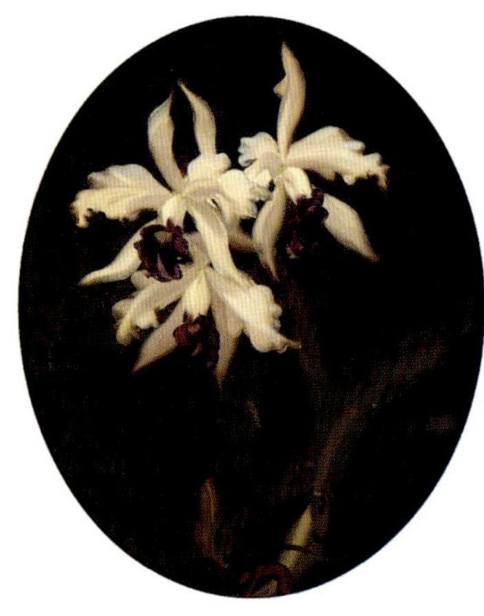

Park, Stuart 1862–1933
Orchids
oil on canvas 50.8 x 40.6
2649

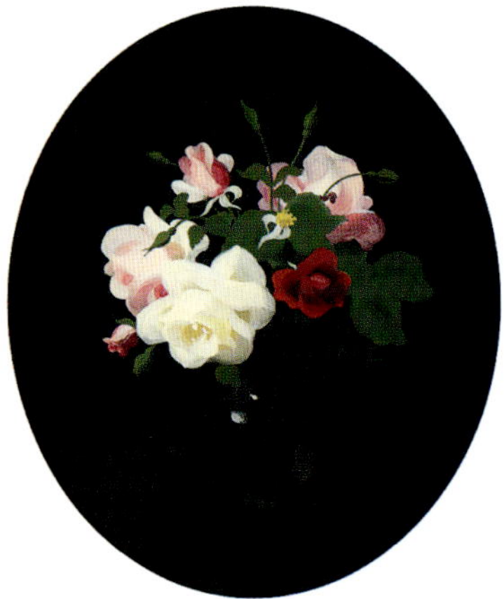

Park, Stuart 1862–1933
Vase of Roses
oil on canvas 59.7 x 49.5
2633

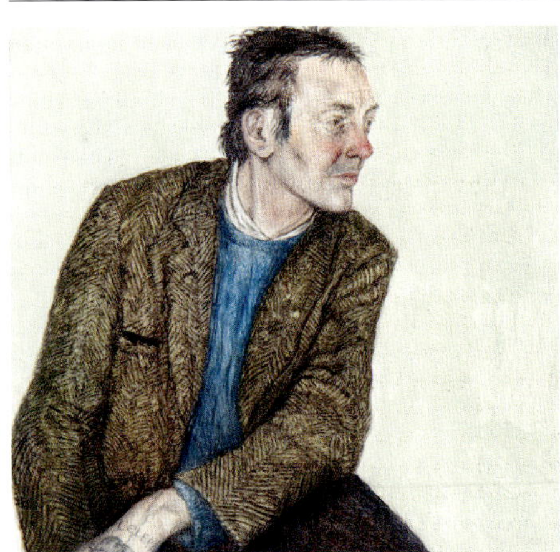

Parker, Alan b.1965
L'éléphant 1995
oil on board 13 x 13.5
3602

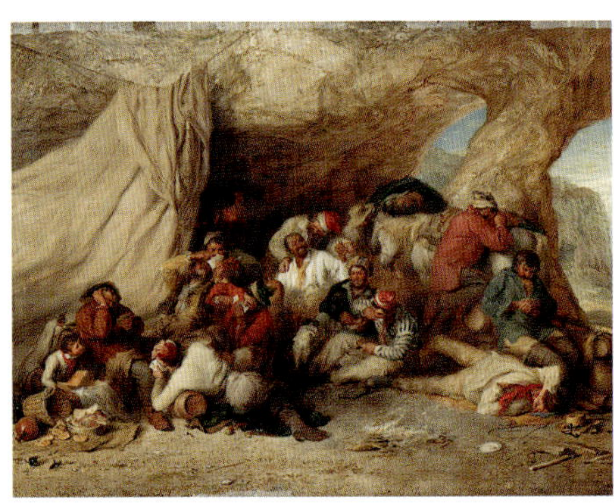

Parker, Henry Perlee 1795–1873
The Smugglers' Cave 1852
oil on canvas 106.7 x 139.7
807

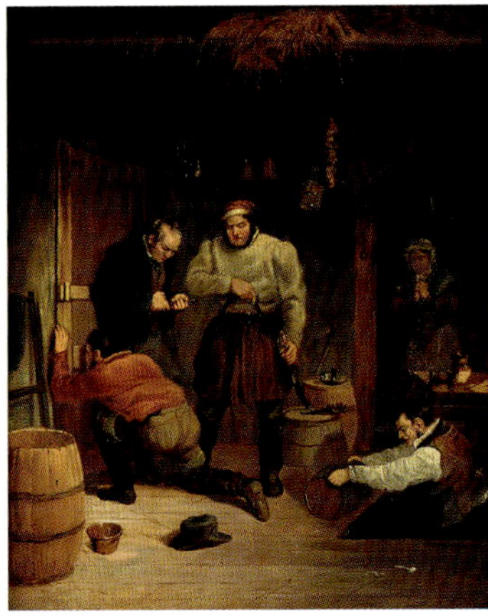

Parker, Henry Perlee (attributed to) 1795–1873
The Smugglers: The Alarm
oil on canvas 52 x 43.2
889

Facing page: Rubens, Peter Paul, 1577–1640, & Brueghel the elder, Jan, 1568–1625, *Nature and Her Followers*, c.1615 (p. 380)

336

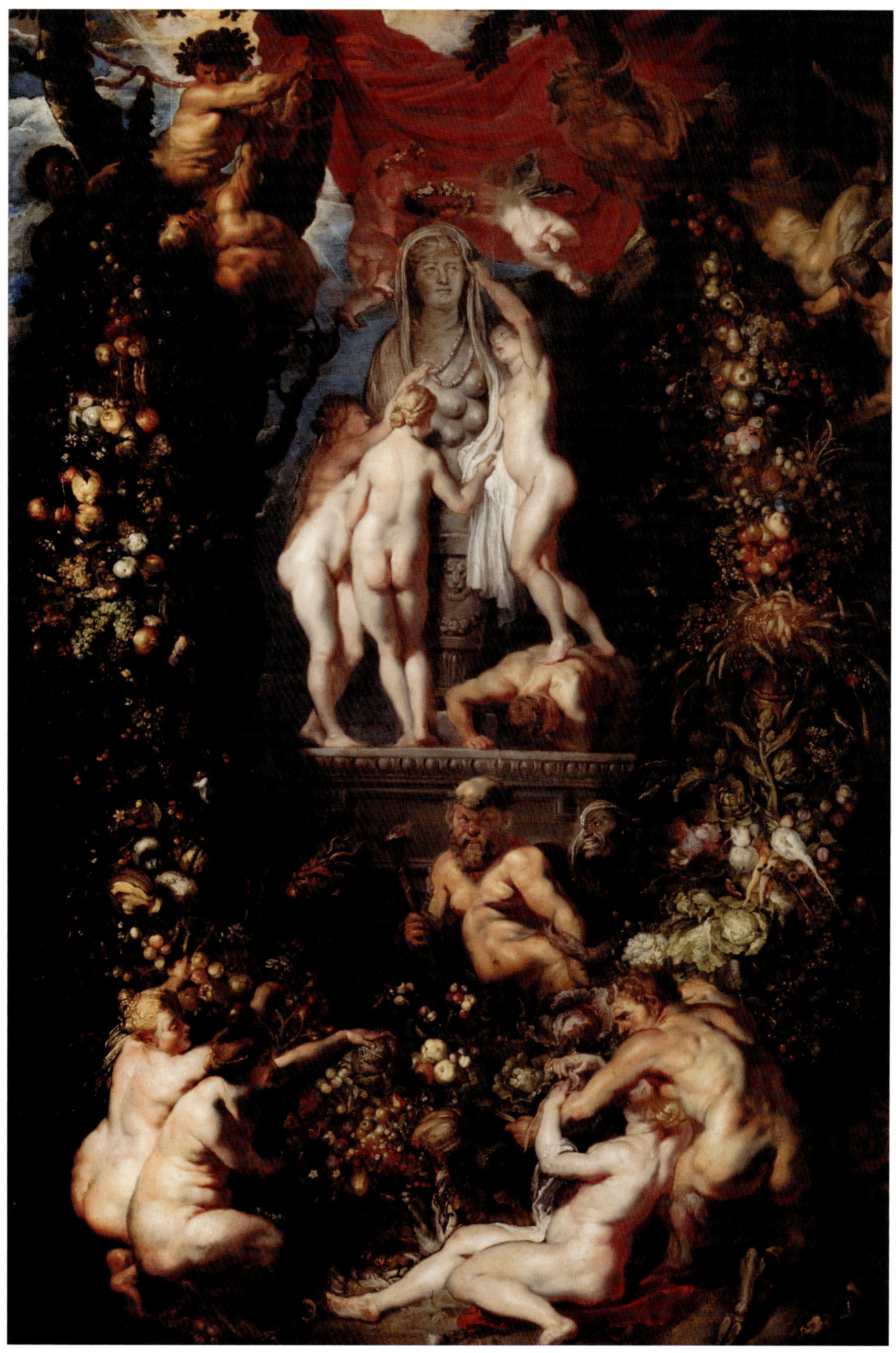

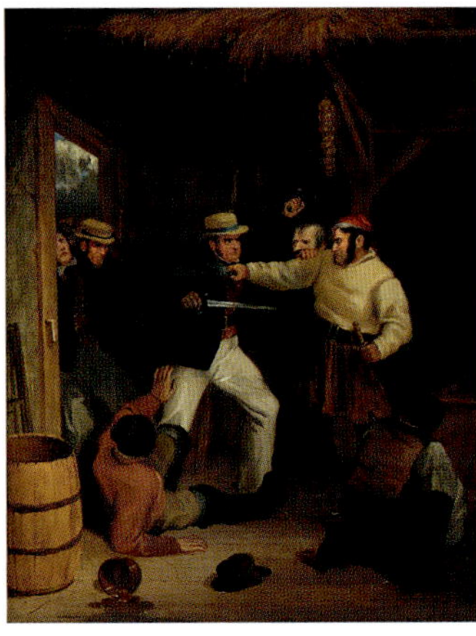

Parker, Henry Perlee (attributed to) 1795–1873
The Smugglers: The Attack
oil on canvas 52 x 43.2
890

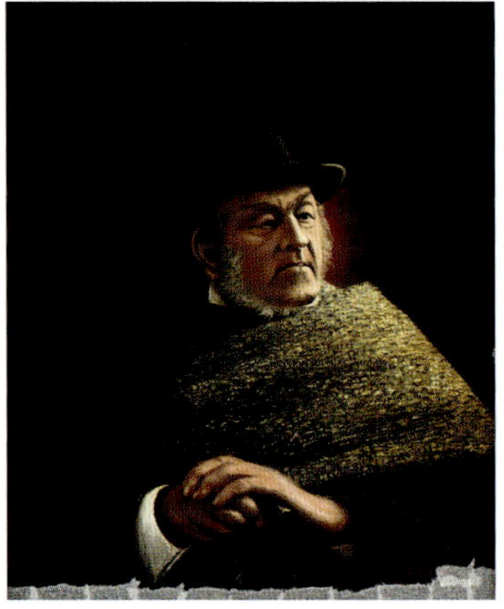

Parker, James (attributed to)
A. B. Todd 1906
oil on canvas 71 x 61
TEMP.14944

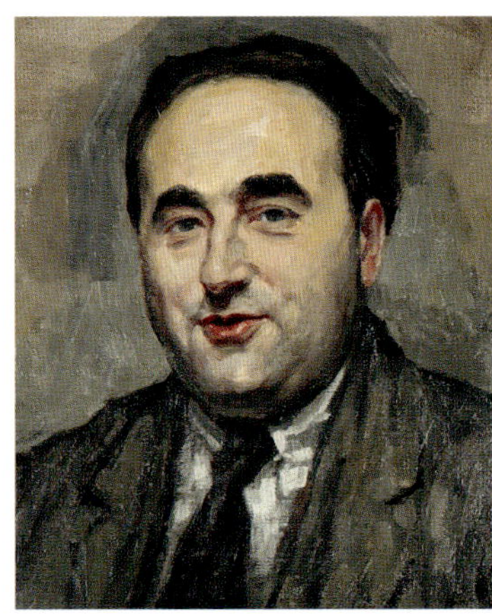

Parkes, Jane active 20th C
Guy Alfred Aldred (1886–1893)
oil on canvas 38 x 31.8
TEMP.2516

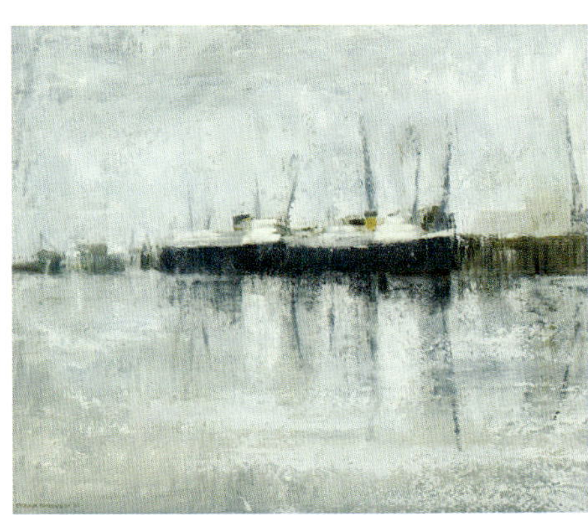

Parkinson, Gerald b.1926
Cross Channel Terminus, Newhaven 1961
oil on hardboard 50.8 x 61.3
3149

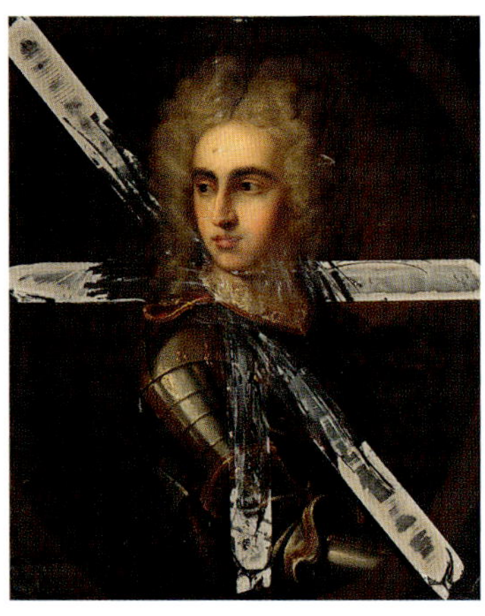

Parrocel, Pierre (after) 1670–1739
George Keith (c.1693–1778), 10th Earl Marischal 18th C
oil on canvas 75.2 x 62.2
1017

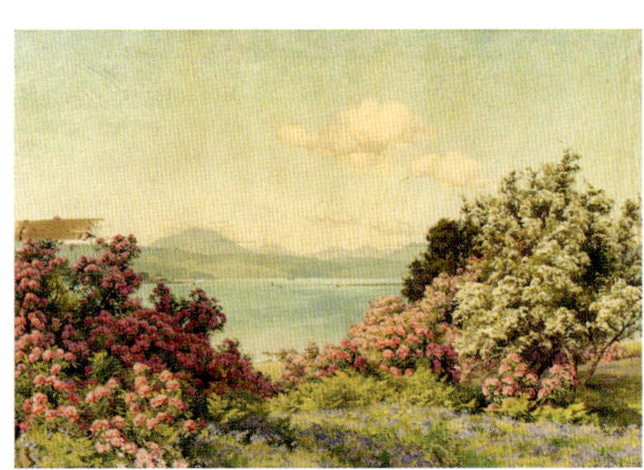

Parsons, Alfred William 1847–1920
The Narrows at Rosneath and the Gareloch
oil on canvas 106.7 x 153
3084

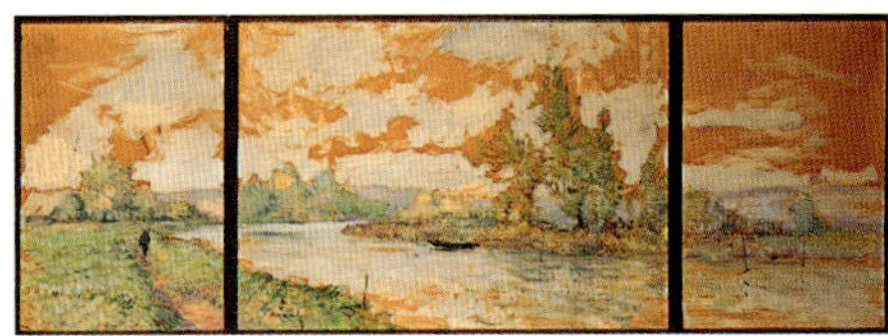

Pascal, Léopold 1900–1957
A River Scene (triptych) 1940–1945
oil on board 59 x 164
2553

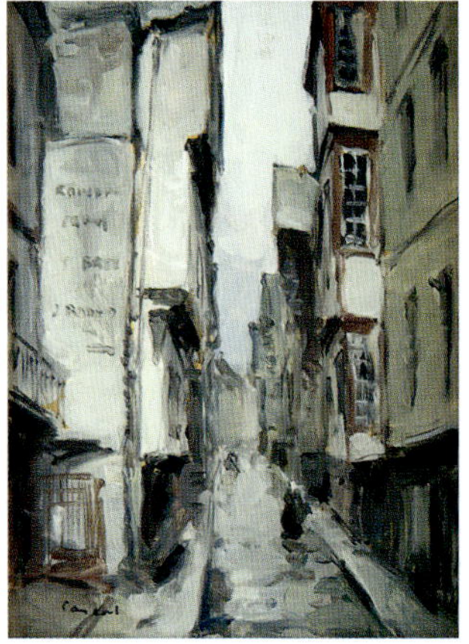

Pascal, Léopold 1900–1957
La Grand'Rue, Morlaix
oil on cardboard 35.5 x 25.5
2348

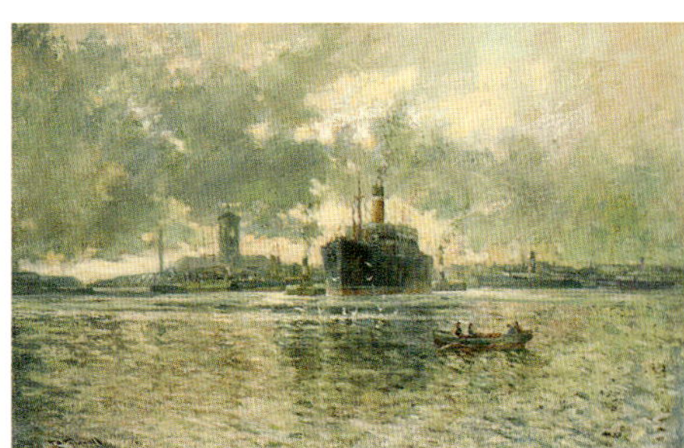

Pasquoll, Robert D. 1881–1927
On the Clyde c.1921
oil on canvas 64 x 90
T.1980.3

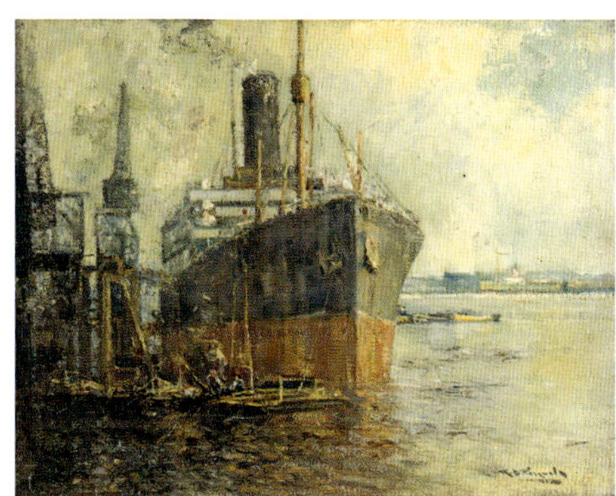

Pasquoll, Robert D. 1881–1927
TSS 'Cameronia'
oil on canvas 41.9 x 52.1
1710

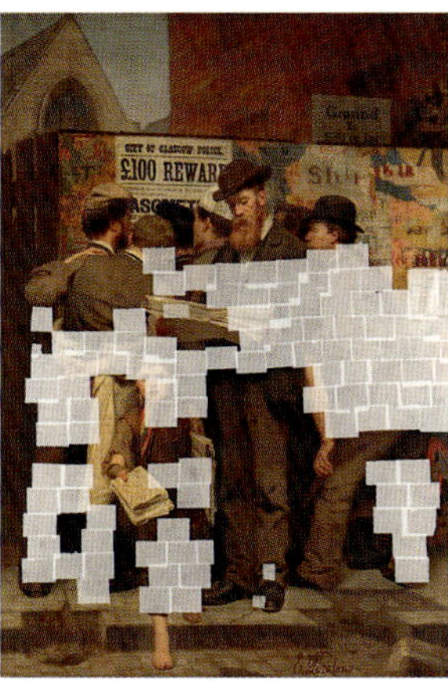

Patalano, Enrico active 1869–1886
Plot to Blow Up the Gasworks
oil on canvas 268 x 177.8
NR.41

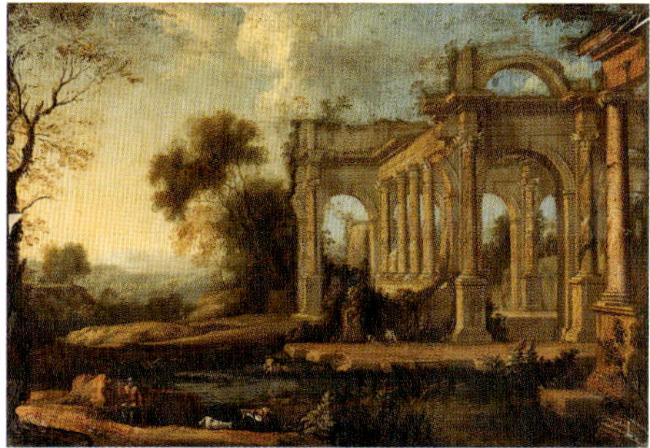

Patel, Pierre I (style of) c.1605–1676
Landscape with Classical Ruins c.1650–1655
oil on canvas 96.2 x 135.9
1451

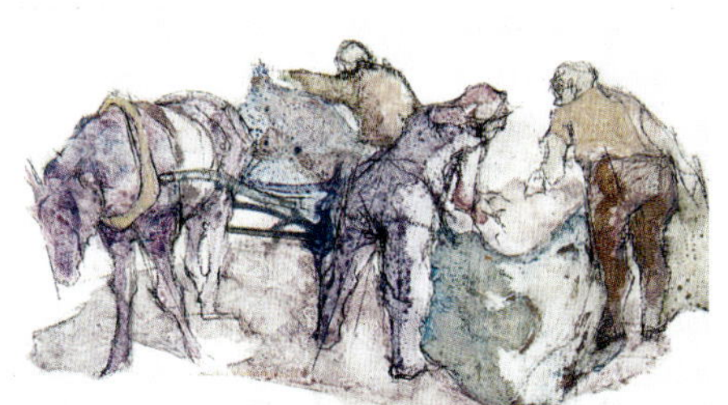

Paterson, Anda b.1935
Saltmarket, Glasgow c.1970
PVA on board 12.9 x 22.5
PP.1988.45.3

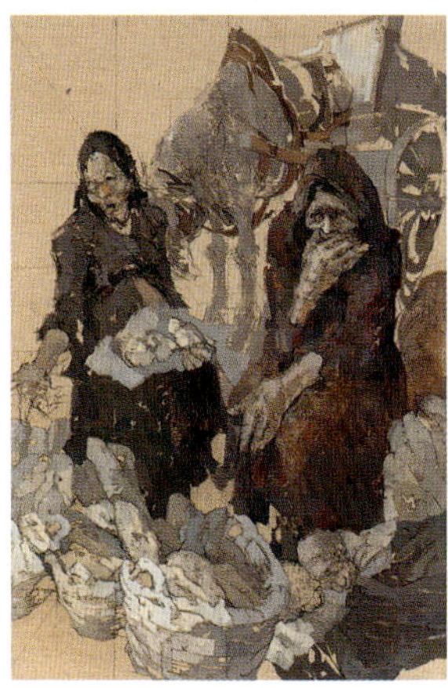

Paterson, Anda b.1935
Bread Seller c.2008
oil & mixed media on canvas 158.6 x 113
3681

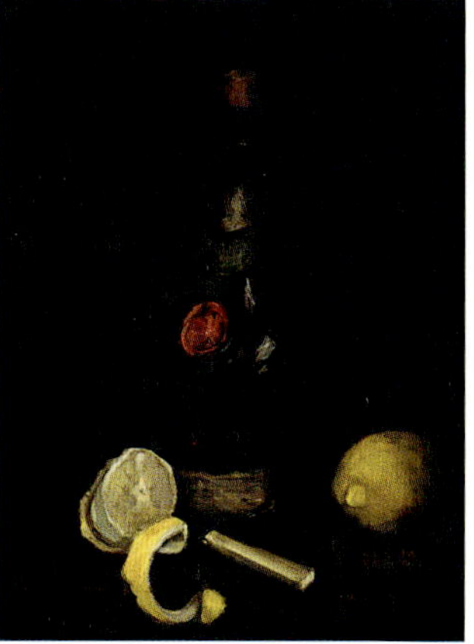

Paterson, Emily Murray 1855–1934
Still Life
oil on canvas on pasteboard 40.6 x 30.5
1906

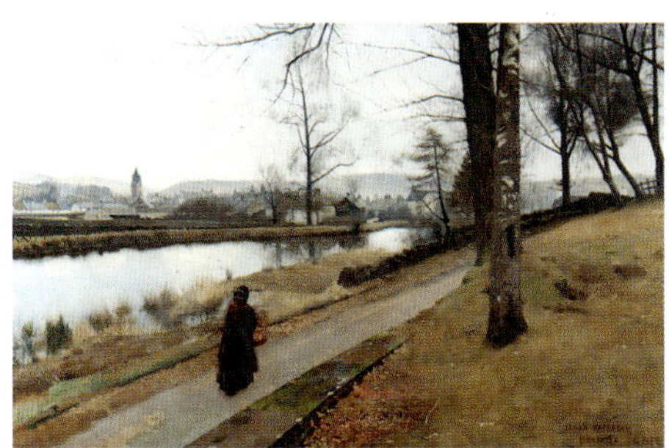

Paterson, James 1854–1932
The Last Turning, Winter, Moniaive 1885
oil on canvas 61.3 x 91.4
3349

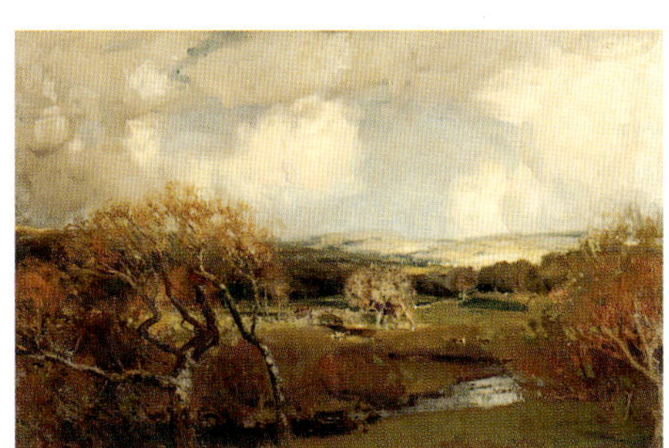

Paterson, James 1854–1932
Borderland c.1896–1898
oil on canvas 121.9 x 182.9
885

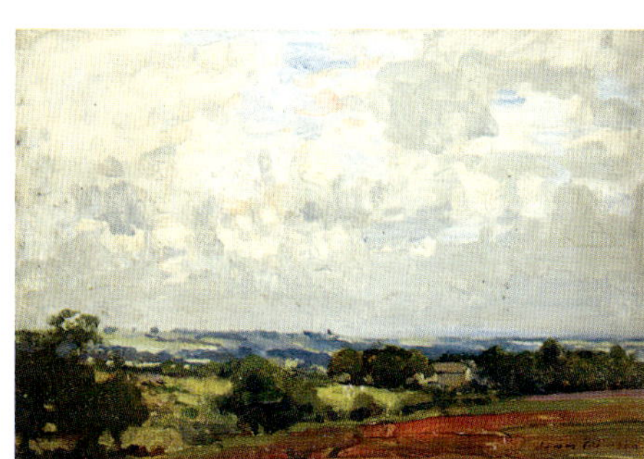

Paterson, James 1854–1932
Barbuie near Moniaive
oil on panel 22.9 x 33.2
3230

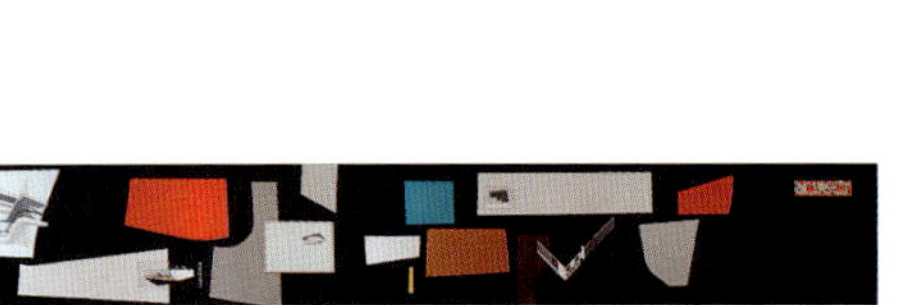

Paterson, Toby b.1974
Black Elegy: Untitled (installation) 2004
acrylic on wall 284 x 1774
ICE.2006.1.1.a

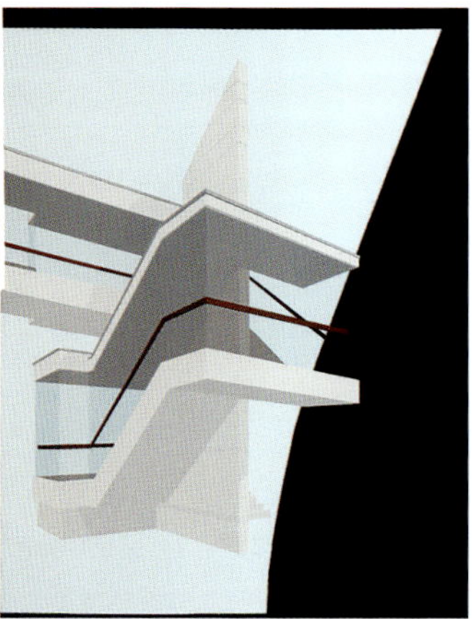

Paterson, Toby b.1974
Black Elegy: Sunlit Emergency Exit (Anderston Version) (installation) 2002–2004
acrylic on wall 149 x 112.3
ICE.2006.1.1.b

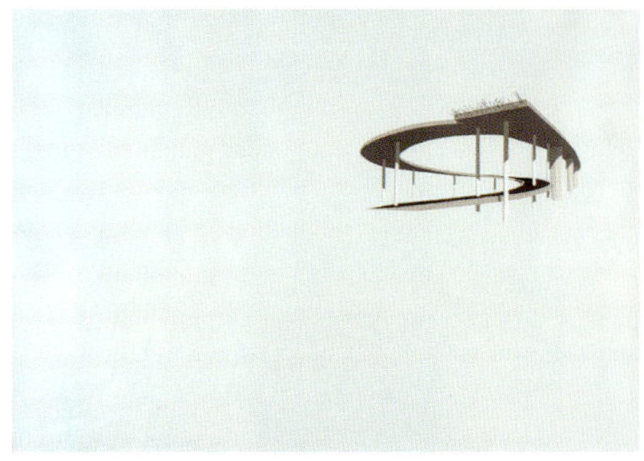

Paterson, Toby b.1974
Black Elegy: Spiral Motif (The Bridge to Nowhere) (installation) 2004
acrylic on paper 99 x 136.4
ICE.2006.1.1.c

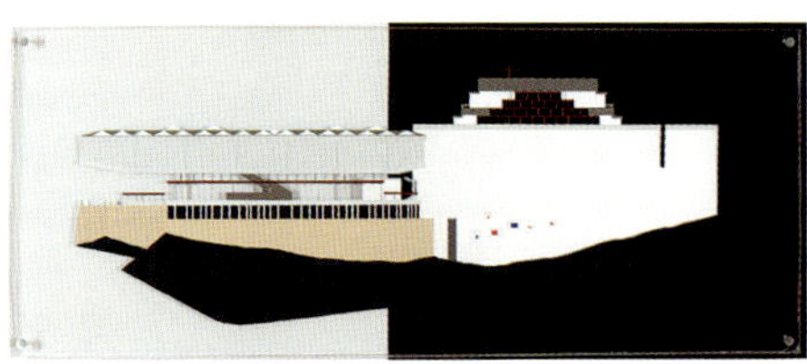

Paterson, Toby b.1974
Black Elegy: Seminary Elevation (installation) 2004
acrylic on perspex 50 x 122
ICE.2006.1.1.d

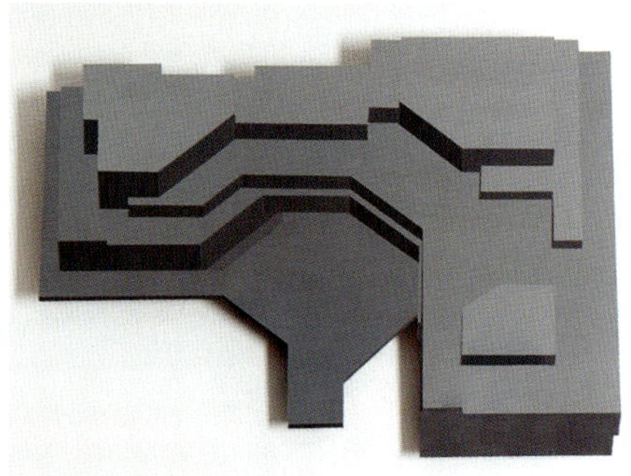

Paterson, Toby b.1974
Black Elegy: Proposed Cultural Centre (installation) 2004
acrylic on perspex 38 x 50
ICE.2006.1.1.e

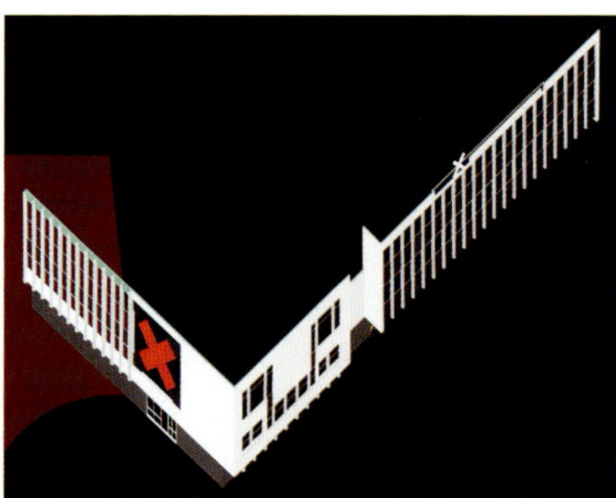

Paterson, Toby b.1974
Black Elegy: Axonometric Facade with Red Cross (installation) 2004
acrylic on wall 126 x 152.5
ICE.2006.1.1.f

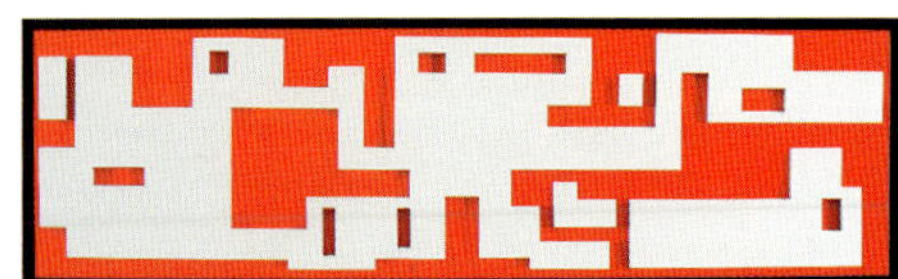

Paterson, Toby b.1974
Black Elegy: Grey and Red Relief (installation) 2004
acrylic on MDF 32 x 110.5
ICE.2006.1.1.g

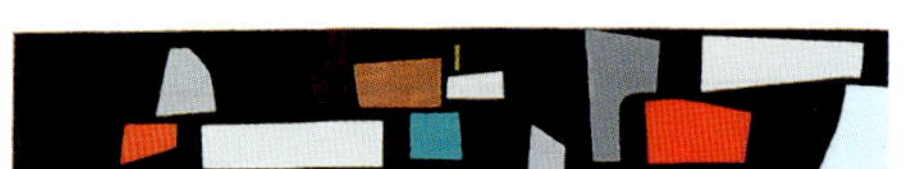

Paterson, Toby b.1974
Working Drawing for 'Black Elegy' 2004
acrylic on paper 10.5 x 36
ICE.2006.1.2

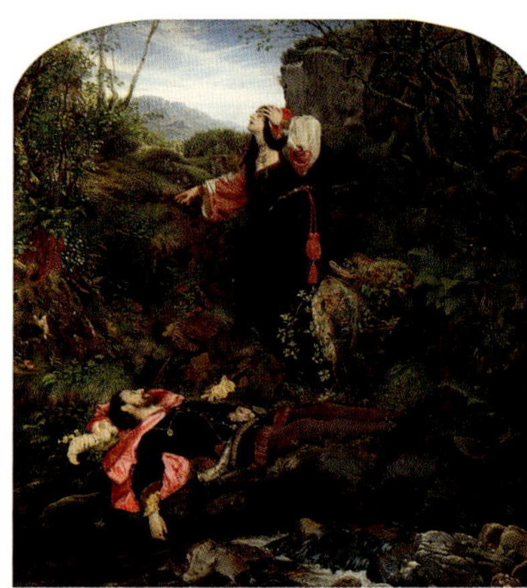

Paton, Joseph Noel 1821–1901
The Bluidie Tryste 1855
oil on canvas 73 x 65.2
3156

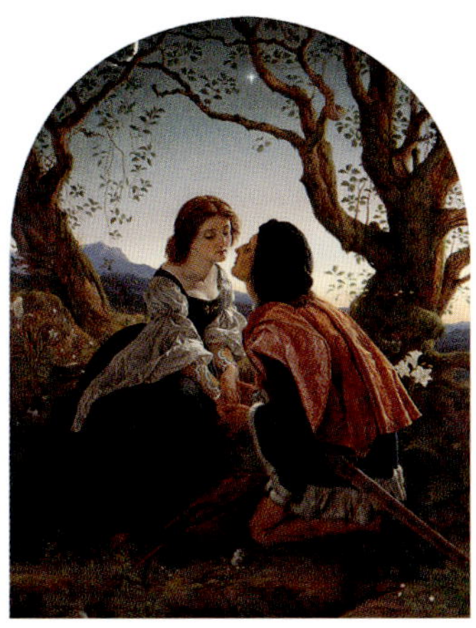

Paton, Joseph Noel 1821–1901
Hesperus, the Evening Star, Sacred to Lovers 1857
oil on millboard 91.4 x 68.6
1033

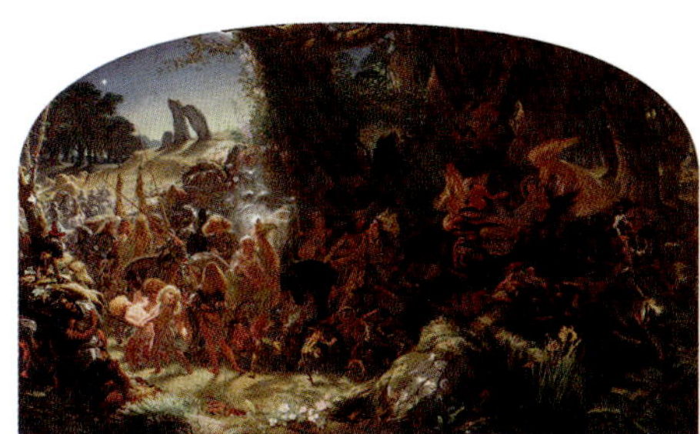

Paton, Joseph Noel 1821–1901
The Fairy Raid: Carrying Off a Changeling, Midsummer Eve 1867
oil on canvas 90.5 x 146.7
3234

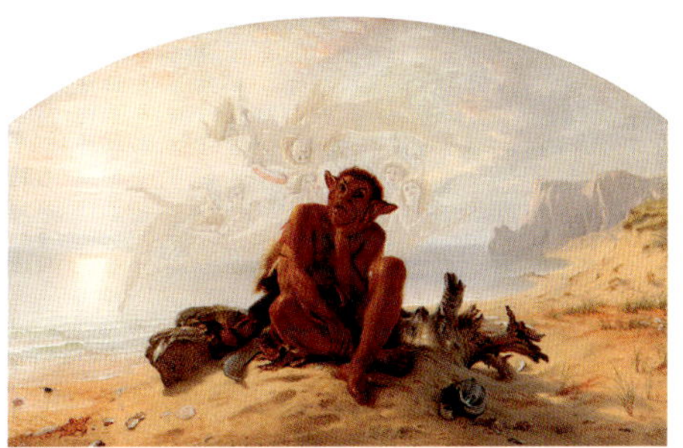

Paton, Joseph Noel 1821–1901
Caliban (from 'The Tempest' by William Shakespeare) 1868
oil on canvas 83.8 x 124.5
1804

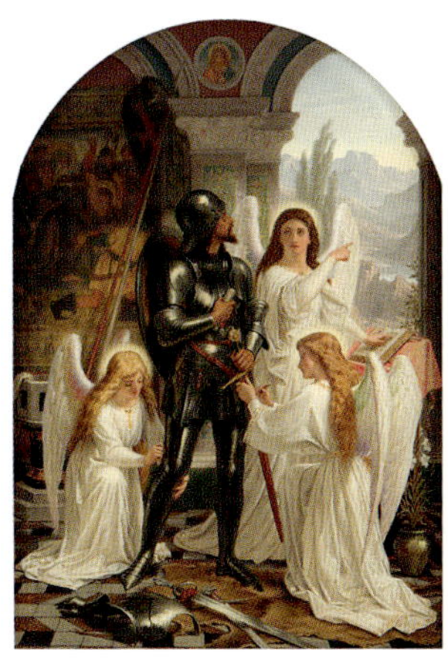

Paton, Joseph Noel 1821–1901
Arming Christian for the Fight (from 'The Pilgrim's Progress' by John Bunyan) 1876
oil on canvas 40.6 x 27.9
2921

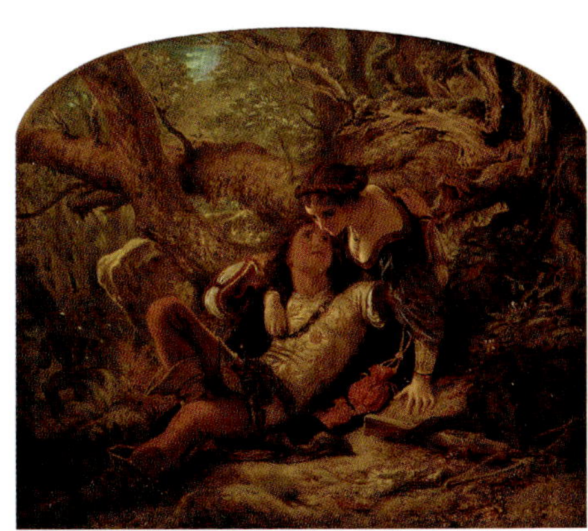

Paton, Joseph Noel 1821–1901
The Tryst
oil on canvas 30.5 x 35.6
2113

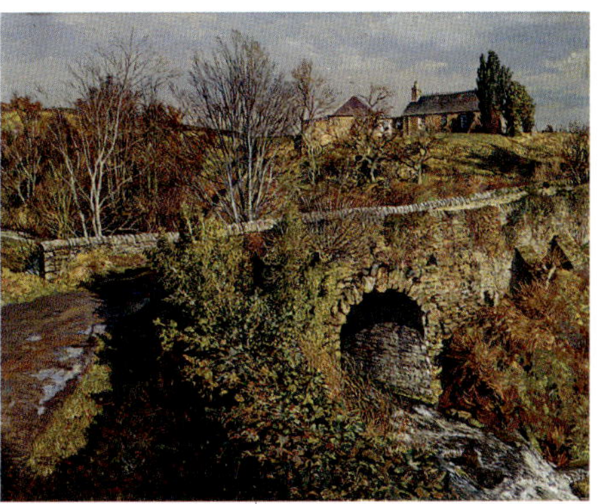

Patrick, James McIntosh 1907–1998
The Bridge, Den of Fowlis, Angus c.1957
oil on canvas 63.3 x 75.7
3076

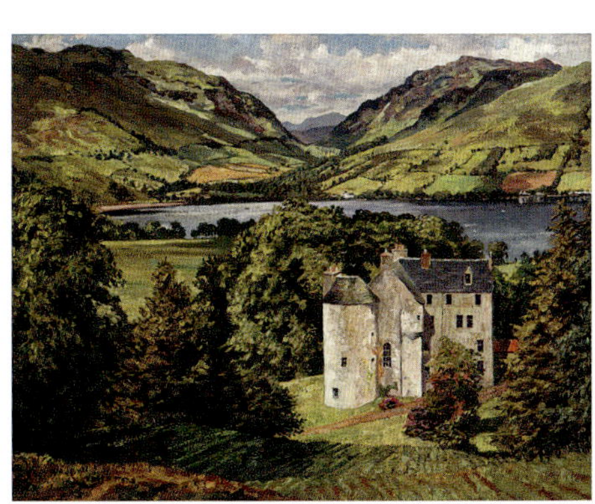

Patrick, James McIntosh 1907–1998
A Castle in Scotland
oil on canvas 41 x 50.8
NR.129

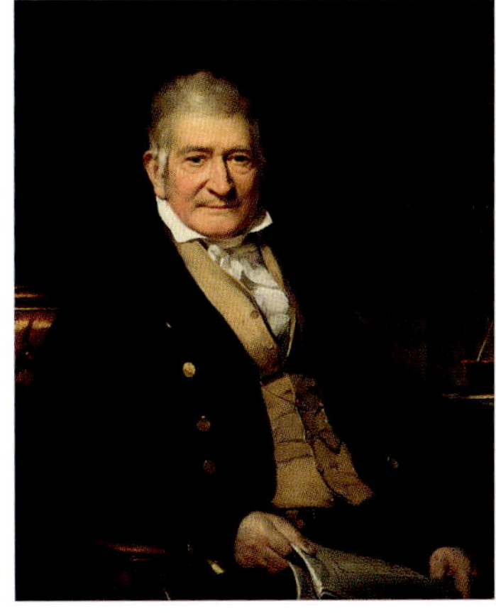

Patten, George 1801–1865
Thomas Telford (1757–1834) 1829
oil on canvas 91.7 x 71.5
3068

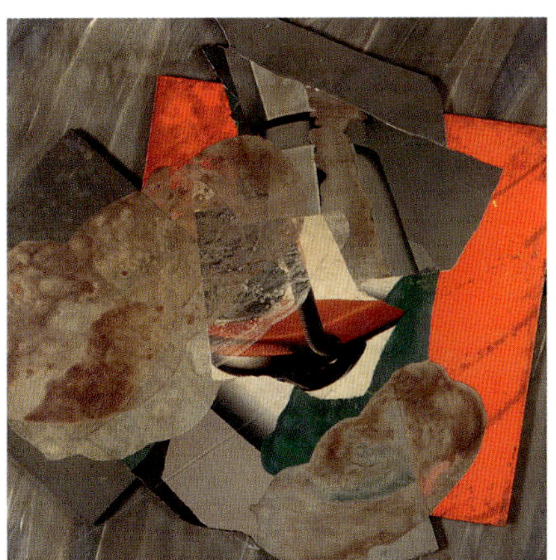

Pattison, Jim b.1955
Untitled c.1990
acrylic, wax, paper & mixed media on fibreboard 60.3 x 60
TEMP.15550

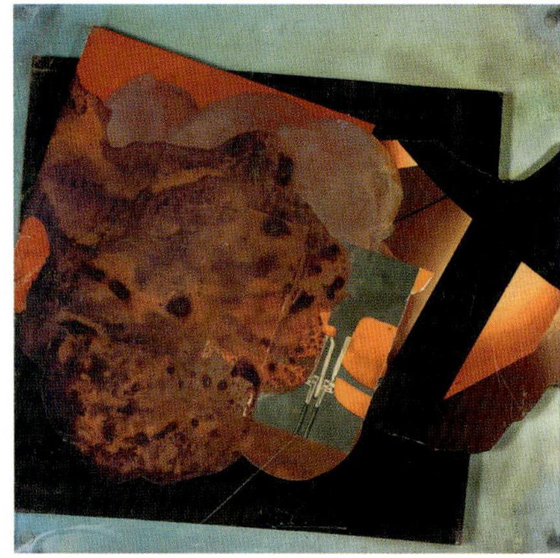

Pattison, Jim b.1955
Untitled c.1990
acrylic, wax, paper & mixed media on
fibreboard 60.3 x 60
TEMP.15552

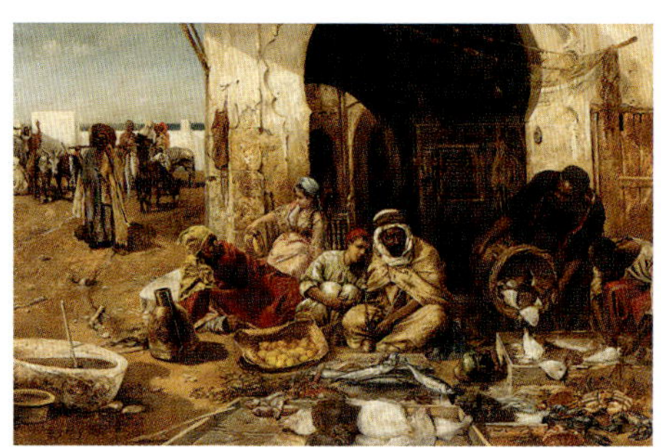

Pavy, Eugène active 1879–c.1900
An Eastern Market Place 1885
oil on canvas 85.3 x 128.5
774

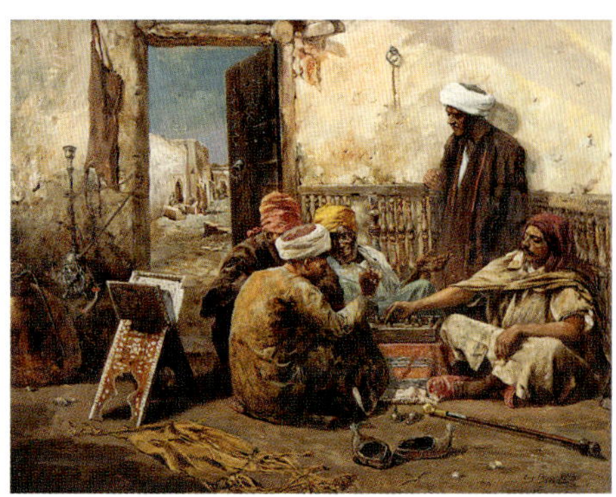

Pavy, Eugène active 1879–c.1900
Eastern Scene 1885
oil on canvas 50.5 x 63.5
871

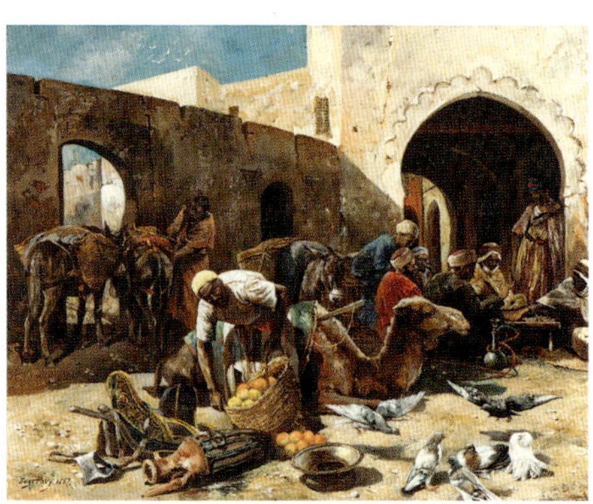

Pavy, Eugène active 1879–c.1900
Eastern Courtyard Scene 1887
oil on panel 49.5 x 60.9
836

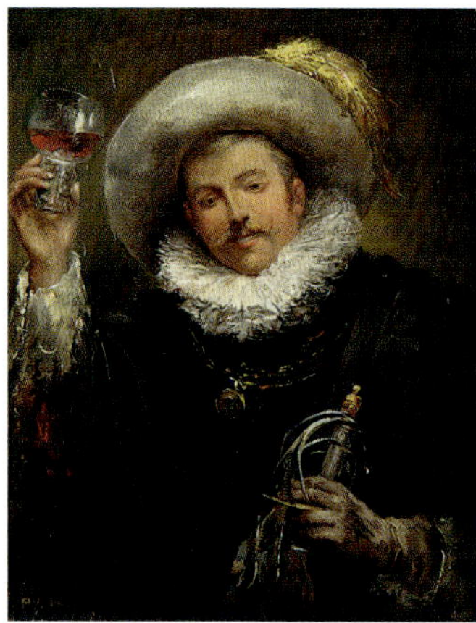

Pavy, Philippe b.1860
The Toast 1880
oil on cardboard 21.9 x 17.1
818

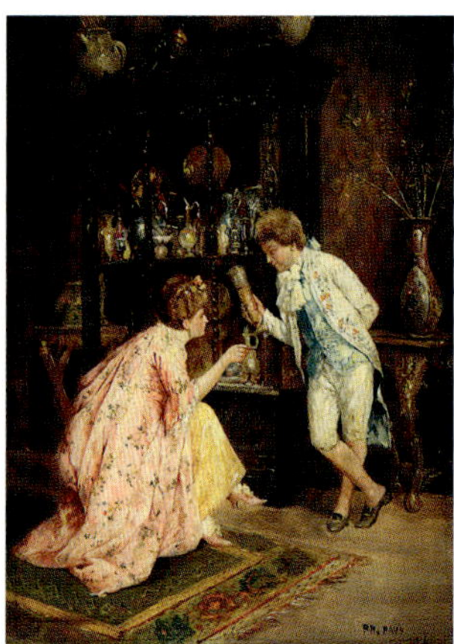

Pavy, Philippe b.1860
The Connoisseur 1881
oil on panel 25.4 x 17.5
827

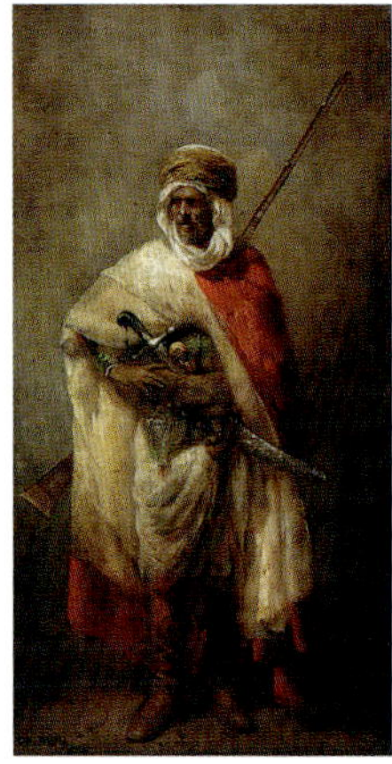

Pavy, Philippe b.1860
A Moroccan Soldier 1885
oil on panel 38.1 x 20
839

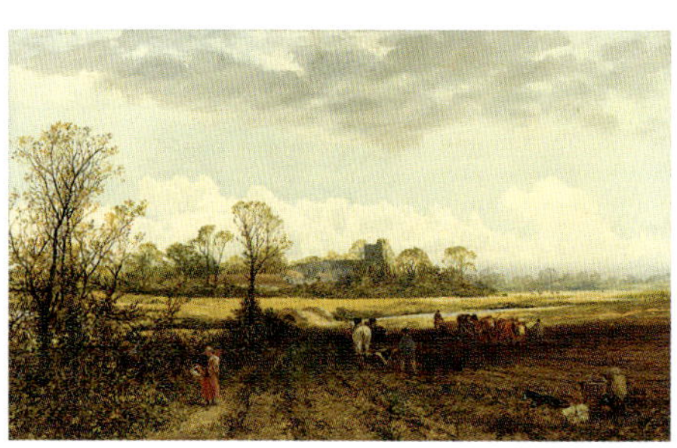

Peel, James 1811–1906
Church Field at Edmonton 1869
oil on canvas 40.6 x 66
926

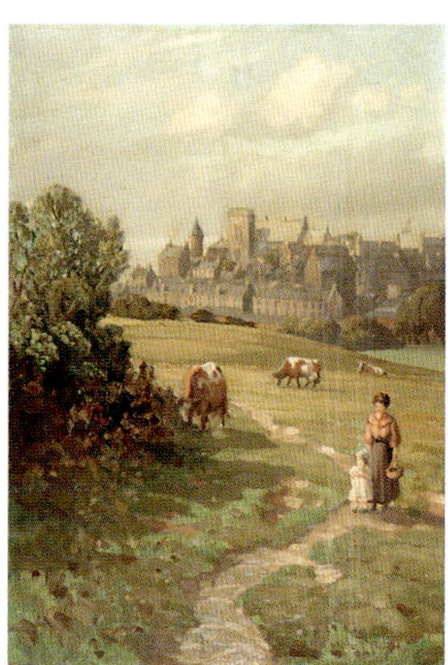

Pender, Walter L. active 1904–1932
Shawhill Pollokshaws c.1924–1932
oil on board 72 x 48.3
NR.171

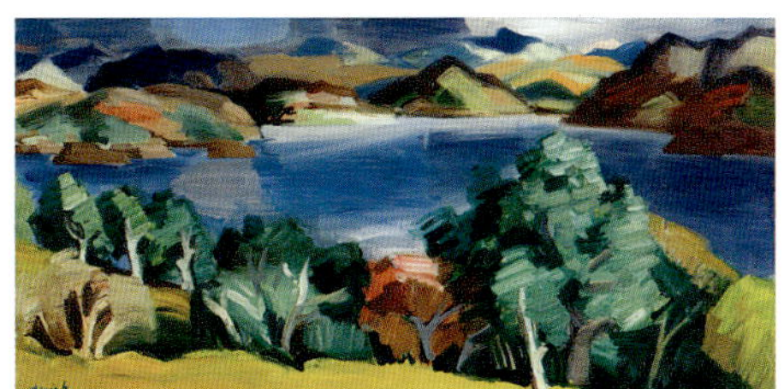

Peploe, Denis Frederic Neal 1914–1993
Oak Trees, Loch Carron 1952
oil on canvas 45.7 x 88.9
2998

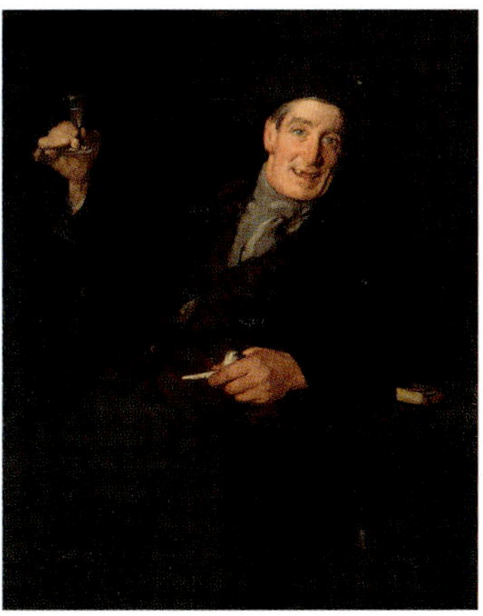

Peploe, Samuel John 1871–1935
Old Tom Morris c.1901
oil on canvas 127 x 101.6
3313

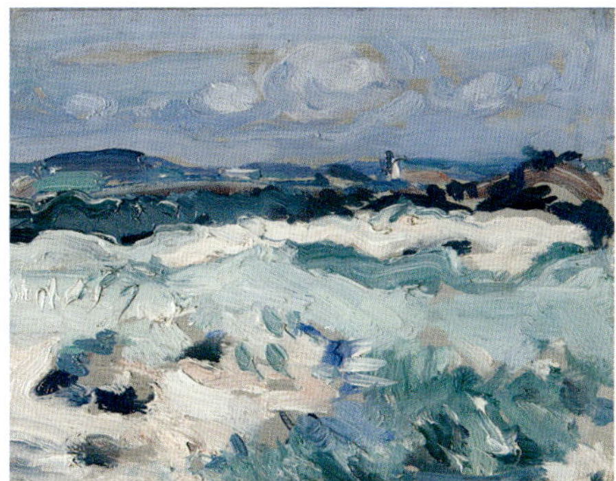

Peploe, Samuel John 1871–1935
Barra c.1902–1903
oil on panel 18.7 x 24.1
3039

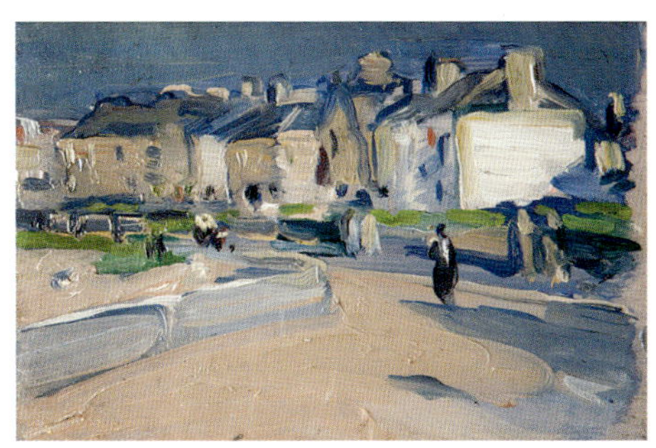

Peploe, Samuel John 1871–1935
Evening, North Berwick c.1903
oil on panel 16 x 23.8
3229

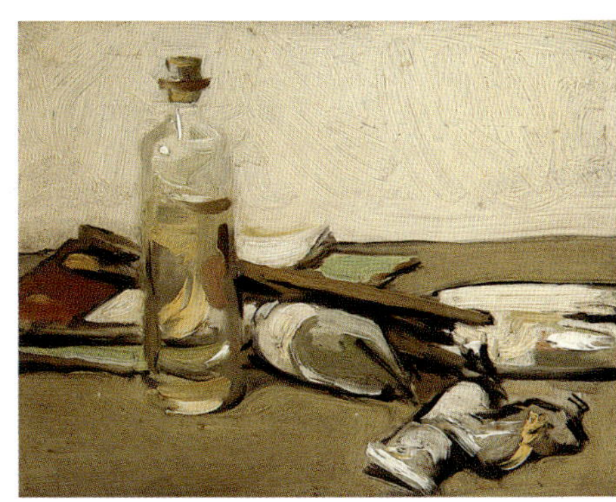

Peploe, Samuel John 1871–1935
Still Life with Paint Tubes c.1903
oil on panel 20 x 25.5
3226

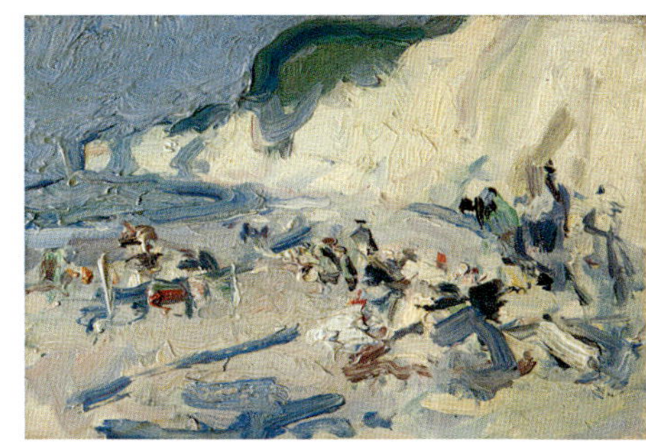

Peploe, Samuel John 1871–1935
Bernaval c.1904–1905
oil on panel 15.9 x 23.5
3228

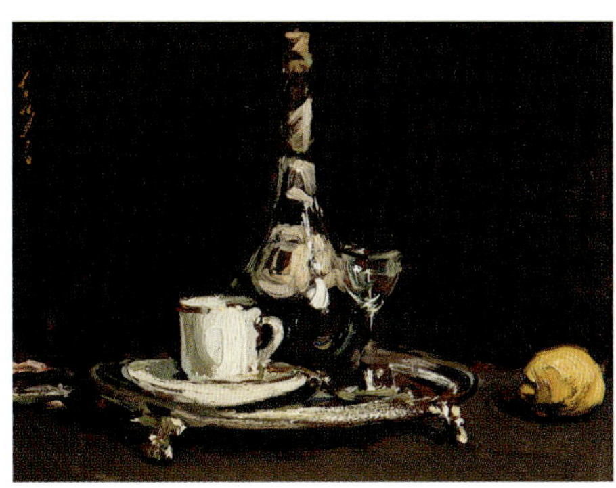

Peploe, Samuel John 1871–1935
Coffee and Liqueur c.1905
oil on panel 26.7 x 34.3
35.586

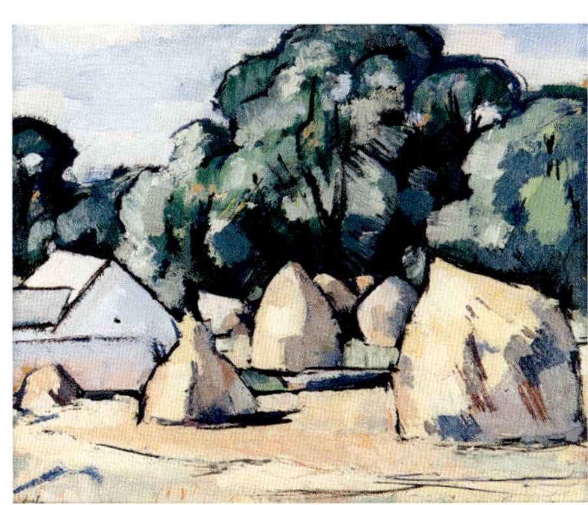

Peploe, Samuel John 1871–1935
Laggan Farm Buildings near Dalbeattie c.1916
oil on panel 31.8 x 38.1
2415

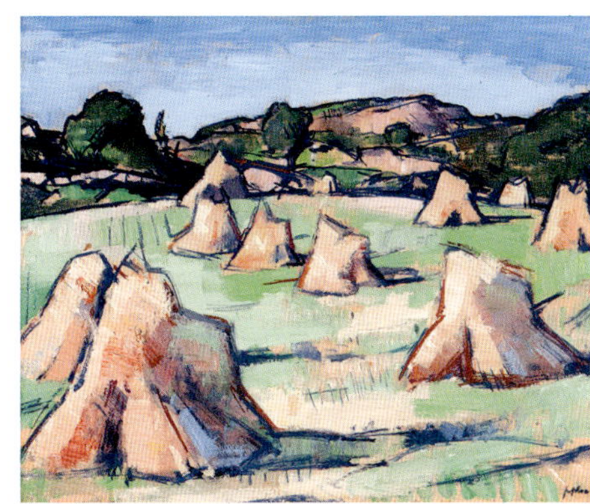

Peploe, Samuel John 1871–1935
The Cornfield, Douglas Hall 1919
oil on panel 33 x 39.4
2416

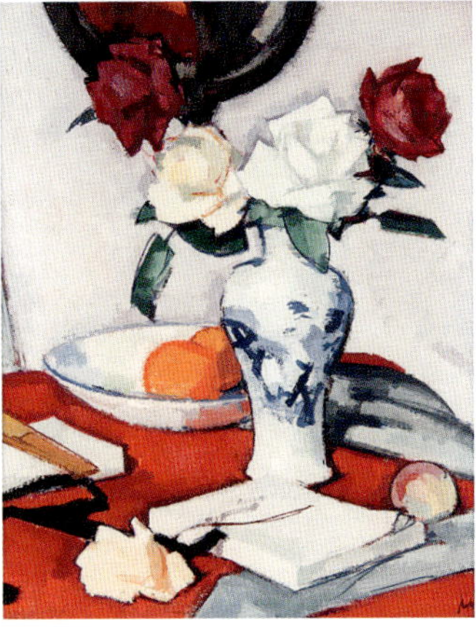

Peploe, Samuel John 1871–1935
Roses c.1920
oil on canvas 50.8 x 40.6
2810

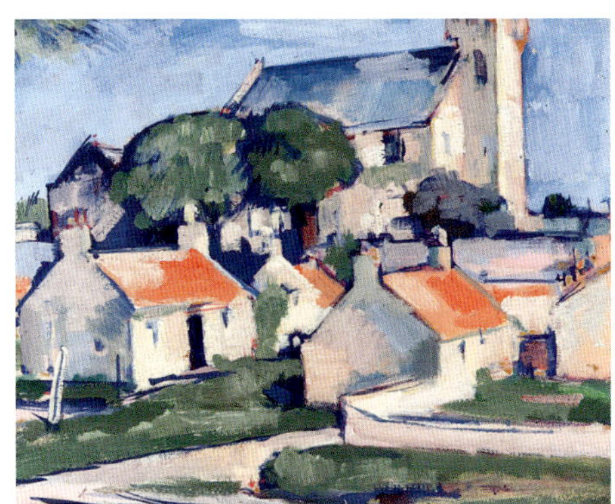

Peploe, Samuel John 1871–1935
Ceres c.1920–1925
oil on panel 33 x 40.9
3225

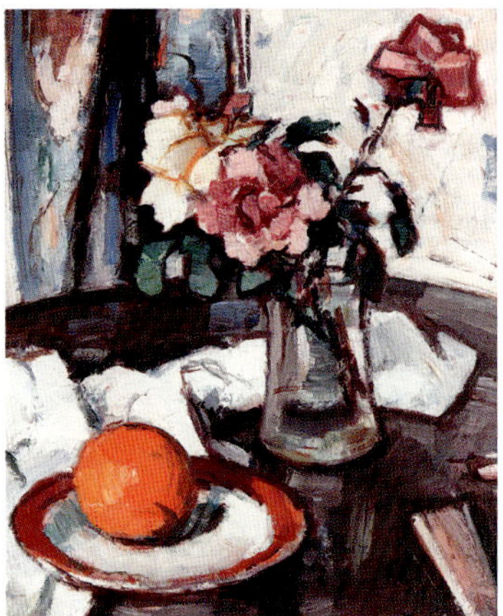

Peploe, Samuel John 1871–1935
Still Life c.1920–1930
oil on canvas 50.8 x 40.6
1839

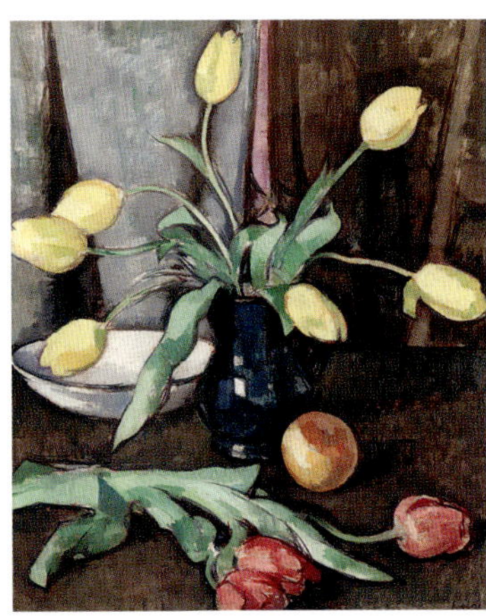

Peploe, Samuel John 1871–1935
Still Life with Tulips c.1920–1930
oil on canvas 54.5 x 45.5
3319

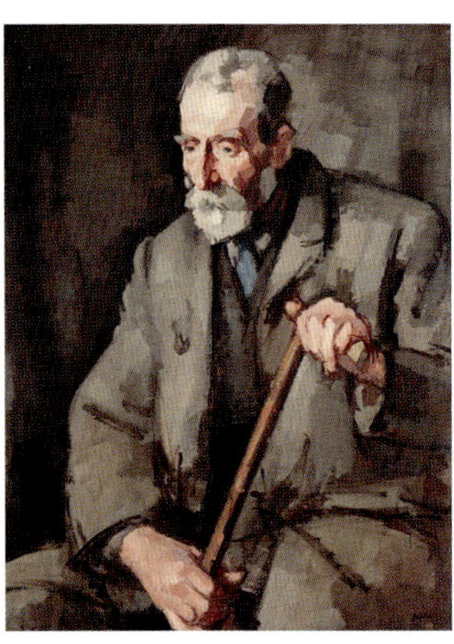

Peploe, Samuel John 1871–1935
Old Duff 1922
oil on canvas 101.6 x 74.9
2686

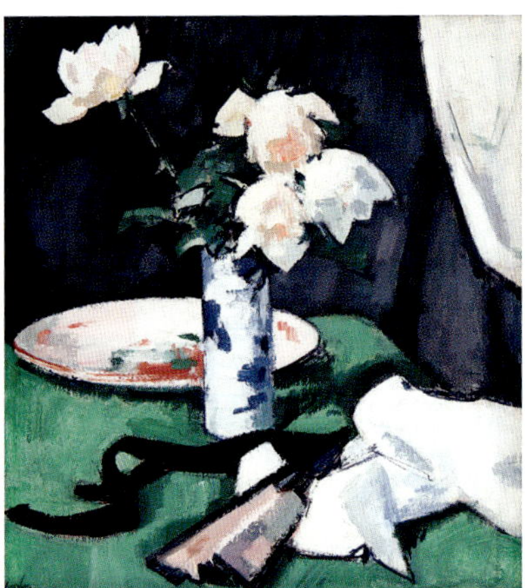

Peploe, Samuel John 1871–1935
Still Life, White Roses c.1925
oil on canvas 45.7 x 40.6
2414

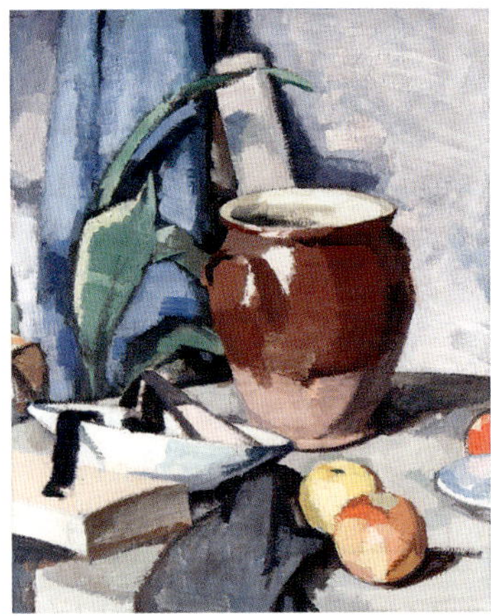

Peploe, Samuel John 1871–1935
The Brown Crock c.1925
oil on canvas 61 x 50.8
2413

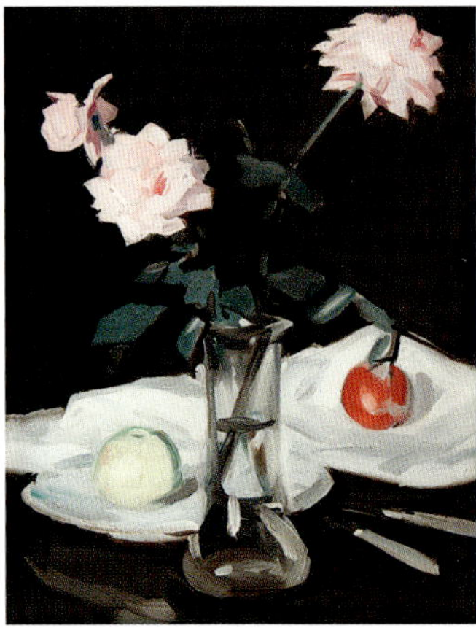

Peploe, Samuel John 1871–1935
Still Life, Pink Roses 1926
oil on canvas 50.8 x 40.6
2412

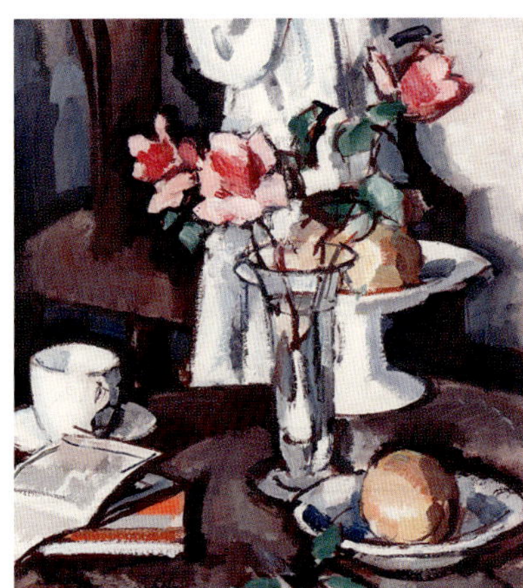

Peploe, Samuel John 1871–1935
Still Life, Red Roses c.1931
oil on canvas 55.9 x 50.8
1824

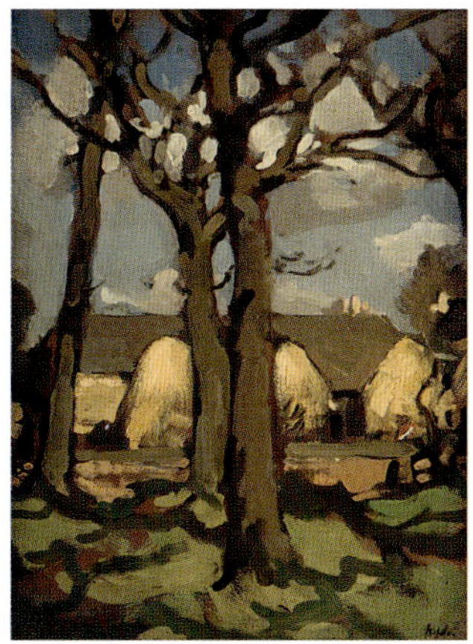

Peploe, Samuel John 1871–1935
Farm Steading
oil on panel 34.7 x 25.7
3227

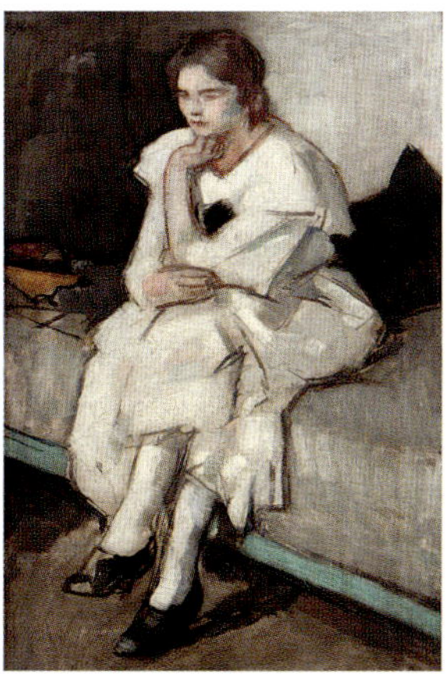

Peploe, Samuel John 1871–1935
Girl in a White Dress
oil on canvas 61 x 40.6
35.587

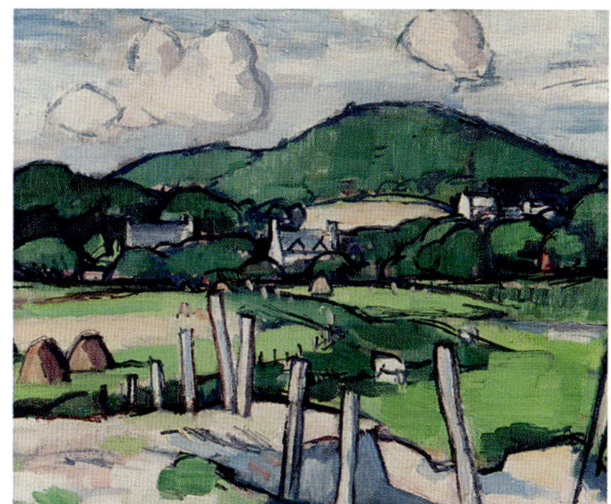

Peploe, Samuel John 1871–1935
Landscape
oil on canvas 33 x 40.6
2338

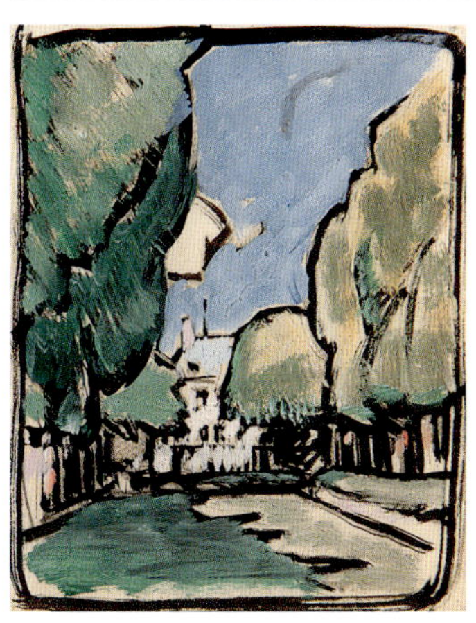

Peploe, Samuel John 1871–1935
Landscape
oil on paper 19.4 x 17.1
2655

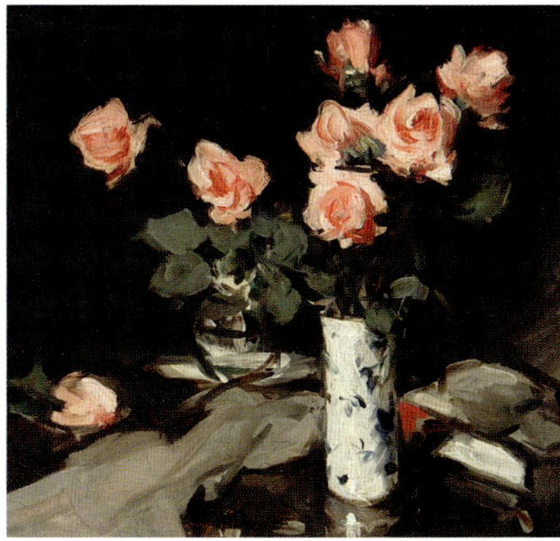

Peploe, Samuel John 1871–1935
Roses
oil on canvas 50.8 x 50.8
35.589

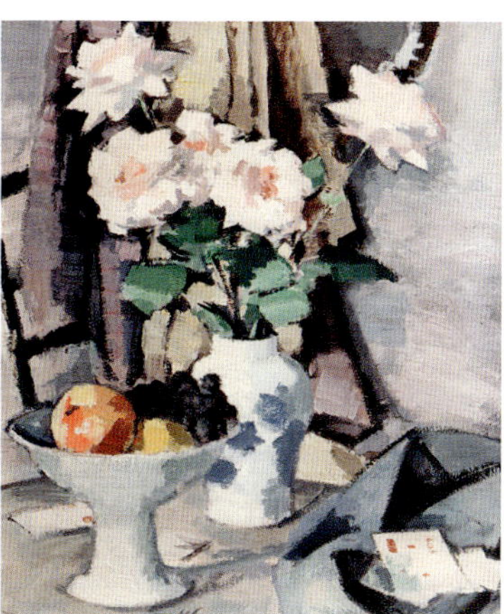

Peploe, Samuel John 1871–1935
Still Life, Pink Roses
oil on canvas 61 x 50.8
35.588

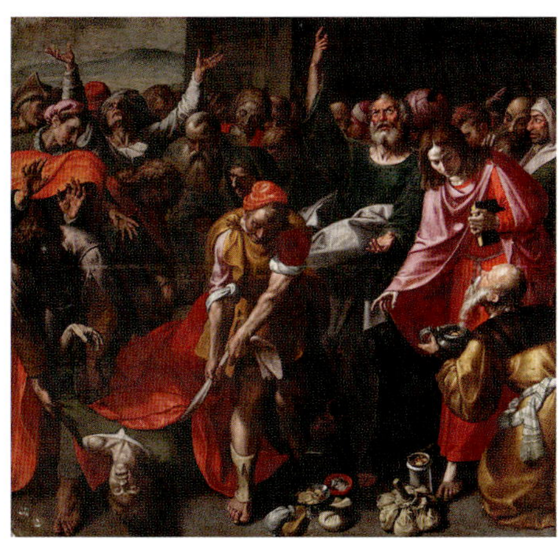

Pepyn, Marten (attributed to) 1575–1643
The Death of Ananias c.1600–1620
oil on canvas 205.7 x 218.7
204

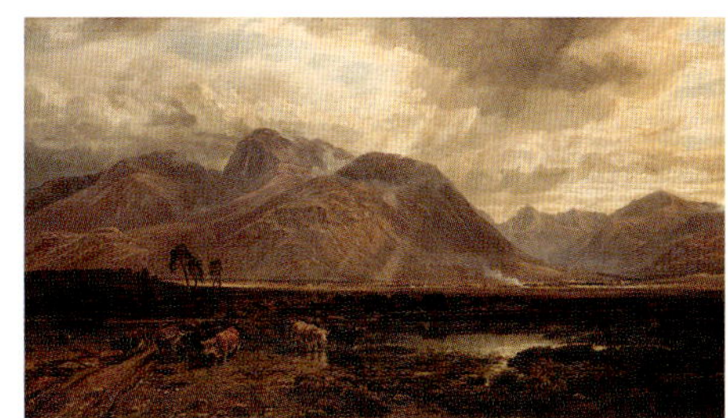

Perigal, Arthur the younger 1816–1884
Banavie Moor 1878
oil on canvas 91.4 x 156.2
2620

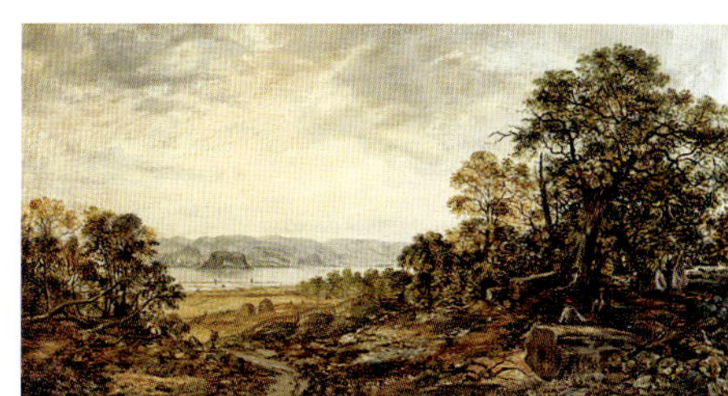

Perigal, Arthur the younger 1816–1884
On the Clyde, Dumbarton 1879
oil on canvas 48.3 x 94
1342

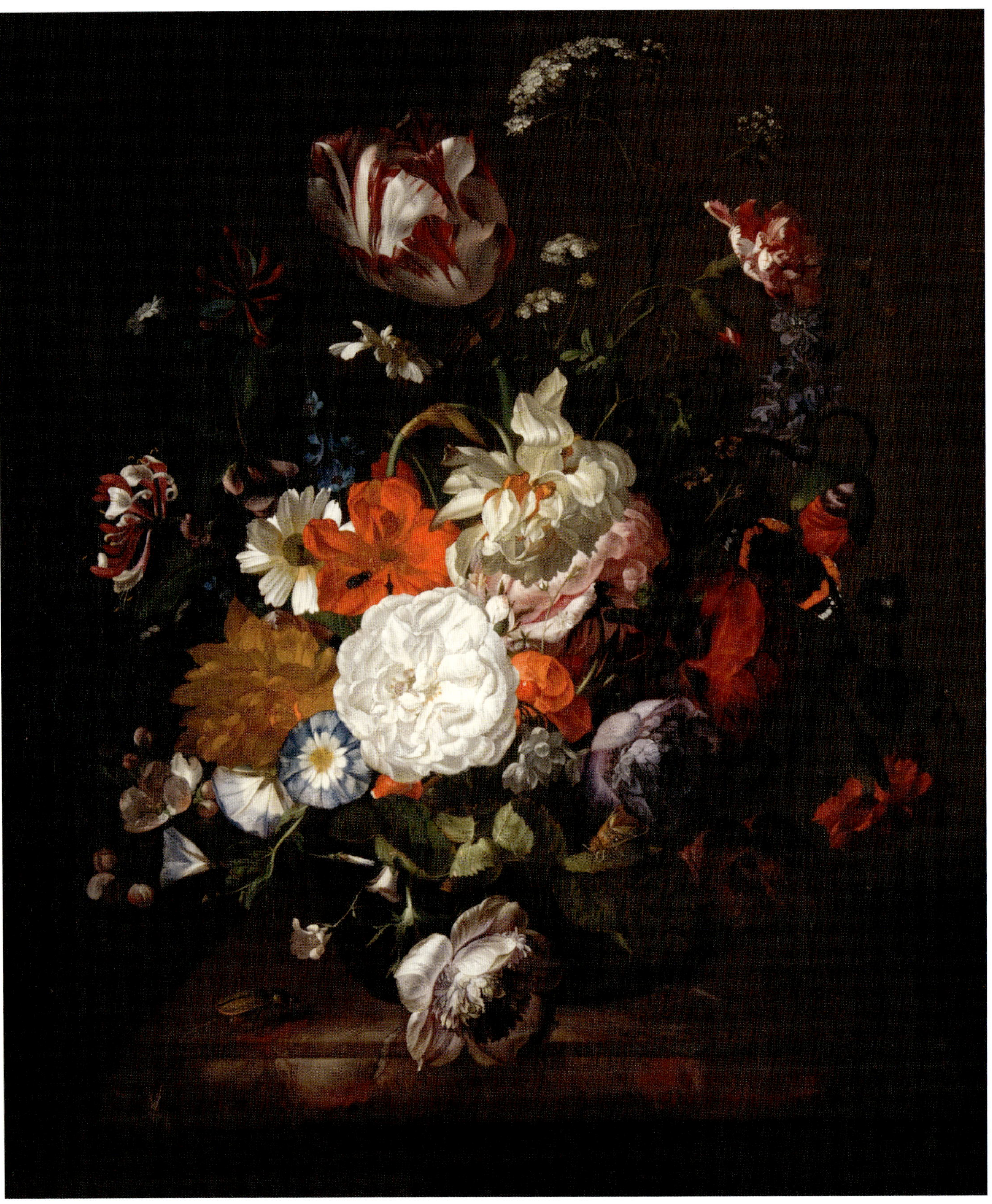

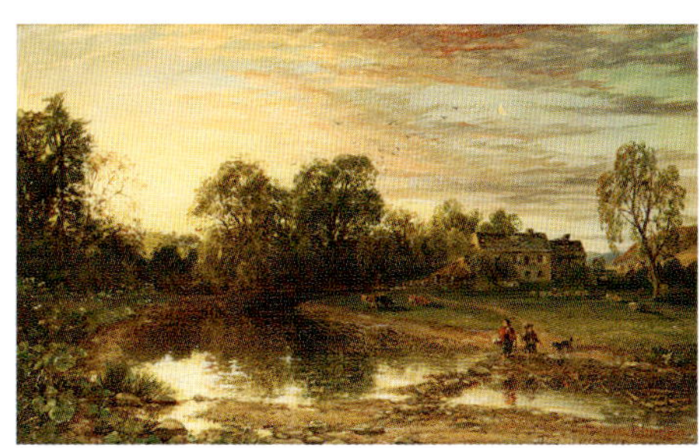

Perigal, Arthur the younger 1816–1884
Stepping Stones on the Jed 1881
oil on canvas 37.7 x 56.5
1853

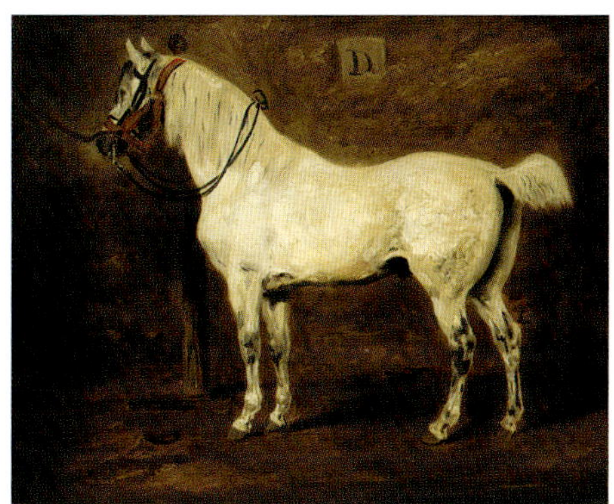

Pérignon, Alexis Joseph 1806–1882
The White Horse
oil on canvas 45.7 x 55.9
35.25

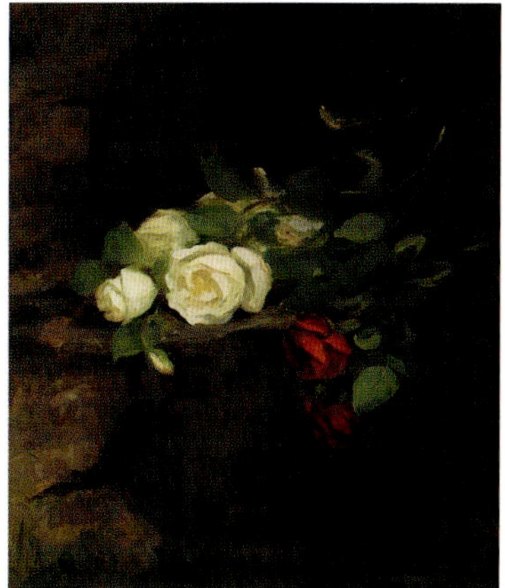

Perman, Louisa Ellen 1854–1921
Red and White Roses
oil on canvas 61 x 50.8
2876

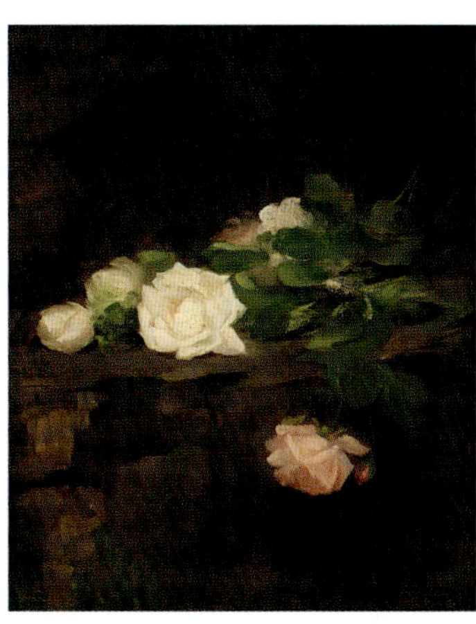

Perman, Louisa Ellen 1854–1921
Roses
oil on canvas 62.2 x 47
1500

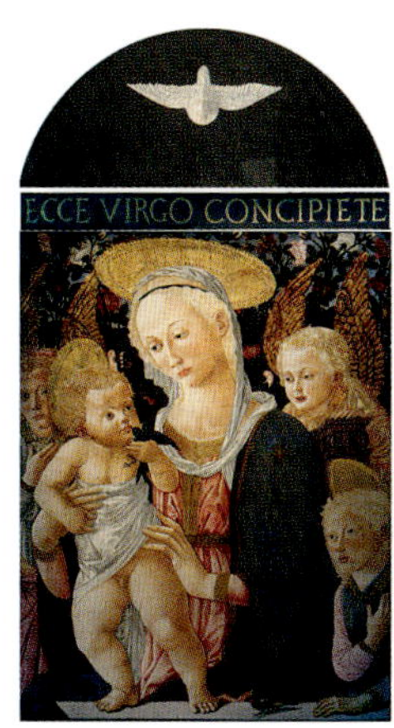

Pesellino, Francesco di Stefano (follower of)
c.1422–1457
Virgin and Child with Angels c.1459
tempera & gold on wood 106 x 69.5 (E)
914

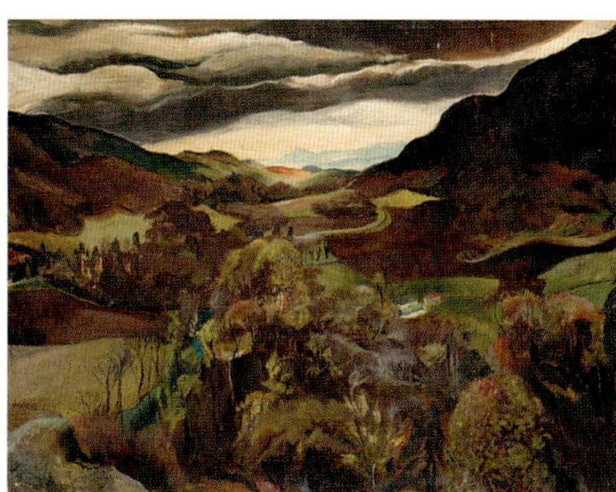

Peters, Joyce
Valley of the Earn c.1941
oil on board 66 x 83.8
2264

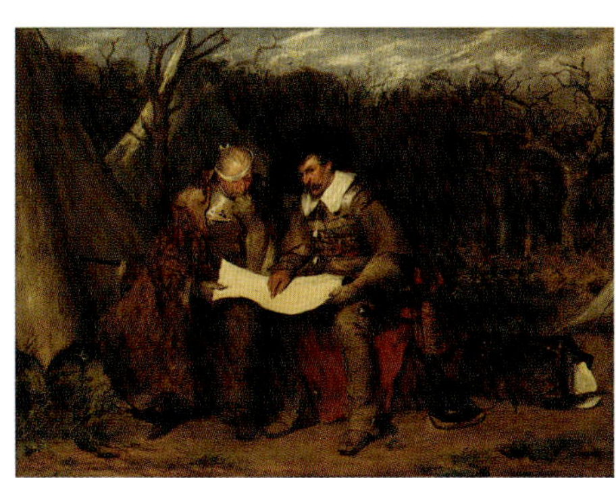

Pettie, John 1839–1893
The Strategists 1864
oil on canvas 39.4 x 52.1
798

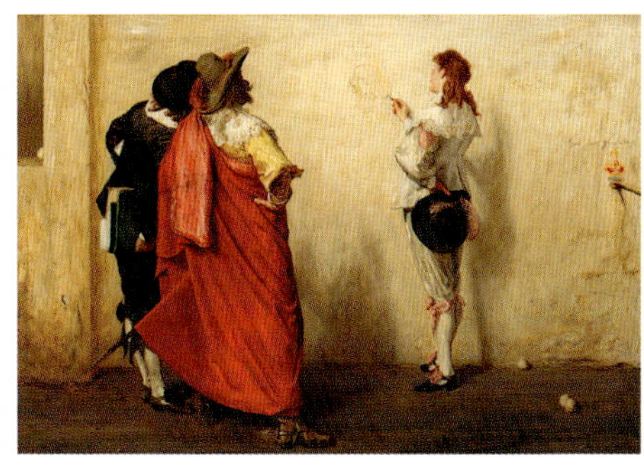

Pettie, John 1839–1893
Ho! Ho! Ho! Old Noll c.1874
oil on canvas 81.3 x 113
2144

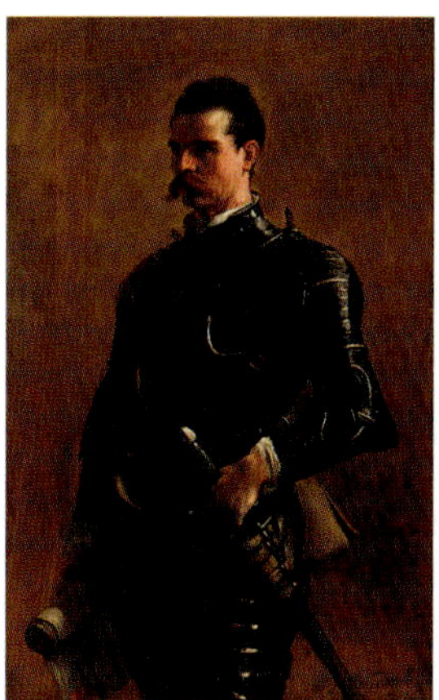

Pettie, John 1839–1893
A Knight of the Seventeenth Century 1877
oil on canvas 123.8 x 80
897

Facing page: Ruysch, Rachel, 1664–1750, *Still Life, Flowers and Insects*, c.1720–1730 (p. 384)

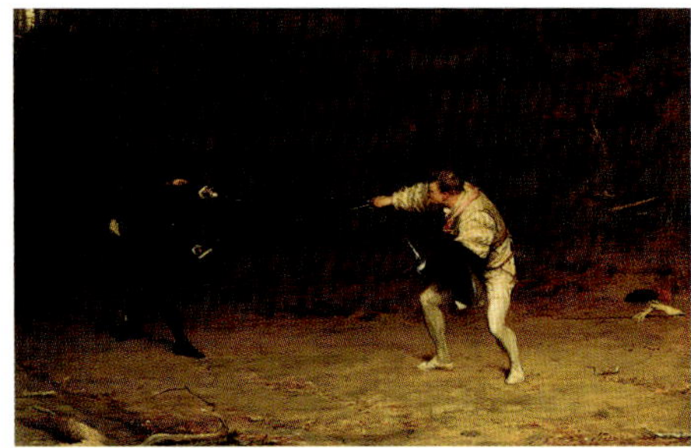

Pettie, John 1839–1893
Sword and Dagger Fight c.1880
oil on canvas 49.5 x 77.5
1140

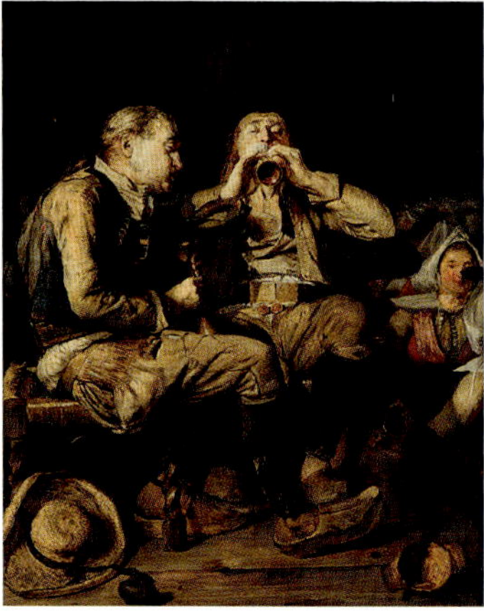

Pettie, John 1839–1893
Brittany Minstrels 1887
oil on canvas 40.6 x 33
779

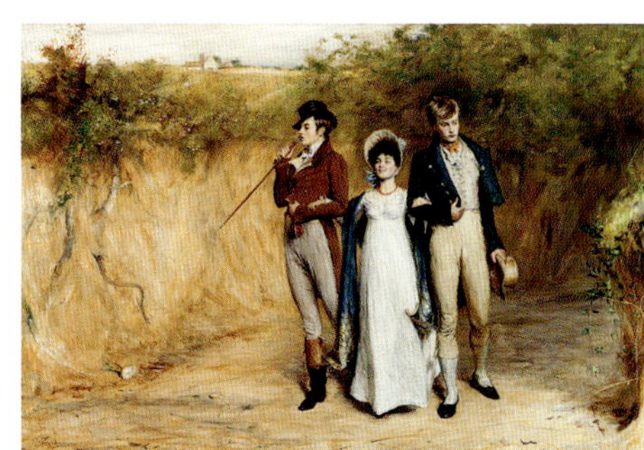

Pettie, John 1839–1893
Two Strings to Her Bow 1887
oil on canvas 82.6 x 119.4
663

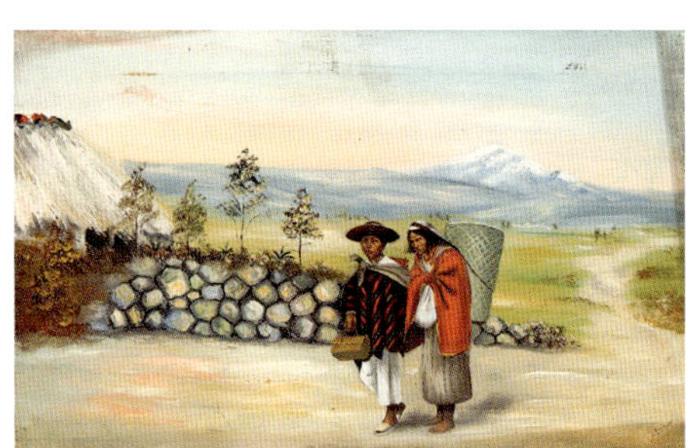

Pevoyeii (attributed to)
Indians on the Trek
oil on canvas 26.7 x 42.5
A.1940.33.e

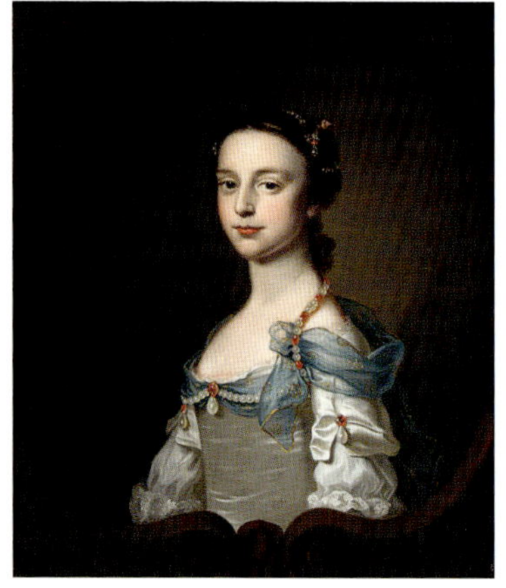

Phelps, Richard (attributed to) 1710–1785
Elizabeth Prowse c.1769
oil on canvas 76.2 x 63.5
35.285

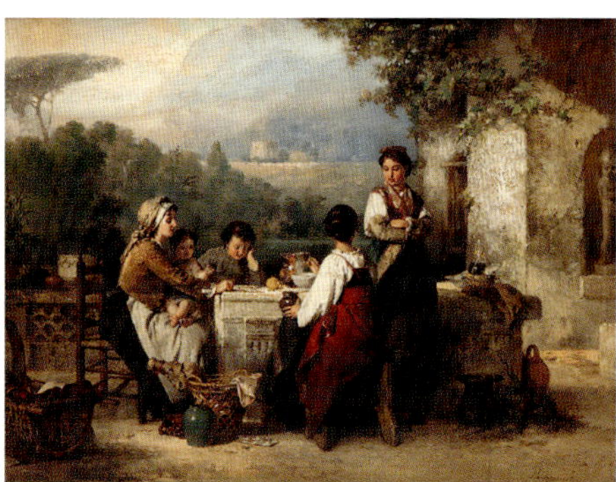

Philippeau, Karel Frans 1825–1897
The Midday Meal
oil on canvas 34.7 x 46.1
972

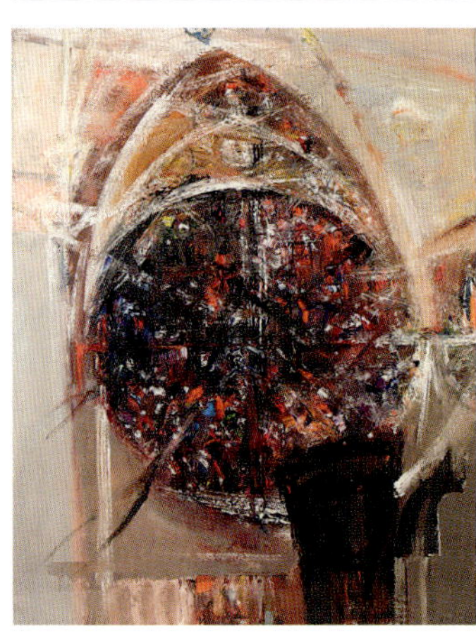

Philipson, Robin 1916–1992
Cathedral Interior 1960
oil on canvas 114.4 x 88.5
3148

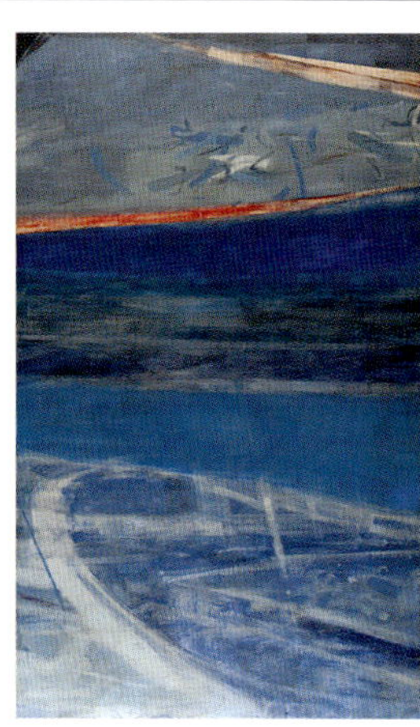

Philipson, Robin 1916–1992
Flight (polyptych, panel 1 of 8) 1966
oil on panel 255.5 x 146.5
3412.1

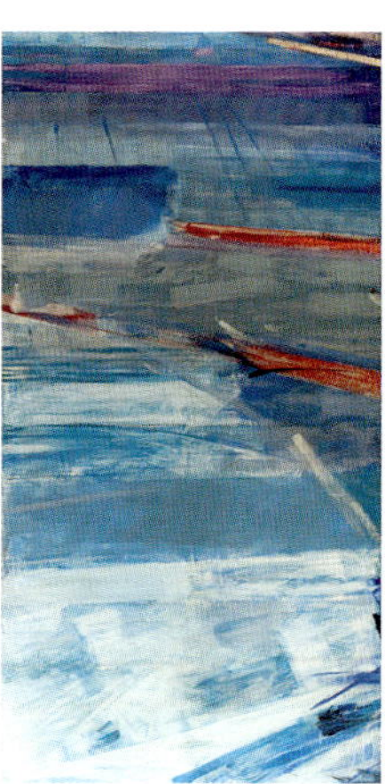

Philipson, Robin 1916–1992
Flight (polyptych, panel 2 of 8) 1966
oil on panel 255.5 x 146.5
3412.2

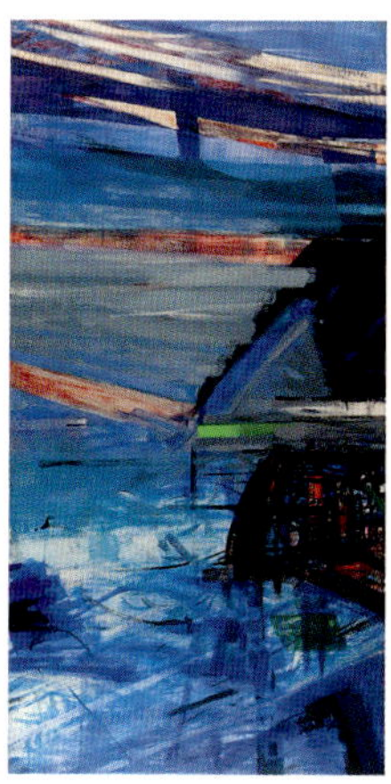

Philipson, Robin 1916–1992
Flight (polyptych, panel 3 of 8) 1966
oil on panel 255.5 x 146.5
3412.3

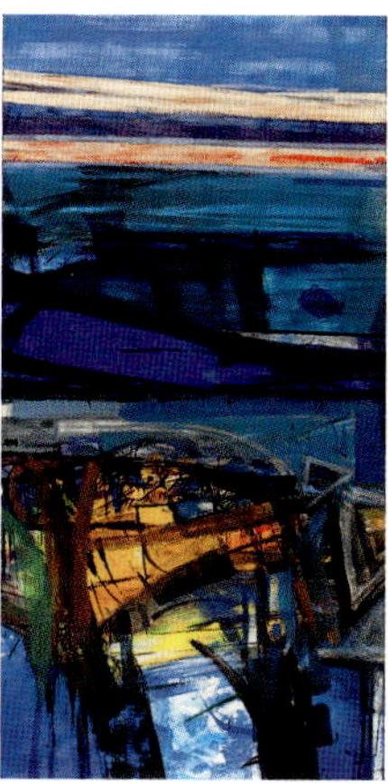

Philipson, Robin 1916–1992
Flight (polyptych, panel 4 of 8) 1966
oil on panel 255.5 x 146.5
3412.4

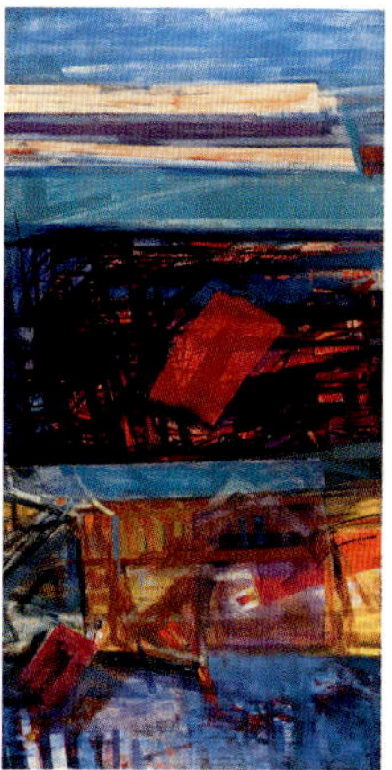

Philipson, Robin 1916–1992
Flight (polyptych, panel 5 of 8) 1966
oil on panel 255.5 x 146.5
3412.5

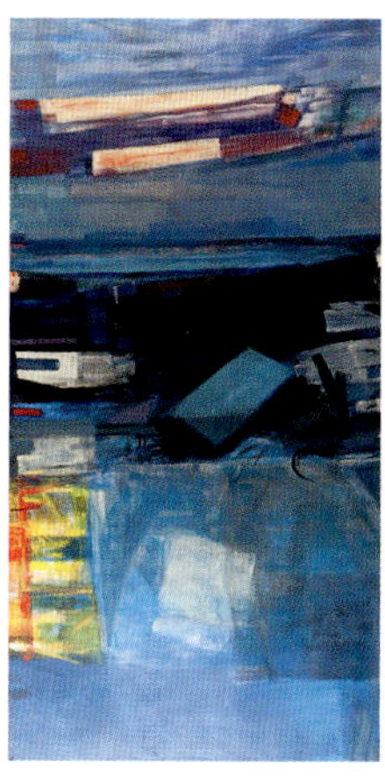

Philipson, Robin 1916–1992
Flight (polyptych, panel 6 of 8) 1966
oil on panel 255.5 x 146.5
3412.6

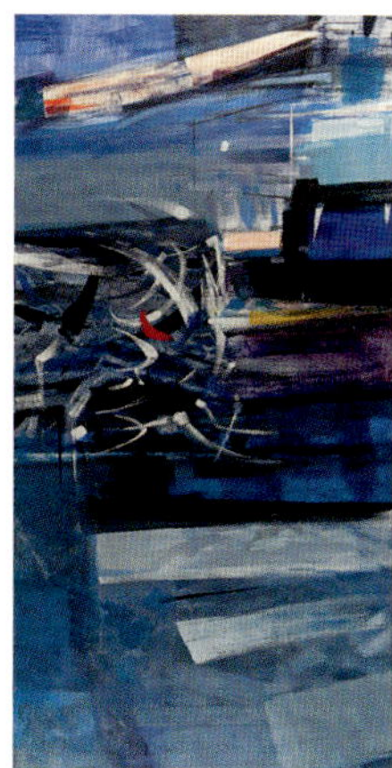

Philipson, Robin 1916–1992
Flight (polyptych, panel 7 of 8) 1966
oil on panel 255.5 x 146.5
3412.7

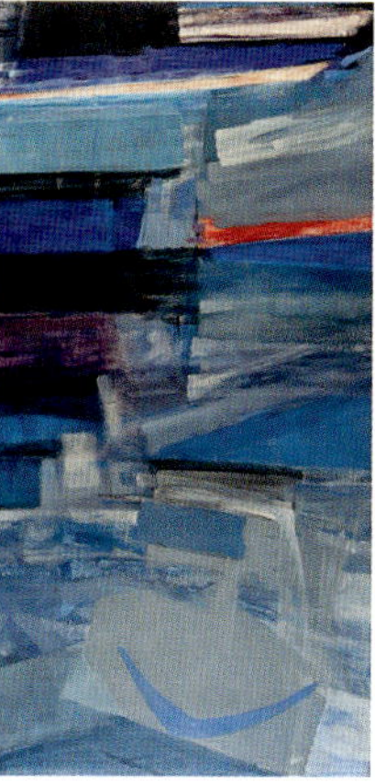

Philipson, Robin 1916–1992
Flight (polyptych, panel 8 of 8) 1966
oil on panel 255.5 x 146.5
3412.8

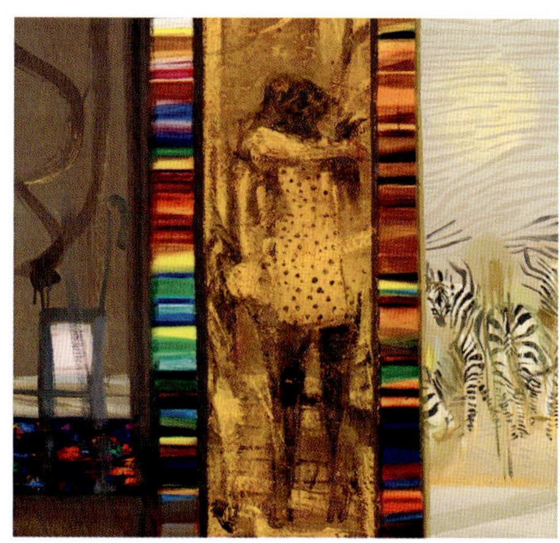

Philipson, Robin 1916–1992
Threnody 1969
oil on canvas 76.2 x 76.2
3395

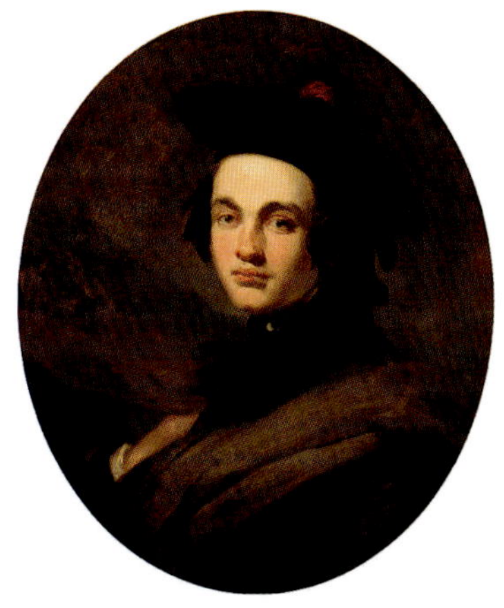

Phillip, John 1817–1867
Self Portrait When a Young Man c.1840
oil on canvas 74.9 x 62.2
1847

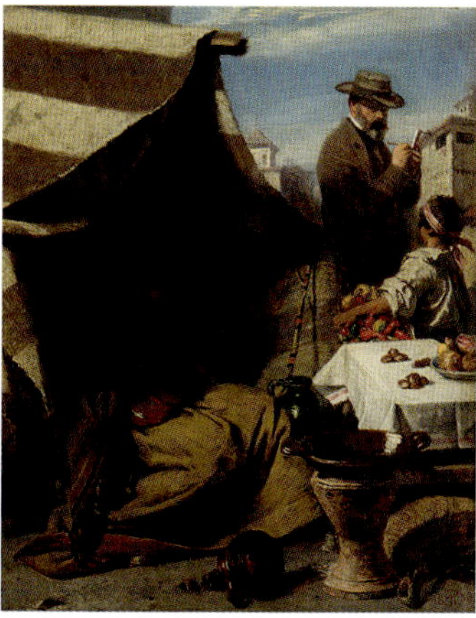

Phillip, John 1817–1867
The Evil Eye 1858
oil on canvas 50.8 x 40.6
1108

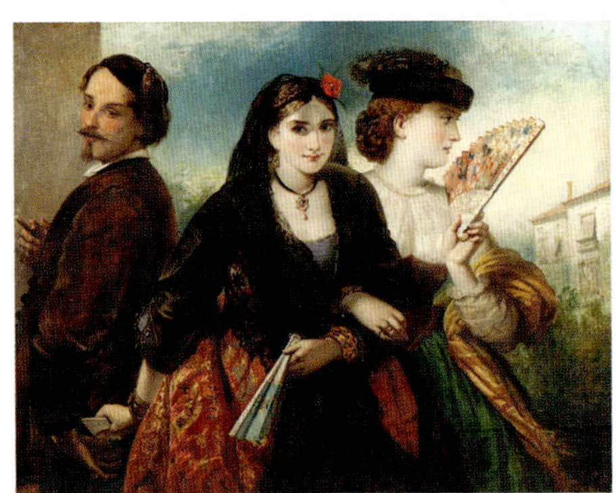

Phillip, John 1817–1867
The Assignation 1859
oil on canvas 101.6 x 128.3
1095

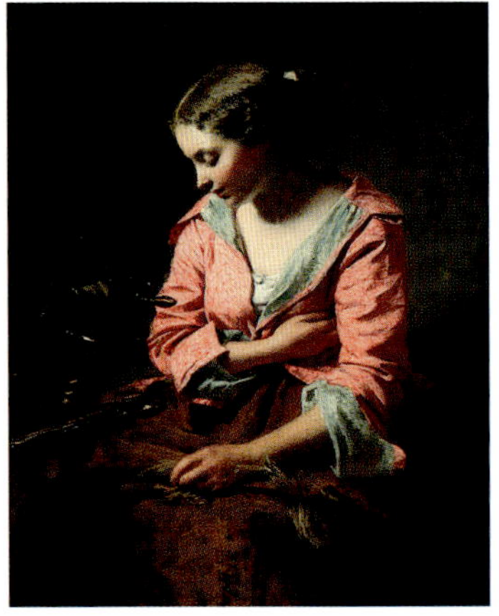

Phillip, John 1817–1867
The Spinning Wheel 1859
oil on canvas 45.7 x 35.6
1551

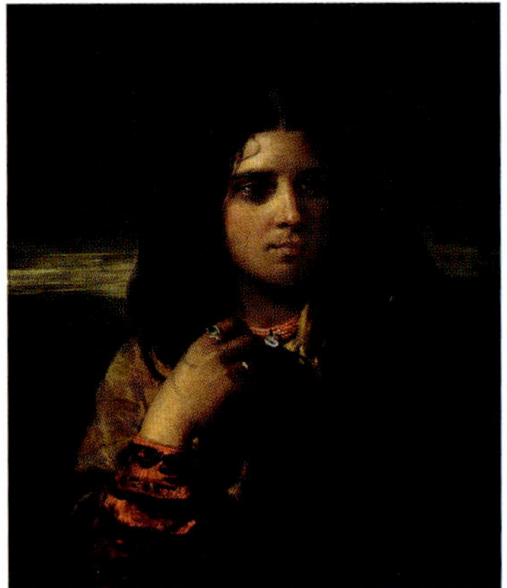

Phillip, John 1817–1867
A Gypsy Girl 1860
oil on canvas 64.8 x 53.3
911

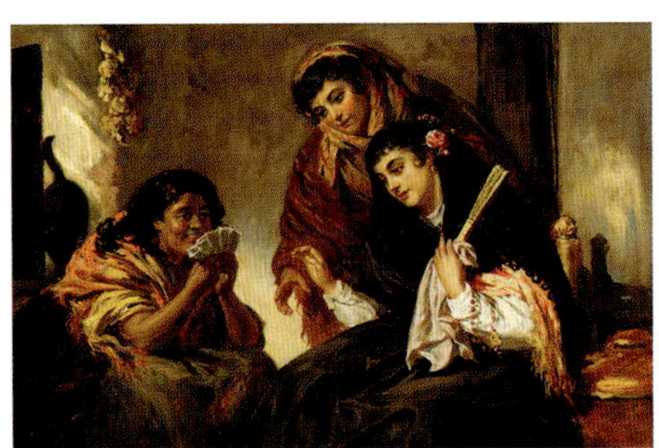

Phillip, John 1817–1867
The Fortune Teller c.1860–1862
oil on canvas 50.8 x 76.2
1749

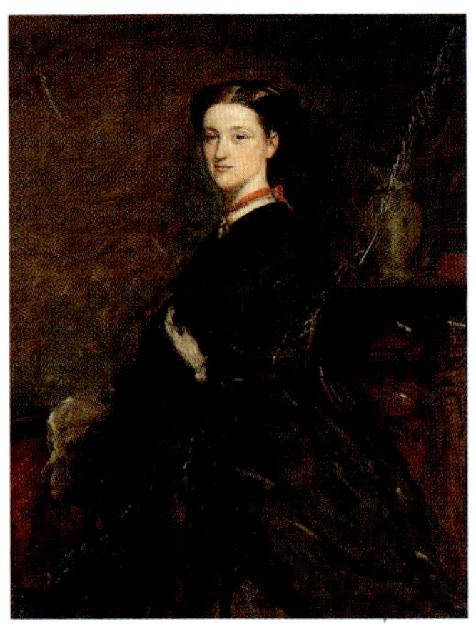

Phillip, John 1817–1867
Mrs Alexander Collie
oil on canvas 127 x 101.6
1846

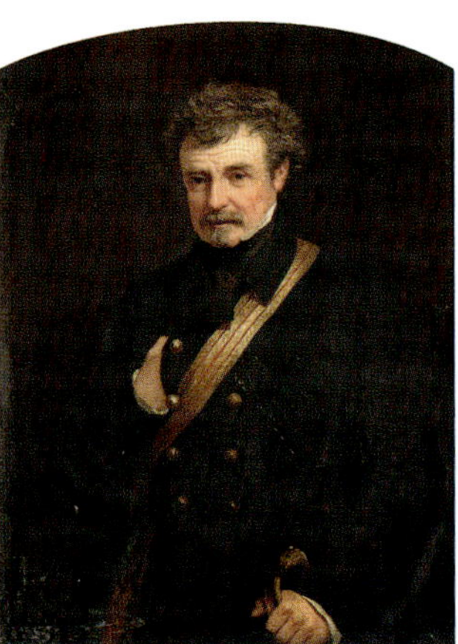

Phillips, Henry Wyndham 1820–1868
Colin Campbell (1792–1863), Lord Clyde
oil on canvas 109.2 x 78.7
488

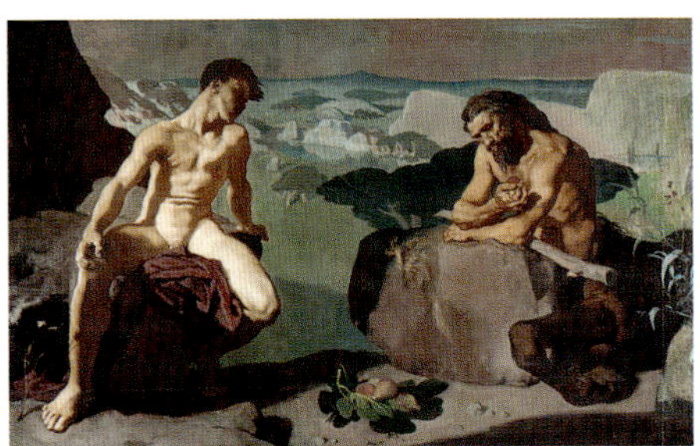

Philpot, Glyn Warren 1884–1937
Melampus and the Centaur 1919
oil on canvas 121.9 x 204.3
1563

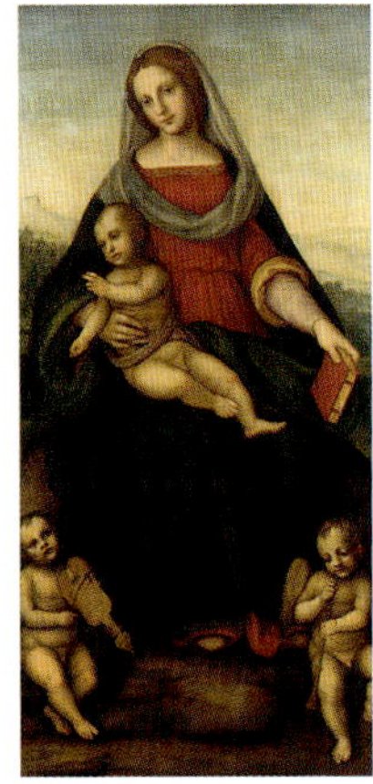

Piazza, Alberto 1490–1528
*Virgin and Child with Two Musician
Angels* c.1520
oil on panel 110.5 x 55.9
35.591

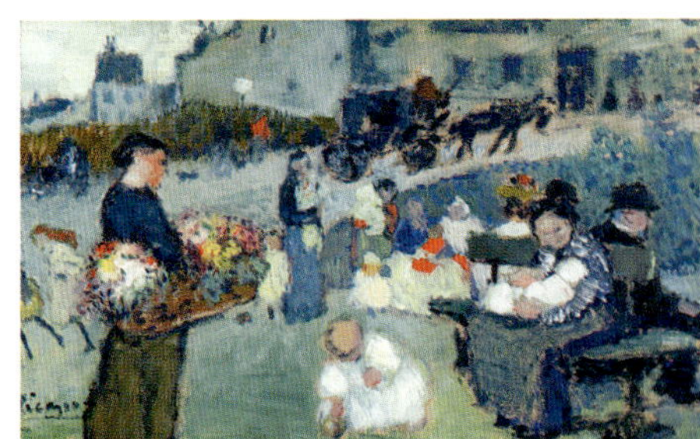

Picasso, Pablo 1881–1973
The Flower Seller 1901
oil on millboard 33.7 x 52.1
2417

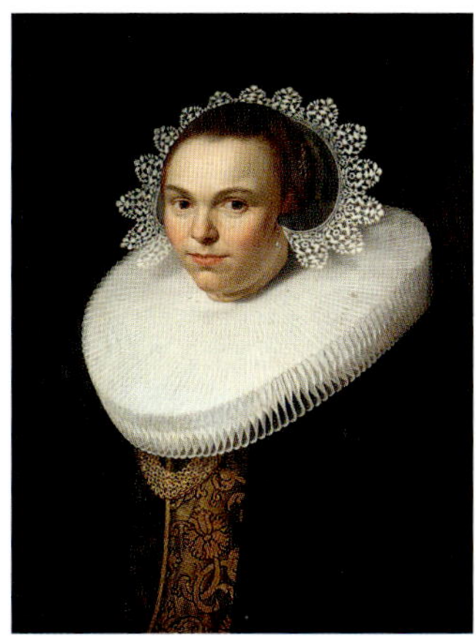

Pickenoy, Nicolaes Eliasz. (attributed to)
c.1588–c.1655
Portrait of a Young Woman c.1625–1635
oil on panel 71.7 x 54.3
576

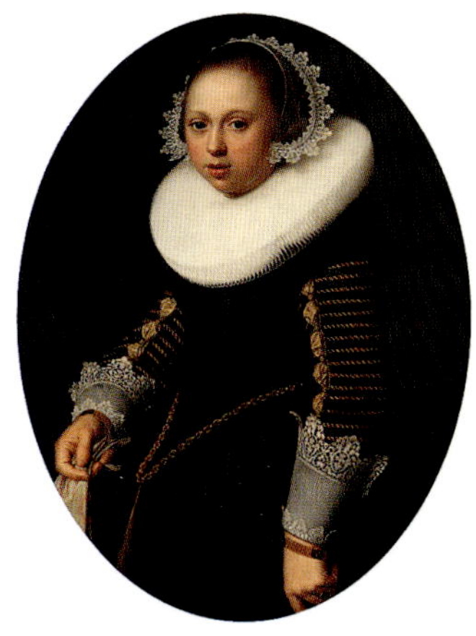

Pickenoy, Nicolaes Eliasz. (circle of)
c.1588–c.1655
Portrait of a Girl Aged 15 1633
oil on panel 69.8 x 53.3
577

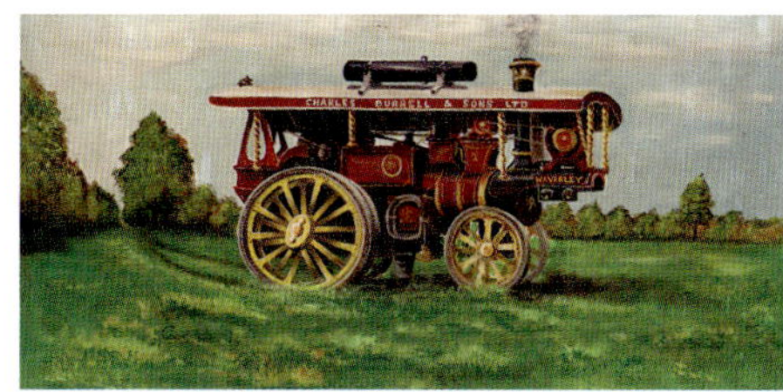

Pinder, Carl
Steam Traction Engine 'Waverley' 1970
oil on board 63.9 x 125.3
TEMP.15476

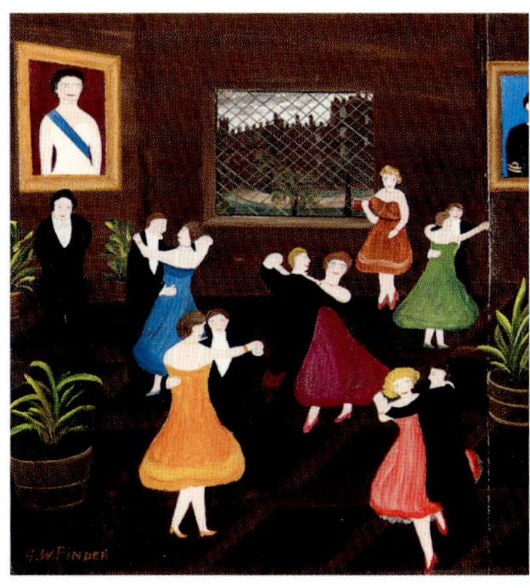

Pinder, George William 1894–1984
The Dance 1964
oil on board 42.9 x 39
3572

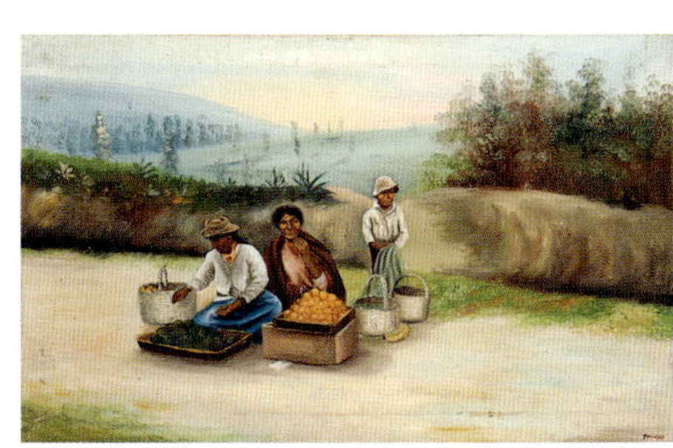

Pinogah (attributed to)
Ecuadorians Selling Fruit by the Road
oil on canvas 26.4 x 42.1
A.1940.33.d

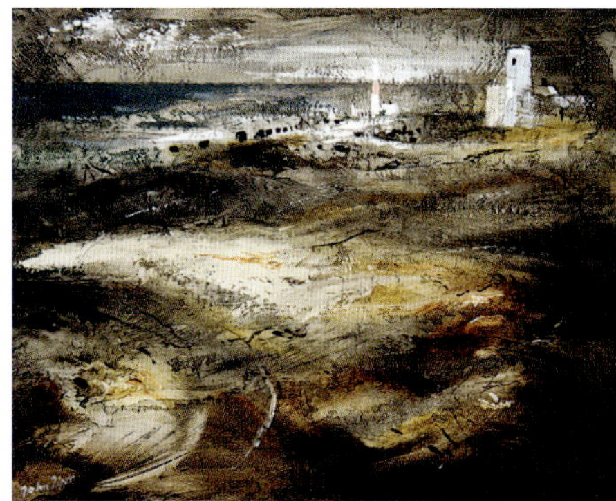

Piper, John 1903–1992
Portland Bill 1950
oil on board 45.7 x 55.9
2966

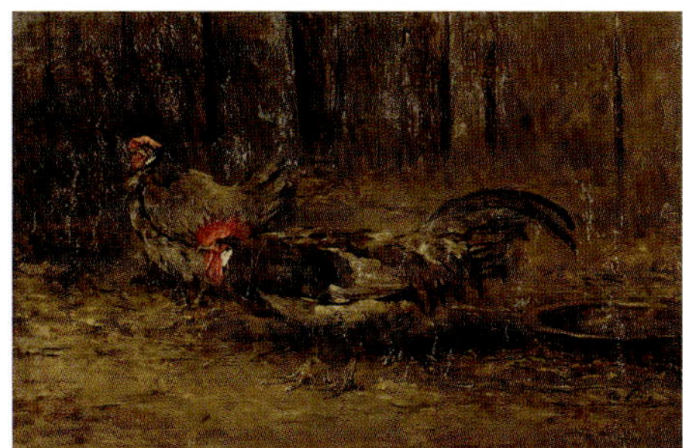

Pirie, George 1863–1946
Birds of a Feather c.1911
oil on canvas 59.7 x 90.2
1276

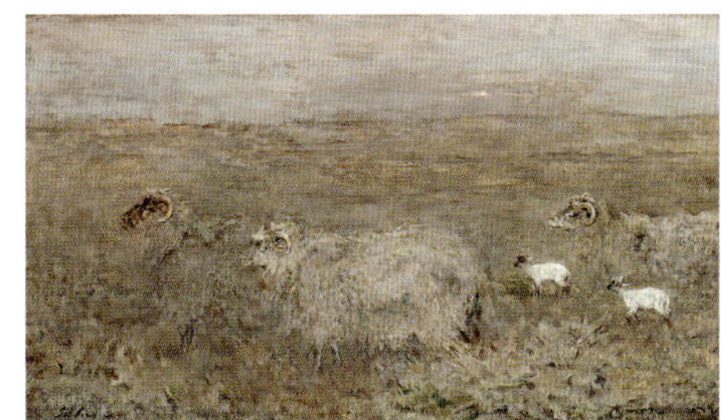

Pirie, George 1863–1946
Hill Ewes 1934
oil on canvas 76.2 x 127
1899

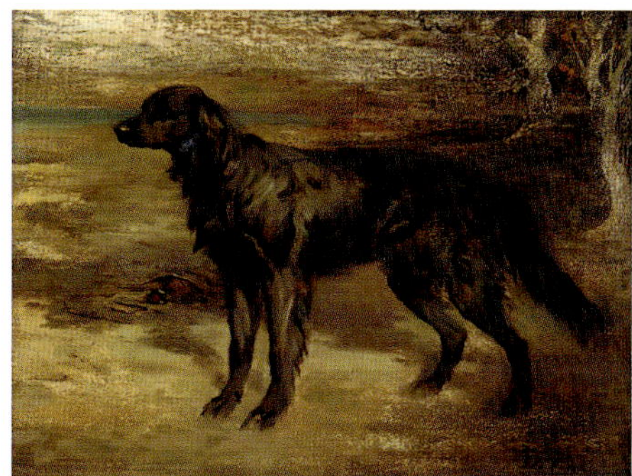

Pirie, George 1863–1946
Black Setter
oil on canvas 52.1 x 67.9
2172

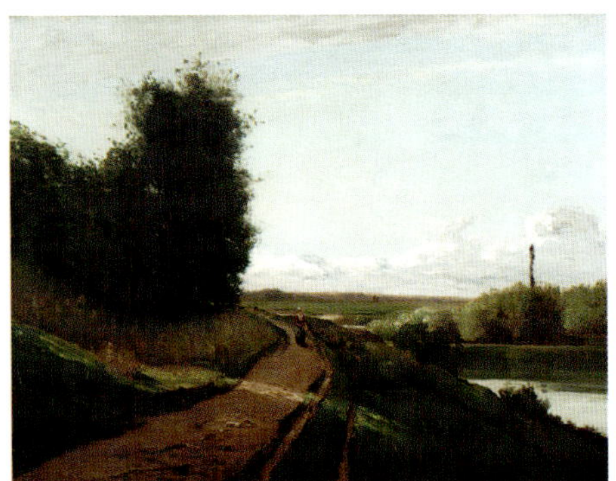

Pissarro, Camille 1831–1903
The Banks of the Marne 1864
oil on canvas 81.9 x 107.9
2934

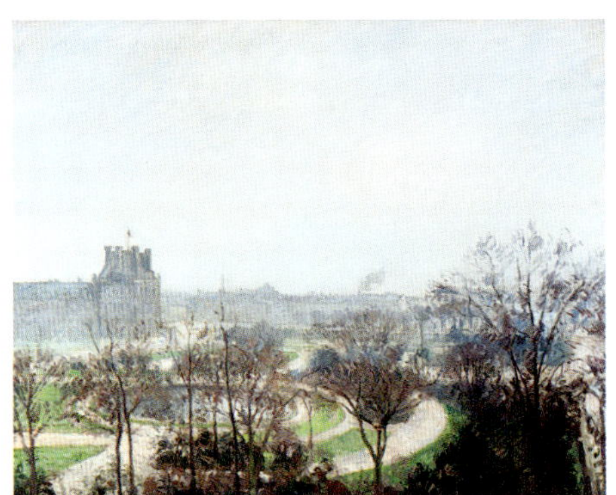

Pissarro, Camille 1831–1903
The Tuileries Gardens, Paris 1900
oil on canvas 73.6 x 92.3
2811

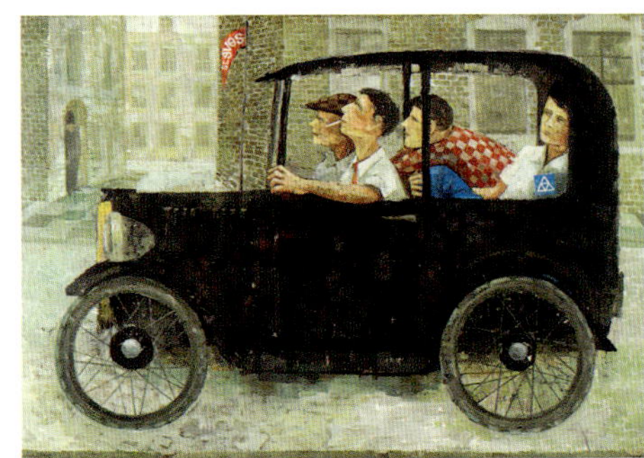

Plosky, Jonas b.1940
My Mate's Car 1962
oil on hardboard 80.9 x 114.6
3180

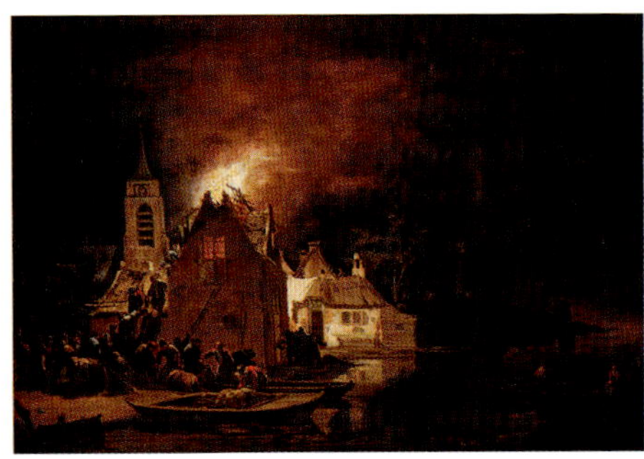

Poel, Egbert Lievensz. van der 1621–1664
A Fire at Night c.1650
oil on canvas 42.2 x 61.5
111

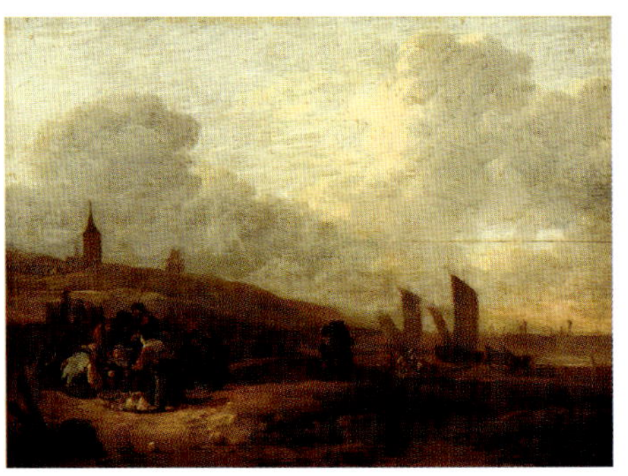

Poel, Egbert Lievensz. van der 1621–1664
*Beach Scene, Scheveningen, The Netherlands,
with a Fish Auction* c.1650–1664
oil on panel 34 x 47
40

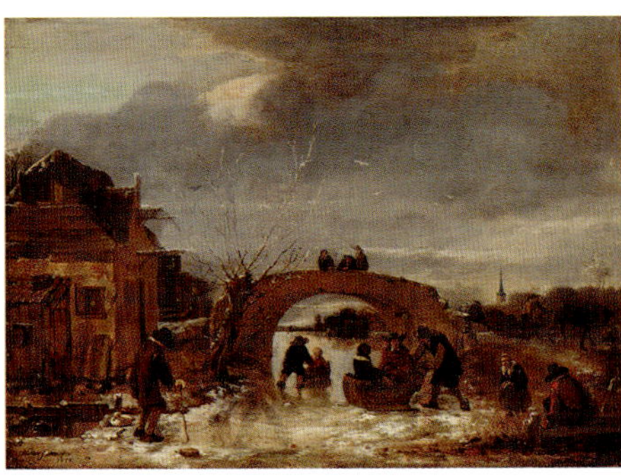

Poel, Egbert Lievensz. van der 1621–1664
Figures on a Frozen Canal c.1652–1662
oil on panel 37.3 x 50.3
89

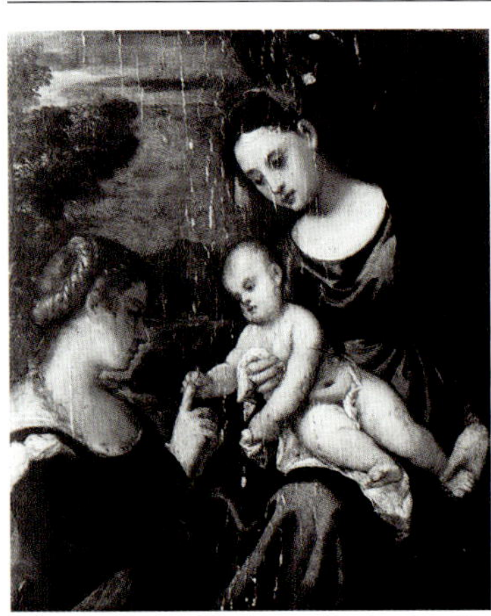

Polidoro da Lanciano c.1515–1565
The Mystic Marriage of Saint Catherine
c.1540–1550
oil on panel 57.2 x 49.8
583

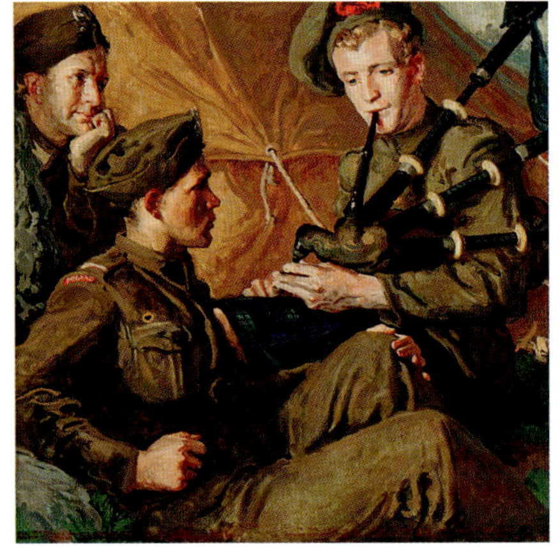

Polish School
A Scottish and Two Polish Soldiers 1940
oil on canvas 101.6 x 101.6
3446

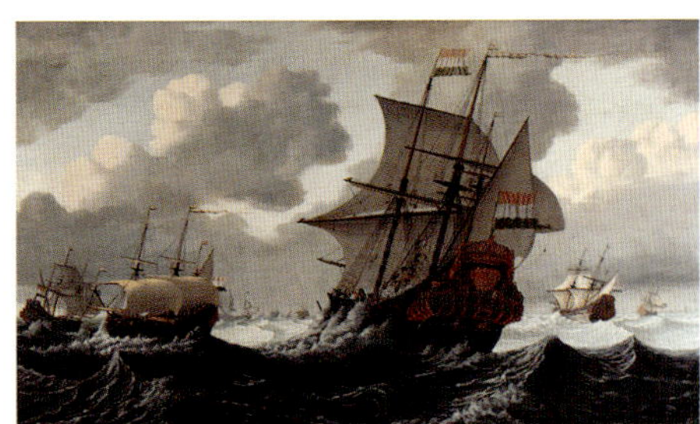

Pompe, Gerrit (attributed to)
c.1640/1650–c.1695/1705
Dutch Men-of-War Beating to Windward
c.1680–1705
oil on canvas 172.1 x 284.2
722

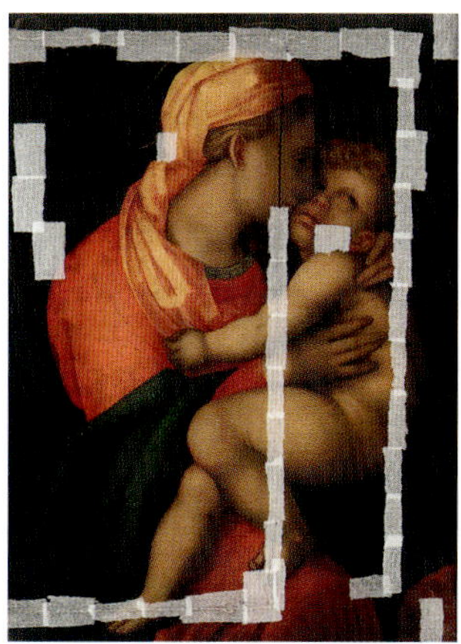

Pontormo, Jacopo Carucci (after) 1494–1556
Virgin and Child 16th C (?)
oil on panel 87.6 x 59.7
3420

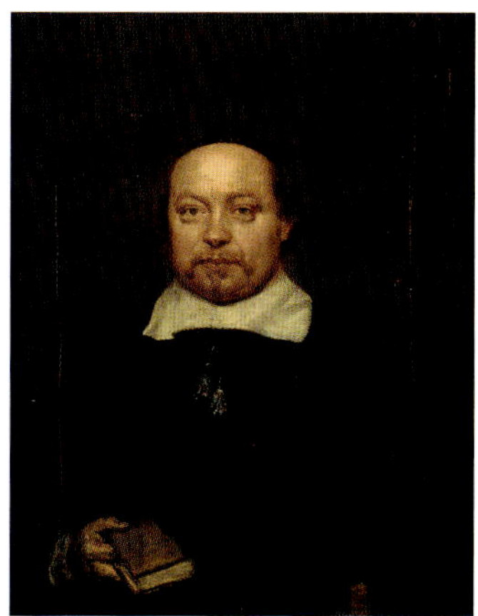

Pot, Hendrik Gerritsz. (attributed to)
c.1585–1657
Portrait of a Man c.1640–1657
oil on panel 29.5 x 23.7
1743

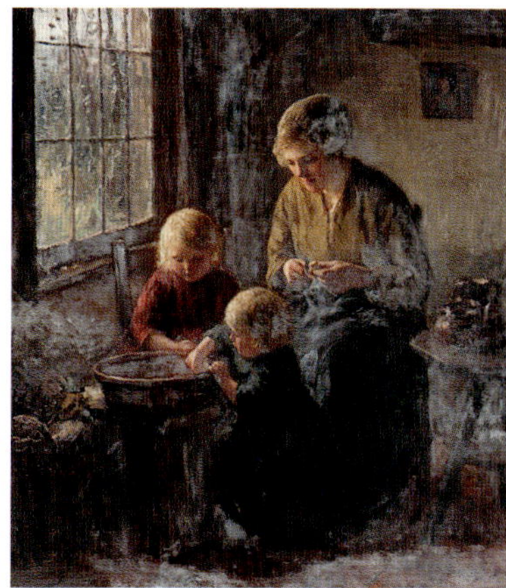

Pothast, Bernard Jean Corneille 1882–1966
Preparing for Dinner c.1900–1921
oil on canvas 74.6 x 65
1522

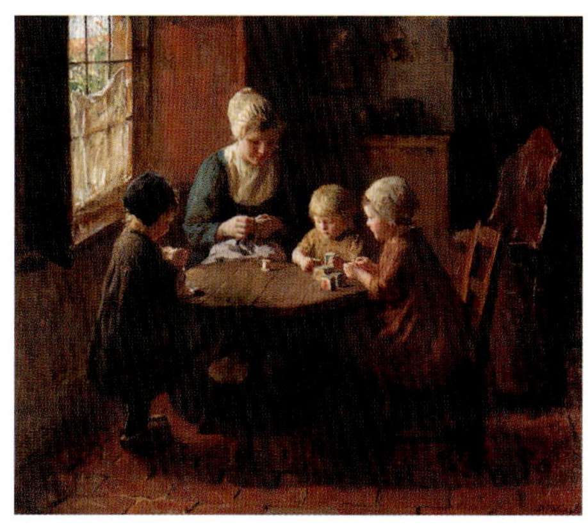

Pothast, Bernard Jean Corneille 1882–1966
Interior with a Woman and Children
oil on canvas 66 x 75.5
2192

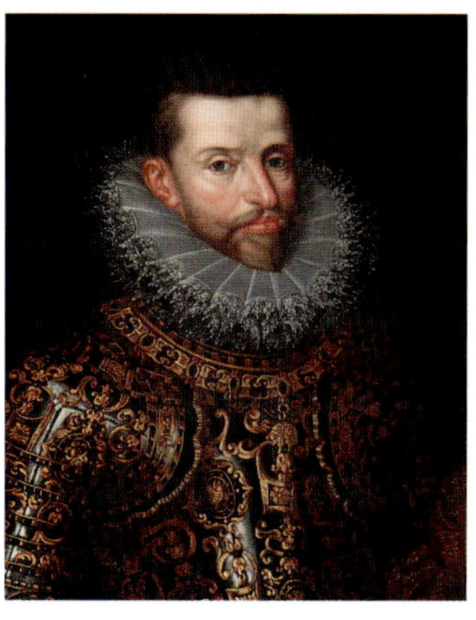

Pourbus, Frans the younger (after)
1569–1622
Archduke Albert of Austria (1559–1621)
17th C
oil on canvas 67.3 x 48.5
PC.74

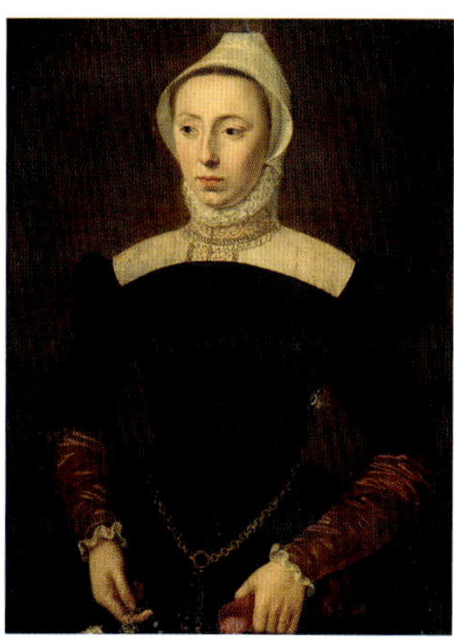

Pourbus, Pieter the younger (circle of)
1524–1584
Portrait of a Lady
oil on panel 68 x 50.8
35.51

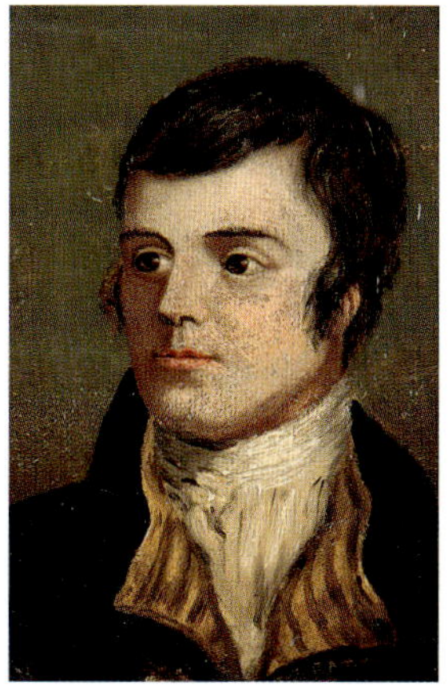

Pratt, D. active 19th C
Robert Burns (1759–1796)
oil on canvas 19 x 13 (E)
1924.15.ah

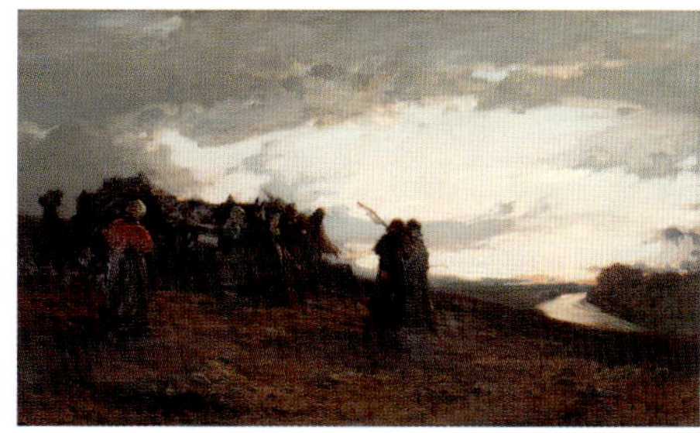

Pratt, William M. 1855–1936
The Close of Day 1915
oil on canvas 85.1 x 135.9
1379

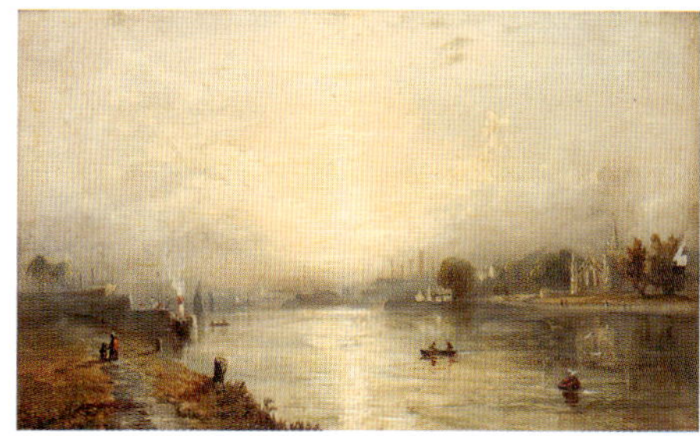

Prentice, J. A. active 19th C
Govan Church, Looking up the Clyde
oil on canvas 24.3 x 36.7
OG.1947.83

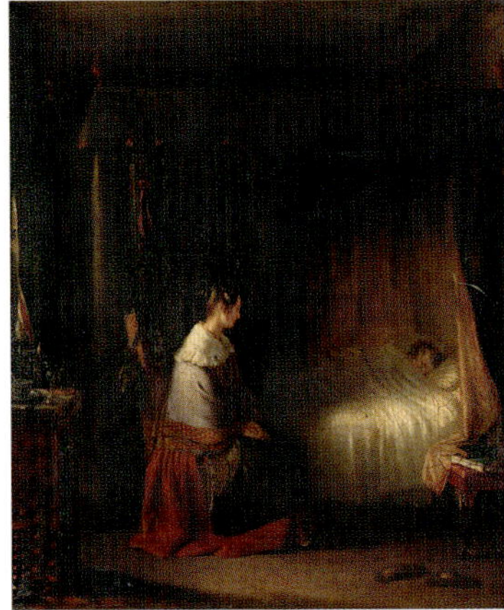

Prentis, Edward 1797–1854
The Sick Bed 1836
oil on canvas 78.7 x 50.8
388

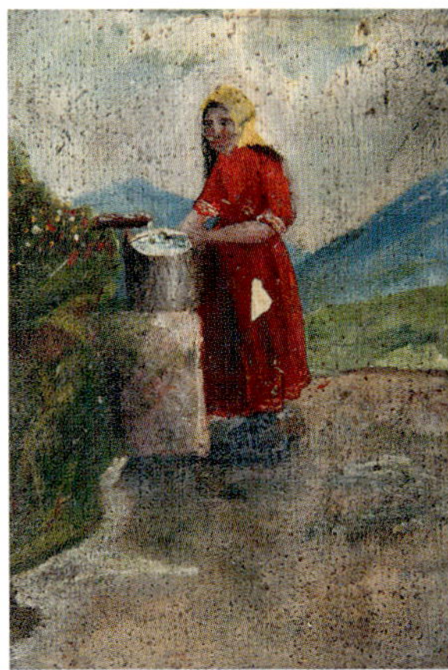

Pringle, John Quinton 1864–1925
Girl at a Well c.1882
oil on card 13 x 8.6
PR.1963.1.au

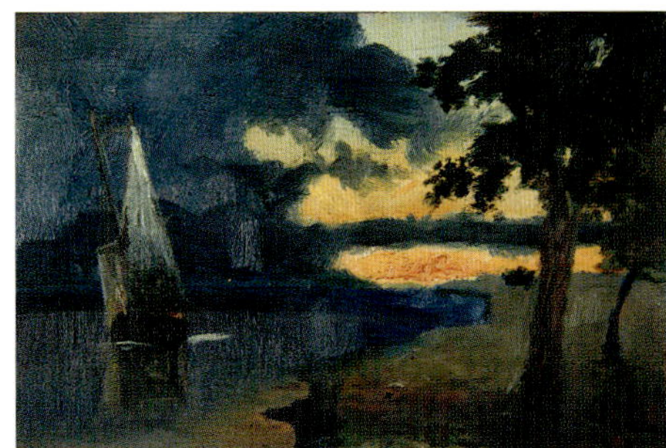

Pringle, John Quinton 1864–1925
Sunset and Approaching Storm 1883
oil on card 10.5 x 16.2
PR.1963.1.d

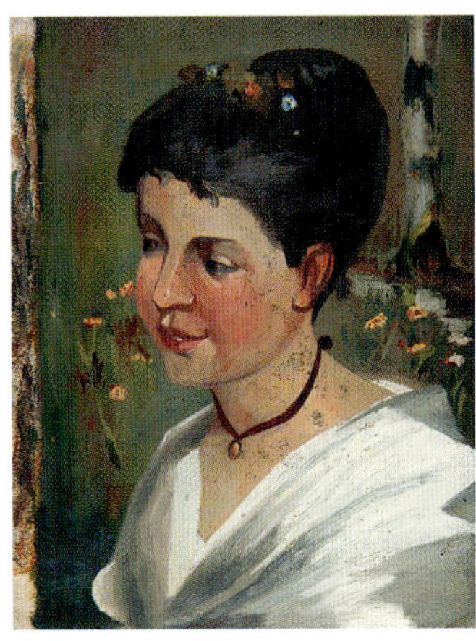

Pringle, John Quinton 1864–1925
Head of a Girl 1885–1886
oil on card 17.8 x 13.3
PR.1963.1.ac

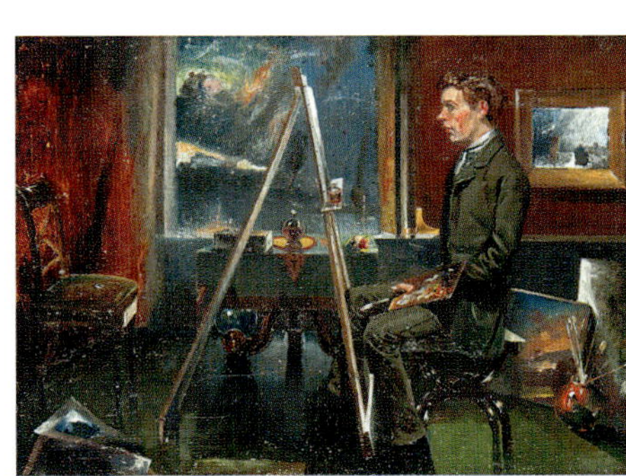

Pringle, John Quinton 1864–1925
Artist at an Easel c.1885
oil on canvas 25.4 x 35.6
2658

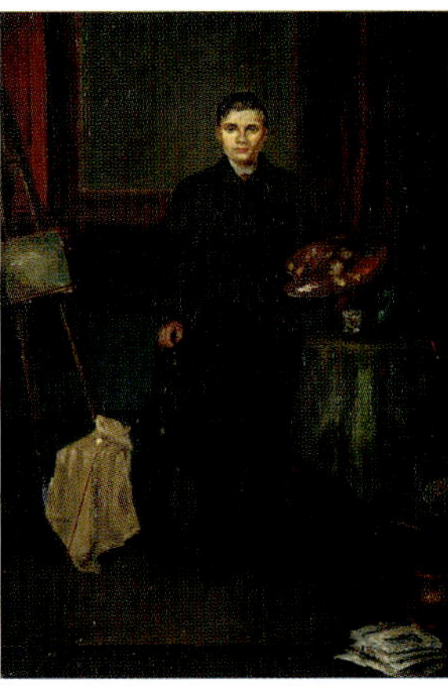

Pringle, John Quinton 1864–1925
Full-Length Figure of the Artist with an Easel
c.1885
oil on canvas 35.6 x 25.1
2665

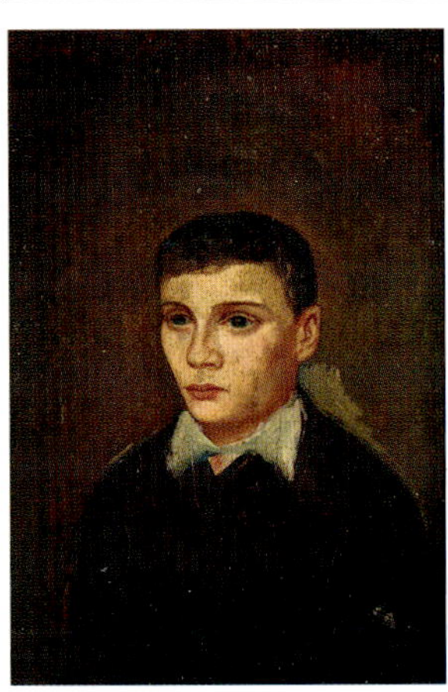

Pringle, John Quinton 1864–1925
Half-Length Figure, a Boy with a White Collar
c.1885
oil on canvas 20.3 x 14.9
2670

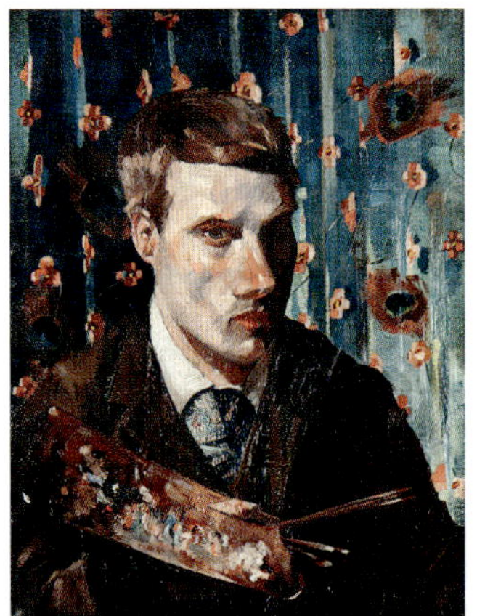

Pringle, John Quinton 1864–1925
Head and Shoulders of the Artist with a Palette
c.1886
oil on canvas 30.5 x 22.5
2661

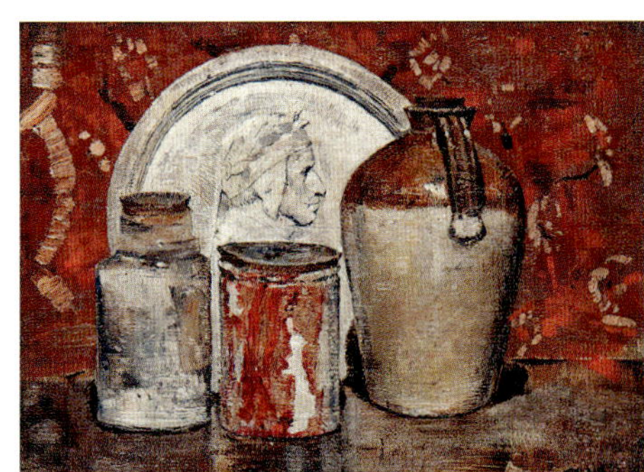

Pringle, John Quinton 1864–1925
Still Life with the Head of Dante c.1886–1890
oil on canvas 15.2 x 20.3
2667

Facing page: Rembrandt van Rijn, 1606–1669, *A Man in Armour*, 1655 (?) (p. 368)

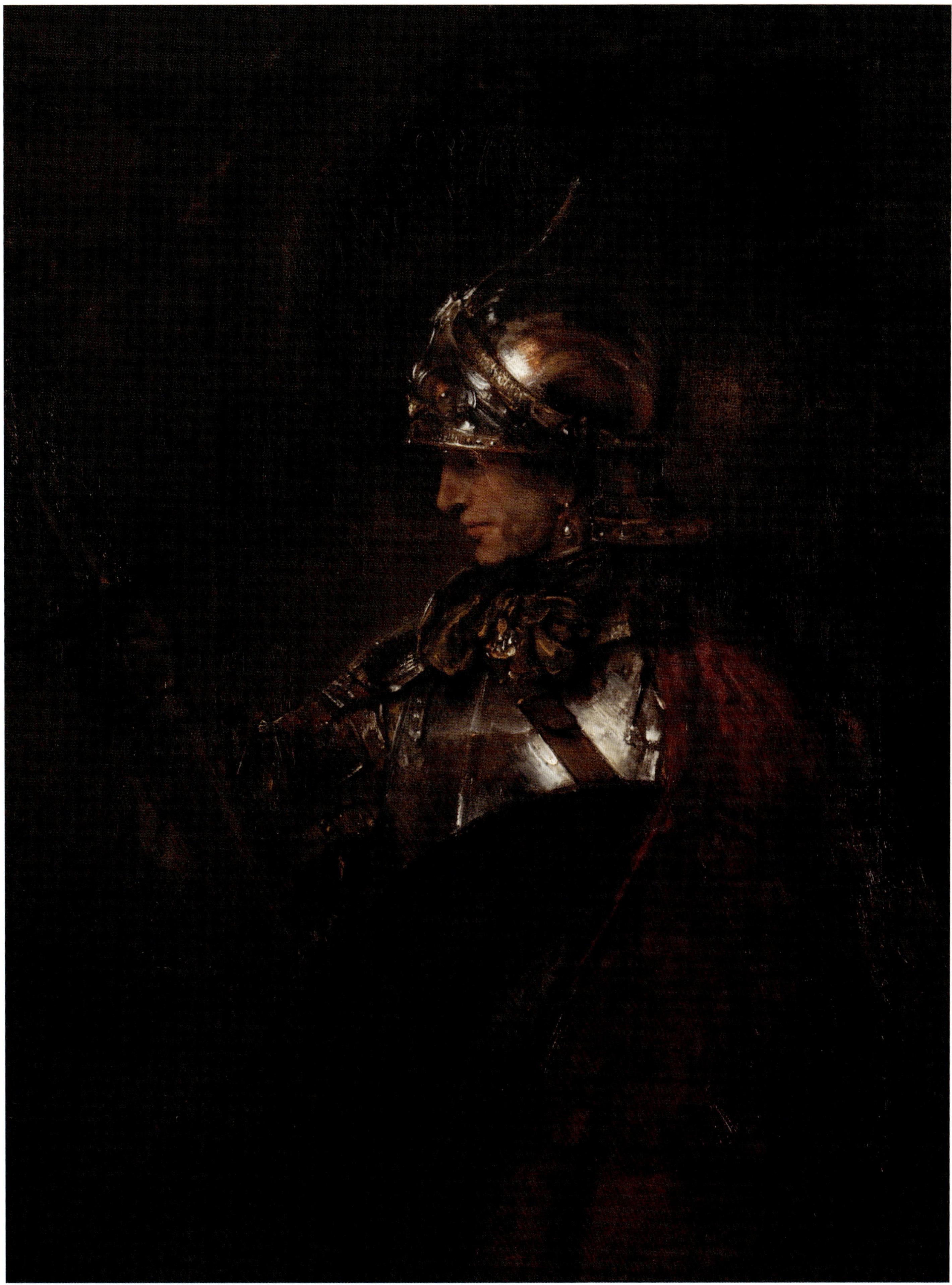

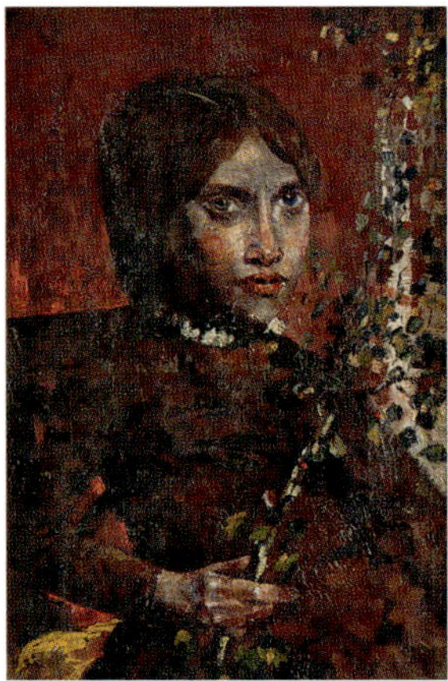

Pringle, John Quinton 1864–1925
Half-Length Figure of a Seated Girl with Flowers c.1888
oil on canvas 25.4 x 17.8
2660

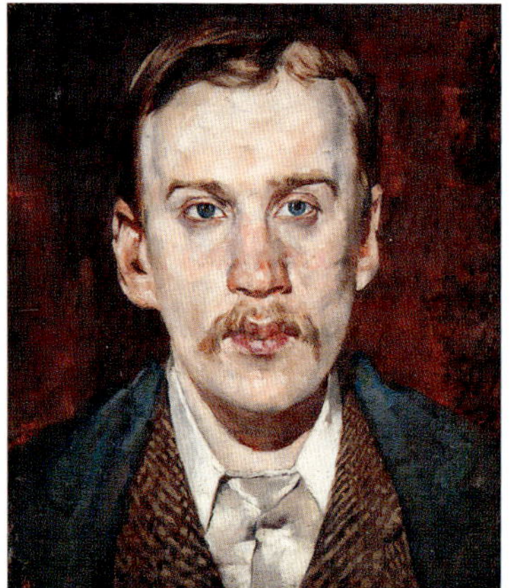

Pringle, John Quinton 1864–1925
Christopher N. Pringle (or James Pringle) 1889
oil on canvas 30.4 x 25.4
3362

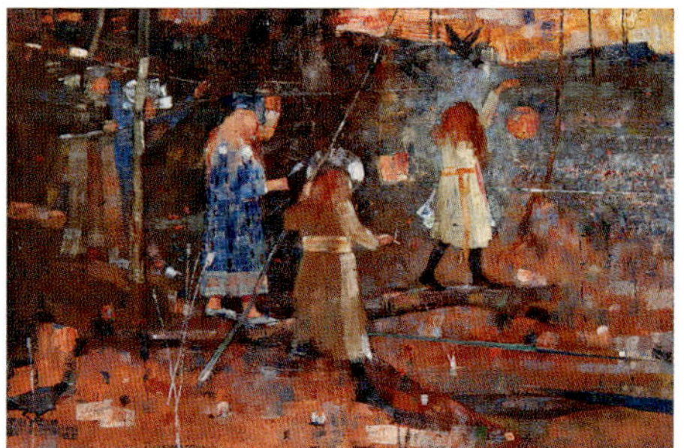

Pringle, John Quinton 1864–1925
Chinese Lanterns c.1889
oil on board 21.6 x 31.7
3346

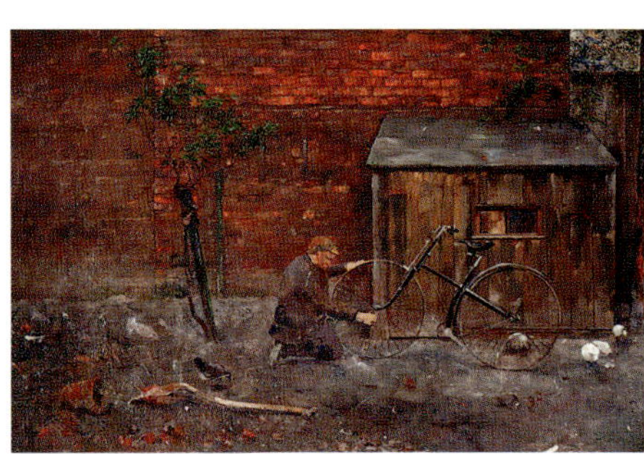

Pringle, John Quinton 1864–1925
Repairing the Bicycle c.1889
oil on canvas 30.5 x 45.7
3214

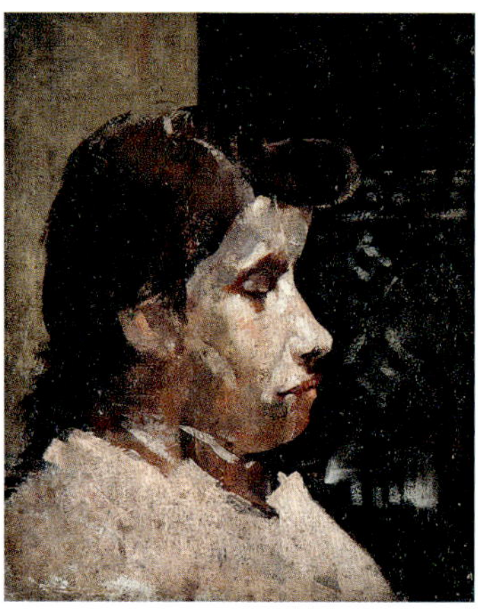

Pringle, John Quinton 1864–1925
Girl's Head c.1890
oil on canvas 25.4 x 20
2659

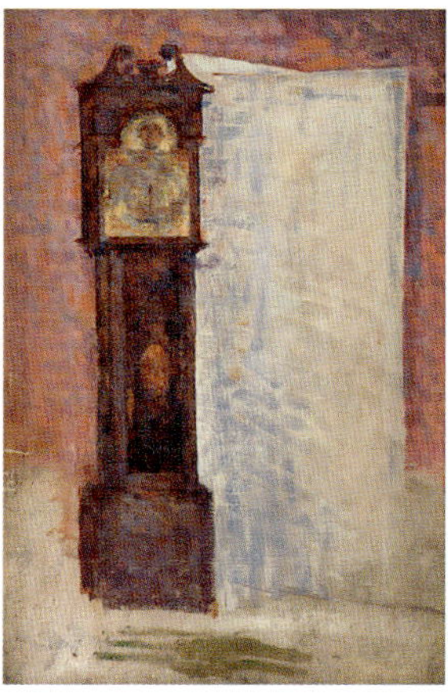

Pringle, John Quinton 1864–1925
The Grandfather Clock c.1890
oil on canvas 45.7 x 30.5
2657

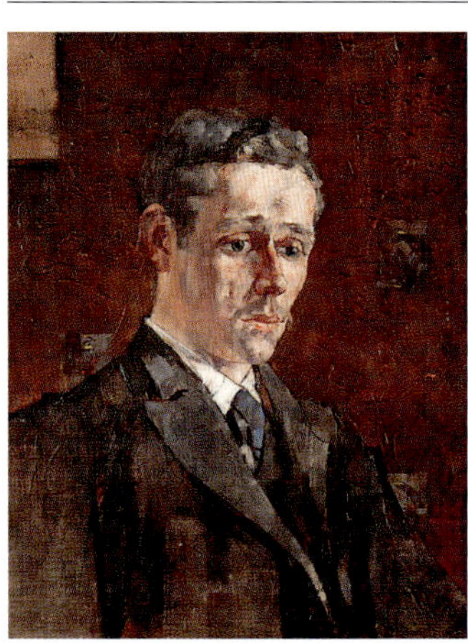

Pringle, John Quinton 1864–1925
William Meldrum (1865–1942) c.1890
oil on canvas 45.4 x 35.2
3241

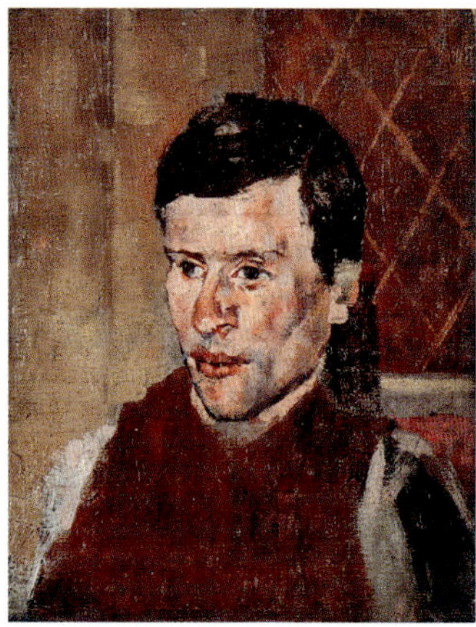

Pringle, John Quinton 1864–1925
Head and Shoulders of an Artisan c.1891
oil on canvas 20.3 x 14.9
2671

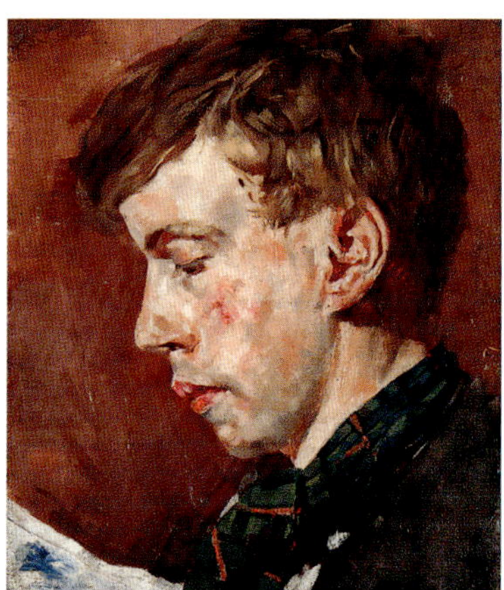

Pringle, John Quinton 1864–1925
Man's Head with a Tartan Scarf c.1892
oil on canvas 30.5 x 25.4
2663

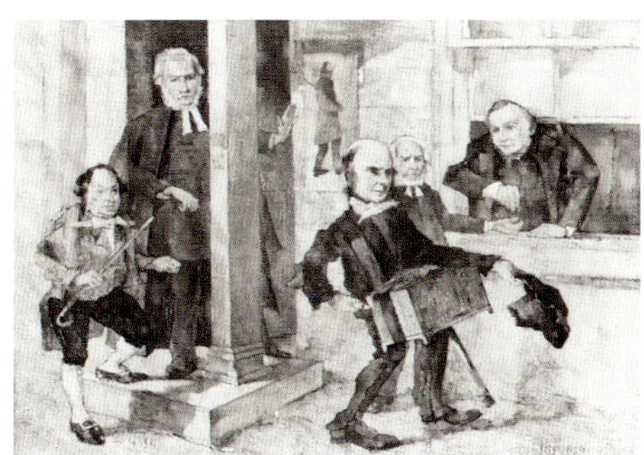

Pringle, John Quinton 1864–1925
The Organ Question 1893
oil on canvas 45.7 x 60.9
3363

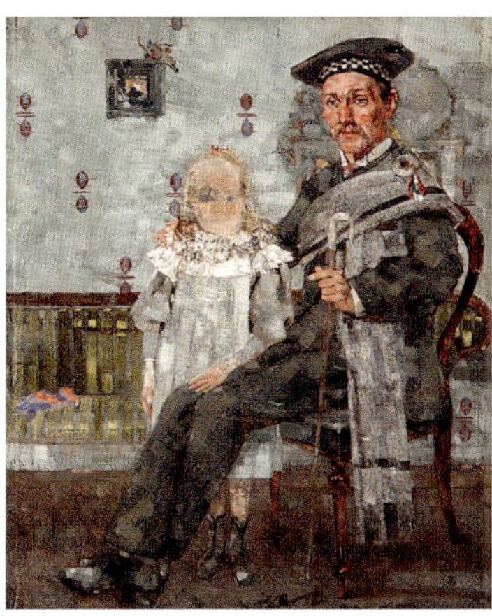

Pringle, John Quinton 1864–1925
Shepherd Seated with a Small Girl c.1896
oil on canvas 61 x 50.8
2675

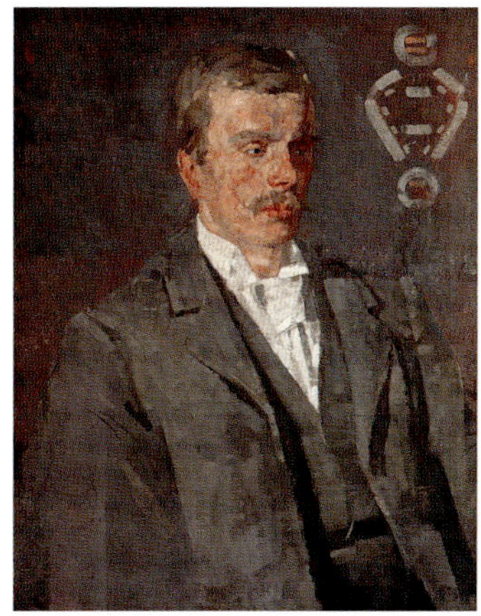

Pringle, John Quinton 1864–1925
Barclay W. Pringle c.1897
oil on canvas 91.4 x 70.8
2676

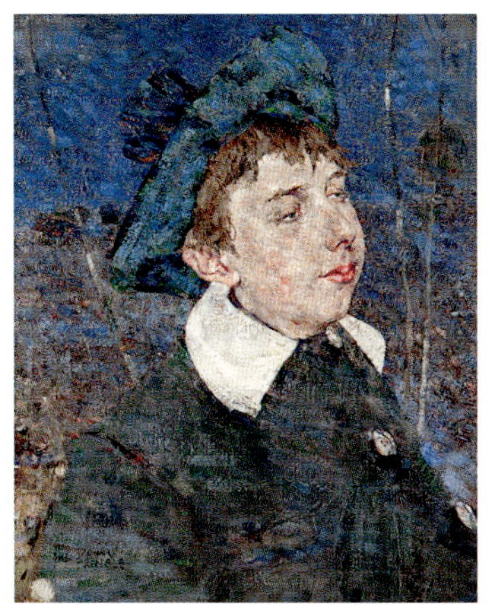

Pringle, John Quinton 1864–1925
*A Boy, Green Hat and Jacket, White
Collar* 1903
oil on canvas 53.3 x 43.2
2682

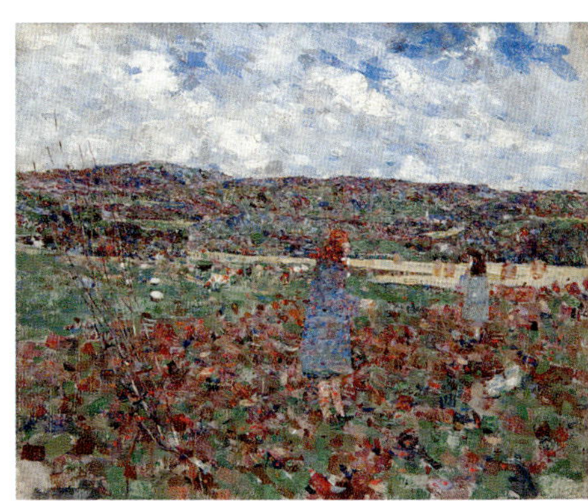

Pringle, John Quinton 1864–1925
Landscape with Two Girls in Blue c.1903
oil on canvas 25.4 x 30.5
2673

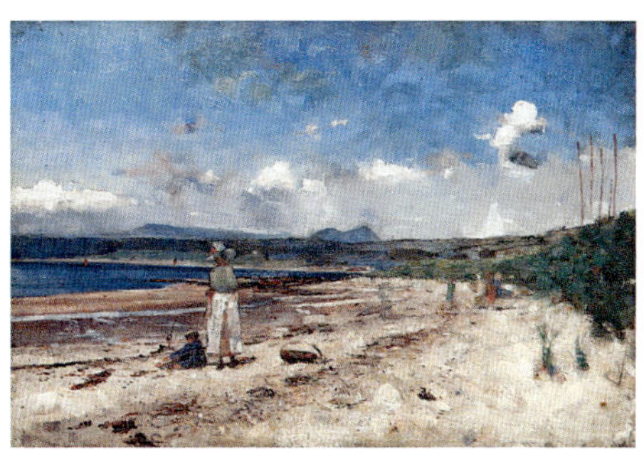

Pringle, John Quinton 1864–1925
*Seascape with Two Figures on a Beach and
Two Boats in a Bay* c.1903
oil on canvas 30.5 x 45.7
2674

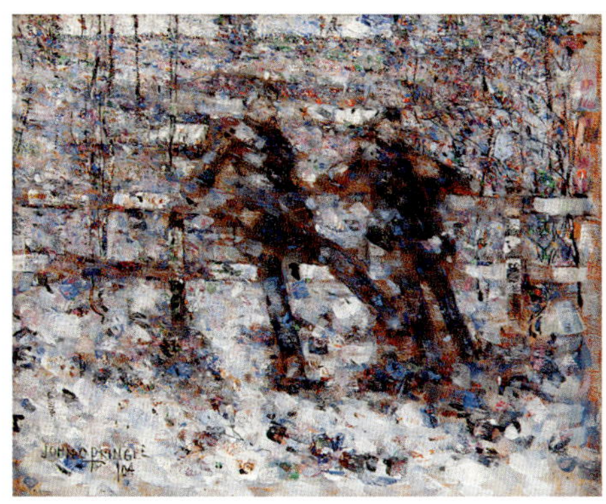

Pringle, John Quinton 1864–1925
Two Figures at a Fence 1904
oil on canvas 25.4 x 30.5
2662

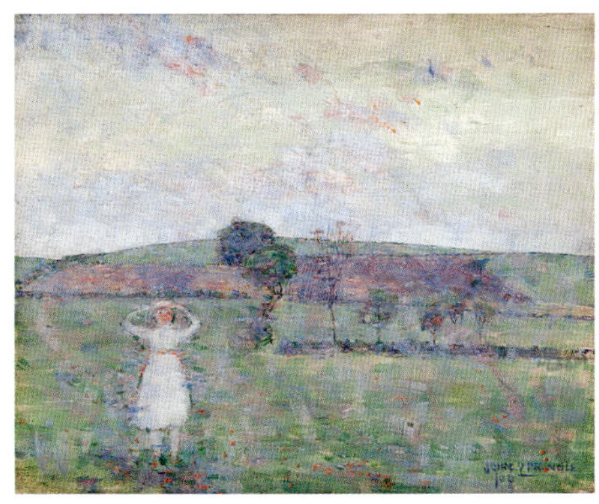

Pringle, John Quinton 1864–1925
*Landscape with Trees and a Girl in
White* 1906
oil on canvas 25.1 x 30.5
2664

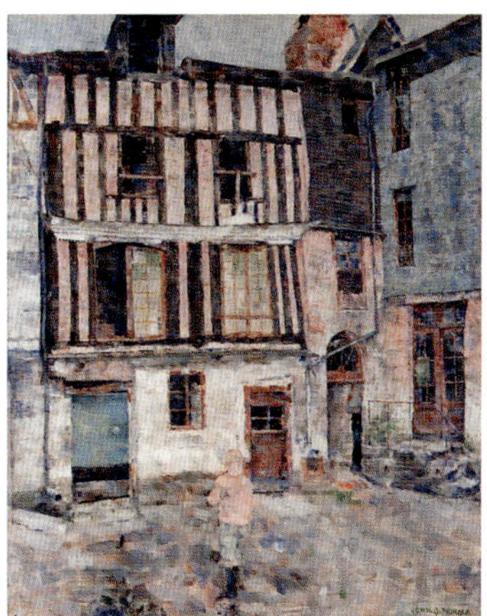

Pringle, John Quinton 1864–1925
Caudebec, Normandy 1910
oil on canvas 53.3 x 43.2
1577

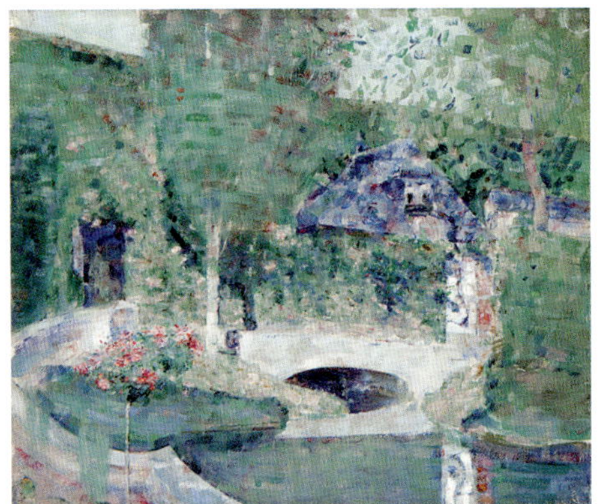

Pringle, John Quinton 1864–1925
Garden and Bridge, Caudebec 1910
oil on canvas 25.4 x 30.5
3383

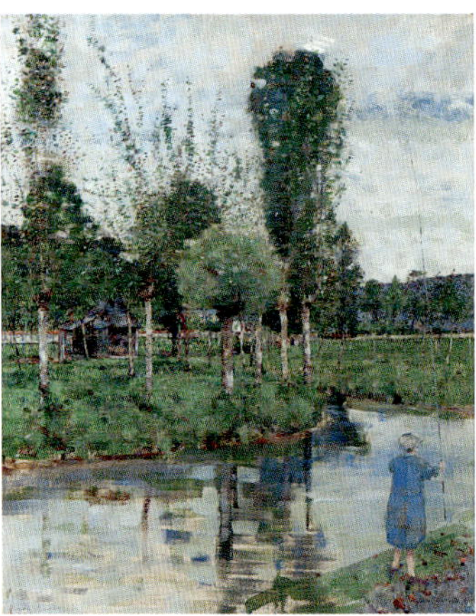

Pringle, John Quinton 1864–1925
*On the River Sainte-Gertrude, Caudebec,
Normandy* 1910
oil on canvas 53.5 x 43
3306

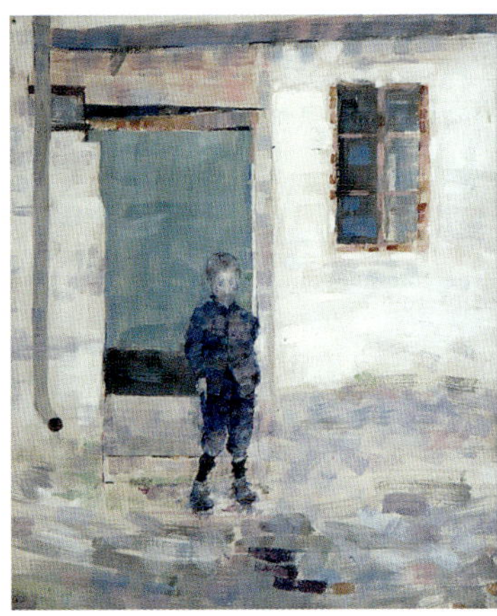

Pringle, John Quinton 1864–1925
Study of a Boy, Caudebec, Normandy 1910
oil on canvas 30.5 x 25.4
3382

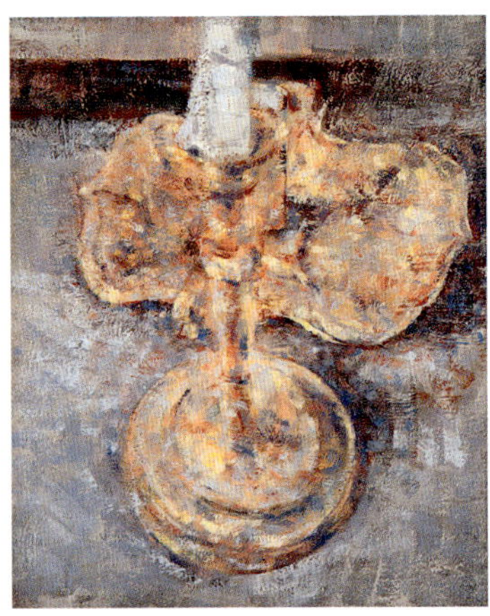

Pringle, John Quinton 1864–1925
Still Life, a Candlestick and a Salver c.1923–
1924
oil on canvas 25.4 x 20.3
2668

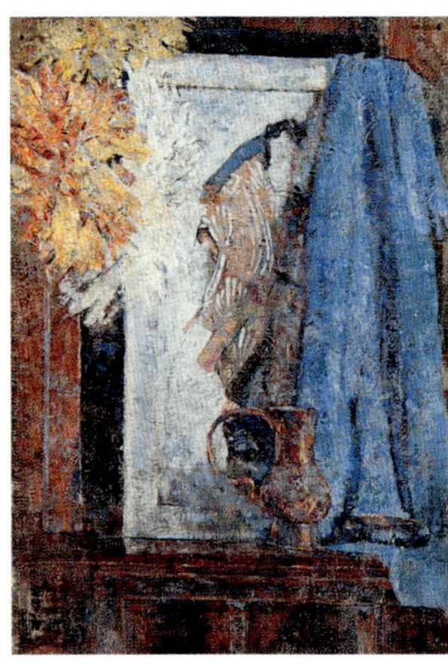

Pringle, John Quinton 1864–1925
*Still Life, a Jug, a Japanese Print and a Blue
Drape* c.1923–1924
oil on canvas 25.4 x 17.5
2669

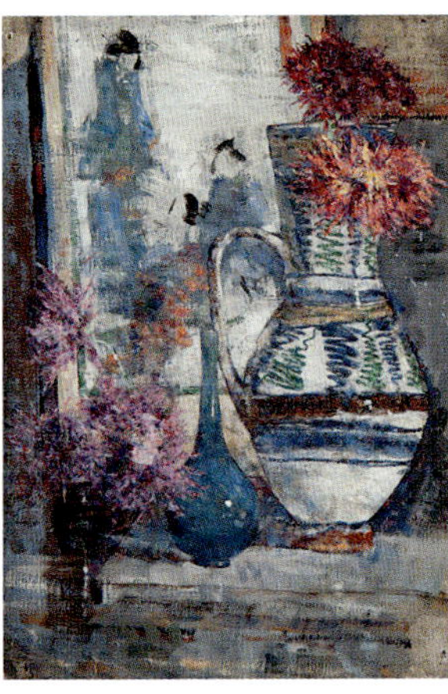

Pringle, John Quinton 1864–1925
*Still Life, a Vase, a Bottle and a Jug with
Flowers* c.1923–1924
oil on canvas 30.5 x 20.3
2666

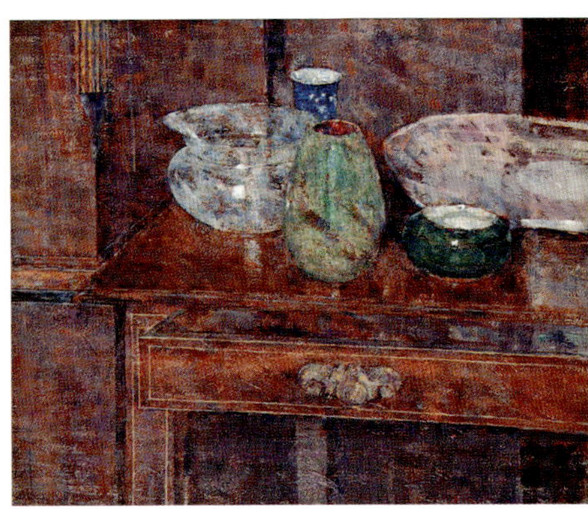

Pringle, John Quinton 1864–1925
Still Life on a Table c.1923–1924
oil on canvas 25.4 x 30.4
3398

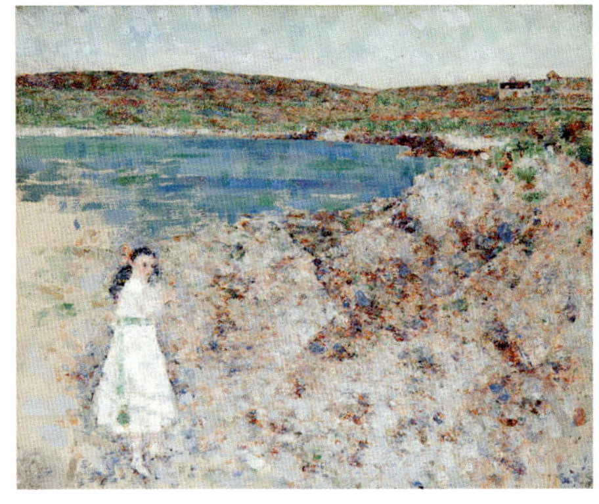

Pringle, John Quinton 1864–1925
Whalsay Bay, with a Girl in White 1924
oil on canvas 25.7 x 30.5
2672

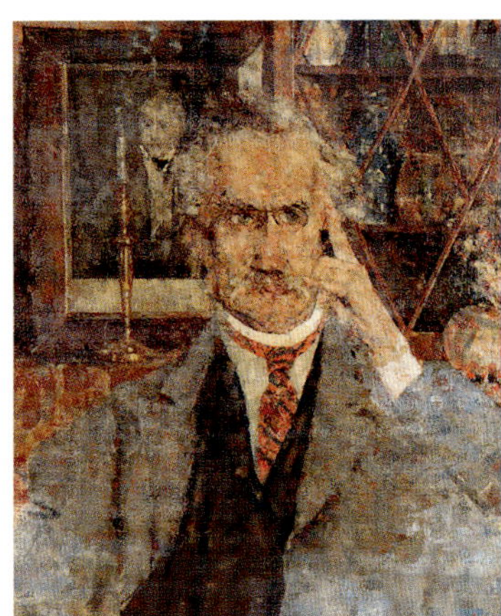

Pringle, John Quinton 1864–1925
Arthur Campbell 1925
oil on canvas 30.4 x 25.4
3388

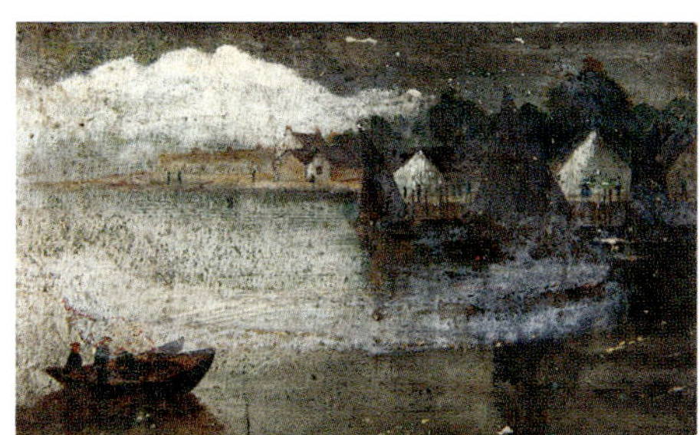

Pringle, John Quinton 1864–1925
Boats at a Small Harbour
oil on card 12.7 x 21.3
PR.1963.1.aq

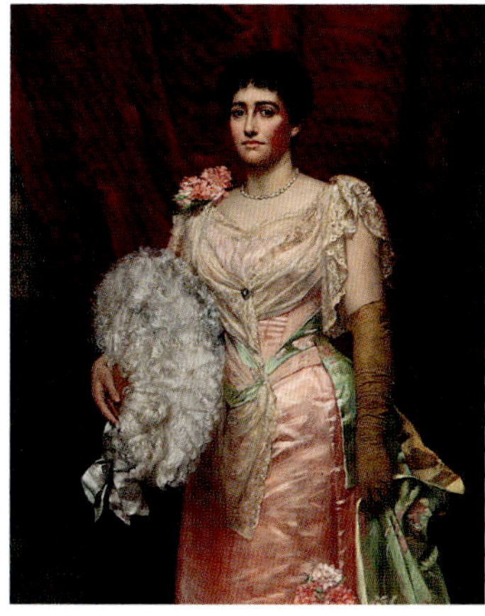

Prinsep, Valentine Cameron 1838–1904
Lady Simpson 1892
oil on canvas 142.2 x 111.8
2997

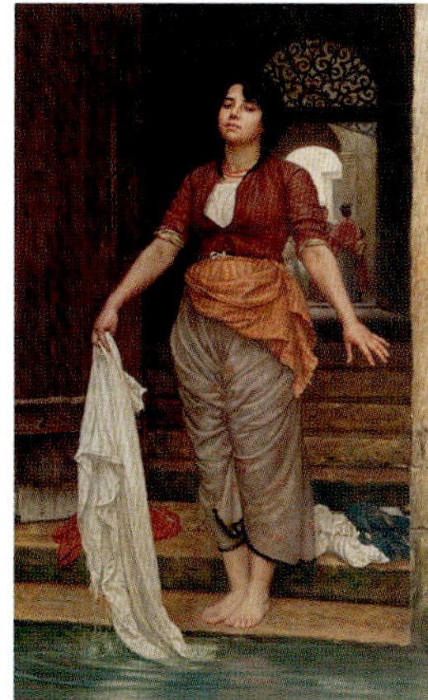

Prinsep, Valentine Cameron 1838–1904
In a Street in Venice c.1904
oil on canvas 152.4 x 94
1562

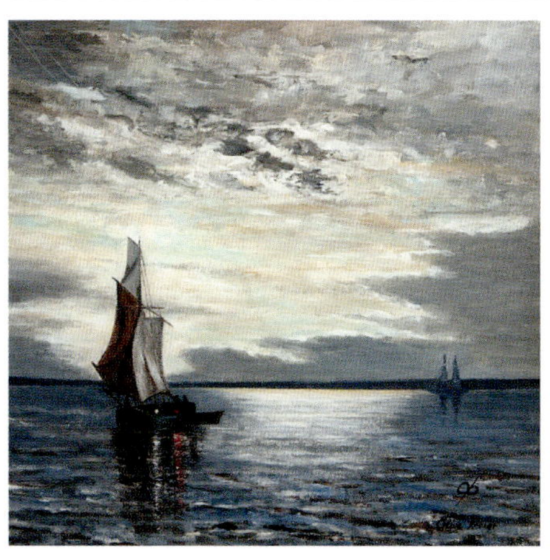

Prior, Olive
Boat at Sea 1990
acrylic/oil on hardboard 60 x 60
TEMP.15519

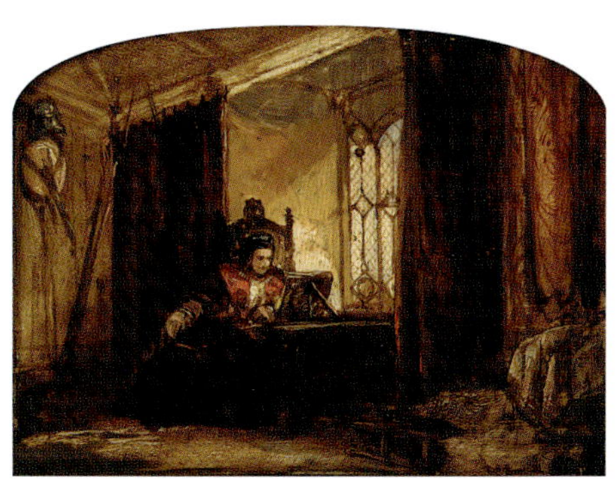

Pritchett, Robert Taylor 1828–1907
The Student
oil on panel 17.8 x 24.1
418

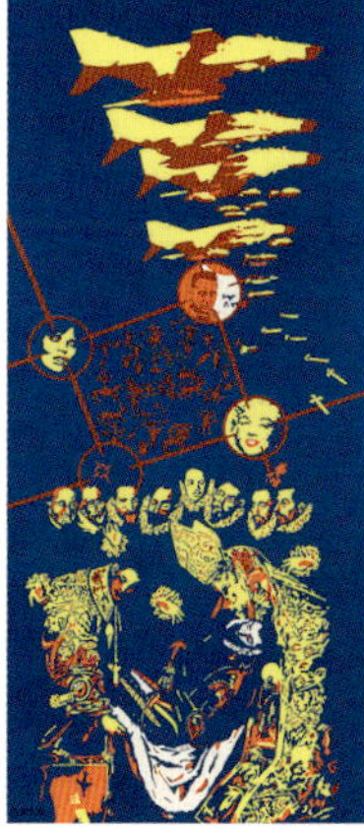

Purves, Ian Hamilton 1938–1975
Count Down Orgaz 1973
acrylic on hardboard 213.3 x 91.5
3304

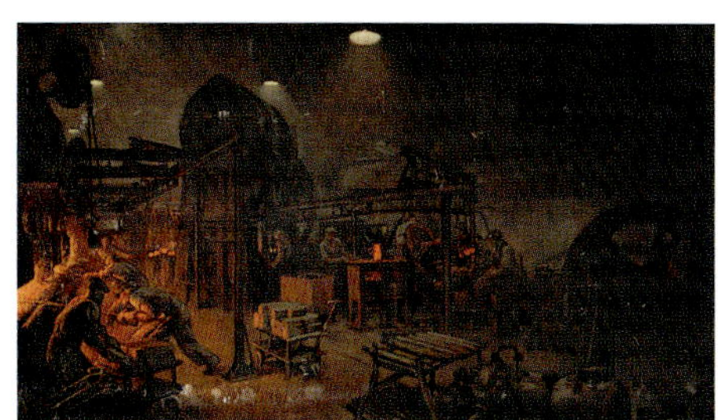

Purvis, Tom 1888–1959
A Factory Interior
oil on board 65 x 119
TEMP.16831

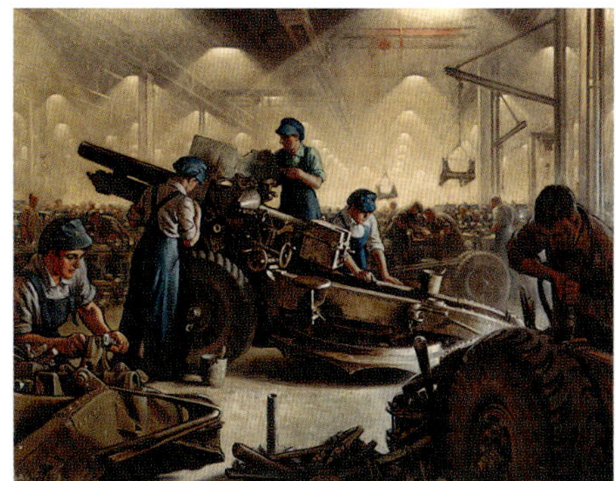

Purvis, Tom 1888–1959
Women Munitions Workers at Weir's Factory
oil on canvas 116 x 141.2
T.2008.8

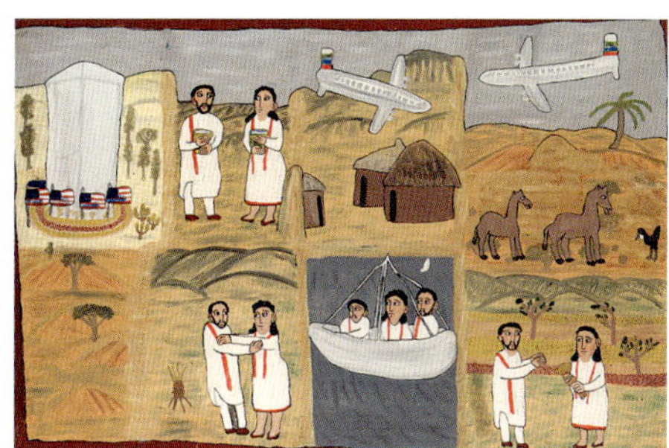

Qaana
Airplane Crash over Lake Tana, Ethiopia, at Night 1970
oil on canvas 83 x 124.5
3549

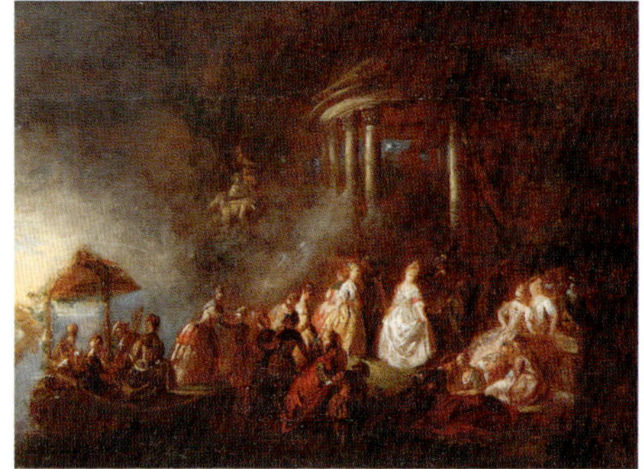

Quillard, Pierre Antoine (follower of)
1701–1733
The Arrival at the Island of Cythera
oil on canvas 26.9 x 32.1
227

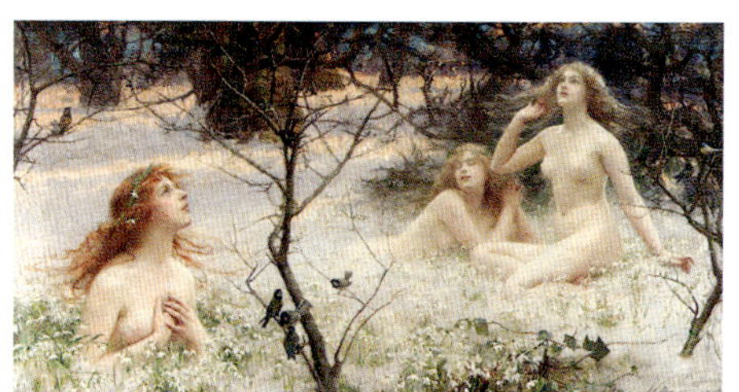

Rae, Henrietta 1859–1928
Spring's Awakening (The Snow Maidens)
1913
oil on canvas 106.7 x 198.1
1822

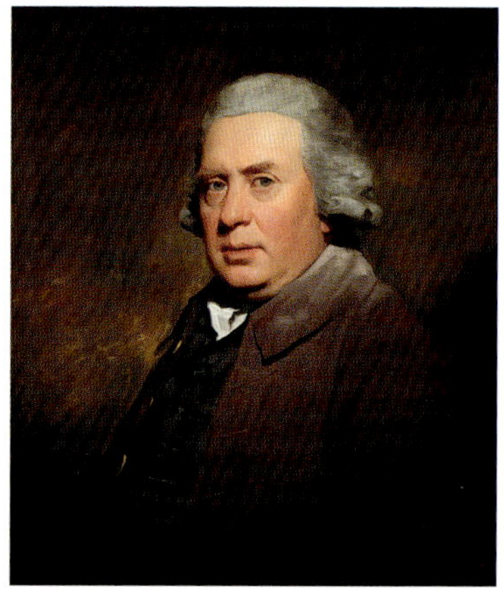

Raeburn, Henry 1756–1823
Colin Campbell of Park (1728–1793)
c.1780–1793
oil on canvas 76.2 x 63.5
1418

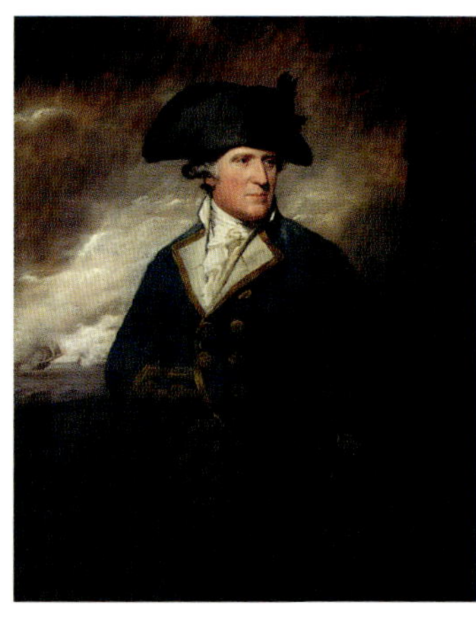

Raeburn, Henry 1756–1823
Portrait of a Captain, RN c.1787
oil on canvas 124.8 x 103.8
3206

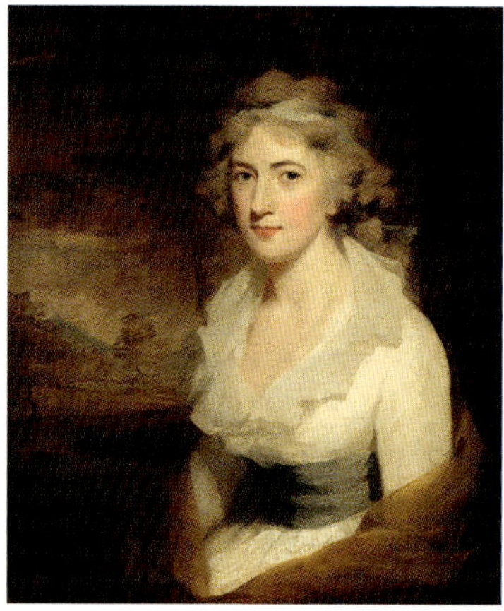

Raeburn, Henry 1756–1823
Miss Macartney 1794
oil on canvas 73.7 x 61
35.646

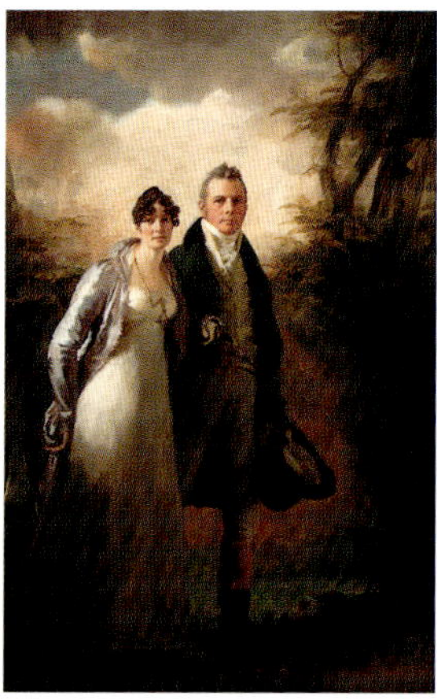

Raeburn, Henry 1756–1823
Mr and Mrs Robert N. Campbell of Kailzie
c.1805
oil on canvas 241.3 x 152.4
1594

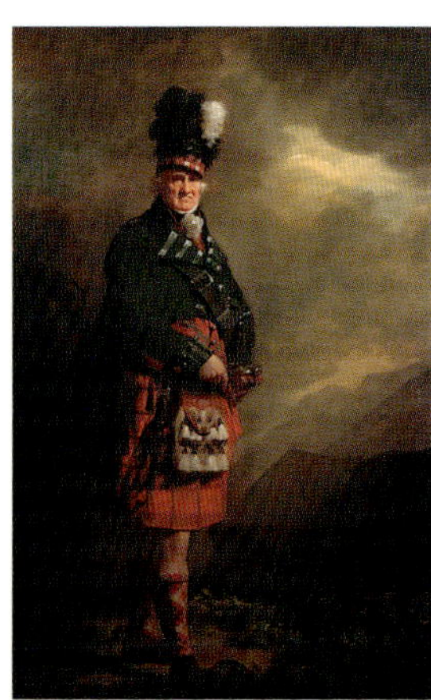

Raeburn, Henry 1756–1823
The MacNab c.1810
oil on canvas 284.5 x 196.8
LI.2005.010.1 (P)

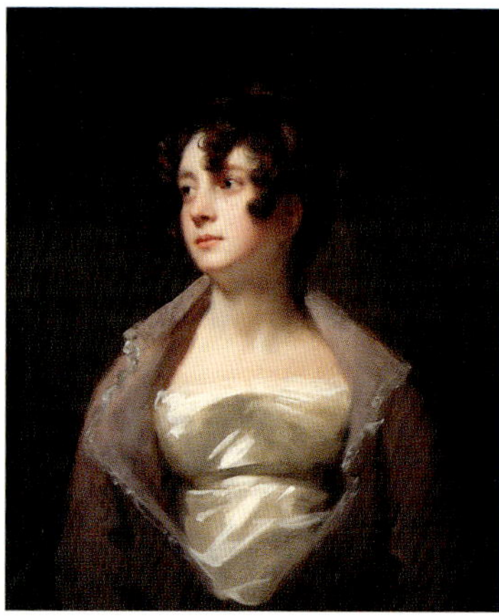

Raeburn, Henry 1756–1823
Mrs William Urquhart (c.1796–1864)
1814–1815
oil on canvas 76.2 x 63.5
904

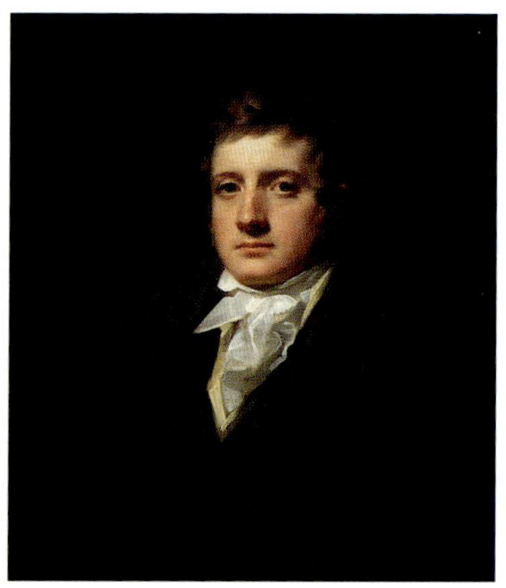

Raeburn, Henry 1756–1823
William Urquhart (c.1794–1840) 1814–1815
oil on canvas 75.6 x 62.9
903

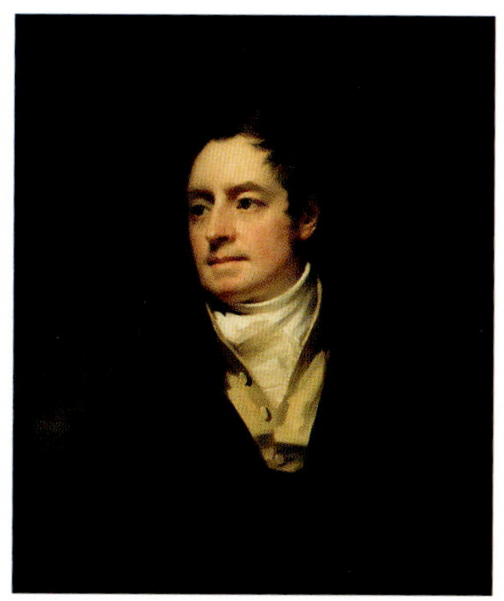

Raeburn, Henry 1756–1823
Alexander Campbell of Hallyards (1768–1817)
oil on canvas 76.2 x 63.5
1902

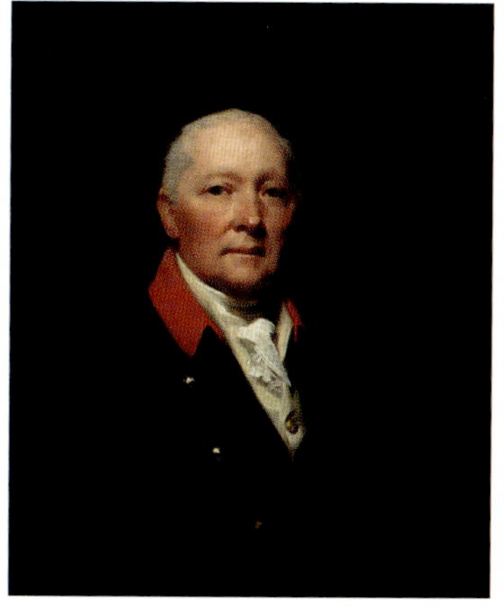

Raeburn, Henry 1756–1823
Colonel Bowes
oil on canvas 76.2 x 63.5
35.594

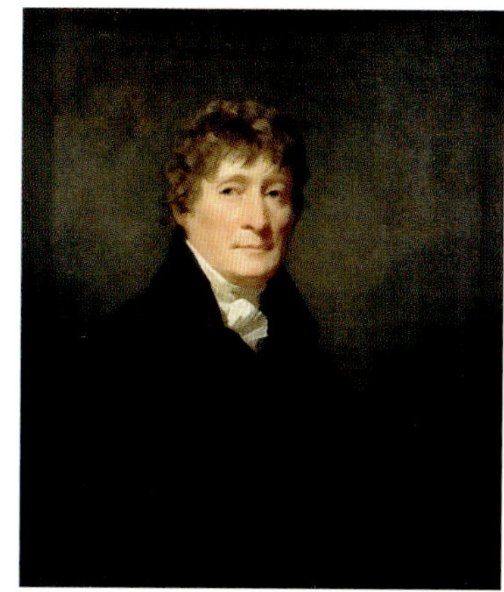

Raeburn, Henry 1756–1823
Henry MacKenzie (1745–1831)
oil on canvas 76.2 x 63.5
35.595

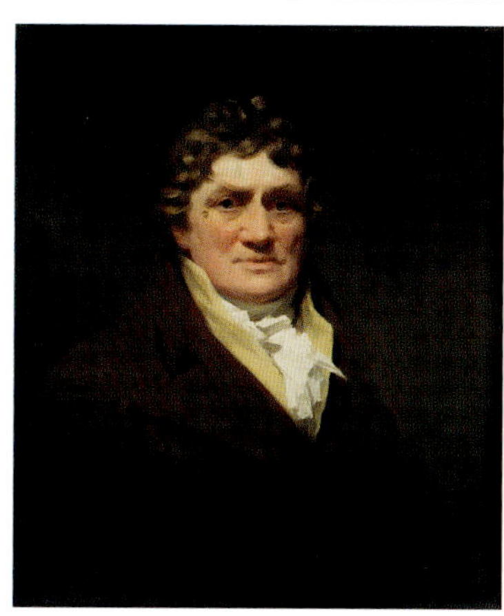

Raeburn, Henry 1756–1823
John Campbell Senior of Morriston (c.1734–1808)
oil on canvas 76.2 x 63.5
1417

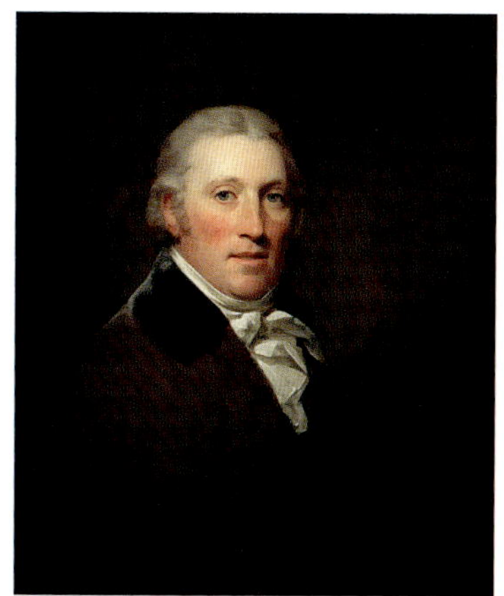

Raeburn, Henry 1756–1823
John Dunlop (1774–1820), Provost of Glasgow (1794–1795)
oil on canvas 74 x 61.9
3277

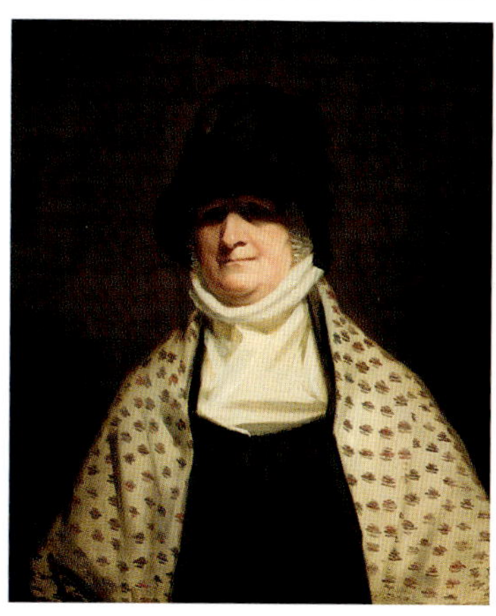

Raeburn, Henry 1756–1823
Mrs Anne Campbell
oil on canvas 76.2 x 63.5
1419

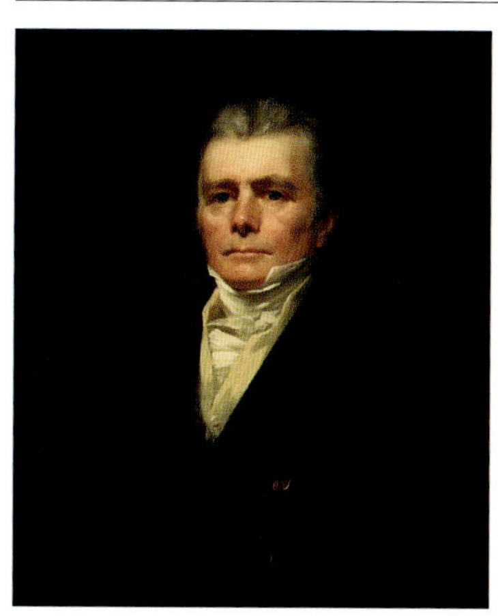

Raeburn, Henry 1756–1823
Robert N. Campbell of Kailzie (c.1761–1845)
oil on canvas 76.2 x 63.5
1424

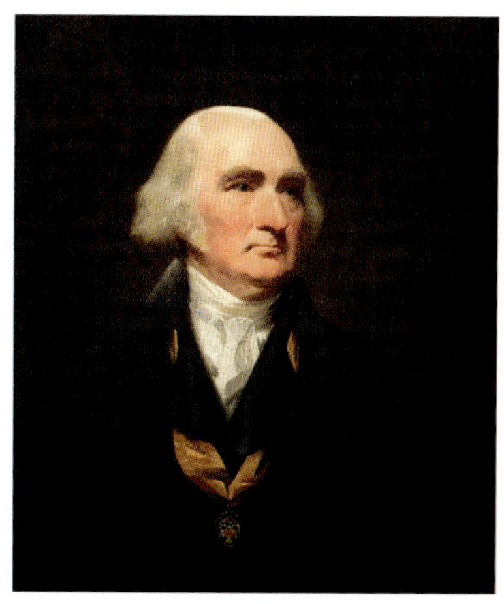

Raeburn, Henry 1756–1823
William Forbes of Pitsligo (1739–1806)
oil on canvas 73.7 x 61
35.596

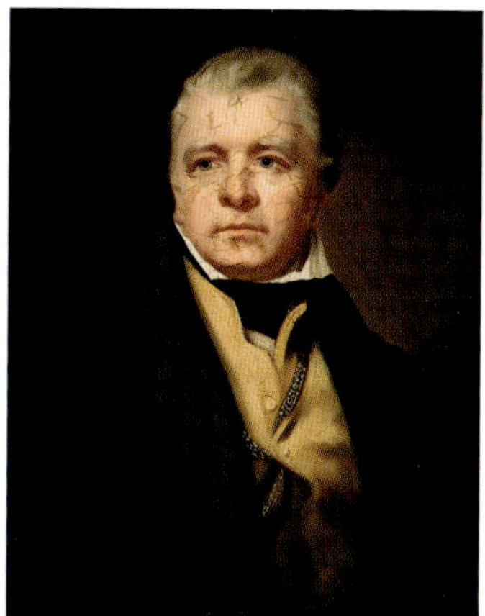

Raeburn, Henry (after) 1756–1823
Sir Walter Scott (1771–1832) 19th C
oil on canvas 34.3 x 28.6
229

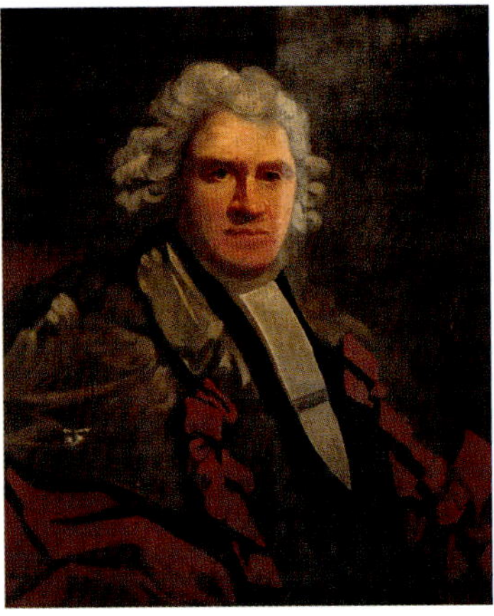

Raeburn, Henry (after) 1756–1823
Lord Moncrieff (1776–1851)
oil on canvas 76.2 x 63.5
2534

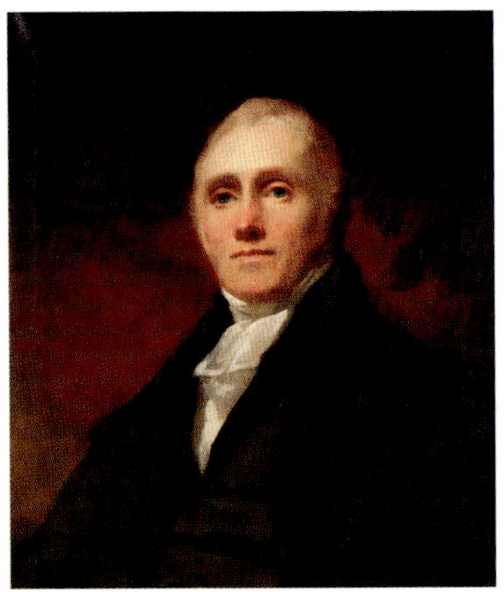

Raeburn, Henry (studio of) 1756–1823
Portrait of a Man with a Clerical Collar
c.1810–1815
oil on canvas 76.2 x 63.5
TEMP.4674

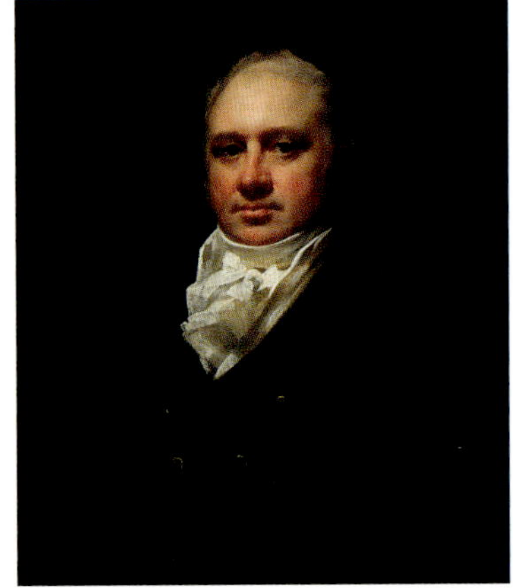

Raeburn, Henry (style of) 1756–1823
William Jamieson, Junior 1805
oil on canvas 76.2 x 63.5
750

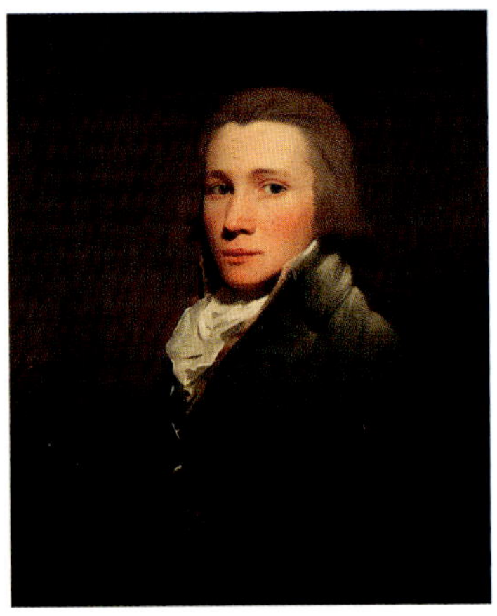

Raeburn, Henry (style of) 1756–1823
Mr Campbell
oil on canvas 76.2 x 63.5
1426

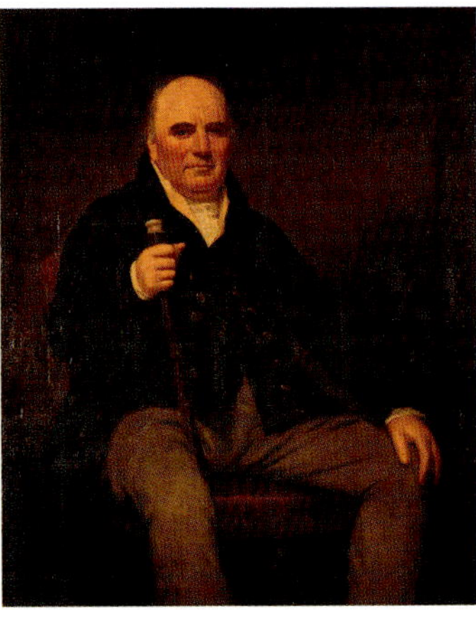

Raeburn, Henry (style of) 1756–1823
William Dixon of Govanhill (1753–1822)
oil on canvas 127 x 101.6
NR.74

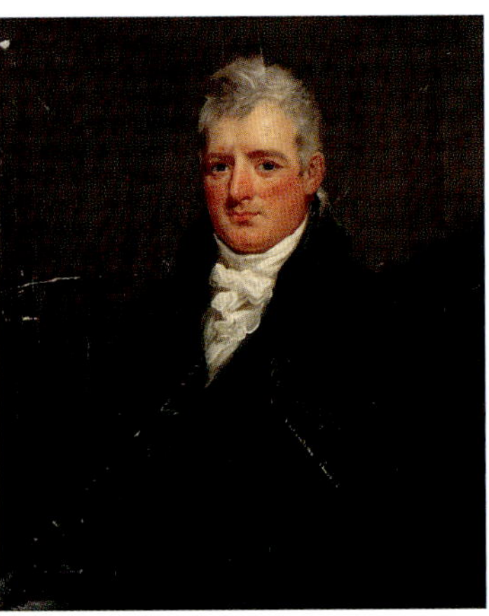

Raeburn, Henry (style of) 1756–1823
William Mills (1776–1857), Lord Provost of Glasgow (1834–1837)
oil on canvas 76.2 x 63.5
689

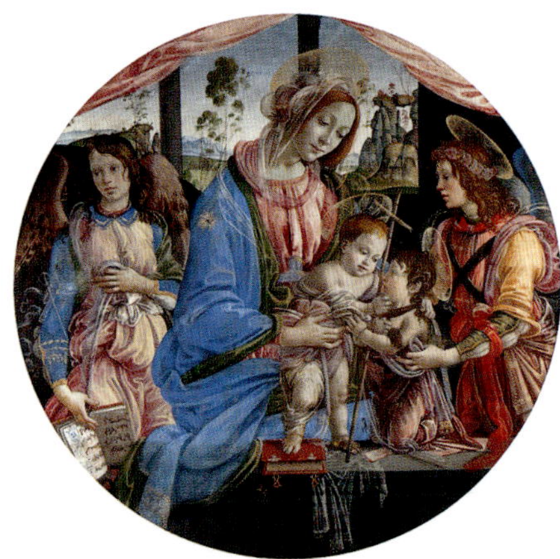

Raffaellino del Garbo c.1470–1527/1528
Virgin and Child with the Child Baptist and Two Angels c.1493–1494
tempera on panel 118.4
1015

Ramsay, Allan 1713–1784
Colonel John Stewart of Stewartfield (d.1750) 1742
oil on canvas 76.2 x 63.2
3204

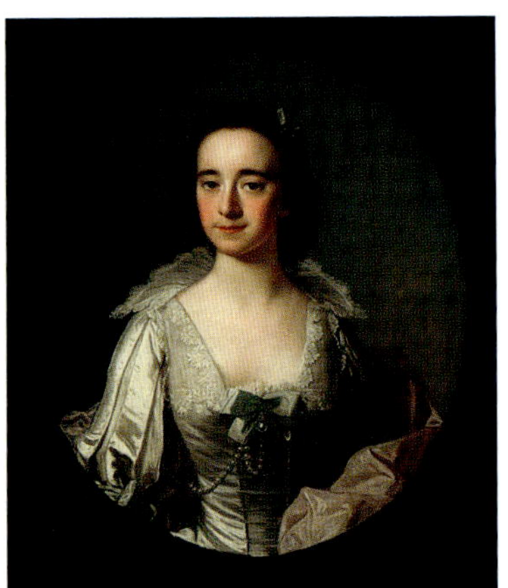

Ramsay, Allan 1713–1784
Portrait of a Lady c.1747
oil on canvas 80.7 x 68.8
3279

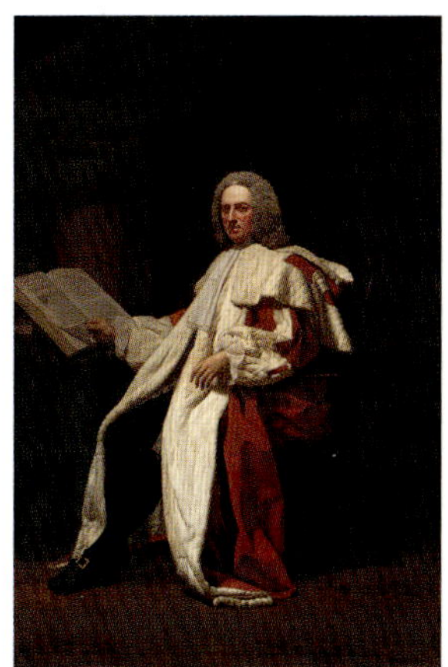

Ramsay, Allan 1713–1784
Archibald Campbell (1682–1761), 3rd Duke of Argyll 1749
oil on canvas 238.8 x 156.2
471

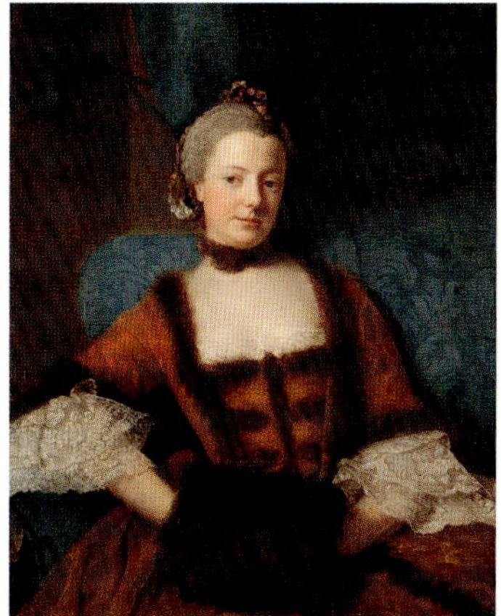

Ramsay, Allan 1713–1784
Henrietta Diana (1728–1761), Dowager Countess of Stafford 1759
oil on canvas 94.6 x 73.7
3026

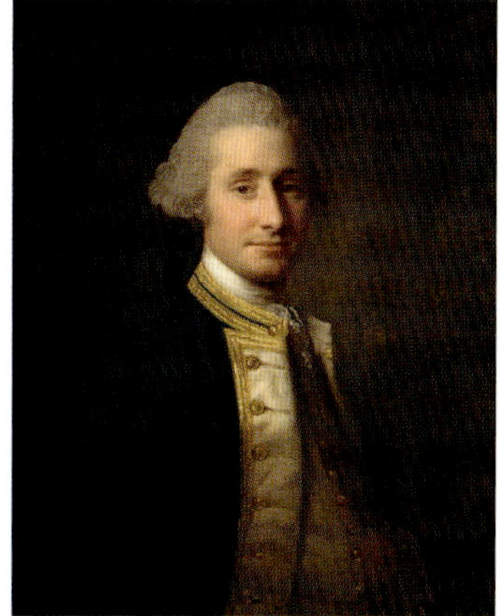

Ramsay, Allan 1713–1784
Captain Sir John Lindsay (1737–1788) c.1768/1769
oil on canvas 76.2 x 63.5
2888

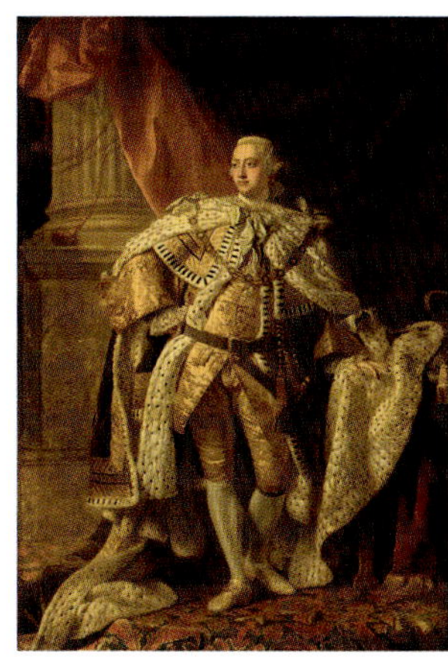

Ramsay, Allan (studio of) 1713–1784
George III (1738–1820) c.1764
oil on canvas 238.8 x 158.8
479

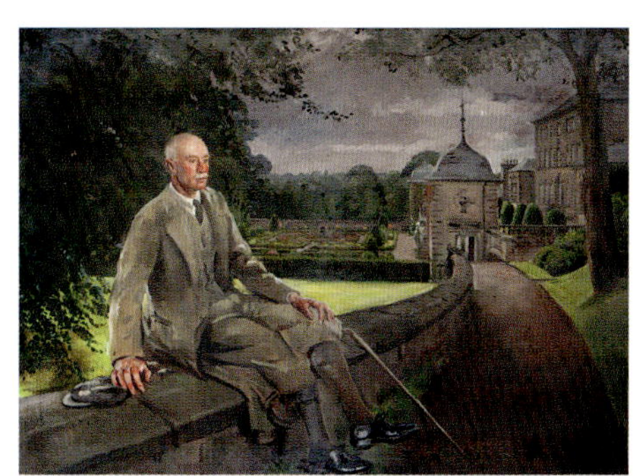

Ranken, William Bruce Ellis 1881–1941
Sir John Stirling Maxwell (1866–1956), 10th Bt 1922
oil on canvas 76.8 x 102.2
PL.20 (P)

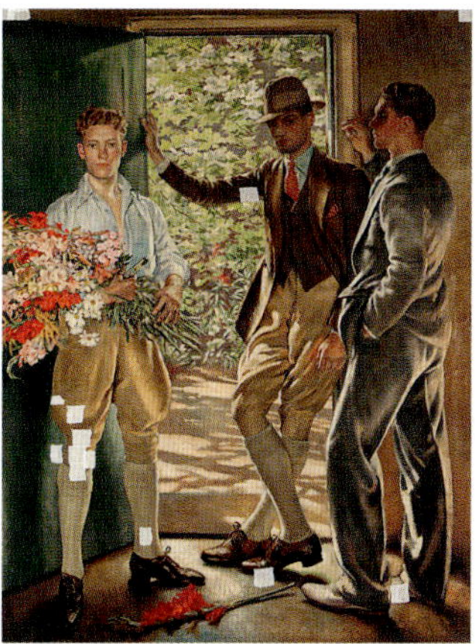

Ranken, William Bruce Ellis 1881–1941
The Garden Door 1926
oil on canvas 218.4 x 162.6
2568

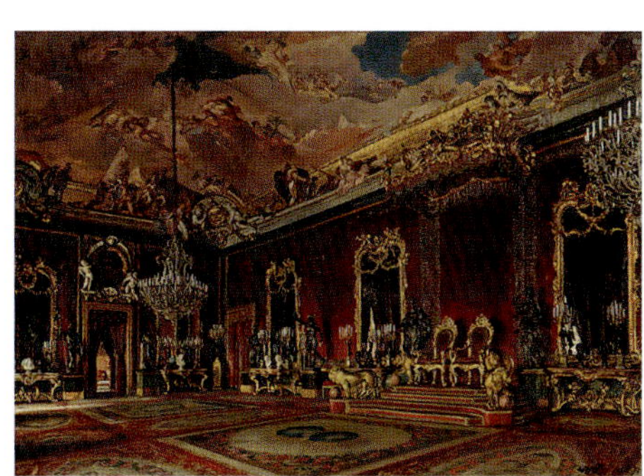

Ranken, William Bruce Ellis 1881–1941
The Throne Room, Madrid 1927
oil on millboard 94 x 128.9
2824

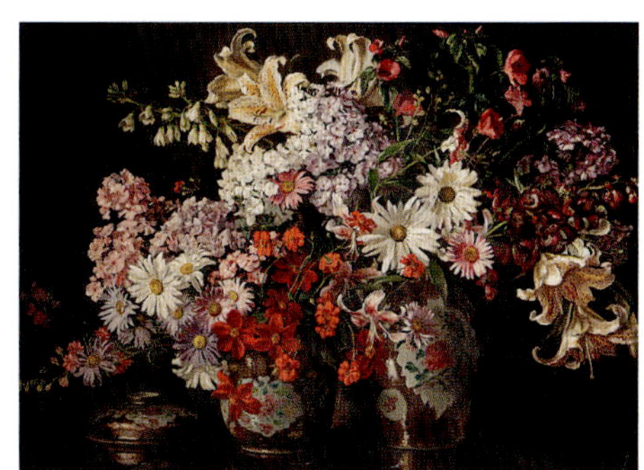

Ranken, William Bruce Ellis 1881–1941
Flower Piece
oil on canvas 79.4 x 109.2
PC.80

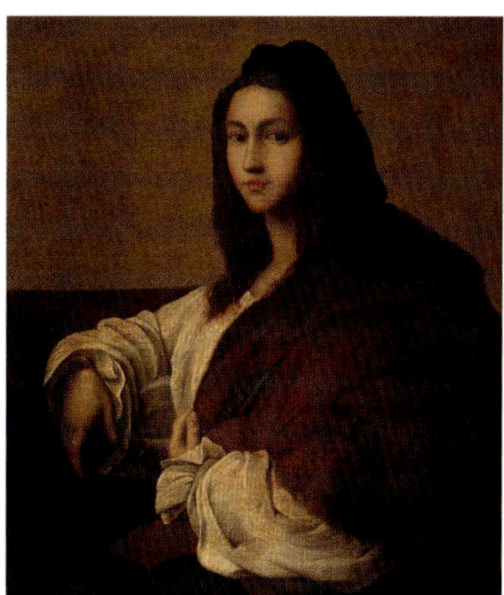

Raphael (after) 1483–1520
Portrait of a Man 17th C–18th C
oil on panel 75.9 x 64.8
PL.101 (P)

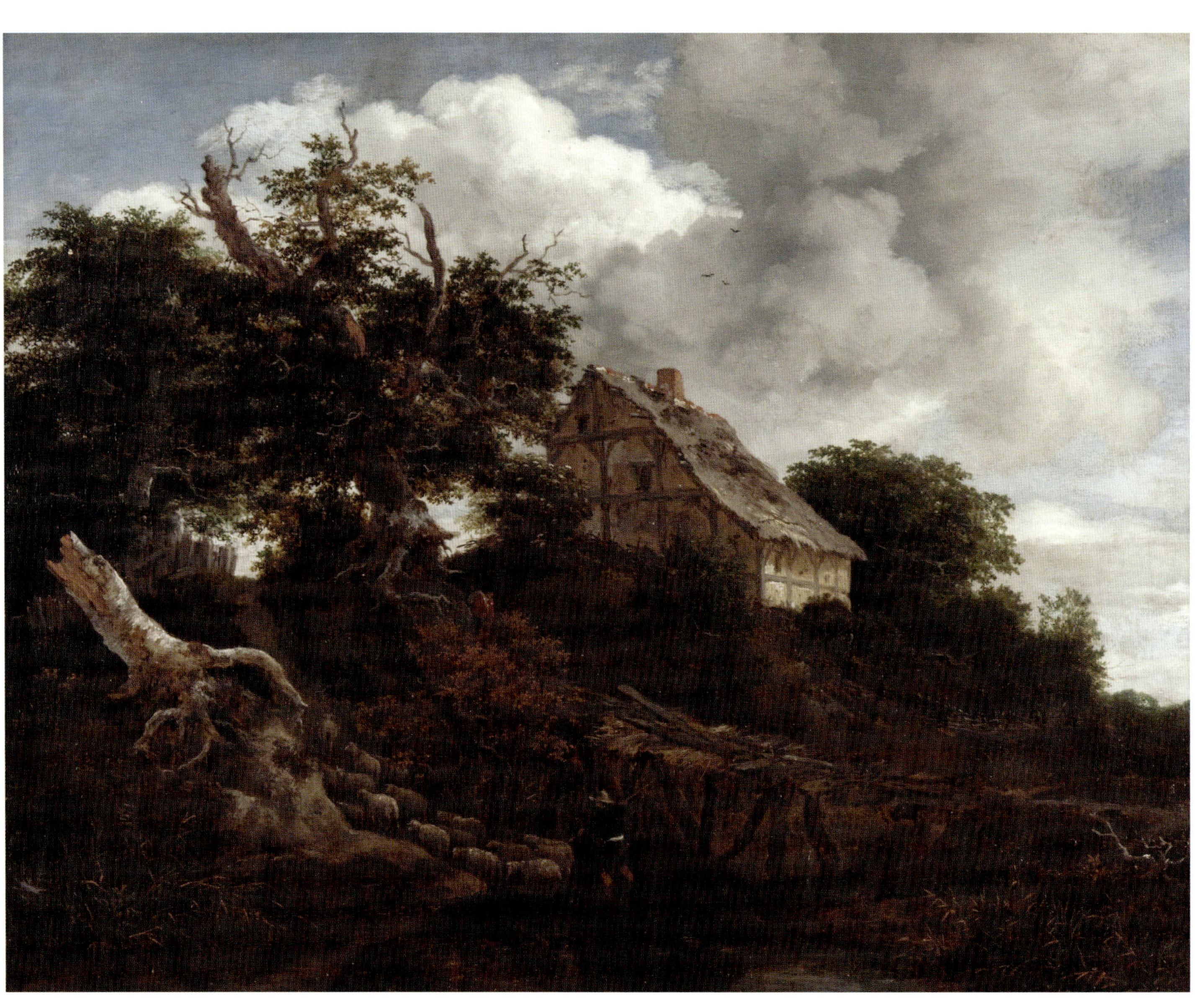

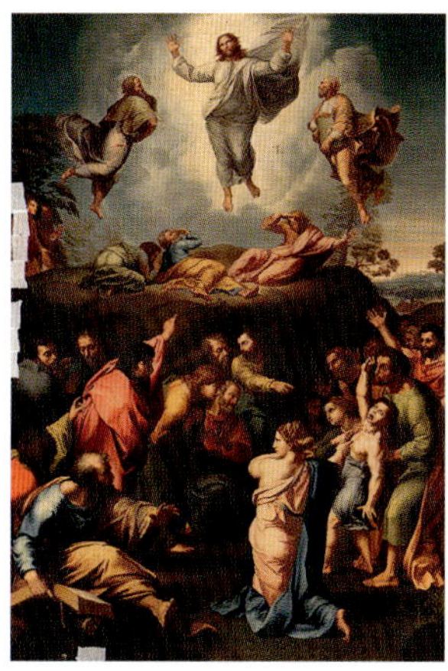

Raphael (after) 1483–1520
The Transfiguration 1820s (?)
oil on canvas 172.7 x 116.8
309

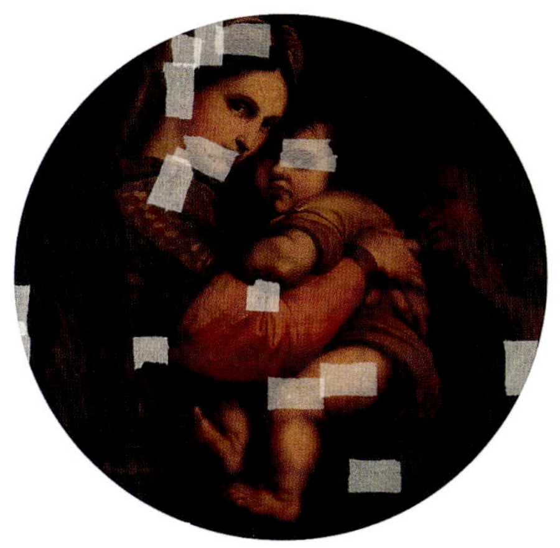

Raphael (after) 1483–1520
Madonna della sedia 19th C
oil on canvas 72.4
3419

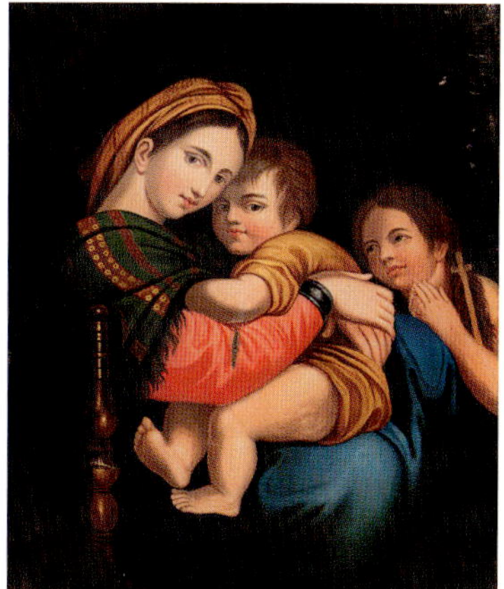

Raphael (after) 1483–1520
Madonna della sedia 19th C
oil on canvas 77.4 x 63.5
NR.109

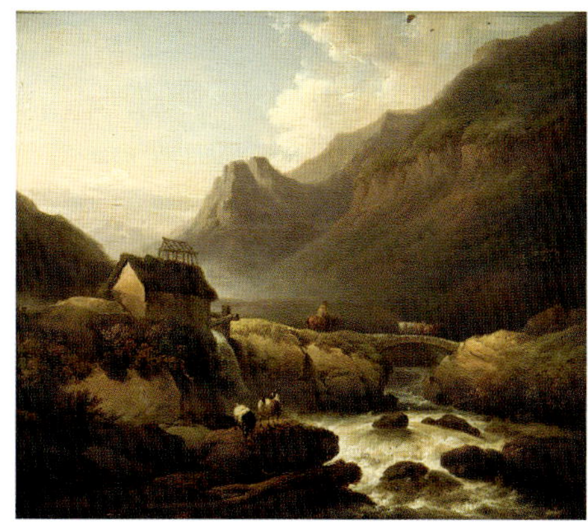

Rathbone, John c.1750–1807
*A Mountain Stream with a Peasant Driving
Cattle over a Rustic Bridge* 1797
oil on panel 29.2 x 32.4
1363

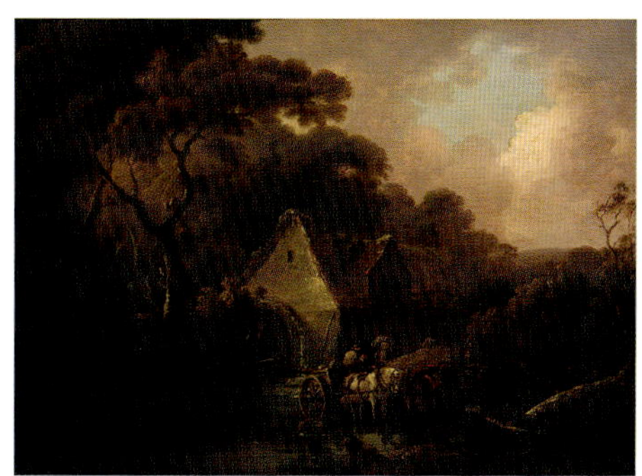

Rathbone, John c.1750–1807
Old Mill and a Farm Cart 1797
oil on panel 29.2 x 40.9
1368

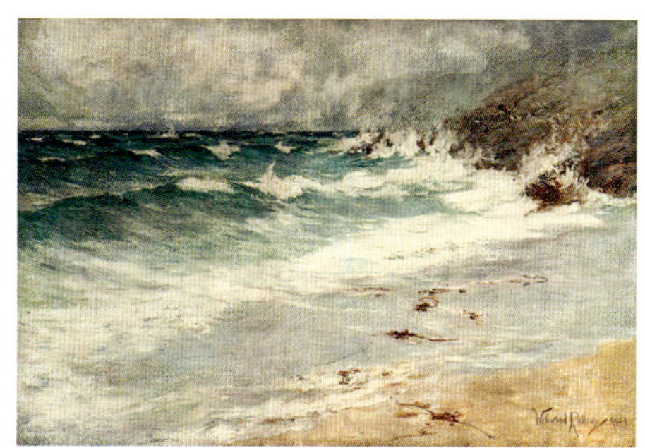

Rattray, Alexander William Wellwood
1849–1902
Seascape, Kintyre c.1896–1902
oil on canvas 86.5 x 127.3
3097

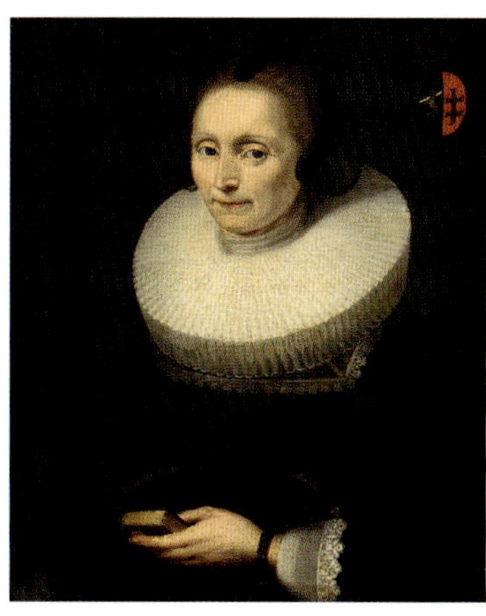

Ravesteyn, Jan Anthonisz. van (style of)
c.1570–1657
Portrait of a Lady 1630s
oil on panel 68.6 x 58.4
35.598

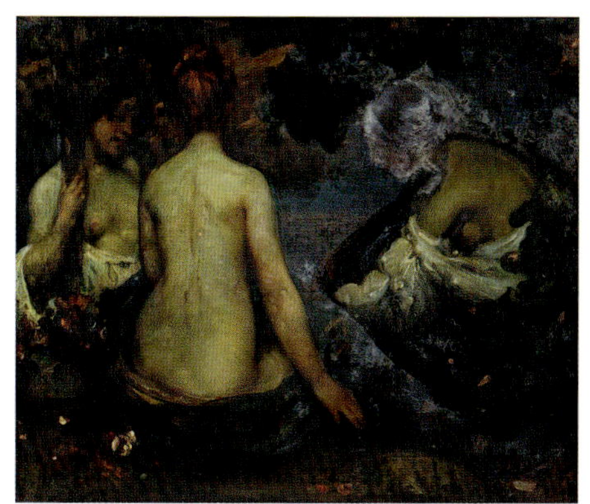

Rea, Cecil William 1860–1935
In Arcady
oil on canvas 55.9 x 66
1712

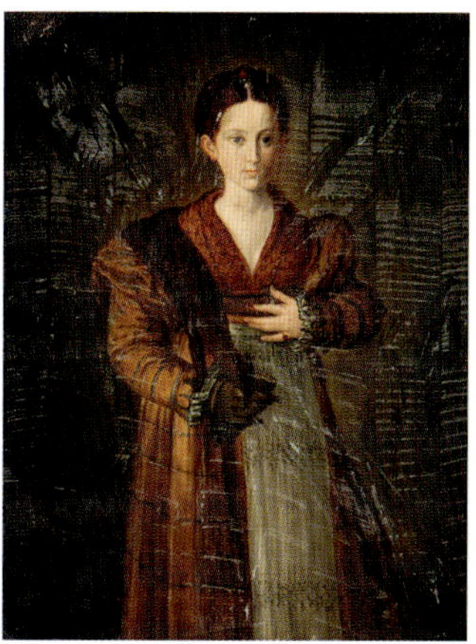

Recupero, Giovanni
Anthea (after Parmigianino) c.1825
oil on canvas 50.2 x 38.7
314

Facing page: Ruisdael, Jacob van, 1628/1629–1682, *Landscape with a Cottage, Bridge and Sheep,*
c.1650–1655 (p. 383)

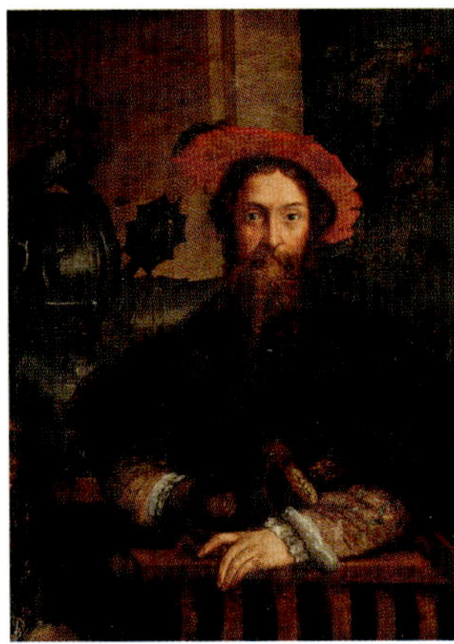

Recupero, Giovanni
Galeazzo Sanvitale (1566–1622) (after
Parmigianino) c.1825
oil on canvas 50.1 x 38.9
313

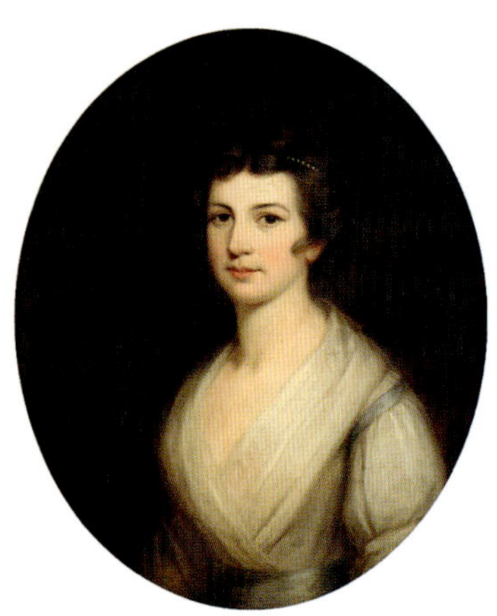

Reddock, A. (attributed to) d.1842
*Lady Hannah Anne Gardiner Maxwell
(1764–1841)*
oil on canvas 75.6 x 62.8
PL.177 (P)

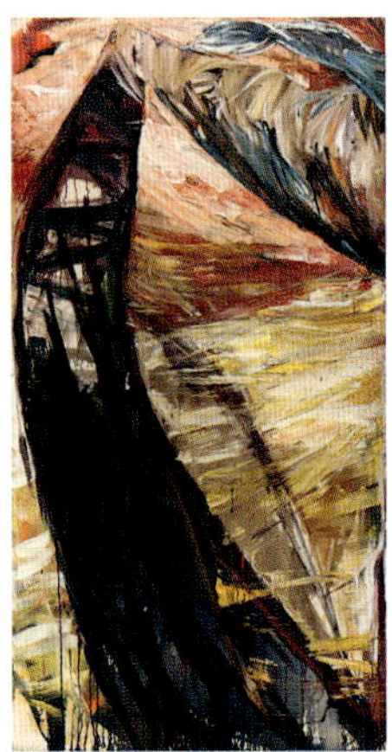

Redfern, June b.1951
The Devil at Llandaff (diptych, left panel)
1984
oil on canvas 245.8 x 123.2
3550.1

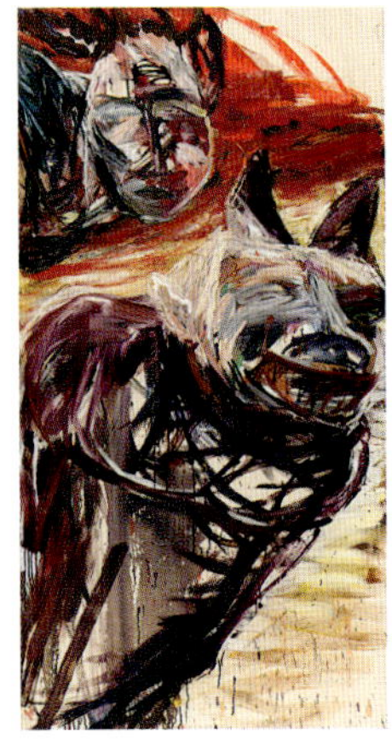

Redfern, June b.1951
The Devil at Llandaff (diptych, right panel)
1984
oil on canvas 245.8 x 123.2
3550.2

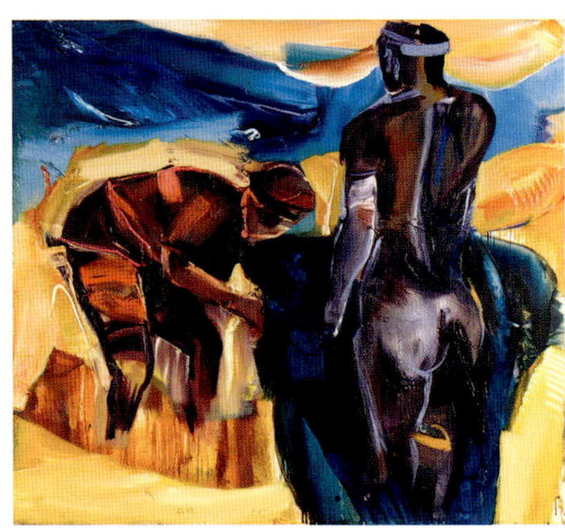

Redfern, June b.1951
From Two Paths 1993–1994
oil on canvas 168.2 x 183.5
3542

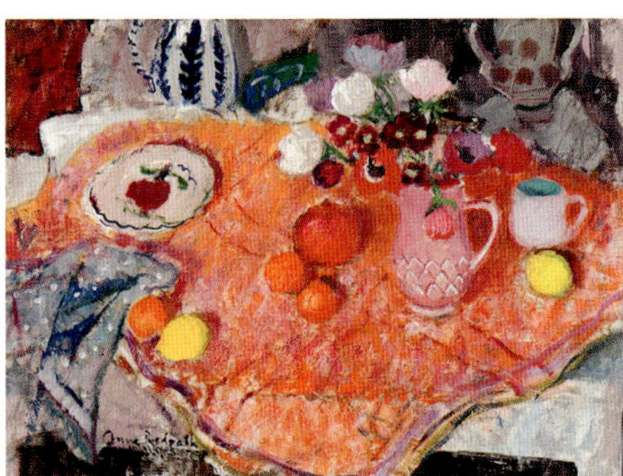

Redpath, Anne 1895–1965
Pinks 1947
oil on canvas 55.9 x 76.2
2777

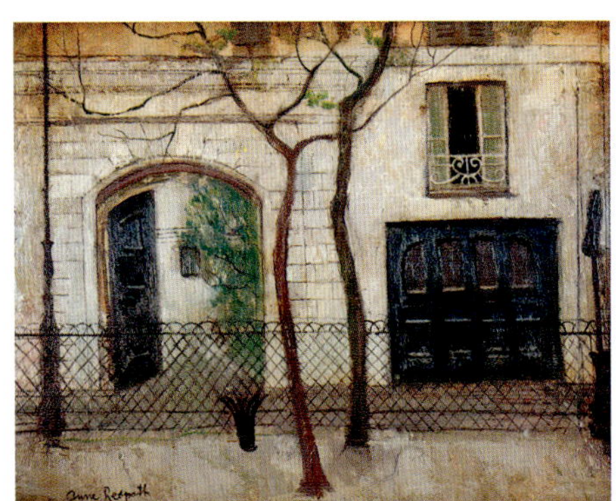

Redpath, Anne 1895–1965
Place de l'Institut, Paris (recto) c.1949
oil on board 68.6 x 86.4
2944

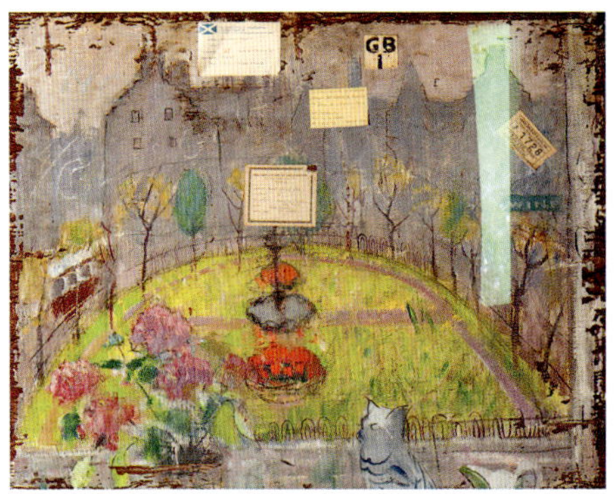

Redpath, Anne 1895–1965
Nicolson Square, Edinburgh (verso) c.1949
oil on board 68.6 x 86.4
2944 (verso)

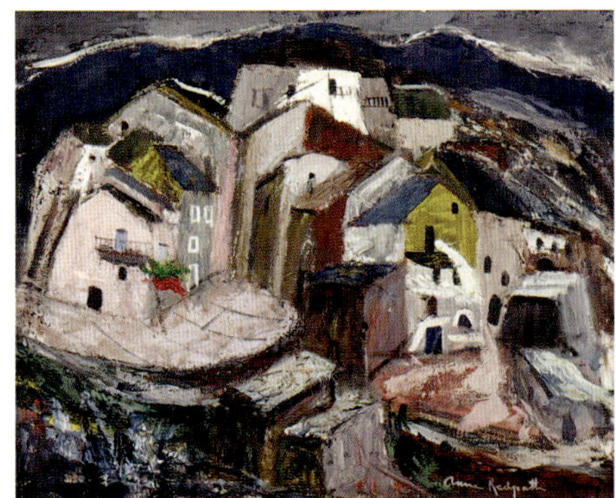

Redpath, Anne 1895–1965
Corsican Village c.1955
oil on canvas 63.5 x 76.2
3659

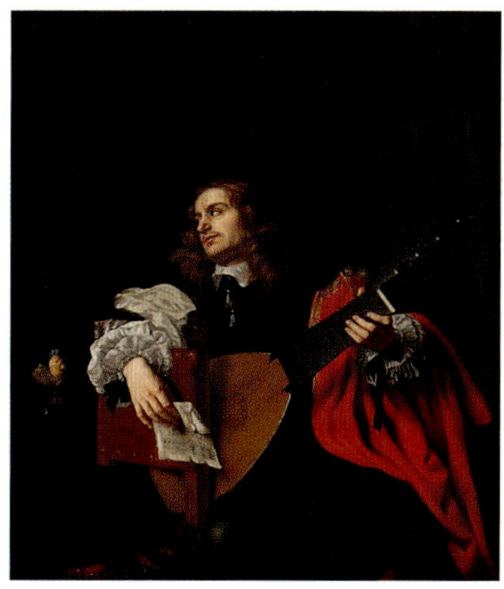

Reesbroeck, Jacob van (attributed to)
1620–1704
Portrait of a Man with a Lute c.1655–1660
oil on canvas 146 x 125.7
443

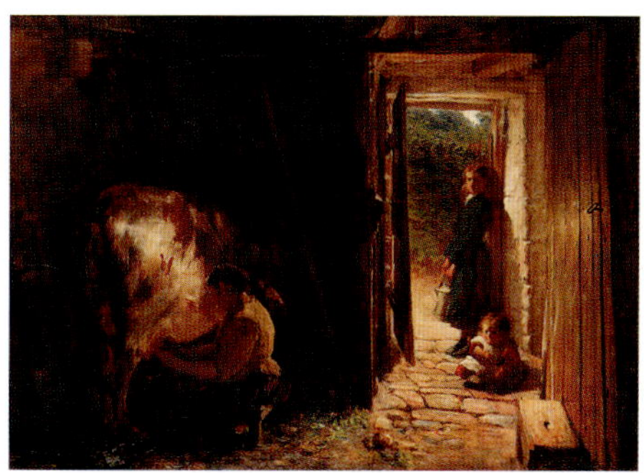

Reid, George 1841–1913
Milking Time 1878
oil on canvas 55.8 x 76.2
2058

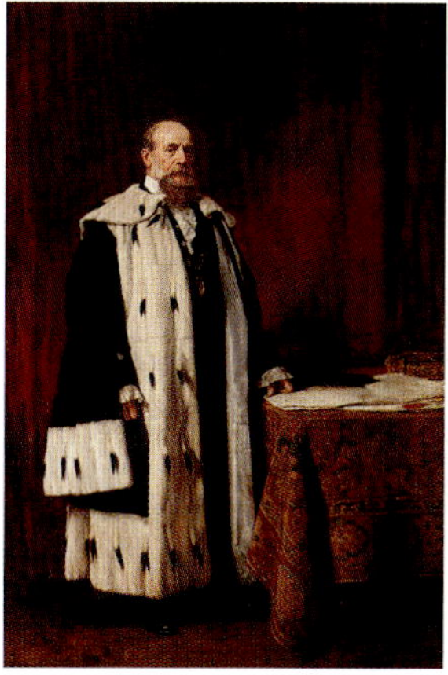

Reid, George 1841–1913
*John Ure (1824–1901), Lord Provost of
Glasgow (1880–1883)* 1885
oil on canvas 238.8 x 147.3
658

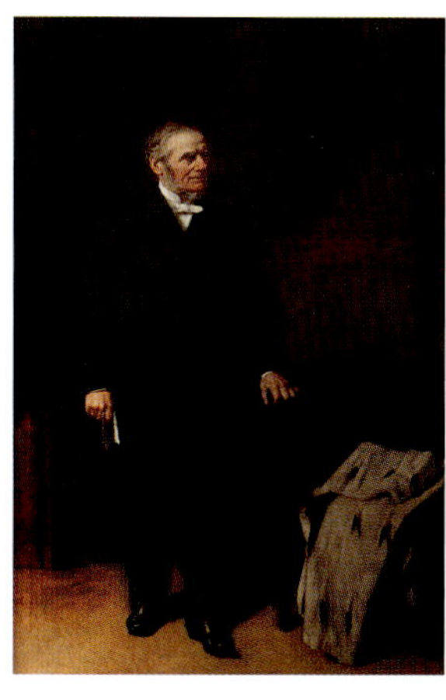

Reid, George 1841–1913
*Sir William McOnie (d.1894), Lord Provost of
Glasgow (1883–1886)* c.1887
oil on canvas 238.8 x 147.3
662

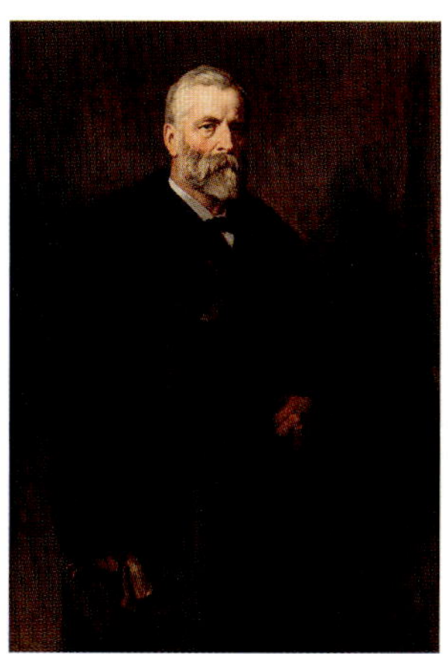

Reid, George 1841–1913
*James Reid (1823–1894), of Auchterarder and
Hydepark Locomotive Works* c.1890
oil on canvas 144.8 x 97.8
760

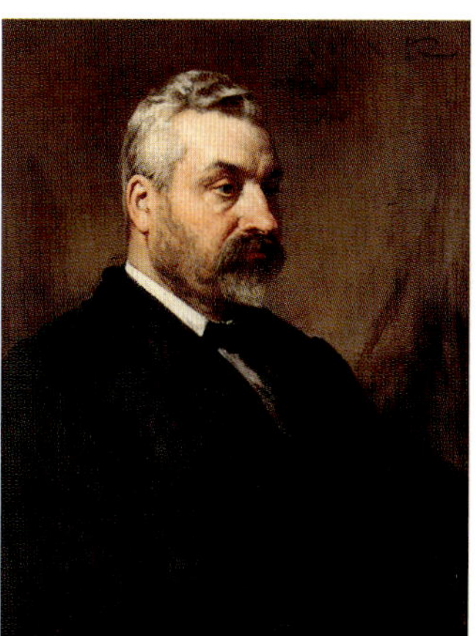

Reid, George 1841–1913
*John Duncan (d.1903), General Manager of
the Glasgow Tramway and Omnibus
Company* c.1893
oil on canvas 75.3 x 56.8
2128

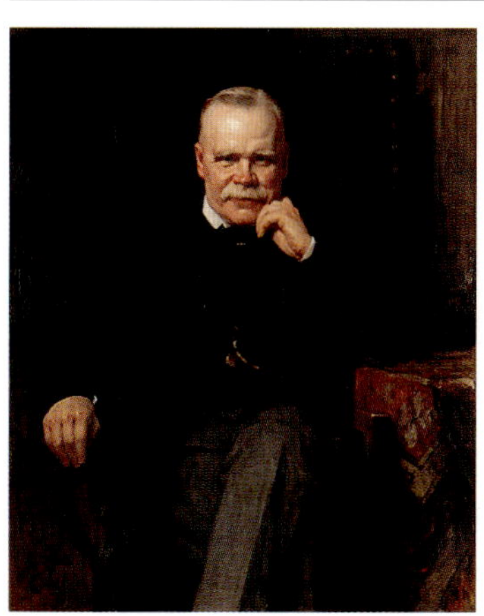

Reid, George 1841–1913
*James Hozier (1851–1929), 2nd Lord
Newlands* c.1908
oil on canvas 110.5 x 87.6
1869

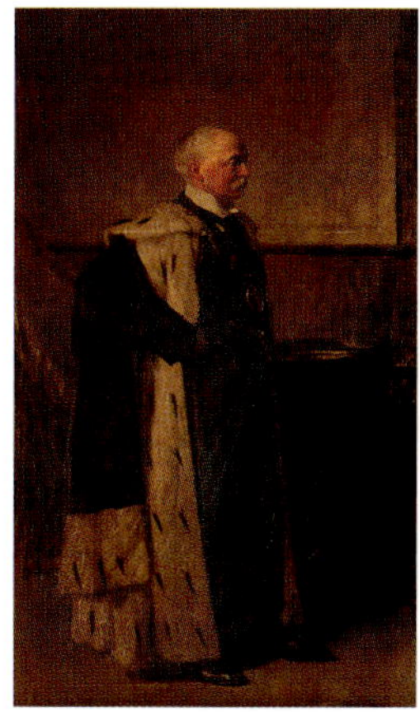

Reid, George 1841–1913
*Sir William Bilsland (b.1847), Lord Provost of
Glasgow (1905–1908)* c.1909
oil on canvas 218.4 x 116.8
1257

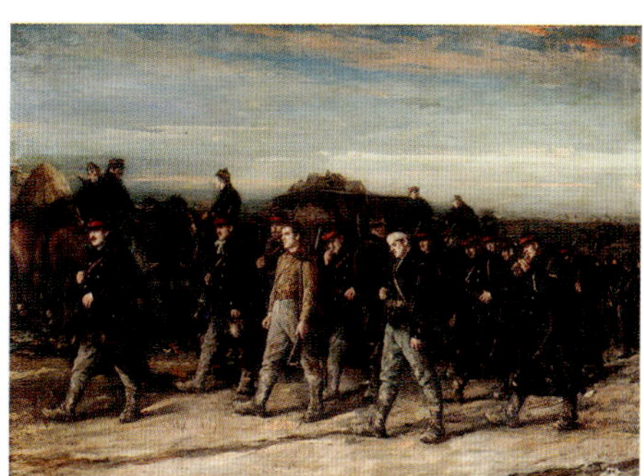

Reid, George Ogilvy 1851–1928
1914: The Belgians on the March
oil on canvas 121.9 x 167.6
2085

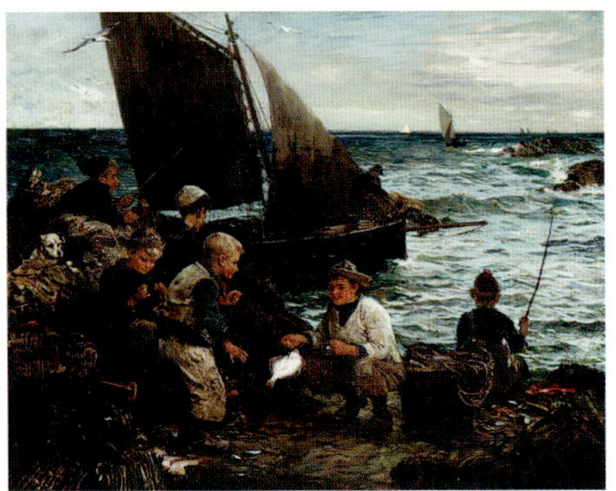

Reid, John Robertson 1852–1926
Sons of the Sea c.1912
oil on canvas 100.3 x 125.7
1292

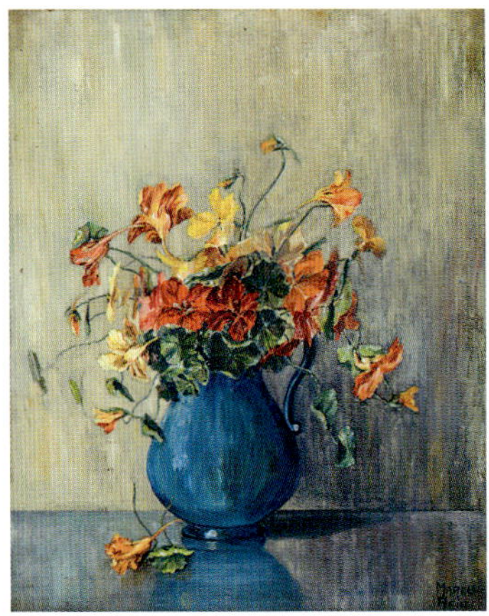

Reid, Marell active 20th C
Flower Piece, Blue Vase
oil on board 55.9 x 45.1
NR.148

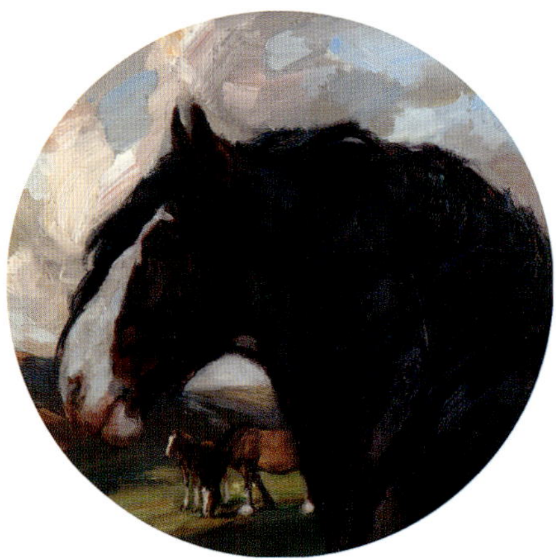

Reid, Stuart 1883–1971
'Baron of Buchlyvie' Horse Portrait c.1910
oil on board 43
NR.26

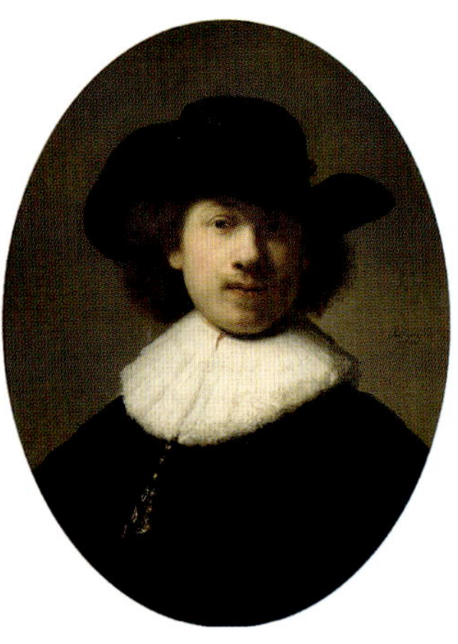

Rembrandt van Rijn 1606–1669
Self Portrait 1632
oil on panel 63.5 x 46.3
35.6

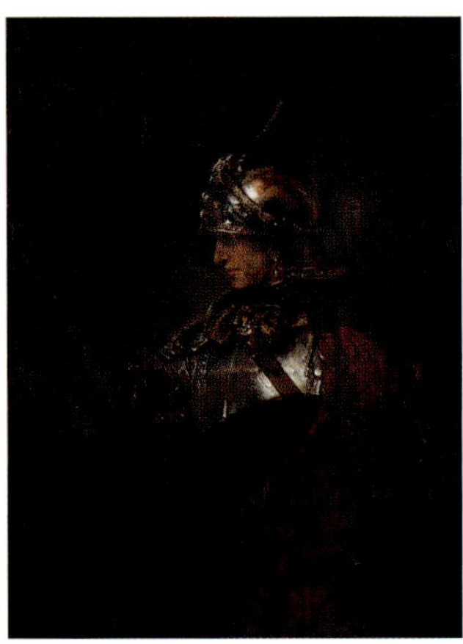

Rembrandt van Rijn 1606–1669
A Man in Armour 1655 (?)
oil on canvas 137.5 x 104.4
601

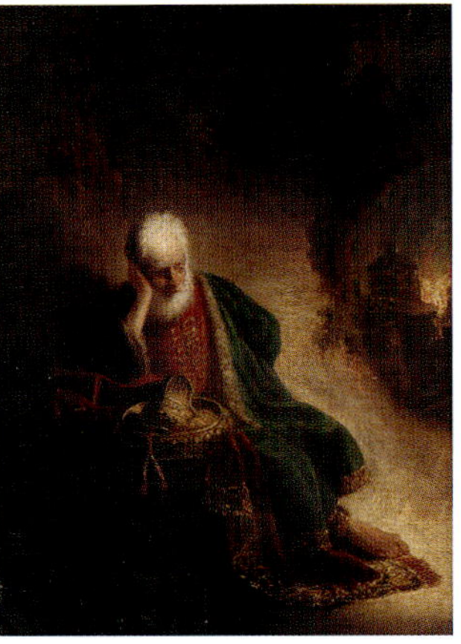

Rembrandt van Rijn (after) 1606–1669
*Jeremiah Mourning the Destruction of
Jerusalem* 18th C
oil on canvas 40.6 x 32.3
305

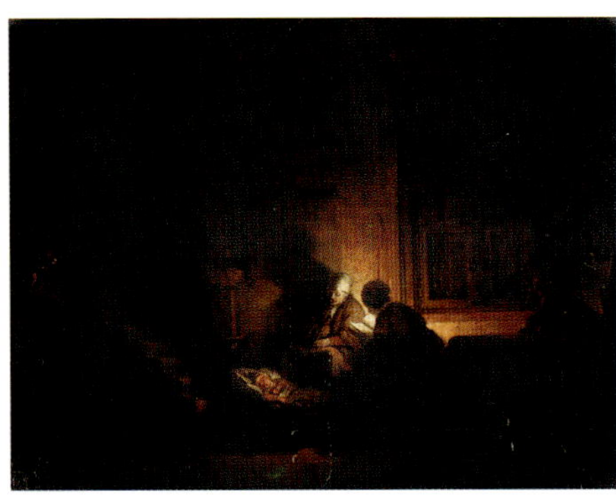

Rembrandt van Rijn (after) 1606–1669
The Holy Family in the Evening
18th C–19th C
oil on canvas 62.5 x 80.3
98

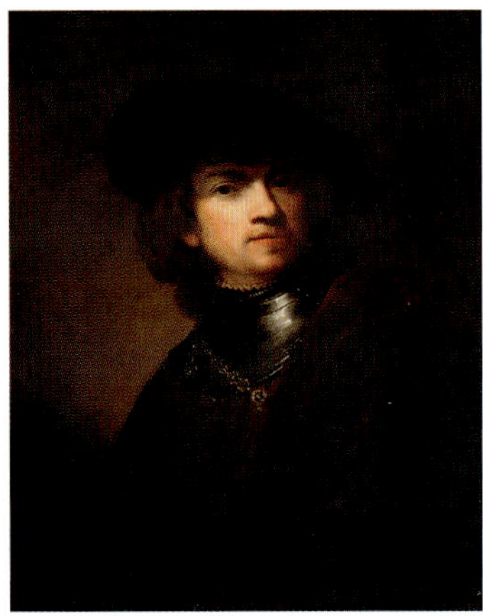

Rembrandt van Rijn (after) 1606–1669
Self Portrait 19th C
oil on canvas 66 x 54.6
754

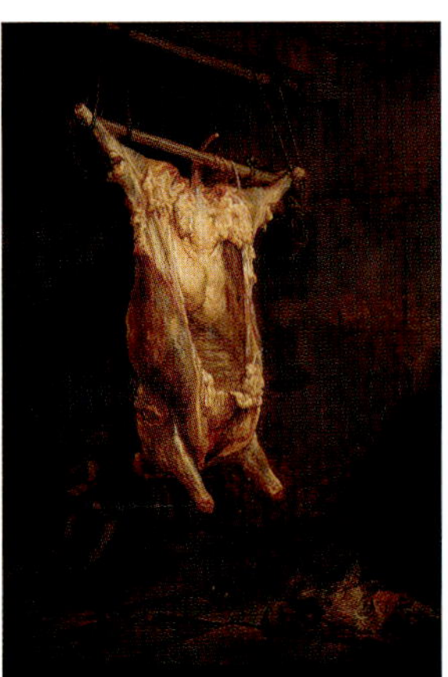

Rembrandt van Rijn (attributed to)
1606–1669
The Carcase of an Ox c.1640–1645
oil on panel 73.3 x 51.7
600

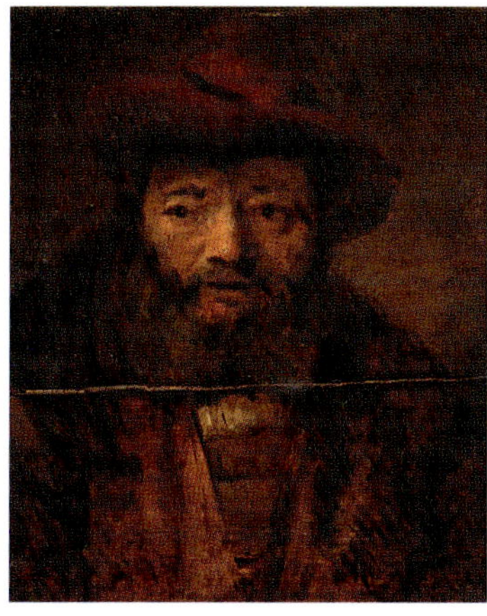

Rembrandt van Rijn (follower of)
1606–1669
Head of a Bearded Man
oil on panel 24.1 x 21.6
599

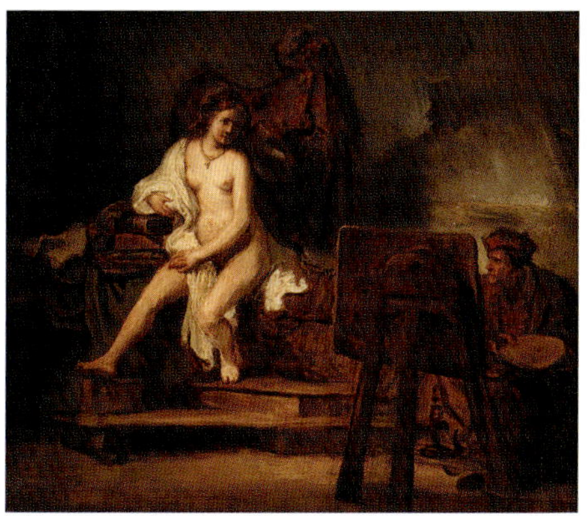

Rembrandt van Rijn (imitator of)
1606–1669
A Painter and His Model late 18th C/early
19th C
oil on panel 53 x 60.6
122

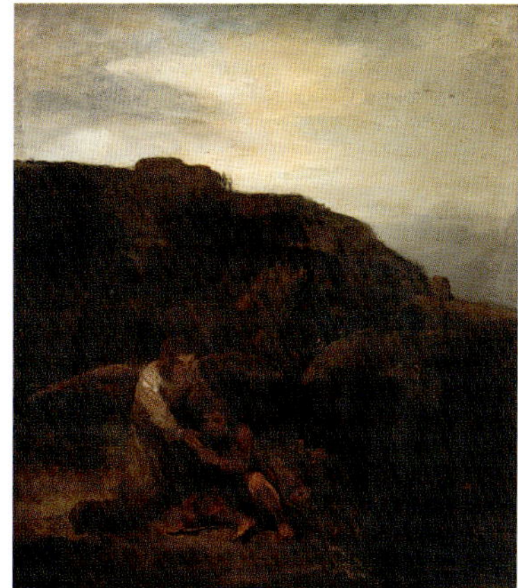

Rembrandt van Rijn (school of) 1606–1669
Landscape with Tobias and the Angel c.1650–
1660
oil on panel 77.1 x 67.3
597

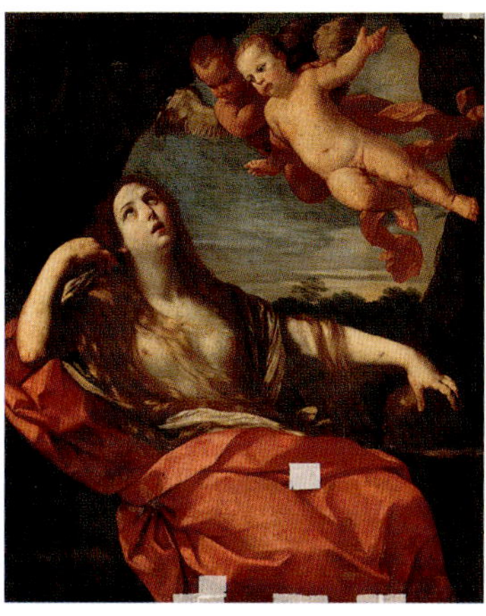

Reni, Guido (after) 1575–1642
Saint Mary Magdalen 17th C
oil on canvas 160 x 129.5
132

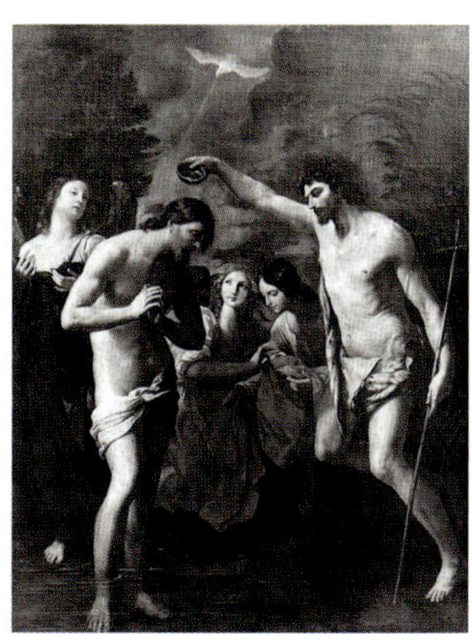

Reni, Guido (after) 1575–1642
The Baptism of Christ 17th C
oil on canvas 257.2 x 193.1
137

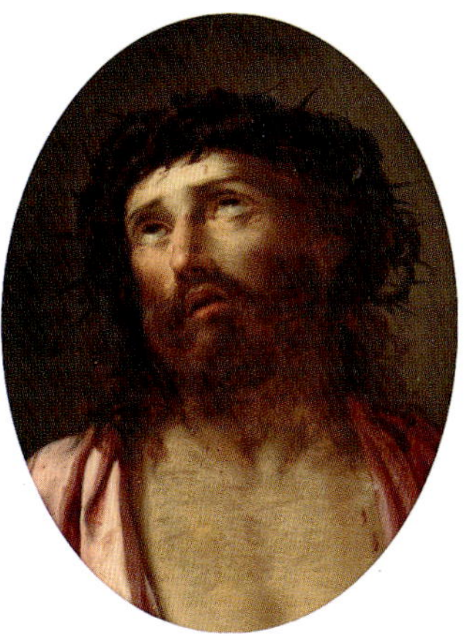

Reni, Guido (after) 1575–1642
Christ Crowned with Thorns 18th C (?)
oil on copper 30.5 x 22.9
157

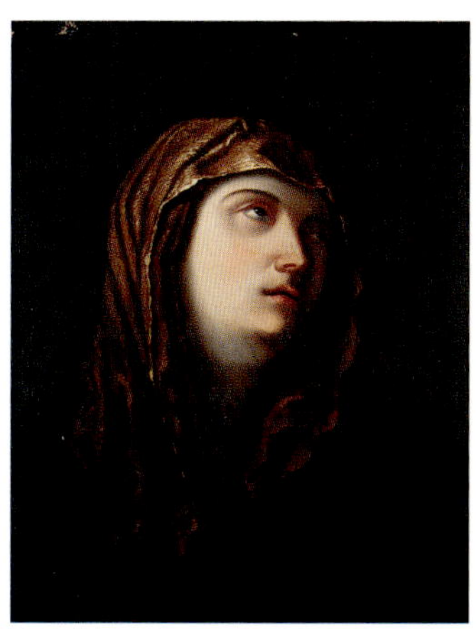

Reni, Guido (after) 1575–1642
Madonna in Grief 19th C (?)
oil on canvas 54.3 x 40.9
138

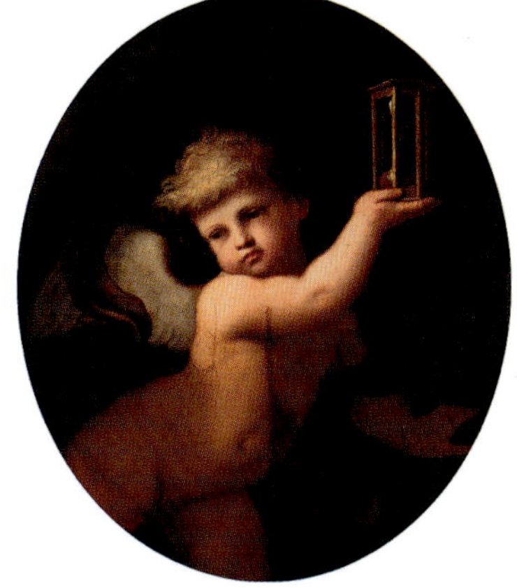

Reni, Guido (follower of) 1575–1642
Cupid with an Hour-Glass 17th C
oil on canvas 82.2 x 70.2
130

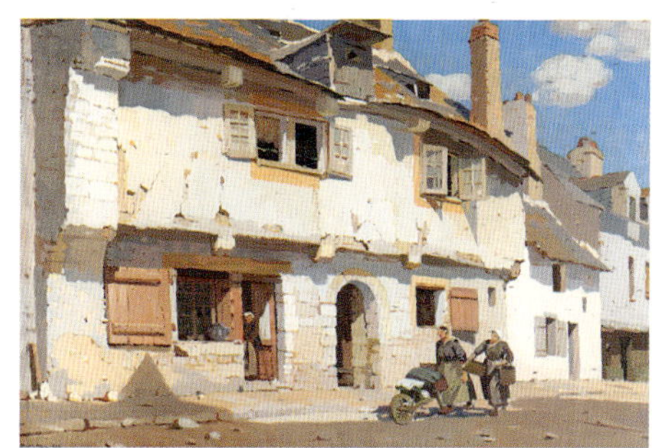

Reni-Mel, Léon 1893–c.1960
Old Vannes 1936
oil on canvas 75.2 x 110.4
2117

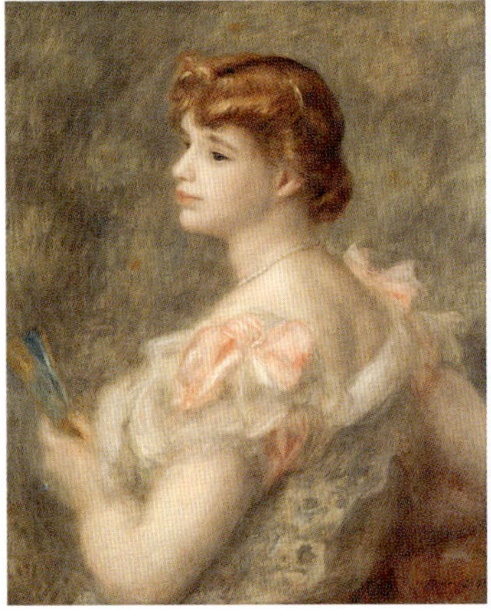

Renoir, Pierre-Auguste 1841–1919
Madame Valentine Fray (1870–1943) 1901
oil on canvas 64.8 x 54
2419

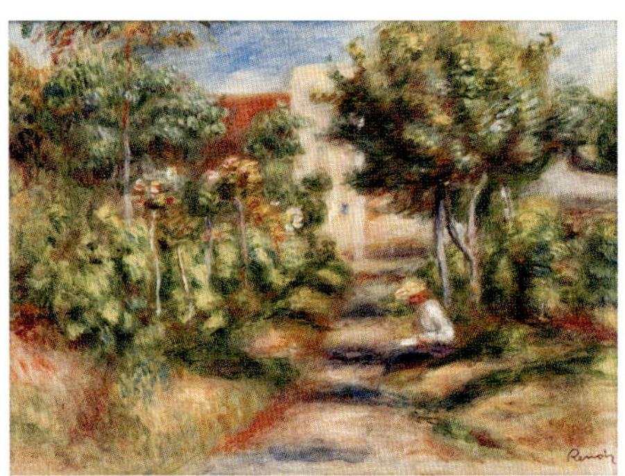

Renoir, Pierre-Auguste 1841–1919
The Painter's Garden c.1903
oil on canvas 33.2 x 46
2418

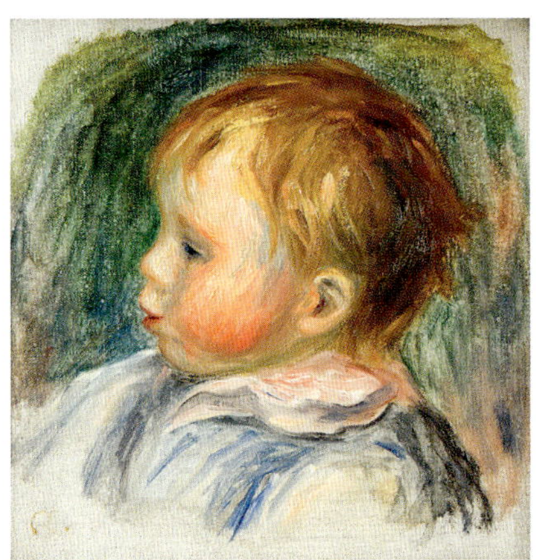

Renoir, Pierre-Auguste 1841–1919
Coco 1905
oil on canvas 21 x 20
3640

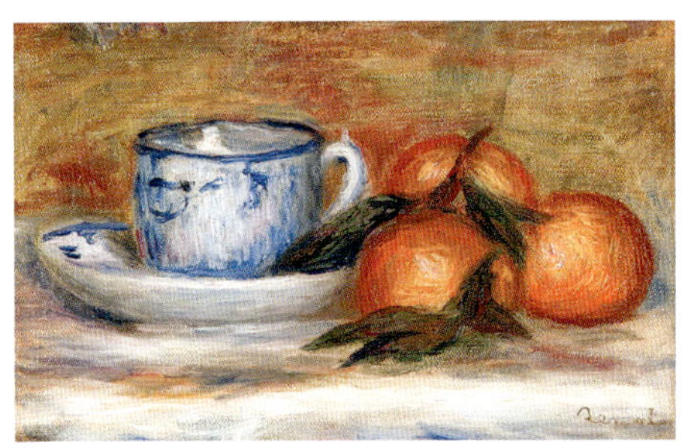

Renoir, Pierre-Auguste 1841–1919
Still Life c.1908
oil on canvas 15.9 x 25.4
2420

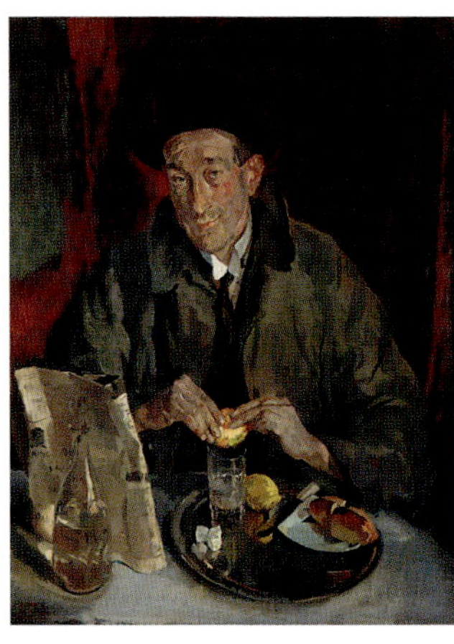

Revel, John Daniel 1884–1967
Happy Days 1944
oil on canvas 101.6 x 76.2
3176

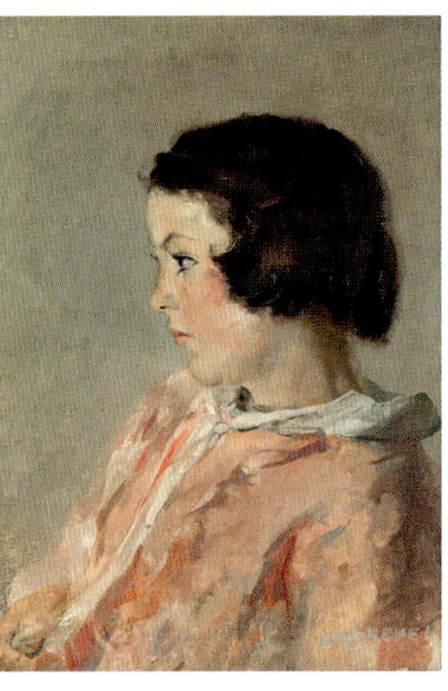

Revel, Lucy Elizabeth Babington 1887–1961
Molly c.1935
oil on plywood 56.2 x 40.3
3177

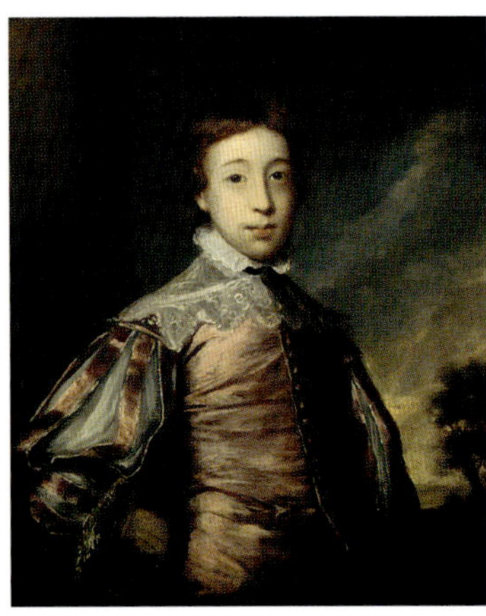

Reynolds, Joshua 1723–1792
A Boy in Van Dyck Dress c.1758
oil on canvas 76.2 x 61
263

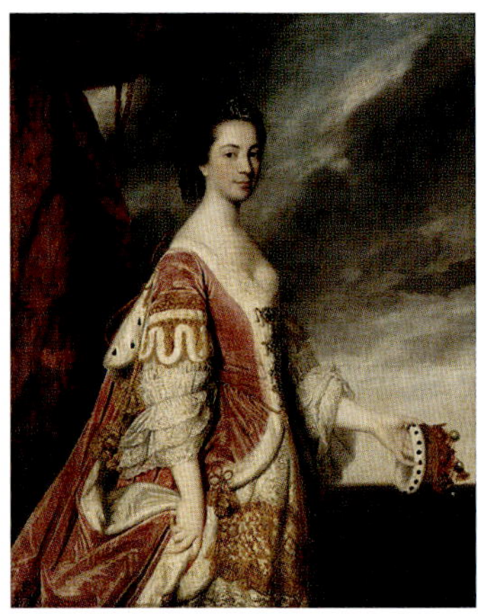

Reynolds, Joshua 1723–1792
Isabella Hay (1742–1808), Countess of Erroll
1763
oil on canvas 129.5 x 102.9
1605

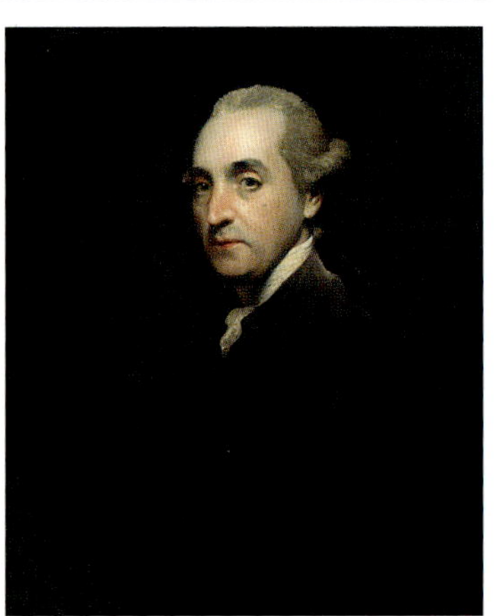

Reynolds, Joshua 1723–1792
Andrew Stuart of Torrance (1725–1801)
c.1778–1779
oil on canvas 74.9 x 62.5
L.2.1972 (P)

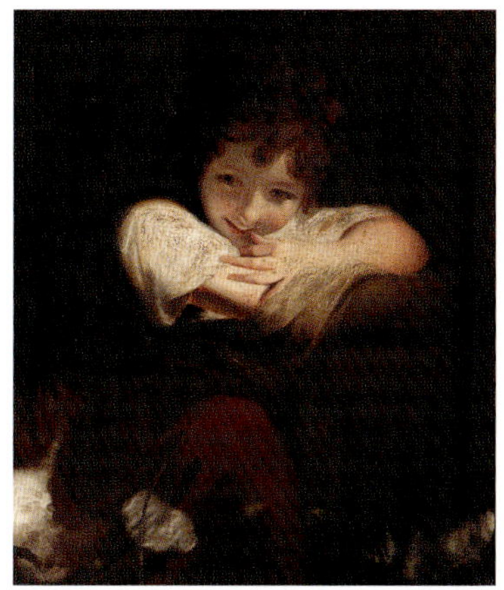

Reynolds, Joshua (after) 1723–1792
A Girl Leaning on a Pedestal (The Laughing Girl) c.1782–1800
oil on canvas 76.2 x 63.5
2785

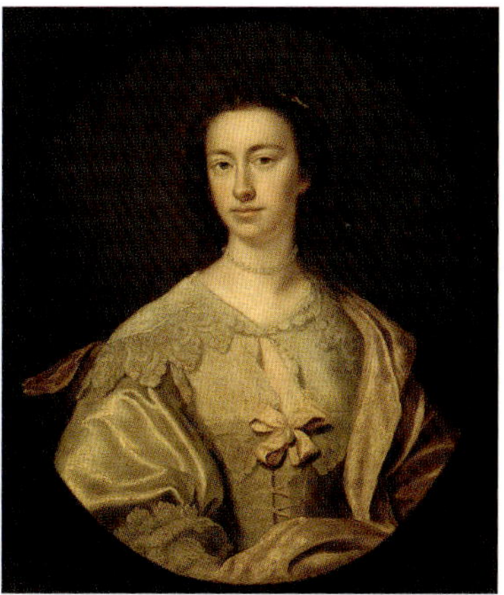

Reynolds, Joshua (attributed to) 1723–1792
Lady Mary Carew (c.1710/1720–before 1762) c.1743–1749
oil on canvas 74.9 x 61
35.602

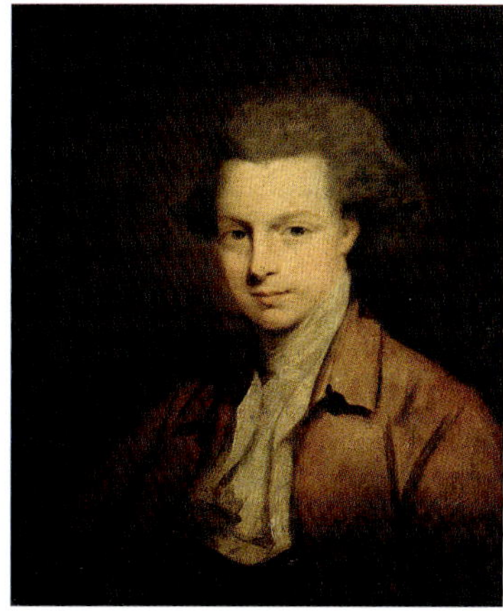

Reynolds, Joshua (attributed to) 1723–1792
Portrait of a Young Man
oil on canvas 63.5 x 53.3
35.604

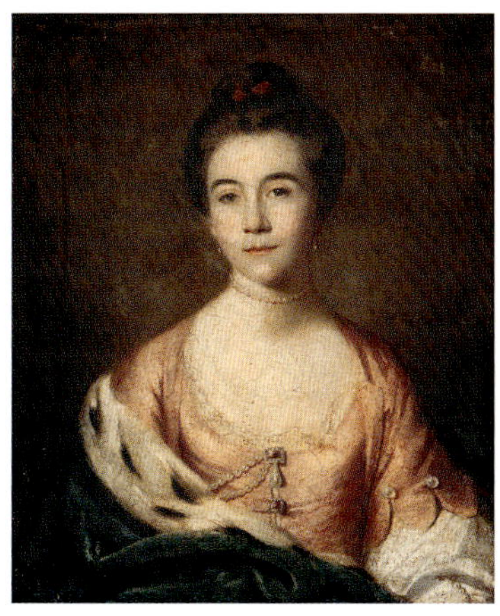

Reynolds, Joshua (style of) 1723–1792
Portrait of a Lady
oil on canvas 76.2 x 63.5
603

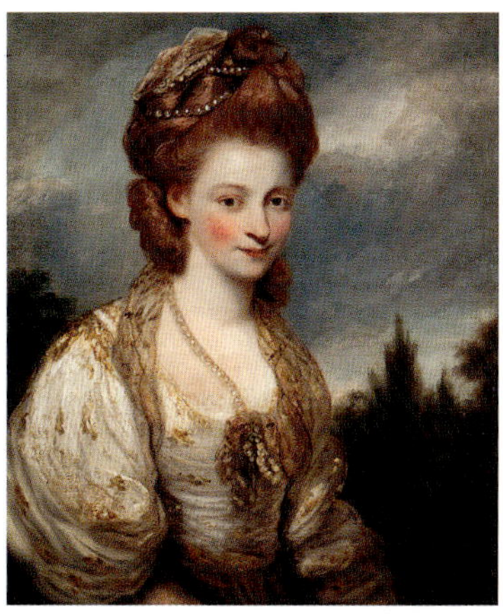

Reynolds, Joshua (style of) 1723–1792
Portrait of a Lady
oil on canvas 75.6 x 62.9
605

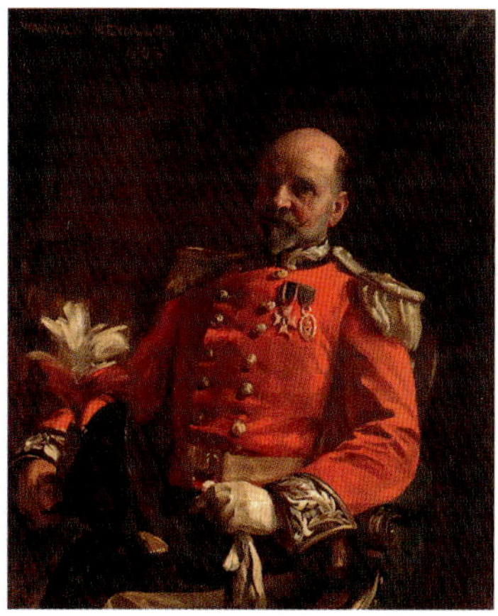

Reynolds, Warwick 1880–1926
Colonel John Macfarlane (1846–1910) 1908
oil on canvas 127 x 101.6
1865

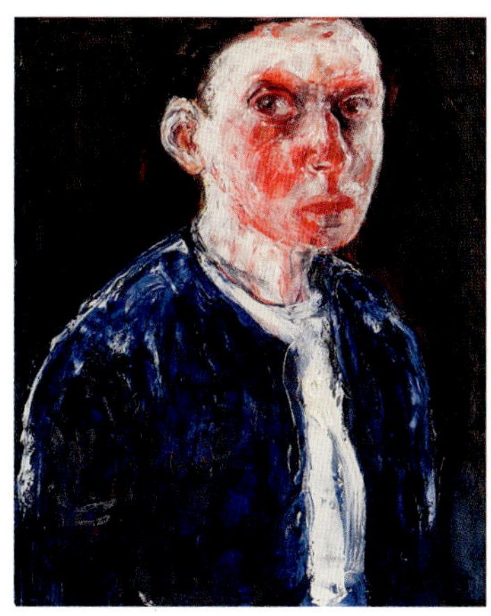

Rhys-James, Shani b.1953
Blue Top 1996
oil on canvas 76.2 x 60.4
3626

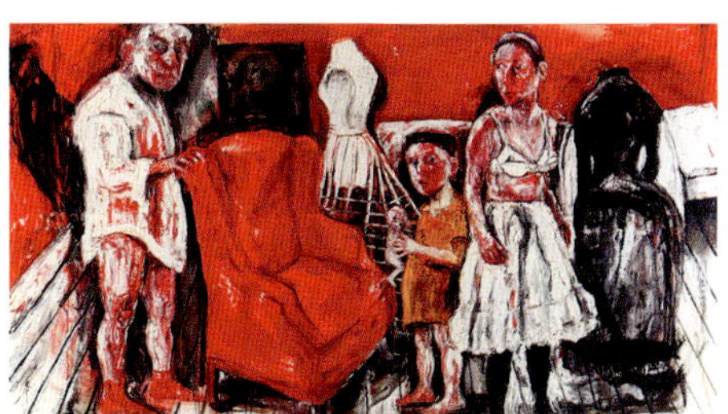

Rhys-James, Shani b.1953
The Boards 1996–1997
oil on canvas 183.5 x 335.3
3627

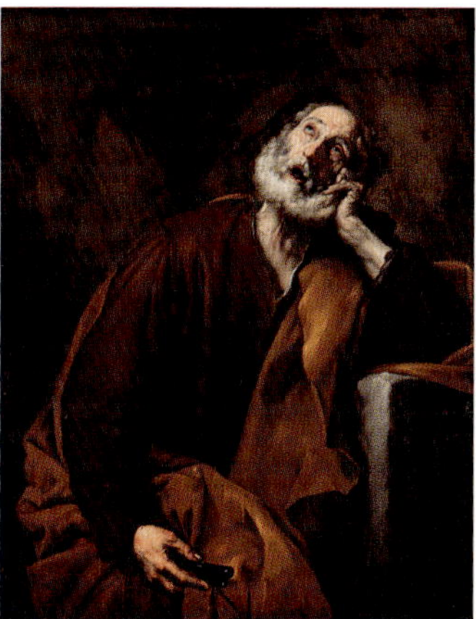

Ribera, Jusepe de (studio of) 1591–1652
Saint Peter Repentant 1628
oil on canvas 124 x 97.8
1075

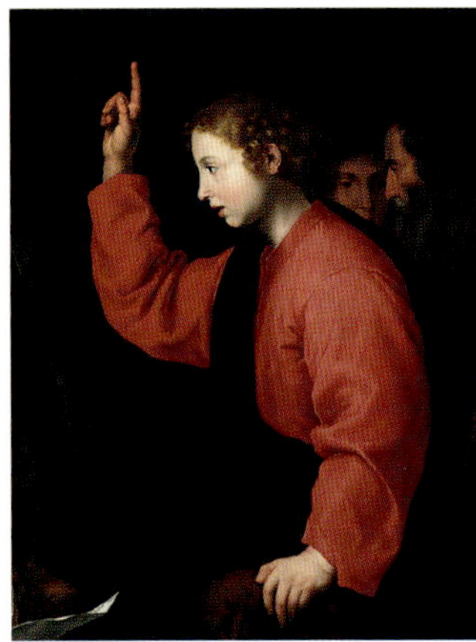

Ribera, Jusepe de (studio of) 1591–1652
Christ Disputing with the Doctors
oil on canvas 108 x 80
35.605

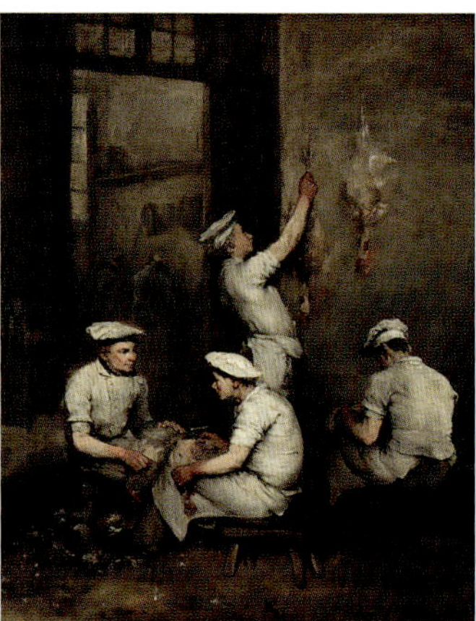

Ribot, Augustin Théodule 1823–1891
The Cooks 1862
oil on canvas 74.3 x 61.6
35.607

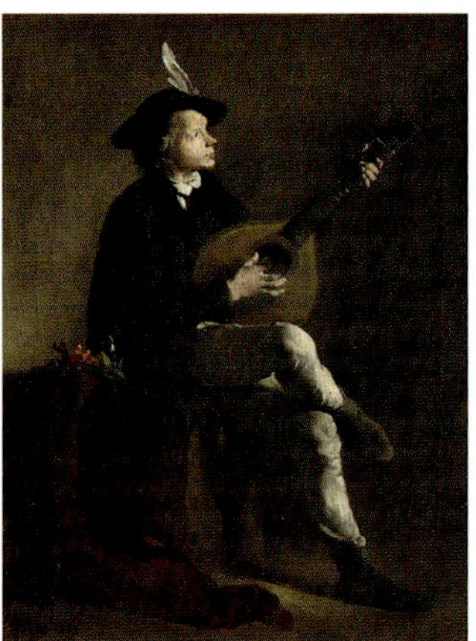

Ribot, Augustin Théodule 1823–1891
The Musician 1862
oil on canvas 40.6 x 33
35.611

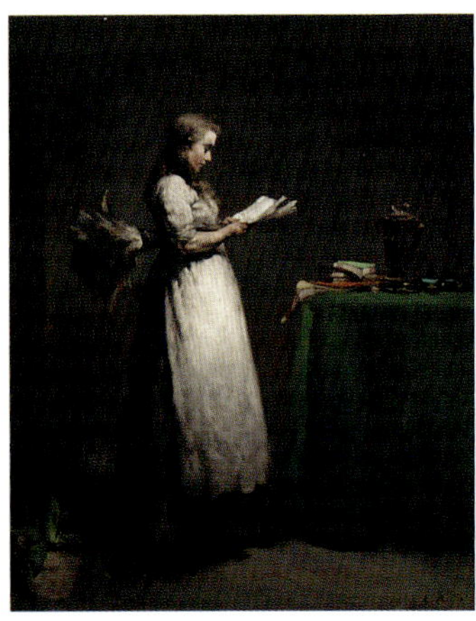

Ribot, Augustin Théodule 1823–1891
The Studious Servant c.1871
oil on canvas 73 x 59.7
35.651

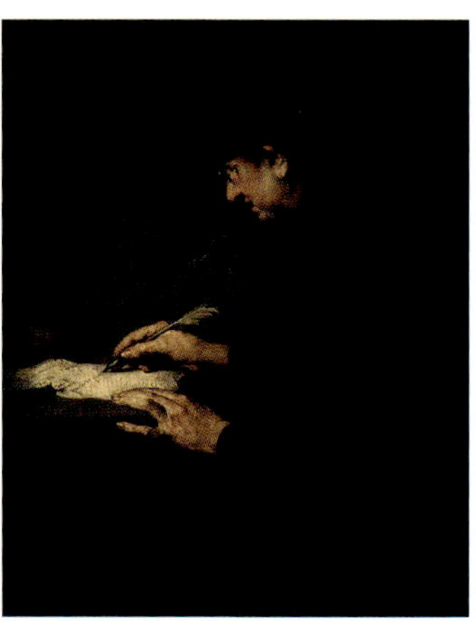

Ribot, Augustin Théodule 1823–1891
The Accountant c.1878
oil on canvas 91.4 x 72.4
35.606

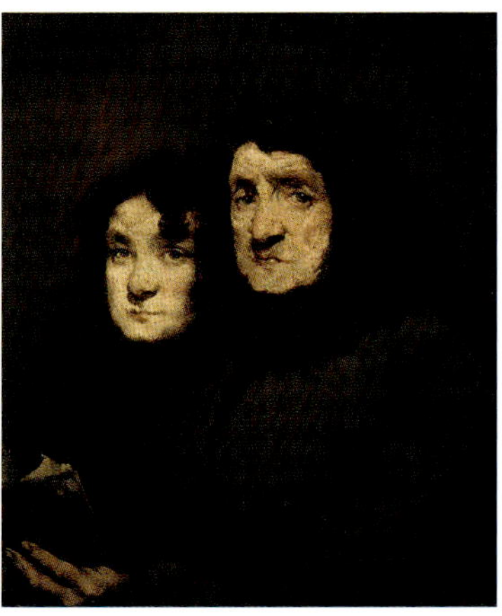

Ribot, Augustin Théodule 1823–1891
Mother and Daughter
oil on canvas 46.4 x 38.7
35.61

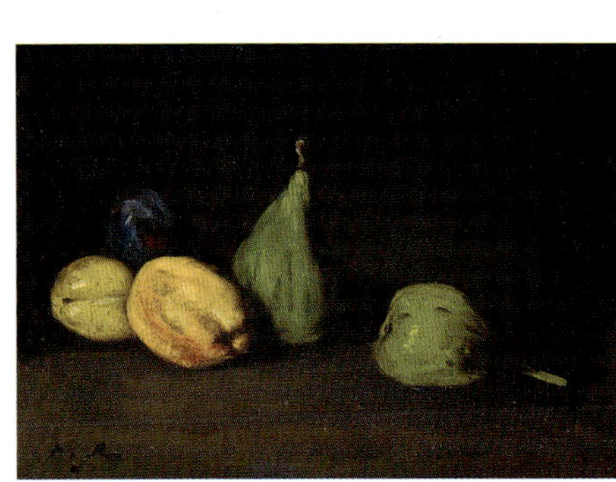

Ribot, Augustin Théodule 1823–1891
Still Life with Fruit, Figs and Apricots
oil on canvas 19.1 x 24.1
35.609

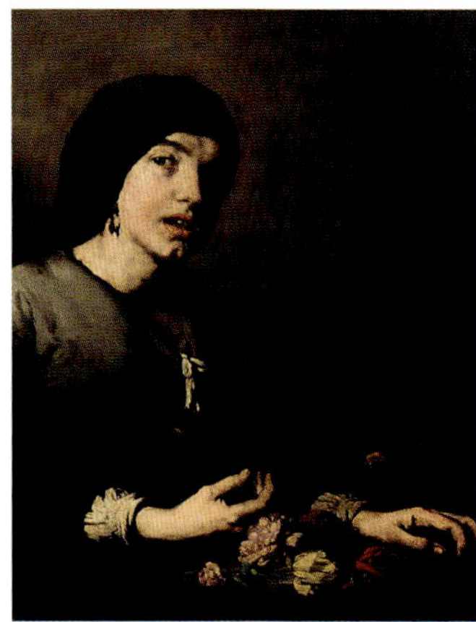

Ribot, Augustin Théodule 1823–1891
The Flower Girl
oil on canvas 73.6 x 61
35.608

Ribot, Augustin Théodule 1823–1891
The Old Fisherman
oil on canvas 73.7 x 61
35.613

Facing page: Brodie, Isabel Babianska, 1920–2006, *Reflection (Self Portrait)*, 1939 (p. 62)

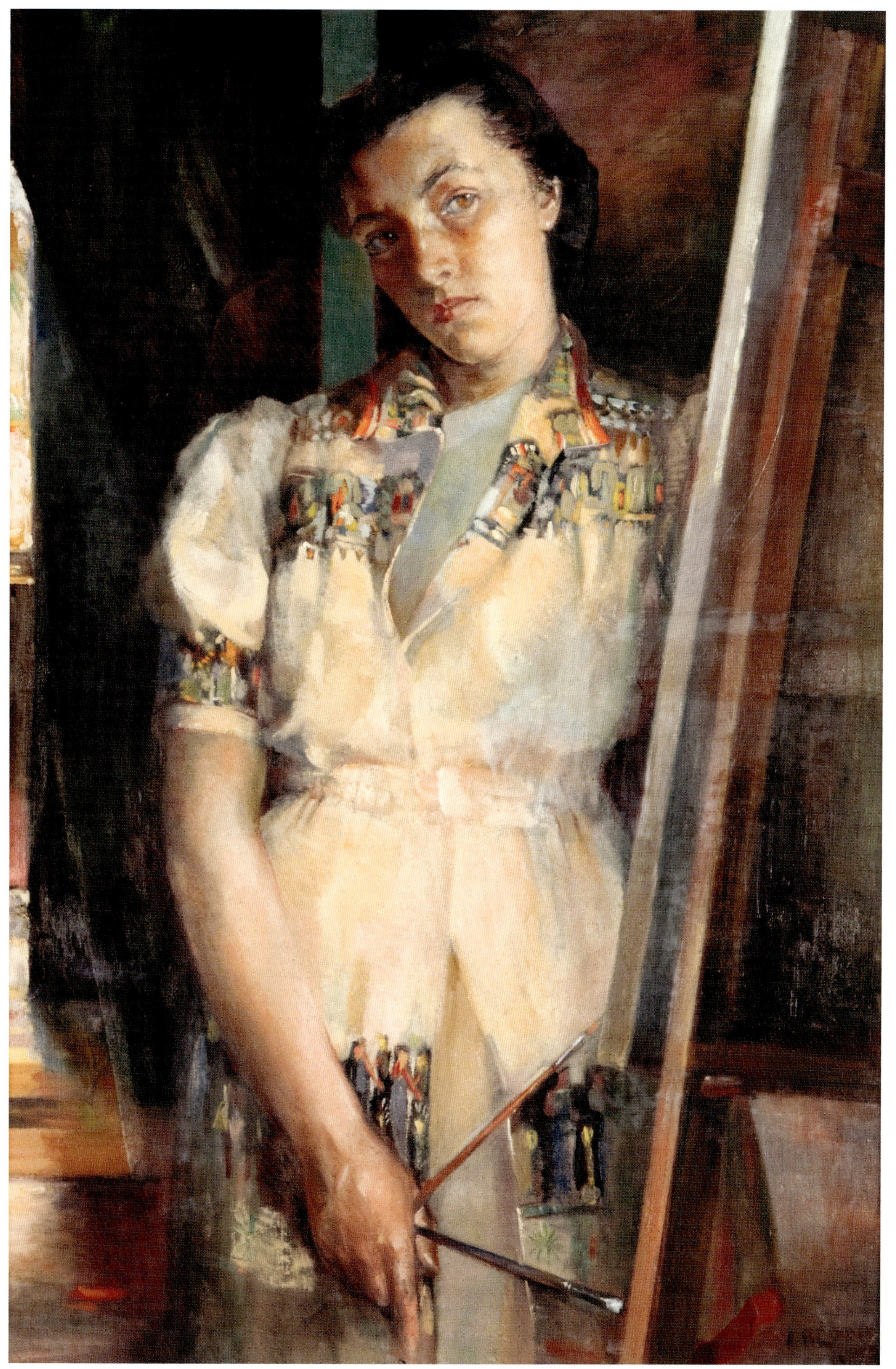

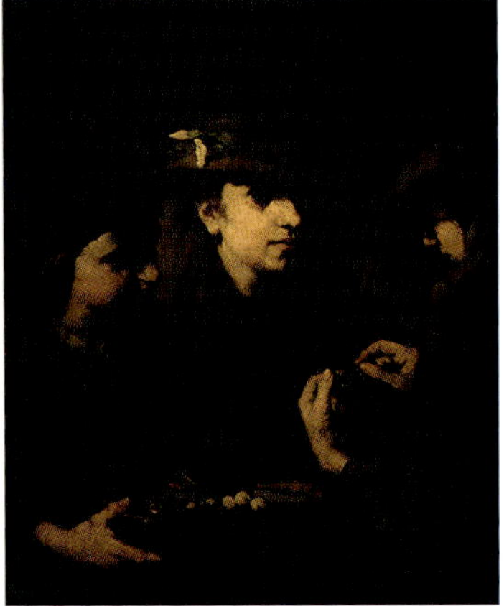

Ribot, Augustin Théodule 1823–1891
The Rosary
oil on canvas 73.7 x 59.7
35.612

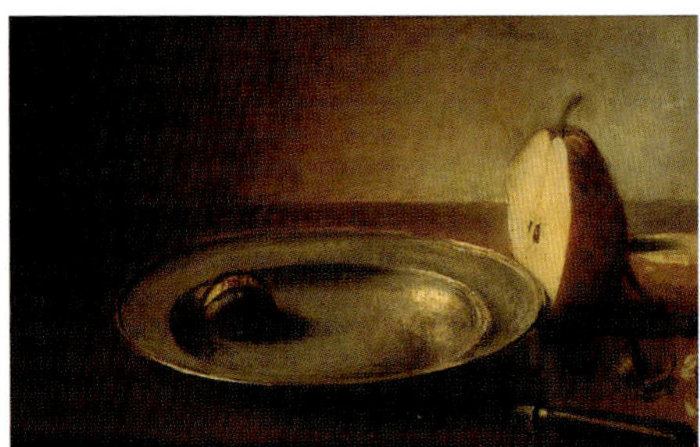

Ricard, Gustave 1823–1873
Still Life, Pear and Plate
oil on panel 26.7 x 38.7
35.615

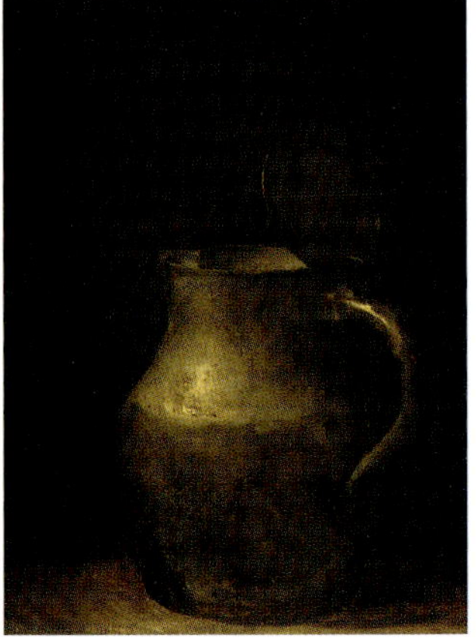

Ricard, Gustave 1823–1873
The Pitcher
oil on panel 32.4 x 24.8
35.614

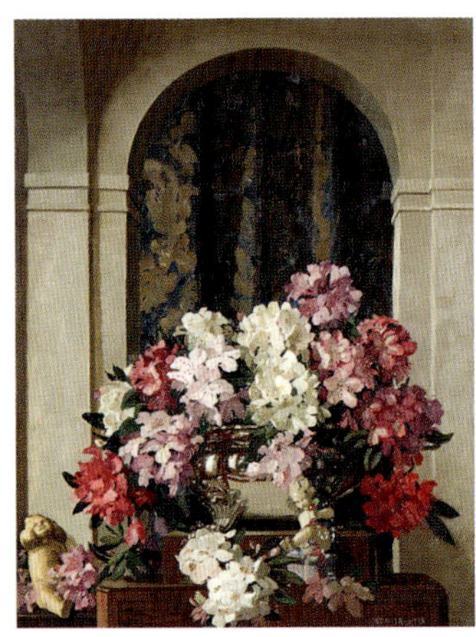

Richter, Herbert Davis 1874–1955
A Festal Day c.1936
oil on canvas 101.6 x 76.2
2069

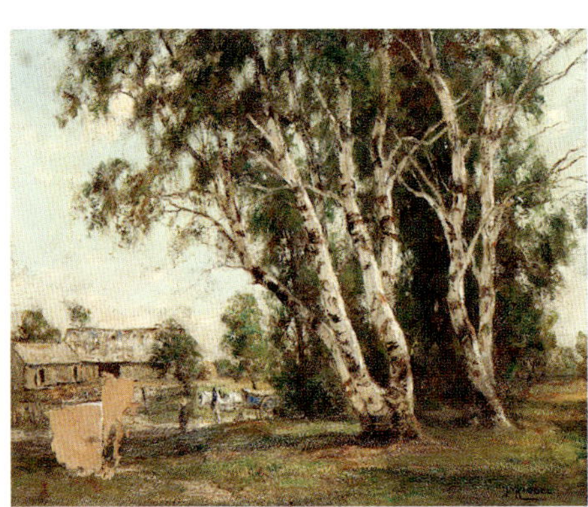

Riddel, James 1857–1928
Man Driving a Cart 1874
oil on canvas 63.5 x 76.2
TEMP.14931

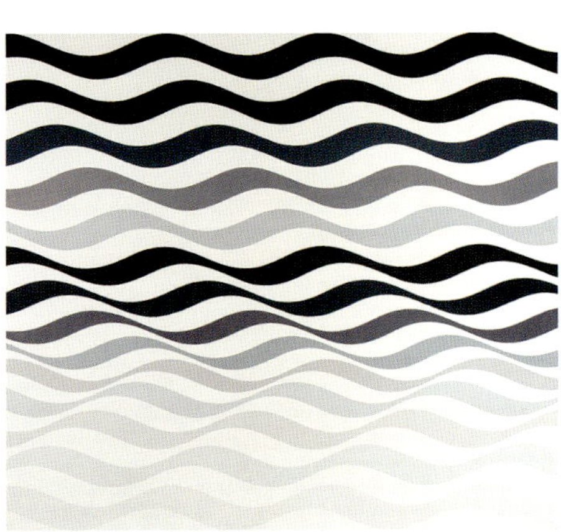

Riley, Bridget b.1931
Arrest III 1965
emulsion on linen 174 x 191.8
3494

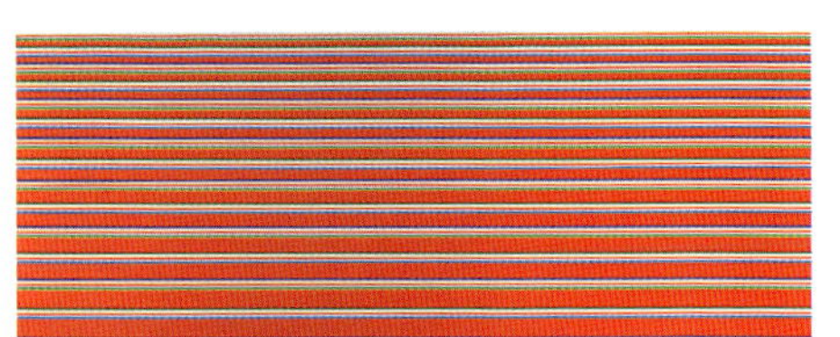

Riley, Bridget b.1931
Punjab 1971
acrylic on canvas 145 x 365
3475

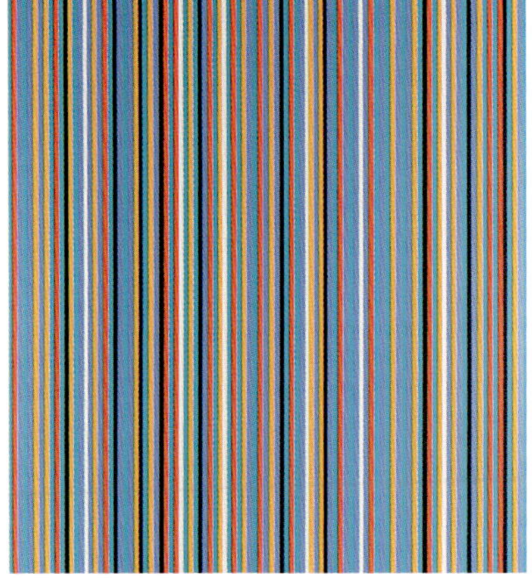

Riley, Bridget b.1931
Luxor 1982
oil on linen 223.5 x 197.5
3474

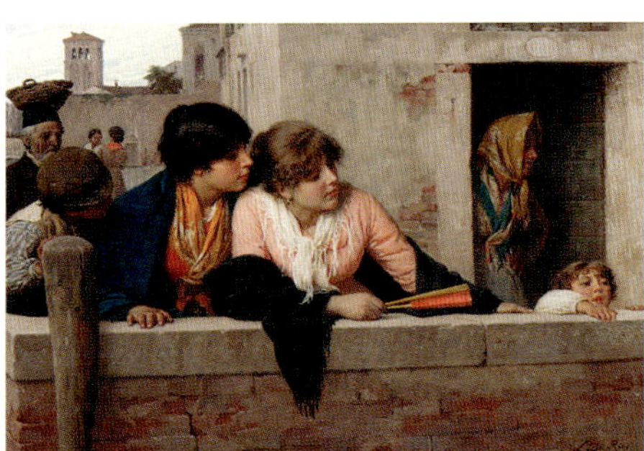

Rios, Luigi da 1844–1892
Overlooking a Canal, Venice 1886
oil on canvas 47.6 x 68.1
787

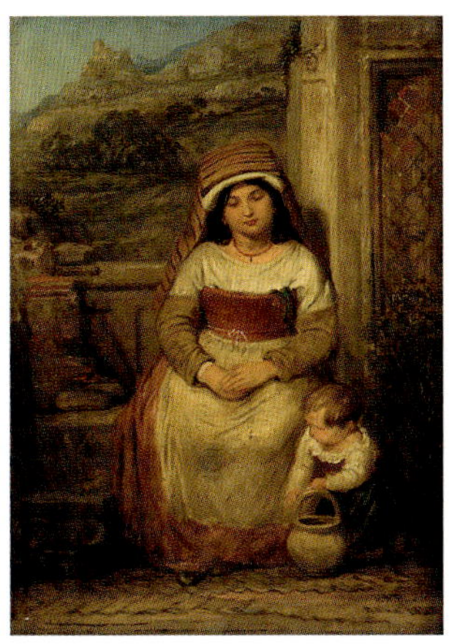

Rippingille, Edward Villiers 1798–1859
Roman Mother and Child 1840
oil on canvas 43.2 x 29.2
372

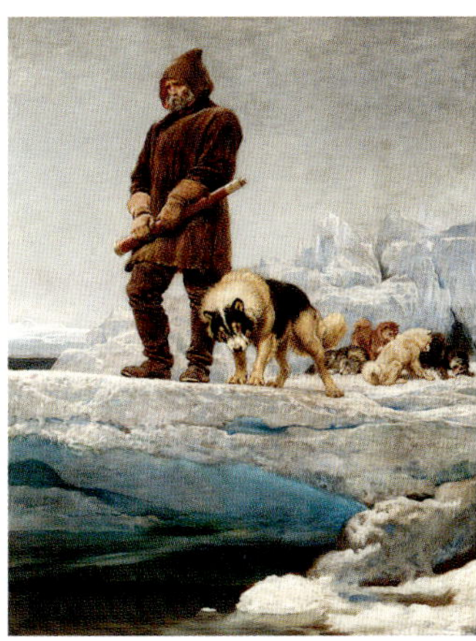

Riviere, Briton 1840–1920
The Last of the Crew 1883
oil on canvas 182.9 x 139.7
1723

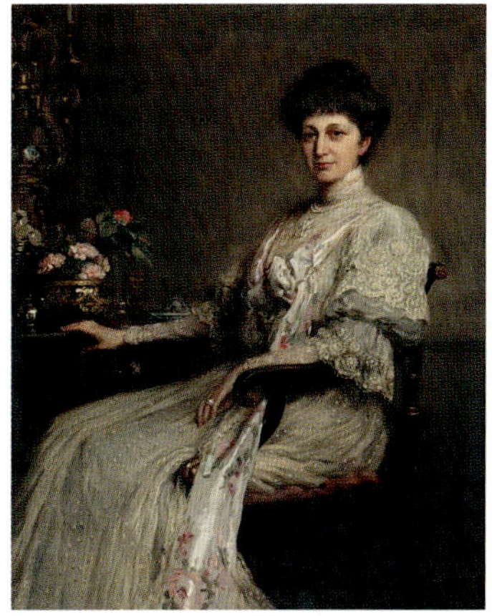

Riviere, Hugh Goldwin 1869–1956
Lady Newlands (d.1930) 1908
oil on canvas 127 x 101.6
1870

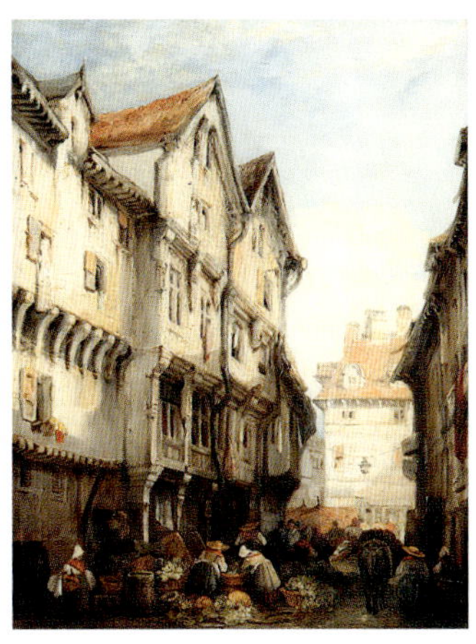

Roberts, David 1796–1864
A Street in Abbeville c.1844
oil on panel 39.4 x 29.2
1369

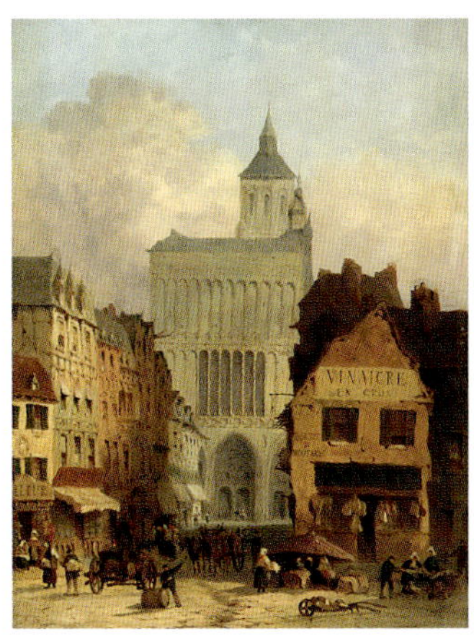

Roberts, David (attributed to) 1796–1864
Church of Notre-Dame, Dijon 1835
oil on canvas 40.3 x 30.3
3112

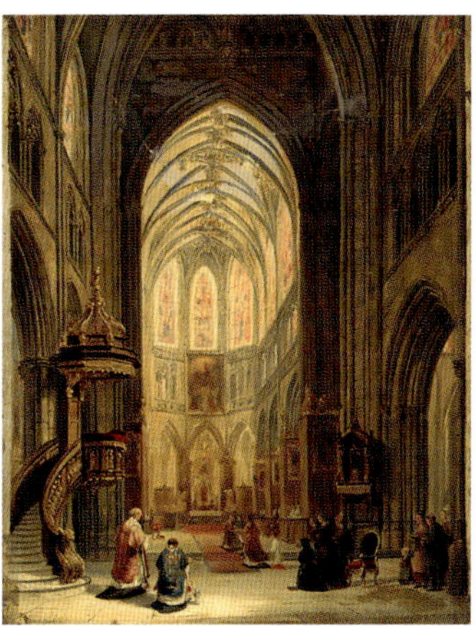

Roberts, David (attributed to) 1796–1864
Interior of a Church
oil on canvas 40.3 x 29.9
3123

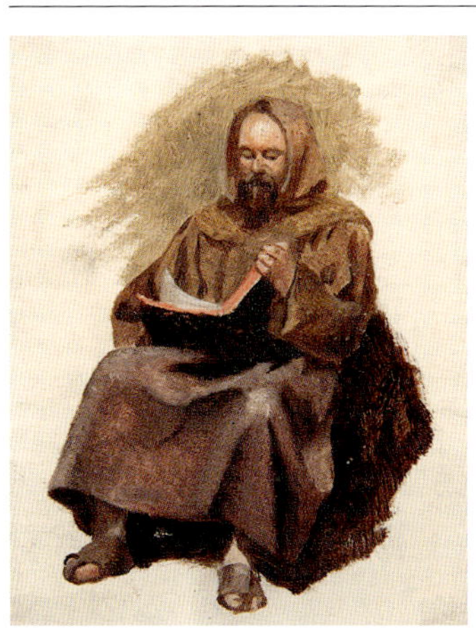

Roberts, David (attributed to) 1796–1864
Study of a Monk
oil on paper 17.2 x 13.1
U.2.h

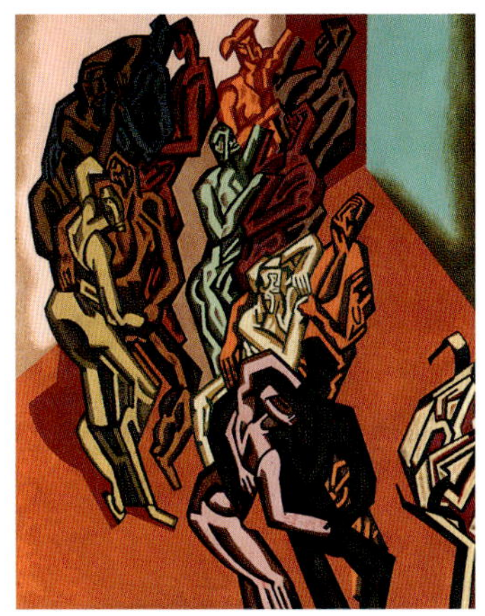

Roberts, William Patrick 1895–1980
The Dancers 1919
oil on canvas 152 x 116.5
3340

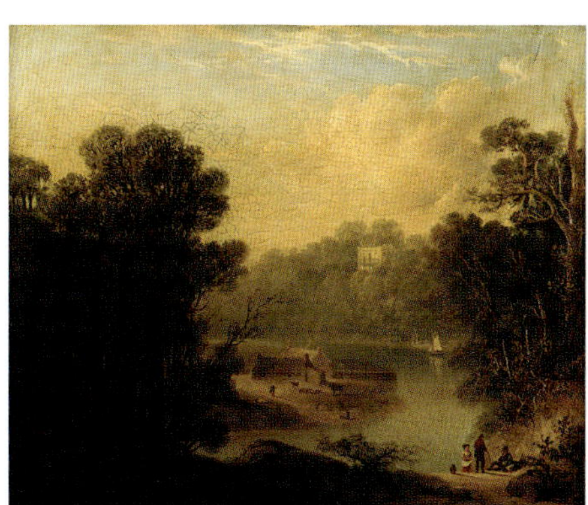

Robertson, Alexander Duff 1807–1886
Woodside House on the Kelvin
oil on canvas 62.2 x 74.9
451

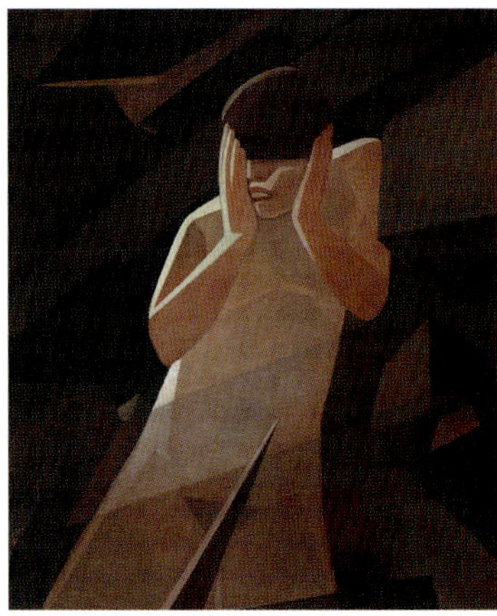

Robertson, Eric Harald Macbeth 1887–1941
Despair 1921
oil on canvas 91.4 x 76.2
3365 🐝

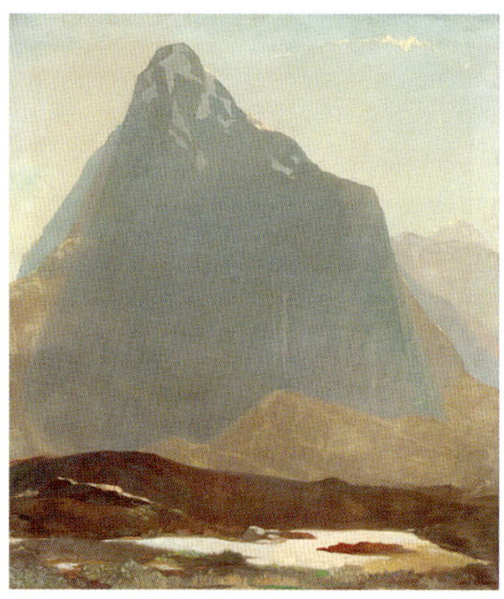

Robertson, Eric Harald Macbeth 1887–1941
Buachaille Etive Mhòr
oil on canvas 106.7 x 91.4
2454 🐝

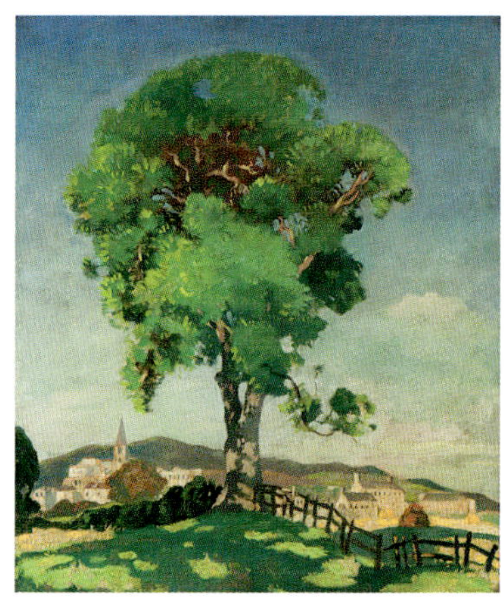

Robertson, Eric Harald Macbeth 1887–1941
Near Wenhaston, Suffolk
oil on canvas 91.4 x 76.2
2455 🐝

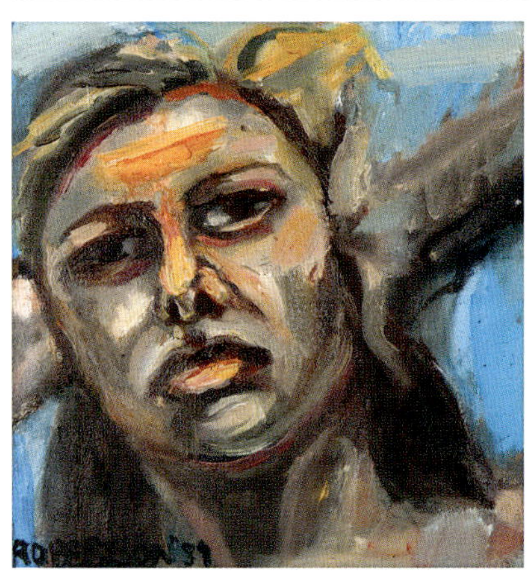

Robertson, Fiona
Hear No Evil 1989
oil on canvas 37.8 x 37.3
3687

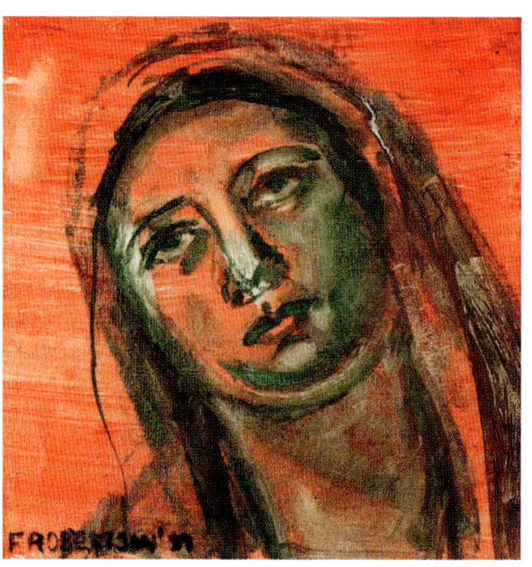

Robertson, Fiona
Madonna 1989
oil on canvas 37.9 x 37.6
3686

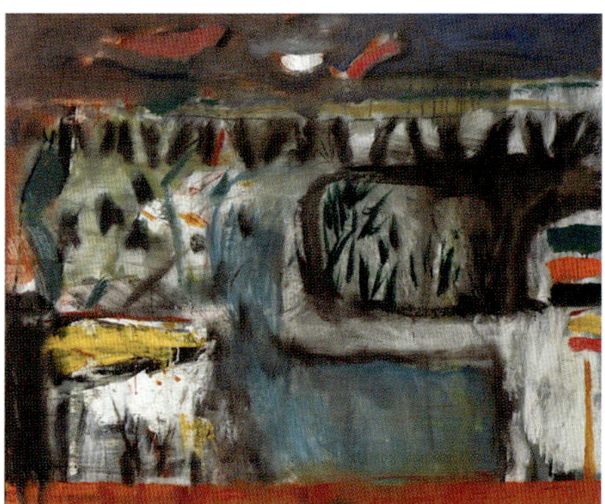

Robertson, James Downie 1931–2010
Landscape 1979
oil on canvas 81.2 x 96.5
3351

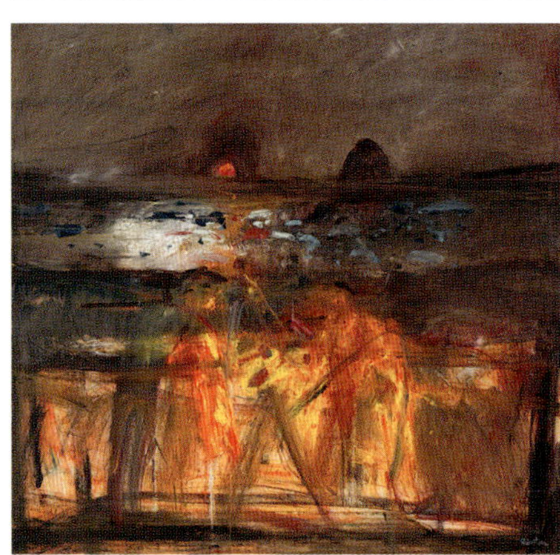

Robertson, James Downie 1931–2010
Sunset 1990
oil on canvas 119.4 x 119.4
3468

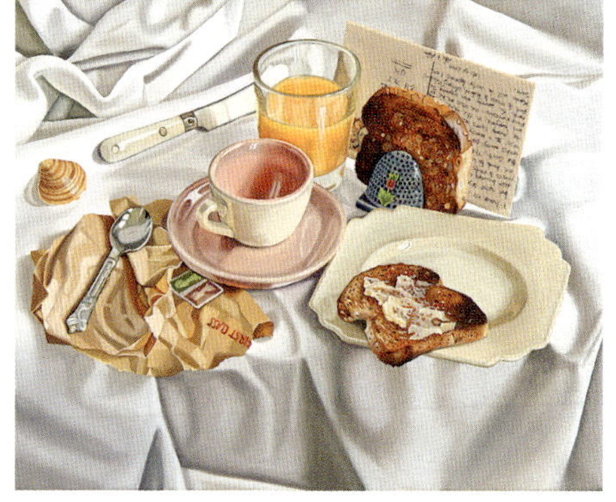

Robertson, Saul b.1978
Surfacing c.2005
oil on canvas 26 x 30
3653

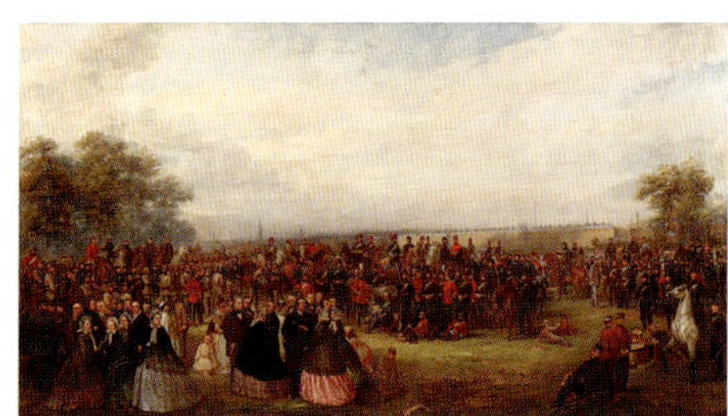

Robertson, Thomas 1822–1866
The Glasgow Volunteers 1861–1866
oil on canvas 160 x 243.8
1857

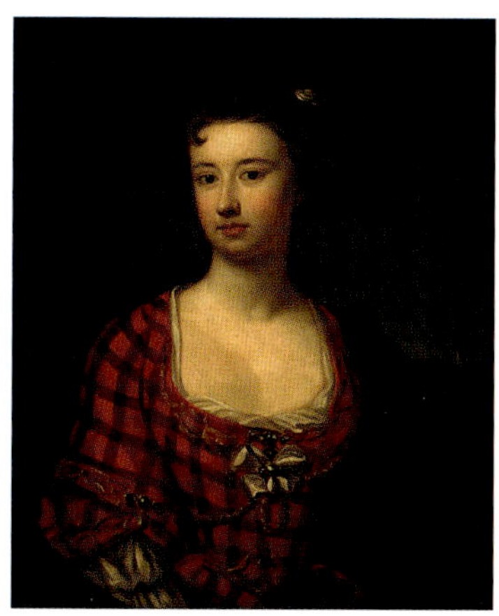

Robertson, William active 1740–1757
Flora Macdonald (1722–1790) 1750
oil on canvas 76.2 x 63.5
655

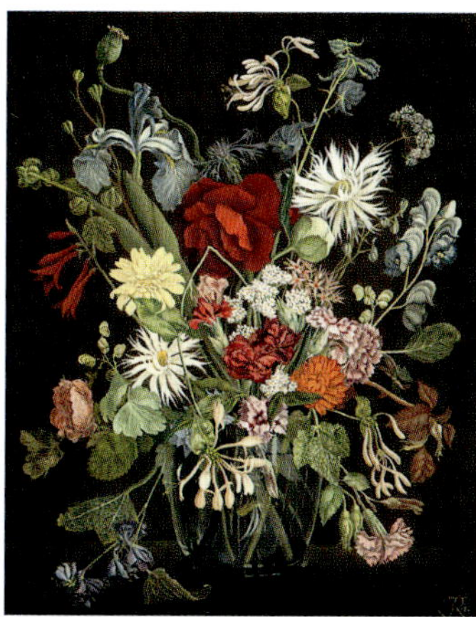

Robinson, Joan active 1943–1966
Flowers 1947
oil on canvas 50.8 x 40.6
2702

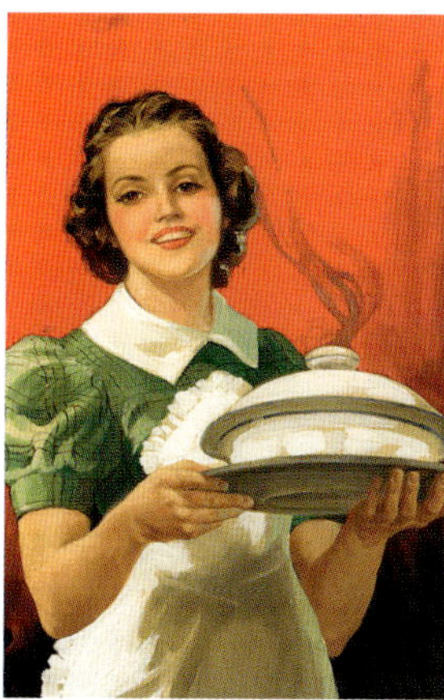

Robinson's of Bristol
Jean MacGregor (1916–1968) 1939
oil on cardboard 71.1 x 48.3
PP.1982.40.1

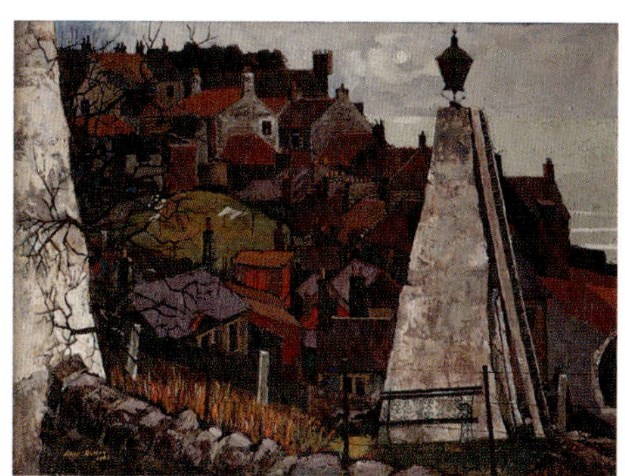

Robson, Adam 1928–2007
Harbour Guides at Crail 1962
oil on canvas 76 x 101.3
3169

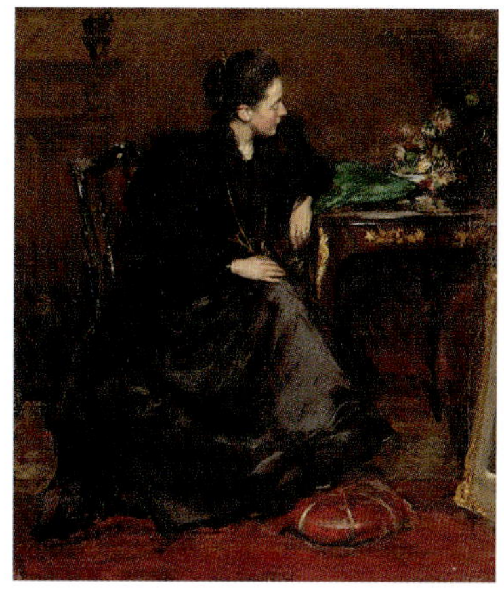

Roche, Alexander Ignatius 1861–1921
Mrs Roberts 1895
oil on canvas 101.6 x 86.4
2967

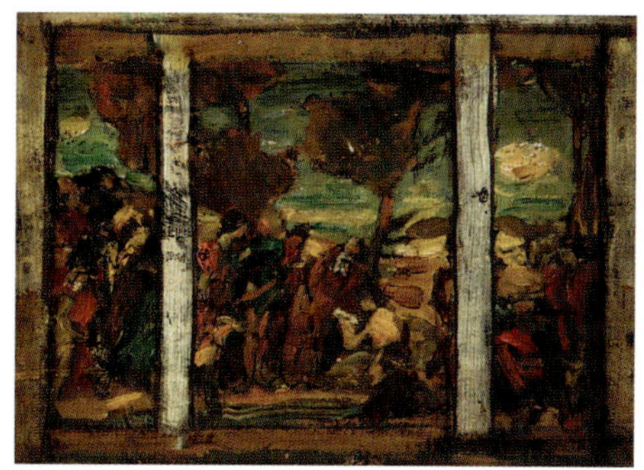

Roche, Alexander Ignatius 1861–1921
Legendary Glasgow: The Finding of Queen Languoreth's Ring (study) c.1899
oil on panel 20.3 x 26.7
3280

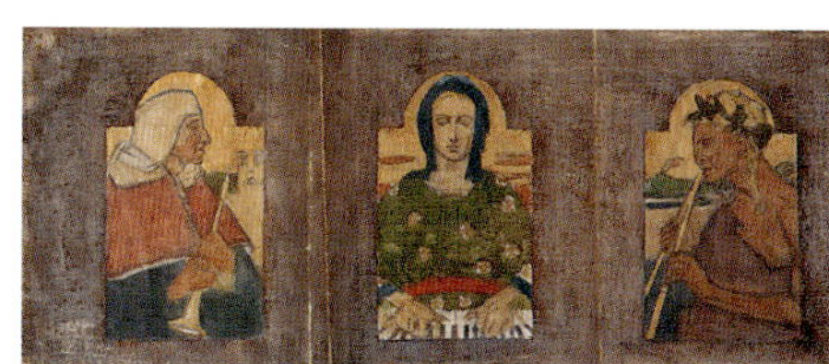

Roche, Alexander Ignatius 1861–1921
Original Study for Glasgow Town Hall Mural c.1899
oil on canvas 20.3 x 50.1
NR.145

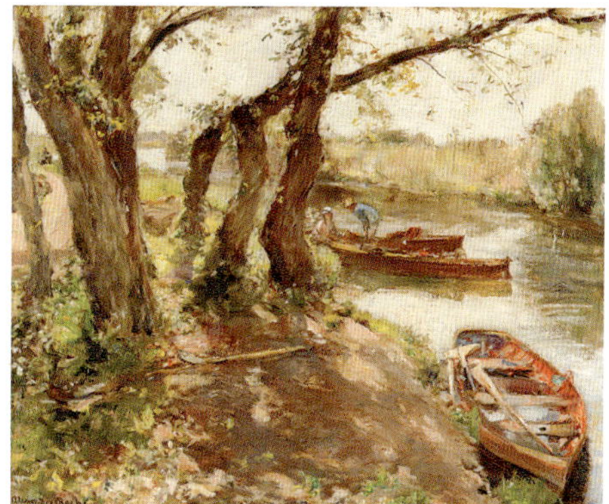

Roche, Alexander Ignatius 1861–1921
River Ouse c.1918
oil on canvas 63.5 x 76.2
1456

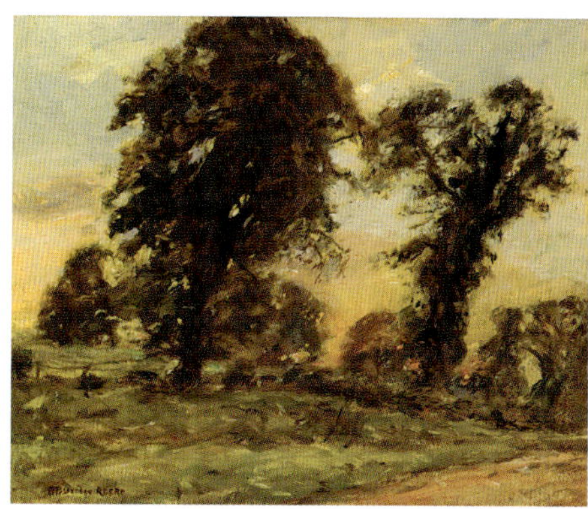

Roche, Alexander Ignatius 1861–1921
Evening
oil on canvas 38.1 x 45.7
2448

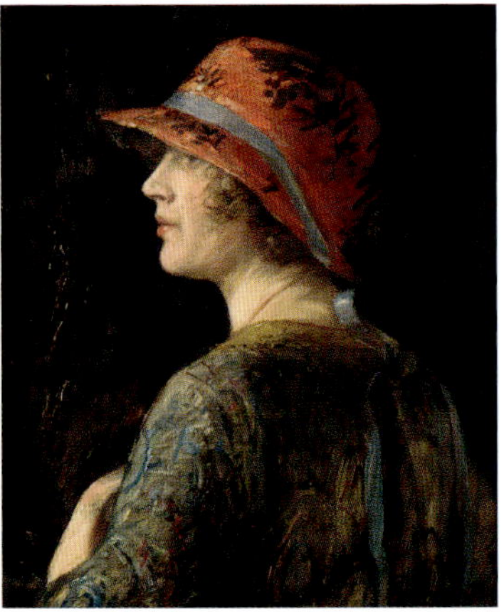

Roche, Alexander Ignatius 1861–1921
Girl in Red Hat
oil on canvas 58.4 x 48.3
2270

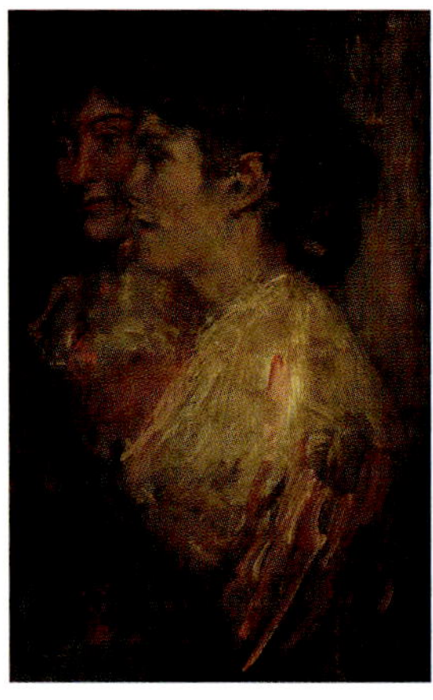

Roche, Alexander Ignatius 1861–1921
Study of Two Female Heads
oil on canvas 53 x 35.2
2856

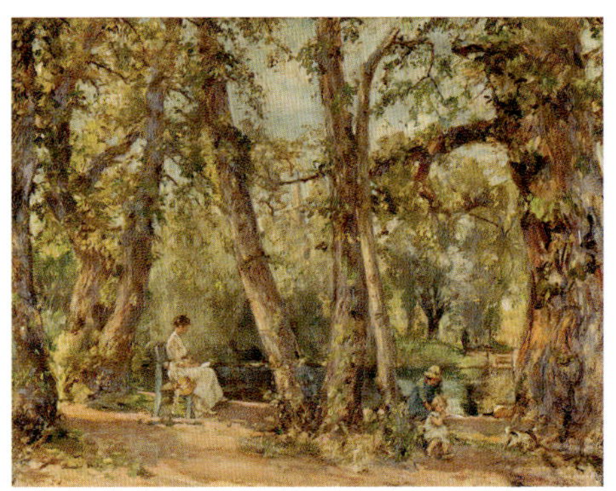

Roche, Alexander Ignatius 1861–1921
Woodland and River
oil on canvas 101.6 x 127
2173

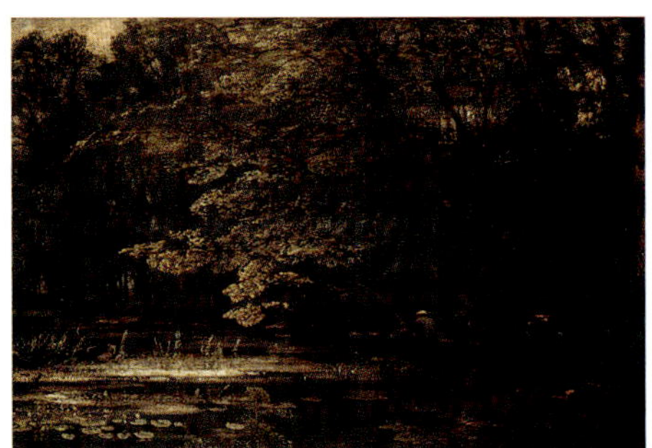

Rodeck, Karl 1841–1909
An Angler by a Woodland Pond c.1880–1881
oil on canvas 75.5 x 110.5
867

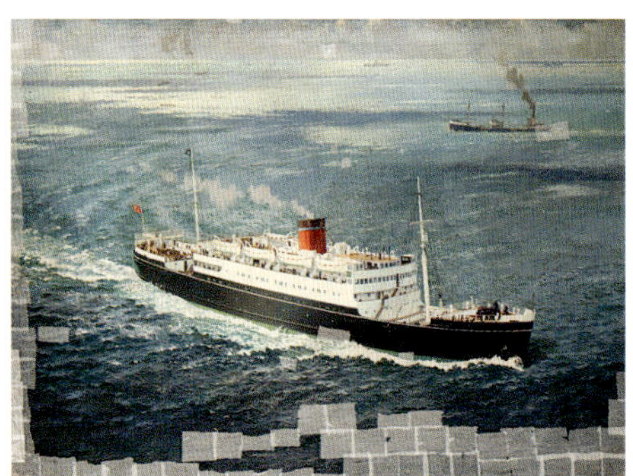

Rodmell, Harry Hudson 1896–1984
'Royal Scotsman'
oil on canvas 107.5 x 142.5
T.1971.11

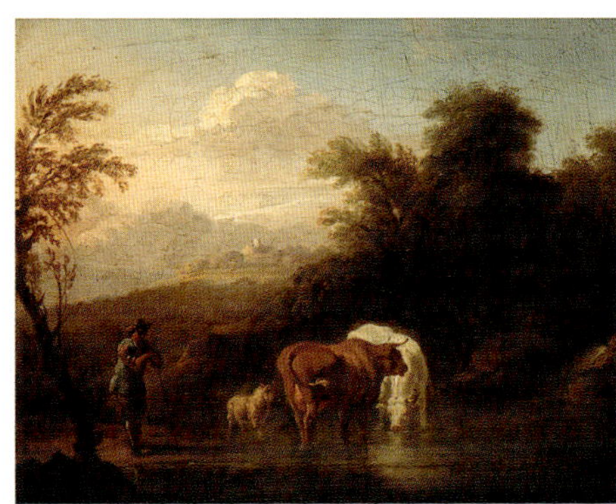

Romeyn, Willem (style of) c.1624–1694
Landscape with Cattle and a Cowherd
late 18th C
oil on canvas 30.5 x 35.5
343

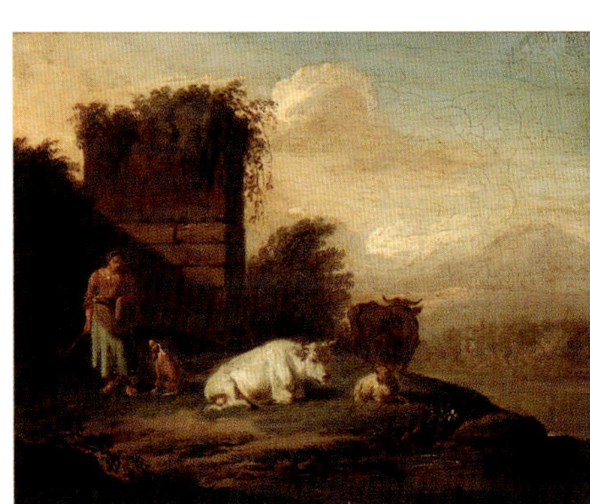

Romeyn, Willem (style of) c.1624–1694
Landscape with Cattle and a Peasant Woman
late 18th C
oil on canvas 30.5 x 35.5
347

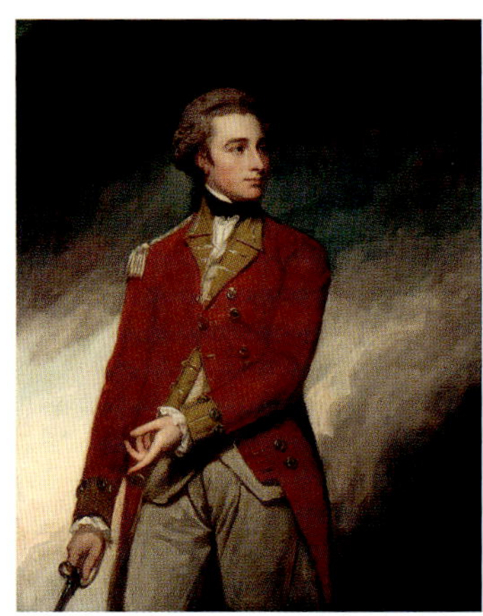

Romney, George 1734–1802
Lieutenant Colonel Sir Charles Stuart
(1753–1801) 1779
oil on canvas 127 x 101.6
2240

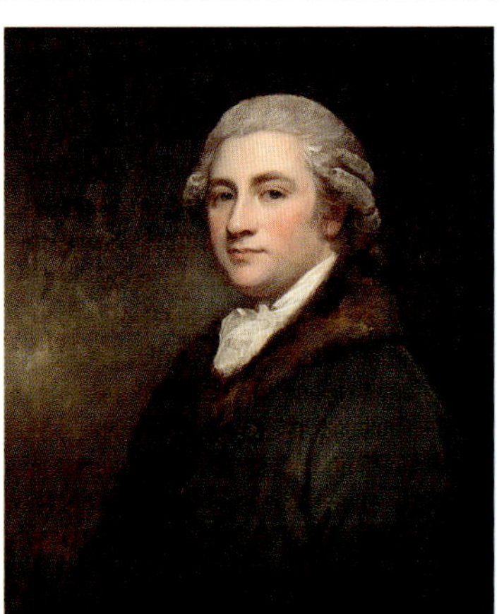

Romney, George 1734–1802
Portrait of a Man
oil on canvas 74.9 x 62.2
35.616

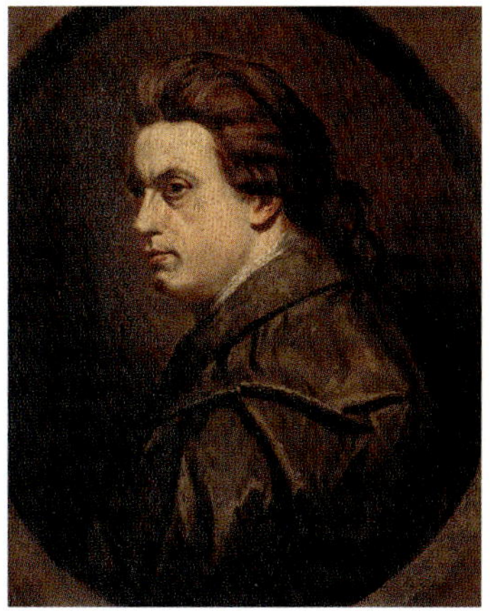

Romney, George 1734–1802
Richard Cumberland (1732–1811)
oil on canvas 33.6 x 26
PC.56

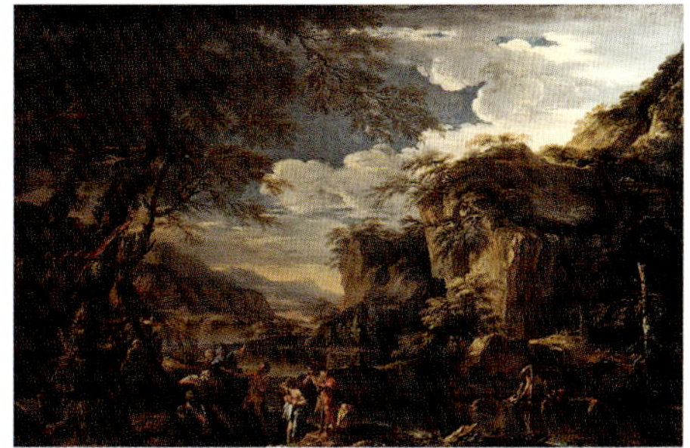

Rosa, Salvator 1615–1673
Saint John the Baptist Baptising Christ in the Jordan c.1655
oil on canvas 173 x 258.7
2987

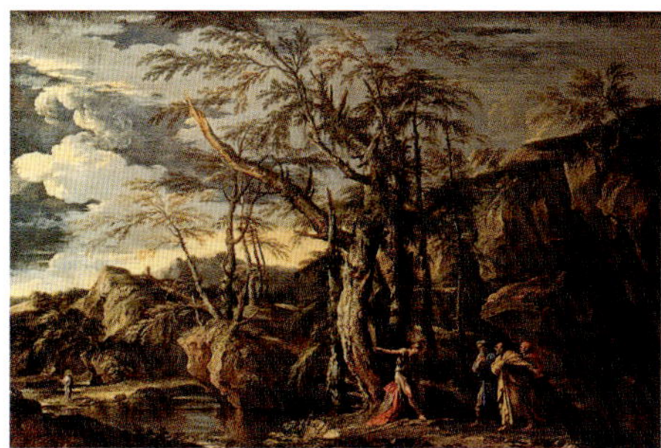

Rosa, Salvator 1615–1673
Saint John the Baptist Revealing Christ to the Disciples c.1655
oil on canvas 173.4 x 260.7
2969

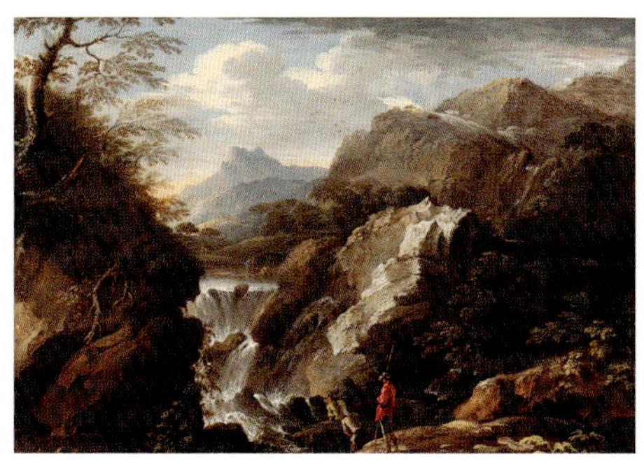

Rosa, Salvator (follower of) 1615–1673
A Mountainous Landscape with a Waterfall c.1660–1670
oil on canvas 99.7 x 136.5
267

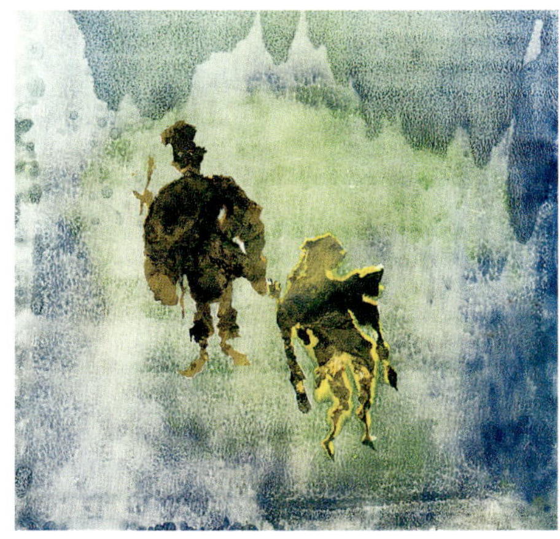

Rosen, Frank b.1918
The Knight and the Squire
oil on canvas 122 x 122
3504

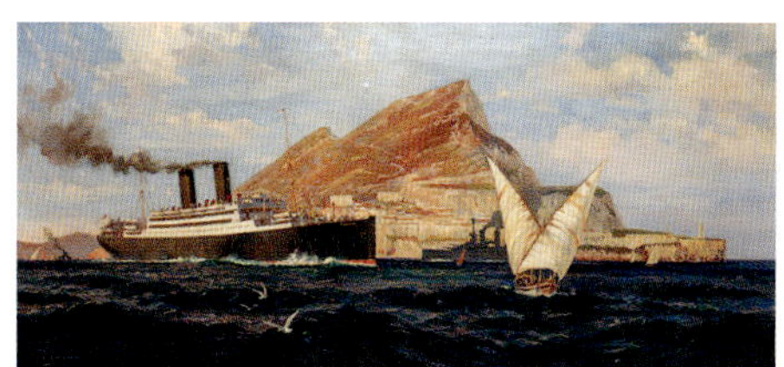

Rosenvinge, Odin 1880–1957
'Tuscania' 1916
oil on canvas 75 x 164
LT.1977.1 (P)

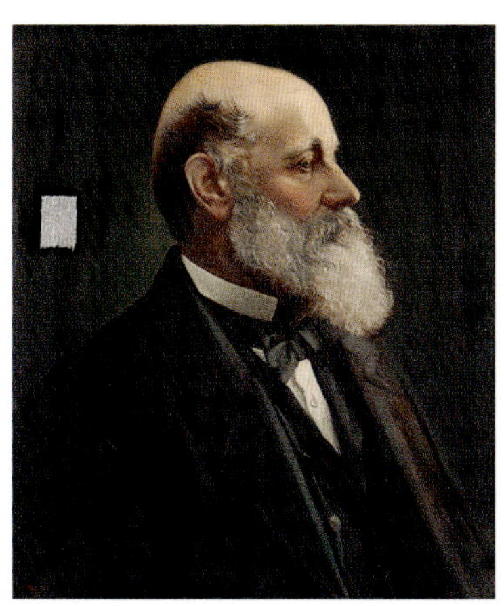

Ross, E. M.
W. A. Jardine, Engineer, NBR 1846–1850
oil on canvas 61.3 x 51
T.1967.33.ah

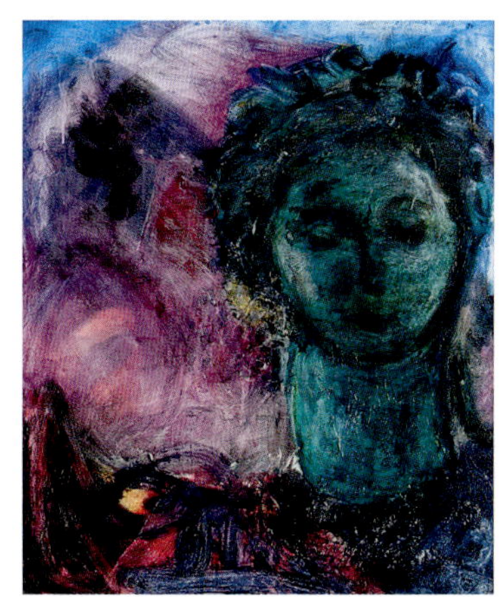

Ross, Lucy b.1961
Isolated Head c.2008
oil on canvas 93.8 x 81.6
3685

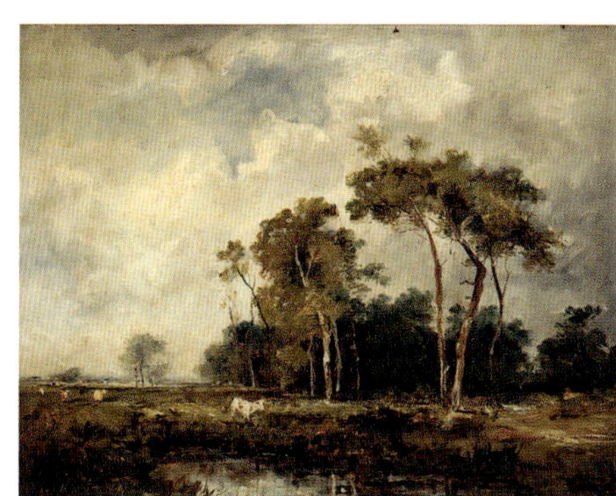

Ross, Malcolm active 19th C
Landscape with Trees and Cattle
oil on canvas 38.1 x 49.5
824

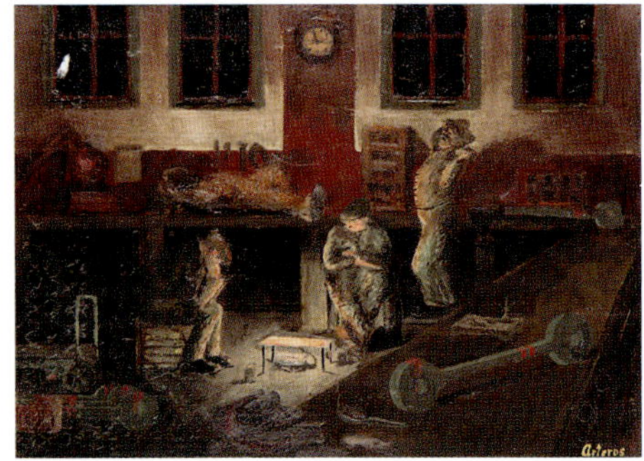

Ross, R.
Nightshift in the Finishing Shop 1944
oil on board 25.8 x 34.9
1988.39

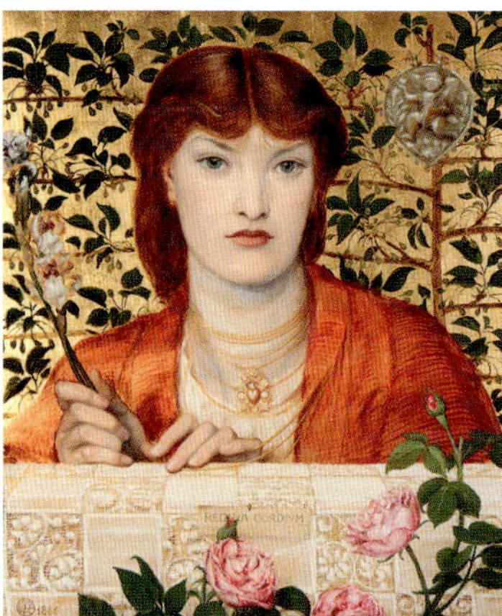

Rossetti, Dante Gabriel 1828–1882
Regina cordium 1866
oil on canvas on panel 59.7 x 49.5
2196

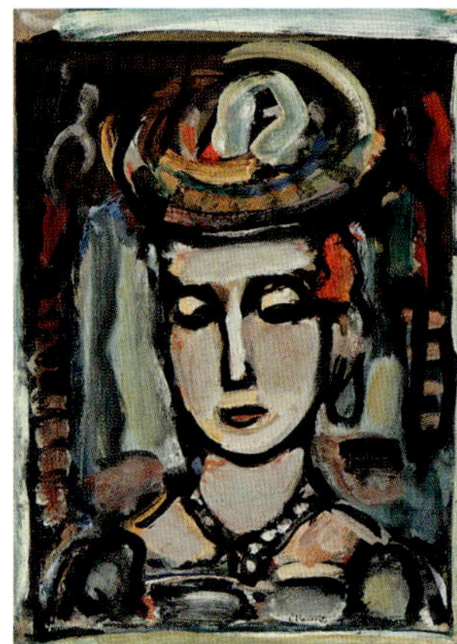

Rouault, Georges 1871–1958
Circus Girl c.1939
oil on canvas 64.3 x 45.3
3101

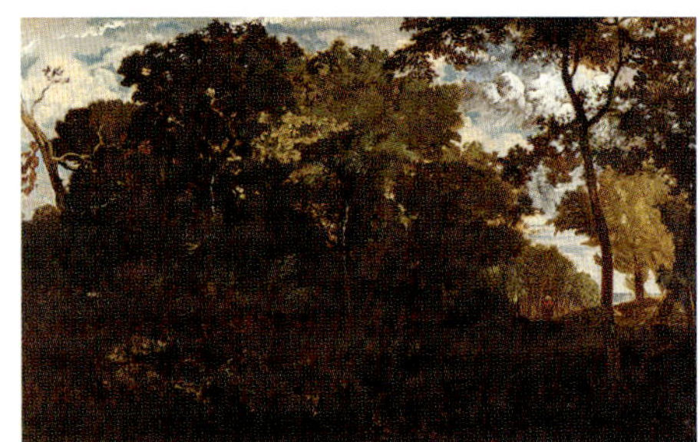

Rousseau, Théodore 1812–1867
The Forest of Clairbois c.1836–1839
oil on canvas 65.4 x 104.1
1124

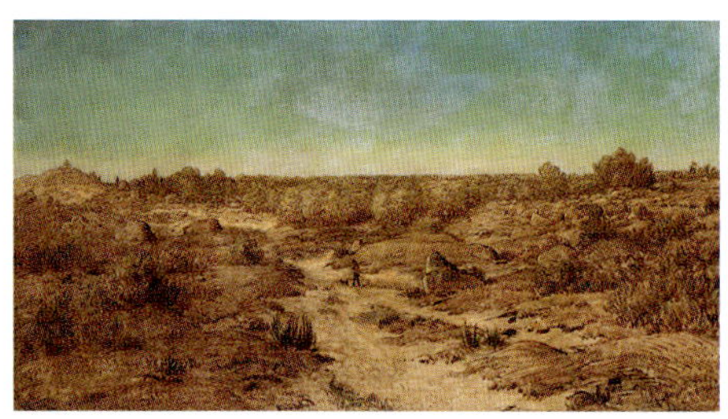

Rousseau, Théodore 1812–1867
Les gorges d'Apremont
oil on canvas 82.2 x 146.4
3062

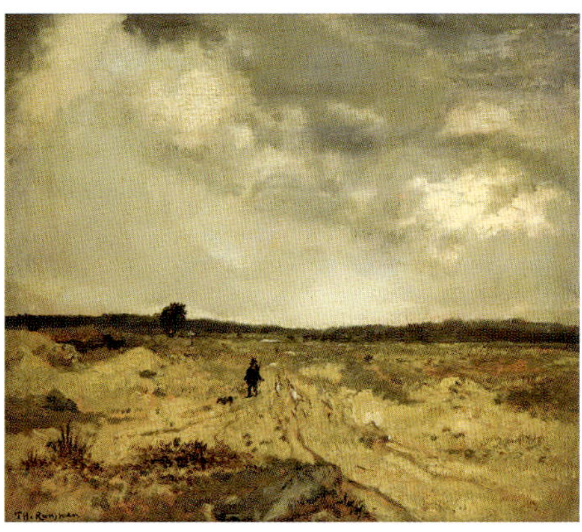

Rousseau, Théodore 1812–1867
The Heath
oil on canvas 29.4 x 33
1122

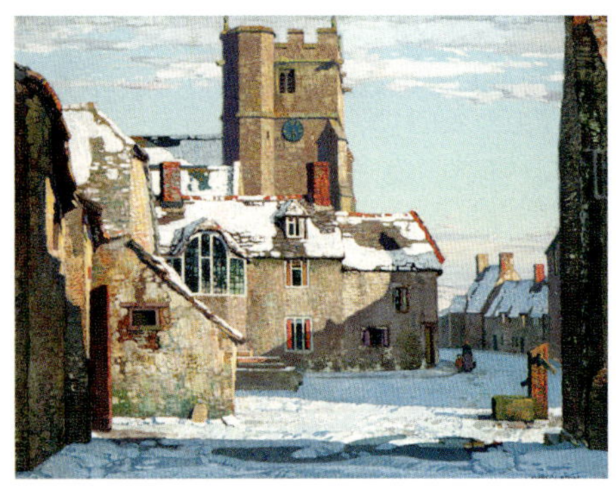

Royle, Stanley 1888–1961
Winter, Corfe Castle Village 1937
oil on canvas 71.1 x 91.4
2153 🐝

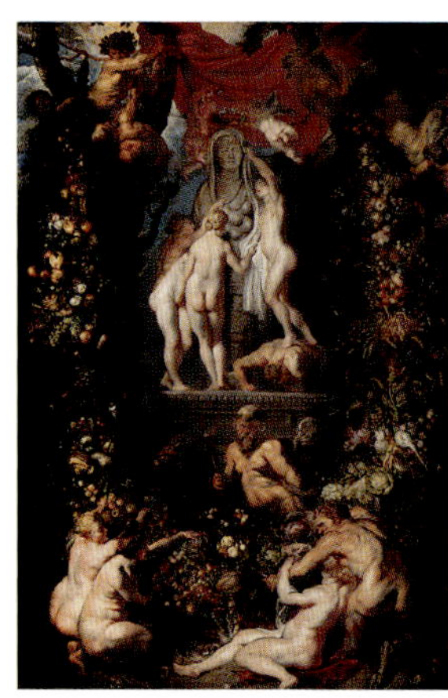

Rubens, Peter Paul 1577–1640 & **Brueghel, Jan the elder** 1568–1625
Nature and Her Followers c.1615
oil on panel 106.7 x 72.4
609

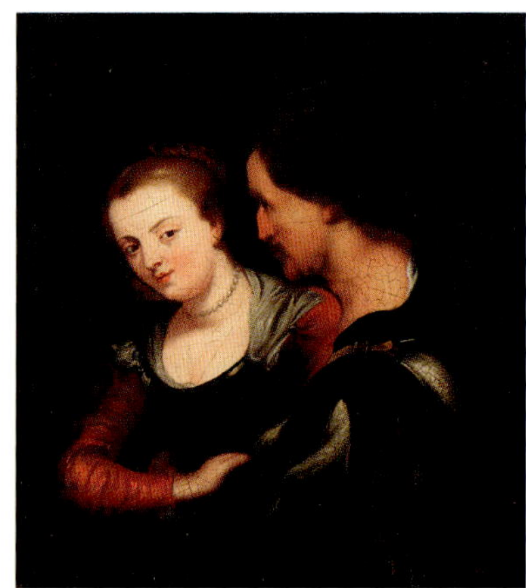

Rubens, Peter Paul (after) 1577–1640
A Man and a Girl 17th C
oil on canvas 31.8 x 28
3428

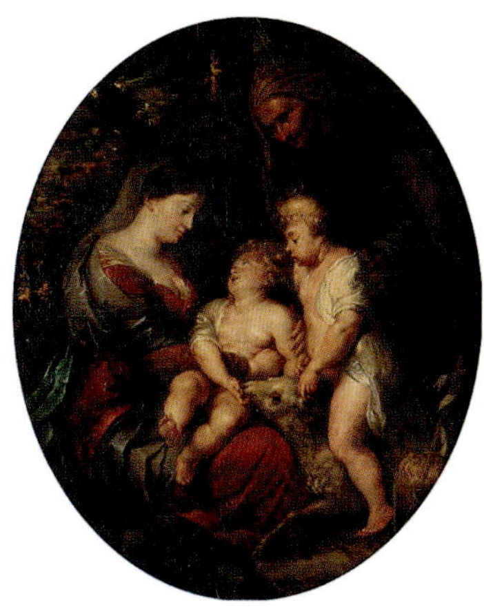

Rubens, Peter Paul (after) 1577–1640
Madonna and Child with Saints Elizabeth and John 17th C
oil on copper 29.2 x 24.1
28

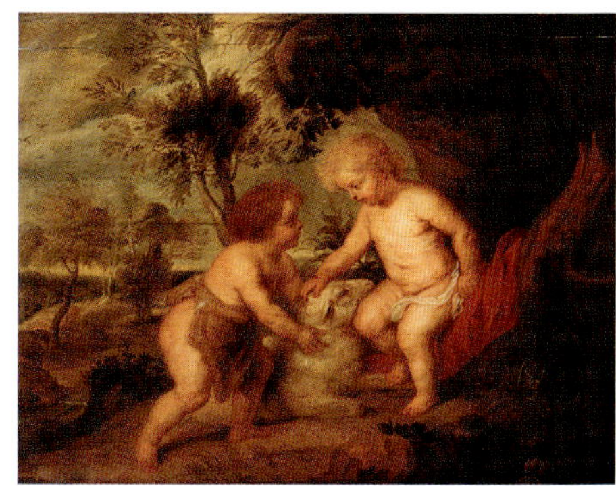

Rubens, Peter Paul (after) 1577–1640
The Infant Christ and Saint John with a Lamb 17th C
oil on panel 48.6 x 63.8
36

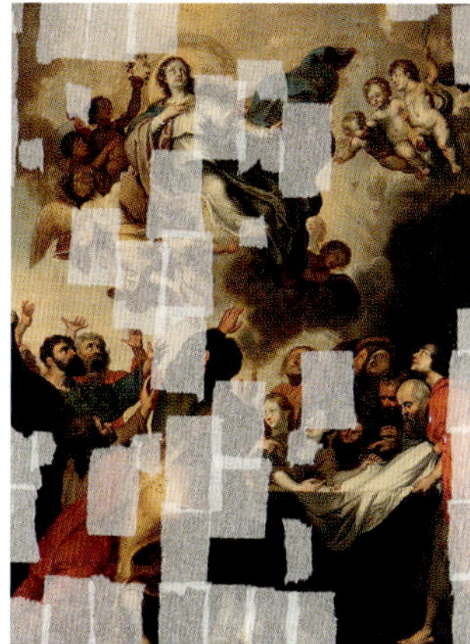

Rubens, Peter Paul (after) 1577–1640
The Assumption of the Virgin 19th C
oil on panel 57.4 x 43.8
408

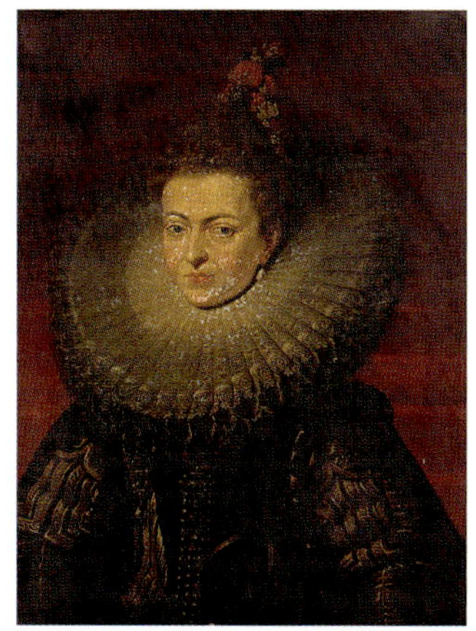

Rubens, Peter Paul (after) 1577–1640
Infanta Isabella Clara Eugenia (1566–1633)
oil on canvas 78.7 x 57.2
PC.73

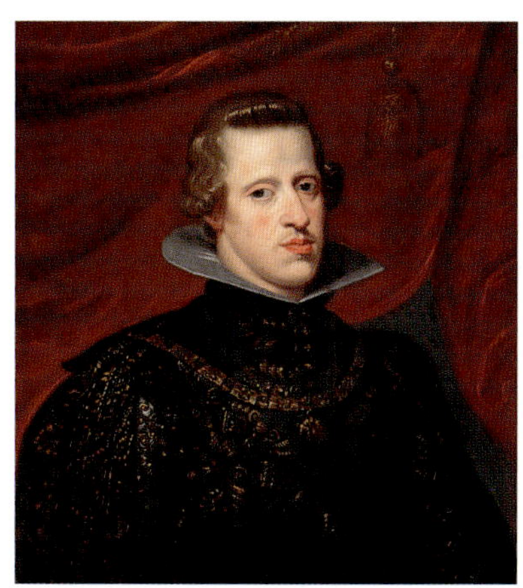

Rubens, Peter Paul (after) 1577–1640
Philip IV of Spain (1605–1665)
oil on canvas 67.6 x 59.7
PC.3

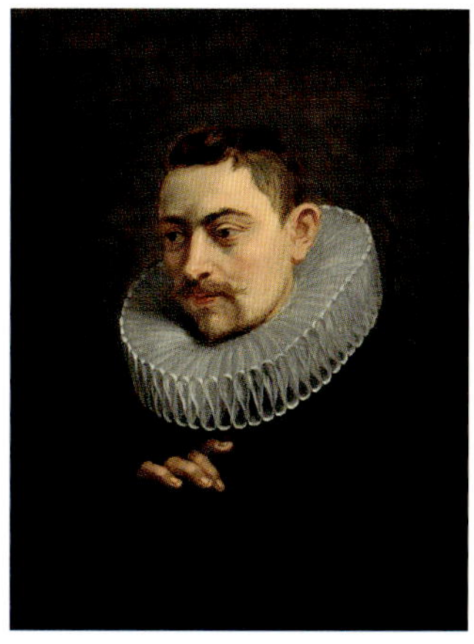

Rubens, Peter Paul (attributed to) 1577–1640
Portrait of a Young Man c.1617–1620
oil on panel 64.8 x 49.8
581

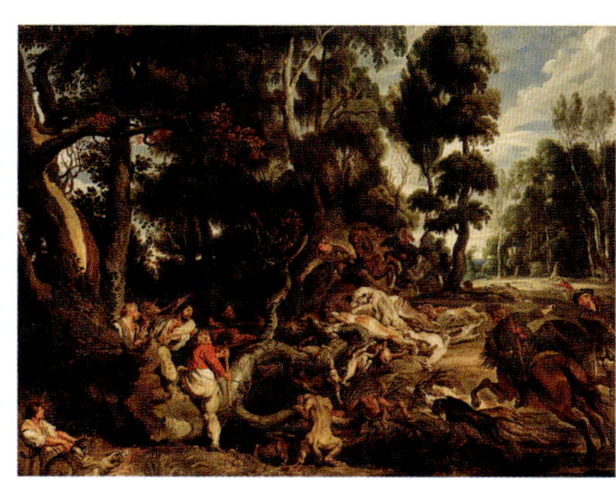

Rubens, Peter Paul (studio of) 1577–1640
Landscape with a Boar Hunt c.1617–1620
oil on panel 135.2 x 167.6
715

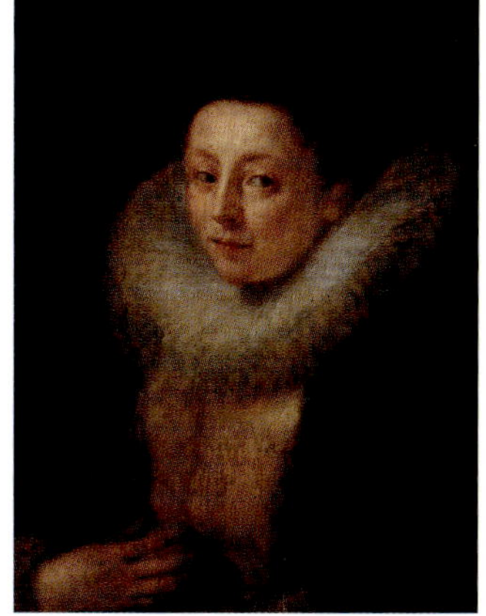

Rubens, Peter Paul (style of) 1577–1640
Portrait of a Young Woman 18th C/early 19th C
oil on panel 65.1 x 49.5
607

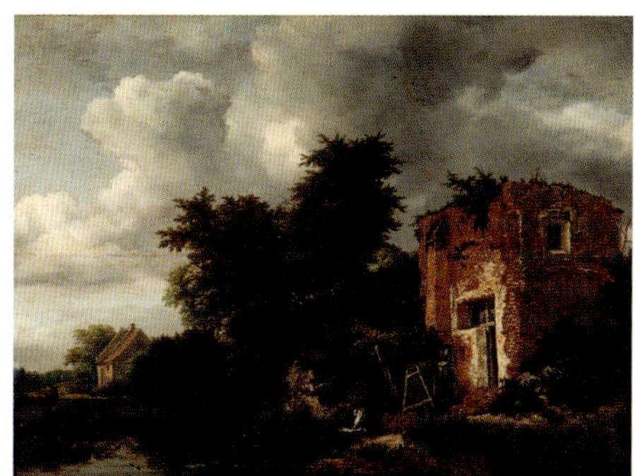

Ruisdael, Jacob van 1628/1629–1682
Landscape with a Ruined Tower c.1646–1648
oil on panel 47 x 63.2
611

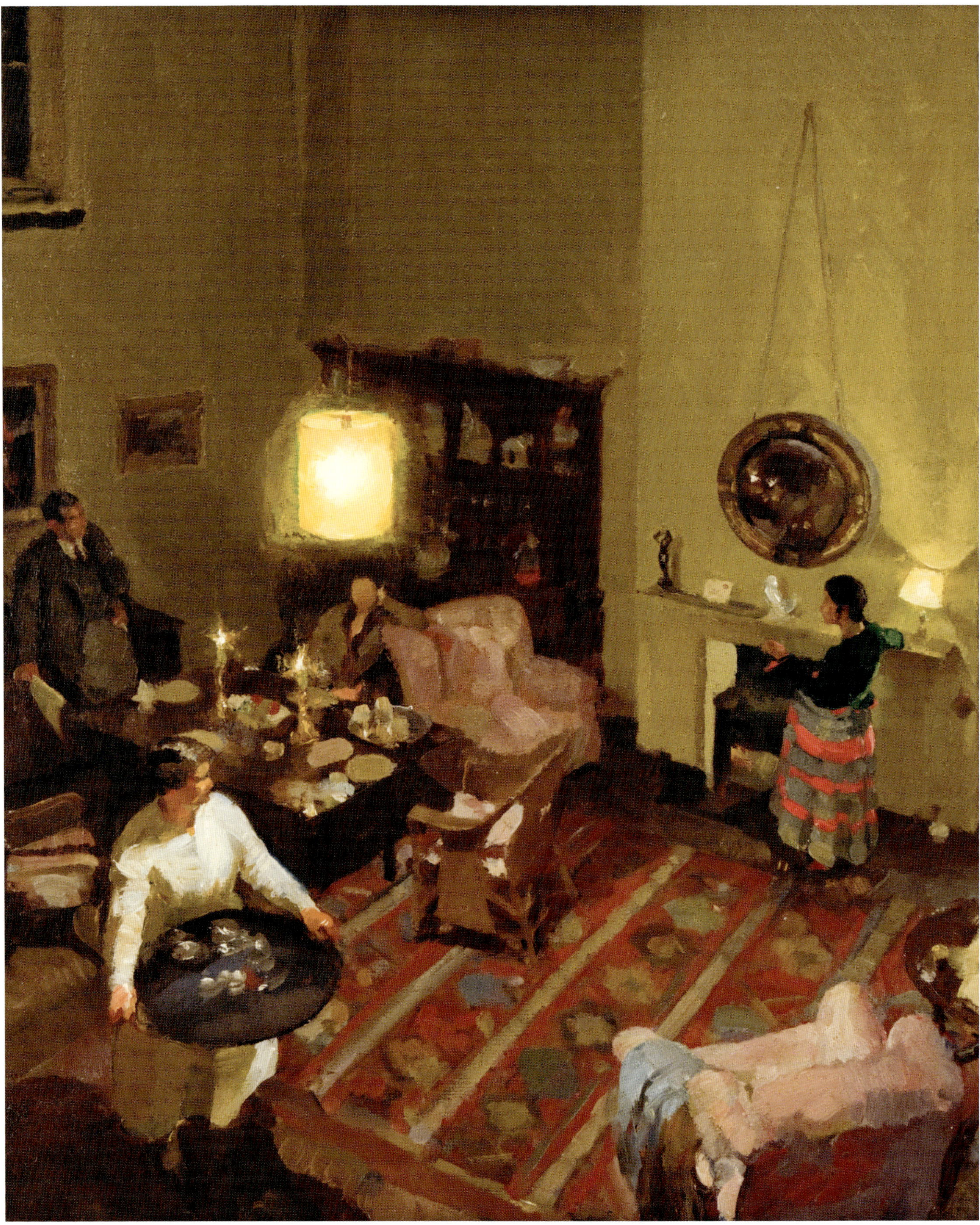

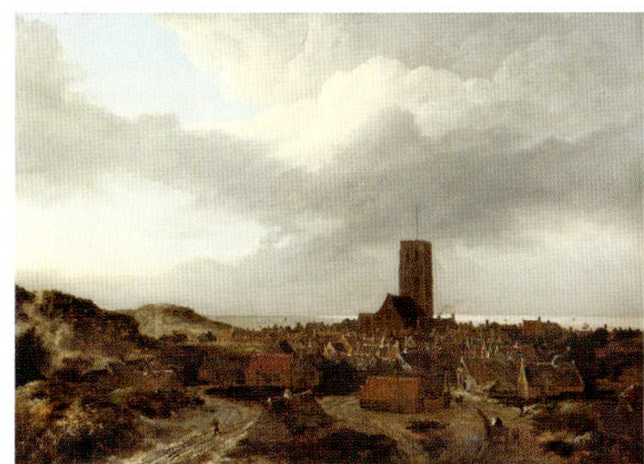

Ruisdael, Jacob van 1628/1629–1682
A View of Egmond aan Zee c.1647–1652
oil on panel 49.8 x 68.3
34

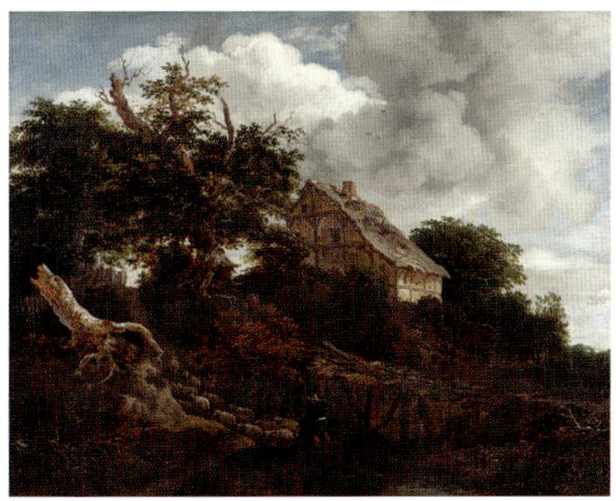

Ruisdael, Jacob van 1628/1629–1682
Landscape with a Cottage, Bridge and Sheep
c.1650–1655
oil on canvas 55.2 x 68.6
612

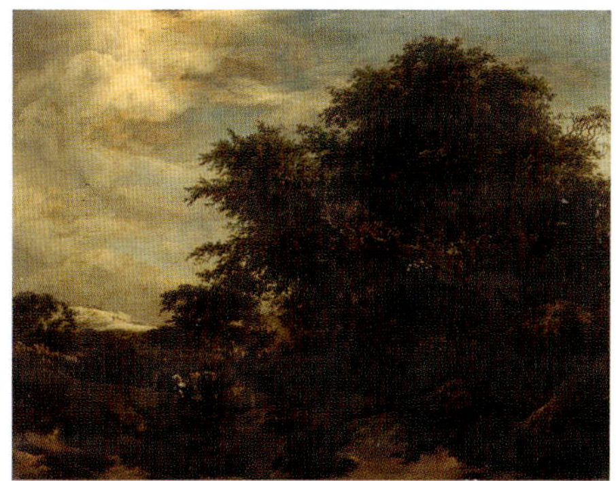

Ruisdael, Jacob van (attributed to)
1628/1629–1682
Landscape with Figures c.1650
oil on panel 52.7 x 67.9
614

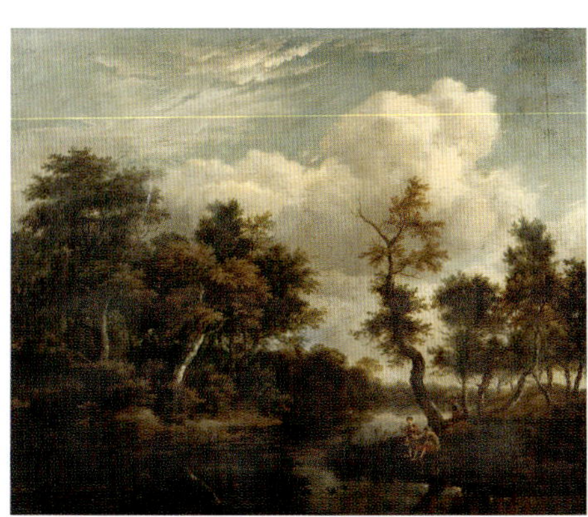

Ruisdael, Jacob van (attributed to)
1628/1629–1682
Wooded Landscape with Fishermen by a Pond
c.1670–1676
oil on canvas 55.2 x 64.1
109

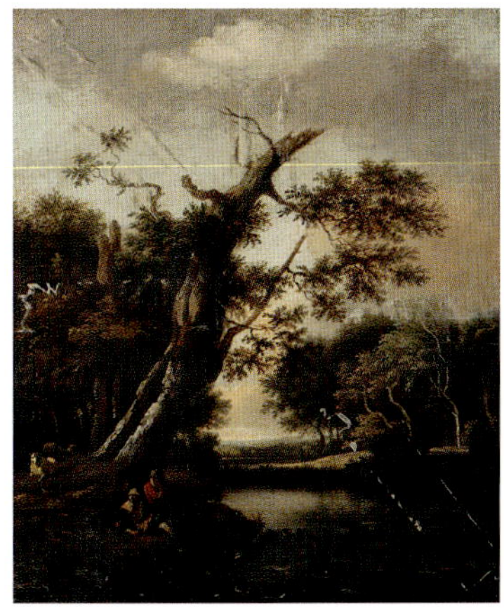

Ruisdael, Jacob van (imitator of)
1628/1629–1682
*Wooded Landscape with Shepherds by a
Stream* 18th C/19th C
oil on canvas 64.1 x 53.3
681

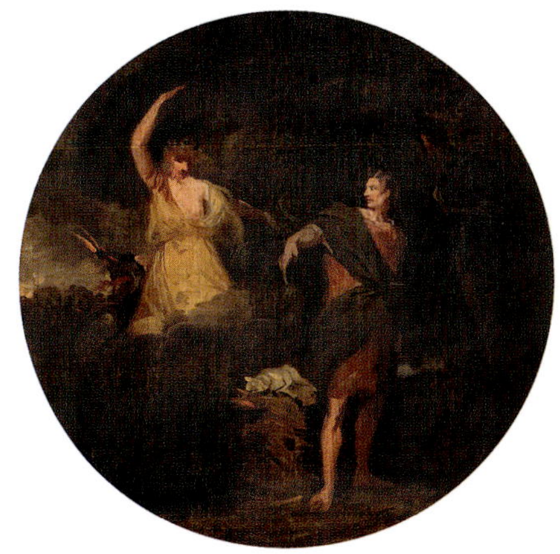

Runciman, Alexander (attributed to)
1736–1785
*A Sacrificial Scene Attended by Demonic
Figures*
oil on canvas 47
3251

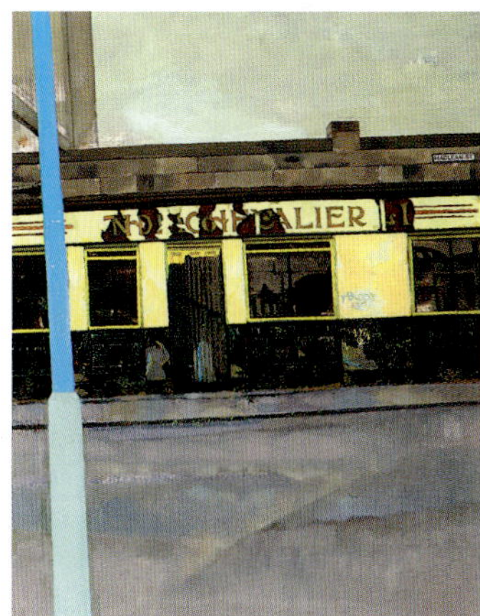

Russell, Peter J. active 1972–c.1980
What Happened to the Cavalier Spirit 1975
oil on canvas 91.4 x 71.1
NR.94

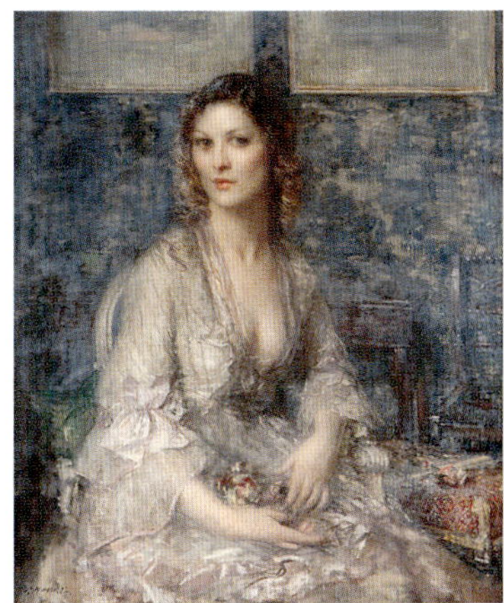

Russell, Walter Westley 1867–1949
Amelia c.1937
oil on canvas 61 x 50.8
2080

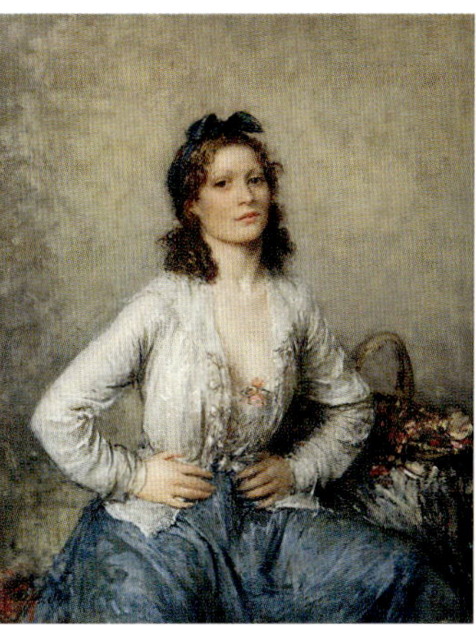

Russell, Walter Westley 1867–1949
The Flower Girl c.1938
oil on canvas 61 x 50.8
2095

Facing page: Browning, Amy Katherine, 1881–1978, *Interior: Studio Supper*, 1930 (p. 64)

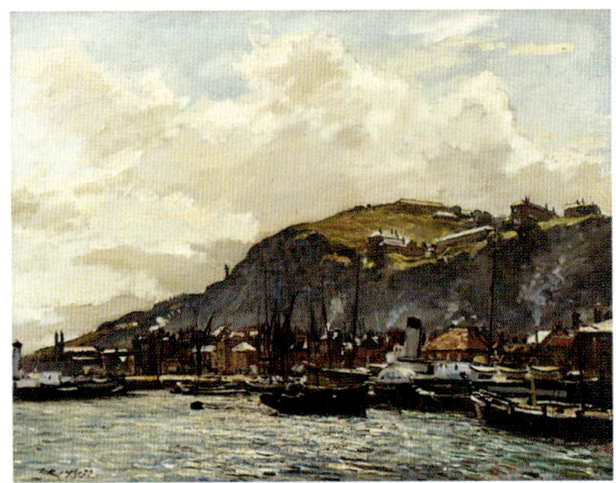

Russell, Walter Westley 1867–1949
Dover
oil on canvas 71.1 x 91.4
2287

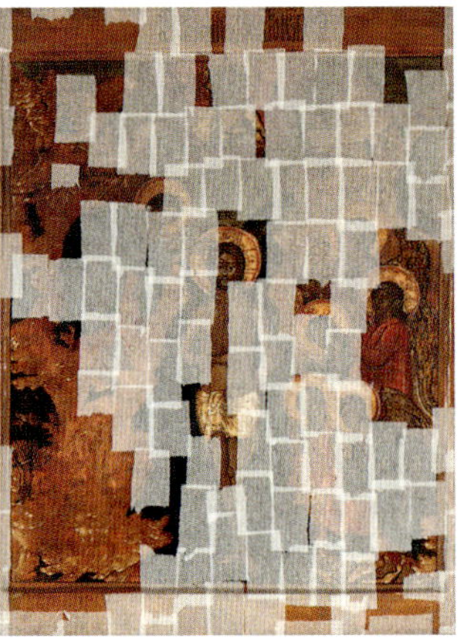

Russian School (attributed to)
16th C–17th C
The Baptism of Christ
oil on panel 72.4 x 54.7
3421

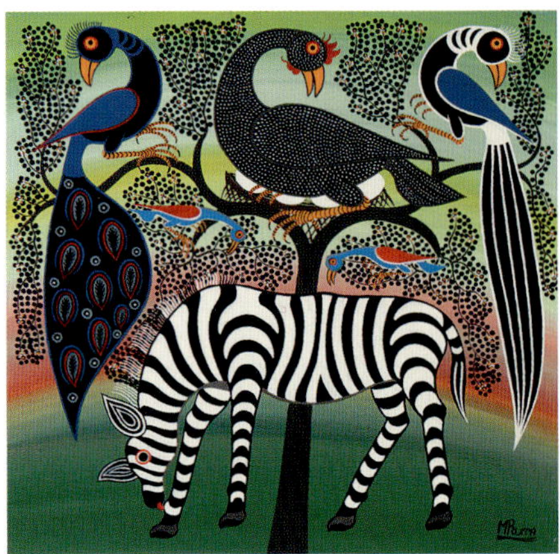

Ruta, M.
Zebra and Birds
enamel on hardboard 62.5 x 62.5
A.1989.23.e

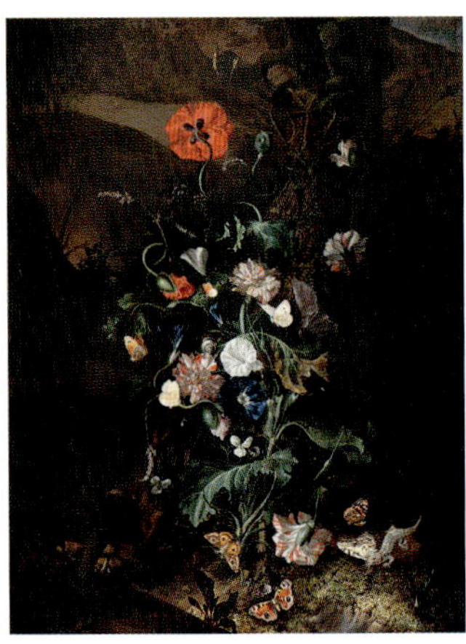

Ruysch, Rachel 1664–1750
An Arrangement of Flowers by a Tree Trunk c.1683
oil on canvas 93.7 x 71.1
45

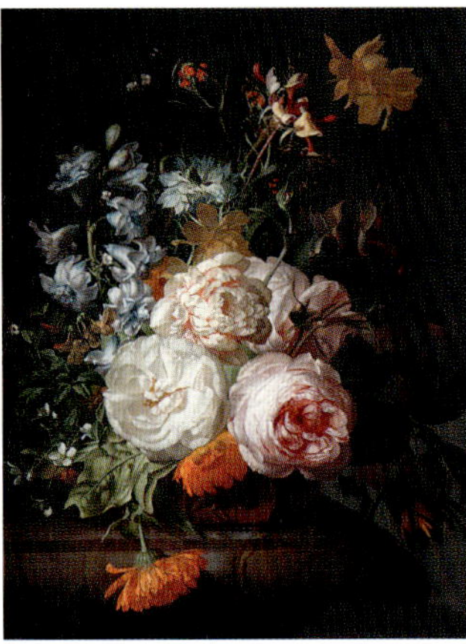

Ruysch, Rachel 1664–1750
Flowers in a Terracotta Vase 1723
oil on canvas 39.4 x 31.4
82

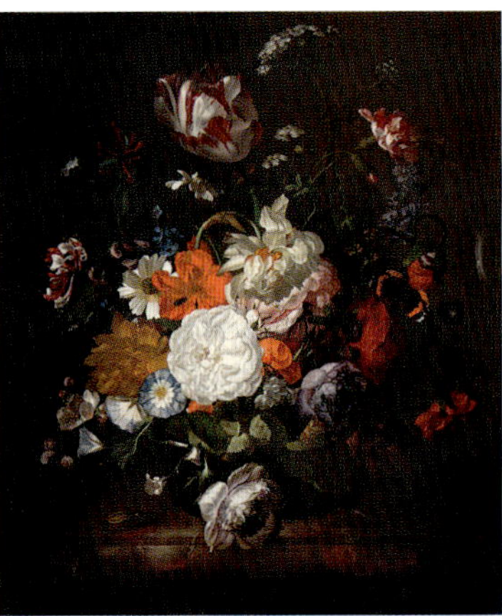

Ruysch, Rachel (attributed to) 1664–1750
Still Life, Flowers and Insects c.1720–1730
oil on canvas 61.2 x 54.1
104

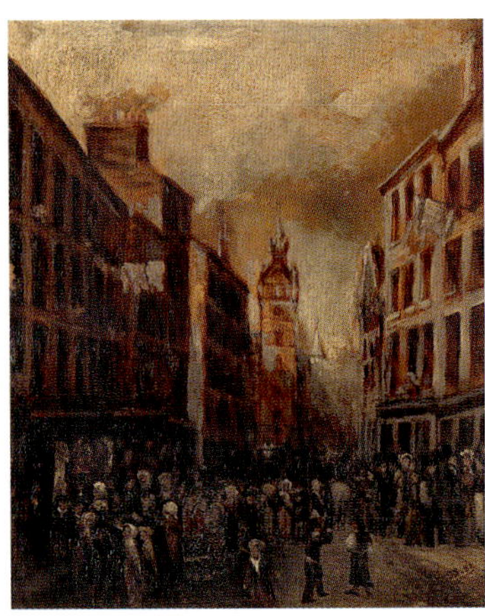

S. S.
Saltmarket and Tron Steeple, Glasgow 1881
oil on canvas 30.4 x 25.1
OG.1951.417.n

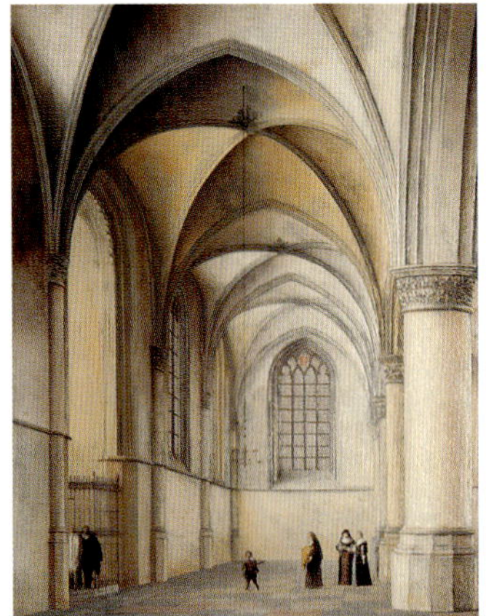

Saenredam, Pieter Jansz. 1597–1665
Interior of St Bavo's, Haarlem, with a Catholic Baptism 1633
oil on panel 39.3 x 33.6
383

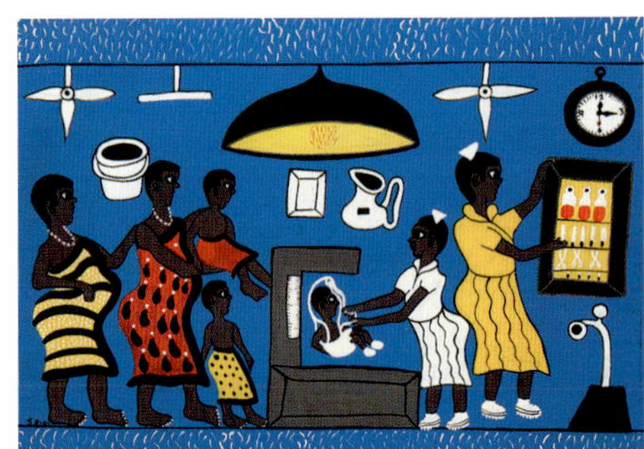

Saidi
Maternity Clinic
enamel on hardboard 46.5 x 63
A.1989.23.b

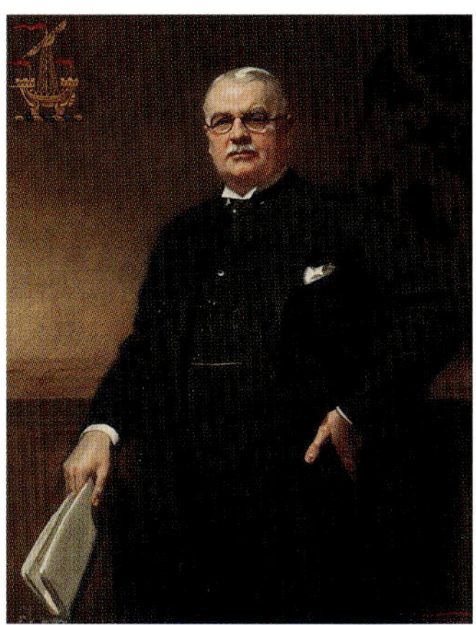

Salisbury, Frank O. 1874–1962
Andrew Weir (1865–1955), Lord Inverforth of Southgate
oil on canvas 127 x 101.6
2310

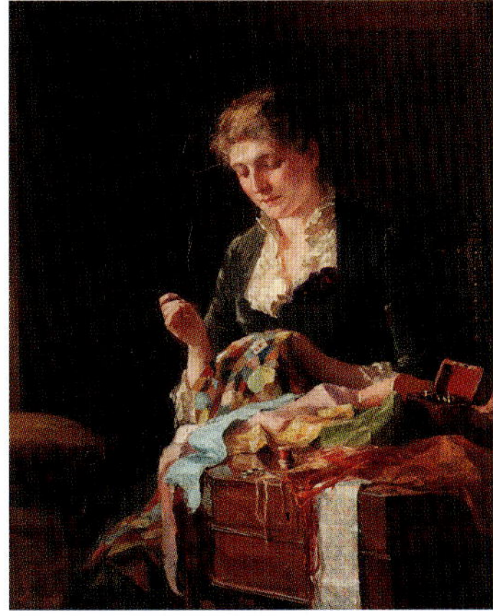

Salmon, Helen Russell 1855–1891
Patchwork 1888
oil on canvas 64.8 x 52.1
1325

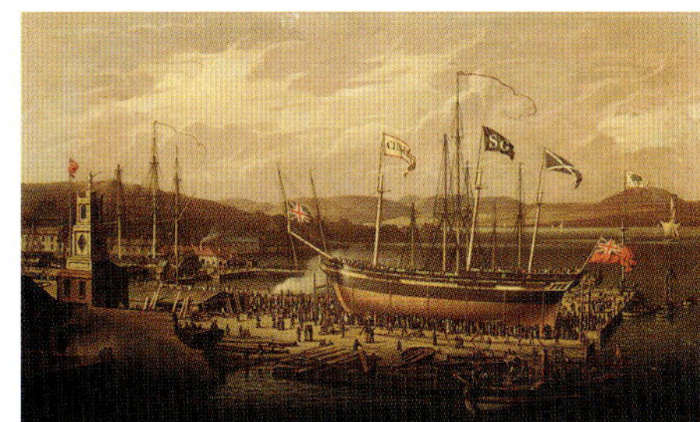

Salmon, Robert W. 1775–1851
Launch of the 'Christian' 1818
oil on canvas 58.2 x 93.4
T.1957.15

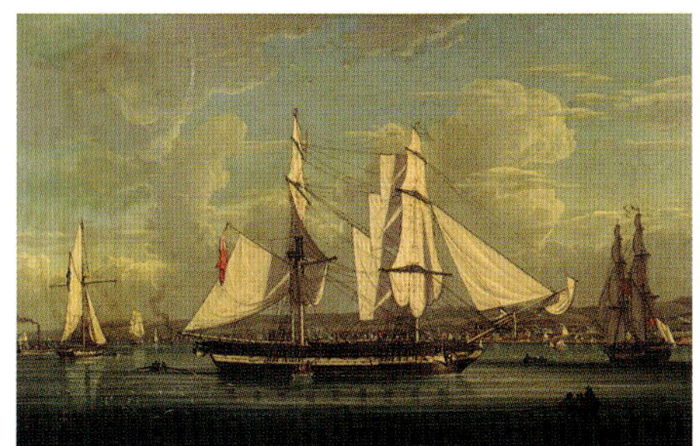

Salmon, Robert W. 1775–1851
A Snow off Greenock
oil on canvas 49 x 75.2
TEMP.14939

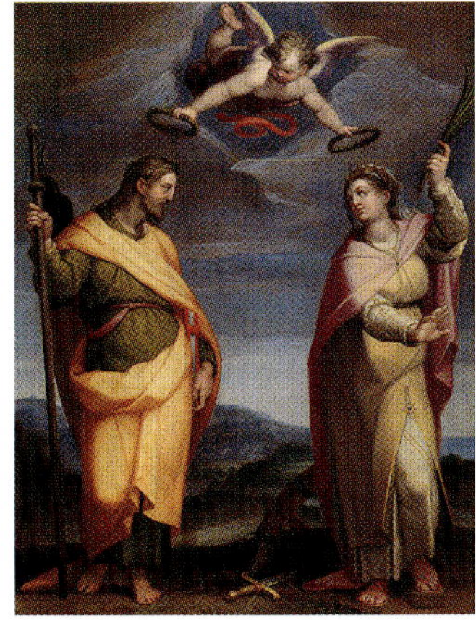

Sammacchini, Orazio 1532–1577
Saint James Major and Saint Catherine of Alexandria c.1565
oil on metal 22.8 x 16.8
164

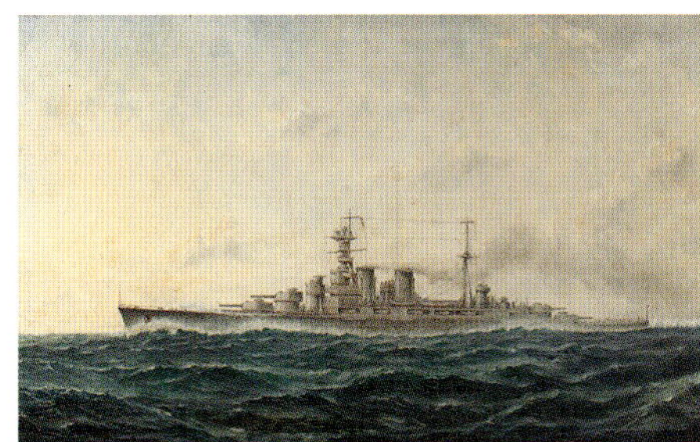

Sampson, J.
HMS 'Hood' 1922
oil on canvas 95 x 178
T.1973.10.ah

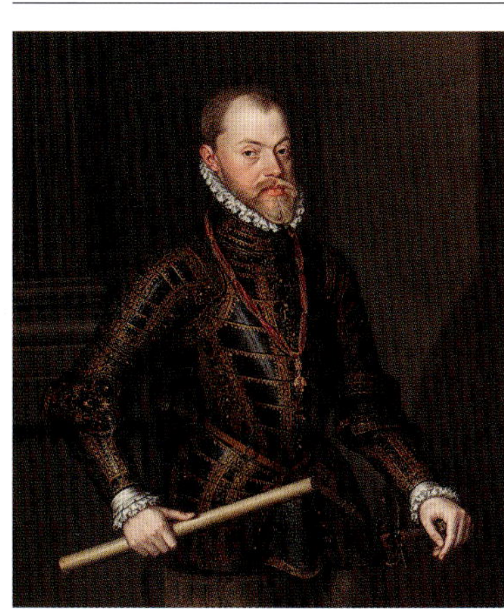

Sánchez Coello, Alonso c.1531–1588
Philip II of Spain (1527–1598) c.1570
oil on canvas 109.5 x 92.4
PC.159

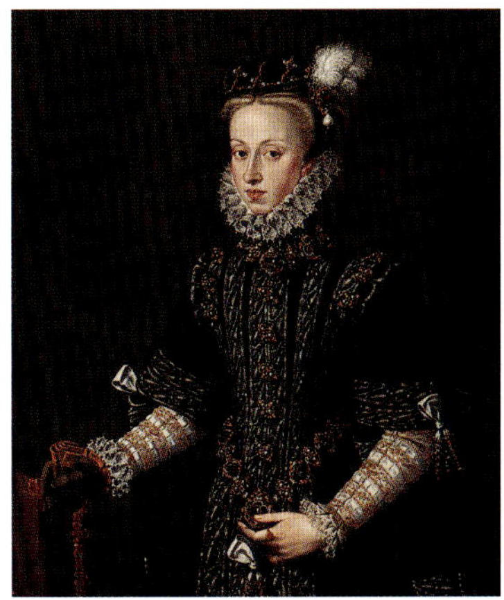

Sánchez Coello, Alonso c.1531–1588
Anne of Austria (1546–1580), Fourth Wife of Philip II c.1570
oil on canvas 109.5 x 93
PC.137

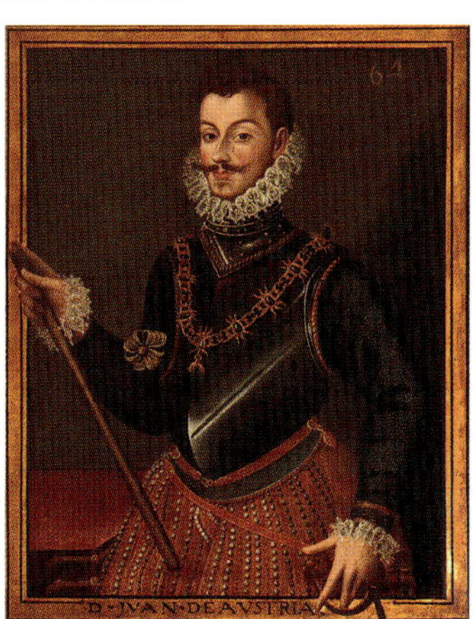

Sánchez Coello, Alonso (after) c.1531–1588
Don John of Austria (1547–1578)
oil on canvas 105.1 x 81.3
PC.8

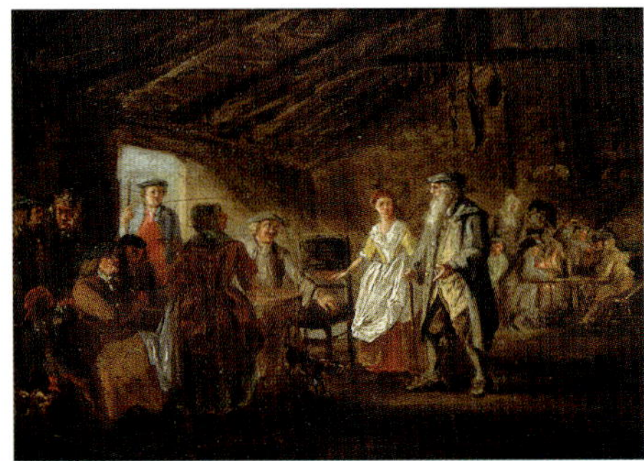

Sandby, Paul 1731–1809
Scene from Allan Ramsay's 'Gentle Shepherd'
c.1750
oil on panel 14.6 x 21
1096

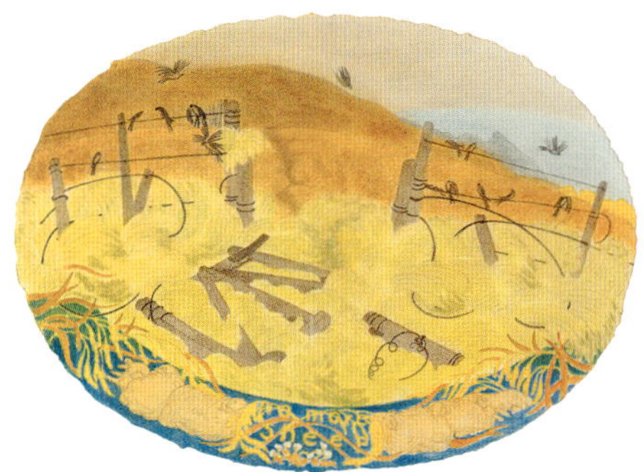

Sandeman, Margot 1922–2009
No More Sheep I 1981
acrylic & ink on paper 49 x 70.5
PR.2004.2.a

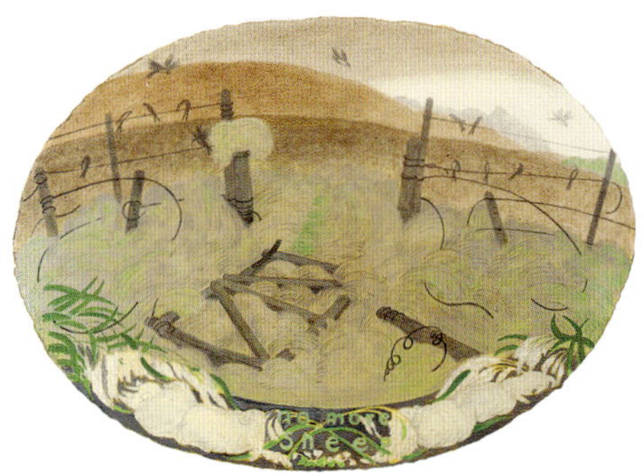

Sandeman, Margot 1922–2009
No More Sheep III 1981
acrylic & ink on paper 44.8 x 68.5
PR.2004.2.b

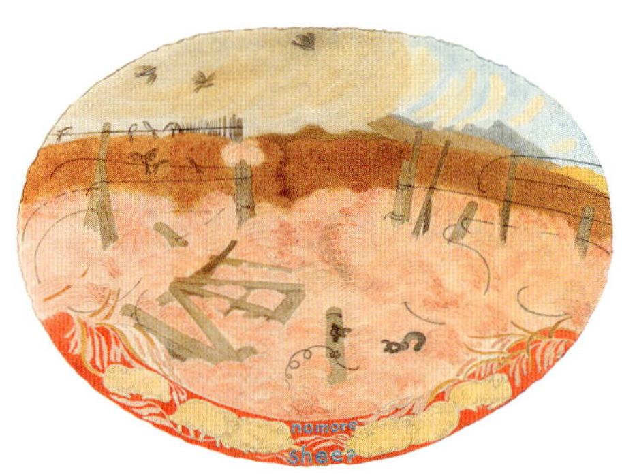

Sandeman, Margot 1922–2009
No More Sheep IV 1981
acrylic & ink on paper 56 x 75.3
PR.2004.2.c

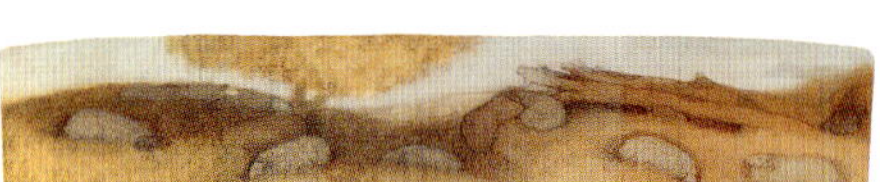

Sandeman, Margot 1922–2009
Sheep Grazing on a Hillside c.1981
acrylic & ink on paper 24.8 x 142.2
PR.2004.2

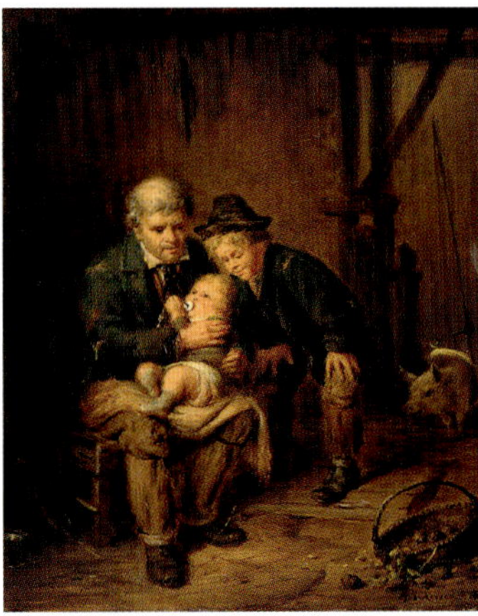

Sanderson, Robert 1848–1908
The Motherless Bairn 1895
oil on panel 30.5 x 25.4
790

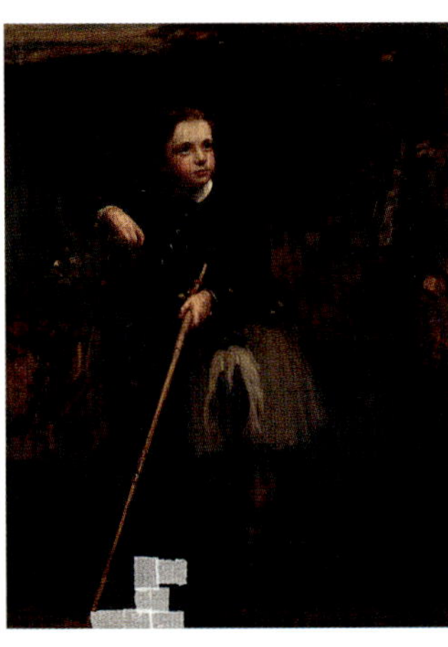

Sant, James 1820–1916
Major Dennistoun as a Boy c.1873
oil on canvas 143.5 x 101.5
3437

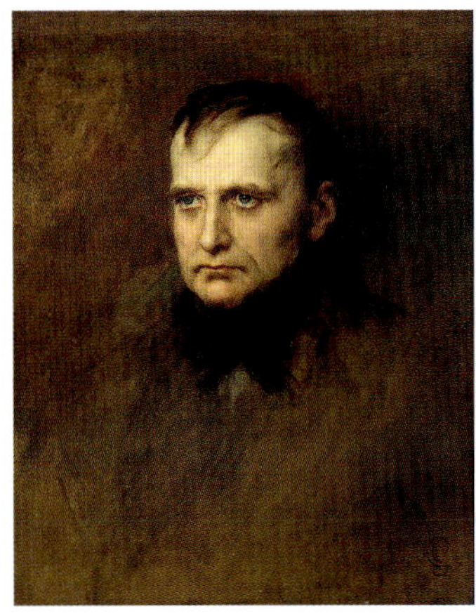

Sant, James 1820–1916
St Helena, the Last Phase c.1900
oil on canvas 63.5 x 48.3
1198

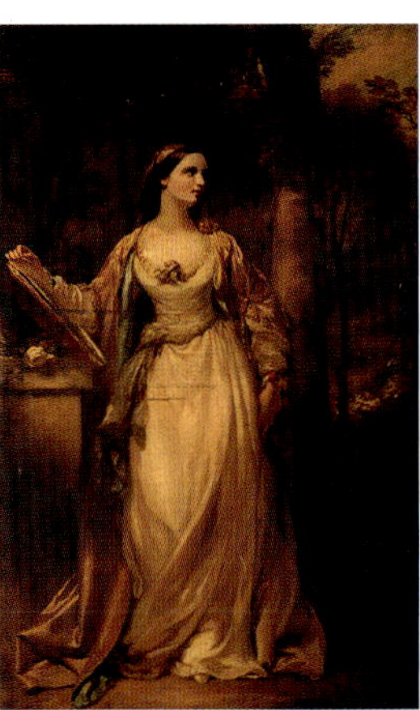

Sant, James 1820–1916
A Lady
oil on canvas 237.5 x 147.3
1391

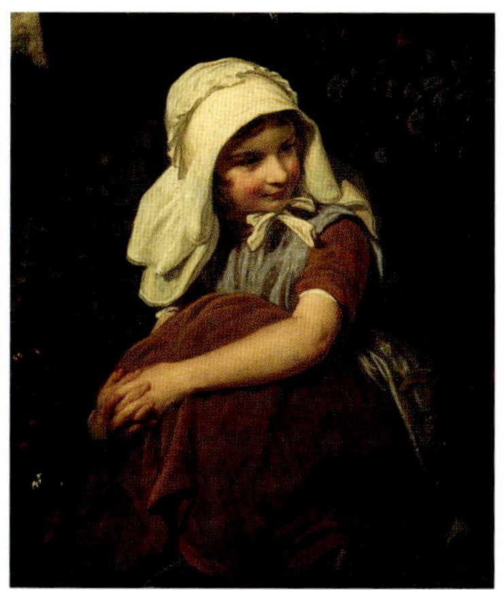

Sant, James 1820–1916
The Gipsy Girl
oil on canvas 76.2 x 62.2
1046

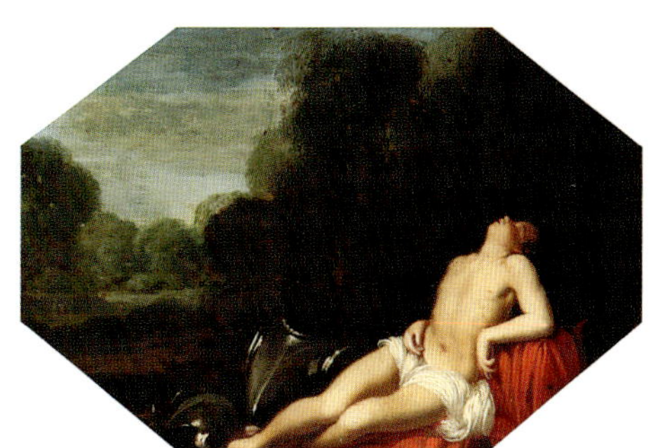

Saraceni, Carlo (studio of) 1579–1620
*Young Warrior Asleep in a Wooded
Landscape* c.1606–1610
oil on copper 12.7 x 18.4
118

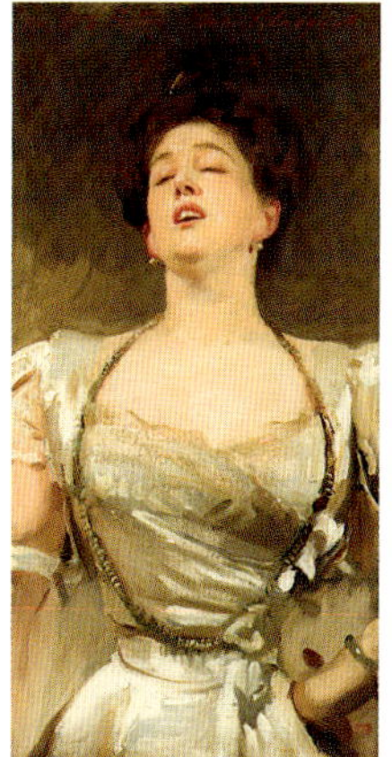

Sargent, John Singer 1856–1925
Mrs George Batten Singing 1895
oil on canvas 88.9 x 43.2
1769

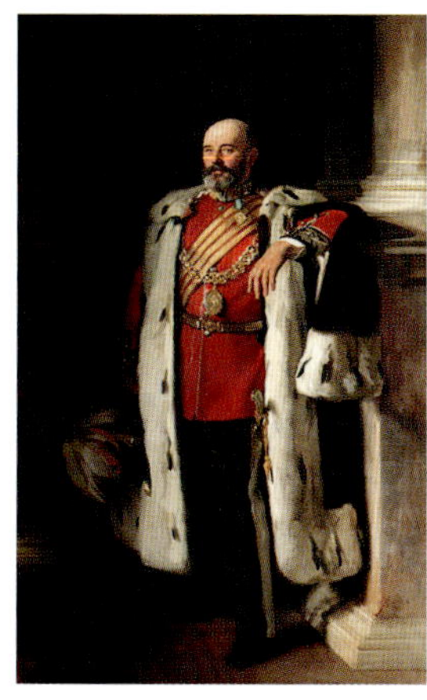

Sargent, John Singer 1856–1925
*Sir David Richmond (1843–1908), Lord
Provost of Glasgow (1896–1899)* c.1899
oil on canvas 243.8 x 134.6
899

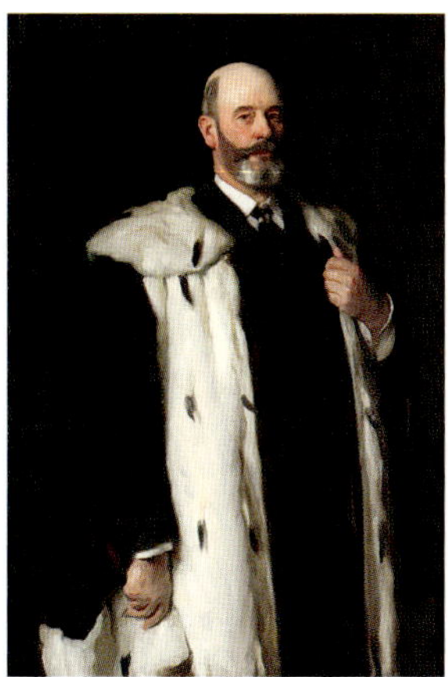

Sargent, John Singer 1856–1925
*Sir David Richmond (1843–1908), Lord
Provost of Glasgow (1896–1899)* c.1899
oil on canvas 147.3 x 96.5
2567

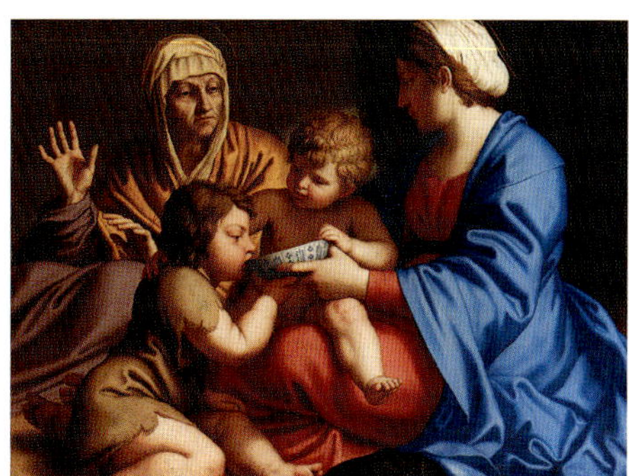

Sassoferrato 1609–1685
*Virgin and Child with Saint Elisabeth and
Child Baptist (after Annibale Carracci)* 1640
(?)
oil on canvas 73.4 x 97.5
584

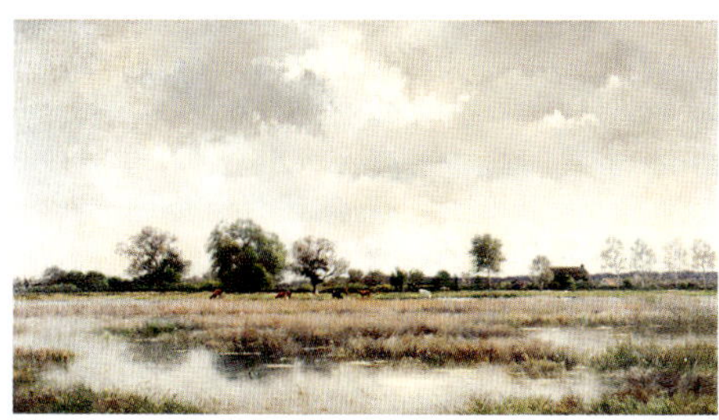

Sauzay, Adrien Jacques 1841–1928
The Pond at Vaugoing, Sologne c.1882
oil on canvas 114.3 x 198.1
843

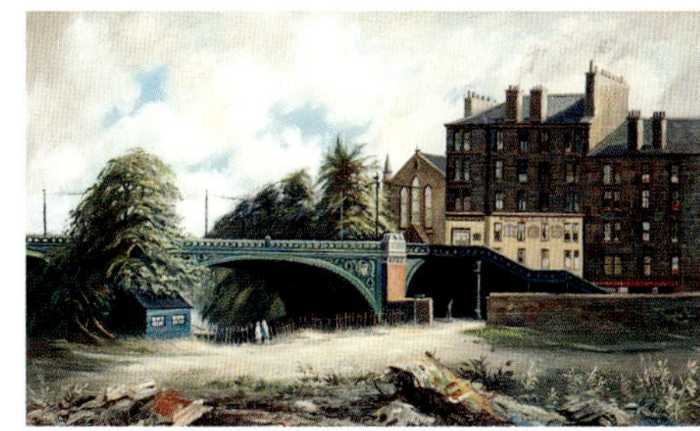

Saville, Paul b.1941
Kelvinbridge 1966
oil on canvas 86.5 x 133
OG.1966.33

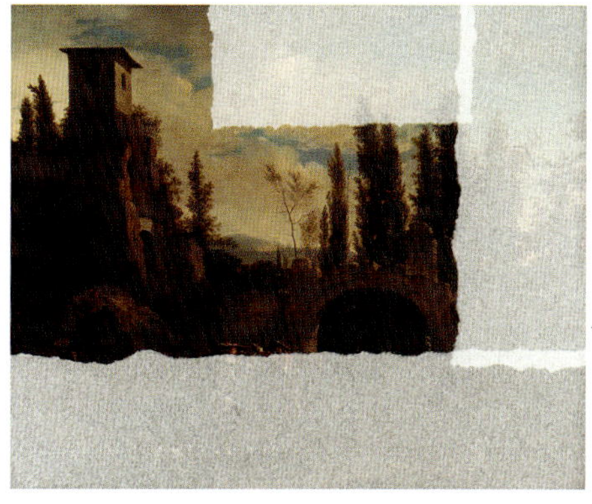

Schellinks, Willem 1627–1678
A Hawking Party by a Ruined Bridge
oil on canvas 62.5 x 78.1
616

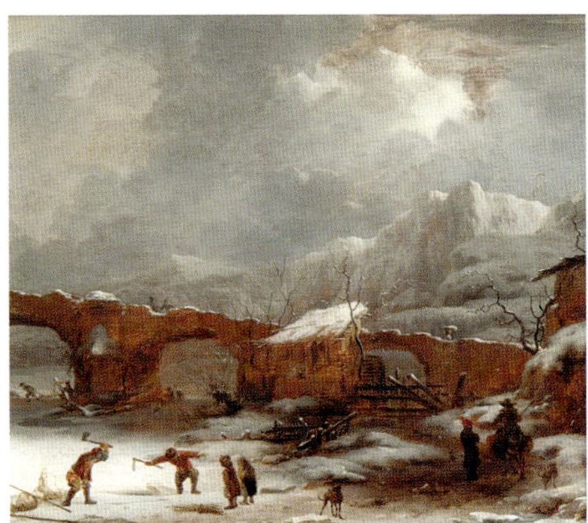

Schellinks, Willem 1627–1678
A Winter Landscape with the Pont du Rhone, Lyons
oil on panel 29 x 32.8
20

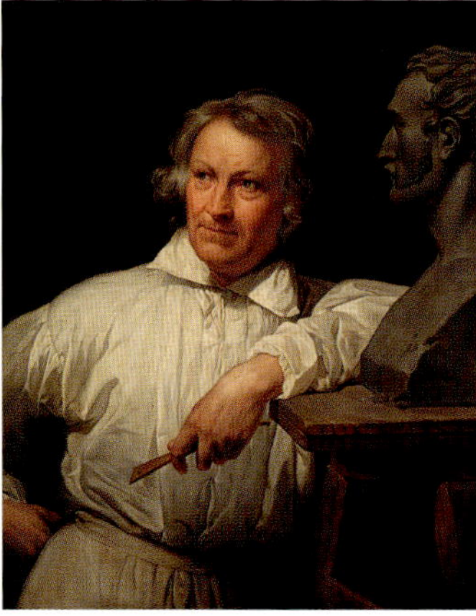

Schenström, Christian Wilhelm 1828–1876
Bertel Thorvaldsen (1770–1844), Sculptor (after Horace Vernet) 1857
oil on canvas 99.1 x 77.8
413

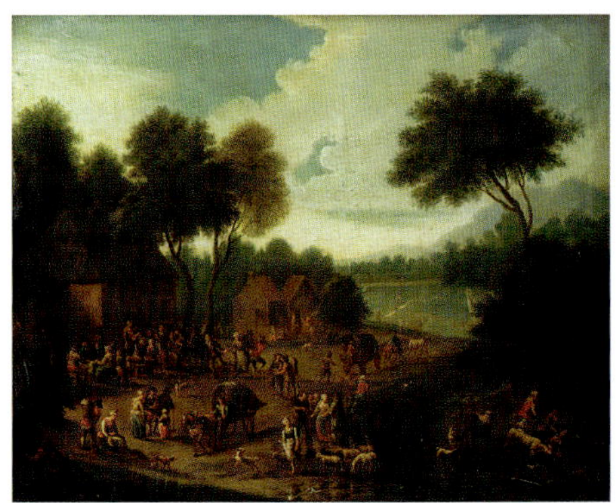

Schoevaerdts, Mathys (attributed to) c.1665–1723
A Village Festival
oil on canvas 38.7 x 46
1465

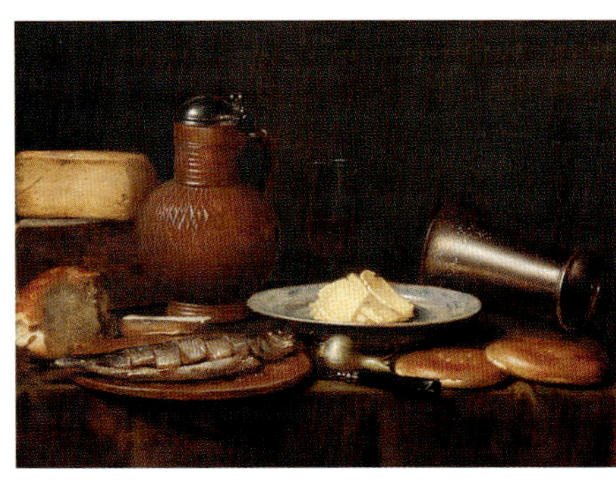

Schooten, Floris Gerritsz. van c.1585–after 1655
Still Life, a Breakfast Piece
oil on panel 40 x 55.9
2478

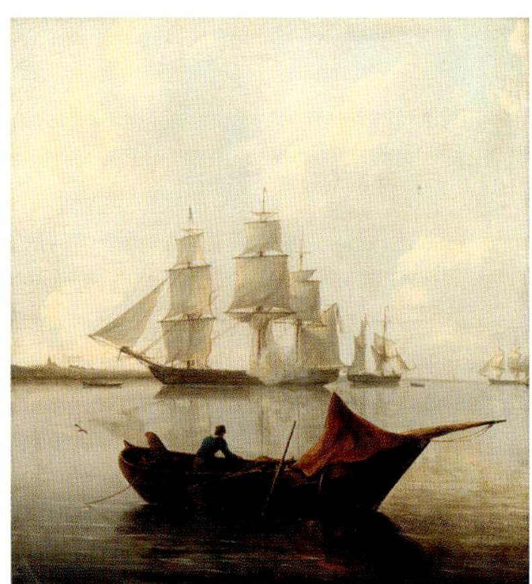

Schouman, Martinus 1770–1848
A Frigate and Other Vessels Becalmed Inshore c.1815–1825
oil on panel 51.4 x 40.6
1209

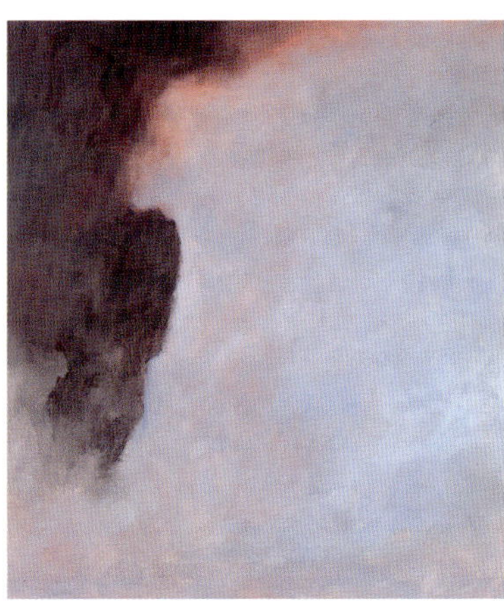

Schueler, Jon 1916–1992
The Search: Black Shadow Blues, IV (...) 1981
oil on canvas 152.4 x 132.1
3372

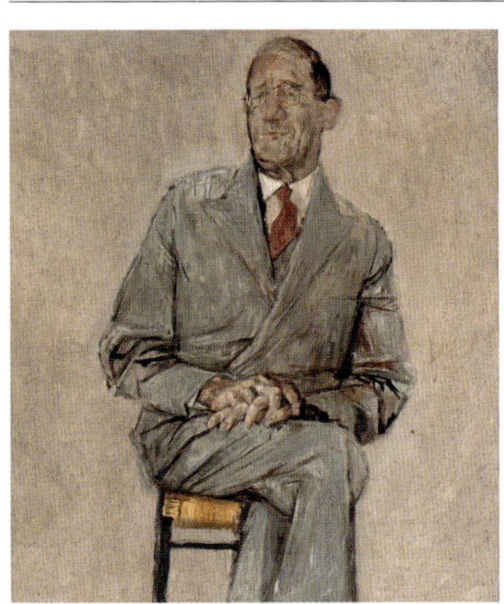

Schwarz, Hans 1922–2003
Sir Eric Ashby (1904–1992), Master of Clare College, Cambridge 1962
oil on hardboard 121.9 x 106.9
3195

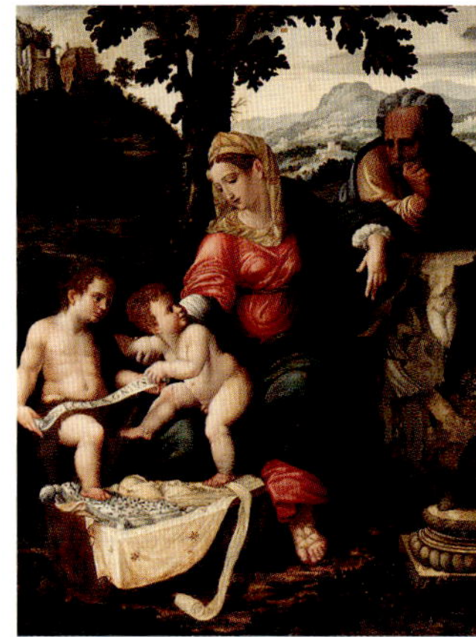

Scorel, Jan van (circle of) 1495–1562
The Holy Family and Saint John the Baptist under an Oak Tree (after Raphael) c.1518–1530
oil on panel 142.2 x 109
279

Scott, David 1806–1849
Nimrod c.1832
oil on canvas 177.8 x 140.3
3369

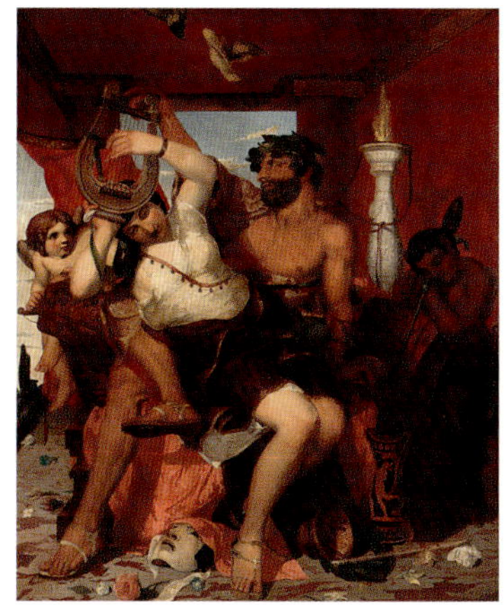

Scott, David 1806–1849
Sappho and Anacreon c.1835
oil on canvas 182 x 145.5
3050

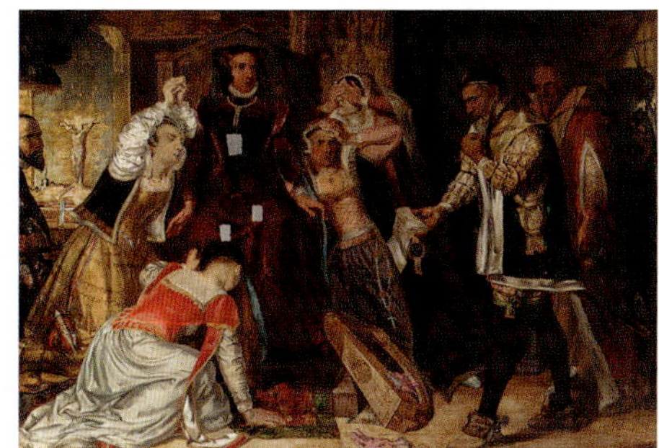

Scott, David 1806–1849
Mary, Queen of Scots, Receiving the Warrant for Her Execution 1840
oil on canvas 188 x 269.2
1687

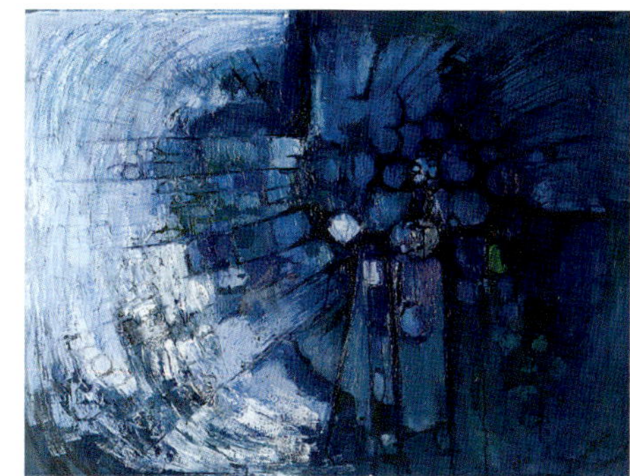

Scott, Frieda Ewart active 1970–2006
Blue Abstract 1970
oil on hardboard 76.2 x 101.3
3275

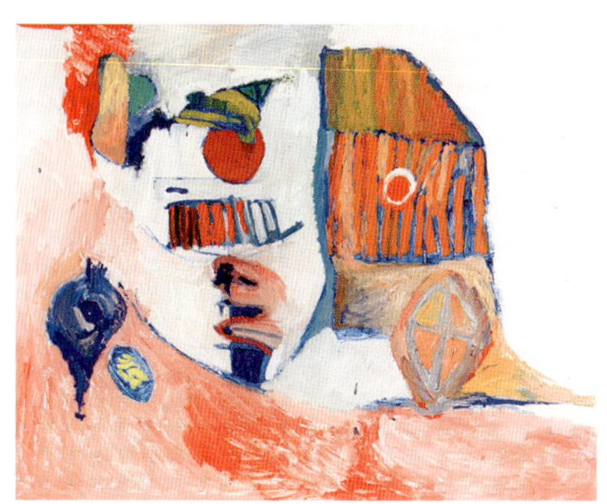

Scott, Lewis
Untitled
oil on canvas 159 x 189
TEMP.14958

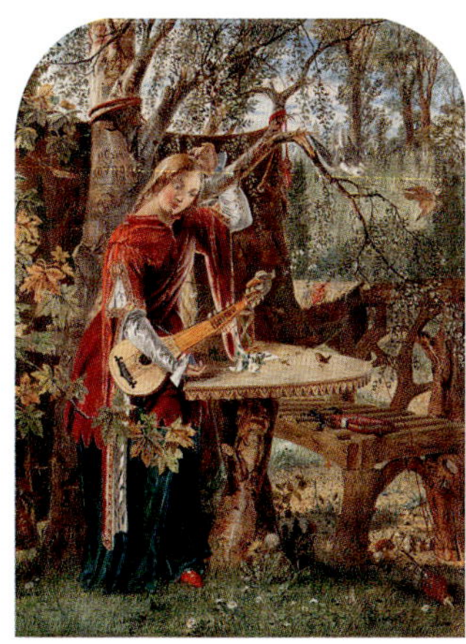

Scott, William Bell 1811–1890
Fair Rosamond Alone in Her Bower c.1853
oil on canvas 68 x 51.4
3387

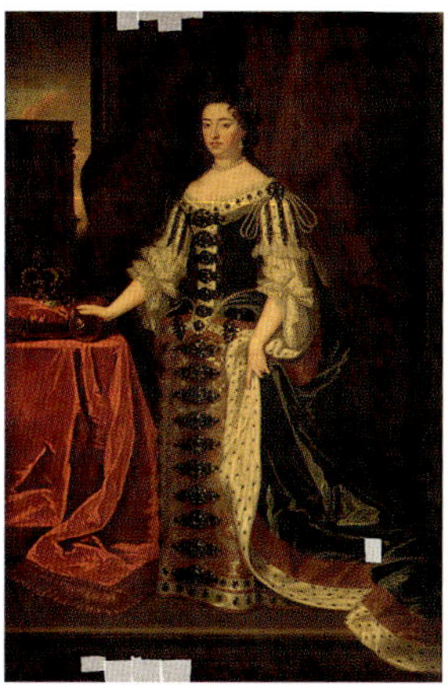

Scougal, John c.1645–1730
Mary II (1662–1694) 1707–1708
oil on canvas 238.8 x 157.4
481

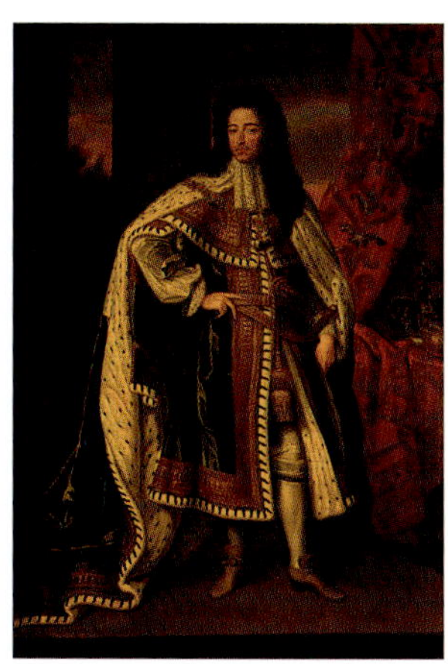

Scougal, John c.1645–1730
William III (1650–1702) 1707–1708
oil on canvas 238.8 x 158.8
480

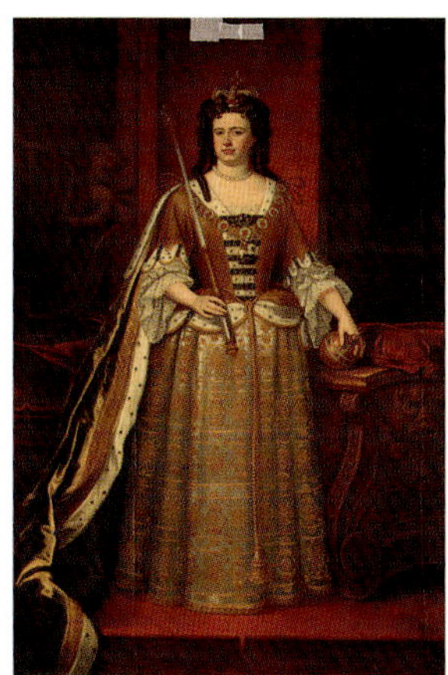

Scougal, John c.1645–1730
Queen Anne (1665–1714) 1712
oil on canvas 238.8 x 156.2
472

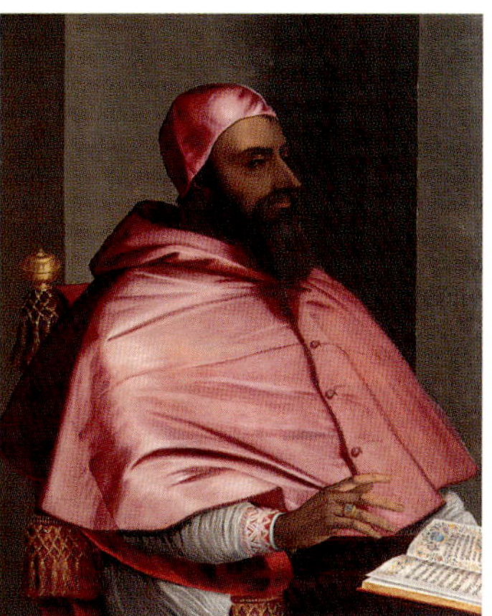

Sebastiano del Piombo (after) c.1485–1547
Pope Clement VII (1478–1534) c.1530–1540
oil on panel 107.5 x 84.8
PC.5

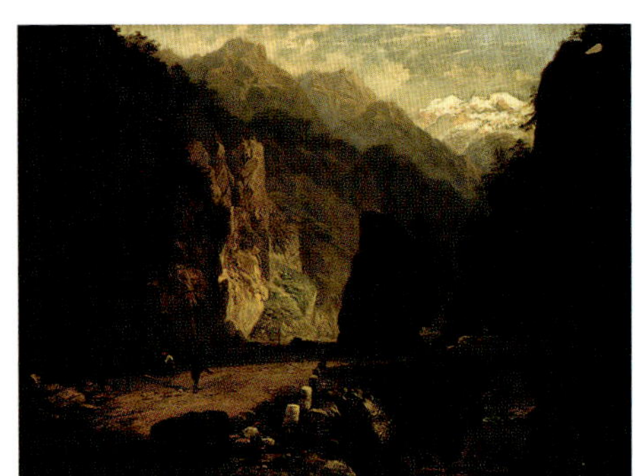

Selous, Henry Courtney 1803–1890
The Pass of the Simeron, Switzerland
oil on canvas 45.7 x 61
445

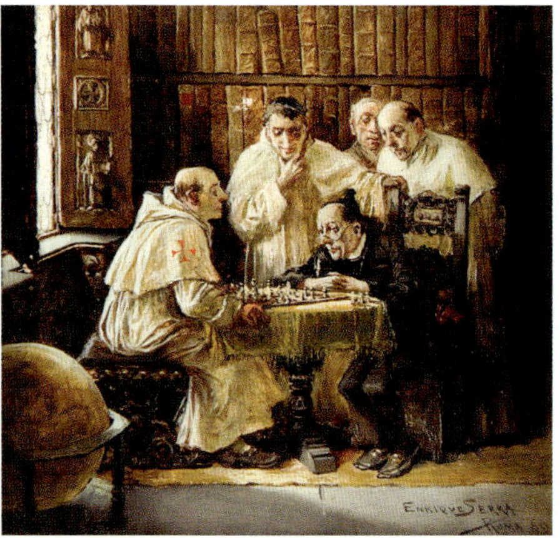

Serra, Enrique 1859–1918
The Chess Players 1889
oil on panel 12.6 x 13.5
1163

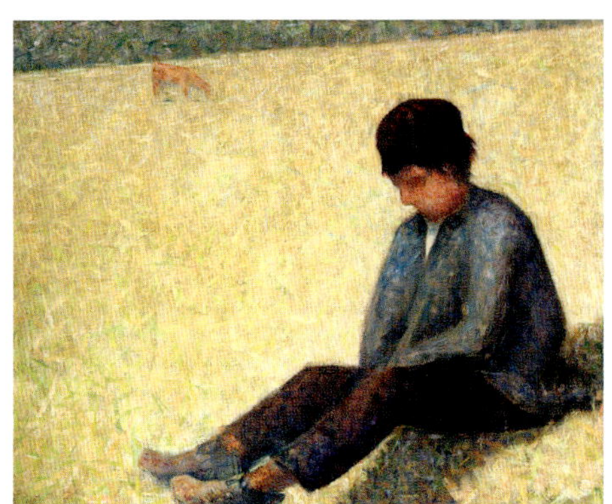

Seurat, Georges 1859–1891
Boy Sitting in a Meadow c.1882–1883
oil on canvas 63.5 x 79.6
2857

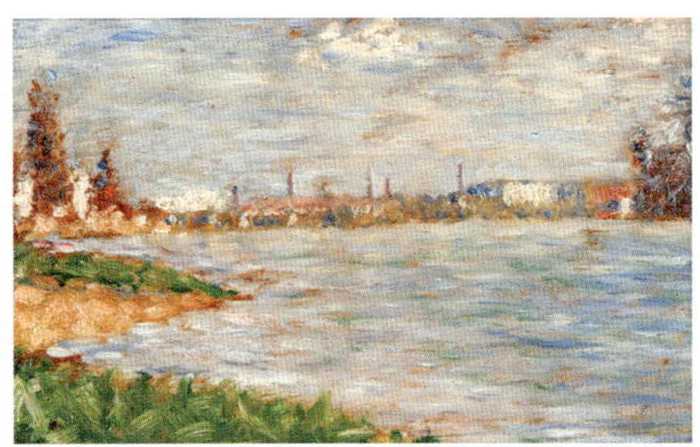

Seurat, Georges 1859–1891
The Riverbanks c.1882–1883
oil on panel 16 x 25
2422

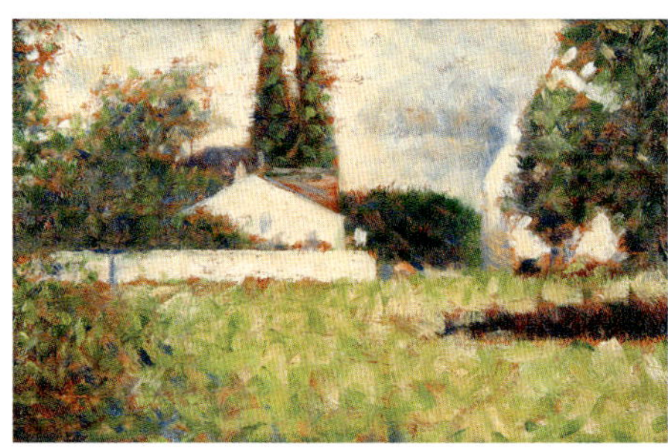

Seurat, Georges 1859–1891
House among Trees c.1883
oil on panel 15.6 x 25.1
2421

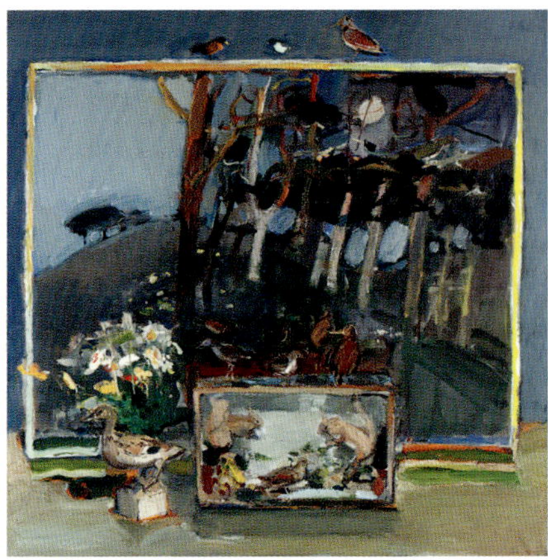

Shanks, Duncan b.1937
Night Wood with Birds and Squirrels 1974
oil on canvas 177.2 x 172.7
3638

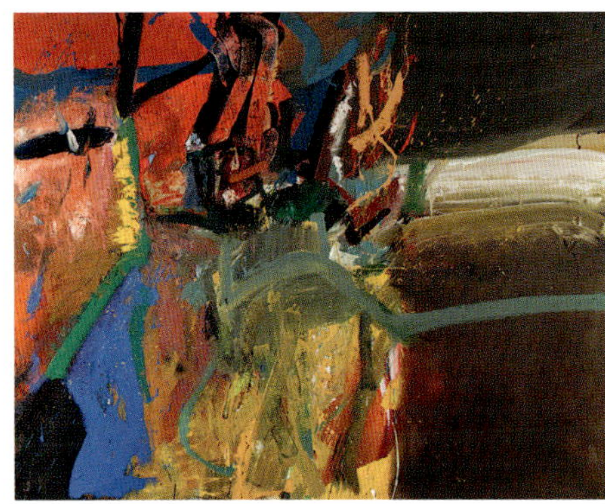

Shanks, Duncan b.1937
Into the Storm c.1982–1984
oil on canvas 198.1 x 243.9
3406

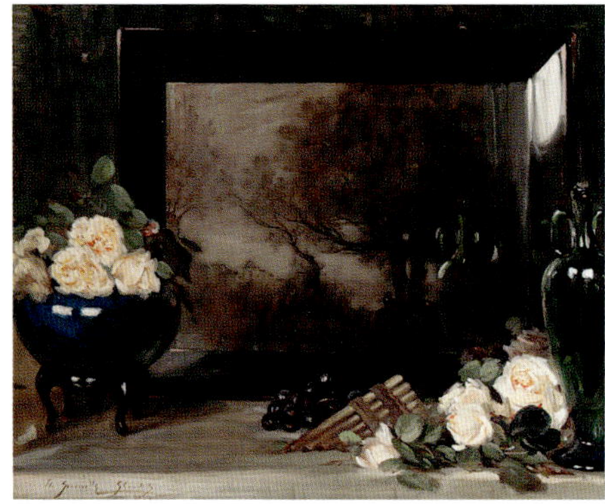

Shanks, William Somerville 1864–1951
Pipes of Pan c.1919
oil on canvas 63.5 x 76.2
1473

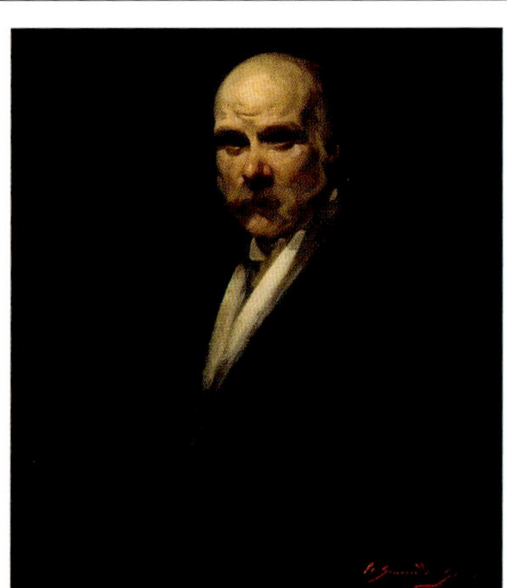

Shanks, William Somerville 1864–1951
John Q. Pringle (1864–1925) c.1920–1924
oil on canvas 76.2 x 63.5
1578

Facing page: Turner, Joseph Mallord William, 1775–1851, *Modern Italy: The Pifferari*, 1838 (p. 420)

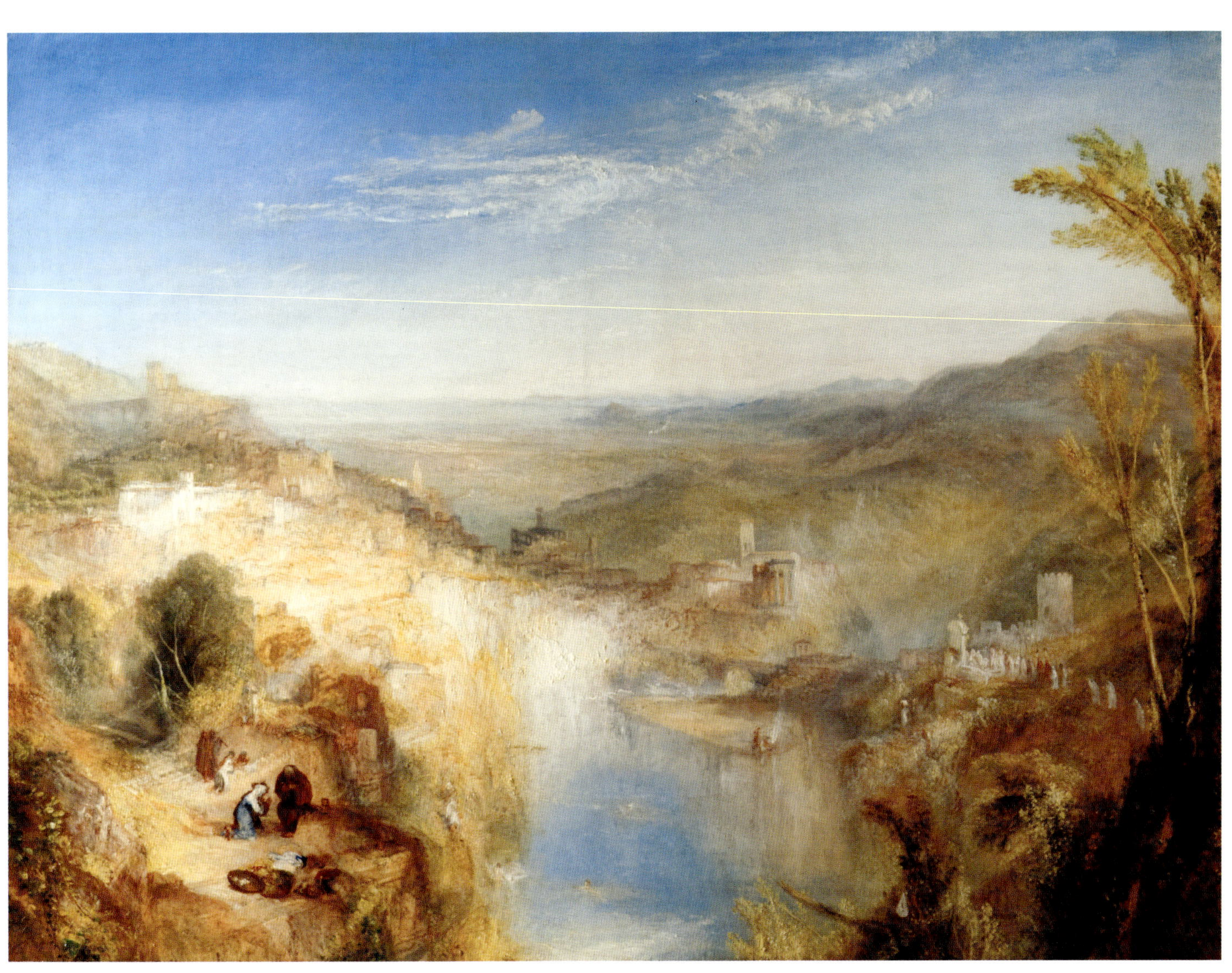

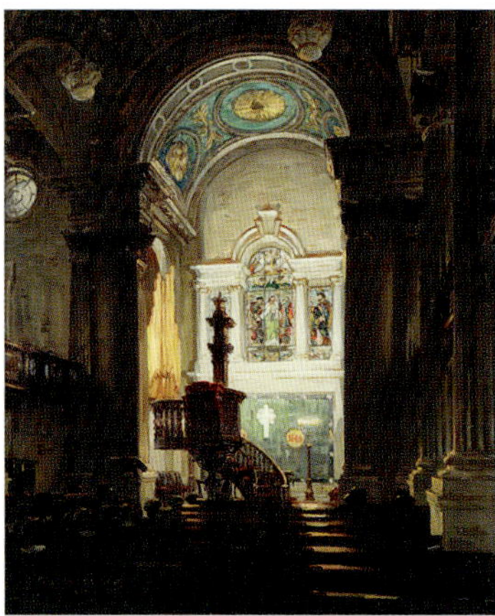

Shanks, William Somerville 1864–1951
*The Chancel, St Andrew's Parish Church,
Glasgow* c.1935
oil on canvas 76.2 x 63.5
1926

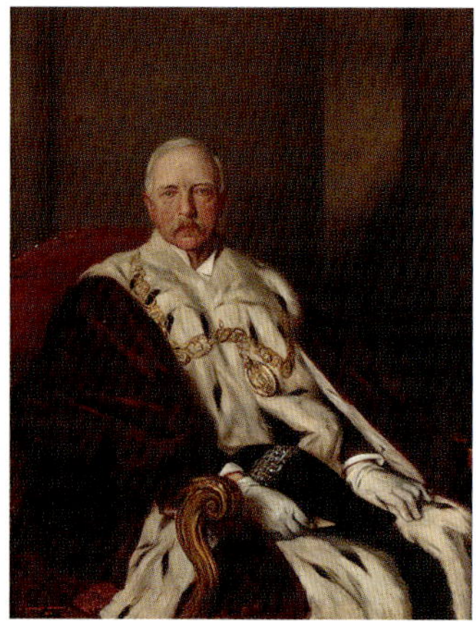

Shannon, Charles Haslewood 1863–1937
*Sir Matthew W. Montgomery (1859–1933),
Lord Provost of Glasgow (1923–1926)* 1926
oil on canvas 127 x 101.6
1684

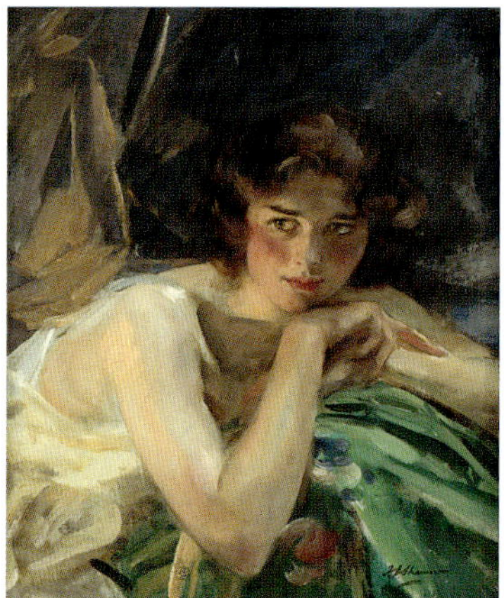

Shannon, James Jebusa 1862–1923
Flora c.1922
oil on canvas 69.9 x 59.7
1756

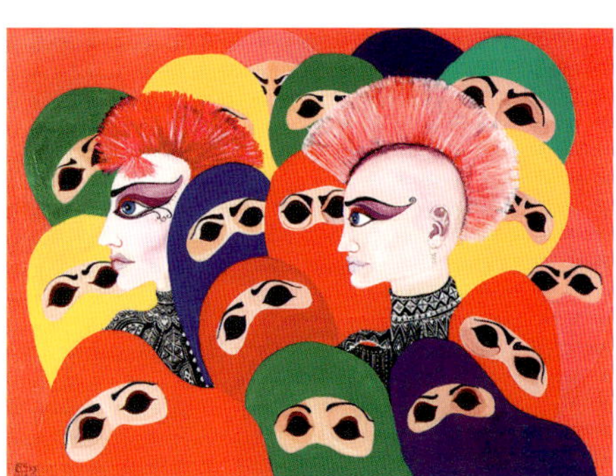

Shawa, Laila b.1940
Aliens? 1988
oil on canvas 76 x 102
3599

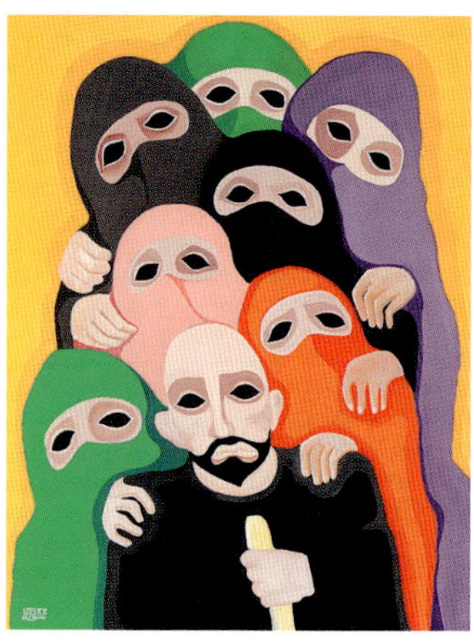

Shawa, Laila b.1940
The Blind Leading the Blind! 1988
oil on canvas 102 x 76
3600

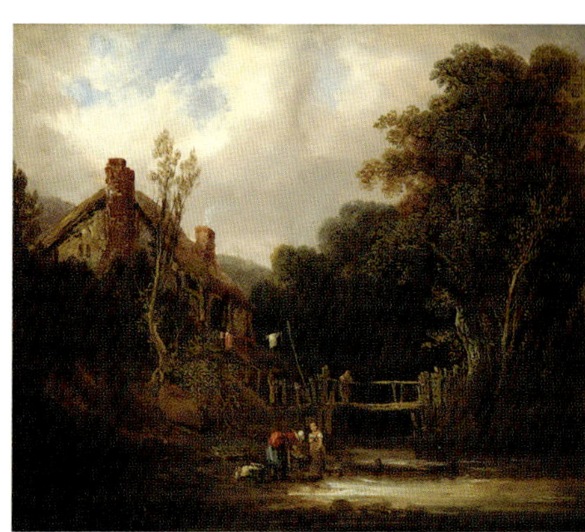

Shayer, William 1788–1879
A Woody Stream 1846
oil on board 24.8 x 29.2
1364

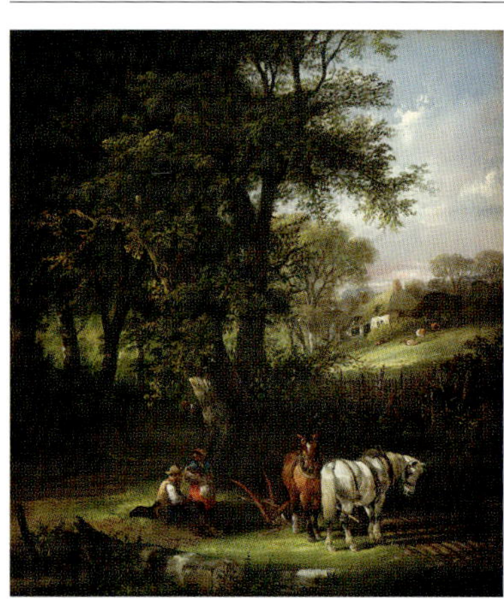

Shayer, William 1788–1879
Ploughing 1846
oil on canvas 34.9 x 29.8
1370

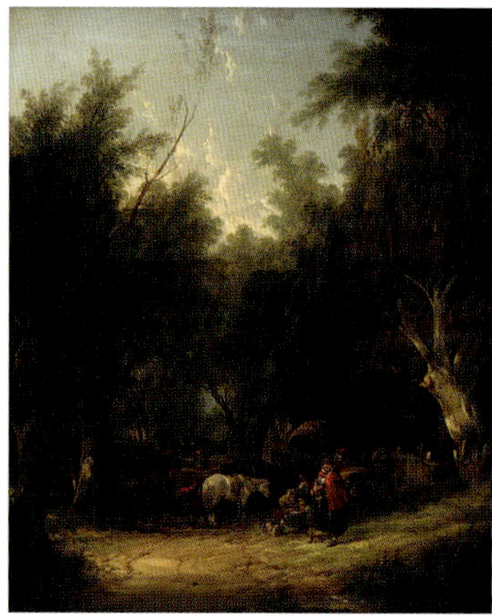

Shayer, William 1788–1879
Gypsy Encampment
oil on canvas 59.1 x 48.9
953

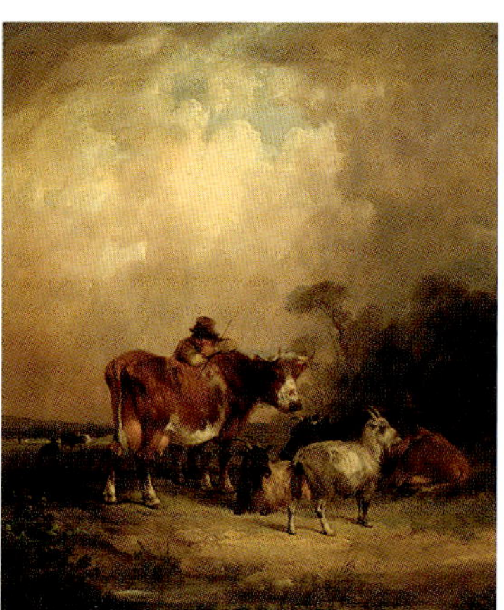

Shayer, William 1788–1879
Landscape with Cattle
oil on panel 34.3 x 29.2
348

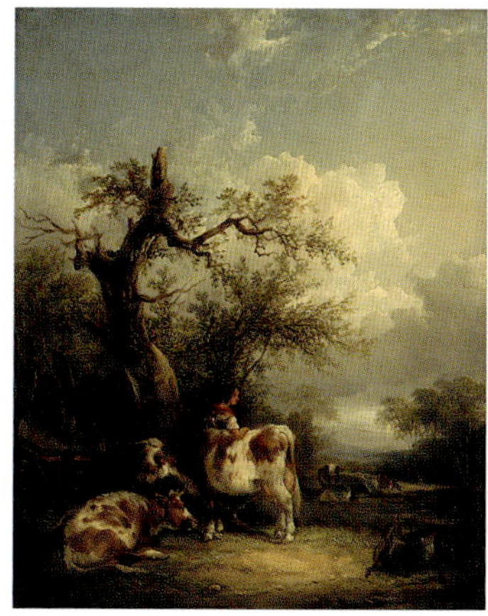

Shayer, William 1788–1879
Landscape with Cattle
oil on millboard 29.8 x 24.1
351

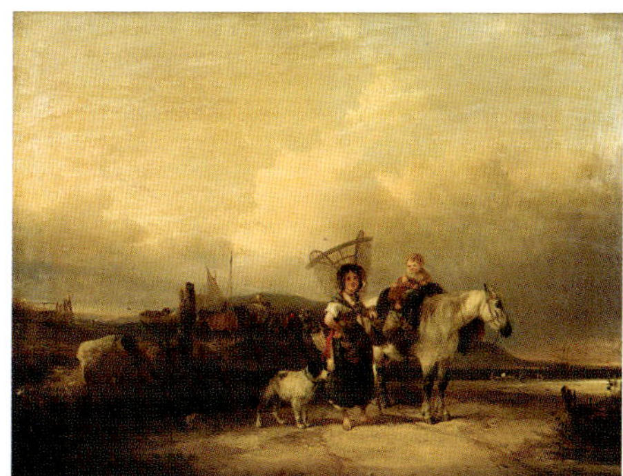

Shayer, William 1788–1879
The Shrimp Girl, Cornish Coast
oil on canvas 68.6 x 88.9
462

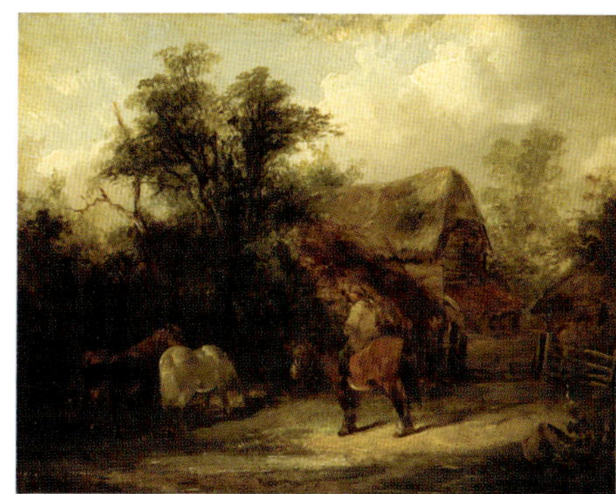

Shayer, William Joseph 1811–1892
A Shady Pool
oil on millboard 13.3 x 17.1
455

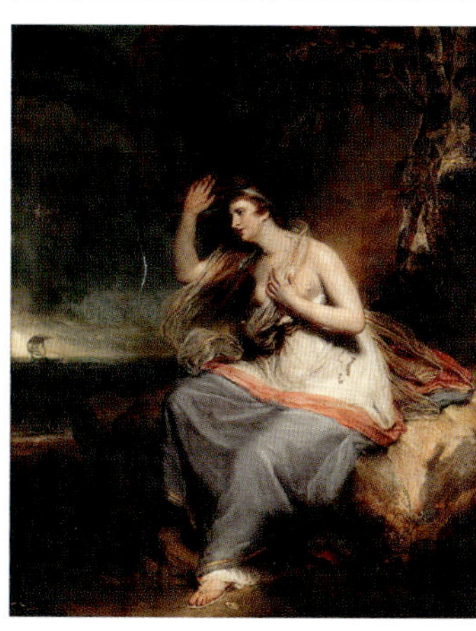

Shee, Martin Archer 1769–1850
Ariadne Deserted by Theseus 1834
oil on canvas 124.5 x 99.1
359

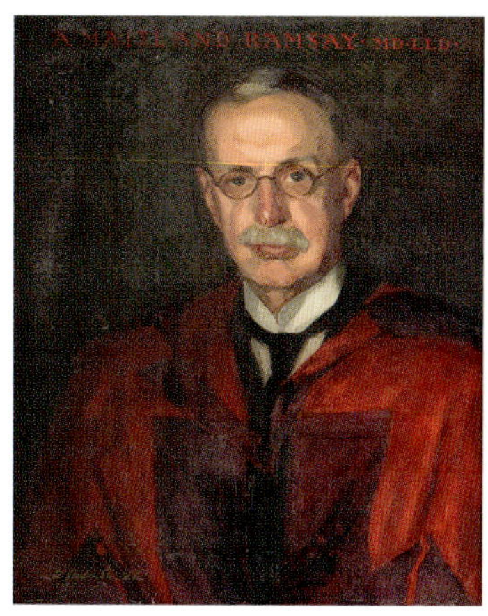

Shields, Douglas Gordon 1888–1943
A. Maitland Ramsay (1859–1946), MD 1927
oil on canvas 61 x 50.8
3006

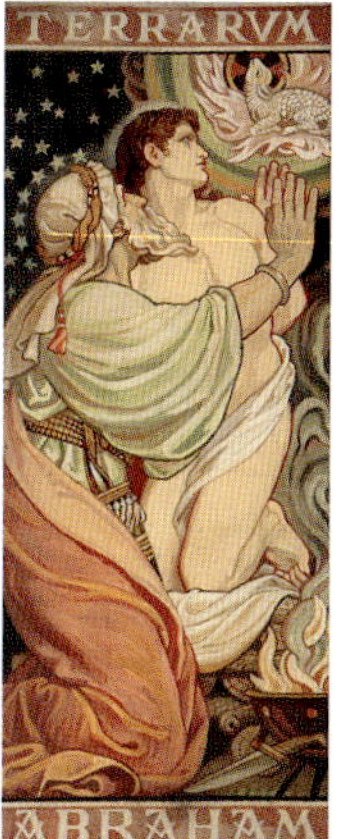

Shields, Frederick James 1833–1911
Abraham
oil on canvas 125.7 x 50.8
PR.1944.12.b

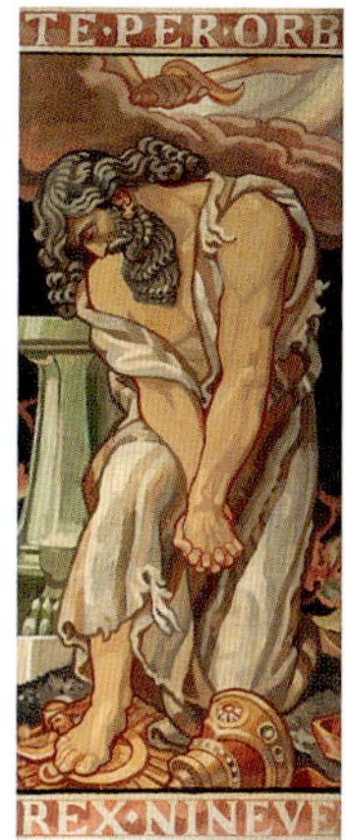

Shields, Frederick James 1833–1911
Rex Nineveh
oil on canvas 125.7 x 50.8
PR.1944.12.a

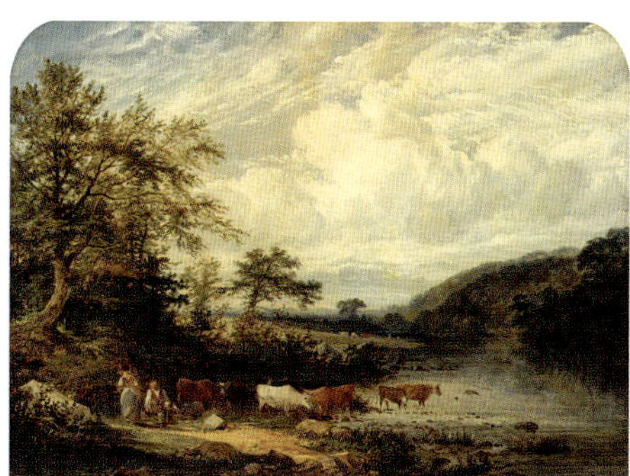

Shipham, Benjamin 1808–1872
Landscape with Cattle and Figures 1862
oil on canvas 47 x 64.8
810

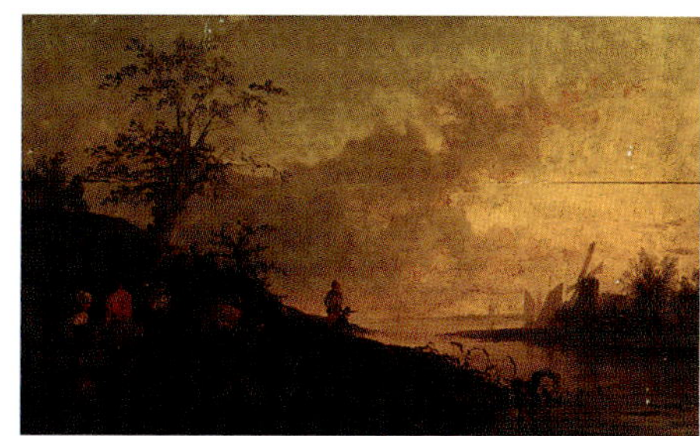

Shirley, Henry d.1870 & **Will, H. B.**
Dutch River Scene
oil on panel 64.8 x 105.4
360

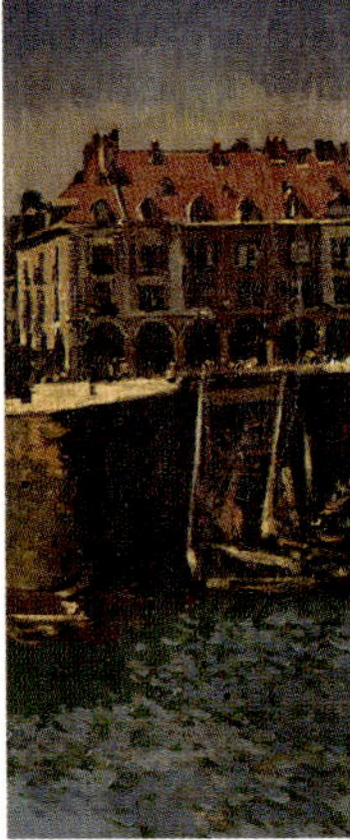

Sickert, Walter Richard 1860–1942
Dieppe Harbour c.1902
oil on canvas 151.1 x 61
2831

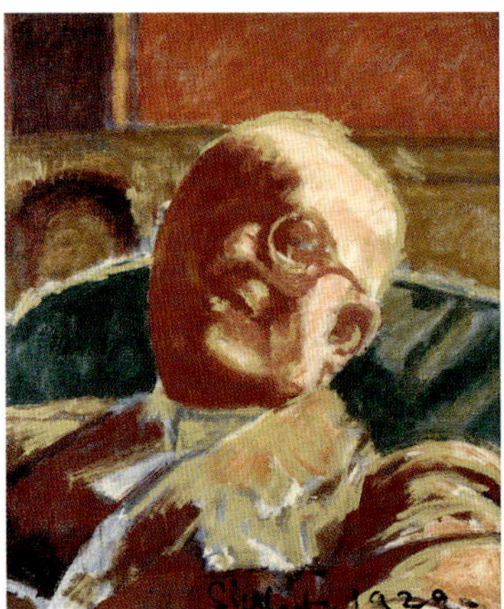

Sickert, Walter Richard 1860–1942
Sir Hugh Walpole (1884–1941) 1929
oil on canvas 76.2 x 63.5
2607

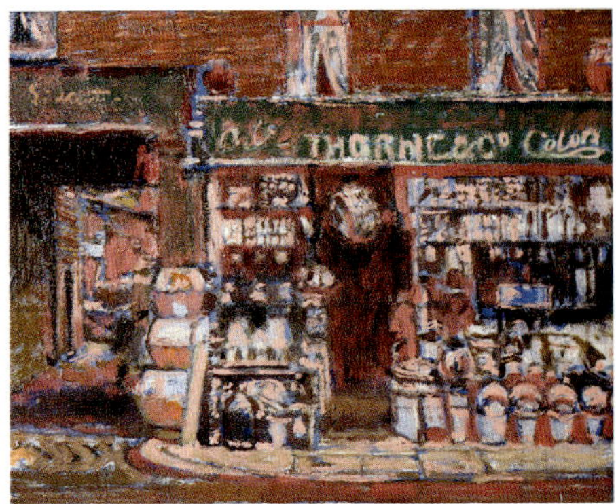

Sickert, Walter Richard 1860–1942
Barnsbury c.1931
oil on canvas 50.8 x 61
1823

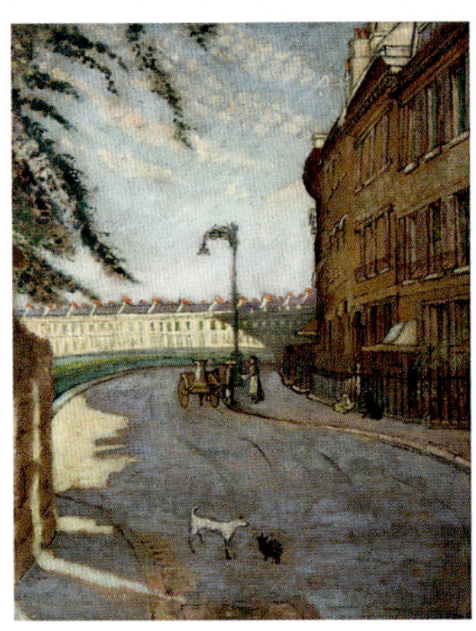

Sickert, Walter Richard (style of)
1860–1942
Lansdowne Crescent, Bath
oil on canvas 65.4 x 50.8
3144

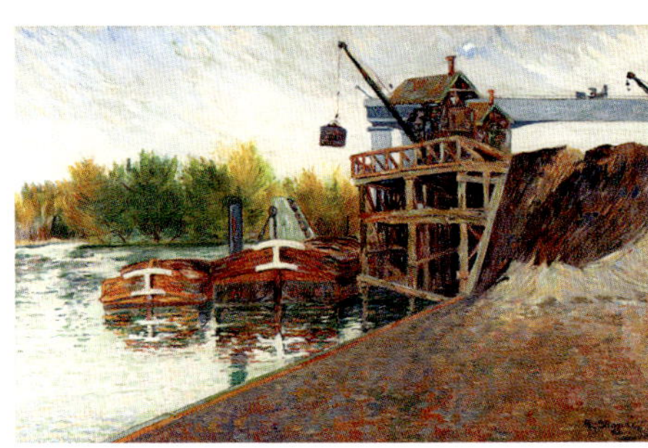

Signac, Paul 1863–1935
Coal Crane, Clichy 1884
oil on canvas 59 x 91.4
2574

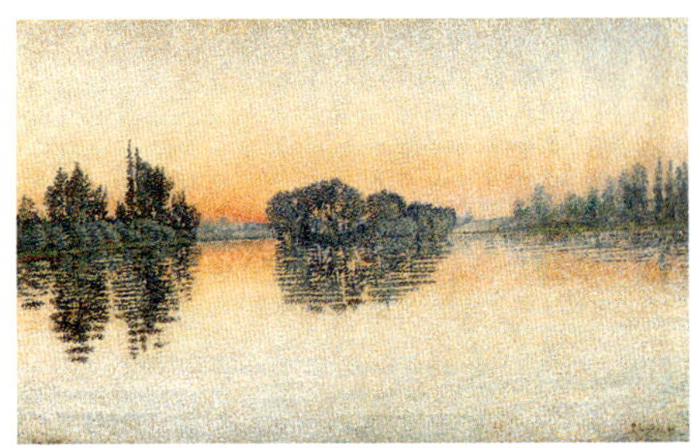

Signac, Paul 1863–1935
Sunset, Herblay, Opus 206 1889
oil on canvas 57.1 x 90
3324

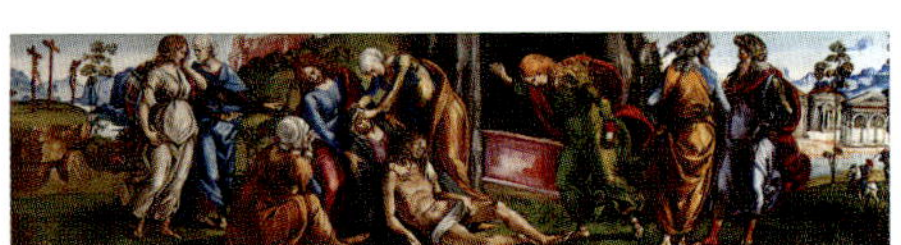

Signorelli, Luca c.1450–1523
Lamentation over the Dead Christ
c.1488–1490
tempera on panel 29.8 x 119.1
PC.25

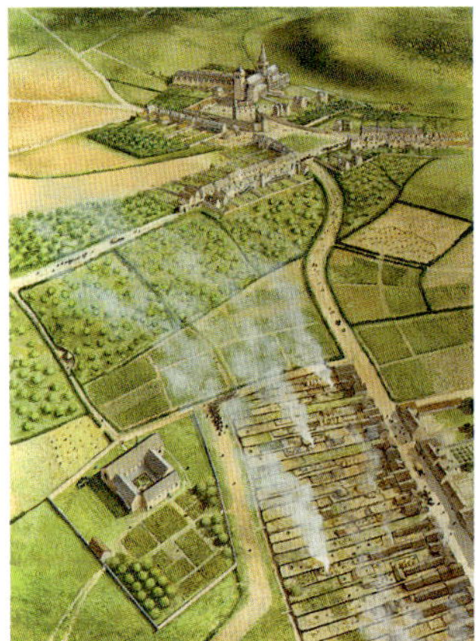

Simon, David active 20th C
*Shuttle Street, Franciscan Friary
Reconstruction Illustration*
oil on paper 91 x 66
SP.2006.89

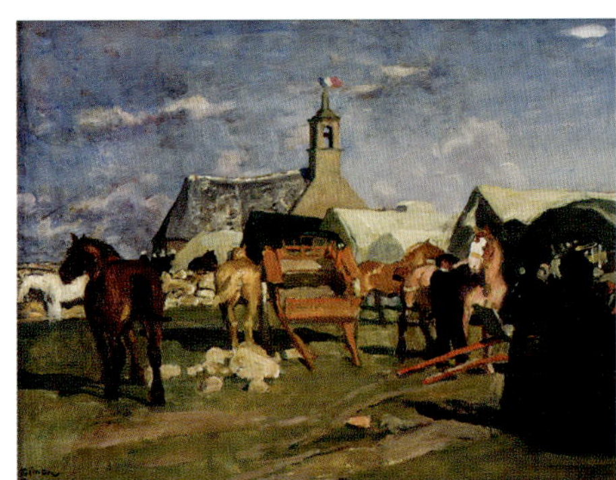

Simon, Lucien 1861–1945
Staging Post c.1913
oil on canvas 48.2 x 62.7
2423

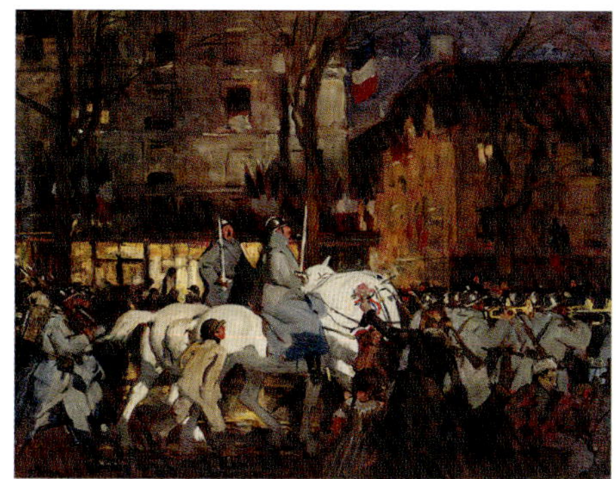

Simon, Lucien 1861–1945
After the War c.1919
oil on canvas 85.2 x 118.5
2794

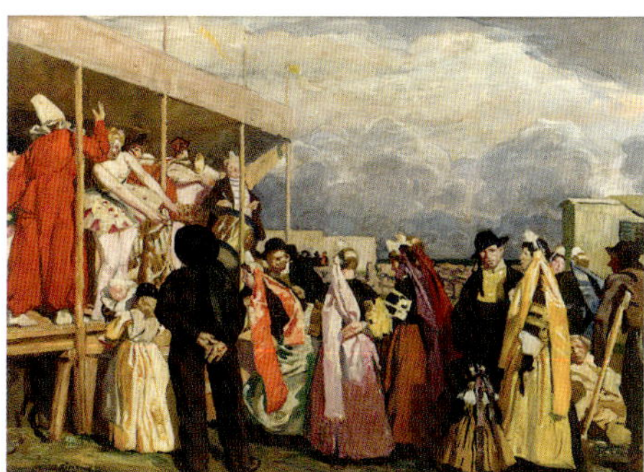

Simon, Lucien 1861–1945
The Fair
oil on canvas 134.6 x 179.1
35.622

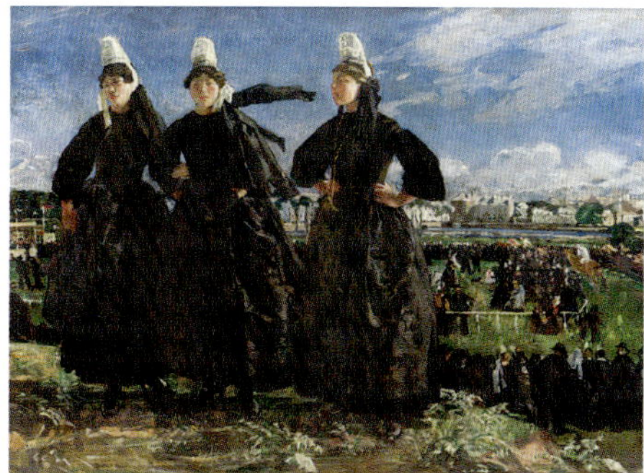

Simon, Lucien 1861–1945
The Races
oil on canvas 134.6 x 182.8
35.623

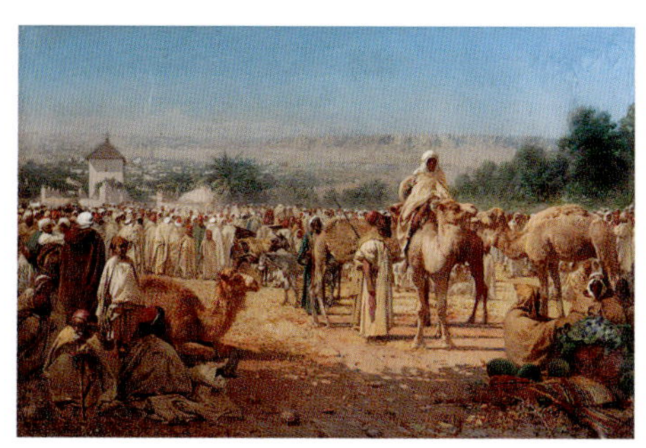

Simoni, Gustavo 1846–1926
Eastern Festival 1883
oil on canvas 58.9 x 86.3
832

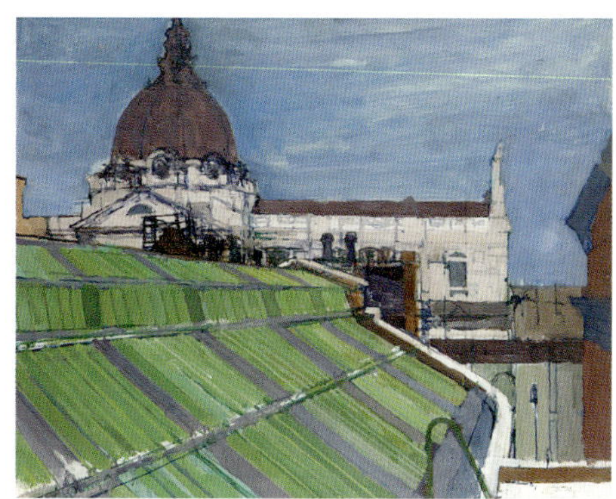

Simpson, Ian 1933–2011
The Green Roof 1963
oil on hardboard 75.9 x 91.4
3178

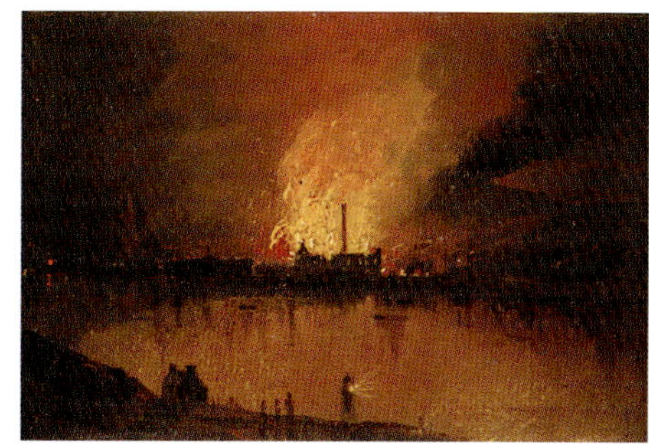

Simpson, Robert
Fire at Trades Lane Warehouses 1870
oil on card 8 x 12
NR.144

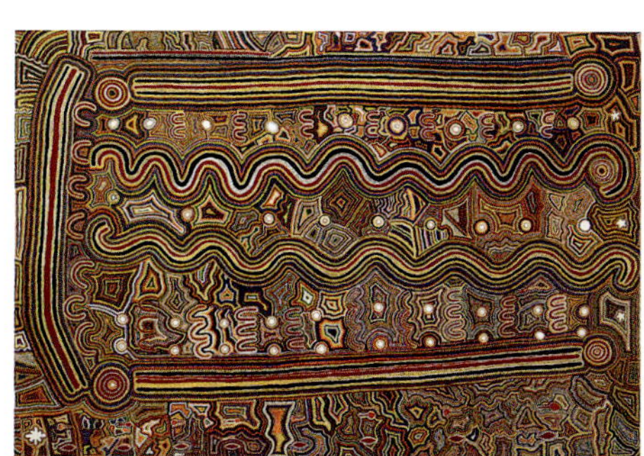

Sims, Paddy Japaljarri b.c.1916
The Night Sky Dreaming 1992
acrylic on canvas 280.5 x 405.7
3520

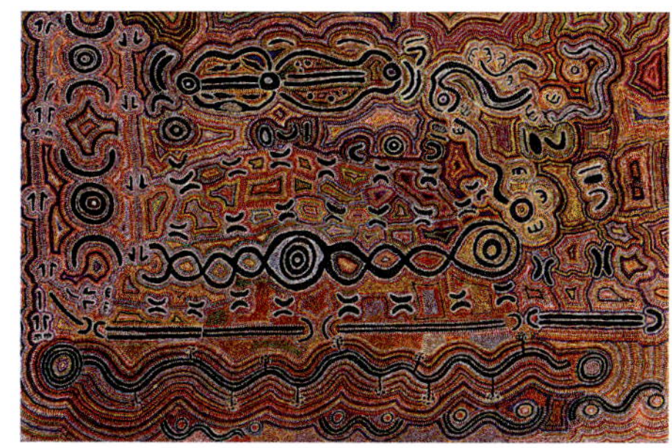

Sims, Paddy Japaljarri b.c.1916 & **Sims, Bessie Nakamarra** b.c.1932
Kangaroo, Wild Cabbage, Cermonial Speer, Possum and Bush Carrot Dreaming 1992
acrylic on canvas 122 x 183
3517

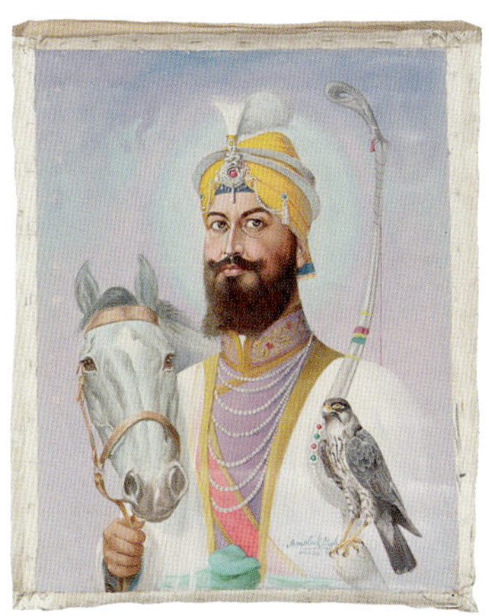

Singh, Amoca active 20th C
Guru Gobind Singh
oil on canvas 92 x 77
A.1993.7.n

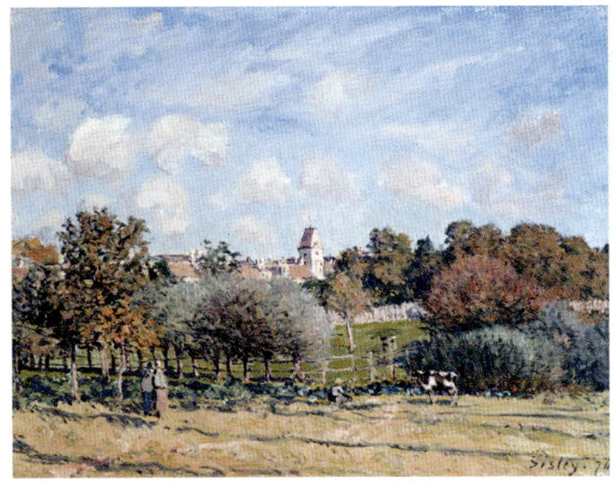

Sisley, Alfred 1839–1899
The Bell Tower at Noisy-le-Roi, Autumn 1874
oil on canvas 45.7 x 61
35.625

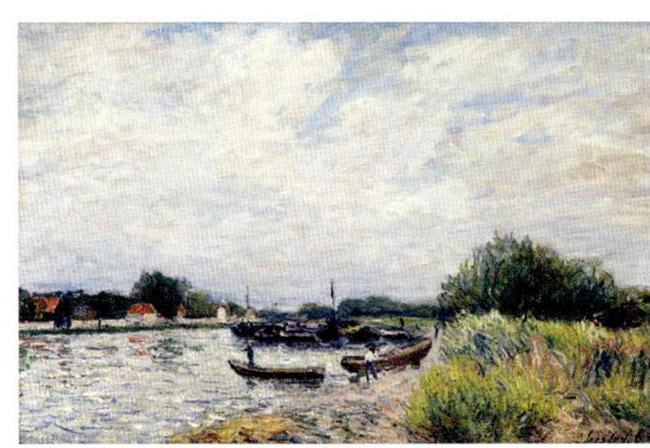

Sisley, Alfred 1839–1899
The Loing at Saint-Mammès 1883
oil on canvas 38.2 x 55.6
3661

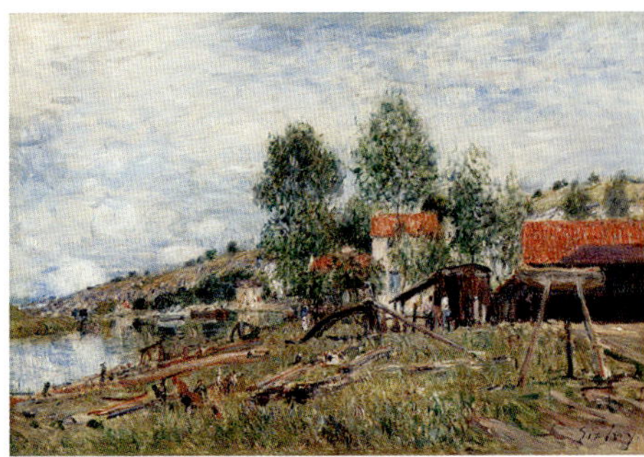

Sisley, Alfred 1839–1899
Boatyard at Saint-Mammès c.1886
oil on canvas 38.1 x 55.8
2464

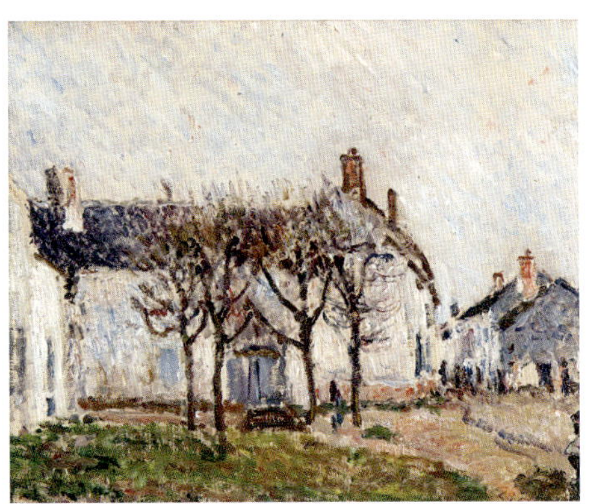

Sisley, Alfred 1839–1899
Village Street, Moret-sur-Loing c.1894
oil on canvas 35.1 x 46
2424

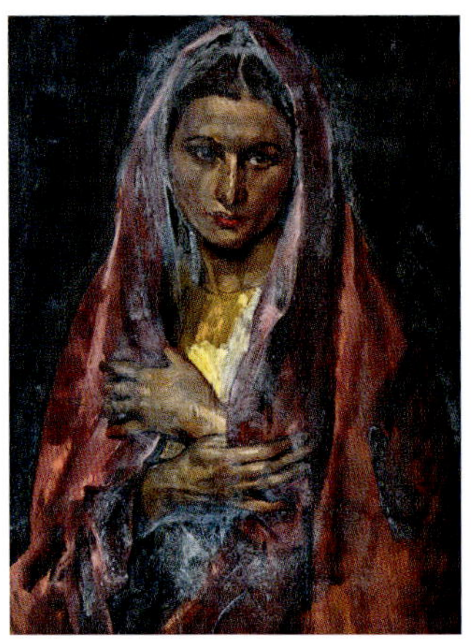

Sivell, Robert 1888–1958
Woman in a Shawl 1939
oil on panel 61 x 45.7
2314

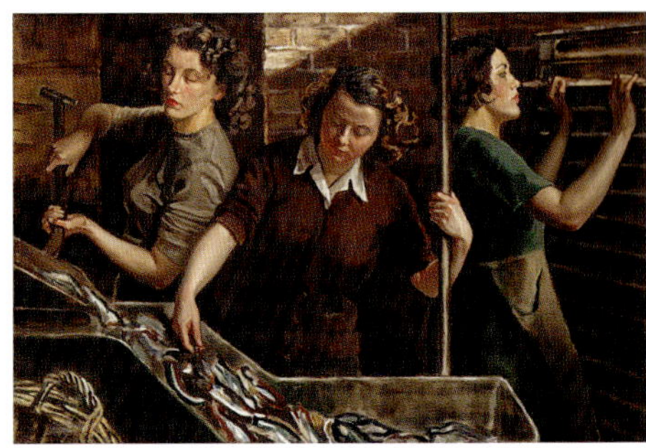

Sivell, Robert 1888–1958
Dehydration of Herrings 1943
oil on canvas 76.2 x 106.7
2769

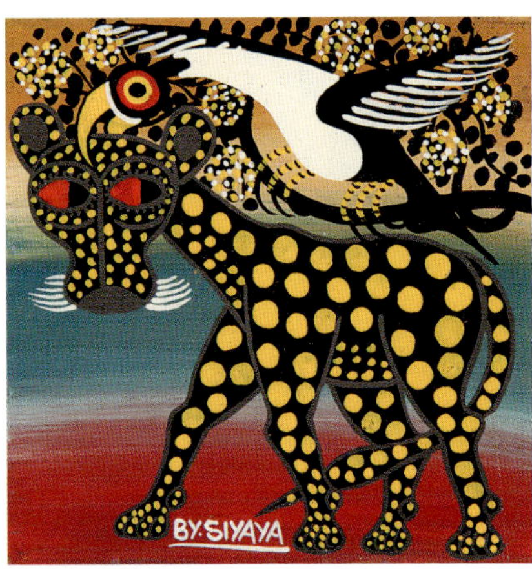

Siyaya, Steven active 20th C
Leopard and Bird in Tree
enamel on hardboard 15.3 x 14.7
A.1989.23.a

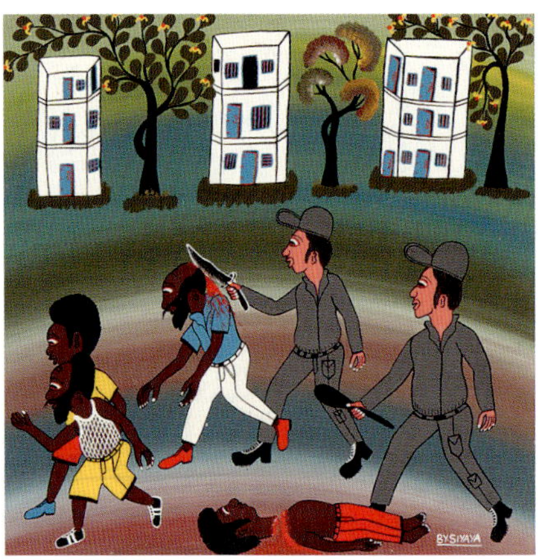

Siyaya, Steven active 20th C
Policemen Murdering African Men
enamel on hardboard 62 x 62
A.1989.23.r

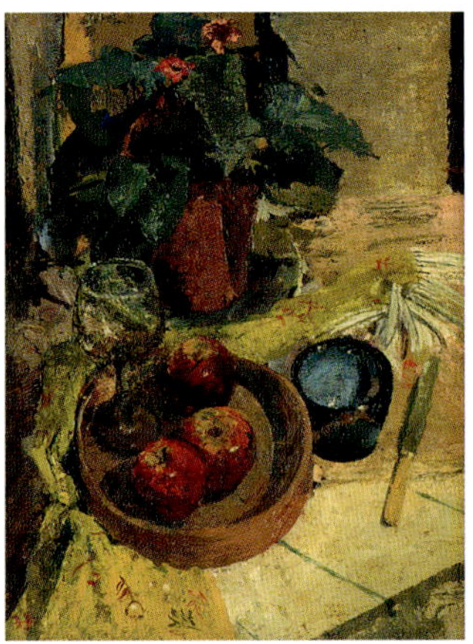

Slaney, Noel b.1915
The Three Red Apples 1953
oil on hardboard 60.3 x 44.8
3037

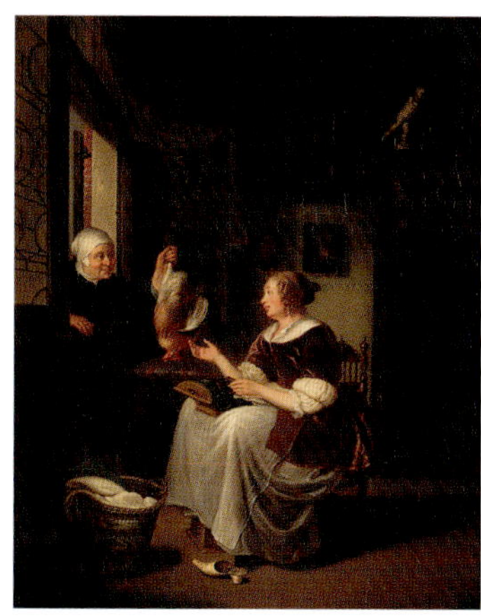

Slingeland, Pieter Cornelisz. van (after)
1640–1691
A Young Woman Rejecting the Offer of a Dead Fowl 19th C
oil on panel 38.4 x 30.2
1892

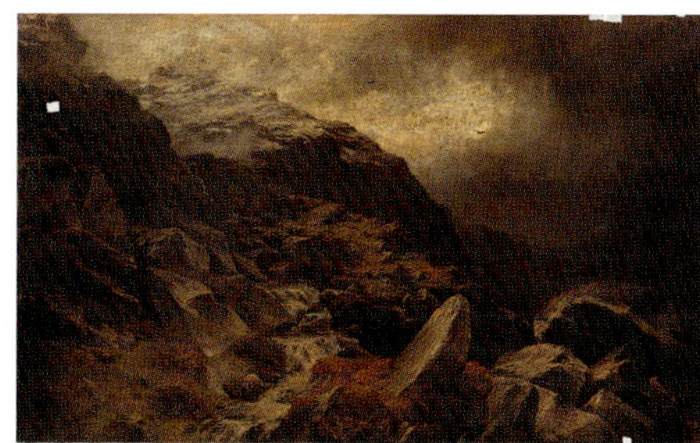

Smart, John 1838–1899
The Gloom of Glen Ogle 1875
oil on canvas 151.1 x 242.5
1066

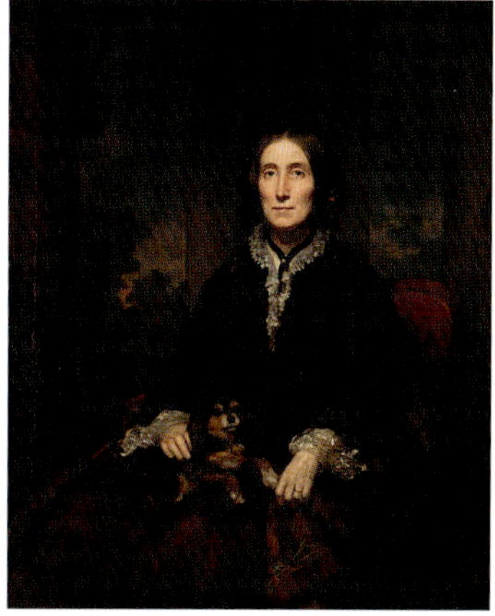

Smith, Colvin 1795–1875
Elizabeth Steven of Polmadie and Bellahouston
oil on canvas 142.2 x 110.5
743

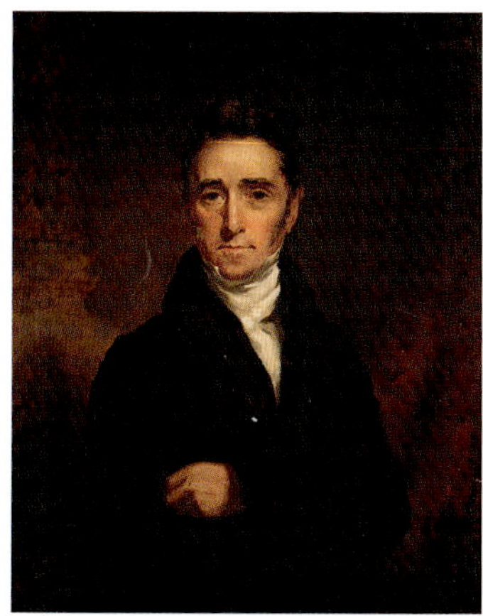

Smith, Colvin 1795–1875
Lord Jeffrey (1773–1850)
oil on canvas 91.4 x 68.6
452

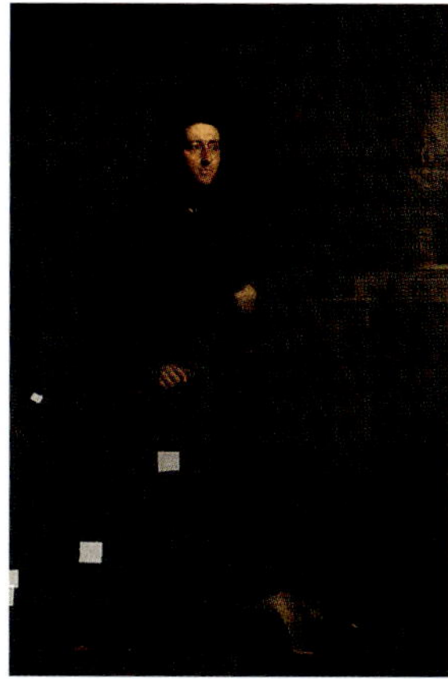

Smith, Colvin 1795–1875
Moses Steven of Polmadie and Bellahouston (1806–1871)
oil on canvas 246.4 x 156.2
742

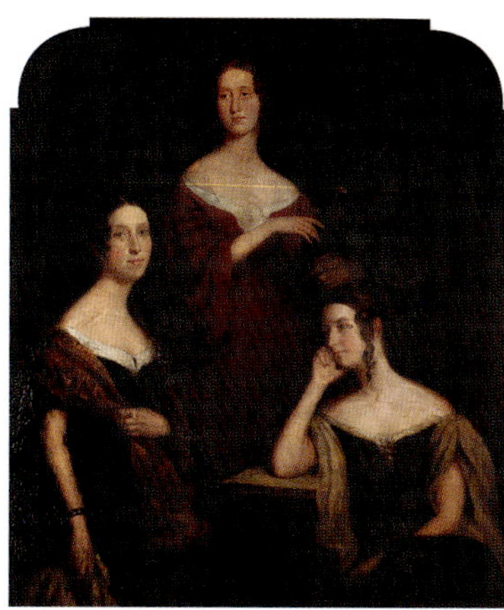

Smith, Colvin 1795–1875
The Daughters of Colin Campbell of Jura
oil on canvas 162.6 x 139.7
2501

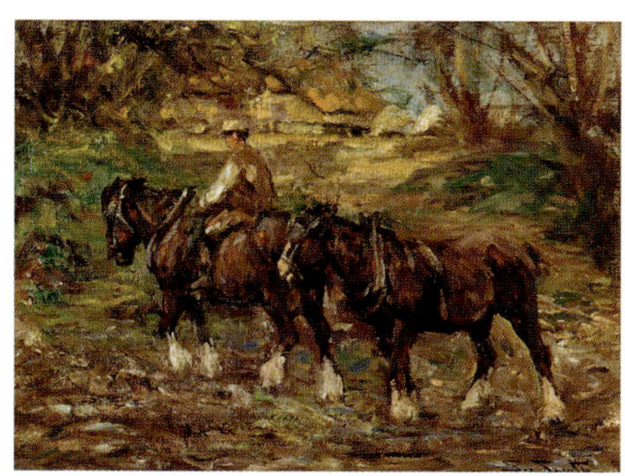

Smith, George 1870–1934
Farm Horses
oil on board 30.5 x 40.6
2837

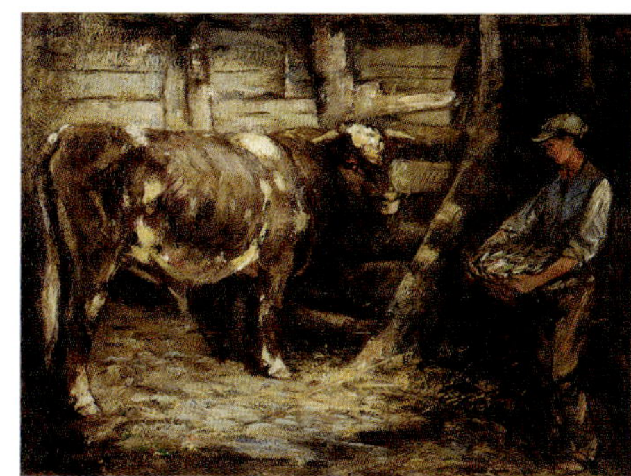

Smith, George 1870–1934
Feeding Time
oil on board 30.5 x 40.6
2836

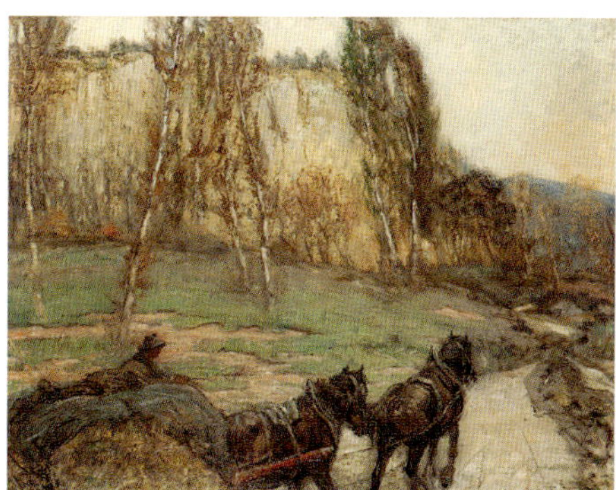

Smith, George 1870–1934
The Winding Road
oil on canvas 101.6 x 127
2123

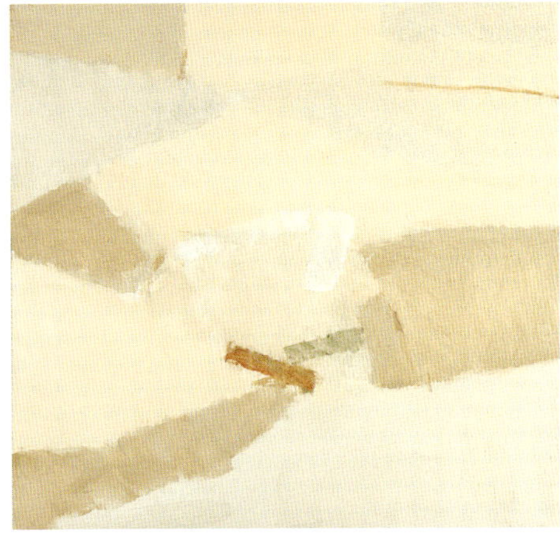

Smith, Ian McKenzie b.1935
West Sea c.1972
oil on canvas 60.8 x 60.8
3301

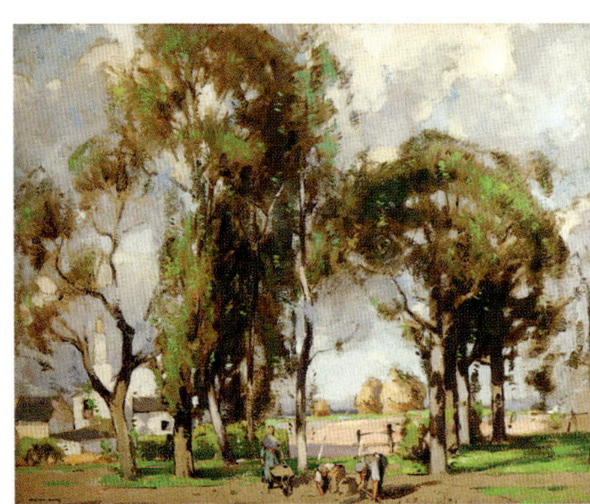

Smith, John Guthrie Spence 1880–1951
A Midlothian Farm c.1925
oil on millboard 63.5 x 76.2
2469

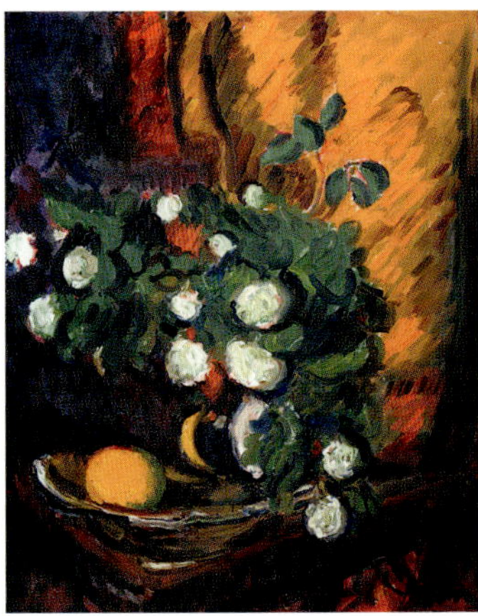

Smith, Matthew Arnold Bracey 1879–1959
Flowers c.1949
oil on canvas 91.4 x 71.1
2982

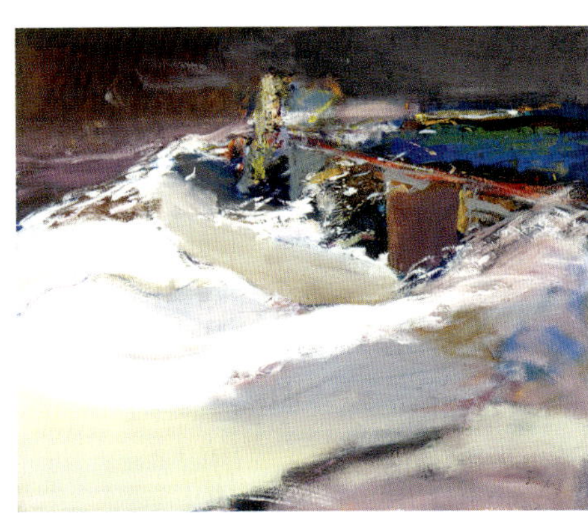

Smith, Ronald F. b.1946
Powerful Sea, St Andrews 1972
oil on canvas 81 x 96.2
3293

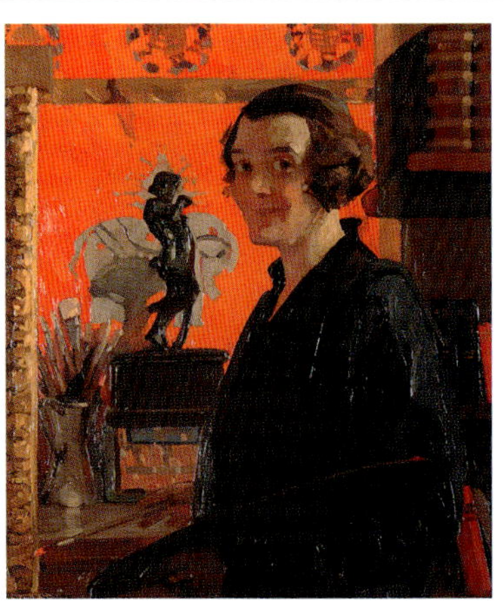

Smyth, Dorothy Carleton 1880–1933
Self Portrait 1921
oil on canvas 76.8 x 68.6
2776

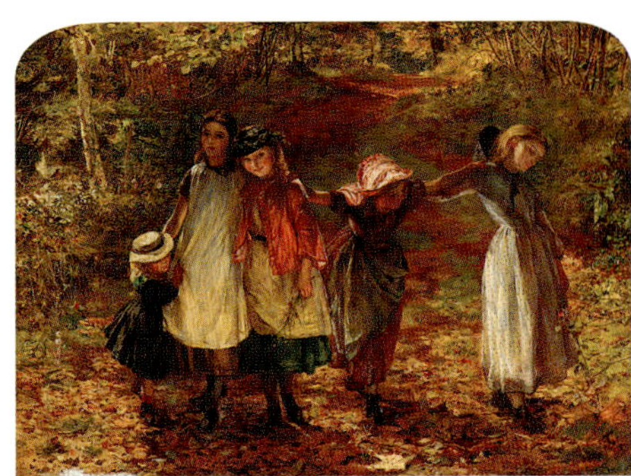

Smythe, Lionel Percy 1839–1918
Children Coming from School 1868
oil on canvas 78.7 x 106.7
1169

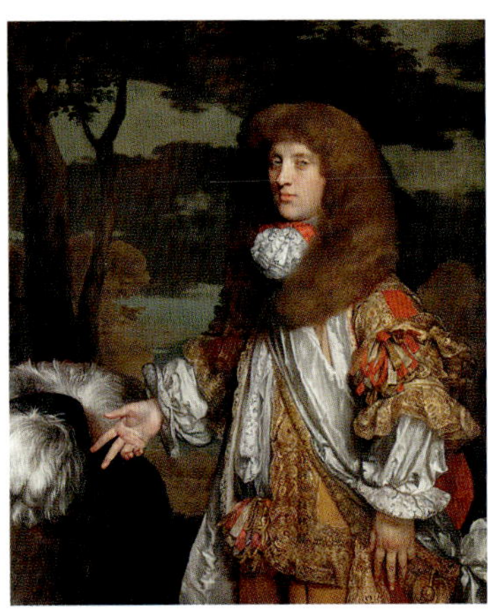

Soest, Gerard c.1600–1681
John Hay (1645–1713), 2nd Marquis of Tweeddale
oil on canvas 125.9 x 105.2
3326

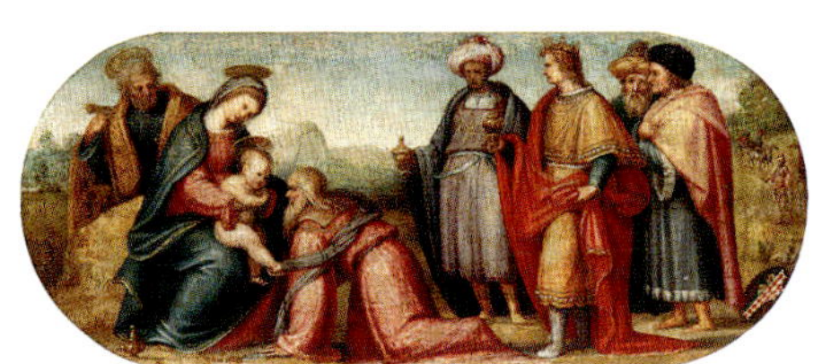

Sogliani, Giovanni Antonio 1492–1544
The Adoration of the Magi c.1515–1520
oil on panel 21.6 x 45.1
214

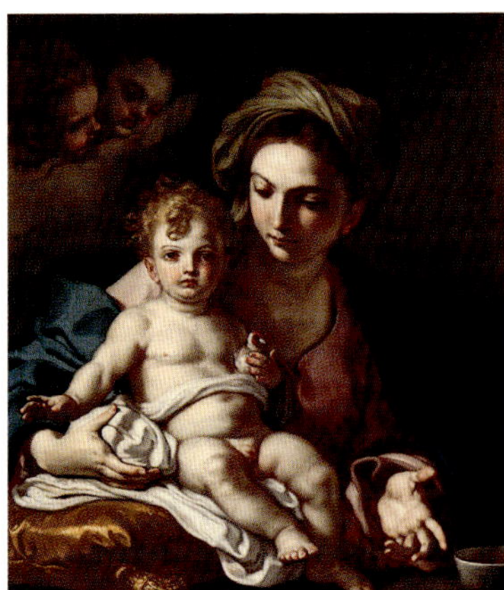

Solimena, Francesco 1657–1747
Virgin and Child c.1720–1730
oil on canvas 74.9 x 62.2
143

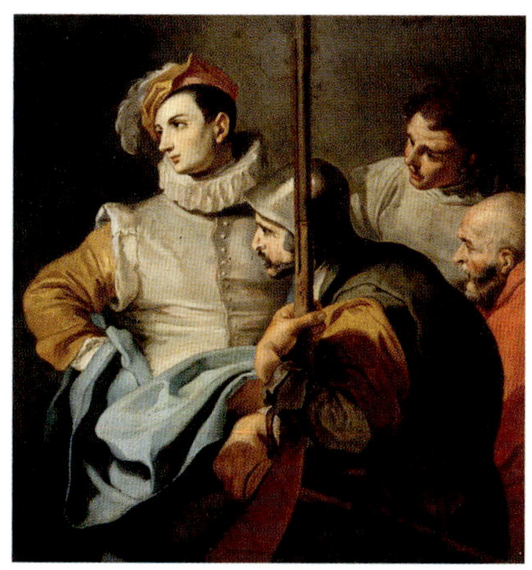

Solimena, Francesco (after) 1657–1747
A Group of Four Men c.1720–1730
oil on panel 34.9 x 32.7
1590

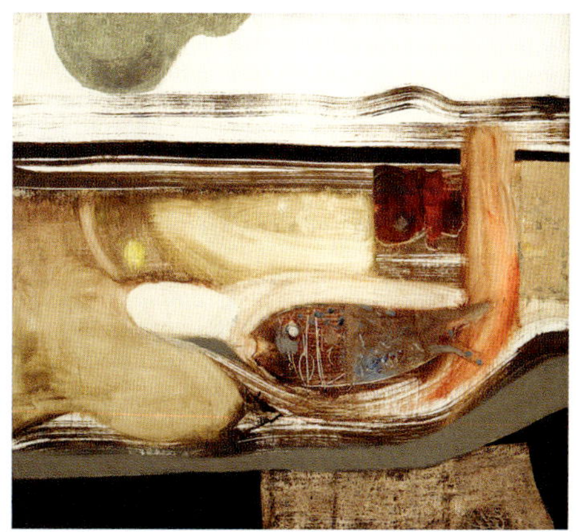

Somerville, Ward O. b.1942
Long Summer 1965
oil on canvas 75.9 x 80.9
3239

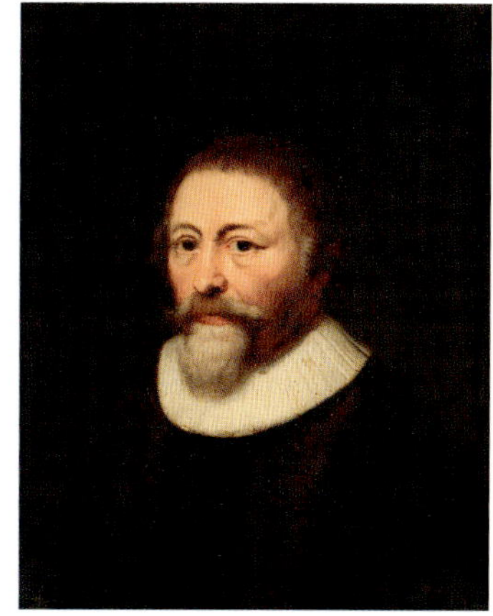

Sorgh, Hendrik Martensz. (after)
1609/1611–1670
Simon Episcopius (1583–1643) 17th C
oil on panel 25.4 x 20
55

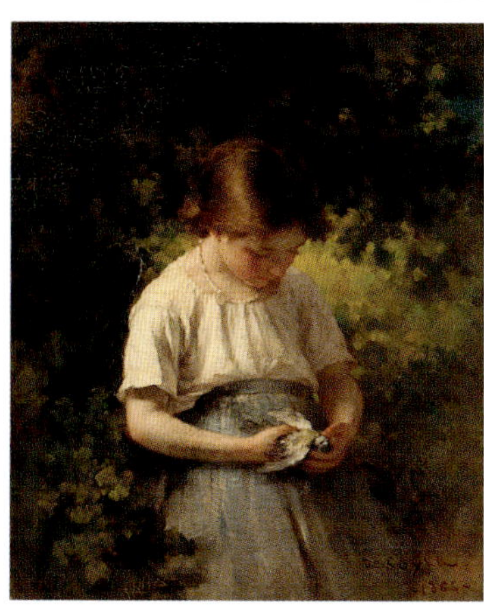

Soyer, Paul Constant 1823–1903
The Dead Bird 1886
oil on canvas 67.3 x 55.9
721

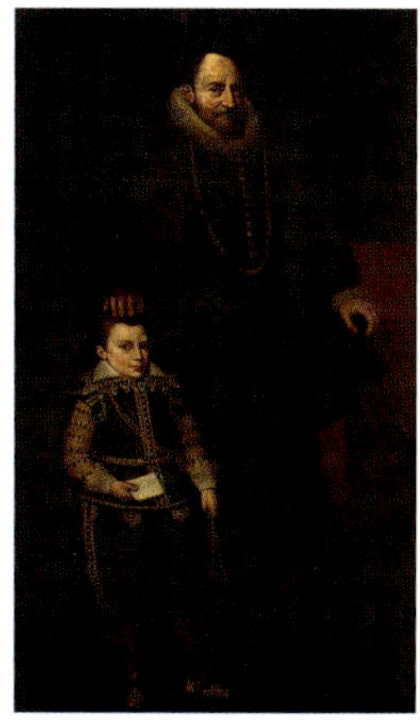

Spanish School
Portrait of a Father and Son c.1625–1635
oil on canvas 196 x 108.6
PC.143

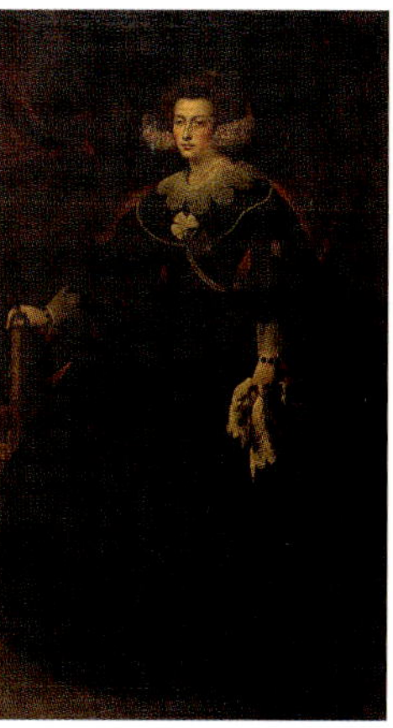

Spanish School
Portrait of a Spanish Lady c.1625–1635
oil on canvas 196.5 x 108.5
PC.130

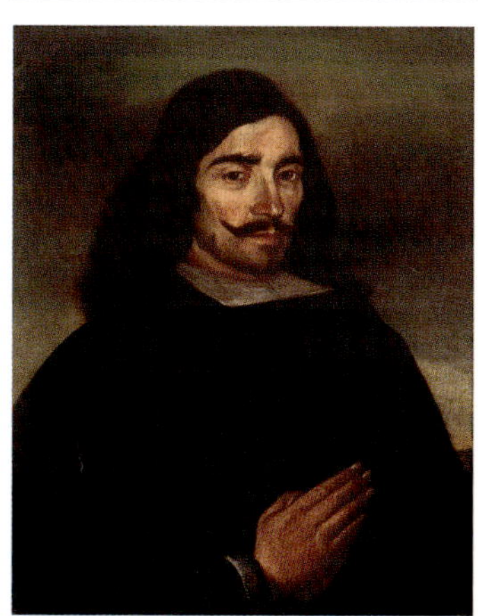

Spanish School
Portrait of a Man at Prayer c.1630–1650
oil on canvas 67.9 x 55.2
PC.72

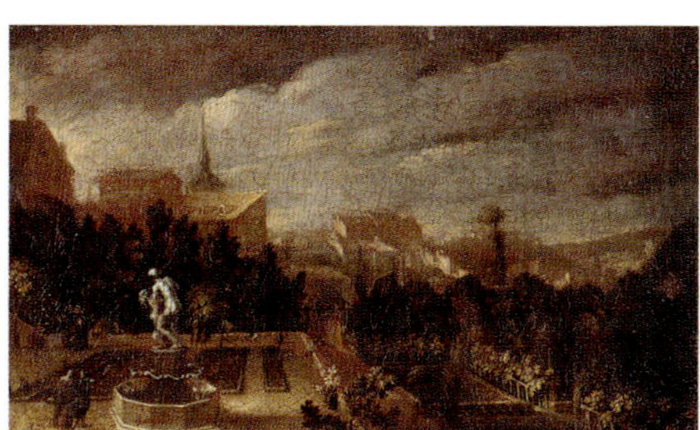

Spanish School 17th C
*The Garden of the Duke of Lerma's Palace,
Madrid*
oil on canvas 27.9 x 45.7
PC.88

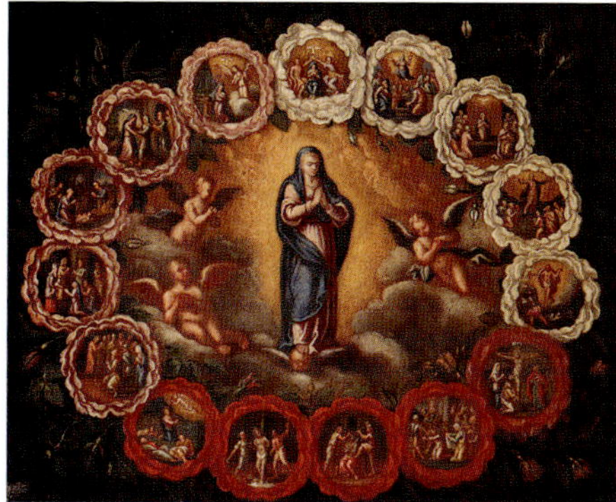

Spanish School 17th C
*The Rosary of Fifteen Joys and Sorrows of the
Virgin*
oil on canvas 49.2 x 61.9
PC.66

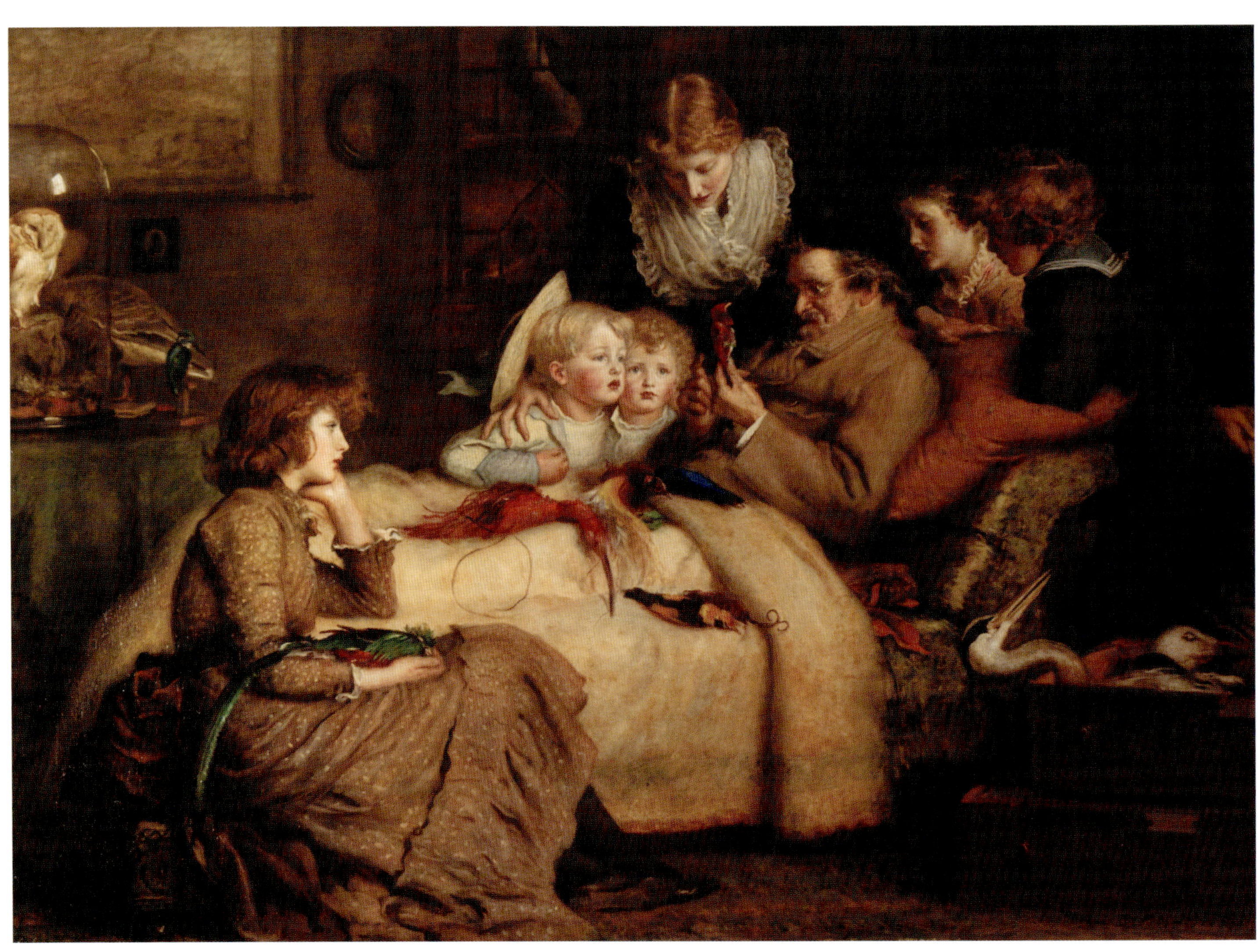

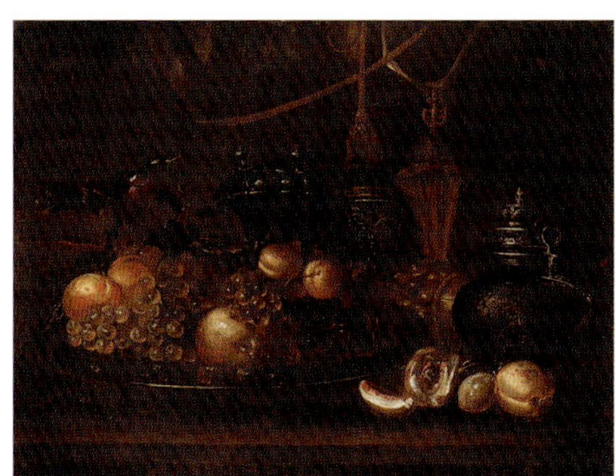

Spanish School (attributed to) 17th C
Still Life
oil on canvas 64.5 x 82.9
PC.7

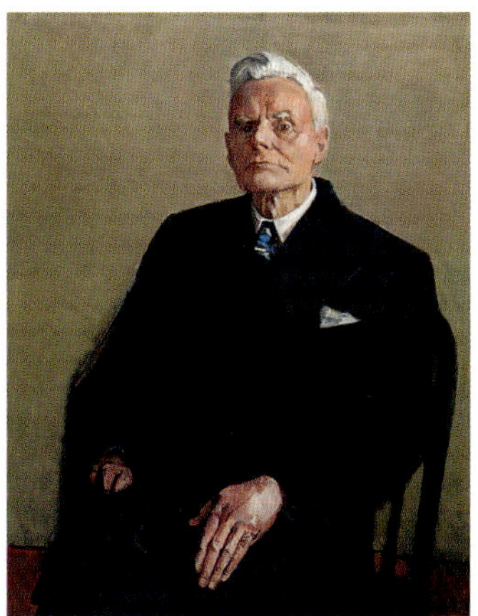

Spear, Ruskin 1911–1990
George B. Primrose (1881–1969), 3rd
Chairman of the Hamilton Trust (1946–1969)
1968
oil on canvas 121.9 x 91.4
3257

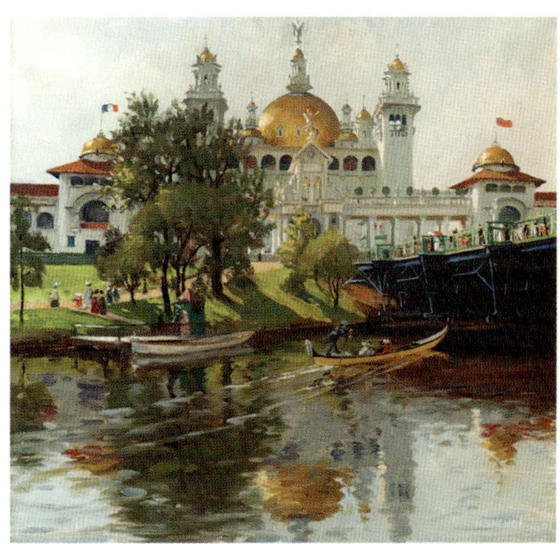

Spence, Harry 1860–1928
The Gondola 1901
oil on canvas 61 x 59.7
1019

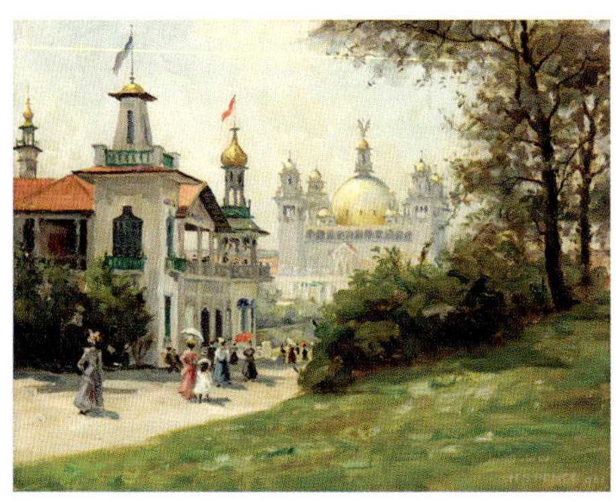

Spence, Harry 1860–1928
View of the Glasgow International Exhibition
1901
oil on canvas 40.1 x 49.5
NR.95

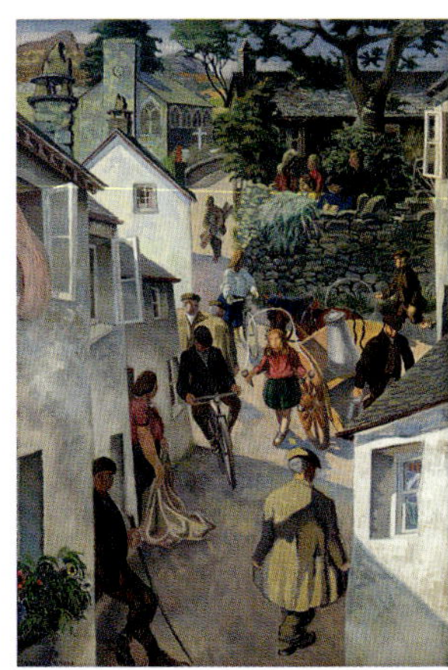

Spencer, Gilbert 1892–1979
The School on Peggy Hill, Ambleside c.1952
oil on canvas 101.6 x 70.5
2978

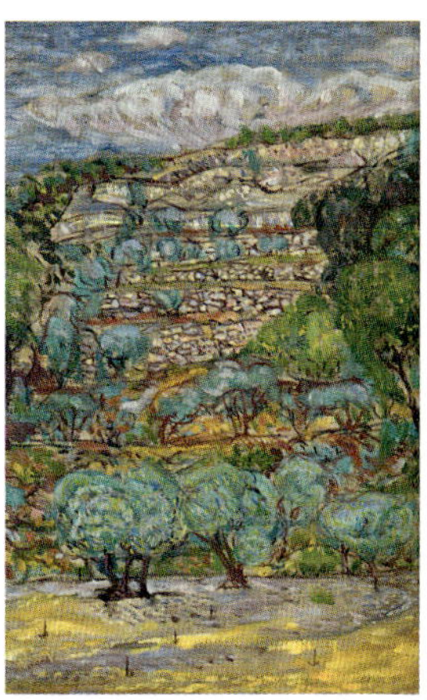

Spencer, John E.
Olive Trees, Montmajour c.1951
oil on canvas 73.7 x 47
2945

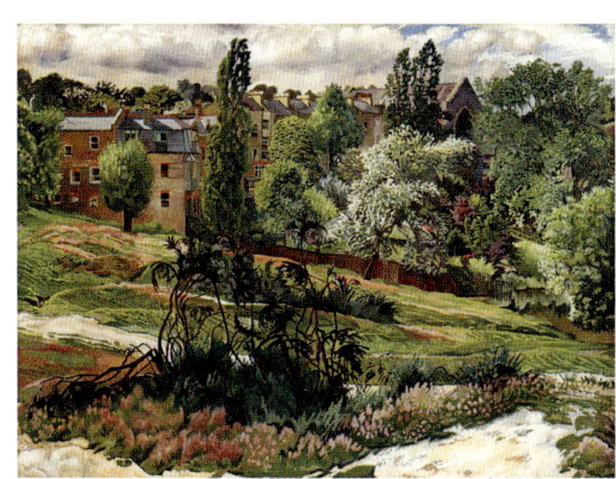

Spencer, Stanley 1891–1959
The Vale of Health, Hampstead, London
c.1940
oil on canvas 61 x 81.3
2215

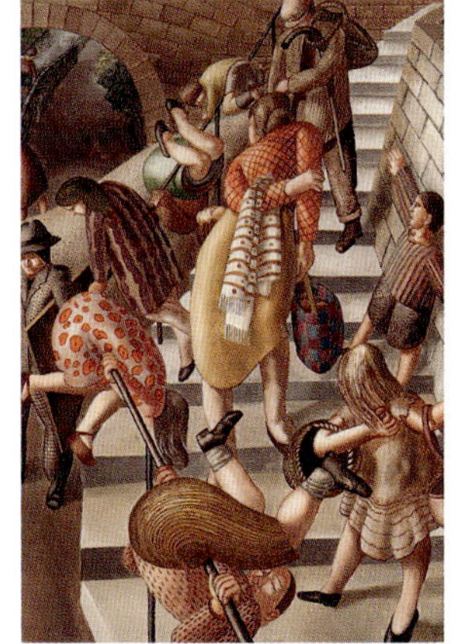

Spencer, Stanley 1891–1959
The Glen, Port Glasgow 1952
oil on canvas 76.2 x 50.9
3009

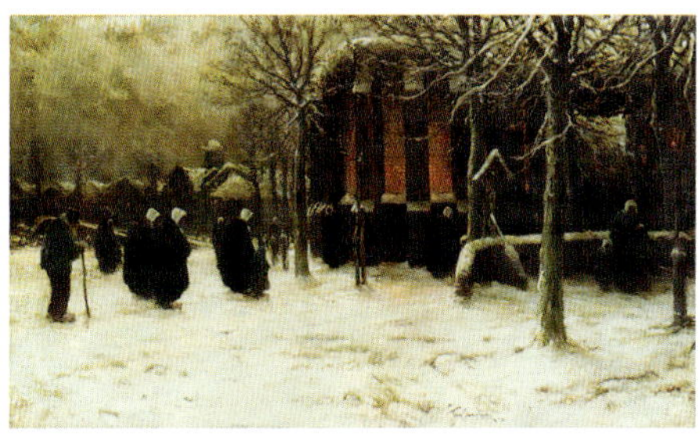

Spenlove-Spenlove, Frank 1866–1933
Vespers, New Year's Eve in the Low Country
1905
oil on canvas 105.4 x 151.1
1222

Facing page: Millais, John Everett, 1829–1896, *The Ornithologist*, 1885 (p. 304)

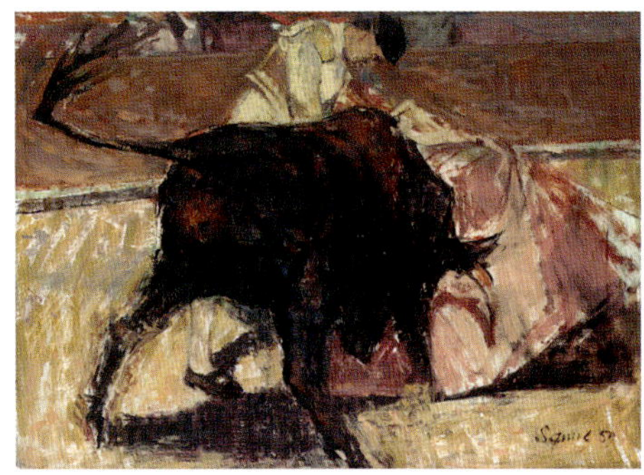

Squire, Geoffrey b.1923
Veronica 1959
oil on board 76.5 x 102
3117

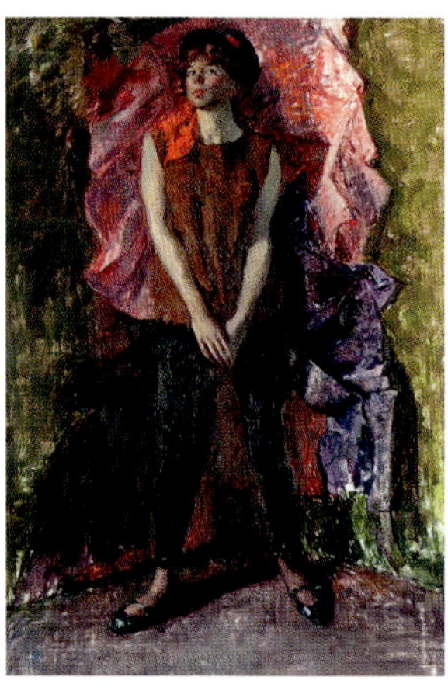

Squire, Geoffrey b.1923
Elsa 1963
oil on hardboard 180.3 x 121.9
3194

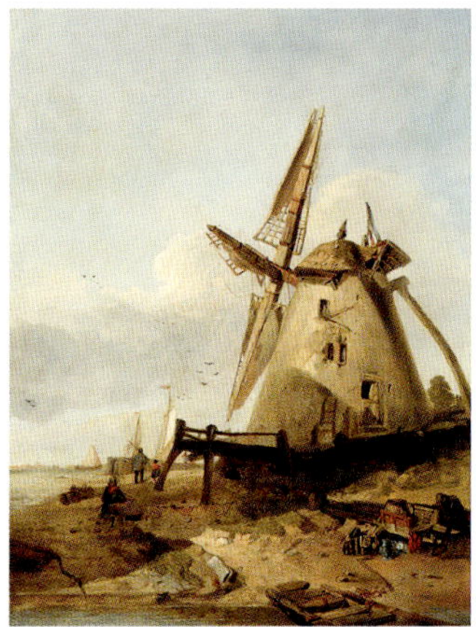

Stanfield, Clarkson 1793–1867
A Dutch Mill
oil on canvas 61 x 45.7
1734

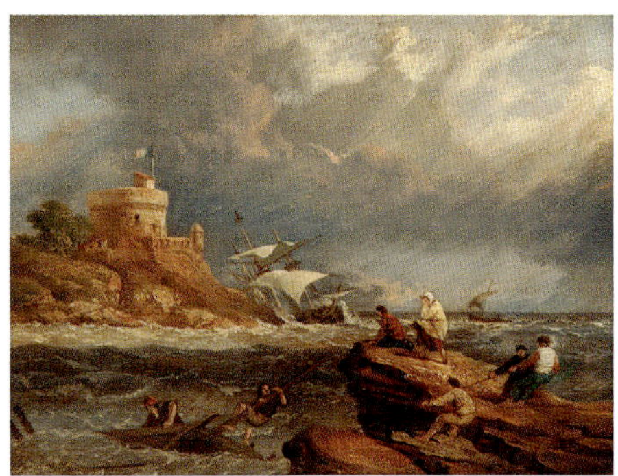

Stanfield, Clarkson 1793–1867
Rocky Seascape with a Shipwreck
oil on cardboard 22.9 x 30.8
3185

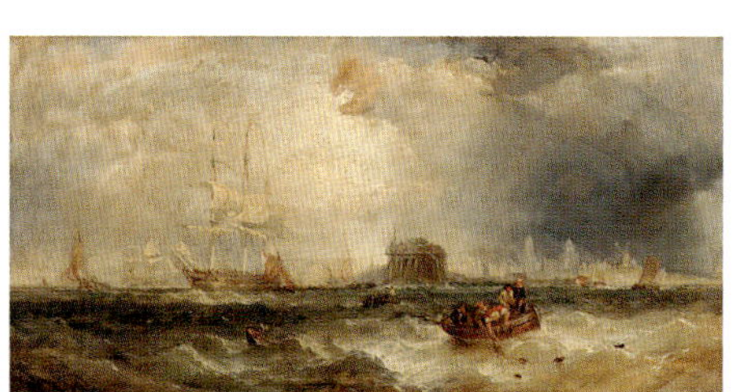

Stanfield, Clarkson 1793–1867
Seascape
oil on canvas 63.5 x 124.5
1506

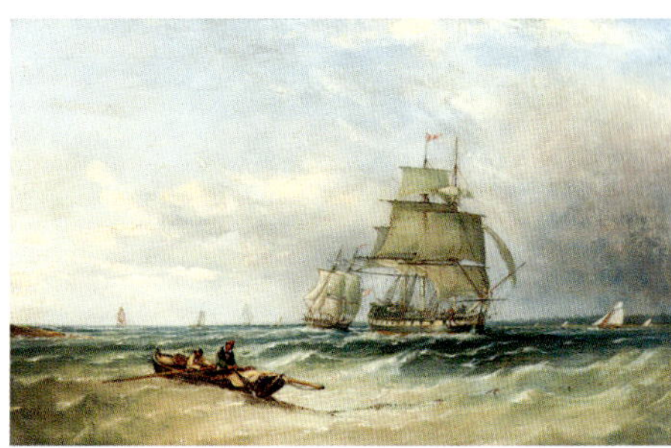

Stanfield, Clarkson 1793–1867
Seascape
oil on canvas 50.8 x 76.2
2911

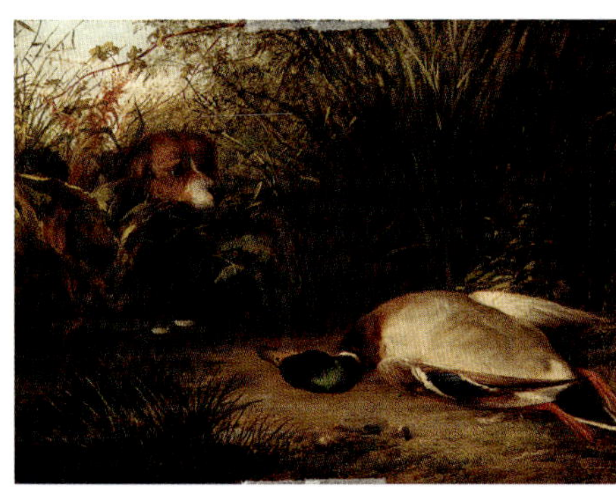

Stark, Arthur James 1831–1902
A Pointer and a Dead Wild Duck 1851
oil on canvas 44.5 x 59.7
870

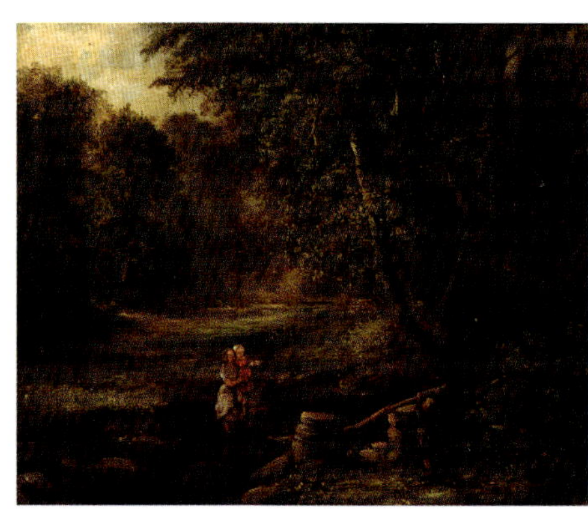

Stark, James 1794–1859
A Burn Side
oil on canvas 26.2 x 31.1
993

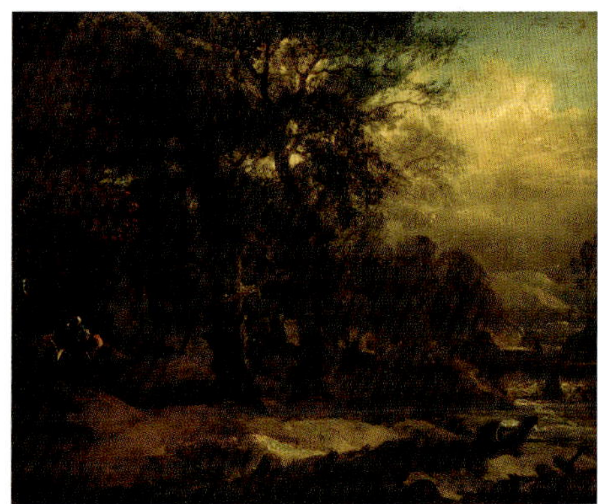

Stark, James 1794–1859
Woodland Scene
oil on panel 22.9 x 28.9
1213

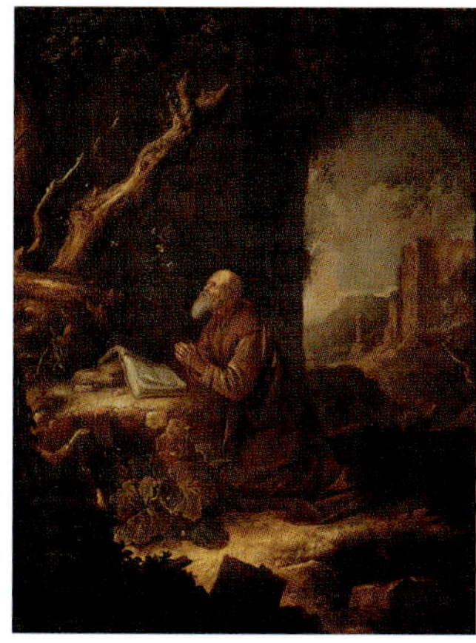

Staveren, Jan Adriaensz. van c.1625–c.1668
A Hermit at Prayer
oil on panel 33.7 x 29.1
442

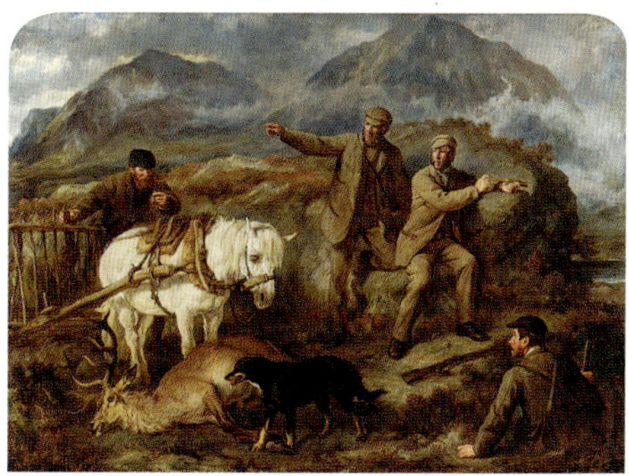

Steell, Gourlay 1819–1894
Deerstalking on Jura c.1870
oil on canvas 142.2 x 185.4
2502

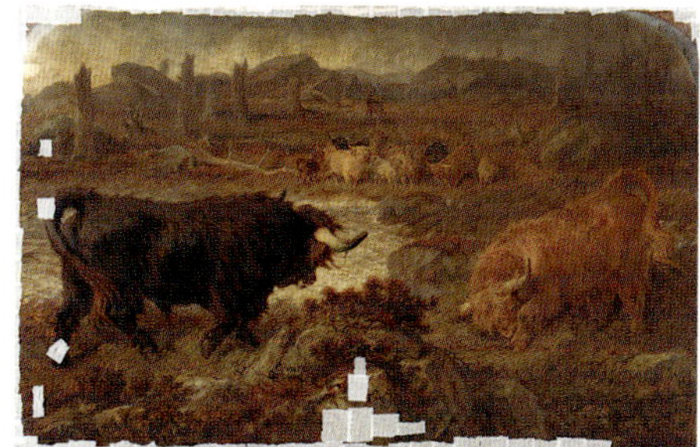

Steell, Gourlay 1819–1894
A Challenge 1876
oil on canvas 112.1 x 167.9
3078

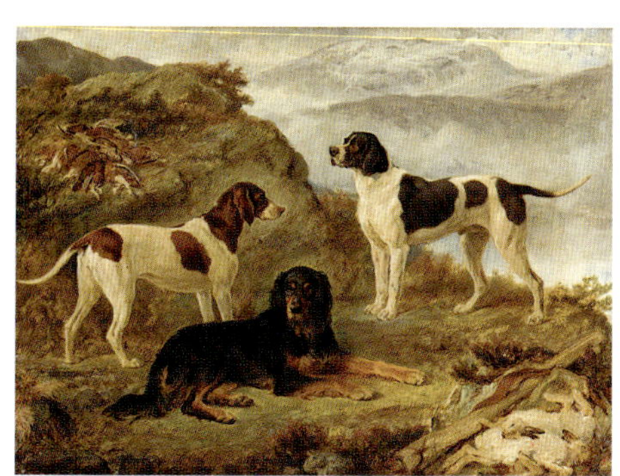

Steell, Gourlay 1819–1894
The Trysting Place
oil on canvas 110.5 x 144.8
823

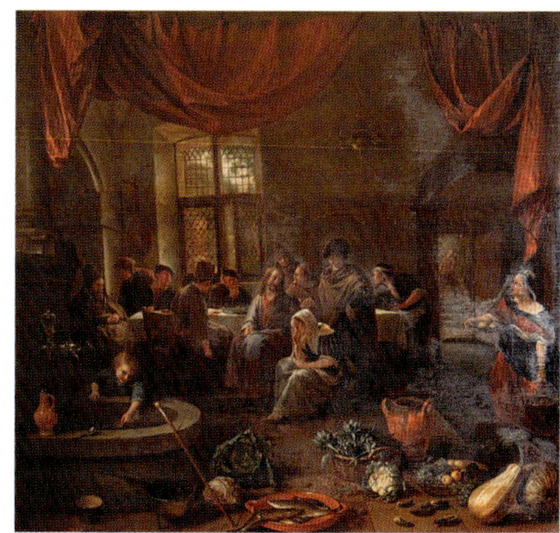

Steen, Jan 1626–1679
Christ in the House of Martha and Mary
oil on panel 73 x 73
PL.96 (P)

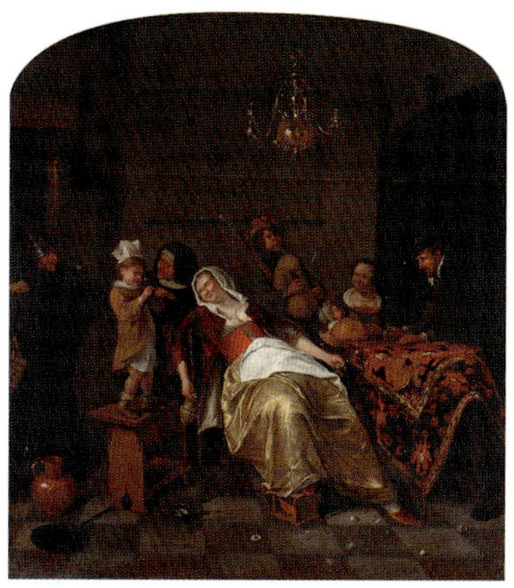

Steen, Jan (imitator of) 1626–1679
A Merry Company late 17th C
oil on canvas 72.4 x 64.8
65

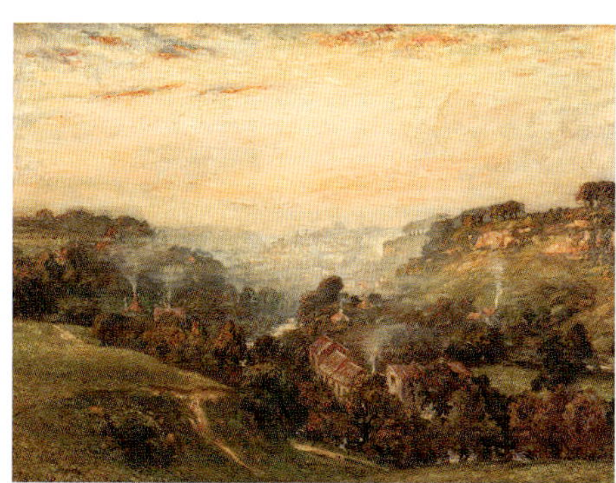

Steer, Philip Wilson 1860–1942
Nidderdale 1900
oil on canvas 85.1 x 111.8
1912

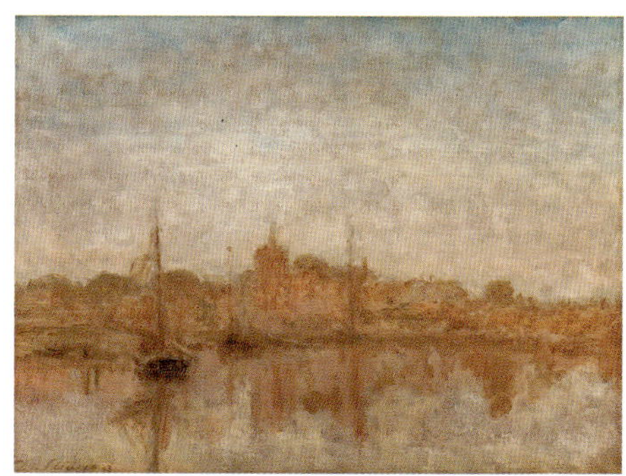

Steer, Philip Wilson 1860–1942
Maldon 1933
oil on canvas 40.7 x 51.5
3358

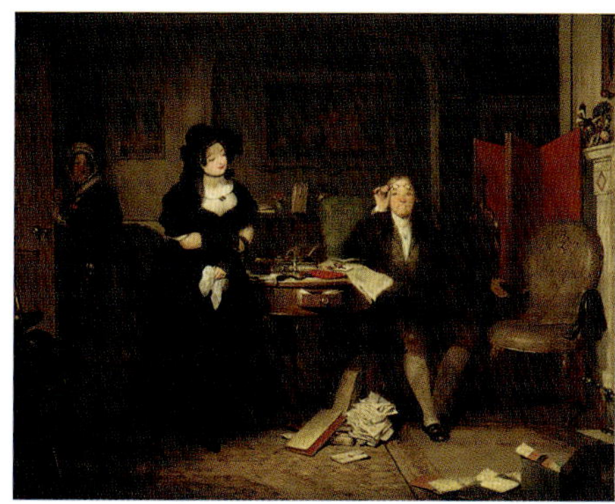

Stephanoff, Francis Philip 1790–1860
Answering the Advertisement c.1841
oil on canvas 62.2 x 74.9
364

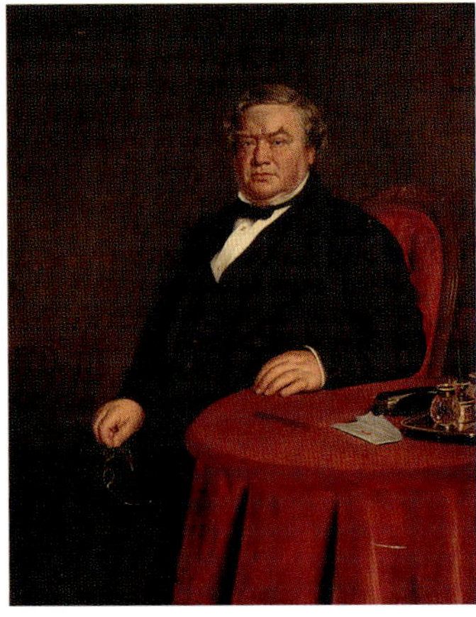

Stevenson active 19th C
Robert Barclay (d.1861), Shipbuilder
oil on canvas 141 x 111.8
NR.79

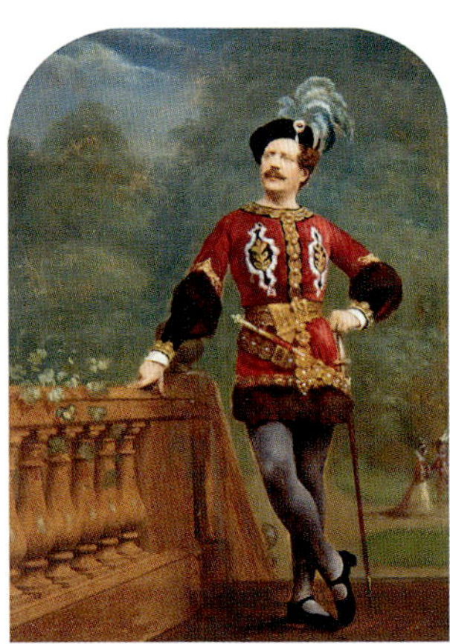

Stevenson, Robert
Harcourt Blair (Beatty) 1869
oil on canvas 18.6 x 14.3
TEMP.1392

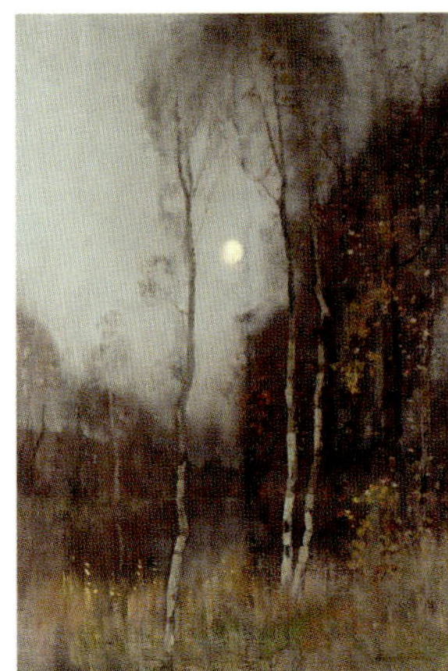

Stevenson, Robert Macaulay 1854–1952
Moonrise c.1892–1900
oil on canvas 111.8 x 76.2
1670

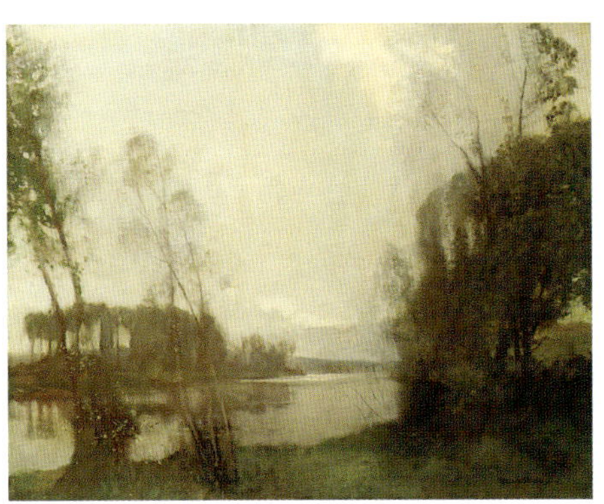

Stevenson, Robert Macaulay 1854–1952
Early Summer on the Seine c.1904
oil on canvas 90.2 x 110.5
1081

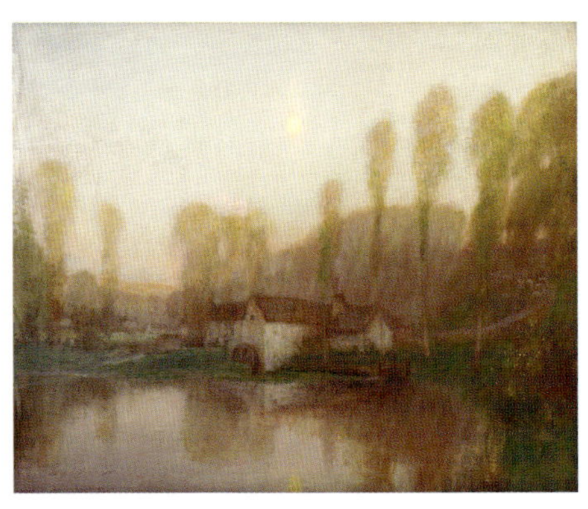

Stevenson, Robert Macaulay 1854–1952
An Old World Mill
oil on canvas 76.2 x 91.4
2587

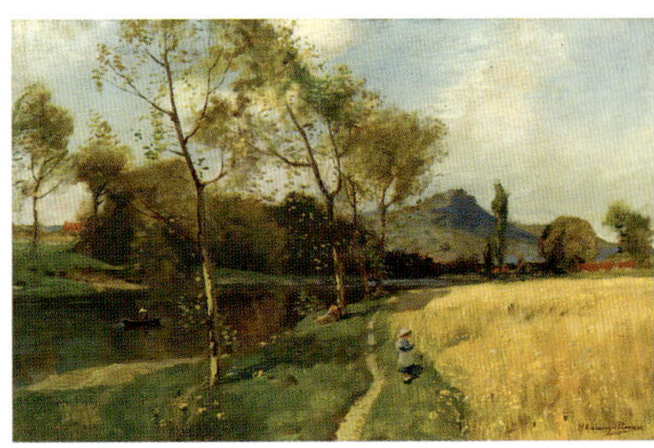

Stevenson, Robert Macaulay 1854–1952
By the River, Harvest-Time
oil on canvas 50.8 x 76.2
3028

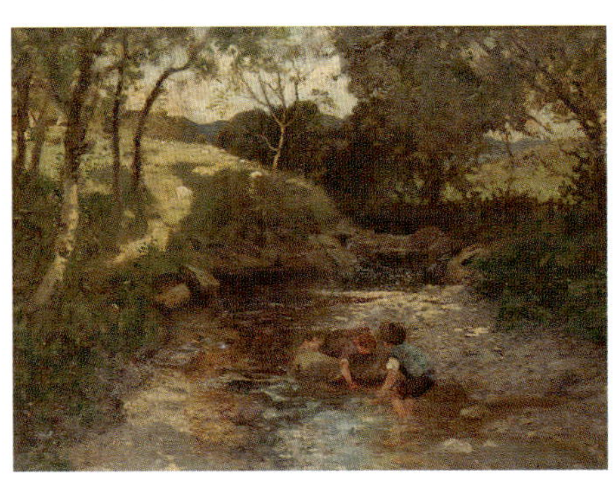

Stevenson, Robert Macaulay 1854–1952
Days of Auld Lang Syne
oil on canvas 81.3 x 106.7
2505

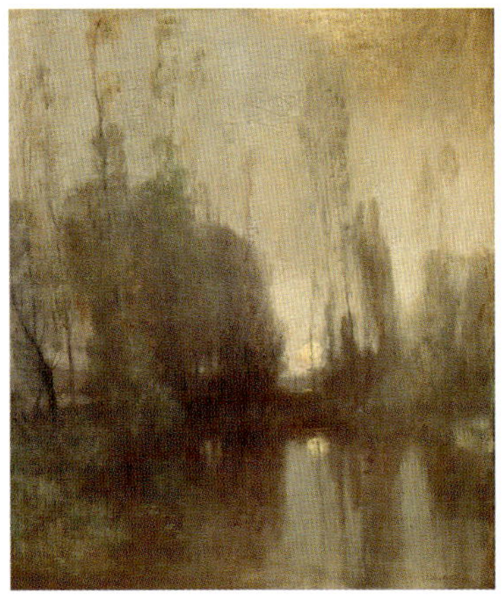

Stevenson, Robert Macaulay 1854–1952
In the Gloaming
oil on canvas 111.8 x 91.4
2586

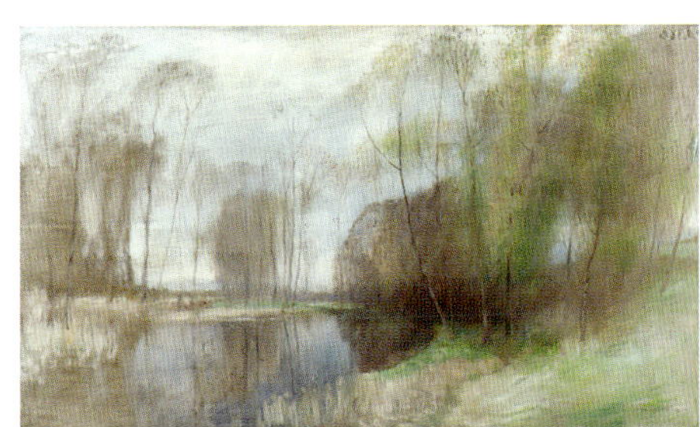

Stevenson, Robert Macaulay 1854–1952
Landscape
oil on canvas 106.7 x 177.8
2339

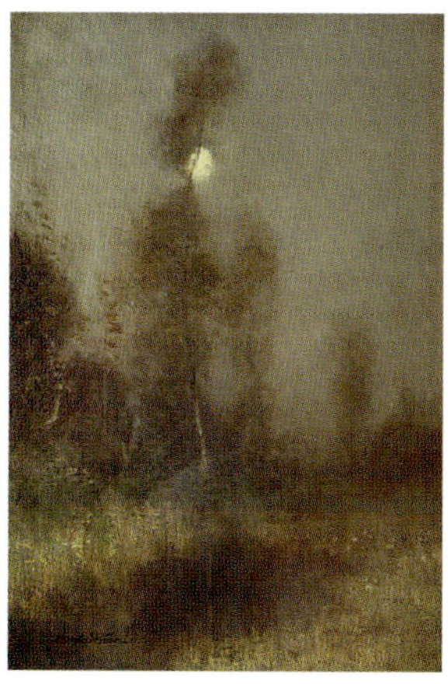

Stevenson, Robert Macaulay 1854–1952
Moonlit Landscape
oil on canvas 61 x 40.6
2473

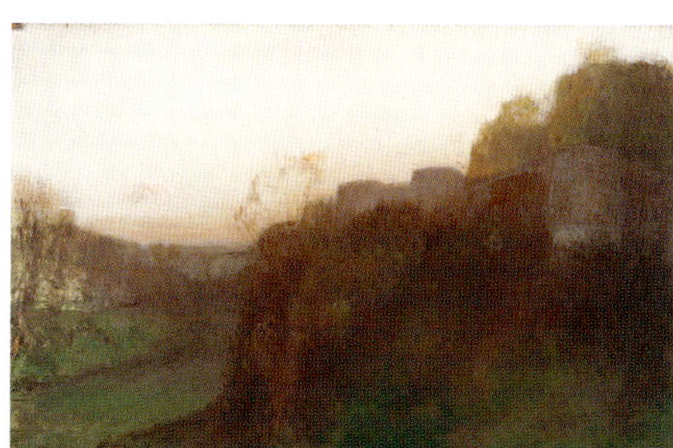

Stevenson, Robert Macaulay 1854–1952
Ramparts of Monteuil
oil on canvas 61 x 91.4
2496

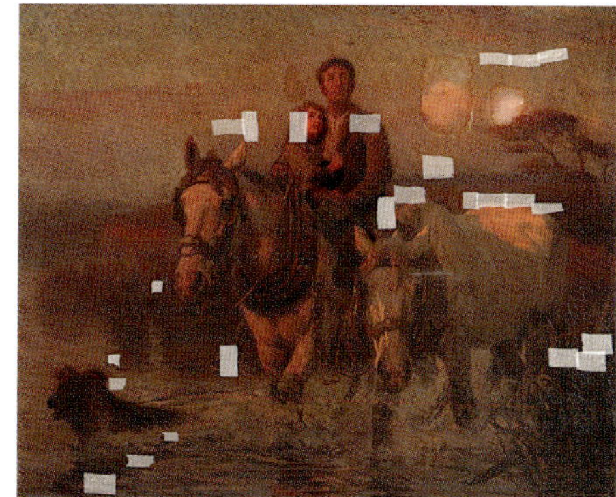

Stewart, Charles Edward active 1887–1938
Crossing the Ford c.1901
oil on canvas 137.2 x 170.2
1093

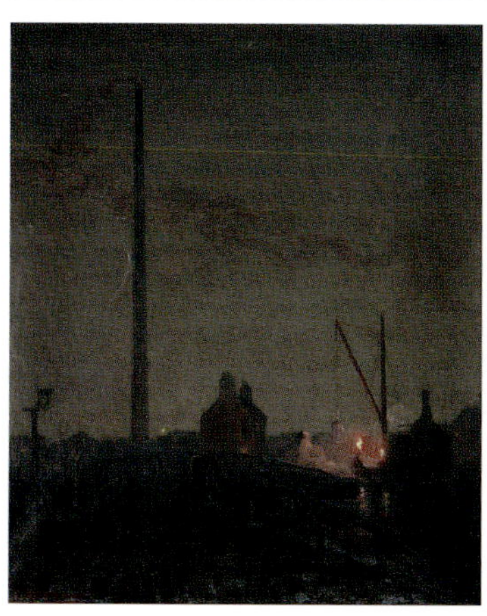

Stewart, Charles Edward active 1887–1938
The Townsend Stalk 1913
oil on canvas 47.5 x 39
OG.1954.161

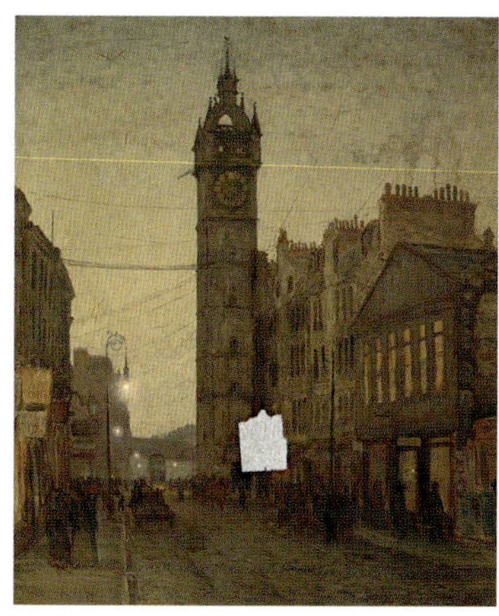

Stewart, Charles Edward active 1887–1938
Tollbooth, Old High Street, Glasgow 1913
oil on canvas 76.2 x 61
TEMP.14956

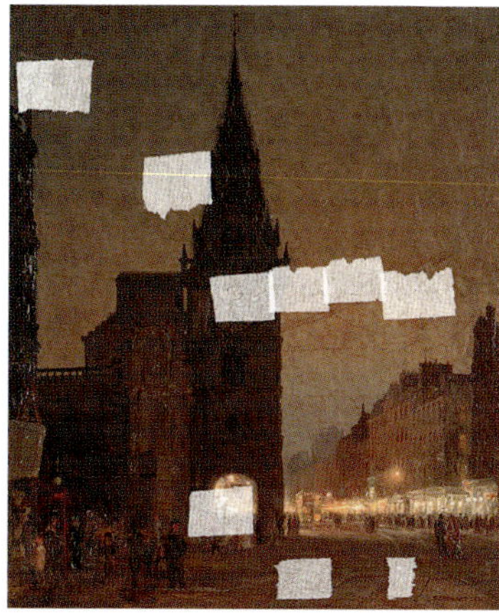

Stewart, Charles Edward (attributed to)
active 1887–1938
Tron Steeple, Glasgow
oil on canvas 76.2 x 61
TEMP.14957

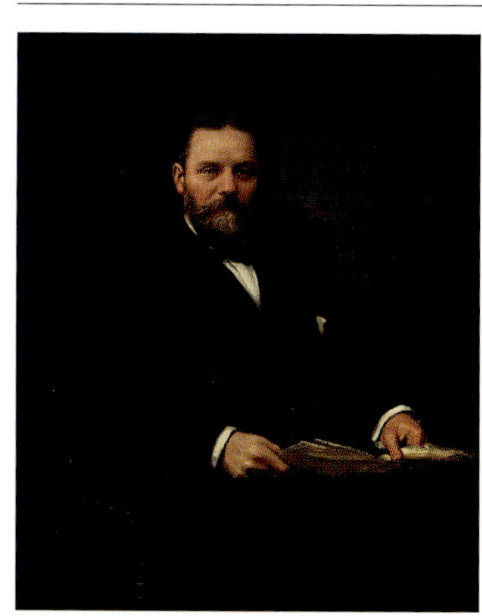

Stewart, J.
John McGill c.1899
oil on canvas 127 x 101.6
NR.42

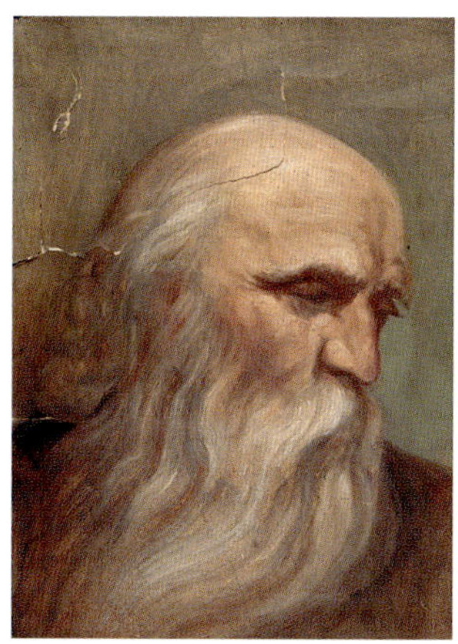

Stewart, J. T. (studio of) active c.1885–1960
& Stewart, Charles Edward (studio of) active
1887–1938
Head of a Bearded Man
oil on card 47.3 x 33.1
TEMP.2661

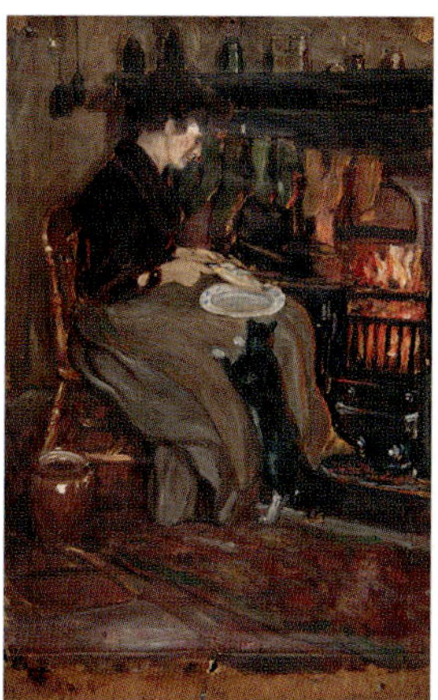

Stewart, J. T. (studio of) active c.1885–1960
& Stewart, Charles Edward (studio of) active
1887–1938
Seated Woman Gutting Fish by a Fire
oil on card 47.6 x 29.7
PP.1980.20.96

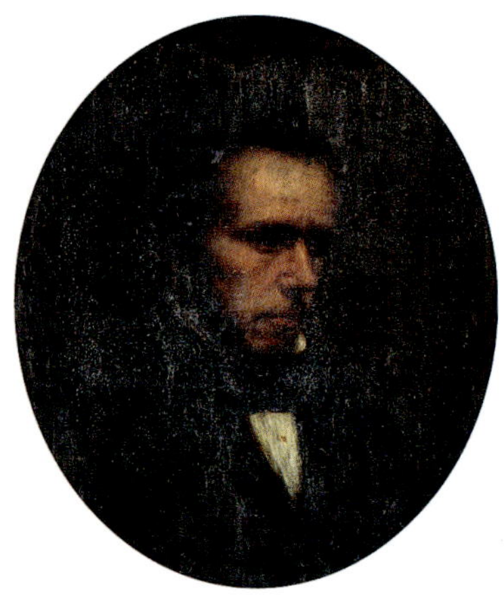

Stewart, James Scott b.c.1832
J. Milne Donald (1819–1866)
oil on canvas 35.6 x 30.5
1227

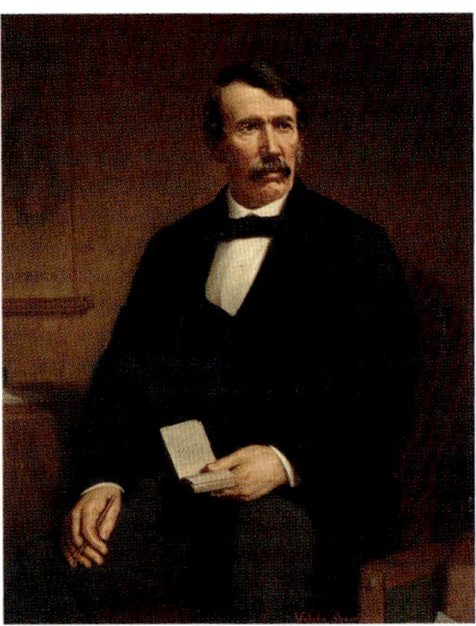

Stewart, Malcolm 1829–1916
Dr Livingstone (1813–1873), Missionary and Explorer 1876
oil on canvas 127 x 100.3
647

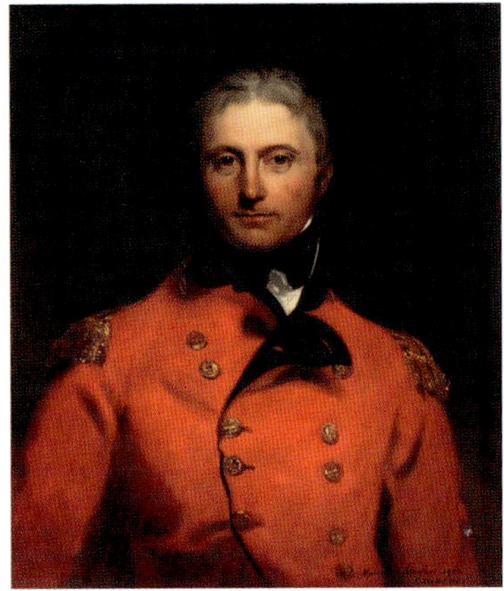

Stewart, Malcolm 1829–1916
Lieutenant-General Sir John Moore (1761–1809) (after Thomas Lawrence) 1902
oil on canvas 76.2 x 63.5
1029

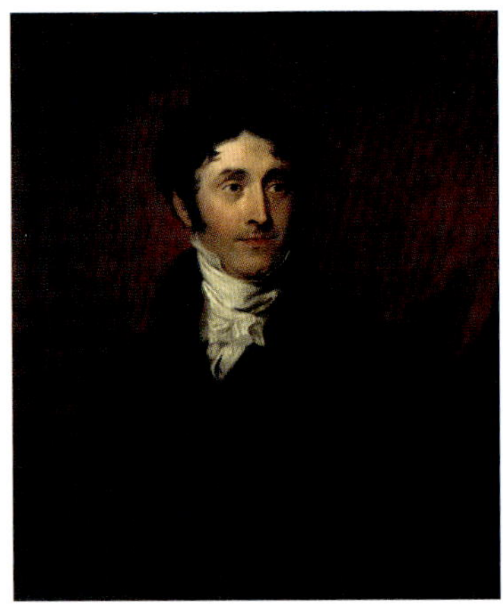

Stewart, Malcolm 1829–1916
Thomas Campbell (1777–1844), Poet 1902
oil on canvas 76.2 x 63.5
1028

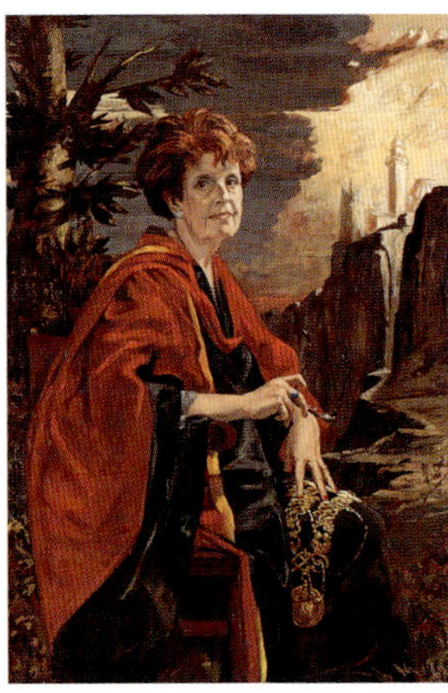

Stoddart, Alexander b.1959
Elizabeth Cameron, Lord Provost of the City of Glasgow (2003–2007) 2008
oil on canvas 155 x 115
3692

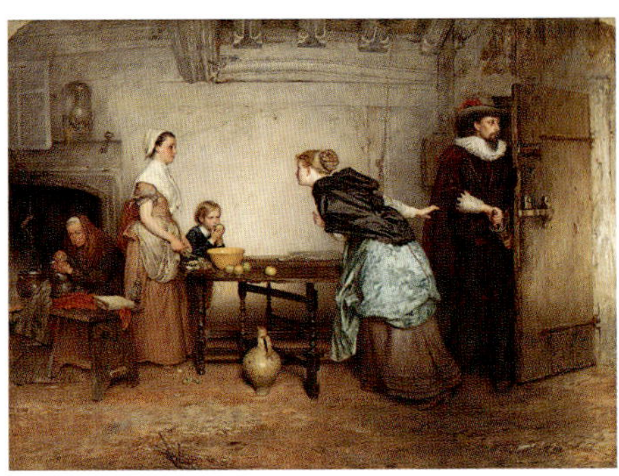

Stone, Marcus C. 1840–1921
Royalists Seeking Safety 1866
oil on canvas 109.2 x 144.8
1155

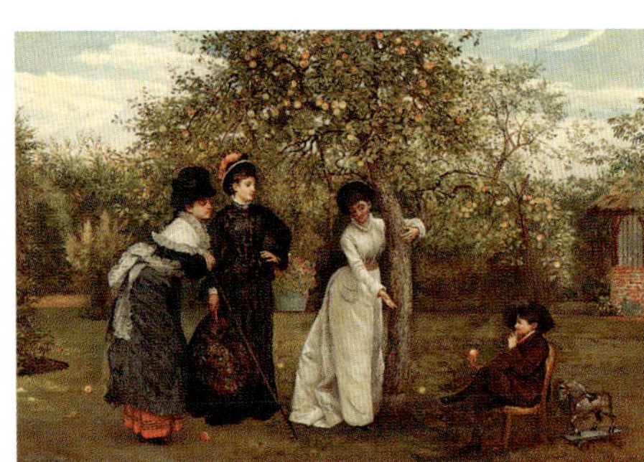

Storey, George Adolphus 1834–1919
The Judgment of Paris 1877
oil on canvas 86.4 x 124.5
1351

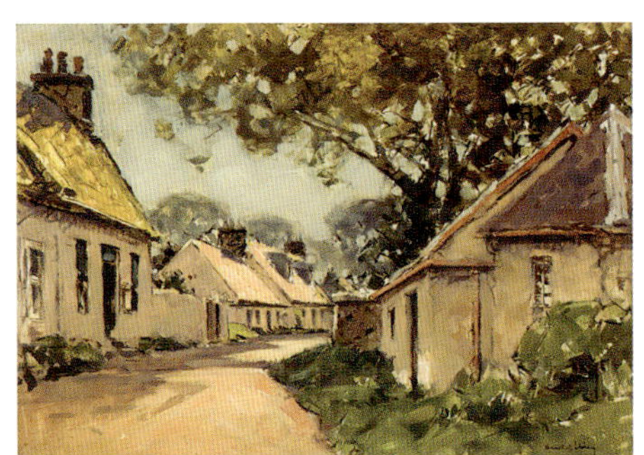

Storey, Harold 1888–1965
Symington, Ayrshire c.1945
oil on millboard 53.3 x 76.2
2472

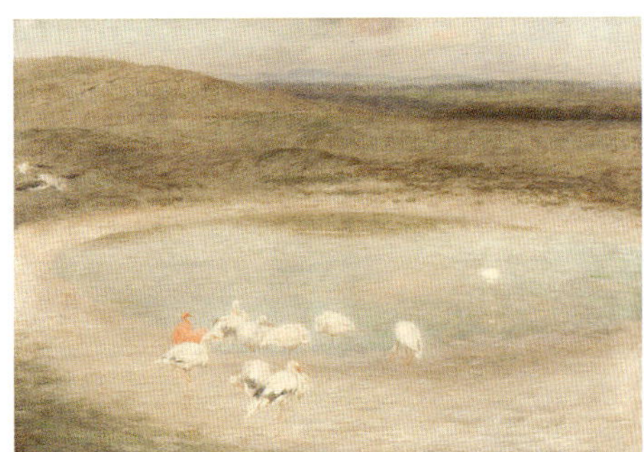

Stott, Edward William 1859–1918
The Sacred Pool
oil on canvas 76.2 x 109.2
1819

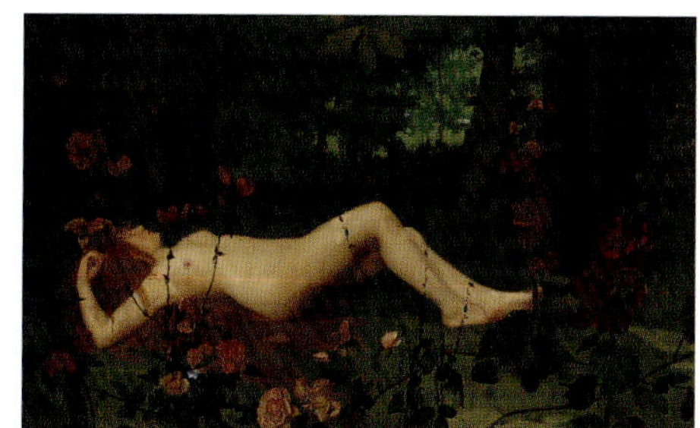

Stott, William 1857–1900
The Nymph 1886
oil on canvas 127 x 203.2
1735

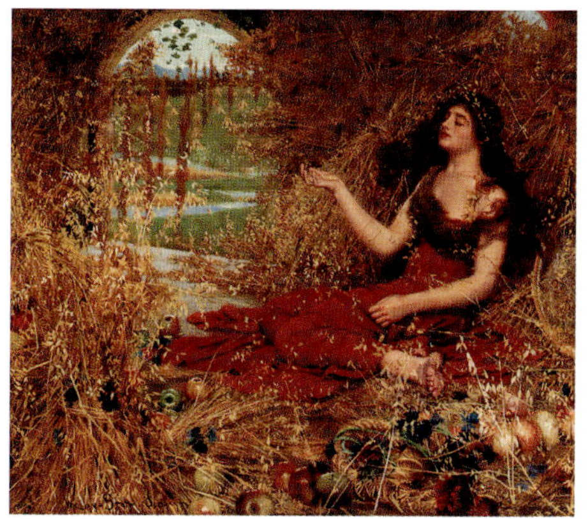

Stott, William 1857–1900
Autumn c.1898
oil on canvas 116.8 x 127
1030

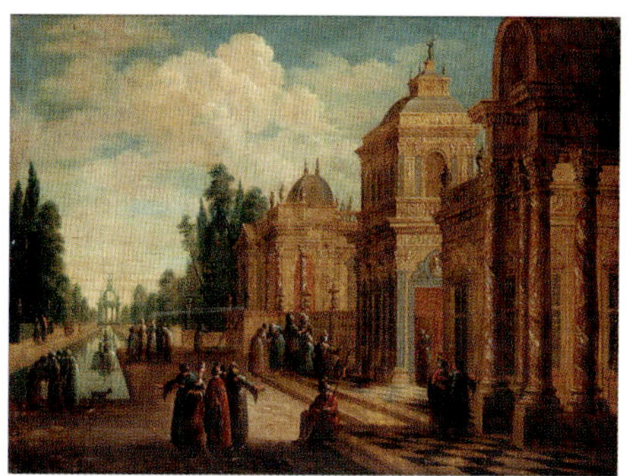

Straeten, Jan van der (attributed to)
1667/1681–1731/1741
An Architectural Fantasy with Figures
oil on canvas 31.8 x 42.2
95

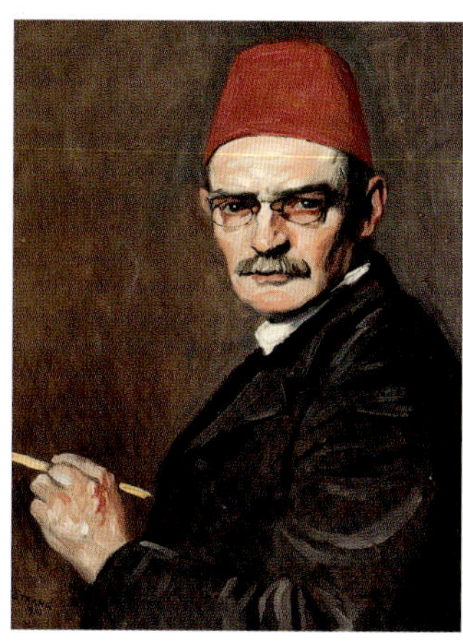

Strang, William 1859–1921
The Red Fez: Self Portrait 1910
oil on canvas 61 x 45.4
1754

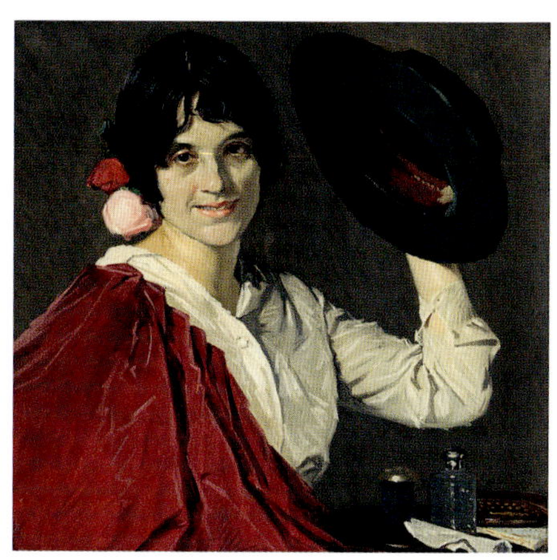

Strang, William 1859–1921
Good Morning, Señor 1913
oil on canvas 61 x 61
2190

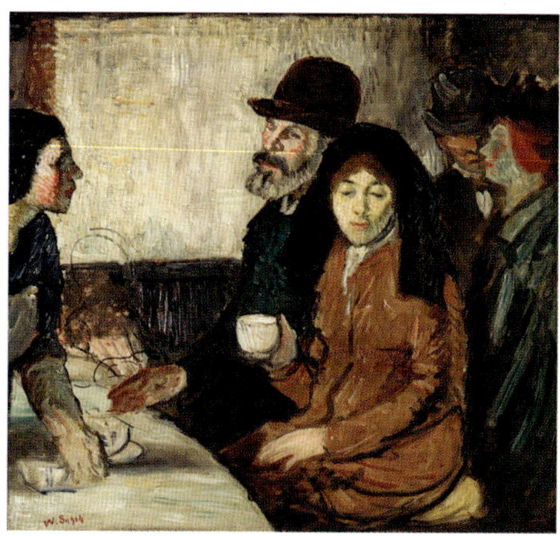

Strang, William 1859–1921
Café Bar (sketch) 1914
oil on canvas 47.3 x 50.5
2826

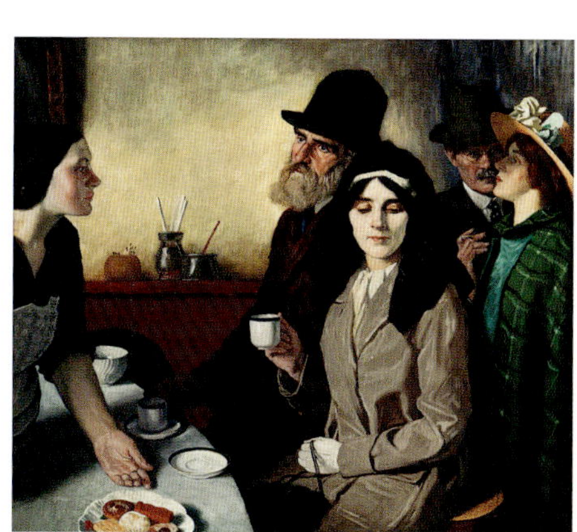

Strang, William 1859–1921
Café Bar 1915
oil on canvas 101.6 x 114.3
2549

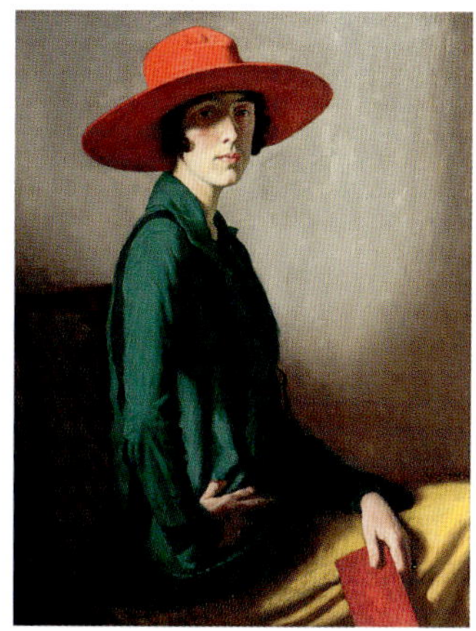

Strang, William 1859–1921
Lady with a Red Hat 1918
oil on canvas 102.9 x 77.5
1470

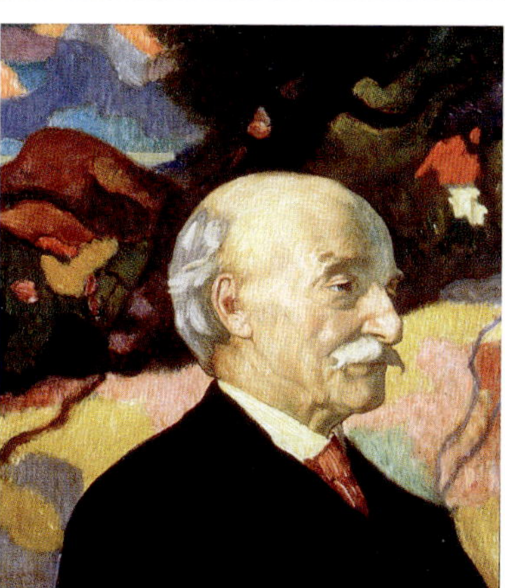

Strang, William 1859–1921
Thomas Hardy (1840–1928), OM 1920
oil on canvas 61 x 50.8
1546

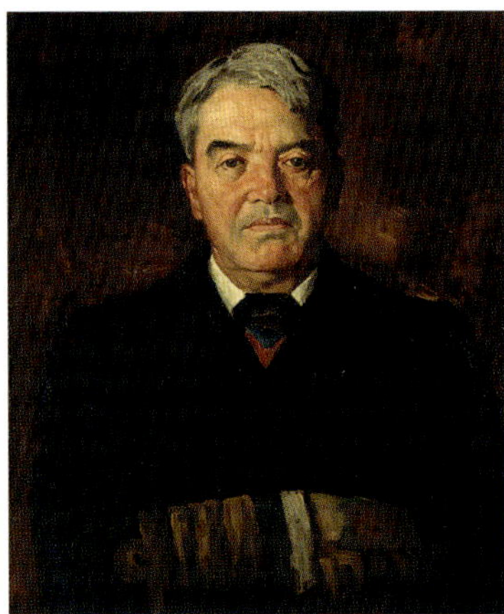

Strang, William 1859–1921
Admiral Sir John Fisher (1841–1920), OM
oil on canvas 61 x 50.9
1595

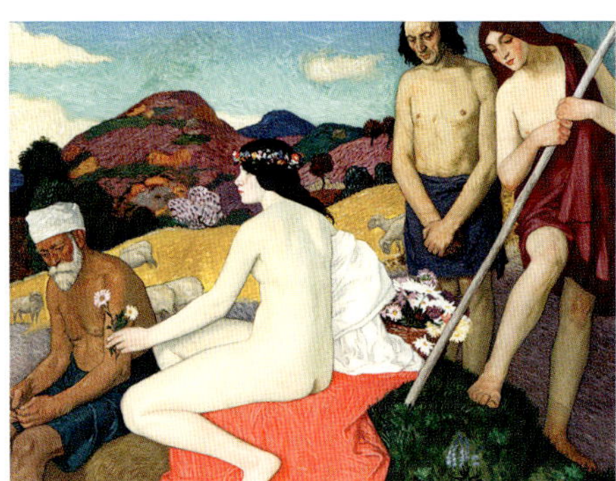

Strang, William 1859–1921
Nymph and Shepherds
oil on canvas 101.6 x 127
1533

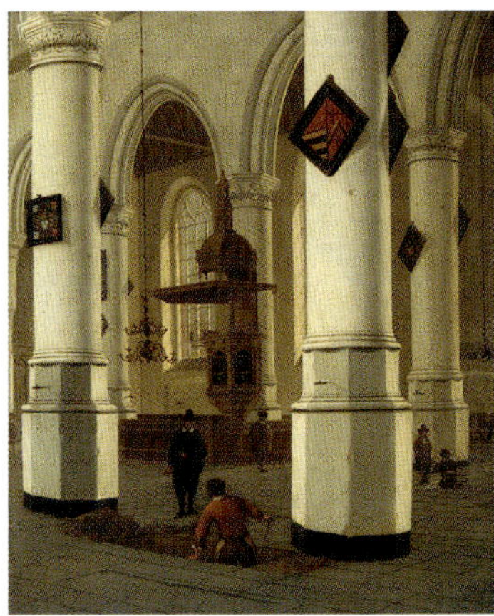

Streeck, Hendrick van (attributed to)
1659–1719
Interior of the Oude Kerk, Delft, with a Gravedigger
oil on canvas 52.1 x 43.2
35.636

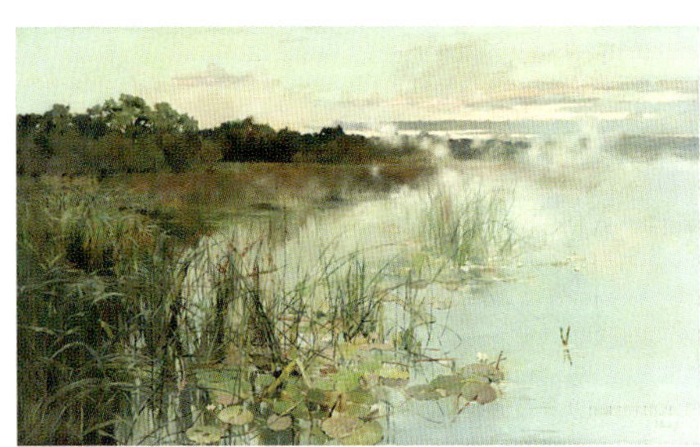

Stretton, Philip Eustace c.1863–c.1930
Landscape and Lily Pond 1889
oil on canvas 76.2 x 127
2145

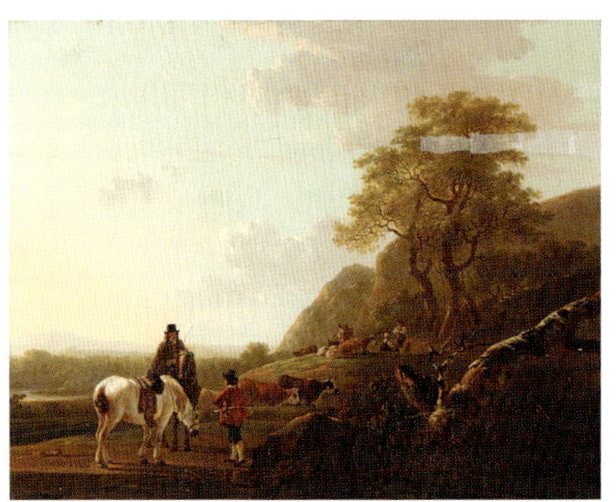

Strij, Jacob van 1756–1815
Landscape with Horsemen and Cattle
oil on panel 71.1 x 87.6
422

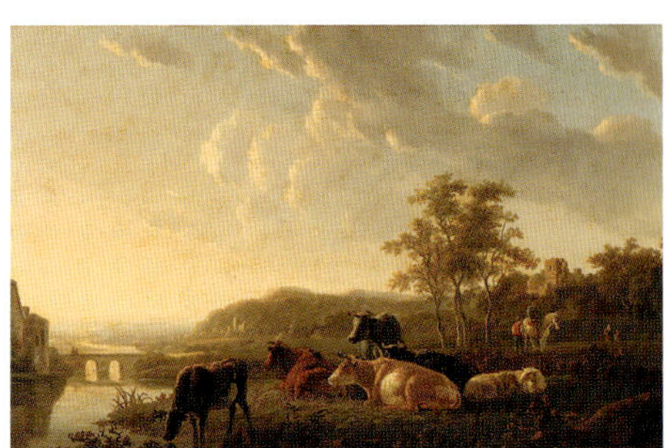

Strij, Jacob van 1756–1815
River Landscape with Cattle, Sheep and Figures
oil on panel 52.3 x 79
456

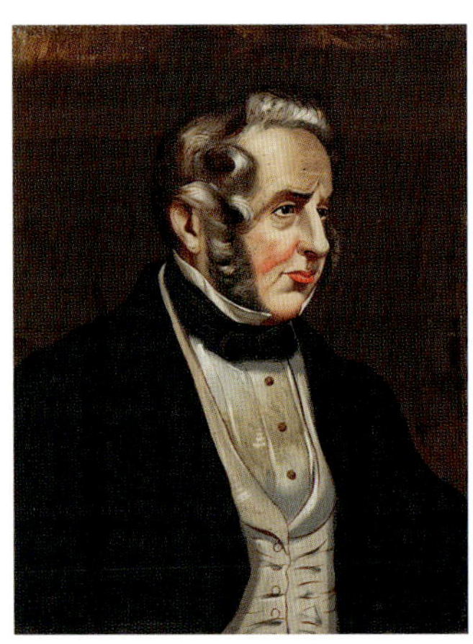

Struthers, A.
Lord Palmerston (1784–1865) 1890
oil on glass 54.6 x 41.3
OG.1948.103.a

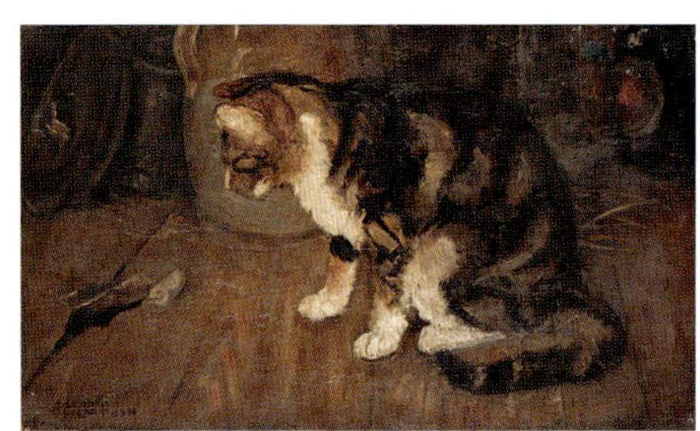

Stuart, Charles Edward 1885–c.1960
Tabby Cat 1901
oil on canvas 30.5 x 50.5
TEMP.1734

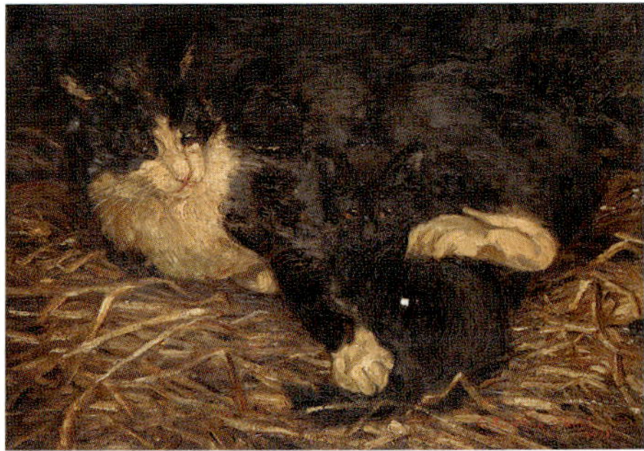

Stuart, Charles Edward 1885–c.1960
Cat and Kitten 1902
oil on canvas 30.1 x 40.7
TEMP.1733

Facing page: Brangwyn, Frank, 1867–1956, *The Burial at Sea*, 1890 (p. 46)

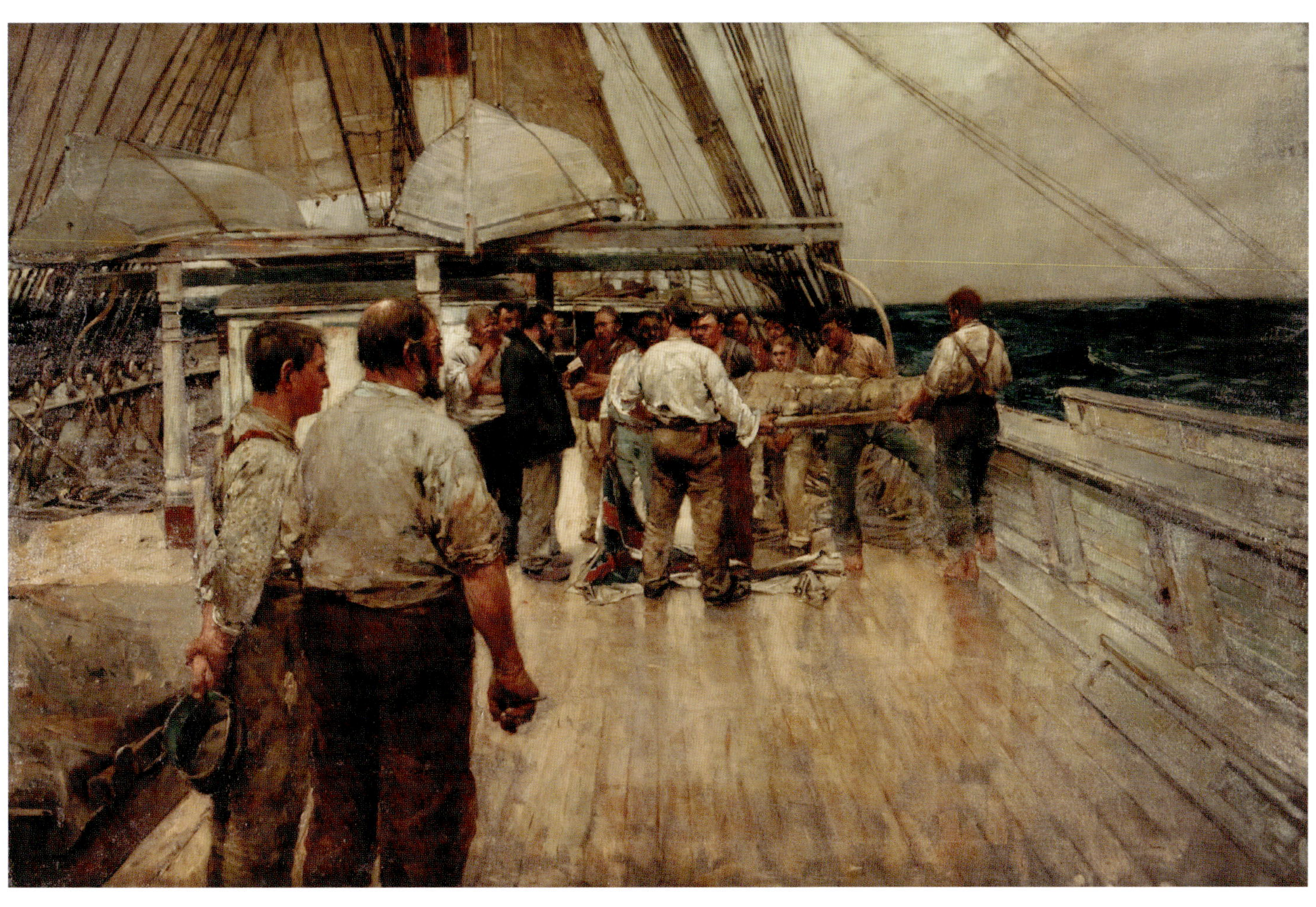

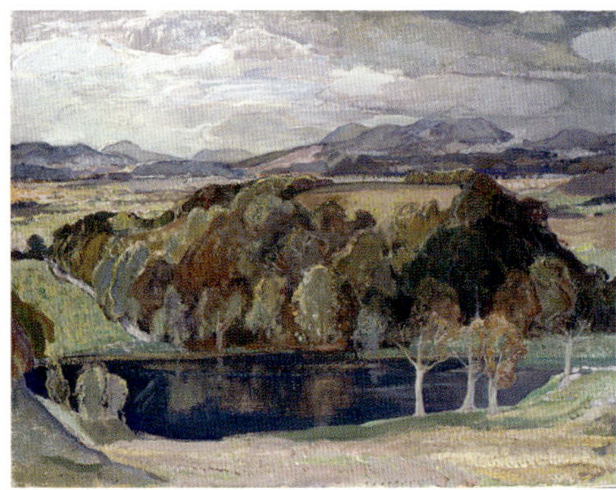

Sturrock, Alick Riddell 1885–1953
Perthshire Panorama c.1949
oil on canvas 71.1 x 91.4
2844

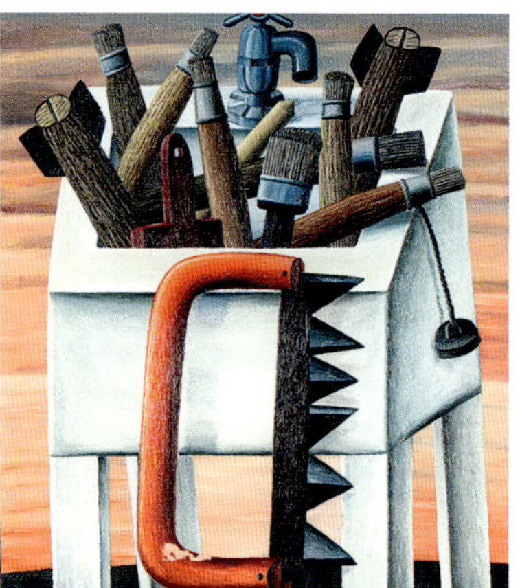

Summerton, Edward b.1962
Sink: Living with an Artist
acrylic on canvas 122 x 107
3679

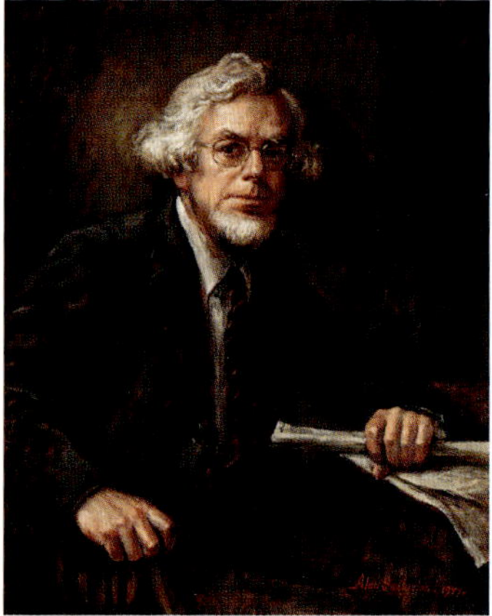

Sutherland, Alan b.1931
Sir William Gray (1928–2000), Lord Provost of Glasgow (1972–1975) 1977
oil on canvas 116.8 x 86.3
3336

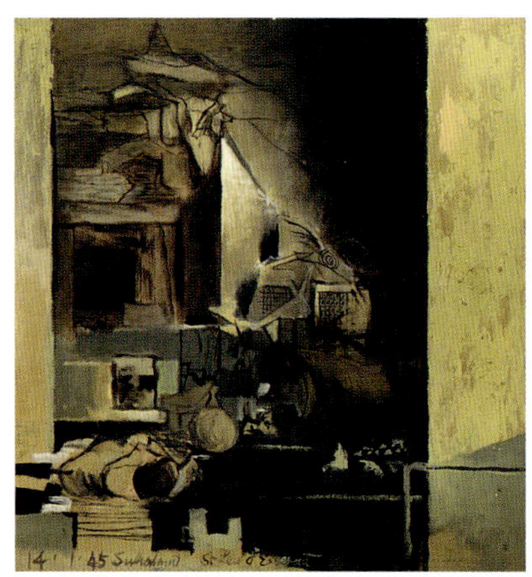

Sutherland, Graham Vivian 1903–1980
Flying Bomb Depot: The Caverns, Saint-Leu-d'Esserent, 14 January 1945 1945
oil on board 96.5 x 88.9
2771

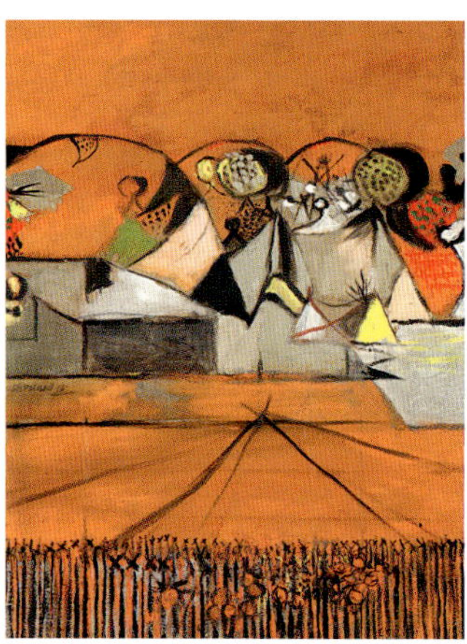

Sutherland, Graham Vivian 1903–1980
Landscape with Rocks 1945
oil on board 94 x 72.4
2983

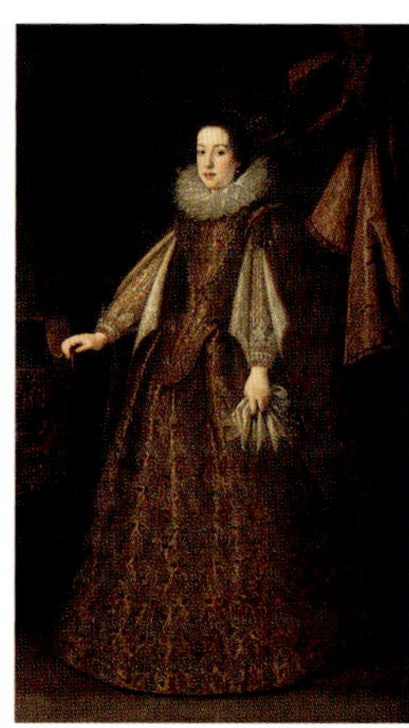

Suttermans, Justus (and studio) 1597–1681
Anna de' Medici (1616–1676), Daughter of Cosimo II de' Medici c.1632–1634
oil on canvas 200 x 113.7
PC.146

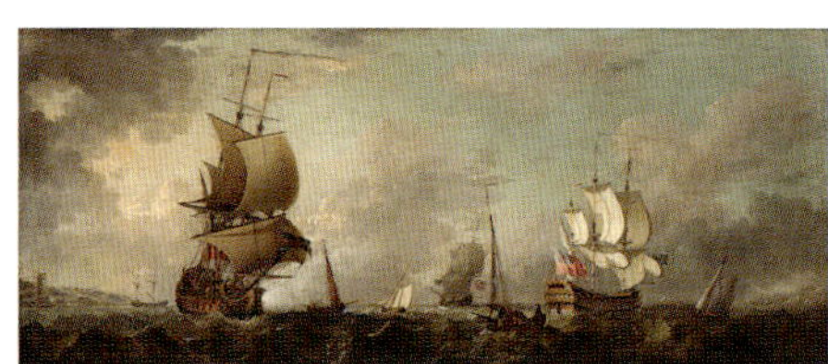

Swaine, Francis (attributed to) 1730–1782
Shipping in a Breeze off the Coast
oil on canvas 67.6 x 154.3
101.b

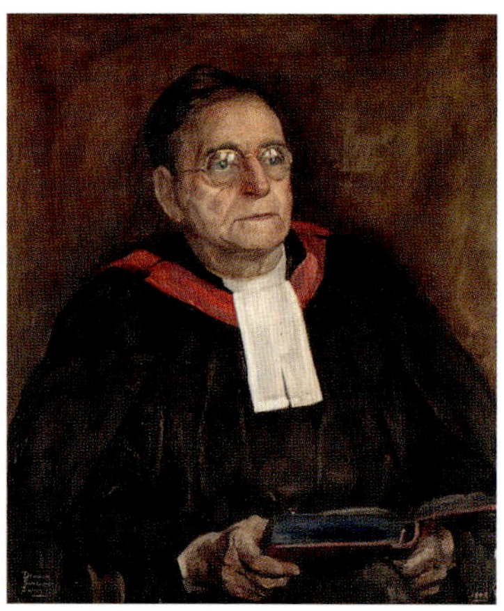

Swan, Donald Sinclair 1918–2004
A Minister 1948
oil on canvas 74.5 x 61.8
PP.1985.222.2.1

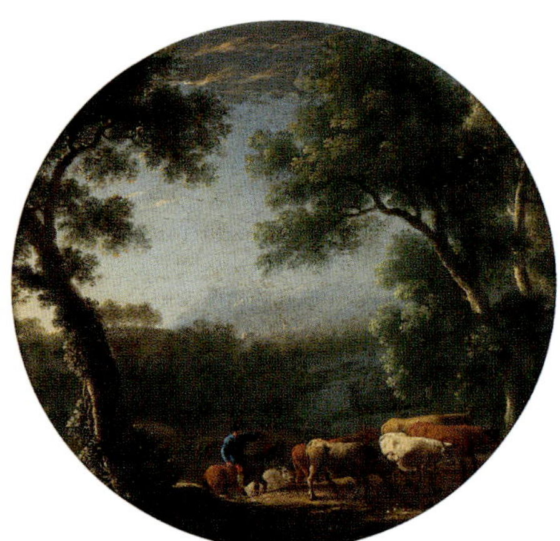

Swanevelt, Herman van c.1600–1665
Wooded Landscape with a Horseman Driving Cattle 1644
oil on canvas 24.8
280

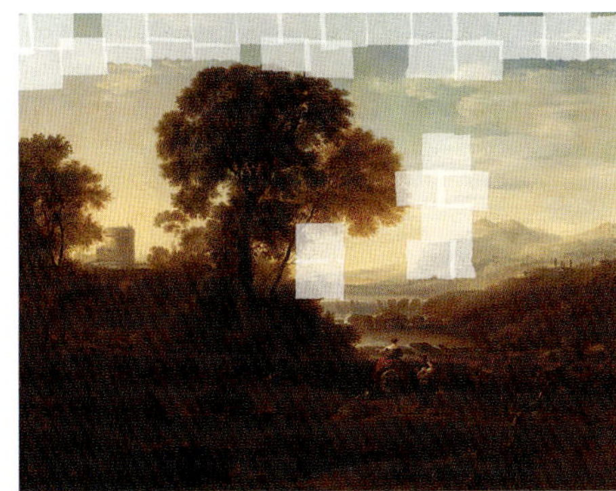

Swanevelt, Herman van c.1600–1665
River Landscape with a Castle and Figures
oil on canvas 86.3 x 107.3
381

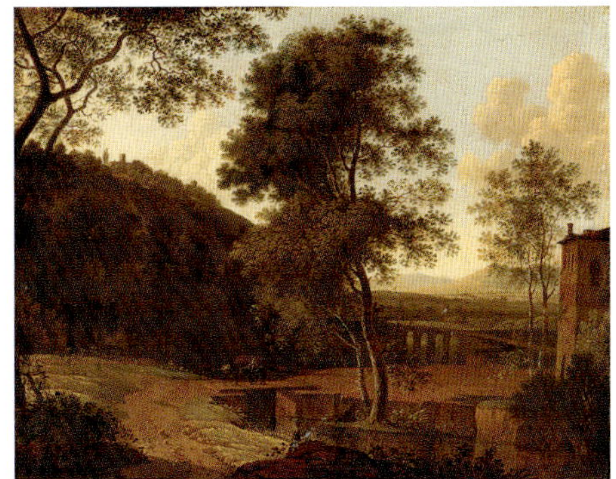

Swanevelt, Herman van (imitator of)
c.1600–1665
River Landscape with Donkeys Crossing a Bridge 19th C
oil on canvas 65.7 x 80.6
428

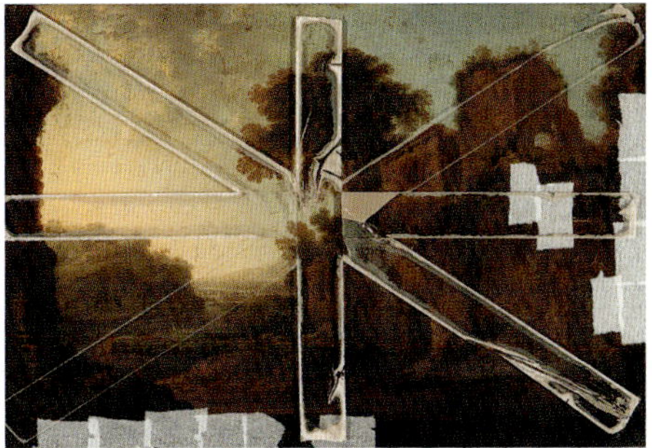

Swanevelt, Herman van (style of)
c.1600–1665
Landscape with Ruins 17th C
oil on canvas 50.2 x 73
617

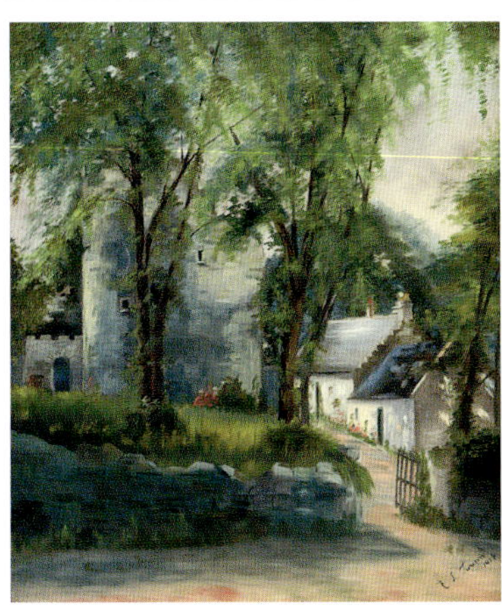

Swann, E. L.
Cathcart Castle 1905
oil on canvas 80 x 70
OG.1957.33

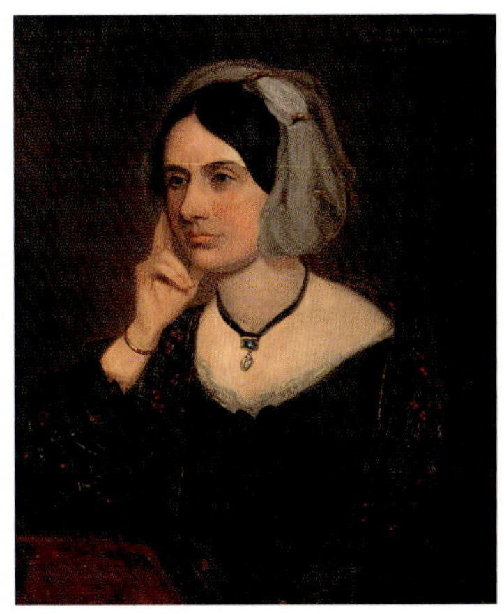

Swinton, James Rannie 1816–1888
Lady Matilda Maxwell (1802–1857), Wife of Sir John Maxwell, 8th Bt
oil on canvas 74.9 x 61.9
PL.127 (P)

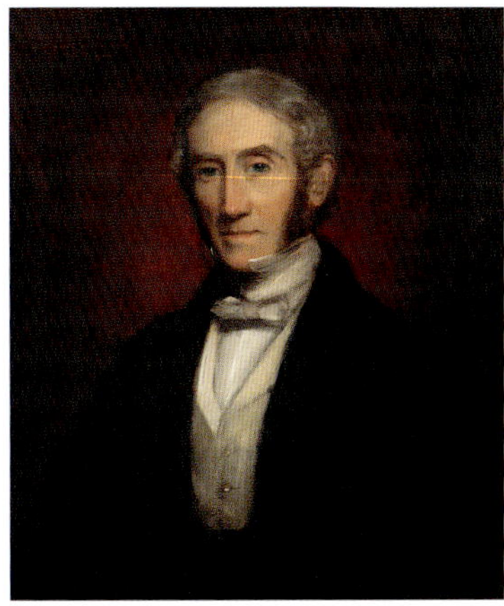

Swinton, James Rannie 1816–1888
Sir John Maxwell (1791–1865), 8th Bt
oil on canvas 72.3 x 62.2
PL.125 (P)

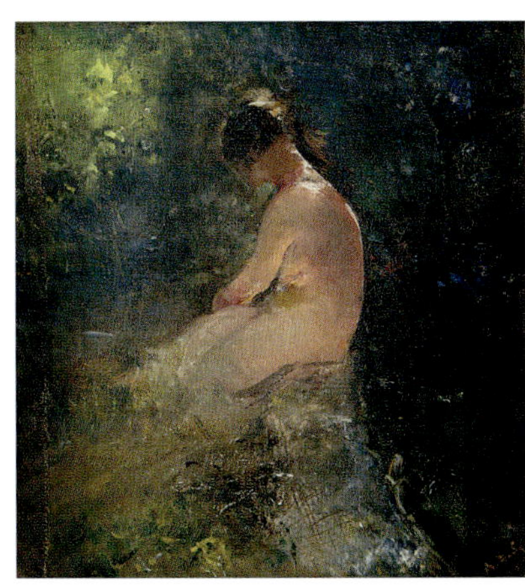

Swynnerton, Annie Louisa 1844–1933
A Dryad
oil on canvas 33 x 29.2
2186

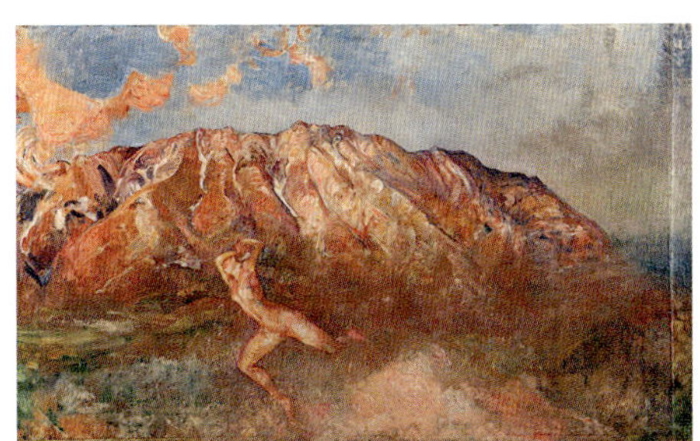

Swynnerton, Annie Louisa 1844–1933
The Soul's Journey: The Soul's Awakening
oil on canvas 100.3 x 161.3
NR.53

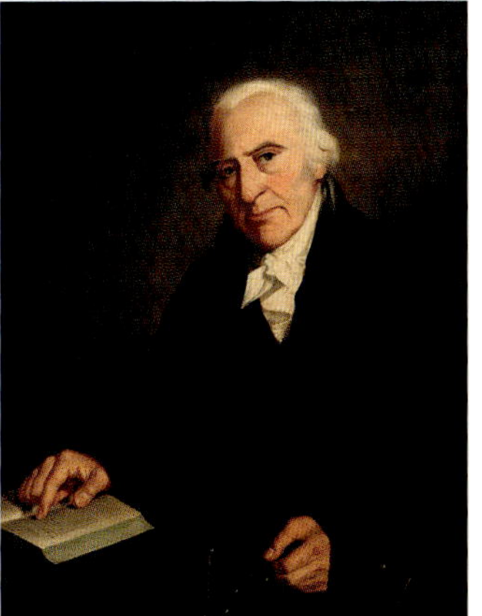

Syme, John S. 1795–1861
J. Bell, MD
oil on canvas 88.9 x 69.9
2205

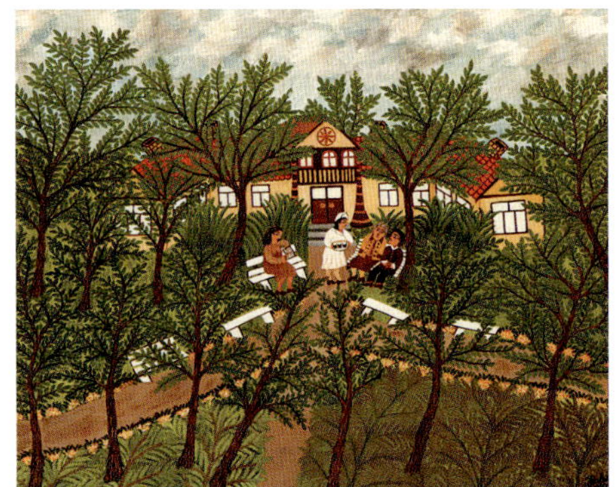

Szubert, Jozef 1898–1984
Convalescence 1980
oil on hardboard 46.6 x 56.6
3581

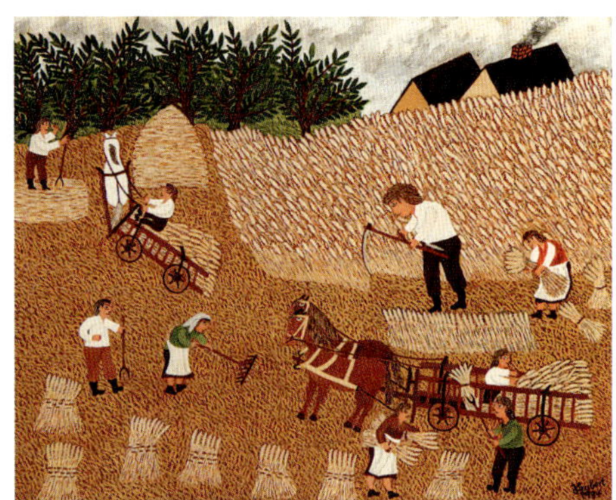

Szubert, Jozef 1898–1984
The Harvest 1984
oil on hardboard 44.5 x 55.2
3580

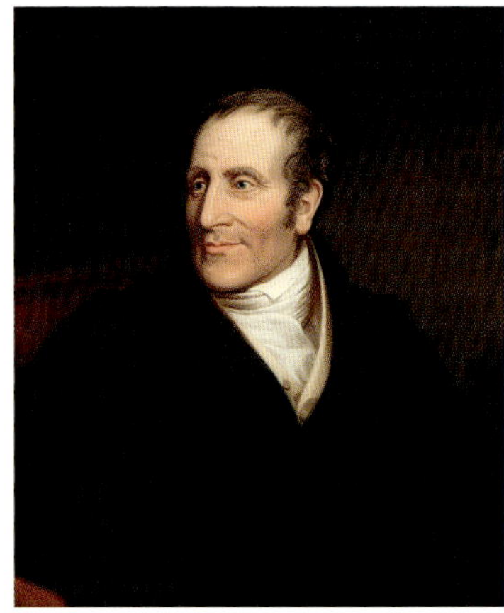

Tannock, James 1784–1863
Henry Bell (1767–1830) 1820s
oil on canvas 76.2 x 63.5
NR.82

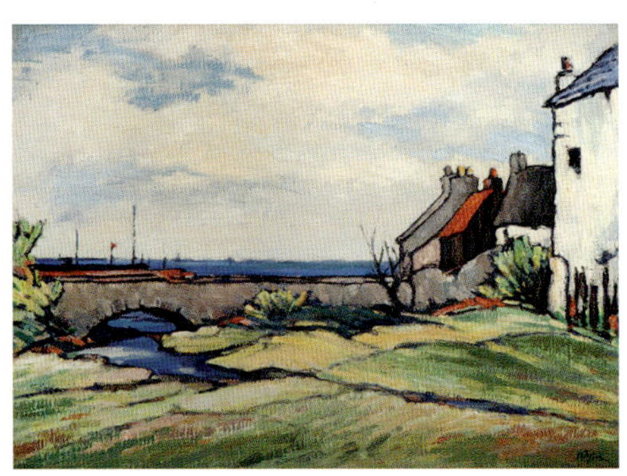

Taylor, Ernest Archibald 1874–1952
Isle of Whithorn c.1941
oil on canvas 61 x 81.3
2261

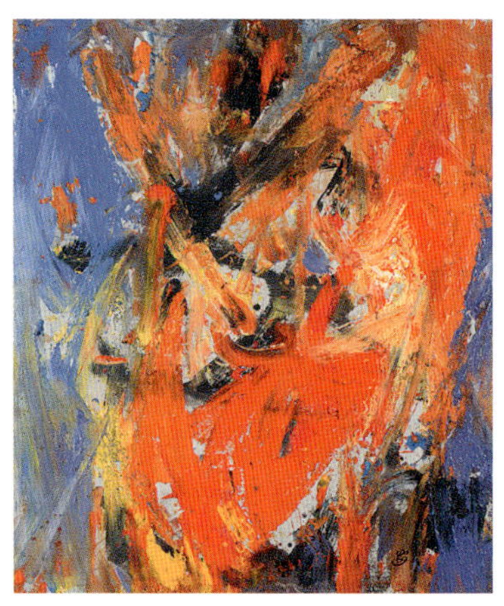

Teh, Hock Aun b.1950
Fitness Is Energy 1986
acrylic on canvas 188 x 152.8
3479

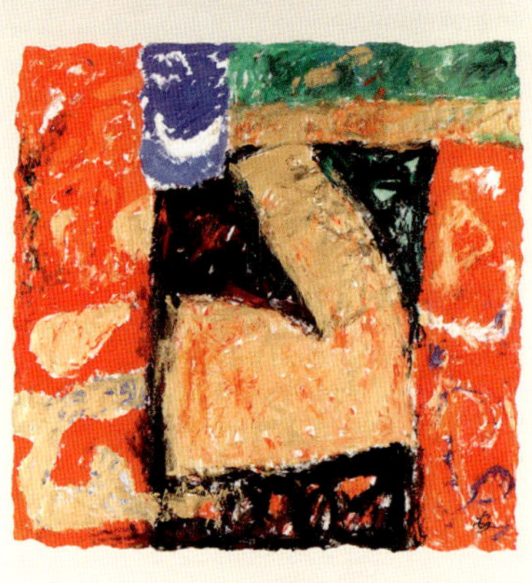

Teh, Hock Aun b.1950
Street Opera at the Temple Festival 1990
acrylic on paper 153 x 151.8
PR.1993.6

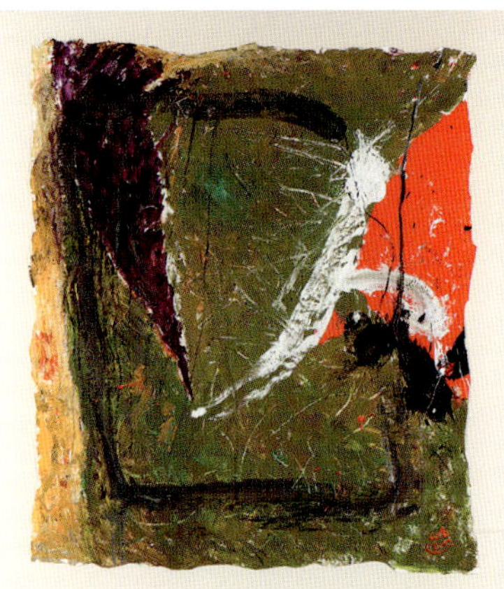

Teh, Hock Aun b.1950
The Legend of Mahsuri 1992
acrylic on paper 151.1 x 125.1
PR.1994.13

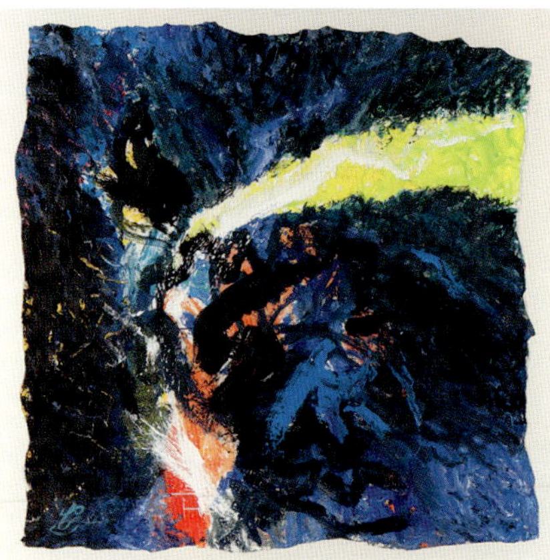

Teh, Hock Aun b.1950
The Milky Way c.1992
acrylic on paper 154.9 x 149.9
PR.1994.15

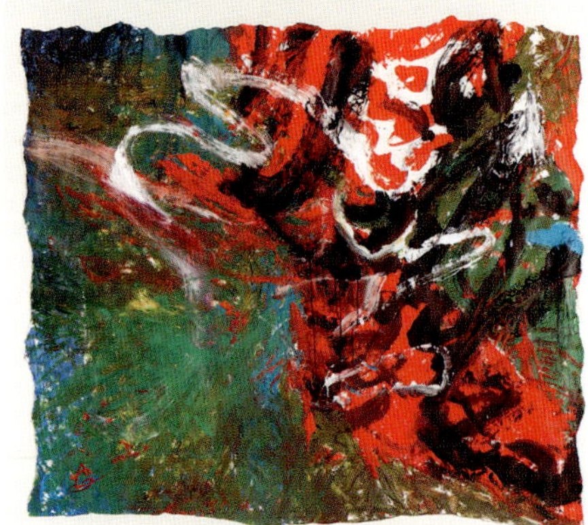

Teh, Hock Aun b.1950
White Snake c.1992
acrylic on paper 138.4 x 149.9
PR.1994.14

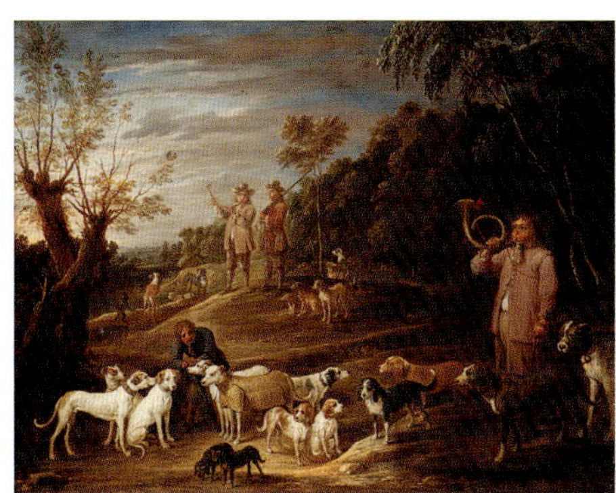

Teniers, David II 1610–1690
Landscape with Huntsmen and Dogs
c.1630–1660
oil on canvas 66 x 82.5
97

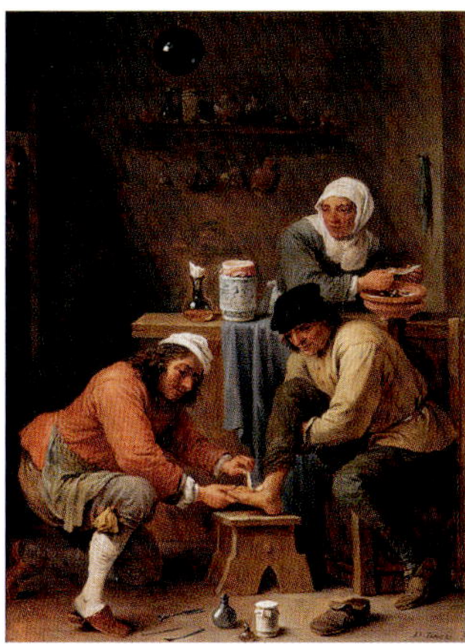

Teniers, David II 1610–1690
A Surgeon Treating a Peasant's Foot 1640s
oil on panel 36.8 x 27.3
13

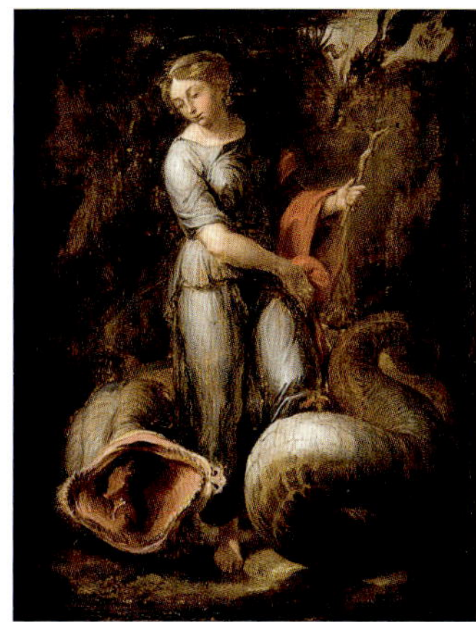

Teniers, David II 1610–1690
Saint Margaret (after Raphael) c.1651–1660
oil on panel 27 x 20.8
37

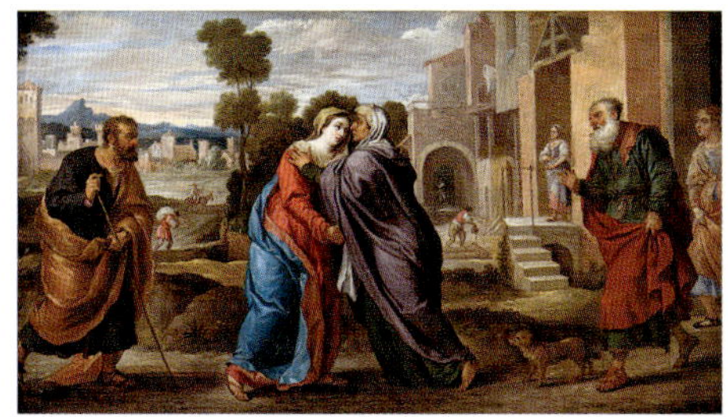

Teniers, David II 1610–1690
The Visitation (after Jacopo Palma il Vecchio)
c.1651–1660
oil on panel 31 x 54.3
27

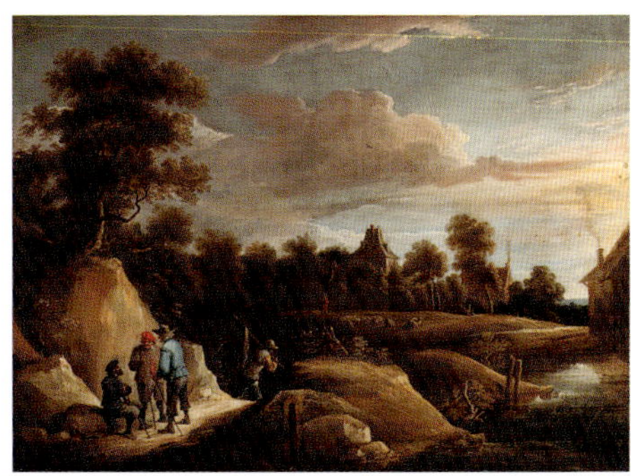

Teniers, David II (after) 1610–1690
Landscape with Peasants on a Pathway
17th C
oil on canvas 105.7 x 145.4
100

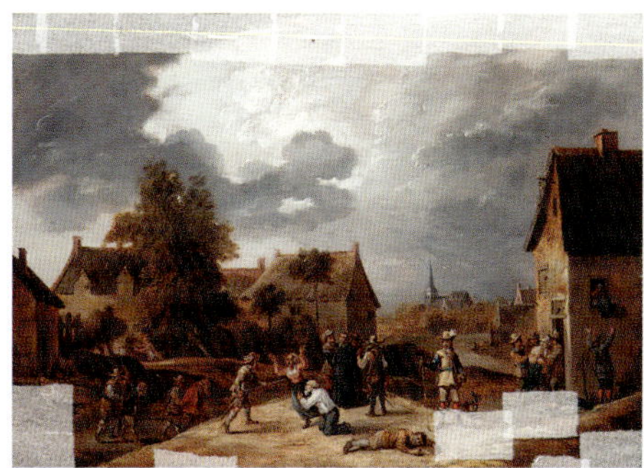

Teniers, David II (after) 1610–1690
Soldiers Plundering a Village 17th C
oil on panel 38.4 x 51.1
86

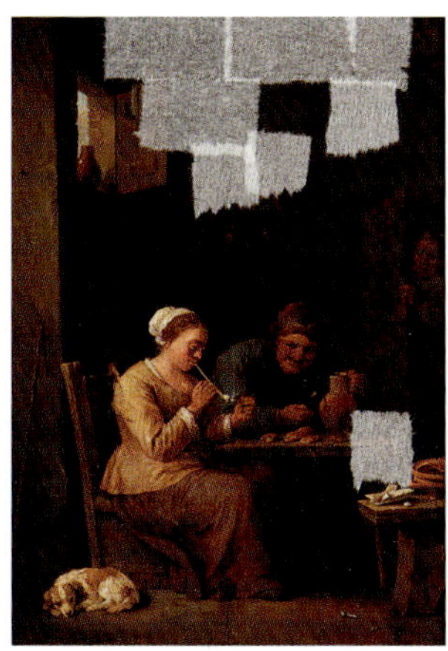

Teniers, David II (attributed to) 1610–1690
Interior with a Man and a Woman at a Table
oil on canvas 36 x 26.7
79

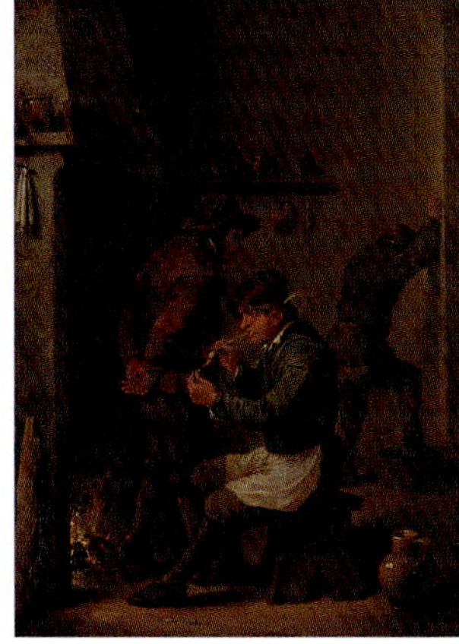

Teniers, David II (attributed to) 1610–1690
Interior with Peasants before a Fire
oil on panel 30.8 x 22.8
106

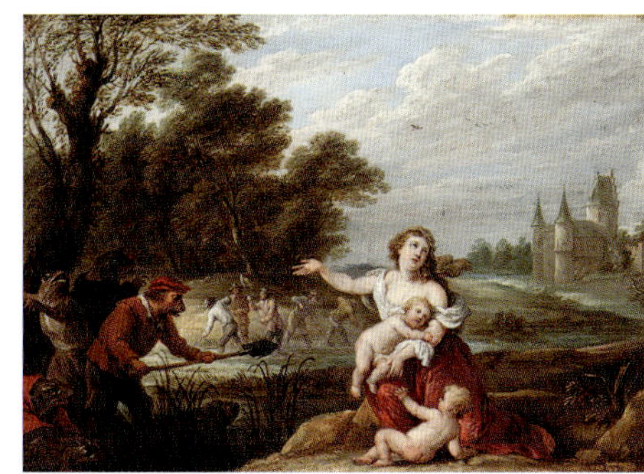

Teniers, David II (attributed to) 1610–1690
Latona and the Lycian Peasants
oil on canvas 33.7 x 45
3

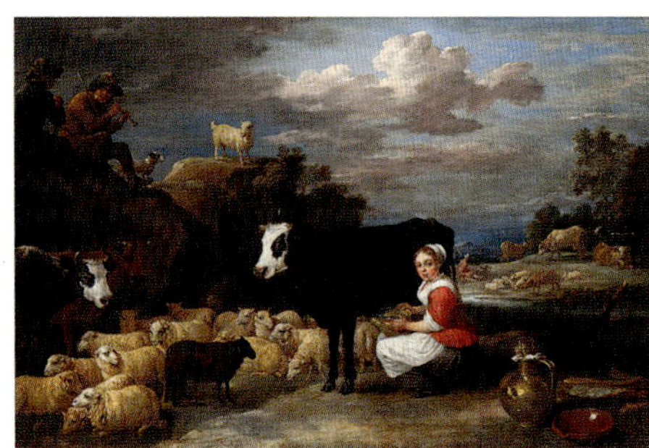

Teniers, David II (attributed to) 1610–1690
The Milk Maid
oil on canvas 41.9 x 61
42

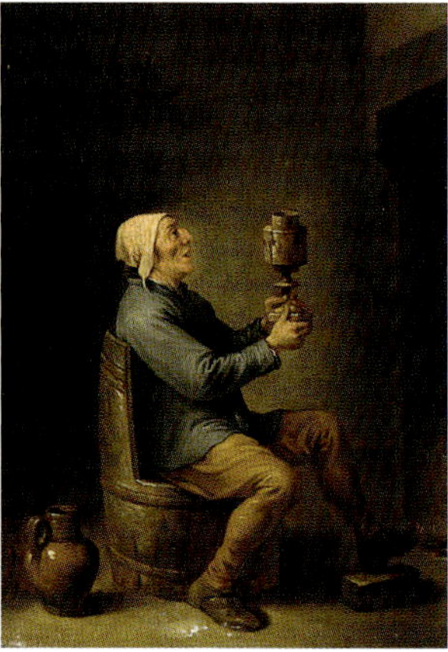

Teniers, David II (follower of) 1610–1690
Boer Seated on a Barrel Chair 17th C
oil on panel 28.5 x 21.6
35.72

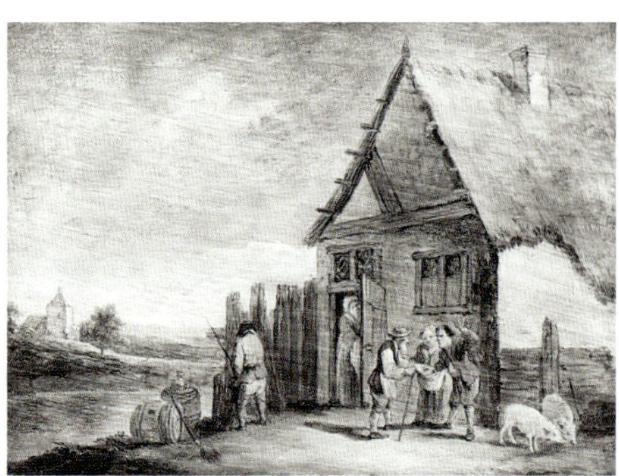

Teniers, David II (follower of) 1610–1690
Landscape with Figures before a Cottage
late 17th C
oil on panel 14.6 x 19.7
72

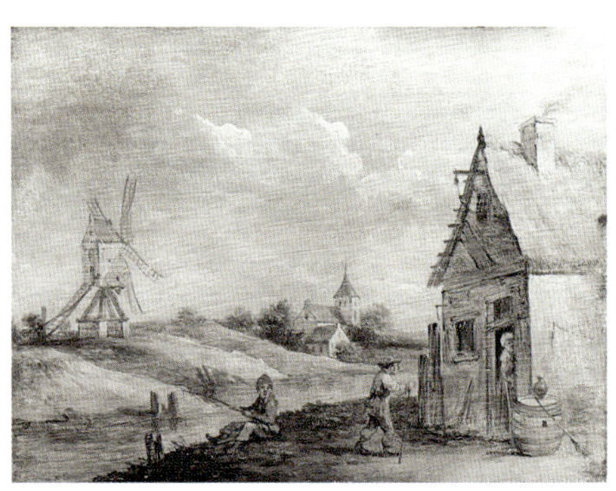

Teniers, David II (follower of) 1610–1690
*Landscape with Figures before a Cottage, and a
Windmill* late 17th C
oil on panel 14.6 x 19.7
73

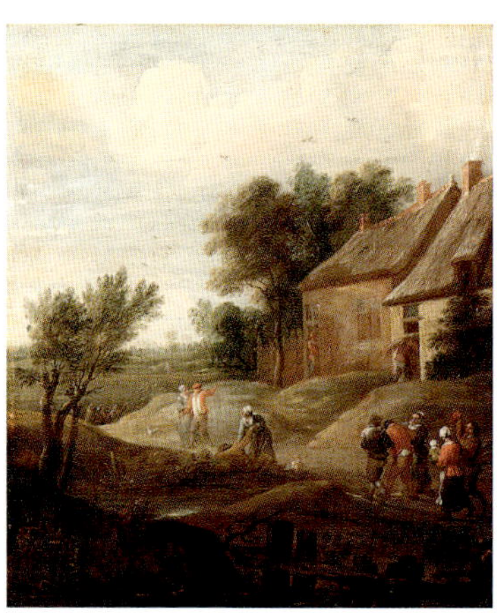

Teniers, David II (imitator of) 1610–1690
Drunken Peasants Going Home
oil on canvas 69.8 x 59.7
87

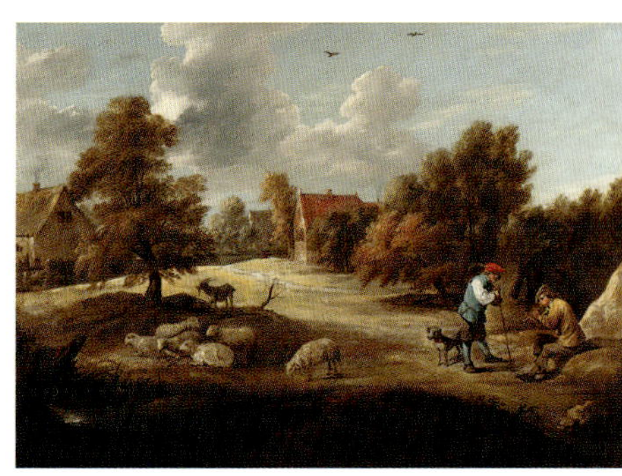

Teniers, David II (imitator of) 1610–1690
Landscape with Shepherds Outside a Village
oil on canvas 99 x 132.7
47

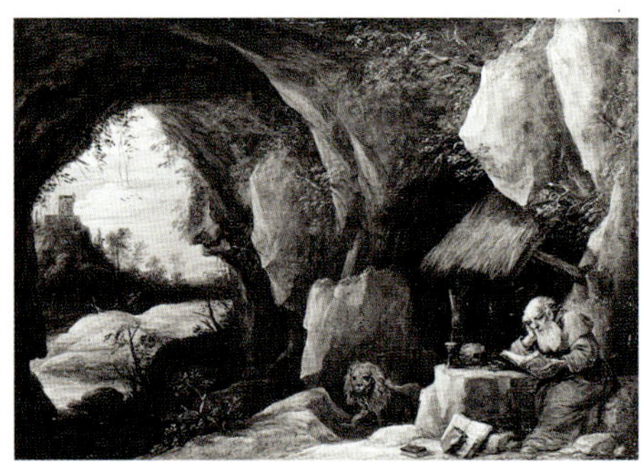

Teniers, David II (studio of) 1610–1690
Saint Jerome in a Rocky Landscape
oil on panel 24.8 x 34.9
6

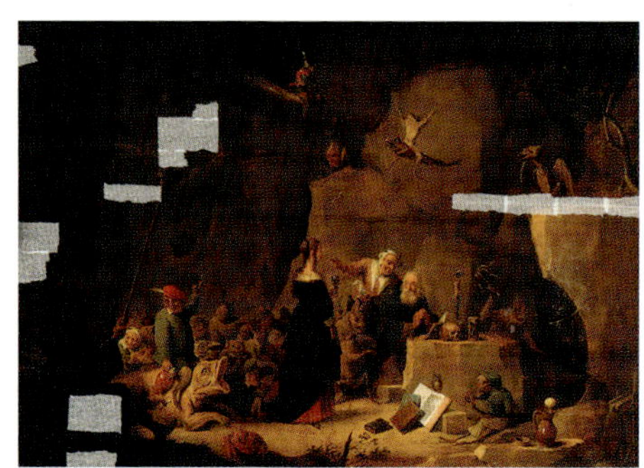

Teniers, David II (studio of) 1610–1690
The Temptation of Saint Anthony
oil on panel 57.8 x 84.1
46

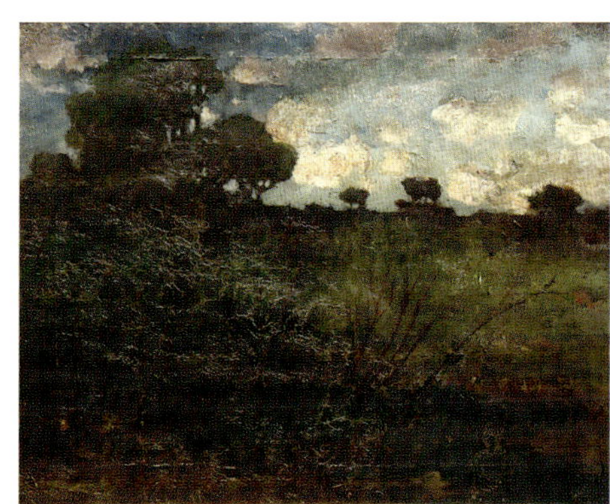

Thomas, Grosvenor 1856–1923
Landscape
oil on canvas 43.2 x 51.4
35.627

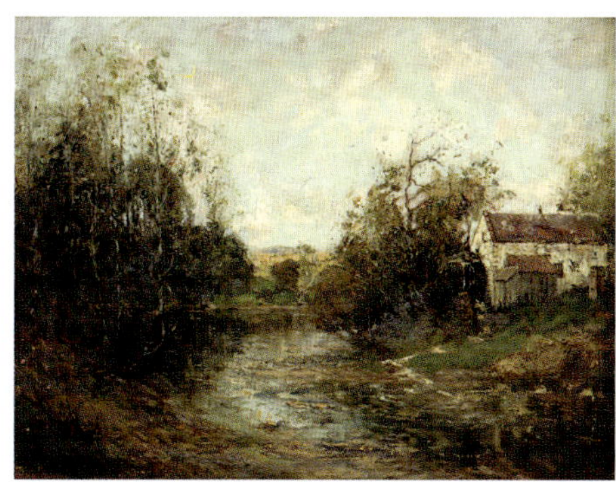

Thomas, Grosvenor 1856–1923
The Mill
oil on canvas 71.1 x 91.4
1917

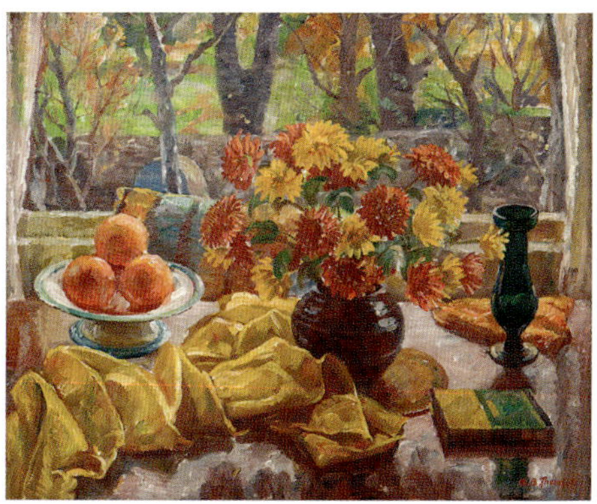

Thomson, Adam Bruce 1885–1976
Still Life at a Window c.1944
oil on canvas 63.5 x 76.2
2468

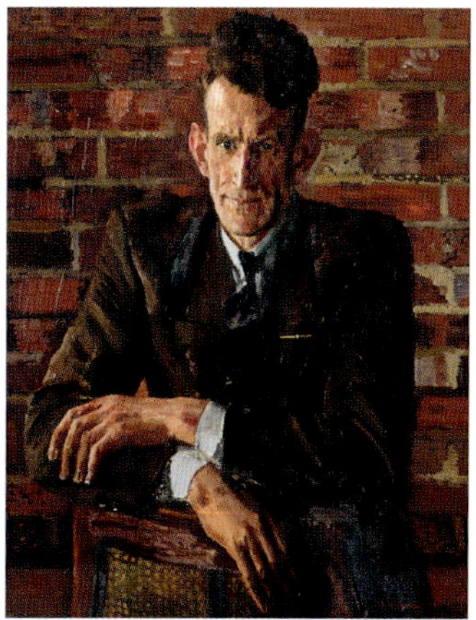

Thomson, Alfred Reginald 1894–1979
E. Court, Esq. c.1941
oil on canvas 91.4 x 71.1
L.1.1942

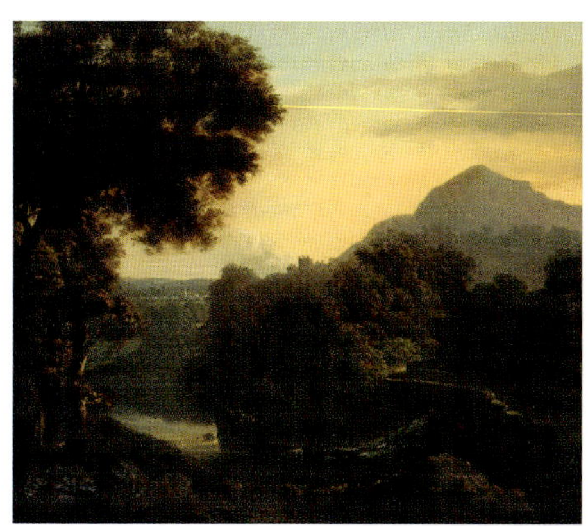

Thomson, John 1778–1840
Craigmillar Castle and Arthur's Seat
oil on canvas 41.5 x 51.1
3046

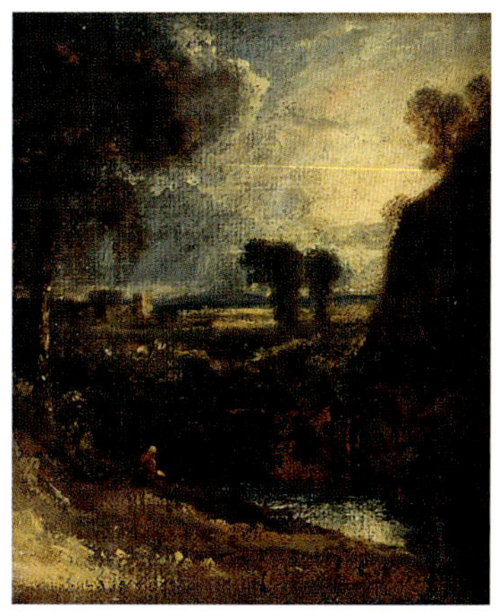

Thomson, John 1778–1840
Landscape
oil on canvas on board 21 x 17.8
430

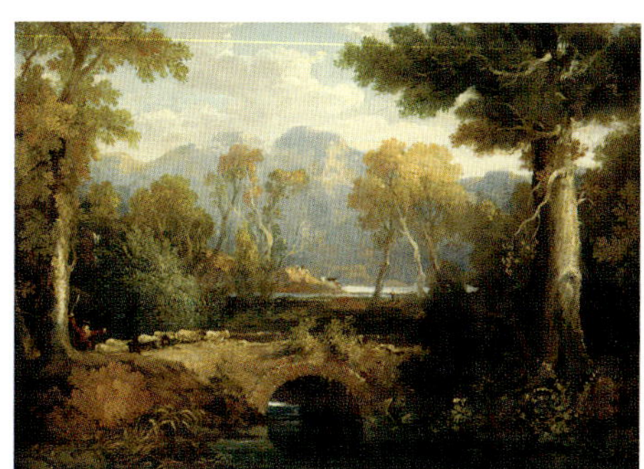

Thomson, John 1778–1840
Landscape with a Bridge
oil on panel 34.9 x 48.9
1071

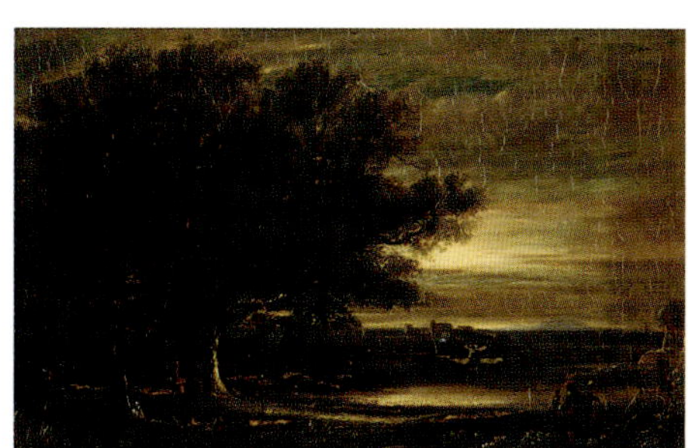

Thomson, John 1778–1840
River Scene
oil on panel 24.1 x 38.1
996

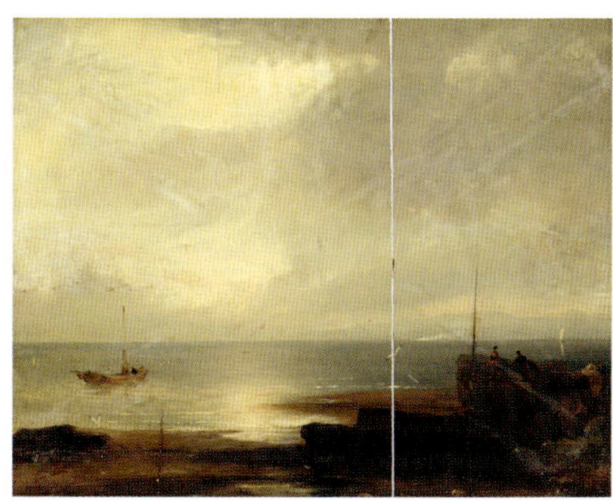

Thomson, John 1778–1840
The Firth of Forth, Morning
oil on panel 36.8 x 47.6
463

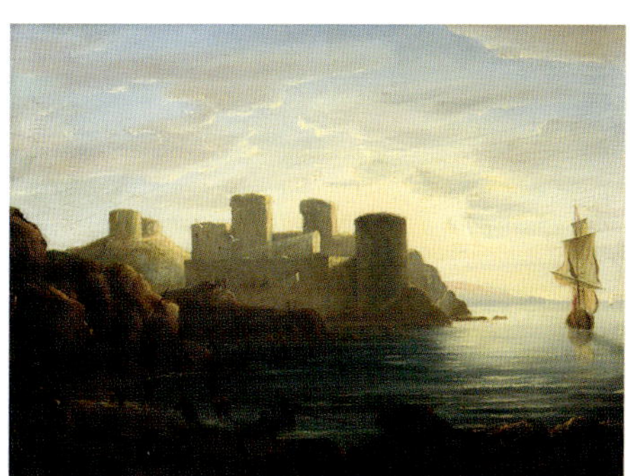

Thomson, John (attributed to) 1778–1840
Tantallon Castle
oil on panel 35 x 47.1
3109

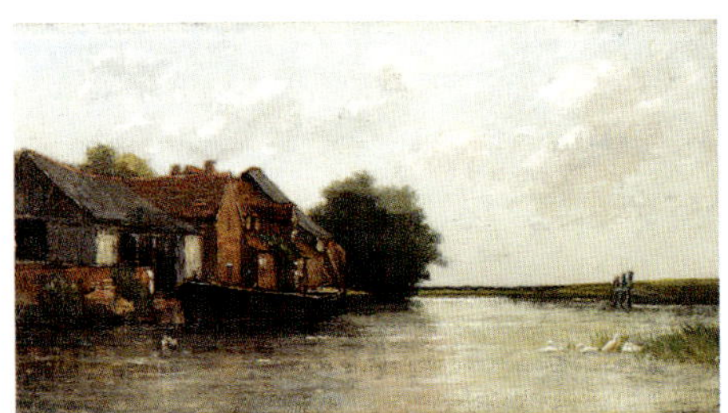

Thomson, John Leslie 1851–1929
A Suffolk River
oil on canvas 27.9 x 50.8
2562

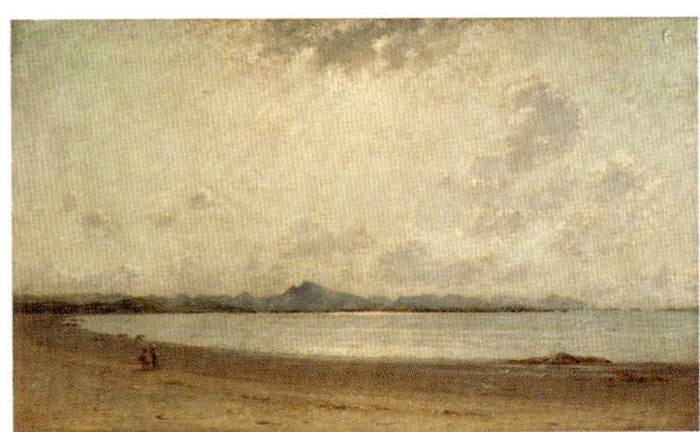

Thomson, John Leslie 1851–1929
Seascape, Anglesey
oil on canvas 91.4 x 152.4
2565

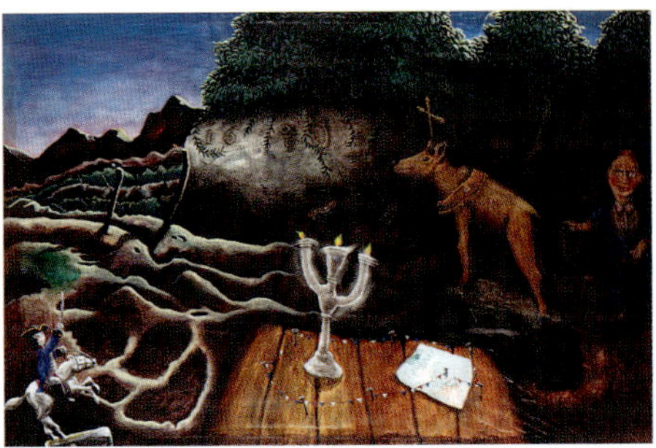

Thomson, Peter b.1962
1690–1990 1989
acrylic on paper 107.5 x 158.5
PR.1998.2.j

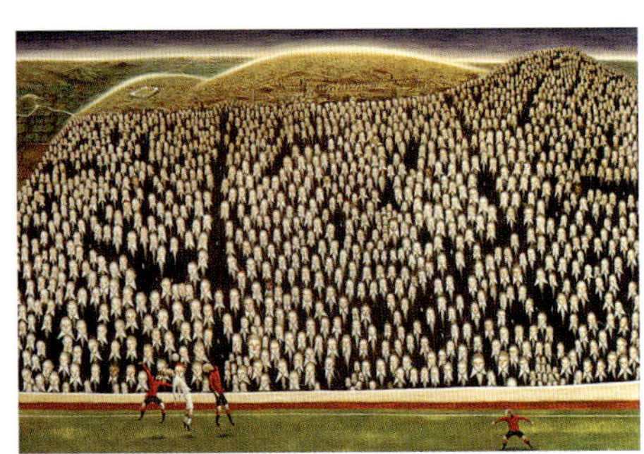

Thomson, Peter b.1962
The Spectacle 1996–1997
acrylic on board 99.5 x 151
3615

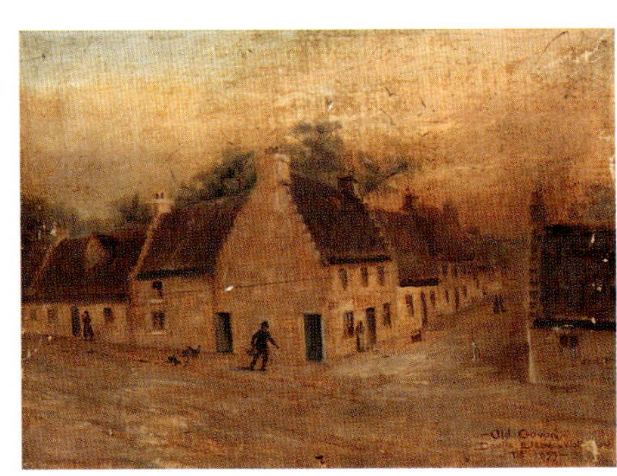

Till
Old Govan, Devil's Elbow and Water Row
1859
oil on canvas 40.5 x 53.4
TEMP.8512

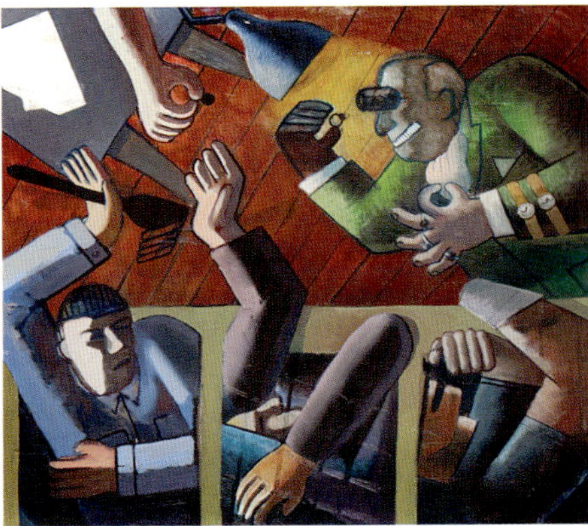

Tinney, Stephen b.1963
The Pawn Shop 1980s
oil on canvas 156 x 176
PP.1986.167

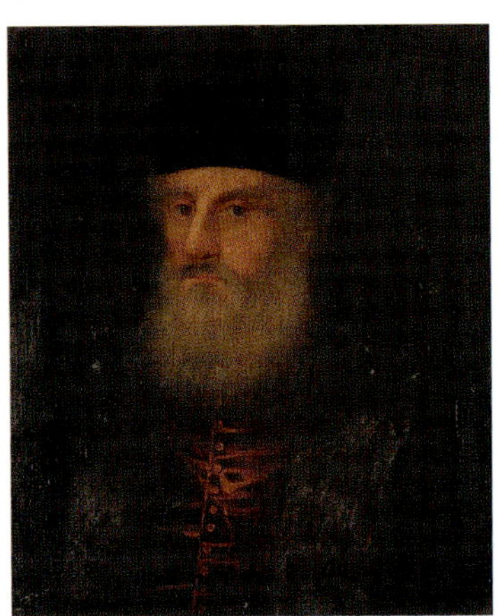

Tintoretto, Jacopo (follower of) 1519–1594
Portrait of a Venetian Senator late 16th C
oil on canvas 66 x 54
NR.29

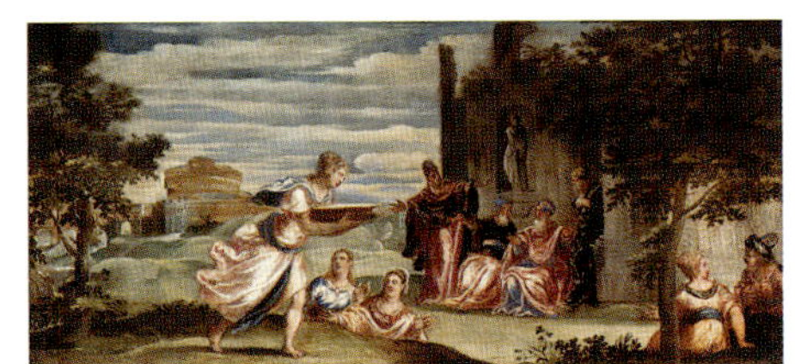

Tintoretto, Jacopo (studio of) 1519–1594
The Ordeal of Tuccia c.1555
oil on canvas 47.6 x 103.2
189

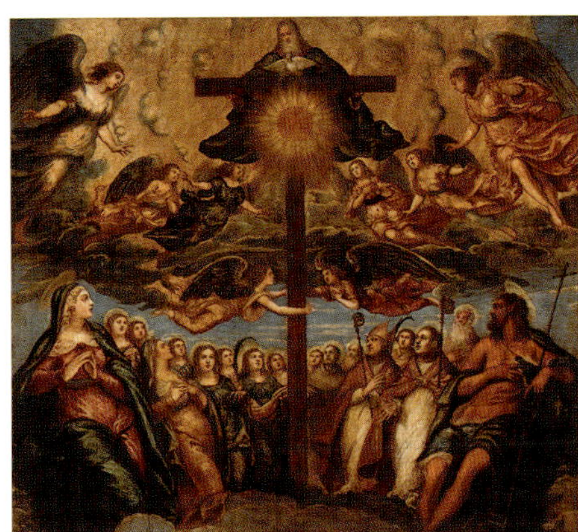

Tintoretto, Jacopo (studio of) 1519–1594
The Trinity Adored by Saints and Angels
c.1580–1585
oil on canvas 158.7 x 165.7
620

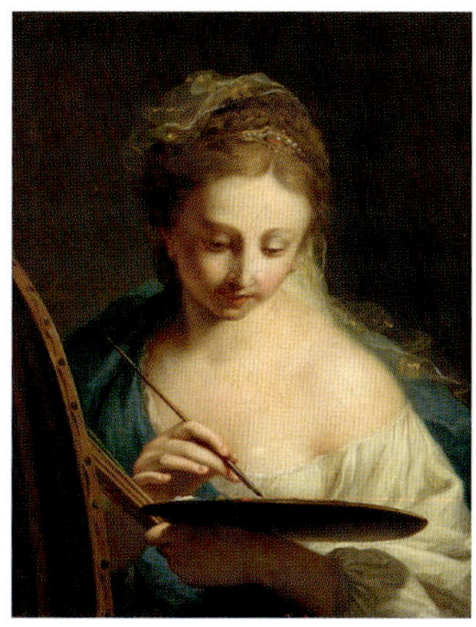

Tischbein, Johann Heinrich I 1722–1789
Young Woman Painting 1758
oil on canvas 56.5 x 45.7
223

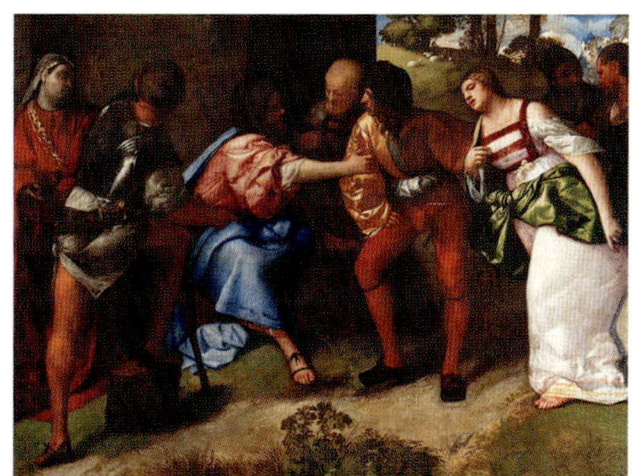

Titian c.1488–1576
Christ and the Adulteress c.1508–1510
oil on canvas 139.3 x 181.7
181

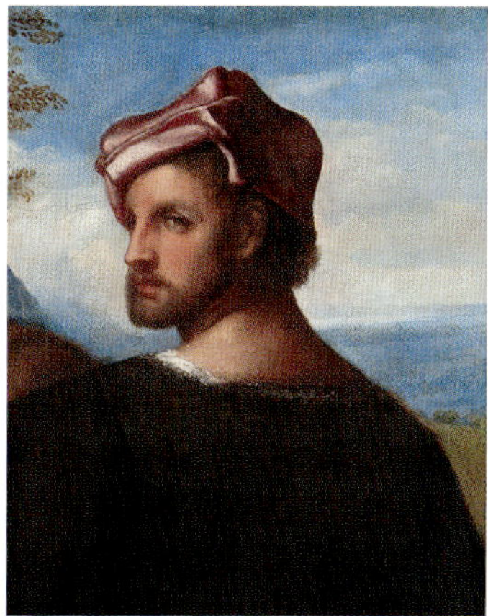

Titian c.1488–1576
Head of a Man (fragment of 'Christ and the
Adulteress') c.1508–1510
oil on canvas 47 x 40.5
3283

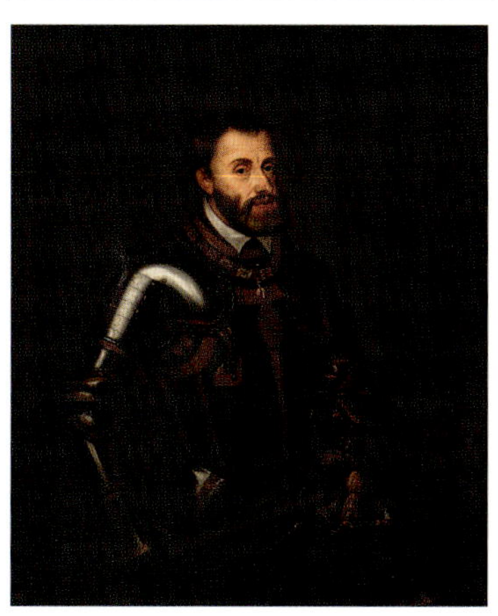

Titian (after) c.1488–1576
Emperor Charles V (1500–1558)
16th C–17th C
oil on canvas 122.9 x 98.7
PC.156

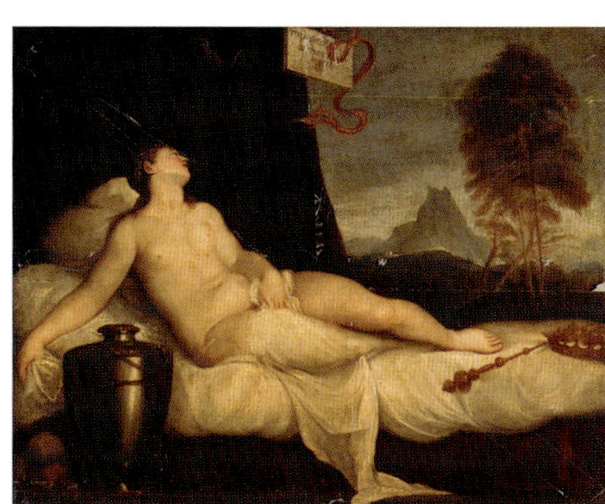

Titian (after) c.1488–1576
Vanitas 18th C (?)
oil on canvas 80.4 x 99.4
190

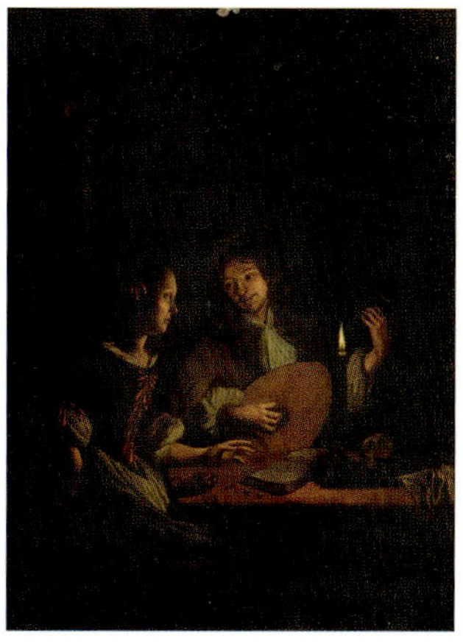

Toorenvliet, Jacob c.1635–1719
The Guitarist and the Listener
oil on copper 43.2 x 31.8
PL.108 (P)

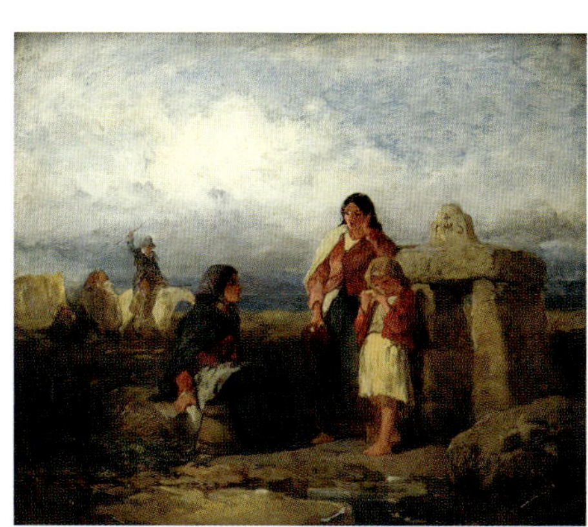

Topham, Francis Williams 1808–1877
At the Holy Well
oil on canvas 38.1 x 45.7
984

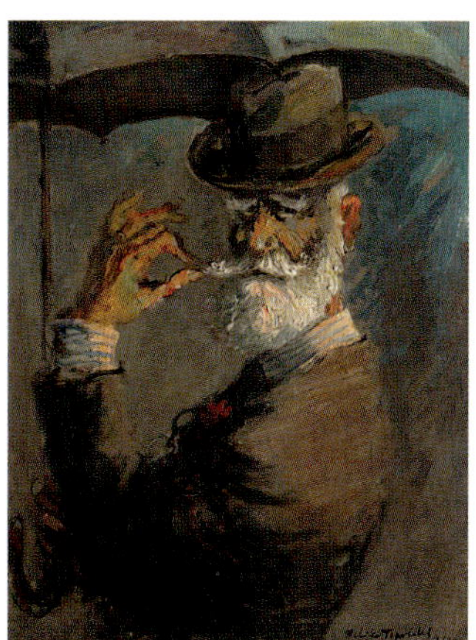

Topolski, Feliks 1907–1989
George Bernard Shaw (1856–1950) 1939
oil on paper on hardboard 81.3 x 61
2257

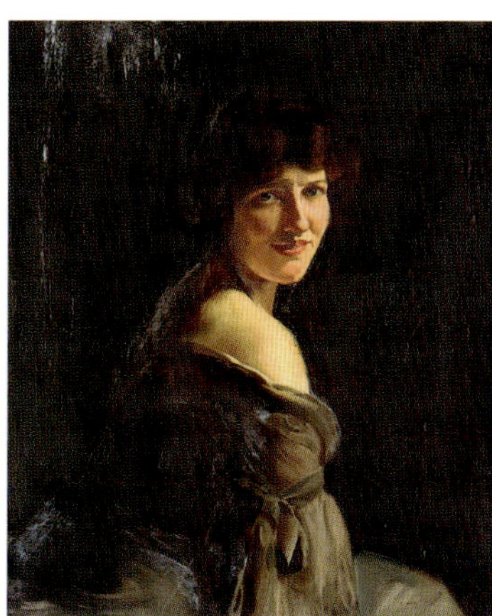

Torrance, James 1859–1916
Head of a Lady late 1890s
oil on canvas 76.2 x 63.5
2125

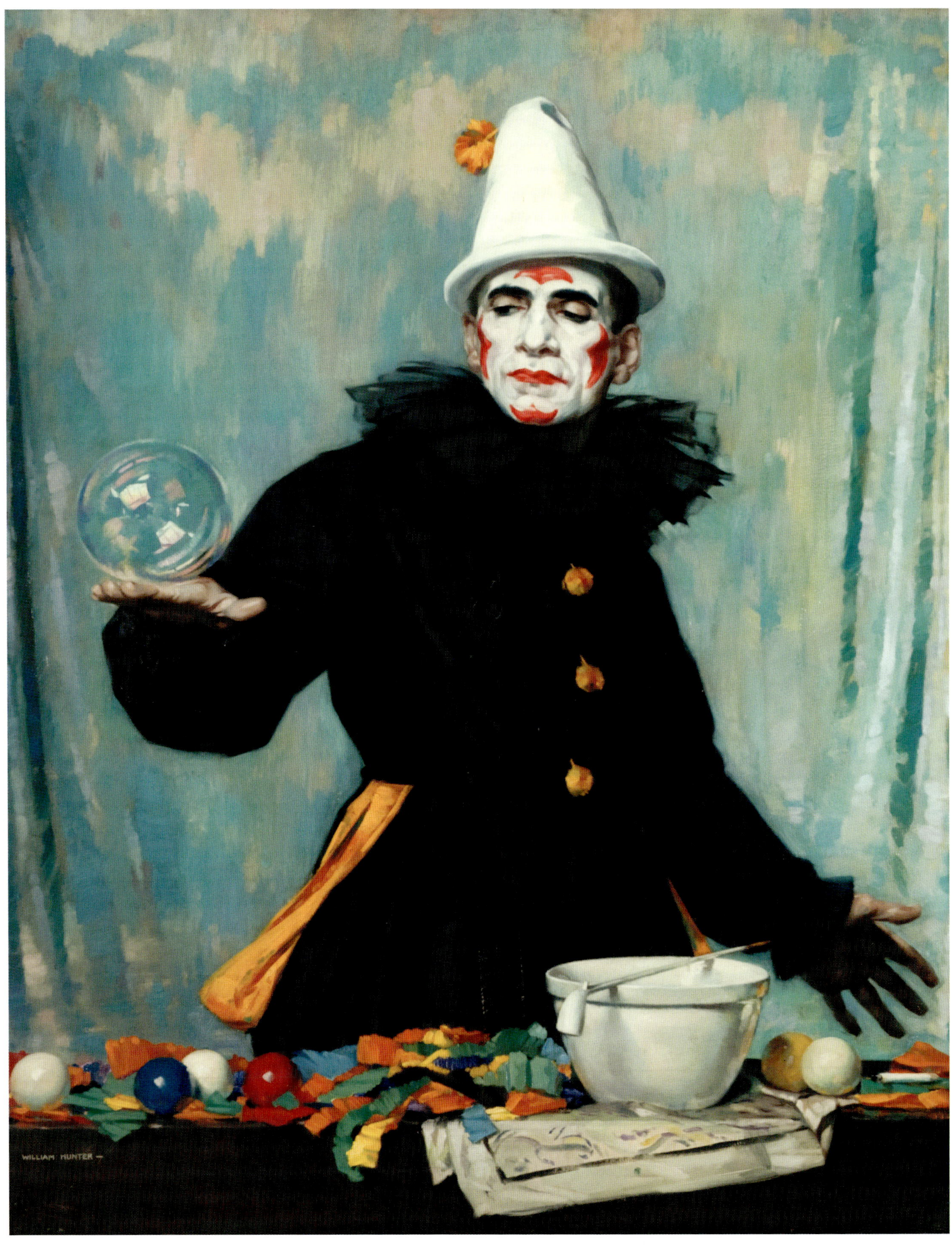

WILLIAM HUNTER

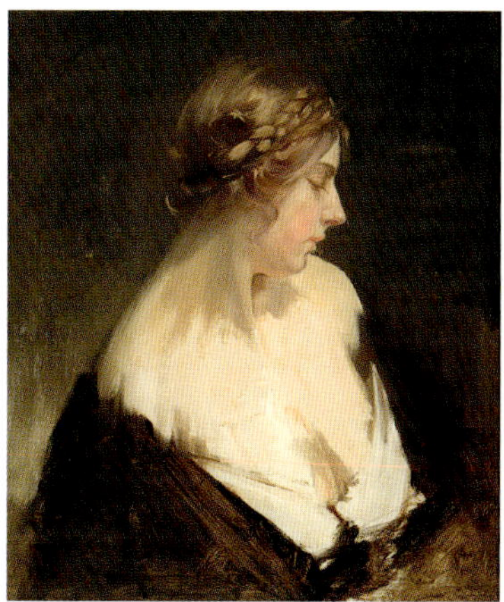

Torrance, James 1859–1916
Kitty
oil on canvas 61 x 50.8
1521

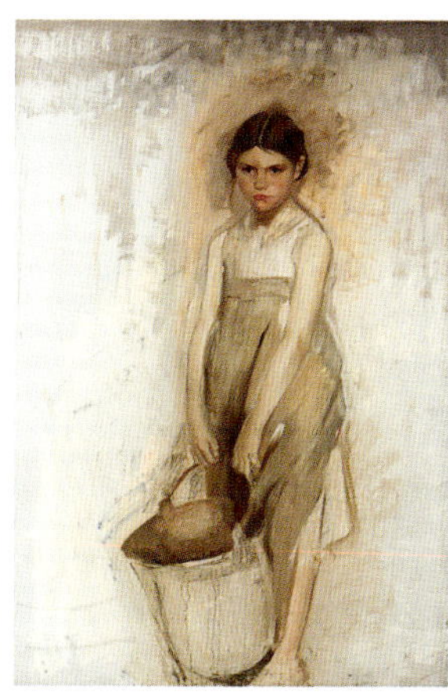

Torrance, James 1859–1916
The Pig-Feeder's Daughter
oil on canvas 119.4 x 79.4
3405

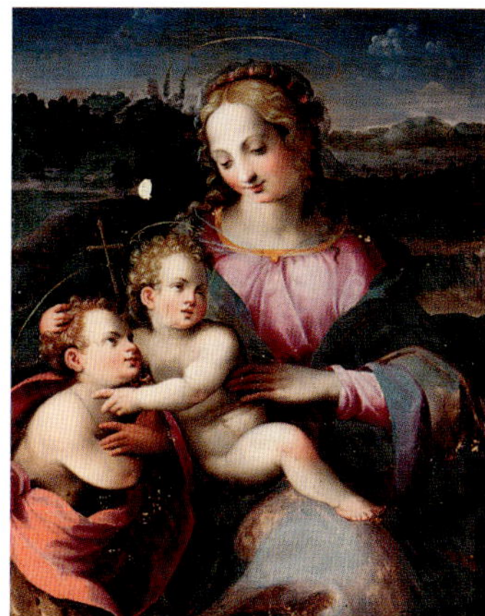

Tosini, Michele (attributed to) 1503–1577
Virgin and Child with the Child Baptist
c.1570
oil on panel 83.5 x 66.4
165

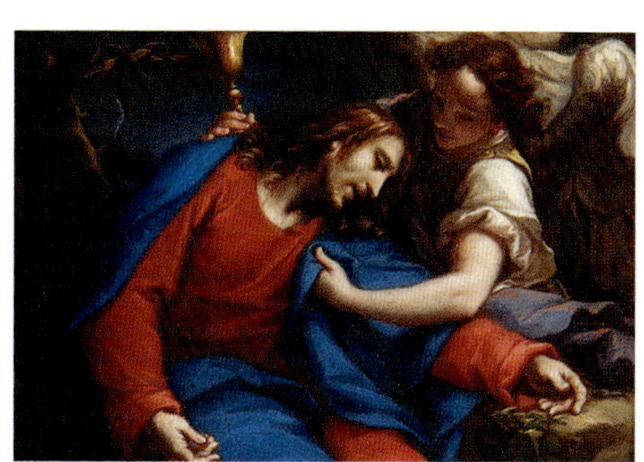

Trevisani, Francesco 1656–1746
The Agony in the Garden 1740
oil on copper 16.2 x 22.6
145

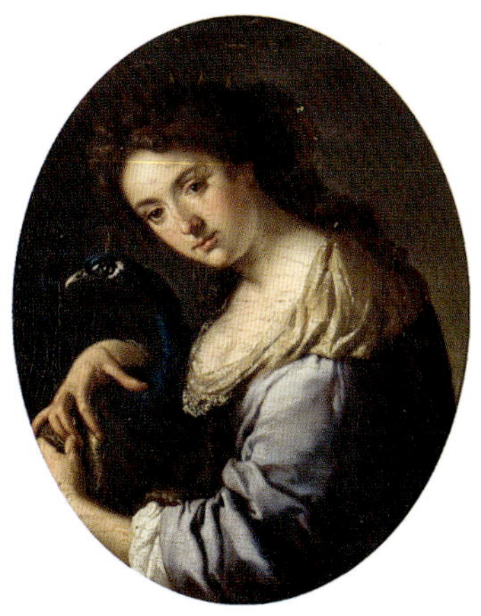

Trevisani, Francesco (circle of) 1656–1746
Portrait of a Woman as Juno c.1690–1710
oil on canvas 75.5 x 59.4
183

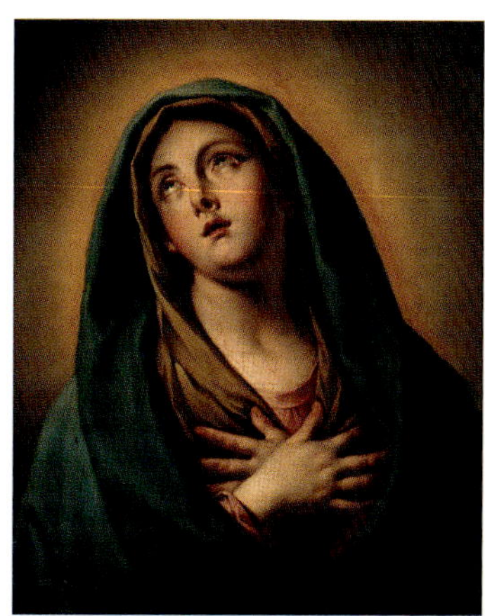

Trevisani, Francesco (studio of) 1656–1746
Mater dolorosa
oil on canvas 68.8 x 58.5
376

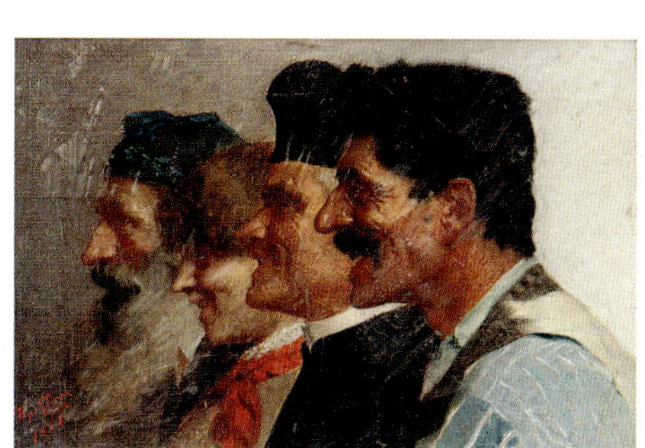

Tricca, Fosco 1856–1918
Looking at the Carnival 1881
oil on canvas 27.1 x 36.8
1161

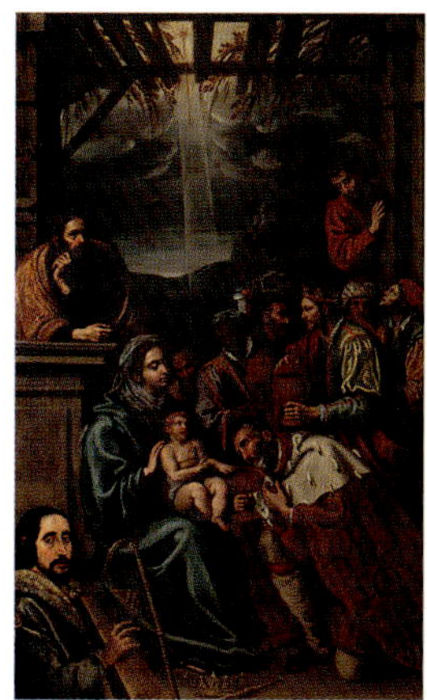

Tristán de Escamilla, Luis 1585–1624
The Adoration of the Magi
oil on canvas 167.4 x 100.3
PC.64

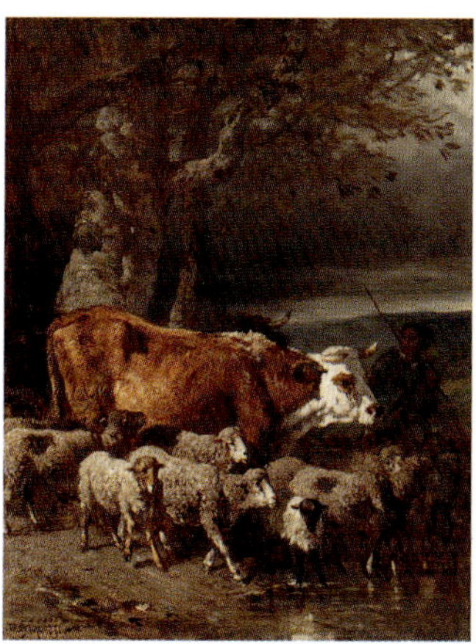

Troyon, Constant 1810–1865
Returning from Market 1851
oil on canvas 92.3 x 73.4
1145

Facing page: Hunter, William, 1890–1967, *The Bubble Reputation*, 1928 (p. 215)

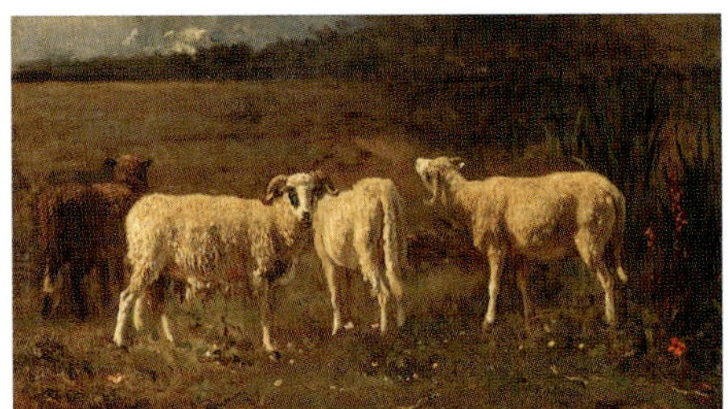

Troyon, Constant 1810–1865
Sheep 1855
oil on canvas 29 x 52.5
1118

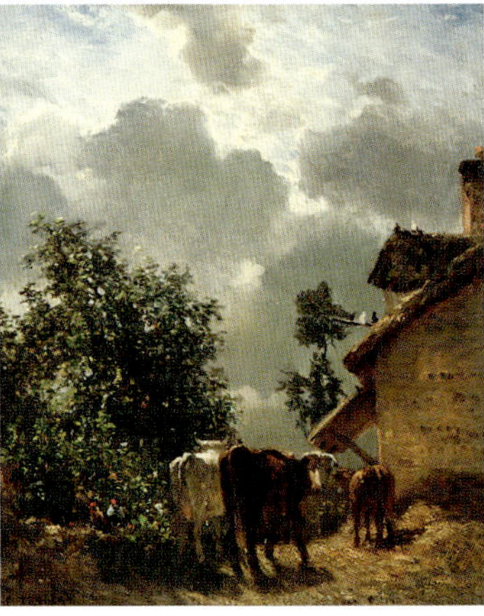

Troyon, Constant 1810–1865
Cattle
oil on canvas 46 x 38
1133

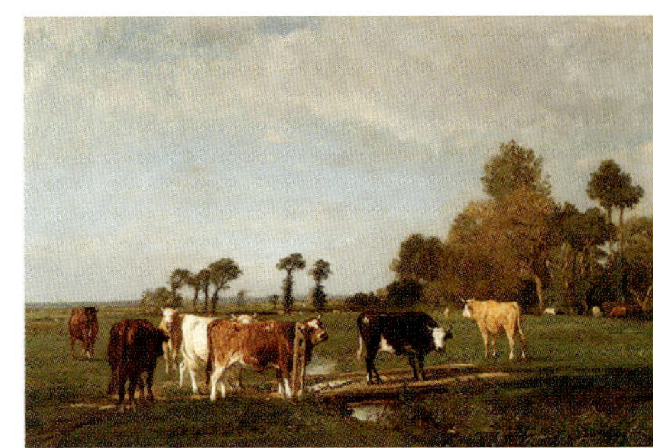

Troyon, Constant 1810–1865
Landscape and Cattle
oil on canvas 65 x 93.1
735

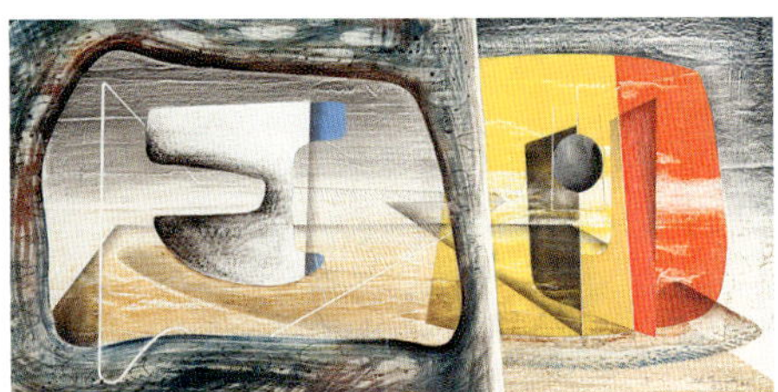

Tunnard, John 1900–1971
Special Device 1945
oil on composite board 30.7 x 60.8
2543

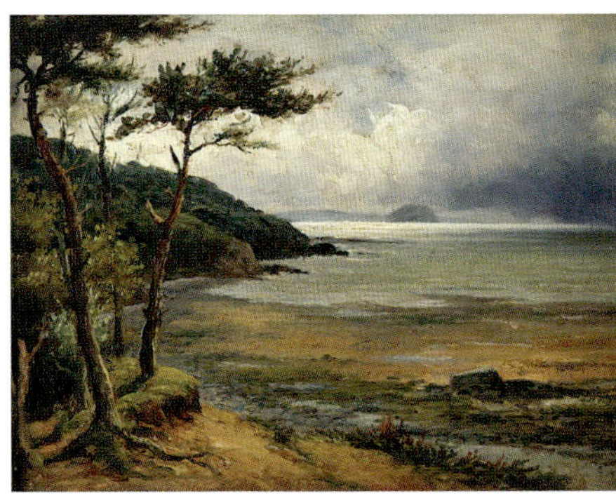

Turner, Francis C.
The River Severn from Weston-super-Mare
1895
oil on millboard 24.1 x 31.8
2097

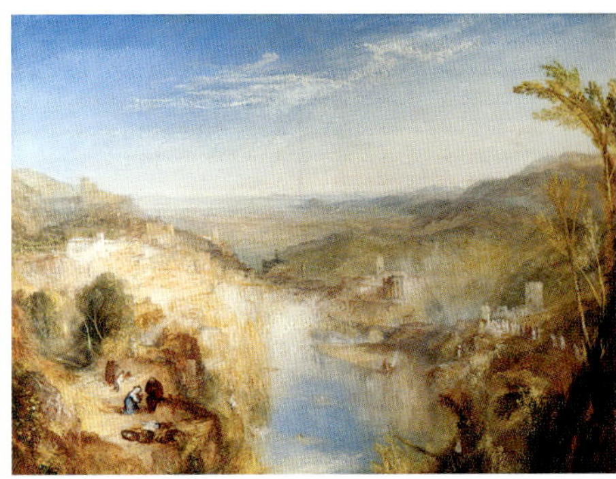

Turner, Joseph Mallord William 1775–1851
Modern Italy: The Pifferari 1838
oil on canvas 92.6 x 123.2
733

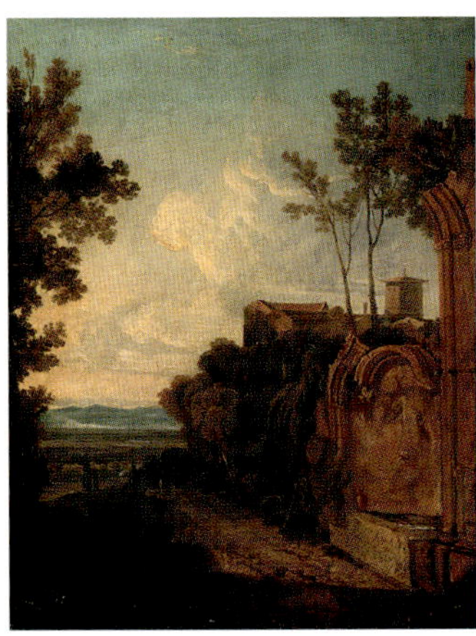

Turner, Joseph Mallord William (attributed to) 1775–1851
Italian Scene
oil on canvas 72.4 x 54.6
1132

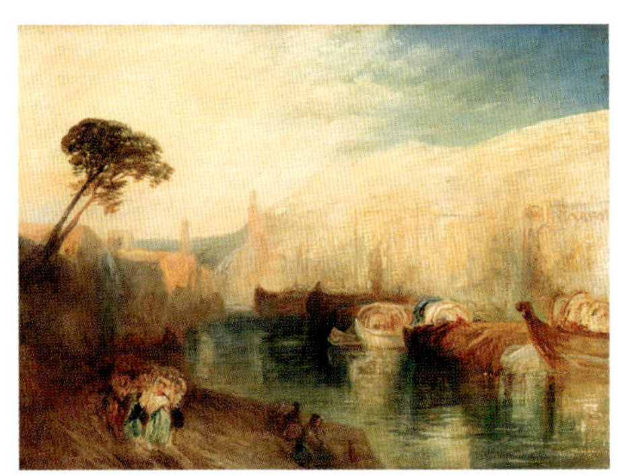

Turner, Joseph Mallord William (imitator of) 1775–1851
Italian Scene with Boats and Figures
oil on canvas 35.6 x 44.5
792

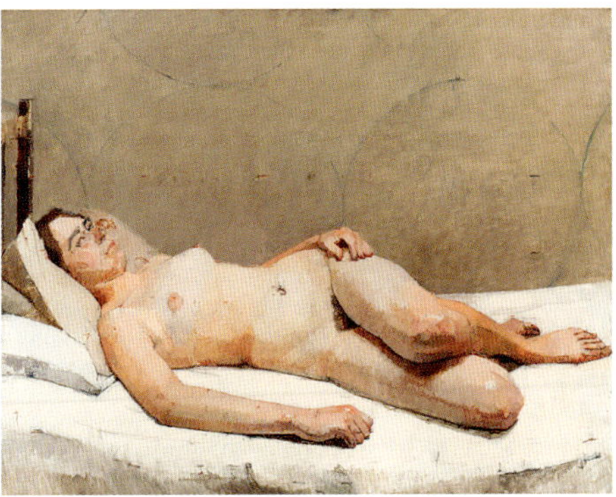

Uglow, Euan 1932–2000
Young Nude Girl 1960
oil on canvas 101.6 x 126.4
3155

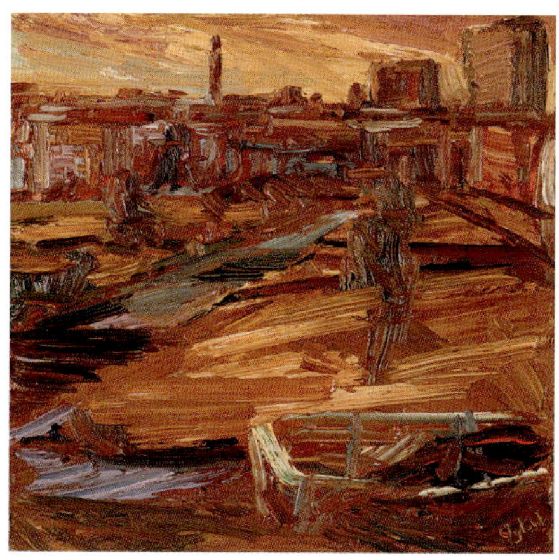

Uglow, Geoff b.1978
Glasgow Green IV 2000
oil on canvas 66.2 x 66.2
PP.2001.40

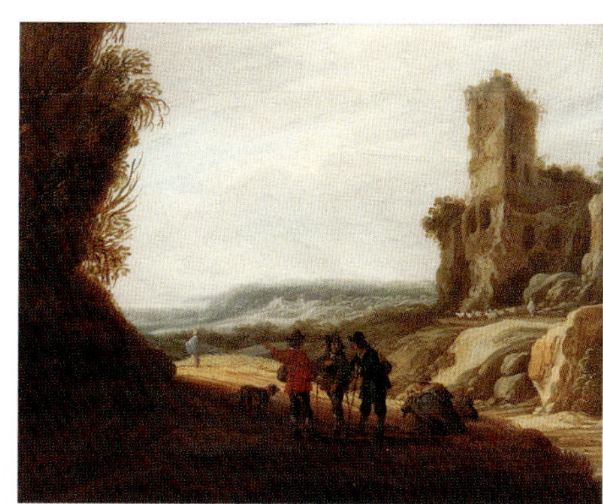

Ulft, Jacob van der (style of) 1627–1689
*Landscape with Figures and a Ruined
Castle* late 17th C
oil on panel 29.2 x 34.3
17

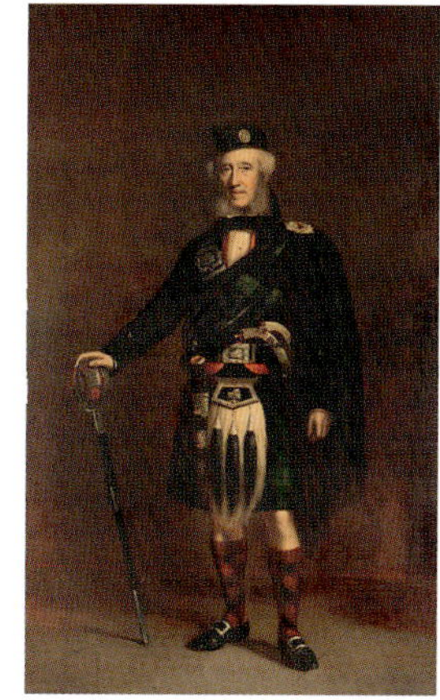

Underhill
William Campbell of Tullichewan (1794–1864)
oil on canvas 231.1 x 134.6
2546

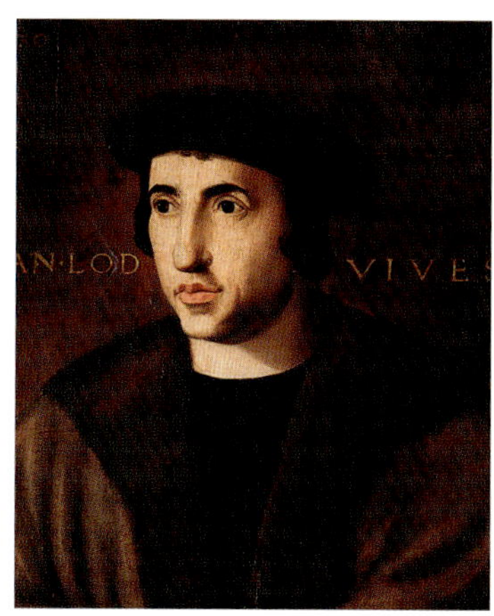

unknown artist
*Juan Luis Vives (1493–1540), the Tutor of
Mary I* 1520s
oil on board 30.5 x 25.4
PL.1927.249

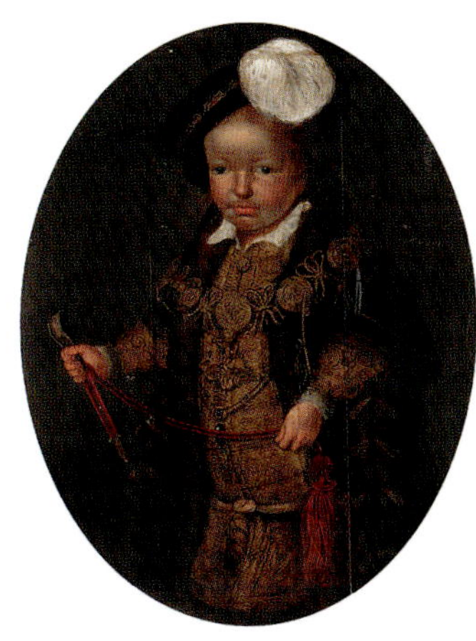

unknown artist
Edward VI (1537–1553) c.1537
oil on board 76.5 x 62
PL.1927.252

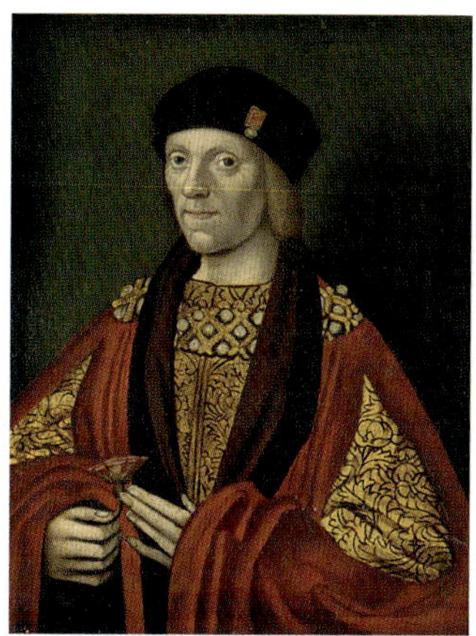

unknown artist 16th C
Henry VII (1457–1509)
oil on panel 34.5 x 27.5
35.632

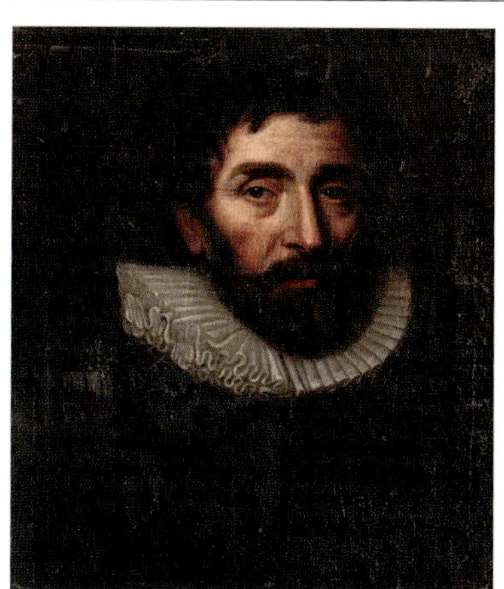

unknown artist 16th C–17th C
Reverend Alexander Henderson (1583–1646)
oil on canvas 55.6 x 48.2
1018

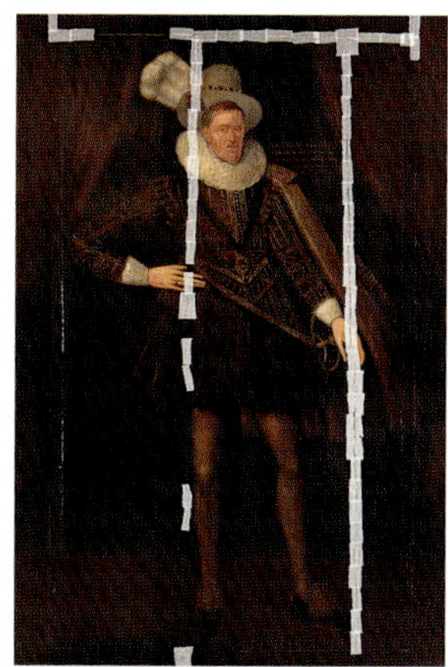

unknown artist
*James VI of Scotland and I of England
(1566–1625)* 1618
oil on panel 238.8 x 156.2
475

unknown artist
*James Graham (1612–1650), 1st Marquis of
Montrose* c.1650–1660
oil on canvas 76 x 64
3077

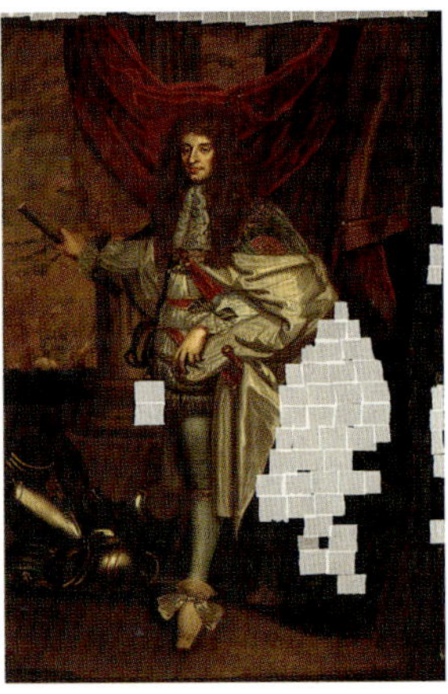

unknown artist
James II (1633–1701) 1683
oil on canvas 238.8 x 156.2
476

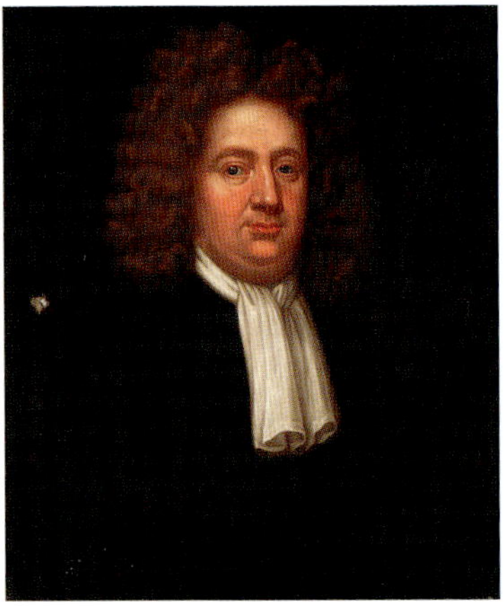

unknown artist
Reverend William Dunlop (1654–1700)
c.1690–1700
oil on canvas 74.3 x 61
OG.1961.10.n

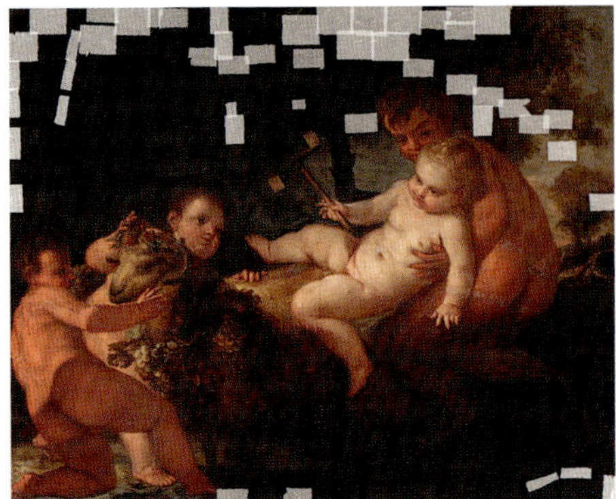

unknown artist 17th C
Four Cherubs in a Landscape with a Sheep
oil on canvas 123.8 x 149.9
NR.120

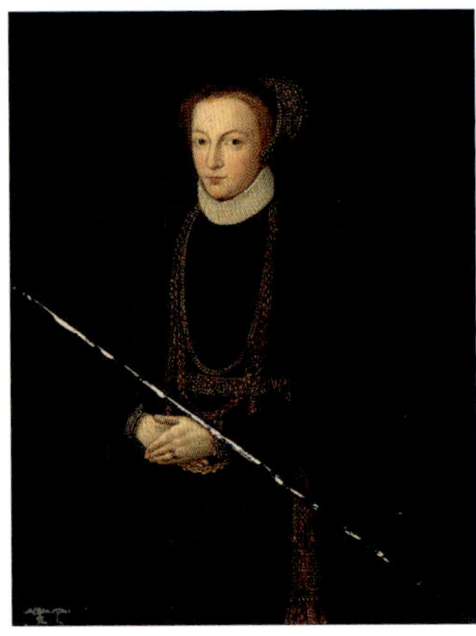

unknown artist 17th C
Mary, Queen of Scots (1542–1587)
oil on panel 102.9 x 79.7
228

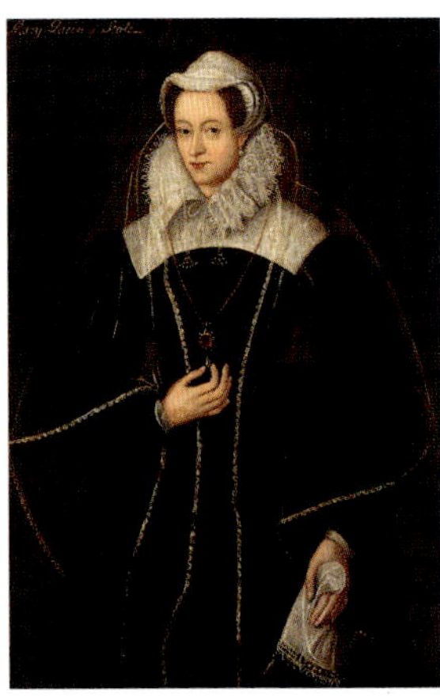

unknown artist 17th C
Mary, Queen of Scots (1542–1587)
oil on panel 114 x 77.9
1685

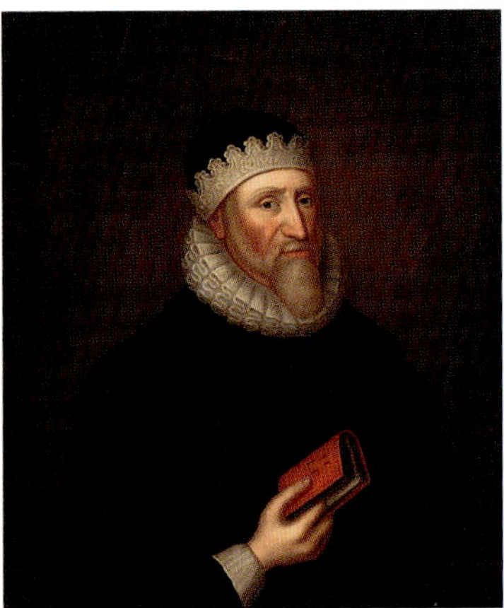

unknown artist 17th C
Reverend John Bell (c.1560–1641)
oil on canvas 74.3 x 61.8
TEMP.9381

unknown artist 17th C–18th C
*James F. Keith (1696–1758), Marshal to the
Prussian Army under Frederick the Great*
oil on canvas 91.4 x 71.1
2784

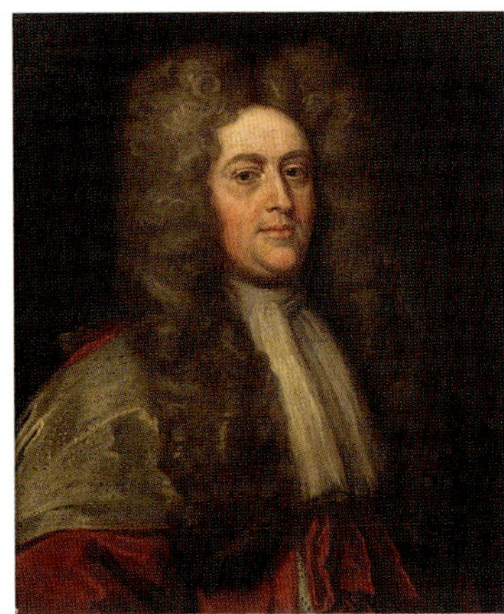

unknown artist 17th C–18th C
Sir John Maxwell (1648–1732)
oil on canvas 74.6 x 61.6
PL.153 (P)

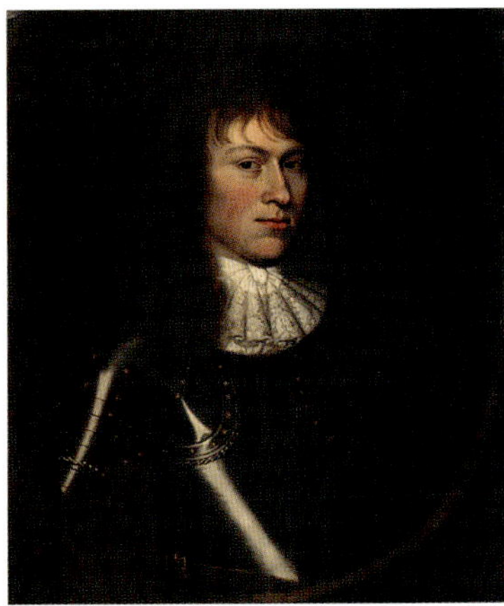

unknown artist 17th C–18th C
Sir John Maxwell, 1st Bt
oil on canvas 76.2 x 62.9
PL.54 (P)

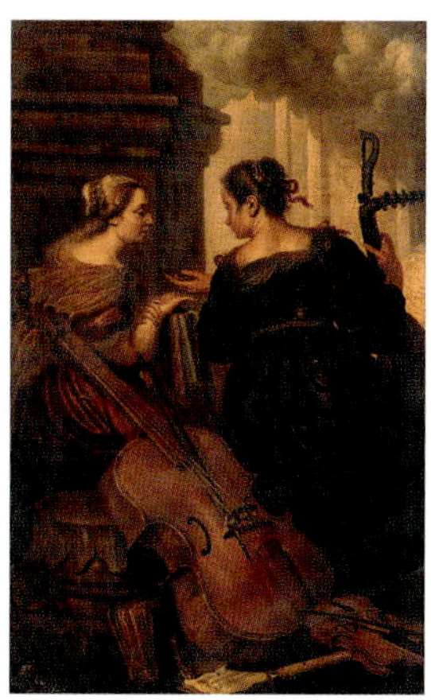

unknown artist late 17th C
Two Seated Women with Musical Instruments
oil on canvas 127.6 x 84.5
3167

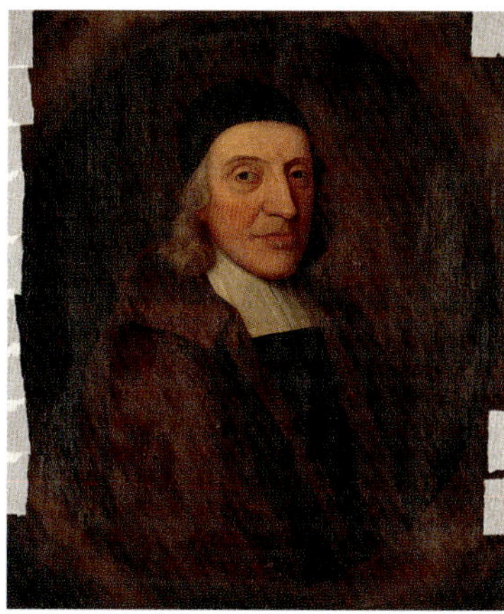

unknown artist
George Bogle of Whiteinch (1682–1707)
c.1700
oil on canvas 76.2 x 63.5
2515

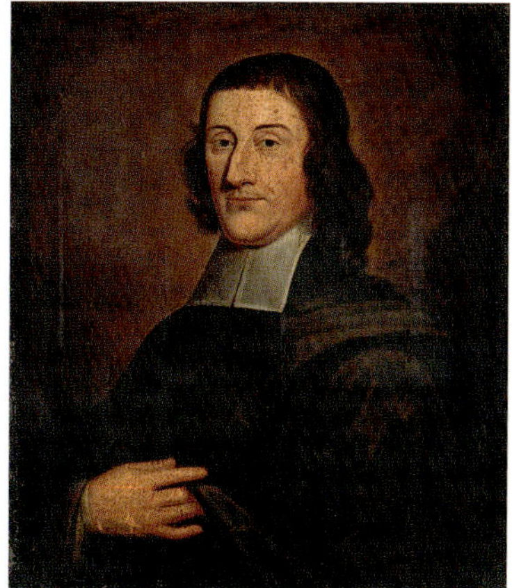

unknown artist
*John Luke the Younger of Claythorn (1665–
1731)* c.1700
oil on canvas 83.8 x 66
678

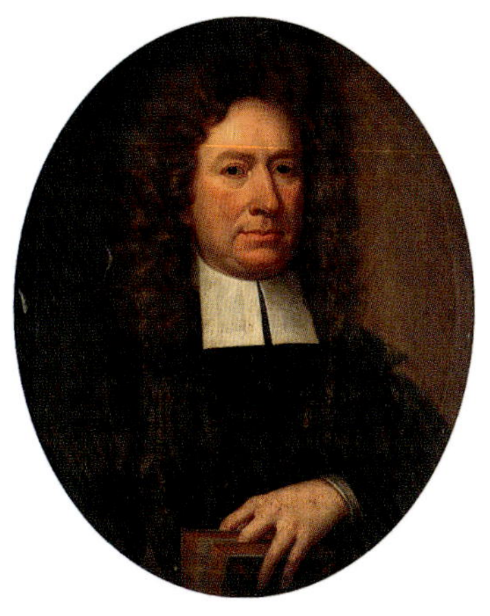

unknown artist
Reverend James Brown, Glasgow Cathedral
c.1700
oil on canvas 76.2 x 63.5
2521

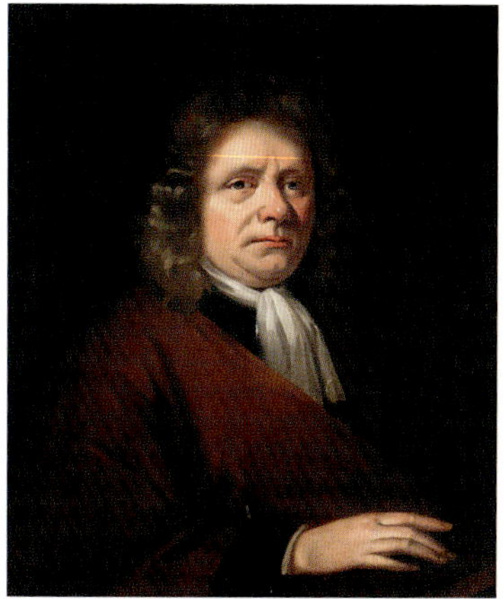

unknown artist
William Carstares (1649–1715) c.1700
oil on canvas 74.3 x 61
OG.1961.10.P

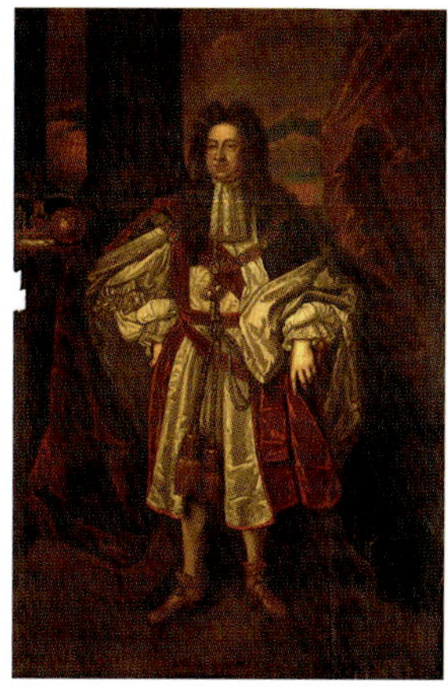

unknown artist
George I (1660–1727) 1717
oil on canvas 238.8 x 156.2
477

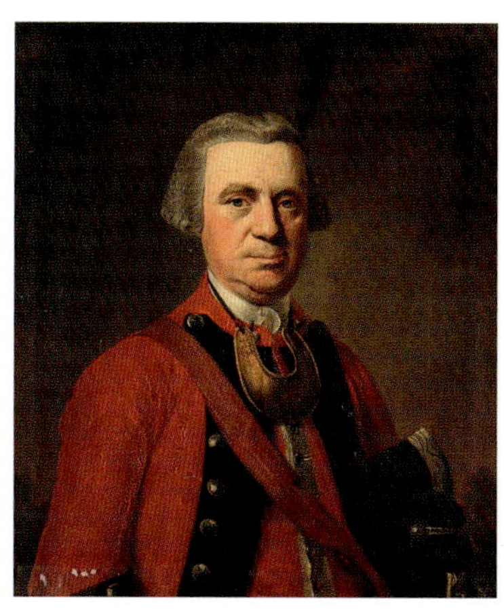

unknown artist
Captain Alexander Campbell (c.1700–1780)
c.1750
oil on canvas 78.1 x 68.6
1421

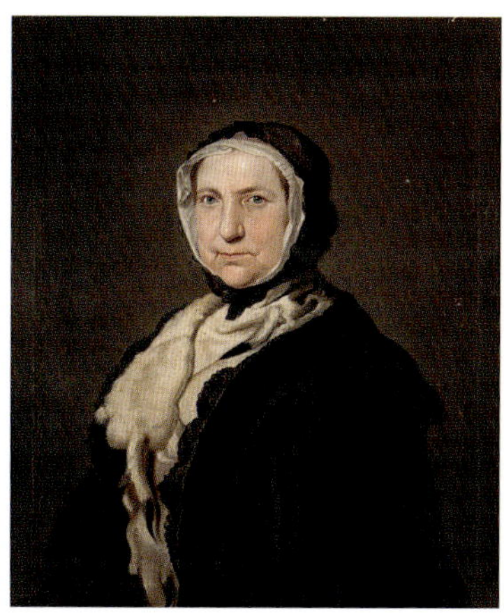

unknown artist
Mrs Helen Campbell of Glen Lyon c.1750
oil on canvas 76.2 x 63.5
1422

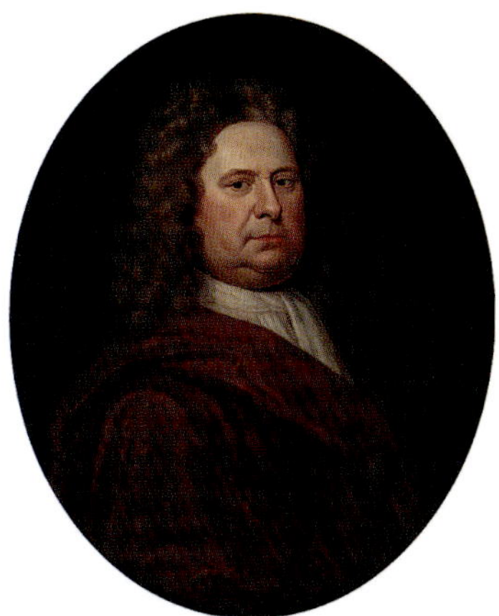

unknown artist
Andrew Cochrane of Brighouse (1693–1777)
1750s–1760s
oil on canvas 73.8 x 60.7
TEMP.10652

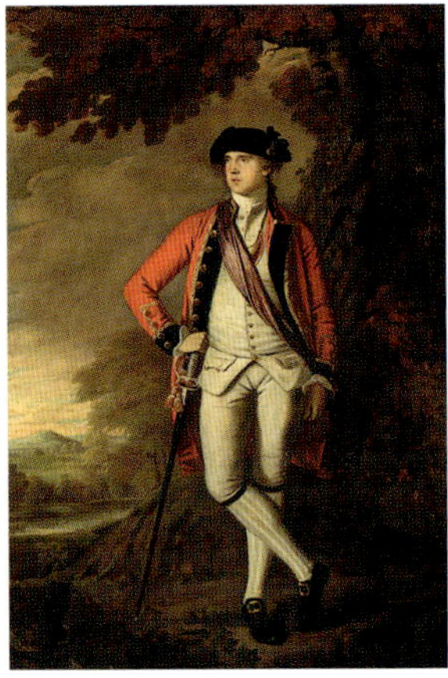

unknown artist
Portrait of a Military Officer c.1765
oil on canvas 229 x 151
674

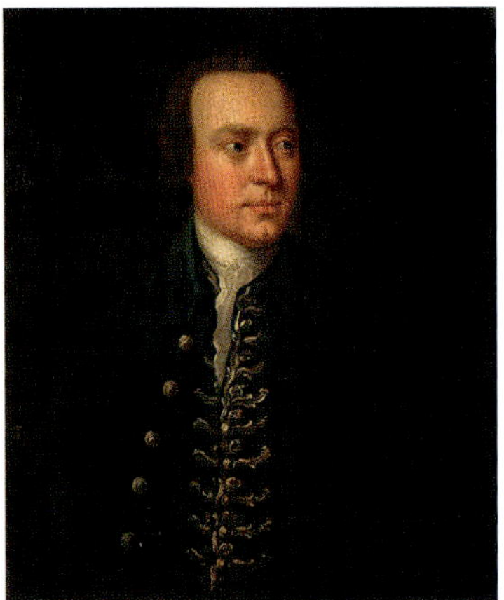

unknown artist
Robert Donald (1724–1803), Provost of Glasgow (1776–1777) c.1777
oil on canvas 76.2 x 63.5
2458

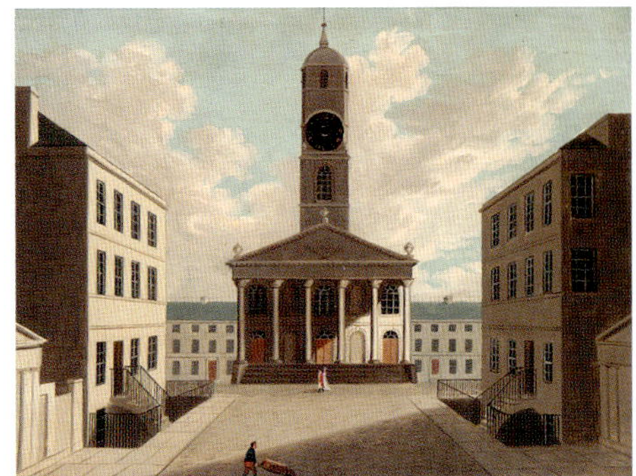

unknown artist
St Andrew's Church c.1798–1805
oil on sheet iron 28.5 x 36.2
A.1940.22.dk

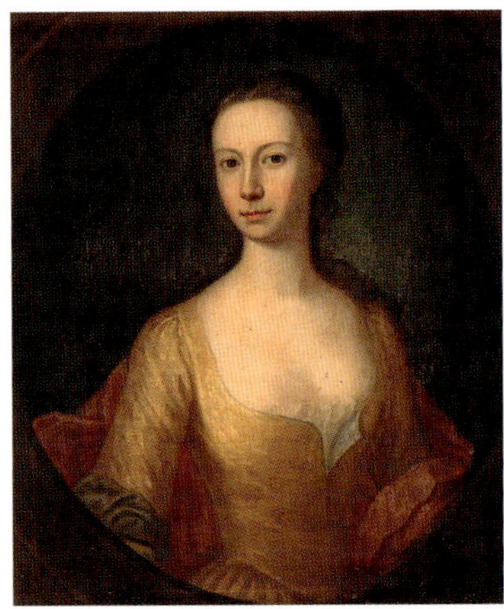

unknown artist 18th C
Ann Sinclair (d.1759), Wife of George Bogle of Daldowie
oil on canvas 76.2 x 63.5
2514

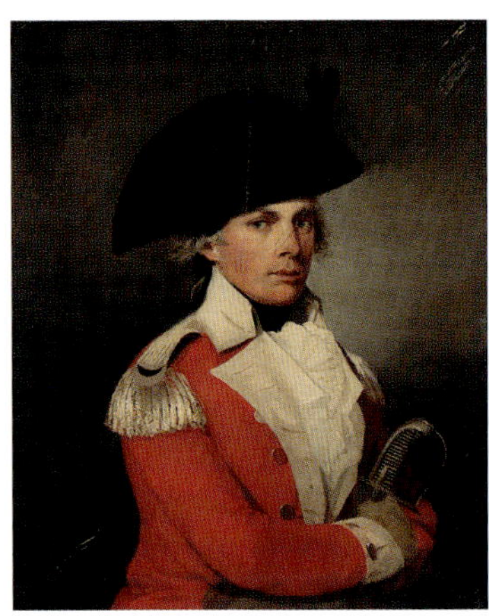

unknown artist 18th C
Colonel Gordon of Aitkenhead
oil on canvas 76.2 x 63.5
1432

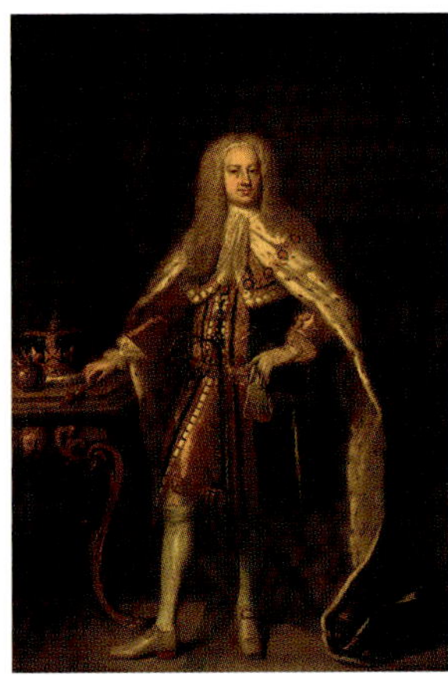

unknown artist 18th C
George II (1683–1760)
oil on canvas 238.8 x 156.2
478

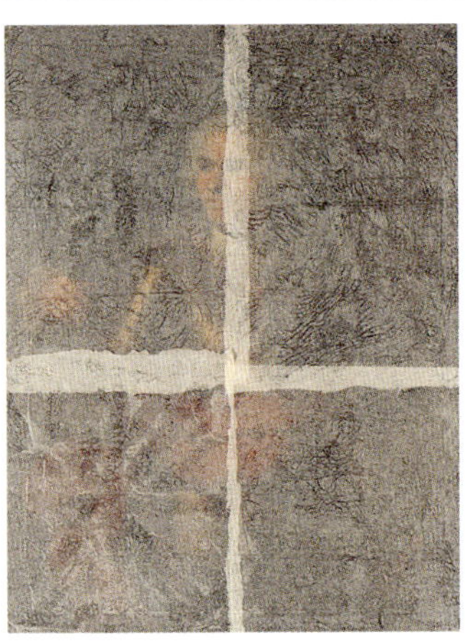

unknown artist 18th C
George Keith (1693–1778), Earl Marischal of Scotland
oil on canvas 121.9 x 91.4
2783

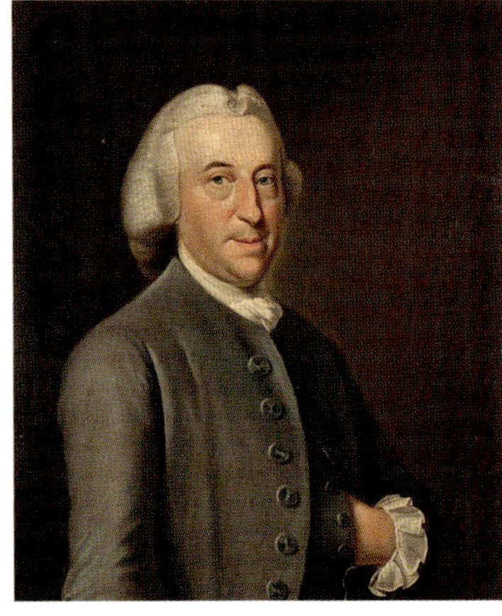

unknown artist 18th C
George McCall (b.1683), Merchant of Glasgow
oil on canvas 76.2 x 63.5
2522

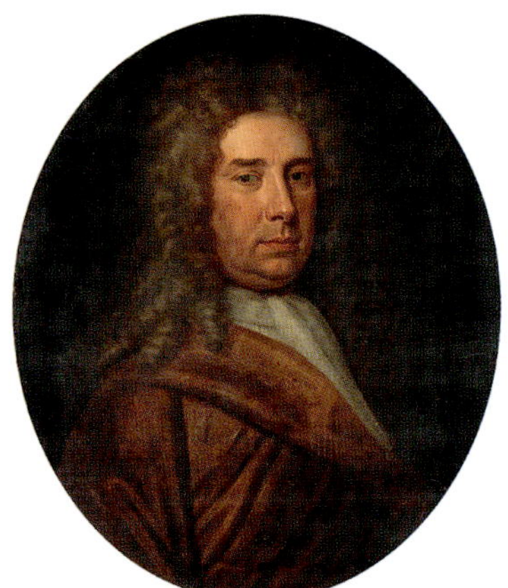

unknown artist 18th C
James Luke of Greenfield (1672–1726), Merchant of Glasgow
oil on canvas 83.8 x 66
676

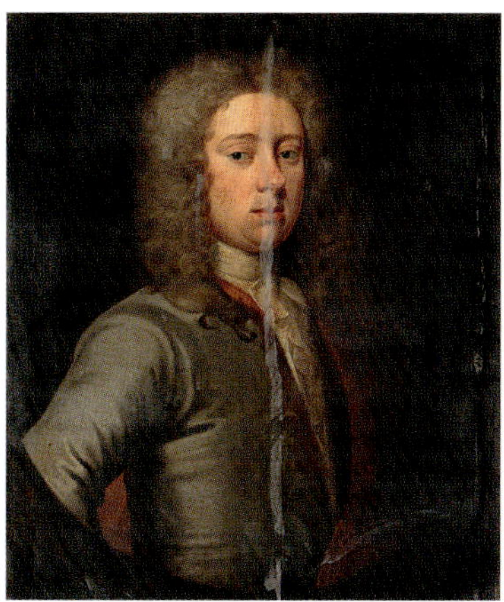

unknown artist 18th C
John Luke (1698–1750)
oil on canvas 88.9 x 66
677

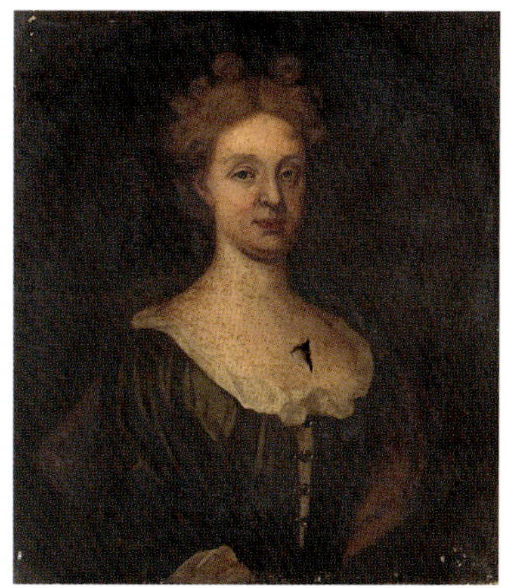

unknown artist 18th C
Lady Barbara Maxwell (d.1737)
oil on canvas 78 x 65.4
PL.154

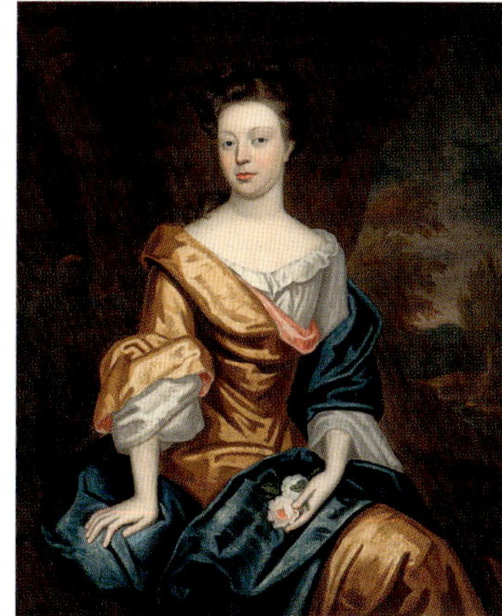

unknown artist 18th C
*Lady Castlehill (1668–1752), Mother of Mrs
George Bogle and Wife of Sir John Sinclair of
Stevenson*
oil on canvas 124.5 x 101.6
2513

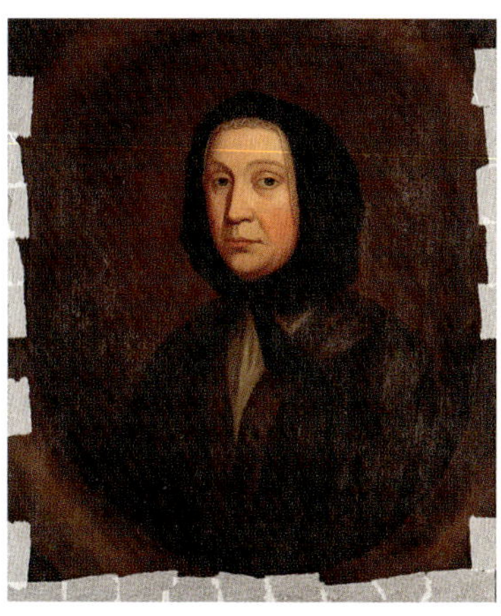

unknown artist 18th C
Mrs George Bogle of Whiteinch
oil on canvas 76.2 x 63.5
2518

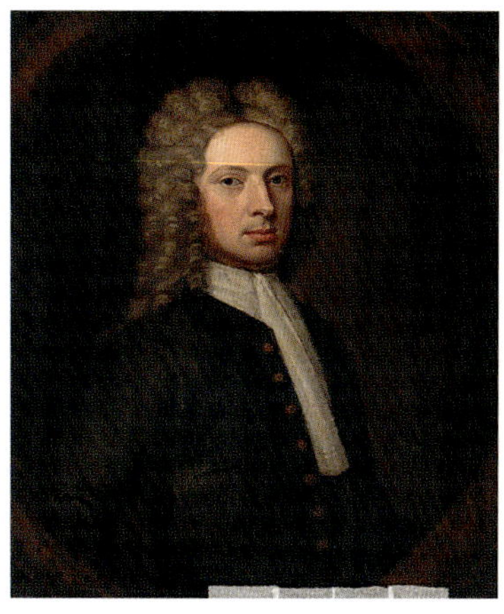

unknown artist 18th C
Portrait of a Gentleman
oil on canvas 73.6 x 61
373

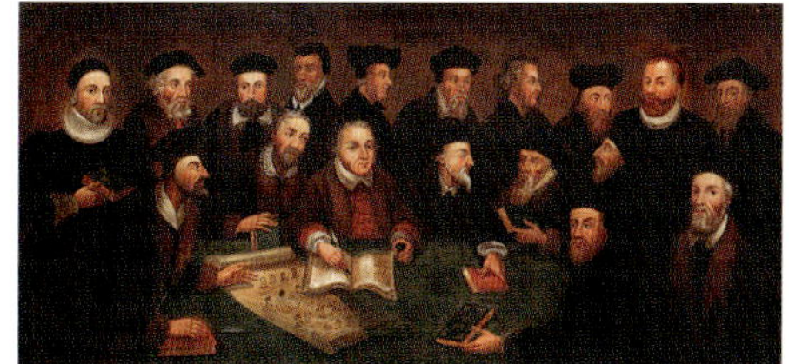

unknown artist 18th C
Protestant Reformers
oil on canvas 63.2 x 130.8
A.2004.2

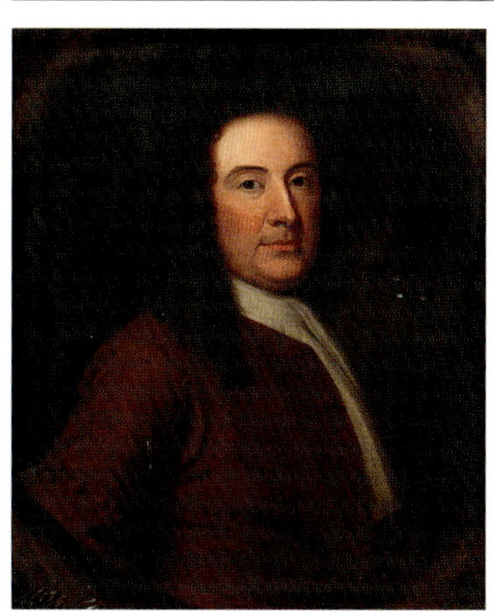

unknown artist 18th C
Robert Bogle of Daldowie (d.1735)
oil on canvas 76.2 x 63.5
2517

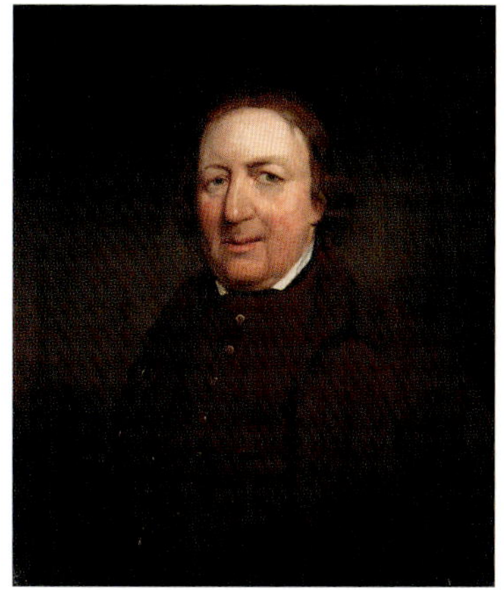

unknown artist 18th C–19th C
John Dunlop (1730–1805), Tide Surveyor
oil on board 74.5 x 62
OG.1961.10.o

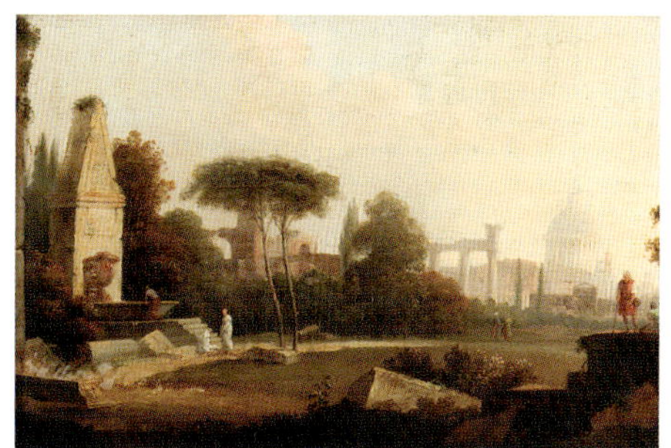

unknown artist 18th C–19th C
*Rome: An Imaginary View of the Forum
Romanum*
oil on panel 43.2 x 63.5
250

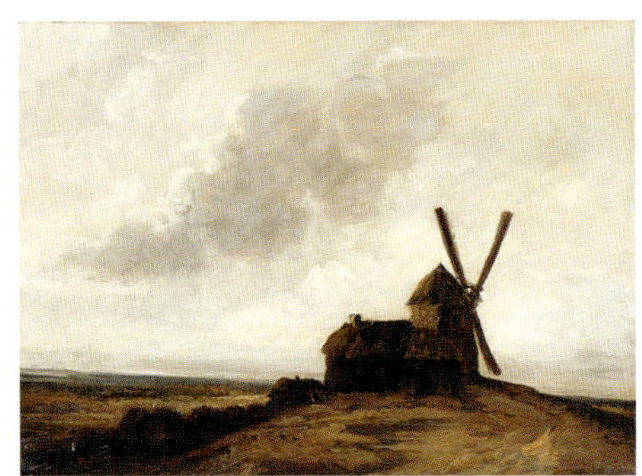

unknown artist 18th C–19th C
The Old Mill
oil on canvas 53.6 x 72.4
3193

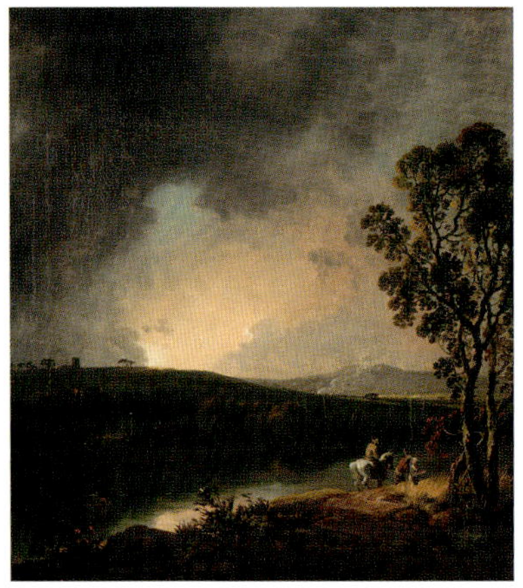

unknown artist 18th C/19th C
Landscape with Figures
oil on panel 53.3 x 48.3
282

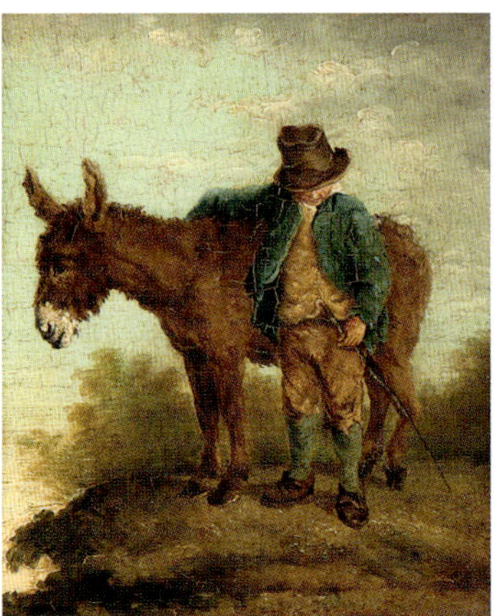

unknown artist 18th C/19th C
Peasant and Donkey
oil on panel 25.4 x 20.3
399

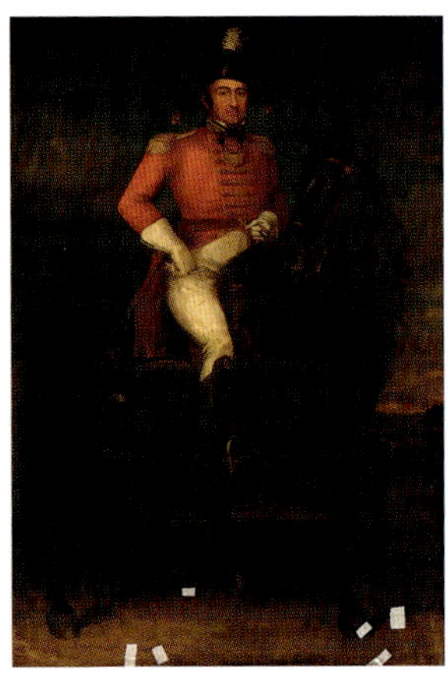

unknown artist
John Geddes, Equestrian Portrait c.1803–1804
oil on canvas 243.9 x 158.8
3559

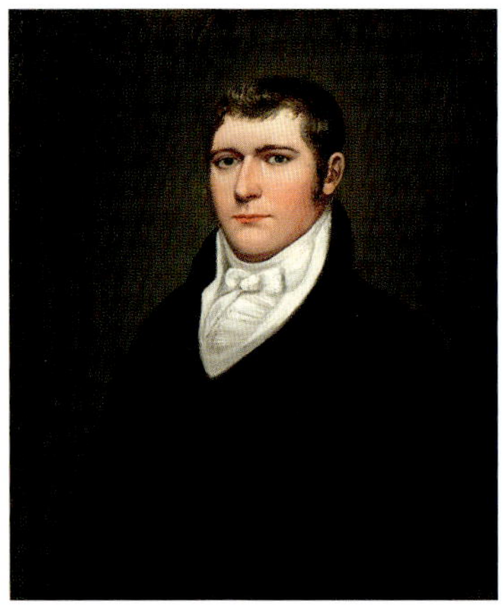

unknown artist
John Robertson (1782–1868) c.1815
oil on canvas 110 x 86
1882.53

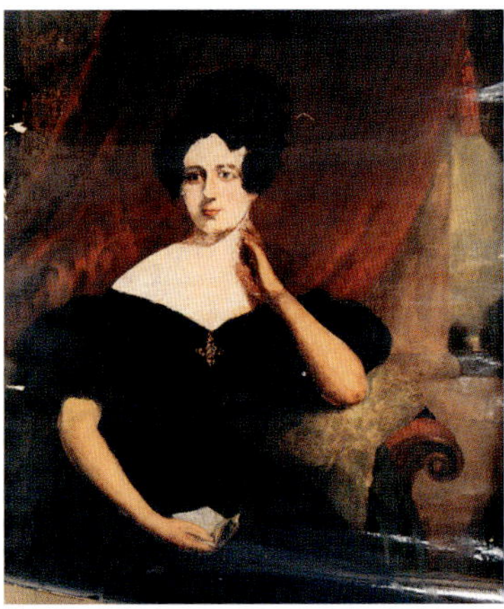

unknown artist
Portrait of a Lady c.1815–1840
oil on canvas 124.4 x 100.3
NR.103

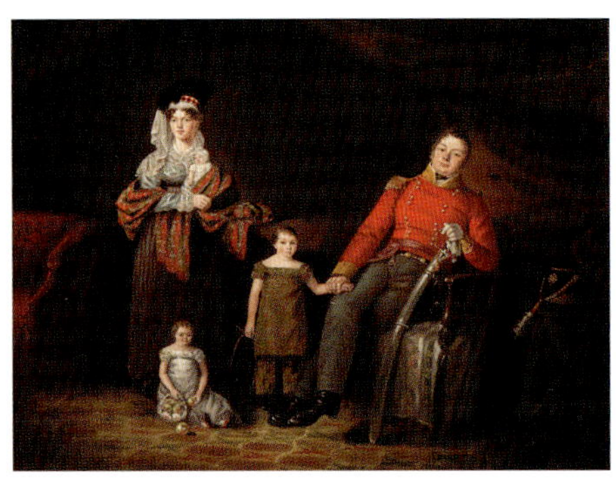

unknown artist
A Soldier with His Family c.1820
oil on canvas 40 x 49.5
NR.135

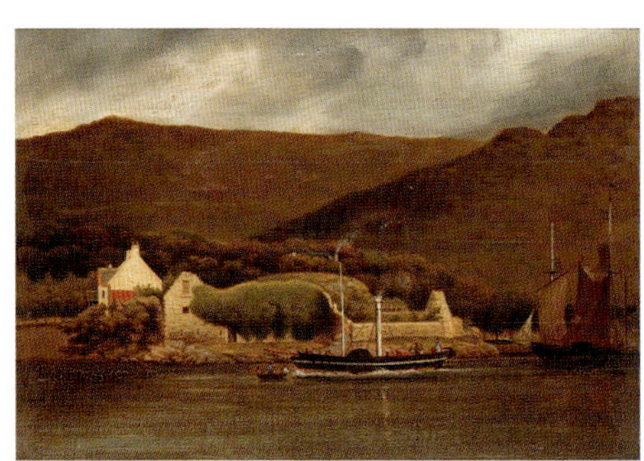

unknown artist
Dunglass Castle on the Clyde c.1825
oil on canvas 28.6 x 38.1
1906.34

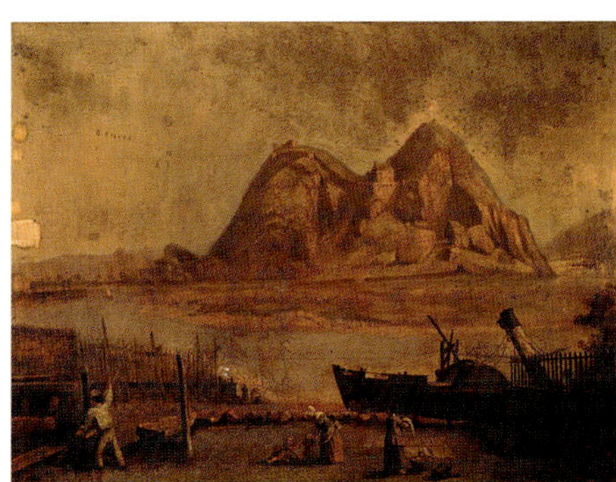

unknown artist
Dumbarton Rock, with a Steamer
c.1830–1840
oil on panel 86.3 x 111.8
3449

Facing page: Knight, Harold, 1874–1961, *A Window in St John's Wood*, c.1932 (p. 231)

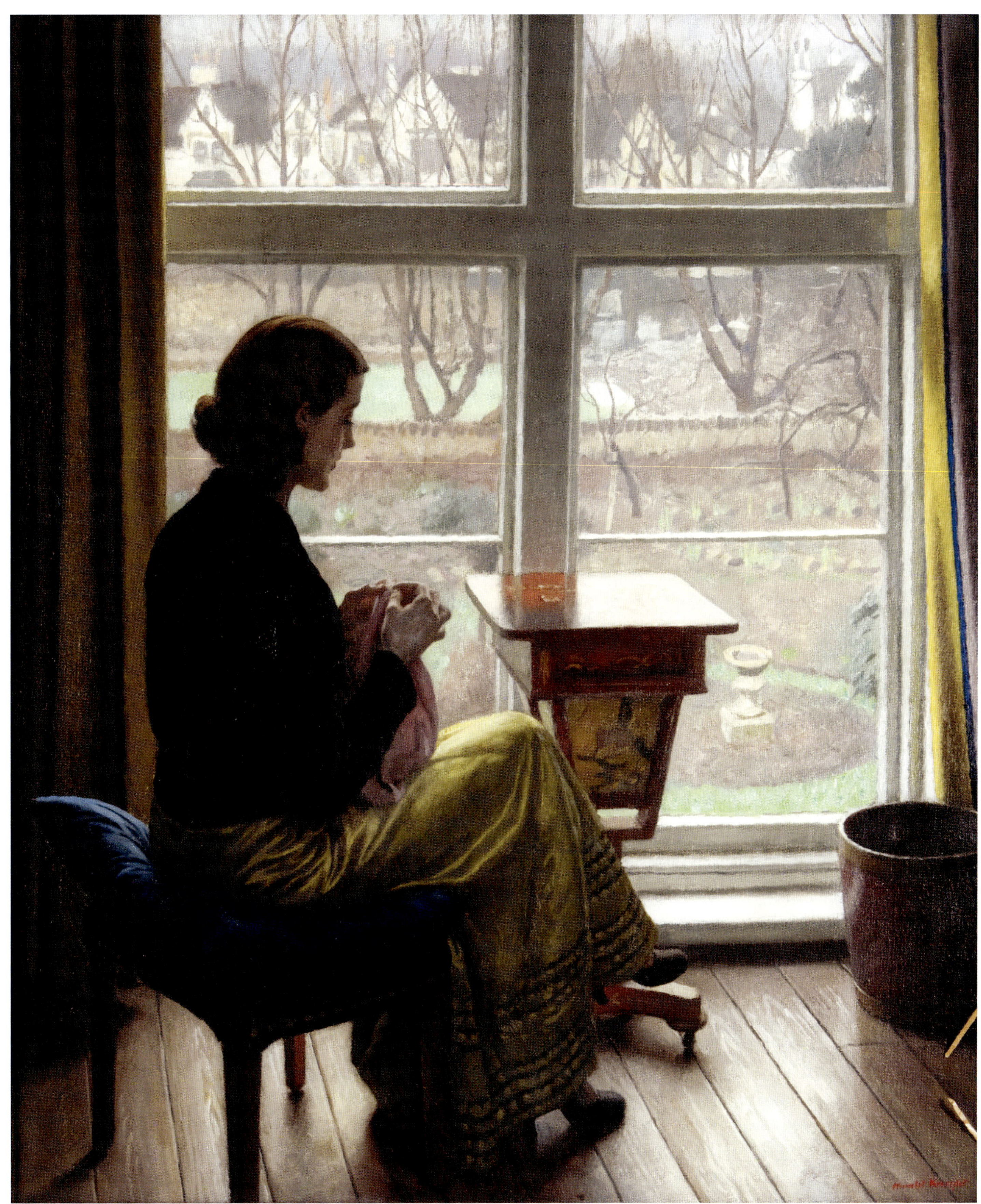

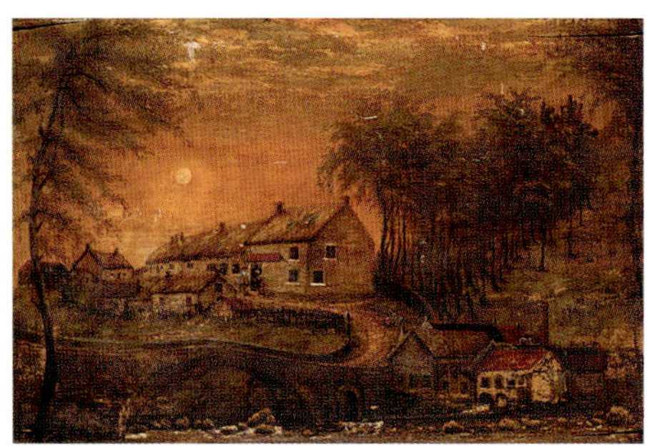

unknown artist
Ye Auld Hoose, Cathcart, Glasgow 1836
oil on oak panel 77.3 x 114.8
PP.2007.4

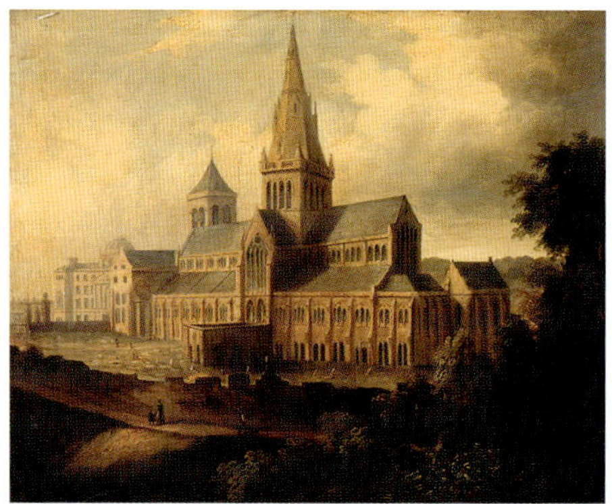

unknown artist
Glasgow Cathedral from the South-East
c.1840
oil on canvas 61 x 76.2
3424

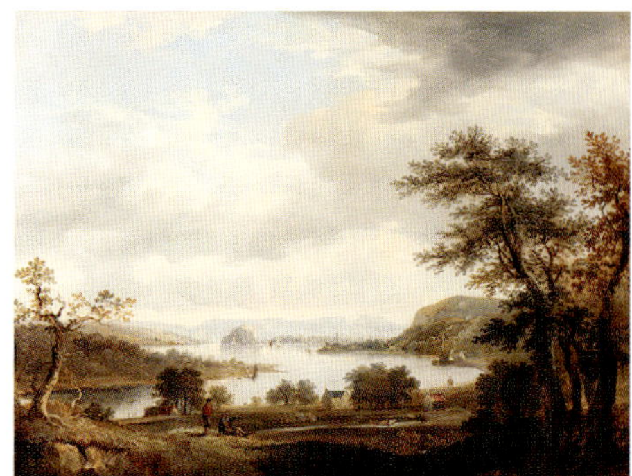

unknown artist
On the Clyde c.1840
oil on canvas 71.1 x 91.4
819

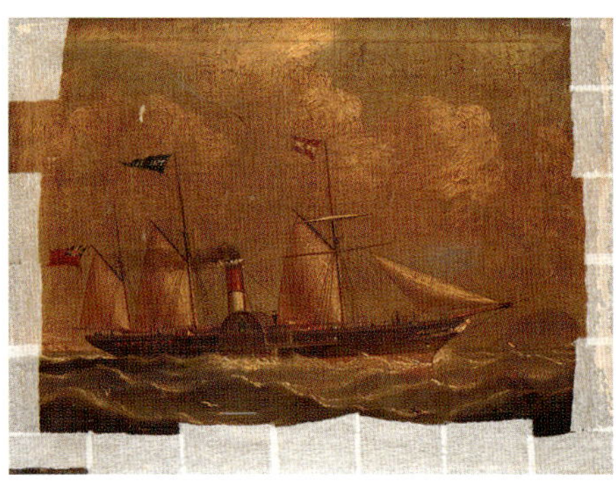

unknown artist
PS 'Thistle' 1840s
oil on canvas 36.5 x 47.8
TEMP.14968

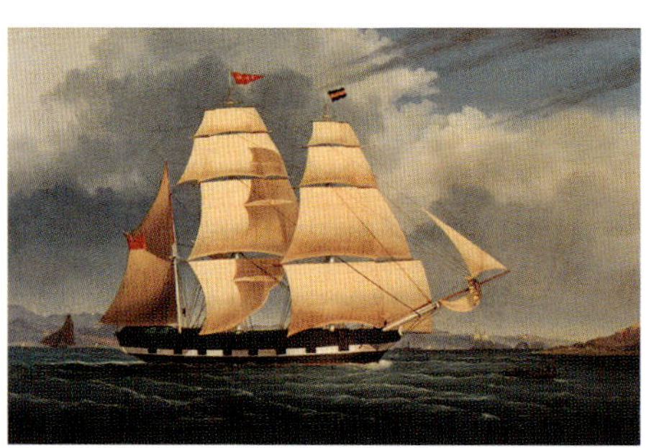

unknown artist
Barque 'Medora' off Greenock c.1840–1850
oil on canvas 61.5 x 91.5
3308

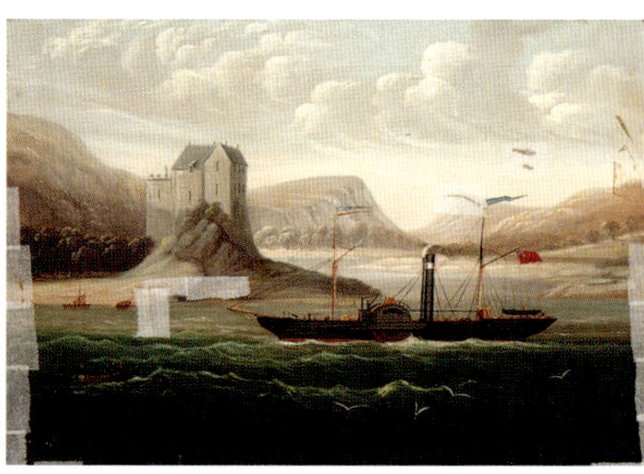

unknown artist
PS 'Duntroon Castle' 1842
oil on canvas 53.4 x 76
T.1940.48

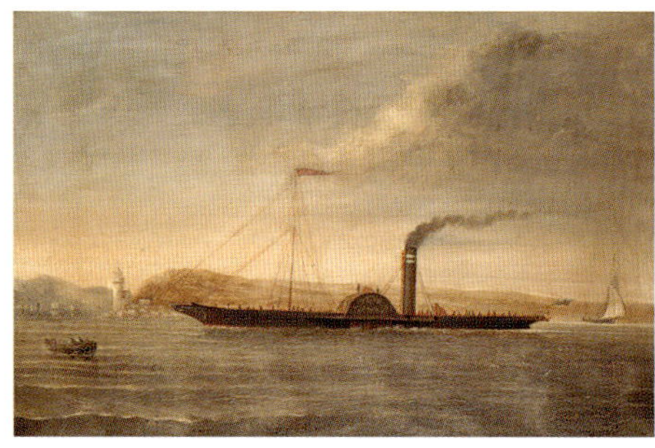

unknown artist
PS 'Mars' on the Clyde 1845
oil on canvas 66.5 x 88.8
T.1958.9

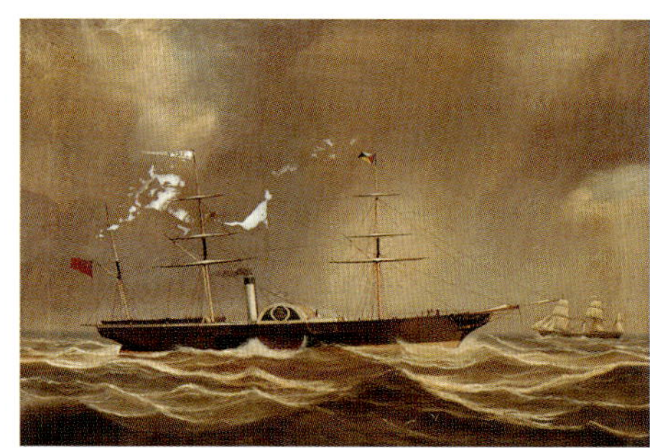

unknown artist
Steamship 'Pekin' c.1850
oil on canvas 102.5 x 139
1909.104

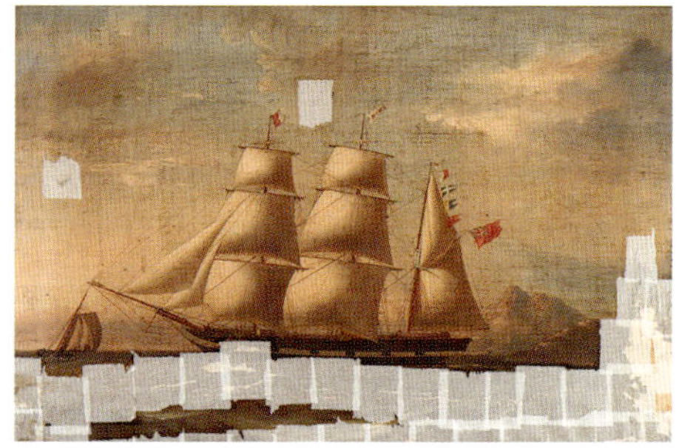

unknown artist
Barque 'Elizabeth Walker' c.1859
oil on canvas 93.5 x 124
T.1952.77

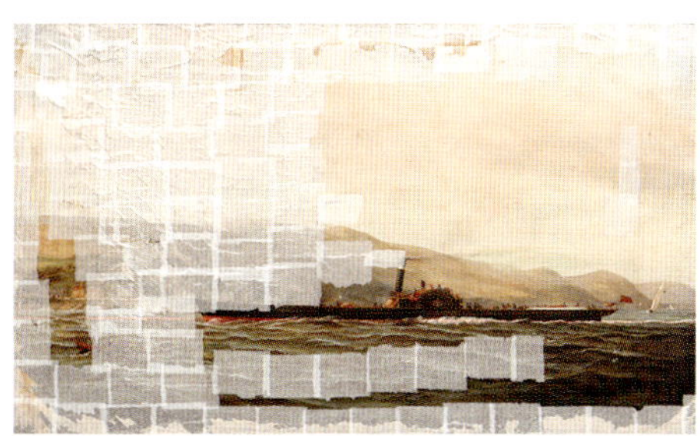

unknown artist
Clyde Steamer PS 'Sultan' 1861
oil on canvas 68.5 x 112
LT.1.1927.d (P)

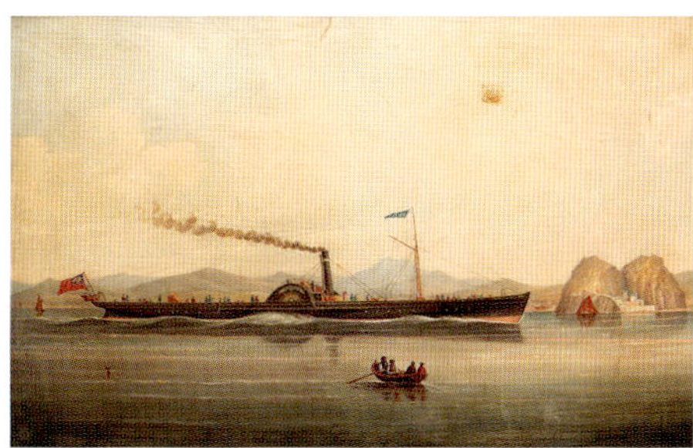

unknown artist
Clyde Steamer PS 'Sultan' 1861
oil on canvas 73.5 x 104
LT.1.1927.e (P)

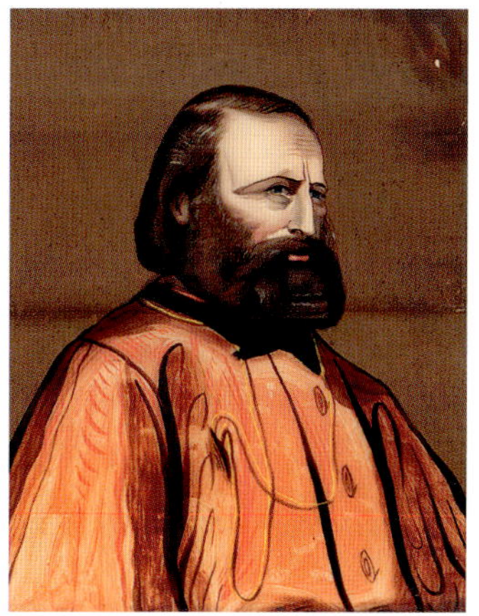

unknown artist
Giuseppe Garibaldi (1807–1882) c.1865
oil on glass 55.5 x 43.5
PP.1987.97

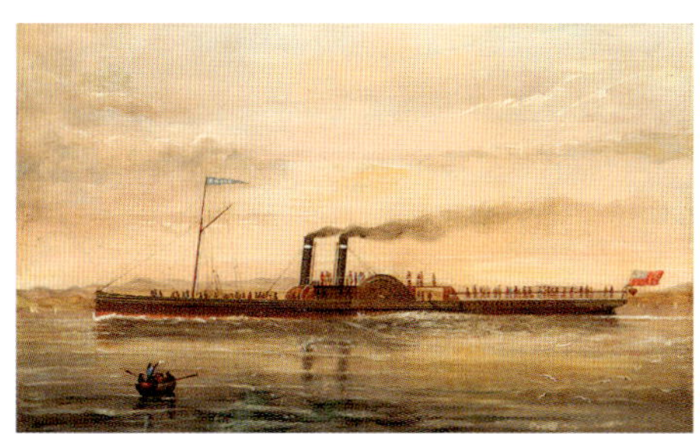

unknown artist
PS 'Eagle' c.1865
oil on canvas 44.2 x 69
TEMP.5882

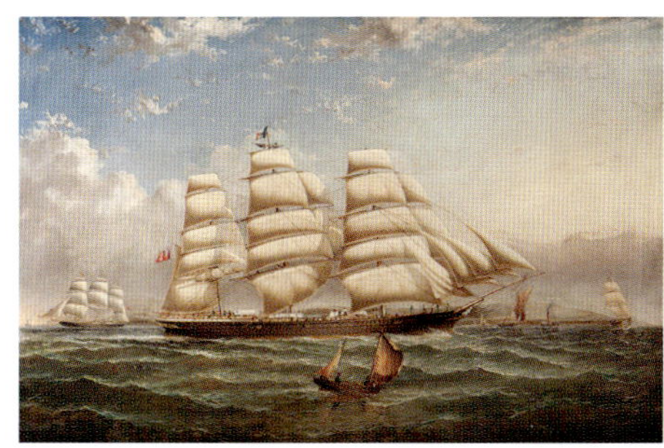

unknown artist
Outward Bound 1866
oil on canvas 101.5 x 148.5
MTEMP.5921

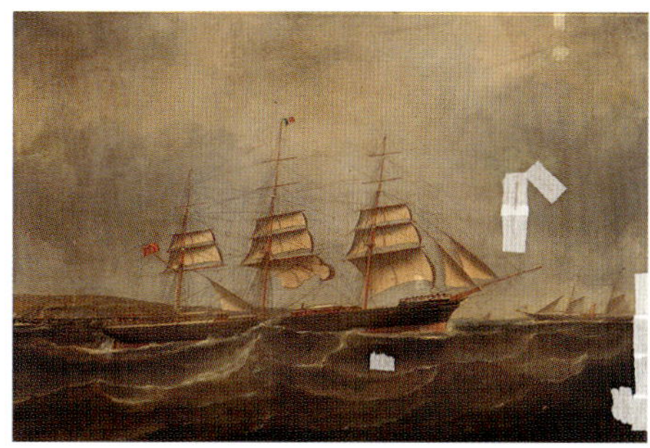

unknown artist
*The Henderson Line Ship 'Ormaru' or
'Timaru'* c.1874
oil on canvas 108.8 x 146.2
TEMP.15478

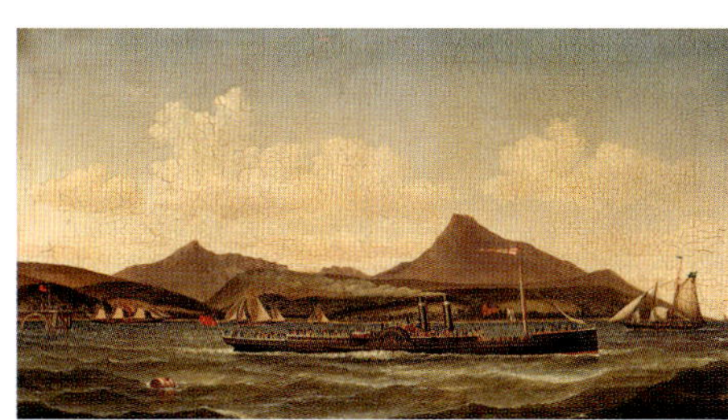

unknown artist
PS 'Brodick Castle' c.1878
oil on canvas 83.2 x 123.5
T.1937.41.a

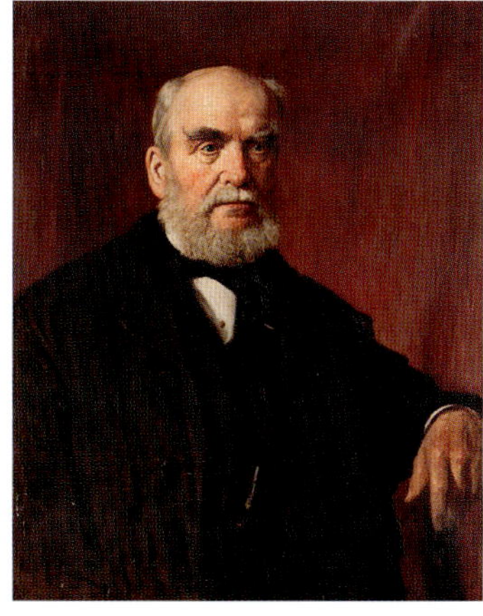

unknown artist
*Sir J. Falshaw (d.1889), Bt, Chairman of the
North British Railway Company (1882–1887)*
1882–1887
oil on canvas 82 x 62
T.1967.33.af

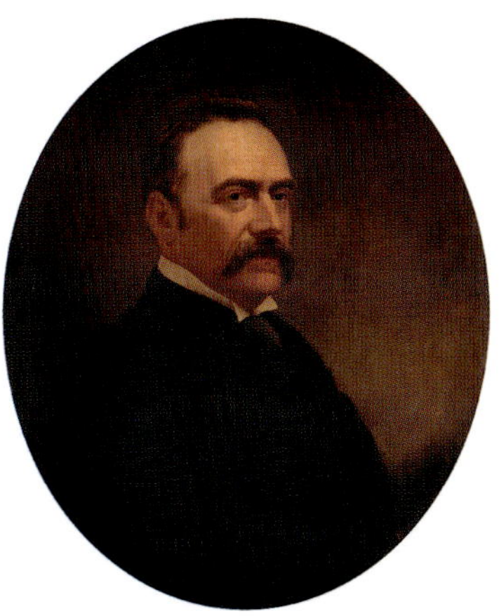

unknown artist
*David Jones (1834–1906), Locomotive
Engineer, Highland Railway* 1887
oil on canvas 66 x 63.6
T.1968.14.a

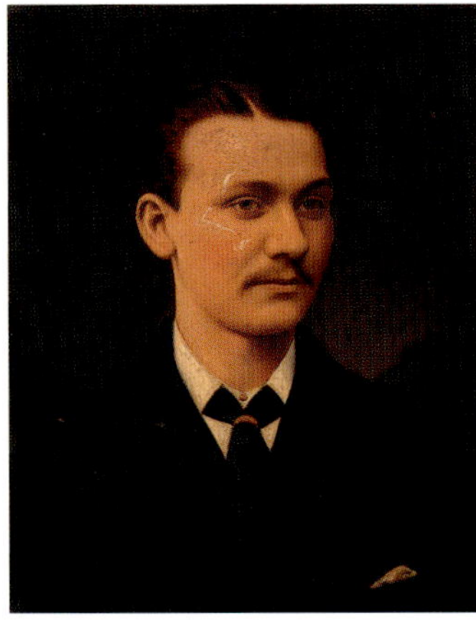

unknown artist
George Kilgour, Slater, Partickhill c.1890
oil on board 47.4 x 37
PP.1981.43.1

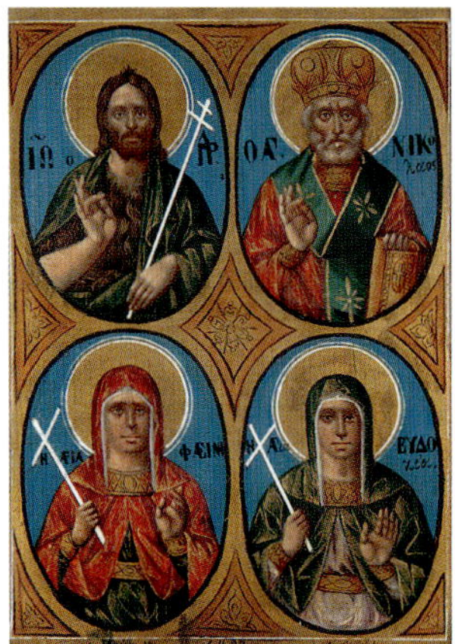

unknown artist
Saint John the Baptist, Saint Nikolaos, Saint Phæina and Saint Eudoxia 1897
oil on panel 31.1 x 23.2
E.1943.59

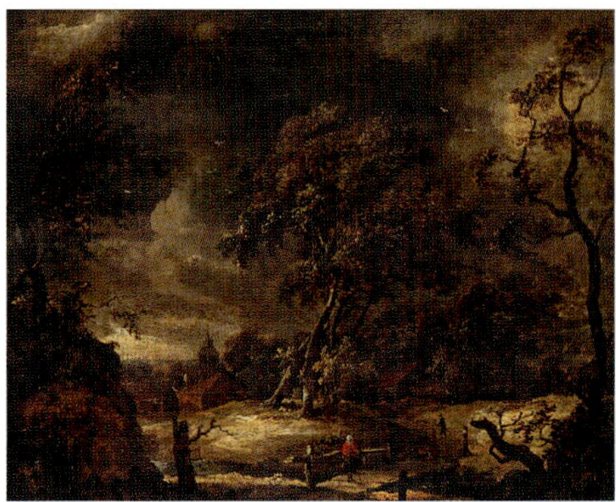

unknown artist 19th C
A Stormy Landscape
oil on canvas 26 x 30.5
582

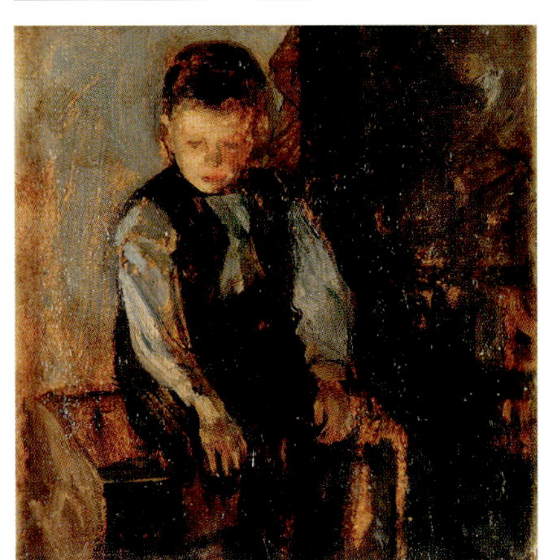

unknown artist 19th C
Boy Sitting on a Box
oil on cardboard 13.7 x 13.3
3162

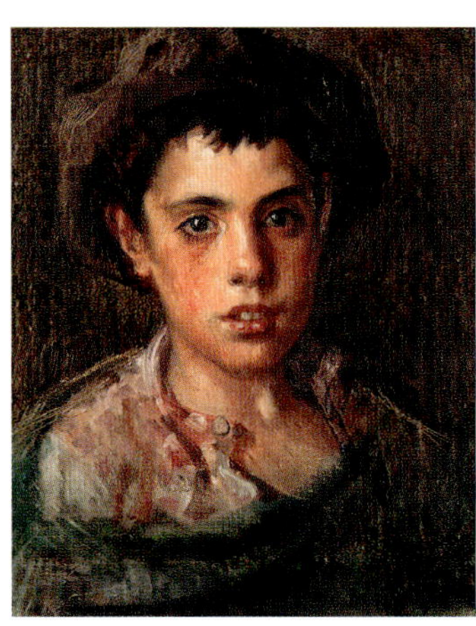

unknown artist 19th C
Boy's Head
oil on canvas 40.6 x 33
2147

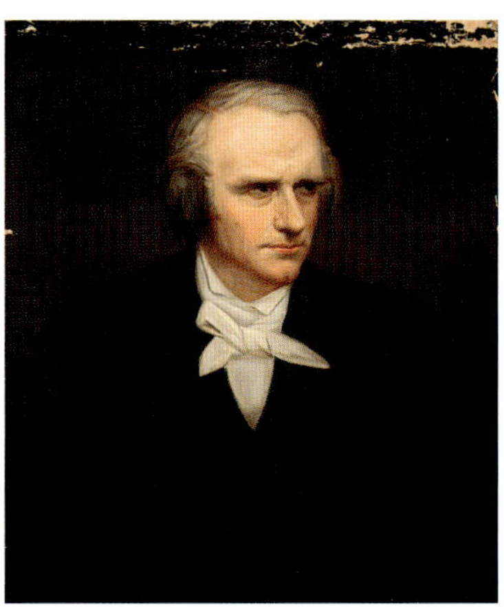

unknown artist 19th C
Dr Guthrie
oil on canvas 75.9 x 63.5
441

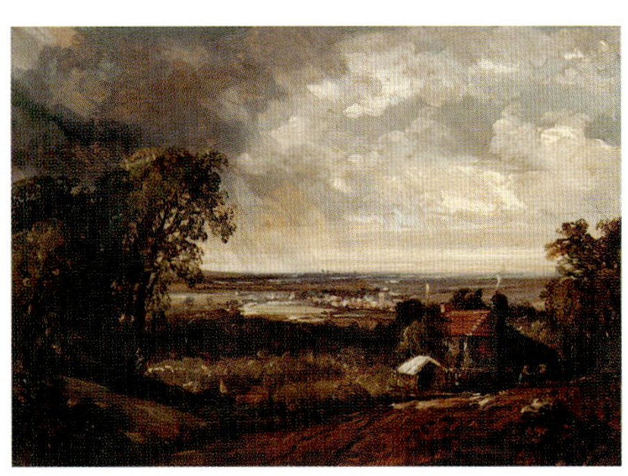

unknown artist 19th C
Extensive Landscape
oil on panel 25.4 x 35.9
3186

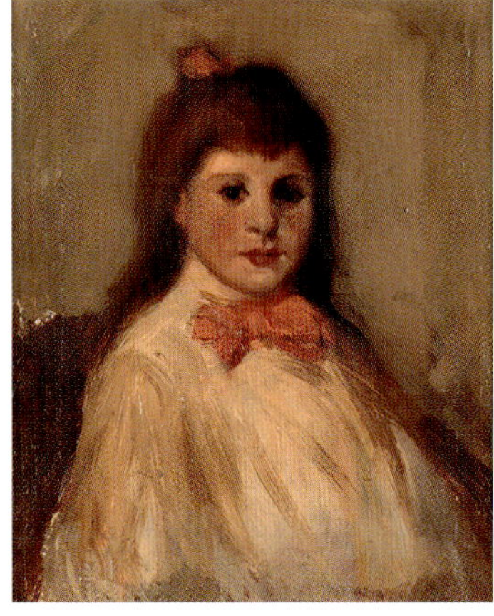

unknown artist 19th C
Girl with a Pink Bow
oil on glass 30.5 x 25.4
3158

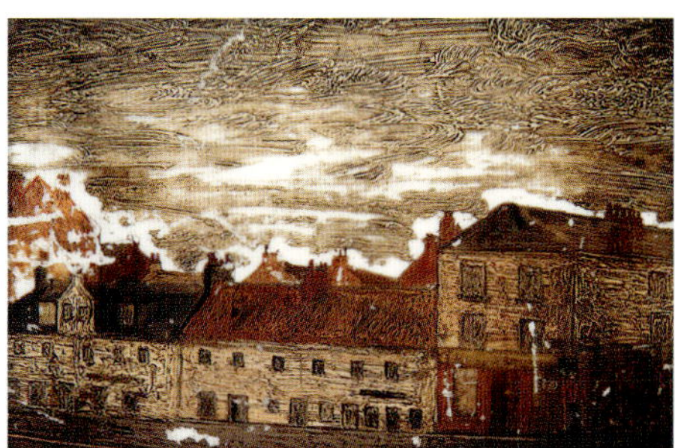

unknown artist 19th C
Gorbals Street and Bedford Row with the 'Rob Roy' Tavern
oil on glass 13 x 19.5
A.1938.75

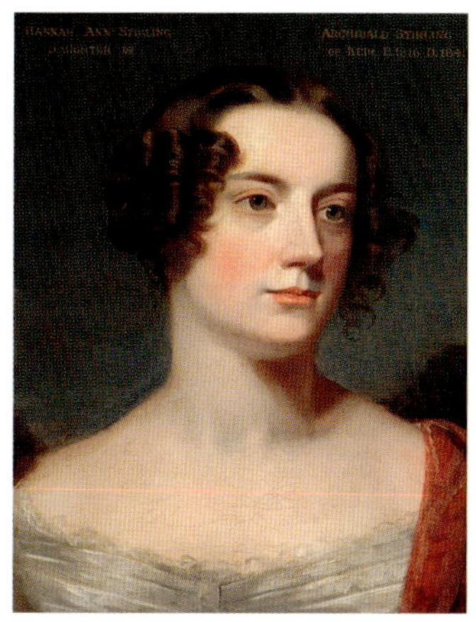

unknown artist 19th C
*Hannah Anne Stirling (1816–1843), Daughter
of Archibald Stirling of Keir*
oil on canvas 44.4 x 34.3
PL.148 (P)

unknown artist 19th C
Hugh Robertson of Gartloch (1777–1853)
oil on canvas 76 x 63
3049

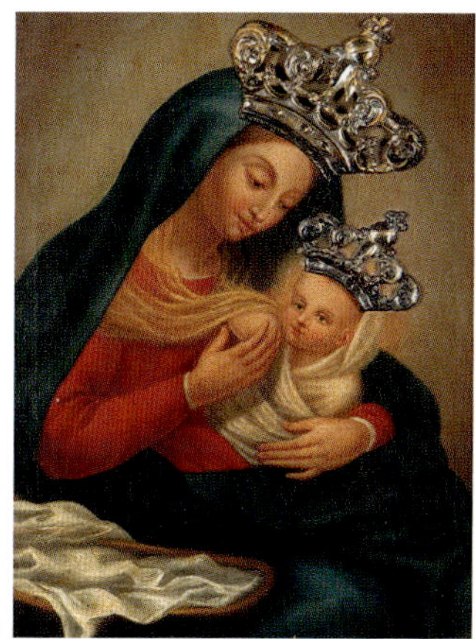

unknown artist 19th C
Ikon, Virgin and Child
oil & metal on canvas 30.4 x 24.2
1912.26

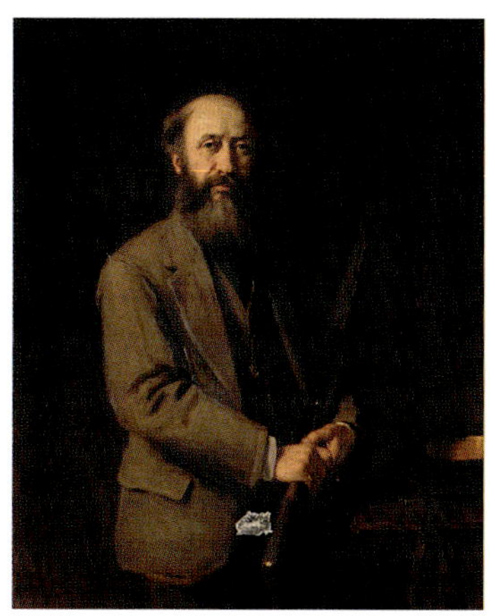

unknown artist 19th C
James Campbell of Tullichewan (1823–1901)
oil on canvas 127 x 101.6
2547

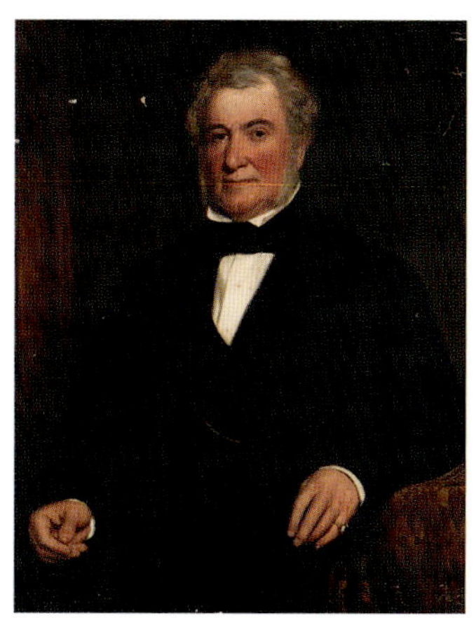

unknown artist 19th C
James Douglas of Barloch
oil on canvas 101.6 x 77
TEMP.2978

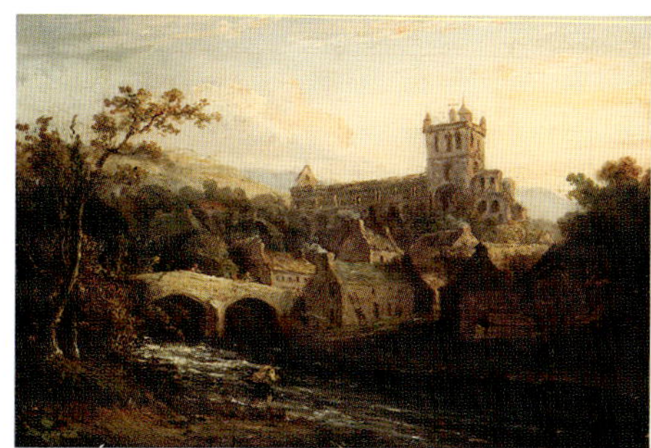

unknown artist 19th C
Jedburgh Abbey
oil on canvas 30.5 x 40.3
3047

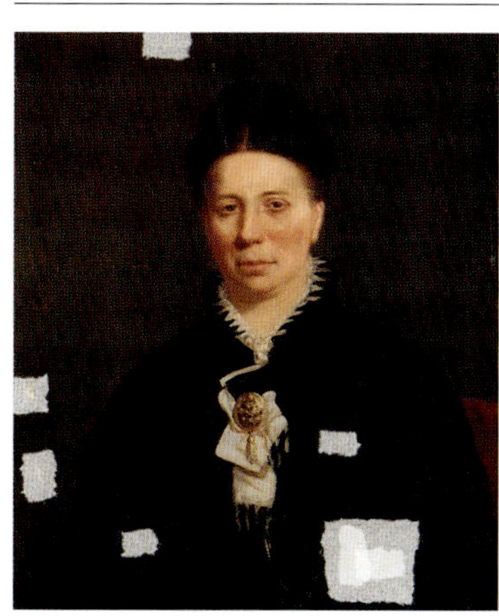

unknown artist 19th C
Portrait of a Lady
oil on canvas 76.2 x 63.5
TEMP.14930

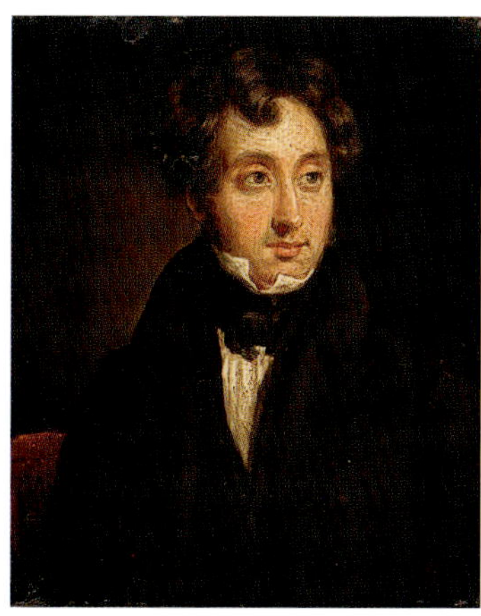

unknown artist 19th C
Portrait of a Man
oil on panel 21 x 16.5
NR.143

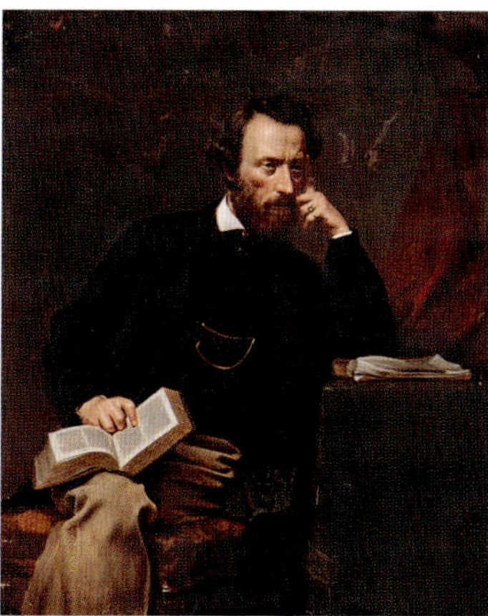

unknown artist 19th C
Portrait of a Victorian Gentleman
oil on panel 30.5 x 25
PP.1983.199

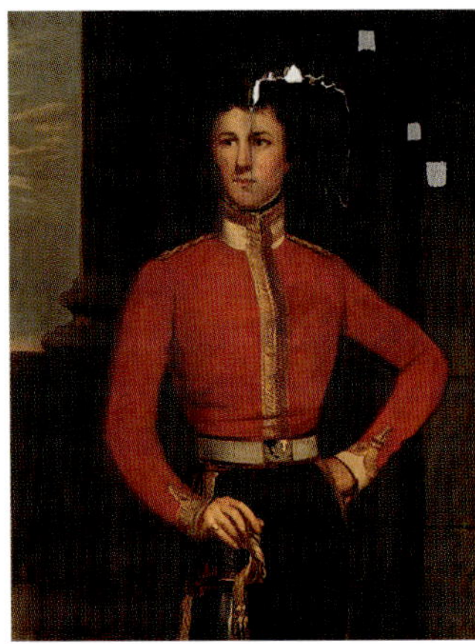

unknown artist 19th C
*Portrait of a Young Man, Nephew of
Lieutenant Colonel A. Hope Pattison*
oil on canvas 119.4 x 90.2
2533

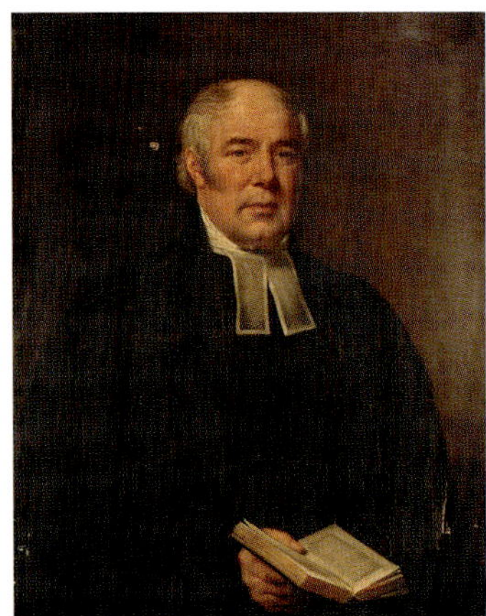

unknown artist 19th C
Reverend A. O. Bear
oil on canvas 92.2 x 72.2
TEMP.2735

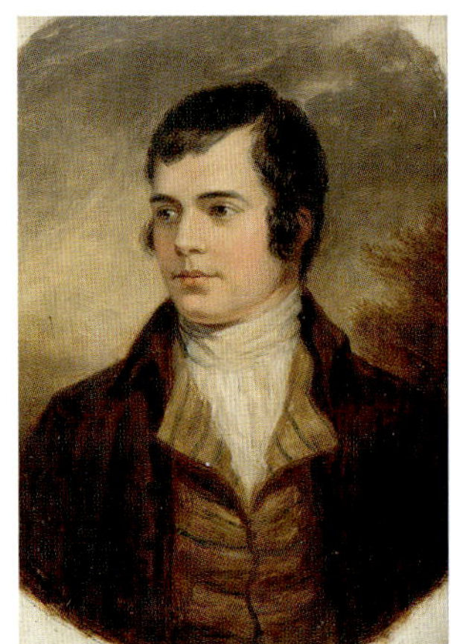

unknown artist 19th C
Robert Burns (1759–1796)
oil on canvas 50.8 x 40.7
3450

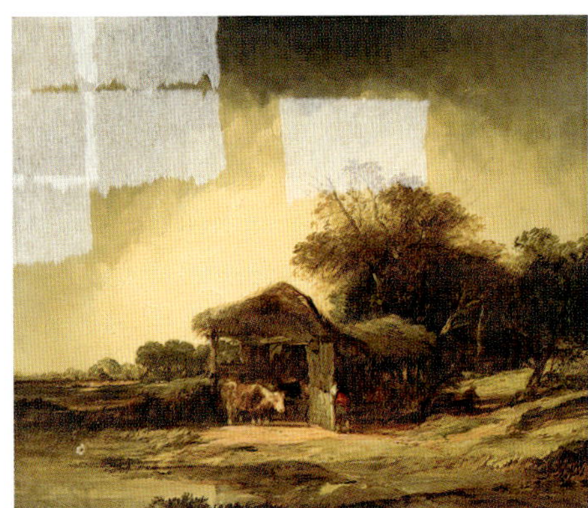

unknown artist 19th C
Scottish Landscape
oil on canvas 24.1 x 29.2
382

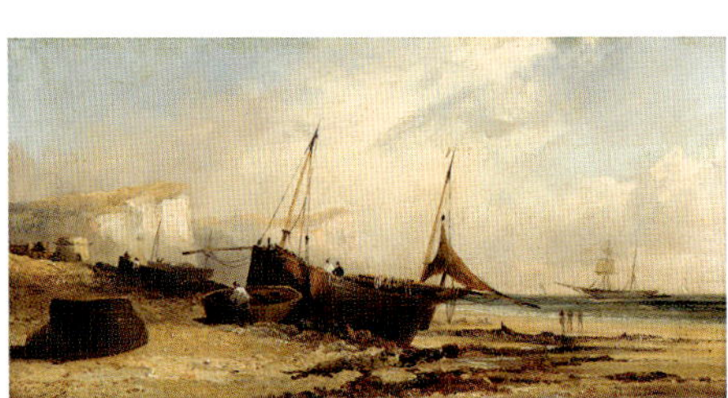

unknown artist 19th C
Sea Piece and Shipping
oil on canvas 19.1 x 40.6
775

unknown artist 19th C
Sir John Maxwell (1648–1732), 1st Bt
oil on canvas 74.6 x 61.6
PL.168 (P)

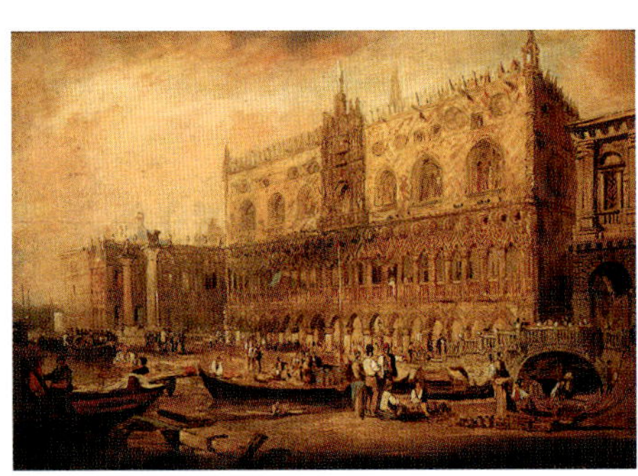

unknown artist 19th C
The Doge's Palace, Venice
oil on cardboard 32.5 x 49.2
3189

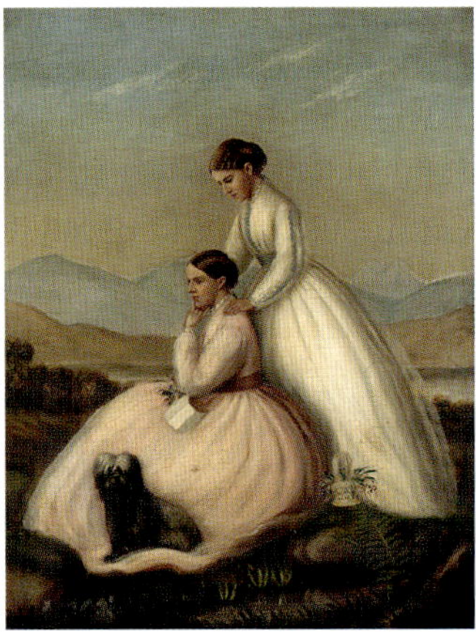

unknown artist 19th C
*The Misses C. and M. Crawford-Cummming
of Rosneath*
oil on canvas 91.4 x 71.1
2947

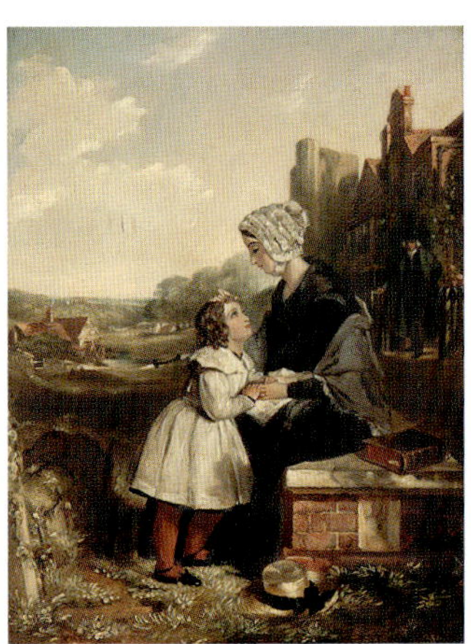

unknown artist 19th C
The Mourners
oil on panel 25.4 x 19.1
429

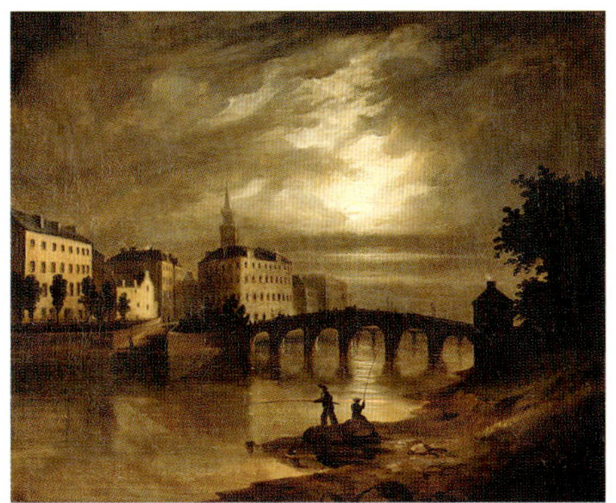

unknown artist 19th C
The Old Stockwell Bridge
oil on canvas 63.3 x 76
1503

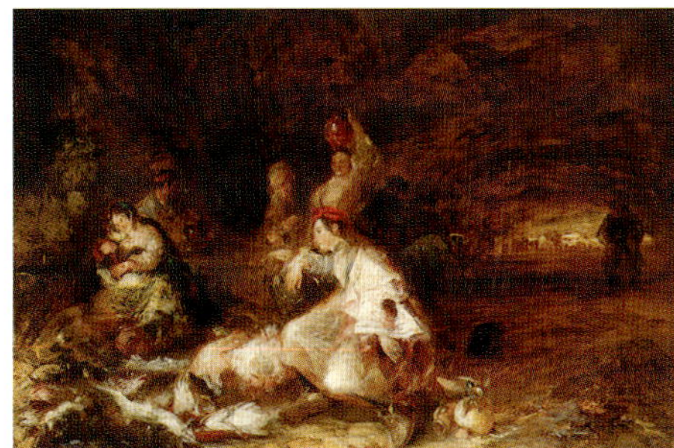

unknown artist 19th C
Travellers Resting in a Cave
oil on panel 44.8 x 64.4
3216

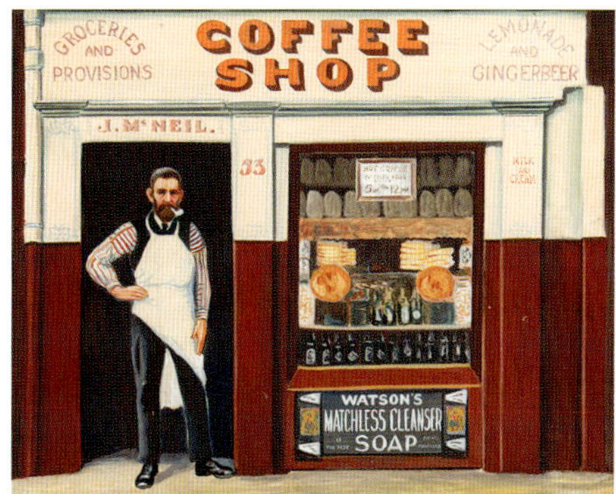

unknown artist
'Coffee John' c.1900
poster paint on cardboard 47.5 x 58.1
OG.1958.34.a

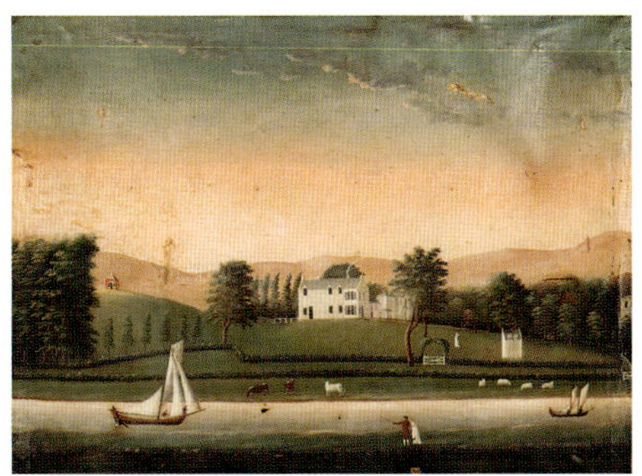

unknown artist
Stobcross House c.1906
oil on canvas 67.5 x 90.5
1906.109

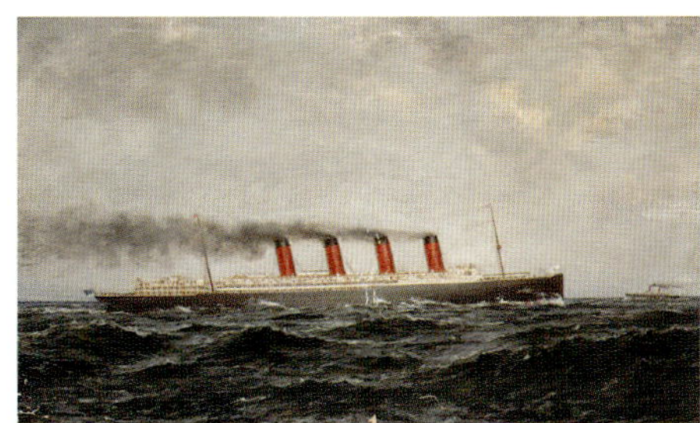

unknown artist
RMS 'Lusitania' c.1911
oil on canvas 111.5 x 183
T.1973.10.ae

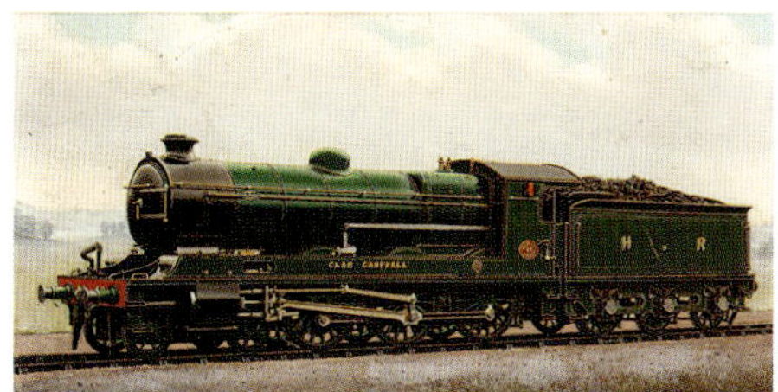

unknown artist
Highland Railway Locomotive No.49, 'Clan Campbell' after 1918
oil on board 33.6 x 61.3
T.1976.4

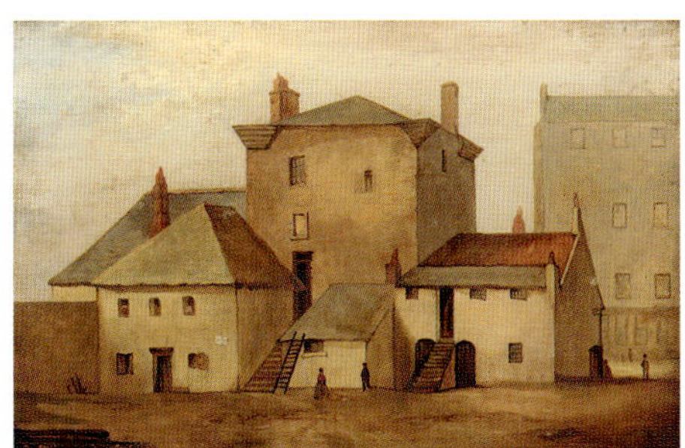

unknown artist
Gorbals Tower c.1919
oil on canvas 30.6 x 46.1
PL.1919.244

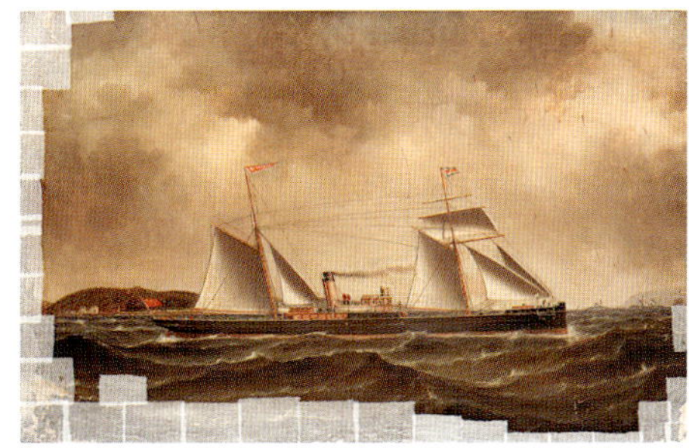

unknown artist
'St George' c.1931
oil on canvas 65.8 x 101.5
LT.4.1931.b (P)

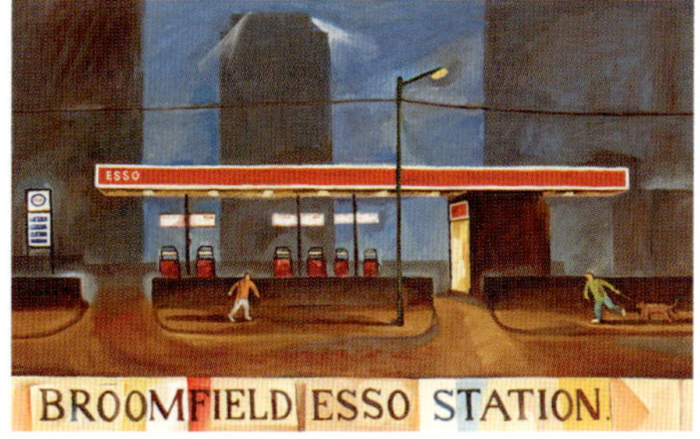

unknown artist
Broomfield Esso Station 1980–1990s
oil on paper 78.5 x 128
TEMP.15459

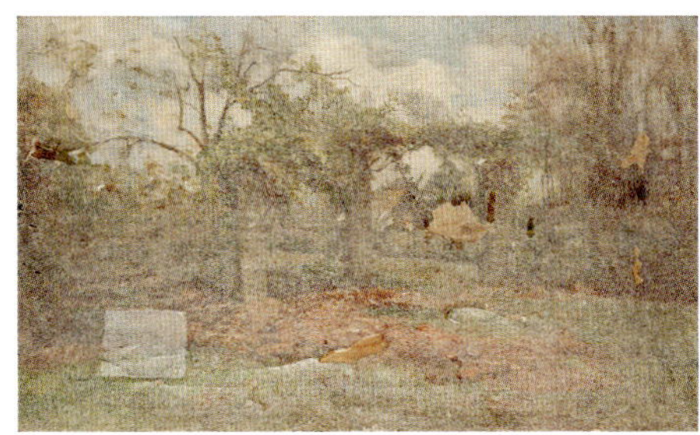

unknown artist
Orchard c.1984
oil on canvas 40.7 x 66
NR.151

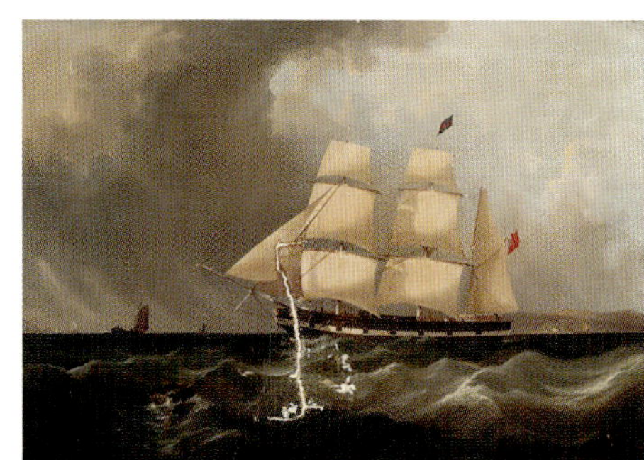

unknown artist
Ships at Sea c.1850
oil on canvas 64.8 x 89.9
TEMP.14950

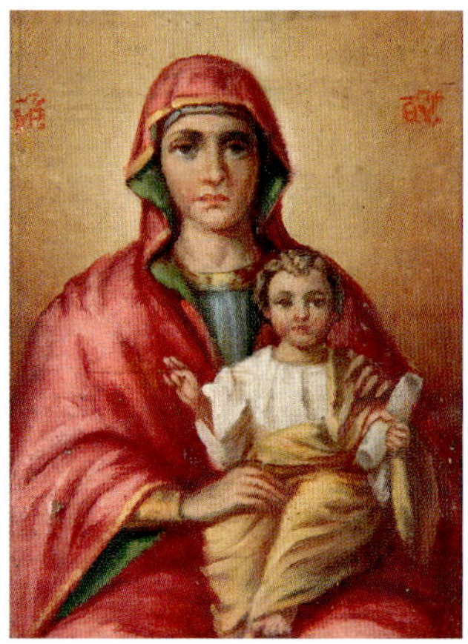

unknown artist 20th C
Virgin and Child
oil on panel 20 x 15.2
TEMP.19218

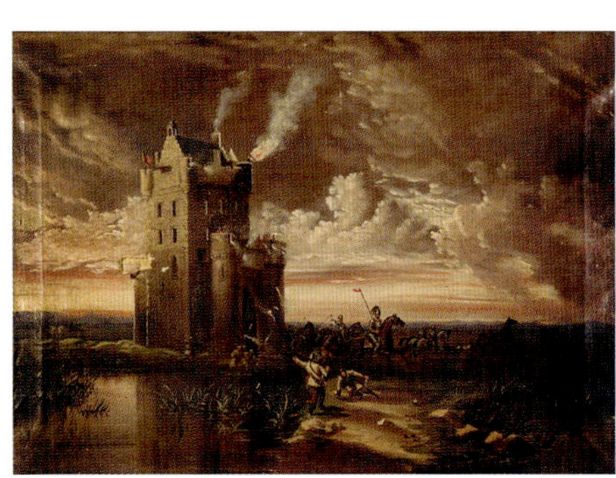

unknown artist
A Castle under Siege
oil on canvas 45.8 x 61.5
DEP.10

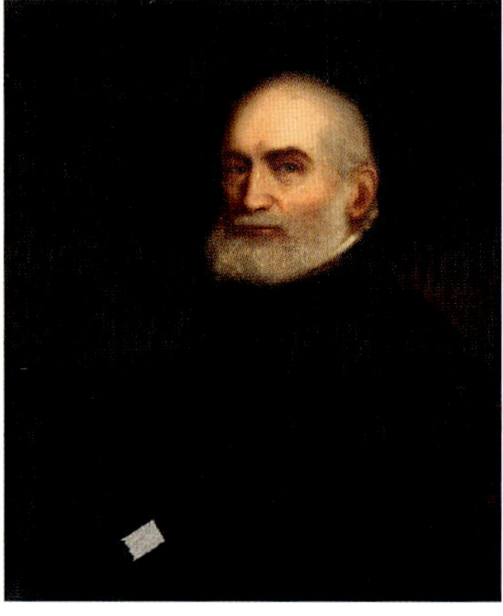

unknown artist
*Alexander Campbell (1796–1870), a Socialist
Co-Operative Pioneer*
oil on canvas 99.5 x 87
LPP.1975.87 (P)

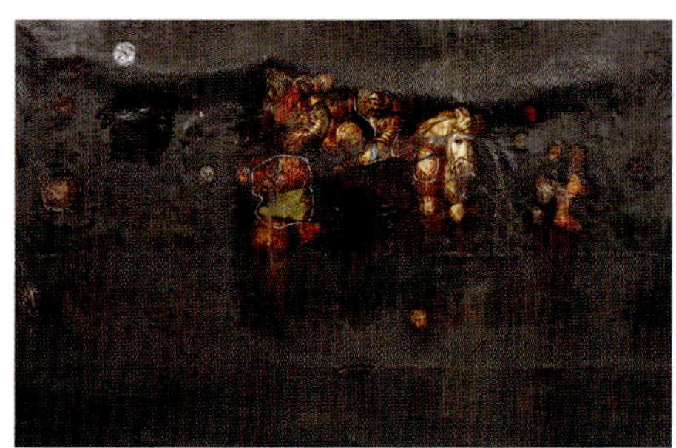

unknown artist
Battle of the Bell o' the Brae
oil on leather 147 x 231
TEMP.19289

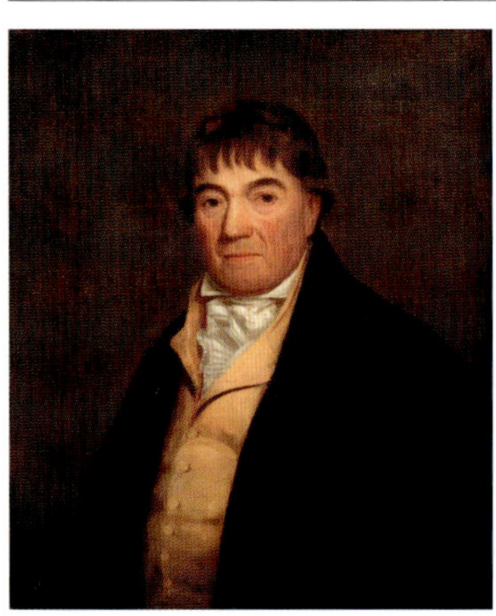

unknown artist
Captain Hugh Morris
oil on canvas 73.7 x 62.2
2905

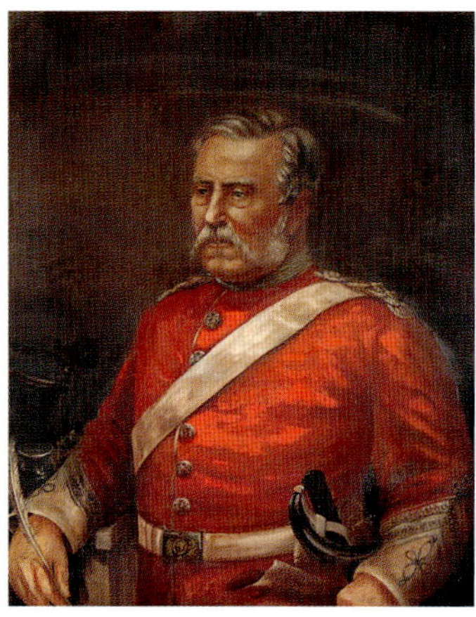

unknown artist
Captain John Crawford
oil on canvas 91.4 x 71.1
TEMP.14926

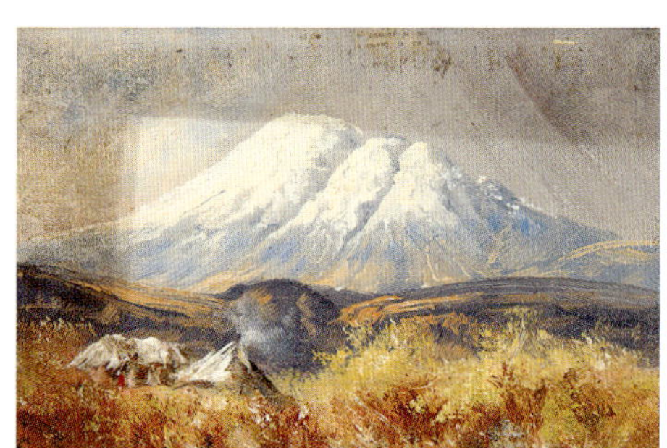

unknown artist
Chimborazo Volcano
oil on canvas 20.3 x 30.5
A.1940.33.c

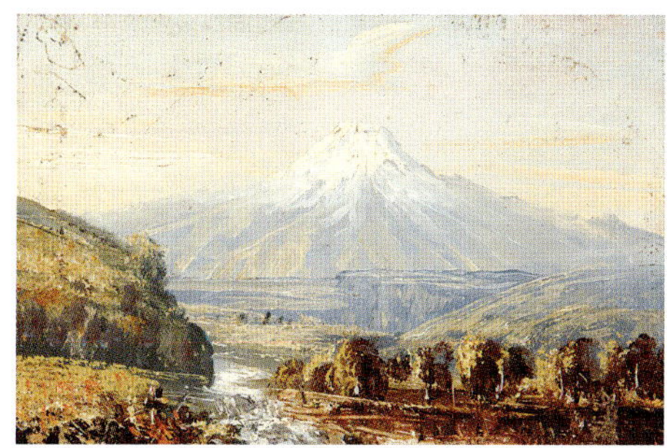

unknown artist
Cumbal Volcano
oil on canvas 19.7 x 29.8
A.1940.33.a

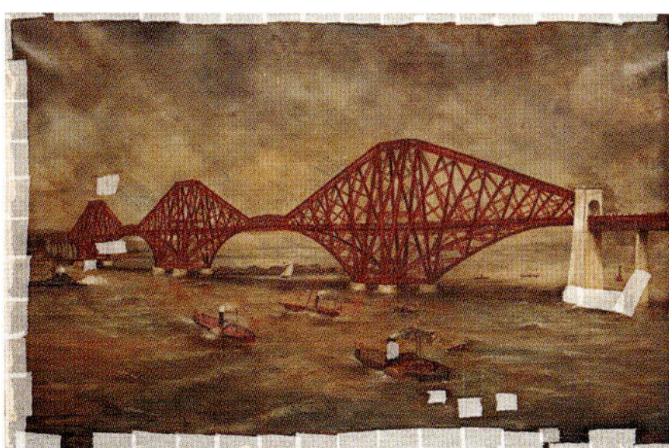

unknown artist
Forth Rail Bridge (Opening Ceremony)
oil on canvas 74.3 x 112
T.1967.33.ak

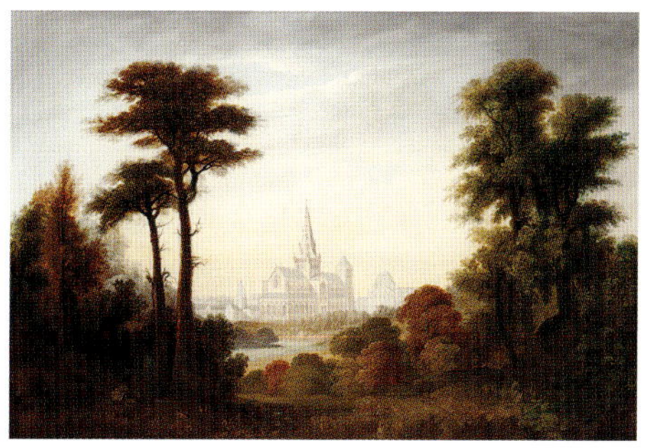

unknown artist
Glasgow Cathedral from the East
oil on canvas 67.7 x 90.2
TEMP.2756

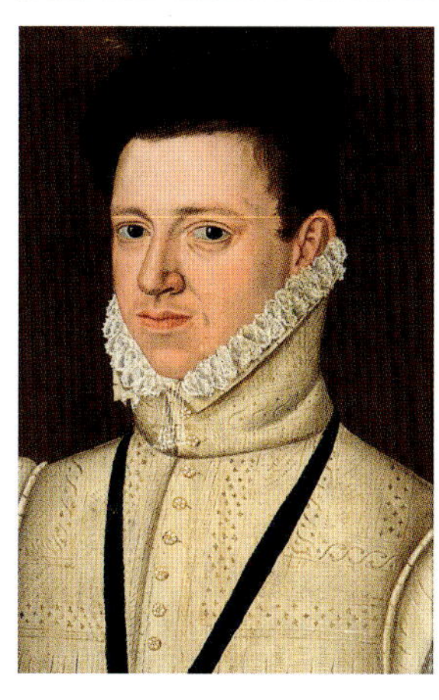

unknown artist
Henry Stuart (1545–1567), Lord Darnley
oil on panel 38.4 x 27.7
PL.1927.248

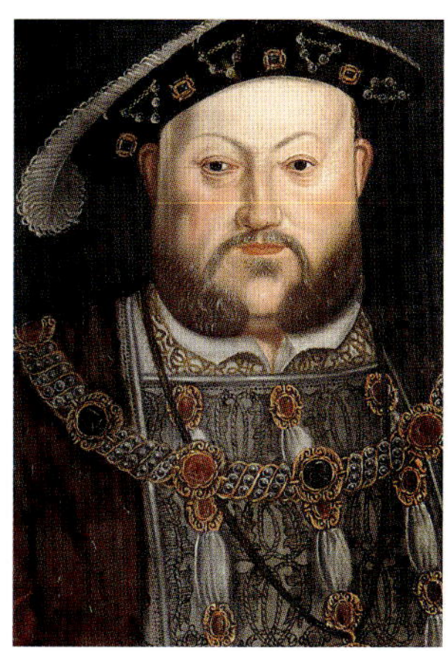

unknown artist
Henry VIII (1491–1547)
oil on board 46.6 x 35.5
PL.1927.250

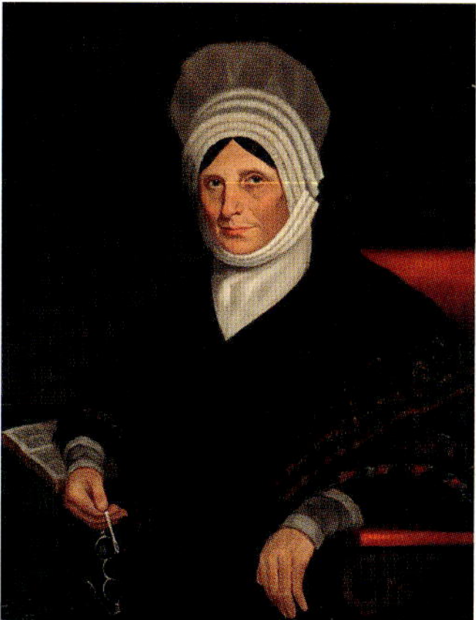

unknown artist
Jean Blackburn, Wife of Robert Swan of Wattison
oil on canvas 91.4 x 71.1
2255

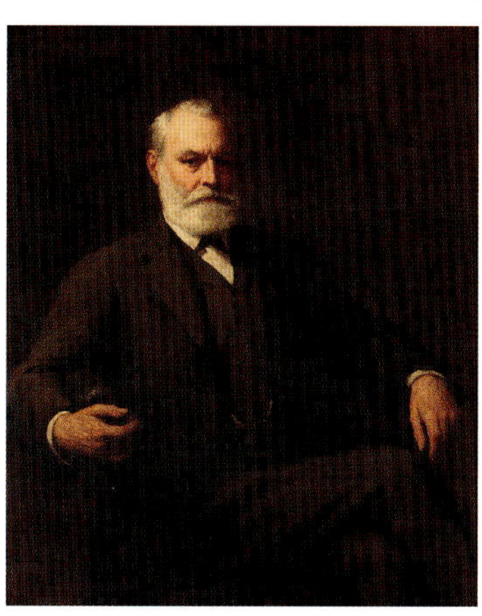

unknown artist
Joseph Cheney Bolton, Esq. (1819–1901), Director of the Royal Bank of Scotland (1868–1901), Chairman of the (...)
oil on canvas 163 x 136
TEMP.14965

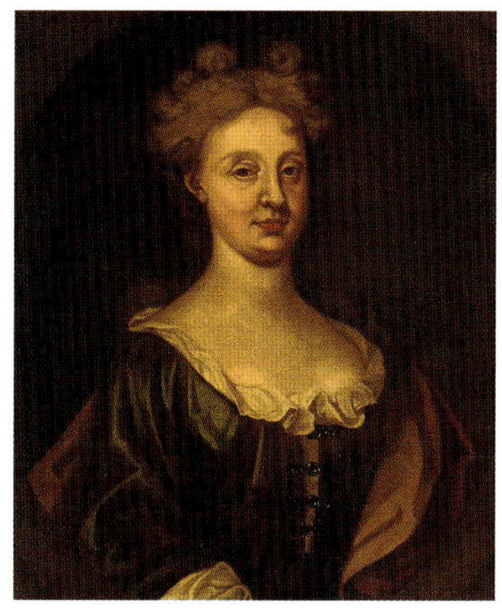

unknown artist
Lady Barbara Maxwell (d.1737)
oil on canvas 75.6 x 61.6
PL.172 (P)

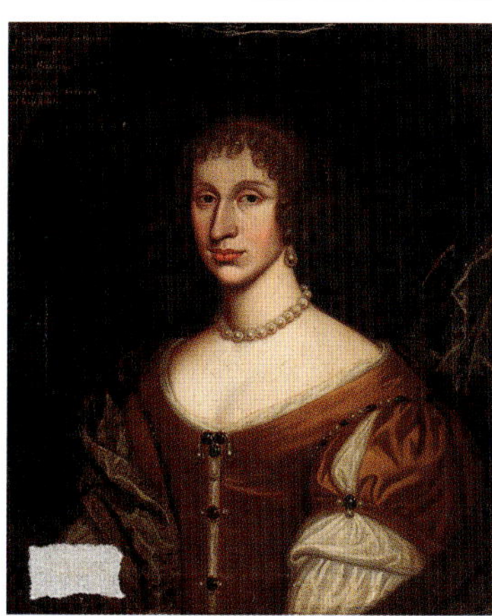

unknown artist
Lady Marian Maxwell (d.1705)
oil on canvas 74.6 x 61.6
PL.151 (P)

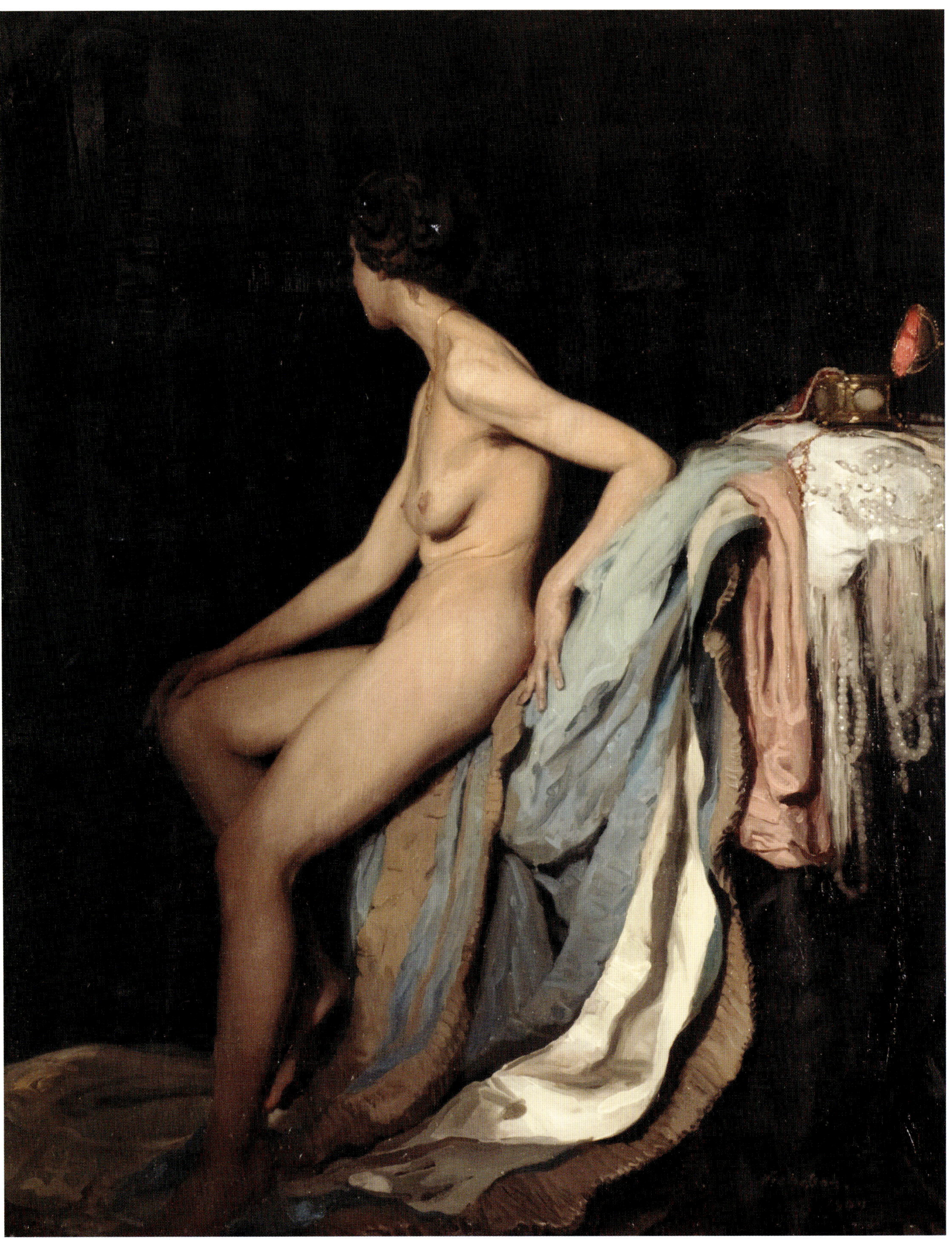

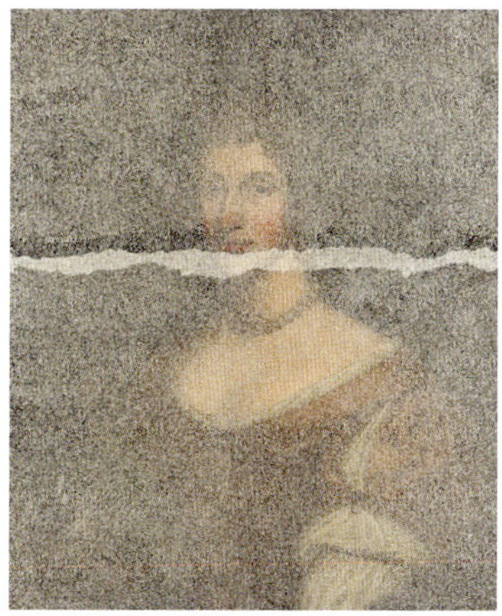

unknown artist
Lady Marian Maxwell (d.1705)
oil on canvas 77 x 63.4
PL.169 (P)

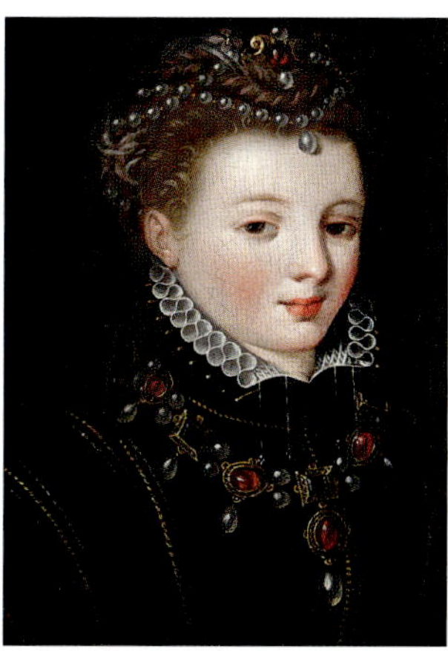

unknown artist
Mary Stuart (1542–1587), Queen of Scots
oil on panel 24.5 x 19.2
PL.1927.253

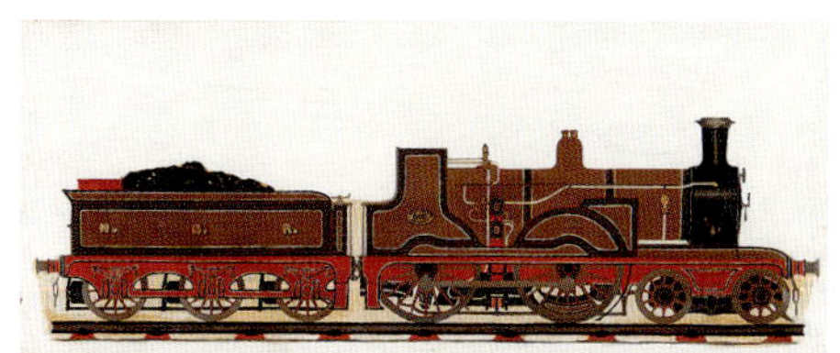

unknown artist
North British Railway Locomotive No.603
oil on paper 43.2 x 101.6
T.1980.26

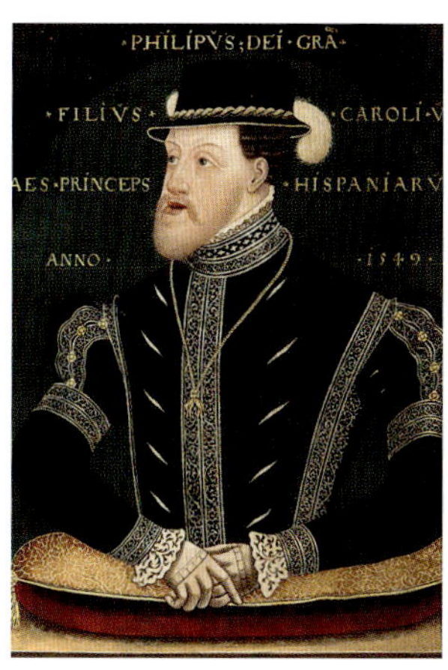

unknown artist
Philip II of Spain (1527–1598)
oil on panel 42.3 x 29.7
PL.1927.247

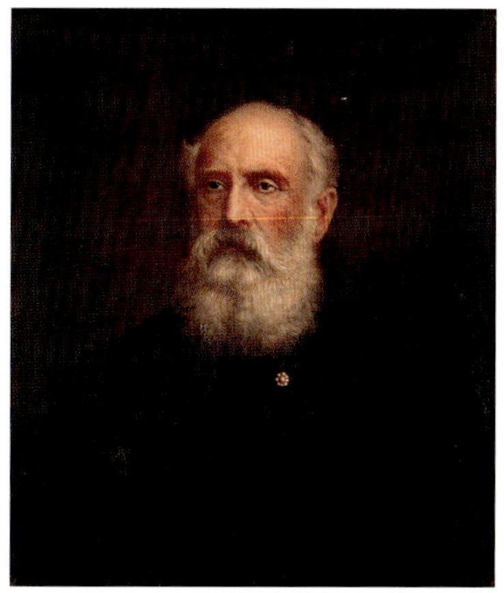

unknown artist
Portrait of a Bearded Man
oil on canvas 76.4 x 64.1
TEMP.17823

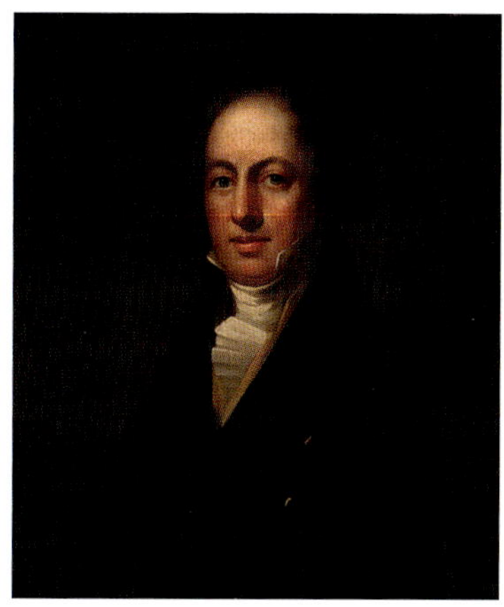

unknown artist
Portrait of a Gentleman
oil on canvas 76.2 x 63.5
2536

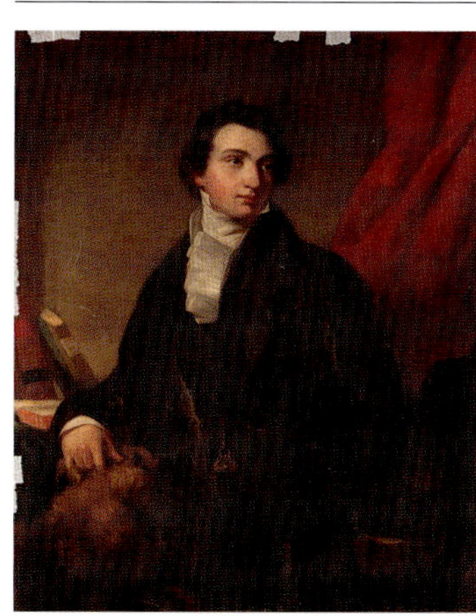

unknown artist
Portrait of a Man
oil on canvas 127 x 101.6
3441

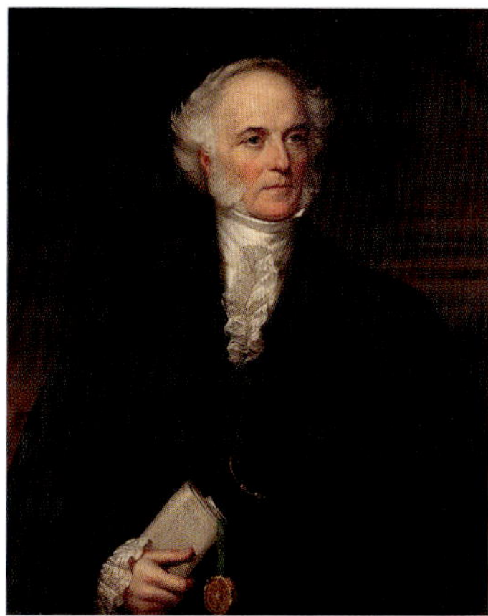

unknown artist
Portrait of a Man with a Lace Cravat
oil on canvas 94 x 73.7
3445

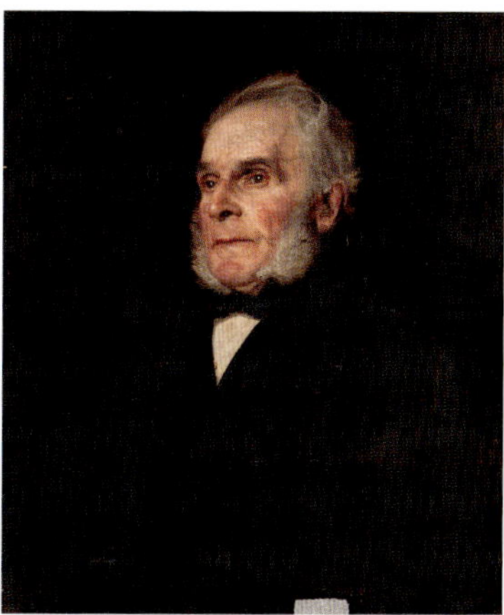

unknown artist
Portrait of a Seated Man
oil on canvas on board 76.7 x 63.2
TEMP.14967

Facing page: Nicholson, William, 1872–1949, *Carlina*, 1909 (p. 327)

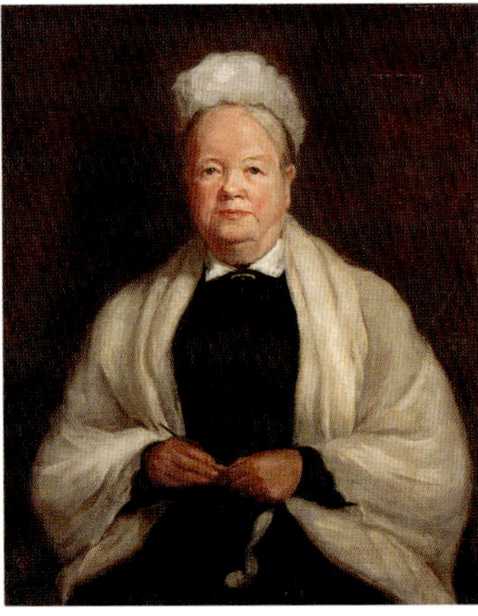

unknown artist
Portrait of a Seated Woman
oil on canvas on board 90.2 x 70.3
TEMP.14966

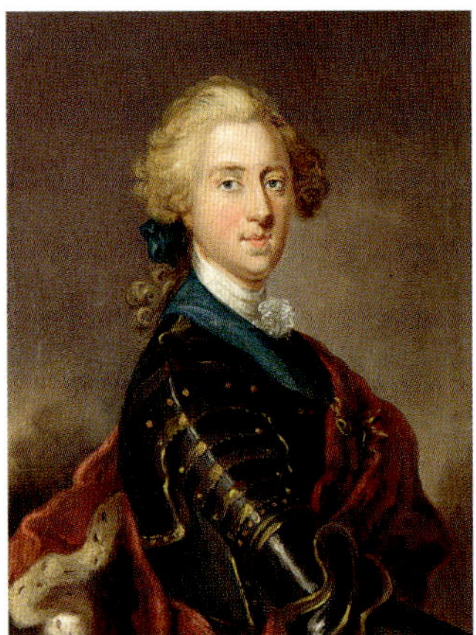

unknown artist
Prince Charles Edward Stuart (1720–1788)
('Bonnie Prince Charlie')
oil on canvas 28.2 x 22.2
PL.1927.251

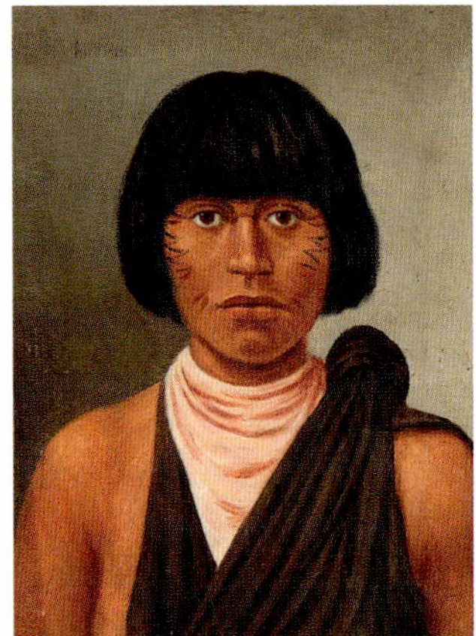

unknown artist
Portrait of an Oriental Indian with a Tattooed
Face
oil on canvas 21.6 x 15.9
A.1940.33.k

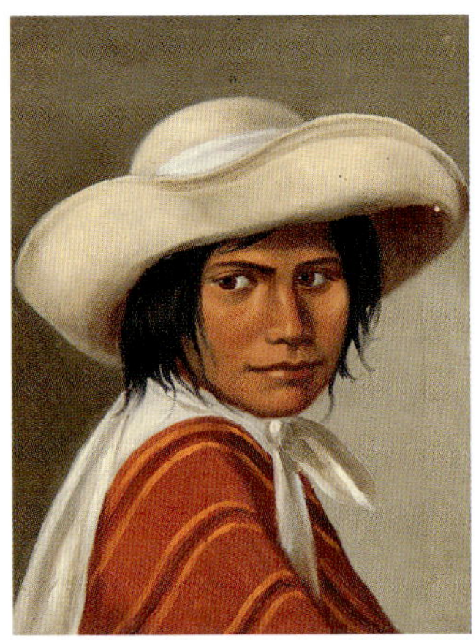

unknown artist
Portrait of a Serrano Indian
oil on canvas 22 x 16
A.1940.33.j

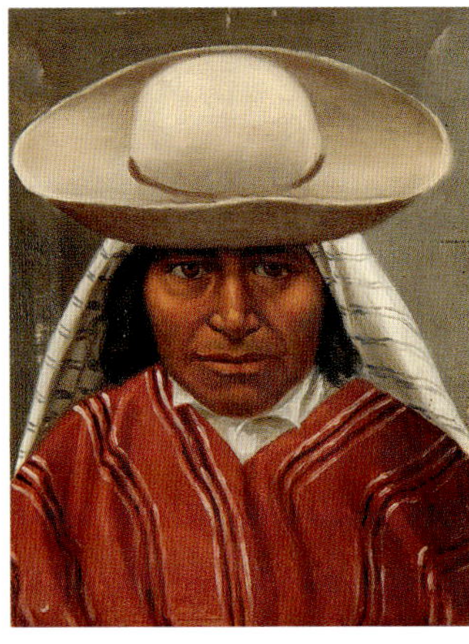

unknown artist
Portrait of a Serrano Indian in a Red Blouse
oil on canvas 22 x 16
A.1940.33.h

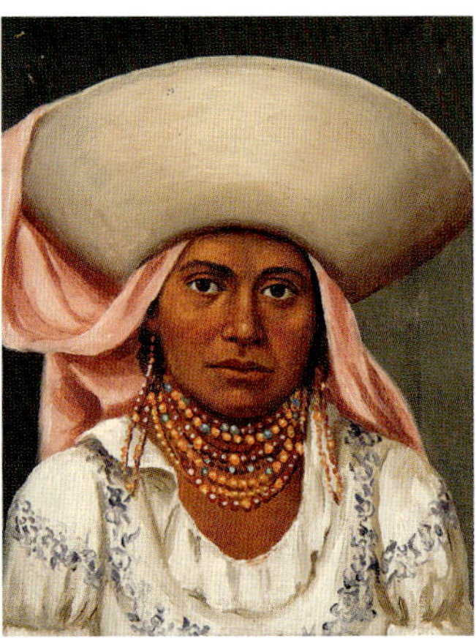

unknown artist
Portrait of a Serrano Indian Woman
oil on canvas 21.6 x 15.9
A.1940.33.i

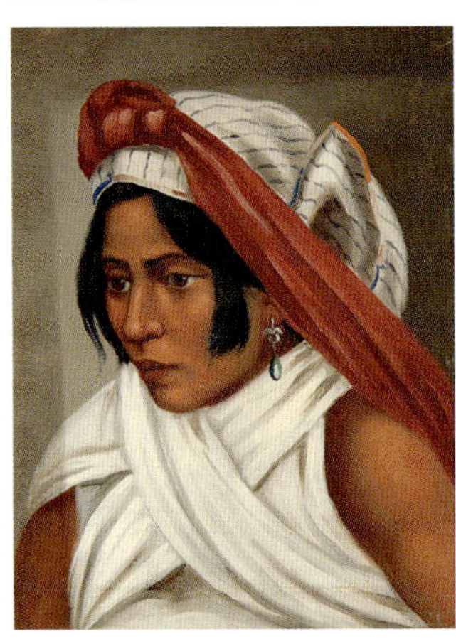

unknown artist
Portrait of a Serrano Indian Woman with a
Red and White Headdress
oil on canvas 21.6 x 15.9
A.1940.33.g

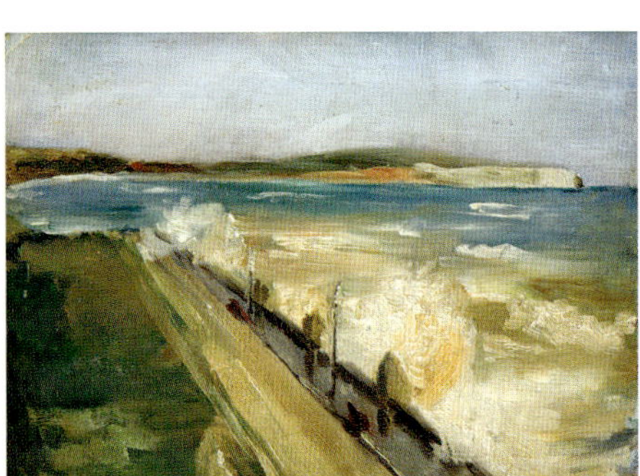

unknown artist
Rough Seas
oil on board 25.4 x 34.9
35.643

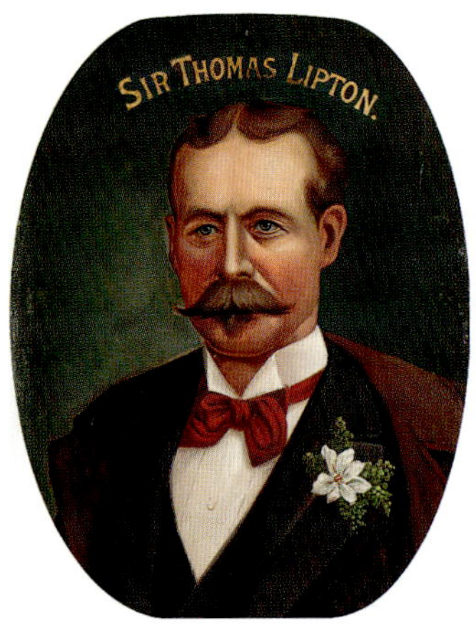

unknown artist
Sir Thomas Lipton (1848–1931)
oil on board 73.5 x 55
PP.1982.235

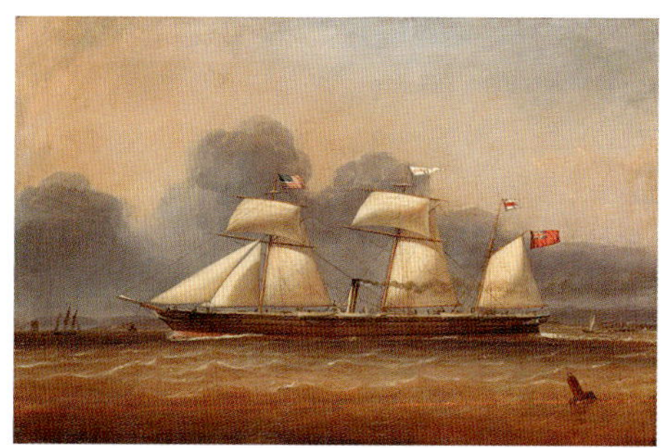

unknown artist
Steamship 'Clyde'
oil on canvas 76.2 x 111.8
TEMP.14927

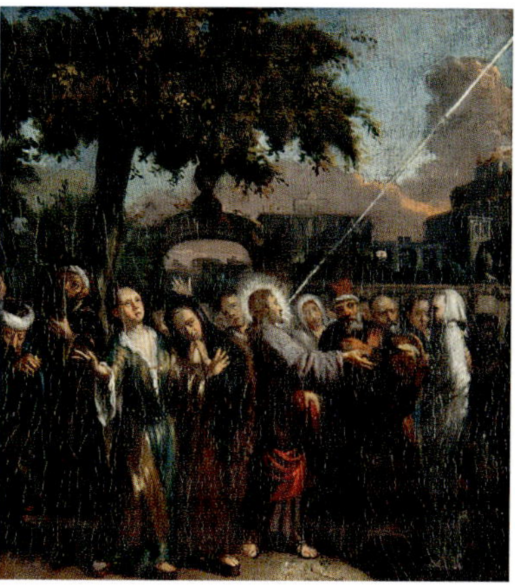

unknown artist
The Raising of Lazarus
oil on canvas on wood 19.1 x 18.4
680

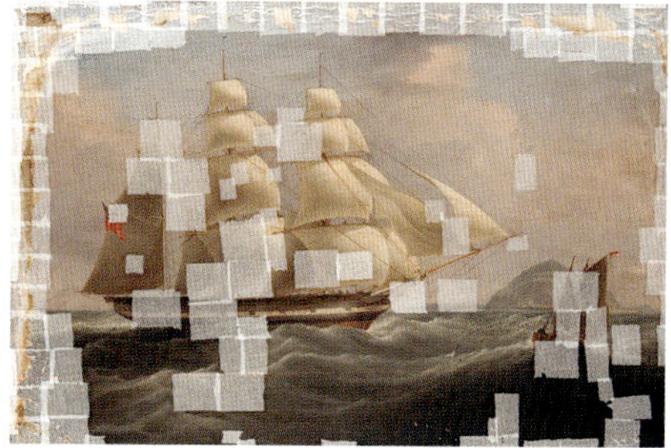

unknown artist
Three-Masted Barque
oil on canvas 86.5 x 127.5
TEMP.14971

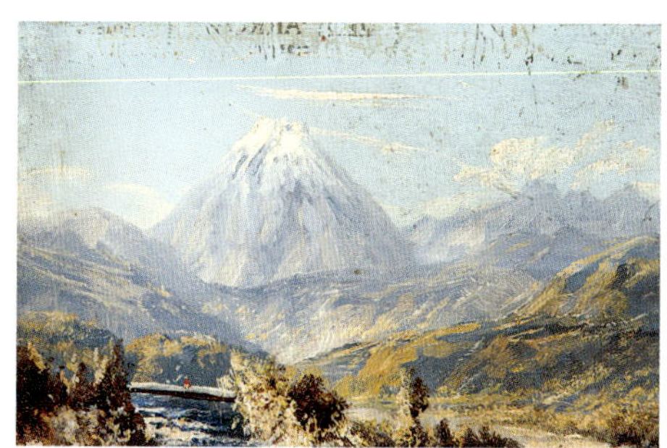

unknown artist
Tungurahua Volcano
oil on canvas 20 x 29.8
A.1940.33.b

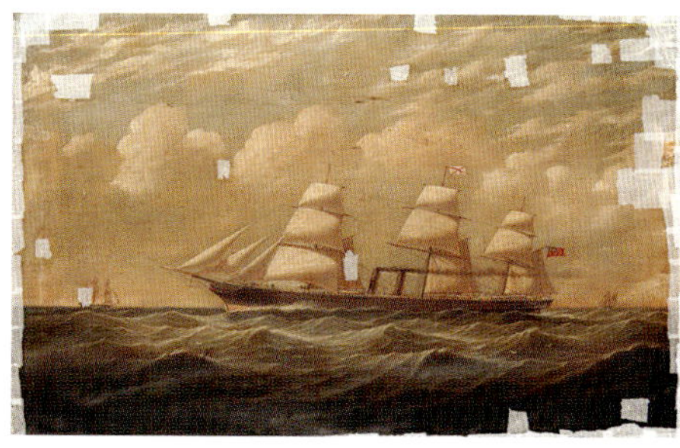

unknown artist
Twin-Funnel Steamship with Auxiliary Sail
oil on canvas 76.5 x 121.5
TEMP.14970

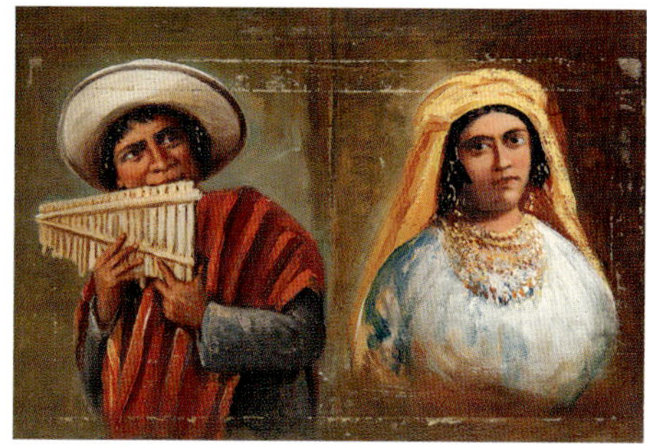

unknown artist
Two Serrano Indians Dressed for Market
oil on canvas 29.5 x 43.5
A.1940.33.f

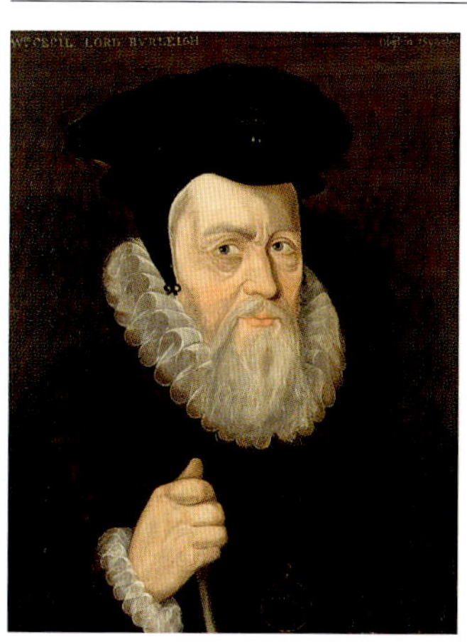

unknown artist
William Cecil (1520–1598), Lord Burghley
oil on panel 58 x 45.6
PL.1927.246

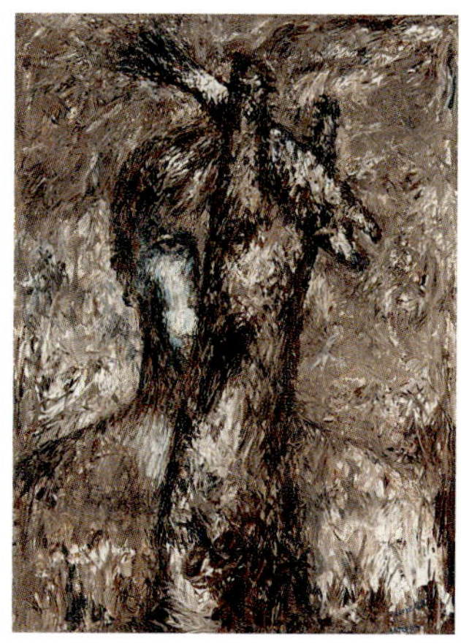

Urie, Joseph b.1947
Man with a Dog 1987
oil on paper 78.5 x 56
PR.2007.2.112

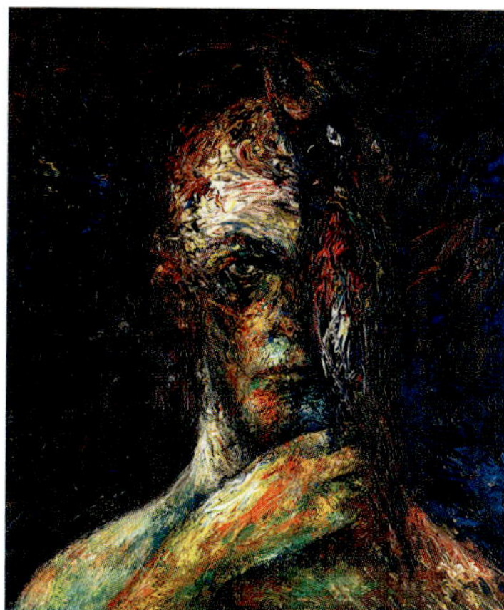

Urie, Joseph b.1947
Man with a Blackbird 1988
oil on canvas 63 x 54
3683

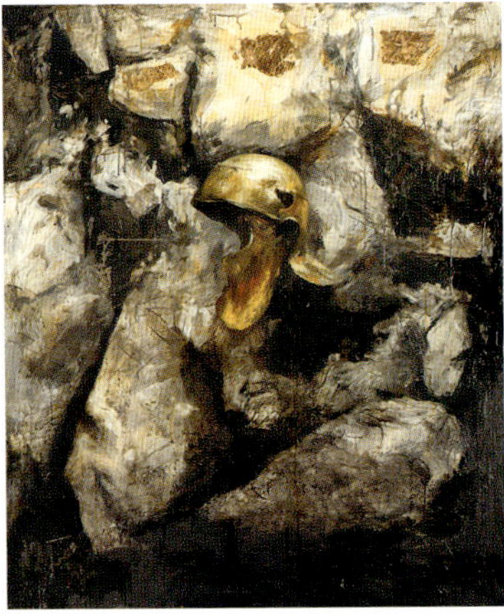

Urquhart, Donald b.1959
Pyrites 1989
oil & gold leaf on canvas 146.5 x 121
3677

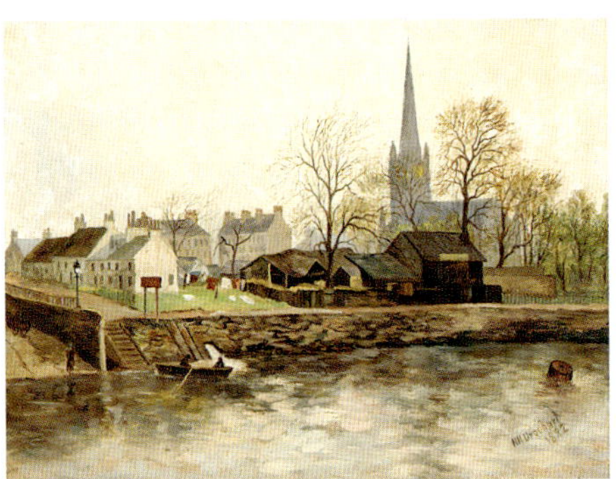

Urquhart, H. H.
Old Govan Water Row 1882
oil on canvas 58 x 70
1934.12

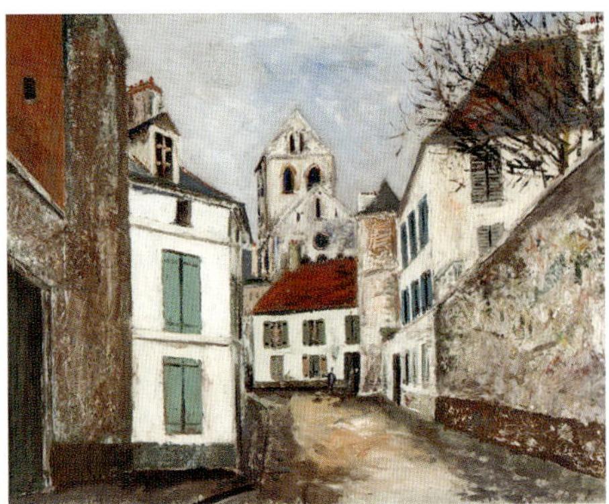

Utrillo, Maurice 1883–1955
Village Street, Auvers-sur-Oise c.1912
oil on canvas 59.4 x 73
2217

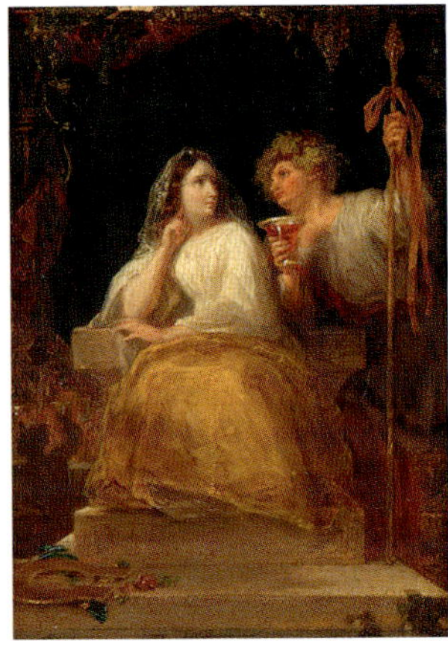

Uwins, Thomas 1782–1857
*Comus Offering the Enchanted Cup to the
Lady* (from the masque by John Milton)
oil on millboard 21.6 x 16.5
366

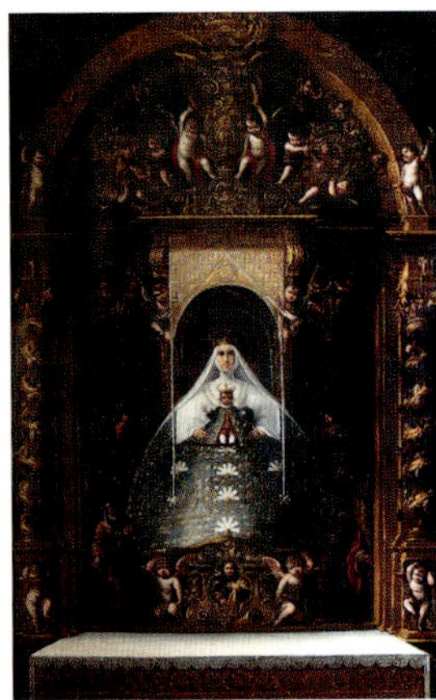

Valdés Leal, Juan de 1622–1690
Madonna and Child
oil on canvas 125.9 x 79.5
PC.62

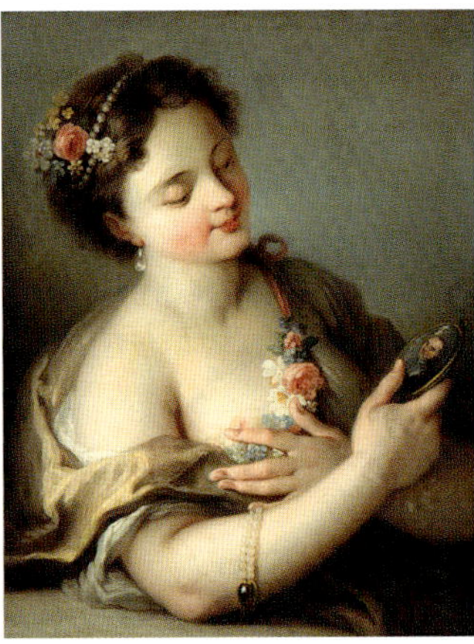

Valory, Caroline de b.c.1790
The Miniature
oil on canvas 58.4 x 48.2
216

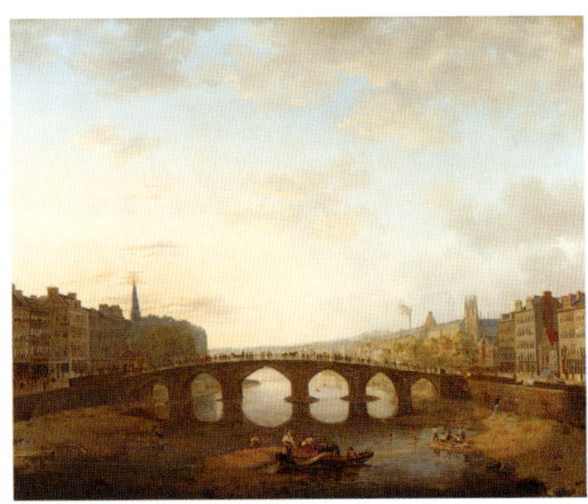

Van der Houten
Stockwell Bridge, Glasgow 1838
oil on canvas 74.5 x 86.6
TEMP.14947

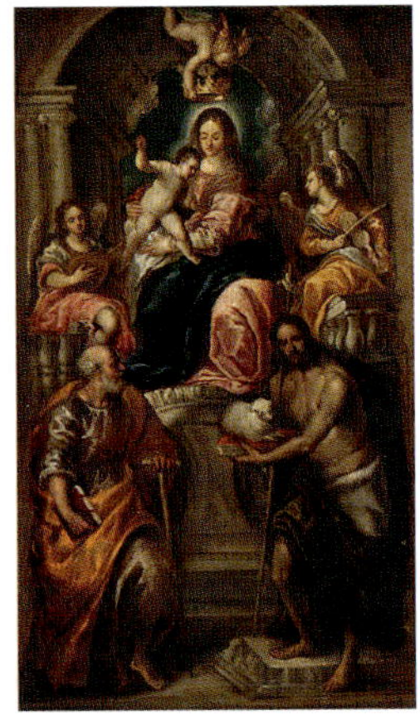

Varotari, Dario 1539–1596
*Madonna and Child Enthroned with Saints
Peter and John the Baptist and Angels* c.1575–
1580
oil on canvas 70.5 x 40.6
33

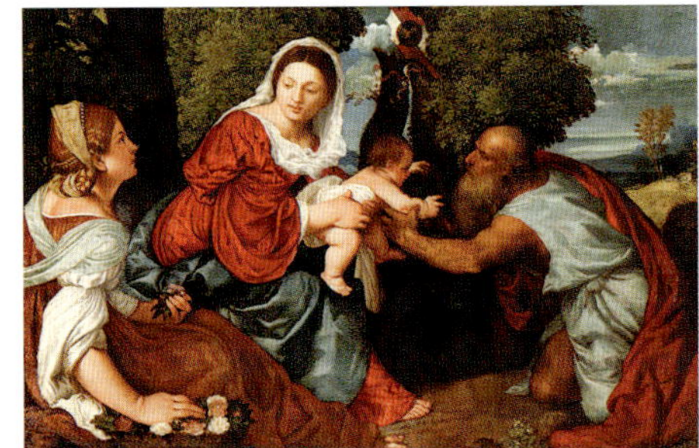

Vecellio, Francesco 1475–1559/1560
*Madonna and Child with Saint Jerome and
Saint Dorothy* c.1520
oil on canvas 60.3 x 88.9
192

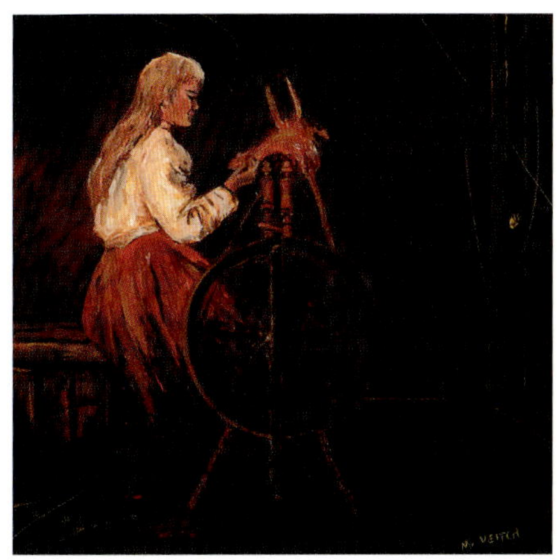

Veitch
Girl at a Spinning Wheel c.1990
acrylic on hardboard 44 x 44.5
TEMP.15554 DUP

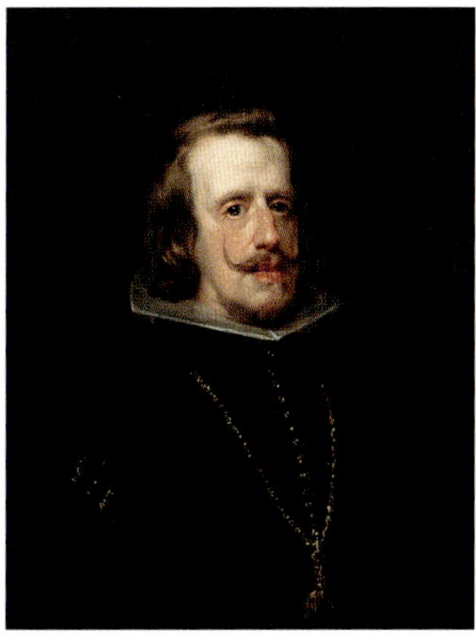

Velázquez, Diego (and studio) 1599–1660
Philip IV of Spain (1605–1665) c.1650–1660
oil on canvas 68.6 x 53.3
1116

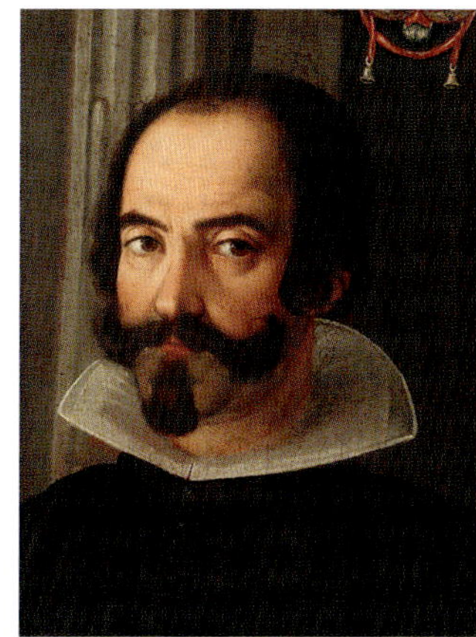

Velázquez, Diego (school of) 1599–1660
Head of a Man: The Conde De Tilly, Johan 't Serclaes (1559–1632) c.1619–1632
oil on canvas 43.8 x 31.4
PC.67

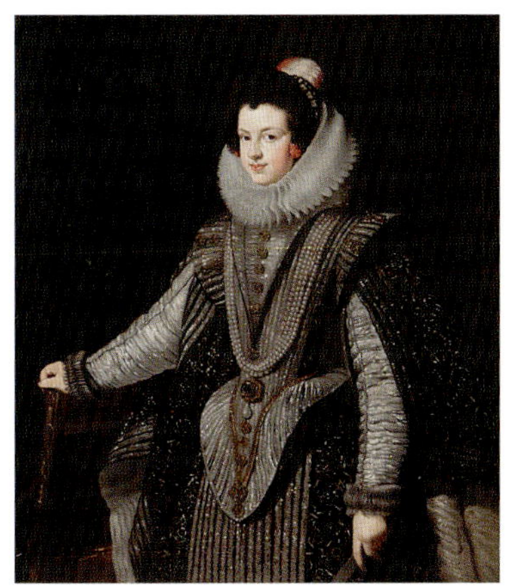

Velázquez, Diego (school of) 1599–1660
Isabella of Bourbon (1603–1644) c.1620
oil on canvas 116.2 x 97.8
PC.10

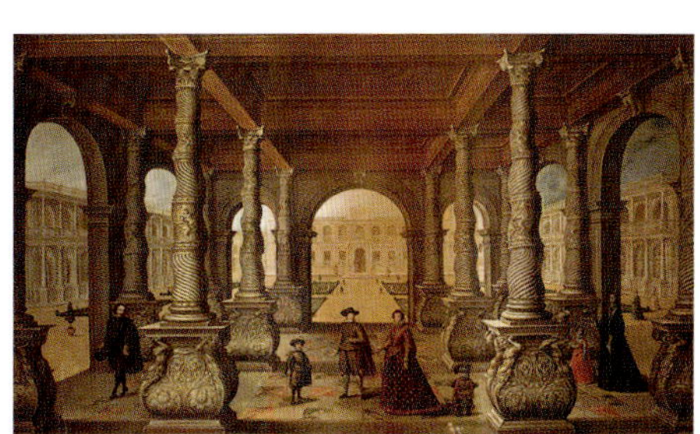

Velázquez, Diego (school of) 1599–1660
Philip IV and His Queen in a Colonnade
oil on canvas 181.1 x 303.8
PC.71

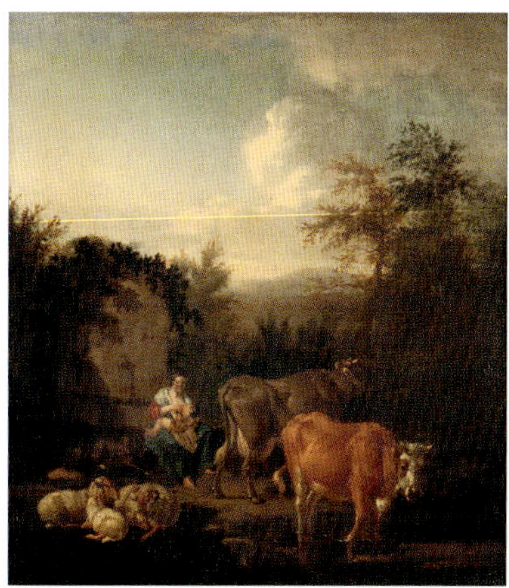

Velde, Adriaen van de 1636–1672
A Woman and a Child, Cattle and Sheep by a Fountain
oil on canvas 25.4 x 22.9
99

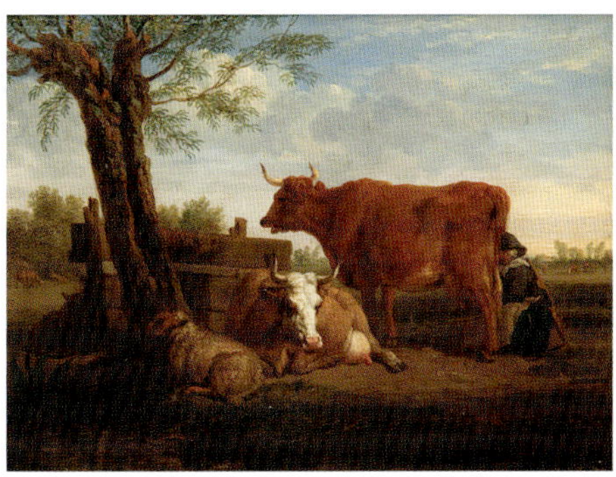

Velde, Adriaen van de (after) 1636–1672
A Meadow with Cattle and a Woman Milking 17th C
oil on panel 14.3 x 18.1
66

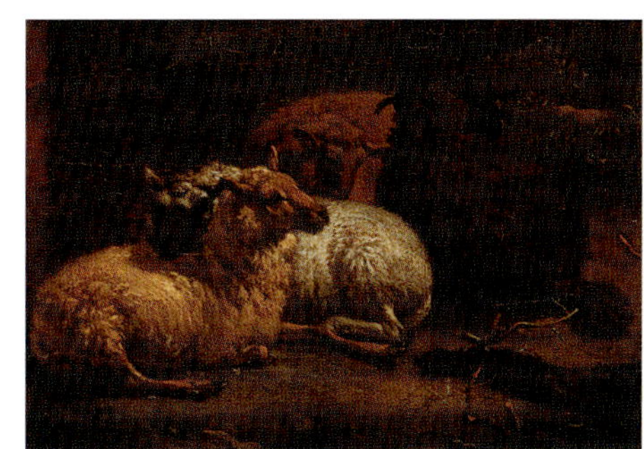

Velde, Adriaen van de (imitator of) 1636–1672
Four Sheep Resting 19th C
oil on canvas 10.2 x 14
424

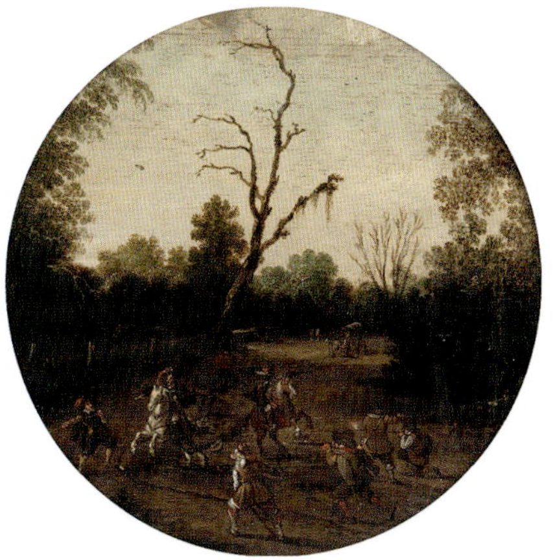

Velde, Esaias van de I 1587–1630
A Military Skirmish 1624
oil on panel 26
70

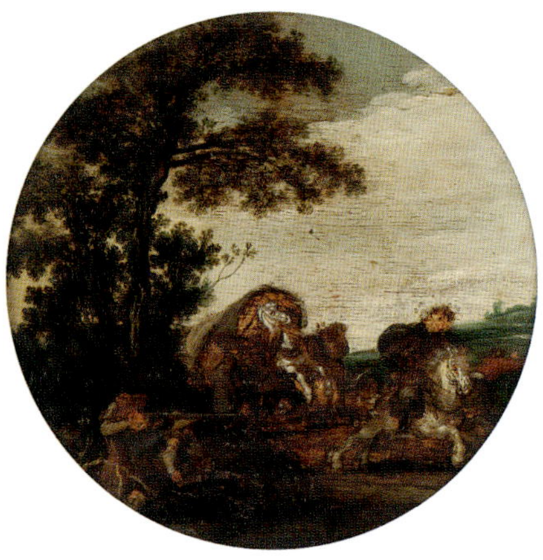

Velde, Esaias van de I 1587–1630
The Ambush of a Wagon Train c.1624
oil on panel 26
71

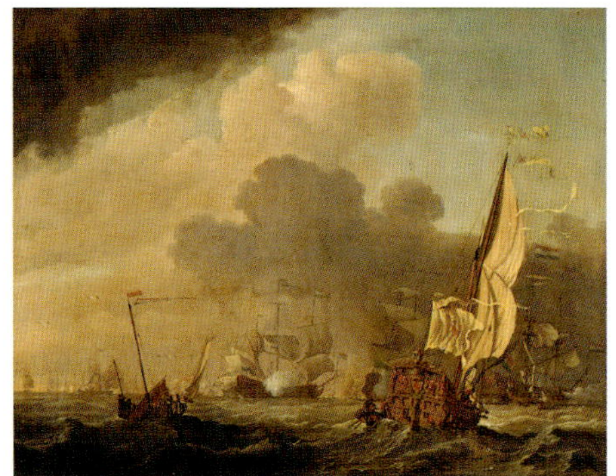

Velde, Willem van de II (after) 1633–1707
A States Yacht Running down towards the Dutch Fleet 17th C–18th C
oil on canvas 73.3 x 93.7
85

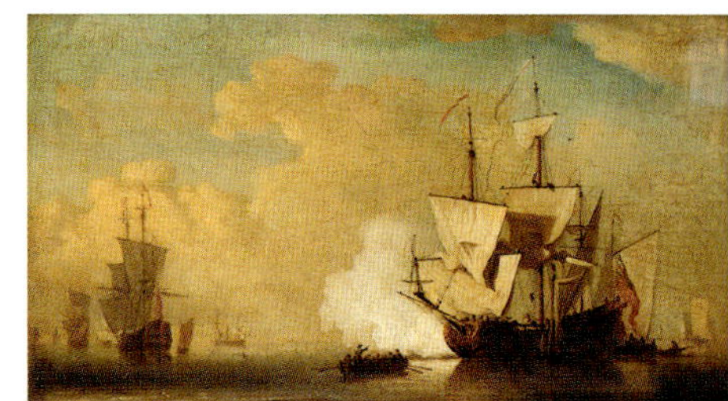

Velde, Willem van de II (after) 1633–1707
An English Ship Becalmed, Firing a Gun
18th C
oil on canvas 35.5 x 57.8
123

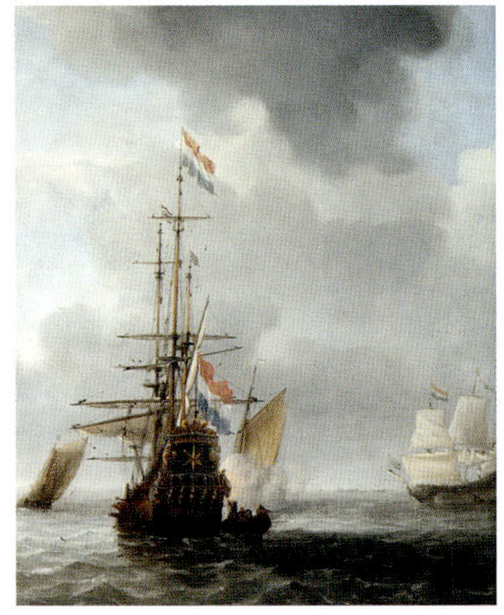

Velde, Willem van de II (attributed to)
1633–1707
The Dutch Man-of-War 'Star' at Anchor
c.1653
oil on panel 28.3 x 24.1
102

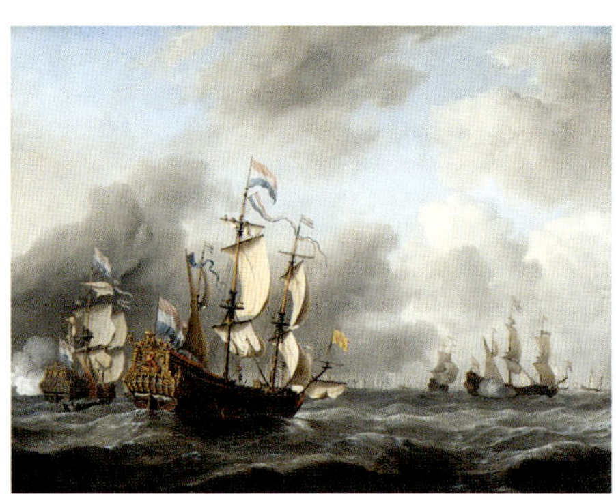

Velde, Willem van de II (attributed to)
1633–1707
The 'Eendracht' and Other Ships of the Dutch Fleet 1673 (?)
oil on canvas 64.7 x 85.4
622

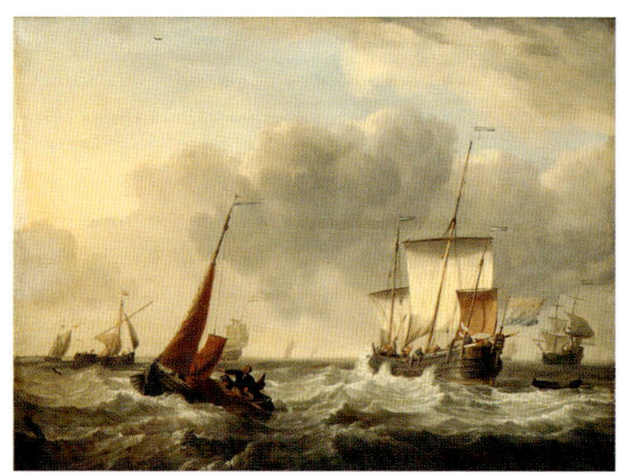

Velde, Willem van de II (attributed to)
1633–1707
A Dutch Fishing Buss under Sail, with Other Vessels in a Breeze c.1670
oil on canvas 34 x 43.2
281

Velde, Willem van de II (studio of)
1633–1707
A Dutch Vessel Pushing Off from Shore with Others under Sail late 17th C
oil on canvas 32.7 x 50.8
9

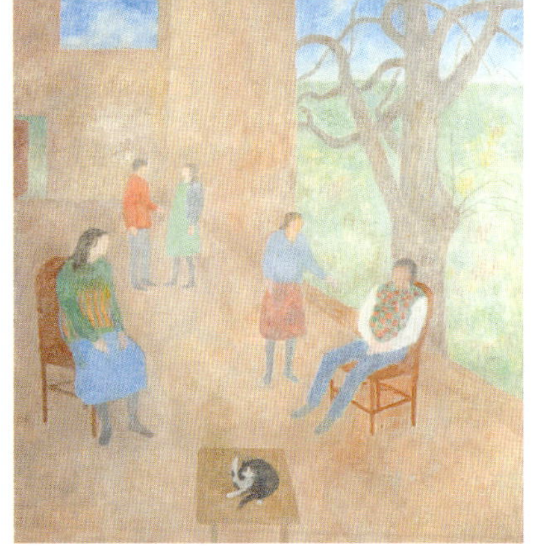

Vellacott, Elisabeth 1905–2002
Conversations, Cat and Pear Tree 1992
oil on board 63.5 x 60.6
3570

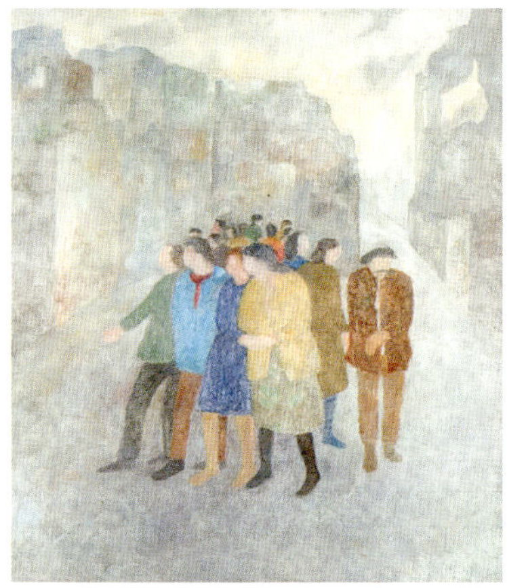

Vellacott, Elisabeth 1905–2002
Raided City 1993
oil on board 60 x 50.5
3571

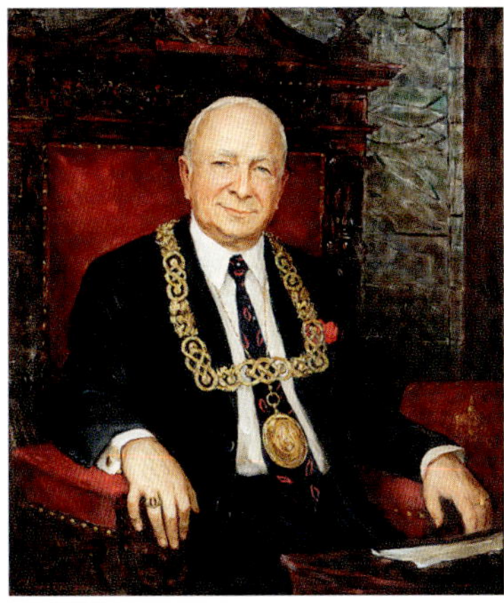

Venskiy, Igor Ivanov
Alex Mosson, Lord Provost of the City of
Glasgow (1999–2003) 2003
oil on canvas 125.7 x 106
3648

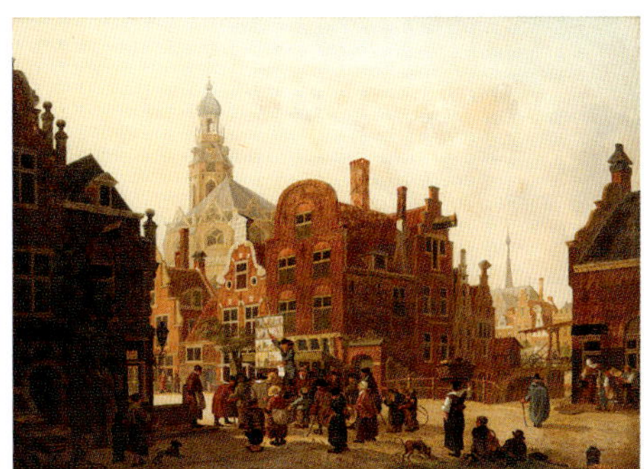

Verheyen, Jan Hendrik 1778–1846
An Imaginary Dutch Street, with a
Huckster 1815
oil on panel 33.3 x 43.2
409

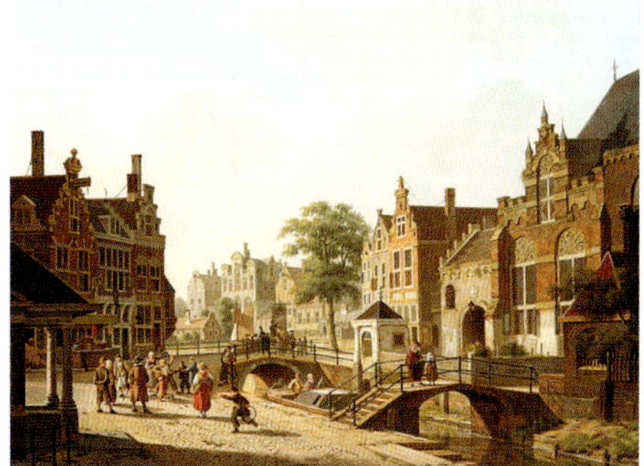

Verheyen, Jan Hendrik 1778–1846
A Dutch Street, with Children Fighting
oil on panel 43.8 x 55.9
458

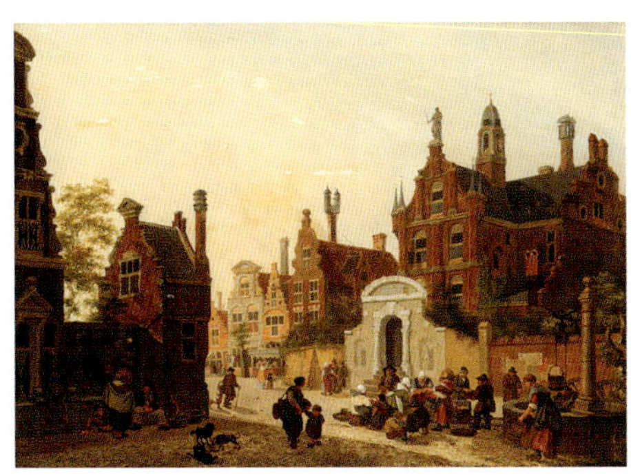

Verheyen, Jan Hendrik 1778–1846
An Imaginary Dutch Street, with Figures by a
Well
oil on panel 33.3 x 43.5
417

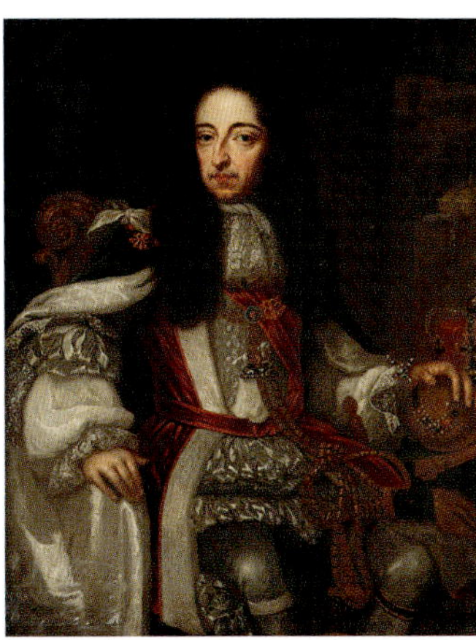

Verkolje, Jan I (imitator of) 1650–1693
William III (1650–1702) 18th C–early 19th C
oil on canvas 53.7 x 43.5
922

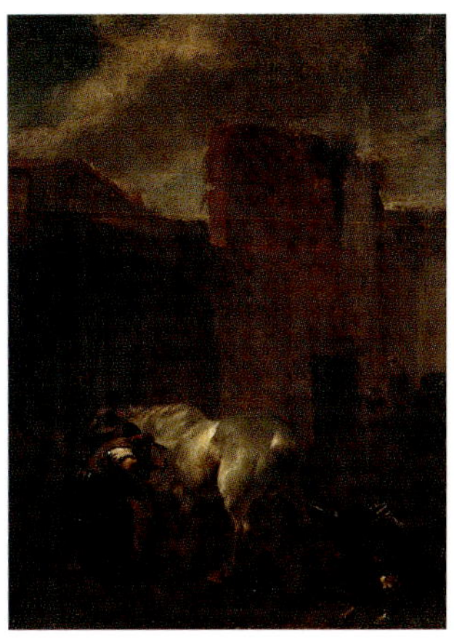

Verschuring, Hendrik (attributed to)
1627–1690
A Horse and a Farrier before an Archway
oil on panel 31.7 x 24.7
627

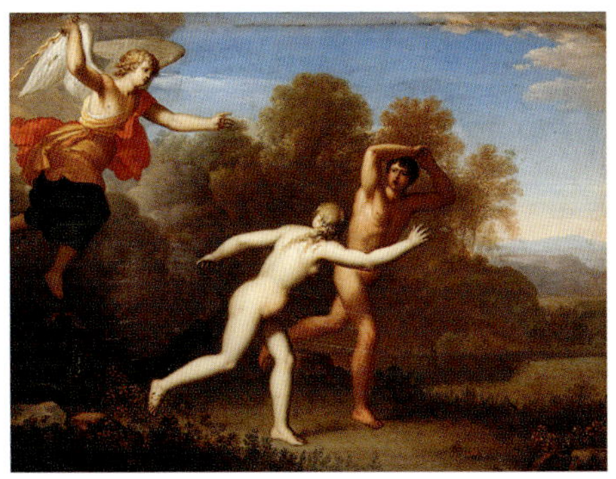

Vertangen, Daniel c.1598–1681/1684
The Expulsion from Paradise c.1640–1650
oil on copper 22.9 x 29.8
26

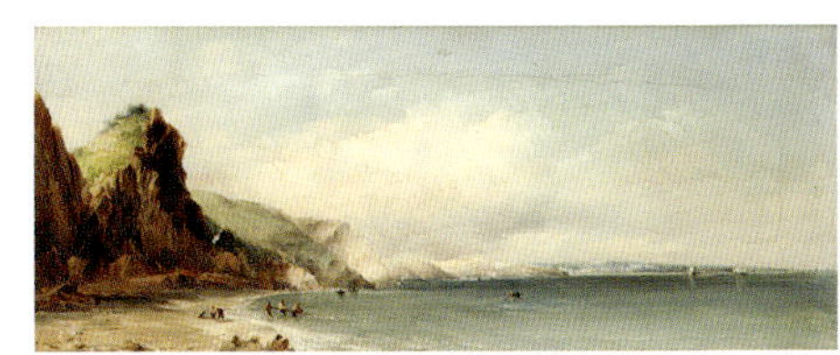

Vickers, Alfred 1786–1868
A Coast Scene
oil on canvas 19.1 x 44.5
389

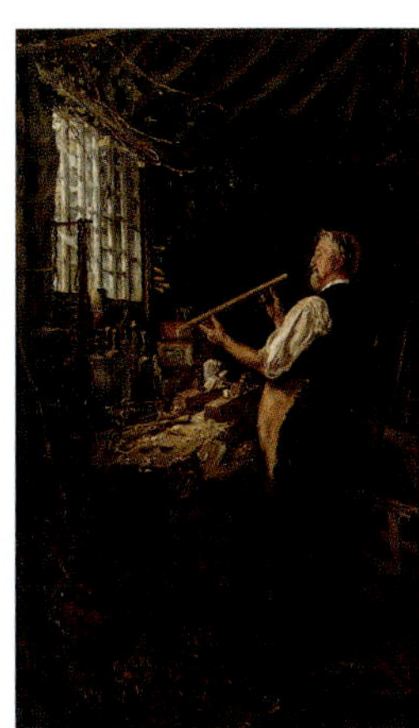

Vinall, Joseph William Topham 1873–1953
The Amateur c.1922
oil on canvas 127 x 76.2
2284

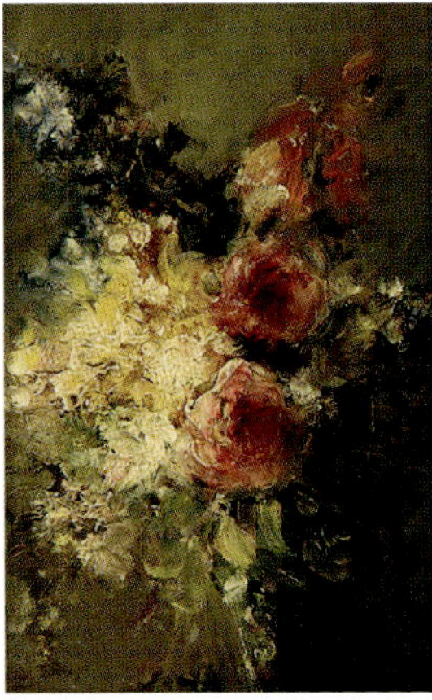

Vincelet, Victor 1840–1871
A Bunch of Flowers
oil on canvas 21.6 x 15.9
2817

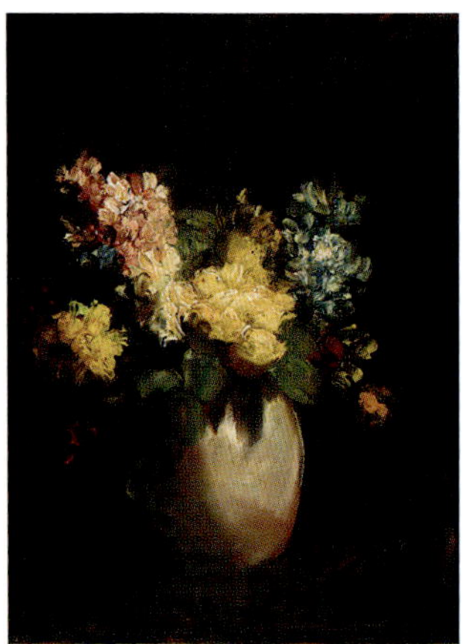

Vincelet, Victor 1840–1871
A Vase of Flowers
oil on canvas 54.5 x 39.3
940

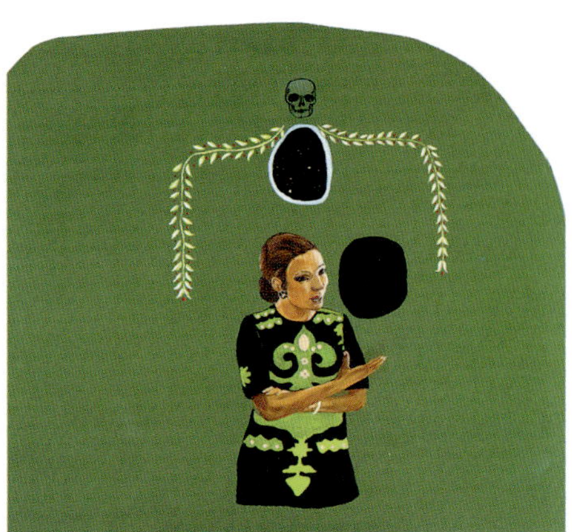

Visnes, Hanneline b.1972
Farah Diba (b.1938) 2003
oil on MDF 59 x 61
3644

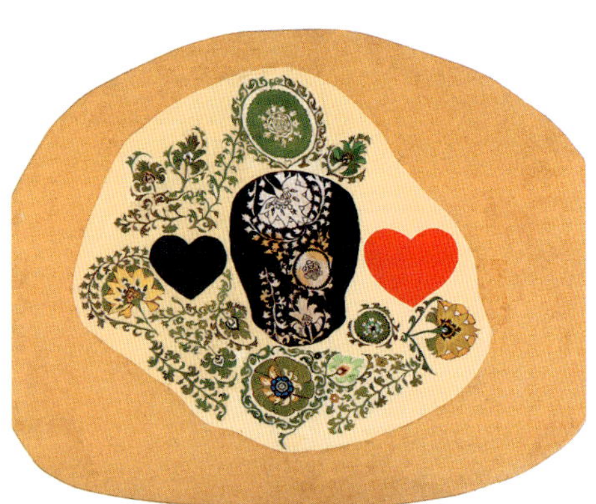

Visnes, Hanneline b.1972
Sisters 2003
oil on MDF 51 x 61
3645.b

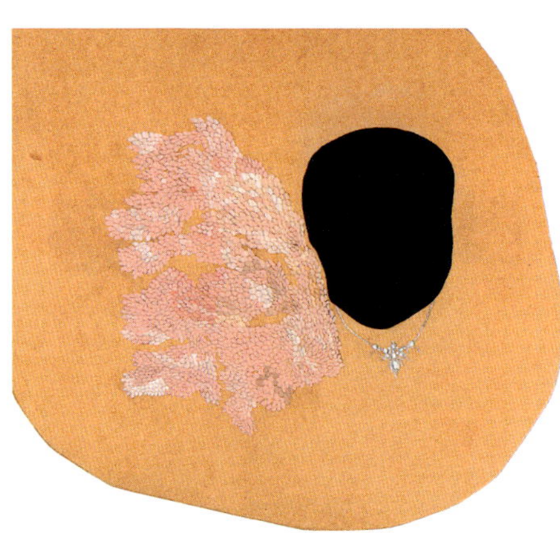

Visnes, Hanneline b.1972
Victoria 2003
oil on MDF 56 x 61
3645.a

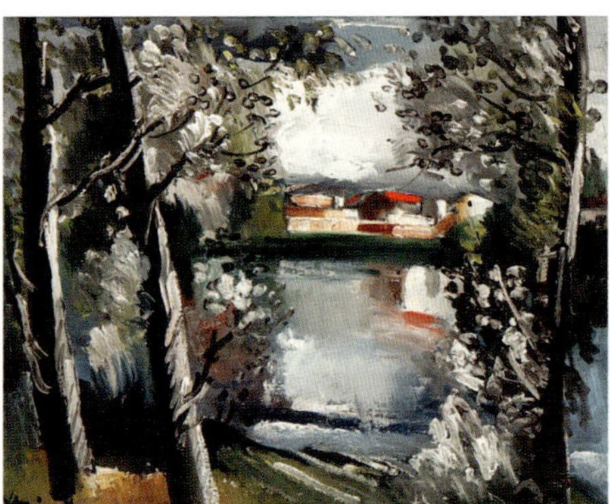

Vlaminck, Maurice de 1876–1958
By the Seine 1912
oil on canvas 46 x 55
3086

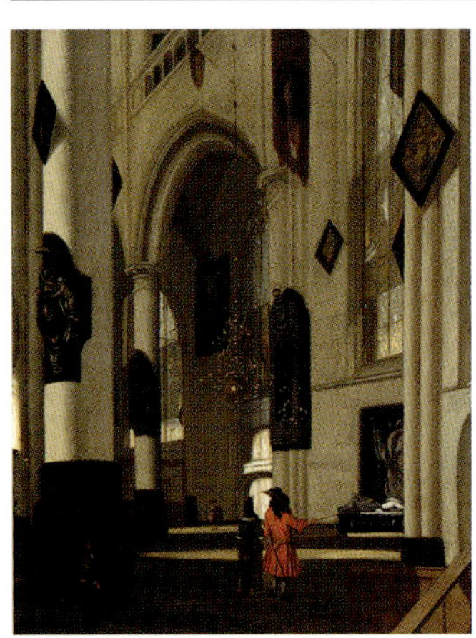

Vliet, Hendrick Cornelisz. van c.1611–1675
Interior of the Oude Kerk, Delft c.1660–1675
oil on canvas 45.7 x 38.1
35.635

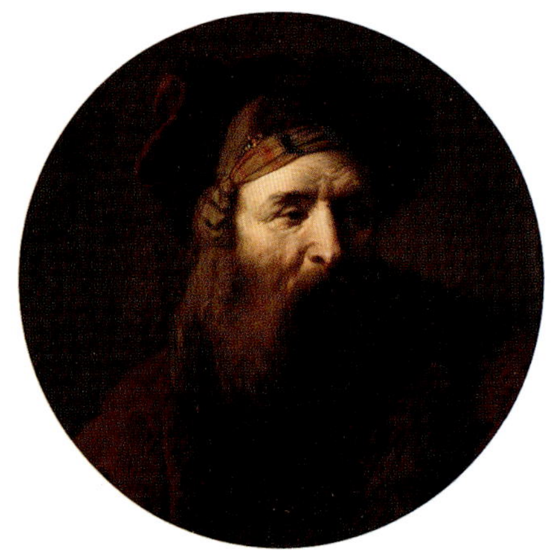

Vois, Ary de c.1632–1680
The Head of a Jew
oil on panel 21.3
625

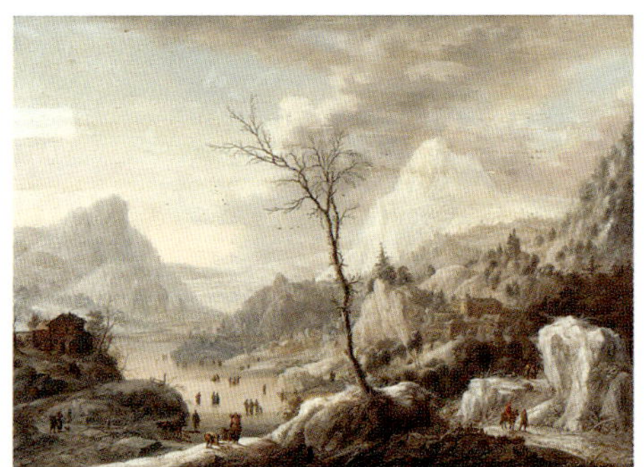

Vollerdt, Johann Christian 1708–1769
A Mountain Landscape in Winter
oil on panel 53.6 x 71.4
374

Facing page: Orpen, William, 1878–1931, *A Saint of the Poor*, c.1905 (p. 332)

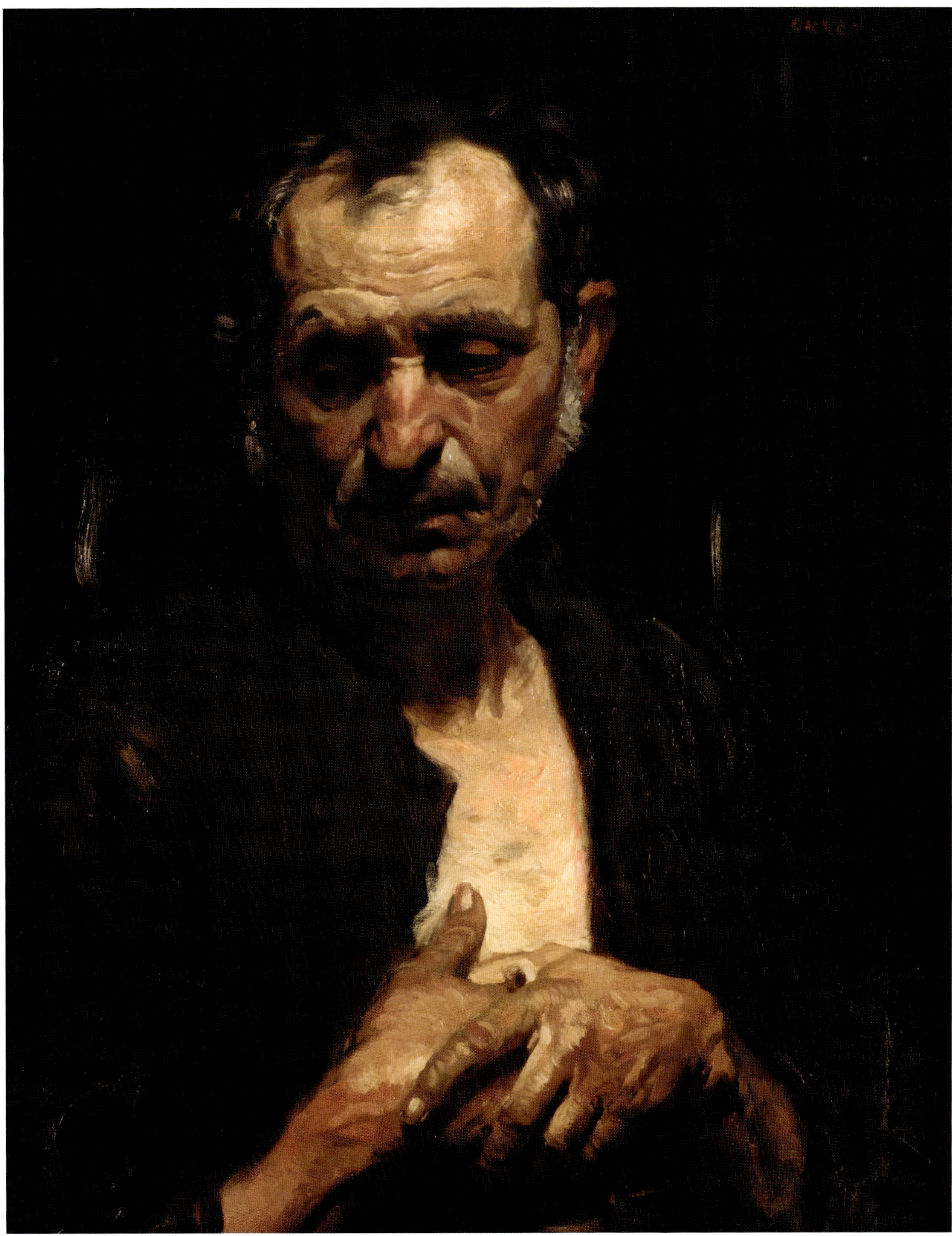

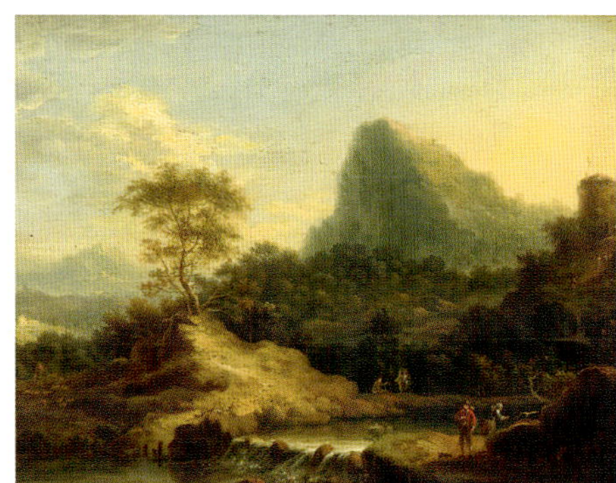

Vollerdt, Johann Christian 1708–1769
A Mountain Landscape with a Waterfall
oil on panel 17.8 x 23.5
341

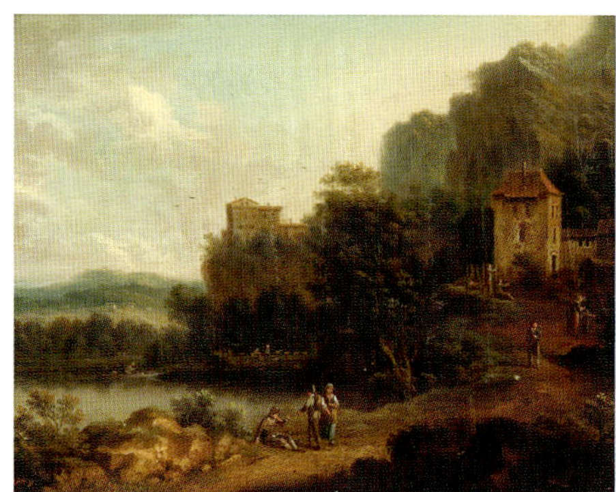

Vollerdt, Johann Christian 1708–1769
Landscape with Buildings and Figures beside a Lake
oil on panel 17.8 x 23.2
340

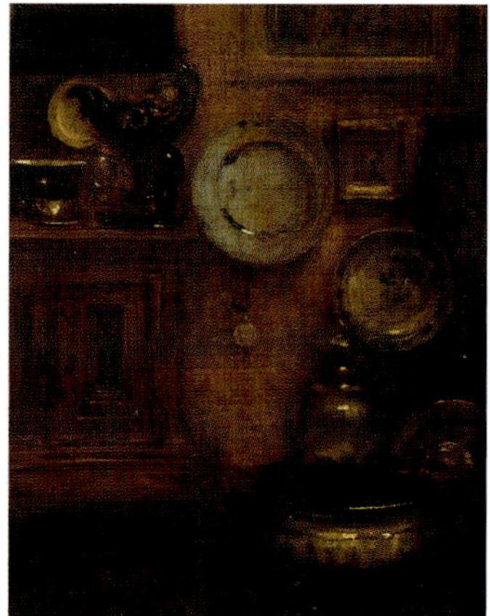

Vollon, Antoine 1833–1900
Still Life c.1865
oil on canvas 45.7 x 35.6
35.637

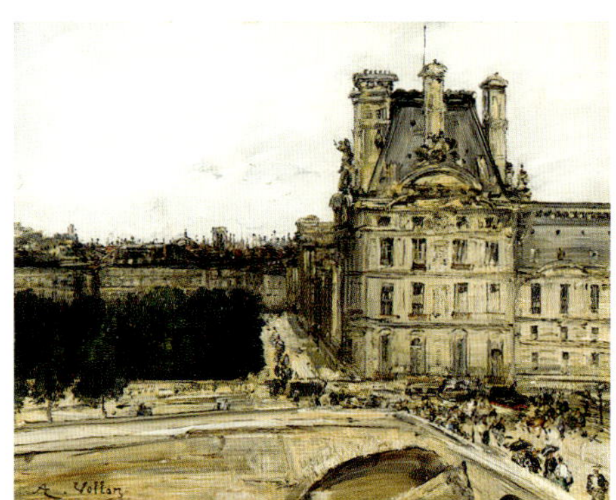

Vollon, Antoine 1833–1900
A Corner of the Louvre c.1872–1885
oil on panel 31.8 x 40
2813

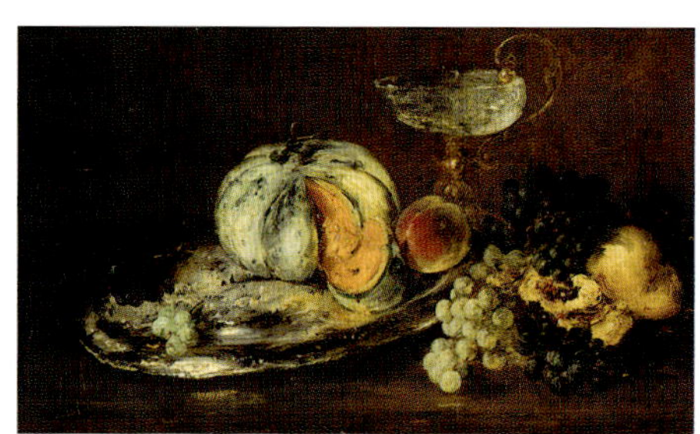

Vollon, Antoine 1833–1900
Still Life with Fruit
oil on panel 42.5 x 72.1
1109

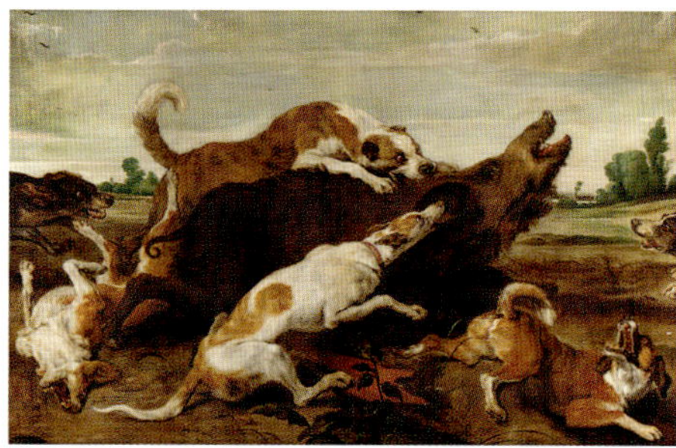

Vos, Paul de (attributed to) 1591–1592 or 1595–1678
Dogs Harrying a Wild Boar
oil on canvas 165.1 x 247
3035

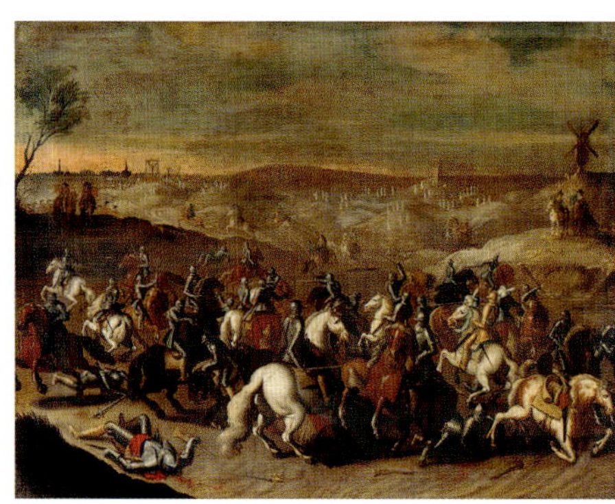

Vrancx, Sebastian (after) 1573–1647
The Battle of Leckerbeetje, 1600 17th C
oil on canvas 132.1 x 162.5
3436

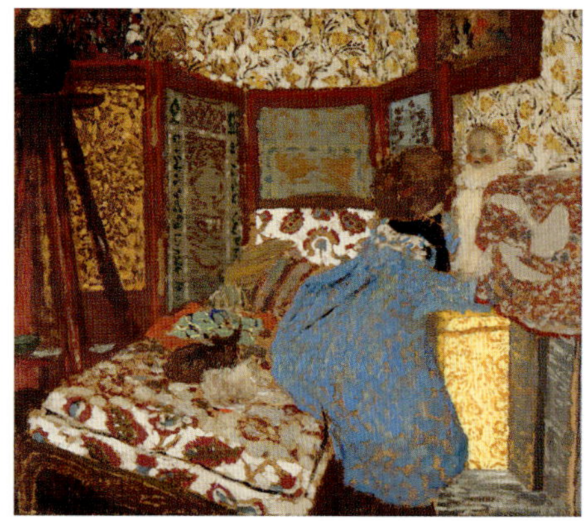

Vuillard, Jean Edouard 1868–1940
Woman in Blue with a Child c.1899
oil on compressed card 48.6 x 56.5
2814

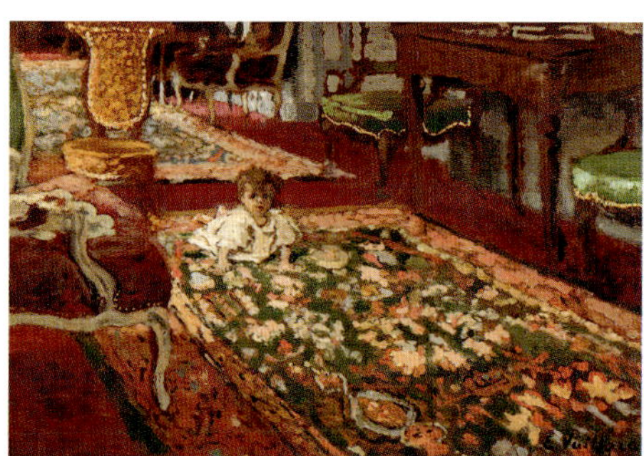

Vuillard, Jean Edouard 1868–1940
Interior: The Drawing Room 1901
oil on compressed card 35.5 x 52.7
2428

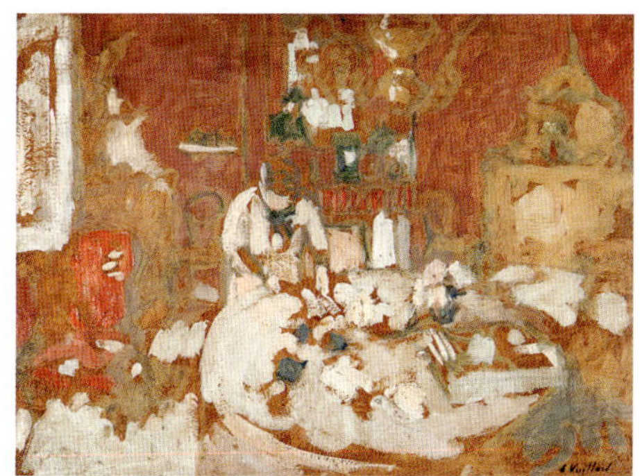

Vuillard, Jean Edouard 1868–1940
The Table 1902
oil on compressed card 25.4 x 34.3
2427

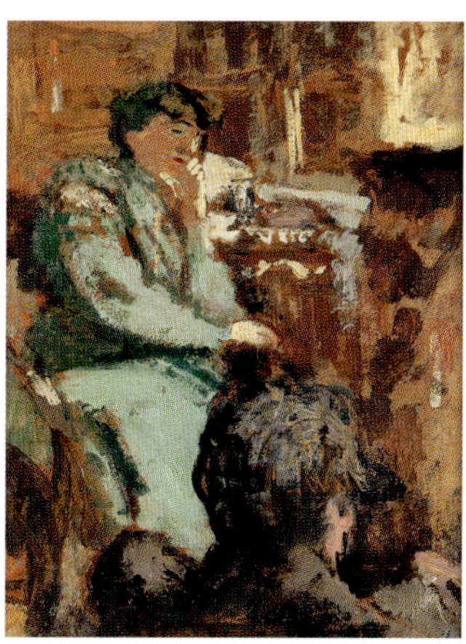

Vuillard, Jean Edouard 1868–1940
Lady in Green 1905
oil on millboard 30.2 x 22.5
2426

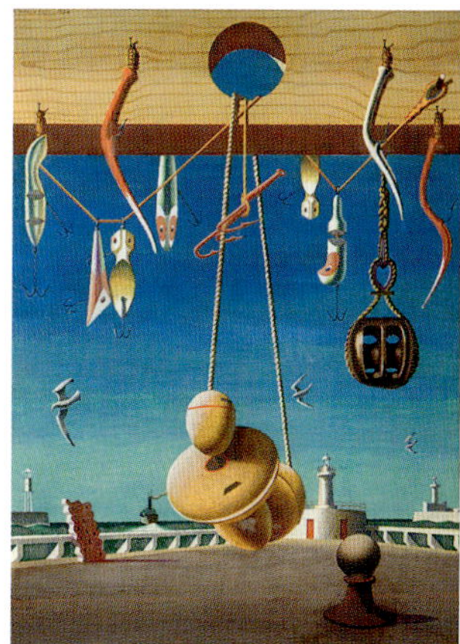

Wadsworth, Edward Alexander 1889–1949
Departure 1938
tempera on panel 88.9 x 63.5
3010

Waitt, Richard (after) d.1732
Alastair Grant Mor, the Castle Grant Champion c.1714
oil on canvas 76.2 x 64.1
2198

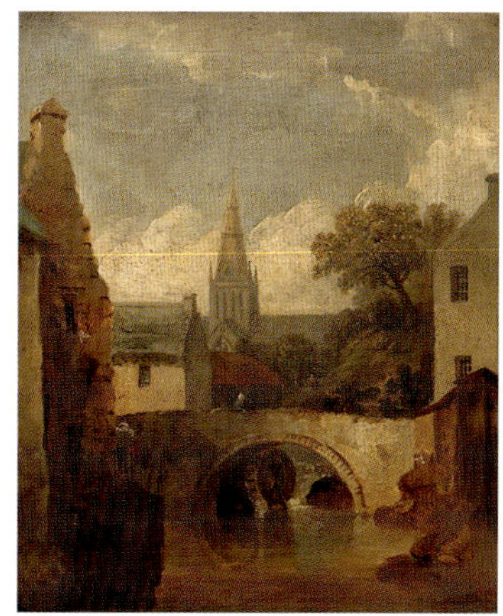

Walker, Elizabeth
Molendinar Burn c.1850
oil on canvas 43.3 x 34.7
OG.1952.80

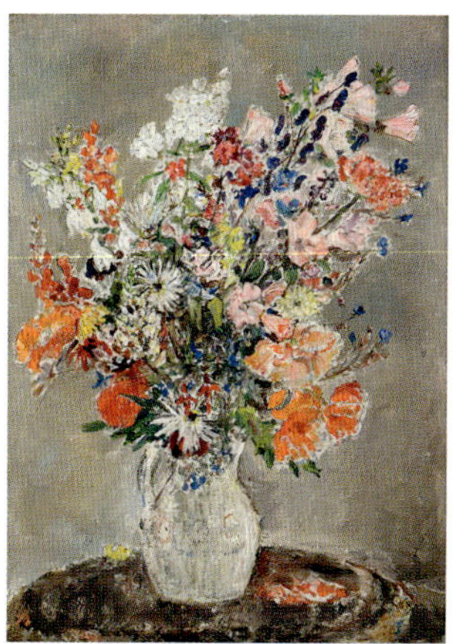

Walker, Ethel 1861–1951
Flower Piece c.1940
oil on canvas 88.9 x 63.5
2212 ☷

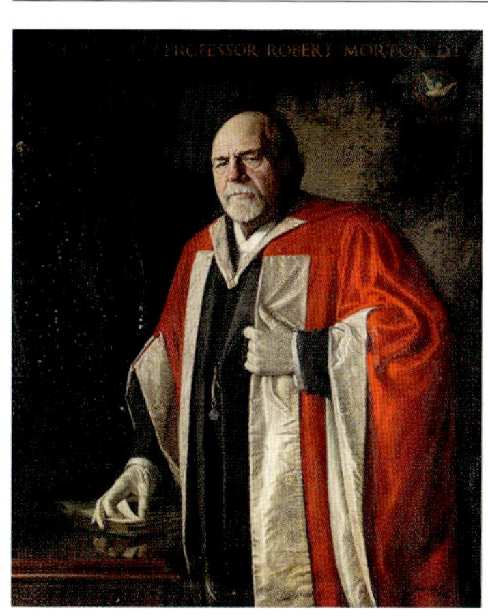

Wallace, James
Reverend Professor Robert Morton, DD 1951
oil on canvas 127.3 x 101.4
PP.1978.121.11

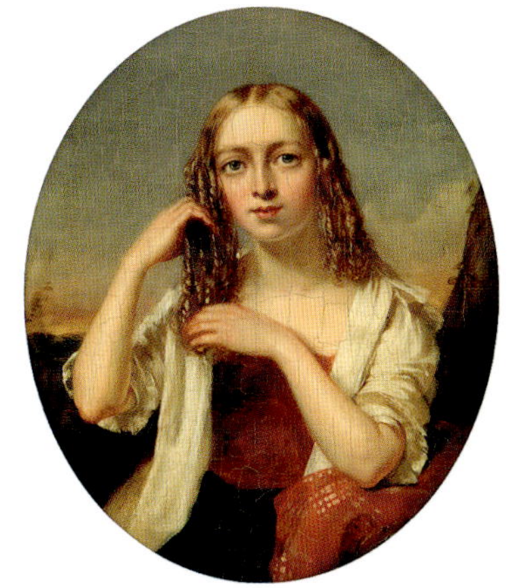

Wallace, William 1801–1866
Annie Laurie
oil on panel 30.5 x 25.4
394

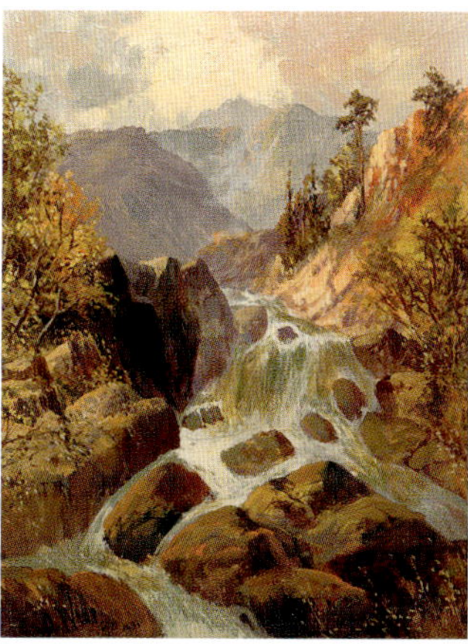

Walls, D.
Falls of Moness, Aberfeldy 1931
oil on board 40.6 x 30.4
NR.138

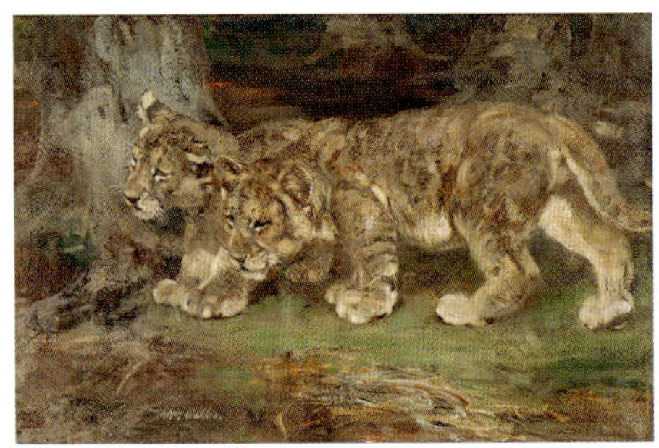

Walls, William 1860–1942
Lion Cubs, Suspicion c.1923
oil on canvas 64.8 x 96.5
1564

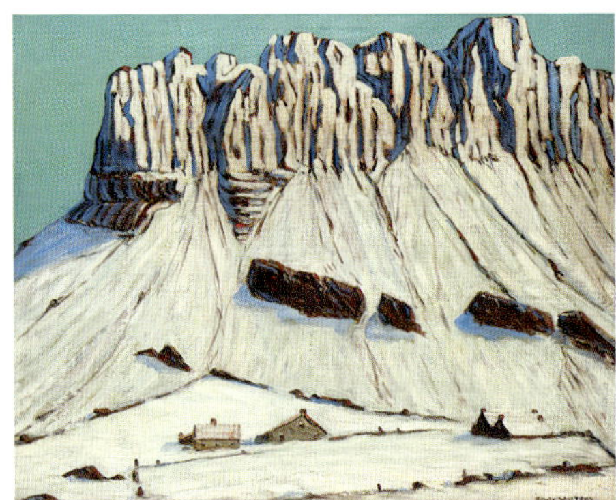

Walters, Emile 1893–1977
The Harp of the Valkyries
oil on canvas 64.1 x 76.8
2847

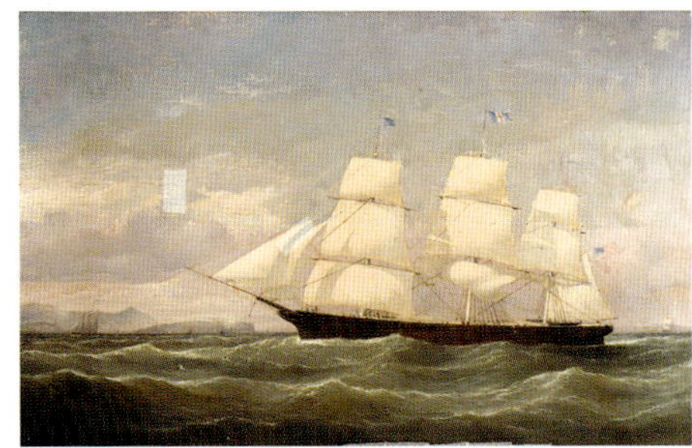

Walters, Samuel 1811–1882
'Red Gauntlet'
oil on canvas 74.5 x 111.8
T.1955.16

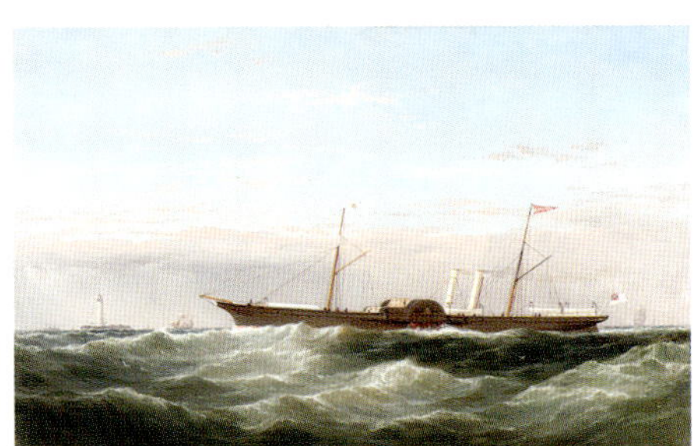

Walters, Samuel (attributed to) 1811–1882
'A. D. Vance' 1860s
oil on canvas 66 x 96
1917.24.c

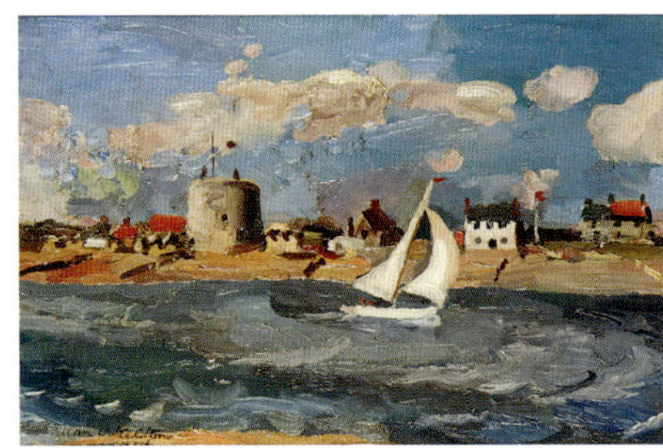

Walton, Allan 1891–1948
Bawdsey
oil on canvas 30.5 x 44.2
3147

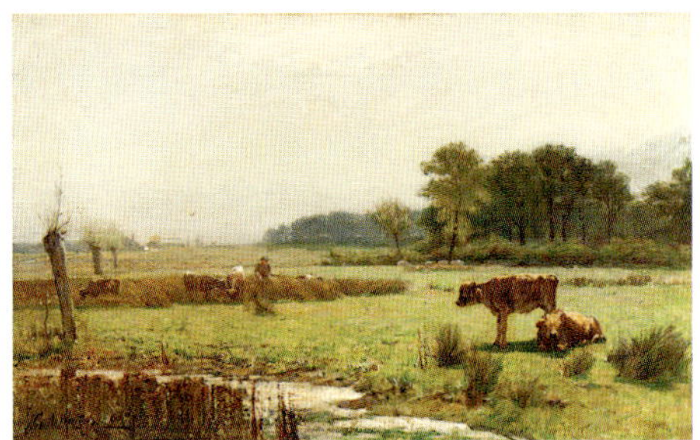

Walton, Edward Arthur 1860–1922
A Surrey Meadow, Morning 1880
oil on canvas 76.8 x 121.9
2485

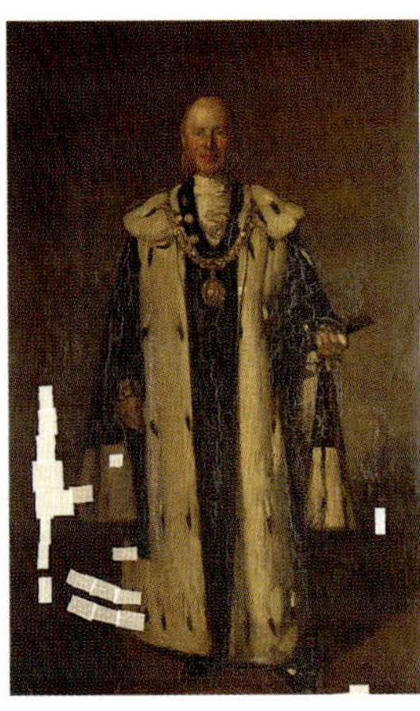

Walton, Edward Arthur 1860–1922
*Sir James King (1830–1911), Lord Provost of
Glasgow (1886–1889)* 1889
oil on canvas 218.4 x 132.1
673

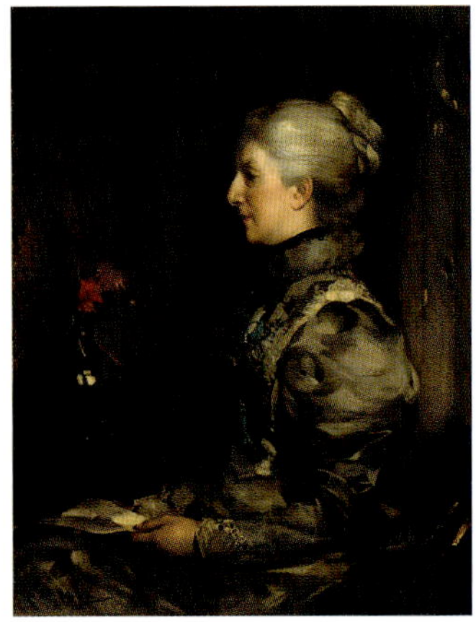

Walton, Edward Arthur 1860–1922
Mrs H. S. Ashbee c.1890–1893
oil on canvas 92.7 x 69.9
2605

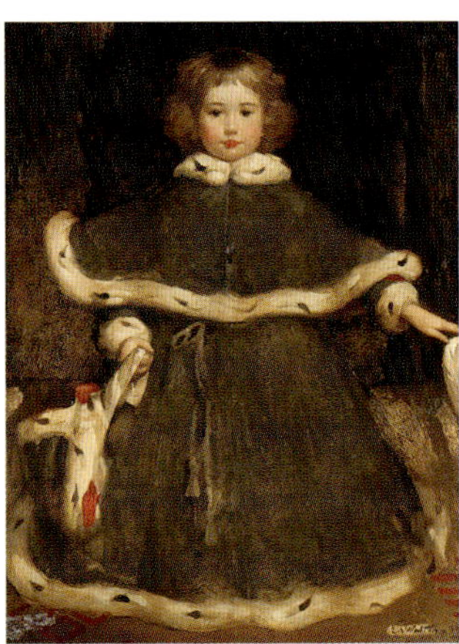

Walton, Edward Arthur 1860–1922
*Cecile Walton (1891–1956), the Artist's Elder
Daughter* 1893
oil on canvas 101.6 x 78.7
2459

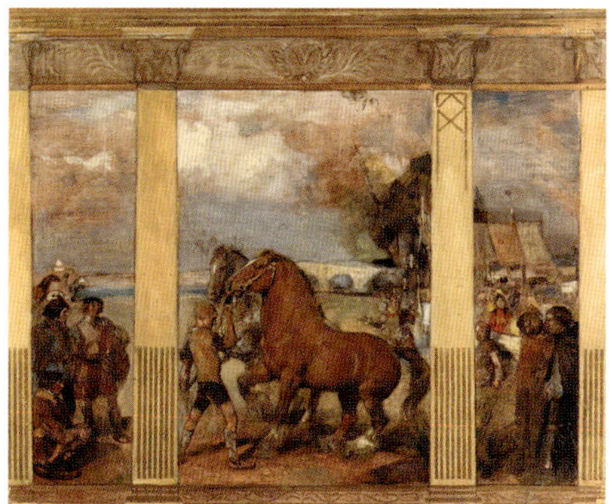

Walton, Edward Arthur 1860–1922
The Horse Fair (sketch) c.1899
oil on canvas 129.5 x 152.4
1883

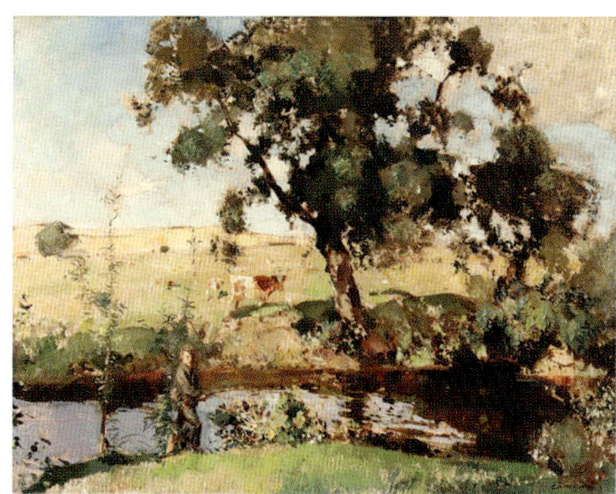

Walton, Edward Arthur 1860–1922
The Amber Pool c.1904–1910
oil on canvas 80 x 104.1
2922

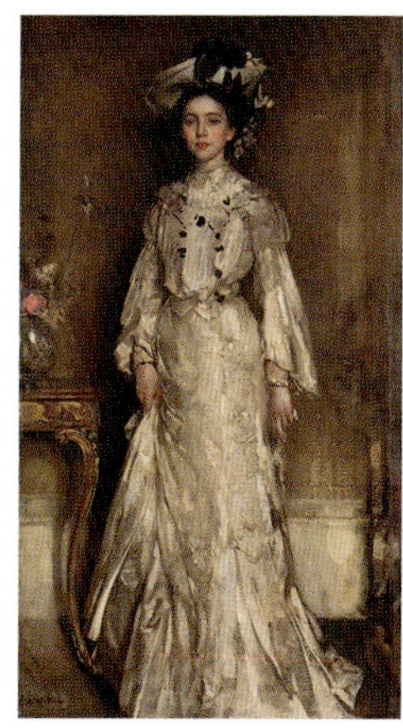

Walton, Edward Arthur 1860–1922
Lilian May Law (d.1882) c.1905
oil on canvas 182.9 x 104.1
NR.93

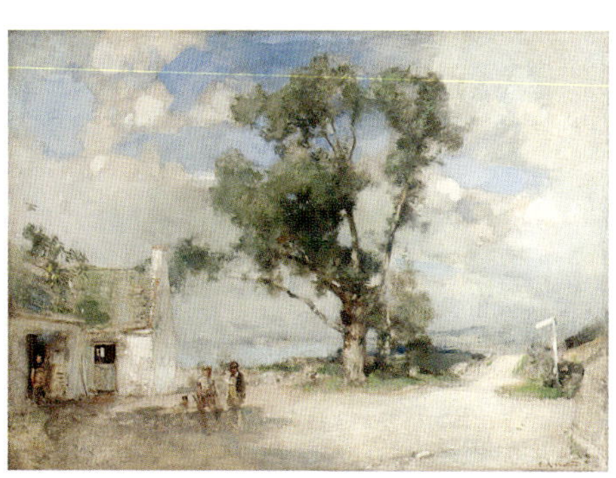

Walton, Edward Arthur 1860–1922
The Smithy at the Crossroads 1921
oil on canvas 81.3 x 109.2
1569

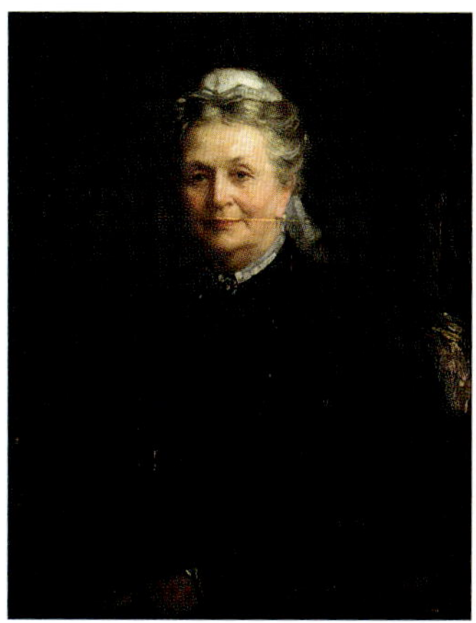

Walton, Edward Arthur 1860–1922
Portrait of a Lady
oil on canvas 91.4 x 71.1
2560

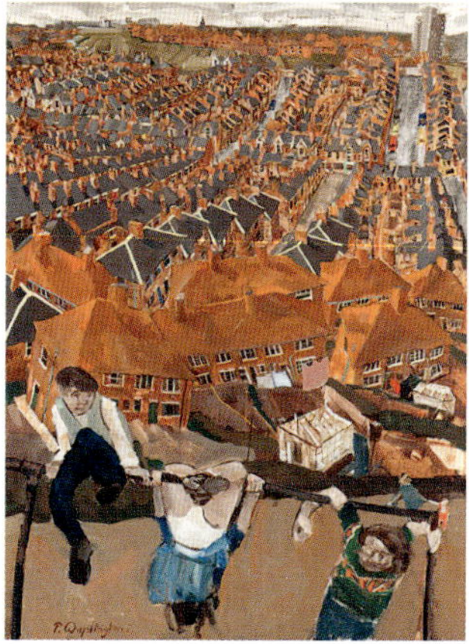

Waplington, Paul Anthony b.1938
View over Sneinton Dale (triptych, left wing) 1983
oil on canvas 175.2 x 126.3
3552 (left)

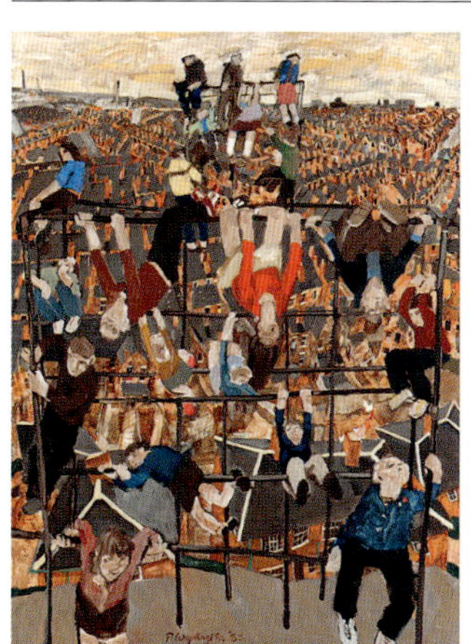

Waplington, Paul Anthony b.1938
View over Sneinton Dale (triptych, centre panel) 1983
oil on canvas 207.5 x 151.5
3552 (centre)

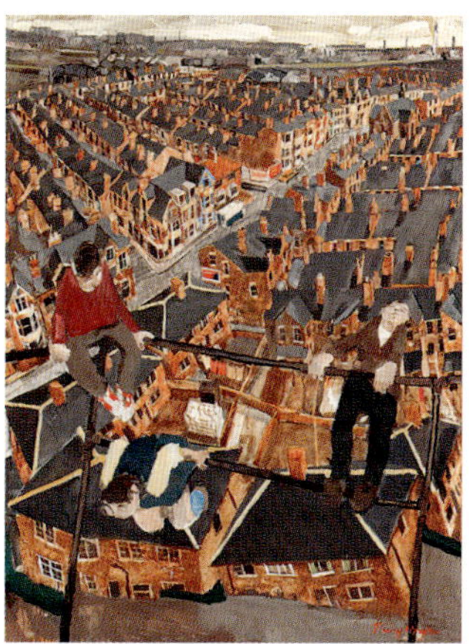

Waplington, Paul Anthony b.1938
View over Sneinton Dale (triptych, right wing) 1983
oil on canvas 175.2 x 126.3
3552 (right)

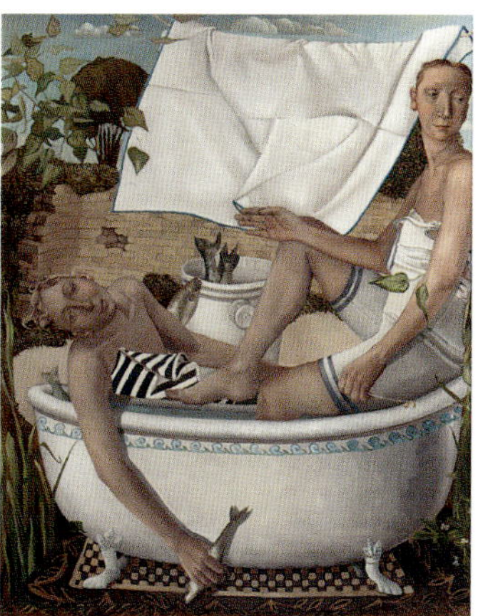

Watt, Alison b.1965
Marat and the Fishes 1990
oil on canvas 152.4 x 122
3463

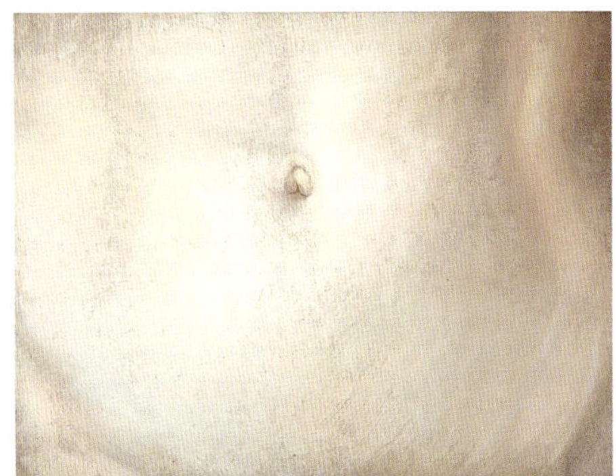

Watt, Alison b.1965
Centre 1996
oil on board 20.5 x 25.6
3604

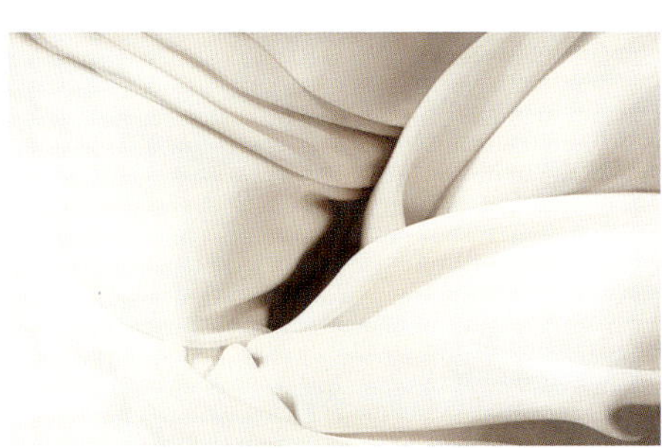

Watt, Alison b.1965
Phantom 2007
oil on canvas 213.4 x 335.3
3663

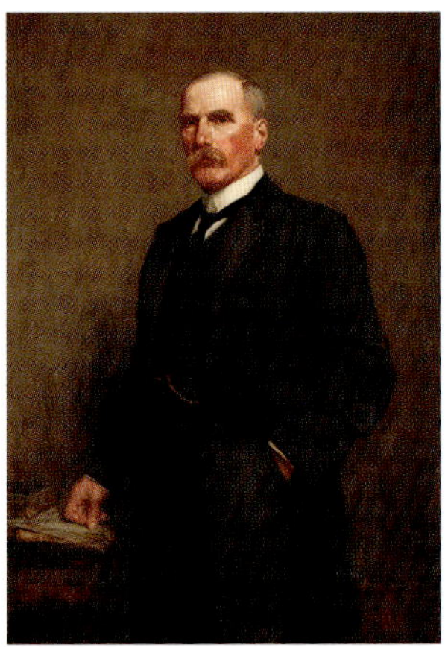

Watt, George Fiddes 1873–1960
*Sir William Alexander Smith (1854–1914),
Founder of the Boys' Brigade* 1909
oil on canvas 124.5 x 83.8
1259

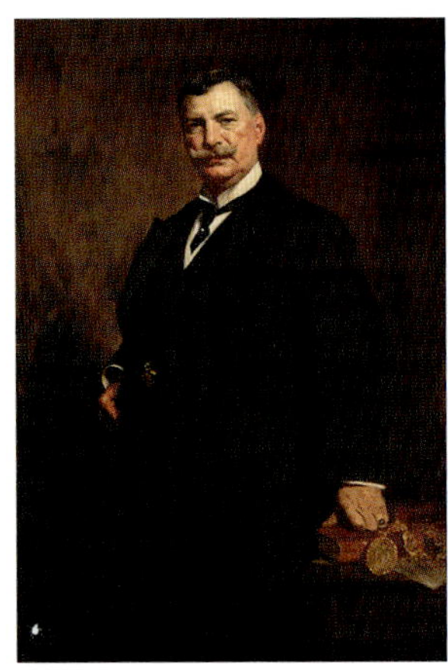

Watt, George Fiddes 1873–1960
*Sir Archibald M. Shaw (b.1862), Lord Provost
of Glasgow (1908–1911)* 1911
oil on canvas 152.4 x 99.1
1281

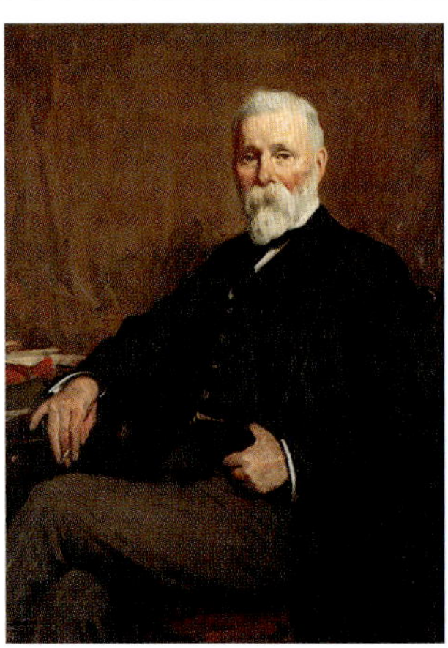

Watt, George Fiddes 1873–1960
Sir William Lorimer (1844–1922) 1914
oil on canvas 117.1 x 88.6
3164

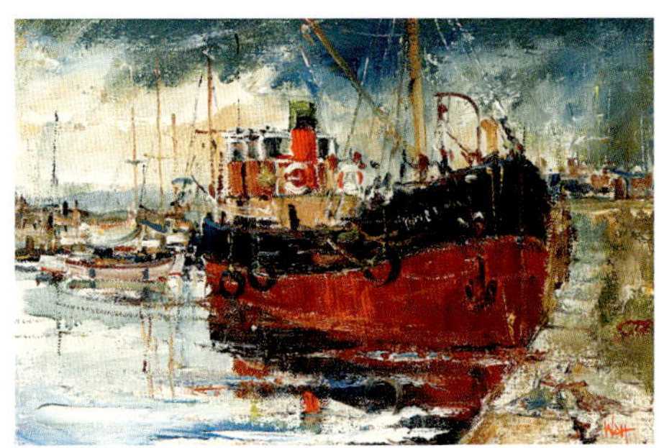

Watt, James b.1931
Ship
oil on canvas 35.5 x 50.5
3666

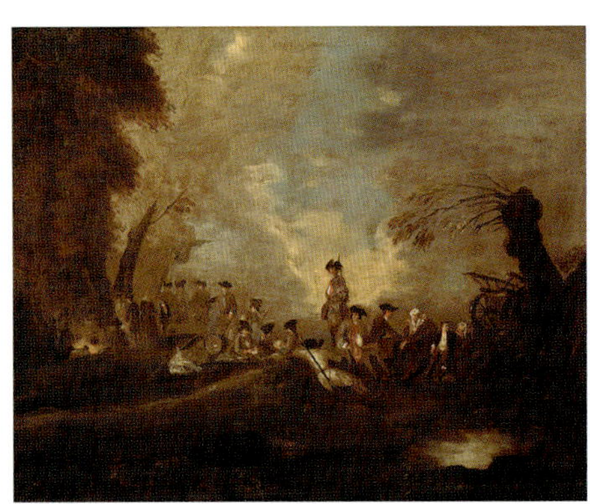

Watteau, Jean-Antoine (after) 1684–1721
Detachment Resting 18th C
oil on canvas 64.2 x 80.3
392

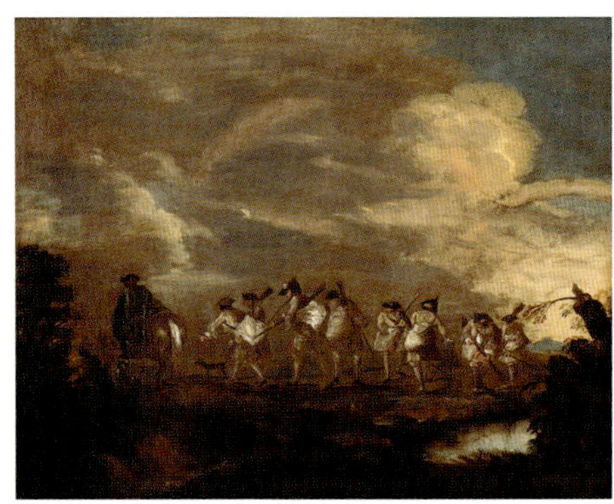

Watteau, Jean-Antoine (after) 1684–1721
Recruits Going to Join the Regiment 18th C
oil on canvas 64 x 80.3
396

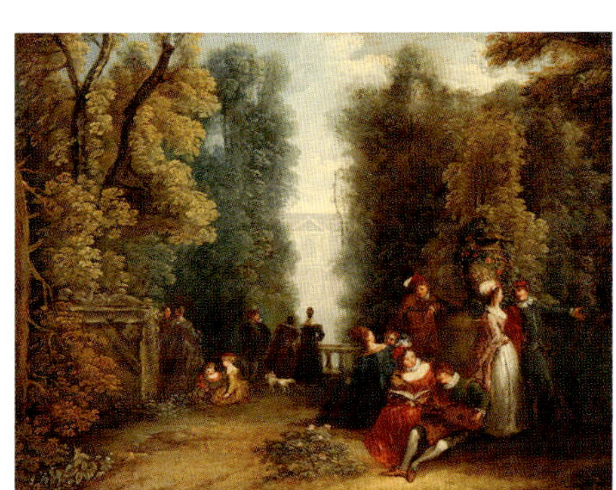

Watteau, Jean-Antoine (after) 1684–1721
Garden Scene 19th C
oil on canvas 36.2 x 46
410

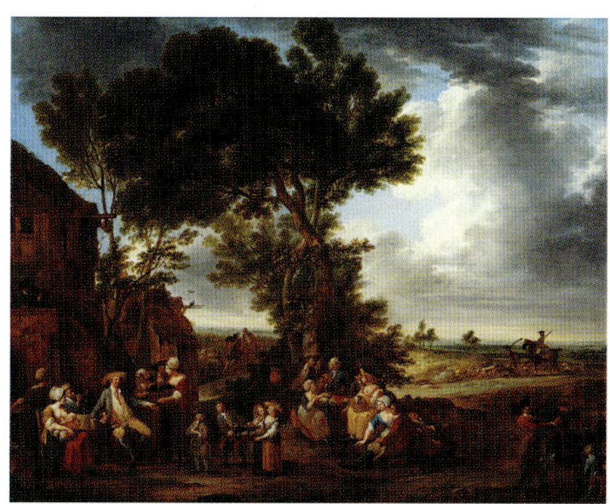

Watteau, Louis Joseph (style of) 1731–1798
The Vintage c.1784
oil on canvas 63.9 x 80.3
219

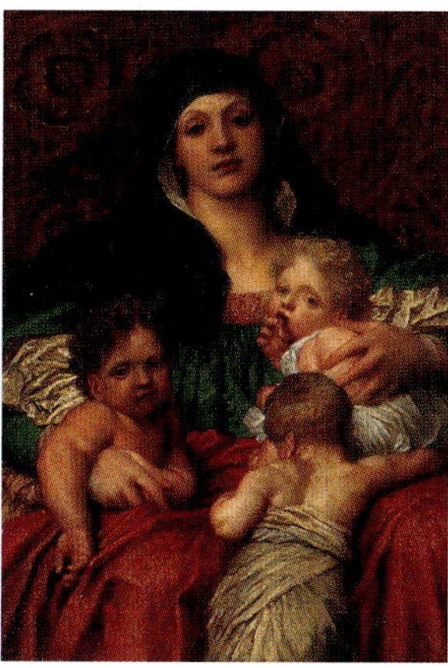

Watts, George Frederick 1817–1904
Charity 1898
oil on canvas 116.9 x 81.3
3418

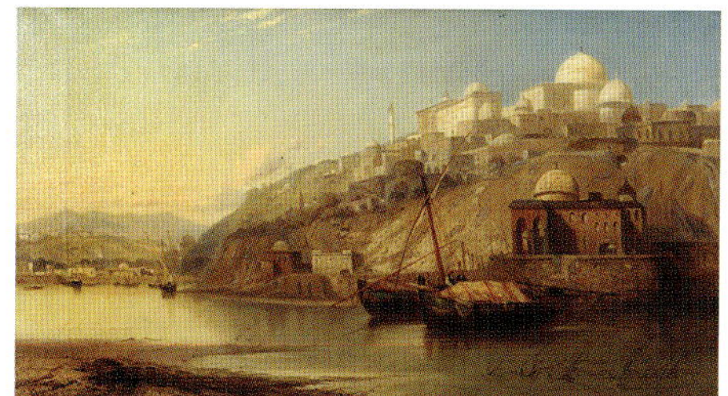

Webb, James 1825–1895
Constantinople 1876
oil on canvas 44.5 x 80
796

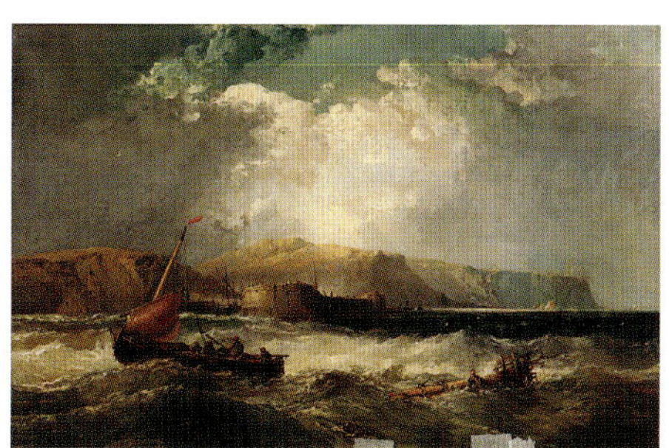

Webb, James 1825–1895
Clovelly, North Devon
oil on canvas 76.2 x 118.1
872

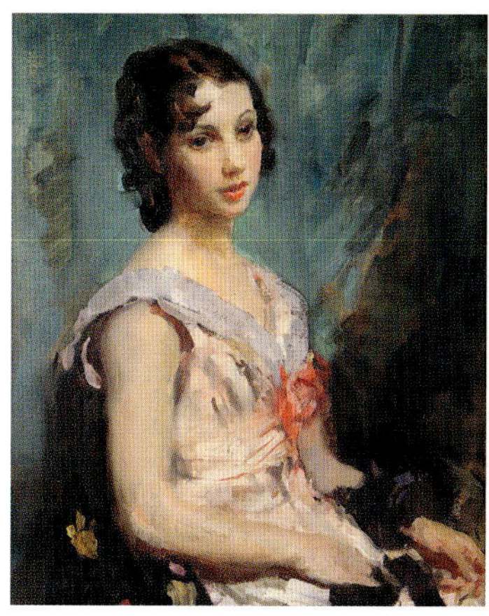

Webster, Walter Ernest 1877–1959
Spanish Girl c.1937
oil on canvas 67.3 x 54.6
2082

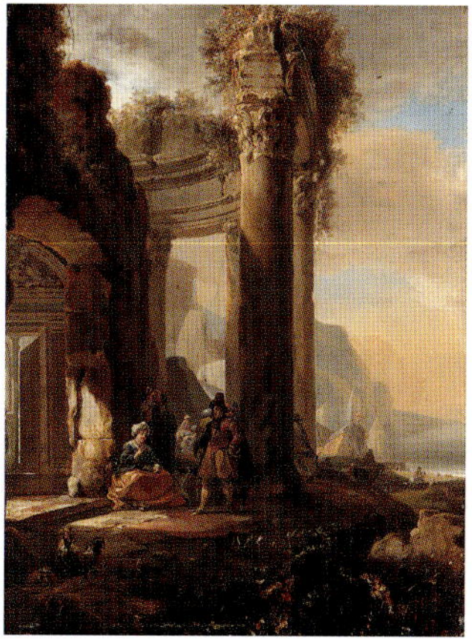

Weenix, Jan 1642–1719
*A Ruined Colonnade and Figures by a
Harbour* c.1660–1665
oil on panel 54.9 x 40.9
8

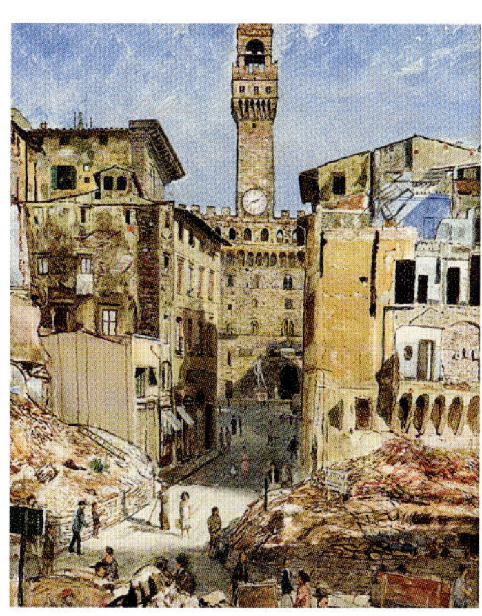

Weight, Carel Victor Morlais 1908–1997
Palazzo Vecchio, Florence, August 1945 1945
oil on canvas 62.2 x 50.8
2774

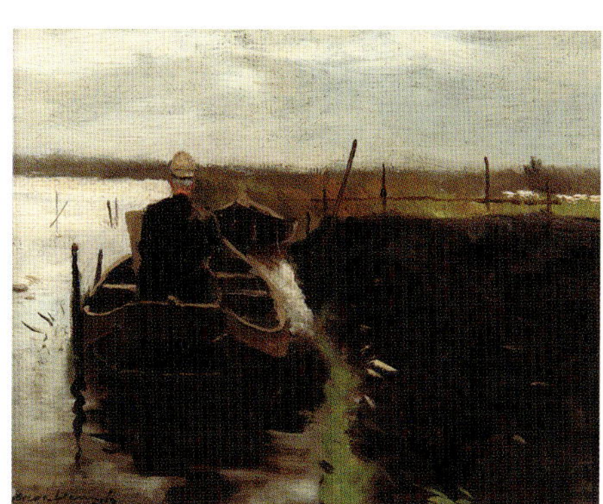

Weissenbruch, Jan Hendrik (attributed to)
1824–1903
An Artist Sketching from a Boat
oil on canvas 24.4 x 29.5
2231

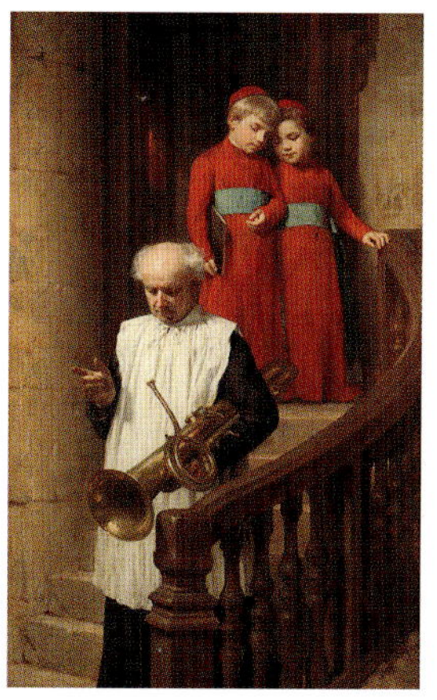

Weisz, Adolphe 1838–1914
Going to Mass 1868
oil on canvas 55.3 x 33
2604

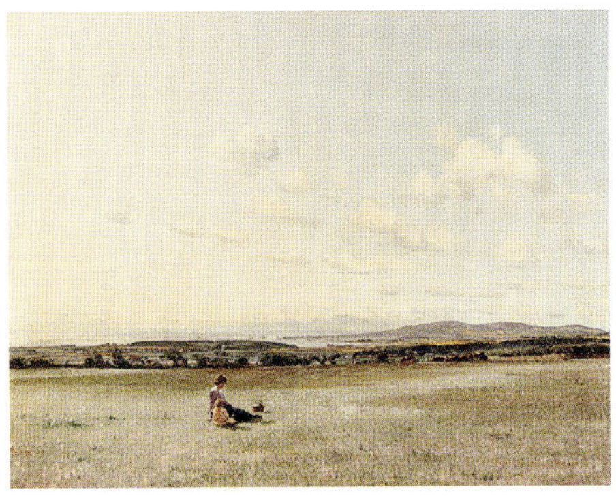

Wells, William Page Atkinson 1872–1923
A Manx Landscape 1912
oil on canvas 100.3 x 125.7
1320

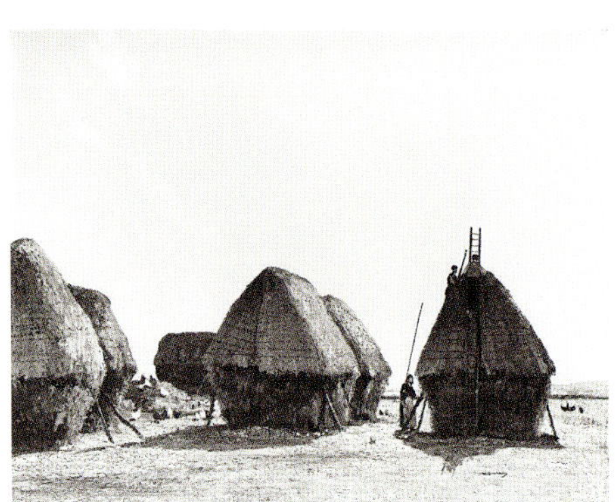

Wells, William Page Atkinson 1872–1923
The Hackett
oil on canvas 81.3 x 101.6
2164

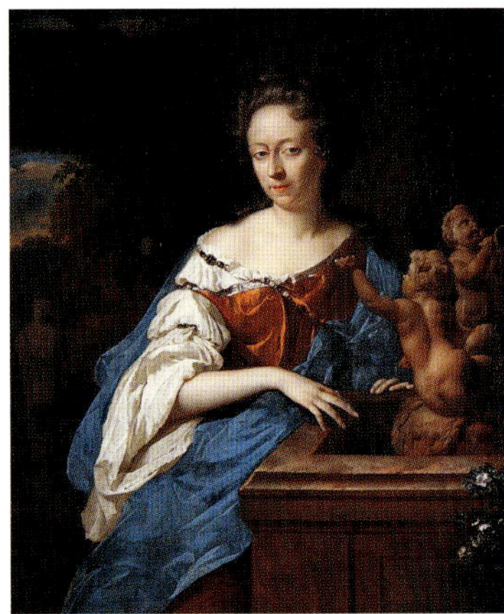

Werff, Adriaen van der 1659–1722
Portrait of a Lady by a Fountain c.1693–1697
oil on canvas 47.9 x 39
629

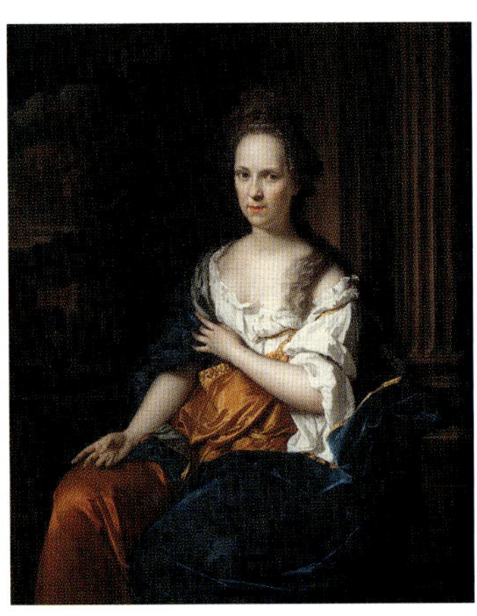

Werff, Adriaen van der 1659–1722
Portrait of a Woman, Aged 33 1695
oil on canvas 47.9 x 39
630

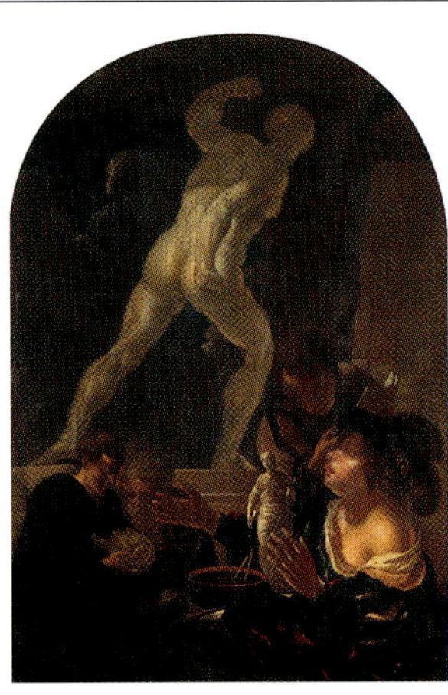

Werff, Adriaen van der (after) 1659–1722
Amateurs of Statuary 17th C–18th C
oil on copper 26 x 21
1537

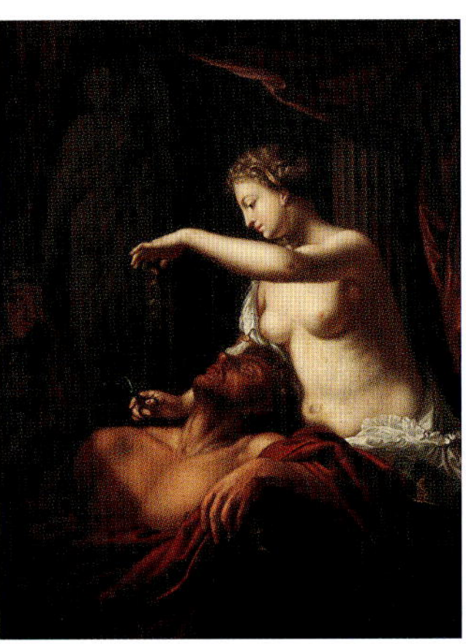

Werff, Adriaen van der (after) 1659–1722
Samson and Delilah 17th C/18th C
oil on panel 35.5 x 28.2
83

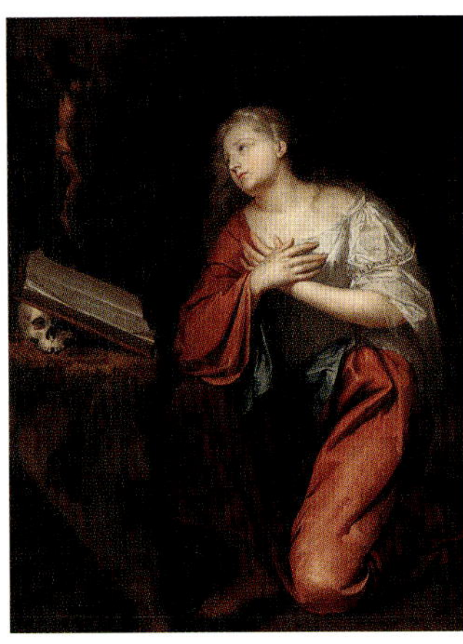

Werff, Adriaen van der (follower of)
1659–1722
The Penitent Magdalen early 18th C
oil on canvas 69.8 x 53
29

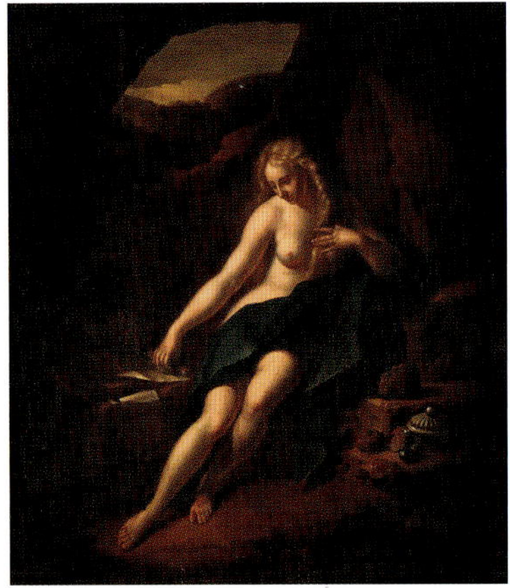

Werff, Pieter van der (attributed to)
1665–1722
Saint Mary Magdalen c.1707–1722
oil on panel 54.3 x 46.7
PC.84

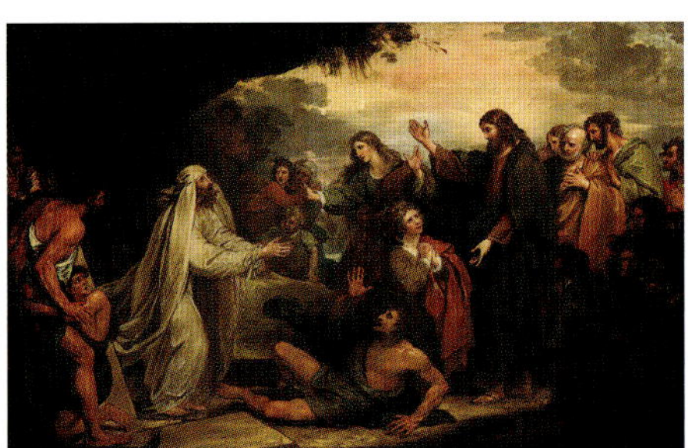

West, Benjamin 1738–1820
The Raising of Lazarus 1788
oil on canvas 72.4 x 116.8
258

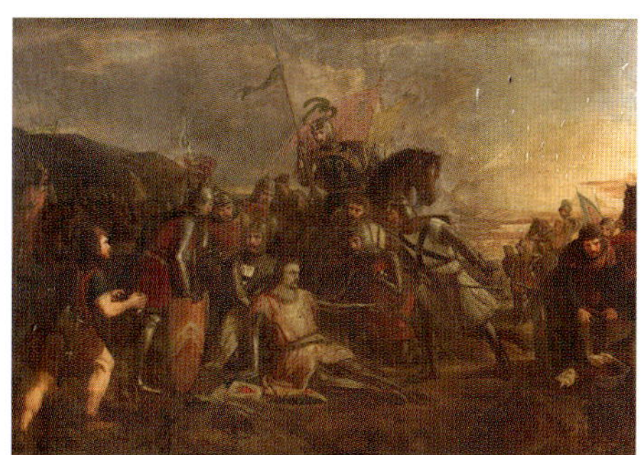

West, Samuel c.1810–after 1881
Battle of Otterburn, 5 August 1388: The Death of Douglas and Capture of Sir Ralph Percy by Sir John Maxwell
oil on canvas 135.9 x 198.1
NR.89

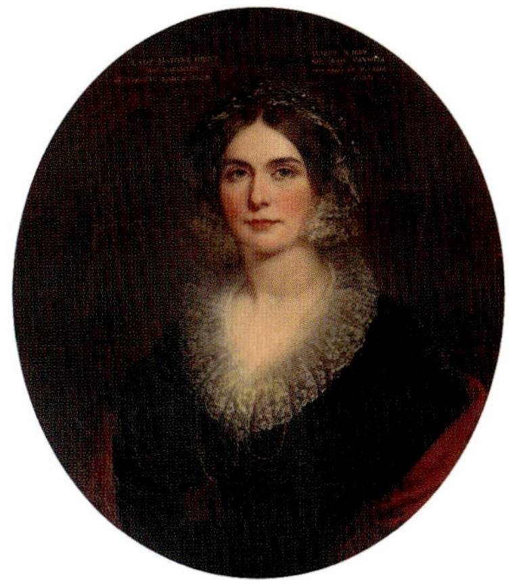

West, Samuel (attributed to) c.1810–after 1881
Lady Matilda Maxwell (1802–1857)
oil on canvas 76 x 63.4
PL.179 (P)

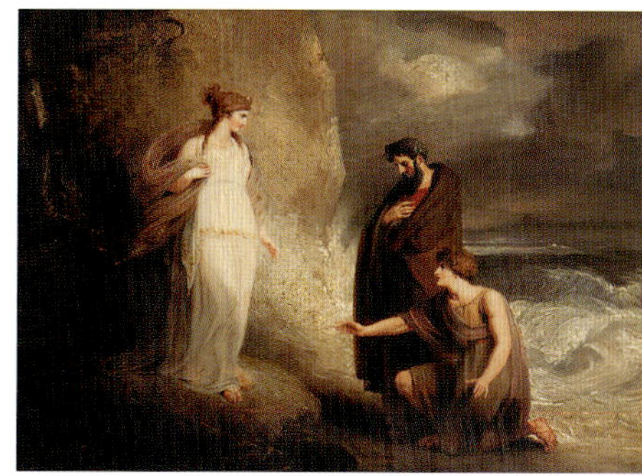

Westall, Richard 1765–1836
Telemachus Landing on the Isle of Calypso (from Homer's 'Odyssey') 1803
oil on panel 54.6 x 74.9
257

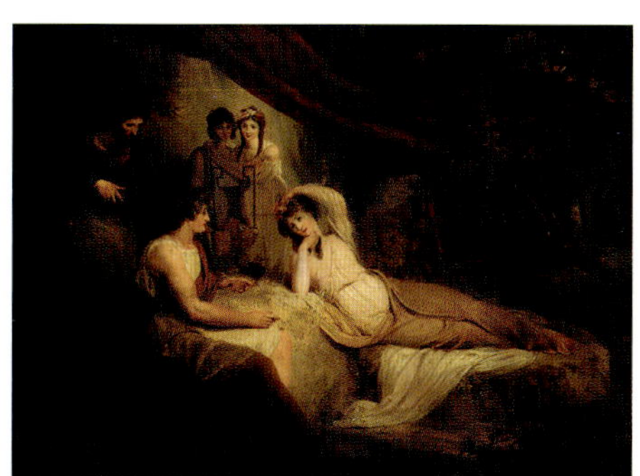

Westall, Richard 1765–1836
Telemachus in the Bower of Calypso (from Homer's 'Odyssey') c.1803
oil on panel 54.6 x 74.9
256

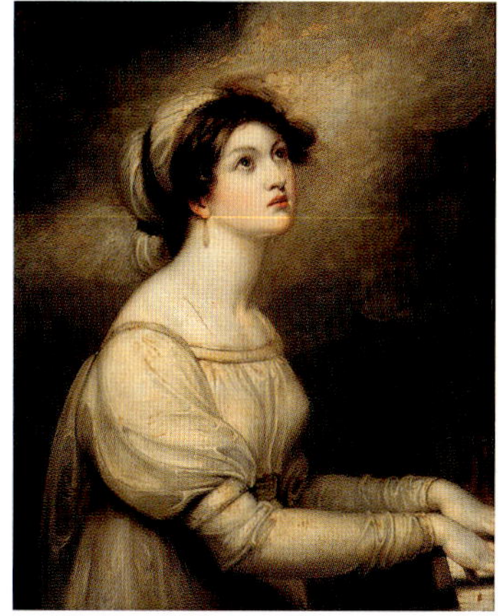

Westall, Richard 1765–1836
Saint Cecilia
oil on canvas 77.5 x 61
446

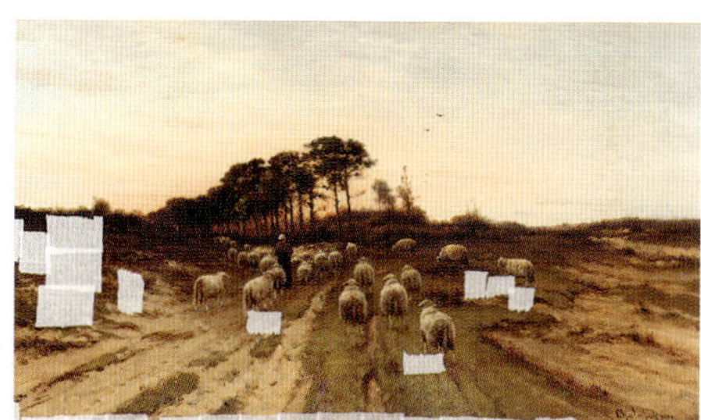

Westerbeek, Cornelis 1844–1903
At the End of the Day 1900
oil on canvas 65 x 110.1
2640

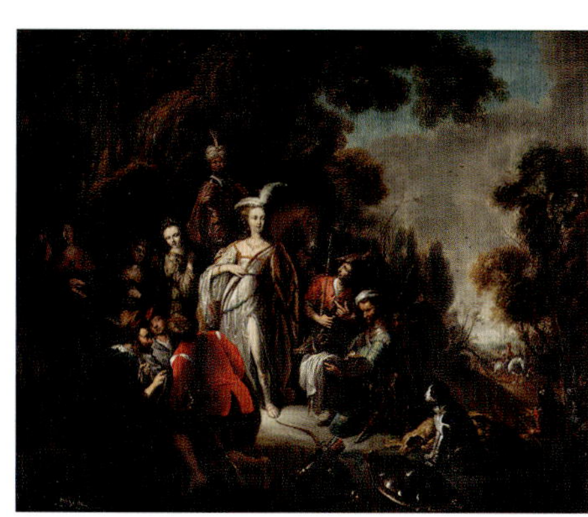

Wet, Gerrit de 1616–1674
Meleager Presents the Calydonian Boar to Atalanta c.1673–1674
oil on canvas 118.1 x 141
1785

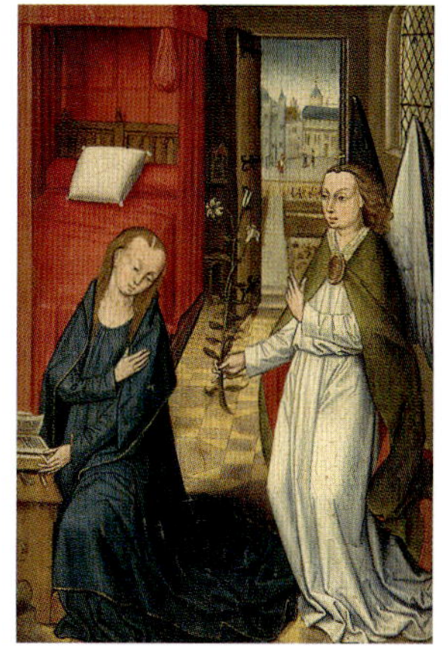

Weyden, Rogier van der (follower of) c.1399–1464
The Annunciation 15th C
oil on panel 29.2 x 19.1
35.64

Whistler, James Abbott McNeill 1834–1903
Nocturne: Grey and Gold, Westminster Bridge c.1871–1872
oil on canvas 71 x 86.4
35.642

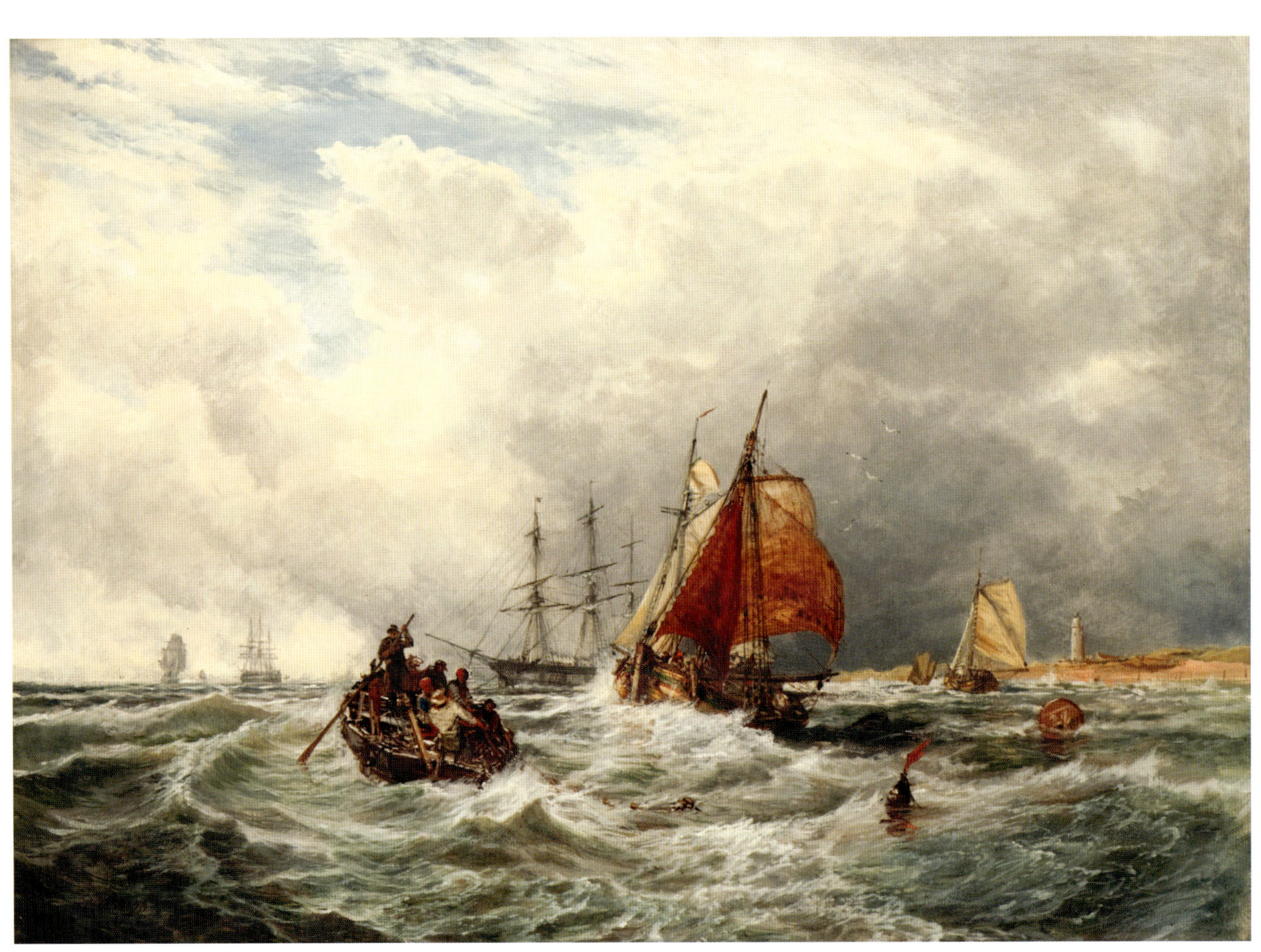

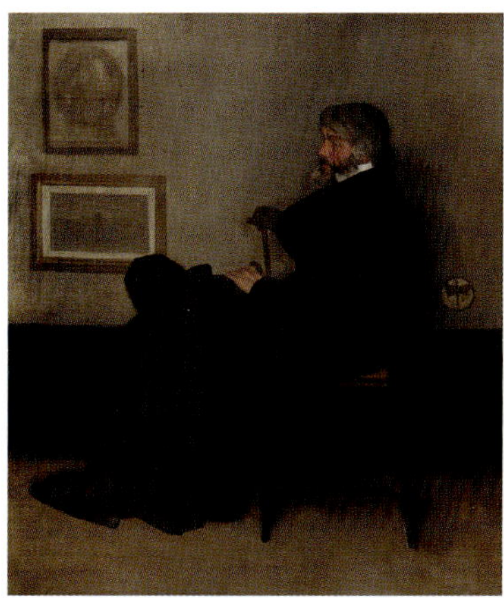

Whistler, James Abbott McNeill 1834–1903
*Arrangement in Grey and Black, No.2: Portrait
of Thomas Carlyle* 1872–1873
oil on canvas 171.1 x 143.5
671

Whiteford, Kate b.1952
Pompeiian Red (diptych, left panel) c.1981
acrylic on canvas 183 x 122
3371.2

Whiteford, Kate b.1952
Pompeiian Red (diptych, right panel) c.1981
acrylic on canvas 183 x 61
3371.1

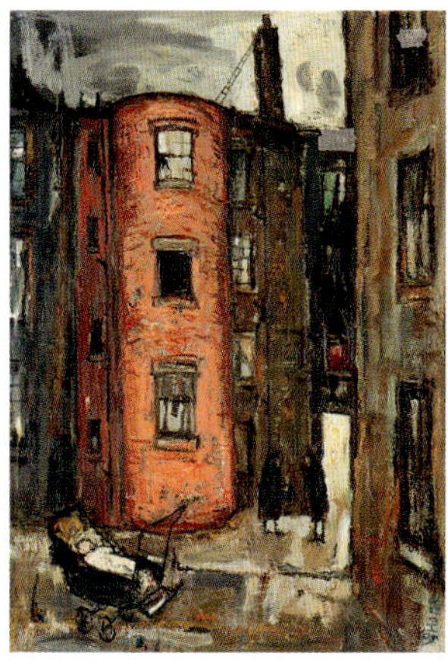

Whone, Herbert Bannister b.1925
Tenements, Anderston 1964
oil on canvas 152.4 x 101.6
3457

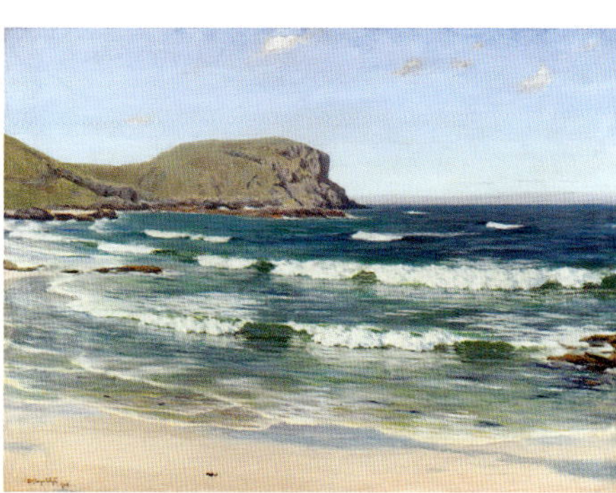

Whyte, Duncan MacGregor 1866–1953
Stalla Hunisgeir c.1949
oil on canvas 78.7 x 106.7
2843

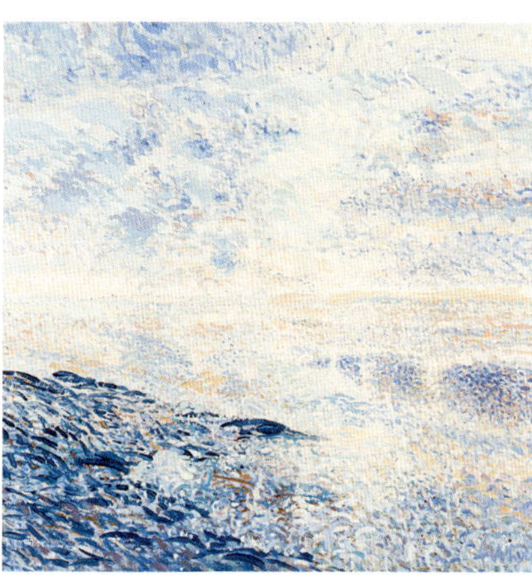

Whyte, Edna b.1930
Distant to North c.2008
oil on board 59.5 x 59.5
3689

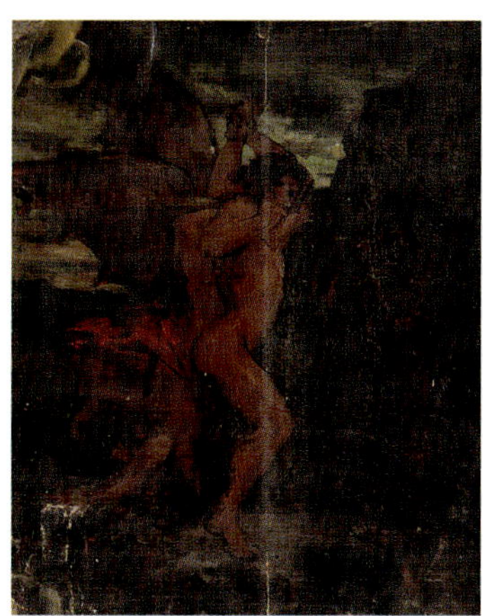

Wiertz, Antoine Joseph 1806–1865
The Devil Carrying Off One of the Damned
oil on canvas 42.8 x 34.6
3061

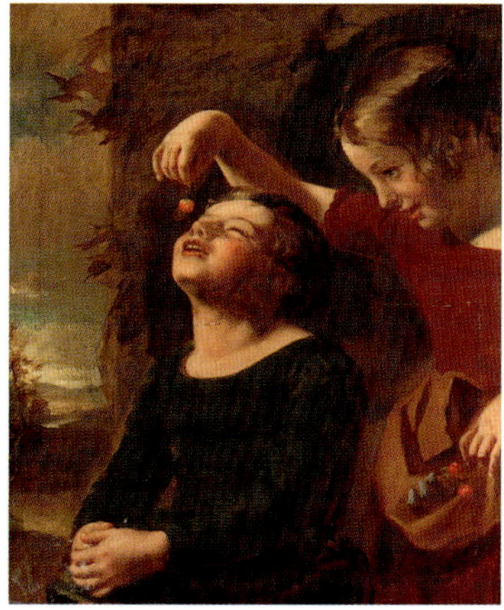

Wighton, William d.1875/1876
Open Your Mouth, and Shut Your Eyes
oil on canvas 76.2 x 63.5
412

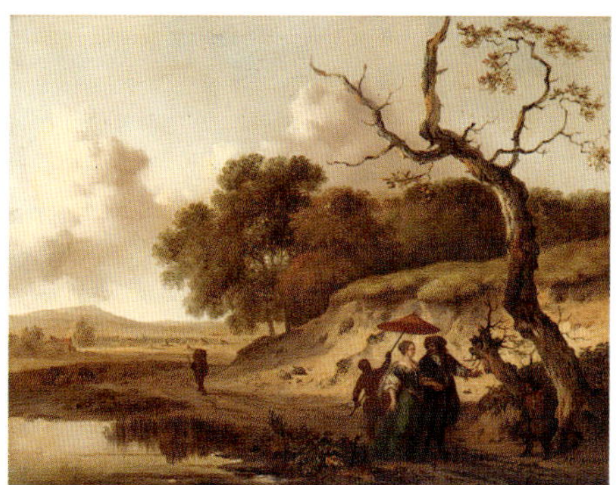

Wijnants, Jan c.1635–1684
*Landscape in Dunes with a Married
Couple* c.1660–1684
oil on panel 32.4 x 39.3
63

Facing page: Bough, Samuel, 1822–1878, *Dutch Lugger Entering the Thames*, (p. 45)

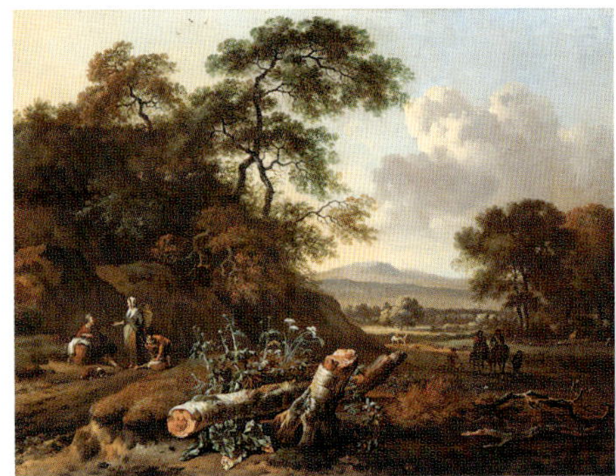

Wijnants, Jan c.1635–1684 & **Lingelbach, Johannes** 1622–1674
Landscape with a Fallen Tree, Peasants and Huntsmen 1672
oil on canvas 49.5 x 64.1
58

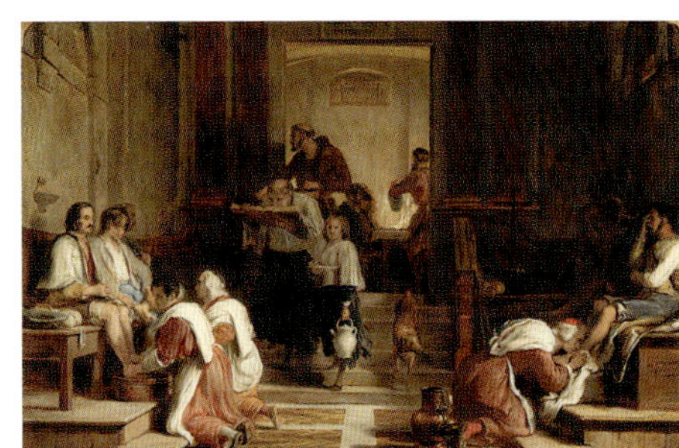

Wilkie, David 1785–1841
Cardinals, Priests and Roman Citizens Washing the Pilgrims' Feet 1827
oil on canvas 49.5 x 73.7
1717

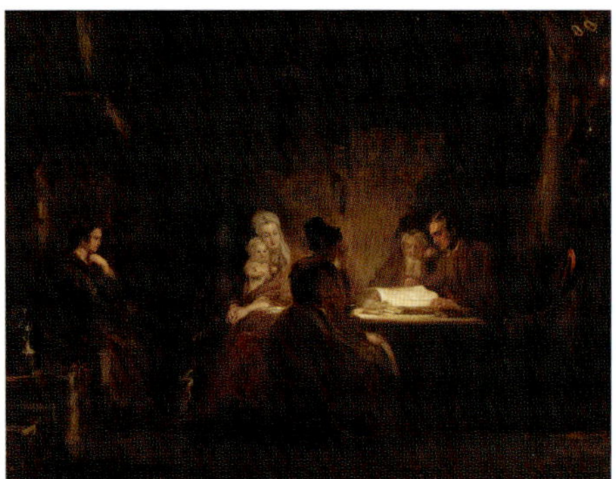

Wilkie, David 1785–1841
The Cottar's Saturday Night 1837
oil on panel 83.8 x 108
2795

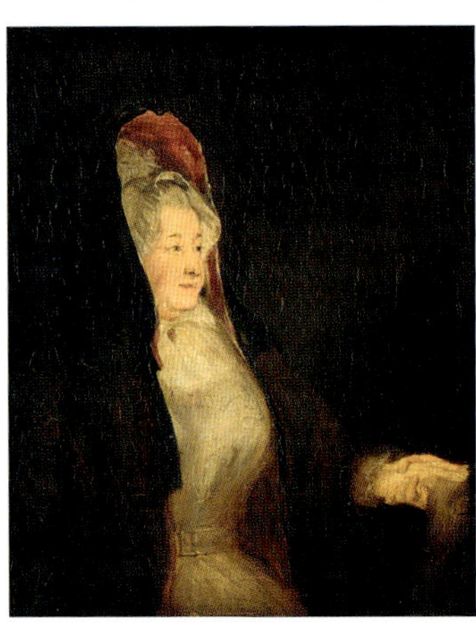

Wilkie, David 1785–1841
Portrait of a Lady (sketch)
oil on panel 30.5 x 25.1
368

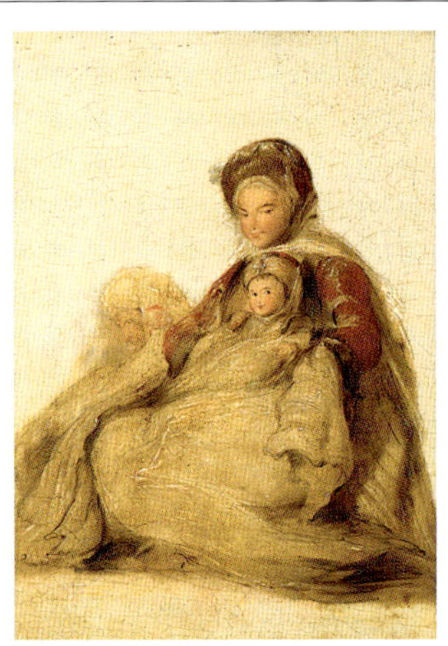

Wilkie, David (after) 1785–1841
Turkish Mother and Child 19th C (?)
oil on panel 32.7 x 26
244

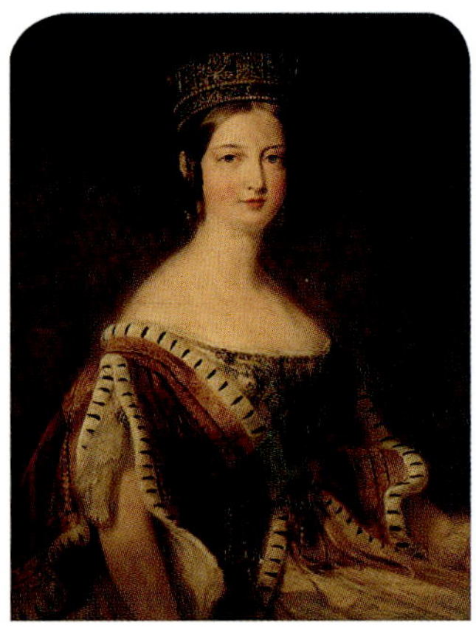

Wilkie, David (attributed to) 1785–1841
Queen Victoria (1819–1901)
oil on canvas 90.2 x 69.9
259

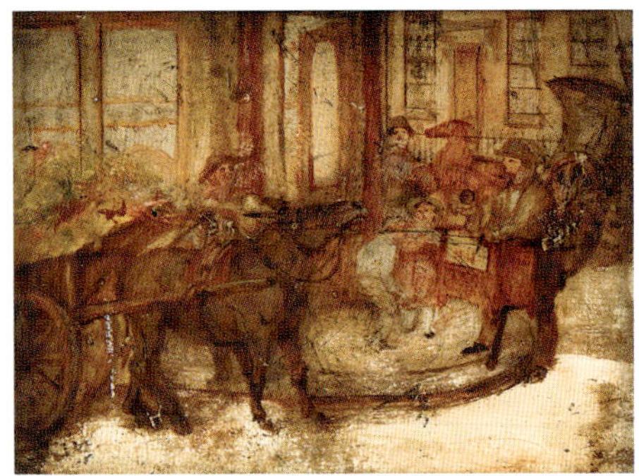

Wilkie, David (imitator of) 1785–1841
City Street Scene (sketch)
oil on panel 20 x 28
NR.133

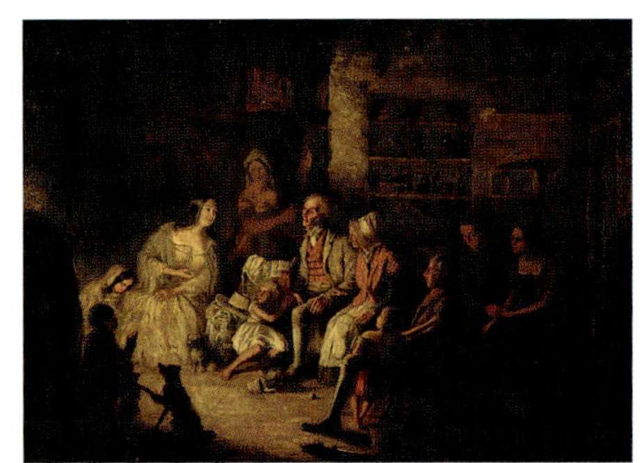

Wilkie, David (style of) 1785–1841
Family Group in an Interior
oil on canvas 66 x 96.5
L.3.1944 (P)

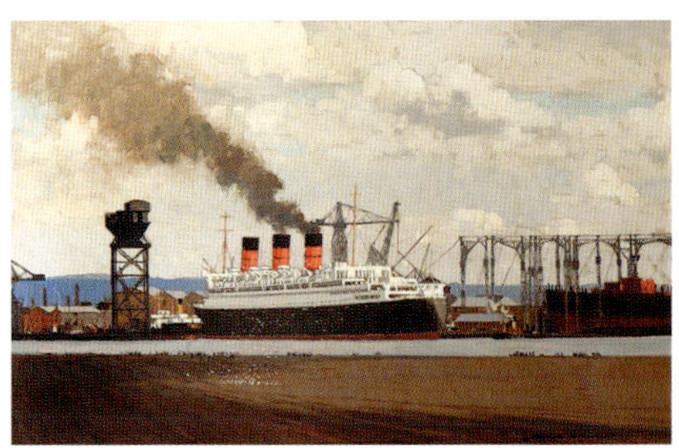

Wilkinson, Norman 1878–1972
Fitting Out: RMS 'Queen Mary' at Clydebank, 1936
oil on canvas 55 x 81
T.1973.10.ag

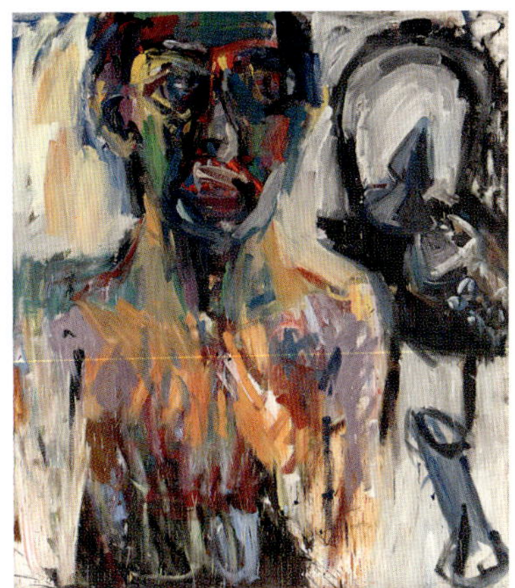

Williams, Andrew b.1954
Self Portrait
oil on canvas 214.2 x 191
3551

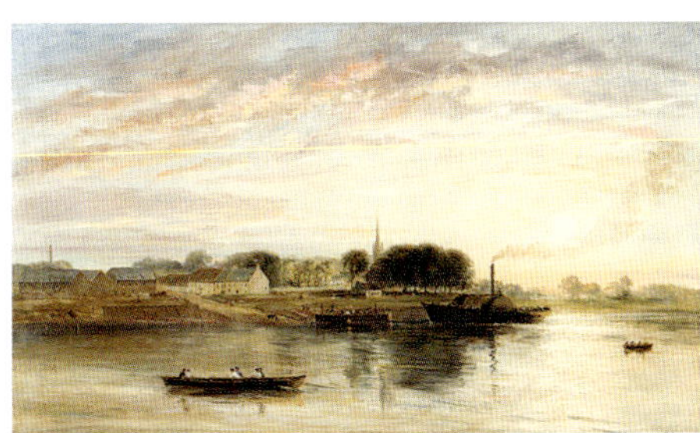

Williams, Hugh William 1773–1829
Govan Ferry c.1820
oil on canvas 45.7 x 76.2
1911.82

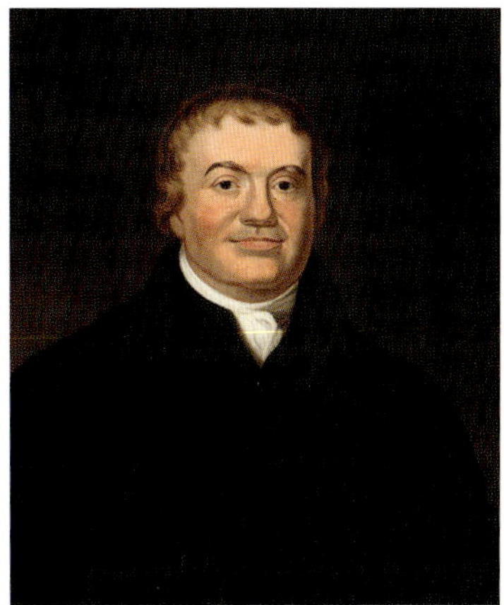

Williams, Hugh William 1773–1829
David Dale (1739–1806)
oil on canvas 76.8 x 63.5
333

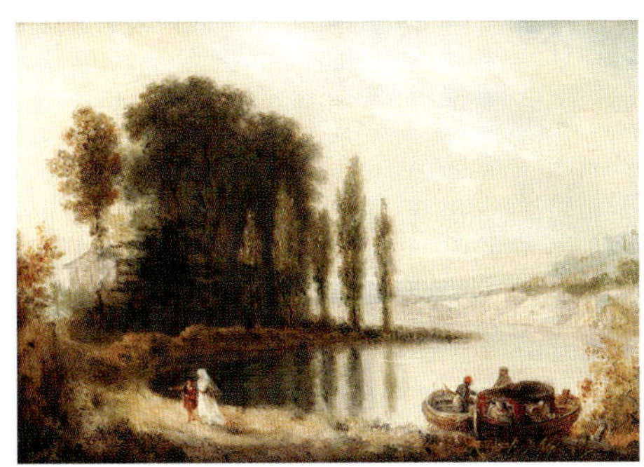

Williams, Hugh William 1773–1829
Landscape
oil on canvas 35.6 x 47
1072

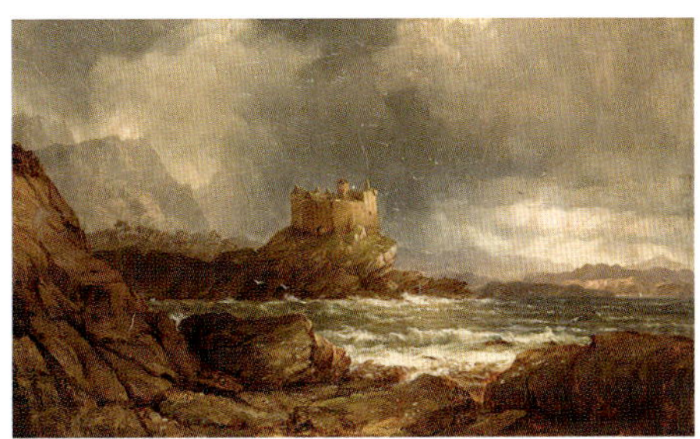

Williams, James Francis 1785–1846
On the West Coast of Inverness-shire 1832
oil on panel 32.4 x 52.4
PC.147

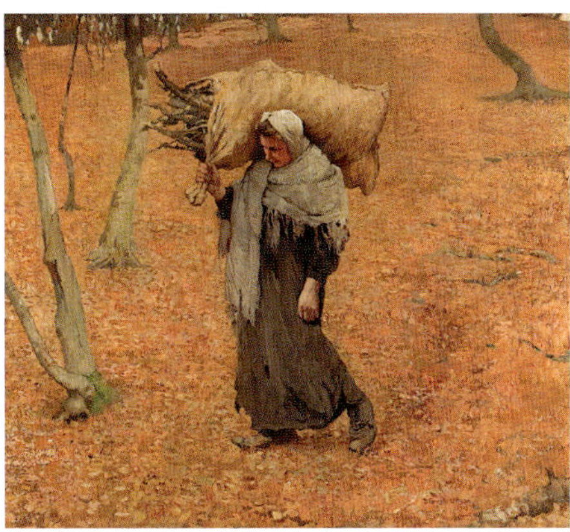

Wilson, David Forrester 1873–1950
Faggots 1915
oil on canvas 120.7 x 135.9
1380

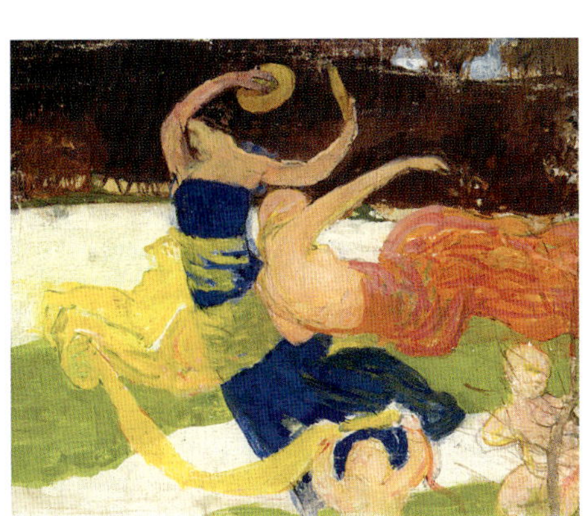

Wilson, David Forrester 1873–1950
The Valley of Melting Snow (sketch) c.1920
oil on canvas 26 x 30.8
3397

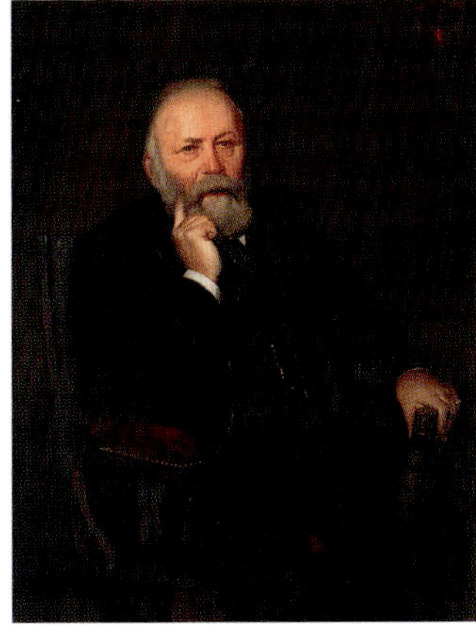

Wilson, Francis 1876–1957
David Fortune (d.1917) 1911
oil on canvas 121.9 x 91.4
1452

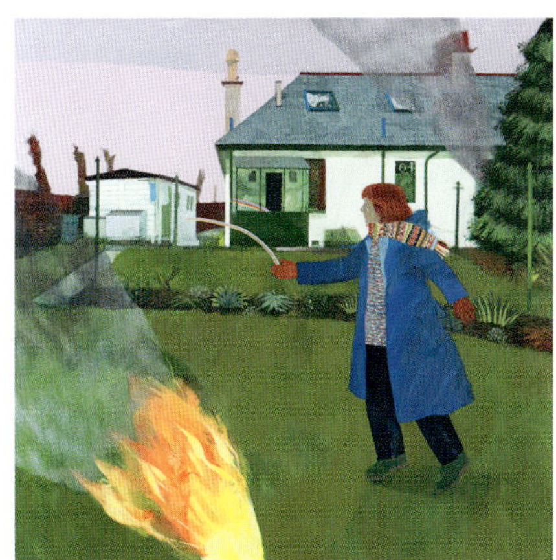

Wilson, Helen F. b.1954
Wednesday Afternoon 1980–1981
oil on canvas 153 x 153
3373

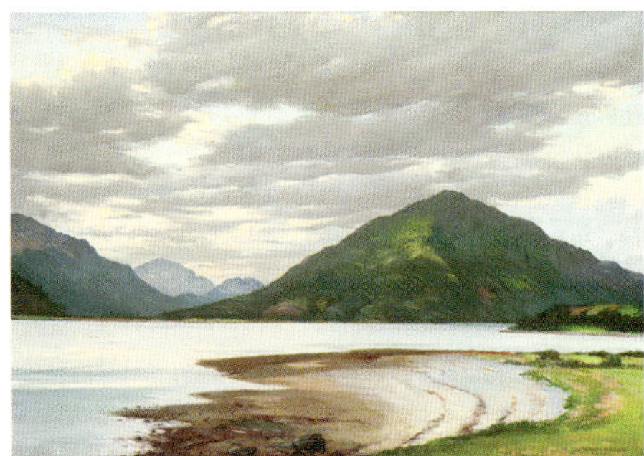

Wilson, Hugh Cameron 1885–1952
Evening Calm c.1952
oil on canvas 55.9 x 76.2
2979

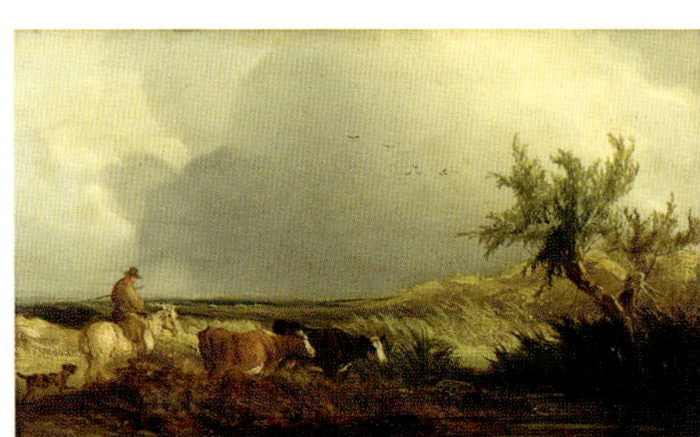

Wilson, John Glen 1774–1855
Landscape and Cattle
oil on panel 20.3 x 35.6
355

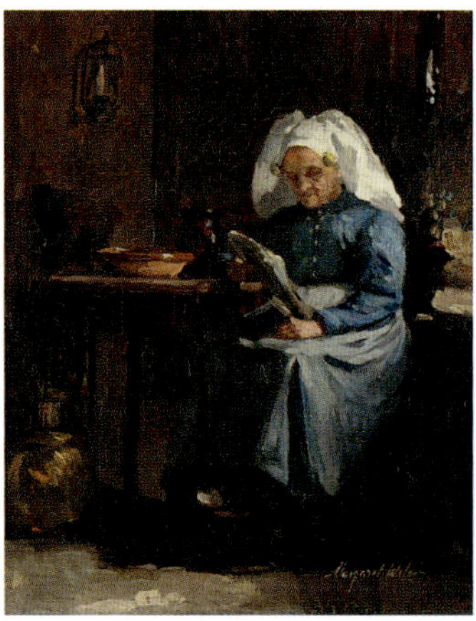

Wilson, Margaret Thomson 1864–1912
A Dutch 'Vrouw'
oil on canvas 50.8 x 40.6
1341

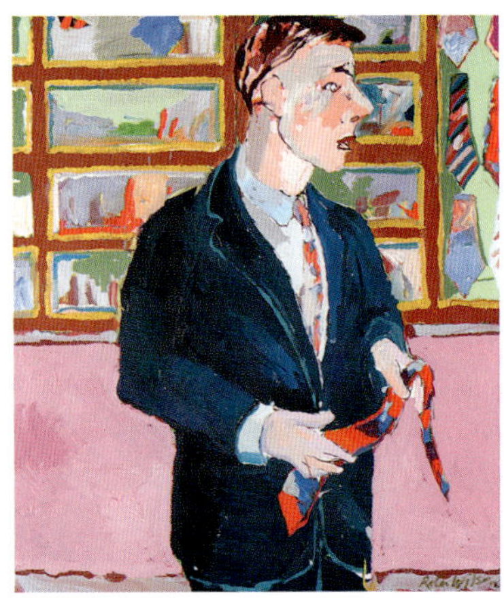

Wilson, Peter b.1940
The Tie Salesman 1978
oil on canvas 107.2 x 90.6
3609

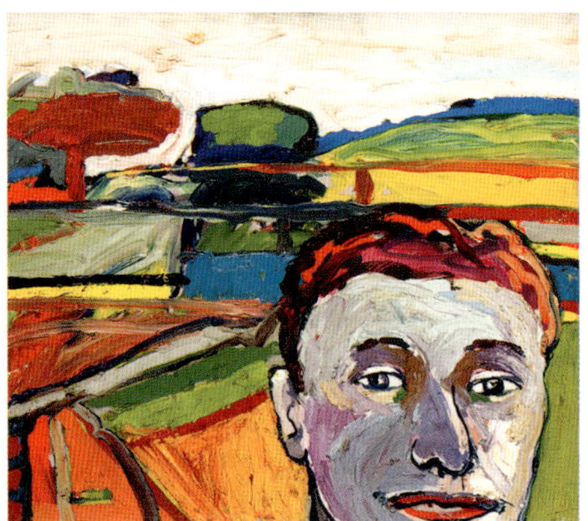

Wilson, Peter b.1940
Headscape from Train II 1983
oil on canvas 45 x 50.1
3409

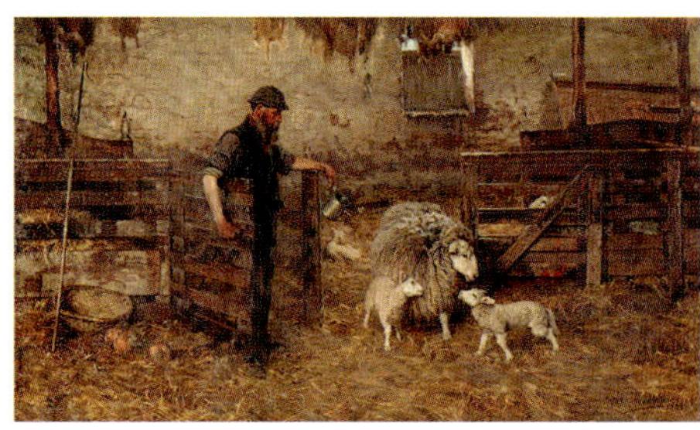

Wilson, Peter MacGregor 1855/1856–1928
The Firstlings of the Flock 1884
oil on canvas 91.4 x 152.4
1761

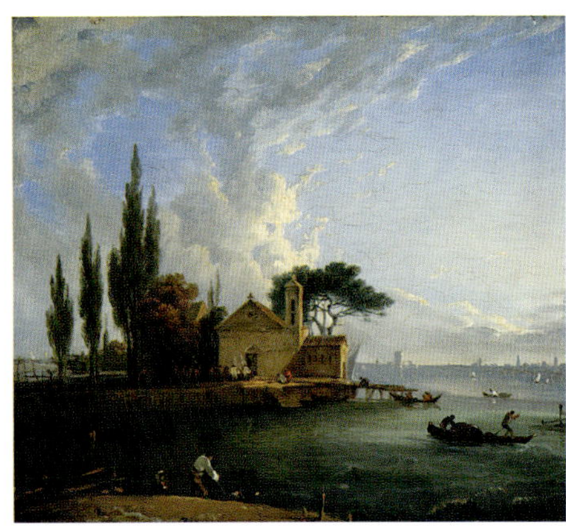

Wilson, Richard (after) 1714–1787
Island of Anconetta, near Mestre 18th C
oil on panel 21.6 x 24.1
242

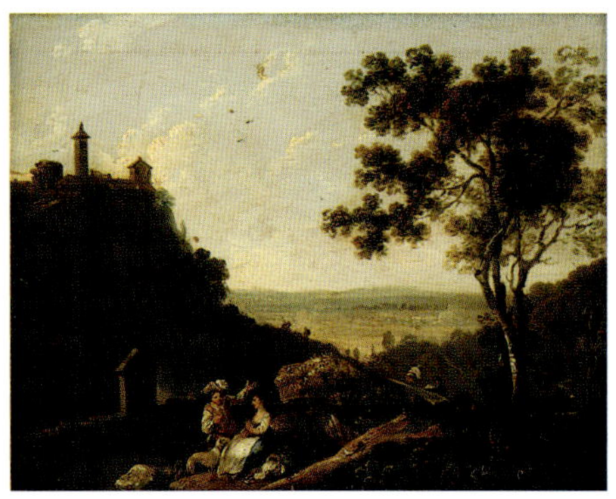

Wilson, Richard (after) 1714–1787
View near Tivoli c.1854
oil on canvas 34.3 x 43.2
249

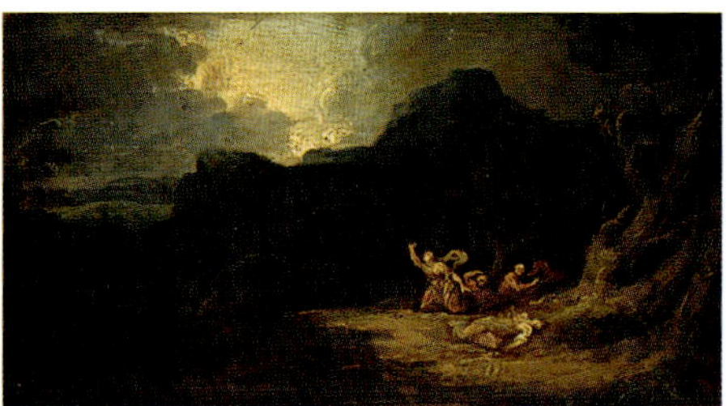

Wilson, Richard (attributed to) 1714–1787
Landscape with Figures
oil on panel 14 x 24.1
245

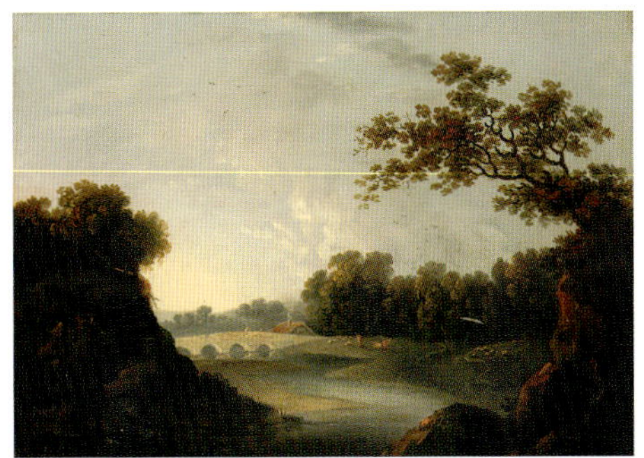

Wilson, Richard (imitator of) 1714–1787
River Scene c.1854
oil on canvas 35.6 x 47
232

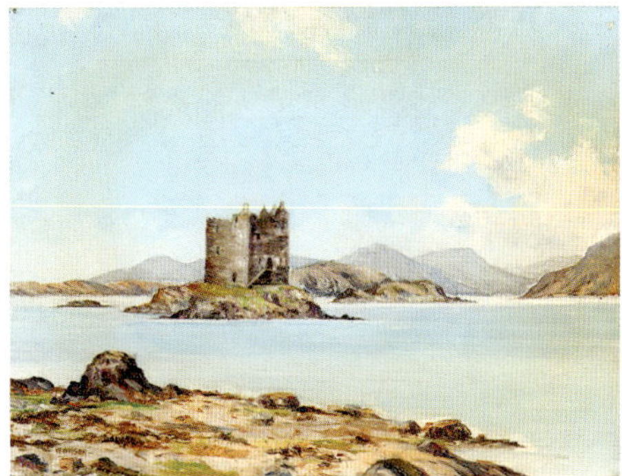

Wilson, W. active 20th C
Castle Stalker
oil on canvas 35.6 x 45.8
NR.173

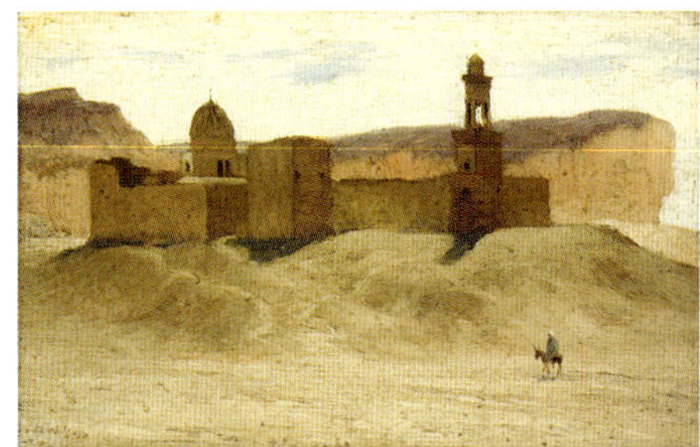

Wilson, William Heath 1849–1927
A Desert Mosque
oil on board 12.7 x 19.7
1766.8

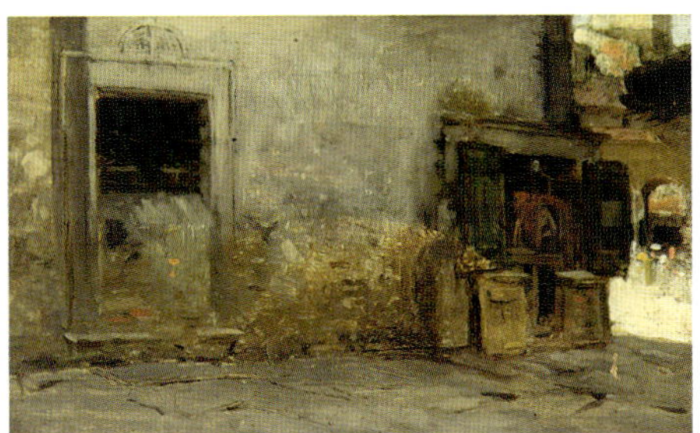

Wilson, William Heath 1849–1927
A Quaint Corner
oil on board 12.7 x 19.7
1766.3

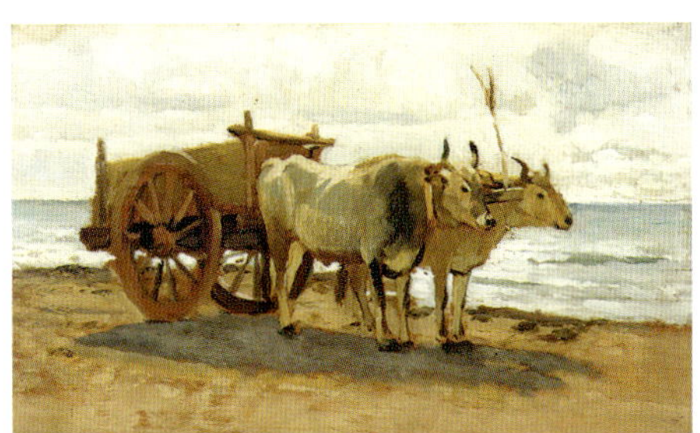

Wilson, William Heath 1849–1927
Bullocks Drawing a Cart
oil on panel 20.3 x 33
1765

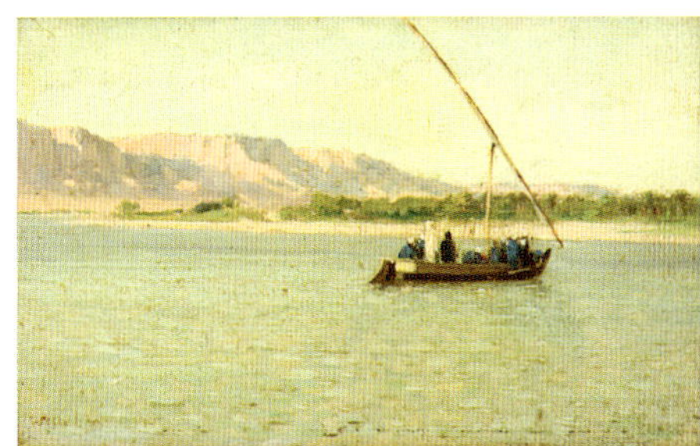

Wilson, William Heath 1849–1927
Egypt, a Ferryboat on the Nile
oil on board 12.7 x 19.7
1766.7

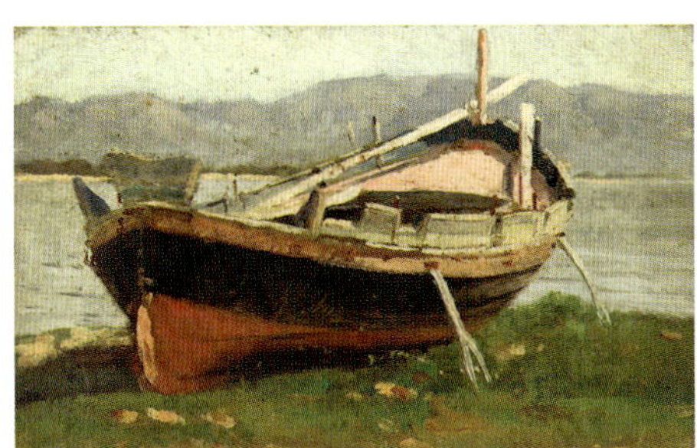

Wilson, William Heath 1849–1927
Old Boat Beached
oil on board 12.7 x 19.7
1766.2

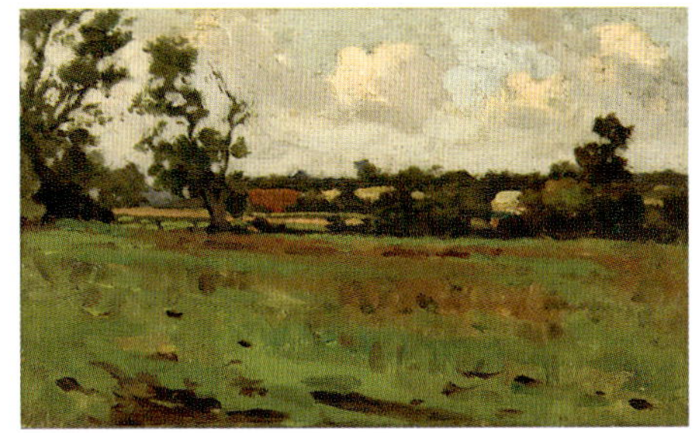

Wilson, William Heath 1849–1927
The Marsh, Wenhaston
oil on board 12.7 x 19.7
1766.1

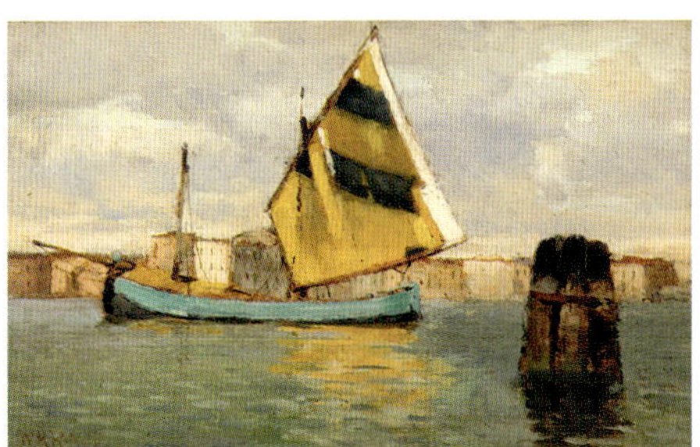

Wilson, William Heath 1849–1927
Venice
oil on board 12.7 x 19.7
1766.6

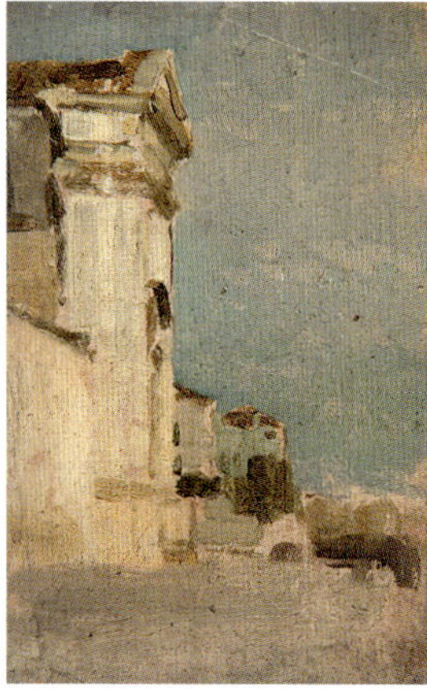

Wilson, William Heath 1849–1927
Venice, along the Zattere
oil on cardboard 12.1 x 7.6
NR.127

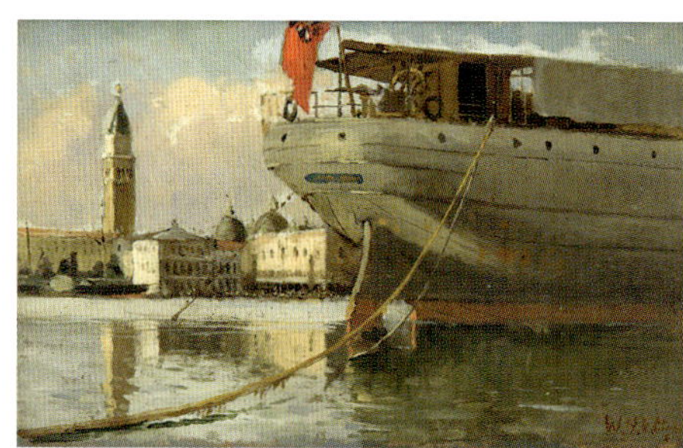

Wilson, William Heath 1849–1927
Venice, the Campanile, St Mark's and Doge's Palace
oil on board 12.7 x 19.7
1766.5

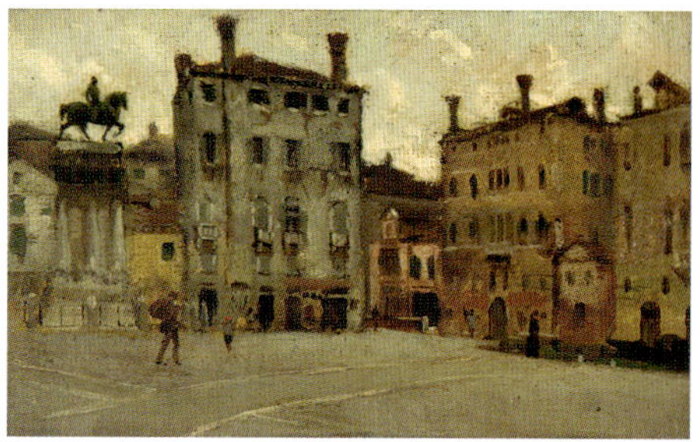

Wilson, William Heath 1849–1927
Venice, the Colleoni Monument
oil on board 12.7 x 19.7
1766.4

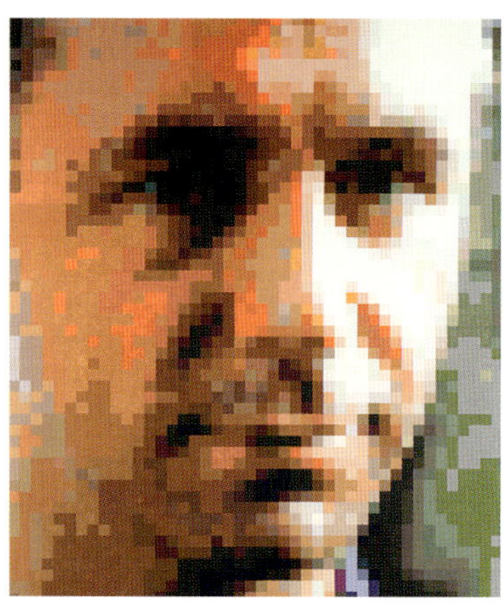

Windle, Michael b.1958
Calum Colvin 1996
acrylic on canvas 210 x 176.5
3610

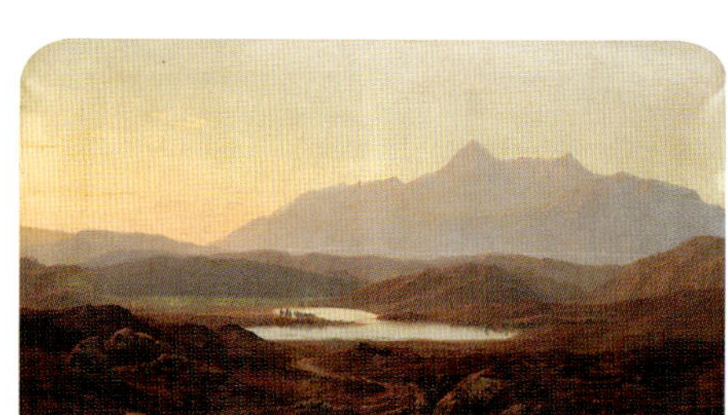

Wingate, James Lawton 1846–1924
Ben Cruachan 1866
oil on canvas 70.5 x 127
3246

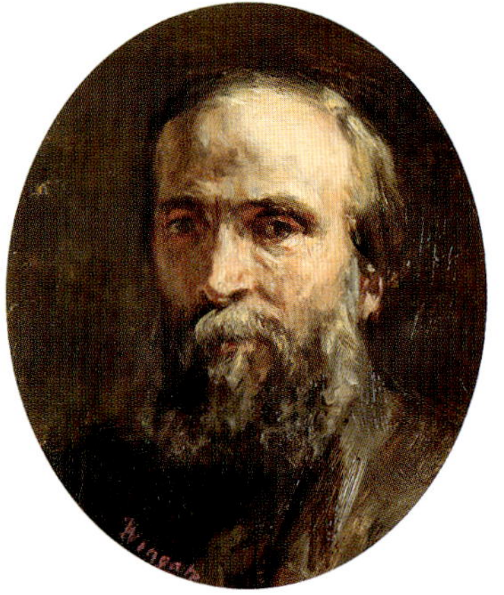

Wingate, James Lawton 1846–1924
Thomas Fairbairn (1820–1885), RSW
c.1870–1880
oil on panel 15.3 x 12.6
1928.34

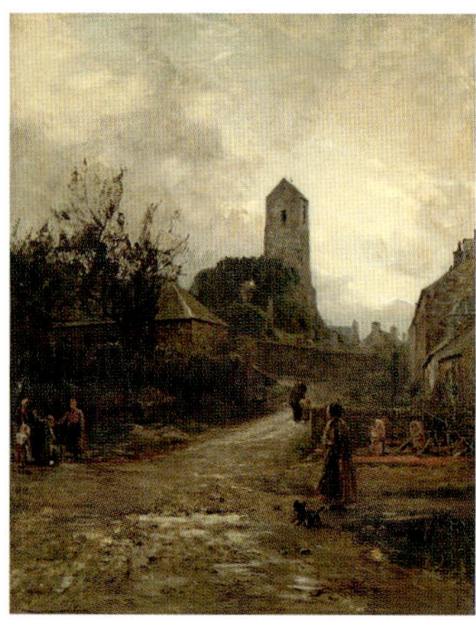

Wingate, James Lawton 1846–1924
Old Church at Muthill 1874
oil on canvas 91.4 x 71.1
928

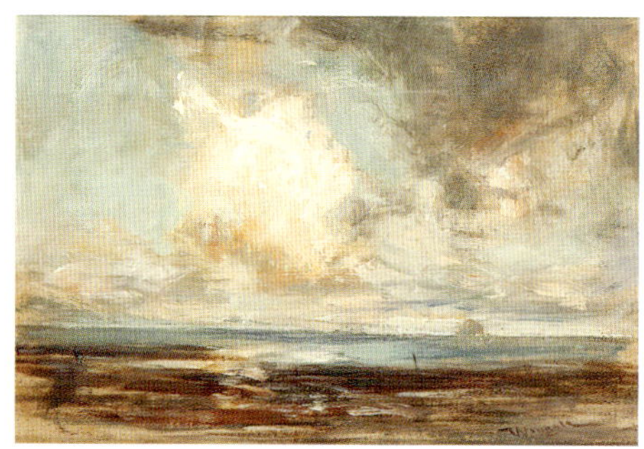

Wingate, James Lawton 1846–1924
Ailsa Craig
oil on canvas 24.6 x 35.3
3231

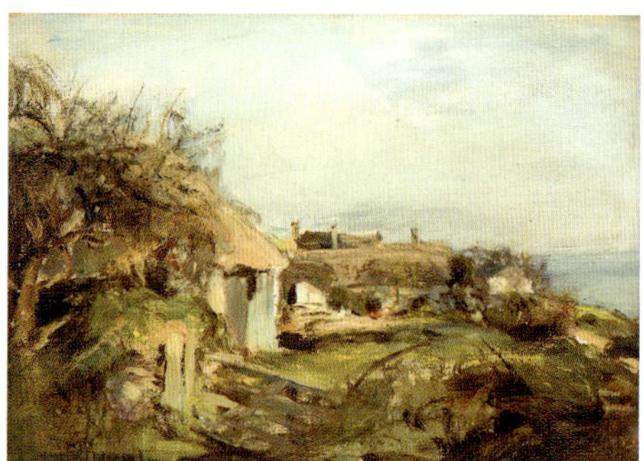

Wingate, James Lawton 1846–1924
Cottages in Arran
oil on canvas 25.4 x 35.6
2430

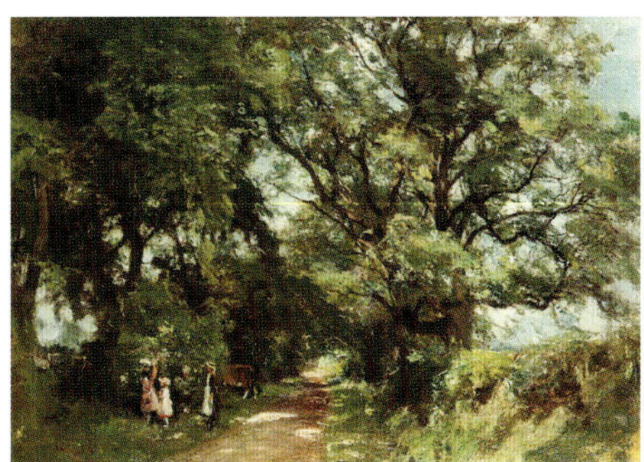

Wingate, James Lawton 1846–1924
The Avenue
oil on canvas 44.5 x 59.7
833

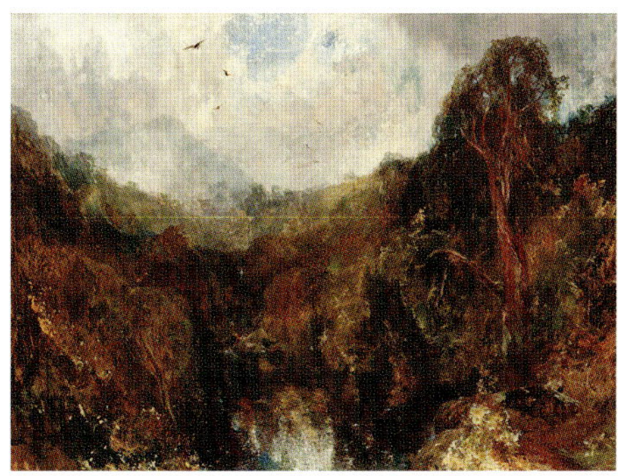

Wintour, John Crawford 1825–1882
Killiecrankie 1878
oil on canvas 68.6 x 90.2
773

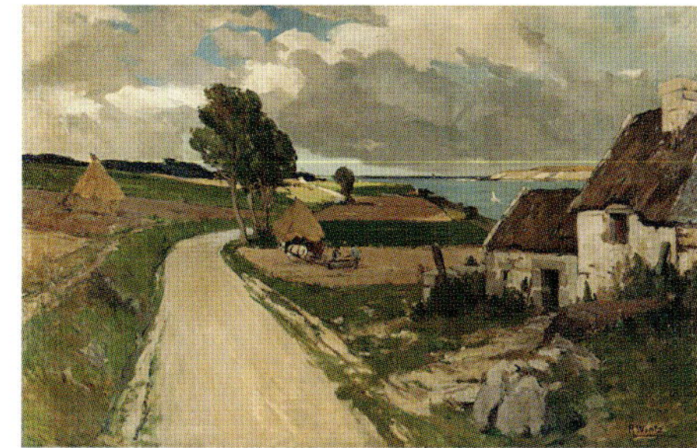

Wintz, Raymond 1884–1956
Along the Coast
oil on canvas 157.5 x 243
2115

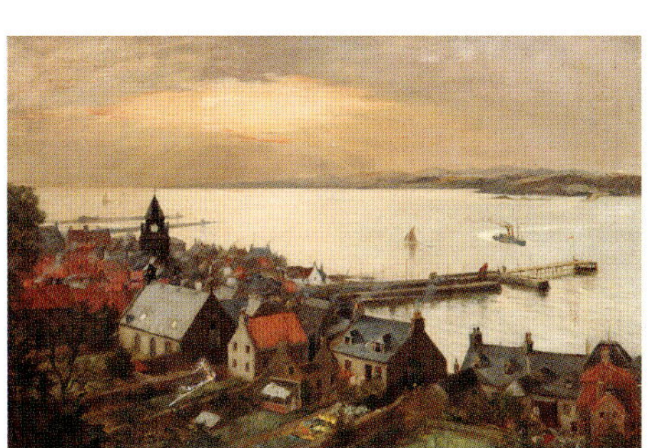

Wirrell, D. (attributed to) active 20th C
Evening Scene on the Clyde
oil on canvas 36.4 x 54
PP.1988.45.4

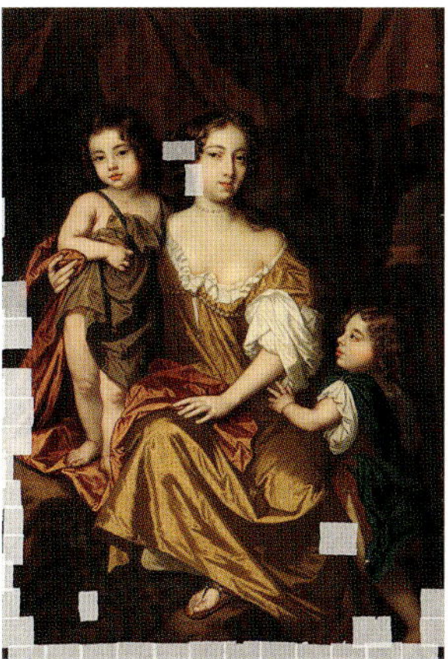

Wissing, Willem (attributed to) 1656–1687
Nell Gwynn (1650–1687), and Her Two Children c.1676–1681
oil on canvas 166.4 x 111.8
251

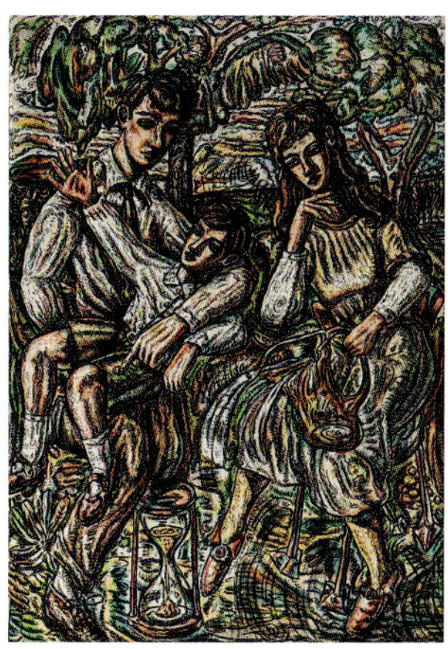

Wiszniewski, Adrian b.1958
Robertson Park 1987
acrylic & ink on paper 26.1 x 18.3
PR.1988.6

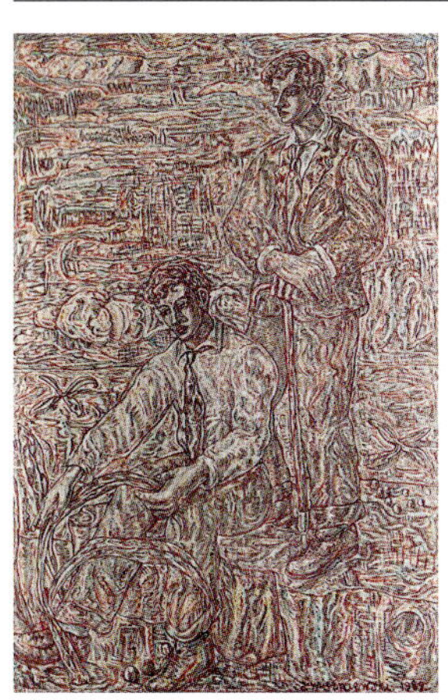

Wiszniewski, Adrian b.1958
Weeds in a Landscape 1989
oil on canvas 346.1 x 213.4
3501

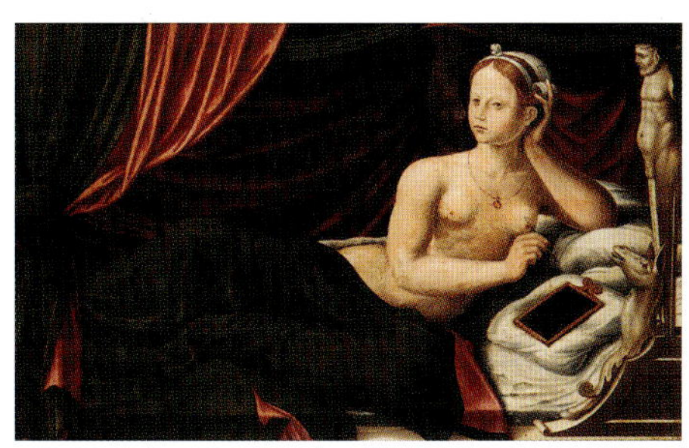

Witz, Konrad (follower of)
c.1400/1410–c.1445/1446
Byblis Writing to Caunus c.1450–1475
oil on panel 49.9 x 74.6
1592

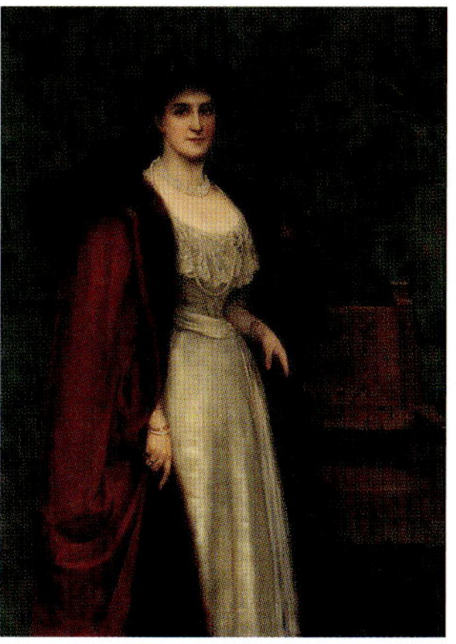

Wontner, William Clarke 1857–1930
Ina Campbell (d.1925), Duchess of Argyll 1897
oil on canvas 160 x 111.8
1663

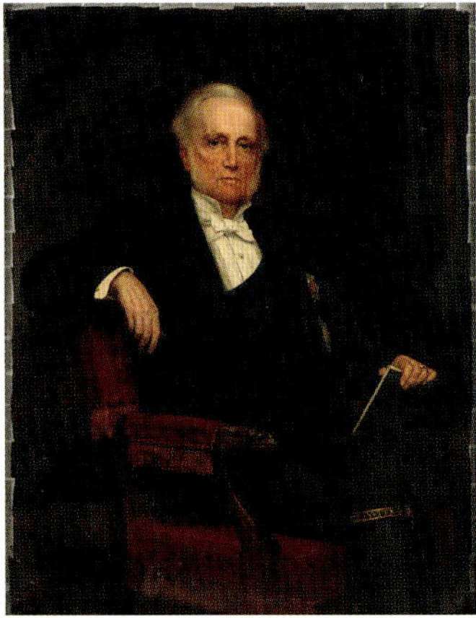

Wontner, William Clarke 1857–1930
*George Campbell (1823–1900), 8th Duke of
Argyll* 1898
oil on canvas 132.1 x 81.3
1662

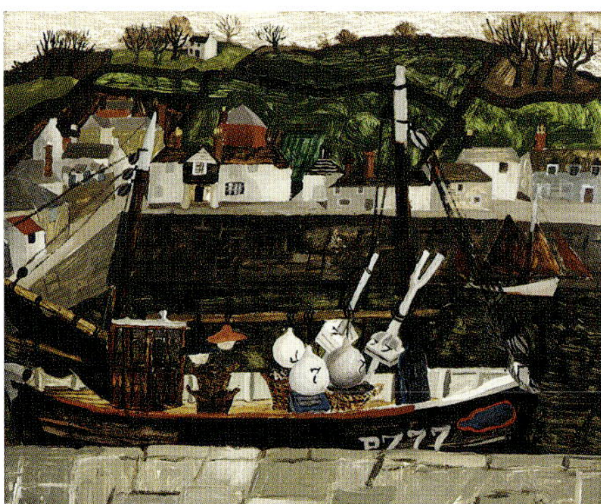

Wood, Christopher 1901–1930
Newlyn 1930
oil on board 48.9 x 63.3
3341

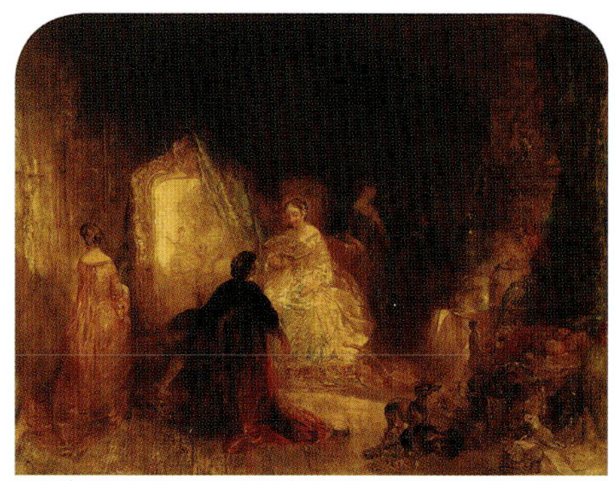

Woolmer, Alfred Joseph 1805–1892
Watteau in His Studio c.1843
oil on canvas 89.5 x 95.3
447

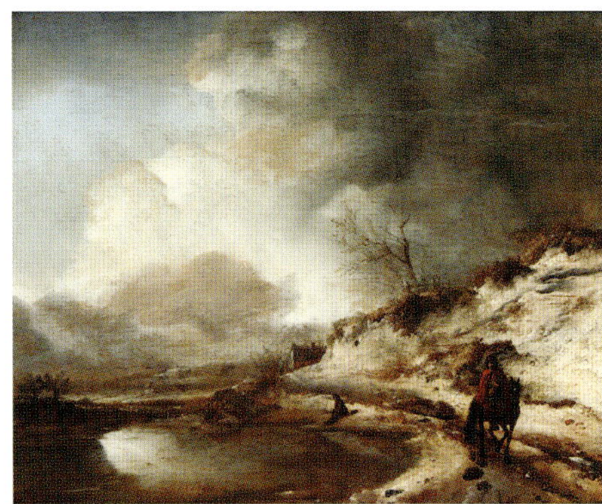

Wouwerman, Philips 1619–1668
A Horseman by a Pond c.1650–1652
oil on panel 35.6 x 41.3
16

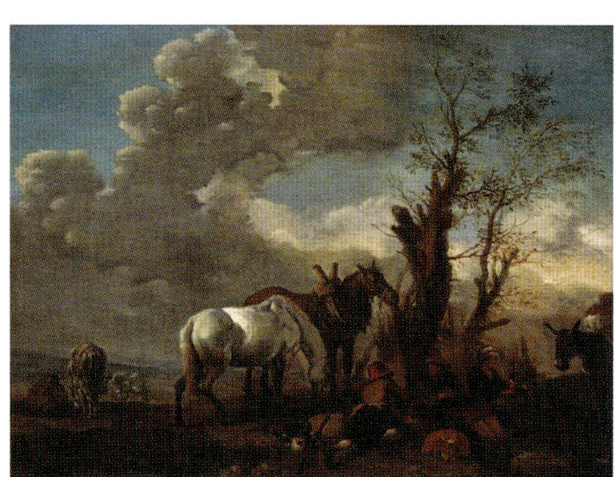

Wouwerman, Philips (after) 1619–1668
A Family of Itinerants Resting 17th C
oil on panel 29.5 x 37.1
39

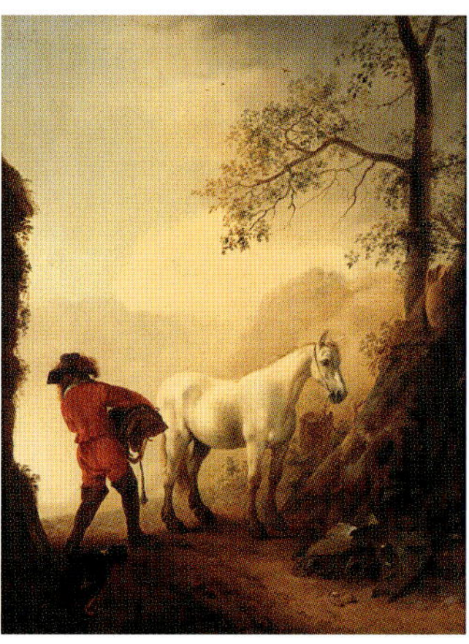

Wouwerman, Philips (after) 1619–1668
A Man Saddling a Tethered Horse 19th C
oil on panel 40 x 32.7
1455

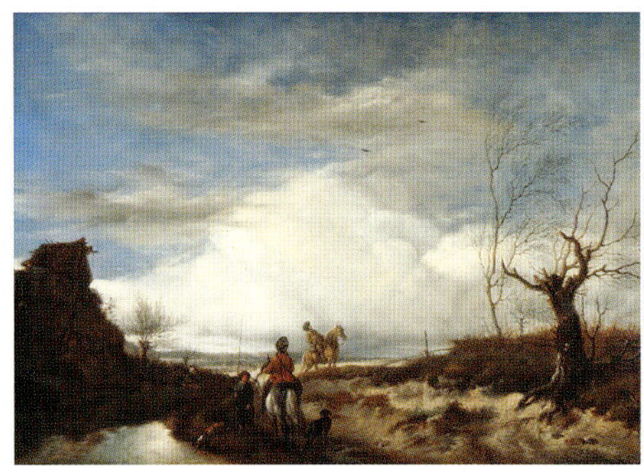

Wouwerman, Philips (attributed to)
1619–1668
Hawking c.1650–1652
oil on panel 31.7 x 45.1
626

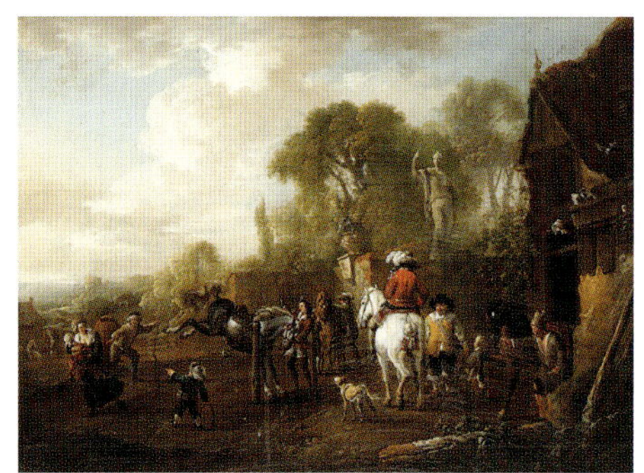

Wouwerman, Philips (follower of)
1619–1668
Departure from a Riding School early 18th C
oil on canvas 49.5 x 63.2
578

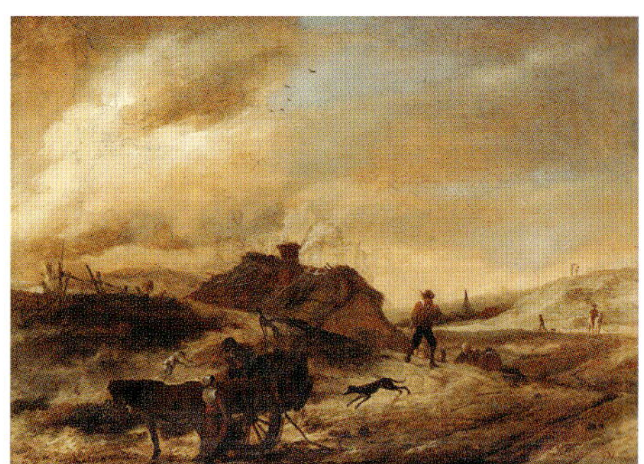

Wouwerman, Philips (style of) 1619–1668
Landscape with a Farm Cart mid-17th C–late
17th C
oil on panel 29.8 x 40.6
12

Facing page: Orchardson, William Quiller, 1832–1910, *Le mariage de convenance*, (p. 332)

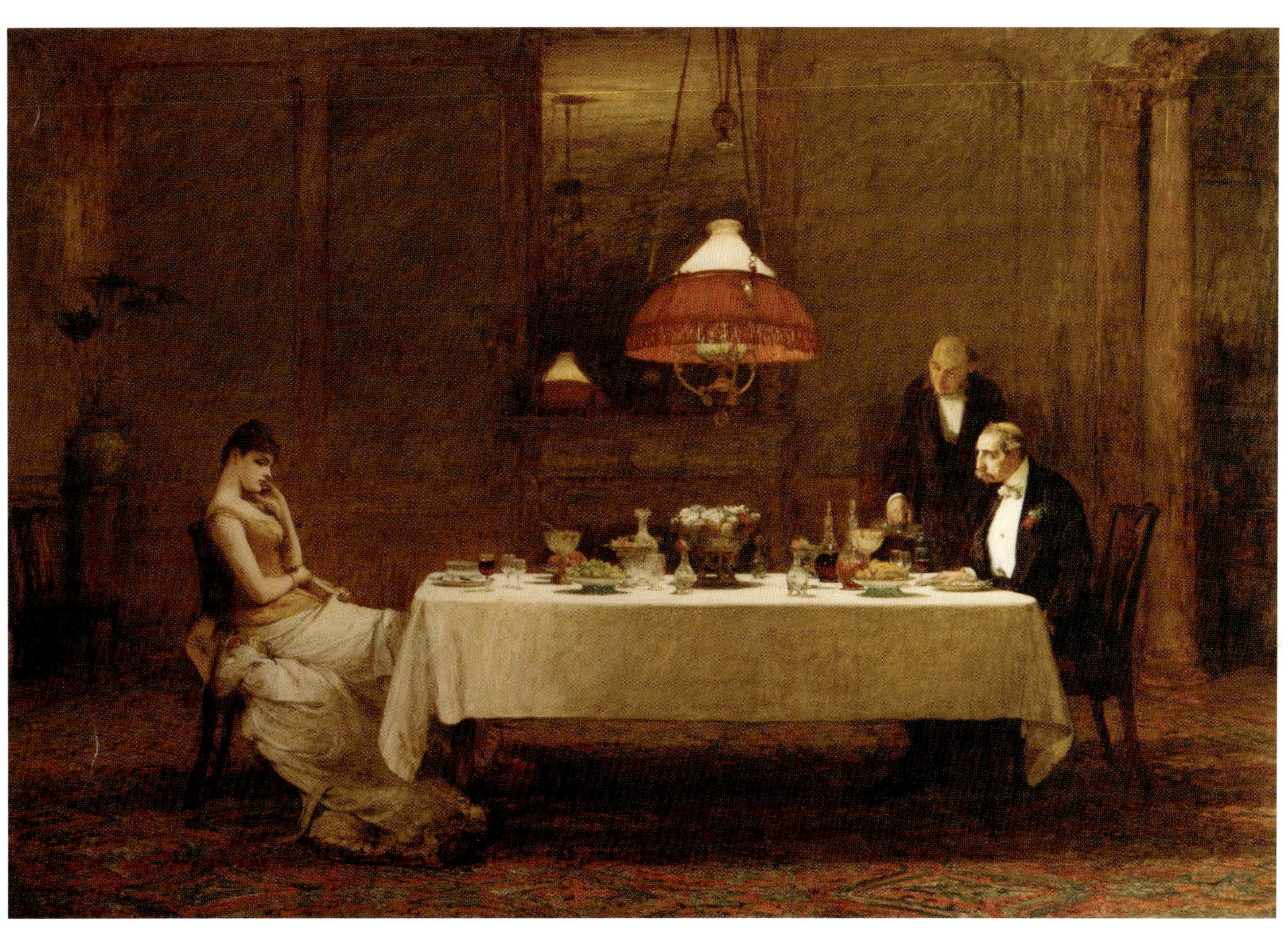

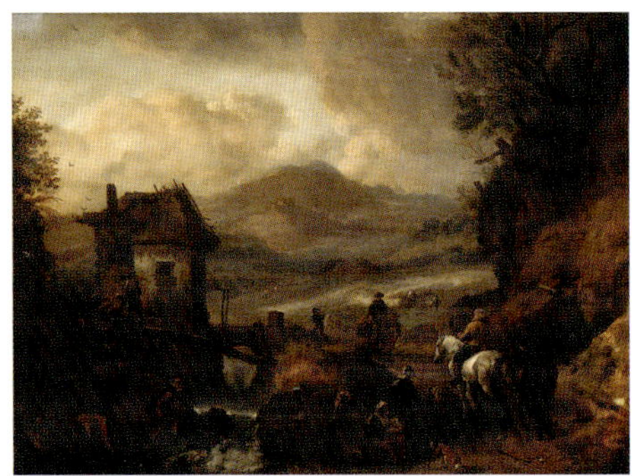

Wouwerman, Philips (style of) 1619–1668
Landscape with a Watermill and Figures
mid-17th C–late 17th C
oil on canvas 40.9 x 55.5
1144

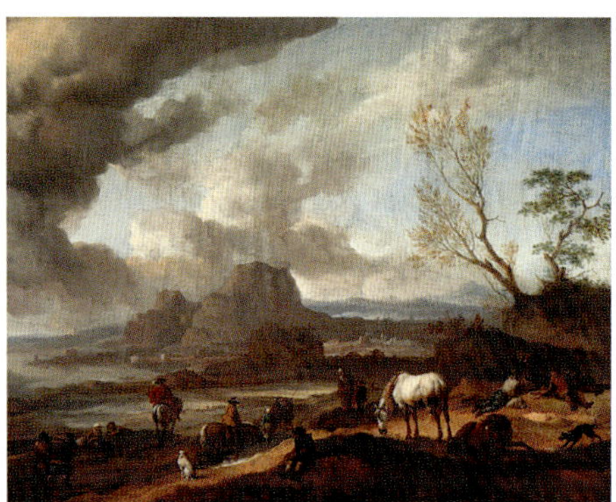

Wouwerman, Philips (style of) 1619–1668
*Landscape with Horses and Figures, with a
Distant View of the Sea*
mid-17th C–late 17th C
oil on canvas 52 x 62.8
64

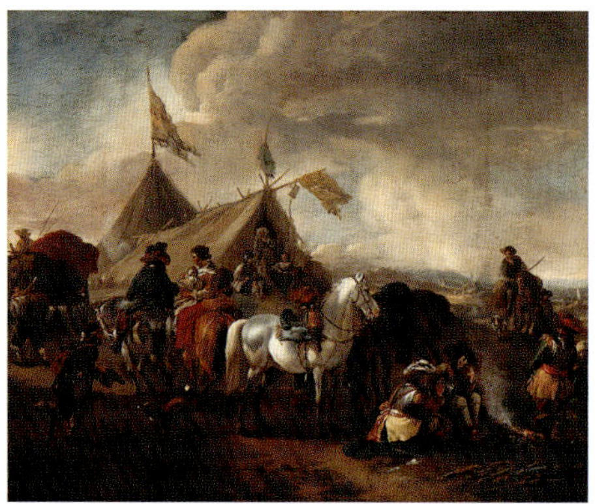

Wouwerman, Pieter 1623–1682
Cavalry Men by a Suttler's Tent
oil on canvas 41.2 x 48.2
628

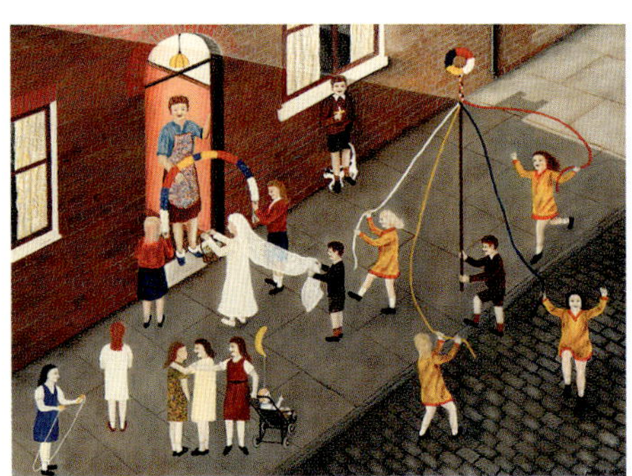

Wright, Arthur 1904–1981
May Day in Town 1974
oil on board 44.4 x 60.3
3596

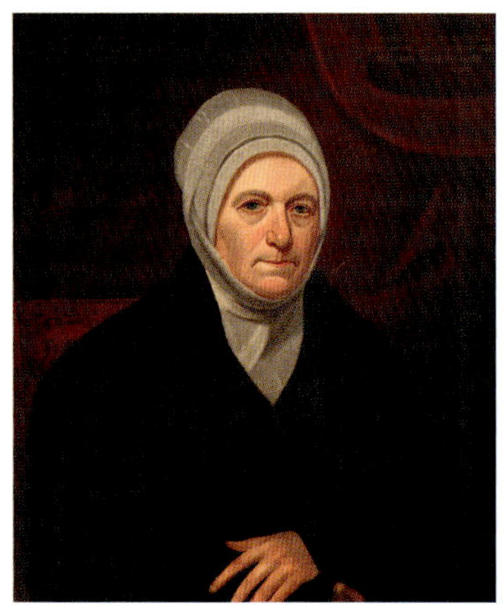

Wright, J. active 18th C
Frances Colquhoun (d.1818), Lady Maxwell
oil on canvas 74.6 x 61.6
PL.173 (P)

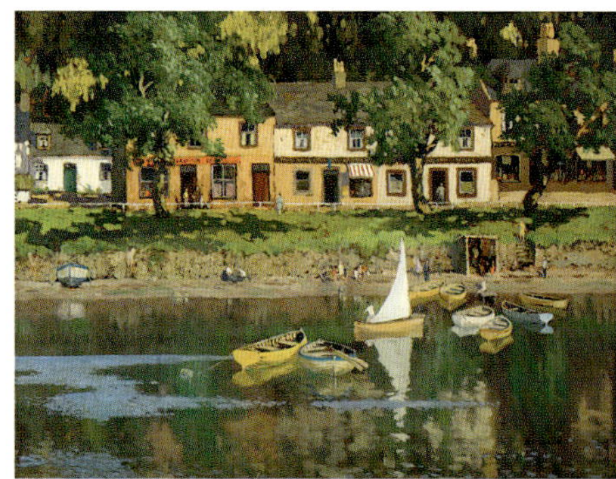

Wright, James 1885–1947
Garelochhead c.1941
oil on canvas 71.1 x 91.4
2259

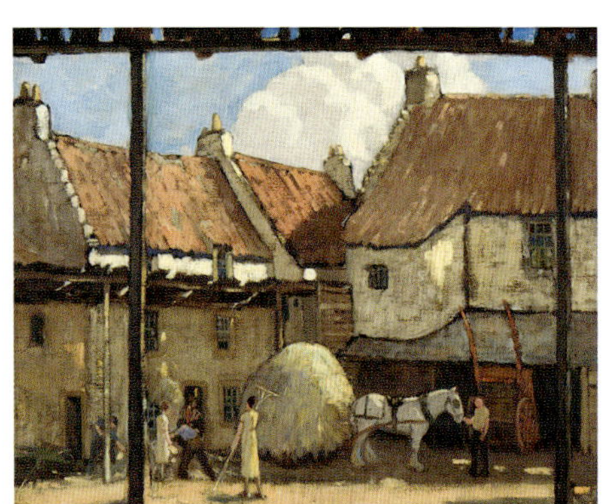

Wright, James 1885–1947
A Sunlit Courtyard, Culross
oil on canvas 50.8 x 61
2122

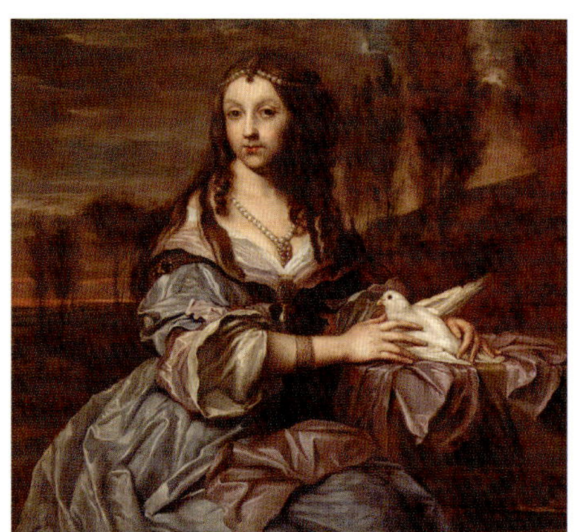

Wright, John Michael 1617–1694
*Frances Cromwell (1638–1720), Daughter of
Oliver Cromwell* c.1658
oil on canvas 101.5 x 112
3393

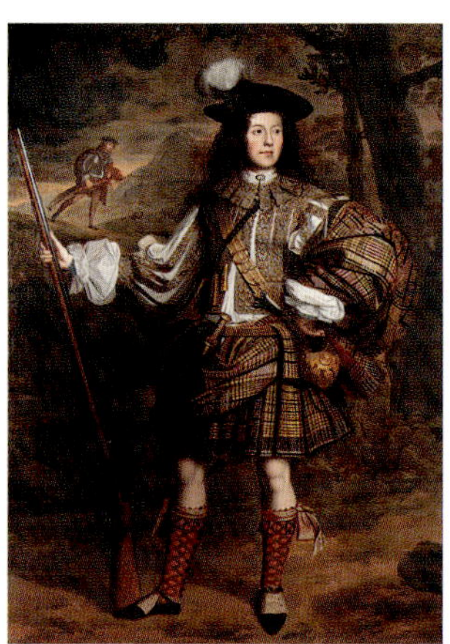

Wright, John Michael 1617–1694
*Lord Mungo Murray (1668–1700), Portrait of
a Highland Chieftain* 1680s
oil on canvas 85 x 60
LI.2005.008.1 (P)

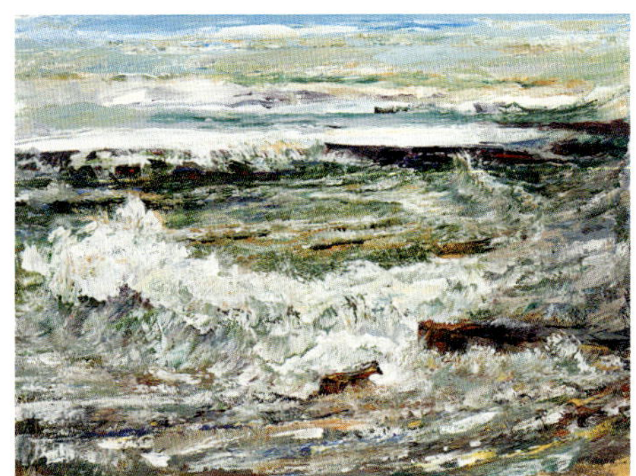

Wuterland, C.
Stormy Sea
acrylic on paper 76 x 92
PR.2007.2.128

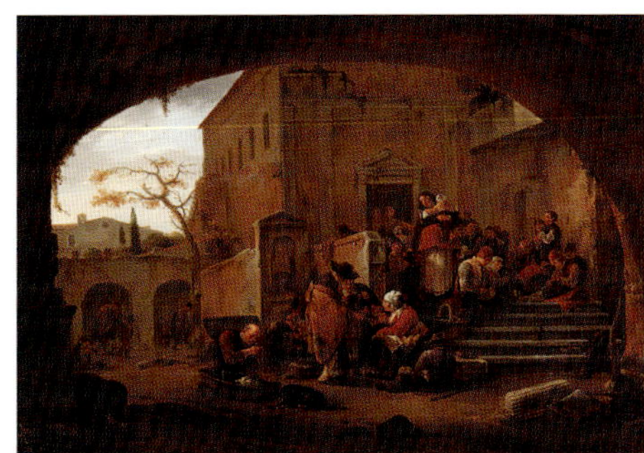

Wyck, Thomas 1616–1677
The Poor Being Fed at a Monastery
oil on panel 49.2 x 72.1
571

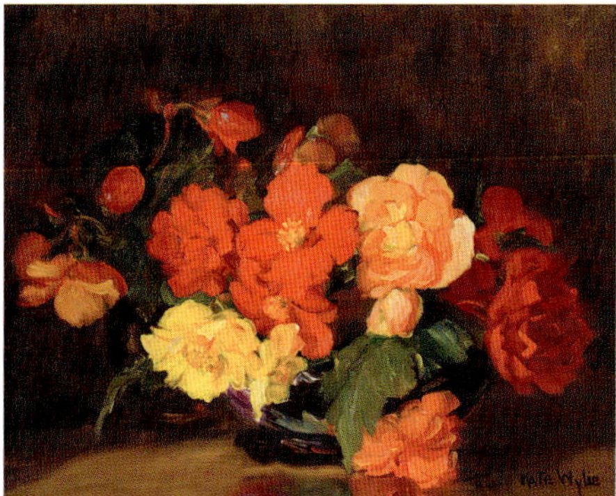

Wylie, Kate 1877–1941
Flowers (Begonias)
oil on canvas 40.6 x 50.8
2246

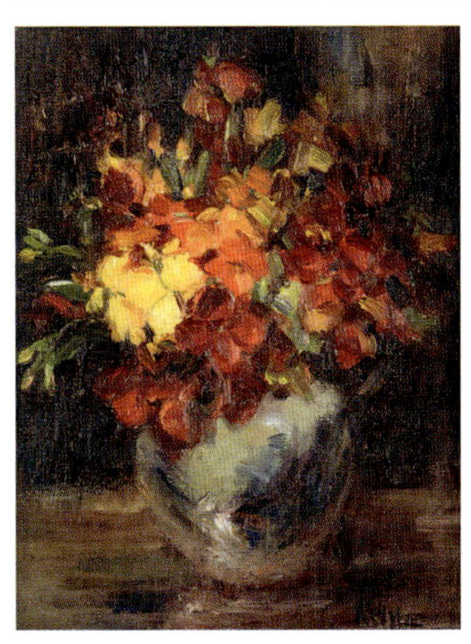

Wylie, Kate 1877–1941
Wallflower
oil on canvas 30.5 x 24.1
2880

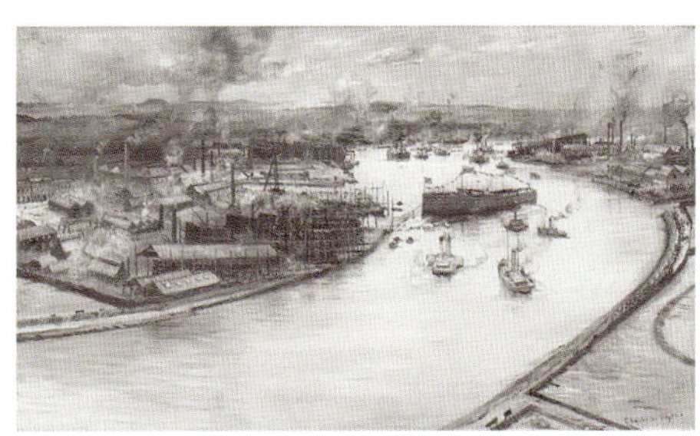

Wyllie, Charles William 1853–1923
The Launch of HMS 'Indomitable', Fairfield
1907
oil on canvas 40.6 x 66
T.1959.3.a

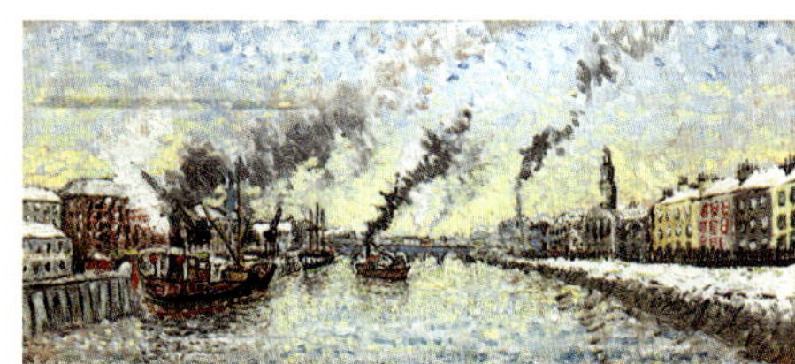

Wyllie, Robin H. active 20th C
The Clyde at Carlton Place
oil on board 35 x 76.1
3071

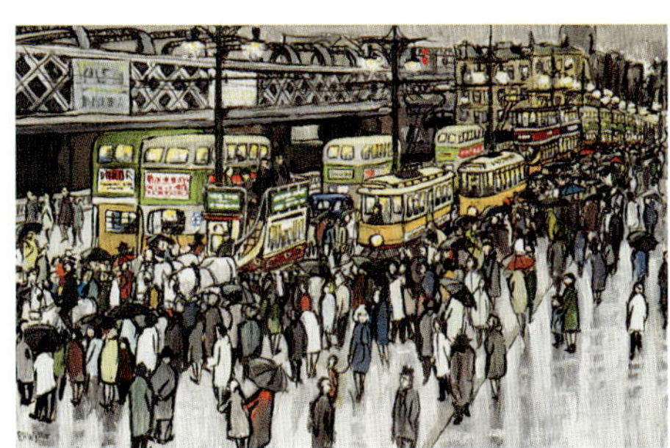

Wyllie, Robin H. active 20th C
The Last Tram Procession
oil on board 64.5 x 89
TEMP.2709

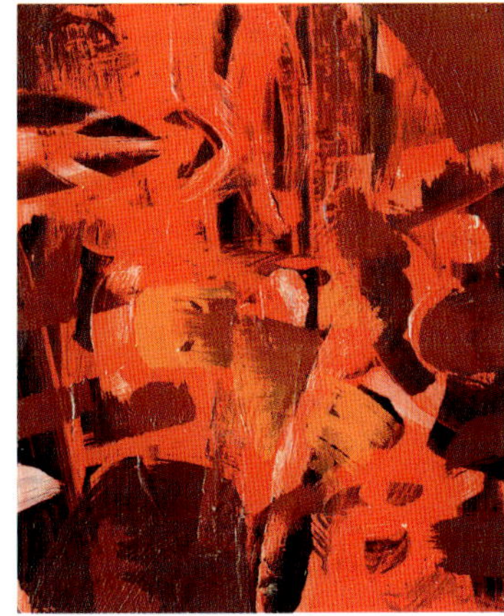

Wynter, Bryan 1915–1975
Small Red 1961
oil on board 18.1 x 14.6
3459

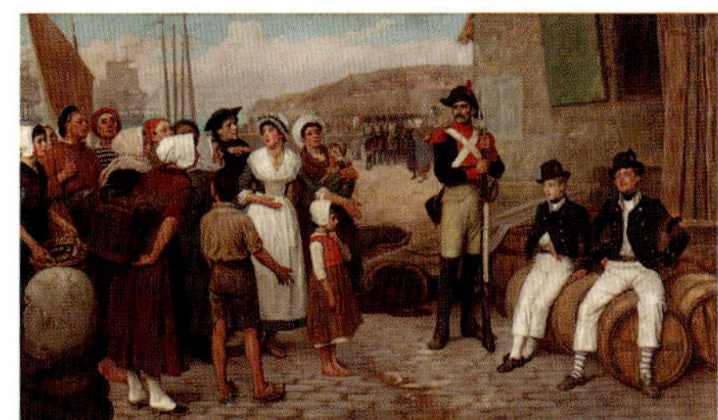

Yeames, William Frederick 1835–1918
Prisoners of War 1885
oil on canvas 152.4 x 256.5
1092

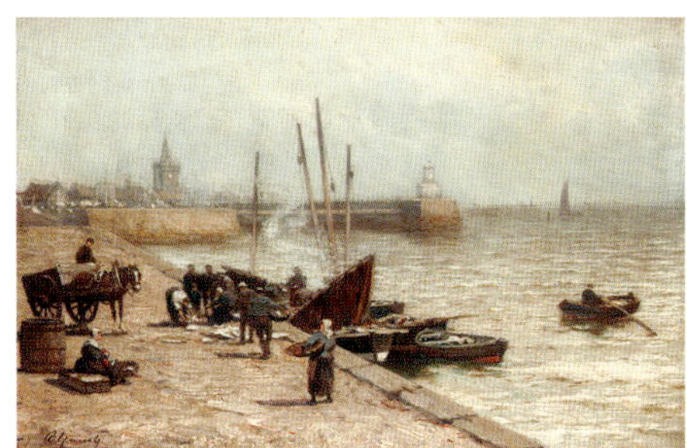

Young, A. active 19th C
Fishing Village
oil on canvas 36.8 x 62.2
1512

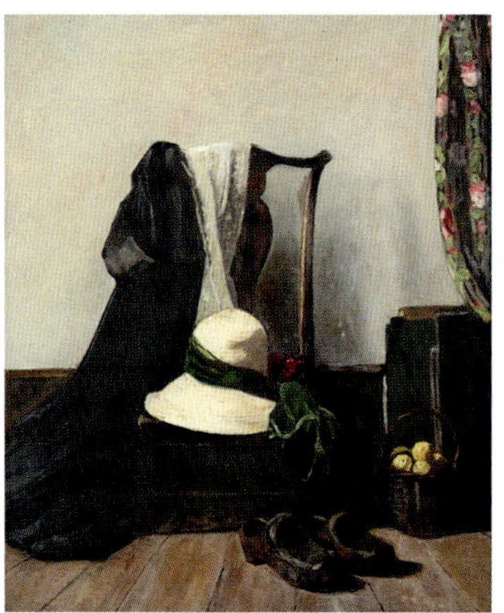

Young, Bessie Innes 1855–1936
The Garden Hat 1927
oil on canvas 55.9 x 45.7
2073

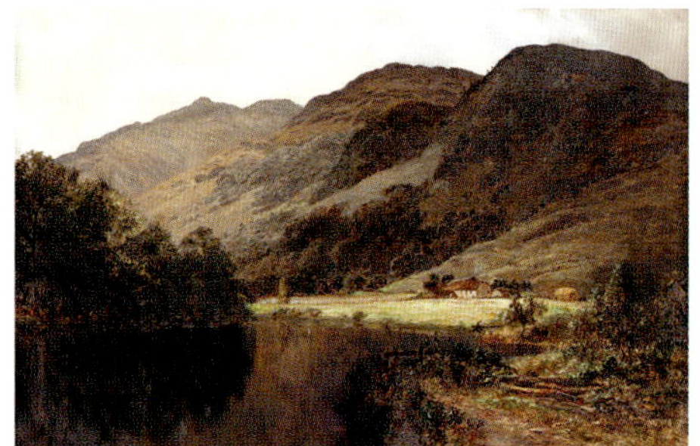

Young, William 1845–1916
Glen Falloch c.1905
oil on canvas 61 x 91.4
1105

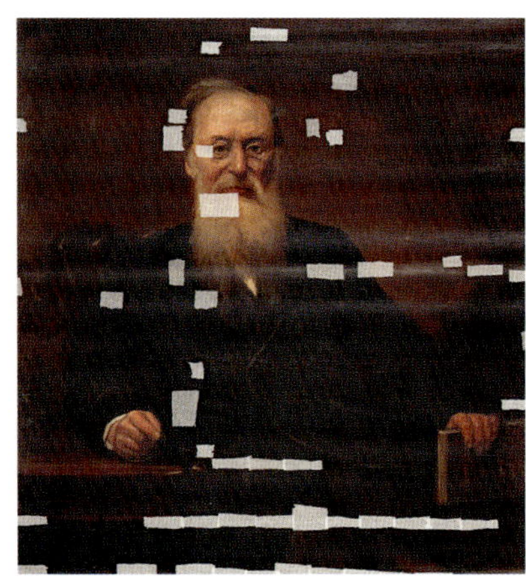

Young, William Drummond 1855–1924
A. D. Muir
oil on canvas 125.7 x 101.6
NR.118

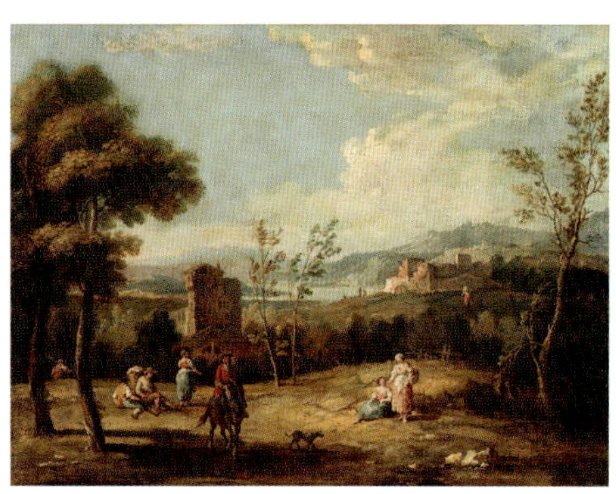

Zais, Giuseppe 1709–1781
Landscape with a Horseman and Peasants
oil on canvas 61.9 x 78.1
404

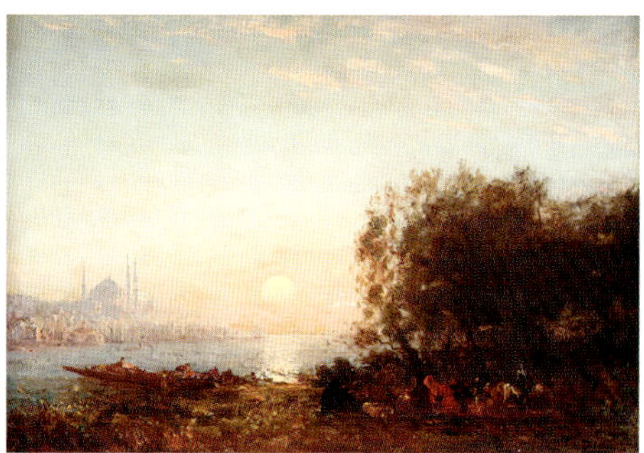

**Ziem, Félix François Georges
Philibert** 1821–1911
Constantinople, Sunset c.1870–1890
oil on panel 53.8 x 76.5
2143

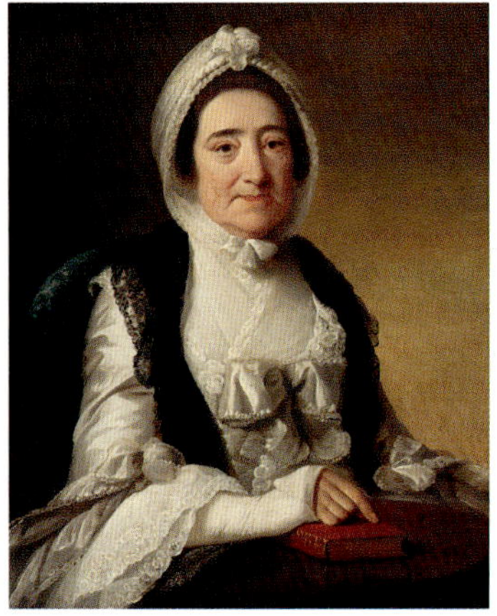

Zoffany, Johann 1733–1810
Mrs Maintrew
oil on canvas 76.1 x 63
3069

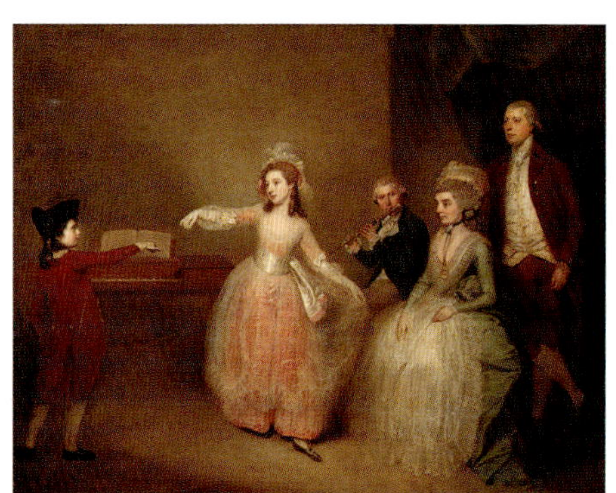

Zoffany, Johann (circle of) 1733–1810
A Family Party: The Minuet c.1780–1783
oil on canvas 99.1 x 124.5
247

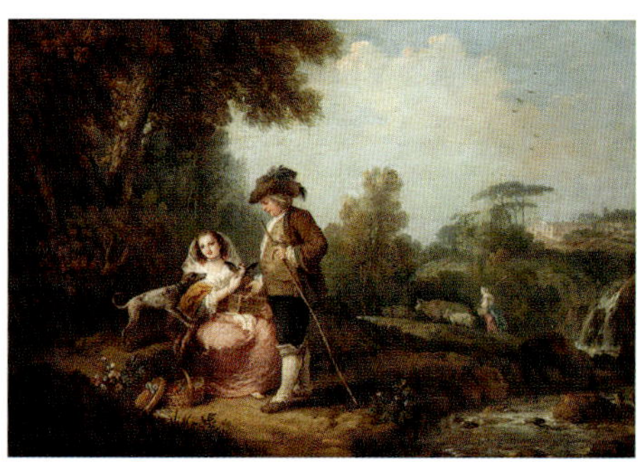

Zuccarelli, Franco 1702–1788
*A Pastoral Landscape with Figures by a
Stream* c.1725–1750
oil on canvas 34 x 46.2
149

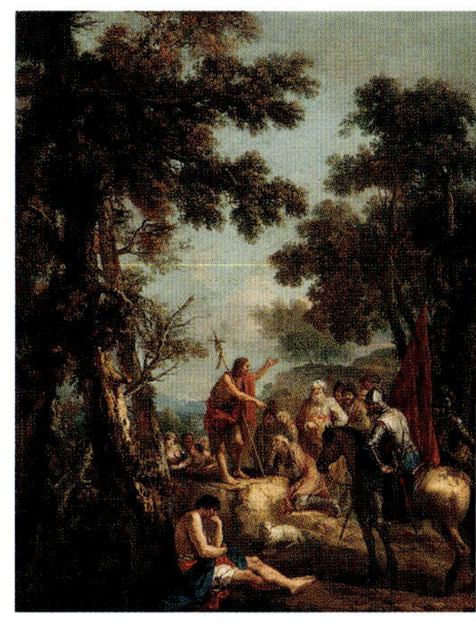

Zuccarelli, Franco 1702–1788
Saint John the Baptist Preaching c.1735–1745
oil on canvas 67.1 x 51.4
166

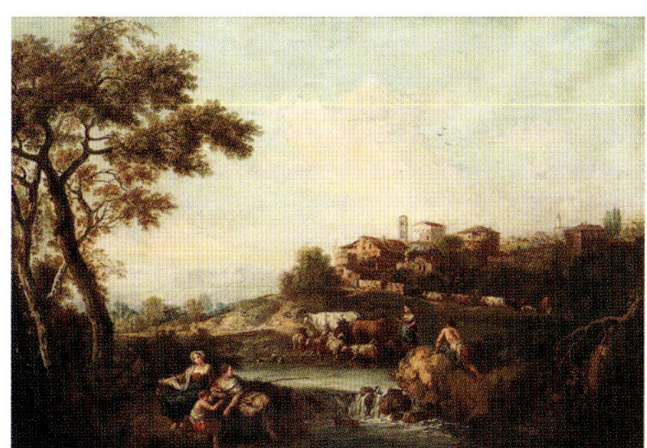

Zuccarelli, Franco 1702–1788
A Watering Place near a Village
oil on canvas 54.6 x 77.7
632

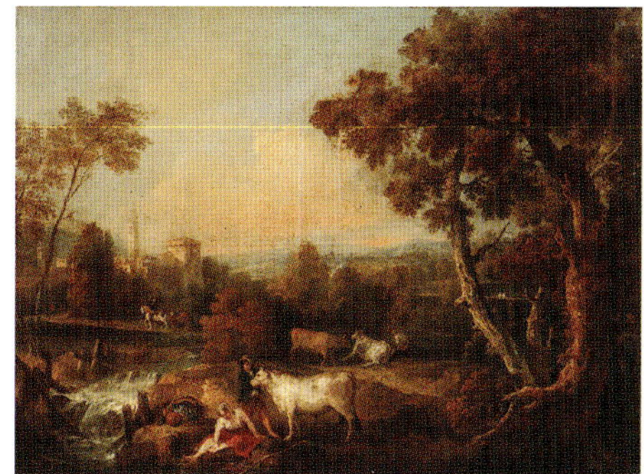

Zuccarelli, Franco 1702–1788
Pastoral Landscape
oil on canvas 57.8 x 78
631

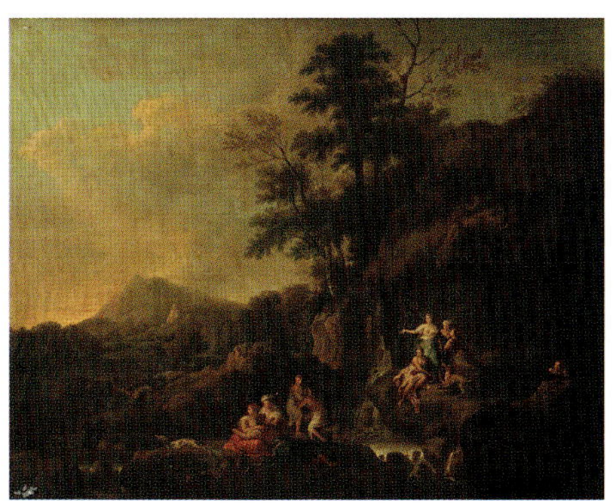

Zuccarelli, Franco (after) 1702–1788
Landscape with Diana and Actaeon
late 18th C
oil on canvas 100.6 x 126
148

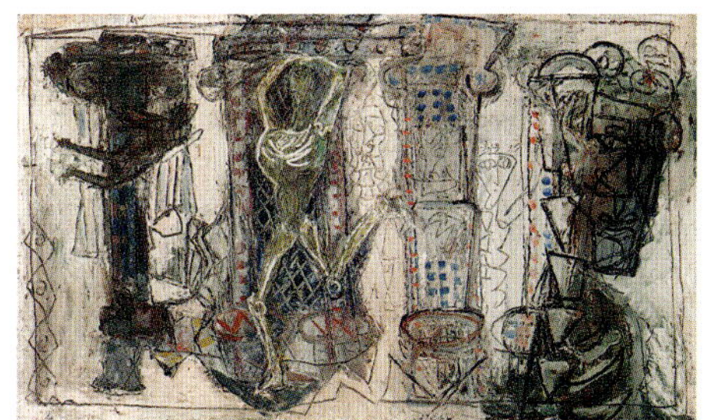

Żyw, Aleksander 1905–1995
The Stage c.1950
oil on canvas 74.5 x 125.5
3625

Paintings Without Reproductions

This section lists all the paintings that have not been included in the main pages of the catalogue. They were excluded as it was not possible to photograph them for this project. Additional information relating to acquisition credit lines or loan details is also included. For this reason the information below is not repeated in the Further Information section.

Glasgow Museums

Alexander, David *George Square, Glasgow* (after Joseph Swan), c.1832, 37.5 x 46.4, oil on canvas, OG.1960.4, not available at the time of photography

Armstrong, James active 1932–1933, *William Carstares Dunlop*, 1932, 73.7 x 55.2, oil on canvas, OG.1961.10.q, gift from John G. Dunlop and the Mercantile Bank, 1961, not available at the time of photography

Bain, Donald 1904–1979, *La baou Saint-Jeannet, Nice*, 1997.72.1, gift from the Scottish Arts Council, 1997, not available at the time of photography

Bain, Donald 1904–1979, *Petite place, Paris*, 1997.72.2, gift from the Scottish Arts Council, 1997, not available at the time of photography

Bain, Donald 1904–1979, *Quayside*, 1997.72.3, gift from the Scottish Arts Council, 1997, not available at the time of photography

Bloemen, Jan Frans van 1662–1749, *Landscape with a Figure*, 41.9 x 20.3, oil on canvas, 918, gift from T. Graham Young, in memory of his father, James Young, 1900, not available at the time of photography

Bloemen, Jan Frans van 1662–1749, *Landscape with a Figure*, 41.9 x 20.3, oil on canvas, 919, gift from T. Graham Young, in memory of his father, James Young, 1900, not available at the time of photography

Brough, Robert 1872–1905, *Edie, Daughter of O. H. Edinger*, 134.6 x 123.2, oil on canvas, 2285, gift from Mrs Geoffrey E. Howard, 1942, not available at the time of photography

Carmichael, John Wilson 1800–1868, *Sea Piece*, oil on canvas, 379, bequeathed by William Euing, 1874, not available at the time of photography

Carrick, John 1819–1890, *Trongate*, oil, OG.1951.409.oj, not available at the time of photography

Docharty, James 1829–1878, *Cathcart from Langside*, 1873, 22.2 x 35.6, oil on canvas, 2539, purchased, 1945, not available at the time of photography

Dolci, Carlo (after) 1616–1686, *The Saviour*, 19th C, 27.9 x 20.3, oil on canvas, 316, bequeathed by Mrs Cecilia Douglas, 1862, not available at the time of photography

Donaldson, Andrew 1790–1846, *View of Trongate, East Corner of Stockwell Street*, 1831, oil, 1906.53, purchased, 1906, not available at the time of photography

Fraser, Alexander *Crewel Gardens*, 1940, 99 x 132, oil on paper, PR.2007.2.40, gift from the BBC Collection, 2008, not available at the time of photography

Graham-Gilbert, John 1794–1866, *John Wilson of Dundyvan (1789–1851)*, 1842, 238.8 x 147.3, oil on canvas, 640, gift from George James Wilson, 1879, not available at the time of photography

Graham-Gilbert, John 1794–1866, *Christ Bearing His Cross*, 25.4 x 35.6, oil on panel, 537, bequeathed by Jane Graham-Gilbert, 1877, not available at the time of photography

Graham-Gilbert, John 1794–1866, *Dr Richardson* (after Henry Raeburn), 22.9 x 17.8, oil on panel, 549, bequeathed by Jane Graham-Gilbert, 1877, not available at the time of photography

Graham-Gilbert, John 1794–1866, *Head of an Old Woman with a Cap, Full Face*, 25.4 x 20.3, oil on panel, 524, bequeathed by Jane Graham-Gilbert, 1877, not available at the time of photography

Graham-Gilbert, John 1794–1866, *La penserosa*, 76.2 x 63.5, oil on canvas, 506, bequeathed by Jane Graham-Gilbert, 1877, not available at the time of photography

Graham-Gilbert, John 1794–1866, *Madonna and Child*, 61 x 22.9, oil on canvas, 533, bequeathed by Jane Graham-Gilbert, 1877, not available at the time of photography

Graham-Gilbert, John 1794–1866, *Madonna and Child* (after Correggio), 29.2 x 15.2, oil on canvas, 308, bequeathed by Mrs Cecilia Douglas, 1862, not available at the time of photography

Graham-Gilbert, John 1794–1866, *Portrait of a Lady*, 213.4 x 144.8, oil on canvas, 522, bequeathed by Jane Graham-Gilbert, 1877, not available at the time of photography

Graham-Gilbert, John 1794–1866, *Portrait of a Lady* (after Henry Raeburn), 58.4 x 48.3, oil on canvas, 550, bequeathed by Jane Graham-Gilbert, 1877, not available at the time of photography

Graham-Gilbert, John 1794–1866, *Portrait of a Lady* (after Joshua Reynolds), 22.2 x 16.5, oil on panel, 556, bequeathed by Jane Graham-Gilbert, 1877, not available at the time of photography

Graham-Gilbert, John 1794–1866, *Reverend Professor John Mitchell (1768–1844), DD*, 142.6 x 112.9, oil on canvas, PP.1978.121.10, acquired, 1978, not available at the time of photography

Graham-Gilbert, John 1794–1866, *Study of a Head* (after Rembrandt van Rijn), 14 x 10.2, oil on panel, 634, bequeathed by Jane Graham-Gilbert, 1877, not available at the time of photography

Graham-Gilbert, John 1794–1866, *The Age of Innocence* (after Joshua Reynolds), 20.3 x 17.1, oil on panel, 555, bequeathed by Jane Graham-Gilbert, 1877, not available at the time of photography

Graham-Gilbert, John 1794–1866, *The Banished Lord* (after Joshua Reynolds), 73.7 x 61, oil on canvas, 554, bequeathed by Jane Graham-Gilbert, 1877, not available at the time of photography

Graham-Gilbert, John 1794–1866, *The Orphan*, 76.2 x 63.5, oil on canvas, 518, bequeathed by Jane Graham-Gilbert, 1877, not available at the time of photography

Graham-Gilbert, John 1794–1866, *Tyrolese Mother*, 76.2 x 62.2, oil on canvas, 502, bequeathed by Jane Graham-Gilbert, 1877, not available at the time of photography

Graham-Gilbert, John (attributed to) 1794–1866, *Cain Slaying Abel*, 73.7 x 63.5, oil on canvas, 633, bequeathed by Jane Graham-Gilbert, 1877, not available at the time of photography

Green, Madeline 1884–1947, *The Model*, oil on canvas, 2121, purchased, 1938, not available at the time of photography

Harlow, George Henry 1787–1819, *Miss Catherine Stephens*, 21.6 x 13, oil on canvas, PC.112, Stirling Maxwell Collection, gift, 1967, not available at the time of photography

Henry, Sam *Mumford's Theatre, Greendyke Street*, 1905, 20.3 x 27.9, oil on millboard, OG.1963.17.b, acquired, 1963, not available at the time of photography

Henry, Sam *'Old Saracen's Head' Inn*, 1905, oil on millboard, OG.1963.17.c, acquired, 1963, not available at the time of photography

Henry, Sam *On the Molendinar*, 1905, oil on millboard, OG.1963.17.a, acquired, 1963, not available at the time of photography

Holland, James 1800–1870, *Grand Canal, Venice*, 30.4, oil on panel, 1138, bequeathed by James Donald, 1905, not available at the time of photography

Hunter, L. & Hunter, H. L. *Old Glasgow Bridge and Surroundings*, c.1830, oil, OG.1959.45, not available at the time of photography

Joets, Jules Arthur 1884–1959, *Military Officer*, 288, oil on canvas, TEMP.14962, not available at the time of photography

Linnell, John 1792–1882, *The Disobedient Prophet*, 259.1 x 198.1, oil on canvas, 1153, bequeathed by Mrs Isabella Elder, 1906, not available at the time of photography

Lucy, Charles 1814–1873, *Cromwell with His Family at Hampton Court*, 1863, 259.1 x 383.5, oil on canvas, 336, gift from William Graham, MP, 1870, not available at the time of photography

MacFarlane, Alasdair 1902–1960, *Millport Bay*, 50.8 x 76.2, oil on canvas, NR.128, not available at the time of photography

Maratti, Carlo 1625–1713, *Madonna and Child Attended by Angels*, oil, 147, Archibald McLellan Collection, purchased, 1856, not available at the time of photography

McDougall, William Brown 1868–1936, *The Ferry Bell, Creeksea, River Crouch*, 35.6 x 45.7, oil on canvas, 2052, gift from Mrs Agnes Watson, 1936, not available at the time of photography

McLaurin, Duncan 1848–1921, *Cattle by the Stream*, 1910, 34.3 x 49.5, oil on canvas, 1274, purchased, 1911, not available at the time of photography

McLellan, Malcolm *Oor Jamie*, 1953, 45.7 x 30.5, oil on canvas, OG.1959.50, not available at the time of photography

McTaggart, William 1835–1910, *Salmon Fishers, Carnoustie*, 1890, 19.1 x 27.9, oil on panel, 2410, bequeathed by William McInnes, 1944, not available at the time of photography

Michel, M. active 19th C, *Fruits of Mauritius*, oil, 1877.92.gy, gift from the Royal Gardens, Kew, 1877, not available at the time of photography

Panini, Giovanni Paolo c.1692–1765, *A Woody Landscape*, oil on canvas, 297, Archibald McLellan Collection, purchased, 1856, not available at the time of photography

Petherbridge *Untitled*, 74.3 x 107, acrylic on paper, TEMP.15447, not available at the time of photography

Ribera, Jusepe de (after) 1591–1652, *Head of a Male Saint with a Sword in His Hand*, 77.5 x 59.7, oil on canvas, NR.105, not available at the time of photography

Scott, R. active 19th C, *The Tail of the Bank*, oil, 1919.59, gift, 1919, not available at the time of photography

Smith, David *Broomielaw*, 1951.456.ch, not available at the time of photography

Spanish School *Madonna and Child Attended by Saints*, c.1855, 26.7 x 21.6, oil on copper, 283, Archibald McLellan Collection, purchased, 1856, not available at the time of photography

Tunigo active 20th C, *Zaire*, 100 x 80, acrylic on canvas, A.1991.6, purchased, 1991, not available at the time of photography

unknown artist *Glasgow Cathedral from the North*, 1810–1820, 30.5 x 41.9, oil on tin, PP.1976.46, gift, 1976, not available at the time of photography

unknown artist *The Clyde at Govan Ferry*, 1820–1830, 32.4 x 47, oil on canvas, PP.1977.126.1, gift, 1977, not available at the time of photography

unknown artist *The Kelvin at the Three-Tree Well*, c.1820–1840, oil, 1933.29, gift from Mrs Elizabeth McKirdy, 1933, not available at the time of photography

unknown artist *William McLean's Children*, c.1833, oil, OG.1965.4, acquired from Montgomerie Flemings Fyfe Maclean and Company, 1965, not available at the time of photography

unknown artist *Reverend Dr Robert Chrystal of Auchinleck*, c.1837, 127 x 101.6, oil on canvas, 2222, presented by the Trustees of William J. Chrystal, 1941, not available at the time of photography

unknown artist *John Beaumont Department (PNBR)*, 1867–1886, oil, T.1967.33.ai, gift from British Rail, London, 1967, not available at the time of photography

unknown artist *Portrait of an Old Glasgow Merchant*, c.1874, oil, 1874.23.1, gift, 1874, not available at the time of photography

unknown artist *Portrait of an Old Glasgow Merchant*, c.1874, oil, 1874.23.2, gift, 1874, not available at the time of photography

unknown artist *Portrait of an Old Glasgow Merchant*, c.1874, oil, 1874.23.3, gift, 1874, not available at the time of photography

unknown artist *Portrait of an Old Glasgow Merchant*, c.1874, oil, 1874.23.4, gift, 1874, not available at the time of photography

unknown artist *Portrait of an Old Glasgow Merchant*, c.1874, oil, 1874.23.5, gift, 1874, not available at the time of photography

unknown artist *Portrait of an Old Glasgow Merchant*, c.1874, oil, 1874.23.6, gift, 1874, not available at the time of photography

unknown artist *Dundee*, c.1877, oil, 1877.137.a, gift from John Napier, 1877, not available at the time of photography

unknown artist *Mango*, c.1877, oil, 1877.129.gl, gift from the Royal Gardens, Kew, 1877, not available at the time of photography

unknown artist *Mangosteen*, c.1877, oil, 1877.9.418, gift from the Royal Gardens, Kew, 1877, not available at the time of photography

unknown artist *Oranges*, c.1877, oil, 1877.9.417, gift from the Royal Gardens, Kew, 1877, not available at the time of photography

unknown artist *The Three-Tree Well on the Kelvin about 40 Years Ago*, c.1884, oil on canvas, 1924.44, not available at the time of photography

unknown artist *Colosseum*, 1887, oil on canvas, OG.1957.23, gift from Arthur Wilson, 1957, not available at the time of photography

unknown artist 19th C, *George Peebles*, 61 x 85.1, OG.1966.1.1, not available at the time of photography

unknown artist 19th C, *Sir George H. B. MacLeod (1828–1892)*, oil on canvas, OG.1962.31, acquired from the Royal Faculty of Physicians and Surgeons, 1962, not available at the time of photography

unknown artist 19th C, *Woodland Scene with Figures*, 23.5 x 29.2, oil on panel, 3053, purchased, 1956, not available at the time of photography

unknown artist *Glasgow Cathedral and Royal Infirmary*, c.1904, oil, 1904.234, presented by James Maclehose and Son, 1904, not available at the time of photography

unknown artist *William Davie*, c.1913, oil, 1913.41.duplicate.2, gift, 1913, not available at the time of photography

unknown artist *Caledonian Railway Locomotive No.729*, 1916, oil, T.2004.99, not available at the time of photography

unknown artist *St John*, c.1933, 1933.50, gift from Corporal Thomas Chalmers, 1933, not available at the time of photography

unknown artist *Mr Crawford in an Old Press Corps of Glasgow Uniform*, c.1949, oil, OG.1949.97, bequeathed by Miss Crawford, 1949, not available at the time of photography

unknown artist *Young Girl*, c.1949, 76.2 x 62.2, oil on canvas, NR.106, temporary identification number allocated, 1979, not available at the time of photography

unknown artist *Madonna and Child*, c.1976, PP.1976.90, gift, 1976, not available at the time of photography

unknown artist *Provand's Lordship*, c.1976, PP.1976.170, gift, 1976, not available at the time of photography

unknown artist *Barber's Shop, Drygate*, 46.5 x 59.7, oil on card, PL.1908.243, gift from the Provand's Lordship Society, 1978, not available at the time of photography

unknown artist *Caledonian Railway Locomotive No.769*, T.2004.101.1, not available at the time of photography

unknown artist *Composition with Three Men*, 52.4 x 55.2, oil on canvas, NR.57, temporary identification number allocated, 1979, not available at the time of photography

unknown artist *Courtship*, 66 x 58.4, oil on canvas (?), 679, not available at the time of photography

unknown artist *Fifty Scenes of Scotland*, oil on board, TEMP.1549, not available at the time of photography

unknown artist *Govan Parish Church from the South Side of the Clyde*, oil, OG.1960.49, gift from A. G. Duncan, 1960, not available at the time of photography

unknown artist *Indian Locomotive*, T.1965.6.1, gift, 1965, not available at the time of photography

unknown artist *Landscape*, 58.4 x 88.9, oil on canvas, NR.63, temporary identification number allocated, 1977, not available at the time of photography

unknown artist *Merchants' House and Briggait Kirk*, oil, OG.1955.52, gift from Mrs Mona Carfrae, 1955, not available at the time of photography

unknown artist *Mule-Drawn Trams*, OG.1954.136.4, purchased, 1954, not available at the time of photography

unknown artist *National Coalboard Locomotive*, T.1965.6.5, gift, 1965, not available at the time of photography

unknown artist *North British Locomotive No.231*, oil, T.1967.33.ae.10, gift from British Rail, London, 1967, not available at the time of photography

unknown artist *Portrait*, oil, PP.1985.222.2.2, gift from Barony Parish Church, 1985, not available at the time of photography

unknown artist *Portrait*, oil, T.1967.33.ag, gift from British Rail, London, 1967, not available at the time of photography

unknown artist *Portrait*, TEMP.1385, not available at the time of photography

unknown artist *Portrait of a Man*, 73.7 x 61, oil on canvas, 1091, not available at the time of photography

unknown artist *Queen Elizabeth I (1533–1603)*, oil, 1518.a, gift, 1921, not available at the time of photography

unknown artist *RMS 'Queen Elizabeth'*, oil, T.1973.10.ad, purchased with the assistance of the National Fund for Acquisitions, 1973, not available at the time of photography

unknown artist *Rutherglen Bridge*, oil, OG.1957.8.2, gift from Dr W. H. Findlay, 1957, not available at the time of photography

unknown artist *South African Railway Locomotive*, T.1965.6.2, gift, 1965, not available at the time of photography

unknown artist *Steamship*, oil, T.1940.20.1, gift from Bruce Murray, 1940, not available at the time of photography

unknown artist *Steamship*, oil, T.1940.20.2, gift from Bruce Murray, 1940, not available at the time of photography

unknown artist *The Clyde at Pointhouse Ferry*, oil, T.1927.18, gift from James Wotherspoon, 1927, not available at the time of photography

Vickers, Alfred 1786–1868, *River Scene, with Cattle and a Figure*, 17.8 x 34.3, oil on panel, 778, bequeathed by Adam Teacher, 1898, not available at the time of photography

Vrancx, Sebastian 1573–1647, *Landscape with Figures*, 11.4 x 17.1, oil on panel, 386, bequeathed by William Euing, 1874, not available at the time of photography

Vroom, Cornelis the younger c.1591–1661, *Trees by a Pool, with Cattle and a Figure*, 12.7 x 15.2, oil on panel, 610, bequeathed by Jane Graham-Gilbert, 1877, not available at the time of photography

Wallace, William 1801–1866, *Andrew Gemmill*, 1836, A.1936.37.a, gift from Miss Margaret Brown, 1936, not available at the time of photography

Ward, Robert active 19th C–20th C, *A Salmon Stream* (after James Docharty), 76.2 x 101.6, oil on canvas, NR.96, temporary identification number allocated, 1978, not available at the time of photography

West, Samuel c.1810–after 1881, *Angus Turner (1800–1876), Town Clerk of Glasgow (1857–1873)*, c.1873, 96.5 x 76.2, oil on canvas, 1778, bequeathed by Mrs Mary de Spofforth, 1929, not available at the time of photography

Wighton, William d.1875/1876, *Robert Burns (1759–1796)*, oil on canvas, 380, bequeathed by William Euing, 1874, not available at the time of photography

Wilson, John Glen 1774–1855, *Seascape, a Gale*, oil, 354, bequeathed by William Euing, 1874, not available at the time of photography

Wilson, Peter MacGregor 1855/1856–1928, *Burgomaster of Antwerp*, 1882, 45.7 x 35.6, oil on canvas, 1767, gift from J. Pasquoll, 1928, not available at the time of photography

STOLEN

Allan, Robert Weir 1852–1942, *On the Berwickshire Coast*, 1875, 44.5 x 59.7, oil on canvas, 865, bequeathed by Adam Teacher, 1898, stolen

Brown, Thomas Austen 1857–1924, *Lost and Found*, 1886, 35.6 x 25.4, oil on millboard, 1446, bequeathed by Mr and Mrs James Caldwell, 1918, stolen

**Gainsborough, Thomas
(attributed to)** 1727–1788,
*Landscape with Figures and
Animals*, 36 x 30.5, oil on canvas,
NR.15, temporary identification
number allocated, 1974, stolen

Hornel, Edward Atkinson
1864–1933, *Japanese Girls*, 1894, 61
x 40.6, oil on canvas, 2390,
bequeathed by William McInnes,
1944, stolen

Lawson, John 1868–1909, *The
Storm*, c.1889–1909, 25.4 x 35.6, oil
on canvas, 1705, gift from Mrs M.
D. Lindsay in memory of Colonel
Barclay Shaw, 1927, stolen

McCulloch, Horatio 1805–1867,
Inchmurrin, Loch Lomond, 1849,
91.4 x 156.2, oil on canvas, 1000,
bequeathed by Mrs Janet Rodger,
1901, stolen

McCutcheon, John 1910–1995,
Flowers and Fruit, 1962, 51.7 x 36.2,
oil on paper on board, 3187,
purchased, 1963, stolen

Park, Stuart 1862–1933, *Red and
White Begonias*, c.1907, 61 x 50.8,
oil on canvas, 1202, purchased,
1907, stolen

unknown artist *Principal Story as a
Child*, 1840s, 24 x 16.5, oil on
canvas, NR.9, deposited during
World War II as part of the Dr
Helen Story Collection, stolen

unknown artist *Port Scene at
Night*, 33 x 42, oil on cardboard,
NR.25, temporary identification
number allocated, 1974, stolen

unknown artist *Village Scene with
a Church in the Background*, 38.1 x
46.4, oil on canvas, 2885, gift from
Jessie W. Craig, 1950, stolen

Weir, William d.1865, *William
Euing, Senior*, 74.9 x 61, oil on
canvas, 459, bequeathed by
William Euing, 1874, stolen

Further Information

The paintings listed in this section have additional information relating to one or more of the five categories outlined below. This extra information is only provided where it is applicable and where it exists. Paintings listed in this section follow the same order as in the illustrated pages of the catalogue.

I   The full name of the artist if this was too long to display in the illustrated pages of the catalogue. Such cases are marked in the catalogue with a (…).

II   The full title of the painting if this was too long to display in the illustrated pages of the catalogue. Such cases are marked in the catalogue with a (…).

III   Acquisition information or acquisition credit lines as well as information about loans, copied from the records of the owner collection.

IV   Artist copyright credit lines where the copyright owner has been traced. Exhaustive efforts have been made to locate the copyright owners of all the images included within this catalogue and to meet their requirements. Any omissions or mistakes brought to our attention will be duly attended to and corrected in future publications.

V   The credit line of the lender of the transparency if the transparency has been borrowed. Bridgeman images are available subject to any relevant copyright approvals from the Bridgeman Art Library at www.bridgemanart.com

All paintings with the word TEMP appearing before the identification number have lost their association with their original accession number and it is hoped through further research to reconcile these works, therefore a credit line is rarely provided.

As a result of the Data Protection Act, Glasgow Museums do not wish to name any donors since 1960.

Glasgow Museums

Aachen, Hans von 1552–1615, *The Holy Family with Angels*, Archibald McLellan Collection, purchased, 1856

Adam, Joseph 1819–1886, *Overlooking Glendaruel, Kyles of Bute*, bequeathed by Adam Teacher, 1898

Adam, Joseph 1819–1886 & **Roe, Robert Henry** 1822–1905 *Strathblane*, bequeathed by Adam Teacher, 1898

Adam, Joseph Denovan 1841–1896, *In Clover*, bequeathed by Adam Teacher, 1898

Adam, Joseph Denovan 1841–1896, *Balmoral, Autumn*, purchased from the Trustees of artist's estate, 1896

Adam, Joseph Denovan 1841–1896, *Calves in the Cabbage Patch*, purchased, 1949

Adam, Joseph Denovan 1841–1896, *December, near Callander*, presented by the family of William Murdoch, 1943

Adam, Patrick William 1854–1929, *Interior: The Signet Library, Edinburgh*, gift from Ossian Donner, 1918

Adler, Jankel 1895–1949, *Composition*, purchased, 1953, © DACS 2013

Aelst, Willem van 1627–after 1687, *Still Life: Herring, Cherries and Glassware*, bequeathed by Mrs Cecilia Douglas, 1862

Agar, Charles d' (attributed to) 1669–1723, *Portrait of a Boy*, gift from Sir William and Lady Burrell to the City of Glasgow, 1944

Ahrens, Carl 1864–1938, *The Glade*, found in store, registered, 1988

Aiken, John MacDonald 1880–1961, *The Seamstress*, purchased, 1940

Aiken, John P. 1919–1966, *Low Tide, Arbroath*, purchased, 1954

Aikman, William 1682–1731, *John Dalrymple (1673–1747), 2nd Earl of Stair or John Campbell (1680–1743), Duke of Argyll and Greenwich*, purchased, 1961

Aikman, William (attributed to) 1682–1731, *Lady Anne Maxwell (d.1720)*, on loan from a private collection

Aikman, William (attributed to) 1682–1731, *Sir John Maxwell (1686–1752), 2nd Bt*, on loan from a private collection

Aitchison, Craigie Ronald John 1926–2009, *Wayney Dead 2*, purchased with the assistance of the National Fund for Acquisitions, 1987, © the artist's estate/Bridgeman Art Library

Aitchison, Craigie Ronald John 1926–2009, *Crucifixion VII*, purchased with the assistance of the National Art Collections Fund and the National Fund for Acquisitions, 1991, © the artist's estate/Bridgeman Art Library

Aitken, Henry *Springburn Tram*

Aitken, James Alfred 1846–1897, *Ben Nevis: The First Snow*, found in store, registered, 1988

Albani, Francesco (after) 1578–1660, *Cupids at Play*, Archibald McLellan Collection, purchased, 1856

Albani, Francesco (studio of) 1578–1660, *Apollo and Daphne*, Archibald McLellan Collection, purchased, 1856

Aldi, Pietro 1852–1888, *A Painter and His Model*, bequeathed by John Charles McIntyre, 1939

Alexander, Ella Hean 1862–1951, *Reverend Dr George Reith (b.1842)*, presented by Mrs R. M. Leishman on behalf of her mother, Dowager Lady Reith, 1972

Alexander, Robert L. 1840–1923, *Head of a Goat*, purchased, 1924

Alfaro y Gámez, Juan de 1643–1688, *Diego Velázquez (1599–1660)*, Stirling Maxwell Collection, gift, 1967

Algie, Jessie 1859–1927, *Rambler Roses*, bequeathed by Jessie W. Craig, 1950

Alison, Henry Young 1889–1972, *Youth*, gift from Sir John Richmond, 1936

Allan, Andrew 1863–1942, *Thistledown*, presented by the artist's widow, 1943

Allan, Archibald Russell Watson 1878–1959, *The Top of the Hill*, purchased, 1924

Allan, Archibald Russell Watson 1878–1959, *Harvest Time*, bequeathed by Miss M. A. W. Thomson, 1947

Allan, David 1744–1796, *The Vestals Attending the Sacred Fire*, purchased with the assistance of the National Fund for Acquisitions, 1985

Allan, David 1744–1796, *Jean Duff (1746–1805), Lady Grant*, purchased, 1940

Allan, Mary Parsons Reid 1917–2002, *Still Life with Fish*, purchased, 1955

Allan, Mary Parsons Reid 1917–2002, *Still Life with Flowers and 'Renoir' Book*, gift from the Park and Laurel Bank Schools Collection (incorporating Laurel Park School), 2006

Allan, Robert Weir 1852–1942, *Doorway and Figures*, bequeathed by Adam Teacher, 1898

Allan, Robert Weir 1852–1942, *Home from the Herring Fishing*, bequeathed by Adam Teacher, 1898

Allan, Robert Weir 1852–1942, *Crail Harbour*, gift from James Carfrae Alston, 1909

Allan, Robert Weir 1852–1942, *The Funeral of Thomas Carlyle*, gift from the artist, 1911

Allan, Robert Weir 1852–1942, *Sheltered from the Stormy Sea*, purchased, 1904

Allan, Robert Weir 1852–1942, *Paris, River Scene*, temporary identification number allocated, 1979

Allan, Robert Weir 1852–1942, *Bathing Scene*, temporary identification number allocated, 1979

Allan, Robert Weir 1852–1942, *Home with a Good Fishing*, temporary identification number allocated, 1979

Allan, Robert Weir 1852–1942, *In from the Sea*, bequeathed by the artist, 1942

Allan, Robert Weir 1852–1942, *Near Athens*, on loan from a private collection

Allan, Robert Weir 1852–1942, *North-Easter Gale*, bequeathed by the artist, 1942

Allan, Robert Weir 1852–1942, *Sea Piece*, bequeathed by the artist, 1942

Allan, Robert Weir 1852–1942, *Seascape, Fishing Boats Returning*, temporary identification number allocated, 1979

Allan, William 1782–1850, *The Bride of Abydos* (from the poem by Byron), Archibald McLellan Collection, purchased, 1856

Allan, William 1782–1850, *Heroism and Humanity*, gift from William S. Steel, 1909

Allori, Alessandro (attributed to) 1535–1607, *Saint John the Baptist*, bequeathed by Sir Claude Phillips, 1924

Alma-Tadema, Lawrence 1836–1912, *A Lover of Art*, presented by the sons of James Reid of Auchterarder, 1896

Amberger, Christoph c.1505–1561/1562, *Portrait of a Lady*, Archibald McLellan Collection, purchased, 1856

Ancill, Joseph 1896–c.1976, *James Welsh, Lord Provost of Glasgow (1943–1945)*, gift from the sitter, 1947

Anderson, Charles *The Barras, Glasgow*, gift, 1986

Anderson, James Bell 1886–1938, *Sir Daniel Macaulay Stevenson (1851–1944), Lord Provost of Glasgow (1911–1914)*, purchased, 1914

Anderson, James Bell 1886–1938, *Miss Muriel Sterling*, gift from the Park and Laurel Bank Schools Collection (incorporating Laurel Park School), 2006

Anderson, James Bell 1886–1938, *Former Bailie James Steele*, purchased, 1928

Anderson, James Bell 1886–1938, *Still Life*, purchased, 1933

Anderson, James Bell 1886–1938, *Still Life*, bequeathed by Miss M. A. W. Thomson, 1947

André, Edmond 1837–1877, *Awaiting Orders*, bequeathed by Adam Teacher, 1898

Andreotti, Federico 1847–1930, *The Violin Teacher*, presented by Miss M. Garroway, 1947

Andrews, Henry 1794–1868, *The Pet Dove*, bequeathed by William Euing, 1874

Andrews, Henry 1794–1868, *The Toilet*, bequeathed by William Euing, 1874

Anesi, Paolo 1697–1773, *View of Ariccia*, Archibald McLellan Collection, purchased, 1856

Angermann, Peter b.1945, *Baggersee*, purchased from the artist, 1995, © DACS 2013

Anglo/Flemish School 17th C, *George Villiers (1592–1628), 1st Duke of Buckingham* (after Peter Paul Rubens), Stirling Maxwell Collection, gift, 1967

Angus, A. M. active 19th C, *Landscape and Cattle*, presented by Miss Russell, 1948

Ankarcrona, Alexis 1825–1901, *Woody Landscape*, presented by the Trustees of the estate of Sir Daniel M. Stevenson, 1945

Annand, Louise Gibson b.1915, *Border Landscape*, purchased, 1943

Apshoven, Thomas van (attributed to) 1622–1664, *A Village Festival*, Archibald McLellan Collection, purchased, 1856

Archer, James 1822–1904, *Classical Subject*, bequeathed by Adam Teacher, 1898

Archer, James 1822–1904, *John Francis Ure (1820–1883)*, bequeathed by Mrs Isabella Elder, 1906

Armfield, George 1810–1893, *Dogs*, bequeathed by William Euing, 1874

Armitage, Edward 1817–1896, *The Christian Martyr*, bequeathed by Adam Teacher, 1898

Armitage, Edward 1817–1896, *Hero*, bequeathed by Mrs Isabella Elder, 1906

Armour, George Denholm 1864–1949, *Two Huntsmen on Horseback, One Blowing a Horn*, purchased, 1964

Armour, Mary 1902–2000, *Rhum from Skye*, gift, 1966, © the artist's estate/Bridgeman Art Library

Armour, Mary 1902–2000, *Still Life (Lustre Jug)*, purchased, 1942, © the artist's estate/Bridgeman Art Library

Armour, Mary 1902–2000, *Ben Ledi*, purchased, 1948, © the artist's estate/Bridgeman Art Library

Armour, Mary 1902–2000, *The Clyde from Corrie, Arran*, purchased, 1964, © Culture and Sport Glasgow (Glasgow Museums)

Armour, Mary 1902–2000, *Green Dish with Melon*, purchased, 1973, © Culture and Sport Glasgow (Glasgow Museums)

Armour, William 1903–1979, *Still Life with Gourd*, purchased, 1958, © with permission of the artist's estate

Armstrong, Anthony b.1935, *Preparing for the Rally*, gift from RAC Scotland, 1990, © the artist

Armstrong, James active 1932–1933, *Portrait of a Man*

Armstrong, John 1893–1973, *Spring and Winter*, purchased with the assistance of the Contemporary Art Society, 1956, © the artist's estate/Bridgeman Art Library

Armstrong, William active 1887–1896, *Provand's Lordship*, gift from the Provand's Lordship Society, 1978

Arthois, Jacques d' 1613–1686, *A Wooded Landscape*, bequeathed by Mrs Isabella Elder, 1906

Arthois, Jacques d' 1613–1686, *Peasants at the Edge of a Forest*, Archibald McLellan Collection, purchased, 1856

Arthur, G. G. *City Chambers Staircase*, gift from Miss R. Arthur, 1954

Artz, David Adolph Constant 1837–1890, *Coming from Church*, bequeathed by George Robb, 1909

Asch, Pieter Jansz. van 1603–1678, *A Hawking Party at the Edge of a Forest*, Archibald McLellan Collection, purchased, 1856

Asselyn, Jan (attributed to) after 1610–1652, *Mountain Landscape with a Castle*, Archibald McLellan Collection, purchased, 1856

Backer, Jacques de 1540/1545–before 1600, *Charity*, Archibald McLellan Collection, purchased, 1856

Backhuysen, Ludolf I (attributed to) 1630–1708, *A Dutch Ship Clawing off a High Coast in a Gale*, Archibald McLellan Collection, purchased, 1856

Backhuysen, Ludolf I (imitator of) 1630–1708, *A Dutch Flagship and Other Vessels Running before a Gale*, Archibald McLellan Collection, purchased, 1856

Backhuysen, Ludolf I (imitator of) 1630–1708, *A Dutch States Yacht Beating to Windward off the Coast, and Other Vessels*, Archibald McLellan Collection, purchased, 1856, photo credit: Glasgow Museums

Backhuysen, Ludolf I (style of) 1630–1708, *Fishing Boats off the Coast in a Gale*, bequeathed by Jane Graham-Gilbert, 1877

Baillie, Charles Cameron 1901–1960, *Self Portrait*, purchased, 1981

Baillie, Martin b.1920, *Painter Drawing from the Model*, gift from the BBC Collection, 2008

Bain, Donald 1904–1979, *Flower Piece*, purchased, 1944

Bain, Donald 1904–1979, *Old Tweed Mill*, purchased from the artist, 1949

Baird, Edward 1904–1949, *Unidentified Aircraft (over Montrose)*, purchased, 1943, © the artist's estate

Baird, Margaret 1891–1979, *School Days*, purchased, 1995

Baird, Margaret 1891–1979, *Sheep Dipping*, purchased, 1995

Baird, Margaret 1891–1979, *Doubles*, purchased, 1995

Baker, Thomas 1809–1869, *Landscape and Cattle*, Archibald McLellan Collection, purchased, 1856

Baldan, Giuseppe active 20th C, *La Faruk Madonna (triptych, left wing)*, gift, 1995

Baldan, Giuseppe active 20th C, *La Faruk Madonna (triptych, centre panel)*, gift, 1995

Baldan, Giuseppe active 20th C, *La Faruk Madonna (triptych, right wing)*, gift, 1995

Balen, Hendrik van I 1575–1632, *Justice and Peace*, Archibald McLellan Collection, purchased, 1856

Balen, Hendrik van I 1575–1632, *A Bacchic Procession*, Archibald McLellan Collection, purchased, 1856

Balen, Hendrik van I 1575–1632, *The Adoration of the Shepherds*, Archibald McLellan Collection, purchased, 1856

Balen, Hendrick van I 1575–1632 & **Brueghel, Jan the younger** 1601–1678 *An Allegory of Abundance*, Archibald McLellan Collection, purchased, 1856

Balen, Jan van (attributed to) c.1611–1654, *The Marriage Feast of Peleus and Thetis*, Archibald McLellan Collection, purchased, 1856

Balestra, Antonio 1666–1740, *Justice and Peace Embracing*, Archibald McLellan Collection, purchased, 1856

Balmer, Barbara b.1929, *Sleeping Fairground*, purchased with the assistance of the National Fund for Acquisitions, 1982, © Culture and Sport Glasgow (Glasgow Museums)

Banks, John 1883–1945, *Fuji San*, gift from the artist in memory of his mother, 1938

Banks, Lesley b.1962, *Leaving*, gift from the BBC Collection, 2008, © the artist

Banks, Lesley b.1962, *The 39th Week – Counting*, purchased, 1995, © the artist

Banner, Delmar Harmond 1896–1983, *On Top of Goatfell, Arran*, gift from the artist, 1948, © the artist's estate

Barber, Joseph Vincent 1788–1838, *Landscape: The Golden Age*, Archibald McLellan Collection, purchased, 1856

Barber, Joseph Vincent 1788–1838, *Landscape with Cattle*, Archibald McLellan Collection, purchased, 1856

Barber, Joseph Vincent 1788–1838, *Landscape with Cattle*, Archibald McLellan Collection, purchased, 1856

Bargue, Charles 1826–1883, *Lady at a Table*, gift from Sir William and Lady Burrell to the City of Glasgow, 1944

Barnes, Mary 1923–2001, *Feeding the Five Thousand*, purchased, 1998

Barnes, Mary 1923–2001, *The Transfiguration*, purchased, 1998

Barnes, Mary 1923–2001, *Crucifixion*, purchased, 1998

Barnes, Mary 1923–2001, *Our Lady*, purchased, 1998

Barnes, Mary 1923–2001, *Tunnel*, purchased, 1998

Barnes, Mary 1923–2001, *Willow*, purchased, 1998

Barnes, Mary 1923–2001, *Heavy Snowfall*, purchased, 1998

Barnes, Mary 1923–2001, *Dancers of the Dunes*

Barns-Graham, Wilhelmina 1912–2004, *November (Collage 179)*, gift, 1988, © by courtesy of the Barns-Graham Charitable Trust

Barnston, J. *Old Lambhill Bridge, Glasgow*, gift, 1972

Barocci, Federico (after) 1535–1612, *The Infant Saviour*, Archibald McLellan Collection, purchased, 1856

Barrie, Mardi 1931–2004, *Across a Dark Wood*, purchased, 1963

Bartolomeo Veneto c.1480–1531, *Saint Catherine*, Archibald McLellan Collection, purchased, 1856

Bassano, Francesco II (after) 1549–1592, *Spring*, Archibald McLellan Collection, purchased, 1856

Bassano, Francesco II (after) 1549–1592, *Summer*, Archibald McLellan Collection, purchased, 1856

Bassano, Francesco II (after) 1549–1592, *Autumn*, Archibald McLellan Collection, purchased, 1856

Bassano, Francesco II (after) 1549–1592, *Winter*, Archibald McLellan Collection, purchased, 1856

Bassano, Jacopo the elder (after) c.1510–1592, *The Adoration of the Magi*

Bassen, Bartholomeus van c.1590–1652, *An Imaginary Church Interior*, Archibald McLellan Collection, purchased, 1856

Bastien-Lepage, Jules 1848–1884, *Poor Fauvette*, purchased, 1913

Bateman, Anthony Robert b.1942, *Gloucester Central*, purchased, 1963, © the artist

Batoni, Pompeo (studio of) 1708–1787, *Virgin Annunciate*, gift from T. Graham Young in memory of his father, James Young, 1900

Baynes, Keith 1887–1977, *Quai des Chartrons, Bordeaux*, purchased, 1950

Bear, George Telfer 1876–1973, *Figures in a Landscape*, temporary identification number allocated, 1979

Bear, George Telfer 1876–1973, *La jeunesse*, purchased, 1940

Bear, George Telfer 1876–1973, *Rhododendron and Icelandic Poppies*, gift from an anonymous donor, 1947

Beattie-Brown, William 1831–1909, *Lochranza Castle*, gift from Miss Russell, 1927

Beattie-Brown, William 1831–1909, *A Mountain Burn, Glen Shieldaig, Ross-shire*, gift from Helen Walker, 1933

Beaubrun, Charles 1604–1692, *Maria Theresa of Spain (1638–1683)*, Stirling Maxwell Collection, gift, 1967

Beaumont, Claudio Francesco (attributed to) 1694–1766, *Moses and the Daughters of Jethro*, Archibald McLellan Collection, purchased, 1856

Beaumont, Hugues de 1874–1947, *Still Life*, bequeathed by William McInnes, 1944

Beavis, Richard 1824–1896, *The Midnight Ride of Deloraine*, bequeathed by Adam Teacher, 1898

Beavis, Richard 1824–1896, *Castle Campbell, near Dollar*, presented by Andrew Lusk, Windsor, 1941

Beechey, William 1753–1839, *Margaret Stirling of Ardoch (c.1754–c.1825)*, on loan from James Everett McDonald Stuart-Stevenson

Begg, Nita b.1920, *Exotic Plant*, purchased, 1968, © the artist

Bonvin, François 1817–1887, *Still Life with a Jug, Cheese, Onions, Fish and a Knife*, gift from Sir William and Lady Burrell to the City of Glasgow, 1944

Bonvin, François 1817–1887, *Woman at a Spinet*, gift from Sir William and Lady Burrell to the City of Glasgow, 1944

Bonvin, François 1817–1887, *'Miss'*, gift from Sir William and Lady Burrell to the City of Glasgow, 1944

Bonvin, François 1817–1887, *Still Life with Game*, gift from William Burrell, 1925

Bonvin, François 1817–1887, *Still Life with a Book and an Ink Well*, gift from William Burrell, 1925

Bonvin, François 1817–1887, *Still Life with Apples and a Silver Goblet*, bequeathed by William McInnes, 1944

Bonvin, François 1817–1887, *Still Life with Oysters, a Wine Bottle and a Glass of Wine*, gift from Sir William and Lady Burrell to the City of Glasgow, 1944

Bonvin, François 1817–1887, *Still Life with a Copper Pot*, gift from Sir William and Lady Burrell to the City of Glasgow, 1944

Bonvin, François 1817–1887, *Oysters*, gift from Sir William and Lady Burrell to the City of Glasgow, 1944

Bonvin, François 1817–1887, *Still Life with a Glass, Pears and a Knife*, gift from Sir William and Lady Burrell to the City of Glasgow, 1944

Bonvin, François 1817–1887, *Still Life with a Tobacco Pot and a Pipe*, gift from Sir William and Lady Burrell to the City of Glasgow, 1944

Bonvin, François 1817–1887, *Still Life with Vegetables and Cooking Utensils*, gift from Sir William and Lady Burrell to the City of Glasgow, 1944

Bonvin, François 1817–1887, *The Violin*, gift from William Burrell, 1925

Boonen, Arnold (attributed to) 1669–1729, *A Woman in Bed Extinguishing a Candle*, Archibald McLellan Collection, purchased, 1856

Bordon, Paris 1500–1571, *Virgin Mary and Child with Saints Jerome and Anthony Abbot and a Donor*, bequeathed by Jane Graham-Gilbert, 1877

Bordon, Paris 1500–1571, *Virgin and Child with Saints John the Baptist, Mary Magdalene and George (?)*, Archibald McLellan Collection, purchased, 1856

Bordon, Paris (after) 1500–1571, *The Mystic Marriage of Saint Catherine*, found in store, registered, 1988

Borthwick, Alfred Edward 1871–1955, *Edward, Prince of Wales (1894–1972), in Highland Costume*, presented by the artist's widow, 1957

Borthwick, Alfred Edward 1871–1955, *Lady Fairfax-Lucy (1866–1943)*, presented by the artist's widow, 1957

Borthwick, Alfred Edward 1871–1955, *Sir Ernest C. MacMillan (1893–1973)*, presented by the artist's widow, 1957

Bosch, Hieronymus (imitator of) c.1450–1516, *Christ Driving the Money-Lenders from the Temple*, bequeathed by Sir Claude Phillips, 1924

Both, Jan (school of) c.1618–1652, *A Mountain Landscape with a River Valley*, bequeathed by Adam Birkmyre, 1906

Both, Jan (style of) c.1618–1652, *Evening Landscape*, on loan from a private collection

Botticelli, Sandro (and studio) 1444/1445–1510, *The Annunciation*, Archibald McLellan Collection, purchased, 1856

Botticelli, Sandro (school of) 1444/1445–1510, *Virgin and Child*, gift from Sir William and Lady Burrell to the City of Glasgow, 1944

Boucher, François (after) 1703–1770, *Amintas Revived by Sylvia*, gift from George Campbell, 1952

Boucher, François (after) 1703–1770, *Sylvia Saved by Amintas*, gift from George Campbell, 1952

Boudin, Eugène Louis 1824–1898, *The Beach at Trouville, the Empress Eugénie*, gift from Sir William and Lady Burrell to the City of Glasgow, 1944

Boudin, Eugène Louis 1824–1898, *The Jetty at Trouville*, gift from Sir William and Lady Burrell to the City of Glasgow, 1944

Boudin, Eugène Louis 1824–1898, *A Dutch Canal*, gift from Sir William and Lady Burrell to the City of Glasgow, 1944

Boudin, Eugène Louis 1824–1898, *The Old Fish Market, Brussels*, gift from Sir William and Lady Burrell to the City of Glasgow, 1944

Boudin, Eugène Louis 1824–1898, *The Port of Portrieux at Low Tide*, gift from William Burrell, 1925

Boudin, Eugène Louis 1824–1898, *The Port of Deauville*, bequeathed by William McInnes, 1944

Boudin, Eugène Louis 1824–1898, *Washerwomen on the Banks of the River Touques*, gift from Sir William and Lady Burrell to the City of Glasgow, 1944

Boudin, Eugène Louis 1824–1898, *A Street in Dordrecht*, bequeathed by William McInnes, 1944

Boudin, Eugène Louis 1824–1898, *Large Sailing Ship in Port, Deauville*, gift from Sir William and Lady Burrell to the City of Glasgow, 1944

Boudin, Eugène Louis 1824–1898, *Trouville, the Jetties at Low Tide*, gift from Sir William and Lady Burrell to the City of Glasgow, 1944

Boudin, Eugène Louis 1824–1898, *Washerwomen on the Banks of the River Touques*, gift from Sir William and Lady Burrell to the City of Glasgow, 1944

Boudin, Eugène Louis 1824–1898, *A Street in Caudebec-en-Caux*, gift from William Burrell, 1925

Boudin, Eugène Louis 1824–1898, *Deauville, the Dock*, gift from Sir William and Lady Burrell to the City of Glasgow, 1944

Boudin, Eugène Louis 1824–1898, *The Shore at Deauville*, bequeathed by George B. Dunlop, 1951

Boudin, Eugène Louis 1824–1898, *Villefranche*, bequeathed by Lord and Lady Fraser of Allander, 2003

Boudin, Eugène Louis 1824–1898, *The Port of Trouville*, bequeathed by Lord and Lady Fraser of Allander, 2003

Boudin, Eugène Louis 1824–1898, *Venice: Santa Maria della Salute and the Dogana Seen from across the Grand Canal*, presented by the family of W. F. Robertson, 1996

Bough, Samuel 1822–1878, *By the Lake, Cumberland*, bequeathed by Mary McKerracher, 1897

Bough, Samuel 1822–1878, *Cadzow Forest*, bequeathed by Mary McKerracher, 1897

Bough, Samuel 1822–1878, *The Mail Coach*, presented by the White Horse Distillery Company, 1927

Bough, Samuel 1822–1878, *In Glen Massan*, bequeathed by Mary McKerracher, 1897

Bough, Samuel 1822–1878, *Dunkirk Harbour*, gift from Sir Charles Tennant, 1901

Bough, Samuel 1822–1878, *Loch Achray*, bequeathed by Mrs Isabella Elder, 1906

Bough, Samuel 1822–1878, *Crosthwaite Bridge, near Keswick*, gift from Miss Anderson, 1921

Bough, Samuel 1822–1878, *Crummock Water, Cumberland*, bequeathed by Mrs Edith M. Anderson, 1953

Bough, Samuel 1822–1878, *Peel Castle, Mona*, bequeathed by Adam Teacher, 1898

Bough, Samuel 1822–1878, *Burn's Cottage, Alloway*, gift from Andrew T. Reid, 1936

Bough, Samuel 1822–1878, *Scottish Landscape*, gift from N. B. Kinnear, 1944

Bough, Samuel 1822–1878, *Dutch Lugger Entering the Thames*, bequeathed by Mary McKerracher, 1897

Bough, Samuel 1822–1878, *Sea Piece*, gift from Miss Anderson, 1921

Bough, Samuel 1822–1878, *The Hayfield, Coming Storm*, bequeathed by Thomas D. Smellie, 1901

Boughton, George Henry 1833–1905, *Girl with Pitchers, Summer Scene*, gift from Miss Kirkpatrick, 1947

Boughton, George Henry 1833–1905, *Girl with a Muff, Winter Scene*, gift from Miss Kirkpatrick, 1947

Boullogne, Bon (after) 1649–1717, *The Annunciation*, Archibald McLellan Collection, purchased, 1856

Bout, Peeter (after) 1658–1719, *Skaters on a Frozen River*, gift from G. B. Sawers, 1919

Boyd, John *The Scaffolders*, purchased, 1980

Brangwyn, Frank 1867–1956, *The Burial at Sea*, purchased, 1904, © the artist's estate/Bridgeman Art Library

Brangwyn, Frank 1867–1956, *Arab Musicians*, presented by the Trustees of the Hamilton Bequest, 1928, © the artist's estate/ Bridgeman Art Library

Brangwyn, Frank 1867–1956, *The Crucifixion*, presented by the Trustees of the Hamilton Bequest, 1930, © the artist's estate/ Bridgeman Art Library

Braque, Georges 1882–1963, *A Dish of Fruit, a Glass and a Bottle*, bequeathed by William McInnes, 1944, © ADAGP, Paris and DACS, London 2013

Bratby, John Randall 1928–1992, *A Carlisle City Councillor with Jean and David Bratby*, purchased, 1959, © Culture and Sport Glasgow (Glasgow Museums)

Breanski, Alfred de 1852–1928, *Evening on a Perthshire River*, temporary identification number allocated, 1979

Breanski, Alfred de 1852–1928, *Highland Loch*, gift from William Ure, 1948

Breton, Jules Adolphe Aimé Louis 1827–1906, *The Reapers*, purchased with the assistance of the Government's Local Museums Purchase Fund, the National Art Collections Fund, the Pilgrim Trust, Glasgow Art Gallery and the Museums Association and public subscription, 1984

Brett, John 1830–1902, *St Ives Bay*, bequeathed by Andrew Lusk, 1928

Bright, Henry 1810–1873, *Rocky Landscape, Val d'Aosta*, bequeathed by William Euing, 1874

Bright, Henry 1810–1873, *A Rock-Bound Coast*, bequeathed by William Euing, 1874

Bril, Paul 1554–1626, *A Mountain Landscape with the Journey to Emmaus*, Archibald McLellan Collection, purchased, 1856

Brissot, Frank active 1879–1881, *Landscape with a Shepherd and Sheep*, bequeathed by Adam Teacher, 1898

Brissot, Frank active 1879–1881, *River Scene*, bequeathed by Reverend H. G. Roberts Hay-Boyd, 1941

British (English) School (attributed to) *Portrait of a Lady*, gift from Sir William and Lady Burrell to the City of Glasgow, 1944

Boughton, George Henry 1833–1905, *Girl with a Muff, Winter Scene*, gift from Miss Kirkpatrick, 1947

British (Scottish) School *John Anderson of Dowhill (1611–1689), Provost*, gift from Mrs C. L. Stirling (Luke Collection) to the Stirling's Library, Glasgow, 1937

British (Scottish) School *John Luke of Claythorn (1627–1686)*, gift from Mrs C. L. Stirling (Luke Collection) to the Stirling's Library, Glasgow, 1937

British (Scottish) School *Robert Cross (or Corse) (1639–1705)*, gift from Mrs C. L. Stirling (Luke Collection) to the Stirling's Library, Glasgow, 1937

British (Scottish) School *William Carstares (1649–1715)*, gift from John G. Dunlop and the Mercantile Bank, 1961

British (Scottish) School *Helen Smith Orr of Barrowfield*, temporary identification number allocated, 1977

British (Scottish) School *George Bogle of Daldowie*, gift from Frances I. Steggall and Katherine E. M. Steggall, 1945

British (Scottish) School *Alexander Dunlop (1682–1747)*, gift from John G. Dunlop and the Mercantile Bank, 1961

British (Scottish) School *Professor William Cullen (1710–1790)*, gift from the Royal Faculty of Physicians & Surgeons, 1962

British (Scottish) School *John McCall of Belvidere and Family (The Dennistoun)*, acquired, 1965

British (Scottish) School *Trongate, Glasgow, Looking West from Glasgow Cross (after the Foulis Academy)*, purchased, 1959

British (Scottish) School *Mungo Campbell of Hundleshope (1731–1793)*, bequeathed by Isabella A. H. J. Campbell, 1917

British (Scottish) School 18th C, *Sir John Maxwell (1648–1732), 1st Bt*, on loan from a private collection

British (Scottish) School *Penny a Week School, Goat Burn*, gift, 1978

British (Scottish) School *George MacIntosh (1739–1807)*, presented by the Glasgow Highland Society, 1903

British (Scottish) School *John Bartholemew*, temporary identification number allocated, 1978

British (Scottish) School *Alex Campbell of Haylodge, Peeblesshire (1780–1849)*, bequeathed by Isabella A. H. J. Campbell, 1917

British (Scottish) School *Barclay Curle's Shipyard at Stobcross*, gift, 1977

British (Scottish) School *Andrew Gemmill*, gift from Miss Brown, 1936

British (Scottish) School *Joseph Reid, Town Clerk Depute of Glasgow (1820–1832)*, temporary identification number allocated, 1978

British (Scottish) School *John Dunlop (1789–1865)*

British (Scottish) School *John Robertson (1782–1863)*, gift from Mrs Yule, 1894

British (Scottish) School *Portrait of a Man*, temporary identification number allocated, 1977

British (Scottish) School *The River Kelvin at, or below, the Pear Tree Well*

British (Scottish) School *John Turnbull, Junior*

British (Scottish) School *Portrait of a Man*, temporary identification number allocated, 1988

British (Scottish) School *John White, Provost of Partick*, temporary identification number allocated, 1996

British (Scottish) School *Principal Robert Herbert Story*, deposited during World War II as part of the Dr Helen Story Collection

British (Scottish) School 19th C, *Bridge Gate*

British (Scottish) School 19th C, *Cottage Scene*

British (Scottish) School 19th C, *Glasgow Cathedral*

British (Scottish) School 19th C, *Glasgow Cathedral from the Necropolis* (after J. A. Houston)

British (Scottish) School 19th C, *Mr Campbell*, on loan from a private collection

British (Scottish) School 19th C, *Salmon Fishing at Govan*

British (Scottish) School 19th C–20th C, *Glasgow Fire Brigade Crossing the Albert Bridge*, gift, 1961

British (Scottish) School 19th C–20th C, *Old Malabar*, gift from George H. Fisher, 1955

British (Scottish) School *Sir Renny Watson of Braco*, temporary identification number allocated, 1977

British (Scottish) School *James Dalrymple*, temporary identification number allocated, 1988

British (Scottish) School *Boating Scene in Queen's Park*, gift, 1977

British (Scottish) School *Dave Willis (1895–1973)*, gift, 1978

British (Scottish) School *Meighan's Premises*, gift, 1977

British (Scottish) School *Fish and Towers*

British (Scottish) School *Turret Tower*

British (Scottish) School *U*

British (Scottish) School *1 IX 9 0*

British (Scottish) School *Culture City Net 1990*

British (Scottish) School *Culture City Net 1990*

British (Scottish) School 20th C, *Loch Landscape*

British (Scottish) School 20th C, *Loch Scene Landscape*

British (Scottish) School 20th C, *Sir George MacLeod*, temporary identification number allocated, 1977

British (Scottish) School 20th C, *The Lower Church of Glasgow Cathedral*

British (Scottish) School *Girl with Sunflowers*

British (Scottish) School *Mrs Elizabeth Campbell*, bequeathed by Isabella A. H. J. Campbell, 1917

British (Scottish) School *Mrs General Campbell*, bequeathed by Isabella A. H. J. Campbell, 1917

British (Scottish) School *Portrait of a Gentleman*, bequeathed by William Euing, 1874

British (Scottish) School *Portrait of a Man* (said to be Henry Frederick Stuart, 1594–1612, Prince of Wales), Stirling Maxwell Collection, gift, 1967

British School 17th C, *Oliver Cromwell (1599–1658)* (after Peter Lely), Stirling Maxwell Collection, gift, 1967

British School 17th C, *Portrait of a Man*, on loan from a private collection

British School 17th C, *Mary Queen of Scots (1542–1587)*, bequeathed by Mrs Galbraith, 1904

British School *Colonel Archer*, temporary identification number allocated, 1979

British School *Portrait of a Lady*, on loan from a private collection

British School *The Woman Shopkeeper*

British School 18th C, *Captain Robert Maxwell (1770–1796)*, on loan from a private collection

British School 18th C, *Elizabeth A. Linley*, Archibald McLellan Collection, purchased, 1856

British School 18th C, *Portrait of a Clergyman, Half-Length*, temporary identification number allocated, 1977

British School 18th C, *Portrait of a Gentleman*, bequeathed by Jane Graham-Gilbert, 1877

British School 18th C, *Portrait of a Man*, on loan from a private collection

British School 18th C, *Portrait of a Man*, temporary identification number allocated, 1977

British School 18th C, *Sir John Maxwell (1686–1752), 2nd Bt*, on loan from a private collection

British School *Portrait of a Man*

British School *Portrait of a Woman in a White Dress*

British School *Mr W. S. Dixon*, temporary identification number allocated, 1974

British School *Portrait of a Man*, temporary identification number allocated, 1977

British School *Portrait of a Man*, temporary identification number allocated, 1979

British School *Portrait of a Man*, deposited during World War II as part of the Dr Helen Story Collection

British School *Portrait of a Gentleman*, temporary identification number allocated, 1988

British School *Portrait of a Man*, temporary identification number allocated, 1977

British School *Portrait of a Man*, temporary identification number allocated, 1977

British School *Portrait of a Man*, temporary identification number allocated, 1977

British School *Portrait of a Man*, temporary identification number allocated, 1974

British School 19th C, *Child with Animals*, temporary identification number allocated, 1977

British School 19th C, *Doctor of Divinity*, acquired, 1978

British School 19th C, *Genre Scene with a Blacksmith*, temporary identification number allocated, 1974

British School 19th C, *George Stephenson (1781–1848)*, temporary identification number allocated, 1979

British School 19th C, *Harbour Scene*, temporary identification number allocated, 1981

British School 19th C, *Landscape*

British School 19th C, *Mrs Stirling of Keir (1793–1822)*, on loan from a private collection

British School 19th C, *Night Scene: Dancing near Classical Ruins*, temporary identification number allocated, 1974

British School 19th C, *Portrait of a Blonde Girl*

British School 19th C, *Portrait of a Lady*, temporary identification number allocated, 1977

British School 19th C, *Portrait of a Man*, deposited during World War II as part of the Dr Helen Story Collection

British School 19th C, *Portrait of a Man*, temporary identification number allocated, 1977

British School 19th C, *Portrait of a Man*, temporary identification number allocated, 1979

British School 19th C, *Portrait of a Man*, acquired, 1978

British School 19th C, *Portrait of a Man*

British School 19th C, *Portrait of a Man*

British School 19th C, *Portrait of a Man with a White Stock*, deposited during World War II as part of the Dr Helen Story Collection

British School 19th C, *Portrait of a Young Minister*

British School 19th C, *Portrait of an Unknown Man*

British School 19th C, *Sir John Maxwell (1791–1865), 8th Bt*, on loan from a private collection

British School 19th C, *Thomas Campbell*, bequeathed by Isabella A. H. J. Campbell, 1917

British School 19th C–20th C, *J. M. Gass*

British School 20th C, *Portrait of a Man*, temporary identification number allocated, 1974

British School 20th C, *Still Life with a Rose and Lilacs*, temporary identification number allocated, 1988

British School *Portrait of a Man*, temporary identification number allocated, 1977

British School *Portrait of a Man*, temporary identification number allocated, 1977

British School *Portrait of a Man*, temporary identification number allocated, 1974

British School 20th C, *Two Profiles of Girls and a Mask*, gift from the BBC Collection, 2008

British School 20th C (?), *Portrait of a Child*

British School *An Old Pilgrim*, bequeathed by William Euing, 1874

British School *Henry Rich (1590–1649), 1st Earl of Holland*, Stirling Maxwell Collection, gift, 1967

British School *Nell Gwynn (1650–1687) (?)*, bequeathed by Mrs Isabella Elder, 1906

British School *Portrait of a Man*, temporary identification number allocated, 1979

British School (attributed to) 18th C (?), *Lobster, Wine Glass and Spoon*, gift from Sir William and Lady Burrell to the City of Glasgow, 1944

British School (attributed to) 19th C, *The Convent (Church of San Vitale, Posillipo, near Naples)*, Archibald McLellan Collection, purchased, 1856

British School (attributed to) 19th C (?), *Portrait of a Sleeping Baby*

British School (attributed to) 20th C, *Pink Flowers*

British School (attributed to) 20th C, *Sunflowers and Foliage*

Brock, Edmond b.1882, *Marion L. Chrystal (b.1855)*, presented by the Trustees of the estate of William J. Chrystal, 1941

Brock, Edmond b.1882, *William J. Chrystal (1854–1921)*, presented by the Trustees of the estate of William J. Chrystal, 1941

Brockhurst, Gerald Leslie 1890–1978, *Gillian*, presented by the Trustees of the Hamilton Bequest, 1935

Brodie, Isabel Babianska 1920–2006, *Reflection (Self Portrait)*, purchased, 1940

Brooker, Peter Alfred 1900–1965, *Emile Plantin*, gift from the Contemporary Art Society, 1938

Brooking, Charles 1723–1759, *Sea Piece*, bequeathed by William Euing, 1874

Brough, Robert 1872–1905, *Miss Maud Lawrence*, gift from Mrs A. H. Pollen, 1951

Brown, Alexander Kellock 1849–1922, *Springtime*, purchased from the artist, 1898

Brown, Alexander Kellock 1849–1922, *A Dagger Day*, gift from Alexander Hill, 1922

Brown, Alexander Kellock 1849–1922, *Ben Lawers*, bequeathed by Thomas Martin, 1926

Brown, Alexander Kellock 1849–1922, *Landscape*, bequeathed by Adam Teacher, 1898

Brown, Ford Madox 1821–1893, *Wycliffe on Trial*, presented by the Trustees of the Hamilton Bequest, 1929

Brown, Mather (attributed to) 1761–1831, *A Girl at a Harpsichord*, purchased, 1952

Brown, Neil Dallas 1938–2003, *Shroud*, presented by the Neil Dallas Brown Trust, 2006, © the artist's estate

Brown, Neil Dallas 1938–2003, *The Indictment*, presented by the Neil Dallas Brown Trust, 2006, © the artist's estate

Brown, Neil Dallas 1938–2003, *Alarm (Danger Zone)*, presented by the Neil Dallas Brown Trust, 2006, © the artist's estate

Brown, Neil Dallas 1938–2003, *Fast Glide (Impact)*, presented by the Neil Dallas Brown Trust, 2006, © the artist's estate

Brown, Thomas Austen 1859–1924, *A Gypsy Encampment*, gift from James Caldwell, 1904

Brown, Thomas Austen 1859–1924, *Feeding the Pigeons*, bequeathed by Mr and Mrs James Caldwell, 1918

Browning, Amy Katherine 1881–1978, *Interior: Studio Supper*, presented by the Trustees of the Hamilton Bequest, 1938, © Joanna Dunham

Brueghel, Jan the elder (attributed to) 1568–1625 & Avont, Peeter van 1600–1652 *The Holy Family in a Wooded Landscape*, Archibald McLellan Collection, purchased, 1856

Brueghel, Jan the elder (attributed to) 1568–1625 & Rottenhammer, Hans I (attributed to) 1564–1625 *A Wooded Landscape with the Rest on the Flight into Egypt*, Archibald McLellan Collection, purchased, 1856

Brydall, Robert 1839–1907, *Lady Anna Stirling Maxwell (d.1874)*, on loan from a private collection

Buchanan, George F. 1800–1864, *Greenan Castle*, Archibald McLellan Collection, purchased, 1856

Bunting, Thomas 1851–1928, *Landscape, Woodland Scene*, gift from Mr and Mrs William Ure, 1948

Burbidge, John active c.1855–1894, *Crinan Canal*, bequeathed by William Euing, 1874

Burgess, Arthur James Wetherall 1879–1957, *The Fairfield Fleet*, gift from Govan Shipbuilders Limited, 1977, © the artist's estate

Burne-Jones, Edward 1833–1898, *The Angel*, bequeathed by Allan McLean, 1928

Burne-Jones, Edward 1833–1898, *Danaë (The Tower of Brass)*, gift from William Connal, 1901

Burnet, John 1784–1868, *Tam o' Shanter*, bequeathed by William Euing, 1874

Burns, William 1921–1972, *Ferryden*, purchased, 1952

Burns, William 1921–1972, *Boats, Gourdon*, purchased, 1954

Burns, William 1921–1972, *Sea-Crane*, purchased, 1984

Burr, Alexander Hohenlohe 1835–1898, *Shuttlecock*,

Burrell to the City of Glasgow, 1944

Chardin, Jean-Baptiste Siméon (style of) 1699–1779, *Still Life*, gift from Sir William and Lady Burrell to the City of Glasgow, 1944

Charinda, Mohamed Wasia b.1947, *Street Scene*, purchased, 1998

Christie, James Elder 1847–1914, *Mr Glover*

Christie, James Elder 1847–1914, *The Red Fisherman*, purchased, 1911

Christie, James Elder 1847–1914, *Vanity Fair* (study of children's heads), purchased, 1980

Christie, James Elder 1847–1914, *Vanity Fair*, purchased from the artist, 1895

Ciardi, Guglielmo 1842–1917, *October in the Venetian Countryside*, purchased, 1904

Cikovsky, Nicolai 1894–1987, *Mandolin and the Old Corcoran Gallery*, purchased, 1945

Cina, Colin b.1943, *MH9*, presented by the Contemporary Art Society, 1983, © the artist

Clark, Georges 1896–1990, *Back of Keppoch*, purchased, 1957

Clark, William 1803–1883, *Paddle Steamer*

Clark, William 1803–1883, *The British and North American Royal Mail Steam Ships 'Europa' and 'Niagara' off the Tail of the Bank*, gift from John Napier, 1877

Clark, William 1803–1883, *HMS 'Hogue'*, purchased, 1960

Clark, William (after) 1803–1883, *'Britannia': First of the Cunard Line*, gift from Robert Duncan, 1882

Clarke, William Hanna 1882–1924, *Flying the Kite*, gift from Mr and Mrs James Johnstone, 1946

Clarkson, Marjorie b.1898, *The Broken Spring*, purchased, 1995

Clausen, George 1852–1944, *La pensée*, gift from Bailie Robert Murdoch, 1895, © Clausen estate

Cleve, Joos van (school of) c.1464–c.1540, *Saint Jerome in His Study*, Stirling Maxwell Collection, gift, 1967

Cleve, Joos van (studio of) c.1464–c.1540, *Virgin and Child*, gift from Sir William and Lady Burrell to the City of Glasgow, 1944

Cleveley, John c.1712–1777, *A Shipyard on the Thames*, purchased with the assistance of Government Grant-in-Aid, 1971

Clouet, François (style of) c.1515–1572, *Portrait of a Lady*, Archibald McLellan Collection, purchased, 1856

Cobbett, Edward John 1815–1899, *Forest Scene*, bequeathed by William Euing, 1874

Cochran, William 1738–1785, *Portrait of a Man* (formerly said to be James Watt), purchased, 1942

Cochran, William 1738–1785, *Sir James Dunbar of Mochrum*

(d.1782), purchased, 1953

Codner, Maurice Frederick 1888–1958, *Sir Hugh Roberton (1874–1952)*, presented by the Glasgow Orpheus Choir, 1946, © the artist's estate

Coecke van Aelst, Pieter the elder (attributed to) 1502–1550, *Christ Taking Leave of His Mother*, Archibald McLellan Collection, purchased, 1856

Coffermans, Marcellus 1520/1530–c.1578, *The Annunciation*, gift from Sir William and Lady Burrell to the City of Glasgow, 1944

Cole, George Vicat 1833–1893, *A Harvest Field*, bequeathed by Mrs A. C. Thorneycroft, 1934

Coleman, William Stephen 1829–1904, *A Naiad*, bequeathed by Adam Teacher, 1898

Colley, Virginia *Peasants at Work*

Colley, Virginia *Peasants at Work*

Collier, Edwaert c.1640–c.1707, *Still Life*, gift from William Burrell, 1925

Collier, John 1850–1934, *The Death of Albine*, presented by the executors of the estate of Professor William Smart, 1921

Collins, Jim b.1947, *Guardians of Helios*, © the artist

Collins, Peter b.1935, *Family Group*, purchased, 1963, © the artist

Collins, Peter b.1935, *The Yellow Bandana*, purchased, 1964, © the artist

Colonia, Adam (attributed to) 1634–1685, *A Landscape with Goats*, bequeathed by William Euing, 1874

Colquhoun, Robert 1914–1962, *Marrowfield, Worcestershire*, gift from the Contemporary Art Society, 1944, © the artist's estate/ Bridgeman Art Library

Colquhoun, Robert 1914–1962, *Encounter*, purchased, 1978, © the artist's estate/Bridgeman Art Library

Colquhoun, Robert 1914–1962, *The Lock Gate*, gift from A. J. McNeill Reid, 1952, © the artist's estate/Bridgeman Art Library

Colquhoun, Robert 1914–1962, *Thea Neu*, gift from Mrs Elizabeth M. Macdonald, 1958, © the artist's estate/Bridgeman Art Library

Conder, Charles 1868–1909, *The Bridge*, gift from Lewis P. Renateau, 1953

Conder, Charles 1868–1909, *The Trellis*, gift from Lewis P. Renateau, 1953

Connard, Philip 1875–1958, *Portrait of a Lady in Grey (Mrs Benge)*, gift from Francis Howard, 1942

Conroy, Stephen b.1964, *Self Portrait 1*, purchased with the assistance of the Art Fund, the Trustees of the Hamilton Bequest, the National Fund for Acquisitions and Muriel Gray, 2006, © the artist

Constable, John 1776–1837, *Hampstead Heath*, presented by

the sons of James Reid of Auchterarder, 1896

Constable, John (imitator of) 1776–1837, *Landscape with Barges on a River*, temporary identification number allocated, 1978

Constable, John (style of) 1776–1837, *House by the Road*, bequeathed by James Donald, 1905

Constable, John (style of) 1776–1837, *On the Wye, Herefordshire*, gift from Miss Kirkpatrick, 1947

Conway, F. J. active 20th C, *Mimosa*, gift from George Campbell, 1950

Cook, Beryl 1926–2008, *By the Clyde*, purchased from the artist, 1993

Cook, Beryl 1926–2008, *Karaoke*, purchased from the artist, 1993

Cook, Beryl 1926–2008, *The Accordion Player*, purchased from the artist, 1993

Cook, Beryl 1926–2008, *Hen Party II*, purchased from the artist, 1996

Cook, David b.1957, *Mask*, purchased, 1994

Cooper, Gladys 1899–1975, *The Bridal Group*, purchased, 1995

Cooper, Gladys 1899–1975, *The New Carpet*, purchased, 1995

Cooper, Gladys 1899–1975, *The Gate*, purchased, 1995

Cooper, Thomas Sidney 1803–1902, *Landscape with Cattle*, bequeathed by Mrs Isabella Elder, 1906

Cooper, Thomas Sidney 1803–1902, *Landscape with Sheep*, bequeathed by Mrs Isabella Elder, 1906

Cooper, Thomas Sidney 1803–1902, *Canterbury Meadows*, bequeathed by Thomas D. Smellie, 1901

Cope, Arthur Stockdale 1857–1940, *Sir John Ure Primrose (1847–1924), Lord Provost of Glasgow (1902–1905)*, purchased, 1906

Copley, John 1875–1950, *String Quartet*, purchased, 1944, © the artist's estate

Corbet, Philip 1801–1877, *Going to Chapel: Edith Corbet (1833–1904)*, bequeathed by William Euing, 1874

Corot, Jean-Baptiste-Camille 1796–1875, *Shipping*, gift from Sir William and Lady Burrell to the City of Glasgow, 1944

Corot, Jean-Baptiste-Camille 1796–1875, *Portrait of a Woman*, gift from Sir William and Lady Burrell to the City of Glasgow, 1944

Corot, Jean-Baptiste-Camille 1796–1875, *The Crayfisher*, bequeathed by James Donald, 1905

Corot, Jean-Baptiste-Camille 1796–1875, *The Woodcutter*, bequeathed by James Donald, 1905

Corot, Jean-Baptiste-Camille 1796–1875, *Peasants' Houses, Fontainebleau*, gift from Sir

William and Lady Burrell to the City of Glasgow, 1944

Corot, Jean-Baptiste-Camille 1796–1875, *The Riverbank*, bequeathed by William McInnes, 1944

Corot, Jean-Baptiste-Camille 1796–1875, *Mademoiselle de Foudras*, presented by the Trustees of the estate of D. W. T. Cargill, 1950

Corot, Jean-Baptiste-Camille 1796–1875, *Pastorale*, presented by the family of the late James Reid of Auchterarder, 1896

Corot, Jean-Baptiste-Camille (attributed to) 1796–1875, *Evening*, bequeathed by James Donald, 1905

Corot, Jean-Baptiste-Camille (attributed to) 1796–1875, *The Bathers*, bequeathed by William J. Chrystal, 1939

Corot, Jean-Baptiste-Camille (attributed to) 1796–1875, *The Lake*, bequeathed by James Donald, 1905

Corot, Jean-Baptiste-Camille (attributed to) 1796–1875, *Wooded Landscape with Figures*, bequeathed by Mrs Isabella Elder, 1906

Correggio (after) c.1489–1534, *Madonna and Child with a Rabbit*, Archibald McLellan Collection, purchased, 1856

Correggio (after) c.1489–1534, *The Mystic Marriage of Saint Catherine*, Archibald McLellan Collection, purchased, 1856

Correggio (after) c.1489–1534, *Madonna of Saint Jerome*, Archibald McLellan Collection, purchased, 1856, photo credit: Glasgow Museums

Correggio (imitator of) c.1489–1534, *Head of an Angel*, Archibald McLellan Collection, purchased, 1856

Cosida, Jerónimo c.1516–1592, *San Ildefonso Receiving the Chasuble*, Stirling Maxwell Collection, gift, 1967

Cossaar, Jacobus Cornelis Wyand 1874–1966, *Interior with Figures*, gift from Sir John Richmond, 1948

Cossiers, Jan (style of) 1600–1671, *A Gambling Party*, Archibald McLellan Collection, purchased, 1856

Cotes, Francis (circle of) 1726–1770, *Henrietta Archer (1754–1794)*, on loan from James Everett McDonald Stuart-Stevenson

Cottrel, A. *Glasgow Cathedral and Infirmary*, temporary identification number allocated, 1977

Couling, Arthur Vivian 1890–1962, *Le bateau à la moustache jaune*, purchased, 1929

Courbet, Gustave 1819–1877, *Baskets of Flowers*, presented by the Trustees of the estate of D. W. T. Cargill, 1950

Courbet, Gustave 1819–1877, *Lily and Gillyflower*, gift from William Burrell, 1925

Courbet, Gustave 1819–1877, *Woman with a Parasol, Mademoiselle Aubé de la Holde*, gift from Sir William and Lady Burrell to the City of Glasgow, 1944

Courbet, Gustave 1819–1877, *The Charity of a Beggar at Ornans*, gift from William Burrell, 1925

Courbet, Gustave 1819–1877, *Pomegranates*, gift from Sir William and Lady Burrell to the City of Glasgow, 1944

Courbet, Gustave 1819–1877, *Apple, Pear and Orange*, bequeathed by William McInnes, 1944

Courbet, Gustave 1819–1877, *Fruit*, gift from Sir William and Lady Burrell to the City of Glasgow, 1944

Courbet, Gustave (attributed to) 1819–1877, *Portrait of a Woman*, presented by the Trustees of the Hamilton Bequest, 1948

Courbet, Gustave (attributed to) 1819–1877, *The Washerwomen*, gift from Sir William and Lady Burrell to the City of Glasgow, 1944

Couture, Thomas 1815–1879, *A Volunteer*, gift from Sir William and Lady Burrell to the City of Glasgow, 1944

Couture, Thomas (attributed to) 1815–1879, *Girl*, gift from Sir William and Lady Burrell to the City of Glasgow, 1944

Coventry, Robert McGown 1855–1914, *The Haven*, purchased, 1908

Cowell, Margaret 1899–1970, *Collecting the Divi*, purchased, 1995

Cowie, James 1886–1956, *Nude*, purchased from the artist, 1947, © the artist's estate

Cowie, James 1886–1956, *The Looking-Glass*, purchased, 1956, © the artist's estate

Cowie, James 1886–1956, *Scottish Policeman*, presented by the War Artists' Advisory Committee through the Imperial War Museum, 1948

Cox, David the elder 1783–1859, *Landscape with a Windmill*, purchased, 1956

Cozza, Francesco 1605–1682, *Music*, Archibald McLellan Collection, purchased, 1856

Craig, Alexander d.1878, *Thomas Campbell (1777–1844), Poet*

Craig, Alexander d.1878, *Dr Livingstone (1813–1873)*, on loan from a private collection

Cranach, Lucas the elder 1472–1553, *Judith with the Head of Holofernes*, purchased by the Trustees of the Burrell Collection with the assistance of the Heritage Lottery Fund and the Art Fund, 1995

Cranach, Lucas the elder (studio of) 1472–1553, *The Stag Hunt*, gift from Sir William and Lady Burrell to the City of Glasgow, 1944

Cranach, Lucas the elder (studio of) 1472–1553, *Venus and Cupid, the Honey Thief*, gift from Sir

William and Lady Burrell to the City of Glasgow, 1944

Crane, Walter 1845–1915, *The Briar Rose* (triptych, left wing), purchased, 1921

Crane, Walter 1845–1915, *The Briar Rose* (triptych, centre panel), purchased, 1921

Crane, Walter 1845–1915, *The Briar Rose* (triptych, right wing), purchased, 1921

Crawford, Hugh Adam 1898–1982, *Sir Patrick Dollan (1885–1963), Lord Provost of Glasgow (1938–1941)*, presented by the War Artists' Advisory Committee through the Imperial War Museum, 1948

Crawford, Hugh Adam 1898–1982, *Sir Alexander King (1888–1973)*, on loan from a private collection, © the artist's estate

Crawford, Robert Cree 1842–1924, *Midday Rest*, gift from the Trustees of Margaret Moore, 1943

Crawford, Robert Cree 1842–1924, *The Water Stoup*, gift from an anonymous donor, 1907

Crawford, Robert Cree 1842–1924, *Woman and Child*, gift from Miss Murray, 1946

Crawford, Robert Cree 1842–1924, *Sir James Thompson, Chairman of the Caledonian Railway (1901–1906)*, gift, 1972

Crawford, Robert Cree 1842–1924, *Former Bailie Walter Paton (1838–1906)*, gift from subscribers, 1905

Crawford, Robert Cree 1842–1924, *Portrait of a Man*, temporary identification number allocated, 2004

Crawford, Robert Cree 1842–1924, *Archibald McLellan (1795–1854)* (after John Graham-Gilbert), purchased, 1906

Crawford, Robert Cree 1842–1924, *Portrait of a Man*, temporary identification number allocated, 1988

Crawford, Robert Cree 1842–1924, *James W. Briggs, Violin Maker in Glasgow*, gift from Henry B. Briggs, 1939

Crawford, Robert Cree 1842–1924, *John Arnott (1814–1898)*, bequeathed by Mrs Arnott, 1943

Crawford, Robert Cree 1842–1924, *Storm at Portincross*, gift from George J. Kidston, 1907

Crawford, Robert Cree 1842–1924, *The Gates of the North*, gift from E. O. Inglis, 1927

Crawhall, Joseph E. 1861–1913, *Landscape with Cattle*, purchased, 1956

Crayer, Gaspar de (and studio) 1584–1669, *Cardinal Infante Fernando of Austria (1609–1641)*, Stirling Maxwell Collection, gift, 1967

Creswick, Thomas 1811–1869, *Coast Scene*, bequeathed by Thomas D. Smellie, 1901

Creswick, Thomas 1811–1869,

Sea-Beach Scene, bequeathed by William Euing, 1874

Cretan School early 17th C, *The Birth of the Virgin*, Archibald McLellan Collection, purchased, 1856

Croft-Smith, David A. b.1934, *Polarization*, purchased, 1972, © the artist

Crosbie, William 1915–1999, *A Kabyle Pot*, © the artist's estate

Crosbie, William 1915–1999, *Hugh MacDiarmid (1892–1978)*, purchased, 1944, © the artist's estate

Crosbie, William 1915–1999, *Composition, Flowers*, purchased, 1961, © the artist's estate

Crosbie, William 1915–1999, *Cambridge from Grantchester*, purchased, 1952, © the artist's estate

Crosbie, William 1915–1999, *Birds and Tree*, purchased, 1970, © the artist's estate

Crosbie, William 1915–1999, *Halbert Tatlock (d.1963)*, gift from Derrick Morley, 1958, © the artist's estate

Crosbie, William 1915–1999, *John Morton, Radio Personality*, © the artist's estate

Crosbie, William 1915–1999, *Moonlight and Flowers*, bequeathed by Mrs Agnes Blake, 1968, © the artist's estate

Crozier, William 1893–1930, *The Well*, purchased, 1929

Crozier, William b.1930, *Fallen Man II*, gift from the Contemporary Art Society, 1965, © William Crozier

Crozier, William b.1930, *Aviator*, gift from the artist, 1967, © William Crozier

Cruickshank, George active 1895–1909, *Girls at a Rabbit Hutch at Ravelston*, purchased, 1962

Cruickshank, R. S. '*Duchess of Montrose*', gift, 1992

Cubley, William Harold 1816–1896, *Killin, Perthshire*, bequeathed by Jane A. Cubley, 1926

Cumming, James 1922–1991, *The Hill Farmer*, purchased, 1963, © the artist's estate

Cumming, James 1922–1991, *Points of Contact*, bequeathed by George and Isobel Neillands, 1988, © the artist's estate

Cundall, Charles Ernest 1890–1971, *The Hipper at Kiel*, presented by the War Artists' Advisory Committee through the Imperial War Museum, 1948, © Culture and Sport Glasgow (Glasgow Museums)

Cuneo, Terence Tenison 1907–1996, *Blue Train at Bowling Harbour*, gift from the British Railways Board through the Heritage Railway Commitee, 2009, © reproduced with kind permission of the Cuneo estate

Cunningham, John 1926–1998, *Flanders Moss*, purchased, 1961, © the artist's estate

Cunningham, John 1926–1998, *Farm near Charolles*, purchased, 1964, © the artist's estate

Currie, Ken b.1960, *Peace*, purchased from the artist, 1984, © the artist

Currie, Ken b.1960, *War*, purchased from the artist, 1984, © the artist

Currie, Ken b.1960, *Weavers' Struggles … The Calton Weavers' Massacre*, commissioned, 1986, © the artist

Currie, Ken b.1960, *Radical Wars … Let Truth and Justice Be Woven Together, Liberty Is Our Fabric*, commissioned, 1986, © the artist

Currie, Ken b.1960, *Great Reform Agitation … Union Is Strength*, commissioned, 1986, © the artist

Currie, Ken b.1960, *The Socialist Vision … Workers of the World*, commissioned, 1986, © the artist

Currie, Ken b.1960, *Red Clyde … 'We Can Make Glasgow a Petrograd, a Revolutionary Storm Centre Second to None'*, commissioned, 1986, © the artist

Currie, Ken b.1960, *Fight or Starve … Wandering through the Thirties*, commissioned, 1986, © the artist

Currie, Ken b.1960, *The UCS*, commissioned, 1986, © the artist

Currie, Ken b.1960, *Unfurling Our History … Our Future!*, commissioned, 1986, © the artist

Currie, Ken b.1960, *Scottish Stoics: A Prostitute* (triptych, left wing), purchased, 1990, © the artist

Currie, Ken b.1960, *Scottish Stoics: A Cripple* (triptych, centre panel), purchased, 1990, © the artist

Currie, Ken b.1960, *Scottish Stoics: A Worker* (triptych, right wing), purchased, 1990, © the artist

Currie, Ken b.1960, *The Bathers*, purchased, 1993, © the artist

Currie, Ken b.1960, *Untitled*, purchased from the artist, 2000, © the artist

Cursiter, Stanley 1887–1976, *Evening on the Loch*, purchased, 1950, © estate of Stanley Cursiter 2013. All Rights Reserved, DACS

Cursiter, Stanley 1887–1976, *Authors in Session*, presented by the Trustees of the Hamilton Bequest, 1951, © estate of Stanley Cursiter 2013. All Rights Reserved, DACS

Cursiter, Stanley 1887–1976, *Andrew Hood, Lord Provost of Glasgow (1955–1958)*, purchased, 1958, © estate of Stanley Cursiter 2013. All Rights Reserved, DACS

Cuylenborch, Abraham van c.1610–1658, *A Tomb in a Grotto*, bequeathed by William Euing, 1874

Cuyp, Aelbert (imitator of) 1620–1691, *Farm Buildings and Figures*, bequeathed by James Donald, 1905

Cuyp, Aelbert (school of) 1620–1691, *Christ Riding into Jerusalem*, Archibald McLellan Collection, purchased, 1856

Cuyp, Aelbert (style of) 1620–1691, *Landscape with Cattle and Figures*, bequeathed by Jane Graham-Gilbert, 1877

Cuyp, Aelbert (style of) 1620–1691, *Landscape with Cattle and Figures*, bequeathed by Jane Graham-Gilbert, 1877

Cuyp, Aelbert (style of) 1620–1691, *The Head of a Cow*, bequeathed by William Euing, 1874

Cuyp, Benjamin Gerritsz. 1612–1652, *The Quack Doctor*, bequeathed by William Euing, 1874

Czedekowski, Bloleslaw Jan 1885–1969, *The Artist's Family*, presented by the Trustees of the Hamilton Bequest, 1928

Dafter, William R. b.1901, *Nearing the End*, purchased, 1995

Dagnan-Bouveret, Pascal Adolphe Jean 1852–1929, *Portrait of a Lady*, presented by Lionel M. Angus-Butterworth through the National Art Collections Fund, 1960

Dahl, Michael I 1656/1659–1743, *Mrs Salisbury*, Stirling Maxwell Collection, gift, 1967

Daiwaille, Alexander Joseph 1818–1888 & **Verboeckhoven, Eugène Joseph** 1799–1881 *Landscape with Cattle*, gift from Miss Anderson, 1921

Dalby, Eva b.1915, *Operation Salvage*, purchased, 1995

Dale, William *Old Partrick Bridge*

Dalí, Salvador 1904–1989, *Christ of St John of the Cross*, purchased, 1952, © Glasgow City Council

Daret, Jean 1613/1615–1668, *A Mountainous Coastal Landscape with Classical Ruins and Shepherds*, Archibald McLellan Collection, purchased, 1856

Daubigny, Charles-François 1817–1878, *Landscape with Cattle*, gift from Sir William and Lady Burrell to the City of Glasgow, 1944

Daubigny, Charles-François 1817–1878, *Château Gaillard, the Seine at Roche Guyon*, gift from Sir William and Lady Burrell to the City of Glasgow, 1944

Daubigny, Charles-François 1817–1878, *Landscape with a Mill*, gift from Sir William and Lady Burrell to the City of Glasgow, 1944

Daubigny, Charles-François 1817–1878, *Lake with Ducks*, bequeathed by James Donald, 1905

Daubigny, Charles-François 1817–1878, *Seascape at Villerville*, bequeathed by William J. Chrystal, 1939

Daubigny, Charles-François 1817–1878, *River Scene with Wooded Banks*, bequeathed by William J. Chrystal, 1939

Daubigny, Charles-François (attributed to) 1817–1878, *River Scene, Sunset*, bequeathed by Reverend H. G. Roberts Hay-Boyd, 1941

Daumier, Honoré 1808–1879, *The Bathers*, gift from Sir William and Lady Burrell to the City of Glasgow, 1944

Daumier, Honoré 1808–1879, *The Miller, His Son and the Ass*, gift from Sir William and Lady Burrell to the City of Glasgow, 1944

Daumier, Honoré 1808–1879, *The Gossip*, bequeathed by William McInnes, 1944

Daumier, Honoré 1808–1879, *The Good Samaritan*, gift from Sir William and Lady Burrell to the City of Glasgow, 1944

Daumier, Honoré 1808–1879, *Susannah and the Elders*, gift from Sir William and Lady Burrell to the City of Glasgow, 1944

Daumier, Honoré 1808–1879, *The Burden*, gift from Sir William and Lady Burrell to the City of Glasgow, 1944

Daumier, Honoré 1808–1879, *The Print Collector*, gift from Sir William and Lady Burrell to the City of Glasgow, 1944

Daumier, Honoré 1808–1879, *Don Quixote and Sancho Panza* (from the novel by Cervantes), gift from Sir William and Lady Burrell to the City of Glasgow, 1944

Daumier, Honoré (attributed to) 1808–1879, *Four Heads*, gift from Sir William and Lady Burrell to the City of Glasgow, 1944

Daumier, Honoré (attributed to) 1808–1879, *The Fugitives*, gift from William Burrell, 1925

Davie, Alan b.1920, *Cornucopia*, purchased with the assistance of the National Art Collections Fund, 1992, © the artist

Davie, Joseph b.1965, *The Poetic Stoker*, gift from the BBC Collection, 2008

Davie, Joseph b.1965, *Apostleship*, purchased, 1991

Davie, Joseph b.1965, *The 37 Bus*, acquired, 1990

Davis, Jason Pyper b.1973, *Flutter*, purchased, 2003, © the artist

De Karlowska, Stanislawa 1876–1952, *Cottages at Cuckfield, Sussex*, gift, 1968, © the artist's estate/Bridgeman Art Library

de la Rua, Jorge active 1552–1578, *Don John of Austria (1547–1578)*, Stirling Maxwell Collection, gift, 1967

de Roelas, Juan (style of) c.1558–1625, *Head of a Female Saint*, temporary identification number allocated, 1974

de Tobar, Alonso Miguel 1678–1758, *The Infant Saint John with the Lamb* (after Bartolomé Esteban Murillo), Stirling Maxwell Collection, gift, 1967

Dean, Fiona b.1962, *Water Dipper*, gift from the BBC Collection, 2008, © the artist

Dean, Stansmore Richmond Leslie 1866–1944, *Jean Macaulay Stevenson*, gift, 1983

Dean, Stansmore Richmond Leslie 1866–1944, *Portrait of a Lady*, gift, 1983

Decamps, Alexandre-Gabriel 1803–1860, *Saint Jerome in the Wilderness*, bequeathed by James Donald, 1905

Decker, Cornelis Gerritsz. (style of) before 1625–1678, *A Landscape*, bequeathed by Jane Graham-Gilbert, 1877

Degas, Edgar 1834–1917, *Girl Looking through Field Glasses*, gift from Sir William and Lady Burrell to the City of Glasgow, 1944

Degas, Edgar 1834–1917, *Horse Tied to a Tree*, gift from Sir William and Lady Burrell to the City of Glasgow, 1944

Degas, Edgar 1834–1917, *The Rehearsal*, gift from Sir William and Lady Burrell to the City of Glasgow, 1944

Degas, Edgar 1834–1917, *In the Tuileries, Woman with a Parasol*, gift from Sir William and Lady Burrell to the City of Glasgow, 1944

Delacroix, Eugène (studio of) 1798–1863, *The Expulsion of Adam and Eve from Paradise*, presented by the Trustees of the Hamilton Bequest, 1933

Denune, William c.1712–1750, *Portrait of a Lady in White*, gift from Sir William and Lady Burrell to the City of Glasgow, 1944

Derain, André 1880–1954, *Blackfriars Bridge, London*, purchased, 1942, © ADAGP, Paris and DACS, London 2013

Derbyshire, Florence Abba 1922–1975, *Black Jack*, purchased, 1995

Desmarées, George (studio of) 1697–1776, *Princess Theresia Benedikta Maria of Bavaria (1725–1743)*, bequeathed by Sir Daniel M. Stevenson, 1944

Diaz de la Peña, Narcisse Virgile 1808–1876, *Roses and Other Flowers*, bequeathed by Mrs Isabella Elder, 1906

Diaz de la Peña, Narcisse Virgile 1808–1876, *Flower Piece*, bequeathed by James Donald, 1905

Diaz de la Peña, Narcisse Virgile 1808–1876, *In the Forest*, bequeathed by James Donald, 1905

Dick, Bill *James Keir Hardie (1856–1915)*, purchased from the artist, 1984

Dick, Bill *Emrys Hughes (1894–1969)*, purchased, 1977

Dicksee, Frank 1853–1928, *Charlotte Mary Emily Nugent-Dunbar (d.1951), Wife of 3rd Baron Inverclyde*, bequeathed by Lord Inverclyde, 1958

Dietrich, Christian Wilhelm Ernst (attributed to) 1712–1774, *A Festive Gathering in a Park*, Archibald McLellan Collection, purchased, 1856

Dixon, Charles 1872–1934, *'Shamrock IV' and 'Victory', 26 May 1914*, presented by the Trustees of the estate of Sir Thomas Lipton, 1932

Dixon, Charles 1872–1934, *'Shamrock IV' Leaving for New York from Portsmouth, 18 July 1914*, presented by the Trustees of the estate of Sir Thomas Lipton, 1932

Dixon, Charles 1872–1934, *SY 'Erin' as a Hospital Ship*, presented by the Trustees of the estate of Sir Thomas Lipton, 1932

Diziani, Gaspare (attributed to) 1689–1767, *Hagar and the Angel*, Archibald McLellan Collection, purchased, 1856

Dobson, Cowan 1894–1980, *Old Lady Reading*, bequeathed by Jessie W. Craig, 1950

Dobson, Cowan 1894–1980, *Mrs Cowan Dobson*, purchased, 1932

Dobson, Henry John 1858–1928, *Mrs Hamilton*

Dobson, Henry John 1858–1928, *George Hamilton (1855–1935)*

Dobson, Henry John 1858–1928, *Dr Livingstone Teaching the Natives*, presented by the Misses Brechin, 1945

Docharty, Alexander Brownlie 1862–1940, *September, Glen Falloch*, gift from Archibald W. Finlayson, 1907

Docharty, Alexander Brownlie 1862–1940, *In the Woods, Early Spring*, gift from the artist, 1917

Docharty, Alexander Brownlie 1862–1940, *Lochiel's Country*, purchased from the artist, 1914

Docharty, Alexander Brownlie 1862–1940, *An Autumn Day*, gift from the artist, 1917

Docharty, Alexander Brownlie 1862–1940, *Springtime, Hawthorn Blossom*, gift from the artist, 1917

Docharty, Alexander Brownlie 1862–1940, *Winter Sunshine*, gift from the artist, 1917

Docharty, Alexander Brownlie 1862–1940, *The Old Clock Tower*, gift from the artist, 1917

Docharty, James 1829–1878, *Head of the Holy Loch*, bequeathed by Adam Teacher, 1898

Docharty, James 1829–1878, *The Heart of the Trossachs*, bequeathed by Adam Teacher, 1898

Docharty, James 1829–1878, *Moorland Road with Cattle*, bequeathed by Thomas D. Smellie, 1901

Docharty, James 1829–1878, *The Lone Shieling on the Misty Island*, bequeathed by Thomas D. Smellie, 1901

Docharty, James 1829–1878, *A Fishing Village, Skye*, gift from J. C. Arnot, 1903

Docharty, James 1829–1878, *In the Trossachs*, gift from Walter N. M. Reid, 1919

Docharty, James 1829–1878, *A Salmon Stream*, gift from J. C. Arnot, 1903

Docharty, James 1829–1878, *Head of Loch Eil*, bequeathed by Mary R. Lang, 1960

Dodd, Francis 1874–1949, *Afternoon in the Parlour*, bequeathed by Mrs Francis Dodd, 1948, © the artist's estate

Dodson, Sarah Paxton Ball 1847–1906, *The Duenna*, gift from R. Ball Dodson, 1920

Dodson, Sarah Paxton Ball 1847–1906, *An Oak Tree, Green Hedges, East Grinstead, Sussex*, gift from R. Ball Dodson, 1920

Dolci, Carlo 1616–1686, *The Adoration of the Magi*, Archibald McLellan Collection, purchased, 1856

Dolci, Carlo 1616–1686, *Salome*, purchased, 1883

Dolci, Carlo (after) 1616–1686, *Head of the Virgin*, bequeathed by Mrs Cecilia Douglas, 1862

Domenichino 1581–1641, *Landscape with Saint Jerome*, Archibald McLellan Collection, purchased, 1856

Domenichino (after) 1581–1641, *The Last Communion of Saint Jerome*, bequeathed by Mrs Cecilia Douglas, 1862

Donald, Anne b.1941, *Abbotsford Lane, Gorbals*, purchased, 1964

Donald, Anne b.1941, *Maryhill, Old and New, January*, gift from the artist, 2001

Donald, George Malcolm b.1943, *Singer*, gift from the BBC Collection, 2008, © the artist

Donald, George Malcolm b.1943, *Red Dragon over West Lake*, gift from the BBC Collection, 2008, © the artist

Donald, George Malcolm b.1943, *Temples*, gift from the BBC Collection, 2008, © the artist

Donald, John Milne 1819–1866, *Moorland Landscape*, bequeathed by Thomas D. Smellie, 1901, photo credit: Glasgow Museums

Donald, John Milne 1819–1866, *Cattle in a Pool*, gift from Miss Kirkpatrick, 1947

Donald, John Milne 1819–1866, *Loch Eck*, bequeathed by W. B. Faulds, 1898

Donald, John Milne 1819–1866, *Autumn Leaves*, bequeathed by W. B. Faulds, 1898

Donald, John Milne 1819–1866, *A Brooding Storm*, bequeathed by Adam Teacher, 1898

Donald, John Milne 1819–1866, *Canal Scene, Boats and Figures*, bequeathed by Adam Teacher, 1898

Donald, John Milne 1819–1866, *Highland Loch Scene*, bequeathed by Adam Teacher, 1898

Donald, John Milne 1819–1866, *Landscape with a Ruined Castle*, gift from Archibald G. Macdonald, 1896

Donald, John Milne 1819–1866, *Landscape with Figures*, bequeathed by Thomas D. Smellie, 1901

Donaldson, Andrew 1790–1846, *Old Theatre Royal, Queen Street, after the Fire in January 1829*, Archibald McLellan Collection, purchased, 1856

Donaldson, Andrew 1790–1846, *A Scotch Highland Village*, Archibald McLellan Collection, purchased, 1856

Donaldson, David Abercrombie 1916–1996, *Maria*, purchased, 1950, © the artist's estate

Donaldson, David Abercrombie 1916–1996, *Miss Barrie*, purchased, 1956, © the artist's estate

Donaldson, David Abercrombie 1916–1996, *White Tulips*, bequeathed by Miss Mary P. R. Allan, 2003, © the artist's estate

Donaldson, David Abercrombie 1916–1996, *Dame Jean Roberts (1895–1988), Lord Provost of Glasgow (1960–1963)*, purchased, 1965, © the artist's estate

Donaldson, David Abercrombie 1916–1996, *Self Portrait*, purchased, 1967, © the artist's estate

Donaldson, David Abercrombie 1916–1996, *Narcissi*, purchased, 1973, © the artist's estate

Donaldson, David Abercrombie 1916–1996, *Montjoi*, presented by Glasgow Art Gallery and the Museums Association with the assistance of Government Grant-in-Aid, 1982, © the artist's estate

Donaldson, David Abercrombie 1916–1996, *Susannah and the Elders*, purchased with the assistance of Glasgow Art Gallery, the Museums Association and the National Fund for Acquisitions, 1982, © the artist's estate

Donaldson, David Abercrombie 1916–1996, *Ronald J. P. Cowan (d.1922), Chairman of the Trustees of the Hamilton Bequest*, presented by the Trustees of the Hamilton Bequest, 1984, © the artist's estate

Doré, Gustave 1832–1883, *Glen Massan*, gift, 1979

Dorigny, Michel (attributed to) 1617–1665, *The Four Seasons*, Archibald McLellan Collection, purchased, 1856

Doughty, William (attributed to) 1757–1782, *Mr Palmer*, gift from William Burrell, 1925

Douglas, William Fettes 1822–1891, *The Recusant's Concealment Discovered*, purchased, 1964

Douglas, William Fettes 1822–1891, *The Rosicrucian*, bequeathed by Sir Alexander Cross, 1963

Douglass, Lilian 1903–1982, *Orchids for the Bride*, purchased, 1995

Douglass, Lilian 1903–1982, *Sundown*, purchased, 1995

Douglass, Lilian 1903–1982, *Who Art in Heaven*, purchased, 1995

Dow, Thomas Millie 1848–1919, *The Hudson River*, bequeathed by Allan McLean, 1928

Dow, Thomas Millie 1848–1919, *St Ives, Cornwall*, bequeathed by Allan McLean, 1928

Dowell, Charles R. c.1876–1935, *Interior of Glasgow Corporation Art Galleries*, purchased from the artist, 1926

Dowell, Charles R. c.1876–1935, *Sir William MacEwan (1848–1924)*, gift from Dr A. Freeland Fergus, 1928

Downie, John Patrick 1871–1945, *John Burns (b.1815), MD*, gift from subscribers, 1898

Downie, Kate b.1958, *Périphérique, la nouvelle ville*, purchased from the artist, 1992, © the artist

Downie, Kate b.1958, *Blue Night, Yellow Roof*, purchased from the artist, 1992, © the artist

Downie, Kate b.1958, *12 Minute Baby*, © the artist

Downie, Kate b.1958, *The Mother Pool*, purchased from the artist, 1994, © the artist

Downie, Patrick 1854–1945, *The Day of Rest, Winter*, purchased, 1906

Downie, Patrick 1854–1945, *Haddock Fishers, Ballantrae*, bequeathed by Mary R. Lang, 1960

Drew, J. P. active 1835–1861, *Study of a Girl*, bequeathed by William Euing, 1874

Drew, J. P. active 1835–1861, *Study of a Boy*, bequeathed by William Euing, 1874

Drummond, James 1816–1877, *The Marriage of Mary, Queen of Scots, and the Earl of Bothwell*, bequeathed by Robert Cochran, 1937

Drummond, Rose Myra active 1833–1849, *Helena Saville Faucit (1817–1898), Lady Martin*, bequeathed by Sir Theodore Martin, 1909

Dufy, Raoul 1877–1953, *The Jetties of Trouville-Deauville*, gift, 1960, © ADAGP, Paris and DACS, London 2013

Dugdale, Thomas Cantrell 1880–1952, *Robert L. Scott (1871–1939)*, presented by the executors of the estate and relatives of R. L. Scott, 1940, © Joanna Dunham

Dugdale, Thomas Cantrell 1880–1952, *Vivien Leigh (1913–1967)*, purchased, 1936, © Joanna Dunham

Dughet, Gaspard 1615–1675, *Ideal Landscape*, bequeathed by Jane Graham-Gilbert, 1877

Dughet, Gaspard 1615–1675, *Landscape with Figures*, Stirling Maxwell Collection, gift, 1967

Duguid, David 1832–1907, *Landscape*

Duguid, David 1832–1907, *Landscape*

Dunbar, Evelyn Mary 1906–1960, *Women's Auxiliary Air Force Store*, presented by the War Artists' Advisory Committee through the Imperial War Museum, 1948, © Culture and Sport Glasgow (Glasgow Museums)

Dunbar, Peter 1929–1983, *Seashore*, gift from the Contemporary Art Society, 1956

Duncan, E. active 20th C, *Peonies*, presented by the Trustees of the Hamilton Bequest, 1935

Duncan, John 1866–1945, *Ivory, Apes and Peacocks (The Queen of Sheba)*, purchased, 1963, © estate of John Duncan. All rights reserved, DACS 2013

Duncan, John 1866–1945, *The Coming of Bride*, purchased, 1918, © estate of John Duncan. All rights reserved, DACS 2013

Duncan, John 1866–1945, *Force and Reason*, bequeathed by the artist, 1945, © estate of John Duncan. All rights reserved, DACS 2013

Duncan, Thomas 1807–1845, *Christina Mitchell McNeil, the Mother of Ina, Dowager Duchess of Argyll*, bequeathed by Ina, Dowager Duchess of Argyll, 1926

Duncan, Thomas 1807–1845, *The Martyrdom of John Brown of Priesthill, 1685*, gift from J. Houldsworth, 1857

Duncan, Thomas 1807–1845, *Lieutenant Colonel A. Hope Pattison (1785–1824)*, gift from Godfrey H. Pattison, 1945

Duncan, Thomas 1807–1845, *The Brother of Ina, Dowager Duchess of Argyll, as a Boy*, bequeathed by Ina, Dowager Duchess of Argyll, 1926

Dunlop, Ronald Ossory 1894–1973, *Walberswick*, presented by the Trustees of the Hamilton Bequest, 1937

Dunlop, Ronald Ossory 1894–1973, *Southwold from Walberswick Beach*, presented by the Trustees of the Hamilton Bequest, 1938

Dunlop, Ronald Ossory 1894–1973, *Myself in a French Hat*, purchased, 1952

Dunn, Patrick S. active 1880–1918, *Renfield Street*

Dunn, William 1862–c.1932, *A Spring Morning in Marshland*, purchased, 1925

Dunn, William 1862–c.1932, *Marshy Land, Kent*, gift from J. D. Roberton, 1946

Duplessis, Jacques Vigoroux 1680–1732, *In a Notary Public's Office*, gift from Mrs Leadbetter, 1937

Dupont, Gainsborough 1754–1797, *Woody Landscape near Bath*, presented by the Trustees of the Hamilton Bequest, 1947

Dupont, Gainsborough (and studio) 1754–1797, *William Pitt the Younger (1759–1806)*, gift from Sir William and Lady Burrell to the City of Glasgow, 1944

Duprà, Domenico 1689–1770, *James Carnegie of Boysack (c.1714–1770)*, purchased, 1954

Dupré, Jules 1811–1889, *The Headland*, bequeathed by James Donald, 1905

Dupré, Léon Victor 1816–1879, *Landscape*, presented by Alexander Hill, 1922

Dürer, Albrecht (imitator of) 1471–1528, *The Head of Christ Crowned with Thorns*, Archibald McLellan Collection, purchased, 1856

Dusart, Cornelis (imitator of) 1660–1704, *A Man and a Woman Making Music*, bequeathed by William Euing, 1874, photo credit: Glasgow Museums

Dutch (Friesland) School *Portrait of a Girl, Aged One, with a Basket of Strawberries*, gift from Sir William and Lady Burrell to the City of Glasgow, 1944

Dutch (Friesland) School *Portrait of a Girl, Aged One, with a Rattle*, gift from Sir William and Lady Burrell to the City of Glasgow, 1944

Dutch School *Portrait of a Bearded Man, Aged 54*, presented by the Trustees of Hutchesons' Hospital, 1913

Dutch School *Portrait of a Boy, Aged Three, with a Large Hat and a Parrot*, gift from Sir William and Lady Burrell to the City of Glasgow, 1944

Dutch School 17th C, *Interior of a Living Room*, bequeathed by William Euing, 1874

Dutch School late 17th C, *A Disused Quarry in a Wood, with Figures*, Archibald McLellan Collection, purchased, 1856

Dutch School (attributed to) *Portrait of a Woman, Aged 46*, Archibald McLellan Collection, purchased, 1856

Dutch School (attributed to) 17th C, *Landscape with Ruins, Figures and Animals*, found in store, registered, 1988

Dutch School (attributed to) 18th C–19th C, *Interior with a Young Woman and a Boy*, Archibald McLellan Collection, purchased, 1856

Dutch School (attributed to) 18th C–19th C, *The Head of a Young Woman*, bequeathed by Mrs A. J. MacLaren, 1940

Duthie, Alexander Spottiswoode active 1885–1930, *Mrs Ruby McLennan*, gift from Mr and Mrs J. Bryce McLennan, 1946

Duverger, Théophile Emmanuel 1821–1901, *Playmates*, bequeathed by Mrs Isabella Elder, 1906

Dyce, William 1806–1864, *Sketch of a Doorway with a Water Barrel*, purchased, 1964

Dyce, William 1806–1864, *Christabel*, presented by the Trustees of the Hamilton Bequest, 1965

Dyck, Abraham van (attributed to) c.1635–1672, *A Bearded Man in a Fur Hat with a Book*, gift from William Burrell, 1925

Dyck, Anthony van (after) 1599–1641, *A Bacchic Procession*, bequeathed by William Euing, 1874

Dyck, Anthony van (after) 1599–1641, *The Rest on the Flight into Egypt*, gift from Sir Andrew Orr, 1856

Dyck, Anthony van (after) 1599–1641, *Infanta Isabella Clara Eugenia (1566–1633)*, Stirling Maxwell Collection, gift, 1967

Dyck, Anthony van (follower of) 1599–1641, *Portrait of a Young Bearded Man*, Archibald McLellan Collection, purchased, 1856

Eadie, Robert 1877–1954, *J. Shaw Maxwell (1855–1928), JP*, gift from the sitter, 1927

Eadie, Robert 1877–1954, *St Vincent Street*, purchased, 1942

Eardley, Joan Kathleen Harding 1921–1963, *Glasgow Kids, a Saturday Matinée Picture Queue*, presented by the Trustees of the Hamilton Bequest, 1966, © the Eardley estate

Eardley, Joan Kathleen Harding 1921–1963, *Catterline Coastguard Cottages*, purchased, 1952, © the Eardley estate

Eardley, Joan Kathleen Harding 1921–1963, *A Glasgow Lodging*, presented by the Trustees of the Hamilton Bequest, 1975, © the Eardley estate

Eardley, Joan Kathleen Harding 1921–1963, *A Stormy Sea No.1*, purchased, 1961, © the Eardley estate

Eardley, Joan Kathleen Harding 1921–1963, *Two Children*, purchased with the assistance of the National Fund for Acquisitions, Glasgow Art Gallery and the Museums Association, 1994, © the Eardley estate

East, Alfred 1844–1913, *Falls of Dochart, Killin*, presented by the Trustees of the estate of George Dickson, 1918

Eastlake, Charles Lock 1793–1865, *Christ Lamenting over Jerusalem*, gift from John Weir, 1928

Edwards *Mary Millar, Dairy Girl*, gift, 1977

Edwards, J. *Portrait of a Girl with a Doll*

Edwards, Lionel D. R. 1878–1966, *John Alan Burns (1897–1957), 4th Lord Inverclyde*, bequeathed by the sitter, 1957, © the artist's estate courtesy of Felix Rosenstiel's Widow & Son Ltd

El Greco 1541–1614, *Lady in a Fur Wrap*, Stirling Maxwell Collection, gift, 1967

El Greco 1541–1614, *Portrait of a Man*, Stirling Maxwell Collection, gift, 1967

Elder, Andrew Taylor 1908–1966, *Scottish Loch*, purchased, 1940

Ellis, Edwin 1841–1895, *On the South Coast of England*, bequeathed by Adam Teacher, 1898

Ellis, Edwin 1841–1895, *Seascape*, presented by the family of D. Brodie MacLeod, 1929

Elwell, Frederick William 1870–1958, *Widdall's*, purchased, 1930

Elwell, Frederick William 1870–1958, *The Squire*, bequeathed by Miss M. A. W. Thomson, 1947

Emsley, Walter 1860–1938, *The Clincher*

Erichsen, Vigilius (after) 1722–1783, *Prince Paul of Russia (1754–1801)*, bequeathed by William Euing, 1874

Es, Jacob Foppens van c.1596–1666, *Still Life with Game and Fruit*, bequeathed by William Euing, 1874

Es, Jacob Foppens van (attributed to) c.1596–1666, *Still Life with Fruit and Crayfish*, Archibald McLellan Collection, purchased, 1856

Esselens, Jacob 1626–1687, *Landscape with a Fowling Party*, Archibald McLellan Collection, purchased, 1856

Etty, William 1787–1849, *The Bathers*, bequeathed by William Euing, 1874

Etty, William 1787–1849, *The Honourable Mrs Caroline Norton (d.1877), Lady Stirling Maxwell*, on loan from a private collection

Etty, William 1787–1849, *The Three Graces*, bequeathed by William Euing, 1874

Eudes de Guimard, Louisa 1827–1904, *Boy Asleep*, bequeathed by William Euing, 1874

Evans, David Pugh b.1942, *North Corridor*, purchased with the assistance of the National Fund for Acquisitions, 1982, © the artist

Evans, Merlyn Oliver 1910–1973, *Wharfside Construction, Morning*, gift from the Contemporary Art Society, 1959, © the artist's estate

Everbroeck, Frans van (attributed to) active 1654–1672, *A Garland of Fruit around the Sculpted Bust of a Girl*, Archibald McLellan Collection, purchased, 1856

Ewart, David Shanks 1901–1965, *A Scots Lady*, purchased, 1929

Ewart, David Shanks 1901–1965, *Sir John Stewart, Lord Provost of Glasgow (1935–1938)*, purchased, 1938

Ewart, David Shanks 1901–1965, *Sir Hector McNeil, Lord Provost of Glasgow (1945–1949)*, gift from the sitter, 1950

Faed, John 1819–1902, *The Death of Burd Ellen*, bequeathed by Thomas D. Smellie, 1901

Faed, John 1819–1902, *View of Gatehouse of Fleet*, purchased with the assistance of the National Fund for Acquisitions, 1978

Faed, John 1819–1902, *The Artist's Wife, Jane Macdonald (1820–1897)*, gift from J. A. Faed, 1953

Faed, John 1819–1902, *Trysting Place, Landscape with Cattle and Sheep*, bequeathed by Adam Teacher, 1898

Faed, Thomas 1826–1900, *Burns and Highland Mary*, presented by the Trustees of the Hamilton Bequest, 1928

Faed, Thomas 1826–1900, *Alexander Dennistoun of Golfhill (1790–1874), and Family*, gift from John F. Carson, 1955

Faed, Thomas 1826–1900, *The Last of the Clan*, purchased with the assistance of the Heritage Fund for Scotland, the National Art Collections Fund, the Pilgrim Trust, Glasgow Print Studio and via public subscription, 1980

Faed, Thomas 1826–1900, *Violets and Primroses*, bequeathed by Adam Teacher, 1898

Faed, Thomas 1826–1900, *Where's My Good Little Girl?*, gift from Dr Douglas White, 1938

Faed, Thomas 1826–1900, *Interior with Figures*, gift from J. A. Faed, 1953

Faed, Thomas 1826–1900, *Spanish Bandits in a Cave*, bequeathed by Adam Teacher, 1898

Faed, Thomas 1826–1900, *Venus and Cupid*, bequeathed by Adam Teacher, 1898

Faed, Thomas (after) 1826–1900, *Three Children Playing in a Wood*, gift from A. S. Gilbert, 1954

Fairbairn, Thomas 1820–1885, *'We twa hae paddled i' the burn'*, bequeathed by Mrs Seller, 1927

Fantin-Latour, Henri 1836–1904, *A Mixed Bunch*, bequeathed by George B. Dunlop, 1951

Fantin-Latour, Henri 1836–1904, *Chrysanthemums*, gift from Sir William and Lady Burrell to the City of Glasgow, 1944

Fantin-Latour, Henri 1836–1904, *Basket of Peaches*, gift from Sir William and Lady Burrell to the City of Glasgow, 1944

Fantin-Latour, Henri 1836–1904, *Still Life*, bequeathed by William McInnes, 1944

Fantin-Latour, Henri 1836–1904, *Spring Flowers*, gift from Sir William and Lady Burrell to the City of Glasgow, 1944

Fantin-Latour, Henri 1836–1904, *Yellow Chrysanthemums*, presented by the Trustees of the Hamilton Bequest, 1929

Fantin-Latour, Henri 1836–1904, *The Bathers*, gift from Miss Rule, 1951

Fantin-Latour, Henri 1836–1904, *Basket of Peaches*, gift from Sir William and Lady Burrell to the City of Glasgow, 1944

Fantin-Latour, Henri 1836–1904, *Larkspur*, bequeathed by William J. Chrystal, 1939

Fantin-Latour, Henri 1836–1904, *Roses 'La France'*, bequeathed by William J. Chrystal, 1939

Fantin-Latour, Henri 1836–1904, *The Dance*, bequeathed by William McInnes, 1944

Fantin-Latour, Henri 1836–1904, *The Bather*, gift from Sir William and Lady Burrell to the City of Glasgow, 1944

Farquharson, David 1839–1907, *The Wayside, Loch Maree*, bequeathed by Mr and Mrs James Caldwell, 1918

Farquharson, David 1839–1907, *On the Achray*, bequeathed by Thomas D. Smellie, 1901

Farquharson, David 1839–1907, *Arran from the Ayrshire Coast*, bequeathed by Adam Teacher, 1898

Fell-Clark, Patricia 1914–2001, *James Maxton (1885–1946), MP*, gift from the James Maxton Memorial Fund, 1955, © the artist's estate

Fellowes, James (attributed to) c.1690–c.1760, *Lady Villiers*, gift from Sir William and Lady Burrell to the City of Glasgow, 1944

Ferguson, Dan 1910–1992, *Flowers in a Jug*, purchased, 1952

Ferguson, Dan 1910–1992, *Breaking Wave*, purchased, 1965

Ferguson, Dan 1910–1992, *Sea Edge*, purchased, 1971

Ferguson, William Gowe c.1632/1633–c.1695, *Still Life*, purchased, 1900

Ferguson, William Gowe c.1632/1633–c.1695, *Still Life*, purchased, 1900

Fergusson, John Duncan 1874–1961, *On the Loing*, gift, 1976, © The Fergusson Gallery, Perth and Kinross Council, Scotland

Fergusson, John Duncan 1874–1961, *On the Beach at Tangier*, purchased, 1962, © The Fergusson Gallery, Perth and Kinross Council, Scotland

Fergusson, John Duncan 1874–1961, *Garden Scene with Clothes Drying on a Line*, purchased, 1962, © The Fergusson Gallery, Perth and Kinross Council, Scotland

Fergusson, John Duncan 1874–1961, *Tenements, Edinburgh*, purchased, 1962, © The Fergusson Gallery, Perth and Kinross Council, Scotland

Fergusson, John Duncan 1874–1961, *Grey Day, Paris Plage*, presented by the Trustees of the Hamilton Bequest, 1981, © The Fergusson Gallery, Perth and Kinross Council, Scotland

Fergusson, John Duncan 1874–1961, *Hat with Bird: Anne Estelle Rice*, gift, 1963, © The Fergusson Gallery, Perth and Kinross Council, Scotland

Fergusson, John Duncan 1874–1961, *The Pink Parasol: Bertha Case*, purchased, 1958, © The Fergusson Gallery, Perth and Kinross Council, Scotland

Fergusson, John Duncan 1874–1961, *Montgeron*, purchased, 1963, © The Fergusson Gallery, Perth and Kinross Council, Scotland

Fergusson, John Duncan 1874–1961, *Torse de femme*, purchased, 1963, © The Fergusson Gallery, Perth and Kinross Council, Scotland

Fergusson, John Duncan 1874–1961, *Head of a Girl*, gift from the Contemporary Art Society, 1923, © The Fergusson Gallery, Perth and Kinross Council, Scotland

Fergusson, John Duncan 1874–1961, *Damaged Destroyer*, presented by Glasgow Art Gallery and the Museums Association, 1976, © The Fergusson Gallery, Perth and Kinross Council, Scotland

Fergusson, John Duncan 1874–1961, *In the Boltons: The Artist's Wife*, gift from William McInnes, 1928, © The Fergusson Gallery, Perth and Kinross Council, Scotland

Fergusson, John Duncan 1874–1961, *Golfe-Juan*, purchased, 1948, © The Fergusson Gallery, Perth and Kinross Council, Scotland

Fergusson, John Duncan 1874–1961, *The Roadman's House, St Fillans*, purchased from the artist, 1948, © The Fergusson Gallery, Perth and Kinross Council, Scotland

Fergusson, John Duncan 1874–1961, *Sun, Wind and Sea, and the Smell of the Pines*, gift from the Contemporary Art Society, 1964, © The Fergusson Gallery, Perth and Kinross Council, Scotland

Findlay, William 1875–1960, *The Liberation of Scotland (The Battle of Bannockburn)*, purchased from the artist, 1914

Finlayson *John and Mary Carmichael*, gift, 1977

Fischetti, Fedele 1734–1789, *The Holy Family with Saints Januarius and Anthony of Padua*, Archibald McLellan Collection, purchased, 1856

Flattely, Alastair Frederick 1922–2009, *View of Stroud, from Rodborough Common*, purchased, 1962, © the artist's estate

Fleming *Captain John Orkney*, gift, 2000

Fleming, Ian 1906–1994, *Arbroath Harbour*, purchased, 1952, © the artist's estate

Fleming, Ian 1906–1994, *Bomb Crater, Knightswood*, gift from the artist, 1986, © the artist's estate

Fleming, Jean 1937–1988, *Self Portrait*, purchased, 1958, © the artist's estate

Fleming, John B. 1792–1845, *View of Greenock*, bequeathed by William Euing, 1874

Flemish School early 17th C, *The Holy Family, Saint John and Angels*, Archibald McLellan Collection, purchased, 1856

Flemish School 17th C, *A Portrait of the Madonna, Supported by Cherubs, with Donors and Saints*, bequeathed by William Euing, 1874

Flemish School 17th C, *Bust of a Bearded Man Wearing a Cap*, bequeathed by Jane Graham-Gilbert, 1877

Flemish School 17th C, *Portrait of a Lady with a Ruff*, Stirling Maxwell Collection, gift, 1967

Flemish School 17th C, *The Arch of Constantine, Rome*, bequeathed by Thomas D. Smellie, 1901

Flemish School 17th C, *The Temple in the Piazza della Bocca della Verità, Rome*, bequeathed by Thomas D. Smellie, 1901

Flemish School *The Triumph of Amphitrite*, Archibald McLellan Collection, purchased, 1856

Flemish School (attributed to) 16th C, *The Mass of Saint Gregory*, found in store, registered, 1988

Flemish School (attributed to) *Portrait of a Boy*, Stirling Maxwell Collection, gift, 1967

Flemish School (attributed to) 17th C, *Italian Landscape with Figures*, Archibald McLellan Collection, purchased, 1856

Flemish School (attributed to) 17th C, *Kermesse*, found in store, registered, 1984

Flemish School (attributed to) 17th C, *The Infant Christ and Saint John in a Landscape*, bequeathed by Jane Graham-Gilbert, 1877

Fletcher, Alan 1936–1958, *Hill Street from George's Road, Glasgow* (recto), gift, 1989

Fletcher, Alan 1936–1958, *Study of an Art School Model* (verso), gift, 1989

Flinck, Govaert 1615–1660, *Self Portrait with Beret*, Archibald McLellan Collection, purchased, 1856

Flinck, Govaert (attributed to) 1615–1660, *Portrait of a Woman (possibly Saskia Uylenburgh, 1612–1642)*, gift from Sir William and Lady Burrell to the City of Glasgow, 1946

Flint, William Russell 1880–1969, *The Four Singers of Vera*, presented by the Trustees of the Hamilton Bequest, 1936, © the artist's estate

Flockhart, Helen b.1963, *Dwelling Place*, purchased, 1999, © the artist

Floris, Frans the elder (follower of) c.1517–1570, *A Pietà, with the Crucifixion and the Entombment*, Archibald McLellan Collection, purchased, 1856

Foggie, David Simpson 1878–1948, *Grandmother Knits*, purchased, 1944, © the artist's estate

Foottet, Frederick Francis 1850–1935, *Barnes, Surrey by Twilight*, gift from Miss A. M. Alexander, 1935

Ford, John A. active 1880–1923, *Lady Barbara Steuart Maxwell (d.1737)*, on loan from a private collection

Ford, John A. active 1880–1924, *Sir John Maxwell (1648–1732), 1st Bt*, on loan from a private collection

Forrester, W. *Waverley Station, Edinburgh*, gift from British Rail, London, 1967

Foschi, Francesco 1710–1780, *A Winter Landscape with Fortified Buildings*, bequeathed by William Euing, 1874

Fragonard, Jean-Honoré (follower of) 1732–1806, *Spring*, gift from F. J. Nettlefold, 1948

Fragonard, Jean-Honoré (follower of) 1732–1806, *Summer*, gift from F. J. Nettlefold, 1948

Fragonard, Jean-Honoré (follower of) 1732–1806, *Autumn*, gift from F. J. Nettlefold, 1948

Fragonard, Jean-Honoré (follower of) 1732–1806, *Winter*, gift from F. J. Nettlefold, 1948,

photo credit: Glasgow Museums

Fragonard, Jean-Honoré (school of) 1732–1806, *A Child's Head*, Archibald McLellan Collection, purchased, 1856

Francia, Francesco c.1450–1517, *The Nativity of Christ*, Archibald McLellan Collection, purchased, 1856

Francken, Frans I (circle of) 1542–1616, *The Adoration of the Shepherds*, Archibald McLellan Collection, purchased, 1856

Francken, Frans II 1581–1642, *The Procession to Calvary*, Archibald McLellan Collection, purchased, 1856

Francken, Frans III (attributed to) 1607–1667, *The Battle of the Amazons (after Peter Paul Rubens)*, Archibald McLellan Collection, purchased, 1856

Franco-Italian (Savoy) School *The Nativity with Saint Sixtus (?), Saint Jerome and a Cardinal*, Archibald McLellan Collection, purchased, 1856

Fraser, Alexander 1827–1899, *A Highland Burn (A Brooklet Stream)*, bequeathed by Adam Teacher, 1898

Fraser, Alexander 1827–1899, *A Highland Croft*, gift from C. B. Sherriff, 1946

Fraser, Alexander 1827–1899, *At North Berwick, Sunshine*, bequeathed by Adam Teacher, 1898

Fraser, Alexander 1827–1899, *Barncluith*, gift from James Carfrae Alston, 1909

Fraser, Alexander 1827–1899, *Cadzow Forest, Autumn*, bequeathed by Adam Teacher, 1898

Fraser, Alexander 1827–1899, *Cadzow Forest in Springtime*, bequeathed by Adam Teacher, 1898

Fraser, Alexander 1827–1899, *Castle Campbell, Springtime*, bequeathed by Adam Teacher, 1898

Fraser, Alexander 1827–1899, *Cathcart Castle*, acquired, 1967

Fraser, Alexander 1827–1899, *Dundarave Castle, Loch Fyne*, bequeathed by Adam Teacher, 1898

Fraser, Alexander 1827–1899, *East Coast Harbour Scene*, bequeathed by Adam Teacher, 1898

Fraser, Alexander 1827–1899, *Gathering Logs in Cadzow Forest*, bequeathed by Adam Teacher, 1898

Fraser, Alexander 1827–1899, *Harvest in the Highlands*, bequeathed by Thomas Binnie, 1912

Fraser, Alexander 1827–1899, *Highland Flitting*, bequeathed by Thomas D. Smellie, 1901

Fraser, Alexander 1827–1899, *Landscape and Cattle*, bequeathed by Adam Teacher, 1898

Fraser, Alexander 1827–1899, *On Loch Fyne*, bequeathed by Adam Teacher, 1898

Fraser, Alexander 1827–1899, *Springtime, Dundarroch, Brig o' Turk*, bequeathed by Adam Teacher, 1898

Fraser, Alexander 1827–1899, *The Bass Rock from Canty Bay*, bequeathed by Adam Teacher, 1898

Fraser, Alexander 1827–1899, *The Salmon Trap*, presented by the family of D. Brodie MacLeod, 1929

Fraser, Alexander 1827–1899, *View in Cadzow Forest*, bequeathed by Adam Teacher, 1898

Fraser, Alexander 1827–1899, *Waterfall*, bequeathed by Adam Teacher, 1898

Fraser, Alexander 1827–1899, *Woodcutters in Cadzow Forest*, bequeathed by Adam Teacher, 1898

Fraser, Alexander (attributed to) 1827–1899, *Landscape with a Rustic Bridge*, temporary identification number allocated, 1974

Fraser, Alexander b.1940, *Celtic Cross and Birds*, purchased, 1962, © the artist

Fraser, Alexander George 1786–1865, *Smoking the Cobbler*, Stirling Maxwell Collection, gift, 1967

Frater, William 1890–1974, *Bush Landscape, Wandong, Victoria*, presented by the Victorian Artists Society, Australia, 1968

French (Amiens) School late 15th C, *Angel of the Annunciation*, gift from Sir William and Lady Burrell to the City of Glasgow, 1944

French School *Figures in a Park*, Archibald McLellan Collection, purchased, 1856

French School (attributed to) *Leda and the Swan*, Archibald McLellan Collection, purchased, 1856

French School (attributed to) 18th C, *The Death of Cleopatra*, Archibald McLellan Collection, purchased, 1856

Frère, Pierre Edouard 1819–1886, *Mother and Children*, bequeathed by James Donald, 1905

Frew, Alexander d.1908, *Landscape*, gift from Edward N. Marshall, 1951

Friesz, Othon 1879–1949, *The Seine at Paris, Pont de Grenelle*, purchased, 1959, © ADAGP, Paris and DACS, London 2013

Frith, William Powell 1819–1909, *A Royal Princess*, gift from Lewis Lyons in memory of his father, 1943

Frood, Millie 1900–1988, *Hayricks*, purchased from the artist, 1942

Frost, George 1754–1821, *Courtship*, bequeathed by William Euing, 1874

Fry, Roger Eliot 1866–1934, *A Provençal Harbour*, purchased, 1959

Fry, Roger Eliot 1866–1934, *Roquebrune and Monte Carlo from*

Palm Beach, purchased, 1969

Fulton, David 1848–1930, *By the Burnside*, purchased, 1912

Fulton, David 1848–1930, *Morning Time, Grogport, Kintyre*, presented by the Misses Fulton Brown, 1936

Fulton, Samuel 1855–1941, *Foxhounds*, purchased, 1910

Gabain, Ethel Leontine 1883–1950, *Stripes and Lace*, gift from John Copley, 1950, © the artist's estate

Gabrielli, Gaspare 1770–1828, *View of the Roman Forum*, bequeathed by Mrs Cecilia Douglas, 1862

Gael, Barend c.1635–1698, *Peasants before a Cottage*, Archibald McLellan Collection, purchased, 1856

Gainsborough, Thomas (after) 1727–1788, *The Blue Boy*, Stirling Maxwell Collection, gift, 1967

Gainsborough, Thomas (attributed to) 1727–1788, *Donkeys in a Storm*, Archibald McLellan Collection, purchased, 1856

Gale, William 1823–1909, *The Dance of Nymphs*, gift from Archibald G. Macdonald, 1896

Gambara, Lattanzio c.1530–1574, *Agrippine Sibyl*, gift from Charles Heath Wilson, 1870

Gardner, A. active 19th C, *Auld Shettleston Road, Glasgow*

Gardner, Alexandra b.1945, *Yellow Pond*, purchased, 1975, © the artist

Gardner, Audrey R. *Mrs Gray, Headmistress of Park School (1995)*, gift from the Park and Laurel Bank Schools Collection (incorporating Laurel Park School), 2006

Gardner, Audrey R. *Mrs Myatt, Headmistress of Park School (1986–1995)*, gift from the Park and Laurel Bank Schools Collection (incorporating Laurel Park School), 2006

Gardner, Daniel 1750–1805, *Agnes Pennington*, gift from A. E. Anderson, 1931

Garofalo c.1481–1559, *Saint Catherine of Alexandria*, Archibald McLellan Collection, purchased, 1856

Garofalo c.1481–1559, *Saint Ursula*, Archibald McLellan Collection, purchased, 1856

Garofalo (after) c.1481–1559, *The Vision of Saint Augustine*, Archibald McLellan Collection, purchased, 1856

Garrido, Leandro Ramón 1868–1909, *The Lady with the Gloves*, purchased, 1904

Garstin, Norman 1847–1926, *The Last Furrow*, gift from Mrs Norman Garstin, 1927

Gartside, Fred *Glasgow University, Sunrise*, gift from Thomas S. Bisset, 1915

Garzi, Luigi 1638–1721, *The Sacrifice of Marcus Curtius*, bequeathed by William Kennedy, 1899

Gatti, Gervasio (attributed to) 1549–1631, *Mother and Child*, gift

from Sir William and Lady Burrell to the City of Glasgow, 1944

Gauguin, Paul 1848–1903, *Østre Anlæg Park, Copenhagen*, presented by the Trustees of the Hamilton Bequest, 1944

Gauld, David 1865–1936, *Portrait Head*, gift from Sir John Richmond, 1948

Gauld, David 1865–1936, *Contentment*, purchased, 1903

Gauld, David 1865–1936, *Robert Stewart, Lord Provost of Glasgow (1851–1854)* (after Daniel Macnee), found in store, registered, 1909

Gauld, David 1865–1936, *Raploch, Stirling*, purchased, 1931

Gauld, David 1865–1936, *A Boy*, gift from J. Norman Lang, 1942

Gauld, David 1865–1936, *East Linton Mill*, gift from Sir John Richmond, 1948

Gauld, David 1865–1936, *Two Calves*, gift from Sir John Richmond, 1948

Gauld, David 1865–1936, *Two Calves*, gift from Mrs K. F. Cameron, Mrs M. C. Smith and their nephews, Patrick, John and David Donaldson, 1958

Gear, William 1915–1997, *Summer Garden*, purchased with the assistance of the National Fund for Acquisitions, 1982, © the artist's estate

Geddes, Andrew 1783–1844, *Portrait of a Lady*, presented by the Trustees of the Hamilton Bequest, 1929

Geddes, Andrew 1783–1844, *Charles Tennant (1768–1838)*, bequeathed by James Couper, 1920

Geddes, Andrew 1783–1844, *Alexander Oswald of Changue (1777–1821)*, presented by the Trustees of the Hamilton Bequest, 1949

Geddes, Andrew 1783–1844, *Child with a Spaniel*, purchased, 1956

Geddes, Andrew 1783–1844, *Jeremiah Greatorex (1768–1877)*, purchased, 1950

Geddes, Andrew 1783–1844, *Portrait of an Old Scottish Lady*, purchased, 1917

Geel, Joost van 1631–1698, *The Queen of Hearts*, bequeathed by Francis J. Eck, 1915

Geeraerts, Marcus the younger (school of) 1561–1635, *William Cecil (1520–1598), Lord Burghley*, gift from Sir William and Lady Burrell to the City of Glasgow, 1944

Geeraerts, Marcus the younger (school of) 1561–1635, *Elizabeth Vernon (1572–1655), Countess of Southampton*, purchased by the Trustees of the Burrell Collection with the assistance of the Heritage Lottery Fund, 1999

Gemmell, A. active 19th C, *The Clyde at Carmyle, Glasgow*

Gérard, Lucien 1852–1935, *Young Man Reading*, presented by Miss M. Garroway, 1947

Géricault, Théodore 1791–1824, *A*

Prancing Grey Horse, gift from Sir William and Lady Burrell to the City of Glasgow, 1944

Géricault, Théodore 1791–1824, *The Trumpeter of the Lancers of the Guard*, gift from Sir William and Lady Burrell to the City of Glasgow, 1944

Géricault, Théodore (after) 1791–1824, *The Stud Farm*, gift from Sir William and Lady Burrell to the City of Glasgow, 1944

Géricault, Théodore (attributed to) 1791–1824, *The Grey Horse 'Telemachus'*, gift from Sir William and Lady Burrell to the City of Glasgow, 1944

Géricault, Théodore (attributed to) 1791–1824, *Two Brown Horses in a Stall*, gift from Sir William and Lady Burrell to the City of Glasgow, 1944

Géricault, Théodore (style of) 1791–1824, *A Piebald Stallion*, gift from Sir William and Lady Burrell to the City of Glasgow, 1944

Géricault, Théodore (style of) 1791–1824, *Grey Charger Harnessed with Blue Trappings*, gift from Sir William and Lady Burrell to the City of Glasgow, 1944

Géricault, Théodore (style of) 1791–1824, *The Stallion*, gift from Sir William and Lady Burrell to the City of Glasgow, 1944

German School *The Emperor Ferdinand I (1503–1564)*, Stirling Maxwell Collection, gift, 1967

German School *Christ and the Pope*, Stirling Maxwell Collection, gift, 1967

German School *The Resurrection*, Archibald McLellan Collection, purchased, 1856

German School 17th C (?), *The Christ Child Sleeping on the Cross, with Saint John*, Archibald McLellan Collection, purchased, 1856

German School (attributed to) 18th C, *A Miser*, gift from Archibald M. Craig, 1944

German School (attributed to) 18th C, *Still Life: Oysters, a Glass and a Decanter*, gift from William Burrell, 1925

Gertler, Mark 1891–1939, *Clytie and Autumn Leaves*, gift from John Mathias, 1951

Gertler, Mark 1891–1939, *After Giotto*, gift from John Mathias, 1951

Gertler, Mark 1891–1939, *Head of a Girl*, gift from the Contemporary Art Society, 1935

Ghezzi, Pier Leone 1674–1755, *The Purification of Aeneas in the River Numicius*, found in store, registered, 1965

Ghisolfi, Giovanni (attributed to) c.1623–1683, *Christ Giving the Keys to Saint Peter*, Archibald McLellan Collection, purchased, 1856

Gibb, Robert II 1845–1932, *Portrait of a Seated Man*, acquired, 1978

Gibb, Robert II 1845–1932, *Alma: Forward the 42nd*, gift from Lord

Woolavington, 1923

Gibbons, Carole b.1935, *Self Portrait with Henry*, purchased from the artist, 1992, © the artist

Gibson, John 1768–1852, *Reverend William Kidston, DD*, acquired, 1978

Gibson, William Alfred 1866–1931, *The Passing of Autumn*, purchased, 1913

Gijsels, Philips (attributed to) active 1642–1663, *Still Life: Lobster, Fruit and Glasses*, gift from Sir William and Lady Burrell to the City of Glasgow, 1944

Gilbert, Arthur 1819–1895, *Landscape*, bequeathed by William Euing, 1874

Gilbert, Arthur 1819–1895, *Landscape*, bequeathed by William Euing, 1874

Gilfillan, James active 20th C, *Ferry off the Antrim Coast*

Gilfillan, John Alexander 1793–1864, *Robinson Crusoe Landing Stores from the Wreck*, bequeathed by William Euing, 1874

Gill, André (attributed to) 1840–1885, *Pierrot voleur*, gift from Sir William and Lady Burrell to the City of Glasgow, 1944

Gillemans, Jan Pauwel I (attributed to) 1618–1675, *Still Life with Fruit and Oysters*, Archibald McLellan Collection, purchased, 1856

Gillies, William George 1898–1973, *Still Life, Flowers and Figures*, purchased, 1943, © the artist's estate

Gillies, William George 1898–1973, *Still Life, Blue and Brown*, presented by Glasgow Art Gallery and the Museums Association, 1953, © the artist's estate

Gillies, William George 1898–1973, *Carrington*, purchased with the assistance of the Trustees of the Hamilton Bequest and the National Fund for Acquisitions, 1983, © the artist's estate

Gillies, William George 1898–1973, *Interior*, purchased, 1965, © Culture and Sport Glasgow (Glasgow Museums)

Gillies, William George 1898–1973, *Storm over Gladhouse*, bequeathed by George and Isobel Neillands, 1988, © the artist's estate

Gilman, Harold 1876–1919, *Contemplation*, purchased, 1974

Giordano, Luca 1634–1705, *The Holy Family with Saint Catherine of Alexandria*, gift from A. G. McDonald, 1896

Giordano, Luca (follower of) 1634–1705, *Elijah and the Widow of Zarephath*, Archibald McLellan Collection, purchased, 1856

Giordano, Luca (follower of) 1634–1705, *Bacchus and Infant Fauns*, Archibald McLellan Collection, purchased, 1856

Giordano, Luca (follower of) 1634–1705, *Cupids at Play*,

Archibald McLellan Collection, purchased, 1856

Giovanni da Asola (attributed to) d.1531, *Musicians in a Landscape*, bequeathed by Jane Graham-Gilbert, 1877

Girling, Fred Jay 1900–1982, *HMS 'Vanguard'*, purchased with the assistance of the National Fund for Acquisitions, 1973, © the artist's estate

Girolamo da Carpi c.1501–1556, *Virgin and Child in a Landscape with the Child Baptist and Saint Catherine of Alexandria*, bequeathed by Sir Claude Phillips, 1924

Glendening, Alfred Augustus 1840–1921, *Lady Place, Hurley-on-Thames*, gift from Miss Anderson, 1921

Glover, Edmund 1816–1860, *Landscape, Moonlight*, bequeathed by William Euing, 1874

Glover, Edmund 1816–1860, *Rothesay Castle, Moonlight*, bequeathed by William Euing, 1874

Glover, Edmund 1816–1860, *Village of Newhaven, near Edinburgh*, bequeathed by William Euing, 1874

Glover, William 1836–1916, *Glasgow Cross from the Saltmarket*, purchased, 1960

Glover, William 1836–1916, *The River Kelvin from the North at the Botanic Gardens*, gift from Sir Thomas Dunlop, 1912

Glover, William 1836–1916, *Castle Street, Glasgow*, purchased, 1960

Glover, William 1836–1916, *Glenboig Clay Mill*, gift from Henry Cornish, 1940

Godward, John William 1861–1922, *A Lady*, bequeathed by Major John Garroway, 1920

Gogh, Vincent van 1853–1890, *The Blute-Fin Windmill, Montmartre*, bequeathed by William McInnes, 1944

Gogh, Vincent van 1853–1890, *Alexander Reid (1854–1928)*, purchased with the assistance of the National Fund for Acquisitions, the National Art Collections Fund, an anonymous donor and public subscription, 1974

Gogin, Charles 1844–1931, *A Road in France*, gift from Mrs Alma Gogin, 1944

Gogin, Charles 1844–1931, *Thelma*, gift from Mrs Alma Gogin, 1944

Goodall, Frederick 1822–1904, *Spanish Peasants Retreating from the French Army*, bequeathed by Mrs Isabella Elder, 1906

Gordon, Cora Josephine 1879–1950, *France: The Village on the Hills*, gift from Mrs Carola Yapp, 1950

Gordon, Jan (Godfrey Jervis) 1882–1944, *The Gipsy Singer*, gift from Mrs Carola Yapp, 1950

Gordon, Jan (Godfrey Jervis) 1882–1944, *The Melon Guzzlers*, gift from Mrs Carola Yapp, 1950

Gordon, John Watson 1788–1864, *Alexander Dunlop of Keppoch (1766–1840)*, gift from John G. Dunlop and the Mercantile Bank, 1961

Gordon, John Watson 1788–1864, *A Boy and a Girl*, bequeathed by Mrs Whyte of Newbury, 1912

Gordon, John Watson 1788–1864, *Elizabeth Galloway (or Grieve), of Sandyhills (d.1826)*, gift from William T. Wilson, 1903

Gordon, John Watson 1788–1864, *The Honourable Mrs Alexander Macalister*, gift from Major T. Ranken, 1949

Gordon, John Watson 1788–1864, *Alexander Macalister of Loup, Torrisdale and Strathaird (1802–1876)*, gift from Major T. Ranken, 1949

Gordon, John Watson 1788–1864, *Andrew Vannan*, gift from Miss J. Dunlop Vannan, 1946

Gordon, John Watson 1788–1864, *Mrs Janet D. Vannan*, gift from Miss J. Dunlop Vannan, 1946

Gordon, John Watson 1788–1864, *Charles Heath Wilson (1809–1882)*, gift from W. Heath Wilson, 1915

Gordon, John Watson 1788–1864, *James Grant*, gift from Mrs Wallace, 1947

Gordon, John Watson 1788–1864, *Mrs James Grant*, gift from Mrs Wallace, 1947

Gordon, John Watson 1788–1864, *John Geddes of Verreville Pottery and Glassworks, Anderston*, on loan from a private collection

Gordon, John Watson 1788–1864, *Portrait of a Gentleman*, gift from Professor G. H. Bell, 1951

Gordon, John Watson 1788–1864, *Portrait of a Lady*, presented by the Misses Kirsop, 1915

Gordon, John Watson 1788–1864, *Mrs William Scott of Sandyfaulds*, bequeathed by D. S. MacColl, 1949

Gordon, John Watson 1788–1864, *William Scott of Sandyfaulds*, bequeathed by D. S. MacColl, 1949

Gossman, Mary Hislop Somerville *Provan Hall, Glasgow*

Goudie, Alexander 1933–2004, *Andrew Hood (b.1887), LLD, Lord Provost of Glasgow (1955–1958)*, gift from Mrs Jean Roberts, 1956, © the artist's estate/Bridgeman Art Library

Goudie, Alexander 1933–2004, *Evening Light, Saint-Lizier*, purchased, 1959, © the artist's estate/Bridgeman Art Library

Goudie, Alexander 1933–2004, *Still Life with a Bowl of Fruit*, purchased, 1964, © the artist's estate/Bridgeman Art Library

Goudie, Alexander 1933–2004, *John Johnston, Lord Provost of Glasgow (1965–1969)*, purchased, 1970, © the artist's estate/ Bridgeman Art Library

Goudie, Alexander 1933–2004, *Après le repas du soir*, purchased, 1972, © the artist's estate/ Bridgeman Art Library

Goulding, Arthur b.1921, *Reflections*, purchased, 1995

Goya, Francisco de 1746–1828, *Boys Playing at See-Saw*, Stirling Maxwell Collection, gift, 1967

Goya, Francisco de 1746–1828, *Boys Playing at Soldiers*, Stirling Maxwell Collection, gift, 1967

Goyen, Jan van 1596–1656, *Cottages and Fishermen by a River*, Archibald McLellan Collection, purchased, 1856

Goyen, Jan van (after) 1596–1656, *Cottages by a Canal*, Archibald McLellan Collection, purchased, 1856

Goyen, Jan van (follower of) 1596–1656, *Shipping Scene*, on loan from a private collection

Goyen, Jan van (style of) 1596–1656, *Landscape with an Old Oak Tree*, bequeathed by Jane Graham-Gilbert, 1877

Graham, Peter 1836–1921, *Along the Cliffs*, bequeathed by Mrs Isabella Elder, 1906

Graham, Peter 1836–1921, *Where Gannets Build*, bequeathed by Mrs A. C. Thorneycroft, 1934

Graham, Thomas Alexander Ferguson 1840–1906, *Venetian Water Girl*, gift from T. Graham Young in memory of his father, James Young, 1900

Graham Bell, Frank 1910–1943, *Miss Pool*, gift from the Contemporary Art Society, 1944, © the artist's estate

Graham-Gilbert, John 1794–1866, *James Hopkirk of Dalbeth (1749–1836)*, bequeathed by Isabella J. Hopkirk, 1899

Graham-Gilbert, John 1794–1866, *Figure of a Lady* (after Jacopo Palma il vecchio), bequeathed by Jane Graham-Gilbert, 1877

Graham-Gilbert, John 1794–1866, *Madonna della scodella* (after Correggio), bequeathed by Jane Graham-Gilbert, 1877

Graham-Gilbert, John 1794–1866, *Madonna with Saint Jerome* (after Correggio), bequeathed by Jane Graham-Gilbert, 1877

Graham-Gilbert, John 1794–1866, *The Martyrdom of Saint Justina* (after Paolo Veronese), bequeathed by Jane Graham-Gilbert, 1877

Graham-Gilbert, John 1794–1866, *A Tyrolese Hunter*, bequeathed by Jane Graham-Gilbert, 1877

Graham-Gilbert, John 1794–1866, *Saint Sebastian*, bequeathed by Jane Graham-Gilbert, 1877

Graham-Gilbert, John 1794–1866, *James Dennistoun, Esq. of Golfhill (1758–1835)*, temporary identification number allocated, 1979

Graham-Gilbert, John 1794–1866, *John T. Alston (1780–1857), Provost of Glasgow (1820–1821)*, gift from Mrs Stella Alston, 1930

Graham-Gilbert, John 1794–1866, *Mrs Hugh Robertson of Gartloch (1798–1846)*, presented by the descendants of Mr and Mrs Hugh Robertson of Gartloch, 1956

Graham-Gilbert, John 1794–1866, *Lord Kelvin William Thomson (1824–1907), at the Age of 22*, gift from Agnes G. K. Hartwell, 1920

Graham-Gilbert, John 1794–1866, *Mrs James Scott of Kelly*, gift from Major Ker, 1946

Graham-Gilbert, John 1794–1866, *The First Born*, bequeathed by Jane Graham-Gilbert, 1877

Graham-Gilbert, John 1794–1866, *Crossing the Ford*, bequeathed by Jane Graham-Gilbert, 1877

Graham-Gilbert, John 1794–1866, *Mrs John Jarvie*, gift from Mrs Helen Percy, 1950

Graham-Gilbert, John 1794–1866, *Going to Market*, bequeathed by Jane Graham-Gilbert, 1877

Graham-Gilbert, John 1794–1866, *Mrs Agnes D'Arcy Jarvie*, gift, 1962

Graham-Gilbert, John 1794–1866, *A Country Maid*, bequeathed by Jane Graham-Gilbert, 1877

Graham-Gilbert, John 1794–1866, *A Girl*, bequeathed by Jane Graham-Gilbert, 1877

Graham-Gilbert, John 1794–1866, *A Grecian Girl*, bequeathed by Jane Graham-Gilbert, 1877

Graham-Gilbert, John 1794–1866, *A Grecian Girl*, bequeathed by Jane Graham-Gilbert, 1877

Graham-Gilbert, John 1794–1866, *A Grecian Girl*, bequeathed by Jane Graham-Gilbert, 1877

Graham-Gilbert, John 1794–1866, *A Lady* (after Henry Raeburn), bequeathed by Jane Graham-Gilbert, 1877, photo credit: Glasgow Museums

Graham-Gilbert, John 1794–1866, *A Lady Sketching*, bequeathed by Jane Graham-Gilbert, 1877

Graham-Gilbert, John 1794–1866, *A Woman of Lonico*, bequeathed by Jane Graham-Gilbert, 1877

Graham-Gilbert, John 1794–1866, *Andrew Stevenson Dalglish (1793–1858)*, temporary identification number allocated, 1977

Graham-Gilbert, John 1794–1866, *Bailie John Alston of Rosemount (1778–1846)*, gift from Reverend J. M. Brodie, 1953

Graham-Gilbert, John 1794–1866, *Christ and the Woman of Samaria*, bequeathed by Jane Graham-Gilbert, 1877

Graham-Gilbert, John 1794–1866, *Christ Appearing to Mary Magdalene*, bequeathed by Jane Graham-Gilbert, 1877

Graham-Gilbert, John 1794–1866, *Cupid* (after Titian), bequeathed by Jane Graham-Gilbert, 1877

Graham-Gilbert, John 1794–1866, *Dr William Hunter (1718–1783)* (after Joshua Reynolds), bequeathed by Jane Graham-Gilbert, 1877

Graham-Gilbert, John 1794–1866, *Female Figure* (after Titian),

bequeathed by Jane Graham-Gilbert, 1877

Graham-Gilbert, John 1794–1866, *Female Figure* (after Titian), bequeathed by Jane Graham-Gilbert, 1877

Graham-Gilbert, John 1794–1866, *Female Portrait*

Graham-Gilbert, John 1794–1866, *Figure Study*, bequeathed by Jane Graham-Gilbert, 1877

Graham-Gilbert, John 1794–1866, *Figure Study*, bequeathed by Jane Graham-Gilbert, 1877

Graham-Gilbert, John 1794–1866, *Gipsy Girl*, bequeathed by Jane Graham-Gilbert, 1877

Graham-Gilbert, John 1794–1866, *Girl Playing the Guitar*, bequeathed by Jane Graham-Gilbert, 1877

Graham-Gilbert, John 1794–1866, *Girls at a Stream*, bequeathed by Jane Graham-Gilbert, 1877

Graham-Gilbert, John 1794–1866, *Head of an Old Woman with a Cap, in Profile to the Right*, bequeathed by Jane Graham-Gilbert, 1877

Graham-Gilbert, John 1794–1866, *Humphrey E. Maclae of Cathkin (1773–1860)*, gift from Mrs A. C. Grahame, 1954

Graham-Gilbert, John 1794–1866, *Ideal Portrait*, bequeathed by Jane Graham-Gilbert, 1877

Graham-Gilbert, John 1794–1866, *Italian Gentleman*, bequeathed by Jane Graham-Gilbert, 1877

Graham-Gilbert, John 1794–1866, *Italian Girl*, bequeathed by Jane Graham-Gilbert, 1877

Graham-Gilbert, John 1794–1866, *Italian Study*, bequeathed by Jane Graham-Gilbert, 1877

Graham-Gilbert, John 1794–1866, *Italian Woman*, bequeathed by Jane Graham-Gilbert, 1877

Graham-Gilbert, John 1794–1866, *James Buchanan of Dowanhill (1756–1844)*, gift from Francis C. Buchanan on behalf of Buchanan, FRS, 1916

Graham-Gilbert, John 1794–1866, *James Dennistoun, Esq. of Golfhill (1758–1835)*, on loan from Captain Dennistoun of Golfhill, since 1912

Graham-Gilbert, John 1794–1866, *James Hamilton*, presented by the Police Commissioners, 1883

Graham-Gilbert, John 1794–1866, *Lady with a Finch*, bequeathed by William Euing, 1874

Graham-Gilbert, John 1794–1866, *Madonna and Child* (after Correggio), bequeathed by Jane Graham-Gilbert, 1877

Graham-Gilbert, John 1794–1866, *Madonna and Child* (after Correggio), bequeathed by Jane Graham-Gilbert, 1877

Graham-Gilbert, John 1794–1866, *Magdalene and Child* (after Correggio), bequeathed by Jane Graham-Gilbert, 1877

Graham-Gilbert, John 1794–1866, *Meditation*, bequeathed by Jane Graham-Gilbert, 1877

Graham-Gilbert, John 1794–1866, *Mungo Campbell*, bequeathed by

Isabella A. H. J. Campbell, 1917

Graham-Gilbert, John 1794–1866, *Mrs Isabella C. Campbell*, bequeathed by Isabella A. H. J. Campbell, 1917

Graham-Gilbert, John 1794–1866, *Nymph with Infant Bacchus* (after Joshua Reynolds), bequeathed by Jane Graham-Gilbert, 1877

Graham-Gilbert, John 1794–1866, *Old Lady Reading*, bequeathed by Jane Graham-Gilbert, 1877

Graham-Gilbert, John 1794–1866, *Old Woman Reading* (after Rembrandt van Rijn), bequeathed by Jane Graham-Gilbert, 1877

Graham-Gilbert, John 1794–1866, *Pope Paul III* (after Titian), bequeathed by Jane Graham-Gilbert, 1877

Graham-Gilbert, John 1794–1866, *Study of a Female Figure*, bequeathed by Jane Graham-Gilbert, 1877

Graham-Gilbert, John 1794–1866, *Study of a Head*, bequeathed by Jane Graham-Gilbert, 1877

Graham-Gilbert, John 1794–1866, *Study of a Head* (after Henry Raeburn), bequeathed by Jane Graham-Gilbert, 1877

Graham-Gilbert, John 1794–1866, *The Beggar Maid*, gift from Archibald Colquhoun, 1873, photo credit: Glasgow Museums

Graham-Gilbert, John 1794–1866, *The Father of Archibald McLellan*, Archibald McLellan Collection, purchased, 1856

Graham-Gilbert, John 1794–1866, *The Gipsy*, bequeathed by Jane Graham-Gilbert, 1877

Graham-Gilbert, John 1794–1866, *The Madonna Adoring the Infant Christ* (after Correggio), bequeathed by Jane Graham-Gilbert, 1877

Graham-Gilbert, John 1794–1866, *The Pet Dove*, bequeathed by Jane Graham-Gilbert, 1877

Graham-Gilbert, John 1794–1866, *The Reading Magdalene* (after Titian), bequeathed by Jane Graham-Gilbert, 1877

Graham-Gilbert, John 1794–1866, *The Young Seamstress*, Archibald McLellan Collection, purchased, 1856

Graham-Gilbert, John (attributed to) 1794–1866, *A Rabbi*, bequeathed by Jane Graham-Gilbert, 1877

Graham-Gilbert, John (attributed to) 1794–1866, *Charles I with M. de St Antoine* (after Anthony van Dyck), bequeathed by Jane Graham-Gilbert, 1877

Graham-Gilbert, John (attributed to) 1794–1866, *Margaretha de Geer, Wife of Jacob Trip* (after Rembrandt van Rijn), bequeathed by Jane Graham-Gilbert, 1877

Graham-Gilbert, John (attributed to) 1794–1866, *Self Portrait* (after Peter Paul Rubens), bequeathed by Jane Graham-Gilbert, 1877

Graham-Gilbert, John (attributed to) 1794–1866, *Self Portrait* (after

(1791–1870), bequeathed by Mrs A. C. Grahame, 1954

Harding, Chester 1792–1866, *John Pattison (1783–1867)*, gift from Godfrey H. Pattison, 1945

Harding, Chester 1792–1866, *Robert Grahame (1759–1851), Lord Provost of Glasgow (1833–1834)*, gift from Mrs Felicia P. Cockerell, 1947

Hargitt, Edward 1835–1895, *Mountain Landscape*, purchased, 1959

Harmar, Fairlie 1876–1945, *Oxen in Brittany*, presented by the Trustees of the Hamilton Bequest, 1938

Harpignies, Henri-Joseph 1819–1916, *Moonrise*, presented by the Trustees of the Hamilton Bequest, 1932

Harris, H. active 19th C, *William C. Honeyman*, gift from an anonymous donor, 1996

Harvey, George 1806–1876, *The Covenanters' Preaching*, gift from John Fleming, 1870

Harvey, George 1806–1876, *Drumclog*, purchased, 1959

Harvey, George 1806–1876, *The Drove Road*, gift from T. Graham Young in memory of his father, James Young, 1900

Harvey, R. *James Watt (1736–1819), Engineer, Greenock*

Harvie, Robert d.1781, *Arthur Connell (1717–1775), Provost of Glasgow (1772–1773)*, gift from Mrs Anne D. Houston, 1947

Harvie, Robert d.1781, *Mrs Magdalene Connell (d.1803)*, gift from Mrs Anne D. Houston, 1947

Harvie, Robert d.1781, *Mrs George McCall*, gift from Frances I. and Katherine E. M. Steggall, 1945

Hassall, John 1868–1948, *Bannockburn*, purchased from the artist, 1915, © the artist's estate

Hawkins, James b.1954, *The Black Rock Falls*, purchased, 1992, © the artist

Hawkins, James b.1954, *Galleon Rock*, purchased from the artist, 1996, © the artist

Hawkins, James b.1954, *Vertigo*, purchased from the artist, 1996, © the artist

Hay, Andrew b.1944, *Michael McGahey (1925–1999)*, purchased from the artist, 1985, © the artist

Hay, Andrew b.1944, *No Vacancies at This Colliery of Any Category*, purchased from the artist, 1985, © the artist

Hay, Andrew b.1944, *Pickets and 'Yuill and Dodds' Lorry*, purchased from the artist, 1985, © the artist

Hay, Andrew b.1944, *Portrait of a Miner*, purchased from the artist, 1985, © the artist

Hay, Andrew b.1944, *Riot Police at the Newsagents*, purchased from the artist, 1985, © the artist

Hay, Andrew b.1944, *The Police and the Picket Lines*, purchased from the artist, 1985, © the artist

Hay, Andrew b.1944, *The Strike Leaders*, purchased from the artist,

1985, © the artist

Hay, Andrew b.1944, *The Strike Leaders and Supporters*, purchased from the artist, 1985, © the artist

Hay, Andrew b.1944, *Harry*, purchased from the artist, 1991, © the artist

Hay, Andrew b.1944, *Self Portrait*, purchased from the artist, 1994, © the artist

Hay, Andrew b.1944, *Streets I Walked with My Father*, purchased from the artist, 1994, © the artist

Hay, Andrew b.1944, *A Mean Wind Wanders through the Backcourt Trash*, purchased from the artist, 2001, © the artist

Hay, Andrew b.1944, *Arthur Scargill (b.1938), Miners' Leader*, purchased from the artist, 1985, © the artist

Hay, Andrew b.1944, *Springburn Tenement*, acquired, 1990, © the artist

Hay, Andrew b.1944, *The Hierarchy of Art*, gift from the artist, 1994, © the artist

Hay, Andrew b.1944, *The Steamie*, on loan from a private collection, © the artist

Haynes-Williams, John 1836–1908, *The Spanish Bride*, bequeathed by W. B. Faulds, 1898

Hayon, Léon-Albert 1840–1895, *Young Woman at Her Window*, presented by the Trustees of the Hamilton Bequest, 1994

Hayter, George 1792–1871, *First State Visit of Queen Victoria to the City of London, November 1837, Passing St Paul's*, gift from Arthur Kay, 1902

Heath, Adrian 1920–1992, *Brown Painting*, gift from the Contemporary Art Society, 1968, © the estate of Adrian Heath

Heem, Cornelis de (attributed to) 1631–1695, *Still Life: Flowers in a Glass Vase*, Archibald McLellan Collection, purchased, 1856

Heindel, Robert 1938–2005, *The Last Obstacle*, gift from the artist, 2004

Heinsius, Johann Ernst (after) 1740–1812, *A Small Boy with a House of Cards*, Archibald McLellan Collection, purchased, 1856

Helst, Bartholomeus van der 1613–1670, *Captain Willem van der Zaan (1621–1669)*, purchased, 1895

Hemy, Charles Napier 1841–1917, *Saved*, gift from R. D. MacGregor, 1927

Hemy, Charles Napier 1841–1917, *Lost*, gift from R. D. MacGregor, 1927

Hemy, Charles Napier 1841–1917, *Limehouse Hole*, purchased, 1911

Henderson, J. *Male in Clerical Dress*

Henderson, John 1860–1924, *The Path by the Stream*, purchased, 1912

Henderson, Joseph 1832–1908, *Haul on the Sands*, bequeathed by Sir George T. Beatson, 1933

Henderson, Joseph 1832–1908,

Sea Piece, bequeathed by Adam Teacher, 1898

Henderson, Joseph 1832–1908, *Sea Piece*, bequeathed by Adam Teacher, 1898

Henderson, Joseph 1832–1908, *James Wilson*, temporary identification number allocated, 1974

Henderson, Joseph 1832–1908, *Councillor Alexander Waddell*, presented by the family of Councillor Waddell, 1896

Henderson, Joseph 1832–1908, *Sir John Muir (1828–1903), Lord Provost of Glasgow (1889–1892)*, commissioned by Glasgow Corporation, 1893

Henderson, Joseph 1832–1908, *James Paton (1843–1921), Superintendent of Glasgow Art Gallery and Museum (1876–1914)*, bequeathed by Dr Edward L. Paton, 1933

Henderson, Joseph 1832–1908, *Portrait of a Man*, temporary identification number allocated, 1978

Henderson, Joseph 1832–1908, *The Right Honourable Lord Charles Scott Dickson (1850–1922), Lord Justice Clerk (1915–1922)*, presented by the representatives of Lady Scott Dickson, 1934

Henderson, Joseph 1832–1908, *The Flowing Tide*, purchased from the artist, 1897

Henderson, Joseph 1832–1908, *Sir Samuel Chisholm (1836–1923), Lord Provost of Glasgow (1899–1902)*, purchased from the artist, 1902

Henderson, Joseph 1832–1908, *A Fresh Breeze*, bequeathed by Mrs Mary Calder, 1936

Henderson, Joseph 1832–1908, *James Docharty (1829–1878)*, purchased, 1927

Henderson, Joseph Morris 1863–1936, *In the Meadow*, purchased, 1909

Henderson, Keith 1883–1982, *Pilot and Navigator Confer*, presented by the War Artists' Advisory Committee through the Imperial War Museum, 1948

Henderson, Keith 1883–1982, *Glen Nevis, Inverness-shire*, purchased, 1944, photo credit: Glasgow Museums

Henderson, Keith 1883–1982, *Spur-Winged Geese*, gift from the artist, 1972

Hendrie, John active 1665–1677, *Charles I (1600–1649) (after Daniel Mytens I)*, commissioned by Glasgow Town Council, 1677

Hennin, Adriaen de active 1664–1710, *Landscape with the Death of Eurydice*, bequeathed by Jane Graham-Gilbert, 1877

Hennin, Adriaen de (attributed to) active 1664–1710, *Pastoral Landscape with Figures*, bequeathed by Jane Graham-Gilbert, 1877

Henry, George 1858–1943, *Brig o' Turk*, presented by the Fine Art Society Limited, 1977

Henry, George 1858–1943, *Head of the Holy Loch*, bequeathed by James Lindsay, 1914

Henry, George 1858–1943, *Autumn*, bequeathed by William McInnes, 1944

Henry, George 1858–1943, *A Galloway Landscape*, presented by the Trustees of Sir Thomas Dunlop, 1940

Henry, George 1858–1943, *Gloamin'*, purchased with the assistance of the National Fund for Acquisitions, 1980

Henry, George 1858–1943 & **Hornel, Edward Atkinson** 1864–1933 *The Druids: Bringing in the Mistletoe*, purchased, 1922

Henry, George 1858–1943 & **Hornel, Edward Atkinson** 1864–1933 *The Star in the East*, purchased, 1960

Henry, George 1858–1943, *Japanese Lady with a Fan*, gift from Mrs M. D. Lindsay in memory of Colonel Barclay Shaw, 1927

Henry, George 1858–1943, *In a Japanese Garden*, gift from Edward N. Marshall, 1944

Henry, George 1858–1943, *Councillor Robert Crawford (b.1845)*, gift from subscribers, 1903

Henry, George 1858–1943, *Mrs Burrell*, gift from Sir William and Lady Burrell to the City of Glasgow, 1944

Henry, George 1858–1943, *Sir John Neilson Cuthbertson (1829–1905), LLD, DL*, gift from subscribers, 1903

Henry, George 1858–1943, *Mrs Isabella Sandilands (1865–1925)*, bequeathed by Mrs Agnes M. L. Lambie, 1974

Henry, George 1858–1943, *Helen Stirling Stuart of Castlemilk (1896–1985)*, gift, 1963

Henry, George 1858–1943, *The Reading*, purchased, 1913

Henry, George 1858–1943, *Sir Thomas Dunlop (1855–1938), Lord Provost of Glasgow (1914–1917)*, purchased, 1917

Henry, George 1858–1943, *Lady in a Green Dress*, bequeathed by David Perry, 1940

Henshaw, Frederick Henry 1807–1891, *Swiss Landscape*, Archibald McLellan Collection, purchased, 1856

Herdman, Robert Inerarity 1829–1888, *Morning*, gift from Archibald G. Macdonald, 1896

Herdman, Robert Inerarity 1829–1888, *Evening*, gift from Archibald G. Macdonald, 1896

Herdman, Robert Inerarity 1829–1888, *Execution of Mary, Queen of Scots*, bequeathed by Adam Teacher, 1898

Herdman, Robert Inerarity 1829–1888, *Sir James David Marwick (1826–1908), Town Clerk of Glasgow (1873–1903)*, purchased, 1933

Herdman, Robert Inerarity 1829–1888, *Pleasures of Hope*,

presented by the Trustees of the estate of Margaret Moore, 1943

Herdman, Robert Inerarity 1829–1888, *Lochiel's Warning*, gift from Reverend John Moore, 1943

Herdman, Robert Inerarity 1829–1888, *Reverend George S. Burns, Minister of Glasgow Cathedral*, gift from subscribers, 1882

Herdman, Robert Inerarity 1829–1888, *Sir William Collins (1817–1895), Lord Provost of Glasgow (1877–1880)*, purchased, 1881

Herdman, Robert Inerarity 1829–1888, *Sir James Watson (1801–1889), Lord Provost of Glasgow (1871–1874)*, gift from subscribers, 1882

Herdman, Robert Inerarity 1829–1888, *Peter Clouston, Lord Provost of Glasgow (1860–1863)*, gift from subscribers, 1883

Herkomer, Hubert von 1849–1914, *Lord Kelvin (1824–1907)*, presented by the J. T. Bottomley Trust, 1926

Herkomer, Hubert von 1849–1914, *Sir James Bell (b.1850), Lord Provost of Glasgow (1892–1896)*, purchased, 1896

Herkomer, Hubert von 1849–1914, *Sir Thomas J. Lipton (1850–1931)*, bequeathed by Sir Thomas J. Lipton, 1932

Herman, Josef 1911–2000, *Blue-Costume for 'Ballet of the Palette'*, purchased, 1980, © Culture and Sport Glasgow (Glasgow Museums)

Herman, Josef 1911–2000, *Pink-Costume for 'Ballet of the Palette'*, purchased, 1980, © Culture and Sport Glasgow (Glasgow Museums)

Herman, Josef 1911–2000, *Set Design for 'Ballet of the Palette'*, purchased, 1980, © Culture and Sport Glasgow (Glasgow Museums)

Herman, Josef 1911–2000, *The Big Brush for 'Ballet of the Palette'*, purchased, 1980, © Culture and Sport Glasgow (Glasgow Museums)

Herman, Josef 1911–2000, *Southern Landscape*, purchased, 1959, © estate of Josef Herman. All rights reserved, DACS 2013

Herman, Josef 1911–2000, *Three Mexican Women*, presented by the Trustees of the Hamilton Bequest, 1973, © estate of Josef Herman. All rights reserved, DACS 2013

Hernández, Daniel 1856–1932, *Pierrette*, bequeathed by Adam Teacher, 1898

Herrera, Francisco de 1622–1685, *The Adoration of the Blessed Sacrament*, Stirling Maxwell Collection, gift, 1967

Herrera, Francisco de (attributed to) 1622–1685, *Saint Jerome (after Jusepe de Ribera)*, Stirling Maxwell Collection, gift, 1967

Herring, John Frederick I 1795–1865, *A Group of Ducks*, bequeathed by William Euing, 1874

Herring, John Frederick I 1795–1865, *The Deer-Stalker*, bequeathed by William Euing, 1874

Herring, John Frederick I 1795–1865, *The Frugal Meal*, gift from Mrs A. C. Thorneycroft, 1924

Herring, John Frederick I 1795–1865, *The Meet*, bequeathed by George Robb, 1909

Herring, John Frederick I 1795–1865, *Two Cows with Goats and Ducks in a Landscape*, bequeathed by Francis J. Eck, 1915

Hervier, Louis Adolphe 1818–1879, *Windmills*, gift from William Burrell, 1925

Hervier, Louis Adolphe 1818–1879, *Village Scene, Barbizon*, bequeathed by William McInnes, 1944

Hervier, Louis Adolphe 1818–1879, *Village Street with Poultry*, gift from Sir William and Lady Burrell to the City of Glasgow, 1944

Heyden, Jan van der (imitator of) 1637–1712, *A Bridge into a Fortified Town*, Archibald McLellan Collection, purchased, 1856

Highmore, Joseph 1692–1780, *Portrait of a Man*, purchased with the assistance of the National Fund for Acquisitions, 1975

Highmore, Joseph (attributed to) 1692–1780, *Portrait of a Man* (said to be William Pitt, 1708–1778, 1st Earl of Chatham), purchased, 1958

Hill, David Octavius 1802–1870, *Kirkoswald, Tam o' Shanter's Grave*, bequeathed by Thomas D. Smellie, 1901

Hill, David Octavius 1802–1870, *Viaduct over the River Almond, West Lothian*, gift from British Rail, London, 1967

Hill, David Octavius 1802–1870, *Ballochmyle Viaduct over the River Ayr*, gift from British Railways, Scottish Region, 1967

Hilliard, Nicholas (attributed to) 1537–1619, *William Cecil (1520–1598), Lord Burghley*, gift from Sir William and Lady Burrell to the City of Glasgow, 1944

Hillier, Tristram Paul 1905–1983, *Hulks*, presented by the Trustees of the Hamilton Bequest, 1959, © the artist's estate/Bridgeman Art Library

Hillingford, Robert Alexander 1825–1904, *'Yet Still a King'*, gift from Charles J. C. Douglas, 1893

Hilton, William (attributed to) active c.1780–1820, *Hannah Anne Gardiner (1764–1841), Lady Maxwell*, on loan from a private collection

Hislop, Andrew active 1880–1903, *The Cart at the Linn*, gift, 1973

Hislop, Margaret 1894–1972, *Jardin du Luxembourg*, purchased, 1955

Hislop, Margaret 1894–1972, *Flower Piece*, purchased, 1948

Hitchens, Ivon 1893–1979, *Garden with a Poppy*, purchased, 1946, © Ivon Hitchens' estate/Jonathan Clark & Co.

Hobbema, Meindert 1638–1709, *River Landscape with Fishermen*, Archibald McLellan Collection, purchased, 1856

Hobbema, Meindert (imitator of) 1638–1709, *A Ruined Cottage*, Archibald McLellan Collection, purchased, 1856

Hobbema, Meindert (imitator of) 1638–1709, *A Wooded Landscape with a Pond*, Archibald McLellan Collection, purchased, 1856

Hobbema, Meindert (school of) 1638–1709, *A Wooded Landscape with Cottages*, Archibald McLellan Collection, purchased, 1856

Hodgkins, Frances 1869–1947, *The Weir*, gift from the Contemporary Art Society, 1950, © the artist's estate

Hogarth, William 1697–1764, *Mrs Ann Lloyd (1717–1757)*, gift from Sir William and Lady Burrell to the City of Glasgow, 1944

Hogarth, William (after) 1697–1764, *James Thomson (1700–1748)*, Stirling Maxwell Collection, gift, 1967

Hogarth, William (attributed to) 1697–1764, *St Peter's Chapel in the Tower of London*, Stirling Maxwell Collection, gift, 1967

Holland, James 1800–1870, *Grand Canal, Venice*, bequeathed by James Donald, 1905

Holosiy, Oleg 1965–1993, *Adagio*, purchased, 1995

Holosiy, Oleg 1965–1993, *Psychedelic Attack of the Blue Rabbits*, purchased, 1991

Holt, S. *Landscape with Trees, a Pond and a Cottage*, temporary identification number allocated, 1984

Holyoake, William 1834–1894, *In the Front Row at the Opera*, bequeathed by Adam Teacher, 1898

Holzhandler, Dora b.1928, *The Sabbath Candles*, purchased, 1993, © the artist/Bridgeman Art Library

Holzhandler, Dora b.1928, *Wedding Night*, purchased, 1995, © the artist/Bridgeman Art Library

Hondecoeter, Melchior de 1636–1695, *Poultry and Pigeons*, Archibald McLellan Collection, purchased, 1856

Hondius, Abraham c.1625–1691, *A Swan Enraged by Dogs*, Archibald McLellan Collection, purchased, 1856

Hone, Nathaniel I 1718–1784, *Antonina Willoughby*, gift from Sir William and Lady Burrell to the City of Glasgow, 1944

Honthorst, Gerrit van (after) 1590–1656, *Frederick Henry (1584–1647), Prince of Orange*, bequeathed by William Euing, 1874

Hood, David *Fiddler's Close*, gift from the Provand's Lordship Society, 1978

Hood, Ernest 1932–1988, *Self Portrait*, purchased with the assistance of the National Art Collections Fund, 1988

Hood, Ernest 1932–1988, *'Castle Vaults'*, purchased, 1978

Hood, Ernest 1932–1988, *The Dairy*, purchased, 1978

Hoog, Bernard de 1867–1943, *Tea Time*, bequeathed by Miss M. A. W. Thomson, 1947

Hope, Robert 1869–1936, *The Charm*, gift from Westwood A. Macneill, 1918

Hope, Robert 1869–1936, *The Return of the Sardine Fishers, Concarneau*, presented by the Trustees of the artist, 1937

Hoppner, John 1758–1810, *Mrs Errington*, presented by the Trustees of the Hamilton Bequest, 1937

Horn, David active 19th C, *Still Life*, gift from Dr Neville Davidson, 1945

Hornel, Edward Atkinson 1864–1933, *The Brownie of Blednoch*, purchased, 1945

Hornel, Edward Atkinson 1864–1933, *The Goatherd*, on loan from a private collection

Hornel, Edward Atkinson 1864–1933, *The Dance of Spring*, purchased, 1960

Hornel, Edward Atkinson 1864–1933, *The Fish Pool*, purchased, 1951

Hornel, Edward Atkinson 1864–1933, *The Coming of Spring*, purchased from the artist, 1900

Hornel, Edward Atkinson 1864–1933, *The Swans*, purchased, 1951

Hornel, Edward Atkinson 1864–1933, *Gathering Snowdrops*, gift from Sir John Richmond, 1948

Hornel, Edward Atkinson 1864–1933, *A Spring Roundelay*, gift from Miss C. S. Howden, 1914

Hornel, Edward Atkinson 1864–1933, *The Lily Pond*, bequeathed by George B. Dunlop, 1951

Hornel, Edward Atkinson 1864–1933, *Blue Flax*, gift from Mrs Maitland Ramsay, 1953

Hornel, Edward Atkinson 1864–1933, *Gathering Primroses*, bequeathed by Mary R. Lang, 1960

Hornel, Edward Atkinson 1864–1933, *Two Girls and Swans at a Pool*, bequeathed by Jessie W. Craig, 1950

Hornel, Edward Atkinson 1864–1933, *Blue Flax*, bequeathed by George B. Dunlop, 1951

Hornel, Edward Atkinson 1864–1933, *Children on the Sands*, bequeathed by Jessie W. Craig, 1950

Hornel, Edward Atkinson (after) 1864–1933, *In a Japanese Garden*, bequeathed by Miss M. A. W. Thomson, 1947

Hornel, Edward Atkinson (after) 1864–1933, *The Paper Hat*, bequeathed by Miss M. A. W. Thomson, 1947

Horsburgh, Edward active 19th C, *David Jones (1834–1906)*

Houston, George 1869–1947, *Ayrshire Landscape*, gift from an anonymous donor, 1904, © the artist's estate

Houston, George 1869–1947, *Heart of Argyll*, purchased, 1936, © the artist's estate

Houston, George 1869–1947, *Dundarave Castle, Loch Fyne*, bequeathed by Mary R. Lang, 1960, © the artist's estate

Houston, George 1869–1947, *Glen Orchy*, bequeathed by Mary R. Lang, 1960, © the artist's estate

Houston, George 1869–1947, *James D. Paterson (1879–1949)*, gift, 1983, © the artist's estate

Houston, George 1869–1947, *Landscape*, gift from Mrs S. Stevenson, 1940, © the artist's estate

Houston, George 1869–1947, *Loch Fyne Head*, bequeathed by Mary R. Lang, 1960, © the artist's estate

Houston, George 1869–1947, *Summer Green, Loch Fyne Side*, bequeathed by Mary R. Lang, 1960, © the artist's estate

Houston, George 1869–1947, *White Sands of Iona*, gift from Dr Alexander Macphail, 1927, © the artist's estate

Houston, George 1869–1947, *Winter Sunshine, Lochgoilhead*, bequeathed by John Fleming, 1923, © the artist's estate

Houston, John 1930–2008, *October Sunset*, purchased, 1973, © Culture and Sport Glasgow (Glasgow Museums)

Houston, John 1930–2008, *Yellow Flowers in a Black Jug*, bequeathed by George and Isobel Neillands, 1994, © the artist's estate

Houston, John Adam 1812–1884, *View of Glasgow and the Cathedral*, gift from A. Dennistoun, 1877

Houston, Robert 1891–1940, *Stirling Brig*

Hove, Edmond Theodor van 1853–1913, *The Botanist*, purchased, 1907

Howard, Francis 1874–1954, *Mrs Francis Howard*, gift from Cathleen S. Mann, 1959

Howard-Jones, Ray 1903–1996, *Homage to James Cowie*, purchased, 1972, © Culture and Sport Glasgow (Glasgow Museums)

Howson, Peter b.1958, *City Bar*, purchased, 1985, © the artist

Howson, Peter b.1958, *The Final Parade*, presented by the Trustees of the Hamilton Bequest, 1987, © Culture and Sport Glasgow (Glasgow Museums)

Howson, Peter b.1958, *Patriots*, purchased with the assistance of the National Fund for Acquisitions, 1993, © the artist

Howson, Peter b.1958, *The Glorious Game*, purchased, 1997, © the artist

Howson, Peter b.1958, *Patrick Lally (b.1926), Lord Provost of the*

City of Glasgow (1996–1999), purchased, 2001, © the artist

Hubert, F. active 19th C, *A Forest Glade*, bequeathed by Adam Teacher, 1898

Hughes, Jean *Echoes*, gift from the BBC Collection, 2008

Hughes, Patrick b.1939, *The Shadow of War*, purchased, 1994, © the artist's estate

Hughes, Patrick b.1939, *Jubilee*, purchased, 1995, © the artist's estate

Hulst, Maerten Fransz. van der (after) 1605–1645, *Fish Selling on the Dunes*, gift from D. Dreghorn, 1856

Hunt, Alfred William 1830–1896, *The Sound of Kerrera*, gift from Archibald G. Macdonald, 1896

Hunt, Thomas 1854–1929, *A Few Remarks*, gift from W. J. I. Muir, 1939

Hunt, Thomas 1854–1929, *Alterations, Corner of Hope Street and Sauchiehall Street, Glasgow*, gift from subscribers, 1917

Hunt, Thomas 1854–1929, *November, Braes of Balquhidder*, purchased, 1914

Hunt, Walter 1861–1941, *Dog in the Manger*, gift from Dr Douglas White, 1938

Hunt, William active 1888–1911, *In Full Blossom*, bequeathed by Adam Teacher, 1898

Hunter, Colin 1841–1904, *Beach Scene*, gift from Miss Birkmyre, 1956

Hunter, Colin 1841–1904, *Sea Piece, Dawn*, bequeathed by Adam Teacher, 1898

Hunter, Colin 1841–1904, *Ebbing Tide*, bequeathed by Adam Teacher, 1898

Hunter, Colin 1841–1904, *Wet Day on the Clyde*, gift from Mrs Maitland Ramsay, 1953

Hunter, Colin 1841–1904, *Falls of Niagara*, bequeathed by Adam Teacher, 1898

Hunter, Colin 1841–1904, *Good-Night to Skye*, purchased from the artist, 1895

Hunter, Colin 1841–1904, *Niagara Rapids* (detail), gift from Sir Donald Currie, 1901

Hunter, Colin 1841–1904, *J. Milne Donald (1819–1866), Sketching*, gift from G. Telfer Bear, 1940

Hunter, George Leslie 1877–1931, *On the Shore*, gift from A. B. Clements, 1940

Hunter, George Leslie 1877–1931, *The Red Jacket*, gift from A. B. Clements, 1940

Hunter, George Leslie 1877–1931, *Mrs Helen Meldrum (1829–1924)*, gift, 1972

Hunter, George Leslie 1877–1931, *A Summer Day, Largo*, bequeathed by William McInnes, 1944

Hunter, George Leslie 1877–1931, *A Village in Fife*, gift, 1970

Hunter, George Leslie 1877–1931, *Old Mill, Fifeshire*, gift from William McInnes, 1921

Hunter, George Leslie 1877–1931, *The Green Bowl*, gift from William McInnes, 1941

Hunter, George Leslie 1877–1931, *Ceres, Fife*, bequeathed by William McInnes, 1944

Hunter, George Leslie 1877–1931, *Doge's Palace, Venice*, bequeathed by William McInnes, 1944

Hunter, George Leslie 1877–1931, *Sails, Venice*, bequeathed by William McInnes, 1944

Hunter, George Leslie 1877–1931, *Souvenir de Venise*, bequeathed by William McInnes, 1944

Hunter, George Leslie 1877–1931, *Houseboat, Loch Lomond*, gift from William McInnes, 1943

Hunter, George Leslie 1877–1931, *Houseboats, Loch Lomond*, bequeathed by William McInnes, 1944

Hunter, George Leslie 1877–1931, *Loch Lomond*, bequeathed by William McInnes, 1944

Hunter, George Leslie 1877–1931, *The Blue Hat*, bequeathed by William McInnes, 1944

Hunter, George Leslie 1877–1931, *The Huntsman*, purchased, 1950

Hunter, George Leslie 1877–1931, *William McInnes (1868–1944)*, purchased, 1985

Hunter, George Leslie 1877–1931, *William McNair*, purchased, 1962

Hunter, George Leslie 1877–1931, *Dr Tom J. Honeyman (1891–1971), Director of Glasgow Art Galleries (1939–1954)*, purchased with the assistance of the Heritage Lottery Fund and the Friends of Glasgow Museums, 2006

Hunter, George Leslie 1877–1931, *Flowers in a Chinese Vase*, presented by the family of Dr T. J. Honeyman, in his memory, 1972

Hunter, George Leslie 1877–1931, *Flowers in a Vase and Fruit*, bequeathed by William McInnes, 1944

Hunter, George Leslie 1877–1931, *Old Dog Seated by a Tree*, gift from Mrs J. MacFarlane, 1946

Hunter, George Leslie 1877–1931, *Roses in a White and Blue Vase*, purchased, 1964

Hunter, George Leslie 1877–1931, *Still Life*, gift from William McInnes, 1921

Hunter, William 1890–1967, *The Bubble Reputation*, purchased, 1939

Hutcheson, Tom 1922–1999, *Red Blaze Bing*, purchased, 1964

Hutcheson, Tom 1922–1999, *Red Landscape, Lanarkshire*, purchased, 1965

Hutcheson, Tom 1922–1999, *Pier, West Coast*, purchased, 1969

Hutchison, George Jackson 1896–1918, *Getting Ready*, gift from R. Gemmell Hutchison, 1918

Hutchison, Robert Gemmell 1855–1936, *A Dutch Mother*, purchased, 1911

Hutchison, Robert Gemmell 1855–1936, *Children Wading*, bequeathed by Mary R. Lang, 1960,

photo credit: Glasgow Museums

Hutchison, Robert Gemmell 1855–1936, *The Dead Seagull*, bequeathed by Mary R. Lang, 1960

Hutchison, Robert Gemmell 1855–1936, *When the Day Is Done*, presented by the Trustees of the Hamilton Bequest, 1929

Hutchison, William Oliphant 1889–1970, *Humoresque, 1919: The Artist's Wife*, gift, 1970, © the artist's estate

Hutchison, William Oliphant 1889–1970, *The Kitchen Bathroom*, purchased, 1936, © the artist's estate

Hutchison, William Oliphant 1889–1970, *Hugh Munro (1870–1916)*, gift from William B. Taylor, 1940, © the artist's estate

Hutchison, William Oliphant 1889–1970, *Sir Victor Warren (1903–1953), Lord Provost of Glasgow (1949–1952)*, purchased, 1953, © the artist's estate

Hutchison, William Oliphant 1889–1970, *J. Gordon Moffat*, acquired, 1978, © the artist's estate

Huysmans, Cornelis 1648–1727, *Wooded Landscape with Figures*, bequeathed by Jane Graham-Gilbert, 1877

Huysmans, Cornelis 1648–1727, *Wooded Landscape with Figures*, bequeathed by Jane Graham-Gilbert, 1877

Huysum, Jan van 1682–1749, *Still Life: Flowers in a Glass Vase*, Archibald McLellan Collection, purchased, 1856

Huysum, Jan van 1682–1749, *Still Life: Flowers in a Terracotta Urn*, Archibald McLellan Collection, purchased, 1856

Hyon, Georges Louis 1840–1909, *An Episode in the Franco-Prussian War*, bequeathed by Major John Garroway, 1920

Ibbetson, Julius Caesar 1759–1817, *Women Washing Clothes in a Welsh Stream*, gift from F. J. Nettlefold, 1948

Irvine, Jennifer b.1956, *Paddy's Market*, gift, 1988, © the artist

Irvine, Olivia b.1960, *Catching the Sky*, gift from the BBC Collection, 2008, © the artist

Israëls, Jozef 1824–1911, *Grief*, bequeathed by Miss M. D. Wylie, 1951

Israëls, Jozef 1824–1911, *The Happy Family*, bequeathed by James Donald, 1905

Israëls, Jozef 1824–1911, *The Frugal Meal*, presented by the family of the late James Reid of Auchterarder, 1896

Italian (Lombard) School 16th C, *The Holy Family with the Child Baptist*, Archibald McLellan Collection, purchased, 1856

Italian (Neapolitan) School 17th C, *Christ's Charge to Saint Peter*, Archibald McLellan Collection, purchased, 1856

Italian (Neapolitan) School *Tobias and the Angel*, Archibald McLellan Collection, purchased, 1856

Italian (Neapolitan) School 18th C, *Landscape with Figures beside a Ruined Colonnade*, gift from T. Graham Young in memory of his father, James Young, 1900

Italian (Neapolitan) School 18th C, *Virgin and Child*, found in store, registered, 1988

Italian (Neapolitan) School (attributed to) 18th C, *Portrait of a Royal Infant*, Stirling Maxwell Collection, gift, 1967

Italian (Roman) School *Engaged*, bequeathed by Adam Teacher, 1898

Italian (Roman) School 19th C, *Madonna and Child in Glory*, Archibald McLellan Collection, purchased, 1856

Italian (Roman) School (attributed to) 17th C, *Rebekah at the Well*, presented by the Governors of the Glasgow and West of Scotland Technical College, 1906

Italian School 17th C, *Portrait of a Man (possibly a cleric)*, Stirling Maxwell Collection, gift, 1967

Italian School early 18th C, *Rocky Landscape with a River and a Bridge*, found in store, registered, 1988

Italian School (attributed to) 16th C/17th C, *Ecce Homo*, bequeathed by Jane Graham-Gilbert, 1877

Italian School (attributed to) late 17th C, *An Allegory of Repentance*, Stirling Maxwell Collection, gift, 1967

Jack, Richard 1866–1952, *The Italian Room, 42 Hyde Park Gate, London*, purchased, 1930, © the artist's estate

Jacob, Julius I 1811–1882, *Alexander Gartshore Stirling of Craigbarnet Returning from Shooting (detail)*, gift from Mr and Mrs Arthur Miller-Stirling, 1948

Jacque, Charles Émile 1813–1894, *The Wane of Day*, presented by the family of the late James Reid of Auchterarder, 1896

Jacque, Charles Émile 1813–1894, *The Knife Grinder*, gift from Sir William and Lady Burrell to the City of Glasgow, 1944

Jacque, Charles Émile 1813–1894, *The Pig*, gift from Sir William and Lady Burrell to the City of Glasgow, 1944

Jamesone, George c.1586–1644, *Portrait of a Man*, purchased, 1956

Jamesone, George (after) c.1586–1644, *John Bell, Minister*, purchased, 1944

Jamesone, George (attributed to) c.1586–1644, *King James VI and I (1566–1625)*, gift from the Provand's Lordship Society, 1978

Jamesone, George (style of) c.1586–1644, *Thomas Hutcheson*, presented by the Trustees of Hutchesons' Hospital, 1913

Jamieson, Alexander 1873–1937, *Our Pond*, purchased, 1937

Jamieson, Florence b.1925, *Mackerel Still Life*, purchased, 1961, © the artist

Jamieson, Robert Kirkland 1881–1950, *Winter*, purchased, 1942

Jansen, Willem George Frederik 1871–1949, *Milking Time*, bequeathed by Miss M. A. W. Thomson, 1947

Janssens van Ceulen, Cornelis 1593–1661, *Portrait of a Woman*, Archibald McLellan Collection, purchased, 1856

Jeremiah, Emanuel b.1975, *Three Birds on a Tree Branch*, purchased, 1989

John, Augustus Edwin 1878–1961, *William Butler Yeats (1865–1939), Irish Poet and Patriot*, presented by the Trustees of the Hamilton Bequest, 1931, © the artist's estate/ Bridgeman Art Library

Johnson, Ben b.1946, *The Keeper*, purchased, 1978, © the artist

Johnson, Frank 1917–1998, *Manor Row, Bradford*, purchased, 1954, © estate of the late Frank Johnson (James Edward George Johnson)

Johnson, W. *Bridge over the River Cart*, gift, 1997

Johnson, W. *Pollok House*, gift, 1997

Johnston, Alexander 1815–1891, *The Marriage of the Covenanter*, gift from Major Caine, 1954

Johnston, Alexander 1815–1891, *Family Devotions*, bequeathed by John Fleming, 1923

Johnstone, William 1897–1981, *Border Farmer*, gift, 1971, © the artist's estate

Johnstone, William 1897–1981, *Border Landscape: The Eildon Hills*, purchased, 1971, © the artist's estate

Jones, George 1786–1869, *Cawnpore, Passage of the Ganges*, gift from Mrs George Jones, 1880

Jones, George 1786–1869, *The Relief of Lucknow*, gift from Mrs George Jones, 1880

Jones, Joe active 20th C, *The Wheat Farmer*, gift from the Encyclopaedia Britannica, 1953

Joney, James W. G. *Bull's Horn with Crab Shell*, gift from the BBC Collection, 2008

Jongh, Ludolf de (attributed to) 1616–1679, *The Huntsman's Toast*, gift from Sir William and Lady Burrell to the City of Glasgow, 1944

Jongkind, Johan Barthold 1819–1891, *Winter Scene in Holland*, bequeathed by William McInnes, 1944

Jongkind, Johan Barthold 1819–1891, *Paris, Demolition of the Rue des Francs-Bourgeois*, gift from Sir William and Lady Burrell to the City of Glasgow, 1944

Jordaens, Jacob 1593–1678, *A Maidservant with a Basket of Fruit and Two Lovers*, Archibald McLellan Collection, purchased, 1856

Jordaens, Jacob (attributed to) 1593–1678, *The Satyr and the Peasant*, Stirling Maxwell Collection, gift, 1967

Joseph, Tam b.1947, *Timespan*, presented by the Contemporary Art Society, 1992, © the artist

Julliotte, Madeleine Camille 1887–1948, *Market in Spain*, bequeathed by Mary R. Lang, 1960

Kalf, Willem 1619–1693, *Still Life: Silver-Gilt Goblet and Bowl of Fruit*, bequeathed by James Donald, 1905

Kalf, Willem 1619–1693, *Still Life: Silver-Gilt Goblet, Porcelain Bowl, Glassware and Peeled Orange*, bequeathed by James Donald, 1905

Kalf, Willem (after) 1619–1693, *Still Life: Fruit, Oyster and Glasses*, gift from Sir William and Lady Burrell to the City of Glasgow, 1944

Kappata, Stephen b.1936, *Likishi*, purchased with the assistance of the National Fund for Acquisitions, 1990

Kauage, Mathias 1944–2003, *Carry Leg*, purchased, 1994, © the artist's estate

Kauage, Mathias 1944–2003, *Suicide*, purchased, 1994, © the artist's estate

Kauage, Mathias 1944–2003, *Buka War*, purchased, 1994, © the artist's estate

Kauage, Mathias 1944–2003, *Burial*, purchased, 1994, © the artist's estate

Kauage, Mathias 1944–2003, *Misis Kwin*, purchased, 1996, © the artist's estate

Kay, Archibald 1860–1935, *The Rhymer's Glen*, purchased, 1909

Kay, Archibald 1860–1935, *Furnace Quarries, Streets of a Great City*, gift from Mrs Margaret Kay, 1936

Kay, Archibald 1860–1935, *Ploughing at Crail*, gift from J. D. Roberton, 1946

Kay, James 1858–1942, *The Launch of the 'Lusitania'*, purchased, 1907

Kay, James 1858–1942, *George Square, Glasgow*

Kay, James 1858–1942, *Harbour Scene*, gift, 1997

Kay, James 1858–1942, *Thaw*, purchased, 1969

Keane, John b.1954, *The Old Lie Café*, purchased from the artist, 1991, © the artist

Keelan, J. active 1994, *Memories of Springburn*, gift from the artist, 1994

Keith, Alexander active 1808–1874, *Reverend Dr Norman McLeod (1780–1866)*, gift from Barony Parish Church, 1985

Keller, Johann Heinrich (attributed to) 1692–1765, *Gottfried Wilhelm Leibniz (1646–1716)*, transferred from the Old Town Hall, 1891, photo credit: Glasgow Museums

Kellner, Hermann II 1849–1926, *The Ravages of War*, bequeathed by Adam Teacher, 1898

Kelly, Gerald Festus 1879–1972, *The Blue Door (Consuelo VII)*, purchased, 1933

Kelly, Gerald Festus 1879–1972, *Dr Ralph Vaughan Williams*

(1872–1958), presented by the Trustees of the Hamilton Bequest, 1959

Kelly, Gerald Festus 1879–1972, *Mademoiselle*, bequeathed by John Keppie, 1945

Kelly, Robert George Talbot 1861–1934, *'In a dry and thirsty land, where no water is'*, bequeathed by Adam Teacher, 1898

Kennedy, William 1859–1918, *The Deserter*, purchased with the assistance of the National Fund for Acquisitions, 1982

Kennedy, William 1859–1918, *Stirling Station*, purchased with the assistance of the Heritage Lottery Fund, the Art Fund, the Trustees of the Hamilton Bequest and the Friends of Glasgow Museums, 2008

Kennedy, William 1859–1918, *The Fur Boa*, purchased, 1944

Kennedy, William 1859–1918, *Homewards*, purchased, 1960

Kennedy, William 1859–1918, *The Highlander*, gift from Bailie J. F. Wilson, 1941

Kennedy, William 1859–1918, *Midday Rest*, purchased, 1963

Kennedy, William 1859–1918, *Evening in Berkshire*, gift from Sir John Richmond, 1948

Kennedy, William 1859–1918, *Moonlight*, gift from W. J. I. Muir, 1939

Kennedy, William 1859–1918, *Restaurant in Tangier*, purchased, 1928

Kennington, Eric Henri 1888–1960, *Mrs George Struthers (1856–1946)*, gift, 1964, © courtesy of the family of the artist

Kerr, Charles Henry Malcolm 1858–1907, *March Winds, the Marble Arch*, gift from Mrs Gertrude Kerr, 1931

Kerry, J. Vincent active 1917–1935, *Provand's Lordship from the East*

Kessel, Jan van II 1641–1680, *Wooded Landscape with an Inn*, Archibald McLellan Collection, purchased, 1856

Kessel, Jan van II (attributed to) 1641–1680, *Landscape with a Waterfall*, bequeathed by William Euing, 1874

Kidd, William 1790–1863, *An Art Connoisseur*, gift from Arthur Kay, 1901

Kilmartin, John b.1964, *Outside the Mission*, purchased, 1994, © the artist

Kilpatrick, *William Ross*, gift from W. R. Stevenson, 1936

King, A. *Glasgow Fair in the Saltmarket*

King, Jessie Marion 1875–1949, *The Frog Prince*, purchased with the assistance of the Heritage Lottery Fund, 2004, © Dumfries and Galloway Council

Kinnear, M. A. *Aircraft in Flight*, gift, 1995

Kirkham, Norman b.1936, *Fran and Anna*, gift from the artist, 1985, © the artist

Kneller, Godfrey (attributed to) 1646–1723, *Thomas Betterton (1635?–1710)*, Stirling Maxwell Collection, gift, 1967

Knight, Harold 1874–1961, *A Window in St John's Wood*, presented by the Trustees of the Hamilton Bequest, 1938, © reproduced with permission of the estate of Dame Laura Knight, DBE, RA, 2013. All rights reserved

Knight, Laura 1877–1970, *A Theatre Dressing Room*, purchased, 1935, © reproduced with permission of the estate of Dame Laura Knight, DBE, RA, 2013. All rights reserved

Knowles, John b.1966, *A Big Cat with a Bit of Writing Underneath*, purchased, 1992, © the artist

Knox, Jack b.1936, *Burning the Heather*, purchased with the assistance of the National Fund for Acquisitions, 1988, © the artist

Knox, John 1778–1845, *The Nelson Monument on Glasgow Green Struck by Lightning*, purchased, 1977

Knox, John 1778–1845, *Old Glasgow Bridge*, purchased, 1955

Knox, John 1778–1845, *First Steamboat on the Clyde*, purchased, 1943

Knox, John 1778–1845, *The Cloch Lighthouse*, presented by the Misses Birrell, 1921

Knox, John 1778–1845, *Old Glasgow Cross or the Trongate*, purchased, 1914

Knox, John 1778–1845, *Govan Ferry*, presented by the Trustees of the Hamilton Bequest, 1975

Knox, John 1778–1845, *North Western View from Ben Lomond*, bequeathed by William Euing, 1874

Knox, John 1778–1845, *South Western View from Ben Lomond*, bequeathed by William Euing, 1874

Knox, John 1778–1845, *Glasgow Green*, gift from John M. Watson, 1950

Knox, John 1778–1845, *Highland Loch Scene*, Stirling Maxwell Collection, gift, 1967

Knox, John 1778–1845, *The Clyde from Dalnottar Hill*, gift from T. F. Donald, 1921

Knox, John 1778–1845, *View of Glencoe*, purchased, 1983

Knox, John *Hilly Landscape*, gift from Edith A. Knox, 1907

Knox, John *Landscape with Trees*, gift from Edith A. Knox, 1907

Koekkoek, Hermanus the elder 1815–1882, *Boats Taking Haven from a Storm*, bequeathed by William Euing, 1874

Koekkoek, Hermanus the younger 1836–1909, *Windmills*, gift from R. D. Macgregor, 1924

Kondracki, Henry b.1953, *Old Man*, purchased, 1995, © the artist

Kondracki, Henry b.1953, *Passing the Butcher Shop*, purchased, 1995, © the artist

Kratké, Charles Louis 1848–1921, *French Army on the March*, bequeathed by Miss M. Garroway, 1947

Kynoch, Kathryn b.1942, *Lillian McDonald, Headmistress of Park School (1944–1962)*, gift from the Park and Laurel Bank Schools Collection (incorporating Laurel Park School), 2006, © the artist

Kynoch, Kathryn b.1942, *Girl in a White Blouse*, purchased, 1966, © Culture and Sport Glasgow (Glasgow Museums)

Kynoch, Kathryn b.1942, *Sir Donald Liddle, Lord Provost of Glasgow (1969–1972)*, commissioned by the Corporation of the City of Glasgow, 1974, © the artist

Kynoch, Kathryn b.1942, *Joan Lightwood, Headmistress of Park School (1962–1974)*, gift from the Park and Laurel Bank Schools Collection (incorporating Laurel Park School), 2006, © the artist

La Fosse, Charles de 1636–1716, *The Assumption of the Virgin*, Archibald McLellan Collection, purchased, 1856

La Thangue, Henry Herbert 1859–1929, *Provençal Winter*, gift from an anonymous donor, 1904

La Thangue, Henry Herbert 1859–1929, *On the Ramparts*, bequeathed by Mrs K. La Thangue, 1942

La Thangue, Henry Herbert 1859–1929, *Roman Campagna*, bequeathed by Mrs K. La Thangue, 1942

La Thangue, Henry Herbert 1859–1929, *Stumping the Cow*, presented by the executors of the estate of Mrs K. La Thangue, 1942

Lacroix de Marseille, Charles François (attributed to) c.1700–1782, *A Storm*, bequeathed by Sir Claude Phillips, 1924

Laing, Annie Rose 1869–1946, *The Mirror*, purchased, 1919

Laing, Annie Rose 1869–1946, *After Rehearsal*, gift from Mrs Margaret F. Ogden, 1959

Lairesse, Gerard de 1640–1711, *An Allegory of the Senses*, purchased with the assistance of the Heritage Lottery Fund, the National Art Collections Fund and the Trustees of the Hamilton Bequest, 2001

Lamb, Henry 1883–1960, *Lieutenant General Le Chevalier Van Strydonck de Burkel (1879–1961)*, presented by the War Artists' Advisory Committee through the Imperial War Museum, 1948, © estate of Henry Lamb

Lamb, Henry 1883–1960, *Driver Abdul Ghani*, presented by the War Artists' Advisory Committee through the Imperial War Museum, 1948, © Culture and Sport Glasgow (Glasgow Museums)

Lamb, Henry 1883–1960, *Breton Peasant*, gift from the Contemporary Art Society, 1928, © estate of Henry Lamb

Lambinet, Emile Charles 1815–1877, *Coast Scene*, bequeathed by Mrs Isabella Elder, 1906

Lander, Heather Rose b.1976, *Take a Seat*, gift from the BBC Collection, 2008, © the artist

László, Philip Alexius de 1869–1937, *Portrait Study: Madame Montague Yaunez*, purchased, 1913

Lauder, Charles James 1841–1920, *Glasgow Bridge*, bequeathed by Sir Alexander Cross, 1963

Lauder, Robert Scott 1803–1869, *Portrait of a Lady*, bequeathed by William Euing, 1874

Laughlin, Alex b.1930, *Untitled*, purchased, 1992

Lauri, Filippo 1623–1694, *The Holy Family*, Archibald McLellan Collection, purchased, 1856

Lavery, John 1856–1941, *A Conquest, a Heart for a Rose*, purchased, 1944, © by courtesy of Felix Rosenstiel's Widow and Son Ltd, London on behalf of the estate of Sir John Lavery

Lavery, John 1856–1941, *A Quiet Day in the Studio*, purchased, 1944, © by courtesy of Felix Rosenstiel's Widow and Son Ltd, London on behalf of the estate of Sir John Lavery

Lavery, John 1856–1941, *George U. Baird*, gift from Mrs Baird, 1944, © by courtesy of Felix Rosenstiel's Widow and Son Ltd, London on behalf of the estate of Sir John Lavery

Lavery, John 1856–1941, *Duchess of Abercorn* (sketch), gift from the artist, 1935, © by courtesy of Felix Rosenstiel's Widow and Son Ltd, London on behalf of the estate of Sir John Lavery

Lavery, John 1856–1941, *Potter at Work*, gift from Bailie W. Graham Greig, 1949, © by courtesy of Felix Rosenstiel's Widow and Son Ltd, London on behalf of the estate of Sir John Lavery

Lavery, John 1856–1941, *The Duke of Abercorn, KP* (sketch), gift from the artist, 1935, © by courtesy of Felix Rosenstiel's Widow and Son Ltd, London on behalf of the estate of Sir John Lavery

Lavery, John 1856–1941, *The Glasgow International Exhibition*, purchased, 1945, © by courtesy of Felix Rosenstiel's Widow and Son Ltd, London on behalf of the estate of Sir John Lavery

Lavery, John 1856–1941, *Woman Painting a Pot*, gift from Bailie W. Graham Greig, 1949, © by courtesy of Felix Rosenstiel's Widow and Son Ltd, London on behalf of the estate of Sir John Lavery

Lavery, John 1856–1941, *Alexander Clapperton* (sketch), gift from the artist, 1935, © by courtesy of Felix Rosenstiel's Widow and Son Ltd, London on behalf of the estate of Sir John Lavery

Lavery, John 1856–1941, *Alexander Osborne* (sketch), gift from the artist, 1935, © by courtesy of Felix Rosenstiel's Widow and Son Ltd, London on behalf of the estate of Sir John Lavery

Lavery, John 1856–1941, *Alexander Stephen* (sketch), gift from the artist, 1935, © by courtesy of Felix Rosenstiel's Widow and Son Ltd, London on behalf of the estate of Sir John Lavery

Lavery, John 1856–1941, *Bailie James Hunter Dickson (b.1824), Vice-Chairman of Glasgow International Exhibition (1888)* (sketch), gift from the artist, 1935, © by courtesy of Felix Rosenstiel's Widow and Son Ltd, London on behalf of the estate of Sir John Lavery

Lavery, John 1856–1941, *Bailie MacLaren* (sketch), gift from the artist, 1935, © by courtesy of Felix Rosenstiel's Widow and Son Ltd, London on behalf of the estate of Sir John Lavery

Lavery, John 1856–1941, *Bailie Simons* (sketch), gift from the artist, 1935, © by courtesy of Felix Rosenstiel's Widow and Son Ltd, London on behalf of the estate of Sir John Lavery

Lavery, John 1856–1941, *Bailie Watson* (sketch), gift from the artist, 1935, © by courtesy of Felix Rosenstiel's Widow and Son Ltd, London on behalf of the estate of Sir John Lavery

Lavery, John 1856–1941, *Captain Shaw, Contractor* (sketch), gift from the artist, 1935, © by courtesy of Felix Rosenstiel's Widow and Son Ltd, London on behalf of the estate of Sir John Lavery

Lavery, John 1856–1941, *Charles Howatson* (sketch), gift from the artist, 1935, © by courtesy of Felix Rosenstiel's Widow and Son Ltd, London on behalf of the estate of Sir John Lavery

Lavery, John 1856–1941, *Colonel Sir D. Matheson, KCB, Grand Marshal* (sketch), gift from the artist, 1935, © by courtesy of Felix Rosenstiel's Widow and Son Ltd, London on behalf of the estate of Sir John Lavery

Lavery, John 1856–1941, *Colonel Walker, ADC* (sketch), gift from the artist, 1935, © by courtesy of Felix Rosenstiel's Widow and Son Ltd, London on behalf of the estate of Sir John Lavery

Lavery, John 1856–1941, *Duncan McPherson* (sketch), gift from the artist, 1935, © by courtesy of Felix Rosenstiel's Widow and Son Ltd, London on behalf of the estate of Sir John Lavery

Lavery, John 1856–1941, *General Gardiner* (sketch), gift from the artist, 1935, © by courtesy of Felix Rosenstiel's Widow and Son Ltd, London on behalf of the estate of Sir John Lavery

Lavery, John 1856–1941, *Harry Younger* (sketch), gift from the artist, 1935, © by courtesy of Felix

Rosenstiel's Widow and Son Ltd, London on behalf of the estate of Sir John Lavery

Lavery, John 1856–1941, *Henry Cook* (sketch), gift from the artist, 1935, © by courtesy of Felix Rosenstiel's Widow and Son Ltd, London on behalf of the estate of Sir John Lavery

Lavery, John 1856–1941, *HRH Prince Henry of Battenberg (1858–1896), KG* (sketch), gift from the artist, 1935, © by courtesy of Felix Rosenstiel's Widow and Son Ltd, London on behalf of the estate of Sir John Lavery

Lavery, John 1856–1941, *HRH Princess Alix of Hesse (1872–1918)* (sketch), gift from the artist, 1935, © by courtesy of Felix Rosenstiel's Widow and Son Ltd, London on behalf of the estate of Sir John Lavery

Lavery, John 1856–1941, *HRH Princess Henry (Beatrice) of Battenberg (1857–1944)* (sketch), gift from the artist, 1935, © by courtesy of Felix Rosenstiel's Widow and Son Ltd, London on behalf of the estate of Sir John Lavery

Lavery, John 1856–1941, *HRH the Grand Duke of Hesse, KG* (sketch), gift from the artist, 1935, © by courtesy of Felix Rosenstiel's Widow and Son Ltd, London on behalf of the estate of Sir John Lavery

Lavery, John 1856–1941, *HRH the Hereditary Grand Duke of Hesse* (sketch), gift from the artist, 1935, © by courtesy of Felix Rosenstiel's Widow and Son Ltd, London on behalf of the estate of Sir John Lavery

Lavery, John 1856–1941, *Hugh Brechin (b.1846)* (sketch), gift from the artist, 1935, © by courtesy of Felix Rosenstiel's Widow and Son Ltd, London on behalf of the estate of Sir John Lavery

Lavery, John 1856–1941, *J. F. X. King (1855–1933)* (sketch), gift from the artist, 1935, © by courtesy of Felix Rosenstiel's Widow and Son Ltd, London on behalf of the estate of Sir John Lavery

Lavery, John 1856–1941, *J. L. Mitchell* (sketch), gift from the artist, 1935, © by courtesy of Felix Rosenstiel's Widow and Son Ltd, London on behalf of the estate of Sir John Lavery

Lavery, John 1856–1941, *J. Wyllie Guild* (sketch), gift from the artist, 1935, © by courtesy of Felix Rosenstiel's Widow and Son Ltd, London on behalf of the estate of Sir John Lavery

Lavery, John 1856–1941, *James B. Russell (1837–1904)* (sketch), gift from the artist, 1935, © by courtesy of Felix Rosenstiel's Widow and Son Ltd, London on behalf of the estate of Sir John Lavery

Lavery, John 1856–1941, *James Barr, Architectural Engineer* (sketch), gift from the artist, 1935,

© by courtesy of Felix Rosenstiel's Widow and Son Ltd, London on behalf of the estate of Sir John Lavery

Lavery, John 1856–1941, *James Black, Provost of Elgin* (sketch), gift from the artist, 1935, © by courtesy of Felix Rosenstiel's Widow and Son Ltd, London on behalf of the estate of Sir John Lavery

Lavery, John 1856–1941, *James Brown, Council Officer* (sketch), gift from the artist, 1935, © by courtesy of Felix Rosenstiel's Widow and Son Ltd, London on behalf of the estate of Sir John Lavery

Lavery, John 1856–1941, *James Muir* (sketch), gift from the artist, 1935, © by courtesy of Felix Rosenstiel's Widow and Son Ltd, London on behalf of the estate of Sir John Lavery

Lavery, John 1856–1941, *James Murray* (sketch), gift from the artist, 1935, © by courtesy of Felix Rosenstiel's Widow and Son Ltd, London on behalf of the estate of Sir John Lavery

Lavery, John 1856–1941, *James Nicol (1833–1911), City Chamberlain, Glasgow* (sketch), gift from the artist, 1935, © by courtesy of Felix Rosenstiel's Widow and Son Ltd, London on behalf of the estate of Sir John Lavery

Lavery, John 1856–1941, *John Boyd, City Treasurer, Edinburgh* (sketch), gift from the artist, 1935, © by courtesy of Felix Rosenstiel's Widow and Son Ltd, London on behalf of the estate of Sir John Lavery

Lavery, John 1856–1941, *John Filshill* (sketch), gift from the artist, 1935, © by courtesy of Felix Rosenstiel's Widow and Son Ltd, London on behalf of the estate of Sir John Lavery

Lavery, John 1856–1941, *John Muir of Deanston (1828–1903), 1st Bt, Lord Provost of Glasgow (1889–1892)* (sketch), gift from the artist, 1935, © by courtesy of Felix Rosenstiel's Widow and Son Ltd, London on behalf of the estate of Sir John Lavery

Lavery, John 1856–1941, *John Neil* (sketch), gift from the artist, 1935, © by courtesy of Felix Rosenstiel's Widow and Son Ltd, London on behalf of the estate of Sir John Lavery

Lavery, John 1856–1941, *John S. Templeton* (sketch), gift from the artist, 1935, © by courtesy of Felix Rosenstiel's Widow and Son Ltd, London on behalf of the estate of Sir John Lavery

Lavery, John 1856–1941, *Lady Octavia Shaw-Stewart* (sketch), gift from the artist, 1935, © by courtesy of Felix Rosenstiel's Widow and Son Ltd, London on behalf of the estate of Sir John Lavery

Lavery, John 1856–1941, *Lady Southampton* (sketch), gift from

the artist, 1935, © by courtesy of Felix Rosenstiel's Widow and Son Ltd, London on behalf of the estate of Sir John Lavery

Lavery, John 1856–1941, *Leonard Gow (1859–1936)* (sketch), gift from the artist, 1935, © by courtesy of Felix Rosenstiel's Widow and Son Ltd, London on behalf of the estate of Sir John Lavery

Lavery, John 1856–1941, *Lieutenant-General Douglas Mackinnon Baillie Hamilton Cochrane (1852–1935), 12th Earl of Dundonald, KGB, KCVO* (sketch), gift from the artist, 1935, © by courtesy of Felix Rosenstiel's Widow and Son Ltd, London on behalf of the estate of Sir John Lavery

Lavery, John 1856–1941, *Mrs Francis Powell* (sketch), gift from the artist, 1935, © by courtesy of Felix Rosenstiel's Widow and Son Ltd, London on behalf of the estate of Sir John Lavery

Lavery, John 1856–1941, *Mrs John Shearer* (sketch), gift from the artist, 1935, © by courtesy of Felix Rosenstiel's Widow and Son Ltd, London on behalf of the estate of Sir John Lavery

Lavery, John 1856–1941, *Mrs Macleod* (sketch), gift from the artist, 1935, © by courtesy of Felix Rosenstiel's Widow and Son Ltd, London on behalf of the estate of Sir John Lavery

Lavery, John 1856–1941, *Mrs Stewart Clark* (sketch), gift from the artist, 1935, © by courtesy of Felix Rosenstiel's Widow and Son Ltd, London on behalf of the estate of Sir John Lavery

Lavery, John 1856–1941, *Peter Bertram* (sketch), gift from the artist, 1935, © by courtesy of Felix Rosenstiel's Widow and Son Ltd, London on behalf of the estate of Sir John Lavery

Lavery, John 1856–1941, *Peter Denny (1821–1895)* (sketch), gift from the artist, 1935, © by courtesy of Felix Rosenstiel's Widow and Son Ltd, London on behalf of the estate of Sir John Lavery

Lavery, John 1856–1941, *Portrait of a Man* (possibly John Martin) (sketch), presented by the executors of the artist's estate, 1941, © by courtesy of Felix Rosenstiel's Widow and Son Ltd, London on behalf of the estate of Sir John Lavery

Lavery, John 1856–1941, *Portrait of a Man* (thought to be Archibald Henderson) (sketch), presented by the executors of the artist's estate, 1941, © by courtesy of Felix Rosenstiel's Widow and Son Ltd, London on behalf of the estate of Sir John Lavery

Lavery, John 1856–1941, *Professor Sir George H. B. Macleod (1828–1892), MD, the Queen's Surgeon* (sketch), gift from the artist, 1935, © by courtesy of Felix

Rosenstiel's Widow and Son Ltd, London on behalf of the estate of Sir John Lavery

Lavery, John 1856–1941, *Reverend Donald Macleod, DD, the Queen's Chaplin* (sketch), gift from the artist, 1935, © by courtesy of Felix Rosenstiel's Widow and Son Ltd, London on behalf of the estate of Sir John Lavery

Lavery, John 1856–1941, *Reverend F. L. Robertson, DD* (sketch), gift from the artist, 1935, © by courtesy of Felix Rosenstiel's Widow and Son Ltd, London on behalf of the estate of Sir John Lavery

Lavery, John 1856–1941, *Reverend George Stewart Burns, DD* (sketch), gift from the artist, 1935, © by courtesy of Felix Rosenstiel's Widow and Son Ltd, London on behalf of the estate of Sir John Lavery

Lavery, John 1856–1941, *Robert Cochrane, Provost of Paisley* (sketch), gift from the artist, 1935, © by courtesy of Felix Rosenstiel's Widow and Son Ltd, London on behalf of the estate of Sir John Lavery

Lavery, John 1856–1941, *Robert Graham* (sketch), gift from the artist, 1935, © by courtesy of Felix Rosenstiel's Widow and Son Ltd, London on behalf of the estate of Sir John Lavery

Lavery, John 1856–1941, *Sir Charles Tennant (1823–1906), Bt* (sketch), gift from the artist, 1935, © by courtesy of Felix Rosenstiel's Widow and Son Ltd, London on behalf of the estate of Sir John Lavery

Lavery, John 1856–1941, *Sir Fleetwood Edwards, KCB* (sketch), gift from the artist, 1935, © by courtesy of Felix Rosenstiel's Widow and Son Ltd, London on behalf of the estate of Sir John Lavery

Lavery, John 1856–1941, *Sir James Bain* (sketch), gift from the artist, 1935, © by courtesy of Felix Rosenstiel's Widow and Son Ltd, London on behalf of the estate of Sir John Lavery

Lavery, John 1856–1941, *Sir James King (1830–1911), Lord Provost of Glasgow (1886–1889)* (sketch), purchased, 1947, © by courtesy of Felix Rosenstiel's Widow and Son Ltd, London on behalf of the estate of Sir John Lavery

Lavery, John 1856–1941, *Sir James Marwick (1826–1908), Town Clerk of Glasgow (1873–1903)* (sketch), gift from the artist, 1935, © by courtesy of Felix Rosenstiel's Widow and Son Ltd, London on behalf of the estate of Sir John Lavery

Lavery, John 1856–1941, *Sir John Neilson Cuthbertson (1829–1905), LLD, DL* (sketch), gift from the artist, 1935, © by courtesy of Felix Rosenstiel's Widow and Son Ltd, London on behalf of the estate of Sir John Lavery

Lavery, John 1856–1941, *Sir Thomas Clark (1832–1900), Bt, Lord Provost of Edinburgh* (sketch), gift from the artist, 1935, © by courtesy of Felix Rosenstiel's Widow and Son Ltd, London on behalf of the estate of Sir John Lavery

Lavery, John 1856–1941, *Stewart Clarke* (sketch), gift from the artist, 1935, © by courtesy of Felix Rosenstiel's Widow and Son Ltd, London on behalf of the estate of Sir John Lavery

Lavery, John 1856–1941, *The Earl of Haddington* (sketch), gift from the artist, 1935, © by courtesy of Felix Rosenstiel's Widow and Son Ltd, London on behalf of the estate of Sir John Lavery

Lavery, John 1856–1941, *The Earl of Lindsay* (sketch), gift from the artist, 1935, © by courtesy of Felix Rosenstiel's Widow and Son Ltd, London on behalf of the estate of Sir John Lavery

Lavery, John 1856–1941, *The Honourable Harriet Lepel Phipps (1841–1922)* (sketch), gift from the artist, 1935, © by courtesy of Felix Rosenstiel's Widow and Son Ltd, London on behalf of the estate of Sir John Lavery

Lavery, John 1856–1941, *The Honourable J. C. Maxwell-Scott* (sketch), gift from the artist, 1935, © by courtesy of Felix Rosenstiel's Widow and Son Ltd, London on behalf of the estate of Sir John Lavery

Lavery, John 1856–1941, *The Honourable Mrs Maxwell-Scott* (sketch), gift from the artist, 1935, © by courtesy of Felix Rosenstiel's Widow and Son Ltd, London on behalf of the estate of Sir John Lavery

Lavery, John 1856–1941, *The Marquis of Lothian, KT* (sketch), gift from the artist, 1935, © by courtesy of Felix Rosenstiel's Widow and Son Ltd, London on behalf of the estate of Sir John Lavery

Lavery, John 1856–1941, *William Ure* (sketch), gift from the artist, 1935, © by courtesy of Felix Rosenstiel's Widow and Son Ltd, London on behalf of the estate of Sir John Lavery

Lavery, John 1856–1941, *William Walls (1819–1893)* (sketch), gift from the artist, 1935, © by courtesy of Felix Rosenstiel's Widow and Son Ltd, London on behalf of the estate of Sir John Lavery

Lavery, John 1856–1941, *Bailie McLennan* (sketch), gift from the artist, 1935, © by courtesy of Felix Rosenstiel's Widow and Son Ltd, London on behalf of the estate of Sir John Lavery

Lavery, John 1856–1941, *William Pettigrew* (sketch), gift from the artist, 1935, © by courtesy of Felix Rosenstiel's Widow and Son Ltd, London on behalf of the estate of Sir John Lavery

Glasgow (1917–1920), purchased, 1921, © by courtesy of Felix Rosenstiel's Widow and Son Ltd, London on behalf of the estate of Sir John Lavery

Lavery, John 1856–1941, *The Right Honourable J. Ramsay Macdonald Addressing the House of Commons*, gift from the artist, 1930, © by courtesy of Felix Rosenstiel's Widow and Son Ltd, London on behalf of the estate of Sir John Lavery

Lavery, John 1856–1941, *Whitewashing*, bequeathed by Mrs A. J. MacLaren, 1940, © by courtesy of Felix Rosenstiel's Widow and Son Ltd, London on behalf of the estate of Sir John Lavery

Lavery, John 1856–1941, *Maidenhead Regatta*, gift from the artist, 1935, © by courtesy of Felix Rosenstiel's Widow and Son Ltd, London on behalf of the estate of Sir John Lavery

Law, Andrew 1873–1967, *The Tron Steeple, Glasgow*, purchased, 1927

Law, Andrew 1873–1967, *Stella Cameron*, purchased, 1956

Law, Andrew 1873–1967, *Chrysanthemums*, purchased, 1944

Lawrence, Thomas 1769–1830, *Mrs John Trower (1782/1783–1809)*, presented by the Trustees of the Hamilton Bequest, 1967

Lawrence, Thomas (attributed to) 1769–1830, *Sketch of a Lady*, gift from Thomas S. Campbell, 1936

Lawson, Cecil Gordon 1851–1882, *Don Saltero's Walk*, gift from Sir William and Lady Burrell to the City of Glasgow, 1944

Lawson, Cecil Gordon 1851–1882, *Barden Moor, Yorkshire*, gift from Mrs Clara Graham, 1924

Lawson, Cecil Gordon 1851–1882, *Landscape with Clouds*, gift from Sir William and Lady Burrell to the City of Glasgow, 1944

Lawson, John 1868–1909, *Killermont House*, found in store, registered, 1951

Lawson, John 1868–1909, *Landscape, Dunlop*, gift from Sir John Richmond, 1948

Lawson, John 1868–1909, *Whitewashed Farmstead*, bequeathed by Mrs Mary A. Lawson, 1950

Lawson, John 1868–1909, *An Ayrshire Stream*, gift from Sir John Richmond, 1948

Lawson, John 1868–1909, *Rhuddlan Castle, North Wales*, purchased, 1910

Le Bas, Edward 1904–1966, *Still Life, No.4*, purchased, 1951

Le Bas, Edward 1904–1966, *Model Resting*, purchased, 1955

Le Nain, Antoine (attributed to) c.1588–1648, *Peasant Children*, gift from Sir William and Lady Burrell to the City of Glasgow, 1944

Le Sidaner, Henri Eugène 1862–1939, *A Beauvais Square by Moonlight*, bequeathed by David Perry, 1940

Le Sidaner, Henri Eugène 1862–1939, *The Snow*, gift from William Burrell, 1925

Le Sidaner, Henri Eugène 1862–1939, *The Lighted Window*, gift from Sir William and Lady Burrell to the City of Glasgow, 1944

Le Sidaner, Henri Eugène 1862–1939, *Rocky Inlets by Moonlight*, gift from Sir William and Lady Burrell to the City of Glasgow, 1944

Leader, Benjamin Williams 1831–1923, *A Golden Eve*, gift from Douglas White, 1939

Leader, Benjamin Williams 1831–1923, *Worcestershire Cottages*, gift from the Misses Anderson, 1921

Lear, Edward 1812–1888, *Launce and His Dog*, bequeathed by William Euing, 1874

Lear, Edward 1812–1888, *Valentine*, bequeathed by William Euing, 1874

Leclerc, Jacques Sébastien (attributed to) c.1734–1785, *Autumn*, bequeathed by William Euing, 1874, photo credit: Glasgow Museums

Leclerc, Jacques Sébastien (attributed to) c.1734–1785, *Summer*, bequeathed by William Euing, 1874, photo credit: Glasgow Museums

Lecomte, Paul Émile 1877–1950, *The End of the Market, Granada, Spain*, purchased, 1937, © ADAGP, Paris and DACS, London 2013

Lee, Sydney 1866–1949, *The Gallery*, presented by the Trustees of the Hamilton Bequest, 1929

Lee-Hankey, William 1869–1952, *Mrs John de la Valette*, purchased, 1934

Legros, Alphonse 1837–1911, *An Approaching Storm*, gift from R. D. McGregor, 1919

Leitch, William Leighton 1804–1883, *Classical Composition*, gift from Archibald G. Macdonald, 1896

Lely, Peter (after) 1618–1680, *The Duchess of Lauderdale*, Archibald McLellan Collection, purchased, 1856

Lely, Peter (after) 1618–1680, *Edward Hyde (1609–1674), Earl of Clarendon*, Stirling Maxwell Collection, gift, 1967

Lely, Peter (attributed to) 1618–1680, *Portrait of a Man*, on loan from a private collection

Lely, Peter (studio of) 1618–1680, *Charles II (1630–1685)*, commissioned by Glasgow Town Council, 1670

Lemmens, Theophile Victor Émile 1821–1867, *Poultry*, bequeathed by Adam Teacher, 1898

Lemoine, François (after) 1688–1737, *Hercules and Omphale*, purchased, 1953

Lemoine, François (after) 1688–1737, *The Guilt of Callisto*, Archibald McLellan Collection, purchased, 1856

Leon, Amanda de b.1908, *Spanish Dancers*, gift from Mr and Mrs E. K. Perry, 1954

Leon, Amanda de b.1908, *The Papaya Tree*, gift from Mr and Mrs E. K. Perry, 1954

Lépine, Stanislas 1835–1892, *The Rue de Norvins, Montmartre*, bequeathed by William McInnes, 1944

Lessore, Thérèse 1884–1945, *ThÈ dansant*, presented by the Sickert Trustees, 1947, © Henry & John Lessore

Lewis, Leonard Avery 1866–1906, *Berkshire Landscape*, gift from J. D. Roberton, 1946

Lewis, Wyndham 1882–1957, *Froanna, the Artist's Wife*, purchased, 1940, © the artist's estate

Leyden, Lucas van (after) c.1494–1533, *Musicians: An Old Man and An Old Woman*, bequeathed by Jane Graham-Gilbert, 1877, photo credit: Glasgow Museums

Lhermitte, Léon-Augustin 1844–1925, *Ploughing with Oxen*, bequeathed by Reverend H. G. Roberts Hay-Boyd, 1941

Lhermitte, Léon-Augustin 1844–1925, *Evening Work*, bequeathed by William J. Chrystal, 1939

Lhote, André 1885–1962, *Negress*, gift from John Mathias, 1951, © ADAGP, Paris and DACS, London 2013

Lhote, André 1885–1962, *Nude*, gift from John Mathias, 1951, © ADAGP, Paris and DACS, London 2013

Lingelbach, Johannes 1622–1674, *An Imaginary Mediterranean Seaport*, bequeathed by Jane Graham-Gilbert, 1877

Lingelbach, Johannes 1622–1674, *A Harbour, with Figures in Oriental Costume*, bequeathed by William Euing, 1874

Linnell, John 1792–1882, *Downward Rays*, presented by the sons of James Reid of Auchterarder, 1896

Linnell, John 1792–1882, *A Coming Storm*, bequeathed by John McGavin, 1881

Lion, Flora 1878–1958, *Mrs Ralph Peto*, presented by the Trustees of the artist, 1961

Lion, Flora 1878–1958, *Mrs Hunter Crawford*, presented by the Trustees of the artist, 1961

Lisse, Dirck van der 1586–1669, *Landscape with Mercury, Argus and Io*, bequeathed by Jane Graham-Gilbert, 1877

Llewellyn, William Samuel Henry 1858–1941, *Sir David Mason (1862–1940), Lord Provost of Glasgow (1926–1929)*, purchased, 1930

Llewellyn, William Samuel Henry 1858–1941, *Sir Hugh Reid (1860–1935)*, acquired from the North British Locomotive Company, 1962

L'Ortolano 1485–c.1527, *Madonna and Child*, bequeathed by Jane Graham-Gilbert, 1877

Locatelli, Andrea 1695–1741, *Landscape and Figures*, Archibald McLellan Collection, purchased, 1856

Locatelli, Andrea 1695–1741, *Landscape with Three Fishermen by a Stream*, Archibald McLellan Collection, purchased, 1856

Locatelli, Andrea 1695–1741, *Landscape with Figures*

Locatelli, Andrea (style of) 1695–1741, *Landscape with a Caprice View of the Temple of Vesta at Tivoli*, purchased, 1956

Lochhead, John 1866–1921, *An Old World Garden*, purchased, 1921

Lochhead, John 1866–1921, *Reverend Monteith*, gift, 1985

Lockhart, William Ewart 1846–1900, *The Right Honourable Arthur J. Balfour (1848–1930), MP*, gift from A. Cameron Corbett, MP (Lord Rowallan), 1898

Lockhart, William Ewart 1846–1900, *The White Cockade*, presented by the executors of the estate of Mrs Mary Lockhart, 1934

Loenen, Johan Cornelisz. van c.1590–c.1643/1663, *Portrait of a Little Girl*, on loan from a private collection

Logan, George 1866–1939, *Lady Lying in a Punt with a Parasol*, gift, 1983

Lokhorst, Dirk Peter van (attributed to) 1848–1894, *Landscape with Cattle*, bequeathed by Adam Teacher, 1898

Lonsdale, James 1777–1839, *Thomas Campbell (1777–1844), Poet*, gift from Miss A. E. Coultate, 1912

Loo, Jacob van c.1614–1670, *Susannah and the Elders*, bequeathed by Jane Graham-Gilbert, 1877

Lorimer, John Henry 1856–1936, *Reverend Peter H. Waddell*, gift from James Waddell, 1903

Loutherbourg, Philip James de 1740–1812, *Horseman and Cattle in a Thunderstorm*, bequeathed by William Euing, 1874

Lowndes, Alan 1921–1978, *Mum Sweeping*, purchased, 1991, © the artist's estate

Lowry, Laurence Stephen 1887–1976, *River Scene*, purchased, 1943, © courtesy of the estate of L. S. Lowry

Lowry, Laurence Stephen 1887–1976, *A Village Square*, presented by George Singleton in memory of his wife, 1965, © courtesy of the estate of L. S. Lowry

Lowry, Laurence Stephen 1887–1976, *VE Day*, purchased, 1946, © courtesy of the estate of L. S. Lowry

Lowry, Laurence Stephen 1887–1976, *Cranes and Ships, Glasgow Docks*, purchased with the assistance of Willie Haughey, the Executive Chairman of City Refrigeration Holdings, and the Art Fund, 2005, © courtesy of the estate of L. S. Lowry

Lowry, Laurence Stephen 1887–1976, *Seascape*, purchased with the assistance of the National Fund for Acquisitions, 1991, © courtesy of the estate of L. S. Lowry

Luce, Maximilien 1858–1941, *Landscape with Willow Trees*, purchased with the assistance of the Lady Moore Bequest and the Local Museums Purchase Fund, 1975, © ADAGP, Paris and DACS, London 2013

Luyckx, Carstian (after) 1623–c.1653, *Still Life with Fruit*, Archibald McLellan Collection, purchased, 1856

D. M. active mid-19th C–mid-20th C, *The Auld Kirk, Trongate*

Macallum, John Thomas Hamilton 1841–1896, *Haymaking in the Highlands*, bequeathed by James Donald, 1905

Macallum, John Thomas Hamilton 1841–1896, *The Draught of Fishes*, gift from R. D. MacGregor, 1927

MacArthur, Lindsay Grandison c.1866–1945, *Pastorale, Evening*, gift from Mrs Lindsay MacArthur, 1946

MacArthur, Lindsay Grandison c.1866–1945, *The Golden Quarry*, gift from Mrs Lindsay MacArthur, 1946

Macbeth, Norman 1821–1888, *Patrick Fairbairn (1805–1874), DD*, acquired, 1978

Macbeth, Norman 1821–1888, *Reverend Robert Buchanan (1802–1875)*, presented by the Trustees and family of the sitter, 1898

Macbeth, Norman 1821–1888, *Alexander Whitelaw (1823–1879), MP*, gift from subscribers, 1880

Macbeth, Norman 1821–1888, *Andrew Galbraith (b.1799), Lord Provost of Glasgow (1857–1860)*, gift from subscribers, 1882

Macbeth, Norman 1821–1888, *John Mossman (1817–1890), Sculptor*, gift from the artist, 1886

Macbeth, Norman 1821–1888, *A Somerset Farm*, found in store, registered, 1900

Macbeth, Norman 1821–1888, *George Thompson of Partick*

Macbeth, Norman 1821–1888, *James Turner of Thrushgrove (1768–1858), a Former Magistrate of the City*, bequeathed by Jessie Turner, 1927

Macbride, William 1856–1913, *Sheep Dipping, River Dee, Kirkcudbright*, purchased, 1907

MacBryde, Robert 1913–1966, *Still Life*, gift from A. J. McNeill Reid, 1952

MacBryde, Robert 1913–1966, *The Backgammon Player*, purchased with the assistance of the National Fund for Acquisitions, 1982

MacColl, Dugald Sutherland 1859–1948, *Wardrope Hard, Tollesbury*, gift from Leonard Gow, 1929, © the artist's estate

MacDonald, Tom 1914–1985, *Still Life with a Plant*, purchased, 1979

MacDougall, Norman McLeod 1849/1850–1937 & **Maris, Matthijs** 1839–1917 *Girls Reading*, gift from Sir William and Lady Burrell to the City of Glasgow, 1944

Macedo, Urbano de b.1912, *Huns and Bersaglieri*, presented by the artist through HM Government, 1950

Macgillivray, James Pittendrigh 1856–1938, *Rhododendrons*, purchased, 1978

MacGregor, William York 1855–1923, *Durham, Evening*, gift from an anonymous donor, 1904

MacGregor, William York 1855–1923, *Westerton, Bridge of Allan*, purchased, 1963

MacGregor, William York 1855–1923, *A Street in Rouen*, bequeathed by Miss Jessie L. Hamilton, 2001

MacGregor, William York 1855–1923, *Oban Bay*, purchased, 1942

MacGregor, William York 1855–1923, *Stirling Castle*, bequeathed by William McInnes, 1944

MacGregor, William York 1855–1923, *The Convent, Twilight*, bequeathed by Mrs W. Y. Macgregor, 1942

MacGregor, William York 1855–1923, *Trees*, purchased, 1942

Mackay, Alexander S. 1832–1899, *Hugh Macdonald (1817–1860), the Glasgow Rambler*, presented by the family of John Cameron, 1923

Mackellar, Duncan 1849–1908, *'The bee that sips the honey gets lost in the sweets'*, purchased, 1940

Mackellar, Duncan 1849–1908, *The Minuet*, purchased, 1908

MacKenzie, David M. active 1832–1875, *Braidburn, near Edinburgh*, Archibald McLellan Collection, purchased, 1856

Mackenzie, James Hamilton 1875–1926, *Fleeting Shadows*, purchased, 1913

Mackenzie, James Hamilton 1875–1926, *Reaper*, bequeathed by William McInnes, 1944

Mackie, Campbell 1886–1952, *Ben Ledi*, purchased, 1944

Mackie, Charles Hodge 1862–1920, *Landscape with Sheep under Trees*, purchased, 1961

Mackintosh, Anne H. b.1944, *Miss Jean Rutherford*, gift from the Park and Laurel Bank Schools Collection (incorporating Laurel Park School), 2006, © the artist

Mackintosh, Charles Rennie 1868–1928, *The Wassail*, acquired by Glasgow Corporation as part of the Ingham Street Tearooms, 1950

Mackintosh, John 1931–1966, *Sunday Afternoon*, purchased, 1956

Mackintosh, Margaret Macdonald 1865–1933, *The May Queen*, gesso, hessian, scrim, twine, glass beads, thread, mother of pearl & tin leaf on panel, acquired by Glasgow Corporation as part of the Ingham Street Tearooms, 1950

Mackintosh, Margaret Macdonald 1865–1933, *'O ye, all ye that walk in Willowwood'*, purchased with the assistance of the National Art Collections Fund, the Heritage Lottery Fund, the Friends of Glasgow Museums and a public appeal, 2001

MacLellan, Malcolm b.1908, *Lochermill, near Bridge of Weir*, purchased, 1957

MacLellan, Malcolm b.1908, *Oor Jamie*

Macnee, Daniel 1806–1882, *Mrs Agnes W. Whyte of Newbury*, bequeathed by Mrs A. Whyte, 1912

Macnee, Daniel 1806–1882, *Horatio McCulloch (1805–1867), RSA*, gift from the artist, 1864

Macnee, Daniel 1806–1882, *Queen Victoria (1819–1901)*, temporary identification number allocated, 1978

Macnee, Daniel 1806–1882, *Mrs Thomas McGuffie (1842–1908)*, gift from Miss McGuffie, 1929

Macnee, Daniel 1806–1882, *Reverend Dr Ralph Wardlaw (1779–1853)*, gift from Elgin Place Congregational Church, Glasgow, 1926

Macnee, Daniel 1806–1882, *John Erskine, Manager of William Dunn's Machine Works, John Street, Glasgow*, gift from Duncan McPherson, 1940

Macnee, Daniel 1806–1882, *Portrait of an Old Lady*, gift from Mrs Wiseman, 1905

Macnee, Daniel 1806–1882, *David Hutcheson (1799–1880)*, bequeathed by the sitter, 1885

Macnee, Daniel 1806–1882, *Lady Macnee*, temporary identification number allocated, 1979

Macnee, Daniel 1806–1882, *Robert Dalglish (1808–1880), MP*, purchased, 1874

Macnee, Daniel 1806–1882, *Robert Dalglish (1808–1880), MP*

Macnee, Daniel 1806–1882, *Bailie James Moir (1806–1880)*, gift from subscribers, 1877

Macnee, Daniel 1806–1882, *John Carrick (1819–1890), Glasgow City Architect*, gift from Ellen T. Carrick, 1920

Macnee, Daniel 1806–1882, *Sam Bough (1822–1878)*, gift from Sir Hugh Reid, 1902

Macnee, Daniel 1806–1882, *Sir James Bain (1818–1898), Lord Provost of Glasgow (1874–1877)*, found in store, registered, 1879

Macnee, Daniel 1806–1882, *James Donaldson, Builder*, purchased, 1957

Macnee, Daniel 1806–1882, *James Fillans (1808–1852), Sculptor*, gift from Miss Fillans, 1870

Macnee, Daniel 1806–1882, *John Aitchison (1769–1859)*, bequeathed by Janet Aitchison, 1886

Macnee, Daniel 1806–1882, *John Elder (1824–1869)*, bequeathed by Mrs Isabella Elder, 1906

Macnee, Daniel 1806–1882, *Mrs Catherine D. Blackie (1774–1847)*, bequeathed by Mrs A. R. B. Black, 1933

Macnee, Daniel 1806–1882, *Mrs George Kerr*, bequeathed by Mary A. C. Maxwell, 1932

Macnee, Daniel 1806–1882, *Reverend Dr William Anderson (1799–1873)*, gift from J. G. Anderson, 1932, photo credit: Glasgow Museums

Macnee, Daniel 1806–1882, *Sir John Whitehead*, temporary identification number allocated, 1977

Macnee, Daniel 1806–1882, *Sketch of a Lady with Two Children*, temporary identification number allocated, 1980

Macnee, Daniel 1806–1882, *Thomas McGuffie (c.1831–1895)*, gift from Miss McGuffie, 1929

Macnee, Daniel 1806–1882, *William Johnstone of Glenorchard (1806–1864)*, gift from E. C. H. Wolff, 1945

Macnee, Daniel 1806–1882, *William Mathieson*, bequeathed by D. S. MacColl, 1949

MacNee, Robert Russell c.1863–1952, *Maytime*, gift from W. J. I. Muir, 1939

MacNicol, Bessie 1869–1904, *A Galloway Landscape*, gift from Edward N. Marshall, 1951

MacNicol, Bessie 1869–1904, *Self Portrait*, bequeathed by John Keppie, 1945

MacNicol, Bessie 1869–1904, *Under the Apple Tree*, purchased, 1963

MacNicol, Bessie 1869–1904, *A Girl of the Sixties*, bequeathed by John Keppie, 1945

MacNicol, Bessie 1869–1904, *Deborah*, purchased, 1908

MacNiven, John 1819–1895, *Glasgow Regatta, the Closing Stages*, gift from former Bailie Charles Carlton, 1924

MacNiven, John 1819–1895, *A Clutha Ferry at Pointhouse*

MacNiven, John 1819–1895, *Launch of the 'County of Roxburgh'*

MacPherson, Neil b.1954, *The Dance Master's Blue Coat*, presented by the Contemporary Art Society, 1989, © the artist

MacPherson, Neil b.1954, *The Washer Woman*, gift from the BBC Collection, 2008, © the artist

MacPherson, Neil b.1954, *Painting of a Cow*, gift from the BBC Collection, 2008, © the artist

MacTaggart, William 1903–1981, *Spring Landscape*, purchased, 1942, © by permission of the artist's family

MacTaggart, William 1903–1981, *The Gay Bouquet*, purchased, 1951, © by permission of the artist's family

MacTaggart, William 1903–1981, *Sunset, Pontarme*, purchased, 1957, © by permission of the artist's family

MacTavish, Grant *Towards Glasgow I*

MacTavish, Grant *Towards Glasgow II*

MacWhirter, John 1839–1911, *Iona by Moonlight*, gift from Sir Stephen P. H. Renshaw, 1944

MacWhirter, John 1839–1911, *Love among the Roses*, found in store, registered, 1988

MacWhirter, John 1839–1911, *Sannox Bay, Arran*, bequeathed by Adam Teacher, 1898

Maes, Nicolaes (attributed to) 1634–1693, *Jacob Trip (1576–1661?)*, gift from Sir William and Lady Burrell to the City of Glasgow, 1944

Maes, Nicolaes (attributed to) 1634–1693, *Portrait of a Man*, bequeathed by Jane Graham-Gilbert, 1877

Maieu, Frank b.1952, *Miss Liberty*, purchased from the artist, 1997

Makinson, Trevor b.1926, *Maryhill Goods Yard*, purchased, 1962

Malleyn, Gerrit 1753–1816, *A Hawking Party Preparing to Depart*, Stirling Maxwell Collection, gift, 1967

Malleyn, Gerrit 1753–1816, *A Boar Hunt*, Stirling Maxwell Collection, gift, 1967

Malleyn, Gerrit 1753–1816, *A Hawking Party*, Stirling Maxwell Collection, gift, 1967

Malleyn, Gerrit 1753–1816, *A Hunting Party at Rest by an Inn*, Stirling Maxwell Collection, gift, 1967

Malleyn, Gerrit 1753–1816, *A Stag Hunt*, Stirling Maxwell Collection, gift, 1967

Malleyn, Gerrit 1753–1816, *An Ambush in the Woods*, Stirling Maxwell Collection, gift, 1967

Mancini, Antonio 1852–1930, *The Sulky Boy*, bequeathed by David Perry, 1940

Manet, Édouard 1832–1883, *The Ham*, gift from Sir William and Lady Burrell to the City of Glasgow, 1944

Manet, Édouard 1832–1883, *Roses in a Champagne Glass*, gift from Sir William and Lady Burrell to the City of Glasgow, 1944

Manet, Édouard (attributed to) 1832–1883, *Fruit*, gift from Sir William and Lady Burrell to the City of Glasgow, 1944

Mann, Alexander 1853–1908, *By the Findhorn*, purchased with the assistance of the Heritage Lottery Fund, the Trustees of the Hamilton Bequest and the Friends of Glasgow Museums, 2004

Mann, Alexander 1853–1908, *Chaff*, purchased, 1908

Mann, Cathleen 1896–1959, *Ballerina*, purchased, 1934, © the artist's estate

Mann, Cathleen 1896–1959, *St James's Park*, purchased, 1944, © the artist's estate

Mann, Cathleen 1896–1959, *A Group of Writers (Shane Leslie, Compton Mackenzie, Henry Green, James Laver and Vyvyan Holland)*, gift from an anonymous donor, 1959, © the artist's estate

Mann, Harrington 1864–1936, *A Young Woman*, presented by the Trustees of Sir Daniel M. Stevenson, 1945

Mann, Harrington 1864–1936, *Jinny Carpenter*, gift, 1960

Mann, Harrington 1864–1936, *Francis Howard*, gift from Mrs Elsie Peache, 1959

Mann, Harrington 1864–1936, *Christine*, purchased, 1935

Mann, Harrington 1864–1936, *Sir John Lavery (1856–1941), RA, RSA*, purchased, 1937

Mann, Harrington 1864–1936, *Alexander Fergusson*, gift from J. I. M. Barr, 1994

Mann, Harrington 1864–1936, *Francis Howard*, gift from Mrs Elsie Peache, 1959

Mann, Harrington 1864–1936, *Study of a Young Girl*, presented by the Trustees of Sir Daniel M. Stevenson, 1945

Mann, Kathleen b.1906, *February*, purchased, 1972

March, Esteban 1610–1660, *Self Portrait*, on loan from a private collection

Marchesi, Giuseppe 1699–1771, *Virgin Adoring the Infant Christ*, Archibald McLellan Collection, purchased, 1856

Marcoussis, Louis 1883–1941, *Still Life in front of a Balcony*, purchased, 1951, © ADAGP, Paris and DACS, London 2013

Marek, Jerzy b.1925, *Still Life*, purchased, 1995, © the artist

Marek, Jerzy b.1925, *The Conspirators*, purchased, 1995, © the artist

Marek, Jerzy b.1925, *Football*, purchased, 1995, © the artist

Marieschi, Michele Giovanni (after) 1710–1743, *Venice: View of the Campo Santa Maria Formosa*, gift from T. Graham Young in memory of his father, James Young, 1900

Maris, Jacob Henricus 1837–1899, *The Pet Goat*, gift from Sir William and Lady Burrell to the City of Glasgow, 1944

Maris, Jacob Henricus 1837–1899, *Breezy Downs*, gift from Sir William and Lady Burrell to the City of Glasgow, 1944

Maris, Jacob Henricus 1837–1899, *A Quiet Berth, Morning Glow*, gift from James Carfrae Alston, 1909

Maris, Jacob Henricus 1837–1899, *Girl with a Peacock Feather*, gift from Sir William and Lady Burrell to the City of Glasgow, 1944

Maris, Jacob Henricus 1837–1899, *A Girl Asleep on a Sofa*, bequeathed by James Donald, 1905

Maris, Jacob Henricus 1837–1899, *Amsterdam*, gift from William Burrell, 1925

Maris, Jacob Henricus 1837–1899, *Beach Scene with a Grounded Boat*, bequeathed by James Donald, 1905
Maris, Jacob Henricus 1837–1899, *Dordrecht*, gift from Sir William and Lady Burrell to the City of Glasgow, 1944
Maris, Jacob Henricus 1837–1899, *A Souvenir of Dordrecht*, gift from Sir William and Lady Burrell to the City of Glasgow, 1944
Maris, Jacob Henricus 1837–1899, *River Scene with a Storm Cloud*, gift from James Carfrae Alston, 1909
Maris, Jacob Henricus 1837–1899, *The Stranded Boat*, gift from William Burrell, 1925
Maris, Jacob Henricus (style of) 1837–1899, *A Dutch Lugger*, purchased, 1970
Maris, Matthijs 1839–1917, *Montmartre*, gift from Sir William and Lady Burrell to the City of Glasgow, 1944
Maris, Matthijs 1839–1917, *Butterflies*, gift from Sir William and Lady Burrell to the City of Glasgow, 1944
Maris, Matthijs 1839–1917, *The Sisters*, gift from Sir William and Lady Burrell to the City of Glasgow, 1944
Maris, Matthijs 1839–1917, *Lessore's Child*, gift from Sir William and Lady Burrell to the City of Glasgow, 1944
Maris, Matthijs 1839–1917, *The Lady of Shalott*, gift from Sir William and Lady Burrell to the City of Glasgow, 1944
Maris, Matthijs 1839–1917, *The Dark Beauty*, gift from Sir William and Lady Burrell to the City of Glasgow, 1951
Maris, Matthijs 1839–1917, *The Fair Beauty*, gift from Sir William and Lady Burrell to the City of Glasgow, 1944
Maris, Matthijs 1839–1917, *Girl with Auburn Hair*, gift from Sir William and Lady Burrell to the City of Glasgow, 1944
Maris, Matthijs 1839–1917, *The Pond*, gift from Sir William and Lady Burrell to the City of Glasgow, 1944
Maris, Matthijs 1839–1917, *Grief*, gift from Sir William and Lady Burrell to the City of Glasgow, 1944
Maris, Matthijs 1839–1917, *Child with a Lemon: Barye Swan*, gift from Sir William and Lady Burrell to the City of Glasgow, 1944
Maris, Matthijs 1839–1917, *The Dreamer*, gift from Sir William and Lady Burrell to the City of Glasgow, 1944
Maris, Matthijs 1839–1917, *Roses*, gift from Sir William and Lady Burrell to the City of Glasgow, 1951
Maris, Matthijs 1839–1917, *At the Altar*, gift from Sir William and Lady Burrell to the City of Glasgow, 1951
Maris, Matthijs 1839–1917, *The Princess*, gift from Sir William and

Lady Burrell to the City of Glasgow, 1944
Maris, Matthijs 1839–1917, *The Prisoners*, gift from Sir William and Lady Burrell to the City of Glasgow, 1944
Maris, Willem 1844–1910, *Dead Bird*, gift from Sir William and Lady Burrell to the City of Glasgow, 1944
Maris, Willem 1844–1910, *Ducks*, gift from William Burrell, 1925
Mark, Brenda 1922–1960, *Conversation at Polperro*, Scottish Arts Council Bequest, 1997, © the artist's estate
Marle, Edward b.1949, *Lotus Eaters*, purchased, 1972, © the artist
Marquet, Albert 1875–1947, *The Port of Algiers*, presented by the Trustees of the Hamilton Bequest, 1955, © ADAGP, Paris and DACS, London 2013
Martin, David 1736/1737–1798, *George Murdoch (1715–1795), Provost of Glasgow (1754–1755 & 1766–1767)*, bequeathed by Kenneth Sanderson, 1943
Martin, David 1736/1737–1798, *Captain Robert Maxwell (1770–1796)*, on loan from a private collection
Martin, Francis Patrick 1883–1966, *The Old Tow Horse*, purchased, 1958
Martin, Francis Patrick 1883–1966, *Maryhill Dock, Forth and Clyde Canal*
Martin, Francis Patrick 1883–1966, *Spring Morning, Blaven*, purchased, 1953
Martin, John 1789–1854, *Adam's First Sight of Eve*, presented by the Imperial Chemical Company, 1946
Martin, John 1789–1854, *Distant View of London*, Archibald McLellan Collection, purchased, 1856
Martínez de Gradilla, Juan active 1660–1682, *Philip IV (1605–1665), King of Spain*, Stirling Maxwell Collection, gift, 1967
Martino, Edoardo de 1838–1912, *Yacht 'Shamrock'*, presented by the Trustees of Sir Thomas Lipton, 1932
Master of Moulins active c.1475–c.1505, *Saint Maurice (or Saint Victor) with a Donor*, Archibald McLellan Collection, purchased, 1856
Master of Paris active c.1440–1460, *The Judgement of Paris*, gift from Sir William and Lady Burrell to the City of Glasgow, 1944
Master of the Beyghem Altarpiece (attributed to) active 16th C, *Saint Adrian*, Archibald McLellan Collection, purchased, 1856
Master of the Brunswick Diptych (attributed to) active c.1480–1510, *The Annunciation*, gift from Sir William and Lady Burrell to the City of Glasgow, 1944
Master of the Glasgow Adoration active c.1490–1520, *The Adoration of the Magi*, bequeathed by Jane

Graham-Gilbert, 1877
Master of the Prado Adoration of the Magi (attributed to) active c.1450–1475, *The Flight into Egypt*, gift from Sir William and Lady Burrell to the City of Glasgow, 1944
Master of the Prado Adoration of the Magi (attributed to) active c.1450–1475, *Virgin Annunciate*, gift from Sir William and Lady Burrell to the City of Glasgow, 1944
Master of the Twelve Apostles active c.1527–1542, *'Noli me tangere'*, Archibald McLellan Collection, purchased, 1856
Masuré, Jules 1819–1910, *Sunset*, gift from Reverend John Moore, 1943
Mateo, José Luis Alonso b.1964, *Reina Isabel*, purchased, 1997, © the artist
Matisse, Henri 1869–1954, *Woman in Oriental Dress*, gift from William McInnes, 1940, © succession H. Matisse/DACS 2013
Matisse, Henri 1869–1954, *The Pink Tablecloth*, bequeathed by William McInnes, 1944, © succession H. Matisse/DACS 2013
Mauve, Anton 1838–1888, *Scheveningen*, gift from Sir William and Lady Burrell to the City of Glasgow, 1944
Mauve, Anton 1838–1888, *Carting Sand*, gift from Sir William and Lady Burrell to the City of Glasgow, 1944
Mauve, Anton 1838–1888, *A Woman Driving Cattle*, gift from F. J. Nettlefold, 1948
Maxwell, John 1905–1962, *Boy with an Accordion*, purchased, 1957
Maxwell, Joseph b.1925, *'Extra Yankee' over the Tay Bridge*, purchased, 1966
Maxwell, Joseph b.1925, *Piper's Brae, Culzean*, purchased, 1970
Mayo, Drummond b.1929, *Vennel*, gift from the BBC Collection, 2008, © the artist
Mayo, Drummond b.1929, *The Visitors*, gift from the BBC Collection, 2008, © the artist
Maze, Paul Lucien 1887–1979, *Regatta at Meulan*, presented by the Contemporary Art Society, 1940, © the artist's estate
Mazo, Juan Bautista Martínez del (after) 1612–1667, *The Infanta Margarita (1651–1673)*, gift from Sir William and Lady Burrell to the City of Glasgow, 1944
Mazo, Juan Bautista Martínez del (attributed to) 1612–1667, *Landscape with Figures*, Stirling Maxwell Collection, gift, 1967
McAdam, Walter 1866–1935, *Flowers in the Meadow*, purchased, 1909
McBey, James 1883–1959, *Sir Harry Lauder (1870–1950)*, gift from the sitter, 1930, © the artist's estate
McBey, James 1883–1959, *Mrs John Arnott*, bequeathed by Mrs Arnott, 1943, © the artist's estate

McCaig, Charles active 20th C, *Train*
McCaig, Charles active 20th C, *Train*
McCance, William 1894–1970, *Conflict*, purchased, 1973, © the artist's estate
McCann, Frank b.1946, *Untitled*, purchased, 1992
McClue, R. *Albert Ernest Pickard (1874–1964), of Albert Ernest Pickard Limited*
McClure, David 1926–1998, *The Shrine*, purchased, 1963, © Culture and Sport Glasgow (Glasgow Museums)
McClymant *William Strang (1859–1921)*, gift, 1975
McCulloch, Horatio 1805–1867, *Bowling*, bequeathed by Mary A. C. Maxwell, 1932
McCulloch, Horatio 1805–1867, *View from the Roman Camp at Dalzell near Hamilton*, purchased with the assistance of the Trustees of the Hamilton Bequest, 1985
McCulloch, Horatio 1805–1867, *The Clyde near Erskine Ferry*, gift from J. H. Downes, 1890
McCulloch, Horatio 1805–1867, *Dunstaffnage Castle*, bequeathed by Mrs Janet Rodger, 1901
McCulloch, Horatio 1805–1867, *The Cuillin from Ord, Skye*, gift from Archibald G. Macdonald, 1896
McCulloch, Horatio 1805–1867, *Kinlochaline Castle, Morvern*, purchased, 1960
McCulloch, Horatio 1805–1867, *Glen Affric*, gift from Miss Russell, 1927
McCulloch, Horatio 1805–1867, *'My heart's in the Highlands'*, bequeathed by Mrs Janet Rodger, 1901
McCulloch, Horatio 1805–1867, *Ross-shire Landscape*, bequeathed by Thomas D. Smellie, 1901
McCulloch, Horatio 1805–1867, *Loch Lomond*, gift from Archibald G. Macdonald, 1896
McCulloch, Horatio 1805–1867, *Glencoe*, bequeathed by Mrs Janet Rodger, 1901
McCulloch, Horatio 1805–1867, *Loch Achray, Evening*, bequeathed by Mrs Janet Rodger, 1901
McCulloch, Horatio 1805–1867, *Loch Achray, Morning*, bequeathed by Mrs Janet Rodger, 1901
McCulloch, Horatio 1805–1867, *Loch Maree*, bequeathed by Mrs Janet Rodger, 1901
McCulloch, Horatio 1805–1867, *Mountain Scenery*, temporary identification number allocated, 1981
McCulloch, Horatio (after) 1805–1867, *Bowling*, gift from McIlwraith, 1942
McCulloch, Horatio (attributed to) 1805–1867, *Abbotsford from the Tweed*, bequeathed by Miss Margaret O. Sibbald, 2005
McCulloch, Horatio (attributed to) 1805–1867, *Landscape*, gift from Mrs Inglis Pollock, 1953

McCulloch, Horatio (attributed to) 1805–1867, *Loch Lomond*, bequeathed by Mrs Margaret H. W. Frame, 1985
McCulloch, Ian b.1935, *Strathclyde (diptych, left panel)*, commissioned by Strathclyde Regional Council, 1990, © the artist
McCulloch, Ian b.1935, *Strathclyde (diptych, right panel)*, commissioned by Strathclyde Regional Council, 1990, © the artist
McDonald, James b.1956, *Whistles*, gift from the BBC Collection, 2008, © the artist
McDougall, Lily Martha Maud 1875–1958, *The Marbled Jug*, purchased, 1955
McEvoy, Ambrose 1878–1927, *Elizabeth Johnson*, presented by the Trustees of the Hamilton Bequest, 1933
McEwan, Thomas 1846–1914, *Interior: The Spinning Wheel*, gift from Dr Arthur Ballantyne, 1942
McEwan, Thomas 1846–1914, *An Interior*, purchased from the artist, 1898
McEwan, Thomas 1846–1914, *Tea Time*, bequeathed by Miss M. A. W. Thomson, 1947
McFadyen, Jock b.1950, *Depression*, purchased, 1991, © the artist
McFarlane, A. *Glasgow Cathedral and Molendinar Burn*
McFarlane, J. *Rendezvous Court*, purchased, 1958
McGarvey, Don *Peripheral Reflection I*, gift from the BBC Collection, 2008
McGarvey, Don *Peripheral Reflection II*, gift from the BBC Collection, 2008
McGarvey, Don *Peripheral Reflection III*, gift from the BBC Collection, 2008
McGarvey, Don *Peripheral Reflection IV*, gift from the BBC Collection, 2008
McGarvey, Don *Peripheral Reflection V*, gift from the BBC Collection, 2008
McGhie, John 1867–1952, *Fresh from the Sea*, purchased, 1911
McGhie, John 1867–1952, *Fisher Girls Landing the Catch*, bequeathed by Miss M. A. W. Thomson, 1947
McGhie, John 1867–1952, *Rocky Seascape*, bequeathed by Jessie W. Craig, 1950
McGlashan, Alexander 1853–1880, *Burnam Beeches*, gift from Mr and Mrs W. S. Anderson, 1929
McGlashan, Alexander 1853–1880, *Midday, Glen Falloch*, gift from Mr and Mrs W. S. Anderson, 1929
McGlashan, Archibald A. 1888–1980, *Self Portrait as a Young Man*, gift, 1976, © the artist's estate
McGlashan, Archibald A. 1888–1980, *Sir Patrick Dollan (1885–1963), Wearing 'The Red Jacket'*, gift, 1969, © the artist's estate

McGlashan, Archibald A. 1888–1980, *Mother and Child*, purchased, 1931, © the artist's estate

McGlashan, Archibald A. 1888–1980, *Lachlan Mackinnon, JP*, temporary identification number allocated, 1988, © the artist's estate

McGlashan, Archibald A. 1888–1980, *Child in a Cot*, purchased, 1955, © the artist's estate

McGlashan, Archibald A. 1888–1980, *Child's Head*, gift from Sir John Richmond, 1948, © the artist's estate

McGoran, Thomas b.1927, *Back Court Games*, purchased from the artist, 1992, © the artist

McGoran, Thomas b.1927, *Bathtime*, purchased from the artist, 1996, © the artist

McGoran, Thomas b.1927, *Bridgeton Cross*, purchased from the artist, 1992, © the artist

McGoran, Thomas b.1927, *Carpet Beaters*, purchased from the artist, 1992, © the artist

McGoran, Thomas b.1927, *Coia's Corner*, purchased from the artist, 1992, © the artist

McGoran, Thomas b.1927, *Half a Kitchen*, purchased from the artist, 1996, © the artist

McGoran, Thomas b.1927, *The Other Half*, purchased from the artist, 1996, © the artist

McGoran, Thomas b.1927, *Night Watchman*, purchased from the artist, 1992, © the artist

McGoran, Thomas b.1927, *Our Daily Bread*, purchased from the artist, 1992, © the artist

McGoran, Thomas b.1927, *Pitch and Toss*, purchased from the artist, 1992, © the artist

McGoran, Thomas b.1927, *Saturday Night at the Movies*, purchased from the artist, 1992, © the artist

McGoran, Thomas b.1927, *Street Games*, purchased from the artist, 1992, © the artist

McGoran, Thomas b.1927, *Sunday Morning*, purchased from the artist, 1996, © the artist

McGoran, Thomas b.1927, *The Big Store*, purchased from the artist, 1992, © the artist

McGoran, Thomas b.1927, *The Bookies' Close*, purchased from the artist, 1992, © the artist

McGoran, Thomas b.1927, *The Pokey Hat Man*, purchased from the artist, 1992, © the artist

McGoran, Thomas b.1927, *Wash Day*, purchased from the artist, 1992, © the artist

McGoran, Thomas b.1927, *Foggy Day in Glasgow*, purchased from the artist, 1992, © the artist

McGregor, Robert 1847–1922, *Doing the Provinces*, bequeathed by Adam Teacher, 1898

McGregor, Robert 1847–1922, *A Smoker*, bequeathed by Adam Teacher, 1898

McGregor, Robert 1847–1922, *Breadwinners*, purchased, 1905

McGuinness, Johnny b.1955, *The Field*

McGuinness, Johnny b.1955, *White Sails*

McInnes, Robert 1801–1886, *An Italian Hostelry*, bequeathed by William Euing, 1874

McIntosh, Archibald Dunbar b.1936, *Windows and Sinks*, purchased, 1966

McIntyre, Keith b.1959, *Psalms of the Shadows Opus II*, purchased, 1992

McKay, William Darling 1844–1924, *The Old Gateway*, bequeathed by Adam Teacher, 1898

McKenzie, Elizabeth H. b.1931, *Noon*, purchased, 1954

McKinna, Mary E. Tait active 1930–1952, *Nasturtiums in a Lustre Jug*, bequeathed by Jessie W. Craig, 1950

McLauchlan, Archibald active 1752–after 1770, *John Glassford (1715–1783), and His Family*, gift from John Duncan, 1950

McLaughlin, Brian b.1966, *Thomas Dingwall, Lord Provost of the City of Glasgow (1995–1996)*, purchased from the artist, 2001

McLean, Bruce b.1944, *Untitled*, purchased with the assistance of the National Fund for Acquisitions, 1985, © the artist

McLean, John b.1939, *Gaillac*, purchased, 1994, © the artist

McLean, John b.1939, *Hunter*, purchased, 1994, © the artist

McLean, John b.1939, *Inchcape*, purchased, 1994, © the artist

McLean, John b.1939, *Peninsula*, purchased, 1994, © the artist

McLean, John b.1939, *Strathspey*, purchased, 1994, © the artist

McLean, Talbert 1906–1992, *Scree*, presented by the Contemporary Art Society, 1983, © John & David McLean

McNairn, Caroline 1955–2010, *In a Foreign Country*, purchased, 1991

McNulty, Tracy b.1970, *Portrait*, purchased, 1992

McTaggart, F. R. active 19th C, *A Port by the Sea*, temporary identification number allocated, 1979

McTaggart, William 1835–1910, *Grandmother's Pet*, bequeathed by John Fleming, 1923

McTaggart, William 1835–1910, *Do Doggies Gang tae Heaven?*, purchased, 1951

McTaggart, William 1835–1910, *Lucy's Flitting*, presented by the family of D. Brodie MacLeod, 1929

McTaggart, William 1835–1910, *Summer Breezes*, presented by the daughters of Sir T. McCall Anderson, 1944

McTaggart, William 1835–1910, *North Wind, Kilbrannan Sound*, bequeathed by William McInnes, 1944

McTaggart, William 1835–1910, *Robert Greenlees (1820–1894)*, gift from Robert Brydall, 1894

McTaggart, William 1835–1910, *Dawn at Sea, Homewards*, presented by the Trustees of the Hamilton Bequest, 1936

McTaggart, William 1835–1910, *Joseph Henderson (1832–1908), RSW*, presented by the family of Joseph Henderson, 1925

McTaggart, William 1835–1910, *The Lilies*, bequeathed by William McInnes, 1944

McTaggart, William 1835–1910, *The Paps of Jura*, gift from Leonard Gow, 1922

McTaggart, William 1835–1910, *Along the Shore*, bequeathed by William McInnes, 1944

McTaggart, William 1835–1910, *Gathering Brambles: Kevoch Mill*, bequeathed by Miss Mary P. R. Allan, 2003

McTaggart, William 1835–1910, *The Ballad*, gift from Mrs Maitland Ramsay, 1953

Meadows, Arthur Joseph 1843–1907, *Venice, Morning*, gift from Miss Anderson, 1921

Meadows, Arthur Joseph 1843–1907, *Venice with the Doge's Palace*, gift from Miss Anderson, 1921

Medina, John Baptist de 1659–1710, *Sir John Maxwell (1648–1732), 1st Bt*, on loan from a private collection

Medina, John Baptist de (after) 1659–1710, *Self Portrait*, Stirling Maxwell Collection, gift, 1967

Meissonier, Jean Louis Ernest 1815–1891, *Pasquale*, bequeathed by Captain R. Allan Ogg, 1943

Mellis, Margaret 1914–2009, *Three Faded Flowers*, purchased, 1991, © the estate of Margaret Mellis

Mellis, Margaret 1914–2009, *Burnt Out*, purchased, 1991, © the estate of Margaret Mellis

Melville, Arthur 1855–1904, *The Tragedy of the Morn*, purchased, 1944

Melville, Arthur 1855–1904, *Night, Spain*, purchased with the assistance of the National Fund for Acquisitions, 1982

Mengs, Anton Raphael 1728–1779, *Girl with a Dove*, on loan from a private collection

Meninsky, Bernard 1891–1950, *Woman with a Basket of Fruit*, purchased, 1950, © the artist's estate/Bridgeman Art Library

Mercier, Philippe (after) 1689–1760, *Frederick, Prince of Wales (1707–1751)*, Stirling Maxwell Collection, gift, 1967

Metsu, Gabriel (after) 1629–1667, *The Doctor's Visit*, Archibald McLellan Collection, purchased, 1856

Mettling, Louis 1847–1904, *Boy's Head*, bequeathed by David Perry, 1940

Mettling, Louis 1847–1904, *Woman Cooking at a Stove*, bequeathed by John Fleming, 1923

Michel, Georges 1763–1843, *Landscape with Cottages*, purchased, 1959

Michel, Georges 1763–1843, *Moorland: The Storm Cloud*, gift from William Burrell, 1925

Michie, David Alan Redpath b.1928, *E. P. N. S. Teapot*, purchased, 1959, © the artist/Bridgeman Art Library

Michie, David Alan Redpath b.1928, *Edge of the Sea*, purchased, 1965, © Culture and Sport Glasgow (Glasgow Museums)

Michonze, Grégoire 1902–1982, *Children at Play*, purchased, 1949, © ADAGP, Paris and DACS, London 2013

Middleton, James Raeburn 1855–1931, *Sir John S. Samuel, Secretary to the Lord Provost of Glasgow*, acquired, 1963

Middleton, James Raeburn 1855–1931, *Alexander Walker*, gift from Alex Walker, 1943

Middleton, James Raeburn 1855–1931, *Jeanie Deans and the Queen*, gift from Mrs E. W. Gow, 1943

Mielich, Hans 1516–1573, *The Conversion of Saint Eustace* (or *Saint Hubert*), Archibald McLellan Collection, purchased, 1856

Mieris, Frans van the elder (after) 1635–1681, *The Music Lesson*, Archibald McLellan Collection, purchased, 1856

Mieris, Frans van the elder (studio of) 1635–1681, *A Sick Woman and Her Doctor*, Archibald McLellan Collection, purchased, 1856

Mieris, Frans van the younger (after) 1689–1763, *A Boy and a Girl at a Window*, bequeathed by Thomas D. Smellie, 1901

Mieris, Frans van the younger (style of) 1689–1763, *A Woman and a Child by a Window*, bequeathed by William Euing, 1874

Millais, John Everett 1829–1896, *William E. Gladstone (1809–1898)*, presented by the family of Agnes Wickham, the sitter's daughter, through the National Art Collections Fund, 1950

Millais, John Everett 1829–1896, *Reverend John Caird (1820–1898), Principal of Glasgow University (1873–1898)*, bequeathed by Mrs Caird, 1913

Millais, John Everett 1829–1896, *The Ornithologist*, purchased, 1907

Millais, John Everett 1829–1896, *Mrs Isabella Elder (1828–1905)*, purchased, 1917

Millais, John Everett 1829–1896, *The Forerunner*, gift from Sir Charles Tennant, 1903

Millar, Jean M. 1932–2006, *Glasgow University from Bunhouse Road*, gift, 1984

Miller, Archibald Elliot Haswell 1887–1979, *The Bridge of St Martin, Toledo*, purchased, 1926

Miller, Barse 1904–1973, *Tattoo Artist*, purchased, 1945

Miller, Charles Keith 1836–1907, *In a Storm*, purchased with the assistance of the National Fund for Acquisitions, 1973

Miller, Charles Keith 1836–1907, *'Marion Inglis'*, gift from Mrs Alexina E. Melville, 1948

Miller, Edmund b.1929, *Sword in the Sky*, gift from Dan Air Services Limited, 1990, © the artist

Miller, John 1911–1975, *Landscape near Fintry*, purchased from the artist, 1945

Miller, John 1911–1975, *Showery Weather, St Andrews*, purchased, 1969

Miller, John 1911–1975, *Spring on the Gareloch*, purchased, 1973

Miller, Walter active 1894–1949, *Memory of the Past*, purchased, 1969

Millet, Jean-François 1814–1875, *A Woman Adjusting Her Stocking*, gift from Sir William and Lady Burrell to the City of Glasgow, 1944

Millet, Jean-François 1814–1875, *A Shepherdess*, gift from Sir William and Lady Burrell to the City of Glasgow, 1944

Millet, Jean-François 1814–1875, *Going to Work*, bequeathed by James Donald, 1905

Milne, John Maclauchlan 1885–1957, *North Glen Sannox*, purchased, 1941

Milne, John Maclauchlan 1885–1957, *Loch Eriboll*, presented by the Trustees of John Tattersall, 1935

Mitchell, Colin Gillespie c.1870–c.1938, *Reflections*, gift from an anonymous donor, 1940

Mitchell, John Campbell 1865–1922, *Cruachan*, gift from Mrs Inglis Pollock, 1953

Mitchell, Meg *Finlay Stone Windows*, gift from the BBC Collection, 2008

Mitchell, T. *The Kelvin at the Three Tree Well*

Moir, John 1776–1857, *John M. Robertson*, bequeathed by Isabella A. H. J. Campbell, 1917

Moir, John 1776–1857, *Mrs J. M. Robertson, Mother of John M. Robertson*, bequeathed by Isabella A. H. J. Campbell, 1917

Moira, Gerald 1867–1959, *Highland Landscape*, purchased, 1933

Molenaer, Klaes (attributed to) c.1630–1676, *The Musicians*, bequeathed by William Euing, 1874

Monamy, Peter 1681–1749, *The Battle of Barfleur, 19 May 1692*, Archibald McLellan Collection, purchased, 1856

Monet, Claude 1840–1926, *Vétheuil*, bequeathed by William McInnes, 1944

Monet, Claude 1840–1926, *View of Ventimiglia*, presented by the Trustees of the Hamilton Bequest, 1943

Montagna, Bartolomeo c.1450–1523, *Virgin and Child Enthroned with Saint James Major and Saint John the Evangelist*, gift from William G. Crum, 1906, photo credit: Glasgow Museums

Montézin, Pierre Eugène 1874–1946, *The Meadow in June*, purchased, 1937, © ADAGP, Paris and DACS, London 2013

Monticelli, Adolphe Joseph Thomas 1824–1886, *The Adoration of the Magi*, bequeathed by James Donald, 1905

Monticelli, Adolphe Joseph Thomas 1824–1886, *Strolling Players*, gift from Sir William and Lady Burrell to the City of Glasgow, 1944

Monticelli, Adolphe Joseph Thomas 1824–1886, *Garden Fête: The White Horse*, gift from James Carfrae Alston, 1909

Monticelli, Adolphe Joseph Thomas 1824–1886, *Autumn in the Field*, gift from Sir William and Lady Burrell to the City of Glasgow, 1944

Monticelli, Adolphe Joseph Thomas 1824–1886, *Scene from 'The Decameron'* (by Giovanni Boccaccio), gift from Sir William and Lady Burrell to the City of Glasgow, 1944

Monticelli, Adolphe Joseph Thomas 1824–1886, *Children Playing in a Park*, gift from Sir William and Lady Burrell to the City of Glasgow, 1948

Monticelli, Adolphe Joseph Thomas 1824–1886, *The Harpist*, gift from Sir William and Lady Burrell to the City of Glasgow, 1944

Monticelli, Adolphe Joseph Thomas 1824–1886, *The New Vintage*, gift from Sir William and Lady Burrell to the City of Glasgow, 1944

Monticelli, Adolphe Joseph Thomas 1824–1886, *Ladies of Quality*, bequeathed by William McInnes, 1944

Monticelli, Adolphe Joseph Thomas 1824–1886, *The Orange Game*, bequeathed by William J. Chrystal, 1939

Monticelli, Adolphe Joseph Thomas 1824–1886, *A Woodland Dance*, gift from Sir William and Lady Burrell to the City of Glasgow, 1953

Monticelli, Adolphe Joseph Thomas 1824–1886, *Alfresco*, gift from Sir William and Lady Burrell to the City of Glasgow, 1944

Monticelli, Adolphe Joseph Thomas 1824–1886, *Fête champêtre*, bequeathed by William J. Chrystal, 1939

Monticelli, Adolphe Joseph Thomas 1824–1886, *Forest Glade*, gift from Sir William and Lady Burrell to the City of Glasgow, 1944

Monticelli, Adolphe Joseph Thomas 1824–1886, *In the Forest*, gift from Sir William and Lady Burrell to the City of Glasgow, 1944

Monticelli, Adolphe Joseph Thomas 1824–1886, *Ladies in a Glade near a Statue of Venus*, gift from Sir William and Lady Burrell to the City of Glasgow, 1944

Monticelli, Adolphe Joseph Thomas 1824–1886, *The Bazaar, Marseilles*, gift from Sir William and Lady Burrell to the City of Glasgow, 1944

Monticelli, Adolphe Joseph Thomas 1824–1886, *The Marriage Procession*, bequeathed by Archibald R. Henderson, 1901

Monticelli, Adolphe Joseph Thomas 1824–1886, *The Ravine*, gift from Sir William and Lady Burrell to the City of Glasgow, 1944

Monticelli, Adolphe Joseph Thomas 1824–1886 & **Maris, Matthijs** 1839–1917 *In the Forest*, gift from Sir William and Lady Burrell to the City of Glasgow, 1944

Moon, Henry George 1857–1905, *The Outlook, Palling, Norfolk*, bequeathed by J. Barnard Davis, 1943

Moore, Albert Joseph 1841–1893, *Reading Aloud*, gift from Andrew T. Reid, 1908

Moore, Henry 1831–1895, *St Alban's Race*, purchased, 1906

Morales, Luis de c.1509–c.1586, *Pietà*, Stirling Maxwell Collection, gift, 1967

More, Jacob 1740–1793, *Evening*, purchased with the assistance of the National Fund for Acquisitions, 1975

More, Jacob 1740–1793, *Morning*, purchased with the assistance of the National Fund for Acquisitions, 1975

Moret, Henry 1856–1913, *Cliffs at Port-Domois, Belle-Île*, presented by the Trustees of the Hamilton Bequest, 1962

Morier, David 1705–1770, *George II (1683–1760)*, Stirling Maxwell Collection, gift, 1967

Morier, David 1705–1770, *HRH William Augustus (1721–1765), Duke of Cumberland*, Stirling Maxwell Collection, gift, 1967

Morland, George 1763–1804, *Sea-Coast Scene, Smugglers*, Archibald McLellan Collection, purchased, 1856

Morland, George (attributed to) 1763–1804, *An English Homestead*, bequeathed by James Stevenson, 1903

Morland, George (attributed to) 1763–1804, *Landscape, an Inland Stream*, Archibald McLellan Collection, purchased, 1856

Morland, George (attributed to) 1763–1804, *Storm and Wreck*, bequeathed by William Euing, 1874

Morland, George (style of) 1763–1804, *Sea Piece*, bequeathed by William Euing, 1874

Morland, Henry Robert c.1716–1797, *The Oyster Seller*,

Archibald McLellan Collection, purchased, 1856

Morley, John b.1942, *Noah and the Animals*, purchased from the artist, 1991, © the artist

Morris, Margaret 1891–1980, *Near Dieppe*, purchased, 1943

Morris, May active 1893–1950, *Rocky Cove*, bequeathed by Jessie W. Craig, 1950

Morrison, James b.1932, *Camp Coffee Works, Charlotte Street, Glasgow*, gift, 1983, © the artist

Morrison, James b.1932, *Binney House*, purchased, 1957, © the artist

Morrison, James b.1932, *Seascape I*, gift from the artist, 1981, © Culture and Sport Glasgow (Glasgow Museums)

Morrison, James b.1932, *Apsley Street, Glasgow*, purchased, 1961, © the artist

Morrison, James b.1932, *Athole Gardens, Glasgow*, purchased, 1965, © Culture and Sport Glasgow (Glasgow Museums)

Morrison, James b.1932, *Half-Demolished Tenements*, temporary identification number allocated, 1984, © the artist

Morrison, James b.1932, *Edge of the Storm, Turtle Lake*, purchased with the assistance of the Trustees of the Hamilton Bequest and the National Fund for Acquisitions, 1988, © Culture and Sport Glasgow (Glasgow Museums)

Morrison, James b.1932, *Tenements*, temporary identification number allocated, 1984, © the artist

Morrison, John b.1904, *Design*, purchased, 1944

Morrocco, Alberto 1917–1998, *The Blue Bedroom*, purchased, 1957, © Culture and Sport Glasgow (Glasgow Museums)

Morton, Cavendish b.1911, *TSS 'Caronia' Fitting Out at Clydebank*, purchased with the assistance of the National Fund for Acquisitions, 1973, © the artist

Morton, Cavendish b.1911, *Passenger-Cargo Motor Vessel 'Rangitane'*, purchased with the assistance of the National Fund for Acquisitions, 1973, © the artist

Morton, Cavendish b.1911, *Rotors Being Hardened, Beardmore Forge, Glasgow*, purchased from the artist, 1991, © the artist

Morton, Cavendish b.1911, *Steam Hammer and Ingot, Beardmore Forge, Glasgow*, purchased from the artist, 1991, © the artist

Morton, Cavendish b.1911, *Stern Iron Being Bored, Beardmore Forge, Glasgow*, purchased from the artist, 1991, © the artist

Morton, Cavendish b.1911, *Passenger-Cargo Motor Vessel 'Ruahine'*, purchased with the assistance of the National Fund for Acquisitions, 1973, © the artist

Morton, Robert Harold 1893–1965, *St Thomas's Well*, purchased, 1948

Morton, Thomas Corsan 1859–1928, *Souvenir de Manet*, gift from William McInnes, 1930

Morton, Thomas Corsan 1859–1928, *A Cathedral City, Durham*, purchased, 1929

Morton, Victoria b.1971, *Compartments for Isis* (diptych, left panel), purchased, 2007, © the artist

Morton, Victoria b.1971, *Compartments for Isis* (diptych, right panel), purchased, 2007, © the artist

Moser, Oswald 1874–1953, *Girl in Red*, purchased, 1930

Moucheron, Frederick de 1633–1686, *Landscape with a Ruined Tower and Figures*, Archibald McLellan Collection, purchased, 1856

Moucheron, Frederick de (attributed to) 1633–1686, *Landscape with a Hawking Party*, Archibald McLellan Collection, purchased, 1856

Mouncey, William 1852–1901, *Autumn in Galloway*, purchased, 1961

Mouncey, William 1852–1901, *Kirkcudbrightshire Landscape*, presented by the executors of the artist, 1939

Mouncey, William 1852–1901, *Landscape*, gift from A. B. Clements, 1942

Mouncey, William 1852–1901, *Wooded Landscape*, gift from Mr and Mrs Julian G. Lusada through the National Art Collections Fund, 1934

Moustafa, Ahmed b.1943, *The Attributes of Divine Perception*, purchased with the assistance of the National Fund for Acquisitions, 1994

Moynihan, Rodrigo 1910–1990, *Sir Garnet Wilson (1885–1975)*, gift from the sitter, 1950, © the artist's estate

Mpetyane, Lindsay Bird b.1935, *Anarkakula*, purchased, 1993, © DACS 2013

Muhrmann, Henry 1854–1916, *Maying*, bequeathed by John Keppie, 1945

Muhrmann, Henry 1854–1916, *The Thames*, gift from William Burrell, 1925

Muir, Anne Davidson 1875–1951, *Primulas in a Blue and White Vase*, bequeathed by Jessie W. Craig, 1950

Muir, Anne Davidson 1875–1951, *Spring Bouquet*, bequeathed by Jessie W. Craig, 1950

Muirhead, David 1867–1930, *Durham Cathedral*, gift from Mrs A. E. Borthwick, 1957

Muirhead, David 1867–1930, *Landscape*, gift from Francis Howard, 1942

Mulier, Pieter the younger (attributed to) c.1637–1701, *Stormy Landscape with a Fallen Tree*, bequeathed by William Willis, 1858

Muller, William James 1812–1845, *Eastern Letter Writer*, bequeathed by James Donald, 1905

Muller, William James 1812–1845, *The Treasure Finders*, purchased, 1907

Mulready, William (attributed to) 1786–1863, *Studies of Italian Organ Boys and Their Monkeys*, purchased with the assistance of the National Fund for Acquisitions, 1976

Munnings, Alfred James 1878–1959, *By the River: A Mare and a Foal*, bequeathed by Lord and Lady Fraser of Allander, 2003, © the artist's estate courtesy of Felix Rosenstiel's Widow & Son Ltd

Munro, Daniel active 1846–1873, *The Shaving Lesson*, bequeathed by William Euing, 1874

Munro, Hugh 1873–1939, *Roses and My Morning Walk*, purchased, 1919

Munro, Hugh 1873–1939, *The Stranger*, purchased, 1931

Murdoch, John S. *A Ruined Cloister*, temporary identification number allocated, 1981

Murillo, Bartolomé Esteban 1618–1682, *Madonna and Child with Infant Saint John, 'La serrana'*, Stirling Maxwell Collection, gift, 1967

Murillo, Bartolomé Esteban (after) 1618–1682, *The Rest on the Flight into Egypt*, Archibald McLellan Collection, purchased, 1856

Murillo, Bartolomé Esteban (after) 1618–1682, *Virgin and Child*, Archibald McLellan Collection, purchased, 1856

Murillo, Bartolomé Esteban (after) 1618–1682, *Girl Drinking with a Child on Her Arm*, Stirling Maxwell Collection, gift, 1967

Murillo, Bartolomé Esteban (after) 1618–1682, *Saint Joseph with the Infant Jesus*, Archibald McLellan Collection, purchased, 1856

Murillo, Bartolomé Esteban (after) 1618–1682, *Santa Justa and Santa Rufina*, Stirling Maxwell Collection, gift, 1967

Murillo, Bartolomé Esteban (attributed to) 1618–1682, *Head of the Madonna*, Stirling Maxwell Collection, gift, 1967

Murray, Charles 1894–1954, *Winter*, purchased, 1951

Murray, Charles 1894–1954, *The Spotted Jug*, purchased, 1964

Murray, Charles 1894–1954, *The Yellow Door*, purchased, 1964

Murray, David 1849–1933, *Landscape with a Figure and Sheep*, bequeathed by Adam Teacher, 1898

Murray, David 1849–1933, *The 'Old Anchor' Inn*, bequeathed by Adam Teacher, 1898

Murray, David 1849–1933, *The Orchard*, bequeathed by Adam Teacher, 1898

Murray, David 1849–1933, *Tarbert, Loch Fyne*, bequeathed by

Philipson, Robin 1916–1992, *Flight* (polyptych, panel 3 of 8), presented by the British Airports Authority, 1976; registered, 1986, © the artist's estate

Philipson, Robin 1916–1992, *Flight* (polyptych, panel 4 of 8), presented by the British Airports Authority, 1976; registered, 1986, © the artist's estate

Philipson, Robin 1916–1992, *Flight* (polyptych, panel 5 of 8), presented by the British Airports Authority, 1976; registered, 1986, © the artist's estate

Philipson, Robin 1916–1992, *Flight* (polyptych, panel 6 of 8), presented by the British Airports Authority, 1976; registered, 1986, © the artist's estate

Philipson, Robin 1916–1992, *Flight* (polyptych, panel 7 of 8), presented by the British Airports Authority, 1976; registered, 1986, © the artist's estate

Philipson, Robin 1916–1992, *Flight* (polyptych, panel 8 of 8), presented by the British Airports Authority, 1976; registered, 1986, © the artist's estate

Philipson, Robin 1916–1992, *Threnody*, bequeathed by Alan Forrest Stark through the Scottish Arts Council, 1984, © the artist's estate

Phillip, John 1817–1867, *Self Portrait When a Young Man*, gift from Mrs C. B. Phillip, 1932

Phillip, John 1817–1867, *The Evil Eye*, bequeathed by James Donald, 1905

Phillip, John 1817–1867, *The Assignation*, gift from Sir Charles Tennant, 1904

Phillip, John 1817–1867, *The Spinning Wheel*, bequeathed by John Fleming, 1923

Phillip, John 1817–1867, *A Gypsy Girl*, purchased, 1900

Phillip, John 1817–1867, *The Fortune Teller*, presented by the Trustees of the Hamilton Bequest, 1928

Phillip, John 1817–1867, *Mrs Alexander Collie*, gift from Mrs C. B. Phillip, 1932

Phillips, Henry Wyndham 1820–1868, *Colin Campbell (1792–1863), Lord Clyde*, gift from John Tennant, c.1870

Philpot, Glyn Warren 1884–1937, *Melampus and the Centaur*, purchased, 1923

Piazza, Alberto 1490–1528, *Virgin and Child with Two Musician Angels*, gift from Sir William and Lady Burrell to the City of Glasgow, 1944

Picasso, Pablo 1881–1973, *The Flower Seller*, bequeathed by William McInnes, 1944, © succession Picasso/DACS 2013

Pickenoy, Nicolaes Eliasz. (attributed to) c.1588–c.1655, *Portrait of a Young Woman*, bequeathed by Jane Graham-Gilbert, 1877

Pickenoy, Nicolaes Eliasz. (circle of) c.1588–c.1655, *Portrait of a Girl Aged 15*, bequeathed by Jane Graham-Gilbert, 1877

Pinder, Carl *Steam Traction Engine 'Waverley'*

Pinder, George William 1894–1984, *The Dance*, purchased, 1995

Pinogah (attributed to) *Ecuadorians Selling Fruit by the Road*, gift from Andrew B. Holmes, 1940

Piper, John 1903–1992, *Portland Bill*, gift from the Contemporary Art Society, 1952, © the artist's estate

Pirie, George 1863–1946, *Birds of a Feather*, purchased, 1911

Pirie, George 1863–1946, *Hill Ewes*, presented by the Trustees of the Hamilton Bequest, 1934

Pirie, George 1863–1946, *Black Setter*, gift from Colonel and Miss Spencer, 1940

Pissarro, Camille 1831–1903, *The Banks of the Marne*, presented by the Trustees of the Hamilton Bequest, 1951

Pissarro, Camille 1831–1903, *The Tuileries Gardens, Paris*, gift from Sir John Richmond, 1948

Plosky, Jonas b.1940, *My Mate's Car*, purchased, 1963, © the artist

Poel, Egbert Lievensz. van der 1621–1664, *A Fire at Night*, Archibald McLellan Collection, purchased, 1856

Poel, Egbert Lievensz. van der 1621–1664, *Beach Scene, Scheveningen, The Netherlands, with a Fish Auction*, Archibald McLellan Collection, purchased, 1856

Poel, Egbert Lievensz. van der 1621–1664, *Figures on a Frozen Canal*, Archibald McLellan Collection, purchased, 1856

Polidoro da Lanciano c.1515–1565, *The Mystic Marriage of Saint Catherine*, bequeathed by Jane Graham-Gilbert, 1877, photo credit: Glasgow Museums

Polish School *A Scottish and Two Polish Soldiers*, presented by the Polish 10th Cavalry Brigade, 1940

Pompe, Gerrit (attributed to) c.1640/1650–c.1695/1705, *Dutch Men-of-War Beating to Windward*, presented by the family of the late Mrs John Henderson of Westbank, 1895

Pontormo, Jacopo Carucci (after) 1494–1556, *Virgin and Child*, gift from Mrs J. G. Coats, 1948

Pot, Hendrik Gerritsz. (attributed to) c.1585–1657, *Portrait of a Man*, bequeathed by Allan McLean, 1928

Pothast, Bernard Jean Corneille 1882–1966, *Preparing for Dinner*, purchased, 1921

Pothast, Bernard Jean Corneille 1882–1966, *Interior with a Woman and Children*, bequeathed by David Perry, 1940

Pourbus, Frans the younger (after) 1569–1622, *Archduke Albert of Austria (1559–1621)*, Stirling Maxwell Collection, gift, 1967

Pourbus, Pieter the younger (circle of) 1524–1584, *Portrait of a Lady*, gift from Sir William and Lady Burrell to the City of Glasgow, 1944

Pratt, D. active 19th C, *Robert Burns (1759–1796)*, gift from Reverend William Blair, 1924

Pratt, William M. 1855–1936, *The Close of Day*, purchased, 1915

Prentice, J. A. active 19th C, *Govan Church, Looking up the Clyde*, gift, 1947

Prentis, Edward 1797–1854, *The Sick Bed*, bequeathed by William Euing, 1874

Pringle, John Quinton 1864–1925, *Girl at a Well*, gift from John W. Pringle, 1947

Pringle, John Quinton 1864–1925, *Sunset and Approaching Storm*, gift from John W. Pringle, 1947

Pringle, John Quinton 1864–1925, *Head of a Girl*, gift from John W. Pringle, 1947

Pringle, John Quinton 1864–1925, *Artist at an Easel*, gift from John W. Pringle, 1947

Pringle, John Quinton 1864–1925, *Full-Length Figure of the Artist with an Easel*, gift from John W. Pringle, 1947

Pringle, John Quinton 1864–1925, *Half-Length Figure, a Boy with a White Collar*, gift from John W. Pringle, 1947

Pringle, John Quinton 1864–1925, *Head and Shoulders of the Artist with a Palette*, gift from John W. Pringle, 1947

Pringle, John Quinton 1864–1925, *Still Life with the Head of Dante*, gift from John W. Pringle, 1947

Pringle, John Quinton 1864–1925, *Half-Length Figure of a Seated Girl with Flowers*, gift from John W. Pringle, 1947

Pringle, John Quinton 1864–1925, *Christopher N. Pringle (or James Pringle)*, presented by Mrs Mary Richmond Blackwood and Miss Jeanie Nisbet Pringle, 1980

Pringle, John Quinton 1864–1925, *Chinese Lanterns*, gift from John W. Pringle, 1947

Pringle, John Quinton 1864–1925, *Repairing the Bicycle*, gift, 1964

Pringle, John Quinton 1864–1925, *Girl's Head*, gift from John W. Pringle, 1947

Pringle, John Quinton 1864–1925, *The Grandfather Clock*, gift from John W. Pringle, 1947

Pringle, John Quinton 1864–1925, *William Meldrum (1865–1942)*, gift, 1966

Pringle, John Quinton 1864–1925, *Head and Shoulders of an Artisan*, gift from John W. Pringle, 1947

Pringle, John Quinton 1864–1925, *Man's Head with a Tartan Scarf*, gift from John W. Pringle, 1947

Pringle, John Quinton 1864–1925, *The Organ Question*, gift from James Meldrum, 1980, photo credit: Glasgow Museums

Pringle, John Quinton 1864–1925,

Pringle, John Quinton 1864–1925, *Barclay W. Pringle*, gift from John W. Pringle, 1947

Pringle, John Quinton 1864–1925, *A Boy, Green Hat and Jacket, White Collar*, gift from John W. Pringle, 1947

Pringle, John Quinton 1864–1925, *Landscape with Two Girls in Blue*, gift from John W. Pringle, 1947

Pringle, John Quinton 1864–1925, *Seascape with Two Figures on a Beach and Two Boats in a Bay*, gift from John W. Pringle, 1947

Pringle, John Quinton 1864–1925, *Two Figures at a Fence*, gift from John W. Pringle, 1947

Pringle, John Quinton 1864–1925, *Landscape with Trees and a Girl in White*, gift from John W. Pringle, 1947

Pringle, John Quinton 1864–1925, *Caudebec, Normandy*, gift from W. Somerville Shanks, 1924

Pringle, John Quinton 1864–1925, *Garden and Bridge, Caudebec*, gift from Mrs Eva Meldrum, in accordance with the wishes of James Meldrum, 1983

Pringle, John Quinton 1864–1925, *On the River Sainte-Gertrude, Caudebec, Normandy*, gift, 1973

Pringle, John Quinton 1864–1925, *Study of a Boy, Caudebec, Normandy*, gift from Mrs Eva Meldrum, in accordance with the wishes of James Meldrum, 1983

Pringle, John Quinton 1864–1925, *Still Life, a Candlestick and a Salver*, gift from John W. Pringle, 1947

Pringle, John Quinton 1864–1925, *Still Life, a Jug, a Japanese Print and a Blue Drape*, gift from John W. Pringle, 1947

Pringle, John Quinton 1864–1925, *Still Life, a Vase, a Bottle and a Jug with Flowers*, gift from John W. Pringle, 1947

Pringle, John Quinton 1864–1925, *Still Life on a Table*, bequeathed by Mrs Eva Meldrum, 1984

Pringle, John Quinton 1864–1925, *Whalsay Bay, with a Girl in White*, gift from John W. Pringle, 1947

Pringle, John Quinton 1864–1925, *Arthur Campbell*, bequeathed by Hector B. Campbell, 1983

Pringle, John Quinton 1864–1925, *Boats at a Small Harbour*, gift from John W. Pringle, 1947

Prinsep, Valentine Cameron 1838–1904, *Lady Simpson*, gift from Lady Florence Willert, 1953

Prinsep, Valentine Cameron 1838–1904, *In a Street in Venice*, gift from F. T. L. Prinsep, 1923

Prior, Olive *Boat at Sea*

Pritchett, Robert Taylor 1828–1907, *The Student*, bequeathed by William Euing, 1874

Purves, Ian Hamilton 1938–1975, *Count Down Orgaz*, purchased, 1973

Purvis, Tom 1888–1959, *A Factory Interior*

Purvis, Tom 1888–1959, *Women Munitions Workers at Weir's Factory*, gift from the Weir Group PLC, 2008

Qaana *Airplane Crash over Lake Tana, Ethiopia, at Night*, purchased, 1994

Quillard, Pierre Antoine (follower of) 1701–1733, *The Arrival at the Island of Cythera*, Archibald McLellan Collection, purchased, 1856

Rae, Henrietta 1859–1928, *Spring's Awakening (The Snow Maidens)*, presented by the family of Ernest Normand, 1931

Raeburn, Henry 1756–1823, *Colin Campbell of Park (1728–1793)*, bequeathed by Isabella A. H. J. Campbell, 1917

Raeburn, Henry 1756–1823, *Portrait of a Captain, RN*, purchased, 1964

Raeburn, Henry 1756–1823, *Miss Macartney*, gift from Sir William and Lady Burrell to the City of Glasgow, 1952

Raeburn, Henry 1756–1823, *Mr and Mrs Robert N. Campbell of Kailzie*, bequeathed by Isabella A. H. J. Campbell, 1917

Raeburn, Henry 1756–1823, *The MacNab*, on loan from Diageo Plc

Raeburn, Henry 1756–1823, *Mrs William Urquhart (c.1796–1864)*, gift from Mrs Caroline Urquhart, 1900

Raeburn, Henry 1756–1823, *William Urquhart (c.1794–1840)*, gift from Mrs Caroline Urquhart, 1900

Raeburn, Henry 1756–1823, *Alexander Campbell of Hallyards (1768–1817)*, presented by the Glasgow Highland Society, 1903

Raeburn, Henry 1756–1823, *Colonel Bowes*, gift from Sir William and Lady Burrell to the City of Glasgow, 1944

Raeburn, Henry 1756–1823, *Henry MacKenzie (1745–1831)*, gift from Sir William and Lady Burrell to the City of Glasgow, 1944

Raeburn, Henry 1756–1823, *John Campbell Senior of Morriston (c.1734–1808)*, bequeathed by Isabella A. H. J. Campbell, 1917

Raeburn, Henry 1756–1823, *John Dunlop (1774–1820), Provost of Glasgow (1794–1795)*, gift, 1971

Raeburn, Henry 1756–1823, *Mrs Anne Campbell*, bequeathed by Isabella A. H. J. Campbell, 1917

Raeburn, Henry 1756–1823, *Robert N. Campbell of Kailzie (c.1761–1845)*, bequeathed by Isabella A. H. J. Campbell, 1917

Raeburn, Henry 1756–1823, *William Forbes of Pitsligo (1739–1806)*, gift from Sir William and Lady Burrell to the City of Glasgow, 1944

Raeburn, Henry (after) 1756–1823, *Sir Walter Scott (1771–1832)*, Archibald McLellan Collection, purchased, 1856

Raeburn, Henry (after) 1756–1823, *Lord Moncrieff*

(1776–1851), gift from Godfrey H. Pattison, 1945

Raeburn, Henry (studio of) 1756–1823, *Portrait of a Man with a Clerical Collar*

Raeburn, Henry (style of) 1756–1823, *William Jamieson, Junior*, purchased, 1897

Raeburn, Henry (style of) 1756–1823, *Mr Campbell*, bequeathed by Isabella A. H. J. Campbell, 1917

Raeburn, Henry (style of) 1756–1823, *William Dixon of Govanhill (1753–1822)*, temporary identification number allocated, 1977

Raeburn, Henry (style of) 1756–1823, *William Mills (1776–1857), Lord Provost of Glasgow (1834–1837)*, presented by the Trustees of George Mills, 1892

Raffaellino del Garbo c.1470–1527/1528, *Virgin and Child with the Child Baptist and Two Angels*, presented by Mrs Mary Ann Walker in memory of her father, James Young, 1902

Ramsay, Allan 1713–1784, *Colonel John Stewart of Stewartfield (d.1750)*, purchased, 1964

Ramsay, Allan 1713–1784, *Portrait of a Lady*, presented by the Trustees of the Hamilton Bequest, 1971

Ramsay, Allan 1713–1784, *Archibald Campbell (1682–1761), 3rd Duke of Argyll*, commissioned by Glasgow Town Council

Ramsay, Allan 1713–1784, *Henrietta Diana (1728–1761), Dowager Countess of Stafford*, presented by the Trustees of the Hamilton Bequest, 1955

Ramsay, Allan 1713–1784, *Captain Sir John Lindsay (1737–1788)*, presented by the Trustees of the Hamilton Bequest, 1950

Ramsay, Allan (studio of) 1713–1784, *George III (1738–1820)*, commissioned by Glasgow Town Council, 1764

Ranken, William Bruce Ellis 1881–1941, *Sir John Stirling Maxwell (1866–1956), 10th Bt*, on loan from a private collection

Ranken, William Bruce Ellis 1881–1941, *The Garden Door*, gift from Mrs Ernest Thesiger, 1946

Ranken, William Bruce Ellis 1881–1941, *The Throne Room, Madrid*, gift from Major T. Ranken, 1949

Ranken, William Bruce Ellis 1881–1941, *Flower Piece*, Stirling Maxwell Collection, gift, 1967

Raphael (after) 1483–1520, *Portrait of a Man*, on loan from a private collection

Raphael (after) 1483–1520, *The Transfiguration*, bequeathed by Mrs Cecilia Douglas, 1862

Raphael (after) 1483–1520, *Madonna della sedia*, gift from Mrs J. G. Coats, 1948

Raphael (after) 1483–1520, *Madonna della sedia*, temporary identification number allocated, 1979

Rathbone, John c.1750–1807, *A Mountain Stream with a Peasant Driving Cattle over a Rustic Bridge*, bequeathed by Francis J. Eck, 1915

Rathbone, John c.1750–1807, *Old Mill and a Farm Cart*, bequeathed by Francis J. Eck, 1915

Rattray, Alexander William Wellwood 1849–1902, *Seascape, Kintyre*, presented by the Royal Army Service Corps and Garrison Officers' Mess, Maryhill Barracks, Glasgow, 1959

Ravesteyn, Jan Anthonisz. van (style of) c.1570–1657, *Portrait of a Lady*, gift from William Burrell, 1925

Rea, Cecil William 1860–1935, *In Arcady*, gift from Miss Russell, 1927

Recupero, Giovanni *Anthea* (after Parmigianino), bequeathed by Mrs Cecilia Douglas, 1862

Recupero, Giovanni *Galeazzo Sanvitale (1566–1622)* (after Parmigianino), bequeathed by Mrs Cecilia Douglas, 1862

Reddock, A. (attributed to) d.1842, *Lady Hannah Anne Gardiner Maxwell (1764–1841)*, on loan from a private collection

Redfern, June b.1951, *The Devil at Llandaff* (diptych, left panel), purchased, 1994, © June Redfern. All rights reserved, DACS 2013

Redfern, June b.1951, *The Devil at Llandaff* (diptych, right panel), purchased, 1994, © June Redfern. All rights reserved, DACS 2013

Redfern, June b.1951, *From Two Paths*, purchased from the artist, 1994, © June Redfern. All rights reserved, DACS 2013

Redpath, Anne 1895–1965, *Pinks*, purchased, 1948, © the artist's estate/Bridgeman Art Library

Redpath, Anne 1895–1965, *Place de l'Institut, Paris* (recto), purchased, 1951, © Culture and Sport Glasgow (Glasgow Museums)

Redpath, Anne 1895–1965, *Nicolson Square, Edinburgh* (verso), purchased, 1951, © Culture and Sport Glasgow (Glasgow Museums)

Redpath, Anne 1895–1965, *Corsican Village*, Scottish Arts Council Bequest, 1997; received, 2006, © the artist's estate/ Bridgeman Art Library

Reesbroeck, Jacob van (attributed to) 1620–1704, *Portrait of a Man with a Lute*, bequeathed by William Euing, 1874

Reid, George 1841–1913, *Milking Time*, gift from Thomas S. Campbell, 1936

Reid, George 1841–1913, *John Ure (1824–1901), Lord Provost of Glasgow (1880–1883)*, purchased, 1885

Reid, George 1841–1913, *Sir William McOnie (d.1894), Lord Provost of Glasgow (1883–1886)*, purchased, 1887

Reid, George 1841–1913, *James Reid (1823–1894), of Auchterarder and Hydepark Locomotive Works*, presented by the sons of the sitter, 1897

Reid, George 1841–1913, *John Duncan (d.1903), General Manager of the Glasgow Tramway and Omnibus Company*, gift from Mrs Jean Fairman, 1939

Reid, George 1841–1913, *James Hozier (1851–1929), 2nd Lord Newlands*, bequeathed by Lady Newlands, 1933

Reid, George 1841–1913, *Sir William Bilsland (b.1847), Lord Provost of Glasgow (1905–1908)*, purchased, 1909

Reid, George Ogilvy 1851–1928, *1914: The Belgians on the March*, gift from Amelia D. Reid, 1937

Reid, John Robertson 1852–1926, *Sons of the Sea*, purchased, 1912

Reid, Marell active 20th C, *Flower Piece, Blue Vase*, temporary identification number allocated, 1982

Reid, Stuart 1883–1971, *'Baron of Buchlyvie' Horse Portrait*, gift from J. Pasquoll, 1927

Rembrandt van Rijn 1606–1669, *Self Portrait*, gift from Sir William and Lady Burrell to the City of Glasgow, 1946

Rembrandt van Rijn 1606–1669, *A Man in Armour*, bequeathed by Jane Graham-Gilbert, 1877

Rembrandt van Rijn (after) 1606–1669, *Jeremiah Mourning the Destruction of Jerusalem*, bequeathed by William Willis, 1858

Rembrandt van Rijn (after) 1606–1669, *The Holy Family in the Evening*, Archibald McLellan Collection, purchased, 1856

Rembrandt van Rijn (after) 1606–1669, *Self Portrait*, gift from Michael Honeyman, 1897

Rembrandt van Rijn (attributed to) 1606–1669, *The Carcase of an Ox*, bequeathed by Jane Graham-Gilbert, 1877

Rembrandt van Rijn (follower of) 1606–1669, *Head of a Bearded Man*, bequeathed by Jane Graham-Gilbert, 1877

Rembrandt van Rijn (imitator of) 1606–1669, *A Painter and His Model*, Archibald McLellan Collection, purchased, 1856

Rembrandt van Rijn (school of) 1606–1669, *Landscape with Tobias and the Angel*, bequeathed by Jane Graham-Gilbert, 1877

Reni, Guido (after) 1575–1642, *Saint Mary Magdalen*, Archibald McLellan Collection, purchased, 1856

Reni, Guido (after) 1575–1642, *The Baptism of Christ*, Archibald McLellan Collection, purchased, 1856, photo credit: Glasgow Museums

Reni, Guido (after) 1575–1642, *Christ Crowned with Thorns*, Archibald McLellan Collection, purchased, 1856

Reni, Guido (after) 1575–1642, *Madonna in Grief*, Archibald McLellan Collection, purchased, 1856

Reni, Guido (follower of) 1575–1642, *Cupid with an Hour-Glass*, Archibald McLellan Collection, purchased, 1856

Reni-Mel, Léon 1893–c.1960, *Old Vannes*, purchased, 1938

Renoir, Pierre-Auguste 1841–1919, *Madame Valentine Fray (1870–1943)*, bequeathed by William McInnes, 1944

Renoir, Pierre-Auguste 1841–1919, *The Painter's Garden*, bequeathed by William McInnes, 1944

Renoir, Pierre-Auguste 1841–1919, *Coco*, bequeathed by Lord and Lady Fraser of Allander, 2003

Renoir, Pierre-Auguste 1841–1919, *Still Life*, bequeathed by William McInnes, 1944

Revel, John Daniel 1884–1967, *Happy Days*, gift from the artist, 1963

Revel, Lucy Elizabeth Babington 1887–1961, *Molly*, gift, 1963

Reynolds, Joshua 1723–1792, *A Boy in Van Dyck Dress*, Archibald McLellan Collection, purchased, 1856

Reynolds, Joshua 1723–1792, *Isabella Hay (1742–1808), Countess of Erroll*, gift from Lord Rothermere, 1925

Reynolds, Joshua 1723–1792, *Andrew Stuart of Torrance (1725–1801)*, on loan from James Everett McDonald Stuart-Stevenson

Reynolds, Joshua (after) 1723–1792, *A Girl Leaning on a Pedestal (The Laughing Girl)*, gift from Mrs Miller-Stirling, 1948

Reynolds, Joshua (attributed to) 1723–1792, *Lady Mary Carew (c.1710/1720–before 1762)*, gift from Sir William and Lady Burrell to the City of Glasgow, 1944

Reynolds, Joshua (attributed to) 1723–1792, *Portrait of a Young Man*, gift from Sir William and Lady Burrell to the City of Glasgow, 1944

Reynolds, Joshua (style of) 1723–1792, *Portrait of a Lady*, bequeathed by Jane Graham-Gilbert, 1877

Reynolds, Joshua (style of) 1723–1792, *Portrait of a Lady*, bequeathed by Jane Graham-Gilbert, 1877

Reynolds, Warwick 1880–1926, *Colonel John Macfarlane (1846–1910)*, gift from Miss G. E. Macfarlane, 1933

Rhys-James, Shani b.1953, *Blue Top*, purchased, 1998, © the artist

Rhys-James, Shani b.1953, *The Boards*, purchased, 1998, © the artist

Ribera, Jusepe de (studio of) 1591–1652, *Saint Peter Repentant*, purchased, 1903

Ribera, Jusepe de (studio of) 1591–1652, *Christ Disputing with the Doctors*, gift from Sir William

and Lady Burrell to the City of Glasgow, 1948

Ribot, Augustin Théodule 1823–1891, *The Cooks*, gift from Sir William and Lady Burrell to the City of Glasgow, 1944

Ribot, Augustin Théodule 1823–1891, *The Musician*, gift from William Burrell, 1925

Ribot, Augustin Théodule 1823–1891, *The Studious Servant*, gift from Sir William and Lady Burrell to the City of Glasgow, 1956

Ribot, Augustin Théodule 1823–1891, *The Accountant*, gift from Sir William and Lady Burrell to the City of Glasgow, 1944

Ribot, Augustin Théodule 1823–1891, *Mother and Daughter*, gift from Sir William and Lady Burrell to the City of Glasgow, 1944

Ribot, Augustin Théodule 1823–1891, *Still Life with Fruit, Figs and Apricots*, gift from Sir William and Lady Burrell to the City of Glasgow, 1944

Ribot, Augustin Théodule 1823–1891, *The Flower Girl*, gift from Sir William and Lady Burrell to the City of Glasgow, 1944

Ribot, Augustin Théodule 1823–1891, *The Old Fisherman*, gift from William Burrell, 1925

Ribot, Augustin Théodule 1823–1891, *The Rosary*, gift from Sir William and Lady Burrell to the City of Glasgow, 1944

Ricard, Gustave 1823–1873, *Still Life, Pear and Plate*, gift from Sir William and Lady Burrell to the City of Glasgow, 1944

Ricard, Gustave 1823–1873, *The Pitcher*, gift from Sir William and Lady Burrell to the City of Glasgow, 1944

Richter, Herbert Davis 1874–1955, *A Festal Day*, purchased, 1936

Riddel, James 1857–1928, *Man Driving a Cart*

Riley, Bridget b.1931, *Arrest III*, purchased, 1992, © the artist

Riley, Bridget b.1931, *Punjab*, purchased with the assistance of the National Art Collections Fund and the National Fund for Acquisitions, 1991, © the artist

Riley, Bridget b.1931, *Luxor*, purchased from the artist, 1991, © the artist

Rios, Luigi da 1844–1892, *Overlooking a Canal, Venice*, bequeathed by Adam Teacher, 1898

Rippingille, Edward Villiers 1798–1859, *Roman Mother and Child*, bequeathed by William Euing, 1874

Riviere, Briton 1840–1920, *The Last of the Crew*, gift from R. D. Macgregor, 1927

Riviere, Hugh Goldwin 1869–1956, *Lady Newlands (d.1930)*, bequeathed by the sitter, 1933, © the artist's estate

Roberts, David 1796–1864, *A Street in Abbeville*, bequeathed by

Francis J. Eck, 1915

Roberts, David (attributed to) 1796–1864, *Church of Notre-Dame, Dijon*, purchased, 1959

Roberts, David (attributed to) 1796–1864, *Interior of a Church*, purchased, 1960

Roberts, David (attributed to) 1796–1864, *Study of a Monk*, gift from Mrs Hyde

Roberts, William Patrick 1895–1980, *The Dancers*, purchased with the assistance of the Monument Fund and the National Art Collections Fund, 1978, © William Roberts Society

Robertson, Alexander Duff 1807–1886, *Woodside House on the Kelvin*, bequeathed by William Euing, 1874

Robertson, Eric Harald Macbeth 1887–1941, *Despair*, purchased, 1980, © the artist's estate/ Bridgeman Art Library

Robertson, Eric Harald Macbeth 1887–1941, *Buachaille Etive Mhòr*, gift from Miss J. M. Robertson, 1944, © the artist's estate/ Bridgeman Art Library

Robertson, Eric Harald Macbeth 1887–1941, *Near Wenhaston, Suffolk*, gift from Miss J. M. Robertson, 1944, © the artist's estate/Bridgeman Art Library

Robertson, Fiona *Hear No Evil*, gift from the BBC Collection, 2008

Robertson, Fiona *Madonna*, gift from the BBC Collection, 2008

Robertson, James Downie 1931–2010, *Landscape*, purchased, 1979, © the artist's estate

Robertson, James Downie 1931–2010, *Sunset*, purchased from the artist, 1990, © the artist's estate

Robertson, Saul b.1978, *Surfacing*, purchased, 2005, © the artist

Robertson, Thomas 1822–1866, *The Glasgow Volunteers*, purchased, 1933

Robertson, William active 1740–1757, *Flora Macdonald (1722–1790)*, gift from Mrs Flora Wylde, 1883

Robinson, Joan active 1943–1966, *Flowers*, purchased, 1948

Robinson's of Bristol *Jean MacGregor (1916–1968)*, gift, 1982

Robson, Adam 1928–2007, *Harbour Guides at Crail*, purchased, 1962, © the artist's estate

Roche, Alexander Ignatius 1861–1921, *Mrs Roberts*, gift from John Roberts, 1952

Roche, Alexander Ignatius 1861–1921, *Legendary Glasgow: The Finding of Queen Languoreth's Ring* (study), found in store, registered, 1971

Roche, Alexander Ignatius 1861–1921, *Original Study for Glasgow Town Hall Mural*, temporary identification number allocated, 1982

Roche, Alexander Ignatius 1861–1921, *River Ouse*, purchased, 1918

Roche, Alexander Ignatius 1861–1921, *Evening*, purchased, 1944

Roche, Alexander Ignatius 1861–1921, *Girl in Red Hat*, gift from Matthew Dickie, 1942

Roche, Alexander Ignatius 1861–1921, *Study of Two Female Heads*, purchased, 1950

Roche, Alexander Ignatius 1861–1921, *Woodland and River*, gift from Sir John and Lady Anderson, 1940

Rodeck, Karl 1841–1909, *An Angler by a Woodland Pond*, bequeathed by Adam Teacher, 1898

Rodmell, Harry Hudson 1896–1984, *'Royal Scotsman'*, gift from Burns and Laird Limited, 1971, © the artist's estate

Romeyn, Willem (style of) c.1624–1694, *Landscape with Cattle and a Cowherd*, bequeathed by William Euing, 1874

Romeyn, Willem (style of) c.1624–1694, *Landscape with Cattle and a Peasant Woman*, bequeathed by William Euing, 1874

Romney, George 1734–1802, *Lieutenant Colonel Sir Charles Stuart (1753–1801)*, presented by the Trustees of the Hamilton Bequest, 1941

Romney, George 1734–1802, *Portrait of a Man*, gift from Sir William and Lady Burrell to the City of Glasgow, 1944

Romney, George 1734–1802, *Richard Cumberland (1732–1811)*, Stirling Maxwell Collection, gift, 1967

Rosa, Salvator 1615–1673, *Saint John the Baptist Baptising Christ in the Jordan*, gift from Alice M. Thom, 1953

Rosa, Salvator 1615–1673, *Saint John the Baptist Revealing Christ to the Disciples*, presented in memory of John Young by his family, 1952

Rosa, Salvator (follower of) 1615–1673, *A Mountainous Landscape with a Waterfall*, Archibald McLellan Collection, purchased, 1856

Rosen, Frank b.1918, *The Knight and the Squire*, bequeathed by Lady Catherine E. M. Archibald, 1992

Rosenvinge, Odin 1880–1957, *'Tuscania'*, on loan from a private collection, © the artist's estate

Ross, E. M. *W. A. Jardine, Engineer, NBR*, gift from British Rail, London, 1967

Ross, Lucy b.1961, *Isolated Head*, gift from the BBC Collection, 2008

Ross, Malcolm active 19th C, *Landscape with Trees and Cattle*, bequeathed by Adam Teacher, 1898

Ross, R. *Nightshift in the Finishing Shop*

Rossetti, Dante Gabriel 1828–1882, *Regina cordium*, presented by the Trustees of the Hamilton Bequest, 1940

Rouault, Georges 1871–1958, *Circus Girl*, presented by the Trustees and residuary beneficiaries of the late Mrs Elizabeth Maud Macdonald, 1959, © ADAGP, Paris and DACS, London 2013

Rousseau, Théodore 1812–1867, *The Forest of Clairbois*, bequeathed by James Donald, 1905

Rousseau, Théodore 1812–1867, *Les gorges d'Apremont*, purchased with the assistance of the Lady Moore Bequest Fund, 1957

Rousseau, Théodore 1812–1867, *The Heath*, bequeathed by James Donald, 1905

Royle, Stanley 1888–1961, *Winter, Corfe Castle Village*, purchased, 1940, © the artist's estate/ Bridgeman Art Library

Rubens, Peter Paul 1577–1640 & **Brueghel, Jan the elder** 1568–1625 *Nature and Her Followers*, bequeathed by Jane Graham-Gilbert, 1877

Rubens, Peter Paul (after) 1577–1640, *A Man and a Girl*, found in store, registered, 1988

Rubens, Peter Paul (after) 1577–1640, *Madonna and Child with Saints Elizabeth and John*, Archibald McLellan Collection, purchased, 1856

Rubens, Peter Paul (after) 1577–1640, *The Infant Christ and Saint John with a Lamb*, Archibald McLellan Collection, purchased, 1856

Rubens, Peter Paul (after) 1577–1640, *The Assumption of the Virgin*, bequeathed by William Euing, 1874

Rubens, Peter Paul (after) 1577–1640, *Infanta Isabella Clara Eugenia (1566–1633)*, Stirling Maxwell Collection, gift, 1967

Rubens, Peter Paul (after) 1577–1640, *Philip IV of Spain (1605–1665)*, Stirling Maxwell Collection, gift, 1967

Rubens, Peter Paul (attributed to) 1577–1640, *Portrait of a Young Man*, bequeathed by Jane Graham-Gilbert, 1877

Rubens, Peter Paul (studio of) 1577–1640, *Landscape with a Boar Hunt*, purchased, 1894

Rubens, Peter Paul (style of) 1577–1640, *Portrait of a Young Woman*, bequeathed by Jane Graham-Gilbert, 1877

Ruisdael, Jacob van 1628/1629–1682, *Landscape with a Ruined Tower*, bequeathed by Jane Graham-Gilbert, 1877

Ruisdael, Jacob van 1628/1629–1682, *A View of Egmond aan Zee*, Archibald McLellan Collection, purchased, 1856

Ruisdael, Jacob van 1628/1629–1682, *Landscape with a Cottage, Bridge and Sheep*, bequeathed by Jane Graham-Gilbert, 1877

Ruisdael, Jacob van (attributed to) 1628/1629–1682, *Landscape with Figures*, bequeathed by Jane Graham-Gilbert, 1877

Ruisdael, Jacob van (attributed to) 1628/1629–1682, *Wooded Landscape with Fishermen by a Pond*, Archibald McLellan Collection, purchased, 1856

Ruisdael, Jacob van (imitator of) 1628/1629–1682, *Wooded Landscape with Shepherds by a Stream*, transferred from the Old Town Hall, 1891

Runciman, Alexander (attributed to) 1736–1785, *A Sacrificial Scene Attended by Demonic Figures*, purchased, 1967

Russell, Peter J. active 1972–c.1980, *What Happened to the Cavalier Spirit*, temporary identification number allocated, 1978

Russell, Walter Westley 1867–1949, *Amelia*, purchased, 1937

Russell, Walter Westley 1867–1949, *The Flower Girl*, presented by the Trustees of the Hamilton Bequest, 1938

Russell, Walter Westley 1867–1949, *Dover*, gift from Francis Howard, 1942

Russian School (attributed to) 16th C–17th C, *The Baptism of Christ*, found in store, registered, 1988

Ruta, M. *Zebra and Birds*, purchased, 1989

Ruysch, Rachel 1664–1750, *An Arrangement of Flowers by a Tree Trunk*, Archibald McLellan Collection, purchased, 1856

Ruysch, Rachel 1664–1750, *Flowers in a Terracotta Vase*, Archibald McLellan Collection, purchased, 1856

Ruysch, Rachel (attributed to) 1664–1750, *Still Life, Flowers and Insects*, Archibald McLellan Collection, purchased, 1856

S. S. *Saltmarket and Tron Steeple, Glasgow*, found in store, registered, 1951

Saenredam, Pieter Jansz. 1597–1665, *Interior of St Bavo's, Haarlem, with a Catholic Baptism*, bequeathed by William Euing, 1874

Saidi *Maternity Clinic*, purchased, 1989

Salisbury, Frank O. 1874–1962, *Andrew Weir (1865–1955), Lord Inverforth of Southgate*, gift from the sitter, 1943, © estate of Frank O. Salisbury. All rights reserved, DACS 2013

Salmon, Helen Russell 1855–1891, *Patchwork*, gift from Thomas Hunt, 1913

Salmon, Robert W. 1775–1851, *Launch of the 'Christian'*, gift, 1957

Salmon, Robert W. 1775–1851, *A Snow off Greenock*

Sammacchini, Orazio 1532–1577, *Saint James Major and Saint Catherine of Alexandria*, Archibald McLellan Collection, purchased, 1856

Sampson, J. *HMS 'Hood'*, purchased with the assistance of the National Fund for Acquisitions, 1973

Landscape with Fishermen by a Pond, Archibald McLellan Collection, purchased, 1856

Sánchez Coello, Alonso c.1531–1588, *Philip II of Spain (1527–1598)*, Stirling Maxwell Collection, gift, 1967

Sánchez Coello, Alonso c.1531–1588, *Anne of Austria (1546–1580), Fourth Wife of Philip II*, Stirling Maxwell Collection, gift, 1967

Sánchez Coello, Alonso (after) c.1531–1588, *Don John of Austria (1547–1578)*, Stirling Maxwell Collection, gift, 1967

Sandby, Paul 1731–1809, *Scene from Allan Ramsay's 'Gentle Shepherd'*, bequeathed by W. A. Sandby, 1905

Sandeman, Margot 1922–2009, *No More Sheep I*, purchased with the assistance of the National Fund for Acquisitions and the Friends of Glasgow Museums, 2004

Sandeman, Margot 1922–2009, *No More Sheep III*, purchased with the assistance of the National Fund for Acquisitions and the Friends of Glasgow Museums, 2004

Sandeman, Margot 1922–2009, *No More Sheep IV*, purchased with the assistance of the National Fund for Acquisitions and the Friends of Glasgow Museums, 2004

Sandeman, Margot 1922–2009, *Sheep Grazing on a Hillside*, purchased with the assistance of the National Fund for Acquisitions and the Friends of Glasgow Museums, 2004

Sanderson, Robert 1848–1908, *The Motherless Bairn*, bequeathed by Adam Teacher, 1898

Sant, James 1820–1916, *Major Dennistoun as a Boy*, found in store, registered, 1988

Sant, James 1820–1916, *St Helena, the Last Phase*, gift from the Earl of Rosebery, 1907

Sant, James 1820–1916, *A Lady*, gift from Captain M. L. Sant, 1916

Sant, James 1820–1916, *The Gipsy Girl*, gift from Archibald G. Macdonald, 1896

Saraceni, Carlo (studio of) 1579–1620, *Young Warrior Asleep in a Wooded Landscape*, Archibald McLellan Collection, purchased, 1856

Sargent, John Singer 1856–1925, *Mrs George Batten Singing*, presented by the Trustees of the Hamilton Bequest, 1929

Sargent, John Singer 1856–1925, *Sir David Richmond (1843–1908), Lord Provost of Glasgow (1896–1899)*, purchased, 1899

Sargent, John Singer 1856–1925, *Sir David Richmond (1843–1908), Lord Provost of Glasgow (1896–1899)*, bequeathed by Mrs A. J. Fairley, 1946

Sassoferrato 1609–1685, *Virgin and Child with Saint Elisabeth and Child Baptist* (after Annibale Carracci), bequeathed by Jane Graham-Gilbert, 1877

Sauzay, Adrien Jacques 1841–1928, *The Pond at Vaugoing*,

Sologne, bequeathed by Adam Teacher, 1898

Saville, Paul b.1941, *Kelvinbridge*, purchased from the artist, 1966

Schellinks, Willem 1627–1678, *A Hawking Party by a Ruined Bridge*, bequeathed by Jane Graham-Gilbert, 1877

Schellinks, Willem 1627–1678, *A Winter Landscape with the Pont du Rhone, Lyons*, Archibald McLellan Collection, purchased, 1856

Schenström, Christian Wilhelm 1828–1876, *Bertel Thorvaldsen (1770–1844), Sculptor* (after Horace Vernet), bequeathed by William Euing, 1874

Schoevaerdts, Mathys (attributed to) c.1665–1723, *A Village Festival*, gift from G. B. Sawers, 1919

Schooten, Floris Gerritsz. van c.1585–after 1655, *Still Life, a Breakfast Piece*, gift from A. B. Clements, 1945

Schouman, Martinus 1770–1848, *A Frigate and Other Vessels Becalmed Inshore*, Archibald McLellan Collection, purchased, 1856

Schueler, Jon 1916–1992, *The Search: Black Shadow Blues, IV, 1981, 152.4cm x 132.1cm (o/c 1155)*, purchased with the assistance of the National Fund for Acquisitions, 1981, © Jon Schueler Estate

Schwarz, Hans 1922–2003, *Sir Eric Ashby (1904–1992), Master of Clare College, Cambridge*, purchased, 1963, © Culture and Sport Glasgow (Glasgow Museums)

Scorel, Jan van (circle of) 1495–1562, *The Holy Family and Saint John the Baptist under an Oak Tree* (after Raphael), Archibald McLellan Collection, purchased, 1856

Scott, David 1806–1849, *Nimrod*, purchased with the assistance of the National Fund for Acquisitions, 1981

Scott, David 1806–1849, *Sappho and Anacreon*, presented by the executors of the estate of the Misses Carfrae, 1956

Scott, David 1806–1849, *Mary, Queen of Scots, Receiving the Warrant for Her Execution*, gift from Rachel McGibbon, 1927

Scott, Frieda Ewart active 1970–2006, *Blue Abstract*, purchased, 1970

Scott, Lewis *Untitled*

Scott, William Bell 1811–1890, *Fair Rosamond Alone in Her Bower*, purchased with the assistance of the Trustees of the Hamilton Bequest and the National Fund for Acquisitions, 1983

Scougal, John c.1645–1730, *Mary II (1662–1694)*, commissioned by Glasgow Town Council, 1707–1708

Scougal, John c.1645–1730, *William III (1650–1702)*, commissioned by Glasgow Town Council, 1707–1708

Scougal, John c.1645–1730, *Queen Anne (1665–1714)*, commissioned by Glasgow Town Council, 1712

Sebastiano del Piombo (after) c.1485–1547, *Pope Clement VII (1478–1534)*, Stirling Maxwell Collection, gift, 1967

Selous, Henry Courtney 1803–1890, *The Pass of the Simeron, Switzerland*, bequeathed by William Euing, 1874

Serra, Enrique 1859–1918, *The Chess Players*, bequeathed by Mrs Isabella Elder, 1906

Seurat, Georges 1859–1891, *Boy Sitting in a Meadow*, presented by the Trustees of D. W. T. Cargill, 1950

Seurat, Georges 1859–1891, *The Riverbanks*, bequeathed by William McInnes, 1944

Seurat, Georges 1859–1891, *House among Trees*, bequeathed by William McInnes, 1944

Shanks, Duncan b.1937, *Night Wood with Birds and Squirrels*, bequeathed by Miss Mary P. R. Allan, 2003, © the artist

Shanks, Duncan b.1937, *Into the Storm*, purchased, 1985, © Culture and Sport Glasgow (Glasgow Museums)

Shanks, William Somerville 1864–1951, *Pipes of Pan*, purchased, 1919

Shanks, William Somerville 1864–1951, *John Q. Pringle (1864–1925)*, gift from an anonymous donor, 1924

Shanks, William Somerville 1864–1951, *The Chancel, St Andrew's Parish Church, Glasgow*, purchased, 1935

Shannon, Charles Haslewood 1863–1937, *Sir Matthew W. Montgomery (1859–1933), Lord Provost of Glasgow (1923–1926)*, purchased, 1926

Shannon, James Jebusa 1862–1923, *Flora*, presented by the Trustees of the Hamilton Bequest, 1928

Shawa, Laila b.1940, *Aliens?*, purchased from the artist, 1996, © the artist/Bridgeman Art Library

Shawa, Laila b.1940, *The Blind Leading the Blind!*, purchased from the artist, 1996, © the artist/ Bridgeman Art Library

Shayer, William 1788–1879, *A Woody Stream*, bequeathed by Francis J. Eck, 1915

Shayer, William 1788–1879, *Ploughing*, bequeathed by Francis J. Eck, 1915

Shayer, William 1788–1879, *Gypsy Encampment*, bequeathed by Thomas D. Smellie, 1901

Shayer, William 1788–1879, *Landscape with Cattle*, bequeathed by William Euing, 1874

Shayer, William 1788–1879, *Landscape with Cattle*, bequeathed by William Euing, 1874

Shayer, William 1788–1879, *The Shrimp Girl, Cornish Coast*, bequeathed by William Euing, 1874

Shayer, William Joseph 1811–1892, *A Shady Pool*, bequeathed by William Euing, 1874

Shee, Martin Archer 1769–1850, *Ariadne Deserted by Theseus*, bequeathed by William Euing, 1874

Shields, Douglas Gordon 1888–1943, *A. Maitland Ramsay (1859–1946), MD*, gift from Mrs Maitland Ramsay, 1953

Shields, Frederick James 1833–1911, *Abraham*, gift from Sir Frank Brangwyn, 1944

Shields, Frederick James 1833–1911, *Rex Nineveh*, gift from Sir Frank Brangwyn, 1944

Shipham, Benjamin 1808–1872, *Landscape with Cattle and Figures*, bequeathed by Adam Teacher, 1898

Shirley, Henry d.1870 & **Will, H. B.** *Dutch River Scene*, bequeathed by William Euing, 1874

Sickert, Walter Richard 1860–1942, *Dieppe Harbour*, presented by the Trustees of the Hamilton Bequest, 1949, © estate of Walter R. Sickert. All rights reserved, DACS 2013

Sickert, Walter Richard 1860–1942, *Sir Hugh Walpole (1884–1941)*, purchased, 1947, © estate of Walter R. Sickert. All rights reserved, DACS 2013

Sickert, Walter Richard 1860–1942, *Barnsbury*, purchased, 1931, © estate of Walter R. Sickert. All rights reserved, DACS 2013

Sickert, Walter Richard (style of) 1860–1942, *Lansdowne Crescent, Bath*, purchased, 1961, © estate of Walter R. Sickert. All rights reserved, DACS 2013

Signac, Paul 1863–1935, *Coal Crane, Clichy*, presented by the Trustees of the Hamilton Bequest, 1946

Signac, Paul 1863–1935, *Sunset, Herblay, Opus 206*, accepted by HM Government in lieu of inheritance tax, 1976

Signorelli, Luca c.1450–1523, *Lamentation over the Dead Christ*, Stirling Maxwell Collection, gift, 1967

Simon, David active 20th C, *Shuttle Street, Franciscan Friary Reconstruction Illustration*, purchased, 2006

Simon, Lucien 1861–1945, *Staging Post*, bequeathed by William McInnes, 1944, © ADAGP, Paris and DACS, London 2013

Simon, Lucien 1861–1945, *After the War*, gift from Marc A. Béra, 1948, © ADAGP, Paris and DACS, London 2013

Simon, Lucien 1861–1945, *The Fair*, gift from Sir William and Lady Burrell to the City of Glasgow, 1944, © ADAGP, Paris and DACS, London 2013

Simon, Lucien 1861–1945, *The Races*, gift from William Burrell, 1925, © ADAGP, Paris and DACS, London 2013

Simoni, Gustavo 1846–1926, *Eastern Festival*, bequeathed by Adam Teacher, 1898

Simpson, Ian 1933–2011, *The Green Roof*, purchased, 1963

Simpson, Robert *Fire at Trades Lane Warehouses*, temporary identification number allocated, 1982

Sims, Paddy Japaljarri b.c.1916, *The Night Sky Dreaming*, commissioned from the Worlukurlanga Artists' Aboriginal Association, 1992, © Warlukurlanga Artists Aboriginal Corporation

Sims, Paddy Japaljarri b.c.1916 & **Sims, Bessie Nakamarra** b.c.1932 *Kangaroo, Wild Cabbage, Cermonial Speer, Possum and Bush Carrot Dreaming*, purchased, 1992, © Warlukurlanga Artists Aboriginal Corporation

Singh, Amoca active 20th C, *Guru Gobind Singh*, purchased, 1993

Sisley, Alfred 1839–1899, *The Bell Tower at Noisy-le-Roi, Autumn*, gift from Sir William and Lady Burrell to the City of Glasgow, 1944

Sisley, Alfred 1839–1899, *The Loing at Saint-Mammès*, bequeathed by Lord and Lady Fraser of Allander; received, 2003

Sisley, Alfred 1839–1899, *Boatyard at Saint-Mammès*, presented by the Trustees of the Hamilton Bequest, 1944

Sisley, Alfred 1839–1899, *Village Street, Moret-sur-Loing*, bequeathed by William McInnes, 1944

Sivell, Robert 1888–1958, *Woman in a Shawl*, purchased, 1943

Sivell, Robert 1888–1958, *Dehydration of Herrings*, presented by the War Artists' Advisory Committee through the Imperial War Museum, 1948, © Culture and Sport Glasgow (Glasgow Museums)

Siyaya, Steven active 20th C, *Leopard and Bird in Tree*, purchased, 1989

Siyaya, Steven active 20th C, *Policemen Murdering African Men*, purchased, 1989

Slaney, Noel b.1915, *The Three Red Apples*, purchased, 1956

Slingeland, Pieter Cornelisz. van (after) 1640–1691, *A Young Woman Rejecting the Offer of a Dead Fowl*, bequeathed by Thomas Craig, 1925

Smart, John 1838–1899, *The Gloom of Glen Ogle*, purchased, 1903

Smith, Colvin 1795–1875, *Elizabeth Steven of Polmadie and Bellahouston*, presented by the Trustees of the Bellahouston Bequest Fund, 1896

Smith, Colvin 1795–1875, *Lord Jeffrey (1773–1850)*, bequeathed by William Euing, 1874

Smith, Colvin 1795–1875, *Moses Steven of Polmadie and Bellahouston (1806–1871)*, presented by the Trustees of the Bellahouston Bequest Fund, 1896

Smith, Colvin 1795–1875, *The Daughters of Colin Campbell of Jura*, gift from Captain Campbell of Jura, 1945

Smith, George 1870–1934, *Farm Horses*, gift from W. G. Campbell, 1949

Smith, George 1870–1934, *Feeding Time*, gift from W. G. Campbell, 1949

Smith, George 1870–1934, *The Winding Road*, gift from Miss M. M. W. Campbell, 1939

Smith, Ian McKenzie b.1935, *West Sea*, purchased, 1973, © Culture and Sport Glasgow (Glasgow Museums)

Smith, John Guthrie Spence 1880–1951, *A Midlothian Farm*, purchased, 1945

Smith, Matthew Arnold Bracey 1879–1959, *Flowers*, purchased, 1953, © by permission of the copyright holder

Smith, Ronald F. b.1946, *Powerful Sea, St Andrews*, purchased, 1972

Smyth, Dorothy Carleton 1880–1933, *Self Portrait*, gift from Olive C. Smyth, 1948

Smythe, Lionel Percy 1839–1918, *Children Coming from School*, bequeathed by Mrs Isabella Elder, 1906

Soest, Gerard c.1600–1681, *John Hay (1645–1713), 2nd Marquis of Tweeddale*, purchased with the assistance of the National Fund for Acquisitions, 1976

Sogliani, Giovanni Antonio 1492–1544, *The Adoration of the Magi*, Archibald McLellan Collection, purchased, 1856

Solimena, Francesco 1657–1747, *Virgin and Child*, Archibald McLellan Collection, purchased, 1856

Solimena, Francesco (after) 1657–1747, *A Group of Four Men*, bequeathed by Sir Claude Phillips, 1924

Somerville, Ward O. b.1942, *Long Summer*, purchased, 1965

Sorgh, Hendrik Martensz. (after) 1609/1611–1670, *Simon Episcopius (1583–1643)*, Archibald McLellan Collection, purchased, 1856

Soyer, Paul Constant 1823–1903, *The Dead Bird*, bequeathed by John Robertson, 1895

Spanish School *Portrait of a Father and Son*, Stirling Maxwell Collection, gift, 1967

Spanish School *Portrait of a Spanish Lady*, Stirling Maxwell Collection, gift, 1967

Spanish School *Portrait of a Man at Prayer*, Stirling Maxwell Collection, gift, 1967

Spanish School 17th C, *The Garden of the Duke of Lerma's Palace, Madrid*, Stirling Maxwell Collection, gift, 1967

Spanish School 17th C, *The Rosary of Fifteen Joys and Sorrows of the Virgin*, Stirling Maxwell Collection, gift, 1967

Spanish School (attributed to) 17th C, *Still Life*, Stirling Maxwell Collection, gift, 1967

Spear, Ruskin 1911–1990, *George B. Primrose (1881–1969), 3rd Chairman of the Hamilton Trust (1946–1969)*, presented by the Trustees of the Hamilton Bequest, 1968, © the artist's estate/ Bridgeman Art Library

Spence, Harry 1860–1928, *The Gondola*, purchased from the artist, 1901

Spence, Harry 1860–1928, *View of the Glasgow International Exhibition*, temporary identification number allocated, 1978

Spencer, Gilbert 1892–1979, *The School on Peggy Hill, Ambleside*, purchased, 1952, © the artist's estate/Bridgeman Art Library

Spencer, John E. *Olive Trees, Montmajour*, purchased, 1952

Spencer, Stanley 1891–1959, *The Vale of Health, Hampstead, London*, purchased, 1941, © the estate of Stanley Spencer 2013. All rights reserved DACS

Spencer, Stanley 1891–1959, *The Glen, Port Glasgow*, purchased, 1953, © Culture and Sport Glasgow (Glasgow Museums)

Spenlove-Spenlove, Frank 1866–1933, *Vespers, New Year's Eve in the Low Country*, purchased, 1908

Squire, Geoffrey b.1923, *Veronica*, purchased, 1959

Squire, Geoffrey b.1923, *Elsa*, purchased, 1963

Stanfield, Clarkson 1793–1867, *A Dutch Mill*, bequeathed by Andrew Lusk, 1928

Stanfield, Clarkson 1793–1867, *Rocky Seascape with a Shipwreck*, purchased, 1963

Stanfield, Clarkson 1793–1867, *Seascape*, gift from Miss Anderson, 1921

Stanfield, Clarkson 1793–1867, *Seascape*, gift from Professor G. H. Bell, 1951

Stark, Arthur James 1831–1902, *A Pointer and a Dead Wild Duck*, bequeathed by Adam Teacher, 1898

Stark, James 1794–1859, *A Burn Side*, bequeathed by Thomas D. Smellie, 1901

Stark, James 1794–1859, *Woodland Scene*, gift from Mrs Wiseman, 1907

Staveren, Jan Adriaensz. van c.1625–c.1668, *A Hermit at Prayer*, bequeathed by William Euing, 1874

Steell, Gourlay 1819–1894, *Deerstalking on Jura*, gift from Captain Campbell of Jura, 1945

Steell, Gourlay 1819–1894, *A Challenge*, gift from Mrs J. Turnbull, 1957

Steell, Gourlay 1819–1894, *The Trysting Place*, bequeathed by Adam Teacher, 1898

Steen, Jan 1626–1679, *Christ in the House of Martha and Mary*, on

loan from a private collection

Steen, Jan (imitator of) 1626–1679, *A Merry Company*, Archibald McLellan Collection, purchased, 1856

Steer, Philip Wilson 1860–1942, *Nidderdale*, presented by the Trustees of the Hamilton Bequest, 1935, © Tate, London 2013

Steer, Philip Wilson 1860–1942, *Maldon*, bequeathed by Miss Marion K. Mitchell, 1980, © Tate, London 2013

Stephanoff, Francis Philip 1790–1860, *Answering the Advertisement*, bequeathed by William Euing, 1874

Stevenson active 19th C, *Robert Barclay (d.1861), Shipbuilder*, temporary identification number allocated, 1977

Stevenson, Robert *Harcourt Blair (Beatty)*

Stevenson, Robert Macaulay 1854–1952, *Moonrise*, bequeathed by C. E. Lichfield-Knox, 1926

Stevenson, Robert Macaulay 1854–1952, *Early Summer on the Seine*, purchased, 1904

Stevenson, Robert Macaulay 1854–1952, *An Old World Mill*, gift from Allan Wilson, 1946

Stevenson, Robert Macaulay 1854–1952, *By the River, Harvest-Time*, purchased, 1955

Stevenson, Robert Macaulay 1854–1952, *Days of Auld Lang Syne*, presented by the Trustees of Sir Daniel M. Stevenson, 1945

Stevenson, Robert Macaulay 1854–1952, *In the Gloaming*, gift from Allan Wilson, 1946

Stevenson, Robert Macaulay 1854–1952, *Landscape*, bequeathed by Samuel M. Mavor, 1943

Stevenson, Robert Macaulay 1854–1952, *Moonlit Landscape*, presented by the Trustees of Sir Daniel M. Stevenson, 1945

Stevenson, Robert Macaulay 1854–1952, *Ramparts of Monteuil*, bequeathed by John Keppie, 1945

Stewart, Charles Edward active 1887–1938, *Crossing the Ford*, gift from T. Cuthbert-Stewart, 1904

Stewart, Charles Edward active 1887–1938, *The Townsend Stalk*, purchased, 1954

Stewart, Charles Edward active 1887–1938, *Tollbooth, Old High Street, Glasgow*

Stewart, Charles Edward (attributed to) active 1887–1938, *Tron Steeple, Glasgow*

Stewart, J. *John McGill*, temporary identification number allocated, 1977

Stewart, J. T. (studio of) active c.1885–1960 & **Stewart, Charles Edward (studio of)** active 1887–1938 *Head of a Bearded Man*

Stewart, J. T. (studio of) active c.1885–1960 & **Stewart, Charles Edward (studio of)** active 1887–1938 *Seated Woman Gutting Fish by a Fire*, gift, 1980

Stewart, James Scott b.c.1832, *J. Milne Donald (1819–1866)*, gift

from the artist, 1908

Stewart, Malcolm 1829–1916, *Dr Livingstone (1813–1873), Missionary and Explorer*, gift, 1881

Stewart, Malcolm 1829–1916, *Lieutenant-General Sir John Moore (1761–1809) (after Thomas Lawrence)*, gift from the artist, 1902

Stewart, Malcolm 1829–1916, *Thomas Campbell (1777–1844), Poet*, gift from the artist, 1902

Stoddart, Alexander b.1959, *Elizabeth Cameron, Lord Provost of the City of Glasgow (2003–2007)*, purchased, 2008, © the artist

Stone, Marcus C. 1840–1921, *Royalists Seeking Safety*, bequeathed by Mrs Isabella Elder, 1906

Storey, George Adolphus 1834–1919, *The Judgment of Paris*, bequeathed by Mrs McLean, 1914

Storey, Harold 1888–1965, *Symington, Ayrshire*, purchased, 1945

Stott, Edward William 1859–1918, *The Sacred Pool*, gift from A. E. Anderson, 1931

Stott, William 1857–1900, *The Nymph*, bequeathed by Allan McLean, 1928

Stott, William 1857–1900, *Autumn*, purchased, 1903

Straeten, Jan van der (attributed to) 1667/1681–1731/1741, *An Architectural Fantasy with Figures*, Archibald McLellan Collection, purchased, 1856

Strang, William 1859–1921, *The Red Fez: Self Portrait*, gift from Leonard Gow, 1928

Strang, William 1859–1921, *Good Morning, Señor*, bequeathed by David Perry, 1940

Strang, William 1859–1921, *Café Bar* (sketch), purchased, 1949

Strang, William 1859–1921, *Café Bar*, gift from Arthur S. L. Young, 1946

Strang, William 1859–1921, *Lady with a Red Hat*, purchased, 1919

Strang, William 1859–1921, *Thomas Hardy (1840–1928), OM*, gift from Sir John Richmond, 1923

Strang, William 1859–1921, *Admiral Sir John Fisher (1841–1920), OM*, gift from Mrs Lawrence Glen, 1925

Strang, William 1859–1921, *Nymph and Shepherds*, purchased, 1922

Streeck, Hendrick van (attributed to) 1659–1719, *Interior of the Oude Kerk, Delft, with a Gravedigger*, gift from Sir William and Lady Burrell to the City of Glasgow, 1944

Stretton, Philip Eustace c.1863–c.1930, *Landscape and Lily Pond*, bequeathed by John C. McIntyre, 1939

Strij, Jacob van 1756–1815, *Landscape with Horsemen and Cattle*, bequeathed by William Euing, 1874

Strij, Jacob van 1756–1815, *River Landscape with Cattle, Sheep and Figures*, bequeathed by William

Euing, 1874

Struthers, A. *Lord Palmerston (1784–1865)*, gift from James Dunlop, 1948

Stuart, Charles Edward 1885–c.1960, *Tabby Cat*

Stuart, Charles Edward 1885–c.1960, *Cat and Kitten*

Sturrock, Alick Riddell 1885–1953, *Perthshire Panorama*, purchased, 1950

Summerton, Edward b.1962, *Sink: Living with an Artist*, gift from the BBC Collection, 2008

Sutherland, Alan b.1931, *Sir William Gray (1928–2000), Lord Provost of Glasgow (1972–1975)*, purchased, 1977

Sutherland, Graham Vivian 1903–1980, *Flying Bomb Depot: The Caverns, Saint-Leu-d'Esserent, 14 January 1945*, presented by the War Artists' Advisory Committee through the Imperial War Museum, 1948, © Culture and Sport Glasgow (Glasgow Museums)

Sutherland, Graham Vivian 1903–1980, *Landscape with Rocks*, purchased, 1953, © estate of Graham Sutherland

Suttermans, Justus (and studio) 1597–1681, *Anna de' Medici (1616–1676), Daughter of Cosimo II de' Medici*, Stirling Maxwell Collection, gift, 1967

Swaine, Francis (attributed to) 1730–1782, *Shipping in a Breeze off the Coast*, Archibald McLellan Collection, purchased, 1856

Swan, Donald Sinclair 1918–2004, *A Minister*, gift from Barony Parish Church, 1985, © the artist's estate

Swanevelt, Herman van c.1600–1665, *Wooded Landscape with a Horseman Driving Cattle*, Archibald McLellan Collection, purchased, 1856

Swanevelt, Herman van c.1600–1665, *River Landscape with a Castle and Figures*, bequeathed by William Euing, 1874

Swanevelt, Herman van (imitator of) c.1600–1665, *River Landscape with Donkeys Crossing a Bridge*, bequeathed by William Euing, 1874

Swanevelt, Herman van (style of) c.1600–1665, *Landscape with Ruins*, bequeathed by Jane Graham-Gilbert, 1877

Swann, E. L. *Cathcart Castle*

Swinton, James Rannie 1816–1888, *Lady Matilda Maxwell (1802–1857), Wife of Sir John Maxwell, 8th Bt*, on loan from a private collection

Swinton, James Rannie 1816–1888, *Sir John Maxwell (1791–1865), 8th Bt*, on loan from a private collection

Swynnerton, Annie Louisa 1844–1933, *A Dryad*, bequeathed by Mrs A. J. MacLaren, 1940

Swynnerton, Annie Louisa 1844–1933, *The Soul's Journey: The Soul's Awakening*, gift from Francis Howard, 1952

Syme, John S. 1795–1861, *J. Bell, MD*, purchased, 1940

Szubert, Jozef 1898–1984, *Convalescence*, purchased, 1995

Szubert, Jozef 1898–1984, *The Harvest*, purchased, 1995

Tannock, James 1784–1863, *Henry Bell (1767–1830)*, temporary identification number allocated, 1977

Taylor, Ernest Archibald 1874–1952, *Isle of Whithorn*, purchased, 1942

Teh, Hock Aun b.1950, *Fitness Is Energy*, purchased, 1991, © the artist

Teh, Hock Aun b.1950, *Street Opera at the Temple Festival*, purchased from the artist, 1993, © the artist

Teh, Hock Aun b.1950, *The Legend of Mahsuri*, purchased from the artist, 1994, © the artist

Teh, Hock Aun b.1950, *The Milky Way*, purchased from the artist, 1994, © the artist

Teh, Hock Aun b.1950, *White Snake*, purchased from the artist, 1994, © the artist

Teniers, David II 1610–1690, *Landscape with Huntsmen and Dogs*, Archibald McLellan Collection, purchased, 1856

Teniers, David II 1610–1690, *A Surgeon Treating a Peasant's Foot*, Archibald McLellan Collection, purchased, 1856

Teniers, David II 1610–1690, *Saint Margaret (after Raphael)*, Archibald McLellan Collection, purchased, 1856

Teniers, David II 1610–1690, *The Visitation (after Jacopo Palma il Vecchio)*, Archibald McLellan Collection, purchased, 1856

Teniers, David II (after) 1610–1690, *Landscape with Peasants on a Pathway*, Archibald McLellan Collection, purchased, 1856

Teniers, David II (after) 1610–1690, *Soldiers Plundering a Village*, Archibald McLellan Collection, purchased, 1856

Teniers, David II (attributed to) 1610–1690, *Interior with a Man and a Woman at a Table*, Archibald McLellan Collection, purchased, 1856

Teniers, David II (attributed to) 1610–1690, *Interior with Peasants before a Fire*, Archibald McLellan Collection, purchased, 1856

Teniers, David II (attributed to) 1610–1690, *Latona and the Lycian Peasants*, Archibald McLellan Collection, purchased, 1856

Teniers, David II (attributed to) 1610–1690, *The Milk Maid*, Archibald McLellan Collection, purchased, 1856

Teniers, David II (follower of) 1610–1690, *Boer Seated on a Barrel Chair*, Archibald McLellan Collection, purchased, 1856

Teniers, David II (follower of) 1610–1690, *Landscape with Figures before a Cottage*, Archibald

unknown artist *PS 'Thistle'*

unknown artist *Barque 'Medora' off Greenock*, gift, 1974

unknown artist *PS 'Duntroon Castle'*, gift from H. Wilkie, 1940

unknown artist *PS 'Mars' on the Clyde*, purchased, 1958

unknown artist *Steamship 'Pekin'*, gift, 1909

unknown artist *Barque 'Elizabeth Walker'*, bequeathed by P. D. Ridge-Beedle, 1952

unknown artist *Clyde Steamer PS 'Sultan'*, on loan from a private collection

unknown artist *Clyde Steamer PS 'Sultan'*, on loan from a private collection

unknown artist *Giuseppe Garibaldi (1807–1882)*, purchased, 1987

unknown artist *PS 'Eagle'*

unknown artist *Outward Bound*

unknown artist *The Henderson Line Ship 'Ormaru' or 'Timaru'*, gift from P. Henderson & Co., 1953

unknown artist *PS 'Brodick Castle'*, presented by Williamson Buchanan Steamers Limited, 1937

unknown artist *Sir J. Falshaw (d.1889), Bt, Chairman of the North British Railway Company (1882–1887)*, gift from British Rail, London, 1967

unknown artist *David Jones (1834–1906), Locomotive Engineer, Highland Railway*, gift from British Rail, 1968

unknown artist *George Kilgour, Slater, Partickhill*, gift, 1981

unknown artist *Saint John the Baptist, Saint Nikolaos, Saint Phæina and Saint Eudoxia*, gift, 1943

unknown artist 19th C, *A Stormy Landscape*, bequeathed by Jane Graham-Gilbert, 1877

unknown artist 19th C, *Boy Sitting on a Box*, purchased, 1962

unknown artist 19th C, *Boy's Head*, gift from Lewis Lyons, 1939

unknown artist 19th C, *Dr Guthrie*, bequeathed by William Euing, 1874

unknown artist 19th C, *Extensive Landscape*, purchased, 1963

unknown artist 19th C, *Girl with a Pink Bow*, purchased, 1962

unknown artist 19th C, *Gorbals Street and Bedford Row with the 'Rob Roy' Tavern*, gift from Superintendant Brown, 1938

unknown artist 19th C, *Hannah Anne Stirling (1816–1843), Daughter of Archibald Stirling of Keir*, on loan from a private collection

unknown artist 19th C, *Hugh Robertson of Gartloch (1777–1853)*, presented by the descendants of Mr and Mrs Hugh Robertson of Gartloch, 1956

unknown artist 19th C, *Ikon, Virgin and Child*, gift from David Alec Wilson, 1912

unknown artist 19th C, *James Campbell of Tullichewan (1823–1901)*, gift from Lieutenant Colonel Alistair Campbell, 1946

unknown artist 19th C, *James Douglas of Barloch*

unknown artist 19th C, *Jedburgh Abbey*, purchased, 1956

unknown artist 19th C, *Portrait of a Lady*

unknown artist 19th C, *Portrait of a Man*

unknown artist 19th C, *Portrait of a Victorian Gentleman*, purchased, 1983

unknown artist 19th C, *Portrait of a Young Man, Nephew of Lieutenant Colonel A. Hope Pattison*, gift from Godfrey H. Pattison, 1945

unknown artist 19th C, *Reverend A. O. Bear*

unknown artist 19th C, *Robert Burns (1759–1796)*, found in store, registered, 1988

unknown artist 19th C, *Scottish Landscape*, bequeathed by William Euing, 1874

unknown artist 19th C, *Sea Piece and Shipping*, bequeathed by Adam Teacher, 1898

unknown artist 19th C, *Sir John Maxwell (1648–1732), 1st Bt*, on loan from a private collection

unknown artist 19th C, *The Doge's Palace, Venice*, bequeathed by Sir Alexander Cross, 1963

unknown artist 19th C, *The Misses C. and M. Crawford-Cummming of Rosneath*, gift from Mrs M. Groome, 1952

unknown artist 19th C, *The Mourners*, bequeathed by William Euing, 1874

unknown artist 19th C, *The Old Stockwell Bridge*, bequeathed by Thomas S. Bisset, 1921

unknown artist 19th C, *Travellers Resting in a Cave*, purchased, 1964

unknown artist *'Coffee John'*, purchased, 1958

unknown artist *Stobcross House*, gift from Mrs Henry Drummond, 1906

unknown artist *RMS 'Lusitania'*, purchased with the assistance of the National Fund for Acquisitions, 1973

unknown artist *Highland Railway Locomotive No.49, 'Clan Campbell'*, gift, 1976

unknown artist *Gorbals Tower*, gift from the Provand's Lordship Society, 1978

unknown artist *'St George'*, on loan from a private collection

unknown artist *Broomfield Esso Station*

unknown artist *Orchard*, temporary identification number allocated, 1984

unknown artist *Ships at Sea*

unknown artist 20th C, *Virgin and Child*

unknown artist *A Castle under Siege*

unknown artist *Alexander Campbell (1796–1870), a Socialist Co-Operative Pioneer*, on loan from a private collection

unknown artist *Battle of the Bell o' the Brae*

unknown artist *Captain Hugh Morris*, bequeathed by Miss Mary Morris, 1951

unknown artist *Captain John Crawford*

unknown artist *Chimborazo Volcano*, gift from Andrew B. Holmes, 1940

unknown artist *Cumbal Volcano*, gift from Andrew B. Holmes, 1940

unknown artist *Forth Rail Bridge (Opening Ceremony)*, gift from British Rail, London, 1967

unknown artist *Glasgow Cathedral from the East*

unknown artist *Henry Stuart (1545–1567), Lord Darnley*, gift from the Provand's Lordship Society, 1978

unknown artist *Henry VIII (1491–1547)*, gift from the Provand's Lordship Society, 1978

unknown artist *Jean Blackburn, Wife of Robert Swan of Wattison*, presented by the sitter's great-granddaughters, the Misses MacLean Brodie, 1941

unknown artist *Joseph Cheney Bolton, Esq. (1819–1901), Director of the Royal Bank of Scotland (1868–1901), Chairman of the Caledonian Railway Company (1880–1897)*

unknown artist *Lady Barbara Maxwell (d.1737)*, on loan from a private collection

unknown artist *Lady Marian Maxwell (d.1705)*, on loan from a private collection

unknown artist *Lady Marian Maxwell (d.1705)*, on loan from a private collection

unknown artist *Mary Stuart (1542–1587), Queen of Scots*, gift from the Provand's Lordship Society, 1978

unknown artist *North British Railway Locomotive No.603*, gift, 1980

unknown artist *Philip II of Spain (1527–1598)*, gift from the Provand's Lordship Society, 1978

unknown artist *Portrait of a Bearded Man*

unknown artist *Portrait of a Gentleman*, gift from Godfrey H. Pattison, 1945

unknown artist *Portrait of a Man*, found in store, registered, 1988

unknown artist *Portrait of a Man with a Lace Cravat*, found in store, registered, 1988

unknown artist *Portrait of a Seated Man*

unknown artist *Portrait of a Seated Woman*

unknown artist *Prince Charles Edward Stuart (1720–1788) ('Bonnie Prince Charlie')*, gift from the Provand's Lordship Society, 1978

unknown artist *Portrait of an Oriental Indian with a Tattooed Face*, gift from Andrew B. Holmes, 1940

unknown artist *Portrait of a Serrano Indian*, gift from Andrew B. Holmes, 1940

unknown artist *Portrait of a Serrano Indian in a Red Blouse*, gift from Andrew B. Holmes, 1940

unknown artist *Portrait of a Serrano Indian Woman*, gift from Andrew B. Holmes, 1940

unknown artist *Portrait of a Serrano Indian Woman with a Red and White Headdress*, gift from Andrew B. Holmes, 1940

unknown artist *Rough Seas*, gift from Sir William and Lady Burrell to the City of Glasgow, 1944

unknown artist *Sir Thomas Lipton (1848–1931)*

unknown artist *Steamship 'Clyde'*

unknown artist *The Raising of Lazarus*, found in store, registered, 1891

unknown artist *Three-Masted Barque*

unknown artist *Tungurahua Volcano*, gift from Andrew B. Holmes, 1940

unknown artist *Twin-Funnel Steamship with Auxiliary Sail*

unknown artist *Two Serrano Indians Dressed for Market*, gift from Andrew B. Holmes, 1940

unknown artist *William Cecil (1520–1598), Lord Burghley*, gift from the Provand's Lordship Society, 1978

Urie, Joseph b.1947, *Man with a Dog*, gift from the BBC Collection, 2008

Urie, Joseph b.1947, *Man with a Blackbird*, gift from the BBC Collection, 2008

Urquhart, Donald b.1959, *Pyrites*, gift from the BBC Collection, 2008, © the artist

Urquhart, H. H. *Old Govan Water Row*, gift from John Service, 1934

Utrillo, Maurice 1883–1955, *Village Street, Auvers-sur-Oise*, presented by the Trustees of the Hamilton Bequest, 1941, © ADAGP, Paris and DACS, London 2013/Jean Fabris 2013

Uwins, Thomas 1782–1857, *Comus Offering the Enchanted Cup to the Lady* (from the masque by John Milton), bequeathed by William Euing, 1874

Valdés Leal, Juan de 1622–1690, *Madonna and Child*, Stirling Maxwell Collection, gift, 1967

Valory, Caroline de b.c.1790, *The Miniature*, Archibald McLellan Collection, purchased, 1856

Van der Houten *Stockwell Bridge, Glasgow*, acquired, 1959

Varotari, Dario 1539–1596, *Madonna and Child Enthroned with Saints Peter and John the Baptist and Angels*, Archibald McLellan Collection, purchased, 1856

Vecellio, Francesco 1475–1559/1560, *Madonna and Child with Saint Jerome and Saint Dorothy*, Archibald McLellan Collection, purchased, 1856

Veitch *Girl at a Spinning Wheel*

Velázquez, Diego (and studio) 1599–1660, *Philip IV of Spain (1605–1665)*, bequeathed by James Donald, 1905

Velázquez, Diego (school of) 1599–1660, *Head of a Man: The Conde De Tilly, Johan 't Serclaes (1559–1632).*, Stirling Maxwell Collection, gift, 1967

Velázquez, Diego (school of) 1599–1660, *Isabella of Bourbon (1603–1644)*, Stirling Maxwell Collection, gift, 1967

Velázquez, Diego (school of) 1599–1660, *Philip IV and His Queen in a Colonnade*, Stirling Maxwell Collection, gift, 1967

Velde, Adriaen van de 1636–1672, *A Woman and a Child, Cattle and Sheep by a Fountain*, Archibald McLellan Collection, purchased, 1856

Velde, Adriaen van de (after) 1636–1672, *A Meadow with Cattle and a Woman Milking*, Archibald McLellan Collection, purchased, 1856

Velde, Adriaen van de (imitator of) 1636–1672, *Four Sheep Resting*, bequeathed by William Euing, 1874

Velde, Esaias van de I 1587–1630, *A Military Skirmish*, Archibald McLellan Collection, purchased, 1856

Velde, Esaias van de I 1587–1630, *The Ambush of a Wagon Train*, Archibald McLellan Collection, purchased, 1856

Velde, Willem van de II (after) 1633–1707, *A States Yacht Running down towards the Dutch Fleet*, Archibald McLellan Collection, purchased, 1856

Velde, Willem van de II (after) 1633–1707, *An English Ship Becalmed, Firing a Gun*

Velde, Willem van de II (attributed to) 1633–1707, *The Dutch Man-of-War 'Star' at Anchor*, Archibald McLellan Collection, purchased, 1856

Velde, Willem van de II (attributed to) 1633–1707, *The 'Eendracht' and Other Ships of the Dutch Fleet*, bequeathed by Jane Graham-Gilbert, 1877

Velde, Willem van de II (attributed to) 1633–1707, *A Dutch Fishing Buss under Sail, with Other Vessels in a Breeze*, Archibald McLellan Collection, purchased, 1856

Velde, Willem van de II (studio of) 1633–1707, *A Dutch Vessel Pushing Off from Shore with Others under Sail*, Archibald McLellan Collection, purchased, 1856

Vellacott, Elisabeth 1905–2002, *Conversations, Cat and Pear Tree*, purchased, 1995, © the artist's estate

Vellacott, Elisabeth 1905–2002, *Raided City*, purchased, 1995, © the artist's estate

Venskiy, Igor Ivanov *Alex Mosson, Lord Provost of the City of Glasgow*

(1999–2003), purchased from the artist, 2003

Verheyen, Jan Hendrik 1778–1846, *An Imaginary Dutch Street, with a Huckster*, bequeathed by William Euing, 1874

Verheyen, Jan Hendrik 1778–1846, *A Dutch Street, with Children Fighting*, bequeathed by William Euing, 1874

Verheyen, Jan Hendrik 1778–1846, *An Imaginary Dutch Street, with Figures by a Well*, bequeathed by William Euing, 1874

Verkolje, Jan I (imitator of) 1650–1693, *William III (1650–1702)*, gift from T. Graham Young in memory of his father, James Young, 1900

Verschuring, Hendrik (attributed to) 1627–1690, *A Horse and a Farrier before an Archway*, bequeathed by Jane Graham-Gilbert, 1877

Vertangen, Daniel c.1598–1681/1684, *The Expulsion from Paradise*, Archibald McLellan Collection, purchased, 1856

Vickers, Alfred 1786–1868, *A Coast Scene*, bequeathed by William Euing, 1874

Vinall, Joseph William Topham 1873–1953, *The Amateur*, gift from the artist, 1942

Vincelet, Victor 1840–1871, *A Bunch of Flowers*, bequeathed by Mrs Anna Walker, 1948

Vincelet, Victor 1840–1871, *A Vase of Flowers*, bequeathed by Archibald R. Henderson, 1901

Visnes, Hanneline b.1972, *Farah Diba (b.1938)*, purchased from the artist, 2003

Visnes, Hanneline b.1972, *Sisters*, purchased from the artist, 2003

Visnes, Hanneline b.1972, *Victoria*, purchased from the artist, 2003

Vlaminck, Maurice de 1876–1958, *By the Seine*, purchased, 1958, © ADAGP, Paris and DACS, London 2013

Vliet, Hendrick Cornelisz. van c.1611–1675, *Interior of the Oude Kerk, Delft*, gift from William Burrell, 1925

Vois, Ary de c.1632–1680, *The Head of a Jew*, bequeathed by Jane Graham-Gilbert, 1877

Vollerdt, Johann Christian 1708–1769, *A Mountain Landscape in Winter*, bequeathed by William Euing, 1874

Vollerdt, Johann Christian 1708–1769, *A Mountain Landscape with a Waterfall*, bequeathed by William Euing, 1874

Vollerdt, Johann Christian 1708–1769, *Landscape with Buildings and Figures beside a Lake*, bequeathed by William Euing, 1874

Vollon, Antoine 1833–1900, *Still Life*, gift from Sir William and Lady Burrell to the City of Glasgow, 1944

Vollon, Antoine 1833–1900, *A*

Corner of the Louvre, gift from Sir John Richmond, 1948

Vollon, Antoine 1833–1900, *Still Life with Fruit*, bequeathed by James Donald, 1905

Vos, Paul de (attributed to) 1591–1592 or 1595–1678, *Dogs Harrying a Wild Boar*, purchased, 1955

Vrancx, Sebastian (after) 1573–1647, *The Battle of Leckerbeetje, 1600*, found in store, registered, 1988

Vuillard, Jean Edouard 1868–1940, *Woman in Blue with a Child*, gift from Sir John Richmond, 1948, © ADAGP, Paris and DACS, London 2013

Vuillard, Jean Edouard 1868–1940, *Interior: The Drawing Room*, bequeathed by William McInnes, 1944, © ADAGP, Paris and DACS, London 2013

Vuillard, Jean Edouard 1868–1940, *The Table*, bequeathed by William McInnes, 1944, © ADAGP, Paris and DACS, London 2013

Vuillard, Jean Edouard 1868–1940, *Lady in Green*, bequeathed by William McInnes, 1944, © ADAGP, Paris and DACS, London 2013

Wadsworth, Edward Alexander 1889–1949, *Departure*, purchased, 1953, © estate of Edward Wadsworth 2013. All rights reserved, DACS

Waitt, Richard (after) d.1732, *Alastair Grant Mor, the Castle Grant Champion*, gift from Mrs Louisa MacGregor, 1940

Walker, Elizabeth *Molendinar Burn*, gift from P. D. Ridge-Beedle, 1952

Walker, Ethel 1861–1951, *Flower Piece*, purchased, 1941, © the artist's estate/Bridgeman Art Library

Wallace, James *Reverend Professor Robert Morton, DD*

Wallace, William 1801–1866, *Annie Laurie*, bequeathed by William Euing, 1874

Walls, D. *Falls of Moness, Aberfeldy*

Walls, William 1860–1942, *Lion Cubs, Suspicion*, purchased, 1923

Walters, Emile 1893–1977, *The Harp of the Valkyries*, gift from Russell Horn, 1950

Walters, Samuel 1811–1882, *'Red Gauntlet'*, gift from the Misses Katherine J. and Margaret McNidder, 1955

Walters, Samuel (attributed to) 1811–1882, *'A. D. Vance'*, gift, 1917

Walton, Allan 1891–1948, *Bawdsey*, purchased, 1961

Walton, Edward Arthur 1860–1922, *A Surrey Meadow, Morning*, purchased, 1945

Walton, Edward Arthur 1860–1922, *Sir James King (1830–1911), Lord Provost of Glasgow (1886–1889)*, purchased, 1889

Walton, Edward Arthur

1860–1922, *Mrs H. S. Ashbee*, gift from Mrs Janet E. Ashbee, 1947

Walton, Edward Arthur 1860–1922, *Cecile Walton (1891–1956), the Artist's Elder Daughter*, gift from Mrs Cecile Walton Gildard, 1944

Walton, Edward Arthur 1860–1922, *The Horse Fair* (sketch), found in store, registered, 1934

Walton, Edward Arthur 1860–1922, *The Amber Pool*, bequeathed by George B. Dunlop, 1951

Walton, Edward Arthur 1860–1922, *Lilian May Law (d.1882)*, temporary identification number allocated, 1978

Walton, Edward Arthur 1860–1922, *The Smithy at the Crossroads*, purchased, 1923

Walton, Edward Arthur 1860–1922, *Portrait of a Lady*, presented by the Trustees of the estate of Leonard Gow, 1946

Waplington, Paul Anthony b.1938, *View over Sneinton Dale* (triptych, left wing), purchased from the artist, 1994, © the artist

Waplington, Paul Anthony b.1938, *View over Sneinton Dale* (triptych, centre panel), purchased from the artist, 1994, © the artist

Waplington, Paul Anthony b.1938, *View over Sneinton Dale* (triptych, right wing), purchased from the artist, 1994, © the artist

Watt, Alison b.1965, *Marat and the Fishes*, presented by the Trustees of the Hamilton Bequest, 1990, © the artist

Watt, Alison b.1965, *Centre*, purchased, 1996, © the artist

Watt, Alison b.1965, *Phantom*, purchased with the assistance of the Art Fund and the National Fund for Acquisitions, 2008, © the artist

Watt, George Fiddes 1873–1960, *Sir William Alexander Smith (1854–1914), Founder of the Boys' Brigade*, gift from subscribers, 1909, © the artist's estate

Watt, George Fiddes 1873–1960, *Sir Archibald M. Shaw (b.1862), Lord Provost of Glasgow (1908–1911)*, purchased, 1911, © the artist's estate

Watt, George Fiddes 1873–1960, *Sir William Lorimer (1844–1922)*, presented by the North British Locomotive Company Limited, 1962, © the artist's estate

Watt, James b.1931, *Ship*, gift from the BBC Collection, 2008, © the artist

Watteau, Jean-Antoine (after) 1684–1721, *Detachment Resting*, bequeathed by William Euing, 1874

Watteau, Jean-Antoine (after) 1684–1721, *Recruits Going to Join the Regiment*, bequeathed by William Euing, 1874

Watteau, Jean-Antoine (after) 1684–1721, *Garden Scene*,

bequeathed by William Euing, 1874

Watteau, Louis Joseph (style of) 1731–1798, *The Vintage*, Archibald McLellan Collection, purchased, 1856

Watts, George Frederick 1817–1904, *Charity*, presented anonymously through the National Art Collections Fund, 1988

Webb, James 1825–1895, *Constantinople*, bequeathed by Adam Teacher, 1898

Webb, James 1825–1895, *Clovelly, North Devon*, bequeathed by Adam Teacher, 1898

Webster, Walter Ernest 1877–1959, *Spanish Girl*, purchased, 1937

Weenix, Jan 1642–1719, *A Ruined Colonnade and Figures by a Harbour*, Archibald McLellan Collection, purchased, 1856

Weight, Carel Victor Morlais 1908–1997, *Palazzo Vecchio, Florence, August 1945*, presented by the War Artists' Advisory Committee through the Imperial War Museum, 1948, © Culture and Sport Glasgow (Glasgow Museums)

Weissenbruch, Jan Hendrik (attributed to) 1824–1903, *An Artist Sketching from a Boat*, bequeathed by Reverend H. G. Roberts Hay-Boyd, 1941

Weisz, Adolphe 1838–1914, *Going to Mass*, bequeathed by Miss M. Garroway, 1947

Wells, William Page Atkinson 1872–1923, *A Manx Landscape*, purchased, 1913

Wells, William Page Atkinson 1872–1923, *The Hackett*, gift from Mrs S. Stevenson, 1940, photo credit: Glasgow Museums

Werff, Adriaen van der 1659–1722, *Portrait of a Lady by a Fountain*, bequeathed by Jane Graham-Gilbert, 1877

Werff, Adriaen van der 1659–1722, *Portrait of a Woman, Aged 33*, bequeathed by Jane Graham-Gilbert, 1877

Werff, Adriaen van der (after) 1659–1722, *Amateurs of Statuary*, purchased, 1922

Werff, Adriaen van der (after) 1659–1722, *Samson and Delilah*, Archibald McLellan Collection, purchased, 1856

Werff, Adriaen van der (follower of) 1659–1722, *The Penitent Magdalen*, Archibald McLellan Collection, purchased, 1856

Werff, Pieter van der (attributed to) 1665–1722, *Saint Mary Magdalen*, Stirling Maxwell Collection, gift, 1967

West, Benjamin 1738–1820, *The Raising of Lazarus*, Archibald McLellan Collection, purchased, 1856

West, Samuel c.1810–after 1881, *Battle of Otterburn, 5 August 1388: The Death of Douglas and Capture of Sir Ralph Percy by Sir John*

Maxwell, temporary identification number allocated, 1977

West, Samuel (attributed to) c.1810–after 1881, *Lady Matilda Maxwell (1802–1857)*, on loan from a private collection

Westall, Richard 1765–1836, *Telemachus Landing on the Isle of Calypso* (from Homer's 'Odyssey'), Archibald McLellan Collection, purchased, 1856

Westall, Richard 1765–1836, *Telemachus in the Bower of Calypso* (from Homer's 'Odyssey'), Archibald McLellan Collection, purchased, 1856

Westall, Richard 1765–1836, *Saint Cecilia*, bequeathed by William Euing, 1874

Westerbeek, Cornelis 1844–1903, *At the End of the Day*, bequeathed by Miss M. A. W. Thomson, 1947

Wet, Gerrit de 1616–1674, *Meleager Presents the Calydonian Boar to Atalanta*, gift from Hugh S. Smith, 1929

Weyden, Rogier van der (follower of) c.1399–1464, *The Annunciation*, gift from Sir William and Lady Burrell to the City of Glasgow, 1944

Whistler, James Abbott McNeill 1834–1903, *Nocturne: Grey and Gold, Westminster Bridge*, gift from Sir William and Lady Burrell to the City of Glasgow, 1944

Whistler, James Abbott McNeill 1834–1903, *Arrangement in Grey and Black, No.2: Portrait of Thomas Carlyle*, purchased from the artist, 1891

Whiteford, Kate b.1952, *Pompeiian Red* (diptych, left panel), purchased with the assistance of the National Fund for Acquisitions, 1981, © the artist

Whiteford, Kate b.1952, *Pompeiian Red* (diptych, right panel), purchased with the assistance of the National Fund for Acquisitions, 1981, © the artist

Whone, Herbert Bannister b.1925, *Tenements, Anderston*, gift from the artist, 1988, © the artist

Whyte, Duncan MacGregor 1866–1953, *Stalla Hunisgeir*, purchased, 1950

Whyte, Edna b.1930, *Distant to North*, gift from the BBC Collection, 2008, © the artist

Wiertz, Antoine Joseph 1806–1865, *The Devil Carrying Off One of the Damned*, purchased, 1956

Wighton, William d.1875/1876, *Open Your Mouth, and Shut Your Eyes*, bequeathed by William Euing, 1874

Wijnants, Jan c.1635–1684, *Landscape in Dunes with a Married Couple*, Archibald McLellan Collection, purchased, 1856

Wijnants, Jan c.1635–1684 & **Lingelbach, Johannes** 1622–1674 *Landscape with a Fallen Tree, Peasants and Huntsmen*, Archibald McLellan Collection, purchased, 1856

Wilkie, David 1785–1841,
*Cardinals, Priests and Roman
Citizens Washing the Pilgrims' Feet*,
presented by the Trustees of the
Hamilton Bequest, 1927
Wilkie, David 1785–1841, *The
Cottar's Saturday Night*, presented
by the Trustees of the Hamilton
Bequest, 1948
Wilkie, David 1785–1841, *Portrait
of a Lady* (sketch), bequeathed by
William Euing, 1874
Wilkie, David (after) 1785–1841,
Turkish Mother and Child,
Archibald McLellan Collection,
purchased, 1856
Wilkie, David (attributed to)
1785–1841, *Queen Victoria
(1819–1901)*, Archibald McLellan
Collection, purchased, 1856
Wilkie, David (imitator of)
1785–1841, *City Street Scene*
(sketch), temporary identification
number allocated, 1981
Wilkie, David (style of)
1785–1841, *Family Group in an
Interior*, on loan from a private
collection
Wilkinson, Norman 1878–1972,
*Fitting Out: RMS 'Queen Mary' at
Clydebank, 1936*, purchased with
the assistance of the National Fund
for Acquisitions, 1973, © the
Norman Wilkinson estate
Williams, Andrew b.1954, *Self
Portrait*, purchased, 1994
Williams, Hugh William
1773–1829, *Govan Ferry*, presented
by an anonymous donor, 1911
Williams, Hugh William
1773–1829, *David Dale
(1739–1806)*, gift from John
Blackie Jnr, 1868
Williams, Hugh William
1773–1829, *Landscape*, gift from J.
C. Arnot, 1903
Williams, James Francis
1785–1846, *On the West Coast of
Inverness-shire*, Stirling Maxwell
Collection, gift, 1967
Wilson, David Forrester
1873–1950, *Faggots*, purchased,
1915
Wilson, David Forrester
1873–1950, *The Valley of Melting
Snow* (sketch), gift, 1984
Wilson, Francis 1876–1957, *David
Fortune (d.1917)*, bequeathed by
the sitter, 1918
Wilson, Helen F. b.1954,
Wednesday Afternoon, purchased
from the artist, 1981, © Glasgow
Museums
Wilson, Hugh Cameron
1885–1952, *Evening Calm*,
purchased, 1952
Wilson, John Glen 1774–1855,
Landscape and Cattle, bequeathed
by William Euing, 1874
Wilson, Margaret Thomson
1864–1912, *A Dutch 'Vrouw'*, gift
from J. Hamilton Mackenzie, 1914
Wilson, Peter b.1940, *The Tie
Salesman*, purchased from the
artist, 1997, © Peter Wilson
Wilson, Peter b.1940, *Headscape
from Train II*, purchased from the
artist, 1986, © Peter Wilson

Wilson, Peter MacGregor
1855/1856–1928, *The Firstlings of
the Flock*, gift from J. Morris
Henderson, 1928
Wilson, Richard (after)
1714–1787, *Island of Anconetta,
near Mestre*, Archibald McLellan
Collection, purchased, 1856
Wilson, Richard (after)
1714–1787, *View near Tivoli*,
Archibald McLellan Collection,
purchased, 1856
Wilson, Richard (attributed to)
1714–1787, *Landscape with Figures*,
Archibald McLellan Collection,
purchased, 1856
Wilson, Richard (imitator of)
1714–1787, *River Scene*, Archibald
McLellan Collection, purchased,
1856
Wilson, W. active 20th C, *Castle
Stalker*, temporary identification
number allocated, 1997
Wilson, William Heath
1849–1927, *A Desert Mosque*, gift
from Miss A. Heath Wilson, 1928
Wilson, William Heath
1849–1927, *A Quaint Corner*, gift
from Miss A. Heath Wilson, 1928
Wilson, William Heath
1849–1927, *Bullocks Drawing a
Cart*, gift from Miss A. Heath
Wilson, 1928
Wilson, William Heath
1849–1927, *Egypt, a Ferryboat on
the Nile*, gift from Miss A. Heath
Wilson, 1928
Wilson, William Heath
1849–1927, *Old Boat Beached*, gift
from Miss A. Heath Wilson, 1928
Wilson, William Heath
1849–1927, *The Marsh, Wenhaston*,
gift from Miss A. Heath Wilson,
1928
Wilson, William Heath
1849–1927, *Venice*, gift from Miss
A. Heath Wilson, 1928
Wilson, William Heath
1849–1927, *Venice, along the
Zattere*
Wilson, William Heath
1849–1927, *Venice, the Campanile,
St Mark's and Doge's Palace*, gift
from Miss A. Heath Wilson, 1928
Wilson, William Heath
1849–1927, *Venice, the Colleoni
Monument*, gift from Miss A.
Heath Wilson, 1928
Windle, Michael b.1958, *Calum
Colvin*, purchased, 1997, © the
artist
Wingate, James Lawton
1846–1924, *Ben Cruachan*, gift
from J. Mackinlay Macleod, 1945
Wingate, James Lawton
1846–1924, *Thomas Fairbairn
(1820–1885), RSW*, gift from Mrs
Thornton, 1928
Wingate, James Lawton
1846–1924, *Old Church at Muthill*,
gift from T. Graham Young in
memory of his father, James
Young, 1900
Wingate, James Lawton
1846–1924, *Ailsa Craig*, purchased,
1965
Wingate, James Lawton
1846–1924, *Cottages in Arran*,

bequeathed by William McInnes,
1944
Wingate, James Lawton
1846–1924, *The Avenue*,
bequeathed by Adam Teacher,
1898
Wintour, John Crawford
1825–1882, *Killiecrankie*,
bequeathed by Adam Teacher,
1898
Wintz, Raymond 1884–1956,
Along the Coast, purchased, 1938
Wirrell, D. (attributed to) active
20th C, *Evening Scene on the Clyde*,
purchased with the assistance of
the National Art Collections Fund,
1988
Wissing, Willem (attributed to)
1656–1687, *Nell Gwynn
(1650–1687), and Her Two
Children*, Archibald McLellan
Collection, purchased, 1856
Wiszniewski, Adrian b.1958,
Robertson Park, purchased with the
assistance of the Local Museum
Purchase Fund, 1988, © the artist
Wiszniewski, Adrian b.1958,
Weeds in a Landscape, purchased,
1992, © the artist
Witz, Konrad (follower of)
c.1400/1410–c.1445/1446, *Byblis
Writing to Caunus*, bequeathed by
Sir Claude Phillips, 1924
Wontner, William Clarke
1857–1930, *Ina Campbell (d.1925),
Duchess of Argyll*, gift from the
sitter, 1925
Wontner, William Clarke
1857–1930, *George Campbell
(1823–1900), 8th Duke of Argyll*,
gift from Ina Campbell, Duchess of
Argyll, 1925
Wood, Christopher 1901–1930,
Newlyn, purchased with the
assistance of the National Fund for
Acquisitions, 1973
Woolmer, Alfred Joseph
1805–1892, *Watteau in His Studio*,
bequeathed by William Euing,
1874
Wouwerman, Philips 1619–1668,
A Horseman by a Pond, Archibald
McLellan Collection, purchased,
1856
Wouwerman, Philips (after)
1619–1668, *A Family of Itinerants
Resting*, Archibald McLellan
Collection, purchased, 1856
Wouwerman, Philips (after)
1619–1668, *A Man Saddling a
Tethered Horse*, gift from R. D.
McGregor, 1918
**Wouwerman, Philips (attributed
to)** 1619–1668, *Hawking*,
bequeathed by Jane Graham-
Gilbert, 1877
**Wouwerman, Philips (follower
of)** 1619–1668, *Departure from a
Riding School*, bequeathed by Jane
Graham-Gilbert, 1877
Wouwerman, Philips (style of)
1619–1668, *Landscape with a Farm
Cart*, Archibald McLellan
Collection, purchased, 1856
Wouwerman, Philips (style of)
1619–1668, *Landscape with a
Watermill and Figures*, bequeathed
by James Donald, 1905

Wouwerman, Philips (style of)
1619–1668, *Landscape with Horses
and Figures, with a Distant View of
the Sea*, Archibald McLellan
Collection, purchased, 1856
Wouwerman, Pieter 1623–1682,
Cavalry Men by a Suttler's Tent,
bequeathed by Jane Graham-
Gilbert, 1877
Wright, Arthur 1904–1981, *May
Day in Town*, purchased, 1995
Wright, J. active 18th C, *Frances
Colquhoun (d.1818), Lady Maxwell*,
on loan from a private collection
Wright, James 1885–1947,
Garelochhead, purchased, 1942
Wright, James 1885–1947, *A Sunlit
Courtyard, Culross*, gift from Mrs
Kathleen McNeil, 1939
Wright, John Michael 1617–1694,
*Frances Cromwell (1638–1720),
Daughter of Oliver Cromwell*,
purchased with the assistance of
the National Fund for
Acquisitions, 1984
Wright, John Michael 1617–1694,
*Lord Mungo Murray (1668–1700),
Portrait of a Highland Chieftain*, on
loan from Allan G. Murray and
Carol E. Murray
Wuterland, C. *Stormy Sea*, gift
from the BBC Collection, 2008
Wyck, Thomas 1616–1677, *The
Poor Being Fed at a Monastery*,
bequeathed by Jane Graham-
Gilbert, 1877
Wylie, Kate 1877–1941, *Flowers
(Begonias)*, purchased, 1941
Wylie, Kate 1877–1941,
Wallflower, bequeathed by Jessie
W. Craig, 1950
Wyllie, Charles William
1853–1923, *The Launch of HMS
'Indomitable', Fairfield*, gift from
Mrs I. R. Gracie, 1959
Wyllie, Robin H. active 20th C,
The Clyde at Carlton Place,
purchased, 1957
Wyllie, Robin H. active 20th C,
The Last Tram Procession,
acquired, 1963
Wynter, Bryan 1915–1975, *Small
Red*, gift, 1988, © Bryan Wynter. All
rights reserved, DACS 2013
Yeames, William Frederick
1835–1918, *Prisoners of War*,
purchased from the artist, 1904
Young, A. active 19th C, *Fishing
Village*, gift from Miss Anderson,
1921
Young, Bessie Innes 1855–1936,
The Garden Hat, gift from
Katherine Young in memory of her
sister, 1937
Young, William 1845–1916, *Glen
Falloch*, purchased, 1905
Young, William Drummond
1855–1924, *A. D. Muir*, temporary
identification number allocated,
1979
Zais, Giuseppe 1709–1781,
*Landscape with a Horseman and
Peasants*, bequeathed by William
Euing, 1874
**Ziem, Félix François Georges
Philibert** 1821–1911,
Constantinople, Sunset, bequeathed
by William J. Chrystal, 1939

Zoffany, Johann 1733–1810, *Mrs
Maintrew*, purchased, 1959
Zoffany, Johann (circle of)
1733–1810, *A Family Party: The
Minuet*, Archibald McLellan
Collection, purchased, 1856
Zuccarelli, Franco 1702–1788, *A
Pastoral Landscape with Figures by
a Stream*, Archibald McLellan
Collection, purchased, 1856
Zuccarelli, Franco 1702–1788,
Saint John the Baptist Preaching,
Archibald McLellan Collection,
purchased, 1856
Zuccarelli, Franco 1702–1788, *A
Watering Place near a Village*,
bequeathed by Jane Graham-
Gilbert, 1877
Zuccarelli, Franco 1702–1788,
Pastoral Landscape, bequeathed by
Jane Graham-Gilbert, 1877
Zuccarelli, Franco (after)
1702–1788, *Landscape with Diana
and Actaeon*, Archibald McLellan
Collection, purchased, 1856
Żyw, Aleksander 1905–1995, *The
Stage*, Scottish Arts Council
Bequest, 1997

Collection Addresses

Glasgow Museums

Glasgow Museums
Glasgow Life, 20 Trongate, Glasgow G1 5ES
Telephone 0141 287 4350
email museums@glasgowlife.org.uk
website www.glasgowlife.org.uk/museums

> Gallery of Modern Art (GoMA)
> Royal Exchange Square, Glasgow G1 3AH
> Telephone 0141 287 3050
>
> Glasgow Museums Resource Centre (GMRC)
> 200 Woodhead Road South Nitshill Industrial
> Estate, Glasgow G53 7NN
> Telephone 0141 276 9300
>
> Kelvingrove Art Gallery and Museum
> Argyle Street, Glasgow G3 8AG
> Telephone 0141 276 9599
>
> People's Palace and Winter Gardens
> Glasgow Green, Glasgow G40 1AT
> Telephone 0141 276 0788
>
> Pollok House
> Pollok Country Par, 2060 Pollokshaws Road
> Glasgow G43 1AT
> Telephone 0141 616 6410
>
> Provand's Lordship
> 3 Castle Street, Glasgow G4 0RB
> Telephone 0141 552 8819
>
> Riverside Museum
> 100 Pointhouse Place, Glasgow G3 8RS
> Telephone 0141 287 2720
>
> Scotland Street School Museum
> 225 Scotland Street, Glasgow G5 8QB
> Telephone 0141 287 0500
>
> St Mungo Museum of Religious Life and Art
> 2 Castle Street, Glasgow G4 0RH
> Telephone 0141 276 1625
>
> The Burrell Collection
> Pollok Country Park, 2060 Pollokshaws Road,
> Glasgow G43 1AT
> Telephone 0141 287 2550

Index of Artists

In this catalogue, artists' names and the spelling of their names follow the preferred presentation of the name in the Getty Union List of Artist Names (ULAN) as of February 2004, if the artist is listed in ULAN.

The page numbers next to each artist's name below direct readers to paintings that are by the artist; are attributed to the artist; or, in a few cases, are more loosely related to the artist being, for example, 'after', 'the circle of' or copies of a painting by the artist. The precise relationship between the artist and the painting is listed in the catalogue.

Acknowledgements

The Public Catalogue Foundation would like to thank the individual artists
and copyright holders for their permission to reproduce for free the paintings
in this catalogue. Exhaustive efforts have been made to locate the copyright
owners of all the images included within this catalogue and to meet their
requirements. Copyright credit lines for copyright owners who have been
traced are listed in the Further Information section.

The Public Catalogue Foundation would like to express its great appreciation
to the following organisations for their kind assistance in the preparation of
this catalogue:

Bridgeman Art Library
Flowers East
Marlborough Fine Art
National Association of Decorative & Fine Arts Societies (NADFAS)
National Gallery, London
National Portrait Gallery, London
Royal Academy of Arts, London
Tate

The Public Catalogue Foundation

The Public Catalogue Foundation is a registered charity. It was launched in 2003 to create a photographic record of the entire national collection of oil, tempera and acrylic paintings in public ownership in the United Kingdom.

Whilst our public galleries and civic buildings hold arguably the greatest collection of oil paintings in the world, over 80 per cent of these are not on view. Few collections have a complete photographic record of their paintings let alone a comprehensive illustrated catalogue. What is publicly owned is not publicly accessible.

The Foundation is publishing a series of fully illustrated, county-by-county catalogues that will cover, eventually, the entire national UK collection. To date, it has published over 30 volumes, presenting over 72,000 paintings.

In partnership with the BBC, the Foundation will make its database of the entire UK collection of 200,000 oil paintings available online through a new website called *Your Paintings*. The website was launched in the summer of 2011.

Your Paintings (*www.bbc.co.uk/arts/yourpaintings*) offers a variety of ways of searching for paintings as well as further information about the paintings and artists, including links to the participating collections' websites. For those interested in paintings and the subjects they portray *Your Paintings* is an unparalleled learning resource.

Collections benefit substantially from the work of the Foundation, not least from the digital images that are given to them for free following photography, and from the increased recognition that the project brings. These substantial benefits come at no financial cost to the collections.

The Foundation is funded by a combination of support from individuals, charitable trusts, companies and the public sector although the latter provides less than 20 per cent of the Foundation's financial support.

Supporters

Master Patrons

The Public Catalogue Foundation is greatly indebted to the following Master Patrons who have helped it in the past or are currently working with it to raise funds for the publication of their county catalogues. All of them have given freely of their time and have made an enormous contribution to the work of the Foundation.

Peter Andreae (*Hampshire*)
Sir Henry Aubrey-Fletcher, Bt, Lord Lieutenant of Buckinghamshire (*Buckinghamshire*)
Sir Nicholas Bacon, DL, High Sheriff of Norfolk (*Norfolk*)
Sir John Bather, Lord Lieutenant of Derbyshire (*Derbyshire*)
The Hon. Mrs Bayliss, JP, Lord Lieutenant of Berkshire (*Berkshire*)
Ian Bonas (*County Durham*)

Peter Bretherton (*West Yorkshire: Leeds*)
Michael Brinton, Lord Lieutenant of Worcestershire (*Worcestershire*)
Sir Hugo Brunner, KCVO, JP (*Oxfordshire*)
Mr John Bush, OBE, Lord-Lieutenant of Wiltshire (*Wiltshire*)
Lady Butler (*Warwickshire*)
Richard Compton (*North Yorkshire*)
George Courtauld, DL, Vice Lord Lieutenant of Essex (*Essex*)

The Countess of Darnley, Lord
Lieutenant of Herefordshire
(Herefordshire)
The Marquess of Downshire *(North
Yorkshire)*
Martin Dunne, Lord Lieutenant of
Warwickshire *(Warwickshire)*
Sir Henry Elwes, KCVO, Lord-
Lieutenant of Gloucestershire
(Gloucestershire)
Jenny Farr, MBE, DL *(Nottinghamshire)*
John Fenwick *(Tyne & Wear
Museums)*
Mark Fisher, MP *(Staffordshire)*
Patricia Grayburn, MBE, DL *(Surrey)*
The Earl of Halifax, KStJ, JP, DL *(East
Riding of Yorkshire)*
Lord Roy Hattersley, PC *(South
Yorkshire: Sheffield*
Algy Heber-Percy, Lord Lieutenant of
Shropshire *(Shropshire)*
The Lady Mary Holborow, Lord
Lieutenant of Cornwall *(Cornwall)*
Sarah Holman *(Warwickshire)*
Tommy Jowitt *(West Yorkshire)*
Alderman Sir David Lewis, The Rt
Hon. The Lord Mayor of London,
2007–2008 *(The City of London)*

Sir Michael Lickiss *(Cornwall)*
Magnus Linklater *(Scotland)*
Lord Marlesford, DL *(Suffolk)*
Dr Bridget McConnell *(Glasgow)*
Lady Sarah Nicholson *(County
Durham)*
Malcolm V. L. Pearce, MP *(Somerset)*
Sir John Riddell, Lord Lieutenant
of Northumberland
(Northumberland)
Venetia Ross Skinner *(Dorset)*
The Most Hon. The Marquess of
Salisbury, PC, DL *(Hertfordshire)*
Julia Somerville *(Government Art
Collection)*
Tim Stevenson, OBE, Lord
Lieutenant of Oxfordshire
(Oxfordshire)
Phyllida Stewart-Roberts, OBE *(East
Sussex)*
Lady Juliet Townsend, Lord
Lieutenant of Northamptonshire
(Northamptonshire)
Leslie Weller, DL *(West Sussex)*
Sir Samuel C. Whitbread, KCVO,
Lord Lieutenant of Bedfordshire
(Bedfordshire)

Financial support

The Public Catalogue Foundation is particularly grateful to the following
organisations and individuals who have given it generous financial support
since the project started in 2003.

National Sponsor

Christie's

Benefactors
(£10,000–£50,000)

The 29th May 1961 Charitable Trust
Arts Council England
The Barbour Trust
Binks Trust
City of Bradford Metropolitan
District Council
Deborah Loeb Brice Foundation
The Bulldog Trust
A. & S. Burton 1960 Charitable Trust
Christie's
City of London Corporation
The John S. Cohen Foundation
Covent Garden London
Creative Scotland
Department for Culture, Media and
Sport

Sir Harry Djanogly, CBE
Mr Lloyd Dorfman
Dunard Fund
The Elmley Foundation
Fenwick Ltd
Fidelity UK Foundation
Marc Fitch Fund
The Foyle Foundation
J. Paul Getty Jr Trust
Hampshire County Council
The Charles Hayward Foundation
Peter Harrison Foundation
Mr Robert Hiscox
Hiscox plc
David Hockney, CH, RA
ICAP plc

G. F. Armitage Family Charitable Trust
Mr Ian Askew
Aurelius Charitable Trust
The Bacon Charitable Trust
Lawrence Banks, CBE, DL
Barlow Robbins LLP
Mr James & Lady Emma Barnard
Basingstoke and Deane Borough Council
Bath & North East Somerset District Council Heritage Services
Robert Baxter, DL
Birmingham Common Good Trust
Sir Christopher Bland
Johnnie Boden
The Charlotte Bonham-Carter Charitable Trust
H. R. Pratt Boorman Family Foundation
A. J. H. du Boulay Charitable Trust
The Bowerman Charitable Trust
Viscountess Boyd Charitable Trust
Lord & Lady Bradbury
Bramdean Asset Management LLP
Peter Bretherton
Brewin Dolphin
J. & M. Britton Charitable Trust
Mrs T. Brotherton-Ratcliffe
Janey Buchan
Mr & Mrs Patrick Burgess
Mr & Mrs Mark Burrell
Arnold J. Burton Charitable Trust
Bushey Museum in Memory of Lavender Watson
Mrs Anne Cadbury, OBE, JP, DL
Roger Cadbury
C. J. R. & Mrs C. L. Calderwood
Sir Ralph Carr-Ellison
Mr & Mrs J. Chambers
Chichester District Council
His Honour Richard Cole, DL & Mrs Sheila Cole
The Timothy Colman Charitable Trust
Mr & Mrs Derek Coombs
The Helen Jean Cope Trust
Mr & Mrs Ian Copesteak
Cornwall County Council
Mr S. J. D. Corsan

Graeme Cottam & Gloriana Marks de Chabris
Coutts Charitable Trust
David Crane Trust
Elaine Craven, Earl Street Employment Consultants Ltd
Harriett Cullen
Culture North East
Rt Hon. Viscount Daventry
N. Davie-Thornhill
Brigadier Mike Dauncey, DSO, DL
De La Rue Charitable Trust
Mr Robert Dean
Deborah Gage (Works of Art) Ltd
Derek Johns Ltd, London
Derby City Council
Derby High School Trust Ltd
Derbyshire Building Society
Derbyshire Community Foundation (The Ashby Fund)
J. N. Derbyshire Trust
The Duke of Devonshire's Charitable Trust
S. Dewhirst Charitable Trust
Sir Harry Djanogly, CBE
Dorset County Council
Lord Douro
Professor Patrick & Dr Grace Dowling
Dunn Family Charitable Trust
East Sussex County Council
Eastbourne Borough Council
EEMLAC, through the Association for Suffolk Museums
Lord & Lady Egremont
Sir John & Lady Elliott
Andrew & Lucy Ellis
Peter & Judy Ellwood
Essex County Council
John & Felicity Fairbairn
Fairfield Charitable Trust
Jenny Farr, MBE, DL
John Feeney Charitable Trust
The Trustees of the Finnis Scott Foundation
The Fishmongers' Company
David & Ann FitzWilliam-Lay
Elizabeth & Val Fleming
The Follett Trust
Richard & Elizabeth Fothergill

Christopher & Catherine Foyle
Freemasons of Derbyshire
The Friends of Historic Essex
The Friends of the Laing Art Gallery
The Friends of the Royal Pavilion,
    Art Gallery & Museums, Brighton
The Friends of Southampton's
    Museums, Archives and Galleries
The Friends of Sunderland Museums
The Friends of York Art Gallery (E. J.
    Swift Bequest)
Philip Gibbs
The Hon. H. M. T. Gibson's Charity
    Trust
Lewis & Jacqueline Golden
The Goldsmiths' Company
Gorringes
Charles Gregson
The Grocers' Company
The Gulland Family
David Gurney
Philip Gwyn
Sir Ernest Hall
The Earl of Halifax, KStJ, JP, DL
The W. A. Handley Charity Trust
The Hartnett Charitable Trust
Hazlitt, Gooden & Fox Ltd
Heartwood Wealth Management Ltd
The Trustees of the King Henry VIII
    Endowed Trust, Warwick
The Rt Hon. the Lord Heseltine, CH,
    PC & Lady Heseltine
The Lady Hind Trust
Hobart Charitable Trust
Edward and Anna Hocknell
David Hockney CH, RA
Patrick Holden & Lin Hinds
Mrs Michael Hollingbery
The Holman Family
Mr & Mrs A. Holman-West
The Honourable Company of
    Gloucestershire
The Hope Scott Trust
David & Prue Hopkinson
Major & Mrs Bill Hutchinson
His Honour Gabriel Hutton
Isle of Wight Council
The J. and S. B. Charitable Trust
Alan & Penny Jerome
James & Lucilla Joll Charitable Trust

Mr & Mrs Peter Jones
Tommy Jowitt
The Keatley Trust
Kent Messenger Group
Garrett Kirk, Jr
Mr John Kirkland, OBE & Mrs
    Sheila Kirkland
Robert Kirkland
Kirklees Council
The David Laing Foundation
Landau Foundation
Lord Lea of Crondall, OBE
The Leche Trust
Leeds Art Collections Fund
Leeds City Council
Leeds Philosophical and Literary
    Society
The Hon. David Legh, DL
Lord Leverhulme's Charitable Trust
Mr & Mrs John Lewis
Mark & Sophie Lewisohn
Tom Lugg & the Lane Family
The Orr Mackintosh Foundation
The MacRobert Trust
Maidstone Borough Council
John Manser
Mr & Mrs Derek Mapp
Walter & Barbara Marais
The Marlay Group
Marshall Charitable Trust
Stephen & Carolyn Martin
Tom & Anne Martin
The Medlock Charitable Trust
The Piet Mendels Foundation
MLA East of England
MLA North East of England
Museums Galleries Scotland
Mr Paul Myners
Rupert Nabarro
Nancie Massey Charitable Trust
Newcastle City Council
Bryan Norman
Lord & Lady Northampton
The University of Northampton
NP Aerospace Ltd
Oakmoor Trust
Jasper & Virginia Olivier
The Orr Mackintosh Foundation
Mr Christopher Oughtred
The Owen Family Trust

First published in 2013 by The Public Catalogue
Foundation, Printed Catalogue Division,
8 Frederick's Place, London, EC2R 8AB

Designed by Sally Jeffery